GEBBIE PRESS
All-In-One*
Directory

Editor & Publisher: Mark Gebbie
Associate Editor: Barbara A. Edelman

2014: 43rd edition
Copyright 2014 Gebbie Press Inc.

Gebbie Press: Box 1000 New Paltz, NY 12561
Phone: 845-255-7560 Fax: 888-345-2790
www.gebbiepress.com

Please note:

* For all newspapers, circulation figures are given in thousands (M)
  For example, 2.5M means 2,500

* For magazines, circulation figures are read as is. TH denotes Twitter handle.

* TV Network abbreviations:

  ABC, CBS, CW, FOX, IND (Independent), ION, MY (My Network TV),
  NBC, PBS, REL (Religious), SPN (Spanish Language)

* Radio format key: format follows call sign in parentheses:

Radio formats: **A**-Adult Contemporary, **B**-Big Band, **C**-Country, **D**-Asian,
E-Ethnic, **F**-Farm, **G**-Gospel, **H**-Contemporary Hits, **I**-International, **J**-Jazz,
K-Business, **L**-Classical, **M**-Middle of the Road, **N**-News, **O**-Oldies,
P-Public Radio, **Q**-Religious, **R**-Rock, **S**-Sports, **T**-Talk,
U-Urban Contemporary, **V**-Educational/College, **W**-Black,
X-Rhythm & Blues, **Y**-Hispanic, **Z**-Easy Listening

Below is a page from the very first edition of the All-In-One Directory, published in 1971. While times and press release delivery methods have changed since then, this advice from Conley Gebbie is as true now as it was then.

Editors change—titles don't.

This fact is the key to setting up efficient and dependable PR contact lists in the print and broadcast fields.

A press release addressed to editors by name may not reach them if they have the day off, if on vacation, out sick or if they are no longer employed.

But a release addressed to "Managing Editor", "Morning Show Producer" or "Business Editor" will always reach the correct news desk surely and swiftly.

Newcomers to public relations tend to see a magic in the use of an editor's name on a press release, but no editors (especially if not there) are impressed by seeing their own name.

The real magic is in the content of your message and the certainty of delivery.

Veteran PR people know the value of editor names and they know that nothing can substitute for personalized attention when circumstances call for first and last names. But editor names properly belong in a PR professional's personal contact book and only rarely should they be used for routine mailings.

To make certain of dependable delivery to the news desk you want to reach...

Use titles—not names.

This page left blank intentionally.

Publication Categories

Advertising-Marketing-Promotion-Public Relations 1
African-American Interest 69h
Agricultural Publications 68
Airline-Travel.. 65a
Appliances 19a
Architecture 3
Arts.. 26a
Auto Clubs & Associations 65d
Auto Sports-Racing... 4a
Automotive... 4
Aviation-Aerospace 5
Baking-Confectionery-Dairy................................. 6
Banking-Financial 7
Beauty-Cosmetics 8
Beverages-Bottling-Brewing 9
Bicycles-Motorcycles.. 4c
Books & Libraries 10a
Building-Bldg. Mgmt.-Real Estate........................ 11
Business 12
Camping.. 65b
Cattle 68g
Cement-Rock-Stone 3a
Ceramics-China-Glass 13
Chemical Industry 14
Children & Teens.. 69e
Clothing-Fashions... 16
Coins 26b
Computers-Info. Technology-Internet................... 19b
Crafts-Arts-Hobbies 26
Dairy.. 68a
Dental 17
Drugs-Pharmaceuticals...................................... 18
Electric-Electronic-Telecommunications 19
Engineering-Construction.................................... 20
Environment & Ecology 28c
Farm Bureau-Grange.. 68b
Farm Electric-Cooperatives 68c
Farm Equipment... 68d
Federal-State-Municipal 28b
Feed-Grain-Milling.. 21
Fertilizers-Soil Science 22
Film-Theater-Amusements................................... 2
Fire Control & Police...28a
Firearms 57
Fish Industry 39a
Fishing-Hunting-Outdoors 61a
Food & Wine..69k
Food Processing-Distribution............................... 23
Footwear-Leather Goods 24
Fraternal-Professional Clubs 25
Fruits-Nuts-Vegetables 68f
Furniture-Interiors... 29
Garden-Nursery-Florists 30
Gay & Lesbian Interest...................................... 69i
General Interest 69
Golf... 61b
Grocery-Supermarkets....................................... 27
Health-Fitness-Nutrition...................................... 69g
Home & Garden..69a
Horses-Breeding-Riding-Show 61c
Hospitals-Nursing 31
Hotels-Motels-Clubs-Restaurants 32
Industrial 33
Insurance 34
Jewelry... 35
Journalism 10b
Laundry-Dry Cleaning 36
Legal.. 37
Lumber-Forestry-Woodworking 38
Marine-Maritime 39
Meat Trade..23a
Medical-Surgical 40
Men's Interest..69c
Metals-Machinery-Tool Making 41
Military 42
Mining-Coal-Ore 43
Mobile Homes-Trailers-Rec. Vehicles...................65c
Mortuary-Cemetery 44
Music-Music Trades 45
Office Equipment & Management 46
Optical.. 47
Packaging.. 48
Paint-Decoration 49
Paper-Paper Products.. 50
Parenting & Babies 69d
Petroleum-Gas 51
Pets-Veterinary 52
Photography-Audio-Visual................................... 53
Plastics 54
Plumbing-Heating-Cooling................................... 55
Poultry..68h
Power-Power Plants... 56

Printing & Publishing.. 10c
Railroad Industry 59
Regional Interest 69f
Religion... 15
Retail..12a
Safety & Security..33a
Schools-Education 60
Science-Research & Development 33b
Senior Citizen Interest 69j
Sheep-Goats-Hogs.. 68i
Spanish Language...69l
Sports 61
Textiles 62
Tobacco 63
Traffic-Warehousing 64
Travel-Tourism.. 65
Trucks-Buses-Fleets..4b
TV-Video-Radio... 58
Vending... 67
Water & Wastes 28d
Water Sports 61d
Winter & Snow Sports 61e
Women's Interest..69b

A

AAA Arizona Highroads 65d
AAA Carolinas Go Magazine 65d
AAA Going Places 65d
AAA Midwest Traveler 65d
AAA Southern Traveler 65d
AAA World 65d
AACN Bold Voices 31
AANA Journal 31
AAOHN Journal 31
AAPG Explorer 51
AARC Times 40
AARP Bulletin Today 69j
AARP The Magazine 69j
AARP Viva 69l
AATCC Review 62
ABA Bank Marketing 7
ABA Banking Journal 7
ABA Journal 37
ABILITY Magazine 69g
Academe 60
ACC Docket 37
Access 17
Accessories Magazine 16
Accounting Today 12
Acoustic Guitar 45
Acres USA 68
Action Pursuit Games 61
ADA News 17
Adcrafter 1
ADDitude 69g
Adhesives & Sealants Industry 33
Adirondack Life 69f
Adoptive Families 69d
Advance For Medical Lab Pros 40
Advance For NPs & PAs 31
Advance For Physical Therapists 40
Advanced Materials & Processes 41
Advancing Philanthropy 69
Adventist Review 15
Adventure Cyclist 4c
Advertising Age 1
Advertising/Communications Times 1
Advisor Today 34
Adweek 1
Aerospace America 5
Aerospace Engineering & Mfg. 5
AFAR Magazine 65
Affordable Housing Finance 11
African American Golfer's Digest 69h
AfterCapture 53
Aftermarket Business World 4
Ag Alert 68b
Ag Professional 22
AGD Impact 17
Agency Sales Magazine 12
Aggregates Manager 3a
Agri Marketing Magazine 1
Agri-News 68
Agri News 68
Agri-View 68
Agronomy Journal 22
AGRR Magazine 4
Agweek 68
AHA News 31
AI Magazine 19b
AIDS Patient Care & STDs 40
Air & Space Smithsonian 5
Air Cargo World 5
Air Classics 5
Air Cond. Heat & Refrig. News 55
Air Force Magazine 5
Air Force Times 42
Air Line Pilot 5
Air Pollution Control 33
Air Transport World 5
Airbrush Action 1
Aircraft Maintenance Technology 5
Airport Business 5
Airport Press 5
Airways Magazine 5
Alabama Cattleman 68g
Alabama Living 68c
Alaska 69f
Alaska Airlines 65a
Alaska Business Monthly 12
All About Beer 9
Allure 69b
Alternative Press 45
Ambush Magazine 69i
America 15
American Agent & Broker 34
American Agriculturist 68
American Angler 61a
American Baby 69d

American Banker 7
American Bee Journal 68
American Biology Teacher 60
American Bungalow 69a
American Cattlemen 68g
American Cemetery 44
Amer. Ceramic Soc. Bulletin 13
American Chiropractor 40
American Christmas Tree Jrnl. 38
American Cinematographer 53
American City & County 28b
American Coin-Op 36
American COP Magazine 28a
American Craft Magazine 26
American Drycleaner 36
American Educator 60
American Family Physician 40
American Farriers Journal 61c
American Field 52
American Fine Art Magazine 26a
American Firearms Industry 57
American Fitness 61
American Forests 38
American Funeral Director 44
The American Gardener 30
American Gas 51
American Handgunner 57
American Heritage 69
American History 69
American Iron 4c
American Jrnl. Cardiology 40
American Jrnl. Clinical Nutrition 40
American Jrnl. Critical Care 31
American Jrnl. Health Education 60
American Jrnl. Health Sys Pharm 18
American Jrnl. Medicine 40
American Jrnl. Nursing 31
American Jrnl. OB/GYN 40
American Jrnl. Occup. Therapy 40
American Jrnl. Orthodontics 17
American Jrnl. Psychiatry 40
American Jrnl. Public Health 40
American Jrnl. Sports Medicine 40
American Jrnl. Transportation 64
American Jrnl. Ophthalmology 47
American Journalism Review 10b
American Laboratory 33b
American Laundry News 36
American Lawyer 37
American Legion Magazine 25
American Libraries 10a
American Mathematical Monthly 60
American Metal Market 41
American Motorcyclist 4c
American Music Teacher 45
American Nurse 31
American Nurseryman 30
The American Organist 45
American Painting Contractor 49
American Photo 53
American Police Beat 28a
American Prospect 69
American Psychologist 40
American Quarter Horse Journal 61c
American Recycler 28c
American Rifleman 57
American Road Magazine 65
American Rose 30
American Salesman 12
American Salon 8
American School & University 60
American School Brd. Jrnl. 60
American Scientist 33b
American Shipper 39
American Songwriter 45
American Spa 8
American Spectator 69
American Square Dance 2
American String Teacher 45
American Teacher 60
American Theatre 2
American Towman 4
American Trucker 4b
American Turf Monthly 61c
American Vegetable Grower 68f
American Veteran 42
American Vineyard 68f
American Waste Digest 28d
American Way 65a
American/Western Fruit Grower 68f
American Woodworker 26
America's Pharmacist 18
Amusement Today 2
ANA Magazine 1
Analytical Chemistry 14

Anesthesiology 40
Angus Icon 68g
Ann Arbor Observer 69f
Annals Of Internal Medicine 40
Antique Trader 26
AntiqueWeek 26
AOA News 47
AOPA Pilot 5
AORN Journal 31
Apartment Finance Today 11
APICS 33
Appaloosa Journal 61c
Apparel 16
Appliance 19a
Appliance Design 19a
Applied Clinical Trials 18
Applied Radiology 40
Applied Spectroscopy 33b
APWA Reporter 28d
Aquatics International 61d
Arabian Horse World 61c
Arbor Age 38
Archaeology 69
Archery Business 61
Architect 3
Architectural Digest 3
Architectural Record 3
Architectural West 3
Architecture Minnesota 3
Archives Internal Medicine 40
Archives Ped/Adolescent Medicine 40
Archives Surgery 40
Area Auto Racing News 4a
Area Development 11
Arizona Business Gazette 12
Arizona Foothills 69f
Arizona Highways 65
Arkansas Business 12
Arkansas Cattle Business 68g
Armchair General 69
Armed Forces Journal 42
Army 42
Army Aviation 42
Army Times 42
Art & Antiques 26a
Art & Auction 26a
Art Education 60
Art In America 26a
Artforum Intl. 26a
Arthritis Self-Management 69g
Arthritis Today 69g
The Artist's Magazine 26a
Artnews 26a
Arts & Activities 60
ASCE News 20
ASDA News 17
ASHRAE Journal 55
ASID Icon 29
Aspen Magazine 69f
Asphalt Contractor 20
Assembly 41
Associations Now 12
Association Meetings 65
Association Trends 12
ASTM Standardization News 14
Astronomy 69
At Home in Arkansas 69f
Athletic Business 60
Athletic Management 60
Atlanta 69f
Atlanta Business Chronicle 12
Atlanta Parent 69d
The Atlantic 69
Atlantic Control St. Bev. Jrnl. 9
ATV Rider 4c
Audience Development 10c
AudioFile 10a
Audrey 69b
Audubon 28c
Autism Asperger's Digest 69d
Auto Glass Journal 4
Auto Exec 4
Auto Laundry News 4
Auto Remarketing 4
Auto Rental News 4
AutoInc. 4
Automatic Merchandiser 67
Automobile Magazine 4
Automotive Body Repair Network 4
Automotive Design & Production 4
Automotive Engineering Intl. 4
Automotive Fleet 4b
Automotive News 4
Automotive Recycling 4
AutoWeek 4

Aviation for Women 5
Aviation Intl. News 5
Aviation Safety 5
Aviation Week & Space Technology 5
Avionics 5
Avionics News 5
AWCI's Construction Dimensions 11

B

Back Home In Kentucky 69f
Back Stage 2
Backcountry 61e
Backpacker 61a
Backyard Pountry 68h
BAI Banking Strategies 7
Baking & Snack 6
Baking Buyer 6
Baltimore Business Journal 12
Baltimore Magazine 69f
Bank Director 7
Bank Investment Consultant 7
Bank Note Reporter 26b
Bank Systems & Technology 7
Bank Technology News 7
BankNews 7
The Bark 52
Barrel Horse News 61c
Barron's 12
Bartender Magazine 9
Baseball America 61
Baseball Digest 61
Basketball Times 61
Bass Player 45
BASS Times 61a
Bassmaster 61a
Bead & Button 26
Bead-It Today 26
BeadStyle 26
Beadwork Magazine 26
Beauty Fashion 8
Beauty Store Business 8
BedTimes 29
Bee Culture 68
Beef 68g
Best's Review 34
Better Homes & Gardens 69a
Better Nutrition 69g
Better Roads 20
BetterInvesting 12
Beverage Dynamics 9
Beverage Industry 9
Beverage World 9
Biblical Archaeology Review 15
Bicycle Retailer & Industry News 4c
Bicycling 4c
Big Builder 11
Big Game Fishing Journal 61a
The Big Picture 10c
Big River 69f
Bike 4c
Biker 4c
Billboard 45
Billiards Digest 61
Bingo Bugle 2
Bio-IT World 33b
Biochemistry 14
Biocycle 28c
Biopharm 18
Bioscience 33b
Bioscience Technology 40
Biosupply Trends Quarterly 40
Biotechniques 33b
Bird Watcher's Digest 52
Birding 52
Birds & Blooms 69a
BirdWatching 52
Birmingham 69f
Birmingham Business Journal 12
Black Belt 61
Black Car News 4b
Black Enterprise 69h
Black Men 69h
Blade Magazine 26
Blood-Horse 61c
Bloomberg BusinessWeek 12
Bluegrass Unlimited 45
BMX Plus! 4c
B'nai B'rith Magazine 15
Board Converting News 48
BoatU.S. 39
Boating Industry 39
Boating 39
Boating World 39
Boca Life 69f
Boca Raton 69f
Bodyshop Business 4
Bon Appetit 69k
Book Links 10a
Booklist 10a
Bookmarks Magazine 10a
BookPage 10a
BoomerTimes & Senior Life 69j
Borough News 28b
Boston 69f
Boston Business Journal 12
Boston Parents' Paper 69d
Bow & Arrow Hunting 61a
Bowhunt America 61a
Bowhunter 61a
Bowhunting World 61a
Bowlers Journal 61
Bowling Center Management 61
Box Office 2
Boys' Life 69e
Brake & Front End 4
Brandpackaging 48
Brew Your Own 69k
Bridal Guide 69b
Brides Magazine 69b
Bridge Bulletin 26
Broadcast Engineering 58
Broadcasting & Cable 58
Broker World 34
Buckeye Farm News 68b
Buckmasters Whitetail Magazine 61a
Budget Travel 65
Bugle 61a
Builder 11
Building Operating Management 11
Building Products Digest 11
Buildings 11
Bulk Transporter 4b
Bus Conversions 65c
Bus Ride 4b
Business Air 5
Business & Commercial Aviation 5
Business Credit 12
Business Facilities 11
Business First Columbus 12
Business First Louisville 12
Business Insurance 34
Business Jet Traveler 5
Business Journal Charlotte 12
Business Journal Milwaukee 12
Business Law Today 37
Business Leader 12
Business Life 12
Business NC 12
Business Officer 60
Business Review 12
Business Solutions 19b
Business TN 12
Business Travel News 65
Bust 69b
Butane-Propane News 51
Byways 65

C

C4ISR Journal 42
CabinetmakerFDM 29
CableFax 58
Cadalyst 19b
Calf News 68g
California Apparel News 16
California Bar Journal 37
California Broker 34
California Builder & Engineer 20
California Cattleman 68g
California Dairy 68a
California Educator 60
California Farmer 68
California Fire Service 28a
California Pharmacist 18
California Real Estate 11
California Riding Magazine 61c
Camp Business 65b
Campaigns & Elections 28b
Camping Magazine 65b
Campus Safety 33a
Campus Technology 60
Cancer 40
Candy Industry 6
Canoe & Kayak 61d
CAP Today 40
Cape Cod Life 69f
Capital Press 68
Capper's 68
Car and Driver 4
Car & Travel 65d
Car Craft 4a
Cardiology News 40
Cardiology Today 40
CardMaker 26
Carolina Business 12
Carolina Country 68c
Carolina-Virginia Farmer 68
Casa & Estilo 69l
Casino Journal 2
Casual Living 29
Cat Fancy 52
Catechist 15
Catering Magazine 32
Catholic Cemetery 44
Catholic Digest 15
Cattle Business in MS. 68g
Cattleman 68g
CDS Review 17
CE News 20
CED 58
Celebrated Living 65a
Cell 33b
Central Penn Business Journal 12
Ceramic Industry 13
Ceramics Monthly 13
Cesar's Way 52
Cessna Owner 5
CFO 7
Chain Drug Review 18
Chain Store Age 12a
Chamber Music 45
Champion 37
Channel Partners 19
Charisma 15
Charleston Magazine 69f
Charlotte Magazine 69f
Cheers 9
Cheese Reporter 6
Chef 32
Chemical & Engineering News 14
Chemical Engineering 14
Chemical Engineering Progress 14
Chemical Processing 14
Chem.Info 14
Chesapeake Bay Magazine 39
Chess Life 26
Chest 40
Chevy High Performance 4a
Chicago 69f
Chicago Lawyer 37
Chicago Parent 69d
Chief Engineer 11
Chief Executive 12
Chief of Police 28a
Childhood Education 60
Children's Ministry 15
Chiropractic Economics 40
Choice 10a
Christian Century 15
Christian Retailing 10a
Christian Science Monitor 69
Christianity Today 15
The Chronicle Higher Education 60
The Chronicle of Philanthropy 12
Chronicle of the Horse 61c
Church Executive 15
Church Production 15
Cigar Aficionado 69c
Cigar Smoker Magazine 69c
Cincinnati Magazine 69f
Cincinnati Parent 69d
CIO 12
Circle Track & Racing Technology 4a
Circuit Cellar 19b
Circuits Assembly 19
Circulation 40
Cities & Villages 28b
Citrus & Vegetable Magazine 68f
Citrus Industry 68f
Civil Engineering 20
Civil War Times 69
Claims 34
Classic Toy Trains 26
Cleaner & Launderer 36
Cleaning & Maintenance Mgmt 11
Clergy Journal 15
Cleveland 69f
Cleveland Clinic Jrnl. Medicine 40
Climbing 61a
Clinical Lab Products 40
Clinical Psychiatry News 40
Clinician Reviews 40
Closets Magazine 29
Cloth Paper Scissors 26
Club Director 32
Club Industry 32
Club Management 32
CM/Cleanfax 33

CMJ New Music Monthly ... 45
Coal Age ... 43
Coal People ... 43
Coast Magazine ... 69f
Coast to Coast Magazine ... 65c
Coastal Living ... 69a
Coatings World ... 49
Coffee Business Solutions ... 9
Coin Prices ... 26b
Coin World ... 26b
Coinage ... 26b
Coins ... 26b
Collections & Credit Risk ... 12
College & Rsch. Libraries News ... 10a
College Planning & Management ... 60
Colorado Expression ... 69f
Colorado Homes & Lifestyles ... 69f
The Colorado Lawyer ... 37
Colorado Springs Business Jrnl. ... 12
ColoradoBiz ... 12
Columbia ... 25
Columbia Journalism Review ... 10b
Columbus CEO ... 12
Columbus Monthly ... 69f
Combat Handguns ... 57
Commentary ... 69
Commercial Building Products ... 11
Commercial Carrier Journal ... 4b
Commercial Construction & Renov. ... 11
Commercial Fisheries News ... 39a
Commercial Integrator ... 19
Commercial Property Executive ... 11
Commonweal ... 69
Communication Arts ... 10c
Communication World ... 1
Communications News ... 19b
Communications of ACM ... 19b
Communications Technology ... 58
Community College Journal ... 60
Community College Week ... 60
Community Oncology ... 40
Complex ... 69c
Compliance Week ... 12
Composites Manufacturing ... 54
Composites Technology ... 54
Compressor Tech Two ... 51
Computer ... 19b
Computer Shopper ... 19b
Computers in Libraries ... 19b
ComputerTalk for the Pharmacist ... 18
Computerworld ... 19b
Concrete Construction ... 3a
Concrete Decor ... 29
Concrete International ... 3a
The Concrete Producer ... 3a
Concrete Products ... 3a
Conde Nast Traveler ... 65
The Conference Board Review ... 12
Connected World ... 19b
Connecticut Law Tribune ... 37
Connecticut Magazine ... 69f
Conservationist ... 28c
Construction/Demolition Recyc. ... 20
Construction Equip. Distribution ... 20
Construction Equipment Guide ... 20
The Construction Specifier ... 20
Consultant ... 40
Consultant Pharmacist ... 18
Consulting-Specifying Engineer ... 20
Consumer Goods Technology ... 12a
Consumer Reports ... 69
Contact Lens Spectrum ... 47
Contemporary OB/GYN ... 40
Contingencies ... 34
Contingent Workforce Strategies ... 12
Contract ... 29
Contract Management ... 12
Contracting Business ... 55
Contractor ... 55
Control ... 20
Control Design ... 20
Control Engineering ... 20
Convene ... 65
Convenience Distribution ... 6
Convenience Store Decisions ... 27
Convenience Store News ... 27
ConventionSouth ... 65
Cooking Light ... 69g
Cooking With Paula Deen ... 69k
Cook's Illustrated ... 69k
The Cooling Journal ... 4
Coonhound Bloodlines ... 52
Cooperative Living ... 68c
Coping with Cancer ... 69g
Corn & Soybean Digest ... 68f
Cornea ... 47
Corporate & Incentive Travel ... 65
Corporate Meetings & Incentives ... 65
Correctional News ... 28a
Corrections Forum ... 28a
Corrections Today ... 28a
Corvette Fever ... 4a
Cosmetic Dermatology ... 40
Cosmetic Surgery Times ... 40
Cosmetic World ... 8
Cosmetics & Toiletries ... 8
Cosmopolitan ... 69b
Cosmopolitan En Espanol ... 69l
Cost Engineering ... 20
Cottages & Bungalows ... 69a
Cotton Farming ... 68
Cotton Grower ... 68
Counselor ... 1
Counterman ... 4
Country Folks ... 68
Country Gardens ... 30
Country Living ... 69a
Country Living Magazine ... 68c
Country Sampler ... 69a
Country Today ... 68
Country Weekly ... 45
Country Woman ... 68
County Magazine ... 28b
Courier ... 65
Cowman ... 68g
The CPA Journal ... 12
CPA Technology Advisor ... 19b
CPU Computer Power User ... 19b
CQ - Amateur Radio ... 58
CQ Weekly ... 28b
Crafts 'N Things ... 26
Crafts Report ... 26
Crain's Chicago Business ... 12
Crain's Cleveland Business ... 12
Crain's Detroit Business ... 12
Crain's NY Business ... 12
Create & Decorate ... 26
Creating Keepsakes ... 26
Creative ... 1
Creative Knitting ... 26
Credit Union Journal ... 7
Credit Union Magazine ... 7
Credit Union Management ... 7
Credit Union Times ... 7
Cremationist of North America ... 44
The Crisis ... 69h
Critical Care Nurse ... 31
CRM/Customer Relationship Mgmt. ... 1
CRN ... 19b
Crochet World ... 26
Crochet! ... 26
Crop Science ... 22
CropLife ... 22
Cross Country Skier ... 61e
Crossties ... 38
Cruise Travel ... 65
Cruising Outpost ... 39
Cruising World ... 39
CSP ... 27
Culture ... 69k
Culture & Travel ... 65
Cure Magazine ... 69g
Curious Parents ... 69d
Current ... 58
Currents ... 60
Curve ... 69i
Custom Classic Trucks ... 4
Custom Home ... 11
Custom Woodworking Business ... 29
Customer Magazine ... 19
Cutis ... 40
Cutting Tool Engineering ... 41
Cycle World ... 4c

D

D Magazine ... 69f
Dairy Foods ... 6
Dairy Goat Journal ... 68i
Dairy Herd Management ... 68a
Dairy Today ... 68a
Dairy World ... 68a
Dallas Business Journal ... 12
Dance Magazine ... 2
Dance Retailer News ... 12a
Dance Spirit ... 2
Dance Teacher ... 2
DAV Magazine ... 42
Dayspa ... 8
DDBC News ... 27
Dealer Communicator ... 10c
Dealernews ... 4c
Dealerscope ... 19
Decor ... 26
Deer & Deer Hunting ... 61a
Defense News ... 42
Defense Systems ... 28b
Defense Transportation Journal ... 64
Delaware Today ... 69f
Delicious Living! ... 69g
Delta Farm Press ... 68
Delta Sky ... 65a
Demolition ... 20
Dental Assistant Journal ... 17
Dental Economics ... 17
Dental Lab Products ... 17
Dental Products Report ... 17
Dental Tribune ... 17
Dentistry Today ... 17
Denver Business Journal ... 12
Dermatology Times ... 40
Des Moines Business Record ... 12
Design Solutions ... 3
Design/Build Business ... 11
Desktop Engineering ... 19b
Details ... 69c
Detroiter ... 12
Development ... 11
Diabetes Forecast ... 40
Diabetes Health Magazine ... 69g
Diabetes Self-Management ... 69g
Diabetic Cooking ... 69g
Diagnostic & Invasive Cardiology ... 40
Diagnostic Imaging ... 40
The Diapason ... 45
Die Casting Engineer ... 41
Diesel & Gas Turbine Worldwide ... 56
Diesel Progress ... 56
Digital Output ... 10c
Digital Photo ... 53
Digital Signage ... 58
Digital Video ... 58
The Director ... 44
Dirt Bike ... 4c
Dirt Sports ... 4a
Dirt Wheels ... 4c
Disaster Recovery Journal ... 12
Discover ... 69
Discovery Girls ... 69e
Display & Design Ideas ... 12a
District Administration ... 60
Dive Training ... 61d
Diverse ... 60
Diversion ... 40
DiversityInc ... 12
DJ Times ... 45
Direct Marketing News ... 1
The DO ... 40
Dr. Dobb's Journal ... 19b
Document ... 46
Dog Fancy ... 52
Doll Reader ... 26
Dollhouse Miniatures ... 26
Dolls ... 26
Doors & Hardware ... 11
Down Beat ... 45
Down East ... 69f
Draft Magazine ... 69k
Drag Racer ... 4a
Dramatics ... 2
Draperies & Window Coverings ... 29
Dressage Today ... 61c
Drilling Contractor ... 51
Drovers ... 68g
Drug Store News ... 18
Drug Topics ... 18
Drum Business ... 45
Drum Corps World ... 45
Ducks Unlimited ... 61a
Dune Buggies & Hot VWs ... 4a
DVM Newsmagazine ... 52
Dwell ... 69a
DWM/Shelter Magazine ... 11
Dynamic Chiropractic ... 40

E

E-The Environmental Magazine ... 28c
EAA Sport Aviation ... 5
Ear, Nose & Throat Journal ... 40
Earth ... 33b
East Bay Monthly ... 69f
Eastern DairyBusiness ... 68a
Eastern PA Business Jrnl ... 12
Easyriders ... 4c
Eating Well ... 69k
Ebony ... 69h
EC&M ... 19
Echo Magazine ... 69i

ECN 19
Eco-Structure 3
EcoHome 11
Economist 12
EContent 19b
Editor & Publisher 10b
Education Digest 60
Education Week 60
Egg Industry 68h
EHS Today 33a
850 Business Magazine 12
El Restaurante Mexicano 32
Electric Consumer 68c
Electric Light & Power 19
Electric Perspectives 19
Electrical Apparatus 19
Electrical Contractor 19
Electrical Wholesaling 19
Electroindustry 19
Electronic Design 19
Electronic House 69a
Electronic Musician 45
Electronic Products 19
Elevator World 11
Elks Magazine 25
Elle 69b
Elle Decor 69a
Emerald Coast 69f
Emergency Management 28b
Emergency Medicine 40
Empire State Report 28b
Employee Benefit News 12
EMS World Magazine 40
Encore Arts Programs 2
Energy Efficiency & Technology 19
Engagement Strategies 1
Engine Builder 4
Engineered Systems 55
Engineering & Mining Journal 43
EnLIGHTenment Magazine 29
ENR-Engineering News-Record 20
The Ensign 39
Entertainment Weekly 69
Environment 28c
Environmental Forum 37
Environmental Protection 28c
Environmental Science & Tech. 28c
EQ 45
Equip & Connect 15
Equipment Today 20
Equipment World 20
Equus 61c
Erosion Control 20
ESPN The Magazine 61
Essence Magazine 69h
European Car 4a
Event Solutions 12
Every Day with Rachael Ray 69k
Exchange and Commissary News 42
Exchange Today 25
Executive Golfer 61b
Exhibit Builder 12a
Eyecare Business 47

F

Fabric Architecture 3
Fabricator 41
Facilities Magazine 11
Facility Care 49
Fader 45
Fairfield Co. Business Journal 12
Fama Magazine 69l
Family Advocate 37
Family Business Magazine 12
Family Circle 69b
Family Dog 52
Family Handyman 69a
Family Magazine 42
Family Motor Coaching 65c
Family Practice Management 40
Family Practice News 40
Family Tree Magazine 26
Fancy Food & Culinary Products 23
Farm & Dairy 68
Farm & Ranch Guide 68
Farm Collector 26
Farm Equipment 68d
Farm Industry News 68
Farm Journal 68
Farm Jrnls. Implement & Tractor 68d
Farm Show 68
Farm Talk 68
Farm World 68
The Farmer-Stockman 68
Farmers' Advance 68
Farming 68
Farmshine 68
FarmWeek 68b
Fast Company 12
Fastener Technology Intl. 41
Federal Computer Week 19b
Federal Times 28b
Feed & Grain 21
Feed Management 21
Feedstuffs 21
Female Patient 40
Fence Post 68
FFA New Horizons 68
Field & Stream 61a
Fight! 61
Film Comment 2
Film Journal International 2
Film Score Monthly 2
Filtration News 33
Financial Analysts Journal 7
Financial Executive 7
Financial Planning 7
Fine Cooking 69k
Fine Gardening 30
Fine Homebuilding 11
Fine Woodworking 26
Finescale Modeler 26
Fire Apparatus & Emergency Equip 28a
Fire Chief 28a
Fire Engineering 28a
Fire Rescue Magazine 28a
Fired Arts & Crafts 13
Firehouse 28a
First For Women 69b
First Glimpse 19b
Fish Alaska 61a
Fish Farming News 39a
Fisheries 39a
Fisherman 61a
Fishermen's News 39a
Fishing Facts 61a
Fishing Tackle Retailer 61a
Fit Pregnancy 69d
Fit Yoga 69g
5280:The Denver Magazine 69f
Fleet Equipment 4b
Fleet Maintenance 4b
Fleet Owner 4b
Flex 69g
Flexible Packaging 48
Flexo 10c
Flight Journal 5
Flight Training 5
Floor Covering Installer 29
Floor Covering News 29
Floor Covering Weekly 29
Floor Focus 29
Floral Management 30
Florida Bar Journal 37
FL Cattleman & Livestock Jrnl. 68g
Florida CPA Today 12
Florida Grower 68f
Florida Monthly 69f
Florida Realtor 11
Florida Sportsman 61a
Florida Trend 12
FloridAgriculture 68b
Florists' Review 30
Flow Control 33
Flowers& Magazine 30
Fluid Power Journal 33
Flute Talk 45
Fly Fisherman 61a
Fly RC 26
Fly Rod & Reel 61a
Fly Tyer 61a
Flying 5
Flying Models 26
Foam 69b
FOAM Magazine 69b
Foghorn 39
Folio Magazine 10b
Food & Beverage Packaging 48
Food & Wine 69k
Food Arts 32
Food Engineering 23
Food Industry News 27
Food Logistics 32
Food Management 32
Food Manufacturing 23
Food Processing 23
Food Product Design 23
Food Quality 23
Food Safety Magazine 23
Foodservice Equipment & Supplies 32
Food Technology 23
Food World 23
Foodservice Director 32
Foodservice East 32
Foodservice Equipment Reports 32
Footwear News 24
Forbes 12
Fore 61b
Foreign Affairs 69
Forest Chemicals Review 38
Foreword Reviews 10a
Forging 41
Form Pioneering Design 3
Formulary 18
Fort Worth Business Press 12
Fortune 12
Foundry Mgmt. & Technology 41
4 Wheel & Off Road 4a
4 Wheel ATV Action Magazine 4c
4 Wheel Drive Magazine 4a
Four Wheeler 4a
FP Foreign Policy 69
FRA Today 42
Frame Building News 11
Freeskier 61e
Fresh Cut 23
Friends & Family 68b
Front Porch 68b
Frozen & Refrigerated Buyer 27
The Fruit Growers News 68f
Fuel Oil News 55
Full Cry 61a
Funworld 2
Fur-Fish-Game 61a
Furniture Today 29
Furniture World 29
Futures 7
The Futurist 69

G

GAMA International Journal 34
Game & Fish Magazine 61a
Game Developer 19b
Game Informer 19b
Games World of Puzzles 26
Garden & Gun 69f
Garden Center Magazine 30
Gardening How-To 30
Gas Engine 26
Gas Oil & Mining Contractor 51
Gas Turbine World 56
GCI 8
Gear Technology 41
General Aviation News 5
General Dentistry 17
General Surgery News 40
Genetic Engineering/Biotech News 33b
Genome Technology 33b
Gentry 69f
Geophysics 51
Georgia Cattleman 68g
Georgia Farm Bureau News 68b
Georgia Trend 12
GFWC Clubwoman 25
Gifted Child Quarterly 69d
Gifts & Decorative Accessories 26
Giftware News 26
Girls' Life 69e
Glamour 69b
Glass Art 13
Glass Craftsman 13
Glass Line 13
Glass Magazine 13
Global Traveler 65
Globe 69
Go 65a
Goat Rancher 68i
Gobbles 68h
Gold Coast Life 69f
Goldmine 45
Golf Business 61b
Golf Course Management 61b
Golf Digest 61b
Golf Getaways 61b
Golf Magazine 61b
Golf Range Magazine 61b
Golf Range Times 61b
Golf Tips 61b
Golf Today NW 61b
Golf World 61b
Golfdom 61b
Golfweek 61b
Good Fruit Grower 68f
Good Housekeeping 69b
Good Old Days 69
Gospel Today 45
Gourmet News 27

Gourmet Retailer 23
Governing 28b
Government Computer News 19b
Government Elearning! 19b
Government Executive 28b
Government Food Service 23
Government Procurement 28b
Government Product News 28b
Government Recreation & Fitness 61
Government Technology 19b
GPS World 5
GQ Gentlemen's Quarterly 69c
Grain Journal 21
Grand Magazine 69j
Grand Rapids Magazine 69f
Grand Rapids Business Journal 12
Graphic Design: USA 10c
Grass & Grain 68
Grassroots Motorsports 4a
Gravure 10c
Gray's Sporting Journal 61a
Great Lakes Boating 39
Greater Charlotte Biz 12
Green Builder 11
Green Building Product Dealer 11
Greenhouse Grower 30
Greenhouse Management 30
Greenhouse Product News 30
GreenSource 11
Greenwich Magazine 69f
Greetings Etc. 12a
Griffin Report 27
Grit Magazine 69
Grocery Headquarters 27
Groomer to Groomer 52
Ground Water 28d
Group 15
Group Travel Leader 65
Grower Talks 30
Growing 68
Guideposts 15
Guitar Player 45
Guitar World 45
Gulfshore Life 69f
Gun Digest 57
Gun Dog 61a
Guns Magazine 57

H

Habitat 11
Hadassah Magazine 15
Hampton Roads 69f
Handball 61
Handloader 57
Hang Gliding & Paragliding 61
HAPPI/Household & PP Industry 14
Hardware Retailing 12a
Hardwood Floors 29
The Harmonizer 45
Harper's Magazine 69
Harvard Business Review 12
Hawaii Business 12
Hawai'i Magazine 69f
Hay & Forage Grower 68
Health 69g
Health Data Management 31
Health Facilities Mgmt. 31
Health Insurance Underwriter 34
Health Management Technology 31
Healthcare Building Ideas 11
Healthcare Executive 31
Healthcare Financial Mgmt. 31
Healthcare IT News 31
Healthcare Jrnl. of New Orleans 40
HealthLeaders 31
Healthy Aging 69j
The Healthy Planet 69g
Hearing Journal 40
Heart & Soul 69h
Hype Hair 69h
Heartland Boating 39
Heavy Duty Trucking 4b
Hemispheres 65a
Hemmings Classic Car 4a
Hemmings Motor News 4a
Hemmings Muscle Machines 4a
Hereford World 68g
HFN Home Furnishings News 29
HGTV Magazine 69a
High Country News 69f
High Plains Journal 68
High Times 69
Highways 65c
Hinduism Today 15
Hispanic Business 12
Hispanic Executive 12

HME Business 40
Hoard's Dairyman 68a
Hobby Farms 26
Hobby Merchandiser 26
Hollywood Reporter 2
Holstein World 68a
Home Business 12
Home Channel News 11
Home Education Magazine 60
Home Healthcare Nurse 31
Home Shop Machinist 26
Home Textiles Today 29
HomeCare 40
Homecoming Magazine 15
Homeland Security Today 28b
HomeWorld Business 29
Homiletic & Pastoral Review 15
Honda Tuning 4a
Honolulu 69f
Hoof Beats 61c
Hoop Magazine 61
Hope Today 15
Horn Book Magazine 10a
Horological Times 35
Horse & Rider 61c
Horse Illustrated 61c
Horseman and Fair World 61c
Horticulture 30
Hospital Pharmacy Journal 18
Hospitality Design 32
Hospitality Technology 32
Hospitals & Health Networks 31
Hot Bike 4c
Hot Rod Magazine 4a
Hotel & Motel Management 32
Hotel Business 32
Hotel Design 32
Hotels Magazine 32
House Beautiful 69a
Houseboat 39
Houston Business Journal 12
How 10c
HPAC Engineering 55
HR Magazine 12
Hudson Valley 69f
Hudson Valley Business Digital 12
Human Resource Executive 12
Hunting Illustrated 61a
HVACR Business 55
Hydraulics & Pneumatics 33
Hydro Review 56
Hydrocarbon Processing 51

I

I Love Cats 52
IAEI News 19
The IAPD Magazine 54
ICCFA Magazine 44
ICIS Chemical Business 14
ICMJ Prospecting & Mining Jrnl. 43
ICS Cleaning Specialist 29
Idea Fitness Journal 61
IEEE Industry Applications 33
IEEE Internet Computing 19b
IEEE Security & Privacy 19b
IEEE Software 19b
IEEE Spectrum 19
IGA Grocergram 27
IHS Chemical Week 14
Illinois Bar Journal 37
Illinois Beef 68g
Illinois Country Living 68c
Illinois Pharmacist 18
Imaging Technology News 40
Imbibe 69k
Import Automotive Parts/Accessor 4
ImportCar 4
Impressions 16
IMSA Journal 28b
IN 34
In-Fisherman 61a
In New York 69f
In-Plant Graphics 10c
In the Wind 4c
In These Times 69
In Touch Weekly 69
Inbound Logistics 64
Inc. Magazine 12
Incentive 1
Independent Agent 34
Independent Banker 7
Independent Cable News 58
The Independent Restaurateur 32
Indiana Beef 68g
Indiana Lawyer 37
Indiana Prairie Farmer 68

Indianapolis Business Journal 12
Indianapolis Monthly 69f
Indoor Comfort Marketing 55
Indoor Comfort News 55
Industrial Engineer 33
Industrial Equipment News 33
Specialty Fabrics Review 62
Industrial Fire World 28a
Industrial Heating 41
Industrial Hygiene News 33a
Industrial Laser Solutions 41
Industrial Maintenance/Plant Op. 33
Industrial Safety & Hygiene News 33a
IndustryWeek 12
Indy's Child Parenting Magazine 69d
Infection Control Today 40
Infectious Disease News 40
Infectious Diseases In Children 40
Inform 14
Information Management 19b
Informationweek 19b
Infostor 19b
Ink World 10c
Inked Magazine 69c
Inland Empire 69f
Inside Gymnastics 61
Inside Pool 61
Inside Self-Storage 64
Inside Supply Management 12
InsideCounsel 37
Instinct 69i
Institutional Investor 7
InStyle 69b
Insurance & Technology 34
Insurance Networking News 34
Intech 19
Interior Design 29
Interiors & Sources 29
Interiorscape 30
Internal Auditor 12
Internal Medicine News 40
Int'l. Bowling Industry 61
International Fiber Journal 62
International Figure Skating 61e
International Musician 45
Internet Retailer 19b
Internet Telephony 19b
Interview Magazine 2
Investment Advisor 7
Investor's Business Daily 12
Iowa Cattleman 68g
Iowa Farmer Today 68
Iowa Outdoors 69f
Iowa Pork Producer 68i
The Iowan 69f
iPhone Life 19b
Iron & Steel Technology 41
IronWorks 4c
Irrigation & Green Industry 30
Islands 65
ISTA Advocate 60

J

J-14 Magazine 69e
Jack O'Dwyer's Newsletter 1
Jacksonville 69f
Jax Fax Travel Marketing 65
Jazziz Magazine 45
JazzTimes 45
JCT CoatingsTech 49
JDMS 19b
Jersey Journal 68a
Jet 69h
Jewelers' Circular-Keystone 35
Jewelry Artist 26
Jewish Action 15
Jewish Exponent 15
Jewish Journal 15
Jewish Post & Opinion 15
Jewish Press 15
Jewish Week 15
JOM 41
Jrnl. Accountancy 12
Jrnl. Advertising Research 1
Jrnl. Amer. Dental Assn. 17
Jrnl. Amer. Dietetic Assn. 31
Jrnl. American Medical Assn. 40
Jrnl. Amer. Osteopathic Assn. 40
Jrnl. Amer. Veterinary Med. Assn 52
Jrnl. AWWA 28d
Jrnl. Bone/Joint Surgery 40
Jrnl. Chemical Education 14
Jrnl. Clinical Orthodontics 17
Jrnl. Clinical Outcomes Mgmt. 40
Jrnl. Commerce 12
Jrnl. Cosmetic Science 8

Jrnl. Court Reporting 46
Jrnl. Emergency Nursing 31
Jrnl. Endodontics 17
Jrnl. Environmental Health 28c
Jrnl. Equine Veterinary Science 52
Jrnl. Family Practice 40
Jrnl. Financial Planning 7
Jrnl. Finan. Svc. Professionals 34
Jrnl. Forestry 38
Jrnl. Gerontological Nursing 31
Jrnl. Light Construction 11
Jrnl. Midwifery & Women's Health 31
Jrnl. Natl. Medical Assn. 40
Jrnl. Nuclear Medicine 40
Jrnl. Nursing Administration 31
Jrnl. Nursing Education 31
Jrnl. Oral/Maxillofacial Surgery 17
Jrnl. Pediatric Nursing 31
Jrnl. Pediatrics 40
Jrnl. Periodontology 17
Jrnl. Petroleum Technology 51
Jrnl. Property Mgmt. 11
Jrnl. Prosthetic Dentistry 17
Jrnl. Protective Coatings/Lining 49
Jrnl. Reproductive Medicine 40
Jrnl. Taxation 7
JTNews 15
Junior Scholastic 69e
Junior Shooters 57
Just CrossStitch 26
Just Jazz Guitar 45
Just Labs 52
Just Out 69i
Justine 69e
Juxtapoz 26a

K

Kansas City Business Journal 12
Kansas Country Living 68c
Kansas Farmer 68
Kansas Stockman 68g
Kashrus Magazine 69k
KC Magazine 69f
KEA News 60
Kentucky Living 68c
Kentucky Monthly 69f
Key Club Magazine 25
Keyboard Magazine 45
Kiplinger's Personal Finance 12
Kitchen & Bath Business 29
Kitchen & Bath Design News 29
KitPlanes 5
Kiwanis Magazine 25
Knit 'N Style 26
Knives Illustrated 61a
KoreAm Journal 69
Kosher Spirit 15
Kyria 15

L

La Cucina Italiana 69k
Lab Animal 33b
Lab Management Today 17
Label & Narrow Web 48
LabMedicine 40
Laboratory Equipment 33b
Lacrosse Magazine 61
Ladies' Home Journal 69b
Lakeland Boating 39
Lancaster Farming 68
Lancet 40
Land 68
Land & Water 28c
Land Line 4b
Landings Magazine 11
Landscape & Irrigation 30
Landscape Architecture 30
Landscape Contractor 30
Landscape Management 30
Laptop 19b
Las Vegas Business Press 12
Laser Focus World 19
Late Model Digest 4a
Latina 69l
Latina Style 69b
LatinFinance 7
Laundry Today 36
Lavender Magazine 69i
Law & Order 28a
Law Enforcement Product News 28a
Law Enforcement Technology 28a
Law Officer Magazine 28a
Law Practice 37
Law Technology News 37
Lawn & Landscape 30
Lawyers USA 37
LC GC North America 33b
LDB Interior Textiles 29
League of Amer. Bicyclists Mag. 4c
Leather Crafters & Saddlers Jrnl 24
Leatherneck 42
Legal Intelligencer 37
Legal Management 37
Lesbian News 69i
LI & Business 12
Library Journal 10a
Library Media Connection 10a
License! 1
Licensing Book 1
Life + Dog 52
Life Extension 69g
Life Insurance Selling 34
Light & Medium Truck 4b
Light Metal Age 41
Light Sport & Ultralight Flying! 5
Lighting Design & Application 19
Lightwave 19
Liguorian 15
Limousin World 68g
Limousine Digest 4b
Links 61b
Linn's Stamp News 26
The LION 25
Live Design 2
Live Steam & Outdoor Railroading 26
Livestock Market Digest 68g
Living Church 15
Living the Country Life 69a
Locksmith Ledger International 33
Locomotive Engineers/Trainmen Ne 59
LocumLife 40
Lodging 32
Log 39
Log Home Living 69a
Loggers World 38
Logistics Management 64
Logistics Today 64
Long Beach Business Journal 12
Long Island Business News 12
Los Angeles Business Journal 12
Los Angeles Lawyer 37
Los Angeles Magazine 69f
Louisiana Country 68c
Louisville 69f
Lovin' Life After 50 .... 69j
Lowrider 4
LPGas 51
Lubes 'N Greases 33
Lucky 69b
The Lutheran 15

M

M Magazine 69e
Machine Design 33
Machinist's Workshop 26
MacLife 19b
MacTech 19b
Macworld 19b
Madison Magazine 69f
Magnet 45
Mailing Systems Technology 46
Maine Educator 60
Maintenance Sales News 11
Maintenance Solutions 11
Maintenance Supplies 11
Maintenance Technology 33
Managed Care 40
Managed Healthcare Executive 31
Manufacturers' Mart 33
Manufacturing Engineering 41
Marie Claire 69b
Marina Dock Age 39
Marine Corps Gazette 42
Marine Corps Times 42
Marine Log 39
Marine News 39
Markee 2.0 2
Market Watch 9
Marketing Management 1
Marketing News 1
Marlin Magazine 61a
Martha Stewart Living 69a
Martha Stewart Weddings 69b
Maryland Physician 40
Maryland/Wash. Beverage Jrnl. 9
Masonry 3a
Mass Market Retailers 12a
Mass Transit 28b
Massachusetts Lawyers Weekly 37
Material Handling & Logistics 33
Material Handling Network 33
Materials Evaluation 33
Maxim 69c
Maximum PC 19b
Mayo Clinic Proceedings 40
MB News 44
MEA-MFT Today 60
MEA Voice 60
Meat & Poultry 23a
Meat Goat Monthly News 68i
Meatingplace 23a
Mechanical Engineering 33
Med Ad News 1
Medical Design 40
Medical Design Technology 40
Medical Device/Diagnostic Ind. 40
Medical Economics 40
Medical Marketing & Media 1
Medical Meetings 40
Meetings & Conventions 1
Memphis 69f
Memphis Business Journal 12
Men of Integrity 15
Men's Fitness 69c
Men's Health 69c
Men's Journal 69c
Mental Floss 69
Mergers & Acquisitions 7
Message Magazine 15
Metal Architecture 3
Metal Center News 41
Metal Construction News 11
Metal Finishing 41
MetalForming 41
Metro Magazine 28b
Metro Parent 69d
MetroKids 69d
Metroline Magazine 69i
Metropolis Magazine 69a
Metropolitan Corporate Counsel 37
Michigan Agent 34
Michigan Farm News 68b
Michigan Farmer 68
Michigan Lawyers Weekly 37
Michigan Milk Messenger 68a
Michigan Out-Of-Doors 61a
Microwave Journal 19
Microwave Product Digest 19
Microwaves & RF 19
Middle School Journal 60
Midstream 15
Midwest Living 69f
Midwest Real Estate News 11
Military 42
Military & Aerospace Electronics 19
Military Club & Hospitality 42
The Military Engineer 20
Military Heritage 69
Military Money 42
Military Officer 42
Military Spouse 42
Military Trader 42
Millimeter 58
Milling & Baking News 6
Milling Journal 21
Milwaukee Magazine 69f
Miners News 43
Mines Magazine 43
Mini Truckin' 4b
Miniature Collector 26
Mining Engineering 43
Ministry Today 15
Minnesota Cities Magazine 28b
Minnesota Monthly 69f
Minority Business Entrepreneur 12
Minority Nurse 31
Mission Critical Magazine 19
Mississippi Business Journal 12
Mississippi Educator 60
Mississippi Farm Country 68b
Mississippi Magazine 69f
Missouri Lawyers Weekly 37
Missouri Life 69f
Missouri Ruralist 68
MIT Technology Review 33b
Mix 58
MJSA Journal 35
MMA Magazine 61
Mobile Beat 45
Mobile Electronics 19
Mobile Enterprise 19b
Model Airplane News 26
Model Cars 26
Model Railroader 26
Model Retailer 26
Modern Casting 41
Modern Healthcare 31

Modern Machine Shop	41
Modern Materials Handling	33
Modern Metals	41
Modern Painters	26a
Modern Salon	8
Modern Steel Construction	20
Modern Tire Dealer	4
Modified	4
Moment Magazine	15
Money	69
Monitor on Psychology	40
Monitoring Times	58
Montana Magazine	69f
Montana Outdoors	69f
Montana Wool Grower	68i
Moose Magazine	25
More	69b
The Morgan Horse	61c
Mortgage Banking	7
Mortgage Servicing News	7
Mortuary Management	44
Mother Earth Living	69a
Mother Earth News	69
Mother Jones	69
Mothering	69d
Motor Age	4
Motor Magazine	4
Motor Trend	4
Motorcycle & Powersports News	4c
Motorcycle Cruiser	4c
Motorcycle Industry	4c
Motorcyclist	4c
MotorHome	65c
Mountain Bike Action	4c
Mountain Living	69a
Mountain Magazine	61a
MovieMaker	2
Movin' Out	4b
Mpls-St. Paul	69f
MR.	16
Ms.	69b
MSW Management	28d
MTA Today	60
Multichannel News	58
Multifamily Executive	11
Muscle & Fitness	61
Mushing	61
Music & Sound Retailer	45
Music Connection	45
Music Educators Journal	45
Music Inc.	45
Music Trades	45
Musical Merchandise Review	45
Modified Mustangs & Fords	4
Mustang Monthly	4
Mutineer Magazine	69k
Muzzleloader	61a
My Daily Visitor	15
NAEDA Equipment Dealer	68d
Nailpro	8
Nails	8
NASA Tech Briefs	5
NASCAR Illustrated	4a
Nashville Business Journal	12
The Nation	69

N

National Catholic Register	15
National Catholic Reporter	15
National Clothesline	36
National Defense	42
National Dipper	6
National Enquirer	69
National Fisherman	39a
National Floor Trends	29
National Geographic	69
National Geographic Kids	69e
National Geographic Traveler	65
National Guard	42
National Hardwood Magazine	38
National Hog Farmer	68i
National Jeweler	35
National Law Journal	37
National Locksmith	33
National Mortgage News	7
National Paralegal Reporter	37
National Petroleum News	51
National Provisioner	23a
National Real Estate Investor	11
National Review	69
National Speed Sport News	4a
Natl. Underwriter-Life & Health	34
The Nation's Health	40
Nation's Restaurant News	32
Native Peoples	69
Natural Food Network	23

Natural Foods Merchandiser	23
Natural Health	69g
Natural History	69
Natural Horse	61c
Natural Solutions	69g
Nature Biotechnology	33b
Naval History	42
Naval Institute Proceedings	42
Navy Times	42
NEA Today	60
Nebraska Cattleman	68g
Nebraska Farm Bureau News	68b
Nebraska Farmer	68
Needlework Retailer	26
Neighbors	68
Nephrology News & Issues	40
Nephrology Nursing Journal	31
Network Computing	19b
The Network Journal	12
Network Marketing Business Jrnl.	12
Network World	19b
Neurology	40
Neurology Now	40
Nevada Magazine	69f
New Accountant	12
New Equipment Digest	33
New Hampshire Business Review	12
New Hampshire Magazine	69f
New Jersey Business	12
New Jersey Countryside	69f
New Jersey Law Journal	37
New Jersey Monthly	69f
New Jersey Municipalities	28b
New Mexico Magazine	69f
New Mexico Stockman	68g
New Mobility	69
New Orleans Magazine	69f
New Physician	40
The New Republic	69
New York Law Journal	37
New York Magazine	69
NY Metro Parents	69d
New York Review of Books	10a
New York Spaces	69a
New York State Bar Jrnl.	37
New York State Dental Jrnl.	17
New Yorker	69
Newport Life	69f
News Photographer	53
Newspapers & Technology	10b
Newsweek	69
Next Magazine	69i
NextStepU	69e
NFPA Journal	28a
Nightclub & Bar	32
9-1-1 Magazine	28a
NJBIZ	12
NJEA Review	60
NonProfit Times	12
Nonwovens Industry	62
North American Fisherman	61a
North American Hunter	61a
North American Whitetail	61a
North American Windpower	56
North Dakota Living	68c
North Shore	69f
Northern Logger/Timber Processor	38
NSEA Voice	60
NSTA Reports	60
Nuclear News	56
Nuclear Plant Journal	56
Numismatic News	26b
Numismatist	26b
Nursery Management	30
Nursery Retailer	30
Nursing Economics	31
Nursing Education Perspectives	31
Nursing Management	31
Nursing2014	31
Nutrition & Foodservice Edge	32
Nutrition Industry Executive	27
Nutrition Today	69g
Nuts & Volts	19
Nylon	69b
Nylon Guys	69c
NYSUT United	60

O

O Gauge Railroading	26
O, The Oprah Magazine	69b
OB. GYN. News	40
OBG Management	40
Obstetrics & Gynecology	40
Occupational Health & Safety	33a
Ocean Drive	69f
Ocean Home	69a

Ocean Navigator	39
Ocean News & Technology	39
O'Dwyer's Magazine	1
Off-Road	4a
Office Technology	46
OfficePro	46
The Officer	42
Offshore	51
Ohio Farmer	68
Ohio Lawyer	37
Ohio Magazine	69f
Ohio Schools	60
Ohio Tavern News	9
Oil & Gas Journal	51
Oil, Gas & Petrochem Equipment	51
Oklahoma Living	68c
Oklahoma Magazine	69f
Old Cars Weekly	4a
Old House Journal	69a
On-Campus Hospitality	32
On Patrol	42
On Premise	9
On Wall Street	7
Oncology News International	40
Oncology Nursing Forum	31
Oncology Times	40
Oncourse	15
OnFitness	69g
Onion World	68f
Opera News	2
Ophthalmology	47
Ophthalmology Times	47
Optics & Photonics News	33b
Optimist	25
Optometric Management	47
Oracle Magazine	19b
Orange Coast Magazine	69f
Orange County Business Journal	12
Orchids	30
Oregon Business	12
Oregon Coast	69f
Oregon Grange Bulletin	68b
Organic Gardening	30
Organic Spa Magazine	65
Origination News	7
Orlando	69f
Orlando Business Journal	12
Orthopedics	40
Our Animals	52
Our Sunday Visitor	15
Our Wisconsin	69f
Out	69i
Out Traveler	69i
Outdoor Life	61a
Outdoor Photographer	53
Outdoor Power Equipment	30
Outreach Magazine	15
Outside	61
Over the Road	4b
Overdrive	4b
Overhaul & Maintenance	5

P

P3 Update	2
Pacific Business News	12
Pacific Fishing	39a
Pacific Nut Producer	68f
Pacific Standard	69
Package Printing	10c
Packaging Digest	48
Packaging World	48
The Packer	68f
Paddling Life	61d
Pageantry	69b
Paint & Coatings Industry	49
Paint & Decorating Retailer	49
The Paint Contractor	49
The Paint Dealer	49
Paint Horse Journal	61c
Painters & Allied Trades Journal	49
PaintWorks	26
Pallet Enterprise	38
Palm Beach Illustrated	69f
Palm Beacher	69f
Palm Springs Life	69f
Panel World	38
Paper Age	50
Paper Crafts Magazine	26
Paper Creations	26
Paper360	50
Paperboard Packaging	48
Papercity Dallas	69f
Papercity Houston	69f
Parabola Magazine	15
Parachutist	61
Paralegal Today	37

Parents Magazine............69d
Parking............20
The Parking Professional............20
Parking Today............20
Parks & Recreation............28b
PassageMaker............39
Paste Magazine............45
Pastel Journal............26a
Pastoral Music............45
Pathfinders Travel............69h
Pavement............20
PC Magazine............19b
PC World............19b
PCI Journal............3a
PDB Magazine............39
PE & RS............20
PE Magazine............20
Peanut Grower............68f
Pecan South............68f
Pediatric News............40
Pediatric Nursing............31
Pediatrics............40
Penn Lines............68c
Pennsylvania Bar News............37
Pennsylvania Township News............28b
Pensions & Investments............7
People............69
People en Espanol............69l
Percussive Notes............45
Performance Racing Industry............4a
Perfumer & Flavorist............14
Perishables Buyer............23
Personal Fitness Professional............69g
Pest Control Technology............11
Pest Management Professional............11
Pet Age............52
Pet Business............52
Pet Product News Intl............52
Petersen's Bowhunting............61a
Petfood Industry............52
Pharma. & Medical Packaging News............48
Pharmaceutical Engineering............18
Pharmaceutical Executive............18
Pharmaceutical Processing............18
Pharmacy and Therapeutics............18
Pharmacy Practice News............18
Pharmacy Times............18
Pharmacy Today............18
Pharmacy Week............18
Pheasants Forever............61a
Phi Delta Kappan............60
Philadelphia Business Journal............12
Philadelphia Magazine............69f
Philadelphia Weekly............69f
Philanthropy............69
Phoenix............69f
Phoenix Home & Garden............69a
Photo District News............53
Photo Technique............53
Photographer's Forum............53
Photoshop User............53
Photovoltaics World............19
Physical Therapy............40
Physical Therapy Products............40
Physicians Practice............40
Physics Teacher............60
Physics Today............33b
PI Magazine............28a
Picture Framing Magazine............26a
PieceWork............26
Pink Magazine............69i
Pink Sheet............18
Pipeline & Gas Journal............51
Pipers Magazine............5
Pipes and Tobaccos............63
Pit and Quarry............3a
Pittsburgh............69f
Pittsburgh Business Times............12
Pizza Today............23
Plane & Pilot............5
Planning............28b
Plant Engineering............33
Plant Services............33
Plantfinder............30
Plastic Surgery News............40
Plastic Surgery Practice............40
Plastics Engineering............54
Plastics News............54
Plastics Technology............54
Plastics Today............54
Plate............32
Plating & Surface Finishing............41
Playbill............2
Playboy............69c
Plumbing & Mechanical............55

Plumbing Engineer............55
PM Engineer............55
PMA Magazine............53
POB Point Of Beginning............20
Podiatry Today............40
Poets & Writers Magazine............10b
Pointe Magazine............2
Police............28a
Police & Security News............28a
Police Chief............28a
Police Fleet Manager............4b
Police Times............28a
Pollution Engineering............28c
Pollution Equipment News............28c
Pool & Spa Living............69a
Pool & Spa News............61d
Popular Communications............58
Popular Hot Rodding............4a
Popular Mechanics............69c
Popular Photography............53
Popular Science............69
Popular Woodworking............26
Pork............68i
Pork Checkoff Report............68i
Porthole Cruise............65
Portland Monthly............69f
Post............2
Potato Grower............68f
Pottery Making Illustrated............13
Poultry Times............68h
Powder............61e
Powder and Bulk Engineering............14
Powder/Bulk Solids............14
Powder Coating............41
Power & Motoryacht............39
Power Engineering............56
Power Equipment Trade............30
PowerGrid International............19
Powerlifting USA............61
Powersports Business............61
POZ............69g
PQ Monthly............69i
PR News............1
PR Week............1
Practical Horseman............61c
Practical Real Estate Lawyer............37
Practical Welding Today............41
PracticeLink Magazine............40
Prairie Farmer............68
Precision Engine............4
Predator Xtreme............61a
Prepared Foods............23
Presbyterians Today............15
Presstime............10b
Prevention............69g
The Priest............15
Primary Care Optometry News............47
Principal............60
Print Magazine............10c
Print Professional............10c
Print Solutions............10c
Printing Impressions............10c
Printing News............10c
Printwear............62
Private Clubs............32
Private Label Buyer............27
Private Label Store Brands............27
Pro............30
Pro Audio Review............58
Pro AV............58
Pro Sound News............58
Probate & Property............37
Processing............14
Produce Business............68f
Produce News............27
Produce Retailer............27
Product Design & Development............33
Products Finishing............41
Professional Artist............26a
Professional BoatBuilder............39
Professional Builder............11
Professional Carwashing/Detail............4
Professional Insurance Agents............34
Professional Mariner............39
Professional Photographer............53
Professional Pilot............5
Professional Remodeler............11
Professional Roofing............11
Professional Safety............33a
Professional Surveyor............20
Professional Tool & Equip. News............4
Profit............12
The Progressive............69
Progressive Farmer............68
Progressive Grocer............27

Progressive Railroading............59
Projection Lights Staging News............2
Promotional Products Business............1
Prosales............11
Providence Business News............12
Provider............40
PSA Journal............53
Psychiatric News............40
Psychiatric Times............40
Psychology Today............69
Psychotherapy Networker............40
PT In Motion............40
Public CIO............28b
Public Gaming International............2
Public Health Reports............40
Public Power............56
Public Relations Tactics............1
Public Utilities Fortnightly............56
Public Works Magazine............28b
Publishers' Auxiliary............10b
Publishers Weekly............10a
Publishing Executive............10c
Pumps & Systems............33

Q

QSR Magazine............32
QST............58
Qualified Remodeler............11
Quality............33
Quality Assurance & Food Safety............23
Quality Progress............33
Que Onda!............69i
Quick Printing............10c
Quill............10b
Quilt Magazine............26
Quilter's World............26
Quintessence Intl............17
Quirks Marketing Rsch Review............1

R

R & D............33b
R&D Directions............18
Racquet Sports Industry............61
Racquetball............61
Radio Control Car Action............26
Radio Ink............58
Radio Magazine............58
Radio World............58
Radiology............40
Ragan Report............1
Railfan & Railroad............59
Railroad Model Craftsman............26
Railway Age............59
Railway Track & Structures............59
Ranch & Rural Living............68i
Rangefinder............53
RC Car............26
RC Driver............26
RDH............17
Reader's Digest............69
The Reading Teacher............60
Reading Today............60
Real Estate Finance & Investment............7
Real Estate Forum............11
Real Estate Magazine............11
Real Estate News............11
Real Fighter............61
Real Living w/Multiple Sclerosis............31
Real Simple............69b
Realtor Magazine............11
Reason Magazine............69
Rebel Ink............69
Recommend............65
Record Stockman............68g
Recording............45
Recreation News............65
Recycling Today............41
Redmond............19b
Reeves Journal............55
Referee............61
Reform Judaism............15
Refrigerated Transporter............4b
Regulation............12
Rehab Management............40
Rehabilitation Counsel. Bulletin............40
Rehabilitation Nursing............31
Religious Conference Manager............15
Reminisce Magazine............69
Remodeling............11
Remodeling News............11
Render............23a
Renewable Energy World............56
Rental Equipment Register............12
Rental Management............12
Rental Product News............12
Replay Magazine............2

Reptiles....52
Research....7
Residential Architect....3
Residential Bldg. Products & Tec....11
Residential Design & Build....11
Residential Lighting....29
Residential Systems....19
Resource....34
Resource Recycling....28c
Respiratory Care....40
Response....1
Restaurant Business....32
Restaurant Development & Design....32
Restaurant Hospitality....32
Restaurant Startup & Growth....32
Restyling....4
Retail Info Systems....12a
Retail Merchandiser....12a
Retail Observer....19a
Retail Traffic....12a
Retailer NOW....29
Retailing Today....12a
REV! Magazine....15
The Review....28b
Revolver....45
Rice Farming....68
Richmond Magazine....69f
Ride BMX....4c
Rider....4c
Rides Magazine....4
Rifle....57
Rinksider....2
Risk & Insurance....34
Risk Management....34
Road & Track....4a
Road King....4b
Roadbike....4c
Roads & Bridges....20
Robb Report....69
Rochester Business Journal....12
Rock & Gem....26
Rock and Dirt....3a
Rock Products....3a
Rod & Custom Magazine....4a
Roller Skating Business....2
Rolling Stone....45
Romantic Homes....69a
Roofing Contractor....11
Rotarian....25
Rotor & Wing....5
Rough Notes....34
RSES Journal....55
RSI Magazine....11
RT....40
Rubber & Plastics News....33
Rubber World....33
Rugby Magazine....61
Runner's World....61
Running Times....61
Rural Builder....11
Rural Electric Magazine....56
Rural Electric Nebraskan....68c
Rural Lifestyle Dealer....68d
Rural Missouri....68c
Rural Montana....68c
Ruralite....68c
RV Business....65c
RV Pro....65c

S

Sacramento....69f
Sacramento Business Journal....12
Saddle & Bridle....61c
SAE Update....4
Safety & Health....33a
Sail....39
Sailing....39
Sailing World....39
St. Anthony Messenger....15
Sales & Marketing Management....1
Salon Today....8
SalonSense Magazine....8
Salt Lake....69f
Salt Water Sportsman....61a
Salute....42
San Antonio Business Journal....12
San Diego Business Journal....12
San Diego Home/Garden Lifestyles....69a
San Diego Magazine....69f
San Diego Metropolitan....12
San Francisco....69f
San Francisco Business Times....12
Sanitary Maintenance....11
Sarasota Magazine....69f
Saturday Evening Post....69g
Saveur Magazine....69k
Scale Auto....26
Scholastic Early Childhood Today....60
Scholastic Parent & Child....69d
School Bus Fleet....4b
School Business Affairs....60
School Library Journal....10a
School Nutrition....60
School Planning & Management....60
SchoolArts....60
Science....33b
Science & Children....60
Science News....33b
The Science Teacher....60
Scientific American....69
Scientific Computing....19b
Scientist....33b
Scouting....69e
Scrap....41
Scrap & Stamp Arts....26
Screen Printing Magazine....10c
Script Magazine....2
Scuba Diving....61d
Sculpture Magazine....26a
Sea Classics....69
Sea Kayaker....61d
Sea Magazine....39
Sea Technology....39
Seafood Business....23
Seapower....42
Seattle Business Monthly....12
Seattle Magazine....69f
Secondary Marketing Executive....7
Security....33a
Security Dealer & Integrator....33a
Security Distributing & Mktg.....33a
Security Management....33a
Security Products....33a
Security Sales & Integration....33a
Security Systems News....33a
Security Technology Executive....33a
Seed World....68
Self....69b
Selling Power....1
Ser Padres....69l
Sergeants Magazine....42
Servo Magazine....19
Seventeen....69e
Sew Beautiful....26
Sew News....26
Shape....69g
She Magazine....69i
Sheep....68i
Sheep Industry News....68i
Shelby Report....27
The Shepherd....68i
Sheriff....28a
Shooting Industry....57
Shooting Sportsman....61a
Shooting Times....57
Shopper Marketing....1
Shopping Center Business....12a
Shopping Centers Today....12a
Shotgun Sports....61a
Shutterbug....53
Siempre Mujer!....69l
Sierra....28c
Sign & Digital Graphics....10c
Sign Builder Illustrated....1
Signal....42
Signalman's Journal....59
Signature Kitchens & Baths....69a
Signcraft....1
Significant Living....15
Signs Of The Times....1
Silent Sports....61
Silicon Vly Business Journal....12
Simply the Best....69f
Sister 2 Sister....69h
Site Selection....11
SKATING Magazine....61e
Skeptical Inquirer....33b
Ski Area Management....61e
Ski Magazine....61e
Ski Racing....61e
Skiing Magazine....61e
Skin & Allergy News....40
Skin & Ink....69
Skin Inc. Magazine....8
Sky & Telescope....26
SLAM....61
Small Business Opportunities....12
Smart Computing....19b
Smart Meetings....12
SmartMoney....69
Smithsonian....69
Smoke....69c
Smokeshop....63
SMPTE Journal....58
Snack Food & Wholesale Bakery....23
Snips Magazine....55
Snowboard Magazine....61e
Snowboarder....61e
SnoWest....61e
Soap Opera Digest....69b
Soccer America....61
Social Education....60
The Social Media Monthly....19b
Softwood Forest Prod. Buyer....38
Soil Science....22
Solid State Technology....19
Sound & Communications....58
Sound & Vibration....20
Sound & Video Contractor....58
Sound & Vision....58
South Carolina Farmer....68b
South Carolina Living....68c
South Dakota Magazine....69f
South Florida Business Journal....12
South Shore Living....69f
Southeast Farm Press....68
Southeast Food Service News....32
Southeastern Peanut Farmer....68f
Southern Beverage Jrnl.....9
Southern Boating....39
Southern Farmer....68
Southern Jewelry News....35
Southern Lady....69b
Southern Living....69a
Southern Loggin' Times....38
Southern Lumberman....38
Southern Medical Journal....40
Southern P-H-C....55
SW Airlines Spirit....65a
Southwest Art....26a
Southwest Farm Press....68
Southwest Food Service News....32
Souvenirs, Gifts & Novelties....26
SpaceNews....5
Special Events....12
SpeciaLiving Magazine....69
Specialty Automotive Magazine....4
Specialty Insider....16
Spectrum Bulletin....10c
Spin....45
Sport Fishing....61a
Sport Rider....4c
Sport Truck....4b
Sporting Classics....61a
Sporting Goods Dealer....61
Sporting News....61
Sports Illustrated....69
Sports Illustrated For Kids....69e
SportsField Management....61
Sportsturf....30
Sportswear International....12a
Spray Technology & Marketing....14
Sprinkler Age....28a
Spudman....68f
St. Louis Business Journal....12
Stable Management....61c
Stamping Journal....41
Standard....34
Star....69
State Legislatures....28b
State News....28b
Stateways....9
Step by Step Wire Jewelry....26
Stereophile....53
Stockman Grass Farmer....68g
Stocks & Commodities....7
Stone Sand & Gravel Review....3a
Stone World....3a
Stores....12a
Strategic Finance....7
Street Chopper....4c
Street Rodder....4a
Strictly Slots....2
Strings Magazine....45
Student Lawyer....37
Studio Monthly....58
Success....12
Successful Farming....68
Successful Meetings....12
Sugar Journal....68f
Sugar Producer....68f
Sugarbeet Grower....68f
Sunflower....68f
Sunset Magazine....69a
Super Chevy....4a
Super Floral Retailing....30

Super Street 4
Superintendent........ 61b
Supermarket News........ 27
Supply & Demand Chain Executive 12
Supply Chain Management Review........ 12
Supply House Times 55
Surface........ 26a
Surface Fabrication........ 3a
Surfer Magazine 61d
Surfing........ 61d
Surgery........ 40
Surgical Products 40
Surplus Record 33
Swap Meet........ 12
Swimming World Magazine........ 61d
Symphony Magazine........ 45
Synergist........ 33a
Systems Contractor News 58

T

T&D Magazine 12
T.H.E. Journal........ 60
Tablet 15
Tablet Magazine 15
Tack 'n Togs Merchandising 12a
Tactical Response........ 28a
Talkers Magazine 58
Tallahassee Magazine 69f
Tampa Bay Business Journal 12
Tampa Bay Magazine 69f
Tanning Trends........ 8
Target Marketing 1
Taste for Life........ 69g
Taste of Home........ 69K
Taste of the South........ 69k
The Tasting Panel 9
Tattoo........ 69
Tax Adviser 7
Tea Time........ 69k
Teacher Magazine 60
Teaching Children Mathematics 60
Teaching Music........ 45
Tech Directions........ 60
Technical Communication 10c
Technical Support........ 19b
Techniques........ 60
Technology & Engineering Teacher........ 60
Technology & Learning........ 60
Teddy Bear & Friends 26
Teen Vogue 69e
TeleRevista........ 69l
Tennessee Farm Bureau News 68b
The Tennessee Magazine........ 68c
Tennis 61
Tennis Life 61
Texas Agriculture........ 68b
Texas Architect 3
Texas Bar Journal 37
Texas Co-op Power 68c
Texas Highways 65
Texas Medicine 40
Texas Monthly........ 69f
Texas Parks & Wildlife........ 65
Texas Realtor 11
Texas Town & City 28b
Textile Services........ 36
Textile World 62
This Old House........ 69a
Thrasher........ 61
Threads 26
The Tidings 15
Timber Harvesting........ 38
Timber Processing........ 38
Timber West........ 38
Timberline 38
Time 69
Time Out New York 69f
Times of the Islands........ 69f
Tire Business 4
Tire Review 4
Toastmaster 25
Tobacco International 63
Tobacco Outlet Business........ 63
Tobacco Reporter 63
Tobacconist 63
Today's Chicago Woman 69b
Today's Black Woman........ 69h
Today's Caregiver........ 69g
Today's Catholic Teacher........ 60
Today's Chiropractic Lifestyle........ 40
Today's Diet & Nutrition........ 69g
Today's Facility Manager 11
Today's Farmer 68
Today's Insurance Professional........ 34
Today's OEA........ 60
Today's Photographer Intl. 53
Toledo Business Journal........ 12
Tools of the Trade........ 11
Top Producer........ 68
Total Food Service........ 32
Total Health........ 69g
Tourist Attractions and Parks........ 2
Tow Times........ 4b
Towing & Recovery Footnotes 4b
Town and Country 69
Toy Book........ 26
Toy Farmer........ 26
Toy Trucker & Contractor 26
TPJ-Tube & Pipe Journal........ 41
Track & Field News........ 61
Traditional Home 69a
Trail & Timberline 61a
Trail Blazer........ 61c
Trailer/Body Builders........ 4b
Trailer Life........ 65c
Training & Simulation Journal........ 42
Trains........ 59
Transmission/Distribution World........ 56
Transmission Digest........ 4
Transport Topics 4b
Transworld SNOWboarding........ 61e
Transworld Surf........ 61d
Transworld Wakeboarding........ 61d
Trap & Field 61a
Trapper & Predator Caller........ 61a
Travel Agent........ 65
Travel & Leisure........ 65
Travel Goods Showcase........ 24
Travel Weekly 65
Travel With Spirit........ 65
Travel World News........ 65
Travelage West 65
Traverse City Business News........ 12
Traverse N MI Magazine........ 69f
Treasures........ 26
Treasury & Risk 7
Tree Care Industry 38
Tree Farmer 38
Tree Services........ 38
Trenchless Technology 20
Trends........ 69f
Tri-State Neighbor 68
Trial........ 37
Triangle Business Journal........ 12
Tribology & Lubrication Tech. 33
Tricycle: The Buddhist Review........ 15
Tropical Fish Hobbyist........ 26
Truck Parts & Service........ 4b
Trucker........ 4b
Truckers News........ 4b
Truckin'........ 4b
True Magazine........ 45
Trustee........ 31
Trusts & Estates 7
Tuff Stuff........ 26
TurboMachinery International 56
Turf 30
Turf News........ 30
Turkey & Turkey Hunting........ 61a
Turkey Country........ 61a
TV Technology........ 58
TVWeek........ 58
Tweeting & Business........ 12
20/20 47
Twice........ 58
Twin Cities Business 12

U

Ultimate MMA........ 61
Ultimate MotorCycling 4c
Ultrapure Water........ 28d
Undercar Digest........ 4
Underground Construction........ 20
Underhood Service........ 4
Unique Homes 69a
United Mine Workers Journal 43
Units........ 11
University Business........ 60
Upholstery Journal 29
Upscale Magazine........ 69h
Urban Farm........ 26
Urban Ink 69h
Urgent Communications........ 58
Urology Times........ 40
US Airways Magazine 65a
US Glass Metal & Glazing........ 13
US Medicine........ 40
US Pharmacist........ 18
US Tech........ 19
US Weekly........ 69
USA Gymnastics........ 61
USA Hockey Magazine........ 61
USA Today Magazine 69
Used Car Dealer 4
Utah Business........ 12
Utility Fleet Professional 56
Utne Reader........ 69
UTU News........ 59
U.U. World 15

V

Vacations........ 65
Value Retail News........ 12a
Valve Magazine........ 33
Vanity Fair 69
Variety 2
The Vegetable Growers News 68f
Vegetarian Times........ 69g
Vending Times........ 67
Veranda 69a
Vermont Magazine........ 69f
Vermont NEA Today 60
Vertical Systems Reseller 19b
Vertiflite........ 5
Veterinary Economics........ 52
Veterinary Medicine........ 52
Veterinary Practice News 52
Veterinary Technician 52
Vette 4a
VFW Magazine........ 25
Via 65d
Vibrant Life........ 15
Victorian Homes........ 69a
Videomaker 58
View Camera 53
Vineyard & Winery Management 9
Vintage Motorsport........ 4a
Virginia Business 12
Virginia Journal Education........ 60
Virginia Review 28b
Virginia Wildlife........ 69f
Vision Monday........ 47
Vision Systems Design 19
Vitamin Retailer........ 27
Vogue 69b
Volleyball Magazine........ 61

W

W 69b
Walking Horse Report 61c
Wall Street & Technology........ 12
Walls & Ceilings 11
Ward's AutoWorld 4
Ward's Dealer Business 4
Washington Business Journal 12
Washington Lawyer........ 37
Washington Technology 19b
Washingtonian Magazine 69f
Waste Age 28d
Waste & Recycling News........ 28d
Waste Handling Equipment News 28d
Waste Management World........ 28d
Watch & Jewelry Review 35
Watch Journal 35
Water & Wastes Digest........ 28d
Water Conditioning/Purification........ 28d
Water Environment & Technology 28d
Water Quality Products 28d
Water Technology 28d
Water Well Journal 28d
Watercolor Artist........ 26a
WaterSki 61d
WaterWorld........ 28d
Watt Poultry USA........ 68h
WEA News........ 60
Weatherwise........ 33b
Website Magazine 19b
The Week........ 69
Weekly Livestock Reporter 68g
Weighing & Measurement 33
Weight Watchers Magazine........ 69g
Welding Design & Fabrication........ 41
Welding Journal 41
Well Servicing 51
West Suburban Dog 52
Westchester........ 69f
Westchester Co. Business Jrnl. 12
Western & English Today........ 24
Western City........ 28b
Western Cowman 68g
Western Farm Press........ 68
Western Farmer-Stockman........ 68
Western Horseman........ 61c
Western Livestock Journal........ 68g
Western Ag Reporter........ 68g
Western Roofing/Insul./Siding 11
Westways 65d
Wfm 25

Wheat Life...68
Where to Retire...65
Whispering Wind..26
Whitetail Journal...61a
WholeFoods Magazine 23
Wholesaler..55
Wichita Business Journal................................12
Wide-Format Imaging 10c
Wildfowl..61a
The Wilson Quarterly.....................................69
Window & Door...11
Window Fashion Vision...................................29
Window Film Magazine...................................13
Windows IT Pro..19b
Wine & Spirits...69k
Wine Business...69k
Wine Enthusiast...69k
Wine Spectator..69k
WineMaker...69k
Wines & Vines...9
Wire & Cable Technology Intl. 33
Wire Journal International 33
Wired..19b
Wireless Design & Development 19
Wisconsin Agriculturist..................................68
Wisconsin Energy Co-op News..........................68c
Wisconsin Lawyer..37
Wisconsin State Farmer 68
Wisconsin Trails...69f
Woman's Day..69b
Woman's World..69b
Women In Business......................................12
Women's Adventure 61
Women's Health...69b
Women's Wear Daily.....................................16
Wood (Better Homes/Gardens)..........................26
Wood & Wood Products.................................38
Woodall's Campground Mgmt. 65b
WoodenBoat...39
Woodshop News...38
Woodworker's Journal...................................26
Word Up!..45
WorkBoat..39
Workforce Management..................................12
Working Mother...69b
Workplace HR & Safety 33a
World Airshow News 5
World Dredging..39
World Fence News.......................................11
World-Generation 56
World Oil...51
WorldRadio Online 58
Worship Leader 15
The Writer...10b
Writer's Digest..10b
WWE Magazine 61
WREN Magazine 68c

X

XXL Magazine 45

Y

Yachting...39
Yachts Intl...39
Yankee Magazine..69f
Yard & Garden 30
Yoga Journal 69g
Young Rider...61c
Your AAA..65d
YouthWorker Journal 15

Advertising-Marketing-Promotion-Public Relations .1

Adcrafter 3011 W Grand Blvd Ste 561 Detroit MI 48202 **Phn:** 313-872-7850 **Fax** 313-872-7858 Melanie D. Davis. Biweekly magazine.
2,600 to members of Ad Club of Detroit; Detroit area advertising/marketing personnel. www.adcraft.org adcraft@adcraft.org

Advertising Age 711 3rd Ave New York NY 10017 **Phn:** 212-210-0100 **Fax** 212-210-0200 Abbey Klaassen. Crain Communications. Weekly tabloid. TH:@amklaassen
56,200 to advertisers, ad agencies; PR, media execs; corporate CEOS; journalists. adage.com fatta-mensah@crain.com

Advertising/Communications Times 29 Bala Ave Ste 114 Bala Cynwyd PA 19004 **Phn:** 484-562-0063 **Fax** 484-562-0068 Joseph Ball. Monthly newspaper.
20,000 to ad industry personnel in Philadelphia, eastern Pennsylvania, New Jersey, Delaware. www.phillybizmedia.com adcomtimes@aol.com

Adweek 770 Broadway New York NY 10003 **Phn:** 212-493-4100 Tony Case. Prometheus Global Media. Weekly magazine. TH:@tonymedia
20,000 to advertising, marketing personnel at agencies, major companies. www.adweek.com tony.case@adweek.com

Agri Marketing Magazine 1422 Elbridge Payne Rd Ste 250 Chesterfield MO 63017 **Phn:** 636-728-1428 **Fax** 636-777-4178 Lynn Henderson. Doane Agricultural Svcs. 10-issue mag.
8,000 to agribusiness mgmt., marketing & communications execs., ag trade assn. members. www.agrimarketing.com lynnh@agrimarketing.com

Airbrush Action PO Box 438 Allenwood NJ 08720 **Phn:** 732-223-7878 **Fax** 732-223-2855 Cliff Stieglitz. Bimonthly. TH:@AirbrushAction
40,000 to professional & amateur artists interested in airbrush technique, instruction, interviews, products. www.airbrushaction.com ceo@airbrushaction.com

ANA Magazine 708 Third Ave Fl 33 New York NY 10017 **Phn:** 212-697-5950 **Fax** 212-687-7310 Ken Beaulieu. Assn. of Natl. Advertisers. Quarterly magazine. TH:@ANAmarketers
10,000 to mktg. mgrs. & directors responsible for all aspects of brandbuilding, integrated marketing, communications. www.ana.net kbeaulieu@ana.net

Communication World 601 Montgomery St Ste 1900 San Francisco CA 94111 **Phn:** 415-544-4700 **Fax** 415-544-4747 Natasha Nicholson. Intl. Assn. Business Communicators. Online only. TH:@IABC
 to communication professionals responsible for strategic business communication mgmt. www.iabc.com/cw/ cwmagazine@iabc.com

Counselor 4800 E Street Rd Trevose PA 19053 **Phn:** 215-942-8600 **Fax** 215-953-3034 Andrew Cohen. Advtg. Specialty Institute. 13-issue magazine. TH:@asicentral
14,500 to specialty advertising industry personnel interested in case studies, research, trade shows, industry news. www.asicentral.com acohen@asicentral.com

Creative 31 Merrick Ave Ste 60 Merrick NY 11566 **Phn:** 516-378-0800 **Fax** 516-378-0884 David Flasterstein. Bimonthly magazine.
15,000 to advertising and sales promotion managers, designers, production and exhibit supvs. www.creativemag.com info@creativemag.com

CRM/Customer Relationship Mgmt. 237 W 35th St Fl 14 New York NY 10001 **Phn:** 212-251-0608 **Fax** 212-779-1152 David Myron. CRM Media. Monthly.
75,000 to executives interested in managing, implementing customer-focused workforces. www.destinationcrm.com dmyron@destinationcrm.com

Direct Marketing News 114 W 26th St Fl 4 New York NY 10001 **Phn:** 646-638-6000 **Fax** 646-638-6159 Ginger Conlon. Haymarket Media. Monthly tabloid. TH:@customeralchemy
45,000 to marketers responsible for direct, database, interactive & online marketing functions. www.dmnews.com ginger.conlon@dmnews.com

Engagement Strategies 520 White Plains Rd Ste 120 Tarrytown NY 10591 **Phn:** 914-591-7600 **Fax** 914-591-7699 Richard Kern. Selling Comms, Inc. Quarterly magazine.
25,000 to managers responsible for sales and performance incentives, motivational meetings. www.engagementstrategiesmag.com rkern@sellingcommunications.com

Incentive 100 Lighting Way Fl 2 Secaucus NJ 07094 **Phn:** 646-380-6247 Vincent Alonzo. Northstar Travel Media. 6-issue magazine.
25,000 to sales, mktg., advertising execs. who use performance incentives; for vendors looking incentive buyers. www.incentivemag.com valonzo@ntmllc.com

Jack O'Dwyer's Newsletter 271 Madison Ave Ste 600 New York NY 10016 **Phn:** 212-679-2471 **Fax** 212-683-2750 Greg Hazley. Weekly newsletter.
30,000 to management level PR personnel; magazine, newspaper, radio, TV professionals. www.odwyerpr.com greg@odwyerpr.com

Jrnl. Advertising Research 432 Park Ave S Fl 6 New York NY 10016 **Phn:** 212-751-5656 **Fax** 212-319-5265 Catherine Gardner. Advertising Rsch. Fndtn. Quarterly.
3,000 to advertisers and marketers interested in research findings and applications. www.thearf.org/jar.php catherine@thearf.org

License! 641 Lexington Ave Fl 8 New York NY 10022 **Phn:** 212-951-6600 **Fax** 212-951-6714 Amanda Peabody. Monthly magazine.
31,700 to licensing personnel interested in licensing arrangements, trends, opportunities. www.licensemag.com apeabody@advanstar.com

Licensing Book 286 5th Ave Fl 3 New York NY 10001 **Phn:** 212-575-4510 **Fax** 212-575-4521 Jackie Breyer. Adventure Publishing. 7-issue magazine.
20,000 to retail mktg. execs. interested in all aspects of successful retail licensing programs. www.licensingbook.com jbreyer@adventurepub.com

Marketing Management 311 S Wacker Dr Ste 5800 Chicago IL 60606 **Phn:** 312-542-9000 **Fax** 312-542-9001 Mary Flory. Amer. Mktg. Assn. Quarterly.
9,100 to mid and senior level mgrs. responsible for marketing strategies and concepts. www.marketingpower.com mflory@ama.org

Marketing News 311 S Wacker Dr Ste 5800 Chicago IL 60606 **Phn:** 312-542-9000 **Fax** 312-542-9001 Elisabeth Sullivan. Amer. Mktg. Assn. 16-issue tab.
22,800 to members of American Marketing Assn.; others in advertising, marketing research. www.marketingpower.com editor@ama.org

Med Ad News 300 American Metro Blvd Ste 125 Hamilton NJ 08619 **Phn:** 609-759-7600 **Fax** 609-759-7676 Christiane Truelove. UBM Canon. Monthly magazine.
16,500 to pharmaceutical marketing personnel interested in news, events, trends. www.pharmalive.com chris.truelove@ubm.com

Medical Marketing & Media 114 W 26th St Fl 3 New York NY 10001 **Phn:** 646-638-6000 **Fax** 646-638-6150 James Chase. Haymarket Media. Monthly.
14,100 to healthcare industry mktg. execs. and govt. regulating agency personnel. www.mmm-online.com james.chase@haymarketmedia.com

Meetings & Conventions 100 Lighting Way Fl 2 Secaucus NJ 07094 **Phn:** 201-902-2000 **Fax** 201-902-2053 Loren G. Edelstein. Northstar Travel Media. Monthly magazine.
50,000 to decision-making meeting planners, both corporate and independent. www.meetings-conventions.com ledelstein@ntmllc.com

O'Dwyer's Magazine 271 Madison Ave Ste 600 New York NY 10016 **Phn:** 646-843-2080 **Fax** 212-683-2750 Greg Hazley. Monthly magazine.
3,500 to public relations personnel interested in trends, news, campaigns. www.odwyerpr.com/magazine/pr-magazine.htm greg@odwyerpr.com

PR News 88 Pine St Ste 510 New York NY 10005 **Phn:** 212-621-4875 **Fax** 212-621-4879 Matthew Schwartz. Access Intelligence. Weekly. TH:@PRNews
25,000 to PR/PA executives interested in case studies, trends, technology developments, events. www.prnewsonline.com mschwartz@accessintel.com

PR Week 114 W 26th St Fl 3 New York NY 10001 **Phn:** 646-638-6030 **Fax** 646-638-6115 Steve Barrett. Haymarket Media. Monthly.
10,000 to PR, corporate communication, public affairs professionals in business and govt. www.prweekus.com steve.barrett@prweek.com

Promotional Products Business 3125 Skyway Cir N Irving TX 75038 **Phn:** 972-258-3084 **Fax** 972-258-3012 Tina Berres Filipski. Promotional Products Assn. Intl. Monthly magazine.
11,400 to promotional product suppliers, distributors interested in news, trends. www.ppbmag.com tinaf@ppa.org

Public Relations Tactics 33 Maiden Ln Fl 11 New York NY 10038 **Phn:** 212-460-1400 **Fax** 212-995-0757 John Elsasser. Public Relations Soc. of Amer. Monthly newspaper.
27,500 to PR practitioners interested in techniques, campaigns, profiles. www.prsa.org john.elsasser@prsa.org

Quirks Marketing Rsch Review 4662 Slater Rd Eagan MN 55122 **Phn:** 651-379-6200 **Fax** 651-379-6205 Joseph Rydholm. Monthly mag.
30,000 to market research buyers, commercial research providers interested in new techniques. www.quirks.com joe@quirks.com

Ragan Report 111 E Wacker Dr Ste 500 Chicago IL 60601 **Phn:** 312-960-4140 **Fax** 312-960-4106 Roula Amire. Lawrence Ragan Comms. Weekly.
10,000 to communications/PR execs interested in expert advice and strategies. www.ragan.com roulaa@ragan.com

Response 201 Sandpointe Ave Ste 500 Santa Ana CA 92707 **Phn:** 714-338-6700 **Fax** 714-338-6710 Thomas Haire. Questex Media. Monthly.
21,500 to direct response marketing and advertising professionals. www.responsemagazine.com thaire@questex.com

Sales & Marketing Management PO Box 247 Excelsior MN 55331 **Phn:** 952-401-1283 Paul Nolan. Lakewood Media Group. 6-issue magazine.
50,000 to executives in advertising, sales promotion, research and development, packaging. www.salesandmarketing.com paul@salesandmarketing.com

Selling Power PO Box 5467 Fredericksburg VA 22403 **Phn:** 540-752-7000 **Fax** 540-752-7001 Larissa Gschwandtner. PSP, Inc. Bimonthly magazine.
145,000 to marketing, sales executives interested in training, motivational systems. www.sellingpower.com editorial@sellingpower.com

Shopper Marketing 7400 Skokie Blvd Skokie IL 60077 **Phn:** 847-675-7400 **Fax** 847-675-7494 Tim Binder. Path to Purchase Inst. Mo. tabloid.
18,200 to marketers, retailers of consumer products interested in ad displays, signs and fixtures. www.shoppermarketingmag.com tbinder@p2pi.org

Sign Builder Illustrated 345 Hudson St Rm 1201 New York NY 10014 **Phn:** 252-355-5806 **Fax** 212-633-1863 Jeff Wooten. Simmons-Boardman. Monthly magazine.
18,800 to sign shop personnel responsible for concept, design, fabrication, installation, service. www.signshop.com jwooten@sbpub.com

Signcraft PO Box 60031 Fort Myers FL 33906 **Phn:** 239-939-4644 **Fax** 239-939-0607 Tom McIlltrot. Bimonthly.
11,400 to sign shop owners interested in all aspects of sign design and production. www.signcraft.com signcraft@signcraft.com

Signs Of The Times 11262 Cornell Park Dr Cincinnati OH 45242 **Phn:** 513-421-2050 **Fax** 513-421-5144 Wade Swormstedt. ST Media Group Intl. Monthly magazine.
18,100 to outdoor advertising, display, electric, commercial, poster and show card sign shops. www.signweb.com
wade.swormstedt@stmediagroup.com

Target Marketing 1500 Spring Garden St Ste 1200 Philadelphia PA 19130 **Phn:** 215-238-5300 **Fax** 215-238-5270 Thorin McGee. North Amer. Publishing. Monthly mag.
47,100 to list brokers/compilers, telemarketers, catalogers, mail order companies, retailers. www.targetmarketingmag.com tmcgee@napco.com

Film--Theater--Amusements .2

American Square Dance 34 E Main St Apopka FL 32703 **Phn:** 407-886-7151 **Fax** 407-886-8464 Bill Boyd. Gramac Printing. Monthly.
21,800 to dancers, callers, teachers, and leaders in the square dance movement. americansquaredance.com americansquaredance@earthlink.net

American Theatre 520 8th Ave Rm 2400 New York NY 10018 **Phn:** 212-609-5900 **Fax** 212-609-5901 Jim O'Quinn. Monthly.
22,000 to working professionals, amateurs, theatre goers interested in current news and information. www.tcg.org at@tcg.org

Amusement Today PO Box 5427 Arlington TX 76005 **Phn:** 817-460-7220 **Fax** 817-265-6397 Gary Slade. Monthly newspaper.
3,000 to intl. amusement industry personnel interested in facility openings, industry news & people. www.amusementtoday.com gslade@amusementtoday.com

Back Stage 770 Broadway New York NY 10003 **Phn:** 646-654-5500 **Fax** 646-654-5743 David Sheward. Weekly newspaper.
10,000 to directors, actors, singers, dancers, entertainment industry personnel. www.backstage.com editorial@backstage.com

Bingo Bugle PO Box 527 Vashon WA 98070 **Phn:** 206-463-5656 Tara Snowden. Monthly newspaper.
856,800 to gambling enthusiasts interested in lotto, bingo, casinos. www.bingobugle.com tara@bingobugle.com

Box Office 9107 Wilshire Blvd Ste 450 Beverly Hills CA 90210 **Phn:** 310-876-9090 Ken Bacon. Monthly magazine. TH:@BoxOffice
10,000 to movie theater operators interested in industry news, film reviews/previews. www.boxoffice.com ken@boxoffice.com

Casino Journal 505 E Capovilla Ave Ste 102 Las Vegas NV 89119 **Phn:** 702-794-0718 **Fax** 702-794-0799 Marian Green. BNP Media. Monthly magazine.
9,000 to casino industry personnel interested in people, products, technology. www.casinojournal.com greenm@bnpmedia.com

Dance Magazine 110 William St Fl 23 New York NY 10038 **Phn:** 646-459-4800 **Fax** 646-459-4900 Hanna Rubin. Macfadden Comms Group. Monthly.
50,800 to students, teachers, professionals interested in technique, dance companies, interviews. www.dancemagazine.com hrubin@dancemagazine.com

Dance Spirit 110 William St Fl 23 New York NY 10038 **Phn:** 646-459-4800 **Fax** 646-459-4900 Kate Lydon. Macfadden Comms Group. Monthly.
52,800 covers dancing techniques, nutrition, choreography and interviews for dancers. www.dancespirit.com klydon@dancemedia.com

Dance Teacher 110 William St Fl 23 New York NY 10038 **Phn:** 646-459-4800 **Fax** 646-459-4900 Joe Sullivan. Macfadden Comms Group. Monthly.
21,800 covers business, includes success stories and business and health articles. www.dance-teacher.com jsullivan@dancemedia.com

Dramatics 2343 Auburn Ave Cincinnati OH 45219 **Phn:** 513-421-3900 **Fax** 513-421-7077 Don Corathers. Educ. Theatre Assn. 9-issue magazine. TH:@schooltheatre
37,300 to performing arts students & teachers interested in theatre skills, career opportunities. schooltheatre.org dcorathers@schooltheatre.org

Encore Arts Programs 425 N 85th St Seattle WA 98103 **Phn:** 206-443-0445 **Fax** 206-443-1246 Paul Heppner. 10-issue magazine.
316,500 to event attendees at performing arts venues in Seattle & San Francisco metro areas. www.encoremediagroup.com paulh@encoremediagroup.com

Film Comment 70 Lincoln Center Plz New York NY 10023 **Phn:** 212-875-5614 **Fax** 212-875-5636 Gavin Smith. Film Society of Lincoln Cen. Bimonthly.
40,000 to Film Society members interested in film criticism, the artform, history. www.filmlinc.com editor@filmlinc.com

Film Journal International 770 Broadway Fl 7 New York NY 10003 **Phn:** 646-654-7680 **Fax** 646-654-7694 Kevin Lally. Monthly magazine.
5,000 to movie production/dist. personnel concerned with all aspects of theatrical release. www.filmjournal.com kevin.lally@filmjournal.com

Film Score Monthly 4470 W Sunset Blvd #705 Los Angeles CA 90027 **Phn:** 646-417-3507 **Fax** 323-461-2241 Jim Lochner. Monthly.
1,500 guide to original film and television music, edited for professionals and enthusiasts alike. fsmonlinemag.com jim@filmscoremonthly.com

Funworld 1448 Duke St Alexandria VA 22314 **Phn:** 703-836-4800 **Fax** 703-836-2824 Amanda Charney. Monthly magazine.
10,000 to amusement park executives interested in industry trends, operations and procedures. www.iaapa.org/industry/funworld/ acharney@iaapa.org

Hollywood Reporter 5700 Wilshire Blvd Los Angeles CA 90036 **Phn:** 323-525-2000 Matthew Belloni. Weekly magazine.
70,000 to intl. entertainment industry members in film, TV, cable, music, home theater. www.hollywoodreporter.com matthew.belloni@thr.com

Interview Magazine 575 Broadway Fl 5 New York NY 10012 **Phn:** 212-941-2800 **Fax** 212-941-2885 Peter Brant, Jr. Brant Publications. 10 issue magazine.
229,000 covers pop culture, fashions, photography; interviews with actors, artists, musicians. www.interviewmagazine.com intervieweditor@brantpub.com

Live Design 249 W 17th St Fl 4 New York NY 10011 **Phn:** 212-462-3300 **Fax** 212-204-4291 Marian Sandberg. Penton Media. 9-issue magazine.
21,700 to visual design professionals responsible for lighting, sound, costumes, special effects. livedesignonline.com msandberg@livedesignonline.com

Markee 2.0 506 Roswell St Ste 220 Marietta GA 30060 **Phn:** 770-431-0867 **Fax** 770-432-6969 Cory Sekine-Pettite. Bimonthly magazine. TH:@MarkeeMag
20,000 to U.S. film/video production personnel interested in industry news, rgnl. & indie productions. www.markeemag.com cory@markeemagazine.com

MovieMaker 8328 De Soto Ave Canoga Park CA 91304 **Phn:** 818-349-2300 **Fax** 818-349-9922 Jennifer M. Wood. Bimonthly magazine.
44,000 to film screenwriters, producers, directors, editors, distributors, educators, festival organizers. www.moviemaker.com jwood@moviemaker.com

Opera News 70 Lincoln Center Plz New York NY 10023 **Phn:** 212-769-7080 **Fax** 212-769-8500 F. Paul Driscoll. Metropolitan Opera Guild. Monthly magazine.
101,000 to opera enthusiasts interested in performers, performances, broadcast & recorded performances, reviews. www.operanews.com info@operanews.com

P3 Update 1438 N Gower St Ste 65 Hollywood CA 90028 **Phn:** 323-315-9477 **Fax** 818-785-8092 James Thompson. Monthly magazine.
19,400 to film, video, digital production, preproduction & post production personnel. www.p3update.com jt@p3update.com

Playbill 575 Fashion Ave # 1801 New York NY 10018 **Phn:** 212-557-5757 **Fax** 212-682-2932 Blake Ross. Monthly magazine.
4,000,000 to theater and concertgoers in major metropolitan areas nationwide. www.playbill.com bross@playbill.com

Pointe Magazine 333 7th Ave Fl 11 New York NY 10001 **Phn:** 212-979-4800 **Fax** 646-674-0103 Brian McTigue. DanceMedia. Bimonthly.
30,400 to ballet students, educators, professional ballet dancers, choreographers. www.pointemagazine.com pointe@dancemedia.com

Post 620 W Elk Ave Glendale CA 91204 **Phn:** 818-291-1100 **Fax** 818-291-1190 Mark Loftus. Monthly tabloid.
30,000 to animation, film, video post production personnel interested in innovations, products. www.postmagazine.com mloftus@postmagazine.com

Projection Lights Staging News 6000 S Eastern Ave Ste 14J Las Vegas NV 89119 **Phn:** 702-932-5585 **Fax** 702-932-5584 William Vanyo. Timeless Comms. Monthly tabloid.
21,300 to lighting, staging, live production industry personnel interested in products, news. www.plsn.com info@plsn.com

Public Gaming International 218 Main St # 203 Kirkland WA 98033 **Phn:** 425-985-3159 **Fax** 800-657-9340 Paul Jason. Monthly.
20,000 to worldwide lottery industry personnel concerned with sales, mktg., new technologies. www.publicgaming.com pjason@publicgaming.com

Replay Magazine PO Box 572829 Tarzana CA 91357 **Phn:** 818-776-2880 **Fax** 818-776-2888 Steve White. Monthly.
4,000 to coin-operated amusement machine, pinball machine, jukebox industry personnel. www.replaymag.com editor@replaymag.com

Rinksider 2470 E Main St Columbus OH 43209 **Phn:** 614-235-1022 **Fax** 614-235-3584 Linda Katz. Target Publishing. Bimonthly tab.
1,500 to rink operators interested in promotions, operations, industry news and information. www.rinksider.com rinksider@rinksider.com

Roller Skating Business 6905 Corporate Dr Indianapolis IN 46278 **Phn:** 317-347-2626 **Fax** 317-347-2636 Beth Grant. Roller Skating Assn. Bimonthly.
1,900 to rink owners and operators responsible for marketing, management, maintenance. www.rollerskating.org editor@rollerskating.com

Script Magazine 5638 Sweet Air Rd Baldwin MO 21013 **Phn:** 888-245-2228 **Fax** 410-592-8062 Shelly Mellott. Final Draft Inc. Bimo.
59,400 informative articles on writing, developing, marketing screenplays and television scripts. www.scriptmag.com mellott@finaldraft.com

Strictly Slots 2860 S Jones Blvd Ste 1 Las Vegas NV 89146 **Phn:** 702-736-8886 **Fax** 702-736-8889 Adam Fine. Monthly magazine.
127,000 to slot and video poker players interested in new machine reviews, strategies. www.casinocenter.com letters@casinocenter.com

Tourist Attractions and Parks 10 E Athens Ave Ste 208 Ardmore PA 19003 **Phn:** 610-645-6940 **Fax** 610-645-6943 Scott C. Borowsky. 7-issue magazine.
32,300 to decision makers at amusement parks, raceways, zoos, museums, fairs, natl. parks, stadiums. tapmag.com editortapmag@kanec.com

Variety 11175 Santa Monica Blvd Los Angeles CA 90025 **Phn:** 323-617-9100 **Fax** 646-746-6977 Timothy Gray. Penske Media. Weekly tabloid. TH:@variety
30,200 to directors, producers, technicians, performers in theater, film, TV, cable, music. www.variety.com news@variety.com

Architecture .3

Architect 1 Thomas Cir NW Ste 600 Washington DC 20005 **Phn:** 202-452-0800 **Fax** 202-785-1974 Ned Cramer. Hanley-Wood. Monthly magazine.
60,000 to practicing architects interested in projects, awards, events, products, practice mgmt.
www.architectmagazine.com
ncramer@hanleywood.com

Architectural Digest 4 Times Sq Fl 18 New York NY 10036 **Phn:** 212-286-2860 **Fax** 212-286-6905 Laurie Sprague. Conde Nast. Monthly magazine.
800,000 to readers interested in interior design, fine arts, antiques; interior designers.
www.architecturaldigest.com
laurie_sprague@condenast.com

Architectural Record 2 Penn Plz New York NY 10121 **Phn:** 212-904-2594 **Fax** 212-904-4256 Elisabeth Broome. McGraw-Hill. Monthly magazine.
115,500 to architects, engineers, building owners, interior and landscape designers.
archrecord.construction.com
elisabeth_broome@mcgraw-hill.com

Architectural West 546 Court St Reno NV 89501 **Phn:** 775-333-1080 **Fax** 775-333-1081 Marcus Dodson. Bimonthly magazine.
21,200 to western U.S. building professionals responsible for building product design, specification, application. www.architecturalwest.com
dottie@architecturalwest.com

Architecture Minnesota 275 Market St Ste 54 Minneapolis MN 55405 **Phn:** 612-338-6763 **Fax** 612-338-7981 Christopher Hudson. Bimonthly magazine.
10,000 to architects, designers, the public, construction professionals in MN, ND, SD, WI and IA.
www.ArchitectureMN.com hudson@aia-mn.org

Design Solutions 46179 Westlake Dr Ste 120 Potomac Falls VA 20165 **Phn:** 571-323-3636 **Fax** 571-323-3630 Elaine Ferri. Quarterly.
24,100 to architects & designers responsible for specifying interior woodwork. www.awinet.org
kallen@awinet.org

Eco-Structure 1 Thomas Cir NW Ste 600 Washington DC 20005 **Phn:** 202-736-3353 **Fax** 202-785-1974 Katie Weeks. Hanley-Wood/Amer. Inst. Architects. Bimonthly mag.
28,100 to architects and designers interested in cool roofing, green housing, conserving energy. www.eco-structure.com kweeks@hanleywood.com

Fabric Architecture 1801 County Road B W Roseville MN 55113 **Phn:** 651-222-2508 **Fax** 651-225-6966 Bruce Wright. Bimonthly.
8,000 to architects and construction fabric specifiers.
www.FabricArchitecture.com fabarch@ifai.com

Form Pioneering Design 512 E Wilson Ave Ste 213 Glendale CA 91206 **Phn:** 818-956-5313 **Fax** 818-956-5904 Caren Kurlander. Balcony Media. Bimonthly magazine.
69,200 to architects & designers intersted in modern design projects in major U.S. urban centers.
www.formmag.net edit@formmag.net

Metal Architecture 7450 Skokie Blvd Skokie IL 60077 **Phn:** 847-674-2200 **Fax** 847-674-3676 Marcy Marro. Modern Trade Comms. Monthly tabloid.
29,100 to architects and engineers who design commercial and industrial buildings.
www.metalarchitecture.com
mmarro@moderntrade.com

Film--Theater--Amusements .2

Residential Architect 1 Thomas Cir NW Ste 600 Washington DC 20005 **Phn:** 202-452-0800 **Fax** 202-785-1974 Claire Conroy. Hanley-Wood. 9-issue magazine.
21,200 to house-designing architects interested in practice mgmt., technology, profiles.
www.residentialarchitect.com cconroy@hanley-wood.com

Texas Architect 500 Chicon St Austin TX 78702 **Phn:** 512-478-7386 **Fax** 512-478-0528 Stephen Sharpe. Bimonthly.
13,400 to national architectural personnel interested in or working on TX projects. texasarchitects.org

Cement--Rock--Stone .3a

Aggregates Manager 2849 Lee Rd Silver Lake OH 44224 **Phn:** 330-920-9737 **Fax** 330-920-9739 Therese Dunphy. James Info. Media. Monthly mag.
19,300 to managers of non-metal mining operations.
www.aggman.com therese@aggman.com

Concrete Construction 8725 W Higgins Rd Ste 600 Chicago IL 60631 **Phn:** 773-824-2400 **Fax** 773-824-2401 Joe Nasvik Hanley-Wood. Monthly magazine.
70,000 to contractors, architects, engineers, designers, mfrs. of highway and building equip.
www.worldofconcrete.com jnasvik@hanleywood.com

Concrete International 38800 Country Club Dr Farmington Hills MI 48331 **Phn:** 248-848-3700 **Fax** 248-848-3701 Rex Donahey. American Concrete Inst. Monthly.
18,000 to concrete design architects, engineers, contractors, Institute members.
www.concreteinternational.com
rex.donahey@concrete.org

The Concrete Producer 8725 W Higgins Rd Ste 600 Chicago IL 60631 **Phn:** 773-824-2400 **Fax** 773-824-2401 Tom Bagsarian. Hanley-Wood. Monthly.
20,000 to producers & distributors of precast, prestressed, ready-mixed concrete & blocks.
www.theconcreteproducer.com tbagsarian@hanley-wood.com

Concrete Products 8751 E Hampden Ave Ste B1 Denver CO 80231 **Phn:** 312-720-9869 **Fax** 303-283-0641 Don Marsh. Mining Media Intl. Monthly magazine.
16,800 to admin. & productions mgrs. in mfg. & distribution of ready mix & precast concrete.
concreteproducts.com dmarsh@mining-media.com

Masonry 506 Roswell St SE Ste 220 Marietta GA 30060 **Phn:** 770-431-0867 **Fax** 770-432-6969 Jennifer Morrell. Mason Contractors Assn of Amer. Monthly.
20,100 to Assn. members and other masonry mgmt., architects, engineers, mfrs., dealers.
masonrymagazine.com jmorrell@lionhrtpub.com

PCI Journal 209 W Jackson Blvd Ste 500 Chicago IL 60606 **Phn:** 312-786-0300 **Fax** 312-786-0353 Michelle Burgess. Quarterly.
7,600 to engineers, architects, mgrs. using precast concrete & interested in project study, rsch.
www.pci.org/publications/journal/index.cfm
mburgess@pci.org

Pit and Quarry 1360 E 9th St Fl 10 Cleveland OH 44114 **Phn:** 855-460-5502 **Fax** 216-706-3711 Darren Constantino. North Coast Media. Monthly magazine.
23,800 to non-metallic mineral mining, quarrying, processing personnel who specify, purchase.
www.pitandquarry.com
dconstantino@northcoastmedia.net

Rock and Dirt PO Box 489 Crossville TN 38557 **Phn:** 931-484-5137 **Fax** 931-484-2532 Mike Stone. TAP Publishing. 36-issue tabloid.
160,400 to construction contractors and other heavy equipment buyers and sellers. www.rockanddirt.com
webmaster@rockanddirt.com

Rock Products PO Box 1025 Medina OH 44258 **Phn:** 330-722-4081 **Fax** 303-283-0641 Mark Kuhar. Mining Media Intl. Monthly magazine.
20,200 to management in the production, distribution of sand, stone, gravel, other rock forms.
rockproducts.com mkuhar@mining-media.com

Stone Sand & Gravel Review 1605 King St Alexandria VA 22314 **Phn:** 703-525-8788 **Fax** 703-525-7782 Peggy Disney. Stone Sand & Gravel Assn. Bimonthly.
6,000 to stone producers and equipment suppliers.
www.nssga.org pdisney@nssga.org

Stone World 210 E State Rt 4 Ste 203 Paramus NJ 07652 **Phn:** 201-291-9001 **Fax** 201-291-9002 Michael Reis. BNP Media. Monthly magazine.
21,000 to architects, producers/users of granite, marble, limestone, slate, sandstone, tiles.
www.stoneworld.com michael@stoneworld.com

Surface Fabrication 1233 Janesville Ave Fort Atkinson WI 53538 **Phn:** 920-563-1694 **Fax** 920-563-1707 Jackie Roembke. Cygnus Business Media. 9-issue magazine.
9,300 to solid surface, stone/quartz surfacing industry personnel interested in installation, mktg.
www.surfacefabrication.com
jackie.roembke@cygnusb2b.com

Automotive .4

Aftermarket Business World 24950 Country Club Blvd Ste 200 North Olmsted OH 44070 **Phn:** 440-891-2746 **Fax** 440-891-2675 Krista McNamara. Advanstar. Online only.
for auto retail, wholesale sr. and middle mgrs. in parts distribution, marketing, purchasing.
aftermarketbusiness.search-autoparts.com
kmcnamara@advanstar.com

AGRR Magazine PO Box 569 Garrisonville VA 22463 **Phn:** 540-720-5584 **Fax** 540-720-5687 Penny Stacey. Key Communications. Bimonthly magazine.
28,000 to owners, mgrs, repair technicians in field of windshield and other auto glass repair.
www.agrrmag.com pstacey@glass.com

American Towman 7 West St Warwick NY 10990 **Phn:** 845-986-4546 **Fax** 845-986-5181 Brendan Dooley. Monthly.
38,000 to owners and business mgrs. in towing, recovery, salvage, service station industries.
www.towman.com scalitri@towman.com

Auto Glass Journal 1088 River Wind Cir Vero Beach FL 32967 **Phn:** 772-232-8888 **Fax** 772-770-2466 Charlene Komar Storey. Monthly.
6,000 to autoglass shop personnel interested in step-by-step glass replacement features, products.
www.bkbpublications.com

Auto Exec 8400 Westpark Dr McLean VA 22102 **Phn:** 703-821-7150 **Fax** 703-821-7234 Peter Craig. Natl Automobile Dealers Assn. Monthly magazine.
20,500 to NADA members interested in all issues affecting auto sales. www.autoexecmag.com
pcraig@nada.org

Auto Laundry News 2125 Center Ave Ste 305 Fort Lee NJ 07024 **Phn:** 201-592-7007 **Fax** 201-592-7171 Stefan Budricks. E.W. Williams Publishing. Monthly mag.
16,000 to carwash owners, managers, buyers; equipment manufacturers, wholesalers, retailers.
www.carwashmag.com alnedit@aol.com

Auto Remarketing 301 Cascade Pointe Ln # 101 Cary NC 27513 **Phn:** 919-674-6020 **Fax** 919-674-6027 Joe Overby. Twice monthly magazine. TH:@AR_JoeOverby
35,000 to used vehicle industry dealers, fleet and rental vehicle managers. www.autoremarketing.com
joverby@autoremarketing.com

Auto Rental News 3520 Challenger St Torrance CA 90503 **Phn:** 310-533-2400 **Fax** 310-533-2507 Chris Brown. Bobit Business Media.
12,000 to car and truck rental industry personnel intersted in news, statistics, industry profiles.
www.autorentalnews.com chris.brown@bobit.com

AutoInc PO Box 929 Bedford TX 76095 **Phn:** 817-358-5219 **Fax** 817-685-0225 Leona Dalavai Scott. Automotive Service Assn. Monthly magazine.
13,300 to repair shop owners interested in technical, business mgmt. info., developments. www.autoinc.org
leonad@asashop.org

Automobile Magazine 120 E Liberty St Frnt 2 Ann Arbor MI 48104 **Phn:** 734-994-3500 **Fax** 734-994-1153 Jean Jennings. Source Interlink Media. Monthly magazine.
555,300 to car enthusiasts interested in car culture, test drives, road trips. www.automobilemag.com feedback@automobilemag.com

Automotive Body Repair Network 24950 Country Club Blvd Ste 200 North Olmsted OH 44070 **Phn:** 440-891-2617 **Fax** 440-891-2675 Bruce Adams. Advanstar. Monthly mag.
41,800 to collision repair industry shop owners, technicians, parts distributors.
www.searchautoparts.com/abrn/
bruce.adams@advanstar.com

Automotive Design & Production 705 S Main St Ste 205 Plymouth MI 48170 **Phn:** 734-416-9705 **Fax** 734-416-9707 Gary Vasilash. Gardner Pubs. Monthly mag.
60,500 to auto industry execs., production mgrs., designers, R&D personnel; purchasing agents.
www.autofieldguide.com gsv@autofieldguide.com

Automotive Engineering Intl. 400 Commonwealth Dr Warrendale PA 15086 **Phn:** 724-772-8509 **Fax** 724-776-9765 Kevin Jost. Soc. Automotive Engineers. Mo. mag.
85,700 to domestic and intl. automotive engineers interested in applied technology.
www.sae.org/mags/aei/ aei@sae.org

Automotive News 1155 Gratiot Ave Detroit MI 48207 **Phn:** 313-446-6000 **Fax** 313-446-0383 Richard Johnson. Crain Communications. Wkly. tabloid.
65,400 to vehicle dealers interested in sales & production numbers, market analyses.
www.autonews.com rjohnson@crain.com

Automotive Recycling 9113 Church St Manassas VA 20110 **Phn:** 571-208-0428 **Fax** 571-208-0430 Caryn Suko-Smith. Bimonthly magazine.
1,200 to managers, owners of auto salvage yards and recycling businesses. www.a-r-a.org
araeditor@comcast.net

AutoWeek 1155 Gratiot Ave Detroit MI 48207 **Phn:** 313-446-6000 **Fax** 313-446-1027 Wes Raynal. Crain Automotive Gp. Biweekly magazine.
275,300 to auto enthusiasts interested in car trends, domestic and imported cars, car travel.
www.autoweek.com wraynal@crain.com

Bodyshop Business 3550 Embassy Pkwy Akron OH 44333 **Phn:** 330-670-1234 **Fax** 330-670-0874 Jason Stahl. Babcox Media. Monthly magazine.
58,800 to body repair/refinishing personnel interested in shop mgmt. and operations.
www.bodyshopbusiness.com jstahl@babcox.com

Brake & Front End 3550 Embassy Pkwy Akron OH 44333 **Phn:** 330-670-1234 **Fax** 330-670-0874 Andrew Markel. Babcox Media. Monthly magazine.
40,000 to specialists in brakes, wheel alignment, suspension, steering, front ends.
www.brakeandfrontend.com amarkel@babcox.com

Car and Driver 1585 Eisenhower Pl Ann Arbor MI 48108 **Phn:** 734-971-3600 **Fax** 734-971-9188 Eddie Alterman. HFMUS. Monthly magazine.
1,304,200 to auto enthusiasts interested in domestic and import test drives and evaluations.
www.caranddriver.com editors@caranddriver.com

The Cooling Journal 3000 Village Run Rd Ste 103 Wexford PA 15090 **Phn:** 724-799-8415 **Fax** 724-934-1036 Wayne Juchno. Natl. Automotive Radiator Svce. Assn. Monthly.
10,000 to automotive thermal energy industry personnel interested in activities, products, networking. narsa.org wjuchno@narsa.org

Counterman 3550 Embassy Pkwy Akron OH 44333 **Phn:** 330-670-1234 **Fax** 330-670-0874 Mark Phillips. Babcox Media. Monthly magazine.
40,300 to employees at all levels of the wholesale and retail parts industries. www.counterman.com mphillips@babcox.com

Custom Classic Trucks 774 S Placentia Ave Placentia CA 92870 **Phn:** 714-939-2400 **Fax** 714-927-7213 Ryan Manson. Source Interlink Media. Monthly magazine.
70,400 to readers interested in pre-1972 vintage pickup/panel trucks, photo essays, restorations.
www.customclassictrucks.com

Engine Builder 3550 Embassy Pkwy Akron OH 44333 **Phn:** 330-670-1234 **Fax** 330-670-0874 Doug Kaufman. Babcox Media. Monthly magazine.
18,000 to engine builders/rebuilders interested in technical info, industry news.
www.enginebuildermag.com dkaufman@babcox.com

Import Automotive Parts/Accessor 799 Camarillo Springs Rd Camarillo CA 93012 **Phn:** 805-445-8881 **Fax** 805-445-8882 Steve Relyea. 9-issue magazine.
30,000 to import dealerships, wholesalers, service and repair shops, sales reps. www.meyerspublishing.com steve@meyerspublishing.com

ImportCar 3550 Embassy Pkwy Akron OH 44333 **Phn:** 330-670-1234 **Fax** 330-670-0874 Mary DellaValle. Babcox Media. Monthly magazine.
28,000 to independent repair shops specializing in repair & service of import vehicles. www.import-car.com mdellavalle@babcox.com

Lowrider 1733 Alton Pkwy Irvine CA 92606 **Phn:** 949-705-3100 Joe Ray. Source Interlink Media. Monthly magazine.
55,400 to lowrider enthusiasts interested in hydraulics, suspensions, photos, how-to articles.
www.lowridermagazine.com joe.ray@sorc.com

Modern Tire Dealer 3515 Massillon Rd Ste 350 Uniontown OH 44685 **Phn:** 330-899-2200 **Fax** 330-899-2209 Robert Ulrich. Bobit Business Media. Monthly magazine.
35,000 to independent retail, commercial & wholesale tire dealers interested in industry news, how-to features. www.moderntiredealer.com
bob.ulrich@bobit.com

Modified 1733 Alton Pkwy Irvine CA 92606 **Phn:** 949-705-3100 Phil McRae. Source Interlink Media. Monthly magazine.
30,800 to import/turbo car enthusiasts; technical articles, installs, project cars. www.modified.com editors@modified.com

Motor Age 24950 Country Club Blvd Ste 200 North Olmsted IL 44070 **Phn:** 440-891-2745 **Fax** 440-891-2675 Tschanen Brandyberry. Advanstar. Monthly magazine.
140,100 to service station/repair shop owners/mechanics interested in technical content. motorage.search-autoparts.com tbrandyberry@advanstar.com

Motor Magazine 1301 W Long Lake Rd Ste 300 Troy MI 48098 **Phn:** 248-312-2700 **Fax** 248-879-8603 John Lypen. Hearst Corp. Monthly magazine.
143,300 to car and truck dealers, repair and service outlets, service stations, automotive suppliers.
www.motor.com jlypen@motor.com

Motor Trend 831 S. Douglas St Ste 100 El Segundo CA 90245 **Phn:** 310-531-9900 Edward Loh. Source Interlink Media. Monthly magazine.
1,135,000 to readers interested in test drives, comparisons, car care, repair Q&A.
www.motortrend.com edward.loh@sorc.com

Modified Mustangs & Fords 9036 Brittany Way Tampa FL 33619 **Phn:** 813-675-3500 **Fax** 813-675-3559 Steve Baur. Source Interlink Media. Monthly magazine.
50,000 to readers interested in vintage (1955-78) Fords, Mercurys & Lincolns.
www.mustangandfords.com steve.baur@sorc.com

Mustang Monthly 9036 Brittany Way Tampa FL 33619 **Phn:** 813-675-3500 **Fax** 813-675-3559 Donald Farr. Source Interlink Media. Monthly magazine.
50,000 to Mustang enthusiasts interested in do-it-yourself Mustang projects. www.mustangmonthly.com inquiries@automotive.com

Precision Engine PO Box 65 Seville OH 44273 **Phn:** 330-435-6347 Mike Mavrigian. Bobit Business Media. Online only.
for owners and managers of engine rebuilding machine shops. www.precisionenginetech.com mike.mavrigian@bobit.com

Professional Carwashing/Detail 19 British American Blvd W Latham NY 12110 **Phn:** 518-783-1281 **Fax** 518-783-1386 Phillip Lawless. NTP Media. Monthly.
18,300 to full/self-service, dual wash station mgrs./owners interested in equipment, labor, sales.
www.carwash.com plawless@grandviewmedia.com

Professional Tool & Equip. News 1233 Janesville Ave Fort Atkinson WI 53538 **Phn:** 920-568-8363 **Fax** 920-563-1699 Jacques Gordon. Cygnus Media. 9 issues.
100,000 to shop owners, technicians interested in methods, products to diagnose & repair.
www.vehicleservicepros.com jgordon@vehicleservicepros.com

Restyling PO Box 1416 Broomfield CO 80038 **Phn:** 303-469-0424 **Fax** 303-469-5730 Alan Farb. Natl. Business Media. Monthly.
21,100 to aftermarket parts installation personnel at restyling shops and truck cap centers.
restylingmag.com afarb@nbm.com

Rides Magazine 1115 Broadway Fl 8 New York NY 10010 **Phn:** 212-807-7100 **Fax** 212-807-0216 Brian Scotto. Harris Publ. Bimonthly magazine.
150,000 to urban auto enthusiasts interested new, custom, classic cars; celebrities' vehicles. www.rides-mag.com ridesonline@harris-pub.com

SAE Update 400 Commonwealth Dr Warrendale PA 15096 **Phn:** 724-772-8509 **Fax** 724-776-9765 Matt Monaghan. Soc. Automotive Engineers. Online only.
for Society members interested in non-technical news, meetings and seminar information. www.sae.org update@sae.org

Specialty Automotive Magazine 799 Camarillo Springs Rd Camarillo CA 93012 **Phn:** 805-445-8881 **Fax** 805-445-8882 Steve Relyea. Bimonthly magazine.
25,000 to car and truck aftermarket product suppliers, distributors and installers. www.meyerspublishing.com steve@meyerspublishing.com

Super Street 831 S Douglas St Ste 100 El Segundo CA 90245 **Phn:** 310-531-9900 Jonathan Wong. Source Interlink Media. Monthly magazine.
52,300 to compact car owners interested in modifying car appearance and performance.
www.superstreetonline.com jonathan.wong@sorc.com

Tire Business 1725 Merriman Rd Ste 300 Akron OH 44313 **Phn:** 330-836-9180 **Fax** 330-836-2831 David Zielasko. Crain Communications. Biweekly tabloid.
31,200 to independent tire dealers, wholesalers, retreaders responsible for tire manufacture & distribution. www.tirebusiness.com dzielasko@crain.com

Tire Review 3550 Embassy Pkwy Akron OH 44333 **Phn:** 330-670-1234 **Fax** 330-670-0874 James Smith. Babcox Media. Monthly magazine.
32,300 to independent tire dealers and retreaders, tire company store managers, distributors.
www.tirereview.com jsmith@babcox.com

Transmission Digest PO Box 2210 Springfield MO 65801 **Phn:** 417-866-3917 **Fax** 417-866-2781 Gary Sifford. MD Publications. Monthly.
16,800 to transmission/powertrain industry personnel interested in business and technical features.
www.transmissiondigest.com editor@transmissiondigest.com

Undercar Digest PO Box 2210 Springfield MO 65801 **Phn:** 417-866-3917 **Fax** 417-866-2781 Jim Wilder. Monthly.
28,800 to undercar service owners/operators interested in technical & business features.
www.undercardigest.com jwilder@undercardigest.com

Underhood Service 3550 Embassy Pkwy Akron OH 44333 **Phn:** 330-670-1234 **Fax** 330-670-0874 Ed Sunkin. Babcox Media. Monthly magazine.
40,500 to owners, managers, professional technicians at high-volume, independent repair shops.
www.underhoodservice.com esunkin@babcox.com

Used Car Dealer 2521 Brown Blvd Arlington TX 76006 **Phn:** 817-640-3838 **Fax** 817-649-2377 Mike Harbour. Natl. Independent Auto Dealers Assn. Monthly.
19,500 to independent used car dealers interested in trends, legislation, auctions.
www.usedcardealermagazine.com/read/account_titles/163463 editor@niada.com

Ward's AutoWorld 3000 Town Ctr Ste 2750 Southfield MI 48075 **Phn:** 248-357-0800 **Fax** 248-357-0810 Drew Winter. Penton Media. Monthly magazine.
68,200 to automotive OEM mfrs./suppliers; purchasing, engineering personnel. waw.wardsauto.com dwinter@wardsauto.com

Ward's Dealer Business 3000 Town Ctr Ste 2750 Southfield MI 48075 **Phn:** 248-799-2664 **Fax** 248-357-0810 Steve Finlay. Penton Media. Monthly magazine.
25,500 to auto dealership mgmt. interested in news, analysis, operations. www.WardsDealer.com sfinlay@wardsauto.com

Auto Sports--Racing .4a

Area Auto Racing News PO Box 8547 Trenton NJ 08650 **Phn:** 609-888-3618 **Fax** 609-888-2538 Len Sammons. Weekly.
28,000 to northeast NASCAR, USAC, other race enthusiasts interested in events, results.
www.aarn.com info@aarn.com

Car Craft 831 S Douglas St Ste 100 El Segundo CA 90245 **Phn:** 310-531-9900 Douglas Glad. Source Interlink Media. Monthly magazine.
203,700 to drag racing & high performance auto enthusiasts interested in how-to articles, tests.
www.carcraft.com douglas.glad@sorc.com

Chevy High Performance 1733 Alton Parkway Ste 100 Irvine CA 92606 **Phn:** 949-705-3100 Henry De Los Santos. Source Interlink Media. Monthly.
123,100 to Chevrolet enthusiasts interested in buying, restoring, modifying performance Chevys.
www.Chevyhiperformance.com
henry.delossantos@sorc.com

Circle Track & Racing Technology 9036 Brittany Way Tampa FL 33619 **Phn:** 813-675-3500 **Fax** 813-675-3556 Rob Fisher. Source Interlink Media. Monthly magazine.
95,600 to oval-track racing enthusiasts interested in all aspects of the sport. www.circletrack.com robert.fisher@sourceinterlink.com

Corvette Fever 9036 Brittany Way Tampa FL 33619 **Phn:** 813-675-3500 **Fax** 813-675-3556 Alan Colvin. Source Interlink Media. Monthly magazine.
34,300 to Corvette enthusiasts interested in new products, test drives, restoration.
www.corvettefever.com

Dirt Sports 53`8 E 2nd St # 542 Long Beach CA 90803 **Phn:** 562-439-3478 **Fax** 562-433-2965 Marty Fiolka. Monthly.
51,000 to off-road, dirt racing enthusiasts interested in drivers, race resulta, gear. dirtsportsnation.com edit@dirtsportsnation.com

Drag Racer 265 S Anita Dr Ste 120 Orange CA 92868 **Phn:** 714-939-9991 **Fax** 714-939-9909 Peter J. Ward. Beckett Media. Bimonthly magazine.
130,000 to readers interested in natl., intl. events for amateur & professional racers.
www.motortopia.com/dragracer/ pward@beckett.com

Dune Buggies & Hot VWs 2950 Airway Ave Ste A7 Costa Mesa CA 92626 **Phn:** 714-979-2560 **Fax** 714-979-3998 history and more. Wright Publishing. Monthly.
53,400 to VW and dune buggy owners interested in restoration, performance, technology, maintenance,
www.hotvws.com bsimurda@hotvws.com

Automotive .4

European Car 1733 Alton Parkway Irvine CA 92606 **Phn:** 949-705-3100 Greg Emmerson. Source Interlink Media. 9-issue magazine. TH:@europeancar
34,400 to European car enthusiasts interested in performance, modifications, history.
www.europeancarweb.com
greg.emmerson@sorc.com

4 Wheel & Off Road 831 S Douglas St Ste 100 El Segundo CA 90245 **Phn:** 310-531-5038 Rick Pewe. Source Interlink Media. Monthly.
318,400 to 4-wheel drive enthusiasts interested in terrain, performance, modification projects.
www.4wheeloffroad.com
rick.pewe@4wheeloffroad.com

4 Wheel Drive Magazine 1733 Alton Parkway Ste 100 Irvine CA 92606 **Phn:** 949-705-3100 Phil Howell. Source Interlink Media. Monthly.
25,800 to 4-wheel drive enthusiasts interested in trails, club events, modification projects.
www.4wdandsportutility.com phil.howell@sorc.com

Four Wheeler 1733 Alton Parkway Ste 100 Irvine CA 92606 **Phn:** 949-705-3100 John Cappa. Source Interlink Media. Monthly magazine.
183,000 to four-wheel drive enthusiasts interested in equipment, evaluations, technical articles.
www.fourwheeler.com john.cappa@sorc.com

Grassroots Motorsports 915 Ridgewood Ave Holly Hill FL 32117 **Phn:** 386-239-0523 **Fax** 386-239-0573 David Wallens. 8-issue magazine.
64,000 to amateur motorsport enthusiasts interested in events, interviews. grassrootsmotorsports.com david@grassrootsmotorsports.com

Hemmings Classic Car 222 Main St Bennington VT 05201 **Phn:** 802-442-3101 **Fax** 802-447-9631 Richard Lentinello. Hemmings Motor News. Monthly mag.
155,000 to vintage auto enthusiasts interested in history, restoration, prices, auctions, road tests.
www.hemmings.com rlentinello@hemmings.com

Hemmings Motor News 222 Main St Bennington VT 05201 **Phn:** 802-442-3101 **Fax** 802-447-9631 Mike McNessor. Hemmings Motor News. Monthly mag.
213,700 to collectors, restorers interested in antique & vintage cars, thousands of classified ads.
www.hemmings.com mmcnessor@hemmings.com

Hemmings Muscle Machines 222 Main St Bennington VT 05201 **Phn:** 802-442-3101 **Fax** 802-447-9631 Terry McGean. Hemmings Motor News. Monthly mag.
137,000 articles about muscle cars, American performance cars, road tests, restoration and buyer's guides. www.hemmings.com tmcgean@hemmings.com

Honda Tuning 1733 Alton Pkwy Irvine CA 92606 **Phn:** 949-705-3100 Matthew Rodriguez. Source Interlink Media. 10-issue magazine.
35,000 to Honda performance enthusiasts interested in parts, projects, vehicle reviews, photos.
www.hondatuningmagazine.com
matthew.rodriguez@sorc.com

Hot Rod Magazine 831 S Douglas St Ste 100 El Segundo CA 90245 **Phn:** 310-531-9900 **Fax** 323-782-2223 David Freiburger. Source Interlink Media. Monthly.
6,100,000 to hot rod enthusiasts interested in performance, events, street rods, muscle cars.
www.hotrod.com david.freiburger@sorc.com

Late Model Digest PO Box 340 Murphy NC 28906 **Phn:** 828-837-9539 **Fax** 828-837-7718 Jim Carson. Biweekly newspaper.
14,000 to pavement short track fans and drivers interested in track coverage. www.latemodeldigest.net jim@latemodeldigest.net

NASCAR Illustrated 120 W Morehead St Ste 320 Charlotte NC 28202 **Phn:** 704-973-1300 **Fax** 704-973-1303 Ben White. Monthly.
112,000 to readers interested in NASCAR stock car racing circuits, race results, drivers.
www.scenedaily.com

Automotive .4

National Speed Sport News PO Box 1210 Harrisburg NC 28075 **Phn:** 704-455-2531 **Fax** 704-455-2605 Chris Economaki. Weekly newspaper.
30,000 to race fans interested in local, regional, natl., intl. auto racing events, driver profiles.
www.nationalspeedsportnews.com
info@nationalspeedsportnews.com

Off-Road 2400 E Katella Ave Ste 1100 Anaheim CA 92806 **Phn:** 714-939-2400 **Fax** 714-978-6390 Jerrod Jones. Source Interlink Media. Monthly magazine.
47,300 to readers interested in modifying light truck & 4-wheel drive vehicles for off-road use. www.off-roadweb.com jerrod.jones@off-roadweb.com

Old Cars Weekly 700 E State St Iola WI 54990 **Phn:** 715-445-2214 **Fax** 715-445-4087 Angelo Van Bogart. F&W Media. Weekly magazine.
65,000 to automobile collectors & hobbyists interested in swap meets, car clubs, shows, auctions.
www.oldcarsweekly.com
angelo.vanbogart@fwpubs.com

Performance Racing Industry 31706 Coast Hwy Laguna Beach CA 92651 **Phn:** 949-499-5413 **Fax** 949-499-0410 John Kilroy. Monthly magazine.
27,000 to performance racing marketers, retailers, engine builders, racing participants.
www.performanceracing.com
mail@performanceracing.com

Popular Hot Rodding 2400 E Katella Ste 1100 Anaheim CA 92806 **Phn:** 714-939-2400 **Fax** 714-978-6390 John Hunkins. Source Interlink Media. Monthly magazine.
107,300 to auto enthusiasts interested in performance engine building, interior/exterior restoration.
www.popularhotrodding.com john.hunkins@sorc.com

Road & Track 1350 Eisenhower Pl Ann Arbor MI 48108 **Phn:** 734-352-8000 Larry Webster. Hearst Corp. Monthly.
604,000 to enthusiasts interested in road tests, design, race coverage, photo features, tech. info.
www.roadandtrack.com lwebster@hearst.com

Rod & Custom Magazine 2400 E Katella Ave Ste 1100 Anaheim CA 92806 **Phn:** 714-939-2400 **Fax** 714-978-6390 Rob Fortier. Source Interlink Media. Monthly.
113,000 to hot rod/custom auto enthusiasts covering all aspects of street rod scene.
www.rodandcustommagazine.com
rob.fortier@sorc.com

Street Rodder 774 S Placentia Ave Placentia CA 92870 **Phn:** 714-939-2589 **Fax** 714-572-1864 Brian Brennan. Source Interlink Media. Monthly.
141,900 to pre-1949 auto enthusiasts interested in modifications, technical info.
www.streetrodderweb.com brian.brennan@sorc.com

Super Chevy 2400 E Katella Ave Ste 1100 Anaheim CA 92806 **Phn:** 714-939-2400 **Fax** 714-978-6390 Nick Schultz. Source Interlink Media. Monthly.
176,600 to Chevrolet car & engine enthusiasts interested in DIY modification, restoration.
www.superchevy.com
jim.campisano@sourceinterlink.com

Vette 9036 Brittany Way Tampa FL 33619 **Phn:** 813-675-3500 **Fax** 813-675-3559 Jay Heath. Source Interlink Media. Monthly.
30,300 to Corvette enthusiasts interested in restoration, modifications, swap meets. www.vetteweb.com jay.heath@sorc.com

Vintage Motorsport PO Box 7200 Lakeland FL 33807 **Phn:** 415-898-5776 **Fax** 863-607-9514 Randy Riggs. Bimonthly.
28,000 to readers interested in history of racing, vintage racing vehicles, shows, book reviews.
www.vintagemotorsport.com
d.randyriggs@comcast.net

American Trucker PO Box 603 Indianapolis IN 46206 **Phn:** 317-297-5500 **Fax** 317-299-1356 Richard White. Penton Media. Monthly magazine.
533,700 in 3 regional editions offering trucks for sale and other services. www.trucker.com atmarketing@penton.com

Automotive Fleet 3520 Challenger St Torrance CA 90503 **Phn:** 310-533-2400 **Fax** 310-533-2503 Michael Antich. Bobit Business Media. Monthly magazine.
20,000 to vehicle fleet owners, managers and maintenance personnel. www.automotive-fleet.com mike.antich@bobit.com

Black Car News 714 Crestbrook Ave Cherry Hill NJ 08003 **Phn:** 856-751-0656 **Fax** 856-751-0657 Neil Weiss. Monthly magazine.
10,000 to NY metro area livery and limousine service, other vehicle-for-hire owners and operators. www.blackcarnews.com neil@blackcarnews.com

Bulk Transporter 4200 S Shepherd Dr Ste 200 Houston TX 77098 **Phn:** 713-523-8124 **Fax** 713-523-8384 Charles Wilson. Penton Media. Monthly.
15,000 to mgmt. personnel of tank motor vehicles transporting liquid, dry or gas cargo. bulktransporter.com charles.wilson@penton.com

Bus Ride 4742 N 24th St Ste 340 Phoenix AZ 85016 **Phn:** 602-265-7600 **Fax** 602-265-4300 David Hubbard. Power Trade Media. Monthly magazine.
36,000 to execs. in private, public bus transport including charter, city, school, rural areas. busride.com david@busride.com

Commercial Carrier Journal 3200 Rice Mine Rd NE Tuscaloosa AL 35406 **Phn:** 205-349-2990 **Fax** 205-750-8070 Dean Smallwood. Randall-Reilly Publishing. Monthly.
96,500 to executives who manage, operate and maintain private, utility, specialty truck fleets. www.etrucker.com dsmallwood@randallpub.com

Fleet Equipment 3550 Embassy Pkwy Akron OH 44333 **Phn:** 330-670-1234 **Fax** 330-670-0874 Carol Birkland. Babcox Media. Monthly magazine.
60,100 to private, contractual, common carrier fleet service and maintenance supervisors. www.fleetequipmentmag.com cbirkland@babcox.com

Fleet Maintenance 1233 Janesville Ave Fort Atkinson WI 53538 **Phn:** 920-563-6388 **Fax** 920-563-1699 Erica Shulz. Cygnus Business Media. 8-issues.
65,000 to truck fleet maintenance mgmt. interested in operations, environmental compliance. www.vehicleservicepros.com erica@vehicleservicepros.com

Fleet Owner 11 Riverbend Dr S Stamford CT 06907 **Phn:** 203-358-9900 **Fax** 203-358-5819 Jim Mele. Penton Media. Monthly magazine.
105,000 to fleet maintenance operations, purchasing and maintenance managers. fleetowner.com jmele@fleetowner.com

Heavy Duty Trucking 38 Executive Park Ste 300 Irvine CA 92614 **Phn:** 847-496-7070 **Fax** 847-485-8667 Deborah Lockridge. Bobit Business Media. Monthly.
115,100 to truck fleet managers operating Class 1 to Class 8 trucks. www.truckinginfo.com dlockridge@truckinginfo.com

Land Line PO Box 1000 Grain Valley MO 64029 **Phn:** 816-229-5791 **Fax** 816-443-2227 Sandi Soendker. Owner-Operator Indep. Drivers Assn. 9-issue magazine.
231,200 to owner/operator truckers, small fleet operators of over-the-road class 8's. www.landlinemag.com information@landlinemag.com

Light & Medium Truck 950 N Glebe Rd Ste 210 Arlington VA 22203 **Phn:** 703-838-1770 **Fax** 703-548-3662 James Galligan. Transport Topics Pubs. Monthly.
62,200 to commercial vehicle mgrs. responsible for purchasing, maintenance, driver training. www.ttnews.com/lmt/ jgalliga@trucking.org

Trucks--Buses--Fleets .4b

Limousine Digest 29 Fostertown Rd Medford NJ 08055 **Phn:** 609-953-4900 **Fax** 609-953-4905 Susan Rose. Monthly magazine.
14,000 to limousine, van/bus fleet, livery car owners interested in marketing, insurance, news. www.limodigest.com info@limodigest.com

Mini Truckin' 1733 Alton Parkway Irvine CA 92606 **Phn:** 949-705-3100 John Mata Jr. Source Interlink Media. Monthly magazine.
20,700 to mini truck building enthusiasts interested in installation tips, truck shows. www.minitruckinweb.com john.mata@sorc.com

Movin' Out PO Box 97 Slippery Rock PA 16057 **Phn:** 724-794-6831 **Fax** 724-794-1314 Pam Pollock. Monthly newspaper.
70,000 to trucking industry personnel interested in news, products, services, regulations. www.movinout.com movinout@zoominternet.net

Over the Road PO Box 549 Roswell GA 30077 **Phn:** 770-587-0311 **Fax** 770-642-8874 Marvin Shefsky. Ramp Publishing. Monthly magazine.
125,000 to professional truck drivers interested in new products, indus. news, job opportunities. rampmediagroup.com pshefsky@otrprotrucker.com

Overdrive 3200 Rice Mine Rd NE Tuscaloosa AL 35406 **Phn:** 205-349-2990 **Fax** 205-750-8070 Max Heine. Randall-Reilly Publishing. Monthly magazine.
90,000 to owners-operators, drivers, small fleet owners of long distance heavy duty trucks. www.overdriveonline.com mheine@randallpub.com

Police Fleet Manager 130 Waukegan Rd Ste 202 Deerfield IL 60015 **Phn:** 847-444-3300 **Fax** 847-444-3333 Ed Sanow. Hendon Publishing. Bimonthly magazine.
17,000 to police fleet shop supervisors, chief mechanics, police and civilian fleet administrators. www.hendonpub.com esanow@hendonpub.com

Refrigerated Transporter PO Box 66010 Houston TX 77266 **Phn:** 713-523-8124 **Fax** 713-523-8384 Jay Miller. Online only.
 for for-hire carriers, supermarket chains, meat packers, frozen foods packers, distributors. refrigeratedtrans.com jay.miller@penton.com

Road King 102 Woodmont Blvd #450 Nashville TN 37205 **Phn:** 615-627-2200 **Fax** 615-627-2197 Nancy Henderson. Parthenon Publishing. Bimonthly magazine.
223,600 to over-the-road truck drivers interested in human interest and lifestyle features. roadking.com submissions@roadking.com

School Bus Fleet 3520 Challenger St Torrance CA 90503 **Phn:** 310-533-2400 **Fax** 310-533-2512 Thomas McMahon. Bobit Business Media. 11-issue magazine.
24,000 to public, private, parochial school transportation officials; bus owners. www.schoolbusfleet.com thomas.mcmahon@bobit.com

Sport Truck 2400 E Katella Ave Anaheim CA 92806 **Phn:** 714-939-2400 **Fax** 714-572-3502 Mike Finnegan. Source Interlink Media. Monthly magazine.
68,500 to owners of 1967-87 light duty trucks interested in performance, equipment, accessories. www.sporttruck.com

Tow Times 203 W State Road 434 Winter Springs FL 32708 **Phn:** 407-327-4817 **Fax** 407-327-2603 Tim Jackson. Monthly magazine.
30,500 to towing industry owners and mgrs. interested in business and mgmt. topics. www.towtimes.com tjackson@towtimes.com

Towing & Recovery Footnotes PO Box 64397 Virginia Beach VA 23467 **Phn:** 877-219-7734 David Abraham. Monthly tabloid.
35,000 to towing, recovery, repossession industry personnel interested in equip., business mgmt. www.trfootnotes.com david@trfootnotes.com

Trailer/Body Builders 4200 S Shepherd Dr Ste 200 Houston TX 77098 **Phn:** 713-523-8124 **Fax** 713-523-8384 Bruce Sauer. Penton Media. Monthly magazine.
15,500 to execs. in truck trailer/body OEM industry interested in sales, regulations, products. trailer-bodybuilders.com bruce.sauer@penton.com

Transport Topics 950 N Glebe Rd Ste 210 Arlington VA 22203 **Phn:** 703-838-1770 **Fax** 703-838-7916 Howard Abramson. Weekly newspaper.
27,100 to trucking and freight transportation industry management personnel. www.ttnews.com habramso@ttnews.com

Truck Parts & Service 2340 S River Rd Ste 202 Des Plaines IL 60018 **Phn:** 847-636-5060 Lucas Deal. Randall-Reilly Publishing. Monthly magazine. TH:@TPSMagazine
25,000 to medium/heavy truck repair and maintenance specialists and aftermarket distributors. www.truckpartsandservice.com editorial@truckpartsandservice.com

Trucker 1123 S University Ave Ste 320 Little Rock AR 72204 **Phn:** 501-666-0500 **Fax** 501-666-0700 Lyndon Finney. Semimonthly newspaper.
180,000 to trucking management and drivers interested in trucking industry breaking news. www.thetrucker.com editor@thetrucker.com

Truckers News 3200 Rice Mine Rd NE Tuscaloosa AL 35406 **Phn:** 205-349-2990 **Fax** 205-750-8070 Max Heine. Randall-Reilly Publishing. Monthly tabloid. TH:@eTruckerStore
100,000 to over-the-road truckers interested in regulations, safety, family & health issues. www.etrucker.com mheine@rrpub.com

Truckin' 1733 Alton Pkwy Irvine CA 92606 **Phn:** 949-705-3100 Dan Ward. Source Interlink Media. Monthly magazine.
92,200 to readers interested in customizing light trucks, aftermarket products, accessories. www.truckinweb.com dan.ward@sorc.com

Motorcycles--Bicycles .4c

Adventure Cyclist PO Box 8308 Missoula MT 59807 **Phn:** 406-721-1776 **Fax** 406-721-8754 Mike Deme. Adventure Cycling Assn. 9 issues.
45,000 to bicycling tourists, fitness cyclists, mountain bikers interested in trails, destinations, gear. www.adventurecycling.org/mag/ magazine@adventurecycling.org

American Iron 1010 Summer St Stamford CT 06905 **Phn:** 203-425-8777 **Fax** 203-425-8775 Joe Knezevic. Tam Communications. Monthly magazine.
133,700 to Harley-Davidson enthusiasts interested in new models, racing, remodel how-tos. www.aimag.com joek@americanironmag.com

American Motorcyclist 13515 Yarmouth Dr Pickerington OH 43147 **Phn:** 614-856-1900 **Fax** 614-856-1935 Grant Parsons. Amer. Motorcycle Assn. Monthly.
242,000 to Assn. members interested in races, events, touring, regulations. www.americanmotorcyclist.com gparsons@ama-cycle.org

ATV Rider 236 Avenida Fabricante #201 San Clemente CA 92672 **Phn:** 949-325-6200 **Fax** 949-325-6196 Eli Madero. GrindMedia. Bimonthly magazine. TH:@ATV_Rider_Mag
27,100 to ATV enthusiasts interested in bike tests, modifying how-tos, gear & accessory reviews, profiles. www.atvrideronline.com atvrider@sorc.com

Bicycle Retailer & Industry News 25431 Cabot Rd Ste 204 Laguna Hills CA 92653 **Phn:** 949-206-1677 **Fax** 949-206-1675 Lynette Carpiet. 18-issue tabloid.
12,500 to equipment, bikewear, accessory manufacturers and retailers. www.bicycleretailer.com lcarpiet@bicycleretailer.com

Bicycling 33 E Minor St Emmaus PA 18098 **Phn:** 610-967-5171 **Fax** 610-967-8960 Peter Flax. Rodale Press. 11-issue magazine.
418,000 to bicyclers interested in new equipment, physical fitness, travel. www.bicycling.com peter.flax@rodale.com

Bike 236 Avenida Fabricante #201 San Clemente CA 92672 **Phn:** 949-325-6200 **Fax** 949-325-6196 Nicole Formosa. GrindMedia. 9-issue magazine.
42,900 to mountain bikers interested in gear, product reviews, locations. www.bikemag.com nicole@bikemag.com

Biker 28210 Dorothy Dr Agoura Hills CA 91301 **Phn:** 818-889-8740 **Fax** 818-889-1252 Dean Shawler. Paisano Publications. 6-issue magazine.
47,000 to adult male bikers interested in biker lifestyle, biker fiction. www.paisanopub.com dshawler@paisanopub.com

BMX Plus! 25233 Anza Dr Valencia CA 91355 **Phn:** 661-295-1910 **Fax** 661-295-1278 Ben Crockett. Hi-Torque Publications. Monthly magazine.
19,000 to bicycle motocross and freestyle riders interested in race coverage, interviews. www.bmxplusmag.com

Cycle World 1499 Monrovia Ave Newport Beach CA 92663 **Phn:** 949-720-5300 **Fax** 949-631-0651 Mark Hoyer. Bonnier Corp. Monthly magazine.
240,000 to street, dirt, dual purpose motorcycle enthusiasts interested in competition, travel, accessories. www.cycleworld.com hotshots@cycleworld.com

Dealernews 2525 Main St Ste 400 Irvine CA 92614 **Phn:** 949-954-8616 **Fax** 949-954-8845 Dennis Johnson. Advanstar. Monthly magazine.
17,500 to motorcycle, ATV, snowmobile dealers interested in merchandising and operations. www.dealernews.com editors@dealernews.com

Dirt Bike 25233 Anza Dr Valencia CA 91355 **Phn:** 661-295-1910 **Fax** 661-295-1278 Ron Lawson. Hi-Torque Publications. Monthly magazine.
60,300 to off-road motorcycle, supercross enthusiasts interested in products, events, tech. info. www.dirtbikemagazine.com rlawson@hi-torque.com

Dirt Wheels 25233 Anza Dr Valencia CA 91355 **Phn:** 661-295-1910 **Fax** 661-295-1278 Dennis Cox. Hi-Torque Publications. Monthly.
134,100 to readers interested in three/four-wheel off-roading, races, products, model kits. www.dirtwheelsmag.com

Easyriders 28210 Dorothy Dr Agoura Hills CA 91301 **Phn:** 818-889-8740 **Fax** 818-889-1252 Dave Nichols. Paisano Publications, Inc. Monthly magazine.
109,400 to adult male custom motorcycle riders w/emphasis on entertainment, humor, lifestyle. www.paisanopub.com dnichols@paisanopub.com

4 Wheel ATV Action Magazine 25233 Anza Dr Valencia CA 91355 **Phn:** 661-295-1910 **Fax** 661-295-1278 Hi-Torque Publications. Monthly magazine.
62,300 to those interested in high-performance, product reviews, race coverage, riding tecnhique. www.atvaction.net

Hot Bike 1733 Alton Pkwy Irvine CA 92606 **Phn:** 949-705-3100 Jeff Holt. Source Interlink Media. Monthly magazine. **TH:**@HotBikeMagazine
113,000 to Harley-Davidson enthusiasts interested in upgrades, road tests, events, products. www.hotbikeweb.com jeff.holt@bonniercorp.com

In the Wind PO Bos 3000 Agoura Hills CA 91376 **Phn:** 818-889-8740 **Fax** 818-889-1252 Kim Peterson. Paisano Publications. Quarterly magazine.
59,700 to motorcyclists interested in photo features, rider rallies, events. www.paisanopub.com kpeterson@paisanopub.com

IronWorks PO Box 1126 Lewisville NC 27023 **Phn:** 336-945-2500 Marilyn Stemp. 9-issue magazine.
45,100 to sophisticated Harley-Davidson enthusiasts interested in travel, vintage/custom bikes. www.ironworksmag.com iwpr@ironworksmag.com

League of Amer. Bicyclists Mag. 1612 K St NW Ste 800 Washington DC 20006 **Phn:** 202-822-1333 **Fax** 202-822-1334 Meghan Cahill. Quarterly.
40,000 to League members interested in bike travel, products, fitness, events. www.bikeleague.org communication@bikeleague.org

Motorcycles--Bicycles .4c

Motorcycle & Powersports News 3550 Embassy Pkwy Akron OH 44333 **Phn:** 330-670-1234 **Fax** 330-670-0874 Sean Donohue. Babcox Media. Monthly.
15,000 to motorcycle, personal watercraft, ATV, snowmobile, powersports retailers. www.motorcyclepowersportsnews.com sdonohue@babcox.com

Motorcycle Cruiser 831 S. Douglas St Ste 100 El Segundo CA 90245 **Phn:** 310-531-9900 Source Interlink Media. Bimonthly magazine.
406,000 to affluent, mature riders interested in classically-styled modern motorcycle cruisers. www.motorcyclecruiser.com cruiser@sorc.com

Motorcycle Industry 1521 Church St Gardnerville NV 89410 **Phn:** 775-782-0222 **Fax** 775-782-0266 Megan Vickers. Monthly magazine.
12,700 to motorcycle, ATV, personal watercraft, snowmobile dealers. www.mimag.com

Motorcyclist 1733 Alton Pkwy Irvine CA 92606 **Phn:** 949-705-3100 **Fax** 310-531-9373 Marc Cook. Source Interlink Media. Monthly.
205,700 to motorcycle riders interested in how-to's, prices and specs, buying advice, road tests. www.motorcyclistonline.com marc.cook@sorc.com

Mountain Bike Action 25233 Anza Dr Valencia CA 91355 **Phn:** 661-295-1910 **Fax** 661-295-1278 Sean McCoy. Hi-Torque Publications. Monthly magazine.
141,000 to mountain bike racers and trail riders interested in tests, products, extreme biking. www.mbaction.com mbaction@hi-torque.com

Ride BMX 2052 Corte Del Nogal Ste 100 Carlsbad CA 92011 **Phn:** 714-247-0077 **Fax** 714-247-0078 Keith Mulligan. Bonnier Corp. 9-issue magazine.
29,400 to freestyle BMX enthusiasts interested in rider profiles, riding locations. bmx.transworld.net keith.mulligan@transworld.net

Rider 2575 Vista Del Mar Dr Ventura CA 93001 **Phn:** 805-667-4100 **Fax** 805-667-4378 Mark Tuttle Jr. Monthly magazine.
140,000 to motorcycle enthusiasts interested in road-riding, sport touring, commuting. www.ridermagazine.com rider@ridermagazine.com

Roadbike 1010 Summer St Stamford CT 06905 **Phn:** 203-425-8777 **Fax** 203-425-8775 Steve Lita. Tam Communications. 11-issue magazine.
55,400 to novice and veteran motorcyclists interested in buying guides, destinations. roadbikemag.com info@roadbikemag.com

Sport Rider 831 S. Douglas Street El Segundo CA 90245 **Phn:** 310-531-9900 Kent Kunitsugu. Source Interlink Media. Monthly magazine.
59,000 to performance motorcycle enthusiasts interested in techniques, trials, training. www.sportrider.com kent.kunitsugu@sorc.com

Street Chopper 1733 Alton Pkwy Irvine CA 92606 **Phn:** 949-705-3100 Jeff Holt. Bonnier Corp. Monthly.
95,000 features tech articles on chopper building, parts, accessories, latest builder's bikes. www.streetchopperweb.com jeff.holt@bonniercorp.com

Ultimate MotorCycling 11087 Vare Ct Moorpark CA 93021 **Phn:** 805-367-4438 **Fax** 805-715-3718 David Morris. Source Interlink Media. Bimonthly magazine.
110,000 to enthusiasts of cruiser, sport, touring, custom and collectible motorcycles and equipment. www.ultimatemotorcycling.com onlineeditor@ultimatemotorcycling.com

Aviation--Aerospace .5

Aerospace America 1801 Alexander Bell Dr Ste 500 Reston VA 20191 **Phn:** 703-264-7580 **Fax** 703-264-7606 Elaine Camhi. Amer. Inst. Aero/Astronautics. 10-issues.
30,000 to Institute members, engineers, technicians. www.AerospaceAmerica.org elainec@aiaa.org

Aerospace Engineering & Mfg 400 Commonwealth Dr Warrendale PA 15086 **Phn:** 724-772-8509 **Fax** 724-776-9765 Jean Broge. Soc. Automotive Engineers. 10-issue mag.
31,200 to design engineers, technical mgmt. in aerospace manufacturing, related industries. www.sae.org/mags/aem/ aero@sae.org

Air & Space Smithsonian 600 Maryland Ave SW # 6001 Washington DC 20024 **Phn:** 202-633-6070 **Fax** 202-633-6085 Linda Shiner. Smithsonian Institution. BimMonthly.
215,100 to readers interested in aviation enterprise, history, current developments. www.airspacemag.com editors@si.edu

Air Cargo World 1080 Holcomb Bridge Rd Bldg 200255 Roswell GA 30076 **Phn:** 704-237-3317 **Fax** 770-642-9982 Steve Prince. Monthly magazine.
14,500 to executives responsible for purchase of transportation services and supplies. www.aircargoworld.com sprince@aircargoworld.com

Air Classics 9509 Vassar Ave Ste A Chatsworth CA 91311 **Phn:** 818-700-6868 **Fax** 818-700-6282 Edwin A. Schnepf. Challenge Publications. Monthly.
75,000 feature coverage of aircraft and pilots that have written history in the skies. www.challengeweb.com moleary@challengeweb.com

Air Force Magazine 1501 Lee Hwy Ste 400 Arlington VA 22209 **Phn:** 703-247-5800 **Fax** 703-247-5855 Adam Hebert. Air Force Assn. Monthly magazine.
127,000 to Air Force Assn. members; aerospace personnel, government air officials, pilots. www.airforce-magazine.com afmag@afa.org

Air Line Pilot 535 Herndon Pkwy Herndon VA 20170 **Phn:** 703-481-4460 **Fax** 703-464-2114 Sharon Vereb. Air Line Pilots Assn. 10-issue magazine.
85,000 to Assn. members interested in safety, union and regulatory issues. www.alpa.org magazine@alpa.org

Air Transport World 8380 Colesville Rd Ste 700 Silver Spring MD 20910 **Phn:** 301-650-2420 **Fax** 301-650-2434 Kathy Young. Penton Media. Monthly mag.
38,100 to commercial airline management, manufacturers, govt. officials. atwonline.com kathy.young@penton.com

Aircraft Maintenance Technology 1233 Janesville Ave Fort Atkinson WI 53538 **Phn:** 920-563-6388 **Fax** 920-563-1702 Barb Zuehlke. Cygnus Business Media. 11 issues.
41,300 to maintenance professionals in corporate, commercial, gen. aviation; aviation schools. www.aviationpros.com editor@amtonline.com

Airport Business 1233 Janesville Ave Fort Atkinson WI 53538 **Phn:** 920-563-6388 **Fax** 920-563-1699 John Infanger. Cygnus Business Media. 10-issue tabloid.
17,800 to managers of airports, airline facilities, fixed base operations, aircraft dealers. www.airportbusiness.com john.infanger@cygnuspub.com

Airport Press PO Box 300879 Jamaica NY 11430 **Phn:** 718-244-6788 **Fax** 718-995-3432 Joe Alba. P.A.T.I Publishing. Monthly newspaper.
19,000 to aviation personnel interested in air cargo, airport operations, passenger segments. www.airportpress.us/ airprtpres@aol.com

Airways Magazine PO Box 1109 Sandpoint ID 83864 **Phn:** 360 457 6485 **Fax** 360-457-6419 John Wegg. Airways International. Monthly.
65,000 news and review of the commercial flight, civil aviation and airline industry. airwaysmag.com airways@airwaysmag.com

AOPA Pilot 421 Aviation Way Frederick MD 21701 **Phn:** 301-695-2350 **Fax** 301-695-2180 Thomas Haines. AOPA Publications. Monthly magazine.
362,500 to members of Aircraft Owners and Pilots Assn.; regulatory air officials; airline executives. www.aopa.org/pilot/ benet.wilson@aopa.org

Aviation for Women 3647 State Route 503 S West Alexandria OH 45381 **Phn:** 937-839-4647 **Fax** 937-839-4645 Amy Laboda. Monthly magazine.
12,000 to women flight attendants, pilots, mechanics, airport, airline executives, teachers. www.wai.org alaboda@wai.org

Aviation Intl. News 214 Franklin Ave Midland Park NJ 07432 **Phn:** 201-444-5075 **Fax** 201-444-4647 Nigel Moll. Convention News Inc. Monthly magazine.
45,000 to corp. and rotary wing aviation, regional airlines personnel interested in news, trends. www.ainonline.com nmoll@ainonline.com

Aviation Safety 7820 Holiday Dr S Ste 315 Sarasota FL 34231 **Phn:** 203-857-3100 **Fax** 203-857-3103 Joseph Burnside. Belvoir Media Group. Bimo.
15,000 Covers risk management and accident prevention for general aviation. www.aviationsafetymagazine.com

Aviation Week & Space Technology 1200 G St NW Ste 922 Washington DC 20005 **Phn:** 202-383-2300 **Fax** 202-383-2347 Joe Anselmo. Weekly magazine.
115,000 to defense technology personnel & to aftermarket operations executives. www.aviationweek.com joe_anselmo@aviationweek.com

Avionics 4 Choke Cherry Rd Fl 2 Rockville MD 20850 **Phn:** 301-354-2000 **Fax** 301-340-8741 Emily Feliz. Access Intelligence. Monthly.
20,000 to engineers, technical personnel in govt. and commercial aviation worldwide. www.aviationtoday.com/av/ efeliz@accessintel.com

Avionics News 3570 NE Ralph Powell Rd Lees Summit MO 64064 **Phn:** 816-347-8400 **Fax** 816-347-8405 Geoff Hill. Monthly magazine.
15,000 covers regulatory updates, technical articles, news, legislative issues, new products. www.aea.net newsreleases@aea.net

Business Air PO Box 1052 Fort Dodge IA 50501 **Phn:** 515-955-1600 **Fax** 515-955-6636 Ken Grams, publisher. Heartland Comm. Group.
28,000 to pilots, owners, dealers seeking to buy, sell or trade aviation equipment. www.businessair.com gale@hlipublishing.com

Business & Commercial Aviation 54 Danbury Rd Ste 327 Ridgefield CT 06877 **Phn:** 203-826-7134 Jessica Salerno. McGraw-Hill. Monthly.
50,600 to operations and mgmt. personnel & pilots at business aviation flight departments. www.aviationweek.com/bca/ jessica_salerno@aviationnow.com

Business Jet Traveler 214 Franklin Ave Midland Park NJ 07432 **Phn:** 201-444-5075 **Fax** 201-444-4647 Jennifer Leach English. Bimonthly tabloid.
35,500 to private jet owners & fractional owners interested in leasing, chartering opportunities. www.bjtonline.com jenglish@bjtonline.com

Cessna Owner PO Box 5000 Iola WI 54945 **Phn:** 715-445-5000 **Fax** 715-445-4053 Maggie Pickart. Jones Publ. Monthly magazine.
7,500 to Cessna aircraft owners interested in maintenance, news, updates, NTSB report. www.cessnaowner.org editor@cessnaowner.org

EAA Sport Aviation 3000 Poberezny Rd Oshkosh WI 54902 **Phn:** 920-426-4800 **Fax** 920-426-4828 Mary Jones. Experimental Aircraft Assn. Monthly magazine.
170,000 to Association members; builders and flyers of home-built aircraft. www.eaa.org editorial@eaa.org

Flight Journal 88 Danbury Rd Ste 2B Wilton CT 06897 **Phn:** 203-431-9000 **Fax** 203-761-8744 Budd Davisson. Bimonthly.
70,300 to readers interested in aviation history, airshows, restorations. www.flightjournal.com flight@airage.com

Aviation--Aerospace .5

Flight Training 421 Aviation Way Frederick MD 21701 **Phn:** 301-695-2350 **Fax** 301-695-2180 Thomas Haines. AOPA Publishing. Monthly magazine.
66,800 to pilots receiving, renewing or upgrading certification interested in operational info. flighttraining.aopa.org/magazine/ benet.wilson@aopa.org

Flying 2 Park Ave Fl 9 New York NY 10016 **Phn:** 212-767-4936 **Fax** 212-767-4932 Bethany Whitfield. Bonnier Corp. Monthly magazine.
203,300 to pilots, plane owners interested in new/used equipment, safety, training, events. www.flyingmag.com editorial@flyingmag.com

General Aviation News PO Box 39099 Lakewood WA 98496 **Phn:** 253-471-9888 **Fax** 253-471-9911 Janice Wood. 24-issue magazine.
42,400 to airplane owners, pilots interested in govt. regulations, safety, trade shows. www.generalaviationnews.com janice@generalaviationnews.com

GPS World 1360 East 9th St Ste 1070 Cleveland OH 44114 **Phn:** 541-984-5312 Alan Cameron. North Coast Media. Monthly magazine.
40,200 to readers using global positioning system applications in geodesy, surveying, military. www.gpsworld.com editor@gpsworld.com

KitPlanes PO Box 1501 Solana Beach CA 92075 **Phn:** 760-487-8075 **Fax** 760-436-4747 Mary Bernard. Belvoir Media Group. Mo.
63,000 to builders, flyers, designers of amateur-built category of manned aircraft. www.kitplanes.com editorial@kitplanes.com

Light Sport & Ultralight Flying! 1085 Bailey Ave Chattanooga TN 37404 **Phn:** 423-629-5375 **Fax** 423-629-5379 Sharon Wilcox. Glider Rider. Monthly tabloid.
13,700 to readers interested in ultralight & light aircraft, hang gliding, human/solar-powered craft. www.ultralightflying.com contact@ultralightflying.com

NASA Tech Briefs 1466 Broadway Ste 910 New York NY 10036 **Phn:** 212-490-3999 **Fax** 212-986-7864 Linda Bell. Associated Business Publications. Monthly.
190,700 to engineering and mgmt. personnel in aerospace, electronic, and technology industries. www.nasatech.com linda@techbriefs.com

Overhaul & Maintenance 1200 G St NW Ste 900 Washington DC 20005 **Phn:** 202-383-2300 **Fax** 202-383-2440 Lee Ann Tegtmeier. Monthly mag.
18,000 to compliance/safety execs. at airlines, corp. flight depts., military. www.aviationweek.com/aw/ o&m@aviationweek.com

Pipers Magazine PO Box 5000 Iola WI 54945 **Phn:** 715-445-5000 **Fax** 715-445-4053 Jennifer Julin Jones Publishing. Mo.
3,200 to members of the Piper Owners Societyinterested in flying, safety and affordability. piperowner.org editor@piperowner.org

Plane & Pilot 12121 Wilshire Blvd Ste 1200 Los Angeles CA 90025 **Phn:** 310-820-1500 **Fax** 310-826-5008 Jessica Ambats. Werner Publishing. Monthly magazine.
101,100 to piston-engine pilots interested in financing, maintenance, destinations. www.planeandpilotmag.com editor@planeandpilotmag.com

Professional Pilot 30 S Quaker Ln Ste 300 Alexandria VA 22314 **Phn:** 703-370-0606 **Fax** 703-370-7082 Phil Rose. Queensmith Comm. Corp. Monthly.
36,200 to corporate, commuter, charter, military and commercial pilots; airport operators. www.propilotmag.com editor@propilotmag.com

Rotor & Wing 4 Choke Cherry Rd Fl 2 Rockville MD 20850 **Phn:** 301-354-2000 **Fax** 301-340-8741 Ernie Stephens. Access Intelligence. Monthly magazine.
30,300 to executives and management in civil and military helicopter industry, dealers, mfrs. www.aviationtoday.com/rw/ estephens@accessintel.com

SpaceNews 6883 Commercial Dr. Springfield VA 22151 **Phn:** 703-658-8418 **Fax** 703-750-8601 Warren Fester. Weekly tabloid. TH:@Space_News_Intl
40,000 to space & satellite industry decisionmakers, including members of Congress, NASA & Dept of Defense officials. www.spacenews.com wferster@spacenews.com

Vertiflite 217 N Washington St Alexandria VA 22314 **Phn:** 703-684-6777 **Fax** 703-739-9279 L. Kim Smith. Amer. Helicopter Soc. Quarterly.
6,000 to Society members, helicoptor manufacturers, military & government personnel. www.vtol.org staff@vtol.org

World Airshow News PO Box 975 East Troy WI 53120 **Phn:** 262-642-2450 **Fax** 262-642-4374 Jeff Parnau. Richardson Ventures Ltd. Bimo.
4,000 serve both airshow fans and airshow people, performers and planners, enthusiasts. www.airshowmag.com jeffparnau@gmail.com

Baking--Confectionery--Dairy .6

Baking & Snack 4800 Main St Ste 100 Kansas City MO 64112 **Phn:** 816-756-1000 **Fax** 816-756-0494 Steve Berne. Sosland Publishing. Monthly magazine.
11,600 to production, R&D personnel engaged in wholesale, baking, snack mfg. www.bakingbusiness.com sberne@sosland.com

Baking Buyer 4800 Main St Ste 100 Kansas City MO 64112 **Phn:** 816-756-1000 **Fax** 816-756-0494 John Unrein. Sosland Publishing. 10-issue magazine.
18,000 to volume baked foods producers, supermarket bakeries, retail stores, distributors. www.bakingbusiness.com junrein@sosland.com

Candy Industry 155 N Pfingsten Rd Ste 205 Deerfield IL 60015 **Phn:** 847-405-4004 **Fax** 847-405-4100 Bernie Pacyniak. BNP Media. Monthly magazine.
6,500 to chocolate and confection mfrs. interested in products, processing, technology. www.candyindustry.com pacyniakb@bnpmedia.com

Cheese Reporter 2810 Crossroads Dr Ste 3000 Madison WI 53718 **Phn:** 608-246-8430 **Fax** 608-246-8431 Dick Groves. Weekly.
1,900 to cheese manufacturers & marketers responsible for sales, technology, pricing, promotion. www.cheesereporter.com news@cheesereporter.com

Convenience Distribution 2750 Prosperity Ave Ste 530 Fairfax VA 22031 **Phn:** 703-208-3358 **Fax** 703-573-5738 Joan R. Fay. AWMA Publications. Bimonthly magazine.
10,500 to Amer. Wholesale Mktrs. Assn. members, candy/snack distributors, retailers, brokers, suppliers. www.conveniencedistributionmagazine.com joanf@awmanet.org

Dairy Foods 155 N Pfingsten Rd Ste 205 Deerfield IL 60015 **Phn:** 630-616-0200 **Fax** 630-227-0527 Jim Carper. BNP Media. Monthly magazine.
22,300 to dairy processors interested in company profiles, technology, operations. www.dairyfoods.com carperj@dairyfoods.com

Milling & Baking News 4800 Main St Ste 100 Kansas City MO 64112 **Phn:** 816-756-1000 **Fax** 816-756-0494 Joshua Sosland. Sosland Publishing. Weekly mag.
3,300 to grain-based food industry execs. responsible for mfg., technology, transportation, labor. www.bakingbusiness.com jsosland@sosland.com

National Dipper 1028 W Devon Ave Elk Grove Vlg IL 60007 **Phn:** 847-301-8400 **Fax** 847-301-8402 Lynda Utterback. US Expo Corp. Bimonthly magazine.
15,000 to ice cream dipping store mgrs. interested in products, events, sales tips. www.nationaldipper.com lynda@nationaldipper.com

ABA Bank Marketing 1120 Connecticut Ave NW Washington DC 20036 **Phn:** 202-663-5428 **Fax** 202-828-4540 Walt Albro. Amer. Bankers Assn. Monthly magazine.
2,900 to financial service & bank mktg. mgmt. responsible for advertising, PR, sales training. www.aba.com/bankmarketing/ walbro@aba.com

ABA Banking Journal 345 Hudson St Rm 1201 New York NY 10014 **Phn:** 212-620-7200 **Fax** 212-633-1165 Steve Cocheo. Simmons-Boardman. Monthly.
31,500 to commercial, mutual savings banks; S&L officers, executives, insurance firms. www.ababj.com ababj@sbpub.com

American Banker 1 State St Fl 26 New York NY 10004 **Phn:** 212-803-8200 **Fax** 212-843-9600 Neil Weinberg. SourceMedia. Daily newspaper.
13,000 to senior bank management and financial service executives. www.americanbanker.com neil.weinberg@sourcemedia.com

BAI Banking Strategies 1 N Franklin St Ste 1000 Chicago IL 60606 **Phn:** 312-553-4600 **Fax** 312-683-2426 Kenneth Cline. Bank Admin. Inst. Online only.
for bankers concerned with economics, regulations, technology planning, human resources. www.bai.org/bankingstrategies/ kcline@bai.org

Bank Director 201 Summit View Dr # 350 Brentwood TN 37027 **Phn:** 615-309-3200 **Fax** 615-371-0899 Jack Milligan. Quarterly magazine.
35,200 to bank directors and CEOs interested in liability, risk and regulatory issues. www.bankdirector.com jmilligan@bankdirector.com

Bank Investment Consultant 1 State St New York NY 10004 **Phn:** 212-803-8200 **Fax** 212-843-9600 Pam Black. SourceMedia. Monthly mag.
26,400 to bank securities & insurance personnel interested in news, regulatory updates. www.bankinvestmentconsultant.com pamela.black@sourcemedia.com

Bank Systems & Technology 240 W 35th St New York NY 10001 **Phn:** 212-600-3000 **Fax** 212-600-3050 Bryan Yurcan. TechWeb. 6-issue magazine.
24,300 to senior bank executives responsible for technology integration, data processing. www.banktech.com byurcan@techweb.com

Bank Technology News 1 State St Fl 27 New York NY 10004 **Phn:** 212-803-8200 **Fax** 212-843-9600 Rebecca Sausner. SourceMedia. Monthly tabloid.
30,000 to bank IT execs. responsible for ATM's, security, check processing systems. www.americanbanker.com/btn_issues/ rebecca.sausner@sourcemedia.com

BankNews PO Box 29156 Shawnee Mission KS 66201 **Phn:** 913-261-7000 **Fax** 913-261-7010 Bill Poquette. Monthly.
12,000 to execs. at community banks, credit unions, thrift banks interested in information, technology, resources. www.banknews.com info@banknews.com

CFO 51 Sleeper St Fl 3 Boston MA 02210 **Phn:** 617-345-9700 **Fax** 617-951-9306 Edward Teach. CFO Publishing Corp. 10-issue magazine.
402,500 to chief financial officers responsible for insurance, technology, employee benefits. www.cfo.com edteach@cfo.com

Credit Union Journal 224 Datura St Ste 615 West Palm Beach FL 33401 **Phn:** 561-832-2929 **Fax** 561-832-2939 Frank Diekmann. SourceMedia. Weekly.
8,100 to credit union decisionmakers responsible for technology, facilities, lending, marketing. www.cujournal.com fdiekmann@cujournal.com

Credit Union Magazine PO Box 431 Madison WI 53701 **Phn:** 608-231-4082 **Fax** 608-232-8024 Steve Rodgers. Credit Union Natl. Assn. Monthly magazine.
30,000 to credit union treasurers, managers, board members; regulatory officials. www.creditunionmagazine.com srodgers@cuna.com

Credit Union Management PO Box 14167 Madison WI 53708 **Phn:** 608-271-2664 **Fax** 608-271-2303 Mary Auestad Arnold. Credit Union Executives Society. Monthly.
8,100 to credit union CEOs, senior execs & and directors in the United States and abroad. www.cumanagement.org editors@cues.org

Credit Union Times 33-41 Newark St Ste 2 Hoboken NJ 07030 **Phn:** 201-526-1230 **Fax** 201-526-1260 Don Shoultz. Weekly tab.
11,800 to credit union mgmt., board members interested in indus. news, conferences, legislation. www.cutimes.com dshoultz@cutimes.com

Financial Analysts Journal 560 Ray C Hunt Dr Charlottesville VA 22903 **Phn:** 434-951-5442 **Fax** 434-951-5290 Richard M. Ennis. CFA Institute. Bimonthly.
81,700 to investment product decisionmakers at banks & insurance cos., portfolio & risk mgrs. www.cfapubs.org faj@cfainstitute.org

Financial Executive 1250 Headquarters Plz W. Tower, flr 7 Morristown NJ 07960 **Phn:** 973-765-1050 **Fax** 973-765-1018 Ellen M. Heffes. Financial Executives Intl. 10-issue magazine.
18,000 to FEI members, financial managers interested in business and management strategies. www.financialexecutives.org eheffes@financialexecutives.org

Financial Planning 1 State St Fl 27 New York NY 10004 **Phn:** 212-803-8200 **Fax** 212-843-9600 Rachel Elson. SourceMedia. Monthly magazine.
115,000 to planners & CPA's interested in news, products, client relations. www.financial-planning.com rachel.elson@sourcemedia.com

Futures 222 S Riverside Plz Ste 620 Chicago IL 60606 **Phn:** 312-846-4600 **Fax** 312-846-4638 Dan Collins. Summit Prof. Networks. Monthly magazine.
60,300 to futures, options, derivatives market traders interested in analysis, strategies, products. www.futuresmag.com dcollins@futuresmag.com

Independent Banker 1615 L St NW Ste 900 Washington DC 20036 **Phn:** 202-659-8111 **Fax** 202-659-1413 Tim Cook. Indep. Community Bankers of Am. Mo. mag.
14,000 to ICBA members, other community bankers interested in mgmt. issues and technology. www.icba.org magazine@icba.org

Institutional Investor 225 Park Ave S Fl 7 New York NY 10003 **Phn:** 212-224-3300 **Fax** 212-224-3171 Michael Peltz. 10-issue magazine. TH:@mppeltz
115,000 to investment professionals, portfolio mgrs., financial mgmt. executives. www.institutionalinvestor.com iieditor@institutionalinvestor.com

Investment Advisor 7009 S Pomotac St Centennial CO 80112 **Phn:** 720-895-3962 Danielle Andrus. Summit Prof. Networks. Monthly magazine.
50,100 to financial advisors selling variable & fixed annuities, life insurance, long-term health care. www.advisorone.com dandrus@boomermarketadvisor.com

Jrnl. Financial Planning 7535 E Hampden Ave Ste 600 Denver CO 80231 **Phn:** 303-759-4900 **Fax** 303-759-0749 Christina Nelson. Financial Planning Assn. Monthly magazine.
44,100 to certified & other financial planners interested in retirement/estate planning, tax and regulatory news. www.fpanet.org/journal/ christina.nelson@fpanet.org

Jrnl. Taxation 195 Broadway Fl 5 New York NY 10007 **Phn:** 212-807-2195 **Fax** 212-337-4186 Joseph Graf. Monthly magazine.
97,900 to tax professionals concerned with legislation, court decisions, IRS developments. ria.thomsonreuters.com/journals/ joseph.graf@thomsonreuters.com

LatinFinance 1101 Brickell Ave Ste 1200 Miami FL 33131 **Phn:** 305-416-5261 **Fax** 305-416-5286 James Crombie. Bimonthly magazine.
25,300 to bankers & investment mgrs. with banking & commercial interests in Latin America. www.latinfinance.com editorial@latinfinance.com

Mergers & Acquisitions 1 State St Fl 27 New York NY 10004 **Phn:** 212-803-8200 **Fax** 212-843-9600 Mary Kathleen Flynn. SourceMedia. Monthly magazine. TH:@TheMiddleMarket
16,000 to M&A decisionmakers in private equity & hedge funds interested in regulatory news, trends, profiles. www.themiddlemarket.com marykathleen.flynn@sourcemedia.com

Mortgage Banking 1717 Rhode Island Ave NW Washington DC 20036 **Phn:** 202-557-2853 **Fax** 202-408-1918 Janet Hewitt. Monthly
10,900 to mortgage bankers/brokers interested in economic and mortgage trends and forecasts. mortgagebankers.org jhewitt@mortgagebankers.org

Mortgage Servicing News 1 State St Fl 26 New York NY 10004 **Phn:** 212-803-8200 **Fax** 212-843-9678 Mark Fogarty. SourceMedia. 11-issue newspaper.
17,000 to residential, commercial mortgage industry members responsible for loan processing. www.mortgageservicingnews.com mark.fogarty@sourcemedia.com

National Mortgage News 1 State St Fl 26 New York NY 10004 **Phn:** 212-803-8200 Bonnie Sinnock. SourceMedia. Weekly newspaper..
8,500 to S&L assn. officers & dept. heads, savings banks, loan assns., credit unions. www.nationalmortgagenews.com bonnie.sinnock@sourcemedia.com

On Wall Street 1 State St Fl 26 New York NY 10004 **Phn:** 212-803-8200 **Fax** 212-843-9678 Kris Frieswick. SourceMedia. Monthly magazine. TH:@Kris_Frieswick
91,000 to brokers interested in news, market analyses, practice management. www.onwallstreet.com kris.frieswick@sourcemedia.com

Origination News 1 State St Fl 26 New York NY 10004 **Phn:** 212-803-8200 **Fax** 212-843-9678 Bonnie Sinnock. SourceMedia. Monthly tabloid.
14,500 to mortgage industry executives responsible for selling loans to mortgage wholesalers. www.originationnews.com bonnie.sinnock@sourcemedia.com

Pensions & Investments 360 N Michigan Ave Fl 4 Chicago IL 60601 **Phn:** 312-649-5407 **Fax** 312-649-5228 Nancy Webman. Crain Communications. 26-issue newspaper.
51,500 to mgrs., administrators, financial execs. of private, union, state, local govt. plans. www.pionline.com nwebman@crain.com

Real Estate Finance & Investment 225 Park Ave S Fl 7 New York NY 10003 **Phn:** 212-224-3300 **Fax** 212-224-3203 Samantha Rowan. Weekly.
6,100 to real estate executives interested in U.S. commercial real estate property & capital markets. www.realestatefinanceintelligence.com srowan@iinews.com

Research 88 Kearny St Ste 1800 San Francisco CA 94108 **Phn:** 415-348-4200 Janet Levaux. Zackin Publications. 11-issue magazine.
14,000 to secondary mortgage bank personnel responsible for negotiating, servicing, approving loans. www.advisorone.com jlevaux@sbmedia.com

Secondary Marketing Executive PO Box 2180 Waterbury CT 06722 **Phn:** 203-262-4670 **Fax** 203-262-4680 Patrick Barnard. Monthly magazine. TH:@MortgageOrb
15,000 to residential, commercial mortgage pros concerned with buying, selling mortgages. www.sme-online.com/sme/ pbarnard@sme-online.com

Stocks & Commodities 4757 California Ave SW Seattle WA 98116 **Phn:** 206-938-0570 Jayanthi Gopalakrishna. Technical Analysis, Inc. Monthly magazine.
10,000 to professional & individual investors in all public markets interested in analysis, tools. www.traders.com editor@traders.com

Strategic Finance 10 Paragon Dr Ste 1 Montvale NJ 07645 **Phn:** 201-573-9000 **Fax** 201-474-1603 Kathy Williams. Institute of Mgmt. Accts. Monthly magazine.
53,800 to finance/IT sr. mgrs. interested in career development, technology, risk mgmt. www.imanet.org kwilliams@imanet.org

Tax Adviser 220 Leigh Farm Rd Durham NC 27707 **Phn:** 919-402-4500 **Fax** 919-490-4329 Alistair Nevius. Amer. Inst. CPAs. Monthly magazine.
22,700 to CPA's, attorneys, financial executives interested in technical analyses. www.aicpa.org anevius@aicpa.org

Treasury & Risk 475 Park Ave S Rm 3300 New York NY 10016 **Phn:** 212-557-7480 **Fax** 212-557-7654 Meg Waters. Summit Prof. Networks. Online only. TH:@TreasuryandRisk
 to CFO's, corporate treasurers, corporate controllers in risk management. www.treasuryandrisk.com mwaters@sbmedia.com

Trusts & Estates 249 W 17th St New York NY 10011 **Phn:** 212-462-3300 **Fax** 212-206-3923 Susan Lipp. Penton Media. Monthly magazine.
10,000 to portfolio mgrs., trust officers, investment mgrs., tax advisors, estate attys. trustsandestates.com susan.lipp@penton.com

Beauty--Cosmetics .8
American Salon 757 3rd Ave Fl 5 New York NY 10017 **Phn:** 212-895-8200 **Fax** 212-895-8219 Marianne Dougherty. Questex Media. Monthly magazine. TH:@AmericanSalon
120,000 Marianne Dougherty.
www.americansalonmag.com
mdougherty@questex.com

American Spa 757 3rd Ave Fl 5 New York NY 10017 **Phn:** 212-895-8200 **Fax** 212-895-8210 Julie Keller. Questex Media. Monthly magazine.
28,200 to spa owners and mgrs. interested in treatment trends, profiles, products. www.americanspamag.com jkeller@questex.com

Beauty Fashion 16 E 40th Ste Ste 700 New York NY 10016 **Phn:** 212-840-8800 **Fax** 212-840-7246 Adelaide Farah. Monthly magazine.
20,500 to cosmetic, fragrance, toiletry buyers interested in mtkg. stats, industry news. www.beautyfashion.com afarah@beautyfashion.com

Beauty Store Business 7628 Densmore Ave Van Nuys CA 91406 **Phn:** 818-782-7328 **Fax** 818-782-7450 Marc Birenbaum. Creative Age Publishing. Monthly magazine.
15,300 to professional beauty supply industry decisionmakers and distributors.
www.beautystorebusiness.com
mbirenbaum@creativeage.com

Cosmetic World 16 E 40th St # 700 New York NY 10016 **Phn:** 212-840-8800 **Fax** 212-840-7246 Geoff Weiss. Bimonthly magazine.
5,700 to cosmetic industry marketing, sales, retailing, technical personnel. www.cosmeticworld.com gweiss@cosmeticworld.com

Cosmetics & Toiletries 336 Gundersen Dr Ste A Carol Stream IL 60188 **Phn:** 630-653-2155 **Fax** 630-597-0118 Rachel Grabenhofer. Allured Business Media. Monthly magazine.
7,400 to cosmetic/toiletry mfrs. interested in technologies, R&D, production.
www.cosmeticsandtoiletries.com
rgrabenhofer@allured.com

Banking--Financial .7
Dayspa 7628 Densmore Ave Van Nuys CA 91406 **Phn:** 818-782-7328 **Fax** 818-782-7450 Linda Kossoff. Creative Age Publishing. Monthly magazine.
30,400 to owners of premium salons and dayspas interested in mgmt. and operations. www.dayspamagazine.com lkossoff@creativeage.com

GCI 336 Gundersen Dr Ste A Carol Stream IL 60188 **Phn:** 630-653-2155 **Fax** 630-653-2192 Jeff Falk. Allured Business Media. Monthly.
16,000 to mfrs., marketers of personal care products, cosmetics, perfumes worldwide.
www.gcimagazine.com jfalk@allured.com

Jrnl. Cosmetic Science 120 Wall St Ste 2400 New York NY 10005 **Phn:** 212-668-1500 **Fax** 212-668-1504 Colleen Rocafort. Society of Cosmetic Chemists. Bimonthly.
4,000 to chemists concerned with science underlying cosmetic preparations. www.scconline.org dscelso@scconline.org

Modern Salon 400 Knightsbridge Pkwy Lincolnshire IL 60069 **Phn:** 847-634-2600 **Fax** 847-634-4342 Laurel Nelson. Vance Publishing. Monthly magazine.
117,000 to salon owners and stylists interested in cut, color, style techniques. www.modernsalon.com ashipley@vancepublishing.com

Nailpro 7628 Densmore Ave Van Nuys CA 91406 **Phn:** 818-782-7328 **Fax** 818-782-7450 Stephanie Yaggy. Creative Age Publishing. Monthly magazine.
60,500 to salon owners, nail technicians and artists, beauty schools, salon suppliers, mfrs.
www.nailpro.com syaggy@creativeage.com

Nails 3520 Challenger St Torrance CA 90503 **Phn:** 310-533-2400 **Fax** 310-533-2504 Hannah Lee. Bobit Business Media. Monthly magazine.
57,300 to nail salon owners and technicians interested in advanced education. www.nailsmag.com hannah.lee@bobit.com

Salon Today 400 Knightsbridge Pkwy Lincolnshire IL 60069 **Phn:** 847-634-2600 **Fax** 847-634-4342 Stacey Soble. Vance Publishing. Monthly.
25,000 to salon/spa owners and managers interested in promotion, decor, marketing.
www.modernsalon.com/SalonToday/
ssoble@vancepublishing.com

SalonSense Magazine PO Box 4778 Chicago IL 60680 **Phn:** 312-951-6699 **Fax** 312-951-5171 Terri Winston. 11-issue magazine.
42,000 to African-Amer. beauty salon owners, mgrs. interested in marketing, styling techniques.
www.salonsense.com terri@salonsense.com

Skin Inc. Magazine 336 Gundersen Dr Ste A Carol Stream IL 60188 **Phn:** 630-653-2155 **Fax** 630-653-2192 Cathy Christensen. Allured Publishing. Monthly magazine.
26,000 to spa owners and estheticians interested in mgmt., products, procedures, training.
www.skininc.com cchristensen@allured.com

Tanning Trends 3101 Page Ave Jackson MI 49203 **Phn:** 517-784-1772 **Fax** 517-787-3940 Jennifer Carter. Intl. Smart Tan Network. Monthly magazine.
20,000 to indoor tanning center and salon mgrs. interested in products, promotion. smarttan.com editor@smarttan.com

Beverages--Bottling--Brewing .9
All About Beer 501 Washington St Ste H Durham NC 27701 **Phn:** 919-530-8150 **Fax** 919-530-8160 Greg Barbera. Bimonthly magazine.
26,000 to readers interested in beer styles & history, brewing techniques, industry info, festival dates. allaboutbeer.com greg@allaboutbeer.com

Atlantic Control St. Bev. Jrnl. 2001 Main St Ste 203 Wheeling WV 26003 **Phn:** 304-232-7620 Arnold Lazarus. Monthly.
6,300 in 3 regional editions to alcohol industry personnel in WV, VA, NC. www.bevnetwork.com bevjournalch@swave.net

Bartender Magazine PO Box 157 Spring Lake NJ 07762 **Phn:** 732-449-4499 **Fax** 732-974-3289 Jaclyn Foley. Foley Publishing. Quarterly mag.
105,000 to bartenders, bar mgrs. & owners at taverns, hotels, clubs interested in recipes, products. www.bartender.com barmag@aol.com

Beverage Dynamics 17 High St Ste 2 Norwalk CT 06851 **Phn:** 203-855-8499 **Fax** 203-855-9446 Richard Brandes. Adams Beverage Group. Bimonthly magazine.
50,100 to alcoholic/non-alcoholic beverage chain, indep. store buyers, merchandisers, owners. bevinfogroup.com rbrandes@m2media360.com

Beverage Industry 155 N Pfingsten Rd Ste 205 Deerfield IL 60015 **Phn:** 847-405-4040 **Fax** 847-405-4100 Jessica Jacobsen. BNP Media. Monthly magazine.
34,000 to management personnel in the beer, spirits, wine, water and juice bottling industries. www.bevindustry.com jacobsenj@bnpmedia.com

Beverage World 200 E Randolph St Ste 7000 Chicago IL 60601 **Phn:** 646-708-7300 **Fax** 646-708-7399 Andrew Kaplan. Ideal Media. Monthly magazine.
34,000 to execs. in soft drink, beer, wine and fruit juices industries; package manufacturers. www.beverageworld.com akaplan@beverageworld.com

Cheers 17 High St Ste 2 Norwalk CT 06851 **Phn:** 415-994-0130 **Fax** 203-855-9446 Melissa Dowling. Beverage Info Grp. 9-issue magazine.
70,000 to owners, managers of high-volume bars, restaurants, clubs interested in food, marketing. bevinfogroup.com mdowling@m2media360.com

Coffee Business Solutions 13511 Skywatch Ln Unit 202 Louisville KY 40245 **Phn:** 502-749-0992 **Fax** 877-737-3936 Jonlyn Scrogham. Bimonthly magazine.
18,500 to specialty coffe & tea retailers interested in suppliers, management & ownership topics. www.coffeebusinesssolutions.com jonlyn@coffeebusinesssolutions.com

Market Watch 387 Park Ave S Fl 8 New York NY 10016 **Phn:** 212-684-4224 **Fax** 212-779-3334 David Fleming. M. Shanken Comms. 9-issue mag.
50,000 to retailers, restaurateurs, food, beverage directors interested in sales, trends, issues. www.mshanken.com dfleming@mshanken.com

Maryland/Wash. Beverage Jrnl. PO Box 59 Hampstead MD 21074 **Phn:** 410-796-5455 **Fax** 410-796-5511 Stephen Patten. Monthly.
7,000 to MD and DC alcohol retailers interested in trends and legislation. www.beerwineliquor.com spatten@beerwineliquor.com

Ohio Tavern News 580 S High St Ste 316 Columbus OH 43215 **Phn:** 614-224-4835 **Fax** 614-224-8649 Chris Bailey. Semi-monthly newspaper.
8,200 to Ohio beverage industry; owners of bars, restaurants, inns, night clubs; distillers. www.OhioTavernNews.com editor@ohiotavernnews.com

On Premise 2817 Fish Hatchery Rd Fitchburg WI 53713 **Phn:** 608-270-8591 **Fax** 608-270-8595 Pete Madland. Tavern League of WI. Bimonthly.
5,000 to alcohol-serving venue personnel interested in promos, laws, news. www.slackattack.com petem@tlw.org

Southern Beverage Jrnl. PO Box 561107 Miami FL 33256 **Phn:** 305-233-7230 **Fax** 305-252-2580 Wanda Rowe. Monthly magazine.
17,000 to wine, spirits licensees in MO, FL, GA, LA, SC, TN, TX interested in merchandising. www.bevnetwork.com sobevjrnl@bevmedia.com

Stateways 17 High St Ste 2 Norwalk CT 06851 **Phn:** 203-855-8499 **Fax** 203-855-9446 Richard Brandes. Adams Beverage Group. Bimonthly magazine.
8,500 to commissioners, board members, store mgrs. in 18 liquor control states. bevinfogroup.com rbrandes@m2media360.com

The Tasting Panel 17203 Ventura Blvd # 5 Encino CA 91316 **Phn:** 818-990-0350 **Fax** 818-990-0390 Meridith May. 11-issue magazine.
79,000 to U.S. alcohol industry personnel interested in news, products, profiles, trade tastings.
www.tastingpanelmag.com
mmay@tastingpanelmag.com

Vineyard & Winery Management PO Box 14459 Santa Rosa CA 95402 **Phn:** 707-577-7700 **Fax** 707-577-7705 Tina Caputo. Bimonthly magazine.
6,200 to wine industry personnel in viticulture, marketing, finance interested in news, photo features.
www.vwm-online.com tcaputo@vwm-online.com

Wines & Vines 65 Mitchell Blvd # A San Rafael CA 94903 **Phn:** 415-453-9700 **Fax** 415-453-2517 Jim Gordon. Monthly. TH:@WinesandVines
5,200 to personnel in the grape growing, wine making and marketing industries. www.winesandvines.com
jim@winesandvines.com

Books .10a
American Libraries 50 E Huron St Chicago IL 60611 **Phn:** 312-944-6780 **Fax** 312-440-0901 Laurie Borman. American Library Assn. Monthly magazine.
66,000 to members of American Library Assn.; public, academic, school, corporate libraries.
americanlibrariesmagazine.org lborman@ala.org

AudioFile PO Box 109 Portland ME 04112 **Phn:** 207-774-7563 **Fax** 207-775-3744 Robin Whitten. Bimonthly magazine.
15,000 to audiobook enthusiasts, librarians, narration talent interested in reviews, author & narrator profiles.
www.audiofilemagazine.com
info@audiofilemagazine.com

Book Links 50 E Huron St Chicago IL 60611 **Phn:** 312-944-6780 **Fax** 312-337-6787 Laura Tillotson. Amer. Library Assn. Bimonthly.
14,000 to elementary and secondary school librarians, teachers, media specialists. www.ala.org
americanlibraries@ala.org

Booklist 50 E Huron St Chicago IL 60611 **Phn:** 312-944-6780 **Fax** 312-337-6787 William Ott. Amer. Library Assn. 22-issue magazine.
20,200 to school, public, special libraries interested in books, videos, software.
www.ala.org/ala/aboutala/offices/publishing/booklist_p ublications/booklist/booklist.cfm bott@ala.org

Bookmarks Magazine 1818 MLK Blvd Ste 181 Chapel Hill NC 27514 **Phn:** 888-356-8107 Jessica Teisch. Bimonthly.
40,000 to general readers, library staff, book group organizers interested in reviews & author profiles.
www.bookmarksmagazine.com
jessica@bookmarksmagazine.com

BookPage 2143 Belcourt Ave Nashville TN 37212 **Phn:** 615-292-8926 **Fax** 615-292-8249 Lynn Green. 11-issue magazine.
440,000 to readers, bookstore buyers, librarians, publishers interested in book reviews & authors.
bookpage.com lynn@bookpage.com

Choice 575 Main St Ste 300 Middletown CT 06457 **Phn:** 860-347-6933 **Fax** 860-704-0465 Irving Rockwood. Assn. College/Research Libraries. Monthly magazine.
3,000 to college and university librarians interested in book reviews and reference databases. www.ala.org
irockwood@ala-choice.org

Christian Retailing 600 Rinehart Rd Lake Mary FL 32746 **Phn:** 407-333-0600 **Fax** 407-333-7133 Christine D. Johnson. Charisma Media. 20-issue tab.
7,000 to Christian bookstore owners concerned with marketing, promotions, trends.
www.christianretailing.com
chris.johnson@charismamedia.com

Beverages--Bottling--Brewing .9
College & Rsch. Libraries News 50 E Huron St Chicago IL 60611 **Phn:** 312-944-6780 **Fax** 312-280-2520 David Free. Amer. Library Assn. 11-issue magazine.
13,700 to academic library staff interested in collections, grants, technology. www.acrl.org
dfree@ala.org

Foreword Reviews 425 Boardman Ave Traverse City MI 49684 **Phn:** 231-933-3699 **Fax** 231-933-3899 Victoria Sutherland. Quarterly magazine. TH:@ForeWordmag
10,000 to librarians & booksellers interested in independent & university press offerings.
www.forewordreviews.com
victoria@forewordmagazine.com

Horn Book Magazine 56 Roland St Ste 200 Boston MA 02129 **Phn:** 617-628-0225 **Fax** 617-628-0882 Roger Sutton. Bimonthly magazine.
8,500 to teachers and school librarians interested in books for children and young adults. www.hbook.com
info@hbook.com

Library Journal 160 Varick St Fl 11 New York NY 10013 **Phn:** 646-380-0700 **Fax** 646-380-0756 Meredith Schwartz. Media Source. 20-issue magazine. TH:@LibraryJournal
17,000 to library decisionmakers responsible for books, technology, furnishings, admin.
www.libraryjournal.com
mschwartz@mediasourceinc.com

Library Media Connection PO Box 204 Vandalia OH 45377 **Phn:** 800-607-4410 **Fax** 937-890-0221 Carol Simpson. Linworth Publishing. Bimo.
3,400 covers operation of K to 12 school libraries, reviews books and other media.
www.librarymediaconnection.com
lmc@librarymediaconnection.com

New York Review of Books 435 Hudson St Rm 300 New York NY 10014 **Phn:** 212-757-8070 **Fax** 212-333-5374 Robert B. Silvers. 20-issue tabloid.
135,100 to readers interested in critical analyses of contemporary books and ideas. www.nybooks.com
editor@nybooks.com

Publishers Weekly 360 Park Ave S New York NY 10010 **Phn:** 646-746-6758 **Fax** 646-746-6631 Michael Coffey. Weekly magazine.
21,700 to book publishers, book wholesalers and retailers, book designers and printers, librarians.
www.publishersweekly.com
mcoffey@publishersweekly.com

School Library Journal 160 Varick St Fl 11 New York NY 10013 **Phn:** 646-380-0700 **Fax** 646-380-0756 Brian Kenney. Media Source. Monthly magazine.
33,900 to librarians responsible for purchasing books for grades Pre-K to 12. www.schoollibraryjournal.com
bkenney@mediasourceinc.com

Journalism .10b
American Journalism Review 1117 Journalism Bldg # 2116 College Park MD 20742 **Phn:** 301-405-8803 **Fax** 301-405-8323 Rem Rieder. Univ of MD/Merrill College of Journalism. Online only. TH:@AmJourReview
to readers interested in actions and impact of U.S. print, broadcast, online media; ethics, technology.
www.ajr.org editor@ajr.org

Columbia Journalism Review 729 7th Ave Fl 3 New York NY 10019 **Phn:** 212-854-1881 **Fax** 212-854-8367 Liz Spayd. Bimonthly magazine. TH:@CJR
25,000 to professionals, others concerned with performance, standards of journalism. www.cjr.org
editors@cjr.org

Editor & Publisher 17782 Cowan Ste A Irvine CA 92614 **Phn:** 949-660-6150 **Fax** 949-660-6172 Kristina Ackermann. Duncan McIntosh. Monthly magazine.
14,000 to online & print newspaper personnel interested in technology, newsroom staffing changes, advertising, equipment. www.editorandpublisher.com
kristina@editorandpublisher.com

Folio Magazine 10 Norden Pl Norwalk CT 06855 **Phn:** 203-854-6730 **Fax** 203-854-6735 Bill Mickey. Red 7 Media. 10-issue magazine.
10,000 to magazine publishers and editors, production, circulation and sales mgrs., art directors.
www.foliomag.com bmickey@red7media.com

Newspapers & Technology 1623 Blake St Ste 250 Denver CO 80202 **Phn:** 303-575-9595 **Fax** 303-575-9555 Chuck Moozakis. Citizen Pubishing. Monthly tabloid.
16,500 to publishers, production, press, prepress mgrs. interested in installations, products.
www.newsandtech.com
cmoozakis@newsandtech.com

Poets & Writers Magazine 90 Broad St Ste 2100 New York NY 10004 **Phn:** 212-226-3586 **Fax** 212-226-3963 Kevin Larimer. Bimonthly.
80,000 to professionals in the literary community, poets, writers, publishing tips, interviews.
www.pw.org/magazine editor@pw.org

Presstime 4401 Wilson Blvd Ste 900 Arlington VA 22203 **Phn:** 571-366-1000 **Fax** 571-366-1195 Joan Mills. Newspaper Assn. of America. Online only.
for newspaper mgmt. responsible for advertising, circulation, printing, content. www.naa.org
joan.mills@naa.org

Publishers' Auxiliary PO Box 7540 Columbia MO 65205 **Phn:** 573-777-4980 **Fax** 573-777-4985 Stan Schwartz. Natl. Newspaper Assn. Monthly newspaper.
4,200 to community newspaper industry personnel interested in methods, mgmt., people.
www.nnaweb.org stan@nna.org

Quill 3909 N Meridian St Indianapolis IN 46208 **Phn:** 317-927-8000 **Fax** 317-920-4789 Scott Leadingham. Soc. Prof. Journalists. Bimonthly magazine.
10,900 to journalists interested in newsroom and news coverage issues. www.spj.org/quill.asp
sleadingham@spj.org

The Writer 85 Quincy Ave. Ste 2 Quincy MA 02169 **Phn:** 617-706-9110 **Fax** 617-706-9110 Jeff Reich. Madavor Media. Monthly magazine.
30,000 to writers at all levels interested in market listings, fiction & nonfiction craft & techniques.
www.writermag.com tweditorial@madavor.com

Writer's Digest 10151 Carver Rd Blue Ash OH 45242 **Phn:** 513-531-2690 **Fax** 513-891-7153 Jennifer Strawser. F&W Media. 8 issues.
110,000 to freelance, technical, aspiring writers interested in markets and craft of writing.
www.writersdigest.com writersdigest@fwmedia.com

Printing & Publishing .10c
Audience Development 10 Norden Pl Ste 2 Norwalk CT 06855 **Phn:** 203-854-6730 **Fax** 203-854-6735 Bill Mickey. Red 7 Media. Quarterly magazine.
9,000 to personnel responsible for print & online audience acquistion & retention.
www.audiencedevelopment.com
bmickey@red7media.com

The Big Picture 11262 Cornell Park Dr Cincinnati OH 45242 **Phn:** 513-421-2050 **Fax** 513-421-5144 Gregory Sharpless. Monthly magazine.
20,300 to sign shop, photo lab, exhibit building staff working with large format digital printing. bigpicture.net
gregory.sharpless@stmediagroup.com

Communication Arts 110 Constitution Dr Menlo Park CA 94025 **Phn:** 650-326-6040 **Fax** 650-326-1648 Robin Alyse Doyle. Coyne & Blanchard. 6-issue magazine. TH:@CommArts
64,700 to graphic designers, art directors, illustrators in advertising, display, printing and arts.
www.commarts.com editorial@commarts.com

Dealer Communicator 1919 N State Road 7 Ste 202 Margate FL 33063 **Phn:** 954-971-4360 **Fax** 954-971-4362 Patricia Leavitt. Fichera Publications. Monthly tabloid.
13,600 to graphic art equipment dealership mgmt. personnel interested in new products, sales.
www.dealercommunicator.com
pat@dealercommunicator.com

Digital Output 100 Cummings Ctr Ste 321E Beverly MA 01915 **Phn:** 978-921-7850 **Fax** 978-921-7870 Melissa Donovan. Rockport Custom Publ. Monthly magazine.
25,000 to electronic publishers & digital imagers interested in technologies, methods, profitability. www.digitaloutput.net edit@digitaloutput.net

Flexo 3920 Veterans Memorial Hwy Ste 9 Bohemia NY 11716 **Phn:** 631-737-6020 **Fax** 631-737-6813 Bob Moran. Monthly.
25,000 to flexographic printing industry managers, press workers, buyers. www.flexography.org rmoran@flexography.org

Graphic Design: USA 89 5th Ave Ste 901 New York NY 10003 **Phn:** 212-696-4380 **Fax** 212-696-4564 Gordon Kaye. Kaye Publishing. Monthly magazine.
27,300 to art directors, ad agency personnel, graphic design firm executives, illustrators. www.gdusa.com editorial@gdusa.com

Gravure PO Box 25617 Rochester NY 14625 **Phn:** 201-523-6042 **Fax** 201-523-6048 Linda Casatelli. Gravure Assn. of Amer. Online only.
to Assn. members, other industry personnel interested in gravure technology, training, history. www.gaa.org lcasatelli@gaa.org

How 10151 Carver Rd Blue Ash OH 45242 **Phn:** 513-531-2690 **Fax** 513-891-7153 Bryn Mooth. F&W Media. Bimonthly magazine.
38,600 to graphic designers interested in creativity, business info, new and successful designers. www.howdesign.com editorial@howdesign.com

In-Plant Graphics 1500 Spring Garden St Ste 1200 Philadelphia PA 19130 **Phn:** 215-238-5300 **Fax** 215-238-5457 Bob Neubauer. N. Amer. Publ. Monthly mag.
23,400 to supervisors at corp., govt., academic inhouse printshops and reprographic facilities. www.inplantgraphics.com bobneubauer@napco.com

Ink World 70 Hilltop Rd Fl 3 Ramsey NJ 07446 **Phn:** 201-825-2552 **Fax** 201-825-0553 David Savastano. Monthly magazine.
5,100 to professionals in the field of letterpress, lithography, gravure, specialty and other inks. www.inkworldmagazine.com dave@rodpub.com

Package Printing 1500 Spring Garden St Ste 1200 Philadelphia PA 19130 **Phn:** 215-238-5300 **Fax** 215-238-5429 Tom Polischuk. N. Amer. Publ. Monthly magazine.
25,000 to producers of flexible packaging, tags, labels, specialty papers, folding cartons. www.packageprinting.com tpolischuk@napco.com

Print Magazine 10151 Carver Rd Ste 200 Blue Ash OH 45242 **Phn:** 513-531-2690 **Fax** 513-891-7153 Sarah Whitman. F&W Media. Bimonthly magazine.
46,300 to designers, art directors, interested in creative, technological developments & visual culture. www.printmag.com info@printmag.com

Print Professional 1500 Spring Garden St Ste 1200 Philadelphia PA 19130 **Phn:** 215-238-5300 **Fax** 215-238-5337 Nichole Stella. N. Amer. Publ. Monthly.
12,600 to printed product distributors and manufacturers interested in new products, technology. www.printprofessionalmag.com nstella@napco.com

Print Solutions 401 N Michigan Ave Ste 2400 Chicago IL 60611 **Phn:** 800-336-4641 **Fax** 312-673-6880 John Delavan. Print Svcs. & Distribution Assn. Monthly.
24,000 to commercial printing industry management responsible for sales and marketing. www.psda.org jdelavan@psda.org

Printing Impressions 1500 Spring Garden St Ste 1200 Philadelphia PA 19130 **Phn:** 215-238-5300 **Fax** 215-238-5484 Mark Michelson. N. Amer. Publ. Monthly tab.
79,900 to printing company management responsible for marketing, equipment, finance. www.piworld.com mmichelson@napco.com

Printing & Publishing .10c

Printing News 3 Huntington Quad Ste 301N Melville NY 11747 **Phn:** 631-845-2700 **Fax** 631-249-5774 Denise Gustavson Cygnus Business Media. Weekly tabloid.
6,300 to graphic arts and printing industry personnel in the New York and NJ metropolitan areas. www.myprintresource.com denise@printingnews.com

Publishing Executive 1500 Spring Garden St Ste 1200 Philadelphia PA 19130 **Phn:** 215-238-5300 **Fax** 215-238-5484 Lynn Rosen. North Amer. Publishing. Bimonthly magazine. TH:@lynn_rosen
17,500 to creative, production & workflow staff working in digital imaging, multimedia publishing. www.pubexec.com lrosen@napco.com

Quick Printing 3 Huntington Quad Ste 301N Melville NY 11747 **Phn:** 800-616-2252 **Fax** 631-845-2741 Karen Hall. Cygnus Business Media. Monthly magazine.
40,000 to copy shops, quick printers, small printers, in-plant printers, binderies, mailhouses. www.myprintresource.com karen@quickprinting.com

Screen Printing Magazine 11262 Cornell Park Dr Blue Ash OH 45242 **Phn:** 513-421-2050 **Fax** 513-421-5144 Ben Rosenfield. ST Media Group. Monthly magazine.
17,600 to management and technical personnel in the screen printing industry. www.screenweb.com ben.rosenfield@stmediagroup.com

Sign & Digital Graphics PO Box 1416 Broomfield CO 80038 **Phn:** 303-469-0424 **Fax** 303-469-5730 Ken Mergentime. Monthly magazine.
31,500 to sign and digital graphics personnel responsible for design, creation & installation. www.sdgmag.com ken.mergentime@nbm.com

Spectrum Bulletin 1600 Duke St Ste 420 Alexandria VA 22314 **Phn:** 703-837-1070 **Fax** 703-837-1072 Chuck Lenatti. IDEAlliance. Bimonthly magazine.
3,800 to content & media producers/creators responsible for workflow, technology, distribution, training. www.ideaalliance.org chuckl8899@aol.com

Technical Communication 9401 Lee Hwy Ste 300 Fairfax VA 22031 **Phn:** 703-301-2299 **Fax** 703-522-2075 Liz Pohland. Society for Technical Comm. Quarterly mag.
13,300 to technical literature writing staff and graphic production personnel. www.stc.org liz.pohland@stc.org

Wide-Format Imaging 3 Huntington Quad Ste 301N Melville NY 11747 **Phn:** 631-845-2700 **Fax** 631-249-5774 Denise Gustavson. Cygnus Business Media. Monthly mag.
17,600 to design and technical personnel responsible for creating blueprints, signage, displays. www.myprintresource.com denise.gustavson@cygnusb2b.com

Building-Bldg. Management-Real Estate .11

Affordable Housing Finance 33 New Montgomery St Ste 290 San Francisco CA 94105 **Phn:** 415-315-1241 **Fax** 415-315-1248 Christine Serlin. Hanley-Wood. Bimonthly.
13,000 to developers, tax credit sponsors, property managers, financers, service providers. www.housingfinance.com/ahf/ cserlin@hanleywood.com

Apartment Finance Today 1 Thomas Cir NW Ste 600 Washington DC 20005 **Phn:** 202-452-0800 **Fax** 202-785-1974 Jahn McManus. Hanley-Wood. 8-isseu magazine.
31,000 to apartment owners, developers of rental property seeking news and information. www.housingfinance.com/aft/ jmcmanus@hanleywood.com

Area Development 400 Post Ave Ste 304 Westbury NY 11590 **Phn:** 516-338-0900 **Fax** 516-338-0100 Geraldine Gambale. Bimonthly magazine.
43,700 to executives responsible for site selections and industrial facility planning. www.areadevelopment.com gerri@areadevelopment.com

AWCI's Construction Dimensions 513 W Broad St Ste 210 Falls Church VA 22046 **Phn:** 703-538-1600 **Fax** 703-534-8307 Laura Porinchak. Assn Wall & Ceiling Industry. Monthly.
33,000 to wall and ceiling subcontractors, builders, general contractors, manufacturers, suppliers. www.awci.org/cd porinchak@awci.org

Big Builder 1 Thomas Cir NW Ste 600 Washington DC 20005 **Phn:** 202-452-0800 **Fax** 202-785-1974 John McManus. Hanley-Wood. Online only.
covers management, finance and operating concerns of America's blue-chip builders. bigbuilderonline.com jmcmanus@hanleywood.com

Builder 1 Thomas Cir NW Ste 600 Washington DC 20005 **Phn:** 202-452-0800 **Fax** 202-785-1974 Boyce Thompson. Natl. Assn. Home Builders. 16-issue magazine.
144,100 to Assn. members interested in design, marketing, mgmt., technology, finance, assn. news. www.builderonline.com bthompso@hanleywood.com

Building Operating Management 2100 W Florist Ave Milwaukee WI 53209 **Phn:** 414-228-7701 **Fax** 414-228-1134 Edward Sullivan. Trade Press Media Group. Monthly.
73,100 to commercial bldg. owners, facilities mgrs. concerned with energy, renovation, security. www.facilitiesnet.net casey.laughman@tradepress.com

Building Products Digest 4500 Campus Dr Ste 480 Newport Beach CA 92660 **Phn:** 949-852-1990 **Fax** 949-852-0231 David Koenig. Cutler Publ. Monthly magazine.
17,500 to bldg. product retailers and wholesalers in states east of the Rocky Mountains. www.building-products.com dkoenig@building-products.com

Buildings PO Box 1888 Cedar Rapids IA 52406 **Phn:** 319-364-6167 **Fax** 319-364-4278 Chris Olson. Stamats Comms. Monthly magazine.
72,000 to building owners, facility mgrs. in charge of 100K+ sq. ft. facilities. www.buildings.com chris.olson@buildings.com

Business Facilities 44 Apple St Ste 3 Tinton Falls NJ 07724 **Phn:** 732-842-7433 **Fax** 732-758-6634 Jack Rogers. Group C Communications. Monthly magazine.
43,000 to executives responsible for plant, office site selections, realtors. businessfacilities.com jrogers@groupc.com

California Real Estate 525 S Virgil Ave Los Angeles CA 90020 **Phn:** 213-739-8200 **Fax** 213-480-7724 Heather Skyler. CA Assn. Realtors. Monthly magazine.
1,930,000 to real estate salespeople, bankers, attorneys interested in all aspects of CA real estate. www.car.org heathers@car.org

Chief Engineer 4701 Midlothian Tpke Ste 4 Crestwood IL 60445 **Phn:** 708-293-1720 **Fax** 708-293-1432 John Fanning. Monthly magazine.
40,300 to facilities mgrs. responsible for heating/cooling/maintenance, security, infrastructure. chiefengineer.org info@chiefengineer.org

Cleaning & Maintenance Mgmt. 19 British American Blvd W Latham NY 12110 **Phn:** 518-783-1281 **Fax** 518-783-1386 Rich DiPaolo. Natl. Trade Publications. Monthly mag.
40,200 to hospital, school, office maintenance mgrs. interested in efficiency, performance. www.cmmonline.com rdipaolo@ntpmedia.com

Commercial Building Products 1300 S Grove Ave Ste 105 Barrington IL 60010 **Phn:** 847-382-8100 **Fax** 847-304-8603 Gary H. Parr. 9-issue tabloid.
41,200 to commercial & institutional bldg. construction industry specifiers, architects, owners. www.cbpmagazine.com info@cbpmagazine.com

Commercial Construction & Renov. PO Box 3908 Suwanee GA 30024 **Phn:** 678-765-6550 **Fax** 678-765-6551 Michael Pallerino. Bimonthly magazine.
10,000 to retail mgmt. responsible for design, construction, renovation of retail facilities. www.ccr-mag.com mikep@ccr-mag.com

Commercial Property Executive 770 Broadway Fl 4 New York NY 10003 **Phn:** 646-654-4500 **Fax** 646-654-4598 Suzann Silverman. Nielsen Business Media. Semimo. tabloid.
35,000 to builders, developers, owners of commercial properties, financial lenders and investors. www.cpexecutive.com ssilverman@cpexecutive.com

Custom Home 1 Thomas Cir NW Ste 600 Washington DC 20005 **Phn:** 202-452-0800 **Fax** 202-785-1974 Claire Conroy. Hanley-Wood. 6-issue magazine.
30,000 to home builders, architects, interior designers of one-of-a-kind, luxury homes. www.hanleywood.com cconroy@hanleywood.com

Design/Build Business 144 Lexington St Woburn MA 01801 **Phn:** 781-937-9265 **Fax** 781-937-9241 William Angelo. McGraw-Hill. 9 issues.
63,700 to builders, architects interested in new construction and remodelling markets. designbuild.construction.com

Development 2201 Cooperative Way Ste 300 Herndon VA 20171 **Phn:** 703-904-7100 **Fax** 703-904-7942 Julie Stern. Natl. Assn. Industrial & Office Parks. Quarterly magazine. TH:@NAIOP
19,000 to commerical real estate development professionals interested in new/redeveloped commercial, retail, warehouse projects www.naiop.org/en/Magazine.aspx stern@naiop.org

Doors & Hardware 14150 Newbrook Dr Ste 200 Chantilly VA 20151 **Phn:** 703-222-2010 **Fax** 703-222-2410 Jesse Madden. Door & Hardware Institute. Monthly magazine.
13,000 to door and hardware industry personnel, architects, specifiers and building code officials. www.dhi.org jmadden@dhi.org

DWM/Shelter Magazine 385 Garrisonville Rd Ste 116 Stafford VA 22554 **Phn:** 540-720-5584 **Fax** 540-720-5687 Tara Taffera. Key Communications. 9-issue magazine.
30,000 to retailers, wholesalers, mfrs. of lumber, hardware, other construction materials. www.dwmmag.com ttaffera@glass.com

EcoHome 1 Thomas Cir NW Ste 600 Washington DC 20005 **Phn:** 202-452-0800 **Fax** 202-785-1974 Rick Schwolsky. Hanley-Wood. Monthly magazine.
30,000 to residential builders, architects interested in green construction standards, practices, products. www.hanleywood.com rschwolsky@hanleywood.com

Elevator World 356 Morgan Ave Mobile AL 36606 **Phn:** 251-479-4514 **Fax** 251-479-7043 Robert Caporale. Monthly.
7,000 to intl. elevator/escalator/moving walk personnel concerned with safety, new technology. www.elevatorworld.com editorial@elevatorworld.com

Facilities Magazine PO Box 970281 Orem UT **Phn:** 801-796-5503 Kelly Lux. Jengo Media. Bimonthly magazine. TH:@FacilitiesMag
50,000 in natl./UT/AZ/OR/CO/WA/Dallas editions to bldg. owners & mgrs. responsible for construction, mgmt., modernization. www.facilitiesmagazine.com kelly@jengomedia.com

Fine Homebuilding 63 S Main St Newtown CT 06470 **Phn:** 203-426-8171 **Fax** 203-270-6753 Brian Pontolilo. Taunton Press. 8-issue magazine.
307,400 to readers interested in information & advice on residential construction & remodeling. www.finehomebuilding.com fh@taunton.com

Florida Realtor PO Box 725025 Orlando FL 32872 **Phn:** 407-438-1400 **Fax** 407-438-1411 Doug Damerst. FL Assn. Realtors. 10-issue magazine.
104,000 to FL real estate salespeople interested in promotional & sales ideas, legal issues. www.floridarealtors.org magazine@floridarealtors.org

Frame Building News 700 E State St Iola WI 54990 **Phn:** 715-445-2214 **Fax** 715-445-4087 Jim Austin. Krause Publications. 5-issue magazine.
24,000 to town, country builders of post-frame commercial, agricultural, residential units. www.constructionmagnet.com jim.austin@fwmedia.com

Building-Bldg. Management-Real Estate .11

Green Builder 9891 Montgomery Rd # 314 Cincinnati OH 45242 **Phn:** **Fax** 866-380-7504 Matt Power. Monthly magazine.
110,000 to contractors & builders interested in environmentally sustainable products, methods. www.greenbuildermag.com admin@greenbuildermag.com

Green Building Product Dealer 11469 Olive Blvd Ste 103 Saint Louis MO 63141 **Phn:** 314-995-3067 Mike Matthews. 10-issue magazine.
21,000 to construction product buyers interested in environmentally friendly building materials. www.gbproductnews.com editor@gbproductnews.com

GreenSource 2 Penn Plz 9th Fl New York NY 10121 **Phn:** 212-904-2594 **Fax** 212-904-4256 Alanna Malone. McGraw-Hill. Bimonthly.
10,000 covers environmentally conscious design for architects, designers, builders, owners. greensource.construction.com alanna_malone@mcgraw-hill.com

Habitat 150 W 30th St Rm 902 New York NY 10001 **Phn:** 212-505-2030 Carol J. Ott. 11-issue magazine.
9,000 to co-op, condo HOA board members, mgrs. responsible for operations, legal, financial areas. www.habitatmag.com jwu@habitatmag.com

Healthcare Building Ideas 3800 Lakeside Ave E Ste 201 Cleveland OH 44114 **Phn:** 216-373-1218 **Fax** 216-391-9200 Jennifer Kovacs. Quarterly magazine.
20,000 to developers, designers, contractors involved in healthcare bldg. construction, expansion. www.healthcarebuildingideas.com jkovacs@vendomegrp.com

Home Channel News 425 Park Ave Fl 6 New York NY 10022 **Phn:** 212-756-5000 Ken Clark. Lebhar-Friedman. Monthly tabloid.
40,200 to home center, bldg. material retailers, wholesalers interested in market rsch., trends. www.homechannelnews.com kclark@homechannelnews.com

Jrnl. Light Construction 186 Allen Brook Ln Williston VT 05495 **Phn:** 802-879-3335 **Fax** 802-879-9384 Don Jackson. Hanley-Wood. Monthly magazine.
68,300 to builders, remodelers interested in design, engineering, energy conservation features. www.jlconline.com jlc-editorial@hanley-wood.com

Jrnl. Property Mgmt. 430 N Michigan Ave Chicago IL 60611 **Phn:** 312-329-6016 **Fax** 312-410-7916 Mariana Toscas. Institute of Real Estate Mgmt. Bimonthly.
19,300 to residential, corporate property mgrs. responsible for asset mgmt., leasing, tenancy. www.irem.org jpm@irem.org

Landings Magazine PO Box 7721 Overland Park KS 66207 **Phn:** 913-709-2228 **Fax** 816-298-6352 Brett Miller. Bimonthly magazine. TH:@magazinepub
250,000 to Kansas City, MO real estate agents & brokers, builders interested in opportunities, news. www.LandingsMag.com brittmiller@kc.rr.com

Maintenance Sales News PO Box 130 Arcola IL 61910 **Phn:** 217-268-4959 **Fax** 217-268-4815 Harrell Kerkhoff. Bimonthly tabloid.
14,800 to maintenance supply distributors interested in management issues, training, product lines. www.maintenancesalesnews.com rankinmag@consolidated.net

Maintenance Solutions 2100 W Florist Ave Milwaukee WI 53209 **Phn:** 414-228-7701 **Fax** 414-228-1134 Dan Hounsell. Trade Press Media Group. Monthly tabloid.
35,100 to maintenance/engineering mgrs. responsible for facilities, grounds, housekeeping. www.facilitiesnet.com/ms dan.hounsell@tradepress.com

Maintenance Supplies 1233 Janesville Ave Fort Atkinson WI 53538 **Phn:** 920-563-1628 **Fax** 920-563-1700 Arlette Sambs. Cygnus Business Media. 9-issue mag.
17,600 to distributors selling maintenance equipment, sanitary supplies, cleaning equipment. www.maintenancesuppliesmag.com arlette.sambs@cygnusb2b.com

Metal Construction News 7450 Skokie Blvd Skokie IL 60077 **Phn:** 847-674-2200 **Fax** 847-674-3676 Mark Robbins. Modern Trade Comm. Monthly tabloid.
29,500 to building systems, panel, metal roofing/siding personnel interested in energy efficiency. www.moderntrade.com mrobins@moderntrade.com

Midwest Real Estate News 415 N State St Chicago IL 60654 **Phn:** 312-644-7800 **Fax** 312-644-5074 Dan Rafter. Monthly tabloid.
17,000 to builders, developers, real estate agents, property managers in the midwest U.S. www.rejournals.com drafter@rejournals.com

Multifamily Executive 1 Thomas Cir NW Ste 600 Washington DC 20005 **Phn:** 202-452-0800 **Fax** 202-785-1974 John McManus. Hanley-Wood. Monthly magazine.
20,700 news and information for senior-level execs. in the multifamily housing industry. www.multifamilyexecutive.com jmcmanus@hanleywood.com

National Real Estate Investor 249 W 17th St New York NY 10011 **Phn:** 212-204-4200 **Fax** 212-206-3622 Susan Piperato. Penton Media. 8-issue magazine.
35,000 to commercial bldg. owners, realtors, appraisers, real estate investors & lawyers, bankers. nreionline.com susan.piperato@penton.com

Pest Control Technology 4020 Kinross Lakes Pkwy Richfield OH 44286 **Phn:** 330-523-5400 **Fax** 330-659-0823 Jodi Dorsch. GIE Media. Monthly magazine.
22,000 to pest control operators, exterminators, fumigators, industry suppliers interested in technology, training, products. www.pctonline.com jdorsch@gie.net

Pest Management Professional 1360 E. 9th St. Fl 10 Cleveland OH 44114 **Phn:** 800-669-1668 **Fax** 216-706-3712 Marty Whitford. North Coast Media. Monthly magazine.
19,000 to pest control specialists in commercial, residential, institutional, health facilities. www.mypmp.net mwhitford@northcoastmedia.net

Professional Builder 3030 W Salt Creek Ln Ste 201 Arlington Hts IL 60005 **Phn:** 847-391-1000 **Fax** 847-390-0408 David Barista. Monthly magazine.
127,000 to owners & managers of building, contracting, architectural & real estate firms. www.housingzone.com dbarista@sgcmail.com

Professional Remodeler 3030 W Salt Creek Ln Ste 201 Arlington Hts IL 60005 **Phn:** 847-391-1000 **Fax** 847-390-0408 Tim Gregorski. Scranton Gillette. Monthly magazine.
83,800 to remodelers interested in business & project mgmt., product comparisons, industry news. www.housingzone.com tgregorski@sgcmail.com

Professional Roofing 10255 W Higgins Rd Ste 600 Rosemont IL 60018 **Phn:** 847-299-9070 **Fax** 847-299-1183 Ambika Bailey. Natl. Prof. Roofing Contractors Assn. Mo.
25,000 to Assn. members; roofing, waterproofing, insulating contractors; suppliers; architects. www.professionalroofing.net abailey@nrca.net

Prosales 1 Thomas Cir NW Ste 600 Washington DC 20005 **Phn:** 202-452-0800 **Fax** 202-785-1974 Craig Webb. Hanley-Wood. Monthly magazine.
34,000 to bldg. product dealers, distributors, wholesalers serving builders' supply needs. www.hanleywood.com cwebb@hanleywood.com

Qualified Remodeler 1233 Janesville Ave Fort Atkinson WI 53538 **Phn:** 920-563-6388 **Fax** 920-563-1707 Andrea Girolamo. Cygnus Business Media. Monthly magazine. TH:@KBDNsustainable
82,500 to remodeling industry personnel interested in design, estimation, installation, marketing.
www.forresidentialpros.com
andrea.girolamo@cygnus.com

Real Estate Forum 120 Broadway Fl 5 New York NY 10271 **Phn:** 212-457-9400 Sule Carranza. ALM. 10-issue magazine.
42,300 to corporate, institutional realty executives, developers, asset managers, brokers.
www.almrealestatemediagroup.com
saygoren@alm.com

Real Estate Magazine 69 East Ave Norwalk CT 06851 **Phn:** 203-855-1234 **Fax** 203-852-7208 Maria Patterson. RIS Media. Monthly magazine.
42,000 to real estate brokers, corp. relocation mgrs. interested in mortgages, buy/sell strategies.
rismedia.com maria@rismedia.com

Real Estate News 3500 W Peterson Ave Ste 403 Chicago IL 60659 **Phn:** 773-866-9900 **Fax** 773-866-9881 Steven Polydoris. Quarterly magazine.
12,500 to real estate industry professionals in Chicago, St. Louis, Milwaukee, Indianapolis, Mpls.
www.realestatenewsusa.com rencorpil@aol.com

Realtor Magazine 430 N Michigan Ave Fl 9 Chicago IL 60611 **Phn:** 312-329-8449 **Fax** 312-329-5978 Stacey Moncrieff. Natl. Assn. of Realtors. 11-issue magazine.
1,300,000 to real estate brokers, sales personnel, land developers, others in related industries.
www.realtor.org smoncrieff@realtors.org

Remodeling 1 Thomas Cir NW Ste 600 Washington DC 20005 **Phn:** 202-452-0800 **Fax** 202-785-1974 Sal Alfano. Hanley-Wood. 13-issue magazine.
80,600 to remodeling contractors interested in mgmt., marketing, design, construction, products.
www.remodeling.hw.net salfano@hanley-wood.com

Remodeling News 700 Godwin Ave Ste 120 Midland Park NJ 07432 **Phn:** 201-389-3838 Renee Rewiski. JSD Comms. 4-issue magazine.
50,000 in 4 editions to Northeast and mid-Atlantic area remodelers and contractors.
www.remodelingnews.com
editor@remodelingnews.com

Residential Bldg. Products & Tec 425 Park Ave New York NY 10022 **Phn:** 212-756-5000 Nigel Maynard. Lebhar-Friedman. Online only. TH:@products_hound
to architects, contractors, lighting & plumbing designers interested in products, trends, industry news, trade shows. residentialbuildingproducts.com
nmaynard@lf.com

Residential Design & Build 3030 W Salt Creek Ln Ste 200 Arlington Hts IL 60005 **Phn:** 847-454-2700 **Fax** 847-454-2759 Rob Heselbarth. Cygnus Media. 9-issue mag.
51,000 to architects, builders and developers creating upper-end, custom homes.
www.forresidentialpros.com
rob.heselbarth@cygnusb2b.com

Roofing Contractor 2401 W Big Beaver Rd Ste 700 Troy MI 48084 **Phn:** 248-244-6497 **Fax** 248-786-1401 Chris King. BNP Media. Monthly magazine.
27,100 to roofers, insulators, contractors interested in equip. comparisons, projects, techniques.
www.roofingcontractor.com kingc@bnpmedia.com

RSI Magazine 600 Superior Ave E Ste 1100 Cleveland OH 44114 **Phn:** 216-706-3700 **Fax** 216-706-3710 Tom Skernivitz. Questex Media. Monthly magazine.
23,700 to roofing, siding, insulation contractors, manufacturers, distributors, engineers, architects.
www.rsimag.com tskernivitz@questex.com

Building-Bldg. Management-Real Estate .11

Rural Builder 700 E State St Iola WI 54990 **Phn:** 715-445-2214 **Fax** 715-445-4087 Sharon Thatcher. F&W Media. 7-issue magazine.
31,400 to rural contractors building light industrial, residential and agricultural structures.
www.constructionmagnet.com
sharon.thatcher@fwmedia.com

Sanitary Maintenance 2100 W Florist Ave Milwaukee WI 53209 **Phn:** 414-228-7701 **Fax** 414-228-1134 Dan Weltin. Trade Press Media Group. Monthly.
16,100 to sanitary supply distribution execs.
responsible for customer service, finance, marketing.
www.cleanlink.com dan.weltin@tradepress.com

Site Selection 6625 The Corners Pkwy Ste 200 Norcross GA 30092 **Phn:** 770-446-6996 **Fax** 770-263-8825 Adam Brunes. Bimonthly magazine.
44,700 to execs. in corporate facility planning, site selection, real estate management.
www.siteselection.com editor@conway.com

Texas Realtor 1115 San Jacinto Blvd Ste 200 Austin TX 78701 **Phn:** 512-480-8200 **Fax** 512-370-2390 Marty Kramer. TX Assn. of Realtors. Monthly magazine.
65,000 to Realtors interested in TX property sales, development, environmental issues, legislation.
www.texasrealtors.com mkramer@texasrealtors.com

Today's Facility Manager 44 Apple St Ste 3 Tinton Falls NJ 07724 **Phn:** 732-842-7433 **Fax** 732-758-6634 Heidi Schwartz. Group C Comms. Monthly tabloid.
50,000 to building owners and mgrs. responsible for facility space usage and design mgmt.
www.TodaysFacilityManager.com
schwartz@groupc.com

Tools of the Trade 1 Thomas Cir NW Ste 600 Washington DC 20005 **Phn:** 202-452-0800 **Fax** 202-785-1974 Rick Schwolsky. Quarterly magazine.
50,000 to renovation and construction professionals interested in tool and equipment reviews.
www.toolsofthetrade.net rschwolsky@hanleywood.com

Units 4300 Wilson Blvd Ste 400 Arlington VA 22203 **Phn:** 703-518-6141 **Fax** 703-248-9440 Paul Bergeron. Natl. Apartment Assn. Monthly magazine.
61,200 to multifamily housing industry personnel concerned with residential property mgmt.
www.naahq.org paul@naahq.org

Walls & Ceilings 2401 W Big Beaver Rd Ste 700 Troy MI 48084 **Phn:** 313-894-7380 **Fax** 248-362-5103 John Wyatt. BNP Media. Monthly mag.
30,000 to contractors in drywall, insulation, lath, stucco, ceiling systems, metal framing.
www.wconline.com wyattj@bnpmedia.com

Western Roofing/Insul./Siding 546 Court St Reno NV 89501 **Phn:** 775-333-1080 **Fax** 775-333-1081 Marc Dodson. Bimonthly magazine.
20,500 to roofing, siding, water proofing, decking, insulation contractors, local trade assns.
www.WesternRoofing.net marc@westernroofing.net

Window & Door 23 E 10th St Apt 101 New York NY 10003 **Phn:** 212-254-5899 **Fax** 212-254-7123 John Swanson. Natl. Glass Assn. 8-issue magazine.
27,000 to fabricators, mfrs. of doors and windows interested in news, products, events.
www.windowanddoor.com jswanson@glass.org

World Fence News 6101 W Courtyard Dr Ste 3-115 Austin TX 78730 **Phn:** 512-349-2536 **Fax** 512-349-2567 Rick Henderson. Monthly newspaper.
12,600 to fence & automatic access control industry personnel interested in products, trade shows, how-to features. www.worldfencenews.com
editor@worldfencenews.com

Business .12

Accounting Today 1 State St Fl 27 New York NY 10004 **Phn:** 212-803-8200 **Fax** 646-264-6830 Daniel Hood. SourceMedia. Monthly tab.
60,000 to decisionmaking tax & accounting personnel interested in news, products and services.
www.accountingtoday.com
daniel.hood@sourcemedia.com

Agency Sales Magazine PO Box 1185 Fairfield CT 06825 **Phn:** 203-258-4628 **Fax** 949-855-2973 Jack Foster. Mfrs. Agents Natl. Assn. Monthly magazine.
8,000 to Assn. members, others interested in market development, sales techniques, training.
www.manaonline.org jfoster@manaonline.org

Alaska Business Monthly 501 W Northern Lights Blvd Ste 100 Anchorage AK 99503 **Phn:** 907-276-4373 **Fax** 907-279-2900 Susan Harrington. Monthly.
12,000 to readers interested in the business of Alaska's economy includes all industries in the state.
www.akbizmag.com press@akbizmag.com

American Salesman 320 Valley St Burlington IA 52601 **Phn:** 319-752-5415 **Fax** 319-752-3421 Todd Darnall. Natl. Research Bureau. Monthly.
1,400 to sales professionals interested in productivity, staff motivation, sales goals, closing techniques.
www.salestrainingandtechniques.com
articles@salestrainingandtechniques.com

Arizona Business Gazette PO Box 194 Phoenix AZ 85001 **Phn:** 602-444-7300 **Fax** 602-444-7363 Mel Melendez. Weekly.
1,800 to readers interested in AZ law, real estate, construction, small businesses.
www.azcentral.com/business/abg/abg_more.html
mel.melendez@arizonarepublic.com

Arkansas Business PO Box 3686 Little Rock AR 72203 **Phn:** 501-372-1443 **Fax** 501-375-7933 Gwen Moritz. Weekly.
7,200 to readers interested in AR agriculture, banking, politics, mfg., technology, tourism.
www.arkansasbusiness.com gmoritz@abpg.com

Associations Now 1575 I St NW Washington DC 20005 **Phn:** 202-626-2708 **Fax** 202-408-9635 Julie Shoop. Amer. Soc. of Assn. Execs. Monthly.
24,000 to Assn. members; execs., managers of business, trade and philanthropic associations.
www.asaecenter.org editorial@asaecenter.org

Association Trends 8120 Woodmont Ave Ste 110 Bethesda MD 20814 **Phn:** 202-464-1662 **Fax** 202-464-1775 Ed Dalere. Monthly magazine.
25,000 to assn. execs. responsible for administration, communications, meetings, mktg., events.
www.associationtrends.com
associationtrends@associationtrends.com

Atlanta Business Chronicle 3423 Piedmont Rd NE Ste 400 Atlanta GA 30305 **Phn:** 404-249-1000 **Fax** 404-249-1048 David Allison. Weekly newspaper.
40,000 to readers interested in Atlanta companies, transportation systems, urban planning, prominent businesspeople. www.bizjournals.com/atlanta/
atlanta@bizjournals.com

Baltimore Business Journal 1 E Pratt St Ste 205 Baltimore MD 21202 **Phn:** 410-576-1161 **Fax** 410-539-8570 Joanna Sullivan. Weekly newspaper.
8,500 to Baltimore business community interested in real estate, construction, education, politics, people.
www.bizjournals.com/baltimore/
baltimore@bizjournals.com

Barron's 1211 Avenue of the Americas New York NY 10036 **Phn:** 212-416-2700 **Fax** 212-416-2829 Fleming Meeks. Dow Jones. Weekly magazine.
305,000 to private investors, money managers, officials in charge of financial affairs. online.barrons.com
fleming.meeks@barrons.com

BetterInvesting PO Box 220 Royal Oak MI 48068 **Phn:** 248-583-6242 **Fax** 248-583-4880 Adam Ritt. Natl. Assn. Investors Corp. Monthly magazine.
60,000 to investment club members interested in corporate analysis, investment education.
www.betterinvesting.org bi@betterinvesting.org

Birmingham Business Journal 2140 11th Ave S Ste 205 Birmingham AL 35205 **Phn:** 205-443-5600 **Fax** 205-322-0040 Joel Welker. Weekly newspaper.
5,500 to Alabama readers interested in Birmingham real estate, banking, healthcare, events.
www.bizjournals.com/birmingham/
birmingham@bizjournals.com

Bloomberg BusinessWeek 731 Lexington Ave New York NY 10022 **Phn:** 212-318-2300 **Fax** 917-369-5000 Ellen Pollack. Bloomberg LLP. Weekly magazine.
675,000 to readers interested in business news, economic trends, technology applications. www.businessweek.com epollock@bloomberg.net

Boston Business Journal 160 Federal St Fl 12 Boston MA 02110 **Phn:** 617-330-1000 **Fax** 617-330-1016 George Donnelly. Weekly.
15,600 to Boston-area businesspeople interested in economic outlook for state, industries, education, healthcare. www.bizjournals.com/boston/ boston@bizjournals.com

Business Credit 8840 Columbia 100 Pkwy Columbia MD 21045 **Phn:** 410-740-5560 **Fax** 410-740-5574 Caroline Zimmerman. Natl. Assn. Credit Mgmt. 9-issue magazine.
16,000 to Assn. members, other business managers with responsibility for extension of credit. www.nacm.org bcm@nacm.org

Business First Columbus 303 W Nationwide Blvd Columbus OH 43215 **Phn:** 614-461-4040 **Fax** 614-365-2967 Dominic Cappa. Weekly newspaper.
9,500 to Ohio businesspeople interested in local companies, natls. based in state, banking, education, healthcare. www.bizjournals.com/columbus/ columbus@bizjournals.com

Business First Louisville 455 S 4th St Ste 278 Louisville KY 40202 **Phn:** 502-583-1731 **Fax** 502-587-1703 Carol Timmons. Weekly newspaper.
9,700 to area businesspeople interested in local companies, business conditions, events, banking. www.bizjournals.com/louisville/ louisville@bizjournals.com

Business Journal Charlotte 1100 S Tryon St Ste 100 Charlotte NC 28203 **Phn:** 704-973-1100 **Fax** 704-973-1102 Robert Morris. Weekly newspaper.
12,400 to area businesspeople concerned with area banks, manufacturers, news, events. www.bizjournals.com/charlotte/ charlotte@bizjournals.com

Business Journal Milwaukee 825 N Jefferson St Ste 200 Milwaukee WI 53202 **Phn:** 414-278-7788 **Fax** 414-278-7028 Mark Kass. Weekly newspaper.
10,600 to area businesspeople interested in Wisconsin manufacturing, healthcare, education, tourism, real estate. www.bizjournals.com/milwaukee/ milwaukee@bizjournals.com

Business Leader 9 Dunwoody Pk Ste 121 Atlanta GA 30338 **Phn:** 866-963-6118 Alison McKinney. Bimonthly magazine.
15,000 in 8 southern U.S. rgnl. Editions to businesspeople interested in banking, real estate, personalities. www.businessleadermedia.com stephen@businessleader.com

Business Life PO Box 2065 Glendale CA 91209 **Phn:** 818-240-7088 **Fax** 818-240-7320 John Krikorian. 7-issue magazine.
17,000 to business, govt., civic leaders in Burbank/Glendale/Pasadena/San Gabriel, San Fernando. businesslife.com editorial@businesslife.com

Business NC 5605 77 Center Dr Ste 101 Charlotte NC 28217 **Phn:** 704-523-6987 **Fax** 704-523-4211 David Kinney. Monthly magazine.
26,400 statewide audience interested in agriculture, banking, insurance, retail, tourism, mfg. www.businessnc.com kinney@businessnc.com

Business Review 40 British American Blvd Ste 3 Latham NY 12110 **Phn:** 518-640-6800 **Fax** 518-640-6836 Neil Springer. Weekly.
7,000 www.bizjournals.com/albany/ albany@bizjournals.com

Business TN 624 Grassmere Park Ste 28 Nashville TN 37211 **Phn:** 615-298-9833 **Fax** 615-298-2780 Drew Ruble. Bimonthly magazine.
35,000 to TN businesspeople interested in public affairs, tourism, utilities, agriculture, healthcare. businesstn.com info@businesstn.com

Carolina Business PO Box 12006 New Bern NC 28561 **Phn:** 252-633-5106 **Fax** 252-633-2836 Cindy Gaskins. Monthly.
32,000 www.carolinabusiness.net taylorpub@embarqmail.com

Central Penn Business Journal 1500 Paxton St Harrisburg PA 17104 **Phn:** 717-236-4300 **Fax** 717-909-0538 Christopher Passante. Weekly newspaper.
11,000 to businesspeople interested in local industries, real estate, technology, news & events. www.centralpennbusiness.com editorial@journalpub.com

Chief Executive 1 Sound Shore Dr Ste 100 Greenwich CT 06830 **Phn:** 203-930-2700 **Fax** 203-930-2701 Mr. J.P. Donlon. Bimonthly magazine.
42,000 to U.S. CEOs interested in features about technology, effectiveness, data analysis, profiles. chiefexecutive.net editorial@chiefexecutive.net

The Chronicle of Philanthropy 1255 23rd St NW Fl 7 Washington DC 20037 **Phn:** 202-466-1200 **Fax** 202-466-2078 Stacy Palmer. 18-issue magazine.
33,400 to foundation mgrs., corporate grant makers, charity donors interested in news, statistics, fundraising ideas. philanthropy.com editor@philanthropy.com

CIO PO Box 9208 Framingham MA 01701 **Phn:** 508-872-0080 **Fax** 508-879-7784 Kim Nash. CXO Media. 18-issue magazine.
140,000 to information execs. interested in management issues, technology, trends, studies. www.cio.com knash@cio.com

Collections & Credit Risk 4709 Golf Rd Ste 600 Skokie IL 60076 **Phn:** 815-463-9008 **Fax** 212-843-9600 Darren Waggoner. SourceMedia. Monthly magazine.
27,000 to credit risk & debt collection personnel interested in legal & technology developments. www.collectionscreditrisk.com darren.waggoner@sourcemedia.com

Colorado Springs Business Jrnl. 31 E Platte Ave Ste 300 Colorado Springs CO 80903 **Phn:** 719-634-5905 **Fax** 719-634-5157 Ralph Routon. Weekly newspaper.
4,300 to readers interested in area real estate, businesspeople, banking, insurance, investments. csbj.com editorial@csbj.com

ColoradoBiz 6160 S Syracuse Way Ste 300 Greenwood Village CO 80111 **Phn:** 303-662-5200 **Fax** 303-397-7619 Mike Taylor. Monthly magazine.
20,500 to readers interested in CO businesspeople, projects, tourism, healthcare, energy, technology. www.cobizmag.com mtaylor@cobizmag.com

Columbus CEO 5255 Sinclair Rd Columbus OH 43229 **Phn:** 614-540-8900 **Fax** 614-848-3838 Julanne Hohbach. Monthly.
24,000 to central OH business owners & executives, medical & legal professionals, govt. executives. www.columbusceo.com pressreleases@columbusceo.com

Compliance Week 77 N Washington St Ste 201 Boston MA 02114 **Phn:** 888-519-9200 **Fax** 800-675-1887 Matt Kelly. Haymarket Media. Monthly magazine.
26,500 to financial, legal, audit, risk & compliance executives at public companies. www.complianceweek.com editor@complianceweek.com

The Conference Board Review 845 3rd Ave New York NY 10022 **Phn:** 212-759-0900 **Fax** 212-836-3828 Matthew Budman. Conference Board Inc. Quarterly magazine.
26,100 to corporate senior management interested in business opinion, ideas, forecasts, research. www.tcbreview.com tcbreview@tcbreview.com

Contingent Workforce Strategies 881 Fremont Ave Ste A3 Los Altos CA 94024 **Phn:** 650-232-2350 **Fax** 650-232-2360 Subadhra Sriram. Staffing Indus. Analysts. 9 issues.
20,000 to human resource managers responsible for contingent staffing decisionmaking. www.staffingindustry.com ssriram@staffingindustry.com

Contract Management 21740 Beaumeade Cir Ste 125 Ashburn VA 20147 **Phn:** 571-382-1107 **Fax** 703-448-0939 Kerry Hansen. Natl. Contract Mgmt. Assn. Monthly.
21,000 to corporate & govt. procurement mgrs. concerned with policy, legislation, ethics. www.ncmahq.org kmckinnon@ncmahq.org

The CPA Journal 3 Park Ave Fl 18 New York NY 10016 **Phn:** 212-719-8300 **Fax** 212-719-3364 Mary-Jo Kranacher. NY State Soc. of CPAs. Monthly magazine.
30,900 to Soc. members, CPA's, corporate accts. responsible for auditing, taxes, mgmt. services. www.cpajournal.com cpaj-editors@nysscpa.org

Crain's Chicago Business 360 N Michigan Ave Fl 7 Chicago IL 60601 **Phn:** 312-649-5411 **Fax** 312-280-3150 Michael Arndt. Weekly tabloid.
45,700 to Chicago-area business & professional people in real estate, finance, business equipment, travel, services. www.chicagobusiness.com marndt@crain.com

Crain's Cleveland Business 700 W Saint Clair Ave Ste 310 Cleveland OH 44113 **Phn:** 216-522-1383 **Fax** 216-522-0625 Mark Dodosh. Weekly tabloid.
16,000 www.crainscleveland.com mdodosh@crain.com

Crain's Detroit Business 1155 Gratiot Ave Detroit MI 48207 **Phn:** 313-446-0419 **Fax** 313-446-1687 Cindy Goodaker. Weekly tabloid.
32,000 to readers interested in Detroit & SE Michigan businesspeople, economic development, automotive industry. www.crainsdetroit.com cgoodaker@crain.com

Crain's NY Business 711 3rd Ave New York NY 10017 **Phn:** 212-210-0100 **Fax** 212-210-0799 Jeremy Smerd. Weekly tabloid.
80,000 www.crainsnewyork.com jsmerd@crainsnewyork.com

Dallas Business Journal 12801 N Central Expy Ste 800 Dallas TX 75243 **Phn:** 214-696-5959 **Fax** 214-361-4045 Juan Elizondo. Weekly newspaper.
15,000 www.bizjournals.com/dallas/ dallas@bizjournals.com

Denver Business Journal 1700 Broadway Ste 515 Denver CO 80290 **Phn:** 303-837-3500 **Fax** 303-837-3535 Neil Westergaard. Weekly newspaper.
14,100 to Denver-area businesspeople interested in real estate, energy regulations, mining, healthcare, events, profiles. www.bizjournals.com/denver/ denvernews@bizjournals.com

Des Moines Business Record 100 4th St Des Moines IA 50309 **Phn:** 515-288-3336 **Fax** 515-288-0309 Chris Conetzkey. Weekly newspaper.
6,500 to Des Moines area businesspeople interested in events, agriculture, utilities, real estate, econ development. businessrecord.com chrisconetzkey@bpcdm.com

Detroiter 1 Woodward Ave Ste 1900 Detroit MI 48226 **Phn:** 313-964-4000 Jim Martinez. Detroit Rgnl. Chamber of Commerce. 6-issue magazine.
20,000 to Chamber members & other readers interested in business people & opportunities in Detroit metro. www.detroitchamber.com/participation/detroiter-online jmartinez@detroitchamber.com

Disaster Recovery Journal PO Box 510110 Saint Louis MO 63151 **Phn:** 636-282-5800 **Fax** 636-282-5802 Jon Seals. Quarterly magazine.
58,000 to managers responsible for corporate contingency and post-disaster continuity planning. www.drj.com jon@drj.com

DiversityInc PO Box 32069 Newark NJ 07102 **Phn:** 973-494-0500 **Fax** 973-494-0525 Gail Zoppo. Bimonthly magazine.
342,000 to sr. mgmt. responsible for hiring & interested in business benefits of diverse workforce. diversityinc.com

Business .12

Eastern PA Business Jrnl 65 E Elizabeth Ave Ste 700 Bethlehem PA 18018 **Phn:** 610-807-9619 **Fax** 610-807-9612 John Moore. Weekly newspaper.
9,800 www.epbj.com epbjnews@epbj.com

Economist 111 W 57th St Fl 9 New York NY 10019 **Phn:** 212-541-0500 **Fax** 212-969-9098 Rosemarie Ward. Weekly magazine.
639,200 to senior business managers, policy makers interested in worldwide business, finance. www.economist.com nyeditorial@economist.com

850 Business Magazine 1932 Miccosukee Rd Tallahassee FL 32308 **Phn:** 850-878-0554 **Fax** 850-807-5037 Linda Kleindienst. Rowland Publishing. Bimonthly.
17,000 to Tallahassee-area business people interested in capital issues, profiles, industry-specific features. www.850businessmagazine.com lkleindienst@rowlandpublishing.com

Employee Benefit News 4401 Wilson Blvd Ste 910 Arlington VA 22203 **Phn:** 202-504-1122 **Fax** 202-772-1448 Andrea Davis. Source Media. 15-issue mag.
70,200 to group benefits decisionmakers interested in health care, retirement, quality of life benefits. ebn.benefitnews.com andrea.davis@sourcemedia.com

Event Solutions PO Box 11660 Tempe AZ 85284 **Phn:** 480-831-5100 **Fax** 480-777-2300 Ann Turner. Monthly magazine.
28,600 to event planners responsible for locating venues and providing products and services. www.event-solutions.com ann@event-solutions.com

Fairfield Co. Business Journal 3 Gannett Dr Ste G7 White Plains NY 10604 **Phn:** 914-694-3600 **Fax** 914-694-3680 Bob Rozycki. Westfair Communications. Weekly.
8,300 to readers interested in local business conditios, people, events. westfaironline.com bobr@westfairinc.com

Family Business Magazine 1845 Walnut St Ste 900 Philadelphia PA 19103 **Phn:** 215-567-3200 **Fax** 215-405-6078 Barbara Spector. 5-issue magazine.
6,800 to family-owned business owners, mgrs. & advisers interested in case studies, profiles, strategies. www.familybusinessmagazine.com bspector@familybusinessmagazine.com

Fast Company 7 World Trade Ctr Fl 29 New York NY 10007 **Phn:** 212-389-5300 **Fax** 212-389-5496 Lori Hoffman. 10-issue magazine.
734,000 to upper level corporate mgmt. responsible for technological innovation, leadership, innovation. www.fastcompany.com pr@fastcompany.com

Florida CPA Today PO Box 5437 Tallahassee FL 32314 **Phn:** 850-224-2727 **Fax** 850-222-8190 Bimonthly magazine.
18,500 to Florida accounting professionals interested in newsmakers, events, state legislation. www.ficpa.org communications@ficpa.org

Florida Trend 490 1st Ave S Fl 8 Saint Petersburg FL 33701 **Phn:** 727-821-5800 **Fax** 727-822-5083 Mark Howard. Monthly magazine.
10,000 to executives and decisionmakers in Florida business, government, industry. www.floridatrend.com mhoward@floridatrend.com

Forbes 60 5th Ave Frnt 1 New York NY 10011 **Phn:** 212-620-2200 **Fax** 212-620-2273 Randall Lane. Bi-weekly magazine.
900,000 to top management in business and industry; presidents, treasurers, controllers, dept. mgrs. www.forbes.com rlane@forbes.com

Fort Worth Business Press 3509 Hulen St Ste 201 Fort Worth TX 76107 **Phn:** 817-336-8300 **Fax** 817-332-3038 Robert Francis. Weekly.
8,700 to readers interested in local banks, real estate, business people and events. www.fwbusinesspress.com rfrancis@bizpress.net

Fortune 1271 Avenue Of The Americas Bsmt SB7 New York NY 10020 **Phn:** 212-522-1212 **Fax** 212-522-0810 Cliff Leaf. Time, Inc. 18-issue magazine. TH:@CliftonLeaf
867,000 to upper level corporate mgmt. interested in personal finance, executive profiles, policy. money.cnn.com/magazines/fortune/ clifton.leaf@fortune.com

Georgia Trend 5880 Live Oak Pkwy Ste 280 Norcross GA 30093 **Phn:** 770-931-9410 **Fax** 770-931-9505 Susan Percy. Monthly.
55,000 to executives and decisionmakers in Georgia business, government, industry. www.georgiatrend.com spercy@georgiatrend.com

Grand Rapids Business Journal 549 Ottawa Ave NW Ste 201 Grand Rapids MI 49503 **Phn:** 616-459-4545 **Fax** 616-459-4800 Carole Valade. Gemini Publs. Weekly newspaper.
7,000 www.grbj.com cvalade@geminipub.com

Greater Charlotte Biz 7300 Carmel Executive Park Dr Ste 115 Charlotte NC 28226 **Phn:** 704-676-5850 **Fax** 704-676-5853 Maryl A. Lane. Monthly magazine.
19,500 to Charlotte, NC area business people interested in products, services, profiles, rgnl. economic issues. www.greatercharlottebiz.com editor@greatercharlottebiz.com

Harvard Business Review 60 Harvard Way Boston MA 02163 **Phn:** 617-783-7410 **Fax** 617-783-7493 Christine Jack. Monthly magazine.
247,600 to management personnel interested in trends, case studies, business concepts. hbr.org hbr_editorial@hbsp.harvard.edu

Hawaii Business PO Box 913 Honolulu HI 96808 **Phn:** 808-537-9500 **Fax** 808-537-6455 Steven Petranik. Monthly.
12,900 to business people interested in state data, trends, profiles, networking opportunities, resources. www.hawaiibusiness.com stevep@hawaiibusiness.com

Hispanic Business 425 Pine Ave Santa Barbara CA 93117 **Phn:** 805-964-4554 **Fax** 805-964-5539 Jesus Chavarria. Online only. TH:@HispanicBizMag
to Hispanic execs., mgrs. interested in rsch., mgmt. trends, profiles, influential Hispanic people. www.hispanicbusiness.com editorial@hbinc.com

Hispanic Executive 205 N Michigan Ave Ste 3200 Chicago IL 60601 **Phn:** 312-447-2370 **Fax** 312-765-8785 Chris Sheppard. Quarterly magazine. TH:@HispanicExecMag
25,000 to execs., mgrs., vendors interested in Latino leadership, markets, research, influential Hispanic people. www.hispanicbusiness.com csheppard@hispanicexecutive.com

Home Business 20711 Holt Ave PMB 807 Lakeville MN 55044 **Phn:** 949-240-7529 **Fax** 714-388-3883 Richard Henderson. Bimonthly magazine. TH:@homebusinessmag
75,000 to home-based business owners interested in technology, marketing, franchising opps, start up how tos. www.homebusinessmag.com customerservice@homebusinessmag.com

Houston Business Journal 1233 West Loop S Ste 1300 Houston TX 77027 **Phn:** 713-688-8811 **Fax** 713-968-8025 Giselle Greenwood. Weekly newspaper. TH:@ggreenwood
15,600 to readers interested in metro Houston area real estate, energy, mfg., tourism, healthcare. www.bizjournals.com/houston/ ggreenwood@bizjournals.com

HR Magazine 1800 Duke St Alexandria VA 22314 **Phn:** 703-548-3440 **Fax** 703-548-9140 Nancy Davis. Soc. Human Resource Mgmt. Monthly magazine.
243,700 to HR management concerned with recruitment, training, benefits, compensation. www.shrm.org hrmag@shrm.org

Hudson Valley Business Digital 86 E Main St Wappingers Falls NY 12590 **Phn:** 845-298-6236 Debbie Kwiatoski. Online only.
to Hudson Valley, NY area business people interested in real estate, legislative decisions, banking, local profiles. www.hvbizjournal.com debhvbj@gmail.com

Human Resource Executive 747 Dresher Rd # 500 Horsham PA 19044 **Phn:** 215-784-0910 **Fax** 215-784-0275 Anne Freedman. LRP Magazine Grp. 12-issue tab.
75,000 to senior-level HR executives interested in strategic issues, HR executive profiles. www.hreonline.com afreedman@lrp.com

Inc. Magazine 7 World Trade Center New York NY 10007 **Phn:** 212-389-5300 **Fax** 212-389-5379 Bobbie Gossage. Monthly magazine.
700,000 to small to mid-sized company CEO's concerned with growth management, mktg. www.inc.com bgossage@inc.com

Indianapolis Business Journal 41 E Washington St Ste 200 Indianapolis IN 46204 **Phn:** 317-634-6200 **Fax** 317-263-5406 Greg Andrews. Weekly newspaper.
16,200 www.ibj.com gandrews@ibj.com

IndustryWeek 1300 E 9th St Cleveland OH 44114 **Phn:** 216-696-7000 **Fax** 216-696-7670 Steve Minter. Penton Media. Monthly magazine. TH:@IndustryWeek
126,200 to manufacturing execs. in administration, production, engineering, marketing. www.industryweek.com sminter@industryweek.com

Inside Supply Management 2055 E Centennial Cir Tempe AZ 85284 **Phn:** 480-752-6276 **Fax** 480-752-7890 Terri Tracey. Institute for Supply Mgmt. Monthly mag.
40,700 to purchasing and materials mgmt. staff interested in case studies and practical strategies. www.ism.ws/ ttracey@ism.ws

Internal Auditor 247 Maitland Ave Altamonte Springs FL 32701 **Phn:** 407-937-1100 **Fax** 407-937-1103 Anne Millage. Inst. Internal Auditors. Bimonthly mag.
90,000 to members of Inst. Internal Auditors; corp. & govt. financial execs. & treasurers. www.theiia.org/intauditor/ editor@theiia.org

Investor's Business Daily 12655 Beatrice St Los Angeles CA 90066 **Phn:** 310-448-6000 **Fax** 310-577-7350 Ed Carson. Daily newspaper.
229,500 www.investors.com ibdnews@investors.com

Jrnl. Accountancy 220 Leigh Farm Rd Durham NC 27707 **Phn:** 919-402-4449 Amelia Rasmus. Amer. Inst. CPA. Monthly magazine.
341,000 to CPA's, other accounting professionals interested in news, analysis, continuing ed. www.journalofaccountancy.com joaed@aicpa.org

Jrnl. Commerce 33 Washington St Fl 13 Newark NJ 07102 **Phn:** 973-848-7000 **Fax** 973-848-7004 Chris Brooks. Weekly magazine.
8,000 to logistics executives responsible for importing, exporting, transportation and routing. www.joc.com cbrooks@joc.com

Kansas City Business Journal 1100 Main St Ste 210 Kansas City MO 64105 **Phn:** 816-421-5900 **Fax** 816-472-4010 Brian Kaberline. Weekly newspaper.
10,500 www.bizjournals.com/kansascity/ kansascity@bizjournals.com

Kiplinger's Personal Finance 1729 H St NW Washington DC 20006 **Phn:** 202-887-6400 **Fax** 202-331-1206 Jeffrey Kosnett. Monthly magazine.
825,000 to readers interested in investments, insurance, taxes, tuition and retirement plans. www.kiplinger.com jkosnett@kiplinger.com

Las Vegas Business Press PO Box 70 Las Vegas NV 89125 **Phn:** 702-871-6780 **Fax** 702-871-3298 Matt Ward. Weekly newspaper.
10,000 www.lvbusinesspress.com mward@lvbusinesspress.com

LI & Business 1301 Skippack Pike Ste 7A-218 Blue Bell PA 19422 **Phn:** 610-879-8828   Nathan Lievman. GSG WorldMedia. Online only. TH:@nathankievman to readers interested in how to leverage LinkedIn's capabilities to create business visibility.
www.socialmediamags.com
editorial@socialmediamags.com

Long Beach Business Journal 2599 E 28th St Ste 212 Signal Hill CA 90755 **Phn:** 562-988-1222 **Fax** 562-988-1239 George Economides. Biweekly newspaper.
33,000 www.lbbusinessjournal.com info@lbbj.com

Long Island Business News 2150 Smithtown Ave Ste 7 Ronkonkoma NY 11779 **Phn:** 631-737-1700 **Fax** 631-737-1890 John Kominicki. Weekly newspaper.
10,800 libn.com editor@libn.com

Los Angeles Business Journal 5700 Wilshire Blvd Ste 170 Los Angeles CA 90036 **Phn:** 323-549-5225 **Fax** 323-549-5262 Laurence Darmiento. Weekly newspaper.
30,000 www.labusinessjournal.com
ldarmiento@labusinessjournal.com

Memphis Business Journal 80 Monroe Ave Ste 600 Memphis TN 38103 **Phn:** 901-523-1000 **Fax** 901-526-5240 Bill Wellborn. Weekly magazine.
7,000 www.bizjournals.com/memphis/
memphis@bizjournals.com

Minority Business Entrepreneur 2120 Dufour Ave Unit 14 Redondo Beach CA 90278 **Phn:** 310-540-9398 **Fax** 310-792-8263 Emily Richwine. Bimonthly.
20,400 to minority, female, disabled veteran business owners interested in govt., corp. contracts.
www.mbemag.com editor@mbemag.com

Mississippi Business Journal 200 N Congress St Ste 400 Jackson MS 39201 **Phn:** 601-364-1000 **Fax** 601-364-1035 Ross Reily. Weekly newspaper.
4,900 msbusiness.com mbj@msbusiness.com

Nashville Business Journal 1800 Church St Ste 300 Nashville TN 37203 **Phn:** 615-248-2222 **Fax** 615-248-6246 Lance Williams. Weekly newspaper.
7,500 www.bizjournals.com/nashville/
nashville@bizjournals.com

The Network Journal 39 Broadway Rm 2120 New York NY 10006 **Phn:** 212-962-3791 **Fax** 212-962-3537 Rosalind McClymont. 10-issue magazine.
26,500 to African-Amer. professionals, business owners interested in growth, success techniques.
www.tnj.com editors@tnj.com

Network Marketing Business Jrnl. 20636 Burl Ct Unit E Joliet IL 60433 **Phn:** 815-726-5555 **Fax** 815-726-5550 Keith Laggos. Monthly newspaper. TH:@nmbj
15,000 to network & multi level marketers, direct salespeople interested in opportunities, entrepreneurial topics. www.nmbj.com editors@nmbj.com

New Accountant 3500 W Peterson Ave Ste 403 Chicago IL 60659 **Phn:** 773-866-9900 **Fax** 773-866-9881 Steven Polydoris. Real Estate News Corp. 6-issue magazine.
65,000 to accounting and finance students interested in careers, practical articles.
www.newaccountantusa.com

New Hampshire Business Review 150 Dow St Manchester NH 03101 **Phn:** 603-624-1442 **Fax** 603-624-1310 Jeff Feingold. Biweekly newspaper.
16,600 www.nhbr.com jfeingold@nhbr.com

New Jersey Business 310 Passaic Ave Fairfield NJ 07004 **Phn:** 973-882-5004 **Fax** 973-882-4648 Anthony Birritteri. Monthly.
27,600 www.njbmagazine.com
a.birritteri@njbmagazine.com

NJBIZ 220 Davidson Ave Ste 302 Somerset NJ 08873 **Phn:** 732-246-7677 **Fax** 732-249-8886 Tom Bergeron. Weekly tabloid. TH:@NJBIZ
15,000 to readers interested in state of NJ real estate, technology, business leader profiles, intl. issues.
www.njbiz.com tomb@njbiz.com

NonProfit Times 201 Littleton Rd Ste 2 Morris Plains NJ 07950 **Phn:** 973-401-0202 **Fax** 973-401-0404 Paul Clolery. Semimonthly tabloid.
36,400 to non-profit managers responsible for technology, human resources, marketing, fundraising.
www.nptimes.com ednchief@nptimes.com

Orange County Business Journal 18500 Von Karman Ave Ste 150 Irvine CA 92612 **Phn:** 949-833-8373 **Fax** 949-833-8751 Jerry Sullivan. Weekly newspaper.
14,700 www.ocbj.com sullivan@ocbj.com

Oregon Business 715 SW Morrison St Ste 800 Portland OR 97205 **Phn:** 503-223-0304 **Fax** 503-221-6544 Monthly.
20,000 www.oregonbusiness.com
editor@oregonbusiness.com

Orlando Business Journal 255 S Orange Ave Ste 700 Orlando FL 32801 **Phn:** 407-649-8470 **Fax** 407-420-1625 Cindy Barth. Weekly newspaper.
8,200 www.bizjournals.com/orlando/
orlando@bizjournals.com

Pacific Business News 1833 Kalakaua Ave Fl 7 Honolulu HI 96815 **Phn:** 808-955-8100 **Fax** 808-955-8051 Jim Kelly. Weekly.
12,500 www.bizjournals.com/pacific/
pbn@bizjournals.com

Philadelphia Business Journal 400 Market St Ste 1200 Philadelphia PA 19106 **Phn:** 215-238-1450 **Fax** 215-238-9489 Bernard Dagenais. Weekly.
11,400 www.bizjournals.com/philadelphia/
philadelphia@bizjournals.com

Pittsburgh Business Times 424 S 27th St Ste 211 Pittsburgh PA 15203 **Phn:** 412-481-6397 **Fax** 412-481-9956 Lauren Lawley Head. Weekly newspaper.
12,100 www.bizjournals.com/pittsburgh/
pittsburgh@bizjournals.com

Profit 500 Oracle Pkwy Ms OPL Redwood City CA 94065 **Phn:** 650-506-5308 **Fax** 650-633-2424 Margaret Lindquist. Oracle Corp. Bimonthly magazine.
516,000 to IT professionals interested in increasing profits through use of Oracle products.
www.oracle.com/us/oramag/
margaret.lindquist@oracle.com

Providence Business News 220 W Exchange St Ste 210 Providence RI 02903 **Phn:** 401-273-2201 **Fax** 401-274-0670 Mark S. Murphy. Weekly newspaper.
9,000 www.pbn.com editor@pbn.com

Regulation 1000 Massachusetts Ave NW Washington DC 20001 **Phn:** 202-842-0200 **Fax** 202-842-3490 Thomas A. Firey. Cato Institute. Quarterly magazine.
50,000 to policymakers, govt. affairs personnel & academics interested in govt. regulation effects on business. www.cato.org/pubs/regulation/
tfirey@cato.org

Rental Equipment Register 17383 W Sunset Blvd # A220 Pacific Palisades CA 90272 **Phn:** 310-230-7177 **Fax** 310-230-7169 Michael Roth. Penton Media. Mo. magazine.
21,200 to owners & mgrs. of tool, truck, construction equip., outdoor power equip. rental ctrs. rermag.com
michael.roth@penton.com

Rental Management 1900 19th St Moline IL 61265 **Phn:** 309-764-2475 **Fax** 309-764-1533 Wayne Walley. Amer. Rental Assn. Monthly magazine.
17,000 to equip. rental business owners interested in industry news, customer service, products.
www.rentalmanagementmag.com
wayne.walley@ararental.org

Rental Product News 1233 Janesville Ave Fort Atkinson WI 53538 **Phn:** 920-563-6388 **Fax** 920-563-1700 Jennifer Lescohier. Cygnus Business Media. 10-issue magazine.
21,000 to construction, industrial equip. rental center owners interested in asset mgmt.
www.forconstructionpros.com
jenny.lescohier@cygnusb2b.com

Rochester Business Journal 45 East Ave Ste 500 Rochester NY 14604 **Phn:** 585-546-8303 **Fax** 585-546-3398 Paul Ericson. Weekly newspaper.
10,000 www.rbj.net rbj@rbj.net

Sacramento Business Journal 1400 X St Sacramento CA 95818 **Phn:** 916-447-7661   Ron Trujillo. Weekly magazine.
13,800 www.bizjournals.com/sacramento/
sacramento@bizjournals.com

San Antonio Business Journal 8200 W Interstate 10 Ste 820 San Antonio TX 78230 **Phn:** 210-341-3202 **Fax** 210-341-3031 Bill Conroy. Weekly newspaper.
7,100 www.bizjournals.com/sanantonio/
sanantonio@bizjournals.com

San Diego Business Journal 4909 Murphy Canyon Rd Ste 200 San Diego CA 92123 **Phn:** 858-277-6359 **Fax** 858-571-3628 Tom York. Weekly newspaper.
15,000 www.sdbj.com tyork@sdbj.com

San Diego Metropolitan 1502 6th Ave San Diego CA 92101 **Phn:** 619-233-4060 **Fax** 619-233-4272 Tim McClain. Monthly magazine.
30,600 to San Diego area execs. in banking, real estate, biotech, finance, hospitality industries.
sandiegometro.com manny@sandiegometro.com

San Francisco Business Times 275 Battery St Ste 940 San Francisco CA 94111 **Phn:** 415-989-2522 **Fax** 415-398-2494 Steve Symanovich. Weekly newspaper.
12,500 www.bizjournals.com/sanfrancisco/
sanfrancisco@bizjournals.com

Seattle Business Monthly 1518 1st Ave S Ste 500 Seattle WA 98134 **Phn:** 206-452-2966 **Fax** 206-284-2550 Leslie Helm. Monthly magazine.
27,600 to mgmt & execs at large and small companies responsible for policy, decisionmaking.
leslie.helm@tigeroak.com

Silicon Vly Business Journal 125 S Market St Fl 11 San Jose CA 95113 **Phn:** 408-295-3800 **Fax** 408-295-5028 Moryt Milo. Weekly.
8,000 www.bizjournals.com/sanjose/
sanjose@bizjournals.com

Small Business Opportunities 1115 Broadway Fl 8 New York NY 10010 **Phn:** 212-807-7100 **Fax** 212-924-8416 Susan Rakowski. Harris Publ. Bimonthly magazine.
251,400 to small business owners interested in legal & financial advice, how-to's. www.sbomag.com
sr@harris-pub.com

Smart Meetings 475 Gate 5 Rd #235 Sausalito CA 94965 **Phn:** 415-339-9355 **Fax** 415-339-9361 Christine Loomis. Bright Business Media. Monthly magazine. TH:@SmartMeetings
40,000 to meeting planners, others responsible for meeting destination, vendor, program selection.
www.smartmeetings.com
christine@smartmeetings.com

South Florida Business Journal 6400 N Andrews Ave Ste 200 Fort Lauderdale FL 33309 **Phn:** 954-949-7600 **Fax** 954-949-7591 Weekly newspaper. TH:@SFlaBizJournal
8,400 www.bizjournals.com/southflorida/
southflorida@bizjournals.com

Special Events 17383 W Sunset Blvd Ste 220 Pacific Palisades CA 90272 **Phn:** 310-230-7179 **Fax** 913-514-3941 Lisa Hurley. Penton Media. Monthly magazine.
25,500 to professionals who provide products, services for parties, meetings, galas of all sizes.
specialevents.com lhurley@specialevents.com

St. Louis Business Journal 815 Olive St Ste 100 Saint Louis MO 63101 **Phn:** 314-421-6200 **Fax** 314-621-5031 Patricia Miller. Weekly newspaper.
18,300 www.bizjournals.com/stlouis/
stlouis@bizjournals.com

Success 200 Swisher Rd Lake Dallas TX 75065 **Phn:** 877-577-6504 **Fax** 940-497-9987 Deborah Heisz. Monthly magazine.
200,000 to entrepreneurs, home-based & small business owners interested in pratical advice, goal setting, time mgmt. www.success.com editor@success.com

Successful Meetings 100 Lighting Way Fl 2 Secaucus NJ 07094 **Phn:** 646-380-6247 Vincent Alonzo. Northstar Travel Media. Monthly magazine.
50,000 to execs. who plan/manage off-premise meetings, conferences, training programs. www.successfulmeetings.com valonzo@ntmllc.com

Supply & Demand Chain Executive 3030 W Salt Lake Creek Ln Ste 200 Arlington Hts IL 60005 **Phn:** 847-454-2700 **Fax** 847-454-2759 Natalia Kosk. Cygnus Business Media. Quarterly magazine.
55,000 to supply chain decisionmakers interested in profiles, case studies, analysis & opinion editorial. www.sdcexec.com nkosk@cygnussecurity.com

Supply Chain Management Review 111 Speen St Ste 200 Framingham MA 01701 **Phn:** 508-663-1500 **Fax** 508-663-1599 Patrick Burnson. EH Publishing Network. 7-issue magazine.
15,000 to supply chain mgmt. responsible for sourcing, procurement, logistics, technology interested in case studies. www.scmr.com pburnson@ehpub.com

Swap Meet 383 E Main St Centerport NY 11721 **Phn:** 631-754-5000 **Fax** 631-754-0630 Forum Publishing. Monthly.
75,000 to serious flea market and swap meet vendors nationally, merchandise suppliers. www.swapmeetmag.com forumpublishing@aol.com

T&D Magazine 1640 King St. #1443 Alexandria VA 22314 **Phn:** 703-683-8100 **Fax** 703-683-9591 Paula Ketter. Amer. Society Training & Development. Monthly.
38,900 to HR professionals and others responsible for corporate training and development. www.astd.org/TD/ submissions@astd.org

Tampa Bay Business Journal 4890 W Kennedy Blvd Ste 850 Tampa FL 33609 **Phn:** 813-873-8225 **Fax** 813-873-0219 Mr. Alexis Muellner. Weekly.
7,600 www.bizjournals.com/tampabay/ tampabay@bizjournals.com

Toledo Business Journal 5301 Southwyck Blvd Ste 104 Toledo OH 43614 **Phn:** 419-865-0972 **Fax** 419-865-2429 Janice Pisello. Monthly.
22,000 to Toledo-area business people interested in mfg., real estate, banking, trade shows, business profiles. www.toledobiz.com editor@toledobiz.com

Traverse City Business News 109 S Union St Ste 305 Traverse City MI 49684 **Phn:** 231-929-7919 **Fax** 231-929-7914 Lynda Twardowski. Monthly magazine.
6,800 www.tcbusinessnews.com lt@tcbusinessnews.com

Triangle Business Journal 3600 Glenwood Ave Ste 100 Raleigh NC 27612 **Phn:** 919-878-0010 **Fax** 919-954-4898 Sougata Mukherjee. Weekly newspaper. TH:@TriBizEditor
8,100 to Raleigh-Durham area readers interested in real estate, banking, education, construction. www.bizjournals.com/triangle/ triangle@bizjournals.com

Tweeting & Business 1301 Skippack Pike Ste 7A-218 Blue Bell PA 19422 **Phn:** 610-879-8828 Jeffrey Hayzlett. GSG WorldMedia. Online only. TH:@JeffreyHayzlett
to readers interested in how to leverage Twitter's capabilities to create awareness of products & services. www.socialmediamags.com editorial@socialmediamags.com

Twin Cities Business 220 S 6th St Ste 500 Minneapolis MN 55402 **Phn:** 612-339-7571 **Fax** 612-336-9220 Dale Kurschner. Monthly magazine.
33,000 mspcommunications.com edit@tcbm.com

Business .12

Utah Business 859 W South Jordan Pkwy Ste 101 South Jordan UT 84095 **Phn:** 801-568-0114 **Fax** 801-568-0812 Dave Kennard. Monthly magazine.
25,000 www.utahbusiness.com dkennard@utahbusiness.com

Virginia Business 1207 E Main St, Ste 100 Richmond VA 23219 **Phn:** 804-225-9262 **Fax** 804-225-0028 Robert Powell. Monthly magazine.
27,500 to readers interested in statewide businesspeople, banking, govt., real estate, mfg. www.virginiabusiness.com rpowell@virginiabusiness.com

Wall Street & Technology 240 W 35th St New York NY 10001 **Phn:** 212-600-3000 **Fax** 212-600-3060 Gregory MacSweeney. InformationWeek. Monthly.
21,000 covering information technology for the securities and investment markets. www.wallstreetandtech.com gmacsweeney@techweb.com

Washington Business Journal 1555 Wilson Blvd Ste 400 Arlington VA 22209 **Phn:** 703-258-0800 **Fax** 703-258-0802 Mike Mills. Weekly newspaper.
17,000 www.bizjournals.com/washington/ washington@bizjournals.com

Westchester Co. Business Jrnl. 3 Gannett Dr Ste G7 White Plains NY 10604 **Phn:** 914-694-3600 **Fax** 914-694-3680 Bob Rozycki. Westfair Communications. Weekly newspaper.
9,100 to area business people interested in local real estate, ventures, businesspeople, events. westfaironline.com bobr@westfairinc.com

Wichita Business Journal 121 N Mead St Ste 100 Wichita KS 67202 **Phn:** 316-267-6406 **Fax** 316-267-8570 Bill Roy. Weekly tab.
5,900 www.bizjournals.com/wichita/ wichita@bizjournals.com

Women In Business 11050 Roe Ave. Ste 200 Overland Park KS 66211 **Phn:** 913-732-5100 **Fax** 913-660-0101 Leigh Elmore. Amer. Business Women's Assn. Quarterly mag.
30,000 to Assn. members & other women interested in business trends, networking, education. www.abwa.org abwa@abwa.org

Workforce Management 4 Executive Cir Ste 185 Irvine CA 92614 **Phn:** 949-255-5340 **Fax** 949-221-8964 Rick Bell. Crain Communications. Monthly mag.
50,400 to human resource executives concerned with how HR functions contribute to profitability. www.workforce.com rbell@workforce.com

Retail .12a

Chain Store Age 425 Park Ave Fl 6 New York NY 10022 **Phn:** 212-756-5252 **Fax** 212-756-5256 Marianne Wilson. Lebhar-Friedman. Monthly magazine.
35,600 to chain store executives responsible for finance, insurance, marketing. www.chainstoreage.com mwilson@chainstoreage.com

Consumer Goods Technology 4 Middlebury Blvd Randolph NJ 07869 **Phn:** 973-607-0010 **Fax** 973-607-1395 Alliston Ackerman. Edgell Inc. Monthly.
20,700 to readers who use IT systems to develop, market and distribute their products to consumers. consumergoods.edgl.com aackerman@edgellmail.com

Dance Retailer News 110 William St Fl 23 New York NY 10038 **Phn:** 646-459-4800 **Fax** 646-459-4900 Libby Dowd. MacFadden Comms Group. Monthly tabloid.
6,000 to dance retail store mgrs. and buyers interested in products, industry news, strategies. www.danceretailernews.com ldowd@dancemedia.com

Display & Design Ideas 1145 Sanctuary Pkwy Ste 100 Alpharetta GA 30009 **Phn:** 770-569-1540 **Fax** 770-569-5105 Jessie Bove. Nielsen Business Media. Monthly tab.
21,500 to display planners, visual merchandisers interested in trends, new products, technology. www.ddionline.com jbove@ddimagazine.com

Exhibit Builder PO Box 4144 Woodland Hills CA 91365 **Phn:** 818-225-0100 **Fax** 818-225-0138 Judy Pomerantz. Bimonthly magazine.
14,600 to exhibit designers and fabricators interested in new products, techniques, case studies. www.exhibitbuilder.net

Greetings Etc. 4 Middlebury Blvd Randolph NJ 07869 **Phn:** 973-607-1300 **Fax** 973-607-1395 Dorothy Creamer. Edgell Inc. Monthly.
21,700 Covers the greeting card and stationery-related marketplace, for retailers. greetings.edgl.com dcreamer@edgellmail.com

Hardware Retailing 6325 Digital Way Ste 300 Indianapolis IN 46278 **Phn:** 317-290-0338 **Fax** 317-328-4354 Jaime Koch. N. Amer. Retail Hardware Assn. Monthly mag.
36,000 to hardware, home center, lumber retailers concerned with marketing, operations, news. www.nrha.org jkoch@nrha.org

Mass Market Retailers 220 5th Ave New York NY 10001 **Phn:** 212-213-6000 **Fax** 212-725-3961 Greg Jacobson. Racher Press. 21-issue tabloid.
22,000 to supermarket, chain drug and discount store executives responsible for operations. www.massmarketretailers.com gjacobson@racherpress.com

Retail Info Systems 4 Middlebury Blvd Randolph NJ 07869 **Phn:** 973-607-1300 **Fax** 973-607-1395 Adam Blair. Edgell Inc. Monthly.
22,700 systems reference magazine for retailers and related businesses. risnews.edgl.com ablair@edgellmail.com

Retail Merchandiser 100 Cumming Ctr Ste 211-C Beverly MA 01915 **Phn:** 978-338-6547 Amy Ingoldsby. Phoenix Media Corp. Bimonthly.
32,500 to retail CEO's, buyers, consultants, merchandisers, store managers. www.retail-merchandiser.com amy.ingoldsby@phoenixmediacorp.com

Retail Traffic 249 W 17th St New York NY 10011 **Phn:** 212-204-4200 **Fax** 212-206-3923 David Bodamer. Penton Media. Monthly.
35,700 to shopping center developers, leasing agents, architects, retailers, contractors, investors. retailtrafficmag.com david.bodamer@penton.com

Retailing Today 3922 Coconut Palm Dr Tampa FL 33619 **Phn:** 813-627-6946 Mike Troy. Lebhar-Friedman. Online only.
for discount retail store, warehouse club, catalog showroom personnel. www.retailingtoday.com mtroy@lf.com

Shopping Center Business 3500 Piedmont Rd NE Ste 415 Atlanta GA 30305 **Phn:** 404-832-8262 **Fax** 404-832-8260 Lindsay Sport. Monthly.
34,100 to shopping ctr. industry mgmt. concerned with retail trends, new construction, leasing. www.shoppingcenterbusiness.com scb@francepublications.com

Shopping Centers Today 1221 Avenue Of The Americas Fl 41 New York NY 10020 **Phn:** 646-728-3800 **Fax** 732-694-1730 Edmund Mander. Intl Cncl. Shopping Ctrs.
62,400 to Council members interested in personnel changes and property sales. www.icsc.org sctweek@icsc.org

Sportswear International 611 Broadway Ste 809 New York NY 10012 **Phn:** 212-727-7337 Christopher Blomquist. Intl. Business Press. 7-issue mag.
50,000 to sportswear retail execs. interested in sales ideas, in-store merchandising, trends. www.sportswearnet.com blomquist@sportswearnet.com

Stores 325 7th St NW Ste 1100 Washington DC 20004 **Phn:** 202-626-8101 **Fax** 202-661-3042 Susan Reda. Natl. Retail Federation. Monthly magazine.
37,500 to execs. of dept. stores, specialty shops, chain stores, home centers, internet retailers. www.stores.org editor@nrf.com

Tack 'n Togs Merchandising 12400 Whitewater Dr Ste 160 Minnetonka MN 55343 **Phn:** 952-930-4390 **Fax** 952-930-4362 Sarah Muirhead. Monthly magazine. **13,600** to boot, tack/saddle, custom saddle shops, riding apparel & rancher supply stores. www.tackntogs.com smuirhead@tackntogs.com

Value Retail News 2519 N McMullen Booth Rd Ste 510-356 Clearwater FL 33761 **Phn:** 727-781-7557 **Fax** 732-694-1753 Linda Humphers. Intl. Cncl. Shopping Ctrs. 10-issue magazine. **TH:**@ValueRetailNews **53,000** to operators/decisionmakers at outlet & value retail centers responsible for leasing, mktg. valueretailnews.com lhumphers@icsc.org

Ceramics--China--Glass .13

Amer. Ceramic Soc. Bulletin 600 N Cleveland Ave Ste 210 Westerville OH 43082 **Phn:** 614-890-4700 **Fax** 614-794-5822 Peter Wray. Amer. Ceramic Soc. Monthly. **15,300** to Society members and others interested in mfg., processes, applications. ceramics.org pwray@ceramics.org

Ceramic Industry 6075 Glick Rd Ste B Powell OH 43065 **Phn:** 614-789-1880 **Fax** 248-502-2033 Susan Sutton. BNP Media. Monthly magazine. **9,600** to operating mgmt. in ceramic mfg. industry interested in technology, processes, equipment. www.ceramicindustry.com suttons@bnpmedia.com

Ceramics Monthly 600 N Cleveland Ave Ste 210 Westerville OH 43082 **Phn:** 614-890-4700 **Fax** 614-891-8960 Sherman Hall. American Ceramic Soc. 10-issue magazine. **30,000** to ceramics craftspeople interested in glazes, firing techniques, expert advice. ceramicartsdaily.org/ceramics-monthly/ editorial@ceramicsmonthly.org

Fired Arts & Crafts PO Box 5000 Iola WI 54945 **Phn:** 715-445-5000 **Fax** 715-445-4053 Joyce Greenholdt. Jones Publ. Monthly magazine. **TH:**@CKeditorial **7,500** to ceramic & pottery artists, teachers, hobbyists interested in projects, shows, products. www.firedartsandcrafts.com joyceg@jonespublishing.com

Glass Art PO Box 630377 Highlands Ranch CO 80163 **Phn:** 303-791-8998 **Fax** 303-791-7739 Shawn Waggoner. Bimonthly. **5,000** to stained/decorative glass industry personnel, collectors, suppliers, retailers. www.glassartmagazine.com editor@glassartmagazine.com

Glass Craftsman PO Box 678 Richboro PA 18954 **Phn:** 215-968-4655 **Fax** 215-968-4766 Joe Porcelli. Arts & Media Publishing. Bimonthly magazine. **10,000** to readers interested in modern stained glass, restoring antique glass, lamps. www.glasscraftsman.com glasscraftsman@gmail.com

Glass Line 1818 E Redwood Ave Anaheim CA 92805 **Phn:** 714-520-0121 **Fax** 714-520-4370 Jim Thingwold. Bimonthly. **5,700** newest techniques, how-to articles on glassblowing, lampworking, glass-beads, safety. www.hotglass.com editor@hotglass.com

Glass Magazine 8200 Greensboro Dr Ste 302 McLean VA 22102 **Phn:** 703-442-4890 **Fax** 703-442-0630 Jenni Chase. Natl. Glass Assn. Monthly mag. **26,000** to architectural glass industry personnel interested in technical info., industry news. www.glassmagazine.com jchase@glass.org

Pottery Making Illustrated 600 N Cleveland Ave Ste 210 Westerville OH 43082 **Phn:** 614-890-4700 **Fax** 614-891-8960 Bill Jones. American Ceramic Soc. Bimonthly. **16,000** covers handbuilding, throwing, glazing, firing techniques, projects, tools, equipment. ceramicartsdaily.org/pottery-making-illustrated/

Retail .12a

US Glass Metal & Glazing PO Box 569 Garrisonville VA 22463 **Phn:** 540-720-5584 **Fax** 540-720-5687 Megan Headley. Key Communications. Monthly magazine. **33,600** to management, merchandising and operations personnel in glass, metal, related industries. www.usglassmag.com mheadley@glass.com

Window Film Magazine PO Box 569 Garrisonville VA 22463 **Phn:** 540-720-5584 **Fax** 540-720-5687 Ellen Rogers. Key Communications. Bimonthly magazine. **13,000** to retailers and suppliers of window, auto, security, solar film and tint. www.windowfilmmag.com erogers@glass.com

Chemical Industry .14

Analytical Chemistry Univ of IL Chem Dept/600 S Mathews Ave Urbana IL 61801 **Phn:** 217-244-7866 **Fax** 217-265-6290 Jonathan Sweedler. Amer. Chemical Soc. Twice monthly. **12,400** to engineers, chemists, life scientists interested in peer-reviewed research, technology. pubs.acs.org/journal/ancham eic@anchem.acs.org

ASTM Standardization News University of Illinois West Conshohocken PA 19428 **Phn:** 610-832-9500 **Fax** 610-832-9623 Maryann Gorman. Bimonthly mag. **28,900** to applied technology engineers and scientists in r&d, quality control, design engineering. www.astm.org mgorman@astm.org

Biochemistry 600 South Mathews Avenue, 63-5 Nashville TN 37232 **Phn:** 615-343-3915 **Fax** 202-354-5420 Richard Armstrong. Amer. Chemical Society. Weekly. **3,900** to the members of the American Chemical Society and other research life scientists. pubs.acs.org/journal/bichaw eic@biochem.acs.org

Chemical & Engineering News 1155 16th St NW Washington DC 20036 **Phn:** 202-872-4600 **Fax** 202-872-8727 William G. Schulz Amer. Chemical Soc. Weekly magazine. **134,000** to chemical process industry personnel interested in policy, technology, employment, education. pubs.acs.org/cen/ w_schulz@acs.org

Chemical Engineering 88 Pine St Ste 510 New York NY 10005 **Phn:** 212-621-4900 **Fax** 212-621-4949 Dorothy Lozowski. Access Intelligence. Monthly. **65,400** to chemical engineers, technical decisionmakers in chemical process industries. www.che.com dlozowski@che.com

Chemical Engineering Progress 3 Park Ave Fl 19 New York NY 10016 **Phn:** 646-495-1300 **Fax** 646-495-1504 Cynthia Fabian Mascone. Amer. Inst. Chem. Eng.. Monthly. **47,700** to Institute members, other engineers working in all depts. of chemical processing plants. www.aiche.org/CEP/ cepedit@aiche.org

Chemical Processing 555 W Pierce Rd Ste 301 Itasca IL 60143 **Phn:** 630-467-1300 **Fax** 630-467-1109 Mark Rosenzweig. Putman Media. Monthly magazine. **55,000** to chemical, pharmaceutical, petrochemical, petrorefining industry mgmt. www.chemicalprocessing.com mrosenzweig@putman.net

Chem.Info 100 Enterprise Dr Bx 912 # 600 Rockaway NJ 07866 **Phn:** 973-920-7000 **Fax** 973-920-7531 Krystal Gabert. Advantage Business Media. Online only. **TH:**@Chem_Info to chemical process industry engineers, plant mgrs., maintenance engineers. www.chem.info/ krystal.gabert@advantagemedia.com

HAPPI/Household & PP Industry 70 Hilltop Rd Fl 3 Ramsey NJ 07446 **Phn:** 201-825-2552 **Fax** 201-825-0553 Thomas Branna. Rodman Publications. Monthly magazine. **16,000** to mktg., production, technical personnel in household, personal product industries. www.happi.com tomb@rodpub.com

ICIS Chemical Business 360 Park Ave S Fl 12 New York NY 10010 **Phn:** 212-791-4200 Joseph Chang. Reed Business Info. Weekly tabloid. **19,600** to chemical industry management responsible for marketing, purchasing, manufacturing. www.icis.com joseph.chang@icis.com

IHS Chemical Week 140 E 45th St Rm 4000 New York NY 10017 **Phn:** 212-884-9528 **Fax** 212-884-9514 Robert Westervelt. Weekly magazine. **20,800** to chemical process industry business mgmt. responsible for profitability & operations. www.chemweek.com rob.westervelt@ihs.com

Inform PO Box 17190 Urbana IL 61803 **Phn:** 217-693-4837 **Fax** 217-693-4880 Jeremy Coulter. Amer. Oil Chemists Society. Monthly magazine. **5,700** to Soc. members, others in fats, oils, related substance research & technical mgmt. www.aocs.org jeremyc@aocs.org

Jrnl. Chemical Education 209 N Brooks St Madison WI 53715 **Phn:** 706-542-6559 **Fax** 706-542-9454 Norbert Pienta. Monthly magazine. **8,000** to chemistry teachers at all levels interested in research, apparatus, teaching methods. pubs.acs.org/journal/jceda8 norbert-pienta@jce.acs.org

Perfumer & Flavorist 336 Gundersen Dr Ste A Carol Stream IL 60188 **Phn:** 630-653-2155 **Fax** 630-653-2192 Jeb Gleason-Allured. Allured Publishing. Monthly magazine. **1,400** to flavor/fragrance industry members interested in materials, processes, industry news. www.PerfumerFlavorist.com perfumer@allured.com

Powder and Bulk Engineering 1155 Northland Dr Saint Paul MN 55120 **Phn:** 651-287-5600 **Fax** 651-287-5650 Terry O'Neill. CSC Publishing. Monthly magazine. **30,100** to engineers, technical mgrs. in processing, packaging, handling dry particulates. www.powderbulk.com powderandbulkengineering@cscpub.com

Powder/Bulk Solids 45 Summit Rd Andover NJ 07821 **Phn:** 973-786-6401 **Fax** 973-786-6471 Kevin Cronin. UBM Canon LLC. Monthly **37,000** to industrial engineers in processing, handling, packaging dry particulates, solids. www.powderbulksolids.com kevin.cronin@ubm.com

Processing 200 Croft St # 1 Birmingham AL 35242 **Phn:** 205-408-3700 **Fax** 205-408-3797 Nick Phillips. Grand View Media. Monthly tabloid. **55,800** to R&D, production, plant mgrs., engineers interested in services, materials. www.processingmagazine.com nphillips@grandviewmedia.com

Spray Technology & Marketing 3621 Hill Rd Parsippany NJ 07054 **Phn:** 973-331-9545 **Fax** 973-331-9547 Ava Caridad. Monthly. **5,900** to spray packaging industry mgmt. responsible for mktg., manufacturing, quality control. www.spraytechnology.com acaridad@spraytechnology.com

Religion .15

Adventist Review 12501 Old Columbia Pike Silver Spring MD 20904 **Phn:** 301-680-6560 **Fax** 301-680-6638 Carlos Medley. Weekly magazine. **30,000** to Church members, others interested in 7th Day theology, spiritual topics, news, issues, profiles. www.adventistreview.org cmedley@adventistreview.org

America 106 W 56th St New York NY 10019 **Phn:** 212-581-4640 **Fax** 212-399-3596 Drew Christiansen. America Press Inc. Weekly magazine. **38,000** to Catholics interested in church current events; book and film reviews. www.americamagazine.org america@americamagazine.org

Biblical Archaeology Review 4710 41st St NW Washington DC 20016 **Phn:** 202-364-3300 **Fax** 202-364-2636 Hershel Shanks. Biblical Archaeology Soc. Bimonthly mag. TH:@BibArch
176,000 to readers interested in secular Bible scholarship, translations, textual matters.
www.biblicalarchaeology.org bas@bib-arch.org

B'nai B'rith Magazine 2020 K St NW Fl 7 Washington DC 20006 **Phn:** 202-857-2701 **Fax** 202-857-2781 Hiram Reisner. B'nai B'rith Intl. Quarterly magazine.
58,300 to Jewish families interested in politics, culture, Israel, personalities. www.bnaibrith.org bbm@bnaibrith.org

Catechist 2621 Dryden Rd Ste 300 Dayton OH 45439 **Phn:** 937-293-1415 **Fax** 937-293-1310 Kass Dotterweich. Peter Li Edu. Grp. 7-issue magazine.
53,400 to Catholic religion teachers and Catholic school administrators. www.catechist.com kdotterweich@peterli.com

Catholic Digest 1 Montauk Ave Ste 2 New London CT 06320 **Phn:** 860-437-3012 **Fax** 860-437-3013 Dan Connors. Bayard USA. Monthly magazine.
200,000 to readers interested in Catholic-oriented general editorial content. www.catholicdigest.com dconnors@catholicdigest.com

Charisma 600 Rinehart Rd Lake Mary FL 32746 **Phn:** 407-333-0600 **Fax** 407-333-7133 Marcus Yoars. Charisma Media. Monthly magazine.
110,000 to Christians in charismatic renewal movement interested in books, music, news.
www.charismamag.com charisma@charismamedia.com

Children's Ministry PO Box 481 Loveland CO 80539 **Phn:** 970-669-3836 **Fax** 970-292-4372 Christine Yount Jones. Group Publishing. Bimonthly. TH:@ChristineYJones
54,000 to Christian Sunday school teachers, youth group leaders, other church based personnel who work with children to age 12.
www.childrensministry.com cyjones@group.com

Christian Century 104 S Michigan Ave Ste 700 Chicago IL 60603 **Phn:** 312-263-7510 **Fax** 312-263-7540 John Buchanan. Biweekly magazine.
32,000 to Christian general public with ecumenical interest in religion, world affairs, the arts.
www.christiancentury.org main@christiancentury.org

Christianity Today 465 Gundersen Dr Carol Stream IL 60188 **Phn:** 630-260-6200 **Fax** 630-260-8428 Mark Galli. Christianity Today Intl. Monthly magazine.
147,900 to clergy, lay leaders, others interested in doctrine, current events, evangelism.
www.christianitytoday.com letters@christianitytoday.com

Church Executive 4742 N 24th St Ste 340 Phoenix AZ 85016 **Phn:** 602-265-7600 **Fax** 602-265-4300 Ron Keener. Power Trade Media. Monthly magazine.
40,000 to Christian church business administrators & directors responsible for finance, equipment, insurance, construction. churchexecutive.com rkeener@churchexecutive.com

Church Production 2610 Wycliff Rd Ste 405 Raleigh NC 27607 **Phn:** 919-325-0120 **Fax** 919-325-0121 Brian Blackmore. Monthly.
33,300 to production oriented houses of worship covering audio, video and lighting technologies.
www.churchproduction.com editorial@churchproduction.com

Clergy Journal 6160 Carmen Ave Inver Grove Heights MN 55076 **Phn:** 651-451-9945 **Fax** 651-457-4617 Sharon Firle. Logos Productions. Bimonthly magazine.
9,000 to mainline Protestant ministers, church administrators and executives.

Equip & Connect 1700 N Brown Rd Ste 102 Lawrenceville GA 30043 **Phn:** 678-825-1100 **Fax** 678-825-1101 Stephen Estock. Presbyterian Church of America. Quarterly.
11,000 to Presbyterian Church of America leaders responsible for church materials, conferences, supplies. www.pcacep.org sestock@pcanet.org

Group PO Box 481 Loveland CO 80539 **Phn:** 970-669-3836 **Fax** 970-292-4372 Rick Lawrence. Group Publishing. Bimonthly magazine. TH:@RickSkip
25,000 to Christian youth leaders responsible for activities, projects, service, fundraising, admn.
www.youthministry.com rlawrence@group.com

Guideposts 16 E 34th St New York NY 10016 **Phn:** 212-251-8100 **Fax** 212-684-0679 Rick Hamlin. Guidepost Associates. Monthly magazine.
2,400,000 to global audience of all faiths interested in inspirational stories. www.guideposts.com/media gpeditors@guideposts.org

Hadassah Magazine 50 W 58th St New York NY 10019 **Phn:** 212-451-6289 **Fax** 212-451-6257 Alan Tigay. Women's Zionist Org. of Amer. Monthly magazine.
239,200 to WZOA members, other American Jewish readers interested in intl. Jewish life and issues.
www.hadassah.org egoldberg@hadassah.org

Hinduism Today 107 Kaholalele Rd Kapaa HI 96746 **Phn:** 808-822-7032 **Fax** 808-822-4351 Paramacharya Palaniswami. Quarterly magazine.
80,000 to Hindu readers and others interested in festivals, observance, intl. communities, history, educational events. www.hinduismtoday.com letters@hindu.org

Homecoming Magazine 402 BNA Dr Ste 400 Nashville TN 37217 **Phn:** 615-386-3011 **Fax** 615-312-4266 Roberta Croteau. Salem Publishing. Bimonthly magazine.
81,800 to readers interested in Christian music, entertainment, family life, southern lifestyle.
magazine.homecomingmagazine.com homecoming@salempublishing.com

Homiletic & Pastoral Review PO Box 297 Ramsey NJ 07446 **Phn:** 201-236-9336 **Fax** 201-236-9362 Catherine Harmon. Online only.
for Catholic clergy and theologians interested in sermons, current moral, dogmatic issues.
www.hprweb.com hpr@jesuits.net

Hope Today 3909 Westpoint Blvd Ste B Winston Salem NC 27103 **Phn:** 336-768-6565 **Fax** 336-768-1404 John Parks. Monthly.
24,600 addresses life's challenges and opportunities on an inspirational level.

Jewish Action 11 Broadway Fl 14 New York NY 10004 **Phn:** 212-613-8146 **Fax** 212-613-0646 Rashel Zywicka. Orthodox Union. Quarterly magazine.
12,000 to Orthodox Jewish readers interested in life & experience articles, art, music, poetry, books, history. www.ou.org/jewish_action/ ja@ou.org

Jewish Exponent 2100 Arch St Philadelphia PA 19103 **Phn:** 215-832-0700 **Fax** 215-569-3389 Lisa Hostein. Weekly newspaper.
42,000 to metro Philadelphia Jewish families interested in local, natl., intl. Jewish issues.
www.jewishexponent.com lhostein@jewishexponent.com

Jewish Journal 3580 Wilshire Blvd Ste 1510 Los Angeles CA 90010 **Phn:** 213-368-1661 **Fax** 213-368-1684 Robert Eshman. Weekly newspaper.
150,000 to Los Angeles area Jewish readers interested in local, regional, national topics.
www.jewishjournal.com editor@jewishjournal.com

Jewish Post & Opinion 1427 W 86th St Ste 228 Indianapolis IN 46260 **Phn:** 317-405-8054 **Fax** 317-405-8054 Jennie Cohen. Monthly newspaper.
10,000 in 2 editions (Indiana & natl.) to Jewish readers interested in state, natl., intl. news.
www.jewishpostopinion.com jpostopinion@gmail.com

Jewish Press 4915 16th Avenue Brooklyn NY 11204 **Phn:** 718-330-1100 **Fax** 718-935-1215 Jason Maoz. Weekly.
67,400 to readers interested in current events & religious commentary from Modern Orthodox Jewish perspective. www.jewishpress.com editor@jewishpress.com

Jewish Week 1501 Broadway Ste 505 New York NY 10036 **Phn:** 212-921-7822 **Fax** 212-921-8420 Robert Goldblum. Weekly newspaper.
275,000 in 5 metro New York area editions to readers interested in local, natl. intl. Jewish issues.
www.thejewishweek.com robert@jewishweek.org

JTNews 2041 3rd Ave Seattle WA 98121 **Phn:** 206-441-4553 Joel Magalnick. Semimonthly.
4,500 to Washington State Jewish families interested in area, natl., intl. Jewish issues. www.jtnews.net editor@jtnews.net

Kosher Spirit 391 Troy Ave Brooklyn NY 11213 **Phn:** 718-771-0100 **Fax** 718-771-0991 Chaim Fogelman. Quarterly. TH:@KosherAlerts
5,000 to readers interested in kosher recipes, nutrition, Jewish law analysis, rabbinical commentaries.
www.kosherspirit.com/about.asp editor@kosherspirit.com

Kyria 465 Gundersen Dr Carol Stream IL 60188 **Phn:** 630-260-6200 **Fax** 630-260-0114 Ginger Kolbaba. Christianity Today Intl. Online only.
for Christian women interested in inspirational and motivational topics. www.kyria.com kyria@christianitytoday.com

Liguorian 1 Liguori Dr Liguori MS 63057 **Phn:** 636-464-2500 Cheryl Plass. 10-issue magazine.
24,600 to Catholics, information about their faith, practical ways to live it, spiritual nourishment.
www.liguorian.org liguorianeditor@liguori.org

Living Church 816 E Juneau Ave Milwaukee WI 53202 **Phn:** 414-276-5420 **Fax** 414-276-7483 Weekly.
9,200 to Episcopal clergy and adult laypeople interested in diocesan and foreign news.
livingchurch.org tlc@livingchurch.org

The Lutheran 8765 W Higgins Rd Fl 5 Chicago IL 60631 **Phn:** 773-380-2540 **Fax** 773-380-2409 Daniel J. Lehmann. Evangelical Lutheran Church in Amer. Monthly magazine.
210,000 to readers interested in Lutheran theology, issues, activities, pastor profiles, organizational information. www.thelutheran.org lutheran@thelutheran.org

Men of Integrity 465 Gundersen Dr Carol Stream IL 60188 **Phn:** 630-260-6200 **Fax** 630-260-9401 Michelle Dowell. Christianity Today Intl. Bimo.
60,000 providing biblical answers to the issues that men face in the modern world.
www.christianitytoday.com/moi/ mail@menofintegrity.net

Message Magazine 55 W Oak Ridge Dr Hagerstown MD 21740 **Phn:** 301-393-4100 **Fax** 301-393-4103 Washington Johnson. Bimonthly magazine.
99,000 to primarily Afr.-Amer. readers interested in contemporary Christian missions, doctrine, devotion, profiles. www.messagemagazine.org wjohnson@rhpa.org

Midstream 633 3rd Ave Fl 21 New York NY 10017 **Phn:** 212-339-6020 **Fax** 212-318-6176 Leo Haber. Theodor Herzl Fndtn. Bimo.
12,000 covers contemporary life, culture, emphasis on the State of Israel, and Zionist ideas.
www.midstreamthf.com midstreamthf@aol.com

Ministry Today 600 Rinehart Rd Lake Mary FL 32746 **Phn:** 407-333-0600 **Fax** 407-333-7133 Marcus Yoars. Charisma Media. Bimonthly.
15,500 to Christian pastors, deacons, church members in ministry leadership positions.
www.ministrytodaymag.com ministrytoday@charismamedia.com

Moment Magazine 4115 Wisconsin Ave NW Ste 102 Washington DC 20016 **Phn:** 202-363-6422 **Fax** 202-362-2514 Nadine Epstein. Bimonthly magazine.
99,000 provides interdisciplinary forum for discussion of modern Jewish experience. www.momentmag.com editor@momentmag.com

My Daily Visitor 200 Noll Plz Huntington IN 46750 **Phn:** 260-356-8400 **Fax** 260-356-8472 Bill Dodds. Our Sunday Visitor. Bimo.
33,500 Pocket-sized bimonthly that gives you the Scripture references for the day. www.osv.com mdvisitor@osv.com

National Catholic Register PO Box 100699 Irondale AL 35210 **Phn:** 205-278-8400 **Fax** 205-278-8401 Debbie Aguiar. EWTN News, Inc. Biweekly newspaper.
25,500 to readers interested in current events, commentary from Roman Catholic perspective. www.ncregister.com editor@ewtn.com

National Catholic Reporter 115 E Armour Blvd Kansas City MO 64111 **Phn:** 816-531-0538 **Fax** 816-968-2280 Joe Feuerherd. Biweekly newspaper.
100,000 to readers interested in current events and religious issues from progressive Roman Catholic perspective. ncronline.org tmalcolm@ncronline.org

Oncourse 1445 N Boonville Ave Springfield MO 65802 **Phn:** 417-862-2781 Amber Weigand-Buckley. Assemblies of God USA. Quarterly magazine. TH:@OnCourseMag; @Barefacedgirl
160,000 to 13-18 Assemblies of God youth interested in making right choices in regard to ethics, sexuality, campus missions. oncourse.ag.org amber@oncourse.ag.org

Our Sunday Visitor 200 Noll Plz Huntington IN 46750 **Phn:** 260-356-8400 **Fax** 260-356-8472 John Norton. Our Sunday Visitor, Inc. Weekly newspaper.
62,500 to Catholic families interested in Catholic belief & practice; TV, movie, book reviews. www.osv.com oursunvis@osv.com

Outreach Magazine 2230 Oak Ridge Way Vista CA 92081 **Phn:** 760-940-0600 Brian Orme. Bimonthly magazine.
30,000 to Protestant senior pastors, church leaders, laity responsible for congregational outreach. www.outreachmagazine.com borme@outreach.com

Parabola Magazine 20 W 20th St New York NY 10011 **Phn:** 212-822-8806 **Fax** 260-356-8472 Dale Fuller. Soc.for the Study of Myth. Qu.
36,500 the world's myths, symbols, and religious traditions, meaning of life, wisdom. www.parabola.org editorial@parabola.org

Presbyterians Today 100 Witherspoon St Louisville KY 40202 **Phn:** 502-569-5520 **Fax** 502-569-8632 Eva Stimson. Presbyterian Church (USA). 10-issue magazine.
38,000 to Presbyterians interested in religious current events, Bible study, church activities. gamc.pcusa.org/ministries/today/ eva.stimson@pcusa.org

The Priest 200 Noll Plz Huntington IN 46750 **Phn:** 260-356-8400 **Fax** 260-356-8472 Fr. Owen Campion. Our Sunday Visitor, Inc. Monthly.
4,500 to Catholic clergymen interested in commentary, viewpoints, theology, pastoral issues. www.osv.com tpriest@osv.com

Reform Judaism 633 3rd Ave Fl 7 New York NY 10017 **Phn:** 212-650-4240 **Fax** 212-650-4249 Joy Weinberg. Quarterly magazine.
305,000 to readers interested in Union for Reformed Judaism matters, education, Israel, theology, lifestyle features. reformjudaismmag.org rjmagazine@urj.org

Religious Conference Manager 10 Fawcett St Ste 500 Cambridge MA 01238 **Phn:** 978-448-0377 Regina McGee. Penton Media. 7-issue magazine. TH:@meetingsnet
4,300 to church leadership, others responsible for planning & execution of religious retreats & conferences. meetingsnet.com rmcgee2125@verizon.net

REV! Magazine PO Box 481 Loveland CO 80539 **Phn:** 970-669-3836 **Fax** 970-292-4372 Lee Sparks. Group Publishing. Bimonthly.
27,000 to senior Christian pastors concerned with leadership issues, sermons. rev.org lsparks@group.com

Religion .15

St. Anthony Messenger 28 W Liberty St Cincinnati OH 45202 **Phn:** 513-241-5615 **Fax** 513-241-0399 Fr. Pat McCloskey. Monthly.
300,000 to Catholic families interested in positive, entertaining, informative editorial content. www.americancatholic.org patm@americancatholic.org

Significant Living PO Box 5000 Iola WI 54945 **Phn:** 715-445-5000 **Fax** 715-445-4053 Diana Jones. 6-issue magazine.
30,000 to older Christian readers interested in inspirational articles, Bible humor, financial advice. www.significantliving.org editor@significantliving.org

Tablet 1712 10th Ave Brooklyn NY 11215 **Phn:** 718-499-9705 **Fax** 800-683-6602 Ed Wilkinson. Brooklyn Diocese. Weekly newspaper.
76,000 to Catholic families in Brooklyn area, church officials, schools, educators, libraries. thetablet.org ewilkinson@diobrook.org

Tablet Magazine 37 W 28th St Fl 8 New York NY 10001 **Phn:** 212-920-3685 **Fax** 212-920-3699 Allison Hoffman. Online only. TH:@tabletmag
to readers interested in Jewish life, culture, news, media, politics. www.tabletmag.com ahoffman@tabletmag.com

The Tidings 3424 Wilshire Blvd Fl 6 Los Angeles CA 90010 **Phn:** 213-637-7360 **Fax** 213-637-6360 Mike Nelson. Catholic Archdiocese of Los Angeles. Weekly.
200,400 to south CA Catholics interested in local, national & international church news & events. www.the-tidings.com mnelson@the-tidings.com

Tricycle: The Buddhist Review 92 Vandam St Fl 3 New York NY 10013 **Phn:** 212-645-1143 **Fax** 212-645-1493 James Shaheen. Quarterly magazine.
60,000 to Western Buddhists interested in intl. Buddhist activities and impact on America. www.tricycle.com editorial@tricycle.com

U.U. World 25 Beacon St Boston MA 02108 **Phn:** 617-948-6108 **Fax** 617-742-7025 Chris Walton. Unitarian Universalist Assn. Quarterly magazine.
125,000 to Unitarian Universalist church members interested in church values and purposes. www.uuworld.org world@uua.org

Vibrant Life 55 W Oak Ridge Dr Hagerstown MD 21740 **Phn:** 301-393-4019 **Fax** 301-393-4055 Linda Starkey. 7th Day Adventist Publications. Bimonthly magazine.
100,000 to Christian readers interested in vegan nutrition, health, exercise, family, environment. www.vibrantlife.com vibrantlife@rhpa.org

Worship Leader 32234 Paseo Adelanto Ste A San Juan Capistrano CA 92675 **Phn:** 949-240-9339 **Fax** 949-240-0038 Jeremy Armstrong. Bimonthly magazine.
35,000 to church worship leaders and music directors interested in resources, products, technology. www.worshipleader.com editor@wlmag.com

YouthWorker Journal 402 BNA Dr Ste 400 Nashville TN 37217 **Phn:** 615-386-3011 **Fax** 615-312-4266 Steve Rabey. Salem Publishing. Bimonthly.
21,000 to Christian church youth & lay ministers interested in resources, activities, music, curricula. www.youthworker.com articles@youthworker.com

Clothing--Fashions .16

Accessories Magazine 1384 Broadway Fl 11 New York NY 10018 **Phn:** 212-686-4412 **Fax** 212-686-6821 Lauren Parker. Business Journals, Inc. Monthly magazine.
25,000 to retailers of shoes, handbags, gloves, belts, jewelry, neckwear, hats, leegwear, eyeware. www.accessoriesmagazine.com laurenp@busjour.com

Apparel 801 Gervais St Ste 101 Columbia SC 29201 **Phn:** 803-771-7500 **Fax** 803-799-1461 Jordan Speer. Edgell Communications. Monthly magazine.
18,100 to clothing mfg. execs., textile mill mgmt. concerned with distribution, sourcing. apparel.edgl.com jspeer@apparelmag.com

California Apparel News 110 E 9th St Ste A777 Los Angeles CA 90079 **Phn:** 213-627-3737 **Fax** 213-623-5707 Alison Nieder. MNM Publishing. Weekly newspaper.
11,200 to West Coast fashion industry manufacturers, retailers, importers and exporters. www.apparelnews.net alison@apparelnews.net

Impressions 1145 Sanctuary Pkwy. #355 Alpharetta GA 30009 **Phn:** 770-569-1540 **Fax** 770-777-8733 Marcia Derryberry. Nielsen Business Media. Monthly.
36,000 to commercial embroiderers interested in business operations, trends, marketing. www.impressionsmag.com mderryberry@impressionsmag.com

MR 1384 Broadway New York NY 10018 **Phn:** 212-686-4412 **Fax** 212-686-6821 Karen Alberg. Business Journals. 9-issue magazine.
18,300 to retailers, corp. buying personnel of men's clothing, furnishings, sportswear. www.mrketplace.com karena@busjour.com

Specialty Insider 114 Sunset Ln Tebafly NJ 06760 **Phn:** 201-602-1722 **Fax** 201-894-0912 Ralph Erardy. Quarterly magazine.
15,000 to luxury & speciality retailers interested in merchandising, marketing, displays, industry news. www.specialtyinsider.com rerardy@specialtyinsider.com

Women's Wear Daily 750 3rd Ave New York NY 10017 **Phn:** 212-630-3500 **Fax** 212-630-3566 Edward Nardoza. Conde Nast/Fairchild. Daily newspaper.
46,700 to women's apparel mfrs., buyers, retailers, fashion writers, press, merchandise mgrs. www.wwd.com wwdedit@fairchildpub.com

Dental .17

Access 444 N Michigan Ave Ste 3400 Chicago IL 60611 **Phn:** 312-440-8900 **Fax** 312-467-1702 Jean Majeski. Amer. Dental Hygienists Assn. 10-issue magazine.
55,000 to dental hygienists interested in professional development, clinical info., employment. www.adha.org communications@adha.net

ADA News 211 E Chicago Ave Fl 21 Chicago IL 60611 **Phn:** 312-440-2780 **Fax** 312-440-3538 Judy Jakush. Amer. Dental Assn. Publications. Semimonthly tab.
152,400 to Assn. members interested in scientific & educational developments, Assn. news. www.ada.org/news/ adanews@ada.org

AGD Impact 211 E Chicago Ave # 900 Chicago IL 60611 **Phn:** 312-440-4322 **Fax** 312-335-3427 Emily Taylor. Acad. General Dentistry Pubs. Monthly magazine.
50,000 to dentists interested in trends and issues relevant to general dental practices. www.AGD.org impact@agd.org

American Jrnl. Orthodontics PO Box 357446 Seattle WA 98195 **Phn:** 206-221-5413 David L. Turpin. Elsevier, Inc. Monthly.
15,800 o orthodontic & dentofacial orthopedic practitioners interested in research, reviews, case reports, clinical material. www.us.elsevierhealth.com dlturpin@aol.com

ASDA News 211 E Chicago Ave Ste 700 Chicago IL 60611 **Phn:** 312-440-2795 **Fax** 312-440-2820 Kim Schneider. Amer. Student Dental Assn. 10-issue newspaper.
18,000 to dental students intersted in Assn. and student news. www.asdanet.org kim@asdanet.org

CDS Review 401 N Michigan Ave Ste 200 Chicago IL 60611 **Phn:** 312-836-7300 **Fax** 312-836-7337 William Conkis. Chicago Dental Society. 7-issue mag.
8,000 to Society members interested in events, local and natl. dental news. www.cds.org review@cds.org

Dental Assistant Journal 35 E Wacker Dr Chicago IL 60601 **Phn:** 312-541-1550 **Fax** 312-541-1496 Michi Trota. Amer. Dental Assts. Assn. Bimonthly magazine.
14,500 to dental assistants interested in clinical issues, practice administration, continuing education. www.dentalassistant.org mtrota@adaa1.com

Dental Economics 1421 S. Sheridan Rd. Tulsa OK 74112 **Phn:** 918-835-3161 **Fax** 918-831-9804 Joseph Blaes DDS. PennWell Publishing. Monthly magazine.
103,700 to dentists, dental office mgrs. interested in technology, insurance, business practices. www.dentaleconomics.com joeb@pennwell.com

Dental Lab Products 641 Lexington Ave Fl 8 New York NY 10022 **Phn:** 212-951-6600 Stan Goff. Monthly tabloid.
18,300 to dental lab owners & mgrs. interested in new product uses & applications, continuing education, industry trends. www.dentalproductsreport.com sgoff@advanstar.com

Dental Products Report 641 Lexington Ave Fl 8 New York NY 10022 **Phn:** 212-951-6600 **Fax** 212-951-6666 Renee Knight. Monthly tabloid.
150,000 to dentists, dental students, dental product mfrs. and distributors. www.dentalproductsreport.com rknight@advanstar.com

Dental Tribune 116 W 23rd St Ste 500 New York NY 10011 **Phn:** 212-244-7181 **Fax** 212-244-7185 Robin Goodman. Monthly newspaper.
100,000 in 2 editions (eastern & western U.S.) to dental professionals interested in profiles, conventions, conferences. www.dental-tribune.com r.goodman@dental-tribune.com

Dentistry Today 100 Passaic Ave Ste 220 Fairfield NJ 07004 **Phn:** 973-882-4700 **Fax** 973-882-3622 Phillip Bonner. Monthly tabloid.
150,000 to practicing dentists interested in successful management practices, clinical trends. www.dentistrytoday.com phillipbonner@hotmail.com

General Dentistry 211 E Chicago Ave # 900 Chicago IL 60611 **Phn:** 312-440-4300 **Fax** 312-335-3427 Cathy McNamara. Acad. General Dentistry Pubs. Bimo. mag.
35,000 to Academy members, other general dentists interested in scientific & clinical information. www.agd.org generaldentistry@agd.org

Jrnl. Amer. Dental Assn. 211 E Chicago Ave Fl 21 Chicago IL 60611 **Phn:** 312-440-2785 **Fax** 312-440-3538 Michael Glick. Monthly magazine.
147,000 to Assn. members interested in programs, clinical reports, continuing education. www.ada.org jadaletters@ada.org

Jrnl. Clinical Orthodontics 1828 Pearl St Boulder CO 80302 **Phn:** 303-443-1720 **Fax** 303-443-9356 David Vogels. Monthly magazine.
8,500 o orthodontists interested in original research, case reports, clinical techniques & aids. www.jco-online.com wendyo@jco-online.com

Jrnl. Endodontics 7703 Floyd Curl Dr San Antonio TX 78229 **Phn:** 210-567-3385 **Fax** 210-567-3389 Kenneth Hargreaves. Monthly.
7,000 to endodontists interested in scientific articles, case reports, materials and methods. www.jendodon.com jendodontics@uthscsa.edu

Jrnl. Oral/Maxillofacial Surgery E Carolina Univ Dental/Lakeside 7/MS 7 Greenville NC 27834 **Phn:** James R. Hupp. Monthly magazine.
8,200 to oral & maxillofacial surgeons interested in case studies, research, conferences. www.joms.org joms@aaoms.org

Jrnl. Periodontology 737 N Michigan Ave Ste 800 Chicago IL 60611 **Phn:** 312-573-3224 **Fax** 312-787-3670 Julie Daw. Monthly.
9,000 to periodontists interested in original clinical research, disease, implant design and testing. www.perio.org julie@perio.org

Jrnl. Prosthetic Dentistry 1120 15th St Augusta GA 30912 **Phn:** 706-721-4558 **Fax** 706-721-4571 Dr. Carol A. Lefebvre. Monthly.
6,000 to practitioners of prosthetic and restorative dentistry interested in original peer-reviewed papers, techniques. www.us.elsevierhealth.com

Dental .17

Lab Management Today 84 S Main St Newtown CT 06470 **Phn:** 203-459-2888 **Fax** 203-459-2889 Kelly F. Carr. 10-issue tabloid.
18,600 to dental lab owners, managers interested in marketing, promotion, financial planning. www.lmtmag.com info@lmtcommunications.com

New York State Dental Jrnl. 20 Corporate Woods Blvd Ste 602 Albany NY 12211 **Phn:** 518-465-0044 **Fax** 518-465-3219 Mary Stoll. 6-issue magazine.
13,200 to Assn. members interested in original peer-reviewed research, Assn. news and events. www.nysdental.org mstoll@nysdental.org

Quintessence Intl. 4350 Chandler Dr Hanover Park IL 60133 **Phn:** 630-736-3600 **Fax** 630-736-3633 Lori Bateman. 10-issue magazine.
16,000 to general practice dentists interested in continuing knowledge in all practice areas. www.quintpub.com lbateman@quintbook.com

RDH 1421 S. Sheridan Rd. Tulsa OK 74112 **Phn:** 918-835-3161 **Fax** 918-831-9804 Mark Hartley. PennWell Publishing. Monthly magazine.
68,300 to dental hygienists interested in practice options, careers, new products. www.rdhmag.com markh@pennwell.com

Drugs--Pharmaceuticals .18

American Jrnl. Health Sys Pharm 7272 Wisconsin Ave Bethesda MD 20814 **Phn:** 301-664-8601 **Fax** 301-634-5701 C. Richard Talley. Semimonthly magazine.
38,000 to hospital, healthcare facility pharmacists interested in clinical trials, news, technology. www.ashp.org ajhp@ashp.org

America's Pharmacist 100 Daingerfield Rd Alexandria VA 22314 **Phn:** 703-683-8200 **Fax** 703-683-3619 Michael Conlan. Natl. Community Pharma. Assn. Monthly mag.
23,000 to independent retail pharmacists interested in merchandising, regulations, products. www.ncpanet.org info@ncpanet.org

Applied Clinical Trials 485 US Highway 1 S Fl 1 # F Iselin NJ 08830 **Phn:** 732-346-3022 **Fax** 732-596-0003 Timothy Denman. Advanstar. Monthly.
18,200 to medical, CRO and pharmaceutical personnel who conduct and monitor clinical trials. appliedclinicaltrialsonline.findpharma.com tdenman@advanstar.com

Biopharm 485 US Highway 1 S Fl 1 # F Iselin NJ 08830 **Phn:** 732-596-0276 **Fax** 732-596-0003 Laura Bush. Advanstar. Monthly.
30,200 to scientists concerned with biopharmaceutical, biotherapeutic development technology. biopharminternational.findpharma.com lbush@advanstar.com

California Pharmacist 4030 Lennane Dr Sacramento CA 95834 **Phn:** 916-779-1400 **Fax** 916-779-1401 Jamie Carota. CA Pharmacists Assn. Quarterly.
6,100 to Assn. members interested in peer-reviewed research, regulatory issues, Assn. events and news. www.cpha.com jcarota@cpha.com

Chain Drug Review 220 5th Ave New York NY 10001 **Phn:** 212-213-6000 **Fax** 212-725-3961 David Pinto. Racher Press. Biweekly tab.
45,000 to chain drugstore mgrs., headquarters exec. staff, merchandisers, buyers. www.chaindrugreview.com rmonks@racherpress.com

ComputerTalk for the Pharmacist 492 Norristown Rd Ste 160 Blue Bell PA 19422 **Phn:** 610-825-7686 **Fax** 610-825-7641 William A. Lockwood Jr. Bimonthly magazine.
32,000 to pharmacists interested in technology products and training, vendor profiles. www.computertalk.com wal@computertalk.com

Consultant Pharmacist 1321 Duke St Alexandria VA 22314 **Phn:** 703-739-1300 **Fax** 703-739-1500 Marlene Bloom. Monthly magazine.
8,000 to pharmacists working in long-term care & assisted living facilities, hospices, other adult care facilities. www.ascp.com mbloom@ascp.com

Drug Store News 425 Park Ave Ste 501 New York NY 10022 **Phn:** 212-756-5000 **Fax** 212-486-1180 Rob Eder. Lebhar-Friedman. 16-issue tab.
37,500 to chain drugstore mgmt. responsible for supplier relationships, merchandise, loss prevention. www.drugstorenews.com jkenlon@drugstorenews.com

Drug Topics 24950 Country Club Blvd Ste 200 North Olmsted OH 44070 **Phn:** 440-891-2733 **Fax** 440-891-2735 Julianne Stein. Advanstar. Monthly magazine.
151,600 to retail, hospital, HMO, mailorder pharmacists interested in managed care trends. drugtopics.modernmedicine.com jstein@advanstar.com

Formulary 24950 Country Club Blvd Ste 200 North Olmsted OH 44070 **Phn:** 440-891-2792 **Fax** 440-891-2683 Julia Talsama. Advanstar. Monthly magazine.
40,500 to physicians, pharmacists, others who select, use drugs in hospitals, HMOs, PPOs, PBMs. formularyjournal.modernmedicine.com jtalsma@advanstar.com

Hospital Pharmacy Journal 255 Jefferson Rd Saint Louis MO 63119 **Phn:** 314-963-7445 **Fax** 314-963-9345 Mary Killion. Thomas Land Publishers. Monthly magazine.
34,000 to hospital & health system pharmacists responsible for drug, IV selection & computer applications. www.thomasland.com/hospitalpharmacy.html mary@thomasland.com

Illinois Pharmacist 204 W Cook St Springfield IL 62704 **Phn:** 217-522-7300 **Fax** 217-522-7349 Stacy Ashbaker. Bimonthly. IL Pharmacist Assn.
2,500 to Assn. members interested in regulatory, legal and pharmacy practice issues. www.ipha.org ipha@ipha.org

Pharmaceutical Engineering 3109 W Dr. M.L. King Jr Blvd Ste 250 Tampa FL 33607 **Phn:** 813-960-2105 **Fax** 813-264-2816 Gloria Hall. Intl. Soc. Pharma. Engs. Bimo. mag.
25,000 to Society members, other industry professionals who buy or specify supplies & services. www.ispe.org ghall@ispe.org

Pharmaceutical Executive 641 Lexington Ave Fl 8 New York NY 10022 **Phn:** 212-951-6600 **Fax** 212-951-6604 William Looney. Advanstar. Monthly.
18,000 to pharmaceutical industry execs. responsible for mktg., sales, legal & regulatory issues. pharmexec.findpharma.com wlooney@advanstar.com

Pharmaceutical Processing 100 Enterprise Dr Box 912 # 600 Rockaway NJ 07866 **Phn:** 973-920-7000 **Fax** 973-920-7542 Mike Auerbach. Monthly tabloid.
31,000 to pharmaceutical industry personnel in development, marketing, packaging, validation. www.pharmpro.com mike.auerbach@advantagemedia.com

Pharmacy and Therapeutics 780 Township Line Rd Yardley PA 19067 **Phn:** 267-685-2788 **Fax** 267-685-2966 Sonja Sherritze. MediMedia USA. Monthly magazine.
70,700 to pharmaceutical, therapeutic committee members at med. ctrs., HMOs, decisonmakers. www.ptcommunity.com ssherritze@medimedia.com

Pharmacy Practice News 545 W 45th St Fl 8 New York NY 10036 **Phn:** 212-957-5300 **Fax** 212-957-7230 David Bronstein. McMahon Pub. Monthly tabloid.
45,500 to hospital pharmacy, HMO directors & staff interested in clinical findings & buying guides. www.pharmacypracticenews.com davidb@mcmahonmed.com

Pharmacy Times 666 Plainsboro Rd Ste 300 Plainsboro NJ 08536 **Phn:** 609-716-7777 **Fax** 609-716-4747 Kirk McKay. Intellisphere. Monthly mag. TH:@Pharmacy_Times
174,100 to pharmacists interested in pharmacy law, drug interactions, new disease treatments. www.pharmacytimes.com kmckay@pharmacytimes.com

Pharmacy Today 2215 Constitution Ave NW Washington DC 20037 **Phn:** 202-429-7583 **Fax** 202-783-2351 Carli Richard. Amer. Pharmacists Assn. Monthly.
146,900 to Association members, others interested in all aspects of pharmacy practice. www.pharmacytoday.org pt@aphanet.org

Pharmacy Week 7780 Elmwood Ave Ste 210 Middleton WI 53562 **Phn:** 608-828-4400 **Fax** 608-828-4401 43-issue magazine.
72,900 to pharmacists interested in employment opportunities and career issues. www.pharmacyweek.com info@pharmacyweek.com

Pink Sheet 5635 Fishers Ln Ste 6000 Rockville MD 20852 **Phn:** 240-221-4500 **Fax** 240-221-4400 Mary Jo Laffler. Weekly magazine.
5,300 to pharmaceutical & biotechnology execs. interested in govt. regulations, new products. thepinksheet.elsevierbi.com pinkeditor@elsevier.com

R&D Directions 828A Newtown Yardley Rd Newtown PA 18940 **Phn:** 215-944-9800 **Fax** 215-867-0053 Michael Christel. Engel Publishing. 10-issue magazine.
12,600 to pharmaceutical industry R&D professionals interested in clinical trials, development. www.pharmalive.com/magazines/randd/

US Pharmacist 160 Chubb Ave Ste 304 Lyndhurst NJ 07071 **Phn:** 201-623-0982 **Fax** 201-623-0921 Harold E. Cohen RPh. Jobson Med Info LLC. Monthly magazine.
127,600 to pharmacists interested in peer-reviewed clinical articles. www.uspharmacist.com editor@uspharmacist.com

Electric--Electronic--Telecommunications .19

Channel Partners 3300 N Central Ave Ste 300 Phoenix AZ 85012 **Phn:** 480-990-1101 Khali Henderson. Virgo Publishing. Monthly magazine.
20,000 to communication distribution channel agents, brokers, VARs, systems integrators. www.channelpartnersonline.com khenderson@vpico.com

Circuits Assembly 2400 Lake Park Dr SE Ste 440 Smyrna GA 30080 **Phn:** 678-589-8800 **Fax** 678-589-8850 Mike Buetow. UP Media. Monthly.
40,000 to printed circuit board assemblers interested in current, expected future technologies. circuitsassembly.com/cms/ mbuetow@upmediagroup.com

Commercial Integrator 111 Speen St Ste 200 Framingham MA 01701 **Phn:** 508-663-1500 **Fax** 508-663-1599 Tom LeBlanc. EH Publishing Network. 9-issue magazine.
25,000 to owners/mgrs. of electronic installation svces. for hospitality, institutional, entertainment facilities. www.commercialintegrator.com tleblanc@ehpub.com

Customer Magazine 800 Connecticut Ave Fl 1E Norwalk CT 06854 **Phn:** 203-852-6800 **Fax** 203-866-3326 Erik Linask. Technology Mktg. Corp. 10-issue magazine.
60,000 to contact center mgrs. concerned with human resources, site selection, database mgmt. www.tmcnet.com elinask@tmcnet.com

Dealerscope 1500 Spring Garden St Ste 1200 Philadelphia PA 19130 **Phn:** 631-427-0604 **Fax** 215-238-5346 Jeff O'Heir. N. Amer. Publ. Monthly tabloid.
20,000 to dealers, distributors, mfrs. of consumer appliances, electronics, telecom equipment. www.dealerscope.com joheir@napco.com

EC&M 9800 Metcalf Ave Overland Park KS 66212 **Phn:** 913-967-1782 **Fax** 913-514-6782 Mike Eby. Penton Media. Monthly magazine.
140,100 to electrical systems designers, contractors, maintenance staff. ecmweb.com mike.eby@penton.com

Drugs--Pharmaceuticals .18

ECN 100 Enterprise Dr Bx 912 # 600 Rockaway NJ 07866 **Phn:** 973-920-7000 **Fax** 973-607-5488 Chris Warner. Advantage Business Media. 15-issue tabloid.
110,000 to design engineers, engineering mgmt. personnel in electronics OEM. www.ecnmag.com chris.warner@advantagemedia.com

Electric Light & Power 1421 S Sheridan Rd Tulsa OK 74112 **Phn:** 918-835-3161 **Fax** 918-831-9834 Kristen Wright. PennWell Publishing. Bimonthly tabloid. TH:@ELPmagazine
21,300 to electric utility industry personnel responsible for regulatory issues, IT, marketing. www.elp.com kristenw@pennwell.com

Electric Perspectives 701 Pennsylvania Ave NW Washington DC 20004 **Phn:** 202-508-5000 **Fax** 202-508-5096 Bruce Cannon. Edison Electric Institute. Bimonthly magazine. TH:@Edison_Electric
15,300 to executive level personnel at investor-owned electric utilities. www.eei.org bcannon@eei.org

Electrical Apparatus 400 N Michigan Ave Ste 900 Chicago IL 60611 **Phn:** 312-321-9440 **Fax** 312-321-1288 Kevin Jones. Monthly.
15,500 to personnel at electric utility, distributor & mfr. plants responsible for engineering & maintenance. eamagazine.com eamagazine@barks.com

Electrical Contractor 3 Bethesda Metro Ctr # 1100 Bethesda MD 20814 **Phn:** 301-657-3110 **Fax** 301-215-4501 Andrea Klee. Natl. Elec. Contractors Assn. Monthly.
85,400 to electrical contractors, engineers, architects, wholesalers, inspectors, trade officials. www.ecmag.com jmazur@necanet.org

Electrical Wholesaling 9800 Metcalf Ave Overland Park KS 66212 **Phn:** 913-341-1300 **Fax** 913-514-6743 Jim Lucy. Penton Media. Monthly magazine.
22,000 to sales and management personnel at wholesale electrical distributorships. ewweb.com jim.lucy@penton.com

Electroindustry 1300 17th St N Ste 1752 Rosslyn VA 22209 **Phn:** 703-841-3200 **Fax** 703-841-3356 Pat Walsh. Natl. Electrical Mfrs. Assn. Monthly.
35,000 to electrical mfg.industry personnel in utility, medical imaging, industrial, residential applications. www.nema.org/media/ei/ communications@nema.org

Electronic Design 249 W 17th St Fl 4 New York NY 10011 **Phn:** 212-204-4368 **Fax** 913-514-7214 Joe Desposito. Penton Media. 15-issue magazine.
115,000 to engineers, mgmt. in design and specification of EOEM products and systems. electronicdesign.com joe.desposito@penton.com

Electronic Products 50 Charles Lindbergh Blvd Ste 100 Uniondale NY 11553 **Phn:** 516-227-1300 **Fax** 516-227-1444 Lauren Leetun. Hearst Business Comm. Monthly. TH:@GatorGrl
123,000 to engineering personnel interested in state of the art electronic product developments. www.electronicproducts.com lleetun@hearst.com

Energy Efficiency & Technology 1300 E 9th St Cleveland OH 44114 **Phn:** 216-696-7000 **Fax** 216-621-8469 Lee Teschler. Penton Media. Bimonthly magazine.
50,000 to engineers responsible for development of devices, circuits & systems related to efficient energy conversion. eetweb.com leland.teschler@penton.com

IAEI News 901 Waterfall Way Ste 602 Richardson TX 75080 **Phn:** 972-235-1455 **Fax** 972-235-3855 Kathryn Ingley. Intl. Assn. of Electrical Inspectors. Bimo.
20,000 to Assn. members and others responsible for electrical code enforcement. www.iaei.org kingley@iaei.org

IEEE Spectrum 3 Park Ave Fl 17 New York NY 10016 **Phn:** 212-419-7555 **Fax** 212-419-7570 Susan Hassler. Inst. Electric/Electronic Engs. Monthly.
385,000 to scientific, engineering pros in govt., industry; engineering universities worldwide. spectrum.ieee.org s.hassler@ieee.org

Intech 67 Alexander Dr Research Triangle Park NC 27709 **Phn:** 919-549-8411 **Fax** 919-549-8288 Susan Colwell. ISA Services. Monthly magazine.
80,000 to engineers and mgrs. responsible for all aspects of instrumentation and control systems. www.isa.org/intech ekovac@isa.org

Laser Focus World 98 Spit Brook Rd Ste LL4 Nashua NH 03062 **Phn:** 603-891-0123 **Fax** 603-891-0574 Carrie Meadows. PennWell Publishing. Monthly magazine.
71,000 to engineers, product researchers interested in opto-electronic technologies, applications. www.optoiq.com carriem@pennwell.com

Lighting Design & Application 120 Wall St Fl 17 New York NY 10005 **Phn:** 212-248-5000 **Fax** 212-248-5017 Paul Tarricone. Illuminating Engineering Society. Monthly.
10,000 to lighting industry professionals interested in energy, products, news, events, projects. www.iesna.org ptarricone@iesna.org

Lightwave 98 Spit Brook Rd Nashua NH 03062 **Phn:** 603-891-0123 **Fax** 603-891-0587 Carrie Meadows. Monthly tabloid.
25,000 to fiberoptic communications personnel interested in new products, industry news. www.lightwaveonline.com carriem@pennwell.com

Microwave Journal 685 Canton St Norwood MA 02062 **Phn:** 781-769-9750 **Fax** 781-769-5037 Pat Hindle. Horizon House Pubs. Monthly magazine.
49,700 to microwave application specialists in electronics manufacturing, R&D and design. www.mwjournal.com mwj@mwjournal.com

Microwave Product Digest 385 Sylvan Ave Ste 16 Englewood Cliffs NJ 07632 **Phn:** 201-569-5870 **Fax** 201-569-6684 Karen Hoppe. Monthly tab.
37,500 to microwave engineers in design and R&D interested in new products, industry news. www.mpdigest.com editor@mpdigest.com

Microwaves & RF 249 W 17th St New York NY 10011 **Phn:** 212-204-4373 **Fax** 913-514-6695 Nancy Friedrich. Penton Media. Monthly magazine.
45,000 to R&D, design, production, purchasing personnel in electronic mfg. industry. www.mwrf.com nancy.friedrich@penton.com

Military & Aerospace Electronics 98 Spit Brook Rd Nashua NH 03062 **Phn:** 603-891-0123 **Fax** 603-891-9146 John Keller. PennWell Publishing. Monthly tabloid.
37,000 to military and aerospace engineers interested in design technologies and standards. www.militaryaerospace.com jkeller@pennwell.com

Mission Critical Magazine 2401 W. Big Beaver Rd. Ste 700 Troy MI 48084 **Phn:** 303-250-2781 **Fax** 248-502-105 Caroline Fritz. BNP Media. 6-issue magazine. TH:@Mcritical
30,000 to data center owners, mgrs., engineers responsible for emergency & backup functions; disaster recovery professionals. www.missioncriticalmagazine.com fritzc@bnpmedia.com

Mobile Electronics 3520 Challenger St Torrance CA 90503 **Phn:** 310-533-2400 **Fax** 310-533-2504 Todd Ramsey. Bobit Business Media. 7-issue magazine.
20,000 to mobile electronics retailers interested in timely news, information, support, products. www.me-mag.com sdaniels@me-mag.com

Nuts & Volts 430 Princeland Ct Corona CA 92879 **Phn:** 951-371-8497 **Fax** 951-371-3052 Bryan Bergeron. T&L Pubs. Monthly.
26,100 covers robotics, circuit design, lasers, home automation, data acquisition, DIY projects. www.nutsvolts.com editor@nutsvolts.com

Photovoltaics World 98 Spit Brook Rd Nashua NH 03062 **Phn:** 603-891-0123 **Fax** 603-891-0597 Peter Singer. PennWell Publishing. Bimonthly magazine.
20,000 to solar mfg./photovoltaic industry personnel responsible for production, research, legal, environmental functions. www.electroiq.com psinger@pennwell.com

PowerGrid International 1421 S Sheridan Rd Tulsa OK 74112 **Phn:** 918-832-9269 Kristen Wright. PennWell Publishing. Monthly magazine. TH:@POWERGRIDmag
44,000 to utility mgmt. and transmission & distribution staff responsible for utility IT and automation. www.elp.com kristenw@pennwell.com

Residential Systems 28 E 28th St Fl 12 New York NY 10016 **Phn:** 212-378-0400 **Fax** 917-281-4704 Jeremy Glowacki. NewBay Media. Monthly tabloid.
20,000 to designers, installers of custom home entertainment/automation/security systems. www.resmagonline.com jglowacki@nbmedia.com

Servo Magazine 430 Princeland Ct Corona CA 92879 **Phn:** 951-371-8497 **Fax** 951-371-3052 Bryan Bergeron. T&L Pubs. Monthly.
23,100 feature articles, interviews, tutorials, DIY projects, hacks, parts for robots and robotics. servomagazine.com editor@servomagazine.com

Solid State Technology 98 Spit Brook Rd Nashua NH 03062 **Phn:** 603-891-0123 **Fax** 603-891-0597 Peter Singer. PennWell Publishing. Monthly magazine.
41,100 to solid state technical staff interested in latest processes, materials, news. www.electroiq.com psinger@pennwell.com

US Tech 10 Gay St Phoenixville PA 19460 **Phn:** 610-783-6100 **Fax** 610-783-0317 Walter Salm. Monthly tabloid.
35,000 to corporate mgrs., design engineers, purchasers, marketers using electronic products, svcs. www.us-tech.com ustech@gim.net

Vision Systems Design 98 Spit Brook Rd Ste LL4 Nashua NH 03062 **Phn:** 603-891-0123 **Fax** 603-891-0574 Carrie Meadows. PennWell Publishing. Monthly magazine.
32,000 covers machine-vision systems, image-processing for industry, military, and science. www.optoiq.com carriem@pennwell.com

Wireless Design & Development 100 Enterprise Dr Bx 912 # 600 Rockaway NJ 07866 **Phn:** 973-920-7053 **Fax** 973-920-7551 Meaghan Ziemba. Monthly tabloid.
36,000 to wireless component and design engineers who design, specify, test wireless products. www.wirelessdesignmag.com meaghan.ziemba@advantagemedia.com

Appliances .19a
Appliance 11444 W Olympic Blvd Los Angeles CA 90064 **Phn:** 310-445-4200 **Fax** 310-445-4299 Tim Somheil. UBM Canon. Online only.
for appliance industry decisionmakers interested in news, technology, statistics, events. www.appliancemagazine.com tim.somheil@ubm.com

Appliance Design 2401 W Big Beaver Rd Ste 700 Troy MI 48084 **Phn:** 440-886-1210 **Fax** 248-362-0317 Richard Babyak. BNP Media. Monthly.
26,200 to design and engineering team members in global appliance mfg. industry. www.appliancedesign.com babyakr@bnpmedia.com

Retail Observer 5542 Monterey Hwy Ste 258 San Jose CA 95138 **Phn:** 408-228-1270 **Fax** 408-360-9371 Moe Lastfogel. Monthly.
13,000 to mgrs., sales personnel at appliance/kitchen/bath retailers in west, midwest, south US. www.retailobserver.com info@retailobserver.com

Computers--Info. Technology--Internet .19b
AI Magazine 445 Burgess Dr Ste 100 Menlo Park CA 94025 **Phn:** 650-328-3123 **Fax** 650-321-4457 David Leake. Amer. Assn. for Artificial Intelligence. Quarterly.
5,600 to scientists, researchers, academics interested in artificial intelligence developments. www.aaai.org aaai@liveoakpress.com

Electric--Electronic--Telecommunications .19
Business Solutions 5340 Fryling Rd Ste 300 Erie PA 16510 **Phn:** 814-897-9000 **Fax** 814-899-5581 Michael Monocello. Jameson Publishing. Monthly magazine.
41,500 to IT product resellers & dealers interested in sales methods and customer service. www.bsminfo.com mike.monocello@jamesonpublishing.com

Cadalyst PO Box 832 Dover MA 02030 **Phn:** 541-343-0678 **Fax** 714-783-3000 Nancy Johnson. Longitude Media. Quarterly magazine.
62,000 to readers interested in CAD-related products, hardware, services, news. www.cadalyst.com editors@cadalyst.com

Circuit Cellar 4 Park St Vernon CT 06066 **Phn:** 860-875-2199 **Fax** 860-871-0411 C.J. Abate. Monthly.
28,400 to hardware and software builders, manufacturers, designers and engineers. www.circuitcellar.com editor@circuitcellar.com

Communications News 2500 Tamiami Trl N Nokomis FL 34275 **Phn:** 941-966-9521 **Fax** 941-966-2590 Vern Nelson. Nelson Publishing. Monthly magazine.
40,000 to IT and network mgrs. responsible for data and voice networks, network monitoring. www.comnews.com vnelson@nelsonpub.com

Communications of ACM 2 Penn Plz Rm 701 New York NY 10121 **Phn:** 212-869-7440 **Fax** 212-869-0481 Diane Crawford. Assn. Computer Machinery. Mo. magazine.
89,000 to software engineers and developers interested in trends, applications and research. cacm.acm.org crawfordd@hq.acm.org

Computer 10662 Los Vaqueros Cir Los Alamitos CA 90720 **Phn:** 714-821-8380 **Fax** 714-821-4010 Judith Prow. IEEE Computer Society. Monthly magazine.
77,000 to Society members, other system designers, developers, programmers. www.computer.org computer@computer.org

Computer Shopper 72 Madison Ave Fl 10 New York NY 10016 **Phn:** 917-326-8700 **Fax** 212-481-0920 John Burek. Online only.
for readers interested in making informed computer purchasing decisions. computershopper.com john.burek@computershopper.com

Computers in Libraries 143 Old Marlton Pike Medford NJ 08055 **Phn:** 609-654-6266 **Fax** 609-654-4309 Victoria Cox Kaser. 10 issues.
6,000 to information professionals responsible for specifying hardware & software for libraries. www.infotoday.com cilnews@infotoday.com

Computerworld PO Box 9171 Framingham MA 01701 **Phn:** 508-879-0700 **Fax** 508-875-8931 Scot Finnie. Weekly tabloid.
180,000 to IT execs. interested in business & technology reporting, career opportunities. www.computerworld.com scot_finnie@computerworld.com

Connected World 135 E Saint Charles Rd Ste D Carol Stream IL 60188 **Phn:** 630-933-0844 **Fax** 630-933-0845 Mike Carrozzo. Specialty Publishing. 6-issue magazine.
300,000 to individuals interested in the latest gadgets, technology developments for work, home, leisure. www.connectedworldmag.com mcarrozzo@connectedworldmag.com

CPA Technology Advisor 420 N Kickapoo Ave Shawnee OK 74801 **Phn:** 405-275-3100 **Fax** 405-275-3101 Melody Wrinkle. 8-issue tab.
42,500 to CPAs responsible for recommending technology and systems to their clients. www.cpapracticeadvisor.com melody.wrinkle@cygnuspub.com

CPU Computer Power User 131 W Grand Dr Lincoln NE 68521 **Phn:** 800-848-1478 **Fax** 402-479-2193 Chris Trumble. Sandhills Publishing. Monthly.
10,000 to computer power users, from IT professionals to at-home technology extremists. www.computerpoweruser.com editor@computerpoweruser.com

CRN 600 Community Dr Manhasset NY 11030 **Phn:** 516-562-5000 **Fax** 516-562-7822 Jane O'Brien. CMP Media. Weekly magazine.
115,000 to VARs, other reseller mgmt. interested in industry news and analysis, product reviews. www.crn.com jobrien@cmp.com

Desktop Engineering PO Box 1039 Dublin NH 03444 **Phn:** 603-563-1631 **Fax** 603-563-8192 Steve Robbins. Level 5 Comms. Monthly.
63,000 to design & mechanical engineers using CAD/CAM, data acquisition & analysis. www.deskeng.com de-editors@deskeng.com

Dr. Dobb's Journal 303 2nd St, South Twr, Ste 900 San Francisco CA 94107 **Phn:** 415-947-6000 **Fax** 415-947-6070 Andrew Binstock. TechWeb. Online only.
for professional developers interested in tools, languages, operating systems. drdobbs.com alb@drdobbs.com

EContent 88 Danbury Rd Ste 1D Wilton CT 06897 **Phn:** 203-761-1466 **Fax** 203-761-1444 Theresa Cramer.. 10-issue magazine.
12,200 to digital publishing, media, marketing executives & professionals in decision-making roles. www.econtentmag.com ecnews@infotoday.com

Federal Computer Week 3141 Fairview Park Dr Ste 777 Falls Church VA 22042 **Phn:** 703-876-5100 **Fax** 703-876-5126 Terri Huck. 1105 Media. 39 issues.
80,000 to Federal, state and local govt. dept. personnel responsible for IT specifying, purchasing. fcw.com thuck@1105govinfo.com

First Glimpse 131 W Grand Dr Lincoln NE 68521 **Phn:** 800-848-1478 **Fax** 402-479-2193 Ashley Kumpula. Sandhills Publishing.
98,000 offers help in buying, using digital cameras, MP3 players, HDTVs, appliances. www.firstglimpsemag.com editor@firstglimpsemag.com

Game Developer 600 Harrison St San Francisco CA 94107 **Phn:** 415-947-6000 Simon Carless. 11-issue magazine.
35,000 to professional game developers interested in products, technical solutions, development. www.gdmag.com scarless@think-services.com

Game Informer 724 N 1st St Fl 3 Minneapolis MN 55401 **Phn:** 612-486-6100 **Fax** 612-486-6101 Andy McNamara. Sunrise Publications. Monthly mag.
5,100,000 to online, video & computer gamers interested in game features, news and reviews. www.gameinformer.com andy@gameinformer.com

Government Computer News 8609 Westwood Center Dr Ste 500 Vienna VA 22182 **Phn:** 703-876-5100 **Fax** 703-876-5126 Paul McCloskey. 1105 Govt. Info. Group. Monthly magazine.
100,000 to government IT & technology mgrs. responsible for technology products, services & systems. gcn.com pmccloskey@gcn.com

Government Elearning! PO Box 5417 Oceanside NY 92052 **Phn:** 888-201-2841 Jerry Roche. B2B Media Co. Bimonthly.
150,000 to govt. personnel responsible for technology training, e-learning program & product selection. gov.2elearning.com editor@2elearning.com

Government Technology 100 Blue Ravine Rd Folsom CA 95630 **Phn:** 916-932-1300 **Fax** 916-932-1470 Steve Towns. e. Republic, Inc. Monthly tabloid.
77,400 to state, county, local govt. staff who specify, purchase, manage and use info systems. www.govtech.com stowns@govtech.net

IEEE Internet Computing 10662 Los Vaqueros Cir Los Alamitos CA 90720 **Phn:** 714-821-8380 **Fax** 714-821-4010 Hazel Kosky. Inst. Electric/Electronic Engs. Bimonthly.
6,500 to Institute members, technology users interested in Internet's impact on engineering. www.computer.org internet@computer.org

IEEE Security & Privacy 10662 Los Vaqueros Cir Los Alamitos CA 90720 **Phn:** 714-821-8380 **Fax** 714-821-4010 Kathy Clark-Fisher. Bimonthly magazine.
9,900 to IT execs. responsible for network infrastructure, implementation of security systems. www.computer.org security@computer.org

IEEE Software 10662 Los Vaqueros Cir Los Alamitos CA 90720 **Phn:** 714-821-8380 **Fax** 714-821-4010 Crystal Shif. Inst. Electric/Electronic Engs. Bimonthly.
11,800 to software professionals interested in engineering, development tools, languages. www.computer.org software@computer.org

Information Management 220 Regency Ct Ste 210 Brookfield WI 53045 **Phn:** 262-784-0444 **Fax** 262-782-9489 Julie Langenkamp. Source Media. Monthly magazine.
75,000 to IT executives in data warehousing, customer relationship mgmt., object technology. www.information-management.com julie.langenkamp@sourcemedia.com

Informationweek 600 Community Dr Manhasset NY 11030 **Phn:** 516-562-5000 **Fax** 516-562-5036 Wyatt Kash. UBM Tech. Online only. TH:@WyattKash
to business technology buyers interested in products, vendors, trends. www.informationweek.com wyatt.kash@ubm.com

Infostor 950 Tower Ln Fl 6 Foster City CA 94404 **Phn:** 650-578-7700 **Fax** 650-350-1423 James Maguire. Quinstreet Enterprises. Online only. TH:@JamesMaguire
for IT personnel responsible for evaluating & specifying storage products & technologies. www.infostor.com jmaguire@quinstreet.com.

Internet Retailer 125 S Wacker Dr Ste 2900 Chicago IL 60606 **Phn:** 312-362-9527 **Fax** 312-362-9532 Paul Demery. Monthly magazine.
43,000 to internet retail mgmt. responsible for fulfillment, marketing, payment processing. www.internetretailer.com paul@verticalwebmedia.com

Internet Telephony 800 Connecticut Ave Flr 1 East Norwalk CT 06854 **Phn:** 203-852-6800 **Fax** 203-866-3326 Paula Bernier. Monthly magazine.
70,000 to IP communications, voice and data communication providers, developers, resellers and end users. www.tmcnet.com/voip/ pbernier@tmcnet.com

iPhone Life 110 N Court St Fairfield IA 52556 **Phn:** 641-472-6330 **Fax** 641-472-1879 Hal Goldstein. Thaddeus Computing. Bimonthly magazine.
110,000 to iPhone, iPad, iPod users interested in apps, tips, tweaks, tech support, reviews. www.iphonelife.com iphone-press@iphonelife.com

JDMS 2598 Fortune Way Ste I Vista CA 92081 **Phn:** 858-277-3888 **Fax** 858-277-3930 Vicki Pate. Quarterly magazine.
3,000 to defense industry computer modeling & simulation community. www.scs.org scs@scs.org

Laptop 1410 Broadway Rm 2101 New York NY 10018 **Phn:** 212-807-8220 **Fax** 212-807-1098 Mark Spoonauer. Bedford Comms. 15-issue magazine.
90,000 to consumers & mobile/IT pros interested in reviews & features about note/netbooks, handhelds, accessories. www.laptopmag.com news@bedfordmags.com

MacLife 4000 Shoreline Ct # 400 South San Francisco CA 94080 **Phn:** 650-872-1642 Susie Ochs. Future US. Monthly.
136,800 to Apple product enthusiasts interested in reviews, ratings, apps, software, demos. www.maclife.com susie@maclife.com

MacTech PO Box 5200 Westlake Village CA 91359 **Phn:** 805-494-9797 **Fax** 805-494-9798 Edward Marczak. Xplain Corp. Monthly magazine.
32,400 to programmers & developers interested in latest Apple trends & technologies. www.mactech.com press_releases@mactech.com

Computers--Info. Technology--Internet .19b

Macworld 501 2nd St Ste 120 San Francisco CA 94107 **Phn:** 415-243-0505 **Fax** 415-243-3545 Jason Snell. Monthly.
351,000 to Apple device users interested in new products, comparisons, how-tos. www.macworld.com news@macworld.com

Maximum PC 4000 Shoreline Ct # 400 South San Francisco CA 94080 **Phn:** 650-872-1642 Katherine Stevenson. Future US. Monthly.
200,000 to affluent PC enthusiasts interested in gaming, peripherals, upgrades. www.maclife.com tips@maximumpc.com

Mobile Enterprise 4 Middlebury Blvd Randolph NJ 07869 **Phn:** 973-607-1300 **Fax** 973-607-1395 Lori Castle. Edgell Communications. Bimonthly magazine.
28,000 to users & specifiers of enterprise-wide cellphone, smartphone, laptop, other mobile device purchase & usage. mobileenterprise.edgl.com lcastle@edgellmail.com

Network Computing 600 Community Dr Manhasset NY 11030 **Phn:** 516-562-5000 **Fax** 516-562-7293 Mike Fratto. TechWeb. Online only.
for network managers interested in new products, technical reviews, workshops. www.networkcomputing.com mfratto@techweb.com

Network World 492 Old Connecticut Path Framingham MA 01701 **Phn:** 508-766-5301 **Fax** 508-626-2705 John Dix. Intl. Data Grp. Weekly tabloid.
107,100 to IS personnel who design and implement large-scale network infrastructures. www.networkworld.com jdix@nww.com

Oracle Magazine 500 Oracle Pkwy MS10BP1 Redwood City CA 94065 **Phn:** 650-506-7000 **Fax** 650-633-2424 Aaron Lazenby. Quarterly magazine.
516,000 to Oracle product users interested in increasing profitability. www.oracle.com/profit aaron.lazenby@oracle.com

PC Magazine 28 E 28th St New York NY 10016 **Phn:** 212-503-3500 Dan Costa. Ziff Davis. Online only.
for technology buyers & decisionmakers interested in product reviews and lab tests. www.pcmag.com dan_costa@pcmag.com

PC World 501 2nd St Ste 120 San Francisco CA 94107 **Phn:** 415-243-0500 **Fax** 415-442-1891 Jon Phillips. Intl. Data Grp. Online only.
to corporate technology mgrs. interested in PC buying guides, education resources. www.pcworld.com jphillips@pcworld.com

Redmond 600 Worcester Rd Ste 204 Framingham MA 01702 **Phn:** 508-875-6644 **Fax** 508-875-6633 Doug Barney. 1105 Media. Monthly.
120,500 to IT professionals working with MS Windows platform computing environment. redmondmag.com doug.barney@redmondmag.com

Scientific Computing 100 Enterprise Dr Bx 912 # 600 Rockaway NJ 07866 **Phn:** 973-920-7000 **Fax** 973-920-7542 Suzanne Tracy. Advantage Business Media. Bimonthly.
42,000 to scientists & engineers interested in computer applications, technologies, products. www.scimag.com suzanne.tracy@advantagemedia.com

Smart Computing 131 W Grand Dr Lincoln NE 68521 **Phn:** 402-479-2199 **Fax** 402-479-2104 Lesa Call. Sandhills Publishing. Monthly magazine.
500,000 to PC users interested in plain English troubleshooting tips, product reviews, tutorials. www.smartcomputing.com editor@smartcomputing.com

The Social Media Monthly 2100 M St NW Ste 170-242 Washington DC 20037 **Phn:** 202-684-6207 Robert Fine. Cool Blue Company, LLC. Monthly magazine. TH:@bobfine
50,000 to readers interested in apps, creative uses for social media, social media's impact on art, polictics, culture. www.thesocialmediamonthly.com bob@thesocialmediamonthly.com

Technical Support 7044 S 13th St Oak Creek WI 53154 **Phn:** 414-768-8000 **Fax** 414-768-8001 Jenny Kasza. Network & System Pro.Assn. Online only.
for corp. technology mgmt. responsible for purchase, implementation, mainframe support. www.naspa.com

Vertical Systems Reseller 4 Middlebury Blvd Randolph NJ 07869 **Phn:** 973-607-1300 **Fax** 973-607-1395 Abigail Lorden. Edgell Communications. Monthly.
30,000 to resellers interested in retail IT marketing opportunities, industry news. vsr.edgl.com/home alorden@edgellmail.com

Washington Technology 3141 Fairview Park Dr Ste 777 Falls Church VA 22042 **Phn:** 703-876-5100 **Fax** 703-876-5126 David Hubler. 11-issue tabloid.
40,100 to systems integrators, contractors, subcontractors active in Federal marketplace. washingtontechnology.com dhubler@1105govinfo.com

Website Magazine 999 E Touhy Ave Des Plaines IL 60018 **Phn:** 773-628-2779 Peter Prestipino. Monthly magazine.
142,700 to IT personnel responsible for SEO & SEM, site design & maintenance, content management, e-commerce, CRM. www.websitemagazine.com peter@websitemagazine.com

Windows IT Pro 221 E 29th St Loveland CO 80538 **Phn:** 970-663-4700 **Fax** 970-667-2321 Lavon Peters. Penton Media. Online only.
to IT executives responsible for Windows NT and 2000 business applications. www.windowsitpro.com lavon.peters@penton.com

Wired 520 3rd St Ste 305 San Francisco CA 94107 **Phn:** 415-276-5000 **Fax** 415-276-5150 Kevin Poulsen. Conde Nast. Monthly magazine.
825,000 to readers interested in people & companies promoting technological trends. www.wired.com kevin_poulsen@wiredmag.com

Engineering--Construction .20

ASCE News 1801 Alexander Bell Dr Reston VA 20191 **Phn:** 703-295-6000 **Fax** 703-295-6276 Doug Scott. Amer. Soc. Civil Engineers. Monthly tabloid.
90,000 to engineers interested in Fed., state, local policies; career & education oppotunities. asce-news.asce.org dscott@asce.org

Asphalt Contractor 1233 Janesville Ave Fort Atkinson WI 53538 **Phn:** 608-583-4107 **Fax** 920-563-1700 Greg Udelhofen. Cygnus Business Media. 10-issue magazine.
10,100 to asphalt producers and contractors interested in how-to features, industry news. www.forconstructionpros.com greg.udelhofen@cygnusb2b.com

Better Roads 3200 Rice Mine Rd Tuscaloosa AL 35406 **Phn:** 205-248-1062 Amanda Bayhi. Randall-Reilly Publishing. Monthly magazine. TH:@BetterRoads
40,000 to state, county, city road engineers, specifiers, buyers; maintenance and highway officials. www.betterroads.com amanda.bayhi@randallreilly.com

California Builder & Engineer 1200 Madison Ave Ste LL20 Indianapolis IN 46225 **Phn:** 951-328-1920 **Fax** 317-423-7094 Chad Dorn. Semimo. magazine.
8,200 to heavy construction contractors, foremen, engineers, suppliers in CA, HI, NV, AZ. www.acppubs.com cbe@acppubs.com

CE News PO Box 1528 Fayetteville AR 72702 **Phn:** 330-966-2454 **Fax** 800-842-1560 Bob Drake. ZweigWhite Media. Monthly.
50,000 to civil engineers interested in mgmt. advice, buying guides, news, technical features. www.cenews.com bdrake@zweigwhite.com

Civil Engineering 1801 Alexander Bell Dr Reston VA 20191 **Phn:** 703-295-6000 **Fax** 703-295-6276 Anne Powell. Amer. Soc. Civil Engineers. Monthly.
89,200 to Soc. members, structural, environmental, geotechnical, infrastructural, civil engineers. www.asce.org cemag@asce.org

Construction/Demolition Recyc. 4020 Kinross Lakes Pkwy Ste 201 Richfield OH 44286 **Phn:** 330-523-5400 **Fax** 330-659-4043 Dan Sandoval. GIE Media. Bimonthly mag.
9,400 to processors and buyers of concrete asphalt, wood, gypsum, ferrous & nonferrous scrap. www.cdrecycler.com dsandoval@gie.net

Construction Equip. Distribution 615 W 22nd St Oak Brook IL 60523 **Phn:** 630-574-0650 **Fax** 630-574-0132 Kim Phelan. Monthly magazine.
5,000 to construction equip. distributorship mgrs. concerned with business practices, operations. www.cedmag.com info@aednet.org

Construction Equipment Guide 470 Maryland Dr Fort Washington PA 19034 **Phn:** 215-885-2900 **Fax** 215-885-2910 Craig Mongeau. Biweekly newspaper.
107,000 in 4 U.S. editions (NE, S. East, S. West, Midwest) to construction equip. decisionmakers. www.constructionequipmentguide.com editorial@cegltd.com

The Construction Specifier 266 Elmwood Ave Ste 289 Buffalo NY 14222 **Phn:** 866-572-5633 **Fax** 866-572-5677 Blair Adams. Monthly magazine.
26,100 to Construction Specifiers Inst. members, architects, engineers, officials, designers. www.constructionspecifier.com editor@constructionspecifier.com

Consulting-Specifying Engineer 1111 W 22nd St Ste 250 Oak Brook IL 60523 **Phn:** 630-571-4070 **Fax** 630-214-4504 Amara Rozgus. CFE Media. 11-issue magazine.
45,500 to engineers responsible for specification/design of mechanical, electrical, plumbing systems. www.csemag.com arozgus@cfemedia.com

Control 555 W Pierce Rd Ste 301 Itasca IL 60143 **Phn:** 630-467-1300 **Fax** 630-467-1124 Walt Boyes. Putman Media. Monthly magazine.
63,000 to engineers responsible for instrumentation, process control within process industries. www.controlglobal.com wboyes@putman.net

Control Design 555 W Pierce Rd Ste 301 Itasca IL 60143 **Phn:** 630-467-1300 **Fax** 630-467-1109 Joe Feeley. Putman Media. Monthly magazine.
45,000 covers automation, control, instrumentation needs of industrial original equipment mfrs. www.controldesign.com jfeeley@putman.net

Control Engineering 1111 W 22nd St Ste 250 Oak Brook IL 60523 **Phn:** 630-571-4070 **Fax** 630-214-4504 Mark Hoske. CFE Media. 12-issue magazine.
86,000 to automation engineers who design, implement, maintain, manage control/instrumentation systems. www.controleng.com mhoske@cfemedia.com

Cost Engineering 209 Prairie Ave Ste 100 Morgantown WV 26501 **Phn:** 304-296-8444 **Fax** 304-291-5728 Marvin Gelhausen. Monthly magazine.
4,800 to engineers and project mgrs. responsible for cost estimates and controls. www.aacei.org mgelhausen@aacei.org

Demolition 16 N Franklin St Ste 203 Doylestown PA 18901 **Phn:** 215-348-8282 **Fax** 215-348-8422 Michael Taylor. Natl. Demolition Assn. Bimonthly mag.
4,700 to demolition contractors, mgrs. responsible for project mgmt., recycling, health & safety. www.demolitionmagazine/com info@demolitionassociation.com

ENR-Engineering News-Record 2 Penn Plz Fl 12 New York NY 10121 **Phn:** 212-904-3507 **Fax** 212-904-2820 Erin Joyce.. McGraw-Hill. Weekly magazine.
70,000 to construction industry mgmt., architects, engineers interested in industry news, events. enr.construction.com erin_joyce@mcgraw-hill.com

Engineering--Construction .20

Equipment Today 1233 Janesville Ave Fort Atkinson WI 53538 **Phn:** 920-563-6388 **Fax** 920-563-1700 Becky Schultz. Cygnus Business Media. Monthly tabloid.
78,000 to contractors responsible for heavy equip. selection, rental, purchase, lease, upkeep. www.forconstructionpros.com becky.schultz@cygnusb2b.com

Equipment World 3200 Rice Mine Rd NE Tuscaloosa AL 35406 **Phn:** 205-349-2990 **Fax** 205-345-5695 Tom Jackson. Randall-Reilly Publishing. Monthly magazine.
80,300 to readers involved in construction, earthmoving, excavating using heavy equipment. www.equipmentworld.com tjackson@randallpub.com

Erosion Control 2946 De La Vina St Santa Barbara CA 93105 **Phn:** 805-682-1300 **Fax** 805-682-0200 Janice Kaspersen. Forester Media. 7-issue magazine.
23,300 to project mgrs. responsible for erosion, sediment control interested in technical articles. www.erosioncontrol.com eceditor@forester.net

The Military Engineer 607 Prince St Alexandria VA 22314 **Phn:** 703-549-3800 **Fax** 703-548-6153 Eileen Erickson. Soc. Amer. Military Engineers. Bimonthly magazine.
31,000 to uniformed service, public & private sector engineers. www.same.org erickson@same.org

Modern Steel Construction 1 E Wacker Dr Ste 700 Chicago IL 60601 **Phn:** 312-670-2400 **Fax** 312-896-9022 Geoff Weisenberger. Amer. Inst. Steel Construction. Monthly magazine.
52,200 to structural steel industry engineers, architects and contractors. www.modernsteel.com weisenberger@aisc.org

Parking 1112 16th St NW Ste 840 Washington DC 20036 **Phn:** 202-296-4336 **Fax** 202-296-3102 Denise Gable. 10-issue magazine.
6,900 to owners, operators of parking facilities concerned with mgmt., insurance, personnel. www.npapark.org denisegable@npapark.org

The Parking Professional PO Box 7167 Fredericksburg VA 22404 **Phn:** 540-371-7535 **Fax** 540-371-8022 Kim Fernandez. Intl Parking Institute. Monthly magazine.
7,500 to airport, hospital, college parking facility mgmt.; planners & architects; industry suppliers. www.parking.org fernandez@parking.org

Parking Today PO Box 66515 Los Angeles CA 90066 **Phn:** 310-390-5277 **Fax** 310-390-4777 John Van Horn. Monthly magazine.
14,900 to parking industry personnel concerned with safety, maintenance and design. www.parkingtoday.com editor@parkingtoday.com

Pavement PO Box 370 La Grange IL 60525 **Phn:** 708-354-7039 **Fax** 708-354-7268 Allan Heydorn. Cygnus Business Media. 8-issue magazine.
19,000 to on and off road asphalt and concrete contractors concerned with equip., supplies. www.forconstructionpros.com allan.heydorn@cygnusb2b.com

PE & RS 5410 Grosvenor Ln Ste 210 Bethesda MD 20814 **Phn:** 301-493-0290 **Fax** 301-493-0208 Kimberly Tilley. Am. Soc. Photogrammetry & Remote Sensing. Mo. mag.
6,500 to photogrammetrc engineering & remote sensing professionals interested in peer-reviewed technical features. www.asprs.org kimt@asprs.org

PE Magazine 1420 King St Alexandria VA 22314 **Phn:** 703-684-2800 **Fax** 703-836-4875 David Siegel. Natl. Soc. Professional Engineers. 10-issue newspaper.
43,000 to engineers in all disciplines interested in business practices, employment opportunities. www.nspe.org/PEmagazine/index.html pemagazine@nspe.org

POB Point Of Beginning 2401 W Big Beaver Rd Ste 700 Troy MI 48084 **Phn:** 248-362-3700 **Fax** 248-362-5103 Christine L. Grahl. BNP Media. Monthly magazine.
39,000 to mappers, surveyors and engineers working with mapping, GPS, GIS. www.pobonline.com pobeditor@bnpmedia.com

Professional Surveyor 20 W 3rd St Frederick MD 21701 **Phn:** 301-682-6101 **Fax** 301-682-6105 Shelly Cox. Monthly magazine.
39,200 to surveying, mapping professionals interested in new products & technologies. www.profsurv.com shelly@profsurv.com

Roads & Bridges 3030 W Salt Creek Ln Ste 201 Arlington Hts IL 60005 **Phn:** 847-391-1000 **Fax** 847-390-0408 Bill Wilson. Scranton Gillette. Monthly magazine.
60,100 to road & hwy. agency personnel who specify equipment, technology, services. www.roadsbridges.com bwilson@sgcmail.com

Sound & Vibration PO Box 40416 Bay Village OH 44140 **Phn:** 440-835-0101 **Fax** 440-835-9303 Jack K. Mowry. Acoustical Publications. Monthly magazine.
8,300 to personnel in noise, vibration control, shock/vibration testing, dynamic measurement. www.sandv.com sv@mindspring.com

Trenchless Technology 1770 Main St Peninsula OH 44264 **Phn:** 330-467-7588 **Fax** 330-468-2289 Jim Rush. Benjamin Media Inc. Monthly magazine.
37,000 to engineers and contractors working with underground construction. www.trenchlessonline.com jrush@benjaminmedia.com

Underground Construction PO Box 941669 Houston TX 77094 **Phn:** 281-558-6930 **Fax** 281-558-7029 Robert Carpenter. Monthly magazine.
38,300 to contractor & engineering firm mgmt. concerned with underground piping construction & rehab infrastructure. www.uconline.com rcarpenter@oildom.com

Feed--Grain--Milling .21

Feed & Grain 1233 Janesville Ave Fort Atkinson WI 53538 **Phn:** 920-563-1628 **Fax** 920-563-1700 Elise Schafer. IDEAg Group. 7-issue magazine. TH:@FeedAndGrainMag
15,700 to grain and feed storing, processing, mixing and marketing industry personnel. www.feedandgrain.com elise.schafer@feedandgrain.com

Feed Management 303 N Main St Ste 500 Rockford IL 61101 **Phn:** 815-966-5400 **Fax** 815-966-6416 Kathleen McLaughlin. Watt Publishing. Bimonthly magazine.
14,000 to US, Canadian animal feed mfrs. & distributors interested in nutrition, market trends. www.wattagnet.com kmclaughlin@wattnet.net

Feedstuffs 12400 Whitewater Dr Ste 160 Hopkins MN 55343 **Phn:** 952-931-0211 **Fax** 952-938-1832 Sarah Muirhead. Miller Publishing. Weekly tabloid.
14,800 to execs. and managers in feed production, distribution and related agribusiness functions. www.feedstuffs.com smuirhead@feedstuffs.com

Grain Journal 3065 Pershing Ct Decatur IL 62526 **Phn:** 217-877-9660 **Fax** 217-877-6647 Ed Zdrojewski. Country Jrnl. Publishing. Bimonthly magazine.
10,900 to grain elevator, feed mill personnel in all areas of grain/feed industry. www.grainnet.com ed@grainnet.com

Milling Journal 3065 Pershing Ct Decatur IL 62526 **Phn:** 217-877-9660 **Fax** 217-877-6647 Mark Avery. Country Jrnl. Publishing. Quarterly.
1,200 to technical personnel in flour milling, grain & oilseed processing industries. www.grainnet.com mark@grainnet.com

Ag Professional 10901 W 84th Ter Ste 200 Lenexa KS 66214 **Phn:** 913-438-8700 **Fax** 913-438-0695 Rich Keller. Vance Publishing. Monthly magazine.
24,000 to crop protection chemical, nutrient, seed salespeople interested in industry news.
www.agprofessional.com
rkeller@vancepublishing.com

Agronomy Journal 677 S Segoe Rd Madison WI 53711 **Phn:** 608-273-8080 **Fax** 608-273-2021 Susan Ernst. Amer. Society of Agronomy. Bimonthly magazine.
2,600 to Soc. members, crop/soil scientists, range/pasture mgrs. interested in research findings.
www.agronomy.org sernst@agronomy.org

Crop Science 5585 Guilford Rd Madison WI 53711 **Phn:** 608-273-8080 **Fax** 608-273-2021 Elizabeth Gebhardt. Bimonthly.
4,200 to readers interested in original research into crop breeding, genetics, physiology, metabolism, mgmt. www.crops.org/publications/cs
egebhardt@sciencesocieties.org

CropLife 37733 Euclid Ave Willoughby OH 44094 **Phn:** 440-942-2000 **Fax** 440-942-0662 Paul Schrimpf. Meister Media. Monthly. TH:@croplifemag
22,000 to ag dealers and distributors interested in market trends, new products, ag technology.
www.croplife.com pjschrimpf@meistermedia.com

Soil Science 14 College Farm Rd New Brunswick NJ 08901 **Phn:** 732-932-9810 **Fax** 732-932-8644 Robert L. Tate III. Monthly magazine.
1,100 to international audience concerned with soil investigation, use of fertilizers. journals.lww.com/soilsci/
soilscience@aesop.rutgers.edu

Food Processing--Distribution .23
Fancy Food & Culinary Products 233 N Michigan Ave Ste 1780 Chicago IL 60601 **Phn:** 312-849-2220 **Fax** 312-849-2174 Stephanie Hunsberger. Talcott Communications. 11-issue magazine.
24,900 to gourmet, specialty food & upscale houseware retailers interested in trends and products.
www.fancyfoodmagazine.com fancyfood@talcott.com

Food Engineering 600 Willowbrook Ln Ste 610 West Chester PA 19382 **Phn:** 610-436-4220 **Fax** 248-502-2059 Joyce Fassl. BNP Media. Monthly magazine.
45,000 to food & beverage processing industry mgrs. in R&D, operations, purchasing, admn.
www.foodengineeringmag.com fasslj@bnpmedia.com

Food Manufacturing 100 Enterprise Dr Box 912 # 600 Rockaway NJ 07866 **Phn:** 973-920-7000 **Fax** 973-920-7542 Krystal Gabert. Advantage Business Media. 10-iss.
40,000 to food indus. personnel responsible for production, plant ops., material handling.
www.foodmanufacturing.com
krystal.gabert@advantagemedia.com

Food Processing 555 W Pierce Rd Ste 301 Itasca IL 60143 **Phn:** 630-467-1300 **Fax** 630-467-1179 Dave Fusaro. Putman Media. Monthly magazine.
62,500 to food processing industry mgmt. responsible for R&D, engineering, marketing, purchasing.
www.foodprocessing.com dfusaro@putman.net

Food Product Design 3300 N Central Ave Ste 300 Phoenix AZ 85012 **Phn:** 480-990-1101 Lynn Kuntz. Weeks Publishing. Monthly.
32,000 to food industry personnel in quality control, research and development, process engineering.
www.foodproductdesign.com lkuntz@vpico.com

Food Quality 111 River St Hoboken NJ 07030 **Phn:** 201-748-6000 **Fax** 201-748-6088 Lisa Dionne. John Wiley & Sons. Bimonthly magazine.
21,000 to food industry personnel responsible for quality assurance/control and plant operations.
www.foodquality.com ldionne@wiley.com

Fertilizers--Soil Science .22
Food Safety Magazine 1945 W Mountain St Glendale CA 91201 **Phn:** 508-210-3149 **Fax** 508-210-3139 Barbara VanRenterghem. Bimonthly magazine.
20,000 to food & beverage safety mgrs. responsible for testing, control, contamination prevention.
www.foodsafetymagazine.com
barbara@foodsafetymagazine.com

Food Technology 525 W Van Buren St Ste 1000 Chicago IL 60607 **Phn:** 312-782-8424 **Fax** 312-782-8348 Bob Swientek. Inst. Food Technologists. Monthly.
21,000 to food processors, packaged foods mfrs., research organizations; mfrs. of food machinery.
www.ift.org bswientek@ift.org

Food World 5537 Twin Knolls Rd Ste 438 Columbia MD 21045 **Phn:** 410-730-5013 **Fax** 410-740-4680 Terri Maloney. Best-Met Publishing. Monthly magazine.
21,500 to industry personnel in DE, MD, PA, VA, DC interested in market studies, broker reports. best-met.com tmaloney@best-met.com

Fresh Cut PO Box 128 Sparta MI 49345 **Phn:** 616-887-9008 **Fax** 616-887-2666 Lee Dean. Great America Publ. Monthly magazine.
16,000 to retail and food service personnel responsible for fresh fruits and vegetables. freshcut.com
fcedit@freshcut.com

Gourmet Retailer PO Box 1417 Miami FL 33134 **Phn:** 239-992-2404 Anna Wolfe. Stagnito Media. 9-issue magazine.
21,000 to buyers at specialty food stores interested in bakeware, confections, small electrics.
www.gourmetretailer.com awolfe@stagnitomedia.com

Government Food Service 825 Old Country Rd Westbury NY 11590 **Phn:** 516-334-3030 **Fax** 516-334-3059 Ken Baglino. Exec. Business Media. Monthly tab.
4,000 to food service professionals facilities serving federal government agencies. www.ebmpubs.com
ken@ebmpubs4.com

Natural Food Network 1030 Higgins Rd Ste 230 Park Ridge IL 60068 **Phn:** 847-720-5600 **Fax** 847-720-5601 Jeremy Nedelka. M2Media360. Bimonthly magazine.
15,000 to instore buyers & mgrs. responsible for organic/natural product selection & merchandising.
www.naturalfoodnet.com jnedelka@specialtyim.com

Natural Foods Merchandiser 1401 Pearl St Ste 200 Boulder CO 80302 **Phn:** 303-939-8440 **Fax** 303-998-9020 Carlotta Mast. New Hope Natural Media. Online only.
for natural and organic food industry personnel interested in products, trends, research.
newhope360.com carlotta.mast@penton.com

Perishables Buyer 155 N Pfingsten Rd Ste 205 Deerfield IL 60015 **Phn:** 847-405-4105 **Fax** 847-405-4100 Douglas J. Peckenpaugh. BNP Media. Monthly magazine.
12,500 to food industry personnel in bakery, dairy, deli, frozen, meat, produce, refrigerated, seafood.
www.perishablesbuyer.com
peckenpaughd@bnpmedia.com

Pizza Today 908 S 8th St Ste 200 Louisville KY 40203 **Phn:** 502-736-9500 **Fax** 502-736-9501 Jeremy White. Natl. Assn. Pizza Operators. Monthly magazine.
40,000 to decision-making personnel at independent and chain pizza operations. www.pizzatoday.com
jwhite@pizzatoday.com

Prepared Foods 155 Pfingsten Rd Ste 205 Deerfield IL 60015 **Phn:** 630-616-0200 **Fax** 630-227-0527 Claudia O'Donnell. BNP Media. Monthly magazine.
43,200 to food and beverage product development personnel responsible for R & D, marketing.
www.preparedfoods.com pfeditors@bnpmedia.com

Quality Assurance & Food Safety 4020 Kinross Lakes Pkwy Ste 201 Richfield OH 44286 **Phn:** 330-523-5400 **Fax** 330-659-0823 Lisa Jo Lupo. GIE Media. Bimo.
20,000 the latest news on food industry quality control.
www.qualityassurancemag.com qanews@gie.net

Seafood Business PO Box 7438 Portland ME 04112 **Phn:** 207-842-5606 **Fax** 207-842-5603 Fiona Robinson. Diversified Business Comms. Monthly tabloid.
14,000 to N. Amer. seafood buyers interested in trends, sourcing, legislation, new products.
www.seafoodbusiness.com frobinson@divcom.com

Snack Food & Wholesale Bakery 155 N Pfingsten Rd Ste 205 Deerfield IL 60015 **Phn:** 847-405-4015 **Fax** 847-405-4100 Dan Malovany. BNP Media. Mo. tabloid.
14,900 to mgmt., mktg., R&D personnel at snack food producers, processors, packers, distributors.
www.snackandbakery.com
malovanyd@bnpmedia.com

WholeFoods Magazine 4041G Hadley Rd Ste 101 South Plainfield NJ 07080 **Phn:** 908-769-1160 **Fax** 908-769-1171 Kaylynn Chiarello-Ebner. Monthly magazine.
15,200 to health & organic food retailers interested in foods, supplements, herbs, homeopathy.
www.wholefoodsmagazine.com
kaylynnebner@wfcinc.com

Meat Trade .23a
Meat & Poultry 4800 Main St Ste 100 Kansas City MO 64112 **Phn:** 816-756-1000 **Fax** 816-756-0494 Joel Crews. Sosland Publishing. Monthly magazine.
21,100 to mgmt. personnel at meat/poultry/seafood packers, processors, wholesalers.
www.meatpoultry.com jcrews@sosland.com

Meatingplace 1415 N. Dayton St. Chicago IL 60642 **Phn:** 312-274-2000 **Fax** 312-266-3363 Tom Johnston. Monthly magazine.
25,000 to mgmt. & technical personnel in red meat packaging and processing industry.
www.meatingplace.com tjohnston@meatingplace.com

National Provisioner 155 N Pfingsten Rd Ste 205 Deerfield IL 60015 **Phn:** 847-405-4000 **Fax** 847-405-4100 Andy Hanacek. BNP Media. Monthly magazine.
23,000 to meat, poultry, seafood industry mgmt. responsible for supply, processing, marketing.
www.provisioneronline.com
hanaceka@bnpmedia.com

Render 2820 Birch Ave Camino CA 95709 **Phn:** 530-644-8428 **Fax** 530-644-8429 Tina Caparella. Sierra Publishing. Bimonthly.
3,400 to meat by-product industry personnel interested in events and news. rendermagazine.com
editors@rendermagazine.com

Footwear--Leather Goods .24
Footwear News 750 3rd Ave Fl 10 New York NY 10017 **Phn:** 212-630-3800 **Fax** 212-630-3796 Michael Atmore. Fairchild Fashion Group. Weekly tabloid.
17,100 to men's/women's/children's footwear industry buyers, wholesalers, designers.
www.wwd.com/footwear-news/
michael_atmore@condenast.com

Leather Crafters & Saddlers Jrnl 222 Blackburn St Rhinelander WI 54501 **Phn:** 715-362-5393 **Fax** 715-362-5391 Dot Reis. Bimonthly magazine.
8,500 to leather workers interested in step-by-step instructions for boots, saddles, harnesses, leathercraft.
www.leathercraftersjournal.com journal@newnorth.net

Travel Goods Showcase 301 N Harrison St # 412 Princeton NJ 08540 **Phn:** 877-842-1938 **Fax** 877-842-1938 Michele Marini Pittenger. Travel Goods Assn. 4 issues.
8,300 to retailers, mfrs., suppliers in luggage, business/computer cases, leather accessories.
www.travel-goods.org info@travel-goods.org

Western & English Today 6688 N Central Expy Ste 650 Dallas TX 75206 **Phn:** 512-431-2013 **Fax** 214-750-4522 Susan Ebert. Bimonthly magazine.
10,000 to Western & English saddle retailers interested in products, trade shows, industry studies.
www.wetoday.com sebert@wetoday.com

American Legion Magazine PO Box 1055 Indianapolis IN 46206 **Phn:** 317-630-1298 **Fax** 317-630-1280 Jeff Stoffer. Monthly magazine.
2,400,000 to readers interested in world events, Legion news, veterans' affairs, patriotism. www.legion.org magazine@legion.org

Columbia 1 Columbus Plz New Haven CT 06510 **Phn:** 203-752-4398 **Fax** 203-752-4109 Alton Pelowski. Knights of Columbus Publications. Monthly.
1,700,000 to members of Knights of Columbus, families; others interested in Catholic content. www.kofc.org

Elks Magazine 425 W Diversey Pkwy Chicago IL 60614 **Phn:** 773-755-4740 **Fax** 773-755-4792 Cheryl Stachura. B.P.O.E. Publication. 10-issue magazine.
870,000 to members of Benevolent & Protective Order of Elks and their families. www.elks.org/elksmag/ elksmag@elks.org

Exchange Today 3050 W Central Ave Toledo OH 43606 **Phn:** 419-535-3232 **Fax** 419-535-1989 Peverley Hormann. Natl. Exchange Club. Quarterly magazine.
25,000 to members of Natl. Exchange Club interested in fundraising ideas & Club activities. www.nationalexchangeclub.org info@nationalexchangeclub.org

GFWC Clubwoman 1734 N St NW Washington DC 20036 **Phn:** 202-347-3168 **Fax** 202-835-0246 Nikki Willoughby. Gen. Fed. of Women's Clubs. Bimo. magazine.
14,400 to clubwomen concerned with education, public affairs, conservation and arts programs. www.gfwc.org gfwc@gfwc.org

Key Club Magazine 3636 Woodview Trce Indianapolis IN 46268 **Phn:** 317-875-8755 **Fax** 317-879-0204 Amberly Peterson. Key Club Intl. 4-issue magazine.
230,000 to Key Club high school service organization members interested in community projects. www.keyclub.org keyclubnews@kiwanis.org

Kiwanis Magazine 3636 Woodview Trce Indianapolis IN 46268 **Phn:** 317-875-8755 **Fax** 317-879-0204 Jack Brockley. Kiwanis Intl. Bimonthly magazine.
225,000 to members of Kiwanis Intl. interested in community matters, business issues. www.kiwanisone.org magazine@kiwanis.org

The LION 300 W 22nd St Oak Brook IL 60523 **Phn:** 630-571-5466 **Fax** 630-571-1685 Jay Copp. Intl. Assn. of Lions Clubs. 11-issue magazine.
446,600 to Lions Club members interested in Club activities and service programs. www.lionsclubs.org/EN/news-and-events/lion-magazine/index.php pr@lionsclubs.org

Moose Magazine 155 S International Dr Rm 2 Mooseheart IL 60539 **Phn:** 630-966-2229 **Fax** 630-966-2225 Kurt Wehrmeister. Loyal Order of Moose Pubs. Quarterly.
876,000 to members of Loyal Order of the Moose and Women of the Moose. www.mooseintl.org kwehrmeister@mooseintl.org (ng@@)

Optimist 4494 Lindell Blvd Saint Louis MO 63108 **Phn:** 314-371-6000 **Fax** 314-371-6006 Krista Grueninger. Optimist Intl. Quarterly magazine.
100,000 www.optimist.org communications@optimist.org

Rotarian 1560 Sherman Ave Evanston IL 60201 **Phn:** 847-866-3000 **Fax** 847-866-9732 Vince Aversano. Rotary Intl. Publications. Monthly magazine.
500,000 to members of Rotary Intl. interested in professional and personal development. www.rotary.org rotarian@rotary.org

Toastmaster PO Box 9052 Mission Viejo CA 92690 **Phn:** 949-858-8255 **Fax** 949-858-1207 Suzanne Frey. Monthly magazine.
250,000 to Toastmaster members interested in effective communication and leadership. www.toastmasters.org sfrey@toastmasters.org

Fraternal--Professional Clubs .25

VFW Magazine 406 W 34th St Kansas City MO 64111 **Phn:** 816-756-3390 **Fax** 816-968-1169 Richard Kolb. Veterans of Foreign Wars. 10-issue magazine.
1,660,000 to VFW members interested in veterans' rights, foreign affairs, military remembrance. www.vfw.org/News-and-Events/Magazine/ magazine@vfw.org

Wfm 1700 Farnam St Omaha NE 68102 **Phn:** 402-342-1890 **Fax** 402-997-7957 Billie Jo Foust. Quarterly.
485,000 to members of Woodmen of the World Life Ins Society and/or Omaha Woodmen Life Ins Society. www.woodmen.org wow@woodmen.org

Crafts--Arts--Hobbies .26

American Craft Magazine 1224 Marshall St NE Ste 200 Minneapolis MN 55413 **Phn:** 612-206-3100 Monica Moses. American Craft Cncl. Bimonthly magazine.
15,000 to readers interested in emerging artists using all kinds of materials & techniques; gallery owners; collectors. www.americancraftmag.org query@craftcouncil.org

American Woodworker 1285 Corporate Center Dr Eagan MN 55121 **Phn:** 952-948-5890 **Fax** 952-948-5895 Randy Johnson. 6-issue magazine.
222,000 to woodworking enthusiasts interested in improving skills, new tools, techniques. americanwoodworker.com aweditor@americanwoodworker.com

Antique Trader 700 E State St Iola WI 54990 **Phn:** 715-445-2214 **Fax** 715-445-4087 Eric D. Bradley. F&W Media. 26-issue magazine.
35,000 to antique collectors and dealers interested in buying, selling, trading. www.antiquetrader.com atnews@fwmedia.com

AntiqueWeek PO Box 90 Knightstown IN 46148 **Phn:** 765-345-5133 **Fax** 800-695-8153 Rachel Shallenberg. MidCountry Media. Weekly tabloid. TH:@antiqueweek
40,000 in 2 editions (eastern and central) to dealers, collectors, auction house staff. www.antiqueweek.com rshallenberg@antiqueweek.com

Bead & Button PO Box 1612 Waukesha WI 53187 **Phn:** 262-796-8776 **Fax** 262-796-1383 Ann Dee Allen. Kalmbach Publishing. Bimonthly magazine.
130,000 to crafters interested in stringing, bead weaving, wire work, bead crochet, supplies, how tos. bnb.jewelrymakingmagazines.com editor@beadandbutton.com

Bead-It Today 7 Waterloo Rd Stanhope NJ 07874 **Phn:** 973-347-6900 **Fax** 973-347-6909 Joanna Tiritilli. Bimonthly magazine. TH:@BeadItToday
100,000 to bead crafters interested in stylish, value-priced beading supplies & projects, beading basics, how tos, reader projec www.bead-it-today.com editor@bead-it-today.com

BeadStyle PO Box 1612 Waukesha WI 53187 **Phn:** 262-796-8776 **Fax** 262-796-1383 Cathy Jakicic. Kalmbach Publishing. Bimonthly magazine.
118,000 to crafters interested in how-to projects, necklaces, bracelets, earrings, other beadwork. www.beadstylemag.com editor@beadstylemag.com

Beadwork Magazine 201 E 4th St Loveland CO 80537 **Phn:** 970-669-7672 **Fax** 970-669-6117 Interweave Press. Bimonthly magazine.
118,000 to crafters interested in stringing, bead weaving, necklaces, bracelets, earrings. www.interweave.com/bead/ beadworksubmissions@interweave.com

Blade Magazine 700 E State St Iola WI 54990 **Phn:** 715-445-2214 **Fax** 715-445-4087 Joe Kertzman. F&W Media. Monthly magazine.
24,900 to knife owners, makers, collectors interested in custom, factory made, antique knives. www.blademag.com bladeeditor@fwmedia.com

Bridge Bulletin 6575 Windchase Blvd Horn Lake MS 38637 **Phn:** 662-253-3156 **Fax** 662-253-3187 Brent Manley. Amer. Contract Bridge League. Monthly magazine.
150,000 to contract bridge enthusiasts interested in news, features, championship schedules. www.acbl.org editor@acbl.org

CardMaker 396 E Parr Rd Berne IN 46711 **Phn:** 260-589-4000 **Fax** 260-589-8093 Tanya Fox. DRG. 6-issue magazine.
80,000 to card making enthusiasts interested in improving skills, new tools, techniques. www.cardmakermagazine.com editor@cardmakermagazine.com

Chess Life PO Box 3967 Crossville TN 38557 **Phn:** 931-787-1234 **Fax** 931-787-1200 Daniel Lucas. US Chess Fed. Mo. magazine.
250,200 covers chess news of national, international significance, analysis, instruction. www.uschess.org dlucas@uschess.org

Classic Toy Trains PO Box 1612 Waukesha WI 53187 **Phn:** 262-796-8776 **Fax** 262-796-1142 Carl Swanson. Kalmbach Publishing. 9-issue magazine.
51,100 to Lionel, MTH, American Flyer, K-Line, Marx and other toy train enthusiasts. trc.trains.com/ctt/ contacteditor@classictoytrains.com

Cloth Paper Scissors 201 E 4th St Loveland CO 80537 **Phn:** 970-669-7672 **Fax** 970-669-6117 Jenn Mason. Interweave Press. Bimonthly magazine.
9,000 to crafters of all levels interested in all types of fiber arts and collage work. www.clothpaperscissors.com

Crafts 'N Things PO Box 1009 Oak Park IL 60304 **Phn:** 937-498-2111 Anne Niemiec. Amos Press. 7-issue magazine.
72,000 covers sewing, beading, embroidery, paper crafts, quilting, decoupage, calligraphy, macrame. www.craftsnthings.com aniemiec@amoscraft.com

Crafts Report PO Box 5000 Iola WI 54945 **Phn:** 715-445-5000 **Fax** 715-445-4053 Dennis Piotrowski. Jones Publishing. Monthly magazine.
25,000 to professional craftspeople & crafts retailers interested in industry news, business how tos, shows. www.craftsreport.com dennisp@jonespublishing.com

Create & Decorate 7 Waterloo Rd Stanhope NJ 07874 **Phn:** 973-347-6900 **Fax** 973-347-6909 Beverly Hotz. All Amer. Crafts. 7-issue magazine.
149,000 to readers interested in designs for needlework, cross stitch, quilting, crochet. www.createanddecorate.com editors@createanddecorate.com

Creating Keepsakes 14850 Pony Express Rd Bluffdale UT 84065 **Phn:** 801-816-8300 **Fax** 801-816-8301 Jennafer Martin. Creative Crafts Group. Bimonthly magazine.
186,000 to scrapbook enthusiasts interested in projects, techniques, products, shows. www.creatingkeepsakes.com editorial@creatingkeepsakes.com

Creative Knitting 306 E Parr Rd Berne IN 46711 **Phn:** 260-589-4000 **Fax** 260-589-8093 Kara Gott Warner. DRG. Bimonthly magazine.
100,000 to knitters of afghans, sweaters, baby gifts, holiday home accents; how-to articles. www.creativeknittingmagazine.com editor@creativeknittingmagazine.com

Crochet World 306 E Parr Rd Berne IN 46711 **Phn:** 260-589-4000 **Fax** 260-589-8093 Carol Alexander. DRG. Bimonthly magazine.
125,000 to readers interested in crocheting toys, blankets, clothing, home needs. www.crochet-world.com editor@crochet-world.com

Crochet! 306 E Parr Rd Berne IN 46711 **Phn:** 260-589-4000 **Fax** 260-589-8093 Carol Alexander. DRG. Bimonthly magazine.
70,000 official magazine of the Crochet Guild of America, covers all aspects of crochet. crochetmagazine.com editor@crochetmagazine.com

Decor 1801 Park 270 Dr Ste 550 Saint Louis MO 63146 **Phn:** 314-824-5500 **Fax** 314-824-5640 Kristin Stefek Brashares. Summit Prof. Networks. Monthly magazine. **24,000** to frame shop, art gallery personnel interested in framing, display how-to's, merchandise. decormagazine.com kstefek@gmail.com

Doll Reader 85 Quincy Ave Ste 2 Quincy MA 02169 **Phn:** 800-437-5828 **Fax** 617-536-0102 Kathryn Peck. Madavor Media. 9-issue magazine. **35,800** to adult doll collectors; doll makers, artists, manufacturers, costumers. www.dollreader.com kpeck@madavor.com

Dollhouse Miniatures 68132 250th Ave Kasson MN 55944 **Phn:** 507-634-3143 **Fax** 507-634-7691 Kelly Rud. Bimonthly magazine. **18,700** to collectors and crafters of scale miniatures, dollhouses, shadow boxes. www.dhminiatures.com usoffice@ashdown.co.uk

Dolls PO Box 5000 Iola WI 54945 **Phn:** 715-445-5000 **Fax** 715-445-4053 Carie Ferg. Jones Publishing. 10-issue magazine. **16,500** to collectors of antique & contemporary dolls interested in shows, sales, restoration. www.dollsmagazine.com editor@dollsmagazine.com

Family Tree Magazine 10151 Carver Rd Blue Ash OH 45242 **Phn:** 513-531-2690 **Fax** 513-891-7153 Allison Dolan. F&W Media. Bimonthly magazine. **70,000** to family history enthusiasts interested in genealogy, family reunions, memoirs, preservation. www.familytreemagazine.com ftmedit@fwmedia.com

Farm Collector 1503 SW 42nd St Topeka KS 66609 **Phn:** 785-274-4300 **Fax** 785-274-4305 Leslie McManus. Ogden Publications. Bimo. **45,000** focuses on antique tractors, gas engines, windmills, hog oilers, implements, tools. www.farmcollector.com editor@farmcollector.com

Fine Woodworking 63 S Main St Newtown CT 06470 **Phn:** 203-426-8171 **Fax** 203-270-6753 Asa Christiana. Taunton Press. 7-issue magazine. **227,000** to beginner and expert woodworkers interested in projects, techniques, tools. www.finewoodworking.com fw@taunton.com

Finescale Modeler PO Box 1612 Waukesha WI 53187 **Phn:** 262-796-8776 **Fax** 262-796-1383 Matthew Usher. Kalmbach Publishing. 10-issue magazine. **52,700** to hobbyists interested in crafting authentic airplane, car, ship models. www.finescale.com editor@finescale.com

Fly RC 650 Danbury Rd Ridgefield CT 06877 **Phn:** 203-431-7787 **Fax** 203-438-0720 Thayer Syme. Monthly magazine. **390,000** for the RC airplane enthusiast, covers the latest RC products and techniques. flyrc.com editors@flyrc.com

Flying Models PO Box 700 Newton NJ 07860 **Phn:** 973-383-3355 **Fax** 973-383-4064 Frank Fanelli. Carstens Publications. Monthly magazine. **24,500** to radio controlled & free flight airplane enthusiasts interested in products, how to's. www.flying-models.com frankf@flying-models.com

Games World of Puzzles 6198 Butler Pike Ste 200 Blue Bell PA 19422 **Phn:** 215-643-6385 **Fax** 215-628-3571 R. Wayne Schmittberger. Bimonthly magazine. **82,000** to readers interested in puzzles, games and brainteasers of all kinds. www.kappapublishing.com games@kappapublishing.com

Gas Engine 1503 SW 42nd St Topeka KS 66609 **Phn:** 785-274-4300 **Fax** 785-274-4305 Richard Backus. Ogden Publications. **21,000** to collectors of antique gas engies, tractor equipment interested in restoration. gasengine.farmcollector.com rbackus@ogdenpubs.com

Gifts & Decorative Accessories 1271 Ave of the Americas Fl 17 New York NY 10020 **Phn:** 917-934-2800 Caroline Kennedy. Progressive Business Media. 10-issue magazine. **TH:**@GiftsandDecMag **27,000** to owners, mgrs., buyers at gift, china, glass, accessory, candle, collectible retail stores. www.giftsanddec.com ckennedy@giftsanddec.com

Giftware News 233 N Michigan Ave Ste 1780 Chicago IL 60601 **Phn:** 312-849-2220 **Fax** 312-849-2174 D. F. von Rabenau. Talcott Communications. Monthly tabloid. **24,300** to owners, mgrs., buyers at gift, stationery, party & paper good retail stores. www.giftwarenews.com dvon@talcott.com

Hobby Farms PO Box 12106 Lexington KY 40580 **Phn:** 949-855-8822 **Fax** 859-252-7480 Stephanie Staton. I-5 Publ. LLC. Bimonthly magazine. **TH:**@HobbyFarmsMag **144,000** to small, part-time farmers looking to profit from farming, finance off-farm lifestyle. www.hobbyfarms.com sstaton@i5publishing.com

Hobby Merchandiser 207 Commercial Ct Morganville NJ 07751 **Phn:** 732-536-5160 **Fax** 732-536-5761 Dennnis McFarlane. Monthly magazine. **5,700** to model hobby industry personnel interested in products, profiles, reviews, merchandising. www.hobbymerchandiser.com hobbymerch@aol.com

Home Shop Machinist PO Box 629 Traverse City MI 49685 **Phn:** 231-946-3712 **Fax** 231-946-6180 George Bullis. Village Press, Inc. Bimonthly. **30,500** to metalwork professionals and hobbyists interested in projects, tools, techniques. www.homeshopmachinist.net gbulliss@villagepress.com

Jewelry Artist 300 Chesterfield Pkwy # 100 Malvern PA 19355 **Phn:** 610-232-5700 **Fax** 610-232-5756 Merle White. Interweave Press. Monthly magazine. **53,600** to gemstone, bead, jewelry collectors and artists interested in shows and projects. www.jewelryartistmagazine.com ljeditorial@interweave.com

Just CrossStitch 1900 International Park Dr Ste 50 Birmingham AL 35243 **Phn:** 205-995-8860 **Fax** 205-991-0071 Lorna Reeves. Hoffman Media. Bimonthly magazine. **50,000** to cross-stitchers of all skill levels interested in new designs, samplers, hangings, wearables. www.just-crossstitch.com cschmitz@hoffmanmedia.com

Knit 'N Style 7 Waterloo Rd Stanhope NJ 07874 **Phn:** 973-347-6900 **Fax** 973-347-6909 Penelope Taylor. All Amer. Crafts. Bimonthly. **58,400** to fashion-conscious knitters interested in creating clothing, home decor, gift items. www.knitnstyle.com editors@knitnstyle.com

Linn's Stamp News PO Box 29 Sidney OH 45365 **Phn:** 937-498-0801 **Fax** 888-304-8388 Michael Baadke. Amos Press. Weekly tabloid. **38,800** to stamp collectors interested in clubs, exhibitions, buy/sell/trade ads. www.linns.com mbaadke@amospress.com

Live Steam & Outdoor Railroading PO Box 1810 Traverse City MI 49685 **Phn:** 231-946-3712 **Fax** 231-946-9588 Clover McKinley. Village Press, Inc. Bimo. mag. **9,700** to locomotive, steam engine enthusiasts interested in locomotive clubs and projects. www.livesteam.net cmckinley@villagepress.com

Machinist's Workshop PO Box 629 Traverse City MI 49685 **Phn:** 231-946-3712 **Fax** 231-946-6180 Daron Klooster. Village Press, Inc. 6-issue magazine. **29,500** to metalwork hobbyists interested in projects, tools, techniques, improving skills. www.homeshopmachinist.net daronklooster@villagepress.com

Miniature Collector 2145 W Sherman Blvd Norton Shores MI 49441 **Phn:** 231-755-2200 **Fax** 231-755-1003 Barbara Aardema. Monthly magazine. **22,300** to serious collectors of miniatures; crafters and artists of scale miniatures. www.scottpublications.com/mcmag/ baardema@scottpublications.com

Model Airplane News 88 Danbury Rd Wilton CT 06897 **Phn:** 203-431-9000 **Fax** 203-761-8744 Debra Cleghorn. Air Age Media. Monthly magazine. **63,300** to airplane model enthusiasts interested in building & flying techniques, plans, products. www.modelairplanenews.com man@airage.com

Model Cars 2403 Champa St Denver CO 80205 **Phn:** 303-296-1600 **Fax** 303-295-2159 Gregg Hutchings. Golden Bell Press. 9-issue magazine. **7,700** to model car collectors & builders interested in how-to's, contests, model car events. www.modelcarsmag.com modelcarsmag@yahoo.com

Model Railroader PO Box 1612 Waukesha WI 53187 **Phn:** 262-796-8776 **Fax** 262-796-1142 Neil Besougloff. Kalmbach Publishing. Monthly magazine. **147,000** to model railroad builders interested in how-tos and projects for all gauges and scales. trc.trains.com/mrr/ mrmag@mrmag.com

Model Retailer PO Box 1612 Waukesha WI 53187 **Phn:** 262-796-8776 **Fax** 262-796-1142 Hal Miller. Kalmbach Publishing. Monthly. **4,200** to model and hobby retailers and suppliers interested in tradeshows and trends. www.modelretailer.com hmiller@modelretailer.com

Needlework Retailer PO Box 2438 Ames IA 50010 **Phn:** 515-232-6507 **Fax** 515-232-0789 Megan Chriswisser. Bimonthly magazine. **9,000** to needlecraft retailers interested in new products, in-store workshops, mgmt. issues. www.needleworkretailer.com info@yarntree.com

O Gauge Railroading 33 Sheridan Rd Poland OH 44514 **Phn:** 330-757-3020 **Fax** 330-757-3771 Allan Miller. 7-issue magazine. **35,000** to O gauge hobbyists interested in how-tos, repair, new products. www.ogaugerr.com editor@ogaugerr.com

PaintWorks 7 Waterloo Rd Stanhope NJ 07874 **Phn:** 973-347-6900 **Fax** 973-347-6909 Linda Heller. All Amer. Crafts. 9-issue magazine. **97,000** to decorative painters of all skill levels interested in patterns, techniques, trends. www.paintworksmag.com editors@paintworksmag.com

Paper Crafts Magazine 14850 Pony Express Rd Bluffdale UT 84065 **Phn:** 801-816-8300 **Fax** 801-816-8301 Jennifer Schaerer. Creative Crafts Group. Online only. **TH:**@PaperCraftsMag to crafters interested in cardmaking, rubber stampging, frames, book covers, invitations. www.papercraftsmag.com editor@papercraftsmag.com

Paper Creations 7 Waterloo Rd Stanhope NJ 07874 **Phn:** 973-347-6900 **Fax** 973-347-6090 Jane Guthrie. All Amer. Crafts. Quarterly magazine. **194,500** to beginning & advanced paper crafters interested in cards, stationery, decorations, gift boxes. www.papercreationsmag.com editors@scrapbookingandbeyondmag.com

PieceWork 201 E 4th St Loveland CO 80537 **Phn:** 970-669-7672 **Fax** 970-669-6117 Jeane Hutchins. Interweave Press. Bimonthly magazine. **17,000** to readers interested in historic & ethnic fabric handwork of many types; projects and instructions. www.interweave.com/needle/ piecework@interweave.com

Popular Woodworking 10151 Carver Rd Blue Ash OH 45242 **Phn:** 513-531-2690 **Fax** 513-891-7196 Robert Lang. F&W Media. 7-issue magazine. **200,000** to hobbyist and pro woodworkers interested in tools, techniques, projects. www.popularwoodworking.com robert.lang@fwpubs.com

Quilt Magazine 46 Rock Creek Rd Cumberland VA 23040 **Phn:** 212-807-7100 **Fax** 212-463-9958 Deborah Hearn. Harris Publications. Bi-mo.
119,000 to quilters interested in traditional quilts, quilting personalities and activities. www.quiltmag.com quiltmag@epix.net

Quilter's World 306 E Parr Rd Berne IN 46711 **Phn:** 260-589-4000 **Fax** 260-589-8093 Carolyn Vagts. DRG. Bimonthly.
125,000 to quilters interested in patterns, shows and events, quilter profiles and stories. www.quiltersworld.com carolyn_vagts@annies-publishing.com

Radio Control Car Action 88 Danbury Rd Wilton CT 06897 **Phn:** 203-431-9000 **Fax** 203-761-8744 John Howell. Air Age Media. Monthly magazine.
81,700 to radio control car enthusiasts interested building & modifying RC cars, events, products. www.rccaraction.com rcca@airage.com

Railroad Model Craftsman PO Box 700 Newton NJ 07860 **Phn:** 973-383-3355 **Fax** 973-383-4064 William Schaumburg. Carstens Publishing. Monthly magazine.
62,400 to model railroad enthusiasts interested in product reviews, modeling techniques. www.rrmodelcraftsman.com bills@rrmodelcraftsman.com

RC Car 25233 Anza Dr Valencia CA 91355 **Phn:** 661-295-1910 **Fax** 661-295-1278 Stephen Bess. Hi-Torque Publications. Monthly magazine.
600,000 to remote control car enthusiasts interested in gear, new models, contests, photos. hi-torque.com

RC Driver 650 Danbury Rd Ridgefield CT 06877 **Phn:** 203-431-7787 **Fax** 203-438-0720 David Baker. Maplegate Media. Monthly magazine.
600,000 to remote control car, truck and racecar enthusiasts interested in races, celebrity rc owners, projects. find.rcdriver.com editorsinbox@rcdriver.com

Rock & Gem 3585 Maple St Ste 232 Ventura CA 93003 **Phn:** 805-644-3824 **Fax** 805-644-3875 Bob Jones. JMiller Media. Monthly.
33,600 information, entertainment for lapidary, mineral hobbyists, rockhounds, diehard diggers. www.rockngem.com editor@rockngem.com

Scale Auto PO Box 1612 Waukesha WI 53187 **Phn:** 262-796-8776 **Fax** 262-796-1383 Jim Haught. Kalmbach Publishing. Bimonthly magazine.
23,600 to scale auto builders and collectors interested in new products. www.scaleautomag.com editor@scaleautomag.com

Scrap & Stamp Arts 2145 W Sherman Blvd Norton Shores MI 49441 **Phn:** 231-755-2200 **Fax** 231-755-1003 Kelly Herrold. Scott Publications. 8-issue magazine.
60,000 to scrapbooking & rubber stamp crafters interested in step-by-step projects, new products, craft shows. www.scottpublications.com/ssa kherrold@scottpublications.com

Sew Beautiful 149 Old Big Cove Rd Brownsboro AL 35741 **Phn:** 256-261-2532 **Fax** 256-534-5486 Kathy Barnard. Bimonthly magazine.
65,000 to sewing and embroidery enthusiasts interested in how-to features, patterns. www.sewbeautifulmag.com editorial@sewbeautifulmag.com

Sew News 741 Corporate Cir Ste A Golden CO 80401 **Phn:** 303-215-5600 **Fax** 303-215-5601 Ellen March. Creative Crafts Group. Bimonthly magazine.
150,000 to home sewers interested in techniques, crafts, home decorating, fabric reviews. www.sewnews.com emarch@creativecraftsgroup.com

Sky & Telescope 90 Sherman St Cambridge MA 02140 **Phn:** 617-864-7360 **Fax** 617-864-6117 Robert Naeye. Sky Publishing. Monthly magazine.
90,100 to astronomy enthusiasts interested in space science, observing tips, sky maps. www.skyandtelescope.com editors@skyandtelescope.com

Crafts--Arts--Hobbies .26

Souvenirs, Gifts & Novelties 10 E Athens Ave Ste 208 Ardmore PA 19003 **Phn:** 610-645-6940 **Fax** 610-645-6943 S.C. Borowsky. 8-issue magazine.
43,100 to gift and souvenir buyers who buy for resorts, theme parks, museums, attractions. www.sgnmag.com editorsgnmag@kanec.com

Step by Step Wire Jewelry 300 Chesterfield Pkwy # 100 Malvern PA 19355 **Phn:** 610-232-5700 **Fax** 610-232-5756 Denise Peck. Interweave Press. Bimo. magazine.
31,600 illustrated bead, gem, pearl projects, for wire jewelry makers of all levels. www.stepbystepwire.com/wire/ dpeck@interweave.com

Teddy Bear & Friends PO Box 5000 Iola WI 54945 **Phn:** 715-445-5000 **Fax** 715-445-4053 Joyce Greenholdt. Jones Publ. 6-issue magazine.
20,600 to teddy bear collectors, experts, artists, manufacturers, retailers. www.teddybearandfriends.com editor@teddybearandfriends.com

Threads 63 S Main St Newtown CT 06470 **Phn:** 203-426-8171 **Fax** 203-426-3434 Deana Tierney. Taunton Press. Bimonthly magazine.
124,700 to readers interested in techniques, materials, designs for garment sewing, embroidery. www.threadsmagazine.com th@taunton.com

Toy Book 307 7th Ave # 1601 New York NY 10001 **Phn:** 212-575-4510 **Fax** 212-575-4521 Jackie Breyer. Monthly tabloid.
19,000 to toy manufacturers worldwide interested in products, marketing and promotions. www.toybook.com jbreyer@adventurepub.com

Toy Farmer 7496 106th Ave SE LaMoure ND 58458 **Phn:** 701-883-5206 **Fax** 701-883-5209 Catherine Scheibe. Monthly.
25,000 to farm toy collectors interested in restoration, shows, buy/sell/trade ads. www.toyfarmer.com info@toyfarmer.com

Toy Trucker & Contractor 7496 106th Ave SE LaMoure ND 58458 **Phn:** 701-883-5206 **Fax** 701-883-5209 Catherine Scheibe. Monthly.
9,500 to collectors of toy trucks, other toy heavy vehicles interested in Tonka topics, shows. www.toytrucker.com info@toyfarmer.com

Treasures 300 Walnut St Ste 6 Des Moines IA 50309 **Phn:** 877-899-9977 **Fax** 319-824-3414 Pioneer Comms. Bimonthly magazine.
7,000 to collectors of antiques, country collectibles interested in prices, shows, flea markets. treasuresmagazine.com mcampbell@pioneermagazines.com

Tropical Fish Hobbyist 1 TFH Plz Neptune City NJ 07753 **Phn:** 732-988-8400 **Fax** 732-988-9635 Albert Connelly. TFH Publications. Mo. mag.
21,800 to readers who maintain tropical fish for pleasure or educational purposes. www.tfhmagazine.com associateeditor@tfh.com

Tuff Stuff 700 E State St Iola WI 54990 **Phn:** 715-445-2214 **Fax** 715-445-4087 Scott Fragale. F&W Media. Monthly magazine.
45,600 to collectors of sports trading cards and other sports collectibles. www.tuffstuff.com

Urban Farm 3 Burroughs Irvine CA 92618 **Phn:** 888-245-3699 **Fax** 859-260-1154 I-5 Publishing. Bimonthly.
122,000 guide to homegrown food, greater self sustainability in urban, limited space settings. www.urbanfarmonline.com uf@bowtieinc.com

Whispering Wind PO Box 1390 Folsom LA 70437 **Phn:** 985-796-5433 **Fax** 985-796-9236 Jack Heriard. Written Heritage. Bimonthly.
23,000 to readers interested in the Amer. Indian past and present way of life, material culture, crafts. www.whisperingwind.com info@whisperingwind.com

Wood (Better Homes/Gardens) 1716 Locust St # LS221 Des Moines IA 50309 **Phn:** 515-284-3502 **Fax** 515-284-2115 Bill Krier. Meredith Corp. 7-issue magazine.
500,000 to woodworkers of all skill levels interested in projects and tools.tools. www.woodmagazine.com woodmail@woodmagazine.com

Woodworker's Journal 4365 Willow Dr Medina MN 55340 **Phn:** 763-478-8201 **Fax** 763-478-8396 Rob Johnstone. Rockler Press. Bimonthly magazine.
218,000 to woodworking hobbyists, professionals seeking new techniques, project ideas. www.woodworkersjournal.com editor@woodworkersjournal.com

Arts .26a

American Fine Art Magazine 7530 E Main St Ste 105 Scottsdale AZ 85251 **Phn:** 480-425-0806 **Fax** 480-425-0724 Joshua Rose. Bimonthly magazine.
50,000 to gallery owners, art collectors, readers interested in events, auctions, exhibitions of Amer. fine art. www.americanfineartmagazine.com editor@americanfineartmagazine.com

Art & Antiques 447 W 24th St New York NY 10011 **Phn:** 910-679-4402 **Fax** 919-869-1864 John Dorfman 10-issue magazine.
30,000 to collectors, galleries, designers interested in painting, sculpture, silver, furniture. www.artandantiquesmag.com johnd@artandantiquesmag.com

Art & Auction 601 W 26th St Rm 410 New York NY 10001 **Phn:** 212-447-9555 **Fax** 212-627-4148 Sarah Hanson. Louise Blouin Media. 11-issue magazine. TH:@artinfodotcom
20,000 to intl. fine arts collectors, dealers, gallery owners, auction houses. www.artinfo.com shanson@artinfo.com

Art In America 575 Broadway Fl 5 New York NY 10012 **Phn:** 212-941-2800 **Fax** 212-941-2819 Lindsay Pollock. Brant Publications. Monthly magazine.
100,000 to painters, sculptors, photographers, curators interested in news and exhibitions. www.artinamericamagazine.com lpollock@brantpub.com

Artforum Intl. 350 7th Ave Fl 19 New York NY 10001 **Phn:** 212-475-4000 **Fax** 212-529-1257 Michelle Kuo. 10-issue magazine.
31,200 to artists, curators, collectors, dealers interested in international contemporary art. www.artforum.com editorial@artforum.com

The Artist's Magazine 10151 Carver Rd Ste 200 Blue Ash OH 45242 **Phn:** 513-531-2690 **Fax** 513-891-7153 Maureen Bloomfield. F&W Media. 10-issue magazine.
167,400 to serious amateur artists interested in tools, materials, techniques, exhibitions. www.artistsnetwork.com/the-artists-magazine tamedit@fwmedia.com

Artnews 48 W 38th St Fl 9 New York NY 10018 **Phn:** 212-398-1690 **Fax** 212-768-4002 Robin Cembalest. 11-issue magazine.
70,100 to artists, collectors, others interested in intl. art world, exhibitions, books, profiles. www.artnews.com editorial@artnews.com

Juxtapoz 1303 Underwood Ave San Francisco CA 94124 **Phn:** 415-822-3083 **Fax** 415-822-8359 Evan Pricco. High Speed Productions. 8-issues.
78,400 covers a new and influential movement in the art world, underground artists. www.juxtapoz.com evan@juxtapoz.com

Modern Painters 601 W 26th St Rm 410 New York NY 10001 **Phn:** 212-447-9555 **Fax** 212-447-5221 Louise Blouin Media. 10 issues.
38,400 covering contemporary visual arts, architecture, and aesthetics, not written by art critics. www.artinfo.com modernpaintersmag@artinfo.com

Pastel Journal 10151 Carver Rd Ste 200 Blue Ash OH 45242 **Phn:** 513-531-2690 **Fax** 513-891-7153 Anne Hevener FW Media. Bimonthly magazine.
28,400 to artists who work in pastels, pro and amateur, offering inspiration and instruction.
www.artistsnetwork.com/PastelJournal
pjedit@fwmedia.com

Picture Framing Magazine 207 Commercial Ct Morganville NJ 07751 **Phn:** 732-536-5160 **Fax** 732-536-5761 Patrick Sarver. Hobby Publications. Monthly.
23,100 to retailers, galleries, manufacturers and suppliers of frames and related supplies.
www.pictureframingmagazine.com
psarver@hobbypub.com

Professional Artist 1500 Park Center Dr Orlando FL 32835 **Phn:** 407-563-7000 **Fax** 407-563-7099 Kim Hall. 10-issue magazine.
17,000 to business-oriented artists interested in income and exhibition opportunities.
www.professionalartistmag.com
khall@professionalartistmag.com

Sculpture Magazine 1633 Connecticut Ave NW Ste 400 Washington DC 20009 **Phn:** 202-234-0555 **Fax** 202-234-2663 Glenn Harper. Monthly magazine.
15,000 to international general readership interested in contemporary 3-dimensional art. www.sculpture.org
gharper@sculpture.org

Southwest Art 1301 Spruce St Boulder CO 80302 **Phn:** 303-442-0427 **Fax** 303-449-0279 Kristin Hoerth. F&W Media. Monthly magazine.
54,000 to general public & art collectors interested in western & southwestern art trends.
www.southwestart.com kristin.hoerth@fwmedia.com

Surface 140 W 26th St Street Level West New York NY 10001 **Phn:** 212-229-1500 Dan Rubenstein. Sandow Media. Bimonthly magazine. TH:@SurfaceMag
130,000 to designers & artists interested in current visual arts trends & influence on fashion, architecture, products. www.surfacemag.com
editorial@surfacemag.com

Watercolor Artist 10151 Carver Rd Ste 200 Blue Ash OH 45242 **Phn:** 513-531-2690 **Fax** 513-891-7153 Kelly Kane. F&W Media. Bimonthly magazine.
52,000 to all levels of watercolorists interested in tools, materials, techniques and instruction.
www.artistsnetwork.com/watercolorartist/
wcamag@fwmedia.com

Coins .26b
Bank Note Reporter 700 E State St Iola WI 54990 **Phn:** 715-445-2214 **Fax** 715-445-4087 Robert Van Ryzin. F&W Media. Monthly magazine.
8,500 to paper money collectors interested in trends and buy/sell/trade marketplace. numismaster.com
robert.vanryzin@fwmedia.com

Coin Prices 700 E State St Iola WI 54990 **Phn:** 715-445-2214 **Fax** 715-445-4087 Robert Van Ryzin. F&W Media. Bimonthly.
51,000 to collectors interested in collection basics, coin grading, current retail values of coins.
numismaster.com coinprices@krause.com

Coin World PO Box 926 Sidney OH 45365 **Phn:** 937-498-0800 **Fax** 937-498-0812 Beth Deisher. Amos Press. Weekly magazine.
73,900 to beginning, intermediate, advanced coin collectors interested in basics, prices, shows.
www.coinworld.com bdeisher@coinworld.com

Coinage PO Box 6925 Ventura CA 93006 **Phn:** 805-644-3824 **Fax** 805-644-3875 Marcy Gibbel. Miller Magazines. Monthly magazine.
70,000 to serious & hobby collectors interested in history, collector profiles, investing, auctions.
coinagemag.com mgibbel@jmillermedia.com

Coins 700 E State St Iola WI 54990 **Phn:** 715-445-2214 **Fax** 715-445-4087 Robert Van Ryzin. F&W Media. Monthly magazine.
51,000 to coin hobbyists interested in collection cataloging, grading, storage, display.
numismaster.com coins@krause.com

Arts .26a
Numismatic News 700 E State St Iola WI 54990 **Phn:** 715-445-2214 **Fax** 715-445-4087 David Harper. F&W Media. Weekly magazine.
33,000 to collectors, investors who buy/sell US coins/bills interested in Mint reports, market info.
www.numismaticnews.net david.harper@fwmedia.com

Numismatist 818 N Cascade Ave Colorado Springs CO 80903 **Phn:** 719-632-2646 **Fax** 719-634-4085 Barbara Gregory. Amer. Numismatic Assn. Monthly.
33,000 to Assn. members, others interested in coins and bills, medal education, Assn. events.
www.money.org/publicationsdept.html
gregory@money.org

Grocery--Supermarkets .27
Convenience Store Decisions 1991 Crocker Rd Ste 200 Westlake OH 44145 **Phn:** 440-250-1583 **Fax** 215-245-4060 John Lofstock. Harbor Comms. Monthly magazine.
41,400 to convenience store decisionmakers responsible for foodservice, security, technology.
www.csdecisions.com jlofstock@csdecisions.com

Convenience Store News 111 Town Square Pl Ste 400 Jersey City NJ 07310 **Phn:** 201-855-7606 **Fax** 646-654-7676 Don Longo. Stagnito Media. 15-issue tabloid.
70,600 to buying & admn. execs. responsible for all aspects of convenience store operations.
www.csnews.com dlongo@csnews.com

CSP 1100 Jorie Blvd Ste 260 Oak Brook IL 60523 **Phn:** 630-574-5201 **Fax** 630-574-5175 Mitch Morrison. 15-issue magazine.
46,200 to C-store & retail petroleum mgmt. interested in conferences, retail case studies, products.
www.cspnet.com mmorrison@cspnet.com

DDBC News PO Box 4533 Huntington Beach CA 92605 **Phn:** 714-375-3900 **Fax** 714-375-3906 Dave Daniel. Deli Council of S. California. 10 issues.
5,000 to S. Calif. deli, dairy, bakery retailers interested in products, personnel, Council events.
www.ddbcsocal.org dave.pacrim@verizon.net

Food Industry News 1440 Renaissance Dr Ste 210 Park Ridge IL 60068 **Phn:** 847-699-3300 **Fax** 847-699-3307 Terry Minnich. Monthly.
24,000 to Chicago area food industry personnel interested in suppliers, trends, news.
www.foodindustrynews.com
terry@foodindustrynews.com

Frozen & Refrigerated Buyer 272 Elm St Norwich VT 05055 **Phn:** 603-252-0507 Warren Thayer. 11-issue magazine.
11,000 to retail grocery frozen & dairy buyers, merchandisers interested in newproducts, strategies, consumer behavior. www.frbuyer.com
warren@frbuyer.com

Gourmet News 1877 N Kolb Rd Tucson AZ 85715 **Phn:** 520-721-1300 **Fax** 520-521-6300 Rocelle Aragon. Oser Comms. Monthly tabloid.
25,100 to gourmet food and cookware industry retailers, distributors, importers.
www.gourmetnews.com rocelle_a@oser.com

Griffin Report PO Box 2826 Duxbury MA 02331 **Phn:** 781-829-4700 **Fax** 781-829-0134 Michael Berger. Griffin Publishing. Monthly tabloid.
30,000 to eastern U.S. food mfrs., distributors, retailers, interested in market & product studies, news, events.
www.griffinpublishing.net
mberger@griffinpublishing.net

Grocery Headquarters 333 7th Ave Rm 1100 New York NY 10001 **Phn:** 212-979-4800 **Fax** 646-674-0102 Seth Mendelson. McFadden Publ. Monthly magazine.
40,000 to supermarket, convenience store, warehouse club, drug chain, other headquarters execs.
www.groceryheadquarters.com
smendelson@groceryheadquarters.com

IGA Grocergram 8745 W Higgins Rd Chicago IL 60631 **Phn:** 773-772-5724 Ashley Page. Quarterly magazine.
11,000 to members of Ind. Grocers' Alliance concerned with all aspects of retail grocery mgmt.
www.iga.com apage@igainc.com

Nutrition Industry Executive 431 Cranbury Rd Ste C E Brunswick NJ 08816 **Phn:** 732-432-9600 **Fax** 732-432-9288 Kate Quackenbush. 18-issue magazine.
14,000 covers news, packaging, legalities, product development for dietary supplement industry.
www.niemagazine.com kateq@vitaminretailer.com

Private Label Buyer 155 N Pfingsten Rd Ste 205 Deerfield IL 60015 **Phn:** 847-405-4000 **Fax** 847-405-4100 Chris Freeman. BNP Media. Monthly.
27,000 to retail executives responsible for marketing private label products. www.privatelabelbuyer.com
freemanc@bnpmedia.com

Private Label Store Brands 570 Lake Cook Rd, Suite 310 Deerfield IL 60015 **Phn:** 224-632-8200 **Fax** 224-632-8266 Randy Hofbauer. Stagnito Media. Monthly magazine.
52,600 to supermarket, drug, warehouse club buyers of generic & private label products. plstorebrands.com
rhofbauer@stagnitomedia.com

Produce News 800 Kinderkamack Rd Ste 100 Oradell NJ 07649 **Phn:** 201-986-7990 **Fax** 201-986-7996 John Groh. Weekly newspaper.
13,100 to fresh produce buyers at retail food chains, wholesale and foodservice operations.
www.theproducenews.com
newsdesk@theproducenews.com

Produce Retailer 10901 W 84th Ter Ste 200 Lenexa KS 66214 **Phn:** 913-438-8700 **Fax** 913-438-0691 Pamela Riemenschneider. Vance Publishing. Monthly.
11,900 to produce retail mgmt. responsible for product selection, marketing, industry news.
www.produceretailer.com
pamelar@produceretailer.com

Progressive Grocer 570 Lake Cook Rd, Suite 310 Deerfield IL 60015 **Phn:** 224-632-8200 **Fax** 224-632-8266 James Dudlicek. Stagnito Media. 10-issue magazine.
35,300 to retail grocery mgmt. concerned with industry news, store design & technology, rsch.
www.progressivegrocer.com
jdudlicek@stagnitomedia.com

Shelby Report 517 Green St NW Gainesville GA 30501 **Phn:** 770-534-8380 **Fax** 678-343-2197 Lorrie Griffith. Monthly tabloid.
15,100 in 6 rgnl. editions to food store owners/operators, brokers, foodservice execs., food assns. & co-ops. www.shelbypublishing.com
editor@shelbypublishing.com

Supermarket News 249 W 17th St Frnt 1 New York NY 10011 **Phn:** 212-204-4342 **Fax** 913-514-9136 David Orgel. Penton Media. Weekly tabloid.
20,000 to supermarket industry decisionmakers overseeing all areas of supermarket operations.
supermarketnews.com david.orgel@penton.com

Vitamin Retailer 431 Cranbury Rd Ste C E Brunswick NJ 08816 **Phn:** 732-432-9600 **Fax** 732-432-9288 Kate Quackenbush. 12-issue magazine.
15,500 to organic, earth-friendly product retailers interested in new products, retailing workshops.
www.vitaminretailer.com kateq@vitaminretailer.com

Fire Control & Police .28a
American COP Magazine 12345 World Trade Dr San Diego CA 92128 **Phn:** 858-605-0244 **Fax** 858-605-0247 Suzi Hintingdon. Publishers Development Corp. Monthly.
50,000 to police officers of all ranks interested in training, equipment, procedures, technology.
www.americancopmagazine.com
editor@americancopmagazine.com

American Police Beat 43 Thorndike St Ste 2 Cambridge MA 02141 **Phn:** 617-491-8878 **Fax** 617-354-6515 Sarah Vallee. Monthly tabloid.
52,300 to police officers of all ranks interested in legislative and social issues, opinion forums.
www.apbweb.com cynthia@apbweb.com

California Fire Service 2701 K St Ste 201 Sacramento CA 95816 **Phn:** 916-410-1394 **Fax** 916-446-9889 Gary Giacomo. 6-issue magazine.
27,500 to CA firefighters concerned with firefighting trends, news, pending legislation. www.csfa.net ggiacomo@csfa.net

Chief of Police 6350 Horizon Dr Titusville FL 32780 **Phn:** 321-264-0911 **Fax** 321-264-0033 Peter Connolly. Natl. Assn. Chiefs of Police. Bimonthly.
7,000 to decisionmakers in police depts. & agencies responsible for promotional exams, legal decisions. www.aphf.org/thechief.html peterc@aphf.org

Correctional News 1241 Andersen Dr Ste N San Rafael CA 94901 **Phn:** 415-460-6185 **Fax** 415-460-6288 Robin Hoey. Bimonthly tabloid.
15,400 to personnel involved in the design, supply and building of jails, prisons, courthouses. www.correctionalnews.com cn@emlenpub.com

Corrections Forum 116 S Catalina Ave # 116 Redondo Beach CA 92077 **Phn:** 310-374-2700 Thomas Kapinos. Bimonthly magazine.
13,000 to local, state, Federal corrections personnel interested in news, products, procedures. www.correctionsforum.net tsk2@me.com

Corrections Today 206 N Washington St Ste 200 Alexandria VA 22314 **Phn:** 703-224-0000 **Fax** 703-224-0179 Susan Clayton. Amer. Correctional Assn. Bimonthly magazine.
125,000 to Assn. members, others at federal, state, county facilities, parole & court systems. www.aca.org/publications/ctmagazine.asp susanc@aca.org

Fire Apparatus & Emergency Equip 21-00 Route 208 South Fair Lawn NJ 07410 **Phn:** 973-251-5040 **Fax** 973-251-5065 Robert Halton. PennWell Publishing. Monthly tabloid.
35,000 to fire dept. purchasers interested in apparatus reviews, recommendations, developments. www.fireapparatusmagazine.com roberth@pennwell.com

Fire Chief 330 N Wabash Ave Ste.2300 Chicago IL 60611 **Phn:** 312-595-1080 **Fax** 312-595-0295 Lisa Allegretti. Penton Media. Monthly magazine.
50,900 to fire dept. chiefs, municipal & state fire admns. responsible for mgmt., equip., operations. firechief.com lisa@firechief.com

Fire Engineering 21-00 State Rt 208 Fair Lawn NJ 07410 **Phn:** 973-251-5040 **Fax** 973-251-5065 Robert Halton. PennWell Publishing. Monthly magazine.
45,800 to fire chiefs, fire marshals & firefighters responsible for training, equipment utilization. www.fireengineering.com roberth@pennwell.com

Fire Rescue Magazine 525 B St Ste 1800 San Diego CA 92101 **Phn:** 619-231-6616 **Fax** 619-699-6396 Tim Sendelbach. Elsevier. Monthly magazine.
54,000 to fire department and rescue squad equipment and service decisionmakers. www.firefighternation.com/magazines frm.editor@elsevier.com

Firehouse 3 Huntington Quad Ste 301N Melville NY 11747 **Phn:** 631-845-2700 **Fax** 631-845-7109 Jeff Barrington. Cygnus Business Media. Monthly magazine.
76,100 to fire dept. personnel responsible for apparatus, training, education, communications. www.Firehouse.com jeff.barrington@cygnus.com

Industrial Fire World PO Box 9161 College Station TX 77842 **Phn:** 979-690-7559 **Fax** 979-690-7562 Anton Riecher. Bimonthly magazine.
24,300 to industrial fire & emergency response mgrs. responsible for industrial facility protection. www.fireworld.com ind@fireworld.com

Law & Order 130 Waukegan Rd Ste 202 Deerfield IL 60015 **Phn:** 847-444-3300 **Fax** 847-444-3333 Ed Sanow. Hendon Publishing. Monthly magazine.
38,100 to police chiefs, training administrators interested in law enforcement methods and trends. www.hendonpub.com/publications/lawandorder/ esanow@hendonpub.com

Fire Control & Police .28a

Law Enforcement Product News 1233 Janesville Ave Fort Atkinson WI 53538 **Phn:** 920-563-6388 **Fax** 920-563-1702 Jonathan Kozlowski. Cygnus Media. 8 issues.
30,000 to field officers, tactical experts, security officials, trainers interested in technology, equipment. www.officer.com jonathan.kozlowski@cygnusb2b.com

Law Enforcement Technology 1233 Janesville Ave Fort Atkinson WI 53538 **Phn:** 800-547-7377 **Fax** 920-563-1702 Tabatha Wethal. Cygnus Business Media. Monthly.
30,000 to police chiefs & sheriffs responsible for communications, training, weaponry, computers. www.officer.com tabatha.wethal@cygnus.com

Law Officer Magazine 525 B St Ste 1900 San Diego CA 92101 **Phn:** 619-231-6616 **Fax** 619-699-6396 Dale Stockton. Elsevier. 11-issue magazine.
41,000 to fire department and rescue squad equipment and service decisionmakers. www.lawofficer.com editor@lawofficermagazine.com

NFPA Journal 1 Batterymarch Park Quincy MA 02169 **Phn:** 617-770-3000 **Fax** 617-984-7004 Scott Sutherland. Natl. Fire Protection Assn. Bimonthly magazine.
85,000 to volunteer and municipal fire services; fire protection system architects and contractors. www.nfpa.org ssutherland@nfpa.org

9-1-1 Magazine 18201 Weston Pl Tustin CA 92780 **Phn:** 714-544-7776 **Fax** 714-838-9233 Randall D. Larson. Online only.
for EMS, fire, police, emergency mgmt. decisionmakers responsible for communications, other technology. www.9-1-1magazine.com publisher@9-1-1magazine.com

PI Magazine PO Box 7198 Freehold NJ 07728 **Phn:** 732-308-3800 **Fax** 732-308-3314 Grace Elting Castle. Bimonthly magazine.
10,000 to private investigators interested in investigator and case profiles. www.pimagazine.com editor@pimagazine.com

Police 3520 Challenger St Torrance CA 90503 **Phn:** 310-533-2400 **Fax** 310-533-2507 David Griffith. Bobit Business Media. Monthly magazine.
48,100 to police officers of all ranks interested in training, equipment, procedures, technology. www.policemag.com info@policemag.com

Police & Security News 1208 Juniper St Quakertown PA 18951 **Phn:** 215-538-1240 **Fax** 215-538-1208 James Devery. Bimonthly tabloid.
22,500 to public & private law enforcement mgrs. responsible for fleet mgmt., training, firearms. policeandsecuritynews.com jdevery@policeandsecuritynews.com

Police Chief 515 N Washington St Alexandria VA 22314 **Phn:** 703-836-6767 **Fax** 703-836-5386 Charles Higginbotham. Intl. Assn. Chiefs of Police. Monthly magazine.
25,000 to Assn. members & other police officers interested in news, products, pending legislation. www.policechiefmagazine.org higginbotham@theiacp.org

Police Times 6350 Horizon Dr Titusville FL 32780 **Phn:** 321-264-0911 **Fax** 321-264-0033 Peter Connolly. Amer. Fed. Police & Concerned Citizens. Quarterly magazine.
104,500 to police personnel interested in training, products, services, technology. www.aphf.org/pt.html peterc@aphf.org

Sheriff 1450 Duke St Alexandria VA 22314 **Phn:** 703-836-7827 **Fax** 703-838-5349 Susan Crow. Natl. Sheriffs' Assn. Bimonthly magazine.
23,000 to sheriffs, deputies, corrections officers interested in training, law enforcement research. www.sheriffs.org scrow@sheriffs.org

Sprinkler Age 12750 Merit Dr Ste 350 Dallas TX 75251 **Phn:** 214-349-5965 **Fax** 214-343-8898 D'Arcy Montalvo. Amer. Fire Sprinkler Assn. Monthly magazine.
3,800 to fire sprinkler contractors, fire marshals, architects, engineers, industrial safety officers. www.firesprinkler.org dmontalvo@firesprinkler.org

Tactical Response 130 Waukegan Rd Ste 202 Deerfield IL 60015 **Phn:** 847-444-3300 **Fax** 847-444-3333 Ed Sanow. Hendon Publishing. Bimonthly magazine.
27,800 to tactical officers interested in counter-terrorism and domestic preparedness. www.hendonpub.com/publications/tacticalresponse/ esanow@hendonpub.com

Federal-State-Municipal .28b

American City & County 6151 Powers Ferry Rd NW Ste 200 Atlanta GA 30339 **Phn:** 770-618-0112 **Fax** 913-514-3887 Bill Wolpin. Penton Media. Mo. mag.
82,500 to state, county, city, town, village elected/appointed officials, policymakers. americancityandcounty.com bill.wolpin@penton.com

Borough News 2941 N Front St Harrisburg PA 17110 **Phn:** 717-236-9526 **Fax** 717-236-8164 Courtney Accurti. PA State Assn of Boroughs. Monthly.
6,100 to state of PA elected & appointed officials responsible for municipal mgmt. & administration. www.boroughs.org/boroughnews/ caccurti@boroughs.org

Campaigns & Elections 1901 N Moore St # 1105 Arlington VA 22209 **Phn:** 703-778-4028 **Fax** 703-778-4024 Shane D'Aprile. Political World Comms. 13-issue magazine.
10,500 to political campaign staffers, elected officials, polling & fundraising personnel, political consultants. www.campaignsandelections.com sdaprile@campaignsandelections.com

Cities & Villages 175 S 3rd St Ste 510 Columbus OH 43215 **Phn:** 614-221-4349 **Fax** 614-221-4390 Cynthia Grant. OH Municipal League. Bimonthly magazine.
9,700 to League members concerned with land use, municipal administration & policies. www.omlohio.org cgrant@omlohio.org

County Magazine PO Box 2131 Austin TX 78768 **Phn:** 512-478-8753 **Fax** 512-481-1240 Maria Sprow. TX Assn. of Counties. Bimonthly magazine.
5,100 to Assn. members responsible for records mgmt., technology, transportion, recycling. www.county.org/resources/library/county_mag/index.asp marias@county.org

CQ Weekly 77 K Street NE Fl 8 Washington DC 20002 **Phn:** 202-650-6500 David Hawkings. Congressional Quarterly, Inc. Weekly magazine.
14,500 to media, govt., business, academic readers interested in Congressional process, events. corporate.cqrollcall.com johncranford@cqrollcall.com

Defense Systems 8609 Westwood Center Dr Ste 500 Vienna VA 22182 **Phn:** 703-876-5100 **Fax** 703-876-5059 Barry Rosenberg. 1105 Govt. Info. Group. 11-issue magazine.
34,000 to govt. defense & intelligence personnel responsible for technology, communications, training, simulation. www.defensesystems.com brosenberg@defensesystems.com

Emergency Management 100 Blue Ravine Rd Folsom CA 95630 **Phn:** 916-932-1300 **Fax** 916-932-1470 Steve Towns. e.Republic, Inc. Quarterly.
40,000 government officials and first responders dealing with emergencies of all kinds. www.emergencymgmt.com pharney@govtech.net

Empire State Report PO Box 9001 Mount Vernon NY 10552 **Phn:** 914-966-3180 **Fax** 914-966-3264 Stephen Acunto Sr. 10-issue magazine.
22,000 to NY State policy decisionmakers concerned with business, labor, finance. www.empirestatereport.com sa@cinn.com

Federal Times 6883 Commercial Dr Springfield VA 22151 **Phn:** 703-642-7300 **Fax** 703-750-8603 Steve Watkins. Weekly tabloid.
40,100 to mgmt. level civilian Federal employees interested in govt. agency programs & services. www.federaltimes.com swatkins@federaltimes.com

Governing 1100 Connecticut Ave NW Ste 1300 Washington DC 20036 **Phn:** 202-862-8802 **Fax** 202-862-0032 Tod Newcombe. Monthly magazine.
83,000 to state, local govt. officials responsible for technology, finance, infrastructure, policy. www.governing.com tnewcombe@governing.com

Government Executive 600 New Hampshire Ave NW Frnt 3 Washington DC 20037 **Phn:** 202-739-8500 **Fax** 202-739-8511 Timothy Clark. 14-issue magazine.
77,300 to Federal govt. mgrs. responsible for technology, defense, finance, administration. www.govexec.com govexec@govexec.com

Government Procurement 6151 Powers Ferry Rd NW # 200 Atlanta GA 30339 **Phn:** 770-618-0193 **Fax** 913-514-3887 Erin Green. Penton Media. Bimonthly magazine. TH:@AmerCityCounty
28,000 to govt. purchasing personnel responsible for purchasing standards and ethics.
americancityandcounty.com/government-procurement erin.greer@penton.com

Government Product News 6151 Powers Ferry Rd NW # 200 Atlanta GA 30339 **Phn:** 770-618-0193 **Fax** 913-514-3887 Erin Green. Penton Media. Monthly tabloid. TH:@AmerCityCounty
60,000 to city, state, Federal purchasing personnel responsible for products, svcs., equip.
americancityandcounty.com/gpn erin.greer@penton.com

Homeland Security Today PO Box 9789 McLean VA 22102 **Phn:** 703-757-0520 **Fax** 866-503-5758 David Silverberg. Monthly magazine.
23,000 to federal, state, local homeland security policymakers, decisionmakers, managers. www.hstoday.us/ editor@hstoday.us

IMSA Journal PO Box 539 Newark NY 14513 **Phn:** 315-331-2182 **Fax** 315-331-8205 Marilyn Lawrence. Intl. Municipal Signal Assn. Bimonthly magazine.
13,000 to traffic signal, roadway lighting personnel interested in installation, maintenance. www.imsasafety.org mel@imsasafety.org

Mass Transit 1233 Janesville Ave Fort Atkinson WI 53538 **Phn:** 920-563-6388 **Fax** 920-563-1699 Fred Jandt. Cygnus Business Media. 8-issue magazine.
20,500 to govt. officials engaged in planning, maintenance of all types of mass transit systems. www.masstransitmag.com fred.jandt@cygnusb2b.com

Metro Magazine 3520 Challenger St Torrance CA 90503 **Phn:** 310-533-2400 **Fax** 310-533-2502 Alex Roman. Bobit Business Media. 10-issue magazine.
20,500 to municipal mass transit system and privately owned bus line management personnel. www.metro-magazine.com alex.roman@bobit.com

Minnesota Cities Magazine 145 University Ave W Saint Paul MN 55103 **Phn:** 651-281-1200 **Fax** 651-281-1299 Claudia Hoffacker. League of MN Cities. 6-issue magazine.
7,300 to MN city managers and elected officials responsible for public safety and infrastructure. www.lmc.org choffacker@lmc.org

New Jersey Municipalities 222 W State St Trenton NJ 08608 **Phn:** 609-695-3481 **Fax** 609-695-0151 Bill Dressel. Monthly magazine.
8,300 to NJ municipal govt. personnel concerned with laws, finance, planning/zoning. www.njslom.com njm@njslom.com

Parks & Recreation 22377 Belmont Ridge Rd Ashburn VA 20148 **Phn:** 703-858-0784 **Fax** 703-858-0794 Gina Mullins-Cohen. Natl. Rec./Park Assn. Monthly magazine. TH:@NRPA_news
40,000 to Assn. members; park mgrs., supervisors responsible for mgmt. & policy. www.nrpa.org gcohen@nrpa.org

Federal-State-Municipal .28b

Pennsylvania Township News 4855 Woodland Dr Enola PA 17025 **Phn:** 717-763-0930 **Fax** 717-763-9732 Ginni Linn. Monthly magazine.
9,500 to PA local govt. officials responsible for roads & bridges, public safety, waste mgmt. www.psats.org glinn@psats.org

Planning 205 N Michigan Ave Ste 1200 Chicago IL 60601 **Phn:** 312-431-9100 **Fax** 312-786-6700 Sylvia Lewis. Amer. Planning Assn. 10-issue magazine.
43,000 to Assn. members, regional planners, architects, civil engineers, environmental consultants. www.planning.org slewis@planning.org

Public CIO 100 Blue Ravine Rd Folsom CA 95630 **Phn:** 916-932-1300 **Fax** 916-932-1470 Tod Newcombe. e.Republic, Inc. Bimonthly.
26,000 to chief executives with IT functions in federal, state, local, international government. www.govtech.com tnewcombe@govtech.com

Public Works Magazine 8725 W Higgins Rd Ste 600 Chicago IL 60631 **Phn:** 773-824-2400 **Fax** 773-824-2401 Victoria K. Sicaras. Hanley-Wood. Monthly magazine.
66,600 to municipal mgrs., public works dept. heads responsible for equip., materials, services. www.pwmag.com vsicaras@hanleywood.com

The Review PO Box 1487 Ann Arbor MI 48106 **Phn:** 734-662-3246 **Fax** 734-662-8083 Kim Cekola. MI Municipal League. Bimonthly magazine.
10,400 to policymakers, administrators concerned with issues facing MI municipalities. www.mml.org kcekola@mml.org

State Legislatures 7700 E 1st Pl Denver CO 80230 **Phn:** 303-364-7700 **Fax** 303-364-7800 Edward Smith. Natl. Conf. State Legislatures. 10-issue magazine.
25,700 to elected and appointed state officials interested in legislative procedures and processes. www.ncsl.org/magazine/ edward.smith@ncsl.org

State News PO Box 11910 Lexington KY 40578 **Phn:** 859-244-8000 **Fax** 859-244-8001 Jack Penchoff. Cncl. State Govts. 10-issue magazine.
15,000 to state, Fed. govt. personnel, press & b'cast media interested in state political activities. www.csg.org press@csg.org

Texas Town & City 1821 Rutherford Ln # 400 Austin TX 78754 **Phn:** 512-231-7400 **Fax** 512-231-7490 Karla Vining. TX Municipal League. 11-issue magazine.
11,300 to mayors, council members, other Texas municipal and government personnel. www.tml.org kvining@tml.org

Virginia Review 7307 Belmont Stakes Dr Midlothian VA 23112 **Phn:** 804-396-4744 James Smith. Online only.
for Virginia state and local officials, purchasing managers, educators. vareview.com virginiareview@gmail.com

Western City 1400 K St # 400 Sacramento CA 95814 **Phn:** 916-978-9877 **Fax** 916-658-8289 Jude Hudson. League of CA Cities. Monthly magazine.
9,000 to CA city municipal mgrs., finance mgrs, city council members, purchasing mgrs., state & federal congress members. www.westerncity.com jude@surewest.net

Environment & Ecology .28c

American Recycler 900 W South Boundary St Bldg 6 Perrysburg OH 43551 **Phn:** 419-931-0737 **Fax** 419-931-0740 Esther G. Fournier. Monthly tabloid.
35,000 to recycling execs. interested in suppliers & customers for all types of recycled material. www.americanrecycler.com news@americanrecycler.com

Audubon 225 Varick St Fl 7 New York NY 10014 **Phn:** 212-979-3000 **Fax** 212-477-9069 David Seideman. Natl. Audubon Society. Bimonthly magazine. TH:@DavidSeideman
434,000 to Society members, others interested in nature, bird life, conservation, biodiversity. www.audubonmagazine.org dseideman@audubon.org

Biocycle 63 S 7th St Ste 2 Emmaus PA 18049 **Phn:** 610-967-4135 **Fax** 610-967-1345 Dan Sullivan. Monthly magazine.
9,900 to waste industry personnel, others interested in composting, renewable energy, sustainability, organic waste mgmt. www.jgpress.com editinfo@jgpress.com

Conservationist 625 Broadway Fl 2 Albany NY 12233 **Phn:** 518-402-8047 **Fax** 518-402-9036 David Nelson. NY State Dept. Environmental Conservation. Bimonthly magazine.
95,000 to readers interested in NY State fishing, hunting, natural history, outdoor recreation. www.theconservationist.org magazine@gw.dec.state.ny.us

E-The Environmental Magazine 28 Knight St Norwalk CT 06851 **Phn:** 203-854-5559 **Fax** 203-866-0602 Doug Moss. Bimonthly magazine. TH:@EEnviroMag
50,000 to readers interested in key environmental issues, grassroots activism and organizations. www.emagazine.com doug@emagazine.com

Environment 325 Chestnut St Ste 800 Philadelphia PA 19106 **Phn:** 215-625-8900 Margaret Benner. Taylor & Francis. 10-issue magazine.
4,300 to policymakers concerned with natural and human ecosystem issues. www.environmentmagazine.org margaret.benner@taylorandfrancis.com

Environmental Protection 14901 Quorum Dr Ste 425 Dallas TX 75254 **Phn:** 972-687-6730 **Fax** 972-687-6770 Brent Dirks. 1105 Media. Online only.
for environmental professionals concerned with EPA regulations, legislative matters. www.eponline.com bdirks@1105media.com

Environmental Science & Tech. 1155 16th St NW Washington DC 20036 **Phn:** 202-872-4582 **Fax** 202-872-4403 Jerald Schnoor. Amer. Chemical Soc. Semimonthly.
7,100 to engineers, scientists, govt. officials responsible for pollution control policy and equipment. pubs.acs.org/journals/esthag est@uiowa.edu

Jrnl. Environmental Health 720 S Colorado Blvd Ste 1000N Denver CO 80246 **Phn:** 303-756-9090 **Fax** 303-691-9490 Kristen Ruby. 10-issue magazine.
5,500 to technical and professional personnel concerned with environment, health, sanitation. www.neha.org kruby@neha.org

Land & Water 320 A St Fort Dodge IA 50501 **Phn:** 515-576-3191 **Fax** 515-576-2606 Amy Dencklau. Bimonthly magazine.
20,000 to consultants & engineers responsible for natural resource mgmt. and restoration. www.landandwater.com landandwater@frontiernet.net

Pollution Engineering 2401 W Big Beaver Rd Ste 700 Troy MI 48084 **Phn:** 248-362-3700 **Fax** 248-786-1356 Roy Bigham. BNP Media. Monthly magazine.
35,000 to pollution control engineers interested in products, new technology, regulations, svcs. www.pollutionengineering.com roy@pollutionengineering.com

Pollution Equipment News 8650 Babcock Blvd Pittsburgh PA 15237 **Phn:** 412-364-5366 **Fax** 412-369-9720 Raquel Rimbach. Bimonthly tabloid.
88,600 to specifiers, purchasers & installers of air/water/hazmat pollution control equipment. www.rimbach.com editorialdept@rimbach.com

Resource Recycling PO Box 42270 Portland OR 97242 **Phn:** 503-233-1305 **Fax** 503-233-1356 Jerry Powell. Monthly magazine.
13,500 to waste recycling/composting personnel interested in news, programs, events. www.resource-recycling.com jpowell@resource-recycling.com

Sierra 85 2nd St Fl 2 San Francisco CA 94105 **Phn:** 415-977-5572 **Fax** 415-977-5794 Bob Sipchen. Sierra Club Inc. Bimonthly magazine.
531,000 to Club members, others interested in wilderness preservation, recycling, environment. www.sierraclub.org/sierra/ bob.sipchen@sierraclub.org

American Waste Digest 226 King St Pottstown PA 19464 **Phn:** 610-326-9480 **Fax** 610-326-9752 Robert Gauthier. Monthly magazine.
16,100 to private waste haulers, equipment dealers, manufacturers and suppliers.
www.americanwastedigest.com
awd@americanwastedigest.com

APWA Reporter 2345 Grand Blvd Ste 700 Kansas City MO 64108 **Phn:** 816-472-6100 **Fax** 816-472-1610 Kevin Clark. Amer. Public Works Assn. Monthly magazine.
34,000 to Assn. members, public works personnel interested in research, training, technology.
www.apwa.net kclark@apwa.net

Ground Water 601 Dempsey Rd Westerville OH 43081 **Phn:** 614-898-7791 **Fax** 614-898-7786 Thad Plumley. Natl. Ground Water Assn. Bimonthly magazine.
12,000 to hydrogeologists interested in peer-reviewed articles, technical research, book reviews.
www.ngwa.org tplumley@ngwa.org

Jrnl. AWWA 6666 W Quincy Ave Denver CO 80235 **Phn:** 303-794-7711 **Fax** 303-794-7310 Marcia Lacey. Monthly magazine.
40,900 to water professionals interested in drinking water related peer-reviewed papers. www.awwa.org journal@awwa.org

MSW Management PO Box 3100 Santa Barbara CA 93130 **Phn:** 805-682-1300 **Fax** 805-682-0200 John Trotti. Solid Waste Mgmt. Assn. 7-issue mag.
25,600 to city, county, state personnel who maintain, supervise municipal solid waste disposal.
www.mswmanagement.com editor@forester.net

Ultrapure Water 60 Golden Eagle Ln Littleton CO 80127 **Phn:** 303-973-6700 Mike Henley. Tall Oaks Publishing. Online only.
for personnel in pharmaceutical, food/beverage, elec. utility industries using pure water. www.talloaks.com mike@ultrapurewater.com

Waste Age 6151 Powers Ferry Rd NW Ste 200 Atlanta GA 30339 **Phn:** 770-618-0201 **Fax** 770-618-0349 Allan Gerlat. Penton Media. Monthly magazine.
51,000 to municipal & private waste mgmt. personnel interested in news, trends, products. waste360.com allan.gerlat@penton.com

Waste & Recycling News 1725 Merriman Rd Ste 300 Akron OH 44313 **Phn:** 330-836-9180 **Fax** 330-836-1692 Peter Fehrenbach. Crain Communications. Biweekly tab.
51,100 to waste processors responsible for transport and disposal of solid & hazardous waste.
www.wasterecyclingnews.com
editorial@wasterecyclingnews.com

Waste Handling Equipment News PO Box 121 Palatine Bridge NY 13428 **Phn:** 518-673-3237 **Fax** 518-673-2381 Jon Casey. Lee Publications. Monthly newspaper.
18,700 to landfill and compost facility operators, recyclers, demolition firms. www.wastehandling.com jcasey@leepub.com

Waste Management World 1421 S Sheridan Rd Tulsa OK 74112 **Phn:** 918-835-3161 **Fax** 918-831-9722 Tom Freyberg. PennWell Publishing. Bimonthly.
18,000 solid waste technology, trends, waste recycling, minimization, transport and collection.
www.waste-management-world.com
wmw@pennwell.com

Water & Wastes Digest 3030 W Salt Creek Ln Ste 201 Arlington Hts IL 60005 **Phn:** 847-391-1000 **Fax** 847-390-0408 Neda Simeonova. Scranton Gillette. Monthly tab.
90,100 to those responsible for treatment and distribution of drinking water; wastewater mgmt.
www.wwdmag.com nsimeonova@sgcmail.com

Water Conditioning/Purification 2800 E Fort Lowell Rd Tucson AZ 85716 **Phn:** 520-323-6144 **Fax** 520-323-7412 Kurt C. Peterson. Monthly magazine.
18,600 to water treatment industry personnel, system retailers, dealers, distributors. www.wcponline.com info@wcponline.com

Water & Wastes .28d
Water Environment & Technology 601 Wythe St Alexandria VA 22314 **Phn:** 703-684-2400 **Fax** 703-684-2492 Melissa Jackson. Monthly magazine.
33,000 to wastewater, environmental mgmt., groundwater, pollution control personnel. www.wef.org mjackson@wef.org

Water Quality Products 3030 W Salt Creek Ln Ste 201 Arlington Hts IL 60005 **Phn:** 847-391-1000 **Fax** 847-390-0408 Kate Cline. Scranton Gillette. Monthly tab.
18,100 to water enhancement system retailers, wholesalers, plumbing contractors, bottlers.
www.wqpmag.com kcline@sgcmail.com

Water Technology 19 British American Blvd W Latham NY 12110 **Phn:** 518-783-1281 **Fax** 518-783-1386 Richard DiPaolo. NTP Media. Monthly.
19,500 to water treatment equip. and bulk bottled water retailers, dealers, wholesalers, specifiers.
www.watertechonline.com rdipaolo@ntpmedia.com

Water Well Journal 601 Dempsey Rd Westerville OH 43081 **Phn:** 614-898-7791 **Fax** 614-898-7786 Thad Plumley. Natl. Ground Water Assn. Monthly magazine.
23,200 to ground water indus. personnel responsible for drilling, rig maintenance, water treatment.
www.ngwa.org tplumley@ngwa.org

WaterWorld 1421 S Sheridan Rd Tulsa OK 74112 **Phn:** 918-835-3161 **Fax** 918-831-9776 James Laughlin. PennWell Publishing. Monthly tabloid.
59,500 to municipal water, wastewater personnel interested in new technology, industry trends.
www.waterworld.com jamesl@pennwell.com

Furniture--Interiors .29
ASID Icon 608 Massachusetts Ave NE Washington DC 20002 **Phn:** 202-546-3480 **Fax** 202-546-3240 Jennifer Lipner. Amer. Soc. Interior Designers. Quarterly magazine.
31,000 to Society members interested in design trends, products, news and business practices. www.asid.org icon@asid.org

BedTimes 501 Wythe St Alexandria VA 22314 **Phn:** 703-683-8371 **Fax** 703-683-4503 Julie Palm. Intl. Sleep Products Assn. Monthly magazine.
3,700 to mattress industry mfrs. and suppliers interested in industry news, events and trends.
www.bedtimesmagazine.com
jpalm@sleepproducts.org

CabinetmakerFDM 303 N Main St Rockford IL 61101 **Phn:** 815-966-5400 **Fax** 815-966-6416 William Sampson. CCI Media. Monthly magazine.
40,000 to wood bath/kitchen cabinet mfrs., panel laminators, fabricators, cabinet designers; furniture mfg. mgmt. www.cabinetmakerfdm.com will.sampson@ccimedia.net

Casual Living 7025 Albert Pick Rd Ste 200 Greensboro NC 27409 **Phn:** 336-605-1122 **Fax** 336-605-1143 Cinde W. Ingram. Progressive Business Media. Monthly magazine. TH:@CasualLiving
11,500 to indoor/outdoor casual furniture retailers, mfrs., designers, buyers, suppliers.
www.casualliving.com cingram@casualliving.com

Closets Magazine PO Box 1400 Lincolnshire IL 60069 **Phn:** 847-634-4347 **Fax** 847-634-4374 Michaelle Bradford. Vance Publishing. Bimo.
19,000 to independent closet manufacturers, large franchisers, builders, remodelers.
www.closetsdaily.com
mbradford@vancepublishing.com

Concrete Decor PO Box 25210 Eugene OR 97402 **Phn:** 541-341-3390 **Fax** 541-341-6443 John Strieder. 8 issues.
56,000 covers architectural finishes and maintenance of new and existing concrete decor.
www.concretedecor.net john@protradepub.com

Contract 770 Broadway New York NY 10003 **Phn:** 646-654-5000 Murrye Bernard. Nielsen Business Media. 10-issue magazine. TH:@contractmag
30,000 to architects, interior designers, specifiers of commercial installations. www.contractdesign.com mbernard@contractdesign.com

Custom Woodworking Business 400 Knightsbridge Pkwy Lincolnshire IL 60069 **Phn:** 847-634-4347 **Fax** 847-634-4374 Bill Esler. Vance Publishing. Monthly.
41,000 to custom woodworking business owners interested in design, architecture, supplies.
www.woodworkingnetwork.com
besler@vancepublishing.com

Draperies & Window Coverings 840 US Highway 1 Ste 330 North Palm Beach FL 33408 **Phn:** 561-627-3393 **Fax** 561-694-6578 Howard Shingle. Monthly magazine.
27,700 to window fashion retailers, wholesalers, manufacturers, designers, workroom personnel.
www.dwconline.com

EnLIGHTenment Magazine 620 W. Germantown Pike Ste 440 Plymouth Meeting PA 19462 **Phn:** 800-774-9861 Linda Longo. Bravo Integrated Media. Monthly magazine.
10,700 to retailers, designers of lamps, fixtures, interested in sales training, showroom display, trends, technology. www.enlightenmentmag.com linda@bravointegratedmedia.com

Floor Covering Installer 22801 Ventura Blvd Ste 115 Woodland Hills CA 91364 **Phn:** 818-224-8035 **Fax** 818-224-8042 Michael Chmielecki. BNP Media. 9-issue magazine.
38,500 to floor installation contractors, retailers, distributors working with all types of flooring materials. www.fcimag.com chmieleckim@bnpmedia.com

Floor Covering News 550 W Old Country Rd Ste 204 Hicksville NY 11801 **Phn:** 516-932-7860 **Fax** 516-932-7639 Matthew Spieler. Ro-El Pubs. Biweekly tabloid.
15,000 to mfrs., retailers, interior designers in carpet, resilient & wood flooring industries. www.fcnews.net fcnewsmatt@yahoo.com

Floor Covering Weekly 50 Charles Lindbergh Blvd Ste 100 Uniondale NY 11553 **Phn:** 516-229-3600 **Fax** 516-227-1342 Alycia Broderick. Hearst Corp. 31-issue tab.
17,200 to floor covering personnel responsible for mfg., technology, merchandising, styling.
www.floorcoveringweekly.com fcwedit@hearst.com

Floor Focus PO Box 3399 Chattanooga TN 37404 **Phn:** 423-752-0400 **Fax** 423-752-0401 Brian Hamilton. 11-issue magazine.
15,000 to floor covering retailers, wholesalers, designers interested in business, technical aspects.
www.floordaily.net info@floorfocus.com

Furniture Today 7025 Albert Pick Rd Ste 200 Greensboro NC 27409 **Phn:** 336-605-1112 **Fax** 336-605-1143 Ray Allegrezza. Progressive Business Media. Weekly tabloid. TH:@rjallegrezza
28,000 to furniture, dept. and chain store execs.; accessory buyers; fashion coordinators.
www.furnituretoday.com
rallegrezza@furnituretoday.com

Furniture World 1333A North Ave # 437 New Rochelle NY 10804 **Phn:** 914-235-3095 **Fax** 914-235-3278 Russell Bienenstock. Towse Publishing. Bimo.
17,500 to furniture retail managers & buyers interested in marketing, finance, sales training. www.furninfo.com russ@furninfo.com

Hardwood Floors 4130 Lien Rd Madison WI 53704 **Phn:** 608-249-0186 **Fax** 608-249-1153 Kim Wahlgren. Natl. Wood Flooring Assn. 7-issue magazine.
25,000 to flooring contractors, retailers interested in hardwood installation, sales & marketing.
hardwoodfloorsmag.com
editors@hardwoodfloorsmag.com

HFN Home Furnishings News 333 7th Ave Fl 11 New York NY 10001 **Phn:** 212-979-4800 **Fax** 646-674-0102 Duke Ratliff. 18-issue tabloid.
18,100 to home furnishings retail mgmt. interested in suppliers, business analyses, marketing.
www.hfnmag.com dratliff@hfnmag.com

Home Textiles Today 1271 Ave of the Americas Fl 17 New York NY 10020 **Phn:** Jennifer Marks. Progressive Business Media. 31-issue tabloid. TH:@HomeTextilesTod
7,200 to marketers, merchandisers, retailers of domestics, furnishings, bedding, bath, textiles. www.hometextilestoday.com jnegley@hometextilestoday.com

HomeWorld Business 45 Research Way Ste 106 East Setauket NY 11733 **Phn:** 631-246-9300 **Fax** 631-246-9496 Peter Gianetti. ICD Publications. 26-issue tab.
12,500 to retailers, mfrs., sales in houseware field concerned with new products, news, forecasts. www.homeworldbusiness.com peterg@homeworldbusiness.com

ICS Cleaning Specialist 2401 W Big Beaver Rd Ste 700 Troy MI 48084 **Phn:** 248-786-1667 **Fax** 248-502-1028 Eric Fish. BNP Media. Bimonthly magazine.
46,300 to floorcare personnel who clean, restore, maintain floors interested in equip. & training. www.icsmag.com fishe@bnpmedia.com

Interior Design 1271 Ave of the Americas Fl 17 New York NY 10020 **Phn:** 917-934-2863 Helene Oberman. Sandow Media. 14-issue magazine. TH:@Interior_Design
73,400 to interior designers & decorators working on residential & commercial interiors. www.interiordesign.net hoberman@interiordesign.net

Interiors & Sources PO Box 1888 Cedar Rapids IA 52406 **Phn:** 319-364-5190 **Fax** 319-364-4278 Erika Templeton. Stamats Comms. Monthly magazine. TH:@erikatempleton
30,500 to commercial interior designers responsible for commercial structure products, services. www.interiorsandsources.com erika.templeton@interiorsandsources.com

Kitchen & Bath Business 770 Broadway New York NY 10003 **Phn:** 646-654-4500 **Fax** 646-654-4417 Chelsie Butler. Nielsen Business Media. Monthly magazine.
34,000 to dealers, designers, wholesalers of countertops, cabinetry & built-in appliances. www.kbbonline.com chelsie.butler@nielsen.com

Kitchen & Bath Design News 3 Huntington Quad Ste 301N Melville NY 11747 **Phn:** 631-845-2700 **Fax** 631-845-7109 Janice Anne Costa. Cygnus Business Media. Monthly.
48,600 to kitchen & bath dealers, designers, wholesalers interested in trends, ideas, products. www.forresidentialpros.com janice.costa@cygnuspub.com

LDB Interior Textiles 370 Lexington Ave Rm 1409 New York NY 10017 **Phn:** 212-661-1516 **Fax** 212-661-1713 Wanda Jankowski. E.W. Williams Pubs. Mo. mag.
10,000 to retailers, buyers of linens, domestics, pillows, decorative fabrics. www.ldbinteriortextiles.com wandaldb@ewwpi.com

National Floor Trends 22801 Ventura Blvd Ste 115 Woodland Hills CA 91364 **Phn:** 818-224-8035 **Fax** 818-224-8042 Michael Chmielecki. BNP Media. Monthly mag.
25,000 to floor covering industry personnel concerned with upscale design trends, installations. www.ntlfloortrends.com chmieleckim@bnpmedia.com

Residential Lighting 3030 W Salt Creek Ln Ste 201 Arlington Hts IL 60005 **Phn:** 847-391-1000 **Fax** 847-390-0408 Laura Van Zeyl. Scranton Gillette. Monthly magazine.
10,000 to home lighting product manufacturers, designers, retailers. www.residentiallighting.com lvanzeyl@sgcmail.com

Retailer NOW 500 Giuseppe Ct Ste 6 Roseville CA 95678 **Phn:** 800-422-3778 Jennifer Billock. N. Amer Home Furnishings Assn. 10-issue magazine. TH:@RetailerNOW
12,100 to executives in home furnishing industry responsible for mgmt., training, retail operations. www.retailernowmag.com jennifer@retailernowmag.com

Furniture--Interiors .29

Upholstery Journal 1801 County Road B W Roseville MN 55113 **Phn:** 651-225-6970 **Fax** 651-225-6966 Chris Tschida. Bimonthly magazine.
12,000 to home, auto, marine upholsterers interested in fabrics, tools, equipment, techniques. upholsteryjournal.com srniemi@ifai.com

Window Fashion Vision 4756 Banning Ave # 206 Saint Paul MN 55110 **Phn:** 651-756-8834 **Fax** 651-756-8141 Grace McNamara McNamara Publishing. Bimonthly magazine.
29,100 to window treatment retailers, designers, mfrs. interested in market reports, trends. www.wf-vision.com grace@wf-vision.com

Horticulture--Garden--Nursery .30

The American Gardener 7931 E Boulevard Dr Alexandria VA 22308 **Phn:** 703-768-5700 **Fax** 703-768-7533 David Ellis. American Horticultural Soc. Bimonthly magazine.
25,000 to professional & advanced amateur gardeners interested in ornamental plants; environmental matters. www.ahs.org dellis@ahs.org

American Nurseryman 374 Emerson Falls Rd Ste 1 Saint Johnsbury VT 05819 **Phn:** 802-748-8908 **Fax** 802-748-1866 Sally Benson. Moose River Media. Monthly magazine. TH:@AmNurseryman
13,200 to garden center, landscaping business owners interested in industry & technical info. www.amerinursery.com sbenson@mooserivermedia.com

American Rose PO Box 30000 Shreveport LA 71130 **Phn:** 318-938-5402 **Fax** 318-938-5405 Beth Smiley. Amer. Rose Society. Bimonthly.
15,000 to rose gardeners interested in new varieties, arrangements, exhibitions. www.ars.org beth@ars-hq.org

Country Gardens 1716 Locust St Des Moines IA 50309 **Phn:** 515-284-3000 **Fax** 515-284-3264 Samantha Thorpe. Meredith Corp. Quarterly magazine.
600,000 to gardeners interested in garden design, plant selection, outdoor entertaining. www.meredith.com samantha.thorpe@meredith.com

Fine Gardening 63 S Main St Newtown CT 06470 **Phn:** 203-426-8171 **Fax** 203-270-6753 Steven Aitken. Taunton Press. Bimonthly magazine.
148,100 to expert gardeners, designers interested in plant selection, techniques and tools. www.finegardening.com fg@taunton.com

Floral Management 1601 Duke St Alexandria VA 22314 **Phn:** 703-836-8700 **Fax** 703-836-8705 Kate Penn. Soc. Amer. Florists. Monthly magazine.
15,800 to floral business mgrs., owners, designers in new products, merchandising, promotion. www.safnow.org fmeditor@safnow.org

Florists' Review PO Box 4368 Topeka KS 66604 **Phn:** 785-266-0888 **Fax** 785-266-0333 David Coake. Monthly magazine.
22,300 to fresh flower and plant retailers & wholesalers responsible for design, business mgmt. www.floristsreview.com dcoake@floristsreview.com

Flowers& Magazine 11444 W Olympic Blvd Los Angeles CA 90064 **Phn:** 310-966-3590 **Fax** 310-966-3610 Bruce Wright. Teleflora, Inc. Monthly magazine.
14,000 to florists, wholesalers, distributors, growers, floral designers, silk & dried flower retailers. www.flowersandmagazine.com bwright@teleflora.com

Garden Center Magazine 4020 Kinross Lakes Pkwy Richfield OH 44286 **Phn:** 800-456-0707 **Fax** 216-651-0830 Karen Varga. GIE Media. 9-issue magazine. TH:@gardencentermag
20,000 to independent garden center owners/mgrs. interested in all aspects of retailing. www.gardencentermag.com kvarga@gie.net

Gardening How-To 12301 Whitewater Dr Minnetonka MN 55343 **Phn:** 952-936-9333 **Fax** 952-988-7486 Kathy Childers. Natl. Home Gardening Club. Bimo. magazine.
600,000 to gardeners interested in practical information on planning, designing, new products. www.gardeningclub.com kchilders@namginc.com

Greenhouse Grower 37733 Euclid Ave Willoughby OH 44094 **Phn:** 440-942-2000 **Fax** 440-942-0662 Robin Siktberg. Meister Media. Monthly magazine. TH:@RobinS_GG
20,500 to commercial greenhouse floriculture growers interested in tools, technology, profitability, industry profiles. www.greenhousegrower.com rasiktberg@meistermedia.com

Greenhouse Management 4020 Kinross Lakes Pkwy U-2 Richfield OH 44286 **Phn:** 800-456-0707 **Fax** 330-659-0823 Joe Jancsurak. GIE Media. Monthly magazine. TH:@JoeJancsurak
21,600 to flower, herb, vegetable greenhouse growers interested in products, news. www.greenhousemag.com jjancsurak@gie.net

Greenhouse Product News 3030 W Salt Creek Ln Ste 201 Arlington Hts IL 60005 **Phn:** 847-391-1000 **Fax** 847-390-0408 Tim Hodson. Scranton Gillette. Mo. tab.
20,100 to commercial floriculture growers interested in new products, seeds and industry trends. www.gpnmag.com thodson@sgcmail.com

Grower Talks PO Box 1660 West Chicago IL 60186 **Phn:** 630-231-3675 **Fax** 630-231-5254 Chris Beytes. Ball Publishing. Monthly magazine.
30,800 to commercial greenhouse growers of bedding plants, pot plants, foliage, cut flowers. www.ballpublishing.com cbeytes@ballpublishing.com

Horticulture 10151 Carver Rd Ste 200 Blue Ash OH 45242 **Phn:** 513-531-2690 **Fax** 513-891-7153 Meghan Shinn. F&W Media. Bimonthly magazine.
90,000 to active home gardeners interested in ornamental plants, garden design. www.hortmag.com edit@hortmag.com

Interiorscape 2873 Saber Dr Clearwater FL 33759 **Phn:** 727-724-0020 **Fax** 727-724-0021 Jill LoCascio. Brantwood Publications. Bimo. magazine.
5,400 to interior landscapers who design, install and maintain plants in businesses and homes. www.interiorscape.com jill@nurseryretailer.com

Irrigation & Green Industry 6925 Canby Ave Ste 104 Reseda CA 91335 **Phn:** 818-342-3204 **Fax** 818-342-0731 Denne Goldstein. ISG Communications. Monthly magazine.
43,500 to landscape, irrigation co. mgmt. interested in industry news and trends, market analyses. www.igin.com denne@igin.com

Landscape & Irrigation 1030 Higgins Rd Ste 230 Park Ridge IL 60068 **Phn:** 847-720-5600 **Fax** 847-720-5601 John Kmitta. M2Media360. 9-issue magazine.
40,000 to landscape architects, contractors; golf course, parks, recreation, irrigation personnel. www.greenmediaonline.com jkmitta@m2media360.com

Landscape Architecture 636 I St NW Washington DC 20001 **Phn:** 202-898-2444 **Fax** 202-898-0062 Lisa Speckhardt. Amer. Soc. Landscape Architects. Monthly.
60,000 to Society members interested in projects, awards, continuing education, environmental issues. www.landscapearchitecturemagazine.org lspeckhardt@asla.org

Landscape Contractor PO Box 909 Naperville IL 60566 **Phn:** 630-637-8632 **Fax** 630-637-8629 Rick Reuland. IL Landscape Contractors Assn. Monthly magazine.
2,500 to Assn. members, others in IL, MI, WI interested in training features, labor news. www.ilca.net information@ilca.net

Landscape Management 1360 E. 9th St. Fl 10 Cleveland OH 44114 **Phn:** 855-460-5502 Marisa Palmieri. North Coast Media. Monthly magazine.
48,300 to landscape contractors, lawn care operators, other grounds care professionals. www.landscapemanagement.net mpalmieri@northcoastmedia.net

Lawn & Landscape 4020 Kinross Lakes Pkwy Ste 201 Richfield OH 44286 **Phn:** 800-456-0707 **Fax** 330-659-0823 Chuck Bowen. GIE Media. Monthly magazine.
80,000 to landscape personnel responsible for lawn, tree installation, seeding, care, design.
www.lawnandlandscape.com cbowen@gie.net

Nursery Management 4020 Kinross Lakes Pkwy Ste 201 Richfield OH 44286 **Phn:** 972-957-0050 **Fax** 817-885-7875 Kelli Rodda. GIE Media. Monthly.
15,200 to plant nursery personnel responsible for products, personnel, industry news.
www.nurserymanagementonline.com krodda@gie.net

Nursery Retailer 2873 Saber Dr Clearwater FL 33759 **Phn:** 727-724-0020 **Fax** 727-724-0021 Jill LoCascio. Brantwood Publications. Bimonthly mag.
26,100 to nursery, garden supply & home ctr. mgrs. interested in merchandise, sales forecasts.
www.nurseryretailer.com jill@nurseryretailer.com

Orchids 16700 A O S Ln Delray Beach FL 33446 **Phn:** 561-404-2040 **Fax** 561-404-2045 James Watson. Amer. Orchid Soc. Monthly magazine.
16,000 to orchid enthusiasts, cultivators interested in techniques, propagation, hybrids, shows. www.aos.org jwatson@aos.org

Organic Gardening 400 S 10th St Emmaus PA 18049 **Phn:** 610-967-5171 Scott Meyer. Rodale Press. Bimonthly magazine.
260,000 to organic home gardeners interested in flowers, vegetables, herbs, ornamentals.
www.organicgardening.com og@rodale.com

Outdoor Power Equipment 1030 Higgins Rd Ste 230 Park Ridge IL 60068 **Phn:** 847-720-5600 **Fax** 847-720-5601 Steve Noe. M2Media360. Monthly magazine.
20,200 to retailers & distributors who sell and/or service outdoor power equipment.
www.greenmediaonline.com snoe@m2media360.com

Plantfinder 7770 Davie Road Ext Hollywood FL 33024 **Phn:** 954-981-2821 **Fax** 954-981-2823 Donna Kurtzer. Monthly magazine.
18,500 to wholesale nursery, landscape personnel interested in plants and plant supplies.
www.plantfinder.com donna@betrock.com

Power Equipment Trade PO Box 2268 Montgomery AL 36102 **Phn:** 334-834-1170 **Fax** 334-834-4525 Dan Shell. 10-issue magazine.
20,700 to lawn, garden equip. dealers, mfrs. concerned with products, surveys, trade shows.
www.powerequipmenttrade.com
dan@hattonbrown.com

Pro 1233 Janesville Ave Fort Atkinson WI 53538 **Phn:** 920-563-6388 **Fax** 920-563-1699 Rod Dickens. Cygnus Business Media. 9-issue tabloid.
55,000 to lawn maintenance, club/hotel lawn care personnel interested in profitable operation.
www.greenindustrypros.com
rod.dickens@cygnusb2b.com

Sportsturf 760 Market St Ste 432 San Francisco CA 94102 **Phn:** 815-479-8547 Eric Schroder. M2Media360. Monthly magazine.
25,100 to sports complex, park, resort, golf course architects, builders, maintenance mgrs.
www.sportsturfonline.com
eschroder@m2media360.com

Super Floral Retailing 3300 SW Van Buren St Topeka KS 66611 **Phn:** 785-266-0888 **Fax** 785-266-0333 Cynthia McGowan. Monthly magazine.
16,200 to traditional and discount floral retailers interested in sales and marketing strategies.
www.superfloralretailing.com
cmcgowan@superfloralretailing.com

Turf 374 Emerson Falls Rd Ste 1 Saint Johnsbury VT 05819 **Phn:** 802-748-8908 **Fax** 802-748-1866 Amy K. Hill. Moose River Publishing. Monthly tabloid. TH:@TurfMagazine
70,500 in 4 regional editions to landscape, lawn care svcs., park & golf course superintendents.
www.turfmagazine.com ahill@mooserivermedia.com

Horticulture--Garden--Nursery .30

Turf News 2 E Main St East Dundee IL 60118 **Phn:** 847-649-5555 **Fax** 847-649-5678 Lynn Grooms. Bimonthly magazine.
1,800 to turfgrass industry personnel responsible for marketing, equipment, personnel, agronomics.
www.turfgrassSod.org info@turfgrasssod.org

Yard & Garden 1233 Janesville Ave Fort Atkinson WI 53538 **Phn:** 920-563-6388 **Fax** 920-563-1699 Gregg Wartgow. Cygnus Business Media. 8-issue magazine.
17,500 to power equipment retailers interested in success stories, mgmt. techniques, products.
www.greenindustrypros.com
gregg.wartgow@cygnusb2b.com

Hospitals--Nursing .31

AACN Bold Voices 101 Columbia Aliso Viejo CA 92656 **Phn:** 949-362-2000 **Fax** 949-362-2049 Richard Howell. Monthly magazine.
94,000 to members of Am. Assn. of Critical-Care Nurses interested in news, treatments, continuing ed.
www.aacn.org/boldvoices aacnboldvoices@aacn.org

AANA Journal 222 S Prospect Ave Park Ridge IL 60068 **Phn:** 847-692-7050 **Fax** 847-518-0938 Sally Aquino. Bimonthly magazine.
38,100 to members of the American Association of Nurse Anesthetists. www.aana.com
publications@aana.com

AAOHN Journal 6900 Grove Rd Thorofare NJ 08086 **Phn:** 856-848-1000 **Fax** 856-853-5991 Joy E. Wachs. Monthly magazine.
9,300 to members of Am. Assn. of Occupational Health nurses interested in mgmt. and rsch.
www.slackjournals.com/aaohn aaohn@slackinc.com

Advance For NPs & PAs 2900 Horizon Dr King Of Prussia PA 19406 **Phn:** 610-278-1400 **Fax** 610-278-1425 Michelle Pronsati. Merion Pubs. Monthly magazine.
67,200 to nurse practitioners & physician assistants interested in clinical features and professional news.
nurse-practitioners-and-physician-assistants.advanceweb.com mpronsati@merion.com

AHA News 325 7th St NW Washington DC 20004 **Phn:** 202-638-1100 **Fax** 202-626-2287 Gary Luggiero. Amer. Hosp Assn. Biweekly newspaper.
22,500 to healthcare executives interested in up-to-the-minute Federal, state health policy news.
www.ahanews.com gluggiero@aha.org

American Jrnl. Critical Care 101 Columbia Aliso Viejo CA 92656 **Phn:** 800-394-5995 **Fax** 949-448-6629 Melissa Jones. Bimonthly peer-reviewed journal
92,000 to critical care personnel in private, public facilities, nursing homes, research labs.
www.ajcconline.org ajcc@aacn.org

American Jrnl. Nursing 333 7th Ave Fl 19 New York NY 10001 **Phn:** 646-674-6600 **Fax** 212-886-1206 Shawn Kennedy. Lippincott Williams & Wilkins. Monthly magazine.
354,600 to Association members, other nurses interested in all aspects of the profession.
journals.lww.com/ajnonline/ ajn@wolterskluwer.com

American Nurse 8515 Georgia Ave Ste 400 Silver Spring MD 20910 **Phn:** 301-628-5027 **Fax** 301-628-5340 Joseph Vallina. Amer. Nurses Assn. Bimonthly.
155,000 to Assn. members, other nurses interested in professional trends, legislative issues.
www.nursingworld.org taneditor@ana.org

AORN Journal 2170 S Parker Rd Ste 400 Denver CO 80231 **Phn:** 303-755-6300 **Fax** 303-750-3441 Patricia C. Seifert Assn. Perioperative Registered Nurses. Monthly mag.
44,000 to Assn. members, other OR nurses interested in OR roles, patient education. www.aorn.org
aornjournal@aorn.org

Critical Care Nurse 101 Columbia Aliso Viejo CA 92656 **Phn:** 949-362-2050 **Fax** 949-362-2049 Rebecka Ryan. Bimonthly magazine.
73,000 to acute and critical care nurses interested in practices, techniques in patient care.
ccn.aacnjournals.org ccn@aacn.org

Health Data Management 4709 Golf Rd Ste 600 Skokie IL 60076 **Phn:** **Fax** 312-913-1959 Greg Gillespie. Monthly magazine.
42,100 to execs. at hospitals, clinics, managed care cos. responsible for healthcare IT.
www.healthdatamanagement.com
greg.gillespie@sourcemedia.com

Health Facilities Mgmt. 1 N Franklin St Ste 2800 Chicago IL 60606 **Phn:** 312-893-6800 **Fax** 312-422-4500 Mike Hrickiewicz. Health Forum. Monthly mag.
33,000 to health care facility mgrs., architects, engineers, construction mgrs., environmental services personnel. www.hfmmagazine.com
mhrickiewicz@healthforum.com

Health Management Technology 2477 Stickney Point Rd. Ste. 221-B Sarasota FL 34231 **Phn:** 941-388-7050 **Fax** 941-388-7490 Michael McBride. NP Publications. Monthly mag.
42,500 to healthcare provider and payor information technology decisionmakers. www.healthmgttech.com
pcolpas@healthmgttech.com

Healthcare Executive 1 N Franklin St Ste 1700 Chicago IL 60606 **Phn:** 312-424-2800 **Fax** 312-424-0023 Nicole Voges. Amer. College Healthcare Execs. Bimo. mag.
30,600 to execs. at hospitals, long-term care facilities concerned with technology, managed care.
www.ache.org he-editor@ache.org

Healthcare Financial Mgmt. 2 Westbrook Corporate Ctr Ste 700 Westchester IL 60154 **Phn:** 708-531-9600 **Fax** 708-531-0032 Eric Reese. Monthly magazine.
31,200 to senior financial management at hospitals, HMOs, physician groups. www.hfma.org
webmaster@hfma.org

Healthcare IT News 71 Pineland Dr Ste 203 New Gloucester ME 04260 **Phn:** 207-688-6270 **Fax** 207-688-6273 Bernie Monegain. Medtech Publ. Monthly magazine.
54,000 to in/out patient healthcare facility IT mgrs. interested in products and services.
www.healthcareitnews.com
editor@healthcareitnews.com

HealthLeaders 5115 Maryland Way Brentwood TN 37027 **Phn:** 615-515-0908 **Fax** 615-515-0910 Jacqueline Fellows. HealthLeaders Media. Monthly magazine.
40,000 to sr. execs. responsible for selecting svces. at healthcare facilities & organizations.
www.healthleadersmedia.com
jfellows@healthleadersmedia.com

Home Healthcare Nurse PO Box 629 Boca Grande FL 33921 **Phn:** 941-697-2900 **Fax** 941-697-2901 Tina Marrelli. 10-issue magazine.
9,300 to home healthcare nurses, community and public health nurses.
journals.lww.com/homehealthcarenurseonline/
news@marrelli.com

Hospitals & Health Networks 1 N Franklin St Ste 2800 Chicago IL 60606 **Phn:** 312-893-6800 **Fax** 312-422-4500 Bill Santamour. Health Forum. Monthly.
70,000 to healthcare senior executives responsible for finance, technology. www.hhnmag.com
bsantamour@healthforum.com

Jrnl. Amer. Dietetic Assn. 120 S Riverside Plz Ste 2000 Chicago IL 60606 **Phn:** 312-899-0040 **Fax** 312-899-4790 Jennifer Herendeen. Monthly magazine.
70,000 to members of American Dietetic Association; nutritionists, home economists, physicians.
www.adajournal.org jherendeen@eatright.org

Jrnl. Emergency Nursing 77 Rolling Ridge Rd Amherst MA 01002 **Phn:** 413-549-1490 **Fax** 413-549-1485 Renee Holleran. Bimonthly magazine.
30,600 to emergency room nurses, dept. mgrs., other trauma staff interested in practical research and reports. www.jenonline.org reneeflightnurse@msn.com

Jrnl. Gerontological Nursing 6900 Grove Rd Thorofare NJ 08086 **Phn:** 856-848-1000 **Fax** 856-848-6091 Kathleen C Buckwalter PhD Slack, Inc. Monthly magazine.
3,500 to nurses caring for older adults interested in community healthcare, health education.
www.slackjournals.com/jgn jgn@slackinc.com

Jrnl. Midwifery & Women's Health 8403 Colesville Rd Ste 1550 Silver Spring MD 20910 **Phn:** 240-485-1800 **Fax** 240-485-1818 Frances Likis. Bimonthly magazine.
7,500 to practitioners interested in contemporary care, new research in midwiferymaternal-child healthcare.
www.jmwh.com jmwh@acnm.org

Jrnl. Nursing Administration 2000 Market St Philadelphia PA 19103 **Phn:** 215-521-8300 Karen S. Hill. 11-issue magazine.
10,000 to nurse executives & directors responsible for personnel, systems and financial management.
journals.lww.com/jonajournal/
drhillassistant@gmail.com

Jrnl. Nursing Education 6900 Grove Rd Thorofare NJ 08086 **Phn:** 856-848-1000 **Fax** 856-848-6091 Betti Bandura. Slack, Inc. Monthly magazine.
3,100 to nursing educators interested in curriculum development, education research, innovation.
www.healio.com/jne jne@slackinc.com

Jrnl. Pediatric Nursing 1540 Alcazar St # 222 Los Angeles CA 90089 **Phn:** Cecily Betz. Bimonthly magazine.
3,800 to staff and management nurses concerned with research, theory, clinical advances.
www.pediatricnursing.org cbetz@hsc.usc.edu

Managed Healthcare Executive 24950 Country Club Blvd Ste 200 North Olmsted OH 44070 **Phn:** 440-243-8100 **Fax** 440-891-2683 Julie Miller. Monthly magazine.
41,800 to healthcare organization executives responsible for quality assurance, cost containment.
managedhealthcareexecutive.modernmedicine.com
julie.miller@advanstar.com

Minority Nurse 211 W Wacker Dr Ste 900 Chicago IL 60606 **Phn:** 312-525-3095 **Fax** 312-429-3336 Pam Chwedyk. Alloy Education. Quarterly magazine.
45,000 to Afr.-Amer, Hispanic, Filipino, Native Amer., Asian-Amer.,male nursing professionals and students.
www.minoritynurse.com editor@minoritynurse.com

Modern Healthcare 150 N Michigan Ave Chicago IL 60601 **Phn:** 312-649-5200 **Fax** 312-280-3183 Gregg Blesch. Crain Communications. Weekly magazine. TH:@MHgblesch
70,100 to hospital executives responsible for managed care, finance, technology, legal, HR.
www.modernhealthcare.com
gblesch@modernhealthcare.com

Nephrology Nursing Journal PO Box 56 Pitman NJ 08071 **Phn:** 856-256-2300 **Fax** 856-589-7463 Beth Ulrich. Bimonthly magazine.
15,500 to nephrology nurses interested in research, practice and education. www.annanurse.org
anna.webeditor@inurse.com

Nursing Economics PO Box 56 Pitman NJ 08071 **Phn:** 856-256-2300 **Fax** 856-589-7463 Donna Nickitas. Bimonthly magazine.
5,500 to nursing execs., mgrs., & educators concerned with managing patient healthcare costs.
www.nursingeconomics.net nejrnl@ajj.com

Nursing Education Perspectives 61 Broadway Fl 33 New York NY 10006 **Phn:** 212-363-5555 **Fax** 212-812-0393 Leslie Block. Natl. League for Nursing. Bimo. mag.
6,000 to healthcare administrators and nursing faculties interested in education and policy.
www.nln.org/nlnjournal/index.htm journal@nln.org

Nursing Management 323 Norristown Rd Ste 200 Ambler PA 19002 **Phn:** 215-646-8700 **Fax** 215-367-2147 Kimberly Gasda. Monthly magazine.
80,000 to supervising nurses, nursing directors, hospital and clinic management.
journals.lww.com/nursingmanagement/
editor@nursingcenter.com

Hospitals--Nursing .31

Nursing2014 323 Norristown Rd Ste 200 Ambler PA 19002 **Phn:** 215-646-8700 **Fax** 215-367-2155 Linda Laskowski-Jones. Lippincott Williams & Wilkins. Monthly mag.
300,000 to nurses interested in skills enrichment; clinical & ethical issues. journals.lww.com/nursing/
nursingeditor@wolterskluwer.com

Oncology Nursing Forum 125 Enterprise Dr Pittsburgh PA 15275 **Phn:** 412-859-6100 **Fax** 412-859-6163 Susan Moore. Bimonthly magazine.
37,000 to oncology nurses interested practice, technology, education, research & leadership.
www.ons.org onfeditor@ons.org

Pediatric Nursing PO Box 56 Pitman NJ 08071 **Phn:** 856-256-2300 **Fax** 856-589-7463 Veronica D. Feeg. Bimonthly magazine.
13,900 to nurses in pediatric practice interested in research, administration, education.
www.ajj.com/services/pblshng/pnj/ pnjrnl@ajj.com

Real Living w/Multiple Sclerosis 323 Norristown Rd Ste 200 Ambler PA 19002 **Phn:** 215-628-6538 **Fax** 215-654-1328 Dan Pastorius. Bimo.
2,100 information on how to cope with the clinical and personal consequences of this disease.
pt.wkhealth.com/pt/re/lms

Rehabilitation Nursing 4700 W Lake Ave Glenview IL 60025 **Phn:** 847-375-4710 **Fax** 888-576-4349 Elaine Miller. Bimonthly magazine.
6,500 to rehab nurses interested in administration, research, resources, education. www.rehabnurse.org
info@rehabnurse.org

Trustee 155 N Wacker Dr Fl 4 Chicago IL 60606 **Phn:** 312-893-6800 **Fax** 312-422-4500 Jane Jeffries. Health Forum. 10-issue magazine.
27,000 to hospital boards responsible for representing their communities' health needs. www.trusteemag.com
jjeffries@healthforum.com

Hotels--Motels--Clubs--Restaurants .32

Catering Magazine 60 E. Rio Salado Pkwy Ste 900 Tempe AZ 85281 **Phn:** 480-366-6025 **Fax** 480-366-5801 Sara Webber. Bimonthly magazine.
10,000 to food & beverage directors, catering mgrs. & owners, event planners interested in news, products, trade shows, educati www.cateringmagazine.com
sara@cateringmagazine.com

Chef 233 N Michigan Ave Ste 1780 Chicago IL 60601 **Phn:** 312-849-2220 **Fax** 312-849-2174 Barbara Wujcik. Talcott Communications. Online only.
to institutional, commercial chefs interested in sourcing, food prep ideas, marketing.
www.chefmagazine.com bwujcik@talcott.com

Club Director 1201 15th St NW # 450 Washington DC 20005 **Phn:** 202-822-9822 **Fax** 202-822-9808 Cindy Vizza. Quarterly magazine.
6,000 to owners, officers, directors and managers of private clubs, golf and yacht clubs.
www.nationalclub.org vizza@nationalclub.org

Club Industry 9800 Metcalf Ave Overland Park KS 66212 **Phn:** 913-341-1300 **Fax** 913-967-7276 Pam Kufahl. Penton Media. Monthly magazine.
30,000 to operators of fitness clubs, YM/YWCA's, corporate rec. programs, hotel clubs. clubindustry.com
pam.kufahl@penton.com

Club Management 5950 NW 1st Pl Gainesville FL 32607 **Phn:** 352-332-1252 **Fax** 352-331-3525 Jill Andreu. Naylor Publs. Bimonthly magazine.
15,500 to management personnel at golf, country, yacht, athletic, military clubs, resorts. www.naylor.com
jandreu@naylor.com

El Restaurante Mexicano PO Box 2249 Oak Park IL 60303 **Phn:** 708-488-0100 **Fax** 708-488-0101 Kathleen Furore. Quarterly magazine.
21,000 Bilingual English/Spanish magazine to operators of Mexican & southwestern menu restaurants. www.restmex.com kfurore@restmex.com

Food Arts 387 Park Ave S New York NY 10016 **Phn:** 212-684-4224 **Fax** 212-779-3334 Beverly Stephen. M. Shanken Comms. Monthly magazine.
55,300 to restaurant chefs, hotel/club food & beverage mgrs., caterers responsible for fine service.
www.foodarts.com bstephen@mshanken.com

Food Logistics 3 Huntington Quad Ste 301N Melville NY 11747 **Phn:** 914-831-9046 **Fax** 866-745-2047 Katherine Doherty. Cygnus Business Media. 9-issue magazine.
20,000 to food distribution industry mgmt. in logistics, supply chain, e-business functions.
www.foodlogistics.com kdoherty@foodlogistics.com

Food Management 1300 E 9th St Ste 316 Cleveland OH 44114 **Phn:** 216-931-9620 John Lawn. Penton Media. Monthly magazine.
47,000 to institutional foodservice directors in schools, nursing homes, hospitals, hotels, resorts. food-management.com john.lawn@penton.com

Foodservice Equipment & Supplies 110 E Schiller St Ste 312 Elmhurst IL 60126 **Phn:** 800-630-4168 **Fax** 800-630-4169 Joe Carbonara. Zoomba Group. Monthly magazine.
22,000 to food equipment & supply mfrs. & providers interested in news about operators, E&S dealers, facility designers. www.fesmag.com
joe@zoombagroup.com

Foodservice Director 1 Tower Ln Ste 200 Oakbrook Terrace IL 60181 **Phn:** 630-574-5075 **Fax** 630-574-5175 Becky Schilling. CSP Business Media. Monthly tabloid. TH:@fsdeditor
45,100 to foodservice professionals in hospitals, nursing homes, schools, military institutions.
www.foodservicedirector.com hp@penton.com

Foodservice East 197 8th St Apt 728 Charlestown MA 02129 **Phn:** 617-242-2217 Susan Holaday. 6-issue tabloid.
14,000 to NE U.S. foodservice managers interested in trend analysis, operational, product info.
www.foodserviceeast.com
susan@foodserviceeast.com

Foodservice Equipment Reports 2906 Central St Ste 175 Evanston IL 60201 **Phn:** 847-673-8675 Megan Hernandez. Monthly magazine.
25,000 to equipment specifiers interested in menus, kitchen layouts, trade shows, news.
www.fermag.com fsreport@fermag.com

Hospitality Design 770 Broadway Fl 5 New York NY 10003 **Phn:** 646-654-4500 **Fax** 646-654-7626 Michael Adams. Nielsen Business Media. 10-issue magazine.
30,100 to designers, architects, contractors for lodging, restaurant chains, casinos, senior facilities.
www.hospitalitydesign.com
madams@hospitalitydesign.com

Hospitality Technology 4 Middlebury Blvd Randolph NJ 07869 **Phn:** 973-252-0100 **Fax** 973-252-9020 Abigail Lorden. Edgell Communications. 9-issue magazine.
16,100 to foodservice, lodging operations mgrs. interested in P-O-S & back office systems.
hospitalitytechnology.edgl.com
alorden@edgellmail.com

Hotel & Motel Management 600 Superior Ave E Ste 1100 Cleveland OH 44114 **Phn:** 216-706-3700 **Fax** 216-706-3711 Paul J. Henry. Questex Media. 15-issue tabloid.
57,600 to lodging execs. responsible for finance, technology, food service, security, design.
www.hotelmanagement.net pheney@questex.com

Hotel Business 45 Research Way Ste 106 East Setauket NY 11733 **Phn:** 631-246-9300 **Fax** 631-246-9496 Stefani C. O'Connor. ICD Publications. Semimonthly tabloid.
40,500 to lodging industry professionals interested in financial analysis pertinent to industry.
www.hotelbusiness.com stefanio@hotelbusiness.com

Hotel Design 757 3rd Ave Fl 5 New York NY 10017 **Phn:** 212-895-8436 Dave Eisen. Questex Media. 8 issues.
12,600 to execs., architects, designers interested in openings, developments, industry events.
www.hotelmanagement.net deisen@questex.com

Hotels Magazine 1415 N Dayton St Chicago IL 60642 **Phn:** 312-266-3311 **Fax** 312-266-3363 Jeffrey Weinstein. Marketing & Technology Group. Monthly magazine.
55,000 to hotel mgmt. staff responsible for design, operations, food serivce, finance, technology.
www.hotelsmag.com jweinstein@hotelsmag.com

The Independent Restaurateur PO Box 917 Newark OH 43058 **Phn:** 740-345-5542 **Fax** 740-345-5557 Mara Miller. Pinnacle Publ. Bimonthly magazine.
46,000 to U.S. independent restaurant owners interested in staffing, menus, equipment, technology, marketing. theindependentrestaurateur.com
editor@theindependentrestaurateur.com

Lodging 385 Oxford Valley Rd Ste 420 Yardley PA 19067 **Phn:** 215-321-9662 **Fax** 215-321-5124 Sean Downey. Amer. Hotel & Lodging Assn. Monthly magazine.
32,000 to Assn. members responsible for technology, real estate, legal, human resources.
Lodgingmagazine.com
sdowney@lodgingmagazine.com

Nation's Restaurant News 1166 Ave of the Americas Fl 10 New York NY 10036 **Phn:** 212-204-4200 **Fax** 212-206-3622 Sarah Lockyer. Penton Media. Biweekly tabloid.
60,000 to mgmt. at restaurants, healthcare facilities, hotels interested in menus, nutrition trends.
www.nrn.com sarah.lockyer@penton.com

Nightclub & Bar 10 Marwood Dr Hauppauge NY 11788 **Phn:** 631-265-3839 **Fax** 261-706-3710 Donna Hood Crecca. Questex Media. Monthly magazine.
35,000 to club operators interested in promotions, market rsch., drink, entertainment trends.
www.nightclub.com dcrecca@questex.com

Nutrition & Foodservice Edge 406 Surrey Woods Dr St Charles IL 60174 **Phn:** 630-587-6336 **Fax** 630-587-6308 Diane Everett. Assn of Nutrition & Foodservice Profs. 10-issue magazine. **TH:**@nourishandgrow
15,000 to institutional foodservice managers responsible for therapeutic menus, health, new product choices. www.anfponline.org deverett@anfponline.org

On-Campus Hospitality 825 Old Country Rd Westbury NY 11590 **Phn:** 516-334-3030 **Fax** 516-334-8958 Gregg Wallis. Exec. Business Media. 9-issue magazine.
9,500 to college, university foodservice professionals responsible for contracts, nutrition. www.ebmpubs.com gregg@ebmpubs4.com

Plate 1415 N. Dayton St. Chicago IL 60642 **Phn:** 312-266-3311 **Fax** 312-266-3363 Bill McDowell. Bimonthly magazine.
25,000 to chefs & foodservice professionals responsible for menu development, food quality.
www.plateonline.com bmcdowell@meatingplace.com

Private Clubs 3030 Lyndon B Johnson Fwy Ste 350 Dallas TX 75234 **Phn:** 972-888-7547 **Fax** 972-888-7338 Don Nichols. ClubCorp Publ. Quarterly.
198,000 to affluent readers who are members of country clubs, resorts, other private clubs.
www.privateclubs.com privateclubs@clubcorp.com

QSR Magazine 4905 Pine Cone Dr Ste 2 Durham NC 27707 **Phn:** 919-489-1916 **Fax** 919-489-4767 Ellen Koteff. Monthly magazine.
30,500 to quick service restaurant mgmt. responsible for F&B, technology, equipment, training.
www.qsrmagazine.com ellen@qsrmagazine.com

Hotels--Motels--Clubs--Restaurants .32

Restaurant Business 90 Broad St Ste 402 New York NY 10004 **Phn:** 503-746-8455 **Fax** 630-574-5175 Kelly Killian. Monthly magazine. **TH:**@RB_magazine
76,100 to restaurant decisionmakers responsible for food, equipment, supplies, services.
www.restaurantbusinessonline.com
kkillian@cspnet.com

Restaurant Development & Design 110 E Schiller St Ste 312 Elmhurst IL 60126 **Phn:** 800-630-4168 **Fax** 800-630-4169 Joe Carbonara. Zoomba Group. Quarterly magazine. **TH:**@RDDmag
20,000 to multi-unit restaurant executives responsible for expansion; architects, contractors & designers.
www.rddmag.com joe@zoombagroup.com

Restaurant Hospitality 1300 E 9th St Cleveland OH 44114 **Phn:** 216-931-9571 **Fax** 216-696-0836 Michael Sanson. Penton Media. Monthly magazine.
100,000 to chefs & restaurant managers responsible for recipes, menus, safety, human resources.
restaurant-hospitality.com mike.sanson@penton.com

Restaurant Startup & Growth 5201 NW Crooked Rd Kansas City MO 64152 **Phn:** 816-741-5151 **Fax** 816-741-6458 Barry Shuster. Monthly magazine.
40,000 to start-up restauranteurs interested in specific how-to features. www.rsgmag.com barry@spc-mag.com

Southeast Food Service News PO Box 1504 Tucker GA 30085 **Phn:** 678-395-6270 John Hayward. SE Publishing. 8-issue tabloid.
19,000 to SE U.S. foodservice personnel at chains, clubs, hotels/motels, schools, caterers. www.sfsn.com jhayward@sfsn.com

Southwest Food Service News 4011 W Plano Pkwy Ste 121 Plano TX 75093 **Phn:** 972-943-1254 **Fax** 972-943-1258 Pat Dodge. Bimonthly tabloid.
16,000 to TX & SW U.S. foodservice personnel at chains, clubs, hotels/motels, schools.
www.southwestfoodservice.com
info@southwestfoodservice.com

Total Food Service 282 Railroad Ave Greenwich CT 06830 **Phn:** 203-661-9090 **Fax** 203-661-9325 Fred Klashman. Monthly tabloid.
30,000 to NY/NJ/CT area restaurant, lodging, healthcare foodservice personnel. www.totalfood.com tfs@totalfood.com

Industrial .33

Adhesives & Sealants Industry PO Box 2148 Ann Arbor MI 48106 **Phn:** 734-332-0541 **Fax** 248-502-2102 Teresa McPherson. BNP Media. Monthly magazine.
15,000 to adhesive/sealant mfrs. concerned with R&D, engineering, administration. www.adhesivesmag.com mcphersont@bnpmedia.com

Air Pollution Control 1155 Northland Drive St. Paul MN 55120 **Phn:** 651-287-5600 **Fax** 651-287-5650 Jan Brenny. CSC Publishing, Inc. 8-issue magazine. **TH:**@APCMagEditor
35,000 to environmental engineers, compliance personnel responsible for air pollution control in industrial settings. www.apcmag.net
jbrenny@cscpub.com

APICS 8430 W Bryn Mawr Ave Ste 1000 Chicago IL 60631 **Phn:** 800-444-2742 **Fax** 773-867-1777 Jennifer Proctor. Assn. for Operations Mgmt. Bimonthly magazine.
50,000 to mid & upper mgmt. in mfg., production, supply chain mgmt., warehousing. www.apics.org editorial@apics.org

CM/Cleanfax 19 British American Blvd W Latham NY 12110 **Phn:** 518-783-1281 **Fax** 518-783-1386 Jeff Cross. NTP Media. Bimo.
25,300 covers cleaning, disaster restoration, smoke, fire, mold, water damage, carpets, ducts.
www.cleanfax.com jcross@cleanfax.com

Filtration News 42400 Grand River Ave Ste 103 Novi MI 48375 **Phn:** 248-347-3486 Ken Norberg. Eagle Publications. Bimonthly magazine.
31,500 to facility mgrs. responsible for air, liquid, gas filtration processes, new technologies.
www.filtnews.com ken@filtnews.com

Flow Control 200 Croft St # 1 Birmingham AL 35242 **Phn:** 205-408-3700 **Fax** 205-408-3797 Matt Migliore. Grand View Media. Monthly.
40,800 covers the technologies that measure, control and contain liquids, gases and powders.
www.flowcontrolnetwork.com
matt@grandviewmedia.com

Fluid Power Journal 3245 Freemansburg Ave Palmer PA 18045 **Phn:** 610-923-0380 **Fax** 610-923-0390 Kristine Coblitz. Innovative Designs & Publ. Bimonthly mag.
28,000 to engineers, technicians, mechanics who design, install, maintain fluid power systems.
www.fluidpowerjournal.com
kcoblitz@fluidpowerjournal.com

Hydraulics & Pneumatics 1300 E 9th St Cleveland OH 44114 **Phn:** 216-696-7000 **Fax** 216-696-1819 Alan Hitchcox. Penton Media. Monthly magazine.
50,400 to fluid power systems engineers, designers, technicians, manufacturers, processors.
www.hydraulicspneumatics.com hp@penton.com

IEEE Industry Applications 445 Hoes Ln Piscataway NJ 08854 **Phn:** 732-981-0060 **Fax** 732-981-1855 Louis Powell. Bimonthly magazine.
10,100 to electronic engineers in petroleum, chemical, plastic, textile, mining industries. www.ieee.org louie.powell@ieee.org

Industrial Engineer 3577 Parkway Ln Ste 200 Norcross GA 30092 **Phn:** 770-449-0461 **Fax** 770-263-8532 Michael Hughes.
15,600 to industrial engineers & mgrs. in mfg. responsible for supply chain mgmt., planning, ergonomics, IT systems. www.iienet.org/IEmagazine mhughes@iienet.org

Industrial Equipment News 90 W Afton Ave Ste 117 Yardley PA 19067 **Phn:** 770-428-6847 **Fax** 888-603-8963 Todd Baker. TCC Media Group. Monthly magazine.
200,000 to mfg. & processing industry personnel interested in new products & services. www.ien.com editorial@ien.com

Industrial Maintenance/Plant Op. 199 E Badger Rd Ste 201 Madison WI 53713 **Phn:** 973-920-7789 **Fax** 608-274-6454 Jeff Reinke. Advantage Business Media. Monthly magazine.
99,900 to plant maintenance, operating, engineering personnel interested in new products.
www.impomag.com jeff.reinke@advantagemedia.com

Locksmith Ledger International 12735 Morris Road Ext Ste 200 Alpharetta GA 30004 **Phn:** 800-547-7377 Emily Pike. Cygnus Business Media. Monthly mag.
11,900 to mfrs., retailers, distributors in physical and electronic security industry. www.locksmithledger.com emily.pike@cygnusb2b.com

Lubes 'N Greases 6105 Arlington Blvd # G Falls Church VA 22044 **Phn:** 703-536-0800 **Fax** 703-536-0803 Lisa Tocci. LNG Publishing. Monthly magazine.
15,800 to personnel working with lubricants for metals, heavy duty vehicles, passenger cars.
www.lngpublishing.com lisa@lngpublishing.com

Machine Design 1300 E 9th St Cleveland OH 44114 **Phn:** 216-696-7000 **Fax** 216-621-8469 Ken Korane. Penton Media. Semimonthly magazine.
180,000 to design engineers interested in current technical coverage, mgmt. information.
machinedesign.com ken.korane@penton.com

Maintenance Technology 1300 S Grove Ave Ste 105 Barrington IL 60010 **Phn:** 847-382-8100 **Fax** 847-304-8603 Jane Alexander. Applied Tech. Pubs. Monthly.
52,100 to engineers and technicians responsible for plant equipment maintenance. www.mt-online.com jalexander@atpnetwork.com

Manufacturers' Mart PO Box 310 Georgetown MA 01833 **Phn:** 800-835-0017 **Fax** 978-352-4829 Phil Cannon. 11-issue newspaper.
18,300 to mgmt., maintenance, purchasing personnel in New England mfg. plants.
www.manufacturersmart.com
info@manufacturersmart.com

Material Handling & Logistics 1300 E 9th St Cleveland OH 44114 **Phn:** 216-696-7000 **Fax** 216-696-2737 Tom Andel. Penton Media. Monthly magazine.
69,400 to personnel responsible for material handling in manufacturing, warehousing, distribution.
mhlnews.com tom.andel@penton.com

Material Handling Network 2407 Washington Rd Ste A Washington IL 61571 **Phn:** 309-699-4431 **Fax** 309-698-0801 Bob Behrens. Monthly tabloid.
9,600 to manufacturers, dealers, suppliers of new and used material handling equipment.
www.mhnetwork.com mhnetwork@wcinet.com

Materials Evaluation PO Box 28518 Columbus OH 43228 **Phn:** 614-274-6003 **Fax** 614-274-6899 Toni Kervina. Monthly magazine.
12,000 to members of Amer. Soc. for Nondestructive Testing; engineers, physicists, R&D staff. www.asnt.org tkervina@asnt.org

Mechanical Engineering 3 Park Ave Fl 22 New York NY 10016 **Phn:** 212-591-7783 Harry Hutchinson. Amer. Soc. Mech. Engineers. Monthly magazine.
100,400 to engineers & execs. working with mechanical & electro-mechanical systems.
www.memagazine.org memag@asme.org

Modern Materials Handling 111 Speen St Ste 200 Framingham MA 01701 **Phn:** 508-663-1500 **Fax** 508-663-1599 Noel Bodenburg. EH Publishing Network. Monthly magazine.
81,000 to mgmt. personnel responsible for transport, import/export, containerization, site selection, warehousing. www.mmh.com modernedit@ehpub.com

National Locksmith 1533 Burgundy Pkwy Streamwood IL 60107 **Phn:** 630-837-2044 **Fax** 630-837-1210 Greg Mango. Monthly magazine.
10,500 to locksmiths, physical security personnel concerned with technical, service information.
www.TheNationalLocksmith.com sales@thenationallocksmith.com

New Equipment Digest 1300 E 9th St Cleveland OH 44114 **Phn:** 216-696-7000 Robert King. Penton Media. Monthly tabloid.
200,000 to industrial admin., production, purchasing personnel interested in new products.
www.newequipment.com bob.king@penton.com

Plant Engineering 1111 W 22nd St Ste 250 Oak Brook IL 60523 **Phn:** 630-571-4070 **Fax** 630-214-4504 Bob Vavra. CFE Media. 10-issue magazine.
70,000 to plant engineering and maintenance mgmt. responsible for materials handling, power, OSHA compliance. www.plantengineering.com bvavra@cfemedia.com

Plant Services 555 W Pierce Rd Ste 301 Itasca IL 60143 **Phn:** 630-467-1300 **Fax** 630-467-0197 Mike Bacidore. Putman Media. Monthly magazine.
80,100 to plant personnel in maintenance, engineering, environment, material handling.
www.plantservices.com mbacidore@putman.net

Product Design & Development 199 E Badger Rd Ste 201 Madison WI 53713 **Phn:** 973-920-7790 **Fax** 608-274-6454 David Mantey. Advantage Business Media. Mo.
140,000 to design engineers interested in components, systems, products. www.pddnet.com david.mantey@advantagemedia.com

Pumps & Systems 1900 28th Ave S Ste 110 Birmingham AL 35209 **Phn:** 205-212-9402 **Fax** 205-212-9452 Michelle Segrest. Monthly mag.
35,400 to buyers and users of industrial pumping systems, distributors and manufacturers. www.pump-zone.com msegrest@pump-zone.com

Quality 1050 Il Route 83 Ste 200 Bensenville IL 60106 **Phn:** 630-616-0200 **Fax** 630-227-0204 Gillian Campbell. BNP Media. Monthly magazine.
64,000 to mfg. and engineering mgrs., chief inspectors, quality assurance mgrs.
www.qualitymag.com campbellg@bnpmedia.com

Industrial .33

Quality Progress 600 N Plankinton Ave Milwaukee WI 53203 **Phn:** 414-272-8575 **Fax** 414-272-1734 Seiche Sanders. Monthly magazine.
84,000 to quality assurance, quality control engineers; inspectors, research directors; educators.
asq.org/qualityprogress/ ssanders@asq.org

Rubber & Plastics News 1725 Merriman Rd Ste 300 Akron OH 44313 **Phn:** 330-836-9180 **Fax** 330-836-2831 Edward Noga. Crain Communications. Biweekly tab.
16,100 to rubber product mfrs. and others in rubber-related industries in the US and Canada.
www.rubbernews.com enoga@crain.com

Rubber World PO Box 5451 Akron OH 44334 **Phn:** 330-864-2122 **Fax** 330-864-5298 Don Smith. Lippincott & Peto, Inc. Monthly magazine.
10,600 to manufacturers of rubber products; machinery and equipment used with rubber; allied fields. www.rubberworld.com don@rubberworld.com

Surplus Record 20 N Wacker Dr Chicago IL 60606 **Phn:** 312-372-9077 **Fax** 312-372-6537 Thomas P. Scanlan. Monthly magazine.
66,700 to industrial machinery and equip. buyers interested in used/surplus items for sale.
www.surplusrecord.com surplus@surplusrecord.com

Tribology & Lubrication Tech. 840 Busse Hwy Park Ridge IL 60068 **Phn:** 847-825-5536 **Fax** 847-825-1456 Karl Phipps. Soc. Tribologists & Lubrication Engineers. Monthly magazine.
7,000 to Society members interested in technical education, professional development, Society news.
www.stle.org kphipps@stle.org

Valve Magazine 1050 17th St NW Ste 280 Washington DC 20036 **Phn:** 202-331-8105 **Fax** 202-296-0378 Judith Tibbs. Valve Mfrs. Assn. of Amer. Quarterly magazine.
24,900 to industrial valve and actuator end users interested new products, applications & maintenance.
www.valvemagazine.com jtibbs@vma.org

Weighing & Measurement PO Box 2247 Hendersonville TN 37077 **Phn:** 615-824-6920 **Fax** 615-824-7092 David Mathieu. Bimonthly magazine.
9,700 to buyers, sellers of industrial measuring and weighing instruments, regulatory officials.
wammag.com

Wire & Cable Technology Intl. 1867 W Market St Akron OH 44313 **Phn:** 330-864-2122 **Fax** 330-864-5298 Michael McNulty. Bimonthly magazine.
10,100 to wire mfg. personnel responsible for production, R&D, quality control, finance, sales.
www.wiretech.com mcnulty@wiretech.com

Wire Journal International PO Box 578 Guilford CT 06437 **Phn:** 203-453-2777 **Fax** 203-453-8384 Mark Marselli. Monthly magazine.
12,400 to mgmt. & technical personnel in manufacture of electrical wire, fiber optic cable. www.wirenet.org

Safety & Security .33a

Campus Safety 111 Speen St Ste 200 Framingham MA 01701 **Phn:** 508-663-1500 **Fax** 508-663-1599 Robin Hattersley Gray. EH Publishing Network. 7-issue magazine. TH:@RobinHattSmiles
18,200 to campus police chiefs, security directors, emergency mgrs. responsible for public safety at colleges, hospitals, schoo
www.campussafetymagazine.com/default.aspx rhattersley@ehpub.com

EHS Today 1300 E 9th St Cleveland OH 44114 **Phn:** 216-696-7000 **Fax** 216-696-8208 Sandy Smith. Penton Media. Monthly magazine.
83,100 to industrial hygiene, safety, security management responsible for OSHA and EPA compliance. ehstoday.com sandy.smith@penton.com

Industrial Hygiene News 8650 Babcock Blvd Pittsburgh PA 15237 **Phn:** 412-364-5366 **Fax** 412-369-9720 Raquel Rimbach. Rimbach Publishing. Bimonthly tabloid.
68,200 to indus. hygiene, health/safety personnel interested in products, services, trade shows.
www.rimbach.com info@rimbach.com

Industrial Safety & Hygiene News 2401 W Big Beaver Rd Ste 700 Troy MI 48084 **Phn:** 610-409-0954 **Fax** 248-502-1087 Maureen Brady. BNP Media. Monthly tabloid.
71,400 to safety, security, accident, fire, mgmt. personnel with purchasing responsibility.
www.ishn.com bradym@bnpmedia.com

Occupational Health & Safety 14901 Quorum Dr Ste 425 Dallas TX 75254 **Phn:** 972-687-6701 **Fax** 972-687-6770 Jerry Laws. 1105 Media. Monthly mag.
80,000 to health & industrial safety mgrs. concerned with workplace injury, illness, hazards. ohsonline.com jlaws@1105media.com

Professional Safety 1800 E Oakton St Des Plaines IL 60018 **Phn:** 847-699-2929 **Fax** 847-296-3769 Sue Trebswether. Amer. Soc. Safety Engineers. Monthly mag.
30,500 to environmental, health, safety personnel interested in regulatory news, best practices.
www.asse.org professionalsafety@asse.org

Safety & Health 1121 Spring Lake Dr Itasca IL 60143 **Phn:** 630-285-1121 **Fax** 630-285-1315 Melissa Ruminski. Natl. Safety Council. Monthly magazine.
71,700 to health and safety specialists in business, government, military, utilities, insurance. www.nsc.org melissa.ruminski@nsc.org

Security 155 Pfingsten Rd, Ste 205 Deerfield IL 60015 **Phn:** 630-616-0200 **Fax** 630-227-0214 Diane Ritchey. BNP Media. Monthly magazine.
35,000 to security mgmt. personnel in corporate, govt., transportation, military environments.
www.securitymagazine.com ritcheyd@bnpmedia.com

Security Dealer & Integrator 12735 Morris Road Ext Ste 200 Alpharetta GA 30004 **Phn:** 800-547-7377 Paul Rothman. Cygnus Business Media. Monthly magazine.
30,000 to alarm industry personnel interested in trends, products, sales, industry news.
www.securityinfowatch.com paul.rothman@cygnus.com

Security Distributing & Mktg. 155 N Pfingsten Rd Ste 205 Deerfield IL 60015 **Phn:** 610-436-4220 **Fax** 248-244-2042 Laura Stepanek. BNP Media. Monthly mag.
28,500 to electronic security installation personnel interested in technical & marketing info.
www.sdmmag.com stepanekl@bnpmedia.com

Security Management 1625 Prince St Alexandria VA 22314 **Phn:** 703-519-6200 **Fax** 703-518-1518 Sherry Harowitz. Amer. Soc. Industrial Security. Monthly magazine.
32,100 to security personnel concerned with exec. protection, access control, physical security.
www.securitymanagement.com smeditorial@asisonline.org

Security Products 14901 Quorum Dr Ste 425 Dallas TX 75254 **Phn:** 972-687-6700 **Fax** 972-687-6770 Ralph Jensen. 1105 Media. Monthly tabloid.
70,100 to industrial, mfg., retail & govt. new technology buyers & specifiers. secprodonline.com rjensen@1105media.com

Security Sales & Integration 111 Speen St Ste 200 Framingham MA 01701 **Phn:** 508-663-1500 **Fax** 508-663-1599 Scott Goldfine. EH Publishing Network. Monthly magazine. TH:@SSIEditor
28,000 to home and commercial security industry sales, marketing, and mgmt. personnel.
www.securitysales.com scott.goldfine@securitysales.com

Security Systems News PO Box 998 Yarmouth ME 04096 **Phn:** 207-846-0600 **Fax** 207-846-0657 Martha Entwistle. Monthly magazine.
28,100 to security & fire system dealers, installers, consultants interested in news & issues.
www.securitysystemsnews.com mentwistle@securitysystemsnews.com

Security Technology Executive 12735 Morris Road Ext Ste 200 Alpharetta GA 30004 **Phn:** 800-547-7377 Paul Rothman. Cygnus Business Media. Monthly. **34,000** to physical security decisionmakers interested in technical features and information. www.securityinfowatch.com paul.rothman@cygnusb2b.com

Synergist 2700 Prosperity Ave Ste 250 Fairfax VA 22031 **Phn:** 703-849-8888 **Fax** 703-207-3561 Ed Rutkowski. Amer. Industrial Hygiene Assn. 11-issue magazine. **10,000** to Assn. members responsible for OSHA/EPA enforcement, ergonomics, risk assessing. www.aiha.org erutkowski@aiha.org

Workplace HR & Safety 8120 Woodmont Ave Bethesda MD 20814 **Phn:** 850-936-0200 **Fax** 850-684-1422 Elizabeth Hintch. Columbia Books, LLC. Online only. TH:@WorkplaceHRSafe for industrial personnel responsible for workplace safety, health, environmental regulations. www.workplacemagazine.com bhintch@columbiabooks.com

Science--Research & Development .33b

American Laboratory 30 Controls Dr Shelton CT 06484 **Phn:** 203-926-9300 **Fax** 203-926-9310 Susan Messinger. Compare Networks, Inc. Online only. to chemists, biologists in applied/basic research fields; scientific instrument mfrs. www.americanlaboratory.com smessinger@americanlaboratory.com

American Scientist PO Box 13975 Research Triangle Park NC 27709 **Phn:** 919-549-0097 **Fax** 919-549-0090 David Schoonmaker. Scientific Research Soc. Bimonthly magazine. **77,000** to Soc. members, other scientists interested in developments in all scientific disciplines. www.americanscientist.org editors@amsci.org

Applied Spectroscopy 5320 Spectrum Dr Ste C Frederick MD 21703 **Phn:** 301-694-8122 **Fax** 301-694-6860 Peter Griffiths. Society for Applied Spectroscopy. Monthly magazine. **2,700** to Society members interested in orginial research, job listings, Society news. www.s-a-s.org office@s-a-s.org

Bio-IT World 250 1st Ave Ste 300 Needham MA 02494 **Phn:** 781-972-5400 **Fax** 781-972-5425 Kevin Davies PhD. Bimonthly. **27,000** to life science R&D/IT decisionmakers responsible for IT infrastructure systems, software, services. www.bio-itworld.com kevin_davies@bio-itworld.com

Bioscience 1444 I St NW Ste 200 Washington DC 20005 **Phn:** 202-628-1500 **Fax** 202-628-1509 Timothy Beardsley. Amer. Inst. of Biological Sciences. Monthly mag. **6,000** to life scientists interested in book reviews, essays, editorials, events. www.aibs.org/bioscience/ tbeardsley@aibs.org

Biotechniques 52 Vanderbilt Ave Fl 7 New York NY 10017 **Phn:** 212-520-2775 **Fax** 212-661-5052 Nathan Blow. Informa Healthcare USA. Monthly mag. **90,400** to lab scientists in basic & applied bioresearch in universities, hospitals, industry. www.biotechniques.com nathan.blow@informausa.com

Cell 600 Technology Sq Ste 5 Cambridge MA 02139 **Phn:** 617-661-7057 **Fax** 617-397-2810 Emilie Marcus. Biweekly magazine. **20,100** to bioscientists in fields of molecular cell biology, immunology, research, new theories. www.cell.com celleditor@cell.com

Earth 4220 King St Alexandria VA 22302 **Phn:** 703-379-2480 **Fax** 703-379-7563 Megan Sever. Amer. Geological Inst. Monthly magazine. **10,000** to geoscientists, earth science educators interested in events, news, research, books. www.earthmagazine.com msever@earthmagazine.org

Safety & Security .33a

Genetic Engineering/Biotech News 140 Huguenot St Fl 3 New Rochelle NY 10801 **Phn:** 914-740-2196 **Fax** 914-740-2201 John Sterling. 21-issue tabloid. **65,000** to R&D scientists interested in govt. & university reports, funding sources, products. www.genengnews.com jsterling@genengnews.com

Genome Technology 40 Fulton St Fl 10 New York NY 10038 **Phn:** 212-269-4747 **Fax** 212-269-3686 Ciara Curtin. GenomeWeb LLC. Monthly magazine. **30,000** to molecular biology scientists interested in research, technology, academia, job opportunities. www.biotechniques.com editorial@genomeweb.com

Lab Animal 75 Varick St Fl 9 New York NY 10013 **Phn:** 212-726-9200 **Fax** 212-696-9481 Monica Harrington. Nature Publishing Group. **10,200** to users of lab animals in biomedical, toxicology, medical education research. www.labanimal.com editors@labanimal.com

Laboratory Equipment 100 Enterprise Dr Ste 600 Rockaway NJ 07866 **Phn:** 973-920-7000 **Fax** 973-920-7542 Tim Studt. Advantage Business Media. Monthly tabloid. **73,000** to specifying and purchasing personnel at industrial, government, educational labs. www.laboratoryequipment.com tim.studt@advantagemedia.com

LC GC North America 485 US Highway 1 S Fl 1 # F Iselin NJ 08830 **Phn:** 732-225-9500 **Fax** 732-596-0003 David Walsh. Advanstar. 13-issue magazine. **50,100** to analytical chemists working with liquid and gas chromatography instrumentation. chromatographyonline.findanalytichem.com lcgcedit@lcgcmag.com

MIT Technology Review 1 Main St Ste 13 Cambridge MA 02142 **Phn:** 617-475-8000 **Fax** 617-475-8042 David Rotman. Mass. Inst. of Tech. Bimo. **181,000** covers emerging technologies, impact for venture capital lenders, sr. technologists, innovators. technologyreview.com kathleen.kennedy@technologyreview.com

Nature Biotechnology 75 Varick St Fl 9 New York NY 10013 **Phn:** 212-726-9200 **Fax** 212-696-9481 Andrew Marshall. Monthly magazine. **14,600** to molecular biologists, microbiologists, immunologists, pharmacologists in R&D. www.nature.com/nbt/ biotech@us.nature.com

Optics & Photonics News 2010 Massachusetts Ave NW Washington DC 20036 **Phn:** 202-223-8130 **Fax** 202-416-6134 Christina Folz. Optical Soc. of Amer. Monthly magazine. **26,200** to Society members in fields of fiber optics, laser science, spectroscopy. www.osa-opn.org opn@osa.org

Physics Today 1 Physics Ellipse College Park MD 20740 **Phn:** 301-209-3040 **Fax** 301-209-0842 Stephen Benka. Amer. Inst. of Physics. Monthly mag. **121,700** to Institute members, physics, nuclear energy researchers, teachers interested in news. www.physicstoday.org pteditors@aip.org

R & D 100 Enterprise Dr Bx 912 # 600 Rockaway NJ 07866 **Phn:** 973-920-7000 **Fax** 973-920-7542 Lindsay Hock. Advantage Business Media. 7-issue magazine. **80,000** to govt. and industry research and development scientists, engineers, technical mgrs. www.rdmag.com lindsay.hock@advantagemedia.com

Science 1200 New York Ave NW Washington DC 20005 **Phn:** 202-326-6500 **Fax** 202-371-9227 Monica Bradford. Amer. Assn. for Advancement of Science. Weekly. **131,300** to scientists, policymakers, journalists interested in developments in scientific disciplines. www.sciencemag.org science_editors@aaas.org

Science News 1719 N St NW Washington DC 20036 **Phn:** 202-785-2255 **Fax** 202-659-0365 Tom Siegfried. Biweekly magazine. **128,400** to readers interested in developments & applications in all fields of science. www.societyforscience.org editors@sciencenews.org

Scientist 415 Madison Ave # 1508 New York NY 10017 **Phn:** 705-526-6888 Mary Beth Aberlin. LabX Media Group. Monthly magazine. **55,000** to research life scientists interested in news, current developments and analysis. www.the-scientist.com eic@the-scientist.com

Skeptical Inquirer PO Box 703 Amherst NY 14226 **Phn:** 716-636-1425 **Fax** 716-636-1733 Benjamin Bradford. Bimonthly. **50,000** covers paranormal and fringe-science claims from a responsible, scientific point of view. www.csicop.org bradford@centerforinquiry.net

Weatherwise 1319 18th St NW Washington DC 20036 **Phn:** 202-296-6267 **Fax** 202-296-5149 Margaret Benner. Bimonthly magazine. **12,500** to general public interested in weather articles, photos, technology. www.weatherwise.org margaret.benner@taylorandfrancis.com

Insurance .34

Advisor Today 2901 Telestar Ct Falls Church VA 22042 **Phn:** 703-770-8100 **Fax** 703-770-8212 Ayo Mseka. Natl. Assn. Insurance & Financial Advisors. Mo. mag. **85,200** to Assn. members, life & health insurance agents interested in mktg. & practice mgmt. vttp://www.advisortoday.com amseka@naifa.org

American Agent & Broker 222 S Riverside Plz Ste 620 Chicago IL 60606 **Phn:** 312-651-0372 **Fax** 312-846-4638 Laura M. Toops. Summit Prof. Networks. Monthly magazine. **40,000** to property/casualty agents and brokers interested in sales, management, technology. www.propertycasualty360.com ltoops@sbmedia.com

Best's Review Ambest Rd Oldwick NJ 08858 **Phn:** 908-439-2200 **Fax** 908-439-3363 Lynna Goch. A.M. Best Publications. Monthly magazine. **48,900** to insurance co. mgmt., agents, brokers interested in product lines, technology, news. www.bestreview.com editor_br@ambest.com

Broker World 9404 Reeds Rd Overland Park KS 66207 **Phn:** 913-383-9191 **Fax** 913-383-1247 Sharon Chace. Insurance Publications, Inc. Monthly magazine. **30,500** to life and health agents, brokers interested in products, sales technology, market developments. www.brokerworldmag.com schace@brokerworldmag.com

Business Insurance 360 N Michigan Ave Chicago IL 60601 **Phn:** 312-649-5398 **Fax** 312-280-3174 Gavin Souter. Crain Communications. Weekly tabloid. **45,600** to execs. responsible for purchase of corp. property, casualty, employee benefit products. www.businessinsurance.com gsouter@businessinsurance.com

California Broker 217 E Alameda Ave Ste 301 Burbank CA 91502 **Phn:** 818-848-2957 **Fax** 818-843-3489 Leila Morris. Monthly magazine. **25,000** to life and health brokers, planners concerned with product development, govt. regulations. www.calbrokermag.com editor@calbrokermag.com

Claims 5081 Olympic Blvd Erlanger KY 41018 **Phn:** 859-692-2198 **Fax** 859-692-2246 Christina Bramlet. Monthly magazine. **15,100** to insurance claims staff, independent adjustors, risk mgrs. responsible for loss reduction. www.propertycasualty360.com cbramlet@sbmedia.com

Contingencies 1850 M St NW Fl 3 Washington DC 20036 **Phn:** 202-223-8196 **Fax** 202-872-1948 Linda Mallon. Amer. Acad. of Actuaries. Bimonthly magazine. **28,000** to insurance, benefit mgrs. interested in non-technical actuarial articles, financial forecasts. www.contingencies.org mallon@actuary.org

GAMA International Journal 2901 Telestar Ct Ste 140 Falls Church VA 22042 **Phn:** 703-770-8184 **Fax** 703-770-8182 Mary Barnes. Gen. Agents & Mgrs. Assn. Bimo. **4,500** to insurance industry execs. responsible for recruitment, communications, marketing. www.gamaweb.com gij@gamaweb.com

Health Insurance Underwriter 2000 14th St N Ste 450 Arlington VA 22201 **Phn:** 703-276-0220 **Fax** 703-841-7797 Martin Carr. Monthly magazine.
30,000 to Natl. Assn. Health Underwriters members interested in legislation, regulation, news. www.hiu-digital.com editor@nahu.org

IN PO Box 68700 Indianapolis IN 46268 **Phn:** 317-875-5250 **Fax** 317-879-8408 Jon Gorman. Natl Assn. Mutual Ins Cos. Quarterly magazine.
2,500 to mgmt., claims, underwriting, financial personnel at property/casualty insurance companies. www.namic.org in@namic.org

Independent Agent 127 S Peyton St Alexandria VA 22314 **Phn:** 703-683-4422 **Fax** 703-683-7556 Katie Butler. Independent Ins. Agents. Monthly magazine.
42,000 to insurance agents, brokers interested in agency technology, office mgmt., products. www.iiaba.net katie.butler@iiaba.net

Insurance & Technology 240 W 35th St Ste 800 New York NY 10001 **Phn:** 212-600-3000 **Fax** 212-600-3060 Katherine Burger. TechWeb. 8-issue magazine.
18,100 to insurance industry decisionmakers who specify & purchase technology products, svcs. www.insurancetech.com kburger@techweb.com

Insurance Networking News 4709 Golf Rd Fl 6 Skokie IL 60076 **Phn:** 847-676-9600 **Fax** 847-933-5199 Pat Speer. Source Media. Monthly.
23,100 to IT managers responsible for claims submission, underwriting, communications technology. www.insurancenetworking.com patricia.speer@sourcemedia.com

Jrnl. Finan. Svc. Professionals 19 Campus Blvd Ste 100 Newtown Sq PA 19073 **Phn:** 610-526-2500 **Fax** 610-527-4010 Mary Anne Mennite. Soc. Fin. Svc. Pros. Bimo.
16,000 to Soc. members, life insurance & planning pros interested in products, agency mgmt. www.financialpro.org journal@financialpro.org

Life Insurance Selling 7009 S Potomac St Ste 200 Centennial CO 80112 **Phn:** 720-895-1529 **Fax** 859-647-4679 Brian Anderson. Summit Prof Networks. Monthly magazine.
50,000 to life/health insurance salespeople interested in sales methods, new products, case study. www.lifehealthpro.com banderson@lifeinsuranceselling.com

Michigan Agent 1141 Centennial Way Lansing MI 48917 **Phn:** 517-323-9473 **Fax** 517-323-1629 Wayne Joubert. MI Assn. of Insurance Agents. 10-issue magazine.
4,500 to property, casualty agents & brokers interested in sales & marketing, industry trends. michagent.org/eweb/ bigimi@michagent.org

Natl. Underwriter-Life & Health 7009 S. Potomac St Ste 200 Centennial CO 80112 **Phn:** 888-265-3616 **Fax** 720-873-8580 Emily Holbrook. Summit Prof. Networks. Biweekly magazine. TH:@LifeHealthPro
50,000 to decisionmakers in life/health insurance & financial services industries. www.lifehealthpro.com eholbrook@sbmedia.com

Professional Insurance Agents PO Box 997 Glenmont NY 12077 **Phn:** 518-434-3111 **Fax** 518-434-2342 Jaye Czupryna. Prof. Ins. Agents Assn. Monthly magazine.
4,700 in 4 regional editions to Association members in NH, NY, NJ, CT. www.pia.org jczupryna@pia.org

Resource 2300 Windy Ridge Pkwy SE # 600 Atlanta GA 30339 **Phn:** 770-951-1770 **Fax** 770-984-6417 Ron Clark. Life Office Mgmt. Assn. Monthly magazine.
19,000 to life insurance co. office managers responsible for operations, finance, IT, HR. www.loma.org/research/resource/resource.aspx resource@loma.org

Risk & Insurance 747 Dresher Rd Ste 500 Horsham PA 19044 **Phn:** 215-784-0910 **Fax** 215-784-0275 Cyril Tuohy. LRP Publications. 14-issue tabloid.
100,000 to execs. responsible for workers' compensation, risk mgmt., loss control. www.riskandinsurance.com ctuohy@lrp.com

Insurance .34

Risk Management 1065 Ave Of The Americas Fl 13 New York NY 10018 **Phn:** 212-655-5919 **Fax** 212-655-2695 Caroline McDonald. Risk & Insurance Mgmt. Soc. 10-issue magazine. TH:@RiskMgmt
18,400 to corporate risk mgrs. responsible for all aspects of protecting corporate assets. www.rmmagazine.com cmcdonald@rims.org

Rough Notes 11690 Technology Dr Carmel IN 46032 **Phn:** 317-582-1600 **Fax** 317-816-1000 Thomas A. McCoy. Monthly magazine.
42,200 to property, casualty ins. agents & brokers interested in technology, products, markets. www.roughnotes.com rnc@roughnotes.com

Standard 155 Federal St Ste 1301 Boston MA 02110 **Phn:** 617-457-0600 **Fax** 617-457-0608 Erin Ayers. Weekly magazine.
5,000 to members of New England ins. industry interested in legislation, news, analysis. www.spcpub.com e.ayers@spcpub.com

Today's Insurance Professional 9343 E 97th Ct S Tulsa OK 74133 **Phn:** 918-294-3700 **Fax** 918-294-3711 Melissa Cobbs. NAIW Int'l. Quarterly magazine.
12,900 to insurance industry women intersted in networking, professional education, Assn news. www.internationalinsuranceprofessionals.org editor@naiw.org

Jewelry .35

Horological Times 701 Enterprise Dr Harrison OH 45030 **Phn:** 513-367-9800 **Fax** 513-367-1414 Amy S. Dunn. Amer. Watch/Clockmakers Inst. Monthly magazine.
3,700 to watch, clockmaking, jewelry personnel interested in technical features, news. www.awci.com adunn@awci.com

Jewelers' Circular-Keystone 400 Madison Ave, Suite 10D New York NY 10017 **Phn:** 646-746-6400 **Fax** 646-746-7431 Rob Bates. Reed Business Info. Monthly magazine.
25,000 to retail jewelers interested in sales and promotion, staffing, security and insurance. www.jckonline.com/jckgroup rbates@jckonline.com

MJSA Journal 57 John L Dietsch Sq Attleboro Falls MA 02763 **Phn:** 401-274-3840 **Fax** 401-274-0265 Tina Snyder. Mfg. Jewelers & Suppliers of Amer. Monthly magazine.
7,800 to mfg. jewelers, suppliers interested in artistic, technical design features, business news. www.mjsa.org tina.snyder@mjsa.org

National Jeweler 770 Broadway Fl 5 New York NY 10003 **Phn:** 646-654-4500 **Fax** 646-654-4949 Whitney Sielaff. Nielsen Business Media. Monthly tabloid.
29,200 to retail jewelers interested in news, events, industry people, products. www.nationaljeweler.com wsielaff@nationaljeweler.com

Southern Jewelry News 2006 New Garden Rd Ste 208 Greensboro NC 27410 **Phn:** 336-389-1950 **Fax** 336-389-1952 Bill Newnam. Monthly newspaper
12,000 to retail jewelers in 17 southern states interested in news, mfrs., shows. southernjewelrynews.com info@southernjewelrynews.com

Watch & Jewelry Review 1838 2nd Ave # 320 New York NY 10128 **Phn:** 212-987-3026 **Fax** 212-987-3027 Dara Hinshaw. Bell Publications. 10-issue magazine.
14,600 to watch/clock designers, mfrs., retailers & repair personnel interested in industry news. www.goldenbellpress.com darah123@aol.com

Watch Journal 3946 Glade Valley Dr Houston TX 77339 **Phn:** 281-359-4385 **Fax** 561-750-0152 Marie Picon. Sandow Media. Bimonthly. TH:@CoutureTimeByWJ
31,600 news and information about new and limited edition watches, both US and International. www.watchjournal.com mpicon@watchjournal.com

Laundry--Dry Cleaning .36

American Coin-Op 566 W Lake St Ste 420 Chicago IL 60661 **Phn:** 312-361-1683 **Fax** 312-361-1685 Bruce Beggs. Amer. Trade Magazines. Monthly magazine.
17,600 to owners, operators, managers of coin-operated laundries and drycleaning stores. www.americancoinop.com bbeggs@americantrademagazines.com

American Drycleaner 566 W Lake St Ste 420 Chicago IL 60661 **Phn:** 312-361-1683 **Fax** 312-361-1685 Bruce Beggs. Amer. Trade Magazines. Monthly magazine.
24,200 to drycleaners, plant owners, managers, suppliers interested in technical, business info. www.americandrycleaner.com bbeggs@americantrademagazines.com

American Laundry News 566 W Lake St STe 420 Chicago IL 60661 **Phn:** 312-361-1683 **Fax** 312-361-1685 Bruce Beggs. Amer. Trade Magazines. Monthly tabloid.
15,200 to linen suppliers, institutional, commercial, industrial laundry mgmt. interested in events & equipment. www.americanlaundrynews.com bbeggs@americantrademagazines.com

Cleaner & Launderer 3236 Estado St Pasadena CA 91107 **Phn:** 626-793-2911 **Fax** 626-793-5540 Randy Wente. Wakefield Publishing. Monthly tabloid.
14,300 to owners/mgrs. of drycleaning plants and stores, coin-op laundries. www.wcl-online.com randy@wcl-online.com

Laundry Today PO Box 361 Eastport NY 11941 **Phn:** 212-644-4344 **Fax** 212-644-4346 Eda Galeno. Monthly tabloid.
14,300 to laundry mgrs., linen service directors, executive housekeepers. www.laundrytoday.com eda@laundrytoday.com

National Clothesline PO Box 340 Willow Grove PA 19090 **Phn:** 215-830-8467 **Fax** 215-830-8490 Hal Horning. BPS Communications. Monthly tabloid.
30,000 to drycleaning, laundry mgmt. interested in trade assn. activities, seminars, new products. www.natclo.com info@natclo.com

Textile Services 1800 Diagonal Rd Ste 200 Alexandria VA 22314 **Phn:** 703-519-0029 **Fax** 703-519-0026 Jack Morgan. Textile Rental Svces. Assn. Monthly magazine.
6,000 to owners and mgrs. of commercial laundries and uniform/linen supply services. www.trsa.org jmorgan@trsa.org

Legal .37

ABA Journal 321 N Clark St Chicago IL 60654 **Phn:** 312-988-5000 **Fax** 312-988-6014 Allen Pusey. Amer. Bar Assn. Monthly magazine.
375,000 to Assn. members, law firm decisionmakers interested in legal news, court decisions. www.abajournal.com releases@americanbar.org

ACC Docket 1025 Connecticut Ave NW Ste 200 Washington DC 20036 **Phn:** 202-293-4103 **Fax** 202-293-4701 Kimberly A. Howard. Assn. of Corp. Counsel. 10-issue magazine.
35,000 to attorneys working as corporate counsels interested in continuing education, industry specific issues. www.acc.com howard@acc.com

American Lawyer 120 Broadway Fl 5 New York NY 10271 **Phn:** 212-457-9400 **Fax** 646-822-5146 Emily Barker. ALM. Monthly magazine.
17,000 to attorneys & firm administrators interested in news, resources, surveys. www.law.com/jsp/tal/index.jsp ebarker@alm.com

Business Law Today 321 N Clark St Chicago IL 60654 **Phn:** 312-988-6122 **Fax** 312-988-6081 John Palmer. Amer. Bar Assn. Online only.
to in-house counsels; attorneys at corporate law practices, banks, financial institutions. apps.americanbar.org/buslaw/blt/ john.palmer@americanbar.org

California Bar Journal 180 Howard St San Francisco CA 94105 **Phn:** 415-538-2504 **Fax** 415-538-2247 Laura Ernde. CA State Bar. Monthly newspaper.
206,600 to CA attorneys interested in Bar news, member profiles, continuing education. www.calbar.ca.gov/ cbj@calbar.ca.gov

Champion 1660 L St NW Fl 12 Washington DC 20036 **Phn:** 202-872-8600 **Fax** 202-872-8690 Quintin Chatman. Natl. Assn. Criminal Defense Lawyers. 10 issues.
15,200 to Assn. members interested in trial strategies and techniques, Assn. news. www.nacdl.org qchatman@nacdl.org

Chicago Lawyer 415 N State St Chicago IL 60654 **Phn:** 312-644-7800 **Fax** 312-644-4255 Pat Milhizer. Monthly.
9,000 to Chicago area attorneys interested in firm news, surveys, trends in all practice areas. www.chicagolawyermagazine.com pmilhizer@lbpc.com

The Colorado Lawyer 1900 Grant St Ste 900 Denver CO 80203 **Phn:** 303-860-1115 **Fax** 303-830-3990 Leona Martinez. Monthly magazine.
16,000 to CO State Bar members intersted in continuing education, Bar news, state laws. www.cobar.org leonamartinez@cobar.org

Connecticut Law Tribune 201 Ann St Fl 4 Hartford CT 06103 **Phn:** 860-527-7900 **Fax** 860-527-7815 Paul Sussman. ALM. Weekly newspaper.
3,000 to CT attorneys interested in state courts, law firms, legislature. www.ctlawtribune.com

Environmental Forum 2000 L St NW Ste 620 Washington DC 20036 **Phn:** 202-939-3815 Stephen Dujack. Bimonthly magazine.
2,900 to environmental professionals interested in opinion pieces and ideas exchange. www.eli.org dujack@eli.org

Family Advocate 1600 Main St Racine WI 53403 **Phn:** 262-619-1334 **Fax** 262-619-1335 Deborah Eisel. Quarterly magazine.
12,000 to family law practitioners concerned with divorce, custody, adoption, elder care. www.americanbar.org/groups/family_law.html eiseld@sbcglobal.net

Florida Bar Journal 651 E Jefferson St Tallahassee FL 32399 **Phn:** 850-561-5686 **Fax** 850-681-3859 Cheryle Dodd. Monthly magazine.
428,000 to FL attorneys interested in practical application of case law, analysis; opinion. www.floridabar.org cdodd@flabar.org

Illinois Bar Journal 424 S 2nd St Springfield IL 62701 **Phn:** 217-525-1760 **Fax** 217-525-0712 Mark Mathewson. Monthly magazine.
33,100 to IL State Bar members interested in practice-oriented features. www.isba.org mmathew@isba.org

Indiana Lawyer 41 E Washington St Ste 200 Indianapolis IN 46204 **Phn:** 317-636-0200 **Fax** 317-263-5259 Kelly Lucas. Twice monthly newspaper.
6,500 to IN attorneys interested in pending legislation, court decisions, opinion pieces. www.theindianalawyer.com klucas@ibj.com

InsideCounsel 222 S Riverside Plz Ste 620 Chicago IL 60606 **Phn:** 312-654-3500 **Fax** 312-654-3525 Cathleen Flahardy. Summit Prof. Networks. Monthly tab.
40,000 to in-house attorneys responsible for strategic planning, law firm/corporation relations. www.insidecounsel.com cflahardy@insidecounsel.com

Law Practice 24476 N Echo Lake Rd Hawthorn Woods IL 60047 **Phn:** 847-550-9790 **Fax** 847-550-9107 Joan Feldman. Amer. Bar Assn. 6-issue magazine.
12,300 to attys. & legal administrators responsible for firm finances, IT, human resources. www.americanbar.org lawpracticemagazine@gmail.com

Law Technology News 120 Broadway Fl 5 New York NY 10271 **Phn:** 212-457-9400 Monica Bay. ALM. Monthly tabloid.
40,000 to law firm partners, IT directors responsible for technology specifying & purchasing. www.law.com lawtech@alm.com

Lawyers USA 10 Milk St Fl 10 Boston MA 02108 **Phn:** 617-218-8191 **Fax** 617-451-1466 Susan Bocamazo. Lawyers Weekly, Inc. Monthly newspaper.
7,900 to attorneys interested in latest case law, practice management, marketing. lawyersusaonline.com susan.bocamazo@lawyersusaonline.com

Legal Intelligencer 1617 John F Kennedy Blvd Ste 1750 Philadelphia PA 19103 **Phn:** 215-557-2300 **Fax** 215-557-2301 Hank Grezlak. American Lawyer Media. Daily newspaper.
4,000 to Philadelphia area attorneys interested in local court decisions, trial dates, law firm news. www.law.com/jsp/pa/ hgrezlak@alm.com

Legal Management 75 Tri State Intl Ste 222 Lincolnshire IL 60069 **Phn:** 847-267-1252 **Fax** 847-267-1329 Amy Dvorak. Assn. Legal Administrators. Bimonthly magazine.
17,000 to attorneys responsibile for practice, financial mgmt., human resources, IT, space plans. www.alanet.org advorak@alanet.org

Los Angeles Lawyer 1055 W 7th St Ste 2700 Los Angeles CA 90017 **Phn:** 213-896-6503 **Fax** 213-833-6715 Samuel Lipsman. Los Angeles County Bar Assn. Monthly magazine.
23,200 to Los Angeles County Bar members interested in continuing education, Assn. member news. www.lacba.org lalawyer@lacba.org

Massachusetts Lawyers Weekly 10 Milk St Ste 1000 Boston MA 02108 **Phn:** 617-451-7300 **Fax** 617-451-7324 Henriette Campagne. Weekly newspaper.
10,800 to MA attorneys interested in state & federal court decisions, case summaries & verdicts. masslawyersweekly.com henriette.campagne@lawyersweekly.com

Metropolitan Corporate Counsel 1180 Wychwood Rd Mountainside NJ 07092 **Phn:** 908-654-4840 **Fax** 908-654-4068 Al Driver. Monthly tabloid.
27,000 to corporate counsels interested in legal developments, career profiles, continuing education. www.metrocorpcounsel.com adriver@metrocorpcounsel.com

Michigan Lawyers Weekly 7013 Orchard Lake Rd Ste 110 West Bloomfield MI 48322 **Phn:** 800-678-5297 **Fax** 248-865-3117 Gary Gosselin. Weekly newspaper.
3,300 to lawyers interested in State of MI court decisions, verdict reports, news. milawyersweekly.com gary.gosselin@mi.lawyersweekly.com

Missouri Lawyers Weekly 319 N 4th St Fl 5 Saint Louis MO 63102 **Phn:** 314-421-1880 **Fax** 314-621-1913 Richard Jackoway. Weekly newspaper.
2,600 to MO attorneys interested in all state court decisions, verdicts & settlements, news. molawyersmedia.com rick.jackoway@molawyersmedia.com

National Law Journal 120 Broadway Fl 5 New York NY 10271 **Phn:** 212-457-9400 **Fax** 646-417-7705 Ruth Singleton. ALM. Weekly newspaper.
17,800 to independent lawyers, members of legal firms, corporate legal personnel, govt. agencies. www.law.com/jsp/nlj/ rsingleton@alm.com

National Paralegal Reporter 13210 Barkley St Leawood KS 66209 **Phn:** 816-942-1600 **Fax** 913-387-4313 Dan O'Leary. Natl. Fed. Paralegal Assns. Bimo.
12,000 to paralegals interested in career opportunities, Assn. activities, continuing education. www.paralegals.org editor@paralegals.org

New Jersey Law Journal PO Box 20081 Newark NJ 07101 **Phn:** 973-642-0075 **Fax** 973-642-0920 Ronald Fleury. Incisive Media. Weekly newspaper.
11,200 to NJ attorneys interested in cases, courts, job listings, news about attorneys in the state. www.law.com/jsp/nj/ rfleury@alm.com

New York Law Journal 120 Broadway Fl 5 New York NY 10271 **Phn:** 212-457-9400 **Fax** 646-822-5146 Kris Fischer. ALM. Weekly newspaper.
12,600 to NY State attorneys interested in verdicts, decisions, settlements, judges. www.law.com/jsp/nylj/ kfischer@alm.com

New York State Bar Jrnl. 1 Elk St Albany NY 12207 **Phn:** 518-463-3200 **Fax** 518-463-8844 Dan McMahon. 9-issue magazine.
72,000 to members of NY State bar interested in practice of law in all specialty areas. www.nysba.org journal@nysba.org

Ohio Lawyer PO Box 16562 Columbus OH 43216 **Phn:** 614-487-2050 **Fax** 614-487-1008 Nina Corbut. OH State Bar Assn. Bimonthly magazine.
30,000 to OH Bar Assn. members interested in verdicts, decisions, courts, Assn. news. www.ohiobar.org ncorbut@ohiobar.org

Paralegal Today 10632 Little Patuxent Pkwy Ste 249 Columbia MD 21044 **Phn:** 410-740-9700 **Fax** 410-740-9771 Sally A. Kane. Conexion Intl Media. Quarterly magazine.
7,500 to paralegals interested in news, techniques, information relative to paralegal practice in all areas. paralegaltoday.com editorparalegal@conexionmedia.com

Pennsylvania Bar News PO Box 186 Harrisburg PA 17108 **Phn:** 717-238-6715 **Fax** 717-238-2342 Patricia Graybill. PA Bar Assn. Biweekly tabloid.
30,000 to PA Bar Assn. members interested in state and federal court opinions, practice advice & commentary. www.pabar.org patricia.graybill@pabar.org

Practical Real Estate Lawyer 4025 Chestnut St Philadelphia PA 19104 **Phn:** 215-243-1600 **Fax** 215-243-1664 Mark Carroll. Bimonthly magazine.
3,400 to attorneys interested in real estate statutes, judgements, document compliance. www.ali-aba.org mcarroll@ali-aba.org

Probate & Property 321 N Clark St Chicago IL 60654 **Phn:** 312-988-6083 **Fax** 312-988-6081 Rick Bright. Amer. Bar Assn. Bimonthly magazine.
29,000 to lawyers whose areas of practice are real estate, wills, trusts, estates. www.americanbar.org/groups/real_property_trust_estate.html rpte@americanbar.org

Student Lawyer 321 N Clark St Chicago IL 60654 **Phn:** 312-988-6048 **Fax** 312-988-6081 Angela Gwizdala. Amer. Bar Assn. 9-issue magazine.
35,000 to law students interested practical advice, law school issues, careers,exam prep, summer placements. www.americanbar.org/publications/student_lawyer/2013-14/september.html studentlawyer@americanbar.org

Texas Bar Journal PO Box 12487 Austin TX 78711 **Phn:** 512-427-1726 **Fax** 512-427-4107 Kevin Priestner. Stae Bar of TX. Monthly magazine.
99,000 to TX private practice attorneys; Federal & state trial and appellate judges. www.texasbar.com/tbj/ tbj@texasbar.com

Trial 777 6th St NW Ste 200 Washington DC 20001 **Phn:** 202-965-3510 **Fax** 202-965-0030 Julie Shoop. Amer. Assn for Justice. Monthly magazine.
28,000 to litigation attorneys interested in developments in case prep, jury selection, practice mgmt. www.justice.org trial@justice.org

Washington Lawyer 1250 H St NW Fl 6 Washington DC 20005 **Phn:** 202-737-4700 **Fax** 202-626-3471 Tim Wells. Washington DC Bar Assn. 11-issue magazine.
80,000 to DC Bar members news, practice mgmt., natl. politics relative to District courts. www.dcbar.org twells@dcbar.org

Wisconsin Lawyer PO Box 7158 Madison WI 53707 **Phn:** 608-257-3838 **Fax** 608-257-5502 Joyce Hastings. Monthly magazine.
22,700 to WI-licensed attorneys interested in legal trends & developments impacting law practice in WI. www.wisbar.org wislawyer@wisbar.org

American Christmas Tree Jrnl. 16020 Swingley Ridge Rd Ste 300 Chesterfield MO 63017 **Phn:** 636-449-5070 **Fax** 636-449-5051 Becky Rasmussen Natl. Christmas Tree Assn. Quarterly mag.
1,200 to Christmas tree farmers, retailers interested in production features, marketing ideas, Assn. news.
www.realchristmastrees.org
info@realchristmastrees.org

American Forests 734 15th St NW Ste 800 Washington DC 20005 **Phn:** 202-737-1944 **Fax** 202-737-2457 Katrina Ma5land. American Forests. Quarterly magazine.
18,000 to environmentalists, arborists, policymakers interested in trees, forests, ecosystem restoration.
www.americanforests.org
kmarland@americanforests.org

Arbor Age 1030 Higgins Rd Ste 230 Park Ridge IL 60068 **Phn:** 815-479-8547 **Fax** 815-479-8548 John Kmitta. M2Media360. Monthly magazine.
18,500 to urban tree industry personnel caring for trees in municipal and institutional settings.
www.greenmediaonline.com
jkmitta@m2media360.com

Crossties PO Box 2267 Gulf Shores AL 36547 **Phn:** 251-968-5300 **Fax** 251-968-4532 Kristen McIntosh. Railway Tie Assn. Bimonthly magazine.
3,400 to wood crosstie producers and marketers interested in industry news, market demands.
www.rta.org kmcintosh@coveypubs.com

Forest Chemicals Review 3803 Cleveland Ave New Orleans LA 70119 **Phn:** 504-482-3914 **Fax** 504-482-4205 Charles Richard. Kriedt Enterprises. Bimonthly.
1,200 Covers by-products of pine & pulp chemicals industry, rosin, terpenes, tall oil.
forestchemicalsreview.com
info@forestchemicalsreview.com

Jrnl. Forestry 5400 Grosvenor Ln Bethesda MD 20814 **Phn:** 301-897-8720 **Fax** 301-897-3690 Matthew Walls. Soc. Amer. Foresters. 8-issue magazine.
15,000 to Soc. members, land mgrs., foresters, loggers interested in forest protection & use.
www.eforester.org/publications/jof/ wallsm@safnet.org

Loggers World 4206 Jackson Hwy Chehalis WA 98532 **Phn:** 360-262-3376 **Fax** 360-262-3337 Michael Crouse. Monthly magazine.
22,000 to loggers, contractors and timber owners in the Western U.S. www.loggersworld.com
logworld@aol.com

National Hardwood Magazine PO Box 34908 Memphis TN 38184 **Phn:** 901-372-8280 **Fax** 901-373-6180 Sue Putman. Monthly magazine.
6,000 to hardwood purchasing agents interested in trade shows, news, end user profiles.
www.millerpublishing.com
editor@millerpublishing.com

Northern Logger/Timber Processor PO Box 69 Old Forge NY 13420 **Phn:** 315-369-3078 **Fax** 315-369-3736 Eric Johnson. Northeast Loggers Assn. Monthly magazine.
11,300 to Assn. members, other loggers, timberland managers, sawmill operators. www.northernlogger.com
eric@northernlogger.com

Pallet Enterprise 10244 Timber Ridge Dr Ashland VA 23005 **Phn:** 804-550-0323 **Fax** 804-550-2181 Chaille Brindley. Monthly magazine.
10,000 to mfrs., sellers, users of wooden pallets interested in machinery, recycling, tech. info.
www.palletenterprise.com chailleb@gmail.com

Panel World PO Box 2268 Montgomery AL 36102 **Phn:** 334-834-1170 **Fax** 334-834-4525 Rich Donnell. Hatton-Brown. Bimonthly magazine.
12,000 to mfrs., distributors, jobbers, salespeople, retailers of veneer, plywood panels.
www.panelworldmag.com rich@hattonbrown.com

Lumber--Forestry--Woodworking .38

Softwood Forest Prod. Buyer PO Box 34908 Memphis TN 38184 **Phn:** 901-372-8280 **Fax** 901-373-6180 Sue Putnam. Bimonthly magazine.
20,000 to sawmill operators, wholesalers and manufacturers of shingles, shakes, millwork.
www.millerpublishing.com
editor@millerpublishing.com

Southern Loggin' Times PO Box 2268 Montgomery AL 36102 **Phn:** 334-834-1170 **Fax** 334-834-4525 D.K. Knight. Hatton-Brown. Monthly tabloid.
14,100 to forest product industry personnel interested in illustrated features, equipment.
www.southernloggintimesmagazine.com
dk@hattonbrown.com

Southern Lumberman PO Box 2268 Montgomery AL 36102 **Phn:** 334-834-1170 **Fax** 334-834-4525 David Abbott. Hatton-Brown. 9-issue magazine.
14,300 to smaller hard & softwood mill owner-operators interested in business mgmt., technology, news.
www.timberprocessing.com rich@hattonbrown.com

Timber Harvesting PO Box 2268 Montgomery AL 36102 **Phn:** 334-834-1170 **Fax** 334-834-4525 D.K. Knight. Hatton-Brown. Bimonthly magazine.
21,100 to loggers and timber dealers interested in technologies, transportation, products.
www.timberharvesting.com rich@hattonbrown.com

Timber Processing PO Box 2268 Montgomery AL 36102 **Phn:** 334-834-1170 **Fax** 334-834-4525 Rich Donnell. Hatton-Brown. 10-issue magazine.
20,000 to mgmt. of sawmills, chipmills, engineered wood product producers, pulp and paper mill processors. www.timberprocessing.com
rich@hattonbrown.com

Timber West PO Box 610 Edmonds WA 98020 **Phn:** 425-778-3388 **Fax** 425-771-3623 Diane Mettler. Bimonthly magazine.
10,000 to log and timber industry personnel in AK, WA, OR, ID, MT, northern CA. www.forestnet.com
timberwest@forestnet.com

Timberline 10244 Timber Ridge Dr Ashland VA 23005 **Phn:** 804-550-0323 **Fax** 804-550-2181 Chaille Brindley. Monthly newspaper.
15,000 to loggers, sawmill operators, pallet and secondary wood mfrs. www.timberlinemag.com
chailleb@gmail.com

Tree Care Industry 136 Harvey Rd Ste 101 Londonderry NH 03053 **Phn:** 603-314-5380 **Fax** 603-314-5386 Amy Tetreault. Tree Care Industry Assn. Monthly magazine.
27,500 to commercial and residential arborists, municipal and utility foresters. www.tcia.org
atetreault@tcia.org

Tree Farmer 1111 19th St NW Ste 780 Washington DC 20036 **Phn:** 202-463-2700 **Fax** 202-463-2461 Brigitte Johnson. Amer. Forest Fndtn. 5-issue magazine.
19,000 to tree farmers interested in sustainable production, responsible stewardship.
www.treefarmsystem.org info@treefarmsystem.org

Tree Services 374 Emerson Falls Rd Saint Johnsbury VT 05819 **Phn:** 802-748-8908 **Fax** 802-748-1866 Katie Meyers. Moose River Publishing. Monthly.
19,500 to arborists, landscapers, utilities contractors and others; all aspects of the tree services.
www.treeservicesmagazine.com
treepr@mooserivermedia.com

Wood & Wood Products 400 Knightsbridge Pkwy Lincolnshire IL 60069 **Phn:** 847-634-4347 **Fax** 847-634-4374 Karen Koenig. Vance Publishing. Monthly mag.
31,000 to senior mgmt. in furniture and cabinet production; other woodworking facilities.
woodworkingnetwork.com
kkoenig@vancepublishing.com

Woodshop News 10 Bokum Rd Essex CT 06426 **Phn:** 860-767-8227 **Fax** 860-767-0645 Todd Riggio. Monthly magazine.
40,000 to professional woodworkers, the news, technology, materials, people & issues that affect them. www.woodshopnews.com
editorial@woodshopnews.com

Marine--Maritime .39

American Shipper PO Box 4728 Jacksonville FL 32201 **Phn:** 904-355-2601 **Fax** 904-791-8836 Gary G. Burrows. Monthly magazine.
13,900 to logistics, freight and shipping executives in air, land and ocean transportation.
www.americanshipper.com releases@shippers.com

BoatU.S. 880 S Pickett St Alexandria VA 22304 **Phn:** 703-461-2864 **Fax** 703-461-2845 Bernadette Bernon. Boat Owners Assn. Bimonthly magazine.
525,000 to recreational power & sailboat owners interested in legislative, regulatory, Assn. news; consumer issues. www.boatus.com
magazine@boatus.com

Boating Industry 6420 Sycamore Ln N Ste 100 Maple Grove MN 55369 **Phn:** 763-383-4400 **Fax** 763-383-4499 Brent Renneke. Affinity Media. Monthly magazine.
26,000 to leisure marine industry personnel interested in financial, regulatory issues, new products.
www.boatingindustry.com
brenneke@boatingindustry.com

Boating 460 N Orlando Ave Ste 200 Winter Park FL 32789 **Phn:** 407-628-4802 **Fax** 407-628-7061 Sue Whitney. Bonnier Corp. 9-issue magazine.
100,000 to recreational boat owners interested in equipment reviews, advice, destinations.
www.boatingmag.com sue.whitney@bonniercorp.com

Boating World 17782 Cowan Ste A Irvine CA 92614 **Phn:** 949-660-6150 **Fax** 949-660-6172 Mike Werling. Duncan McIntosh. 9-issue magazine.
101,000 to family/cruising boaters, fishermen interested in new boats, marine products.
www.boatingworld.com alan@boatingworld.com

Chesapeake Bay Magazine 1819 Bay Ridge Ave Ste 180 Annapolis MD 21403 **Phn:** 410-263-2662 **Fax** 410-267-6924 Tim Sayles. Monthly magazine.
35,500 to Chesapeake Bay residents and visitors interested in power and sail boating, marinas.
www.chesapeakeboating.net
editor@chesapeakeboating.net

Cruising Outpost 909 Marina Village Pkwy, #351 Alameda CA 94501 **Phn:** Bob Bitchin. Quarterly magazine.
to world cruisers interested in tips on sailing with children and pets; at-sea repairs.
www.cruisingoutpost.com bob@cruisingoutpost.com

Cruising World 55 Hammarlund Way Middletown RI 02842 **Phn:** 401-845-5100 **Fax** 401-845-5180 Mark Pillsbury. Bonnier Corp. Monthly magazine.
135,000 to sailboat owners interested in safety, navigation skills, sailing lifestyle.
www.cruisingworld.com
mark.pillsbury@cruisingworld.com

The Ensign PO Box 31664 Raleigh NC 27622 **Phn:** 919-821-0892 **Fax** 919-836-0813 Yvonne Hill. U.S. Power Squadrons. Quarterly magazine.
28,000 to Squadron members interested in boat handling & navigation, safety, equipment.
www.theensign.org ensign@hq.usps.org

Foghorn 2201 W Commodore Way Seattle WA 98199 **Phn:** 301-869-9777 **Fax** 206-284-0391 Karen Rainbolt. Passenger Vessel Assn. Monthly.
1,800 to commercial passenger vessel owners & operators interested in regulatory & safety matters, profitability. www.foghornmagazine.com
pvafoghorn@aol.com

Great Lakes Boating 1032 N La Salle Dr Chicago IL 60610 **Phn:** 312-266-8400 Karen Malonis. Bimonthly.
30,000 to the Great Lakes area and inland waterway power boating and sailing enthusiasts.
www.greatlakesboating.com
kmalonis@greatlakesboating.com

Heartland Boating 319 N 4th St Ste 650 Saint Louis MO 63102 **Phn:** 314-241-4310 **Fax** 314-241-4207 Lee Braff. 8-issue magazine.
11,900 to sail & power boaters interested in boating mid-U.S. lakes and river systems.
www.heartlandboating.com
lbraff@heartlandboating.com

Houseboat 360 B St Idaho Falls ID 83402 **Phn:** 208-524-7000 **Fax** 208-522-5241 Brady L. Kay. Harris Publ. Monthly magazine.
24,200 to houseboat owners and renters interested in boat models, destinations, maintenance.
www.houseboatmagazine.com
hbeditor@harrispublishing.com

Lakeland Boating 727 S Dearborn St Ste 812 Chicago IL 60605 **Phn:** 312-276-0610 **Fax** 312-276-0619 Lindsey Johnson O'Meara-Brown Inc. 11-issue magazine.
42,000 to Great Lakes boaters interested in maintenance, testing, navigation.
www.lakelandboating.com
ljohnson@lakelandboating.com

Log 17782 Cowan Ste A Irvine CA 92614 **Phn:** 949-660-6150 **Fax** 949-660-6172 Eston Ellis. Duncan McIntosh. Biweekly tabloid.
55,100 in 3 California editions to power & sailboaters interested in events, races, news. www.thelog.com
eston@goboating.com

Marina Dock Age 6600 W Touhy Ave Niles IL 60714 **Phn:** 847-647-2900 **Fax** 847-647-1155 Anna Townshend. Preston Pubs. 8-issue magazine.
17,200 to marine and boatyard owners, managers, designers and builders. www.marinadockage.com
atownshend@marinadockage.com

Marine Log 345 Hudson St New York NY 10014 **Phn:** 212-620-7200 **Fax** 212-633-1165 John Snyder. Simmons-Boardman. Monthly magazine.
26,600 to maritime industry execs. responsible for oceangoing, offshore, commercial shipping.
www.marinelog.com marinelog@sbpub.com

Marine News 118 E 25th St Fl 2 New York NY 10010 **Phn:** 212-477-6700 **Fax** 212-254-6271 Greg Trauthwein. Monthly tabloid.
33,600 to vessel operations, oil drilling, ship building & repair, naval architecture, port officials.
www.marinelink.com trauthwein@marinelink.com

Ocean Navigator 58 Fore St Portland ME 04101 **Phn:** 207-772-2466 **Fax** 207-772-2879 Tim Queeney. Navigator Publishing. 7-issue magazine.
40,400 to large sailboat, poweryacht owners interested in technical features, product news.
www.oceannavigator.com
editors@oceannavigator.com

Ocean News & Technology 360 Park Ave S New York NY 10010 **Phn:** 772-221-7720 **Fax** 772-221-7715 Dan White. Technology Systems Corp. Bimo.
3,200 covers ocean industry news, including defense, offshore oil & gas, environment, recreation.
www.ocean-news.com techsystems@sprintmail.com

PassageMaker 105 Eastern Ave Ste 203 Annapolis MD 21403 **Phn:** 410-990-9086 **Fax** 410-990-9095 Kelly Fong. 8-issue magazine. TH:@PassageMakerMag
41,000 to readers interested in power cruiseboats, destinations, boat & equipment reviews, safety.
www.passagemaker.com kfong@aimmedia.com

PDB Magazine 360 B St Idaho Falls ID 83402 **Phn:** 208-524-7000 **Fax** 208-522-5241 Brady Kay. 11-issue magazine.
76,200 to owners of pontoon/deck boats interested in new models, destinations, maintenance.
www.pdbmagazine.com blk@harrispublishing.com

Power & Motoryacht 261 Madison Ave Fl 6 New York NY 10016 **Phn:** 212-915-4000 **Fax** 212-915-4327 George Sass. Active Interest Media. Monthly magazine.
130,700 to owners of 24-foot+ powerboats interested in cruising, chartering, sport fishing.
www.powerandmotoryacht.com

Marine--Maritime .39

Professional BoatBuilder PO Box 78 Brooklin ME 04616 **Phn:** 207-359-4651 **Fax** 207-359-8920 Paul Lazarus. Bimonthly magazine.
25,400 to professional boatbuilders, repairers, designers and surveyors. www.proboat.com
proboat@proboat.com

Professional Mariner 58 Fore St Portland ME 04101 **Phn:** 207-772-2466 **Fax** 207-772-2879 Dom Yanchunas. Navigator Publishing. 11-issue magazine. TH:@ProMarinerMag
23,000 to owners, operators of commercial maritime industry businesses in North America.
www.professionalmariner.com
dyanchunas@professionalmariner.com

Sail 98 N Washington St Ste 107 Boston MA 02114 **Phn:** 617-720-8600 **Fax** 617-723-0911 Peter Nielsen. Source Interlink Media. Monthly magazine. TH:@sailmagazine
101,000 to beginning and expert sailors interested in cruising, racing, events, product reviews.
www.sailmag.com pnielsen@sailmagazine.com

Sailing 125 E Main St Port Washington WI 53074 **Phn:** 262-284-3494 **Fax** 262-284-7764 Greta Schanen. Monthly magazine.
40,000 to sailors interested in technical features, racing, large-format sailing photos.
www.sailingmagazine.net
editorial@sailingmagazine.net

Sailing World 55 Hammarlund Way Unit A Middletown RI 02842 **Phn:** 401-845-5100 **Fax** 401-845-5180 David Reed. Bonnier Corp. 9-issue magazine.
41,300 to experienced racing sailors interested in tips, tactics, events, equipment. www.sailingworld.com
editor@sailingworld.com

Sea Magazine 17782 Cowan Ste A Irvine CA 92614 **Phn:** 949-660-6150 **Fax** 949-660-6172 Lysa Christopher. Duncan McIntosh. Monthly magazine.
50,500 to Western U.S. & Mexican coast boaters interested in people, news, events.
www.seamagazine.com
editor@goboatingamerica.com.

Sea Technology 1501 Wilson Blvd Ste 1001 Arlington VA 22209 **Phn:** 703-524-3136 **Fax** 703-841-0852 Chris Knight. Compass Publications. Monthly magazine.
13,000 to marine industry designers, engineers, researchers, scientists, technicians, academics.
www.sea-technology.com oceanbiz@sea-technology.com

Southern Boating 330 N Andrews Ave Fort Lauderdale FL 33301 **Phn:** 954-522-5515 **Fax** 954-522-2260 Liz Pasch. Monthly magzine.
41,000 to boat owners who cruise and sail the waters of Florida, the Bahamas and the Caribbean.
southernboating.com liz@southernboating.com

WoodenBoat PO Box 78 Brooklin ME 04616 **Phn:** 207-359-4651 **Fax** 207-359-8920 Matthew Murphy. WoodenBoat Pubs. Bimonthly magazine.
88,800 to wooden boat owners, builders, designers; maintenance, repair, restoration personnel.
www.woodenboat.com carl@woodenboat.com

WorkBoat 121 Free St Portland ME 04101 **Phn:** 207-842-5600 **Fax** 207-842-5611 Ken Hocke. Diversified Business Communications.
25,100 to owners, operators, managers and captains of vessels less than 400 feet in length.
www.workboat.com khocke@divcom.com

World Dredging PO Box 17479 Irvine CA 92623 **Phn:** 949-553-0386 **Fax** 949-863-9261 Steve Richardson. World Dredging Inc. Bimo.
2,400 to dredging, mining & marine construction industry personnel interested in technical topics.
www.worlddredging.com wdmcsteve@aol.com

Yachting 2 Park Ave Fl 9 New York NY 10016 **Phn:** 212-779-5000 **Fax** 212-779-5479 Mary South. Bonnier Corp. Monthly magazine.
121,400 to owners, builders, brokers, designers, mfrs., dealers of boats, engines, parts.
www.yachtingmagazine.com
mary.south@bonniercorp.com

Yachts Intl 1850 SE 17th St Ste 107A Ft Lauderdale FL 33316 **Phn:** 954-761-8777 **Fax** 954-761-8890 Kenny Wooton. Active Interest Media. Monthly magazine. TH:@kbwooton
42,000 to yacht owners (60 ft. & over) and enthusiasts interested in shows, products, shipyards, destinations.
www.yachtsmagazine.com kwooton@aimmedia.com

Fish Industry .39a

Commercial Fisheries News PO Box 600 Deer Isle ME 04672 **Phn:** 207-367-2396 **Fax** 207-367-2490 Lorelei Stevens. Compass Publications. Monthly newspaper.
7,000 to Atlantic fishing industry personnel interested in waterfront news, gear, markets, prices. www.fish-news.com/cfn/ lstevens@fish-news.com

Fish Farming News PO Box 600 Deer Isle ME 04672 **Phn:** 207-367-2396 **Fax** 207-367-2490 Lorelei Stevens. Compass Publications. 7-issue newspaper.
7,600 to aquaculturists interested in fish health, fish farm profiles, regulatory news, marketing. www.fish-news.com/ffn.htm/ lstevens@fish-news.com

Fisheries 5410 Grosvenor Ln Ste 110 Bethesda MD 20814 **Phn:** 301-897-8616 **Fax** 301-897-8096 Sarah Gilbert Fox. Amer. Fisheries Society. Monthly magazine.
10,000 to industry personnel interested in technical topics, events and Society news. www.fisheries.org sgilbertfox@fisheries.org

Fishermen's News 2201 W Commodore Way Seattle WA 98199 **Phn:** 206-284-8285 **Fax** 206-284-0391 Chris Philips. Monthly tabloid.
3,500 to fishing vessel owners in the Pacific; salmon, tuna seiners, trollers; equip. mfrs.
www.fishermensnews.com
editor@fishermensnews.com

National Fisherman PO Box 7438 Portland ME 04112 **Phn:** 207-842-5606 **Fax** 207-842-5611 Jerry Fraser. Diversified Publications, Inc. Monthly tabloid.
38,400 to Amer. commercial fishing and boatbuilding industry personnel. www.nationalfisherman.com
jfraser@divcom.com

Pacific Fishing 1000 Andover Park E Seattle WA 98188 **Phn:** 206-324-5644 **Fax** 206-324-8939 Don McManman. Monthly magazine.
5,000 to Pacific coastal commercial fishing industry personnel from California to the Bering Sea.
www.pacificfishing.com editor@pacificfishing.com

Medical--Surgical .40

AARC Times 9425 N Macarthur Blvd Ste 100 Irving TX 75063 **Phn:** 972-243-2272 **Fax** 972-484-2720 Marsha Cathcart. Amer. Assn Respiratory Care. Monthly mag.
34,700 to cardiopulmonary staff, respiratory therapists, managers, supervisors. www.aarc.org
cathcart@aarc.org

Advance For Medical Lab Pros 2900 Horizon Dr King Of Prussia PA 19406 **Phn:** 610-278-1400 **Fax** 610-278-1425 Lynn Nace. Merion Matters. 10pissue magazine.
42,000 to medical laboratory staff interested in educational, regulatory & society news, scientific developments. laboratorian.advanceweb.com
lnace@advanceweb.com

Advance For Physical Therapists 2900 Horizon Dr King Of Prussia PA 19406 **Phn:** 610-278-1400 **Fax** 610-278-1425 Lisa Lombardo. Merion Pub. Biweekly magazine.
85,000 to therapists interested in career opportunities, continuing education, news. physical-therapy.advanceweb.com llombardo@merion.com

AIDS Patient Care & STDs 140 Huguenot St Fl 3 New Rochelle NY 10801 **Phn:** 914-740-2100 **Fax** 914-740-2101 Maxine Langweil. Mary Ann Liebert, Inc. Mo. magazine.
5,600 to medical staff responsible for AIDS & STD diagnosis, treatment, prevention, education.
www.liebertpub.com info@liebertpub.com

American Chiropractor 8619 NW 68th St Ste CO138 Miami FL 33166 **Phn:** 305-434-8865 **Fax** 305-716-9212 Jaclyn Busch Touzard. Monthly magazine.
50,000 to chiropractors interested in peer-reviewed papers about current research and therapies.
www.theamericanchiropractor.com
pr@amchiropractor.com

American Family Physician 11400 Tomahawk Creek Pkwy Leawood KS 66211 **Phn:** 913-906-6000 **Fax** 913-906-6080 Joyce Merriman. Semimonthly magazine.
167,000 to family/primary care physicians interested in latest diagnostic and therapeutic techniques.
www.aafp.org afpedit@aafp.org

American Jrnl. Cardiology 3600 Gaston Ave Ste 457 Dallas TX 75246 **Phn:** 214-826-8252 **Fax** 214-826-2855 William C. Roberts. Elsevier Science. Semi-mo.
27,200 to physicians interested in drugs, diagnosis and treatment of cardiovascular disease.
www.ajconline.org

American Jrnl Clinical Nutrition 1100 Bates Ave Houston TX 77030 **Phn:** 713-798-7022 **Fax** 713-798-7046 Dennis M. Bier. Monthly magazine.
4,600 to clinicians interested in original research studies relevant to human nutrition. www.ajcn.org
dbier@nutrition.org

American Jrnl. Medicine 1840 E River Rd # E120 Tucson AZ 85718 **Phn:** 520-207-9415 **Fax** 520-207-9418 Joseph S. Alpert. Elsevier Science. Monthly magazine.
129,200 to Assn. of Professors of Medicine members concerned with academic rsch. only.
www.amjmed.com editors@amjmed.org

American Jrnl. OB/GYN 5228 Bressler Dr Hilliard OH 43026 **Phn:** 614-527-3820 **Fax** 614-527-3821 Donna Stroud. Monthly magazine.
44,700 to ob-gyn practioners interested in maternal-fetal medicine, assisted reproductin, gyn oncology.
www.ajog.org ajog@rrohio.com

American Jrnl. Occup. Therapy 4720 Montgomery Ln Ste 600 Bethesda MD 20814 **Phn:** 301-652-6611 **Fax** 301-652-7711 Sharon A. Gutman. Bimonthly magazine.
55,000 to Amer. Occ. Therapy Assn. members interested in new techniques, research. www.aota.org
cdavis@aota.org

American Jrnl. Psychiatry 1000 Wilson Blvd Ste 1825 Arlington VA 22209 **Phn:** 703-907-7300 **Fax** 703-907-1093 Kathy Stein. Amer. Psychiatric Assn. Monthly mag.
34,500 to Assn. members interested in mental illness diagnosis & treatment; Assn. activities. www.psych.org
ajp@psych.org

American Jrnl. Public Health 800 I St NW Washington DC 20001 **Phn:** 202-777-2742 **Fax** 202-777-2531 Nina Tristani. Monthly magazine.
28,000 to public health professionals interested in disease prevention, promoting public health.
www.apha.org comments@apha.org

American Jrnl. Sports Medicine 6300 N River Rd Ste 500 Rosemont IL 60018 **Phn:** 847-292-4900 **Fax** 847-653-8001 Bruce Reider. Monthly magazine.
9,000 to orthopaedic sports practitioners interested in peer-reviewed research. ajs.sagepub.com
breider@ajsm.org

American Psychologist 750 1st St NE Washington DC 20002 **Phn:** 202-336-5500 **Fax** 202-336-5549 Gary R. VandenBos. Amer. Psychological Assn. 9-issue magazine.
93,000 to APA members interested in academic articles on psychology, practice, public interest.
www.apa.org/pubs/journals/amp/index.aspx
apeditor@apa.org

Anesthesiology 200 Hawkins Dr Iowa City IA 52242 **Phn:** 319-356-4601 **Fax** 319-353-6817 James C Eisenach MD Lippincott Williams & Wilkins. Mo. magazine.
40,000 to members of Amer. Soc. of Anesthesiologists; clinical pharmacologists, ICU attendants.
journals.lww.com/anesthesiology/ editorial-office@anesthesiology.org

Medical--Surgical .40

Annals Of Internal Medicine 190 N Independence Mall W Philadelphia PA 19106 **Phn:** 215-351-2400 **Fax** 215-351-2644 Christine Laine. Semimonthly magazine.
102,000 to physicians in internal medicine, related fields; public health officials; libraries. www.annals.org
annals@acponline.org

Applied Radiology 180 Glenside Ave Scotch Plains NJ 07076 **Phn:** 908-301-1995 **Fax** 908-301-1997 Cristen Bolan. 10-issue magazine.
22,000 to radiologists, nuclear medicine physicians, technologists interested in peer-reviewed clinical articles. www.appliedradiology.com
cristen@appliedradiology.com

Archives Internal Medicine 3333 California St Ste 430/UCSF San Francisco CA 94118 **Phn:** 415-476-3545 **Fax** 415-476-8990 Philip Greenland. AMA. 22-issue magazine.
75,600 to physicians practicing internal medicine; other specialists practicing adult medicine.
archinte.ama-assn.org archinternmed@jama-archives.org

Archives Ped/Adolescent Medicine 6200 NE 74th St Ste 120B Seattle WA 98115 **Phn:** 206-685-3573 **Fax** 206-685-3572 Frederick P. Rivara. AMA. Mo. mag.
20,600 to pediatricians concerned with infant, child, adolescent health rsch. & developments.
archpedi.ama-assn.org archpediatrics@jama-archives.org

Archives Surgery 720 Rutland Ave Baltimore MD 21205 **Phn:** 443-287-0026 **Fax** 410-502-3131 Julie Ann Freischlag. Monthly magazine.
14,600 to surgeons interested in original acacemic papers, authoritative commentary. archsurg.ama-assn.org archsurg@jama-archives.org

Bioscience Technology 100 Enterprise Dr Ste 600 Rockaway NJ 07866 **Phn:** 973-920-7000 **Fax** 973-920-7542 Robert Fee. Advantage Business Media. Monthly.
55,000 to research scientists in hospitals, industry, universities, government, pharmaceuticals.
www.biosciencetechnology.com
robert.fee@advantagemedia.com

Biosupply Trends Quarterly 41093 County Center Dr Temecula CA 92591 **Phn:** 800-843-7477 Ronale Tucker Rhodes. FFF Enterprises. Quarterly magazine.
50,000 to primary care physicians, hospital & clinic buyers, pharmacy buyers responsible for biopharma product purchase. laboratorian.advanceweb.com
rrhodes@fffenterprises.com

Cancer 250 Williams St NW Atlanta GA 30303 **Phn:** 404-327-6411 **Fax** 404-551-5650 Carissa Gilman. Amer. Cancer Soc. 24-issue journal .
8,200 to oncology clinicians interested in peer-reviewed research. canceronlinejournal.com
canceredoff@cancer.org

CAP Today 325 Waukegan Rd Northfield IL 60093 **Phn:** 847-832-7000 **Fax** 847-832-8873 Sherrie Rice. College of American Pathologists. Monthly tabloid.
51,000 to College members, other pathologists, laboratory managers, hospital administrators.
www.cap.org captoday@sbcglobal.net

Cardiology News 5635 Fishers Ln Ste 6000 Rockville MD 20852 **Phn:** 240-221-4500 **Fax** 240-221-4400 Mary Jo Dales. Monthly tabloid.
25,200 to cardiologists interested in clinical developments, impacts of healthcare policy.
www.ecardiologynews.com
cardiologynews@elsevier.com

Cardiology Today 6900 Grove Rd Thorofare NJ 08086 **Phn:** 856-848-1000 **Fax** 856-848-6091 Stephanie Arasim Portnoy. Slack, Inc. Monthly magazine. TH:@GoHealio
55,900 to cardiologists & cardiology subspecialists interested in clinical issues, therapies, conferences.
www.cardiologytoday.com
editor@cardiologytoday.com

Chest 3300 Dundee Rd Northbrook IL 60062 **Phn:** 847-498-1400 **Fax** 847-498-5460 Jean Rice. Amer. College Chest Physicians. Monthly magazine.
20,500 to clinicians in pulmonology, thoracic, airways disease, other chest related medicine.
chestjournal.chestpubs.org editor@chestnet.org

Chiropractic Economics 5150 Palm Valley Rd #103 Ponte Vedra Beach FL 32082 **Phn:** 904-285-6020 **Fax** 904-567-1539 Daniel Sosnoski. 20-issue magazine. TH:@ChiroEcoMag
30,000 to chiropractors interested in practice mgmt., marketing, technology, patient care, continuing ed.
www.chiroeco.com dsosnoski@chiroeco.com

Circulation 560 Harrison Ave # 502 BU Boston MA 02118 **Phn:** 617-542-5100 **Fax** 617-542-6539 Joseph Loscalzo. Weekly magazine.
24,000 to cardiologists and internists interested in cardiovascular clinical and lab research.
circ.ahajournals.org circ@circulationjournal.org

Cleveland Clinic Jrnl. Medicine 9500 Euclid Ave # NA32 Cleveland OH 44195 **Phn:** 216-444-2661 **Fax** 216-444-9385 Dr. Brian Mandell. Monthly magazine.
101,600 to internists & cardiologists interested in drug trials, clinical matters. www.ccjm.org ccjm@ccf.org

Clinical Lab Products 6100 Center Dr Ste 1000 Los Angeles CA 90045 **Phn:** 310-642-4400 **Fax** 310-641-4444 Suzanne Clancy. Allied Media. Monthly tabloid.
45,000 to supervisory personnel in hospitals & independent labs, buyers of hospital & lab equipment.
www.clpmag.com sclancy@allied360.com

Clinical Psychiatry News 5635 Fishers Ln Ste 6000 Rockville MD 20852 **Phn:** 240-221-4500 **Fax** 240-221-4400 Mary Jo Dales. Elsevier Science. Monthly tabloid.
42,700 to practicing psychiatrists interested in clinical developments, news, commentary, health care policy.
www.clinicalpsychiatrynews.com
m.dales@elsevier.com

Clinician Reviews 7 Century Dr Ste 302 Parsippany NJ 07054 **Phn:** 973-206-3434 **Fax** 973-206-9378 Ann M. Hoppel. Frontline Medical Comms. Monthly magazine. TH:@ClinRev
125,000 to physician assts., nurse practitioners interested in current developments & news.
www.clinicianreviews.com
ahoppel@frontlinemedcom.com

Community Oncology 330 S Service Rd Ste 124 Melville NY 11747 **Phn:** 631-424-8900 **Fax** 631-424-8905 Randi Gould. Biolink Comms. Monthly magazine.
33,000 to oncologists, nurses, pharmacists interested in research, quality of care, practice mgmt.
www.communityoncology.net r.gould@elsevier.com

Consultant 535 Connecticut Ave Norwalk CT 06854 **Phn:** 203-523-7000 **Fax** 203-523-6776 Julie Bowen. CMPMedica. 14-issue magazine.
250,000 to physicians in all fields interested in diagnostic tips, patient education.
www.consultantlive.com
consultantedit@cmpmedica.com

Contemporary OB/GYN 24950 Country Club Blvd Ste 200 North Olmsted OH 44070 **Phn:** 440-243-8100 **Fax** 440-891-2651 Catherine M. Radwan. Advanstar. Monthly magazine.
47,000 to specialists and physicians in obstetrics and gynecology; nurse, supervisory staff.
www.modernmedicine.com cradwan@advanstar.com

Cosmetic Dermatology 7 Century Dr Ste 302 Parsippany NJ 07054 **Phn:** 973-206-3434 **Fax** 973-206-9251 Alicia Wendt. . Frontline Medical Comms. Monthly magazine. TH:@CSTNow
13,300 to dermatologists who practice cosmetic dermatology interested in articles, case study.
www.cosderm.com
alicia.wendt@frontlinemedcom.com

Cosmetic Surgery Times 24950 Country Club Blvd Ste 200 North Olmsted OH 44070 **Phn:** 440-243-8100 **Fax** 440-891-2651 Teresa McNulty. Advanstar. Bimonthly.
11,500 leading technology, surgical and noninvasive techniques, and practice management. cosmeticsurgerytimes.modernmedicine.com tmcnulty@advanstar.com

Cutis 7 Century Dr Ste 302 Parsippany NJ 07054 **Phn:** 973-206-3434 **Fax** 973-206-9251 Melissa Steiger. Frontline Medical Comms. Monthly magazine. TH:@CutisJournal
32,100 to physicians interested only in original clinical articles on dermatology, skin allergies. www.cutis.com msteiger@frontlinemedcom.com

Dermatology Times 24950 Country Club Blvd Ste 200 North Olmsted OH 44070 **Phn:** 440-243-8100 **Fax** 440-891-2651 Sarah Thuerk. Advanstar. Monthly tabloid. TH:@DermTimesNow
21,000 to practicing dermatologists interested in diagnosis and treatment analyses. dermatologytimes.modernmedicine.com sthuerk@advanstar.com

Diabetes Forecast 1701 N Beauregard St Alexandria VA 22311 **Phn:** 703-549-1500 **Fax** 703-253-4870 Kelly Rawlings. Amer. Diabetes Assn. Monthly magazine.
484,200 to diabetes patients & their families interested in all aspects of care & treatment, latest rsch. www.forecast.diabetes.org krawlings@diabetes.org

Diagnostic & Invasive Cardiology 3030 W Salt Creek Ln Ste 201 Arlington Hts IL 60005 **Phn:** 847-391-1000 **Fax** 847-390-0408 Dave Fornell. Scranton Gillette. Bimo. tab.
27,900 to cardiac care medical professionals responsible for technology specification. www.dicardiology.com dfornell@sgcmail.com

Diagnostic Imaging 600 Harrison St San Francisco CA 94107 **Phn:** 415-947-6000 **Fax** 415-947-6099 Sara Michael. CMP Medica. Online only.
for radiology & imaging professionals interested in imaging news & developments, job listings, conferences. www.diagnosticimaging.com sara.michael@ubm.com

Diversion 300 W 57th St New York NY 10019 **Phn:** 212-969-7500 Cathy Cavender. Hearst Corp. Online only.
for physicians interested in travel, recreation, food & wine, entertainment, lifestyle news. ccavender@hearst.com

The DO 142 E Ontario St Chicago IL 60611 **Phn:** 312-202-8000 **Fax** 312-202-8204 Patrick Sinco. Amer. Osteopathic Assn. Monthly magazine.
64,000 to Assn. members, osteopathic physicians interested in practice mgmt., meetings/events. www.do-online.org/TheDO/ psinco@osteopathic.org

Dynamic Chiropractic 5406 Bolsa Ave Huntington Beach CA 92649 **Phn:** 714-230-3150 **Fax** 714-899-4273 Peter Crownfield. Semimonthly tabloid.
70,000 to chiropractors interested in scientific, student, college, association news. www.chiroweb.com editorial@mpamedia.com

Ear, Nose & Throat Journal 1721 Pine St Philadelphia PA 19103 **Phn:** 215-732-6100 **Fax** 215-735-2725 Robert Sataloff. Monthly magazine.
11,200 to clinicians in ENT & otolaryngology practice interested in original research, reports, reviews. www.entjournal.com entjournal@phillyent.com

Emergency Medicine 7 Century Dr Ste 302 Parsippany NJ 07054 **Phn:** 973-206-3434 **Fax** 973-206-9542 Maura Griffin. Quadrant HealthCom. Monthly magazine.
34,000 to office- and hospital-based emergency medicine physicians and urgent care practitioners. www.emedmag.com maura.griffin@qhc.com

EMS World Magazine 1233 Janesville Ave Fort Atkinson WI 53538 **Phn:** 920-563-6388 **Fax** 866-436-2375 Nancy Perry. Monthly magzine.
48,000 to emergency medical svce. providers interested in clinical skills, equip., legal issues. www.emsworld.com nancy.perry@emsworld.com

Family Practice Management PO Box 11210 Overland Park KS 66207 **Phn:** 913-906-6000 **Fax** 913-906-6010 Leigh Ann Backer. Bimonthly magazine. TH:@FPMJournal
150,000 to primary care physicians interested in govt. regulations, practice mgmt., quality care. www.aafp.org/journals/fpm.html lbacker@aafp.org

Family Practice News 5635 Fishers Ln Ste 6000 Rockville MD 20852 **Phn:** 240-221-4500 **Fax** 240-221-4400 Mary Jo Dales. 21-issue tabloid.
80,300 to GPs with interest in family practice, news, trends in general practice medicine. www.efamilypracticenews.com fpnews@elsevier.com

Female Patient 7 Century Dr Ste 302 Parsippany NJ 07054 **Phn:** 973-206-3434 **Fax** 973-206-9251 John Hawes. Frontline Medical Comms.. 10-issue magazine. TH:@femalepatient
55,000 to obstetricians, gynecologists, physicians interested in new procedures & products. www.femalepatient.com john.hawes@qhc.com

General Surgery News 545 W 45th St Fl 8 New York NY 10036 **Phn:** 212-957-5300 **Fax** 212-957-7230 Kevin Horty. McMahon Publishing. Monthly newspaper.
37,600 to general surgeons interested in conventions, drug approvals, journal summaries. www.generalsurgerynews.com khorty@mcmahonmed.com

Healthcare Jrnl. of New Orleans 17732 Highland Rd Ste G-137 Baton Rouge LA 70810 **Phn:** 225-302-7500 Karen Stassi. Bimonthly magazine.
27,000 to New Orleans area healthcare professionals interested in news, interviews, local facilities, legal issues. www.healthcarejournalno.com editor@healthcarejournalno.com

Hearing Journal 333 7th Ave, Fl 19 New York NY 10001 **Phn:** 646-674-6561 **Fax** 646-674-6500 Lisa Hoffman. Lippincott Williams & Wilkins. Monthly mag.
22,000 to audiologists, ENT physicians, clinics, retail hearing aid specialists. journals.lww.com/thehearingjournal/ hj@wolterskluwer.com

HME Business 16261 Laguna Canyon Rd Irvine CA 92618 **Phn:** 949-265-1561 David Kopf. HME Media Group. Monthly tabloid.
17,300 to home medical equipment dealers & providers interested in markets, trends, news. hme-business.com dkopf@hmemediagroup.com

HomeCare 1900 28th Ave S Ste 110 Birmingham AL 35209 **Phn:** 205-212-9402 **Fax** 205-212-9452 Russ Willcutt. Cahaba Media Group. Monthly magazine. TH:@HomeCareSCPmags
17,100 to medical equipment providers of in-home equipment & svces. (wheelchairs, oxygen devices, infustion therapy, etc. www.homecaremag.com rwillcutt@cahabamedia.com

Imaging Technology News 3030 W Salt Creek Ln Ste 201 Arlington Hts IL 60005 **Phn:** 847-391-1000 **Fax** 847-390-0408 Dave Fornell. Scranton Gillette. 9-issue tabloid.
36,000 to medical imaging & radiation oncology personnel responsible for technology purchasing & administration. www.itnonline.com dfornell@sgcmail.com

Infection Control Today 3300 N Central Ave Ste 300 Phoenix AZ 85012 **Phn:** 480-990-1101 Kelly Pyrek. Virgo Publishing. Monthly magazine.
31,000 to infection preventionists in operating rooms, sterile processing, environmental services. www.infectioncontroltoday.com kpyrek@vpico.com

Infectious Disease News 6900 Grove Rd Thorofare NJ 08086 **Phn:** 856-848-1000 **Fax** 856-853-5991 Jay Lewis. Slack, Inc. Monthly tabloid.
8,900 to infectious disease professionals interested in clinical issues and medical therapies. www.infectiousdiseasenews.com idn@slackinc.com

Infectious Diseases In Children 6900 Grove Rd Thorofare NJ 08086 **Phn:** 856-848-1000 **Fax** 856-853-5991 Colleen Zacharyczuk. Slack, Inc. Monthly tabloid.
65,800 to pediatricians interested in new drugs, procedures, vaccines, treatment. www.pediatricsupersite.com editor@pediatricsupersite.com

Internal Medicine News 5635 Fishers Ln Ste 6000 Rockville MD 20852 **Phn:** 240-221-4500 **Fax** 240-221-4400 21-issue tabloid.
120,100 to internists, cardiologists, gastroenterologists interested in conventions & developments. www.internalmedicinenews.com imnews@elsevier.com

Jrnl. American Medical Assn. 515 N. State St. Chicago IL 60654 **Phn:** 312-464-2400 **Fax** 312-464-5824 Amer. Medical Assn. Weekly magazine.
311,600 to Assn. members, physicians in all types of practice, medical schools. www.ama-assn.org jama-comments@ama-assn.org

Jrnl. Amer. Osteopathic Assn. 142 E Ontario St Chicago IL 60611 **Phn:** 312-202-8166 **Fax** 312-202-8466 Audrey D. Lusher. Am. Osteopathic Assn. Mo. mag.
62,600 to Assn. members, osteopathic physicians interested only in research & scientific papers. www.jaoa.org jaoa@osteopathic.org

Jrnl. Bone/Joint Surgery 20 Pickering St Needham MA 02492 **Phn:** 781-449-9780 **Fax** 781-449-9787 Vernon Tolo. Monthly magazine.
38,300 to orthopaedic surgeons interested only in original academic & research papers. www.jbjs.org editorial@jbjs.org

Jrnl. Clinical Outcomes Mgmt. 125 Strafford Ave Ste 220 Wayne PA 19087 **Phn:** 610-975-4541. **Fax** 610-975-4564 Bobbie Lewis. Turner-White. Monthly magazine.
54,600 to managed-care decisionmakers & primary care physicians interested in evidence-based clinical care reviews. www.turner-white.com blewis@turner-white.com

Jrnl. Family Practice 110 Summit Ave Montvale NJ 07645 **Phn:** 201-391-9100 **Fax** 201-391-2778 Marya Ostrowski. Frontline Medical Comms. Monthly magazine. TH:@JFamPract
95,400 to office & hospital-based practitioners of family medicine; interns, residents, staffs. www.jfponline.com mostrowski@frontlinemedcom.com

Jrnl. Natl. Medical Assn. 1012 10th St NW Washington DC 20001 **Phn:** 202-347-1895 **Fax** 202-371-1162 Eddie Hoover. Monthly magazine.
43,500 to physicians & policymakers interested in health & medical needs of inner-city residents. www.nmanet.org editorjnma@nmanet.org

Jrnl. Nuclear Medicine 1850 Samuel Morse Dr Reston VA 20190 **Phn:** 703-708-9000 **Fax** 703-708-9018 Susan Alexander. Monthly magazine.
15,000 to medical imaging professionals interested in peer-reviewed papers. jnm.snmjournals.org eic_jnm@mednet.ucla.edu

Jrnl. Pediatrics 3333 Burnet Ave # D3.50 Cincinnati OH 45229 **Phn:** 513-636-7140 **Fax** 513-636-7141 William Balistreri. Mosby, Inc. Monthly magazine.
4,900 to physicians concerned with disorders of infants, children & adolescents. www.jpeds.com journal.pediatrics@cchmc.org

Jrnl. Reproductive Medicine 8342 Olive Blvd Saint Louis MO 63132 **Phn:** 314-991-4440 **Fax** 314-991-4654 Donna Kessel. Monthly magazine.
36,500 to specialists, residents in obstetrics & gynecology interested in clinical reviews, case study. www.reproductivemedicine.com editor@reproductivemedicine.com

LabMedicine 33 W Monroe St Ste 1600 Chicago IL 60603 **Phn:** 312-541-4999 **Fax** 312-541-4998 Molly Strzelecki. Amer. Soc. Clinical Pathology. Monthly magazine.
8,800 to clinical pathology lab personnel interested in lab science, education, procedures.
labmed.ascpjournals.org labmed@ascp.org

Lancet 360 Park Ave S New York NY 10010 **Phn:** 212-633-3810 **Fax** 212-633-3850 Maja Zecevic. Weekly magazine.
53,800 to North Amer. physicians interested in medical breakthroughs, global perspectives.
www.thelancet.com m.zecevic@lancet.com

LocumLife 24950 Country Club Blvd Ste 200 North Olmsted OH 44070 **Phn:** 440-891-2702 **Fax** 440-891-2735 David Bennett. Advanstar. Online only. TH:@LocumLife
to physicians interested in temporary practice alternative, staffing firms, contracts.
locumlife.modernmedicine.com
dbennett@advanstar.com

Managed Care 780 Township Line Rd Yardley PA 19067 **Phn:** 267-685-2788 **Fax** 267-685-2966 John Marcille. MediMedia USA. Monthly magazine.
43,700 to clinical managers and senior level executives at health plans. www.managedcaremag.com
editors@managedcaremag.com

Maryland Physician PO Box 1663 Millersville MD 21108 **Phn:** 443-837-6948 Jacquie Roth. Mojo Media, LLC. Bimonthly magazine. TH:@mdphysicianmag
8,000 to Maryland physicians & healthcare administrators responsible for practice management & patient care. www.mdphysicianmag.com
editor@mdphysicianmag.com

Mayo Clinic Proceedings 200 1st St SW Rochester MN 55905 **Phn:** 507-284-2094 **Fax** 507-284-0252 Dr. William Lanier. Monthly magazine.
124,100 to general & specialized practitioners interested only in physician-submitted articles.
www.mayoclinicproceedings.com
proceedings@mayo.edu

Medical Design 1300 E 9th St Cleveland OH 44114 **Phn:** 216-931-9636 **Fax** 216-931-9616 Michael Browne. Penton Media. 10-issue magazine.
35,100 to engineers, designers, decisionmakers in medical device mfg., diagnostic device mfg., pharmaceutical mfg. medicaldesign.com
michael.browne@penton.com

Medical Design Technology 100 Enterprise Dr Bx 912 # 600 Rockaway NJ 07866 **Phn:** 973-920-7054 **Fax** 973-920-7542 Sean Fenske. Advantage Business Media. Mo. tab.
41,000 to design engineers, technical staff at medical device mfrs., in vitro diagnostic firms.
www.mdtmag.com
sean.fenske@advantagemedia.com

Medical Device/Diagnostic Ind. 11444 W Olympic Blvd Los Angeles CA 90064 **Phn:** 310-445-4200 **Fax** 310-445-4269 Heather Thompson. UMB Canon. Monthly magazine.
48,000 to medical device, in vitro diagnostic, biotech product mfg. mgmt. & technical personnel.
www.mddionline.com heather.thompson@ubm.com

Medical Economics 24950 Country Club Blvd Ste 200 North Olmsted OH 44070 **Phn:** 440-243-8100 **Fax** 440-891-2651 Donna Marbury. Advanstar. 24-issue magazine. TH:@MedEconomics
181,400 to physicians concerned with practice & personal financial mgmt. www.MedicalEconomics.com
dmarbury@advanstar.com

Medical Meetings 10 Fawcett St Ste 500 Cambridge MA 01238 **Phn:** 978-448-0377 Sue Pelletier. Penton Media. 7-issue magazine.
12,100 to personnel responsible for planning & execution of healthcare conferences, CME programs, related conventions. meetingsnet.com
spelletier@meetingsnet.com

Monitor on Psychology 750 1st St NE Washington DC 20002 **Phn:** 202-336-5500 **Fax** 202-336-6103 Sara Martin. Am. Psychological Assn. Monthly magazine.
106,200 to psychologists interested in updates on scientific, legislative, mental health news.
www.apa.org/monitor/ smartin@apa.org

The Nation's Health 800 I St NW Washington DC 20001 **Phn:** 202-777-2438 **Fax** 202-777-2534 Michele Late. Amer. Public Health Assn. 10-issue tabloid.
24,000 to Assn. members; media, members of Congress, health officials in private and public fields.
thenationshealth.aphapublications.org
nations.health@apha.org

Nephrology News & Issues 200 Croft St # 1 Birmingham AL 35242 **Phn:** 205-408-3700 **Fax** 205-408-3797 Rebecca Zumoff. Grand View Media. Monthly.
26,500 to nephrologists, other renal care personnel responsible for care, research, policy setting.
nephnews.com

Neurology 1080 Montreal Ave Saint Paul MN 55116 **Phn:** 651-695-2782 **Fax** 651-332-8608 Robert A. Gross MD Weekly journal.
20,200 to neurologists interested in peer-reviewed research applicable to their practices.
www.neurology.org journal@neurology.org

Neurology Now 530 Walnut St Philadelphia PA 19106 **Phn:** 646-674-6560 **Fax** 646-674-6500 Mike Smolinsky. Bimonthly magazine. TH:@NeurologyNow
500,000 to readers with neurological conditions, their caregivers & families, interested in treatment, research, products.
journals.lww.com/neurologynow/pages/default.aspx
mike.smolinsky@wolterskluwer.com

New Physician 45610 Woodland Rd #300 Sterling VA 20166 **Phn:** 703-620-6600 **Fax** 703-620-6445 Pete Thomson. Amer. Med. Student Assn. 6-issue magazine.
28,000 to Assn. members, med. & pre-med. students interested in educational issues & healthcare news.
www.amsa.org/tnp/ tnp@amsa.org

OB. GYN. News 5635 Fishers Ln Ste 6000 Rockville MD 20852 **Phn:** 240-221-4500 **Fax** 240-221-4400 Mary Jo Dales. Elsevier Science. 24-issue tabloid.
40,000 to family practitioners, obstetricians, gynecologists interested in clinical matters.
www.obgynnews.com obnews@elsevier.com

OBG Management 7 Century Dr # 302 Parsippany NJ 07054 **Phn:** 07054-460942 **Fax** 973-206-9251 Robert L. Barbieri MD. Frontline Medical Comms. Monthly magazine. TH:@obgmanagement
112,400 to ob gyn practitioners interested in clinical developments, legal issues, practice mgmt.
www.obgmanagement.com
rbarbieri@frontlinemedcom.com

Obstetrics & Gynecology 423 Wakara Way Ste 201 Salt Lake City UT 84108 **Phn:** 801-583-6000 **Fax** 801-583-6010 James R. Scott. Amer. College Obstetrics & Gynecology. Mo. mag.
45,900 to practitioners interested in all aspects of clinical practice, ACOG news.
journals.lww.com/greenjournal/
obgyn@greenjournal.com

Oncology News International 600 Community Dr Manhasset NY 11030 **Phn:** 516-734-2004 **Fax** 516-734-2018 Rachel Warren. CMP Medica. Monthly tabloid.
26,800 to cancer clinicians interested in news and meetings in fields of hematology and oncology.
www.cancernetwork.com rachel.warren@ubm.com

Oncology Times 333 7th Ave Fl 19 New York NY 10001 **Phn:** 646-674-6544 **Fax** 646-674-6500 Serena Stockwell. Lippincott Williams & Wilkins. Twice-monthly tabloid.
45,400 to cancer physicians & nurses interested in latest international news and research.
journals.lww.com/oncology-times/ ot@lwwny.com

Orthopedics 6900 Grove Rd Thorofare NJ 08086 **Phn:** 856-848-1000 **Fax** 856-848-6091 Robin Vadel. Slack, Inc. Monthly magazine.
29,500 to physicians interested in clinical articles about orthopedic surgery and treatments.
www.orthosupersite.com ortho@slackinc.com

Pediatric News 5635 Fishers Ln Ste 6000 Rockville MD 20852 **Phn:** 240-221-2385 **Fax** 240-221-4400 Catherine Nellist. Elsevier Science. Monthly tabloid.
54,400 to practicing pediatricians interested in news, clinical developments, health care policy.
www.pediatricnews.com

Pediatrics 141 Northwest Point Blvd Elk Grove Vlg IL 60007 **Phn:** 847-434-7895 **Fax** 847-434-8000 Alain Park. Amer. Acad. of Pediatrics. Monthly magazine.
61,600 to pediatricians and other physicians interested in original clinical and research papers.
pediatrics.aappublications.org apark@aap.org

Physical Therapy 1111 N Fairfax St Alexandria VA 22314 **Phn:** 703-706-3194 **Fax** 703-706-3169 Jan Reynolds. Amer. Phys. Therapy Assn. Monthly.
70,000 to Assn. members & other physical therapists interested in case studies & methodology.
www.apta.org janreynolds@apta.org

Physical Therapy Products 6100 Center Dr Ste 1000 Los Angeles CA 90045 **Phn:** 310-642-4400 **Fax** 310-641-1511 Frank Long. Ascend Media. 9-issue mag.
30,000 to physical therapy practioners, pt facility business mgrs. & owners interested in products & services. www.ptproductsonline.com
flong@allied360.com

Physicians Practice 5523 Research Park Dr Ste 220 Baltimore MD 21228 **Phn:** 443-543-5100 **Fax** 443-543-5170 Pamela Moore. CMP Medica. 10-issue magazine.
255,000 to physicians interested in legal, financial, technology aspects of their practices.
www.physicianspractice.com
info@physicianspractice.com

Plastic Surgery News 444 E Algonquin Rd Arlington Heights IL 60005 **Phn:** 847-228-9900 **Fax** 847-228-9131 Mike Stokes. Amer. Soc. Plastic Srgns. 11-issue tab.
6,600 to plastic & reconstructive surgeons interested in new procedures, symposia, meetings.
www.plasticsurgery.org mss@plasticsurgery.org

Plastic Surgery Practice 6100 Center Dr Ste 1000 Los Angeles CA 90045 **Phn:** 310-642-4400 **Fax** 310-641-1511 Denise Mann. Ascend Media. Monthly magazine.
12,000 to plastic surgeons interested in practice mgmt., products, technologies, news.
www.plasticsurgerypractice.com
ddmann@allied360.com

Podiatry Today 83 General Warren Blvd Ste 100 Malvern PA 19355 **Phn:** 610-560-0500 **Fax** 610-560-0502 Jeff Hall. HMP Comms. Monthly magazine.
11,600 to practicing podiatrists interested in conditions, treatments, technology.
www.podiatrytoday.com
jhall@hmpcommunications.com

PracticeLink Magazine 214 S 8th St Ste 502 Louisville KY 40202 **Phn:** 502-589-8250 **Fax** 502-587-0848 Laura Hammond. Quarterly magazine.
80,000 to physicians interested in career development, practice searches, placements. practicelink.com
laura.hammond@practicelink.com

Provider 1201 L St NW Washington DC 20005 **Phn:** 202-842-4444 **Fax** 202-842-3860 Joanne Erickson. Amer. Health Care Assn. Monthly magazine.
50,300 to long-term healthcare facility directors, medical & nursing staff. www.providermagazine.com
jpewing@ahca.org

Psychiatric News 1000 Wilson Blvd Ste 1825 Arlington VA 22209 **Phn:** 703-907-8570 **Fax** 703-907-1091 Jeffrey Borenstein. Amer. Psychiatric Assn. Semimonthly tab.
31,400 to Assn. members, psychiatric residents and interns, others in mental health field.
psychiatryonline.org pnews@psych.org

Psychiatric Times 535 Connecticut Ave Ste 300 Norwalk CT 06854 **Phn:** 203-523-7000 **Fax** 203-662-6776 Natalie Timoshin. CMP Medica. Monthly magazine.
39,600 to psychiatrists and physicians interested in mental health issues. www.psychiatrictimes.com ptedit@cmpmedica.com

Psychotherapy Networker 5135 MacArthur Blvd NW Washington DC 20016 **Phn:** 202-537-8950 **Fax** 202-537-6869 Livia Kent. Bimonthly. TH:@pnetworker
45,000 to professional counselors, social workers, marriage/family therapists, psychotherapists. www.psychotherapynetworker.org lkent@psychnetworker.org

PT In Motion 1111 N Fairfax St Alexandria VA 22314 **Phn:** 703-706-3194 **Fax** 703-706-3169 Donald Tepper. Amer. Phys. Therapy Assn. Monthly.
75,000 to Assn. members & other physical therapists interested in healthcare, news, research. www.apta.org/ptinmotion ptmag@apta.org

Public Health Reports 1101 15th St NW Ste 910 Washington DC 20005 **Phn:** 202-296-1099 **Fax** 202-296-1252 Julie Keefe. U.S. Public Health Svc. Bimo. magazine.
6,500 to medical, political community interested in disease prevention & control, public policy. www.publichealthreports.org jak2@cdc.gov

Radiology 800 Boylston St. Boston MA 02199 **Phn:** 617-236-7376 **Fax** 630-571-7837 John Humpal. Radiological Soc. of N. Amer. Monthly magazine.
28,600 to radiologists, radiation oncologists, medical physicists interested in peer-reviewed clinical information. www.rsna.org radiology@rsna.org

Rehab Management 6100 Center Dr Ste 1020 Los Angeles CA 90045 **Phn:** 310-642-4400 **Fax** 310-641-4444 Frank Long. Allied Media. 9 issues.
20,000 to physical & occupational therapists interested in facility reports, news, products, services. rehabpub.com flong@allied360.com

Rehabilitation Counsel. Bulletin 100 Ball Hall Univ Of Memphis Memphis TN 38152 **Phn:** 901-678-2841 **Fax** 901-678-5114 Douglas C. Strohmer. Quarterly mag.
1,500 to rehabilitation counselors interested only in original research, case studies. www.proedinc.com dstrohmr@memphis.edu

Respiratory Care 9425 N Macarthur Blvd Ste 100 Irving TX 75063 **Phn:** 972-243-2272 **Fax** 972-484-2720 Ray Masferrer. Monthly magazine.
29,000 to respiratory care clinicians interested in diagnosis, prevention & mgmt. of conditions; technologies. www.rcjournal.com masferrer@aarc.org

RT 6100 Center Dr Ste 1020 Los Angeles CA 90045 **Phn:** 310-642-4400 **Fax** 310-641-0831 Marian Benjamin. Allied Media. Monthly magazine.
20,000 to respiratory clinicians & mgrs. interested in case studies, news, events, features. www.rtmagazine.com mbenjamin@allied360.com

Skin & Allergy News 5635 Fishers Ln Ste 6000 Rockville MD 20852 **Phn:** 240-221-4500 **Fax** 240-221-4400 Mary Jo Dales. Elsevier Science. Monthly tabloid.
14,800 to dermatologists interested in news about clinical developments, healthy care policy, practice mgmt. www.skinandallergynews.com sknews@elsevier.com

Southern Medical Journal PO Box 70429 Johnson City TN 37614 **Phn:** 423-439-8091 **Fax** 423-979-3438 Ronald Hamdy. Southern Med. Assn. Monthly magazine.
11,000 to primary care & specialist doctors interested in natl. and regional medical issues; Assn. news. sma.org/smj smj@sma.org

Surgery 20 North St Ste 1 Plymouth MA 02360 **Phn:** 508-732-6767 **Fax** 508-732-6766 David Newcombe. Stellar Medical Pubs. Monthly magazine.
3,300 to practicing general surgeons interested clinical/experimental surgery academic papers. www.surgjournal.com surgery@stellarmed.com

Medical--Surgical .40

Surgical Products 199 E. Badger Rd. Ste 201 Madison WI 53713 **Phn:** 973-920-7000 **Fax** 973-920-7542 Jon Minnick. Advantage Business Media. Monthly.
60,000 to surgeons, O.R. staff, purchasing mgrs. interested in new techniques and equipment. www.surgicalproductsmag.com jon.minnick@advantagemedia.com

Texas Medicine 401 W 15th St Ste 100 Austin TX 78701 **Phn:** 512-370-1300 **Fax** 512-370-1630 Larry BeSaw. TX Medical Assn. Monthly magazine.
34,200 to TX physicians interested in public health, medicolegal & economic issues. www.texmed.org editor@texmed.org

Today's Chiropractic Lifestyle 450 Northridge Pkwy Ste 202 Atlanta GA 30350 **Phn:** 770-650-1102 **Fax** 770-650-2848 Katie Brown. Bimonthly magazine.
38,000 to practitioners interested in chiropractic healthcare, nutrition, diagnostics, instruments. www.todayschiropractic.com editor@todayschiropractic.com

Urology Times 24950 Country Club Blvd Ste 200 North Olmsted OH 44070 **Phn:** 440-243-8100 **Fax** 440-891-2651 Patricia M. Fernberg. Advanstar. Monthly magazine.
10,500 advances in surgical and non-surgical techniques, treatments, and practice management. www.modernmedicine.com/modernmedicine/Urology/home/40184 ut@advanstar.com

US Medicine 39 York St Lambertville NJ 08530 **Phn:** 609-397-5522 **Fax** 609-397-4237 Brenda L. Mooney. Marathon Medical Comms. Monthly tabloid.
34,600 to Federal, state, municipal, military, V.A. physicians interested in clinical, legislative news. www.usmedicine.com mooney@usmedicine.com

Metals--Machinery--Toolmaking .41

Advanced Materials & Processes 9639 Kinsman Rd Materials Park OH 44073 **Phn:** 440-338-5151 **Fax** 440-338-4634 Ed Kubel. ASM Intl. Monthly magazine.
25,200 to metallurgists, engineers responsible for materials testing, fabrication, manufacture. www.asminternational.org ed.kubel@asminternational.org

American Metal Market 225 Park Ave S Fl 7 New York NY 10003 **Phn:** 646-274-6230 **Fax** 212-213-6617 Anne Riley. Monthly magazine.
7,800 to senior mgmt. and procurement personnel in metal fabricating, distributing, producing. www.amm.com ariley@amm.com

Assembly 1050 Il Route 83 Ste 200 Bensenville IL 60106 **Phn:** 630-616-0200 **Fax** 630-227-0204 John Sprovieri. BNP Media. 13-issue magazine.
56,100 to OEM market manufacturing and engineering professionals. www.assemblymag.com h rovierij@bnpmedia.com

Cutting Tool Engineering 40 Skokie Blvd Ste 450 Northbrook IL 60062 **Phn:** 847-714-0175 **Fax** 847-559-4444 Alan Richter. CTE Publications. Monthly magazine.
47,500 to metalworking industry mgrs., engineers, purchasers, equipment mfrs., wholesalers. www.ctemag.com alanr@jwr.com

Die Casting Engineer 241 Holbrook Dr Wheeling IL 60090 **Phn:** 847-279-0001 **Fax** 847-279-0002 Andrew Ryzner. N. Amer. Die Casting Assn. Bimonthly.
2,500 to Assn. members, other die casting industry personnel interested in markets, design, plant operations. www.diecasting.org/dce/ dce@diecasting.org

Fabricator 833 Featherstone Rd Rockford IL 61107 **Phn:** 815-399-8700 Dan Davis. FMA Comms. Inc. Monthly tabloid.
58,000 to owners, execs., supervisors, engineers, foremen at forming/fabricated metals plants. www.thefabricator.com press_releases@thefabricator.com

Fastener Technology Intl. 1867 W Market St Ste C3 Akron OH 44313 **Phn:** 330-864-2122 **Fax** 330-864-5298 Michael McNulty. Initial Publications. Bimonthly.
13,100 to fastener, cold heading industries mgrs. interested in new products & equipment. www.fastenertech.com mcnulty@fastenertech.com

Forging 1300 E 9th St Cleveland OH 44114 **Phn:** 216-696-7000 **Fax** 216-931-9524 Robert Brooks. Penton Media.
35,000 to owners, operators, managers, engineers, researchers, technicians, in the forging field. www.forgingmagazine.com robert.brooks@penton.com

Foundry Mgmt. & Technology 1300 E 9th St Cleveland OH 44114 **Phn:** 216-696-7000 **Fax** 216-931-9524 Robert Brooks. Penton Media. Monthly magazine.
17,000 to mgmt., production, engineering, personnel in foundries and metal casting departments. www.foundrymag.com robert.brooks@penton.com

Gear Technology 1840 Jarvis Ave Elk Grove Village IL 60007 **Phn:** 847-437-6604 **Fax** 847-437-6618 Michael Goldstein. Randall Publishing. 8-issue magazine.
10,800 to gearing industry design, manufacturing, engineering, executive personnel. www.geartechnology.com wrs@geartechnology.com

Industrial Heating 1910 Cochran Rd Ste 450 Pittsburgh PA 15220 **Phn:** 412-531-3370 **Fax** 412-531-3375 Reed Miller. BNP Media. Monthly magazine.
23,000 to mfg. personnel responsible for thermal energy systems and delivery. www.industrialheating.com reed@industrialheating.com

Industrial Laser Solutions 98 Spit Brook Rd Nashua NH 03062 **Phn:** 603-891-0123 **Fax** 603-891-0574 Carrie Meadows. PennWell Publishing. Monthly magazine.
15,200 to laser materials processing personnel interested in products, technology, industry developments. www.optoiq.com carriem@pennwell.com

Iron & Steel Technology 186 Thorn Hill Rd Warrendale PA 15086 **Phn:** 724-814-3032 **Fax** 724-814-3033 Janet McConnell. Assn. for Iron & Steel Tech. Monthly magazine.
12,300 to iron and steel industry personnel working in metallurgy, engineering, operations. www.aist.org jmcconnell@aist.org

JOM 184 Thorn Hill Rd Warrendale PA 15086 **Phn:** 724-776-9000 **Fax** 724-776-3770 Maureen Byko. Minerals/Metals/Material Soc. Monthly magazine.
6,900 to materials science & engineering professionals in industry, research, academia. www.tms.org/pubs/journals/JOM/ jom@tms.org

Light Metal Age 170 S Spruce Ave Ste 120 South San Francisco CA 94080 **Phn:** 650-588-8832 **Fax** 650-588-0901 Joseph Benedyk. Bimonthly magazine.
3,300 to aluminum and non-ferrous metals industry personnel interested in technical content. www.lightmetalage.com lma@lightmetalage.com

Manufacturing Engineering PO Box 930 Dearborn MI 48121 **Phn:** 313-271-1500 **Fax** 313-425-3417 Brian Hogan. Soc. Mfg. Engineers. Monthly magazine.
92,700 to mfg. engineers, owners, plant mgrs., designers, researchers, technicians. www.sme.org bhogan@sme.org

Metal Center News 1100 Jorie Blvd Ste 207 Oak Brook IL 60523 **Phn:** 630-571-1067 **Fax** 630-572-0689 Tim Triplett. Sackett Business Media. Monthly magazine.
15,700 to mgmt., sales, production, purchasing personnel in metal distribution industry. www.metalcenternews.com dmarkham@metalcenternews.com

Metal Finishing 360 Park Ave S New York NY 10010 **Phn:** 212-633-3100 **Fax** 212-633-3140 Drew Amorosi. Elsevier. 11-issue magazine.
25,800 to electroplating & coating industry personnel interested in problem solving, products, technologies. www.metalfinishing.com d.amorosi@elsevier.com

MetalForming 6363 Oak Tree Blvd Independence OH 44131 **Phn:** 216-901-8800 **Fax** 216-901-9190 Brad Kuvin. PMA Services. Monthly magazine.
60,000 to engineers, production & purchasing mgrs. in precision metalforming industry.
www.metalformingmagazine.com bkuvin@pma.org

Modern Casting 1695 N Penny Ln Schaumburg IL 60173 **Phn:** 847-824-0181 **Fax** 847-824-7848 Alfred Spada. Amer. Foundry Soc. Monthly magazine.
16,500 to foundry managers responsible for production, operations and marketing.
www.moderncasting.com aspada@afsinc.org

Modern Machine Shop 6915 Valley Ln Cincinnati OH 45244 **Phn:** 513-527-8800 **Fax** 513-527-8801 Mark Albert. Gardner Publications. Monthly magazine.
102,000 to operations and production mgrs. in metalworking plants of all sizes and types.
www.mmsonline.com press@gardnerweb.com

Modern Metals 625 N Michigan Ave Ste 1100 Chicago IL 60611 **Phn:** 312-654-2300 **Fax** 312-654-2323 Lauren Duensing. Trend Publishing. 11-issue magazine.
35,000 to metal component plant mgrs., engineers, production & purchasing personnel.
www.modernmetals.com lduensing@modernmetals.com

Plating & Surface Finishing 1155 15th St NW Ste 500 Washington DC 20005 **Phn:** 202-457-8401 **Fax** 202-530-0659 Jim Lindsey. Nat'l Assn for Surface Finishing. 10-issue mag.
4,500 to Assn. members interested in continuing education, industry networking, Assn. news.
www.nasf.org editorjasf@yahoo.com

Powder Coating 1155 Northland Dr Saint Paul MN 55120 **Phn:** 651-287-5600 **Fax** 651-287-5650 Peggy Koop. 10-issue magazine.
22,000 to engineers, managers, technicians in powder coating system operation or production.
www.pcoating.com pkoop@cscpub.com

Practical Welding Today 833 Featherstone Rd Rockford IL 61107 **Phn:** 815-399-8700 **Fax** 815-484-7700 Amanda Carlson. FMA Comms. Inc. Bimonthly.
30,000 to welders interested in hands-on technical news, metallurgy, machinery, tools.
www.thefabricator.com press_releases@thefabricator.com

Products Finishing 6915 Valley Ln Cincinnati OH 45244 **Phn:** 513-527-8800 **Fax** 513-527-8801 Kate Hand. Gardner Publishing. Monthly magazine.
35,000 to engineers and managers in metal, plastic, wood finishing process function. www.pfonline.com khand@pfonline.com

Recycling Today 4020 Kinross Lakes Pkwy Ste 201 Richfield OH 44286 **Phn:** 330-523-5400 **Fax** 216-925-5038 Brian Taylor. G.I.E. Media. Monthly magazine.
14,800 to recycling personnel concerned with marketing on natl., state, municipal levels.
www.recyclingtoday.com btaylor@gie.net

Scrap 1615 L St NW Ste 600 Washington DC 20036 **Phn:** 202-662-8543 **Fax** 202-626-0943 Rachel Pollack. Inst. Scrap Recycling Industries. Bimonthly magazine.
11,300 to processors, brokers, users of metal, paper, glass, textile, rubber, electronic, plastic scrap.
www.scrap.org rachelpollack@scrap.org

Stamping Journal 833 Featherstone Rd Rockford IL 61107 **Phn:** 815-399-8700 **Fax** 815-381-1370 Kate Bachman. FMA Comms. Inc. Bimonthly magazine.
34,000 to metal stamping industry personnel interested in technical information, equipment & product reviews.
www.fma-communications.com/SJ/ press_releases@thefabricator.com

TPJ-Tube & Pipe Journal 833 Featherstone Rd Rockford IL 61107 **Phn:** 815-399-8700 **Fax** 815-399-8618 Eric Lundin. FMA Comms. Inc. 8-issue magazine.
28,000 to metal tube & pipe mfg. industry personnel interested in technical articles. www.thefabricator.com press_releases@thefabricator.com

Metals--Machinery--Toolmaking .41

Welding Design & Fabrication 1300 E 9th St Cleveland OH 44114 **Phn:** 216-696-7000 **Fax** 216-931-9524 Robert Brooks. Penton Media. Online only.
for designers, engineers, managers, supervisors, and buyers in plants and field sites. weldingdesign.com robert.brooks@penton.com

Welding Journal 550 NW 42nd Ave Miami FL 33126 **Phn:** 305-443-9353 **Fax** 305-443-7404 Andrew Cullison. Amer. Welding Society. Monthly magazine.
49,900 to Soc. members, others in welding interested in testing, training, products, events. www.aws.org/wj/ cullison@aws.org

Military .42

Air Force Times 6883 Commercial Dr. Springfield VA 22151 **Phn:** 703-750-8699 **Fax** 703-750-8601 Markie Harwood. Army Times Publishing. Weekly newspaper.
54,200 to USAF servicepeople & their families interested in careers, benefits, lifestyle.
www.airforcetimes.com airlet@airforcetimes.com

American Veteran 4647 Forbes Blvd. Lanham MD 20706 **Phn:** 877-726-8387 **Fax** 202-318-7653 Brittany Barry. AMVETS. Quarterly magazine. TH:@AMVETSNational
216,000 to veterans & their families interested in VA affairs, veterans' legislation, assistance, community programs, local even www.amvets.org/american-veteran-magazine/ bbarry@amvets.org

Armed Forces Journal 6883 Commercial Dr Springfield VA 22151 **Phn:** 703-750-7312 **Fax** 703-750-8601 Brad Peniston. Monthly magazine.
23,400 to senior career military officers; members of Department of Defense, govt. officials.
www.armedforcesjournal.com bpeniston@atpco.com

Army 2425 Wilson Blvd Ste 100 Arlington VA 22201 **Phn:** 703-841-4300 **Fax** 703-841-3505 Mary Blake French. Assn. of US Army. Monthly magazine.
84,700 to Assn. members, military defense staff, defense industry personnel, members of Congress.
www.ausa.org mfrench@ausa.org

Army Aviation 755 Main St Ste 4D Monroe CT 06468 **Phn:** 203-268-2450 **Fax** 203-268-5870 James Bullinger. Army Aviation Assn. 10-issue magazine.
17,100 to Assn. members interested in Army Aviation news, technology, developments. www.quad-a.org editor@quad-a.org

Army Times 6883 Commercial Dr. Springfield VA 22151 **Phn:** 703-750-8619 **Fax** 703-750-8612 Richard Sandza. Army Times Publishing. Weekly newspaper.
54,200 to officers & enlisted personnel & their families interested in benefits, pay, lifestyle.
www.armytimes.com rsandza@militarytimes.com

C4ISR Journal 6883 Commercial Dr. Springfield VA 22151 **Phn:** 703-750-9000 **Fax** 703-658-8410 Ben Iannotta. Army Times Publishing. 10 issues.
18,000 covers high-tech realm of military intelligence, surveillance and reconnaissance programs.
www.c4isrjournal.com tnaegele@atpco.com

DAV Magazine 807 Maine Ave SW Washington DC 20024 **Phn:** 202-554-3501 **Fax** 202-863-0233 David Autry. Disabled American Veterans. Bimonthly magazine.
1,300,000 to members of Disabled American Veterans Org., their families; press, legislators. www.dav.org dautry@davmail.org

Defense News 6883 Commercial Dr. Springfield VA 22151 **Phn:** 703-642-7300 **Fax** 703-642-7386 Vago Muradian. Military Times Group/Gannett. Weekly newspaper.
36,500 to Amer. and intl. defense policymakers; military & defense contractors. www.defensenews.com vmuradian@defensenews.com

Exchange and Commissary News 825 Old Country Rd Westbury NY 11590 **Phn:** 516-334-3030 **Fax** 516-334-8958 Phil Gray. Exec. Business Media. Monthly tab.
8,000 to buyers & mgrs. at the Armed Forces post exchanges and commissary retail stores.
www.ebmpubs.com phil-eandcnews@ebmpubs4.com

Family Magazine 370 Old Country Rd Ste C20 Garden City NY 11530 **Phn:** 516-746-2000 **Fax** 516-746-2023 Dina Santorelli. Military Family Comms. Monthly magazine.
500,000 to military spouses interested in relocation issues, children, careers, money-saving tips.
www.familymedia.com editor@familymedia.com

FRA Today 125 N West St Alexandria VA 22314 **Phn:** 703-683-1400 **Fax** 703-549-6610 Eileen Murphy. Fleet Reserve Assn. Monthly.
155,000 to Fleet Reserve Association members interested in personnel & policy issues. www.fra.org eileen@fra.org

Leatherneck PO Box 1775 Quantico VA 22134 **Phn:** 703-640-6161 **Fax** 703-640-0823 Col. W.G. Ford. Marine Corps Assn. Monthly magazine.
79,000 to active/retired members of Corps, others interested in Corps history, training, equipment.
www.mca-marines.org/leatherneck/ leatherneck@mca-marines.org

Marine Corps Gazette PO Box 1775 Quantico VA 22134 **Phn:** 703-640-6161 **Fax** 703-630-9147 Col. John Keenan. Marine Corps Assn. Monthly magazine.
28,400 to Assn. members; publication is professional journal of the U.S. Marines. www.mca-marines.org/gazette/ gazette@mca-marines.org

Marine Corps Times 6883 Commercial Dr Springfield VA 22151 **Phn:** 703-750-8640 **Fax** 703-750-8767 Andrew deGrandpre. Military Times Group/Gannett. Weekly newspaper.
30,100 to Marine Corps members and their families interested in careers, benefits, lifestyle.
www.marinecorpstimes.com adegrandpre@militarytimes.com

Military 2120 28th St Sacramento CA 95818 **Phn:** 916-457-8990 **Fax** 916-457-7339 John Shank. Monthly magazine.
16,500 to American combat veterans WWII to present interested in veteran-written features. milmag.com editor@milmag.com

Military Club & Hospitality 825 Old Country Rd Westbury NY 11590 **Phn:** 516-334-3030 **Fax** 516-334-8958 Cory Harris. 8-issue magazine.
8,500 to military club mgmt. responsible for menu development, purchasing, entertainment, upkeep, lodging. ebmpubs.com cory@ebmpubs4.com

Military Money 5750 Major Blvd, Ste 310 Orlando FL 32819 **Phn:** 407-532-5745 Karen Carlson. Online only. TH:@InChargeDotOrg
to active, reserve & retired military staff & families interested in saving, investing, insurance, home ownership, retir www.militarymoney.com kcarlson@incharge.org

Military Officer 201 N Washington St Alexandria VA 22314 **Phn:** 703-549-2311 **Fax** 703-838-8179 Warren Lacy. Monthly magazine.
324,800 to active and retired officers of United States uniformed services and their families.
www.moaa.org/magazine editor@moaa.org

Military Spouse PO Box 26 Sewickley PA 15143 **Phn:** 412-269-1663 **Fax** 412-291-3375 Babette Maxwell. Victory Media. Monthly.
59,000 provides advice, information and support to military spouses. www.milspouse.com editorial@milspouse.com

Military Trader 700 E State St Iola WI 54990 **Phn:** 715-445-2214 **Fax** 715-445-4087 John Adams-Graf. F&W Media. Monthly tabloid.
7,500 to military collectible dealers and enthusiasts interested in shows, events, prices.
www.militarytrader.com john.adams-graf@fwpubs.com

National Defense 2111 Wilson Blvd Ste 400 Arlington VA 22201 **Phn:** 703-522-1820 **Fax** 703-522-1885 Sandra Erwin. Natl. Defense Industry Assn. Monthly magazine.
50,200 to buyers, specifiers in all military branches, defense-related govt. agencies, contractors.
www.ndia.org serwin@ndia.org

National Guard 1 Massachusetts Ave NW Washington DC 20001 **Phn:** 202-789-0031 **Fax** 202-682-9358 John Goheen. Natl. Guard Assn. of US. Monthly mag.
45,000 to Assn. members interested in Reserves policy & legislation, Assn. news. www.ngaus.org john.goheen@ngaus.org

Naval History 291 Wood Rd Annapolis MD 21402 **Phn:** 410-268-6110 **Fax** 410-295-1049 Richard G. Latture. Bimonthly magazine.
60,000 to active duty Navy members interested in 1st person Navy action accounts, art and photographs. www.usni.org rlatture@usni.org

Naval Institute Proceedings 291 Wood Rd Annapolis MD 21402 **Phn:** 410-268-6110 **Fax** 410-295-1049 Paul Merzlak. Monthly magazine.
75,000 to Coast Guard, Navy, Marine personnel interested in strategy, geopolitics, law. www.usni.org pmerzlak@usni.org

Navy Times 6883 Commercial Dr. Springfield VA 22151 **Phn:** 703-750-8698 **Fax** 703-750-8767 Kevin Lilley. Military Times Group/Gannett. Monthly newspaper. TH:@KRLilley
55,800 to Navy members and families interested in career, benefits, lifestyle. www.navytimes.com klilley@militarytimes.com

The Officer 1 Constitution Ave NE Washington DC 20002 **Phn:** 202-479-2200 **Fax** 202-547-1641 Chris Prawdzik. Reserve Officer Assn. 6-issue magazine.
60,000 to Association members interested in policy & legislation that impacts on the Reserves. www.roa.org cprawdzik@roa.org

On Patrol 2111 Wilson Blvd Ste 1200 Arlington VA 22201 **Phn:** 703-908-6400 Samantha L. Quigley. USO. Quarterly magazine. TH:@USOonPatrol
100,000 to servicepeople and their families interested in inspirational features, details about programs for military personnel. usoonpatrol.org editoronpatrol@uso.org

Salute 370 Old Country Rd Ste C20 Garden City NY 11530 **Phn:** 516-746-2000 **Fax** 516-746-2023 Dina Santorelli. Military Forces Features. Bimonthly magazine.
200,000 to singles in all branches of the military interested in sports, music, travel, lifestyle. www.familymedia.com/salute/ editor@familymedia.com

Seapower 2300 Wilson Blvd Ste 200 Arlington VA 22201 **Phn:** 703-528-1775 **Fax** 703-528-2333 Amy Wittman. Navy League of US. Monthly magazine.
55,000 to Navy, Marine Corps, Coast Guard, Dept. of Defense procurement decisionmakers. www.navyleague.org awittman@navyleague.org

Sergeants Magazine 5211 Auth Rd Suitland MD 20746 **Phn:** 301-899-3500 **Fax** 301-899-8136 John R. McCauslin. Air Force Sergeants Assn. 6-issue magazine.
135,000 to career enlisted men & women in US Air Force, USAF Reserves & their families. www.hqafsa.org staff@hqafsa.org

Signal 4400 Fair Lakes Ct Fairfax VA 22033 **Phn:** 703-631-6192 **Fax** 703-631-6188 Robert K. Ackerman. Armed Forces Communications & Electronics Assn. Monthly mag.
33,000 www.afcea.org/signal/ signalnews@afcea.org

Training & Simulation Journal 6883 Commercial Dr. Springfield VA 22151 **Phn:** 703-750-7312 **Fax** 703-750-8601 Brad Peniston. Military Times Group/Gannett. Bimonthly.
14,200 products and opportunities in the global military training and simulation market. www.tsjonline.com bpeniston@atpco.com

Mining--Coal--Ore .43
Coal Age 11555 Central Pkwy Ste 401 Jacksonville FL 32224 **Phn:** 904-721-2925 **Fax** 904-721-2930 Steve Fiscor. Mining Media. Monthly magazine.
14,700 to coal industry managers in surface/underground mining and coal preparation. www.mining-media.com sfiscor@mining-media.com

Military .42
Coal People PO Box 6247 Charleston WV 25362 **Phn:** 304-342-4129 **Fax** 304-343-3124 Al Skinner. 10-issue magazine.
13,000 to coal industry executives interested in industry profiles, history, conferences, technology. www.coalpeople.com alskinner@ntelos.net

Engineering & Mining Journal 11555 Central Pkwy Ste 401 Jacksonville FL 32224 **Phn:** 904-721-2925 **Fax** 904-721-2930 Steve Fiscor. Mining Media. Monthly mag.
20,900 to executive, production, engineering staffs in ore/mineral mining and processing worldwide. www.mining-media.com sfiscor@mining-media.com

ICMJ Prospecting & Mining Jrnl. PO Box 2260 Aptos CA 95001 **Phn:** 831-479-1500 **Fax** 831-479-4385 Scott Harn. Monthly magazine.
10,000 to independent mining operators and recreational miners interested in methods, equipment. www.icmj.com editor@icmj.com

Miners News PO Box 4965 Boise ID 83711 **Phn:** 208-658-0047 **Fax** 208-658-4901 Arnie Weber. Bimonthly newspaper.
3,900 to mining industry personnel interested in news, trends, products, safety, company profiles. www.minersnews.com arnie_weber@msn.com

Mines Magazine PO Box 1410 Golden CO 80402 **Phn:** 303-273-3294 **Fax** 303-273-3583 Nick Sutcliffe. Quarterly magazine.
20,000 to Colorado School of Mines alumni interested in people, news, events. www.mines.edu/magazine/ nick.sutcliffe@is.mines.edu

Mining Engineering 12999 E Adam Aircraft Cir Englewood CO 80112 **Phn:** 303-948-4200 **Fax** 303-973-3845 Steve Kral. Society of Mining Engineers. Monthly magazine.
15,000 to geologists, metallurgists, engineers & mgmt. interested in features, technical content. me.smenet.org kral@smenet.org

United Mine Workers Journal 8315 Lee Hwy Fl 5 Fairfax VA 22031 **Phn:** 703-208-7241 **Fax** 703-208-7227 Phil Smith. United Mine Workers of Amer. Bimo. tab.
200,000 to UMWA current and retired members, labor leaders, legislators. www.umwa.org

Mortuary--Cemetery .44
American Cemetery 3349 State Route 138 Bldg D # D Wall Township NJ 07719 **Phn:** 800-500-4585 **Fax** 732-730-2515 Thomas Parmalee. Kates-Boylston. Monthly magazine.
5,200 to cemetery owners and managers interested in industry news, vendors, technology. www.katesboylston.com editorial@katesboylston.com

American Funeral Director 3349 State Route 138 Bldg D # D Wall Township NJ 07719 **Phn:** 800-500-4585 **Fax** 732-730-2515 Thomas Parmalee. Kates-Boylston. Monthly magazine.
10,800 to funeral directors, embalmers, casket mfrs., salespeople, mortuary colleges. www.katesboylston.com editorial@katesboylston.com

Catholic Cemetery 1400 S Wolf Rd # 3 Hillside IL 60162 **Phn:** 708-202-1242 **Fax** 708-202-1255 Christine Kohut. Catholic Cemetery Conference. Monthly.
2,000 www.catholiccemeteryconference.org cakohut@catholiccemeteryconference.org

Cremationist of North America 401 N Michigan Ave Chicago IL 60611 **Phn:** 312-673-4889 **Fax** 312-321-4098 Amie Shak. Quarterly magazine.
1,400 to crematory owners, cemeteries and mortuaries covering ethical policies, procedures. www.cremationassociation.org ashak@cremationassociation.org

The Director 13625 Bishops Dr Brookfield WI 53005 **Phn:** 262-789-1880 **Fax** 262-789-6977 Edward J Defort. Natl. Funeral Dirs. of Amer. Monthly magazine.
13,400 to funeral service professionals interested in education, counseling, mgmt., public relations. www.nfda.org edefort@nfda.org

ICCFA Magazine 107 Carpenter Dr Ste 100 Sterling VA 20164 **Phn:** 703-391-8400 **Fax** 703-391-8416 Susan Loving. Intl. Cemetery & Funeral Assn. 10-issue mag.
8,000 to cemeterians and funeral directors interested in products, services, Assn. activities. www.iccfa.com sloving@iccfa.com

MB News 136 S Keowee St Dayton OH 45402 **Phn:** 800-233-4472 **Fax** 937-222-5794 Don Mounce. Monument Builders of N. Amer. Monthly mag.
1,000 to monument building industry personnel interested in design, programs, products. www.monumentbuilders.org mbnews@monumentbuilders.org

Mortuary Management 2361 Horseshoe Dr W Bloomfield MI 48322 **Phn:** 248-737-9294 **Fax** 248-737-9296 Jon St. John. Monthly magazine.
10,200 to funeral directors, industry personnel interested in mortuary science, policies, laws. www.abbottandhast.com info@abbottandhast.com

Music--Music Trades .45
Acoustic Guitar PO Box 767 San Anselmo CA 94979 **Phn:** 415-485-6946 **Fax** 415-485-0831 Scott Nygaard. String Letter Publishing. Monthly magazine.
60,000 to amateurs, professionals interested in instructional articles, transcriptions, buying guides. www.acousticguitar.com editors.ag@stringletter.com

Alternative Press 1305 W 80th St # 214 Cleveland OH 44102 **Phn:** 216-631-1510 **Fax** 216-631-1016 Annie Zaleski. Monthly.
121,000 covering youth and music culture, latest releases and music news, indie bands. www.altpress.com news@altpress.com

American Music Teacher 441 Vine St Ste 3100 Cincinnati OH 45202 **Phn:** 513-421-1420 **Fax** 513-421-2503 Marcie Lindsey. Bimonthly magazine.
24,000 to Music Teachers Assn. members interested in teaching trends, technology, resources. www.mtna.org amt@mtna.org

The American Organist 475 Riverside Dr Ste 1260 New York NY 10115 **Phn:** 212-870-2310 **Fax** 212-870-2163 Todd Sisley. Amer. Guild of Organists. Monthly mag.
22,500 to Guild members, church musicians, choirmasters, composers, organ builders. www.agohq.org info@agohq.org

American Songwriter 1303 16th Ave S 2nd Fl Nashville TN 37212 **Phn:** 615-321-6096 **Fax** 615-321-6097 Matthew Shearon. Bimonthly magazine.
40,800 fatures pictorials, interviews and lifestyles of singers and songwriters. www.americansongwriter.com info@americansongwriter.com

American String Teacher 4155 Chain Bridge Rd Fairfax VA 22030 **Phn:** 703-279-2113 **Fax** 703-279-2114 Mary Jane Dye. Amer. String Teachers Assn. Quarterly mag.
1,900 covers various string teaching methods; reviews of conferences, new books and music. www.astaweb.com asta@astaweb.com

Bass Player 1111 Bayhill Dr Ste 125 San Bruno CA 94066 **Phn:** 650-238-0300 **Fax** 650-238-0263 Brian Fox. NewBay Media. Monthly magazine. TH:@BassPlayerNow
28,400 to electric and acoustic bass players interested in lessons, interviews, gear, repair. www.bassplayer.com bfox@musicplayer.com

Billboard 770 Broadway New York NY 10003 **Phn:** 646-654-5500 **Fax** 646-654-4674 Joe Levy. Prometheus Global Media. Weekly tabloid.
20,200 to sales, mktg., merchandising personnel in music, video, home entertainment industries. www.billboard.com joe.levy@billboard.com

Bluegrass Unlimited PO Box 771 Warrenton VA 20188 **Phn:** 540-349-8181 **Fax** 540-341-0011 Peter Kuykendall. Monthly magazine.
19,000 to bluegrass/oldtime country music enthusiasts & musicians interested in reviews, festivals, profiles.
www.bluegrassmusic.com
editor@bluegrassmusic.com

Chamber Music 305 7th Ave Rm 502 New York NY 10001 **Phn:** 212-242-2022 **Fax** 212-242-7955 Ellen Goldensohn. Chamber Music America. Bimonthly magazine.
10,000 to chamber music enthusiasts, players, teachers, students, concertgoers. www.chamber-music.org egoldensohn@chamber-music.org

CMJ New Music Monthly 151 W 25th St Fl 12 New York NY 10001 **Phn:** 917-606-1908 **Fax** 917-606-1914 Kenny Herzog. Monthly magazine.
40,700 to music enthusiasts interested in all contemporary music, reviews, profiles, pop culture. www.cmj.com

Country Weekly 118 16th Ave S Ste 230 Nashville TN 37203 **Phn:** 615-259-1111 **Fax** 615-255-1110 Lisa Konicki. American Media. Weekly magazine.
449,800 to readers interested in country music artists, rising stars, concert schedules, reviews.
www.countryweekly.com lkonicki@countryweekly.com

The Diapason 3030 W Salt Creek Ln Ste 201 Arlington Hts IL 60005 **Phn:** 847-391-1045 **Fax** 847-390-0408 Jerome Butera. Scranton Gillette. Monthly magazine.
4,600 to readers interested in organ, harpsichord, carillon, church music. www.thediapason.com jbutera@sgcmail.com

DJ Times 25 Willowdale Ave Port Washington NY 11050 **Phn:** 516-767-2500 **Fax** 516-767-9335 Jim Tremayne. Testa Communications. Monthly tabloid.
27,700 to club and mobile DJ's interested in equipment features, interviews, remix tips. www.djtimes.com djtimes@testa.com

Down Beat 102 N Haven Rd Elmhurst IL 60126 **Phn:** 630-941-2030 **Fax** 630-941-3210 Ed Enright. Maher Publications. Monthly magazine.
68,000 to amateur and professional jazz musicians interested in interviews, news, reviews.
www.downbeat.com editor@downbeat.com

Drum Business 12 Old Bridge Rd Cedar Grove NJ 07009 **Phn:** 973-239-4140 **Fax** 973-239-7139 Kevin Kearns. Bimonthly tabloid.
5,800 to instore mgmt. & sales staff in retail sales of acoustic & electronic percussion.
www.moderndrummer.com
info@moderndrummer.com

Drum Corps World 56 Golf Course Rd Madison WI 53704 **Phn:** 608-241-2292 **Fax** 608-241-4974 Steve Vickers. Online only.
for drum & bugle corps members, enthusiasts interested in events, scores, news, products.
www.drumcorpsworld.com
publisher@drumcorpsworld.com

Electronic Musician 1111 Bayhill Dr Ste 125 San Bruno CA 94066 **Phn:** 650-238-0300 **Fax** 650-238-0263 Sarah Jones. NewBay Media. Monthly magazine.
37,000 to musicians recording or producing in personal studios interested in technology & equip.
emusician.com sjones@musicplayer.com

EQ 1111 Bayhill Dr Ste 125 San Bruno CA 94066 **Phn:** 650-238-0300 **Fax** 650-238-0263 Kylee Swenson. NewBay Media. Monthly magazine.
35,000 to musicians, engineers, producers interested in recording & sound technique how-to's.
www.eqmag.com eqeditor@musicplayer.com

Fader 71 W 23rd St Fl 13 New York NY 10010 **Phn:** 212-741-7100 **Fax** 212-656-1416 Matthew Schnipper. Bimonthly magazine. TH:@mattschnipper
105,000 to readers interested in emerging artists/trends in hip-hop, indie rock, folk, grime, dancehall and R&B music forms.
www.fadermedia.com/the-fader-magazine/
editorial@thefader.com

Flute Talk 200 Northfield Rd Northfield IL 60093 **Phn:** 847-446-5000 **Fax** 847-446-6263 Victoria Jicha. Instrumentalist Publishing Co. 10-issues.
13,000 to serious flutists, teachers, performers, adult amateurs, H.S. and college flutists.
www.theinstrumentalist.com/magazine-flutetalk/
editor@flutetalkmagazine.com

Goldmine 700 E State St Iola WI 54990 **Phn:** 715-445-2214 **Fax** 715-445-4087 Peter Linblad. F&W Media. Biweekly tabloid.
9,400 to vinyl/CD collectors of all types of music 1940-present, buy/sell/trade listings.
www.goldminemag.com goldmine@krause.com

Gospel Today PO Box 1009 Hendersonville TN 37077 **Phn:** 770-719-4825 **Fax** 770-716-2660 Teresa Hairston. Bimonthly magazine.
65,000 to readers interested in African-American gospel music and church music. mygospeltoday.com gteditorial@aol.com

Guitar Player 1111 Bayhill Dr Ste 125 San Bruno CA 94066 **Phn:** 650-238-0300 **Fax** 650-238-0263 Michael Molenda. NewBay Media. Monthly magazine.
153,400 to serious guitarists interested in equipment, songwriting, career info, profiles.
www.guitarplayer.com mmolenda@nbmedia.com

Guitar World 149 5th Ave New York NY 10010 **Phn:** 212-768-2966 **Fax** 212-944-9279 Brad Tolinski. NewBay Media. Monthly magazine.
175,000 to pro, semi-pro, amateur guitarists interested in all music styles, instruments, lifestyle.
www.guitarworld.com brad@guitarworld.com

The Harmonizer 110 7th Ave N Nashville TN 37203 **Phn:** 800-876-7464 **Fax** 615-313-7615 Lorin May. Bimonthly magazine. Barbershop Harmony Society.
30,000 to Society members interested in Society news and member activities. www.barbershop.org harmonizer@barbershop.org

International Musician 120 Walton St Ste 300 Syracuse NY 13202 **Phn:** 315-422-0900 **Fax** 315-422-3837 Antoinette Follett. Amer. Fed. of Musicians. Monthly tabloid.
115,800 to Fed. members, other professional musicians in both recording and live settings.
www.internationalmusician.org afollett@afm.org

Jazziz Magazine PO Box 880189 Boca Raton FL 33488 **Phn:** 561-893-6868 **Fax** 561-910-5535 Michael Fagien. Jazziz Omnimedia. Quarterly magazine.
197,000 covering the jazz world, documenting musical innovations, charting industry trends. www.jazziz.com service@jazziz.com

JazzTimes 10801 Margate Rd Silver Spring MD 20901 **Phn:** 617-315-9154 **Fax** 617-536-0102 Lee Mergner. 10-issue magazine.
78,100 to jazz enthusiasts, musicians interested in personalities, jazz & social issues, CD reviews.
jazztimes.com lmergner@jazztimes.com

Just Jazz Guitar PO Box 76053 Atlanta GA 30358 **Phn:** 404-250-9298 **Fax** 404-250-9951 Ed Benson. Quarterly magazine.
75,000 to jazz guitar enthusiasts, musicians interested in players, lessons, instruments. justjazzguitar.com justjazzguitar@mindspring.com

Keyboard Magazine 1111 Bayhill Dr Ste 125 San Bruno CA 94066 **Phn:** 650-238-0300 **Fax** 650-238-0263 Stephen Fortner. NewBay Media. Monthly magazine.
45,500 to keyboardists & musicians who use technology to make music. www.keyboardmag.com sfortner@musicplayer.com

Magnet 1218 Chestnut St Ste 508 Philadelphia PA 19107 **Phn:** 215-413-8570 Eric T. Miller. Monthly mag. TH:@MAGNETMagazine
50,000 to indie music enthusiasts interested in profiles, reviews, features, photography.
www.magnetmagazine.com
eric@magnetmagazine.com

Mobile Beat PO Box 42365 Urbandale IA 50323 **Phn:** 515-986-3300 **Fax** 515-986-3344 Dan Walsh. LA Communications. Bimonthly.
15,800 to wedding, party, dance, event DJ's, equipment reviews, how to boost bookings.
www.mobilebeat.com dwalsh@mobilebeat.com

Music & Sound Retailer 25 Willowdale Ave Port Washington NY 11050 **Phn:** 516-767-2500 **Fax** 516-767-9335 Dan Ferrisi. Testa Communications. Monthly tabloid.
11,800 to musical instrument & sound product retail store owners, mgrs., sales staff. www.msretailer.com dferrisi@testa.com

Music Connection 14654 Victory Blvd Fl 1 Van Nuys CA 91411 **Phn:** 818-995-0101 **Fax** 818-995-9235 Mark Nardone. Monthly.
75,000 to recording artists, producers, engineers, record company executives, music publishers.
musicconnection.com markn@musicconnection.com

Music Educators Journal 1806 Robert Fulton Dr Reston VA 20191 **Phn:** 703-860-4000 **Fax** 703-860-4826 Patrick K. Freer. Sage Publications. Quarterly.
71,700 to music educators interested in instructional philosophies, techniques, resources. www.menc.org pfreer@gsu.edu

Music Inc. 102 N Haven Rd Elmhurst IL 60126 **Phn:** 630-941-2030 **Fax** 630-941-3210 Zach Phillips. Maher Publications. Monthly magazine.
9,700 to musical instrument and equipment retailers, manufacturers, wholesalers, music publishers.
www.musicincmag.com editor@musicincmag.com

Music Trades 80 West St Englewood NJ 07631 **Phn:** 201-871-1965 **Fax** 201-871-0455 Brian Majeski. Monthly magazine.
6,100 to music industry retailers and wholesalers interested in sales and promotional methods.
www.musictrades.com brian@musictrades.com

Musical Merchandise Review 21 Highland Cir Ste 1 Needham MA 02494 **Phn:** 781-453-9310 **Fax** 781-453-9389 Christian Wissmuller. Symphony Publishing. Monthly magazine.
9,300 to musical instrument and related merchandise retail managers. www.mmrmagazine.com cwissmuller@symphonypublishing.com

Paste Magazine 2852 E College Ave #E Decatur GA 30030 **Phn:** 404-207-2100 **Fax** 404-378-8872 Josh Jackson Monthly.
205,000 covers broad range of music, rock, alternative, indie genres, film, DVD, books.
www.pastemagazine.com editor@pastemagazine.com

Pastoral Music 962 Wayne Ave Ste 210 Silver Spring MD 20910 **Phn:** 240-247-3000 **Fax** 240-247-3001 Gordon Truitt. 5-issue magazine.
9,700 to clergy and parish musicians interested in sung worship, events, career opportunities.
www.npm.org npmedit@npm.org

Percussive Notes 110 W Washington St Ste A Indianapolis IN 46204 **Phn:** 317-974-4488 **Fax** 317-974-4499 Rick Mattingly. Bimonthly.
8,800 to educators, performers, students, enthusiasts covering all facets of percussion. www.pas.org percarts@pas.org

Recording 5408 Idylwild Trl Boulder CO 80301 **Phn:** 303-516-9118 **Fax** 303-516-9119 Lorenz Rychner. Music Maker Publications. Monthly magazine.
28,000 to musicians interested in home and project recording studio set up and gear.
www.recordingmag.com lorenz@recordingmag.com

Revolver 149 5th Ave Fl 9 New York NY 10010 **Phn:** 212-768-2966 **Fax** 212-944-9279 Brandon Geist. NewBay Media. Monthly magazine.
150,000 to young male readers interested in concerts & profiles of metal, punk, classic rock bands.
www.revolvermag.com geist@revolvermag.com

Rolling Stone 1290 Avenue of the Americas New York NY 10104 **Phn:** 212-484-1616 **Fax** 212-484-1644 Will Dana. Wenner Media. 24-issue magazine.
1,462,100 to readers interested in music, film, fashion, politics, American culture. www.rollingstone.com rseditors@rollingstone.com

Spin 408 Broadway Fl 4 New York NY 10013 **Phn:** 212-231-7400 **Fax** 212-231-7312 Jem Aswad. Online only. TH:@jemaswad
to teens & young adults interested in music, fashion, technology, politics, art. www.spin.com

Strings Magazine PO Box 767 San Anselmo CA 94979 **Phn:** 415-485-6946 **Fax** 415-485-0831 Greg Cahill. 10-issues.
11,000 written by and for players, instructors of bow-stringed instruments, interviews. www.allthingsstrings.com greg@stringletter.com

Symphony Magazine 33 W 60th St Fl 5 New York NY 10023 **Phn:** 212-262-5161 **Fax** 212-262-5198 Robert Sandla. Amer. Symphony Orch League. Bimonthly.
18,400 to symphony orchestra mgrs., conductors, musicians, directors, fundraisers. www.americanorchestras.org orchnews@americanorchestras.org

Teaching Music 1806 Robert Fulton Dr Reston VA 20191 **Phn:** 703-860-4000 **Fax** 703-860-4826 Ella Wilcox. Natl. Assn. for Music Education. Bimonthly magazine. TH:@NAfME
70,000 to music educators interested in teaching methods, news, resources. musiced.nafme.org ellaw@nafme.org

True Magazine 11033 Hartsook St N Hollywood CA 91601 **Phn:** 818-505-8162 Dave Hill. Monthly.
187,000 covers the independent and underground artist/labels, hip hop, fashion, lifestyle. www.true-magazine.com dmh@dmhmedianetwork.com

Word Up! 210 E State Rt 4 Ste 211 Paramus NJ 07652 **Phn:** 201-843-4004 **Fax** 201-843-8775 Mary Ann Cassata. Bimonthly magazine.
78,400 to readers interested in African-Amer. entertainment, music, film, television. www.wordupmag.com editor@wordupmag.com

XXL Magazine 1115 Broadway Fl 8 New York NY 10010 **Phn:** 212-807-7100 **Fax** 212-807-0216 Vanessa Satten. Harris Publ. Monthly magazine.
100,000 to hip-hop fans interested in profiles, new releases, djs, fashion, lifestyle. www.xxlmag.com xxl@harris-pub.com

Office Equipment & Management .46

Document 2901 International Ln Madison WI 53704 **Phn:** 608-241-8777 **Fax** 608-241-8666 Allison Lloyd. Online only. RB Publishing.
for high-volume document processors interested in industry trends, new technologies. www.documentmedia.com allison.l@rbpub.com

Jrnl. Court Reporting 8224 Old Courthouse Rd Vienna VA 22182 **Phn:** 703-556-6272 **Fax** 703-556-6291 Jacqueline Schmidt. Natl. Court Reporters Assn. 10-issue mag.
23,200 to Assn. members, other court & deposition reporters, b'cast captioners, TTY operators. www.ncraonline.org jschmidt@ncrahq.org

Mailing Systems Technology 2901 International Ln Ste 100 Madison WI 53704 **Phn:** 608-241-8777 **Fax** 608-241-8666 Amanda Armendariz. RB Publishing. 6-issue magazine.
22,000 to mailing, express, delivery mgmt. personnel interested in equip., technology, regulations. Mailingsystemstechnology.com amanda.c@rbpub.com

Office Technology 12411 Wornall Rd Kansas City MO 64145 **Phn:** 816-941-3100 **Fax** 816-303-4056 Brent Hoskins. Business Technology Assn. Monthly magazine.
3,500 to imaging technology dealers & resellers interested in management skills development. www.bta.org brent@bta.org

Music--Music Trades .45

OfficePro PO Box 20404 Kansas City MO 64195 **Phn:** 816-891-6600 **Fax** 816-891-9118 Emily Allen. Intl. Assn. Admin. Professionals. 9-issue magazine.
32,600 to Assn. members, secretaries, office mgrs interested in meetings, computer skills, supplies. www.iaap-hq.org eallen@iaap-hq.org

Optical .47

American Jrnl. Ophthalmology 4500 San Pablo Rd S Jacksonville FL 32224 **Phn:** 904-953-2555 **Fax** 904-953-2551 Sarah Duncan. Monthly magazine.
7,600 to ophthalmologic practitioners interested in peer-reviewed clinical research. www.ajo.com ajo@mayo.edu

AOA News 243 N Lindbergh Blvd Saint Louis MO 63141 **Phn:** 314-991-4100 **Fax** 314-991-4101 Robert Foster. Amer. Optometric Assn. 18-issue tabloid.
29,000 to optometrists interested in rsch., Assn. news and events, new techniques, products. www.aoa.org rafoster@aoa.org

Contact Lens Spectrum 323 Norristown Rd Ste 200 Ambler PA 19002 **Phn:** 215-646-8700 Lisa Starcher. Wolters Kluwer. Monthly.
31,500 to optometrists, ophthalmologists, opticians concerned with lens fitting, patient care. www.clspectrum.com lisa.starcher@wolterskluwer.com

Cornea 875 Johnson Ferry Rd NE Ste 100 Atlanta GA 30342 **Phn:** 404-778-6166 **Fax** 404-778-6165 R. Doyle Stulting. Lippincott Williams & Wilkins. 8-issue magazine.
1,200 to ophthalmologists interested in peer-reviewed papers, clinical research. journals.lww.com/corneajrnl/ cornea@emory.edu

Eyecare Business 323 Norristown Rd Ste 200 Ambler PA 19002 **Phn:** 215-646-8700 Amy Spiezio. Pentavision. Monthly magazine. TH:@eyecarebusiness
45,000 to optometrists & opticians interested in glasses, frames, contact lens, ancillary product marketing and sales. www.eyecarebusiness.com amy.spiezio@pentavisionmedia.com

Ophthalmology 1550 Orleans St CRB II #1M50 Baltimore MD 21231 **Phn:** 443-287-2445 **Fax** 443-287-2448 Veronica Doyle. Monthly magazine.
26,500 to ophthamologists interested in clinical studies, peer-reviewed investigations, techniques and treatments. www.ophsource.org vdoyle@jhmi.edu

Ophthalmology Times 7500 Old Oak Blvd Cleveland OH 44130 **Phn:** 440-243-8100 **Fax** 440-891-2735 Mark Dlugoss. Biweekly tabloid.
17,100 to ophthalmologists interested in clinical insights, knowledge and discoveries. www.modernmedicine.com mdlugoss@advanstar.com

Optometric Management 323 Norristown Rd Ste 200 Ambler PA 19002 **Phn:** 215-646-8700 Jim Thomas. Pentavision. Monthly mag.
33,400 to optometrists interested in practice and patient management. www.optometricmanagement.com james.thomas@pentavisionmedia.com

Primary Care Optometry News 6900 Grove Rd Thorofare NJ 08086 **Phn:** 856-848-1000 **Fax** 856-848-6091 Nancy Hemphill. Slack, Inc. Monthly tabloid.
40,100 to optometrists interested in clinical issues, legislative affairs, techniques and treatments. www.pconsupersite.com editor@pconsupersite.com

20/20 100 Avenue Of The Americas Fl 9 New York NY 10013 **Phn:** 212-274-7000 **Fax** 212-274-0392 James Spina. Jobson Publishing. 14-issue tabloid.
49,500 to optometrists, opticians, retailers interested in eyewear merchandising & store design. www.2020mag.com jspina@jobson.com

Vision Monday 100 Avenue Of The Americas Fl 9 New York NY 10013 **Phn:** 212-274-7000 **Fax** 212-274-0392 Marge Axelrad. Jobson Publishing. 14-issue tabloid.
20,000 to opticians, optometrists, eyewear mgmt. interested in industry news, events, products. www.visionmonday.com maxelrad@jobson.com

Packaging .48

Board Converting News 43 Main St Avon by the Sea NJ 07717 **Phn:** 518-366-9017 Len Prazych. Weekly magazine.
3,900 to owners, mfg./production/corporate mgmt. at corrugated and folding carton plants. www.nvpublications.com lprazych@nvpublications.com

Brandpackaging 155 Pfingsten Rd Ste 205 Deerfield IL 60015 **Phn:** 847-405-4000 **Fax** 847-405-4100 Laura Zielinski. BNP Media. 10-issue magazine.
30,000 to brand and category mgrs. responsible for developing packaging strategies and concepts. www.brandpackaging.com zielinskil@bnpmedia.com

Flexible Packaging 155 N Pfingsten Rd Ste 205 Deerfield IL 60015 **Phn:** 847-405-4000 **Fax** 847-405-4100 Erin J. Wolford. BNP Media. 9-issue magazine.
10,000 to flexible packaging mfg. personnel interested in trends, materials, equipment, suppliers. www.flexpackmag.com wolforde@bnpmedia.com

Food & Beverage Packaging 155 N Pfingsten Rd Ste 205 Deerfield IL 60015 **Phn:** 847-405-4000 **Fax** 847-405-4100 Elisabeth Cuneo. BNP Media. 10-issue magazine.
64,400 to buyers & vendors of packaging machinery, equipment, containers, materials, services. www.foodandbeveragepackaging.com cuneo@bnpmedia.com

Label & Narrow Web 70 Hilltop Rd Fl 3 Ramsey NJ 07446 **Phn:** 201-825-2552 **Fax** 201-825-0553 Jack Kenny. Rodman Publications. 8-issue magazine.
10,400 to narrow web press mfrs. interested in products, company profiles, industry issues. www.labelandnarrowweb.com skatz@rodpub.com

Packaging Digest 1200 Jorie Blvd Ste 230 Oak Brook IL 60523 **Phn:** 630-990-2311 **Fax** 630-990-8894 Lisa McTigue Pierce. UBM Canon LLC. Monthly tabloid.
90,000 to industrial and consumer goods packagers interested in materials and machinery. www.packagingdigest.com lisa.pierce@ubm.com

Packaging World 330 N Wabash Ave Ste 2401 Chicago IL 60611 **Phn:** 312-222-1010 **Fax** 312-222-1310 Patrick Reynolds. Summit Media Group. Monthly magazine.
77,200 to users of packaging machinery, materials, svcs. interested in technology & products. www.packworld.com reynolds@packworld.com

Paperboard Packaging 2835 N Sheffield Ave Ste 226 Chicago IL 60657 **Phn:** 419-806-5716 **Fax** 773-880-2244 Esther Hertzfeld. RISI. Quarterly magazine.
10,200 to corp. and production mgrs. in paperboard converting interested in market, tech. data. www.packaging-online.com ehertzfeld@risi.com

Pharma. & Medical Packaging News 11444 W Olympic Blvd Ste 900 Los Angeles CA 90064 **Phn:** 310-445-4200 **Fax** 310-445-4299 Daphne Allen. UBM Canon. Monthly mag.
20,000 to mfg., R&D, packaging and purchasing personnel responsible for packaging operations. www.pmpnews.com daphne.allen@ubm.com

Paint--Decoration .49

American Painting Contractor 8120 Woodmont Ave Bethesda MD 20814 **Phn:** 850-936-0200 **Fax** 850-684-1422 Emily Howard. Columbia Books, LLC. 9-issue magazine. TH:@PaintMag
25,000 to painting contractors, paperhangers interested in equip., decorating trends, market rsch. www.paintmag.com ehoward@columbiabooks.com

Coatings World 70 Hilltop Rd Fl 3 Ramsey NJ 07446 **Phn:** 201-825-2552 **Fax** 201-825-0553 Tim Wright. Rodman Publications. Monthly magazine.
17,700 to worldwide industry personnel interested in new coating, paint, sealant products. www.coatingsworld.com twright@rodpub.com

Facility Care 2807 N Parham Rd Ste 200 Richmond VA 23294 **Phn:** 850-936-0200 **Fax** 850-936-0206 Emily Howard. Briefings Media. Bimo.
21,000 covers planning, constructing, operating a safe environment for employees, patients, visitors. www.facilitycare.com ehoward@briefingsmediagroup.com

JCT CoatingsTech 492 Norristown Rd Blue Bell PA 19422 **Phn:** 610-940-0777 **Fax** 610-940-0292 Patricia Zeigler. 11-issue magazine.
5,700 to coatings industry technical, scientific, production personnel in research and engineering. www.paint.org publications@paint.org

Jrnl. Protective Coatings/Lining 2100 Wharton St Ste 310 Pittsburgh PA 15203 **Phn:** 412-431-8300 **Fax** 412-431-5428 Karen Kapsanis. Technology Publishing/PaintSquare. Mo. mag.
15,000 to personnel responsible for protective coatings on bridges, railroads, new construction. www.paintsquare.com kkapsanis@protectivecoatings.com

Paint & Coatings Industry 1907 Farmbrook Dr Troy MI 48098 **Phn:** 248-641-0592 Kristin Johansson. BNP Media. Monthly mag.
20,000 to mfrs., end users & distributors of paints, coatings, adhesives, sealants, printing inks. www.pcimag.com johanssonk@bnpmedia.com

Paint & Decorating Retailer 1401 Triad Center Dr Saint Peters MO 63376 **Phn:** 636-326-2636 **Fax** 636-229-4750 Diane Capuano. Monthly magazine.
50,000 to owners, mgrs., employees at decorating, hardware, wallpaper, window covering, flooring retailers. www.pdra.org dianecapuano@sbcglobal.net

The Paint Contractor 111A N Kirkwood Rd Saint Louis MO 63122 **Phn:** 314-984-0800 **Fax** 314-984-0866 Jerry Rabushka. Mugler Publications. Monthly magazine.
30,000 to prof. painting contractors interested in mgmt. issues, industry news, profitability, new products. www.paintdealer.com/paintcontractor/ jrabushka@paintdealer.com

The Paint Dealer 111A N Kirkwood Rd Saint Louis MO 63122 **Phn:** 314-984-0800 **Fax** 314-984-0866 Jerry Rabushka. Mugler Publications. Monthly magazine.
18,000 to retailers interested in store mgmt., industry news, profitability, new products. www.paintdealer.com jrabushka@paintdealer.com

Painters & Allied Trades Journal 1750 New York Ave NW Fl 8 Washington DC 20006 **Phn:** 202-637-0700 **Fax** 202-637-0771 James Williams. Quarterly.
117,000 to members of Intl. Brotherhood of Painters & Allied Trades union. www.iupat.org askthegeneralpresident@iupat.org

Paper--Paper Products .50

Paper Age 20 Schofield Rd Cohasset MA 02025 **Phn:** 781-378-2126 **Fax** 781-923-1389 John O'Brien. Bimonthly magazine.
14,000 to pulp and paper industry executives, marketers, operators, technicians, superintendents and consultants. www.paperage.com jobrien@paperage.com

Paper360 15 Technology Pkwy S Norcross GA 30092 **Phn:** 770-446-1400 **Fax** 770-446-6947 Glenn Ostle. Tech. Assn. Paper/Pulp Industry. Monthly.
38,500 to pulp & paper converting industry mgmt., technical, engineering, purchasing staff. www.tappi.org/Publications/Paper-360.aspx gostle@tappi.org

Petroleum--Gas .51

AAPG Explorer PO Box 979 Tulsa OK 74101 **Phn:** 918-560-2657 **Fax** 918-560-2636 Vern Stefanic. Amer. Assn. Petroleum Geologists. Monthly tab.
31,000 to Assn. members interested in features about all aspects of energy exploration. www.aapg.org vstefan@aapg.org

Paint--Decoration .49

American Gas 400 N Capitol St NW Ste 450 Washington DC 20001 **Phn:** 202-824-7000 **Fax** 202-824-7216 Sherri Hamm. Amer. Gas Assn. 10-issue magazine.
10,200 to gas industry executives responsible for IT, distribution, operations. www.aga.org shamm@aga.org

Butane-Propane News PO Box 660698 Arcadia CA 91066 **Phn:** 626-357-2168 **Fax** 626-303-2854 John Needham. Monthly magazine.
13,500 to personnel engaged in sale, distribution of liquefied petroleum gas and appliances. www.bpnews.com john@bpnews.com

Compressor Tech Two 20855 Watertown Rd Ste 220 Waukesha WI 53186 **Phn:** 262-754-4100 **Fax** 262-754-4175 Brent Haight. 10-issue magazine.
13,300 to natural gas industry personnel responsible for transporation, storage, processing. www.compressortech2.com bhaight@dieselpub.com

Drilling Contractor 10370 Richmond Ave Ste 760 Houston TX 77042 **Phn:** 713-292-1945 **Fax** 713-292-1946 Mike Killalea. Intl. Assn. Drilling Contractors. Bimonthly.
34,500 to global oil drilling industry contractors, natural gas producers, oilfield service staff. www.drillingcontractor.org drilling.contractor@iadc.org

Gas Oil & Mining Contractor PO Box 220 Three Lakes WI 54562 **Phn:** 715-546-3346 **Fax** 715-546-3786 Jim Kneiszel. Monthly magazine. TH:@GOMCmag
15,800 to land-based gas, oil, mining operations personnel responsible for equipment, maintenance, training, systems. www.gomcmag.com editor@gomcmag.com

Geophysics 8801 S Yale Ave Ste 500 Tulsa OK 74137 **Phn:** 918-497-5500 **Fax** 918-497-5557 Jennifer Cobb. Soc. Exploration Geophysicists. Bimonthly magazine.
3,100 to Soc. members, other geophysicists concerned with petro. & other mineral exploration. www.segdl.org/geophysics/ jcobb@seg.org

Hydrocarbon Processing PO Box 2608 Houston TX 77252 **Phn:** 713-529-4301 **Fax** 713-520-4433 Les Kane. Gulf Publishing. Monthly magazine.
30,100 to execs., plant mgrs., engineers, superintendents in hydrocarbon processing industry. www.hydrocarbonprocessing.com hpeditorial@gulfpub.com

Jrnl. Petroleum Technology 10777 Westheimer Rd Ste 335 Houston TX 77042 **Phn:** 713-779-9595 **Fax** 713-779-4216 John Donnelly. Soc. of Petro. Eng. Mo. mag.
59,000 to petroleum industry engineers interested in drilling & exploration features, indus. issues. www.spe.org jpt@spe.org

LPGas 1360 E. 9th St. Fl 10 Cleveland OH 44114 **Phn:** 855-460-5502 Brian Richesson. North Coast Media. Monthly magazine.
15,000 to liquified petroleum (propane) industry mgmt., dealers, operating personnel, equip. mfrs. www.lpgasmagazine.com brichesson@northcoastmedia.net

National Petroleum News 1030 Higgins Rd Ste 230 Park Ridge IL 60068 **Phn:** 847-720-5600 **Fax** 847-720-5610 Keith Reid. M2Media360. 9-issue magazine.
22,500 to marketing and operations management in petroleum & convenience store retailing. www.npnweb.com kreid@m2media360.com

Offshore 1455 West Loop S Ste 400 Houston TX 77027 **Phn:** 713-621-9720 **Fax** 713-963-6228 Eldon Ball. PennWell Publishing. Monthly magazine.
41,700 to offshore/marine oil and gas industry personnel, equipment manufacturers, suppliers. www.offshore-mag.com eldonb@pennwell.com

Oil & Gas Journal 1455 West Loop S Ste 400 Houston TX 77027 **Phn:** 713-621-9720 **Fax** 713-963-6285 Bob Tippee. PennWell Publishing. Weekly magazine.
109,000 to oil & gas company management responsible for technology, operations, finance. www.ogj.com news@ogjonline.com

Oil, Gas & Petrochem Equipment 1421 S Sheridan Rd Tulsa OK 74112 **Phn:** 918 832 9351 **Fax** 918-832-9201 J.B. Avants. PennWell Publishing. Monthly tabloid.
30,000 to product and service decisionmakers in oil/gas drilling, production, refining, processing. www.ogpe.com jba@pennwell.com

Pipeline & Gas Journal PO Box 941669 Houston TX 77094 **Phn:** 281-558-6930 **Fax** 281-558-7029 Jeff Share. Oildom Publishing. Monthly magazine.
28,400 to oil/gas pipeline transmission mgmt., engineering, mktg. personnel. www.oildom.com jshare@oildom.com

Well Servicing 14531 Fm 529 Rd Ste 250 Houston TX 77095 **Phn:** 713-781-0758 **Fax** 713-781-7542 Patty Jordan. Bimonthly magazine.
10,000 to petro. production industry mgmt. & operations personnel interested in news, tech. info. www.wellservicingmagazine.com pjordan@aesc.net

World Oil PO Box 2608 Houston TX 77252 **Phn:** 713-529-4301 **Fax** 713-520-4433 Gulf Publishing Co. Monthly magazine.
35,300 to owners, operating mgrs., drilling contractors, production engineers, geologists. www.worldoil.com editorial@worldoil.com

Pets--Veterinary .52

American Field 542 S Dearborn Ste 1350 Chicago IL 60605 **Phn:** 312-663-9797 **Fax** 312-663-5557 B.J. Matthys. American Field Pub. Weekly tabloid.
8,300 to pointer dog owners, breeders and trainers; operators of kennels, field trial clubs. americanfield.villagesoup.com amfieldedit@att.net

The Bark 2810 8th St Berkeley CA 94710 **Phn:** 510-704-0827 **Fax** 510-704-0933 Claudia Kawczynska. Bimonthly magazine.
150,000 to readers interested in fiction, poetry, essays, news, books reviews about dogs. www.thebark.com editor@thebark.com

Bird Watcher's Digest PO Box 110 Marietta OH 45750 **Phn:** 740-373-5285 **Fax** 740-373-8443 William Thompson III Pardson Corp. Bimonthly magazine.
45,600 to readers interested in how to attract birds by using plantings, feeders, housing. www.birdwatchersdigest.com editor@birdwatchersdigest.com

Birding 4945 N 30th St Ste 200 Colorado Spgs CO 80919 **Phn:** 303-444-6365 **Fax** 719-578-1480 Ted Floyd. Amer. Birding Assn. Bimonthly magazine.
15,800 to active field birders interested in conservation, field trips, photographing birds. www.aba.org tfloyd@aba.org

BirdWatching 85 Quincy Ave, Suite 2 Quincy MA 02169 **Phn:** 617-706-9110 **Fax** 617-706-9110 Chuck Hagner. Madavor Media. Bimonthly magazine.
25,000 to readers interested in birding travel and locales, identifying, attracting bird species. www.birdwatchingdaily.com chagner@madavor.com

Cat Fancy 3 Burroughs Irvine CA 92618 **Phn:** 949-855-8822 **Fax** 949-855-3045 Susan Logan. I-5 Publishing. Monthly magazine. TH:@CATeditor
238,300 to cat owners, breeders, exhibitors interested in behavior, diet, cat rescue, grooming, lifestyle. www.catchannel.com slogan@i5publishing.com

Cesar's Way 333 7th Ave Fl 11 New York NY 10001 **Phn:** 212-979-4800 **Fax** 646-674-0102 Steve Legrice. MacFadden Comms Group. Bimonthly magazine. TH:@cesarmillan
150,000 to readers interested in Cesar Milan's dog training methods, travel with dogs, canine health, fitness, grooming. www.cesarsway.com editor@cesarswaymag.com

Coonhound Bloodlines 100 E Kilgore Rd Portage MI 49002 **Phn:** 269-343-9020 **Fax** 269-343-7037 Vicki Rand. United Kennel Club. Monthly magazine.
16,000 to trail hound enthusiasts interested in hunt training, field trials, products and news. ukcdogs.com vrand@ukcdogs.com

Dog Fancy 3 Burroughs Irvine CA 92618 **Phn:** 949-855-8822 **Fax** 949-855-3045 Ernie Slone. I-5 Publishing. Monthly magazine. TH:@DOGeditor
247,500 to dog owners, breeders, groomers, exhibitors interested in diet, health, shows, products.
www.dogchannel.com eslone@i5publishing.com

DVM Newsmagazine 8033 Flint St Lenexa KS 66214 **Phn:** 800-255-6864 **Fax** 913-871-3808 Kristi Reimer. Advanstar. Monthly tabloid.
58,000 in 3 editions to small animal, equine and food animal veterinarians in private practice.
veterinarynews.dvm360.com
products@advanstar.com

Family Dog 260 Madison Ave New York NY 10016 **Phn:** 212-696-8295 **Fax** 212-696-8239 Erica Mansourian. Amer. Kennel Club. Bimonthly magazine.
40,000 to dog owners & enthusiasts interested in training, behavior, healthcare, dog stories & features.
www.akc.org/pubs/familydog/ familydog@akc.org

Groomer to Groomer 970 W Trindle Rd Mechanicsburg PA 17055 **Phn:** 717-691-3388 **Fax** 717-691-3381 Deb Becker. Barkleigh Productions. 9 issues.
25,000 to professional pet groomers interested in marketing, client relations, industry news.
www.groomertogroomer.com dbecker@barkleigh.com

I Love Cats 908 Oak Tree Ave Ste H South Plainfield NJ 07080 **Phn:** 908-222-0990 **Fax** 908-222-8228 Lisa Allmendinger. Bimonthly magazine.
20,000 to cat owners interested in nutrition & veterinary advice, stories by cat owners, products.
www.iluvcats.com ilovecatseditor@sbcglobal.net

Jrnl. Amer. Veterinary Med. Assn 1931 N Meacham Rd Ste 100 Schaumburg IL 60173 **Phn:** 847-925-8070 **Fax** 847-925-9329 Kurt J. Matushek. Semimonthly magazine.
80,000 to veterinarians interested in diagnostics, research findings, conference reports. www.avma.org news@avma.org

Jrnl. Equine Veterinary Science Univ Of Ky Gluck Equine Rese Lexington KY 40506 **Phn:** 859-257-4757 **Fax** 859-257-8542 Edward L. Squires. Monthly magazine.
5,900 to equine health practitioners interested in original research, clinical techniques, news, conferences. www.j-evs.com elsq222@uky.edu

Just Labs 2779 Aero Park Dr Traverse City MI 49686 **Phn:** 231-946-3712 **Fax** 231-946-9588 Jill Swan. Village Press. Bimonthly.
35,000 to owners of America's favorite breed-the black, yellow or chocolate Labrador Retriever.
www.justlabsmagazine.com jswan@villagepress.com

Life + Dog 7 Switchboard Pl #192-210 The Woodlands TX 77380 **Phn:** 832-592-7204 Ryan Rice. Monthly magazine. TH:@RyanRice
22,500 to dog lovers who treat them as part of the family, fashion, photo & lifestyle features.
www.lifeanddog.com editor@lifeanddog.com

Our Animals 2500 16th St San Francisco CA 94103 **Phn:** 415-554-3029 **Fax** 415-901-5977 Tina Ahn. San Francisco SPCA. Quarterly.
55,500 to readers interested in features and photos about S.F. SPCA programs, people, animals.
www.sfspca.org publicinfo@sfspca.org

Pet Age 220 Davidson Ave Ste 302 Somerset NJ 08873 **Phn:** 732-339-3700 **Fax** 732-846-0421 Michelle Maskaly. Journal Multimedia. Monthly magazine. TH:@petagemag
26,000 to pet industry retailers and buyers interested in sales, new products, pet care trends.
www.petage.com michellem@journalmultimedia.com

Pet Business 333 7th Ave Rm 1100 New York NY 10001 **Phn:** 212-979-4800 **Fax** 646-674-0102 Mark Kalaygian. Monthly magazine.
24,100 to US and Canadian pet industry retailers interested in new products, merchandising.
www.petbusiness.com mkalaygian@petbusiness.com

Pets--Veterinary .52

Pet Product News Intl. 3 Burroughs Irvine CA 92618 **Phn:** 949-855-8822 **Fax** 949-855-3045 Ken Niedziela. I-5 Publ. LLC. Monthly tabloid. TH:@VetPetNews
26,400 to pet store retailers, wholesalers, distributors interested in products, business strategies.
www.petproductnews.com
kniedziela@i5publishing.com

Petfood Industry 303 N Main St Ste 500 Rockford IL 61101 **Phn:** 815-966-5400 **Fax** 815-968-0941 Debbie Phillips-Donaldson. Watt Publishing. Monthly magazine.
11,000 to petfood industry decisionmakers responsible for marketing, planning, profitability.
www.petfoodindustry.com dphillips@wattnet.net

Reptiles 3 Burroughs Irvine CA 92618 **Phn:** 949-855-8822 **Fax** 949-855-3045 Russ Case. I-5 Publishing. Monthly magazine. TH:@REPTILESMag
40,500 to readers who have reptile pets and are interested in feeding, healthcare, breeders.
www.reptilechannel.com reptiles@i5publishing.com

Veterinary Economics 8033 Flint St Lenexa KS 66214 **Phn:** 913-871-3800 **Fax** 913-871-3808 Kristi Reimer. Monthly magazine.
58,900 to veterinarians in small animal practice concerned with practice management.
veterinarybusiness.dvm360.com ve@advanstar.com

Veterinary Medicine 8033 Flint St Lenexa KS 66214 **Phn:** 913-492-4300 **Fax** 913-871-3808 Margaret Rampey. Monthly.
171,600 to small animal veterinarians interested in research, clinical topics, case studies.
veterinarymedicine.dvm360.com
mrampey@advanstar.com

Veterinary Practice News 3 Burroughs Irvine CA 92618 **Phn:** 949-855-8822 **Fax** 949-855-3045 Elisa Jordan. I-5 Publishing. Monthly tabloid. TH:@VetPetNews
55,300 to veterinarians and support staff interested in practice mgmt., industry news & events.
www.veterinarypracticenews.com
kniedziela@i5publishing.com

Veterinary Technician 780 Township Line Rd Yardley PA 19067 **Phn:** 267-685-2300 **Fax** 267-685-1221 Tracey Giannouris. MediMedia. Online only.
for vet. technicians, other vet staff interested in techniques and procedures, client relations.
www.vetlearn.com editor@compendiumvet.com

West Suburban Dog PO Box 4915 Naperville IL 60567 **Phn:** 630-857-9228 **Fax** 630-596-0892 Brooke Keane. 6-issue magazine. TH:@WestSuburbanDog
7,500 to Naperville, IL & other Chicago western suburbs dog owners interested in services, products, photo features. www.westsuburbandog.com
info@westsuburbandog.com

Photography--Audio Visual .53

AfterCapture 6255 Sunset Blvd Fl 19 Los Angeles CA 90028 **Phn:** 310-846-4770 **Fax** 310-846-4995 Bill Hurter. Monthly magazine.
41,000 to post photo production professionals interested in how tos, photographer profiles, alternative processes. www.rangefinderonline.com
bhurter@rfpublishing.com

American Cinematographer PO Box 2230 Hollywood CA 90078 **Phn:** 323-969-4333 **Fax** 323-876-4973 Stephen Pizzello. Amer. Soc Cinematography. Mo. magazine.
34,100 to film and video production directors interested in technical and creative features.
www.theasc.com newproducts@ascmag.com

American Photo 2 Park Ave New York NY 10016 **Phn:** 212-779-5000 Miriam Leuchter. Bonnier Corp. Bimonthly magazine.
150,000 to photography enthusiasts interested in shoots, exhibitions, methods, photographer profiles.
www.americanphotomag.com
miriam.leuchter@bonniercorp.com

Digital Photo 12121 Wilshire Blvd Ste 1200 Los Angeles CA 90025 **Phn:** 310-820-1500 **Fax** 310-826-5008 Wes Pitts. Werner Publishing. 8-issue magazine.
191,000 to digital photo enthusiasts interested in cameras, lenses, software, hardware, techniques.
www.dpmag.com editors@dpmag.com

News Photographer 3200 Croasdaile Dr Ste 306 Durham NC 27705 **Phn:** 919-383-7246 **Fax** 919-383-7261 Donald Winslow. Natl. Press Photographers Assn. Monthly magazine.
9,000 to news photographers interested in profiles, industry news, trade shows, books. www.nppa.org
magazine@nppa.org

Outdoor Photographer 12121 Wilshire Blvd Ste 1200 Los Angeles CA 90025 **Phn:** 310-820-1500 **Fax** 310-826-5008 Chris Robinson. Werner Pub. 11-issue magazine. TH:@OPRobinson
217,400 to outdoor, travel, nature, sports photography enthusiasts interested in techniques, equipment, destinations. www.outdoorphotographer.com
editor@outdoorphotographer.com

Photo District News 770 Broadway Fl 7 New York NY 10003 **Phn:** 646-654-5800 **Fax** 646-654-5813 Holly Hughes. Nielsen Business News. Monthly magazine.
20,000 to pro photographers interested in business practices, legal issues, new products.
www.pdnonline.com hhughes@pdnonline.com

Photo Technique 6600 W Touhy Ave Niles IL 60714 **Phn:** 847-647-2900 **Fax** 847-647-1155 Wendy Erickson. Preston Publications. Bimonthly magazine.
14,600 to photographers interested in film & digital composition, lighting, scanning.
www.phototechmag.com wendy@phototechmag.com

Photographer's Forum 813 Reddick St Santa Barbara CA 93103 **Phn:** 805-963-0439 **Fax** 805-965-0496 Glen R. Serbin. Quarterly magazine.
33,000 to student photographers, emerging professional photographers interested in interviews, contests, business opportunities pfmagazine.com
admin@serbin.com

Photoshop User 333 Douglas Rd E Oldsmar FL 34677 **Phn:** 813-433-5000 **Fax** 813-433-5015 Scott Kelby. Natl. Assn. Photoshop Professionals. 8-issue mag.
95,000 to graphic and multimedia designers, photographers using Adobe Photoshop.
www.photoshopuser.com
skelby@kelbymediagroup.com

PMA Magazine 2282 Springport Rd Ste F Jackson MI 49202 **Phn:** 517-788-8100 **Fax** 517-788-8371 Jennifer Kruger. Photo Marketing Assn. Monthly magazine.
82,400 to personnel at photo/video retail minilabs, wholesale finishers, professional image labs.
www.pmai.org/magazine/ jkruger@pmai.org

Popular Photography 2 Park Ave New York NY 10016 **Phn:** 212-779-5463 Miriam Leuchter. Bonnier Corp. Monthly magazine.
350,000 to amateur, professional photographers interested in technique, product tests, advice.
www.popphoto.com
miriam.leuchter@bonniercorp.com

Professional Photographer 229 Peachtree St NE Ste 2200 Atlanta GA 30303 **Phn:** 404-522-8600 **Fax** 404-614-6406 Ms. Cameron Bishopp. Prof. Photographers Assn. Mo.
50,300 to PPA members, photographers interested in composition, lighting, products, marketing.
www.ppmag.com cbishopp@ppa.com

PSA Journal 2728 Cashion Pl Oklahoma City OK 73112 **Phn:** 405-943-7019 **Fax** 405-843-1438 Donna Brennan. Photographic Soc. of Am. Mo.
6,500 to PSA members interested in equipment, book reviews, Society news. psa-photo.org editor@psa-photo.org

Rangefinder 6255 Sunset Blvd Fl 19 Los Angeles CA 90028 **Phn:** 310-846-4770 **Fax** 310-846-4995 Bill Hurter. Monthly magazine.
61,000 to pro photographers interested in equipment tests, tech. applications, business practices.
www.rangefinderonline.com bhurter@rfpublishing.com

Shutterbug 1415 Chaffee Dr Ste 10 Titusville FL 32780 **Phn:** 321-269-3120 **Fax** 321-225-3149 George Schaub. Source Interlink Media. Monthly magazine.
107,200 to advanced hobbyists, pro. photographers interested in how-to's, products, business. www.shutterbug.com editorial@shutterbug.com

Stereophile 261 Madison Ave Fl 6 New York NY 10016 **Phn:** 212-915-4156 **Fax** 212-915-4167 John Atkinson. Source Interlink Media. Monthly magazine.
74,300 to owners of high-end audio systems interested in equip. reports, developments in sound. www.stereophile.com john.atkinson@sorc.com

Today's Photographer Intl. PO Box 777 Lewisville NC 27023 **Phn:** 336-945-9867 **Fax** 336-945-3711 Vonda Blackburn. American Image, Inc. Quarterly magazine.
78,000 to pro & amateur photographers interested in methods, techniques, how to sell photos. www.aipress.com homeoffice@ainewsservice.net

View Camera PO Box 2328 Corrales NM 87048 **Phn:** 505-899-8054 **Fax** 505-899-7977 Steve Simmons. Bimonthly.
16,000 to large format photographers interested in equip., darkrooms, how-to articles, reviews. www.viewcamera.com largformat@aol.com

Plastics .54

Composites Manufacturing 1010 N Glebe Rd Ste 450 Arlington VA 22201 **Phn:** 703-525-0511 **Fax** 703-525-0743 Melinda Skea. Monthly magazine.
11,500 to fiberglass, composites, parts mfg. personnel responsible for operations & processes. www.acmanet.org/CM/ mskea@acmanet.org

Composites Technology 6915 Valley Ln Cincinnati OH 45244 **Phn:** 513-527-8800 **Fax** 513-527-8801 Michael Musselman. Gardner Publications. Bimonthly magazine.
20,000 to engineers & mfg. personnel working in reinforced plastics industry. www.gardnerweb.com/composites/ mike@compositesworld.com

The IAPD Magazine 6734 W 121st St Overland Park KS 66209 **Phn:** 913-345-1005 **Fax** 913-345-1006 Janet Thill. Intl. Assn. Plastics Distribution. Bimonthly magazine.
10,000 to purchasing decisionmakers in plastics distribution, mfg., fabrication & OEM. www.theiapdmagazine.com iapd@iapd.org

Plastics Engineering 13 Church Hill Rd Newtown CT 06470 **Phn:** 203-775-0471 **Fax** 203-775-8490 Daniel Domoff. Soc. Plastics Engineers. Monthly magazine.
26,400 to Society members; technical execs. in plastics production, design, R&D. www.plasticsengineering.org djdomoff@4spe.org

Plastics News 1725 Merriman Rd Akron OH 44313 **Phn:** 330-836-9180 **Fax** 330-836-2322 Donald Loepp. Crain Communications. Weekly tabloid. TH:@plasticsnews
60,500 to N. Amer. plastics processing industry personnel & customers. www.plasticsnews.com dloepp@crain.com

Plastics Technology 7 Penn Plz Ste 1003 New York NY 10001 **Phn:** 646-827-4848 **Fax** 646-827-4859 Matthew Naitove. Gardner Publications. Monthly mag.
47,200 to plastic processors interested in business & technical information. www.ptonline.com mnaitove@ptonline.com

Plastics Today 11444 W Olympic Blvd Ste 900 Los Angeles CA 90064 **Phn:** 310-445-4200 **Fax** 310-445-4269 Tony Deligio. UBM Canon. Online only.
for plastics industry decisionmakers in medical, automotive, packaging, other industries. www.plasticstoday.com tony.deligio@ubm.com

Plumbing--Heating--Cooling .55

Air Cond. Heat & Refrig. News 2401 W Big Beaver Rd Ste 700 Troy MI 48084 **Phn:** 248-362-3700 **Fax** 248-362-0317 Mike Murphy. BNP Media. Weekly tabloid.
30,700 to mfrs., wholesalers, distributors, contractors concerned with all industry aspects. www.achrnews.com mikemurphy@achrnews.com

Photography--Audio Visual .53

ASHRAE Journal 1791 Tullie Cir NE Atlanta GA 30329 **Phn:** 404-636-8400 **Fax** 404-321-5478 Fred Turner. Amer. Soc. Heating Refrigeration Air Cond. Engineers. Mo. mag.
60,000 to non-residential bldg. HVACR professionals interested application focused articles. www.ashrae.org/Journal fturner@ashrae.org

Contracting Business 1300 E 9th St Cleveland OH 44114 **Phn:** 216-696-7000 **Fax** 216-696-7932 Mike Weil. Penton Media. Monthly magazine.
49,000 to HVACR contractors & retailers interested in new construction, replacement, service. contractingbusiness.com mike.weil@penton.com

Contractor 330 N Wabash Ave Ste 2300 Chicago IL 60611 **Phn:** 312-840-8404 **Fax** 312-755-1128 Robert P. Mader. Penton Media. Monthly tabloid.
50,000 to plumbing/heating/cooling industry mgmt. interested in markets, technology, jobsites. contractormag.com robert.mader@penton.com

Engineered Systems PO Box 2600 Troy MI 48007 **Phn:** 434-974-6986 **Fax** 248-502-1038 Robert Beverly. BNP Media. Monthly magazine.
52,200 to specifiers, installers, buyers of commercial/industrial/institutional HVAC/R systems. www.esmagazine.com beverlyr@bnpmedia.com

Fuel Oil News 5600 N River Rd Ste 800 Rosemont IL 60018 **Phn:** 760-318-7000 **Fax** 415-398-3511 Keith Reid. M2Media360. Monthly.
15,200 to heating oil, diesel, alternative fuel dealers interested in equipment, case histories. www.fueloilnews.com kreid@m2media360.com

HPAC Engineering 1300 E 9th St Cleveland OH 44114 **Phn:** 216-931-9980 **Fax** 913-514-6315 Scott Arnold. Penton Media. Monthly mag.
35,000 to mechanical systems engineers who design, operate, maintain HVACR systems. hpac.com scott.arnold@penton.com

HVACR Business PO Box 451310 Westlake OH 44145 **Phn:** 440-234-3542 **Fax** 440-234-3698 Tonya Vinas. Monthly tab.
49,600 HVACR contracting mgrs. responsible for finance, sales, marketing, training, insurance. www.hvacrbusiness.com tvinas@hvacrbusiness.com

Indoor Comfort Marketing 3621 Hill Rd Parsippany NJ 07054 **Phn:** 973-331-9545 **Fax** 973-331-9547 Michael SanGiovanni. Monthly magazine.
14,400 to local oil heat co. owners, managers interested in research, repair, customer service. www.indoorcomfortmarketing.com editor@indoorcomfortmarketing.com

Indoor Comfort News 454 W Broadway Glendale CA 91204 **Phn:** 818-551-1555 **Fax** 818-551-1115 Al Stewart. Inst. of Heating & AC Industries. Monthly tab.
25,000 to HVACR personnel interested in green technologies, industry news, market trends, business issues. www.indoorcomfortnews.com ihaci@ihaci.org

Plumbing & Mechanical 155 N Pfingsten Rd Ste 205 Deerfield IL 60015 **Phn:** 847-405-4041 **Fax** 248-502-1006 Kelly Faloon. BNP Media. Monthly mag.
49,000 to plumbing, piping, hydronic heating, solar thermal and mechanical contractors. www.pmmag.com faloonk@bnpmedia.com

Plumbing Engineer 2165 Shermer Rd Ste A Northbrook IL 60062 **Phn:** 847-564-1127 **Fax** 847-564-1264 Jim Schneider. TMB Publishing. Monthly magazine.
25,300 to plumbing engineers, designers interested in tech. info, codes, standards, new products. www.plumbingengineer.com editor@plumbingengineer.com

PM Engineer 155 N Pfingsten Rd Ste 205 Deerfield IL 60015 **Phn:** 630-694-4011 **Fax** 248-283-6547 Jim Camillo. BNP Media. Monthly magazine.
26,500 to fire protection, hydronics engineers working with water-based systems for commercial, multi-family residences. www.pmengineer.com camilloj@bnpmedia.com

Reeves Journal 23421 S Pointe Dr Ste 280 Laguna Hills CA 92653 **Phn:** 949-830-0881 **Fax** 949-859-7845 Jack Sweet. BNP Media. Monthly.
13,500 to western U.S. plumbing, heating, cooling contractors, engineers, architects, suppliers. www.reevesjournal.com jack@reevesjournal.com

RSES Journal 1666 Rand Rd Des Plaines IL 60016 **Phn:** 847-297-6464 **Fax** 847-297-5038 Lori Kasallis. Refrigeration Svce. Engineers Society. Monthly.
17,200 to Society members interested in technical articles, new products, industry news. www.rses.org lkasallis@rses.org

Snips Magazine 2401 W Big Beaver Rd Ste 700 Troy MI 48084 **Phn:** 248-362-3700 **Fax** 248-362-0317 Mike McConnell. BNP Media. Monthly magazine.
20,800 to sheet metal, cooling, heating, ventilation contractors, dealers and installers. www.snipsmag.com mcconnellm@bnpmedia.com

Southern P-H-C PO Box 7344 Greensboro NC 27417 **Phn:** 336-235-3084 **Fax** 877-496-0676 Charles Cheek. Southern Trade Publications. Bimonthly magazine.
11,300 to plumbing, heating, air conditioning contractors & wholesalers in 14 southern U.S. states. www.southernphc.com charlie@southernphc.com

Supply House Times 155 N Pfingsten Rd Ste 205 Deerfield IL 60015 **Phn:** 630-694-4006 **Fax** 248-502-1007 Jim Olsztynski. BNP Media. Monthly mag.
30,000 to P&H, AC, industrial piping wholesale mgmt. personnel interested in products, forecasts, trends, co. profiles. www.supplyht.com olsztynskij@bnpmedia.com

Wholesaler 1838 Techny Ct Northbrook IL 60062 **Phn:** 847-564-1127 **Fax** 847-564-1264 Mary Jo Martin. TMB Publishing. Monthly tabloid.
31,700 to owners & mgrs. at plumbing-heating-cooling wholesale distributorships. www.thewholesaler.com editor@thewholesaler.com

Power--Power Plants .56

Diesel & Gas Turbine Worldwide 20855 Watertown Rd Ste 220 Waukesha WI 53186 **Phn:** 832-205-3047 **Fax** 262-754-4175 Brent Haight. 10-issue magazine.
20,000 to end users, engineers, designers of industrial, military and aircraft gas turbines. www.dieselgasturbine.com bhaight@dieselpub.com

Diesel Progress 20855 Watertown Rd Ste 220 Waukesha WI 53186 **Phn:** 262-754-4100 **Fax** 262-754-4175 Michael Brezonick. Monthly.
28,100 to engine power and transmission system technology industry personnel. www.dieselprogress.com mbrezonick@dieselpub.com

Gas Turbine World PO Box 447 Southport CT 06890 **Phn:** 203-259-1812 **Fax** 203-254-3431 Robert Farmer. Bimonthly.
10,300 to engineering and corporate mgmt. in combustion and steam turbine-using industries. www.gtwbooks.com gtwnews@gmail.com

Hydro Review 1421 S Sheridan Rd Tulsa OK 74112 **Phn:** 918-835-3161 **Fax** 918-831-9834 Marla Barnes. PennWell Publishing. 8-issue magazine.
3,500 to hydroelectric industry personnel interested in technical and environmental developments. www.pennwell.com marlab@pennwell.com

North American Windpower PO Box 2180 Waterbury CT 06722 **Phn:** 203-262-4670 **Fax** 203-262-4680 Michael Bates. Zackin Publications. Monthly magazine.
17,100 to wind energy industry personnel interested in regional profiles, innovations, projects. www.nawindpower.com bates@nawindpower.com

Nuclear News 555 N Kensington Ave La Grange Park IL 60526 **Phn:** 708-352-6611 **Fax** 708-352-6464 Betsy Tompkins. Amer. Nuclear Society. Monthly magazine.
10,700 to Soc. members, nuclear scientists, engineers interested in career opportunities, products. www.ans.org nucnews@ans.org

Nuclear Plant Journal 799 Roosevelt Rd Bldg 6 # 208 Glen Ellyn IL 60137 **Phn:** 630-858-6161 **Fax** 630-858-8787 Michelle Gaylord. EQES, Inc. Bimo. magazine.
14,000 to tech. mgrs., engineers in global nuclear power industry interested in info. exchange.
www.nuclearplantjournal.com michelle@goinfo.com

Power Engineering 1421 S Sheridan Rd Tulsa OK 74112 **Phn:** 918-835-3161 **Fax** 918-831-9834 David Wagman. PennWell Publishing. Monthly.
60,100 to executives responsible for design, use, maintenance of public, private power facilities.
www.power-eng.com pe-editor@pennwell.com

Public Power 1875 Connecticut Ave NW Ste 1200 Washington DC 20009 **Phn:** 202-467-2900 **Fax** 202-467-2910 Jeanne LaBella. Amer. Public Power Assn. Bimonthly mag.
21,000 to management of locally-owned electric utilities interested in R&D, Assn. activities.
www.publicpower.org jlabella@appanet.org

Public Utilities Fortnightly 8229 Boone Blvd Ste 400 Vienna VA 22182 **Phn:** 703-847-7720 **Fax** 703-847-0683 Michael Burr. Monthly magazine.
3,500 to electric, gas, water & telephone utility senior mgmt., engineers, govt. regulators.
www.fortnightly.com burr@pur.com

Renewable Energy World 98 Spit Brook Rd Ste LI-1 Nashua NH 03062 **Phn:** 603-924-4405 **Fax** 603-924-4451 Jennifer Runyan. PennWell Publishing. Monthly.
20,100 covers renewable energy technology industry, policy, technology, finance, and news.
www.renewableenergyworld.com
rewnews@pennwell.com

Rural Electric Magazine 4301 Wilson Blvd Arlington VA 22203 **Phn:** 703-907-5500 **Fax** 703-907-5519 Scot Hoffman. Natl. Rural Elec. Co-op Assn. Monthly.
25,700 to rural electric co-op managers, employees interested in legal, marketing, training news.
remagazine.cooperative.com
scot.hoffman@nreca.coop

Transmission/Distribution World 9800 Metcalf Ave Overland Park KS 66212 **Phn:** 913-341-1300 **Fax** 913-514-6743 Richard Bush. Penton Media. Monthly mag.
36,600 to electric power utility engineers & operating mgrs. interested in technical topics & products.
tdworld.com rbush@tdworld.com

TurboMachinery International PO Box 5550 Norwalk CT 06856 **Phn:** 323-660-4862 **Fax** 203-852-8175 Drew Robb. Business Journals, Inc. 7-issue magazine.
11,100 to energy industry mgrs. responsible for maintenance/operation of turbines, compressors.
www.turbomachinerymag.com drew@busjour.com

Utility Fleet Professional 360 Memorial Dr Ste 10 Crystal Lake IL 60014 **Phn:** 203-272-7644 **Fax** 847-620-0662 Seth Skydel. 5-issue magazine.
5,500 to utility, utility contractor, communications provider, publics works fleet equipment & maintenance managers. www.utilityfleetprofessional.com
seth@utilityfleetprofessional.com

World-Generation 2 Penn Plz Rm 1500 New York NY 10121 **Phn:** 212-292-5009 **Fax** 212-292-5023 Richard Flanagan. Bimonthly tabloid.
7,100 to worldwide power plant mgmt. responsible for plant design, operation, maintenance. www.world-gen.com flanagan@world-gen.com

Firearms .57

American Firearms Industry 2620 Alamanda Ct Fort Lauderdale FL 33301 **Phn:** 954-467-9994 **Fax** 954-463-2501 Andrew Molchan. Monthly.
24,200 to firearms retailers interested in new products, industry news and analysis. www.amfire.com
webmaster@amfire.com

American Handgunner 12345 World Trade Dr San Diego CA 92128 **Phn:** 858-605-0200 **Fax** 858-605-0247 Roy Huntington. Publishers Development Corp. Bimo. mag.
106,500 to handgun collectors, hobbyists and handgun hunters novice to expert.
www.americanhandgunner.com
ed@americanhandgunner.com

Power--Power Plants .56

American Rifleman 11250 Waples Mill Rd Ste 4 Fairfax VA 22030 **Phn:** 703-267-1379 **Fax** 703-267-3971 Mark Keefe. NRA Publications. Monthly magazine.
1,500,000 to shooting hobbyists interested in equipment, techniques, safety.
www.americanrifleman.org publications@nrahq.org

Combat Handguns 1115 Broadway New York NY 10010 **Phn:** 212-807-7100 **Fax** 212-807-1479 Linus Cernauskas. Harris Outdoor Grp. Bimo.
83,000 Covers the use of handguns in combat situations. www.tactical-life.com

Gun Digest 700 E State St Iola WI 54990 **Phn:** 715-445-2214 **Fax** 715-445-4087 Andy Belmas. F&W Media. Bi-weekly magazine.
58,000 to gun enthusiasts interested in firearm news, pricing, guns for sale, product reviews.
www.gundigest.com gundigestonline@fwmedia.com

Guns Magazine 12345 World Trade Dr San Diego CA 92128 **Phn:** 858-605-0200 **Fax** 858-605-0247 Jeff John. Publishers Development Corp. Monthly.
89,300 to hunters, hobbyists, collectors interested in equipment, techniques, pending legislation.
www.gunsmagazine.com ed@gunsmagazine.com

Handloader 2625 Stearman Rd Ste A Prescott AZ 86301 **Phn:** 928-445-7810 **Fax** 928-778-5124 Roberta Scovill. Bimonthly.
133,800 to members of Intl. Handloader Assn. and others interested in technical features.
www.handloadermagazine.com
wolfepub@riflemag.com

Junior Shooters 7154 W State St #377 Boise ID 83714 **Phn:** 208-629-8967 Andy Fink. Quarterly.
30,000 to readers interested in gun safety, events, clubs, equipment for tweens & teens.
www.juniorshooters.net articles@juniorshooters.net

Rifle 2625 Stearman Rd Ste A Prescott AZ 86301 **Phn:** 928-445-7810 **Fax** 928-778-5124 Roberta Scovill. Bimonthly magazine.
135,000 to affluent rifle hunters and shooters.
www.riflemagazine.com wolfepub@riflemag.com

Shooting Industry 12345 World Trade Dr San Diego CA 92128 **Phn:** 858-605-0200 **Fax** 858-605-0247 Russ Thurman. Publishers Development Corp. Monthly.
17,700 to gun dealers interested in news, products, sales techniques, mfg. developments.
www.shootingindustry.com
russ@shootingindustry.com

Shooting Times 2 News Plz Fl 2 Peoria IL 61614 **Phn:** **Fax** 309-682-7394 Joseph von Benedikt. InterMedia Outdoors. Monthly magazine.
174,600 to novice and experienced gun enthusiasts interested in shooting sports. www.shootingtimes.com
shootingtimes@imoutdoors.com

TV--Video--Radio .58

Broadcast Engineering 9800 Metcalf Ave Overland Park KS 66212 **Phn:** 913-341-1300 **Fax** 913-967-1905 Brad Dick. Penton Media. Monthly magazine.
33,300 to broadcast engineering & operations mgmt. responsible for equip. selection, operation.
broadcastengineering.com brad.dick@penton.com

Broadcasting & Cable 28 E 28th St Fl 12 New York NY 10016 **Phn:** 212-378-0400 **Fax** 917-281-4704 Dade Hayes. NewBay Media. Weekly magazine.
23,100 to TV/radio industry personnel including b'cast, cable, satellite, emerging technology.
www.broadcastingcable.com dhayes@nbmedia.com

CableFax 4 Choke Cherry Rd Fl 2 Rockville MD 20850 **Phn:** 301-354-2000 **Fax** 301-738-8453 Kaylee Hultgren. Access Intelligence. Quarterly magazine. TH:@CableFAX
60,000 to cable and broadband personnel responsible for programming, operations, marketing.
www.cablefax.com/cablefaxmag/
khultgren@accessintel.com

CED 100 Enterprise Dr Ste 600 Rockaway NJ 07866 **Phn:** 973-920-7000 **Fax** 973-920-7542 Brian Santo. Advantage Business Media. Monthly.
22,400 to broadband communications technology specifying engineers. www.cedmagazine.com
brian.santo@advantagemedia.com

Communications Technology 4 Choke Cherry Rd Fl 2 Rockville MD 20850 **Phn:** 301-354-2000 **Fax** 301-738-8453 Debra Baker. PBI Media. Monthly.
18,000 to engineering personnel in MSO, independent cable systems; contractors, brokers.
www.cable360.net/ct/ dbaker@accessintel.com

CQ - Amateur Radio 25 Newbridge Rd Hicksville NY 11801 **Phn:** 516-681-2922 **Fax** 516-681-2926 Richard Moseson. Monthly magazine.
50,000 to amateur operators worldwide who build, operate and experiment with radio equipment.
www.cq-amateur-radio.com w2vu@cq-amateur-radio.com

Current 6930 Carroll Ave Ste 350 Takoma Park MD 20912 **Phn:** 301-270-7240 **Fax** 301-270-7241 Karen Everhart. 23-issue tabloid.
4,000 to public radio/TV station, network personnel interested in programming, regulatory issues.
www.current.org karen@current.org

Digital Signage 28 E 28th St Fl 12 New York NY 10016 **Phn:** 512-480-9473 **Fax** 512-480-9255 David Keene. NewBay Media. Bimonthly magazine. TH:@DigiSignageMag
21,000 to marketing, operations & technology personnel responsible for digital signage specs, creation, installation. www.digitalsignageweekly.com
jdavidkeene@gmail.com

Digital Video 28 E 28th St Fl 12 New York NY 10016 **Phn:** 212-378-0400 **Fax** 917-281-4704 Katie Makal. NewBay Media. Monthly magazine.
60,000 to professionals involved in the production, postproduction and delivery of digital video.
www.dv.com kmakal@nbmedia.com

Independent Cable News 40 W Littleton Blvd # 210-110 Littleton CO 80120 **Phn:** 303-730-3006 **Fax** 303-797-0276 Robert Searle. Monthly magazine.
3,000 to executives at independent and small multi-system cable operations. www.independentcable.com
rsearle@searlepub.com

Millimeter 9800 Metcalf Ave Overland Park KS 66212 **Phn:** 913-967-1300 **Fax** 913-967-1898 Susan Anderson. Penton Media. Online only.
for film, TV and commercial producers, camera operators, post-production staff.
digitalcontentproducer.com
susan.anderson@penton.com

Mix 1111 Bayhill Dr Ste 125 San Bruno CA 94066 **Phn:** 650-238-0300 **Fax** 650-238-0263 Tom Kenny. NewBay Media. Monthly magazine.
40,000 to audio production studio personnel interested in recording studios, equip., industry news.
mixonline.com tkenny@nbmedia.com

Monitoring Times 7540 Highway 64 W Brasstown NC 28902 **Phn:** 828-837-9200 **Fax** 828-837-2216 Ken Reitz. Grove Ents. Monthly.
10,000 to amateur radio operators, radio hobbyists, shortwave listeners, scanner monitors.
www.monitoringtimes.com
editor@monitoringtimes.com

Multichannel News 28 E 28th St Fl 12 New York NY 10016 **Phn:** 212-378-0400 **Fax** 917-281-4704 Kent Gibbons. NewBay Media. Weekly tabloid.
18,000 to programming, marketing, finance mgrs. in global cable TV, telecom industries.
www.multichannel.com kgibbons@nbmedia.com

Popular Communications 25 Newbridge Rd Ste 309 Hicksville NY 11801 **Phn:** 516-681-2922 **Fax** 516-681-2926 Edith Lennon. CQ Communications. Monthly mag.
40,000 to radio communication, b'cast, radio restoration enthusiasts, pirate radio broadcasters.
www.popular-communications.com editor@popular-communications.com

Pro Audio Review 28 E 28th St Fl 27 New York NY 10016 **Phn:** 212-378-0400 **Fax** 917-281-4704 Frank Wells. NewBay Media. Monthly magazine.
28,000 to professional audio equip. buyers interested in product reviews, user reports, tech. info.
www.proaudioreview.com fwells@nbmedia.com

Pro AV 1 Thomas Cir NW Ste 600 Washington DC 20005 **Phn:** 202-452-0800 **Fax** 202-785-1974 Brad Grimes. Hanley-Wood. Bimonthly.
20,000 to dealers, sound and video contractors, engineers, consultants and end-users.
www.proavmagazine.com
dmmoran@hanleywood.com

Pro Sound News 28 E 28th St Fl 12 New York NY 10016 **Phn:** 212-378-0400 **Fax** 917-281-4704 Clive Young. NewBay Media. Monthly tabloid.
24,300 to audio industry personnel interested in business trends, new products and technology.
www.prosoundnetwork.com cyoung@nbmedia.com

QST 225 Main St Newington CT 06111 **Phn:** 860-594-0200 **Fax** 860-594-0259 Steve Ford. Amer. Radio Relay League. Monthly magazine.
156,300 to amateur radio operators interested in equipment, events, public service. www.arrl.org qst@arrl.org

Radio Ink 1901 S. Congress Ave Ste 118 Boynton Beach FL 33426 **Phn:** 561-655-8778 **Fax** 561-655-6164 Ed Ryan. 20-issue magazine. TH:@Radio_Ink
5,000 to radio station, radio group owners, operators, mgrs. responsible for sales, programming.
www.radioink.com edryantheeditor@gmail.com

Radio Magazine 5285 Shawnee Rd Ste 100 Alexandria VA 22312 **Phn:** 212-378-0400 Chriss Scherer. NewBay Media. Monthly.
9,000 to radio station engineers, mgrs. responsible for equip. specifying, purchasing, installation.
radiomagonline.com cscherer@radiomagonline.com

Radio World 5285 Shawnee Rd Ste 100 Alexandria VA 22312 **Phn:** 703-852-4600 **Fax** 703-852-4585 Paul McLane. Biweekly tabloid.
10,000 to engineering and technical personnel in radio broadcast industry. www.rwonline.com
pmclane@nbmedia.com

SMPTE Journal 3 Barker Ave White Plains NY 10601 **Phn:** 914-761-1100 **Fax** 914-761-3115 Dianne Purrier. Soc. Motion Pic/TV Eng. 8-issue magazine.
8,000 to Society members, technicians, engineers, execs. in TV and related fields. www.smpte.org dpurrier@smpte.org

Sound & Communications 25 Willowdale Ave Port Washington NY 11050 **Phn:** 516-767-2500 **Fax** 516-767-9335 David A. Silverman. Testa Communications. Monthly.
27,100 to audio and audio-visual system designers, specifiers, installers.
www.soundandcommunications.com
dsilverman@testa.com

Sound & Video Contractor 28 E 28th St Fl 12 New York NY 10016 **Phn:** 818-236-3667 **Fax** 917-281-4704 Cynthia Wisehart. NewBay Media. Monthly.
20,000 to sound/video contractors, design consultants interested in how-to's, new technology. svconline.com cwisehart@nbmedia.com

Sound & Vision 2 Park Ave Fl 10 New York NY 10016 **Phn:** 212-779-5000 **Fax** 212-779-5200 Rob Sabin. Bonnier Corp. 8-issue magazine. TH:@RobFSabin
230,000 to readers interested in all aspects of home theater, surround sound, new releases, audio/video/multimedia products.
www.soundandvisionmag.com
rob.sabin@hometheater.com

Studio Monthly 110 William St Fl 11 New York NY 10038 **Phn:** 212-621-4900 **Fax** 212-621-4879 Beth Marchant. Access Intelligence. Online only.
for corporate/organizational producers interested in emerging technologies, production.
www.studiodaily.com/studiomonthly/
bmarchant@accessintel.com

TV--Video--Radio .58

Systems Contractor News 28 E 28th St Fl 12 New York NY 10016 **Phn:** 212-378-0400 **Fax** 917-281-4704 Kirsten Nelson. NewBay Media. Bimonthly.
18,000 to A/V, multimedia, security, access control, telecom, life safety, networks installers.
www.systemscontractor.com knelson@nbmedia.com

Talkers Magazine 650 Belmont Ave Springfield MA 01108 **Phn:** 413-739-8255 **Fax** 413-746-6786 Michael Harrison. 10-issue magazine.
12,000 to talk media industry personnel in all broadcast fields interested in trends, research.
www.talkers.com info@talkers.com

TV Technology 28 E 28th St Fl 12 New York NY 10016 **Phn:** 212-378-0400 **Fax** 917-281-4704 Tom Butts. NewBay Media. 26 issues.
31,000 to TV station production, engineering & operations personnel interested in equip. & tech. info.
www.tvtechnology.com tbutts@nbmedia.com

TVWeek 711 3rd Ave New York NY 10017 **Phn:** 212-210-0706 **Fax** 212-210-0200 Chuck Ross. Crain Communications. Online only.
for industry personnel in the broadcast, cable & digital media fields interested in events & technology.
www.tvweek.com chkross@tvweek.com

Twice 28 E 28th St Fl 12 New York NY 10016 **Phn:** 212-378-0400 **Fax** 917-281-4704 Stephen Smith. NewBay Media. 26-issue tabloid.
20,000 to consumer electronics retailers interested in sales statistics, new products. www.twice.com ssmith@nbmedia.com

Urgent Communications 330 N Wabash Ave Ste 2300 Chicago IL 60611 **Phn:** 312-595-1080 **Fax** 312-595-0296 Glenn Bischoff. Penton Media. Online only. TH:@UrgentComm
to public safety, utility, transportation industry personnel using mobile communications equip.
urgentcomm.com glenn.bischoff@penton.com

Videomaker PO Box 4591 Chico CA 95927 **Phn:** 530-891-8410 Matt York. York Publishing. Monthly magazine.
50,000 to video producers working in business & education settings, video production hobbyists.
www.videomaker.com editor@videomaker.com

WorldRadio Online 25 Newbridge Rd Hicksville NY 11801 **Phn:** 516-681-2922 **Fax** 516-681-2926 Nancy Kott. CQ Communications. Online only.
for amateur radio operators interested in emergency communications, public service. www.cq-amateur-radio.com worldradioeditor@cq-amateur-radio.com

Railroad Industry .59

Locomotive Engineers/Trainmen Ne 1370 Ontario St Cleveland OH 44113 **Phn:** 216-241-2630 **Fax** 216-241-6516 John Bentley. Brotherhood of Locomotive Engineers.
53,300 to railroad union members interested in union news, benefits, rail technology and operations.
www.ble-t.org presstaff@ble-t.org

Progressive Railroading 2100 W Florist Ave Milwaukee WI 53209 **Phn:** 414-228-7701 **Fax** 414-228-1134 Pat Foran. Trade Press Media Group. Monthly magazine.
25,000 to freight, transit execs. responsible for way maintenance, equipment operations, gov. affairs.
www.progressiverailroading.com
pat.foran@tradepress.com

Railfan & Railroad 108 Phil Hardin Rd Newton NJ 07860 **Phn:** 973-383-3355 **Fax** 973-383-4064 Steve Barry. Carstens Publications. Monthly magazine.
41,400 to readers interested in all aspects of railroading and all types of trains. www.railfan.com steveb@railfan.com

Railway Age 345 Hudson St Rm 1201 New York NY 10014 **Phn:** 212-620-7200 **Fax** 212-633-1863 William C. Vantuono. Simmons-Boardman. Monthly mag.
18,700 to railway management responsible for all aspects of passenger, freight, light rail operations.
www.railwayage.com wvantuono@sbpub.com

Railway Track & Structures 20 S Clark St Ste 2450 Chicago IL 60603 **Phn:** 312-683-0130 **Fax** 312-683-0131 Mischa Wanek-Libman. Simmons-Boardman. Monthly magazine.
8,000 to railroad industry engineering department managers responsible for track, structures.
www.rtands.com mischa@sbpub-chicago.com

Signalman's Journal 917 Shenandoah Shores Rd Front Royal VA 22630 **Phn:** 540-622-6522 **Fax** 540-622-6532 Jerry Boles. Brotherhood Railroad Signalmen. Quarterly.
14,000 to railroad signal industry union members interested in union news, railroad project. www.brs.org signalman@brs.org

Trains PO Box 1612 Waukesha WI 53187 **Phn:** 262-796-8776 **Fax** 262-798-6468 Jim Wrinn. Kalmbach Publishing. Monthly magazine.
93,300 to railroad enthusiasts interested in rail operations, train technology, railroad history.
trc.trains.com/trn/ editor@trainsmag.com

UTU News 24950 Country Club Blvd # 340 North Olmsted OH 44070 **Phn:** 216-228-9400 **Fax** 216-228-5755 Mike Futhey. Monthly.
95,000 to active and retired members of United Transportation Union. utu.org president_td@smart-union.org

Schools--Education .60

Academe 1133 19th St NW Ste 200 Washington DC 20036 **Phn:** 202-737-5900 **Fax** 202-737-5526 Michael Ferguson. Amer. Assn. Univ. Professors. Bimonthly.
45,000 to university faculty interested in tenure, distance education, academic news. www.aaup.org mferguson@aaup.org

American Biology Teacher 1313 Dolley Madison Blvd Ste 402 McLean VA 22101 **Phn:** 703-264-9696 **Fax** 703-264-7778 Cheryl S. Merrill. Natl. Assn. Biology Teachers. 9 iss.
12,300 to biology teachers (elementary-college) interested in curriculum development. www.nabt.org office@nabt.org

American Educator 555 New Jersey Ave NW Washington DC 20001 **Phn:** 202-879-4420 **Fax** 202-879-4534 Lisa Hansel. Amer. Fed. Teachers. Quarterly.
850,000 to Federation members interested in education issues nationally and internationally.
www.aft.org/ae amered@aft.org

American Jrnl. Health Education 1900 Association Dr Reston VA 20191 **Phn:** 703-476-3400 **Fax** 703-476-9527 Linda M. Moore. Bimonthly magazine.
12,000 to health and safety directors, educators, athletic directors, coaches, school nurses.
www.aahperd.org lmoore@aahperd.org

American Mathematical Monthly 1529 18th St NW Washington DC 20036 **Phn:** 202-387-5200 **Fax** 202-265-2384 Harry Waldman. Math. Assn. Amer. 10-issue mag.
18,000 to Assn. members, college level math instructors interested in book reviews, analyses.
www.maa.org monthly@shsu.edu

American School & University 9800 Metcalf Ave Overland Park KS 66212 **Phn:** 913-341-1300 **Fax** 913-514-9250 Joe Agron. Penton Media. 13-issue magazine.
65,000 to school & college administrators, business mgrs., architects, facility planners. asumag.com jagron@asumag.com

American School Brd. Jrnl. 1680 Duke St Alexandria VA 22314 **Phn:** 703-838-6722 **Fax** 703-549-6719 Kathleen Vail. Natl. School Boards Assn. Monthly magazine. TH:@ASBJMagazine
90,000 to school superintendents, principals, board of education members. www.asbj.com kvale@nsba.org

American Teacher 555 New Jersey Ave NW Washington DC 20001 **Phn:** 202-879-4400 **Fax** 202-783-2014 Roger Glass. Amer. Fed. Teachers. 5-issue tabloid.
915,000 to Federation members interested in classroom tips, technology, union news. www.aft.org online@aft.org

Schools--Education .60

Art Education 1916 Association Dr Reston VA 20191 **Phn:** 703-860-8000 **Fax** 703-860-2960 Lynn Ezell. Natl. Art Education Assn. Bimonthly magazine.
23,000 to art instructors at elementary through adult level interested in teaching methods.
www.arteducators.org info@arteducators.org

Arts & Activities 12345 World Trade Dr San Diego CA 92128 **Phn:** 858-605-0200 **Fax** 858-605-0247 Maryellen Bridge. Monthly magazine.
19,200 to classroom & art teachers, school libraries, teachers' colleges. www.artsandactivities.com ed@artsandactivities.com

Athletic Business 4130 Lien Rd Madison WI 53704 **Phn:** 608-249-0186 **Fax** 608-249-1153 Monthly magazine.
40,000 to athletic, recreation, fitness program admins. responsible for operations, finances.
athleticbusiness.com editors@athleticbusiness.com

Athletic Management 31 Dutch Mill Rd Ithaca NY 14850 **Phn:** 607-257-6970 **Fax** 607-257-7328 Eleanor Frankel.
32,100 to H.S. & college athletic decisionmakers responsible for equip., operations, team travel.
www.AthleticManagement.com
ef@momentummedia.com

Business Officer 1110 Vermont Ave NW Ste 800 Washington DC 20005 **Phn:** 202-861-2500 **Fax** 202-861-2583 Dorothy Wagener. Natl. Assn. College/Univ. Business Officers. Monthly magazine.
28,500 to educational administrators in accounting, finance, technology, facilities. www.nacubo.org
editor@nacubo.org

California Educator 1705 Murchison Dr Burlingame CA 94010 **Phn:** 650-697-1400 **Fax** 650-552-5002 Dave Carpenter. CA Teachers Assn. 9-issue magazine.
314,500 to CA teachers and administrators interested in trends, policy decisions, local and state news.
www.cta.org

Campus Technology 9121 Oakdale Ave Ste 101 Chatsworth CA 91311 **Phn:** 818-734-1520 **Fax** 818-734-1522 Rhea Kelly. 1105 Media. Online only.
to administrators, IT personnel responsible for technology in high school and post-h.s.
campustechnology.com rkelly@1105media.com

Childhood Education 17904 Georgia Ave Ste 215 Olney MD 20832 **Phn:** 301-570-2111 **Fax** 301-570-2212 Anne Bauer. Bimonthly magazine.
8,500 to preschool through early adolescence educators interested in classroom practices, research.
www.acei.org abauer@acei.org

The Chronicle Higher Education 1255 23rd St NW Ste 700 Washington DC 20037 **Phn:** 202-466-1000 **Fax** 202-452-1033 Liz McMillen. Weekly tabloid.
76,700 to professors, administrators at universities interested in news & analysis about higher ed.
chronicle.com newseditor@chronicle.com

College Planning & Management 2621 Dryden Rd Ste 300 Dayton OH 45439 **Phn:** 937-293-1415 **Fax** 937-293-1310 Shannon O'Connor. Peter Li Edu. Grp. Monthly.
27,000 to college mgmt. responsible for construction, facilities, technology purchasing decisions.
www.peterli.com/cpm/ soconnor@peterli.com

Community College Journal 1 Dupont Cir NW Ste 410 Washington DC 20036 **Phn:** 202-728-0200 **Fax** 202-223-9390 Norma Kent. Bimonthly magazine.
10,000 to administrators, directors, faculties of community, jr., technical colleges in U.S. and abroad.
www.aacc.nche.edu/ nkent@aacc.nche.edu

Community College Week PO Box 1305 Fairfax VA 22038 **Phn:** 703-978-3535 **Fax** 703-978-3933 Paul Bradley. 25-issue magazine.
35,000 to 2-year college faculty, administrators, trustees interested in news, trends, statistics, technology. www.ccweek.com editor@ccweek.com

Currents 1307 New York Ave NW Ste 1000 Washington DC 20005 **Phn:** 202-328-5900 **Fax** 202-387-4973 Liz Reilly. Cncl. Adv. & Support of Edu. 9-issue magazine. TH:@CASEAdvance
19,000 to college advancement & development personnel responsible for fundraising, alum relations, research, surveys. www.case.org reilly@case.org

District Administration 488 Main Ave Norwalk CT 06851 **Phn:** 203-663-0100 **Fax** 203-663-0148 Angela Pascopella. Monthly magazine. TH:@apascopella
144,000 to K-12 curriculum specialists, superintendents, tech. dirs., school board presidents.
www.districtadministration.com
apascopella@districtadministration.com

Diverse 10520 Warwick Ave Ste B8 Fairfax VA 22030 **Phn:** 703-385-2981 **Fax** 703-385-1839 Toni Coleman. Biweekly magazine.
40,000 to college, university personnel interested in news, trends, statistics regarding minorities.
diverseeducation.com editor@diverseeducation.com

Education Digest PO Box 8623 Ann Arbor MI 48107 **Phn:** 734-975-2800 **Fax** 734-975-2787 Pamela Moore. Monthly magazine.
9,300 to teachers, administrators interested in new policies, curriculum, research, technology.
eddigest.com pam@eddigest.com

Education Week 6935 Arlington Rd Ste 100 Bethesda MD 20814 **Phn:** 301-280-3100 **Fax** 301-280-3200 Greg Chronister. Editorial Projects in Edu. 37-issue tabloid.
40,000 to public, private, elementary, secondary school educators interested in news, trends.
www.edweek.org ew@epe.org

Home Education Magazine PO Box 1083 Tonasket WA 98855 **Phn:** 509-486-1531 Helen Hegener. Bimonthly.
50,000 to homeschooling families interested in resources, learning, children, family living, legal issues.
homeedmag.com info@homeedmag.com

ISTA Advocate 150 W Market St Ste 900 Indianapolis IN 46204 **Phn:** 317-263-3400 **Fax** 317-655-3700 Mark Shoup. IN State Teachers Assn. Quarterly magazine.
50,000 to members of IN State Teachers Assn members intersted in local, state, natl. issues.
www.ista-in.org mshoup@ista-in.org

KEA News 401 Capitol Ave Frankfort KY 40601 **Phn:** 502-875-2889 **Fax** 502-227-8062 Charles Main. KY Education Assn. 5 issues.
38,000 to KY educators and administrators interested in local, state education issues, news. www.kea.org
cmain@kea.org

Maine Educator 35 Community Dr Augusta ME 04330 **Phn:** 207-622-5866 **Fax** 207-623-2129 Keith Harvie. 9 issues.
21,000 to Maine teachers and administrators interested in state and local issues and news.
www.maine.nea.org kharvie@nea.org

MEA-MFT Today 1232 E 6th Ave Helena MT 59601 **Phn:** 406-442-4250 **Fax** 406-443-5081 Sanna Porte. MT Education Assn./MT Federation Teachers. Bimonthly.
10,500 to Montana teachers and administrators interested in local and state issues. www.mea-mft.org
sporte@mea-mft.org

MEA Voice 1216 Kendale Blvd East Lansing MI 48823 **Phn:** 517-332-6551 **Fax** 517-337-5414 Karen Schulz. MI Education Assn. Quarterly tab.
160,000 to MEA members interested in state issues, Assn. news. www.mea.org kschulz@mea.org

Middle School Journal 4151 Executive Pkwy Ste 300 Westerville OH 43081 **Phn:** 614-895-4730 **Fax** 614-895-4750 David Virtue. Assn. for Middle Level Edu. 5-issue magazine.
22,000 to Assn. members interested in topics relevant to promotion & improvement of education of 10-15 year olds. www.amle.org howmanc@amle.org

Mississippi Educator 775 N State St Jackson MS 39202 **Phn:** 601-354-4463 **Fax** 601-352-7054 Barbara Kidd. Quarterly.
9,000 to Mississippi educators interested in state and local topics. maetoday.nea.org bkidd@nea.org

MTA Today 20 Ashburton Pl Boston MA 02108 **Phn:** 617-878-8000 **Fax** 617-742-7046 Jim Sacks. MA Teachers Assn. 5-issue tabloid. TH:@massteacher
107,000 to Massachusetts teachers interested in local and state educational issues. www.massteacher.org
jsacks@massteacher.org

NEA Today 1201 16th St NW Washington DC 20036 **Phn:** 202-822-7207 **Fax** 202-822-7206 Doug Walker. Natl. Education Assn. 8-issue tabloid.
2,872,000 to teachers, NEA members interested in classroom practices, new ideas and materials.
www.nea.org dwalker@nea.org

NJEA Review PO Box 1211 Trenton NJ 08607 **Phn:** 609-599-4561 **Fax** 609-392-6321 Lisa Galley. NJ Education Assn. 9 issues.
200,000 to NJ teachers and administrators interested in classroom and career issues. www.njea.org
lgalley@njea.org

NSEA Voice 605 S 14th St Lincoln NE 68508 **Phn:** 402-475-7611 **Fax** 402-475-2630 Al Koontz. NE State Education Assn. 9 issues.
25,000 to Nebraska teachers interested in legislative affairs, state news, union matters. www.nsea.org
al.koontz@nsea.org

NSTA Reports 1840 Wilson Blvd Arlington VA 22201 **Phn:** 703-312-9243 **Fax** 703-243-7177 Debra Shapiro. Natl. Science Teachers Assn. 9-issue newspaper.
75,000 to teachers interested in science materials, student/teacher programs, Assn. activities.
www.nsta.org nstareports@nsta.org

NYSUT United 800 Troy Schenectady Rd Latham NY 12110 **Phn:** 518-213-6000 **Fax** 518-213-6415 Mary Fran Gleason. NY State United Teachers. Biweekly newspaper.
550,000 to NYSUT members interested in union news, legislative issues. nysut.org united@nysutmail.org

Ohio Schools PO Box 2550 Columbus OH 43216 **Phn:** 614-228-4526 **Fax** 614-228-8771 Julie Newhall. 7-issue magazine.
135,000 to OH teachers and administrators interested in state and local news; classroom resources.
www.ohea.org communic@ohea.org

Phi Delta Kappan 408 N Union St Bloomington IN 47405 **Phn:** 812-339-1156 **Fax** 812-339-0018 Joan Richardson. 10-issue magazine.
65,400 to pre-K to post-high school educators interested in research-based school reform.
www.pdkintl.org kappan@pdkintl.org

Physics Teacher Appa St U Physics Asu Box 32142 Boone NC 28608 **Phn:** 828-262-7497 **Fax** 828-262-7329 Karl Mamola. Amer. Assn. Physics Teachers. 9-issue magazine.
7,300 to teachers of introductory physics at all levels interested in curriculum development, lab equipment.
tpt.aapt.org tpt@appstate.edu

Principal 1615 Duke St Alexandria VA 22314 **Phn:** 703-684-3345 **Fax** 703-548-6021 Vanessa St. Gerard. 5-issue magazine.
29,800 to elementary, secondary school principals interested in trends, professional news.
www.naesp.org publications@naesp.org

The Reading Teacher PO Box 8139 Newark DE 19714 **Phn:** 302-731-1600 **Fax** 302-368-2449 Robert Cooter. Intl. Reading Assn. 8-issue magazine.
54,200 to reading teachers interested in assessment methods, technology, literature reviews.
www.reading.org rcooter@bellarmine.edu

Reading Today PO Box 8139 Newark DE 19714 **Phn:** 302-731-1600 **Fax** 302-368-2449 Dan Mangan. Intl. Reading Assn. Bimonthly magazine.
89,100 to reading teachers from pre-K through adult education interested in books, curriculum, conferences. www.reading.org publications@reading.org

Scholastic Early Childhood Today 557 Broadway Fl 5 New York NY 10012 **Phn:** 212-343-6100 **Fax** 212-343-4801 Tia Disick. Online only.
for child care professionals, educators interested in development, nutrition, health, play. teacher.scholastic.com/products/ect/index.htm

School Business Affairs 11401 North Shore Dr Reston VA 20190 **Phn:** 703-478-0405 **Fax** 703-478-0205 11-issue magazine.
5,200 to school finance mgrs., asst superintendents of business, purchasing personnel. asbointl.org asbosba@asbointl.org

School Nutrition 120 Waterfront St Ste 300 Oxon Hill VA 20745 **Phn:** 301-686-3100 **Fax** 301-686-3155 Patricia Fitzgerald. Monthly magazine.
49,300 to School Nutrition Assn. members, K-12 school food service/nutrition mgrs. www.schoolnutrition.org snmagazine@schoolnutrition.org

School Planning & Management 2621 Dryden Rd Ste 300 Dayton OH 45439 **Phn:** 937-293-1415 **Fax** 937-293-1310 Jerry Enderle. Peter Li Edu. Grp. Monthly magazine.
75,200 to school district facility, business, IT managers; other top-level school administrators. www.peterli.com/spm/ jenderle@peterli.com

SchoolArts 50 Portland St Worcester MA 01608 **Phn:** 800-533-2847 **Fax** 508-753-3834 Jackie Gothing. Davis Publications. 9-issue magazine. TH:@DavisPub
20,000 to school, museum, student art teachers interested in lesson plans, activities, products, services.
www.davisart.com/Portal/SchoolArts/SADefault.aspx jgothing@davisart.com

Science & Children 1840 Wilson Blvd Arlington VA 22201 **Phn:** 703-243-7100 **Fax** 703-243-7177 Valynda Mayes. 9 issues.
21,000 to elementary school teachers interested in science education resources and techniques. www.nsta.org vmayes@nsta.org

The Science Teacher 1840 Wilson Blvd Arlington VA 22201 **Phn:** 703-243-7100 **Fax** 703-243-7177 Scott Stuckey. 9 issues.
28,500 to secondary school biology, chemistry, physics, astronomy, earth science teachers. www.nsta.org sstuckey@nsta.org

Social Education 8555 16th St Ste 500 Silver Spring MD 20910 **Phn:** 301-588-1800 **Fax** 301-588-2049 Michael Simpson. Natl. Cncl. Social Studies. 5 issues.
24,000 to Council members, other social studies teachers interested in methods & materials. www.socialstudies.org msimpson@ncss.org

T.H.E. Journal 9121 Oakdale Ave Ste 101 Chatsworth CA 91311 **Phn:** 818-814-5200 **Fax** 818-734-1522 Therese Mageau. 1105 Media. Online only. TH:@Therese1105Edu
to educators interested in technology aided instruction, classroom management. thejournal.com tmageau@1105media.com

Teacher Magazine 6935 Arlington Rd Ste 100 Bethesda MD 20814 **Phn:** 301-280-3100 **Fax** 301-280-3150 Anthony Rebora. Editorial Projects, Inc. 6-issue tab.
94,900 to teachers interested in curriculum, research, teacher profiles, career development. www.edweek.org/tm/ arebora@epe.org

Teaching Children Mathematics 1906 Association Dr Reston VA 20191 **Phn:** 703-620-9840 **Fax** 703-715-9536 Beth Skipper. Natl. Cncl. Teachers of Mathematics. 9-issue mag.
27,700 to elementary school math teachers interested in curriculum development, research. www.nctm.org/publications/ bskipper@nctm.org

Schools--Education .60

Tech Directions PO Box 8623 Ann Arbor MI 48107 **Phn:** 734-975-2800 **Fax** 734-975-2787 Susanne Peckham. Prakken Publications. 10-issue magazine.
41,800 to vocational, technical, industrial school program administrators and teachers. www.techdirections.com susanne@techdirections.com

Techniques 1410 King St Alexandria VA 22314 **Phn:** 703-683-3111 **Fax** 703-683-7424 Margaret Mitchell. Assn. for Career/Tech. Edu. 8-issue magazine.
30,000 to H.S., college level career and technical teachers, dept. heads, guidance counselors. www.acteonline.org mmitchell@acteonline.org

Technology & Engineering Teacher 1914 Association Dr Ste 201 Reston VA 20191 **Phn:** 703-860-2100 **Fax** 703-860-0353 Kathleen de la Paz. 8-issue magazine.
5,000 to technology educators at elementary through college level interested in products, reviews, curriculum. www.iteea.org kdelapaz@iteea.org

Technology & Learning 1111 Bayhill Dr Ste 125 San Bruno CA 94066 **Phn:** 650-238-0300 **Fax** 650-238-0263 Christine Weiser. NewBay Media. Monthly magazine.
80,500 to technology-using educators and administrators working with grades K-12. www.techlearning.com cweiser@nbmedia.com

Today's Catholic Teacher 2621 Dryden Rd Ste 300 Dayton OH 45439 **Phn:** 937-293-1415 **Fax** 937-293-1310 Elizabeth Shepard. Peter Li Edu. Grp. 6-issue magazine.
50,000 to Catholic school admins., supvs., teachers, principals, superintendents; officials. www.catholicteacher.com bshepard@peterli.com

Today's OEA 6900 SW Atlanta St Portland OR 97223 **Phn:** 503-684-3300 **Fax** 503-684-8063 Meg Krugel. OR Education Assn. 5 issues.
40,000 to Oregon educators and administrators interested in state & local issues, union news. www.oregoned.org meg.krugel@oregoned.org

University Business 488 Main Ave Norwalk CT 06851 **Phn:** 203-663-0100 **Fax** 203-663-0148 Tim Goral. Prof. Media Grp. 10-issue magazine.
46,200 to administrators in all areas of higher education management. www.universitybusiness.com tgoral@universitybusiness.com

Vermont NEA Today 10 Wheelock St Montpelier VT 05602 **Phn:** 802-223-6375 **Fax** 802-223-1253 Darren Allen. VT Natl. Education Assn. 11 issues.
10,000 to Vermont educations and administrators interested in union news, state news. www.vtnea.org dallen@vtnea.org

Virginia Journal Education 116 S 3rd St Richmond VA 23219 **Phn:** 804-648-5801 **Fax** 804-775-8379 Thomas Allen. 8 issues.
59,000 to Virginia educators and administrators interested in state and local policy issues. www.veanea.org tallen@veanea.org

WEA News 115 E 22nd St Ste 1 Cheyenne WY 82001 **Phn:** 307-634-7991 **Fax** 307-778-8161 Erin Cochran. WY Education Assn. 4 issues.
7,500 to Wyoming educators and administrators interested in union news, state and local education issues. www.wyoea.org ecochran@nea.org

Sports .61

Action Pursuit Games 2400 E Katella Ave Ste 300 Anaheim CA 92806 **Phn:** 714-939-9991 **Fax** 714-939-9909 Doug Jeffrey. Beckett Media. Monthly.
68,000 to paint ball game players, technical reviews, upgrades and accessories. www.actionpursuitgames.com djeffrey@beckett.com

American Fitness 15250 Ventura Blvd Ste 200 Sherman Oaks CA 91403 **Phn:** 818-884-6800 **Fax** 818-595-0463 Meg Jordan.
42,000 to professionals, enthusiasts covering innovations/trends in aerobics, exercise and health. www.americanfitness.com americanfitness@afaa.com

Archery Business 5959 Baker Rd Ste 300 Minnetonka MN 55345 **Phn:** 763-473-5800 **Fax** 763-473-5801 Mark Melotik. Grand View Media Group. Bimonthly magazine.
11,100 to archery retailers interested in products, merchandising tips, retailer and supplier profiles. www.grandviewoutdoors.com/bowhunting markm@grandviewmedia.com

Baseball America 4319 S Alston Ave Ste 103 Durham NC 27713 **Phn:** 919-682-9635 **Fax** 919-682-2880 Will Lingo. Biweekly.
40,500 to fans, players, coaches, scouts interested in major, minor, college, high school leagues. www.baseballamerica.com willlingo@baseballamerica.com

Baseball Digest 990 Grove St Ste 400 Evanston IL 60201 **Phn:** 847-491-6440 **Fax** 847-491-0459 Mark Healey. Lakeside Publishing. Bimonthly.
125,800 to readers interested in big league baseball, player profiles, scouting reports. www.centurysports.net cs@centurysports.net

Basketball Times PO Box 1437 Matthews NC 28106 **Phn:** 704-443-9104 John Akers. Monthly magazine.
5,000 to college basketball enthusiasts, coaches, scouts interested in players, stats, high school prospects. www.basketballtimes.com johna19081@gmail.com

Billiards Digest 122 S Michigan Ave Ste 1506 Chicago IL 60603 **Phn:** 312-341-1110 **Fax** 312-341-1180 Nicholas Leider. Luby Publishing. Monthly.
16,800 to billiard players and enthusiasts interested in competitions, events, player profiles. www.billiardsdigest.com

Black Belt 300 Continental Blvd Ste 650 El Segundo CA 90245 **Phn:** 310-356-4100 **Fax** 310-356-4110 Robert W. Young. AIM Media. Monthly magazine.
80,000 to martial artists, beginner to expert, detailed information on every style of self-defense. www.blackbeltmag.com byoung@aimmedia.com

Bowlers Journal 122 S Michigan Ave Ste 1506 Chicago IL 60603 **Phn:** 312-341-1110 **Fax** 312-341-1180 Jim Dressel. Luby Publishing. Monthly.
22,000 to bowling enthusiasts & industry personnel interested in players, products, tournaments. www.bowlersjournal.com email@bowlersjournal.com

Bowling Center Management 122 S Michigan Ave Ste 1506 Chicago IL 60603 **Phn:** 312-341-1110 **Fax** 312-341-1180 Michael Mazek. Luby Publishing. Monthly magazine.
9,500 to bowling center owners and managers interested in products, suppliers, financial and employee mgmt. www.bcmmag.com mikem@lubypublishing.com

ESPN The Magazine 545 Middle St Bristol CT 06010 **Phn:** 860-766-2000 **Fax** 212-515-1285 Chad Millman. Biweekly magazine.
2,000,000 to sports fans interested in which match-ups, players to watch; field news. espn.go.com chad.x.millman@espn.com

Fight! 1200 Lake Hearn Dr NE Ste 450 Atlanta GA 30319 **Phn:** 404-250-1798 **Fax** 404-250-1943 Donovan Craig. Bluff Media. Monthly magazine.
115,000 covers competitors and personalities in the mixed martial arts sports arena. www.fightmagazine.com todd@bluffmedia.com

Government Recreation & Fitness 825 Old Country Rd Westbury NY 11590 **Phn:** 516-334-3030 **Fax** 516-334-3059 Paul Ragusa. Executive Business Media.
9,500 to management of recreation and fitness facilities at government agencies. www.ebmpubs.com paul@ebmpubs4.com

Handball 2333 N Tucson Blvd Tucson AZ 85716 **Phn:** 520-795-0434 **Fax** 520-795-0465 US Handball Assn. Bimo.
8,100 to handball enthusiasts who are members of the US Handball Association. www.ushandball.org info@ushandball.org

Hang Gliding & Paragliding PO Box 1330 Colorado Springs CO 80901 **Phn:** 719-632-8300 **Fax** 719-632-6417 CJ Sturtevant. US Hang Gliding Assn. Mo.
9,100 for hang gliding and paragliding enthusiasts, covers skills, safety, www.ushpa.aero/ editor@ushpa.aero

Hoop Magazine 519 8th Ave 25th Fl New York NY 10018 **Phn:** 212-697-1460 **Fax** 646-753-9481 Ming Wong. Monthly magazine.
200,000 Covers the NBA for the adult reader, full-color action photos, player interviews. www.nba.com/hoop/ hoop@pspsports.com

Idea Fitness Journal 10455 Pacific Center Ct San Diego CA 92121 **Phn:** 858-535-8979 **Fax** 858-535-8234 Sandra Webster. 10-issue magazine.
19,000 to fitness club mgrs. & trainers interested in exercise program design, equipment news. www.ideafit.com websters@ideafit.com

Inside Gymnastics PO Box 88605 Atlanta GA 30356 **Phn:** 770-394-7160 **Fax** 770-394-7720 Lindsay Kaplan. Bimonthly.
47,000 covers news, event coverage, profiles of athletes, and the latest in gym wear. www.insidegymnastics.com

Inside Pool PO Box 972 Kittanning PA 16201 **Phn:** 724-543-3700 **Fax** 877-349-2119 Sally Timko. Monthly magazine.
25,300 covers tournaments, professional instruction and techniques for pool players. www.insidepoolmag.com publisher@insidepoolmag.com

Int'l. Bowling Industry 13245 Riverside Dr Ste 501 Sherman Oaks CA 91423 **Phn:** 818-789-2695 **Fax** 818-789-2812 Fred Groh. Crown Publishing. Mo.
9,000 to bowling center proprietors, manufacturers, distributors, and sports shop owners. www.bowlingindustry.com groh@bowlingindustry.com

Lacrosse Magazine 113 W University Pkwy Baltimore MD 21210 **Phn:** 410-235-6882 **Fax** 410-366-6735 Paul Krome. U.S. Lacrosse Inc.
235,000 feature articles, coaching and playing techniques and general lacrosse news. www.laxmagazine.com pkrome@uslacrosse.org

MMA Magazine 5252 Orange Ave Ste 109 Cypress CA 90630 **Phn:** 714-226-0585 **Fax** 714-226-0583 Chris Staab. Bimonthly magazine.
225,000 to mixed martial arts fans, fighters, trainers, fighter interviews, fight results. mmaworldwide.com info@mmaworldwide.com

Muscle & Fitness 4 New York Plz New York NY 10004 **Phn:** 212-545-4800 **Fax** 818-595-0463 Brian Good. American Media. Monthly. TH:@muscle_fitness
400,000 to readers interested in strength, body building, fitness, diet & nutrition. www.muscleandfitness.com bgood@amilink.com

Mushing PO Box 1195 Willow AK 99688 **Phn:** 907-495-2468 Greg Sellentin. Smelly Dog Media, Inc. Bimo.
6,100 Dog-powered sports information, including dog breeds and new sports equipment. www.mushing.com editor@mushing.com

Outside 400 Market St Santa Fe NM 87501 **Phn:** 505-989-7100 **Fax** 505-989-4700 Will Palmer. Mariah Media. Monthly magazine.
675,000 to readers interested in hang gliding, camping, rock climbing, skiing, rafting. www.outsideonline.com wpalmer@outsidemag.com

Parachutist 5401 Southpoint Centre Blvd Fredericksburg VA 22407 **Phn:** 540-604-9740 **Fax** 540-604-9741 Laura Sharp. U.S. Parachute Assn. Monthly.
33,000 to skydiving enthusiasts interested in instruction, destinations, equipment, photography. www.uspa.org communications@uspa.org

Powerlifting USA PO Box 467 Camarillo CA 93011 **Phn:** 800-448-7693 **Fax** 805-987-4275 Mike Lambert. Monthly magazine.
13,500 Covering powerlifting, with contest results, training techniques and athlete profiles. www.powerliftingusa.com lambertplusa@aol.com

Powersports Business 6420 Sycamore Ln N Ste 100 Maple Grove MN 55369 **Phn:** 763-383-4400 **Fax** 763-383-4499 Neil Pascale. Ehlert Publishing. 16-issue tab.
12,200 to retailers, mfrs., distributors of ATVs, snowmobiles, personal watercraft. www.powersportsbusiness.com npascale@affinitygroup.com

Racquet Sports Industry 75 Painter Hill Rd Woodbury CT 06798 **Phn:** 203-263-5243 Peter Francesconi. 10-issue magazine.
18,000 to tennis industry retailers, tennis schools, clubs, resorts; tennis equipment mfrs. www.racquetsportsindustry.com rsi@racquettech.com

Racquetball 1685 W Uintah St Colorado Springs CO 80904 **Phn:** 719-635-5396 **Fax** 719-635-0685 Steve Czarnecki. U.S. Racquetball Assn. Quarterly.
60,000 to Assn. members interested in tournaments, player and team profiles, equipment, news. usra.org magazine@usra.org

Real Fighter 11050 Santa Monica Blvd Los Angeles CA 90025 **Phn:** 310-445-7500 **Fax** 310-445-7583 Mike Carlson. Basic Media Group. Bimonthly magazine.
231,200 to MMA fans interested in fighters, training, interviews, behind the scenes info. www.realfightermag.com editor@realfightermag.com

Referee PO Box 161 Franksville WI 53126 **Phn:** 262-632-8855 **Fax** 262-632-5460 Bill Topp. Monthly magazine.
28,700 to football, baseball, basketball, soccer officials interested in rules, news. www.referee.com btopp@referee.com

Rugby Magazine 433 Kings Hwy Orangeburg NY 10962 **Phn:** 845-359-4225 **Fax** 845-359-4698 Ed Hagerty. Rugby Press. Bimo.
12,000 covers rugby, player profiles, coaching, refereeing, nutrition, position play, skills. www.rugbymag.com rugbymag@aol.com

Runner's World 135 N 6th St Emmaus PA 18049 **Phn:** 610-967-5171 **Fax** 610-967-8883 David Willey. Rodale Press. Monthly magazine.
642,300 to pleasure, health & competition runners interested in nutrition, training, runner profiles. www.runnersworld.com david.willey@rodale.com

Running Times 135 N 6th St Emmaus PA 18049 **Phn:** 610-967-5171 **Fax** 610-967-8963 Jonathan Beverly. Rodale Press. Monthly magazine.
108,300 to runners interested in training, racing, sports medicine, news, runner profiles. www.runningtimes.com editor@runningtimes.com

Silent Sports PO Box 558 Rhinelander WI 54501 **Phn:** 715-258-5546 **Fax** 715-258-8162 Joel Patenaude. Multi Media Channels. Monthly magazine. TH:@SilentSportsEd
10,000 to cross-country skiers, bikers, runners, paddlers, hikers in the upper midwest U.S. interested in events, equipment. www.silentsports.net jpatenaude@mmclocal.com

SLAM 1115 Broadway Fl 8 New York NY 10010 **Phn:** 212-807-7100 **Fax** 212-924-2352 Ben Osborne. Harris Publishing. 10-issues.
198,000 covers entire spectrum of basketball, its culture, from H.S., college to NBA. www.slamonline.com susan@harris-pub.com

Soccer America 1140 Broadway New York NY 10001 **Phn:** 212-849-2901 **Fax** 212-204-2032 Paul Kennedy. Monthly magazine.
25,000 to U.S. soccer enthusiasts interested in players, tournaments, teams, feature stories. www.socceramerica.com paul@socceramerica.com

Sporting Goods Dealer 2151 Hawkins St Ste 200 Charlotte NC 28203 **Phn:** 704-987-3450 **Fax** 704-987-3455 Jim Hartford. Bi-mo. magazine.
8,000 to wholesalers, retailers selling to college, H.S., local, pro teams, team dealers, mfrs. www.sportsonesource.com editor@sportsonesource.com

Sporting News 120 W Morehead St Ste 310 Charlotte NC 28202 **Phn:** 704-973-1000 Garry D. Howard. Online only. TH:@sportingnews
to baseball, pro & college football, hockey, pro & college basketball, NASCAR fans. aol.sportingnews.com

SportsField Management 374 Emerson Falls Rd Saint Johnsbury VT 05819 **Phn:** 802-748-8908 **Fax** 802-748-1866 Katie Meyers. Moose River Publishing. Monthly.
19,500 Focuses on the management of sports fields, including soccer, football, baseball. www.sportsfieldmanagementmagazine.com sfmpr@mooserivermedia.com

Tennis 79 Madison Ave Fl 8 New York NY 10016 **Phn:** 212-636-2700 **Fax** 212-636-2720 Stephen Tignor. Tennis Media Group. 8-issue magazine.
600,000 to tennis enthusiasts interested in player profiles, tips, tournaments, photos. www.tennis.com stephen.tignor@tennis.com

Tennis Life 18213 30th St Lutz FL 33559 **Phn:** 813-949-0006 **Fax** 813-433-5181 Deb Goldman. Goldman Group. Bimonthly.
180,000 to tennis enthusiasts, covers ATP, WTA and ITF events, tips, instructional articles. www.tennislife.com eb

Thrasher 1303 Underwood Ave San Francisco CA 94124 **Phn:** 415-822-3083 **Fax** 415-822-8359 Jake Phelps. High Speed Productions. Monthly.
170,000 covering international skateboarding, team tours, band interviews, culture, gear. www.thrashermagazine.com stanislaus@thrashermagazine.com

Track & Field News 2570 W El Camino Real Ste 220 Mountain View CA 94040 **Phn:** 650-948-8188 **Fax** 650-948-9445 E. Garry Hill. Monthly.
19,000 to readers interested in high school, college, club, olympic level track & field events www.trackandfieldnews.com editorial@trackandfieldnews.com

Ultimate MMA 22840 Savi Ranch Pkwy # 200 Yorba Linda CA 92887 **Phn:** 714-939-9991 **Fax** 714-939-9909 Doug Jeffrey. Beckett Media. Monthly.
78,000 make ultimate fighting readily understandable to beginners as well as professionals. www.ultimatemmamag.com djeffrey@beckett.com

USA Gymnastics 132 E Washington St Ste 700 Indianapolis IN 46204 **Phn:** 317-237-5050 **Fax** 317-237-5069 Luan Peszek. Bimonthly magazine.
100,000 to readers interested in gymnastics, exercise, fitness, safety, competitions, Olympics. usagym.org lpeszek@usagym.org

USA Hockey Magazine 1775 Bob Johnson Dr Colorado Springs CO 80906 **Phn:** 719-576-8724 **Fax** 719-538-1160 Harry Thompson. 10-issue magazine.
410,500 to hockey-playing youth, coaches, refs interested in player bios, league news, games. www.usahockeymagazine.com harryt@usahockey.org

Volleyball Magazine 85 Quincy Ave Quincy MA 02169 **Phn:** 617-706-9110 **Fax** 617-536-0102 Aubrey Everett. Madavor Media. 9-issues.
30,000 particular emphasis on the US national teams, pro tour and collegiate competition. www.volleyballmag.com aeverett@madavor.com

Women's Adventure 3005 Center Green Dr Ste 225 Boulder CO 80301 **Phn:** 303-541-1539 **Fax** 303-443-9687 Jennifer Olson. Quarterly magazine. TH:@womensadventure
20,000 to women who participate in outdoor, all-season sports, including running, biking, climbing, snowboarding. www.womensadventuremagazine.com jennifer@womensadventuremagazine.com

WWE Magazine 1241 E Main St Stamford CT 06902 **Phn:** 203-352-8600 **Fax** 203-353-2855 Tony Romando. 13-issue magazine.
250,000 to World Wrestling Entertainment fans. www.wwe.com

Fishing--Hunting--Outdoors .61a

American Angler 735 Broad St Augusta GA 30901 **Phn:** 706-823-3739 **Fax** 706-724-3873 Russ Lumpkin. Morris Comms. Bimonthly.
33,000 to fly fishing enthusiasts interested in solid, practical fly-fishing information, products. www.americanangler.com mike.floyd@morris.com

Backpacker 2520 55th St Boulder CO 80301 **Phn:** 303-625-1600 **Fax** 310-356-4110 Jonathan Dorn. Active Interest Media. 9-issue magazine.
340,000 to readers interested in overnight N. American backcountry low-impact foot travel. www.backpacker.com jdorn@backpacker.com

BASS Times 3500 Blue Lake Dr Ste 330 Birmingham AL 35243 **Phn:** 205-313-0900 Dave Precht. Monthly.
113,200 to bass fishing enthusiasts interested in bait, techniques, destinations, types of bass. www.bassmaster.com editorial@bassmaster.com

Bassmaster 3500 Blue Lake Dr Ste 330 Birmingham AL 35243 **Phn:** 205-313-0900 James Hall. 11-issue magazine.
541,900 to expert, intermediate, beginner fresh water bass fishing enthusiasts. www.bassmaster.com editorial@bassmaster.com

Big Game Fishing Journal 1800 Bay Ave Point Pleasant Boro NJ 08742 **Phn:** 732-840-4900 **Fax** 732-223-2449 Len Belcaro. Offshore Info. Publs. Bimonthly.
50,000 to sport fishermen interested in billfish, tuna, shark, other large saltwater game fish. www.biggamefishingjournal.com captlen@biggamefishingjournal.com

Bow & Arrow Hunting 22840 Savi Ranch Pkwy Ste 200 Yorba Linda CA 92887 **Phn:** 714-200-1900 **Fax** 800-249-7761 Joe Bell. Beckett Media. 9-issue magazine.
20,700 to bowhunting enthusiasts interested in how-to's and technical advice. bowandarrowhunting.com jbell@beckett.com

Bowhunt America 2960 N Academy Blvd Ste 101 Colorado Springs CO 80917 **Phn:** 877-499-9988 **Fax** 719-495-8899 Jace Bauserman. Zebra Publishing. 9-issue magazine.
101,000 to bowhunting enthusiasts interested in how-to's, technical advice, tactics, gear. www.bowhuntamerica.com support@bowhuntamerica.com

Bowhunter 6385 Flank Dr Ste 800 Harrisburg PA 17112 **Phn:** 717-695-8085 **Fax** 717-545-2527 Jeff Waring. InterMedia Outdoors. 9-issue magazine.
156,000 to bowhunters interested in basics, news, activities, new products, game forecasts. www.bowhunter.com jeff.waring@imoutdoors.com

Bowhunting World 5959 Baker Rd Ste 300 Minnetonka MN 55345 **Phn:** 763-473-5800 **Fax** 763-473-5801 Grand View Media. 9-issue mag.
96,600 to bowhunters interested in techniques, gear, safety, hunting trip feature articles. www.grandviewoutdoors.com/bowhunting

Buckmasters Whitetail Magazine PO Box 244022 Montgomery AL 36124 **Phn:** 334-215-3337 **Fax** 334-215-3535 Ken Piper. 6-issue magazine.
367,300 to deer hunters interested in techniques for rifle, pistol, muzzleloader, bow & arrow. www.buckmasters.com kpiper@buckmasters.com

Bugle 5705 Grant Creek Rd Missoula MT 59808 **Phn:** 406-523-4500 **Fax** 406-523-4581 Dan Crockett. Rocky Mtn. Elk Foundation. Bimonthly.
161,000 to readers interested in fiction & non-fiction about elk habitat conservation & hunting. www.rmef.org bugle@rmef.org

Sports .61

Climbing 2520 55th St Boulder CO 80301 **Phn:** 303-625-1600 **Fax** 303-440-3618 Shannon Davis. Active Interest Media. Monthly magazine.
25,000 to climbers interested in mountaineering, bouldering, indoor, competition climbing, sport climbing. www.urbanclimbermag.com sdavis@climbing.com

Deer & Deer Hunting 700 E State St Iola WI 54990 **Phn:** 715-445-2214 **Fax** 715-445-4087 Dan Schmidt. F&W Media. 10-issue magazine.
113,100 to white-tailed deer hunters interested in hunting techniques, deer biology and habitat. www.deeranddeerhunting.com dan.schmidt@fwmedia.com

Ducks Unlimited 1 Waterfowl Way Memphis TN 38120 **Phn:** 901-758-3825 **Fax** 901-758-3850 Matt Young.. Bimonthly magazine.
546,100 to hunters, conservationists, game officials interested in waterfowl habitat restoration. www.ducks.org myoung@ducks.org

Field & Stream 2 Park Ave New York NY 10016 **Phn:** 212-779-5000 **Fax** 212-779-5114 Anthony Licata. Bonnier Corp. 11-issue magazine.
1,543,700 to hunting, fishing, camping, outdoors sportspeople interested in gear & conservation. www.fieldandstream.com anthony.licata@bonniercorp.com

Fish Alaska PO Box 113403 Anchorage AK 99511 **Phn:** 907-345-4337 **Fax** 907-345-2087 Troy Letherman. 10-issue magazine.
53,000 offers how-to-fish articles, regional features, trip-planning advice, gear reviews. www.fishalaskamagazine.com info@fishalaskamagazine.com

Fisherman 14 Ramsey Rd Shirley NY 11967 **Phn:** 631-345-5200 **Fax** 631-345-5304 Fred Golofaro. L.I.F. Publishing. Weekly magazines.
98,800 in 4 E. Coast editions to fresh, saltwater anglers interested in fishing locations, technique. fgolofaro@thefisherman.com

Fishing Facts 111 Shore Dr Burr Ridge IL 60527 **Phn:** 630-887-7722 **Fax** 630-887-1958 Gene Laulunen. Midwest Outdoors, Ltd. Bimonthly magazine.
28,500 to anglers interested in improving skills, fish behavior, new products. www.fishingfacts.com info@midwestoutdoors.com

Fishing Tackle Retailer PO Box 10000 Lake Buena Vista FL 32830 **Phn:** 717-543-8427 **Fax** 407-566-2072 Clem Dippel. ESPN/B.A.S.S. 11-issue magazine.
16,500 to sportfishing equipment retailers, wholesalers and manufacturers. espn.go.com/outdoors/bassmaster/ clem.dippel@centurytel.net

Florida Sportsman 2700 S Kanner Hwy Stuart FL 34994 **Phn:** 772-219-7400 **Fax** 772-219-6900 Jeff Weakley. Intermedia Outdoors. Monthly.
105,200 to anglers who fish Florida's inshore and offshore. www.floridasportsman.com jeff@floridasportsman.com

Fly Fisherman 6385 Flank Dr Ste 800 Harrisburg PA 17112 **Phn:** 717-695-8073 **Fax** 717-545-2527 Ross Purnell. InterMedia Outdoors. Bimonthly magazine.
111,700 to fly rod anglers interested in techniques, destinations, conservation, new products. www.flyfisherman.com ross.purnell@imoutdoors.com

Fly Rod & Reel PO Box 370 Camden ME 04843 **Phn:** 207-549-9544 **Fax** 207-594-5144 Joe Healy. Down East Enterprises. Bimonthly.
54,200 to fly fishermen interested in conservation, equipment, travel, fish habitat. www.flyrodreel.com editors@flyrodreel.com

Fly Tyer PO Box 1207 Augusta GA 30903 **Phn:** 706-724-0851 Russ Lumpkin. MCC Magazines. Quarterly.
42,800 to fly tyers of all skill levels interested in step-by-step, illustrated tying instructions. flytyer.com russ.lumpkin@morris.com

Full Cry PO Box 777 Sesser IL 62884 **Phn:** 618-625-2711 **Fax** 618-625-6221 Terry Walker. C&N Publications. Monthly magazine.
19,000 to coon and tree hound hunting enthusiasts interested in field trials, training. www.americancooner.com fullcry@mychoice.net

Fur-Fish-Game 2878 E Main St Columbus OH 43209 **Phn:** 614-231-9585 Mitch Cox. A.R. Harding Publications. Monthly magazine.
115,500 to U.S. & Canadian amateur & professional outdoorsmen, trappers and hunters. www.furfishgame.com editor@furfishgame.com

Game & Fish Magazine 2250 New Market Pkwy SE Ste 110 Marietta GA 30067 **Phn:** 770-953-9222 Ken Dunwoody. InterMedia Outdoors. Monthly mag.
428,100 in 17 editions, each designed for the hunters and anglers in that particular state or region www.gameandfishmag.com ken.dunwoody@imoutdoors.com

Gray's Sporting Journal 735 Broad St Augusta GA 30901 **Phn:** 706-722-6060 **Fax** 706-724-3873 Russ Lumpkin. MCC Magazines. Bimonthly magazine.
30,200 to sophisticated outdoorspeople interested in fine sporting photography, conservation. www.graysportingjournal.com russ.lumpkin@morris.com

Gun Dog PO Box 35803 Des Moines IA 50315 **Phn:** 515-287-0312 Rick Van Etten. Intermedia Outdoors. 7-issue magazine.
41,300 to upland bird and waterfowl hunters working with pointing, flushing and retrieving breeds. www.gundogmag.com rick.vanetten@imoutdoors.com

Hunting Illustrated 192 E. 100 N. Fayette UT 84630 **Phn:** 435-528-7999 Dave King. Christensen Arms. Bimonthly.
43,000 covers hunting of mule deer, elk, predators, pronghorn, moose, sheep and more. www.huntingillustrated.com editor@huntingillustrated.com

In-Fisherman 7819 Highland Scenic Rd Baxter MN 56425 **Phn:** 218-829-1648 **Fax** 218-829-2371 Doug Stange. InterMedia Outdoors. 8-issue magazine.
254,100 to freshwater anglers of all skill levels interested in destinations, awards. www.in-fisherman.com dstange@in-fisherman.com

Knives Illustrated 2400 E Katella Ave Ste 300 Anaheim CA 92806 **Phn:** 714-939-9991 **Fax** 714-456-0146 Beckett Media. Bi-mo. magazine.
41,700 to knife collectors, makers, those who use knifes for sport, product reviews. www.knivesillustrated.com bvoyles@beckett.com

Marlin Magazine 460 N Orlando Ave Ste 200 Winter Park FL 32789 **Phn:** 407-628-4802 **Fax** 407-628-7061 Dave Ferrell. Bonnier Corp. 8-issue magazine.
40,000 reviews of the newest boats, fish-fighting techniques, latest equipment for billfishing. www.marlinmag.com dave.ferrell@bonniercorp.com

Michigan Out-Of-Doors PO Box 30235 Lansing MI 48909 **Phn:** 517-371-1041 **Fax** 517-371-1505 Tony Hansen. MI United Conservation Clubs. Monthly.
74,400 to conservation-minded hunters, hikers, campers, anglers. www.mucc.org thansen@mucc.org

Mountain Magazine 3121-A Longhorn Rd Boulder CO 80302 **Phn:** 303-815-1080 Marc Peruzzi. Mountain Media. 5-issue magazine. TH:@mountainmag
125,000 to N. Amer. mountain enthusiasts interested in skiing, biking, alpine activities, environmental advocacy, photography. www.mountainonline.com/mountain-magazine marc@mtnmedia.com

Muzzleloader 1293 Myrtle Springs Rd Texarkana TX 75503 **Phn:** 903-832-4726 **Fax** 903-831-3177 Linda Scurlock. Scurlock Publishing. Bimo.
16,000 articles on hunting, shooting, gunsmithing, projects for traditional black powder shooters. muzzleloadermag.com custserv@scurlockpublishing.com

North American Fisherman 12301 Whitewater Dr # 260 Hopkins MN 55343 **Phn:** 952-936-9333 **Fax** 952-988-7486 Kurt Beckstrom. 8-issue magazine.
456,300 to freshwater/saltwater fishing enthusiasts interested in species-specific techniques. www.fishingclub.com kbeckstrom@namginc.com

North American Hunter 12301 Whitewater Dr # 260 Hopkins MN 55343 **Phn:** 952-352-7530 Gordy Krahn. North Amer. Hunting Club. 8-issue magazine.
860,200 to N. Amer. multi-species hunters interested in gear, tactics, techniques, destinations. www.huntingclub.com gkrahn@namginc.com

North American Whitetail 2250 New Market Pkwy SE Ste 110 Marietta GA 30067 **Phn:** 770-953-9222 Pat Hogan. InterMedia Outdoors. 8-issue mag.
144,800 to deer hunters, deer population mgmt. officials interested in hunting, conservation. www.northamericanwhitetail.com whitetail@imoutdoors.com

Outdoor Life 2 Park Ave Fl 9 New York NY 10016 **Phn:** 212-779-5000 **Fax** 212-779-5366 Gerry Bethge. Bonnier Corp. 10-issue magazine.
944,800 to hunting and fishing enthusiasts interested in techniques, equipment. www.outdoorlife.com olletters@bonniercorp.com

Petersen's Bowhunting 6385 Flank Dr Harrisburg PA 17112 **Phn:** 717-695-8171 Christian Berg. Intermedia Outdoors.9-issue magazine.
158,300 to bowhunting enthusiasts and archery industry personnel. www.bowhuntingmag.com bowhunting@imoutdoors.com

Pheasants Forever 1783 Buerkle Cir Saint Paul MN 55110 **Phn:** 651-773-2000 **Fax** 651-773-5500 Mark Herwig. 5 issues.
97,900 to pheasant hunters and enthusiasts interested in conservation, upland birds. www.pheasantsforever.org herwig@pheasantsforever.org

Predator Xtreme 200 Croft St # 1 Birmingham AL 35242 **Phn:** 205-408-3700 **Fax** 205-408-3797 Bob Robb. Grand View Media. Bimonthly.
76,800 to predator, varmint hunters interested in technical info about guns, habitats. www.grandviewoutdoors.com/predator-hunting brobb@grandviewmedia.com

Salt Water Sportsman 460 N Orlando Ave Winter Park FL 32789 **Phn:** 407-628-4800 **Fax** 407-628-7061 John Brownlee. Bonnier Corp. Monthly magazine.
169,500 to saltwater fishermen interested in U.S. and intl. destinations, boats, products. www.saltwatersportsman.com editor@saltwatersportsman.com

Shooting Sportsman PO Box 1357 Camden ME 04843 **Phn:** 207-594-9544 **Fax** 207-594-5144 Ed Carroll. Down East Enterprise. Bimonthly.
32,800 covers wingshooting, shotguns, gunmakers, sporting clays, destinations, game recipes. shootingsportsman.com ecarroll@shootingsportsman.com

Shotgun Sports PO Box 6810 Auburn CA 95604 **Phn:** 530-889-2220 **Fax** 530-889-9106 Johnny Cantu. Monthly magazine.
106,000 to readers interested in waterfowl, upland birds, small game hunting, trap/skeet shooting. www.shotgunsportsmagazine.com shotgun@shotgunsportsmagazine.com

Sport Fishing 460 N Orlando Ave Ste 200 Winter Park FL 32789 **Phn:** 407-571-4635 **Fax** 407-628-7061 Doug Olander. Bonnier Corp. 9-issue magazine. TH:@SportFishingMag
115,600 to fishing enthusiasts interested in boats, gear, destinations, techniques. www.sportfishingmag.com editor@sportfishingmag.com

Fishing--Hunting--Outdoors .61a

Sporting Classics PO Box 23707 Columbia SC 29224 **Phn:** 803-736-2424 **Fax** 803-736-3404 Chuck Wechsler. Bimonthly magazine.
25,000 edited for discovering the best in hunting and fishing worldwide, firearms, tackle. www.sportingclassics.com chuck@sportingclassics.com

Trail & Timberline 710 10th St., Ste 200 Golden CO 80401 **Phn:** 303-279-3080 **Fax** 303-279-9690 Christian Green. Colorado Mountain Club. Quarterly magazine. TH:@ColoradoMtnClub
8,000 to Club members, others interested in CO mtn., other Rocky Mtn. area expeditions, photography, conservation. www.cmc.org/About/Newsroom/TrailandTimberline.aspx editor@cmc.org

Trap & Field 1000 Waterway Blvd Indianapolis IN 46202 **Phn:** 317-633-8800 **Fax** 317-633-8813 Terry Heeg. Amateur Trapshooting Assn. Monthly magazine.
15,300 to trapshooting enthusiasts and Assn. members interested in equipment, shoot results, club news. www.trapandfield.com terry@trapandfield.com

Trapper & Predator Caller 700 E State St Iola WI 54990 **Phn:** 715-445-2214 **Fax** 715-445-4087 Jared Blohm. F&W Media. 10-issue magazine.
40,000 to fur trappers, animal and predator control trappers, fur ranchers. www.trapperpredatorcaller.com jared.blohm@fwmedia.com

Turkey & Turkey Hunting 700 E State St Iola WI 54990 **Phn:** 715-445-2214 **Fax** 715-445-4087 Brian Lovett. F&W Media. 6-issue magazine.
30,700 to turkey hunters at all skill levels interested in state conditions, guns, calls, gear. www.turkeyandturkeyhunting.com brian.lovett@fwmedia.com

Turkey Country PO Box 530 Edgefield SC 29824 **Phn:** 803-637-3106 **Fax** 803-637-0034 Karen Lee. Natl. Wild Turkey Federation. Bimonthly magazine.
235,000 to wild turkey enthusiasts interested in lawful, ethical hunting and wildlife management. www.urbanclimbermag.com klee@nwtf.net

Whitetail Journal 200 Croft St # 1 Birmingham AL 35242 **Phn:** 205-408-3700 **Fax** 205-408-3797 Hilary Dyer. Grand View Media. Bimonthly.
50,800 for enjoyment and education of whitetail hunters who dream of taking trophy bucks. www.grandviewoutdoors.com hilary@grandviewmedia.com

Wildfowl 7819 Highland Scenic Rd Baxter MN 56425 **Phn:** 218-829-1648 **Fax** 218-829-2371 Paul Wait. InterMedia Outdoors. 6-issue magazine.
39,600 to duck and goose hunting enthusiasts interested in regional conditions around U.S., equipment. www.wildfowlmag.com paul.wait@imoutdoors.com

Golf .61b

Executive Golfer 2171 Campus Dr Irvine CA 92612 **Phn:** 949-752-6474 **Fax** 949-752-0398 Joyce Stevens. Bimonthly.
103,000 to private country club golfers interested in course architecture, golf resort reviews. www.executivegolfermagazine.com joyce@executivegolfermagazine.com

Fore 3740 Cahuenga Blvd Studio City CA 91604 **Phn:** 818-980-3630 **Fax** 818-980-1808 Frank Moore. SoCal Golf Assn. Quarterly magazine. TH:@thescga
160,000 to golf & country club members in S. Calif. interested in tournament news, personalities, travel, lifestyle. www.scga.org/fore/ fmoore@scga.org

Golf Business 291 Seven Farms Dr Charleston SC 29492 **Phn:** 800-933-4262 **Fax** 843-856-3288 Ronnie Musselwhite. Natl. Golf Course Owners Assn. Monthly mag. TH:@GolfBusiness
18,000 to golf course owners & operators responsible for pro shop, food, turf equipment purchasing, personnel, grounds. www.golfbusinessmagazine.com rmusselwhite@ngcoa.org

Golf Course Management 1421 Research Park Dr Lawrence KS 66049 **Phn:** 785-832-4456 **Fax** 785-832-3665 Scott Hollister. Monthly magazine.
28,600 to superintendents, greens chairmen, club presidents, course designers, architects. www2.gcsaa.org/gcm/ shollister@gcsaa.org

Golf Digest PO Box 850 Wilton CT 06897 **Phn:** 203-761-5100 **Fax** 203-761-5129 Ashley Mayo. Conde Nast. Monthly magazine.
1,700,000 to golfers of all ability levels interested in techniques, rankings, players. www.golfdigest.com ashley.mayo@golfdigest.com

Golf Getaways 85 Quincy Ave Ste 2 Quincy MA 02169 **Phn:** 617-706-9110 **Fax** 617-706-9110 Darin Bunch. Madavor Media. Bimonthly magazine.
75,000 to golfers interested in destinations, course details, resorts, restaurants, celebrity golfer profiles. playgolfgetaways.com dbunch@madavor.com

Golf Magazine 2 Park Ave New York NY 10016 **Phn:** 212-779-5000 **Fax** 212-467-2915 David Clarke. Time Inc. Monthly magazine.
1,416,600 to golfers, spectators interested in personalities, instructor ratings, destinations, products. www.golf.com golfletters@golfonline.com

Golf Range Magazine PO Box 240 Georgetown CT 06829 **Phn:** 203-938-2720 **Fax** 203-938-2721 Mark Silverman. Monthly magazine.
28,600 to owners, operators, managers of driving ranges, indoor, outdoor golf teaching facilities. www.golfrange.org pcherry@golfrange.org

Golf Range Times PO Box 3106 Glen Allen VA 23058 **Phn:** 804-447-7258 **Fax** 866-543-0784 Bill Edwards. Bimonthly magazine.
6,000 to owners, operators, managers of driving ranges, indoor, outdoor golf teaching facilities. www.forecastgolf.com info@forecastgolf.com

Golf Tips 12121 Wilshire Blvd Ste 1200 Los Angeles CA 90025 **Phn:** 310-820-1500 **Fax** 310-826-5008 Ryan Knoll. Werner Publishing. 7-issue magazine.
221,200 to amateur golfers interested in instructions, equipment, buyer guides, techniques. www.golftipsmag.com editors@golftipsmag.com

Golf Today NW 2020 Maltby Rd Ste 7 PMB 344 Bothell WA 98021 **Phn:** 425-941-9946 Cameron Healey, Online only.
to WA, OR & ID area golfers interested in destinations, equipment, player profiles. www.golftodaynw.com cameron@golftodaynw.com

Golf World PO Box 850 Wilton CT 06897 **Phn:** 203-761-5100 **Fax** 203-761-5148 Geoff Russell. Golf Digest Cos. 42-issue magazine.
203,500 to serious amateur, pro golfers interested in tournament coverage, player profiles. www.golfdigest.com/golfworld/ editor@golfworld.com

Golfdom 1360 E. 9th St. Fl 10 Cleveland OH 44114 **Phn:** 855-460-5502 Seth Jones. North Coast Media. Monthly magazine.
31,600 to superintendents, greens chairmen, club presidents, course designers, architects. www.golfdom.com sjones@northcoastmedia.net

Golfweek 1500 Park Center Dr Orlando FL 32835 **Phn:** 407-563-7000 **Fax** 407-563-7077 Jeff Babineau. Weekly tabloid.
158,500 to readers interested in PGA, LPGA, senior PGA, PGA Europe, amateur tour coverage. www.golfweek.com jbabineau@golfweek.com

Links 10 Executive Park Rd Ste 202 Hilton Head Island SC 29928 **Phn:** 843-842-6200 **Fax** 843-842-6233 Nancy Purcell. Purcell Enterprises. Quarterly magazine.
253,000 to affluent golfers interested in courses, destinations, gear. www.linksmagazine.com npurcell@linksmagazine.com

Superintendent 374 Emerson Falls Rd Saint Johnsbury VT 05819 **Phn:** 802-748-8908 **Fax** 802-748-1866 Larry Aylward. Moose River Publishing. Monthly.
19,500 News, information and product guides for the golf course industry, superintendents. www.superintendentmagazine.com superpr@mooserivermedia.com

Horses--Breeding--Riding--Show .61c

American Farriers Journal PO Box 624 Brookfield WI 53008 **Phn:** 262-782-4480 **Fax** 262-782-1252 Frank Lessiter. 8-issue magazine.
7,200 to horse-shoers, others involved in equine health, horse leg and foot care. www.americanfarriers.com info@lesspub.com

American Quarter Horse Journal PO Box 32470 Amarillo TX 79120 **Phn:** 806-376-4888 **Fax** 806-349-6400 Christine Hamilton. Amer. Quarter Horse Assn. Mo. mag.
59,600 to owners, trainers, breeders, exhibitors of registered Quarter Horses. www.aqha.com aqhajrnl@aqha.org

American Turf Monthly 747 Middle Neck Rd Great Neck NY 11024 **Phn:** 516-773-4075 **Fax** 516-773-2944 Joe Girardi. Monthly magazine.
30,000 American Turf Monthly has been helping horseplayers pick winners for six decades. www.americanturf.com editor@americanturf.com

Appaloosa Journal 2720 W Pullman Rd Moscow ID 83843 **Phn:** 208-882-5578 **Fax** 208-882-8150 Dana Russell. Appaloosa Horse Club. Monthly.
20,000 to Club members interested in breed health, racing, riding and care information. www.appaloosajournal.com journal@appaloosajournal.com

Arabian Horse World 1316 Tamsen St Ste 101 Cambria CA 93428 **Phn:** 805-771-2300 **Fax** 805-927-6522 Denise Hearst. AIM Equine Network. Monthly.
7,100 to Arabian breed enthusiasts interested in champion profiles, worldwide competitions. www.arabianhorseworld.com info@arabianhorseworld.com

Barrel Horse News 2112 Montgomery St Fort Worth TX 76107 **Phn:** 817-737-6397 **Fax** 817-737-9455 Bonnie Wheatley. Monthly magazine.
11,000 variety of barrel racing information including event coverage and comprehensive calendars. www.barrelhorsenews.com bhneditorial@cowboypublishing.com

Blood-Horse 3101 Beaumont Centre Cir Ste 100 Lexington KY 40513 **Phn:** 859-278-2361 **Fax** 859-276-4450 Tom LaMarra. Weekly.
23,700 to thoroughbred racing & breeding industry personnel, racing fans. www.bloodhorse.com tlamarra@bloodhorse.com

California Riding Magazine 8622 Argent St Ste A Santee CA 92071 **Phn:** 619-258-1570 **Fax** 619-258-1726 Cheryl Erpelding. Monthly magazine.
30,000 to California equestrians interested in state news about all breeds and all disciplines. www.ridingmagazine.com alicia@ridingmagazine.com

Chronicle of the Horse PO Box 46 Middleburg VA 20118 **Phn:** 540-687-6341 **Fax** 540-687-3937 Tricia Booker Weekly magazine.
16,500 to horse lovers interested in horse care, training, breeding, events, fox hunting. www.chronofhorse.com

Dressage Today 656 Quince Orchard Rd Ste 600 Gaithersburg MD 20878 **Phn:** 301-977-3900 **Fax** 301-977-7473 Patricia Lasko. AIM Equine Network. Monthly magazine.
45,000 to dressage riders interested in training techniques, showing strategies, international news. www.equisearch.com/magazines/dressage-today/ dressage.today@equinetwork.com

Golf .61b

Equus 656 Quince Orchard Rd Ste 600 Gaithersburg MD 20878 **Phn:** 301-977-3900 **Fax** 301-990-9015 Laurie Prinz. AIM Equine Network. Monthly magazine.
145,000 to horse owners interested in training, care, performance, stable mgmt. www.equisearch.com/magazines/equus/ eqletters@equinetwork.com

Hoof Beats 750 Michigan Ave Columbus OH 43215 **Phn:** 614-224-2291 **Fax** 614-222-6791 Dan Leary. U.S. Trotting Assn. Monthly magazine.
13,000 to harness racing participants, spectators interested in trainers, riders, tracks, events. www.hoofbeatsmagazine.com dan.leary@ustrotting.com

Horse & Rider 2520 55th St # 210 Boulder CO 80301 **Phn:** 303-625-5460 **Fax** 303-413-1602 Juli S. Thorson. AIM Equine Network. Monthly magazine.
162,800 to Western riders interested in training, advice, how tos. www.equisearch.com/magazines/horse-and-rider/ horseandrider@aimmedia.com

Horse Illustrated PO Box 8237 Lexington KY 40533 **Phn:** 859-260-9800 **Fax** 859-260-1154 Elizabeth Moyer. I-5 Publishing. Monthly magazine. **TH:**@HI_mag
191,800 to English & Western riding enthusiasts interested in horse care, riding lifestyle. www.horsechannel.com horseillustrated@bowtieinc.com

Horseman and Fair World PO Box 8480 Lexington KY 40533 **Phn:** 859-276-4026 **Fax** 859-277-8100 Kathy Parker. Monthly magazine.
5,500 covers track harness racing including features, statistics, race results, horse sales. www.harnessracing.com kparker@harnessracing.com

The Morgan Horse 4066 Shelburne Rd Ste 5 Shelburne VT 05482 **Phn:** 802-985-4944 **Fax** 802-985-8897 Stephen Kinney. Monthly magazine.
4,000 breed publication covering management, breeding, history, uses, training and promotion. www.morganhorse.com stephen@morganhorse.com

Natural Horse PO Box 758 Leesport PA 19533 **Phn:** 610-926-0427 **Fax** 610-926-0238 Randi Peters. Monthly magazine.
4,500 humane, natural care for horse maintenance, alternative therapies, humane training. www.naturalhorse.com publisher@naturalhorse.com

Paint Horse Journal PO Box 961023 Fort Worth TX 76161 **Phn:** 817-834-2742 **Fax** 817-222-8466 Jessica Hein. American Paint Horse Assn. Monthly.
12,000 to paint horse enthusiasts interested in horse care, health, shows, competitions. www.painthorsejournal.com jhein@apha.com

Practical Horseman 656 Quince Orchard Rd Ste 600 Gaithersburg MD 20878 **Phn:** 301-977-3900 **Fax** 301-990-9015 Sandy Oliynyk. Source Interlink Media. Monthly magazine.
60,600 to English-style riders interested in breeding, racing, training for show, hunting, dressage. www.equisearch.com/magazines/practical-horseman/ practical.horseman@equinetwork.com

Saddle & Bridle 375 Jackson Ave Saint Louis MO 63130 **Phn:** 314-725-9115 Jeffrey Thompson. Monthly.
4,500 to horse show enthusiasts interested in results, photos, prominent horse people. saddleandbridle.com saddlebr@saddleandbridle.com

Stable Management PO Box 644 Woodbury CT 06798 **Phn:** 203-263-0888 **Fax** 203-266-0452 Jennifer Rowan. 8-issue magazine.
19,300 to equine facility owners & operators interested in nutrition, health, marketing, finance. www.stable-management.com jenn@stable-management.com

Trail Blazer PO Box 27243 Prescott Valley AZ 86312 **Phn:** 928-759-7045 **Fax** 866-458-4537 Susana Gibson. Monthly magazine.
48,000 for the equestrian trail rider, distance rider, campers, trail riders, skill tips. www.trailblazermagazine.us/ editor@trailblazermagazine.us

Walking Horse Report 730 Madison St Shelbyville TN 37160 **Phn:** 931-684-8123 **Fax** 931-684-8196 Kasi Hensley. Online only.
 to owners, breeders, enthusiasts of the Tennessee Walking Horse breed. www.walkinghorsereport.com hensley@horseworld.net

Western Horseman PO Box 470725 Fort Worth TX 76147 **Phn:** 719-633-5524 **Fax** 719-633-1392 Ross Hecox. Monthly magazine.
198,000 to horse owners & breeders, Western-style riders, riding club members, rodeo fans. www.westernhorseman.com edit@westernhorseman.com

Young Rider PO Box 12106 Lexington KY 40580 **Phn:** 949-855-8822 **Fax** 949-855-3045 Lesley Ward. I-5 Publishing. Bimonthly. **TH:**@YoungRiderMag
78,000 to young riders interested in horse care and riding lessons. www.youngrider.com yreditor@bowtieinc.com

Water Sports .61d

Aquatics International 6222 Wilshire Blvd Ste 600 Los Angeles CA 90048 **Phn:** 323-801-4900 **Fax** 323-801-4986 Kendra Kozen. Hanley-Wood. 10-issue magazine.
25,000 to swimming pool designers, mgrs., maintenance staff at parks, resorts, clubs, camps. www.aquaticsintl.com kkozen@hanleywood.com

Canoe & Kayak 236 Avenida Fabricante #201 San Clemente CA 92672 **Phn:** 949-325-6200 **Fax** 949-325-6196 Jeff Moag. GrindMedia. 7-issue magazine.
50,000 to readers interested in canoeing, kayaking, river rafting, water paddlesports. www.canoekayak.com jeff@canoekayak.com

Dive Training 5201 NW Crooked Rd Parkville MO 64152 **Phn:** 816-741-5151 **Fax** 816-741-6458 Cathryn Castle. Dive Training Ltd. Monthly magazine.
90,700 to instructors and novice divers interested in safety, new equipment, events. www.dtmag.com cccastle@gorge.net

Paddling Life PO Box 775589 Steamboat Spgs CO 80477 **Phn:** 970-870-0880 Eugene Buchanan. Online only. **TH:**@PaddlingLife
 for advanced kayakers & canoers interested in destinations, challenges, gear, competitions, conferences. www.paddlinglife.net eugene@paddlinglife.net

Pool & Spa News 6222 Wilshire Blvd Ste 600 Los Angeles CA 90048 **Phn:** 323-801-4900 **Fax** 323-801-4986 Erika Taylor. Hanley-Wood. Semimonthly mag.
16,000 to pool, spa, hot tub industry personnel interested in news, trends, products. poolspanews.com etaylor@hanley-wood.com

Scuba Diving 460 N Orlando Ave Ste 200 Winter Park FL 32789 **Phn:** 407-628-4802 **Fax** 407-628-7061 Ty Sawyer. Bonnier Corp. 11-issue magazine.
201,000 to scuba enthusiasts interested in gear, destinations, photography, training. www.sportdiver.com editor@sportdiver.com

Sea Kayaker PO Box 17029 Seattle WA 98127 **Phn:** 206-789-9536 **Fax** 206-781-1141 Christopher Cunningham. Bimonthly magazine.
17,000 to kayakers of all skill levels interested in destinations, coastal navigation, gear. www.seakayakermag.com editorial@seakayakermag.com

Surfer Magazine 236 Avenida Fabricante #201 San Clemente CA 92672 **Phn:** 949-325-6200 **Fax** 949-235-6196 Brendan Thomas. GrindMedia. Monthly.
92,300 to surfers interested in surfer profiles, equipment, contests, locations. www.surfermag.com brendon@surfermag.com

Surfing 236 Avenida Fabricante #201 San Clemente CA 92672 **Phn:** 949-325-6200 **Fax** 949-325-6196 Taylor Paul. GrindMedia. Monthly magazine.
88,800 to surfers, enthusiasts interested in action photos, board design, surf champion interviews. www.surfingmagazine.com taylor@surfingmagazine.com

Swimming World Magazine PO Box 20337 Sedona AZ 86341 **Phn:** 928-284-4005 **Fax** 928-284-2477 Jason Marsteller. Monthly magazine.
50,000 to coaches and swimmers at all ages and levels of competitive swimming.
www.swimmingworldmagazine.com
jasonm@swimmingworldmagazine.com

Transworld Surf 2052 Corte Del Nogal Ste B Carlsbad CA 92011 **Phn:** 760-722-7777 **Fax** 760-722-0653 Casey Koteen. Bonnier Corp. Monthly magazine.
73,000 to young surfers interested in tips, surfer profiles, action photos. surf.transworld.net
casey.koteen@transworld.net

Transworld Wakeboarding 460 N Orlando Ave Ste 200 Winter Park FL 32789 **Phn:** 407-628-4802 **Fax** 407-628-7061 Shawn Perry. Bonnier Corp. 8-issue magazine.
40,000 equipment reviews and extensive technical instruction, youth, style and culture.
wakeboardingmag.com
shawn.perry@bonniercorp.com

WaterSki 460 N Orlando Ave Ste 200 Winter Park FL 32789 **Phn:** 407-628-4802 **Fax** 407-628-7061 Todd Ristorcelli. Bonnier Corp.
50,000 to all skill level enthusiasts interested in technique, boats, destinations, equipment.
waterskimag.com todd.ristorcelli@bonniercorp.com

Winter & Snow Sports .61e
Backcountry 60 Main St Suite 201 Jeffersonville VT 05464 **Phn:** 802-644-6606 **Fax** 802-644-6328 Adam Howard. 5-issue magazine.
16,000 features on remote skiing areas for those who like to stay off the beaten track.
backcountrymagazine.com
jon@backcountrymagazine.com

Cross Country Skier PO Box 550 Cable WI 54821 **Phn:** 715-798-5500 **Fax** 715-798-3599 Ron Bergin. 3-issue magazine.
25,000 to cross country skiers interested in technique, destinations, news, equipment.
www.crosscountryskier.com
info@crosscountryskier.com

Freeskier 137 2nd Avenue Niwot CO 80544 **Phn:** 303-834-9775 **Fax** 303-834-9781 Matthew Harvey. Storm Mtn. Publishing. 6-issues.
73,000 to 18-34 year old skiers covering lifestyles, the sport, learning new tricks. freeskier.com
harvey@freeskier.com

International Figure Skating 85 Quincy Ave Ste 2 Quincy MA 02169 **Phn:** 617-706-9110 **Fax** 617-536-0102 Susan Russell. Madavor Media. Monthly magazine.
85,000 to those interested in figure skating from the competitive to professional levels.
www.ifsmagazine.com srussell@madavor.com

Powder 236 Avenida Fabricante #201 San Clemente CA 92672 **Phn:** 949-325-6200 **Fax** 949-325-6196 John Stifter. GrindMedia. 6-issue magazine.
122,000 to expert skiers interested in deep powder & back-country skiing, products & equipment.
www.powdermag.com john@powder.com

SKATING Magazine 20 1st St Colorado Springs CO 80906 **Phn:** 719-635-5200 **Fax** 719-635-9548 Troy Schwindt. U.S. Figure Skating Assn. 10-issue magazine.
42,000 to Association members, recreational and competitive skaters, spectators.
www.usfsa.org/Magazine.asp
tschwindt@usfigureskating.org

Ski Area Management PO Box 644 Woodbury CT 06798 **Phn:** 203-263-0888 **Fax** 203-266-0452 Rick Kahl. Bimonthly magazine.
3,800 to ski resort personnel responsible for slope operations, machinery, food service, equipment & lodging. www.saminfo.com news@saminfo.com

Water Sports .61d
Ski Magazine 5720 Flatiron Pkwy Boulder CO 80301 **Phn:** 303-253-6300 **Fax** 303-253-6377 Kendall Hamilton. Bonnier Corp. 7-issue magazine.
400,000 to skiers interested in high-end ski travel, luxury resorts, apres ski events. www.skinet.com/ski/ editor@skimag.com

Ski Racing PO Box 1467 Ketchum ID 83340 **Phn:** 801-556-9988 Sarah Tuff. Monthly magazine.
30,000 to ski and snowboard racers, coaches, fans interested in courses, gear, results. www.skiracing.com stuff@skiracing.com

Skiing Magazine 5720 Flatiron Pkwy Boulder CO 80301 **Phn:** 303-253-6300 **Fax** 303-253-6377 Jake Bogoch. 7-issue magazine.
408,500 to younger skiers interested in destinations, parties, techniques, new equipment.
www.skinet.com/skiing/ editor@skiingmag.com

Snowboard Magazine PO Box 789 Niwot CO 80544 **Phn:** 303-834-9775 Nate Deschenes. Storm Mtn. Publishing. 6-issue magazine.
62,800 products, personalities, places that make snowboarding, not just a sport, but a culture.
snowboardmag.com nate@snowboard-mag.com

Snowboarder 236 Avenida Fabricante #201 San Clemente CA 92672 **Phn:** 949-325-6200 **Fax** 949-325-6196 Tom Monterosso. GrindMedia. 9-issue magazine. TH:@Snowboardermag
70,000 to snowboarding enthusiasts interested in pro boarder profiles, products, travel.
www.snowboardermag.com
tom@snowboardermag.com

SnoWest 360 B St Idaho Falls ID 83402 **Phn:** 208-524-7000 **Fax** 208-522-5241 Lane Lindstrom. Harris Publ. 6-issue magazine.
89,300 to readers interested in snowmobiling in western U.S., equipment reviews, racing.
www.snowest.com lindstrm@snowest.com

Transworld SNOWboarding 2052 Corte del Nogal Ste B Carlsbad CA 92011 **Phn:** 760-722-7777 **Fax** 760-722-0653 Gerhard Gross. GrindMedia. 9-issue magazine. TH:@GerhardGross
115,800 to snowboarding enthusiasts interested in profiles, techniques & equipment.
snowboarding.transworld.net
gerhard.gross@grindmedia.com

Textiles--Knits .62
AATCC Review PO Box 12215 Durham NC 27709 **Phn:** 919-549-8141 **Fax** 919-549-8933 Glenna Musante. Amer. Assn. Textile Chemists/Colorists. Bimonthly.
3,000 to textile design, materials processing, testing personnel interested in technical and news features.
www.aatcc.org musanteg@aatcc.org

Specialty Fabrics Review 1801 County Road B W Roseville MN 55113 **Phn:** 651-225-6928 **Fax** 651-225-6966 Galynn Nordstrom. Monthly.
13,000 to managers & owners of specialty fabric mfg. businesses such as awnings, canopies, protective materials. specialtyfabricsreview.com review@ifai.com

International Fiber Journal 6000 Fairview Rd Ste 1200 Charlotte NC 28210 **Phn:** 704-552-3708 **Fax** 704-552-3705 Ken Norberg. Bimonthly.
9,000 to producers of man-made fibers, non-woven manufacturers and yarn spinners. www.ifj.com ifj@ifj.com

Nonwovens Industry 70 Hilltop Rd Fl 3 Ramsey NJ 07446 **Phn:** 201-825-2552 **Fax** 201-825-0553 Karen McIntyre. Rodman Publications. Monthly magazine.
10,400 to producers, distributors of fabrics created by mechanical, chemical, thermal means.
www.nonwovens-industry.com
nonwovens@rodpub.com

Printwear PO Box 1416 Broomfield CO 80038 **Phn:** 303-469-0424 **Fax** 303-469-5730 Emily Andre. Natl. Business Media. Monthly magazine.
35,000 to garment screen printers, embroiderers, retailers interested in sourcing, educational features.
printwearmag.com pweditor@nbm.com

Textile World 2100 Riveredge Pkwy NW Ste 1200 Atlanta GA 30328 **Phn:** 770-955-5656 **Fax** 770-952-0669 James Borneman. Billian Publishing. Bimonthly.
15,000 to textile industry decisionmakers responsible for plant operations, manufacturing, mgmt.
www.textileworld.com

Tobacco .63
Pipes and Tobacco 3101 Poplarwood Ct Ste 115 Raleigh NC 27604 **Phn:** 919-872-5040 **Fax** 919-876-6531 Chuck Stanion. SpecComm Pubs. Mo.
23,000 articles on pipes, pipe-making, pipe smoking, history, personalities, and companies.
pipesandtobaccosmagazine.com rperkins@pt-magazine.com

Smokeshop 26 Broadway # 9M New York NY 10004 **Phn:** 212-391-2060 **Fax** 212-827-0945 Ted Hoyt. Lockwood Trade Jrnl. Co. Bimonthly magazine.
8,300 to tobacco retailers concerned with merchandising, advertising, trends, legislation.
www.smokeshopmag.com
editor@smokeshopmag.com

Tobacco International 26 Broadway # 9M New York NY 10004 **Phn:** 212-391-2060 **Fax** 212-827-0945 Emerson Leonard. Lockwood Trade Jrnl. Co. Monthly.
5,200 to tobacco industry mgmt. personnel worldwide interested in mfr. profilesequipment reviews & leaf reports. www.tobaccointernational.com
editor@tobaccointernational.com

Tobacco Outlet Business 8311 Six Forks Rd Ste 211 Raleigh NC 27615 **Phn:** 877-702-4427 **Fax** 919-844-6866 Jennifer Pellet. Bimonthly magazine.
16,500 to tobacco industry retailers and wholesalers interested in industry and legislative news.
tobaccooutletbusinessonline.com
info@tmginternational.com

Tobacco Reporter 3101 Poplarwood Ct Ste 115 Raleigh NC 27604 **Phn:** 919-872-5040 **Fax** 919-876-6531 Taco Tuinstra. SpecComm Pubs. Monthly mag.
5,500 to international tobacco industry executives, growers, dealers/processors.
www.tobaccoreporter.com taco@tobaccoreporter.com

Tobacconist 3101 Poplarwood Ct Ste 115 Raleigh NC 27604 **Phn:** 919-872-5040 **Fax** 919-876-6531 Phil Bowling. SpecComm Pubs. Bimonthly.
4,700 to tobacco retailers interested in product mix, promotions, industry news.
www.tobacconistmagazine.com
phil@tobacconistmagazine.com

Traffic--Warehousing .64
American Jrnl. Transportation 116 Court St Ste 5 Plymouth MA 02360 **Phn:** 508-927-4188 **Fax** 508-927-4189 George Lauriat. Weekly tab.
7,700 to shipping industry personnel interested in air/sea/land transit issues. www.ajot.com glauriat@ajot.com

Defense Transportation Journal 50 S Pickett St Ste 220 Alexandria VA 22304 **Phn:** 703-751-5011 **Fax** 703-823-8761 Karen Schmitt. Natl. Defense Transport. Asn. Bimo.
9,000 to Assn. members responsible for defense system delivery logistics and research.
www.ndtahq.com karen@ndtahq.com

Inbound Logistics 5 Penn Plz Fl 12 New York NY 10001 **Phn:** 212-629-1560 **Fax** 212-629-1565 Felecia Stratton. Thomas Publishing. Monthly magazine.
60,000 to business logistics mgrs. responsible for inventory control, warehousing, delivery.
www.inboundlogistics.com
editor@inboundlogistics.com

Inside Self-Storage 3300 N Central Ave Ste 300 Phoenix AZ 85012 **Phn:** 480-990-1101 Teri Lanza. Virgo Publishing. Monthly mag.
19,300 to self-storage facility owners, operators interested in construction, marketing, mgmt.
www.insideselfstorage.com tlanza@vpico.com

Logistics Management 111 Speen St Ste 200 Framingham MA 01701 **Phn:** 508-663-1500 **Fax** 508-663-1599 Michael Levans. EH Publishing Network. Monthly magazine.
72,000 to mgmt. personnel responsible for transport, import/export, containerization, site selection, warehousing. www.electronichouse.com mlevans@ehpub.com

Logistics Today 1300 E 9th St Cleveland OH 44114 **Phn:** 216-696-7000 **Fax** 216-696-2737 David Blanchard. Penton Media. Monthly.
75,000 to logistics pros responsible for warehousing, distribution, fulfillment, supply chain mgmt. mhlnews.com editor@logisticstoday.com

Travel--Tourism .65

AFAR Magazine 394 Pacific Ave Fl 2 San Francisco CA 94111 **Phn:** 415 814-1400 **Fax** 415 391-1566 Julia Cosgrove. Bimonthly.
111,000 covers travel as cultural experiences, not escapist vacations for an affluent audience. www.afar.com julia@afar.com

American Road Magazine PO Box 46519 Mount Clemens MI 48046 **Phn:** 877-285-5434 Thomas Arthur Repp. Mock Turtle Press. Quarterly magazine.
21,000 to readers interested in U.S. 2-lane highways, past & present, attractions, photos. www.americanroadmagazine.com editor@americanroadmagazine.com

Arizona Highways 2039 W Lewis Ave Phoenix AZ 85009 **Phn:** 602-712-2000 **Fax** 602-254-4505 Robert Stieve. AZ Dept. Transportation. Monthly.
300,000 to traveling public interested in Arizona for recreational, business purposes. www.arizonahighways.com editor@arizonahighways.com

Association Meetings 125 Cambridgepark Dr Ste 202 Cambridge MA **Phn:** 978-448-0582 **Fax** 913-514-6950 Betsy Bair. Penton Media. Bimonthly magazine.
19,300 to association meeting, exposition, training planners responsible for site selection, logistics. meetingsnet.com bbair@meetingsnet.com

Budget Travel 469 7th Ave Fl 3 New York NY 10018 **Phn:** 646-695-6700 **Fax** 646-695-6704 Gillian Telling. IntelliTravel Media. 6-issue magazine.
676,100 covers planning wide array of affordable destinations for domestic, international travel. www.budgettravel.com gillian.telling@budgettravel.com

Business Travel News 770 Broadway New York NY 10003 **Phn:** 646-654-5400 **Fax** 646-654-4455 David Meyer. Northstar Travel Media. 17-issue tabloid.
54,700 to travel mgrs. who plan, purchase, manage corporate business travel & meetings. www.businesstravelnews.com dmeyer@btnonline.com

Byways 42 Cabin Hill Ln Mount Jackson VA 22842 **Phn:** 540-477-3202 **Fax** 540-477-3858 Stephen Kirchner. Online only.
to motorcoach charter/tour passengers, group leaders, company owners, agents. bywaysmagazine.com smk@motorcoach.com

Conde Nast Traveler 4 Times Sq Bsmt C1B New York NY 10036 **Phn:** 212-286-2860 **Fax** 212-286-2190 Hanya Yanagihara. Conde Nast. Monthly magazine.
TH:@CNTraveler
798,300 to readers interested in art, architecture, fashion, cuisine of vacation areas. www.cntraveler.com hanga_yanagihara@condenast.com

Convene 2301 S Lake Shore Dr # 1001 Chicago IL 60616 **Phn:** 312-423-7262 **Fax** 312-423-7222 Michelle Russell. Prof. Convention Mgmt. Assn. Monthly magazine.
34,000 to meeting planners & mgrs. responsible for non-profit assn. conventions & meetings. www.pcma.org convene@pcma.org

Traffic--Warehousing .64

ConventionSouth PO Box 2267 Gulf Shores AL 36547 **Phn:** 251-968-5300 **Fax** 251-968-4532 Kristen McIntosh. Covey Communications. Monthly tab.
18,200 to planners of meetings, conventions, seminars sited in southern U.S. www.conventionsouth.com info@conventionsouth.com

Corporate & Incentive Travel 2700 N Military Trl Ste 120 Boca Raton FL 33431 **Phn:** 561-989-0600 **Fax** 561-989-9509 Susan Fell. Coastal Comms. Mo. mag.
40,000 to meeting planners responsible for all aspects of conferences, events, incentive travel. www.themeetingmagazines.com cceditor1@att.net

Corporate Meetings & Incentives 10 Fawcett St Ste 500 Cambridge MA 02138 **Phn:** 978-448-8211 Barbara Scofidio. Penton Media. 11-issue magazine.
36,300 to planners responsible for meetings & incentive travel interested in motivational trends. meetingsnet.com bscofidio@meetingsnet.com

Courier 546 E Main St Lexington KY 40508 **Phn:** 859-226-4444 **Fax** 859-226-4447 Penny Whitman. Natl. Tour Assn. Monthly magazine.
6,000 to N. American packaged travel and tour operators and suppliers. www.ntaonline.com penny.whitman@ntastaff.com

Cruise Travel 990 Grove St Ste 400 Evanston IL 60201 **Phn:** 847-491-6440 **Fax** 847-491-0459 Charles Doherty. Bimonthly magazine.
145,500 to readers interested in learning about or taking a cruise, deck plans, destinations, costs. www.cruisetravelmag.com cs@centurysports.net

Culture & Travel 601 W 26th St Rm 410 New York NY 10001 **Phn:** 212-447-9555 **Fax** 212-447-5221 Louise Blouin Media. 10-issues.
28,400 covers culture and travel for affluent readers, cities, museums, architecture. cultureandtravelmag@artinfo.com

Global Traveler 310 Floral Vale Blvd Yardley PA 19067 **Phn:** 267-364-5811 **Fax** 267-364-5796 Lisa Matte. FXExpress Publications. Monthly.
107,000 news, articles, city guides, travel deals, and hotel, airline and restaurant info. globaltravelerusa.com letters@globaltravelerusa.com

Group Travel Leader 301 E High St Lexington KY 40507 **Phn:** 859-253-0455 **Fax** 859-253-0499 Herbert Sparrow. Monthly newspaper.
30,000 to group travel organizers interested in destinations, festivals, marketing, products & services. www.grouptravelleader.com hsparrow@grouptravelleader.com

Islands 460 N Orlando Ave Ste 200 Winter Park FL 32789 **Phn:** 407-628-4802 **Fax** 407-628-7061 Eddy Patricelli. Bonnier Corp. 10-issue magazine.
250,000 to readers interested in cultural, historic, leisure aspects of worldwide island travel. www.islands.com editor@islands.com

Jax Fax Travel Marketing 52 W Main St Milford CT 06460 **Phn:** 203-301-0255 **Fax** 203-301-0250 Doug Cooke. Monthly.
20,800 to travel agency sales and mgmt. personnel, tour packagers, travel incentive organizers. www.jaxfaxmagazine.com editor@jaxfax.com

National Geographic Traveler 1145 17th St NW Washington DC 20036 **Phn:** 202-857-7030 **Fax** 202-429-5712 Norie Quintos. 8-issue magazine.
715,100 to readers interested in destinations, ecotourism, restaurants, travel essays. travel.nationalgeographic.com nquintos@ngs.org

Organic Spa Magazine 1564 Greenbriar Blvd. Boulder CO 80305 **Phn:** 303-554-1333 **Fax** 440-331-7860 Robyn Griggs Lawrence. Bimonthly magazine.
125,000 to spa consumers, staff interested in environmentally responsible spa destinations, products. www.organicspamagazine.com robynl@organicspamagazine.com

Porthole Cruise 4517 NW 31st Ave Fort Lauderdale FL 33309 **Phn:** 954-377-7777 **Fax** 954-377-7000 Bill Panoff. Panoff Publishing. Bimonthly.
200,000 to ship cruising enthusiasts interested in destinations, food, ship reviews, amenities, travel tips. www.porthole.com editorial@ppigroup.com

Recommend 5979 NW 151st St Ste 120 Miami Lakes FL 33014 **Phn:** 305-828-0123 **Fax** 305-826-6950 Paloma Villaverde de Rico. Worth Intl. Monthly magazine.
50,500 to retail and corporate travel agents interested in destination info and selling tools. www.recommend.com paloma@recommend.com

Recreation News 1713 Grafton Ridge Ct Forest Hill MD 21050 **Phn:** 410-638-6901 **Fax** 410-638-6902 Marvin Bond. Monthly magazine.
100,000 to federal, military & corp. personnel interested in mid-Atlantic states travel ideas, planning, sites. recreationnews.com editor@recreationnews.com

Texas Highways PO Box 141009 Austin TX 78714 **Phn:** 512-486-5858 **Fax** 512-486-5879 Jill Lawless. TX Dept. of Transportation. Monthly.
222,800 to readers interested in TX events, destinations, photography. www.texashighways.com letters05@texashighways.com

Texas Parks & Wildlife 4200 Smith School Rd Bldg D Austin TX 78744 **Phn:** 512-389-8706 **Fax** 512-389-8397 Louie Bond. Texas Parks & Wildlife Dept. Monthly.
147,800 to readers interested in vacationing, camping, exploring the landscape, recreation in TX. tpwmagazine.com magazine@tpwd.state.tx.us

Travel Agent 757 3rd Ave Fl 5 New York NY 10017 **Phn:** 212-895-8200 **Fax** 212-895-8210 Ruthanne Terrero. Questex Media. Biweekly magazine.
50,300 to travel agents, tour operators, executives and officials of govt., state tourist bureaus. www.travelagentcentral.com rterrero@questex.com

Travel & Leisure 1120 Avenue Of The Americas Fl 9 New York NY 10036 **Phn:** 212-382-5600 **Fax** 212-768-1568 Jennifer Barr. Time, Inc. Monthly mag.
967,200 to luxury leisure and business travelers interested in hotels, restaurants, destinations. www.travelandleisure.com tleditor@aexp.com

Travel Weekly 100 Lighting Way Secaucus NJ 07094 **Phn:** 201-902-2000 **Fax** 201-902-2034 Rebecca Tobin. Northstar Travel Media. Weekly tab.
39,000 to travel agency staff, tour operators interested in hotels, resorts, cruises, airlines, packages. www.travelweekly.com tweditorial@ntmllc.com

Travel With Spirit PO Box 1318 Sunset Beach FL 90742 **Phn:** 714-442-9973 **Fax** 714-795-2033 Honnie Korngold. Travel Network Group. Quarterly magazine.
20,000 to readers interested in Christian, faith-based travel, missions, family friendly destinations. www.travelwithspirit.com hkorngold@christiantravelfinder.com

Travel World News 28 Knight St Norwalk CT 06851 **Phn:** 203-286-6679 **Fax** 203-286-6681 Jennifer Lane. Travel Industry Network. Online only.
for industry personnel interested in promotions, destinations, suppliers, industry news. www.travelworldnews.com editor@travelworldnews.com

Travelage West 11400 W Olympic Blvd Ste 325 Los Angeles CA 90064 **Phn:** 310-954-2500 **Fax** 310-954-2520 Kenneth Shapiro. Northstar Travel Media. Biwkly. tabloid.
26,000 to western U.S. travel agency mgrs. interested in industry news, market reports, sales tips. www.travelagewest.com travelagewest@ntmllc.com

Vacations 5851 San Felipe St Ste 500 Houston TX 77057 **Phn:** 713-974-6903 **Fax** 713-974-0445 Elizabeth Armstrong. Bimonthly magazine.
197,500 to readers interested in practical, budget-oriented U.S. travel advice, recommendations. www.vacationsmagazine.com contact@vacationsmagazine.com

Where to Retire 5851 San Felipe St Ste 500 Houston TX 77057 **Phn:** 713-974-6903 **Fax** 713-974-0445 Mary Lu Abbott. Vacation Publications. Bimo.
207,000 helps retirees find the ideal setting for their new life, city and town profiles. wheretoretire.com contact@wheretoretire.com

Airline-Travel .65a

Alaska Airlines 2701 1st Ave Ste 250 Seattle WA 98121 **Phn:** 206-441-5871 **Fax** 206-448-6939 Paul Frichtl. Paradigm Comms. Group. Monthly.
300,000 to Alaska Airlines passengers interested in business and destination editorial, photo features. www.alaskaairlinesmagazine.com info@paradigmcg.com

American Way 4333 Amon Carter Blvd MD5374 Fort Worth TX 76155 **Phn:** 817-967-1804 **Fax** 817-967-1571 Adam Pitluk. 24-issue magazine.
333,400 to all classes of American Airlines passengers interested in lifestyle, business, travel editorial. www.americanwaymag.com editor@americanwaymag.com

Celebrated Living 4333 Amon Carter Blvd MD5374 Fort Worth TX 76155 **Phn:** 817-967-1804 **Fax** 817-967-1571 Lori Stacy Quarterly magazine.
170,000 to American Airlines first- & business-class passengers interested in style, resort, food & wine editorial. www.celebratedliving.com lori.stacy@aa.com

Delta Sky 220 S 6th St Ste 500 Minneapolis MN 55402 **Phn:** 612-339-5571 **Fax** 612-339-5806 Liz Doyle. MSP Comms. Monthly.
381,000 to passengers flying with Delta Airlines. deltaskymag.delta.com edit@deltaskymag.com

Go 68 Jay St Ste 315 Brooklyn NY 11201 **Phn:** 347-294-1220 **Fax** 917-591-6247 Orion Ray-Jones. Ink Global Monthly. TH:@AirTranGo
2,000,000 to AirTran Airways airline passengers interested in destination editorial, travel how tos. www.airtranmagazine.com orion@ink-global.com

Hemispheres 68 Jay St Ste 315 Brooklyn NY 11201 **Phn:** 347-294-1220 **Fax** 917-591-6247 Joe Keohane. Monthly.
400,000 to United Airlines passengers. www.hemispheresmagazine.com joe.keohane@ink-publishing.com

SW Airlines Spirit 2811 McKinney Ave Ste 360 Dallas TX 75204 **Phn:** 214-580-8070 **Fax** 214-580-2491 Brad Cope. Monthly.
480,300 to Southwest Airlines passengers interested in celebrity profiles, pop culture, technology. www.spiritmag.com ideas@spiritmag.com

US Airways Magazine 1301 Carolina St Greensboro NC 27401 **Phn:** 336-378-6065 **Fax** 336-378-8278 Lance Elko. Pace Communications. Monthly magazine.
350,000 to business and first-class class passengers flying with US Airways. www.usairwaysmag.com edit@usairwaysmag.com

Camping .65b

Camp Business PO Box 1166 Medina OH 44258 **Phn:** 330-721-9126 **Fax** 330-723-6598 Rodney Auth. Northstar Publishing. 6-issue magazine.
10,000 to children's camp managers responsible for outdoor, sports, special programs. www.northstarpubs.com editor@northstarpubs.com

Camping Magazine 5000 State Road 67 N Martinsville IN 46151 **Phn:** 765-342-8456 **Fax** 765-342-2065 Harriet Lowe. Amer. Camping Assn. Bimonthly.
7,000 to camp directors responsible for equipment, feeding, staffing, recreation, organization. www.acacamps.org/camping-magazine magazine@acacamps.org

Woodall's Campground Mgmt. 8073 E Constitution Dr Syracuse NY 46567 **Phn:** 574-457-3370 **Fax** 574-457-8295 Sherman Goldenberg. Monthly.
14,000 to owners, mgrs. of private campgrounds, RV parks; state, Federal parks mgmt. www.woodallscm.com info@woodallpub.com

Travel--Tourism .65
Mobile Homes--Trailers--Recreational Vehicles .65c

Bus Conversions 7246 Garden Grove Blvd. Westminster CA 92683 **Phn:** 714-799-0042 **Fax** 877-783-1667 Chad Laines. Monthly.
8,000 to RV and bus owners interested in installing, operating and repairing vehicle systems. www.busconversions.com info@busconversions.com

Coast to Coast Magazine 2575 Vista Del Mar Dr Ventura CA 93001 **Phn:** 805-667-4100 **Fax** 805-667-4363 Valerie Law. Good Sam Enterprises. Quarterly.
50,000 to visitors at Coast to Coast brand resorts interested in destinations, RV-related articles. www.coastresorts.com editor@coastresorts.com

Family Motor Coaching 8291 Clough Pike Cincinnati OH 45244 **Phn:** 513-474-3622 **Fax** 513-474-2332 Robbin Gould. Family Motor Coaching Assn. Monthly magazine.
132,800 to Assn. members, motor coach owners interested in travel, products, Assn. activities. www.fmcmagazine.com rgould@fmca.com

Highways 650 Three Springs Rd Bowling Green KY 42104 **Phn:** 800-626-6189 **Fax** 270-781-2775 Justin Hurst. 5-issue magazine.
1,300,000 to members of Good Sam Club, the intl. org. of RV owners; & members of the Coast to Coast camping org. www.highwaysmag.com jhurst@campingworld.com

MotorHome 2575 Vista Del Mar Dr Ventura CA 93001 **Phn:** 805-667-4100 **Fax** 805-667-4484 Eileen Hubbard. Affinity Group,Inc. Monthly magazine.
144,500 to motorhome owners, prospective buyers interested in tests, equipment, accessories. www.motorhomemagazine.com info@motorhomemagazine.com

RV Business 2901 E Bristol St Ste B Elkhart IN 46514 **Phn:** 574-266-7980 **Fax** 574-266-7984 Bruce Hampson. G&G Media Group. Monthly magazine.
25,000 to dealers, manufacturers, service and supply personnel in retail and marketing of RVs. www.rvbusiness.com bhampson@rvbusiness.com

RV Pro PO Box 1416 Broomfield CO 80038 **Phn:** 303-469-0424 **Fax** 303-465-3424 Bradley Worrell. Natl. Business Media, Inc. Monthly magazine. TH:@RVPROMagazine
15,000 to recreational vehicle industry decisionmakers interested in services, aftermarket parts, dealership news, sales/mktg. rv-pro.com bworrell@rv-pro.com

Trailer Life 2575 Vista Del Mar Dr Ventura CA 93001 **Phn:** 805-667-4100 **Fax** 805-667-4484 Kris Bunker. Affinity Group Inc. Monthly magazine.
370,300 to owners of rec. vehicles, trailers, campers, motorhomes interested in RV lifestyle. www.trailerlife.com info@trailerlife.com

Auto Clubs & Associations .65d

AAA Arizona Highroads 3144 N 7th Ave Phoenix AZ 85013 **Phn:** 602-650-2732 **Fax** 602-241-2917 Jill Schildhouse. Bimonthly magazine.
470,000 to AZ AAA Club members interested in local destinations, vehicle reviews. www.aaaaz.com highroads@arizona.aaa.com

AAA Carolinas Go Magazine 6600 AAA Dr Charlotte NC 28212 **Phn:** 704-569-7733 **Fax** 704-569-7815 Tom Crosby. Bimonthly newspaper.
1,025,000 to NC & SC AAA members interested in destinations, travel discounts, vehicle care. www.aaagomagazine.com trcrosby@mailaaa.com

AAA Going Places 1515 N West Shore Blvd Tampa FL 33607 **Phn:** 813-289-1391 **Fax** 813-289-6245 Sandy Klim. Bimonthly magazines.
2,500,000 to members of 30 Eastern U.S. AAA Clubs. www.aaagoingplaces.com editor@aaagoingplaces.com

AAA Midwest Traveler 12901 N 40 Dr Saint Louis MO 63141 **Phn:** 314-523-7350 **Fax** 314-523-6982 Michael Right. Bimonthly magazine.
504,000 to AAA members in MO, southern IL, southern IN, eastern KS interested in travel, auto safety, Assn benefits. www.ouraaa.com/traveler/ mright@aaamissouri.com

AAA Southern Traveler 12901 N 40 Dr Saint Louis MO 63141 **Phn:** 314-523-7350 **Fax** 314-523-6982 Deborah Reinhardt. AAA Publications. Bimonthly.
179,700 to AAA members in Louisiana and Mississippi. www.ouraaa.com/traveler/ dreinhardt@aaamissouri.com

AAA World 1 River Pl Wilmington DE 19801 **Phn:** 302-299-4270 **Fax** 302-230-2758 John Moyer. Bimonthly magazine.
2,106,700 to AAA members in mid-Atlantic U.S. states. midatlantic.aaa.com jcm@aaaworld.com

Car & Travel 1415 Kellum Pl Garden City NY 11530 **Phn:** 516-746-7730 **Fax** 516-873-2216 Peter F. Crescenti. AAA Publications. 10-issue magazine.
939,000 to metropolitan NY AAA members interested in car, road, travel, safety information. www.aaa.com/CarandTravel/ carandtravel@aaany.com

Via 3055 Oak Rd Ms B508 Walnut Creek CA 94597 **Phn:** 925-279-2441 Bruce Anderson. CA State Auto Assn. Bimonthly.
2,826,600 to north & central California, Nevada & Utah American Automobile Assn. members. www.aaa.com/via/ viamail@viamagazine.com

Westways 3333 Fairview Rd # A327 Costa Mesa CA 92626 **Phn:** 714-885-2376 **Fax** 714-885-2335 John Lehrer. Automobile Club of S. CA. Bimonthly magazine.
3,754,700 to southern CA Club members intersted in West Coast & Alaska desinations, vehicle info, Club discounts. www.calif.aaa.com/westways/ westways@aaa-calif.com

Your AAA 1 Hanover Rd Florham Park NJ 07932 **Phn:** 973-245-4861 **Fax** 973-377-2979 Shani Jarvis. Bimonthly newspaper.
225,000 to NJ AAA members interested in destinations, Assn. member benefits, auto insurance. www.youraaamagazine.com njacpr@njac.aaa.com

Vending .67

Automatic Merchandiser 1233 Janesville Ave Fort Atkinson WI 53538 **Phn:** 216-360-0050 **Fax** 920-563-1700 Elliot Maras. Cygnus Business Media. Monthly.
15,700 to vending operation owners & mgrs.; coffee service operators. www.vendingmarketwatch.com elliot.maras@vendingmarketwatch.com

Vending Times 55 Maple Ave Ste 102 Rockville Centre NY 11570 **Phn:** 516-442-1850 **Fax** 516-442-1849 Tim Sanford. Monthly tabloid.
16,300 to vending machine, coffee service, music, game machine operators. www.vendingtimes.com editor@vendingtimes.net

Farm Publications .68

Acres USA PO Box 91299 Austin TX 78709 **Phn:** 512-892-4400 **Fax** 512-892-4448 Fred Walters. Monthly newspaper.
18,000 to farmers interested in sustainable agriculture including organic growing, insect control, marketing, livestock care. www.acresusa.com editor@acresusa.com

Agri-News 420 2nd St La Salle IL 61301 **Phn:** 815-223-2558 **Fax** 815-223-5997 James Henry. Weekly newspaper.
54,600 in 2 editions (IL & IN) to farmers interested in crop/livestock issues, new products, markets, political issues. www.agrinews-pubs.com editorial@agrinews-pubs.com

Agri News 18 1st Ave SE Rochester MN 55904 **Phn:** 507-285-7600 **Fax** 507-281-7474 Mychal Wilmes. Post-Bulletin Co. Weekly newspaper.
17,800 to ranch and farm families in Minnesota and northern Iowa agribusiness operations. www.agrinews.com wilmes@agrinews.com

Farm Publications .68

Agri-View PO Box 8457 Madison WI 53708 **Phn:** 608-250-4320 **Fax** 608-250-4155 Shannon Hayes. Madison Newspapers. Weekly newspaper.
38,800 to Wisconsin farmers working 100+ acres interested in marketing, production, politics. www.agriview.com agriview@madison.com

Agweek PO Box 6008 Grand Forks ND 58206 **Phn:** 701-780-1236 **Fax** 701-780-1211 Kim Deats. Grand Forks Herald. Weekly newspaper.
26,600 to farm operators in ND, SD, MN, MT interested in local & intl. markets, farm news, policies, programs. www.agweek.com kdeats@agweek.com

American Agriculturist 5227B Baltimore Pike Littlestown PA 17340 **Phn:** 717-359-0150 **Fax** 717-359-0250 John Vogel. Penton Ag. Grp. Monthly.
30,100 to dairy, alfalfa, vegetable, fruit, cattle, corn farmers in northeastern U.S. mobile.americanagriculturist.com jvogel@farmprogress.com

American Bee Journal 51 S 2nd St Hamilton IL 62341 **Phn:** 217-847-3324 **Fax** 217-847-3660 Joe M. Graham. Dadant & Sons, Inc. Monthly.
14,000 to beekeepers interested in hive mgmt., honey production & markets, disease control. www.americanbeejournal.com info@americanbeejournal.com

Bee Culture PO Box 706 Medina OH 44258 **Phn:** 330-725-6677 **Fax** 330-725-5624 Kim Flottum. A.I. Root Co. Monthly magazine.
17,300 to beginner and hobbyist beekeepers interested in how-to's, research, production. www.beeculture.com kim@beeculture.com

California Farmer 125 Ryan Industrial Ct Ste 107 San Ramon CA 94583 **Phn:** 925-855-9409 **Fax** 925-855-9578 Len Richardson. Penton Ag. Grp. Monthly mag.
30,000 to CA & AZ beef, dairy, grape, lettuce, cotton, cantaloupe, greenhouse, nursery farmers. mobile.californiafarmer.com lrichardson@farmprogress.com

Capital Press PO Box 2048 Salem OR 97308 **Phn:** 503-364-4431 **Fax** 503-370-4383 Joe Beach. Weekly.
37,700 to farmers/ranchers interested in water issues, machinery testing, crop/livestock features. www.capitalpress.com jbeach@capitalpress.com

Capper's 1503 SW 42nd St Topeka KS 66609 **Phn:** 785-274-4300 **Fax** 785-274-4305 Hank Will. Ogden Publications. Monthly magazine.
90,000 to small-town families interested in general lifestyle content with rural slant. cappers.grit.com hwill@ogdenpubs.com

Carolina-Virginia Farmer 700 Privette St NE Wilson NC 27893 **Phn:** 252-237-4422 **Fax** 252-237-8999 Richard Davis. Penton Ag. Grp. Monthly magazine.
21,800 to tobacco, cotton, corn, nursery, greenhouse, hog, beef farmers in NC, SC, VA, WV. mobile.carolinavirginiafarmer.com rdavis@farmprogress.com

Cotton Farming 1010 June Rd Ste 102 Memphis TN 38119 **Phn:** 901-767-4020 **Fax** 901-767-4026 Tommy Horton. One Grower Publishing. Monthly magazine.
30,000 to cotton growers in the southern U.S. interested in production, marketing, equipment. www.cottonfarming.com thorton@onegrower.com

Cotton Grower 65 Germantown Ct Ste 202 Cordova TN 38018 **Phn:** 901-756-8822 **Fax** 901-756-8879 Mike McCue. Meister Media. Online only. TH:@CottonGrowerMag
 to 100-acre+ cotton producers, growers, ginners, managers. www.cotton247.com mmccue@meistermedia.com

Country Folks PO Box 121 Palatine Bridge NY 13428 **Phn:** 518-673-3237 **Fax** 518-673-2699 Gary Elliott. Lee Publications. Weekly newspaper.
24,000 in 3 editions to farmers in the northeast U.S. interested in natl. & rgnl. agriculture news. www.countryfolks.com cfeditor@leepub.com

Country Today 701 S Farwell St Eau Claire WI 54701 **Phn:** 715-833-9270 **Fax** 715-858-7307 Jim Massey. Eau Claire Press. Weekly newspaper.
21,700 to WI farmers, agribusiness personnel interested in markets, mgmt., weather forecasts. www.thecountrytoday.com thecountrytoday@ecpc.com

Country Woman 5400 S 60th St Greendale WI 53129 **Phn:** 414-423-0100 **Fax** 414-423-8463 Joanne Wied. RDA Milwaukee. Bimonthly magazine.
1,500,000 to rural women interested in home decorating, gardening, health, cooking, crafts. countrywomanmagazine.com editors@countrywomanmagazine.com

Delta Farm Press PO Box 1420 Clarksdale MS 38614 **Phn:** 662-624-8503 **Fax** 662-627-1137 Elton Robinson. Penton Media. Weekly tabloid.
27,000 to diversified farmers in Mississippi Delta regions of MS, AR, TN, LA, MO. deltafarmpress.com erobinson@farmpress.com

Farm & Dairy PO Box 38 Salem OH 44460 **Phn:** 330-337-3419 **Fax** 330-337-9550 Susan Crowell. Weekly magazine.
30,300 to farmers in OH, PA, WV interested in experimental ag. rsch., markets, lifestyle features. www.farmanddairy.com editor@farmanddairy.com

Farm & Ranch Guide PO Box 1977 Bismarck ND 58502 **Phn:** 701-255-4905 **Fax** 701-255-2312 Mark Conlon. Agri-Media. Biweekly tabloid.
28,200 to farmers, ranchers in ND, SD, MN & MT interested in small grain, row crops, livestock. www.farmandranchguide.com mconlon@farmandranchguide.com

Farm Industry News 7900 International Dr Ste 300 Minneapolis MN 55425 **Phn:** 952-851-4680 **Fax** 952-851-4601 Karen McMahon. Penton Media. 11-issue mag.
232,000 to large-scale soybean, sorghum, corn, wheat growers interested in products, technology. farmindustrynews.com fin@penton.com

Farm Journal PO Box 958 Mexico MO 65265 **Phn:** 573-581-9641 **Fax** 573-581-9646 Charlene Finck. Farm Journal Media. 12-issue magazine.
433,000 in 4 regional editions covering continental U.S. to crop, livestock, dairy farmers & ranchers. www.Agweb.com cfinck@farmjournal.com

Farm Show PO Box 1029 Lakeville MN 55044 **Phn:** 952-469-5572 **Fax** 952-469-5575 Mark Newhall. Bimonthly magazine.
201,000 focuses on latest new agricultural products, and product evaluations. www.farmshow.com

Farm Talk PO Box 601 Parsons KS 67357 **Phn:** 620-421-9450 **Fax** 620-421-9473 Danielle Beard. Weekly newspaper. TH:@danibeard
10,400 to farmers and ranchers in AR, KS, MO, OK interested in agribusiness issues. farmtalknewspaper.com farmtalk@terraworld.net

Farm World PO Box 90 Knightstown IN 46148 **Phn:** 765-345-5133 **Fax** 800-318-1055 Dave Blower Jr. MidCountry Media. Weekly newspaper.
34,400 to IN, IL, OH, KY farmers, agribusiness people, FFA & 4H members. www.farmworldonline.com davidb@farmworldonline.com

The Farmer-Stockman PO Box 459 Tuscola TX 79562 **Phn:** 325-554-7388 **Fax** 325-554-7389 J.T. Smith. Penton Ag. Grp. Monthly.
34,500 to beef, wheat, dairy, cotton, peanut, hog farmers in OK, TX, NM. mobile.thefarmerstockman.com jtsmith@farmprogress.com

Farmers' Advance 331 E Bell St Camden MI 49232 **Phn:** 517-368-0365 **Fax** 517-368-5131 Erin Robinstine. Camden Publications. Weekly newspaper.
16,000 to MI, IN, OH row crop, livestock, dairy, vegetable farmers interested in crops, weather. www.farmersadvance.com erobinstine@gannett.com

Farming 374 Emerson Falls Rd #1 Saint Johnsbury VT 05819 **Phn:** 802-748-8908 **Fax** 802-748-1866 Bob Montgomery. Moose River Publishing. Monthly tabloid.
44,800 to northeastern U.S. farmers interested in all aspects of area agriculture. www.farmingmagazine.com farmingpr@mooserivermedia.com

Farmshine PO Box 219 Brownstown PA 17508 **Phn:** 717-656-8050 **Fax** 717-656-8188 Dieter Krieg. Weekly tab.
15,000 to PA, MD, NY, DE, OH dairy farmers interested in local, regional farm news, dairy shows. www.farmshine.net cowsrus1@ptd.net

Fence Post PO Box 1690 Greeley CO 80632 **Phn:** 970-686-5691 **Fax** 970-352-7164 Amiella Dietz. Greeley Publ. Co. Monthly magazine.
24,000 to Rocky Mtn. farmers & ranchers interested in local livestock & crop market reports. www.thefencepost.com adietz@thefencepost.com

FFA New Horizons PO Box 68960 Indianapolis IN 46268 **Phn:** 615-261-2091 Kim Newsom. Natl. FFA Org. Bimonthly magazine.
538,000 to Future Farmers of Amer. members ages 14-21 in all 50 states. www.ffa.org

Grass & Grain PO Box 1009 Manhattan KS 66505 **Phn:** 785-539-7558 **Fax** 785-539-2679 Beth Gaines-Riffel. Weekly newspaper.
15,500 to KS farmers and farm families interested in ag mgmt., family matters, economy. www.grassandgrain.com gandgeditor@agpress.com

Growing 374 Emerrson Falls Rd #1 Saint Johnsbury VT 05819 **Phn:** 802-748-8908 **Fax** 802-748-1866 Bob Montgomery. Moose River Publishing. Monthly magazine.
34,600 in 3 regional editions (NE, Central, SE) to East US commercial fruit & vegetable growers. www.growingmagazine.com growingpr@mooserivermedia.com

Hay & Forage Grower 7900 International Dr Ste 300 Minneapolis MN 55425 **Phn:** 952-851-4677 **Fax** 952-851-4601 Neil Tietz. Penton Media. 8-issue magzine.
83,500 to large alfalfa, grass hay, silage, pasture growers interested in production, harvest. hayandforage.com ntietz@hayandforage.com

High Plains Journal PO Box 760 Dodge City KS 67801 **Phn:** 620-227-7171 **Fax** 620-227-7173 Holly Martin. Weekly tabloid.
50,600 in 6 regional editions to High Plains & midwest farmers & ranchers interested in agribusiness news. www.hpj.com journal@hpj.com

Indiana Prairie Farmer PO Box 247 Franklin IN 46131 **Phn:** 317-738-0565 **Fax** 317-738-5441 Tom Bechman. Penton Ag. Grp. Monthly magazine.
23,100 to IN corn, soybean, hay, dairy, hog farmers. mobile.indianaprairiefarmer.com tbechman@farmprogress.com

Iowa Farmer Today 1065 Sierra Ct NE Ste B Cedar Rapids IA 52402 **Phn:** 319-398-2640 **Fax** 319-398-2696 Kevin Blind. Lee Agri-Media. Weekly newspaper.
68,800 to IA crop and livestock farmers concerned with production, technology, finance. www.iowafarmertoday.com news@iowafarmertoday.com

Kansas Farmer 6716 E Bainbridge Rd Wichita KS 67226 **Phn:** 316-681-2100 **Fax** 316-681-2102 Phyllis Griekspoor. Penton Ag. Grp. Monthly magazine.
19,100 to KS farmers producing cattle, wheat, corn, sorghum, soybeans. mobile.kansasfarmer.com pgriekspoor@farmprogress.com

Lancaster Farming PO Box 609 Ephrata PA 17522 **Phn:** 717-394-3047 **Fax** 717-733-6058 Dennis Larison. Weekly.
57,000 to dairy, field crop, produce, poultry, livestock farmers in New England, PA, MD, NJ, DE, OH, NY, VA. www.lancasterfarming.com farming@lancasterfarming.com

Land PO Box 3169 Mankato MN 56002 **Phn:** 507-345-4523 Kevin Schulz. Free Press Co. Biweekly tabloid.
33,400 to MI, MN and IA farm residents interested in new farming techniques, family life.
www.thelandonline.com editor@thelandonline.com

Michigan Farmer 710 W Park St Saint Johns MI 48879 **Phn:** 989-224-1235 Jennifer Vincent. Penton Ag. Grp. Monthly tabloid.
12,100 to Michigan dairy, corn, soybean, wheat, beef and cattle farmers and ranchers.
mobile.michiganfarmer.com
jvincent@farmprogress.com

Missouri Ruralist 5555 SW Peak Dr Polo MO 64671 **Phn:** 816-586-5555 **Fax** 816-586-2727 Jerilyn Johnson. Penton Ag Grp. Monthly magazine.
20,200 to MO soybean, beef, corn, hog, broiler farmers and ranchers. mobile.missouriruralist.com
jjohnson@farmprogress.com

Nebraska Farmer 5625 O St Ste 5 Lincoln NE 68510 **Phn:** 402-489-9331 **Fax** 402-489-9335 Don McCabe. Penton Ag. Grp. Monthly magazine.
30,300 to NE cattle, corn, soybean, hog, wheat farmers and ranchers. mobile.nebraskafarmer.com
dmccabe@farmprogress.com

Neighbors PO Box 11000 Montgomery AL 36191 **Phn:** 334-288-3900 **Fax** 334-284-3957 Jeff Helms. Alabama Farmers Federation. Monthly magazine.
107,200 to AL farmers and farm families interested in agtech, women's editorial, news. www.alfafarmers.org
jhelms@alfafarmers.org

Ohio Farmer 117 W Main St Ste 202 Lancaster OH 43130 **Phn:** 740-654-6500 **Fax** 740-654-9367 Tim White. Penton Ag. Grp. Monthly magazine.
20,200 to OH soybean, corn, dairy, hog farmers.
mobile.ohiofarmer.com twhite@farmprogress.com

Prairie Farmer 515 W Wildwood Dr Mt Zion IL 62549 **Phn:** 217-864-3264 **Fax** 217-864-3042 Josh Flint. Penton Ag. Grp. Monthly magazine.
40,400 to Illinois corn, soybean, hog, cattle, dairy farmers and ranchers. mobile.prairiefarmer.com
jflint@farmprogress.com

Progressive Farmer 2100 Lakeshore Dr Birmingham AL 35209 **Phn:** 205-445-6000 Jack Odle. Southern Progress Corp. 10-issue magazine.
626,000 in 2 regional editions to southern & midwestern farmers interested in production & mgmt.
www.dtnprogressivefarmer.com
jodle@progressivefarmer.com

Rice Farming 1010 June Rd Ste 102 Memphis TN 38119 **Phn:** 901-767-4020 **Fax** 901-767-4026 Ms. Carroll Smith. One Grower Publishing. 7-issue magazine.
8,700 to rice farmers interested in crop profitability and management, govt. issues. www.ricefarming.com
csmith@onegrower.com

Seed World PO Box 360 Grand Forks ND 58201 **Phn:** 877-710-3222 **Fax** 204-475-5247 Lindsay Hoffman. 6-issue magazine.
5,500 to seed industry personnel interested in crop mktg. & forecasts, meetings, industry news.
www.seedworld.com lhoffman@issuesink.com

Southeast Farm Press PO Box 1420 Clarksdale MS 38614 **Phn:** 662-624-8503 **Fax** 662-627-1137 Paul Hollis. Penton Media. 28-issue tabloid.
47,700 to SE U.S. growers & agribusiness mgrs. interested in environmental & regulatory issues.
southeastfarmpress.com phollis@farmpress.com

Southern Farmer 111 Lonnie Jack Dr Crestview FL 32536 **Phn:** 850-682-0608 **Fax** 850-689-6661 Pam Golden. Penton Ag. Grp. Monthly.
22,400 to cotton, peanut, tobacco, wheat, cattle farmers & ranchers in GA, AL, FL, KY, eastern TN.
mobile.southernfarmer.com
pgolden@farmprogress.com

Farm Publications .68

Southwest Farm Press PO Box 1420 Clarksdale MS 38614 **Phn:** 662-624-8503 **Fax** 662-627-1137 Ron Smith. Penton Media. 24-issue tabloid.
32,100 to SW U.S. growers & agribusiness mgrs. interested in environmental & regulatory issues.
southwestfarmpress.com rsmith@farmpress.com

Successful Farming 1716 Locust St Des Moines IA 50309 **Phn:** 515-284-2903 **Fax** 515-284-3127 David Kurns. Meredith Corp. 13-issue magazine.
TH:@davekurns
420,000 to crop farmers & farm families interested in markets, machinery, mgmt., production.
www.agriculture.com david.kurns@meredith.com

Today's Farmer 201 Ray Young Dr Columbia MO 65201 **Phn:** 573-876-5524 **Fax** 573-876-5505 Steve Fairchild. MFA Inc. 9-issue magazine.
38,000 to Assn. members, farmers interested in ag rsch., farm mgmt. & trends, legislation.
todaysfarmermagazine.com todaysfarmer@mfa-inc.com

Top Producer 30 S 15th St Ste 900 Philadelphia PA 19102 **Phn:** 816-873-3070 **Fax** 816-873-3025 Julie Douglas. Farm Journal Media. 9-issue magazine.
171,400 to major crop category producers concerned with mgmt., marketing, capital strategies.
www.agweb.com jdouglas@farmjournal.com

Tri-State Neighbor 309 W 43rd St Ste 103 Sioux Falls SD 57105 **Phn:** 605-335-7300 **Fax** 605-335-8141 Bruce Falk. Lee Agri-Media. Biweekly tabloid.
30,000 to farmers & ranchers in SD, IA, NE & MN interested in local, regional agricultural news.
www.tristateneighbor.com bfalk@tristateneighbor.com

Western Farm Press PO Box 1420 Clarksdale MS 38614 **Phn:** 662-624-8503 **Fax** 662-627-1137 Cary Blake. Penton Media. 24-issue tabloid.
21,300 to western U.S. growers & agribusiness mgrs. interested in environmental & regulatory issues.
westernfarmpress.com cblake@farmpress.com

Western Farmer-Stockman 12309 NE 21st St Vancouver WA 98684 **Phn:** 360-546-2433 **Fax** 360-546-2977 T.J. Burnham. Penton Ag. Grp. Monthly.
30,100 to livestock, dairy, potato, onion, wheat, hay and fruit farmers in the western U.S.
mobile.westernfarmerstockman.com
tburnham@farmprogress.com

Wheat Life 109 E 1st Ave Ritzville WA 99169 **Phn:** 509-659-0611 **Fax** 509-659-4302 Lisa Urbat. WA Assn. Wheat Growers. 11-issue magazine.
14,500 to Pacific NW wheat & barley industry personnel interested in rsch., nutrition, legislation.
www.wawg.org l_urbat@yahoo.com

Wisconsin Agriculturist PO Box 236 Brandon WI 53919 **Phn:** 920-346-2285 Fran O'Leary. Penton Ag. Grp. Monthly magazine.
25,200 to dairy, corn, alfalfa, soybean and hog farmers in Wisconsin. mobile.wisconsinagriculturist.com
foleary@farmprogress.com

Wisconsin State Farmer PO Box 152 Waupaca WI 54981 **Phn:** 715-258-5546 **Fax** 715-258-8162 Carla Gunst. Waupaca Publishing. Weekly newspaper.
27,500 to Wisconsin farmers interested in economics and technology of running a profitable farm.
www.wisfarmer.com cgunst@jcpgroup.com

Dairy .68a

California Dairy PO Box 626 Clovis CA 93613 **Phn:** 559-298-6675 **Fax** 559-323-6016 Patrick Cavanaugh. Monthly magazine.
5,100 to CA dairy producers interested in industry news, research, events. www.malcolmmedia.com
malcolmmed@aol.com

Dairy Herd Management 10901 W 84th Ter Ste 200 Lenexa KS 66214 **Phn:** 913-438-8700 **Fax** 913-438-0695 Tom Quaife. Vance Publishing. Monthly magazine.
61,000 to progressive dairy mgrs. concerned with increasing profits via technology, better mgmt.
www.dairyherd.com tquaife@vancepublishing.com

Dairy Today PO Box 1167 Monticello MN 55362 **Phn:** 763-271-3363 **Fax** 763-271-3360 Jim Dickrell. Farm Journal, Inc. 10-issue magazine.
20,000 to dairy producers with 200+ cows interested in nutrition, health, industry news.
www.agweb.com/livestock/dairy/
jdickrell@farmjournal.com

Dairy World 19 River St Millbury MA 01527 **Phn:** 508-865-2507 **Fax** 508-865-5891 Julie Norberg. Independent Buyers Assn. Bimonthly magazine.
118,500 to dairy farmers interested in health, sanitation, milk production, mktg., govt. regulations.
dairyworld@ibaprintshop.com

Eastern DairyBusiness 6437 Collamer Rd East Syracuse NY 13057 **Phn:** 315-703-7979 **Fax** 315-703-7988 Dave Natzke. Multi Ag Media. Monthly.
15,400 to eastern U.S. dairy cattle raisers interested in herd mgmt., milk prices, govt. regulations.
dairybusiness.com dnatzke@dairybusiness.com

Hoard's Dairyman 28 Milwaukee Ave W Fort Atkinson WI 53538 **Phn:** 920-563-5551 **Fax** 920-563-7298 Steven Larson. 20-issue tabloid.
78,900 to dairy farmers interested in cow feeding, breeding, health, farm management. www.hoards.com
hoards@hoards.com

Holstein World 6437 Collamer Rd East Syracuse NY 13057 **Phn:** 315-703-7979 **Fax** 315-703-7988 Karen Knutsen. Multi Ag Media. Monthly magazine.
8,000 to high-income dairy farmers who own or manage registered Holstein dairy cattle.
www.holsteinworld.com kknutsen@dairybusiness.com

Jersey Journal 6486 E Main St Reynoldsburg OH 43068 **Phn:** 614-861-3636 **Fax** 614-861-8040 Kim Billman. Amer. Jersey Cattle Assn. Monthly magazine.
17,200 to Jersey breed cattle raisers interested in prices, shows, feeding, health.
jerseyjournal.usjersey.com kbillman@usjersey.com

Michigan Milk Messenger PO Box 8002 Novi MI 48376 **Phn:** 248-474-6672 **Fax** 248-442-5695 Laura Moser. MI Milk Producers Assn. Online only.
for Association members, dairy farmers interested in prices, handling, production. www.mimilk.com
moser@mimilk.com

Farm Bureau--Grange .68b

Ag Alert 2300 River Plaza Dr Sacramento CA 95833 **Phn:** 916-561-5570 **Fax** 916-561-5695 Dave Kranz. CA Farm Bureau Fed. Weekly.
36,000 to CA farmers and ranchers interested in agricultural legislation, labor matters, taxes.
www.agalert.com agalert@cfbf.org

Buckeye Farm News 280 N High St Fl 6 Columbus OH 43215 **Phn:** 614-249-2400 **Fax** 614-249-2200 Joe Cornely. OH Farm Bureau Federation. 16-issue newspaper.
60,200 to OH farmers interested in local & lifestyle features. ofbf.org jcornely@ofbf.org

FarmWeek 1701 Towanda Ave Bloomington IL 61701 **Phn:** 309-557-2239 **Fax** 309-557-3185 Dave McClelland. IL Farm Bureau. Weekly newspaper.
79,700 to Illinois farmers interested in legislative issues, quality of life. farmweek.ilfb.org
dmcclelland@ilfb.org

FloridAgriculture PO Box 147030 Gainesville FL 32614 **Phn:** 352-374-1521 **Fax** 352-374-1530 Ed Albanesi. Monthly. FL Farm Bureau Federation.
140,000 to FL crop & livestock farmers interested in economic and informational features.
www.floridagriculture.org ed.albanesi@ffbf.org

Friends & Family PO Box 11000 Montgomery AL 36191 **Phn:** 334-288-3900 **Fax** 334-284-3957 Debra Davis. Quarterly.
310,000 to Alabama farmers and other owners of Alabama Farmers Fed. insurance policies.
www.alfafarmers.org ddavis@alfafarmers.org

Front Porch PO Box 31 Little Rock AR 72203 **Phn:** 501-224-4400 **Fax** 501-228-1557 Steve Eddington. AR Farm Bureau Federation. Bimonthly.
212,000 to Federation members interested in general editorial content about Arkansas. www.arfb.com frontporch@arfb.com

Georgia Farm Bureau News PO Box 7068 Macon GA 31209 **Phn:** 478-474-8411 **Fax** 478-474-8750 Jennifer Whittaker. Bimonthly magazine.
63,000 to GA agribusiness professionals interested in current & emerging crops , technology, state & local news. www.gfb.org jawhittaker@gfb.org

Michigan Farm News 7373 W Saginaw Hwy Lansing MI 48917 **Phn:** 517-323-7000 **Fax** 517-323-6541 Paul Jackson. MI Farm Bureau. 20-issue newspaper.
48,500 to Michigan farmers interested in market analysis, regulatory & legislative issues, farm programs. www.michiganfarmnews.com mfneditor@michfb.com

Mississippi Farm Country PO Box 1972 Jackson MS 39215 **Phn:** 601-977-4153 **Fax** 601-977-4808 Glynda Phillips. MS Farm Bureau Federation. Bimonthly.
180,000 to Mississippi farmers intersted in agricultural issues at natl., state & local level. www.msfb.com gphillips@msfb.com

Nebraska Farm Bureau News PO Box 80299 Lincoln NE 68501 **Phn:** 402-421-4400 **Fax** 402-421-4761 Tina Henderson. 11 issues.
49,000 to NE farmers interested in crop news, state & federal regulatory topics, & readers interested in food production. www.nefb.org tinah@nefb.org

Oregon Grange Bulletin 643 Union St NE Salem OR 97301 **Phn:** 503-316-0106 **Fax** 503-316-0109 Chris Rea. Monthly.
17,500 to OR Grange members interested in member news, local and state activities. www.orgrange.org gbulletin@orgrange.org

South Carolina Farmer PO Box 754 Columbia SC 29202 **Phn:** 803-796-6700 **Fax** 803-936-4452 Larry Smith. SC Farm Bureau. Quarterly.
115,000 to South Carolina farmers interested in education, legislation, member activities. www.scfb.org lsmith@scfb.org

Tennessee Farm Bureau News PO Box 313 Columbia TN 38402 **Phn:** 931-388-7872 **Fax** 931-388-5818 Pettus Read. Bimonthly newspaper.
117,000 to TN farmers interested in crop and livestock marketing & mgmt, state & federal govt. issues. www.tnfarmbureau.org pread@tfbf.org

Texas Agriculture PO Box 2689 Waco TX 76702 **Phn:** 254-751-2246 **Fax** 254-772-1766 Gene Hall. Semimonthly newspaper.
84,600 to TX farmers and ranchers interested in regulatory and legislative issues, animal health, marketing. www.texasfarmbureau.org ghall@txfb.org

Farm Electric--Cooperatives .68c
Alabama Living 340 TechnaCenter Dr Montgomery AL 36117 **Phn:** 334-215-2732 **Fax** 334-215-2733 Darryl Gates. AL Rural Elec Assn. Monthly.
382,300 to Alabama electric co-op consumers interested in energy use & conservation, lifestyle features. www.areapower.coop/ dgates@areapower.coop

Carolina Country PO Box 27306 Raleigh NC 27611 **Phn:** 919-875-3062 **Fax** 919-878-3970 Michael Gery. Monthly.
572,500 to readers interested in North Carolina rural culture, business, electric co-op news. www.carolinacountry.com editor@carolinacountry.com

Cooperative Living PO Box 2340 Glen Allen VA 23058 **Phn:** 804-346-3344 **Fax** 804-346-3448 William Sherrod. VA-MD-DE Assn. Elec. Co-ops. 10 issues.
397,000 to VA, MD, DE electric co-op consumers interested in electrical usage, lifestyle features, local events. www.co-opliving.com bsherrod@odec.com

Farm Bureau--Grange .68b
Country Living Magazine PO Box 26036 Columbus OH 43226 **Phn:** 614-846-5757 **Fax** 614-846-7108 Rich Warren. OH Rural Elec. Co-op, Inc. Monthly.
287,100 to Buckeye Power electric co-o consumers interested in conservation, current events, lifestyle features. www.buckeyepower.com editor@buckeyepower.com

Electric Consumer PO Box 24517 Indianapolis IN 46224 **Phn:** 317-487-2220 **Fax** 317-247-5220 Emily Schilling. IN Statewide Assn. of Rural Elec. Coops. Monthly.
230,000 to IN electric co-op consumers interested in local and state events, environmental issues, co-op news. www.electricconsumer.org ec@isa.coop

Illinois Country Living PO Box 3787 Springfield IL 62708 **Phn:** 217-529-5561 **Fax** 217-529-5810 John Lowrey. Monthly.
151,800 to IL electric co-op consumers interested in conservation, gardening, state & local events. www.icl.coop/ aiecinfo@aiec.coop

Kansas Country Living PO Box 4267 Topeka KS 66604 **Phn:** 785-478-4554 **Fax** 785-478-4852 Larry Freeze. Monthly magazine.
74,000 to Kansas electric co-op consumers interested in energy issues, seasonal features, food, travel. www.kec.coop/ lfreeze@kec.org

Kentucky Living PO Box 32170 Louisville KY 40232 **Phn:** 502-451-2430 **Fax** 502-459-1611 Paul Wesslund. Monthly.
490,000 to Kentucky electric co-op consumers interested in conservation, recipes, gardening, events. www.kentuckyliving.com pwesslund@kentuckyliving.com

Louisiana Country 10725 Airline Hwy Baton Rouge LA 70816 **Phn:** 225-293-3450 **Fax** 225-296-0924 Billy Gibson. Monthly.
135,000 to Louisiana electric co-op consumers interested in energy conservation & usage, recipes, travel. www.alec.coop/ bgibson@alec.coop

North Dakota Living PO Box 727 Mandan ND 58554 **Phn:** 701-663-6501 **Fax** 701-663-3745 Kent Brick. ND Assn. Rural Elec./Rural Telephone Co-ops. Monthly.
73,000 to N. Dakota electric co-op consumers interested in energy usage, weather, lifestyle features. www.ndarec.com kbrick@ndarec.com

Oklahoma Living PO Box 54309 Oklahoma City OK 73154 **Phn:** 405-478-1455 **Fax** 405-478-0246 Chelsey Simpson. OK Assn. Elec. Co-ops. Monthly.
310,000 to Oklahoma electric co-op consumers interested in energy conservation & consumption, gardening, travel. www.ok-living.coop/ editor@ok-living.coop

Penn Lines PO Box 1266 Harrisburg PA 17108 **Phn:** 717-233-5704 **Fax** 717-234-1309 Peter Fitzgerald. PA Rural Elec. Assn. Monthly.
148,200 to PA electric co-op consumers interested in rural social & political issues, electricity consumption. www.prea.com peter_fitzgerald@prea.com

Rural Electric Nebraskan PO Box 82048 Lincoln NE 68501 **Phn:** 402-475-4988 **Fax** 402-475-0835 Wayne Price. Monthly.
68,000 to Nebraska electric co-op consumers interested in electric usage, conservation, lifestyle features. www.nrea.org

Rural Missouri PO Box 1645 Jefferson City MO 65102 **Phn:** 573-635-6857 **Fax** 573-636-9499 Jim McCarty. MO Electric Co-ops. Monthly.
490,000 to Missouri electric co-op consumers interested in conservation, state history, lifestyle features. www.ruralmissouri.coop/ mailbag@ruralmissouri.org

Rural Montana PO Box 3469 Great Falls MT 59403 **Phn:** 406-761-8333 **Fax** 406-761-8339 James V. Smith. Monthly.
113,000 to Montana electric co-op consumers interested in energy usage, rural features, photography, recipes. montanaco-ops.com rural@mtco-ops.com

Ruralite PO Box 558 Forest Grove OR 97116 **Phn:** 503-357-2105 **Fax** 503-357-8615 Curtis Condon. Monthly.
303,500 to consumers of publicly-owned electric utility power in NW US, Alaska & Arizona. www.ruralite.org editor@ruralite.org

South Carolina Living 808 Knox Abbott Dr Cayce SC 29033 **Phn:** 803-926-3175 **Fax** 803-796-6064 John Bruce. Elec. Co-ops of SC, Inc. 11 issues.
500,000 to SC electric co-op consumers interested in conservation, outdoors, cooking, events, destinations. www.ecsc.org/livinginsc.htm john.bruce@ecsc.org

The Tennessee Magazine PO Box 100912 Nashville TN 37224 **Phn:** 615-367-9284 **Fax** 615-367-2495 Robin Conover. TN Elec. Co-op Assn. Monthly.
547,000 to TN co-op customers interested in state travel, recipes, history, resident profiles. www.tnelectric.org rconover@tnelectric.org

Texas Co-op Power 1122 Colorado St 24th Fl Austin TX 78701 **Phn:** 512-486-6243 **Fax** 512-763-3410 Carol Moczgemba. Monthly.
1,222,000 to TX elec. co-op consumers interested state travel, economic development, history, small town businesses. www.texascooppower.com letters@texas-ec.org

Wisconsin Energy Co-op News 1 S Pinckney St Ste 810 Madison WI 53703 **Phn:** 608-258-4400 **Fax** 608-258-4407 Perry Baird. WI Federation of Co-ops. Monthly.
158,000 to Wisconsin electric co-op consumers interested in energy usage, statewide issues, lifestyle features. www.wecnmagazine.com perry.baird@cooperativenetwork.coop

WREN Magazine 2312 Carey Ave Cheyenne WY 82001 **Phn:** 307-634-0727 **Fax** 307-634-0728 Shawn Taylor. WY Rural Elec. Assn. 11 issues.
35,600 to Wyoming electric co-op consumers interested in energy usage, rural lifestyle features, state politics. www.wyomingrea.org wren@wyomingrea.org

Farm Equipment .68d
Farm Equipment 225 Regency Ct Ste 200 Brookfield WI 53045 **Phn:** 262-782-4480 **Fax** 262-782-1252 Dave Kanicki. Lessiter Publs. 8-issue magazine.
11,200 to farm equipment dealers interested in marketing, mgmt., industry news. www.farm-equipment.com dkanicki@lesspub.com

Farm Jrnls. Implement & Tractor PO Box 958 Mexico MO 65265 **Phn:** 573-581-8689 **Fax** 573-581-9646 Margy Fischer. Bimonthly.
1,200 to agricultural equipment dealers, mfrs., wholesalers, consultants. www.agweb.com/farmjournal/ mfischer@farmjournal.com

NAEDA Equipment Dealer 1195 Smizer Mill Rd Fenton MO 63026 **Phn:** 636-349-5000 **Fax** 636-349-5443 Joann Klump. N. Amer. Equip. Dealers Assn. 11-issue mag.
8,600 to Assn. members, agricultural equip. retailers interested in merchandising & mgmt. www.naeda.com klumpj@naeda.com

Rural Lifestyle Dealer 225 Regency Ct Ste 200 Brookfield WI 53045 **Phn:** 262-782-4480 **Fax** 262-782-1252 Dave Kanicki. Lessiter Publs. Quarterly magazine.
13,200 to retailers serving part time rural residents, hobby farmers and large property owners. www.rurallifestyledealer.com dkanicki@lesspub.com

Fruits--Nuts--Vegetables .68f
American Vegetable Grower 37733 Euclid Ave Willoughby OH 44094 **Phn:** 440-942-2000 **Fax** 440-942-0662 Ana Reho. Meister Media. Monthly mag. TH:@GrowingProduce
26,100 to commercial vegetable growers interested in all aspects of growing, packing, marketing. www.growingproduce.com/vegetables/ aireho@meistermedia.com

American Vineyard PO Box 626 Clovis CA 93613 **Phn:** 559-298-6675 **Fax** 559-323-6016 Dan Malcolm. Monthly magazine.
10,200 to CA growers of grapes for wine, raisin, juice, table interested in rsch., industry news. www.malcolmmedia.com dan@malcolmmedia.com

American/Western Fruit Grower 37733 Euclid Ave Willoughby OH 44094 **Phn:** 440-942-2000 **Fax** 440-942-0662 Brian Sparks. Meister Media. Monthly magazine. TH:@GrowingProduce
14,800 to U.S. fruit growers & processors interested in all aspects of commercial fruit production. www.growingproduce.com/fruits-nuts bdsparks@meistermedia.com

Citrus & Vegetable Magazine 10901 W 84th Ter Ste 200 Lenexa KS 66214 **Phn:** 913-438-8700 **Fax** 913-438-0691 Vicky Boyd. Vance Publishing. 9-issue magazine.
9,300 to FL commercial citrus, fruit, vegetable growers/packers, shippers, processors, buyers. www.thegrower.com/news/regions/florida

Citrus Industry 5053 NW Highway 225A Ocala FL 34482 **Phn:** 352-671-1909 **Fax** 352-671-1364 Ernie Neff. Monthly.
8,600 to Florida citrus growers, suppliers, packers, processors, researchers. www.citrusindustry.net ernie@southeastagnet.com

Corn & Soybean Digest 7900 International Dr Ste 300 Minneapolis MN 55425 **Phn:** 952-851-9329 **Fax** 952-851-4601 Kurt Lawton. Penton Media. 11-issue magazine.
147,000 to soybean, corn, cotton, wheat, sorghum growers interested in marketing, profitability. cornandsoybeandigest.com klawton@csdigest.com

Florida Grower 1555 Howell Branch Rd Ste C204 Winter Park FL 32789 **Phn:** 407-539-6552 **Fax** 407-539-6544 Frank Giles. Meister Media. Monthly magazine.
12,000 to vegetable/citrus growers interested in harvesting, processing, marketing issues. www.meistermedia.com fgiles@meistermedia.com

The Fruit Growers News PO Box 128 Sparta MI 49345 **Phn:** 616-887-9008 **Fax** 616-887-2666 Matt Milkovitch. Great American Publ. Monthly magazine.
14,600 to tree/small fruit & grape growers selling via farm & roadside markets, U-pick operations. fruitgrowersnews.com news@fruitgrowersnews.com

Good Fruit Grower 105 S 18th St Ste 217 Yakima WA 98901 **Phn:** 509-853-3520 **Fax** 509-454-4186 Jim Black. WA State Fruit Commission. 17-issue tabloid.
10,900 to WA State apple, cherry, pear, peach, plum, nectarine, apricot and grape growers. www.goodfruit.com growing@goodfruit.com

Onion World 8405 Ahtanum Rd Yakima WA 98903 **Phn:** 509-949-0550 **Fax** 509-248-4056 D. Brent Clement. Columbia Publishing. 8 issues.
5,000 to onion growers and shippers interested in research, markets, conventions. www.onionworld.net dbrent@columbiapublications.com

Pacific Nut Producer PO Box 626 Clovis CA 93613 **Phn:** 559-298-6675 **Fax** 559-323-6016 Dan Malcolm. 10-issue magazine.
9,100 to Pacific almond, walnut, pistachio, pecan, chestnut, hazelnut and macadamia growers. www.malcolmmedia.com dan@malcolmmedia.com

The Packer 10901 W 84th Ter Ste 200 Lenexa KS 66214 **Phn:** 913-438-8700 **Fax** 913-438-0691 Chris Koger. Vance Publishing. Weekly newspaper.
12,300 to fresh fruit, vegetable industry personnel interested in pricing, availability, transport. www.thepacker.com news@thepacker.com

Peanut Grower 1010 June Rd Ste 102 Memphis TN 38119 **Phn:** 352-486-7006 **Fax** 352-486-7009 Amanda Huber. One Grower Publishing. 8 issues.
13,500 to peanut farmers interested in production practices, research findings, industry news. www.peanutgrower.com ahuber@svic.net

Fruits--Nuts--Vegetables .68f

Pecan South 4348 Carter Creek Pkwy Ste 101 Bryan TX 77802 **Phn:** 979-846-3285 **Fax** 979-846-1752 Blair Krebs TX Pecan Growers Assn. Monthly.
4,200 to Texas pecan growers and industry personnel interested in forecasts, marketing, Assn. news. www.tpga.org blair@tpga.org

Potato Grower 360 B St Idaho Falls ID 83402 **Phn:** 208-542-2259 **Fax** 208-522-5241 Tyler Baum. Harris Publ. Monthly magazine.
11,700 to U.S. potato growers, packers, shippers, buyers, processors, suppliers. www.potatogrower.com tbaum@potatogrower.com

Produce Business PO Box 810425 Boca Raton FL 33481 **Phn:** 561-994-1118 **Fax** 561-994-1610 Ken Whitacre. Phoenix Media. Monthly.
21,300 to produce industry personnel responsible for marketing, management, supplier relations. www.producebusiness.com kwhitacre@phoenixmedianet.com

Southeastern Peanut Farmer PO Box 967 Tifton GA 31793 **Phn:** 229-386-3690 **Fax** 229-386-3501 Joy Carter. 6 issues.
8,200 to GA, FL, AL, MS & SC peanut growers interested in research, industry news, crop promotion. www.gapeanuts.com joycarter@gapeanuts.com

Spudman PO Box 128 Sparta MI 49345 **Phn:** 616-887-9008 **Fax** 616-887-2666 Bill Schaefer. Great American Publ. 9-issue magazine.
14,800 to potato growers, processors, shippers, buyers, sales & mkting. personnel. spudman.com spudedit@spudman.com

Sugar Journal PO Box 19084 New Orleans LA 70179 **Phn:** 504-482-3914 **Fax** 504-482-4205 Charley Richard. Kriedt Enterprises. Monthly.
3,700 covers global trends in production, processing, refining of cane, beet and corn. www.sugarjournal.com charley@sugarjournal.com

Sugar Producer 360 B St Idaho Falls ID 83402 **Phn:** 208-524-7000 **Fax** 208-522-5241 Nancy I. Sanchez. Harris Publ. 9-issue magazine.
10,300 to sugarbeet growers, processors, equip. mfrs. & distributors. www.sugarproducer.com ageditor@harrispublishing.com

Sugarbeet Grower 4601 16th Ave N Fargo ND 58102 **Phn:** 701-476-2111 **Fax** 701-476-2182 Don Lilleboe. Sugar Publications. 6-issue magazine.
10,800 to sugarbeet growers/processors interested in research, production, industry news. www.sugarpub.com sugar@forumprinting.com

Sunflower 2401 46th Ave SE Ste 206 Mandan ND 58554 **Phn:** 701-328-5100 John Sandbakken. Natl. Sunflower Assn. Bimonthly magazine.
26,300 to sunflower growers interested in markets, forecasts, research, education. www.sunflowernsa.com johns@sunflowernsa.com

The Vegetable Growers News PO Box 128 Sparta MI 49345 **Phn:** 616-887-9008 **Fax** 616-887-2666 Matt Milkovich. Great American Publ. Monthly.
15,200 to U.S. vegetable growers interested in markets, equipment, crop-specific features, farm mgmt. vegetablegrowersnews.com vgnedit@vegetablegrowersnews.com

Cattle .68g

Alabama Cattleman PO Box 2499 Montgomery AL 36102 **Phn:** 334-265-1867 **Fax** 334-834-5326 William Powell. AL Cattlemen's Assn. Monthly.
13,000 to Alabama beef cattle raisers interested in food safety, international gtrade, legislation & regulations. www.bamabeef.org bpowell@bamabeef.org

American Cattlemen 919 2nd Ave SW Spencer IA 51301 **Phn:** 712-264-4100 **Fax** 712-264-4125 Rick Thomas. Heartland Comms Group. Monthly magazine.
30,200 to cattle owners & operators interested in equipment, markets, animal health, best practices. www.americancattlemen.com rick@hlipublishing.com

Angus Icon 9960 Business Park Dr Ste 170 Sacramento CA 95693 **Phn:** 916-837-1432 Sherry Danekas. Western States Angus Assn. 10 issues.
4,200 to Angus cattle ranchers & producers from Dakota to Pacific states interested in Assn. news, shows, sales. angusthemagazine.com jdainc@cwo.com

Arkansas Cattle Business 310 Executive Ct Little Rock AR 72205 **Phn:** 501-224-2114 **Fax** 501-224-5377 Carson Horn. AR Cattlemen's Assn. Monthly.
9,500 to AR cattle raisers & operators interested in Assn. and industry news, local and state issues. www.arbeef.org carson@arbeef.org

Beef 7900 International Dr Ste 300 Minneapolis MN 55425 **Phn:** 952-851-4669 **Fax** 913-514-3718 Joe Roybal. Penton Media. Monthly magazine.
97,000 to commercial beef production industry personnel concerned with operational aspects. beefmagazine.com jroybal@beef-mag.com

Calf News 1531 Kensington Blvd Garden City KS 67846 **Phn:** 620-272-6862 **Fax** 316-462-5678 Betty Jo Gigot. Bimonthly magazine.
7,500 to large (more than one thousand head) U.S. cattle feeding operations. www.calfnews.com dgigot1@cox.net

California Cattleman 1221 H St Sacramento CA 95814 **Phn:** 916-444-0845 **Fax** 916-444-2194 Stevie Ipsen. 11 issues.
4,500 to California ranchers interested in state & federal regulations, education, markets. www.calcattlemen.org stevie@calcattlemen.org

Cattle Business in MS. 680 Monroe St Ste A Jackson MS 39202 **Phn:** 601-354-8951 **Fax** 601-355-7128 LeAnne Peters. MS Cattlemen's Assn. 10-issue magazine.
4,000 to Mississippi ranchers & operators interested in sales, Assn. news, education, legislation. www.mscattlemen.org mscattle@telepak.net

Cattleman 1301 W 7th St Fort Worth TX 76102 **Phn:** 817-332-7155 **Fax** 817-332-5446 Ellen Brisendine. Texas & SW Cattle Raisers Assn. Monthly magazine.
19,300 to beef cattle ranchers, feeders, breeders interested in cattle & land mgmt. techniques. www.thecattlemanmagazine.com ehbrisendine@tscra.org

Cowman 2500 Exchange Ave Oklahoma City OK 73108 **Phn:** 405-235-4391 **Fax** 405-235-3608 Chisolm Kinder. OK Cattleman's Assn. Monthly.
4,600 to Oklahoma cattle raisers interested in events, legislation, education, research. www.okcattlemen.org ckinder@okcattlemen.org

Drovers 10901 W 84th Ter Ste 200 Lenexa KS 66214 **Phn:** 913-438-8700 **Fax** 913-438-0695 Greg Henderson. Vance Publishing. Monthly magazine.
91,800 to beef cattle producers interested in marketing, management, industry news. www.cattlenetwork.com ghenderson@food360.com

FL Cattleman & Livestock Jrnl. PO Box 421403 Kissimmee FL 34742 **Phn:** 407-846-8025 **Fax** 407-933-8209 Jim Handley. FL Cattleman's Assn. Monthly.
4,600 to Florida cattle raisers interested in research, breeds, markets, health, Assn. activities and news. www.floridacattlemen.org fbcfcajimhandley@aol.com

Georgia Cattleman PO Box 27990 Macon GA 31211 **Phn:** 478-474-6560 **Fax** 478-474-5732 Dallas Duncan. Monthly.
5,500 to Georgia ranchers and raisers interested in breeds, sales, markets, conventions. www.gabeef.org magazine@gabeef.org

Hereford World PO Box 14059 Kansas City MO 64101 **Phn:** 816-842-8878 **Fax** 816-842-6931 Angie Denton. Hereford Publications. 11-issue magazine.
10,000 to members of Amer. Hereford Assn., Hereford owners & breeders. www.hereford.org adenton@hereford.org

Illinois Beef 2060 W Iles Ave Ste B Springfield IL 62704 **Phn:** 217-787-4280 **Fax** 217-793-3605 Maralee Johnson. IL Beef Assn. Bimonthly.
6,200 to Illinois raisers & operators interested in research, health, state & federal legislation & issues. www.illinoisbeef.com maralee@illinoisbeef.com

Indiana Beef 5738 W 74th St Indianapolis IN 46278 **Phn:** 317-293-2333 **Fax** 317-295-8421 Jennifer Biesecker. IN Beef Cattle Assn. 5-issue magazine.
5,000 to Indiana beef cattle industry interested in farm quality of life, markets, management, consumer demands. www.indianabeef.org jbiesecker@indianabeef.org

Iowa Cattleman 2055 Ironwood Ct Ames IA 50014 **Phn:** 515-296-2266 **Fax** 515-296-2261 Jackie Ditsworth. 9 issues.
9,700 to Iowa beef producers interested in state & federal regulations, markets, education. www.iacattlemen.org jackie@iabeef.org

Kansas Stockman 6031 SW 37th St Topeka KS 66614 **Phn:** 785-273-5115 **Fax** 785-273-3399 Todd Domer. KS Livestock Assn. 10 issues.
5,600 to KS cattle & livestock industry personnel interested in news, analysis, goods & services. www.kla.org todd@kla.org

Limousin World 2005 Ruhl Dr Guthrie OK 73044 **Phn:** 405-260-3775 **Fax** 405-260-3766 Kyle Haley. Monthly.
10,500 to Limousin beef cattle breeders and breed enthusiasts interested in shows, sales, mgmt. www.limousinworld.com limousin@limousinworld.com

Livestock Market Digest PO Box 7458 Albuquerque NM 87194 **Phn:** 505-243-9515 **Fax** 505-998-6236 Lee Pitts. Monthly tabloid.
22,500 to producers & feeders interested in market conditions, livestock transportation & health. www.aaalivestock.com itsdapitts@charter.net

Nebraska Cattleman 1010 Lincoln Mall Ste 101 Lincoln NE 68508 **Phn:** 402-475-2333 **Fax** 402-475-0822 Mike Fitzgerald. 10 issues.
15,000 to Nebraska cattle producers interested in issues, production and marketing, legal issues. www.nebraskacattlemen.org mfitzgerald@necattlemen.org

New Mexico Stockman PO Box 7127 Albuquerque NM 87194 **Phn:** 505-243-9515 **Fax** 505-998-6236 Caren Cowan. NM Cattle Growers Assn. Monthly.
10,700 to New Mexico cattle raisers interested in state & federal legislation, assn. activities, breeds. www.aaalivestock.com caren@aaalivestock.com

Record Stockman PO Box 1209 Wheat Ridge CO 80034 **Phn:** 303-420-1500 **Fax** 303-420-1888 Chris Brooks. Weekly.
20,000 to breeders, stockmen of cattle interested in market prices, marketing, USDA regulations.

Stockman Grass Farmer PO Box 2300 Ridgeland MS 39158 **Phn:** 800-748-9808 **Fax** 601-853-8087 Glinda Davenport. Monthly tabloid.
11,000 to farmers & ranchers who raise grass-fed livestock interested in education, profitability, farmer profiles. www.stockmangrassfarmer.com sgfsample@aol.com

Weekly Livestock Reporter PO Box 7655 Fort Worth TX 76111 **Phn:** 817-831-3147 **Fax** 817-831-3117 Phil Stoll. Weekly.
10,400 to livestock buyers, sellers interested in marketing news, equipment, real estate, feed, grain. www.weeklylivestock.com service@weeklylivestock.com

Western Cowman PO Box 410 Wilton CA 95693 **Phn:** 916-837-1432 Sherry Danekas. 10 issues.
7,700 to Western U.S. cattle industry personnel interested in lifestyle, market development. www.jdaonline.com jdainc@cwo.com

Cattle .68g
Western Livestock Journal 7355 E Orchard Rd Ste 300 Greenwood Village CO 80111 **Phn:** 303-722-7600 **Fax** 303-722-0155 John Robinson. Crow Pubs. Weekly newspaper.
17,800 to cattle industry personnel concerned with marketing, sales, show reports. www.wlj.net editorial@wlj.net

Western Ag Reporter PO Box 30758 Billings MT 59107 **Phn:** 406-259-4589 **Fax** 406-259-6888 Linda Grosskopf. Weekly newspaper.
11,000 to livestock owners, mgrs., producers, purebred breeders, feeders, buyers, marketers. www.cattleplus.com wlrpubs@imt.net

Poultry .68h
Backyard Pountry 145 Industrial Dr Medford WI 54451 **Phn:** 715-785-7979 **Fax** 715-785-7414 Elaine Belanger. 6-issue magazine.
75,000 to small flock poultry raisers interested in breeds, health & nutrition, housing, news. www.backyardpoultrymag.com byp@tds.net

Egg Industry 303 N Main St Ste 500 Rockford IL 61101 **Phn:** 815-966-5400 **Fax** 815-968-0941 Terrence O'Keefe. Watt Publishing. Monthly.
2,200 to worldwide egg operations mgmt. interested in case studies, technology. www.wattagnet.com tokeefe@wattnet.net

Gobbles 108 Marty Dr Buffalo MN 55313 **Phn:** 763-682-2171 **Fax** 763-682-5546 Lara Durben. MN Turkey Growers Assn. Monthly.
900 minnesotaturkey.com lara@minnesotaturkey.com

Poultry Times PO Box 1338 Gainesville GA 30503 **Phn:** 770-536-2476 **Fax** 770-532-4894 David Strickland. Morris Multimedia. Biweekly tabloid.
8,700 to natl. poultry industry personnel with emphasis on broiler, turkey, egg production. www.poultryandeggnews.com dstrickland@poultryandeggnews.com

Watt Poultry USA 303 N Main St Ste 500 Rockford IL 61101 **Phn:** 815-966-5400 **Fax** 815-968-0941 Gary Thornton. Watt Publishing. Monthly magazine.
12,800 to N. Amer. poultry industry mgmt. responsible for production, processing, marketing. www.wattagnet.com gthornton@wattnet.net

Sheep--Goats--Hogs .68i
Dairy Goat Journal 145 Industrial Dr Medford WI 54451 **Phn:** 715-785-7979 **Fax** 715-785-7414 Jennifer Stultz. Bimonthly.
5,000 to dairy and meat goat owners interested in animal health and nutrition, marketing. www.dairygoatjournal.com dairygoatjournal@tds.net

Goat Rancher 225 Hankins Rd Sarah MS 38665 **Phn:** 662-562-9529 **Fax** 662-562-9529 Terry Hankins. Monthly.
6,000 to Boer and meat goat owners interested in breeding, nutrition, health, showing. www.goatrancher.com goatrancher@hughes.net

Iowa Pork Producer PO Box 71009 Clive IA 50325 **Phn:** 515-225-7675 **Fax** 515-225-0563 Ron Birkenholz. IA Pork Producers Assn. Bimonthly magazine.
20,000 to IA producers of feeder pigs, market hogs, breeding stock interested in rsch. & mktg. www.iowapork.org info@iowapork.org

Meat Goat Monthly News PO Box 2678 San Angelo TX 76902 **Phn:** 325-655-4434 **Fax** 325-658-8250 Gary Cutrer. Monthly.
1,500 to Boer and meat goat breeders interested in news, products, buy/sell listings. www.ranchmagazine.com/mgn.html info@ranchmagazine.com

Montana Wool Grower PO Box 1693 Helena MT 59624 **Phn:** 406-442-1330 Brent Roeder. MT Wool Growers Assn. 4-issue magazine.
800 to Montana sheep and wool growers interested in govt. affairs, land use issues, market reports www.mtsheep.org mwga@mtsheep.org

National Hog Farmer 7900 International Dr Ste 300 Minneapolis MN 55425 **Phn:** 952-851-4661 **Fax** 952-851-4601 Dale Miller. Penton Media. Monthly magazine.
26,400 to commercial swine producers marketing 3000+ hogs & pigs annually. nationalhogfarmer.com dpmiller@nationalhogfarmer.com

Pork 10901 W 84th Ter Ste 200 Lenexa KS 66214 **Phn:** 913-438-8700 **Fax** 913-438-0695 Marlys Miller. Vance Publishing. Monthly magazine.
17,900 to hog producers interested in production practices, methods, mktg., industry news. www.porknetwork.com mmpork@aol.com

Pork Checkoff Report PO Box 9114 Des Moines IA 50306 **Phn:** 515-223-2600 **Fax** 515-223-2646 Jan Jorgensen. Natl. Pork Board. Quarterly magazine.
92,000 to pork raisers, producers interested in govt. developments, consumer, market trends. www.pork.org jjorgensen@pork.org

Ranch & Rural Living PO Box 2678 San Angelo TX 76902 **Phn:** 325-655-4434 **Fax** 325-658-8250 Gary Cutrer. Monthly.
12,000 to SW U.S. Angora, meat & Boer goat raisers/breeders; sheep & cattle raisers & ranchers. www.ranchmagazine.com info@ranchmagazine.com

Sheep HCR 68 Box 185 Trout WV 24991 **Phn:** 715-785-7979 **Fax** 715-785-7414 Nathan Griffith. Bimonthly magazine.
10,000 to U.S. & Canadian readers interested in practical info about sheep, wool, woolcrafts. www.sheepmagazine.com sheepmag@tds.net

Sheep Industry News 9785 Maroon Cir Ste 360 Englewood CO 80112 **Phn:** 303-771-3500 **Fax** 303-771-8200 Amy Trinidad. Amer. Sheep Industry Assn. Monthly.
9,200 to sheep raisers & ranchers interested in markets, federal legislation, Assn. news & events. sheepindustrynews.org amy@sheepusa.org

The Shepherd PO Box 168 Farson WY 82932 **Phn:** Cat Urbigkit. Long Draw Publishing. Monthly magazine.
5,000 to domestic sheep & goat industry personnel interested in breeding, nutrition, mgmt., marketing, health, R&D. theshepherdmagazine.com editor@theshepherdmagazine.com.

General Interest Magazines .69
Advancing Philanthropy 4300 Wilson Blvd Ste 300 Arlington VA 22203 **Phn:** 703-684-0410 **Fax** 703-684-0540 Marie Reed. NSFRE. Bimonthly.
23,000 practical information and useful tools to help fundraisers at every level. www.afpnet.org afp@afpnet.org

American Heritage 416 Hungerford Dr Ste 216 Rockville MD 20850 **Phn:** 240-453-0902 Edward Grosvenor. Quarterly magazine.
369,000 to readers interested in historical viewpoint on politics, art, business, intl. affairs. www.americanheritage.com editor@americanheritage.com

American History 19300 Promenade Dr Leesburg VA 20176 **Phn:** 703-771-9400 **Fax** 703-779-8345 Nan Siegel. Weider History Group. Bimonthly.
80,600 to readers interested in authoritative American history topics presented in entertaining, information format. www.historynet.com americanhistory@weiderhistorygroup.com

American Prospect 1710 Rhode Island Ave NW Fl 12 Washington DC 20036 **Phn:** 202-776-0730 Bob Moser. Bimonthly magazine. TH:@rkuttner
45,000 to readers interested in progressive/liberal policies, domestic & intl. issues, economics. prospect.org bmoser@prospect.org

American Spectator 1611 N Kent St Ste 901 Arlington VA 22209 **Phn:** 703-807-2011 **Fax** 703-807-2013 R. Emmett Tyrell, Jr. 10-issue magazine.
50,000 to readers interested in wide range of commentary; business, political, cultural coverage. spectator.org editor@spectator.org

Archaeology 3636 33rd St Ste 301 Long Island City NY 11106 **Phn:** 718-472-3050 **Fax** 718-472-3051 Claudia Valentino. Archaeological Inst. of America. Bimonthly magazine.
255,200 to readers interested in the study of ancient cultures, current excavations. www.archaeology.org editorial@archaeology.org

Armchair General 2060 E Avenida De Los Arboles Ste 373 Thousand Oaks CA 91362 **Phn:** Jerry D. Morlock Weider History Network. Bimonthly.
27,000 to military enthusiasts interested in historic & contemporary battle analysis, command, interactivity. www.armchairgeneral.com press02@armchairgeneral.com

Astronomy PO Box 1612 Waukesha WI 53187 **Phn:** 262-796-8776 **Fax** 262-798-6468 Dave Eicher. Kalmbach Publishing. Monthly.
131,300 to readers interested in astronomy equipment and techniques. www.astronomy.com editor@astronomy.com

The Atlantic 600 New Hampshire Ave NW Fl 4 Washington DC 20037 **Phn:** 202-266-6000 **Fax** 202-266-6001 Scott Stossel. 10-issue magazine.
428,000 to readers interested in politics, government, current events, business, economics. www.theatlantic.com sstossel@theatlantic.com

Christian Science Monitor 210 Massachusetts Ave Boston MA 02115 **Phn:** 617-450-2300 **Fax** 617-450-2707 Amelia Newcomb. Weekly magazine. TH:@csmonitor
100,000 to readers interested in independent, in-depth editorial about natl. and intl. topics. www.csmonitor.com nutgraf@csmonitor.com

Civil War Times 19300 Promenade Dr Leesburg VA 20176 **Phn:** 703-771-9400 **Fax** 703-779-8345 Dana Shoaf. Weider History Group. Bimonthly magazine.
72,400 to Civil War enthusiasts interested in battle details, profiles of soliers and politicians. www.historynet.com civilwartimes@weiderhistorygroup.com

Commentary 165 E 56th St New York NY 10022 **Phn:** 212-751-4000 **Fax** 212-891-6700 Jonathan S. Tobin. Amer. Jewish Committee. 11-issue magazine.
25,000 to readers interested in world affairs, domestic policy, arts, culture, Jewish affairs. www.commentarymagazine.com editorial@commentarymagazine.com

Commonweal 475 Riverside Dr Rm 405 New York NY 10115 **Phn:** 212-662-4200 **Fax** 212-662-4183 Paul Baumann. Biweekly.
19,500 to readers interested in public affairs commentary from point of view of Catholic laity. www.commonwealmagazine.org editors@commonwealmagazine.org

Consumer Reports 101 Truman Ave Yonkers NY 10703 **Phn:** 914-378-2000 **Fax** 914-378-2904 Kimberly Kleman. Consumers Union. 13-issue magazine.
4,000,000 to readers interested in buying guides, reports for home/office products, cars, svcs. www.consumerreports.org klemki@consumer.org

Discover 275 7th Ave Fl 21 New York NY 10001 **Phn:** 212-624-4800 **Fax** 212-624-4813 Stephen George. Kalmbach Publishing. 10-issue magazine.
600,000 to readers interested in broad range of scientific, technological information. discovermagazine.com editorial@discovermagazine.com

Entertainment Weekly 135 W 50th St New York NY 10020 **Phn:** 212-522-5600 **Fax** 212-522-4482 Jess Cagle. Time, Inc. Weekly magazine.
1,777,000 to readers interested in reviews & features on TV, movies, music, DVDs. www.ew.com/ew/ jess_cagle@ew.com

Foreign Affairs 58 E 68th St New York NY 10065 **Phn:** 212-585-5800 Jonathan Tepperman. Cncl. on Foreign Relations. Bimonthly magazine. TH:@Justin_Vogt
154,000 to readers interested in Amer. foreign policy, intl. economy & politics, finance, academia. www.foreignaffairs.com editor@foreignaffairs.com

FP Foreign Policy 1899 L St NW Ste 550 Washington DC 20036 **Phn:** 202-728-7300 **Fax** 202-728-7342 Noah Shachtman. Slate Group. Bimonthly. TH:@NoahShachtman
101,300 global politics, economics as seen by leading journalists, thinkers, and practitioners. www.foreignpolicy.com editor@foreignpolicy.com

The Futurist 7910 Woodmont Ave Ste 450 Bethesda MD 20814 **Phn:** 301-656-8274 **Fax** 301-951-0394 Edward Cornish. World Future Society. Bimonthly magazine.
13,400 to readers interested in five-50 years' out projections of culture, technology, politics, economics, health. www.americanheritage.com cwagner@wfs.org

Globe 1000 American Media Way Boca Raton FL 33464 **Phn:** 561-997-7733 **Fax** 561-989-1004 Tony Frost. American Media. Weekly magazine.
487,100 to readers interested in contemporary human-interest accounts. www.globemagazine.com tfrost@globefl.com

Good Old Days 306 E Parr Rd Berne IN 46711 **Phn:** 260-589-4000 **Fax** 260-589-8093 Ken Tate. DRG. Bimonthly.
175,000 to readers interested in American folklore, nostalgia and history from 1930s to 1960s. www.goodolddaysmagazine.com editor@goodolddaysmagazine.com

Grit Magazine 1503 SW 42nd St Topeka KS 66609 **Phn:** 785-274-4300 **Fax** 785-274-4305 Oscar Will. Ogden Publications. Monthly magazine.
223,000 presenting the positive side of rural American life and traditions, real-life stories. www.grit.com hwill@grit.com

Harper's Magazine 666 Broadway Fl 11 New York NY 10012 **Phn:** 212-420-5720 **Fax** 212-228-5889 Ellen Rosenbush. Monthly magazine.
217,000 to readers interested in political, social, cultural essays and fiction. www.harpers.org harpers@harpers.org

High Times 419 Park Ave S Fl 16 New York NY 10016 **Phn:** 212-387-0500 **Fax** 212-475-7684 Dan Skye. Trans-High Corp. Monthly.
251,000 news, interviews, photographs, growing tips, legal and drug testing information. hightimes.com hteditor@hightimes.com

In These Times 2040 N Milwaukee Ave Chicago IL 60647 **Phn:** 773-772-0100 **Fax** 773-772-4180 Joel Bleifuss. Inst. for Public Affairs. Monthly.
21,000 News analysis and opinion covering social, environmental and economic issues. inthesetimes.com joel@inthesetimes.com

In Touch Weekly 270 Sylvan Ave Englewood Cliffs NJ 07632 **Phn:** 201-569-6699 **Fax** 201-569-3584 Jo Piazza. Bauer Publishing. Weekly.
650,000 to readers interested in picture-driven, upbeat coverage of celebrities & their lifestyles. intouchweekly.com jpiazza@bauerpublishing.com

KoreAm Journal 17000 S Vermont Ave Ste A Gardena CA 90247 **Phn:** 310-769-4913 **Fax** 310-769-4903 Julie Ha. Monthly magazine.
37,000 news, issues, stories, culture magazine aimed at Korean Americans published in English. iamkoream.com julie@iamkoream.com

Mental Floss 2821 2nd Ave S Ste. L Birmingham AL 35233 **Phn:** 205-254-3770 Jessanne Collins. Bimonthly magazine. TH:@jessanne
150,000 to readers interested in learning about both simple & complex issues in clever, engaging words & images. www.mentalfloss.com jessanne@mentalfloss.com

Military Heritage 6731 Whittier Ave Ste A100 McLean VA 22101 **Phn:** 703-964-0361 **Fax** 703-964-0366 Roy Morris. Sovereign Media Co. Bimo.
121,000 military history related to human history, thoughtfully written, well researched articles. www.militaryheritagemagazine.com editor@militaryheritagemagazine.com

Money 1271 Avenue of the Americas New York NY 10020 **Phn:** 212-522-1212 **Fax** 212-522-0189 Craig Matters. Time, Inc. Monthly magazine.
2,000,000 to readers interested in investments, finances, careers, taxes, budgets. money.cnn.com managing_editor@moneymail.com

Mother Earth News 1503 SW 42nd St Topeka KS 66609 **Phn:** 785-274-4300 **Fax** 785-274-4305 Cheryl Long. Ogden Publications. Bimonthly magazine.
500,000 to readers interested in country lifestyle, do-it-yourself living, gardening, environment. www.motherearthnews.com letters@motherearthnews.com

Mother Jones 222 Sutter St Ste 600 San Francisco CA 94108 **Phn:** 415-321-1700 **Fax** 415-321-1749 Clint Hendler. Bimonthly.
233,800 to readers interested in progressive viewpoint reporting on environment, politics, society. motherjones.com chendler@motherjones.com

The Nation 33 Irving Pl Fl 8 New York NY 10003 **Phn:** 212-209-5400 **Fax** 212-982-9000 Betsy Reed. Weekly magazine.
186,500 to readers interested in political, economic, social analysis from liberal viewpoint. www.thenation.com betsy@thenation.com

National Enquirer 1000 American Media Way Boca Raton FL 33464 **Phn:** 561-997-7733 **Fax** 561-989-1004 Tony Frost. American Media. Weekly tabloid.
1,150,000 to readers interested in celebrity news, human interest stories, diet and health. www.nationalenquirer.com tfrost@globefl.com

National Geographic 1145 17th St NW Washington DC 20036 **Phn:** 202-857-7000 **Fax** 202-828-6667 Victoria Pope. Natl. Geographic Soc. Monthly.
5,100,000 to readers interested in exploration, geography, global culture. www.nationalgeographic.com ngsforum@nationalgeographic.com

National Review 215 Lexington Ave Fl 4 New York NY 10016 **Phn:** 212-679-7330 **Fax** 212-849-2835 Jay Nordlinger. Biweekly magazine.
160,000 to readers interested in political, economic, social analysis from conservative viewpoint. www.nationalreview.com submissions@nationalreview.com

Native Peoples 5333 N 7th St Ste C224 Phoenix AZ 85014 **Phn:** 602-265-4855 **Fax** 602-265-3113 Daniel Gibson. Media Concepts. Bimonthly.
47,000 to readers interested in Amer. Indian arts, history, culture, music, books, travel, foods. www.nativepeoples.com editorial@nativepeoples.com

Natural History 36 W 25th St Fl 5 New York NY 10010 **Phn:** 646-356-6500 **Fax** 646-356-6511 Vittorio Maestro. Amer. Museum Natural History. 10 issues.
225,200 to readers interested in social, natural sciences, human environment, wildlife. www.naturalhistorymag.com nhmag@naturalhistorymag.com

New Mobility PO Box 220 Horsham PA 19044 **Phn:** 215-675-9133 **Fax** 215-675-9376 Tim Gilmer. Monthly magazine.
24,000 to wheelchair-using readers interested in relationships, travel, work, parenting. www.newmobility.com

The New Republic 525 9th St NW Washington DC 20004 **Phn:** 202-508-4444 **Fax** 202-204-4871 Franklin Foer. Biweekly magazine. TH:@FranklinFoer
49,000 to readers interested in public affairs, domestic and international issues. www.newrepublic.com ffoer@tnr.com

New York Magazine 75 Varick St Fl 4 New York NY 10013 **Phn:** 212-508-0700 **Fax** 212-583-7507 Adam Moss. 26-issue magazine.
429,200 to readers interested in NY City, style, art, business, local & natl. politics. nymag.com contactus@nymag.com

New Yorker 4 Times Sq New York NY 10036 **Phn:** 212-286-5400 **Fax** 212-286-5024 David Remnick. Conde Nast. Weekly magazine.
1,070,000 to readers interested in metropolitan ideas & events, theater, fiction, poetry. www.newyorker.com themail@newyorker.com

Newsweek 7 Hanover Sq Fl 5 New York NY 10004 **Phn:** 646-867-7100 Kira Bindrim. IBT Media. Online only TH:@kirabind
to readers interested in current events, natl. & intl. politics, social trends, lifestyle topics, commentary. mag.newsweek.com editorial@newsweekdailybeast.com

Pacific Standard PO Box 698 Santa Barbara CA 93102 **Phn:** 818-487-2076 **Fax** 818-487-4550 Maria Streshinsky. Bimonthly magazine. TH:@Mstreshinsky
100,000 to readers interested in public policy topics based on both academic research & realtime reporting. www.miller-mccune.com theeditor@miller-mccune.com

People 1271 Avenue of the Americas New York NY 10020 **Phn:** 212-522-1212 **Fax** 212-522-1359 Larry Hackett. Time, Inc. Weekly magazine.
3,750,500 to readers interested in celebrities, human interest stories, movies, TV. www.people.com editor@people.com

Philanthropy 1150 17th St NW Ste 503 Washington DC 20036 **Phn:** 202-822-8333 **Fax** 202-822-8325 Christopher Levenick. Philanthropy Round Table. Mo.
43,000 Information on issues facing philanthropic donors and advice on foundation management. www.philanthropyroundtable.org main@philanthropyroundtable.org

Popular Science 2 Park Ave Fl 9 New York NY 10016 **Phn:** 212-779-5000 **Fax** 212-779-5108 Jacob Ward. Bonnier Corp. Monthly magazine.
1,300,000 to readers interested in how science/technology developments impact everyday life. www.popsci.com jacob.ward@bonniercorp.com

The Progressive 409 E Main St Madison WI 53703 **Phn:** 608-257-4626 Matthew Rothschild. Monthly magazine.
66,000 to readers interested in politics, economics, social issues from left-wing editorial viewpoint. www.progressive.org editorial@progressive.org

Psychology Today 115 E 23rd St Fl 9 New York NY 10010 **Phn:** 212-260-7210 **Fax** 212-260-7445 Jane Nussbaum. Sussex Publishing. Bimonthly magazine.
301,700 to readers interested in self improvement, stress mgmt., research, advice. www.psychologytoday.com jane.nussbaum@psychologytoday.com

Reader's Digest Readers Digest Rd Pleasantville NY 10570 **Phn:** 914-238-1000 Courtenay Smith. Monthly magazine.
8,000,000 to readers in U.S. & abroad interested in original & abridged features. www.rd.com courtenay_smith@rd.com

Reason Magazine 3415 S Sepulveda Blvd Ste 400 Los Angeles CA 90034 **Phn:** 310-391-2245 **Fax** 310-391-4395 Jesse Walker. Reason Fndtn. 11-issues.
55,000 public policy, research with a libertarian viewpoint, Pacific Rim, local, state issues. reason.com jwalker@reason.com

Rebel Ink 210 E State Rt 4 Ste 211 Paramus NJ 07652 **Phn:** 201-843-4004 **Fax** 201-843-8775 Paul Gambino. Enoble Media. Bimonthly.
27,000 focuses on hardcore ink, featuring people who are covered head-to-toe with body art. rebelinkmag.com editor@rebelinkmag.com

Reminisce Magazine 5400 S 60th St Greendale WI 53129 **Phn:** 414-423-0100 **Fax** 414-423-1143 Matthew Phenix. Reiman/Readers' Digest. Bimonthly.
75,000 takee a stroll down memory lane, features stories and pictures of times gone by. www.reminisce.com editors@reminisce.com

General Interest Magazines .69

Robb Report 1 Acton Pl Acton MA 01720 **Phn:** 978-264-7500 **Fax** 978-264-7505 Larry Bean. CurtCo Robb Media. Monthly.
103,600 to affluent intl. readers interested in luxury lifestyle, travel, art, jewelry. www.robbreport.com editorial@robbreport.com

Scientific American 75 Varick St Fl 9 New York NY 10013 **Phn:** 212-754-0550 **Fax** 212-755-1976 Seth Fletcher. Monthly magazine. TH:@seth_fletcher
486,100 to technical/professional general public interested in broad range of scientific disciplines. www.scientificamerican.com editors@sciam.com

Sea Classics 9509 Vassar Ave Ste A Chatsworth CA 91311 **Phn:** 818-700-6868 **Fax** 818-700-6282 Edwin A. Schnepf. Challenge Publications. Monthly.
65,000 covers world's major sea battles, first-hand accounts from the men who fought them. www.challengeweb.com mail@challengeweb.com

Skin & Ink 210 E State Rt 4 Ste 211 Paramus NJ 07652 **Phn:** 201-843-4004 Dan Brown. Monthly magazine.
96,000 to those interested in tattoo art, best designs, techniques, lasting designs, photos. www.skinink.com

SmartMoney 1211 Avenue Of The Americas New York NY 10036 **Phn:** Dow Jones & Co. Online only.
to readers interested in investments, spending, saving, financial trends, corporate info. www.smartmoney.com letters@smartmoney.com

Smithsonian PO Box 37012 Washington DC 20013 **Phn:** 202-633-6090 Michael Caruso. Smithsonian Institution. Monthly mag.
2,100,000 to Institution supporters, other readers interested in culture, arts, history. www.smithsonianmag.com carusom@si.edu

SpeciaLiving Magazine PO Box 1000 Bloomington IL 61702 **Phn:** 309-962-2003 Betty Garee. Quarterly.
12,000 to disabled readers interested in travel & housing accessibility, medical & social news. www.specialiving.com gareeb@aol.com

Sports Illustrated 1271 Avenue Of The Americas New York NY 10020 **Phn:** 212-522-1212 **Fax** 212-522-4543 Matt Bean. Time, Inc. Weekly magazine.
3,238,100 to readers interested in sports news, features, information, recreation. sportsillustrated.cnn.com newsbureau@simail.com

Star 4 New York Plz New York NY 10004 **Phn:** 212-545-4800 **Fax** 212-448-9510 James Heidenry. American Media. Weekly magazine.
1,458,100 to readers interested in celebrity personalities, news and lifestyles. www.starmagazine.com jheidenry@amilink.com

Tattoo 28210 Dorothy Dr Agoura Hills CA 91301 **Phn:** 818-889-8740 **Fax** 818-889-1252 Billy Tinney. Paisano Publications. Mo. magazine.
91,000 coverst today's artists, their living canvases, conventions, events of interest. www.paisanopub.com tporter@paisanopub.com

Time 1271 Avenue of the Americas New York NY 10020 **Phn:** 212-522-1212 **Fax** 212-522-0991 Michael Duffy. Time, Inc. Weekly magazine.
3,400,000 to readers interested in national and international current events, society, business. www.time.com/time/ michael_duffy@timemagazine.com

Town and Country 300 W 57th St New York NY 10019 **Phn:** 212-903-5000 **Fax** 646-280-1054 Jay Fielden. Hearst Corp. Monthly magazine. TH:@JayFielden
475,000 to affluent readers interested in travel, fashions, home, social fundraising events. www.townandcountrymag.com tnc@hearst.com

US Weekly 1290 Avenue of the Americas New York NY 10104 **Phn:** 212-484-1616 **Fax** 212-651-7890 Michael Steele. Wenner Media, Inc. Weekly magazine.
1,900,000 to readers interested in entertainment news, celebrity photos, youthful fashion. www.usmagazine.com michael.steele@usmagazine.com

USA Today Magazine 500 Bi County Blvd Ste 203 Farmingdale NY 11735 **Phn:** 631-293-4343 **Fax** 631-293-4321 Wayne Barrett. Monthly.
256,000 to readers interested in politics, foreign affairs, business, health, religion, media. www.usatodaymagazine.net infousa@usatodaymagazine.net

Utne Reader 1503 SW 42nd St Topeka KS 66609 **Phn:** 785-274-4300 **Fax** 785-274-4305 Christian Williams. Ogden Publications. Bimonthly magazine.
215,000 to readers interested in provocative writing from diverse perspectives, art, media. www.utne.com cwilliams@utne.com

Vanity Fair 4 Times Sq New York NY 10036 **Phn:** 212-286-2860 **Fax** 212-286-7094 Jane Sarkin. Conde Nast. Monthly magazine.
1,153,500 to young, affluent readers interested in business, entertainment, politics, art, media. www.vanityfair.com jane_sarkin@condenast.com

The Week 1040 Avenue Of The Americas New York NY 10018 **Phn:** 212-302-2626 William Falk. Weekly magazine.
542,000 to readers interested in news, opinions, ideas culled from U.S. and international press. theweek.com editor@theweekmagazine.com

The Wilson Quarterly 1300 Pennsylvania Ave NW Washington DC 20004 **Phn:** 202-691-4200 Steven Lagerfeld. Online only.
to readers interested in essays on politics, social sciences, foreign affairs, history. www.wilsonquarterly.com steve.lagerfeld@wilsoncenter.org

Home & Garden .69a

American Bungalow PO Box 756 Sierra Madre CA 91025 **Phn:** 800-350-3363 Kathleen Donahue. Quarterly magazine. TH:@AmBungalow
120,000 to readers interested in Arts & Crafts bungalow-style homes, renovations, furniture, collectibles. www.americanbungalow.com editors@ambungalow.com

Better Homes & Gardens 1716 Locust St Des Moines IA 50309 **Phn:** 515-284-3000 **Fax** 515-284-3684 Oma Blaise Ford. Meredith Corp. Monthly magazine.
7,676,000 to readers interested in homes, gardens, cooking, decorating, travel, entertaining. www.bhg.com oma.ford@meredith.com

Birds & Blooms 5400 S 60th St Greendale WI 53129 **Phn:** 414-423-0100 Stacy Tornio. Reiman/Readers' Digest. agazine.
8,000,000 to readers interested in flower gardening, garden designs, backyard birding, photos. www.birdsandblooms.com editors@birdsandblooms.com

Coastal Living 2100 Lakeshore Dr Birmingham AL 35209 **Phn:** 205-445-6000 **Fax** 205-445-6700 Jennifer Slaton. 10-issue magazine. TH:@coastalliving
3,800,000 to readers interested U.S. coastal (ocean & lakeside) house decor, gardening, recipes, travel. www.coastalliving.com jennifer_slaton@timeinc.com

Cottages & Bungalows 22840 Savi Ranch Pkwy Ste 200 Yorba Linda CA 92887 **Phn:** 714-939-9991 **Fax** 714-939-9909 APG Media. 10-issue magazine.
54,000 to cottage decor enthusiasts, owners of small historic homes, restoration articles. www.cottagesandbungalowsmag.com jtorres@beckett.com

Country Living Birmingham AL **Phn:** Rachel Hardage Barrett. Hearst Corp. Monthly magazine. TH:@CountryLiving
1,626,000 to city & suburban readers interested in country style home decor & renovations. www.countryliving.com countryliving@hearst.com

Country Sampler 707 Kautz Rd Saint Charles IL 60174 **Phn:** 630-377-8000 **Fax** 630-377-8194 Donna Marcel. DRG/Annie's. Bimonthly magazine.
300,000 to readers interested in antique and country-style decor editorial and catalog content. www.countrysampler.com editors@countrysampler.com

Dwell 550 Kearny St Ste 710 San Francisco CA 94108 **Phn:** 415-373-5100 **Fax** 415-373-5181 Diana Budds. 10-issue magazine. TH:@DianaBudds
325,000 to young affluent readers interested in modern design and architecture. www.dwell.com diana@dwell.com

Electronic House 111 Speen St Ste 200 Framingham MA 01701 **Phn:** 508-663-1500 **Fax** 508-663-1599 Arlen Schweiger. EH Publishing Network. 10-issue magazine.
79,900 to homeowners interested in home theater, networking, audio, wiring, wireless systems. www.electronichouse.com aschweiger@ehpub.com

Elle Decor 1271 Ave of the Americas Fl 41 New York NY 10020 **Phn:** 212-767-5830 **Fax** 212-489-4241 Michael Boodro. Hearst Corp. 10-issue magazine.
573,000 to affluent readers interested in design resources, decorator & designer profiles, showroom info. www.elledecor.com elledecor@hearst.com

Family Handyman 2915 Commers Dr Ste 700 Eagan MN 55121 **Phn:** 651-454-9200 **Fax** 651-994-2250 Ken Collier. 10-issue magazine.
1,184,900 to homeowners interested in improving, maintaining, repairing their homes. www.familyhandyman.com editors@thefamilyhandyman.com

HGTV Magazine 300 W 57th St New York NY 10019 **Phn:** 212-903-5000 Sara Peterson. Hearst Corp. 10-issue magazine. TH:@HGTVMagSara
700,000 to readers interested in home décor, organizing, gardening ideas inspired by HGTV show personalities & concepts. www.hgtv.com hgtvmagazine@hearst.com

House Beautiful 300 W 57th St Fl 24 New York NY 10019 **Phn:** 212-903-5000 Shax Riegler. Hearst Corp. Monthly magazine. TH:@ShaxRiegler
873,300 to affluent readers interested in interior design, antiques, food, entertaining. www.housebeautiful.com sriegler@hearst.com

Living the Country Life 1716 Locust St Des Moines IA 50309 **Phn:** 515-284-3000 **Fax** 515-284-3264 Betsy Freese. Meredith Corp. Bimo. magazine.
20,000 covers lifestyle issues for affluent ruralpolitans, upscale consumers living in rural areas. www.livingthecountrylife.com staff@livingthecountrylife.com

Log Home Living 4125 Lafayette Center Dr Ste 100 Chantilly VA 20151 **Phn:** 703-222-9411 **Fax** 703-222-3209 Roland Sweet. Monthly.
114,300 to those readers who are planning, building or living in log homes. www.loghome.com rsweet@homebuyerpubs.com

Martha Stewart Living 11 W 42nd St New York NY 10036 **Phn:** 212-827-8000 **Fax** 212-827-8194 Eric Pike. Monthly magazine. TH:@MS_Living
2,000,000 to women interested in improving homes by gardening, renovating, cooking, collecting. www.marthastewart.com eapike@marthastewart.com

Metropolis Magazine 61 W 23rd St Fl 4 New York NY 10010 **Phn:** 212-627-9977 **Fax** 212-627-9988 Susan S. Szenasy. 11-issue magazine.
61,000 to readers interested in design, architecture, product design, urban preservation. www.metropolismag.com edit@metropolismag.com

Mother Earth Living 1503 SW 42nd St Topeka KS 66609 **Phn:** 785-274-4300 **Fax** 785-274-4305 Jessica Kellner. Ogden Publications. Bimonthly magazine. TH:@mthrearthliving
286,000 to readers interested in earth-friendly home décor & cooking, sustainable living, natural remedies. www.motherearthliving.com editor@motherearthliving.com

Mountain Living 1777 S Harrison St Ste 903 Denver CO 80210 **Phn:** 303-248-2060 **Fax** 303-248-2064 Christine DeOrio. Network Communications. 7-issues.
50,700 to affluent readers who live, visit, and dream of being in the mountains. www.mountainliving.com cdeorio@mountainliving.com

Home & Garden .69a

New York Spaces 1440 Broadway Ste 501 New York NY 10018 **Phn:** 212-315-0800 **Fax** 212-271-2239 Jason Kronos. Davler Media Group. 9-issue magazine. TH:@nyspacesmag
56,000 to metro NY area readers interested in photo features of luxurious area homes, where to purchase high-end home goods. www.newyorkspacesmag.com jkontos@davlermedia.com

Ocean Home 300 Brickstone Sq Ste 904 Andover MA 01810 **Phn:** 978-623-8020 **Fax** 978-824-3975 RMS Media Group. TH:@oceanhomemag
54,700 to affluent luxury oceanfront property, estate, island owners and oceanfront home buyers. oceanhomemag.com editor@oceanhomemag.com

Old House Journal 4125 Lafayette Center Dr Ste 100 Chantilly VA 20151 **Phn:** 703-222-9411 **Fax** 703-222-3209 Demetra Aposporos. Active Interest Media. Bimonthly.
103,700 to readers interested in restoring houses built prior to 1960. www.oldhousejournal.com daposporos@homebuyerpubs.com

Phoenix Home & Garden 15169 N Scottsdale Rd Ste 310 Scottsdale AZ 85254 **Phn:** 480-664-3960 **Fax** 480-664-3961 Linda Barkman. Monthly.
100,000 to affluent readers interested in Southwest style decor, homes, food, entertaining. www.phgmag.com lbarkman@citieswestpub.com

Pool & Spa Living 880 Louis Dr Warminster PA 18974 **Phn:** 215-259-1700 **Fax** 215-259-0295 Debra Maurer. Online only. TH:@PoolSpaOutdoor
to pool and spa owners interested in selection, financing, pool and spa accessories. www.poolspaoutdoor.com dmaurer@poolspaliving.com

Romantic Homes 2400 E Katella Ave Ste 300 Anaheim CA 92806 **Phn:** 714-939-9991 **Fax** 714-939-9909 Jacqueline deMontravel. Beckett Media. Monthly mag.
78,000 to women interested in casually elegant home decor, how-to's, remodeling, gardening. www.romantichomes.com

San Diego Home/Garden Lifestyles PO Box 719001 San Diego CA 92171 **Phn:** 858-571-0529 **Fax** 858-634-4413 Eva Ditler. Monthly.
40,400 to readers interested in San Diego area notable homes, decorators, fine stores, restaurants. www.sdhg.net ditler@sdhg.net

Signature Kitchens & Baths 1909 Woodall Rodgers Fwy Ste 300 Dallas TX 75201 **Phn:** 214-525-6700 **Fax** 214-525-6795 Haley Owens. Bimonthly magazine.
110,000 to affluent homeowners seeking creative designs for their kitchen or bath spaces. signaturekitchensandbaths.com haley.owens@gmail.com

Southern Living 2100 Lakeshore Dr Birmingham AL 35209 **Phn:** 205-445-6000 **Fax** 205-445-6700 M. Lindsay Bierman. 13-issue magazine.
2,824,100 to readers interested in southern U.S. homes, gardens, food, travel. www.southernliving.com sl_online@timeinc.com

Sunset Magazine 80 Willow Rd Menlo Park CA 94025 **Phn:** 650-321-3600 **Fax** 650-327-7537 Peggy Northrop. Monthly magazine.
1,300,000 to readers in 13 western states interested in home improvements, gardening, food, travel. www.sunset.com northropp@sunset.com

This Old House 135 W 50th St Fl 10 New York NY 10020 **Phn:** 212-522-9465 **Fax** 212-522-9435 Scott Omelianuk. Time4 Media. 10-issue magazine.
959,100 to home renovation enthusiasts interested in landscaping, plumbing, carpentry. www.thisoldhouse.com/toh/ online_editor@thisoldhouse.com

Traditional Home 1716 Locust St Des Moines IA 50309 **Phn:** 515-284-3000 **Fax** 515-284-2083 Marsha Raisch. Meredith Corp. 8-issue magazine.
850,000 to readers interested in classic American-style architecture, interiors, gardens. www.traditionalhome.com marsha.raisch@meredith.com

Unique Homes 327 Wall St Princeton NJ 08540 **Phn:** 609-688-1110 Kathleen Russell. Bimonthly.
45,000 to readers interested in luxury real estate, architecture & landscaping; emerging markets. www.uniquehomes.com krussell@uniquehomes.com

Veranda 300 W 57th St New York NY 10019 **Phn:** 212-649-2000 Clinton Smith. Hearst Corp. Bimnthly magazine. TH:@VERANDAmag
440,000 to readers interested in high-end, one-of-a-kind home decor, accessories, gardens, luxury goods, travel. www.veranda.com

Victorian Homes 2400 E Katella Ave Ste 300 Anaheim CA 92806 **Phn:** 714-939-9991 **Fax** 714-939-9909 Meryl Schoenbaum. Beckett Media. Bimonthly.
41,700 to readers interested in Victorian-style restoration, decoration, products. www.victorianhomesmag.com

Women's Interest .69b

Allure 4 Times Sq New York NY 10036 **Phn:** 212-286-7441 **Fax** 212-286-2690 Kristin Perrotta. Conde Nast. Monthly magazine.
1,091,000 to women interested in cosmetics, skin care, fashion, hair care, fitness. www.allure.com kristin_perrotta@condenast.com

Audrey 17000 S Vermont Ave Ste A Gardena CA 90247 **Phn:** 310-769-4913 **Fax** 310-769-4903 Anna Park. Bimonthly magazine.
10,000 to Asian-American women interested in fashion, beauty, decor, relationships, careers. audreymagazine.com anna@audreymagazine.com

Bridal Guide 330 7th Ave Fl 10 New York NY 10001 **Phn:** 212-838-7733 **Fax** 212-308-7165 Amy Morgan. Bimonthly.
173,200 to brides-to-be interested in wedding fashions, beauty, decor, etiquette. www.bridalguide.com editorial@bridalguide.com

Brides Magazine 750 3rd Ave New York NY 10017 **Phn:** 212-286-2860 **Fax** 212-286-5535 Keija Minor. Fairchild Publs. Bimonthly magazine.
360,800 to brides-to-be interested in weddings, honeymoons, homes, finances, trousseaus. www.brides.com keija_minor@condenast.com

Bust PO Box 1016 Cooper Stn New York NY 10276 **Phn:** 212-675-1707 Debbie Stoller. Bimonthly magazine. TH:@bust_magazine
100,000 to young women interested in pop culture, arts, fashion, books, entertainment, sex, feminist topics. www.bust.com debbie@bust.com

Cosmopolitan 300 W 57th St New York NY 10019 **Phn:** 212-649-3570 Marina Khidekel. Hearst Corp. Monthly magazine.
3,000,000 to young women interested in dating, sex, celebrities, beauty, career, fitness. www.cosmopolitan.com mkhidekel@hearst.com

Elle 1633 Broadway New York NY 10019 **Phn:** 212-767-5800 Roberta Meyers. Hearst Corp. Monthly magazine.
1,125,000 to style-conscious women interested in fashion, beauty, food, shopping. www.elle.com awelch@hearst.com

Family Circle 375 Lexington Ave Bsmt 3 New York NY 10017 **Phn:** 212-499-2000 **Fax** 212-499-1987 Linda Fears. 15-issue magazine.
4,000,000 to women interested in self improvement, health, decorating, finance, food. www.familycircle.com linda.fears@meredith.com

First For Women 270 Sylvan Ave Ste 210 Englewood Cliffs NJ 07632 **Phn:** 201-569-6699 **Fax** 201-569-6264 Carol Brooks. Bauer Publishing. 17-issue magazine.
1,200,000 to women 30+ interested in family, recipes, health, home decorating, appearance.
www.myfirstforwomen.com
cbrooks@bauerpublishing.com

Foam 1309 Pico Ave Suite E Santa Monica CA 90405 **Phn:** 617-706-9110 **Fax** 617-536-0102 Sari Tuschman. Madavor Media. Bimonthly magazine. TH:@FoamMag
100,000 to young women interested in travel, celebrities, fashion, designers, careers, music, sports.
www.foammagazine.com
stuschman@foammagazine.com

FOAM Magazine 1309 Pico Ave Ste E Santa Monica CA 90405 **Phn:** 424-238-5394 **Fax** 617-536-0102 Sari Tuschman. Madavor Media. Bimonthly. TH:@sarituschmanLA
70,000 Features fashion, ocean, art and music (FOAM) for girls who love the beach. foammagazine.com
editorial@foammagazine.com

Glamour 4 Times Sq New York NY 10036 **Phn:** 212-286-2860 **Fax** 212-286-8336 Robert Campos. Conde Nast. Monthly magazine.
2,301,700 to young women interested in beauty, fashion, health, travel, dating. www.glamour.com

Good Housekeeping 300 W 57th St New York NY 10019 **Phn:** 212-649-2200 **Fax** 212-649-2340 Sarah Scrymser. Hearst Corp. Monthly magazine. TH:@GHrosemary
4,741,400 to women interested in homemaking, child care, family issues, personal stories.
www.goodhousekeeping.com sscrymser@hearst.com

InStyle 1271 Avenue Of The Americas Fl 26 New York NY 10020 **Phn:** 212-522-4455 **Fax** 212-522-0867 Ariel Foxman. Time, Inc. Monthly magazine.
1,780,700 to women interested in lifestyles of celebrities and their families. www.instyle.com/instyle/letters@instylemag.com

Ladies' Home Journal 125 Park Ave Fl 20 New York NY 10017 **Phn:** 212-499-2003 **Fax** 212-455-1212 Kathleen Krems. Meredith Corp. 11-issue magazine.
11,000,000 to women interested in parenting, home decor, food, self-help articles, fashion. www.lhj.com
kathleen.krems@meredith.com

Latina Style 106 E Broad St # B Falls Church VA 22046 **Phn:** 703-531-1424 **Fax** 703-312-7062 Robert Bard. Bimonthly. TH:@LATINAStyleMag
150,000 to professional Latinas interested in career & investment advice, business news, technology reviews.
www.latinastyle.com editor@latinastyle.com

Lucky 4 Times Sq Bsmt C1B New York NY 10036 **Phn:** 212-286-7528 **Fax** 212-286-4986 Eva Chen. Conde Nast. Monthly magazine. TH:@evachen212
1,100,000 to women interested in shopping resources for clothing, home, beauty products.
www.luckymag.com eva_chen@condenast.com

Marie Claire 300 W 57th St Fl 34 New York NY 10019 **Phn:** 212-903-5000 Riza Cruz. Hearst Corp. Monthly.
982,000 American version of the French fashion and beauty publication. www.marieclaire.com
rizacruz@hearst.com

Martha Stewart Weddings 11 W 42nd St New York NY 10036 **Phn:** 212-827-8000 **Fax** 212-827-8194 Eleni Gage. 6-issue magazine. TH:@elenigage
257,700 to women planning weddings and interested in jewelry, dresses, cakes, entertainment, honeymoon destinations. www.marthastewart.com
egage@marthastewart.com

More 375 Lexington Ave Bsmt 3 New York NY 10017 **Phn:** 212-499-2000 **Fax** 212-455-1244 Lesley Jane Seymour. Meredith Corp. 10-issue magazine.
1,300,000 to sophisticated women age 40+ interested in style, money, travel, home, family. www.more.com
more@meredith.com

Women's Interest .69b

Ms. 433 S Beverly Dr Beverly Hills CA 90212 **Phn:** 310-556-2515 **Fax** 310-556-2514 Michele Kort. Feminist Majority Fndtn. Quarterly magazine.
110,000 to women interested in feminism, its relation to current events, workplace, health.
www.msmagazine.com mkort@msmagazine.com

Nylon 110 Greene St Ste 607 New York NY 10012 **Phn:** 212-226-6454 **Fax** 212-226-7738 Ashley Baker. 10-issue magazine.
198,000 to young women interested in trendsetting fashion, beauty, celebrity interviews.
www.nylonmag.com ashley@nylonmag.com

O, The Oprah Magazine 300 W 57th St Fl 34 New York NY 10019 **Phn:** 212-903-5366 **Fax** 212-903-5388 Lucy Kaylin. Hearst Corp. Monthly magazine.
2,436,700 to women interested Oprah Winfrey's vision of personal growth, health, careers. www.oprah.com
lkaylin@hearst.com

Pageantry PO Box 160307 Altamonte Springs FL 32716 **Phn:** 407-260-2262 **Fax** 407-260-5131 Ashley Burns. Quarterly magazine.
50,000 to women interested in beauty pageants contestants, results, model training, pageant fashion.
www.pageantrymagazine.com
editor@pageantrymag.com

Real Simple 1271 Avenue Of The Americas, 9th Fl New York NY 10020 **Phn:** 212-522-1212 **Fax** 212-467-1584 Kristin van Ogtrop. Time, Inc. Monthly magazine.
1,950,000 to women interested in simplifying & enjoying home, career, family. www.realsimple.com
letters@realsimple.com

Self 4 Times Sq New York NY 10036 **Phn:** 212-286-2860 **Fax** 212-286-7704 Lucy Danziger. Conde Nast. Monthly magazine.
1,500,000 to young women interested in style trends, exercise, nutrition, relationships, fashion. www.self.com
letters@self.com

Soap Opera Digest 4 New York Plz New York NY 10004 **Phn:** 212-545-4800 Stephanie Sloane. American Media. Weekly magazine.
500,000 to women interested in plots, personalities, stars acting in soap operas.
www.soapoperadigest.com ssloane@amilink.com

Southern Lady 1900 International Park Dr Ste 50 Birmingham AL 35243 **Phn:** 205-995-8860 **Fax** 205-991-0071 Ande Fanning. Hoffman Media. Bimonthly magazine.
100,000 to women interested in traditional Southern U.S. lifestyle, culture, entertaining, recipes.
www.southernladymagazine.com
bgoff@hoffmanmedia.com

Today's Chicago Woman 150 E Huron St Ste 1001 Chicago IL 60611 **Phn:** 312-951-7600 **Fax** 312-951-9083 Carrie Williams. Monthly magazine. TH:@TCWmag
50,000 to Chicago-area professional women interested in careers, finance, fitness, fashion, events.
www.tcwmag.com cwilliams@tcwmag.com

Vogue 4 Times Sq New York NY 10036 **Phn:** 212-286-2860 **Fax** 212-286-6878 Eve MacSweeney. Conde Nast. Monthly magazine. TH:@voguemagazine
1,301,600 to women interested in fashion, style, world affairs, health and wellness. www.vogue.com
eve_macsweeney@vogue.com

W 750 3rd Ave New York NY 10017 **Phn:** 212-630-4000 **Fax** 212-630-3566 Jamie Rosen. Conde Nast. Monthly magazine.
470,000 to women interested in insider view of fashion, affluent lifestyle, beauty, society. www.wmagazine.com
wcomments@condenast.com

Woman's Day 1271 Ave of the Americas New York NY 10020 **Phn:** 212-767-6000 **Fax** 212-767-5610 Sara Lyle. Hearst Corp. Monthly magazine.
4,000,000 to women interested in health, fashion, family, fitness, decorating, gardening.
www.womansday.com slyle@hearst.com

Woman's World 270 Sylvan Ave Englewood Cliffs NJ 07632 **Phn:** 201-569-6699 **Fax** 201-569-3584 Stephanie Saible. Bauer Publishing. Weekly magazine.
1,600,000 to women interested in food, fashion, parenting, true-life features, crafts.
winit.womansworldmag.com
dearww@bauerpublishing.com

Women's Health 33 E Minor St Emmaus PA 18098 **Phn:** 610-967-5171 **Fax** 610-967-7725 Amy Kelly Laird. Rodale Press. 10-issue magazine. TH:@WomensHealthMag
1,500,000 to women interested in fitness, health, nutrition, fashion, relationships.
www.womenshealthmag.com amy.laird@rodale.com

Working Mother 2 Park Ave Fl 10 New York NY 10016 **Phn:** 212-779-5000 **Fax** 212-779-5200 Irene Chang. Bonnier Corp. 6-issue magazine.
750,000 to working mothers at home, in the community, bridging parenting and lifestyle.
www.workingmother.com
irene.chang@workingmother.com

Men's Interest .69c

Cigar Aficionado 387 Park Ave S Fl 8 New York NY 10016 **Phn:** 212-684-4224 **Fax** 212-684-5424 Gordon Mott. M. Shanken Comms. Bimonthly magazine.
260,100 to affluent men interested in fine cigars, dining, sports, travel, fashion.
www.cigaraficionado.com caonline@mshanken.com

Cigar Smoker Magazine PO Box 2323 Glen Ellyn IL 60138 **Phn:** 630-790-3433 **Fax** 630-790-3077 Ann Wilson. Jonathan Scott. Qu.
80,000 directory of tobacconists, cigar friendly restaurants, and parlors. www.cigarsmokermag.com
dadsmag@aol.com

Complex 40 W 23rd St Fl 2 New York NY 10010 **Phn:** 866-438-7539 Noah Callahan-Bever. Bimonthly.
3,500,000 to men interested in hip-hop artists, actors, sports stars, models, fashion, products.
www.complex.com info@complex.com

Details 4 Times Sq New York NY 10036 **Phn:** 212-286-2860 **Fax** 212-286-3005 Diane Benbasset. Conde Nast. 11-issue magazine.
458,500 to young men interested in fashion, sports, fitness, grooming, travel. www.details.com
detailsletters@condenast.com

GQ Gentlemen's Quarterly 4 Times Sq New York NY 10036 **Phn:** 212-286-2860 **Fax** 212-286-2685 Jim Nelson. Conde Nast. Monthly magazine.
1,005,000 to men interested in fashion trends, grooming, food, entertaining, technology. www.gq.com
gq100@gq.com

Inked Magazine 12 W 27th St Fl 10 New York NY 10001 **Phn:** 646-454-9192 **Fax** 646-454-1865 Rocky Rakovic. Quadra Media. 10-issue magazine.
171,000 to men interested in tattoo art, pop and music culture, celebrity interviews, photos.
www.inkedmag.com rocky@inkedmag.com

Maxim 415 Madison Ave Fl3 New York NY 10017 **Phn:** 212-302-2626 **Fax** 212-302-2635 Dan Bova. Alpha Media Group. 10-issue magazine.
2,000,000 to young men interested in fashion, cars, finance, hi-tech gadgets, dating, sex. www.maxim.com
dbova@alphamediagroup.com

Men's Fitness 4 New York Plz New York NY 10004 **Phn:** 212-545-4800 **Fax** 212-448-9890 Dean Stattmann. American Media. 10-issue magazine. TH:@MensFitness
550,000 to men interested in the active lifestyle, gear, exercise, diet, sports, relationships.
www.mensfitness.com dstattmann@mensfitness.com

Men's Health 33 E Minor St Emmaus PA 18098 **Phn:** 610-967-5171 **Fax** 610-967-7725 Bill Phillips. Rodale Press. 10-issue magazine.
1,816,700 to active men interested in fitness, sports training, nutrition, fashion, relationships.
www.menshealth.com bill.phillips@rodale.com

Men's Journal 1290 Avenue Of The Americas New York NY 10104 **Phn:** 212-484-1616 **Fax** 212-484-3433 Brad Wieners. Wenner Media, Inc. 11-issue magazine.
713,100 to men interested in participatory sports, travel, fitness, adventure, leisure time.
www.mensjournal.com letters@mensjournal.com

Nylon Guys 110 Greene St Ste 607 New York NY 10012 **Phn:** 212-226-6454 **Fax** 212-226-7738 10 issue magazine.
198,000 to young men interested in trendsetting fashion, beauty, celebrity interviews.
www.nylonguysmag.com office@nylonmag.com

Playboy 680 N Lake Shore Dr Chicago IL 60611 **Phn:** 312-751-8000 **Fax** 312-751-2818 Leopold Froehlich. Playboy Enterprises. Monthly magazine.
1,500,000 to men interested in photos of women, fashion, music, cars, celebrity interviews.
www.playboy.com/magazine/ lfroehlich@playboy.com

Popular Mechanics 300 W 57th St New York NY 10019 **Phn:** 212-649-2000 **Fax** 212-649-3742 James Meigs. Hearst Corp. Monthly magazine.
1,230,000 to men interested in home improvement, technology, electronics, car projects.
www. popularmechanics. com
pmwebmaster@hearst.com

Smoke 26 Broadway # 9M New York NY 10004 **Phn:** 212-391-2060 **Fax** 212-827-0945 Murdoch McBride. Quarterly magazine.
12,900 to affluent professionals interested in cigar smoking, travel, sports, fashion, finance.
www.smokemag.com editor@smokemag.com

Parenting & Babies .69d
Adoptive Families 39 W 37th St Fl 15 New York NY 10018 **Phn:** 646-366-0830 **Fax** 646-366-0842 Susan Caughman. New Hope Media. Bimonthly magazine.
33,900 to pre- & post-adoptive families interested in legal & policy news, parent to parent stories.
www.adoptivefamilies.com
susan@adoptivefamilies.com

American Baby 375 Lexington Ave New York NY 10017 **Phn:** 212-499-2000 **Fax** 212-499-1590 Meredith Corp. Monthly magazine.
1,600,000 to expectant & new parents interested in pregnancy, baby care, health & development.
www.parents.com/american-baby-magazine/

Atlanta Parent 2346 Perimeter Park Dr Ste 101 Atlanta GA 30341 **Phn:** 770-454-7599 **Fax** 770-454-7699 Kate Parrott. Monthly.
109,900 to Atlanta, GA area families interested in activities, camps, schools, parenting articles.
www.atlantaparent.com editor@atlantaparent.com

Autism Asperger's Digest PO Box 2257 Burlington NC 27216 **Phn:** 336-222-0442 Kim Fields. 6 issues.
5,000 covers behavior problems, reinforcement, motor skills, social skills, curriculum planning, teaching.
www.autismdigest.com kfields@autismdigest.com

Boston Parents' Paper 639 Granite St Ste 25 Braintree MA 02184 **Phn:** 617-522-1515 **Fax** 617-522-1694 Diedre Wilson. Monthly.
71,400 to Boston area parents interested in activities, schools, camps, events. boston.parenthood.com deirdre.wilson@parenthood.com

Chicago Parent 141 S Oak Park Ave Oak Park IL 60302 **Phn:** 708-386-5555 Tamara O'Shaughnessy. Monthly.
121,100 www.chicagoparent.com
chiparent@chicagoparent.com

Cincinnati Parent 9435 Waterstone Blvd Ste 140 Cincinnati OH 45249 **Phn:** 513-443-2015 **Fax** 317-722-8510 Megan Kirschner. Midwest Parenting Publications. Monthly.
47,000 to area parents, child caregivers interested in activities and resources. www.cincinnatiparent.com editor@cincinnatiparent.com

Men's Interest .69c
Curious Parents 2345 Bethel Ave Merchantville NJ 08109 **Phn:** 856-608-8700 **Fax** 856-608-1902 Monthly magazine.
120,000 in 3 editions covering NJ and PA to parents interested in resources, events.
www.curiousparents.com editor@curiousparents.com

Fit Pregnancy 21100 Erwin St Woodland Hills CA 91367 **Phn:** 818-884-6800 **Fax** 818-992-6895 Laura Kalehoff. American Media. Bimonthly. TH:@fitpregnancy
500,000 to readers interested in pregnancy nutrition, exercise, food, fashion & beauty editorial.
www.fitpregnancy.com lkalehoff@amilink.com

Gifted Child Quarterly 2455 Teller Rd Thousand Oaks CA 91320 **Phn:** 805-499-0721 **Fax** 805-499-8096 D. Betsy McCoach. Sage Pubs. Quarterly.
35,000 covers creative insight, giftedness and talent development in the school, home, society.
gcq.sagepub.com gcquarterly@uconn.edu

Indy's Child Parenting Magazine 921 E 86th St Ste 130 Indianapolis IN 46240 **Phn:** 317-722-8500 **Fax** 317-722-8510 Megan Kirschner. Midwest Parenting Publications. Monthly.
50,000 to area parents, educators, child caregivers interested in arts, camps, activities, health, schools.
www.indyschild.com editor@indyschild.com

Metro Parent 22041 Woodward Ave Ferndale MI 48220 **Phn:** 248-398-3400 **Fax** 248-399-4215 Julia Elliott. Monthly.
59,300 to Detroit-area families with children interested in local activities and events. www.metroparent.com jelliott@metroparent.com

MetroKids 1412 Pine St 1414 Philadelphia PA 19102 **Phn:** 215-291-5560 **Fax** 215-291-5563 Tom Livingston. Monthly tabloid.
130,000 in 3 editions -- PA, south NJ, DE -- to parents interested in recreational & educational activities.
www.metrokids.com editor@metrokids.com

Mothering PO Box 1690 Santa Fe NM 87504 **Phn:** 505-984-8116 **Fax** 505-986-8335 Peggy O'Mara. Bimonthly magazine.
85,000 to parents interested in attachment parenting, homeschooling, organic food, alternative medicine.
www.mothering.com peggyo@mothering.com

NY Metro Parents 1440 Broadway Ste 501 New York NY 10018 **Phn:** 212-315-0800 Dawn Roode. Davler Media Group. Monthly.
224,000 in 8 NY-area editions to parents interested in activities for children. www.nymetroparents.com droode@davlermedia.com

Parents Magazine 375 Lexington Ave New York NY 10017 **Phn:** 212-499-2000 **Fax** 212-499-2083 Jessica Wohlgemuth. Meredith Corp. Monthly magazine.
2,204,000 to parents interested in all aspects of raising happy, healthy children.
www.parents.com/common/magazine/
jessie.wohlgemuth@meredith.com

Scholastic Parent & Child 557 Broadway New York NY 10012 **Phn:** 212-343-6100 **Fax** 212-343-6945 Elizabeth Anne Shaw. Scholastic. 88-issue magazine. TH:@elizanneshaw
7,344,000 to parents of 0-12 year old children interested in family activities, child development, food, travel, health.
www.scholastic.com/parents/resources/collection/parent-child-magazine eshaw@scholastic.com

Children & Teens .69e
Boys' Life 1325 W Walnut Hill Ln Irving TX 75038 **Phn:** 972-580-2000 **Fax** 972-580-2079 Mike Goldman. Boy Scouts of America. Monthly magazine.
1,122,000 to Boy Scouts, other boys ages 6-17 interested in sports, outdoors, hobbies, history.
boyslife.org mike.goldman@scouting.org

Discovery Girls PO Box 110760 Campbell CA 95011 **Phn:** 408-554-0081 **Fax** 408-554-0085 Bimonthly magazine.
207,000 for girls 7-12 with articles ranging from fashion to technology and more. www.discoverygirls.com

Girls' Life 4529 Harford Rd Baltimore MD 21214 **Phn:** 410-426-9600 **Fax** 410-254-0991 Karen Bokram. Bimonthly.
400,000 to girls ages 10-15 interested in friendships, improvement, fashions, music, health, fitness.
www.girlslife.com trish@girlslife.com

J-14 Magazine 270 Sylvan Ave Englewood Cliffs NJ 07632 **Phn:** 201-569-6699 **Fax** 201-569-5503 Molly MacDermot. Bauer Publishing. 10-issues.
402,000 comprehensive celebrity and entertainment news magazine for the teen market today. www.j-14.com

Junior Scholastic 557 Broadway New York NY 10012 **Phn:** 212-343-6100 **Fax** 212-343-6945 Suzanne McCabe. Scholastic. 18-issue magazine.
535,000 to students ages 11-14 interested in current events, world cultures, US history. www.scholastic.com junior@scholastic.com

Justine 6263 Poplar Ave Ste 1154 Memphis TN 38119 **Phn:** 901-761-2845 **Fax** 901-761-2855 Jana Kerr Pettey. Bimonthly magazine.
252,000 coverss style, fashion, beauty in a realistic way, devoid of mixed messages. justinemagazine.com jpetty@justinemagazine.com

M Magazine 270 Sylvan Ave Englewood Cliffs NJ 07632 **Phn:** 201-569-6699 **Fax** 201-567-1901 Jacqueline Fulton. Bauer Publishing. 10-issue magazine.
225,000 to girls ages 8-14 interested in celebrities, pop music, fashion, quizzes, horoscopes. www.mmm-mag.com jfulton@bauerpublishing.com

National Geographic Kids 1145 17th St NW Washington DC 20036 **Phn:** 202-828-6651 **Fax** 202-775-6112 Melina G. Bellows. 10-issue magazine.
1,351,300 to 6-14 year olds interested in animals, science, technology, environment.
kids.nationalgeographic.com/kids/ mbellows@ngs.org

NextStepU 2 W Main St Ste 200 Victor NY 14564 **Phn:** 585-742-1260 **Fax** 585-742-1263 Diana Fisher. 5-issue magazine.
306,600 to high school students interested in college, technical school, military, life skills, career choices, financing. www.nextstepu.com diana@nextstepu.com

Scouting 1325 W Walnut Hill Ln Irving TX 75038 **Phn:** 972-580-2367 **Fax** 972-580-2079 Scott Daniels. Boy Scouts of America. 5-issue magazine.
1,000,000 to Boy Scouts of America adult volunteers interested in programs and activities.
scoutingmagazine.org scott.daniels@scouting.org

Seventeen 300 W 57th St New York NY 10019 **Phn:** 212-649-3100 Bethany Heitman. Hearst Corp. Monthly magazine.
2,052,660 to teenage girls interested in fashion, beauty, dating, college. www.seventeen.com bheitman@hearst.com

Sports Illustrated For Kids 1271 Avenue Of The Americas New York NY 10020 **Phn:** 212-522-1212 **Fax** 212-467-4695 Bob Der. Time, Inc. Monthly.
1,004,200 to 8-15 year olds interested in athletes, teams, sports cards, posters, video games.
www.sikids.com sikids_inbox@sikids.com

Teen Vogue 4 Times Sq New York NY 10036 **Phn:** 212-286-2860 Amy Astley. Conde Nast. 10-issue magazine.
1,005,430 to sophisticated teenage girls interested in fashion, beauty, decor, celebrities.
www.teenvogue.com amy_astley@condenast.com

Regional Interest .69f
Adirondack Life PO Box 410 Jay NY 12941 **Phn:** 518-946-2191 **Fax** 518-946-7461 Annie Stoltie. 8-issue magazine.
43,100 to readers interested in Adirondack Park (NY) regional issues and trends. www.adirondacklife.com aledit@adirondacklife.com

Regional Interest .69f

Alaska 301 Arctic Slope Ave Ste 300 Anchorage AK 99518 **Phn:** 907-272-6070 **Fax** 907-258-5360 Debbie Cutler. Morris Comms. 10-issue magazine.
140,900 to resident/tourist public interested in last-frontier life, natural resources, diversion.
www.alaskamagazine.com
debbie.cutler@alaskamagazine.com

Ann Arbor Observer 201 Catherine St Ann Arbor MI 48104 **Phn:** 734-769-3175 **Fax** 734-769-3375 John Hilton. Monthly.
60,000 to area residents & visitors interested in restaurants, events, news. annarborobserver.com
editor@arborweb.com

Arizona Foothills 8132 N 87th Pl Scottsdale AZ 85258 **Phn:** 480-460-5203 **Fax** 480-443-1517 Michael Dee. Monthly magazine.
57,900 to readers interested in leisure and cultural aspects of desert Foothills communities.
www.arizonafoothillsmagazine.com
publisher@mediathatdeelivers.com

Aspen Magazine PO Box 4577 Aspen CO 81612 **Phn:** 970-300-3071 Alan Klein. Bimonthly. TH:@AspenMagazine
17,000 to readers interested in luxury aspects of Aspen, including real estate, restaurants, people, events. modernluxury.com/aspen
aklein@modernluxury.com

At Home in Arkansas 2207 Cottondale Ln Ste 3 Little Rock AR 72202 **Phn:** 501-666-5510 Tiffany Burgess. Network Comms. 11 issues. TH:@tiffburgess
28,500 to Arkansas residents, others interested in area home design, gardens, weddings, events, arts.
www.athomearkansas.com
tburgess@athomearkansas.com

Atlanta 260 Peachtree St NW Ste 300 Atlanta GA 30303 **Phn:** 404-527-5500 **Fax** 404-527-5585 Steve Fennessey. Emmis Comm. Grp. Monthly magazine.
69,100 to readers in metro Atlanta interested in government, education, arts, sports, home and garden.
www.atlantamagazine.com
atlantamagletters@atlantamag.emmis.com

Back Home In Kentucky PO Box 1555 Shelbyville KY 40066 **Phn:** 502-633-7766 **Fax** 502-633-7850 Bill Matthews. Quarterly magazine.
18,000 to readers interested in Kentucky's heritage, history, people and places. historickentuckyinc.com
bilmatt@aol.com

Baltimore Magazine 1000 Lancaster St Ste 400 Baltimore MD 21202 **Phn:** 410-752-4200 **Fax** 410-625-0280 Richard Basoco. Monthly.
53,100 to readers interested in Baltimore metro area people, events, restaurants, entertainment.
www.baltimoremagazine.net
bdick@baltimoremagazine.net

Big River PO Box 204 Winona MN 55987 **Phn:** 507-454-5949 Reggie McLeod. Open River Press. Bimonthly.
4,500 Provides articles on the history, ecology and wildlife along the upper Mississippi.
bigrivermagazine.com editors@bigrivermagazine.com

Birmingham 2201 4th Ave N Birmingham AL 35203 **Phn:** 205-241-8180 **Fax** 205-324-2847 Julie Keith. Monthly.
19,200 to readers interested in area restaurants, personalities, events, cultural event.
www.bhammag.com jkeith@bhammag.com

Boca Life 800 E Broward Blvd Ste 506 Ft Lauderdale FL 33301 **Phn:** 954-462-4488 **Fax** 954-462-5588 Nila Do. Gulfstream Media. 10-issues.
24,900 covers arts, economy, real estate, sports, food, fashion, shopping, real estate.
www.gulfstreammediagroup.com
nila@gulfstreammediagroup.com

Boca Raton 5455 N Federal Hwy Ste M Boca Raton FL 33487 **Phn:** 561-997-8683 **Fax** 561-997-8909 Kevin Kaminski. 7-issue magazine.
22,900 to readers interested in Boca area restaurants, cultural events, shopping, real estate.
www.bocamag.com kevin@bocamag.com

Boston 300 Massachusetts Ave Boston MA 02115 **Phn:** 617-262-9700 **Fax** 617-267-1774 John Wolfson. Monthly.
94,300 to readers interested in local trends, business, economy, events, investigative reporting.
www.bostonmagazine.com
jwolfson@bostonmagazine.com

Cape Cod Life PO Box 1439 Mashpee MA 02649 **Phn:** 508-419-7381 **Fax** 508-477-1225 Susan Dewey. 8-issue magazine.
37,400 to readers interested in Cape Cod events, environmental issues, restaurants, shopping, real estate. capecodlife.com sdewey@capecodlife.com

Charleston Magazine PO Box 1794 Mount Pleasant SC 29465 **Phn:** 843-971-9811 **Fax** 843-971-0121 Darcy Shankland. 10-issue magazine.
26,300 to residents & visitors interested in cultural events, dining, shopping, social news.
www.charlestonmag.com
dshankland@charlestonmag.com

Charlotte Magazine 309 E Morehead St Ste 50 Charlotte NC 28202 **Phn:** 704-335-7181 **Fax** 704-335-3757 Richard Thurmond. Morris Communications. Monthly.
38,000 features on sports, art, entertainment, politics, fashion, business and education.
www.charlottemagazine.com
richard.thurmond@morris.com

Chicago 435 N Michigan Ave Ste 1100 Chicago IL 60611 **Phn:** 312-222-8999 **Fax** 312-222-0699 Elizabeth Fenner. Chicago Tribune. Monthly magazine.
150,000 to readers interested in Chicago's culture, dining, local personalities. www.chicagomag.com
bfenner@chicagomag.com

Cincinnati Magazine 441 Vine St Ste 200 Cincinnati OH 45202 **Phn:** 513-421-4300 **Fax** 513-562-2746 Jay Stowe. Monthly magazine.
41,700 to readers interested in Cincinnati area events, dining, places, attractions.
www.cincinnatimagazine.com
linda@cincinnatimagazine.com

Cleveland 1422 Euclid Ave Ste 730 Cleveland OH 44115 **Phn:** 216-771-2833 **Fax** 216-781-6318 Steve Gleydura. Great Lakes Pub. Co. Monthly magazine.
43,700 to readers interested in northeast Ohio's people, issues, nightlife, events.
www.clevelandmagazine.com
editorial@clevelandmagazine.com

Coast Magazine 625 N Grand Ave Fl 2 Santa Ana CA 92701 **Phn:** 949-644-4700 **Fax** 714-796-6781 Justine Amodeo. Monthly.
49,400 to affluent Orange County, CA residents interested in arts, fashion, real estate.
www.coastmagazine.com coast@coastmagazine.com

Colorado Expression 3600 S Beeler St Ste 100 Denver CO 80237 **Phn:** 303-694-1289 **Fax** 303-694-6939 Terry Vitale. Bimonthly.
25,000 to affluent readers interested in society news & parties, real estate, dining.
www.coloradoexpression.com
info@coloradoexpression.com

Colorado Homes & Lifestyles 1777 S Harrison St Ste 903 Denver CO 80210 **Phn:** 303-248-2060 **Fax** 303-248-2066 Hilary Oswald. 8-issues.
32,900 covers upscale architecture, home decorating, gardening, luxury real estate.
www.coloradohomesmag.com
hoswald@coloradohomesmag.com

Columbus Monthly 34 S 3rd St Columbus OH 43215 **Phn:** 614-888-4567 **Fax** 614-461-8746 Kristen Schmidt. Monthly.
33,700 to readers interested in area lifestyle features, music, sports, cultural events.
www.columbusmonthly.com
kschmidt@columbusmonthly.com

Connecticut Magazine 40 Sargent Drive New Haven CT 06511 **Phn:** 203-789-5300 Matt DeRienzo. Monthly. TH:@mattderienzo
88,000 to CT residents interested in local politics, shopping, travel, recreation, events.
www.connecticutmag.com
editor@connecticutmag.com

D Magazine 750 N Saint Paul St Ste 2100 Dallas TX 75201 **Phn:** 214-939-3636 **Fax** 214-748-4579 Bradford Pearson Monthly magazine. TH:@BradfordPearson
58,400 to active, affluent Dallas-Ft Worth residents interested in performing arts, events, dining, local personalities. www.dmagazine.com
bradford.pearson@dmagazine.com

Delaware Today 3301 Lancaster Pike Ste 5C Wilmington DE 19805 **Phn:** 302-656-1809 **Fax** 302-656-5843 Mark Nardone. Monthly magazine.
27,300 to readers interested in statewide dining, nightlight, events, decorating, gardening.
www.delawaretoday.com
mnardone@delawaretoday.com

Down East PO Box 679 Camden ME 04843 **Phn:** 207-594-9544 **Fax** 207-594-7215 Paul Doiron. Monthly magazine.
103,700 to State of Maine residents and others interested in Maine people, events, history.
www.downeast.com editorial@downeast.com

East Bay Monthly 1301 59th St Emeryville CA 94608 **Phn:** 510-658-9811 **Fax** 510-658-9902 Sarah Weld. Monthly tabloid.
81,000 to upscale San Francisco Bay Area readers interested in politics, health, shopping, sports.
www.themonthly.com editorial@themonthly.com

Emerald Coast 1932 Miccosukee Rd Tallahassee FL 32308 **Phn:** 850-878-0554 **Fax** 850-807-5037 Zandra Wolfgram. Rowland Publishing. Bimonthly.
21,000 to affluent readers interested FL's Emerald Coast area history, lifestyle, events.
www.emeraldcoastmagazine.com
zwolfgram@rowlandpublishing.com

5280:The Denver Magazine 1515 Wazee St Ste 400 Denver CO 80202 **Phn:** 303-832-5280 **Fax** 303-832-0470 Max Potter. Monthly magazine.
85,900 to Denver residents and visitors interested in dining, arts, local new. www.5280.com
news@5280.com

Florida Monthly 999 Douglas Ave Ste 3301 Altamonte Springs FL 32714 **Phn:** 407-816-9596 **Fax** 407-816-9373 Kristen Cifers. Monthly.
213,400 to statewide audience interested in travel, retirement, events. www.floridamagazine.com
editorial@floridamagazine.com

Garden & Gun 409 King St 2nd Fl Charleston SC 29403 **Phn:** 843-795-1195 **Fax** 843-795-1512 David DiBenedetto. 6-issue magazine.
225,000 to readers interested in southern U.S. sporting culture, food, music, landscaping, conservation.
gardenandgun.com editorial@gardenandgun.com

Gentry 618 Santa Cruz Ave Menlo Park CA 94025 **Phn:** 650-324-1818 **Fax** 650-324-1888 Stefanie Beasley. Monthly.
33,800 in 2 regional Bay area editions to affluent readers interested in social, community event
www.gentrymagazine.com info@18media.com

Gold Coast Life 800 E Broward Blvd Ste 506 Ft Lauderdale FL 33301 **Phn:** 954-462-4488 **Fax** 954-462-5588 Nila Do. Gulfstream Media. 10-issues.
24,900 covers arts, economy, real estate, sports, food, fashion, shopping, real estate.
www.gulfstreammediagroup.com
nila@gulfstreammediagroup.com

Grand Rapids Magazine 549 Ottawa Ave NW Ste 201 Grand Rapids MI 49503 **Phn:** 616-459-4545 **Fax** 616-459-4800 Carole Valade Copenhaver. Monthly.
18,000 to readers interested in W. Michigan real estate, restaurants, events, features, recreation.
www.grmag.com cvalade@geminipub.com

Greenwich Magazine 205 Main St Ste 1 Westport CT 06880 **Phn:** 203-222-0600 **Fax** 203-222-0937 Ann Kaiser. Monthly magazine.
10,500 to readers interested in Greenwich, CT social events, restaurants, fashion, home & garden. www.mofflymedia.com annk@mofflymedia.com

Gulfshore Life 3560 Kraft Rd Ste 301 Naples FL 34105 **Phn:** 239-449-4111 **Fax** 239-449-4163 David Sendler. Open Sky Media. 11-issue magazine.
94,000 to readers interested in SW FL real estate, cultural events, luxury lifestyle. www.gulfshorelife.com dsendler@gulfshorelife.com

Hampton Roads 1264 Perimeter Pkwy Virginia Beach VA 23454 **Phn:** 757-422-8979 **Fax** 757-422-9092 Melissa Stewart. Vista Graphics. 8-issues.
39,900 city and lifestyle magazine that informs, enlightens and entertais its readers. www.hrmagonline.com melissa@hrmag.com

Hawai'i Magazine 1000 Bishop St Ste 405 Honolulu HI 96813 **Phn:** 808-537-9500 **Fax** 808-537-6455 Derek Paiva. Bimonthly magazine.
74,000 to readers interested in Hawaii destinations, culture, food, music, environment. www.hawaiimagazine.com derekp@hawaiimagazine.com

High Country News PO Box 1090 Paonia CO 81428 **Phn:** 970-527-4898 **Fax** 970-527-4897 Ray Ring. Biweekly magazine.
21,000 to readers interested in Rocky Mtn, Pacific NW environment, political issues, photos. www.hcn.org rayring@hcn.org

Honolulu 1000 Bishop St Ste 405 Honolulu HI 96813 **Phn:** 808-537-9500 **Fax** 808-537-6455 Michael Keany. Pacific Basin Comm. Monthly. TH:@HonoluluMag
29,200 to Hawaii residents and frequent visitors interested in state issues, trends, politics. www.honolulumagazine.com mike@pacificbasin.net

Hudson Valley 2678 South Rd Ste 202 Poughkeepsie NY 12601 **Phn:** 845-463-0542 **Fax** 845-463-1544 Olivia Abel. Monthly.
28,900 to readers interested in restaurants, travel, events in NY State's Hudson Valley region. www.hvmag.com oabel@hvmag.com

In New York 79 Madison Ave Fl 8 New York NY 10016 **Phn:** 212-716-8562 **Fax** 212-716-2786 Lois Anzelowitz. Monthly magazine.
135,100 to New York City visitors interested in attractions, dining, shopping, art, Broadway. innewyork.com lois.levine@morris.com

Indianapolis Monthly 40 Monument Cir Ste 100 Indianapolis IN 46204 **Phn:** 317-237-9288 **Fax** 317-684-2080 Amanda Heckert. Monthly.
50,000 to readers interested in area dining, nightlife, real estate, sports, events. www.indianapolismonthly.com aheckert@indymonthly.emmis.com

Inland Empire 3769 Tibbetts St Ste A Riverside CA 92506 **Phn:** 951-682-3026 **Fax** 951-682-0246 Donald Lorenzi. Monthly magazine.
34,900 to Riverside, San Bernardino, Ontario,Temecula area residents interested in lifestyle topics. www.inlandempiremagazine.com iemail@iemag.bz

Iowa Outdoors 502 E 9th St Des Moines IA 50319 **Phn:** 515-281-5918 **Fax** 515-281-6794 Alan Foster. Iowa Dept. Natural Rscs. 6-issues.
65,000 Iowa's outdoor recreation opportunities, fish, wildlife, parks, environmental issues. www.iowadnr.gov/Recreation/IowaOutdoorsMagazine alan.foster@dnr.iowa.gov

The Iowan 218 6th Ave Ste 610 Des Moines IA 50309 **Phn:** 515-246-0402 **Fax** 515-282-0125 Beth Wilson. Bimonthly.
20,500 to readers interested in State of Iowa photography, events, people. www.iowan.com editor@iowan.com

Regional Interest .69f

Jacksonville 1261 King St Jacksonville FL 32204 **Phn:** 904-389-3622 **Fax** 904-389-3628 Joseph White. Monthly.
21,500 to readers interested in area real estate, music scene, beaches, food, fashion. www.jacksonvillemag.com joe@jacksonvillemag.com

KC Magazine 7101 College Blvd Ste 400 Overland Park KS 66210 **Phn:** 913-894-6923 **Fax** 913-894-6932 Katie Van Luchene. Monthly magazine. TH:@KatieVanLuchene
29,000 to Kansas City area readers interested in events, dining, travel, arts. www.kcmag.com kvanluchene@anthempublishing.com

Kentucky Monthly PO Box 559 Frankfort KY 40602 **Phn:** 502-227-0053 **Fax** 502-227-5009 Stephen Vest. Vested Interest Pubs. 10-issue magazine.
40,000 to readers interested in Kentucky's heritage, history, people and places. www.kentuckymonthly.com steve@kentuckymonthly.com

Los Angeles Magazine 5900 Wilshire Blvd Ste 910 Los Angeles CA 90036 **Phn:** 323-801-0100 **Fax** 323-801-0105 Kari Mozena. Emmis Comm. Grp. Monthly magazine.
150,000 to readers interested in Los Angeles news, lifestyles, arts, events, personalities. www.lamag.com kmozena@lamag.com

Louisville 137 W Muhammad Ali Blvd Ste 101 Louisville KY 40202 **Phn:** 502-625-0100 **Fax** 502-625-0107 Kane Webb. Monthly. TH:@LouisvilleMag
24,000 to residents of metro Louisville interested in local and regional personalities and events. www.loumag.com kwebb@loumag.com

Madison Magazine 7025 Raymond Rd Madison WI 53719 **Phn:** 608-270-3600 **Fax** 608-270-3636 Brennan Nardi. Monthly.
19,900 to readers interested in area restaurants, gallery exhibits, cultural events, real estate, shopping. www.madisonmagazine.com bnardi@madisonmagazine.com

Memphis 460 Tennessee St Uppr Memphis TN 38103 **Phn:** 901-521-9000 **Fax** 901-521-0129 Frank Murtaugh. Monthly magazine.
20,000 to readers interested in music scene, restaurants, cultural events, shopping, real estate. www.memphismagazine.com murtaugh@memphismagazine.com

Midwest Living 1716 Locust St Des Moines IA 50309 **Phn:** 515-284-3000 **Fax** 515-284-3836 Greg Philby. Meredith Corp. Bimonthly magazine.
967,000 to Midwesterners interested in regional lifestyles, dining, homes, travel, gardening. www.midwestliving.com greg.philby@meredith.com

Milwaukee Magazine 126 N Jefferson St Ste 100 Milwaukee WI 53202 **Phn:** 414-273-1101 **Fax** 414-287-4373 Kurt Chandler. Monthly. TH:@milwaukeemag
33,500 to southeastern WI residents interested in area social, political, business, lifestyle features. www.milwaukeemag.com/Home kurt.chandler@milwaukeemag.com

Minnesota Monthly 730 2nd Ave S Ste 600 Minneapolis MN 55402 **Phn:** 612-371-5843 **Fax** 612-371-5801 Rachel Hutton. Monthly magazine. TH:@rachel_hutton
69,500 to readers interested in people, issues, travel, arts in Minnesota. www.minnesotamonthly.com rhutton@mnmo.com

Mississippi Magazine 5 Lakeland Cir Jackson MS 39216 **Phn:** 601-982-8418 **Fax** 601-982-8447 Melanie M. Ward. Bimonthly.
42,800 to readers interested in state-wide events, garden features, sports, heritage features. www.mismag.com editor@mismag.com

Missouri Life 501 High St #A Boonville MO 65233 **Phn:** 660-882-9898 **Fax** 660-882-9899 Danita Wood. Bimonthly magazine.
19,000 travel and lifestyle features focusing on arts and culture, cuisine, history. www.missourilife.com info@missourilife.com

Montana Magazine PO Box 5630 Helena MT 59604 **Phn:** 406-444-5100 **Fax** 406-443-5480 Butch Larcombe. Bimonthly magazine.
32,000 to readers interested in Montana travel, people, history, wildlife. www.montanamagazine.com editor@montanamagazine.com

Montana Outdoors PO Box 200701 Helena MT 59620 **Phn:** 406-495-3257 **Fax** 406-495-3259 Tom Dickson. MT Dept. Wildlife. Bimo.
42,000 wildlife management, environmental issues, natural history, and fisheries management. fwp.mt.gov/mtoutdoors/ tdickson@mt.gov

Mpls-St. Paul 220 S 6th St Ste 500 Minneapolis MN 55402 **Phn:** 612-339-7571 **Fax** 612-339-5806 Adam Platt. Monthly.
74,700 to Twin Cities metro area residents interested in local politics, business, lifestyle. www.mspmag.com edit@mspmag.com

Nevada Magazine 401 N Carson St Carson City NV 89701 **Phn:** 775-687-5416 **Fax** 775-687-6159 Matthew B. Brown. NV Commission on Tourism. Bimonthly.
20,000 to readers interested in statewide travel, dining, events, entertainment, history. www.nevadamagazine.com editor@nevadamagazine.com

New Hampshire Magazine 150 Dow St Ste 202 Manchester NH 03101 **Phn:** 603-624-1442 **Fax** 603-624-1310 Richard Broussard. Monthly.
23,500 to readers intersted in statewide politics, real estate, events, people, restaurants. www.nhmagazine.com editor@nhmagazine.com

New Jersey Countryside 134 S Finley Ave Basking Ridge NJ 07920 **Phn:** 908-221-1171 **Fax** 908-221-1656 Victoria Scavo. Bimonthly.
34,000 covers, food, wine, interior design, art, travel, statewide events, environment. www.njcountryside.com me@njcountryside.com

New Jersey Monthly PO Box 920 Morristown NJ 07963 **Phn:** 973-539-8230 **Fax** 973-538-2953 Ken Schlager. Monthly.
92,600 to affluent NJ residents interested in people, places and events. njmonthly.com research@njmonthly.com

New Mexico Magazine 495 Old Santa Fe Trl Santa Fe NM 87501 **Phn:** 505-827-7447 **Fax** 505-827-6496 Dave Herndon. State of NM. Monthly magazine.
100,000 to NM residents, visitors interested in state's history, architecture, recreation, scenery. www.nmmagazine.com queries@nmmagazine.com

New Orleans Magazine 110 Veterans Memorial Blvd Ste 123 Metairie LA 70005 **Phn:** 504-828-1380 **Fax** 504-828-1385 Errol Laborde. Monthly.
35,500 to readers interested in area music, musicians, chefs, restaurants, theater, social events. www.myneworleans.com errol@renpubllc.com

Newport Life 101 Malbone Rd Newport RI 02840 **Phn:** 401-841-0200 **Fax** 401-849-3335 Annie Sherman. Sherman Publishing. Bimo.
11,000 covers, food, wine, interior design, art, travel, statewide events, environment. newportlifemagazine.com magazine@newportri.com

North Shore 3701 W Lake Ave Glenview IL 60026 **Phn:** 847-486-0600 **Fax** 847-486-7427 Sherry Thomas. Monthly magazine.
51,700 to residents of Chicago's north & NW suburbs interested in arts, culture, home design, travel. www.makeitbetter.net info@makeitbetter.net

Ocean Drive 404 Washington Ave Ste 650 Miami Beach FL 33139 **Phn:** 305-532-2544 **Fax** 305-532-4366 Jared Shapiro. 10-issue magazine.
50,000 to south FL residents interested in local arts, entertainment, social events, business. oceandrive.com info@nichemediallc.com

Ohio Magazine 1422 Euclid Ave Ste 730 Cleveland OH 44115 **Phn:** 216-771-2833 **Fax** 216-781-6318 Richard Osborne. Monthly magazine.
72,600 to readers interested in statewide travel, history, food, events. www.ohiomagazine.com editorial@ohiomagazine.com

Oklahoma Magazine PO Box 14204 Tulsa OK 74159 **Phn:** 918-744-6205 **Fax** 918-748-5772 Thom Golden. Monthly magazine.
26,700 to OK residents, visitors interesting in dining, entertainment, events, business. www.okmag.com editor@okmag.com

Orange Coast Magazine 3701 Birch St Ste 100 Newport Beach CA 92660 **Phn:** 949-862-1133 **Fax** 949-862-0133 Martin Smith. Monthly.
56,500 to Orange County, CA area residents interested in celebrity profiles, dining, travel, home decor. www.orangecoast.com gespinoza@orangecoastmagazine.com

Oregon Coast 4969 Highway 101 Unit 2 Florence OR 97439 **Phn:** 541-997-8401 **Fax** 541-902-0400 Alicia Spooner. Bimonthly.
40,000 to readers interested in coastal Oregon travel, real estate, restaurants, hotels, events. www.northwestmagazines.com alicia@nwmags.com

Orlando 801 N Magnolia Ave Ste 201 Orlando FL 32803 **Phn:** 407-423-0618 **Fax** 407-237-6258 Barry Glenn. Monthly.
38,000 to readers interested in Orlando, FL area travel, destinations, dining, trends. www.orlandomagazine.com barry.glenn@orlandomagazine.com

Our Wisconsin PO Box 208 Presque Isle WI 54557 **Phn:** 414-423-3085 Mike Beno. Bimonthly magazine.
20,000 to readers interested in life in Wisconsin, photos, reader-generated content, short stories, people, events, humor. ourwisconsinmag.com editors@ourwisconsinmag.com

Palm Beach Illustrated PO Box 3344 Palm Beach FL 33480 **Phn:** 561-659-0210 **Fax** 561-659-1736 Daphne Nikolopoulos. 11-issue magazine.
37,600 to readers interested in Palm Beach area social events, fashion, resorts, luxury shopping. www.palmbeachillustrated.com info@palmbeachillustrated.com

Palm Beacher 800 E Broward Blvd Ste 506 Ft Lauderdale FL 33301 **Phn:** 954-462-4488 **Fax** 954-462-5588 Nila Do. Gulfstream Media. 10-issues.
24,900 luxury publication featuring personalities, cuisine, travel, art, homes, lifestyles. www.gulfstreammediagroup.com nila@gulfstreammediagroup.com

Palm Springs Life 303 N Indian Canyon Dr Palm Springs CA 92262 **Phn:** 760-325-2333 **Fax** 760-325-7008 Steven Biller. Monthly magazine.
17,200 to Palm Springs residents, visitors interested in community's social and economic life. www.palmspringslife.com

Papercity Dallas 3303 Lee Pkwy Ste 340 Dallas TX 75219 **Phn:** 214-521-3439 **Fax** 214-521-3178 Amy Adams. Monthly.
91,100 to Dallas, TX residents interested in social and charity events, entertaining, fashion. www.papercitymag.com amy@papercitymag.com

Papercity Houston 3411 Richmond Ave Ste 600 Houston TX 77046 **Phn:** 713-524-0606 **Fax** 713-524-0680 Laurann Claridge. Monthly.
85,800 to Houston, TX residents interested in social and charity events, entertaining, fashion. www.papercitymag.com laurann@papercitymag.com

Philadelphia Magazine 1818 Market St Ste 3600 Philadelphia PA 19103 **Phn:** 215-564-7700 **Fax** 215-656-3502 Jason Sheehan. Monthly.
126,700 to readers interested in area attractions, dining, schools, real estate, events, politics. www.phillymag.com jsheehan@phillymag.com

Regional Interest .69f

Philadelphia Weekly 1500 Sansom St Fl 3 Philadelphia PA 19102 **Phn:** 215-563-7400 Stephen Segal. Weekly magazine. TH:@PhillyWeekly
88,000 to young readers interested in area clubs, fashion, personalities, events, civic issues. www.philadelphiaweekly.com ssegal@philadelphiaweekly.com

Phoenix 15169 N Scottsdale Rd Ste C310 Scottsdale AZ 85254 **Phn:** 480-664-3960 **Fax** 480-664-3963 Ashley Deahl. Monthly.
77,700 to readers interested in area personalities, retail, restaurants, events, real estate. www.phoenixmag.com phxmag@citieswestpub.com

Pittsburgh 600 Waterfront Dr Ste 100 Pittsburgh PA 15222 **Phn:** 412-304-0900 **Fax** 412-304-0938 Cindi Lash. Monthly.
47,000 to metro Pittsburgh residents interested in area restaurants, sports, shopping, entertainment. www.pittsburghmagazine.com clash@pittsburghmagazine.com

Portland Monthly 623 SW Oak St Ste 300 Portland OR 97205 **Phn:** 503-222-5144 **Fax** 503-227-8777 Randy Gragg. Monthly magazine.
57,200 to readers intersted in area dining, events, gardening, arts, outdoor activities. www.portlandmonthlymag.com news@portlandmonthlymag.com

Richmond Magazine 2201 W Broad St Ste 105 Richmond VA 23220 **Phn:** 804-355-0111 **Fax** 804-355-8939 Susan Winiecki. Monthly.
55,000 to readers interested in area personalities, attractions, arts, music, real estate, politics. richmag.com editor@richmag.com

Sacramento 706 56th St Ste 210 Sacramento CA 95819 **Phn:** 916-452-6200 **Fax** 916-452-6061 Krista Minard. Monthly.
53,600 to readers intersted in area restaurants, real estate, attractions, arts, events. www.sacmag.com krista@sacmag.com

Salt Lake 515 S 700 E Ste 3I Salt Lake City UT 84102 **Phn:** 801-485-5100 **Fax** 801-485-5133 Jeremy Pugh. Bimonthly.
9,000 to Utah residents and visitors interested in regional events, issues, recreation. www.saltlakemagazine.com editor@saltlakemagazine.com

San Diego Magazine 707 Broadway Ste 1100 San Diego CA 92101 **Phn:** 619-230-9292 **Fax** 619-230-0490 Erin Chambers Smith. Monthly magazine.
49,100 to readers interested in area restaurants, politics, destinations, prominent residents. www.sandiegomagazine.com erin@sandiegomagazine.com

San Francisco 243 Vallejo St San Francisco CA 94111 **Phn:** 415-398-2800 **Fax** 415-398-6777 Modern Luxury Media. Monthly.
115,800 to Bay Area residents & visitors interested in fashion, food, performing & visual arts. www.sanfranmag.com sdinkelspiel@sanfranmag.com

Sarasota Magazine 330 S Pineapple Ave Ste 205 Sarasota FL 34236 **Phn:** 800-881-2394 **Fax** 941-366-0026 Kay Kipling. 12-issue magazine.
19,500 to readers interested in area attractions, shopping, beach life, real estate, restaurants. www.sarasotamagazine.com kayk@sarasotamagazine.com

Seattle Magazine 1518 1st Ave S Ste 500 Seattle WA 98134 **Phn:** 206-284-1750 **Fax** 206-284-2550 Rachel Hart. Tiger Oak Publications. Monthly.
54,000 to upscale residents & visitors interested in the city & Northwest lifestyles, arts, nightlife. www.seattlemag.com rachel.hart@tigeroak.com

Simply the Best 301 NE 51st St Ste 1240 Boca Raton FL 33431 **Phn:** 561-210-4411 **Fax** 561-994-6693 Jenny Bart. Bimonthly.
44,000 to upscale South Florida readers, covering, art, travel, fashion, dining, homes. simplythebestmagazine.com jenny@goodpresspublishing.com

South Dakota Magazine PO Box 175 Yankton SD 57078 **Phn:** 605-665-6655 Bernie Hunhoff. Bimonthly.
45,000 covers interesting people, places that define SD culture, heritage, arts, nature. southdakotamagazine.com

South Shore Living PO Box 208 Yarmouth Port MA 02675 **Phn:** 508-771-6549 **Fax** 508-771-3769 Maria Ferri. Rabideau Publishing. 9-issues.
14,500 covers the lifestyle, interests and activities of the Boston area's South Shore. www.ssliving.com

Tallahassee Magazine 1932 Miccosukee Rd Tallahassee FL 32308 **Phn:** 850-878-0554 **Fax** 850-807-5037 Rosanne Dunkelberger. Rowland Publishing. Bimonthly.
18,000 to readers interested in area business news & general interest articles. www.tallahasseemagazine.com rdunkelberger@rowlandpublishing.com

Tampa Bay Magazine 2531 Landmark Dr Ste 101 Clearwater FL 33761 **Phn:** 727-791-4800 **Fax** 727-796-0527 Aaron Fodiman. Bimonthly.
35,000 to Tampa Bay, FL area residents interested in dining, art, events, real estate. www.tampabaymagazine.com

Texas Monthly PO Box 1569 Austin TX 78767 **Phn:** 512-320-6900 **Fax** 512-476-9007 Erica Grieder. Emmis Publishing. Monthly.
800,000 to residents of TX cities interested in politics, sports, arts, business, culture. www.texasmonthly.com jsilverstein@texasmonthly.com

Time Out New York 475 10th Ave Fl 12 New York NY 10018 **Phn:** 646-432-3000 **Fax** 646-432-3160 Ethan LaCroix. Weekly magazine.
142,700 to readers interested in NYC dining, theater, attractions, cultural events, shopping. newyork.timeout.com elacroix@timeoutny.com

Times of the Islands PO Box 1227 Sanibel FL 33957 **Phn:** 239-472-0205 **Fax** 239-395-2125 Beth Luberecki. TOTI Media. Bimonthly.
24,900 to residents & resort visitors in southern Lee Cty., FL interested in upscale lifestyle & luxury topics. www.timesoftheislands.com fnjaeger@toti.com

Traverse N MI Magazine 148 E Front St Traverse City MI 49684 **Phn:** 231-941-8174 **Fax** 231-941-8391 Jeffrey D. Smith. Monthly magazine.
26,000 to readers interested in northern Michigan people, places, events, history, recreation. www.mynorth.com smith@traversemagazine.com

Trends 6045 N Scottsdale Rd Ste 205 Scottsdale AZ 85250 **Phn:** 480-990-9007 **Fax** 480-990-0048 Bill Macomber. 11-issue tabloid.
40,000 to Phoenix area residents interested in fashion, luxury goods, black tie events. www.trendspublishing.com bmacomber@trendspublishing.com

Vermont Magazine PO Box 900 Arlington VT 05250 **Phn:** 802-375-1366 **Fax** 518-677-8066 Phil Jordan. Bimonthly.
15,300 to readers interested in Vermont farms, towns, history, heritage, homes and lifestyle. www.vermontmagazine.com editor@vermontmagazine.com

Virginia Wildlife PO Box 11104 Richmond VA 23230 **Phn:** 804-367-1000 VA Dept. of Game. Monthly.
40,900 covers animals, editorials, education, news about wildlife conservation and DNR programs. www.dgif.virginia.gov/virginia-wildlife/

Washingtonian Magazine 1828 L St NW Ste 200 Washington DC 20036 **Phn:** 202-296-3600 **Fax** 202-862-3526 Garrett M. Graff. Monthly magazine.
140,300 to metro Wash. DC residents interested in nightlife, restaurants, art, Fed. & local politics. www.washingtonian.com editorial@washingtonian.com

Westchester 100 Clearbrook Rd Elmsford NY 10523 **Phn:** 914-345-0601 **Fax** 914-345-8123 John Bruno Turiano. Monthly. TH:@WestchesterMag
61,400 to readers interested in area real estate, towns, politics, restaurants, cultural events.
www.westchestermagazine.com
jturiano@westchestermagazine.com

Wisconsin Trails 333 W State St Milwaukee WI 53203 **Phn:** 414-224-2600 **Fax** 414-647-4723 Jill Williams. Bimonthly magazine.
42,900 covers tourist destinations, magnificent landscape, wildlife photography, best kept secrets.
www.wisconsintrails.com jwilliams@jrn.com

Yankee Magazine PO Box 520 Dublin NH 03444 **Phn:** 603-563-8111 **Fax** 603-563-8252 Mel Allen. Yankee, Inc. Bimonthly magazine.
506,000 to readers interested in New England places, culture, events, history, travel.
www.yankeemagazine.com mela@yankeepub.com

Health--Fitness--Nutrition .69g

ABILITY Magazine PO Box 10878 Costa Mesa CA 92627 **Phn:** 949-854-8700 **Fax** 949-548-5966 C2 Publishing. Bimonthly.
165,000 featuring celebrity interviews with emphasis on health and disABILITY issues. abilitymagazine.com
editorial@abilitymagazine.com

ADDitude 39 W 37th St Fl 15 New York NY 10018 **Phn:** 646-366-0830 Susan Caughman. New Hope Media. 5-issue magazine.
50,000 to parents of children with ADD, adults with ADD interested in diagnosis, treatment, social skills, parenting. www.additudemag.com
susan@additudemag.com

Arthritis Self-Management 150 W 22nd St Fl 8 New York NY 10011 **Phn:** 212-989-0200 **Fax** 212-989-4786 Katharine Davis. R.A. Rapaport Publishing. Bimonthly mag.
400,000 to people with arthritis interested in day-to-day care, long-term aspects, new developments.
www.arthritisselfmanagement.com
editor@rapaportpublishing.com

Arthritis Today 1330 W Peachtree St NW Ste 100 Atlanta GA 30309 **Phn:** 404-872-7100 **Fax** 404-872-9559 Jill Tyrer. Arthritis Fndtn. Bimonthly magazine.
727,700 to readers interested in arthritis research, care and treatment options. www.arthritistoday.org
jtyrer@arthritis.org

Better Nutrition 300 Continental Blvd Ste 650 El Segundo CA 90245 **Phn:** 310-356-4100 **Fax** 310-356-4110 Nicole Brechka. Active Interest Media. Monthly mag.
350,000 to health food consumers interested in diet, homeopathy, vitamins, fitness. www.betternutrition.com
nbrechka@aimmedia.com

Cooking Light PO Box 1748 Birmingham AL 35201 **Phn:** 205-445-6000 **Fax** 205-445-6600 Scott Mowbray. Southern Progress. 11-issue magazine.
1,750,000 to readers interested in nutrition, healthy living, recipes, exercise. www.cookinglight.com
cl_web@timeinc.com

Coping with Cancer PO Box 682268 Franklin TN 37068 **Phn:** 615-790-2400 **Fax** 615-794-0179 Laura Shipp. Media America. Bimonthly.
90,000 covers research, treatment, survivor profiles, news for people who have been touched by cancer.
copingmag.com info@copingmag.com

Cure Magazine 3102 Oak Lawn Ave Suite 610 Dallas TX 75219 **Phn:** 214-367-3500 **Fax** 214-367-3306 Dr. Debu Tripathy. Cure Media Group. Quarterly magazine. TH:@cure_magazine
325,000 to cancer patients & their caregivers interested in treatment options, practical & emotional issues. curetoday.com editor@curetoday.com

Delicious Living! 1401 Pearl St Ste 200 Boulder CO 80302 **Phn:** 303-939-8440 **Fax** 303-939-9886 Lori Howard. New Hope Natural Media. Monthly magazine.
350,000 to readers interested in natural foods, nutrition, herbs, vitamins, natural living. newhope360.com
lori.howard@penton.com

Regional Interest .69f

Diabetes Health Magazine 365 Bel Marin Keys Blvd Ste 100 Novato CA 94949 **Phn:** 415-883-1990 **Fax** 415-883-1932 Nadia Al-Samarrie. Bimonthly.
645,000 to diabetics interested news and information on living healthfully with diabetes.
www.diabeteshealth.com editor@diabeteshealth.com

Diabetes Self-Management 150 W 22nd St Fl 8 New York NY 10011 **Phn:** 212-989-0200 **Fax** 212-989-4786 Ingrid Strauch. R.A. Rapaport Publishing. Bimonthly mag.
418,400 to people with diabetes interested in day-to-day care, long-term aspects, new developments.
www.diabetesselfmanagement.com
editor@rapaportpublishing.com

Diabetic Cooking 7373 N Cicero Ave Lincolnwood IL 60712 **Phn:** 847-676-3470 **Fax** 847-676-3671 Sandy Sfikas. Bimonthly magazine.
285,000 to readers interested in nutritious, tasty recipes, menu mgmt., shopping & baking tips.
www.diabeticcooking.com ssfikaswolner@pubint.com

Fit Yoga 250 W 57th St Ste 710 New York NY 10107 **Phn:** 212-262-2247 **Fax** 212-262-2279 Rita Trieger. Goodman Media Group. 8-issue magazine.
75,000 to readers interested in yoga practice at all skill levels, instructors, studios, nutrition. www.fityoga.com
ritatude@yahoo.com

Flex 4 New York Plz New York NY 10004 **Phn:** 212-545-4800 **Fax** 818-595-0463 Robbie Durand. American Media. Monthly. TH:@RobbieDurand
75,000 to serious bodybuilders and weight trainers interested in workout routines, nutrition.
www.flexonline.com rdurand@flexmagazine.com

Health 2100 Lakeshore Dr Birmingham AL 35209 **Phn:** 205-445-6000 **Fax** 205-445-5123 Southern Progress. 10-issue magazine.
1,373,300 to women interested in wellness, food, nutrition, fitness, spirituality, relationships.
www.health.com/health/ askhealth@timeinc.com

The Healthy Planet 20 N Gore Ave Ste 200 Saint Louis MO 63119 **Phn:** 314-962-7748 **Fax** 314-962-0728 J.B. Lester. Monthly magazine.
90,000 to St. Louis area readers interested in health, wellness, organic foods, earth-friendly products/services. thehealthyplanet.com
jbl44@aol.com

Life Extension PO Box 407189 Fort Lauderdale FL 33340 **Phn:** 954-544-4440 **Fax** 954-491-5306 Sheldon Baker. Life Extension Fndtn. Monthly magazine.
300,000 to readers interested in new discoveries in vitamins, nutrition, hormones, anti-aging supplements, diseases. www.lifeextension.com
sbaker@lifeextension.com

Natural Health 1 Park Ave Fl 3 New York NY 10016 **Phn:** 212-545-4800 **Fax** 646-521-2830 Laura Kalehoff. American Media. 6-issue magazine. TH:@_NaturalHealth
300,000 to readers interested in natural health, whole foods, fitness, homeopathy.
www.naturalhealthmag.com lkalehoff@amilink.com

Natural Solutions 1270 Eagan Industrial Road Ste 190 Eagan MN 55121 **Phn:** 651-251-9617 **Fax** 651-686-0366 Meghan Rabbitt. InnoVision Health Media. 10-issues.
301,000 to those interested ins the field of alternative medicine and natural health.
www.naturalsolutionsmag.com
editor@naturalsolutionsmag.com

Nutrition Today 530 Walnut St Philadelphia PA 19106 **Phn:** 215-521-8772 Johanna Dwyer. Lippincott Williams & Wilkins. Bimo.
301,000 covers nutrition science, biotechnology, obesity, behavioral issues, government policies.
journals.lww.com/nutritiontodayonline/

OnFitness PO Box 271 Kahuku HI 96731 **Phn:** 808-232-2082 **Fax** 216-803-4528 Joseph Grassadoniia. Bimonthly.
10,500 to those passionate about achieving peak health and fitness through a natural approach.
www.onfitnessmag.com sid@onfitnessmag.com

Personal Fitness Professional 2901 International Ln Ste 100 Madison WI 53704 **Phn:** 608-241-8777 **Fax** 608-241-8666 Mike Beacom. RB Publishing. 7-issue magazine.
37,000 to personal trainers interested in business/financial advice & resources; training.
www.fit-pro.com mike@rbpub.com

POZ 462 7th Ave Fl 19 New York NY 10018 **Phn:** 212-242-2163 **Fax** 212-675-8505 Oriol Gutierrez. 8-issue magazine.
175,000 to readers living with HIV or AIDS interested in treatment options & latest research. www.poz.com
oriolg@poz.com

Prevention 733 3rd Ave New York NY 10017 **Phn:** 212-697-2040 **Fax** 212-297-1534 Siobhan O'Connor. Rodale Press. Monthly magazine. TH:@PreventionMag
2,800,000 to readers interested in disease prevention, mgmt., medical care, nutrition, fitness.
www.prevention.com siobhan.o'connor@rodale.com

Saturday Evening Post 1100 Waterway Blvd Indianapolis IN 46202 **Phn:** 317-636-8881 **Fax** 317-637-0126 Steven Slon. Bimonthly. TH:@StevePostEditor
357,000 to readers interested in food & drink, travel, history, humor, celebrity profiles, popular history.
www.saturdayeveningpost.com
editor@saturdayeveningpost.com

Shape 1 Park Ave Fl 10 New York NY 10016 **Phn:** 212-545-4800 **Fax** 646-521-2830 Tara Kraft. Monthly magazine. TH:@TaraShapeEditor
1,600,000 to women interested in exercise, nutrition, health, fitness, psychology, beauty. www.shape.com
shapemagazinecontact@gmail.com

Taste for Life 100 Emerald St Keene NH 03431 **Phn:** 603-283-0034 **Fax** 603-283-0141 Donna Moxley. Connell Communications. Monthly.
749,000 to natural product consumers interested in food, vitamins, homeopathy, herbs, recipes.
www.tasteforlife.com donna.moxley@tasteforlife.com

Today's Caregiver 3350 Griffin Rd Fort Lauderdale FL 33312 **Phn:** 954-893-0550 **Fax** 954-893-1779 Gary Barg. Bimonthly magazine.
52,000 to professional and family caregivers interested in pain mgmt., nutrition, new treatments.
www.caregiver.com gary@caregiver.com

Today's Diet & Nutrition 4135 Conashaugh Lk Milford PA 18337 **Phn:** 610-948-9500 **Fax** 610-948-4202 Kate Jackson. Great Valley Publishing. Bimonthly mag.
100,000 to readers interested in healthy lifestyle through food, fitness and timely information. www.tdn-digital.com tdnkate@ptd.net

Total Health 165 N 100 E Ste 2 St George UT 84770 **Phn:** 435-673-1789 **Fax** 435-634-9336 Lyle Hurd. Bi-monthly.
53,500 to those interested in anti-aging, longevity and self managed natural health.
www.totalhealthmagazine.com twip2010@gmail.com

Vegetarian Times 300 Continental Blvd Ste 650 El Segundo CA 90245 **Phn:** 310-356-4100 **Fax** 310-356-4110 Elizabeth Turner. Active Interest Media. 9 issues.
315,000 to readers interested in vegetarian nutrition, lifestyle, recipes, alternative healthcare.
www.vegetariantimes.com
editor@vegetariantimes.com

Weight Watchers Magazine 11 Madison Ave Fl 17 New York NY 10010 **Phn:** 212-589-2700 **Fax** 212-589-2600 Michele Shapiro. W/W Twentyfirst Corp. Bimo.
1,200,000 for women committed to change, healthy lifestyle, weight loss and weight management.
www.weightwatchers.com
wwmeditor@weightwatchers.com

Yoga Journal 475 Sansome St Ste 850 San Francisco CA 94111 **Phn:** 415-591-0555 **Fax** 415-591-0733 Carin Gorrell. Active Interest Media. 7-issue magazine. TH:@caringorrell
375,000 to yoga practioners, instructors, students interested in health, practice, equipment, travel.
www.yogajournal.com cgorrell@yjmag.com

African American Golfer's Digest 80 Wall St Ste 720 New York NY 10005 **Phn:** 212-571-6559 **Fax** 212-571-1943 Debert Cook. 4-issue magazine.
10,400 news and events in golf for African Americans, tips, equipment review, golfer profiles.
africanamericangolfersdigest.com
editors@africanamericangolfersdigest.com

Black Enterprise 130 5th Ave Fl 10 New York NY 10011 **Phn:** 212-242-8000 **Fax** 212-886-9610 Derek Dingle. Earl Graves Publications. 10-issue magazine.
523,000 to African-Amer. corporate execs., entrepreneurs interested in career issues, profiles.
www.blackenterprise.com
dingled@blackenterprise.com

Black Men 210 E State Rt 4 Ste 211 Paramus NJ 07652 **Phn:** 201-843-4004 **Fax** 201-843-8775 Kate Ferguson. Enoble Media. 8-issue magazine.
103,000 covers sports, business news, relationships, grooming, celebrities, lifestyles. enoblemedia.com
ehonig@enoblemedia.com

The Crisis 7600 Georgia Ave NW Ste 405 Washington DC 20012 **Phn:** 202-829-5700 **Fax** 202-829-2050 Victoria Valentine. NAACP. Bimonthly magazine.
250,400 to NAACP members, other readers interested in issues of importance to people of color.
www.thecrisismagazine.com jasim@naacpnet.org

Ebony 820 S Michigan Ave Chicago IL 60605 **Phn:** 312-322-9200 **Fax** 312-322-9375 Amy DuBois Barnett. Johnson Publishing. Monthly magazine. TH:@EBONYMag
1,250,000 to African-Americans interested in current events, politics, arts, entertainment. www.ebony.com amy@ebony.com

Essence Magazine 135 W 50th St Fl 4 New York NY 10020 **Phn:** 212-522-1212 Vanessa Bush. Monthly. TH:@Vanessa_KBush
1,075,600 to Afr.-Amer women interested in fashion, personal finance, fitness, dating, travel.
www.essence.com vbush@essence.com

Heart & Soul 2514 Maryland Ave Baltimore MD 21218 **Phn:** 410-662-4590 **Fax** 410-662-4596 Kendra Lee. Bimonthly magazine.
309,300 Living and wellness magazine for African-American women, fitness, fashion, relationships.
www.heartandsoul.com info@heartandsoul.com

Hype Hair 210 E State Rt 4 Ste 211 Paramus NJ 07652 **Phn:** 201-843-4004 **Fax** 201-843-8636 Adrienne Moore. Enoble Media Group. 9-issues.
74,000 covers the hottest hairstyles, beauty tips, and celebrity looks. www.hypehair.com
editor@hypehair.com

Jet 820 S Michigan Ave Chicago IL 60605 **Phn:** 312-322-9200 Mitzi Miller. Johnson Publishing. Biweekly magazine.
700,000 to black readers interested in news, features, sports, education, African affairs. www.jetmag.com
mmiller@jetmagazine.com

Pathfinders Travel 6325 Germantown Ave Philadelphia PA 19144 **Phn:** 215-438-2140 Ms. P.J. Thomas. Quarterly magazine. TH:@PJThomas807
100,000 to affluent African-Amer. readers interested in dining, destinations, spas, cruises, reunion planning.
www.pathfinderstravel.com
pjthomas@pathfinderstravel.com

Sister 2 Sister 9301 Annapolis Rd Ste 205 Lanham MD 20706 **Phn:** 301-306-0100 **Fax** 301-306-0104 Jamie Foster Brown. Monthly magazine.
182,000 fan magazine covering the hottest movie, music, and television celebrities. s2smagazine.com
info@s2smail.com

Today's Black Woman 210 E State Rt 4 Ste 211 Paramus NJ 07652 **Phn:** 201-843-4004 **Fax** 201-843-8775 Kate Ferguson. Bimonthly magazine.
43,900 to black women interested in fashion, careers, relationships, celebrity profiles.
www.todaysblackwoman.com
editor@todaysblackwoman.com

African-American Interest .69h

Upscale Magazine 600 Bronner Bros Way SW Atlanta GA 30310 **Phn:** 404-758-7467 **Fax** 404-448-3153 Sheila Bronner. 9-issue magazine.
182,300 to African-Americans interested in career, health, personal development, fashion.
www.upscalemagazine.com info@upscalemag.com

Urban Ink 210 E State Rt 4 Ste 211 Paramus NJ 07652 **Phn:** 201-843-4004 **Fax** 201-843-8775 Paul Gambino. Enoble Media. 8-issue magazine.
38,400 to people of color interested in tattoos, celebrity interviews, photos of tattoos. www.urbanink.com
pgambino@mail.enoblemedia.com

Gay & Lesbian Interest .69i

Ambush Magazine 828 Bourbon St New Orleans LA 70116 **Phn:** 504-522-8049 **Fax** 415-863-1609 Rip Naquin-Delain. Monthly.
19,700 News and event listings for the New Orleans lesbian, gay, bi and transgender community.
www.ambushmag.com info@ambushmag.com

Curve PO Box 467 New York NY 10034 **Phn:** 415-863-6538 **Fax** 415-863-1609 Rachel Shatto. 10-issue magazine.
69,700 to readers interested in lesbian-oriented pop culture, style, celebrity profiles, travel.
www.curvemag.com editor@curvemag.com

Echo Magazine PO Box 16630 Phoenix AZ 85011 **Phn:** 602-266-0550 **Fax** 602-266-0773 Glenn Gullickson. Ace Publishing. Monthly.
15,700 News and event listings for the Arizona lesbian, gay, bi and transgender community.
www.echomag.com editor@echomag.com

Instinct 303 N Glenoaks Blvd Ste L120 Burbank CA 91502 **Phn:** 818-286-0071 **Fax** 818-286-0077 Mike Wood. 10-issue magazine.
115,000 to gay men interested in relationships, careers, health, travel, finance. instinctmagazine.com
mwood@instinctmag.com

Just Out PO Box 10609 Portland OR 97296 **Phn:** 503-828-3034 **Fax** 503-828-3034 Alley Hector. Monthly magazine. TH:@JustOutPortland
60,000 to Portland-area LGBT readers interested in first-person profiles, products, events, politics, fashion.
www.justout.com editor@justout.com

Lavender Magazine 3715 Chicago Ave Minneapolis MN 55407 **Phn:** 612-436-4660 **Fax** 612-436-4685 Monthly.
65,700 News, event listings for the Twin Cities lesbian, gay, bi and transgender community.
www.lavendermagazine.com
info@lavendermagazine.com

Lesbian News PO Box 55 Torrance CA 90507 **Phn:** 310-548-9888 **Fax** 310-548-9588 Ella Matthes. LN Publishing. Monthly.
35,000 vehicle for the experience of women's art, music, literature, films and history.
www.lesbiannews.com ellalnmag@gmail.com

Metroline Magazine 495 Farmington Ave Hartford CT 06105 **Phn:** 860-231-8845 **Fax** 860-233-8338 Joe DaBrow. Monthly.
10,600 News, event listings for the New England lesbian, gay, bi and transgender community.
www.metroline-online.com editor@metroline-online.com

Next Magazine 121 Varick St Fl 7 New York NY 10013 **Phn:** 212-627-0165 Alex Erikson. Weekly magazine. TH:@NextMagazineNY
58,000 to gay men, others interested in New York City gay nightlife, events, personalities, politics, fashion, celebrities. www.nextmagazine.com
editor@nextmagazine.net

Out PO Box 1253 New York NY 10113 **Phn:** 212-242-8100 **Fax** 212-242-1344 Jerry Portwood. Here Media, Inc. Monthly magazine.
158,700 to upscale gay men interested in culture, design, music, arts, fitness. www.out.com
editor@outtraveler.com

Out Traveler 245 W 17th St Ste 1250 New York NY 10011 **Phn:** 212-242-6115 **Fax** 212-242-8338 Jerry Portwood. Here Media. Monthly.
251,000 Presents the travel experience from a gay perspective, destinations, reviews, articles.
www.outtraveler.com editor@outtraveler.com

Pink Magazine PO Box 408374 Chicago IL 60640 **Phn:** 773-765-4712 David Cohen. Quarterly magazine. TH:@TweetPINKMag
50,000 to LGBT readers in 6 editions (Chicago, Denver, NY, San Francisco, LA, Seattle) interested in events, businesses. www.pinkmag.com
david@pinkmag.com

PQ Monthly PO Box 306 Portland OR 97207 **Phn:** 503-228-3139 Julie Cortez. Monthly. TH:@PQmonthly
50,000 to Pacific NW area readers interested in gay & lesbian activities, personalities, issues, arts & culture.
www.pqmonthly.com julie@pqmonthly.com

She Magazine 6511 Nova Dr Ste 173 Davie FL 33317 **Phn:** 954-354-9751 Tina Sordellini. She Girls LLC. Monthly. TH:@shemagazine
15,000 to southern FL LGBT women, others interested in celebrity interviews, opinion columns, political coverage. www.shemag.com info@shemag.com

Senior Citizen Interest .69j

AARP Bulletin Today 601 E St NW Washington DC 20049 **Phn:** 202-434-3340 **Fax** 202-434-6451 Michael Hedges. AARP. 10-issue magazine. TH:@aarpbulletin
23,361,300 to readers age 50+ interested in legislative, political, economic issues affecting them.
www.aarp.org/bulletin/ mhedges@aarp.org

AARP The Magazine 601 E St NW Washington DC 20049 **Phn:** 202-434-6880 **Fax** 202-434-6883 William Horne AARP. Bimonthly magazine. TH:@WWHorne
24,000,000 in 3 age-specific editions (50-59; 60-69; 70+) to readers interested in finance, health, travel, lifestyle. www.aarp.org/magazine/ whorne@aarp.org

BoomerTimes & Senior Life 1515 Federal Hwy. #300 Boca Raton FL 33432 **Phn:** 561-736-8925 **Fax** 561-369-1476 Bill Finley. Monthly.
180,000 to active, mature adults in Florida's Palm Beach, Broward and northern Dade counties.
www.babyboomers-seniors.com srlife@gate.net

Grand Magazine 4791 Baywood Point Dr S St. Petersburg FL 33711 **Phn:** 727-327-9039 **Fax** 727-323-9587 Christine Crosby. Bimonthly digital magazine.
250,000 to grandparents interested in grandparents' rights, education, travel, entertainment, finances, health. www.grandmagazine.com
ccrosby@grandmagazine.com

Healthy Aging PO Box 442 Unionville PA 19375 **Phn:** 610-793-0979 **Fax** 619-793-0978 Carolyn Worthington. Quarterly magazine. TH:@healthyagingnet
800,000 to 45 years+ higher income readers interested in travel, mental & physical health, financial well being.
www.healthyaging.net editor@healthyaging.net

Lovin' Life After 50 3200 N Hayden Ste 210 Scottsdale AZ 85251 **Phn:** 602-438-1566 **Fax** 602-438-0369 Shanna Hogan. Monthly newspaper.
125,000 in Phoenix & Tucson area adults ages 50+ interested in housing, health, travel. www.lovinlife.com
lovinlifeedit@gmail.com

Food & Wine .69k

Bon Appetit 4 Times Sq Fl 5 New York NY 10036 **Phn:** 212-286-2860 **Fax** 212-286-2860 Adam Rapoport. Conde Nast. Monthly magazine. TH:@rapo4
1,500,000 to readers interested in restaurants, chefs, food trends, entertaining. www.bonappetit.com
adam_rapoport@bonappetit.com

Brew Your Own 5515 Main St Manchester Center VT 05255 **Phn:** 802-362-3981 **Fax** 802-362-2377 Betsy Parks. 8-issue magazine. TH:@BrewYourOwn
60,000 to readers interested in home beer brewing, tips, projects and recipes for beginners and experts.
www.byo.com edit@byo.com

Cooking With Paula Deen 1900 International Park Dr Ste 50 Birmingham AL 35243 **Phn:** 205-995-8860 **Fax** 205-991-0071 Alyce Head. Hoffman Media. Bimonthly magazine. TH:@Paula_Deen
725,000 to readers interested in Deen's Southern U.S.-influenced recipes & restaurant; lifstlye & travel features. www.pauladeenmagazine.com ahead@hoffmanmedia.com

Cook's Illustrated 17 Station St Brookline MA 02445 **Phn:** 617-232-1000 **Fax** 617-232-1572 Christopher Kimball. Boston Common Press. Bimonthly magazine. TH:@TestKitchen
900,000 to serious home cooks interested in basic & in-depth procedures, cookware, tastings. www.cooksillustrated.com cooks@americastestkitchen.com

Culture PO Box 1064 Lynnfield MA 01940 **Phn:** 641-715-3900 **Fax** 641 715 1212 Katie Aberbach. Quarterly magazine. TH:@culturecheese
50,000 to readers interested in local & artisanal cheeses; cheesemaking operations; cheese photography. www.culturecheesemag.com editor@culturecheesemag.com

Draft Magazine PO Box 15769 Phoenix AZ 85060 **Phn:** 602-374-2376 **Fax** 602-334-1176 Jessica Daynor. Bimonthly magazine. TH:@draftmag
270,000 covers pubs, breweries, food, travel and more, connected to the beer lovers lifestyle. draftmag.com jessica.daynor@draftmag.com

Eating Well 6221 Shelburne Rd Ste 100 Shelburne VT 05482 **Phn:** 802-985-4500 **Fax** 802-985-4501 Jessie Price. Bimonthly magazine. TH:@jessieprice73
750,000 to readers interested in food journalism, healthful recipes, cooking tips, nutrition. www.eatingwell.com jessie@eatingwell.com

Every Day with Rachael Ray 805 3rd Ave. New York NY 10022 **Phn:** 212-499-2000 **Fax** 212-499-1987 Lauren Purcell. Meredith Corp. 10-issue magazine. TH:@RachaelRaymag
1,700,000 to readers interested in simple recipes and entertaining, travel, celebrity food lifestyles. www.rachaelraymag.com lauren.purcell@meredith.com

Fine Cooking 63 S Main St Newtown CT 06470 **Phn:** 203-426-8171 **Fax** 203-426-3434 Jennifer Armentrout. Taunton Press. Bimonthly magazine. TH:@FC_Jen
238,300 to readers interested in recipes; the hows & whys of cooking techniques & preparation. www.finecooking.com jarmentrout@taunton.com

Food & Wine 1120 Avenue Of The Americas Fl 9 New York NY 10036 **Phn:** 212-382-5600 **Fax** 212-382-5887 Dana Cowin. Amer. Express Corp. Monthly magazine. TH:@fwscout
948,000 to readers interested in upscale dining, travel, wine reviews, chef profiles. www.foodandwine.com

Imbibe 1028 SE Water Ave Ste 285 Portland OR 97214 **Phn:** 503-595-0144 **Fax** 503-595-0122 Karen Foley. Bimonthly magazine. TH:@imbibe
50,000 to readers interested in all aspects of wine, beer, spirits, coffee and tea including recipes. www.imbibemagazine.com editorial@imbibemagazine.com

Kashrus Magazine PO Box 204 Brooklyn NY 11204 **Phn:** 718-336-8544 **Fax** 718-336-8550 Yosef Wikler. Kashrus Inst. Bimo.
10,000 covers Kosher food for consumers, food trade, vegetarian, health care industries. kashrusmagazine.com editorial@kashrusmagazine.com

La Cucina Italiana 11 W 42nd St Fl 17 New York NY 10036 **Phn:** 800-584-2043 Michael Wilson. Quadratum Publishing. 8-issues. TH:@LCI_Magazine
120,000 to readers interested in Italian cooking & cuisine & lifestyle, recipes, tips and techniques, menus. lacucinaitalianamagazine.com info@quadratumusa.com

Food & Wine .69k

Mutineer Magazine 7510 Sunset Blvd Los Angeles CA 90046 **Phn:** 212-695-4660 **Fax** 212-695-2920 Alan Kropf. Quarterly magazine. TH:@alankropf
60,000 to readers age 21-34 interested in fine wine, cocktails; bartenders, industry personnel. www.mutineermagazine.com/blog/ press@mutineermagazine.com

Saveur Magazine 15 E 32nd St Fl 12 New York NY 10016 **Phn:** 212-219-7400 Sophie Brickman. Bonnier Corp. 9-issue magazine. TH:@SAVEURMAG
325,000 to readers interested in recipes & stories about U.S. and world traditional foods. www.saveur.com sophie.brickman@bonniercorp.com

Taste of Home 5400 S 60th St Greendale WI 53129 **Phn:** 414-423-0100 **Fax** 414-423-1143 Bettina Miller. Reader's Digest. 6-issue magazine. TH:@tasteofhome
3,200,000 to readers interested in reader-generated & editor-tested recipes, entertaining, holiday cooking. www.tasteofhome.com jeanne_ambrose@rd.com

Taste of the South 1900 International Park Dr Ste 50 Birmingham AL 35243 **Phn:** 205-995-8860 **Fax** 205-991-0071 Brooke Bell. Hoffman Media. Bimo. magazine. TH:@TasteMag
70,000 to readers interested in traditional southern recipes, profiles of Southern restaurants. www.tasteofthesouthmagazine.com bbell@hoffmanmedia.com

Tea Time 1900 International Park Dr Ste 50 Birmingham AL 35243 **Phn:** 205-995-8860 **Fax** 205-991-0071 Anna Reeves. Hoffman Media. Bimonthly magazine. TH:@TeaTimeMag
65,000 to tea enthusiasts interested in tea tasting reviews, products, tea-related travel. www.teatimemagazine.com lreeves@hoffmanmedia.com

Wine & Spirits 2 W 32nd St Ste 601 New York NY 10001 **Phn:** 212-695-4660 **Fax** 212-695-2920 Joshua Greene. Winestate Publications. 8-issue magazine.
90,000 to wine consumers and marketers interested in reviews, recipes, tastings. www.wineandspiritsmagazine.com info@wineandspiritsmagazine.com

Wine Business 110 W Napa St Sonoma CA 95476 **Phn:** 707-939-0822 **Fax** 707-939-0833 Cyril Penn. Monthly.
27,000 to wine industry personnel responsible for sales, mktg., windmaking, grape growing, industry news & people. www.winebusiness.com cyrilpenn@winebusiness.com

Wine Enthusiast 333 N Bedford Rd Mount Kisco NY 10549 **Phn:** 914-345-8463 **Fax** 914-218-9186 Joe Czerwinski. 13-issue magazine. TH:@JoeCz
197,000 to readers interested in ratings and recommendations, vineyards, winemaker profiles. www.winemag.com jczerwin@wineenthusiast.net

Wine Spectator 387 Park Ave S Fl 8 New York NY 10016 **Phn:** 212-481-8610 **Fax** 212-684-5424 Thomas Matthews. M. Shanken Comms. 16-issue tabloid. TH:@WineSpectator
408,000 to readers interested in fine wine and dining, cooking, travel, entertaining, arts. www.winespectator.com winespec@mshanken.com

WineMaker 5515 Main St Manchester Center VT 05255 **Phn:** 802-362-3981 **Fax** 802-362-2377 Betsy Parks. Battenkill Communications. Bimonthly. TH:@WineMakerMag
35,000 covers home brewing of wine, tips, projects and recipes for beginners and experts. www.winemakermag.com edit@winemakermag.com

Spanish Language .69l

AARP Viva 601 E St NW Washington DC 20049 **Phn:** 202-434-6880 **Fax** 202-434-6883 Gabriela Zabalua-Goddard. AARP. Quarterly bilingual mag. TH:@AARPenEspanol
400,000 to Spanish-speaking readers ages 50+ interested in finance, health, leisure. www.aarp.org/espanol/ segundajuventud@aarp.org

Casa & Estilo 12182 SW 128th St Miami FL 33186 **Phn:** 305-378-4466 **Fax** 305-378-9951 Jose Nino. Bimonthly magazine.
200,000 to affluent readers interested in interior design, architecture, art, lifestyle. www.casaestilo.com janino@casayestilo.com

Cosmopolitan En Espanol 6355 NW 36th St Miami FL 33166 **Phn:** 305-871-6400 **Fax** 305-871-4939 Monthly. TH:@Cosmopolitan_US
158,000 to women interested in men, dating, fashion, beauty. www.cosmoenespanol.com cosmopolitanweb@cosmohispano.com

Fama Magazine 247 SW 8th St # 123 Miami FL 33130 **Phn:** 305-649-7924 Al Vazquez. Monthly.
210,000 covers cultural, entertainment news, interviews, reviews, Latin art, Spanish food, anrts. www.famaweb.com al@famaweb.com

Latina 625 Madison Ave Frnt 3 New York NY 10022 **Phn:** 212-642-0200 **Fax** 212-575-3088 Damarys Ocaña. 10-issue magazine. TH:@DamarysLatina
500,000 to Latinas interested in fashion, beauty, parenting, entertainment, celebrities. www.latina.com editor@latina.com

People en Espanol 1271 Avenue of the Americas New York NY 10020 **Phn:** 212-522-9411 **Fax** 212-467-2945 Armando Correa. Time, Inc. 11-issue magazine. TH:@ArmandoCorrea
567,000 to Spanish-speaking U.S. readers interested in celebrities, human interest stories, music. www.peopleenespanol.com espanol@people.com

Que Onda! PO Box 692150 Houston TX 77269 **Phn:** 713-880-1133 **Fax** 713-880-2322 Lilia Esparza. Weekly tabloid.
110,000 in 3 city editions (DFW, Houston, San Antonio) to Latinos interested in news, sports. www.queondamagazine.com staff@queondamagazine.com

Ser Padres 375 Lexington Ave New York NY 10017 **Phn:** 212-499-2000 **Fax** 212-499-2077 Alberto Oliva. Meredith Corp. 8-issue magazine. TH:@Serpadres_es
700,000 to Hispanic parents interested in infant care, family life, food. www.serpadres.es/ alberto.oliva@meredith.com

Siempre Mujer! 1716 Locust St Des Moines IA 50309 **Phn:** 515-284-3000 **Fax** 515-284-3264 Zuania Capo-Ramos. Meredith Corp. Bimonthly magazine. TH:@zuaniacapo
550,000 to Latinas interested in health, beauty, relationships, fashion, travel. siempremujer.com zuania.capo@meredith.com

TeleRevista 304 Indian Trce # 238 Weston FL 33326 **Phn:** 954-689-2428 Salvatore Trimarchi. Latino Publishing. Monthly. TH:@TELEREVISTA
75,000 Information on the Spanish-language entertainment world. telerevista.com salvatore@telerevista.com

ASSOCIATED PRESS BUREAUS

AK Anchorage 750 W. 2nd Ave. #102 99501 **Phn:** 907-272-7549 **Fax:** 907-274-2189

AL Montgomery 201 Monroe St. #1940 36104 **Phn:** 334-262-5947 **Fax:** 334-265-7177

AR Little Rock 10810 Executive Ctr. Dr. #308 72211 **Phn:** 501-225-3668 **Fax:** 501-225-3249

AZ Phoenix 1850 N. Central Ave. #640 85004 **Phn:** 602-258-8934 **Fax:** 602-254-9573

CA Los Angeles 221 S. Figueroa St. #300 90012 **Phn:** 213-626-1200 **Fax:** 213-346-0200

CA San Francisco 303 2nd St. #680N 94107 **Phn:** 415-495-1708 **Fax:** 415-495-4967

CO Denver 1444 Wazee St. #130 80202 **Phn:** 303-825-0123 **Fax:** 303-892-5927

CT Hartford 10 Columbus Blvd. Fl. 9 06106 **Phn:** 860-246-6876 **Fax:** 860-727-4003

DC Washington 2021 K St. NW #606 20006 **Phn:** 202-776-9400 **Fax:** 202-776-9570

FL Miami 9100 NW 36th St. #111 33178 **Phn:** 305-594-5825 **Fax:** 305-594-9265

GA Atlanta 101 Marietta St. #2450 30303 **Phn:** 404-522-8971 **Fax:** 404-524-4639

HI Honolulu 500 Ala Moana Blvd. #7-590 96813 **Phn:** 808-536-5510 **Fax:** 808-531-1213

IA Des Moines 505 5th Ave. #1000 50309 **Phn:** 515-243-3281 **Fax:** 515-243-3884

IL Chicago 10 S. Wacker Dr. #2500 60606 **Phn:** 312-781-0500 **Fax:** 312-781-1989

IN Indianapolis 251 N. Illinois St. #1600 46204 **Phn:** 317-639-5501 **Fax:** 317-638-4611

KS Topeka 300 SW 10th St. #047G-E 66612 **Phn:** 785-234-5654 **Fax:** 785-234-2614

KY Louisville 525 W. Broadway 40202 **Phn:** 502-583-7718 **Fax:** 502-589-4831

LA New Orleans 1515 Poydras St. #2500 70112 **Phn:** 504-523-3931 **Fax:** 504-586-0531

MA Boston 184 High St. 02110 **Phn:** 617-357-8100 **Fax:** 617-338-8125

MD Baltimore 218 N. Charles St. #330 21201 **Phn:** 410-837-8315 **Fax:** 410-837-4291

MI Detroit 300 River Pl. #2400 48207 **Phn:** 313-259-0650 **Fax:** 313-259-4966

MN Minneapolis 511 11th Ave. S. #460 55415 **Phn:** 612-332-2727 **Fax:** 612-342-5299

MO Kansas City 215 W. Pershing Rd. #221 64108 **Phn:** 816-421-4844 **Fax:** 816-421-3590

MS Jackson 125 S. Congress #1330 39201 **Phn:** 601-948-5897 **Fax:** 601-948-7975

MT Helena 825 Great Northern Blvd. #203 59601 **Phn:** 406-442-7440 **Fax:** 406-442-5162

NC Raleigh 4800 Six Forks Rd. #210 27609 **Phn:** 919-833-8687 **Fax:** 919-834-1078

NE Omaha 909 N. 96th St. #104 68114 **Phn:** 402-391-0031 **Fax:** 402-391-1412

NH Concord 2 Capitol Plz. #400 03301 **Phn:** 603-224-3327 **Fax:** 603-226-0883

NJ Trenton 50 W. State St. #1114 08608 **Phn:** 609-392-3622 **Fax:** 609-392-3525

NV Las Vegas 300 S. 4th St. #810 89101 **Phn:** 702-382-7440 **Fax:** 702-382-0790

NY New York 450 W 33rd St. 10001 **Phn:** 212-621-1500 **Fax:** 212-621-1679

NY Albany PO Box 11010 12211 **Phn:** 518-458-7821 **Fax:** 518-438-5891

OH Columbus 1103 Schrock Rd. #300 43229 **Phn:** 614-885-2727 **Fax:** 614-885-3248

OK Oklahoma City 525 Central Park Dr. #202 73105 **Phn:** 405-525-2121 **Fax:** 405-524-7465

OR Portland 121 SW Salmon St. #1450 97204 **Phn:** 503-228-2169 **Fax:** 503-228-5514

PA Philadelphia 1835 Market St. #1700 19103 **Phn:** 215-561-1133 **Fax:** 215-561-3544

RI Providence 10 Dorrance St. #601 02903 **Phn:** 401-274-2270 **Fax:** 401-272-5644

SC Columbia 1311 Marion St. 29201 **Phn:** 803-799-6418 **Fax:** 803-252-2913

SD Sioux Falls PO Box 1125 57101 **Phn:** 605-332-2111 **Fax:** 605-332-3931

TX Dallas 4851 LBJ Fwy. #300 75244 **Phn:** 972-991-2100 **Fax:** 972-991-7207

UT Salt Lake City 30 E. 100 S. #200 84111 **Phn:** 801-322-3405 **Fax:** 801-322-0051

VA Richmond 600 E. Main St. #1250 23219 **Phn:** 804-643-6646 **Fax:** 804-643-6223

WA Seattle 3131 Elliott Ave. #750 98121 **Phn:** 206-682-1812 **Fax:** 206-621-1948

WI Milwaukee 111 E. Wisconsin Ave. #1925 53202 **Phn:** 414-225-3580 **Fax:** 414-225-3599

WV Charleston 500 Virginia St. E. #1150 25301 **Phn:** 304-346-0897 **Fax:** 304-345-5282

NOTE: Send or fax your release to ONLY ONE of the AP bureaus, the one closest to you. Do not send or fax to more than one bureau.

NEWS SYNDICATES & SERVICES

African American Newswire 682 Sumner Ave. Springfield MA 01108 **Phn:** 413-734-6444 **Fax:** 413-737-1458

Agence France-Presse 1500 K St NW #600 Washington DC 20005 **Phn:** 202-289-0700 **Fax:** 202-414-0635

Ampersand Communications 2311 S. Bayshore Dr. Miami FL 33133 **Phn:** 305-285-2200 **Fax:**

Artists & Writers Syndicate 582 Brummel Ct. NW Washington DC 20012 **Phn:** 202-882-8882 **Fax:**

Black Press Service 166 Madison Ave. #4 New York NY 10016 **Phn:** 212-686-6850 **Fax:** 212-686-7308

Bloomberg News 731 Lexington Ave. New York NY 10022 **Phn:** 212-318-2300 **Fax:** 212-893-5999

Business Wire 44 Montgomery St. Fl 39 San Francisco CA 94104 **Phn:** 415-986-4422 **Fax:** 415-788-5335

Canadian Press 529 14th St. NW #1128 Washington DC 20045 **Phn:** 202-638-3367 **Fax:** 202-638-3369

Capitol News Service 530 Bercut Dr. #E Sacramento CA 95814 **Phn:** 916-445-6336 **Fax:** 916-443-5871

Catholic News Service 3211 4th St. NE Washington DC 20017 **Phn:** 202-541-3250 **Fax:** 202-541-3255

Copley News Service PO Box 120190 San Diego CA 92112 **Phn:** 619-293-1818 **Fax:** 619-293-2647

Corbis 902 Broadway New York NY 10010 **Phn:** 212-777-6200 **Fax:** 212-375-7700

Creators Syndicate 5777 W. Century Blvd. #700 Los Angeles CA 90045 **Phn:** 310-337-7003 **Fax:** 310-337-7625

Dow Jones Newswires Harborside/800 Plz 2 Fl 8 Jersey City NJ 07311 **Phn:** 201-938-5400 **Fax:** 201-938-5600

DPA (Germany's News Agency) 969 Natl. Press Bldg. Washington DC 20045 **Phn:** 202-662-1241 **Fax:** 202-662-1270

E&E Publishing 122 C St NW #722 Washington DC 20001 **Phn:** 202-628-6500 **Fax:** 202-737-5299

EFE (Spain's News Agency) News 1252 Nat'l. Press Bldg. Washington DC 20045 **Phn:** 202-745-7692 **Fax:** 202-393-4118

Entertainment News Syndicate PO Box 276 New York NY 10156 **Phn:** 212-679-9968 **Fax:** 212-679-9969

Environmental Media Svcs. 1320 18th St NW Washington DC 20036 **Phn:** 202-463-6670 **Fax:** 202-463-6671

Family Features Syndicate 5825 Dearborn St. Mission KS 66202 **Phn:** 913-722-0055 **Fax:** 913-789-9228

Feature Photo Svc. 1071 Ave of Americas Fl 7 New York NY 10018 **Phn:** 212-944-1060 **Fax:** 212-944-7801

Gannett News Service 7950 Jones Branch Dr. McLean VA 22107 **Phn:** 703-854-5800 **Fax:** 703-854-2152

Global Info. Network 146 W. 29th St. #7E New York NY 10001 **Phn:** 212-244-3123 **Fax:** 212-244-3522

Hearst News Service 1850 K St NW #1000 Washington DC 20006 **Phn:** 202-263-6400 **Fax:** 202-263-6441

Hispanic Link News Svc. 1420 N St. NW Washington DC 20005 **Phn:** 202-234-0280 **Fax:** 202-234-4090

Jewish Telegraphic Agncy. 330 7th Ave. Fl 17 New York NY 10001 **Phn:** 212-643-1890 **Fax:** 212-643-8498

King Features 300 W. 57th St. Fl 15 New York NY 10019 **Phn:** 212-969-7550 **Fax:**

Kyodo News Intl. 747 3rd Ave. #1803 New York NY 10017 **Phn:** 212-508-5440 **Fax:** 212-508-5441

LA Times-Wash. Post News Svc. 1150 15th St. NW Washington DC 20071 **Phn:** 202-334-6173 **Fax:** 202-334-5096

Market News Intl. 40 Fulton St. Fl 5 New York NY 10038 **Phn:** 212-669-6400 **Fax:** 212-608-3024

Mature Life Features PO Box 9720 San Diego CA 92169 **Phn:** 858-483-3412 **Fax:**

McClatchy-Tribune News Service 700 12th St NW #1000 Washington DC 20005 **Phn:** 202-383-6080 **Fax:** 202-383-6181

Motor Matters 4635 Bailey Dr. Wilmington DE 19808 **Phn:** 302-998-1650 **Fax:** 302-998-1319

New England News Svc. 66 Alexander Rd. Newton MA 02461 **Phn:** 617-969-4102 **Fax:**

Newhouse News Service 1101 CT Ave. NW #300 Washington DC 20036 **Phn:** 202-383-7800 **Fax:** 202-296-9537

News USA 2841 Hartland Rd. #301 Falls Church VA 22043 **Phn:** 703-734-6300 **Fax:** 703-734-6314

NY Times News Svc. 620 8th Ave. New York NY 10018 **Phn:** 212-556-1927 **Fax:** 212-556-3535

Pacific News Service 275 9th St. San Francisco CA 94103 **Phn:** 415-503-4170 **Fax:** 415-503-0970

PR Newswire 810 7th Ave. Fl 32 New York NY 10019 **Phn:** 212-596-1500 **Fax:** 212-596-1571

Religion News Service 1101 CT Ave. NW #350 Washington DC 20036 **Phn:** 202-463-8777 **Fax:** 202-463-0033

Reuters - CA 445 S. Figueroa #2000 Los Angeles CA 90071 **Phn:** 213-380-2014 **Fax:** 213-622-0056

Reuters - DC 1333 H St. NW #500 Washington DC 20005 **Phn:** 202-898-8300 **Fax:** 202-898-8383

Reuters - IL 311 S. Wacker #1170 Chicago IL 60606 **Phn:** 312-408-8500 **Fax:** 312-983-7351

Reuters - MA 53 State St. Fl 14 Boston MA 02109 **Phn:** 617-367-4106 **Fax:** 617-248-9563

Reuters - NY 3 Times Sq. New York NY 10036 **Phn:** 646-223-4000 **Fax:** 646-223-6001

Scripps-Howard News Svc 1090 VT Ave. NW Fl 10 Washington DC 20005 **Phn:** 202-408-1484 **Fax:** 202-408-5950

Senior Wire News Service 2377 Elm St. Denver CO 80207 **Phn:** 303-355-3882 **Fax:** 303-355-2720

Sports Network 2200 Byberry Rd. Hatboro PA 19040 **Phn:** 215-441-8444 **Fax:** 215-441-5767

Syndicated News Svc. 232 Post Ave. Rochester NY 14619 **Phn:** 585-328-2144 **Fax:** 585-328-7018

Tribune Media Svcs. 435 N. Michigan #1500 Chicago IL 60611 **Phn:** 312-222-4444 **Fax:** 312-222-3459

United Media 200 Madison Ave. Fl 4 New York NY 10016 **Phn:** 212-293-8500 **Fax:** 212-293-8760

United Press Intl 1510 H St. NW #600 Washington DC 20005 **Phn:** 202-898-8000 **Fax:** 202-898-8048

Universal Press Syndicate 4520 Main St. #700 Kansas City MO 64111 **Phn:** 816-932-6600 **Fax:** 816-932-6658

Whitegate Features Synd. 71 Faunce Dr. #1 Providence RI 02906 **Phn:** 401-274-2149 **Fax:**

Wieck Media 12801 N Central Expy. #770 Dallas TX 75243 **Phn:** 972-392-0888 **Fax:** 972-934-8848

NATIONAL

McLean USA Today (2114M) 7950 Jones Branch Dr McLean VA 22108 **Phn:** 703-854-3400 **Fax:** 703-854-2130 www.usatoday.com editor@usatoday.com

New York Wall Street Journal (2100M) 1 World Financial Ctr # 200 New York NY 10281 **Phn:** 212-416-3131 **Fax:** 212-416-2653 online.wsj.com newseditors@wsj.com

ALABAMA

Alexander City Alexander City Outlook (5.1M) PO Box 999 Alexander City AL 35011 **Phn:** 256-234-4281 **Fax:** 256-234-6550 www.alexcityoutlook.com austin.nelson@alexcityoutlook.com

Andalusia Andalusia Star-News (3.4M) PO Box 430 Andalusia AL 36420 **Phn:** 334-222-2402 **Fax:** 334-222-6597 www.andalusiastarnews.com editor@andalusiastarnews.com

Anniston Anniston Star (23.2M) PO Box 189 Anniston AL 36202 **Phn:** 256-236-1551 **Fax:** 256-241-1991 www.annistonstar.com speakout@annistonstar.com

Athens The News Courier (6M) PO Box 670 Athens AL 35612 **Phn:** 256-232-2720 **Fax:** 256-233-7753 enewscourier.com kelly@athensnews-courier.com

Birmingham The Birmingham News (163.5M) PO Box 2553 Birmingham AL 35202 **Phn:** 205-325-2444 **Fax:** 205-325-2283 www.al.com/birminghamnews sdiel@bhamnews.com

Clanton Clanton Advertiser (5M) PO Box 1379 Clanton AL 35046 **Phn:** 205-755-5747 **Fax:** 205-755-5857 www.clantonadvertiser.com newsroom@clantonadvertiser.com

Cullman Cullman Times (10.1M) 300 4th Ave SE Cullman AL 35055 **Phn:** 256-734-2131 **Fax:** 256-736-2972 www.cullmantimes.com editor@cullmantimes.com

Decatur Decatur Daily (19.8M) PO Box 2213 Decatur AL 35609 **Phn:** 256-353-4612 **Fax:** 256-340-2392 decaturdaily.com news@decaturdaily.com

Demopolis Demopolis Times (2.8M) PO Box 860 Demopolis AL 36732 **Phn:** 334-289-4017 **Fax:** 334-289-4019 www.demopolistimes.com news@demopolistimes.com

Dothan Dothan Eagle (35M) PO Box 1968 Dothan AL 36302 **Phn:** 334-792-3141 **Fax:** 334-712-7979 www.dothaneagle.com news@dothaneagle.com

Enterprise Enterprise Ledger (7.1M) PO Box 311130 Enterprise AL 36331 **Phn:** 334-347-9533 **Fax:** 334-347-0825 www.dothaneagle.com/enterprise_ledger news@eprisenow.com

Florence Times Daily (25.2M) PO Box 797 Florence AL 35631 **Phn:** 256-766-3434 **Fax:** 256-740-4717 www.timesdaily.com sherhonda.allen@timesdaily.com

Fort Payne Times-Journal (5M) PO Box 680349 Fort Payne AL 35968 **Phn:** 256-845-2550 **Fax:** 256-845-7459 times-journal.com news@times-journal.com

Gadsden Gadsden Times (21.9M) PO Box 188 Gadsden AL 35902 **Phn:** 256-549-2000 **Fax:** 256-549-2105 www.gadsdentimes.com ron.reaves@gadsdentimes.com

Huntsville Huntsville Times (32.5M) PO Box 1487 Huntsville AL 35807 **Phn:** 256-532-4000 **Fax:** 256-532-4420 www.al.com/huntsvilletimes htimes@htimes.com

Jasper Daily Mountain Eagle (10.2M) PO Box 1469 Jasper AL 35502 **Phn:** 205-221-2840 **Fax:** 205-221-6203 www.mountaineagle.com ron.harris@mountaineagle.com

Lanett Valley Times-News (6.8M) PO Box 850 Lanett AL 36863 **Phn:** 334-644-1101 **Fax:** 334-644-5587 www.valleytimes-news.com news@valleytimes-news.com

DAILY NEWSPAPERS

Mobile Mobile Press-Register (95.7M) PO Box 2488 Mobile AL 36652 **Phn:** 251-433-1551 **Fax:** 251-219-5799 www.al.com/press-register manderson@press-register.com

Montgomery Montgomery Advertiser (46.1M) 425 Molton St Montgomery AL 36104 **Phn:** 334-262-1611 **Fax:** 334-261-1521 www.montgomeryadvertiser.com

Opelika Opelika-Auburn News (13.5M) PO Box 2208 Opelika AL 36803 **Phn:** 334-749-6271 **Fax:** 334-749-1228 www.oanow.com editors@oanow.com

Scottsboro Daily Sentinel (5.5M) PO Box 220 Scottsboro AL 35768 **Phn:** 256-259-1020 **Fax:** 256-259-2709 thedailysentinel.com dsnews@thedailysentinel.com

Selma Selma Times-Journal (5.5M) PO Box 611 Selma AL 36702 **Phn:** 334-875-2110 **Fax:** 334-872-4588 www.selmatimesjournal.com tim.reeves@selmatimesjournal.com

Talladega Daily Home (8.9M) PO Box 977 Talladega AL 35161 **Phn:** 256-362-1000 **Fax:** 256-299-2192 www.dailyhome.com jkeith@dailyhome.com

Troy Troy Messenger (3M) PO Box 727 Troy AL 36081 **Phn:** 334-566-4270 **Fax:** 334-566-4281 www.troymessenger.com stacy.graning@troymessenger.com

Tuscaloosa Tuscaloosa News (33.2M) PO Box 20587 Tuscaloosa AL 35402 **Phn:** 205-345-0505 **Fax:** 205-722-0187 www.tuscaloosanews.com michael.james@tuscaloosanews.com

ALASKA

Anchorage Anchorage Daily News (51.8M) PO Box 149001 Anchorage AK 99514 **Phn:** 907-257-4300 **Fax:** 907-258-2157 www.adn.com newsroom@adn.com

Fairbanks Fairbanks Daily News-Miner (13M) PO Box 70710 Fairbanks AK 99707 **Phn:** 907-456-6661 **Fax:** 907-452-7917 newsminer.com newsroom@newsminer.com

Juneau Juneau Empire (5M) 3100 Channel Dr Ste 1 Juneau AK 99801 **Phn:** 907-586-3740 **Fax:** 907-586-3028 juneauempire.com john.moses@juneauempire.com

Kenai Peninsula Clarion (6.4M) PO Box 3009 Kenai AK 99611 **Phn:** 907-283-7551 **Fax:** 907-283-3299 www.peninsulaclarion.com news@peninsulaclarion.com

Ketchikan Ketchikan News (3.8M) PO Box 7900 Ketchikan AK 99901 **Phn:** 907-225-3157 **Fax:** 907-225-1096 www.ketchikandailynews.com news@ketchikandailynews.com

Kodiak Kodiak Daily Mirror (3.3M) 1419 Selig St Kodiak AK 99615 **Phn:** 907-486-3227 **Fax:** 907-486-3088 www.kodiakdailymirror.com info@kodiakdailymirror.com

Sitka Daily Sitka Sentinel (2M) 112 Barracks St Sitka AK 99835 **Phn:** 907-747-3219 **Fax:** 907-747-8898 www.sitkasentinel.com news@sitkasentinel.com

ARIZONA

Bullhead City Mohave Valley Daily News (10M) PO Box 21209 Bullhead City AZ 86439 **Phn:** 928-763-2505 **Fax:** 928-763-2369 www.mohavedailynews.com mvdnews@mohavedailynews.com

Casa Grande Casa Grande Dispatch (10M) PO Box 15002 Casa Grande AZ 85130 **Phn:** 520-836-7461 **Fax:** 520-836-0343 trivalleycentral.com dkramerjr@trivalleycentral.com

Douglas Daily Dispatch (2.2M) 530 E 11th St Douglas AZ 85607 **Phn:** 520-364-3424 **Fax:** 520-364-6750 www.douglasdispatch.com editor@douglasdispatch.com

Flagstaff Arizona Daily Sun (11.3M) PO Box 1849 Flagstaff AZ 86002 **Phn:** 928-774-4545 **Fax:** 928-773-1934 azdailysun.com azdsnews@azdailysun.com

Kingman Kingman Daily Miner (10M) 3015 N Stockton Hill Rd Kingman AZ 86401 **Phn:** 928-753-6397 **Fax:** 928-753-3796 www.kingmandailyminer.com webmaster@kingmandailyminer.com

Lake Havasu City Today's News Herald (13.3M) 2225 Acoma Blvd W Lake Havasu City AZ 86403 **Phn:** 928-453-4237 **Fax:** 928-855-2637 www.havasunews.com news@havasunews.com

Phoenix Arizona Republic (390M) PO Box 2245 Phoenix AZ 85002 **Phn:** 602-444-8000 **Fax:** 602-444-8044 www.azcentral.com/arizonarepublic newstips@arizonarepublic.com

Prescott Daily Courier (17.3M) PO Box 312 Prescott AZ 86302 **Phn:** 928-445-3333 **Fax:** 928-445-2062 www.dcourier.com editorial@prescottaz.com

Sierra Vista Sierra Vista Herald (20M) 102 Fab Ave Sierra Vista AZ 85635 **Phn:** 520-458-9440 **Fax:** 520-459-0120 www.svherald.com svhnews@transedge.com

Sun City Daily News-Sun (12.6M) 10102 W Santa Fe Dr Sun City AZ 85351 **Phn:** 623-977-8351 **Fax:** 623-876-3698 www.yourwestvalley.com dmccarthy@yourwestvalley.com

Tucson Arizona Daily Star (90M) 4850 S Park Ave Tucson AZ 85714 **Phn:** 520-573-4220 **Fax:** 520-573-4107 azstarnet.com metro@azstarnet.com

Yuma Yuma Sun (21M) PO Box 271 Yuma AZ 85366 **Phn:** 928-783-3333 **Fax:** 928-782-7369 www.yumasun.com tross@yumasun.com

ARKANSAS

Arkadelphia Daily Siftings Herald (2.4M) PO Box 10 Arkadelphia AR 71923 **Phn:** 870-246-5525 **Fax:** 870-246-6556 www.siftingsherald.com siftingsherald@yahoo.com

Batesville Batesville Daily Guard (3.2M) PO Box 2036 Batesville AR 72503 **Phn:** 870-793-2383 **Fax:** 870-793-9268 www.guardonline.com news@guardonline.com

Benton The Saline Courier (5.5M) PO Box 207 Benton AR 72018 **Phn:** 501-315-8228 **Fax:** 501-315-1920 www.bentoncourier.com publisher@bentoncourier.com

Bentonville Benton Co. Daily Record (10M) PO Box 929 Bentonville AR 72712 **Phn:** 479-271-3700 **Fax:** 479-271-3744 www.nwaonline.com

Blytheville Blytheville Courier-News (3.3M) PO Box 1108 Blytheville AR 72316 **Phn:** 870-763-4461 **Fax:** 870-763-6874 www.couriernews.net aweld@couriernews.net

Camden Camden News (4M) PO Box 798 Camden AR 71711 **Phn:** 870-836-8192 **Fax:** 870-837-1414 www.camdenarknews.com camdennews@camdenarknews.com

Conway Log Cabin Democrat (10M) PO Box 969 Conway AR 72033 **Phn:** 501-327-6621 **Fax:** 501-327-6787 thecabin.net mail@thecabin.net

El Dorado El Dorado News-Times (9M) PO Box 912 El Dorado AR 71731 **Phn:** 870-862-6611 **Fax:** 870-862-9482 www.eldoradonews.com shwilson@eldoradonews.com

Fayetteville Northwest Arkansas Times (18M) PO Box 1607 Fayetteville AR 72702 **Phn:** 479-442-1700 **Fax:** 479-442-1714 www.nwaonline.com

Forrest City Times-Herald (4.5M) PO Box 1699 Forrest City AR 72336 **Phn:** 870-633-3130 **Fax:** 870-633-0599 www.thnews.com tamjohns@thnews.com

Fort Smith Times Record (37.8M) PO Box 1359 Fort Smith AR 72902 **Phn:** 479-785-7700 **Fax:** 479-784-0413 www.swtimes.com jgill@swtimes.com

Harrison Harrison Daily Times (9.9M) PO Box 40 Harrison AR 72602 **Phn:** 870-741-2325 **Fax:** 870-741-5632 harrisondaily.com news@harrisondaily.com

Helena Daily World (2.2M) PO Box 340 Helena AR 72342 **Phn:** 870-338-9181 **Fax:** 870-338-9184 www.helena-arkansas.com editorial@helena-arkansas.com

Hope Hope Star (3M) PO Box 648 Hope AR 71802 **Phn:** 870-777-8841 **Fax:** 870-777-3311 www.hopestar.com kmclemore2@yahoo.com

Hot Springs Sentinel-Record (17M) PO Box 580 Hot Springs AR 71902 **Phn:** 501-623-7711 **Fax:** 501-623-2984 www.hotsr.com

Jonesboro Jonesboro Sun (20.7M) PO Box 1249 Jonesboro AR 72403 **Phn:** 870-935-5525 **Fax:** 870-935-5823 www.jonesborosun.com newsroom@jonesborosun.com

Little Rock Arkansas Democrat-Gazette (227M) PO Box 2221 Little Rock AR 72203 **Phn:** 501-378-3400 **Fax:** 501-372-4765 www.arkansasonline.com news@arkansasonline.com

Magnolia Banner-News (3.9M) PO Box 100 Magnolia AR 71754 **Phn:** 870-234-5130 **Fax:** 870-234-2551 www.bannernews.net news@bannernews.net

Malvern Malvern Daily Record (5M) PO Box 70 Malvern AR 72104 **Phn:** 501-337-7523 **Fax:** 501-337-1226 www.malvern-online.com editor@malvern-online.com

Mountain Home Baxter Bulletin (11M) PO Box 1750 Mountain Home AR 72654 **Phn:** 870-425-3133 **Fax:** 870-508-8020 www.baxterbulletin.com newsroom@baxterbulletin.com

Paragould Paragould Daily Press (5.3M) PO Box 38 Paragould AR 72451 **Phn:** 870-239-8562 **Fax:** 870-239-8565 www.paragoulddailypress.com newsinfo@paragoulddailypress.com

Pine Bluff Pine Bluff Commercial (18.5M) PO Box 6469 Pine Bluff AR 71611 **Phn:** 870-534-3400 **Fax:** 870-534-0113 www.pbcommercial.com pbcnews@pbcommercial.com

Russellville The Courier (10.7M) PO Box 887 Russellville AR 72811 **Phn:** 479-968-5252 **Fax:** 479-968-4037 www.couriernews.com editor@couriernews.com

Searcy Daily Citizen (6M) PO Box 1379 Searcy AR 72145 **Phn:** 501-268-8621 **Fax:** 501-268-6277 www.thedailycitizen.com editor@thedailycitizen.com

Searcy Daily Citizen (6M) PO Box 1379 Searcy AR 72145 **Phn:** 501-268-8621 **Fax:** 501-268-6277 www.thedailycitizen.com editor@thedailycitizen.com

Springdale Morning News of NW AR (30M) PO Box 7 Springdale AR 72765 **Phn:** 479-751-6200 **Fax:** 479-872-5055 www.nwaonline.com news@nwaonline.com

Stuttgart Stuttgart Daily Leader (2.4M) 111 W 6th St Stuttgart AR 72160 **Phn:** 870-673-8533 **Fax:** 870-673-3671 www.stuttgartdailyleader.com editor@stuttgartdailyleader.com

West Memphis Evening Times (5M) PO Box 459 West Memphis AR 72303 **Phn:** 870-735-1010 **Fax:** 870-735-1020 www.theeveningtimes.com

CALIFORNIA

Auburn Auburn Journal (10.8M) PO Box 5910 Auburn CA 95604 **Phn:** 530-885-5656 **Fax:** 530-887-1231 www.auburnjournal.com ajournal@goldcountrymedia.com

Bakersfield Bakersfield Californian (144M) PO Box 440 Bakersfield CA 93302 **Phn:** 661-395-7500 **Fax:** 661-395-7519 www.bakersfield.com local@bakersfield.com

ARKANSAS DAILY NEWSPAPERS

Barstow Desert Dispatch (4.5M) 130 Coolwater Ln Barstow CA 92311 **Phn:** 760-256-2257 **Fax:** 760-256-0685 www.desertdispatch.com klovato@desertdispatch.com

Benicia Benicia Herald (3.4M) 820 1st St Benicia CA 94510 **Phn:** 707-745-0733 **Fax:** 707-745-8583 beniciaherald.me beniciaherald@gmail.com

Camarillo Ventura County Star (78M) PO Box 6006 Camarillo CA 93011 **Phn:** 805-437-0000 **Fax:** 805-482-6167 www.vcstar.com feedback@venturacountystar.com

Chico Chico Enterprise-Record (31M) PO Box 9 Chico CA 95927 **Phn:** 530-891-1234 **Fax:** 530-342-3617 www.chicoer.com localnews@chicoer.com

Costa Mesa Daily Pilot (24.5M) 1375 Sunflower Ave Costa Mesa CA 92626 **Phn:** 714-966-4600 **Fax:** 714-966-4667 www.dailypilot.com john.canalis@latimes.com

Crescent City Daily Triplicate (5.3M) PO Box 277 Crescent City CA 95531 **Phn:** 707-464-2141 **Fax:** 707-465-6369 www.triplicate.com rwiens@triplicate.com

Davis Davis Enterprise (10.3M) 315 G St Davis CA 95616 **Phn:** 530-756-0800 **Fax:** 530-756-1668 www.davisenterprise.com newsroom@davisenterprise.net

El Centro Imperial Valley Press (12M) 205 N 8th St El Centro CA 92243 **Phn:** 760-337-3400 **Fax:** 760-353-3003 www.ivpressonline.com rbrown@ivpressonline.com

Escondido North County Times (87M) 207 E Pennsylvania Ave Escondido CA 92025 **Phn:** 760-839-3333 **Fax:** 760-745-3769 www.utsandiego.com/news/communities/north-county metro@utsandiego.com

Eureka Times-Standard (19.9M) PO Box 3580 Eureka CA 95502 **Phn:** 707-441-0500 **Fax:** 707-441-0501 www.times-standard.com newsdesk@times-standard.com

Fairfield Daily Republic (17M) PO Box 47 Fairfield CA 94533 **Phn:** 707-425-4646 **Fax:** 707-425-5924 www.dailyrepublic.com gfaison@dailyrepublic.net

Fremont The Argus (26.4M) 39737 Paseo Padre Pkwy Fremont CA 94538 **Phn:** 510-353-7001 **Fax:** 510-353-7029 www.insidebayarea.com/argus bangcirc@bayareanewsgroup.com

Fresno Fresno Bee (149M) 1626 E St Fresno CA 93786 **Phn:** 559-441-6111 **Fax:** 559-441-6436 www.fresnobee.com metro@fresnobee.com

Gilroy The Dispatch (4.3M) PO Box 22365 Gilroy CA 95021 **Phn:** 408-842-6400 **Fax:** 408-842-2206 www.gilroydispatch.com

Glendale Glendale News-Press (36M) 221 N Brand Blvd Glendale CA 91203 **Phn:** 818-637-3200 **Fax:** 818-241-1975 www.glendalenewspress.com jason.wells@latimes.com

Grass Valley The Union (15.9M) 464 Sutton Way Grass Valley CA 95945 **Phn:** 530-273-9561 **Fax:** 530-477-4292 www.theunion.com letters@theunion.com

Hanford Hanford Sentinel (14M) PO Box 9 Hanford CA 93232 **Phn:** 559-582-0471 **Fax:** 559-587-1876 www.hanfordsentinel.com kkennedy@hanfordsentinel.com

Hollister Free Lance (3M) PO Box 1417 Hollister CA 95023 **Phn:** 831-637-5566 **Fax:** 831-637-4104 www.sanbenitocountytoday.com editor@freelancenews.com

Lakeport Lake County Record-Bee (7.3M) PO Box 849 Lakeport CA 95453 **Phn:** 707-263-5636 **Fax:** 707-263-0600 www.record-bee.com mfeder@record-bee.com

Lodi Lodi News-Sentinel (16.4M) PO Box 1360 Lodi CA 95241 **Phn:** 209-369-2761 **Fax:** 209-369-6706 www.lodinews.com news@lodinews.com

Long Beach Press-Telegram (87.6M) 300 Oceangate Long Beach CA 90844 **Phn:** 562-435-1161 **Fax:** 562-499-1232 www.presstelegram.com robert.meeks@presstelegram.com

Los Angeles Los Angeles Times (723M) 202 W 1st St Los Angeles CA 90012 **Phn:** 213-237-5000 **Fax:** 213-237-4712 www.latimes.com metrodesk@latimes.com

Madera Madera Tribune (5.3M) PO Box 269 Madera CA 93639 **Phn:** 559-674-2424 **Fax:** 559-673-6526 www.maderatribune.com

Manteca Manteca Bulletin (7M) PO Box 1958 Manteca CA 95336 **Phn:** 209-249-3500 **Fax:** 209-249-3559 www.mantecabulletin.com news@mantecabulletin.com

Marysville Appeal-Democrat (20M) 1530 Ellis Lake Dr Marysville CA 95901 **Phn:** 530-741-2345 **Fax:** 530-741-0140 www.appeal-democrat.com evodden@appealdemocrat.com

Menlo Park Palo Alto Daily News (30M) 255 Constitution Dr Menlo Park CA 94025 **Phn:** 650-391-1000 **Fax:** 650-391-1333 www.mercurynews.com/peninsula kmclaughlin@mercurynews.com

Merced Merced Sun-Star (19.4M) 3033 G St Merced CA 95340 **Phn:** 209-722-1511 **Fax:** 209-385-2460 www.mercedsunstar.com dhill@mercedsun-star.com

Modesto Modesto Bee (79.6M) PO Box 5256 Modesto CA 95352 **Phn:** 209-578-2000 **Fax:** 209-578-2207 www.modbee.com local@modbee.com

Monterey Monterey County Herald (29.6M) PO Box 271 Monterey CA 93942 **Phn:** 831-372-3311 **Fax:** 831-372-8401 www.montereyherald.com rcalkins@montereyherald.com

Napa Napa Valley Register (15M) PO Box 150 Napa CA 94559 **Phn:** 707-226-3711 **Fax:** 707-224-3963 napavalleyregister.com michael.donnelly@lee.net

Oakland Oakland Tribune (52.7M) 7677 Oakport St Ste 950 Oakland CA 94621 **Phn:** 510-208-6400 **Fax:** 510-208-6477 www.insidebayarea.com/oaklandtribune mreynolds@bayareanewsgroup.com

Ontario Inland Valley Daily Bulletin (55M) PO Box 4000 Ontario CA 91761 **Phn:** 909-987-6397 **Fax:** 909-948-9038 www.dailybulletin.com ben.demers@inlandnewspapers.com

Oroville Mercury-Register (7M) 2124 5th Ave Oroville CA 95965 **Phn:** 530-533-3131 **Fax:** 530-533-3127 www.orovillemr.com fcrosthwaite@chicoer.com

Palm Springs Desert Sun (45M) PO Box 2734 Palm Springs CA 92263 **Phn:** 760-322-8889 **Fax:** 760-778-4654 www.mydesert.com localnews@thedesertsun.com

Palmdale Antelope Valley Press (21M) PO Box 4050 Palmdale CA 93590 **Phn:** 661-273-2700 **Fax:** 661-947-4870 www.avpress.com editor@avpress.com

Pasadena Pasadena Star-News (29.7M) 911 E Colorado Blvd Ste 100 Pasadena CA 91106 **Phn:** 626-578-6300 **Fax:** 626-432-5248 www.pasadenastarnews.com news.star-news@sgvn.com

Placerville Mountain Democrat (12.5M) PO Box 1088 Placerville CA 95667 **Phn:** 530-622-1255 **Fax:** 530-622-7894 www-new.mtdemocrat.com mtdemo@mtdemocrat.net

Pleasanton Tri-Valley Herald (33.4M) 127 Spring St Pleasanton CA 94566 **Phn:** 925-734-8600 **Fax:** 925-847-2189 www.insidebayarea.com/trivalleyherald srichards@bayareanewsgroup.com

Porterville Porterville Recorder (9.1M) PO Box 151 Porterville CA 93258 **Phn:** 559-784-5000 **Fax:** 559-784-1689 www.recorderonline.com gfaison@portervillerecorder.com

Red Bluff Red Bluff Daily News (6.8M) PO Box 220 Red Bluff CA 96080 **Phn:** 530-527-2151 **Fax:** 530-527-9251 www.redbluffdailynews.com editor@redbluffdailynews.com

Redding Record Searchlight (33.5M) PO Box 492397 Redding CA 96049 **Phn:** 530-243-2424 **Fax:** 530-225-8236 www.redding.com letters@redding.com

Redlands Redlands Daily Facts (6.5M) 700 Brookside Ave Redlands CA 92373 **Phn:** 909-793-3221 **Fax:** 909-793-9588 www.redlandsdailyfacts.com frank.pine@inlandnewspapers.com

Ridgecrest Daily Independent (7M) 224 E Ridgecrest Blvd Ridgecrest CA 93556 **Phn:** 760-375-4481 **Fax:** 760-375-4880 www.ridgecrestca.com

Riverside Press-Enterprise (171M) 3450 14th St Riverside CA 92501 **Phn:** 951-684-1200 **Fax:** 951-368-9023 www.pe.com news@pe.com

Sacramento Sacramento Bee (274M) PO Box 15779 Sacramento CA 95852 **Phn:** 916-321-1001 **Fax:** 916-321-1109 www.sacbee.com jterhaar@sacbee.com

Salinas The Salinas Californian (19.3M) 123 W Alisal St Salinas CA 93901 **Phn:** 831-754-4260 **Fax:** 831-754-4293 www.thecalifornian.com newsroom@thecalifornian.com

San Bernardino San Bernardino Sun (62.3M) 4030 Georgia Blvd San Bernardino CA 92407 **Phn:** 909-889-9666 **Fax:** 909-885-8741 www.sbsun.com citydesk@inlandnewspapers.com

San Diego San Diego Union-Tribune (261M) PO Box 120191 San Diego CA 92112 **Phn:** 619-299-3131 **Fax:** 619-293-1896 www.utsandiego.com metro@utsandiego.com

San Francisco San Francisco Chronicle (312M) 901 Mission St San Francisco CA 94103 **Phn:** 415-777-1111 **Fax:** 415-896-1107 www.sfgate.com eallday@sfchronicle.com

San Francisco San Francisco Examiner (165M) 71 Stevenson St San Francisco CA 94124 **Phn:** 415-359-2600 **Fax:** 415-359-2766 www.sfexaminer.com newstips@sfexaminer.com

San Jose San Jose Mercury-News (229M) 750 Ridder Park Dr San Jose CA 95190 **Phn:** 408-920-5000 **Fax:** 408-288-8060 www.mercurynews.com mfrankel@mercurynews.com

San Luis Obispo The Tribune (37.4M) PO Box 112 San Luis Obispo CA 93406 **Phn:** 805-781-7800 **Fax:** 805-781-7905 www.sanluisobispo.com newsroom@thetribunenews.com

San Mateo San Mateo County Times (29.4M) 477 9th Ave Ste 110 San Mateo CA 94402 **Phn:** 650-348-4321 **Fax:** 650-348-4446 www.mercurynews.com local@mercurynews.com

San Mateo San Mateo Daily Journal (14.8M) 800 S Claremont St Ste 210 San Mateo CA 94402 **Phn:** 650-344-5200 **Fax:** 650-344-5290 www.smdailyjournal.com news@smdailyjournal.com

San Rafael Marin Independent Journal (33M) 4000 Civic Center Dr Ste 301 San Rafael CA 94903 **Phn:** 415-883-8600 **Fax:** 415-382-7209 www.marinij.com localnews@marinij.com

Santa Ana Long Beach Register (287M) PO Box 11626 Santa Ana CA 92711 **Phn:** 714-796-7000 **Fax:** 714-796-3681 www.lbregister.com connect@ocregister.com

Santa Ana Orange County Register (287M) PO Box 11626 Santa Ana CA 92711 **Phn:** 714-796-7000 **Fax:** 714-796-3681 www.ocregister.com epaper@ocregister.com

CALIFORNIA DAILY NEWSPAPERS

Santa Barbara Santa Barbara News-Press (39.3M) PO Box 1359 Santa Barbara CA 93102 **Phn:** 805-564-5200 **Fax:** 805-966-6258 www.newspress.com news@newspress.com

Santa Clarita The Signal (9.2M) PO Box 801870 Santa Clarita CA 91380 **Phn:** 661-259-1234 **Fax:** 661-254-8068 www.signalscv.com lila@signalscv.com

Santa Maria Lompoc Record (6.6M) PO Box 400 Santa Maria CA 93456 **Phn:** 805-736-2313 **Fax:** 805-735-5118 www.lompocrecord.com jscully@lompocrecord.com

Santa Maria Santa Maria Times (19.3M) PO Box 400 Santa Maria CA 93456 **Phn:** 805-925-2691 **Fax:** 805-928-5657 www.santamariatimes.com lwood@santamariatimes.com

Santa Monica Santa Monica Daily Press (19M) 1640 5th St St 218 Santa Monica CA 90401 **Phn:** 310-458-7737 **Fax:** 310-576-9913 www.smdp.com editor@smdp.com

Santa Rosa Press Democrat (82.7M) PO Box 910 Santa Rosa CA 95402 **Phn:** 707-546-2020 **Fax:** 707-521-5330 www.pressdemocrat.com

Scotts Valley Santa Cruz Sentinel (24.4M) 1800 Green Hills Rd Ste 210 Scotts Valley CA 95066 **Phn:** 831-423-4242 **Fax:** 831-429-9620 www.santacruzsentinel.com dmiller@santacruzsentinel.com

Sonora Union Democrat (11.8M) 84 S Washington St Sonora CA 95370 **Phn:** 209-532-7151 **Fax:** 209-532-6451 www.uniondemocrat.com editor@uniondemocrat.com

South Lake Tahoe Tahoe Daily Tribune (7.7M) 3079 Harrison Ave South Lake Tahoe CA 96150 **Phn:** 530-541-3880 **Fax:** 530-541-0373 www.tahoedailytribune.com editor@tahoedailytribune.com

Stockton The Record (58.3M) PO Box 900 Stockton CA 95201 **Phn:** 209-943-6397 **Fax:** 209-547-8186 www.recordnet.com jcriesi@recordnet.com

Torrance Daily Breeze (65.6M) 21250 Hawthorne Blvd Ste 170S Torrance CA 90503 **Phn:** 310-540-5511 **Fax:** 310-540-6272 www.dailybreeze.com newsroom@dailybreeze.com

Tracy Tracy Press (7.7M) PO Box 419 Tracy CA 95378 **Phn:** 209-835-3030 **Fax:** 209-835-0655 www.tracypress.com tpnews@tracypress.com

Tulare Tulare Advance-Register (7M) PO Box 31 Tulare CA 93279 **Phn:** 559-688-0521 **Fax:** 559-688-5580 www.visaliatimesdelta.com news@visaliatimesdelta.com

Ukiah Ukiah Daily Journal (7M) PO Box 749 Ukiah CA 95482 **Phn:** 707-468-3500 **Fax:** 707-468-5780 www.ukiahdailyjournal.com udj@pacific.net

Vacaville The Reporter (17.9M) 916 Cotting Ln Vacaville CA 95688 **Phn:** 707-448-6401 **Fax:** 707-451-5210 www.thereporter.com rmiller@thereporter.com

Vallejo Vallejo Times-Herald (17.3M) 440 Curtola Pkwy Vallejo CA 94590 **Phn:** 707-644-1141 **Fax:** 707-553-6851 www.timesheraldonline.com tvollmer@timesheraldonline.com

Victorville Daily Press (30.4M) PO Box 1389 Victorville CA 92393 **Phn:** 760-241-7744 **Fax:** 760-241-1860 www.vvdailypress.com vvnews@vvdailypress.com

Visalia Visalia Times-Delta (19.7M) PO Box 31 Visalia CA 93279 **Phn:** 559-735-3200 **Fax:** 559-735-3399 www.visaliatimesdelta.com news@visaliatimesdelta.com

Walnut Creek Contra Costa Times (160M) PO Box 8099 Walnut Creek CA 94596 **Phn:** 925-935-2525 **Fax:** 925-943-8362 www.contracostatimes.com ccnnewsrelease@bayareanewsgroup.com

Watsonville Register-Pajaronian (5.2M) 100 Westridge Dr Watsonville CA 95076 **Phn:** 831-761-7300 **Fax:** 831-761-7338 www.register-pajaronian.com newsroom@register-pajaronian.com

West Covina San Gabriel Valley Tribune (42.6M) 1210 N Azusa Canyon Rd West Covina CA 91790 **Phn:** 626-962-8811 **Fax:** 626-814-4729 www.sgvtribune.com news.tribune@sgvn.com

Whittier Whittier Daily News (16.3M) 7612 Greenleaf Ave Whittier CA 90602 **Phn:** 562-698-0955 **Fax:** 562-698-0450 www.whittierdailynews.com steve.hunt@sgvn.com

Woodland Daily Democrat (9.4M) 711 Main St Woodland CA 95695 **Phn:** 530-662-5421 **Fax:** 530-406-6262 www.dailydemocrat.com news@dailydemocrat.com

Woodland Hills Daily News (151M) PO Box 4200 Woodland Hills CA 91365 **Phn:** 818-713-3000 **Fax:** 818-713-0058 www.dailynews.com dnmetro@dailynews.com

Yreka Siskiyou Daily News (5.6M) PO Box 129 Yreka CA 96097 **Phn:** 530-842-5777 **Fax:** 530-842-6787 www.siskiyoudaily.com clynch@siskiyoudaily.com

COLORADO

Alamosa Valley Courier (6M) PO Box 1099 Alamosa CO 81101 **Phn:** 719-589-2553 **Fax:** 719-589-6573 www.alamosanews.com news@alamosanews.com

Aspen Aspen Daily News (12.5M) 517 E Hopkins Ave Ste 206 Aspen CO 81611 **Phn:** 970-925-2220 **Fax:** 970-920-2118 www.aspendailynews.com sack@aspendailynews.com

Aspen Aspen Times (11M) 310 E Main St Aspen CO 81611 **Phn:** 970-925-3414 **Fax:** 970-925-6240 www.aspentimes.com mail@aspentimes.com

Boulder Colorado Daily (20M) 5450 Western Ave Boulder CO 80301 **Phn:** 303-473-1111 **Fax:** www.coloradodaily.com editor@coloradodaily.com

Boulder Daily Camera (29.9M) PO Box 591 Boulder CO 80306 **Phn:** 303-442-1202 **Fax:** 303-449-9358 www.dailycamera.com newsroom@dailycamera.com

Canon City Daily Record (8M) 701 S 9th St Canon City CO 81212 **Phn:** 719-275-7565 **Fax:** 719-275-1353 www.canoncitydailyrecord.com

Colorado Springs The Gazette (98.1M) 30 S Prospect St Colorado Springs CO 80903 **Phn:** 719-632-5511 **Fax:** 719-636-0202 www.gazette.com citydesk@gazette.com

Craig Craig Daily Press (3.4M) PO Box 5 Craig CO 81626 **Phn:** 970-824-7031 **Fax:** 970-824-6810 www.craigdailypress.com editor@craigdailypress.com

Denver Denver Post (372M) 101 W Colfax Ave Denver CO 80202 **Phn:** 303-954-1010 **Fax:** 303-954-1369 www.denverpost.com newsroom@denverpost.com

Durango Durango Herald (9M) PO Box A Durango CO 81302 **Phn:** 970-247-3504 **Fax:** 970-259-5011 www.durangoherald.com herald@durangoherald.com

Fort Collins Fort Collins Coloradoan (27.4M) 1300 Riverside Ave Fort Collins CO 80524 **Phn:** 970-493-6397 **Fax:** 970-224-7899 www.coloradoan.com joshuaawtry@coloradoan.com

Fort Morgan Fort Morgan Times (4M) 329 Main St Fort Morgan CO 80701 **Phn:** 970-867-5651 **Fax:** 970-867-7448 www.fortmorgantimes.com editor@fmtimes.com

Frisco Summit Daily News (9.7M) PO Box 329 Frisco CO 80443 **Phn:** 970-668-3998 **Fax:** 970-668-0755 www.summitdaily.com news@summitdaily.com

Glenwood Springs Glenwood Springs Post-Independent (5.1M) 824 Grand Ave Glenwood Springs CO 81601 **Phn:** 970-945-8515 **Fax:** 970-945-4487 www.postindependent.com dmunro@postindependent.com

Grand Junction Daily Sentinel (30.5M) PO Box 668 Grand Junction CO 81502 **Phn:** 970-242-5050 **Fax:** 970-244-8578 www.gjsentinel.com laurena.davis@gjsentinel.com

Greeley Greeley Daily Tribune (25.2M) 501 8th Ave Greeley CO 80631 **Phn:** 970-352-0211 **Fax:** 970-356-5780 www.greeleytribune.com rbangert@greeleytribune.com

La Junta La Junta Tribune-Democrat (3.7M) PO Box 500 La Junta CO 81050 **Phn:** 719-384-4475 **Fax:** 719-384-5999 www.lajuntatribunedemocrat.com editor@ljtdmail.com

Longmont Daily Times-Call (20.3M) PO Box 299 Longmont CO 80502 **Phn:** 303-776-2244 **Fax:** 303-678-8615 www.timescall.com pressrelease@times-call.com

Loveland Daily Reporter-Herald (15M) 201 E 5th St Loveland CO 80537 **Phn:** 970-669-5050 **Fax:** 970-667-1111 www.reporterherald.com news@reporter-herald.com

Montrose Montrose Daily Press (5.4M) PO Box 850 Montrose CO 81402 **Phn:** 970-249-3444 **Fax:** 970-249-2370 www.montrosepress.com katharhynnh@montrosepress.com

Pueblo Pueblo Chieftain (40.5M) 825 W 6th St Pueblo CO 81003 **Phn:** 719-544-3520 **Fax:** www.chieftain.com city@chieftain.com

Rocky Ford Rocky Ford Daily Gazette (3M) PO Box 430 Rocky Ford CO 81067 **Phn:** 719-254-3351 **Fax:** 719-254-3354

Salida Mountain Mail (3.5M) PO Box 189 Salida CO 81201 **Phn:** 719-539-6691 **Fax:** 719-539-6630 themountainmail.com staff@themountainmail.com

Steamboat Springs Steamboat Today & Pilot (5.8M) PO Box 774827 Steamboat Springs CO 80477 **Phn:** 970-879-1502 **Fax:** 970-879-2888 www.steamboattoday.com editor@steamboattoday.com

Sterling Journal-Advocate (3.2M) PO Box 1272 Sterling CO 80751 **Phn:** 970-522-1990 **Fax:** 970-522-2320 www.journal-advocate.com jtonsing@journal-advocate.com

Telluride Telluride Daily Planet (3.8M) PO Box 2315 Telluride CO 81435 **Phn:** 970-728-9788 **Fax:** 970-728-9793 www.telluridenews.com editor@telluridenews.com

Trinidad Chronicle News (3.3M) PO Box 763 Trinidad CO 81082 **Phn:** 719-846-3311 **Fax:** 719-846-3612 www.thechronicle-news.com asheumaker@gmail.com

Vail Vail Daily (10.5M) PO Box 81 Vail CO 81658 **Phn:** 970-949-0555 **Fax:** 970-949-7096 www.vaildaily.com newsroom@vaildaily.com

CONNECTICUT

Bridgeport Connecticut Post (74M) 410 State St Bridgeport CT 06604 **Phn:** 203-333-0161 **Fax:** 203-367-8158 www.ctpost.com edit@ctpost.com

Bristol Bristol Press (9.4M) 188 Main St Bristol CT 06010 **Phn:** 860-584-0501 **Fax:** 860-584-2192 bristolpress.com editor@bristolpress.com

Danbury News-Times (28.2M) 333 Main St Danbury CT 06810 **Phn:** 203-744-5100 **Fax:** 203-792-8730 www.newstimes.com jsmith@newstimes.com

Hartford Hartford Courant (179M) 285 Broad St Hartford CT 06115 **Phn:** 860-241-6200 **Fax:** 860-241-3865 www.courant.com dhaar@courant.com

COLORADO DAILY NEWSPAPERS

Manchester Journal Inquirer (40M) PO Box 510 Manchester CT 06045 **Phn:** 860-646-0500 **Fax:** 860-646-9867 www.journalinquirer.com news@journalinquirer.com

Meriden Record-Journal (21.7M) 11 Crown St Meriden CT 06450 **Phn:** 203-235-1661 **Fax:** 203-639-0210 www.myrecordjournal.com newsroom@record-journal.com

Middletown Middletown Press (7.3M) 386 Main St Ste 101 Middletown CT 06457 **Phn:** 860-347-3331 **Fax:** 860-347-4425 www.ctcentral.com editor@middletownpress.com

New Britain The Herald (11.4M) 1 Court St 4th Floor New Britain CT 06051 **Phn:** 860-225-4601 **Fax:** 860-223-8171 www.newbritainherald.com mbatterson@newbritainherald.com

New Haven New Haven Register (80.2M) 40 Sargent Dr New Haven CT 06511 **Phn:** 203-789-5200 **Fax:** 203-865-7894 www.ctcentral.com mbrackenbury@nhregister.com

New London The Day (37M) PO Box 1231 New London CT 06320 **Phn:** 860-442-2200 **Fax:** 860-442-5599 www.theday.com tips@theday.com

Norwalk The Hour (15.7M) PO Box 790 Norwalk CT 06852 **Phn:** 203-846-3281 **Fax:** 203-840-1802 www.thehour.com news@thehour.com

Norwich Norwich Bulletin (23.6M) 66 Franklin St Norwich CT 06360 **Phn:** 860-887-9211 **Fax:** 860-887-9666 www.norwichbulletin.com news@norwichbulletin.com

Old Greenwich Greenwich Time (10.4M) 1455 E Putnam Ave Ste 101 Old Greenwich CT 06870 **Phn:** 203-625-4400 **Fax:** 203-964-2345 www.greenwichtime.com thomas.mellana@scni.com

Stamford Stamford Advocate (23.9M) 9 Riverbend Dr S Bldg A Stamford CT 06907 **Phn:** 203-964-2257 **Fax:** 203-964-2345 www.stamfordadvocate.com john.breunig@scni.com

Torrington Register Citizen (7.5M) 59 Field St Torrington CT 06790 **Phn:** 860-489-3121 **Fax:** 860-489-6790 www.registercitizen.com editor@registercitizen.com

Waterbury Waterbury Republican-American (51.7M) 389 Meadow St Waterbury CT 06702 **Phn:** 203-574-3636 **Fax:** 203-596-9277 www.rep-am.com releases@rep-am.com

Willimantic The Chronicle (9.5M) PO Box 148 Willimantic CT 06226 **Phn:** 860-423-8466 **Fax:** 860-423-6585 thechronicle.com editor@thechronicle.com

DELAWARE

Dover Delaware State News (16M) 110 Galaxy Dr Dover DE 19901 **Phn:** 302-674-3600 **Fax:** delaware.newszap.com newsroom@newszap.com

Wilmington News Journal (113M) PO Box 15505 Wilmington DE 19850 **Phn:** 302-324-2500 **Fax:** 302-324-5509 www.delawareonline.com dledford@delawareonline.com

DISTRICT OF COLUMBIA

Washington Washington Post (665M) 1150 15th St NW Washington DC 20071 **Phn:** 202-334-6000 **Fax:** 202-334-5672 www.washingtonpost.com national@washpost.com

Washington Washington Times (100M) 3600 New York Ave NE Washington DC 20002 **Phn:** 202-636-3000 **Fax:** 202-832-0659 www.washingtontimes.com

FLORIDA

Bradenton Bradenton Herald (46.8M) PO Box 921 Bradenton FL 34206 **Phn:** 941-748-0411 **Fax:** 941-745-7097 www.bradenton.com jkrauter@bradentonherald.com

Brooksville Hernando Today (15.1M) 15299 Cortez Blvd Brooksville FL 34613 **Phn:** 352-544-5200 **Fax:** 352-799-5246 www.hernandotoday.com mterry@hernandotoday.com

Cape Coral Cape Coral Daily Breeze (2M) 2510 Del Prado Blvd S Cape Coral FL 33904 **Phn:** 239-574-1110 **Fax:** 239-574-5693 www.breezenewspapers.com vharring@breezenewspapers.com

Crystal River Citrus Co. Chronicle (27.1M) 1624 N Meadowcrest Blvd Crystal River FL 34429 **Phn:** 352-563-6363 **Fax:** 352-563-3280 www.chronicleonline.com newsdesk@chronicleonline.com

Daytona Beach Daytona Beach News-Journal (102M) PO Box 2831 Daytona Beach FL 32120 **Phn:** 386-252-1511 **Fax:** 386-258-8465 www.news-journalonline.com metro@news-jrnl.com

Englewood Englewood Sun (5M) 120 W Dearborn St Englewood FL 34223 **Phn:** 941-681-3000 **Fax:** 941-681-3008 www.yoursun.com porter@sun-herald.com

Fort Lauderdale S. Florida Sun-Sentinel (235M) 200 E Las Olas Blvd Fort Lauderdale FL 33301 **Phn:** 954-356-4000 **Fax:** 954-356-4559 www.sun-sentinel.com dbanker@sun-sentinel.com

Fort Myers News-Press (88.6M) PO Box 10 Fort Myers FL 33902 **Phn:** 239-335-0200 **Fax:** 239-334-0708 www.news-press.com publisher@news-press.com

Fort Pierce The Tribune (102M) 600 Edwards Rd Fort Pierce FL 34982 **Phn:** 772-461-2050 **Fax:** 772-461-4447 www.tcpalm.com

Fort Walton Beach NW Florida Daily News (37.8M) PO Box 2949 Fort Walton Beach FL 32549 **Phn:** 850-863-1111 **Fax:** 850-863-7834 www.nwfdailynews.com clipnicky@nwfdailynews.com

Gainesville Gainesville Sun (47.2M) PO Box 147147 Gainesville FL 32614 **Phn:** 352-374-5000 **Fax:** 352-338-3128 gainesvillesun.com levinej@gvillesun.com

Jacksonville Florida Times-Union (155M) PO Box 1949 Jacksonville FL 32231 **Phn:** 904-359-4111 **Fax:** 904-359-4478 jacksonville.com scott.butler@jacksonville.com

Key West Key West Citizen (9M) PO Box 1800 Key West FL 33041 **Phn:** 305-292-7777 **Fax:** 305-295-8013 keysnews.com sfrederick@keysnews.com

Lake City Lake City Reporter (9M) PO Box 1709 Lake City FL 32056 **Phn:** 386-752-1293 **Fax:** 386-752-9400 www.lakecityreporter.com news@lakecityreporter.com

Lakeland The Ledger (70.5M) PO Box 408 Lakeland FL 33802 **Phn:** 863-802-7000 **Fax:** 863-802-7809 www.theledger.com newstips@theledger.com

Leesburg Daily Commercial (22.9M) PO Box 490007 Leesburg FL 34749 **Phn:** 352-365-8200 **Fax:** 352-365-1951 www.dailycommercial.com news@dailycommercial.com

Marianna Jackson Co. Floridan (6.5M) PO Box 520 Marianna FL 32447 **Phn:** 850-526-3614 **Fax:** 850-482-4478 www.jcfloridan.com editorial@jcfloridan.com

Melbourne Florida Today (81.8M) PO Box 419000 Melbourne FL 32941 **Phn:** 321-242-3500 **Fax:** 321-242-6620 www.floridatoday.com gkaiser@brevard.gannett.com

Miami Miami Herald (280M) 3511 NW 91st Ave Miami FL 33172 **Phn:** 305-350-2111 **Fax:** 305-376-5287 www.miamiherald.com heralded@miamiherald.com

Naples Naples Daily News (58.2M) 1100 Immokalee Rd Naples FL 34110 **Phn:** 239-262-3161 **Fax:** 239-435-3451 www.naplesnews.com news@naplesnews.com

New Smyrna Beach The Observer (2M) PO Box 1396 New Smyrna Beach FL 32170 **Phn:** 386-427-1000 **Fax:** 386-424-9858 editor@nsbobserver.com

North Port North Port Sun (40M) 13487 Tamiami Trl North Port FL 34287 **Phn:** 941-429-3000 **Fax:** 941-429-3007 www.yoursun.com lorraines@sun-herald.com

Ocala Star-Banner (49.2M) 2121 SW 19th Avenue Rd Ocala FL 34471 **Phn:** 352-867-4010 **Fax:** 352-867-4018 www.ocala.com jim.ross@starbanner.com

Okeechobee Okeechobee News (2.6M) 107 SW 17th St Ste D Okeechobee FL 34974 **Phn:** 863-763-3134 **Fax:** 863-763-5901 florida.newszap.com okeenews@newszap.com

Orlando Orlando Sentinel (222M) 633 N Orange Ave Orlando FL 32801 **Phn:** 407-420-5000 **Fax:** 407-420-5350 www.orlandosentinel.com mrussell@orlandosentinel.com

Palatka Daily News (12.1M) PO Box 777 Palatka FL 32178 **Phn:** 386-312-5200 **Fax:** 386-312-5226 www.palatkadailynews.com rstarr@palatkadailynews.com

Palm Beach Palm Beach Daily News (6.3M) 400 Royal Palm Way Ste 100 Palm Beach FL 33480 **Phn:** 561-820-3800 **Fax:** 561-655-4594 www.palmbeachdailynews.com adavis@pbdailynews.com

Panama City Panama City News Herald (29.6M) 501 W 11th St Panama City FL 32401 **Phn:** 850-747-5000 **Fax:** 850-747-5097 www.newsherald.com mmcazalas@pcnh.com

Pensacola Pensacola News Journal (60.7M) PO Box 12710 Pensacola FL 32591 **Phn:** 850-435-8500 **Fax:** 850-435-8633 www.pnj.com helpdesk@pnj.com

Port Charlotte Charlotte Sun (43.1M) 23170 Harborview Rd Port Charlotte FL 33980 **Phn:** 941-206-1000 **Fax:** 941-629-2085 www.yoursun.com porter@sun-herald.com

Saint Augustine St. Augustine Record (18.3M) PO Box 1630 Saint Augustine FL 32085 **Phn:** 904-829-6562 **Fax:** 904-819-3558 staugustine.com editor@staugustinerecord.com

Saint Petersburg Tampa Bay Times (283M) 490 1st Ave S Saint Petersburg FL 33701 **Phn:** 727-893-8111 **Fax:** 727-893-8675 www.tampabay.com biznews@tampabay.com

Sarasota Sarasota Herald-Tribune (76.6M) 1741 Main St Sarasota FL 34236 **Phn:** 941-953-7755 **Fax:** 941-361-4880 www.heraldtribune.com advocate@heraldtribune.com

Sebring Highlands Today (16.6M) 315 US Highway 27 N Sebring FL 33870 **Phn:** 863-386-5800 **Fax:** 863-382-1076 www.highlandstoday.com rhensley@highlandstoday.com

Stuart Treasure Coast News/Press Tribune (102M) PO Box 9009 Stuart FL 34995 **Phn:** 772-287-1550 **Fax:** 772-221-4246 www.tcpalm.com dennis.durkee@scripps.com

Tallahassee Tallahassee Democrat (48.7M) 277 N Magnolia Dr Tallahassee FL 32301 **Phn:** 850-599-2100 **Fax:** 850-599-2223 www.tallahassee.com rcantley@tallahassee.com

Tampa Tampa Tribune (220M) PO Box 191 Tampa FL 33601 **Phn:** 813-259-7711 **Fax:** 813-259-7676 tbo.com info@tbo.com

The Villages The Villages Daily Sun (27.8M) 1100 Main St The Villages FL 32159 **Phn:** 352-753-1119 **Fax:** 352-753-7787 www.thevillagesdailysun.com ldcroom@aol.com

Vero Beach Press Journal (35.1M) PO Box 1268 Vero Beach FL 32961 **Phn:** 772-562-2315 **Fax:** 866-894-9851 www.tcpalm.com feedback@tcpalm.com

FLORIDA DAILY NEWSPAPERS

West Palm Beach Palm Beach Post (168M) PO Box 24700 West Palm Beach FL 33416 **Phn:** 561-820-4100 **Fax:** 561-820-4407 www.palmbeachpost.com pb_metro@pbpost.com

Winter Haven News Chief (9.8M) 455 6th St NW Winter Haven FL 33881 **Phn:** 863-401-6900 **Fax:** 863-401-6999 www.newschief.com bill.blocher@newschief.com

GEORGIA

Albany Albany Herald (24.8M) PO Box 48 Albany GA 31702 **Phn:** 229-888-9300 **Fax:** 229-888-9357 www.albanyherald.com jim.hendricks@albanyherald.com

Americus Americus Times-Recorder (7M) PO Box 1247 Americus GA 31709 **Phn:** 229-924-2751 **Fax:** 229-928-6344 americustimesrecorder.com beth.alston@gaflnews.com

Athens Athens Banner-Herald (26M) 1 Press Pl Athens GA 30601 **Phn:** 706-549-0123 **Fax:** 706-208-2246 www.onlineathens.com donnie.fetter@onlineathens.com

Atlanta Atlanta Journal-Constitution (262M) 223 Perimeter Center Pkwy NE Atlanta GA 30346 **Phn:** 404-526-7003 **Fax:** 404-526-5746 www.ajc.com newstips@ajc.com

Augusta Augusta Chronicle (74.2M) PO Box 1928 Augusta GA 30903 **Phn:** 706-724-0851 **Fax:** 706-722-7403 chronicle.augusta.com newsroom@augustachronicle.com

Brunswick Brunswick News (15.7M) PO Box 1557 Brunswick GA 31521 **Phn:** 912-265-8320 **Fax:** 912-280-0926 www.thebrunswicknews.com newsroom@thebrunswicknews.com

Canton Cherokee Tribune (5M) 521 E Main St Canton GA 30114 **Phn:** 770-479-1441 **Fax:** 770-479-3505 www.cherokeetribune.com bwilson@cherokeetribune.com

Carrollton Times-Georgian (8.5M) PO Box 460 Carrollton GA 30112 **Phn:** 770-834-6631 **Fax:** 770-830-9425 www.times-georgian.com kcampbell@times-georgian.com

Cartersville Daily Tribune News (7.3M) PO Box 70 Cartersville GA 30120 **Phn:** 770-382-4545 **Fax:** 770-382-2711 www.daily-tribune.com jessica.loeding@daily-tribune.com

Columbus Columbus Ledger-Enquirer (42.3M) PO Box 711 Columbus GA 31902 **Phn:** 706-324-5526 **Fax:** 706-576-6290 www.ledger-enquirer.com dkholmes@ledger-enquirer.com

Conyers Rockdale Citizen (16.2M) PO Box 136 Conyers GA 30012 **Phn:** 770-483-7108 **Fax:** 770-483-5797 www.rockdalecitizen.net news@rockdalecitizen.com

Cordele Cordele Dispatch (4.6M) PO Box 1058 Cordele GA 31010 **Phn:** 229-273-2277 **Fax:** 229-273-7239 cordeledispatch.com peggy.king@gaflnews.com

Covington Newton Citizen (5.9M) 7121 Turner Lake Rd NW Covington GA 30014 **Phn:** 770-787-7303 **Fax:** 770-787-8603 www.newtoncitizen.com news@newtoncitizen.com

Cumming Forsyth County News (14M) PO Box 210 Cumming GA 30028 **Phn:** 770-887-3126 **Fax:** 770-889-6017 www.forsythnews.com editor@forsythnews.com

Dalton Daily Citizen (12.8M) PO Box 1167 Dalton GA 30722 **Phn:** 706-217-6397 **Fax:** 706-275-6641 daltondailycitizen.com

Douglasville Douglas Co. Sentinel (4.2M) 8501 Bowden St Douglasville GA 30134 **Phn:** 770-942-6571 **Fax:** 770-949-7556 douglascountysentinel.com newseditor@douglascountysentinel.com

Dublin Courier Herald (9.7M) 115 S Jefferson St Dublin GA 31021 **Phn:** 478-272-5522 **Fax:** 478-272-2189 www.courier-herald.com news@courier-herald.com

Fayetteville Fayette County News (22.2M) PO Box 96 Fayetteville GA 30214 **Phn:** 770-461-6317 **Fax:** 770-460-8172 www.fayette-news.com geneva@fayette-news.com

Gainesville The Times (19.4M) PO Box 838 Gainesville GA 30503 **Phn:** 770-532-1234 **Fax:** 770-532-0457 www.gainesvilletimes.com news@gainesvilletimes.com

Griffin Griffin Daily News (8.7M) PO Box M Griffin GA 30224 **Phn:** 770-227-3276 **Fax:** 770-412-1678 www.griffindailynews.com tim@griffindailynews.com

Jonesboro Clayton News Daily/Henry Daily Herald (4.6M) PO Box 368 Jonesboro GA 30237 **Phn:** 770-478-5753 **Fax:** 770-473-9032 www.news-daily.com

LaGrange LaGrange Daily News (13.4M) PO Box 929 LaGrange GA 30241 **Phn:** 706-884-7311 **Fax:** 706-884-8712 www.lagrangenews.com tepperson@civitasmedia.com

Lawrenceville Gwinnett Daily Post (64.1M) PO Box 603 Lawrenceville GA 30046 **Phn:** 770-963-9205 **Fax:** 770-339-8081 www.gwinnettdailyonline.com news@gwinnettdailypost.com

Macon Macon Telegraph (56.3M) PO Box 4167 Macon GA 31208 **Phn:** 478-744-4200 **Fax:** 478-744-4385 www.macon.com obrown@macon.com

Marietta Marietta Daily Journal (17M) PO Box 449 Marietta GA 30061 **Phn:** 770-428-9411 **Fax:** 770-422-9533 www.mdjonline.com kisaza@mdjonline.com

Milledgeville Union-Recorder (7.4M) PO Box 520 Milledgeville GA 31059 **Phn:** 478-452-0567 **Fax:** 478-453-1459 unionrecorder.com ndavis@unionrecorder.com

Moultrie Moultrie Observer (7.2M) PO Box 2349 Moultrie GA 31776 **Phn:** 229-985-4545 **Fax:** 229-985-3569 moultrieobserver.com dwain.walden@gaflnews.com

Newnan Newnan Times-Herald (11M) PO Box 1052 Newnan GA 30264 **Phn:** 770-253-1576 **Fax:** 770-253-2538 www.times-herald.com news@newnan.com

Perry Houston Home Journal (10.2M) PO Box 1910 Perry GA 31069 **Phn:** 478-987-1823 **Fax:** 478-988-1181 www.hhjnews.com kriner@sunmulti.com

Rome Rome News-Tribune (17.5M) PO Box 1633 Rome GA 30162 **Phn:** 706-290-5252 **Fax:** 706-234-6478 www.northwestgeorgianews.com/rome romenewstribune@rn-t.com

Savannah Savannah Morning News (49.6M) PO Box 1088 Savannah GA 31402 **Phn:** 912-236-9511 **Fax:** 912-525-0795 savannahnow.com chris.thompson@savannahnow.com

Statesboro Statesboro Herald (7.7M) PO Box 888 Statesboro GA 30459 **Phn:** 912-764-9031 **Fax:** 912-489-8181 www.statesboroherald.com jhealy@statesboroherald.com

Thomasville Thomasville Times-Enterprise (9.3M) PO Box 650 Thomasville GA 31799 **Phn:** 229-226-2400 **Fax:** 229-228-5863 timesenterprise.com mark.lastinger@gaflnews.com

Tifton Tifton Gazette (6.7M) PO Box 708 Tifton GA 31793 **Phn:** 229-382-4321 **Fax:** 229-387-7322 tiftongazette.com angye.morrison@gaflnews.com

Valdosta Valdosta Daily Times (15.4M) PO Box 968 Valdosta GA 31603 **Phn:** 229-244-1880 **Fax:** 229-244-2560 valdostadailytimes.com vdt.editorial@gaflnews.com

Waycross Waycross Journal-Herald (9.6M) PO Box 219 Waycross GA 31502 **Phn:** 912-283-2244 **Fax:** 912-283-2815 www.wjhnews.com newsroom@wjhnews.com

HAWAII

Hilo Hawaii Tribune-Herald (20.2M) PO Box 767 Hilo HI 96721 **Phn:** 808-935-6621 **Fax:** 808-961-3680 www.hawaiitribune-herald.com

Honolulu Honolulu Star-Advertiser (59.5M) 500 Ala Moana Blvd Ste 7-210 Honolulu HI 96813 **Phn:** 808-529-4700 **Fax:** 808-529-4750 www.staradvertiser.com webmaster@staradvertiser.com

Kailua Kona West Hawaii Today (14.1M) PO Box 789 Kailua Kona HI 96745 **Phn:** 808-329-9311 **Fax:** 808-329-4860 www.westhawaiitoday.com wht@aloha.net

Lihue The Garden Island (9.1M) PO Box 231 Lihue HI 96766 **Phn:** 808-245-3681 **Fax:** 808-245-5286 thegardenisland.com editor@thegardenisland.com

Wailuku Maui News (19.7M) PO Box 550 Wailuku HI 96793 **Phn:** 808-244-3981 **Fax:** 808-242-9087 www.mauinews.com citydesk@mauinews.com

IDAHO

Blackfoot Morning News (3.8M) PO Box 70 Blackfoot ID 83221 **Phn:** 208-785-1100 **Fax:** 208-785-4239 www.am-news.com mnews@cableone.net

Boise Idaho Statesman (63.5M) PO Box 40 Boise ID 83707 **Phn:** 208-377-6200 **Fax:** 208-377-6449 www.idahostatesman.com bjensen@idahostatesman.com

Coeur D Alene Coeur d'Alene Press (20.5M) 201 N 2nd St Coeur D Alene ID 83814 **Phn:** 208-664-8176 **Fax:** 208-664-0212 www.cdapress.com editor@cdapress.com

Idaho Falls Post Register (26.5M) 333 Northgate Mile Idaho Falls ID 83401 **Phn:** 208-522-1800 **Fax:** 208-529-9683 www.postregister.com mlaorange@postregister.com

Lewiston Lewiston Morning Tribune (19.2M) PO Box 957 Lewiston ID 83501 **Phn:** 208-743-9411 **Fax:** 208-746-1185 www.lmtribune.com city@lmtribune.com

Moscow Moscow-Pullman Daily News (5.5M) 409 S Jackson St Ste 1 Moscow ID 83843 **Phn:** 208-882-5561 **Fax:** 208-883-8205 www.dnews.com briefs@dnews.com

Nampa Idaho Press-Tribune (18.7M) PO Box 9399 Nampa ID 83652 **Phn:** 208-467-9251 **Fax:** 208-467-9562 www.idahopress.com newsroom@idahopress.com

Osburn Shoshone News-Press (3.3M) PO Box 589 Osburn ID 83849 **Phn:** 208-783-1107 **Fax:** 208-784-6791 www.shoshonenewspress.com ddrewry@shoshonenewspress.com

Pocatello Idaho State Journal (16.7M) PO Box 431 Pocatello ID 83204 **Phn:** 208-232-4161 **Fax:** 208-233-8007 www.idahostatejournal.com pressrelease@journalnet.com

Sandpoint Bonner Co. Daily Bee (4.5M) PO Box 159 Sandpoint ID 83864 **Phn:** 208-263-9534 **Fax:** 208-263-9091 www.bonnercountydailybee.com bcdailybee@bonnercountydailybee.com

Twin Falls Times-News (20.5M) 132 Fairfield St W Twin Falls ID 83301 **Phn:** 208-733-0931 **Fax:** 208-734-5538 www.magicvalley.com letters@magicvalley.com

ILLINOIS

Alton The Telegraph (25.1M) PO Box 278 Alton IL 62002 **Phn:** 618-463-2500 **Fax:** 618-463-2578 www.thetelegraph.com telegraph_pub@hotmail.com

Arlington Heights Daily Herald (151M) PO Box 280 Arlington Heights IL 60006 **Phn:** 847-427-4300 **Fax:** 847-427-1301 www.dailyherald.com editorial@dailyherald.com

HAWAII DAILY NEWSPAPERS

Aurora Beacon News (25.6M) 495 N Commons Dr Ste 200 Aurora IL 60504 **Phn:** 630-978-8168 **Fax:** 630-978-8184 beaconnews.suntimes.com beaconviewpoint@scn1.com

Aurora Courier-News (12.6M) 495 N Commons Dr Ste 200 Aurora IL 60504 **Phn:** 847-888-7800 **Fax:** 847-888-7836 www.suburbanchicagonews.com pharth@stmedianetwork.com

Aurora Naperville Sun (17.1M) 495 N Commons Dr Ste 200 Aurora IL 60504 **Phn:** 630-978-8880 **Fax:** 630-978-8509 napervillesun.suntimes.com thesun@stmedianetwork.com

Belleville Belleville News-Democrat (52M) PO Box 427 Belleville IL 62222 **Phn:** 618-234-1000 **Fax:** 618-234-9597 www.bnd.com newsroom@bnd.com

Belvidere Belvidere Daily Republican (13.6M) 130 S State St Ste 101 Belvidere IL 61008 **Phn:** 815-547-0084 **Fax:** 815-547-3045 www.belvideredailyrepublican.net bdrnews@rvpublishing.com

Benton Benton Evening News (3.5M) PO Box 877 Benton IL 62812 **Phn:** 618-438-5611 **Fax:** 618-435-2413 www.bentoneveningnews.com dianaw@clearwave.com

Bloomington The Pantagraph (46.4M) PO Box 2907 Bloomington IL 61702 **Phn:** 309-829-9411 **Fax:** 309-829-7000 www.pantagraph.com newsroom@pantagraph.com

Canton Daily Ledger (5.4M) PO Box 540 Canton IL 61520 **Phn:** 309-647-5100 **Fax:** 309-647-4665 www.cantondailyledger.com editor@cantondailyledger.com

Carbondale Southern Illinoisan (26.8M) PO Box 2108 Carbondale IL 62902 **Phn:** 618-529-5454 **Fax:** 618-457-2935 thesouthern.com mark.fitton@thesouthern.com

Carmi The Times (2.7M) PO Box 190 Carmi IL 62821 **Phn:** 618-382-4176 **Fax:** 618-384-2163 www.carmitimes.com carmitimes@clearwave.com

Centralia Centralia Morning Sentinel (14.3M) PO Box 627 Centralia IL 62801 **Phn:** 618-532-5604 **Fax:** 618-532-1212 www.morningsentinel.com news@morningsentinel.com

Champaign News-Gazette (39.4M) PO Box 677 Champaign IL 61824 **Phn:** 217-351-5252 **Fax:** 217-351-5374 www.news-gazette.com jbeck@news-gazette.com

Chicago Chicago Sun-Times (312M) 350 N Orleans St Fl 10 Chicago IL 60654 **Phn:** 312-321-3000 **Fax:** 312-321-3084 www.suntimes.com metro@suntimes.com

Chicago Chicago Tribune (501M) 435 N Michigan Ave Chicago IL 60611 **Phn:** 312-222-3232 **Fax:** 312-222-4674 www.chicagotribune.com metro@tribune.com

Chicago Redeye (150M) 435 N Michigan Ave Chicago IL 60611 **Phn:** 312-222-4970 **Fax:** 312-222-2407 www.redeyechicago.com redeyeeditor@tribune.com

Crystal Lake Northwest Herald (37.8M) PO Box 250 Crystal Lake IL 60039 **Phn:** 815-459-4040 **Fax:** 815-459-5640 www.nwherald.com webmaster@nwherald.com

Danville Commercial News (13.8M) 17 W North St Danville IL 61832 **Phn:** 217-446-1000 **Fax:** 217-446-6648 commercial-news.com lsmith@dancomnews.com

Decatur Herald & Review (32.9M) 601 E William St Decatur IL 62523 **Phn:** 217-429-5151 **Fax:** 217-421-7965 www.herald-review.com hrnews@herald-review.com

Dekalb Daily Chronicle (9.7M) PO Box 587 Dekalb IL 60115 **Phn:** 815-756-4841 **Fax:** 815-758-5059 www.daily-chronicle.com jkelleher@daily-chronicle.com

Du Quoin Du Quoin Evening Call (3.8M) PO Box 184 Du Quoin IL 62832 **Phn:** 618-542-2133 **Fax:** 618-542-2726 www.duquoin.com duquoin@frontier.com

Edwardsville Edwardsville Intelligencer (4.6M) PO Box 70 Edwardsville IL 62025 **Phn:** 618-656-4700 **Fax:** 618-659-1677 www.theintelligencer.com btucker@edwpub.net

Effingham Effingham Daily News (12.1M) PO Box 370 Effingham IL 62401 **Phn:** 217-347-7151 **Fax:** 217-342-9315 effinghamdailynews.com driley-gordon@cnhi.com

Freeport Journal-Standard (12.3M) PO Box 330 Freeport IL 61032 **Phn:** 815-232-1171 **Fax:** 815-232-0105 www.journalstandard.com frontdoor@journalstandard.com

Galesburg Register-Mail (13.8M) PO Box 310 Galesburg IL 61402 **Phn:** 309-343-7181 **Fax:** 309-343-2382 www.galesburg.com jredfern@register-mail.com

Harrisburg Daily Register (4.6M) PO Box 248 Harrisburg IL 62946 **Phn:** 618-253-7146 **Fax:** 618-252-0863 www.dailyregister.com editor@yourclearwave.com

Jacksonville Jacksonville Journal-Courier (14M) PO Box 1048 Jacksonville IL 62651 **Phn:** 217-245-6121 **Fax:** 217-245-1226 www.myjournalcourier.com news@myjournalcourier.com

Joliet Herald-News (41.1M) 3109 W Jefferson St Joliet IL 60435 **Phn:** 815-729-6100 **Fax:** 815-439-7527 www.suburbanchicagonews.com heraldnews@scn1.com

Kankakee Daily Journal (28.3M) 8 Dearborn Sq Kankakee IL 60901 **Phn:** 815-937-3300 **Fax:** 815-937-3876 www.daily-journal.com webmaster@daily-journal.com

Kewanee Star-Courier (4.7M) PO Box A Kewanee IL 61443 **Phn:** 309-852-2181 **Fax:** 309-852-0010 www.starcourier.com editor@starcourier.com

La Salle News Tribune (17.6M) 426 2nd St La Salle IL 61301 **Phn:** 815-223-3200 **Fax:** 815-224-6443 www.newstrib.com ntnews@newstrib.com

Lawrenceville Daily Record (2.9M) PO Box 559 Lawrenceville IL 62439 **Phn:** 618-943-2331 **Fax:** 618-943-3976 www.lawdailyrecord.com lawnews@lawdailyrecord.com

Lincoln The Courier (5.9M) PO Box 740 Lincoln IL 62656 **Phn:** 217-732-2101 **Fax:** 217-732-7039 www.lincolncourier.com courier@lincolncourier.com

Litchfield News-Herald (5.2M) PO Box 160 Litchfield IL 62056 **Phn:** 217-324-2121 **Fax:** 217-324-2122 lfdnews@litchfieldil.com

Macomb McDonough County Voice (3.8M) 26 West Side Sq Macomb IL 61455 **Phn:** 309-833-2345 **Fax:** 309-833-2346 www.mcdonoughvoice.com jsmith@mcdonoughvoice.com

Marion Marion Daily Republican (4M) PO Box 490 Marion IL 62959 **Phn:** 618-993-2626 **Fax:** 618-993-8326 www.dailyrepublicannews.com editor@dailyrepublicannews.com

Mattoon Journal-Gazette (10M) 100 Broadway Ave Mattoon IL 61938 **Phn:** 217-235-5656 **Fax:** 217-238-6886 jg-tc.com editorial@jg-tc.com

Moline The Dispatch & The Rock Island Argus (31.7M) 1720 5th Ave Moline IL 61265 **Phn:** 309-764-4344 **Fax:** 309-797-0317 www.qconline.com press@qconline.com

Monmouth Daily Review Atlas (3.2M) PO Box 650 Monmouth IL 61462 **Phn:** 309-734-3176 **Fax:** 309-734-7649 www.reviewatlas.com communitynews@reviewatlas.com

Morris Morris Daily Herald (6M) 1804 N Division St Morris IL 60450 **Phn:** 815-942-3221 **Fax:** 815-942-0988 www.morrisdailyherald.com news@morrisdailyherald.com

Mount Carmel Daily Republican Register (3.4M) PO Box 550 Mount Carmel IL 62863 **Phn:** 618-262-5144 **Fax:** 618-263-4437 www.tristate-media.com news@mtcarmelregister.com

Mount Vernon Register-News (10.3M) PO Box 489 Mount Vernon IL 62864 **Phn:** 618-242-0113 **Fax:** 618-242-8286 register-news.com your.news@register-news.com

Olney Olney Daily Mail (4.3M) PO Box 340 Olney IL 62450 **Phn:** 618-393-2931 **Fax:** 618-392-2953 www.olneydailymail.com news@olneydailymail.com

Ottawa Daily Times (15.5M) 110 W Jefferson St Ottawa IL 61350 **Phn:** 815-433-2000 **Fax:** 815-433-1639 www.mywebtimes.com newsroom@mywebtimes.com

Paris Paris Beacon-News (5M) PO Box 100 Paris IL 61944 **Phn:** 217-465-6424 **Fax:** 217-466-5078 www.parisbeacon.com news@parisbeacon.com

Paxton Paxton Daily Record (3.2M) 208 N Market St Paxton IL 60957 **Phn:** 217-379-2356 **Fax:** 217-379-3104 www.paxtonrecord.net wbrumleve@news-gazette.com

Pekin Pekin Daily Times (10.8M) PO Box 430 Pekin IL 61555 **Phn:** 309-346-1111 **Fax:** 309-346-1446 www.pekintimes.com mteheux@pekintimes.com

Peoria Journal Star (66.5M) 1 News Plz Peoria IL 61643 **Phn:** 309-686-3000 **Fax:** 309-686-3296 www.pjstar.com news@pjstar.com

Pontiac Daily Leader (4.8M) 318 N Main St Pontiac IL 61764 **Phn:** 815-842-1153 **Fax:** 815-842-4388 www.pontiacdailyleader.com ldreditor@mchsi.com

Quincy Quincy Herald-Whig (20.5M) PO Box 909 Quincy IL 62306 **Phn:** 217-223-5100 **Fax:** 217-221-3395 www.whig.com whig@whig.com

Robinson Daily News (6M) PO Box 639 Robinson IL 62454 **Phn:** 618-544-2101 **Fax:** 618-544-9533 www.robdailynews.com gbilbrey@robdailynews.com

Rockford Rockford Register-Star (59.1M) 99 E State St Rockford IL 61104 **Phn:** 815-987-1200 **Fax:** 815-987-1365 www.rrstar.com local@rrstar.com

Shelbyville Daily Union (3.5M) 100 W Main St Shelbyville IL 62565 **Phn:** 217-774-2161 **Fax:** 217-774-5732 shelbyvilledailyunion.com news@shelbyvilledailyunion.com

Springfield State Journal-Register (51.8M) PO Box 219 Springfield IL 62705 **Phn:** 217-788-1300 **Fax:** 217-788-1551 www.sj-r.com sjr@sj-r.com

St Charles Kane Co. Chronicle (12.3M) 333 N Randall Rd Ste 2 St Charles IL 60174 **Phn:** 630-232-9222 **Fax:** 630-444-1645 www.kcchronicle.com editorial@kcchronicle.com

Sterling Daily Gazette/Telegraph (19.8M) PO Box 498 Sterling IL 61081 **Phn:** 815-625-3600 **Fax:** 815-625-9390 www.saukvalley.com news@svnmail.com

Taylorville Breeze Courier (5.8M) PO Box 440 Taylorville IL 62568 **Phn:** 217-824-2233 **Fax:** 217-824-2026 breezecourier.com breezenews@ctitech.com

Tinley Park SouthtownStar (48.8M) 6901 159th St Tinley Park IL 60477 **Phn:** 708-633-6700 **Fax:** 708-633-5999 southtownstar.suntimes.com jbiesk@southtownstar.com

Watseka Times-Republic (2.4M) 1492 E Walnut St Watseka IL 60970 **Phn:** 815-432-5227 **Fax:** 815-432-5159 www.newsbug.info/watseka_times_republic editor@rensselaerrepublican.com

ILLINOIS DAILY NEWSPAPERS

West Frankfort Daily American (3.5M) PO Box 617 West Frankfort IL 62896 **Phn:** 618-932-2146 **Fax:** 618-937-6006 www.dailyamericannews.com editor@dailyamericannews.com

INDIANA

Anderson Herald-Bulletin (22M) 1133 Jackson St Anderson IN 46016 **Phn:** 765-622-1212 **Fax:** 765-640-4815 heraldbulletin.com newsroom@heraldbulletin.com

Angola Herald-Republican (4.7M) 45 S Public Sq Angola IN 46703 **Phn:** 260-665-3117 **Fax:** 260-665-2322 www.kpcnews.com mikem@kpcnews.net

Auburn Evening Star (6.8M) 118 W 9th St Auburn IN 46706 **Phn:** 260-925-2611 **Fax:** 260-925-2625 www.kpcnews.com dkurtz@kpcmedia.com

Bedford Times-Mail (12.6M) PO Box 849 Bedford IN 47421 **Phn:** 812-275-3355 **Fax:** 812-277-3472 www.tmnews.com mikel@tmnews.com

Bloomington Herald-Times (27.3M) PO Box 909 Bloomington IN 47402 **Phn:** 812-332-4401 **Fax:** 812-331-4383 www.heraldtimesonline.com rzaltsberg@heraldt.com

Bluffton News-Banner (4.7M) PO Box 436 Bluffton IN 46714 **Phn:** 260-824-0224 **Fax:** 260-824-0700 www.news-banner.com email@news-banner.com

Brazil Brazil Times (4.6M) PO Box 429 Brazil IN 47834 **Phn:** 812-446-2216 **Fax:** 812-446-0938 www.thebraziltimes.com scoop1j@gmail.com

Chesterton Chesterton Tribune (5.1M) PO Box 919 Chesterton IN 46304 **Phn:** 219-926-1131 **Fax:** 219-926-6389 chestertontribune.com news@chestertontribune.com

Clinton Daily Clintonian (5.1M) PO Box 309 Clinton IN 47842 **Phn:** 765-832-2443 **Fax:** 765-832-2560 www.ccc-clintonian.com gbcarey@mikes.net

Columbia City Post & Mail (4.1M) 927 W Connexion Way Columbia City IN 46725 **Phn:** 260-244-5153 **Fax:** 260-244-7598 www.thepostandmail.com editor@thepostandmail.com

Columbus The Republic (21.2M) 333 2nd St Columbus IN 47201 **Phn:** 812-372-7811 **Fax:** 812-379-5711 www.therepublic.com editorial@therepublic.com

Connersville Connersville News-Examiner (6.5M) PO Box 287 Connersville IN 47331 **Phn:** 765-825-0581 **Fax:** 765-825-4599 www.connersvillein.com newsexaminer@newsexaminer.com

Crawfordsville Journal Review (9.5M) PO Box 512 Crawfordsville IN 47933 **Phn:** 765-362-1200 **Fax:** 765-364-5424 www.journalreview.com webmaster@jrpress.com

Decatur Decatur Daily Democrat (5.1M) 141 S 2nd St Decatur IN 46733 **Phn:** 260-724-2121 **Fax:** 260-724-7981 www.decaturdailydemocrat.com bob@decaturdailydemocrat.com

Elkhart Elkhart Truth (29M) PO Box 487 Elkhart IN 46515 **Phn:** 574-294-1661 **Fax:** 574-294-3895 www.elkharttruth.com newsroom@etruth.com

Elwood Call-Leader (3.1M) PO Box 85 Elwood IN 46036 **Phn:** 765-552-3355 **Fax:** 765-552-3358 www.elwoodpublishing.com elpub@elwoodpublishing.com

Evansville Evansville Courier & Press (66.2M) PO Box 268 Evansville IN 47702 **Phn:** 812-424-7711 **Fax:** 812-422-8196 www.courierpress.com baumannb@courierpress.com

Fort Wayne Journal Gazette (49M) PO Box 88 Fort Wayne IN 46801 **Phn:** 260-461-8773 **Fax:** 260-461-8648 www.journalgazette.net jgnews@jg.net

Fort Wayne News-Sentinel (27.3M) PO Box 88 Fort Wayne IN 46801 **Phn:** 260-461-8222 **Fax:** 260-461-8817 www.fortwayne.com/mld/newssentinel nsmetro@news-sentinel.com

Frankfort The Times (6.2M) 211 N Jackson St Frankfort IN 46041 **Phn:** 765-659-4622 **Fax:** 765-654-7031 www.chronicle-tribune.com/ftimes news@ftimes.com

Franklin Daily Journal (17.1M) PO Box 699 Franklin IN 46131 **Phn:** 317-736-7101 **Fax:** 317-736-2766 www.dailyjournal.net newstips@dailyjournal.net

Goshen Goshen News (16.1M) PO Box 569 Goshen IN 46527 **Phn:** 574-533-2151 **Fax:** 574-534-8830 goshennews.com news@goshennews.com

Greencastle Banner-Graphic (6.6M) PO Box 509 Greencastle IN 46135 **Phn:** 765-653-5151 **Fax:** 765-653-2063 www.bannergraphic.com news@bannergraphic.com

Greenfield Daily Reporter (11.4M) 22 W New Rd Greenfield IN 46140 **Phn:** 317-462-5528 **Fax:** 317-467-6017 www.greenfieldreporter.com editorial@greenfieldreporter.com

Greensburg Greensburg Daily News (5.6M) PO Box 106 Greensburg IN 47240 **Phn:** 812-663-3111 **Fax:** 812-662-7552 greensburgdailynews.com

Hartford City News-Times (1.5M) PO Box 690 Hartford City IN 47348 **Phn:** 765-348-0110 **Fax:** 765-348-0112 www.hartfordcitynewstimes.com newstimes@comcast.net

Huntington Huntington Herald-Press (6.4M) 7 N Jefferson St Huntington IN 46750 **Phn:** 260-356-6700 **Fax:** 260-356-9026 www.chronicle-tribune.com/hp_online hpnews@h-ponline.com

Indianapolis Indianapolis Star (259M) PO Box 145 Indianapolis IN 46206 **Phn:** 317-444-4000 **Fax:** 317-444-6600 www.indystar.com jenny.green@indystar.com

Jasper The Herald (12.6M) PO Box 31 Jasper IN 47547 **Phn:** 812-482-2424 **Fax:** 812-482-5241 duboiscountyherald.com news@dcherald.com

Jeffersonville Evening News (7.2M) 221 Spring St Jeffersonville IN 47130 **Phn:** 812-283-6636 **Fax:** 812-206-4598 newsandtribune.com newsroom@newsandtribune.com

Kendallville News-Sun (8.6M) PO Box 39 Kendallville IN 46755 **Phn:** 260-347-0400 **Fax:** 260-347-2693 www.kpcnews.com mattg@kpcnews.net

Kokomo Kokomo Tribune (20.9M) PO Box 9014 Kokomo IN 46904 **Phn:** 765-459-3121 **Fax:** 765-854-6733 kokomotribune.com jeff.kovaleski@kokomotribune.com

Lafayette Journal & Courier (35.9M) 217 N 6th St Lafayette IN 47901 **Phn:** 765-423-5511 **Fax:** 765-420-5246 www.jconline.com bbloom@journalandcourier.com

LaPorte Herald-Argus (12.5M) 701 State St LaPorte IN 46350 **Phn:** 219-362-2161 **Fax:** 219-362-2166 www.heraldargus.com newsroom@heraldargus.com

Lebanon The Reporter (5.3M) 117 E Washington St Lebanon IN 46052 **Phn:** 765-482-4650 **Fax:** 765-482-4652 reporter.net news@reporter.net

Linton Greene Co. Daily World (3M) PO Box 129 Linton IN 47441 **Phn:** 812-847-4487 **Fax:** 812-847-9513 www.gcdailyworld.com cpruett@dailycitizen.com

Logansport Pharos-Tribune (9.3M) PO Box 210 Logansport IN 46947 **Phn:** 574-722-5000 **Fax:** 574-732-5070 pharostribune.com ptnews@pharostribune.com

Madison Madison Courier (8.8M) 310 Courier Sq Madison IN 47250 **Phn:** 812-265-3641 **Fax:** 812-273-6903 madisoncourier.com editor@madisoncourier.com

Marion Chronicle-Tribune (17.1M) PO Box 309 Marion IN 46952 **Phn:** 765-664-5111 **Fax:** 765-668-4256 www.chronicle-tribune.com ctreport@att.net

Martinsville Reporter-Times (5.5M) PO Box 1636 Martinsville IN 46151 **Phn:** 765-342-3311 **Fax:** 765-342-1446 www.reporter-times.com rhawkins@reportert.com

Michigan City News-Dispatch (10.7M) 121 W Michigan Blvd Michigan City IN 46360 **Phn:** 219-874-7211 **Fax:** 219-872-8511 thenewsdispatch.com news@thenewsdispatch.com

Monticello Herald Journal (5.1M) PO Box 409 Monticello IN 47960 **Phn:** 574-583-5121 **Fax:** 574-583-4241 www.newsbug.info/monticello_herald_journal wriggs@thehj.com

Muncie Star-Press (32M) PO Box 2408 Muncie IN 47307 **Phn:** 765-213-5700 **Fax:** 765-213-5858 www.thestarpress.com news@muncie.gannett.com

Munster The Times (81.2M) 601 45th Ave Munster IN 46321 **Phn:** 219-933-3200 **Fax:** 219-933-3249 www.nwitimes.com william.nangle@nwi.com

New Albany Tribune (12.2M) 303 Scribner Dr New Albany IN 47150 **Phn:** 812-944-6481 **Fax:** 812-949-6585 newsandtribune.com newsroom@newsandtribune.com

New Castle Courier-Times (9.2M) 201 S 14th St New Castle IN 47362 **Phn:** 765-529-1111 **Fax:** 765-528-1731 thecouriertimes.com editor@thecouriertimes.com

Noblesville Noblesville Daily Times (6M) PO Box 579 Noblesville IN 46061 **Phn:** 317-773-9960 **Fax:** 317-770-9376 thetimes24-7.com news@thetimes24-7.com

Peru Peru Tribune (6.4M) 26 W 3rd St Peru IN 46970 **Phn:** 765-473-6641 **Fax:** 765-472-4438 www.chronicle-tribune.com/peru_tribune gstamper@perutribune.com

Plymouth Pilot-News (6.2M) PO Box 220 Plymouth IN 46563 **Phn:** 574-936-3101 **Fax:** 574-936-3844 www.thepilotnews.com news@thepilotnews.com

Portland Commercial-Review (4.8M) PO Box 1049 Portland IN 47371 **Phn:** 260-726-8141 **Fax:** 260-726-8143 thecr.com cr.news@comcast.net

Princeton Princeton Daily Clarion (6.3M) PO Box 30 Princeton IN 47670 **Phn:** 812-385-2525 **Fax:** 812-386-6199 www.tristate-media.com news@pdclarion.com

Rensselaer Rensselaer Republican (2.1M) 117 N Van Rensselaer St Rensselaer IN 47978 **Phn:** 219-866-5111 **Fax:** 219-866-3775 www.newsbug.info/rensselaer_republican editor@rensselaerrepublican.com

Richmond Palladium-Item (16.8M) 1175 N A St Richmond IN 47374 **Phn:** 765-962-1575 **Fax:** 765-973-4570 www.pal-item.com palitem@richmond.gannett.com

Rochester Rochester Sentinel (3.8M) PO Box 260 Rochester IN 46975 **Phn:** 574-223-2111 **Fax:** 574-223-5782 www.rochsent.com wsw@rochsent.com

Rushville Rushville Republican (2.7M) PO Box 189 Rushville IN 46173 **Phn:** 765-932-2222 **Fax:** 765-932-4358 rushvillerepublican.com rushvillerepublican@rushvillerepublican.

Seymour The Tribune (8.9M) PO Box 447 Seymour IN 47274 **Phn:** 812-522-4871 **Fax:** 812-522-3371 www.tribtown.com ddavis@tribtown.com

Shelbyville Shelbyville News (8.3M) PO Box 750 Shelbyville IN 46176 **Phn:** 317-398-6631 **Fax:** 317-398-0194 www.shelbynews.com shelbynews@shelbynews.com

South Bend South Bend Tribune (69.6M) 225 W Colfax Ave South Bend IN 46626 **Phn:** 574-235-6161 **Fax:** 574-236-1765 www.southbendtribune.com sbtnews@sbtinfo.com

INDIANA DAILY NEWSPAPERS

Spencer Spencer Evening World (3.6M) PO Box 226 Spencer IN 47460 **Phn:** 812-829-2255 **Fax:** 812-829-4666 www.spencereveningworld.com editor@spencereveningworld.com

Sullivan Sullivan Daily Times (4.1M) PO Box 130 Sullivan IN 47882 **Phn:** 812-268-6356 **Fax:** 812-268-3110 www.sullivan-times.com editor@sullivan-times.com

Terre Haute Tribune-Star (24.6M) PO Box 149 Terre Haute IN 47808 **Phn:** 812-231-4200 **Fax:** 812-231-4321 tribstar.com max.jones@tribstar.com

Tipton Tipton Co. Tribune (2.5M) PO Box 248 Tipton IN 46072 **Phn:** 765-675-2115 **Fax:** 765-675-4147 www.elwoodpublishing.com tiptontribune@elwoodpublishing.com

Vincennes Vincennes Sun-Commercial (9.5M) PO Box 396 Vincennes IN 47591 **Phn:** 812-886-9955 **Fax:** 812-885-2235 www.suncommercial.com vscnews@suncommercial.com

Wabash Wabash Plain Dealer (6.6M) 123 W Canal St Wabash IN 46992 **Phn:** 260-563-2131 **Fax:** 260-563-0816 www.chronicle-tribune.com/wabashplaindealer news@wabashplaindealer.com

Warsaw Times-Union (10.9M) PO Box 1448 Warsaw IN 46581 **Phn:** 574-267-3111 **Fax:** 574-267-7784 www.timesuniononline.com news@timesuniononline.com

Washington Washington Times-Herald (8.8M) 102 E Van Trees St Washington IN 47501 **Phn:** 812-254-0480 **Fax:** 812-254-7517 washtimesherald.com

Winchester News-Gazette (3.7M) PO Box 429 Winchester IN 47394 **Phn:** 765-584-4501 **Fax:** 765-584-3066 www.winchesternewsgazette.com newsgazette@comcast.net

IOWA

Ames The Tribune (10.1M) PO Box 380 Ames IA 50010 **Phn:** 515-232-2160 **Fax:** 515-232-2364 www.amestribune.com news@amestrib.com

Atlantic Atlantic News-Telegraph (3.4M) PO Box 230 Atlantic IA 50022 **Phn:** 712-243-2624 **Fax:** 712-243-4988 swiowanewssource.com news@ant-news.com

Boone Boone News-Republican (2.5M) PO Box 100 Boone IA 50036 **Phn:** 515-432-6694 **Fax:** 515-432-7811 www.newsrepublican.com news@newsrepublican.com

Burlington Hawk Eye (18.8M) PO Box 10 Burlington IA 52601 **Phn:** 319-754-8461 **Fax:** 319-754-6824 www.thehawkeye.com news@thehawkeye.com

Carroll Daily Times-Herald (6.3M) PO Box 546 Carroll IA 51401 **Phn:** 712-792-3573 **Fax:** 712-792-5218 www.carrollspaper.com newspaper@carrollspaper.com

Cedar Rapids The Gazette (60M) PO Box 511 Cedar Rapids IA 52406 **Phn:** 319-398-8211 **Fax:** 319-398-5846 thegazette.com gazcohr@gazettecommunications.com

Centerville Daily Iowegian (2.8M) PO Box 610 Centerville IA 52544 **Phn:** 641-856-6336 **Fax:** 641-856-8118 dailyiowegian.com iowegianeditor@mchsi.com

Charles City Charles City Press (2.8M) PO Box 397 Charles City IA 50616 **Phn:** 641-228-3211 **Fax:** 641-228-2641 www.charlescitypress.com editor@charlescitypress.com

Cherokee Chronicle Times (2.4M) 111 S 2nd St Cherokee IA 51012 **Phn:** 712-225-5111 **Fax:** 712-225-2910 www.chronicletimes.com editor@ctimes.biz

Clinton Clinton Herald (11.7M) 221 6th Ave S Clinton IA 52732 **Phn:** 563-242-7101 **Fax:** 563-242-7147 clintonherald.com scottlevine@clintonherald.com

Council Bluffs Daily Nonpareil (14.1M) 535 W Broadway Ste 300 Council Bluffs IA 51503 **Phn:** 712-328-1811 **Fax:** 712-325-5776 www.nonpareilonline.com editorial@nonpareilonline.com

Creston Creston News-Advertiser (5.5M) PO Box 126 Creston IA 50801 **Phn:** 641-782-2141 **Fax:** 641-782-6628 www.crestonnewsadvertiser.com editor@crestonnews.com

Davenport Quad-City Times (50.4M) 500 E 3rd St Davenport IA 52801 **Phn:** 563-383-2200 **Fax:** 563-383-2370 qctimes.com newsroom@qctimes.com

Des Moines Des Moines Register (148M) 400 Locust St # 500 Des Moines IA 50309 **Phn:** 515-284-8000 **Fax:** 515-286-2504 www.desmoinesregister.com kbolten@dmreg.com

Dubuque Telegraph-Herald (28.3M) PO Box 688 Dubuque IA 52004 **Phn:** 563-588-5611 **Fax:** 563-588-5745 www.thonline.com thonline@wcinet.com

Estherville Estherville Daily News (2.3M) 10 N 7th St Estherville IA 51334 **Phn:** 712-362-2622 **Fax:** 712-362-2624 www.esthervilledailynews.com editor@esthervilledailynews.com

Fairfield Fairfield Ledger (3.2M) PO Box 110 Fairfield IA 52556 **Phn:** 641-472-4130 **Fax:** 641-472-1916 fairfield-ia.villagesoup.com news@ffledger.com

Fort Dodge The Messenger (16.6M) PO Box 659 Fort Dodge IA 50501 **Phn:** 515-573-2141 **Fax:** 515-574-4529 messengernews.net editor@messengernews.net

Fort Madison Daily Democrat (5.1M) PO Box 160 Fort Madison IA 52627 **Phn:** 319-372-6421 **Fax:** 319-372-3867 www.dailydem.com editor@dailydem.com

Iowa City Iowa City Press-Citizen (13.6M) PO Box 2480 Iowa City IA 52244 **Phn:** 319-337-3181 **Fax:** 319-834-1083 www.press-citizen.com online@press-citizen.com

Keokuk Daily Gate City (4.9M) PO Box 430 Keokuk IA 52632 **Phn:** 319-524-8300 **Fax:** 319-524-4363 www.dailygate.com gatecity@dailygate.com

Le Mars Le Mars Daily Sentinel (3.1M) PO Box 930 Le Mars IA 51031 **Phn:** 712-546-7031 **Fax:** 712-546-7035 www.lemarssentinel.com sentinel@lemarscomm.net

Marshalltown Times-Republican (10.2M) PO Box 1300 Marshalltown IA 50158 **Phn:** 641-753-6611 **Fax:** 641-753-7221 timesrepublican.com news@timesrepublican.com

Mason City Globe-Gazette (14.7M) PO Box 271 Mason City IA 50402 **Phn:** 641-421-0500 **Fax:** 641-421-7108 www.globegazette.com news@globegazette.com

Mount Pleasant Mt. Pleasant News (2.7M) 215 W Monroe St Mount Pleasant IA 52641 **Phn:** 319-986-5186 **Fax:** 319-385-8048 mt-pleasant-ia.villagesoup.com news@mpnews.net

Muscatine Muscatine Journal (7.6M) 301 E 3rd St Muscatine IA 52761 **Phn:** 563-263-2331 **Fax:** 563-262-8042 www.muscatinejournal.com rusty.schrader@muscatinejournal.com

Newton Newton Daily News (5.5M) PO Box 967 Newton IA 50208 **Phn:** 641-792-3121 **Fax:** 641-792-5505 www.newtondailynews.com jnelson@newtondailynews.com

Oelwein Daily Register (2.8M) PO Box 511 Oelwein IA 50662 **Phn:** 319-283-2144 **Fax:** 319-283-3268 communitynewspapergroup.com editor@oelweindailyregister.com

Oskaloosa Oskaloosa Herald (3.4M) PO Box 530 Oskaloosa IA 52577 **Phn:** 641-672-2581 **Fax:** 641-672-1264 oskaloosa.com oskynews@oskyherald.com

Ottumwa Ottumwa Courier (13.5M) 213 E 2nd St Ottumwa IA 52501 **Phn:** 641-684-4611 **Fax:** 641-684-7326 ottumwacourier.com lcarrell@ottumwacourier.com

Shenandoah Valley News Today (2.4M) PO Box 369 Shenandoah IA 51601 **Phn:** 712-246-3097 **Fax:** 712-246-3099 southwestiowanews.com editorial@valleynewstoday.com

Sioux City Sioux City Journal (40.6M) PO Box 118 Sioux City IA 51102 **Phn:** 712-293-4250 **Fax:** 712-279-5059 www.siouxcityjournal.com bwalker@siouxcityjournal.com

Spencer Spencer Daily Reporter (4M) PO Box 197 Spencer IA 51301 **Phn:** 712-262-6610 **Fax:** 712-262-3044 www.spencerdailyreporter.com news@spencerdailyreporter.com

Washington Washington Evening Journal (3.5M) 111 N Marion Ave Washington IA 52353 **Phn:** 319-653-2191 **Fax:** 319-653-7524 washington-ia.villagesoup.com news@washjrnl.com

Waterloo Waterloo Courier (41.5M) PO Box 540 Waterloo IA 50704 **Phn:** 319-291-1460 **Fax:** 319-291-2069 wcfcourier.com newsroom@wcfcourier.com

Webster City Daily Freeman-Journal (2.9M) PO Box 490 Webster City IA 50595 **Phn:** 515-832-4350 **Fax:** 515-832-2314 www.freemanjournal.net editor@freemanjournal.net

KANSAS

Abilene Abilene Reflector-Chronicle (4M) PO Box 8 Abilene KS 67410 **Phn:** 785-263-1000 **Fax:** 785-263-1645 www.abilene-rc.com news@abilene-rc.com

Arkansas City Arkansas City Traveler (4.8M) PO Box 988 Arkansas City KS 67005 **Phn:** 620-442-4200 **Fax:** 620-442-7483 www.arkcity.net arkcity@arkcity.net

Augusta Augusta Daily Gazette (2.2M) PO Box 9 Augusta KS 67010 **Phn:** 316-775-2218 **Fax:** 316-775-3220 www.augustagazette.com blarsen@augustagazette.com

Chanute Chanute Tribune (4.4M) PO Box 559 Chanute KS 66720 **Phn:** 620-431-4100 **Fax:** 620-431-2635 www.chanute.com shanna@chanute.com

Clay Center Clay Center Dispatch (3.1M) PO Box 519 Clay Center KS 67432 **Phn:** 785-632-2127 **Fax:** 785-632-6526 www.ccenterdispatch.com dispatch@claycenter.com

Coffeyville Coffeyville Journal (4.1M) PO Box 849 Coffeyville KS 67337 **Phn:** 620-251-3300 **Fax:** 620-251-1905

Colby Colby Free Press (2.1M) 155 W 5th St Colby KS 67701 **Phn:** 785-462-3963 **Fax:** 785-462-7749 www.nwkansas.com colby.editor@nwkansas.com

Columbus Columbus Daily Advocate (2.2M) PO Box 231 Columbus KS 66725 **Phn:** 620-429-2773 **Fax:** 620-429-3223 www.sekvoice.com editorial@columbusdailyadv.com

Concordia Blade-Empire (2.4M) PO Box 309 Concordia KS 66901 **Phn:** 785-243-2424 **Fax:** 785-243-4407 www.bladeempire.com bladeempire@nckcn.com

Council Grove Council Grove Republican (2.1M) 208 W Main St Council Grove KS 66846 **Phn:** 620-767-5123 **Fax:** 620-767-5124 cgnews@cgtelco.net

Dodge City Dodge City Daily Globe (9.7M) PO Box 820 Dodge City KS 67801 **Phn:** 620-225-4151 **Fax:** 620-225-4154 www.dodgeglobe.com jkazar@dodgeglobe.com

El Dorado El Dorado Times (3.4M) PO Box 694 El Dorado KS 67042 **Phn:** 316-321-1120 **Fax:** 316-321-7722 www.eldoradotimes.com eldoradotimes@eldoradotimes.com

Emporia Emporia Gazette (7.7M) PO Box C Emporia KS 66801 **Phn:** 620-342-4800 **Fax:** 620-342-8108 www.emporiagazette.com newsroom@emporiagazette.com

Fort Scott Fort Scott Tribune (3.8M) PO Box 150 Fort Scott KS 66701 **Phn:** 620-223-1460 **Fax:** 620-223-1469 www.fstribune.com editor@fstribune.com

Garden City Garden City Telegram (8.6M) PO Box 958 Garden City KS 67846 **Phn:** 620-275-8500 **Fax:** 620-275-5165 www.gctelegram.com newsroom@gctelegram.com

Great Bend Great Bend Tribune (6.2M) PO Box 228 Great Bend KS 67530 **Phn:** 620-792-1211 **Fax:** 620-792-8381 www.gbtribune.com email@gbtribune.com

Hays Hays Daily News (12.5M) PO Box 857 Hays KS 67601 **Phn:** 785-628-1081 **Fax:** 785-628-8186 www.hdnews.net rfields@dailynews.net

Hutchinson Hutchinson News (27M) PO Box 190 Hutchinson KS 67504 **Phn:** 620-694-5700 **Fax:** 620-662-4186 www.hutchnews.com newsrelease@hutchnews.com

Independence Independence Daily Reporter (6.7M) PO Box 869 Independence KS 67301 **Phn:** 620-331-3550 **Fax:** 620-331-3550

Iola Iola Register (3.7M) PO Box 767 Iola KS 66749 **Phn:** 620-365-2111 **Fax:** 620-365-6289 www.iolaregister.com news@iolaregister.com

Junction City Daily Union (4.3M) 222 W 6th St Junction City KS 66441 **Phn:** 785-762-5000 **Fax:** 785-762-4584 www.yourdu.net m.editor@thedailyunion.net

Lawrence Journal-World (19M) 609 New Hampshire Lawrence KS 66044 **Phn:** 785-843-1000 **Fax:** 785-843-4512 www.ljworld.com news@ljworld.com

Leavenworth Leavenworth Times (5.6M) 422 Seneca St Leavenworth KS 66048 **Phn:** 913-682-0305 **Fax:** 913-682-1114 www.leavenworthtimes.com rmcconiga@leavenworthtimes.com

Liberal Leader & Times (4.3M) PO Box 889 Liberal KS 67905 **Phn:** 620-626-0840 **Fax:** 620-624-9854 leaderandtimes.com denasa@hpleader.com

Lyons Lyons Daily News (2.3M) PO Box 768 Lyons KS 67554 **Phn:** 620-257-2368 **Fax:** 620-257-2369 www.midksnews.com jmisunas@ldn.kscoxmail.com

Manhattan Manhattan Mercury (11.5M) PO Box 787 Manhattan KS 66505 **Phn:** 785-776-2200 **Fax:** 785-776-8807 www.themercury.com news@themercury.com

McPherson McPherson Sentinel (4.2M) PO Box 926 McPherson KS 67460 **Phn:** 620-241-2422 **Fax:** 620-241-2425 www.mcphersonsentinel.com sentinel@sbcglobal.net

Newton Newton Kansan (7.6M) PO Box 268 Newton KS 67114 **Phn:** 316-283-1500 **Fax:** 316-283-2471 www.thekansan.com news@thekansan.com

Olathe Olathe News (4.5M) 514 S Kansas Ave Olathe KS 66061 **Phn:** 913-764-2211 **Fax:** 913-764-2251 www.theolathenews.com respinoza@theolathenews.com

Ottawa Herald (5.8M) 104 S Cedar St Ottawa KS 66067 **Phn:** 785-242-4700 **Fax:** 785-242-9420 www.ottawaherald.com news@ottawaherald.com

Parsons Parsons Sun (5.4M) PO Box 836 Parsons KS 67357 **Phn:** 620-421-2000 **Fax:** 620-421-2217 www.parsonssun.com rnolting@parsonssun.com

Pittsburg Morning Sun (10.3M) PO Box H Pittsburg KS 66762 **Phn:** 620-231-2600 **Fax:** 620-231-0645 www.morningsun.net stephen.wade@morningsun.net

Pratt Pratt Tribune (2.2M) PO Box 909 Pratt KS 67124 **Phn:** 620-672-5511 **Fax:** 620-672-5514 www.pratttribune.com editor@pratttribune.com

Salina Salina Journal (27.8M) PO Box 740 Salina KS 67402 **Phn:** 785-823-6363 **Fax:** 785-827-6363 www.salina.com news@salina.com

Topeka Topeka Capital-Journal (44.1M) 616 SE Jefferson St Topeka KS 66607 **Phn:** 785-295-1111 **Fax:** 785-295-1230 cjonline.com news@cjonline.com

Wellington Wellington Daily News (3.2M) PO Box 368 Wellington KS 67152 **Phn:** 620-326-3326 **Fax:** 620-326-3290 www.wellingtondailynews.com nate.jones@wellingtondailynews.com

Wichita Wichita Eagle (83.8M) PO Box 820 Wichita KS 67201 **Phn:** 316-268-6000 **Fax:** 316-268-6627 www.kansas.com wenews@wichitaeagle.com

Winfield Winfield Daily Courier (4.3M) PO Box 543 Winfield KS 67156 **Phn:** 620-221-1100 **Fax:** 620-221-1101 www.winfieldcourier.com courier@winfieldcourier.com

KENTUCKY

Ashland Independent (17.4M) PO Box 311 Ashland KY 41105 **Phn:** 606-326-2600 **Fax:** 606-326-2678 dailyindependent.com mreliford@dailyindependent.com

Bowling Green Daily News (19.8M) PO Box 90012 Bowling Green KY 42102 **Phn:** 270-781-1700 **Fax:** 270-783-3237 www.bgdailynews.com adennis@bgdailynews.com

Corbin Times-Tribune (6.2M) PO Box 516 Corbin KY 40702 **Phn:** 606-528-2464 **Fax:** 606-528-9850 thetimestribune.com bkillian@thetimestribune.com

Danville Advocate-Messenger (10.5M) PO Box 149 Danville KY 40423 **Phn:** 859-236-2551 **Fax:** 859-236-9566 www-new.mtdemocrat.com johnn@amnews.com

Elizabethtown News-Enterprise (16M) 408 W Dixie Ave Elizabethtown KY 42701 **Phn:** 270-769-2312 **Fax:** 270-769-6965 www.thenewsenterprise.com ne@thenewsenterprise.com

Frankfort State Journal (8.3M) PO Box 368 Frankfort KY 40602 **Phn:** 502-227-4556 **Fax:** 502-227-2831 www.state-journal.com cwest@state-journal.com

Ft Mitchell Kentucky Enquirer (21.5M) 226 Grandview Dr Ft Mitchell KY 41017 **Phn:** 859-578-5555 **Fax:** 859-578-5565 nky.cincinnati.com cwashburn@enquirer.com

Glasgow Glasgow Daily Times (8.5M) PO Box 1179 Glasgow KY 42142 **Phn:** 270-678-5171 **Fax:** 270-678-3372 glasgowdailytimes.com jbrown@glasgowdailytimes.com

Harlan Harlan Daily Enterprise (6.9M) PO Box 1155 Harlan KY 40831 **Phn:** 606-573-4510 **Fax:** 606-573-0042 www.harlandaily.com dcaldwell@heartlandpublications.com

Henderson The Gleaner (10.5M) PO Box 4 Henderson KY 42419 **Phn:** 270-827-2000 **Fax:** 270-827-2765 www.courierpress.com/news/gleaner ddixon@thegleaner.com

Hopkinsville Kentucky New Era (10.4M) PO Box 729 Hopkinsville KY 42241 **Phn:** 270-886-4444 **Fax:** 270-887-3222 www.kentuckynewera.com editor@kentuckynewera.com

Lexington Lexington Herald-Leader (108M) 100 Midland Ave Lexington KY 40508 **Phn:** 859-231-3100 **Fax:** 859-231-3224 www.kentucky.com hlnews@herald-leader.com

Louisville Courier-Journal (210M) PO Box 740031 Louisville KY 40201 **Phn:** 502-582-4011 **Fax:** 502-582-4200 www.courier-journal.com jporter@courier-journal.com

Madisonville The Messenger (7.7M) PO Box 529 Madisonville KY 42431 **Phn:** 270-821-6833 **Fax:** 270-825-3733 www.the-messenger.com newsroom@the-messenger.com

Mayfield The Mayfield Messenger (5.5M) PO Box 709 Mayfield KY 42066 **Phn:** 270-247-1515 **Fax:** 270-247-6336 mayfieldmessenger@kyn.twcbc.com

Maysville Ledger Independent (8.6M) PO Box 518 Maysville KY 41056 **Phn:** 606-564-9091 **Fax:** 606-564-6893 www.maysville-online.com marla.toncray@lee.net

Middlesboro Daily News (5.9M) PO Box 579 Middlesboro KY 40965 **Phn:** 606-248-1010 **Fax:** 606-248-7614 www.middlesborodailynews.com dcaldwell@civitasmedia.com

Murray Murray Ledger & Times (7.5M) PO Box 1040 Murray KY 42071 **Phn:** 270-753-1916 **Fax:** 270-753-1927 murrayledger.com editor@murrayledger.com

Owensboro Owensboro Messenger-Inquirer (27.3M) PO Box 1480 Owensboro KY 42302 **Phn:** 270-926-0123 **Fax:** 270-686-7868 www.messenger-inquirer.com news@messenger-inquirer.com

Paducah Paducah Sun (24.6M) PO Box 2300 Paducah KY 42002 **Phn:** 270-575-8600 **Fax:** 270-442-7859 www.paducahsun.com rclark@paducahsun.com

Richmond Richmond Register (6.1M) PO Box 99 Richmond KY 40476 **Phn:** 859-623-1669 **Fax:** 859-623-7408 richmondregister.com news@richmondregister.com

Somerset Commonwealth-Journal (9.5M) PO Box 859 Somerset KY 42502 **Phn:** 606-678-8191 **Fax:** 606-679-9225 somerset-kentucky.com jneal@somerset-kentucky.com

Winchester Winchester Sun (7.2M) 20 Wall St Winchester KY 40391 **Phn:** 859-744-3123 **Fax:** 859-745-0638 www.centralkynews.com/winchestersun sschurz@amnews.com

LOUISIANA

Abbeville Abbeville Meridional (5.4M) PO Box 400 Abbeville LA 70511 **Phn:** 337-893-4223 **Fax:** 337-898-9022 vermiliontoday.com abbnews@bellsouth.net

Alexandria Alexandria Daily Town Talk (32.8M) PO Box 7558 Alexandria LA 71306 **Phn:** 318-487-6397 **Fax:** 318-487-6488 www.thetowntalk.com pcarty@thetowntalk.com

Bastrop Bastrop Daily Enterprise (4.2M) 119 E Hickory Bastrop LA 71220 **Phn:** 318-281-4421 **Fax:** 318-283-1699 www.bastropenterprise.com dtubbs@bastropenterprise.com

Baton Rouge The Advocate (92.6M) PO Box 588 Baton Rouge LA 70821 **Phn:** 225-383-1111 **Fax:** 225-388-0371 www.theadvocate.com credman@theadvocate.com

Bogalusa Daily News (6.2M) PO Box 820 Bogalusa LA 70429 **Phn:** 985-732-2565 **Fax:** 985-732-4006 www.gobogalusa.com dailynews@wickcommunications.com

Crowley Crowley Post-Signal (4.5M) PO Box 1589 Crowley LA 70527 **Phn:** 337-783-3450 **Fax:** 337-788-0949 www.crowleypostsignal.com cityeditor@bellsouth.net

Deridder Beauregard Daily News (13.5M) PO Box 698 Deridder LA 70634 **Phn:** 337-462-0616 **Fax:** 337-463-5347 www.beauregarddailynews.net ampowers.news@gmail.com

Franklin Franklin Banner-Tribune (3.3M) PO Box 566 Franklin LA 70538 **Phn:** 337-828-3706 **Fax:** 337-828-2874 www.banner-tribune.com editor@banner-tribune.com

Hammond Daily Star (9.7M) PO Box 1149 Hammond LA 70404 **Phn:** 985-254-7827 **Fax:** 985-543-0006 www.hammondstar.com editor@hammondstar.com

Houma The Courier (16.8M) PO Box 2717 Houma LA 70361 **Phn:** 985-850-1100 **Fax:** 985-857-2244 www.houmatoday.com news@houmatoday.com

KENTUCKY DAILY NEWSPAPERS

Jennings Jennings Daily News (4.8M) PO Box 910 Jennings LA 70546 **Phn:** 337-824-3011 **Fax:** 337-824-3019 www.jenningsdailynews.net jdneditor@bellsouth.net

Lafayette Daily Advertiser (43.1M) PO Box 3268 Lafayette LA 70502 **Phn:** 337-289-6300 **Fax:** 337-289-6443 www.theadvertiser.com bdecker@lafayette.gannett.com

Lake Charles American Press (36.2M) PO Box 2893 Lake Charles LA 70602 **Phn:** 337-433-3000 **Fax:** 337-494-4070 www.americanpress.com news@americanpress.com

Leesville Leesville Daily Leader (3.8M) PO Box 619 Leesville LA 71496 **Phn:** 337-239-3444 **Fax:** 337-238-1152 www.leesvilledailyleader.com akunkle@leesvilledailyleader.com

Minden Minden Press-Herald (5M) PO Box 1339 Minden LA 71058 **Phn:** 318-377-1866 **Fax:** 318-377-1895 www.press-herald.com

Monroe News-Star (34.7M) PO Box 1502 Monroe LA 71210 **Phn:** 318-322-5161 **Fax:** 318-362-0273 www.thenewsstar.com news@thenewsstar.com

Morgan City Daily Review (6M) PO Box 948 Morgan City LA 70381 **Phn:** 985-384-8370 **Fax:** 985-384-4255 www.stmarynow.com news@daily-review.com

Natchitoches Natchitoches Times (4.8M) PO Box 448 Natchitoches LA 71458 **Phn:** 318-352-3618 **Fax:** 318-352-7842 www.natchitochestimes.com news@natchitochestimes.com

New Iberia Daily Iberian (13.5M) PO Box 9290 New Iberia LA 70562 **Phn:** 337-365-6773 **Fax:** 337-367-9640 www.iberianet.com don.shoopman@daily-iberian.com

New Orleans Times-Picayune (262M) 3800 Howard Ave New Orleans LA 70125 **Phn:** 504-826-3279 **Fax:** 504-826-3007 www.nola.com letters@nola.com

Opelousas Daily World (9M) PO Box 2389 Opelousas LA 70571 **Phn:** 337-942-4971 **Fax:** 337-948-6572 www.dailyworld.com wjohnson@dailyworld.com

Ruston Ruston Daily Leader (5.6M) PO Box 520 Ruston LA 71273 **Phn:** 318-255-4353 **Fax:** 318-255-4006 www.rustonleader.com elizabeth@rustonleader.com

Shreveport The Times (55.4M) 222 Lake St Shreveport LA 71101 **Phn:** 318-459-3200 **Fax:** 318-459-3301 shreveporttimes.com shreveportopinion@gannett.com

Sulphur Southwest Daily News (4.6M) PO Box 1999 Sulphur LA 70664 **Phn:** 337-527-7075 **Fax:** 337-528-3044 www.sulphurdailynews.com sdneditorial@yahoo.com

Thibodaux Daily Comet (10.6M) PO Box 5238 Thibodaux LA 70302 **Phn:** 985-448-7600 **Fax:** 985-448-7606 www.dailycomet.com news@dailycomet.com

MAINE

Augusta Kennebec Journal (15M) 36 Anthony Ave Ste 101 Augusta ME 04330 **Phn:** 207-623-3811 **Fax:** 207-623-2220 www.kjonline.com smonroe@mainetoday.com

Bangor Bangor Daily News (59.8M) PO Box 1329 Bangor ME 04402 **Phn:** 207-990-8000 **Fax:** 207-941-9476 www.bangordailynews.com bdnnews@bangordailynews.com

Biddeford Journal Tribune (7.3M) PO Box 627 Biddeford ME 04005 **Phn:** 207-282-1535 **Fax:** 207-282-3138 www.journaltribune.com jtcommunity@journaltribune.com

Brunswick Times Record (9.9M) PO Box 10 Brunswick ME 04011 **Phn:** 207-729-3311 **Fax:** 207-721-3151 www.timesrecord.com news@timesrecord.com

Lewiston Sun Journal (34M) PO Box 4400 Lewiston ME 04243 **Phn:** 207-784-5411 **Fax:** 207-777-3436 www.sunjournal.com rrhoades@sunjournal.com

Portland Portland Daily Sun (14.5M) 181 State St Portland ME 04101 **Phn:** 207-699-5801 **Fax:** 207-899-4963 portlanddailysun.me david@portlanddailysun.me

Portland Press Herald/ME Sunday Telegram (72.4M) 390 Congress St Portland ME 04101 **Phn:** 207-791-6650 **Fax:** 207-791-6920 www.pressherald.com amuhs@mainetoday.com

Waterville Morning Sentinel (19.7M) 31 Front St Waterville ME 04901 **Phn:** 207-873-3341 **Fax:** 207-861-9191 www.onlinesentinel.com jevans@centralmaine.com

MARYLAND

Annapolis The Capital (44.6M) PO Box 911 Annapolis MD 21404 **Phn:** 410-268-5000 **Fax:** 410-280-5953 www.capitalgazette.com sgunn@capgaznews.com

Baltimore Baltimore Sun (236M) 501 N Calvert St Baltimore MD 21278 **Phn:** 410-332-6100 **Fax:** 410-752-6049 www.baltimoresun.com publiceditor@baltsun.com

Cumberland Cumberland Times-News (28.8M) PO Box 1662 Cumberland MD 21501 **Phn:** 301-722-4600 **Fax:** 301-722-5270 times-news.com jpalderton@times-news.com

Easton Star-Democrat (16.7M) PO Box 600 Easton MD 21601 **Phn:** 410-822-1500 **Fax:** 410-770-4019 www.stardem.com stardem@chespub.com

Elkton Cecil Whig (13.3M) PO Box 429 Elkton MD 21922 **Phn:** 410-398-3311 **Fax:** 410-398-4044 www.cecildaily.com chamilton@cecilwhig.com

Frederick Frederick News-Post (39.3M) 351 Ballenger Center Dr Frederick MD 21703 **Phn:** 301-662-1177 **Fax:** 301-662-8299 www.fredericknewspost.com stripler@newspost.com

Hagerstown Herald-Mail (12.4M) 100 Summit Ave Hagerstown MD 21740 **Phn:** 301-733-5131 **Fax:** 301-714-0245 www.heraldmailmedia.com news@herald-mail.com

Salisbury Daily Times (25.5M) PO Box 1937 Salisbury MD 21802 **Phn:** 410-749-7171 **Fax:** 410-749-7290 www.delmarvanow.com bpenserga@smgpo.gannett.com

Westminster Carroll Co. Times (24.2M) PO Box 346 Westminster MD 21158 **Phn:** 410-848-4400 **Fax:** 410-857-8749 www.carrollcountytimes.com jim.lee@carrollcountytimes.com

MASSACHUSETTS

Athol Athol Daily News (4.7M) PO Box 1000 Athol MA 01331 **Phn:** 978-249-3535 **Fax:** 978-249-9630 atholdailynews.com newsroom@atholdailynews.com

Attleboro Sun Chronicle (17.7M) 34 S Main St Attleboro MA 02703 **Phn:** 508-222-7000 **Fax:** 508-236-0462 www.thesunchronicle.com mkirby@thesunchronicle.com

Beverly Salem News (30M) 32 Dunham Rd Beverly MA 01915 **Phn:** 978-922-1234 **Fax:** 978-927-4524 www.salemnews.com kandreas@ecnnews.com

Boston Boston Globe (303M) PO Box 55819 Boston MA 02205 **Phn:** 617-929-2000 **Fax:** 617-929-3192 www.boston.com newstip@globe.com

Boston Boston Herald (204M) PO Box 55843 Boston MA 02205 **Phn:** 617-426-3000 **Fax:** 617-619-6450 bostonherald.com mperigard@bostonherald.com

Boston Metro Boston (171M) 320 Congress St Fl 5 Boston MA 02210 **Phn:** 617-210-7905 **Fax:** 617-357-4706 www.readmetro.com pat.healy@metro.us

Brockton The Enterprise (31.7M) 1324 Belmont St Ste 102 Brockton MA 02301 **Phn:** 508-586-6200 **Fax:** 508-586-6506 www.enterprisenews.com newsroom@enterprisenews.com

Fall River Herald News (20.6M) 207 Pocasset St Fall River MA 02721 **Phn:** 508-676-8211 **Fax:** 508-676-2566 www.heraldnews.com news@heraldnews.com

Fitchburg Sentinel & Enterprise (15.2M) PO Box 730 Fitchburg MA 01420 **Phn:** 978-343-6911 **Fax:** 978-342-1158 www.sentinelandenterprise.com news@sentinelandenterprise.com

Framingham MetroWest Daily News (23M) 33 New York Ave Framingham MA 01701 **Phn:** 508-626-3800 **Fax:** 508-626-4400 www.metrowestdailynews.com rlodge@wickedlocal.com

Gardner Gardner News (6.1M) PO Box 340 Gardner MA 01440 **Phn:** 978-632-8000 **Fax:** 978-630-5410 www.thegardnernews.com editorial@thegardnernews.com

Gloucester Gloucester Daily Times (10.4M) 36 Whittemore St Gloucester MA 01930 **Phn:** 978-283-7000 **Fax:** 978-282-4397 www.gloucestertimes.com gdt@ecnnews.com

Greenfield The Recorder (12M) PO Box 1367 Greenfield MA 01302 **Phn:** 413-772-0261 **Fax:** 413-774-5020 www.recorder.com news@recorder.com

Hyannis Cape Cod Times (49.4M) 319 Main St Hyannis MA 02601 **Phn:** 508-775-1200 **Fax:** 508-771-3292 www.capecodonline.com news@capecodonline.com

Lowell The Sun (44.3M) PO Box 1477 Lowell MA 01853 **Phn:** 978-458-7100 **Fax:** 978-970-4600 www.lowellsun.com kpisarik@lowellsun.com

Lynn Daily Item (13.8M) PO Box 951 Lynn MA 01903 **Phn:** 781-593-7700 **Fax:** 781-598-2891 itemlive.com contactus@itemlive.com

Malden Malden Evening News/Medford Mercury (11.4M) 277 Commercial St Malden MA 02148 **Phn:** 781-321-8000 **Fax:** 781-321-8008 editor@maldennews.com

Milford Milford Daily News (8.6M) 159 S Main St Milford MA 01757 **Phn:** 508-473-1111 **Fax:** 508-634-7514 www.milforddailynews.com milforddailynews@wickedlocal.com

New Bedford Standard-Times (31.6M) 25 Elm St New Bedford MA 02740 **Phn:** 508-979-4440 **Fax:** 508-997-7491 www.southcoasttoday.com newsroom@s-t.com

Newburyport Daily News of Newburyport (13M) 23 Liberty St Newburyport MA 01950 **Phn:** 978-462-6666 **Fax:** 978-465-8505 www.newburyportnews.com ndn@ecnnews.com

North Adams North Adams Transcript (6.1M) 124 American Legion Dr North Adams MA 01247 **Phn:** 413-663-3741 **Fax:** 413-662-2792 www.theTranscript.com news@thetranscript.com

North Andover Eagle-Tribune (46.6M) 100 Turnpike St North Andover MA 01845 **Phn:** 978-685-1000 **Fax:** 978-687-6045 www.eagletribune.com jmacone@eagletribune.com

Northampton Daily Hampshire Gazette (17.5M) PO Box 299 Northampton MA 01061 **Phn:** 413-584-5000 **Fax:** 413-585-5299 www.gazettenet.com newsroom@gazettenet.com

Pittsfield Berkshire Eagle (27.5M) PO Box 1171 Pittsfield MA 01202 **Phn:** 413-447-7311 **Fax:** 413-499-3419 www.BerkshireEagle.com kmoran@berkshireeagle.com

Quincy Patriot Ledger (52.7M) PO Box 699159 Quincy MA 02269 **Phn:** 617-786-7000 **Fax:** 617-786-7025 www.patriotledger.com newsroom@ledger.com

MASSACHUSETTS DAILY NEWSPAPERS

Southbridge Southbridge Evening News (5.1M) PO Box 90 Southbridge MA 01550 **Phn:** 508-764-4325 **Fax:** 508-764-8015 www.southbridgeeveningnews.com charlton@stonebridgepress.com

Springfield The Republican (83.3M) PO Box 2350 Springfield MA 01102 **Phn:** 413-788-1000 **Fax:** 413-788-1301 www.masslive.com/republican news@repub.com

Taunton Taunton Daily Gazette (9.5M) PO Box 111 Taunton MA 02780 **Phn:** 508-880-9000 **Fax:** 508-967-3101 www.tauntongazette.com newsroom@tauntongazette.com

Wakefield Wakefield Daily Item (4M) 26 Albion St Wakefield MA 01880 **Phn:** 781-245-0080 **Fax:** 781-246-0061 www.wakefielditem.com news@wakefielditem.com

Westfield The Westfield News (5.2M) 62 School St Westfield MA 01085 **Phn:** 413-562-4181 **Fax:** 413-562-4185 www.TheWestfieldNews.com

Woburn Daily Times Chronicle (10.1M) 1 Arrow Dr Woburn MA 01801 **Phn:** 781-933-3700 **Fax:** 781-932-3321 www.woburnonline.com news@woburnonline.com

Worcester Telegram & Gazette (88.9M) 20 Franklin St Worcester MA 01608 **Phn:** 508-793-9100 **Fax:** 508-793-9281 www.telegram.com newstips@telegram.com

MICHIGAN

Adrian Daily Telegram (14.5M) PO Box 647 Adrian MI 49221 **Phn:** 517-265-5111 **Fax:** 517-263-4152 www.lenconnect.com editor@lenconnect.com

Alpena Alpena News (10.6M) PO Box 367 Alpena MI 49707 **Phn:** 989-354-3111 **Fax:** 989-354-1793 www.thealpenanews.com newsroom@thealpenanews.com

Bad Axe Huron Daily Tribune (7M) 211 N Heisterman St Bad Axe MI 48413 **Phn:** 989-269-6461 **Fax:** 989-269-9435 www.michigansthumb.com hdt_news@hearstnp.com

Battle Creek Battle Creek Enquirer (22.6M) 77 Michigan Ave E Ste 100 Battle Creek MI 49017 **Phn:** 269-964-7161 **Fax:** 269-964-0299 www.battlecreekenquirer.com ccarlson@battlecreekenquirer.com

Bay City Bay City Times (32.7M) 311 5th St Bay City MI 48708 **Phn:** 989-895-8551 **Fax:** 989-893-0649 www.mlive.com/bctimes rclark2@mlive.com

Big Rapids Big Rapids Pioneer (5.2M) 115 N Michigan Ave Big Rapids MI 49307 **Phn:** 231-796-4831 **Fax:** 231-796-1152 www.pioneergroup.com info@pioneergroup.com

Cadillac Cadillac News (10.2M) PO Box 640 Cadillac MI 49601 **Phn:** 231-775-6565 **Fax:** 231-775-8790 www.cadillacnews.com mseward@cadillacnews.com

Cheboygan Cheboygan Daily Tribune (4.9M) 308 N Main St Cheboygan MI 49721 **Phn:** 231-627-7144 **Fax:** 231-627-5331 www.cheboygannews.com richard@cheboygantribune.com

Coldwater Coldwater Daily Reporter (5.3M) 15 W Pearl St Coldwater MI 49036 **Phn:** 517-278-2318 **Fax:** 517-278-6041 www.thedailyreporter.com editor@thedailyreporter.com

Detroit Detroit Free Press (291M) 615 W Lafayette Blvd Detroit MI 48226 **Phn:** 313-222-6400 **Fax:** 313-222-5981 www.freep.com dfpcity@freepress.com

Detroit Detroit News (202M) 615 W Lafayette Blvd Detroit MI 48226 **Phn:** 313-222-2300 **Fax:** 313-222-2335 www.detroitnews.com newsroom@detroitnews.com

Dowagiac Dowagiac Daily News (1.8M) PO Box 30 Dowagiac MI 49047 **Phn:** 269-687-7706 **Fax:** 269-782-5290 www.dowagiacnews.com aly.gibson@leaderpub.com

Escanaba Daily Press (9M) PO Box 828 Escanaba MI 49829 **Phn:** 906-786-2021 **Fax:** 906-786-9006 www.dailypress.net news@dailypress.net

Flint Flint Journal (83.5M) 200 E 1st St Flint MI 48502 **Phn:** 810-766-6100 **Fax:** 810-767-7518 www.mlive.com/flintjournal mraymer@mlive.com

Ft Clinton Twsp Macomb Daily (40.6M) 19176 Hall Rd Ft Clinton Twsp MI 48038 **Phn:** 586-469-4510 **Fax:** 586-469-2892 www.macombdaily.com bruce.macleod@macombdaily.com

Grand Haven Grand Haven Tribune (9.9M) 101 N 3rd St Grand Haven MI 49417 **Phn:** 616-842-6400 **Fax:** 616-842-9584 www.grandhaventribune.com news@grandhaventribune.com

Grand Rapids Grand Rapids Press (132M) 169 Monroe Ave NW # 100 Grand Rapids MI 49503 **Phn:** 616-222-2400 **Fax:** 616-458-2579 www.mlive.com/grpress grnews@mlive.com

Greenville Daily News (8.4M) 109 N Lafayette St Greenville MI 48838 **Phn:** 616-754-9301 **Fax:** 616-754-8559 www.thedailynews.cc

Hillsdale Hillsdale Daily News (7.3M) 3 McCollum St Hillsdale MI 49242 **Phn:** 517-437-7351 **Fax:** 517-437-6397 www.hillsdale.net

Holland Holland Sentinel (18.4M) 54 W 8th St Holland MI 49423 **Phn:** 616-546-4200 **Fax:** 616-392-3526 www.hollandsentinel.com newsroom@hollandsentinel.com

Houghton Daily Mining Gazette (9.5M) PO Box 368 Houghton MI 49931 **Phn:** 906-482-1500 **Fax:** 906-482-2726 www.mininggazette.com archy@mininggazette.com

Howell Daily Press & Argus (13.7M) 323 E Grand River Ave Howell MI 48843 **Phn:** 517-548-2000 **Fax:** 517-548-3005 www.livingstondaily.com business@livingstondaily.com

Ionia Sentinel-Standard (2.9M) 114 N Depot St Ionia MI 48846 **Phn:** 616-527-2100 **Fax:** 616-527-6860 www.sentinel-standard.com newsroom@sentinel-standard.com

Iron Mountain Daily News (9.1M) PO Box 460 Iron Mountain MI 49801 **Phn:** 906-774-2772 **Fax:** 906-774-1285 www.ironmountaindailynews.com news@ironmountaindailynews.com

Ironwood Daily Globe (6.5M) PO Box 548 Ironwood MI 49938 **Phn:** 906-932-2211 **Fax:** 906-932-4211 yourdailyglobe.com news@yourdailyglobe.com

Jackson Jackson Citizen Patriot (33M) 214 S Jackson St Jackson MI 49201 **Phn:** 517-787-2300 **Fax:** 517-787-9711 mlive.com/jackson

Kalamazoo Kalamazoo Gazette (52.4M) 401 S Burdick St Kalamazoo MI 49007 **Phn:** 269-345-3511 **Fax:** 269-388-8447 www.mlive.com/kalamazoo news@kalamazoogazette.com

Lansing Lansing State Journal (63M) 120 E Lenawee St Lansing MI 48919 **Phn:** 517-377-1000 **Fax:** 517-377-1298 www.lansingstatejournal.com sreifert@lsj.com

Ludington Ludington Daily News (8.7M) PO Box 340 Ludington MI 49431 **Phn:** 231-845-5181 **Fax:** 231-843-4011 www.shorelinemedia.net ldn@ludingtondailynews.com

Manistee Manistee News-Advocate (5M) PO Box 317 Manistee MI 49660 **Phn:** 231-723-3592 **Fax:** 231-723-4733 www.pioneergroup.com info@pioneergroup.com

Marquette Mining Journal (14.6M) PO Box 430 Marquette MI 49855 **Phn:** 906-228-2500 **Fax:** 906-228-2617 www.miningjournal.net bsargent@miningjournal.net

Midland Midland Daily News (16M) 124 S McDonald St Midland MI 48640 **Phn:** 989-835-7171 **Fax:** 989-835-9151 www.ourmidland.com info@mdn.net

Monroe Monroe Evening News (20.8M) PO Box 1176 Monroe MI 48161 **Phn:** 734-242-1100 **Fax:** 734-242-0937 www.monroenews.com saul@monroenews.com

Mount Pleasant Morning Sun (10.2M) 711 W Pickard St Ste P Mount Pleasant MI 48858 **Phn:** 989-779-6000 **Fax:** 989-779-6051 www.themorningsun.com rmills@michigannewspapers.com

Muskegon Muskegon Chronicle (42.8M) PO Box 59 Muskegon MI 49443 **Phn:** 231-722-3161 **Fax:** 231-722-2552 www.mlive.com/muskegon dgaydou@mlive.com

Niles Niles Daily Star (2.4M) 217 N 4th St Niles MI 49120 **Phn:** 269-687-7720 **Fax:** 269-683-2175 www.leaderpub.com craig.haupert@leaderpub.com

Owosso Argus-Press (11.2M) 201 E Exchange St Owosso MI 48867 **Phn:** 989-725-5136 **Fax:** 989-725-6376 www.argus-press.com news@argus-press.com

Petoskey Petoskey News-Review (10.6M) 319 State St Petoskey MI 49770 **Phn:** 231-347-2544 **Fax:** 231-347-5461 www.petoskeynews.com petoskeynews@petoskeynews.com

Pontiac Oakland Press (66.6M) PO Box 436009 Pontiac MI 48343 **Phn:** 248-332-8181 **Fax:** 248-332-8885 www.theoaklandpress.com glenn.gilbert@oakpress.com

Port Huron Times Herald (26.1M) 911 Military St Port Huron MI 48060 **Phn:** 810-985-7171 **Fax:** 810-989-6294 www.thetimesherald.com newsroom@thetimesherald.com

Royal Oak Detroit Daily Press (200M) 210 E 3rd St Royal Oak MI 48067 **Phn:** 248-542-6397 **Fax:** 248-543-7608 www.detdailypress.com

Saint Joseph Herald-Palladium (22.2M) PO Box 128 Saint Joseph MI 49085 **Phn:** 269-429-2400 **Fax:** 269-429-4398 www.heraldpalladium.com localnews@heraldpalladium.com

Sault Sainte Marie Evening News (6.8M) 109 Arlington St Sault Sainte Marie MI 49783 **Phn:** 906-632-2235 **Fax:** 906-632-1222 www.sooeveningnews.com edit@sooeveningnews.com

Sturgis Sturgis Journal (6.3M) PO Box 660 Sturgis MI 49091 **Phn:** 269-651-5407 **Fax:** 269-651-2296 www.sturgisjournal.com newsroom@sturgisjournal.com

Three Rivers Three Rivers Commercial-News (2M) PO Box 130 Three Rivers MI 49093 **Phn:** 269-279-7488 **Fax:** 269-279-6007 www.threeriversnews.com news@threeriversnews.com

Traverse City Traverse City Record-Eagle (27.7M) 120 W Front St Traverse City MI 49684 **Phn:** 231-946-2000 **Fax:** 231-946-8632 record-eagle.com mtyree@record-eagle.com

MINNESOTA

Albert Lea Albert Lea Tribune (6.3M) 808 W Front St Albert Lea MN 56007 **Phn:** 507-373-1411 **Fax:** 507-373-0333 www.albertleatribune.com news@albertleatribune.com

Austin Austin Daily Herald (6.5M) 310 2nd St NE Austin MN 55912 **Phn:** 507-433-8851 **Fax:** 507-437-8644 www.austindailyherald.com newsroom@austindailyherald.com

Bemidji The Pioneer (9.5M) PO Box 455 Bemidji MN 56619 **Phn:** 218-333-9200 **Fax:** 218-333-9819 www.bemidjipioneer.com news@bemidjipioneer.com

MICHIGAN DAILY NEWSPAPERS

Brainerd Brainerd Daily Dispatch (13.6M) PO Box 974 Brainerd MN 56401 **Phn:** 218-829-4705 **Fax:** 218-829-0211 brainerddispatch.com keith.hansen@brainerddispatch.com

Crookston Crookston Daily Times (1.8M) 124 S Broadway Crookston MN 56716 **Phn:** 218-281-2730 **Fax:** 218-281-7234 www.crookstontimes.com editor@gvtel.com

Duluth Duluth News-Tribune (40.9M) 424 W 1st St Duluth MN 55802 **Phn:** 218-723-5281 **Fax:** 218-720-4120 www.duluthnewstribune.com cityeditors@duluthnews.com

Fairmont Sentinel (6.9M) PO Box 681 Fairmont MN 56031 **Phn:** 507-235-3303 **Fax:** 507-235-3718 fairmontsentinel.com news@fairmontsentinel.com

Faribault Faribault Daily News (6.4M) 514 Central Ave N Faribault MN 55021 **Phn:** 507-333-3100 **Fax:** 507-333-3103 www.southernminn.com/faribault_daily_news spope@faribault.com

Fergus Falls Daily Journal (8.4M) 914 E Channing Ave Fergus Falls MN 56537 **Phn:** 218-736-7511 **Fax:** 218-736-5919 www.fergusfallsjournal.com newsroom@fergusfallsjournal.com

Hibbing Hibbing Daily Tribune (4.9M) PO Box 38 Hibbing MN 55746 **Phn:** 218-262-1011 **Fax:** 218-262-4318 www.hibbingmn.com kgrinsteinner@hibbingdailytribune.net

International Falls The Journal (3.7M) 1602 Highway 71 International Falls MN 56649 **Phn:** 218-285-7411 **Fax:** 218-285-7206 www.ifallsjournal.com laurel@ifallsjournal.com

Mankato Free Press (22.3M) 418 S 2nd St Mankato MN 56001 **Phn:** 507-625-4451 **Fax:** 507-388-4355 mankatofreepress.com editor@mankatofreepress.com

Marshall Marshall Independent (7.5M) PO Box 411 Marshall MN 56258 **Phn:** 507-537-1551 **Fax:** 507-537-1557 marshallindependent.com news@marshallindependent.com

Minneapolis Star Tribune (320M) 425 Portland Ave Minneapolis MN 55488 **Phn:** 612-673-4000 **Fax:** 612-673-4359 www.startribune.com business@startribune.com

New Ulm The Journal (8.4M) PO Box 487 New Ulm MN 56073 **Phn:** 507-359-2911 **Fax:** 507-359-7362 www.nujournal.com online@nujournal.com

Owatonna Owatonna People's Press (7.3M) 135 W Pearl St Owatonna MN 55060 **Phn:** 507-451-2840 **Fax:** 507-444-2382 www.southernminn.com/owatonna_peoples_press editor@owatonna.com

Red Wing Republican-Eagle (6.8M) PO Box 15 Red Wing MN 55066 **Phn:** 651-388-8235 **Fax:** 651-388-3404 www.republican-eagle.com news@republican-eagle.com

Rochester Post-Bulletin (44.6M) PO Box 6118 Rochester MN 55903 **Phn:** 507-285-7600 **Fax:** 507-285-7772 www.postbulletin.com news@postbulletin.com

Saint Cloud St. Cloud Times (26.8M) PO Box 768 Saint Cloud MN 56302 **Phn:** 320-255-8700 **Fax:** 320-255-8775 www.sctimes.com newsroom@stcloudtimes.com

Saint Paul St. Paul Pioneer Press (184M) 345 Cedar St Saint Paul MN 55101 **Phn:** 651-222-5011 **Fax:** 651-228-5500 www.twincities.com bshaw@pioneerpress.com

Stillwater Stillwater Gazette (3.3M) 1931 Curve Crest Blvd W Stillwater MN 55082 **Phn:** 651-439-3130 **Fax:** 651-439-4713 www.stillwatergazette.com

Virginia Mesabi Daily News (9.3M) PO Box 956 Virginia MN 55792 **Phn:** 218-741-5544 **Fax:** 218-741-1005 www.virginiamn.com bhanna@mesabidailynews.net

Willmar West Central Tribune (16.8M) PO Box 839 Willmar MN 56201 **Phn:** 320-235-1150 **Fax:** 320-235-6769 www.wctrib.com news@wctrib.com

Winona Winona Daily News (11.2M) PO Box 5147 Winona MN 55987 **Phn:** 507-453-3500 **Fax:** 507-453-3517 www.winonadailynews.com circulation@winonadailynews.com

Worthington Daily Globe (9.1M) PO Box 639 Worthington MN 56187 **Phn:** 507-376-9711 **Fax:** 507-376-5202 www.dglobe.com rmcgaughey@dglobe.com

MISSISSIPPI

Biloxi Sun Herald (44M) PO Box 4567 Biloxi MS 39535 **Phn:** 228-896-2100 **Fax:** 228-896-2104 www.sunherald.com kmagandy@sunherald.com

Brookhaven Daily Leader (6.6M) 128 N Railroad Ave Brookhaven MS 39601 **Phn:** 601-833-6961 **Fax:** 601-833-6714 dailyleader.com news@dailyleader.com

Clarksdale Clarksdale Press Register (5.2M) 128 E 2nd St Clarksdale MS 38614 **Phn:** 662-627-2201 **Fax:** 662-624-5125 www.pressregister.com news@pressregister.com

Cleveland Bolivar Commercial (6.3M) PO Box 1050 Cleveland MS 38732 **Phn:** 662-843-4241 **Fax:** 662-843-1830 www.bolivarcom.com news@bolivarcommercial.com

Columbus Commercial Dispatch (13.3M) PO Box 511 Columbus MS 39703 **Phn:** 662-328-2424 **Fax:** 662-329-8937 www.cdispatch.com birney@cdispatch.com

Corinth Daily Corinthian (6.7M) PO Box 1800 Corinth MS 38835 **Phn:** 662-287-6111 **Fax:** 662-287-3525 www.dailycorinthian.com news@dailycorinthian.com

Greenville Delta Democrat Times (10.1M) PO Box 1618 Greenville MS 38702 **Phn:** 662-335-1155 **Fax:** 662-378-0777 www.ddtonline.com ddtnews@ddtonline.com

Greenwood Greenwood Commonwealth (7.3M) PO Box 8050 Greenwood MS 38935 **Phn:** 662-453-5312 **Fax:** 662-453-2908 www.gwcommonwealth.com commonwealth@gwcommonwealth.com

Hattiesburg Hattiesburg American (19.4M) 825 N Main St Hattiesburg MS 39401 **Phn:** 601-582-4321 **Fax:** 601-584-3130 www.hattiesburgamerican.com ejkosnac@hattiesburgamerican.com

Jackson Clarion-Ledger (90.1M) 201 S Congress St Jackson MS 39201 **Phn:** 601-961-7000 **Fax:** 601-961-7211 www.clarionledger.com dskipper@clarionledger.com

McComb Enterprise-Journal (8M) PO Box 2009 McComb MS 39649 **Phn:** 601-684-2421 **Fax:** 601-684-0836 www.enterprise-journal.com news@enterprise-journal.com

Meridian Meridian Star (14.7M) PO Box 1591 Meridian MS 39302 **Phn:** 601-693-1551 **Fax:** 601-485-1275 meridianstar.com hreynolds@themeridianstar.com

Natchez Natchez Democrat (8.4M) PO Box 1447 Natchez MS 39121 **Phn:** 601-442-9101 **Fax:** 601-442-7315 www.natchezdemocrat.com julie.finley@natchezdemocrat.com

Oxford Oxford Eagle (5M) PO Box 866 Oxford MS 38655 **Phn:** 662-234-4331 **Fax:** 662-234-4351 oxfordeagle.com webmaster@oxfordeagle.com

Pascagoula Mississippi Press (16.1M) PO Box 849 Pascagoula MS 39568 **Phn:** 228-762-1111 **Fax:** 228-934-1474 www.gulflive.com/mississippipress mseditor@themississippipress.com

Picayune Picayune Item (4.5M) PO Box 580 Picayune MS 39466 **Phn:** 601-798-4766 **Fax:** 601-798-8602 picayuneitem.com picayuneitem@bellsouth.net

Starkville Starkville Daily News (7.1M) PO Box 1068 Starkville MS 39760 **Phn:** 662-323-1642 **Fax:** 662-323-6586 www.starkvilledailynews.com sdneditor@bellsouth.net

Tupelo NE Mississippi Daily Journal (36.5M) PO Box 909 Tupelo MS 38802 **Phn:** 662-842-2611 **Fax:** 662-842-2233 djournal.com stephanie.rebman@journalinc.com

Vicksburg Vicksburg Post (13.1M) PO Box 821668 Vicksburg MS 39182 **Phn:** 601-636-4545 **Fax:** 601-634-0897 www.vicksburgpost.com post@vicksburg.com

West Point Daily Times Leader (2.9M) PO Box 1176 West Point MS 39773 **Phn:** 662-494-1422 **Fax:** 662-494-1414 www.dailytimesleader.com dtleditor@bellsouth.net

MISSOURI

Boonville Boonville Daily News (2.8M) PO Box 47 Boonville MO 65233 **Phn:** 660-882-5335 **Fax:** 660-882-2256 www.boonvilledailynews.com bdnedward@gmail.com

Branson Branson Tri-Lakes News (11.2M) PO Box 1900 Branson MO 65615 **Phn:** 417-334-3161 **Fax:** 417-334-1460 bransontrilakesnews.com mhoney@bransontrilakesnews.com

Camdenton Lake Sun Leader (4.4M) 918 N Business Route 5 Camdenton MO 65020 **Phn:** 573-346-2132 **Fax:** 573-346-4045 www.lakenewsonline.com newsroom@lakesunonline.com

Cape Girardeau Southeast Missourian (15.9M) PO Box 699 Cape Girardeau MO 63702 **Phn:** 573-335-6611 **Fax:** 573-334-7288 www.semissourian.com msanders@semissourian.com

Carthage Carthage Press (2.5M) PO Box 678 Carthage MO 64836 **Phn:** 417-358-2191 **Fax:** 417-358-7428 www.carthagepress.com news@carthagepress.com

Chillicothe Chillicothe Constitution-Tribune (3.5M) PO Box 707 Chillicothe MO 64601 **Phn:** 660-646-2411 **Fax:** 660-646-2028 www.chillicothenews.com ctnews@chillicothenews.com

Clinton Clinton Daily Democrat (4.2M) PO Box 586 Clinton MO 64735 **Phn:** 660-885-2281 **Fax:** 660-885-2265

Columbia Columbia Daily Tribune (18.2M) PO Box 798 Columbia MO 65205 **Phn:** 573-815-1500 **Fax:** 573-815-1701 www.columbiatribune.com editor@tribmail.com

Columbia Columbia Missourian (7M) PO Box 917 Columbia MO 65205 **Phn:** 573-882-5700 **Fax:** 573-882-5702 www.columbiamissourian.com editor@columbiamissourian.com

Dexter Daily Statesman (2.5M) PO Box 579 Dexter MO 63841 **Phn:** 573-624-4545 **Fax:** 573-624-7449 www.dailystatesman.com nhyslop@dailystatesman.com

Fulton Fulton Sun (3.9M) 115 E 5th St Fulton MO 65251 **Phn:** 573-642-7272 **Fax:** 573-642-0656 www.fultonsun.com news@fultonsun.com

Hannibal Hannibal Courier-Post (7.7M) PO Box A Hannibal MO 63401 **Phn:** 573-221-2800 **Fax:** 573-221-5800 www.hannibal.net marylou.montgomery@courierpost.com

Independence The Examiner (14M) 410 S Liberty St Independence MO 64050 **Phn:** 816-254-8600 **Fax:** 816-254-0211 www.examiner.net sheila.davis@examiner.net

Jefferson City News Tribune (16.9M) PO Box 420 Jefferson City MO 65102 **Phn:** 573-636-3131 **Fax:** 573-761-0235 www.newstribune.com nt@newstribune.com

Joplin Joplin Globe (29.4M) PO Box 7 Joplin MO 64802 **Phn:** 417-623-3480 **Fax:** 417-623-8598 www.joplinglobe.com news@joplinglobe.com

---

Kansas City Kansas City Star (255M) 1729 Grand Blvd Kansas City MO 64108 **Phn:** 816-234-4141 **Fax:** 816-234-4926 www.kansascity.com pbacker@kcstar.com

Kennett Daily Dunklin Democrat (5M) PO Box 669 Kennett MO 63857 **Phn:** 573-888-4505 **Fax:** 573-888-5114 www.dddnews.com

Kirksville Kirksville Daily Express (4.3M) PO Box 809 Kirksville MO 63501 **Phn:** 660-665-2808 **Fax:** 660-665-2608 www.kirksvilledailyexpress.com dailyexpresseditor@gmail.com

Lebanon Lebanon Daily Record (4.5M) 100 E Commercial St Lebanon MO 65536 **Phn:** 417-532-9131 **Fax:** 417-532-8140 www.lebanondailyrecord.com jturner@lebanondailyrecord.com

Macon Macon Chronicle-Herald (2.3M) 204 W Bourke St Macon MO 63552 **Phn:** 660-385-3121 **Fax:** 660-385-3082 www.maconch.com chnews@centurytel.net

Marshall Marshall Democrat-News (3.1M) PO Box 100 Marshall MO 65340 **Phn:** 660-886-2233 **Fax:** 660-886-8544 www.marshallnews.com ecrump@marshallnews.com

Maryville Maryville Daily Forum (3.5M) 111 E Jenkins St Maryville MO 64468 **Phn:** 660-562-2424 **Fax:** 660-562-2823 www.maryvilledailyforum.com

Mexico Mexico Ledger (5M) PO Box 8 Mexico MO 65265 **Phn:** 573-581-1111 **Fax:** 573-581-2029 www.mexicoledger.com news@mexicoledger.com

Moberly Moberly Monitor-Index (5.3M) 218 N WIlliams Moberly MO 65270 **Phn:** 660-263-4123 **Fax:** 660-263-3626 www.moberlymonitor.com dvandyke@moberlymonitor.com

Monett Monett Times (4M) PO Box 40 Monett MO 65708 **Phn:** 417-235-3135 **Fax:** 417-235-8852 www.monett-times.com editor@monett-times.com

Neosho Neosho Daily News (3.5M) PO Box 848 Neosho MO 64850 **Phn:** 417-451-1520 **Fax:** 417-451-6408 www.neoshodailynews.com editor@neoshodailynews.com

Nevada Nevada Daily Mail/Sunday Herald (2.8M) PO Box 247 Nevada MO 64772 **Phn:** 417-667-3344 **Fax:** 417-667-3817 www.nevadadailymail.com editorial@nevadadailymail.com

Park Hills Daily Journal (8.1M) PO Box 9 Park Hills MO 63601 **Phn:** 573-431-2010 **Fax:** 573-431-7640 dailyjournalonline.com editorial@dailyjournalonline.com

Poplar Bluff Daily American Republic (12.9M) PO Box 7C Poplar Bluff MO 63902 **Phn:** 573-785-1414 **Fax:** 573-785-2706 info.darnews.com sberry@darnews.com

Richmond Daily News (3M) PO Box 100 Richmond MO 64085 **Phn:** 816-776-5454 **Fax:** 816-470-6397 www.richmond-dailynews.com editor@richmond-dailynews.com

Rolla Rolla Daily News (4.9M) PO Box 808 Rolla MO 65402 **Phn:** 573-364-2468 **Fax:** 573-341-5847 www.therolladailynews.com paulhackbarth@therolladailynews.com

Saint Joseph St. Joseph News-Press (34.5M) PO Box 29 Saint Joseph MO 64502 **Phn:** 816-271-8500 **Fax:** 816-271-8692 www.newspressnow.com newspressnow@npgco.com

Saint Louis St. Louis Post-Dispatch (277M) 900 N Tucker Blvd Saint Louis MO 63101 **Phn:** 314-340-8000 **Fax:** 314-340-3050 www.stltoday.com siteeditor@stltoday.com

Sedalia Sedalia Democrat (11.9M) PO Box 848 Sedalia MO 65302 **Phn:** 660-826-1000 **Fax:** 660-826-0400 www.sedaliademocrat.com news@sedaliademocrat.com

---

Sikeston Standard Democrat (6.5M) 205 S New Madrid St Sikeston MO 63801 **Phn:** 573-471-1137 **Fax:** 573-471-6981 www.standard-democrat.com standem@yahoo.com

Springfield Springfield News-Leader (58.2M) PO Box 798 Springfield MO 65801 **Phn:** 417-836-1100 **Fax:** 417-837-1381 www.news-leader.com webeditor@news-leader.com

Trenton Republican-Times (3M) PO Box 548 Trenton MO 64683 **Phn:** 660-359-2212 **Fax:** 660-359-4414

Warrensburg Daily Star-Journal (6.3M) PO Box 68 Warrensburg MO 64093 **Phn:** 660-747-8123 **Fax:** 660-747-8741 www.dailystarjournal.com jackmiles@npgco.com

Waynesville Daily Guide (1.8M) PO Box 578 Waynesville MO 65583 **Phn:** 573-336-3711 **Fax:** 573-336-4640 www.waynesvilledailyguide.com editor@waynesvilledailyguide.com

West Plains West Plains Daily Quill (9.1M) PO Box 110 West Plains MO 65775 **Phn:** 417-256-9191 **Fax:** 417-256-9196 home.centurytel.net/westplainsdailyquill wpqnews@centurytel.net

MONTANA

Billings Billings Gazette (43M) PO Box 36300 Billings MT 59107 **Phn:** 406-657-1200 **Fax:** 406-657-1208 billingsgazette.com citynews@billingsgazette.com

Bozeman Bozeman Daily Chronicle (18.4M) PO Box 1190 Bozeman MT 59771 **Phn:** 406-587-4491 **Fax:** 406-582-2656 www.bozemandailychronicle.com citydesk@dailychronicle.com

Butte Montana Standard (14.2M) PO Box 627 Butte MT 59703 **Phn:** 406-496-5510 **Fax:** 406-496-5551 mtstandard.com editor@mtstandard.com

Great Falls Great Falls Tribune (49.1M) PO Box 5468 Great Falls MT 59403 **Phn:** 406-791-1444 **Fax:** 406-791-1431 www.greatfallstribune.com tribbiz@greatfallstribune.com

Hamilton Ravalli Republic (5.3M) 232 W Main St Hamilton MT 59840 **Phn:** 406-363-3300 **Fax:** 406-363-1767 www.ravallirepublic.com editor@ravallirepublic.com

Havre Havre Daily News (4.3M) PO Box 431 Havre MT 59501 **Phn:** 406-265-6796 **Fax:** 406-265-6798 www.havredailynews.com editorial@havredailynews.com

Helena Independent Record (11.3M) PO Box 4249 Helena MT 59604 **Phn:** 406-447-4000 **Fax:** 406-447-4052 helenair.com holly.michels@lee.net

Kalispell Daily Inter Lake (20.5M) PO Box 7610 Kalispell MT 59904 **Phn:** 406-755-7000 **Fax:** 406-752-6114 www.dailyinterlake.com newsed@dailyinterlake.com

Livingston Livingston Enterprise (2.7M) PO Box 2000 Livingston MT 59047 **Phn:** 406-222-2000 **Fax:** 406-222-8580 www.livingstonenterprise.com enterprise@livent.net

Miles City Miles City Star (3.1M) PO Box 1216 Miles City MT 59301 **Phn:** 406-234-0450 **Fax:** 406-234-6687 www.milescitystar.com mceditor@midrivers.com

Missoula Missoulian (29.3M) PO Box 8029 Missoula MT 59807 **Phn:** 406-523-5200 **Fax:** 406-523-5294 missoulian.com newsdesk@missoulian.com

NEBRASKA

Alliance Alliance Times-Herald (3M) PO Box G Alliance NE 69301 **Phn:** 308-762-3060 **Fax:** 308-762-3063 www.alliancetimes.com athnews@alliancetimes.com

Beatrice Beatrice Daily Sun (7.7M) 200 N 7th St Beatrice NE 68310 **Phn:** 402-223-5233 **Fax:** 402-228-3571 beatricedailysun.com beatrice.news@lee.net

Columbus Columbus Telegram (8.9M) PO Box 648 Columbus NE 68602 **Phn:** 402-564-2741 **Fax:** 402-563-7500 columbustelegram.com telegram@megavision.com

Fremont Fremont Tribune (8.2M) PO Box 9 Fremont NE 68026 **Phn:** 402-721-5000 **Fax:** 402-721-8047 fremonttribune.com fremont.newsroom@lee.net

Grand Island Grand Island Independent (21.1M) PO Box 1208 Grand Island NE 68802 **Phn:** 308-382-1000 **Fax:** 308-382-8129 www.theindependent.com newsdesk@theindependent.com

Hastings Hastings Tribune (12M) PO Box 788 Hastings NE 68902 **Phn:** 402-462-2131 **Fax:** 402-462-2184 www.hastingstribune.com tribune@hastingstribune.com

Holdrege Holdrege Daily Citizen (2.9M) PO Box 344 Holdrege NE 68949 **Phn:** 308-995-4441 **Fax:** 308-995-5992

Kearney Kearney Hub (12.2M) PO Box 1988 Kearney NE 68848 **Phn:** 308-237-2152 **Fax:** 308-233-9745 www.kearneyhub.com news@kearneyhub.com

Lincoln Lincoln Journal Star (76.5M) PO Box 81689 Lincoln NE 68501 **Phn:** 402-475-4200 **Fax:** 402-473-7291 journalstar.com citydesk@journalstar.com

McCook McCook Daily Gazette (5.9M) PO Box 1268 McCook NE 69001 **Phn:** 308-345-4500 **Fax:** 308-345-7881 www.mccookgazette.com cityed@ocsmccook.com

Norfolk Norfolk Daily News (16.7M) PO Box 977 Norfolk NE 68702 **Phn:** 402-371-1020 **Fax:** 402-371-5802 www.norfolkdailynews.com editor@norfolkdailynews.com

North Platte North Platte Telegraph (12.5M) PO Box 370 North Platte NE 69103 **Phn:** 308-532-6000 **Fax:** 308-532-9268 www.nptelegraph.com webmaster@nptelegraph.com

Omaha Omaha World-Herald (178M) 1314 Douglas St Ste 700 Omaha NE 68102 **Phn:** 402-444-1000 **Fax:** 402-345-0183 www.omaha.com news@owh.com

Scottsbluff Star-Herald (14.8M) PO Box 1709 Scottsbluff NE 69363 **Phn:** 308-632-9000 **Fax:** 308-632-9003 www.starherald.com news@starherald.com

Sidney Sidney Sun-Telegraph (2.6M) PO Box 193 Sidney NE 69162 **Phn:** 308-254-2818 **Fax:** 308-254-3925 suntelegraph.com editor@suntelegraph.com

York York News-Times (4.7M) PO Box 279 York NE 68467 **Phn:** 402-362-4478 **Fax:** 402-362-6748 www.yorknewstimes.com news@yorknewstimes.com

NEVADA

Carson City Nevada Appeal (16.5M) 580 Mallory Way Carson City NV 89701 **Phn:** 775-882-2111 **Fax:** 775-887-2420 www.nevadaappeal.com editor@nevadaappeal.com

Elko Elko Daily Free Press (7.4M) 3720 E Idaho St Elko NV 89801 **Phn:** 775-738-3118 **Fax:** 775-778-3131 elkodaily.com editor@elkodaily.com

Henderson Las Vegas Sun (24.2M) 2360 Corporate Cir Fl 3 Henderson NV 89074 **Phn:** 702-385-3111 **Fax:** 702-383-7264 www.lasvegassun.com tom.gorman@lasvegassun.com

Las Vegas Las Vegas Review-Journal (168M) PO Box 70 Las Vegas NV 89125 **Phn:** 702-383-0211 **Fax:** 702-383-4676 www.reviewjournal.com kkistner@reviewjournal.com

Reno Reno Gazette-Journal (61.8M) PO Box 22000 Reno NV 89520 **Phn:** 775-788-6200 **Fax:** 775-788-6458 www.rgj.com news@rgj.com

Sparks Daily Sparks Tribune (5M) 1002 C St Sparks NV 89431 **Phn:** 775-358-8061 **Fax:** 775-359-3837 dailysparkstribune.com tribunenews@dailysparkstribune.com

NEW HAMPSHIRE

Berlin Berlin Daily Sun (8.8M) 164 Main St Ste 1 Berlin NH 03570 **Phn:** 603-752-5858 **Fax:** 866-475-4429 www.berlindailysun.com bds@berlindailysun.com

Claremont Eagle-Times (8.4M) 401 River Rd Claremont NH 03743 **Phn:** 603-543-3100 **Fax:** 603-542-9705 www.eagletimes.com news@eagletimes.com

Concord Concord Monitor (19.9M) PO Box 1177 Concord NH 03302 **Phn:** 603-224-5301 **Fax:** 603-224-8120 www.concordmonitor.com news@cmonitor.com

Dover Foster's Daily Democrat (20M) 150 Venture Dr Dover NH 03820 **Phn:** 603-742-4455 **Fax:** 603-749-7079 www.fosters.com mprowland@fosters.com

Hudson The Telegraph (25.5M) 17 Executive Dr Hudson NH 03051 **Phn:** 603-882-2741 **Fax:** 603-882-2681 www.nashuatelegraph.com news@nashuatelegraph.com

Keene Keene Sentinel (13M) PO Box 546 Keene NH 03431 **Phn:** 603-352-1234 **Fax:** 603-352-9700 www.sentinelsource.com news@keenesentinel.com

Laconia Laconia Daily Sun (18M) 1127 Union Ave Laconia NH 03246 **Phn:** 603-527-9299 **Fax:** 603-527-0056 www.laconiadailysun.com news@laconiadailysun.com

Laconia The Citizen (7.7M) 171 Fair St Laconia NH 03246 **Phn:** 603-524-3800 **Fax:** 603-527-3593 www.citizen.com news@citizen.com

Manchester Union-Leader/NH Sunday News (55.8M) PO Box 9555 Manchester NH 03108 **Phn:** 603-668-4321 **Fax:** 603-668-0382 www.unionleader.com avellucci@unionleader.com

North Conway Conway Daily Sun (16.1M) PO Box 1940 North Conway NH 03860 **Phn:** 603-356-3456 **Fax:** 603-356-8360 www.conwaydailysun.com news@conwaydailysun.com

Portsmouth Portsmouth Herald (12.9M) 111 Nh Ave Portsmouth NH 03801 **Phn:** 603-436-1800 **Fax:** 603-433-5760 www.seacoastonline.com news@seacoastonline.com

NEW JERSEY

Bridgeton News of Cumberland County (7.4M) 100 E Commerce St Bridgeton NJ 08302 **Phn:** 856-451-1000 **Fax:** 856-455-3098 www.nj.com/bridgeton mgray@sjnewsco.com

Cherry Hill Courier-Post (68.8M) PO Box 5300 Cherry Hill NJ 08034 **Phn:** 856-663-6000 **Fax:** 856-663-2831 www.courierpostonline.com cpedit@courierpostonline.com

East Brunswick Home News Tribune (59M) 35 Kennedy Blvd East Brunswick NJ 08816 **Phn:** 732-246-5500 **Fax:** 732-565-7208 www.mycentraljersey.com pgrzella@njpressmedia.com

Jersey City Jersey Journal (24.8M) 30 Journal Sq Ste 1 Jersey City NJ 07306 **Phn:** 201-653-1000 **Fax:** 201-653-1414 www.nj.com margaret.schmidt@jjournal.com

Neptune Asbury Park Press (149M) PO Box 1550 Neptune NJ 07754 **Phn:** 732-922-6000 **Fax:** 732-643-4014 www.app.com dcarmody@njpressmedia.com

Newark Star-Ledger (287M) 1 Star Ledger Plz Newark NJ 07102 **Phn:** 973-392-4141 **Fax:** 973-392-5845 www.nj.com/starledger metro@starledger.com

Newton New Jersey Herald (15M) PO Box 10 Newton NJ 07860 **Phn:** 973-383-1500 **Fax:** 973-383-8477 www.njherald.com btomlinson@njherald.com

Parsippany Daily Record (38.2M) PO Box 217 Parsippany NJ 07054 **Phn:** 973-428-6200 **Fax:** 973-428-6666 www.dailyrecord.com mvandyk@njpressmedia.com

Pleasantville Press of Atlantic City (70.8M) 11 Devins Ln Pleasantville NJ 08232 **Phn:** 609-272-7000 **Fax:** 609-272-7224 www.pressofatlanticcity.com spage@pressofac.com

Somerville Courier News (34.5M) 92 E Main St Ste 202 Somerville NJ 08876 **Phn:** 908-243-6600 **Fax:** 908-243-6645 www.mycentraljersey.com pgrzella@mycentraljersey.com

Toms River Ocean County Observer (14.2M) 1451 Route 37 W Toms River NJ 08755 **Phn:** 732-349-3000 **Fax:** 732-557-5758 www.app.com business@app.com

Trenton The Times (59.3M) PO Box 847 Trenton NJ 08605 **Phn:** 609-989-5454 **Fax:** 609-394-2819 www.nj.com/times news@njtimes.com

Trenton The Trentonian (41.7M) 600 Perry St Trenton NJ 08618 **Phn:** 609-989-7800 **Fax:** 609-393-6072 www.trentonian.com editor@trentonian.com

Vineland Daily Journal (17.4M) 891 E Oak Rd Vineland NJ 08360 **Phn:** 856-691-5000 **Fax:** 856-563-5308 www.thedailyjournal.com djlocalnews@vineland.gannett.com

Willingboro Burlington Co. Times (31.9M) 4284 Route 130 Willingboro NJ 08046 **Phn:** 609-871-8000 **Fax:** 609-871-0490 www.phillyburbs.com aharvin@phillyburbs.com

Woodbury South Jersey Times (22.5M) 309 S Broad St Woodbury NJ 08096 **Phn:** 856-845-3300 **Fax:** 856-845-5480 www.nj.com/southjerseytimes news@southjerseymedia.com

Woodland Park Herald News (49M) 1 Garret Mountain Plz Woodland Park NJ 07424 **Phn:** 973-569-7100 **Fax:** 201-457-2520 www.northjersey.com newsroom@northjersey.com

Woodland Park The Record (166M) 1 Garret Mountain Plz Woodland Park NJ 07424 **Phn:** 201-646-4000 **Fax:** 201-457-2520 www.northjersey.com newsroom@northjersey.com

NEW MEXICO

Alamogordo Alamogordo Daily News (6.7M) 518 24th St Alamogordo NM 88310 **Phn:** 575-437-7120 **Fax:** 575-437-7795 www.alamogordonews.com mjohnson@alamogordonews.com

Albuquerque Albuquerque Journal (104M) PO Box J Albuquerque NM 87103 **Phn:** 505-823-7777 **Fax:** 505-823-3994 www.abqjournal.com cmoore@abqjournal.com

Artesia Artesia Daily Press (3.6M) PO Box 190 Artesia NM 88211 **Phn:** 575-746-3524 **Fax:** 575-746-8795 www.artesianews.com news@artesianews.com

Carlsbad Carlsbad Current-Argus (7.2M) PO Box 1629 Carlsbad NM 88221 **Phn:** 575-887-5501 **Fax:** 575-885-1066 www.currentargus.com marthamauritson@currentargus.com

Clovis Clovis News-Journal (7M) PO Box 1689 Clovis NM 88102 **Phn:** 575-763-3431 **Fax:** 575-762-0153 www.cnjonline.com dstevens@cnjonline.com

Deming Deming Headlight (3.5M) PO Box 881 Deming NM 88031 **Phn:** 575-546-2611 **Fax:** 575-546-8116 www.demingheadlight.com barmendariz@demingheadlight.com

Farmington Daily Times (16.8M) PO Box 450 Farmington NM 87499 **Phn:** 505-325-4545 **Fax:** 505-564-4630 www.daily-times.com croberts@daily-times.com

Gallup Gallup Independent (15.4M) 500 N 9th St Gallup NM 87301 **Phn:** 505-863-6811 **Fax:** 505-722-5750 gallupindependent.com barryheifner@yahoo.com

Hobbs News-Sun (9.3M) 201 N Thorp St Hobbs NM 88240 **Phn:** 575-393-2123 **Fax:** 575-393-5724 www.hobbsnews.com editor@hobbsnews.com

Las Cruces Las Cruces Sun-News (21.7M) PO Box 1749 Las Cruces NM 88004 **Phn:** 575-541-5400 **Fax:** 575-541-5498 www.lcsun-news.com jlawitz@lcsun-news.com

Las Vegas Las Vegas Optic (6M) PO Box 2670 Las Vegas NM 87701 **Phn:** 505-425-6796 **Fax:** 505-425-1005 www.lasvegasoptic.com

Los Alamos Los Alamos Monitor (5.1M) PO Box 1268 Los Alamos NM 87544 **Phn:** 505-662-4185 **Fax:** 505-662-4334 www.lamonitor.com

Lovington Lovington Daily Leader (2.1M) PO Box 1717 Lovington NM 88260 **Phn:** 575-396-2844 **Fax:** 575-396-5775 lovingtonleaderonline.com

Portales Portales News-Tribune (2.8M) PO Box 848 Portales NM 88130 **Phn:** 575-356-4481 **Fax:** 575-356-3630 www.pntonline.com dstevens@cnjonline.com

Roswell Roswell Daily Record (13.1M) PO Box 1897 Roswell NM 88202 **Phn:** 575-622-7710 **Fax:** 575-625-0421 www.roswell-record.com editorial@roswell-record.com

Santa Fe Santa Fe New Mexican (24.8M) PO Box 2048 Santa Fe NM 87504 **Phn:** 505-983-3303 **Fax:** 505-986-9147 www.santafenewmexican.com newsroom@sfnewmexican.com

Silver City Silver City Daily Press & Independent (7.8M) PO Box 740 Silver City NM 88062 **Phn:** 575-388-1576 **Fax:** 575-388-1196 www.scdailypress.com dthompson@silvercitydailypress.net

NEW YORK

Albany Times Union (95.5M) PO Box 15000 Albany NY 12212 **Phn:** 518-454-5420 **Fax:** 518-454-5628 www.timesunion.com rsmith@timesunion.com

Amsterdam The Recorder (9.2M) 1 Venner Rd Amsterdam NY 12010 **Phn:** 518-843-1100 **Fax:** 518-843-6580 www.recordernews.com news@recordernews.com

Auburn The Citizen (11.6M) 25 Dill St Auburn NY 13021 **Phn:** 315-253-5311 **Fax:** 315-253-6031 auburnpub.com citizennews@lee.net

Batavia Daily News (12.5M) PO Box 870 Batavia NY 14021 **Phn:** 585-343-8000 **Fax:** 585-343-2623 thedailynewsonline.com news@batavianews.com

Binghamton Press & Sun-Bulletin (52M) PO Box 1270 Binghamton NY 13902 **Phn:** 607-798-1234 **Fax:** 607-798-1113 www.pressconnects.com bgm-newsroom@gannett.com

Brooklyn Brooklyn Daily Eagle (10.1M) 16 Court St Brooklyn NY 11241 **Phn:** 718-858-2300 **Fax:** 718-858-4483 www.brooklyneagle.com news@brooklyneagle.net

Buffalo Buffalo News (145M) PO Box 100 Buffalo NY 14240 **Phn:** 716-849-3434 **Fax:** 716-856-5150 www.buffalonews.com

Canandaigua Daily Messenger (11.7M) 73 Buffalo St Canandaigua NY 14424 **Phn:** 585-394-0770 **Fax:** 585-394-4160 www.mpnnow.com acooper@messengerpostmedia.com

Catskill Daily Mail (3.4M) 414 Main St Catskill NY 12414 **Phn:** 518-943-2100 **Fax:** 518-943-2063 www.registerstar.com/the_daily_mail editorial@thedailymail.net

Corning The Leader (12.8M) PO Box 1017 Corning NY 14830 **Phn:** 607-936-4651 **Fax:** 607-936-9939 www.the-leader.com sdupree@the-leader.com

Cortland Cortland Standard (10.3M) 110 Main St Cortland NY 13045 **Phn:** 607-756-5665 **Fax:** 607-756-4758 www.cortlandstandard.net news@cortlandstandard.net

Dunkirk The Observer (9.1M) PO Box 391 Dunkirk NY 14048 **Phn:** 716-366-3000 **Fax:** 716-366-2389 observertoday.com editorial@observertoday.com

Elmira Star-Gazette (26.3M) PO Box 285 Elmira NY 14902 **Phn:** 607-734-5151 **Fax:** 607-733-4408 www.stargazette.com sgnews@gannett.com

Geneva Finger Lakes Times (15.6M) PO Box 393 Geneva NY 14456 **Phn:** 315-789-3333 **Fax:** 315-789-4077 www.fltimes.com fltimes@fltimes.com

Glens Falls Post-Star (33.3M) PO Box 2157 Glens Falls NY 12801 **Phn:** 518-792-3131 **Fax:** 518-761-1255 poststar.com tingley@poststar.com

Gloversville Leader-Herald (10.2M) 8 E Fulton St Gloversville NY 12078 **Phn:** 518-725-8616 **Fax:** 518-725-7407 www.leaderherald.com editor@leaderherald.com

Herkimer Evening Telegram (6.7M) PO Box 551 Herkimer NY 13350 **Phn:** 315-866-2220 **Fax:** 315-866-5913 www.herkimertelegram.com news@herkimertelegram.com

Herkimer The Times (4M) PO Box 551 Herkimer NY 13350 **Phn:** 315-823-3680 **Fax:** 315-823-4086 www.littlefallstimes.com news@littlefallstimes.com

Hornell Evening Tribune (4.2M) 32 Broadway Hornell NY 14843 **Phn:** 607-324-1425 **Fax:** 607-324-2317 www.eveningtribune.com news@eveningtribune.com

Hudson Register-Star (5.2M) PO Box 635 Hudson NY 12534 **Phn:** 518-828-1616 **Fax:** 518-828-3870 www.registerstar.com editorial@registerstar.com

Ithaca Ithaca Journal (16.4M) 123 W State St Ithaca NY 14850 **Phn:** 607-272-2321 **Fax:** 607-272-4248 orig.theithacajournal.com dbohrer@ithaca.gannett.com

Jamestown Post-Journal (18.6M) PO Box 190 Jamestown NY 14702 **Phn:** 716-487-1111 **Fax:** 716-664-5305 post-journal.com post-journal@oweb.com

Kingston Daily Freeman (19.3M) 79 Hurley Ave Kingston NY 12401 **Phn:** 845-331-5000 **Fax:** 845-331-3557 www.dailyfreeman.com news@freemanonline.com

Lockport Journal-Register (2.7M) 170 East Ave Lockport NY 14094 **Phn:** 585-798-1400 **Fax:** 585-798-0290 journal-register.com john.hopkins@journal-register.com

Lockport Union-Sun & Journal (11.5M) 170 East Ave Lockport NY 14094 **Phn:** 716-439-9222 **Fax:** 716-439-9249 lockportjournal.com john.hopkins@lockportjournal.com

Malone Malone Telegram (5.6M) 469 E Main St Ste 4 Malone NY 12953 **Phn:** 518-483-2000 **Fax:** 518-483-8579 www.mymalonetelegram.com news@mtelegram.com

Massena Daily Courier-Observer (4.9M) PO Box 300 Massena NY 13662 **Phn:** 315-769-2451 **Fax:** 315-764-0337 rmartin@ogd.com

Melville Newsday (368M) 235 Pinelawn Rd Melville NY 11747 **Phn:** 631-843-2020 **Fax:** 631-843-2953 www.newsday.com editor@newsday.com

Middletown Times Herald Record (79.1M) 40 Mulberry St Middletown NY 10940 **Phn:** 845-341-1100 **Fax:** 845-343-2170 www.recordonline.com dosenenko@th-record.com

New York AM New York (267M) 330 W 34th St Fl 17 New York NY 10001 **Phn:** 212-239-5555 **Fax:** 212-239-2828 www.amny.com pcatapano@am-ny.com

New York Daily News (603M) 450 W 33rd St New York NY 10001 **Phn:** 212-210-2100 **Fax:** 212-643-7831 www.nydailynews.com webmaster@web.nydailynews.com

New York Metro New York (327M) 44 Wall St Fl 8 New York NY 10005 **Phn:** 212-952-1500 **Fax:** 212-952-1245 www.metro.us/newyork pat.healy@metro.us

New York New York Post (704M) 1211 Avenue Of The Americas New York NY 10036 **Phn:** 212-930-8000 **Fax:** 212-930-8542 www.nypost.com cshaw@nypost.com

New York New York Times (1040M) 620 8th Ave New York NY 10018 **Phn:** 212-556-1234 **Fax:** 212-556-5999 www.nytimes.com news-tips@nytimes.com

Niagara Falls Niagara Gazette (18.9M) PO Box 549 Niagara Falls NY 14302 **Phn:** 716-282-2311 **Fax:** 716-286-3895 niagara-gazette.com matt.winterhalter@niagara-gazette.com

North Tonawanda Tonawanda News (8M) PO Box 668 North Tonawanda NY 14120 **Phn:** 716-693-1000 **Fax:** 716-693-8573 tonawanda-news.com newsroom@tonawanda-news.com

Norwich Evening Sun (5M) PO Box 151 Norwich NY 13815 **Phn:** 607-334-3276 **Fax:** 607-334-8273 www.evesun.com jgenung@evesun.com

Ogdensburg Ogdensburg Journal (5.8M) PO Box 409 Ogdensburg NY 13669 **Phn:** 315-393-1000 **Fax:** 315-393-5108 www.ogd.com ckelly@ogd.com

Olean Times-Herald (14M) 639 W Norton Dr Olean NY 14760 **Phn:** 716-372-3121 **Fax:** 716-373-6397 www.oleantimesherald.com jeckstrom@oleantimesherald.com

Oneida Oneida Daily Dispatch (6.6M) 130 Broad St Oneida NY 13421 **Phn:** 315-363-5100 **Fax:** 315-363-9832 www.oneidadispatch.com kwanfried@oneidadispatch.com

Oneonta Daily Star (15.9M) PO Box 250 Oneonta NY 13820 **Phn:** 607-432-1000 **Fax:** 607-432-5707 thedailystar.com news@thedailystar.com

Oswego Oswego Palladium-Times (7.3M) 140 W 1st St Oswego NY 13126 **Phn:** 315-343-3800 **Fax:** 315-343-0273 www.palltimes.com smccrobie@palltimes.com

Plattsburgh Press Republican (20M) PO Box 459 Plattsburgh NY 12901 **Phn:** 518-561-2300 **Fax:** 518-561-3362 pressrepublican.com lclermont@pressrepublican.com

Poughkeepsie Poughkeepsie Journal (37.7M) 85 Civic Center Plz Poughkeepsie NY 12601 **Phn:** 845-454-2000 **Fax:** 845-437-4921 www.poughkeepsiejournal.com sshinske@poughkee.gannett.com

Rochester Democrat & Chronicle (156M) 55 Exchange Blvd Rochester NY 14614 **Phn:** 585-232-7100 **Fax:** 585-258-2237 www.democratandchronicle.com editor@democratandchronicle.com

Rome Daily Sentinel (13.7M) PO Box 471 Rome NY 13442 **Phn:** 315-337-4000 **Fax:** 315-339-6281 romesentinel.com release@rny.com

Salamanca Salamanca Press (2M) PO Box 111 Salamanca NY 14779 **Phn:** 716-945-1644 **Fax:** 716-945-4283 www.salamancapress.com salpressnews@verizon.net

Saranac Lake Adirondack Daily Enterprise (4.1M) PO Box 318 Saranac Lake NY 12983 **Phn:** 518-891-2600 **Fax:** 518-891-2756 www.adirondackdailyenterprise.com adenews@adirondackdailyenterprise.com

Saratoga Springs The Saratogian (10.3M) 20 Lake Ave Saratoga Springs NY 12866 **Phn:** 518-584-4242 **Fax:** 518-587-7750 www.saratogian.com news@saratogian.com

Schenectady Daily Gazette (52M) PO Box 1090 Schenectady NY 12301 **Phn:** 518-374-4141 **Fax:** 518-395-3089 www.dailygazette.com news@dailygazette.net

Staten Island Staten Island Advance (58M) 950 W Fingerboard Rd Staten Island NY 10305 **Phn:** 718-981-1234 **Fax:** 718-981-5679 www.silive.com/advance editor@siadvance.com

Syracuse Post-Standard (114M) PO Box 4915 Syracuse NY 13221 **Phn:** 315-470-0010 **Fax:** 315-470-3081 www.syracuse.com citynews@syracuse.com

Troy The Record (15.2M) 501 Broadway Troy NY 12180 **Phn:** 518-270-1200 **Fax:** 518-270-1202 www.troyrecord.com newsroom@troyrecord.com

Utica Observer-Dispatch (41M) 221 Oriskany St E Utica NY 13501 **Phn:** 315-792-5000 **Fax:** 315-792-5033 www.uticaod.com news@uticaod.com

Watertown Watertown Daily Times (29.5M) 260 Washington St Watertown NY 13601 **Phn:** 315-782-1000 **Fax:** 315-661-2523 www.watertowndailytimes.com news@wdt.net

Wellsville Daily Reporter (4.5M) 159 N Main St Wellsville NY 14895 **Phn:** 585-593-5300 **Fax:** 585-593-5303 www.wellsvilledaily.com editor@wellsvilledaily.com

White Plains Journal News (122M) 1 Gannett Dr White Plains NY 10604 **Phn:** 914-694-9300 **Fax:** 914-694-5018 www.lohud.com metro@lohud.com

NORTH CAROLINA

Asheboro Courier-Tribune (13.9M) PO Box 340 Asheboro NC 27204 **Phn:** 336-625-2101 **Fax:** 336-626-7074 courier-tribune.com ajordan@courier-tribune.com

Asheville Asheville Citizen-Times (34M) PO Box 2090 Asheville NC 28802 **Phn:** 828-252-5611 **Fax:** 828-251-0585 www.citizen-times.com communitynews@citizen-times.com

Burlington Times-News (24.9M) PO Box 481 Burlington NC 27216 **Phn:** 336-227-0131 **Fax:** 336-229-2463 www.thetimesnews.com blancaster@thetimesnews.com

Charlotte Charlotte Observer (207M) PO Box 30308 Charlotte NC 28230 **Phn:** 704-358-5000 **Fax:** 704-358-5036 www.charlotteobserver.com localnews@charlotteobserver.com

Clinton Sampson Independent (8M) PO Box 89 Clinton NC 28329 **Phn:** 910-592-8137 **Fax:** 910-592-8756 www.clintonnc.com smatthews@civitasmedia.com

Concord Independent Tribune (17.2M) PO Box 608 Concord NC 28026 **Phn:** 704-782-3155 **Fax:** 704-786-0645 www.independenttribune.com news@independenttribune.com

Dunn Daily Record (8.6M) PO Box 1448 Dunn NC 28335 **Phn:** 910-891-1234 **Fax:** 910-891-4445 www.mydailyrecord.com news@mydailyrecord.com

Durham Herald-Sun (39.2M) PO Box 2092 Durham NC 27702 **Phn:** 919-419-6500 **Fax:** 919-419-6889 www.heraldsun.com bashley@heraldsun.com

Elizabeth City Daily Advance (10.4M) PO Box 588 Elizabeth City NC 27907 **Phn:** 252-335-0841 **Fax:** 252-335-4415 www.dailyadvance.com mgoodman@dailyadvance.com

Fayetteville Fayetteville Observer (50.8M) PO Box 849 Fayetteville NC 28302 **Phn:** 910-486-3500 **Fax:** 910-486-3545 www.fayobserver.com news@fayobserver.com

Forest City Daily Courier (9.3M) PO Box 1149 Forest City NC 28043 **Phn:** 828-245-6431 **Fax:** 828-248-2790 www.thedigitalcourier.com bgreene@thedigitalcourier.com

Gastonia Gaston Gazette (29.3M) PO Box 1538 Gastonia NC 28053 **Phn:** 704-864-3291 **Fax:** 704-867-5751 www.gastongazette.com gastongazette@gastongazette.com

Goldsboro Goldsboro News-Argus (19.2M) PO Box 10629 Goldsboro NC 27532 **Phn:** 919-778-2211 **Fax:** 919-778-5408 www.newsargus.com news@newsargus.com

Greensboro News & Record (85.5M) 200 E Market St Greensboro NC 27420 **Phn:** 336-373-7000 **Fax:** 336-373-7067 www.news-record.com people@news-record.com

Greenville Daily Reflector (21M) PO Box 1967 Greenville NC 27835 **Phn:** 252-752-6166 **Fax:** 252-754-8140 www.reflector.com aclark@reflector.com

Henderson The Daily Dispatch (7.5M) 304 S Chestnut St Henderson NC 27536 **Phn:** 252-436-2700 **Fax:** 252-430-0125 www.hendersondispatch.com news@hendersondispatch.com

Hendersonville Times-News (18.6M) PO Box 490 Hendersonville NC 28793 **Phn:** 828-692-0505 **Fax:** 828-693-5581 www.blueridgenow.com

Hickory Hickory Daily Record (21M) PO Box 968 Hickory NC 28603 **Phn:** 828-322-4510 **Fax:** 828-324-8179 www.hickoryrecord.com news@hickoryrecord.com

High Point High Point Enterprise (21.2M) PO Box 1009 High Point NC 27261 **Phn:** 336-888-3500 **Fax:** 336-888-3644 hpe.com vwheeler@hpe.com

Jacksonville Daily News (19.9M) PO Box 196 Jacksonville NC 28541 **Phn:** 910-353-1171 **Fax:** 910-353-7316 www.jdnews.com

Kinston Free Press (11.1M) PO Box 129 Kinston NC 28502 **Phn:** 252-527-3191 **Fax:** 252-527-9407 www.kinston.com

Laurinburg Laurinburg Exchange (8.2M) PO Box 805 Laurinburg NC 28353 **Phn:** 910-276-2311 **Fax:** 910-276-3815 www.laurinburgexchange.com switten@civitasmedia.com

Lenoir News-Topic (8.7M) PO Box 1100 Lenoir NC 28645 **Phn:** 828-758-7381 **Fax:** 828-754-0110 newstopic.net nathankey@newstopic.net

Lexington The Dispatch (10.7M) PO Box 908 Lexington NC 27293 **Phn:** 336-249-3981 **Fax:** 336-249-0712 www.the-dispatch.com info@the-dispatch.com

Lumberton The Robesonian (12.6M) PO Box 1028 Lumberton NC 28359 **Phn:** 910-739-4322 **Fax:** 910-739-6553 www.robesonian.com ddouglas@bellsouth.net

Marion McDowell News (4.7M) PO Box 610 Marion NC 28752 **Phn:** 828-652-3313 **Fax:** 828-655-1246 www.mcdowellnews.com news@mcdowellnews.com

Monroe Enquirer-Journal (7.8M) PO Box 5040 Monroe NC 28111 **Phn:** 704-289-1541 **Fax:** 704-289-2929 www.enquirerjournal.com news@theej.com

Morganton News Herald (10.7M) 301 Collett St Morganton NC 28655 **Phn:** 828-437-2161 **Fax:** 828-437-5372 www.morganton.com news@morganton.com

Mount Airy Mount Airy News (9.3M) 319 N Renfro St Mount Airy NC 27030 **Phn:** 336-786-4141 **Fax:** 336-789-2816 www.mtairynews.com wbyerlywood@civitasmedia.com

New Bern Sun Journal (14.6M) PO Box 13948 New Bern NC 28561 **Phn:** 252-638-8101 **Fax:** 252-638-4580 www.newbernsj.com sjnewsroom@newbernsj.com

Newton Observer-News-Enterprise (2.3M) PO Box 48 Newton NC 28658 **Phn:** 828-464-0221 **Fax:** 828-464-1267 www.observernewsonline.com onenews@observernewsonline.com

Raleigh News & Observer (165M) PO Box 191 Raleigh NC 27602 **Phn:** 919-829-4500 **Fax:** 919-829-4529 www.newsobserver.com john.drescher@newsobserver.com

Roanoke Rapids The Daily Herald (11.2M) PO Box 520 Roanoke Rapids NC 27870 **Phn:** 252-537-2505 **Fax:** 252-537-2384 www.rrdailyherald.com ksmith@rrdailyherald.com

Rockingham Richmond County Daily Journal (8M) PO Box 190 Rockingham NC 28380 **Phn:** 910-997-3111 **Fax:** 910-997-4321 www.yourdailyjournal.com rbacon@heartlandpublications.com

Rocky Mount Rocky Mount Telegram (14.2M) PO Box 1080 Rocky Mount NC 27802 **Phn:** 252-446-5161 **Fax:** 252-446-4057 www.rockymounttelegram.com jherrin@rmtelegram.com

Salisbury Salisbury Post (21.4M) PO Box 4639 Salisbury NC 28145 **Phn:** 704-633-8950 **Fax:** 704-639-0003 www.salisburypost.com ecook@salisburypost.com

Sanford Sanford Herald (9.2M) PO Box 100 Sanford NC 27331 **Phn:** 919-708-9000 **Fax:** 919-708-9001 www.sanfordherald.com bhorner3@sanfordherald.com

Shelby Shelby Star (14.2M) PO Box 48 Shelby NC 28151 **Phn:** 704-484-7000 **Fax:** 704-484-0805 www.shelbystar.com do not email

Statesville Statesville Record & Landmark (14.5M) 222 E Broad St Statesville NC 28687 **Phn:** 704-873-1451 **Fax:** 704-872-3150 www.statesville.com news@statesville.com

Tarboro Daily Southerner (3.7M) PO Box 1199 Tarboro NC 27886 **Phn:** 252-823-3106 **Fax:** 252-823-4599 dailysoutherner.com

Tryon Tryon Daily Bulletin (5M) 16 N Trade St Tryon NC 28782 **Phn:** 828-859-9151 **Fax:** 828-859-5575 www.tryondailybulletin.com betty.ramsey@tryondailybulletin.com

Washington Washington Daily News (8.8M) PO Box 1788 Washington NC 27889 **Phn:** 252-946-2144 **Fax:** 252-946-9795 www.thewashingtondailynews.com mike.voss@thewashingtondailynews.com

Wilmington Star-News (51.5M) 1003 S 17th St Wilmington NC 28401 **Phn:** 910-343-2000 **Fax:** 910-343-2227 www.starnewsonline.com pam.sander@starnewsonline.com

Wilson The Wilson Times (13M) PO Box 2447 Wilson NC 27894 **Phn:** 252-243-5151 **Fax:** 252-243-7501 www.wilsontimes.com editor@wilsontimes.com

Winston Salem Winston-Salem Journal (82.2M) PO Box 3159 Winston Salem NC 27102 **Phn:** 336-727-7211 **Fax:** 336-727-7315 www.journalnow.com news@wsjournal.com

NORTH DAKOTA

Bismarck Bismarck Tribune (26M) PO Box 5516 Bismarck ND 58506 **Phn:** 701-223-2500 **Fax:** 701-223-2063 bismarcktribune.com jessica.holdman@bismarcktribune.com

Devils Lake Devils Lake Journal (3.5M) PO Box 1200 Devils Lake ND 58301 **Phn:** 701-662-2127 **Fax:** 701-662-3115 www.devilslakejournal.com news@devilslakejournal.com

Dickinson Dickinson Press (6M) PO Box 1367 Dickinson ND 58602 **Phn:** 701-225-8111 **Fax:** 701-225-6653 www.thedickinsonpress.com newsroom@thedickinsonpress.com

Fargo The Forum (45M) PO Box 2020 Fargo ND 58107 **Phn:** 701-235-7311 **Fax:** 701-241-5487 www.inforum.com news@forumcomm.com

Grand Forks Grand Forks Herald (28M) PO Box 6008 Grand Forks ND 58206 **Phn:** 701-780-1100 **Fax:** 701-780-1123 www.grandforks.com mjacobs@gfherald.com

Jamestown Jamestown Sun (6M) PO Box 1760 Jamestown ND 58402 **Phn:** 701-252-3120 **Fax:** 701-952-8477 jamestownsun.com js@jamestownsun.com

Minot Minot Daily News (18M) PO Box 1150 Minot ND 58702 **Phn:** 701-857-1900 **Fax:** 701-857-1961 www.minotdailynews.com mdnews@ndweb.com

Valley City Valley City Times-Record (2.7M) 146 3rd St NE Valley City ND 58072 **Phn:** 701-845-0463 **Fax:** 701-845-0175 www.times-online.com treditor@times-online.com

Wahpeton Daily News (2.6M) PO Box 760 Wahpeton ND 58074 **Phn:** 701-642-8585 **Fax:** 701-642-1501 www.wahpetondailynews.com editor@wahpetondailynews.com

Williston Williston Daily Herald (4.4M) PO Box 1447 Williston ND 58802 **Phn:** 701-572-2165 **Fax:** 701-572-9563 www.willistonherald.com news@willistonherald.com

OHIO

Akron Akron Beacon Journal (119M) PO Box 640 Akron OH 44309 **Phn:** 330-996-3000 **Fax:** 330-996-3033 www.ohio.com bwinges@thebeaconjournal.com

Alliance The Review (11.8M) 40 S Linden Ave Alliance OH 44601 **Phn:** 330-821-1200 **Fax:** 330-821-8258 www.the-review.com mkpatter@aol.com

Ashland Ashland Times-Gazette (11.9M) 40 E 2nd St Ashland OH 44805 **Phn:** 419-281-0581 **Fax:** 419-281-5591 www.times-gazette.com newsroom@times-gazette.com

Ashtabula Star-Beacon (17.6M) PO Box 2100 Ashtabula OH 44005 **Phn:** 440-998-2323 **Fax:** 440-998-7938 starbeacon.com nfeditor@suite224.net

Athens Athens Messenger (11.3M) PO Box 4210 Athens OH 45701 **Phn:** 740-592-6612 **Fax:** 740-592-4647 www.athensohiotoday.com jhiggins@athensmessenger.com

Bellefontaine Bellefontaine Examiner (8.9M) PO Box 40 Bellefontaine OH 43311 **Phn:** 937-592-3060 **Fax:** 937-592-4463 www.examiner.org news@examiner.org

Bellevue Bellevue Gazette (2.8M) PO Box 309 Bellevue OH 44811 **Phn:** 419-483-4190 **Fax:** 419-483-3737 thebellevuegazette.com news@gazettepublishingco.com

Bowling Green Sentinel-Tribune (11.3M) PO Box 88 Bowling Green OH 43402 **Phn:** 419-352-4611 **Fax:** 419-354-0314 www.sent-trib.com local_news@sentinel-tribune.com

Bryan Bryan Times (10.2M) PO Box 471 Bryan OH 43506 **Phn:** 419-636-1111 **Fax:** 419-636-8937 bryantimes.com news@bryantimes.com

Bucyrus Telegraph-Forum (6.2M) PO Box 471 Bucyrus OH 44820 **Phn:** 419-562-3333 **Fax:** 419-562-9162 www.bucyrustelegraphforum.com dkennard@gannett.com

Cambridge Daily Jeffersonian (12.7M) PO Box 10 Cambridge OH 43725 **Phn:** 740-439-3531 **Fax:** 740-432-6219 www.daily-jeff.com newsroom@daily-jeff.com

Canton The Repository (64.1M) 500 Market Ave S Canton OH 44702 **Phn:** 330-580-8300 **Fax:** 330-454-5745 www.cantonrep.com newsroom@cantonrep.com

NORTH DAKOTA DAILY NEWSPAPERS

Celina Daily Standard (11M) PO Box 140 Celina OH 45822 **Phn:** 419-586-2371 **Fax:** 419-586-6271 www.dailystandard.com newsdept@dailystandard.com

Chillicothe Chillicothe Gazette (14.5M) 50 W Main St Chillicothe OH 45601 **Phn:** 740-773-2111 **Fax:** 740-772-9505 www.chillicothegazette.com gaznews@nncogannett.com

Cincinnati Cincinnati Enquirer (198M) 312 Elm St Cincinnati OH 45202 **Phn:** 513-721-2700 **Fax:** 513-768-8340 news.cincinnati.com localnews@enquirer.com

Circleville Circleville Herald (5M) 120 Wall St Circleville OH 43113 **Phn:** 740-474-3131 **Fax:** 740-474-9525 www.circlevilletoday.com webstar@circlevileherald.com

Cleveland Plain Dealer (292M) 1801 Superior Ave E Cleveland OH 44114 **Phn:** 216-999-4800 **Fax:** 216-999-6354 www.cleveland.com dasimmon@plaind.com

Columbus Columbus Dispatch (217M) 34 S 3rd St Columbus OH 43215 **Phn:** 614-461-5000 **Fax:** 614-461-7580 www.dispatch.com bmarrison@dispatch.com

Coshocton Coshocton Tribune (6.2M) PO Box 10 Coshocton OH 43812 **Phn:** 740-622-1122 **Fax:** 740-295-3460 www.coshoctontribune.com coshocton@nncogannett.com

Dayton Dayton Daily News (123M) 1611 S Main St Dayton OH 45409 **Phn:** 937-225-2000 **Fax:** 937-225-2489 www.daytondailynews.com jerickson@daytondailynews.com

Defiance Crescent-News (17.3M) PO Box 249 Defiance OH 43512 **Phn:** 419-784-5441 **Fax:** 419-782-2944 www.crescent-news.com dvan@crescent-news.com

Delaware Delaware Gazette (8.4M) PO Box 100 Delaware OH 43015 **Phn:** 740-363-1161 **Fax:** 740-363-6262 delgazette.com newsroom@delgazette.com

Delphos Delphos Daily Herald (3.3M) 405 N Main St Delphos OH 45833 **Phn:** 419-695-0015 **Fax:** 419-692-7704 www.delphosherald.com nspencer@delphosherald.com

East Liverpool The Review (9.3M) 210 E 4th St East Liverpool OH 43920 **Phn:** 330-385-4545 **Fax:** 330-385-8142 www.reviewonline.com newsroom@reviewonline.com

Elyria Chronicle-Telegram (24.4M) 225 East Ave Elyria OH 44035 **Phn:** 440-329-7000 **Fax:** 440-329-7282 chronicle.northcoastnow.com ctnews@chroniclet.com

Findlay The Courier (21.2M) PO Box 609 Findlay OH 45839 **Phn:** 419-422-5151 **Fax:** 419-427-8480 www.thecourier.com news@thecourier.com

Fostoria Review Times (4.1M) PO Box 947 Fostoria OH 44830 **Phn:** 419-435-6641 **Fax:** 419-435-9073 www.reviewtimes.com rtnews@reviewtimes.com

Fremont News-Messenger (12M) PO Box 1230 Fremont OH 43420 **Phn:** 419-332-5511 **Fax:** 419-332-9750 www.thenews-messenger.com vguerrie@fremont.gannett.com

Galion Galion Inquirer (3.9M) PO Box 648 Galion OH 44833 **Phn:** 419-468-1117 **Fax:** 419-468-7255 galioninquirer.com

Gallipolis Gallipolis Daily Tribune (4.5M) PO Box 469 Gallipolis OH 45631 **Phn:** 740-446-2342 **Fax:** 740-446-3008 www.mydailytribune.com mdtnews@mydailytribune.com

Greenville Daily Advocate (6.5M) PO Box 220 Greenville OH 45331 **Phn:** 937-548-3151 **Fax:** 937-548-3913 dailyadvocate.com

Hamilton Journal-News (20.3M) 228 Court St Hamilton OH 45011 **Phn:** 513-863-8200 **Fax:** 513-896-9489 www.journal-news.com cshamilton@coxohio.com

Hillsboro Times Gazette (5M) 108 Gov Trimble Pl Hillsboro OH 45133 **Phn:** 937-393-3456 **Fax:** 937-393-2059 www.timesgazette.com info@timesgazette.com

Ironton Ironton Tribune (5.2M) PO Box 647 Ironton OH 45638 **Phn:** 740-532-1441 **Fax:** 740-532-1506 www.irontontribune.com mike.caldwell@irontontribune.com

Kenton Kenton Times (7.2M) PO Box 230 Kenton OH 43326 **Phn:** 419-674-4066 **Fax:** 419-673-1125 www.kentontimes.com kteditor@kentontimes.com

Lancaster Eagle-Gazette (13.2M) 138 W Chestnut St Lancaster OH 43130 **Phn:** 740-654-1321 **Fax:** 740-681-4456 www.lancastereaglegazette.com cburnett@nncogannett.com

Lima Lima News (32.9M) 3515 Elida Rd Lima OH 45807 **Phn:** 419-223-1010 **Fax:** 419-229-2926 www.limaohio.com limanews@limanews.com

Lisbon Morning Journal (11.8M) 308 Maple St Lisbon OH 44432 **Phn:** 330-424-9541 **Fax:** 330-424-7093 www.morningjournalnews.com news@mojonews.com

Logan Logan Daily News (4.2M) PO Box 758 Logan OH 43138 **Phn:** 740-385-2107 **Fax:** 740-385-4514 www.logandaily.com ggregory@logandaily.com

London Madison Press (5.5M) PO Box 390 London OH 43140 **Phn:** 740-852-1616 **Fax:** 740-852-1620 www.madison-press.com meditor@madison-press.com

Lorain Morning Journal (26.7M) 1657 Broadway Lorain OH 44052 **Phn:** 440-245-6901 **Fax:** 440-245-6912 www.morningjournal.com news@morningjournal.com

Mansfield News Journal (29.1M) 70 W 4th St Mansfield OH 44903 **Phn:** 419-522-3311 **Fax:** 419-521-7415 www.mansfieldnewsjournal.com dkennard@gannett.com

Marietta Marietta Times (10.7M) 700 Channel Ln Marietta OH 45750 **Phn:** 740-373-2121 **Fax:** 740-376-5475 www.mariettatimes.com news@mariettatimes.com

Marion Marion Star (12.4M) 150 Court St Marion OH 43302 **Phn:** 740-387-0400 **Fax:** 740-375-5188 www.marionstar.com tgraser@marionstar.com

Martins Ferry Times-Leader (16.1M) 200 S 4th St Martins Ferry OH 43935 **Phn:** 740-633-1131 **Fax:** 740-633-1122 www.timesleaderonline.com timesleader@timesleaderonline.com

Marysville Marysville Journal-Tribune (6M) PO Box 226 Marysville OH 43040 **Phn:** 937-644-9111 **Fax:** 937-644-9211 www.marysvillejt.com chad@marysvillejt.com

Massillon The Independent (12.2M) 50 North Ave NW Massillon OH 44647 **Phn:** 330-833-2631 **Fax:** 330-834-3373 www.indeonline.com indenews@indeonline.com

Medina Medina County Gazette (14.4M) 885 W Liberty St Medina OH 44256 **Phn:** 800-633-4623 **Fax:** 330-725-4299 medinagazette.northcoastnow.com areanews@medina-gazette.com

Middletown Middletown Journal (18.3M) 1 N Main St Lower LEFT Middletown OH 45042 **Phn:** 513-422-3611 **Fax:** 513-705-2818 www.middletownjournal.com mdgoodwin@coxohio.com

Mount Vernon Mount Vernon News (9.2M) PO Box 791 Mount Vernon OH 43050 **Phn:** 740-397-5333 **Fax:** 740-397-1321 www.mountvernonnews.com fmain@mountvernonnews.com

Napoleon Northwest Signal (5.7M) 595 E Riverview Ave Napoleon OH 43545 **Phn:** 419-592-5055 **Fax:** 419-592-9778 www.northwestsignal.net briank@northwestsignal.net

New Philadelphia Times Reporter (19.1M) PO Box 667 New Philadelphia OH 44663 **Phn:** 330-364-5577 **Fax:** 330-364-8416 www.timesreporter.com melissa.griffy@timesreporter.com

Newark The Advocate (19.4M) 22 N 1st St Newark OH 43055 **Phn:** 740-345-4053 **Fax:** 740-328-8581 www.newarkadvocate.com mshearer@newarkadvocate.com

Norwalk Norwalk Reflector (8.8M) 61 E Monroe St Norwalk OH 44857 **Phn:** 419-668-3771 **Fax:** 419-668-2424 www.norwalkreflector.com news@norwalkreflector.com

Piqua Piqua Daily Call (6.1M) 310 Spring St Piqua OH 45356 **Phn:** 937-773-2721 **Fax:** 937-773-4225 www.dailycall.com shartley@dailycall.com

Pomeroy The Daily Sentinel (3.5M) 111 Court St Pomeroy OH 45769 **Phn:** 740-992-2156 **Fax:** 740-992-2157 www.mydailysentinel.com sfilson@civitasmedia.com

Port Clinton News-Herald (5.2M) PO Box 550 Port Clinton OH 43452 **Phn:** 419-734-3141 **Fax:** 419-734-1850 www.portclintonnewsherald.com jhaun@gannett.com

Portsmouth Portsmouth Daily Times (12.4M) 637 6th St Portsmouth OH 45662 **Phn:** 740-353-3101 **Fax:** 740-353-4676 www.portsmouth-dailytimes.com news@portsmouth-dailytimes.com

Ravenna Record-Courier (17.9M) 126 N Chestnut St Ravenna OH 44266 **Phn:** 330-296-9657 **Fax:** 330-296-2698 www.recordpub.com editor@recordpub.com

Saint Marys The Evening Leader (4.5M) 102 E Spring St Saint Marys OH 45885 **Phn:** 419-394-7414 **Fax:** 419-394-7202 www.theeveningleader.com editor@theeveningleader.com

Salem Salem News (6.1M) 161 N Lincoln Ave Salem OH 44460 **Phn:** 330-332-4601 **Fax:** 330-332-1441 salemnews.net salemnews@salemnews.net

Sandusky Sandusky Register (22.2M) 314 W Market St Sandusky OH 44870 **Phn:** 419-625-5500 **Fax:** 419-625-3007 www.sanduskyregister.com mattwesterhold@sanduskyregister.com

Shelby Daily Globe (4M) PO Box 647 Shelby OH 44875 **Phn:** 419-342-4276 **Fax:** 419-342-4246 www.sdgnewsgroup.com globe@sdgnewsgroup.com

Sidney Sidney Daily News (13M) 1451 N Vandemark Rd Sidney OH 45365 **Phn:** 937-498-8088 **Fax:** 937-498-5991 www.sidneydailynews.com jbilliel@civitasmedia.com

Springfield Springfield News-Sun (25.7M) 202 N Limestone St Springfield OH 45503 **Phn:** 937-328-0300 **Fax:** 937-328-0328 www.springfieldnewssun.com pprofeta@coxohio.com

Steubenville Herald-Star (13.2M) 401 Herald Sq Steubenville OH 43952 **Phn:** 740-283-4711 **Fax:** 740-284-7355 www.hsconnect.com newsroom@hsconnect.com

Tiffin Advertiser-Tribune (9.8M) PO Box 778 Tiffin OH 44883 **Phn:** 419-448-3200 **Fax:** 419-447-3274 www.advertiser-tribune.com newsroom@advertiser-tribune.com

Toledo The Blade (123M) 541 N Superior St Toledo OH 43660 **Phn:** 419-724-6000 **Fax:** 419-724-6439 www.toledoblade.com kfranck@theblade.com

Troy Troy Daily News (9.3M) 224 S Market St Troy OH 45373 **Phn:** 937-335-5634 **Fax:** 937-440-5286 www.tdn-net.com dfong@civitasmedia.com

Upper Sandusky Daily Chief-Union (3.8M) PO Box 180 Upper Sandusky OH 43351 **Phn:** 419-294-2332 **Fax:** 419-294-5608 www.dailychiefunion.com

Urbana Urbana Daily Citizen (5.6M) PO Box 191 Urbana OH 43078 **Phn:** 937-652-1331 **Fax:** 937-652-1336 www.urbanacitizen.com info@urbanacitizen.com

Van Wert Times-Bulletin (6.4M) PO Box 271 Van Wert OH 45891 **Phn:** 419-238-2285 **Fax:** 419-238-0447 www.timesbulletin.com info@timesbulletin.com

Wapakoneta Wapakoneta Daily News (5M) 520 Industrial Dr Wapakoneta OH 45895 **Phn:** 419-738-2128 **Fax:** 419-738-5352 www.wapakdailynews.com blaney@wapakwdn.com

Warren Tribune Chronicle (30.6M) 240 Franklin St SE Warren OH 44483 **Phn:** 330-841-1600 **Fax:** 330-841-1717 www.tribtoday.com frobinson@tribtoday.com

Washington Court House Record-Herald (5.2M) 320 Washington Sq Washington Court House OH 43160 **Phn:** 740-335-3611 **Fax:** 740-335-5728 www.recordherald.com info@recordherald.com

Willoughby News-Herald (40.6M) 7085 Mentor Ave Willoughby OH 44094 **Phn:** 440-951-0000 **Fax:** 440-975-2293 www.news-herald.com editor@news-herald.com

Wilmington Wilmington News Journal (7.4M) 47 S South St Wilmington OH 45177 **Phn:** 937-382-2574 **Fax:** 937-382-4392 www.wnewsj.com info@wnewsj.com

Wooster Daily Record (21.6M) PO Box 918 Wooster OH 44691 **Phn:** 330-264-1125 **Fax:** 330-264-1132 www.the-daily-record.com lwhite@the-daily-record.com

Xenia Fairborn Daily Herald (4M) 30 S Detroit St Xenia OH 45385 **Phn:** 937-372-4444 **Fax:** 937-372-1951 www.fairborndailyherald.com acrowe@fairborndailyherald.com

Xenia Xenia Daily Gazette (5.9M) 30 S Detroit St Xenia OH 45385 **Phn:** 937-372-4444 **Fax:** 937-372-1951 www.xeniagazette.com editor@xeniagazette.com

Youngstown The Vindicator (58.3M) PO Box 780 Youngstown OH 44501 **Phn:** 330-747-1471 **Fax:** 330-747-6712 www.vindy.com news@vindy.com

Zanesville Times Recorder (18M) 34 S 4th St Zanesville OH 43701 **Phn:** 740-452-4561 **Fax:** 740-450-6759 www.zanesvilletimesrecorder.com rszabrak@nncogannett.com

OKLAHOMA

Ada Ada Evening News (7.9M) PO Box 489 Ada OK 74821 **Phn:** 580-332-4433 **Fax:** 580-332-8841 theadanews.com adanewseditor@cableone.net

Altus Altus Times (4.6M) PO Box 578 Altus OK 73522 **Phn:** 580-482-1221 **Fax:** 580-482-5709 www.altustimes.com fbush@civitasmedia.com

Alva Alva Review-Courier (1.6M) 620 Choctaw St Alva OK 73717 **Phn:** 580-327-2200 **Fax:** 580-327-2454 www.alvareviewcourier.com news@alvareviewcourier.net

Anadarko Anadarko Daily News (9.7M) PO Box 548 Anadarko OK 73005 **Phn:** 405-247-3331 **Fax:** 405-247-5571

Ardmore Daily Ardmoreite (9.7M) PO Box 1328 Ardmore OK 73402 **Phn:** 580-223-2200 **Fax:** 580-226-0050 www.ardmoreite.com yournews@ardmoreite.com

Bartlesville Examiner-Enterprise (8.5M) 4125 Nowata Rd Bartlesville OK 74006 **Phn:** 918-335-8200 **Fax:** 918-335-0601 examiner-enterprise.com kwilliams@examiner-enterprise.com

Chickasha Express-Star (5.3M) PO Box E Chickasha OK 73023 **Phn:** 405-224-2600 **Fax:** 405-224-7087 chickashanews.com editor@chickashanews.com

Claremore Claremore Daily Progress (6M) PO Box 248 Claremore OK 74018 **Phn:** 918-341-1101 **Fax:** 918-341-1131 claremoreprogress.com editor@claremoreprogress.com

Clinton Clinton Daily News (4.6M) 522 Avant Ave Clinton OK 73601 **Phn:** 580-323-5151 **Fax:** 580-323-5154 www.clintondailynews.com cdnews@swbell.net

Duncan Duncan Banner (7.2M) PO Box 1268 Duncan OK 73534 **Phn:** 580-255-5354 **Fax:** 580-255-8889 duncanbanner.com toni.hopper@duncanbanner.com

Durant Durant Daily Democrat (6.8M) PO Box 250 Durant OK 74702 **Phn:** 580-924-4388 **Fax:** 580-924-6026 www.durantdemocrat.com editor@durantdemocrat.com

Edmond Edmond Sun (3.4M) PO Box 2470 Edmond OK 73083 **Phn:** 405-341-2121 **Fax:** 405-340-7363 www.edmondsun.com news@edmondsun.com

Elk City Elk City Daily News (5.7M) PO Box 1009 Elk City OK 73648 **Phn:** 580-225-3000 **Fax:** 580-243-2414 ecdnnews@cableone.net

Enid Enid News & Eagle (17.8M) PO Box 1192 Enid OK 73702 **Phn:** 580-233-6600 **Fax:** 580-548-8121 enidnews.com enidnews@enidnews.com

Grove The Grove Sun (6M) 16 W 3rd St Grove OK 74344 **Phn:** 918-786-2228 **Fax:** 918-786-2156 www.grandlakenews.com news@grovesun.com

Guthrie Guthrie News Leader (2.6M) PO Box 879 Guthrie OK 73044 **Phn:** 405-282-2222 **Fax:** 405-282-7378 www.guthrienewsleader.net gnlnews@yahoo.com

Guymon Guymon Daily Herald (2.3M) PO Box 19 Guymon OK 73942 **Phn:** 580-338-3355 **Fax:** 580-338-5000 www.guymondailyherald.com editor@guymondailyherald.com

Hugo Hugo Daily News (2.9M) 128 E Jackson St Hugo OK 74743 **Phn:** 580-326-3311 **Fax:** 580-326-6397 www.hugonews.com editor@sbcglobal.net

Idabel McCurtain Daily Gazette (5.9M) PO Box 179 Idabel OK 74745 **Phn:** 580-286-3321 **Fax:** 580-286-2208 www.mccurtain.com paper@mccurtain.com

Lawton Lawton Constitution (21.5M) PO Box 2069 Lawton OK 73502 **Phn:** 580-353-0620 **Fax:** 580-585-5140 www.swoknews.com dhale@lawton-constitution.com

McAlester McAlester News-Capital (9.6M) PO Box 987 McAlester OK 74502 **Phn:** 918-423-1700 **Fax:** 918-426-3082 mcalesternews.com editor@mcalesternews.com

Miami Miami News-Record (6M) PO Box 940 Miami OK 74355 **Phn:** 918-542-5533 **Fax:** 918-542-1903 www.miamiok.com news@miaminewsrecord.com

Muskogee Muskogee Phoenix (15.9M) PO Box 1968 Muskogee OK 74402 **Phn:** 918-684-2828 **Fax:** 918-684-2865 muskogeephoenix.com mcarrels@muskogeephoenix.com

Norman Norman Transcript (13.8M) PO Box 1058 Norman OK 73070 **Phn:** 405-321-1800 **Fax:** 405-366-3516 normantranscript.com dparker@normantranscript.com

Oklahoma City Daily Oklahoman (202M) PO Box 25125 Oklahoma City OK 73125 **Phn:** 405-475-3311 **Fax:** 405-475-3183 www.newsok.com mshannon@opubco.com

Okmulgee Okmulgee Daily Times (4.5M) PO Box 1218 Okmulgee OK 74447 **Phn:** 918-756-3600 **Fax:** 918-756-8197 drtimes@rapfire.net

Pauls Valley Pauls Valley Daily Democrat (2.5M) PO Box 790 Pauls Valley OK 73075 **Phn:** 405-238-6464 **Fax:** 405-238-3042 paulsvalleydailydemocrat.com emann@paulsvalleydailydemocrat.com

Perry Perry Daily Journal (3.3M) PO Box 311 Perry OK 73077 **Phn:** 580-336-2222 **Fax:** 580-336-3222 www.pdjnews.com gloriapdjnews@yahoo.com

Ponca City Ponca City News (8.9M) PO Box 191 Ponca City OK 74602 **Phn:** 580-765-3311 **Fax:** 580-765-7800 www.poncacitynews.com news@poncacitynews.com

Poteau Poteau Daily News (3.9M) PO Box 1237 Poteau OK 74953 **Phn:** 918-647-3188 **Fax:** 918-647-8198 www.poteaudailynews.com poteaudailynews.editor@gmail.com

Pryor Daily Times (3.8M) PO Box 308 Pryor OK 74362 **Phn:** 918-825-3292 **Fax:** 918-825-1965 pryordailytimes.com prynews@swbell.net

Sapulpa Sapulpa Daily Herald (4.5M) PO Box 1370 Sapulpa OK 74067 **Phn:** 918-224-5185 **Fax:** 918-224-5196 www.sapulpaheraldonline.com editor@sapulpaheraldonline.com

Seminole Seminole Producer (5.6M) PO Box 431 Seminole OK 74818 **Phn:** 405-382-1100 **Fax:** 405-382-1104 www.seminoleproducer.com news@seminoleproducer.com

Shawnee Shawnee News-Star (8.8M) PO Box 1688 Shawnee OK 74802 **Phn:** 405-273-4200 **Fax:** 405-273-4207 www.news-star.com michael.mccormick@news-star.com

Stillwater News Press (8.6M) PO Box 2288 Stillwater OK 74076 **Phn:** 405-372-5000 **Fax:** 405-372-3112 www.stwnewspress.com editor@stwnewspress.com

Tahlequah Tahlequah Daily Press (6.9M) PO Box 888 Tahlequah OK 74465 **Phn:** 918-456-8833 **Fax:** 918-456-2019 tahlequahdailypress.com news@tahlequahdailypress.com

Tulsa Tulsa World (118M) PO Box 1770 Tulsa OK 74102 **Phn:** 918-581-8300 **Fax:** 918-581-8353 www.tulsaworld.com mary.bishop@tulsaworld.com

Vinita Vinita Daily Journal (4.3M) PO Box 328 Vinita OK 74301 **Phn:** 918-256-6422 **Fax:** 918-256-7100 vdjnews@cableone.net

Weatherford Weatherford Daily News (5.6M) 118 S Broadway Weatherford OK 73096 **Phn:** 580-772-3301 **Fax:** 580-772-7329 www.wdnonline.com wdn@wdnonline.com

Woodward Woodward News (5M) PO Box 928 Woodward OK 73802 **Phn:** 580-256-2200 **Fax:** 580-254-2159 woodwardnews.net editor@woodwardnews.net

OREGON

Albany Democrat-Herald (15.1M) PO Box 130 Albany OR 97321 **Phn:** 541-926-2211 **Fax:** 541-926-4799 democratherald.com news@dhonline.com

Astoria Daily Astorian (8.3M) PO Box 210 Astoria OR 97103 **Phn:** 503-325-3211 **Fax:** 503-325-6573 www.dailyastorian.com astorian@dailyastorian.com

Baker City Baker City Herald (3.3M) PO Box 807 Baker City OR 97814 **Phn:** 541-523-3673 **Fax:** 541-523-6426 www.bakercityherald.com news@bakercityherald.com

Bend The Bulletin (32.3M) PO Box 6020 Bend OR 97708 **Phn:** 541-382-1811 **Fax:** 541-385-5804 www.bendbulletin.com bulletin@bendbulletin.com

Coos Bay The World (12.4M) PO Box 1840 Coos Bay OR 97420 **Phn:** 541-269-1222 **Fax:** 541-269-5071 theworldlink.com news@theworldlink.com

Corvallis Corvallis Gazette-Times (11M) PO Box 368 Corvallis OR 97339 **Phn:** 541-753-2641 **Fax:** 541-758-9505 www.gazettetimes.com mike.mcinally@lee.net

Eugene The Register-Guard (68.5M) PO Box 10188 Eugene OR 97440 **Phn:** 541-485-1234 **Fax:** 541-683-7631 www.registerguard.com dave.baker@registerguard.com

Grants Pass Daily Courier (15.8M) PO Box 1468 Grants Pass OR 97528 **Phn:** 541-474-3700 **Fax:** 541-474-3824 www.thedailycourier.com news@thedailycourier.com

OKLAHOMA DAILY NEWSPAPERS

Klamath Falls Herald & News (16.6M) PO Box 788 Klamath Falls OR 97601 **Phn:** 541-885-4410 **Fax:** 541-885-4456 www.heraldandnews.com news@heraldandnews.com

La Grande The Observer (6M) 1406 5th St La Grande OR 97850 **Phn:** 541-963-3161 **Fax:** 541-963-7804 www.lagrandeobserver.com news@lagrandeobserver.com

Medford Ashland Daily Tidings (5M) 111 N Fir St Medford OR 97501 **Phn:** 541-482-3456 **Fax:** 541-482-3688 www.dailytidings.com bhunter@mailtribune.com

Medford Mail Tribune (30.7M) PO Box 1108 Medford OR 97501 **Phn:** 541-776-4411 **Fax:** 541-776-4376 www.mailtribune.com news@mailtribune.com

Ontario Argus Observer (6.7M) 1160 SW 4th St Ontario OR 97914 **Phn:** 541-889-5387 **Fax:** 541-889-3347 www.argusobserver.com editor@argusobserver.com

Pendleton East Oregonian (8M) 211 SE Byers Ave Pendleton OR 97801 **Phn:** 541-276-2211 **Fax:** 541-276-8314 www.eastoregonian.com kbbrown@eastoregonian.com

Portland The Oregonian (268M) 1320 SW Broadway Portland OR 97201 **Phn:** 503-221-8327 **Fax:** 503-227-5306 www.oregonlive.com newsroom@oregonian.com

Roseburg News-Review (18.6M) PO Box 1248 Roseburg OR 97470 **Phn:** 541-672-3321 **Fax:** 541-957-4270 www.nrtoday.com vmenard@nrtoday.com

Salem Statesman Journal (50.2M) PO Box 13009 Salem OR 97309 **Phn:** 503-399-6611 **Fax:** 503-399-6706 www.statesmanjournal.com newsroom@statesmanjournal.com

The Dalles The Dalles Daily Chronicle (4.6M) PO Box 1910 The Dalles OR 97058 **Phn:** 541-296-2141 **Fax:** 541-298-1365 www.thedalleschronicle.com

PENNSYLVANIA

Allentown Morning Call (108M) 101 N 6th St Allentown PA 18101 **Phn:** 610-820-6500 **Fax:** 610-820-6693 www.mcall.com news@mcall.com

Altoona Altoona Mirror (31.5M) 301 Cayuga Ave Altoona PA 16602 **Phn:** 814-946-7411 **Fax:** 814-946-7540 www.altoonamirror.com news@altoonamirror.com

Beaver Beaver County Times (39.6M) 400 Fair Ave Beaver PA 15009 **Phn:** 724-775-3200 **Fax:** 724-775-4180 www.timesonline.com timesnews@timesonline.com

Bedford Bedford Gazette (10.1M) PO Box 671 Bedford PA 15522 **Phn:** 814-623-1151 **Fax:** 814-623-5055 www.bedfordgazette.com gazetteeditor@embarqmail.com

Bloomsburg Press-Enterprise (21.1M) 3185 Lackawanna Ave Bloomsburg PA 17815 **Phn:** 570-784-2121 **Fax:** 570-784-9226 www.pressenterpriseonline.com webmaster@pressenterprise.net

Bradford Bradford Era (10.5M) PO Box 365 Bradford PA 16701 **Phn:** 814-368-3173 **Fax:** 814-362-6510 www.bradfordera.com news@bradfordera.com

Butler Butler Eagle (27.8M) PO Box 271 Butler PA 16003 **Phn:** 724-282-8000 **Fax:** 724-282-4180 www.butlereagle.com news@butlereagle.com

Carlisle The Sentinel (14.6M) PO Box 130 Carlisle PA 17013 **Phn:** 717-243-2611 **Fax:** 717-243-3121 cumberlink.com frontdoor@cumberlink.com

Chambersburg Public Opinion (17.1M) PO Box 499 Chambersburg PA 17201 **Phn:** 717-264-6161 **Fax:** 717-264-0377 www.publicopiniononline.com bbennett@publicopinionnews.com

Clearfield The Progress (12.2M) PO Box 291 Clearfield PA 16830 **Phn:** 814-765-5581 **Fax:** 814-765-5165 www.theprogressnews.com news@theprogressnews.com

Connellsville Daily Courier (7.5M) 127 W Apple St Connellsville PA 15425 **Phn:** 724-628-2000 **Fax:** 724-626-3567 www.pittsburghlive.com dailycourier@tribweb.com

Corry Corry Journal (3.5M) 28 W South St Corry PA 16407 **Phn:** 814-665-8291 **Fax:** 814-664-2288 www.thecorryjournal.com bwilliams@thecorryjournal.com

Danville Danville News (2.6M) 345 Mill St Danville PA 17821 **Phn:** 570-275-3235 **Fax:** 570-275-7624 dailyitem.com news@thedanvillenews.com

Doylestown Intelligencer Record (39.5M) PO Box 858 Doylestown PA 18901 **Phn:** 215-345-3000 **Fax:** 215-345-3150 www.phillyburbs.com

Du Bois Courier-Express/Tri-County Sunday (9.7M) PO Box 407 Du Bois PA 15801 **Phn:** 814-371-4200 **Fax:** 814-371-3241 www.thecourierexpress.com newsroom@thecourierexpress.com

Easton Express-Times (40M) 30 N Fourth St Easton PA 18042 **Phn:** 610-258-7171 **Fax:** 610-258-7130 www.lehighvalleylive.com news@express-times.com

Ellwood City Ellwood City Ledger (5.3M) 835 Lawrence Ave Ellwood City PA 16117 **Phn:** 724-758-5573 **Fax:** 724-758-2410 www.ellwoodcityledger.com eclnews@ellwoodcityledger.com

Erie Erie Times-News (62.3M) 205 W 12th St Erie PA 16534 **Phn:** 814-870-1600 **Fax:** 814-870-1808 www.goerie.com newsdesk@timesnews.com

Gettysburg Gettysburg Times (11.2M) PO Box 3669 Gettysburg PA 17325 **Phn:** 717-334-1131 **Fax:** 717-334-7408 www.gettysburgtimes.com editor@gburgtimes.com

Greensburg Tribune-Review (101M) 622 Cabin Hill Dr Greensburg PA 15601 **Phn:** 724-834-1151 **Fax:** 724-838-5171 www.pittsburghlive.com fcraig@tribweb.com

Greenville Record-Argus (5.3M) PO Box 711 Greenville PA 16125 **Phn:** 724-588-5000 **Fax:** 724-588-4691

Hanover Evening Sun (19.5M) PO Box 514 Hanover PA 17331 **Phn:** 717-637-3736 **Fax:** 717-637-0900 www.eveningsun.com news@eveningsun.com

Harrisburg Patriot-News (95.2M) 812 Market St Harrisburg PA 17101 **Phn:** 717-255-8100 **Fax:** 717-255-8456 www.pennlive.com newstips@pennlive.com

Hazleton Standard-Speaker (17M) 21 N Wyoming St Hazleton PA 18201 **Phn:** 570-455-3636 **Fax:** 570-455-4408 standardspeaker.com editorial@standardspeaker.com

Honesdale Wayne Independent (4.2M) 220 8th St Honesdale PA 18431 **Phn:** 570-253-3055 **Fax:** 570-253-5387 www.wayneindependent.com editor@wayneindependent.com

Huntingdon Daily News (10M) PO Box 384 Huntingdon PA 16652 **Phn:** 814-643-4040 **Fax:** 814-643-0376 huntingdondailynews.com dnews@huntingdondailynews.com

Indiana Indiana Gazette (15.6M) 899 Water St Indiana PA 15701 **Phn:** 724-465-5555 **Fax:** 724-465-8267 www.indianagazette.com mepetersen@indianagazette.net

Johnstown Tribune-Democrat (39.1M) PO Box 340 Johnstown PA 15907 **Phn:** 814-532-5199 **Fax:** 814-539-1409 tribune-democrat.com

Kane Kane Republican (2M) 200 N Fraley St Kane PA 16735 **Phn:** 814-837-6000 **Fax:** 814-837-2227 www.kanerepublican.com editor3@zitomedia.net

Kittanning Leader-Times (8.1M) PO Box 978 Kittanning PA 16201 **Phn:** 724-543-1303 **Fax:** 724-545-6768 www.pittsburghlive.com leadertimes@tribweb.com

Lancaster Intelligencer Journal (41.3M) PO Box 1328 Lancaster PA 17608 **Phn:** 717-291-8811 **Fax:** 717-399-6507 lancasteronline.com pmekeel@lnpnews.com

Lancaster Lancaster New Era (42.3M) PO Box 1328 Lancaster PA 17608 **Phn:** 717-291-8811 **Fax:** 717-399-6506 lancasteronline.com newera@lnpnews.com

Lancaster Sunday News (250M) PO Box 1328 Lancaster PA 17608 **Phn:** 717-291-8811 **Fax:** 717-291-4950 lancasteronline.com sunnews@lnpnews.com

Lansdale The Reporter (14M) 307 Derstine Ave Lansdale PA 19446 **Phn:** 215-855-8440 **Fax:** 215-855-3432 www.thereporteronline.com citydesk@thereporteronline.com

Latrobe Latrobe Bulletin (7.8M) PO Box 111 Latrobe PA 15650 **Phn:** 724-537-3351 **Fax:** 724-537-0489

Lebanon Daily News (19.8M) 718 Poplar St Lebanon PA 17042 **Phn:** 717-272-5611 **Fax:** 717-274-1608 www.ldnews.com citydesk@ldnews.com

Lehighton Times News (13.7M) PO Box 239 Lehighton PA 18235 **Phn:** 610-377-2051 **Fax:** 610-826-9608 www.tnonline.com timesnews@tnonline.com

Levittown Bucks Co. Courier Times (59M) 8400 Rte 13 Levittown PA 19057 **Phn:** 215-949-4000 **Fax:** 215-949-4177 www.phillyburbs.com djralis@yahoo.com

Lewistown The Sentinel (12.5M) PO Box 588 Lewistown PA 17044 **Phn:** 717-248-6741 **Fax:** 717-248-3481 lewistownsentinel.com sentinel@lewistownsentinel.com

Lock Haven The Express (8.7M) PO Box 208 Lock Haven PA 17745 **Phn:** 570-748-6791 **Fax:** 570-748-1544 lockhaven.com news@lockhaven.com

McKeesport Daily News (19.7M) 409 Walnut St McKeesport PA 15132 **Phn:** 412-664-9161 **Fax:** 412-664-3974 triblive.com/neighborhoods jsisk@tribweb.com

Meadville Meadville Tribune (13.9M) 947 Federal Ct Meadville PA 16335 **Phn:** 814-724-6370 **Fax:** 814-724-8755 meadvilletribune.com tribune@meadvilletribune.com

Milton Standard-Journal (2.1M) 21 N Arch St Milton PA 17847 **Phn:** 570-742-9671 **Fax:** 570-742-9876 www.standard-journal.com newsroom@standard-journal.com

Monessen Valley Independent (13.2M) 19 Eastgate Monessen PA 15062 **Phn:** 724-684-5200 **Fax:** 724-684-2603 www.pittsburghlive.com bburke@tribweb.com

New Castle New Castle News (17.4M) PO Box 60 New Castle PA 16103 **Phn:** 724-654-6651 **Fax:** 724-654-5976 www.ncnewsonline.com ncnews@ncnewsonline.com

Norristown Times Herald (14.4M) PO Box 591 Norristown PA 19404 **Phn:** 610-272-2500 **Fax:** 610-272-0660 www.timesherald.com shuskey@timesherald.com

Oil City News-Herald (7.4M) PO Box 928 Oil City PA 16301 **Phn:** 814-676-7444 **Fax:** 814-677-8351 www.thederrick.com newsroom.thederrick@gmail.com

Oil City The Derrick (18.3M) PO Box 928 Oil City PA 16301 **Phn:** 814-676-7444 **Fax:** 814-677-8347 www.thederrick.com newsroom.thederrick@gmail.com

Philadelphia Philadelphia Daily News (112M) PO Box 7788 Philadelphia PA 19101 **Phn:** 215-854-2000 **Fax:** 215-854-5910 www.philly.com philly_feedback@phillynews.com

Philadelphia Philadelphia Inquirer (288M) PO Box 8263 Philadelphia PA 19101 **Phn:** 215-854-2000 **Fax:** 215-854-5099 www.philly.com cmccoy@phillynews.com

PENNSYLVANIA DAILY NEWSPAPERS

Philadelphia Philadelphia Metro (149M) 30 S 15th St Ste 1400 Philadelphia PA 19102 **Phn:** 215-717-2600 **Fax:** 215-717-2627 www.metro.us/philadelphia letters@metro.us

Phoenixville The Phoenix (3M) 225 Bridge St Phoenixville PA 19460 **Phn:** 610-933-8926 **Fax:** 610-933-1187 www.phoenixvillenews.com editor@phoenixvillenews.com

Pittsburgh Pittsburgh Post-Gazette (212M) 34 Blvd Of The Allies Pittsburgh PA 15222 **Phn:** 412-263-1100 **Fax:** 412-391-8452 www.post-gazette.com ssmith2@post-gazette.com

Pittsburgh Pittsburgh Tribune Review (100M) 503 Martindale St Pittsburgh PA 15212 **Phn:** 412-321-6460 **Fax:** 412-320-7965 www.triblive.com business@tribweb.com

Pottstown The Mercury (22.1M) 24 N Hanover St Pottstown PA 19464 **Phn:** 610-323-3000 **Fax:** 610-323-0682 www.pottsmerc.com nmarch@pottsmerc.com

Pottsville Pottsville Republican & Herald (26M) 111 Mahantongo St Pottsville PA 17901 **Phn:** 570-622-3456 **Fax:** 570-628-6068 republicanherald.com pbanko@republicanherald.com

Primos Delaware Co. Daily Times (44.1M) 500 Mildred Ave Primos PA 19018 **Phn:** 610-622-8800 **Fax:** 610-622-8887 www.delcotimes.com newsroom@delcotimes.com

Punxsutawney Punxsutawney Spirit (5.5M) PO Box 444 Punxsutawney PA 15767 **Phn:** 814-938-8740 **Fax:** 814-938-3794 www.punxsutawneyspirit.com editor@punxsutawneyspirit.com

Reading Reading Eagle (59.5M) PO Box 582 Reading PA 19603 **Phn:** 610-371-5000 **Fax:** 610-371-5098 readingeagle.com news@readingeagle.com

Ridgway Ridgway Record (2.7M) 325 Main St Ridgway PA 15853 **Phn:** 814-773-3161 **Fax:** 814-776-1086 www.ridgwayrecord.com editor3@zitomedia.net

Sayre Morning Times (6.2M) 201 N Lehigh Ave Sayre PA 18840 **Phn:** 570-888-9643 **Fax:** 570-888-5554 www.morning-times.com whoweler@morning-times.com

Scranton Scranton Times-Tribune (53.2M) 149 Penn Ave Scranton PA 18503 **Phn:** 570-348-9100 **Fax:** 570-348-9135 thetimes-tribune.com yesdesk@timesshamrock.com

Shamokin News-Item (10.1M) PO Box 587 Shamokin PA 17872 **Phn:** 570-644-6397 **Fax:** 570-648-7581 newsitem.com nieditor@ptd.net

Sharon The Herald (20.1M) PO Box 51 Sharon PA 16146 **Phn:** 724-981-6100 **Fax:** 724-981-5116 sharonherald.com jraykie@sharonherald.com

Somerset Daily American (13.5M) 334 W Main St Somerset PA 15501 **Phn:** 814-444-5900 **Fax:** 814-444-5966 www.dailyamerican.com news@dailyamerican.com

St Marys Daily Press (5.1M) 245 Brusseles St St Marys PA 15857 **Phn:** 814-781-1596 **Fax:** 814-834-7473 www.smdailypress.com smnews@smdailypress.com

State College Centre Daily Times (24M) PO Box 89 State College PA 16804 **Phn:** 814-238-5000 **Fax:** 814-238-1811 www.centredaily.com ssmith@centredaily.com

Stroudsburg Pocono Record (19.6M) 511 Lenox St Stroudsburg PA 18360 **Phn:** 570-421-3000 **Fax:** 570-421-6284 www.poconorecord.com newsroom@poconorecord.com

Sunbury Daily Item (24.2M) PO Box 607 Sunbury PA 17801 **Phn:** 570-286-5671 **Fax:** 570-286-7695 dailyitem.com dstello@dailyitem.com

Tarentum Valley News Dispatch (28.1M) 210 E 4th Ave Tarentum PA 15084 **Phn:** 724-224-4321 **Fax:** 724-226-4677 www.pittsburghlive.com jdomenick@tribweb.com

Titusville Titusville Herald (3.5M) PO Box 328 Titusville PA 16354 **Phn:** 814-827-3634 **Fax:** 814-827-2512 www.titusvilleherald.com webmaster@titusvilleherald.com

Towanda Daily Review (9M) 116 Main St Towanda PA 18848 **Phn:** 570-265-2151 **Fax:** 570-265-1647 thedailyreview.com reviewnews@thedailyreview.com

Tyrone Daily Herald (1.7M) PO Box 246 Tyrone PA 16686 **Phn:** 814-684-4000 **Fax:** 814-684-4238

Uniontown Herald-Standard (25.2M) PO Box 848 Uniontown PA 15401 **Phn:** 724-439-7500 **Fax:** 724-439-7559 www.HeraldStandard.com mokeefe@heraldstandard.com

Warren Warren Times-Observer (10.8M) 205 Pennsylvania Ave W Warren PA 16365 **Phn:** 814-723-8200 **Fax:** 814-723-6922 www.timesobserver.com editorial@timesobserver.com

Washington Observer-Reporter (32.4M) 122 S Main St Washington PA 15301 **Phn:** 724-222-2200 **Fax:** 724-225-2077 www.observer-reporter.com newsroom@observer-reporter.com

Waynesboro Waynesboro Record-Herald (8M) PO Box 271 Waynesboro PA 17268 **Phn:** 717-762-2151 **Fax:** 717-762-3824 www.therecordherald.com news@therecordherald.com

West Chester Daily Local News (27M) 250 N Bradford Ave West Chester PA 19382 **Phn:** 610-696-1775 **Fax:** 610-430-1180 www.dailylocal.com news@dailylocal.com

Wilkes Barre Citizens' Voice (31.5M) 75 N Washington St Wilkes Barre PA 18701 **Phn:** 570-821-2000 **Fax:** 570-821-2247 citizensvoice.com citydesk@citizensvoice.com

Wilkes Barre Times Leader (39.2M) 15 N Main St Wilkes Barre PA 18701 **Phn:** 570-829-7100 **Fax:** 570-829-5537 www.timesleader.com news@timesleader.com

Williamsport Williamsport Sun-Gazette (26M) 252 W 4th St Williamsport PA 17701 **Phn:** 570-326-1551 **Fax:** 570-326-0314 www.sungazette.com news@sungazette.com

York York Daily Record/Sunday News (47M) 1891 Loucks Rd York PA 17408 **Phn:** 717-771-2000 **Fax:** 717-771-2009 www.ydr.com news@ydr.com

York York Dispatch (32.7M) 205 N George St York PA 17401 **Phn:** 717-854-1575 **Fax:** 717-843-2814 www.yorkdispatch.com news@yorkdispatch.com

PUERTO RICO

Catano Primera Hora (114M) PO Box 2009 Catano PR 00963 **Phn:** 787-641-5454 **Fax:** 787-641-4472 www.primerahora.com

San Juan El Nuevo Dia (203M) PO Box 9067512 San Juan PR 00906 **Phn:** 787-641-8000 **Fax:** 787-641-3924 www.elnuevodia.com opinion@elnuevodia.com

San Juan El Vocero (259M) PO Box 9067515 San Juan PR 00906 **Phn:** 787-721-2300 **Fax:** 787-725-8422 www.vocero.com opinion@vocero.com

RHODE ISLAND

Newport Newport Daily News (12M) PO Box 420 Newport RI 02840 **Phn:** 401-849-3300 **Fax:** 401-849-3306 www.newportdailynews.com editor@newportri.com

Pawtucket The Times (8.7M) 23 Exchange St Pawtucket RI 02860 **Phn:** 401-722-4000 **Fax:** 401-727-9280 www.pawtuckettimes.com editor@pawtuckettimes.com

Providence Providence Journal (153M) 75 Fountain St Providence RI 02902 **Phn:** 401-277-7300 **Fax:** 401-277-7346 www.providencejournal.com pjnews@providencejournal.com

West Warwick Kent Co. Daily Times (2M) PO Box 589 West Warwick RI 02893 **Phn:** 401-821-7400 **Fax:** 401-828-0810 www.ricentral.com/news kceditor@ricentral.com

Westerly Westerly Sun (9.4M) PO Box 520 Westerly RI 02891 **Phn:** 401-348-1000 **Fax:** 401-348-5080 www.thewesterlysun.com dtranchida@thewesterlysun.com

Woonsocket The Call (10.1M) PO Box A Woonsocket RI 02895 **Phn:** 401-762-3000 **Fax:** 401-765-2834 www.woonsocketcall.com news@woonsocketcall.com

SOUTH CAROLINA

Aiken Aiken Standard (15M) PO Box 456 Aiken SC 29802 **Phn:** 803-648-2311 **Fax:** 803-648-6052 www.aikenstandard.com editorial@aikenstandard.com

Anderson Anderson Independent-Mail (34.8M) PO Box 2507 Anderson SC 29622 **Phn:** 864-224-4321 **Fax:** 864-260-1276 www.independentMail.com huffjrj@independentmail.com

Beaufort Beaufort Gazette (12.4M) PO Box 399 Beaufort SC 29901 **Phn:** 843-524-3183 **Fax:** 843-524-8728 www.islandpacket.com/beaufortgazette gazette@beaufortgazette.com

Bluffton Bluffton Today (19.2M) PO Box 486 Bluffton SC 29910 **Phn:** 843-815-0800 **Fax:** 843-815-0828 www.blufftontoday.com kathy.nelson@blufftontoday.com

Charleston Post & Courier (95.7M) 134 Columbus St Charleston SC 29403 **Phn:** 843-577-7111 **Fax:** 843-937-5579 www.postandcourier.com rnelson@postandcourier.com

Columbia The State (105M) PO Box 1333 Columbia SC 29202 **Phn:** 803-771-8415 **Fax:** 803-771-8430 www.thestate.com state@thestate.com

Florence Morning News (30.6M) PO Box 100528 Florence SC 29502 **Phn:** 843-317-6397 **Fax:** 843-317-7292 www.scnow.com news@scnow.com

Greenville Greenville News (82.7M) PO Box 1688 Greenville SC 29602 **Phn:** 864-298-4100 **Fax:** 864-298-4395 www.greenvilleonline.com cweston@greenvillenews.com

Greenwood Index-Journal (14M) PO Box 1018 Greenwood SC 29648 **Phn:** 864-223-1411 **Fax:** 864-223-7331 www.indexjournal.com newsrelease@indexjournal.com

Hilton Head Island Island Packet (19.3M) PO Box 5727 Hilton Head Island SC 29938 **Phn:** 843-706-8100 **Fax:** 843-706-3070 www.islandpacket.com newsroom@islandpacket.com

Myrtle Beach Sun News (48.1M) PO Box 406 Myrtle Beach SC 29578 **Phn:** 843-626-8555 **Fax:** 843-626-0356 www.myrtlebeachonline.com sneditors@thesunnews.com

Orangeburg Times & Democrat (17.1M) PO Box 1766 Orangeburg SC 29116 **Phn:** 803-533-5500 **Fax:** 803-533-5595 www.thetandd.com webmaster@timesanddemocrat.com

Rock Hill The Herald (30.1M) PO Box 11707 Rock Hill SC 29731 **Phn:** 803-329-4000 **Fax:** 803-329-4021 www.heraldonline.com posmundson@heraldonline.com

Seneca Daily Journal (9M) 210 W N 1st St Seneca SC 29678 **Phn:** 864-882-2375 **Fax:** 864-882-2381 www.upstatetoday.com

Spartanburg Herald-Journal (45.4M) PO Box 1657 Spartanburg SC 29304 **Phn:** 864-582-4511 **Fax:** 864-594-6350 www.goupstate.com citydesk@shj.com

Sumter The Item (19.1M) PO Box 1677 Sumter SC 29151 **Phn:** 803-774-1200 **Fax:** 803-774-1210 www.theitem.com citydesk@theitem.com

Union Union Daily Times (6.4M) PO Box 749 Union SC 29379 **Phn:** 864-427-1234 **Fax:** 864-427-1237 www.uniondailytimes.com cwarner@uniondailytimes.com

SOUTH DAKOTA

Aberdeen American News (15.9M) PO Box 4430 Aberdeen SD 57402 **Phn:** 605-225-4100 **Fax:** 605-225-0421 www.aberdeennews.com americannews@aberdeennews.com

Brookings Brookings Register (4.7M) PO Box 177 Brookings SD 57006 **Phn:** 605-692-6271 **Fax:** 605-692-2979 www.brookingsregister.com dkott@brookingsregister.com

Huron The Plainsman (6.1M) PO Box 1278 Huron SD 57350 **Phn:** 605-352-6401 **Fax:** 605-352-7754 www.plainsman.com editor.plainsman@midconetwork.com

Madison Madison Daily Leader (3M) PO Box 348 Madison SD 57042 **Phn:** 605-256-4555 **Fax:** 605-256-6190 madisonet.com news@madisondailyleader.com

Mitchell Daily Republic (12.3M) PO Box 1288 Mitchell SD 57301 **Phn:** 605-996-5514 **Fax:** 605-996-5020 www.mitchellrepublic.com dailynews@mitchellrepublic.com

Pierre Capital Journal (5M) PO Box 878 Pierre SD 57501 **Phn:** 605-224-7301 **Fax:** 605-224-9210 www.capjournal.com news@capjournal.com

Rapid City Rapid City Journal (29.2M) PO Box 450 Rapid City SD 57709 **Phn:** 605-394-8300 **Fax:** 605-394-8463 www.rapidcityjournal.com claudia.laws@rapidcityjournal.com

Sioux Falls Argus Leader (51.1M) PO Box 5034 Sioux Falls SD 57117 **Phn:** 605-331-2200 **Fax:** 605-331-2294 www.argusleader.com plalley@argusleader.com

Spearfish Black Hills Pioneer (4.2M) PO Box 7 Spearfish SD 57783 **Phn:** 605-642-2761 **Fax:** 605-642-9060 www.bhpioneer.com news@bhpioneer.com

Watertown Watertown Public Opinion (12.5M) PO Box 10 Watertown SD 57201 **Phn:** 605-886-6901 **Fax:** 605-886-4280 www.thepublicopinion.com

Yankton Yankton Daily Press & Dakotan (7.9M) PO Box 56 Yankton SD 57078 **Phn:** 605-665-7811 **Fax:** 605-665-1721 www.yankton.net newsroom@yankton.net

TENNESSEE

Athens Daily Post-Athenian (10.5M) PO Box 340 Athens TN 37371 **Phn:** 423-745-5664 **Fax:** 423-745-8295 www.dailypostathenian.com doug.headrick@dailypostathenian.com

Chattanooga Chattanooga Times Free Press (69.4M) 400 East 11th St Chattanooga TN 37401 **Phn:** 423-756-6900 **Fax:** 423-757-6383 www.timesfreepress.com djohnson@timesfreepress.com

Clarksville Leaf-Chronicle (20.4M) PO Box 31029 Clarksville TN 37040 **Phn:** 931-552-1808 **Fax:** 931-552-5859 www.theleafchronicle.com chrissmith@theleafchronicle.com

Cleveland Cleveland Daily Banner (13.3M) PO Box 3600 Cleveland TN 37320 **Phn:** 423-472-5041 **Fax:** 423-614-6529 www.clevelandbanner.com news@clevelandbanner.com

Columbia Daily Herald (11M) PO Box 1425 Columbia TN 38402 **Phn:** 931-388-6464 **Fax:** 931-388-1003 columbiadailyherald.com cfletcher@c-dh.net

Cookeville Herald-Citizen (11.3M) PO Box 2729 Cookeville TN 38502 **Phn:** 931-526-9715 **Fax:** 931-526-1209 www.herald-citizen.com editor@herald-citizen.com

Dyersburg State Gazette (7M) PO Box 808 Dyersburg TN 38025 **Phn:** 731-285-4091 **Fax:** 731-286-2602 www.stategazette.com crimel@stategazette.com

Elizabethton Elizabethton Star (9.4M) PO Box 1960 Elizabethton TN 37644 **Phn:** 423-542-4151 **Fax:** 423-542-2004 www.starhq.com rhardin@starhq.com

Greeneville Greeneville Sun (14.3M) PO Box 1630 Greeneville TN 37744 **Phn:** 423-638-4181 **Fax:** 423-638-3645 www.greenevillesun.com sunbusiness@xtn.net

Jackson Jackson Sun (34.1M) PO Box 1059 Jackson TN 38302 **Phn:** 731-427-3333 **Fax:** 731-425-9639 www.jacksonsun.com jbuie@jacksonsun.com

Johnson City Johnson City Press (29.6M) PO Box 1717 Johnson City TN 37605 **Phn:** 423-929-3111 **Fax:** 423-929-7484 www.johnsoncitypress.com newsroom@johnsoncitypress.com

Kingsport Daily News (6.2M) 310 E Sullivan St Kingsport TN 37660 **Phn:** 423-246-4800 **Fax:** 423-247-2502 www.kingsportdailynews.com sd@kingsportdailynews.com

Kingsport Kingsport Times-News (41.8M) PO Box 479 Kingsport TN 37662 **Phn:** 423-246-8121 **Fax:** 423-392-1385 www.timesnews.net tcomo@timesnews.net

Knoxville Knoxville News-Sentinel (116M) 2332 News Sentinel Dr Knoxville TN 37921 **Phn:** 865-521-8181 **Fax:** 865-342-6400 www.knoxnews.com editor@knoxnews.com

Lebanon Lebanon Democrat (8.8M) PO Box 430 Lebanon TN 37088 **Phn:** 615-444-3952 **Fax:** 615-444-1358 www.lebanondemocrat.com

Maryville Daily Times (22.6M) PO Box 9740 Maryville TN 37802 **Phn:** 865-981-1100 **Fax:** 865-981-1175 www.thedailytimes.com frank.trexler@thedailytimes.com

Memphis Commercial Appeal (154M) 495 Union Ave Memphis TN 38103 **Phn:** 901-529-2345 **Fax:** 901-529-6476 www.commercialappeal.com letters@commercialappeal.com

Morristown Citizen Tribune (18.3M) 1609 W 1st North St Morristown TN 37814 **Phn:** 423-581-5630 **Fax:** 423-581-8863 www.citizentribune.com lpidmd@lcs.net

Murfreesboro Daily News-Journal (14.8M) 224 N Walnut St Murfreesboro TN 37130 **Phn:** 615-893-5860 **Fax:** 615-893-4186 www.dnj.com tloyal@gannett.com

Nashville The Tennessean (165M) 1100 Broadway Nashville TN 37203 **Phn:** 615-259-8000 **Fax:** 615-259-8093 www.tennessean.com madowney@tennessean.com

Newport Newport Plain Talk (6.5M) PO Box 279 Newport TN 37822 **Phn:** 423-623-6171 **Fax:** 423-625-1995 www.newportplaintalk.com nhull@xtn.net

Oak Ridge Oak Ridger (7.6M) 785 Oak Ridge Tpke Oak Ridge TN 37830 **Phn:** 865-482-1021 **Fax:** 865-482-7834 www.oakridger.com editor@oakridger.com

Paris Paris Post-Intelligencer (6.1M) 208 E Wood St Paris TN 38242 **Phn:** 731-642-1162 **Fax:** 731-642-1165 www.parispi.net news@parispi.net

Sevierville Mountain Press (7.8M) PO Box 4810 Sevierville TN 37864 **Phn:** 865-428-0746 **Fax:** 865-453-4913 www.themountainpress.com editor@themountainpress.com

Shelbyville Shelbyville Times-Gazette (7.4M) PO Box 380 Shelbyville TN 37162 **Phn:** 931-684-1200 **Fax:** 931-684-3228 www.t-g.com editor@t-g.com

Union City Daily Messenger (8.3M) PO Box 430 Union City TN 38281 **Phn:** 731-885-0744 **Fax:** 731-885-0782 www.nwtntoday.com dcritch@ucmessenger.com

TEXAS

Abilene Abilene Reporter-News (30.1M) PO Box 30 Abilene TX 79604 **Phn:** 325-673-4271 **Fax:** 325-670-5242 www.reporternews.com jaklewiczg@reporternews.com

Alice Alice Echo-News Journal (3.9M) PO Box 1610 Alice TX 78333 **Phn:** 361-664-6588 **Fax:** 361-668-1030 www.alicetx.com ofelia.hunter@aliceechonews.com

Amarillo Amarillo Globe-News (49.1M) PO Box 2091 Amarillo TX 79166 **Phn:** 806-376-4488 **Fax:** 806-373-0810 amarillo.com matthew.hutchison@amarillo.com

Athens Athens Daily Review (4.9M) PO Box 32 Athens TX 75751 **Phn:** 903-675-5626 **Fax:** 903-675-9450 www.athensreview.com editor@athensreview.com

Austin Austin American-Statesman (169M) PO Box 670 Austin TX 78767 **Phn:** 512-445-3500 **Fax:** 512-445-1736 www.statesman.com news@statesman.com

Baytown Baytown Sun (10.8M) PO Box 90 Baytown TX 77522 **Phn:** 281-422-8302 **Fax:** 281-427-6283 baytownsun.com sunnews@baytownsun.com

Beaumont Beaumont Enterprise (50M) PO Box 3071 Beaumont TX 77704 **Phn:** 409-833-3311 **Fax:** 409-880-0757 www.beaumontenterprise.com localnews@beaumontenterprise.com

Big Spring Big Spring Herald (4.3M) PO Box 1431 Big Spring TX 79721 **Phn:** 432-263-7331 **Fax:** 432-264-7205 www.bigspringherald.com editor@bigspringherald.com

Borger Borger News-Herald (4.5M) PO Box 5130 Borger TX 79008 **Phn:** 806-273-5611 **Fax:** 806-273-2552 www.borgernewsherald.com editor@borgernewsherald.com

Brenham Brenham Banner-Press (5.8M) PO Box 585 Brenham TX 77834 **Phn:** 979-836-7956 **Fax:** 979-830-8577 www.brenhambanner.com arthur@brenhambanner.com

Brownsville Brownsville Herald (16.3M) 1135 E Van Buren St Brownsville TX 78520 **Phn:** 956-542-4301 **Fax:** 956-542-0840 www.brownsvilleherald.com dmaldonado@brownsvilleherald.com

Brownwood Brownwood Bulletin (7.1M) PO Box 1189 Brownwood TX 76804 **Phn:** 325-646-2541 **Fax:** 325-646-6835 www.brownwoodtx.com news@brownwoodbulletin.com

Bryan The Eagle (22.1M) PO Box 3000 Bryan TX 77805 **Phn:** 979-776-4444 **Fax:** 979-776-8923 www.theeagle.com editorial@theeagle.com

Cleburne Cleburne Times-Review (6.7M) PO Box 1569 Cleburne TX 76033 **Phn:** 817-645-2441 **Fax:** 817-645-4020 www.cleburnetimesreview.com dgosser@trcle.com

Clute The Facts (16.8M) PO Box 549 Clute TX 77531 **Phn:** 979-265-7411 **Fax:** 979-265-9052 thefacts.com news@thefacts.com

Conroe Conroe Courier (10.8M) PO Box 609 Conroe TX 77305 **Phn:** 936-756-6671 **Fax:** 936-521-3302 www.yourhoustonnews.com couriernews@hcnonline.com

Corpus Christi Corpus Christi Caller-Times (50.5M) PO Box 9136 Corpus Christi TX 78469 **Phn:** 361-884-2011 **Fax:** 361-886-3732 www.caller.com metrodesk@caller.com

Corsicana Corsicana Daily Sun (7.1M) PO Box 622 Corsicana TX 75151 **Phn:** 903-872-3931 **Fax:** 903-872-6878 corsicanadailysun.com rlinex@corsicanadailysun.com

Dallas Dallas Morning News (332M) PO Box 655237 Dallas TX 75265 **Phn:** 214-977-8222 **Fax:** 214-977-8319 www.dallasnews.com metro@dallasnews.com

Del Rio Del Rio News-Herald (5.1M) 2205 N Bedell Ave Del Rio TX 78840 **Phn:** 830-775-1551 **Fax:** 830-774-2610 delrionewsherald.com newsroom@delrionewsherald.com

Denton Denton Record-Chronicle (17.4M) PO Box 369 Denton TX 76202 **Phn:** 940-387-3811 **Fax:** 940-566-6888 www.dentonrc.com lmcbride@dentonrc.com

DeSoto Focus Daily News (28.6M) 1337 Marilyn Ave DeSoto TX 75115 **Phn:** 972-223-9175 **Fax:** 972-223-9202 focusdailynews.com

El Paso El Paso Times (69M) 300 N Campbell St El Paso TX 79901 **Phn:** 915-546-6100 **Fax:** 915-546-6415 www.elpasotimes.com bmoore@elpasotimes.com

Ennis Ennis Daily News (3.2M) 213 N Dallas St Ennis TX 75119 **Phn:** 972-875-3801 **Fax:** 972-875-9747 www.ennisdailynews.com editor@ennisdailynews.com

Fort Worth Fort Worth Star-Telegram (207M) PO Box 1870 Fort Worth TX 76101 **Phn:** 817-390-7400 **Fax:** 817-390-7789 www.dfw.com newsroom@star-telegram.com

Gainesville Gainesville Daily Register (5.7M) PO Box 309 Gainesville TX 76241 **Phn:** 940-665-5511 **Fax:** 940-665-1499 www.gainesvilleregister.com jperry@ntin.net

Galveston Galveston Co. Daily News (24M) PO Box 628 Galveston TX 77553 **Phn:** 409-683-5200 **Fax:** 409-740-3421 galvestondailynews.com newsroom@galvnews.com

Greenville Herald-Banner (8M) PO Box 6000 Greenville TX 75403 **Phn:** 903-455-4220 **Fax:** 903-455-6281 heraldbanner.com dprice@cnhi.com

Harlingen Valley Morning Star (20.3M) 1310 S Commerce St Harlingen TX 78550 **Phn:** 956-430-6200 **Fax:** 956-430-6233 www.valleymorningstar.com charlenev@valleystar.com

Henderson Henderson Daily News (6M) PO Box 30 Henderson TX 75653 **Phn:** 903-657-2501 **Fax:** 903-657-0056 www.hendersondailynews.com county@hendersondailynews.com

Hereford Hereford Brand (2.8M) PO Box 673 Hereford TX 79045 **Phn:** 806-364-2030 **Fax:** 806-364-8364 www.herefordbrand.com hbnews@wtrt.net

Houston Houston Chronicle (425M) PO Box 4260 Houston TX 77210 **Phn:** 713-220-7171 **Fax:** 713-362-6806 www.chron.com news@chron.com

Huntsville Huntsville Item (5.7M) PO Box 539 Huntsville TX 77342 **Phn:** 936-295-5407 **Fax:** 936-435-0135 itemonline.com ltrow@itemonline.com

Jacksonville Jacksonville Daily Progress (4.2M) PO Box 711 Jacksonville TX 75766 **Phn:** 903-586-2236 **Fax:** 903-586-0987 jacksonvilleprogress.com editor@jacksonvilleprogress.com

Kerrville Kerrville Daily Times (8.9M) PO Box 291428 Kerrville TX 78029 **Phn:** 830-896-7000 **Fax:** 830-895-4060 dailytimes.com news@dailytimes.com

Kilgore Kilgore News Herald (2.7M) PO Box 1210 Kilgore TX 75663 **Phn:** 903-984-2593 **Fax:** 903-984-7462 www.kilgorenewsherald.com knhedit@kilgorenewsherald.com

Killeen Killeen Daily Herald (18.6M) PO Box 1300 Killeen TX 76540 **Phn:** 254-634-2125 **Fax:** 254-200-7640 www.kdhnews.com dmiller@kdhnews.com

Laredo Laredo Morning Times (18.3M) PO Box 2129 Laredo TX 78044 **Phn:** 956-728-2500 **Fax:** 956-724-3036 www.lmtonline.com rmontoya@lmtonline.com

Longview Longview News-Journal (27.5M) PO Box 1792 Longview TX 75606 **Phn:** 903-757-3311 **Fax:** 903-757-3742 www.news-journal.com gstratton@news-journal.com

Lubbock Lubbock Avalanche-Journal (51M) 710 Avenue J Lubbock TX 79401 **Phn:** 806-762-8844 **Fax:** 806-744-9603 lubbockonline.com terry.greenberg@lubbockonline.com

Lufkin Lufkin Daily News (14.4M) PO Box 1089 Lufkin TX 75902 **Phn:** 936-632-6631 **Fax:** 936-632-6655 lufkindailynews.com news@lufkindailynews.com

Marshall Marshall News Messenger (6.7M) PO Box 730 Marshall TX 75671 **Phn:** 903-935-7914 **Fax:** 903-935-6242 www.marshallnewsmessenger.com info@marshallnewsmessenger.com

McAllen The Monitor (39M) PO Box 3267 McAllen TX 78502 **Phn:** 956-686-4343 **Fax:** 956-683-4401 www.themonitor.com news@themonitor.com

McKinney McKinney Courier-Gazette (5.2M) PO Box 400 McKinney TX 75070 **Phn:** 972-542-2631 **Fax:** 972-529-1684 starlocalmedia.com/mckinneycouriergazette rmann@starlocalmedia.com

Mexia Mexia Daily News (2.3M) PO Box 431 Mexia TX 76667 **Phn:** 254-562-2868 **Fax:** 254-562-3121 www.mexiadailynews.com news@themexianews.com

Midland Midland Reporter-Telegram (19.4M) 201 E Illinois Ave Midland TX 79701 **Phn:** 432-682-5311 **Fax:** 432-570-7650 www.mywesttexas.com sdoreen@mrt.com

Mineral Wells Mineral Wells Index (4.9M) 300 S.E. 1st St. Mineral Wells TX 76067 **Phn:** 940-325-4465 **Fax:** 940-325-2020 mineralwellsindex.com editor@mineralwellsindex.com

Mount Pleasant Mount Pleasant Daily Tribune (5M) PO Box 1177 Mount Pleasant TX 75456 **Phn:** 903-572-1705 **Fax:** 903-572-6026 www.dailytribune.net news@dailytribune.net

Nacogdoches Daily Sentinel (7.9M) PO Box 630068 Nacogdoches TX 75963 **Phn:** 936-564-8361 **Fax:** 936-560-4267 dailysentinel.com dryan@dailysentinel.com

New Braunfels New Braunfels Herald-Zeitung (8M) PO Box 311328 New Braunfels TX 78131 **Phn:** 830-625-9144 **Fax:** 830-606-3413 herald-zeitung.com news@herald-zeitung.com

Odessa Odessa American (24.3M) PO Box 2952 Odessa TX 79760 **Phn:** 432-337-4661 **Fax:** 432-333-7742 www.oaoa.com oanews@oaoa.com

Orange Orange Leader (5M) PO Box 1028 Orange TX 77631 **Phn:** 409-883-3571 **Fax:** 409-883-6342 orangeleader.com editorial@orangeleader.com

Palestine Palestine Herald-Press (7.5M) PO Box 379 Palestine TX 75802 **Phn:** 903-729-0281 **Fax:** 903-729-0284 palestineherald.com editor@palestineherald.com

Pampa The Pampa News (5.3M) PO Box 2198 Pampa TX 79066 **Phn:** 806-669-2525 **Fax:** 806-669-2520 www.thepampanews.com thowsare@thepampanews.com

Paris Paris News (9.3M) PO Box 1078 Paris TX 75461 **Phn:** 903-785-8744 **Fax:** 903-785-1263 theparisnews.com editor@theparisnews.com

Pasadena Pasadena Citizen (5.1M) PO Box 6192 Pasadena TX 77506 **Phn:** 713-477-0221 **Fax:** 713-477-4172 www.yourhoustonnews.com/pasadena thepasadenacitizen@hcnonline.com

Plainview Plainview Daily Herald (6.5M) PO Box 1240 Plainview TX 79073 **Phn:** 806-296-1300 **Fax:** 806-296-1363 www.myplainview.com dmcdonough@hearstnp.com

Plano Plano Star Courier (8.3M) PO Box 860248 Plano TX 75086 **Phn:** 972-398-4200 **Fax:** 972-801-3265 www.planostar.com rmann@starlocalnews.com

Port Arthur Port Arthur News (12.5M) PO Box 789 Port Arthur TX 77641 **Phn:** 409-721-2400 **Fax:** 409-724-6854 panews.com panews@panews.com

Rosenberg Fort Bend Herald (7.7M) PO Box 1088 Rosenberg TX 77471 **Phn:** 281-232-3737 **Fax:** 281-342-3219 www.fbherald.com newsroom@fbherald.com

San Angelo San Angelo Standard Times (25M) PO Box 5111 San Angelo TX 76902 **Phn:** 325-653-1221 **Fax:** 325-659-8173 www.gosanangelo.com creative@gosanangelo.com

San Antonio San Antonio Express-News (224M) PO Box 2171 San Antonio TX 78297 **Phn:** 210-250-3000 **Fax:** 210-250-3105 www.mysanantonio.com citydesk@express-news.net

San Marcos San Marcos Daily Record (5.1M) PO Box 1109 San Marcos TX 78667 **Phn:** 512-392-2458 **Fax:** 512-392-4655 www.sanmarcosrecord.com

Seguin Seguin Gazette-Enterprise (4.8M) PO Box 1200 Seguin TX 78156 **Phn:** 830-379-5402 **Fax:** 830-379-8328 seguingazette.com editor@seguingazette.com

Sherman Herald Democrat (20M) PO Box 1128 Sherman TX 75091 **Phn:** 903-893-8181 **Fax:** 903-868-2106 www.heralddemocrat.com news@heralddemocrat.com

Snyder Snyder Daily News (3.6M) PO Box 949 Snyder TX 79550 **Phn:** 325-573-5486 **Fax:** 325-573-0044 snyderdailynews.com editor1@snyderdailynews.com

Stephenville Stephenville Empire-Tribune (4.2M) PO Box 958 Stephenville TX 76401 **Phn:** 254-965-3124 **Fax:** 254-965-4269 www.yourstephenvilletx.com sara.vandenberge@empiretribune.com

Sulphur Springs Sulphur Springs News-Telegram (5.7M) 401 Church St Sulphur Springs TX 75482 **Phn:** 903-885-8663 **Fax:** 903-885-8768 www.myssnews.com news@ssecho.com

Sweetwater Sweetwater Reporter (3.1M) PO Box 750 Sweetwater TX 79556 **Phn:** 325-236-6677 **Fax:** 325-235-4967 www.sweetwaterreporter.com editor@sweetwaterreporter.com

Taylor Taylor Daily Press (4.7M) PO Box 1040 Taylor TX 76574 **Phn:** 512-352-8535 **Fax:** 512-352-2227 www.taylordailypress.net news@taylordailypress.net

Temple Temple Daily Telegram (19.4M) PO Box 6114 Temple TX 76503 **Phn:** 254-778-4444 **Fax:** 254-778-0634 www.tdnews.com tdt@temple-telegram.com

Terrell Terrell Tribune (2.5M) PO Box 669 Terrell TX 75160 **Phn:** 972-563-6476 **Fax:** 972-563-0340 www.terrelltribune.com ttrib@swbell.net

Texarkana Texarkana Gazette (29.6M) PO Box 621 Texarkana TX 75504 **Phn:** 903-794-3311 **Fax:** 903-794-3315 www.texarkanagazette.com lminor@texarkanagazette.com

Tyler Tyler Morning Telegraph (38.5M) 410 W Erwin St Tyler TX 75702 **Phn:** 903-597-8111 **Fax:** 903-595-0335 www.tylerpaper.com dvberry@tylerpaper.com

Vernon Vernon Daily Record (4.3M) 3214 Wilbarger St Vernon TX 76384 **Phn:** 940-552-5454 **Fax:** 940-553-4823 www.vernonrecord.com editor@vernonrecord.com

Victoria Victoria Advocate (33.5M) PO Box 1518 Victoria TX 77902 **Phn:** 361-575-1451 **Fax:** 361-574-1220 www.victoriaadvocate.com feedback@vicad.com

Waco Waco Tribune-Herald (38.1M) PO Box 2588 Waco TX 76702 **Phn:** 254-757-5757 **Fax:** 254-757-0302 www.wacotrib.com news@wacotrib.com

Waxahachie Waxahachie Daily Light (4.8M) PO Box 877 Waxahachie TX 75168 **Phn:** 972-937-3310 **Fax:** 972-937-1139 www.waxahachietx.com neal.white@wninews.com

Weatherford Weatherford Democrat (6.2M) 512 Palo Pinto St Weatherford TX 76086 **Phn:** 817-594-7447 **Fax:** 817-594-9734 weatherforddemocrat.com editor@weatherforddemocrat.com

TEXAS DAILY NEWSPAPERS

Wichita Falls Times Record News (29.6M) PO Box 120 Wichita Falls TX 76307 **Phn:** 940-767-8341 **Fax:** 940-767-1741 www.timesrecordnews.com watsond@timesrecordnews.com

UTAH

Logan Herald Journal (14.9M) 75 W 300 N Logan UT 84321 **Phn:** 435-752-2121 **Fax:** 435-753-6642 news.hjnews.com hjnews@hjnews.com

Ogden Standard-Examiner (65M) PO Box 12790 Ogden UT 84412 **Phn:** 801-625-4200 **Fax:** 801-625-4299 www.standard.net ahowell@standard.net

Provo Daily Herald (31.8M) PO Box 717 Provo UT 84603 **Phn:** 801-373-5050 **Fax:** 801-344-2985 www.heraldextra.com jtolman@heraldextra.com

Saint George The Spectrum (22.8M) 275 E Saint George Blvd Saint George UT 84770 **Phn:** 435-674-6200 **Fax:** 435-674-6270 www.thespectrum.com tseifert@thespectrum.com

Salt Lake City Deseret News (71.4M) PO Box 1257 Salt Lake City UT 84110 **Phn:** 801-237-2100 **Fax:** 801-237-2121 www.deseretnews.com news@desnews.com

Salt Lake City Salt Lake Tribune (131M) 90 S 400 W Ste 700 Salt Lake City UT 84101 **Phn:** 801-257-8742 **Fax:** 801-257-8525 www.sltrib.com news@sltrib.com

VERMONT

Barre Times-Argus (8.8M) PO Box 707 Barre VT 05641 **Phn:** 802-479-0191 **Fax:** 802-479-4096 www.timesargus.com news@timesargus.com

Bennington Bennington Banner (7.1M) 425 Main St Bennington VT 05201 **Phn:** 802-447-7567 **Fax:** 802-442-3413 www.BenningtonBanner.com news@benningtonbanner.com

Brattleboro Brattleboro Reformer (9.2M) 62 Black Mountain Rd Brattleboro VT 05301 **Phn:** 802-254-2311 **Fax:** 802-257-1305 www.reformer.com mwinters@reformer.com

Burlington Burlington Free Press (45.3M) PO Box 10 Burlington VT 05402 **Phn:** 802-863-3441 **Fax:** 802-660-1802 www.burlingtonfreepress.com metro@burlingtonfreepress.com

Newport Newport Daily Express (3.8M) PO Box 347 Newport VT 05855 **Phn:** 802-334-6568 **Fax:** 802-334-6891 www.newportvermontdailyexpress.com editor@newportvermontdailyexpress.com

Rutland Rutland Herald (18.2M) PO Box 668 Rutland VT 05702 **Phn:** 802-747-6121 **Fax:** 802-773-0311 www.rutlandherald.com pressreleases@rutlandherald.com

Saint Albans St. Albans Messenger (5.1M) 281 N Main St Saint Albans VT 05478 **Phn:** 802-524-9771 **Fax:** 802-527-1948 www.samessenger.com news@samessenger.com

Saint Johnsbury The Caledonian-Record (10M) PO Box 8 Saint Johnsbury VT 05819 **Phn:** 802-748-8121 **Fax:** 802-748-1613 caledonianrecord.com news@caledonian-record.com

White River Junction Valley News (16.8M) PO Box 877 White River Junction VT 05001 **Phn:** 603-298-8711 **Fax:** 603-298-0212 www.vnews.com webmaster@vnews.com

VIRGINIA

Bristol Bristol Herald-Courier (38.2M) 320 Bob Morrison Blvd Bristol VA 24201 **Phn:** 276-669-2181 **Fax:** 276-669-3696 www.tricities.com features@bristolnews.com

Charlottesville Daily Progress (28.7M) PO Box 9030 Charlottesville VA 22906 **Phn:** 434-978-7200 **Fax:** 434-978-7252 www.dailyprogress.com rwolverton@dailyprogress.com

Covington Virginian Review (7.4M) PO Box 271 Covington VA 24426 **Phn:** 540-962-2121 **Fax:** 540-962-5072 www.thevirginianreview.com virginianreview@aol.com

Culpeper Star-Exponent (7.3M) 471 James Madison Hwy Ste 201 Culpeper VA 22701 **Phn:** 540-825-0771 **Fax:** 540-825-0778 www.dailyprogress.com/starexponent

Danville Danville Register & Bee (20.9M) 700 Monument St Danville VA 24541 **Phn:** 434-793-2311 **Fax:** 434-797-2299 www.godanriver.com news@registerbee.com

Fredericksburg Free Lance-Star (45.8M) 616 Amelia St Fredericksburg VA 22401 **Phn:** 540-374-5000 **Fax:** 540-373-8455 fredericksburg.com newsroom@freelancestar.com

Harrisonburg Daily News-Record (31.1M) PO Box 193 Harrisonburg VA 22803 **Phn:** 540-574-6200 **Fax:** 540-433-9112 www.dnronline.com kirkwood@dnronline.com

Lynchburg News & Advance (35.3M) PO Box 10129 Lynchburg VA 24506 **Phn:** 434-385-5400 **Fax:** 434-385-5538 www.newsadvance.com news@newsadvance.com

Martinsville Martinsville Bulletin (16.5M) PO Box 3711 Martinsville VA 24115 **Phn:** 276-638-8801 **Fax:** 276-638-7409 www.martinsvillebulletin.com info@martinsvillebulletin.com

Newport News Daily Press (86.1M) 7505 Warwick Blvd Newport News VA 23607 **Phn:** 757-247-4600 **Fax:** 757-245-8618 www.dailypress.com townsquare@dailypress.com

Norfolk Virginian-Pilot (183M) 150 W Brambleton Ave Norfolk VA 23510 **Phn:** 757-446-2000 **Fax:** 757-446-2414 pilotonline.com maria.carrillo@pilotonline.com

Petersburg Progress-Index (13.1M) 15 Franklin St Petersburg VA 23803 **Phn:** 804-732-3456 **Fax:** 804-732-8417 progress-index.com newsroom@progress-index.com

Pulaski Southwest Times (5.7M) PO Box 391 Pulaski VA 24301 **Phn:** 540-980-5220 **Fax:** 540-980-3618 www.southwesttimes.com melinda@southwesttimes.com

Richmond Richmond Times-Dispatch (181M) PO Box 85333 Richmond VA 23293 **Phn:** 804-649-6000 **Fax:** 804-775-8059 www.timesdispatch.com news@timesdispatch.com

Roanoke Roanoke Times (88.9M) PO Box 2491 Roanoke VA 24010 **Phn:** 540-981-3100 **Fax:** 540-981-3346 www.roanoke.com michael.stowe@roanoke.com

Staunton News Leader (17.7M) 11 N Central Ave Staunton VA 24401 **Phn:** 540-885-7281 **Fax:** 540-885-1904 www.newsleader.com localnews@newsleader.com

Strasburg Northern Virginia Daily (15.7M) 152 N Holliday St Strasburg VA 22657 **Phn:** 540-465-5137 **Fax:** 540-465-6164 www.nvdaily.com info@nvdaily.com

Suffolk Suffolk News-Herald (4.3M) PO Box 1220 Suffolk VA 23439 **Phn:** 757-539-3437 **Fax:** 757-539-8804 www.suffolknewsherald.com res.spears@suffolknewsherald.com

Waynesboro News-Virginian (7.3M) 1300 W Main St Waynesboro VA 22980 **Phn:** 540-949-8213 **Fax:** 540-942-4542 www.dailyprogress.com/newsvirginian

Winchester Winchester Star (20.6M) 2 N Kent St Winchester VA 22601 **Phn:** 540-667-3200 **Fax:** 540-667-1649 www.winchesterstar.com news@winchesterstar.com

Woodbridge Potomac News (13.8M) PO Box 2470 Woodbridge VA 22195 **Phn:** 703-878-8000 **Fax:** 703-878-8099 www.insidenova.com

WASHINGTON

Aberdeen Daily World (14.1M) PO Box 269 Aberdeen WA 98520 **Phn:** 360-532-4000 **Fax:** 360-533-6039 www.thedailyworld.com press_releases@thedailyworld.com

Bellingham Bellingham Herald (23.2M) 1155 N State St Bellingham WA 98225 **Phn:** 360-676-2600 **Fax:** 360-756-2826 www.bellinghamherald.com newsroom@bellinghamherald.com

Bremerton The Sun (29.3M) PO Box 259 Bremerton WA 98337 **Phn:** 360-377-3711 **Fax:** 360-415-2681 www.kitsapsun.com sunnews@kitsapsun.com

Centralia The Chronicle (13.9M) 321 N Pearl St Centralia WA 98531 **Phn:** 360-736-3311 **Fax:** 360-736-4796 www.chronline.com news@chronline.com

Ellensburg Daily Record (5.5M) 401 N Main St Ellensburg WA 98926 **Phn:** 509-925-1414 **Fax:** 509-925-5696 dailyrecordnews.com mgallagher@kvnews.com

Everett Daily Herald (49M) PO Box 930 Everett WA 98206 **Phn:** 425-339-3000 **Fax:** 425-339-3435 www.heraldnet.com newstips@heraldnet.com

Kennewick Tri-City Herald (31M) 333 W Canal Dr Kennewick WA 99336 **Phn:** 509-582-1500 **Fax:** 509-582-1510 www.tri-cityherald.com news@tricityherald.com

Longview Daily News (21.5M) PO Box 189 Longview WA 98632 **Phn:** 360-577-2500 **Fax:** 360-577-2538 tdn.com myantis@tdn.com

Moses Lake Columbia Basin Herald (8.1M) PO Box 910 Moses Lake WA 98837 **Phn:** 509-765-4561 **Fax:** 509-765-8659 www.columbiabasinherald.com editor@columbiabasinherald.com

Mount Vernon Skagit Valley Herald (18M) PO Box 578 Mount Vernon WA 98273 **Phn:** 360-424-3251 **Fax:** 360-428-0400 www.goskagit.com cweeks@skagitpublishing.com

Olympia The Olympian (32.8M) PO Box 407 Olympia WA 98507 **Phn:** 360-754-5400 **Fax:** 360-357-0202 www.theolympian.com news@theolympian.com

Port Angeles Peninsula Daily News (16.8M) PO Box 1330 Port Angeles WA 98362 **Phn:** 360-452-2345 **Fax:** 360-417-3521 www.peninsuladailynews.com news@peninsuladailynews.com

Seattle Seattle Post-Intelligencer (Online only) (240M) PO Box 1909 Seattle WA 98111 **Phn:** 206-448-8000 **Fax:** www.seattlepi.com citydesk@seattlepi.com

Seattle Seattle Times (213M) PO Box 70 Seattle WA 98111 **Phn:** 206-464-2111 **Fax:** 206-464-2261 seattletimes.com business@seattletimes.com

Spokane Spokesman-Review (93.1M) PO Box 2160 Spokane WA 99210 **Phn:** 509-459-5000 **Fax:** 509-459-5098 www.spokesman.com news@spokesman.com

Sunnyside Daily Sun News (3.8M) PO Box 878 Sunnyside WA 98944 **Phn:** 509-837-4500 **Fax:** 509-837-6397 www.dailysunnews.com

Tacoma News Tribune (116M) PO Box 11000 Tacoma WA 98411 **Phn:** 253-597-8742 **Fax:** 253-597-8274 www.thenewstribune.com newstips@thenewstribune.com

Vancouver The Columbian (45M) PO Box 180 Vancouver WA 98666 **Phn:** 360-694-3391 **Fax:** 360-735-4598 www.columbian.com lou.brancaccio@columbian.com

Walla Walla Walla Walla Union-Bulletin (13.8M) PO Box 1358 Walla Walla WA 99362 **Phn:** 509-525-3300 **Fax:** 509-525-1232 union-bulletin.com rickdoyle@wwub.com

WASHINGTON DAILY NEWSPAPERS

Wenatchee Wenatchee World (24.6M) PO Box 1511 Wenatchee WA 98807 **Phn:** 509-663-5161 **Fax:** 509-665-1183 www.wenatcheeworld.com newsroom@wenatcheeworld.com

Yakima Yakima Herald-Republic (37.1M) PO Box 9668 Yakima WA 98909 **Phn:** 509-248-1251 **Fax:** 509-577-7767 www.yakimaherald.com news@yakimaherald.com

WEST VIRGINIA

Beckley Register-Herald (27.9M) PO Box 2398 Beckley WV 25802 **Phn:** 304-255-4400 **Fax:** 304-256-5625 www.register-herald.com fwood@register-herald.com

Bluefield Bluefield Daily Telegraph (17.9M) PO Box 1599 Bluefield WV 24701 **Phn:** 304-327-2811 **Fax:** 304-327-6179 bdtonline.com editor@bdtonline.com

Charleston Charleston Daily Mail (23.3M) 1001 Virginia St E Charleston WV 25301 **Phn:** 304-348-5129 **Fax:** 304-348-4847 www.dailymail.com dmnews@dailymail.com

Charleston Charleston Gazette (36M) 1001 Virginia St E Charleston WV 25301 **Phn:** 304-348-5140 **Fax:** 304-348-1233 www.wvgazette.com gazette@wvgazette.com

Clarksburg Exponent-Telegram (15.4M) PO Box 2000 Clarksburg WV 26302 **Phn:** 304-626-1400 **Fax:** 304-624-4188 www.exponent-telegram.com news@exponent-telegram.com

Elkins The Inter-Mountain (10.5M) PO Box 1339 Elkins WV 26241 **Phn:** 304-636-2124 **Fax:** 304-636-8252 theintermountain.com newsroom@theintermountain.com

Fairmont Times West Virginian (10.6M) PO Box 2530 Fairmont WV 26555 **Phn:** 304-367-2500 **Fax:** 304-367-2565 timeswv.com timeswv@timeswv.com

Huntington Herald-Dispatch (27.6M) PO Box 2017 Huntington WV 25720 **Phn:** 304-526-4000 **Fax:** 304-526-2857 www.herald-dispatch.com editor@herald-dispatch.com

Keyser Mineral Daily News-Tribune (4M) PO Box 879 Keyser WV 26726 **Phn:** 304-788-3333 **Fax:** 304-788-3398 www.newstribune.info newsroom@newstribune.info

Lewisburg West Virginia Daily News (4.4M) PO Box 471 Lewisburg WV 24901 **Phn:** 304-645-1206 **Fax:** 304-645-7104 wvdailynews.net wvdailynews@suddenlinkmail.com

Logan Logan Banner (9.6M) PO Box 720 Logan WV 25601 **Phn:** 304-752-6950 **Fax:** 304-752-1239 www.loganbanner.com drolen@civitasmedia.com

Martinsburg The Journal (17.8M) PO Box 807 Martinsburg WV 25402 **Phn:** 304-263-8931 **Fax:** 304-267-2903 journal-news.net news@journal-news.net

Morgantown Dominion Post (21.1M) 1251 Earl L Core Rd Morgantown WV 26505 **Phn:** 304-292-6301 **Fax:** 304-291-2326 www.dominionpost.com editor@dominionpost.com

Moundsville Moundsville Daily Echo (3.9M) PO Box 369 Moundsville WV 26041 **Phn:** 304-845-2660 **Fax:** 304-845-2661 mdsvecho@gmail.com

Parkersburg Parkersburg News & Sentinel (3.6M) 519 Juliana St Parkersburg WV 26101 **Phn:** 304-485-1891 **Fax:** 304-485-5122 newsandsentinel.com editorial@newsandsentinel.com

Point Pleasant Point Pleasant Register (3.9M) 200 Main St Point Pleasant WV 25550 **Phn:** 304-675-1333 **Fax:** 304-675-5234 www.mydailyregister.com gdtnews@civitasmedia.com

Wayne Wayne Co. News (5.1M) 310 Central Ave Wayne WV 25570 **Phn:** 304-272-3433 **Fax:** 304-272-6516 www.waynecountynews.com editor@waynecountynews.com

Weirton Weirton Daily Times (8.3M) PO Box 2830 Weirton WV 26062 **Phn:** 304-748-0606 **Fax:** 304-748-2202 www.weirtondailytimes.com chowell@weirtondailytimes.com

Wheeling The Intelligencer (14M) 1500 Main St Wheeling WV 26003 **Phn:** 304-233-0100 **Fax:** 304-232-1399 www.theintelligencer.net webmaster@theintelligencer.net

Williamson Williamson Daily News (8M) PO Box 1660 Williamson WV 25661 **Phn:** 304-235-4242 **Fax:** 304-235-0730 www.williamsondailynews.com jbyers@civitasmedia.com

WISCONSIN

Antigo Antigo Daily Journal (6.8M) 612 Superior St Antigo WI 54409 **Phn:** 715-623-4191 **Fax:** 715-623-4193 www.antigodailyjournal.com adj@dwave.net

Appleton Post-Crescent (50.9M) PO Box 59 Appleton WI 54912 **Phn:** 920-993-1000 **Fax:** 920-733-1945 www.postcrescent.com jmara@postcrescent.com

Ashland Daily Press (6.2M) PO Box 313 Ashland WI 54806 **Phn:** 715-682-2313 **Fax:** 715-682-4699 www.ashlandwi.com ashlandwieditorial@gmail.com

Baraboo Baraboo News-Republic (4.2M) PO Box 9 Baraboo WI 53913 **Phn:** 608-356-4808 **Fax:** 608-356-0344 www.wiscnews.com bnr-news@capitalnewspapers.com

Beaver Dam Daily Citizen (10M) PO Box 558 Beaver Dam WI 53916 **Phn:** 920-887-0321 **Fax:** 920-887-8790 www.wiscnews.com dc-news@capitalnewspapers.com

Beloit Beloit Daily News (14.2M) 149 State St Beloit WI 53511 **Phn:** 608-365-8811 **Fax:** 608-365-1420 www.beloitdailynews.com dbehling@beloitdailynews.com

Chippewa Falls Chippewa Herald (6.9M) PO Box 69 Chippewa Falls WI 54729 **Phn:** 715-723-5515 **Fax:** 715-723-9644 chippewa.com editor@chippewa.com

Eau Claire Leader-Telegram (25M) PO Box 570 Eau Claire WI 54702 **Phn:** 715-833-9200 **Fax:** 715-858-7308 www.leadertelegram.com don.huebscher@ecpc.com

Fond Du Lac The Reporter (15.5M) PO Box 630 Fond Du Lac WI 54936 **Phn:** 920-922-4600 **Fax:** 920-922-5388 www.fdlreporter.com pbreister@fdlreporter.com

Fort Atkinson Daily Jefferson Co. Union (7.5M) 28 Milwaukee Ave W Fort Atkinson WI 53538 **Phn:** 920-563-5553 **Fax:** 920-563-2329 dailyunion.com dailyunion@dailyunion.com

Green Bay Green Bay Press-Gazette (55M) PO Box 23430 Green Bay WI 54305 **Phn:** 920-431-8400 **Fax:** 920-431-8379 www.greenbaypressgazette.com jash@greenbaypressgazette.com

Janesville Janesville Gazette (21.7M) PO Box 5001 Janesville WI 53547 **Phn:** 608-754-3311 **Fax:** 608-755-8349 www.gazetteextra.com newsroom@gazetteextra.com

Kenosha Kenosha News (24.8M) 5800 7th Ave Kenosha WI 53140 **Phn:** 262-657-1000 **Fax:** 262-657-8455 www.kenoshanews.com newsroom@kenoshanews.com

La Crosse La Crosse Tribune (31.9M) 401 3rd St N La Crosse WI 54601 **Phn:** 608-782-9710 **Fax:** 608-782-9723 lacrossetribune.com rcunningham@lacrossetribune.com

Madison Wisconsin State Journal (87.5M) PO Box 8058 Madison WI 53708 **Phn:** 608-252-6100 **Fax:** 608-252-6119 host.madison.com/wsj wsjcity@madison.com

Manitowoc Herald Times Reporter (14.1M) 902 Franklin St Manitowoc WI 54220 **Phn:** 920-684-4433 **Fax:** 920-686-2103 www.htrnews.com rbudzisz@htrnews.com

Marinette Eagle Herald (10.1M) PO Box 77 Marinette WI 54143 **Phn:** 715-735-6611 **Fax:** 715-735-0229 www.eagleherald.com news@eagleherald.com

Marshfield Marshfield News-Herald (11.6M) 111 W 3rd St Marshfield WI 54449 **Phn:** 715-384-3131 **Fax:** 715-387-4175 www.marshfieldnewsherald.com jgneiser@marshfieldnewsherald.com

Milwaukee Milwaukee Journal-Sentinel (231M) PO Box 371 Milwaukee WI 53201 **Phn:** 414-224-2000 **Fax:** 414-224-2047 www.jsonline.com jsmetro@journalsentinel.com

Monroe Monroe Times (5.2M) 1065 4th Ave W Monroe WI 53566 **Phn:** 608-328-4202 **Fax:** 608-328-4217 www.themonroetimes.com editor@themonroetimes.com

Oshkosh Oshkosh Northwestern (20.8M) 224 W 8th Ave Oshkosh WI 54902 **Phn:** 920-235-7700 **Fax:** 920-426-6600 www.thenorthwestern.com jfitzhen@thenorthwestern.com

Portage Daily Register (5M) PO Box 470 Portage WI 53901 **Phn:** 608-745-3500 **Fax:** 608-742-8346 www.wiscnews.com pdr-news@capitalnewspapers.com

Racine Journal Times (28.4M) 212 4th St Racine WI 53403 **Phn:** 262-634-3322 **Fax:** 262-631-1780 www.journaltimes.com tom.farley@lee.net

Rhinelander Northwoods River News (5.3M) 232 S Courtney St Rhinelander WI 54501 **Phn:** 715-365-6397 **Fax:** 715-365-6367 www.rivernewsonline.com news@rivernewsonline.com

Shawano Shawano Leader (6.6M) 1464 E Green Bay St Shawano WI 54166 **Phn:** 715-526-2121 **Fax:** 715-524-3941 www.shawanoleader.com news@shawanoleader.com

Sheboygan Sheboygan Press (20.9M) 632 Center Ave Sheboygan WI 53081 **Phn:** 920-457-7711 **Fax:** 920-457-3573 www.sheboyganpress.com mknuth@sheboyganpress.com

Stevens Point Stevens Point Journal (11.4M) 1200 3rd St Stevens Point WI 54481 **Phn:** 715-344-6100 **Fax:** 715-345-2069 www.stevenspointjournal.com bkowalski@stevenspoint.gannett.com

Watertown Watertown Daily Times (9.3M) PO Box 140 Watertown WI 53094 **Phn:** 920-261-5161 **Fax:** 920-261-5102 www.wdtimes.com news@wdtimes.com

Waukesha The Freeman (12.8M) PO Box 7 Waukesha WI 53187 **Phn:** 262-542-2501 **Fax:** 262-542-8259 www.gmtoday.com webmaster@conleynet.com

Wausau Wausau Daily Herald (20.9M) PO Box 1286 Wausau WI 54402 **Phn:** 715-842-2101 **Fax:** 715-848-9361 www.wausaudailyherald.com akimmes@wdhprint.com

West Bend Daily News (9.6M) PO Box 478 West Bend WI 53095 **Phn:** 262-306-5000 **Fax:** 262-338-1984 www.gmtoday.com webmaster@conleynet.com

Wisconsin Rapids Daily Tribune (11.2M) 220 1st Ave S Wisconsin Rapids WI 54495 **Phn:** 715-423-7200 **Fax:** 715-421-1545 www.wisconsinrapidstribune.com allen.hicks@cwnews.net

WYOMING

Casper Star-Tribune (31.6M) PO Box 80 Casper WY 82602 **Phn:** 307-266-0500 **Fax:** 307-266-0568 trib.com ron.gullberg@trib.com

Cheyenne Wyoming Tribune-Eagle (15.3M) 702 W Lincolnway Cheyenne WY 82001 **Phn:** 307-634-3361 **Fax:** 307-633-3189 www.wyomingnews.com news@wyomingnews.com

WISCONSIN DAILY NEWSPAPERS

Gillette News-Record (6.5M) PO Box 3006 Gillette WY 82717 **Phn:** 307-682-9306 **Fax:** 307-686-9306 www.gillettenewsrecord.com news@gillettenewsrecord.com

Laramie Laramie Boomerang (5.2M) 320 E Grand Ave Laramie WY 82070 **Phn:** 307-742-2176 **Fax:** 307-721-2973 www.laramieboomerang.com news@laramieboomerang.com

Rawlins Rawlins Daily Times (3.1M) PO Box 370 Rawlins WY 82301 **Phn:** 307-324-3411 **Fax:** 307-324-2797 www.rawlinstimes.com news@rawlinstimes.com

Riverton Riverton Ranger (7.1M) PO Box 993 Riverton WY 82501 **Phn:** 307-856-2244 **Fax:** 307-856-0189 www.dailyranger.com ranger@wyoming.com

Rock Springs Rocket-Miner (8.1M) PO Box 98 Rock Springs WY 82902 **Phn:** 307-362-3736 **Fax:** 307-382-2763 www.rocketminer.com publisher@rocketminer.com

Sheridan Sheridan Press (6.6M) PO Box 2006 Sheridan WY 82801 **Phn:** 307-672-2431 **Fax:** 307-672-7950 www.thesheridanpress.com editor@thesheridanpress.com

Worland Northern Wyoming Daily News (3.5M) PO Box 508 Worland WY 82401 **Phn:** 307-347-3241 **Fax:** 307-347-4267 www.wyodaily.com bobv@wyodaily.com

This page left blank intentionally.

ALABAMA

WEEKLY NEWSPAPERS

Abbeville Abbeville Herald (2.5M) PO Box 609 Abbeville AL 36310 **Phn:** 334-585-2331 **Fax:** 334-585-6835 heraldnews@centurytel.net

Albertville Sand Mountain Reporter (10.6M) PO Box 1729 Albertville AL 35950 **Phn:** 256-840-3000 **Fax:** 256-840-2987 www.sandmountainreporter.com news@sandmountainreporter.com

Alexander City Dadeville Record (2.0M) PO Box 999 Alexander City AL 35011 **Phn:** 256-234-4281 **Fax:** 256-234-6550 www.alexcityoutlook.com/category/dadeville

Anniston Jacksonville News (3.0M) PO Box 189 Anniston AL 36202 **Phn:** 256-236-1551 **Fax:** 256-241-1991 www.annistonstar.com/news_jacksonville jalred@jaxnews.com

Anniston Piedmont Journal (3.5M) PO Box 189 Anniston AL 36202 **Phn:** 256-236-1551 **Fax:** 256-241-1991 www.annistonstar.com/news_piedmont jalred@jaxnews.com

Arab Arab Tribune (7.2M) PO Box 605 Arab AL 35016 **Phn:** 256-586-3188 **Fax:** 256-586-3190 www.thearabtribune.com

Atmore Atmore Advance (3.6M) PO Box 28 Atmore AL 36504 **Phn:** 251-368-2123 **Fax:** 251-368-2124 www.atmoreadvance.com kerry.bean@atmoreadvance.com

Atmore Atmore News (4.0M) 128 S Main St Atmore AL 36502 **Phn:** 251-368-6397 **Fax:** 251-368-3397 www.atmorenews.com sherry@atmorenews.com

Auburn Auburn Villager (3.5M) PO Box 1633 Auburn AL 36831 **Phn:** 334-501-0600 **Fax:** 334-826-7700 www.auburnvillager.com editorial@auburnvillager.com

Auburn Corner News (10.0M) 117 N College St Auburn AL 36830 **Phn:** 334-821-7150 **Fax:** 334-887-0037 www.thecornernews.com dbrown@thecornernews.com

Bay Minette Baldwin Times (3.0M) PO Box 519 Bay Minette AL 36507 **Phn:** 251-937-2511 **Fax:** 251-937-1831 gulfcoastnewstoday.com timeseditor@gulfcoastnewspapers.com

Bessemer Western Star (6.5M) PO Box 1900 Bessemer AL 35021 **Phn:** 205-424-7827 **Fax:** 205-424-8118

Birmingham Alabama Messenger (1.5M) 205 20th St N Ste 706 Birmingham AL 35203 **Phn:** 205-252-3672 **Fax:** 205-252-3679 www.alabamamessenger.com alamsgr@bellsouth.net

Birmingham Birmingham Weekly (30.0M) 2014 6th Ave N Birmingham AL 35203 **Phn:** 205-939-4030 **Fax:** 205-212-1005 www.bhamweekly.com editor@bhamweekly.com

Birmingham Over the Mountain Jrnl. (40.0M) 2016 Columbiana Rd Birmingham AL 35216 **Phn:** 205-823-9646 **Fax:** 205-824-1246 www.otmj.com editorial@otmj.com

Brewton Brewton Standard (3.3M) PO Box 887 Brewton AL 36427 **Phn:** 251-867-4876 **Fax:** 251-867-4877 www.brewtonstandard.com newsroom@brewtonstandard.com

Camden Wilcox Progressive Era (3.1M) PO Box 100 Camden AL 36726 **Phn:** 334-682-4422 **Fax:** 334-682-5163 progressiveera@mchsi.com

Carbon Hill Corridor Messenger (15.0M) PO Box 290 Carbon Hill AL 35549 **Phn:** 205-282-4500 **Fax:** 205-942-0040 www.corridormessenger.com tanya@corridormessenger.com

Carrollton Pickens County Herald (4.5M) PO Box 390 Carrollton AL 35447 **Phn:** 205-367-2217 pcherald.com pickenscnty@centurytel.net

Centre Cherokee County Herald (3.4M) 1460-E West Main St Centre AL 35960 **Phn:** 256-927-5037 **Fax:** 256-927-4853 www.northwestgeorgianews.com/cherokee_county tdean@cherokeeherald.com

Centre Cherokee Post (15.0M) 100 E Main St Centre AL 35960 **Phn:** 256-927-4476 **Fax:** 256-927-7678 www.postpaper.com swright@postpaper.com

Centreville Centreville Press (4.2M) PO Box 127 Centreville AL 35042 **Phn:** 205-926-9769 **Fax:** 205-926-9760 lorrie@centrevillepress.com

Chatom Washington County News (4.0M) PO Box 510 Chatom AL 36518 **Phn:** 251-847-2599 **Fax:** 251-847-3847 www.washcountynews.com williegray@thecallnews.com

Citronelle Call-News (4.2M) 7870 State St Citronelle AL 36522 **Phn:** 251-866-5998 **Fax:** 251-866-5981 www.thecallnews.com williegray@thecallnews.com

Clanton Chilton County News (3.0M) PO Box 189 Clanton AL 35046 **Phn:** 205-755-0110 http:/www.ChiltonCountyNews.com newscc@bellsouth.net

Clayton Clayton Record (2.5M) PO Box 69 Clayton AL 36016 **Phn:** 334-775-3254 **Fax:** 334-775-8554 www.theclaytonrecordonline.com claytonrecord@earthlink.net

Columbiana Shelby County Reporter (15.6M) PO Box 947 Columbiana AL 35051 **Phn:** 205-669-3131 **Fax:** 205-669-4217 www.shelbycountyreporter.com tim.prince@shelbycountyreporter.com

Cullman Cullman Tribune (15.0M) 219 2nd Ave SE Cullman AL 35055 **Phn:** 256-739-1351 **Fax:** 256-739-4422

Daphne Daphne Bulletin (6.6M) PO Box 1560 Daphne AL 36526 **Phn:** 251-626-9300 **Fax:** 251-626-0144 www.gulfcoastnewstoday.com/the_bulletin bulletin@gulfcoastnewspapers.com

Daphne The Sun (3.5M) PO Box 1560 Daphne AL 36526 **Phn:** 251-626-9300 **Fax:** 251-626-0144 www.baldwincountynow.com

Demopolis Demopolis Times (5.0M) PO Box 860 Demopolis AL 36732 **Phn:** 334-289-4017 **Fax:** 334-289-4019 www.demopolistimes.com

Dothan Dothan Progress (25.5M) PO Box 1968 Dothan AL 36302 **Phn:** 334-792-3141 **Fax:** 334-712-7979 www.dothaneagle.com/news/dothan_progress ebrackin@dothanprogress.com

Elba Elba Clipper (3.2M) PO Box 677 Elba AL 36323 **Phn:** 334-897-2823 **Fax:** 334-897-3434 www.elba-clipper.com clipper@alaweb.com

Enterprise The Southeast Sun/Daleville Sun Courier (6.5M) PO Box 311546 Enterprise AL 36331 **Phn:** 334-393-2969 **Fax:** 334-393-2987 www.southeastsun.com news@southeastsun.com

Eufaula Eufaula Tribune (6.5M) PO Box 628 Eufaula AL 36072 **Phn:** 334-687-3506 **Fax:** 334-687-3229 www.dothaneagle.com/eufaula_tribune editorial@eufaulatribune.com

Eutaw Greene County Democrat (3.5M) PO Box 598 Eutaw AL 35462 **Phn:** 205-372-3373 **Fax:** 205-372-2243 greenecountydemocrat.com jzippert@aol.com

Eutaw Greene County Independent (1.2M) 106 Main St Eutaw AL 35462 **Phn:** 205-372-2232 **Fax:** 205-372-1082 greenecoind@aol.com

Evergreen Evergreen Courant (3.8M) PO Box 440 Evergreen AL 36401 **Phn:** 251-578-1492 **Fax:** 251-578-1496 evergreencourant@earthlink.net

Fairhope Fairhope Courier (4.7M) PO Box 549 Fairhope AL 36533 **Phn:** 251-928-2321 **Fax:** 251-928-9963 www.baldwincountynow.com courier@gulfcoastnewspapers.com

Fayette The Times Record (5.0M) PO Box 159 Fayette AL 35555 **Phn:** 205-932-6271 **Fax:** 205-932-6998 www.mytrpaper.com trnews@centurytel.net

Flomaton Tri-City Ledger (5.4M) PO Box 1916 Flomaton AL 36441 **Phn:** 251-296-3491 **Fax:** 251-296-0010 newsroom@tricityledger.com

Florala Florala News (1.6M) 1155 5th St Florala AL 36442 **Phn:** 334-858-3342 **Fax:** 334-858-3786 floralanews@fairpoint.net

Florence Courier Journal (62.8M) 1828 Darby Dr Florence AL 35630 **Phn:** 256-764-4268 **Fax:** 256-760-9618 www.courierjournal.net editor@courierjournal.net

Foley The Onlooker (4.6M) 217 N McKenzie St Foley AL 36535 **Phn:** 251-943-2151 **Fax:** 251-943-3441 www.baldwincountynow.com onlooker@gulfcoastnewspapers.com

Fort Payne De Kalb Advertiser (6.0M) PO Box 680559 Fort Payne AL 35968 **Phn:** 256-845-6156 **Fax:** 256-845-1105

Fort Payne The Weekly Post (5.0M) PO Box 680349 Fort Payne AL 35968 **Phn:** 256-638-4027 **Fax:** 256-638-2329

Gadsden The Gadsden Messenger (6.1M) 630 Broad St Gadsden AL 35901 **Phn:** 256-547-1049 **Fax:** 256-547-1011 www.gadsdenmessenger.com editor@gadsdenmessenger.com

Gardendale North Jefferson News (6.0M) PO Box 849 Gardendale AL 35071 **Phn:** 205-631-8716 **Fax:** 205-631-9902 www.njeffersonnews.com newsroom@njeffersonnews.com

Geneva Geneva County Reaper (2.5M) PO Box 160 Geneva AL 36340 **Phn:** 334-684-2280 **Fax:** 334-684-3099 oppnewsonline.com genevacountyreaper@centurytel.net

Geneva Hartford News Herald (0.8M) PO Box 160 Geneva AL 36340 **Phn:** 334-684-2280 **Fax:** 334-684-3099 oppnewsonline.com news@genevareaper.com

Geneva Samson Ledger (0.8M) PO Box 160 Geneva AL 36340 **Phn:** 334-684-2280 **Fax:** 334-684-3099 oppnewsonline.com news@genevareaper.com

Georgiana Butler County News (2.0M) PO Box 620 Georgiana AL 36033 **Phn:** 334-382-3111 **Fax:** 334-382-7104 www.boonenewspapers.com

Gilbertown Choctaw Sun-Advocate (4.2M) PO Box 269 Gilbertown AL 36908 **Phn:** 251-843-6397 **Fax:** 251-843-3233 choctawsun.com letters@choctawsun.com

Greensboro The Greensboro Watchman (2.8M) PO Box 550 Greensboro AL 36744 **Phn:** 334-624-8323 **Fax:** 334-624-8327 gwatchman@bellsouth.net

Greenville Greenville Advocate (13.0M) PO Box 507 Greenville AL 36037 **Phn:** 334-382-3111 **Fax:** 334-382-7104 www.greenvilleadvocate.com andy.brown@greenvilleadvocate.com

Greenville Lowndes Signal (1.9M) PO Box 507 Greenville AL 36037 **Phn:** 334-382-3111 **Fax:** 334-382-7104 www.boonenewspapers.com/community/lowndes.shtml

Grove Hill Clarke County Democrat (5.0M) PO Box 39 Grove Hill AL 36451 **Phn:** 251-275-3375 **Fax:** 251-275-3060 www.clarkecountydemocrat.com clarkecountydem@tds.net

Gulf Shores The Islander (4.0M) PO Box 1128 Gulf Shores AL 36547 **Phn:** 251-968-6414 **Fax:** 251-968-5233 www.baldwincountynow.com theislander@gulfcoastnewspapers.com

Guntersville The Advertiser-Gleam (11.7M) PO Box 190 Guntersville AL 35976 **Phn:** 256-582-3232 www.advertisergleam.com news@advertisergleam.com

Haleyville Northwest Alabaman (7.5M) PO Box 430 Haleyville AL 35565 **Phn:** 205-486-9461 **Fax:** 205-486-4849 www.mynwapaper.com nwamoore@centurytel.net

Hamilton Journal Record (8.3M) PO Box 1477 Hamilton AL 35570 **Phn:** 205-921-3104 **Fax:** 205-921-3105 myjrpaper.com jrpaper@centurytel.net

Hanceville The Blount Banner (5.0M) PO Box 290 Hanceville AL 35077 **Phn:** 256-352-4775 **Fax:** 256-352-0224 heraldt@bellsouth.net

Hanceville The Clarion (1.5M) PO Box 290 Hanceville AL 35077 **Phn:** 256-352-4775 **Fax:** 256-352-0224 www.bannerheraldnewspapers.com/c heraldt@bellsouth.net

Hanceville The News-Herald (5.0M) PO Box 290 Hanceville AL 35077 **Phn:** 256-352-4775 **Fax:** 256-352-0224 www.bannerheraldnewspapers.com/c heraldt@bellsouth.net

Hartselle Hartselle Enquirer (7.0M) PO Box 929 Hartselle AL 35640 **Phn:** 256-773-6566 **Fax:** 256-773-1953 www.hartselleenquirer.com news@hartselleenquirer.com

Heflin The Cleburne News (3.5M) PO Box 67 Heflin AL 36264 **Phn:** 256-463-2872 **Fax:** 256-463-7127 www.annistonstar.com/news_cleburne news@cleburnenews.com

Jackson The South Alabamian (4.8M) PO Box 68 Jackson AL 36545 **Phn:** 251-246-4494 **Fax:** 251-246-7486 www.southalabamian.com news@thesouthalabamian.com

Lafayette Lafayette Sun (3.0M) PO Box 378 Lafayette AL 36862 **Phn:** 334-864-8885 **Fax:** 334-864-8310

Leeds Leeds News (5.5M) 8024 Parkway Dr Leeds AL 35094 **Phn:** 205-699-2214 **Fax:** 205-699-3157 www.theleedsnews.net

Linden The Democrat-Reporter (8.0M) PO Box 480040 Linden AL 36748 **Phn:** 334-295-5224 **Fax:** 334-295-5563 dreporter2@yahoo.com

Lineville Clay Times Journal (4.0M) PO Box 97 Lineville AL 36266 **Phn:** 256-396-5760 www.theclaytimesjournal.com timesjournal@centurytel.net

Livingston Sumter Co. Record Journal (5.1M) PO Box B Livingston AL 35470 **Phn:** 205-652-6100 **Fax:** 205-652-4466 www.recordjournal.net scrjmedia@yahoo.com

Luverne Luverne Journal (9.3M) PO Box 152 Luverne AL 36049 **Phn:** 334-335-3541 **Fax:** 334-335-4299 www.greenvilleadvocate.com/category/luverne regina.grayson@luvernejournal.com

Madison Madison Record (12.0M) PO Box 859 Madison AL 35758 **Phn:** 256-772-6677 **Fax:** 256-772-6655 www.madisoncountyrecord.com news@madisoncountyrecord.com

Marion Marion Times-Standard (2.3M) PO Box 418 Marion AL 36756 **Phn:** 334-683-6318 **Fax:** 334-683-4616

Millbrook Millbrook Independent (8.0M) PO Box 566 Millbrook AL 36054 **Phn:** 334-285-1299 **Fax:** 334-285-1468 news@millbrookindependent.com

Millport West Alabama Gazette (4.2M) PO Box 249 Millport AL 35576 **Phn:** 205-662-4296 **Fax:** 205-662-4740 gazettenews@frontiernet.net

Mobile Mobile Beacon (5.0M) PO Box 1407 Mobile AL 36633 **Phn:** 251-479-0629 **Fax:** 251-479-0610 mobilebeaconinc@bellsouth.net

ALABAMA WEEKLY NEWSPAPERS

Monroeville Monroe Journal (7.7M) PO Box 826 Monroeville AL 36461 **Phn:** 251-575-3282 **Fax:** 251-575-3284 www.monroejournal.com news@monroejournal.com

Montgomery Montgomery Independent (6.3M) 141 Market Pl Montgomery AL 36117 **Phn:** 334-265-7323 **Fax:** 334-265-7320 www.themontgomeryindependent.com bob@montgomeryindependent.com

Moulton The Moulton Advertiser (13.0M) PO Box 517 Moulton AL 35650 **Phn:** 256-974-1114 **Fax:** 256-974-3097 www.moultonadvertiser.com editor@moultonadvertiser.com

Moundville Moundville Times (1.6M) PO Box 683 Moundville AL 35474 **Phn:** 205-371-2488 **Fax:** 205-371-2788 times@mound.net

Northport Northport Gazette (8.0M) 401 20th Ave Ste 5 Northport AL 35476 **Phn:** 205-759-3091 **Fax:** 205-759-5449 www.northportgazette.com northportgazette@northportgazette.com

Oneonta Blount Countian (6.7M) PO Box 310 Oneonta AL 35121 **Phn:** 205-625-3231 **Fax:** 205-625-3239 www.blountcountian.com robrice@otelco.net

Opp The Opp News (5.5M) PO Box 870 Opp AL 36467 **Phn:** 334-493-3595 **Fax:** 334-493-4901 oppnewsonline.com opppublisher@centurytel.net

Ozark The Southern Star (4.7M) PO Box 1729 Ozark AL 36361 **Phn:** 334-774-2715 **Fax:** 334-774-9619

Pell City St. Clair News-Aegis (6.0M) PO Box 750 Pell City AL 35125 **Phn:** 205-884-2310 **Fax:** 205-884-2312 www.newsaegis.com editor@newsaegis.com

Pell City St. Clair Times (36.0M) 1911 Martin St S Ste 7 Pell City AL 35128 **Phn:** 205-884-3400 **Fax:** 205-814-9194 www.dailyhome.com jkeith@dailyhome.com

Phenix City The Citizen of East Alabama (16.5M) 2400 Sportsman Dr Phenix City AL 36867 **Phn:** 334-664-0145 **Fax:** 334-298-0833

Prattville Prattville Progress (8.0M) 152 W 3rd St Prattville AL 36067 **Phn:** 334-365-6739 **Fax:** 334-365-1400 progress.montgomeryadvertiser.com tmanning@gannett.com

Red Bay The News (3.5M) PO Box 1339 Red Bay AL 35582 **Phn:** 256-356-2148 **Fax:** 256-356-2787 rbnews@hiwaay.net

Roanoke Randolph Leader (6.8M) PO Box 1267 Roanoke AL 36274 **Phn:** 334-863-2819 **Fax:** 334-863-4006 www.therandolphleader.com john@therandolphleader.com

Robertsdale The Independent (2.7M) PO Box 509 Robertsdale AL 36567 **Phn:** 251-947-7318 **Fax:** 251-947-7652 www.baldwincountynow.com independent@gulfcoastnewspapers.com

Rockford Coosa County News (1.4M) PO Box 99 Rockford AL 35136 **Phn:** 256-377-2525 **Fax:** 256-377-2422 www.coosanews.com

Rogersville East Lauderdale News (4.5M) PO Box 479 Rogersville AL 35652 **Phn:** 256-247-5565 **Fax:** 256-247-1902 elnewsrog@aol.com

Russellville Franklin County Times (5.0M) PO Box 1088 Russellville AL 35653 **Phn:** 256-332-1881 **Fax:** 256-332-1883 www.franklincountytimes.com jonathan.willis@franklincountytimes.com

Stevenson North Jackson Progress (5.0M) PO Box 625 Stevenson AL 35772 **Phn:** 256-437-2395 **Fax:** 256-437-2592 njprogresslog@aol.com

Sulligent Lamar Leader (3.4M) PO Box 988 Sulligent AL 35586 **Phn:** 205-698-8148 **Fax:** 205-698-8146 lamarleader@yahoo.com

Tallassee Tallassee Tribune (4.0M) 301 Gilmer Ave Tallassee AL 36078 **Phn:** 334-283-6568 **Fax:** 334-283-6569 editor@tallasseetribune.com

Thomasville Thomasville Times (3.7M) PO Box 367 Thomasville AL 36784 **Phn:** 334-636-2214 **Fax:** 334-636-9822 www.thethomasvilletimes.com newsroom@thethomasvilletimes.com

Tuscaloosa T-News Weekly (22.0M) 315 28th Ave Tuscaloosa AL 35401 **Phn:** 205-345-0505 **Fax:** 205-722-0187 www.tuscaloosanews.com robert.dewitt@tuscaloosanews.com

Tuscumbia Colbert County Reporter (4.5M) PO Box 969 Tuscumbia AL 35674 **Phn:** 256-383-8471 **Fax:** 256-383-8476 colbertcountyreporter@earthlink.net

Tuscumbia Standard & Times (1.2M) PO Box 969 Tuscumbia AL 35674 **Phn:** 256-383-8471 **Fax:** 256-383-8476 colbertcountyreporter@earthlink.net

Union Springs The Herald (3.1M) PO Box 600 Union Springs AL 36089 **Phn:** 334-738-2360 **Fax:** 334-738-2342

Vernon Lamar Democrat (3.0M) PO Box 587 Vernon AL 35592 **Phn:** 205-695-7029 **Fax:** 205-695-9501

Wetumpka Eclectic Observer (1.2M) PO Box 99 Wetumpka AL 36092 **Phn:** 334-567-7811 **Fax:** 334-567-3284 www.thewetumpkaherald.com/eclectic_observer news@thewetumpkaherald.com

Wetumpka Wetumpka Herald (5.6M) PO Box 99 Wetumpka AL 36092 **Phn:** 334-567-7811 **Fax:** 334-567-3284 www.thewetumpkaherald.com news@thewetumpkaherald.com

ALASKA

Anchorage Anchorage Press (20.0M) 540 E 5th Ave Anchorage AK 99501 **Phn:** 907-561-7737 **Fax:** 907-561-7777 www.anchoragepress.com editor@anchoragepress.com

Anchorage Arctic Sounder (2.5M) PO Box 241582 Anchorage AK 99524 **Phn:** 907-348-2432 **Fax:** 907-770-0822 www.thearcticsounder.com crestino@reportalaska.com

Anchorage Dutch Harbor Fisherman (1.2M) 500 W International Airport Rd # F Anchorage AK 99518 **Phn:** 907-770-0820 **Fax:** 907-770-0822 www.thedutchharborfisherman.com jpaulin@reportalaska.com

Anchorage Seward Phoenix Log (2.0M) 301 Calista Ct Ste B Anchorage AK 99518 **Phn:** 907-348-2428 **Fax:** 907-272-9512 www.thesewardphoenixlog.com ahall@alaskanewspapers.com

Anchorage Tundra Drums (4.2M) 301 Calista Ct Ste B Anchorage AK 99518 **Phn:** 907-272-9830 **Fax:** 907-272-9512 www.thetundradrums.com ahall@alaskanewspapers.com

Cordova Cordova Times (1.1M) PO Box 200 Cordova AK 99574 **Phn:** 907-424-7181 **Fax:** 907-424-5799 www.thecordovatimes.com cdvtimes@alaskanewspapers.com

Delta Junction Delta Wind (1.3M) PO Box 986 Delta Junction AK 99737 **Phn:** 907-895-5115 **Fax:** 907-895-5116 editor@deltawindonline.com

Dillingham Bristol Bay Times (1.6M) PO Box 1770 Dillingham AK 99576 **Phn:** 907-348-2432 **Fax:** 907-272-9512 www.thebristolbaytimes.com baytimes@alaskanewspapers.com

Eagle River Alaska Star (8.5M) 16941 N Eagle River Loop Rd Eagle River AK 99577 **Phn:** 907-694-2727 **Fax:** 907-694-1545 www.alaskastar.com news@alaskastar.com

Haines Chilkat Valley News (1.1M) PO Box 630 Haines AK 99827 **Phn:** 907-766-2688 **Fax:** 907-766-2689 www.chilkatvalleynews.com cvn@chilkatvalleynews.com

Homer Homer News (4.0M) 3482 Landings St Homer AK 99603 **Phn:** 907-235-7767 **Fax:** 907-235-4199 www.homernews.com news@homernews.com

Homer Homer Tribune (4.5M) 435 E Pioneer Ave Homer AK 99603 **Phn:** 907-235-3714 **Fax:** 907-235-3716 homertribune.com

Juneau Capital City Weekly (10.0M) 134 N Franklin St Juneau AK 99801 **Phn:** 907-789-4144 **Fax:** 907-789-0987 capitalcityweekly.com editor@capweek.com

Kenai Clarion Dispatch (10.0M) PO Box 3009 Kenai AK 99611 **Phn:** 907-283-7551 **Fax:** 907-283-8144 www.peninsulaclarion.com leslie.talent@peninsulaclarion.com

Nome Nome Nugget (6.0M) PO Box 610 Nome AK 99762 **Phn:** 907-443-5235 **Fax:** 907-443-5112 www.nomenugget.net nugget@nomenugget.com

Petersburg Petersburg Pilot (1.6M) PO Box 930 Petersburg AK 99833 **Phn:** 907-772-9393 **Fax:** 907-772-4871 www.petersburgpilot.com psgpub@gci.net

Skagway Skagway News (1.2M) PO Box 498 Skagway AK 99840 **Phn:** 907-983-2354 **Fax:** 907-983-2356 www.skagwaynews.com skagnews@aptalaska.net

Thorne Bay The Island News (2.0M) PO Box 19430 Thorne Bay AK 99919 **Phn:** 907-828-3377 **Fax:** 907-828-3351 www.smalltownpapers.com islandnews@starband.net

Tok Mukluk News (0.7M) 90 Midnight Sun Dr Tok AK 99780 **Phn:** 907-883-2571

Valdez Valdez Star (2.0M) PO Box 2949 Valdez AK 99686 **Phn:** 907-835-3881 **Fax:** 907-835-3882 valdezstar.net info@valdezstar.net

Wasilla Frontiersman (4.0M) PO Box 873509 Wasilla AK 99687 **Phn:** 907-352-2250 **Fax:** 907-352-2277 www.frontiersman.com news@frontiersman.com

Wrangell Wrangell Sentinel (1.4M) PO Box 798 Wrangell AK 99929 **Phn:** 907-874-2301 **Fax:** 907-874-2303 www.wrangellsentinel.com wrgsent@gmail.com

ARIZONA

Ajo Ajo Copper News (1.7M) PO Box 39 Ajo AZ 85321 **Phn:** 520-387-7688 **Fax:** 520-387-7505 www.cunews.info cunews@cunews.info

Apache Junction Apache Junction News (23.0M) 1075 S Idaho Rd # 102 Apache Junction AZ 85119 **Phn:** 480-982-6397 **Fax:** 480-982-3707 www.ajnews.com ajnews@ajnews.com

Apache Junction Apache Junction/Gold Canyon Independent (18.0M) 850 S Ironwood Dr Ste 112 Apache Junction AZ 85120 **Phn:** 480-982-7799 **Fax:** 480-671-0016 arizona.newszap.com ajeditor@newszap.com

Apache Junction East Mesa Independent (25.0M) 850 S Ironwood Dr Ste 112 Apache Junction AZ 85120 **Phn:** 480-982-7799 **Fax:** 480-671-0016 www.newszap.com emesanews@newszap.com

Avondale West Valley View (79.0M) 1050 E Riley Dr Avondale AZ 85323 **Phn:** 623-535-8439 **Fax:** 623-935-2103 www.westvalleyview.com editor@westvalleyview.com

Benson San Pedro Valley News-Sun (3.7M) PO Box 1000 Benson AZ 85602 **Phn:** 520-586-3382 **Fax:** 520-586-2382 www.bensonnews-sun.com newssun@bensonnews-sun.com

Bisbee Bisbee Observer (2.2M) 7 Bisbee Rd Ste L Bisbee AZ 85603 **Phn:** 520-432-7254 **Fax:** 520-432-4192 www.thebisbeeobserver.com bisbeeobserver@cableone.net

Buckeye Buckeye Star (5.0M) 111 E Monroe Ave # 101 Buckeye AZ 85326 **Phn:** 623-374-4303 **Fax:** 623-322-9686 thebuckeyestar.net publisher@thebuckeyestar.net

Buckeye Buckeye Valley News (2.7M) PO Box 217 Buckeye AZ 85326 **Phn:** 623-386-4426 **Fax:** 623-386-4427 www.buckeyevalleynews.net bvalnews@buckeyevalleynews.org

Bullhead City Bullhead City Bee (2.0M) 1905 Lakeside Dr Bullhead City AZ 86442 **Phn:** 928-763-9339 **Fax:** 928-763-1510 www.bullheadcity-bee.com buzzybee3@bullheadcity-bee.com

Camp Verde Camp Verde Journal (2.4M) PO Box 2048 Camp Verde AZ 86322 **Phn:** 928-567-3341 **Fax:** 928-567-2373 www.journalaz.com cveditor@larsonnewspapers.com

Carefree Desert Advocate (35.0M) PO Box 1380 Carefree AZ 85377 **Phn:** 480-488-1204

Cave Creek Sonoran News (38.5M) 6702 E Cave Creek Rd Ste 3 Cave Creek AZ 85331 **Phn:** 480-488-2021 **Fax:** 480-488-6216 www.sonorannews.com sonnews@aol.com

Chandler SanTan Sun News (38.0M) PO Box 23 Chandler AZ 85244 **Phn:** 480-732-0250 **Fax:** 480-883-8714 www.santansun.com news@santansun.com

Clifton The Copper Era (2.7M) 1 Ward Canyon Rd Clifton AZ 85533 **Phn:** 928-865-3162 **Fax:** 928-428-4901 www.eacourier.com/copper_era editor@eacourier.com

Coolidge Coolidge Examiner (2.3M) 353 W Central Ave Coolidge AZ 85128 **Phn:** 520-723-5441 **Fax:** 520-723-7899 www.trivalleycentral.com coolidgeexaminer@yahoo.com

Cottonwood Cottonwood Journal Extra (8.4M) PO Box 2266 Cottonwood AZ 86326 **Phn:** 928-634-8551 **Fax:** 928-634-0823 www.journalaz.com editor@larsonnewspapers.com

Cottonwood Verde Independent (3.2M) PO Box 429 Cottonwood AZ 86326 **Phn:** 928-634-2241 **Fax:** 928-634-2312 verdenews.com dengler@verdevalleynews.com

Eloy Enterprise (1.0M) PO Box 668 Eloy AZ 85131 **Phn:** 520-466-7333 **Fax:** 520-466-7334 trivalleycentral.com editor@eloyenterprise.com

Flagstaff Flagstaff Live (8.3M) 1751 S Thompson St Flagstaff AZ 86001 **Phn:** 928-774-4545 **Fax:** 928-773-1934 www.flaglive.com calendar@flaglive.com

Flagstaff Navajo Hopi Observer (15.0M) 2217 N 4th St Ste 110 Flagstaff AZ 86004 **Phn:** 928-226-9696 **Fax:** 928-226-1115 www.nhonews.com nhoeditorial@nhonews.com

Florence Florence Reminder (1.6M) PO Box 910 Florence AZ 85132 **Phn:** 520-868-5897 **Fax:** 520-868-5898 www.trivalleycentral.com info@florencereminder.com

Fountain Hills Fountain Hills Times (5.5M) PO Box 17869 Fountain Hills AZ 85269 **Phn:** 480-837-1925 **Fax:** 480-837-1951 www.fhtimes.com mike@fhtimes.com

Gila Bend Gila Bend Sun (12.4M) PO Box Z Gila Bend AZ 85337 **Phn:** 928-683-2393 **Fax:** 623-386-7495 gilabendsun.com gilasun@earthlink.net

Glendale Glendale Star (12.0M) 7122 N 59th Ave Glendale AZ 85301 **Phn:** 623-842-6000 **Fax:** 623-842-6013 www.glendalestar.com cdryer@star-times.com

Glendale Peoria Times (8.0M) 7122 N 59th Ave Glendale AZ 85301 **Phn:** 623-842-6000 **Fax:** 623-842-6013 www.peoriatimes.com cdryer@star-times.com

Globe Apache Moccasin (1.9M) PO Box 31 Globe AZ 85502 **Phn:** 928-425-7121 **Fax:** 928-425-7001 www.silverbelt.com news@silverbelt.com

Globe Arizona Silver Belt (5.0M) PO Box 31 Globe AZ 85502 **Phn:** 928-425-7121 **Fax:** 928-425-7001 www.silverbelt.com news@silverbelt.com

Globe Copper County News (20.0M) 1776 E Ash St Ste B Globe AZ 85501 **Phn:** 928-425-0355 **Fax:** 928-425-6535 globeccn@yahoo.com

Goodyear The Wester (30.0M) 14950 W Indian School Rd Ste 140 Goodyear AZ 85395 **Phn:** 623-584-2992 **Fax:** 623-584-0950

Green Valley Green Valley News-Sun (12.0M) PO Box 567 Green Valley AZ 85622 **Phn:** 520-625-5511 **Fax:** 520-625-1603 www.gvnews.com dshearer@gvnews.com

Green Valley Sahuarita Sun (13.4M) PO Box 567 Green Valley AZ 85622 **Phn:** 520-625-5511 **Fax:** 520-625-8046 www.gvnews.com/sahuarita_sun editorial@gvnews.com

Heber Mogollon Connection (1.8M) PO Box 43 Heber AZ 85928 **Phn:** 928-535-5791 **Fax:** 928-535-6210 www.azalert.com/mc mogollonconnection@yahoo.com

Holbrook Holbrook Tribune-News (5.8M) PO Box 670 Holbrook AZ 86025 **Phn:** 928-524-6203 **Fax:** 928-524-3541 www.azjournal.com tribunenews@cableone.net

Holbrook Silver Creek Herald (2.0M) PO Box 670 Holbrook AZ 86025 **Phn:** 928-524-6203 **Fax:** 928-524-3541 www.azjournal.com lkor@cableone.net

Kearny Copper Basin News (2.5M) PO Box 579 Kearny AZ 85137 **Phn:** 520-363-5554 **Fax:** 520-363-9663 www.copperarea.com mineeditor@gmail.com

Maricopa Maricopa Monitor (3.6M) PO Box 1347 Maricopa AZ 85139 **Phn:** 520-568-4198 **Fax:** 520-568-4729 www.trivalleycentral.com sridenour@trivalleycentral.com

New River Foothills Focus (30.0M) 46641 N Black Canyon Hwy Ste 1 New River AZ 85087 **Phn:** 623-465-5808 **Fax:** 623-465-1363 www.thefoothillsfocus.com foothillsfocus@qwestoffice.net

Nogales Nogales International (5.0M) 260 W View Point Dr Nogales AZ 85621 **Phn:** 520-375-5763 **Fax:** 520-761-3115 www.nogalesinternational.com editorial@nogalesinternational.com

Nogales The Bulletin (1.5M) 268 W View Point Dr Nogales AZ 85621 **Phn:** 520-455-4776 **Fax:** 520-455-5351 www.nogalesinternational.com editorial@nogalesinternational.com

Page Lake Powell Chronicle (3.0M) PO Box 1716 Page AZ 86040 **Phn:** 928-645-8888 **Fax:** 928-645-2209 www.lakepowellchronicle.com leepulaski@lakepowellchronicle.com

Parker Parker Pioneer (4.9M) PO Box 3365 Parker AZ 85344 **Phn:** 928-669-2275 **Fax:** 928-669-9624 www.parkerpioneer.net quinn@havasunews.com

Payson Payson Roundup (7.0M) PO Box 2520 Payson AZ 85547 **Phn:** 928-474-5251 **Fax:** 928-474-1893 www.paysonroundup.com editor@payson.com

Payson Rim County Gazette (5.0M) 7736 N Toya Vista Rd Payson AZ 85541 **Phn:** 928-474-8787 www.rimcountrygazette.blogspot.com peoplesgazette@gmail.com

Phoenix Ahwatukee Foothills News (33.0M) 10631 S 51st St Ste 1 Phoenix AZ 85044 **Phn:** 480-898-7900 **Fax:** 480-893-1684 www.ahwatukee.com ewhitmore@ahwatukee.com

Phoenix Arizona Capitol Times (5.0M) PO Box 2260 Phoenix AZ 85002 **Phn:** 602-258-7026 **Fax:** 602-253-7636 azcapitoltimes.com editor@azcapitoltimes.com

Prescott Big Bug News (3.6M) PO Box 312 Prescott AZ 86302 **Phn:** 928-445-3333 **Fax:** 928-772-3393 bigbugnews.com hdfoster@prescottaz.com

Prescott Chino Valley Review (7.6M) PO Box 312 Prescott AZ 86302 **Phn:** 928-445-3333 **Fax:** 928-772-3393 www.cvrnews.com hdfoster@prescottaz.com

Prescott Prescott Valley Tribune (15.3M) PO Box 312 Prescott AZ 86302 **Phn:** 928-445-3333 **Fax:** 928-772-3393 pvtrib.com hdfoster@prescottaz.com

Safford Eastern Arizona Courier (10.0M) 301 E Hwy 70 # A Safford AZ 85546 **Phn:** 928-428-2560 **Fax:** 928-428-4901 www.eacourier.com editor@eacourier.com

San Manuel San Manuel Miner (3.5M) PO Box 60 San Manuel AZ 85631 **Phn:** 520-385-2266 **Fax:** 520-385-4666 www.copperarea.com minereditor@gmail.com

Scottsdale Independent Newspapers (35.5M) 11000 N Scottsdale Rd Ste 210 Scottsdale AZ 85254 **Phn:** 480-483-0977 **Fax:** 480-948-0496 arizona.newszap.com/northvalley nscottsdalenews@newszap.com

Scottsdale Times Publications (35.5M) 3200 N Hayden # 210 Scottsdale AZ 85251 **Phn:** 480-348-0343 **Fax:** 480-348-2109 www.timespublications.com info@timespublications.com

Sedona Red Rock News (8.0M) PO Box 619 Sedona AZ 86339 **Phn:** 928-282-7795 **Fax:** 928-282-6011 www.redrocknews.com

Show Low White Mountain Independent (8.7M) PO Box 1570 Show Low AZ 85902 **Phn:** 928-537-5721 **Fax:** 928-537-1780 www.wmicentral.com sdieterich@wmicentral.com

Sierra Vista Mountain View News (8.0M) 1835 Paseo San Luis Sierra Vista AZ 85635 **Phn:** 520-458-3340 **Fax:** 520-458-9338 www.mtviewnews.com mvnews@c2i2.com

Sun City Independent Newspapers (79.0M) 17720 N Boswell Blvd # L101 Sun City AZ 85373 **Phn:** 623-972-6101 **Fax:** 623-974-6004 arizona.newszap.com publishyournews@newszap.com

Sun City Surprise Today (39.0M) PO Box 1779 Sun City AZ 85372 **Phn:** 623-977-8351 **Fax:** 623-876-3689

Superior Superior Sun (1.3M) 467 W Main St Superior AZ 85173 **Phn:** 520-363-5554 **Fax:** 520-363-9663 www.copperarea.com

Tempe Wrangler News (20.0M) 2145 E Warner Rd Ste 102 Tempe AZ 85284 **Phn:** 480-966-0845 www.wranglernews.com editor@wranglernews.com

Tombstone Tombstone News (1.0M) PO Box 1760 Tombstone AZ 85638 **Phn:** 520-457-3086 **Fax:** 520-457-3126 thetombstonenews.com editor@thetombstonenews.com

Tucson Explorer Newspaper (47.0M) 7225 N Mona Lisa Rd Ste 125 Tucson AZ 85741 **Phn:** 520-797-4384 **Fax:** 520-575-8891 explorernews.com editor@explorernews.com

Tucson Marana Weekly News (6.0M) 3029 S Kinney Rd Tucson AZ 85713 **Phn:** 520-578-1505 **Fax:** 520-908-0455 www.maranaweeklynews.com news@maranaweeklynews.com

Tucson Tucson Observer (5.0M) PO Box 50733 Tucson AZ 85703 **Phn:** 520-622-7176 www.tucsonobserver.com

Tucson Tucson Weekly (50.0M) PO Box 27087 Tucson AZ 85726 **Phn:** 520-294-1200 **Fax:** 520-294-4040 www.tucsonweekly.com mailbag@tucsonweekly.com

Vail Vail Sun (14.0M) PO Box 746 Vail AZ 85641 **Phn:** 520-762-0038 **Fax:** 520-762-0128

Whiteriver Ft. Apache Scout (3.0M) PO Box 890 Whiteriver AZ 85941 **Phn:** 928-338-4813 **Fax:** 928-338-1894 zenyks74@yahoo.com

Wickenburg The Wickenburg Sun (3.8M) 180 N Washington St Wickenburg AZ 85390 **Phn:** 928-684-5454 **Fax:** 928-684-3185 www.wickenburgsun.com editor@wickenburgsun.com

Willcox Arizona Range News (3.2M) PO Box 1155 Willcox AZ 85644 **Phn:** 520-384-3571 **Fax:** 520-384-3572 www.willcoxrangenews.com rangenews@willcoxrangenews.com

Williams Williams Grand Canyon News (3.2M) PO Box 667 Williams AZ 86046 **Phn:** 928-635-4426 **Fax:** 928-635-4887 www.williamsnews.com editorial@williamsnews.com

Window Rock Navajo Times (25.0M) PO Box 310 Window Rock AZ 86515 **Phn:** 928-871-1130 **Fax:** 928-871-1159 navajotimes.com tarviso@navajotimes.com

ARKANSAS

Ashdown Little River News (3.0M) PO Box 608 Ashdown AR 71822 **Phn:** 870-898-3462 **Fax:** 870-898-6213 www.littlerivernews.net littlerivernews@sbcglobal.net

Atkins Atkins Chronicle (2.4M) PO Box 188 Atkins AR 72823 **Phn:** 479-641-7161 **Fax:** 479-641-1604 www.atkinschronicle.com news@atkinschronicle.com

Bald Knob Bald Knob Banner (1.8M) PO Box 1480 Bald Knob AR 72010 **Phn:** 501-724-0398 **Fax:** 501-724-6362

Bald Knob White County Record (1.7M) PO Box 1480 Bald Knob AR 72010 **Phn:** 501-724-0398 **Fax:** 501-724-6362

Batesville Arkansas Weekly (21.2M) 920 Harrison St # C Batesville AR 72501 **Phn:** 870-793-4196 **Fax:** 870-793-5222 www.arkansasweekly.net rgmax99@yahoo.com

Beebe The Beebe News (2.5M) PO Box 910 Beebe AR 72012 **Phn:** 501-882-5414 **Fax:** 501-882-3576 beebenews.com tbn@beebenews.com

Bella Vista The Weekly Vista (4.8M) 313 Town Ctr W Bella Vista AR 72714 **Phn:** 479-855-3724 **Fax:** 479-855-6992 www.nwaonline.com/weeklies

Bentonville Rogers Hometown News (12.0M) PO Box 929 Bentonville AR 72712 **Phn:** 479-619-2511

Berryville Carroll County News (4.5M) PO Box 232 Berryville AR 72616 **Phn:** 870-423-6636 **Fax:** 870-423-6640 www.carrollconews.com ccneditor@cox-internet.com

Booneville Booneville Democrat (3.0M) PO Box 208 Booneville AR 72927 **Phn:** 479-675-4455 **Fax:** 479-675-5457 www.boonevilledemocrat.com news@boonevilledemocrat.com

Brinkley Brinkley Argus (2.2M) PO Box 711 Brinkley AR 72021 **Phn:** 870-734-1056 **Fax:** 870-734-1494 brinkleyargus@sbcglobal.net

Cabot Cabot Star-Herald (8.0M) PO Box 1058 Cabot AR 72023 **Phn:** 501-843-3534 **Fax:** 501-843-6447 lonokenews.net/cabot-star-herald news@cabotstarherald.com

Calico Rock White River Current (1.5M) PO Box 570 Calico Rock AR 72519 **Phn:** 870-297-3010 **Fax:** 870-297-3070 www.whiterivercurrent.com wrcnews@centurytel.net

Carlisle Carlisle Independent (1.7M) PO Box 47 Carlisle AR 72024 **Phn:** 870-552-3111 **Fax:** 870-552-3111 lonokenews.net/carlisle-independent news@carlisleindependent.com

Charleston Charleston Express (2.2M) PO Box 39 Charleston AR 72933 **Phn:** 479-965-7368 **Fax:** 479-965-7206 www.charlestonexpress.com pgramlich@charlestonexpress.com

Clarendon Monroe County Sun (1.6M) PO Box 315 Clarendon AR 72029 **Phn:** 870-747-3373 **Fax:** 870-734-1494

Clarksville Johnson County Graphic (8.2M) PO Box 289 Clarksville AR 72830 **Phn:** 479-754-2005 **Fax:** 479-754-2098 www.thegraphic.org news@thegraphic.org

Clinton Van Buren County Democrat (4.1M) PO Box 119 Clinton AR 72031 **Phn:** 501-745-5175 **Fax:** 501-745-8865 www.vanburencountydem.com editor@vanburencountydem.com

Corning Clay County Courier (3.5M) PO Box 85 Corning AR 72422 **Phn:** 870-857-3531 **Fax:** 870-857-5204 fredmartin@jvrhomes.com

Crossett Ashley News Observer (4.4M) PO Box 798 Crossett AR 71635 **Phn:** 870-364-5186 **Fax:** 870-364-2116 ashleynewsobserver.com news@ashleynewsobserver.com

Danville Yell County Record (4.7M) PO Box 189 Danville AR 72833 **Phn:** 479-495-2354 **Fax:** 479-495-3501 www.theyellcountyrecord.com ycrecord@arkwest.com

Dardanelle Post-Dispatch (2.2M) PO Box 270 Dardanelle AR 72834 **Phn:** 479-229-2250 **Fax:** 479-229-1159 postdispatch@centurytel.net

De Queen De Queen Bee (3.5M) PO Box 1000 De Queen AR 71832 **Phn:** 870-642-2111 **Fax:** 870-642-3138 dequeenbee.com editor@dequeenbee.com

De Witt DeWitt Era-Enterprise (2.7M) PO Box 678 De Witt AR 72042 **Phn:** 870-946-3933 **Fax:** 870-946-3949 www.dewitt-ee.com manager@dewitt-ee.com

Decatur Decatur Herald (1.8M) PO Box 7 Decatur AR 72722 **Phn:** 479-752-3675 **Fax:** 479-736-8352 www.nwaonline.com

Des Arc White River Journal (2.5M) PO Box 1051 Des Arc AR 72040 **Phn:** 870-256-4254

Dover Dover Times (1.6M) PO Box 547 Dover AR 72837 **Phn:** 479-331-3875 **Fax:** 479-331-4728 www.atkinschronicle.com

Dumas Dumas Clarion (3.2M) Po Box 220 Dumas AR 71639 **Phn:** 870-382-4925 **Fax:** 870-382-6421 thawkins@centurytel.net

England England Democrat (1.6M) PO Box 250 England AR 72046 **Phn:** 501-842-3111 **Fax:** 501-842-3081 englanddemo@centurytel.net

Eureka Springs Lovely Co. Citizen (6.0M) PO Box 679 Eureka Springs AR 72632 **Phn:** 479-253-0070 **Fax:** 479-253-0080 www.lovelycitizen.com citizen.editor@yahoo.com

Fairfield Bay Fairfield Bay News (3.0M) PO Box 1370 Fairfield Bay AR 72088 **Phn:** 501-884-6012 **Fax:** 501-884-6019 www.fairfieldbaynews.com editor@fairfieldbaynews.com

Farmington Washington Co. Enterprise Leader (9.5M) PO Box 864 Farmington AR 72730 **Phn:** 479-267-6502 **Fax:** 479-267-5540

Fayetteville The Free Weekly (12.0M) PO Box 1607 Fayetteville AR 72702 **Phn:** 479-571-6419 **Fax:** 479-442-1714 www.freeweekly.com tbaker@nwaonline.com

Flippin Mountaineer Echo (0.9M) PO Box 1199 Flippin AR 72634 **Phn:** 870-453-3731 **Fax:** 870-453-3071 www.flippinonline.com estesd@suddenlinkmail.com

Fordyce Fordyce News-Advocate (3.0M) PO Box 559 Fordyce AR 71742 **Phn:** 870-352-3144 **Fax:** 870-352-8091 newsadvo@windstream.net

ARKANSAS WEEKLY NEWSPAPERS

Franklin Pacesetting Times (1.5M) PO Box 132 Franklin AR 72536 **Phn:** 870-670-6397 **Fax:** 870-670-7223 pacesetting@centurytel.net

Glenwood Glenwood Herald (2.1M) PO Box 1130 Glenwood AR 71943 **Phn:** 870-356-2111 **Fax:** 870-356-4400 swarkansasnews.com gwherald@windstream.net

Gravette Westside Eagle Observer (1.8M) PO Box 640 Gravette AR 72736 **Phn:** 479-787-5300 **Fax:** 479-787-5332 www.nwaonline.com rmoll@nwaonline.com

Greenwood Greenwood Democrat (2.1M) PO Box 398 Greenwood AR 72936 **Phn:** 479-996-4494 **Fax:** 479-996-4122 www.greenwooddemocrat.com

Hamburg Ashley County Ledger (3.1M) PO Box 471 Hamburg AR 71646 **Phn:** 870-853-2424 www.ashleycountyledger.com editor@ashleycountyledger.com

Hampton South Arkansas Sun (1.3M) 305 E Main Hampton AR 71744 **Phn:** 870-798-3786 www.southarkansassun.com publisher@southarkansassun.com

Harrisburg The Modern News (2.2M) PO Box 400 Harrisburg AR 72432 **Phn:** 870-578-2121 **Fax:** 870-578-9415 modernnews@pcsii.com

Hazen Grand Prairie Herald (1.8M) PO Box 370 Hazen AR 72064 **Phn:** 870-255-4538 **Fax:** 870-255-4539 www.herald-publishing.com editor@herald-publishing.com

Heber Springs Sun-Times (5.8M) PO Box 669 Heber Springs AR 72543 **Phn:** 501-362-2425 **Fax:** 501-362-5877 www.thesuntimes.com news@thesuntimes.com

Hot Springs Village Hot Springs Village Voice (7.5M) PO Box 8508 Hot Springs Village AR 71910 **Phn:** 501-984-6224 **Fax:** 501-623-3131 www.hsvvoice.com news@hsvvoice.com

Huntsville Madison County Record (5.6M) PO Box A Huntsville AR 72740 **Phn:** 479-738-2141 **Fax:** 479-738-1250 www.mcrecordonline.com editor@mcrecordonline.com

Imboden Ozark Journal (1.6M) PO Box 598 Imboden AR 72434 **Phn:** 870-869-2220

Jacksonville Jacksonville Patriot (3.5M) PO Box 5329 Jacksonville AR 72078 **Phn:** 501-982-6506 **Fax:** 501-843-6447 pulaskinews.net news@jacksonvillepatriot.com

Jacksonville The Leader (28.0M) 404 Graham Rd Jacksonville AR 72076 **Phn:** 501-982-9421 **Fax:** 501-985-0026 www.arkansasleader.com editor@arkansasleader.com

Jasper Newton County Times (3.2M) PO Box 453 Jasper AR 72641 **Phn:** 870-446-2645 **Fax:** 870-446-6286 harrisondaily.com/news news@harrisondaily.com

Lake Village Chicot County Spectator (1.8M) 105 N Court St Lake Village AR 71653 **Phn:** 870-265-2071 **Fax:** 870-265-2807 www.chicotnewspapers.com news@chicotnewspapers.com

Lake Village Eudora Enterprise (1.0M) 105 N Court St Lake Village AR 71653 **Phn:** 870-265-2071 **Fax:** 870-265-2807 news@chicotnewspapers.com

Lincoln Farmington Post (2.2M) 219 S Main Ave Lincoln AR 72744 **Phn:** 479-824-3263 **Fax:** 479-824-5540

Lincoln Prairie Grove Enterprise (2.2M) 219 S Main Ave Lincoln AR 72744 **Phn:** 479-824-3263 **Fax:** 479-824-5540 www.stephensmedia.com/newspapers

Little Rock Arkansas Times (3.0M) PO Box 34010 Little Rock AR 72203 **Phn:** 501-375-2985 **Fax:** 501-375-3623 www.arktimes.com arktimes@arktimes.com

Lonoke Lonoke Democrat (2.6M) 402 N Center St Lonoke AR 72086 **Phn:** 501-676-2463 **Fax:** 501-676-6231 lonokenews.net/lonoke-democrat news@lonokedemocrat.com

Manila The Town Crier (2.7M) PO Box 1326 Manila AR 72442 **Phn:** 870-561-4634 **Fax:** 870-561-3602 www.thetown-crier.com towncrier@centurytel.net

Marianna Courier Index (2.5M) PO Box 569 Marianna AR 72360 **Phn:** 870-295-2521 **Fax:** 870-295-9662 cinews@sbcglobal.net

Marshall Mountain Wave (3.0M) PO Box 220 Marshall AR 72650 **Phn:** 870-448-3321 **Fax:** 870-448-5659 mmw@windstream.net

Maumelle Maumelle Monitor (2.0M) PO Box 13230 Maumelle AR 72113 **Phn:** 501-851-6220 **Fax:** 501-851-6397 pulaskinews.net editor@maumellemonitor.com

Mc Crory Woodruff County Leader (2.2M) PO Box 898 Mc Crory AR 72101 **Phn:** 870-731-2263 **Fax:** 870-731-5899 wcm@centurytel.net

Mc Gehee Times-News (3.4M) PO Box 290 Mc Gehee AR 71654 **Phn:** 870-222-3922 **Fax:** 870-222-3726 themcgeheetimes.com editor@themcgeheetimes.com

Melbourne The Melbourne Times (2.6M) PO Box 308 Melbourne AR 72556 **Phn:** 870-368-4421 **Fax:** 870-368-3259 thetimes@centurytel.net

Mena Mena Star (3.3M) PO Box 1307 Mena AR 71953 **Phn:** 479-394-1900 **Fax:** 479-394-1908 www.menastar.com joeben@menastar.com

Monticello Advance Monticellonian (3.5M) PO Box 486 Monticello AR 71657 **Phn:** 870-367-5325 **Fax:** 870-367-6612 www.mymonticellonews.net editor@monticellonews.net

Morrilton Headlight Newspapers (6.5M) PO Box 540 Morrilton AR 72110 **Phn:** 501-354-2451 **Fax:** 501-354-4225 www.headlightnews.com pjch@suddenlinkmail.com

Mount Ida Montgomery County News (2.0M) PO Box 187 Mount Ida AR 71957 **Phn:** 870-867-2821 swarkansasnews.com montcnews2@windstream.net

Mountain View Stone County Leader (5.0M) PO Box 509 Mountain View AR 72560 **Phn:** 870-269-3841 **Fax:** 870-269-2171 www.stonecountyleader.com leader@mvtel.net

Murfreesboro The Diamond (1.8M) PO Box 550 Murfreesboro AR 71958 **Phn:** 870-285-2723 **Fax:** 870-285-3820 www.nashvillenews.org mdiamond.editor@windstream.net

Nashville Nashville Leader (8.4M) 119 N Main St Nashville AR 71852 **Phn:** 870-845-0600 **Fax:** 870-845-0602 www.nashvilleleader.com jrs@nashvilleleader.com

Nashville Nashville News (3.0M) PO Box 297 Nashville AR 71852 **Phn:** 870-845-2010 **Fax:** 870-845-5091 www.nashvillenews.org

Newport Newport Independent (2.6M) PO Box 1750 Newport AR 72112 **Phn:** 870-523-5855 **Fax:** 870-523-6540 www.newportindependent.com news@newportindependent.com

North Little Rock The Times (9.0M) PO Box 428 North Little Rock AR 72115 **Phn:** 501-370-8300 **Fax:** 501-370-8391 pulaskinews.net editor@nlrtimes.com

Osceola Osceola Times (2.8M) PO Box 408 Osceola AR 72370 **Phn:** 870-563-2615 **Fax:** 870-563-2616 www.osceolatimes.com timesnews@osceolatimes.com

Ozark Ozark Spectator (5.8M) 207 W Main St Ozark AR 72949 **Phn:** 479-667-2136 **Fax:** 479-667-4365 www.ozarkspectator.com spectator@centurytel.net

Paris Paris Express (3.6M) PO Box 551 Paris AR 72855 **Phn:** 479-963-2901 **Fax:** 479-963-3062 www.paris-express.com vwiggins@paris-express.com

Pea Ridge Times of NE Benton County (2.0M) PO Box 25 Pea Ridge AR 72751 **Phn:** 479-451-1196 **Fax:** 479-451-9456 tnebc.nwaonline.com prtnews@nwaonline.com

Piggott Piggott Times (3.1M) 209 W Main St Piggott AR 72454 **Phn:** 870-598-2201 **Fax:** 870-598-5189 www.cctimesdemocrat.com piggotttimes@centurytel.net

Pine Bluff White Hall Progress (5.0M) PO Box 6469 Pine Bluff AR 71611 **Phn:** 870-534-3400 **Fax:** 870-534-0113 www.pbcommercial.com khall@whprogress.com

Pocahontas Pocahontas Star-Herald (5.0M) PO Box 608 Pocahontas AR 72455 **Phn:** 870-892-4451 **Fax:** 870-892-4453 starherald@jvrhomes.com

Prescott Gurdon Times (1.9M) 100 E Elm St Prescott AR 71857 **Phn:** 870-353-4482 **Fax:** 870-887-2949 www.thegurdontimes.com gurdontimes@yahoo.com

Prescott Nevada County Picayune (2.4M) 100 E Elm St Prescott AR 71857 **Phn:** 870-887-2002 **Fax:** 870-887-2949 www.picayune-times.com

Rector Clay County Democrat (3.0M) 306 S Main St Rector AR 72461 **Phn:** 870-595-3549 **Fax:** 870-595-3611 www.cctimesdemocrat.com ccd@centurytel.net

Rison Cleveland County Herald (2.5M) PO Box 657 Rison AR 71665 **Phn:** 870-325-6412 **Fax:** 870-325-6127 clevelandcountyherald.com ccherald@tds.net

Salem The News (2.5M) PO Box 248 Salem AR 72576 **Phn:** 870-895-3207 **Fax:** 870-895-4277 www.areawidenews.com news@areawidenews.com

Salem Villager Journal (2.2M) PO Box 248 Salem AR 72576 **Phn:** 870-895-3207 **Fax:** 870-895-4277 www.areawidenews.com villagerjournal@centurytel.net

Sheridan Sheridan Headlight (4.0M) PO Box 539 Sheridan AR 72150 **Phn:** 870-942-2142 **Fax:** 870-942-8823 www.thesheridanheadlight.com info@thesheridanheadlight.com

Sherwood Sherwood Voice (2.6M) PO Box 6166 Sherwood AR 72124 **Phn:** 501-370-8300 **Fax:** 501-370-8391 pulaskinews.net news@sherwoodvoice.com

Siloam Springs Herald-Leader (5.0M) 101 N Mount Olive St Siloam Springs AR 72761 **Phn:** 479-524-5144 hl.nwaonline.com

Stamps Lafayette County Press (1.6M) 221 Main St Stamps AR 71860 **Phn:** 870-533-4708 **Fax:** 870-533-1368 www.lafayettecountypress.com lcpress@sbcglobal.net

Star City Lincoln Ledger (2.4M) 216 W Bradley St Star City AR 71667 **Phn:** 870-628-4161 **Fax:** 870-628-3802

Trumann Democrat Tribune (1.6M) PO Box 5 Trumann AR 72472 **Phn:** 870-483-6317 **Fax:** 870-483-6031 www.democrattribune.com ccd@centurytel.net

Van Buren Alma Journal (5.1M) PO Box 369 Van Buren AR 72957 **Phn:** 479-474-5215 **Fax:** 479-471-5607 www.pressargus.com/alma_journal jmcclure@pressargus.com

Van Buren Press-Argus-Courier (5.1M) PO Box 369 Van Buren AR 72957 **Phn:** 479-474-5215 **Fax:** 479-471-5607 www.pressargus.com jmcclure@pressargus.com

Waldron Waldron News (2.5M) PO Box 745 Waldron AR 72958 **Phn:** 479-637-4161 **Fax:** 479-637-4162 www.waldronnews.com joeben@menastar.com

Walnut Ridge Times-Dispatch (4.0M) PO Box 389 Walnut Ridge AR 72476 **Phn:** 870-886-2464 **Fax:** 870-886-9369 www.thetd.com editor@thetd.com

Warren Eagle-Democrat (4.0M) 200 W Cypress St Warren AR 71671 **Phn:** 870-226-5831 **Fax:** 870-226-6601 eaglepub@sbcglobal.net

White Hall White Hall Journal (2.3M) 7400 Dollarway Rd White Hall AR 71602 **Phn:** 870-247-4700 **Fax:** 870-247-4755 www.whitehalljournal.com tbennett@whitehalljournal.com

White Hall White Hall Progress (3.0M) PO Box 6469 White Hall AR 71611 **Phn:** 870-534-3400 **Fax:** 870-534-0113 pbcommercial.com/white-hall khall@pbcommercial.com

Wynne Wynne Progress (4.0M) PO Box 308 Wynne AR 72396 **Phn:** 870-238-2375 **Fax:** 870-238-4655 wynnenews@cablelynx.com

CALIFORNIA

Agoura Hills Acorn Newspapers (144.0M) 30423 Canwood St Ste 108 Agoura Hills CA 91301 **Phn:** 818-706-0266 **Fax:** 818-707-7848 www.theacornonline.com jr@theacorn.com

Alameda Alameda Sun (20.0M) 3215 Encinal Ave Ste J Alameda CA 94501 **Phn:** 510-263-1470 **Fax:** 510-263-1473 www.alamedasun.com editor@alamedasun.com

Alameda Hills Newspapers (60.0M) 1516 Oak St Alameda CA 94501 **Phn:** 510-748-1683 **Fax:** 510-748-1680 www.contracostatimes.com voice@cctimes.com

Alpine Alpine Sun (2.3M) PO Box 1089 Alpine CA 91903 **Phn:** 619-445-3288 **Fax:** 619-445-6776 www.thealpinesun.com editor@thealpinesun.com

Alturas Modoc County Record (4.3M) PO Box 531 Alturas CA 96101 **Phn:** 530-233-2632 **Fax:** 530-233-5113 www.modocrecord.com record1@modocrecord.com

American Canyon American Canyon Eagle (5.0M) 3860 Broadway St Ste 202 American Canyon CA 94503 **Phn:** 707-256-2210 **Fax:** 707-254-3240 napavalleyregister.com/eagle editor@americancanyoneagle.com

Anaheim OC Register Papers North (135.0M) 1771 S Lewis St Anaheim CA 92805 **Phn:** 714-634-1471 **Fax:** 714-704-3714 www.ocregister.com kbrusic@ocregister.com

Arcata Arcata Eye (4.0M) PO Box 451 Arcata CA 95518 **Phn:** 707-826-7000 www.arcataeye.com news@arcataeye.com

Atascadero Atascadero News (7.2M) PO Box 6068 Atascadero CA 93423 **Phn:** 805-466-2585 **Fax:** 805-466-2714 www.atascaderonews.com editor@atascaderonews.com

Auburn Placer Sentinel (20.0M) 1226 High St Auburn CA 95603 **Phn:** 530-823-2463 **Fax:** 916-773-2999 www.placersentinel.com publisher@placersentinel.com

Avalon Avalon Bay News (3.0M) PO Box 1809 Avalon CA 90704 **Phn:** 310-510-1500 **Fax:** 310-510-1371

Avalon Catalina Islander (5.0M) PO Box 428 Avalon CA 90704 **Phn:** 310-510-0500 **Fax:** 310-510-2882

Bakersfield Bakersfield Voice (55.0M) PO Box 2344 Bakersfield CA 93303 **Phn:** 661-716-8640 **Fax:** 661-716-8631 www.bakersfieldvoice.com ogarcia@bakersfield.com

Bakersfield Lamont Reporter (5.6M) 5409 Aldrin Ct Bakersfield CA 93313 **Phn:** 661-845-3704 **Fax:** 661-845-5907

Bakersfield Observer Group (97.0M) PO Box 3624 Bakersfield CA 93385 **Phn:** 661-324-9466 observernews@gmail.com

Banning Record Gazette (2.6M) PO Box 727 Banning CA 92220 **Phn:** 951-849-4586 **Fax:** 951-849-2437 www.recordgazette.net

Berkeley Berkeley Planet (25.0M) PO Box 5534 Berkeley CA 94705 **Phn:** 510-841-5600 **Fax:** 510-845-8440 www.berkeleydailyplanet.com news@berkeleydailyplanet.com

Beverly Hills Beverly Hills Weekly (15.0M) 140 S Beverly Dr Ste 201 Beverly Hills CA 90212 **Phn:** 310-887-0788 **Fax:** 310-887-0789 www.bhweekly.com editor@bhweekly.com

Beverly Hills Canyon News (40.0M) 260 S Beverly Dr Beverly Hills CA 90212 **Phn:** 310-277-6017 www.canyon-news.com staff@canyon-news.com

Beverly Hills The Beverly Hills Courier (40.0M) 8840 W Olympic Blvd Beverly Hills CA 90211 **Phn:** 310-278-1322 **Fax:** 310-271-5118 www.bhcourier.com editorial@bhcourier.com

Big Bear Lake Grizzly & Life (9.0M) PO Box 1789 Big Bear Lake CA 92315 **Phn:** 909-866-3456 **Fax:** 909-866-2302 www.bigbeargrizzly.net jbowers.grizzly@gmail.com

Bishop Inyo Register (5.9M) 1180 N Main St Ste 108 Bishop CA 93514 **Phn:** 760-873-3535 **Fax:** 760-873-3591 www.inyoregister.com editor@inyoregister.com

Blythe Palo Verde Valley Times (4.0M) PO Box 1159 Blythe CA 92226 **Phn:** 760-922-3181 **Fax:** 760-922-3184 www.paloverdevalleytimes.com webmaster@westernnews.com

Boonville Anderson Valley Advertiser (3.0M) PO Box 459 Boonville CA 95415 **Phn:** 707-895-3016 **Fax:** 707-895-3355 theava.com ava@pacific.net

Borrego Springs Borrego Sun (4.0M) PO Box 249 Borrego Springs CA 92004 **Phn:** 760-767-5338 **Fax:** 760-767-4971 borregosun.com generalmail@borregosun.com

Brentwood The Press for Antioch, Brentwood, Discov (42.0M) 248 Oak St Brentwood CA 94513 **Phn:** 925-634-1441 **Fax:** 925-634-1975 www.thepress.net editor@brentwoodpress.com

Burbank The Burbank Times (20.0M) 3917 W Riverside Dr Burbank CA 91505 **Phn:** 818-841-6397

Burney Intermountain News (3.3M) PO Box 1030 Burney CA 96013 **Phn:** 530-725-0925 **Fax:** 530-303-1528 www.theimnews.com news@burneyfalls.co

California City Mojave Desert News (5.0M) PO Box 2698 California City CA 93504 **Phn:** 760-373-4812 **Fax:** 760-373-2941 www.desertnews.com

Calistoga Weekly Calistogan (2.5M) PO Box 385 Calistoga CA 94515 **Phn:** 707-942-4035 **Fax:** 707-942-4134 napavalleyregister.com/calistogan editor@weeklycalistogan.com

Cambria The Cambrian (4.2M) 2442 Main St Cambria CA 93428 **Phn:** 805-927-8895 **Fax:** 805-927-4708 www.sanluisobispo.com/northcoast newsroom@thetribunenews.com

Campbell Campbell Express (2.7M) 334 E Campbell Ave Frnt Campbell CA 95008 **Phn:** 408-374-9700 **Fax:** 408-374-0813 www.campbellexpress.net news@campbellexpress.net

Canyon Lake The Friday Flyer (6.0M) 31558 Railroad Canyon Rd Ste 2 Canyon Lake CA 92587 **Phn:** 951-244-1966 **Fax:** 951-244-2748 fridayflyer.com news@goldingpublications.com

Capistrano Beach San Clemente Times (20.0M) 3492 Calle Del Sol # B Capistrano Beach CA 92624 **Phn:** 949-388-7700 **Fax:** 949-388-9977 www.sanclementetimes.com info@sanclementetimes.com

Carmel Carmel Pine Cone (22.0M) PO Box G1 Carmel CA 93921 **Phn:** 831-624-0162 **Fax:** 831-375-5018 www.pineconearchive.com mail@carmelpinecone.com

Carmichael Carmichael Times (10.0M) PO Box 14 Carmichael CA 95609 **Phn:** 916-773-1111 **Fax:** 916-773-2999 www.carmichaeltimes.com publisher@carmichaeltimes.com

Carpinteria Coastal View (6.8M) 4856 Carpinteria Ave Carpinteria CA 93013 **Phn:** 805-684-4428 www.coastalview.com news@coastalview.com

Ceres Ceres Courier (19.0M) PO Box 7 Ceres CA 95307 **Phn:** 209-537-5032 **Fax:** 209-537-0543 cerescourier.com

Cerritos Community News (35.0M) 13047 Artesia Blvd Ste C102 Cerritos CA 90703 **Phn:** 562-407-3873 **Fax:** 562-921-1915

Chester Chester Progressive (3.1M) PO Box 557 Chester CA 96020 **Phn:** 530-258-3115 **Fax:** 530-258-2365 www.plumasnews.com chesternews@plumasnews.com

Chico Chico News & Review (42.0M) 353 E 2nd St Chico CA 95928 **Phn:** 530-894-2300 **Fax:** 530-894-0143 www.newsreview.com/chico chiconewstips@newsreview.com

Chino Champion Newspapers (42.0M) PO Box 607 Chino CA 91708 **Phn:** 909-628-5501 **Fax:** 909-590-1217 www.championnewspapers.com news@championnewspapers.com

Chowchilla Chowchilla News (2.2M) 340 Robertson Blvd Chowchilla CA 93610 **Phn:** 559-665-5751 **Fax:** 559-665-5462 www.thechowchillanews.com pmandrell@mercedsun-star.com

Chula Vista The Star-News (33.5M) 296 3rd Ave Chula Vista CA 91910 **Phn:** 619-427-3000 **Fax:** 619-426-6346 www.thestarnews.com publisher@thestarnews.com

Claremont Claremont Courier (6.0M) 1420 N Claremont Blvd Ste 205B Claremont CA 91711 **Phn:** 909-621-4761 **Fax:** 909-621-4072 www.claremont-courier.com pweinberger@claremont-courier.com

Clipper Mills Rabbit Creek Journal (2.1M) PO Box 309 Clipper Mills CA 95930 **Phn:** 530-675-2270 daysnews@rcj.net

Cloverdale Cloverdale Reveille (2.3M) PO Box 157 Cloverdale CA 95425 **Phn:** 707-894-3339 **Fax:** 707-894-3343 www.cloverdalereveille.com reveille@cloverdalereveille.com

Colfax Colfax Record (1.8M) PO Box 755 Colfax CA 95713 **Phn:** 530-346-2232 **Fax:** 530-346-2700 www.colfaxrecord.com marthag@goldcountrymedia.com

Colton Inland Empire Newspapers (20.0M) PO Box 110 Colton CA 92324 **Phn:** 909-381-9898 **Fax:** 909-384-0406 www.iecn.com iecn1@mac.com

Colusa Sun Herald (1.8M) 249 5th St Colusa CA 95932 **Phn:** 530-458-2121 **Fax:** 530-458-5711 www.colusa-sun-herald.com thansen@tcnpress.com

Corcoran Corcoran Journal (2.4M) PO Box 487 Corcoran CA 93212 **Phn:** 559-992-3115 **Fax:** 559-992-5543 www.thecorcoranjournal.net jmstnews@yahoo.com

Corning Corning Observer (6.0M) 1208 Solano St Corning CA 96021 **Phn:** 530-824-5464 **Fax:** 530-824-4804 www.corning-observer.com thansen@tcnpress.com

Corona Sentinel Weekly News (11.0M) 1307B W 6th St Ste 119C Corona CA 92882 **Phn:** 951-737-9784 **Fax:** 951-737-9785 www.thesentinelweekly.com sentinelweekly@aol.com

Coronado Coronado Eagle & Journal (12.5M) 1116 10th St Coronado CA 92118 **Phn:** 619-437-8800 **Fax:** 619-437-8635 www.coronadonewsca.com editor@eaglenewsca.com

CALIFORNIA WEEKLY NEWSPAPERS

Costa Mesa Huntington Beach Independent (31.0M) 1375 Sunflower Ave Costa Mesa CA 92626 **Phn:** 714-966-4600 **Fax:** 714-966-4678 www.hbindependent.com john.canalis@latimes.com

Costa Mesa Independent (65.0M) 1375 Sunflower Ave Costa Mesa CA 92626 **Phn:** 714-966-4600 **Fax:** 714-966-4663 www.hbindependent.com hbindependent@latimes.com

Costa Mesa OC Weekly (68.0M) 2975 Red Hill Ave Ste 150 Costa Mesa CA 92626 **Phn:** 714-550-5900 **Fax:** 714-550-5908 www.ocweekly.com

Coto de Caza Mission News Group (21.5M) 23472 Vista Del Verde # 6 Coto de Caza CA 92679 **Phn:** 949-589-9990 cotodecazanews.com newseditorials@yahoo.com

Crestline The Alpenhorn News (2.8M) PO Box 4572 Crestline CA 92325 **Phn:** 909-337-1848 **Fax:** 909-338-5553 alpenhornnews.com thealpenhornnews@aol.com

Culver City Culver City News (11.0M) 4351 Sepulveda Blvd Culver City CA 90230 **Phn:** 310-437-4401 **Fax:** 310-391-9068 www.culvercitynews.org editor@culvercitynews.org

Culver City Culver City Observer (10.0M) PO Box 2764 Culver City CA 90231 **Phn:** 310-398-6397 **Fax:** 310-398-7099 culvercityobserver.com ccobserver@aol.com

Culver City LA Weekly (214.0M) 3861 Sepulveda Blvd Culver City CA 90230 **Phn:** 310-574-7100 www.laweekly.com editor@laweekly.com

Cypress Event News (28.0M) 9559 Valley View St Cypress CA 90630 **Phn:** 714-220-0292 **Fax:** 714-220-1787

Del Mar Del Mar Times (17.0M) 3702 Via De La Valle Ste 202W Del Mar CA 92014 **Phn:** 858-756-1451 **Fax:** 858-756-9912 www.delmartimes.net editor@delmartimes.net

Delano Delano Record (4.6M) 1625 Cecil Ave Delano CA 93215 **Phn:** 661-725-0600 **Fax:** 661-725-4373

Dinuba Dinuba Sentinel (3.0M) 145 S L St Dinuba CA 93618 **Phn:** 559-591-4632 **Fax:** 559-591-1322 dinubasentinel@sbcglobal.net

Dixon Dixon Tribune (5.6M) 145 E A St Dixon CA 95620 **Phn:** 707-678-5594 **Fax:** 707-678-5404 editor@dixontribune.com

Dixon Independent Voice (4.5M) PO Box 1106 Dixon CA 95620 **Phn:** 707-678-8917 www.independentvoice.com staff@independentvoice.com

Dos Palos Dos Palos Sun (1.0M) 1533 Center Ave Dos Palos CA 93620 **Phn:** 209-392-3921 **Fax:** 209-392-2200

Downey Downey Patriot (25.0M) 8301 Florence Ave Ste 100 Downey CA 90240 **Phn:** 562-904-3668 www.thedowneypatriot.com downeypatriot@yahoo.com

Downieville Mountain Messenger (2.4M) PO Box A Downieville CA 95936 **Phn:** 530-289-3262 mtnmess@cwo.com

El Cajon East Co. Californian (32.0M) 119 N Magnolia Ave El Cajon CA 92020 **Phn:** 619-441-0400 **Fax:** 619-441-0020

El Cajon East Co. Gazette (15.0M) 1130 Broadway El Cajon CA 92021 **Phn:** 619-444-5774 **Fax:** 619-444-5779 www.eastcountygazette.com editor@ecgazette.com

El Monte Mid-Valley News (15.0M) 11401 Valley Blvd Ste 207 El Monte CA 91731 **Phn:** 626-443-1753 **Fax:** 626-443-2245 www.midvalleynews.com editor@midvalleynews.com

El Segundo Herald Publications (42.0M) PO Box 188 El Segundo CA 90245 **Phn:** 310-322-1830 **Fax:** 310-322-2787 www.heraldpublications.com

Elk Grove Elk Grove Citizen (12.0M) PO Box 1777 Elk Grove CA 95759 **Phn:** 916-685-3945 **Fax:** 916-686-6675 www.egcitizen.com egnews@herburger.net

Encinitas Coast News Group (88.0M) PO Box 232550 Encinitas CA 92023 **Phn:** 760-436-9737 thecoastnews.com editor@coastnewsgroup.com

Escondido North County Spectrum (2.0M) 210 S Juniper St Ste 211 Escondido CA 92025 **Phn:** 619-747-8911 **Fax:** 619-747-8912 www.mnc.net news@metnews.com

Eureka Humboldt Beacon (4.5M) 930 6th St Eureka CA 95501 **Phn:** 707-441-0554 **Fax:** 707-441-0501 www.humboldtbeacon.com kwear@times-standard.com

Eureka North Coast Journal (21.0M) 310 F St Eureka CA 95501 **Phn:** 707-442-1400 **Fax:** 707-442-1401 www.northcoastjournal.com editor@northcoastjournal.com

Exeter Foothills Sun-Gazette (3.0M) PO Box 7 Exeter CA 93221 **Phn:** 559-592-3171 **Fax:** 559-592-4308 www.fsgnews.com news@thesungazette.com

Fall River Mills Mountain Echo (3.5M) PO Box 224 Fall River Mills CA 96028 **Phn:** 530-336-6262 www.mountainecho.com mtecho@frontiernet.net

Fallbrook Anza Valley Outlook (2.2M) 127 W Elder St Fallbrook CA 92028 **Phn:** 760-723-7319 **Fax:** 760-723-9606 www.anzavalleyoutlook.com editor@anzavalleyoutlook.com

Fallbrook Fallbrook Village News (13.0M) 127 W Elder St Fallbrook CA 92028 **Phn:** 760-723-7319 **Fax:** 760-723-9606 www.thevillagenews.com editor@thevillagenews.com

Ferndale Ferndale Enterprise (1.5M) PO Box 1066 Ferndale CA 95536 **Phn:** 707-786-4611 **Fax:** 707-786-4311 ferndaleenterprise.us editor@ferndaleenterprise.us

Fillmore Fillmore Gazette (3.0M) PO Box 865 Fillmore CA 93016 **Phn:** 805-524-2481 **Fax:** 805-524-1164 www.fillmoregazette.com wanda@fillmoregazette.com

Folsom The Telegraph (15.0M) 921 Sutter St Ste 100 Folsom CA 95630 **Phn:** 916-985-2581 **Fax:** 916-985-0720 www.folsomtelegraph.com donc@goldcountrymedia.com

Fontana Herald News (11.5M) PO Box 549 Fontana CA 92334 **Phn:** 909-822-2231 **Fax:** 909-355-9358 www.fontanaheraldnews.com ringold@fontanaheraldnews.com

Fort Bragg Advocate-News (5.4M) 450 N Franklin St Fort Bragg CA 95437 **Phn:** 707-964-5642 **Fax:** 707-964-0424 www.advocate-news.com advocatenews@mcn.org

Fort Bragg Mendocino Beacon (2.5M) 450 N Franklin St Fort Bragg CA 95437 **Phn:** 707-964-5642 **Fax:** 707-964-0424 www.mendocinobeacon.com beacon@mcn.org

Fort Jones Pioneer Press Papers (14.0M) PO Box 400 Fort Jones CA 96032 **Phn:** 530-468-5355 **Fax:** 530-468-5356

Foster City Islander (6.0M) 1185 Chess Dr Ste B Foster City CA 94404 **Phn:** 650-574-5952

Fountain Valley OC Register Papers West (113.0M) 17777 Newhope St Fountain Valley CA 92708 **Phn:** 714-445-6680 www.ocregister.com kbrusic@ocregister.com

Frazier Park Mountain Enterprise (3.1M) PO Box 610 Frazier Park CA 93225 **Phn:** 661-245-3794 **Fax:** 661-245-5620 www.mountainenterprise.com publisher@mountainenterprise.com

Fremont Tri-City Voice (35.7M) 39120 Argonaut Way # 335 Fremont CA 94538 **Phn:** 510-494-1999 **Fax:** 510-796-2462 www.tricityvoice.com tricityvoice@aol.com

Fullerton Fullerton Observer (9.0M) PO Box 7051 Fullerton CA 92834 **Phn:** 714-525-6402 www.fullertonobserver.com

Galt Galt Herald (12.0M) PO Box 307 Galt CA 95632 **Phn:** 209-745-1551 **Fax:** 209-745-4492 galtheraldonline.com editor_galtherald@herburger.net

Galt Grapevine Independent (11.0M) PO Box 307 Galt CA 95632 **Phn:** 209-745-1551 **Fax:** 916-361-0491 www.grapevineindependent.com rherburger@herburger.net

Garden Grove Garden Grove Journal (8.4M) 12866 Main St Ste 203 Garden Grove CA 92840 **Phn:** 714-539-6018 **Fax:** 714-539-6079 ggjournal.com ggjournal@ggjournal.com

Garden Grove Westminster Journal (4.5M) 7441 Garden Grove Blvd Ste G Garden Grove CA 92841 **Phn:** 714-895-3484 **Fax:** 714-894-0809

Gardena Gardena Valley News (5.0M) 15005 S Vermont Ave Gardena CA 90247 **Phn:** 310-329-6351 **Fax:** 310-329-7501 www.gardenavalleynews.org gvneditorial@gardenavalleynews.org

Georgetown Georgetown Gazette (1.6M) PO Box 49 Georgetown CA 95634 **Phn:** 530-333-4481 **Fax:** 530-333-0152 editor@gtgazette.com

Greenville Indian Valley Record (1.3M) PO Box 469 Greenville CA 95947 **Phn:** 530-284-7800 **Fax:** 530-283-3952 www.plumasnews.com mail@plumasnews.com

Gridley Gridley Herald (1.8M) PO Box 68 Gridley CA 95948 **Phn:** 530-846-3661 **Fax:** 530-846-4519 www.gridleyherald.com publisher@gridleyherald.com

Gualala Independent Coast Observer (3.0M) PO Box 1200 Gualala CA 95445 **Phn:** 707-884-3501 **Fax:** 707-884-1710 www.mendonoma.com news@mendonoma.com

Half Moon Bay The Review (7.0M) PO Box 68 Half Moon Bay CA 94019 **Phn:** 650-726-4424 **Fax:** 650-726-7054 www.hmbreview.com clay@hmbreview.com

Hanford Lemoore Advance (7.0M) PO Box 9 Hanford CA 93232 **Phn:** 559-924-5361 **Fax:** 559-924-6220

Healdsburg Sonoma West Times & News/Healdsburg Trib (6.0M) PO Box 518 Healdsburg CA 95448 **Phn:** 707-823-7845 **Fax:** 707-431-2623 www.sonomawest.com news@sonomawest.com

Hemet Valley Chronicle (40.0M) 2091 W Florida Ave Ste 140 Hemet CA 92545 **Phn:** 951-652-6529 **Fax:** 951-652-4009 www.thevalleychronicle.com

Hermosa Beach Beach Reporter (52.0M) 2615 Pacific Coast Hwy # 329 Hermosa Beach CA 90254 **Phn:** 310-372-0388 **Fax:** 310-372-6113 www.tbrnews.com estitt@tbrnews.com

Hermosa Beach Easy Reader Inc (58.0M) PO Box 427 Hermosa Beach CA 90254 **Phn:** 310-372-4611 **Fax:** 310-318-6292 www.easyreadernews.com mark@easyreadernews.com

Hesperia Hesperia Star (19.0M) 15550 Main St Ste C11 Hesperia CA 92345 **Phn:** 760-956-7827 **Fax:** 760-956-6803 www.hesperiastar.com editor@hesperiastar.com

Hesperia Valley Wide Newspapers (20.0M) 16295 Main St Hesperia CA 92345 **Phn:** 760-244-0021 **Fax:** 760-244-6609 www.valleywidenewspaper.com

Highland Highland Community News (14.6M) 27000 Base Line #G Highland CA 92346 **Phn:** 909-862-1771 **Fax:** 909-862-1787 www.highlandnews.net editor@highlandnews.net

CALIFORNIA WEEKLY NEWSPAPERS

Hollister The Pinnacle (19.0M) 380 San Benito St Hollister CA 95023 **Phn:** 831-637-6300 **Fax:** 831-637-8174 www.sanbenitocountytoday.com letters@pinnaclenews.com

Holtville Hometown Publishing (11.0M) 570 Holt Ave Holtville CA 92250 **Phn:** 760-356-2995 **Fax:** 760-356-4915 www.tribwekchron.com ivnews@tribwekchron.com

Huntington Beach The Local News (25.0M) 5901 Warner Ave # 429 Huntington Beach CA 92649 **Phn:** 714-914-9797 www.myhbgold.com hbnews1@aol.com

Idyllwild Idyllwild Town Crier (3.7M) PO Box 157 Idyllwild CA 92549 **Phn:** 951-659-2145 **Fax:** 951-659-2071 www.towncrier.com itc@towncrier.com

Imperial Beach Eagle & Times (6.5M) PO Box 748 Imperial Beach CA 91933 **Phn:** 619-429-5555 **Fax:** 619-429-5556 www.imperialbeachnewsca.com editor@eaglenewsca.com

Irvine Irvine World News (55.0M) 2006 McGaw Ave Irvine CA 92614 **Phn:** 949-553-2900 **Fax:** 949-553-2925 www.ocregister.com/sections/city-pages/irvine kbrusic@ocregister.com

Jackson Amador Ledger Dispatch (8.4M) PO Box 1328 Jackson CA 95642 **Phn:** 209-223-1767 **Fax:** 209-223-1264 www.ledger-dispatch.com editor@ledger-dispatch.com

Julian Julian News (2.5M) PO Box 639 Julian CA 92036 **Phn:** 760-765-2231 **Fax:** 760-765-1838 www.juliannews.com editor@juliannews.com

Kenwood Kenwood Press (8.0M) PO Box 277 Kenwood CA 95452 **Phn:** 707-833-5155 **Fax:** 707-833-5175 www.kenwoodpress.com info@kenwoodpress.com

Kerman Kerwest Inc (12.0M) PO Box 336 Kerman CA 93630 **Phn:** 559-846-6689 **Fax:** 559-846-8045 www.kerwestnewspapers.com kerwest@msn.com

King City South County Newspapers (5.6M) PO Box 710 King City CA 93930 **Phn:** 831-385-4880 **Fax:** 831-385-4799 www.kingcityrustler.com editor@southcountynewspapers.com

Kingsburg Kingsburg Recorder (3.3M) PO Box 128 Kingsburg CA 93631 **Phn:** 559-897-2993 **Fax:** 559-897-4868 www.hanfordsentinel.com/kingsburg_recorder jmcgill@hanfordsentinel.com

La Canada La Canada Outlook (11.5M) PO Box 578 La Canada CA 91012 **Phn:** 818-790-7500 **Fax:** 818-790-2039 outlooknewspapers.com outlooknews@outlooknewspapers.com

La Canada Pasadena Outlook (19.6M) PO Box 578 La Canada CA 91012 **Phn:** 626-398-7800 **Fax:** 818-790-2039 www.outlooknewspapers.com outlooknews@outlooknewspapers.com

La Habra La Habra Journal (10.0M) PO Box 44 La Habra CA 90633 **Phn:** 562-697-5473 **Fax:** 562-691-4570 www.lhj90631.com jwilliams@lhj90631.com

La Jolla La Jolla Light (18.0M) 565 Pearl St Ste 300 La Jolla CA 92037 **Phn:** 858-459-4201 **Fax:** 858-459-5250 www.lajollalight.com susandemaggio@lajollalight.com

Laguna Beach Coastline Pilot (12.5M) PO Box 248 Laguna Beach CA 92652 **Phn:** 949-380-4321 www.coastlinepilot.com john.canalis@latimes.com

Laguna Beach Laguna Beach Independent (15.0M) 250 Broadway St Laguna Beach CA 92651 **Phn:** 949-715-4100 **Fax:** 949-715-4106 www.lagunabeachindy.com editor@lbindy.com

Lake Arrowhead Crestline Courier News (3.5M) PO Box 2410 Lake Arrowhead CA 92352 **Phn:** 909-336-3555 **Fax:** 909-337-5275 www.mountain-news.com editor@mountain-news.com

Lake Arrowhead Mountain News (7.5M) PO Box 2410 Lake Arrowhead CA 92352 **Phn:** 909-336-3555 **Fax:** 909-337-5275 www.mountain-news.com editor@mountain-news.com

Lake Isabella Kern Valley Sun (6.5M) PO Box 3074 Lake Isabella CA 93240 **Phn:** 760-379-3667 **Fax:** 760-379-4343 www.kernvalleysun.com editor@kvsun.com

Lakeport Lake County Record-Bee (1.8M) PO Box 849 Lakeport CA 95453 **Phn:** 707-263-5636 **Fax:** 707-263-0600 www.record-bee.com mfeder@record-bee.com

Lamont Arvin Tiller (2.5M) PO Box 548 Lamont CA 93241 **Phn:** 661-845-3704 **Fax:** 661-845-5907

Laytonville Mendocino County Observer (3.0M) PO Box 490 Laytonville CA 95454 **Phn:** 707-984-6223 **Fax:** 707-984-8118 observer@pacific.net

Lincoln News-Messenger (6.3M) 553 F St Lincoln CA 95648 **Phn:** 916-645-7733 **Fax:** 916-645-2776 www.lincolnnewsmessenger.com messenger@goldcountrymedia.com

Linden Linden Herald (1.2M) PO Box 929 Linden CA 95236 **Phn:** 209-887-3112

Livermore The Independent (49.0M) PO Box 1198 Livermore CA 94551 **Phn:** 925-447-8700 **Fax:** 925-447-0212 www.independentnews.com editmail@compuserve.com

Long Beach Beachcomber (42.0M) PO Box 15679 Long Beach CA 90815 **Phn:** 562-597-8000 **Fax:** 562-597-9410 www.longbeachcomber.com editor@longbeachcomber.com

Long Beach Downtown Gazette (23.0M) 5225 E 2nd St Long Beach CA 90803 **Phn:** 562-433-2000 **Fax:** 562-434-8826 www.gazettes.com editor@gazettes.com

Long Beach Grunion Gazette (42.5M) 5225 E 2nd St Long Beach CA 90803 **Phn:** 562-433-2000 **Fax:** 562-434-8826 www.gazettes.com editor@gazettes.com

Long Beach Long Beach Times (45.0M) 121 Linden Ave Long Beach CA 90802 **Phn:** 562-715-5641 **Fax:** 562-628-1907 www.longbeachtimes.org lbtimes@aol.com

Long Beach The Reporter (8.0M) 3010 E Anaheim St Long Beach CA 90804 **Phn:** 562-438-5641 **Fax:** 562-438-7086 reporter.lb@verizon.net

Loomis Loomis News (1.1M) PO Box 125 Loomis CA 95650 **Phn:** 916-652-7939 **Fax:** 916-652-7879 www.theloomisnews.com marthag@goldcountrymedia.com

Los Alamitos News-Enterprise (32.0M) PO Box 1010 Los Alamitos CA 90720 **Phn:** 562-431-1397 **Fax:** 562-493-2310 newsenterprise.net editor@newsenterprise.net

Los Altos Town Crier (16.0M) 138 Main St Los Altos CA 94022 **Phn:** 650-948-9000 **Fax:** 650-948-6647 losaltosonline.com levernec@latc.com

Los Angeles Beverly Press & Park LaBrea News (13.0M) PO Box 36036 Los Angeles CA 90036 **Phn:** 323-933-5518 www.parklabreanewsbeverlypress.com editor@beverlypress.com

Los Angeles Burbank Leader (21.5M) 202 W 1st St Los Angeles CA 90012 **Phn:** 818-637-3200 **Fax:** 818-241-1975 www.burbankleader.com burbankleader@latimes.com

Los Angeles Eastern Group Publications (116.0M) 111 South Avenue 59 Los Angeles CA 90042 **Phn:** 323-341-7970 **Fax:** 323-341-7976 egpnews.com editorial@egpnews.com

Los Angeles La Canada Valley Sun (10.0M) 202 W 1st ST Los Angeles CA 90112 **Phn:** 818-495-4440 **Fax:** 818-790-5690 www.lacanadaonline.com lcnews@valleysun.net

Los Angeles LA Downtown News (49.0M) 1264 W 1st St Los Angeles CA 90026 **Phn:** 213-481-1448 **Fax:** 213-250-4617 www.LADowntownNews.com realpeople@downtownnews.com

Los Banos Los Banos Enterprise (4.5M) 907 6th St Los Banos CA 93635 **Phn:** 209-826-3831 **Fax:** 209-826-2005 www.losbanosenterprise.com kyancey@losbanosenterprise.com

Los Gatos Los Gatos Weekly Times (19.0M) 634 N Santa Cruz Ave Ste 208 Los Gatos CA 95030 **Phn:** 408-354-3110 **Fax:** 408-354-3917 www.mercurynews.com/los-gatos dsparrer@community-newspapers.com

Los Gatos Saratoga News (9.5M) 634 N Santa Cruz Ave Ste 208 Los Gatos CA 95030 **Phn:** 408-354-3110 **Fax:** 408-354-3917 www.mercurynews.com/saratoga dsparrer@community-newspapers.com

Loyalton Sierra Booster (3.5M) PO Box 8 Loyalton CA 96118 **Phn:** 530-993-4379 **Fax:** 530-993-1732 sierrabooster.com jbuck@psln.com

Lucerne Valley The Leader (2.8M) PO Box 299 Lucerne Valley CA 92356 **Phn:** 760-248-7878 **Fax:** 760-248-2042 www.lucernevalleyleader.com

Malibu Malibu Surfside News (13.5M) PO Box 903 Malibu CA 90265 **Phn:** 310-457-2112 **Fax:** 310-457-9908 www.malibusurfsidenews.com editor@malibusurfsidenews.com

Malibu Malibu Times (12.0M) 3864 Las Flores Canyon Rd Malibu CA 90265 **Phn:** 310-456-5507 **Fax:** 310-456-8986 www.malibutimes.com agyork@malibutimes.com

Mammoth Lakes Mammoth Times (4.2M) PO Box 3929 Mammoth Lakes CA 93546 **Phn:** 760-934-3929 **Fax:** 760-934-3951 mammothtimes.com editor@mammothtimes.com

Marina Del Rey The Argonaut (42.0M) PO Box 11209 Marina Del Rey CA 90295 **Phn:** 310-822-1629 **Fax:** 310-823-0616 argonautnews.com joe@argonautnews.com

Mariposa Mariposa Gazette (5.4M) PO Box 38 Mariposa CA 95338 **Phn:** 209-966-2500 **Fax:** 209-966-3384 www.mariposagazette.com mariposagazette@mariposagazette.com

Martinez Martinez News-Gazette (14.0M) PO Box 151 Martinez CA 94553 **Phn:** 925-228-6400 **Fax:** 925-228-1536

Middletown Middletown Times-Star (2.5M) PO Box 608 Middletown CA 95461 **Phn:** 707-987-3602 **Fax:** 707-987-3901 timesstar@gmail.com

Milpitas Milpitas Post (66.0M) 59 Marylinn Dr Milpitas CA 95035 **Phn:** 408-262-2454 **Fax:** 408-263-9710 www.mercurynews.com/milpitas news@themilpitaspost.com

Monrovia Beacon Media News (99.0M) 125 E Chestnut Ave Monrovia CA 91016 **Phn:** 626-301-1010 **Fax:** 626-301-0445 beaconmedianews.com editorial@coremg.net

Montecito Montecito Journal (20.0M) 1206 Coast Village Cir Ste D Montecito CA 93108 **Phn:** 805-565-1860 **Fax:** 805-969-6654 montecitojournal.net news@montecitojournal.net

Morgan Hill Times (4.0M) 30 E 3rd St Ste 100 Morgan Hill CA 95037 **Phn:** 408-779-4106 **Fax:** 408-779-3886 www.morganhilltimes.com editor@morganhilltimes.com

Mount Shasta Mt. Shasta Newspapers (9.8M) PO Box 127 Mount Shasta CA 96067 **Phn:** 530-926-5214 **Fax:** 530-926-4166 www.mtshastanews.com news@mtshastanews.com

Napa Napa Sentinel (15.0M) PO Box 2399 Napa CA 94558 **Phn:** 707-320-7362 napavalleyregister.com pjensen@napanews.com

CALIFORNIA WEEKLY NEWSPAPERS

Needles Needles Desert Star (4.0M) 800 W Broadway Ste E Needles CA 92363 **Phn:** 760-326-2222 **Fax:** 760-326-3480 www.thedesertstar.com publisher@nwppub.com

Newman Gustine Press Standard (1.5M) 1021 Fresno St Newman CA 95360 **Phn:** 209-862-2222 **Fax:** 209-862-4133 www.mattosnews.com

Newman West Side Index (2.1M) 1021 Fresno St Newman CA 95360 **Phn:** 209-862-2222 **Fax:** 209-862-4133 www.mattosnews.com news@mattosnews.com

Newport Beach Balboa Beacon (6.0M) PO Box 4336 Newport Beach CA 92661 **Phn:** 949-673-9575 www.balboabeacon.com balboabeacon@roadrunner.com

Novato Commuter Times (12.0M) PO Box V Novato CA 94948 **Phn:** 415-892-1510 **Fax:** 415-899-9685

Novato Marin Scope Newspapers (33.0M) 1301B Grant Ave Novato CA 94945 **Phn:** 415-892-1516 **Fax:** 415-897-0904 www.marinscope.com editor@marinscope.com

Novato Novato Advance (16.5M) PO Box 8 Novato CA 94948 **Phn:** 415-892-1516 **Fax:** 415-897-0940 marinscope.com/novato_advance editor@marinscope.com

Oakdale Escalon Times (11.0M) 122 S 3rd Ave Oakdale CA 95361 **Phn:** 209-838-7043 **Fax:** 209-847-9750 www.escalontimes.com mjackson@oakdaleleader.com

Oakdale Oakdale Leader (6.0M) 122 S 3rd Ave Oakdale CA 95361 **Phn:** 209-847-3021 **Fax:** 209-847-9750 www.oakdaleleader.com mjackson@oakdaleleader.com

Oakhurst Sierra Star (5.0M) PO Box 305 Oakhurst CA 93644 **Phn:** 559-683-4464 **Fax:** 559-683-8102 www.sierrastar.com editorial@sierrastar.com

Oakland East Bay Express (50.0M) 620 3rd St Oakland CA 94607 **Phn:** 510-879-3700 **Fax:** 510-879-3794 www.eastbayexpress.com editor@eastbayexpress.com

Oakland Post News Group (50.0M) 405 14th St Ste 1215 Oakland CA 94612 **Phn:** 510-287-8200 **Fax:** 510-287-8247 www.postnewsgroup.com

Ojai Ojai Valley News (11.0M) PO Box 277 Ojai CA 93024 **Phn:** 805-646-1476 **Fax:** 805-646-4281 www.ojaivalleynews.com editor@ojaivalleynews.com

Pacific Grove Hometown Bulletin (6.5M) 505 Lighthouse Ave Ste 202 Pacific Grove CA 93950 **Phn:** 831-647-1988 **Fax:** 831-647-1999

Pacific Palisades Palisadian-Post (4.8M) PO Box 725 Pacific Palisades CA 90272 **Phn:** 310-454-1321 **Fax:** 310-454-1078 www.palisadespost.com editor@palipost.com

Pacifica Pacifica Tribune (7.0M) PO Box 1189 Pacifica CA 94044 **Phn:** 650-359-6666 **Fax:** 650-359-3821 www.mercurynews.com/pacifica jnorthrop@bayareanewsgroup.com

Palm Desert Desert Mobile Home News (12.0M) 41995 Boardwalk Ste L2 Palm Desert CA 92211 **Phn:** 760-568-6633 **Fax:** 760-568-0603 news@dmhnews.com

Palm Springs The Desert Sun (20.0M) PO Box 2734 Palm Springs CA 92263 **Phn:** 760-322-8889 **Fax:** 760-778-4654 www.mydesert.com business@thedesertsun.com

Palmdale Antelope Valley Journal (1.0M) 3166 E Palmdale Blvd Ste 107 Palmdale CA 93550 **Phn:** 661-947-5009 **Fax:** 661-947-5208 avjournal@gmail.com

Palo Alto Mountain View Voice (18.0M) 450 Cambridge Ave Palo Alto CA 94306 **Phn:** 650-964-6300 **Fax:** 650-964-0294 www.mv-voice.com editor@mv-voice.com

Palo Alto Palo Alto Weekly (48.0M) 450 Cambridge Ave Palo Alto CA 94306 **Phn:** 650-326-8210 **Fax:** 650-326-3928 www.paloaltoonline.com editor@paweekly.com

Palo Alto The Almanac (15.0M) 450 Cambridge Ave Palo Alto CA 94306 **Phn:** 650-223-6525 **Fax:** 650-223-7525 www.almanacnews.com editor@almanacnews.com

Paradise Paradise Post (9.3M) PO Box 70 Paradise CA 95967 **Phn:** 530-877-4413 **Fax:** 530-877-1326 www.paradisepost.com newsroom@paradisepost.com

Pasadena Pasadena Weekly (35.0M) 50 S De Lacey Ave Ste 200 Pasadena CA 91105 **Phn:** 626-584-1500 **Fax:** 626-795-0149 www.pasadenaweekly.com andrec@pasadenaweekly.com

Paso Robles Paso Robles Press (7.5M) PO Box 427 Paso Robles CA 93447 **Phn:** 805-237-6060 **Fax:** 805-237-6066 www.pasoroblespress.com news@pasoroblespress.com

Patterson Patterson Irrigator (7.5M) 26 N 3rd St Patterson CA 95363 **Phn:** 209-892-6187 **Fax:** 209-892-3761 www.pattersonirrigator.com news@pattersonirrigator.com

Perris Perris Progress/Perris City News (3.5M) PO Box 128 Perris CA 92572 **Phn:** 951-657-1810 **Fax:** 951-940-1832 www.theperrisprogress.com perriscitynews@aol.com

Petaluma The Argus Courier (10.0M) PO Box 750308 Petaluma CA 94975 **Phn:** 707-762-4541 **Fax:** 707-776-8482 www.petaluma360.com argus@arguscourier.com

Placerville Village Life (12.0M) PO Box 1088 Placerville CA 95667 **Phn:** 530-622-1255 **Fax:** 530-622-7894 www.villagelife.com editor@villagelife.com

Pleasanton Pleasanton Weekly (18.0M) 5506 Sunol Blvd Ste 100 Pleasanton CA 94566 **Phn:** 925-600-0840 **Fax:** 925-600-9559 www.pleasantonweekly.com editor@pleasantonweekly.com

Point Reyes Station Point Reyes Light (3.3M) PO Box 210 Point Reyes Station CA 94956 **Phn:** 415-663-8404 **Fax:** 415-663-8458 www.ptreyeslight.com editor@ptreyeslight.com

Point Reyes Station West Marin Citizen (1.9M) PO Box 158 Point Reyes Station CA 94956 **Phn:** 415-723-6948 www.westmarincitizen.com

Porterville Southern Sierra Messenger (4.0M) 1660 N Newcomb St Porterville CA 93257 **Phn:** 888-201-8728 **Fax:** 800-539-3174

Poway Pomerado Newspapers (43.0M) 13475 Danielson St Ste 110 Poway CA 92064 **Phn:** 858-748-2311 **Fax:** 858-748-7695 www.pomeradonews.com editor@pomeradonews.com

Quincy Feather River Bulletin (3.5M) PO Box B Quincy CA 95971 **Phn:** 530-283-0800 **Fax:** 530-283-3952 www.plumasnews.com mail@plumasnews.com

Ramona Ramona Sentinel (5.5M) 425 10th St Ste A Ramona CA 92065 **Phn:** 760-789-1350 **Fax:** 760-789-4057 www.ramonasentinel.com maureen@ramonasentinel.com

Rancho Santa Fe Ranch Coast Newspapers (7.0M) PO Box 9077 Rancho Santa Fe CA 92067 **Phn:** 858-756-1451

Redding Anderson Valley Post (15.1M) 1101 Twin View Blvd Redding CA 96003 **Phn:** 530-365-2797 **Fax:** 530-365-2829 www.andersonvalleypost.com news@andersonvalleypost.com

Reedley Orange Cove & Mtn. Times (14.0M) PO Box 432 Reedley 93654 **Phn:** 559-638-2244 **Fax:** 559-638-5021 www.reedleyexponent.com ocm@reedleyexponent.com

Reedley Parlier Post (14.0M) PO Box 432 Reedley CA 93654 **Phn:** 559-638-2244 **Fax:** 559-638-5021 www.reedleyexponent.com parlier@reedleyexponent.com

Reedley Reedley Exponent (14.0M) PO Box 432 Reedley CA 93654 **Phn:** 559-638-2244 **Fax:** 559-638-5021 www.reedleyexponent.com editor@reedleyexponent.com

Ridgecrest News Review (7.5M) 109 N Sanders St Ridgecrest CA 93555 **Phn:** 760-371-4301 **Fax:** 760-371-4304 www.newsreviewiwv.com newsreview@iwvisp.com

Rio Vista River News-Herald (4.9M) PO Box 786 Rio Vista CA 94571 **Phn:** 707-374-6431 **Fax:** 707-374-6322 rveditor@citlink.net

Ripon Ripon Record (3.0M) 130 W Main St Ripon CA 95366 **Phn:** 209-599-2194 **Fax:** 209-599-2195 www.riponrecordnews.com editor@riponrecordnews.com

Riverside Riverside County Record (3.0M) PO Box 3187 Riverside CA 92519 **Phn:** 951-685-6191 **Fax:** 951-685-2961 www.countyrecordnews.com

Rocklin The Placer Herald (15.0M) 5055 Pacific St Rocklin CA 95677 **Phn:** 916-624-9713 **Fax:** 916-624-7469 www.placerherald.com krissik@goldcountrymedia.com

Rohnert Park Community Voice (13.0M) PO Box 2038 Rohnert Park CA 94927 **Phn:** 707-584-2222 **Fax:** 707-584-2233 www.thecommunityvoice.com news@thecommunityvoice.com

Rolling Hills Estates Peninsula News (15.0M) 550 Deep Valley Dr Ste 293B Rolling Hills Estates CA 90274 **Phn:** 310-377-6877 **Fax:** 310-377-4522 www.thepennews.com pennews@wcnet.org

Rosamond Rosamond News (11.0M) PO Box 848 Rosamond CA 93560 **Phn:** 661-256-0149 **Fax:** 661-269-2139 joycemediainc.com rosamondnews@rosamondnews.com

Roseville Press Tribune (7.0M) 188 Cirby Way Roseville CA 95678 **Phn:** 916-786-8746 **Fax:** 916-783-1183 www.thepresstribune.com pteditor@goldcountrymedia.com

Sacramento Sacramento Gazette (1.7M) 555 University Ave Ste 126 Sacramento CA 95825 **Phn:** 916-567-9654 **Fax:** 916-567-9653 www.sacgazette.com sacgazette@aol.com

Sacramento Sacramento News & Review (85.0M) 1124 Del Paso Blvd Sacramento CA 95815 **Phn:** 916-498-1234 **Fax:** 916-498-7920 www.newsreview.com sactonewstips@newsreview.com

Sacramento Valley Community Newspapers (15.0M) 2709 Riverside Blvd Sacramento CA 95818 **Phn:** 916-429-9901 **Fax:** 916-429-9906 www.valcomnews.com susan@valcomnews.com

Saint Helena St. Helena Star (4.5M) PO Box 346 Saint Helena CA 94574 **Phn:** 707-963-2731 **Fax:** 707-963-8957 napavalleyregister.com/star editor@sthelenastar.com

San Andreas Calaveras Newspapers (29.0M) PO Box 1197 San Andreas CA 95249 **Phn:** 209-754-3861 **Fax:** 209-754-4396 www.calaverasenterprise.com editor@calaverasenterprise.com

San Bernardino Precinct Reporter Group (80.0M) 1677 W Base Line St San Bernardino CA 92411 **Phn:** 909-889-0597 **Fax:** 909-889-1706 www.precinctreporter.com

San Clemente Sun Post (10.0M) 95 Avenida del Mar San Clemente CA 92672 **Phn:** 949-492-4316 **Fax:** 949-492-0401 www.ocregister.com kbrusic@ocregister.com

CALIFORNIA WEEKLY NEWSPAPERS

San Diego Community Newspaper Group (80.0M) 1621 Grand Ave Fl 2 San Diego CA 92109 **Phn:** 858-270-3103 **Fax:** 858-270-9325 www.sdnews.com mail@sdnews.com

San Diego San Diego Reader (169.0M) PO Box 85803 San Diego CA 92186 **Phn:** 619-235-3000 **Fax:** 619-231-0489 www.sandiegoreader.com

San Fernando San Fernando Sun (10.0M) 601 S Brand Blvd Ste 202 San Fernando CA 91340 **Phn:** 818-365-3111 **Fax:** 818-898-7135 www.sanfernandosun.com editor@sanfernandosun.com

San Francisco Bay Guardian (153.0M) 135 Mississippi St San Francisco CA 94107 **Phn:** 415-255-3100 **Fax:** 415-255-8955 www.sfbg.com listings@sfbg.com

San Francisco SF Weekly (116.0M) 225 Bush St Flr 17 San Francisco CA 94104 **Phn:** 415-536-8100 **Fax:** 415-541-9096 www.sfweekly.com

San Jose Almaden Times (21.5M) 1310 Tully Rd Ste 112 San Jose CA 95122 **Phn:** 408-494-7000 **Fax:** 408-494-7078 www.timesmediainc.com times@timesmediainc.com

San Jose Metro Newspapers (83.0M) 550 S 1st St San Jose CA 95113 **Phn:** 408-298-8000 **Fax:** 408-298-0602 www.metronews.com letters@metronews.com

San Jose Silicon Valley Community Newspapers (126.0M) 1095 The Alameda San Jose CA 95126 **Phn:** 408-200-1000 **Fax:** 408-200-1013 www.mercurynews.com/my-town dbryant@community-newspapers.com

San Leandro Times (46.0M) 2060 Washington Ave San Leandro CA 94577 **Phn:** 510-614-1555 **Fax:** 510-483-4209 www.ebpublishing.com jimk@ebpublishing.com

San Luis Obispo The Bay News (18.5M) 615 Clarion Ct Ste 2 San Luis Obispo CA 93401 **Phn:** 805-543-6397 **Fax:** 805-543-3698 www.tolosapress.com editor@tolosapress.com

San Luis Obispo The Coast News (25.0M) 615 Clarion Ct Ste 2 San Luis Obispo CA 93401 **Phn:** 805-543-6397 **Fax:** 805-543-3698 tolosapress.com editor@tolosapress.com

San Luis Obispo The New Times (42.0M) 1010 Marsh St San Luis Obispo CA 93401 **Phn:** 805-546-8208 **Fax:** 805-546-8641 www.newtimesslo.com aschwellenbach@newtimesslo.com

San Marcos Sun Newspapers (8.0M) PO Box 789 San Marcos CA 92079 **Phn:** 760-729-7698 thesunpapers@yahoo.com

San Marino San Marino Tribune (15.0M) 1441 San Marino Ave San Marino CA 91108 **Phn:** 626-792-6397 **Fax:** 626-792-4920 www.sanmarinotribune.com smtribune@earthlink.net

San Pedro Random Lengths (30.0M) PO Box 731 San Pedro CA 90733 **Phn:** 310-519-1016 **Fax:** 310-832-1000 www.randomlengthsnews.com editor@randomlengthsnews.com

San Rafael Pacific Sun (36.0M) 835 4th St Ste B San Rafael CA 94901 **Phn:** 415-485-6700 **Fax:** 415-485-6226 www.pacificsun.com jwalsh@pacificsun.com

Sanger Fowler Ensign (1.2M) 740 N St Sanger CA 93657 **Phn:** 559-875-2511 **Fax:** 559-875-2521 www.reedleyexponent.com/publications/fowler_ensign reedleyexponent@yahoo.com

Sanger Sanger Herald (2.5M) 740 N St Sanger CA 93657 **Phn:** 559-875-2511 **Fax:** 559-875-2521 thesangerherald.com sangerherald@gmail.com

Santa Barbara Santa Barbara Independent (40.0M) 122 W Figueroa St Santa Barbara CA 93101 **Phn:** 805-965-5205 **Fax:** 805-965-5518 www.independent.com news@independent.com

Santa Clara Santa Clara Weekly (15.0M) 3000 Scott Blvd Ste 105 Santa Clara CA 95054 **Phn:** 408-243-2000 **Fax:** 408-243-1408 Www.SantaClaraWeekly.com scweekly@ix.netcom.com

Santa Cruz Good Times (45.0M) 1205 Pacific Ave Ste 301 Santa Cruz CA 95060 **Phn:** 831-458-1100 **Fax:** 831-458-1295 gtweekly.com letters@gtweekly.com

Santa Cruz Metro Santa Cruz (34.0M) 115 Cooper St Santa Cruz CA 95060 **Phn:** 831-457-9000 **Fax:** 831-457-5828 www.santacruzweekly.com

Santa Maria Adobe Press & Times Press Recorder (7.5M) PO Box 400 Santa Maria CA 93456 **Phn:** 805-925-2691 www.theadobepress.com eslater@timespressrecorder.com

Santa Maria The Sun (20.0M) 3130 Skyway Dr Ste 603 Santa Maria CA 93455 **Phn:** 805-347-1968 **Fax:** 805-347-9889 www.santamariasun.com mail@santamariasun.com

Santa Monica Observer (20.0M) 1844 Lincoln Blvd Santa Monica CA 90404 **Phn:** 310-452-9900 **Fax:** 310-388-1235 www.smobserver.com alyssa@smobserver.com

Santa Monica Santa Monica Mirror (20.0M) 3435 Ocean Park Blvd #210 Santa Monica CA 90405 **Phn:** 310-310-2627 **Fax:** 424-744-8821 www.smmirror.com tj@smmirror.com

Santa Paula Santa Paula Times (9.0M) PO Box 431 Santa Paula CA 93061 **Phn:** 805-525-1890 **Fax:** 805-309-2278 www.santapaulatimes.com santapaulatimes@mac.com

Santa Rosa North Bay Bohemian (25.0M) 847 5th St Santa Rosa CA 95404 **Phn:** 707-527-1200 **Fax:** 707-527-1288 www.bohemian.com

Scotts Valley Press Banner (20.0M) 5215 Scotts Valley Dr Ste F Scotts Valley CA 95066 **Phn:** 831-438-2500 **Fax:** 831-438-4114 www.pressbanner.com peter@pressbanner.com

Seal Beach Leisure World Golden Rain News (9.0M) PO Box 2338 Seal Beach CA 90740 **Phn:** 562-430-0534 **Fax:** 562-598-1617 www.lwsb.com grf@lwsb.com

Seal Beach Seal Beach Sun (30.0M) 216 Main St Seal Beach CA 90740 **Phn:** 562-430-7555 **Fax:** 562-430-3469 dennis@sunnews.org

Seaside Monterey Co. Weekly (43.0M) 668 Williams Ave Seaside CA 93955 **Phn:** 831-394-5656 **Fax:** 831-394-2909 www.montereycountyweekly.com mark@mcweekly.com

Selma Selma Enterprise (11.7M) PO Box 100 Selma CA 93662 **Phn:** 559-896-1976 **Fax:** 559-896-9160 www.hanfordsentinel.com/selma_enterprise jmcgill@selmaenterprise.com

Shafter Shafter Press & Wasco Tribune (2.3M) PO Box 1600 Shafter CA 93263 **Phn:** 661-746-4942 **Fax:** 661-746-5571

Shasta Lake Shasta Lake Bulletin (1.4M) PO Box 8025 Shasta Lake CA 96019 **Phn:** 530-275-1716 **Fax:** 530-275-1699 www.shastalake.ws slb@shasta.com

Shingletown Ridge Rider News (1.2M) PO Box 210 Shingletown CA 96088 **Phn:** 530-474-3434 **Fax:** 530-474-3448 editor@shingletownrrn.com

Sierra Madre Mountain Views News (20.0M) 80 W Sierra Madre Blvd # 327 Sierra Madre CA 91024 **Phn:** 626-355-2737 **Fax:** 626-609-3285 mtnviewsnews.com editor@mtnviewsnews.com

Signal Hill Signal Tribune (25.0M) 939 E 27th St Signal Hill CA 90755 **Phn:** 562-595-7900 **Fax:** 562-595-7911 www.signaltribunenewspaper.com newspaper@signaltribune.com

Solvang Santa Ynez Valley News (7.5M) PO Box 647 Solvang CA 93464 **Phn:** 805-688-5522 **Fax:** 805-688-7685 www.syvnews.com jscully@syvnews.com

Sonoma Sonoma Index Tribune (10.2M) 117 W Napa St Sonoma CA 95476 **Phn:** 707-938-2111 **Fax:** 707-938-1600 www.sonomanews.com managingeditor@sonomanews.com

Sonoma Sonoma Valley Sun (15.0M) 158 W Napa St Sonoma CA 95476 **Phn:** 707-933-0101 **Fax:** 707-933-1573 news.sonomaportal.com news@sonomasun.com

South Pasadena South Pasadena Review (4.0M) 1020 C Mission St South Pasadena CA 91030 **Phn:** 626-799-1161 **Fax:** 626-799-2892 south.pasadenanow.com bglazier@southpasadenareview.com

Stockton The Record (35.0M) 530 E Market St Stockton CA 95202 **Phn:** 209-943-6397 **Fax:** 209-547-8186 www.recordnet.com mklocke@recordnet.com

Susanville Lassen County Times (11.0M) 100 Grand Ave Susanville CA 96130 **Phn:** 530-257-5321 **Fax:** 530-257-0408 www.lassennews.com lctimes@lassennews.com

Taft Midway Driller (4.6M) 800 Center St Taft CA 93268 **Phn:** 661-763-3171 **Fax:** 661-763-5638 www.taftmidwaydriller.com editor@bak.rr.com

Tahoe City Tahoe World (4.8M) PO Box 138 Tahoe City CA 96145 **Phn:** 530-583-3488 **Fax:** 530-583-7109 www.tahoe.com rslabaugh@swiftcom.com

Tehachapi Tehachapi News (6.0M) 411 N Mill St Tehachapi CA 93561 **Phn:** 661-822-6828 **Fax:** 661-822-4053 www.tehachapinews.com editorial@tehachapinews.com

Three Rivers Kaweah Commonwealth (3.5M) PO Box 806 Three Rivers CA 93271 **Phn:** 559-561-3627 **Fax:** 559-561-0118 www.kaweahcommonwealth.com 3rnews@kaweahcommonwealth.com

Tiburon The Ark (3.2M) PO Box 1054 Tiburon CA 94920 **Phn:** 415-435-2652 **Fax:** 415-435-0849 www.thearknewspaper.com editor@thearknewspaper.com

Toluca Lake Tolucan Times (40.0M) 10701 Riverside Dr Ste A Toluca Lake CA 91602 **Phn:** 818-762-2171 **Fax:** 818-980-1900 tolucantimes.info editorial@tolucantimes.com

Truckee Sierra Sun (6.5M) 12315 Deerfield Dr Ste 1 Truckee CA 96161 **Phn:** 530-587-6061 **Fax:** 530-587-3763 www.tahoedailytribune.com/NorthShore editor@sierrasun.com

Turlock Turlock Journal (6.0M) 138 S Center St Turlock CA 95380 **Phn:** 209-634-9141 **Fax:** 209-632-8813 www.turlockjournal.com dwyatt@mantecabulletin.com

Twentynine Palms The Desert Trail (3.5M) 6396 Adobe Rd Twentynine Palms CA 92277 **Phn:** 760-367-3577 **Fax:** 760-367-1798 hidesertstar.com/the_desert_trail news@deserttrail.com

Valley Center Valley Roadrunner (3.5M) PO Box 1529 Valley Center CA 92082 **Phn:** 760-749-1112 **Fax:** 760-749-1688 www.valleycenter.com editor@valleycenter.com

Valley Springs The News (1.1M) 1906 Vista Del Lago Dr #L Valley Springs CA 95252 **Phn:** 209-772-2234 **Fax:** 209-772-2244 www.valleyspringsnews.com newsroom@valleyspringsnews.com

Ventura Ventura County Reporter (35.0M) 700 E Main St Ventura CA 93001 **Phn:** 805-648-2244 **Fax:** 805-648-2245 www.vcreporter.com david@vcreporter.com

Walnut Creek Concord Transcript (27.0M) 2640 Shadelands Dr Walnut Creek CA 94598 **Phn:** 925-943-8300 **Fax:** 925-943-8362 transcript@bayareanewsgroup.com

Walnut Creek Contra Costa Sun & Walnut Creek Journal (15.0M) PO Box 8099 Walnut Creek CA 94596 **Phn:** 925-952-2648 **Fax:** 925-933-0239 www.contracostatimes.com ccsun@cctimes.com

Walnut Creek Rossmoor News (6.8M) PO Box 2190 Walnut Creek CA 94595 **Phn:** 925-988-7800 **Fax:** 925-935-8348 www.rossmoornews.com morourke@rossmoor.com

Weaverville Trinity Journal (4.3M) PO Box 340 Weaverville CA 96093 **Phn:** 530-623-2055 **Fax:** 530-623-5382 www.trinityjournal.com trinityjournal@dcacable.net

West Covina San Gabriel Valley Tribune (40.0M) 1210 N Azusa Canyon rd West Covina CA 91790 **Phn:** 626-544-0811 www.sgvtribune.com news.tribune@sgvn.com

West Sacramento The News Ledger (2.3M) PO Box 463 West Sacramento CA 95691 **Phn:** 916-371-8030 **Fax:** 916-371-8055 www.westsac.com/news-ledger

West Sacramento West Sacramento Press (6.0M) 830 Jefferson Blvd Ste 60 West Sacramento CA 95691 **Phn:** 916-371-2397 **Fax:** 916-371-9113

Westminster Westminster Herald (4.0M) PO Box 428 Westminster CA 92684 **Phn:** 714-893-4501 **Fax:** 714-893-4502 westmherald@aol.com

Westwood Westwood Pine Press (1.4M) PO Box 790 Westwood CA 96137 **Phn:** 530-256-2277 **Fax:** 530-257-0408 www.lassennews.com lctimes@lassennews.com

Willits Willits News (3.1M) PO Box 628 Willits CA 95490 **Phn:** 707-459-4643 **Fax:** 707-459-1664 www.willitsnews.com lwilliams@willitsnews.com

Willows Orland Press-Register (2.4M) 130 N Butte St # A Willows CA 95988 **Phn:** 530-934-6800 **Fax:** 530-934-6815 www.willows-journal.com editor@tcnpress.com

Willows Sacramento Valley Mirror (2.9M) 138 W Sycamore St Willows CA 95988 **Phn:** 530-934-9511 **Fax:** 530-934-9208 valleymirror@pulsarco.com

Willows Willows Journal (8.0M) 130 N Butte St Willows CA 95988 **Phn:** 530-934-6800 **Fax:** 530-934-6815 www.willows-journal.com editor@tcnpress.com

Wilton River Valley Times (5.5M) PO Box 209 Wilton CA 95693 **Phn:** 916-687-4832 www.rivervalleytimes.com rvt@herburger.net

Winters Winters Express (2.6M) 312 Railroad Ave Winters CA 95694 **Phn:** 530-795-4551 www.wintersexpress.com news@wintersexpress.com

Winton Mid-Valley Publications (35.0M) PO Box 65 Winton CA 95388 **Phn:** 209-358-5311 **Fax:** 209-358-7108 www.midvalleypublications.com kellythomas@midvalleypub.com

Woodland Hills Valley News Group (20.0M) 23009 Ventura Blvd Woodland Hills CA 91364 **Phn:** 818-223-9545 **Fax:** 818-223-9552 www.valleynewsgroup.com wnrcnews@instanet.com

Wrightwood Mountaineer Progress (4.3M) 3407 State Highway 2 Wrightwood CA 92397 **Phn:** 760-249-3245 **Fax:** 760-249-4021 www.mtprogress.net newsroom@mtprogress.net

Yucaipa Yucaipa News-Mirror (20.3M) PO Box 760 Yucaipa CA 92399 **Phn:** 909-797-9101 **Fax:** 909-797-0502 www.newsmirror.net cteeters@newsmirror.net

Yucca Valley Hi-Desert Star (11.0M) PO Box 880 Yucca Valley CA 92286 **Phn:** 760-365-3315 **Fax:** 760-365-8686 www.hidesertstar.com news@hidesertstar.com

COLORADO

Akron The News-Reporter (2.4M) 69 Main Ave Akron CO 80720 **Phn:** 970-345-2296 **Fax:** 970-345-6638 www.akronnewsreporter.com

Aspen Times Weekly (10.0M) 310 E Main St Aspen CO 81611 **Phn:** 970-925-3414 **Fax:** 970-925-6240 www.aspentimes.com mail@aspentimes.com

Aurora Aurora Sentinel (26.0M) 14305 E Alameda Ave Ste 200 Aurora CO 80012 **Phn:** 303-750-7555 **Fax:** 303-750-7699 www.aurorasentinel.com news@aurorasentinel.com

Bailey Park County Republican & Fairplay Flume (2.5M) PO Box 460 Bailey CO 80421 **Phn:** 303-838-4423 **Fax:** 303-838-8414 theflume.com

Bayfield Pine River Times (1.5M) PO Box 830 Bayfield CO 81122 **Phn:** 970-884-2331 **Fax:** 970-884-4385 www.pinerivertimes.com prt@pinerivertimes.com

Berthoud Berthoud Weekly Surveyor (2.0M) 440 Mountain Ave Berthoud CO 80513 **Phn:** 970-532-2252 **Fax:** 970-532-5424 www.berthoudsurveyor.com editor@berthoudsurveyor.com

Black Hawk Weekly Register-Call (1.9M) PO Box 93 Black Hawk CO 80422 **Phn:** 303-582-0133 www.gilpincountynews.com

Boulder Boulder Weekly (25.0M) 690 S Lashley Ln Boulder CO 80305 **Phn:** 303-494-5511 **Fax:** 303-494-2585 www.boulderweekly.com editorial@boulderweekly.com

Brighton Metro West Publishing (35.0M) 139 N Main St Brighton CO 80601 **Phn:** 303-659-2522 **Fax:** 303-659-2901 www.metrowestfyi.com news@metrowestnewspapers.com

Broomfield Broomfield Enterprise (18.5M) 3400 Industrial Ln Unit 2 Broomfield CO 80020 **Phn:** 303-448-9898 **Fax:** 303-466-8168 www.broomfieldenterprise.com baxterj@broomfieldenterprise.com

Brush Brush News-Tribune (2.3M) PO Box 8 Brush CO 80723 **Phn:** 970-842-5516 **Fax:** 970-842-5519 www.brushnewstribune.com horner@brushnewstribune.com

Buena Vista Chaffee County Times (3.0M) PO Box 2048 Buena Vista CO 81211 **Phn:** 719-395-8621 **Fax:** 719-395-8623 www.chaffeecountytimes.com editor@chaffeecountytimes.com

Burlington Burlington Record (3.0M) PO Box 459 Burlington CO 80807 **Phn:** 719-346-5381 **Fax:** 719-346-5514 www.burlington-record.com brecordeditor@plainstel.com

Castle Rock CO Community Newspapers (90.0M) PO Box 1270 Castle Rock CO 80104 **Phn:** 303-688-3128 **Fax:** 303-660-4826 www.ourcoloradonews.com news@ourcoloradonews.com

Castle Rock Elbert County News (3.0M) 125 Stephanie Pl Castle Rock CO 80109 **Phn:** 303-688-3128 www.ourcoloradonews.com pressreleases@ourcoloradonews.com

Castle Rock Parker Chronicle (17.0M) 125 Stephanie Pl Castle Rock CO 80109 **Phn:** 303-688-3128 www.ourcoloradonews.com pressreleases@ourcoloradonews.com

Cheyenne Wells The Range Ledger (1.5M) PO Box 684 Cheyenne Wells CO 80810 **Phn:** 719-767-5615 **Fax:** 719-767-5113 rangeledger@rmi.net

Colorado Springs Black Forest News (0.9M) PO Box 88088 Colorado Springs CO 80908 **Phn:** 719-495-8750 **Fax:** 719-495-8758 www.blackforestnews-co.com blackforestnews@earthlink.net

Colorado Springs The Colorado Springs Independent (36.5M) 235 S Nevada Ave Colorado Springs CO 80903 **Phn:** 719-577-4545 **Fax:** 719-577-4107 www.csindy.com newsroom@csindy.com

Colorado Springs Westside Pioneer (5.0M) 526 S 26th St Colorado Springs CO 80904 **Phn:** 719-471-6776 www.westsidepioneer.com editor@westsidepioneer.com

Commerce City Commerce City Beacon (14.0M) 7631 Brighton Blvd Commerce City CO 80022 **Phn:** 303-289-4600 **Fax:** 303-288-3344 commercecitybeacon.net unionnorm@qwestoffice.net

Cortez Animas Publishing (9.1M) 123 E Roger Smith Ave Cortez CO 81321 **Phn:** 970-565-8527 **Fax:** 970-565-8532 cortezjournal.com webnews@cortezjournal.com

Crested Butte Crested Butte News (5.2M) PO Box 369 Crested Butte CO 81224 **Phn:** 970-349-0500 **Fax:** 970-349-9876 www.crestedbuttenews.com editorial@crestedbuttenews.com

Crested Butte Crested Butte Weekly (4.0M) PO Box 1609 Crested Butte CO 81224 **Phn:** 970-349-1710 **Fax:** 970-349-1706 www.crestedbuttenews.com editorial@crestedbuttenews.com

Deer Trail Tri-County Tribune (0.6M) PO Box 220 Deer Trail CO 80105 **Phn:** 303-769-4646 **Fax:** 303-769-4650 rbell357@aol.com

Delta Delta County Independent (7.0M) PO Box 809 Delta CO 81416 **Phn:** 970-874-4421 **Fax:** 970-874-4424 www.deltacountyindependent.com editor@deltacountyindependent.com

Denver Colorado Statesman (13.0M) PO Box 18129 Denver CO 80218 **Phn:** 303-837-8600 **Fax:** 303-837-9015 www.coloradostatesman.com info@coloradostatesman.com

Denver Denver Herald-Dispatch (1.2M) 2200 S Federal Blvd Unit 6 Denver CO 80219 **Phn:** 303-936-7778 **Fax:** 303-936-0994 nancy@hdnewspaper.com

Denver North Denver Tribune (20.0M) PO Box 12009 Denver CO 80212 **Phn:** 303-273-0488 **Fax:** 303-273-0490 www.northdenvertribune.com news@northdenvertribune.com

Denver The Colorado Leader (2.4M) 4661 S Utica St Denver CO 80236 **Phn:** 303-922-0589 **Fax:** 303-922-2106 www.coloradoleader.com jayne@coloradoleader.com

Denver Westword (100.0M) PO Box 5970 Denver CO 80217 **Phn:** 303-296-7744 **Fax:** 303-296-5416 www.westword.com editorial@westword.com

Dove Creek Dove Creek Press (1.3M) PO Box 598 Dove Creek CO 81324 **Phn:** 970-677-2214 **Fax:** 970-677-3002 www.dovecreekpress.com dcpress@centurytel.net

Eads Kiowa County Press (0.8M) PO Box 248 Eads CO 81036 **Phn:** 719-438-5800 www.kiowacountypress.com release@kiowacountypress.com

Eagle Eagle Valley Enterprise (2.1M) PO Box 450 Eagle CO 81631 **Phn:** 970-328-6656 **Fax:** 970-328-6393 www.vaildaily.com/News/EagleValley pboyd@eaglevalleyenterprise.com

Eaton North Weld Herald (1.7M) PO Box 235 Eaton CO 80615 **Phn:** 970-454-3466 nwherald.qwestoffice.net

Estes Park Estes Park News (6.5M) PO Box 508 Estes Park CO 80517 **Phn:** 970-586-5800 www.estesparknews.com info@estesparknews.com

Estes Park Estes Park Trail Gazette (5.8M) PO Box 1707 Estes Park CO 80517 **Phn:** 970-586-3356 **Fax:** 970-586-9532 www.eptrail.com tgeditor@eptrail.com

COLORADO WEEKLY NEWSPAPERS

Evergreen Evergreen Newspapers (13.4M) 27902 Meadow Dr Unit 200 Evergreen CO 80439 **Phn:** 303-674-5534 **Fax:** 303-674-4104 www.canyoncourier.com news@evergreenco.com

Flagler Flagler News (1.4M) PO Box 188 Flagler CO 80815 **Phn:** 719-765-4466 **Fax:** 719-765-4517

Florence Florence Citizen (1.0M) 200 S Pikes Peak Ave Florence CO 81226 **Phn:** 719-784-6383 **Fax:** 719-784-6384 www.florencecitizen.com florencecitizen@aol.com

Fountain El Paso County Advertiser-News (4.8M) PO Box 400 Fountain CO 80817 **Phn:** 719-382-5611 **Fax:** 719-382-5614

Fountain Fountain Valley News (4.8M) PO Box 400 Fountain CO 80817 **Phn:** 719-382-5611 **Fax:** 719-382-5614

Fowler Fowler Tribune (1.2M) 112 E Cranston Ave Fowler CO 81039 **Phn:** 719-263-5311 **Fax:** 719-263-5900 www.fowlertribune.com fowlereditor@ljtdmail.com

Frisco Leadville Chronicle (4.5M) PO Box 709 Frisco CO 80443 **Phn:** 719-486-3666 www.summitdaily.com rwondercheck@swiftcom.com

Fruita Fruita Times (1.5M) 217 E Aspen Ave Fruita CO 81521 **Phn:** 970-858-3924 **Fax:** 970-858-7658 www.fruitatimes.com info@fruitatimes.com

Golden Mile High Newspapers (50.2M) PO Box 17270 Golden CO 80402 **Phn:** 303-279-5541 **Fax:** 303-468-2592 www.ourcoloradonews.com mkelly@ourcoloradonews.com

Granby Middle Park Times (3.0M) PO Box 409 Granby CO 80446 **Phn:** 970-887-3334 **Fax:** 970-887-3204 www.skyhidailynews.com news@skyhidailynews.com

Granby Sky-Hi News (7.5M) PO Box 409 Granby CO 80446 **Phn:** 970-887-3334 **Fax:** 970-887-3204 www.skyhidailynews.com news@skyhidailynews.com

Grand Junction Grand Junction Free Press (20.0M) 145 N 4th St Grand Junction CO 81501 **Phn:** 970-243-2200 www.postindependent.com/News/Grandjunction editor@gjfreepress.com

Greenwood Village The Villager (6.2M) 8933 E Union Ave Ste 230 Greenwood Village CO 80111 **Phn:** 303-773-8313 **Fax:** 303-773-8456 www.villagerpublishing.com editorial@villagerpublishing.com

Gunnison Country Times (3.8M) 218 N Wisconsin St Gunnison CO 81230 **Phn:** 970-641-1414 **Fax:** 970-641-6515 www.gunnisontimes.com editor@gunnisontimes.com

Haxtun Haxtun Herald (1.4M) PO Box 128 Haxtun CO 80731 **Phn:** 970-774-6118 **Fax:** 970-774-7690 www.hfherald.com news@hfherald.com

Holyoke Holyoke Enterprise (1.8M) PO Box 297 Holyoke CO 80734 **Phn:** 970-854-2811 **Fax:** 970-854-2232 www.holyokeenterprise.com

Idaho Springs Clear Creek Courant (2.1M) PO Box 2020 Idaho Springs CO 80452 **Phn:** 303-567-4491 **Fax:** 303-567-0520 www.clearcreekcourant.com couranteditor@evergreenco.com

Johnstown Johnstown Breeze (1.6M) PO Box 400 Johnstown CO 80534 **Phn:** 970-587-4525 myjohnstownbreeze.com

Julesburg Julesburg Advocate (2.0M) 108 Cedar St Julesburg CO 80737 **Phn:** 970-474-3388 **Fax:** 970-474-3389 www.julesburgadvocate.com

Kersey The Voice (2.5M) 326 1st St Kersey CO 80644 **Phn:** 970-356-7176

La Veta The Signature (2.6M) PO Box 154 La Veta CO 81055 **Phn:** 719-742-5591 **Fax:** 719-742-3183 www.signaturenewspaper.com editor@signaturenewspaper.com

Lake City Lake City Silver World (1.5M) PO Box 100 Lake City CO 81235 **Phn:** 970-944-2515 **Fax:** 970-944-7009 www.lakecitysilverworld.com silverw@centurytel.net

Lamar Lamar Ledger (2.6M) 310 S 5th St Lamar CO 81052 **Phn:** 719-336-2266 **Fax:** 719-336-2526 www.lamarledger.com editor@lamarledger.com

Las Animas Bent County Democrat (1.9M) PO Box 467 Las Animas CO 81054 **Phn:** 719-456-1333 **Fax:** 719-456-1420 www.bcdemocratonline.com bcd@ljtdmail.com

Leadville The Herald Democrat (3.0M) PO Box 980 Leadville CO 80461 **Phn:** 719-486-0641 **Fax:** 719-486-0611 www.leadvilleherald.com allnews@leadvilleherald.com

Limon Eastern Colorado Plainsman & Limon Leader (1.5M) PO Box 1300 Limon CO 80828 **Phn:** 719-743-2371 **Fax:** 719-775-9082 www.easterncoloradoplainsman.com editor@thelimonleader.com

Littleton Colorado Community Newspapers (47.0M) 2329 W Main St Ste 103 Littleton CO 80120 **Phn:** 303-794-7877 www.ourcoloradonews.com pressreleases@ccnewspapers.com

Littleton Columbine Courier (20.0M) 5868 S Rapp St # 119 Littleton CO 80120 **Phn:** 303-933-2233 **Fax:** 303-933-4449 www.columbinecourier.com news@evergreenco.com

Longmont Hometown Newspapers (18.0M) PO Box 929 Longmont CO 80501 **Phn:** 303-666-6576 **Fax:** 303-666-6602 www.coloradohometownweekly.com news@coloradohometown.com

Lyons Lyons Recorder (0.9M) PO Box 1729 Lyons CO 80540 **Phn:** 303-823-6625 www.lyonsrecorder.com editor@lyonsrecorder.com

Manitou Springs Pikes Peak Bulletin (1.0M) 329 Manitou Ave Ste 103 Manitou Springs CO 80829 **Phn:** 719-685-9690 **Fax:** 719-685-9705 www.pikespeakpublishing.com news@pikespeakpublishing.com

Meeker Rio Blanco Herald Times (3.0M) PO Box 720 Meeker CO 81641 **Phn:** 970-878-4017 **Fax:** 970-878-4016 www.theheraldtimes.com bobby@theheraldtimes.com

Monte Vista Valley Publishing (1.5M) PO Box 607 Monte Vista CO 81144 **Phn:** 719-852-3531 **Fax:** 719-852-3387 www.montevistajournal.com valleypubs@amigo.net

Monument Tri-Lakes/Monument Tribune (4.5M) 47 3rd St Monument CO 80132 **Phn:** 719-481-3423 **Fax:** 719-481-9005 www.ourcoloradonews.com rboldrey@ourcoloradonews.com

Nederland The Mountain-Ear (2.5M) PO Box 99 Nederland CO 80466 **Phn:** 303-258-7075 **Fax:** 303-258-7250 themtnear.com bhz@themountainear.com

Norwood Norwood Post (1.2M) PO Box 400 Norwood CO 81423 **Phn:** 970-729-1681 telluridenews.com/norwood_post norwoodpost@yahoo.com

Nucla San Miguel Basin Forum (1.5M) PO Box 9 Nucla CO 81424 **Phn:** 970-864-7425 smalltownpapers.com

Ordway Ordway New Era (1.1M) 223 Main St Ordway CO 81063 **Phn:** 719-267-3576 **Fax:** 719-267-4661 news@rockyforddailygazette.com

Ouray Ouray County Plaindealer (1.9M) PO Box 607 Ouray CO 81427 **Phn:** 970-325-4412 **Fax:** 970-325-4413 www.ouraynews.com plaindealer@ouraynews.com

Pagosa Springs Pagosa Springs Sun (4.5M) PO Box 9 Pagosa Springs CO 81147 **Phn:** 970-264-2101 **Fax:** 970-264-2103 www.pagosasun.com editor@pagosasun.com

Palisade Palisade Tribune (4.8M) PO Box 8 Palisade CO 81526 **Phn:** 970-464-5614 www.palisadetribune.com info@palisadetribune.com

Pueblo Colorado Tribune (0.4M) 447 Park Dr Pueblo CO 81005 **Phn:** 719-561-4008 **Fax:** 719-561-4007 www.tribuneusa.net colotrib@coyotenet.net

Pueblo West Pueblo West View (11.5M) 215 S Purcell Blvd Pueblo West CO 81007 **Phn:** 719-547-9606 **Fax:** 719-547-4380 www.pueblowestview.com comments@pueblowestview.com

Rifle The Citizen Telegram (3.5M) 125 W 4th St Ste 206 Rifle CO 81650 **Phn:** 970-625-3245 **Fax:** 970-625-3628 www.postindependent.com/News/Rifle news@citizentelegram.com

San Luis Costilla County Free Press (0.3M) PO Box 306 San Luis CO 81152 **Phn:** 719-672-3764 **Fax:** 719-672-3895 costillafreepress@gmail.com

Silverton Silverton Standard/Miner (1.4M) PO Box 8 Silverton CO 81433 **Phn:** 970-387-5477 www.silvertonstandard.com editor@silvertonstandard.com

Simla Ranchland News (4.0M) PO Box 307 Simla CO 80835 **Phn:** 719-541-2288 **Fax:** 719-541-2289 www.ranchland-news.com ranchland@bigsandytelco.com

Snowmass Village Snowmass Village Sun (3.0M) PO Box 5770 Snowmass Village CO 81615 **Phn:** 970-429-9196 www.aspentimes.com/News/Snowmass jbeathard@snowmasssun.com

Springfield The Plainsman Herald (2.0M) PO Box 158 Springfield CO 81073 **Phn:** 719-523-6254 **Fax:** 719-523-4010 plainsmanherald@hotmail.com

Strasburg Eastern Colorado News (1.1M) PO Box 829 Strasburg CO 80136 **Phn:** 303-622-9796 **Fax:** 303-622-9794 www.i-70scout.com dclaussen@i-70scout.com

Stratton Stratton Spotlight (0.6M) PO Box 2 Stratton CO 80836 **Phn:** 719-348-5913 strattonspotlight@yahoo.com

Telluride Telluride Watch (6.0M) PO Box 2042 Telluride CO 81435 **Phn:** 970-728-4496 www.watchnewspapers.com editor@watchnewspapers.com

Walden Jackson County Star (1.4M) PO Box 397 Walden CO 80480 **Phn:** 970-723-4404 **Fax:** 970-723-4474

Walsenburg Huerfano World (3.1M) PO Box 346 Walsenburg CO 81089 **Phn:** 719-738-1720 **Fax:** 719-738-1727

Westcliffe Wet Mountain Tribune (3.0M) PO Box 300 Westcliffe CO 81252 **Phn:** 719-783-2361 **Fax:** 719-783-3725 www.wetmountaintribune.com editor@wetmountaintribune.com

Westminster Metro North News (5.5M) 8703 Yates Dr # 210 Westminster CO 80031 **Phn:** 303-426-6000 **Fax:** 303-426-4209 www.ourcoloradonews.com mkelly@ourcoloradonews.com

Windsor Windsor Beacon (1.8M) 425 Main St Windsor CO 80550 **Phn:** 970-686-9646 **Fax:** 970-686-9647 www.windsorbeacon.com editor@windsorbeacon.com

Woodland Park Mountain Jackpot (7.0M) PO Box 116 Woodland Park CO 80866 **Phn:** 719-687-0803 **Fax:** 719-684-2515 www.mountainjackpot.com

Woodland Park Pikes Peak Courier View (1.2M) PO Box 340 Woodland Park CO 80866 **Phn:** 719-687-3006 **Fax:** 719-687-3009 www.ourcoloradonews.com/tellercounty rcarrigan@ourcoloradonews.com

Wray Wray Gazette (3.0M) PO Box 7 Wray CO 80758 **Phn:** 970-332-4846 **Fax:** 970-332-4065

Yuma Yuma Pioneer (2.9M) PO Box 326 Yuma CO 80759 **Phn:** 970-848-2174 **Fax:** 970-848-2895 www.yumapioneer.com yumapioneer@centurytel.net

CONNECTICUT

Cheshire Cheshire Herald (7.2M) PO Box 247 Cheshire CT 06410 **Phn:** 203-272-5316 **Fax:** 203-250-7145 www.cheshireherald.com news@cheshireherald.com

Darien Darien Times (8.0M) 10 Corbin Dr Ste 212 Darien CT 06820 **Phn:** 203-656-4230 **Fax:** 203-656-4240 www.darientimes.com editor@darientimes.com

Darien Greenwich Post (15.0M) 10 Corbin Dr Fl 3 Darien CT 06820 **Phn:** 203-861-9191 **Fax:** 203-861-0023 greenwich-post.com editor@greenwich-post.com

East Hartford The Gazette (19.0M) 1406 Main St Ste 2 East Hartford CT 06108 **Phn:** 860-289-6468 **Fax:** 860-289-6469 ehgazette.com editor@ehgazette.com

Fairfield The Citizen-News (10.5M) 220 Carter Henry Dr Fairfield CT 06824 **Phn:** 203-255-4561 **Fax:** 203-255-0456 www.fairfieldcitizenonline.com jdoody@bcnnew.com

Fairfield Westport News (11.1M) 220 Carter Henry Dr Fairfield CT 06824 **Phn:** 203-255-4561 **Fax:** 203-255-0456 www.westport-news.com awinchester@bcnnew.com

Georgetown Redding Pilot (2.5M) PO Box 389 Georgetown CT 06829 **Phn:** 203-894-3331 **Fax:** 203-438-3395 www.thereddingpilot.com pilot@thereddingpilot.com

Glastonbury Glastonbury Citizen (9.0M) PO Box 373 Glastonbury CT 06033 **Phn:** 860-633-4691 **Fax:** 860-657-3258 www.glcitizen.com citizen@snet.net

Hartford Hartford Advocate (55.0M) 121 Wawarme Ave Hartford CT 06114 **Phn:** 860-548-9300 **Fax:** 860-548-9335 www.ct.com/news/advocates editor@hartfordadvocate.com

Hartford Hartford News (25.0M) 563 Franklin Ave Hartford CT 06114 **Phn:** 860-296-6128 **Fax:** 866-875-3785 www.greaterhartford.com hartfordnews@aol.com

Hartford The Journal (15.0M) 563 Franklin Ave Hartford CT 06114 **Phn:** 860-296-6128 **Fax:** 866-875-3785 www.greaterhartford.com hartfordnews@aol.com

Lakeville Lakeville Journal (5.5M) PO Box 1688 Lakeville CT 06039 **Phn:** 860-435-9873 **Fax:** 860-435-4802 www.tricornernews.com editor@lakevillejournal.com

Madison Shore Publishing (70.0M) PO Box 1010 Madison CT 06443 **Phn:** 203-245-1877 **Fax:** 203-245-9773 www.shorepublishing.com news@shorepublishing.com

Meriden North Haven Citizen (10.3M) 11 Crown St Meriden CT 06450 **Phn:** 203-235-1661 **Fax:** 203-639-0210 www.northhavencitizen.com news@thenorthhavencitizen.com

Meridien Berlin Citizen (12.5M) 11 Crown St Meridien CT 06450 **Phn:** 203-235-1661 **Fax:** 203-639-0210 www.berlincitizen.com news@theberlincitizen.com

Meridien Southington Citizen (25.0M) 11 Crown St Meridien CT 06450 **Phn:** 203-235-1661 www.southingtoncitizen.com news@thesouthingtoncitizen.com

COLORADO WEEKLY NEWSPAPERS

Meridien The Plainville Citizen (9.0M) 11 Crown St Meridien CT 06450 **Phn:** 203-235-1661 www.plainvillecitizen.com news@plainvillecitizen.com

Meridien Town Times (6.0M) 11 Crown St Meridien CT 06450 **Phn:** 203-235-1661 **Fax:** 203-639-0210 www.towntimes.com news@towntimes.com

Middletown West Hartford News (47.0M) 386 Main St Fl 4 Middletown CT 06457 **Phn:** 860-347-3331 **Fax:** 860-347-3380 www.westhartfordnews.com westhartfordnews@ctcentral.com

Mystic Mystic River Press (12.0M) 15 Holmes St Ste 3 Mystic CT 06355 **Phn:** 860-536-9577 **Fax:** 860-572-8946 www.mysticriverpress.com news@themysticriverpress.com

Naugatuck Citizens News (3.4M) 71 Weid Dr Naugatuck CT 06770 **Phn:** 203-729-2228 **Fax:** 203-729-9099 www.mycitizensnews.com editor@mycitizensnews.com

New Canaan New Canaan Advertiser (7.0M) 42 Vitti St New Canaan CT 06840 **Phn:** 203-966-9541 **Fax:** 203-966-8006 www.ncadvertiser.com editor@ncadvertiser.com

New Canaan News-Review (5.4M) 161 Cherry St Ste 6 New Canaan CT 06840 **Phn:** 203-972-4405 **Fax:** 203-972-4404 www.dariennewsonline.com avarese@bcnnew.com

New Fairfield Citizen News (7.9M) PO Box 8048 New Fairfield CT 06812 **Phn:** 203-746-4669 **Fax:** 203-746-5606 citizennews@aol.com

New Haven Fairfield County Weekly (36.0M) 900 Chapel St Ste 1100 New Haven CT 06510 **Phn:** 203-789-0010 **Fax:** 203-787-1418 www.ct.com/news/advocates

New Haven New Haven Advocate (50.0M) 900 Chapel St Ste 1100 New Haven CT 06510 **Phn:** 203-789-0010 **Fax:** 203-787-1418 www.ct.com/news/advocates editor@hartfordadvocate.com

New Haven Westport Minuteman (15.0M) 40 Sargent Dr New Haven CT 06511 **Phn:** 203-752-2711 **Fax:** 203-789-5309 minutemannewscenter.com editor@westportminuteman.com

New London Times Community News Group (70.0M) 47 Eugene Oneill Dr New London CT 06320 **Phn:** 860-701-1023 **Fax:** 860-442-5599 theday.com tips@theday.com

New Milford New Milford Spectrum (21.0M) 45 Main St # B New Milford CT 06776 **Phn:** 860-354-2273 **Fax:** 860-350-6794 www.newmilfordspectrum.com jsmith@newstimes.com

Newtown Newtown Bee (10.0M) PO Box 5503 Newtown CT 06470 **Phn:** 203-426-3141 **Fax:** 203-426-5169 www.newtownbee.com editor@thebee.com

North Haven The Advisor (30.0M) PO Box 460 North Haven CT 06473 **Phn:** 203-239-5404 **Fax:** 203-239-7097 www.advisor-newspaper.com

Norwalk Wilton Villager (6.5M) 346 Main Ave Norwalk CT 06851 **Phn:** 203-846-3281 **Fax:** 203-840-1802 www.thehour.com/wilton_villager news@wiltonvillager.com

Old Greenwich Greenwich Citizen (21.0M) 1455 E Putnam Ave Ste 102 Old Greenwich CT 06870 **Phn:** 203-625-4460 **Fax:** 203-625-4472 www.greenwichcitizen.com gcitizen@bcnnew.com

Putnam Putnam Town Crier & Northeast Ledger (10.7M) 158 Main St Ste 9 Putnam CT 06260 **Phn:** 860-963-1050 putnamtowncrier.com ptcrier@gmail.com

Ridgefield Ridgefield Press (6.4M) 16 Bailey Ave Ridgefield CT 06877 **Phn:** 203-438-6544 **Fax:** 203-438-3395 TheRidgefieldPress.com news@theridgefieldpress.com

Ridgefield Wilton Bulletin (5.4M) 16 Bailey Ave Ridgefield CT 06877 **Phn:** 203-894-3330 **Fax:** 203-438-3395 wiltonbulletin.com newsroom@wiltonbulletin.com

Shelton Huntington Herald (108.0M) 1000 Bridgeport Ave Shelton CT 06484 **Phn:** 203-402-2332 **Fax:** 203-926-2091 sheltonherald.com huntingtonherald@hersamacorn.com

Southbury Heritage Villager (2.7M) 77 Main St S Unit 207 Southbury CT 06488 **Phn:** 203-264-0123 **Fax:** 203-264-9467 editor@heritagevillager.com

Southbury Voices the Newspaper (32.0M) PO Box 383 Southbury CT 06488 **Phn:** 203-262-6631 **Fax:** 203-262-6658 www.voicesnews.com newsdesk@ctvoices.com

Southington The Observer (5.6M) 213 Spring St Southington CT 06489 **Phn:** 860-621-6751 **Fax:** 860-621-1841 www.southingtonobserver.com eharris@southingtonobserver.com

Stonington The Resident (30.0M) PO Box 269 Stonington CT 06378 **Phn:** 860-599-1221 **Fax:** 860-599-1400 www.theresident.com alexis@theresident.com

Vernon Reminder Press Inc (242.0M) PO Box 27 Vernon CT 06066 **Phn:** 860-875-3366 **Fax:** 860-875-2089 www.remindernews.com info@remindernet.com

Watertown Town Times (9.3M) PO Box 1 Watertown CT 06795 **Phn:** 860-274-8851 **Fax:** 860-945-3116 www.towntimesnews.com

Westfield Enfield Press (2.5M) 62 School St Westfield MA 01085 **Phn:** 413-562-4181 newstips@theenfieldpress.com

Weston Weston Forum (4.0M) PO Box 1185 Weston CT 06883 **Phn:** 203-894-3332 **Fax:** 203-438-3395 www.thewestonforum.com editor@thewestonforum.com

Westport Fairfield Minuteman (24.0M) 1175 Post Rd E Ste 3B Westport CT 06880 **Phn:** 203-752-2711 **Fax:** 203-789-5309 minutemannewscenter.com editor@fairfieldminuteman.com

Winsted Winsted Journal (2.0M) PO Box 835 Winsted CT 06098 **Phn:** 860-738-4418 **Fax:** 860-738-3709 www.tricornernews.com winstedjournal@sbcglobal.net

Woodstock Villager Newspapers (20.7M) PO Bo 196 Woodstock CT 06281 **Phn:** 860-928-1818 **Fax:** 860-928-5946 www.villagernewspapers.com aminor@villagernewspapers.com

DELAWARE

Bethany Beach Delaware Coast Press & Beachcomber (18.0M) PO Box 1420 Bethany Beach DE 19930 **Phn:** 302-227-9466 **Fax:** 302-227-9469 www.delmarvanow.com dcp@gannett.com

Bethany Beach The Delaware Wave (22.0M) PO Box 1420 Bethany Beach DE 19930 **Phn:** 302-537-1881 **Fax:** 302-537-9705 www.delmarvanow.com wave@dmg.gannett.com

Dover Dover Post Co (26.0M) 1196 S Little Creek Rd Dover DE 19901 **Phn:** 302-678-3616 **Fax:** 302-678-8291 www.doverpost.com ben.mace@doverpost.com

Dover Milford Beacon (8.0M) PO Box 664 Dover DE 19903 **Phn:** 302-422-6025 **Fax:** 302-422-2717 www.milfordbeacon.com

Dover Sussex Countian (3.5M) 1196 S Little Creek Rd Dover DE 19901 **Phn:** 302-856-0026 **Fax:** 302-856-0925 www.sussexcountian.com editor@sussexcountian.com

Hockessin Hockessin Community News (50.0M) 24 W Main St Hockessin DE 19709 **Phn:** 302-378-9531 www.hockessincommunitynews.com jesse.chadderdon@doverpost.com

Lewes Cape Gazette (12.0M) PO Box 213 Lewes DE 19958 **Phn:** 302-645-7700 **Fax:** 302-645-1664 capegazette.villagesoup.com newsroom@capegazette.com

Middletown Middletown Transcript (6.0M) 24 W Main St Middletown DE 19709 **Phn:** 302-378-9531 **Fax:** 302-378-0647 www.middletowntranscript.com editor@middletowntranscript.com

Milford Milford Chronicle (8.5M) 37A N Walnut St Milford DE 19963 **Phn:** 302-422-1200 **Fax:** 302-422-1208 delaware.newszap.com/milfordchronicle mc@newszap.com

New Castle New Castle Weekly (1.2M) 203 Delaware St New Castle DE 19720 **Phn:** 302-328-6005

Newark The Newark Post (12.0M) 218 E Main St Ste 109 Newark DE 19711 **Phn:** 302-737-0724 **Fax:** 302-737-9019 www.newarkpostonline.com mcorrigan@chespub.com

Ocean View Coastal Point (15.0M) PO Box 1324 Ocean View DE 19970 **Phn:** 302-539-1788 **Fax:** 302-539-3777 www.thecoastalpoint.com darin.mccann@coastalpoint.com

Seaford Laurel Star (3.3M) PO Box 1000 Seaford DE 19973 **Phn:** 302-629-9788 **Fax:** 302-629-9243 www.laurelstar.com publisher@seafordstar.com

Seaford Seaford Star (4.3M) PO Box 1000 Seaford DE 19973 **Phn:** 302-629-9788 **Fax:** 302-629-9243 www.seafordstar.com publisher@seafordstar.com

Smyrna Smyrna/Clayton Sun-Times (3.7M) PO Box 327 Smyrna DE 19977 **Phn:** 302-653-2083 **Fax:** 302-653-8821 www.scsuntimes.com ben.mace@doverpost.com

DISTRICT OF COLUMBIA

Washington American Free Press (38.0M) 645 Pennsylvania Ave SE Ste 100 Washington DC 20003 **Phn:** 202-544-5977 americanfreepress.net

Washington City Paper (88.0M) 2390 Champlain St NW Fl 3 Washington DC 20009 **Phn:** 202-332-2100 **Fax:** 202-332-8500 www.washingtoncitypaper.com contact@washingtoncitypaper.com

Washington Current Newspapers (65.1M) PO Box 40400 Washington DC 20016 **Phn:** 202-244-7223 **Fax:** 202-244-5924 www.currentnewspapers.com newsdesk@currentnewspapers.com

Washington The Georgetowner (40.0M) 1054 Potomac St NW Washington DC 20007 **Phn:** 202-338-4833 **Fax:** 202-338-4834 www.georgetowner.com editorial@georgetowner.com

FLORIDA

Anna Maria Island Sun (15.0M) PO Box 1189 Anna Maria FL 34216 **Phn:** 941-778-3986 **Fax:** 941-778-6988 www.amisun.com amisun@tampabay.rr.com

Apalachicola Apalachicola Times (4.0M) PO Box 820 Apalachicola FL 32329 **Phn:** 850-653-8868 **Fax:** 850-653-8036 www.apalachtimes.com tcroft@starfl.com

Apalachicola Apalachicola Times (3.5M) PO Box 820 Apalachicola FL 32329 **Phn:** 850-653-8868 **Fax:** 850-653-8036 www.apalachtimes.com dadlerstein@starfl.com

Apopka Apopka Chief (5.0M) 400 N Park Ave Apopka FL 32712 **Phn:** 407-886-2777 **Fax:** 407-889-4121 www.theapopkachief.com news@theapopkachief.com

Arcadia Arcadian (3.2M) 108 S Polk Ave Arcadia FL 34266 **Phn:** 863-494-7600 **Fax:** 863-494-3533 www.yoursun.com shoffman@sun-herald.com

Bartow Polk County Democrat (4.3M) 190 S Florida Ave Bartow FL 33830 **Phn:** 863-533-4183 **Fax:** 863-533-0402 www.polkcountydemocrat.com jroslow@heartlandnewspapers.com

DELAWARE WEEKLY NEWSPAPERS

Belleview Voice Of South Marion (2.7M) PO Box 700 Belleview FL 34421 **Phn:** 352-245-3161 **Fax:** 352-347-7444 thevosm.net vosminfo@aol.com

Big Pine Key News Barometer (10.0M) PO Box 431639 Big Pine Key FL 33043 **Phn:** 305-872-0106 **Fax:** 305-515-2939 newsbarometer.com info@newsbarometer.com

Blountstown The County Record (3.0M) PO Box 366 Blountstown FL 32424 **Phn:** 850-674-5041 **Fax:** 850-674-5008 www.thecountyrecord.net editor@thecountyrecord.net

Boca Grande Boca Beacon (7.0M) PO Box 313 Boca Grande FL 33921 **Phn:** 941-964-2995 **Fax:** 941-964-0372 www.bocabeacon.com mshortuse@bocabeacon.com

Boca Grande Gasparilla Gazette (5.0M) PO Box 929 Boca Grande FL 33921 **Phn:** 941-964-2728 **Fax:** 941-964-2850 bocabeacon.com

Bokeelia Pine Island Eagle (8.5M) 10700 Stringfellow Rd Ste 60 Bokeelia FL 33922 **Phn:** 239-283-2022 **Fax:** 239-283-0232 www.pineisland-eagle.com pineisland@breezenewspapers.com

Bonifay Holmes Co. Times-Advertiser (3.0M) PO Box 67 Bonifay FL 32425 **Phn:** 850-547-9414 **Fax:** 850-547-9418 www.chipleypaper.com news@chipleypaper.com

Bonita Springs The Banner (30.0M) 26381 S Tamiami Trl Ste 116 Bonita Springs FL 34134 **Phn:** 239-213-6000 **Fax:** 239-213-6088 www.naplesnews.com/news/bonita letters@naplesnews.com

Bristol Calhoun Liberty Journal (4.9M) PO Box 536 Bristol FL 32321 **Phn:** 850-643-3333 **Fax:** 888-400-5810 www.cljnews.com thejournal@fairpoint.net

Bronson Levy County Journal (3.1M) PO Box 159 Bronson FL 32621 **Phn:** 352-486-2312 **Fax:** 352-486-5042 levyjournalonline.com editor@levyjournal.com

Bushnell Sumter County Times (3.2M) 204 E McCollum Ave Bushnell FL 33513 **Phn:** 352-793-2161 **Fax:** 352-793-1486 www.sumtercountytimes.com breichman@sctnews.com

Callahan Nassau County Record (5.0M) PO Box 609 Callahan FL 32011 **Phn:** 904-879-2727 **Fax:** 904-879-5155 www.nassaucountyrecord.com editor@nassaucountyrecord.com

Cedar Key Cedar Key Beacon (1.4M) PO Box 532 Cedar Key FL 32625 **Phn:** 352-543-5701 **Fax:** 352-543-5928 www.cedarkeybeacon.com editor@cedarkeybeacon.com

Chattahoochee Twin City News (2.0M) PO Box 505 Chattahoochee FL 32324 **Phn:** 850-663-2255 **Fax:** 850-663-8102 tcnews@fairpoint.net

Chiefland Chiefland Citizen (4.2M) PO Box 980 Chiefland FL 32644 **Phn:** 352-493-4796 **Fax:** 352-493-9336 www.chieflandcitizen.com editor@chieflandcitizen.com

Chipley Washington County News (4.0M) PO Box 627 Chipley FL 32428 **Phn:** 850-638-0212 **Fax:** 850-547-9414 www.chipleypaper.com news@chipleypaper.com

Clermont News Leader (18.0M) 628 8th St Clermont FL 34711 **Phn:** 352-242-9819 **Fax:** 352-242-9820 www.clermontnewsleader.com thenewsleader@cfl.rr.com

Clermont South Lake Press (2.0M) 732 W Montrose St Clermont FL 34711 **Phn:** 352-394-2183 **Fax:** 352-394-8001 www.southlakepress.com roxannebrown@dailycommercial.com

Clewiston Clewiston News (8.0M) PO Box 1236 Clewiston FL 33440 **Phn:** 863-983-9148 **Fax:** 863-983-7537 florida.newszap.com/clewistonnews clewnews@newszap.com

Coral Springs Our Town News (45.0M) 11874 Wiles Rd Coral Springs FL 33076 **Phn:** 954-344-5156 **Fax:** 954-344-0107

Crawfordville The Wakulla News (6.0M) PO Box 307 Crawfordville FL 32326 **Phn:** 850-926-7102 **Fax:** 850-926-3815 www.thewakullanews.com kblackmar@thewakullanews.net

Crescent City Putnam Co. Courier Journal (2.7M) 330 N Summit St Crescent City FL 32112 **Phn:** 386-698-1644 **Fax:** 386-698-1994 news@cjnewsfl.com

Crestview Crestview News Bulletin (4.5M) 705 Ashley Dr Crestview FL 32536 **Phn:** 850-682-6524 **Fax:** 850-682-2246 www.crestviewbulletin.com news@crestviewbulletin.com

Crestview News Extra (14.0M) 295 W James Lee Blvd Crestview FL 32536 **Phn:** 850-682-6524 **Fax:** 850-682-2246

Cross City Dixie County Advocate (4.3M) PO Box 5030 Cross City FL 32628 **Phn:** 352-498-3312 **Fax:** 352-498-0420 dcadvocate.net editor@dcadvocate.net

Dade City Wesley Chapel News-Leader (4.8M) 13032 US Highway 301 Dade City FL 33525 **Phn:** 352-567-5639 **Fax:** 352-567-5640

Deerfield Beach The Observer (20.0M) 201 N Federal Hwy Ste 103 Deerfield Beach FL 33441 **Phn:** 954-428-9045 **Fax:** 954-428-9096 observernewspaperonline.com observernews@comcast.net

Defuniak Springs Defuniak Herald (6.6M) PO Box 1546 Defuniak Springs FL 32435 **Phn:** 850-892-3232 **Fax:** 850-892-2270 defuniakherald.com bruce@defuniakherald.com

Deland West Volusia Beacon (9.0M) PO Box 2397 Deland FL 32721 **Phn:** 386-734-4622 **Fax:** 386-734-4641 www.beacononlinenews.com info@beacononlinenews.com

Destin Destin Log (7.7M) PO Box 339 Destin FL 32540 **Phn:** 850-837-2828 **Fax:** 850-654-5982 www.thedestinlog.com pgriffin@thedestinlog.com

Dunnellon Riverland News (2.8M) 20441 E Pennsylvania Ave Dunnellon FL 34432 **Phn:** 352-489-2731 **Fax:** 352-489-6593 www.riverlandnews.com editor@riverlandnews.com

Englewood Englewood Review (10.0M) 370 W Dearborn St Ste B Englewood FL 34223 **Phn:** 941-474-4351 **Fax:** 941-474-8317 www.englewoodreview.com pr@englewoodreview.com

Fernandina Beach The News-Leader (12.0M) PO Box 766 Fernandina Beach FL 32035 **Phn:** 904-261-3696 **Fax:** 904-261-3698 www.fbnewsleader.com mparnell@fbnewsleader.com

Fleming Island Clay Today (8.0M) 3513 US Highway 17 Fleming Island FL 32003 **Phn:** 904-264-3200 **Fax:** 904-264-3285 claytodayonline.com eric@opcfla.com

Fort Lauderdale New Times Broward (60.0M) 16 NE 4th St Ste 200 Fort Lauderdale FL 33301 **Phn:** 954-233-1600 **Fax:** 954-233-1521 www.browardpalmbeach.com

Fort Meade Ft. Meade Leader (1.0M) 25 W Broadway Fort Meade FL 33841 **Phn:** 863-285-8625 **Fax:** 863-285-7634 www.fortmeadeleader.com news@fortmeadeleader.com

Fort Myers River Weekly News (8.0M) 1609 Hendry St Ste 15 Fort Myers FL 33901 **Phn:** 239-415-7732 **Fax:** 239-415-7702 www.islandsunnews.com press@riverweekly.com

Fort Myers Beach Ft. Myers Beach Bulletin (12.5M) 19260 San Carlos Blvd Fort Myers Beach FL 33931 **Phn:** 239-765-0400 **Fax:** 239-765-0846 www.fortmyersbeachtalk.com mschneider@breezenewspapers.com

FLORIDA WEEKLY NEWSPAPERS

Fort Myers Beach Island Sand Paper (10.0M) 1661 Estero Blvd # 4A Fort Myers Beach FL 33931 **Phn:** 239-463-4461 **Fax:** 239-463-1380 www.islandsandpaper.com islandsandpaper@earthlink.net

Fort Myers Beach The Observer (14.0M) 19260 San Carlos Blvd Fort Myers Beach FL 33931 **Phn:** 239-765-0400 **Fax:** 239-765-0846 fortmyersbeachtalk.com rpetcher@breezenewspapers.com

Fort Pierce Hometown News (102.0M) 5059 Turnpikefeeder Rd Fort Pierce FL 34951 **Phn:** 772-465-5656 **Fax:** 772-465-5301 www.myhometownnews.net info@hometownnewsol.com

Frostproof Frostproof News (1.5M) 14 W Wall St Frostproof FL 33843 **Phn:** 863-635-2171 www.frostproofnews.net backley@heartlandnewspapers.com

Gainesville The Record (5.0M) 620 N Main St Gainesville FL 32601 **Phn:** 352-377-2444 **Fax:** 352-338-1986 record620@aol.com

Graceville Graceville News (1.3M) PO Box 187 Graceville FL 32440 **Phn:** 850-263-6015 **Fax:** 850-263-1042 gvnews@wfeca.net

Gulf Breeze Gulf Breeze News (37.0M) PO Box 1414 Gulf Breeze FL 32562 **Phn:** 850-932-8986 **Fax:** 850-932-8794 www.gulfbreezenews.com news@gulfbreezenews.com

Gulfport The Gabber (14.0M) 1419 49th St S Gulfport FL 33707 **Phn:** 727-321-6965 **Fax:** 727-327-7830 www.thegabber.com news@thegabber.com

Hallandale Beach South FL Sun Times (50.0M) 305 NW 10th Ter Hallandale Beach FL 33009 **Phn:** 954-458-0635 **Fax:** 954-458-0765 www.southfloridasun.net sfsuntimes@aol.com

Havana Havana Herald (2.8M) 103 W 7th Ave Havana FL 32333 **Phn:** 850-539-6586 **Fax:** 850-539-0454 www.havanaherald.net hava0454@bellsouth.net

Holmes Beach The Islander (15.0M) 5404B Marina Dr Holmes Beach FL 34217 **Phn:** 941-778-7978 **Fax:** 866-362-9821 islander.org news@islander.org

Homestead South Dade News Leader (12.0M) PO Box 900340 Homestead FL 33090 **Phn:** 305-245-2311 **Fax:** 305-248-0596 www.southdadenewsleader.com mdill@calkins-media.com

Jacksonville Folio Weekly (50.0M) 9456 Philips Hwy Ste 11 Jacksonville FL 32256 **Phn:** 904-260-9770 **Fax:** 904-260-9773 www.folioweekly.com themail@folioweekly.com

Jacksonville Beach Beaches Leader & Ponte Vedre Leader (12.0M) 1114 Beach Blvd Jacksonville Beach FL 32250 **Phn:** 904-249-9033 **Fax:** 904-249-1501 www.beachesleader.com editor@beachesleader.com

Key Biscayne The Islander News (3.6M) 104 Crandon Blvd Ste 301 Key Biscayne FL 33149 **Phn:** 305-361-3333 **Fax:** 305-361-5051 www.islandernews.com editor@islandernews.com

Key Largo Ocean Reef Press (4.0M) 6 Fishing Village Dr Key Largo FL 33037 **Phn:** 305-367-4911 **Fax:** 305-367-2191

Key West The Newspaper (9.0M) PO Box 567 Key West FL 33041 **Phn:** 305-292-2108 **Fax:** 305-292-1882 kwtn.com thebluepaper@kwtn.com

Kissimmee Osceola News-Gazette (30.0M) 160 Church St Kissimmee FL 34741 **Phn:** 407-846-7600 **Fax:** 407-933-6856 www.aroundosceola.com bmcbride@osceolanewsgazette.com

Labelle Caloosa Belle (7.0M) 22 Fort Thompson Ave Labelle FL 33975 **Phn:** 863-675-2541 **Fax:** 863-675-1449 florida.newszap.com/caloosabelle

Lake Placid Lake Placid Journal (5.0M) 231 N Main Ave Lake Placid FL 33852 **Phn:** 863-465-2522 **Fax:** 863-699-0331 www.lakeplacidjournal.net lakeplacideditor@gmail.com

Lake Wales Lake Wales News (3.5M) 140 E Stuart Ave Lake Wales FL 33853 **Phn:** 863-676-3467 **Fax:** 863-678-1297 www.lakewalesnews.com news@lakewalesnews.com

Lake Worth Herald/Coastal Observer (30.0M) 130 S H St Lake Worth FL 33460 **Phn:** 561-585-9387 **Fax:** 561-585-5434 lwherald@bellsouth.net

Land O'Lake Community News Publications (144.0M) 3632 Land O'Lakes Blvd # 102 Land O'Lake FL 34639 **Phn:** 813-909-2800 **Fax:** 813-909-2802 cnewspubs.com news@cnewspubs.com

Largo Clearwater Gazette (17.0M) 2401 West Bay Dr Ste 125 Largo FL 33770 **Phn:** 727-446-6723 **Fax:** 727-461-5659 www.clearwatergazette.com pollicks@aol.com

Lehigh Acres Citizen (10.0M) 411 Lee Blvd Ste 1 Lehigh Acres FL 33936 **Phn:** 239-368-3944 **Fax:** 239-368-2775 www.lehighacrescitizen.com lehighcitizen@breezenewspapers.com

Lehigh Acres Lehigh News-Star (19.0M) PO Box 908 Lehigh Acres FL 33970 **Phn:** 239-369-2191 **Fax:** 239-369-1396 www.news-press.com news@lehighnewsstar.com

Live Oak Jasper News (1.9M) PO Box 370 Live Oak FL 32064 **Phn:** 800-525-4182 **Fax:** 386-364-5578 jaspernews1@windstream.net

Live Oak Suwanee Democrat (5.0M) 211 Howard St E Live Oak FL 32064 **Phn:** 386-362-1734 **Fax:** 386-364-5578 suwanneedemocrat.com jeff.waters@gaflnews.com

Longboat Key Longboat Observer (14.5M) PO Box 8100 Longboat Key FL 34228 **Phn:** 941-383-5509 **Fax:** 941-383-7193 www.yourobserver.com rhartill@yourobserver.com

Macclenny The Baker County Press (6.0M) PO Box 598 Macclenny FL 32063 **Phn:** 904-259-2400 **Fax:** 904-259-6502 www.bakercountypress.com editor@bakercountypress.com

Madison Enterprise-Recorder (3.5M) PO Box 772 Madison FL 32341 **Phn:** 850-973-4141 **Fax:** 850-973-4121 www.greenepublishing.com news@greenepublishing.com

Madison Madison County Carrier (3.5M) PO Box 772 Madison FL 32341 **Phn:** 850-973-4141 **Fax:** 850-973-4121 www.greenepublishing.com news@greenepublishing.com

Marathon Florida Keys Keynoter (13.0M) PO Box 500158 Marathon FL 33050 **Phn:** 305-743-5551 **Fax:** 305-743-6397 www.keysnet.com lkahn@keynoter.com

Marathon Free Press (11.0M) 6363 Overseas Hwy Ste 3 Marathon FL 33050 **Phn:** 305-743-8766 **Fax:** 305-743-9977 cookecommunications.com marathon@keysnews.com

Marathon Key West Keynoter (11.0M) 3015 Overseas Hwy Marathon FL 33050 **Phn:** 305-743-5551 **Fax:** 305-743-6397 www.keysnet.com lkahn@keynoter.com

Marco Island Marco Eagle (11.0M) PO Box 579 Marco Island FL 34146 **Phn:** 239-213-5300 www.marconews.com mail@marcoeagle.com

Marco Island Sun Times (12.0M) 1857 San Marco Rd Unit 216 Marco Island FL 34145 **Phn:** 239-394-4050 **Fax:** 239-394-3390 www.marcoislandflorida.com joe@misuntimes.com

Mayo Mayo Free Press (1.7M) PO Box 370 Mayo FL 32066 **Phn:** 386-362-1734 **Fax:** 386-362-6827 www.suwanneedemocrat.com/mayo mayofreepress@windstream.net

Melbourne Florida Today (61.0M) PO Box 419000 Melbourne FL 32941 **Phn:** 321-242-3500 **Fax:** 321-242-6620 www.floridatoday.com bstover@floridatoday.com

Melbourne Hometown News (80.0M) 380 N Wickham Rd Ste F Melbourne FL 32935 **Phn:** 321-242-1013 **Fax:** 321-242-1281 www.myhometownnews.net news@hometownnewsol.com

Miami Coral Gables Gazette (8.8M) PO Box 143667 Miami FL 33114 **Phn:** 305-460-9010 **Fax:** 305-460-9020

Miami Miami Community Papers (154.0M) 6796 SW 62nd Ave Miami FL 33143 **Phn:** 305-669-7030 **Fax:** 305-662-6980 www.communitynewspapers.com michael@communitynewspapers.com

Miami Miami New Times (110.0M) PO Box 11591 Miami FL 33101 **Phn:** 305-576-8000 **Fax:** 305-571-7677 www.miaminewtimes.com feedback@miaminewtimes.com

Miami Miami Today (28.6M) 2000 S Dixie Hwy # 100 Miami FL 33133 **Phn:** 305-358-2663 **Fax:** 305-358-4811 www.miamitodaynews.com editor@miamitodaynews.com

Miami Beach The SunPost (45.0M) PO Box 191870 Miami Beach FL 33119 **Phn:** 305-758-1660 sunpostweekly.com kim@miamisunpost.com

Miami Lakes Miami Laker (16.5M) 15450 New Barn Rd Ste 103 Miami Lakes FL 33014 **Phn:** 305-817-4028 **Fax:** 305-817-4197 miamilaker1@aol.com

Milton Santa Rosa Press Gazette (16.0M) 6629 Elva St Milton FL 32570 **Phn:** 850-623-2120 **Fax:** 850-623-2007 www.srpressgazette.com news@srpressgazette.com

Milton The Free Press (7.0M) 6629 Elva St Milton FL 32570 **Phn:** 850-623-2120 **Fax:** 850-623-9308 www.srpressgazette.com news@srpressgazette.com

Monticello Monticello News & Jefferson Co. Journal (3.0M) PO Box 428 Monticello FL 32345 **Phn:** 850-997-3568 **Fax:** 850-997-3774 monticellonews@embarqmail.com

Naples Collier Citizen (17.0M) 1100 Immokalee Rd Naples FL 34110 **Phn:** 239-213-6077 **Fax:** 239-213-6076 www.naplesnews.com/news/citizen news@colliercitizen.com

Naples Naples Sun Times (18.0M) 32 12th St N Naples FL 34102 **Phn:** 239-213-6077 **Fax:** 239-513-2342 www.naplesnews.com news@naplesnews.com

Navarre Navarre Press (7.5M) 7502 Harvest Village Ct Navarre FL 32566 **Phn:** 850-939-8040 **Fax:** 850-939-4575 www.navarrepress.com news@navarrepress.com

New Port Richey The Suncoast News (117.0M) 6214 US Highway 19 New Port Richey FL 34652 **Phn:** 727-815-1060 **Fax:** 727-847-2902 suncoastnews.com mterry@suncoastnews.com

Niceville Bay Beacon (15.5M) 1181 John Sims Pkwy E Niceville FL 32578 **Phn:** 850-678-1080 **Fax:** 850-729-3225 www.baybeacon.com do not email

Ocala South Marion Citizen (15.0M) 8810 SW Highway 200 Unit 103 Ocala FL 34481 **Phn:** 352-854-3986 **Fax:** 352-854-9277 www.smcitizen.com editor@smcitizen.com

Orlando Orlando Weekly (50.0M) 1505 E Colonial Dr Orlando FL 32803 **Phn:** 407-377-0400 **Fax:** 407-377-0420 orlandoweekly.com esullivan@orlandoweekly.com

Orlando Seminole Voice (10.0M) 1500 Park Center Dr Orlando FL 32835 **Phn:** 407-563-7026 **Fax:** 407-563-7099 www.seminolevoice.com editor@turnstilemediagroup.com

Orlando SW Orlando Bulletin (32.5M) 7901 Kingspointe Pkwy Ste 28 Orlando FL 32819 **Phn:** 407-351-1573 **Fax:** 407-363-3954 www.southwestorlandobulletin.com lisa@kearneypublishing.com

Orlando Winter Park/Maitland Observer (5.3M) 1500 Park Center Dr Orlando FL 32835 **Phn:** 407-563-7000 **Fax:** 407-563-7099 www.wpmobserver.com ibabcock@turnstilemediagroup.com

Palmetto North River News (8.0M) 604 6th St W Palmetto FL 34221 **Phn:** 941-722-1088 **Fax:** 866-745-4633 www.northrivernewsonline.com nr.news@verizon.net

Pensacola Escambia Sun Press (1.9M) 605 S Old Corry Field Rd Pensacola FL 32507 **Phn:** 850-456-3121 **Fax:** 850-456-0103 www.escambiasunpress.com stories@escambiasunpress.com

Pensacola Independent News (25.0M) PO Box 12082 Pensacola FL 32591 **Phn:** 850-438-8115 **Fax:** 850-438-0228 inweekly.net info@inweekly.net

Pensacola The Pelican (15.0M) PO Box 12710 Pensacola FL 32591 **Phn:** 850-202-9821 **Fax:** 850-202-2248 www.pnj.com bayers@gannett.com

Perry Perry News-Herald (5.1M) PO Box 888 Perry FL 32348 **Phn:** 850-584-5513 **Fax:** 850-838-1566

Perry Perry Taco Times (5.1M) PO Box 888 Perry FL 32348 **Phn:** 850-584-5513 **Fax:** 850-838-1566 www.perrynewspapers.com newsdesk@perrynewspapers.com

Pompano Beach Forum Newspapers (41.0M) 1701 Green Rd Ste B Pompano Beach FL 33064 **Phn:** 561-791-7790 **Fax:** 954-421-9002 www.sun-sentinel.com/news/broward/cities dfwhite@tribune.com

Pompano Beach Pompano Pelican (4.0M) 1500 E Atlantic Blvd Ste A Pompano Beach FL 33060 **Phn:** 954-783-8700 **Fax:** 954-783-0093 pompanopelican.com siren2415@gmail.com

Pompano Beach The Sentry (5.0M) 2500 SE 5th Ct Pompano Beach FL 33062 **Phn:** 954-532-2000 www.flsentry.com editor@flsentry.com

Ponte Vedra Beach Ponte Vedra Recorder (5.5M) PO Box 501 Ponte Vedra Beach FL 32004 **Phn:** 904-285-8831 **Fax:** 904-285-7232 www.pontevedrarecorder.com pvrecorder@opcfla.com

Port Saint Joe The Star (5.0M) 135 W Highway 98 Port Saint Joe FL 32456 **Phn:** 850-227-1278 **Fax:** 850-227-7212 www.starfl.com

Quincy Gadsden County Times (3.5M) 15 S Madison St Quincy FL 32351 **Phn:** 850-627-7649 **Fax:** 850-627-7191 www.gadcotimes.com editor@gadcotimes.com

Royal Palm Beach Palms West Press (20.0M) 10646 Aquarius Ln Royal Palm Beach FL 33411 **Phn:** 561-793-8596

Ruskin The SCC Observer (39.0M) 210 Woodland Estates Ave Ruskin FL 33570 **Phn:** 813-645-3111 **Fax:** 813-645-4118 www.observernews.net editor@observernews.net

Sanford The Sanford Herald (5.0M) PO Box 1667 Sanford FL 32772 **Phn:** 407-322-2611 **Fax:** 407-323-9408 www.mysanfordherald.com rdelinski@mysanfordherald.com

Sanibel Captiva Current (2.0M) PO Box 809 Sanibel FL 33957 **Phn:** 239-472-1587 **Fax:** 239-472-8398 www.captivasanibel.com vharring@breezenewspapers.com

Sanibel Captiva Islander (6.0M) PO Box 809 Sanibel FL 33957 **Phn:** 239-472-1587 **Fax:** 239-472-8398 www.captivasanibel.com mcassidy@breezenewspapers.com

Sanibel Island Reporter (6.0M) PO Box 809 Sanibel FL 33957 **Phn:** 239-472-1587 **Fax:** 239-472-8398 www.captivasanibel.com jlinette@breezenewspapers.com

FLORIDA WEEKLY NEWSPAPERS

Sanibel Island Sun (12.0M) 1640 Periwinkle Way Ste 2 Sanibel FL 33957 **Phn:** 239-395-1213 **Fax:** 239-395-2299 www.islandsunnews.com press@islandsunnews.com

Santa Rosa Beach Beach Breeze (7.0M) 4401 US Highway 98 E Santa Rosa Beach FL 32459 **Phn:** 850-231-0918 **Fax:** 850-231-0928 defuniakherald.com beachbreezenews@gmail.com

Santa Rosa Beach Walton Sun (12.0M) PO Box 2363 Santa Rosa Beach FL 32459 **Phn:** 850-267-4555 **Fax:** 850-267-0929 www.waltonsun.com news@waltonsun.com

Sarasota East County Observer (22.0M) 1970 Main St 4th flr Sarasota FL 34236 **Phn:** 941-366-3468 **Fax:** 941-362-4808 www.yourobserver.com eastcountynews@yourobserver.com

Sarasota Pelican Press (24.0M) 5011 Ocean Blvd Ste 206 Sarasota FL 34242 **Phn:** 941-349-4949 **Fax:** 941-346-7118 www.yourobserver.com mwalsh@yourobserver.com

Sarasota The Observer Group (20.0M) PO Box 3619 Sarasota FL 34230 **Phn:** 941-366-3468 **Fax:** 941-362-4808 www.yourobserver.com longboatnews@yourobserver.com

Sebring Sebring News-Sun (17.0M) 2227 US Highway 27 S Sebring FL 33870 **Phn:** 863-385-6155 **Fax:** 863-385-1954 www.newssun.com editor@newssun.com

Seminole Tampa Bay Newspapers (120.0M) 9911 Seminole Blvd Seminole FL 33772 **Phn:** 727-397-5563 **Fax:** 727-397-5900 www.tbnweekly.com editorial@tbnweekly.com

Starke Bradford County Telegraph (11.0M) 131 W Call St Starke FL 32091 **Phn:** 904-964-6305 **Fax:** 904-964-8628 www.bctelegraph.com editor@bctelegraph.com

Stuart Jupiter Courier (31.0M) PO Box 9009 Stuart FL 34995 **Phn:** 772-461-2050 www.tcpalm.com/news/news/local/north-palm-beach-county feedback@tcpalm.com

Tampa Tampa Free Press (1.1M) 1010 W Cass St Tampa FL 33606 **Phn:** 813-254-5888 **Fax:** 813-251-0511 cmarshalsea@4freepress.com

Tampa Tampa Record (22.0M) 501 N Falkenburg Rd # E-17 Tampa FL 33619 **Phn:** 813-655-1400 **Fax:** 813-864-4463

Tavernier Free Press (10.0M) 91731 Overseas Hwy Tavernier FL 33070 **Phn:** 305-853-7277 **Fax:** 305-853-0575 www.keysnews.com dcampbell@keysnews.com

Tavernier The Reporter (10.0M) PO Box 1197 Tavernier FL 33070 **Phn:** 305-852-3216 **Fax:** 305-852-0199 www.keysnet.com dgoodhue@keysreporter.com

Trenton Gilchrist County Journal (4.0M) 207 N Main St Trenton FL 32693 **Phn:** 352-463-7135 **Fax:** 352-463-7393 www.gilchristcountyjournal.net gilchristjournal@bellsouth.net

Umatilla North Lake Outpost (2.5M) PO Box 1099 Umatilla FL 32784 **Phn:** 352-669-2430 **Fax:** 352-669-4644

Venice Venice Gondolier (12.0M) 200 E Venice Ave Venice FL 34285 **Phn:** 941-207-1000 **Fax:** 941-484-8460 www.yoursun.com bmudge@venicegondolier.com

Vero Beach Hometown News (23.0M) 1020 Old Dixie Hwy Vero Beach FL 32960 **Phn:** 772-569-6767 **Fax:** 772-569-6268 www.myhometownnews.net news@hometownnewsol.com

Vero Beach Sebastian Sun (15.0M) PO Box 1268 Vero Beach FL 32961 **Phn:** 772-978-2371 **Fax:** 772-978-2364 www.tcpalm.com/news/news/local/sebastian-sun dennis.durkee@scripps.com

Wauchula Herald-Advocate (5.5M) PO Box 338 Wauchula FL 33873 **Phn:** 863-773-3255 **Fax:** 863-773-0657 editor@theheraldadvocate.com

West Palm Beach Condo News (13.0M) PO Box 109 West Palm Beach FL 33402 **Phn:** 561-471-0329 www.condonewsonline.com info@condonewsonline.com

Williston Williston Pioneer (2.5M) 37 S Main St #F Williston FL 32696 **Phn:** 352-528-3343 **Fax:** 352-528-2820 www.willistonpioneer.com editor@willistonpioneer.com

Winter Garden The West Orange Times (9.0M) 720 S Dillard St Winter Garden FL 34787 **Phn:** 407-656-2121 **Fax:** 407-656-6075 www.wotimes.com wotimes@aol.com

Zephyrhills Zephyrhills News (5.0M) 38333 5th Ave Zephyrhills FL 33542 **Phn:** 813-782-1558 **Fax:** 813-788-7987 www.zephyrhillsnews.com readznews@aol.com

GEORGIA

Adairsville North Bartow News (6.5M) PO Box 374 Adairsville GA 30103 **Phn:** 770-773-3754 **Fax:** 770-773-3757 cheryl.ray@daily-tribune.com

Adel Adel News Tribune (3.5M) PO Box 1500 Adel GA 31620 **Phn:** 229-896-2233 **Fax:** 229-896-7237 www.adelnewstribune.com adelnews@windstream.net

Albany Albany Journal (7.0M) PO Box 71371 Albany GA 31708 **Phn:** 229-435-6222 **Fax:** 229-435-0557 thealbanyjournal.com ajournal@thealbanyjournal.com

Alma Alma Times (3.1M) PO Box 428 Alma GA 31510 **Phn:** 912-632-7201 **Fax:** 912-632-4156 www.thealmatimes.com mail@thealmatimes.com

Alpharetta Appen Newspapers Inc (85.0M) 319 N Main St Alpharetta GA 30009 **Phn:** 770-442-3278 **Fax:** 770-475-1216 www.northfulton.com news@northfulton.com

Ashburn The Wiregrass Farmer (3.3M) PO Box 309 Ashburn GA 31714 **Phn:** 229-567-3655 **Fax:** 229-567-4402 www.thewiregrassfarmer.com wiregrassfarmer@yahoo.com

Atlanta Creative Loafing (120.0M) 384 Northyards Blvd NW Ste 600 Atlanta GA 30313 **Phn:** 404-688-5623 **Fax:** 404-614-3599 clatl.com happenings@creativeloafing.com

Atlanta Dunwoody Crier (24.5M) PO Box 888044 Atlanta GA 30356 **Phn:** 770-451-4147 **Fax:** 770-451-4223 www.thecrier.net thecrier@mindspring.com

Atlanta Neighbor Newspapers (27.0M) 1317 Dunwoody Village Pkwy Atlanta GA 30338 **Phn:** 770-454-9388 **Fax:** 770-454-9131 www.neighbornewspapers.com dekalb@neighbornewspapers.com

Atlanta Northside Neighbor (35.0M) 5290 Roswell Rd Ste M Atlanta GA 30342 **Phn:** 404-256-3100 **Fax:** 404-256-3292 www.neighbornewspapers.com nside@neighbornewspapers.com

Atlanta Rockdale Neighbor (16.0M) 3060 Mercer University Dr Ste 210 Atlanta GA 30341 **Phn:** 770-454-9388 **Fax:** 770-454-9131 www.neighbornewspapers.com rockdale@neighbornewspapers.com

Atlanta The Sunday Paper (75.0M) 763 Trabert Ave NW Ste D Atlanta GA 30318 **Phn:** 404-351-5797 **Fax:** 404-351-2350

Bainbridge The Post-Searchlight (7.3M) PO Box 277 Bainbridge GA 39818 **Phn:** 229-246-2827 **Fax:** 229-246-7665 www.thepostsearchlight.com news@thepostsearchlight.com

Barnesville The Herald-Gazette (5.0M) PO Box 220 Barnesville GA 30204 **Phn:** 770-358-0754 **Fax:** 770-358-0756 www.barnesville.com news@barnesville.com

Baxley Baxley News-Banner (5.0M) PO Box 410 Baxley GA 31515 **Phn:** 912-367-2468 **Fax:** 912-367-0277 www.baxleynewsbanner.com mail@baxleynewsbanner.com

Blackshear Blackshear Times (3.5M) PO Box 410 Blackshear GA 31516 **Phn:** 912-449-6693 **Fax:** 912-449-1719 www.theblacksheartimes.com mail@theblacksheartimes.com

Blairsville North Georgia News (10.1M) PO Box 2029 Blairsville GA 30514 **Phn:** 706-745-6343 **Fax:** 706-745-1830 www.nganews.com northgeorgianews@hotmail.com

Blakely Early County News (11.4M) PO Box 748 Blakely GA 39823 **Phn:** 229-723-4376 **Fax:** 229-723-6097 www.earlycountynews.com ecnews@windstream.net

Blue Ridge News Observer (8.9M) PO Box 989 Blue Ridge GA 30513 **Phn:** 706-632-2019 **Fax:** 706-632-2577 www.thenewsobserver.com news@thenewsobserver.com

Bremen Haralson Gateway Beacon (4.2M) PO Box 685 Bremen GA 30110 **Phn:** 770-537-2434 **Fax:** 770-537-8816 www.times-georgian.com kcampbell@times-georgian.com

Brunswick Harbor Sound (30.0M) PO Box 606 Brunswick GA 31521 **Phn:** 912-264-4521 **Fax:** 912-264-4531 harborsoundedit@yahoo.com

Buena Vista Tri-County Journal & Chronicle (2.0M) PO Box 850 Buena Vista GA 31803 **Phn:** 229-649-6397 www.tjournal.com tjournal@windstream.net

Butler Taylor County News (2.5M) PO Box 550 Butler GA 31006 **Phn:** 478-862-5101 **Fax:** 478-862-9668 tcnews@pstel.net

Cairo Cairo Messenger (13.0M) PO Box 30 Cairo GA 39828 **Phn:** 229-377-2032 **Fax:** 229-377-4640 www.cairomessenger.com news@cairomessenger.com

Calhoun Calhoun Times (9.0M) 301 S Park Ave Calhoun GA 30701 **Phn:** 706-629-2231 **Fax:** 706-625-0899 www.northwestgeorgianews.com/calhoun_times alennon@calhountimes.com

Camilla The Camilla Enterprise (3.0M) PO Box 365 Camilla GA 31730 **Phn:** 229-336-5265 **Fax:** 229-336-8476 www.thecamillaenterprise.com camillaenterprise@camillaga.net

Carrollton Carroll Star News (10.6M) PO Box 680 Carrollton GA 30112 **Phn:** 770-214-9900 **Fax:** 770-214-9600 suehorn@bellsouth.net

Carrollton Carroll Weekly (20.0M) PO Box 460 Carrollton GA 30112 **Phn:** 770-834-6631 **Fax:** 770-830-9425 www.times-georgian.com kcampbell@times-georgian.com

Cedartown Cedartown Standard (3.4M) PO Box 308 Cedartown GA 30125 **Phn:** 770-748-1520 **Fax:** 770-748-1524 www.northwestgeorgianews.com/polkfishwrap amadden@npco.com

Cedartown Rockmart Journal (3.3M) 213 Main St Cedartown GA 30125 **Phn:** 770-684-7811 **Fax:** 770-684-8468 www.northwestgeorgianews.com/polkfishwrap amadden@npco.com

Chatsworth Chatsworth Times (5.6M) PO Box 130 Chatsworth GA 30705 **Phn:** 706-695-4646 **Fax:** 706-695-7181 www.chatsworthtimes.com news@chatsworthtimes.com

Claxton Claxton Enterprise (4.2M) PO Box 218 Claxton GA 30417 **Phn:** 912-739-2132 **Fax:** 912-739-2140 www.claxtonenterprise.com editor@claxtonenterprise.com

Clayton Clayton Tribune (8.0M) PO Box 425 Clayton GA 30525 **Phn:** 706-782-3312 **Fax:** 706-782-4230 www.theclaytontribune.com tribune@theclaytontribune.com

Cleveland White County News (7.4M) 13 E Jarrard St Cleveland GA 30528 **Phn:** 706-865-4718 **Fax:** 706-865-3048 www.whitecountynews.net news@whitecountynews.net

Cochran Cochran Journal (3.5M) PO Box 856 Cochran GA 31014 **Phn:** 478-934-6303 **Fax:** 478-934-6800 cochranjournal@yahoo.com

Colquitt Miller County Liberal (3.0M) PO Box 37 Colquitt GA 39837 **Phn:** 229-758-5549 **Fax:** 229-758-5540 www.millercountyliberal.com millercountyliberal@gmail.com

Cornelia The Northeast Georgian (9.1M) PO Box 1555 Cornelia GA 30531 **Phn:** 706-778-4215 **Fax:** 706-778-4114 www.thenortheastgeorgian.com news@thenortheastgeorgian.com

Covington Covington News (7.3M) PO Box 1249 Covington GA 30015 **Phn:** 770-787-6397 **Fax:** 770-786-6451 www.covnews.com news@covnews.com

Cumming Forsyth Co. News (15.5M) PO Box 210 Cumming GA 30028 **Phn:** 770-887-3126 **Fax:** 770-889-6017 www.forsythnews.com circ@forsythnews.com

Dahlonega Dahlonega Nugget (6.9M) PO Box 36 Dahlonega GA 30533 **Phn:** 706-864-3613 **Fax:** 706-864-4360 www.thedahloneganugget.com iamshall@yahoo.com

Dallas Dallas New Era (5.5M) 121 W Spring St Dallas GA 30132 **Phn:** 770-445-3379 **Fax:** 770-445-5726 newerapr@bellsouth.net

Danielsville Madison County Journal (4.9M) PO Box 658 Danielsville GA 30633 **Phn:** 706-795-2567 **Fax:** 706-795-2765 www.mainstreetnews.com news@mainstreetnews.com

Darien Darien News (3.0M) PO Box 496 Darien GA 31305 **Phn:** 912-437-4251 **Fax:** 912-437-2299 www.thedariennews.net news@thedariennews.net

Dawson Dawson News (2.8M) PO Box 350 Dawson GA 39842 **Phn:** 229-995-2175 **Fax:** 229-995-2176 news@thedawsonnews.com

Dawsonville Community News (4.5M) PO Box 1600 Dawsonville GA 30534 **Phn:** 706-265-3384 **Fax:** 706-265-3276 www.dawsonnews.com

Dawsonville News & Advertiser (5.4M) PO Box 225 Dawsonville GA 30534 **Phn:** 706-265-2345 **Fax:** 706-265-7842 www.dawsonadvertiser.com kboim@dawsonadvertiser.com

Decatur The Champion (19.0M) PO Box 1347 Decatur GA 30031 **Phn:** 404-373-7779 **Fax:** 404-373-3903 thechampionnewspaper.com kathy@dekalbchamp.com

Donalsonville Donalsonville News (3.6M) PO Box 338 Donalsonville GA 39845 **Phn:** 229-524-2343 bo@donalsonvillenews.com

Douglas Douglas Enterprise (8.0M) PO Box 750 Douglas GA 31534 **Phn:** 912-384-2323 **Fax:** 912-383-0218 www.douglasenterprise.net publisher@douglasenterprise.net

Douglasville Paulding County Sentinel (11.5M) PO Box 1586 Douglasville GA 30133 **Phn:** 770-942-6571 **Fax:** 770-949-7556 www.douglascountysentinel.com pcsentinel@douglascountysentinel.com

Eastman Dodge County News (5.2M) PO Box 69 Eastman GA 31023 **Phn:** 478-374-6397 **Fax:** 478-374-0361 www.dodgecountynews.com publisher@dodgecountynews.com

Eatonton Eatonton Messenger (5.4M) Po Box 4027 Eatonton GA 31024 **Phn:** 706-485-3501 **Fax:** 706-485-4166 www.msgr.com editor@msgr.com

Elberton The Elberton Star (6.0M) PO Box 280 Elberton GA 30635 **Phn:** 706-283-8500 **Fax:** 706-283-9700 www.elberton.com starexaminer@elberton.com

Ellijay Times-Courier (6.9M) PO Box 1076 Ellijay GA 30540 **Phn:** 706-635-4313 **Fax:** 706-635-7006 www.timescourier.com news@timescourier.com

Evans Columbia Co. News Times (19.0M) 4272 Washington Rd Ste 3B Evans GA 30809 **Phn:** 706-863-6165 **Fax:** 706-868-9824 newstimes.augusta.com

Fayetteville The Citizen (23.5M) PO Drawer 1719 Fayetteville GA 30214 **Phn:** 770-719-1880 **Fax:** 770-719-1976 www.thecitizen.com editor@thecitizen.com

Fitzgerald The Herald Leader (5.4M) PO Box 40 Fitzgerald GA 31750 **Phn:** 229-423-9331 **Fax:** 229-423-6533 www.herald-leader.net tandersonherald@gmail.com

Folkston Charlton County Herald (3.0M) PO Box 398 Folkston GA 31537 **Phn:** 912-496-3585 **Fax:** 912-496-4585 www.charltoncountyherald.com ccheditor@windstream.net

Forest Park Neighbor Papers (104.0M) 5300 Frontage Rd Ste B Forest Park GA 30297 **Phn:** 404-363-8484 **Fax:** 404-363-0212 www.neighbornewspapers.com smetro@neighbornewspapers.com

Forsyth Monroe County Reporter (4.2M) PO Box 795 Forsyth GA 31029 **Phn:** 478-994-2358 **Fax:** 478-994-2359 www.mymcr.net publisher@mymcr.net

Fort Valley Leader-Tribune (4.0M) 109 Anderson Ave Fort Valley GA 31030 **Phn:** 478-825-2432 **Fax:** 478-825-4130 evansnewspapers.com devans@evansnewspapers.com

Glennville Glenville Sentinel (4.6M) PO Box 218 Glennville GA 30427 **Phn:** 912-654-2515 **Fax:** 912-654-2527 www.glennvillesentinel.net editor@glennvillesentinel.net

Gray The Jones Co. News (5.5M) PO Box 1538 Gray GA 31032 **Phn:** 478-986-3929 **Fax:** 478-986-1935 www.jcnews.com articles@jcnews.com

Greensboro Greensboro Herald-Journal & Advocate-Dem (0.8M) PO Box 149 Greensboro GA 30642 **Phn:** 706-453-7988 **Fax:** 706-453-2311 editor@heraldjournal.net

Greensboro Lake Oconee News (6.7M) 1106 Market St Greensboro GA 30642 **Phn:** 706-454-1290 **Fax:** 706-454-1292 www.msgr.com/lake_oconee_news ksears@gmail.com

Hartwell The Hartwell Sun (7.4M) PO Box 700 Hartwell GA 30643 **Phn:** 706-376-8025 **Fax:** 706-376-3016 www.thehartwellsun.com hartwellsun@hartcom.net

Hawkinsville Dispatch & News (3.0M) PO Box 30 Hawkinsville GA 31036 **Phn:** 478-783-1291 **Fax:** 478-783-1293 pulaskinews@comsouth.net

Hazlehurst Jeff Davis Ledger (3.8M) PO Box 460 Hazlehurst GA 31539 **Phn:** 912-375-4225 **Fax:** 912-375-3704 www.jdledger.com news@jdledger.com

Hiawassee Towns County Herald (3.5M) PO Box 365 Hiawassee GA 30546 **Phn:** 706-896-4454 **Fax:** 706-896-1745

Hinesville The Coastal Courier (5.0M) PO Box 498 Hinesville GA 31310 **Phn:** 912-876-0156 **Fax:** 912-368-6329 www.coastalcourier.com pwatkins@coastalcourier.com

Hiram Douglas Neighbor (20.0M) 4471 Jimmy Lee Smith Pkwy Ste 200 Hiram GA 30141 **Phn:** 770-942-1611 **Fax:** 770-942-4348 www.neighbornewspapers.com douglas@neighbornewspapers.com

Hiram Paulding Neighbor (19.0M) 4471 Jimmy Lee Smith Pkwy Ste 200 Hiram GA 30141 **Phn:** 770-445-9401 **Fax:** 770-445-0565 www.neighbornewspapers.com paulding@neighbornewspapers.com

Homer Banks County News (3.5M) PO Box 920 Homer GA 30547 **Phn:** 706-677-3491 **Fax:** 706-677-3263 www.mainstreetnews.com news@mainstreetnews.com

Homerville Clinch County News (2.2M) PO Box 377 Homerville GA 31634 **Phn:** 912-487-5337 **Fax:** 912-487-3227 www.theclinchcountynews.com lrobbins@theclinchcountynews.com

Homerville Echols County Echo (1.7M) PO Box 377 Homerville GA 31634 **Phn:** 912-487-5337 **Fax:** 912-487-3227 echolsecho@windstream.net

Irwinton Wilkinson County Post (1.0M) PO Box 224 Irwinton GA 31042 **Phn:** 478-946-7272 **Fax:** 478-946-7220 post@windstream.net

Jackson Jackson Progress-Argus (4.2M) PO Box 249 Jackson GA 30233 **Phn:** 770-775-3107 **Fax:** 770-775-3855 www.jacksonprogress-argus.com

Jasper Pickens County Progress (6.5M) PO Box 67 Jasper GA 30143 **Phn:** 706-253-2457 **Fax:** 706-253-9738 www.pickensprogress.com news@pickensprogress.com

Jefferson Commerce News (3.1M) PO Box 908 Jefferson GA 30549 **Phn:** 706-367-5233 **Fax:** 706-367-8056 www.mainstreetnews.com news@mainstreetnews.com

Jefferson Jackson Herald (3.4M) PO Box 908 Jefferson GA 30549 **Phn:** 706-367-5233 **Fax:** 706-367-9355 www.mainstreetnews.com news@mainstreetnews.com

Jesup The Press Sentinel (7.2M) 252 W Walnut St Jesup GA 31545 **Phn:** 912-427-3757 **Fax:** 912-427-4092 www.thepress-sentinel.com edenty@bellsouth.net

La Fayette Walker County Messenger (4.7M) 102 N Main St La Fayette GA 30728 **Phn:** 706-638-1859 **Fax:** 706-638-7045 www.northwestgeorgianews.com/catwalkchatt walkercountymessenger@walkermessenger.co

Lakeland Lanier County Advocate (1.3M) PO Box 476 Lakeland GA 31635 **Phn:** 229-482-1045 **Fax:** 229-482-1075 www.laniercountyadvocate.com editor@laniercountyadvocate.com

Lakeland Lanier County News (1.2M) PO Box 216 Lakeland GA 31635 **Phn:** 229-896-2233 **Fax:** 229-896-7237

Lavonia Franklin County Citizen (4.7M) PO Box 580 Lavonia GA 30553 **Phn:** 706-356-8557 **Fax:** 706-356-2008 www.franklincountycitizen.com fccitizen@windstream.net

Leesburg Lee County Ledger (3.8M) PO Box 715 Leesburg GA 31763 **Phn:** 229-759-2413 **Fax:** 229-759-6599 www.leecountyledger.com jim@leecountyledger.com

Lexington Oglethorpe Echo (3.0M) PO Box 268 Lexington GA 30648 **Phn:** 706-743-3111 editor@oglethorpeecho.com

Lincolnton Lincoln Journal (3.0M) PO Box 399 Lincolnton GA 30817 **Phn:** 706-359-3229 **Fax:** 706-359-2884 www.lincolnjournalonline.com journal@nu-z.net

Louisville News & Farmer (5.0M) PO Box 487 Louisville GA 30434 **Phn:** 478-625-7722 **Fax:** 478-625-8816 www.thenewsandfarmer.com news@thenewsandfarmer.com

Madison Morgan County Citizen (5.0M) 235 S Main St Madison GA 30650 **Phn:** 706-342-7440 **Fax:** 706-342-2140 morgancountycitizen.com

Manchester Harris Co. Journal (10.0M) PO Box 426 Manchester GA 31816 **Phn:** 706-846-3188 **Fax:** 706-846-2206

Manchester Star-Mercury Publications (9.0M) PO Box 426 Manchester GA 31816 **Phn:** 706-846-3188 **Fax:** 706-846-2206

Marietta Neighbor Newspapers (98.0M) 580 Fairground St Marietta GA 30060 **Phn:** 770-428-9411 **Fax:** 770-428-7945 www.neighbornewspapers.com douglas@neighbornewspapers.com

Mc Rae Telfair Enterprise (3.2M) PO Box 269 Mc Rae GA 31055 **Phn:** 229-868-6015 **Fax:** 229-868-5486 www.thetelfairenterprise.com telfaireditor@windstream.net

McDonough Henry County Times (7.5M) PO Box 2407 McDonough GA 30253 **Phn:** 770-957-6314 www.henrycountytimes.com editor@henrycountytimes.com

Metter Metter Advertiser (3.0M) PO Box 8 Metter GA 30439 **Phn:** 912-685-6566 **Fax:** 912-685-4901 www.metteradvertiser.com news@metteradvertiser.com

Milledgeville Baldwin Bulletin (3.0M) 136 S Wayne St Milledgeville GA 31061 **Phn:** 478-452-1777 **Fax:** 478-452-8464 www.heraldpublishingcompany.com weeklies@courier-herald.com

Millen Millen News (2.0M) 856 Cotton Ave Ste A Millen GA 30442 **Phn:** 478-982-5460 **Fax:** 478-982-1785 www.themillennews.com themillennews@gmail.com

Monroe Walton Tribune (5.5M) PO Box 808 Monroe GA 30655 **Phn:** 770-267-8371 **Fax:** 770-267-7780 waltontribune.com tribstaff@waltontribune.com

Montezuma The Citizen Georgian (2.9M) 305 S Dooly St Montezuma GA 31063 **Phn:** 478-472-0189 **Fax:** 478-472-5753 evansnewspapers.com thecitizengeorgian@gmail.com

Monticello Monticello News (2.8M) PO Box 30 Monticello GA 31064 **Phn:** 706-468-6511 **Fax:** 706-468-6576 themonticellonews.com editor@themonticellonews.com

Nahunta Brantley Enterprise (2.5M) PO Box 454 Nahunta GA 31553 **Phn:** 912-462-6776 enterkom.com/enterprise editor@brantleyenterprise.com

Nashville The Berrien Press (4.8M) PO Box 455 Nashville GA 31639 **Phn:** 229-686-3523 **Fax:** 229-686-7771 www.theberrienpress.com localnews@windstream.net

Ocilla Ocilla Star (2.0M) PO Box 25 Ocilla GA 31774 **Phn:** 229-468-5433 **Fax:** 229-468-5045 www.theocillastar.com ocillastar@windstream.net

Pearson Atkinson County Citizen (1.5M) PO Box 398 Pearson GA 31642 **Phn:** 912-422-3824 **Fax:** 912-422-6050

Pelham The Pelham Journal (1.5M) PO Box 666 Pelham GA 31779 **Phn:** 229-336-5265 **Fax:** 229-336-8476 camillaenterprise@camillaga.net

Quitman Free Press (3.6M) PO Box 72 Quitman GA 31643 **Phn:** 229-263-4615 **Fax:** 229-263-5282

Reidsville Tattnall Journal (4.2M) PO Box 278 Reidsville GA 30453 **Phn:** 912-557-6761 **Fax:** 912-557-4132 www.tattnalljournal.com mail@tattnalljournal.com

Richland Stewart Webster Journal Patriot Citizen (4.0M) PO Box 250 Richland GA 31825 **Phn:** 229-887-3674 **Fax:** 229-887-2800 swjpc@bellsouth.net

Richmond Hill Bryan County News (3.2M) PO Box 1239 Richmond Hill GA 31324 **Phn:** 912-756-2668 **Fax:** 912-756-5907 www.bryancountynews.net mgriffin@bryancountynews.net

Rincon Effingham Herald (3.0M) 586 S Columbus Ave # 13 Rincon GA 31326 **Phn:** 912-826-5012 **Fax:** 912-826-0381 www.effinghamherald.net pdonahue@effinghamherald.net

Ringgold Catoosa County News (3.6M) 7513 Nashville St Ringgold GA 30736 **Phn:** 706-935-2621 **Fax:** 706-965-5934 www.northwestgeorgianews.com/catwalkchatt catoosacountynews@catoosanews.com

Roberta The Georgia Post (3.0M) PO Box 860 Roberta GA 31078 **Phn:** 478-836-3195 **Fax:** 478-836-9634

Roswell Alpharetta Neighbor (23.0M) 10930 Crabapple Rd Ste 9 Roswell GA 30075 **Phn:** 770-993-7400 **Fax:** 770-518-6062 www.neighbornewspapers.com nfulton@neighbornewspapers.com

Roswell Neighbor (18.0M) 10930 Crabapple Rd Ste 9 Roswell GA 30075 **Phn:** 770-993-7400 **Fax:** 770-518-6062 www.neighbornewspapers.com nfulton@neighbornewspapers.com

Saint Marys Tribune & Georgian (7.6M) PO Box 6960 Saint Marys GA 31558 **Phn:** 912-882-4927 **Fax:** 912-882-6519 www.tribune-georgian.com editor1@tds.net

Saint Simons Island The Islander (4.0M) PO Box 20539 Saint Simons Island GA 31522 **Phn:** 912-265-9654 **Fax:** 912-265-3699 www.theislanderonline.com ssislander@bellsouth.net

Sandersville Sandersville Progress (4.8M) PO Box 431 Sandersville GA 31082 **Phn:** 478-552-3161 **Fax:** 478-552-5177 waconews@att.net

Shellman Citizen News (8.0M) 282 Buford St Shellman GA 39886 **Phn:** 229-679-5569 thecitizen.biz

Soperton Herald Publishing (5.0M) PO Box 527 Soperton GA 30457 **Phn:** 912-529-6624 **Fax:** 912-529-5399 sopertonnews@nlamerica.com

Sparta Sparta Ishmaelite (2.7M) PO Box 308 Sparta GA 31087 **Phn:** 706-444-5330

Summerville Chattooga Press (11.0M) PO Box 485 Summerville GA 30747 **Phn:** 706-857-5433 **Fax:** 706-290-5219

Summerville Summerville News (8.0M) PO Box 310 Summerville GA 30747 **Phn:** 706-857-2494 **Fax:** 706-857-2393 www.thesummervillenews.com jasonespy@thesummervillenews.com

Swainsboro Forest Blade (6.0M) PO Box 938 Swainsboro GA 30401 **Phn:** 478-237-9971 **Fax:** 478-237-9451 www.forest-blade.com news@forest-blade.com

Sylvania Sylvania Telephone (4.5M) PO Box 10 Sylvania GA 30467 **Phn:** 912-564-2045 **Fax:** 912-564-7055 www.sylvaniatelephone.com enoch.autry@morris.com

Sylvester Sylvester Local News (3.8M) PO Box 387 Sylvester GA 31791 **Phn:** 229-776-7713 **Fax:** 229-776-4607

Thomaston Thomaston Times (5.0M) PO Box 430 Thomaston GA 30286 **Phn:** 706-647-5414 **Fax:** 706-647-2833 www.thomastontimes.com editorial1@thomastontimes.com

Thomson McDuffie Mirror (4.0M) 108 Railroad St Thomson GA 30824 **Phn:** 706-597-0335 **Fax:** 706-843-9295 mirror.augusta.com

Thomson McDuffie Progress (3.2M) PO Box 1090 Thomson GA 30824 **Phn:** 706-595-1601 **Fax:** 706-597-8974 www.mcduffieprogress.com editor@mcduffieprogress.com

Toccoa Toccoa Record (7.3M) PO Box 1069 Toccoa GA 30577 **Phn:** 706-886-9476 **Fax:** 706-886-2161 www.thetoccoarecord.com toccoarecord@windstream.net

Trenton Dade County Sentinel (3.6M) PO Box 277 Trenton GA 30752 **Phn:** 706-657-6182 **Fax:** 706-657-4970 www.dadesentinel.com editor@dadesentinel.com

Vidalia The Advance (7.0M) PO Box 669 Vidalia GA 30475 **Phn:** 912-537-3131 **Fax:** 912-537-4899 www.theadvancenews.com theadvance@bellsouth.net

Vienna The News Observer (2.4M) PO Box 186 Vienna GA 31092 **Phn:** 229-268-2096 **Fax:** 229-268-1924

Villa Rica Villa Rican (3.0M) 210B W Montgomery St Villa Rica GA 30180 **Phn:** 770-459-0510 **Fax:** 770-456-9769 www.times-georgian.com/villa-rican kcampbell@times-georgian.com

Warrenton The Warrenton Clipper (3.3M) PO Box 306 Warrenton GA 30828 **Phn:** 706-465-3395 thewarrentonclipper@yahoo.com

Washington The News-Reporter (3.8M) PO Box 340 Washington GA 30673 **Phn:** 706-678-2636 **Fax:** 706-678-3857 www.news-reporter.com editor@news-reporter.com

Watkinsville Oconee Enterprise (4.3M) PO Box 535 Watkinsville GA 30677 **Phn:** 706-769-5175 **Fax:** 706-769-8532 www.oconeeenterprise.com oconeeenterprise@mindspring.com

Waynesboro The True Citizen (5.2M) PO Box 948 Waynesboro GA 30830 **Phn:** 706-554-2111 **Fax:** 706-526-4779 www.thetruecitizen.com lizbillips@yahoo.com

Winder Barrow County News (6.8M) PO Drawer C Winder GA 30680 **Phn:** 770-867-7557 **Fax:** 770-867-1034 www.barrowcountynews.com news@barrowcountynews.com

Woodstock Cherokee Ledger-News (30.0M) PO Box 2369 Woodstock GA 30188 **Phn:** 770-928-0706 **Fax:** 770-928-3152 www.ledgernews.com editor@ledgernews.com

Wrightsville Wrightsville Headlight (1.6M) PO Box 290 Wrightsville GA 31096 **Phn:** 478-864-3528 **Fax:** 478-864-2166

Zebulon Pike Co. Journal-Reporter (3.0M) PO Box 789 Zebulon GA 30295 **Phn:** 770-567-3446 **Fax:** 770-567-8814 www.pikecountygeorgia.com news@pikecountygeorgia.com

HAWAII

Hilo Hawaii Island Journal (175.0M) 116 Kamehameha Ave Ste 3 Hilo HI 96720 **Phn:** 808-961-1200 www.hawaiiislandjournal.com

Honolulu Honolulu Weekly (37.5M) 1111 Fort Street Mall 2nd Fl Honolulu HI 96813 **Phn:** 808-528-1475 **Fax:** 808-528-3144 honoluluweekly.com editorial@honoluluweekly.com

Honolulu Island Weekly (175.0M) PO Box 3350 Honolulu HI 96801 **Phn:** 808-525-8000 **Fax:** 808-525-8037

Honolulu Midweek (268.0M) 500 Ala Moana Blvd Ste 7-500 Honolulu HI 96813 **Phn:** 808-529-4865 **Fax:** 808-583-6324 www.midweek.com thefner@midweek.com

Kailua Oahu Island News (28.0M) PO Box 1501 Kailua HI 96734 **Phn:** 808-263-3535 www.oahuislandnews.com editor@oahuislandnews.com

Kamuela North Hawaii News (4.0M) 65-1279 Kawaihae Rd Ste 217 Kamuela HI 96743 **Phn:** 808-885-8818 **Fax:** 808-885-0601 www.northhawaiinews.com editor@northhawaiinews.net

Kaunakakai Molokai Dispatch (5.0M) PO Box 482219 Kaunakakai HI 96748 **Phn:** 808-552-2781 **Fax:** 808-552-2334 www.themolokaidispatch.com editor@themolokaidispatch.com

Kihei Maui Weekly (10.0M) 411 Huku Lii Pl Ste 303 Kihei HI 96753 **Phn:** 808-875-1700 **Fax:** 808-875-1800 www.mauiweekly.com editor@mauiweekly.com

Lahaina Lahaina News (12.0M) PO Box 10427 Lahaina HI 96761 **Phn:** 808-667-7866 **Fax:** 808-667-2726 www.lahainanews.com lahnews@maui.net

Paia Haleakala Times (15.0M) PO Box 791051 Paia HI 96779 **Phn:** 808-579-8020 **Fax:** 808-579-8026 www.mauiweekly.com haltimes@hawaii.rr.com

Wailuku Maui Time Weekly (18.0M) 33 N Market St Ste 201 Wailuku HI 96793 **Phn:** 808-244-0777 **Fax:** 808-244-0446 www.mauitime.com editor@mauitime.com

IDAHO

Aberdeen Aberdeen Times (1.2M) PO Box 856 Aberdeen ID 83210 **Phn:** 208-397-4440 www.press-times.com times1@dcdi.net

American Falls Power County Press (2.0M) PO Box 547 American Falls ID 83211 **Phn:** 208-226-5294 **Fax:** 208-226-5295 www.press-times.com press1@press-times.com

Arco Arco Advertiser (1.8M) PO Box 803 Arco ID 83213 **Phn:** 208-527-3038 **Fax:** 208-527-8210 arcoadv@aol.com

Boise Boise Weekly (32.0M) 523 W Broad St Boise ID 83702 **Phn:** 208-344-2055 **Fax:** 208-342-4733 www.boiseweekly.com editor@boiseweekly.com

Boise Idaho World (1.5M) PO Box 50248 Boise ID 83705 **Phn:** 208-429-1606 **Fax:** 208-445-2110 idahoworld.com editor@idahoworld.com

Bonners Ferry Bonners Ferry Herald (4.2M) PO Box 539 Bonners Ferry ID 83805 **Phn:** 208-267-5521 **Fax:** 208-267-5523 www.bonnersferryherald.com ljohnson@bonnersferryherald.com

Buhl Buhl Herald (2.8M) PO Box 312 Buhl ID 83316 **Phn:** 208-543-4335 **Fax:** 208-543-6834 buhlherald@cableone.net

Cambridge Upper Country News-Reporter (0.8M) PO Box 9 Cambridge ID 83610 **Phn:** 208-257-3515 **Fax:** 208-257-3540 reporter@ctcweb.net

Cascade Long Valley Advocate (5.0M) PO Box 1079 Cascade ID 83611 **Phn:** 208-382-3233

Challis Challis Messenger (1.9M) PO Box 405 Challis ID 83226 **Phn:** 208-879-4445 **Fax:** 208-879-5276 www.challismessenger.com info@challismessenger.com

Cottonwood Cottonwood Chronicle (1.0M) PO Box 157 Cottonwood ID 83522 **Phn:** 208-962-3851 **Fax:** 208-962-7131 www.cottonwoodchronicle.com editor@cottonwoodchronicle.com

Council Adams County Record (1.6M) PO Box R Council ID 83612 **Phn:** 208-253-6961 **Fax:** 208-253-6801 www.theadamscountyrecord.com record@ctcweb.net

Driggs Teton Valley News (2.9M) 75 N Main St Driggs ID 83422 **Phn:** 208-354-8101 **Fax:** 208-354-8621 www.tetonvalleynews.net editor@tetonvalleynews.net

Emmett Messenger Index (7.0M) PO Box 577 Emmett ID 83617 **Phn:** 208-365-6066 **Fax:** 208-365-6068 www.messenger-index.com newsroom@messenger-index.com

Fort Hall Sho-Ban News (2.5M) PO Box 900 Fort Hall ID 83203 **Phn:** 208-478-3888 **Fax:** 208-478-3702 www.shobannews.com shobnews@ida.net

Grangeville Idaho County Free Press (4.0M) PO Box 690 Grangeville ID 83530 **Phn:** 208-983-1200 **Fax:** 208-983-1336 www.idahocountyfreepress.com

Homedale Owyhee Avalanche (1.6M) PO Box 97 Homedale ID 83628 **Phn:** 208-337-4681 **Fax:** 208-337-4867 www.owyheepublishing.com owyheeavalanche@cableone.net

Island Park Island Park News (5.0M) PO Box 410 Island Park ID 83429 **Phn:** 208-558-0267 ipnews@mac.com

Kamiah Clearwater Progress (4.2M) PO Box 428 Kamiah ID 83536 **Phn:** 208-935-0838 **Fax:** 208-935-0973 www.clearwaterprogress.com progress@clearwaterprogress.com

Ketchum Idaho Mountain Express (13.5M) PO Box 1013 Ketchum ID 83340 **Phn:** 208-726-8060 **Fax:** 208-726-2329 www.mtexpress.com news@mtexpress.com

Kuna Kuna Melba News (2.3M) PO Box 373 Kuna ID 83634 **Phn:** 208-922-3008 **Fax:** 208-922-3009 kunamelba.com editor@kunamelba.com

Malad City Idaho Enterprise (1.4M) PO Box 205 Malad City ID 83252 **Phn:** 208-766-4773 **Fax:** 208-766-4774 www.idahoenterprise.com idahoenterprise@atcnet.net

McCall The Star-News (4.4M) 1000 N 1st St McCall ID 83638 **Phn:** 208-634-2123 **Fax:** 208-634-4950 www.mccallstarnews.com starnews@frontier.com

Montpelier News-Examiner (1.5M) PO Box 278 Montpelier ID 83254 **Phn:** 208-847-0552 **Fax:** 208-847-0553 www.news-examiner.net newseditor@news-examiner.net

Mountain Home Glenns Ferry Gazette (2.3M) PO Box 1330 Mountain Home ID 83647 **Phn:** 208-587-3331 **Fax:** 208-587-9205 gfgazette@aol.com

Mountain Home Mountain Home News (3.5M) PO Box 1330 Mountain Home ID 83647 **Phn:** 208-587-3331 **Fax:** 208-587-9205 www.mountainhomenews.com keveritt@mountainhomenews.com

Nezperce Lewis County Herald (0.9M) PO Box 159 Nezperce ID 83543 **Phn:** 208-937-2671 **Fax:** 208-962-7131 editor@cottonwoodchronicle.com

Orofino Clearwater Tribune (3.0M) PO Box 71 Orofino ID 83544 **Phn:** 208-476-4571 **Fax:** 208-476-0765 www.clearwatertribune.com cleartrib@cebridge.net

Payette Independent-Enterprise (2.4M) 124 S Main St Payette ID 83661 **Phn:** 208-642-3357 **Fax:** 208-642-3560 argusobserver.com/indent/news ienterprise1@qwestoffice.net

Preston Preston Citizen (2.5M) 77 S State St Preston ID 83263 **Phn:** 208-852-0155 **Fax:** 208-852-0158 www.prestoncitizen.com editor@prestoncitizen.com

Priest River Priest River Times (9.0M) PO Box 10 Priest River ID 83856 **Phn:** 208-448-2431 **Fax:** 208-448-2938 www.priestrivertimes.com tivie@priestrivertimes.com

Rathdrum The Rathdrum Star (10.0M) PO Box 1374 Rathdrum ID 83858 **Phn:** 208-687-8228 **Fax:** 208-687-1328 therathdrumstar.com tom@therathdrumstar.com

Saint Maries Gazette-Record (3.5M) 610 Main Ave Saint Maries ID 83861 **Phn:** 208-245-4538 **Fax:** 208-245-4011 gazetterecord.com dan@smgazette.com

Salmon The Recorder Herald (3.4M) PO Box 310 Salmon ID 83467 **Phn:** 208-756-2221 **Fax:** 208-756-2222

Shelley The Shelley Pioneer (1.7M) PO Box P Shelley ID 83274 **Phn:** 208-357-7661 **Fax:** 208-357-3435 www.theshelleypioneer.com news@theshelleypioneer.com

Soda Springs Caribou County Sun (3.0M) PO Box 815 Soda Springs ID 83276 **Phn:** 208-547-3260 **Fax:** 208-547-4422 ccsun10@aol.com

Weiser Weiser Signal American (2.2M) PO Box 709 Weiser ID 83672 **Phn:** 208-549-1717 **Fax:** 208-549-1718 www.signalamerican.org news@signalamerican.org

ILLINOIS

Abingdon Argus-Sentinel (2.0M) 507 N Monroe St Ste 3 Abingdon IL 61410 **Phn:** 309-462-3189 **Fax:** 309-462-3221 www.eaglepublications.com

Albion Navigator & Journal Register (4.0M) PO Box 10 Albion IL 62806 **Phn:** 618-445-2355 **Fax:** 618-445-3459 www.navigatorjournal.com navigator@nwcable.net

Aledo The Times-Record (4.0M) PO Box 309 Aledo IL 61231 **Phn:** 309-582-5112 **Fax:** 309-582-5319 www.aledotimesrecord.com rblackford@aledotimesrecord.com

Altamont Altamont News (1.0M) PO Box 315 Altamont IL 62411 **Phn:** 618-483-6176 **Fax:** 618-483-5177 altnewsban.com altnewsban@frontiernet.net

Amboy Amboy News (2.4M) 219 E Main St Amboy IL 61310 **Phn:** 815-857-2311 **Fax:** 815-857-2517 www.amboynews.com editor@mendotareporter.com

Anna The Gazette-Democrat (5.2M) PO Box 529 Anna IL 62906 **Phn:** 618-833-2158 **Fax:** 618-833-5813 www.annanews.com reppert@midwest.net

Arcola Arcola Record-Herald (2.2M) PO Box 217 Arcola IL 61910 **Phn:** 217-268-4950 **Fax:** 217-268-4938 slackpub@consolidated.net

Arthur Arthur Graphic-Clarion (3.0M) 113 E Illinois St Arthur IL 61911 **Phn:** 217-543-2151 **Fax:** 217-543-2152 www.thearthurgraphic.com arthurgraphic@consolidated.net

Ashton Ashton Gazette (1.0M) 813 Main St Ashton IL 61006 **Phn:** 815-453-2551 **Fax:** 815-453-2422 www.ashtongazette.com monetta@ashtongazette.com

Assumption Golden Prairie News (2.5M) 301 S Chestnut St Assumption IL 62510 **Phn:** 217-226-3721 **Fax:** 217-226-3579 angelagpnews@gmail.com

Astoria Astoria South Fulton Argus (2.0M) 100 N Pearl St POB 590 Astoria IL 61501 **Phn:** 309-329-2151 **Fax:** 309-329-2344 www.kkspc.com/argus argus@kkspc.com

Auburn South County Publications (7.1M) 110 N 5th St Auburn IL 62615 **Phn:** 217-438-6155 **Fax:** 217-438-6156 www.southcountypublications.com southco@royell.org

Aurora Sun Publications (77.0M) 495 N Commons Dr Ste 200 Aurora IL 60504 **Phn:** 630-355-8014 **Fax:** 630-978-8509 www.suburbanchicagonews.com thesun@scn1.com

Bartlett Examiner Publications (48.5M) 4N781 Gerber Rd Bartlett IL 60103 **Phn:** 630-830-4145 www.examinerpublications.com enews@examinerpublications.com

Beardstown Cass County Star-Gazette (2.9M) PO Box 79 Beardstown IL 62618 **Phn:** 217-323-1010 **Fax:** 217-323-1644 www.beardstownnewspapers.com stargazette@casscomm.com

Beardstown Cass County Star-Gazette (3.4M) PO Box 79 Beardstown IL 62618 **Phn:** 217-323-1010 **Fax:** 217-323-5402 www.beardstownnewspapers.com stargazette@casscomm.com

Beecher City Beecher City Journal (1.5M) PO Box 38 Beecher City IL 62414 **Phn:** 618-487-5634 **Fax:** 618-487-5180 bcj@frontiernet.net

Belleville Journal-Messenger (3.0M) 120 S Illinois St Belleville IL 62220 **Phn:** 618-239-2526 **Fax:** 618-239-9597 www.bnd.com jcouch@bnd.com

IDAHO WEEKLY NEWSPAPERS

Belleville O'Fallon Progress (5.7M) 120 S Illinois St Belleville IL 62220 **Phn:** 618-239-2688 **Fax:** 618-632-6438 www.bnd.com/465 ofprogress@bnd.com

Belvidere Boone County Journal (10.5M) 419 S State St Ste A Belvidere IL 61008 **Phn:** 815-544-4430 **Fax:** 815-544-4330 www.boonecountyjournal.com boonecountyjournal@gmail.com

Bloomington Community News (14.0M) PO Box 2907 Bloomington IL 61702 **Phn:** 309-829-9000 **Fax:** 309-829-7000

Bloomington Farmer City Journal (1.7M) PO Box 2907 Bloomington IL 61702 **Phn:** 309-829-9000 **Fax:** 309-829-7000 www.pantagraph.com newsroom@pantagraph.com

Blue Mound Blue Mound Leader (0.9M) PO Box 318 Blue Mound IL 62513 **Phn:** 217-692-2323 bmleader1@yahoo.com

Bourbonnais The Herald (4.0M) 500 Brown Blvd Bourbonnais IL 60914 **Phn:** 815-933-1131 **Fax:** 815-933-3785 www.bbherald.com news@bbherald.com

Breese Breese Journal (6.3M) PO Box 405 Breese IL 62230 **Phn:** 618-526-7211 **Fax:** 618-526-2590 www.breesepub.com bjpc@breesepub.com

Bunker Hill Gazette News (1.6M) 150 N Washington St Bunker Hill IL 62014 **Phn:** 618-585-4411 **Fax:** 618-585-3354

Bushnell McDonough-Democrat (5.0M) PO Box 269 Bushnell IL 61422 **Phn:** 309-772-2129 **Fax:** 309-772-3994 www.themcdonoughdemocrat.com info@themcdonoughdemocrat.com

Cairo Cairo Citizen (3.3M) 231 16th St Cairo IL 62914 **Phn:** 618-734-4242 **Fax:** 618-734-4244 thecairocitizen.com

Cambridge Cambridge Chronicle (1.0M) 119 W Exchange St Cambridge IL 61238 **Phn:** 309-937-3303 www.cambridgechron.com chronicle@geneseorepublic.com

Canton Fulton Democrat (5.0M) 31 S Main St Canton IL 61520 **Phn:** 309-647-9501 **Fax:** 309-647-9511 www.fultondemocrat.com fultondemocrat@att.net

Carbondale Carbondale Times (7.5M) 701 W Main St Carbondale IL 62901 **Phn:** 618-457-4084 **Fax:** 618-549-3664 ctimes@midwest.net

Carlinville Macoupin Co. Enquirer Democrat (5.5M) PO Box 200 Carlinville IL 62626 **Phn:** 217-854-2534 **Fax:** 217-854-2535 enquirerdemocrat.com mcednews@enquirerdemocrat.com

Carlyle Carlyle Union Banner (6.7M) 671 10th St Carlyle IL 62231 **Phn:** 618-594-3131 **Fax:** 618-594-3115 news@unionbanner.net

Carrollton Greene Prairie Press (3.0M) PO Box 265 Carrollton IL 62016 **Phn:** 217-942-9100 **Fax:** 217-942-6543

Carthage Hancock County Journal Pilot (4.2M) PO Box 478 Carthage IL 62321 **Phn:** 217-357-2149 **Fax:** 217-357-2177 www.journalpilot.com editor@journalpilot.com

Casey Lincoln Trail Publishing (3.5M) PO Box 158 Casey IL 62420 **Phn:** 217-932-5211 **Fax:** 217-932-5214 news@rr1.net

Champaign County Star (2.0M) PO Box 677 Champaign IL 61824 **Phn:** 217-351-5678 **Fax:** 217-351-5291 www.county-star.com cwalsh@news-gazette.com

Chester Randolph Co. Herald Tribune (2.6M) PO Box 269 Chester IL 62233 **Phn:** 618-826-2385 **Fax:** 618-826-5181 www.randolphcountyheraldtribune.com tribuneeditor@frontier.com

Chicago Beverly Review (6.4M) 10546 S Western Ave Chicago IL 60643 **Phn:** 773-238-3366 **Fax:** 773-238-1492 beverlyreview.net cconnors@beverlyreview.net

Chicago Bridgeport News (25.0M) 3506 S Halsted St Chicago IL 60609 **Phn:** 773-927-0025 **Fax:** 773-337-6995 www.bridgeportnews.net jrbridgeportnews@aol.com

Chicago Brighton Park Life (25.0M) 2949 W Pope John Paul II Dr Chicago IL 60632 **Phn:** 773-523-3663 **Fax:** 773-523-3983 brightonparklife@aol.com

Chicago Chicago Reader (129.0M) 11 E Illinois St Chicago IL 60611 **Phn:** 312-828-0350 **Fax:** 312-828-9926 www.chicagoreader.com mail@chicagoreader.com

Chicago Hyde Park Herald (32.0M) 1435 E Hyde Park Blvd Chicago IL 60615 **Phn:** 773-643-8533 **Fax:** 773-643-8542 www.hpherald.com herald@hpherald.com

Chicago Inside (50.0M) 6221 N Clark St Chicago IL 60660 **Phn:** 773-465-9700 www.insideonline.com insidepublicationschicago@gmail.com

Chicago Nadig Newspapers (30.0M) 4937 N Milwaukee Ave Chicago IL 60630 **Phn:** 773-286-6100 **Fax:** 773-286-8151 www.nadignewspapers.com nadignewspapers@aol.com

Chicago New City (40.0M) 47 Wt Polk St # 100 Chicago IL 60605 **Phn:** 312-243-8786 newcity.com mike@newcity.com

Chicago Southwest News-Herald Papers (61.0M) 5639 W 63rd St Chicago IL 60638 **Phn:** 773-476-4800 **Fax:** 773-476-7811 www.swnewsherald.com vonpub@aol.com

Chillicothe Chillicothe Independent (2.0M) 916 N 2nd St Chillicothe IL 61523 **Phn:** 309-274-6800 **Fax:** 309-274-6801 www.chillicotheindependent.com editor@mycinews.com

Chrisman Chrisman Leader (1.0M) 340 N New York St Chrisman IL 61924 **Phn:** 217-269-2811 **Fax:** 217-269-3611 chrismanleader@comcast.net

Christopher The Progress (1.2M) PO Box A Christopher IL 62822 **Phn:** 618-724-9423

Cissna Park Cissna Park News & Rankin Independent (1.5M) PO Box 8 Cissna Park IL 60924 **Phn:** 815-457-2245 **Fax:** 815-457-3245 rickbaier@yahoo.com

Clifton Clifton Advocate (2.1M) PO Box 548 Clifton IL 60927 **Phn:** 815-694-2122 **Fax:** 815-694-2649 www.cliftonadvocate.com cliftonadvocate@gmail.com

Clinton Clinton Journal (1.7M) PO Box 615 Clinton IL 61727 **Phn:** 217-935-3171 **Fax:** 217-935-6086 www.theclintonjournal.com gwoods@theclintonjournal.com

Clinton The DeWitt Co. Constitution (2.2M) PO Box 31 Clinton IL 61727 **Phn:** 217-935-0207 **Fax:** 217-935-9797

Coal City Coal City Courant (2.0M) PO Box 215 Coal City IL 60416 **Phn:** 815-634-0315 **Fax:** 815-634-0317 freepressnewspapers.com ann.gill@cbcast.com

Collinsville Suburban Journals (51.0M) 2 Executive Dr Collinsville IL 62234 **Phn:** 618-344-0264 **Fax:** 618-344-3611 www.stltoday.com/suburban-journals chollway@stltoday.com

Danville The Independent News (17.0M) 137 N Walnut Danville IL 61832 **Phn:** 217-443-8484 **Fax:** 217-443-8490 www.the-independent-news.com indnews@news-gazette.com

Decatur Decatur Tribune (7.5M) PO Box 1490 Decatur IL 62525 **Phn:** 217-422-9702 **Fax:** 217-422-7320 www.decaturtribune.com decaturtrb@aol.com

DeKalb Midweek (30.0M) 1586 Barber Greene Rd DeKalb IL 60115 **Phn:** 815-758-4841 **Fax:** 815-756-5069 www.midweeknews.com dherra@shawmedia.com

ILLINOIS WEEKLY NEWSPAPERS

Delavan Delavan Times (1.5M) PO Box 199 Delavan IL 61734 **Phn:** 309-244-7111

Des Plaines Journal & Topics Newspapers (52.0M) 622 Graceland Ave Des Plaines IL 60016 **Phn:** 847-299-5511 **Fax:** 847-298-8549 www.journal-topics.com journalnews@mail.com

Dongola Tri-County Record (1.2M) PO Box 189 Dongola IL 62926 **Phn:** 618-827-4353 **Fax:** 618-827-4193

Downers Grove Liberty Suburban Papers (23.0M) 1101 31st St Ste 100 Downers Grove IL 60515 **Phn:** 630-368-1100 **Fax:** 630-969-0228 www.mysuburbanlife.com rterrell@shawmedia.com

Downers Grove Life Newspapers (210.0M) 101 W 31st St # 1000 Downers Grove IL 60515 **Phn:** 630-368-1100 **Fax:** 630-969-0228 www.mysuburbanlife.com rterrell@shawmedia.com

Downers Grove Reporter/Progress Papers (30.0M) 1101 31st St Ste 100 Downers Grove IL 60515 **Phn:** 630-368-1100 **Fax:** 630-969-0228 www.mysuburbanlife.com dlemery@shawmedia.com

Du Quoin Ashley News (0.3M) PO Box 184 Du Quoin IL 62832 **Phn:** 618-542-2133 **Fax:** 618-542-2726 dqsociety@frontier.com

Durand The Volunteer (1.6M) PO Box 369 Durand IL 61024 **Phn:** 815-248-4407 **Fax:** 815-248-9176 volunteer@stateline-isp.com

Dwight The Paper (10.0M) 204 E Chippewa St Dwight IL 60420 **Phn:** 815-584-1901 **Fax:** 815-584-2196 thepaper1901.com thepaper1901@sbcglobal.net

Earlville Earlville Post (1.0M) PO Box 487 Earlville IL 60518 **Phn:** 815-246-4600 **Fax:** 815-246-6000 www.earlvillepost.com editor@earlvillepost.com

East Dubuque East Dubuque Register (0.8M) 141 Sinsinawa Ave East Dubuque IL 61025 **Phn:** 815-747-3171 **Fax:** 815-747-3215 www.thonline.com/home triniker@wcinet.com

Edinburg The Herald-Star (0.7M) 103 N Eaton St Edinburg IL 62531 **Phn:** 217-623-5523

El Paso El Paso Journal (1.2M) 51 W Front St El Paso IL 61738 **Phn:** 309-527-8595 **Fax:** 309-527-8850 www.fairpoint.net/~journal journal@elpaso.net

Elburn Elburn Herald (4.1M) 525 N Main St Elburn IL 60119 **Phn:** 630-365-6446 **Fax:** 630-365-2251 elburnherald.com info@elburnherald.com

Elizabethtown Hardin County Independent (2.7M) PO Box 328 Elizabethtown IL 62931 **Phn:** 618-287-2361 etownnews@yahoo.com

Elmwood Elmwood Publishing (2.0M) PO Box 289 Elmwood IL 61529 **Phn:** 309-742-2521 **Fax:** 309-742-2511 homeshopper@mchsi.com

Eureka Woodford County Journal (2.5M) PO Box 36 Eureka IL 61530 **Phn:** 309-467-3314 **Fax:** 309-467-4563

Evanston Evanston Roundtable (18.0M) 1124 Florence Ave Ste 3 Evanston IL 60202 **Phn:** 847-864-7741 **Fax:** 847-864-7749 www.evanstonroundtable.com info@evanstonroundtable.com

Fairbury The Blade (3.4M) 125 W Locust St Fairbury IL 61739 **Phn:** 815-692-2366 **Fax:** 815-692-3782 bladenews@mchsi.com

Fairfield Wayne County Press (7.5M) 213 E Main St Fairfield IL 62837 **Phn:** 618-842-2662 **Fax:** 618-842-7912

Flora Clay Co. Advocate-Press (2.9M) 105 W North Ave Flora IL 62839 **Phn:** 618-662-2108 **Fax:** 618-662-2939 www.advocatepress.com editor@advocatepress.com

Flora Hometown Journal (3.0M) PO Box 100 Flora IL 62839 **Phn:** 618-662-6622 **Fax:** 618-662-2343

Forest Park West Suburban Journal (10.0M) 409 Beloit Ave Ste 1 Forest Park IL 60130 **Phn:** 708-771-5975 **Fax:** 708-865-2461 www.westsuburbanjournal.com editor@westsuburbanjournal.com

Franklin Franklin Times (0.9M) 208 Main St Franklin IL 62638 **Phn:** 217-675-2461 **Fax:** 217-675-2470 www.franklinillinois.net/franklintimes.htm ira@dtnspeed.net

Freeburg Freeburg Tribune (2.9M) 820 S State St Freeburg IL 62243 **Phn:** 618-539-3320 **Fax:** 618-539-3346 www.freeburgtribune.com newsroom@freeburgtribune.com

Fulton Fulton Journal (2.2M) PO Box 30 Fulton IL 61252 **Phn:** 815-589-2424 **Fax:** 815-589-2714

Galena Galena Gazette (5.0M) PO Box 319 Galena IL 61036 **Phn:** 815-777-0019 **Fax:** 815-777-3809 galenagazette.com

Galesburg The Zephyr (2.1M) PO Box 1 Galesburg IL 61402 **Phn:** 309-342-2010 **Fax:** 309-342-2728 www.thezephyr.com

Galva Galva News (1.9M) 348 Front St Galva IL 61434 **Phn:** 309-932-2103 **Fax:** 309-932-3282 galvanews@mchsi.com

Geneseo Geneseo Republic (4.2M) 108 W 1st St Geneseo IL 61254 **Phn:** 309-944-2119 **Fax:** 309-944-5615 www.geneseorepublic.com editor@geneseorepublic.com

Georgetown Independent News (17.0M) 201 N Main St # B Georgetown IL 61846 **Phn:** 217-662-2556 **Fax:** 217-662-2484

Gibson City Gibson City Courier (1.8M) PO Box 549 Gibson City IL 60936 **Phn:** 217-784-4244 **Fax:** 217-784-4246 dbenter_gc@sbcglobal.net

Gillespie South County News (3.0M) 302 S Macoupin St Gillespie IL 62033 **Phn:** 217-839-2130 **Fax:** 217-839-2139

Gilman Gilman Star (2.7M) PO Box 7 Gilman IL 60938 **Phn:** 815-265-7332 **Fax:** 815-265-7880

Glasford Glasford Gazette (1.2M) 309 W Main St Glasford IL 61533 **Phn:** 309-389-2811 **Fax:** 309-389-4949

Glenview Pioneer Press (54.0M) 3701 W Lake Ave Glenview IL 60026 **Phn:** 847-486-9200 **Fax:** 847-486-7451 pioneerlocal.suntimes.com jthomas@pioneerlocal.com

Golconda Herald-Enterprise (1.7M) PO Box 400 Golconda IL 62938 **Phn:** 618-683-3531 **Fax:** 618-683-3831 herald@shawneelink.net

Goreville Goreville Gazette (0.8M) PO Box 70 Goreville IL 62939 **Phn:** 618-995-9445 www.johnsoncountyil.com/goreville gorevillegazette@frontier.com

Granville Putnam County Record (3.0M) PO Box 48 Granville IL 61326 **Phn:** 815-339-2321 **Fax:** 815-339-6727

Grayslake Lakeland Journal (10.0M) PO Box 268 Grayslake IL 60030 **Phn:** 847-223-8161 **Fax:** 847-223-8810

Greenup Greenup Press (1.6M) PO Box 127 Greenup IL 62428 **Phn:** 217-923-3704 thepress@rr1.net

Greenville Greenville Advocate (5.1M) PO Box 9 Greenville IL 62246 **Phn:** 618-664-3144 **Fax:** 618-664-1613 www.greenvilleadvocate.com advocateil@sbcglobal.net

Havana Mason County Democrat (6.3M) PO Box 380 Havana IL 62644 **Phn:** 309-543-3311 **Fax:** 309-543-6844 www.masoncountydemocrat.com mcdemo@havanaprint.com

Henry Henry News-Republican (2.0M) PO Box 190 Henry IL 61537 **Phn:** 309-364-3250 **Fax:** 309-364-3858 henrynews@frontier.com

Herrin The Spokesman (2.3M) PO Box 128 Herrin IL 62948 **Phn:** 618-942-5000 **Fax:** 618-993-8326 www.dailyrepublicannews.com/herrin_news editor@dailyrepublicannews.com

Herscher Herscher Pilot (2.2M) PO Box 709 Herscher IL 60941 **Phn:** 815-426-2132 www.herscherpilot.com editor@herscherpilot.com

Highland Highland News Leader (6.0M) PO Box 250 Highland IL 62249 **Phn:** 618-654-2366 **Fax:** 618-654-1181 hnlnews@bnd.com

Hillsboro The Journal-News (7.0M) PO Box 100 Hillsboro IL 62049 **Phn:** 217-532-3933 **Fax:** 217-532-3632 www.thejournal-news.net thejournal-news@consolidated.net

Hinsdale Doings Newspapers (20.0M) 920 N York Rd Ste 200 Hinsdale IL 60521 **Phn:** 630-320-5400 **Fax:** 630-320-5460 hinsdale.suntimes.com doingsnews@pioneerlocal.com

Homer The Leader (7.0M) 115 Lacey Ln Homer IL 61849 **Phn:** 217-582-2373 www.leaderlandnews.com

Hoopeston The Chronicle (2.1M) 308 E Main St Hoopeston IL 60942 **Phn:** 217-283-5111 **Fax:** 217-283-5846 newsbug.info/hoopeston_chronicle chronreporter@frontier.com

Illiopolis The Sentinel (1.3M) PO Box 300 Illiopolis IL 62539 **Phn:** 217-486-6496 www.illiopolis.com/pages/members/illiopolis_sentinel.htm

Jerseyville Jersey County Journal (11.5M) 823 S State St Jerseyville IL 62052 **Phn:** 618-498-1234 jerseycountyjournal.com jcjnews@campbellpublications.net

Jerseyville Jersey County Star (1.6M) 722 W County Rd Ste B Jerseyville IL 62052 **Phn:** 618-498-3377 jcstar@gtec.com

Joliet Farmers Weekly Review (13.6M) 100 Manhattan Rd Joliet IL 60433 **Phn:** 815-727-4811 **Fax:** 815-727-5570 www.farmers-weekly-review.com farmersweekly@sbcglobal.net

Joliet The Times Weekly (28.0M) PO Box 2277 Joliet IL 60434 **Phn:** 815-723-0325 **Fax:** 815-723-0326 thetimesweekly.com news@thetimesweekly.com

Lacon Home Journal (2.2M) 204 S Washington St Lacon IL 61540 **Phn:** 309-246-2865 **Fax:** 309-246-3214 sonbtp@aol.com

Lanark Prairie Advocate (16.2M) 446 S Broad St Lanark IL 61046 **Phn:** 815-493-2560 **Fax:** 815-493-2561 www.pacc-news.com pa@pacc-news.com

Lawrenceville Lawrence County News (0.5M) PO Box 559 Lawrenceville IL 62439 **Phn:** 618-943-2331 **Fax:** 618-943-3976 www.lawdailyrecord.com lawnews@lawdailyrecord.com

Le Roy Le Roy Journal (1.2M) 119 E Center St Le Roy IL 61752 **Phn:** 309-962-4441 **Fax:** 309-962-2037

Lebanon Lebanon Advertiser (1.4M) PO Box 126 Lebanon IL 62254 **Phn:** 618-537-4498

Lena The Scoop Today (8.6M) 213 S Center St Lena IL 61048 **Phn:** 815-947-3353 **Fax:** 815-369-9093 rvpublishing.com scoopshopper@rvpublishing.com

Liberty Elliott Publishing (3.6M) PO Box 198 Liberty IL 62347 **Phn:** 217-645-3033 **Fax:** 217-645-3083 justjans.com/elliottpublishing libertyb@adams.net

ILLINOIS WEEKLY NEWSPAPERS

Lombard The Lombardian & Villa Park Review (13.5M) 116 S Main St Lombard IL 60148 **Phn:** 630-627-7010 **Fax:** 630-627-7027 www.lombardian.info lombardian@sbcglobal.net

Louisville Clay County Republican (1.3M) PO Box B Louisville IL 62858 **Phn:** 618-665-3135 ccrnews@wabash.net

Machesney Park The Post Journal (30.0M) 11512 N 2nd St Machesney Park IL 61115 **Phn:** 815-877-4044 **Fax:** 815-654-4857 rvpublishing.com mbradley@rvpublishing.com

Macomb Eagle Publications (18.0M) 210 S Randolph St Ste A Macomb IL 61455 **Phn:** 309-837-4428 **Fax:** 309-837-7188 www.eaglepublications.com

Mahomet Mahomet Citizen (2.5M) PO Box 919 Mahomet IL 61853 **Phn:** 217-586-2512 **Fax:** 217-586-4821 www.mcitizen.com

Marion Weekly Review (7.5M) 1120 N Carbon St Ste 100 Marion IL 62959 **Phn:** 618-997-2222 **Fax:** 618-997-4018 review@horizonpublicationsinc.com

Marshall Strohm Newspapers Inc (2.0M) PO Box 433 Marshall IL 62441 **Phn:** 217-826-3600 **Fax:** 217-826-3700 www.strohmnews.com strohmnews@joink.com

Mascoutah Herald Publications (13.0M) PO Box C Mascoutah IL 62258 **Phn:** 618-566-8282 **Fax:** 618-566-8283 www.heraldpubs.com heraldpubs@heraldpubs.com

Mason City Banner Times (18.0M) PO Box 71 Mason City IL 62664 **Phn:** 217-482-3276 **Fax:** 217-482-3277 btpublications@frontiernet.net

Mc Leansboro McLeansboro Times-Leader (3.2M) 200 S Washington St Mc Leansboro IL 62859 **Phn:** 618-643-2387 mcleansborotimesleader.com paul.lorenz@mcleansborotimesleader.com

Mendota Mendota Reporter (4.5M) PO Box 300 Mendota IL 61342 **Phn:** 815-539-9396 **Fax:** 815-539-7862 www.mendotareporter.com editor@mendotareporter.com

Metamora Hubbell Publishing (15.8M) PO Box 229 Metamora IL 61548 **Phn:** 309-367-2335 **Fax:** 309-367-4277

Metropolis Metropolis Planet (4.8M) PO Box 820 Metropolis IL 62960 **Phn:** 618-524-2141 **Fax:** 618-524-4727 www.metropolisplanet.com news@metropolisplanet.com

Midlothian SW Messenger Newspapers (63.0M) PO Box 548 Midlothian IL 60445 **Phn:** 708-388-2425 **Fax:** 708-385-7811 spressnews@aol.com

Momence Progress-Reporter (2.0M) 110 W River St Momence IL 60954 **Phn:** 815-472-2000 **Fax:** 815-472-3877 momenceprogressreporter.com m.reporter@mchsi.com

Monticello Journal-Republican (3.9M) 118 E Washington St Monticello IL 61856 **Phn:** 217-762-2511 **Fax:** 217-762-8591 journal@journal-republican.com

Morrison Whiteside News Sentinel (3.0M) 100 E Main St Morrison IL 61270 **Phn:** 815-772-7244 **Fax:** 815-772-4105 www.whitesidesentinel.com sentinel@whitesidesentinel.com

Morrisonville Morrisonville Times (1.0M) PO Box 16 Morrisonville IL 62546 **Phn:** 217-526-3323 pananews@consolidated.net

Mount Carroll Mirror-Democrat (2.2M) PO Box 191 Mount Carroll IL 61053 **Phn:** 815-244-2411 **Fax:** 815-244-2965 mirrordem@grics.net

Mount Olive Mount Olive Herald (1.6M) PO Box 300 Mount Olive IL 62069 **Phn:** 217-999-3941 moherald1880@yahoo.com

Mount Sterling The Democrat Message (2.7M) 110 W Main St Mount Sterling IL 62353 **Phn:** 217-773-3371

Mount Zion Mt. Zion Publications (1.4M) PO Box 79 Mount Zion IL 62549 **Phn:** 217-864-4212 **Fax:** 217-864-4711 mtzionregionnews@comcast.net

Murphysboro Murphysboro American (11.0M) PO Box 550 Murphysboro IL 62966 **Phn:** 618-684-5833 **Fax:** 618-684-5080 www.murphysboroamerican.com

Nashville Nashville News (5.0M) PO Box 47 Nashville IL 62263 **Phn:** 618-327-3411 **Fax:** 618-327-3299 nashnews@sbcglobal.net

Nauvoo The New Independent (0.6M) PO Box 415 Nauvoo IL 62354 **Phn:** 217-453-6771 newindependent@frontiernet.net

New Berlin County Tribune (0.6M) PO Box 409 New Berlin IL 62670 **Phn:** 217-488-3005 **Fax:** 217-435-4511 journaltrib@mchsi.com

Newman Newman Independent (0.5M) PO Box 417 Newman IL 61942 **Phn:** 217-837-2414 **Fax:** 217-837-2071 news1@tni-news.com

Newton Press-Mentor (1.7M) 700 W Washington St Newton IL 62448 **Phn:** 618-783-2324 **Fax:** 618-783-2325 www.pressmentor.com mommaeditor@yahoo.com

Nokomis Free Press-Progress (2.5M) 112 W State St Nokomis IL 62075 **Phn:** 217-563-2115 **Fax:** 217-563-7464 www.nokomisonline.com/fp-p.html admin@nokomisonline.com

Normal Normalite Newspaper Group (4.0M) PO Box 67 Normal IL 61761 **Phn:** 309-454-5476 www.normalite.com thenormalite@gmail.com

Norris City Norris City Banner (1.3M) PO Box 400 Norris City IL 62869 **Phn:** 618-378-3014

Oak Park Pioneer Press (28.0M) 1010 Lake St Ste 104 Oak Park IL 60301 **Phn:** 708-383-3200 **Fax:** 708-383-3678 www.pioneerlocal.com jclark@pioneerlocal.com

Oak Park Wednesday Journal Publishing (47.0M) 141 S Oak Park Ave Oak Park IL 60302 **Phn:** 708-524-8300 **Fax:** 708-524-0447 www.oakpark.com spedersen@wjinc.com

Okawville Okawville Times (2.1M) PO Box 68 Okawville IL 62271 **Phn:** 618-243-5563 www.okawvilletimes.com news1@okawvilletimes.com

Onarga Lone Tree Leader (1.2M) 111 W Seminary Ave Onarga IL 60955 **Phn:** 815-268-4770 **Fax:** 815-839-7441 www.lonetreeleader.net lonetreeleader@sbcglobal.net

Oquawka Oquawka Current (1.0M) PO Box 606 Oquawka IL 61469 **Phn:** 309-867-2515 **Fax:** 309-867-6215

Oregon Ogle Co. Life (13.0M) 311 W Washington St Oregon IL 61061 **Phn:** 815-732-2156 **Fax:** 815-732-6154 news@oglecountylife.com

Oregon Ogle Co. Newspapers (4.8M) PO Box 8 Oregon IL 61061 **Phn:** 815-732-6166 **Fax:** 815-732-4238 www.oglecountynews.com news@oglecountynews.com

Orion Orion Gazette (1.7M) PO Box 400 Orion IL 61273 **Phn:** 309-526-8085 **Fax:** 309-526-3065 www.oriongazette.com editor@geneserepublic.com

Palos Heights Reporter Newspapers (39.0M) 12247 S Harlem Ave Palos Heights IL 60463 **Phn:** 708-448-6161 **Fax:** 708-448-4012 www.thereporteronline.net thereporter@comcast.net

Pana News-Palladium (4.0M) PO Box 200 Pana IL 62557 **Phn:** 217-562-2113 **Fax:** 217-562-3729 pananews@consolidated.net

Paxton Paxton Record (4.0M) PO Box 73 Paxton IL 60957 **Phn:** 217-379-2356 **Fax:** 217-379-3104 www.paxtonrecord.net wbrumleve@paxtonrecord.net

Pecatonica The Gazette (6.8M) 111 W 4th St Pecatonica IL 61063 **Phn:** 815-239-1028 **Fax:** 815-239-9198 rvpublishing.com news@rvpublishing.com

Peoria Times Newspapers (30.0M) PO Box 9426 Peoria IL 61612 **Phn:** 309-692-6600 www.woodfordtimes.com wt@timestoday.com

Peotone Russell Publications (16.0M) PO Box 429 Peotone IL 60468 **Phn:** 708-258-3473 **Fax:** 708-258-6295 www.russell-publications.com

Percy The County Journal (7.9M) PO Box 369 Percy IL 62272 **Phn:** 618-497-8272 **Fax:** 618-497-2607 countyjournalnews.com

Petersburg Petersburg Observer & Menard County Revi (3.1M) PO Box 350 Petersburg IL 62675 **Phn:** 217-632-2236 **Fax:** 217-632-2237 observer@gcctv.com

Pittsfield Pike Press (14.0M) 115 W Jefferson St Pittsfield IL 62363 **Phn:** 217-285-2345 **Fax:** 217-285-5222 pikepress.com ppnews@campbellpublications.net

Plainfield Bugle Newspapers (30.0M) PO Box 1613 Plainfield IL 60544 **Phn:** 815-436-2431 **Fax:** 815-436-2592 voyagernewspapers.com publisher@buglenewspapers.com

Plainfield The Enterprise (7.0M) 23856 Andrew Rd Plainfield IL 60585 **Phn:** 815-436-2431 **Fax:** 815-436-2592 www.buglenewspapers.com/enterprise sweditor@buglenewspapers.com

Pontiac Flanagan Home Times (0.8M) 318 N Main St Pontiac IL 61764 **Phn:** 815-842-1153 **Fax:** 815-842-4388 ldrnews@mchsi.com

Port Byron The Review (2.0M) PO Box 575 Port Byron IL 61275 **Phn:** 309-659-2761 **Fax:** 309-659-7751 review@whitesidesentinel.com

Princeton Bureau County Republican (7.9M) PO Box 340 Princeton IL 61356 **Phn:** 815-875-4461 **Fax:** 815-875-1235 www.bcrnews.com news@bcrnews.com

Prophetstown The Echo (1.7M) PO Box 7 Prophetstown IL 61277 **Phn:** 815-537-5107 **Fax:** 815-537-2658

Ramsey Ramsey News-Journal (1.6M) PO Box 218 Ramsey IL 62080 **Phn:** 618-423-2411 **Fax:** 618-423-2514 www.ramseynewsjournal.com newsj2@frontiernet.net

Rantoul Rantoul Press (9.0M) PO Box 5110 Rantoul IL 61866 **Phn:** 217-892-9613 **Fax:** 217-892-9451 www.rantoulpress.com dhinton@rantoulpress.com

Red Bud North County News (4.2M) PO Box 68 Red Bud IL 62278 **Phn:** 618-282-3803 **Fax:** 618-282-6134 www.blossomcity.com/ncn ncnews@htc.net

Riverton South County Publications (2.0M) 715 N 7th St Riverton IL 62561 **Phn:** 217-629-9221 **Fax:** 217-629-9223 www.southcountypublications.com southcountypub@att.net

Robinson Robinson Constitution (0.4M) PO Box 639 Robinson IL 62454 **Phn:** 618-544-2101 **Fax:** 618-544-9533 www.robdailynews.com news@robdailynews.com

Rochelle Rochelle News Leader (4.7M) 211 E II Route 38 Rochelle IL 61068 **Phn:** 815-562-4171 **Fax:** 815-562-2161 www.rochellenews-leader.com patduffy@rochellenews-leader.com

Rockford Rock River Times (22.0M) 128 N Church St Rockford IL 61101 **Phn:** 815-964-9767 **Fax:** 815-964-9825 rockrivertimes.com contact@rockrivertimes.com

Rockton The Herald (8.8M) 1107 N Blackhawk Rockton IL 61072 **Phn:** 815-624-6211 **Fax:** 815-624-8018 www.rvpublishing.com mbradley@rvpublishing.com

Roseville Roseville Independent (0.8M) 140 N Main St Roseville IL 61473 **Phn:** 309-426-2255 www.eaglepublications.com

Rushville Rushville Times (3.6M) PO Box 226 Rushville IL 62681 **Phn:** 217-322-3321 **Fax:** 217-322-2770 www.rushvilletimes.com editor@rushvilletimes.com

Saint Anne Record Press (0.4M) 6980 S State Route 1 Saint Anne IL 60964 **Phn:** 815-427-6734 **Fax:** 815-427-6751

Saint Charles Suburban Life Media (60.0M) 3755 E Main St Ste 170 Saint Charles IL 60174 **Phn:** 630-368-1100 **Fax:** 630-969-0228 www.mysuburbanlife.com rterrell@shawmedia.com

Saint Elmo St. Elmo Banner (1.0M) PO Box 10 Saint Elmo IL 62458 **Phn:** 618-483-6176 **Fax:** 618-483-5177 altnewsban.com altnewsban@frontiernet.net

Salem Salem Times-Commoner (5.3M) 120 S Broadway Ave Salem IL 62881 **Phn:** 618-548-3330 **Fax:** 618-548-3593

Savanna Savanna Times-Journal (2.3M) PO Box 218 Savanna IL 61074 **Phn:** 815-273-2277 **Fax:** 815-273-2715 savtj@grics.net

Shawneetown Gallatin Democrat & Ridgeway News (1.5M) PO Box 545 Shawneetown IL 62984 **Phn:** 618-269-3147 gallatin@yourclearwave.com

Sidell Sidell Reporter (0.8M) PO Box 475 Sidell IL 61876 **Phn:** 217-288-9365 www.thesidellreporter.com editor@thesidellreporter.com

Sparta News-Plaindealer (4.8M) PO Box 427 Sparta IL 62286 **Phn:** 618-443-2145 **Fax:** 618-443-2780

Springfield Illinois Times (30.0M) PO Box 5256 Springfield IL 62705 **Phn:** 217-753-2226 **Fax:** 217-753-2281 www.illinoistimes.com ffarrar@illinoistimes.com

Staunton Kwik Konnection (4.0M) PO Box 67 Staunton IL 62088 **Phn:** 618-635-3172 **Fax:** 618-635-3171 www.kwikkonnection.com editor@kwikkonnection.com

Staunton Star-Times (3.9M) PO Box 180 Staunton IL 62088 **Phn:** 618-635-2000 **Fax:** 618-635-5281 www.stauntonstartimes.com startime@madisontelco.com

Stronghurst Henderson County Quill (2.7M) PO Box 149 Stronghurst IL 61480 **Phn:** 309-924-1871 **Fax:** 309-924-1212 www.quillnewspaper.com quill@hcil.net

Sullivan Moultrie Co. News-Progress (4.0M) 100 W Monroe St Sullivan IL 61951 **Phn:** 217-728-7381 **Fax:** 217-728-2020 www.newsprogress.com keith@newsprogress.com

Summit Des Plaines Valley News (5.0M) PO Box 348 Summit IL 60501 **Phn:** 708-594-9340 **Fax:** 708-594-9494 www.desplainesvalleynews.com editor@desplainesvalleynews.com

Sumner Sumner Press (2.2M) PO Box 126 Sumner IL 62466 **Phn:** 618-936-2212 **Fax:** 618-936-2858 www.sumnerpress.com editor@sumnerpress.com

Teutopolis Teutopolis Press (1.3M) PO Box 667 Teutopolis IL 62467 **Phn:** 217-857-3116 **Fax:** 217-857-3623 www.teutopolispress.com tpress@frontiernet.net

Thomson Carroll County Review (2.0M) PO Box 369 Thomson IL 61285 **Phn:** 815-259-2131 **Fax:** 815-259-3226 ccreview@grics.net

Tinley Park Star Newspapers (57.0M) 6901 159th St Tinley Park IL 60477 **Phn:** 708-633-4800 **Fax:** 708-633-5999 southtownstar.suntimes.com/neighborhoodstar news@southtownstar.com

Tiskilwa Bureau Valley Chief (1.7M) PO Box 476 Tiskilwa IL 61368 **Phn:** 815-646-4731 **Fax:** 815-646-4376

ILLINOIS WEEKLY NEWSPAPERS

Toledo Toledo Democrat (1.9M) PO Box 7 Toledo IL 62468 **Phn:** 217-849-2000 **Fax:** 217-849-3237 tdnews@cell1net.net

Tonica Tonica News (1.0M) PO Box 67 Tonica IL 61370 **Phn:** 815-442-8419 pcrtnews.com

Trenton Trenton Sun (1.5M) PO Box 118 Trenton IL 62293 **Phn:** 618-224-9422 **Fax:** 618-224-2646 www.trentonsun.net mike@trentonsun.net

Troy Troy Times-Tribune (3.4M) 201 E Market St Troy IL 62294 **Phn:** 618-667-3111 **Fax:** 618-667-3128 troynews@aol.com

Vandalia Vandalia Leader-Union (5.8M) PO Box 315 Vandalia IL 62471 **Phn:** 618-283-3374 **Fax:** 618-283-0977 www.leaderunion.com rbauer@leaderunion.com

Vienna Vienna Times (2.6M) PO Box 457 Vienna IL 62995 **Phn:** 618-658-4321 **Fax:** 618-658-4322 theviennatimes.com viennatimes@frontier.com

Villa Grove Villa Grove News (1.5M) 5 S Main St Villa Grove IL 61956 **Phn:** 217-832-4201 **Fax:** 217-832-4001 www.villagrovenews.com

Virden Gold Nugget Publications (6.2M) PO Box 440 Virden IL 62690 **Phn:** 217-965-3355 **Fax:** 217-965-4512 editor@gnnews.net

Walnut Walnut Leader (2.5M) PO Box 280 Walnut IL 61376 **Phn:** 815-379-9290 **Fax:** 815-379-2659 wleader@mchsi.com

Washington Courier Newspapers (20.0M) PO Box 349 Washington IL 61571 **Phn:** 309-444-3139 **Fax:** 309-444-8505 www.mtco.com/~joi67/washington/washington.html haglnews@mtco.com

Waterloo Republic-Times (3.3M) PO Box 147 Waterloo IL 62298 **Phn:** 618-939-3814 **Fax:** 618-939-3815 www.republictimes.net

Waukegan Pioneer Press-Lake Shore (41.0M) 2382 N Delany Rd Waukegan IL 60087 **Phn:** 847-599-6900 **Fax:** 847-599-6902 www.pioneerlocal.com lake@pioneerlocal.com

Waverly Waverly Journal (1.4M) PO Box 78 Waverly IL 62692 **Phn:** 217-435-9221 **Fax:** 217-435-4511 journaltrib@mchsi.com

West Salem Edwards County Times-Advocate (1.3M) PO Box 427 West Salem IL 62476 **Phn:** 618-456-8808 **Fax:** 618-456-8809 www.ectimesadvocate.com ectanewspaper@gmail.com

Wilmington Braidwood Journal & Free Press Advocate (2.2M) PO Box 327 Wilmington IL 60481 **Phn:** 815-476-7966 **Fax:** 815-476-7002 freepressnewspapers.com eric.fisher@cbcast.com

Winchester Scott County Times (2.2M) PO Box 138 Winchester IL 62694 **Phn:** 217-742-3313 sctnews@campbellpublications.net

Woodstock Woodstock Independent (3.1M) 671 E Calhoun St Woodstock IL 60098 **Phn:** 815-338-8040 **Fax:** 815-338-8177 thewoodstockindependent.com news@thewoodstockindependent.com

Worden Madison County Chronicle (1.0M) PO Box 490 Worden IL 62097 **Phn:** 618-459-3655

Yorkville Kendall Co. Record Inc (16.0M) PO Box J Yorkville IL 60560 **Phn:** 630-553-7034 **Fax:** 630-553-7085 www.kcrecord.com kcrecord@aol.com

Zion Zion/Benton News (22.0M) PO Box 111 Zion IL 60099 **Phn:** 847-746-9000 **Fax:** 847-746-9150 www.zion-bentonnews.com mona@zion-bentonnews.com

INDIANA

Albion New Era (2.0M) PO Box 25 Albion IN 46701 **Phn:** 260-636-2727 **Fax:** 260-636-2042 www.app-printing.com jlecount@app-printing.com

Alexandria Alexandria Times-Tribune (2.1M) PO Box 330 Alexandria IN 46001 **Phn:** 765-724-4469 **Fax:** 765-724-4460 www.elwoodpublishing.com alextribune@elwoodpublishing.com

Attica Fountain County Neighbor (2.2M) 113 S Perry St Attica IN 47918 **Phn:** 765-762-2411 **Fax:** 765-762-1547 newsbug.info/fountain_county_neighbor atticaeditor@sbcglobal.net

Avon Hendricks Co Flyer (83.0M) 8109 Kingston St Ste 500 Avon IN 46123 **Phn:** 317-272-5800 **Fax:** 317-272-5887 flyergroup.com kathy.linton@flyergroup.com

Batesville The Herald-Tribune (4.0M) 475 N Huntersville Rd Batesville IN 47006 **Phn:** 812-934-4343 **Fax:** 812-934-6406 batesvilleheraldtribune.com bryan.helvie@batesvilleheraldtribune.com

Beech Grove Southside Times (22.5M) 301 Main St Beech Grove IN 46107 **Phn:** 317-787-3291 **Fax:** 317-787-3325 www.ss-times.com rhuntzin@ss-times.com

Berne Berne Tri-Weekly News (2.5M) 153 S Jefferson St Berne IN 46711 **Phn:** 260-589-2101 **Fax:** 260-589-8614 www.bernetriweekly.com news@bernetriweekly.com

Boonville Boonville Standard & Newburgh Register (4.5M) PO Box 266 Boonville IN 47601 **Phn:** 812-897-2330 **Fax:** 812-897-3703 www.tristate-media.com newsroom@warricknews.com

Bremen Advance-News (2.2M) 126 E Plymouth St Ste 1 Bremen IN 46506 **Phn:** 574-209-1184 **Fax:** 574-546-5170 www.thepilotnews.com news@thepilotnews.com

Bremen Bremen Enquirer (1.8M) 126 E Plymouth St Bremen IN 46506 **Phn:** 574-546-2941 **Fax:** 574-546-5170 www.thepilotnews.com enquirer@fourway.net

Brookville Brookville American-Democrat (1.2M) PO Box 38 Brookville IN 47012 **Phn:** 765-647-4221 **Fax:** 765-647-4811 www.whitewaterpub.com info@whitewaterpub.com

Brownstown Jackson County Banner (3.0M) PO Box G Brownstown IN 47220 **Phn:** 812-358-2111 **Fax:** 812-358-5606 www.thebanner.com news@thebanner.com

Butler Butler Bulletin (1.0M) PO Box 39 Butler IN 46721 **Phn:** 260-868-5501 **Fax:** 260-925-2625 www.kpcnews.com jeffj@kpcnews.net

Cambridge City Nettle Creek Gazette (1.0M) PO Box 337 Cambridge City IN 47327 **Phn:** 765-478-5448 **Fax:** 765-478-5155 western-wayne-news.com nettlecreekgazette@frontier.com

Cambridge City Western Wayne News (2.7M) PO Box 337 Cambridge City IN 47327 **Phn:** 765-478-5448 **Fax:** 765-478-5155 western-wayne-news.com westernwaynenews@frontier.com

Cayuga Cayuga Herald News (0.8M) PO Box 158 Cayuga IN 47928 **Phn:** 765-492-4401

Charlestown The Leader (13.0M) 382 Main Cross St Charlestown IN 47111 **Phn:** 812-256-3377 newsroom@gbpnews.com

Churubusco The News (2.2M) PO Box 8 Churubusco IN 46723 **Phn:** 260-693-3949 **Fax:** 260-693-6545 www.app-printing.com cheditor@app-printing.com

Clay City Clay City News (2.0M) PO Box 38 Clay City IN 47841 **Phn:** 812-939-2163 **Fax:** 812-939-2286

Cloverdale Hoosier Topics (20.0M) PO Box 496 Cloverdale IN 46120 **Phn:** 765-795-4438 **Fax:** 765-795-3121 htopics@ccrtc.com

INDIANA WEEKLY NEWSPAPERS

Corydon Clarion News & Corydon Democrat (15.0M) 301 N Capitol Ave Corydon IN 47112 **Phn:** 812-738-2211 **Fax:** 812-738-1909 www.clarionnews.net cadams@clarionnews.net

Crawfordsville The Weekly (7.0M) PO Box 272 Crawfordsville IN 47933 **Phn:** 765-361-0100 **Fax:** 765-361-1882 www.thepaper24-7.com news@thepaper24-7.com

Crothersville Crothersville Times (2.3M) 510 Moore St # 100 Crothersville IN 47229 **Phn:** 812-793-2188 crothersvilletimes.com

Crown Point Crown Point Star (2.7M) 112 W Clark St Crown Point IN 46307 **Phn:** 219-663-4212 **Fax:** 219-663-0137 posttrib.suntimes.com/crownpointstar

Dale Spencer County Leader (2.0M) PO Box 206 Dale IN 47523 **Phn:** 812-937-2100 **Fax:** 812-937-4988 www.ferdinandnews.com sclreporter@psci.net

Danville Danville Republican (1.6M) PO Box 149 Danville IN 46122 **Phn:** 317-745-2777 therepublican@sbcglobal.net

Demotte Kankakee Valley Post News (3.3M) PO Box 110 Demotte IN 46310 **Phn:** 219-987-5111 **Fax:** 219-987-5119 newsbug.info editor@rensselaerrepublican.com

Dunkirk Dunkirk News & Sun (1.2M) PO Box 59 Dunkirk IN 47336 **Phn:** 765-768-6022 **Fax:** 765-768-1618

Ellettsville The Journal (2.5M) PO Box 98 Ellettsville IN 47429 **Phn:** 812-876-2254 **Fax:** 812-876-2853 scribe@bluemarble.net

Fairmount Fairmount News Sun (4.4M) PO Box 25 Fairmount IN 46928 **Phn:** 765-948-4164

Ferdinand Ferdinand News (3.1M) PO Box 38 Ferdinand IN 47532 **Phn:** 812-367-2041 **Fax:** 812-367-2371 www.ferdinandnews.com ferdnews@psci.net

Flora Carroll County Comet (5.0M) PO Box 26 Flora IN 46929 **Phn:** 574-967-4135 **Fax:** 574-967-3384 www.carrollcountycomet.com editor@carrollcountycomet.com

Fort Branch South Gibson Star Times (5.1M) PO Box 70 Fort Branch IN 47648 **Phn:** 812-753-3553 **Fax:** 812-753-4251 news@sgstartimes.com

Fort Wayne Fort Wayne Ink (25.0M) 1301 Lafayette St Ste 202 Fort Wayne IN 46802 **Phn:** 260-420-3200 **Fax:** 260-420-3210 inknewspaper.com editor@inknewsonline.com

Fort Wayne Fort Wayne Reader (25.0M) 1301 Lafayette St Ste 202 Fort Wayne IN 46802 **Phn:** 260-420-8580 **Fax:** 260-420-3210 www.fortwaynereader.com mikes@fortwaynereader.com

Fort Wayne Waynedale News (10.0M) 2700 Lower Huntington Rd Fort Wayne IN 46809 **Phn:** 260-747-4535 **Fax:** 260-747-5529 thewaynedalenews.com news@waynedalenews.com

Fowler Benton Review (3.0M) PO Box 527 Fowler IN 47944 **Phn:** 765-884-1902 **Fax:** 765-884-8110 bentonreview@sbcglobal.net

Francesville Francesville Tribune (0.9M) PO Box 458 Francesville IN 47946 **Phn:** 219-567-2221

Frankfort Frankfort Times (2.6M) 211 N Jackson St Frankfort IN 46041 **Phn:** 765-659-4622 **Fax:** 765-654-7031 www.chronicle-tribune.com/ftimes news@ftimes.com

French Lick Springs Valley Herald (2.2M) 8481 W College St French Lick IN 47432 **Phn:** 812-936-9630 **Fax:** 812-723-2592 springsvalleyherald.com svh@bluemarble.net

Garrett Garrett Clipper (1.8M) PO Box 59 Garrett IN 46738 **Phn:** 260-357-4123 **Fax:** 260-925-2625 www.kpcnews.com garrettclipper@kpcnews.net

Gas City Indiana Newspaper Group (5.0M) 787 E Main St Gas City IN 46933 **Phn:** 765-674-0070 **Fax:** 765-674-3496

Grabill East Allen Courier (7.2M) PO Box 77 Grabill IN 46741 **Phn:** 260-627-2728 **Fax:** 260-627-2519 courier@tk7.net

Greensburg Greensburg Times (0.7M) PO Box 106 Greensburg IN 47240 **Phn:** 812-663-3111 **Fax:** 812-663-2985 greensburgdailynews.com

Greenwood Franklin Challenger (3.6M) PO Box 708 Greenwood IN 46142 **Phn:** 317-888-3376 **Fax:** 317-888-3377 www.challengernewspapers.com news@indychallenger.com

Greenwood Southside Challenger (4.2M) PO Box 708 Greenwood IN 46142 **Phn:** 317-888-3376 **Fax:** 317-888-3377 www.challengernewspapers.com news@indychallenger.com

Hamilton Hamilton News (1.0M) 3750 E Church St Hamilton IN 46742 **Phn:** 260-488-3780 **Fax:** 260-488-4326 www.hamilton-news.com

Hope Star Journal (1.0M) PO Box 65 Hope IN 47246 **Phn:** 812-546-4940 **Fax:** 812-546-4944 www.hopestarjournal.com news@hopestarjournal.com

Huntertown Northwest News (1.5M) 15605 Lima Rd Huntertown IN 46748 **Phn:** 260-637-9003 **Fax:** 260-637-8598 www.app-printing.com nweditor@app-printing.com

Huntingburg Huntingburg Press (2.0M) PO Box 260 Huntingburg IN 47542 **Phn:** 812-683-5899 **Fax:** 812-683-5897 hbgpress@insightbb.com

Huntington Huntington County TAB (15.5M) PO Box 391 Huntington IN 46750 **Phn:** 260-356-1107 **Fax:** 260-356-1177 www.huntingtoncountytab.com tabnewsroom@comcast.net

Indianapolis Franklin Township Informer (5.0M) 8822 Southeastern Ave Indianapolis IN 46239 **Phn:** 317-862-1774 **Fax:** 317-862-1775 www.ftcivicleague.org ftinformer@sbcglobal.net

Indianapolis West Indianapolis Community News (15.0M) 608 S Vine St Indianapolis IN 46241 **Phn:** 317-241-7363 **Fax:** 317-240-6397 commnews@in-motion.net

Kendallville Advance Leader (3.0M) PO Box 39 Kendallville IN 46755 **Phn:** 260-894-3102 www.kpcnews.com leader@kpcnews.net

Kentland Community Media Group (4.0M) PO Box 107 Kentland IN 47951 **Phn:** 219-474-5532 **Fax:** 219-474-5354 newsbug.info editor@rensselaerrepublican.com

Kewanna The Observer (0.6M) PO Box 307 Kewanna IN 46939 **Phn:** 574-653-2101 **Fax:** 574-653-3418

Knightstown Knightstown Banner (2.0M) PO Box 116 Knightstown IN 46148 **Phn:** 765-345-2292 **Fax:** 765-345-2113 www.thebanneronline.com bannergm@comcast.net

Knox The Leader (2.5M) 15 N Main St Ste 2 Knox IN 46534 **Phn:** 574-772-2101 **Fax:** 574-772-7041

Kokomo Kokomo Herald (0.5M) PO Box 6488 Kokomo IN 46904 **Phn:** 765-452-5942 **Fax:** 765-452-3037 www.kokomoherald.com koherald@iquest.net

Kokomo Kokomo Perspective (31.0M) 209 N Main St Kokomo IN 46901 **Phn:** 765-452-0055 **Fax:** 765-457-7209 www.kokomoperspective.com editor@kokomoperspective.com

Lafayette Lafayette Leader (2.0M) 401 Main St Ste 2F Lafayette IN 47901 **Phn:** 765-428-8123 **Fax:** 765-428-8124 newsbug.info/lafayette_leader

Lagrange Lagrange Publishing (34.0M) PO Box 148 Lagrange IN 46761 **Phn:** 260-463-2166 **Fax:** 260-463-2734 www.lagrangepublishing.com lagpubco@kuntrynet.com

Lawrenceburg Register Publications (14.0M) PO Box 4128 Lawrenceburg IN 47025 **Phn:** 812-537-0063 **Fax:** 812-537-5576

Lebanon Sun Times (7.0M) 222 W South St Lebanon IN 46052 **Phn:** 765-482-3333 **Fax:** 765-482-1333

Liberty Liberty Herald (2.6M) PO Box 10 Liberty IN 47353 **Phn:** 765-458-5114 **Fax:** 765-458-5115

Liberty Union County Review (4.6M) PO Box 10 Liberty IN 47353 **Phn:** 765-458-5114 **Fax:** 765-458-5115

Loogootee The Tribune (3.0M) PO Box 277 Loogootee IN 47553 **Phn:** 812-295-2500 **Fax:** 812-295-5221 advertising@loogooteetribune.com

Lowell Pilcher Publishing (8.8M) PO Box 248 Lowell IN 46356 **Phn:** 219-696-7711 **Fax:** 219-696-7713 www.thelowelltribune.com tribune@pilcherpublishing.com

Middletown Middletown News (2.0M) 106 N 5th St Middletown IN 47356 **Phn:** 765-354-2221 www.themiddletownnews.com frontpage@themiddletownnews.com

Milford The Papers Inc (71.5M) PO Box 188 Milford IN 46542 **Phn:** 574-658-4111 **Fax:** 800-886-3796 www.the-papers.com jseely@the-papers.com

Mishawaka The Enterprise (1.8M) PO Box 584 Mishawaka IN 46546 **Phn:** 574-255-4789 mishawakanews@aol.com

Monon The News & Review (1.3M) PO Box 98 Monon IN 47959 **Phn:** 219-253-6234 www.smalltownpapers.com

Monroeville The Monroeville News (1.2M) 115 E South St Monroeville IN 46773 **Phn:** 260-623-3316 **Fax:** 260-623-3966 loisternet@yahoo.com

Mount Vernon Mt. Vernon Democrat (3.9M) PO Box 767 Mount Vernon IN 47620 **Phn:** 812-838-4811 **Fax:** 812-838-3696 www.mvdemocrat.com editor@mvdemocrat.com

Nashville Brown County Democrat (4.4M) PO Box 277 Nashville IN 47448 **Phn:** 812-988-2221 **Fax:** 812-988-6502 www.bcdemocrat.com newsroom@bcdemocrat.com

New Harmony Posey County News (4.8M) PO Box 397 New Harmony IN 47631 **Phn:** 812-682-3950 **Fax:** 812-682-3944 www.poseycountynews.com dpearce263@poseycountynews.com

New Palestine New Palestine Press (3.0M) PO Box 407 New Palestine IN 46163 **Phn:** 317-861-4242 **Fax:** 317-861-4201 nppress407@aol.com

North Manchester The Manchester Monitor (1.1M) 116 E Main St North Manchester IN 46962 **Phn:** 260-982-9828 **Fax:** 260-982-9880

North Manchester The News-Journal (1.8M) PO Box 368 North Manchester IN 46962 **Phn:** 260-982-6383 **Fax:** 260-982-8233 news@nmpaper.com

North Vernon North Vernon Plain Dealer (7.0M) PO Box 988 North Vernon IN 47265 **Phn:** 812-346-3973 **Fax:** 812-346-8368 plaindealer-sun.com pds@northvernon.com

North Vernon North Vernon Sun (6.0M) PO Box 988 North Vernon IN 47265 **Phn:** 812-346-3973 **Fax:** 812-346-8368 www.northvernon.com pds@northvernon.com

Odon The Journal (2.8M) PO Box 307 Odon IN 47562 **Phn:** 812-636-7350 **Fax:** 812-636-7359 journal@rtccom.net

Orleans Progress-Examiner (2.1M) PO Box 225 Orleans IN 47452 **Phn:** 812-865-3242   penews@blueriver.net

Ossian Ossian Journal (0.7M) PO Box 365 Ossian IN 46777   **Phn:** 260-622-4108   **Fax:** 260-622-6439 ossianj@adamswells.com

Paoli Orange Co. Publishing (19.0M) PO Box 190 Paoli IN 47454 **Phn:** 812-723-2572 **Fax:** 812-723-2592 paolinewsrepublican.com ocpinc@ocpnews.com

Pekin Green Banner Publications (66.0M) PO Box 38 Pekin IN 47165 **Phn:** 812-967-3176 **Fax:** 812-967-3194 www.gbpnews.com newsroom@gbpnews.com

Pendleton Times-Post (1.0M) PO Box 9 Pendleton IN 46064 **Phn:** 765-778-2324 **Fax:** 765-778-7152 www.pendletontimespost.com sslade@ptlpnews.com

Petersburg Press Dispatch (5.7M) PO Box 68 Petersburg IN 47567 **Phn:** 812-354-8500 **Fax:** 812-354-2014 news@pressdispatch.net

Plymouth Bourbon News-Mirror (1.3M) 214 N Michigan St Plymouth IN 46563 **Phn:** 574-952-1514 **Fax:** 574-936-3844   www.thepilotnews.com newsmirror@thepilotnews.com

Plymouth Culver Citizen (1.8M) 214 N Michigan St Plymouth IN 46563 **Phn:** 574-216-0075 **Fax:** 574-936-3844 www.thepilotnews.com citizen@culcom.net

Princeton Oakland City Journal (0.8M) PO Box 30 Princeton IN 47670 **Phn:** 812-385-2525 **Fax:** 812-386-6199   andrea@pdclarion.com

Rising Sun News Sun Recorder (2.0M) PO Box 128 Rising Sun IN 47040 **Phn:** 812-438-2011 **Fax:** 812-438-3228   risingsun@registerpublications.com

Rockport Spencer County Journal Democrat (6.0M) PO Box 6 Rockport IN 47635 **Phn:** 812-649-9196 **Fax:** 812-649-9197   www.spencercountyjournal.com news@spencercountyjournal.com

Rockville Parke County Sentinel (4.5M) PO Box 187 Rockville IN 47872 **Phn:** 765-569-2033 **Fax:** 765-569-1424

Royal Center Royal Centre Record (1.0M) PO Box 638 Royal Center IN 46978 **Phn:** 574-643-3165 **Fax:** 574-643-9440 www.smalltownpapers.com

Salem Salem Democrat (6.1M) PO Box 506 Salem IN 47167 **Phn:** 812-883-3281 **Fax:** 812-883-4446 www.salemleader.com office@salemleader.com

Salem Salem Leader (6.1M) PO Box 506 Salem IN 47167 **Phn:** 812-883-3281 **Fax:** 812-883-4446 www.salemleader.com stephanie@salemleader.com

Shoals Shoals News (2.7M) PO Box 240 Shoals IN 47581 **Phn:** 812-247-2828 **Fax:** 812-247-2243

South Bend Tri County News (1.0M) PO Box 6666 South Bend IN 46660 **Phn:** 574-243-4664 **Fax:** 574-243-4916   www.tricountynewsinc.com admin@tricountynewsinc.com

South Whitley Tribune-News (1.5M) 113 S State St South Whitley IN 46787 **Phn:** 260-723-4771

Speedway The Press Newspapers (8.5M) 1538 Main St Speedway IN 46224 **Phn:** 317-241-4345 **Fax:** 317-241-4386 thepress@in-motion.net

Spencer Owen Leader (0.4M) PO Box 22 Spencer IN 47460 **Phn:** 812-829-2255 **Fax:** 812-829-4666

Tell City The Perry County News (7.4M) PO Box 309 Tell City IN 47586 **Phn:** 812-547-3424 **Fax:** 812-547-2847   www.perrycountynews.com editor@perrycountynews.com

Versailles Osgood Journal (5.3M) PO Box 158 Versailles IN 47042 **Phn:** 812-689-6364 **Fax:** 812-689-6508 publication@ripleynews.com

Versailles Versailles Republican (5.0M) PO Box 158 Versailles IN 47042 **Phn:** 812-689-6364 **Fax:** 812-689-6508   www.ripleynews.com publication@ripleynews.com

Vevay Reveille-Enterprise (2.9M) PO Box 157 Vevay IN 47043 **Phn:** 812-427-2311 **Fax:** 812-427-2793 www.vevaynewspapers.com

Vevay Switzerland Democrat (0.6M) PO Box 157 Vevay IN   47043   **Phn:**   812-427-2311 www.vevaynewspapers.com

Wabash Paper of Wabash County (16.0M) PO Box 603 Wabash IN 46992 **Phn:** 260-563-8326 **Fax:** 260-563-2863   www.thepaperofwabash.com ads@thepaperofwabash.com

Wakarusa Wakarusa Tribune (1.4M) PO Box 507 Wakarusa   IN   46573   **Phn:**   574-862-2179 editorwaka@aol.com

Warren Warren Weekly (3.2M) PO Box 695 Warren IN 46792   **Phn:**   260-375-3531   **Fax:**   260-247-2426 wwkly@citznet.com

Westville Regional News (2.0M) PO Box 828 Westville IN 46391 **Phn:** 219-785-2234 **Fax:** 219-785-2442 wvindicator@aol.com

Westville Westville Indicator (2.0M) PO Box 828 Westville IN 46391 **Phn:** 219-785-2234 **Fax:** 219-785-2442

Williamsport The Review-Republican (3.5M) PO Box 216 Williamsport IN 47993 **Phn:** 765-762-3322 newsbug.info/williamsport_review_republican editor@rensselaerrepublican.com

Winamac Pulaski County Journal (3.7M) PO Box 19 Winamac IN 46996 **Phn:** 574-946-6628 **Fax:** 574-946-7471   www.pulaskijournal.com news@pulaskijournal.com

Winfield Winfield American (5.0M) 7590 E 109th Ave Winfield   IN   46307   **Phn:**   219-662-8888 winfieldamerican.com news@winfieldamerican.com

Wolcott The New Wolcott Enterprise (0.7M) PO Box 78 Wolcott   IN   47995   **Phn:**   219-279-2167 wolcottenterprise@centurylink.net

Zionsville Zionsville Times Sentinel (4.2M) 250 S Elm St Zionsville IN 46077 **Phn:** 317-873-6397 **Fax:** 317-873-6259 timessentinel.com news@timessentinel.com

IOWA

Ackley Ackley World-Journal (4.6M) 736 Main St Ackley IA 50601 **Phn:** 641-847-2592 **Fax:** 641-847-3010 www.ackleyworldjournal.com news@iafalls.com

Adair Adair News (1.4M) PO Box 8 Adair IA 50002 **Phn:**   641-742-3241   **Fax:**   641-742-3489 www.iowanewspapersonline.com

Adel Dallas County News (2.0M) PO Box 190 Adel IA 50003   **Phn:**   515-993-4233   **Fax:**   515-993-4235 adelnews.com news@adelnews.com

Afton Afton Star Enterprise (1.2M) PO Box 128 Afton IA 50830   **Phn:**   641-347-8721 aftonstar@iowatelecom.net

Akron Akron Hometowner (1.5M) 110 Reed St Akron IA 51001   **Phn:**   712-568-2208   **Fax:**   712-568-2271 www.akronhometowner.com akronht@hickorytech.net

Albia Monroe County News (6.2M) PO Box 338 Albia IA 52531   **Phn:**   641-932-7121   **Fax:**   641-932-2822 www.albianews.com theresa@albianews.com

Albia Union-Republican (6.0M) PO Box 338 Albia IA 52531   **Phn:**   641-932-7121   **Fax:**   641-932-2822 www.albianews.com dave@albianews.com

Algona Upper Des Moines (4.9M) PO Box 400 Algona IA 50511 **Phn:** 515-295-3535 **Fax:** 515-295-7217 algona.com news@algona.com

Allison Butler County Tribune-Journal (1.8M) PO Box 8 Allison   IA   50602   **Phn:**   319-267-2731 butlercountytribune.com startj@netins.net

Anamosa Journal Eureka (2.7M) PO Box 108 Anamosa IA 52205 **Phn:** 319-462-3511 **Fax:** 319-462-4540 www.journal-eureka.com/news/anamosa editorial@anamosaje.com

Anita Anita Tribune (1.3M) PO Box 216 Anita IA 50020 **Phn:** 712-762-4188 **Fax:** 712-762-4189

Anthon Sioux Valley News (1.3M) PO Box 299 Anthon IA   51004   **Phn:**   712-373-5571 siouxvalleynews@ruralwaves.us

Armstrong Community Publications (2.0M) PO Box 289 Armstrong IA 50514 **Phn:** 712-868-3460 **Fax:** 712-868-3028

Audubon Audubon Advocate Journal (2.0M) PO Box 268 Audubon IA 50025 **Phn:** 712-563-2741 **Fax:** 712-563-2740 swiowanewssource.com/audubon_advocate_journal news@auduboncountynews.com

Avoca Avoca Journal-Herald (1.6M) PO Box 308 Avoca IA 51521 **Phn:** 712-343-2154 **Fax:** 712-343-2262 avocajh@iowatelecom.net

Avoca Oakland Herald (1.6M) PO Box 308 Avoca IA 51521 **Phn:** 712-343-2154 **Fax:** 712-343-2262

Bancroft Bancroft Register (1.2M) PO Box 175 Bancroft IA 50517 **Phn:** 515-885-2531 **Fax:** 515-885-2771 bancroftregister@yahoo.com

Bayard Scranton Journal (1.0M) PO Box 130 Bayard IA 50029   **Phn:**   712-651-2321   **Fax:**   712-651-2599 ciapub@netins.net

Bayard The News Gazette (2.2M) PO Box 130 Bayard IA 50029 **Phn:** 712-651-2321 **Fax:** 712-651-2599 www.iowanewspapersonline.com ciapub@netins.net

Bedford Bedford Times-Press (2.0M) PO Box 108 Bedford   IA   50833   **Phn:**   712-523-2525 www.bedfordtimes-press.com btimespress@gmail.com

Bellevue Bellevue Herald-Leader (2.9M) 118 S 2nd St Bellevue IA 52031 **Phn:** 563-872-4159 **Fax:** 563-872-4298   bhleader@bellevueheraldleader.com

Belmond Belmond Independent (2.0M) 215 E Main St Belmond IA 50421 **Phn:** 641-444-3333 **Fax:** 641-444-7777   www.belmondnews.com belmondnews@frontiernet.net

Bettendorf Bettendorf News (10.0M) PO Box 460 Bettendorf IA 52722 **Phn:** 563-355-2644 **Fax:** 563-383-2370 qctimes.com bettnews@qctimes.com

Bloomfield Bloomfield Democrat (2.7M) PO Box 19 Bloomfield IA 52537 **Phn:** 641-664-2334 **Fax:** 641-664-2316 www.bdemo.com bdemo@netins.net

Breda Breda News (0.7M) PO Box 183 Breda IA 51436 **Phn:** 712-673-2318 **Fax:** 712-673-4246

Britt Britt News-Tribune (2.9M) PO Box 38 Britt IA 50423   **Phn:**   641-843-3851   **Fax:**   641-843-3307 www.globegazette.com/brittnewstribune editor@brittnewstribune.com

Buffalo Center Buffalo Center Tribune (1.5M) PO Box 367 Buffalo Center IA 50424 **Phn:** 641-562-2606 **Fax:** 641-562-2636   thebuffalocentertribune.com bctrib@wctatel.net

Carlisle Carlisle Citizen (1.7M) 210 S 1st St Carlisle IA 50047   **Phn:**   515-989-0525   **Fax:**   515-989-0743 carlislecitizen@mchsi.com

Carroll Carroll Today (1.5M) PO Box 593 Carroll IA 51401 **Phn:** 712-792-2179 **Fax:** 712-792-2309

Cascade Cascade Pioneer (1.8M) PO Box 9 Cascade IA 52033 **Phn:** 563-852-3217 **Fax:** 563-852-7188 dceditor@wcinet.com

IOWA WEEKLY NEWSPAPERS

Central City Linn News-Letter (4.0M) PO Box 501 Central City IA 52214 **Phn:** 319-438-1313 **Fax:** 319-438-1838 linnnewsletter@iowatelecom.net

Chariton Chariton Herald-Patriot (3.0M) PO Box 651 Chariton IA 50049 **Phn:** 641-774-2137 **Fax:** 641-774-2139 www.charitonleader.com charnews@charitonleader.com

Chariton Chariton Leader (3.0M) PO Box 651 Chariton IA 50049 **Phn:** 641-774-2137 **Fax:** 641-774-2139 www.charitonleader.com charnews@charitonleader.com

Clarinda Clarinda Herald-Journal (2.6M) PO Box 278 Clarinda IA 51632 **Phn:** 712-542-2181 **Fax:** 712-542-5424 southwestiowanews.com news@clarindaherald.com

Clarion Wright County Monitor (1.6M) PO Box 153 Clarion IA 50525 **Phn:** 515-532-2871 **Fax:** 515-532-2872 www.clarionnewsonline.com cmonitor@mchsi.com

Clarksville Clarksville Star (1.2M) PO Box 788 Clarksville IA 50619 **Phn:** 319-278-4641 butlercountytribune.com startj@netins.net

Clear Lake Mirror-Reporter (3.5M) 12 N 4th St Clear Lake IA 50428 **Phn:** 641-357-2131 **Fax:** 641-357-2133 www.clreporter.com marianne@clreporter.com

Colfax Jasper County Tribune (2.1M) PO Box 7 Colfax IA 50054 **Phn:** 515-674-3591

Columbus Junction Columbus Gazette (1.4M) PO Box 267 Columbus Junction IA 52738 **Phn:** 319-728-2413 **Fax:** 319-728-3272 www.thecolumbusgazette.com

Conrad Conrad Record (1.2M) PO Box 190 Conrad IA 50621 **Phn:** 641-366-2020 www.therecord.biz news@therecord.biz

Corning Adams County Free Press (1.9M) PO Box 26 Corning IA 50841 **Phn:** 641-322-3161 **Fax:** 641-322-3461 acfreepress.com editor@acfreepress.com

Corydon New Era (1.1M) PO Box 258 Corydon IA 50060 **Phn:** 641-872-1234 **Fax:** 641-872-1965 rbennett@corydontimes.com

Corydon Times-Republican (3.3M) PO Box 258 Corydon IA 50060 **Phn:** 641-872-1234 **Fax:** 641-872-1965 www.corydontimes.com rbennett@corydontimes.com

Cresco Times-Plain Dealer (12.0M) PO Box 350 Cresco IA 52136 **Phn:** 563-547-3601 www.crescotimes.com

Danbury Danbury Review (0.7M) PO Box 207 Danbury IA 51019 **Phn:** 712-893-2001 www.danbury-ia.com/review review@danbury-ia.com

Davenport River Cities Reader (21.0M) 532 W 3rd St Davenport IA 52801 **Phn:** 563-324-0049 **Fax:** 563-323-3101 www.rcreader.com

Dayton Dayton Review (0.9M) PO Box 6 Dayton IA 50530 **Phn:** 515-547-2811 **Fax:** 515-547-2337 www.iowanewspapersonline.com daytonreview@lvcta.com

De Witt De Witt Observer (4.3M) PO Box 49 De Witt IA 52742 **Phn:** 563-659-3121 **Fax:** 563-659-3778 www.dewittobserver.com observer@iowatelecom.net

Decorah Decorah Journal (6.0M) PO Box 350 Decorah IA 52101 **Phn:** 563-382-4221 **Fax:** 563-382-5949 www.decorahnewspapers.com news@decorahnewspapers.com

Decorah Decorah Public Opinion (6.5M) PO Box 350 Decorah IA 52101 **Phn:** 563-382-4221 **Fax:** 563-382-5949 www.decorahnewspapers.com news@decorahnewspapers.com

Denison Denison Bulletin Review (4.0M) PO Box 550 Denison IA 51442 **Phn:** 712-263-2123 **Fax:** 712-263-2125 www.DBRnews.com editor@bulletinreview.com

Denver Denver Forum (0.6M) PO Box 509 Denver IA 50622 **Phn:** 319-984-6179 **Fax:** 319-984-6282 www.denveriaforum.com news@denveriaforum.com

Des Moines Altoona Herald & Mitchellville Index (5.0M) 715 Locust St Des Moines IA 50309 **Phn:** 515-699-7000 **Fax:** 515-284-8419 altoonaherald.desmoinesregister.com adwilson@dmreg.com

Des Moines Cityview (28.0M) 416 61st St Des Moines IA 50312 **Phn:** 515-953-4822 **Fax:** 515-953-1394 www.dmcityview.com editor@dmcityview.com

Des Moines Press Citizen (18.0M) PO Box 957 Des Moines IA 50306 **Phn:** 515-964-0639 **Fax:** 515-964-7019 www.desmoinesregister.com dbelt@dmreg.com

Diagonal Diagonal Progress (0.5M) 1729 County Hwy J23 Diagonal IA 50845 **Phn:** 641-734-5507 **Fax:** 641-734-5002 www.thediagonalprogress.com dprogress@iowatelecom.net

Doon Doon Press (3.2M) PO Box 100 Doon IA 51235 **Phn:** 712-726-3313 **Fax:** 712-726-3134 pressgal@hickorytech.net

Dubuque Dubuque Leader (4.0M) PO Box 817 Dubuque IA 52004 **Phn:** 563-556-6625

Dunlap Dunlap Reporter (1.2M) 114 Iowa Ave Dunlap IA 51529 **Phn:** 712-643-5380 **Fax:** 712-643-2173 reporter@iowatelecom.net

Dyersville Dyersville Commercial (4.2M) PO Box 350 Dyersville IA 52040 **Phn:** 563-875-7131 **Fax:** 563-875-2279 www.dyersvillecommercial.com dceditor@wcinet.com

Dysart Dysart Reporter (1.0M) PO Box 70 Dysart IA 52224 **Phn:** 319-476-3550 **Fax:** 319-476-2813 www.dysartreporter.com editor@dysartreporter.com

Eagle Grove Eagle Grove Eagle (1.8M) PO Box 6 Eagle Grove IA 50533 **Phn:** 515-448-4745 **Fax:** 515-448-3182 theeaglegroveeagle.com egeagle@goldfieldaccess.net

Earlham Earlham Advocate (0.7M) PO Box 327 Earlham IA 50072 **Phn:** 515-577-5532 **Fax:** 515-758-3086 editor@earlhamadvocate.com

Edgewood Edgewood Reminder (1.5M) PO Box 458 Edgewood IA 52042 **Phn:** 563-928-6876 edgewood.reminder@yahoo.com

Eldora Eldora Herald-Ledger (3.2M) 1513 Edgington Ave Eldora IA 50627 **Phn:** 641-939-5051 **Fax:** 641-939-5541 editor@eldoranewspaper.com

Eldora Hardin Co. Index (3.2M) 1513 Edgington Ave Eldora IA 50627 **Phn:** 641-939-5051 **Fax:** 641-939-5541

Eldridge North Scott Press (5.6M) PO Box 200 Eldridge IA 52748 **Phn:** 563-285-8111 **Fax:** 563-285-8114 www.northscottpress.com scampbell@northscottpress.com

Elgin Elgin Newspapers (3.1M) PO Box 97 Elgin IA 52141 **Phn:** 563-426-5591 www.newspapersoffayettecounty.com jduren@fayettepublishing.com

Elk Horn Danish Villages Voice (1.0M) PO Box 469 Elk Horn IA 51531 **Phn:** 712-764-4800 thevoice@metc.net

Elkader Clayton County Register (2.8M) PO Box 130 Elkader IA 52043 **Phn:** 563-245-1311 **Fax:** 563-245-1312 ccrnews@alpinecom.net

Emmetsburg Democrat & Reporter (5.7M) PO Box 73 Emmetsburg IA 50536 **Phn:** 712-852-2323 **Fax:** 712-852-3184 www.emmetsburgnews.com jwhitmore@emmetsburgnews.com

Everly Everly/Royal News (1.1M) PO Box 77 Everly IA 51338 **Phn:** 712-834-2388 sentinel@tcaexpress.net

Farmington Leader Record (1.7M) PO Box 155 Farmington IA 52626 **Phn:** 319-878-4111 leaderec@netins.net

Fontanelle Fontanelle Observer (1.2M) PO Box 248 Fontanelle IA 50846 **Phn:** 641-745-3161 **Fax:** 641-745-1201

Forest City Forest City Summit (5.0M) PO Box 350 Forest City IA 50436 **Phn:** 641-585-2112 **Fax:** 641-585-4442 www.globegazette.com/forestcitysummit news@forestcitysummit.com

Garner Garner Leader & Signal (2.2M) 365 State St Garner IA 50438 **Phn:** 641-923-2684 **Fax:** 641-923-2685 theleaderonline.net gleadernews@qwestoffice.net

George Lyon County News (0.9M) PO Box 68 George IA 51237 **Phn:** 712-475-3351 **Fax:** 712-475-3353 lyonconews@mtcnet.net

Gladbrook Northern Sun Print (1.2M) PO Box 340 Gladbrook IA 50635 **Phn:** 641-473-2102 **Fax:** 641-473-1004 www.northernsunprint.com editor@northernsunprint.com

Glenwood Glenwood Opinion Tribune (3.9M) PO Box 191 Glenwood IA 51534 **Phn:** 712-527-3191 **Fax:** 712-527-3193 www.opinion-tribune.com news@opinion-tribune.com

Glidden Glidden Graphic (0.6M) PO Box 607 Glidden IA 51443 **Phn:** 712-659-3144 **Fax:** 712-659-3143 gliddengraphic@iowatelecom.net

Gowrie Gowrie News (1.8M) PO Box 473 Gowrie IA 50543 **Phn:** 515-352-3325 **Fax:** 515-352-3309 gnews@wccta.net

Graettinger Graettinger Times (0.8M) PO Box 118 Graettinger IA 51342 **Phn:** 712-859-3780 **Fax:** 712-859-3039 grtimes@rvtc.net

Graettinger Ruthven Zipcode (0.4M) PO Box 118 Graettinger IA 51342 **Phn:** 712-859-3780 **Fax:** 712-859-3039

Greene Greene Recorder (1.4M) PO Box 370 Greene IA 50636 **Phn:** 641-816-4525 greenerecorder.dotphoto.com news@greenerecorder.com

Greenfield Adair County Free Press (2.4M) PO Box 148 Greenfield IA 50849 **Phn:** 641-743-6121 **Fax:** 641-743-6378 fpnewsed@iowatelecom.net

Grinnell Grinnell Herald-Register (4.0M) PO Box 360 Grinnell IA 50112 **Phn:** 641-236-3113 **Fax:** 641-236-5135 pinder@pcpartner.net

Grinnell Montezuma Republican (1.8M) 925 Broad St Grinnell IA 50112 **Phn:** 641-623-5116 **Fax:** 641-623-5580

Griswold Griswold American (1.1M) PO Box 687 Griswold IA 51535 **Phn:** 712-778-4337 **Fax:** 712-778-4350 grisamer@netins.net

Grundy Center Grundy Register (3.0M) PO Box 245 Grundy Center IA 50638 **Phn:** 319-824-6958 **Fax:** 319-824-6288 register@gcmuni.net

Guthrie Center The Times (2.2M) PO Box 217 Guthrie Center IA 50115 **Phn:** 641-332-2380 **Fax:** 641-332-2382 www.guthrian.com gctimes@netins.net

Guttenberg Guttenberg Press (2.7M) PO Box 937 Guttenberg IA 52052 **Phn:** 563-252-2421 **Fax:** 563-252-1275 www.guttenbergpress.com gbpress@alpinecom.net

Hamburg Hamburg Reporter (1.4M) 1510 Main St Hamburg IA 51640 **Phn:** 712-382-1234 www.hamburgreporter.com

Hampton Hampton Chronicle (2.9M) PO Box 29 Hampton IA 50441 **Phn:** 641-456-2585 **Fax:** 641-456-2587 hamptonchronicle.com chroniclenews@iowaconnect.com

IOWA WEEKLY NEWSPAPERS

Harlan Harlan News-Advertiser (4.2M) PO Box 721 Harlan IA 51537 **Phn:** 712-755-3111 **Fax:** 712-755-3324 www.harlanonline.com news2@harlanonline.com

Harlan Harlan Tribune (4.2M) PO Box 721 Harlan IA 51537 **Phn:** 712-755-3111 **Fax:** 712-755-3324 www.harlanonline.com news2@harlanonline.com

Hartley Hartley Sentinel (1.7M) 71 1st St SE Hartley IA 51346 **Phn:** 712-928-2223 sentinel@tcaexpress.net

Hawarden Hawarden Independent/Ireton Examiner (1.8M) PO Box 31 Hawarden IA 51023 **Phn:** 712-551-1051 **Fax:** 712-551-1057 independent@longlines.com

Hinton Hinton Times (0.4M) 33599 Jade Ave Hinton IA 51024 **Phn:** 712-239-5758 hintontimes@juno.com

Holstein The Advance (1.3M) PO Box 550 Holstein IA 51025 **Phn:** 712-368-4368 **Fax:** 712-368-4369 mari_b15@yahoo.com

Hopkinton Delaware County Leader (1.1M) PO Box 128 Hopkinton IA 52237 **Phn:** 563-926-2626 **Fax:** 563-926-2045

Hospers Siouxland Press (1.7M) PO Box 278 Hospers IA 51238 **Phn:** 712-752-8401 **Fax:** 712-752-8405 siouxlandpress@hotmail.com

Hubbard Signal Review (1.6M) PO Box 457 Hubbard IA 50122 **Phn:** 641-864-2288 sigrev@netins.net

Hudson Hudson Herald (1.5M) PO Box 210 Hudson IA 50643 **Phn:** 319-988-3855

Hull Sioux County Index-Reporter (1.4M) PO Box 420 Hull IA 51239 **Phn:** 712-439-1075 **Fax:** 712-439-2001 www.ncppub.com hulleditor@ncppub.com

Humboldt Humboldt Independent (4.5M) PO Box 157 Humboldt IA 50548 **Phn:** 515-332-2514 **Fax:** 515-332-1505 www.humboldtnews.com independent@humboldtnews.com

Ida Grove Ida County Courier (3.0M) PO Box 249 Ida Grove IA 51445 **Phn:** 712-364-3131 **Fax:** 712-364-3010 www.idacountycourier.com editor@idacountycourier.com

Independence Bulletin Journal (4.7M) PO Box 290 Independence IA 50644 **Phn:** 319-334-2557 **Fax:** 319-334-6752 communitynewspapergroup.com/bulletin-journal editor@bulletinjournal.com

Indianola Record-Herald & Tribune (6.5M) 112 N Howard St Indianola IA 50125 **Phn:** 515-961-2511 **Fax:** 515-961-4833 indianolarecordherald.desmoinesregister.com mrolands@dmreg.com

Iowa Falls Times-Citizen (3.7M) PO Box 640 Iowa Falls IA 50126 **Phn:** 641-648-2521 **Fax:** 641-648-4765 www.timescitizen.com

Jefferson Jefferson Bee (7.8M) PO Box 440 Jefferson IA 50129 **Phn:** 515-386-4161 **Fax:** 515-386-4162

Jefferson Jefferson Herald (3.2M) PO Box 440 Jefferson IA 50129 **Phn:** 515-386-4161 **Fax:** 515-386-4162

Jesup Jesup Citizen-Herald (1.1M) PO Box 545 Jesup IA 50648 **Phn:** 319-827-1128 **Fax:** 319-827-1125 www.jesupcitizenherald.com news@jesupcitizenherald.com

Jewell The Record-News (1.0M) PO Box 130 Jewell IA 50130 **Phn:** 515-827-5931 **Fax:** 515-827-5760 shrecnew@netins.net

Kalona Kalona News (3.0M) PO Box 430 Kalona IA 52247 **Phn:** 319-656-2273 **Fax:** 319-656-2299 www.kalonanews.com news@kalonanews.com

Kanawha The Reporter (0.8M) PO Box 190 Kanawha IA 50447 **Phn:** 641-762-3994

Keota Keota Eagle (1.2M) PO Box 18 Keota IA 52248 **Phn:** 641-636-2309 keotaeagle.com keoeagle@iowatelecom.net

Kingsley Kingsley News-Times (1.0M) PO Box 459 Kingsley IA 51028 **Phn:** 712-378-2770 **Fax:** 712-378-2274

Knoxville Knoxville Journal-Express (2.1M) PO Box 458 Knoxville IA 50138 **Phn:** 641-842-2155 **Fax:** 641-842-2929 journalexpress.net

La Porte City Progress-Review (1.4M) 213 Main St La Porte City IA 50651 **Phn:** 319-342-2429 **Fax:** 319-342-2433 www.theprogressreview.co

Lake City Lake City Graphic (1.5M) PO Box 121 Lake City IA 51449 **Phn:** 712-464-3188 thegraphic-advocate.com lcgraphic@iowatelecom.net

Lake Mills Lake Mills Graphic (2.7M) PO Box 127 Lake Mills IA 50450 **Phn:** 641-592-4222 **Fax:** 641-592-6397 graphic@wctatel.net

Lake View Lake View Resort (1.4M) PO Box 470 Lake View IA 51450 **Phn:** 712-657-8588 **Fax:** 712-657-2495 lakeviewresort@netins.net

Lamoni Lamoni Chronicle (1.0M) PO Box 40 Lamoni IA 50140 **Phn:** 641-784-6397 **Fax:** 641-784-7669 newnews@grm.net

Lamont Leader (0.9M) PO Box 260 Lamont IA 50650 **Phn:** 563-924-2361 **Fax:** 562-924-2159 lamontleader@iowatelecom.net

Laurens Laurens Sun (1.4M) 210 Byron St Laurens IA 50554 **Phn:** 712-841-4541

Lenox Lenox Time Table (1.0M) 101 1/2 E Temple St Lenox IA 50851 **Phn:** 641-333-2810 **Fax:** 641-333-2303 timetable@lenoxia.com

Leon Leon Journal-Reporter (2.1M) PO Box 580 Leon IA 50144 **Phn:** 641-446-4151 **Fax:** 641-446-7645 jrnews@grm.net

Lime Springs Lime Springs Herald (0.8M) PO Box 187 Lime Springs IA 52155 **Phn:** 563-566-2687

Little Rock Little Rock Free Lance (1.0M) PO Box 185 Little Rock IA 51243 **Phn:** 712-479-2270 **Fax:** 712-479-2273 vksc@mtcnet.net

Logan Logan Herald-Observer (1.4M) PO Box 148 Logan IA 51546 **Phn:** 712-644-2705 **Fax:** 712-644-2788 www.loganwoodbine.com news@heraldobserver.com

Lone Tree Lone Tree Reporter (0.9M) PO Box 13 Lone Tree IA 52755 **Phn:** 319-656-2273 **Fax:** 319-656-2299 www.kalonanews.com/lone_tree news@kalonanews.com

Lowden Lowden Sun-News (0.9M) PO Box 370 Lowden IA 52255 **Phn:** 563-886-2131 **Fax:** 563-886-6466 tcadvertising@yahoo.com

Madrid Madrid Register-News (1.4M) PO Box 167 Madrid IA 50156 **Phn:** 515-795-2730 **Fax:** 515-795-2012 www.wilcoxprinting.com info@wilcoxprinting.com

Malvern Malvern Leader (1.2M) PO Box 129 Malvern IA 51551 **Phn:** 712-624-8512 **Fax:** 712-624-9250

Manchester Manchester Press (4.7M) PO Box 245 Manchester IA 52057 **Phn:** 563-927-2020 **Fax:** 563-927-4945 www.manchesterpress.com mpeditor@mchsi.com

Manilla The Manilla Times (1.2M) PO Box 365 Manilla IA 51454 **Phn:** 712-654-2911 **Fax:** 712-654-2910 irwinmtimes@fmctc.com

Manly Manly Signal (1.1M) PO Box 179 Manly IA 50456 **Phn:** 641-454-2216

Manning Manning Monitor (1.5M) 411 Main St Manning IA 51455 **Phn:** 712-653-3854 **Fax:** 712-653-9430

Manson Journal-Herald (1.5M) PO Box 40 Manson IA 50563 **Phn:** 712-469-3381 **Fax:** 712-469-2648 www.journalherald.com journal@journalherald.com

Mapleton Mapleton Press (1.7M) PO Box 187 Mapleton IA 51034 **Phn:** 712-881-1101 **Fax:** 712-881-1330 www.enterprisepub.com/mapleton mpress@longlines.com

Mapleton Schleswig Leader (0.8M) PO Box 187 Mapleton IA 51034 **Phn:** 712-676-3414 **Fax:** 712-881-1330

Maquoketa The Sentinel-Press (5.2M) 108 W Quarry St Maquoketa IA 52060 **Phn:** 563-652-2441 **Fax:** 563-652-6094 mspress.jimdo.com dmelvold@mspress.net

Marengo Iowa County Papers (2.5M) PO Box 208 Marengo IA 52301 **Phn:** 319-642-5506 **Fax:** 319-642-5509 showcase.netins.net/web/bpunion publish@netins.net

Marion Marion Times (1.0M) PO Box 506 Marion IA 52302 **Phn:** 319-377-7037 **Fax:** 319-377-9535

McGregor North Iowa Times (0.8M) 220 Main St McGregor IA 52157 **Phn:** 563-873-2210 **Fax:** 608-326-2443 www.northiowatimes.com niteditor@yahoo.com

Mediapolis Mediapolis News (1.5M) PO Box 548 Mediapolis IA 52637 **Phn:** 319-394-3174 **Fax:** 319-394-3134 mediapolisnews.com meponews@mepotelco.net

Missouri Valley Misouri Valley Times News (2.1M) PO Box 159 Missouri Valley IA 51555 **Phn:** 712-642-2791 **Fax:** 712-642-2595 www.enterprisepub.com/movalley news@missourivalleytimes.com

Monona The Outlook (2.2M) PO Box 310 Monona IA 52159 **Phn:** 563-539-4554 **Fax:** 563-539-4585 outlook@neitel.net

Monroe Monroe Legacy (0.9M) PO Box 340 Monroe IA 50170 **Phn:** 641-259-2708 mmml@iowatelecom.net

Monticello Monticello Express (3.4M) 111 E Grand St Monticello IA 52310 **Phn:** 319-465-3555 **Fax:** 319-465-4611 www.monticelloexpress.com kbrooks@monticelloexpress.com

Moravia Moravia Union (1.2M) PO Box 190 Moravia IA 52571 **Phn:** 641-724-3224 moraviaunion@sirisonline.com

Moravia Moulton Tribune (0.8M) Po Box 190 Moravia IA 52571 **Phn:** 641-724-3224 moraviaunion@sirisonline.com

Mount Ayr Mt. Ayr Record-News (2.3M) PO Box 346 Mount Ayr IA 50854 **Phn:** 641-464-2440 **Fax:** 641-464-2229 mtayrnews.com recnews@iowatelecom.net

Mount Vernon The Sun (1.8M) PO Box 129 Mount Vernon IA 52314 **Phn:** 319-895-6216 **Fax:** 319-895-6217 www.mvlsun.com news@mtvernonlisbonsun.com

Moville Moville Record (1.5M) PO Box 546 Moville IA 51039 **Phn:** 712-873-3141 **Fax:** 712-873-3142 movillerecord.com record@wiatel.net

Nashua The Reporter (1.0M) PO Box 67 Nashua IA 50658 **Phn:** 641-435-4151 www.nhtrib.com tribune@nhtrib.com

Neola Neola Gazette (1.8M) PO Box 7 Neola IA 51559 **Phn:** 712-485-2276 **Fax:** 712-485-2277 thegazette.com editorial@gazcomm.com

Nevada Nevada Journal (3.1M) PO Box 89 Nevada IA 50201 **Phn:** 515-382-2161 **Fax:** 515-382-4299 nevadaiowajournal.com results@nevadaiowajournal.com

Nevada Tri-County Times (3.0M) PO Box 89 Nevada IA 50201 **Phn:** 515-382-2161 **Fax:** 515-382-4299 tricountytimes.com mbarker@nevadaiowajournal.com

IOWA WEEKLY NEWSPAPERS

New Hampton New Hampton Tribune (3.1M) PO Box 380 New Hampton IA 50659 **Phn:** 641-394-2111 **Fax:** 641-394-2113 www.nhtrib.com tribune@nhtrib.com

Newell Buena Vista County Journal (1.2M) PO Box 666 Newell IA 50568 **Phn:** 712-335-3553

North Liberty North Liberty Leader (0.9M) PO Box 288 North Liberty IA 52317 **Phn:** 319-665-2199 **Fax:** 319-624-1356 www.northlibertyleader.com hybrid@southslope.net

Northwood Northwood Anchor (5.5M) PO Box 107 Northwood IA 50459 **Phn:** 641-324-1051 **Fax:** 641-324-2432 www.northwoodanchor.com anchor@northwoodanchor.net

Norwalk Town & County News (1.5M) PO Box 325 Norwalk IA 50211 **Phn:** 515-981-0406

Oakland The Herald (1.6M) PO Box 556 Oakland IA 51560 **Phn:** 888-343-2154 avocajh@iowatelecom.net

Ocheyedan Ocheyedan Press (1.2M) PO Box 456 Ocheyedan IA 51354 **Phn:** 712-758-3140 **Fax:** 712-758-3186 www.thepress-news.com pressinc@nethtc.net

Odebolt Thet Chronicle (3.8M) PO Box 485 Odebolt IA 51458 **Phn:** 712-668-2253 **Fax:** 712-668-4364 paper@netins.net

Ogden Ogden Reporter (2.0M) PO Box R Ogden IA 50212 **Phn:** 515-275-4101 **Fax:** 515-275-2678 www.ogdenreporter.com kspierce@netins.net

Onawa Onawa Democrat (3.0M) PO Box 418 Onawa IA 51040 **Phn:** 712-423-2411 democrat@longlines.com

Onawa Onawa Sentinel (1.0M) PO Box 208 Onawa IA 51040 **Phn:** 712-423-2021 **Fax:** 712-423-3038 vsawyer@longlines.com

Orange City Sioux County Democrat (2.4M) 113 Central Ave SE Orange City IA 51041 **Phn:** 712-737-4266 **Fax:** 712-737-3896 www.siouxcountynews.com pluimpub@orangecitycomm.net

Osage Mitchell County Press News (3.5M) PO Box 60 Osage IA 50461 **Phn:** 641-732-3721 **Fax:** 641-732-5689 www.globegazette.com/mcpress editor@mcpress.com

Osceola Sentinel-Tribune (4.0M) 111 E Washington St Osceola IA 50213 **Phn:** 641-342-2131 **Fax:** 641-342-2060 www.osceolaiowa.com ccpnews@osceolaiowa.com

Ossian Ossian Bee (1.2M) PO Box 96 Ossian IA 52161 **Phn:** 563-532-9113 **Fax:** 563-426-5766 www.newspapersoffayettecounty.com jduren@fayettepublishing.com

Panora Guthrie County Vedette (1.1M) PO Box 38 Panora IA 50216 **Phn:** 641-755-2115 **Fax:** 641-755-2425 www.guthrian.com gctimes@netins.net

Parkersburg Eclipse-News-Review (2.3M) PO Box 340 Parkersburg IA 50665 **Phn:** 319-346-1461 pburgeclipse@aol.com

Paullina Paullina Times (1.3M) PO Box 637 Paullina IA 51046 **Phn:** 712-949-3622

Pella Pella Chronicle (3.6M) PO Box 126 Pella IA 50219 **Phn:** 641-628-3882 **Fax:** 641-628-3905 pellachronicle.com chroniclenews@iowatelecom.net

Perry Perry Chief (3.2M) PO Box 98 Perry IA 50220 **Phn:** 515-465-4666 **Fax:** 515-465-3087

Peterson Peterson Patriot (0.6M) PO Box 126 Peterson IA 51047 **Phn:** 712-295-7711 thepetepatriot@hotmail.com

Pleasantville Marion County News (1.3M) PO Box 561 Pleasantville IA 50225 **Phn:** 515-848-5614

Pocahontas Record-Democrat (9.0M) PO Box 128 Pocahontas IA 50574 **Phn:** 712-335-3553 **Fax:** 712-335-3856

Postville Herald-Leader (9.5M) PO Box 100 Postville IA 52162 **Phn:** 563-864-3333 **Fax:** 563-864-3400

Prairie City Prairie City News (1.0M) PO Box 249 Prairie City IA 50228 **Phn:** 515-994-2349 **Fax:** 515-994-3169 news@myprairiecitynews.com

Preston Preston Times (1.0M) PO Box 9 Preston IA 52069 **Phn:** 563-689-3841 **Fax:** 563-689-3842 prestontimes@netins.net

Primghar O'Brien County Bell (0.9M) PO Box 478 Primghar IA 51245 **Phn:** 712-957-4055

Red Oak Red Oak Express (9.0M) PO Box 377 Red Oak IA 51566 **Phn:** 712-623-2566 **Fax:** 712-623-2568 news@redoakexpress.com

Reinbeck Reinbeck Courier (1.8M) 107 Broad St Reinbeck IA 50669 **Phn:** 319-345-2031 **Fax:** 319-345-6767 www.reinbeckcourier.com editor@reinbeckcourier.com

Remsen Remsen Bell-Enterprise (1.1M) PO Box 10 Remsen IA 51050 **Phn:** 712-786-1196 **Fax:** 712-786-1257 remsenbell@midlands.net

Riceville Riceville Recorder (1.5M) PO Box A Riceville IA 50466 **Phn:** 641-985-2142 **Fax:** 641-985-4185

Rock Rapids Lyon-Sioux Press (5.2M) PO Box 28 Rock Rapids IA 51246 **Phn:** 712-472-2525 **Fax:** 712-472-3414 www.ncppub.com jhoog@ncppub.com

Rock Valley Rock Valley Bee (1.0M) PO Box 157 Rock Valley IA 51247 **Phn:** 712-476-2795 **Fax:** 712-476-2796 pam@rockpublishingco.com

Rockwell Pioneer Enterprise (1.3M) PO Box 203 Rockwell IA 50469 **Phn:** 641-822-3193 thesheffieldpress.com

Rockwell City Calhoun County Advocate (1.0M) PO Box 31 Rockwell City IA 50579 **Phn:** 712-297-7544 advocate@iowatelecom.net

Sac City Sac Sun (1.9M) PO Box 426 Sac City IA 50583 **Phn:** 712-662-7161 **Fax:** 712-662-4198 sacsuneditor@frontiernet.net

Saint Ansgar St. Ansgar Enterprise (1.5M) PO Box 310 Saint Ansgar IA 50472 **Phn:** 641-713-4541 **Fax:** 641-713-2399 staej@iowatelecom.net

Sanborn Sanborn Pioneer (0.8M) PO Box 280 Sanborn IA 51248 **Phn:** 712-729-3201 spioneer@tcaexpress.net

Schaller Schaller Herald (0.9M) PO Box 129 Schaller IA 51053 **Phn:** 712-275-4229 herald@schallertel.net

Scranton Scranton Journal (1.0M) PO Box 187 Scranton IA 51462 **Phn:** 712-651-2321 **Fax:** 712-651-2599 www.iowanewspapersonline.com ciapub@netins.net

Seymour Seymour Herald (1.5M) 206 N 4th St Seymour IA 52590 **Phn:** 641-898-7554

Sheffield Sheffield Press (1.1M) PO Box 36 Sheffield IA 50475 **Phn:** 641-892-4636 jzpress@frontiernet.net

Sheldon N'West Iowa Review (7.0M) PO Box 160 Sheldon IA 51201 **Phn:** 712-324-5347 **Fax:** 712-324-2345 www.nwestiowa.com editor@iowainformation.com

Sheldon Sheldon Mail-Sun (2.0M) PO Box 160 Sheldon IA 51201 **Phn:** 712-324-5347 **Fax:** 712-324-2345 editor@iowainformation.com

Shenandoah Essex Independent (0.4M) PO Box 369 Shenandoah IA 51601 **Phn:** 712-246-3097 **Fax:** 712-246-3099 editorial@valleynewstoday.com

Sibley Gazette Tribune (1.5M) 201 9th St Sibley IA 51249 **Phn:** 712-754-2551 **Fax:** 712-754-2552 gtnews@nethtc.net

Sidney Sidney Argus-Herald (1.2M) PO Box 190 Sidney IA 51652 **Phn:** 712-374-2251 argusherald@iowatelecom.net

Sigourney Sigourney News-Review (2.8M) PO Box 285 Sigourney IA 52591 **Phn:** 641-622-3110 **Fax:** 641-622-2766 sigourneynewsreview.com signred@lisco.com

Sioux Center Sioux Center News (2.5M) 67 3rd St NE Sioux Center IA 51250 **Phn:** 712-722-0741 **Fax:** 712-722-0507 www.siouxcenternews.com editor@siouxcenternews.com

Solon Solon Economist (1.4M) PO Box 249 Solon IA 52333 **Phn:** 319-624-2233 **Fax:** 319-624-1356 www.soloneconomist.com hybrid@southslope.net

Stacyville Monitor-Review (1.1M) PO Box 236 Stacyville IA 50476 **Phn:** 641-710-2119 **Fax:** 641-710-3119

State Center Mid Iowa Enterprise (1.4M) PO Box 634 State Center IA 50247 **Phn:** 641-483-2120 **Fax:** 641-483-2938 midiowaenterprise@yahoo.com

Storm Lake Pilot-Tribune (3.5M) PO Box 1187 Storm Lake IA 50588 **Phn:** 712-732-3130 **Fax:** 712-732-3152 www.stormlakepilottribune.com dlarsen@stormlakepilottribune.com

Storm Lake Storm Lake Times (3.2M) PO Box 487 Storm Lake IA 50588 **Phn:** 712-732-4991 **Fax:** 712-732-4331 www.stormlake.com times@stormlake.com

Story City Story City Herald (2.0M) 511 Broad St Story City IA 50248 **Phn:** 515-733-4318 **Fax:** 515-733-4319 scherald@storycity.com

Stratford Stratford Courier (0.4M) PO Box 169 Stratford IA 50249 **Phn:** 515-838-2494 **Fax:** 515-838-2958 shrecnew@netins.net

Strawberry Point Press-Journal (1.8M) PO Box 70 Strawberry Point IA 52076 **Phn:** 563-933-4370 pressj@iowatelecom.net

Stuart Stuart Herald (1.6M) Po Box 608 Stuart IA 50250 **Phn:** 515-523-1010 **Fax:** 515-523-2825 thestuartherald.com news@thestuartherald.com

Sumner Sumner Gazette (1.7M) PO Box 208 Sumner IA 50674 **Phn:** 563-578-3351 **Fax:** 563-578-3352 sgazette@mchsi.com

Tabor Beacon Enterprise (0.9M) PO Box 299 Tabor IA 51653 **Phn:** 712-629-2255 **Fax:** 712-624-9250 leaderbeacon@qwestoffice.net

Tama Tama News-Herald (3.5M) PO Box 118 Tama IA 52339 **Phn:** 641-484-2841 **Fax:** 641-484-5705 www.tamatoledonews.com editor@tamatoledonews.com

Tama Toledo Chronicle (3.5M) PO Box 118 Tama IA 52339 **Phn:** 641-484-2841 **Fax:** 641-484-5705 www.tamatoledonews.com editor@tamatoledonews.com

Thompson Thompson Courier (1.0M) PO Box 318 Thompson IA 50478 **Phn:** 641-584-2770 **Fax:** 641-584-2802

Tipton Tipton Conservative (4.8M) PO Box 271 Tipton IA 52772 **Phn:** 563-886-2131 **Fax:** 563-886-6466 www.tiptonconservative.com stuartc108@aol.com

Titonka Titonka Topic (0.6M) PO Box 329 Titonka IA 50480 **Phn:** 515-928-2723 **Fax:** 515-928-2506 www.topix.com/city/titonka-ia titonkatopic@netins.net

Traer Star Clipper (2.2M) PO Box 156 Traer IA 50675 **Phn:** 319-478-2323 **Fax:** 319-478-2818 www.traerstarclipper.com editor@traerstarclipper.com

Tripoli Tripoli Leader (1.2M) PO Box 39 Tripoli IA 50676 **Phn:** 319-882-4207 **Fax:** 319-882-4200 tripolileader@butler-bremer.com

Villisca Review & Stanton Viking (1.3M) PO Box 7 Villisca IA 50864 **Phn:** 712-826-2142 **Fax:** 712-826-8888

Vinton Vinton Newspapers (3.0M) PO Box 468 Vinton IA 52349 **Phn:** 319-472-2311 **Fax:** 319-472-4811 www.communitynewspapergroup.com news@vintonnewspapers.com

Walnut Walnut Bureau (0.7M) PO Box 468 Walnut IA 51577 **Phn:** 712-784-3575 **Fax:** 712-784-3219 thewb@walnutel.net

Wapello Louisa Publishing (16.0M) PO Box 306 Wapello IA 52653 **Phn:** 319-523-4631 **Fax:** 319-523-8167 lpc@louisacomm.net

Waukon The Standard (4.0M) PO Box 286 Waukon IA 52172 **Phn:** 563-568-3431 **Fax:** 563-568-4242 www.waukonstandard.com news@waukonstandard.com

Waverly Bremer County Independent (6.5M) PO Box 858 Waverly IA 50677 **Phn:** 319-352-3334 **Fax:** 319-352-5135 www.communitynewspapergroup.com news@waverlynewspapers.com

Waverly Waverly Democrat (6.5M) PO Box 858 Waverly IA 50677 **Phn:** 319-352-3334 **Fax:** 319-352-5135 www.communitynewspapergroup.com news@waverlynewspapers.com

Wellman Wellman Advance (1.1M) PO Box I Wellman IA 52356 **Phn:** 319-646-2712 **Fax:** 319-646-5904 wellnews@netins.net

West Bend West Bend Journal (0.8M) PO Box 47 West Bend IA 50597 **Phn:** 515-887-4141 wjournal@ncn.net

West Branch West Branch Times (1.4M) PO Box 368 West Branch IA 52358 **Phn:** 319-643-2131 www.westbranchtimes.com wbtimes@lcom.net

West Liberty West Liberty Index (1.8M) PO Box 96 West Liberty IA 52776 **Phn:** 319-627-2814 **Fax:** 319-627-2110 www.westlibertyindex.com indexnews@lcom.net

West Point Bee/Star Community Paper (0.6M) PO Box 66 West Point IA 52656 **Phn:** 319-837-6232 **Fax:** 319-837-6913 editor@dailydem.com

West Point West Point Bee (0.6M) PO Box 66 West Point IA 52656 **Phn:** 319-837-6232

West Union Fayette County Union (3.2M) PO Box 153 West Union IA 52175 **Phn:** 563-422-3888 **Fax:** 563-422-3488 www.westunionfayettecountyunion.com mvansickle@thefayettecountyunion.com

Westside The Observer (1.2M) PO Box 156 Westside IA 51467 **Phn:** 712-663-4362 **Fax:** 712-663-4363 observer@win-4-u.net

What Cheer New Sharon Sun (0.7M) PO Box 414 What Cheer IA 50268 **Phn:** 641-622-3110 whatcheerpaper.com

What Cheer What Cheer Paper (2.8M) PO Box 414 What Cheer IA 50268 **Phn:** 641-622-3110 whatcheerpaper.com

Whittemore Whittemore Independent (0.6M) PO Box 237 Whittemore IA 50598 **Phn:** 515-884-2648 wjournal@ncn.net

Williamsburg Journal Tribune (2.0M) PO Box 690 Williamsburg IA 52361 **Phn:** 319-668-1240 **Fax:** 319-668-9112

Wilton Wilton Advocate News (3.0M) PO Box 40 Wilton IA 52778 **Phn:** 563-732-2029 **Fax:** 563-732-3144 northscottpress.com scampbell@northscottpress.com

IOWA WEEKLY NEWSPAPERS

Winfield Winfield Beacon (1.8M) PO Box F Winfield IA 52659 **Phn:** 319-257-6813 **Fax:** 319-257-6902 newspapers2@iowatelecom.net

Winterset Winterset Madisonian (3.6M) PO Box 350 Winterset IA 50273 **Phn:** 515-462-2101 **Fax:** 515-462-2102 www.wintersetmadisonian.com madisonianeditor@gmail.com

Winthrop The Winthrop News (2.0M) PO Box 9 Winthrop IA 50682 **Phn:** 319-935-3027 www.thewinthropnews.com news@thewinthropnews.com

Woodbine Woodbine Twiner (1.5M) PO Box 16 Woodbine IA 51579 **Phn:** 712-647-2821 **Fax:** 712-647-3081 www.loganwoodbine.com news@woodbinetwiner.com

Wyoming Midland Times (1.0M) 301 W Webster St Wyoming IA 52362 **Phn:** 563-488-2281 midtimes@netins.net

KANSAS

Abilene Andover Journal Advocate (2.4M) 304 Wheatridge Pl Abilene KS 67410 **Phn:** 316-733-2002

Alma Wabaunsee Co. Signal Enterprise (1.3M) PO Box 158 Alma KS 66401 **Phn:** 785-765-3327 **Fax:** 785-765-3384 signal@embarqmail.com

Andale Mt. Hope Clarion (2.0M) PO Box 337 Andale KS 67001 **Phn:** 316-661-2697 **Fax:** 316-667-2406

Anthony Anthony Republican (2.7M) PO Box 31 Anthony KS 67003 **Phn:** 620-842-5129 **Fax:** 620-842-5115 anthonyrepublican@att.net

Ashland Clark County Clipper (1.4M) PO Box 457 Ashland KS 67831 **Phn:** 620-635-2312 **Fax:** 620-635-2643

Atchison Atchison Globe (3.3M) PO Box 247 Atchison KS 66002 **Phn:** 913-367-0583 **Fax:** 913-367-7531 atchisonglobeonline.com joewarren@npgco.com

Atwood Rawlins County Square Deal (2.3M) PO Box 371 Atwood KS 67730 **Phn:** 785-626-3600 **Fax:** 785-626-9299 www.squaredealnews.com squaredeal114@sbcglobal.net

Baldwin City Baldwin City Signal (1.3M) PO Box 970 Baldwin City KS 66006 **Phn:** 785-594-7080 **Fax:** 785-594-7084 signal.baldwincity.com editor@baldwincity.com

Baxter Springs Cherokee Co.News Advocate (2.0M) 1242 Military Ave Baxter Springs KS 66713 **Phn:** 620-856-4081 **Fax:** 620-856-4051 www.sekvoice.com publisher@sekvoice.com

Belle Plaine Belle Plaine News (1.0M) PO Box 128 Belle Plaine KS 67013 **Phn:** 620-488-2234 **Fax:** 620-488-3241

Belle Plaine Oxford Register (0.5M) PO Box 128 Belle Plaine KS 67013 **Phn:** 620-488-2234 **Fax:** 620-488-3241 bpnews@oldwiz.net

Belleville Belleville Telescope (3.0M) 1805 N St Belleville KS 66935 **Phn:** 785-527-2244 **Fax:** 785-527-2225 thebellevilletelescope.com dhadachek@gmail.com

Beloit Beloit Call (1.6M) PO Box 366 Beloit KS 67420 **Phn:** 785-738-3537 **Fax:** 785-738-6442

Bird City Bird City Times (1.2M) PO Box 220 Bird City KS 67731 **Phn:** 785-332-3162 **Fax:** 785-332-3001 www.nwkansas.com karen.k@nwkansas.com

Bonner Springs Chieftain-Sentinel Publishing (11.0M) PO Box 256 Bonner Springs KS 66012 **Phn:** 913-422-4048 **Fax:** 913-422-4233 www.basehorinfo.com editor@basehorinfo.com

Bucklin Bucklin Banner (0.5M) PO Box 98 Bucklin KS 67834 **Phn:** 620-826-3311

Burlington Coffey County Republican (3.0M) PO Box A Burlington KS 66839 **Phn:** 620-364-5325 **Fax:** 620-364-2607 www.coffeycountyonline.com ccrepublican@gmail.com

Caldwell Caldwell Messenger (1.3M) PO Box 313 Caldwell KS 67022 **Phn:** 620-845-2320 **Fax:** 620-845-6461 messenger@kanokla.net

Caney Montgomery County Chronicle (2.7M) PO Box 186 Caney KS 67333 **Phn:** 620-879-2156 **Fax:** 620-879-2855 www.taylornews.org rudy@taylornews.org

Cawker City Cawker City Ledger (1.0M) PO Box 7 Cawker City KS 67430 **Phn:** 785-781-4831 **Fax:** 785-454-3866 downsnews@ruraltel.net

Cheney Times Sentinel (3.0M) PO Box 544 Cheney KS 67025 **Phn:** 316-540-0500 www.tsnews.com news@tsnews.com

Cherryvale County Chronicle (3.8M) PO Box 156 Cherryvale KS 67335 **Phn:** 620-336-2100 **Fax:** 620-336-2101

Cimarron Jacksonian (1.2M) PO Box 528 Cimarron KS 67835 **Phn:** 620-855-3902 **Fax:** 620-855-2489

Clyde Clyde Republican (1.0M) PO Box 397 Clyde KS 66938 **Phn:** 785-446-2201 clyderepublican@hotmail.com

Colby The Northwest Journal (7.0M) 560 N Franklin Ave Colby KS 67701 **Phn:** 785-460-7337

Coldwater Western Star (1.0M) PO Box 518 Coldwater KS 67029 **Phn:** 620-582-2101

Conway Springs Norwich News (0.4M) PO Box 194 Conway Springs KS 67031 **Phn:** 620-456-2232

Conway Springs Star & Argonia Argosy (1.3M) PO Box 158 Conway Springs KS 67031 **Phn:** 620-456-2473

Cottonwood Falls Chase County Leader News (1.3M) PO Box K Cottonwood Falls KS 66845 **Phn:** 620-273-6391 **Fax:** 620-273-8674

Courtland Courtland Journal (0.6M) 420 Main St Courtland KS 66939 **Phn:** 785-374-4428 **Fax:** 785-374-4209 cjournal@courtland.net

Cunningham Cunningham Courier (0.7M) PO Box 416 Cunningham KS 67035 **Phn:** 620-298-2659 www.cunninghamks.com

Dighton Dighton Herald (1.5M) PO Box 426 Dighton KS 67839 **Phn:** 620-397-5347 dherald@st-tel.net

Downs Downs News (0.8M) 717 Railroad St Downs KS 67437 **Phn:** 785-454-3514 **Fax:** 785-454-3866

Elkhart Elkhart Tri-State News (1.8M) PO Box 777 Elkhart KS 67950 **Phn:** 620-697-4716 **Fax:** 620-697-2411 tristate@elkhart.com

Ellinwood Ellinwood Leader (1.0M) PO Box 487 Ellinwood KS 67526 **Phn:** 620-564-3116 **Fax:** 620-564-2550 www.midksnews.com theellinwoodleadernews@yahoo.com

Erie Erie Record (1.5M) PO Box 159 Erie KS 66733 **Phn:** 620-244-3371 news@erierecord.com

Eudora Eudora News (1.1M) 1402 Church St Ste B Eudora KS 66025 **Phn:** 785-542-2747 **Fax:** 785-542-3290 www.eudoranews.com editor@eudoranews.com

Eureka Eureka Herald (3.3M) PO Box 590 Eureka KS 67045 **Phn:** 620-583-5721 www.eurekaherald.com news@eurekaherald.com

Fairview Fairview Enterprise (0.6M) PO Box 98 Fairview KS 66425 **Phn:** 785-467-3461

Frankfort Frankfort Area News (0.8M) PO Box 156 Frankfort KS 66427 **Phn:** 785-292-4726 fan@bluevalley.net

KANSAS WEEKLY NEWSPAPERS

Fredonia Wilson County Citizen (4.0M) PO Box 330 Fredonia KS 66736 **Phn:** 620-378-4415 **Fax:** 620-378-4688 news@wilsoncountycitizen.com

Galena Galena Sentinel Times (1.3M) 511 S Main St Galena KS 66739 **Phn:** 620-783-5034 **Fax:** 620-783-1388 www.sentineltimes.com gstimes@kans.com

Gardner Spring Hill New Era (1.0M) PO Box 303 Gardner KS 66030 **Phn:** 913-856-7615 **Fax:** 913-856-6707 www.gardnernews.com submissions@gardnernews.com

Gardner The Gardner News (2.0M) PO Box 303 Gardner KS 66030 **Phn:** 913-856-7615 **Fax:** 913-856-6707 www.gardnernews.com submissions@gardnernews.com

Garnett Anderson County Advocate (1.5M) PO Box 403 Garnett KS 66032 **Phn:** 785-448-7000 **Fax:** 785-448-9800

Garnett Anderson County Review (3.6M) PO Box 409 Garnett KS 66032 **Phn:** 785-448-3121 **Fax:** 785-448-6253

Girard Girard Press (2.6M) PO Box 126 Girard KS 66743 **Phn:** 620-724-4426 **Fax:** 620-724-4493 www.morningsun.net stephen.wade@morningsun.net

Goodland Goodland Star-News (1.9M) 1205 Main St Goodland KS 67735 **Phn:** 785-899-2338 **Fax:** 785-899-6186 www.nwkansas.com star.news@nwkansas.com

Greensburg Kiowa County Signal (1.4M) PO Box 368 Greensburg KS 67054 **Phn:** 620-723-2115 **Fax:** 620-723-1031 www.kiowacountysignal.com jkeene@kiowacountysignal.com

Halstead Harvey Co. Independent (2.1M) PO Box 71 Halstead KS 67056 **Phn:** 316-835-2235 **Fax:** 316-835-3357 www.hcindependent.com robb@hcindependent.com

Hanover Hanover News (1.0M) PO Box 278 Hanover KS 66945 **Phn:** 785-337-2242 **Fax:** 785-337-2261

Harper Harper Advocate (1.9M) PO Box 36 Harper KS 67058 **Phn:** 620-896-7311 **Fax:** 620-896-2754

Herington Herington Times (2.1M) PO Box 310 Herington KS 67449 **Phn:** 785-258-2211 **Fax:** 785-258-2400

Hesston Hesston Record (1.2M) PO Box 340 Hesston KS 67062 **Phn:** 620-327-4831 **Fax:** 620-327-4830 www.hesstonrecord.com bob@hesstonrecord.com

Hiawatha Hiawatha World (0.4M) 607 Utah St Hiawatha KS 66434 **Phn:** 785-742-2111 **Fax:** 785-742-2276

Hill City Hill City Times (2.6M) PO Box 308 Hill City KS 67642 **Phn:** 785-421-5700 **Fax:** 785-421-5712 times@ruraltel.net

Hillsboro Hillsboro Free Press (7.4M) 116 S Main St Hillsboro KS 67063 **Phn:** 620-947-5702 **Fax:** 620-947-5940 www.hillsborofreepress.com don@hillsborofreepress.com

Hillsboro Hillsboro Star-Journal (2.9M) PO Box 10 Hillsboro KS 67063 **Phn:** 620-947-3975 **Fax:** 620-382-2262 www.starj.com starj@starj.com

Hoisington Hoisington Dispatch (2.2M) PO Box 330 Hoisington KS 67544 **Phn:** 620-653-4154 **Fax:** 620-653-4720 www.midksnews.com hdispatch@ruraltel.net

Holton Holton Recorder (4.8M) PO Box 311 Holton KS 66436 **Phn:** 785-364-3141 **Fax:** 785-364-3422 www.holtonrecorder.com

Horton Horton Headlight (1.5M) PO Box 269 Horton KS 66439 **Phn:** 785-486-2512 headlight@carsoncomm.com

Hoxie Hoxie Sentinel (1.9M) PO Box 78 Hoxie KS 67740 **Phn:** 785-675-3321 **Fax:** 785-675-3421

Hugoton Hugoton Hermes (2.4M) 522 S Main St Hugoton KS 67951 **Phn:** 620-544-4321 **Fax:** 620-544-7321 hugotonhermesnews.com hermes10@pid.com

Independence Independence News (0.6M) 2230 Kelly Ln Independence KS 67301 **Phn:** 620-331-4711

Jetmore Jetmore Republican (1.0M) PO Box 337 Jetmore KS 67854 **Phn:** 620-357-8316 **Fax:** 620-357-8464

Johnson Johnson Pioneer (1.0M) PO Box 10 Johnson KS 67855 **Phn:** 620-492-6244 **Fax:** 620-492-6245 rondaf@pld.com

Kansas City The Record (8.5M) PO Box 6197 Kansas City KS 66106 **Phn:** 913-362-1988 www.recordnews.com news@recordnews.com

Kansas City Wyandotte Echo (2.5M) PO Box 2305 Kansas City KS 66110 **Phn:** 913-342-2444

Kansas City Wyandotte Weekly (10.0M) PO Box 12003 Kansas City KS 66112 **Phn:** 913-788-5565 **Fax:** 913-788-9812 www.wyandottedailynews.com news@wyandottepublishing.com

Kingman Kingman Leader Courier (2.2M) PO Box 353 Kingman KS 67068 **Phn:** 620-532-3151 **Fax:** 620-532-3152 news@lc.kscoxmail.com

Kinsley Edwards County Sentinel (2.0M) 218 E 6th St Kinsley KS 67547 **Phn:** 620-659-2080 **Fax:** 620-659-3370 edcsentinel@hotmail.com

Kiowa The Kiowa News (1.5M) 614 Main St Kiowa KS 67070 **Phn:** 620-825-4229 www.kiowanews.com kionews@sctelcom.net

Lakin Lakin Independent (1.7M) PO Box 45 Lakin KS 67860 **Phn:** 620-355-6162 **Fax:** 620-355-6300 indpndt@pld.com

Larned Tiller & Toiler (2.0M) PO Box 206 Larned KS 67550 **Phn:** 620-285-3111 **Fax:** 620-285-6062 www.midksnews.com tiller@star.kscoxmail.com

Lawrence De Soto Explorer (1.1M) 645 New Hampshire St Lawrence KS 66044 **Phn:** 785-542-2747 **Fax:** 785-542-3290 www.desotoexplorer.com editor@desotoexplorer.com

Leavenworth Kansas City Kansan (Online only) (8.5M) 422 Seneca St Leavenworth KS 66048 **Phn:** 913-371-4300 **Fax:** 913-342-8620 www.kckansan.com nick@kansascitykansan.com

Lebanon Lebanon Times (0.6M) 409 Walnut St Lebanon KS 66952 **Phn:** 785-389-6631

Leoti Leoti Standard (1.0M) PO Box N Leoti KS 67861 **Phn:** 620-375-2631 standard@fairpoint.net

Lincoln Lincoln Sentinel-Republican (1.6M) PO Box 67 Lincoln KS 67455 **Phn:** 785-524-4200 **Fax:** 785-524-4242 www.lincolnsentinel.com johnbaetz@gmail.com

Lindsborg News-Record (2.9M) PO Box 31 Lindsborg KS 67456 **Phn:** 785-227-3348 **Fax:** 785-227-3740 lnr@lnr.kscoxmail.com

Linn Linn-Palmer Record (1.1M) PO Box 324 Linn KS 66953 **Phn:** 785-348-5481 tommlpr@bluevalley.net

Little River The Monitor Journal (0.5M) PO Box 68 Little River KS 67457 **Phn:** 620-897-6234 **Fax:** 620-897-6287 themonitor@lrmutual.com

Logan Logan Republican (1.0M) PO Box 97 Logan KS 67646 **Phn:** 785-689-4339 **Fax:** 785-689-4338 loganrep@ruraltel.net

Louisburg Louisburg Herald (2.3M) PO Box 99 Louisburg KS 66053 **Phn:** 913-837-4321 **Fax:** 913-837-4322 www.herald-online.com herald@herald-online.com

Lucas Lucas-Sylvan News (0.9M) PO Box 337 Lucas KS 67648 **Phn:** 785-525-6355 **Fax:** 785-525-6356

Lyons Lyons News (1.0M) PO Box 768 Lyons KS 67554 **Phn:** 620-257-2368 **Fax:** 620-257-2369 www.midksnews.com news@ldn.kscoxmail.com

Madison Madison News (0.7M) PO Box 217 Madison KS 66860 **Phn:** 620-437-2433

Marion Marion County Record (2.7M) PO Box 278 Marion KS 66861 **Phn:** 620-382-2165 **Fax:** 620-382-2262 www.marionrecord.com news@marionrecord.com

Marquette Marquette Tribune (0.8M) PO Box 308 Marquette KS 67464 **Phn:** 785-472-5085 **Fax:** 785-472-5087

Marysville Marysville Advocate (5.3M) PO Box 271 Marysville KS 66508 **Phn:** 785-562-2317 **Fax:** 785-562-5589

Meade Meade County News (1.8M) PO Box 310 Meade KS 67864 **Phn:** 620-873-2118 **Fax:** 620-873-5456 www.mcnewsonline.com mcnews@mcnewsonline.com

Medicine Lodge Gyp Hill Premiere (1.3M) PO Box 127 Medicine Lodge KS 67104 **Phn:** 620-886-5654 **Fax:** 620-886-5655 www.gyphillpremiere.com knoland@cyberlodg.com

Miltonvale Miltonvale Record (0.6M) 12 W Spruce St Miltonvale KS 67466 **Phn:** 785-427-2680

Minneapolis Minneapolis Messenger (2.9M) 108 N Concord St Minneapolis KS 67467 **Phn:** 785-392-2129 **Fax:** 785-392-2026 www.mymessengerks.com submit@mymessengerks.com

Minneola Clark Co. Gazette (0.7M) PO Box 463 Minneola KS 67865 **Phn:** 620-885-5040 **Fax:** 620-873-5456 www.clarkcountygazette.com gazette@clarkcountygazette.com

Montezuma Montezuma Press (1.3M) PO Box 188 Montezuma KS 67867 **Phn:** 620-846-2312 montepress@ucom.net

Moundridge The Ledger (1.2M) PO Box 720 Moundridge KS 67107 **Phn:** 620-345-6353 **Fax:** 620-345-2170 ledgernewspaper.net editor@ledgernewspaper.net

Mulberry Mulberry Advance (0.2M) PO Box 267 Mulberry KS 66756 **Phn:** 620-764-3831

Mulvane Mulvane News (1.9M) PO Box 157 Mulvane KS 67110 **Phn:** 316-777-4233

Mulvane Rose Hill Reporter (0.9M) PO Box 157 Mulvane KS 67110 **Phn:** 316-777-4233

Natoma Natoma Independent (2.5M) PO Box 126 Natoma KS 67651 **Phn:** 785-885-4582 natomanews@ruraltel.net

Ness City Ness County News (2.0M) PO Box C Ness City KS 67560 **Phn:** 785-798-2213 **Fax:** 785-798-2214 nessnews@gbta.net

Norton Norton Telegram (4.8M) 215 S Kansas Ave Norton KS 67654 **Phn:** 785-877-3361 **Fax:** 785-877-3732 www.nwkansas.com dpaxton@nwkansas.com

Oakley Oakley Graphic (1.2M) 118 Center Ave Oakley KS 67748 **Phn:** 785-672-3228 **Fax:** 785-672-3229

Oberlin Oberlin Herald (2.1M) 170 S Penn Ave Oberlin KS 67749 **Phn:** 785-475-2206 **Fax:** 785-475-2800 www.nwkansas.com k.davis@nwkansas.com

Onaga Onaga Herald (1.0M) PO Box 309 Onaga KS 66521 **Phn:** 785-889-4681 oherald@bluevalley.net

Osage City Osage Co. Herald-Chronicle (4.0M) 527 Market St Osage City KS 66523 **Phn:** 785-528-3511 **Fax:** 785-528-4811 www.och-c.com ochcnews@gmail.com

Osawatomie Osawatomie Graphic (4.8M) PO Box 99 Osawatomie KS 66064 **Phn:** 913-755-4151 **Fax:** 913-755-6544 www.graphic-online.com graphic@graphic-online.com

Osborne Osborne County Farmer (2.8M) 210 W Main St Osborne KS 67473 **Phn:** 785-346-5424 **Fax:** 785-346-5400 ospubco@ruraltel.net

Oskaloosa Oskaloosa Independent (2.2M) PO Box 278 Oskaloosa KS 66066 **Phn:** 785-863-2520 **Fax:** 785-863-2730 www.jeffcountynews.com independent@centurylink.net

Oswego Taylor Publishing (3.0M) PO Box 269 Oswego KS 67356 **Phn:** 620-795-2550 www.taylornews.org

Overland Park Sun Publications (122.0M) 4370 W 109th St Ste 300 Overland Park KS 66211 **Phn:** 913-381-1010 **Fax:** 913-381-1130 www.kccommunitynews.com/johnson-county-sun sunpublications@npgco.com

Paola Miami County Republic (5.4M) PO Box 389 Paola KS 66071 **Phn:** 913-294-2311 **Fax:** 913-294-5318 www.republic-online.com republic@miconews.com

Parsons County Line (6.4M) PO Box 836 Parsons KS 67357 **Phn:** 620-421-2000 **Fax:** 620-421-2217

Peabody Gazette-Bulletin (1.4M) 113 N Walnut St Peabody KS 66866 **Phn:** 620-983-2185 **Fax:** 620-983-2700 www.peabodykansas.com gazette@peabodykansas.com

Phillipsburg Advocate (2.0M) PO Box 327 Phillipsburg KS 67661 **Phn:** 785-543-2349 **Fax:** 785-543-2364 theadvocate@ruraltel.net

Phillipsburg Phillips County Review (2.0M) PO Box 446 Phillipsburg KS 67661 **Phn:** 785-543-5242 **Fax:** 785-543-5243 www.phillipscountyreview.com news@phillipscountyreview.com

Plainville Plainville Times (1.5M) 400 W Mill St Plainville KS 67663 **Phn:** 785-434-4525 **Fax:** 785-434-2527 mainstreetmedia.us pvtimes@ruraltel.net

Pleasanton Linn County News (2.8M) PO Box 478 Pleasanton KS 66075 **Phn:** 913-352-6235 **Fax:** 913-352-6607 www.linncountynews.net lcn@ckt.net

Pratt Barber County Index (1.5M) PO Box 909 Pratt KS 67124 **Phn:** 620-886-5617 **Fax:** 620-886-3457 bcinews@sbcglobal.net

Pretty Prairie Ninnescah Valley News (0.8M) PO Box 327 Pretty Prairie KS 67570 **Phn:** 620-459-6322

Protection Protection Press (0.8M) PO Box 567 Protection KS 67127 **Phn:** 620-622-4288 **Fax:** 620-622-4370 propress@unitedwireless.com

Quinter Gove County Advocate (1.8M) PO Box 365 Quinter KS 67752 **Phn:** 785-754-3651 **Fax:** 785-754-3878 advocate@ruraltel.net

Riley Riley Countian (1.2M) PO Box 333 Riley KS 66531 **Phn:** 785-485-2290 countian@twinvalley.net

Russell Russell County News (2.3M) PO Box 513 Russell KS 67665 **Phn:** 785-483-2116 **Fax:** 785-483-4012 mainstreetmedia.us russell@mainstreetmedia.us

Sabetha Sabetha Herald (2.6M) PO Box 208 Sabetha KS 66534 **Phn:** 785-284-3300 **Fax:** 785-284-2320 www.sabethaks.com sabethaherald@sbcglobal.net

Saint Francis St. Francis Herald (1.3M) PO Box 1050 Saint Francis KS 67756 **Phn:** 785-332-3162 **Fax:** 785-332-3001 www.nwkansas.com karen.k@nwkansas.com

Saint Marys St. Marys Star (2.0M) PO Box 190 Saint Marys KS 66536 **Phn:** 785-437-2935 www.thesmstar.com star@oct.net

Sedan Sedan Times-Star (2.4M) PO Box 417 Sedan KS 67361 **Phn:** 620-725-3176 **Fax:** 620-725-3272

Seneca Seneca Courier-Tribune (3.2M) PO Box 100 Seneca KS 66538 **Phn:** 785-336-2175 **Fax:** 785-336-3475 ctseneca@nvcs.com

Sharon Springs Western Times (4.2M) PO Box 279 Sharon Springs KS 67758 **Phn:** 785-852-4900 www.thewesterntimes.com westerntimes@wbsnet.org

Smith Center Smith County Pioneer (3.2M) 201 S Main St Smith Center KS 66967 **Phn:** 785-282-3371 **Fax:** 785-282-6383 mainstreetmedia.us pioneer@ruraltel.net

Spearville Spearville News (0.8M) PO Box 127 Spearville KS 67876 **Phn:** 620-385-2200 **Fax:** 620-385-2610 spnews@ucom.net

St John St. John News (1.0M) PO Box 488 St John KS 67576 **Phn:** 620-549-3201 **Fax:** 620-549-3829 www.sjnewsonline.com tspradley@sjnewsonline.com

Stafford Stafford Courier (1.8M) PO Box 276 Stafford KS 67578 **Phn:** 620-234-5241 **Fax:** 620-234-5242 www.staffordcourier.com franklys1@sbcglobal.net

Sterling Sterling Bulletin (1.5M) PO Box 97 Sterling KS 67579 **Phn:** 620-278-2114 **Fax:** 620-278-2330 sterlingbulletin.net news@sterlingbulletin.com

Stockton Stockton Sentinel (2.0M) PO Box 521 Stockton KS 67669 **Phn:** 785-425-6354 **Fax:** 785-425-7292 www.stocktonsentinel.com stkpaper@ruraltel.net

Sublette Haskell County Monitor (1.0M) PO Box 489 Sublette KS 67877 **Phn:** 620-675-2204 **Fax:** 620-675-8717

Syracuse Syracuse Journal (1.0M) PO Box 1137 Syracuse KS 67878 **Phn:** 620-384-5640 **Fax:** 620-384-5228 www.thesyracusejournal.com editor@thesyracusejournal.com

Tonganoxie Tonganoxie Mirror (2.8M) PO Box 920 Tonganoxie KS 66086 **Phn:** 913-845-2222 **Fax:** 913-845-9451 www.tonganoxiemirror.com mirror@tonganoxiemirror.com

Topeka Metro News (1.4M) PO Box 1794 Topeka KS 66601 **Phn:** 785-232-8600 **Fax:** 785-235-8707 www.topekametronews.com metro@topekametro.com

Tribune Greeley County Republican (1.6M) PO Box 610 Tribune KS 67879 **Phn:** 620-376-4264 **Fax:** 620-376-2433 newspaper@sunflowertelco.com

Turon The Record (0.8M) PO Box 38 Turon KS 67583 **Phn:** 620-497-6448 record@sctelcom.net

Ulysses Grant Co. Gazette (1.3M) PO Box 279 Ulysses KS 67880 **Phn:** 620-356-1033 **Fax:** 620-424-2772

Ulysses Ulysses News (2.4M) PO Box 706 Ulysses KS 67880 **Phn:** 620-356-1201 **Fax:** 620-356-4610 ulynews@pld.com

Valley Center Ark Valley News (2.2M) PO Box 120 Valley Center KS 67147 **Phn:** 316-755-0821 **Fax:** 316-755-0644 www.arkvalleynews.com news@arkvalleynews.com

Valley Falls Valley Falls Vindicator (2.2M) PO Box 187 Valley Falls KS 66088 **Phn:** 785-945-3257 **Fax:** 785-945-3444 www.jeffcountynews.com vindicator@embarqmail.com

WaKeeney Western Kansas World (1.5M) PO Box 218 WaKeeney KS 67672 **Phn:** 785-743-2155 **Fax:** 785-743-5340 westernkansasworld@yahoo.com

Wamego Smoke Signal (10.0M) PO Box 267 Wamego KS 66547 **Phn:** 785-456-2602 **Fax:** 785-456-8484 www.thewamegosmokesignal.com smokesig@wamego.net

Wamego Wamego Times (4.0M) PO Box 247 Wamego KS 66547 **Phn:** 785-456-7838

Washington Clifton Clyde Tribune (0.6M) PO Box 316 Washington KS 66968 **Phn:** 785-455-3466

Washington Washington County News (3.0M) PO Box 316 Washington KS 66968 **Phn:** 785-325-2219 **Fax:** 785-325-3255 editor@bluevalley.net

Wathena Kansas Chief (2.5M) PO Box 368 Wathena KS 66090 **Phn:** 785-989-4415 **Fax:** 785-989-4416 kschief@carsoncomm.com

Wellington Wellington News (3.2M) PO Box 368 Wellington KS 67152 **Phn:** 620-326-3326 **Fax:** 620-326-3290

Westmoreland Westmoreland Recorder (1.0M) PO Box 343 Westmoreland KS 66549 **Phn:** 785-457-3411 **Fax:** 785-457-3461

White City Prairie Post (1.1M) PO Box 326 White City KS 66872 **Phn:** 785-349-5516 ppost@tctelco.net

Yates Center Yates Center News (1.5M) PO Box 285 Yates Center KS 66783 **Phn:** 620-625-2181 **Fax:** 620-625-2081 ycn@sekansas.com

KENTUCKY

Albany Clinton County News (3.5M) PO Box 360 Albany KY 42602 **Phn:** 606-387-5144 **Fax:** 606-387-7949 clintonnews.net

Barbourville Mountain Advocate (7.3M) PO Box 190 Barbourville KY 40906 **Phn:** 606-546-9225 **Fax:** 606-546-3175

Bardstown Kentucky Standard (10.0M) 110 W Stephen Foster Ave Bardstown KY 40004 **Phn:** 502-348-9003 **Fax:** 502-349-3005 www.kystandard.com news@kystandard.com

Bardwell Carlisle County News (1.8M) PO Box 309 Bardwell KY 42023 **Phn:** 270-628-5490 **Fax:** 270-628-3167 www.ky-news.com kpikelly@gmail.com

Bardwell Carlisle Weekly (1.0M) PO Box 301 Bardwell KY 42023 **Phn:** 270-562-3032 www.carlisleweekly.com weekly@ccky.net

Beattyville Beattyville Enterprise (1.2M) PO Box 126 Beattyville KY 41311 **Phn:** 606-464-2444 **Fax:** 606-464-8858 beattyill@bellsouth.net

Beattyville Three Forks Tradition (3.5M) PO Box 557 Beattyville KY 41311 **Phn:** 606-464-2888 **Fax:** 606-464-2388 www.threeforkstradition.com

Bedford Trimble Banner (1.7M) PO Box 289 Bedford KY 40006 **Phn:** 502-255-3205 **Fax:** 502-255-7797 www.mytrimblenews.com tbeditor@bellsouth.net

Benton The Tribune Courier (5.2M) PO Box 410 Benton KY 42025 **Phn:** 270-527-3162 **Fax:** 270-527-4567 www.tribunecourier.com editor@tribunecourier.com

Berea Berea Citizen (5.2M) PO Box 207 Berea KY 40403 **Phn:** 859-986-0959 **Fax:** 859-986-0960 www.bereacitizen.net bereacitizen@windstream.net

Brandenburg Meade County Messenger (5.6M) PO Box 678 Brandenburg KY 40108 **Phn:** 270-422-2155 **Fax:** 270-422-2110 www.meadecountymessenger.com messenger@bbtel.com

Brooksville Bracken County News (3.0M) PO Box 68 Brooksville KY 41004 **Phn:** 606-735-2198 **Fax:** 606-735-2199 thebrackencountynews.com bcnews@ekns.net

Brownsville Edmonson News (4.0M) PO Box 69 Brownsville KY 42210 **Phn:** 270-597-3115

Burkesville Cumberland Co. News (3.7M) PO Box 307 Burkesville KY 42717 **Phn:** 270-864-3891 **Fax:** 270-864-3497 www.burkesville.com ccn@burkesville.com

Cadiz Cadiz Record (4.8M) PO Box 1670 Cadiz KY 42211 **Phn:** 270-522-6605 **Fax:** 270-522-3001 www.cadizrecord.com news@cadizrecord.com

Calhoun McLean County News (3.2M) PO Box 266 Calhoun KY 42327 **Phn:** 270-273-3287 **Fax:** 270-273-3544 www.mcleannews.com news@mcleannews.com

KENTUCKY WEEKLY NEWSPAPERS

Calvert City The Lake News (3.0M) PO Box 498 Calvert City KY 42029 **Phn:** 270-395-5858 thelakenews.net news@thelakenews.net

Campbellsville Central KY News Journal (7.5M) PO Box 1138 Campbellsville KY 42719 **Phn:** 270-465-8111 **Fax:** 270-465-2500 www.cknj.com publisher@cknj.com

Carrollton News-Democrat (3.5M) PO Box 60 Carrollton KY 41008 **Phn:** 502-732-4261 **Fax:** 502-732-0453 www.mycarrollnews.com ndeditor@bellsouth.net

Central City Central City Times-Argus (2.4M) PO Box 31 Central City KY 42330 **Phn:** 270-754-2331 **Fax:** 270-754-1805 timesargus@bellsouth.net

Clinton Hickman County Gazette (2.1M) PO Box 200 Clinton KY 42031 **Phn:** 270-653-3381 **Fax:** 270-653-3322 gazette3322@bellsouth.net

Columbia Adair Progress (4.9M) PO Box 595 Columbia KY 42728 **Phn:** 270-384-6471 www.adairprogress.com editorial@adairprogress.com

Corbin Corbin News Journal (9.0M) PO Box 1524 Corbin KY 40702 **Phn:** 606-528-9767 **Fax:** 606-528-9779 thenewsjournal.net tknuckles@corbinnewsjournal.com

Cromona Community News-Press (2.8M) PO Box 217 Cromona KY 41810 **Phn:** 606-855-4541 **Fax:** 606-855-9290

Cumberland Tri-City News (2.5M) 105 Central St Cumberland KY 40823 **Phn:** 606-589-2588 **Fax:** 606-589-2589 tricitynews@yahoo.com

Cynthiana Cynthiana Democrat (5.6M) PO Box 160 Cynthiana KY 41031 **Phn:** 859-234-1035 **Fax:** 859-234-8096 www.cynthianademocrat.com bbarnes@cynthianademocrat.com

Dawson Springs Dawson Springs Progress (2.4M) PO Box 460 Dawson Springs KY 42408 **Phn:** 270-797-3271 www.dawsonspringsprogress.com progress@vci.net

Eddyville Herald Ledger (2.0M) PO Box 747 Eddyville KY 42038 **Phn:** 270-388-2269 **Fax:** 270-388-5540 www.heraldledger.com office@heraldledger.com

Edmonton Edmonton Herald-News (2.6M) PO Box 87 Edmonton KY 42129 **Phn:** 270-432-3291 **Fax:** 270-432-4414 heraldnews@jpinews.com

Elizabethtown Hardin County Independent (5.0M) PO Box 1117 Elizabethtown KY 42702 **Phn:** 270-737-5585 **Fax:** 270-737-6634

Elkton Todd County Standard (2.5M) PO Box 308 Elkton KY 42220 **Phn:** 270-265-2439 www.tcstandard.com tcstandard@kypress.com

Eminence Henry County Local (4.3M) 18 S Penn Ave Eminence KY 40019 **Phn:** 502-845-2858 **Fax:** 502-845-2921 www.hclocal.com editor@hclocal.com

Falmouth Falmouth Outlook (4.2M) PO Box 111 Falmouth KY 41040 **Phn:** 859-654-3333 **Fax:** 859-654-4365 www.falmouthoutlook.com news@falmouthoutlook.com

Flemingsburg Flemingsburg Gazette (3.0M) PO Box 32 Flemingsburg KY 41041 **Phn:** 606-845-9211 **Fax:** 606-845-3299

Fort Mitchell Recorder Newspapers (67.0M) 228 Grandview Dr Fort Mitchell KY 41017 **Phn:** 859-283-0404 **Fax:** 859-283-7285 news.communitypress.com ndaly@communitypress.com

Franklin Franklin Favorite (5.5M) 103 N High St Franklin KY 42134 **Phn:** 270-586-4481 **Fax:** 270-586-6031 www.franklinfavorite.com jjohnson@franklinfavorite.com

Fulton Fulton Leader (2.6M) PO Box 1200 Fulton KY 42041 **Phn:** 270-472-1121 **Fax:** 270-472-1129 www.magicvalleypublishing.com leadernews@bellsouth.net

Georgetown Georgetown News Graphic (5.5M) 1481 Cherry Blossom Way Georgetown KY 40324 **Phn:** 502-863-1111 **Fax:** 502-863-6296 www.news-graphic.com news@news-graphic.com

Grayson Journal-Enquirer (8.0M) 211 S Carol Malone Blvd Grayson KY 41143 **Phn:** 606-474-5101 **Fax:** 606-474-0013 journal-times.com

Greensburg Record-Herald (7.9M) PO Box 130 Greensburg KY 42743 **Phn:** 270-932-4381 **Fax:** 270-932-4441 www.record-herald.com news@record-herald.com

Greenup Greenup News-Times (3.0M) 203 Harrison St Greenup KY 41144 **Phn:** 606-473-9851 **Fax:** 606-473-7591 cathieshaffer@zoominternet.net

Hardinsburg Breckinridge Herald-News (6.0M) PO Box 6 Hardinsburg KY 40143 **Phn:** 270-756-2109 **Fax:** 270-756-1003 editorialthn@bbtel.com

Harrodsburg Harrodsburg Herald (5.8M) PO Box 68 Harrodsburg KY 40330 **Phn:** 859-734-2726 **Fax:** 859-734-0737 www.harrodsburgherald.com newsroom@harrodsburgherald.com

Hartford Andy Anderson Corp (16.0M) PO Box 226 Hartford KY 42347 **Phn:** 270-298-7100 **Fax:** 270-298-9572 www.octimesnews.com editor@octimesnews.com

Hawesville Hancock Clarion (3.8M) PO Box 39 Hawesville KY 42348 **Phn:** 270-927-6945 **Fax:** 270-927-6947 www.hancockclarion.com

Hazard Hazard Herald (6.5M) PO Box 869 Hazard KY 41702 **Phn:** 606-436-5771 **Fax:** 606-436-3140 www.hazard-herald.com hheditor@hazard-herald.com

Hickman Hickman Courier (2.0M) PO Box 70 Hickman KY 42050 **Phn:** 270-236-2726

Hindman Troublesome Creek Times (4.5M) PO Box 1500 Hindman KY 41822 **Phn:** 606-785-5134 **Fax:** 606-785-0105 www.troublesomecreektimes.com tct@troublesomecreektimes.com

Hodgenville LaRue Co. Herald News (4.6M) 40 Shawnee Dr Hodgenville KY 42748 **Phn:** 270-358-3118 **Fax:** 270-358-4852 www.laruecountyherald.com editor@laruecountyherald.com

Horse Cave Jobe Publishing Inc (42.0M) PO Box 340 Horse Cave KY 42749 **Phn:** 270-786-2676 **Fax:** 270-786-4470 jpinews.com print@jpinews.com

Hyden Leslie County News (3.8M) PO Box 967 Hyden KY 41749 **Phn:** 606-672-2841 **Fax:** 606-672-7409

Hyden Thousandsticks News (3.5M) PO Box 967 Hyden KY 41749 **Phn:** 606-672-3399 **Fax:** 606-672-7409

Inez Mountain Citizen (6.0M) PO Box 1029 Inez KY 41224 **Phn:** 606-298-7570 **Fax:** 606-298-3711 mountaincitizen@bellsouth.net

Irvine Citizen Voice & Times (7.0M) PO Box 660 Irvine KY 40336 **Phn:** 606-723-5161 **Fax:** 606-723-5509 www.cvt-news.com cvtnews@hatfieldnewspapers.com

Irvine Estill County Tribune (2.0M) 6135 Winchester Rd Irvine KY 40336 **Phn:** 606-723-5012

La Grange Oldham Era (7.0M) PO Box 5 La Grange KY 40031 **Phn:** 502-222-7183 **Fax:** 502-222-7194 www.oldhamera.com editor@oldhamera.com

Lancaster Garrard Central Record (4.5M) PO Box 800 Lancaster KY 40444 **Phn:** 859-792-2831 **Fax:** 859-792-3448 www.garrardcentralrecord.com news@garrardcentralrecord.com

Lawrenceburg The Anderson News (6.1M) PO Box 410 Lawrenceburg KY 40342 **Phn:** 502-839-6906 **Fax:** 502-839-3118 www.theandersonnews.com news@theandersonnews.com

Lebanon Lebanon Enterprise (6.0M) 119 S Proctor Knott Ave Lebanon KY 40033 **Phn:** 270-692-6026 **Fax:** 270-692-2118 www.lebanonenterprise.com

Leitchfield Grayson News Gazette (5.0M) PO Box 305 Leitchfield KY 42755 **Phn:** 270-259-9622 **Fax:** 270-259-5537 www.gcnewsgazette.com tarmstrong@gcnewsgazette.com

Leitchfield Leitchfield Record (3.0M) 209 W White Oak St # C Leitchfield KY 42754 **Phn:** 270-259-6061 **Fax:** 270-230-8405

Lexington Ace Weekly (20.0M) 185 Jefferson St Lexington KY 40508 **Phn:** 859-225-4889 www.aceweekly.com editor@aceweekly.com

Liberty Casey County News (7.0M) PO Box 40 Liberty KY 42539 **Phn:** 606-787-7171 **Fax:** 606-787-8306 www.caseynews.net lrowell@caseynews.net

London London Sentinel Echo (9.9M) PO Box 830 London KY 40743 **Phn:** 606-878-7400 **Fax:** 606-878-7404 www.sentinel-echo.com jdill@sentinel-echo.com

Louisa The Big Sandy News (11.0M) PO Box 766 Louisa KY 41230 **Phn:** 606-788-9962 **Fax:** 606-638-9949 www.bigsandynews.com tony@bigsandynews.com

Louisville Eccentric Observer (40.0M) 640 S 4th St Ste 100 Louisville KY 40202 **Phn:** 502-895-9770 **Fax:** 502-895-9779 leoweekly.com leo@leoweekly.com

Louisville The Voice Tribune (13.5M) 130 Saint Matthews Ave Ste 300 Louisville KY 40207 **Phn:** 502-897-8900 **Fax:** 502-897-8915 www.voice-tribune.com lynnallen@voice-tribune.com

Madisonville Pennyrile Plus (7.0M) PO Box 529 Madisonville KY 42431 **Phn:** 270-824-3300 **Fax:** 270-825-3733 dperryman@the-messenger.com

Manchester Manchester Enterprise (7.0M) PO Box 449 Manchester KY 40962 **Phn:** 606-598-6174 **Fax:** 606-598-2330 manchesterenterprise.proboards.com jphilpot@themanchesterenterprise.com

Marion Crittenden Press (4.5M) PO Box 191 Marion KY 42064 **Phn:** 270-965-3191 **Fax:** 270-965-2516 crittendenpress.blogspot.com information@the-press.com

Mc Kee Jackson County Sun (4.4M) PO Box 130 Mc Kee KY 40447 **Phn:** 606-287-7197 **Fax:** 606-287-7196 www.thejacksoncountysun.com tammy@thejacksoncountysun.com

Monticello Wayne County Outlook (6.0M) PO Box 432 Monticello KY 42633 **Phn:** 606-348-3338 **Fax:** 606-348-8848 wcoutlook.com

Morehead Morehead News (6.6M) 722 W 1st St Morehead KY 40351 **Phn:** 606-784-4116 **Fax:** 606-784-7337 themoreheadnews.com sockerman@themoreheadnews.com

Morganfield Union County Advocate (4.8M) PO Box 370 Morganfield KY 42437 **Phn:** 270-389-1833 **Fax:** 270-389-3926 www.ucadvocate.com

Morgantown Banner-Republican (6.0M) PO Box 219 Morgantown KY 42261 **Phn:** 270-526-4151 **Fax:** 270-526-3111

Mount Sterling Mt. Sterling Advocate (7.0M) PO Box 406 Mount Sterling KY 40353 **Phn:** 859-498-2222 **Fax:** 859-498-2228 www.msadvocate.com news@msadvocate.com

Mount Vernon The Banner (9.5M) 35 Lovell Ln Mount Vernon KY 40456 **Phn:** 606-256-9144 www.thebanner.us bannernewspaper@aol.com

Nicholasville Jessamine Journal (6.4M) 507 N Main St Nicholasville KY 40356 **Phn:** 859-885-5381 **Fax:** 859-887-2966 www.centralkynews.com/jessaminejournal news@jessaminejournal.com

Olive Hill Olive Hill Times (6.0M) PO Box 484 Olive Hill KY 41164 **Phn:** 606-286-4201   journal-times.com circulation@journal-times.com

Owenton The News Herald (4.4M) PO Box 219 Owenton KY 40359 **Phn:** 502-484-3431 **Fax:** 502-484-3221   www.owentonnewsherald.com jwhitlock@owentonnewsherald.com

Owingsville Bath County News Outlook (3.5M) PO Box 577 Owingsville KY 40360 **Phn:** 606-674-2181 **Fax:** 606-674-9994

Paducah Kentucky Publishing Inc (39.0M) PO Box 1135 Paducah KY 42002 **Phn:** 270-442-7389 **Fax:** 270-442-5220 ky-news.com kpikelly@gmail.com

Paintsville Paintsville Herald (6.0M) PO Box 1547 Paintsville KY 41240 **Phn:** 606-789-5315 **Fax:** 606-789-9717   www.paintsvilleherald.com news@paintsvilleherald.com

Paris Bourbon County Citizen (3.0M) PO Box 158 Paris KY 40362 **Phn:** 859-987-1870 **Fax:** 859-987-3729

Pineville Sun-Cumberland Courier (3.0M) PO Box 250 Pineville KY 40977 **Phn:** 606-337-2333 **Fax:** 606-337-2360

Prestonsburg Floyd County Times (8.6M) PO Box 390 Prestonsburg KY 41653 **Phn:** 606-886-8506 **Fax:** 606-886-3603   www.floydcountytimes.com web@floydcountytimes.com

Princeton The Times-Leader (6.1M) PO Box 439 Princeton KY 42445 **Phn:** 270-365-5588 **Fax:** 270-365-7299 www.timesleader.net newsroom@timesleader.net

Providence The Journal-Enterprise (4.8M) PO Box 190 Providence KY 42450 **Phn:** 270-667-2068 **Fax:** 270-667-9160   journalenterprise.com matt@journalenterprise.com

Radcliff The Sentinel (3.4M) 1558 Hill St Radcliff KY 40160 **Phn:** 270-351-4407

Russell Springs Russell County News (9.0M) PO Box 190 Russell Springs KY 42642 **Phn:** 270-866-3191 **Fax:** 270-866-3198 russellcounty.net

Russell Springs The Times Journal (4.6M) PO Box 190 Russell Springs KY 42642 **Phn:** 270-866-3191 **Fax:** 270-866-3198 russellcounty.net

Russellville News Democrat & Leader (6.8M) PO Box 270 Russellville KY 42276 **Phn:** 270-726-8394 **Fax:** 270-726-8398   www.newsdemocratleader.com ccooper@newsdemocratleader.com

Salyersville Salyersville Independent (4.8M) PO Box 29 Salyersville KY 41465 **Phn:** 606-349-2915 **Fax:** 888-704-6789   salyersvilleindependent.com heather@salyersvilleindependent.com

Scottsville The Citizen Times (5.6M) PO Box 310 Scottsville KY 42164 **Phn:** 270-237-3441 **Fax:** 270-237-4943 www.thecitizen-times.com ctimes@nctc.com

Sebree Sebree Banner (3.8M) PO Box 36 Sebree KY 42455 **Phn:** 270-835-7521 **Fax:** 270-835-9521 sebreebanner@bellsouth.net

Shelbyville Sentinel News (7.8M) PO Box 399 Shelbyville KY 40066 **Phn:** 502-633-2526 **Fax:** 502-633-2618   www.sentinelnews.com sdoyle@sentinelnews.com

Shepherdsville The Pioneer News (8.4M) PO Box 98 Shepherdsville KY 40165 **Phn:** 502-543-2288 **Fax:** 502-955-9704   www.pioneernews.net editor@pioneernews.net

Springfield Springfield Sun (4.5M) PO Box 31 Springfield KY 40069 **Phn:** 859-336-3716 **Fax:** 859-336-7718   www.thespringfieldsun.com editor@thespringfieldsun.com

KENTUCKY WEEKLY NEWSPAPERS

Stanford The Interior Journal (4.2M) 713 E Main St # A Stanford KY 40484 **Phn:** 606-365-2104 **Fax:** 606-365-2105   www.centralkynews.com/theinteriorjournal sschurz@amnews.com

Stanton Clay City Times (3.6M) PO Box 547 Stanton KY 40380 **Phn:** 606-663-5540 **Fax:** 606-663-6397 www.claycity-times.com cctimesnews@bellsouth.net

Sturgis Sturgis News (3.5M) PO Box 218 Sturgis KY 42459 **Phn:** 270-333-5545 **Fax:** 270-835-9521

Taylorsville Spencer Magnet (3.1M) PO Box 219 Taylorsville KY 40071 **Phn:** 502-477-2239 **Fax:** 502-477-2110   www.spencermagnet.com editor@spencermagnet.com

Tompkinsville Tompkinsville News (4.6M) 105 N Main St Tompkinsville KY 42167 **Phn:** 270-487-5576 www.tompkinsvillenews.com catchall@tompkinsvillenews.com

Vanceburg Lewis County Herald (4.4M) 187 Main St Vanceburg KY 41179 **Phn:** 606-796-2331 **Fax:** 606-796-3110   www.lewiscountyherald.com heraldadvertising@yahoo.com

Versailles Woodford Sun (5.5M) PO Box 29 Versailles KY 40383 **Phn:** 859-873-4131 **Fax:** 859-873-0300 www.woodfordsun.com news@woodfordsun.com

Warsaw Gallatin County News (3.0M) PO Box 435 Warsaw KY 41095 **Phn:** 859-567-5051 **Fax:** 859-567-6397 galnews@zoomtown.com

West Liberty Courier Publishing (8.0M) PO Box 187 West Liberty KY 41472 **Phn:** 606-743-3551 **Fax:** 606-743-3565

Whitesburg Mountain Eagle (6.8M) PO Box 808 Whitesburg KY 41858 **Phn:** 606-633-2252 **Fax:** 606-633-2843   www.themountaineagle.com mtneagle@bellsouth.net

Whitley City McCreary County Record (5.4M) PO Box 9 Whitley City KY 42653 **Phn:** 606-376-5356 **Fax:** 606-376-9565   mccrearyrecord.com news@mccrearyrecord.com

Whitley City McCreary County Voice (6.0M) PO Box 190 Whitley City KY 42653 **Phn:** 606-376-5500 **Fax:** 606-376-8609 https://sites.google.com/site/themccrearycountyvoice editor@tmcvoice.com

Williamstown Grant County News (5.0M) PO Box 247 Williamstown KY 41097 **Phn:** 859-824-3344 **Fax:** 859-824-5888 www.grantky.com kstone@grantky.com

LOUISIANA

Amite Tangi Digest (2.0M) PO Box 698 Amite LA 70422 **Phn:** 985-748-7156 **Fax:** 985-748-7104 www.tangilena.com mark.mathes@tangilena.com

Arabi St. Bernard Voice (22.0M) 234 Mehle St Arabi LA 70032 **Phn:** 504-279-7488 **Fax:** 504-309-5532 thestbernardvoice.com terri@thestbernardvoice.com

Arabi St. Bernard Voice (3.0M) PO Box 88 Arabi LA 70032 **Phn:** 504-279-7488 **Fax:** 504-309-5532 thestbernardvoice.com terri@thestbernardvoice.com

Arcadia Bienville Democrat (3.1M) PO Box 29 Arcadia LA 71001 **Phn:** 318-263-2922 **Fax:** 318-263-8897

Arcadia Ringgold Progress (10.0M) PO Box 29 Arcadia LA 71001 **Phn:** 318-263-2922

Basile Basile Weekly (1.4M) PO Box 578 Basile LA 70515 **Phn:** 337-432-6807 thebasileweekly@hotmail.com

Belle Chasse Plaquemines Gazette (3.5M) PO Box 700 Belle Chasse LA 70037 **Phn:** 504-392-1619 **Fax:** 504-392-7526   plaqueminesgazette.com ads@plaqueminesgazette.com

Bernice The Banner (2.5M) 227 Boyette Rd Bernice LA 71222 **Phn:** 318-285-7424 **Fax:** 318-285-7420 bernicebanner@oeccwildblue.com

Bossier City Bossier Press-Tribune (20.0M) 4250 Viking Dr Bossier City LA 71111 **Phn:** 318-747-7900 **Fax:** 318-747-5298   www.bossierpress.com dspecht@bossierpress.com

Boutte St Charles Herald Guide (6.0M) PO Box 1199 Boutte LA 70039 **Phn:** 985-758-2795 **Fax:** 985-758-7000 www.heraldguide.com editor@heraldguide.com

Bunkie Bunkie Record (1.5M) PO Box 179 Bunkie LA 71322 **Phn:** 318-346-7251 **Fax:** 318-346-7253 bunkierecord@yahoo.com

Church Point Church Point News (1.6M) PO Box 319 Church Point LA 70525 **Phn:** 337-684-5711 **Fax:** 337-684-5793 cpnews@centurytel.net

City of Central Central Speaks (8.0M) PO Box 78137 City of Central LA 70837 **Phn:** 225-262-3730 **Fax:** 888-220-8396   www.centralspeaks.com editor@centralspeaks.com

Clinton East Feliciana Watchman (7.0M) PO Box 368 Clinton LA 70722 **Phn:** 225-683-5195 bmstaton808@yahoo.com

Colfax The Chronicle (2.8M) 305 Main St Colfax LA 71417 **Phn:** 318-627-3737 **Fax:** 318-627-3019 mwchronicle@aol.com

Columbia Caldwell Watchman (2.0M) PO Box 1269 Columbia LA 71418 **Phn:** 318-649-6411 **Fax:** 318-649-7776

Columbia News Journal (8.0M) PO Box 911 Columbia LA 71418 **Phn:** 318-649-7136 **Fax:** 318-649-7776 caldwellwatchman@bellsouth.net

Coushatta Coushatta Citizen (3.0M) PO Box 1365 Coushatta LA 71019 **Phn:** 318-932-4201 **Fax:** 318-932-4285 news@coushattacitizen.com

Covington St. Tammany Farmer (4.1M) PO Box 269 Covington LA 70434 **Phn:** 985-892-2323 **Fax:** 985-892-2325

Denham Springs Livingston Parish News (10.5M) PO Box 1529 Denham Springs LA 70727 **Phn:** 225-665-5176 **Fax:** 225-667-0167 livingstonparishnews.com editor@livingstonparishnews.com

DeQuincy Cameron Parish Pilot (3.8M) PO Box 995 DeQuincy LA 70633 **Phn:** 337-786-8004 **Fax:** 337-786-8131   www.dequincynews.com deqnews@centurytel.net

Dequincy De Quincy News (4.0M) PO Box 995 Dequincy LA 70633 **Phn:** 337-786-8004 **Fax:** 337-786-8131   www.dequincynews.com deqnews@centurytel.net

Donaldsonville Donaldsonville Chief (2.5M) PO Box 309 Donaldsonville LA 70346 **Phn:** 225-473-3101 **Fax:** 225-473-4060   www.donaldsonvillechief.com editor@dvillechief.brcoxmail.com

Eunice Eunice News (3.4M) PO Box 989 Eunice LA 70535 **Phn:** 337-457-3061 **Fax:** 337-457-3122 www.eunicetoday.com

Farmerville Farmerville Gazette (3.8M) PO Box 722 Farmerville LA 71241 **Phn:** 318-368-9732 **Fax:** 318-368-7331 www.fgazette.com fgazette@bellsouth.net

Ferriday Concordia Sentinel (4.7M) PO Box 1485 Ferriday LA 71334 **Phn:** 318-322-3161 **Fax:** 318-757-3001   www.hannapub.com/concordiasentinel hostmaster@hannapub.com

Franklinton Franklinton Era-Leader (3.6M) PO Box F Franklinton LA 70438 **Phn:** 985-839-9077 **Fax:** 985-839-9096

Gonzales Weekly Citizen (4.5M) 231 W Cornerview St Gonzales LA 70737 **Phn:** 225-644-6397 **Fax:** 225-644-2069 www.weeklycitizen.com editor@weeklycitizen.com

Greenwell Springs Central City News (5.0M) PO Box 1 Greenwell Springs LA 70739 **Phn:** 225-261-5055 **Fax:** 225-261-5022 centralcitynews@hotmail.com

Gueydan Gueydan Journal (1.0M) PO Box 536 Gueydan LA 70542 **Phn:** 337-536-6016 **Fax:** 337-536-9997 gueydanjournal@bellsouth.net

Homer Haynesville News (2.4M) PO Box 117 Homer LA 71040 **Phn:** 318-927-3721 news@haynesvillenews.com

Homer The Guardian Journal (3.0M) PO Box 119 Homer LA 71040 **Phn:** 318-927-3541 **Fax:** 318-927-3542 guardianjournal@aol.com

Jena Jena Times-Signal (4.5M) PO Box 3050 Jena LA 71342 **Phn:** 318-992-4121 **Fax:** 318-992-2287 www.thejenatimes.net editor@thejenatimes.net

Jonesboro Jackson Independent (3.5M) 624 Hudson Ave Jonesboro LA 71251 **Phn:** 318-259-2551 **Fax:** 318-259-8537

Jonesville Catahoula News Booster (3.0M) PO Box 188 Jonesville LA 71343 **Phn:** 318-339-7242 **Fax:** 318-339-7243 newsbooster@bellsouth.net

Kaplan Kaplan Herald (1.9M) 219 N Cushing Ave Kaplan LA 70548 **Phn:** 337-643-8002 **Fax:** 337-643-1382 www.kaplantoday.com

Kentwood News Ledger (1.2M) PO Box 930 Kentwood LA 70444 **Phn:** 985-229-8607 **Fax:** 985-229-8698 www.kentwoodtoday.com editor.newsledger@tangilena.com

Kinder Kinder Courier-News (1.3M) PO Box AK Kinder LA 70648 **Phn:** 337-738-5642 **Fax:** 337-738-5630 kindernews@centurytel.net

La Place L'Observateur (5.0M) 116 Newspaper Dr La Place LA 70068 **Phn:** 985-652-9545 **Fax:** 985-652-3885 www.lobservateur.com lobnews@bellsouth.net

Lafayette The Independent Weekly (21.0M) 551 Jefferson St Lafayette LA 70501 **Phn:** 337-988-4607 **Fax:** 337-983-0150 www.theind.com indbox@theind.com

Lafayette Times Of Acadiana (32.0M) 1100 Bertrand Dr Lafayette LA 70506 **Phn:** 337-237-3560 **Fax:** 337-289-6443 www.theadvertiser.com news@theadvertiser.com

Lake Arthur Sun-Times (1.0M) PO Box 670 Lake Arthur LA 70549 **Phn:** 337-774-2527 **Fax:** 337-774-3121 www.lakearthurtoday.com

Lake Charles The Times of SW LA (16.0M) 617 Drew St Lake Charles LA 70601 **Phn:** 337-439-0995 **Fax:** 337-439-0418 www.timessw.com

Lake Providence The Banner-Democrat (2.2M) 313 Lake St Lake Providence LA 71254 **Phn:** 318-559-2750

Larose La Fourche Gazette (14.9M) PO Box 1450 Larose LA 70373 **Phn:** 985-693-7229 **Fax:** 985-693-8282 tlgnewspaper.com news@tlgnewspaper.com

Lutcher Lutcher News Examiner (3.9M) PO Box 460 Lutcher LA 70071 **Phn:** 225-869-5784 **Fax:** 225-869-4386

Mansfield Enterprise & Interstate Progress (4.5M) PO Box 840 Mansfield LA 71052 **Phn:** 318-872-4120 **Fax:** 318-872-6038 enterprise@wnonline.net

Many The Sabine Index (6.5M) PO Box 25 Many LA 71449 **Phn:** 318-256-3495 **Fax:** 318-256-9151 www.thesabineindex.com

Marksville Avoyelles Journal (16.0M) PO Box 36 Marksville LA 71351 **Phn:** 318-253-5413 **Fax:** 318-253-7223 avoyellesjournal@yahoo.com

Marksville Marksville Weekly News (2.3M) PO Box 36 Marksville LA 71351 **Phn:** 318-253-5413 **Fax:** 318-253-7223

Morgan City St. Mary Journal (10.0M) PO Box 31 Morgan City LA 70381 **Phn:** 985-384-1350 **Fax:** 985-384-4255

Napoleonville Assumption Pioneer (2.7M) PO Box 460 Napoleonville LA 70390 **Phn:** 985-369-7153 **Fax:** 985-369-7157 www.theassumptionpioneer.com assumptionpio172@bellsouth.net

New Orleans Gambit (40.0M) 3923 Bienville St New Orleans LA 70119 **Phn:** 504-486-5900 **Fax:** 504-483-3116 www.bestofneworleans.com response@gambitweekly.com

New Roads Pointe Coupee Banner (5.0M) PO Box 400 New Roads LA 70760 **Phn:** 225-638-7155 **Fax:** 225-638-8442

Oak Grove West Carroll Gazette (2.5M) PO Box 1007 Oak Grove LA 71263 **Phn:** 318-428-3207 **Fax:** 318-428-2747

Oakdale Oakdale Journal (2.1M) 231 E 6th Ave Oakdale LA 71463 **Phn:** 318-335-0635 **Fax:** 318-335-0431 oakdalejournal@bellsouth.net

Pierre Part Cajun Gazette (2.5M) PO Box 160 Pierre Part LA 70339 **Phn:** 985-252-6835 **Fax:** 985-252-3836

Plaquemine Post South (4.5M) PO Box 589 Plaquemine LA 70765 **Phn:** 225-687-3288 **Fax:** 225-687-1814 www.postsouth.com

Ponchatoula Ponchatoula Enterprise (2.1M) PO Box 218 Ponchatoula LA 70454 **Phn:** 985-386-6537

Ponchatoula The Ponchatoula Times (7.2M) PO Box 743 Ponchatoula LA 70454 **Phn:** 985-386-2877 **Fax:** 985-386-0458 www.ponchatoula.com/ptimes editor@ponchatoula.com

Port Allen West Side Journal (3.5M) PO Box 260 Port Allen LA 70767 **Phn:** 225-343-2540 **Fax:** 225-344-0923 www.thewestsidejournal.com editor@thewestsidejournal.com

Rayne Rayne Acadian Tribune (2.6M) PO Box 260 Rayne LA 70578 **Phn:** 337-334-3186 **Fax:** 337-334-8474 www.raynetoday.com raynenews@cox-internet.com

Rayne Rayne Independent (3.8M) PO Box 428 Rayne LA 70578 **Phn:** 337-334-2128 **Fax:** 337-334-2120

Rayville Delhi Dispatch (1.2M) PO Box 209 Rayville LA 71269 **Phn:** 318-728-2250 **Fax:** 318-728-5991

Rayville Richland News (3.0M) PO Box 209 Rayville LA 71269 **Phn:** 318-728-2250 **Fax:** 318-728-5991

Ruston Morning Paper (4.0M) PO Box 883 Ruston LA 71273 **Phn:** 318-255-3747

Saint Francisville The St. Francisville Democrat (2.0M) PO Box 1876 Saint Francisville LA 70775 **Phn:** 225-635-3366 **Fax:** 225-635-3398 www.felicianatoday.com erin.foster@felicianatoday.com

Saint Joseph Tensas Gazette (0.8M) PO Box 25 Saint Joseph LA 71366 **Phn:** 318-766-3258 **Fax:** 318-766-4273 tensasgazette@bellsouth.net

Saint Martinville Breaux Bridge Marketplace (9.6M) PO Box 69 Saint Martinville LA 70582 **Phn:** 337-394-6232 **Fax:** 337-394-7511 t_news@bellsouth.net

Saint Martinville Teche News (5.7M) PO Box 69 Saint Martinville LA 70582 **Phn:** 337-394-6232 **Fax:** 337-394-7511 techetoday.com t_news@bellsouth.net

Shreveport The Inquisitor (12.8M) 7781 Highway 1 Shreveport LA 71107 **Phn:** 318-929-5152 **Fax:** 318-309-8966 www.theinquisitor.com dannylawler@cmaaccess.com

Springhill Springhill Press (4.0M) PO Box 669 Springhill LA 71075 **Phn:** 318-539-3511 **Fax:** 318-539-3512 nattimes@wnonline.net

Sulphur Vinton News (2.3M) PO Box 1999 Sulphur LA 70664 **Phn:** 337-527-7075 **Fax:** 337-528-3044 sdneditorial@yahoo.com

Tallulah Madison Journal (2.8M) PO Box 791 Tallulah LA 71284 **Phn:** 318-574-1404 **Fax:** 318-574-4219 www.madisonjournal.com

Vacherie Vacherie Enterprise (1.7M) PO Box 9 Vacherie LA 70090 **Phn:** 225-265-2120

Ville Platte Acadian Press (2.5M) PO Box 220 Ville Platte LA 70586 **Phn:** 337-363-3939 **Fax:** 337-363-2841 vpgaz@centurytel.net

Ville Platte Ville Platte Gazette (4.0M) PO Box 220 Ville Platte LA 70586 **Phn:** 337-363-3939 **Fax:** 337-363-2841 villeplattetoday.com publisher.vp@centurytel.net

Vivian Caddo Citizen (1.3M) 203 S Spruce St Vivian LA 71082 **Phn:** 318-375-3294 **Fax:** 318-375-3308 caddocitizen@centurytel.net

Welsh Welsh Citizen (2.5M) PO Box 706 Welsh LA 70591 **Phn:** 337-734-2891 **Fax:** 337-734-4457 www.welshtoday.com

West Monroe Ouachita Citizen (5.4M) 1400 N 7th St West Monroe LA 71291 **Phn:** 318-322-3161 **Fax:** 318-325-2285 www.hannapub.com/ouachitacitizen news@ouachitacitizen.com

Winnfield Winn Parish Enterprise (3.8M) PO Box 750 Winnfield LA 71483 **Phn:** 318-628-2712 **Fax:** 318-628-6196 news@winnparishenterprise.com

Winnsboro Franklin Sun (6.0M) 514 Prairie St Winnsboro LA 71295 **Phn:** 318-435-4521 **Fax:** 318-435-9220 www.hannapub.com/franklinsun hostmaster@hannapub.com

Zachary Baker Observer (0.5M) 5333 Main St Zachary LA 70791 **Phn:** 225-775-2315

Zachary Zachary Plainsman (2.0M) 2060 Church St Zachary LA 70791 **Phn:** 225-654-6841 **Fax:** 225-654-8271 zacharytoday.com stacy.gill@zacharytoday.com

MAINE

Auburn Twin City Times (25.0M) 33 Dunn St Auburn ME 04210 **Phn:** 207-795-5017 **Fax:** 207-782-9579 www.twincitytimes.com editor@twincitytimes.com

Augusta Capital Weekly (4.4M) PO Box 2788 Augusta ME 04338 **Phn:** 207-621-6000 **Fax:** 207-621-6006

Bangor The Weekly (40.0M) PO Box 1329 Bangor ME 04402 **Phn:** 207-990-8139 **Fax:** 207-941-9476 www.bangordailynews.com weekly@bangordailynews.com

Bar Harbor Bar Harbor Times (8.0M) 74 Cottage St Bar Harbor ME 04609 **Phn:** 207-288-3311 **Fax:** 207-288-5813

Bar Harbor Mount Desert Islander (5.0M) 310 Main St Bar Harbor ME 04609 **Phn:** 207-288-0556 **Fax:** 207-288-0559 mdislander.com news@mdislander.com

Bath Coastal Journal (20.0M) 97 Commercial St Bath ME 04530 **Phn:** 207-443-6241 **Fax:** 207-443-5605 www.coastaljournal.com editor@coastaljournal.com

Bath Maine Switch (18.0M) 832 Washington St Ste 3 Bath ME 04530 **Phn:** 207-781-2283

Belfast Republican Journal (27.0M) PO Box 327 Belfast ME 04915 **Phn:** 207-338-3333 **Fax:** 207-338-5498

Belfast Village Soup Citizen (14.0M) 71 High St Belfast ME 04915 **Phn:** 207-338-0484 **Fax:** 207-338-3491 www.villagesoup.com news@villagesoup.com

Belfast Waldo County Independent (5.0M) PO Box 327 Belfast ME 04915 **Phn:** 207-338-5100

Bethel Bethel Citizen (3.2M) PO Box 109 Bethel ME 04217 **Phn:** 207-824-2444 **Fax:** 207-824-2426 www.bethelcitizen.com news@bethelcitizen.com

Biddeford Mainley Newspapers (75.0M) PO Box 1894 Biddeford ME 04005 Phn: 207-282-4337 **Fax:** 207-282-4339 www.mainelymediallc.com news@inthecourier.com

Blue Hill The Weekly Packet (2.1M) PO Box 646 Blue Hill ME 04614 **Phn:** 207-374-2341 **Fax:** 207-374-2343 www.penobscotbaypress.com wp@penobscotbaypress.com

Boothbay Harbor Boothbay Register (5.7M) PO Box 357 Boothbay Harbor ME 04538 **Phn:** 207-633-4620 **Fax:** 207-633-7123 www.boothbayregister.com kburnham@boothbayregister.com

Bridgton The Bridgton News (7.2M) PO Box 244 Bridgton ME 04009 **Phn:** 207-647-2851 **Fax:** 207-647-5001 bnews@roadrunner.com

Bucksport The Bucksport Enterprise (2.3M) PO Box 829 Bucksport ME 04416 **Phn:** 207-469-6722 **Fax:** 207-469-2114

Calais Calais Advertiser (4.5M) PO Box 660 Calais ME 04619 **Phn:** 207-454-3561 **Fax:** 207-454-3458 www.thecalaisadvertiser.com calaisadvertiser@myfairpoint.net

Camden Camden Herald (5.4M) PO Box 248 Camden ME 04843 **Phn:** 207-236-8511 **Fax:** 207-236-2816

Cape Elizabeth The Cape Courier (4.6M) PO Box 6242 Cape Elizabeth ME 04107 **Phn:** 207-767-5023 www.capecourier.com editor@capecourier.com

Caribou Aroostook Republican (5.2M) PO Box 608 Caribou ME 04736 **Phn:** 207-496-3251 **Fax:** 207-492-4351 republican@nepublish.com

Castine Castine Patriot (0.9M) PO Box 205 Castine ME 04421 **Phn:** 207-326-9300 **Fax:** 207-326-4383 penobscotbaypress.com cp@penobscotbaypress.com

Cutler Downeast Coastal Press (3.5M) 2413 Cutler Rd Cutler ME 04626 **Phn:** 207-259-7751 **Fax:** 207-259-2026 downeastcoastal@earthlink.net

Damariscotta Lincoln County News (7.5M) PO Box 36 Damariscotta ME 04543 **Phn:** 207-563-3171 **Fax:** 207-563-3127 lincolncountynewsonline.com lcn@lincoln.midcoast.com

Dexter The Eastern Gazette (17.0M) PO Box 306 Dexter ME 04930 **Phn:** 207-924-7402

Dover Foxcroft Piscataquis Observer (4.2M) PO Box 30 Dover Foxcroft ME 04426 **Phn:** 207-564-8355 **Fax:** 207-564-7056 observer@nepublish.com

Eastport Quoddy Tides (5.0M) PO Box 213 Eastport ME 04631 **Phn:** 207-853-4806 **Fax:** 207-853-4095 www.quoddytides.com qtides@midmaine.com

Ellsworth The Ellsworth American (11.0M) 30 Water St Ellsworth ME 04605 **Phn:** 207-667-2576 **Fax:** 207-667-7656 ellsworthamerican.com news@ellsworthamerican.com

Falmouth The Forecaster (60.0M) 5 Fundy Rd Ste 1 Falmouth ME 04105 **Phn:** 207-781-3661 **Fax:** 207-781-2060 www.theforecaster.net editor@theforecaster.net

Farmingdale Community Advertiser (13.0M) 20 Peter Path Farmingdale ME 04344 **Phn:** 207-582-8486 www.comadvertiser.com ads@comadvertiser.com

Farmington The Franklin Journal (4.2M) PO Box 750 Farmington ME 04938 **Phn:** 207-778-2075 **Fax:** 207-778-6970 editor@thefranklinjournal.com

MAINE WEEKLY NEWSPAPERS

Gorham Gorham Times (4.2M) PO Box 401 Gorham ME 04038 **Phn:** 207-839-8390 www.gorhamtimes.com gtimes@maine.rr.com

Gray Gray News (4.0M) PO Box 433 Gray ME 04039 **Phn:** 207-657-2200

Greenville Junction Moosehead Messenger (5.0M) PO Box 400 Greenville Junction ME 04442 **Phn:** 207-695-3077 **Fax:** 207-695-3780

Houlton Houlton Pioneer Times (5.1M) PO Box 456 Houlton ME 04730 **Phn:** 207-532-2281 **Fax:** 207-532-2403 www.pioneertimes-me.com pioneertimes@nepublish.com

Kennebunk York County Coast Star (9.0M) PO Box 979 Kennebunk ME 04043 **Phn:** 207-985-5915 **Fax:** 207-985-9050 www.seacoastonline.com yccs@seacoastonline.com

Kingfield Original Irregular (3.5M) PO Box 616 Kingfield ME 04947 **Phn:** 207-265-2773 **Fax:** 207-265-2775 www.theirregular.com theirregular@tds.net

Lincoln Lincoln News (6.3M) PO Box 35 Lincoln ME 04457 **Phn:** 207-794-6532 **Fax:** 207-794-2004 lincnews.com news@lincnews.com

Livermore Falls Livermore Falls Advertiser (2.0M) PO Box B Livermore Falls ME 04254 **Phn:** 207-897-4321 **Fax:** 207-897-4322

Machias Machias Valley News-Observer (2.5M) PO Box 357 Machias ME 04654 **Phn:** 207-255-6561 **Fax:** 207-255-4058 www.machiasnews.com editor@machiasnews.com

Madawaska St. John Valley Times (6.5M) PO Box 419 Madawaska ME 04756 **Phn:** 207-728-3336 **Fax:** 207-728-3825 www.sjvalley-times.com publisher@sjvalley-times.com

Millinocket Katahdin Press (3.6M) 70 Spring St Millinocket ME 04462 **Phn:** 207-723-8118

Newport Rolling Thunder Express (16.0M) PO Box 480 Newport ME 04953 **Phn:** 207-368-2028 **Fax:** 207-368-5513 www.rollingthunderexpress.com info@rollingthunderexpress.com

Norway Advertiser Democrat (5.0M) PO Box 269 Norway ME 04268 **Phn:** 207-743-7011 **Fax:** 207-743-2256 www.advertiserdemocrat.com asheehan@advertiserdemocrat.com

Old Town Penobscott Times (4.5M) PO Box 568 Old Town ME 04468 **Phn:** 207-827-4451 **Fax:** 207-827-2280

Portland Portland Phoenix (40.0M) 16 York St Ste 102 Portland ME 04101 **Phn:** 207-773-8900 **Fax:** 207-773-8905 thephoenix.com letters@phx.com

Presque Isle Star Herald (7.0M) PO Box 510 Presque Isle ME 04769 **Phn:** 207-768-5431 **Fax:** 207-764-7585 www.starherald-me.com starherald@nepublish.com

Rangeley Rangeley Highlander (2.5M) PO Box 542 Rangeley ME 04970 **Phn:** 207-864-3756 **Fax:** 207-864-2447 info@therangeleyhighlander.com

Rockland Courier Gazette (8.2M) PO Box 249 Rockland ME 04841 **Phn:** 207-594-4401 **Fax:** 207-596-6981

Rockland The Free Press (13.0M) 8 N Main St Rockland ME 04841 **Phn:** 207-596-0055 **Fax:** 207-596-6698 www.freepressonline.com freepress@freepressonline.com

Rockland Village Soup (16.0M) PO Box 249 Rockland ME 04841 **Phn:** 207-594-5351 **Fax:** 207-594-5481 www.villagesoup.com news@villagesoup.com

Rumford Rumford Falls Times (5.1M) 69 Congress St Rumford ME 04276 **Phn:** 207-364-7893 **Fax:** 207-369-0170 www.rumfordfallstimes.com editor@rumfordfallstimes.com

Saco Weekly Observer (14.0M) 26 Common St Saco ME 04072 **Phn:** 207-283-1878 **Fax:** 207-854-0018 www.keepmecurrent.com bbragdon@keepmecurrent.com

Sanford Sanford News (6.5M) 835 Main St Sanford ME 04073 **Phn:** 207-324-5986 **Fax:** 207-490-1431 news@sanfordnews.com

South China Town Line (15.0M) PO Box 89 South China ME 04358 **Phn:** 207-445-2234 **Fax:** 207-445-2265 townline.org townline@fairpoint.net

Stonington Island Ad-Vantages (2.7M) PO Box 36 Stonington ME 04681 **Phn:** 207-367-2200 **Fax:** 207-367-6397 www.penobscotbaypress.com ia@penobscotbaypress.com

Westbrook American Journal (7.0M) PO Box 840 Westbrook ME 04098 **Phn:** 207-854-2577 **Fax:** 207-854-0018 www.keepmecurrent.com

Westbrook Suburban Weekly (10.0M) 840 Main St Westbrook ME 04092 **Phn:** 207-892-1166 **Fax:** 207-854-0018 www.keepmecurrent.com

Westbrook Sun Chronicle (20.0M) PO Box 840 Westbrook ME 04098 **Phn:** 207-283-1878 **Fax:** 207-854-0018 www.keepmecurrent.com news@keepmecurrent.com

Westbrook The Current (13.0M) PO Box 840 Westbrook ME 04098 **Phn:** 207-854-2577 **Fax:** 207-856-5530 www.keepmecurrent.com

Windham The Independent (9.0M) 57 Tandberg Trl Ste 2 Windham ME 04062 **Phn:** 207-892-6063 **Fax:** 207-892-6058 www.independentpub.com cgilding@independentpub.com

Wiscasset Wicasset Newspaper (1.4M) PO Box 429 Wiscasset ME 04578 **Phn:** 207-882-6355 **Fax:** 207-633-7123 www.wiscassetnewspaper.com newsdesk@wiscassetnewspaper.com

Yarmouth The Notes (14.0M) PO Box 905 Yarmouth ME 04096 **Phn:** 207-846-4112 **Fax:** 207-846-6828 www.thenotes.org thenotes@maine.rr.com

York York Independent (2.4M) 4 Market Place Dr Ste 215 York ME 03909 **Phn:** 207-363-8484 **Fax:** 207-363-9797 www.yorkindependent.net news@hippopress.com

York York Weekly (5.3M) PO Box 7 York ME 03909 **Phn:** 207-363-4343 **Fax:** 207-351-2849 www.seacoastonline.com yorkweekly@seacoastonline.com

MARYLAND

Alexandria Potomac Almanac (17.0M) 1606 King St Alexandria VA 22314 **Phn:** 703-778-0410 **Fax:** 703-778-9445 www.connectionnewspapers.com smauren@connectionnewspapers.com

Annapolis Bay Weekly (20.0M) 1160 Spa Rd # 1A Annapolis MD 21403 **Phn:** 410-626-9888 **Fax:** 410-626-0008 bayweekly.com editor@bayweekly.com

Annapolis Bowie Blade-News (13.5M) 2000 Capital Dr Annapolis MD 21401 **Phn:** 410-280-5954 **Fax:** 410-280-5953 www.capitalgazette.com demanuel@bladenews.com

Annapolis Maryland Gazette (33.0M) 2000 Capital Dr Annapolis MD 21401 **Phn:** 410-766-3700 **Fax:** 410-766-7031 www.capitalgazette.com rhutzell@capitalgazette.com

Annapolis West County News (15.0M) PO Box 911 Annapolis MD 21404 **Phn:** 410-268-5000 **Fax:** 410-280-5953 www.capitalgazette.com commnews@capgaznews.com

Baltimore Baltimore City Paper (91.0M) 812 Park Ave Baltimore MD 21201 **Phn:** 410-523-2300 **Fax:** 410-523-2222 citypaper.com editorial@citypaper.com

Baltimore Baltimore Guide (40.0M) 526 S Conkling St Baltimore MD 21224 **Phn:** 410-732-6600 **Fax:** 410-732-6604 baltimoreguide.com newsroom@baltimoreguide.com

Baltimore East County Times (36.0M) 513 Eastern Blvd Baltimore MD 21221 **Phn:** 410-780-3303 **Fax:** 410-780-2616 www.eastcountytimesonline.com ecteditorial@comcast.net

Baltimore Times Herald (32.0M) 526 S Conkling St Baltimore MD 21224 **Phn:** 410-529-1006

Bel Air Bel Air Aegis (58.5M) PO Box 189 Bel Air MD 21014 **Phn:** 410-838-4400 **Fax:** 410-838-7867 www.baltimoresun.com news@theaegis.com

Bel Air The Record (4.0M) 139 N Main St Ste 203 Bel Air MD 21014 **Phn:** 410-939-4040 **Fax:** 410-939-2390 news@theaegis.com

Bel Air The Weekender (91.0M) 139 N Main St Ste 203 Bel Air MD 21014 **Phn:** 410-838-4400 **Fax:** 410-838-7867

Berlin Bayside Gazette (10.0M) 11 S Main Sr Berlin MD 21811 **Phn:** 410-641-0039 **Fax:** 410-641-0085 www.baysideoc.com editor@baysidegazette.com

Berlin The Coast Dispatch (25.0M) PO Box 467 Berlin MD 21811 **Phn:** 410-641-4561 **Fax:** 410-641-0966 www.mdcoastdispatch.com editor@mdcoastdispatch.com

Bowie Crofton News-Crier (15.5M) PO Box 770 Bowie MD 20718 **Phn:** 301-262-3700 **Fax:** 301-464-7027 www.capitalgazette.com rhiaasen@capgaznews.com

Brunswick The Brunswick Citizen (3.2M) 101 W Potomac St Brunswick MD 21716 **Phn:** 301-834-7722 **Fax:** 301-834-7876

Brunswick Valley Citizen (3.2M) 101 W Potomac St Brunswick MD 21716 **Phn:** 301-834-7722 citizen@mip.net

Cambridge Banner (3.6M) PO Box 580 Cambridge MD 21613 **Phn:** 410-228-3131 **Fax:** 410-228-6547 www.newszap.com bannernews@newszap.com

Centreville Queen Annes Record Observer (4.5M) 114 Broadway Centreville MD 21617 **Phn:** 410-758-1400 **Fax:** 410-758-1701 www.myeasternshoremd.com

Chestertown Kent County News (8.0M) PO Box 30 Chestertown MD 21620 **Phn:** 410-778-2011 **Fax:** 410-778-6522 www.myeasternshoremd.com

Columbia Catonsville Times (13.0M) 10750 Little Patuxent Pkwy Columbia MD 21044 **Phn:** 410-788-4500 patuxent.com kmeisel@patuxent.com

Columbia Howard County Times (29.0M) 10750 Little Patuxent Pkwy Columbia MD 21044 **Phn:** 410-730-3620 **Fax:** 410-997-4564 www.patuxent.com pmilton@patuxent.com

Columbia Laurel Leader (29.0M) 10750 Little Patuxent Pkwy Columbia MD 21044 **Phn:** 301-725-2000 **Fax:** 301-317-8736 www.baltimoresun.com laurelleadernews@patuxent.com

Crisfield Crisfield Times (2.5M) 914 W Main St Crisfield MD 21817 **Phn:** 410-968-1188 **Fax:** 410-968-1197 www.newszap.com

Cumberland Garrett County Weekender (16.0M) PO Box 1662 Cumberland MD 21501 **Phn:** 301-387-8925 **Fax:** 301-359-0377

Denton Times-Record (5.5M) PO Box 160 Denton MD 21629 **Phn:** 410-479-1800 **Fax:** 410-479-3174

Dundalk Dundalk Eagle (19.5M) PO Box 8936 Dundalk MD 21222 **Phn:** 410-288-6060 **Fax:** 410-288-2712 www.dundalkeagle.com info@dundalkeagle.net

MARYLAND WEEKLY NEWSPAPERS

Easton Chesapeake Publishing (21.0M) PO Box 600 Easton MD 21601 **Phn:** 410-822-1500 **Fax:** 410-770-4019 www.chespub.com eastonedit@chespub.com

Gaithersburg Gazette Newspapers-Montgomery Co. (59.0M) 9030 Comprint Ct Gaithersburg MD 20877 **Phn:** 301-948-3120 **Fax:** 301-670-7183 www.gazette.net editor@gazette.net

Greenbelt Greenbelt News Review (10.5M) 15 Crescent Rd Ste 100 Greenbelt MD 20770 **Phn:** 301-474-4131 greenbelt.com/newsreview

Hancock Hancock News (2.0M) 263 N Pennsylvania Ave Hancock MD 21750 **Phn:** 301-678-6255 **Fax:** 301-678-5520 news@hancocknews.us

Landover Gazette Newspapers-Prince Georges Co. (200.0M) 8201 Corporate Dr Ste 1200 Landover MD 20785 **Phn:** 301-731-2100 **Fax:** 301-731-2141 www.gazette.net princegeorges@gazette.net

Laurel Enquirer Gazette (3.5M) 13501 Virginia Manor Rd Laurel MD 20707 **Phn:** 240-473-7500 **Fax:** 240-473-7501 www.somdnews.com

Lexington Park The Enterprise (16.0M) PO Box 700 Lexington Park MD 20653 **Phn:** 301-862-2111 **Fax:** 301-737-1665 www.somdnews.com rboyd@somdnews.com

Mount Airy Gazette Newspapers-Carroll Co. (10.0M) 218 S Main St Mount Airy MD 21771 **Phn:** 301-831-0047 **Fax:** 301-829-9101 www.gazette.net kbrick@gazette.net

North Beach Voice of South Maryland (3.0M) PO Box 499 North Beach MD 20714 **Phn:** 410-257-6768 **Fax:** 410-257-6445 voice91@aol.com

Oakland The Republican (9.2M) PO Box 326 Oakland MD 21550 **Phn:** 301-334-3963 **Fax:** 301-334-5904 www.therepublicannews.com newsroom@therepublicannews.com

Ocean City Worcester Co. Times (20.0M) 12417 Ocean Gtwy Ste 7 Ocean City MD 21842 **Phn:** 410-213-9442 **Fax:** 410-213-9459 www.delmarvanow.com mkilian@dmg.gannett.com

Prince Frederick The Calvert Recorder (10.0M) PO Box 485 Prince Frederick MD 20678 **Phn:** 410-535-1214 **Fax:** 410-535-5883 www.somdnews.com scraton@somdnews.com

Princess Anne Somerset Herald (3.0M) PO Box 310 Princess Anne MD 21853 **Phn:** 410-651-1600 **Fax:** 410-651-3785 www.delmarvanow.com lholland@dmg.gannett.com

Rockville Montgomery County Sentinel (10.0M) PO Box 1272 Rockville MD 20849 **Phn:** 301-838-0788 **Fax:** 301-838-3458 www.thesentinel.com lynn@thesentinel.com

Seabrook Prince Georges Sentinel (20.0M) 9458 Lanham Severn Rd Ste 200 Seabrook MD 20706 **Phn:** 301-306-9500 **Fax:** 301-306-9596 www.thesentinel.com lynn@thesentinel.com

Stevensville Bay Times (6.0M) 1101 Butterworth Ct Ste 100 Stevensville MD 21666 **Phn:** 410-643-7770 **Fax:** 410-643-8374 www.myeasternshoremd.com baytimes@kibaytimes.com

Towson Arbutus Times (5.4M) 409 Washington Ave Ste 400 Towson MD 21204 **Phn:** 410-995-1667 baltimoresunmediagroup.com kmeisel@patuxent.com

Towson Patuxent Publishing (140.0M) 409 Washington Ave Ste 400 Towson MD 21204 **Phn:** 410-337-2400 **Fax:** 410-337-2490 www.patuxent.com lperl@patuxent.com

Waldorf Maryland Independent (24.0M) 7 Industrial Park Dr Waldorf MD 20602 **Phn:** 301-645-9480 **Fax:** 301-645-2175 somdnews.com abreck@somdnews.com

Westminster Community Times (13.0M) PO Box 203 Westminster MD 21158 **Phn:** 410-875-5449 **Fax:** 410-875-5401 www.carrollcountytimes.com jim.lee@carrollcountytimes.com

MASSACHUSETTS

Amherst Amherst Bulletin (14.0M) 9 E Pleasant St Amherst MA 01002 **Phn:** 413-549-2000 **Fax:** 413-549-8181 www.gazettenet.com editor@gazettenet.com

Andover Andover Townsman (7.5M) PO Box 1986 Andover MA 01810 **Phn:** 978-475-7000 **Fax:** 978-470-2819 www.andovertownsman.com svartabedian@andovertownsman.com

Ashburnham The Community Journal (4.0M) PO Box 67 Ashburnham MA 01430 **Phn:** 978-827-3386 **Fax:** 978-827-3200 www.thecommunityjournal.com

Ayer Nashoba Publishing (5.3M) PO Box 362 Ayer MA 01432 **Phn:** 978-772-0777 **Fax:** 978-772-4012 www.nashobapublishing.com editor@nashobapub.com

Barre Barre Gazette (2.7M) PO Box 448 Barre MA 01005 **Phn:** 978-355-4000 **Fax:** 978-355-6274 www.turley.com edowner@turley.com

Belchertown The Sentinel (10.0M) PO Box 601 Belchertown MA 01007 **Phn:** 413-323-5999 **Fax:** 413-323-9424 www.belchertownsentinelonline.com ahenderson@turley.com

Boston Bay Windows (39.0M) 46 Plympton St Ste 5 Boston MA 02118 **Phn:** 617-266-6670 **Fax:** 617-266-5973 www.baywindows.com news.baywindows@gmail.com

Boston Beacon Hill Times (13.0M) 25 Myrtle St Boston MA 02114 **Phn:** 617-523-9490 **Fax:** 617-523-8668 beaconhilltimes.com editor@beaconhilltimes.com

Boston Boston Phoenix (218.0M) 126 Brookline Ave Boston MA 02215 **Phn:** 617-536-5390 **Fax:** 617-859-8201 thephoenix.com letters@phx.com

Boston Boston Post Gazette (26.0M) 5 Prince St Boston MA 02113 **Phn:** 617-227-8929 **Fax:** 617-227-5307 www.bostonpostgazette.com postgazette@aol.com

Boston South Boston Tribune (20.0M) 314 W Broadway Boston MA 02127 **Phn:** 617-268-3440 **Fax:** 617-268-6420 southbostonnews.com editor@southbostonnews.com

Boston South End News (17.0M) 46 Plympton St Ste 5 Boston MA 02118 **Phn:** 617-266-6670 **Fax:** 617-266-5973 www.mysouthend.com letters@southendnews.com

Canton Canton Citizen (3.5M) 866 Washington St Canton MA 02021 **Phn:** 781-821-4418 **Fax:** 781-821-4419 cancitizen@aol.com

Carlisle Carlisle Mosquito (1.7M) 662A Bedford Rd Carlisle MA 01741 **Phn:** 978-369-8313 **Fax:** 978-369-3569 www.carlislemosquito.org mail@carlislemosquito.org

Charlestown Charlestown Patriot-Bridge (9.0M) 1 Thompson Sq Ste 107 Charlestown MA 02129 **Phn:** 617-241-8500 charlestownbridge.com editor@charlestownbridge.com

Chatham Cape Cod Chronicle (10.3M) 60 Munson Meeting Way Ste C Chatham MA 02633 **Phn:** 508-945-2220 **Fax:** 508-945-2579 www.capecodchronicle.com twood@capecodchronicle.com

Chicopee Holyoke Sun (10.0M) 333 Front St Chicopee MA 01013 **Phn:** 413-612-2310 **Fax:** 413-592-3568 www.holyokesunonline.com kwill@turley.com

Clinton Coulter Press (30.0M) 156 Church St Ste 1 Clinton MA 01510 **Phn:** 978-368-0176 **Fax:** 978-368-1151 www.telegram.com/section/coulter clintonitem@yahoo.com

Clinton The Banner (30.0M) 156 Church St Ste 1 Clinton MA 01510 **Phn:** 978-368-0176 **Fax:** 978-368-1151 www.telegram.com bannews@yahoo.com

Cohasset Tinytown Gazette (2.5M) 172 S Main St Cohasset MA 02025 **Phn:** 781-383-6704 **Fax:** 781-383-9115 www.tinytowngazette.com tinytown@comcast.net

Concord Action Unlimited (113.0M) 100 Domino Dr # 1 Concord MA 01742 **Phn:** 978-371-2442 www.actionunlimited.com articles@actionunlimited.com

Concord Bolton Common (1.5M) 150 Baker Avenue Ext Ste 105 Concord MA 01742 **Phn:** 978-456-8122 **Fax:** 978-371-5214 www.wickedlocal.com bolton@wickedlocal.com

Concord Community Newspaper Co.-NW (67.0M) PO Box 9191 Concord MA 01742 **Phn:** 978-371-5200 **Fax:** 978-371-5212 www.wickedlocal.com concord@wickedlocal.com

Concord Harvard Post (4.0M) 150 Baker Avenue Ext Ste 105 Concord MA 01742 **Phn:** 978-456-3342 **Fax:** 978-456-3341 www.wickedlocal.com harvard@wickedlocal.com

Concord Times & Courier (4.0M) PO Box 9191 Concord MA 01742 **Phn:** 978-365-8040 **Fax:** 978-365-8041 www.wickedlocal.com/lancaster times-courier@wickedlocal.com

Danvers Community Newspaper Co. (162.0M) 75 Sylvan St Ste C105 Danvers MA 01923 **Phn:** 978-739-1300 **Fax:** 978-739-8501 danvers@wickedlocal.com

Dartmouth The Chronicle (5.6M) PO Box 80268 Dartmouth MA 02748 **Phn:** 508-992-1522 **Fax:** 508-992-1689 www.southcoasttoday.com newsroom@s-t.com

Dedham Dedham Times (3.0M) 395 Washington St Ste 7 Dedham MA 02026 **Phn:** 781-329-5553 **Fax:** 781-329-8291 dtimes@rcn.com

Dorchester Dorchester Reporter (22.0M) 150 Mount Vernon St Ste 120 Dorchester MA 02125 **Phn:** 617-436-1222 **Fax:** 617-825-5516 www.dotnews.com news@dotnews.com

Duxbury Duxbury Clipper (4.6M) PO Box 1656 Duxbury MA 02331 **Phn:** 781-934-2811 **Fax:** 781-934-5917 www.eduxbury.com editor@duxburyclipper.com

East Longmeadow Reminder Publications (26.0M) 280 N Main St East Longmeadow MA 01028 **Phn:** 413-525-6661 **Fax:** 413-525-5882 www.thereminder.com news@reminderpublications.com

Easthampton Valley Advocate (55.0M) 116 Pleasant St Ste 335 Easthampton MA 01027 **Phn:** 413-529-2840 **Fax:** 413-529-2844 valleyadvocate.com editor@valleyadvocate.com

Edgartown Vineyard Gazette (13.5M) PO Box 66 Edgartown MA 02539 **Phn:** 508-627-4311 **Fax:** 508-627-7444 www.mvgazette.com news@mvgazette.com

Everett Advocate Newspapers Inc (33.5M) 573 Broadway Everett MA 02149 **Phn:** 617-387-2200 **Fax:** 617-381-0800 advocatenews.net matt@advocatenews.net

Everett Everett Leader-Herald (15.5M) 28 Church St Everett MA 02149 **Phn:** 617-387-4570 **Fax:** 617-387-0409 everettleader@comcast.net

Fairhaven The Advocate (3.0M) PO Box 711 Fairhaven MA 02719 **Phn:** 508-961-2243 **Fax:** 508-992-2333 www.southcoasttoday.com

Fall River Fall River Spirit (10.0M) PO Box 2530 Fall River MA 02722 **Phn:** 508-674-3581 **Fax:** 508-677-1210 www.southcoasttoday.com alittlefield@s-t.com

Falmouth Falmouth Publishing (25.0M) 50 Depot Ave Falmouth MA 02540 **Phn:** 508-548-4700 **Fax:** 508-540-8407 www.capenews.net bhough@capenews.net

MASSACHUSETTS WEEKLY NEWSPAPERS

Feeding Hills Agawam Advertiser News (12.0M) 23 Southwick St Feeding Hills MA 01030 **Phn:** 413-786-7747 **Fax:** 413-786-8457 www.agawamnewsonline.com jwroblewski@turley.com

Foxboro Foxboro Reporter (4.4M) PO Box 289 Foxboro MA 02035 **Phn:** 508-543-4851 **Fax:** 508-543-4888 www.foxbororeporter.com foxboroeditor@yahoo.com

Framingham Community Newspaper Co. (34.0M) 33 New York Ave Framingham MA 01701 **Phn:** 508-626-3923 **Fax:** 508-626-4400 www.wickedlocal.com metrowest@wickedlocal.com

Great Barrington Berkshire Record (4.5M) PO Box 868 Great Barrington MA 01230 **Phn:** 413-528-5380 www.berkshirerecord.net berkrec@bcn.net

Greenfield The Greenfield Athol-Orange Town Crier (12.0M) 393 Main St Greenfield MA 01301 **Phn:** 413-774-7226 **Fax:** 413-774-6809 www.reformer.com/greenfield news@vermontobserver.com

Groton The Groton Herald (1.8M) PO Box 610 Groton MA 01450 **Phn:** 978-448-6061 www.grotonherald.com newseditor@grotonherald.com

Hanson Whitman-Hanson Express (2.1M) PO Box 60 Hanson MA 02341 **Phn:** 781-293-0420 **Fax:** 781-293-0956 www.whitmanhansonexpress.com editor@whitmanhansonexpress.com

Haverhill Haverhill Gazette (6.7M) PO Box 991 Haverhill MA 01831 **Phn:** 978-374-0321 **Fax:** 978-521-6790 www.hgazette.com editor@hgazette.com

Holden The Landmark (9.0M) PO Box 546 Holden MA 01520 **Phn:** 508-829-5981 **Fax:** 508-829-5389 www.thelandmark.com editor@thelandmark.com

Hopkinton Hopkinton Independent (6.1M) 6 Fenton St Hopkinton MA 01748 **Phn:** 508-435-5188 **Fax:** 508-435-5107 www.hopkintonindependent.com hopkintonindependent@verizon.net

Hull The Hull Times (3.0M) 41 Highland Ave Hull MA 02045 **Phn:** 781-925-9266 **Fax:** 781-925-0336 hulltimes.com hulltimeseditor@aol.com

Huntington Country Journal (3.3M) PO Box 429 Huntington MA 01050 **Phn:** 413-667-3211 **Fax:** 413-667-3011 www.turley.com countryjournal@turley.com

Hyannis Barnstable Patriot (5.0M) PO Box 1208 Hyannis MA 02601 **Phn:** 508-771-1427 **Fax:** 508-790-3997 barnstablepatriot.com news@barnstablepatriot.com

Hyde Park Bulletin Newspapers (45.0M) 1 Westinghouse Plz Hyde Park MA 02136 **Phn:** 617-361-8400 **Fax:** 617-361-1933 www.bulletinnewspapers.com news@bulletinnewspapers.com

Jamaica Plain Jamaica Plain Gazette (16.5M) PO Box 301119 Jamaica Plain MA 02130 **Phn:** 617-524-2626 **Fax:** 617-524-3921 jamaicaplaingazette.com news@jamaicaplaingazette.com

Jamaica Plain Mission Hill Gazette (6.7M) PO Box 301119 Jamaica Plain MA 02130 **Phn:** 617-524-2626 **Fax:** 617-524-3921 MissionHillGazette.com news@jamaicaplaingazette.com

Leominster Leominster Champion (9.0M) 285 Central St Ste 202B Leominster MA 01453 **Phn:** 978-534-6006 **Fax:** 978-534-6004 www.leominsterchamp.com editor@leominsterchamp.com

Lexington Community Newspaper Co (30.0M) 9 Meriam St Lexington MA 02420 **Phn:** 781-674-7720 **Fax:** 781-674-7735 www.wickedlocal.com lexington@wickedlocal.com

Lowell Dispatch News (14.5M) 491 Dutton St Lowell MA 01854 **Phn:** 978-458-7100 **Fax:** 978-970-4600 www.thevalleydispatch.com jcampanini@lowellsun.com

Lynnfield Lynnfield Villager (1.7M) 590 Main St # A Lynnfield MA 01940 **Phn:** 781-334-6319 lynnfieldnews@aol.com

Manchester The Manchester Cricket (2.3M) PO Box 357 Manchester MA 01944 **Phn:** 978-526-7131 **Fax:** 978-526-8193 themanchestercricket.com news@cricketpress.com

Mansfield Buzz Newspapers (41.0M) 125 High St Ste 10B Mansfield MA 02048 **Phn:** 508-337-6228 **Fax:** 508-337-6477 thebuzznewspapers.com buzznewsads@yahoo.com

Marlborough Community Newspaper Co. (15.0M) 40 Mechanic St Marlborough MA 01752 **Phn:** 508-490-7450 **Fax:** 508-490-7471 www.wickedlocal.com marlborough@wickedlocal.com

Marshfield Community Newspaper Co. (40.0M) 165 Enterprise Dr Marshfield MA 02050 **Phn:** 781-837-3500 **Fax:** 781-837-4543 www.wickedlocal.com abington@wickedlocal.com

Mattapoisett The Wanderer (12.0M) PO Box 102 Mattapoisett MA 02739 **Phn:** 508-758-9055 **Fax:** 508-758-4845 www.wanderer.com news@wanderer.com

Medfield Hometown Weeklies (36.0M) 29 Janes Ave Medfield MA 02052 **Phn:** 508-359-2200 **Fax:** 508-359-2224 hometownweekly.net news@hometownweekly.net

Medford Medford Transcript (9.0M) 57 High St Medford MA 02155 **Phn:** 781-396-1982 **Fax:** 781-393-1821 www.wickedlocal.com medford@wickedlocal.com

Middleboro Middleboro Gazette (6.0M) PO Box 551 Middleboro MA 02346 **Phn:** 508-947-1760 **Fax:** 508-947-9426 www.southcoasttoday.com/gazette newsroom@s-t.com

Middleton Village Reporter (4.0M) 12 School St Middleton MA 01949 **Phn:** 978-887-0077 **Fax:** 978-887-0770 editor@villagereporter.com

Milford Gatehouse Media (43.0M) 159 S Main St Milford MA 01757 **Phn:** 508-634-7500 **Fax:** 508-634-7514 www.wickedlocal.com gazette@wickedlocal.com

Millbury Sutton Chronicle (2.8M) 117 Elm St Millbury MA 01527 **Phn:** 508-865-1645

Milton Milton Times (4.5M) PO Box 444 Milton MA 02186 **Phn:** 617-696-7758 www.miltontimes.com editor@miltontimes.com

Nantucket Inquirer & Mirror (11.0M) PO Box 1198 Nantucket MA 02554 **Phn:** 508-228-0001 **Fax:** 508-325-5089 www.ack.net newsroom@inkym.com

Needham Community Newspaper Co. (112.0M) PO Box 9113 Needham MA 02492 **Phn:** 781-433-8200 **Fax:** 781-433-8202 www.wickedlocal.com allston-brighton@wickedlocal.com

North Adams The Advocate (10.0M) 124 American Legion Dr North Adams MA 01247 **Phn:** 413-664-6900 **Fax:** 413-664-7900 www.advocateweekly.com news@advocateweekly.com

North Attleboro The Free Press (17.0M) PO Box 1047 North Attleboro MA 02761 **Phn:** 508-699-6755 **Fax:** 508-699-8545 www.wickedlocal.com news@nafreepress.com

North Grafton 79 Worcester St (3.6M) PO Box 457 North Grafton MA 01536 **Phn:** 508-839-2259 **Fax:** 508-839-5235

North Reading North Reading Transcript (4.5M) PO Box 7 North Reading MA 01864 **Phn:** 978-664-4761 **Fax:** 978-664-4954

Norton Hometown News (6.0M) PO Box 612 Norton MA 02766 **Phn:** 508-285-7766 www.smalltownpapers.com/listHMT.htm

Norwood Community Newspapers (11.0M) 1091 Washington St Norwood MA 02062 **Phn:** 781-433-8307 **Fax:** 781-433-8375 www.wickedlocal.com onlineeditor@wickedlocal.com

Orleans The Cape Codder (9.0M) 5 Namskaket Rd Orleans MA 02653 **Phn:** 508-255-2121 **Fax:** 508-247-3201 www.wickedlocal.com capecodder@wickedlocal.com

Palmer Turley Publications (39.0M) 24 Water St Palmer MA 01069 **Phn:** 413-283-8393 **Fax:** 413-289-1977 www.turley.com pkillough@turley.com

Peabody Peabody Citizen (8.0M) PO Box 4233 Peabody MA 01961 **Phn:** 978-531-0407 **Fax:** 978-531-5347

Peabody Weekly News (20.5M) PO Box 6039 Peabody MA 01961 **Phn:** 978-532-5880 **Fax:** 978-532-4250 weeklynews.net bsmith@weeklynews.net

Pittsfield Pittsfield Gazette (7.5M) PO Box 2236 Pittsfield MA 01202 **Phn:** 413-443-2010 **Fax:** 413-443-2445 pittsfieldgazette.com pittsfieldgazette@verizon.net

Provincetown Provincetown Banner (8.0M) PO Box 977 Provincetown MA 02657 **Phn:** 508-487-7400 **Fax:** 508-487-7144 www.wickedlocal.com/provincetown editor@provincetownbanner.com

Quincy Quincy Sun (7.0M) 1372 Hancock St Quincy MA 02169 **Phn:** 617-471-3100 **Fax:** 617-472-3963

Raynham Call Newspapers (32.0M) 370 Paramount Dr Raynham MA 02767 **Phn:** 508-967-3500 **Fax:** 508-967-3501

Revere Revere Newspaper Group (64.0M) 385 Broadway Revere MA 02151 **Phn:** 781-284-2400 **Fax:** 781-289-5352 www.reverejournal.com editor@reverejournal.com

Rowley The Town Common (7.0M) 77 Wethersfield St Rowley MA 01969 **Phn:** 978-948-8696 www.thetowncommon.com editor@thetowncommon.com

Shelburne Falls West County News (2.7M) 8 Deerfield Ave Shelburne Falls MA 01370 **Phn:** 413-625-4660 **Fax:** 413-625-4661

Somerset Somerset Spectator (6.0M) PO Box 427 Somerset MA 02726 **Phn:** 508-674-4656 **Fax:** 508-677-1210 www.southcoasttoday.com news@hathawaypublishing.com

Somerville Cambridge Chronicle (6.6M) 20 Holland St # 404 Somerville MA 02144 **Phn:** 617-629-3385 **Fax:** 617-629-3381 www.wickedlocal.com cambridge@wickedlocal.com

Somerville Somerville Journal (6.7M) 20 Holland St # 404 Somerville MA 02144 **Phn:** 617-629-3385 **Fax:** 617-629-3381 www.wickedlocal.com/somerville somerville@wickedlocal.com

Somerville Somerville News (10.0M) 21 College Ave Somerville MA 02144 **Phn:** 617-666-4010 **Fax:** 617-591-0362 www.thesomervillenews.com somervillenews@aol.com

South Hadley Town Reminder (12.0M) 138 College St Ste 2 South Hadley MA 01075 **Phn:** 413-536-5333 **Fax:** 413-536-5334 www.townreminderonline.com

Southbridge Auburn News (2.4M) PO Box 90 Southbridge MA 01550 **Phn:** 508-832-2222 **Fax:** 508-832-2431 www.southbridgeeveningnews.com aminor@stonebridgepress.com

Southbridge Spencer New Leader (3.3M) 25 Elm St Southbridge MA 01550 **Phn:** 508-885-5041 **Fax:** 508-885-4213 www.spencernewleader.com ddore@stonebridgepress.com

MASSACHUSETTS WEEKLY NEWSPAPERS

Southbridge Webster Times (5.0M) 25 Elm St Southbridge MA 01550 **Phn:** 508-885-5041 **Fax:** 508-885-4213 www.webstertimes.net

Stoneham Stoneham Independent (3.5M) 200F Main St # 343 Stoneham MA 02180 **Phn:** 781-438-1660 **Fax:** 781-438-6762 homenewshere.com news@stonehamindependent.com

Turners Falls Montague Reporter (2.0M) 58 4th St Turners Falls MA 01376 **Phn:** 413-863-8666 **Fax:** 413-863-3050 www.montaguema.net

Upton Town Crier (5.5M) 48 Mechanic St Upton MA 01568 **Phn:** 508-529-7791 **Fax:** 508-529-6397 www.towncrier.us towncriereditor@gmail.com

Vineyard Haven Martha's Vineyard Times (15.0M) PO Box 518 Vineyard Haven MA 02568 **Phn:** 508-693-6100 **Fax:** 508-693-6000 www.mvtimes.com mvt@mvtimes.com

W Springfield Chicopee Register (13.0M) 380 Union St W Springfield MA 01089 **Phn:** 413-592-3599 **Fax:** 413-592-3568 www.chicopeeregisteronline.com kmitchell@turley.com

Walpole Walpole Times (6.2M) 7 West St Ste 2 Walpole MA 02081 **Phn:** 508-668-0243 **Fax:** 508-668-5174 editor@walpoletimes.com

Ware Ware River News (4.0M) 80 Main St Ware MA 01082 **Phn:** 413-967-3505 **Fax:** 413-967-6009 www.warenewsonline.com

Webster Webster Patriot (3.5M) PO Box 310 Webster MA 01570 **Phn:** 508-943-8784 **Fax:** 508-943-8129 www.patriotnewspaper.com news@patriotnewspaper.com

Wellesley Wellesley Townsman (7.0M) 310 Washington St Ste 201 Wellesley MA 02481 **Phn:** 781-431-2000 **Fax:** 781-431-2001 www.wickedlocal.com/wellesley wellesley@wickedlocal.com

West Newbury West Newbury News (7.0M) PO Box 778 West Newbury MA 01985 **Phn:** 978-363-2297 **Fax:** 978-363-1166

West Springfield West Springfield Record (5.6M) PO Box 357 West Springfield MA 01090 **Phn:** 413-736-1587 **Fax:** 413-739-2477

Westborough Community Advocate (24.0M) 32 South St Westborough MA 01581 **Phn:** 508-366-5500 **Fax:** 508-366-2812 www.communityadvocate.com news@communityadvocate.com

Westborough Westborough News (4.4M) 10 E Main St Westborough MA 01581 **Phn:** 508-366-1511 **Fax:** 508-366-5265 www.wickedlocal.com/westborough westboro@wickedlocal.com

Westfield Longmeadow News (2.1M) PO Box 930 Westfield MA 01086 **Phn:** 413-562-4181 **Fax:** 413-562-4185

Weymouth Weymouth News (8.7M) 91 Washington St Weymouth MA 02188 **Phn:** 781-682-4850 **Fax:** 781-682-4851 www.wickedlocal.com weymouth@wickedlocal.com

Whitinsville Blackstone Valley Tribune (3.8M) 110 Church St Whitinsville MA 01588 **Phn:** 508-234-2107 **Fax:** 508-234-7506 www.blackstonevalleytribune.com ddore@stonebridgepress.com

Winchendon Winchendon Courier (2.0M) 91 Central St Winchendon MA 01475 **Phn:** 978-297-0050 **Fax:** 978-297-2177 www.winchendoncourier.com ruth@stonebridgepress.com

Woburn Town Crier (6.3M) 1 Arrow Dr Woburn MA 01801 **Phn:** 978-658-2346 **Fax:** 978-658-2266 www.homenewshere.com office@yourtowncrier.com

MICHIGAN

Albion Albion Recorder (1.1M) 125 E Cass St Albion MI 49224 **Phn:** 517-629-0041 **Fax:** 517-629-5210 therecorder@frontiernet.net

Allegan Allegan County News (5.5M) PO Box 189 Allegan MI 49010 **Phn:** 269-673-5534 **Fax:** 269-673-5535 www.allegannews.com editor@allegannews.com

Atlanta Montmorency Tribune (4.5M) PO Box 186 Atlanta MI 49709 **Phn:** 989-785-4214 **Fax:** 989-785-3118 www.montmorencytribune.com office@montmorencytribune.com

Bad Axe Newsweekly (5.0M) 55 Westland Dr Bad Axe MI 48413 **Phn:** 989-883-3100 **Fax:** 989-883-9211

Bay City Bay City Democrat (0.8M) PO Box 278 Bay City MI 48707 **Phn:** 989-893-6344 **Fax:** 989-893-2991 bclegalnews.com bcdem@sbcglobal.net

Bay City Valley Farmer (1.2M) 905 S Henry St Bay City MI 48706 **Phn:** 989-893-6507

Bellaire Antrim Review (4.4M) PO Box 313 Bellaire MI 49615 **Phn:** 231-533-5651 **Fax:** 231-533-4662

Belleville Belleville Area Independent (7.0M) 152 Main St Ste 9 Belleville MI 48111 **Phn:** 734-699-9020 **Fax:** 734-699-8962 www.bellevilleareaindependent.com mail@bellevilleareaindependent.com

Belleville Ypsilanti Courier (7.0M) 159 Main St Belleville MI 48111 **Phn:** 734-482-3385 **Fax:** 734-697-4610 www.heritage.com/ypsilanti_courier editor@ypsilanticourier.com

Berrien Springs The Journal Era (1.8M) PO Box 98 Berrien Springs MI 49103 **Phn:** 269-473-5421 **Fax:** 269-471-1362 thejournalera@yahoo.com

Big Rapids Pioneer Group (4.9M) 115 N Michigan Ave Big Rapids MI 49307 **Phn:** 231-796-4831 **Fax:** 231-796-1152 www.pioneergroup.com info@pioneergroup.com

Blissfield Blissfield Advance (2.7M) 121 Newspaper St Blissfield MI 49228 **Phn:** 517-486-2400 **Fax:** 517-486-4675 www.blissfieldadvance.com news@blissfieldadvance.com

Brooklyn The Brooklyn Exponent (6.0M) 160 S Main St Brooklyn MI 49230 **Phn:** 517-592-2122 **Fax:** 517-592-3241 www.theexponent.com news@theexponent.com

Brown City Brown City Banner (2.9M) PO Box 250 Brown City MI 48416 **Phn:** 810-346-2753 **Fax:** 810-346-2579 www.mihomepaper.com bcbanner@mihomepaper.com

Buchanan Berrien County Record (2.4M) PO Box 191 Buchanan MI 49107 **Phn:** 269-695-3878 **Fax:** 269-695-3880 www.bcrnews.net bcrnews@bcrnews.net

Cadillac Northern Michigan News (22.0M) PO Box 640 Cadillac MI 49601 **Phn:** 231-775-6565 **Fax:** 231-775-8790 www.cadillacnews.com thuckle@cadillacnews.com

Caro Tuscola County Advertiser (10.0M) PO Box 106 Caro MI 48723 **Phn:** 989-673-3181 **Fax:** 989-673-5662 murphy@tcadvertiser.com

Cass City Cass City Chronicle (3.8M) PO Box 115 Cass City MI 48726 **Phn:** 989-872-2010 **Fax:** 989-872-3810 www.ccchronicle.net tom@ccchronicle.net

Cedar Springs Cedar Springs Post (5.0M) PO Box 370 Cedar Springs MI 49319 **Phn:** 616-696-3655 **Fax:** 616-696-9010 cedarspringspost.com newsreleases@cedarspringspost.com

Charlevoix Charlevoix Courier (3.1M) PO Box 117 Charlevoix MI 49720 **Phn:** 231-547-6558 **Fax:** 231-547-4992 www.petoskeynews.com/charlevoix news@charlevoixcourier.com

MICHIGAN WEEKLY NEWSPAPERS

Charlotte Lansing Community Newspapers (30.0M) 239 S Cochran Ave Charlotte MI 48813 **Phn:** 517-627-6085 **Fax:** 517-627-3497

Cheboygan Mackinaw Journal (1.1M) 308 N Main St Cheboygan MI 49721 **Phn:** 231-627-7144 **Fax:** 231-627-5331

Chesaning Tri-County Citizen (18.0M) PO Box 158 Chesaning MI 48616 **Phn:** 989-845-7403 **Fax:** 989-845-4397 tricountycitizen.mihomepaper.com tccnews@mihomepaper.com

Clare Clare County Review (10.0M) 2141 E Ludington Dr Clare MI 48617 **Phn:** 989-386-4414 **Fax:** 989-386-2412 www.clarecountyreview.com info@clarecountyreview.com

Clare Clare Sentinel (3.3M) PO Box 237 Clare MI 48617 **Phn:** 989-386-9937 **Fax:** 989-386-9311

Climax Climax Crescent (1.0M) 150 N Main St Climax MI 49034 **Phn:** 269-746-4331

Clinton Clinton Local (2.1M) PO Box B Clinton MI 49236 **Phn:** 517-456-4100 **Fax:** 517-456-6372

Clinton Township Advisor & Source Newspapers (125.0M) 19176 Hall Rd # 200 Clinton Township MI 48038 **Phn:** 586-716-8100 **Fax:** 586-716-8533 www.sourcenewspapers.com jody.mcveigh@advisorsource.com

Coldwater Patriot Publications (6.0M) 15 W Pearl St Coldwater MI 49036 **Phn:** 517-278-2318 **Fax:** 517-278-6041

Coopersville Coopersville Observer (8.0M) PO Box 111 Coopersville MI 49404 **Phn:** 616-997-5049 **Fax:** 616-997-9235 www.coopersvilleobserver.com cvobserve@aol.com

Davison Davison Index (11.0M) 220 N Main St Davison MI 48423 **Phn:** 810-653-3511 **Fax:** 810-653-3077 davisonindex.mihomepaper.com editor@mihomepaper.com

Dearborn Times Herald (27.0M) 13730 Michigan Ave Dearborn MI 48126 **Phn:** 313-584-4000 **Fax:** 313-584-1357

Decatur Decatur Republican (1.7M) PO Box 36 Decatur MI 49045 **Phn:** 269-423-2411 www.marcellusnews.com editor@marcellusnews.com

Deckerville Deckerville Recorder (1.5M) 3520 Main St Deckerville MI 48427 **Phn:** 810-376-3805 **Fax:** 810-376-4058 sanduskytribune.com deckervillerecorder@gmail.com

Detroit Metro Times (100.0M) 733 Saint Antoine St Detroit MI 48226 **Phn:** 313-961-4060 **Fax:** 313-961-6598 metrotimes.com cguyette@metrotimes.com

Dundee The Independent (2.8M) 112 Park Pl Dundee MI 48131 **Phn:** 734-529-2688 **Fax:** 734-529-3086 www.dundeeonline.com editor@dundeeonline.com

East Tawas Iosco County News-Herald (6.5M) PO Box 72 East Tawas MI 48730 **Phn:** 989-362-3456 **Fax:** 989-362-6601 www.iosconews.com editor@iosconews.com

Fenton Tri-County Times (24.0M) 256 N Fenway Dr Fenton MI 48430 **Phn:** 810-629-8282 **Fax:** 810-629-9227 www.tctimes.com news@tctimes.com

Flint Suburban Newspaper Group (93.0M) 200 E 1st St Flint MI 48502 **Phn:** 810-766-6100 **Fax:** 810-767-2278 www.mlive.com/communitynewspapers

Frankenmuth Frankenmuth News (4.8M) PO Box 252 Frankenmuth MI 48734 **Phn:** 989-652-3246 **Fax:** 989-652-2417 www.frankenmuthnews.com frankenmuthnews@airadv.net

Frankfort Benzie Co Record Patriot (4.7M) PO Box 673 Frankfort MI 49635 **Phn:** 231-352-9659 **Fax:** 231-352-7874 www.pioneergroup.com info@pioneergroup.com

Freeport Freeport News (1.0M) PO Box 25 Freeport MI 49325 **Phn:** 616-765-8511

Fremont Fremont Times Indicator (7.5M) PO Box 7 Fremont MI 49412 **Phn:** 231-924-4400 **Fax:** 231-924-4066 www.timesindicator.com news@ncats.net

Garden City The Citizen (13.0M) 29956 Rosslyn Ave Garden City MI 48135 **Phn:** 313-365-9500 **Fax:** 313-365-8660 hamtramckcitizen@comcast.net

Gaylord Gaylord Herald Times (7.0M) 2058 S Otsego Ave Gaylord MI 49735 **Phn:** 989-732-1111 **Fax:** 989-732-3490 www.petoskeynews.com/gaylord editor@gaylordheraldtimes.com

Gladwin Gladwin County Record (7.2M) PO Box 425 Gladwin MI 48624 **Phn:** 989-426-9411 **Fax:** 989-426-2023 www.gladwinmi.com mdrey@thegladwincountyrecord.com

Grand Haven The News-Review (6.0M) 101 N 3rd St Grand Haven MI 49417 **Phn:** 616-842-6410 **Fax:** 616-842-9584 lpainter@grandhaventribune.com

Grand Rapids Grand Rapids Times (5.0M) PO Box 7258 Grand Rapids MI 49510 **Phn:** 616-245-8737 **Fax:** 616-245-1026 www.grtimes.com staff@grtimes.com

Grand Rapids Kalamazoo Times (5.0M) PO Box 7258 Grand Rapids MI 49510 **Phn:** 616-245-8737 **Fax:** 616-245-1026

Grayling Crawford County Avalanche (5.3M) PO Box 490 Grayling MI 49738 **Phn:** 989-348-6811 **Fax:** 989-348-6806 www.crawfordcountyavalanche.com avalanche@i2k.net

Greenville Carson City Gazette (8.7M) PO Box 340 Greenville MI 48838 **Phn:** 616-754-9303 **Fax:** 616-754-8559 www.thedailynews.cc rstafford@staffordgroup.com

Grosse Pointe Farms Grosse Pointe News (15.0M) 96 Kercheval Ave Grosse Pointe Farms MI 48236 **Phn:** 313-882-6900 **Fax:** 313-882-1585 www.grossepointenews.com editor@grossepointenews.com

Harbor Springs Harbor Light (2.2M) 211 E 3rd St Harbor Springs MI 49740 **Phn:** 231-526-2191 **Fax:** 231-526-7634 www.harborlightnews.com news@ncpublish.com

Harrison Clare County Cleaver (5.0M) PO Box 436 Harrison MI 48625 **Phn:** 989-539-7496 **Fax:** 989-539-5901 www.clarecountycleaver.net ccleaver@sbcglobal.net

Harrisville Alcona County Review (3.4M) PO Box 548 Harrisville MI 48740 **Phn:** 989-724-6384 **Fax:** 989-724-6655 www.alconareview.com editor@alconareview.com

Hart Oceana's Herald-Journal (7.2M) PO Box 190 Hart MI 49420 **Phn:** 231-873-5602 **Fax:** 231-873-4775 www.shorelinemedia.net editor@oceanaheraldjournal.com

Hastings J-Ad Graphics (48.0M) PO Box 188 Hastings MI 49058 **Phn:** 269-945-9554 **Fax:** 269-945-5192 www.j-adgraphics.com

Highland Spinal Column Newsweekly (50.0M) 1103 S Millford Rd Highland MI 48357 **Phn:** 248-360-7355 **Fax:** 248-360-1220 spinalcolumnonline.com editor@scnmail.com

Hillsdale County Sampler (5.0M) PO Box 287 Hillsdale MI 49242 **Phn:** 517-437-7351 **Fax:** 517-437-3963 www.hillsdale.net avanauker@thedailyreporter.com

Holly Community Voice (4.0M) 304 S Broad St Ste B Holly MI 48442 **Phn:** 248-634-9211

Homer Homer Index (1.8M) PO Box 236 Homer MI 49245 **Phn:** 517-568-4646 **Fax:** 517-568-4346 www.homerindex.com news@homerindex.com

Houghton Lake Houghton Lake Resorter (7.4M) PO Box 248 Houghton Lake MI 48629 **Phn:** 989-366-5341 **Fax:** 989-366-4472 www.houghtonlakeresorter.com news@houghtonlakeresorter.com

Hudson Hudson Post-Gazette (1.6M) PO Box 70 Hudson MI 49247 **Phn:** 517-448-2611 www.hudsonpg.net editor@hudsonpg.net

Imlay City Tri-City Times (6.3M) PO Box 278 Imlay City MI 48444 **Phn:** 810-724-2615 **Fax:** 810-724-8552

Indian River Community Voice (1.7M) 4725 Sherwood Dr Indian River MI 49749 **Phn:** 906-495-5207 **Fax:** 906-495-5604

Indian River Straitsland Resorter (2.2M) PO Box 579 Indian River MI 49749 **Phn:** 231-238-7362 **Fax:** 231-238-1290 www.resorter.com editor@resorter.com

Iron River Iron Co Reporter (6.0M) PO Box 311 Iron River MI 49935 **Phn:** 906-265-9927 **Fax:** 906-265-5755 www.ironcountyreporter.com news@ironcountyreporter.com

Ithaca Gratiot County Herald (8.0M) PO Box 10 Ithaca MI 48847 **Phn:** 989-875-4151 **Fax:** 989-875-3159 www.gcherald.com gcherald@gcherald.com

Jenison Advance Newspapers (189.0M) PO Box 9 Jenison MI 49429 **Phn:** 616-669-2700 **Fax:** 616-669-4848 www.mlive.com/advancenewspapers

Kalamazoo The Commercial-Express (2.0M) 401 S Burdick St Kalamazoo MI 49007 **Phn:** 269-649-2333 **Fax:** 269-649-2335

Kalkaska Leader & Kalkaskian (3.0M) 318 N Cedar St Kalkaska MI 49646 **Phn:** 231-258-4600 **Fax:** 231-258-4603 morningstarpublishing.com dmansfield@michigannewspapers.com

Lake City Missaukee Sentinel (2.5M) 130 N Main St Lake City MI 49651 **Phn:** 231-839-5400 **Fax:** 231-839-5500 www.missaukeesentinel.com editor@missaukeesentinel.com

Lake Leelanau Leelanau Enterprise (7.7M) 7200 E Duck Lake Rd Lake Leelanau MI 49653 **Phn:** 231-256-9827 **Fax:** 231-256-7705 www.leelanaunews.com info@leelanaunews.com

Lambertville Bedford Now (12.0M) 8336 Monroe Rd Rm 119 Lambertville MI 48144 **Phn:** 734-850-2669 **Fax:** 734-850-2023

Lambertville Bedford Press (15.0M) 3363 Hemmingway Ln Lambertville MI 48144 **Phn:** 734-856-6680 **Fax:** 734-856-2925 bedfordpress@aol.com

Lanse L'Anse Sentinel (3.9M) PO Box 7 Lanse MI 49946 **Phn:** 906-524-6194 **Fax:** 906-524-6197 www.lansesentinel.com sentinel@up.net

Lansing City Pulse (20.0M) 1905 E Michigan Ave Lansing MI 48912 **Phn:** 517-371-5600 **Fax:** 517-371-5800 www.lansingcitypulse.com andy@lansingcitypulse.com

Lapeer County Line Reminder (8.3M) PO Box 220 Lapeer MI 48446 **Phn:** 248-627-2843 **Fax:** 248-627-3473

Lapeer LA View (35.0M) 1521 Imlay City Rd Lapeer MI 48446 **Phn:** 810-245-9343 **Fax:** 810-245-9375 www.mihomepaper.com laveditor@mihomepaper.com

Lapeer The County Press (16.5M) PO Box 220 Lapeer MI 48446 **Phn:** 810-664-0811 **Fax:** 810-664-5852 thecountypress.mihomepaper.com editor@mihomepaper.com

Livonia Observer & Eccentric Newspapers (172.0M) 36251 Schoolcraft Rd Livonia MI 48150 **Phn:** 734-591-2300 **Fax:** 734-591-7279 www.hometownlife.com oeletters@hometownlife.com

MICHIGAN WEEKLY NEWSPAPERS

Lowell Lowell Ledger (3.0M) PO Box 128 Lowell MI 49331 **Phn:** 616-897-9261 **Fax:** 616-897-4809 lowellbuyersguide.com

Manistique Pioneer Tribune (3.8M) 212 Walnut St Manistique MI 49854 **Phn:** 906-341-5200 **Fax:** 906-341-5914 www.pioneertribune.com newsroom@pioneertribune.com

Marcellus Marcellus News (1.6M) PO Box 277 Marcellus MI 49067 **Phn:** 269-646-2101 www.marcellusnews.com editor@marcellusnews.com

Marion Marion Press (0.8M) 301 S Mill St Marion MI 49665 **Phn:** 231-743-2481 **Fax:** 231-743-9501 yourmarionpress@gmail.com

Marlette Marlette Leader (2.1M) PO Box 338 Marlette MI 48453 **Phn:** 989-635-2435 **Fax:** 989-635-3769 www.michigansthumb.com/marlette_leader hdt_news@hearstnp.com

Minden City Minden City Herald (1.5M) 1524 Main St Minden City MI 48456 **Phn:** 989-864-3630 **Fax:** 989-864-5363 mcherald@echoicemi.com

Mio Oscoda County Herald (2.6M) PO Box 397 Mio MI 48647 **Phn:** 989-826-5047 **Fax:** 989-826-3037 oscodaherald.com editor@oscodaherald.com

Morenci State Line Observer (2.4M) 120 North St Morenci MI 49256 **Phn:** 517-458-6811 statelineobserver.com editor@statelineobserver.com

Mount Morris Genesee County Herald (3.8M) PO Box 127 Mount Morris MI 48458 **Phn:** 810-686-3840 **Fax:** 810-686-9181

Munising Munising News (2.7M) 132 E Superior St Munising MI 49862 **Phn:** 906-387-3282 **Fax:** 906-387-4054

Muskegon Norton-Lakeshore Examiner (3.0M) 950 W Norton Ave Ste 402 Muskegon MI 49441 **Phn:** 231-739-6397 **Fax:** 231-737-1520

New Baltimore Voice Newspapers (80.0M) 51180 Bedford St New Baltimore MI 48047 **Phn:** 586-716-8100 **Fax:** 586-716-8918 www.voicenews.com editor@voicenews.com

New Buffalo Harbor Country News (19.0M) 122 N Whittaker St New Buffalo MI 49117 **Phn:** 269-469-1410 **Fax:** 269-469-3029 www.harborcountry-news.com djohnson@harborcountry-news.com

New Buffalo New Buffalo Times (5.5M) PO Box 369 New Buffalo MI 49117 **Phn:** 269-469-1100 **Fax:** 269-469-6397

Newberry Newberry News (3.6M) PO Box 46 Newberry MI 49868 **Phn:** 906-293-8401 **Fax:** 906-293-8815

Niles Cassopolis Vigilant (0.6M) 217 N 4th St Niles MI 49120 **Phn:** 269-683-2100 **Fax:** 269-683-2175 leaderpub.com michael.bennett@leaderpub.com

Niles Edwardsburg Argus (0.9M) 217 N 4th St Niles MI 49120 **Phn:** 269-683-2100 **Fax:** 269-683-2175 leaderpub.com scott.novak@leaderpub.com

Norway The Current (1.5M) 400 Main St Ste 5 Norway MI 49870 **Phn:** 906-563-5212

Onaway Onaway Outlook (2.0M) PO Box 176 Onaway MI 49765 **Phn:** 989-733-6543 **Fax:** 989-733-6572 www.piadvance.com editor@piadvance.com

Ontonagon Ontonagon Herald (3.8M) 326 River St Ontonagon MI 49953 **Phn:** 906-884-2826 www.ontonagonherald.com maureen@ontonagonherald.com

Oscoda Oscoda Press (6.0M) PO Box 663 Oscoda MI 48750 **Phn:** 989-739-2055 **Fax:** 989-739-3201 www.iosconews.com/oscoda_press editor1@oscodapress.com

Owosso Sunday Independent (34.0M) 1907 W M 21 Owosso MI 48867 **Phn:** 989-723-1118 **Fax:** 989-725-1834 www.owossoindependent.com news@owossoindependent.com

Oxford Sherman Publications (62.0M) PO Box 108 Oxford MI 48371 **Phn:** 248-628-4801 **Fax:** 248-628-9750 www.oxfordleader.com shermanpub@aol.com

Parma County Press (1.5M) PO Box 279 Parma MI 49269 **Phn:** 517-531-4542 **Fax:** 517-531-3576 countypress@aol.com

Paw Paw The Courier Leader (3.0M) PO Box 129 Paw Paw MI 49079 **Phn:** 269-657-3072 **Fax:** 269-657-5723 www.pawpawcourierleader.com vineyardpress@vineyardpress.biz

Petoskey The Graphic (14.0M) 319 State St Petoskey MI 49770 **Phn:** 231-347-2544 **Fax:** 231-347-6833

Pinconning Pinconning Journal (2.0M) PO Box 626 Pinconning MI 48650 **Phn:** 989-879-3811 **Fax:** 989-879-5529 pinconningjrnl@centurytel.net

Plainwell Union Enterprise (0.6M) PO Box 417 Plainwell MI 49080 **Phn:** 269-685-5985 www.allegannews.com/union_enterprise editor@allegannews.com

Plymouth Associated Newspapers (32.0M) 502 Forest Ave Plymouth MI 48170 **Phn:** 734-467-1900 **Fax:** 734-729-1840 www.associatednewspapers.net editor@journalgroup.com

Rockford Rockford Squire (12.0M) 331 Northland Dr Rockford MI 49341 **Phn:** 616-866-4465 **Fax:** 616-866-3810 rockfordsquire.com squiremail@aol.com

Rogers City Presque Isle Co. Advance (3.8M) PO Box 50 Rogers City MI 49779 **Phn:** 989-734-2105 **Fax:** 989-734-3053 www.piadvance.com editor@piadvance.com

Romeo Romeo Observer (6.7M) PO Box 96 Romeo MI 48065 **Phn:** 586-752-3524 **Fax:** 586-752-0548 www.romeoobserver.com news@romeoobserver.com

Royal Oak The New Monitor (35.0M) PO Box 1078 Royal Oak MI 48068 **Phn:** 248-439-1863 **Fax:** 248-439-185 thenewmonitor@gmail.com

Saginaw Saginaw News (35.0M) 100 S Michigan Ave Ste 3 Saginaw MI 48602 **Phn:** 989-752-7171 **Fax:** 989-752-3115 www.mlive.com/saginaw rclark2@mlive.com

Saginaw Saginaw Press (0.5M) PO Box 1836 Saginaw MI 48605 **Phn:** 989-793-8070 **Fax:** 989-401-3440 saginawpress2004@yahoo.com

Saginaw The Township Times (5.0M) 1668 Midland Rd Saginaw MI 48638 **Phn:** 989-799-3200 **Fax:** 989-799-7085 twptimes.com nicole@twptimes.com

Saint Ignace St. Ignace News (6.6M) PO Box 277 Saint Ignace MI 49781 **Phn:** 906-643-9150 **Fax:** 906-643-9122

Saline Belleville View (2.9M) 106 W Michigan Ave Saline MI 48176 **Phn:** 734-697-8255 **Fax:** 734-697-4610 heritage.com mrogers@heritage.com

Saline Chelsea Standard (5.0M) 106 W Michigan Ave Saline MI 48176 **Phn:** 734-475-1371 **Fax:** 734-475-1413 heritage.com editor@chelseastandard.com

Saline Heritage Newspapers (20.0M) 106 W Michigan Ave Saline MI 48176 **Phn:** 734-475-1371 **Fax:** 734-429-3621 www.heritage.com mrogers@heritage.com

Saline Manchester Enterprise (2.4M) 106 W Michigan Ave Saline MI 48176 **Phn:** 734-428-8173 **Fax:** 734-428-9044 heritage.com editor@manchesterenterprise.com

Sandusky Sanilac County News (8.2M) PO Box 72 Sandusky MI 48471 **Phn:** 810-648-4000 **Fax:** 810-648-4002 sanilaccountynews.mihomepaper.com scneditor@mihomepaper.com

Saugatuck Commercial Record (1.7M) PO Box 246 Saugatuck MI 49453 **Phn:** 269-857-2570 **Fax:** 269-857-4637 www.allegannews.com/commercial_record editorcommrec@allegannews.com

Shepherd Shepherd Argus (1.8M) PO Box 459 Shepherd MI 48883 **Phn:** 989-828-6360 **Fax:** 989-828-5361

South Haven Tribune (14.0M) 255 Center St South Haven MI 49090 **Phn:** 269-637-1104 **Fax:** 269-637-8415

South Lyon Milford Times (7.2M) 101 N Lafayette St South Lyon MI 48178 **Phn:** 248-685-1507 **Fax:** 248-685-2892 www.hometownlife.com news@milfordtimes.com

South Lyon Northville Record (6.5M) 101 N Lafayette St South Lyon MI 48178 **Phn:** 248-349-1700 **Fax:** 248-349-9832

South Lyon Novi News (6.4M) 101 N Lafayette St South Lyon MI 48178 **Phn:** 248-349-1700 **Fax:** 248-349-9832 www.hometownlife.com cstone@hometownlife.com

South Lyon South Lyon Herald (6.6M) 101 N Lafayette St South Lyon MI 48178 **Phn:** 248-437-2011 **Fax:** 248-437-3386 www.hometownlife.com oenews@hometownlife.com

Southgate Dearborn Press & Guide (19.0M) 1 Heritage Dr Ste 100 Southgate MI 48195 **Phn:** 313-359-7820 **Fax:** 313-359-7822 www.pressandguide.com editor@pressandguide.com

Southgate Heritage Newspapers (123.0M) 1 Heritage Dr Ste 100 Southgate MI 48195 **Phn:** 734-246-0800 **Fax:** 734-246-2727 www.heritage.com editor@thenewsherald.com

Southgate The Ile Camera (3.7M) 1 Heritage Dr Ste 100 Southgate MI 48195 **Phn:** 734-676-0515 **Fax:** 734-676-0638 thenewsherald.com/ile_camera editor@ilecamera.com

Springport Springport Signal (1.4M) PO Box 157 Springport MI 49284 **Phn:** 517-857-2500 **Fax:** 517-857-2887

Standish Arenac County Independent (6.1M) PO Box 699 Standish MI 48658 **Phn:** 989-846-4531 **Fax:** 989-846-9868 www.arenacindependent.com news@arenacindependent.com

Stephenson Menominee County Journal (5.4M) PO Box 247 Stephenson MI 49887 **Phn:** 906-753-2296 **Fax:** 906-753-4009 www.greatnorthernconn.com/papers/menominee.html journal@alphacomm.net

Stockbridge Stockbridge Town Crier (10.0M) PO Box 548 Stockbridge MI 49285 **Phn:** 517-851-7833 **Fax:** 517-851-4641

Sunfield Sunfield Sentinel (0.5M) PO Box 8 Sunfield MI 48890 **Phn:** 517-566-8500 susentinel@aol.com

Tecumseh Tecumseh Herald (6.0M) PO Box 218 Tecumseh MI 49286 **Phn:** 517-423-2174 **Fax:** 517-423-6258 www.tecumsehherald.com hollie@tecumsehherald.com

Traverse City Grand Traverse Insider (1.1M) 410 S Union St Traverse City MI 49684 **Phn:** 231-946-3055 **Fax:** 231-946-2613 www.morningstarpublishing.com news@grandtraverseinsider.com

Traverse City Northern Express (30.0M) PO Box 209 Traverse City MI 49685 **Phn:** 231-947-8787 **Fax:** 231-947-2425 info@northernexpress.com

Troy Troy-Somerset Gazette (25.0M) PO Box 482 Troy MI 48099 **Phn:** 248-524-4868 **Fax:** 248-524-9140 www.troy-somersetgazette.com editor@troy-somersetgazette.com

Vassar Vassar Pioneer-Times (1.8M) 113 S Main St Vassar MI 48768 **Phn:** 989-823-8579 **Fax:** 989-823-8778 vptimes@sbcglobal.net

Wakefield Wakefield News (1.4M) 405 Sunday Lake St Wakefield MI 49968 **Phn:** 906-224-9561

Warren C & G Newspapers (545.0M) 13650 E 11 Mile Rd Warren MI 48089 **Phn:** 586-498-8000 **Fax:** 586-498-9631 hwww.candgnews.com jmalavolti@candgnews.com

Watervliet Tri-City Record (2.7M) PO Box 7 Watervliet MI 49098 **Phn:** 269-463-6397 **Fax:** 269-463-8329 www.tricityrecord.com record@tricityrecord.com

Wayland Penasee Globe (16.0M) 206 S Main St Wayland MI 49348 **Phn:** 269-792-2271 **Fax:** 269-792-2030 www.advancenewspapers.com advancenewssubmissions@mlive.com

West Branch Ogemaw County Herald (7.5M) PO Box 247 West Branch MI 48661 **Phn:** 989-345-0044 **Fax:** 989-345-5609 editor@ogemawherald.com

Whitehall White Lake Beacon (11.0M) PO Box 98 Whitehall MI 49461 **Phn:** 231-894-5356 **Fax:** 231-894-2174 www.shorelinemedia.net editor@whitelakebeacon.com

Yale Yale Expositor (2.7M) 21 S Main St Yale MI 48097 **Phn:** 810-387-2300 yalexpo@greatlakes.net

Zeeland Zeeland Record (1.5M) 16 S Elm St Zeeland MI 49464 **Phn:** 616-772-2131 **Fax:** 616-772-9771 zrnews@chartermi.net

MINNESOTA

Ada Norman County Index (2.3M) PO Box 148 Ada MN 56510 **Phn:** 218-784-2541 **Fax:** 218-784-2551 nci@loretel.net

Adams Monitor Review (1.4M) PO Box 823 Adams MN 55909 **Phn:** 507-582-3542

Adrian Nobles County Review (1.3M) PO Box 160 Adrian MN 56110 **Phn:** 507-483-2213 **Fax:** 507-483-2219 noblescountyreview.net ncreview@myclearwave.net

Aitkin Independent Age (5.7M) 213 Minnesota Ave N Aitkin MN 56431 **Phn:** 218-927-3761 **Fax:** 218-927-3763 www.messagemedia.co/aitkin news@aitkinage.com

Albany Stearns-Morrison Enterprise (2.1M) PO Box 310 Albany MN 56307 **Phn:** 320-845-2700 **Fax:** 320-845-4805 www.albanyenterprise.com emily@albanyenterprise.com

Alden Alden Advance (0.9M) PO Box 485 Alden MN 56009 **Phn:** 507-874-3440

Alexandria Osakis Review (1.7M) PO Box 5 Alexandria MN 56308 **Phn:** 320-859-2143 **Fax:** 320-859-2054 www.theosakisreview.com achaffins@theosakisreview.com

Alexandria The Echo Press (10.0M) PO Box 549 Alexandria MN 56308 **Phn:** 320-763-3133 **Fax:** 320-763-3258 www.echopress.com echo@echopress.com

Annandale Annandale Advocate (2.7M) PO Box D Annandale MN 55302 **Phn:** 320-274-3052 **Fax:** 320-274-2301 annandaleadvocate.com news@annandaleadvocate.com

Anoka ABC Newspapers (11.0M) PO Box 99 Anoka MN 55303 **Phn:** 763-421-4444 **Fax:** 763-712-3519 abcnewspapers.com peter.bodley@ecm-inc.com

Apple Valley Thisweek Newspapers (70.0M) 15322 Galaxie Ave # 219 Apple Valley MN 55124 **Phn:** 952-894-1111 **Fax:** 952-846-2010 sunthisweek.com tad.johnson@ecm-inc.com

MICHIGAN WEEKLY NEWSPAPERS

Appleton Appleton Press (4.5M) 241 W Snelling Ave Appleton MN 56208 **Phn:** 320-289-1323 **Fax:** 320-289-2702 news@appletonpress.com

Arlington Arlington Enterprise (1.5M) PO Box 388 Arlington MN 55307 **Phn:** 507-964-5547 **Fax:** 507-964-2423 www.arlingtonmnnews.com info@arlingtonmnnews.com

Askov Askov American (2.0M) PO Box 275 Askov MN 55704 **Phn:** 320-838-3151 **Fax:** 320-838-3152 askovamerican@scicable.com

Bagley Farmers Independent (2.4M) PO Box 130 Bagley MN 56621 **Phn:** 218-694-6265 **Fax:** 218-694-6015

Balaton Press-Tribune (0.6M) PO Box 310 Balaton MN 56115 **Phn:** 507-734-5421 **Fax:** 507-734-5457 balatonpublishing@yahoo.com

Barnesville Record-Review (2.1M) PO Box 70 Barnesville MN 56514 **Phn:** 218-354-2606 **Fax:** 218-354-2246 newsrecordreview@bvillemn.net

Battle Lake Battle Lake Review (2.2M) PO Box 99 Battle Lake MN 56515 **Phn:** 218-864-5952 **Fax:** 218-864-5212 blreview@arvig.net

Baudette Northern Light (1.5M) PO Box 1134 Baudette MN 56623 **Phn:** 218-634-2700 **Fax:** 218-634-2777 www.page1publications.com norlight@wiktel.com

Becker Sherburne County Citizen (10.5M) PO Box 217 Becker MN 55308 **Phn:** 763-261-5880 **Fax:** 763-261-5884 www.citizennewspaper.com citizennewspaper@sherbtel.net

Belgrade Belgrade Observer (1.2M) PO Box 279 Belgrade MN 56312 **Phn:** 320-254-8250 **Fax:** 320-254-3215 www.belgradearea.com observer@belgradearea.com

Belle Plaine Belle Plaine Herald (3.6M) PO Box 7 Belle Plaine MN 56011 **Phn:** 952-873-2261 **Fax:** 952-873-2262 www.belleplaineherald.com bpherald@frontiernet.net

Benson Swift Country Monitor (2.9M) 101 12th St S Benson MN 56215 **Phn:** 320-843-4111 **Fax:** 320-843-3246 www.swiftcountymonitor.com reed@monitor-news.com

Big Lake West Sherburne Tribune (13.0M) PO Box 276 Big Lake MN 55309 **Phn:** 763-263-3602 **Fax:** 763-263-8458 www.westsherburnetribune.com westrib@sherbtel.net

Bird Island Bird Island Union (1.2M) PO Box 160 Bird Island MN 55310 **Phn:** 320-365-3266 **Fax:** 320-848-2249 union@willmar.com

Biwabik Range Times (1.8M) PO Box 169 Biwabik MN 55708 **Phn:** 218-865-6265 **Fax:** 218-865-7007

Blackduck The American (1.2M) PO Box 100 Blackduck MN 56630 **Phn:** 218-835-4211 **Fax:** 218-835-6992

Blooming Prairie Blooming Prairie Times (1.5M) PO Box 247 Blooming Prairie MN 55917 **Phn:** 507-583-4431 **Fax:** 507-583-4445 bloomingprairieonline.com bptimes@frontiernet.net

Blue Earth Faribault Co Register (9.5M) PO Box 98 Blue Earth MN 56013 **Phn:** 507-526-7324 **Fax:** 507-526-4080 www.faribaultcountyregister.com fcnews@bevcomm.net

Bovey Scenic Range NewsForum (1.9M) PO Box 70 Bovey MN 55709 **Phn:** 218-245-1422 **Fax:** 218-245-1698 www.scenicrangenewsforum.com editor@scenicrangenewsforum.com

Brandon West Douglas County Record (1.0M) PO Box 86 Brandon MN 56315 **Phn:** 320-834-4999

Brooten Bonanza Valley Voice (1.2M) PO Box 280 Brooten MN 56316 **Phn:** 320-346-2400 **Fax:** 320-346-2379 bonanzavalvoice@tds.net

Browerville Browerville Blade (1.5M) PO Box 245 Browerville MN 56438 **Phn:** 320-594-2911 **Fax:** 320-594-6111 bladepublishing.net staff@bladepublishing.net

Buffalo Wright County Journal Press (6.0M) PO Box 159 Buffalo MN 55313 **Phn:** 763-682-1221 **Fax:** 763-682-5458 www.thedrummer.com business@thedrummer.com

Byron Byron Review (1.2M) PO Box 39 Byron MN 55920 **Phn:** 507-775-6180 **Fax:** 507-374-9327 www.communitynewscorp.com byronreview@frontiernet.net

Caledonia Caledonia Argus (3.1M) 314 W Lincoln St Caledonia MN 55921 **Phn:** 507-724-3475 **Fax:** 507-725-8610 hometownargus.com charlie.warner@ecm-inc.com

Cambridge Isanti County News (12.0M) 234 Main St S Cambridge MN 55008 **Phn:** 763-689-1981 **Fax:** 763-689-4372 isanticountynews.com editor.countynews@ecm-inc.com

Cambridge Isanti-Chisago Co. Star (16.0M) 930 Cleveland St S Cambridge MN 55008 **Phn:** 763-689-1181 **Fax:** 763-689-1185 www.presspubs.com/isanti editor@countystar.com

Canby Canby News (3.0M) 123 1st St E Canby MN 56220 **Phn:** 507-223-5303 **Fax:** 507-223-5404 cnews@frontiernet.net

Cannon Falls Cannon Falls Beacon (4.6M) PO Box 366 Cannon Falls MN 55009 **Phn:** 507-263-3991 **Fax:** 507-263-2300 www.cannonfalls.com beacon@cannonfalls.com

Cass Lake Cass Lake Times (1.5M) PO Box 398 Cass Lake MN 56633 **Phn:** 218-335-2290 www.lakeandpine.com cltimes2@arvig.net

Chanhassen Chanhassen Villager (6.2M) PO Box 99 Chanhassen MN 55317 **Phn:** 952-934-5045 **Fax:** 952-934-7960 www.chanvillager.com editor@chanvillager.com

Chaska Chaska Herald (5.0M) PO Box 113 Chaska MN 55318 **Phn:** 952-448-2650 **Fax:** 952-448-3146 www.chaskaherald.com editor@chaskaherald.com

Chatfield Chatfield News (1.6M) 220 Main St S Chatfield MN 55923 **Phn:** 507-867-3870 www.hometown-pages.com chatfieldnews@bluffcountrynews.com

Chisholm Tribune Free Press (2.2M) 327 W Lake St Chisholm MN 55719 **Phn:** 218-254-4432 **Fax:** 218-254-7141

Chokio Chokio Review (1.0M) PO Box 96 Chokio MN 56221 **Phn:** 320-324-2405 **Fax:** 320-324-2449 www.chokioreview.com chreview@fedtel.net

Clara City Clara City Herald (1.7M) PO Box 458 Clara City MN 56222 **Phn:** 320-847-3130 **Fax:** 320-847-2630

Clarissa Independent News Herald (2.6M) PO Box 188 Clarissa MN 56440 **Phn:** 218-756-2131 **Fax:** 218-756-2126 www.inhnews.com jeremy@inhnews.com

Clinton Northern Star (1.9M) PO Box 368 Clinton MN 56225 **Phn:** 320-325-5152 **Fax:** 320-325-5280 northernstar@mchsi.com

Cloquet Pine Journal (6.5M) 122 Avenue C Cloquet MN 55720 **Phn:** 218-879-1950 **Fax:** 218-879-2078 www.pinejournal.com news@pinejournal.com

Cokato Enterprise Dispatch (3.0M) PO Box 969 Cokato MN 55321 **Phn:** 320-286-2118 **Fax:** 320-286-2119 www.dasselcokato.com news@dasselcokato.com

MINNESOTA WEEKLY NEWSPAPERS

Cold Spring Cold Spring Record (3.8M) PO Box 456 Cold Spring MN 56320 **Phn:** 320-685-8621 **Fax:** 320-685-8885 www.csrecord.net csrecord@midconetwork.com

Comfrey Comfrey Times (1.0M) PO Box 122 Comfrey MN 56019 **Phn:** 507-877-2281 **Fax:** 507-877-2251 comfreytimes@frontiernet.net

Cook Cook News-Herald (3.0M) PO Box 1179 Cook MN 55723 **Phn:** 218-666-5944 **Fax:** 218-666-5609 cooknewsherald.com gda@accessmn.com

Cottage Grove South Washington Co Bulletin (7.0M) 7584 80th St S Cottage Grove MN 55016 **Phn:** 651-459-3434 **Fax:** 651-459-9491 www.swcbulletin.com editor@swcbulletin.com

Cottonwood Tri-County News (1.4M) PO Box 76 Cottonwood MN 56229 **Phn:** 507-423-6239 **Fax:** 507-423-6230 tcedit@mvtvwireless.com

Crosby Crosby-Ironton Courier (4.5M) PO Box 67 Crosby MN 56441 **Phn:** 218-546-5029 **Fax:** 218-546-8352 www.cicourierinc.com courier@crosbyironton.net

Dawson Dawson Sentinel (1.9M) PO Box 1015 Dawson MN 56232 **Phn:** 320-769-2497 **Fax:** 320-769-2459 www.dawsonmn.com rbm2@frontiernet.net

Deer River Western Itasca Review (1.3M) PO Box 427 Deer River MN 56636 **Phn:** 218-246-8533 **Fax:** 218-246-8540 www.deerriverreviewmn.com drpub@paulbunyan.net

Detroit Lakes Detroit Lakes Newspapers (38.0M) PO Box 826 Detroit Lakes MN 56502 **Phn:** 218-847-3151 **Fax:** 218-847-9409 www.dl-online.com recordtribune@dlnewspapers.com

Dodge Center Star-Herald (2.0M) PO Box 279 Dodge Center MN 55927 **Phn:** 507-374-6531 **Fax:** 507-374-9327 www.communitynewscorp.com communitynewscorp@kmtel.com

Duluth Duluth Budgeteer News (40.0M) 424 W 1st St Duluth MN 55802 **Phn:** 218-723-5212 **Fax:** 218-279-5592 www.duluthnewstribune.com budgeteer@duluthbudgeteer.com

East Grand Forks The Exponent (2.4M) PO Box 285 East Grand Forks MN 56721 **Phn:** 218-773-2808 **Fax:** 218-773-9212 www.page1publications.com exponent@rrv.net

Eden Prairie Eden Prairie News (13.0M) 250 Prairie Center Dr # 211 Eden Prairie MN 55344 **Phn:** 952-445-3333 **Fax:** 952-942-7975 www.edenprairienews.com editor@edenprairienews.com

Eden Prairie Sun Newspapers (225.0M) 10917 Valley View Rd Eden Prairie MN 55344 **Phn:** 952-829-0797 **Fax:** 952-392-6868 www.ecm-inc.com keith.anderson@ecm-inc.com

Eden Valley Journal Patriot (2.0M) PO Box 347 Eden Valley MN 55329 **Phn:** 320-453-2460

Edgerton Edgerton Enterprise (1.8M) 831 Main St Ste 2 Edgerton MN 56128 **Phn:** 507-442-6161 edgent@iw.net

Elbow Lake Grant County Herald (2.1M) PO Box 2019 Elbow Lake MN 56531 **Phn:** 218-685-5326 **Fax:** 218-685-5327 www.grantherald.com gcanne@runestone.net

Elk River Elk River Star News (21.5M) 506 Freeport Ave NW Ste A Elk River MN 55330 **Phn:** 763-441-3500 **Fax:** 763-441-6401 erstarnews.com editor.erstarnews@ecm-inc.com

Ely Ely Echo (4.0M) 15 E Chapman St Ely MN 55731 **Phn:** 218-365-3141 **Fax:** 218-365-3142 www.elyecho.com thepub@elyecho.com

Elysian Elysian Enterprise (0.4M) PO Box 119 Elysian MN 56028 **Phn:** 507-267-4323 **Fax:** 507-362-4458 lrlife@frontiernet.net

Erskine Erskine Echo (1.0M) PO Box A Erskine MN 56535 **Phn:** 218-687-3775 **Fax:** 218-687-3744

Eveleth Eveleth Scene (2.4M) PO Box 588 Eveleth MN 55734 **Phn:** 218-741-4445 **Fax:** 218-749-1515 esgh@2z.net

Fairfax Fairfax Standard-Gazette (1.8M) PO Box 589 Fairfax MN 55332 **Phn:** 507-426-7235 **Fax:** 507-426-7264 fxstandard@mchsi.com

Fairmont Fairmont Photo Press (11.8M) PO Box 973 Fairmont MN 56031 **Phn:** 507-238-9456 **Fax:** 507-238-9457 fairmontphotopress.com editor@fairmontphotopress.com

Farmington Farmington Independent (2.7M) 312 Oak St Farmington MN 55024 **Phn:** 651-460-6606 **Fax:** 651-463-7730 www.farmingtonindependent.com editor@farmingtonindependent.com

Farmington Rosemont Town Pages (1.7M) 312 Oak St Farmington MN 55024 **Phn:** 651-460-6606 **Fax:** 651-463-7730 www.rosemounttownpages.com editor@rosemounttownpages.com

Fertile Fertile Journal (1.6M) PO Box 128 Fertile MN 56540 **Phn:** 218-945-6120 **Fax:** 218-945-6125 fertjou@gvtel.com

Floodwood The Forum (1.0M) PO Box 286 Floodwood MN 55736 **Phn:** 218-476-2232 **Fax:** 218-476-2782 theforum@scicable.com

Foley Benton County News (2.8M) PO Box 187 Foley MN 56329 **Phn:** 320-968-7220

Forest Lake Forest Lake Times (12.0M) 880 15th St SW Forest Lake MN 55025 **Phn:** 651-464-4601 **Fax:** 651-464-4605 forestlaketimes.com editor.forestlaketimes@ecm-inc.com

Forest Lake St. Croix Valley Peach (32.0M) 880 15th St SW Forest Lake MN 55025 **Phn:** 651-464-4601 **Fax:** 651-464-4605 www.forestlaketimes.com editor.forestlaketimes@ecm-inc.com

Fosston Thirteen Towns (3.0M) PO Box 57 Fosston MN 56542 **Phn:** 218-435-1313 **Fax:** 218-435-1309 13towns@gvtel.com

Frazee Frazee Forum (2.1M) PO Box 187 Frazee MN 56544 **Phn:** 218-334-3566 **Fax:** 218-334-3567 www.frazeeforum.com fforum@loretel.net

Fulda Fulda Free Press (1.2M) PO Box 439 Fulda MN 56131 **Phn:** 507-425-2303 **Fax:** 507-425-2501 www.fuldafreepress.net text@fuldafreepress.net

Gaylord Gaylord Hub (1.5M) PO Box 208 Gaylord MN 55334 **Phn:** 507-237-2476 gaylordhub.com news@gaylordhub.com

Gilbert Gilbert Herald (1.1M) PO Box 488 Gilbert MN 55741 **Phn:** 218-741-4445 **Fax:** 218-749-1515 esgh@2z.net

Glencoe Glencoe Enterprise (2.5M) PO Box 97 Glencoe MN 55336 **Phn:** 320-864-4715

Glencoe McLeod County Chronicle (3.9M) PO Box 188 Glencoe MN 55336 **Phn:** 320-864-5518 **Fax:** 320-864-5510 www.glencoenews.com richg@glencoenews.com

Glenwood Pope County Tribune (4.2M) PO Box 157 Glenwood MN 56334 **Phn:** 320-634-4571 **Fax:** 320-634-5522 www.pctribune.com news@pctribune.com

Gonvick Richards Publishing (5.2M) PO Box 159 Gonvick MN 56644 **Phn:** 218-487-5225 **Fax:** 218-487-5251 richards@gvtel.com

Grand Marais Cook County News Herald (4.3M) PO Box 757 Grand Marais MN 55604 **Phn:** 218-387-1025 **Fax:** 218-387-2539 www.cookcountynews-herald.com star@boreal.org

Grand Meadow Meadow Area News (3.0M) PO Box 509 Grand Meadow MN 55936 **Phn:** 507-754-5486 **Fax:** 507-754-5151

Grand Rapids Herald-Review (8.0M) PO Box 220 Grand Rapids MN 55744 **Phn:** 218-326-6623 **Fax:** 218-326-6627 www.grandrapidsmn.com news@grandrapidsheraldreview.net

Granite Falls Advocate-Tribune (3.3M) PO Box 99 Granite Falls MN 56241 **Phn:** 320-564-2126 **Fax:** 320-564-4293 www.granitefallsnews.com tribeditor@mvtvwireless.com

Greenbush Greenbush Tribune (1.4M) PO Box F Greenbush MN 56726 **Phn:** 218-782-2275 **Fax:** 218-782-2277 www.page1publications.com tribune@wiktel.com

Greenbush New River Record (0.5M) PO Box F Greenbush MN 56726 **Phn:** 218-782-2275 **Fax:** 218-782-2277 www.page1publications.com tribune@wiktel.com

Hallock Kittson County Enterprise (2.2M) PO Box 730 Hallock MN 56728 **Phn:** 218-843-2868 **Fax:** 218-843-2312 www.kittsonarea.com kce@invisimax.com

Halstad Valley Journal (3.0M) PO Box 267 Halstad MN 56548 **Phn:** 218-456-2133 **Fax:** 218-456-2567 valleyjournal@rrv.net

Hancock Hancock Record (1.0M) PO Box 425 Hancock MN 56244 **Phn:** 320-392-5527 hrecord@fedteldirect.net

Harmony Mabel News Record (1.6M) 350 Main Ave N Ste 4 Harmony MN 55939 **Phn:** 507-346-7365 **Fax:** 507-346-7366 www.bluffcountrynews.com news-record@bluffcountrynews.com

Hastings Hastings Star-Gazette (6.5M) PO Box 277 Hastings MN 55033 **Phn:** 651-437-6153 **Fax:** 651-437-5911 www.hastingsstargazette.com news@hastingsstargazette.com

Hawley Hawley Herald (2.5M) PO Box 709 Hawley MN 56549 **Phn:** 218-483-3306 **Fax:** 218-483-4457 marc@hawleyherald.net

Hawley Lake Park Journal (2.1M) PO Box 709 Hawley MN 56549 **Phn:** 218-483-3306 **Fax:** 218-483-4457

Hector Hector News Mirror (2.5M) PO Box 278 Hector MN 55342 **Phn:** 320-848-2248 **Fax:** 320-848-2249 newsmir@hcctel.net

Henderson Henderson Independent (1.0M) PO Box 8 Henderson MN 56044 **Phn:** 507-248-3223 **Fax:** 507-248-3611 hendersonindependent.com hendersonind@frontiernet.net

Hendricks Hendricks Herald (0.2M) PO Box 5 Hendricks MN 56136 **Phn:** 507-275-3342 tribute@tylertribute.com

Hendricks Hendricks Pioneer (0.7M) PO Box 5 Hendricks MN 56136 **Phn:** 507-275-3197 **Fax:** 507-275-3108

Herman Herman Review (1.2M) PO Box E Herman MN 56248 **Phn:** 320-677-2229 www.hermanreview.com hcreview@runestone.net

Hermantown Star (2.0M) 4850 Miller Trunk Hwy Ste 4B Hermantown MN 55811 **Phn:** 218-727-0419 **Fax:** 218-722-5821 www.hermantownstar.com news@hermantownstar.com

Heron Lake Tri County News (1.0M) PO Box 227 Heron Lake MN 56137 **Phn:** 507-793-2327 www.tricountynewsmn.net tcnews@roundlk.net

Hinckley Hinckley News (1.8M) PO Box 310 Hinckley MN 55037 **Phn:** 320-384-6188 **Fax:** 320-384-7844

Hoffman Hoffman Tribune (1.3M) PO Box 247 Hoffman MN 56339 **Phn:** 320-986-2851 hofftrib@runestone.net

MINNESOTA WEEKLY NEWSPAPERS

Houston Houston Banner (0.6M) PO Box 326 Houston MN 55943 **Phn:** 507-896-2107 **Fax:** 507-896-2107 banner@acegroup.cc

Hutchinson Leader (5.5M) 36 Washington Ave W Hutchinson MN 55350 **Phn:** 320-587-5000 **Fax:** 320-587-6104 www.hutchinsonleader.com news@hutchinsonleader.com

Isle Mille Lacs Messenger (5.5M) PO Box 26 Isle MN 56342 **Phn:** 320-676-3123 **Fax:** 320-676-8450 www.messagemedia.co/millelacs mlm@millelacsmessenger.com

Ivanhoe Ivanhoe Times (1.1M) PO Box 100 Ivanhoe MN 56142 **Phn:** 507-694-1246 ivanhoetimes.freeservers.com luminamin@yahoo.com

Jackson Jackson County Pilot (2.7M) PO Box 208 Jackson MN 56143 **Phn:** 507-847-3771 **Fax:** 507-847-5822 www.jacksoncountypilot.com dallasl@livewireprinting.com

Jasper Jasper Journal (1.0M) PO Box 188 Jasper MN 56144 **Phn:** 507-348-4176 **Fax:** 507-825-2168 journal@pipestonestar.com

Jordan Jordan Independent (2.1M) 109 Rice St S Jordan MN 55352 **Phn:** 952-492-2224 www.jordannews.com editor@jordannews.com

Karlstad North Star News (2.0M) PO Box 158 Karlstad MN 56732 **Phn:** 218-436-2157 **Fax:** 218-436-3271 www.page1publications.com norstar@wiktel.com

Kasson Dodge County Independent (1.8M) 105 1st Ave NW Kasson MN 55944 **Phn:** 507-634-7503 **Fax:** 507-634-4446 www.dcinews.com dci@kmtel.com

Kenyon Kenyon Leader (2.1M) 638 2nd St Kenyon MN 55946 **Phn:** 507-789-6161 **Fax:** 507-789-5040 www.southernminn.com/the_kenyon_leader kjacobson@thekenyonleader.com

Kerkhoven Kerkhoven Banner (1.1M) PO Box 148 Kerkhoven MN 56252 **Phn:** 320-264-3071 **Fax:** 320-264-3070 kbanner@midstate.tds.net

Kiester The Courier-Sentinel (1.9M) PO Box 250 Kiester MN 56051 **Phn:** 507-294-3400

Kimball Tri-County News (1.8M) PO Box 220 Kimball MN 55353 **Phn:** 320-398-5000 **Fax:** 320-398-5000 www.tricountynews.mn news@tricountynews.mn

La Crosse Houston County News (2.5M) 401 N 3rd St La Crosse MN 54615 **Phn:** 608-791-8411 **Fax:** 608-791-8238 lacrossetribune.com/houstonconews ryan.henry@lee.net

Lafayette Lafayette-Nicollet Ledger (1.2M) PO Box 212 Lafayette MN 56054 **Phn:** 507-228-8985 **Fax:** 507-228-8779 ledger@prairiepublishingmn.com

Lake Benton Lake Benton Valley Journal (1.1M) PO Box 328 Lake Benton MN 56149 **Phn:** 507-368-4604 **Fax:** 507-368-4605 www.lbvalleyjournal.com lbnews@itctel.com

Lake City Lake City Graphic (3.3M) PO Box 469 Lake City MN 55041 **Phn:** 651-345-3316 graphic@rconnect.com

Lake Crystal Lake Crystal Tribune (1.5M) PO Box 240 Lake Crystal MN 56055 **Phn:** 507-726-2133 **Fax:** 507-726-2265 tribune@hickorytech.net

Lakefield Lakefield Standard (1.9M) PO Box 249 Lakefield MN 56150 **Phn:** 507-662-5555 **Fax:** 507-662-6770 www.lakefieldstandard.com connier@livewireprinting.com

Lakeville Lakeville Life & Times (20.0M) PO Box 549 Lakeville MN 55044 **Phn:** 952-469-2181 **Fax:** 952-469-2184 www.thisweek-online.com lakeville.thisweek@ecm-inc.com

Lamberton Lamberton News (1.7M) PO Box 308 Lamberton MN 56152 **Phn:** 507-752-7181

Le Center Le Center Leader (1.4M) PO Box 68 Le Center MN 56057 **Phn:** 507-357-2233 **Fax:** 507-357-6656 www.southernminn.com/le_center_leader srook@lecenter.com

Le Roy Le Roy Independent (1.3M) PO Box 89 Le Roy MN 55951 **Phn:** 507-324-5325 **Fax:** 507-324-5267

Le Sueur Le Sueur News-Herald (2.0M) 101 Bridge St # B Le Sueur MN 56058 **Phn:** 507-665-3332 **Fax:** 507-665-3334 www.southernminn.com/le_sueur_news_herald srook@lesueurnews-herald.com

Lewiston Lewiston Journal (1.2M) PO Box 608 Lewiston MN 55952 **Phn:** 507-523-2119 **Fax:** 507-932-5537

Lindstrom Chisago County Press (4.0M) PO Box 748 Lindstrom MN 55045 **Phn:** 651-257-5115 **Fax:** 651-257-5500 www.chisagocountypress.com chisago@citlink.net

Litchfield Independent-Review (3.9M) PO Box 307 Litchfield MN 55355 **Phn:** 320-693-3266 **Fax:** 320-693-9177 www.independentreview.net news@independentreview.net

Little Falls Morrison Co Record (19.0M) 216 1st St SE Little Falls MN 56345 **Phn:** 320-632-2345 **Fax:** 320-632-2348 mcrecord.com mcr@mcrecord.com

Long Prairie Long Prairie Leader (3.1M) PO Box 479 Long Prairie MN 56347 **Phn:** 320-732-2151 **Fax:** 320-732-2152 www.lpleader.com lpleader@rea-alp.com

Longville Press-Citizen (7.7M) PO Box 401 Longville MN 56655 **Phn:** 218-363-2002 **Fax:** 218-363-3043 pineconepresscitizen.com presscit@eot.com

Luverne Hills Crescent (0.8M) PO Box 837 Luverne MN 56156 **Phn:** 507-962-3230 **Fax:** 507-283-2335 editor@star-herald.com

Luverne Rock County Star-Herald (3.0M) PO Box 837 Luverne MN 56156 **Phn:** 507-283-2333 **Fax:** 507-283-2335 www.star-herald.com editor@star-herald.com

Madelia Times-Messenger (1.4M) 112 W Main St Madelia MN 56062 **Phn:** 507-642-3636 **Fax:** 507-642-3535 www.prairiepublishingmn.com tm@prairiepublishingmn.com

Madison Western Guard (1.9M) 216 6th Ave Madison MN 56256 **Phn:** 320-598-7521 **Fax:** 320-598-7523 westerng@frontiernet.net

Madison Lake Lake Region Times (1.0M) PO Box 128 Madison Lake MN 56063 **Phn:** 507-243-3031 **Fax:** 507-243-3122 lakeregiontimes@gmail.com

Mahnomen Mahnomen Pioneer (2.9M) PO Box 219 Mahnomen MN 56557 **Phn:** 218-935-5296 **Fax:** 218-935-2555 mahpioneer@arvig.net

Maple Lake Maple Lake Messenger (1.6M) PO Box 817 Maple Lake MN 55358 **Phn:** 320-963-3813 **Fax:** 320-963-6114 www.maplelakemessenger.com publisher@maplelakemessenger.com

Mapleton Maple River Messenger (1.7M) PO Box 425 Mapleton MN 56065 **Phn:** 507-524-3212 **Fax:** 507-524-4249 www.prairiepublishingmn.com mrm@prairiepublishingmn.com

McGregor Voyageur Press (1.0M) PO Box 59 McGregor MN 55760 **Phn:** 218-768-3405 **Fax:** 218-768-7046 www.thevoyageurpress.com vpofmg@frontiernet.net

Melrose Melrose Beacon (2.4M) 408 E Main St Melrose MN 56352 **Phn:** 320-256-3240 **Fax:** 320-256-3363 melrosebeacon.com news@melrosebeacon.com

Milaca Mille Lacs County Times (3.1M) 225 2nd St Sw Milaca MN 56353 **Phn:** 320-983-6111 **Fax:** 320-983-6112 millelacscountytimes.com editor.millelacscotimes@ecm-inc.com

Minneapolis City Pages (125.0M) 401 N 3rd St Ste 550 Minneapolis MN 55401 **Phn:** 612-375-1015 **Fax:** 612-372-3737 www.citypages.com

Minneapolis Downtown Journal (35.0M) 1115 Hennepin Ave Minneapolis MN 55403 **Phn:** 612-825-9205 **Fax:** 612-825-0929 www.journalmpls.com smckenzie@mnpubs.com

Minneapolis The Northeaster (32.5M) 2844 Johnson St NE Minneapolis MN 55418 **Phn:** 612-788-9003 **Fax:** 612-788-3299 nenorthnews.com contact@nenorthnews.com

Minneota Minneota Mascot (1.2M) PO Box 9 Minneota MN 56264 **Phn:** 507-872-6492 **Fax:** 507-872-6840 www.theminneotamascot.com news@starpoint.net

Minnesota Lake Minnesota Lake Tribune (0.7M) PO Box 214 Minnesota Lake MN 56068 **Phn:** 507-462-3321 mltrib@bevcomm.net

Montevideo American News (4.8M) 223 S 1st St Montevideo MN 56265 **Phn:** 320-269-2156 **Fax:** 320-269-2159 www.montenews.com editor@montenews.com

Montgomery Montgomery Messenger (2.5M) 310 1st St S Montgomery MN 56069 **Phn:** 507-364-8601 **Fax:** 507-364-8602 mpaper@frontiernet.net

Monticello Monticello Times (3.0M) PO Box 420 Monticello MN 55362 **Phn:** 763-295-3131 **Fax:** 763-295-3080 monticellotimes.com sam.aselstine@ecm-inc.com

Moose Lake Arrowhead Leader (3.6M) PO Box 506 Moose Lake MN 55767 **Phn:** 218-485-8420 **Fax:** 218-485-5904

Moose Lake Star Gazette (2.5M) PO Box 449 Moose Lake MN 55767 **Phn:** 218-485-4406 **Fax:** 218-485-0237 www.mlstargazette.com evergreen@mlstargazette.com

Mora Kanabec County Times (3.0M) 107 Park St S Mora MN 55051 **Phn:** 320-679-2661 **Fax:** 320-679-2663 www.presspubs.com/kanabec editor@moraminn.com

Morgan Morgan Messenger (1.0M) PO Box 38 Morgan MN 56266 **Phn:** 507-249-3130 **Fax:** 507-249-3131 morganmess@yahoo.com

Morris Morris Sun Tribune (3.0M) PO Box 470 Morris MN 56267 **Phn:** 320-589-2525 **Fax:** 320-589-4357 www.morrissuntribune.com news@morrissuntribune.com

Mound The Laker & Pioneer (13.2M) PO Box 82 Mound MN 55364 **Phn:** 952-442-4414 **Fax:** 952-442-6815 lakerpioneer.com todd.moen@ecm-inc.com

Mountain Lake Observer/Advocate (2.3M) PO Box 429 Mountain Lake MN 56159 **Phn:** 507-427-2725 **Fax:** 507-427-2724 www.mtlakenews.com observer@mtlakenews.com

Nevis Northwoods Press (1.7M) PO Box 28 Nevis MN 56467 **Phn:** 218-652-3475 www.lakeandpine.com info@northwoodspress.com

New London Lakes Area Review (6.4M) PO Box 838 New London MN 56273 **Phn:** 320-354-2945 **Fax:** 320-354-6300 lakesareareview@tds.net

New Prague The New Prague Times (4.5M) PO Box 25 New Prague MN 56071 **Phn:** 952-758-4435 **Fax:** 952-758-4135 www.newpraguetimes.com news@newpraguetimes.com

New Richland New Richland Star (1.5M) PO Box 248 New Richland MN 56072 **Phn:** 507-463-8112 **Fax:** 507-463-0504 newstar@hickorytech.net

North Branch ECM Post Review (2.4M) PO Box 366 North Branch MN 55056 **Phn:** 651-674-7025 **Fax:** 651-674-7026 ecmpostreview.com editor.postreview@ecm-inc.com

MINNESOTA WEEKLY NEWSPAPERS

North Saint Paul Lillie Newspapers (97.0M) 2515 7th Ave E North Saint Paul MN 55109 **Phn:** 651-777-8800 **Fax:** 651-777-8288 lillienews.com

North St Paul Bulletin Newspapers (25.0M) 2515 7th Ave E North St Paul MN 55109 **Phn:** 651-777-8800 **Fax:** 651-777-8288 bulletin-news.com bulletin@lillienews.com

Northfield Northfield News (4.9M) 115 5th St W Northfield MN 55057 **Phn:** 507-645-5615 **Fax:** 507-645-6005 www.southernminn.com/northfield_news jcsmith@northfieldnews.com

Norwood Norwood Young America Times (2.5M) PO Box 10 Norwood MN 55368 **Phn:** 952-467-2271 **Fax:** 952-467-2294 sunpatriot.com adam.gruenewald@ecm-inc.com

Olivia Star Farmer News (2.0M) 816 E Lincoln Ave Olivia MN 56277 **Phn:** 320-523-2032 **Fax:** 320-523-2033 oproduction@rencopub.com

Ortonville Ortonville Independent (3.3M) PO Box 336 Ortonville MN 56278 **Phn:** 320-839-6163 **Fax:** 320-839-3761 ortonvilleindependent.com mail@ortonvilleindependent.com

Osseo Sun Focus Newspapers (53.0M) PO Box 280 Osseo MN 55369 **Phn:** 763-706-0890 **Fax:** 763-424-7388 focus.mnsun.com sarah.peterson@ecm-inc.com

Osseo Sun Press & News Papers (40.5M) PO Box 280 Osseo MN 55369 **Phn:** 763-425-3323 **Fax:** 763-425-4299 www.pressnews.com sunpressnews@ecm-inc.com

Park Rapids The Park Rapids Enterprise (6.0M) PO Box 111 Park Rapids MN 56470 **Phn:** 218-732-3364 **Fax:** 218-732-8757 www.parkrapidsenterprise.com roryp@parkrapidsenterprise.com

Parkers Prairie Parkers Prairie Independent (1.5M) PO Box 42 Parkers Prairie MN 56361 **Phn:** 218-338-2741 **Fax:** 218-338-2745 www.ppindependent.net ppinews@me.com

Paynesville Paynesville Press (2.8M) PO Box 54 Paynesville MN 56362 **Phn:** 320-243-3772 **Fax:** 320-243-4492 www.paynesvillearea.com editor@paynesvillepress.com

Pelican Rapids Pelican Rapids Press (3.0M) PO Box 632 Pelican Rapids MN 56572 **Phn:** 218-863-1421 **Fax:** 218-863-1423 prpress@loretel.net

Pequot Lakes Lake Country Echo (4.7M) PO Box 240 Pequot Lakes MN 56472 **Phn:** 218-568-8521 **Fax:** 218-568-5407 www.pineandlakes.com nancy.vogt@pequotlakesecho.com

Perham Enterprise Enterprise (2.9M) PO Box 288 Perham MN 56573 **Phn:** 218-346-5900 **Fax:** 218-346-5901 www.eotfocus.com editor@eot.com

Perham Perham Focus (3.0M) 222 2nd Ave SE Perham MN 56573 **Phn:** 218-385-2275 **Fax:** 218-385-3626 www.perhamfocus.com editor@eotfocus.com

Pine City Pine City Pioneer (3.5M) 405 2nd Ave SE Pine City MN 55063 **Phn:** 320-629-6771 **Fax:** 320-629-6772 www.presspubs.com/pine_city editor@pinecitymn.com

Pine River Pine River Journal (1.9M) PO Box 370 Pine River MN 56474 **Phn:** 218-587-2360 **Fax:** 218-587-2331 www.pineandlakes.com pete.mohs@pequotlakesecho.com

Pipestone Pipestone County Star (4.0M) PO Box 277 Pipestone MN 56164 **Phn:** 507-825-3333 **Fax:** 507-825-2168 www.pipestonestar.com editor@pipestonestar.com

Plainview Plainview News (2.8M) 409 W Broadway Plainview MN 55964 **Phn:** 507-534-3121 **Fax:** 507-534-3920

Preston Fillmore Co Journal (11.0M) PO Box 496 Preston MN 55965 **Phn:** 507-765-2151 **Fax:** 507-765-2468 www.fillmorecountyjournal.com news@fillmorecountyjournal.com

Preston Republican Leader (1.5M) PO Box 27 Preston MN 55965 **Phn:** 507-765-2752 www.bluffcountrynews.com republican-leader@bluffcountrynews.com

Princeton Union-Eagle (3.2M) PO Box 278 Princeton MN 55371 **Phn:** 763-389-1222 **Fax:** 763-389-1728 unioneagle.com pueproduction@ecm-inc.com

Prior Lake The American (7.0M) PO Box 538 Prior Lake MN 55372 **Phn:** 952-447-6669 **Fax:** 952-447-6671 www.plamerican.com editor@plamerican.com

Proctor Proctor Journal (1.8M) 215 5th St Proctor MN 55810 **Phn:** 218-624-3344 **Fax:** 218-624-7037 www.proctorjournal.com journal@proctormn.com

Raymond Raymond-Prinsburg News (0.8M) PO Box 157 Raymond MN 56282 **Phn:** 320-967-4244

Red Lake Falls Red Lake Falls Gazette (1.6M) PO Box 370 Red Lake Falls MN 56750 **Phn:** 218-253-2594 **Fax:** 218-253-4114 rlfgaz@gvtel.com

Redwood Falls Redwood Falls Gazette (4.6M) PO Box 299 Redwood Falls MN 56283 **Phn:** 507-637-2929 **Fax:** 507-637-3175 www.redwoodfallsgazette.com editor@redwoodfallsgazette.com

Renville Renville Co. Register (2.1M) PO Box 468 Renville MN 56284 **Phn:** 320-329-3324 **Fax:** 320-329-3432 editor@rencopub.com

Roseau Roseau Times-Region (3.7M) PO Box 220 Roseau MN 56751 **Phn:** 218-463-1521 **Fax:** 218-463-1530 rtr@mncable.net

Rushford Tri-County Record (1.7M) PO Box 429 Rushford MN 55971 **Phn:** 507-864-7700 **Fax:** 507-864-2356 www.rushford.net tricopub@rushford.net

Saint Charles St. Charles Press (1.9M) PO Box 617 Saint Charles MN 55972 **Phn:** 507-932-3663 **Fax:** 507-932-5537 scpress@hbcsc.net

Saint James St. James Plaindealer (2.1M) PO Box 67 Saint James MN 56081 **Phn:** 507-375-3161 **Fax:** 507-375-3221 www.stjamesnews.com ddurheim@stjamesnews.com

Saint Joseph The Newsleaders (12.0M) PO Box 324 Saint Joseph MN 56374 **Phn:** 320-363-7741 **Fax:** 320-363-4195 www.thenewsleaders.net news@thenewsleaders.com

Saint Paul Minnesota Women's Press (35.0M) 970 Raymond Ave # 201 Saint Paul MN 55114 **Phn:** 651-646-3968 **Fax:** 651-646-2186 www.womenspress.com editor@womenspress.com

Saint Paul The Wanderer (30.0M) 201 Ohio St Saint Paul MN 55107 **Phn:** 651-224-5733 **Fax:** 651-224-9666 www.thewandererpress.com editorial@thewandererpress.com

Saint Peter St. Peter Herald (3.5M) 311 S Minnesota Ave Saint Peter MN 56082 **Phn:** 507-931-4520 **Fax:** 507-931-4522 www.southernminn.com/st_peter_herald shill@stpeterherald.com

Sandstone Pine County Courier (2.1M) PO Box 230 Sandstone MN 55072 **Phn:** 320-245-2368 **Fax:** 320-245-2438 courier@pinenet.com

Sauk Centre Dairyland Peach (30.0M) PO Box 285 Sauk Centre MN 56378 **Phn:** 320-352-6569 **Fax:** 320-352-6181 www.dairylandpeach.com print.saukcentre@ecm-inc.com

Sauk Centre Sauk Centre Herald (3.0M) 522 Sinclair Lewis Ave Sauk Centre MN 56378 **Phn:** 320-352-6577 **Fax:** 320-352-5647 www.saukherald.com bryan@saukherald.com

Sauk Rapids Sauk Rapids Herald (1.3M) PO Box 8 Sauk Rapids MN 56379 **Phn:** 320-251-1971

Savage Pacer (5.2M) PO Box 376 Savage MN 55378 **Phn:** 952-440-1234 **Fax:** 952-447-6671 www.savagepacer.com editor@savagepacer.com

Scandia Country Messenger (1.3M) PO Box 96 Scandia MN 55073 **Phn:** 651-433-3845 **Fax:** 715-755-3314 www.presspubs.com/messenger editor@countrymessenger.com

Sebeka Review Messenger (3.4M) PO Box 309 Sebeka MN 56477 **Phn:** 218-837-5558 **Fax:** 218-837-5560 www.lakeandpine.com remess@wcta.net

Shakopee Shakopee Valley News (5.1M) PO Box 8 Shakopee MN 55379 **Phn:** 952-445-3333 **Fax:** 952-445-3335 www.shakopeenews.com editor@shakopeenews.com

Sherburn Martin Co. Star (1.4M) PO Box 820 Sherburn MN 56171 **Phn:** 507-764-6681 **Fax:** 507-764-2756 mcstar@frontiernet.net

Silver Lake Silver Lake Leader (1.2M) PO Box 343 Silver Lake MN 55381 **Phn:** 320-327-2216 **Fax:** 320-327-2530

Slayton Murray County News (7.5M) PO Box 288 Slayton MN 56172 **Phn:** 507-836-8929 **Fax:** 507-836-6162 www.murraycountynews.net mcnews@frontiernet.net

Slayton Wheel/Herald (7.2M) PO Box 263 Slayton MN 56172 **Phn:** 507-836-8726 **Fax:** 507-836-8942 wheelherald@iw.net

Sleepy Eye Herald-Dispatch (2.8M) PO Box 499 Sleepy Eye MN 56085 **Phn:** 507-794-3511 **Fax:** 507-794-5031 www.sleepyeyenews.com publisher@sleepyeyenews.com

Spring Grove Spring Grove Herald (1.4M) PO Box 68 Spring Grove MN 55974 **Phn:** 507-498-3868 **Fax:** 507-498-6397 www.bluffcountrynews.com sgherald@bluffcountrynews.com

Spring Valley Spring Valley Tribune (1.9M) PO Box 112 Spring Valley MN 55975 **Phn:** 507-346-7365 **Fax:** 507-346-7366 www.bluffcountrynews.com svtribune@bluffcountrynews.com

Springfield Advance Press (2.7M) PO Box 78 Springfield MN 56087 **Phn:** 507-723-4225 **Fax:** 507-723-4400 aps@newulmtel.com

Staples Staples World (2.4M) PO Box 100 Staples MN 56479 **Phn:** 218-894-1112 **Fax:** 218-894-3570 www.staplesworld.com info@staplesworld.com

Starbuck Starbuck Times (1.7M) PO Box 457 Starbuck MN 56381 **Phn:** 320-634-4571 **Fax:** 320-634-5522 www.pctribune.com news@pctribune.com

Stephen Stephen Messenger (2.0M) PO Box 48 Stephen MN 56757 **Phn:** 218-478-2210 messenger@wiktel.com

Stewartville Stewartville Star (2.2M) PO Box 35 Stewartville MN 55976 **Phn:** 507-533-4271 **Fax:** 507-533-4272 thinkstewartville.com starnews@stewiestar.com

Thief River Falls Northern Watch (23.0M) PO Box 100 Thief River Falls MN 56701 **Phn:** 218-681-4450 **Fax:** 218-681-4455 www.trftimes.com/news trftimes@trftimes.com

Thief River Falls Thief River Falls Times (5.0M) PO Box 100 Thief River Falls MN 56701 **Phn:** 218-681-4450 **Fax:** 218-681-4455 www.trftimes.com trftimes@trftimes.com

Tower The Timberjay (7.7M) PO Box 636 Tower MN 55790 **Phn:** 218-753-2950 **Fax:** 218-753-2916 www.timberjay.com editor@timberjay.com

Tower Tower News (2.2M) PO Box 447 Tower MN 55790 **Phn:** 218-753-7777 **Fax:** 218-753-7778

Tracy Headlight Herald (2.0M) 207 4th St Tracy MN 56175 **Phn:** 507-629-4300 **Fax:** 507-629-4301 www.headlightherald.com tracypublishing@headlightherald.com

Truman Truman Tribune (1.0M) PO Box 98 Truman MN 56088 **Phn:** 507-776-2751

Twin Valley Twin Valley Times (1.5M) PO Box 478 Twin Valley MN 56584 **Phn:** 218-584-5195 **Fax:** 218-584-5196 tvtimes@tvutel.com

Two Harbors Lake County News-Chronicle (3.5M) PO Box 158 Two Harbors MN 55616 **Phn:** 218-834-2141 **Fax:** 218-834-2144 www.twoharborsmn.com chronicle@lcnewschronicle.com

Tyler Buffalo Ridge Gazette (0.6M) PO Box Q Tyler MN 56178 **Phn:** 507-658-3919 **Fax:** 507-658-3404

Tyler Tyler Tribune (1.5M) PO Box Q Tyler MN 56178 **Phn:** 507-247-5502 www.tylertribune.com tribute@tylertribute.com

Ulen Clay Co. Union (1.3M) PO Box 248 Ulen MN 56585 **Phn:** 218-596-8813 **Fax:** 218-861-6708

Verndale Verndale Sun (1.0M) PO Box E Verndale MN 56481 **Phn:** 218-445-6397 inhnews.com verndalesun@inhnews.com

Wabasha Wabasha County Herald (3.0M) PO Box 109 Wabasha MN 55981 **Phn:** 651-565-3368 **Fax:** 651-565-4736

Wabasso Wabasso Standard (0.8M) PO Box 70 Wabasso MN 56293 **Phn:** 507-342-5143 **Fax:** 507-342-5144

Waconia Waconia Patriot (3.9M) PO Box 5 Waconia MN 55387 **Phn:** 952-442-4414 **Fax:** 952-442-6815 sunpatriot.com todd.moen@ecm-inc.com

Wadena Wadena Pioneer Journal (4.1M) PO Box 31 Wadena MN 56482 **Phn:** 218-631-2561 **Fax:** 218-631-1621 www.wadenapj.com editorial@wadenapj.com

Walker The Pilot-Independent (3.1M) PO Box 190 Walker MN 56484 **Phn:** 218-547-1000 **Fax:** 218-547-3000 www.walkermn.com

Warren Warren Sheaf (3.1M) PO Box 45 Warren MN 56762 **Phn:** 218-745-5174 **Fax:** 218-745-5175

Waseca Janesville Argus (1.0M) 213 2nd St NW Waseca MN 56093 **Phn:** 507-234-6651 **Fax:** 507-231-6390

Waseca Waseca County News (9.0M) PO Box 465 Waseca MN 56093 **Phn:** 507-835-3380 **Fax:** 507-835-3435 www.southernminn.com/waseca_county_news jfrazier@wasecacountynews.com

Watertown Carver County News (2.1M) PO Box 188 Watertown MN 55388 **Phn:** 952-955-1111 **Fax:** 952-955-2241

Waterville Lake Region Life (1.5M) 115 3rd St S Waterville MN 56096 **Phn:** 507-362-4495 **Fax:** 507-362-4458 lrlife@frontiernet.net

Wayzata Lakeshore Weekly News (25.0M) 1001 Twelve Oaks Center Dr Ste 1017 Wayzata MN 55391 **Phn:** 952-473-0890 **Fax:** 952-473-0895 www.weeklynews.com editor@weeklynews.com

Wells Wells Mirror (1.8M) 40 W Franklin St Wells MN 56097 **Phn:** 507-553-3131 **Fax:** 507-553-3132 wellsmir@bevcomm.net

West Concord News-Enterprise (0.7M) PO Box 8 West Concord MN 55985 **Phn:** 507-527-2492 **Fax:** 507-527-8942

MINNESOTA WEEKLY NEWSPAPERS

Westbrook Westbrook Sentinel-Tribune (1.2M) PO Box 98 Westbrook MN 56183 **Phn:** 507-274-6136 **Fax:** 507-274-6137 www.ncppub.com sentrib@ncppub.com

Wheaton Wheaton Gazette (2.7M) 1114 Broadway Wheaton MN 56296 **Phn:** 320-563-8146 **Fax:** 320-563-8147 wgazette@frontiernet.net

White Bear Lake Press Publications (50.0M) 4779 Bloom Ave White Bear Lake MN 55110 **Phn:** 651-407-1200 **Fax:** 651-429-1242 www.presspubs.com news@presspubs.com

Windom Cottonwood County Citizen (3.8M) PO Box 309 Windom MN 56101 **Phn:** 507-831-3455 **Fax:** 507-831-3740 www.windomnews.com citizen@windomnews.com

Winona Winona Post (25.0M) PO Box 27 Winona MN 55987 **Phn:** 507-452-1262 **Fax:** 507-454-6409 www.winonapost.com winpost@winonapost.com

Winsted Herald Journal (1.5M) PO Box 129 Winsted MN 55395 **Phn:** 320-485-2535 **Fax:** 320-485-2878 www.herald-journal.com news@heraldjournal.com

Winthrop Winthrop News (1.4M) PO Box L Winthrop MN 55396 **Phn:** 507-647-5357 **Fax:** 507-647-5358 winnews@means.net

Woodbury Woodbury Bulletin (10.0M) 8420 City Centre Dr Woodbury MN 55125 **Phn:** 651-730-4007 **Fax:** 651-702-0977 www.woodburybulletin.com editor@woodburybulletin.com

Zumbrota News-Record (3.4M) PO Box 97 Zumbrota MN 55992 **Phn:** 507-732-7617 **Fax:** 507-732-7619 www.zumbrota.com news@zumbrota.com

MISSISSIPPI

Ackerman Choctaw Plaindealer (2.8M) PO Box 910 Ackerman MS 39735 **Phn:** 662-285-6248 **Fax:** 662-285-6695 www.choctawplaindealer.com newsroom@winstoncountyjournal.com

Baldwyn Baldwyn News (2.5M) PO Box 130 Baldwyn MS 38824 **Phn:** 662-365-3232 **Fax:** 662-365-7989 thebaldwynnews@dixie-net.com

Batesville The Panolian (18.0M) PO Box 1616 Batesville MS 38606 **Phn:** 662-563-4591 **Fax:** 662-563-5610 thepanolian@panola.com

Bay Saint Louis Sea Coast Echo (6.8M) PO Box 2009 Bay Saint Louis MS 39521 **Phn:** 228-467-5474 **Fax:** 228-467-0333 www.seacoastecho.com rponder@seacoastecho.com

Bay Springs Jasper County News (2.8M) PO Box 449 Bay Springs MS 39422 **Phn:** 601-764-3104 **Fax:** 601-764-3106 bni@teleclipse.net

Bay Springs Smith Co. Reformer (2.8M) PO Box 449 Bay Springs MS 39422 **Phn:** 601-764-3104 **Fax:** 601-764-3106 bni@teleclipse.net

Belmont Belmont & Tishomingo Journal (2.2M) PO Box 70 Belmont MS 38827 **Phn:** 662-454-7196 **Fax:** 662-454-0055 jrnlb@bellsouth.net

Belzoni The Belzoni Banner (1.4M) PO Box 610 Belzoni MS 39038 **Phn:** 662-247-3373 **Fax:** 662-247-3372 www.thebelzonibanner.com banner@belzonicable.com

Biloxi Biloxi-D'Iberville Press (3.5M) PO Box 1209 Biloxi MS 39533 **Phn:** 228-435-0720 **Fax:** 228-436-7737 getthepress.com

Booneville Banner-Independent (5.4M) PO Box 10 Booneville MS 38829 **Phn:** 662-728-6214 **Fax:** 662-728-1636 boonevillebanner@bellsouth.net

Brandon Rankin County News (8.0M) 207 E Government St Brandon MS 39042 **Phn:** 601-825-8333 **Fax:** 601-825-8334 rankincn@aol.com

Brandon Rankin Record (4.5M) PO Box 5507 Brandon MS 39047 **Phn:** 601-992-4869 **Fax:** 601-992-7825 www.rankinrecord.com news@rankinrecord.com

Bruce Calhoun County Journal (4.7M) PO Box 278 Bruce MS 38915 **Phn:** 662-983-2570 **Fax:** 662-983-7667 www.calhouncountyjournal.com joelmcneece@gmail.com

Carthage Carthaginian (5.7M) 122 W Franklin St Carthage MS 39051 **Phn:** 601-267-4501 **Fax:** 601-267-5290 www.thecarthaginian.com news@thecarthaginian.com

Charleston Charleston Sun-Sentinel (2.4M) PO Box 250 Charleston MS 38921 **Phn:** 662-647-8462 **Fax:** 662-647-3830 clay@charlestonsun.net

Cleveland News Leader (2.2M) PO Box 972 Cleveland MS 38732 **Phn:** 662-588-6397 **Fax:** 662-843-5364

Clinton Clinton News (11.0M) 104 Green Forest Dr Clinton MS 39056 **Phn:** 601-924-7142 www.clintonnews.com news@clintonnews.com

Coffeeville Coffeeville Courier (2.2M) PO Box 607 Coffeeville MS 38922 **Phn:** 662-675-2446 **Fax:** 662-675-2416

Collins The News-Commercial (3.2M) PO Box 1299 Collins MS 39428 **Phn:** 601-765-8275 **Fax:** 601-765-6952

Columbia Columbian-Progress (5.5M) PO Box 1171 Columbia MS 39429 **Phn:** 601-736-2611 **Fax:** 601-736-4507 www.columbianprogress.com news@columbianprogress.com

Crystal Springs Crystal Springs Meteor (3.0M) PO Box 353 Crystal Springs MS 39059 **Phn:** 601-892-2581 **Fax:** 601-892-2249

De Kalb Kemper County Messenger (2.3M) PO Box 546 De Kalb MS 39328 **Phn:** 601-743-5760 **Fax:** 601-743-4430 kempercountymessenger.com rocky@kempercountymessenger.com

Eupora Webster Progress-Times (2.4M) 58 N Dunn St Eupora MS 39744 **Phn:** 662-258-7532 **Fax:** 662-258-6474 www.websterprogresstimes.com news@websterprogresstimes.com

Forest Scott County Times (7.0M) PO Box 89 Forest MS 39074 **Phn:** 601-469-2561 **Fax:** 601-469-2004 www.sctonline.net cbaker@sctonline.net

Fulton Itawamba County Times (4.8M) 106 W Main St Fulton MS 38843 **Phn:** 662-862-3141 **Fax:** 662-862-7804 itawambatimes.com news1@itawamba360.com

Gloster Wilk-Amite Record (2.4M) PO Box 130 Gloster MS 39638 **Phn:** 601-384-2484 **Fax:** 601-384-2276

Grenada Grenada Star (5.6M) 50 Corporate Row Grenada MS 38901 **Phn:** 662-226-4321 **Fax:** 662-226-8310 www.grenadastar.com editor@grenadastar.com

Hattiesburg Hattiesburg Publishing Inc. (18.0M) 126 Westover Dr Hattiesburg MS 39402 **Phn:** 601-268-2331 **Fax:** 601-268-2965 www.hubcityspokes.com beth@hubcityspokes.com

Hazlehurst Copiah County Courier (4.5M) PO Box 351 Hazlehurst MS 39083 **Phn:** 601-894-3141 **Fax:** 601-894-3144 www.copiahcountycourier.com editor@bellsouth.net

Hernando DeSoto Times-Tribune (9.0M) 2445 Highway 51 S Hernando MS 38632 **Phn:** 662-429-6397 **Fax:** 662-429-5229 desototimes.com editor@desototimestribune.com

Holly Springs South Reporter (5.2M) PO Box 278 Holly Springs MS 38635 **Phn:** 662-252-4261 **Fax:** 662-252-3388 www.southreporter.com southreporter@dixie-net.com

Houston Journal & Times-Post (2.2M) PO Box 629 Houston MS 38851 **Phn:** 662-456-3771 **Fax:** 662-456-5202 chickasawjournal.com news@chickasaw360.com

Indianola Enterprise-Tocsin (4.0M) PO Box 650 Indianola MS 38751 **Phn:** 662-887-2222 **Fax:** 662-887-2999 news@enterprise-tocsin.com

Iuka Tishomongo County News (6.5M) PO Box 70 Iuka MS 38852 **Phn:** 662-423-2211 **Fax:** 662-423-2214

Jackson Northside Sun (10.0M) PO Box 16709 Jackson MS 39236 **Phn:** 601-957-1122 **Fax:** 601-957-1533 www.northsidesun.com jimmye@northsidesun.com

Jackson Rankin Ledger (48.0M) 201 S Congress St Jackson MS 39201 **Phn:** 601-360-4600 **Fax:** 601-961-7111 www.rankinledger.com news@rankinledger.com

Kosciusko Kosciusko Star-Herald (7.0M) 207 N Madison St Kosciusko MS 39090 **Phn:** 662-289-2251 **Fax:** 662-289-2254 starherald.net editor@starherald.net

Leakesville Greene County Herald (3.1M) PO Box 220 Leakesville MS 39451 **Phn:** 601-394-5070 **Fax:** 601-394-4389 www.greenecountyheraldonline.com herald@tds.net

Leland Leland Progress (1.2M) PO Box 72 Leland MS 38756 **Phn:** 662-686-4081 **Fax:** 662-686-9076

Lexington Holmes County Herald (3.2M) PO Box 60 Lexington MS 39095 **Phn:** 662-834-1151 **Fax:** 662-834-1074 www.holmescountyherald.com hcherald@bellsouth.net

Liberty The Southern Herald (1.2M) PO Box 674 Liberty MS 39645 **Phn:** 601-657-4818 thesouthernherald@telepak.net

Louisville Winston County Journal (3.2M) PO Box 469 Louisville MS 39339 **Phn:** 662-773-6241 **Fax:** 662-773-6242 www.winstoncountyjournal.com newsroom@winstoncountyjournal.com

Lucedale George County Times (5.5M) PO Box 238 Lucedale MS 39452 **Phn:** 601-947-2967 **Fax:** 601-947-6828 gctimes@bellsouth.net

Macon Macon Beacon (3.1M) PO Box 32 Macon MS 39341 **Phn:** 662-726-4747 **Fax:** 662-726-4742 maconbeacon@aol.com

Madison Madison County Herald (14.0M) 574 US 51 N # B Madison MS 39110 **Phn:** 601-853-2899 **Fax:** 601-853-8720 www.mcherald.com aoeth@jackson.gannett.com

Magee Magee Courier (3.8M) PO Box 338 Magee MS 39111 **Phn:** 601-849-3434 **Fax:** 601-849-6828 mageecourier-countynews.com mcourier@bellsouth.net

Magnolia Magnolia Gazette (1.4M) 280 Magnolia St Magnolia MS 39652 **Phn:** 601-783-2441 **Fax:** 601-783-2091 magnoliagazette.com magnoliagazette@bellsouth.net

Marks Quitman County Democrat (1.5M) PO Box 328 Marks MS 38646 **Phn:** 662-326-2181 quitmancodemocrat@att.net

McComb Southwest Sun (8.8M) PO Box 2009 McComb MS 39649 **Phn:** 601-684-2421 **Fax:** 601-684-0836 news@enterprise-journal.com

Meadville Franklin Advocate (3.4M) PO Box 576 Meadville MS 39653 **Phn:** 601-384-2484 **Fax:** 601-384-2276

Mendenhall Simpson County News (2.7M) PO Box 97 Mendenhall MS 39114 **Phn:** 601-847-2525 **Fax:** 601-847-2571 mageecourier-countynews.com mcourier@bellsouth.net

Monticello Lawrence County Press (3.0M) PO Box 549 Monticello MS 39654 **Phn:** 601-587-2781 **Fax:** 601-587-2794 press@bellsouth.net

MISSISSIPPI WEEKLY NEWSPAPERS

New Albany New Albany Gazette (6.5M) PO Box 300 New Albany MS 38652 **Phn:** 662-534-6321 **Fax:** 662-534-6355 www.newalbanygazette.com editor@newalbanygazette.com

Newton Newton Record (2.4M) PO Box 60 Newton MS 39345 **Phn:** 601-683-2001

Ocean Springs Ocean Springs Record (3.0M) 807B Holcomb Blvd Ocean Springs MS 39564 **Phn:** 228-207-4709 **Fax:** 228-207-4678 news@osrecord.com

Okolona Okolona Messenger (2.6M) 249 W Main St Okolona MS 38860 **Phn:** 662-447-5501 **Fax:** 662-447-5571

Philadelphia Neshoba Democrat (7.5M) PO Box 30 Philadelphia MS 39350 **Phn:** 601-656-4000 **Fax:** 601-656-6379 neshobademocrat.com dmyers@neshobademocrat.com

Pontotoc Pontotoc Progress (6.8M) PO Box 210 Pontotoc MS 38863 **Phn:** 662-489-3511 **Fax:** 662-489-1369 pontotoc-progress.com pontotoc.news@journalinc.com

Poplarville Poplarville Democrat (1.6M) PO Box 549 Poplarville MS 39470 **Phn:** 601-795-2247 **Fax:** 601-795-2232 thedemocrat@bellsouth.net

Port Gibson Pt. Gibson Reveille (2.5M) PO Box 1002 Port Gibson MS 39150 **Phn:** 601-437-5103 **Fax:** 601-437-4410

Prentiss Prentiss Headlight (2.5M) PO Box 1257 Prentiss MS 39474 **Phn:** 601-792-4221 **Fax:** 601-792-4222 dailyleader.com/prentiss editor@prentissheadlight.com

Quitman Clarke County Tribune (4.0M) PO Box 900 Quitman MS 39355 **Phn:** 601-776-3726 **Fax:** 601-776-5793

Raleigh Smith County Reformer (3.0M) PO Box 187 Raleigh MS 39153 **Phn:** 601-782-4358

Raymond Hinds County Gazette (2.2M) PO Box 729 Raymond MS 39154 **Phn:** 601-857-8071 **Fax:** 601-857-5095 hcgazette@aol.com

Richton Richton Dispatch (1.7M) PO Box 429 Richton MS 39476 **Phn:** 601-788-6031

Ridgeland Madison County Journal (5.0M) PO Box 219 Ridgeland MS 39158 **Phn:** 601-853-4222 **Fax:** 601-856-9419 www.onlinemadison.com letters@onlinemadison.com

Ripley Southern Sentinel (7.3M) PO Box 558 Ripley MS 38663 **Phn:** 662-837-8111 **Fax:** 662-837-4504 suburbancommunitynews.com

Rolling Fork Deer Creek Pilot (1.6M) PO Box 398 Rolling Fork MS 39159 **Phn:** 662-873-4354 **Fax:** 662-873-4355 deercreekpilot@bellsouth.net

Sardis The Southern Reporter (2.3M) PO Box 157 Sardis MS 38666 **Phn:** 662-487-1551 **Fax:** 662-487-1552 southernreporter@bellsouth.net

Senatobia The Democrat (5.2M) 219 E Main St Senatobia MS 38668 **Phn:** 662-562-4414 **Fax:** 662-562-8866 www.thedemocrat.com pageeditor@thedemocrat.com

Taylorsville Taylorsville Post (2.0M) PO Box 100 Taylorsville MS 39168 **Phn:** 601-785-4333 tvillepost@bellsouth.net

Tunica Tunica Times (2.1M) PO Box 308 Tunica MS 38676 **Phn:** 662-363-1511 **Fax:** 662-363-9969 www.tunicatimes.com news@tunicatimes.com

Tylertown Tylertown Times (3.9M) PO Box 72 Tylertown MS 39667 **Phn:** 601-876-5111 **Fax:** 601-876-5280 www.thetylertowntimes.org tylertowntimes@bellsouth.net

Union The Newton Co. Appeal (3.0M) 105 Main St Union MS 39365 **Phn:** 601-774-9433 **Fax:** 601-774-8301 jrt@newtoncountyappeal.com

Water Valley North Mississippi Herald (2.9M) PO Box 648 Water Valley MS 38965 **Phn:** 662-473-1473 **Fax:** 662-473-9133 yalnews.com dhowl@bellsouth.net

Waynesboro Wayne County News (4.5M) PO Box 509 Waynesboro MS 39367 **Phn:** 601-735-4341 **Fax:** 601-735-1111 www.thewaynecountynews.com publisher@thewaynecountynews.com

Wiggins Stone County Enterprise (3.6M) PO Box 157 Wiggins MS 39577 **Phn:** 601-928-4802 **Fax:** 601-928-2191 www.stonecountyenterprise.com news@stonecountyenterprise.com

Winona The Conservative (1.3M) PO Box 151 Winona MS 38967 **Phn:** 662-283-1131 **Fax:** 662-283-5374 www.winonatimes.com editor@winonatimes.com

Winona Winona Times (3.2M) PO Box 151 Winona MS 38967 **Phn:** 662-283-1131 **Fax:** 662-283-5374 www.winonatimes.com editor@winonatimes.com

Woodville Woodville Republican (2.6M) PO Box 696 Woodville MS 39669 **Phn:** 601-888-4293 **Fax:** 601-888-6156 wrepublican@bellsouth.net

Yazoo City Yazoo Herald (4.0M) PO Box 720 Yazoo City MS 39194 **Phn:** 662-746-4911 **Fax:** 662-746-4915 www.yazooherald.net jason@yazooherald.net

MISSOURI

Adrian Adrian Journal (1.7M) PO Box 128 Adrian MO 64720 **Phn:** 816-297-2100 adrianjournal@usa.net

Albany Albany Ledger (1.6M) PO Box 247 Albany MO 64402 **Phn:** 660-726-3998 **Fax:** 660-726-3997 www.aledger.net news@aledger.net

Alma Santa Fe Times (0.8M) PO Box 76 Alma MO 64001 **Phn:** 660-674-2250 safetnews@yahoo.com

Appleton City The Journal (1.5M) PO Box 7 Appleton City MO 64724 **Phn:** 660-476-5566 **Fax:** 660-646-8015

Ash Grove Ash Grove Commonwealth (1.8M) PO Box 277 Ash Grove MO 65604 **Phn:** 417-751-2322 **Fax:** 417-751-3499

Ashland Boone County Journal (1.7M) PO Box 197 Ashland MO 65010 **Phn:** 573-657-2334 **Fax:** 573-657-2002 www.bocojo.com bruce@bocojo.com

Aurora Aurora Advertiser (2.2M) PO Box 509 Aurora MO 65605 **Phn:** 417-678-2115 **Fax:** 417-678-2117 www.auroraadvertiser.net jdingman@auroraadvertiser.net

Ava Douglas County Herald (5.0M) PO Box 577 Ava MO 65608 **Phn:** 417-683-4181 **Fax:** 417-683-4102 www.douglascountyherald.com editor@douglascountyherald.com

Belle Tri-County Newspapers (5.3M) PO Box 711 Belle MO 65013 **Phn:** 573-859-3328 **Fax:** 573-859-6274 kjl@socket.net

Bethany Republican-Clipper (3.5M) PO Box 351 Bethany MO 64424 **Phn:** 660-425-6325 **Fax:** 660-425-3441 www.bethanyclipper.com rclipper@grm.net

Bloomfield North Stoddard Countian (3.0M) PO Box 680 Bloomfield MO 63825 **Phn:** 573-568-3310 elfreda_c@yahoo.com

Bolivar Herald-Free Press (6.8M) PO Box 330 Bolivar MO 65613 **Phn:** 417-326-7636 **Fax:** 417-326-7643 bolivarmonews.com news@bolivarmonews.com

Boonville Boonville Record (10.0M) PO Box 47 Boonville MO 65233 **Phn:** 660-882-5335 **Fax:** 660-882-2256

MISSOURI WEEKLY NEWSPAPERS

Bowling Green Bowling Green Times (3.2M) PO Box 110 Bowling Green MO 63334 **Phn:** 573-324-2222 **Fax:** 573-324-3991 www.bowlinggreentimes.com bgteditor@sbcglobal.net

Bowling Green The People's Tribune (8.5M) PO Box 440 Bowling Green MO 63334 **Phn:** 573-324-2551 thepeoplestribune.com april@thepeoplestribune.com

Branson Taney Co. Times (4.0M) PO Box 6670 Branson MO 65615 **Phn:** 417-334-2285 **Fax:** 417-334-4789

Brookfield Linn Co. Ledaer (2.5M) PO Box 40 Brookfield MO 64628 **Phn:** 660-258-7237 **Fax:** 660-258-7238 www.linncountyleader.com news@linncountyleader.com

Brunswick The Brunswicker (1.8M) 118 E Broadway St Brunswick MO 65236 **Phn:** 660-548-3171 **Fax:** 660-388-6688 ps@cvalley.net

Buffalo Buffalo Reflex (5.8M) PO Box 770 Buffalo MO 65622 **Phn:** 417-345-2224 **Fax:** 417-345-2235 buffaloreflex.com paulc@buffaloreflex.com

Buffalo County Courier LLC (2.5M) PO Box 440 Buffalo MO 65622 **Phn:** 417-345-2323 **Fax:** 417-345-6800

Butler Butler News-Xpress (3.0M) PO Box 210 Butler MO 64730 **Phn:** 660-679-6126 **Fax:** 660-679-4905 www.yourxgroup.com butler@yourxgroup.com

Cabool Cabool Enterprise (1.8M) PO Box 40 Cabool MO 65689 **Phn:** 417-962-4411 **Fax:** 417-962-4455 www.thecaboolenterprise.com cabent@centurytel.net

California California Democrat (4.0M) PO Box 126 California MO 65018 **Phn:** 573-796-2135 **Fax:** 573-796-4220 www.californiademocrat.com editor@californiademocrat.com

Cameron Cameron Citizen Observer (2.5M) 403 E Evergreen Cameron MO 64429 **Phn:** 816-632-6543 **Fax:** 816-632-4508 www.mycameronnews.com editor@mycameronnews.com

Canton Press News Journal (3.0M) PO Box 227 Canton MO 63435 **Phn:** 573-288-5668 **Fax:** 573-288-0000 www.lewispnj.com news@lewispnj.com

Carrollton Carrollton Democrat (2.7M) PO Box 69 Carrollton MO 64633 **Phn:** 660-542-0881 **Fax:** 660-542-2580 www.carolnet.com/CDN democrat@carolnet.com

Caruthersville Democrat Argus (2.5M) PO Box 1059 Caruthersville MO 63830 **Phn:** 573-333-4336 **Fax:** 573-333-2307 www.democratargus.com

Cassville Barry County Advertiser (12.0M) PO Box 488 Cassville MO 65625 **Phn:** 417-847-4475 **Fax:** 417-847-4523 www.4bcaonline.com editor@4bca.com

Cassville Cassville Democrat (13.2M) PO Box 486 Cassville MO 65625 **Phn:** 417-847-2610 **Fax:** 417-847-3092 cassville-democrat.com editor@cassville-democrat.com

Centralia Fireside Guard (3.4M) PO Box 7 Centralia MO 65240 **Phn:** 573-682-2133 **Fax:** 573-682-3361 www.firesideguard.com cfgmgr@lcs.net

Chaffee Scott Co Signal (7.8M) PO Box 97 Chaffee MO 63740 **Phn:** 573-887-3636 **Fax:** 573-887-3637

Charleston Mississippi County Times (2.5M) PO Box 443 Charleston MO 63834 **Phn:** 573-683-6689 **Fax:** 573-683-4291 countytimes@sbcglobal.net

Charleston The Enterprise-Courier (3.0M) PO Box 69 Charleston MO 63834 **Phn:** 573-683-3351 **Fax:** 573-683-2217 www.enterprisecourier.com kevin@enterprisecourier.com

Chesterfield Suburban Journals (62.0M) 14522 S Outer 40 Rd Chesterfield MO 63017 **Phn:** 636-296-1800 **Fax:** 636-931-2638 www.stltoday.com/suburban-journals sclubb@yourjournal.com

Clarence Clarence Courier (1.7M) PO Box 10 Clarence MO 63437 **Phn:** 660-699-2344 **Fax:** 660-699-2194

Clinton Clinton Eye (0.7M) PO Box 586 Clinton MO 64735 **Phn:** 660-885-2281 **Fax:** 660-885-2265

Concordia The Concordian (3.0M) PO Box 999 Concordia MO 64020 **Phn:** 660-463-7522 **Fax:** 660-463-7942

Crane Crane Chronicle (2.8M) PO Box 401 Crane MO 65633 **Phn:** 417-723-5248 **Fax:** 417-723-8490 www.cc-scrnews.com

Cuba Cuba Free Press (2.5M) PO Box 568 Cuba MO 65453 **Phn:** 573-885-7460 **Fax:** 573-885-3803 www.threeriverspublishing.com news@cubafreepress.com

Cuba Steelville Star (2.9M) PO Box 568 Cuba MO 65453 **Phn:** 573-885-7460 **Fax:** 573-885-3803 www.threeriverspublishing.com stvlstar@misn.com

Dixon Dixon Pilot (2.2M) PO Box V Dixon MO 65459 **Phn:** 573-759-2127 **Fax:** 573-759-6226 www.dixonpilot.com dixonpilotnews@yahoo.com

Doniphan Prospect-News (3.5M) PO Box 367 Doniphan MO 63935 **Phn:** 573-996-2103 **Fax:** 573-996-2217 pnpaper@windstream.net

Drexel Drexel Star (0.8M) PO Box 378 Drexel MO 64742 **Phn:** 816-657-2222 www.drexelstar.com adrianjournal@usa.net

Edina Edina Sentinel (2.3M) PO Box 270 Edina MO 63537 **Phn:** 660-397-2226 **Fax:** 660-397-3558 www.nemonews.net themedia@centurytel.net

El Dorado Springs El Dorado Springs Sun (3.8M) PO Box 71 El Dorado Springs MO 64744 **Phn:** 417-876-3841 **Fax:** 417-876-3848 www.eldoradospringsmo.com sunnews@socket.net

El Dorado Springs The Star (8.0M) PO Box 269 El Dorado Springs MO 64744 **Phn:** 417-876-2500 **Fax:** 417-876-5986 thestar@socket.net

Eldon Eldon Advertiser (4.0M) PO Box 315 Eldon MO 65026 **Phn:** 573-392-5658 **Fax:** 573-392-7755 www.vernonpublishing.com advertiser@vernonpublishing.com

Ellington Reynolds Co Courier (2.3M) PO Box 130 Ellington MO 63638 **Phn:** 573-663-2243 **Fax:** 573-663-2763 www.waynecojournalbanner.com rccreporter@mac.com

Elsberry Elsberry Democrat (1.6M) PO Box 105 Elsberry MO 63343 **Phn:** 573-898-2318 **Fax:** 573-898-2173 www.elsberrydemocrat.com elsberrydemocrat@sbcglobal.net

Eminence The Current Wave (2.0M) PO Box 728 Eminence MO 65466 **Phn:** 573-226-5229 **Fax:** 573-226-3335 www.shannoncountycurrentwave.com cwave128@gmail.com

Excelsior Springs The Standard (2.6M) PO Box 70 Excelsior Springs MO 64024 **Phn:** 816-637-3147 **Fax:** 816-637-8411 www.excelsiorspringsstandard.com eric@leaderpress.com

Fairfax Fairfax Forum (1.0M) 304 Main St Fairfax MO 64446 **Phn:** 660-686-2741 **Fax:** 660-686-3442 www.farmerpublishing.com forum@fairfaxmo.net

Farmington Farmington Press (4.5M) PO Box 70 Farmington MO 63640 **Phn:** 573-756-8927 **Fax:** 573-756-9160 www.dailyjournalonline.com/farmington-press editorial@dailyjournalonline.com

Fayette Fayette Advertiser (2.3M) PO Box 32 Fayette MO 65248 **Phn:** 660-248-2235 **Fax:** 660-248-1200 www.fayettenewspapers.com news@fayettenews.com

Fayette The Democrat-Leader (2.3M) PO Box 32 Fayette MO 65248 **Phn:** 660-248-2235 **Fax:** 660-248-1200 www.fayettenewspapers.com news@fayettenews.com

Festus Leader Publications (57.0M) PO Box 159 Festus MO 63028 **Phn:** 636-931-7560 **Fax:** 636-931-2226

Florissant Independent News (30.0M) 25 Saint Anthony Ln Florissant MO 63031 **Phn:** 314-831-4645 **Fax:** 314-831-4566 www.flovalleynews.com independentnws@aol.com

Fredericktown Democrat-News (3.5M) PO Box 471 Fredericktown MO 63645 **Phn:** 573-783-3366 **Fax:** 573-783-6890 www.dailyjournalonline.com/democrat-news dn@democratnewsonline.com

Gainesville Ozark County Times (3.7M) PO Box 188 Gainesville MO 65655 **Phn:** 417-679-4641 **Fax:** 417-679-3423 www.ozarkcountytimes.com editor@ozarkcountytimes.com

Gallatin North Missourian (2.0M) 609 S Main St # B Gallatin MO 64640 **Phn:** 660-663-2154 **Fax:** 660-663-2498 www.gallatinnorthmissourian.com news@gpcink.com

Glasgow Glasgow Missourian (1.7M) PO Box 248 Glasgow MO 65254 **Phn:** 660-338-2195 **Fax:** 660-338-2494 glasgow@mcmsys.com

Grandview Jackson County Advocate (4.5M) PO Box 620 Grandview MO 64030 **Phn:** 816-761-6200 **Fax:** 816-761-8215 jcadvocate.com mwilson@jcadvocate.com

Grant City The Times-Tribune (1.5M) PO Box 130 Grant City MO 64456 **Phn:** 660-564-3603

Greenfield The Vedette (2.0M) PO Box 216 Greenfield MO 65661 **Phn:** 417-637-2712 **Fax:** 417-637-2232 www.greenfieldvedette.com greenfieldvedettegraphics@mchsi.com

Hale Hale Horizons (0.6M) PO Box 36 Hale MO 64643 **Phn:** 660-565-2555 **Fax:** 660-565-2556 halehorizons@cvalley.net

Hamilton The Caldwell Co. News (2.0M) PO Box 187 Hamilton MO 64644 **Phn:** 816-583-2116 **Fax:** 816-583-2118 www.mycaldwellcounty.com news@mycaldwellcounty.com

Hannibal Salt River Journal (10.0M) PO Box A Hannibal MO 63401 **Phn:** 573-221-2800 **Fax:** 573-221-1568 www.hannibal.net marylou.montgomery@courierpost.com

Harrisonville Cass County Democrat (6.5M) PO Box 329 Harrisonville MO 64701 **Phn:** 816-380-3228 **Fax:** 816-380-7650 www.demo-mo.com

Hermann Lakeway Publishers (5.3M) PO Box 350 Hermann MO 65041 **Phn:** 573-486-5418 **Fax:** 573-486-5524 www.hermannadvertisercourier.com

Hermitage The Index (4.6M) PO Box 127 Hermitage MO 65668 **Phn:** 417-745-6404 **Fax:** 417-745-2222 theindex@positech.net

Higginsville Higginsville Advance (2.1M) PO Box 422 Higginsville MO 64037 **Phn:** 660-584-3611 **Fax:** 660-584-7966 higvladv@ctcis.net

Holden Holden Image (7.6M) PO Box 8 Holden MO 64040 **Phn:** 816-732-5552 **Fax:** 816-732-4696 www.holdenimage.com

Hopkins Hopkins Journal (0.9M) PO Box 170 Hopkins MO 64461 **Phn:** 660-778-3205 hopkinsjournal@hotmail.com

Houston Houston Herald (4.3M) PO Box 170 Houston MO 65483 **Phn:** 417-967-2000 **Fax:** 417-967-2096 www.houstonherald.com editor@houstonherald.com

Humansville Humansville Star-Leader (1.8M) PO Box 40 Humansville MO 65674 **Phn:** 417-754-2228

MISSOURI WEEKLY NEWSPAPERS

Ironton Mountain Echo (3.0M) PO Box 25 Ironton MO 63650 **Phn:** 573-546-3917 **Fax:** 573-546-3919

Jackson Cash Book Journal (10.0M) PO Box 369 Jackson MO 63755 **Phn:** 573-243-3515 **Fax:** 573-243-3517 www.jacksonmo.com/cashbook cashbook@mvp.net

Jamesport Tri-County Weekly (1.6M) PO Box 137 Jamesport MO 64648 **Phn:** 660-684-6515 www.jamesporttricountyweekly.com

Joplin Joplin Herald (15.0M) PO Box 7 Joplin MO 64802 **Phn:** 417-623-3480 **Fax:** 417-623-8598

Kahoka Hometown Journal (1.2M) 258 W Main St Kahoka MO 63445 **Phn:** 660-727-3383 **Fax:** 660-727-3522

Kahoka The Media (2.0M) PO Box 230 Kahoka MO 63445 **Phn:** 660-727-3395 **Fax:** 660-727-2475 www.nemonews.net themedia@centurytel.net

Kahola La Belle Star (0.8M) PO Box 230 Kahola MO 63445 **Phn:** 660-213-3848

Kansas City Missouri State Post (30.0M) PO Box 414662 Kansas City MO 64141 **Phn:** 816-561-7500

Kansas City Northeast News (12.5M) 5715 Saint John Ave Kansas City MO 64123 **Phn:** 816-241-0765 **Fax:** 816-241-3255 www.northeastnews.net northeastnews@socket.net

Kansas City Pitch Weekly (80.0M) 1701 Main St Kansas City MO 64108 **Phn:** 816-561-6061 **Fax:** 816-756-0502 www.pitch.com

Kansas City Wednesday Magazine (30.0M) 404 E Bannister Rd Ste E Kansas City MO 64131 **Phn:** 816-822-1366 **Fax:** 816-822-1856 guyt@townsendprint.com

Kearney Kearney Courier (3.0M) PO Box 140 Kearney MO 64060 **Phn:** 816-628-6010 **Fax:** 816-628-4422 www.kearneycourier.com kearneynews@kearneycourier.com

Kimberling City Stone County Gazette (2.5M) PO Box 1150 Kimberling City MO 65686 **Phn:** 417-739-3237 **Fax:** 417-739-9417

King City Tri-County News (1.8M) PO Box 428 King City MO 64463 **Phn:** 660-535-4313 **Fax:** 660-535-6133

Knob Noster Knob Noster Item (1.0M) PO Box 188 Knob Noster MO 65336 **Phn:** 660-563-3606 knobnosteritem@sbcglobal.net

La Plata The Home Press (1.2M) PO Box 57 La Plata MO 63549 **Phn:** 660-332-4431 **Fax:** 660-332-7561

Lamar Lamar Democrat (4.0M) PO Box 458 Lamar MO 64759 **Phn:** 417-682-5529 **Fax:** 417-682-5595 www.lamardemocrat.com info@lamardemocrat.com

Lathrop Rural Reporter (1.0M) PO Box 488 Lathrop MO 64465 **Phn:** 816-740-4444 **Fax:** 816-528-4310 www.ruralreporter.com lpubl@aol.com

Lawson Lawson Review (2.1M) PO Box 125 Lawson MO 64062 **Phn:** 816-296-3412

Lees Summit Lee's Summit Tribune (11.0M) 219 SE Douglas St Lees Summit MO 64063 **Phn:** 816-524-0061 **Fax:** 816-600-6102 www.lstribune.net linda@lstribune.net

Lees Summit Lees Summit Journal (25.0M) PO Box 387 Lees Summit MO 64063 **Phn:** 816-524-2345 **Fax:** 816-524-5136 www.lsjournal.com editor@lsjournal.com

Lexington Lexington News (2.0M) PO Box 279 Lexington MO 64067 **Phn:** 660-259-2266 **Fax:** 660-259-2267 www.lexington-news.com lexingtonnews@embarqmail.com

Liberal Liberal News (1.0M) PO Box 6 Liberal MO 64762 **Phn:** 417-843-5315

Liberty Liberty Tribune (10.5M) 104 N Main St Liberty MO 64068 **Phn:** 816-781-4941 **Fax:** 816-781-0909 www.libertytribune.com libtrib@libertytribune.com

Licking Licking News (2.3M) PO Box 297 Licking MO 65542 **Phn:** 573-674-2412 **Fax:** 573-674-4892 www.thelickingnews.com news_ads@thelickingnews.com

Linn Unterrified Democrat (4.6M) PO Box 109 Linn MO 65051 **Phn:** 573-897-3150 **Fax:** 573-897-0076 udna@socket.net

Louisiana Louisiana Press-Journal (3.2M) 3408 Georgia St Louisiana MO 63353 **Phn:** 573-754-5566 **Fax:** 573-754-4749 www.louisianapressjournal.com lpjed@lcs.net

Macon Macon Journal (11.0M) PO Box 7 Macon MO 63552 **Phn:** 660-385-3121 **Fax:** 660-385-3082 www.maconch.com chnews@centurytel.net

Malden Delta News Citizen (11.0M) PO Box 701 Malden MO 63863 **Phn:** 573-276-5148 **Fax:** 573-276-3687

Mansfield Mirror Republican (1.8M) PO Box 197 Mansfield MO 65704 **Phn:** 417-924-3226 **Fax:** 417-924-3227 www.mansfieldmirror.com larry@mansfieldmirror.com

Marble Hill Marble Hill Banner Press (4.2M) PO Box 109 Marble Hill MO 63764 **Phn:** 573-238-2821 **Fax:** 573-238-0020 www.semissourian.com lpresson@semissourian.com

Marshfield Marshfield Mail (5.5M) PO Box A Marshfield MO 65706 **Phn:** 417-468-2013 **Fax:** 417-859-7930 marshfieldmail.com news@marshfieldmail.com

Maryville Nodaway News Leader (3.3M) PO Box 373 Maryville MO 64468 **Phn:** 660-562-4747 **Fax:** 660-562-3607 www.nodawaynews.com nodawaynews@socket.net

Maysville Dekalb County Record Herald (1.8M) PO Box 98 Maysville MO 64469 **Phn:** 816-449-2121 **Fax:** 816-449-2808

Memphis Memphis Democrat (2.4M) 121 S Main St Memphis MO 63555 **Phn:** 660-465-7016 www.memphisdemocrat.com memdemoc@nemr.net

Mercer The Mirror (1.4M) PO Box 557 Mercer MO 64661 **Phn:** 660-382-4204 **Fax:** 660-382-4205

Milan Milan Standard (2.6M) PO Box 276 Milan MO 63556 **Phn:** 660-265-4244 **Fax:** 660-265-3180 milanstd@nemr.net

Monroe City Lake Gazette (2.4M) PO Box 187 Monroe City MO 63456 **Phn:** 573-735-3300 **Fax:** 573-735-3261 lakegazette.net lgeditor@lakegazette.net

Montgomery City Montgomery Standard (3.5M) PO Box 190 Montgomery City MO 63361 **Phn:** 573-564-2339 **Fax:** 573-564-2313 standard@socket.net

Mound City Mound City News (2.6M) PO Box 175 Mound City MO 64470 **Phn:** 660-442-5423 www.moundcitynews.com moundcitynews@socket.net

Mount Vernon Lawrence County Record (3.7M) PO Box 348 Mount Vernon MO 65712 **Phn:** 417-466-2185 **Fax:** 417-466-7865 www.lawrencecountyrecord.com lcrecord@centurytel.net

Mountain Grove News-Journal (4.0M) PO Box 530 Mountain Grove MO 65711 **Phn:** 417-926-5148 **Fax:** 417-926-6648 www.news-journal.net

Mountain View Standard News (1.4M) PO Box 79 Mountain View MO 65548 **Phn:** 417-934-2025 **Fax:** 417-934-1591 standardnews@centurytel.net

Neosho Neosho Post (1.5M) PO Box 848 Neosho MI 64850 **Phn:** 417-451-1520 **Fax:** 417-451-6408

Nevada Sunday Herald (4.7M) PO Box 247 Nevada MO 64772 **Phn:** 417-667-3344 **Fax:** 417-667-3817

New London Ralls Co. Herald Enterprise (1.3M) PO Box 426 New London MO 63459 **Phn:** 573-985-5531 rche@tds.net

New Madrid The Weekly Record (1.0M) 218 Main St New Madrid MO 63869 **Phn:** 573-748-2120 **Fax:** 573-748-5435 www.weeklyrecord.net ed@weeklyrecord.net

Nixa Nixa XPress (4.7M) PO Box 594 Nixa MO 65714 **Phn:** 417-725-3745 **Fax:** 417-725-3683 nixaxpress.com editor@nixaxpress.com

Norborne Norborne Democrat-Leader (1.4M) 208A S Pine St Norborne MO 64668 **Phn:** 660-593-3712 democrat@carolnet.com

O Fallon Community News (21.0M) 2139 Bryan Valley Commercial Dr O Fallon MO 63366 **Phn:** 636-379-1775 **Fax:** 636-379-1632 mycnews.com info@mycnews.com

Oak Grove Focus on Oak Grove (2.2M) 103 SE 12th St Oak Grove MO 64075 **Phn:** 816-690-7218 **Fax:** 816-690-7219 www.theodessan.net focus@iland.net

Odessa The Odessan (4.9M) PO Box 80 Odessa MO 64076 **Phn:** 816-230-5311 www.theodessan.net spaar@iland.net

Oregon Oregon Times-Observer (1.6M) PO Box 317 Oregon MO 64473 **Phn:** 660-446-3331 **Fax:** 660-446-3409 brlogos@ofmlive.net

Osceola St. Clair County Courier (3.0M) PO Box 580 Osceola MO 64776 **Phn:** 417-646-2211 **Fax:** 417-646-8015

Owensville Gasconade County Republican (3.4M) PO Box 540 Owensville MO 65066 **Phn:** 573-437-2323 **Fax:** 573-437-3033 www.gasconadecountyrepublican.com wardpub@fidnet.com

Ozark Christian Co. Headliner News (5.0M) PO Box 490 Ozark MO 65721 **Phn:** 417-581-3541 **Fax:** 417-581-3577 cchheadliner.com donnao@ccheadliner.com

Palmyra Palmyra Spectator (2.7M) PO Box 391 Palmyra MO 63461 **Phn:** 573-769-3111 **Fax:** 573-769-3554 www.palmyra-spectator.com news@palmyra-spectator.com

Paris Monroe County Appeal (2.2M) PO Box 207 Paris MO 65275 **Phn:** 660-327-4192 **Fax:** 660-327-4847 www.monroecountyappeal.com appeal@parismo.net

Parkville Parkville Luminary (2.5M) 5215 NW Crooked Rd Parkville MO 64152 **Phn:** 816-885-0504 parkvilleluminary.com markvasto@gmail.com

Perryville The Republic Monitor (5.5M) PO Box 367 Perryville MO 63775 **Phn:** 573-547-4567 **Fax:** 573-547-1643 www.perryvillenews.com alayton@perryvillenews.com

Piedmont Wayne County Journal-Banner (3.3M) PO Box 97 Piedmont MO 63957 **Phn:** 573-223-7122 **Fax:** 573-223-7871 www.waynecojournalbanner.com harold@waynecojournalbanner.com

Pineville McDonald Newspapers (6.1M) PO Box 266 Pineville MO 64856 **Phn:** 417-223-4675 **Fax:** 417-223-4049 www.press-info.com

Platte City Platte County Citizen (9.3M) PO Box 888 Platte City MO 64079 **Phn:** 816-858-5154 **Fax:** 816-858-2154 www.plattecountycitizen.com editor@plattecountycitizen.com

Platte City The Platte Co. Landmark (4.0M) PO Box 410 Platte City MO 64079 **Phn:** 816-858-0363 **Fax:** 816-858-2313 www.plattecountylandmark.com news@plattecountylandmark.com

Plattsburg Clinton County Leader (2.4M) 102 E Maple St Plattsburg MO 64477 **Phn:** 816-539-2111 **Fax:** 816-539-3530 www.clintoncountyleader.com leader@centurytel.net

Pleasant Hill Pleasant Hills Times (2.2M) PO Box 8 Pleasant Hill MO 64080 **Phn:** 816-540-3500 **Fax:** 816-987-5699 www.phtimes.net phtimes@comcast.net

Portageville Missourian News (1.7M) PO Box 456 Portageville MO 63873 **Phn:** 573-379-5355 **Fax:** 573-379-5488

Potosi The Independent Journal (5.3M) PO Box 340 Potosi MO 63664 **Phn:** 573-438-5141 **Fax:** 573-438-4472 ijnews@centurytel.net

Princeton Princeton Post Telegraph (1.5M) PO Box 286 Princeton MO 64673 **Phn:** 660-748-3266 **Fax:** 660-748-3267

Puxico Puxico Press (3.6M) PO Box 277 Puxico MO 63960 **Phn:** 573-222-3243 **Fax:** 573-222-6327

Raymore The Journal (4.0M) PO Box 1391 Raymore MO 64083 **Phn:** 816-322-6002 **Fax:** 816-322-6009

Raytown Dispatch-Tribune (12.0M) 10227 E 61st St Raytown MO 64133 **Phn:** 816-358-6398 **Fax:** 816-358-5141 www.kccommunitynews.com raytrib@sbcglobal.net

Raytown Raytown Post (12.0M) 10800 E 79th St Raytown MO 64138 **Phn:** 816-353-5545

Republic Republic Monitor (3.2M) 249 US Highway 60 W Republic MO 65738 **Phn:** 417-732-2525 **Fax:** 417-732-2980 republicmonews.com news@republicmonews.com

Rich Hill Mining Review (1.8M) PO Box 29 Rich Hill MO 64779 **Phn:** 417-395-4131 **Fax:** 417-395-4366

Rock Port Atchinson County Mail (2.5M) PO Box 40 Rock Port MO 64482 **Phn:** 660-744-6245 **Fax:** 660-744-2645 www.farmerpublishing.com amail@rpt.coop

Saint James Leader-Journal (1.8M) 104 N Jefferson St Saint James MO 65559 **Phn:** 573-265-3321 **Fax:** 573-265-3197 www.leaderjournal.com leaderjournalnews@gmail.com

Saint Louis Call Publishing (171.0M) 9977 Lin Ferry Dr Saint Louis MO 63123 **Phn:** 314-843-0102 **Fax:** 314-843-0508 www.callnewspapers.com wmilligan@callnewspapers.com

Saint Louis Ladue News (40.0M) 8811 Ladue Rd Ste D Saint Louis MO 63124 **Phn:** 314-863-3737 **Fax:** 314-863-4445 www.laduenews.com pressreleases@laduenews.com

Saint Louis Riverfront Times (80.0M) 6358 Delmar Blvd Ste 200 Saint Louis MO 63130 **Phn:** 314-754-5966 **Fax:** 314-754-5955 www.riverfronttimes.com tom.finkel@riverfronttimes.com

Saint Louis South County Times (36.0M) 122 W Lockwood Ave Saint Louis MO 63119 **Phn:** 314-968-2699 www.southcountytimes.com newsroom@timesnewspapers.com

Saint Louis Webster-Kirkwood Times (40.0M) 122 W Lockwood Ave Saint Louis MO 63119 **Phn:** 314-968-2699 www.websterkirkwoodtimes.com newsroom@timesnewspapers.com

Saint Robert Ft. Leonard Wood Patriot (7.5M) 555 Marshall Dr Saint Robert MO 65584 **Phn:** 573-336-7620 **Fax:** 573-336-7619

Saint Robert Pulaski County Mirror (1.2M) 555 Marshall Dr Saint Robert MO 65584 **Phn:** 573-336-5359 **Fax:** 573-336-7619 www.pulaskicountymirror.com ssmith@pulaskicountymirror.com

Sainte Genevieve Ste. Genevieve Herald (4.7M) PO Box 447 Sainte Genevieve MO 63670 **Phn:** 573-883-2222 **Fax:** 573-883-2833 www.stegenherald.com tcarrig@stegenherald.com

Salem Salem News (3.8M) PO Box 798 Salem MO 65560 **Phn:** 573-729-4126 **Fax:** 573-729-4920 www.thesalemnewsonline.com salemnews@thesalemnewsonline.com

Salisbury Press-Spectator (2.5M) PO Box 313 Salisbury MO 65281 **Phn:** 660-388-6131 **Fax:** 660-388-6688 ps@cvalley.net

Sarcoxie Sarcoxie Publishing (3.0M) PO Box 400 Sarcoxie MO 64862 **Phn:** 417-548-3311 **Fax:** 417-548-3312

Savannah Savannah Reporter (3.8M) PO Box 299 Savannah MO 64485 **Phn:** 816-324-3149 **Fax:** 816-324-3632

Sedalia Sedalia News Journal (5.8M) PO Box 1086 Sedalia MO 65302 **Phn:** 660-827-2425 **Fax:** 660-827-2427 sedalianewsjournal.com news@sedalianewsjournal.com

Seneca Seneca News Dispatch (1.9M) PO Box 1110 Seneca MO 64865 **Phn:** 417-776-2236 **Fax:** 417-776-2204 thenewsdispatch.net editor@senecanewsdispatch.com

Seymour Webster County Citizen (2.3M) PO Box 190 Seymour MO 65746 **Phn:** 417-935-2257 **Fax:** 417-935-2487 www.webstercountycitizen.com

Shelbina Shelbina Democrat (1.3M) 115 S Center St Shelbina MO 63468 **Phn:** 573-588-2133 **Fax:** 573-588-2134

Shelbyville Shelby County Herald (2.0M) PO Box 225 Shelbyville MO 63469 **Phn:** 573-633-2261 **Fax:** 573-633-2133 www.shelbycountyherald.com news@shelbycountyherald.com

Slater Slater Main Street News (1.6M) 222 Main St Slater MO 65349 **Phn:** 660-529-2249 **Fax:** 660-529-2474 slaternews@socket.net

Smithville The Smithville Herald (2.7M) 1001 S Commercial Ave Smithville MO 64089 **Phn:** 816-532-4444 **Fax:** 816-532-4918 www.smithvilleherald.com smithvillenews@smithvilleherald.com

Steele Steele Enterprise (2.2M) PO Box 60 Steele MO 63877 **Phn:** 573-695-3415 **Fax:** 573-695-2114 steelenews@steelemoenterprise.com

Steelville Steelville Star (3.1M) PO Box BG Steelville MO 65565 **Phn:** 573-775-5454 **Fax:** 573-775-2668 threeriverspublishing.com stvlstar@misn.com

Stockton Cedar County Republican (3.3M) PO Box 1018 Stockton MO 65785 **Phn:** 417-276-4211 **Fax:** 417-276-5760 cedarrepublican.com news@cedarrepublican.com

Stover Morgan County Press (1.5M) PO Box 130 Stover MO 65078 **Phn:** 573-377-4616 **Fax:** 573-377-4512 www.vernonpublishing.com press@vernonpublishing.com

Sullivan Sullivan Independent News (6.2M) PO Box 268 Sullivan MO 63080 **Phn:** 573-468-6511 **Fax:** 573-468-4046 www.mysullivannews.com nuz4u@fidnet.com

Sweet Springs Sweet Springs Herald (1.1M) 238 Main St Sweet Springs MO 65351 **Phn:** 660-335-6366 **Fax:** 660-335-6962

Tarkio Tarkio Avalanche (2.0M) 521 Main St Tarkio MO 64491 **Phn:** 660-736-4111 **Fax:** 660-736-5700 www.farmerpublishing.com avalanche@rpt.coop

Thayer South Missourian News (1.5M) 109 Chestnut St Thayer MO 65791 **Phn:** 417-264-3085 **Fax:** 417-264-3814 www.areawidenews.com rirby@areawidenews.com

Tipton Tipton Times (2.0M) PO Box U Tipton MO 65081 **Phn:** 660-433-5721 **Fax:** 660-433-2222 www.vernonpublishing.com times@vernonpublishing.com

Town and Country Suburban Journals (132.0M) 14522 S Outer 40 Rd Ste 300 Town and Country MO 63017 **Phn:** 314-821-1110 **Fax:** 314-821-0843 www.stltoday.com/suburban-journals dbundy@yourjournal.com

Troy Lincoln Co Journal (14.0M) 20 Business Park Dr Troy MO 63379 **Phn:** 636-528-9550 **Fax:** 636-528-6694 www.lincolncountyjournal.com

Troy Troy Free Press (1.8M) 20 Business Park Dr Troy MO 63379 **Phn:** 636-528-9550 **Fax:** 636-528-6694

Unionville Unionville Republican (1.7M) PO Box 365 Unionville MO 63565 **Phn:** 660-947-2222 **Fax:** 660-947-2223 www.unionvillerepublicanonline.com urep@nemr.net

Van Buren The Current Local (2.1M) PO Box 100 Van Buren MO 63965 **Phn:** 573-323-4515

Vandalia Vandalia Leader (2.3M) PO Box 239 Vandalia MO 63382 **Phn:** 573-594-2222 **Fax:** 573-594-6741 www.vandalialeader.com tvlgenmgr@lcs.net

Versailles Leader-Statesman (3.7M) PO Box 348 Versailles MO 65084 **Phn:** 573-378-5441 **Fax:** 573-378-4292 www.vernonpublishing.com bjones@vernonpublishing.com

Viburnum Quad Co. Star (2.7M) PO Box 347 Viburnum MO 65566 **Phn:** 573-244-5206 **Fax:** 573-244-5207 quadstar@misn.com

Warrenton Warren Co. Record (2.5M) 103 E Booneslick Rd Warrenton MO 63383 **Phn:** 636-456-6397 **Fax:** 636-456-6150 recnews@centurytel.net

Warsaw Benton County Enterprise (5.2M) PO Box 128 Warsaw MO 65355 **Phn:** 660-438-6312 **Fax:** 660-438-3464 www.bentoncountyenterprise.com jameswhite@bentoncountyenterprise.com

Washington Missourian Publishing (25.0M) PO Box 336 Washington MO 63090 **Phn:** 636-239-7701 **Fax:** 636-239-0915 www.emissourian.com washnews@emissourian.com

Webb City Webb City Sentinel (2.1M) PO Box 150 Webb City MO 64870 **Phn:** 417-673-2421 **Fax:** 417-673-5308

Wellsville Wellsville Optic-News (1.8M) PO Box 73 Wellsville MO 63384 **Phn:** 573-684-2929 opticnews@socket.net

Weston Weston Chronicle (1.9M) PO Box 6 Weston MO 64098 **Phn:** 816-640-2251 **Fax:** 816-386-2251 www.plattechronicle.com wcnews@embarqmail.com

Willard Cross Co Times (1.7M) PO Box 216 Willard MO 65781 **Phn:** 417-685-4328 **Fax:** 417-685-4145

Windsor Osage Valley Newspapers (4.0M) PO Box 23 Windsor MO 65360 **Phn:** 660-647-2121 **Fax:** 660-647-2122

MONTANA

Anaconda Anaconda Leader (4.0M) 121 Main St Anaconda MT 59711 **Phn:** 406-563-5283 **Fax:** 406-563-5284 www.anacondaleader.com leadernews@anacondaleader.com

Baker Fallon County Times (1.7M) PO Box 679 Baker MT 59313 **Phn:** 406-778-3344 **Fax:** 406-778-3347 fctimes@midrivers.com

Belgrade Belgrade News (9.0M) 29 W Main St Belgrade MT 59714 **Phn:** 406-388-5101 **Fax:** 406-388-5103 www.belgrade-news.com mtucker@belgrade-news.com

Big Sandy The Mountaineer (1.0M) PO Box 529 Big Sandy MT 59520 **Phn:** 406-378-2176 retigpub@ttc-cmc.net

MONTANA WEEKLY NEWSPAPERS

Big Sky Lone Peak Lookout (4.0M) PO Box 160123 Big Sky MT 59716 **Phn:** 406-995-4133 **Fax:** 406-995-4099 www.lonepeaklookout.com editor@lonepeaklookout.com

Big Timber Big Timber Pioneer (1.8M) PO Box 830 Big Timber MT 59011 **Phn:** 406-932-5298 **Fax:** 406-932-4931

Bigfork Bigfork Eagle (1.7M) PO Box 406 Bigfork MT 59911 **Phn:** 406-837-5131 **Fax:** 406-837-1132 www.flatheadnewsgroup.com/bigforkeagle editor@bigforkeagle.com

Billings Billings Outpost (9.0M) 2501 Montana Ave #9 Billings MT 59102 **Phn:** 406-248-1616 **Fax:** 406-248-2414 www.billingsnews.com editor@billingsnews.com

Billings Billings Times (1.2M) 2919 Montana Ave Billings MT 59101 **Phn:** 406-245-4994 **Fax:** 406-245-5115

Boulder The Boulder Monitor (1.6M) PO Box 66 Boulder MT 59632 **Phn:** 406-225-3821 jeffersoncountycourier.com janderson@jeffersoncountycourier.com

Broadus Powder River Examiner (1.0M) PO Box 328 Broadus MT 59317 **Phn:** 406-436-2244

Browning Glacier Reporter (2.4M) PO Box 349 Browning MT 59417 **Phn:** 406-338-2090 **Fax:** 406-338-2410 cutbankpioneerpress.com glacrptr@3rivers.net

Butte Butte Weekly (8.3M) 32 S Main St Ste A Butte MT 59701 **Phn:** 406-782-3820 **Fax:** 406-782-3754

Cascade Cascade Courier (0.8M) 103 1st St S Cascade MT 59421 **Phn:** 406-468-9231 **Fax:** 406-468-3030 www.cascademontana.com/courier.htm cascadecourier@mcn.net

Chester Liberty County Times (1.1M) PO Box 689 Chester MT 59522 **Phn:** 406-759-5355 **Fax:** 406-759-5261 www.libertycountytimes.net lctimes@itstriangle.com

Chinook Journal News-Opinion (2.8M) PO Box 279 Chinook MT 59523 **Phn:** 406-357-3573 **Fax:** 406-357-3736 bcjnews@ttc-cmc.net

Choteau Choteau Acantha (2.0M) PO Box 320 Choteau MT 59422 **Phn:** 406-466-2403 www.choteauacantha.com acantha@3rivers.net

Circle Circle Banner (1.1M) PO Box 308 Circle MT 59215 **Phn:** 406-974-3409 **Fax:** 406-485-2330 www.circlebanner.com banner@midrivers.com

Columbia Falls Hungry Horse News (7.6M) PO Box 189 Columbia Falls MT 59912 **Phn:** 406-892-2151 **Fax:** 406-892-5600 www.flatheadnewsgroup.com/hungryhorsenews newsdesk@hungryhorsenews.com

Columbus Stillwater Co News (2.2M) PO Box 659 Columbus MT 59019 **Phn:** 406-322-5212 **Fax:** 406-322-5391 www.stillwatercountynews.com editor@stillwatercountynews.com

Conrad Independent Observer (1.9M) PO Box 966 Conrad MT 59425 **Phn:** 406-271-5561 **Fax:** 406-271-5562 www.theindependentobserver.com indobserv@3rivers.net

Culbertson The Searchlight (1.2M) PO Box 496 Culbertson MT 59218 **Phn:** 406-787-5821 northeastmontananews.com

Cut Bank Cut Bank Pioneer Press (1.7M) PO Box 847 Cut Bank MT 59427 **Phn:** 406-873-2201 **Fax:** 406-873-2443 cutbankpioneerpress.com cbpress@bresnan.net

Cut Bank The Valierian (0.5M) PO Box 847 Cut Bank MT 59427 **Phn:** 406-279-3440 **Fax:** 406-873-2443 cutbankpioneerpress.com valierian@bresnan.net

Deer Lodge Silver State Post (1.9M) PO Box 111 Deer Lodge MT 59722 **Phn:** 406-846-2424 **Fax:** 406-846-2453 www.sspmt.com mgr@sspmt.com

Dillon Dillon Tribune (2.6M) PO Box 911 Dillon MT 59725 **Phn:** 406-683-2331 **Fax:** 406-683-2332 www.dillontribune.com editor@dillontribune.com

Ennis The Madisonian (2.3M) PO Box 365 Ennis MT 59729 **Phn:** 406-682-7755 **Fax:** 406-682-5013 www.madisoniannews.com editor@madisoniannews.com

Eureka Tobacco Valley News (2.2M) PO Box 307 Eureka MT 59917 **Phn:** 406-297-2514 **Fax:** 406-297-7807 www.tobaccovalleynews.com eurekaeditor@gmail.com

Fairfield Fairfield Sun Times (1.7M) PO Box 578 Fairfield MT 59436 **Phn:** 406-467-2334 **Fax:** 406-467-3354 www.fairfieldsuntimes.com suntimes@3rivers.net

Forsyth Independent Press (1.2M) PO Box 106 Forsyth MT 59327 **Phn:** 406-346-2149 **Fax:** 406-346-2140 ip-news@rangeweb.net

Fort Benton The River Press (2.0M) PO Box 69 Fort Benton MT 59442 **Phn:** 406-622-3311 **Fax:** 406-622-5446 riverpress@live.com

Glasgow Glasgow Courier (2.7M) 341 3rd Ave S Glasgow MT 59230 **Phn:** 406-228-9301 **Fax:** 406-228-2665 www.glasgowcourier.com courier@glasgowcourier.com

Glendive Ranger Review (3.5M) PO Box 61 Glendive MT 59330 **Phn:** 406-377-3303 **Fax:** 406-377-5435 www.rangerreview.com rrnews@rangerreview.com

Hardin Big Horn Co News (2.5M) PO Box 926 Hardin MT 59034 **Phn:** 406-665-1008 **Fax:** 406-665-1012 www.bighorncountynews.com news@bighorncountynews.com

Harlowton The Times-Clarion (1.3M) PO Box 307 Harlowton MT 59036 **Phn:** 406-632-5633 **Fax:** 406-632-5644 harlotms@mtintouch.net

Helena Queen City News (8.0M) 311 Jackson St Helena MT 59601 **Phn:** 406-443-3678 **Fax:** 406-443-3699

Huntley Yellowstone County News (3.7M) PO Box 395 Huntley MT 59037 **Phn:** 406-348-2649 **Fax:** 406-348-2302 info@yellowstonecountynews.com

Jordan Jordan Tribune (0.6M) PO Box 322 Jordan MT 59337 **Phn:** 406-557-2337 **Fax:** 406-557-6284 tradwind@midrivers.com

Laurel Laurel Outlook (3.7M) PO Box 278 Laurel MT 59044 **Phn:** 406-628-4412 **Fax:** 406-628-8260 www.laureloutlook.com news@laureloutlook.com

Lewistown Lewistown News-Argus (5.0M) PO Box 900 Lewistown MT 59457 **Phn:** 406-535-3401 **Fax:** 406-535-3405 www.lewistownnews.com newsstaff@lewistownnews.com

Libby The Montanian (3.6M) PO Box 946 Libby MT 59923 **Phn:** 406-293-8202 news@montanian.com

Libby Western News (3.8M) PO Box 1377 Libby MT 59923 **Phn:** 406-293-4124 **Fax:** 406-293-7187 www.thewesternnews.com thewesternnews@gmail.com

Malta Phillips County News (2.5M) PO Box 850 Malta MT 59538 **Phn:** 406-654-2020 **Fax:** 406-654-1410 phillips_county_news@yahoo.com

Missoula Missoula Independent (25.0M) PO Box 8275 Missoula MT 59807 **Phn:** 406-543-6609 **Fax:** 406-543-4367 missoulanews.bigskypress.com sbrowning@missoulanews.com

Philipsburg Philipsburg Mail (1.2M) PO Box 160 Philipsburg MT 59858 **Phn:** 406-859-3223 www.pburgmail.com news@pburgmail.com

Plains Clark Fork Valley Press (1.4M) PO Box 667 Plains MT 59859 **Phn:** 406-826-3402 **Fax:** 406-826-5577 www.vp-mi.com editor@vp-mi.com

Plains Mineral Independent (1.1M) PO Box 667 Plains MT 59859 **Phn:** 406-826-3402 **Fax:** 406-826-5577 www.vp-mi.com editor@vp-mi.com

Plentywood Sheridan Co News (2.3M) 115 N Main St Plentywood MT 59254 **Phn:** 406-765-2190 **Fax:** 406-765-3333

Polson Leader Advertiser (6.0M) PO Box 1090 Polson MT 59860 **Phn:** 406-883-4343 **Fax:** 406-883-4349 leaderadvertiser.com editor@leaderadvertiser.com

Red Lodge Carbon County News (3.0M) PO Box 970 Red Lodge MT 59068 **Phn:** 406-446-2222 www.carboncountynews.com news@carboncountynews.com

Roundup Roundup Record Tribune (2.0M) PO Box 350 Roundup MT 59072 **Phn:** 406-323-1105 **Fax:** 406-323-1761 rrtnews@midrivers.com

Scobey Daniels County Leader (1.5M) PO Box 850 Scobey MT 59263 **Phn:** 406-487-5303 northeastmontananews.com 2leader@nemont.net

Seeley Lake Seeley Swan Pathfinder (1.5M) PO Box 702 Seeley Lake MT 59868 **Phn:** 406-677-2022 www.seeleyswanpathfinder.com pathfinder@montana.com

Shelby Shelby Promoter (2.1M) PO Box 610 Shelby MT 59474 **Phn:** 406-434-5171 **Fax:** 406-434-5955 cutbankpioneerpress.com promoter@3rivers.net

Sidney Sidney Herald-Leader (3.7M) 310 2nd Ave NE Sidney MT 59270 **Phn:** 406-433-2403 **Fax:** 406-433-7802 www.sidneyherald.com editor@sidneyherald.com

Stanford Judith Basin Press (1.0M) PO Box 507 Stanford MT 59479 **Phn:** 406-566-2471 press@ttc-cmc.net

Stevensville Bitterroot Star (7.0M) PO Box 8 Stevensville MT 59870 **Phn:** 406-777-3928 **Fax:** 406-777-4265 www.bitterrootstar.com editor@bitterrootstar.com

Terry Terry Tribune (0.9M) PO Box 127 Terry MT 59349 **Phn:** 406-635-5513 **Fax:** 406-635-2149 www.terrytribune.com tribune@midrivers.com

Thompson Falls Sanders County Ledger (2.8M) PO Box 219 Thompson Falls MT 59873 **Phn:** 406-827-3421 **Fax:** 406-827-4375 www.scledger.net ledgernews@blackfoot.net

Three Forks Three Forks Herald (1.3M) PO Box 586 Three Forks MT 59752 **Phn:** 406-285-3414 **Fax:** 406-285-3413 andy@threeforksherald.com

Townsend Townsend Star (1.7M) PO Box 1011 Townsend MT 59644 **Phn:** 406-266-3333 **Fax:** 406-266-5440 www.townsendstar.net tstarmt@mt.net

West Yellowstone West Yellowstone News (1.7M) PO Box 969 West Yellowstone MT 59758 **Phn:** 406-646-9719 **Fax:** 406-646-4023 www.westyellowstonenews.com news@westyellowstonenews.com

White Sulphur Springs Meagher County News (1.2M) PO Box 349 White Sulphur Springs MT 59645 **Phn:** 406-547-3831 **Fax:** 406-547-3832 www.meagher-county-news.com mcnews1@ttc-cmc.net

Whitefish Whitefish Pilot (4.6M) PO Box 488 Whitefish MT 59937 **Phn:** 406-862-3505 **Fax:** 406-862-3636 www.flatheadnewsgroup.com/whitefishpilot editor@whitefishpilot.com

Whitehall Whitehall Ledger (1.3M) PO Box 1169 Whitehall MT 59759 **Phn:** 406-287-5301 **Fax:** 406-287-5352 whitehallledger.com whledger@gmail.com

Wibaux Wibaux Pioneer-Gazette (1.0M) PO Box 218 Wibaux MT 59353 **Phn:** 406-796-2218 wibaux@midrivers.com

Wolf Point Wolf Point Herald-News (2.0M) PO Box 639 Wolf Point MT 59201 **Phn:** 406-653-2222 **Fax:** 406-653-2221 www.wolfpointherald.com herald@nemont.net

NEBRASKA

Ainsworth Ainsworth Star-Journal (2.0M) PO Box 145 Ainsworth NE 69210 **Phn:** 402-387-2844 **Fax:** 402-387-1234

Albion Albion News (3.2M) 328 W Church St Albion NE 68620 **Phn:** 402-395-2115 **Fax:** 402-395-2772

Alma Harlan County Journal (1.5M) PO Box 9 Alma NE 68920 **Phn:** 308-928-2143 **Fax:** 308-928-9914 mainstreetmedia.us journal@frontiernet.net

Arapahoe Arapahoe Public Mirror (1.4M) PO Box 660 Arapahoe NE 68922 **Phn:** 308-962-7261 **Fax:** 308-962-7865 www.arapahoemirror.com

Arthur Arthur Enterprise (0.5M) PO Box 165 Arthur NE 69121 **Phn:** 308-764-2402 artent@neb-sandhills.net

Ashland Ashland Gazette (1.9M) PO Box 127 Ashland NE 68003 **Phn:** 402-944-3397 **Fax:** 402-944-3398 www.wahoo-ashland-waverly.com/ashland teresa.livers@ashland-gazette.com

Atkinson Atkinson Graphic (2.2M) PO Box 159 Atkinson NE 68713 **Phn:** 402-925-5411 www.atkinsongraphic.com news@atkinsongraphic.com

Auburn Auburn Press Tribune (3.5M) PO Box 250 Auburn NE 68305 **Phn:** 402-274-3185 **Fax:** 402-274-3273

Auburn Nemaha County Herald (3.5M) PO Box 250 Auburn NE 68305 **Phn:** 402-274-3185 **Fax:** 402-274-3273 www.anewspaper.net news@anewspaper.net

Aurora Aurora News-Register (4.0M) PO Box 70 Aurora NE 68818 **Phn:** 402-694-2131 **Fax:** 402-694-2133 www.auroranewsregister.com newsregister@hamilton.net

Bassett Rock County Leader (1.7M) PO Box 488 Bassett NE 68714 **Phn:** 402-684-3771

Bayard Bayard Transcript (1.2M) PO Box 626 Bayard NE 69334 **Phn:** 308-586-1313 **Fax:** 308-586-2312

Beaver City Beaver City Times-Tribune (1.1M) PO Box 258 Beaver City NE 68926 **Phn:** 308-268-2205 **Fax:** 308-268-4000

Bellevue Bellevue Leader (4.1M) 604 Fort Crook Rd N Bellevue NE 68005 **Phn:** 402-733-7300 **Fax:** 402-733-9116 www.omaha.com ron.petak@bellevueleader.com

Benkelman Benkelman Post (1.2M) PO Box 800 Benkelman NE 69021 **Phn:** 308-423-2337 **Fax:** 308-423-5555 bpost@bwtelcom.net

Bertrand The Bertrand Herald (0.9M) PO Box 425 Bertrand NE 68927 **Phn:** 308-472-3217 **Fax:** 308-472-5165 bertrandherald@atcjet.com

Blair Enterprise Publishing (10.0M) PO Box 328 Blair NE 68008 **Phn:** 402-426-2122 **Fax:** 402-426-2227 www.enterprisepub.com news@enterprisepub.com

Bloomfield Bloomfield Monitor (1.7M) PO Box 367 Bloomfield NE 68718 **Phn:** 402-373-2332 **Fax:** 402-373-2887 bmonitor@yahoo.com

Blue Hill Blue Hill Leader (1.4M) PO Box 38 Blue Hill NE 68930 **Phn:** 402-756-2077 **Fax:** 402-756-2097 bhleader@gtmc.net

Bridgeport News-Blade (1.9M) PO Box 400 Bridgeport NE 69336 **Phn:** 308-262-0675

MONTANA WEEKLY NEWSPAPERS

Broken Bow Custer County Chief (3.2M) PO Box 190 Broken Bow NE 68822 **Phn:** 308-872-2471 **Fax:** 308-872-2415 www.custercountychief.com chiefnews@custercountychief.com

Burwell Burwell Tribune (1.9M) PO Box 547 Burwell NE 68823 **Phn:** 308-346-4504 **Fax:** 308-346-4018 www.tribune2000.com bwtrib@tribune2000.com

Burwell Sargent Leader (0.7M) PO Box 547 Burwell NE 68823 **Phn:** 308-346-4504 **Fax:** 308-346-4018 www.tribune2000.com bwtrib@tribune2000.com

Cairo Cairo Record (0.8M) PO Box 700 Cairo NE 68824 **Phn:** 308-485-0137

Callaway Callaway Courier (0.9M) PO Box 69 Callaway NE 68825 **Phn:** 308-836-2200 ccourier@gpcom.net

Cambridge Cambridge Clarion (1.5M) PO Box 70 Cambridge NE 69022 **Phn:** 308-697-3326 www.cambridgeclarion.com clarion@cambridgeclarion.com

Central City Republican Nonpareil (2.3M) PO Box 26 Central City NE 68826 **Phn:** 308-946-3081 **Fax:** 308-946-3082 jensenpub@hamilton.net

Chadron Chadron Record (2.1M) PO Box 1141 Chadron NE 69337 **Phn:** 308-432-5511 **Fax:** 308-432-2385 www.rapidcityjournal.com/thechadronnews george.ledbetter@lee.net

Chappell Chappell Register (1.1M) PO Box 528 Chappell NE 69129 **Phn:** 308-874-2207

Clarkson Colfax County Press (3.9M) PO Box 266 Clarkson NE 68629 **Phn:** 402-892-3544

Coleridge Coleridge Blade (0.9M) PO Box 8 Coleridge NE 68727 **Phn:** 402-283-4267 www.northeastnebraskanews.com ccnews@hartel.net

Cozad Cozad Free Press (0.5M) PO Box 6 Cozad NE 69130 **Phn:** 308-784-3644 **Fax:** 308-784-3647 www.tricitytrib.com news@tricitytrib.com

Cozad Tri-City Trib (3.3M) PO Box 6 Cozad NE 69130 **Phn:** 308-784-3644 **Fax:** 308-784-3647 www.tricitytrib.com news@tricitytrib.com

Crawford Crawford Clipper/Sun (1.4M) 435 2nd St Crawford NE 69339 **Phn:** 308-665-2310

Creighton Creighton News (1.6M) PO Box 55 Creighton NE 68729 **Phn:** 402-358-5220 **Fax:** 402-358-5132 crenews@gpcom.net

Crete Crete News (4.5M) PO Box 40 Crete NE 68333 **Phn:** 402-826-2147 **Fax:** 402-826-5072 newsdesk@cretenews.net

Crofton Crofton Journal (1.0M) PO Box 339 Crofton NE 68730 **Phn:** 402-388-4355 **Fax:** 402-388-4336 journal@gpcom.net

Crofton Niobrara Tribune (0.5M) PO Box 339 Crofton NE 68730 **Phn:** 402-388-4355 **Fax:** 402-388-4336 journal@gpcom.net

Curtis Hi-Line Enterprise (1.2M) PO Box 85 Curtis NE 69025 **Phn:** 308-367-4144 **Fax:** 308-367-8616 www.hilineenterprise.com editor@hilineenterprise.com

David City Banner-Press (3.0M) PO Box 407 David City NE 68632 **Phn:** 402-367-3054 **Fax:** 402-367-3055 news@thebanner-press.com

Deshler Deshler Rustler (1.8M) PO Box 647 Deshler NE 68340 **Phn:** 402-365-7221 **Fax:** 402-365-4439 deshlerrustler@gpcom.net

Dodge Dodge Criterion (1.3M) PO Box 68 Dodge NE 68633 **Phn:** 402-693-2415

Elgin Elgin Review (1.2M) 116 S 2nd St Elgin NE 68636 **Phn:** 402-843-5500 **Fax:** 402-843-5422 www.elginreview.com elgnrev@gpcom.net

Elkhorn Douglas Co Post-Gazette (2.8M) PO Box 677 Elkhorn NE 68022 **Phn:** 402-289-2329 **Fax:** 402-289-0861 www.dcpostgazette.com editor@dcpostgazette.com

Elm Creek Beacon-Observer (1.3M) PO Box 219 Elm Creek NE 68836 **Phn:** 308-856-4770 **Fax:** 308-987-2452

Elwood Elwood Bulletin (1.0M) PO Box 115 Elwood NE 68937 **Phn:** 308-785-2251 www.arapahoemirror.com

Fairbury Fairbury Journal-News (4.5M) PO Box 415 Fairbury NE 68352 **Phn:** 402-729-6141 **Fax:** 402-729-5652 fairburyjournalnews.com rvcheck@hotmail.com

Falls City Falls City Journal (3.8M) PO Box 128 Falls City NE 68355 **Phn:** 402-245-2431 **Fax:** 402-245-4404

Franklin Franklin Co Chronicle (1.5M) PO Box 271 Franklin NE 68939 **Phn:** 308-425-3481 **Fax:** 308-425-6823 mainstreetmedia.us frcochron@gtmc.net

Friend Friend Sentinel (1.6M) PO Box 228 Friend NE 68359 **Phn:** 402-947-2391 **Fax:** 402-947-3631 www.pioneerpub.com pioneerpublishing@galaxycable.net

Fullerton Nance County Journal (1.2M) PO Box 10 Fullerton NE 68638 **Phn:** 308-536-3100

Geneva Nebraska Signal (3.5M) PO Box 233 Geneva NE 68361 **Phn:** 402-759-3117 **Fax:** 402-759-4214

Gering Gering Courier (2.3M) PO Box 70 Gering NE 69341 **Phn:** 308-436-2222 **Fax:** 308-436-7127 www.starherald.com/gering steve.frederick@starherald.com

Gibbon Gibbon Reporter (1.0M) PO Box 820 Gibbon NE 68840 **Phn:** 308-468-5393 www.clipperpubco.com info@clipperpubco.com

Gordon Sheridan Journal Star (2.2M) 210 N Main St Gordon NE 69343 **Phn:** 308-282-0118 **Fax:** 308-282-0119

Gothenburg Gothenburg Times (2.1M) PO Box 385 Gothenburg NE 69138 **Phn:** 308-537-3636 **Fax:** 308-537-7554 www.gothenburgtimes.com news@gothenburgtimes.com

Grant Grant Tribune-Sentinel (1.8M) PO Box 67 Grant NE 69140 **Phn:** 308-352-4211 **Fax:** 308-352-4101 www.granttribune.com grantrib@gpcom.net

Greeley Greeley Citizen (1.1M) PO Box 268 Greeley NE 68842 **Phn:** 308-428-2915 **Fax:** 308-428-5585

Gretna Gretna Guide (1.2M) PO Box 240 Gretna NE 68028 **Phn:** 402-332-3232 **Fax:** 402-332-4733 www.gretnaguide.com editor@gretnaguide.com

Hartington Cedar County News (1.0M) PO Box 977 Hartington NE 68739 **Phn:** 402-254-3997 **Fax:** 402-254-3999 hartington.net ccnews@hartel.net

Hayes Center Times-Republican (0.9M) PO Box 7 Hayes Center NE 69032 **Phn:** 308-286-3325

Hebron Hebron Journal Register (2.9M) 318 Lincoln Ave Hebron NE 68370 **Phn:** 402-768-7214 **Fax:** 402-768-7354

Hemingford The Ledger (1.3M) PO Box 7 Hemingford NE 69348 **Phn:** 308-487-3334 **Fax:** 308-487-3347 www.starherald.com/hemingford jchytka@ledgeronline.com

Henderson Henderson News (0.5M) PO Box 606 Henderson NE 68371 **Phn:** 402-723-5861 **Fax:** 402-723-5863 servpress@mainstaycomm.net

Hickman The Voice-News (2.5M) PO Box 148 Hickman NE 68372 **Phn:** 402-792-2255 **Fax:** 402-792-2256 www.voicenewsnebraska.com voicenews@inebraska.com

NEBRASKA WEEKLY NEWSPAPERS

Howells Howells Journal (0.9M) PO Box 335 Howells NE 68641 **Phn:** 402-986-1777

Humboldt Humboldt Standard (1.3M) PO Box 627 Humboldt NE 68376 **Phn:** 402-862-2200 **Fax:** 402-862-2209

Humphrey Humphrey Democrat (1.6M) PO Box 158 Humphrey NE 68642 **Phn:** 402-923-1400

Hyannis Grant County News (0.7M) PO Box 308 Hyannis NE 69350 **Phn:** 308-458-2425 gcn@neb-sandhills.net

Imperial Imperial Republican (2.5M) PO Box 727 Imperial NE 69033 **Phn:** 308-882-4453 **Fax:** 308-882-5167 www.imperialrepublican.com

Indianola Indianola News (0.5M) PO Box 130 Indianola NE 69034 **Phn:** 308-364-2130 olanews@swnebr.com

Kimball West Nebraska Observer (2.0M) 118 E 2nd St Kimball NE 69145 **Phn:** 308-235-3631 **Fax:** 308-235-3632 observer@megavision.com

Laurel Laurel Advocate (1.1M) PO Box 688 Laurel NE 68745 **Phn:** 402-256-3200 www.northeastnebraskanews.com ccnews@hartel.net

Lexington Lexington Clipper Herald (3.2M) PO Box 599 Lexington NE 68850 **Phn:** 308-324-5511 **Fax:** 308-324-5240 www.lexch.com news@lexch.com

Lincoln Neighborhood Extra (36.0M) 926 P St Lincoln NE 68508 **Phn:** 402-473-7150 **Fax:** 402-473-7159 journalstar.com/niche/neighborhood-extra dennis.buckley@lee.net

Loup City Sherman County Times (1.7M) PO Box 430 Loup City NE 68853 **Phn:** 308-745-1260 **Fax:** 308-745-0541

Lyons Lyons Mirror-Sun (1.3M) PO Box 59 Lyons NE 68038 **Phn:** 402-687-2616 **Fax:** 402-687-2617

Madison Madison Star-Mail (1.5M) PO Box 487 Madison NE 68748 **Phn:** 402-454-3818

Milford Milford Times (1.1M) PO Box 723 Milford NE 68405 **Phn:** 402-761-2911

Minden Minden Courier (2.8M) PO Box 379 Minden NE 68959 **Phn:** 308-832-2220 **Fax:** 308-832-2221 mindencourier@gtmc.net

Mitchell The Index (1.1M) PO Box 158 Mitchell NE 69357 **Phn:** 308-623-1322

Mullen Hooker County Tribune (0.9M) PO Box 125 Mullen NE 69152 **Phn:** 308-546-2242 **Fax:** 308-546-2722 tribune@nebnet.net

Nebraska City Nebraska City News-Press (2.3M) PO Box 757 Nebraska City NE 68410 **Phn:** 402-873-3334 **Fax:** 402-873-5436 www.ncnewspress.com

Neligh Clearwater Record (0.7M) PO Box 46 Neligh NE 68756 **Phn:** 402-887-4840 **Fax:** 402-887-4711

Neligh Neligh News & Leader (2.3M) PO Box 46 Neligh NE 68756 **Phn:** 402-887-4840 **Fax:** 402-887-4711

Nelson Nelson Gazette (0.7M) PO Box 285 Nelson NE 68961 **Phn:** 402-225-2301

Newman Grove Newman Grove Reporter (1.3M) PO Box 476 Newman Grove NE 68758 **Phn:** 402-447-6012 ngreporter.com/site reporter@megavision.com

North Bend North Bend Eagle (1.6M) PO Box 100 North Bend NE 68649 **Phn:** 402-652-8312

North Platte North Platte Bulletin (3.5M) 1300 E 4th St Ste F North Platte NE 69101 **Phn:** 308-696-0052 **Fax:** 308-696-0053 www.northplattebulletin.com george@northplattebulletin.com

Oakland Oakland Independent (1.9M) 217 N Oakland Ave Oakland NE 68045 **Phn:** 402-685-5624 **Fax:** 402-685-5625

Ogallala Keith County News (4.3M) PO Box 359 Ogallala NE 69153 **Phn:** 308-284-4046 **Fax:** 308-284-4048 newsboy@ogallalakcnews.com

Omaha The Reader (20.0M) PO Box 7360 Omaha NE 68107 **Phn:** 402-341-7323 **Fax:** 402-341-6967 www.thereader.com letters@thereader.com

Oneill Holt County Independent (5.0M) 114 N 4th St Oneill NE 68763 **Phn:** 402-336-1220 **Fax:** 402-336-1222 www.holtindependent.com

Orchard Orchard News (0.8M) PO Box 130 Orchard NE 68764 **Phn:** 402-893-2535 orchardnews@juno.com

Ord Ord Quiz (2.5M) 305 S 16th St Ord NE 68862 **Phn:** 308-728-3262 **Fax:** 308-728-5715 www.ordquiz.com quiz@frontiernet.net

Oshkosh Garden County News (2.0M) PO Box 290 Oshkosh NE 69154 **Phn:** 308-772-3555 **Fax:** 308-772-4475 www.gardencountynews.com gcnews@embarqmail.com

Osmond Osmond Republican (1.0M) PO Box 428 Osmond NE 68765 **Phn:** 402-748-3666 **Fax:** 402-748-3354 www.northeastnebraskanews.com osmondnews@huntel.net

Overton The Beacon-Observer (1.5M) PO Box 330 Overton NE 68863 **Phn:** 308-987-2451 **Fax:** 308-987-2452 beacon@atcjet.net

Oxford Oxford Standard (1.2M) PO Box 125 Oxford NE 68967 **Phn:** 308-824-3582

Palmer Palmer Journal (0.9M) PO Box 218 Palmer NE 68864 **Phn:** 308-894-3025

Papillion Suburban News (12.0M) 1413 S Washington St Ste 300 Papillion NE 68046 **Phn:** 402-339-3331 **Fax:** 402-537-2997 www.omaha.com ron.petak@bellevueleader.com

Pawnee City Pawnee Republican (2.0M) PO Box 111 Pawnee City NE 68420 **Phn:** 402-852-2575 pawneerepublican.com ronald@pawneenews.com

Pender Pender Times (1.4M) PO Box 280 Pender NE 68047 **Phn:** 402-385-3013 ptimes@huntel.net

Petersburg Petersburg Press (0.7M) PO Box 177 Petersburg NE 68652 **Phn:** 402-386-5384

Pierce Pierce County Leader (2.2M) 109 E Main St Pierce NE 68767 **Phn:** 402-329-4665 **Fax:** 402-329-6337 pierceleader@ptcnet.net

Plainview Plainview News (1.9M) PO Box 9 Plainview NE 68769 **Phn:** 402-582-4921 **Fax:** 402-582-4922 www.theplainviewnews.com plvwnews@plvwtelco.net

Plattsmouth Plattsmouth Journal (5.8M) 410 Main St Plattsmouth NE 68048 **Phn:** 402-296-2141 **Fax:** 402-296-3401 fremonttribune.com/cass-news pattijo.peterson@lee.net

Ponca Nebraska Journal Leader (1.8M) PO Box 545 Ponca NE 68770 **Phn:** 402-755-2204 **Fax:** 402-755-2205 joeditor@gpcom.net

Ralston Ralston Recorder (1.8M) PO Box 27072 Ralston NE 68127 **Phn:** 402-331-6300 **Fax:** 402-733-9116 www.omaha.com adam.klinker@ralstonrecorder.com

Randolph Randolph Times (1.4M) PO Box 97 Randolph NE 68771 **Phn:** 402-337-0488

Ravenna Ravenna News (1.4M) PO Box 110 Ravenna NE 68869 **Phn:** 308-452-3411 **Fax:** 308-452-3511 ranews@cornhusker.net

Red Cloud Red Cloud Chief (2.0M) PO Box 484 Red Cloud NE 68970 **Phn:** 402-746-3700 **Fax:** 402-746-2368 mainstreetmedia.us chief@gpcom.net

Saint Edward St. Edward Advance (0.7M) PO Box 287 Saint Edward NE 68660 **Phn:** 402-678-2771 **Fax:** 402-678-2556

Saint Paul Phonograph Herald (2.5M) PO Box 27 Saint Paul NE 68873 **Phn:** 308-754-4401 **Fax:** 308-754-4498

Schuyler Schuyler Sun (3.2M) 1112 C St Schuyler NE 68661 **Phn:** 402-352-2424 **Fax:** 402-352-3332

Scribner Rustler Sentinel (2.0M) PO Box 370 Scribner NE 68057 **Phn:** 402-664-3198 **Fax:** 402-664-3141 rustlernews@gpcom.net

Seward Seward County Independent (3.8M) PO Box 449 Seward NE 68434 **Phn:** 402-643-3676 **Fax:** 402-643-6774 sewardindependent.com scinews@sewardindependent.com

Shelton Shelton Clipper (0.9M) PO Box 640 Shelton NE 68876 **Phn:** 308-647-5158 www.clipperpubco.com info@clipperpubco.com

South Sioux City Dakota County Star (4.8M) PO Box 159 South Sioux City NE 68776 **Phn:** 402-494-4264 **Fax:** 402-494-2414

Spalding Cedar Rapids Press (0.6M) PO Box D Spalding NE 68665 **Phn:** 308-497-2153 crpress@hotmail.com

Spalding Spalding Enterprise (0.7M) PO Box D Spalding NE 68665 **Phn:** 308-497-2153 spalding2002@hotmail.com

Spencer Butte Gazette (0.6M) PO Box 187 Spencer NE 68777 **Phn:** 402-589-1010

Spencer Spencer Advocate (1.1M) PO Box 187 Spencer NE 68777 **Phn:** 402-589-1010

Springview Springview Herald (0.9M) PO Box 369 Springview NE 68778 **Phn:** 402-497-3651 **Fax:** 402-497-2651 herald91@threeriver.net

Stanton Stanton Register (1.8M) PO Box 719 Stanton NE 68779 **Phn:** 402-439-2173 **Fax:** 402-439-2273

Stapleton Creative Printers (2.7M) PO Box 98 Stapleton NE 69163 **Phn:** 308-636-2444 **Fax:** 308-636-2445 creativeprinters@gpcom.net

Superior Jewell County Record (1.0M) PO Box 408 Superior NE 68978 **Phn:** 402-879-3291 **Fax:** 402-879-3463 tse@superiorinet.net

Superior Superior Express (3.2M) PO Box 408 Superior NE 68978 **Phn:** 402-879-3291 **Fax:** 402-879-3463 www.superiorne.com tse@superiorne.com

Sutherland Sutherland Courier-Times (1.3M) PO Box 367 Sutherland NE 69165 **Phn:** 308-386-4617 **Fax:** 308-386-2437

Sutton Clay County News (3.0M) PO Box 405 Sutton NE 68979 **Phn:** 402-773-5576 **Fax:** 402-773-5577 www.claycountynewsonline.com

Syracuse Syracuse Journal-Democrat (2.3M) PO Box O Syracuse NE 68446 **Phn:** 402-269-2135

Tecumseh Tecumseh Chieftain (2.8M) PO Box 809 Tecumseh NE 68450 **Phn:** 402-335-3394 news@tecumsehchieftain.com

Tekamah Burt County Plaindealer (2.5M) PO Box 239 Tekamah NE 68061 **Phn:** 402-374-2225 **Fax:** 402-374-2739 www.midwestmessenger.com/burt_county support@midwestmessenger.com

Thedford Thomas County Herald (0.6M) PO Box 271 Thedford NE 69166 **Phn:** 308-645-2403

Tilden Tilden Citizen (15.0M) PO Box 280 Tilden NE 68781 **Phn:** 402-368-5315

Trenton Hitchcock County News (1.4M) PO Box 278 Trenton NE 69044 **Phn:** 308-334-5226 hcn@gpcom.net

Valentine Midland News (2.1M) PO Box 448 Valentine NE 69201 **Phn:** 402-376-2833 **Fax:** 402-376-1946

Verdigre Verdigre Eagle (1.5M) PO Box 309 Verdigre NE 68783 **Phn:** 402-668-2242

Wahoo Wahoo Newspaper (4.3M) PO Box 147 Wahoo NE 68066 **Phn:** 402-443-4162 **Fax:** 402-443-4459 omahanewsstand.com kristin.byars@wahoonewspaper.com

Wakefield Wakefield Republican (1.2M) PO Box 110 Wakefield NE 68784 **Phn:** 402-287-2323

Wauneta Wauneta Breeze (0.8M) PO Box 337 Wauneta NE 69045 **Phn:** 308-394-5389 **Fax:** 308-394-5931 www.waunetanebraska.com waunetabreeze@bwtelcom.net

Wausa Wausa Gazette (2.1M) PO Box G Wausa NE 68786 **Phn:** 402-586-2661 www.northeastnebraskanews.com

Waverly Waverly News (1.8M) PO Box 100 Waverly NE 68462 **Phn:** 402-786-2344 **Fax:** 402-786-2343 omahanewsstand.com news@newswaverly.com

Wayne Wayne Herald (2.6M) PO Box 70 Wayne NE 68787 **Phn:** 402-375-2600 **Fax:** 402-375-1888 mywaynenews.com melissa@wayneherald.com

West Point West Point News (4.0M) PO Box 40 West Point NE 68788 **Phn:** 402-372-2461 **Fax:** 402-372-3530 www.wpnews.com wpnewseditor@cableone.net

Wilber De Witt Times-News (0.8M) PO Box 457 Wilber NE 68465 **Phn:** 402-821-2586 **Fax:** 402-821-3586

Wilber Wilber Republican (1.5M) PO Box 457 Wilber NE 68465 **Phn:** 402-821-2586 **Fax:** 402-821-3586

Wisner Wisner News Chronicle (2.2M) PO Box 460 Wisner NE 68791 **Phn:** 402-529-3229 **Fax:** 402-529-3279 wisnews@gpcom.net

Wolbach Wolbach Messenger (0.4M) PO Box 38 Wolbach NE 68882 **Phn:** 308-754-4401 **Fax:** 308-754-4498

Wood River Wood River Sunbeam (1.1M) PO Box 356 Wood River NE 68883 **Phn:** 308-583-0124 www.clipperpubco.com wrsunbeam@clipperpubco.com

Wymore Arbor State (1.8M) PO Box 327 Wymore NE 68466 **Phn:** 402-645-3344 **Fax:** 402-645-3345

NEVADA

Battle Mountain Battle Mountain Bugle (1.8M) 113 Carson Rd Ste 5 Battle Mountain NV 89820 **Phn:** 775-635-2230 **Fax:** 775-635-2644 insidenorthernnevada.com bmb.office@winnemuccapublishing.net

Boulder City Boulder City News (5.4M) PO Box 60065 Boulder City NV 89006 **Phn:** 702-293-2302 **Fax:** 702-294-0977 editor@hbcpub.com

Caliente Lincoln County Record (1.7M) PO Box 750 Caliente NV 89008 **Phn:** 775-726-3333 **Fax:** 775-726-3331

Ely Ely Times (2.7M) PO Box 150820 Ely NV 89315 **Phn:** 775-289-4491 **Fax:** 775-289-4566 www.elynews.com elytimes.dave@gmail.com

Ely Eureka Sentinel (0.4M) PO Box 150820 Ely NV 89315 **Phn:** 775-289-4491 **Fax:** 775-289-4566 www.elynews.com elytimes.lukas@gmail.com

Fallon Lahontan Valley News (3.5M) PO Box 1297 Fallon NV 89407 **Phn:** 775-423-6041 **Fax:** 775-423-0474 www.nevadaappeal.com/News/LahontanValley sranson@lahontanvalleynews.com

NEBRASKA WEEKLY NEWSPAPERS

Fernley Fernley Leader (3.1M) 25 E Main St Ste 4 Fernley NV 89408 **Phn:** 775-575-4999 **Fax:** 775-575-5145 www.rgj.com

Gardnerville The Record-Courier (5.6M) 1503 US Highway 395 N Ste G Gardnerville NV 89410 **Phn:** 775-782-5121 **Fax:** 775-782-6132 www.recordcourier.com editor@recordcourier.com

Hawthorne Mineral Co. Independent News (2.8M) PO Box 1270 Hawthorne NV 89415 **Phn:** 775-945-2414 **Fax:** 775-945-1270 hbunchmcin@gmail.com

Henderson Henderson Home News (14.0M) 2290 Corporate Cir Ste 250 Henderson NV 89074 **Phn:** 702-990-8942 **Fax:** 702-990-8950

Incline Village N Lake Tahoe Bonanza (8.0M) 25 Tahoe Blvd # 206 Incline Village NV 89452 **Phn:** 775-831-4666 **Fax:** 775-831-4222 www.tahoedailytribune.com/NorthShore kmacmillan@tahoebonanza.com

Las Vegas City Life (72.0M) PO Box 98375 Las Vegas NV 89193 **Phn:** 702-871-6780 **Fax:** 702-871-3298 www.lasvegascitylife.com ssebelius@lvcitylife.com

Las Vegas Las Vegas Tribune (40.0M) 820 E Charleston Blvd Las Vegas NV 89104 **Phn:** 702-699-8100 lasvegastribune.net newsdesk@lasvegastribune.net

Las Vegas Penny Press (3.0M) 5010 Spencer St Las Vegas NV 89119 **Phn:** 702-740-5588 **Fax:** 702-947-0741 www.pennypresslv.com pennypress@gmail.com

Las Vegas View Newspapers (40.0M) PO Box 70 Las Vegas NV 89125 **Phn:** 702-383-0264 **Fax:** 702-383-4676 www.lvrj.com/view gmeurer@viewnews.com

Laughlin Nevada Times (8.0M) PO Box 29909 Laughlin NV 89028 **Phn:** 702-298-6090 **Fax:** 702-298-3626 www.laughlintimes.com lntedit@cmaaccess.com

Mesquite Desert Valley Times (7.8M) 355 W Mesquite Blvd Ste C10 Mesquite NV 89027 **Phn:** 702-346-7495 **Fax:** 702-346-7494 www.thespectrum.com/section/dvtonline news@dvtnv.com

Overton Moapa Valley Progress (5.0M) PO Box 430 Overton NV 89040 **Phn:** 702-397-6246 **Fax:** 702-397-6247 mvprogress.com progress@mvdsl.com

Pahrump Pahrump Valley Times (7.5M) 2160 E Calvada Blvd Ste A Pahrump NV 89048 **Phn:** 775-727-5102 **Fax:** 775-727-5309 www.pahrumpvalleytimes.com mward@pvtimes.com

Reno Reno News & Review (30.0M) 708 N Center St Ste 200 Reno NV 89501 **Phn:** 775-324-4440 **Fax:** 775-324-4572 www.newsreview.com

Tonopah Tonopah Times-Bonanza/Goldfield News (1.8M) PO Box 1112 Tonopah NV 89049 **Phn:** 775-482-3365 **Fax:** 775-482-5042 tonopahtimes.com broberts@tonopahtimes.com

Virginia City Comstock Chronicle (1.0M) PO Box 530 Virginia City NV 89440 **Phn:** 775-847-0765 **Fax:** 775-847-0799 storeystories@gmail.com

Winnemucca Elko Independent (13.0M) 1022 Grass Valley Rd Winnemucca NV 89445 **Phn:** 775-753-8200 **Fax:** 775-753-2432

Winnemucca Humboldt Sun (4.5M) 1022 Grass Valley Rd Winnemucca NV 89445 **Phn:** 775-623-5011 **Fax:** 775-623-5243 insidenorthernnevada.com bmb.office@winnemuccapublishing.net

Winnemucca Lovelock Review-Miner (1.4M) 1022 Grass Valley Rd Winnemucca NV 89445 **Phn:** 775-273-7245 **Fax:** 775-273-0500 www.insidenorthernnevada.com lrm.office@winnemuccapublishing.net

Yerington Mason Valley News (4.0M) PO Box 841 Yerington NV 89447 **Phn:** 775-463-4242 **Fax:** 775-463-5547 www.rgj.com ktrout@masonvalleynews.com

NEW HAMPSHIRE

Amherst Amherst Citizen (6.2M) PO Box 291 Amherst NH 03031 **Phn:** 603-672-9444 **Fax:** 603-672-8153 www.amherstcitizen.com news@amherstcitizen.com

Claremont Argus Champion (4.7M) 401 River Rd Claremont NH 03743 **Phn:** 603-526-4620 **Fax:** 603-526-4650

Colebrook Colebrook Chronicle (3.1M) PO Box 263 Colebrook NH 03576 **Phn:** 603-246-8998 **Fax:** 603-246-9918 www.colebrookchronicle.com nnhmag@ncia.net

Colebrook The News & Sentinel (5.1M) PO Box 39 Colebrook NH 03576 **Phn:** 603-237-5501 **Fax:** 603-237-5060 www.colbsent.com karenhladd@colebrooknewsandsentinel.com

Conway Carroll County Independent (4.0M) PO Box 530 Conway NH 03818 **Phn:** 603-447-6336 **Fax:** 603-447-5474 www.newhampshirelakesandmountains.com cci@salmonpress.com

Derry Derry News (7.3M) PO Box 307 Derry NH 03038 **Phn:** 603-437-7000 **Fax:** 603-432-4510 www.derrynews.com editor@derrynews.com

Dover Rochester Times (15.0M) 150 Venture Dr Dover NH 03820 **Phn:** 603-332-2300 **Fax:** 603-330-3162 www.fosters.com news@fosters.com

Dover York Times (14.0M) 150 Venture Dr Dover NH 03820 **Phn:** 603-742-4455 **Fax:** 603-749-7079 www.fosters.com letters@fosters.com

Franconia Ammonoosuc Times (5.0M) PO Box 153 Franconia NH 03580 **Phn:** 603-444-7283 **Fax:** 603-444-0028 www.whitemtregion.com/amm_times.php editor@ammtimes.com

Hampton The Atlantic News (9.0M) PO Box 592 Hampton NH 03843 **Phn:** 603-926-4557

Hampton The Beach News (15.0M) PO Box 592 Hampton NH 03843 **Phn:** 603-926-4557

Hillsboro The Messenger (10.0M) PO Box 1190 Hillsboro NH 03244 **Phn:** 603-464-3388 **Fax:** 603-464-4106 leighb@tds.net

Hillsborough NH Weekly Contender (10.0M) PO Box 324 Hillsborough NH 03244 **Phn:** 603-464-4830

Hollis Hollis Times (1.6M) PO Box 148 Hollis NH 03049 **Phn:** 603-465-2051 **Fax:** 603-465-7722 hollistimes@tds.net

Hudson Area News Group (32.0M) 17 Executive Dr Hudson NH 03051 **Phn:** 603-880-1516 **Fax:** 603-879-9707 www.areanewsgroup.com len@areanewsgroup.com

Keene Keene Sentinel Weeklies (12.0M) PO Box 546 Keene NH 03431 **Phn:** 603-352-1234 **Fax:** 603-352-0437 www.sentinelsource.com news@keenesentinel.com

Kingston Carriage Towne News (26.0M) PO Box 100 Kingston NH 03848 **Phn:** 603-642-4499 **Fax:** 603-642-7750 www.carriagetownenews.com info@carriagetownenews.com

Laconia Weirs Times (30.0M) PO Box 5458 Laconia NH 03247 **Phn:** 603-366-8463 **Fax:** 603-366-7301 www.weirs.com info@weirs.com

Lancaster Berlin Reporter (5.0M) 79 Main St Lancaster NH 03584 **Phn:** 603-752-1200 **Fax:** 603-752-2339 www.newhampshirelakesandmountains.com frank@salmonpress.com

Lancaster Coos County Democrat (7.5M) PO Box 29 Lancaster NH 03584 **Phn:** 603-788-4939 **Fax:** 603-788-3022 www.newhampshirelakesandmountains.com frank@salmonpress.com

Littleton The Courier (7.2M) PO Box 230 Littleton NH 03561 **Phn:** 603-444-3927 **Fax:** 603-444-3920 www.newhampshirelakesandmountains.com amcgrath@salmonpress.com

Londonderry Londonderry Times (9.9M) 2 Litchfield Rd Londonderry NH 03053 **Phn:** 603-537-2760 **Fax:** 603-537-2765 www.nutpub.net dpaul@nutpub.net

Londonderry Nutfield News (10.0M) 2 Litchfield Rd Londonderry NH 03053 **Phn:** 603-537-2760 **Fax:** 603-537-2765 www.nutpub.net dpaul@nutpub.net

Lowell The Broadcaster (67.0M) 491 Dutton St Ste 1 Lowell NH 01854 **Phn:** 603-886-6075 **Fax:** 603-886-8180

Manchester Neighborhood News Inc. (50.0M) 100 William Loeb Dr Manchester NH 03109 **Phn:** 603-206-7800 www.newhampshire.com amy@unionleader.com

Manchester The Hippo (32.0M) 49 Hollis St Ste 2 Manchester NH 03101 **Phn:** 603-625-1855 **Fax:** 603-625-2422 www.hippopress.com news@hippopress.com

Meredith Plymouth Record Enterprise (7.0M) PO Box 729 Meredith NH 03253 **Phn:** 603-279-4516 **Fax:** 603-279-3331 www.newhampshirelakesandmountains.com record@salmonpress.com

Meredith Salmon Press (15.0M) PO Box 729 Meredith NH 03253 **Phn:** 603-279-4516 **Fax:** 603-279-3331 www.newhampshirelakesandmountains.com mnews@salmonpress.com

Milford Cabinet Press (30.0M) 54 School St Milford NH 03055 **Phn:** 603-673-3100 **Fax:** 603-673-8250 www.cabinet.com

North Conway The Mountain Ear (15.0M) PO Box 1890 North Conway NH 03860 **Phn:** 603-447-6336 **Fax:** 603-447-5474 www.newhampshirelakesandmountains.com earnews@salmonpress.com

North Sutton Intertown Record (3.0M) PO Box 162 North Sutton NH 03260 **Phn:** 603-927-4028 www.intertownrecord.com info@intertownrecord.com

Peterborough Monadnock Ledger-Transcript (8.5M) PO Box 36 Peterborough NH 03458 **Phn:** 603-924-7172 **Fax:** 603-924-3681 www.ledgertranscript.com news@ledgertranscript.com

Pittsfield Suncook Valley Sun (10.0M) PO Box 156 Pittsfield NH 03263 **Phn:** 603-435-6291 **Fax:** 603-435-7383 www.suncookvalleysun.com svsun@aol.com

Portsmouth Portsmouth Times (19.0M) 8 Market Sq Portsmouth NH 03801 **Phn:** 603-842-8010 **Fax:** 603-749-7079 www.fosters.com

Portsmouth Seacoast Newspapers (2.0M) 111 Nh Ave Portsmouth NH 03801 **Phn:** 603-772-6000 **Fax:** 603-772-3830 www.seacoastonline.com news@seacoastonline.com

Windham Independent (2.4M) 233 Range Rd Windham NH 03087 **Phn:** 603-898-7874

Wolfeboro Falls Granite State News (6.0M) PO Box 250 Wolfeboro Falls NH 03896 **Phn:** 603-569-3126 **Fax:** 603-569-4743 www.newhampshirelakesandmountains.com grunter@salmonpress.com

NEW JERSEY

Allentown Packet Publications (13.0M) PO Box 446 Allentown NJ 08501 **Phn:** 609-259-7778 **Fax:** 609-259-1182 centraljersey.com ckilleen@centraljersey.com

NEW HAMPSHIRE WEEKLY NEWSPAPERS

Asbury Park The Coaster (4.5M) 1011 Main St Ste B Asbury Park NJ 07712 **Phn:** 732-775-6379 **Fax:** 732-775-8345 thecoaster.net editor@thecoaster.net

Bayonne Community News (28.0M) 13 E 21st St Bayonne NJ 07002 **Phn:** 201-437-2460 **Fax:** 201-437-7127 www.hudsonreporter.com

Bernardsville Bernardsville News (9.3M) PO Box 687 Bernardsville NJ 07924 **Phn:** 908-766-3900 **Fax:** 908-766-6365 newjerseyhills.com pnardone@recordernewspapers.com

Blackwood Cam-Glo Newspapers (12.0M) PO Box 1609 Blackwood NJ 08012 **Phn:** 856-228-7300 **Fax:** 856-227-1207

Brigantine Beach Comber News (5.0M) 3824 Atlantic Brigantine Blvd Brigantine NJ 08203 **Phn:** 609-266-1860 **Fax:** 609-266-3599

Browns Mills The Community News (4.5M) 350 Lakehurst Rd Browns Mills NJ 08015 **Phn:** 609-893-4585 **Fax:** 609-654-8237 www.southjerseylocalnews.com news@medfordcentralrecord.com

Caldwell Recorder Community Papers (19.0M) PO Box 72 Caldwell NJ 07006 **Phn:** 973-226-8900 **Fax:** 973-226-0553 newjerseyhills.com pnardone@recordernewspapers.com

Chester Recorder Publishing (17.0M) PO Box 600 Chester NJ 07930 **Phn:** 908-879-4100 **Fax:** 908-879-0799 newjerseyhills.com pgarber@recordernewspapers.com

Clifton Clifton Insider (15.0M) PO Box 764 Clifton NJ 07015 **Phn:** 973-865-7691 **Fax:** 973-773-8035 cliftoninsider.com nveliky@cliftoninsider.com

Clifton Clifton Journal (30.0M) 935 Allwood Rd Ste 200 Clifton NJ 07012 **Phn:** 973-778-2500 **Fax:** 973-778-2525 www.northjersey.com/towns cliftonjournal@northjersey.com

Clifton North Jersey Prospector (82.0M) 479 Grove St Clifton NJ 07013 **Phn:** 973-773-8300

Clifton Post Eagle (13.0M) PO Box 2127 Clifton NJ 07015 **Phn:** 973-473-5414 **Fax:** 973-473-3211 www.posteaglenewspaper.com posteagle@aol.com

Clinton Hunterdon Review (5.5M) PO Box 5308 Clinton NJ 08809 **Phn:** 908-735-4081 **Fax:** 908-735-2945 newjerseyhills.com pnardone@recordernewspapers.com

Collingswood The Retrospect (5.6M) PO Box 296 Collingswood NJ 08108 **Phn:** 856-854-1400 **Fax:** 856-854-8790 theretrospect.com editor@theretrospect.com

Cresskill N Jersey Community Papers (86.0M) 210 Knickerbocker Rd Cresskill NJ 07626 **Phn:** 201-894-6700 **Fax:** 201-568-4360 www.northjersey.com suburbanite@northjersey.com

Dayton Cranbury Press (3.0M) PO Box 309 Dayton NJ 08810 **Phn:** 732-329-9214 **Fax:** 732-329-8291 centraljersey.com ahuston@centraljersey.com

Denville The Citizen (6.4M) 124 E Main St Denville NJ 07834 **Phn:** 973-627-0400 **Fax:** 973-627-0403 newjerseyhills.com eparker@recordernewspapers.com

Egg Harbor Township The Current Newspapers (58.0M) 3129 Fire Rd Ste 2 Egg Harbor Township NJ 08234 **Phn:** 609-383-8994 **Fax:** 609-383-0056 www.catamaranmedia.com current@catamaranmedia.com

Elizabeth CMD Media (33.0M) 1139 E Jersey St Ste 503 Elizabeth NJ 07201 **Phn:** 908-352-3100 **Fax:** 908-469-1210 njtoday.net cmdeditor@gmail.com

Elizabeth Elizabeth Reporter (7.0M) 144 Elmora Ave Elizabeth NJ 07202 **Phn:** 908-352-5000 **Fax:** 908-352-5005

Elmer Elmer Times (2.2M) 21 State St Elmer NJ 08318 **Phn:** 856-358-6171 elmertimes@hotmail.com

Flemington Hunterdon Democrat (24.0M) 8 Minneakoning Rd Flemington NJ 08822 **Phn:** 908-782-4747 **Fax:** 908-782-4706 www.nj.com/hunterdon news@hcdemocrat.com

Flemington Hunterdon Observer (48.0M) 8 Minneakoning Rd Flemington NJ 08822 **Phn:** 908-782-4747 **Fax:** 908-782-4706 www.nj.com news@hcdemocrat.com

Flemington Suburban News (70.0M) 8 Minneakoning Rd Flemington NJ 08822 **Phn:** 732-396-4227 **Fax:** 732-574-2613 www.nj.com subnews@njnpublishing.com

Franklinville Sentinel of Gloucester County (2.0M) PO Box 367 Franklinville NJ 08322 **Phn:** 856-694-1600 **Fax:** 856-694-0469 www.thenjsentinel.com ftsentinel@comcast.net

Freehold Greater Media Papers (230.0M) PO Box 5001 Freehold NJ 07728 **Phn:** 732-358-5200 **Fax:** 732-780-4192 www.gmnews.com gmntnews@gmnews.com

Garfield The Messenger (3.5M) 48 Harrison Ave Garfield NJ 07026 **Phn:** 973-473-1927 **Fax:** 973-546-4233 majorpress@aol.com

Gloucester City Gloucester City News (3.8M) PO Box 151 Gloucester City NJ 08030 **Phn:** 856-456-1199 **Fax:** 856-456-1330 gcneditor@verizon.net

Hackensack County Seat (35.0M) 77 Hudson St Ste 3 Hackensack NJ 07601 **Phn:** 201-488-5795 **Fax:** 201-343-8720 www.cntyseat.com info@cntyseat.com

Hackettstown Warren Reporter (4.6M) PO Box 500 Hackettstown NJ 07840 **Phn:** 908-852-1212 **Fax:** 908-852-9320 www.nj.com/warrenreporter warrenpr@njnpublishing.com

Haddonfield Sun Newspapers (7.0M) 108 Kings Hwy E Haddonfield NJ 08033 **Phn:** 856-427-0933 **Fax:** 856-427-0934 sj.sunne.ws/haddonfield info@sunne.ws

Hammonton Atlantic Co. Weeklies (35.0M) PO Box 596 Hammonton NJ 08037 **Phn:** 609-561-2300 **Fax:** 609-567-2249

Hammonton Hammonton Gazette (8.0M) PO Box 1228 Hammonton NJ 08037 **Phn:** 609-704-1939 **Fax:** 609-704-1938 www.hammontongazette.com

Hasbrouck Heights The Observer (3.0M) PO Box 445 Hasbrouck Heights NJ 07604 **Phn:** 201-288-0333 **Fax:** 201-288-1847

Hawthorne Hawthorne Press (9.5M) PO Box 1 Hawthorne NJ 07507 **Phn:** 973-427-3330 **Fax:** 973-427-8781 hawthornepress@optonline.net

Hoboken Hudson Reporter Newspapers (130.0M) 1400 Washington St Hoboken NJ 07030 **Phn:** 201-798-7800 **Fax:** 201-798-0018 www.hudsonreporter.com editorial@hudsonreporter.com

Kearny The Observer (32.0M) 531 Kearny Ave Kearny NJ 07032 **Phn:** 201-991-1600 **Fax:** 201-991-8941 www.theobserver.com editorial@theobserver.com

Livingston West Essex Tribune (7.5M) PO Box 65 Livingston NJ 07039 **Phn:** 973-992-1771 **Fax:** 973-992-7015 www.LivingstonNavigator.com tribuneeditorial@verizon.net

Madison Recorder Publishing (14.0M) PO Box 160 Madison NJ 07940 **Phn:** 973-377-2000 **Fax:** 973-377-7721 newjerseyhills.com eparker@recordernewspapers.com

Manahawkin Times/Beacon Newspapers (16.0M) 345 E Bay Ave Ste A Manahawkin NJ 08050 **Phn:** 609-597-3211 **Fax:** 609-978-4592 www.app.com editors@app.com

Manasquan Manasquan Coast Star (15.5M) 13 Broad St Manasquan NJ 08736 **Phn:** 732-223-0076 **Fax:** 732-223-8212 starnewsgroup.com news@thecoaststar.com

Manchester Advance News (20.0M) 2048 Route 37 Manchester NJ 08759 **Phn:** 732-657-8936 **Fax:** 732-657-2970

Maplewood Irvington Herald (3.1M) PO Box 158 Maplewood NJ 07040 **Phn:** 973-763-0700 **Fax:** 973-763-2557 www.localsource.com editorial@thelocalsource.com

Maplewood Worrall Community Newspapers (12.0M) PO Box 158 Maplewood NJ 07040 **Phn:** 973-763-0700 **Fax:** 973-763-2557 www.localsource.com editorial@thelocalsource.com

Maywood Our Town (4.5M) 19 W Pleasant Ave Maywood NJ 07607 **Phn:** 201-843-5700 **Fax:** 201-843-5781 www.ourtownnewsonline.com rtownmaywoodrp@aol.com

Medford The Central Record (12.0M) PO Box 1027 Medford NJ 08055 **Phn:** 609-654-5000 **Fax:** 609-654-0391 www.southjerseylocalnews.com news@medfordcentralrecord.com

Middletown The Courier (9.0M) PO Box 399 Middletown NJ 07748 **Phn:** 732-957-0070 **Fax:** 732-957-0143 www.bayshorenews.com bayshorenews.denise@gmail.com

Midland Park Villadom Times (56.0M) PO Box 96 Midland Park NJ 07432 **Phn:** 201-652-0744 **Fax:** 201-670-4745

Millburn Millburn Item (4.7M) 343 Millburn Ave # 100 Millburn NJ 07041 **Phn:** 973-921-6451 **Fax:** 973-921-6458 www.northjersey.com/millburn-shorthills theitem@northjersey.com

Millville Cumberland County Reminder (24.0M) PO Box 1600 Millville NJ 08332 **Phn:** 856-825-8811 **Fax:** 856-825-0011 www.reminderusa.net editor@remindernewspaper.net

Montclair Montclair Times (12.0M) 130 Valley Rd Montclair NJ 07042 **Phn:** 973-233-5000 **Fax:** 973-233-5032 www.northjersey.com/towns contactus@montclairtimes.com

Moorestown Maple Shade Progress (2.6M) 301 Mill St Moorestown NJ 08057 **Phn:** 856-231-7600 **Fax:** 856-231-4333 www.southjerseylocalnews.com news@medfordcentralrecord.com

New Egypt New Egypt Press (3.0M) PO Box 188 New Egypt NJ 08533 **Phn:** 609-758-2112 **Fax:** 609-758-1816 www.southjerseylocalnews.com news@medfordcentralrecord.com

New Milford Palisadian (53.0M) 626 McCarthy Dr New Milford NJ 07646 **Phn:** 201-385-2000

New Providence Independent Press (35.0M) 309 South St Ste 1 New Providence NJ 07974 **Phn:** 908-464-1025 **Fax:** 908-464-9085 www.nj.com/independentpress ipeditors@njnpublishing.com

Newtown Pennington Post (4.0M) 203 S State St Newtown NJ 18940 **Phn:** 609-737-3379 **Fax:** 609-737-8126 www.buckslocalnews.com/pennington_post pennpost@ingnews.com

Nutley North Jersey Papers (12.0M) 90 Centre St Nutley NJ 07110 **Phn:** 973-667-2100 **Fax:** 973-667-3904 www.northjersey.com/towns nutleysun@northjersey.com

Ocean City Ocean City Sentinel (10.0M) PO Box 238 Ocean City NJ 08226 **Phn:** 609-399-5411 **Fax:** 609-399-0416 www.ocsentinel.com oceancitysentinel@comcast.net

Palisades Park Bergen News Publishing (52.0M) PO Box 616 Palisades Park NJ 07650 **Phn:** 201-947-5000 **Fax:** 201-947-6968

NEW JERSEY WEEKLY NEWSPAPERS

Princeton Hillsborough Beacon (4.3M) PO Box 350 Princeton NJ 08542 **Phn:** 732-329-9214 **Fax:** 732-329-8291 centraljersey.com ahuston@centraljersey.com

Princeton Manville News (1.3M) PO Box 350 Princeton NJ 08542 **Phn:** 732-329-9214 **Fax:** 732-329-8291 centraljersey.com grobbins@centraljersey.com

Princeton Princeton Packet (14.0M) PO Box 350 Princeton NJ 08542 **Phn:** 609-924-3244 **Fax:** 609-924-3842 centraljersey.com ckilleen@centraljersey.com

Princeton South Brunswick Post (3.8M) PO Box 350 Princeton NJ 08542 **Phn:** 732-329-9214 **Fax:** 732-329-8291 centraljersey.com hkalet@centraljersey.com

Princeton Town Topics (14.0M) 305 Witherspoon St Princeton NJ 08542 **Phn:** 609-924-2200 **Fax:** 609-924-8818 www.towntopics.com pressreleases@towntopics.com

Princeton Valley News (10.0M) PO Box 350 Princeton NJ 08542 **Phn:** 609-466-1190 **Fax:** 609-466-2123 centraljersey.com rluse@centraljersey.com

Pt Pleasant Beach The Ocean Star (4.3M) 421 River Ave Pt Pleasant Beach NJ 08742 **Phn:** 732-899-7606 **Fax:** 732-899-9778 starnewsgroup.com editor@theoceanstar.com

Red Bank Monmouth Journal (10.0M) 46 English Plz Ste D Red Bank NJ 07701 **Phn:** 732-747-7007 **Fax:** 732-747-5445 themonmouthjournal.com

Red Bank Two River Times (10.0M) 75 W Front St Ste 2 Red Bank NJ 07701 **Phn:** 732-219-5788 **Fax:** 732-747-7213 www.trtnj.com editor@tworivertimes.com

Ridgewood NJ Media Group (70.0M) 41 Oak St Ridgewood NJ 07450 **Phn:** 973-569-7100 **Fax:** 201-457-2520 www.northjersey.com oates@northjersey.com

Rio Grande Cape May County Herald (32.0M) 1508 Route 47 Rio Grande NJ 08242 **Phn:** 609-886-8600 **Fax:** 609-886-1879 www.capemaycountyherald.com newsdesk@cmcherald.com

Rockaway Neighbor News (62.0M) 100 Commons Way Rockaway NJ 07866 **Phn:** 973-586-8190 **Fax:** 973-586-8199 www.northjersey.com/towns neighbor@northjersey.com

Rutherford Leader Newspapers (40.0M) PO Box 71 Rutherford NJ 07070 **Phn:** 201-438-8700 **Fax:** 201-438-9022 leadernewspapers.net jsoltes@leadernewspaper.com

Rutherford South Bergenite (25.0M) 33 Lincoln Ave Ste 4 Rutherford NJ 07070 **Phn:** 201-933-1166 **Fax:** 201-933-5496 www.northjersey.com/towns southbergenite@northjersey.com

Seaville Catamaran Media (46.0M) 2087 Shore Rd flr 2 Seaville NJ 08230 **Phn:** 609-624-8900 **Fax:** 609-624-3470 www.catamaranmedia.com current@catamaranmedia.com

Secaucus Secaucus Home News (4.5M) PO Box 1100 Secaucus NJ 07096 **Phn:** 201-867-2071 **Fax:** 201-865-3806 shn1910@aol.com

Somerville North Jersey Newspapers (57.0M) PO Box 699 Somerville NJ 08876 **Phn:** 908-575-6660 **Fax:** 908-948-1052 www.nj.com

Sparta Straus Newspapers (43.0M) 1A Main St Sparta NJ 07871 **Phn:** 973-300-0890 **Fax:** 973-300-0418 www.strausnews.com editor.pn@strausnews.com

Stirling Echoes-Sentinel (6.7M) PO Box 216 Stirling NJ 07980 **Phn:** 908-647-0412 **Fax:** 908-647-5952 newjerseyhills.com dkelly@recordernewspapers.com

Surf City The Sandpaper (29.0M) 1816 Long Beach Blvd Surf City NJ 08008 **Phn:** 609-494-5900 **Fax:** 609-494-1437 www.catamaranmedia.com current@catamaranmedia.com

Toms River Observer & Community Reporter (97.0M) 1451 Route 37 W Toms River NJ 08755 **Phn:** 732-349-3000 **Fax:** 732-557-5758

Union Worrall Comm. Newspapers (25.0M) PO Box 3109 Union NJ 07083 **Phn:** 908-686-7700 **Fax:** 908-686-6681 www.localsource.com editorial@thelocalsource.com

West Caldwell Reboli Newspapers (31.0M) PO Box 6123 West Caldwell NJ 07007 **Phn:** 973-227-4433

West Cape May Cape May Star & Wave (6.5M) 600 Park Blvd # 4-28 West Cape May NJ 08204 **Phn:** 609-884-3466 **Fax:** 609-884-2893 www.starandwave.com cmstarwave@comcast.net

West Paterson Verona-Cedar Grove Times (5.3M) PO Box 471 West Paterson NJ 07424 **Phn:** 973-569-7341 **Fax:** 973-569-7344 www.northjersey.com/towns vcgtimes@northjersey.com

Westfield Scotch Plains-Fanwood Times (1.9M) PO Box 250 Westfield NJ 07091 **Phn:** 908-232-4407 **Fax:** 908-232-0473 www.goleader.com press@goleader.com

Westfield Westfield Leader (5.7M) PO Box 250 Westfield NJ 07091 **Phn:** 908-232-4407 **Fax:** 908-232-0473 www.goleader.com editor@goleader.com

Westwood Community Life (25.0M) 372 Kinderkamack Rd Ste 5 Westwood NJ 07675 **Phn:** 201-664-2501 **Fax:** 201-664-1332 www.northjersey.com/towns pvcommunitylife@northjersey.com

NEW MEXICO

Albuquerque Health City Sun (2.0M) PO Box 1517 Albuquerque NM 87103 **Phn:** 505-242-3010 **Fax:** 505-842-5464 www.healthcitysun.com legal@healthcitysun.com

Albuquerque Weekly Alibi (40.0M) 413 Central NW Albuquerque NM 87102 **Phn:** 505-346-0660 **Fax:** 505-256-9651 alibi.com letters@alibi.com

Angel Fire Sangre de Cristo Chronicle (2.8M) PO Box 209 Angel Fire NM 87710 **Phn:** 575-377-2358 **Fax:** 575-377-2679 www.sangrechronicle.com news@sangrechronicle.com

Belen Valencia News-Bulletin (21.0M) PO Box 25 Belen NM 87002 **Phn:** 505-864-4472 **Fax:** 505-864-3549 www.news-bulletin.com cgarcia@news-bulletin.com

Clayton Union County Leader (2.3M) PO Box 486 Clayton NM 88415 **Phn:** 575-374-2587 **Fax:** 575-374-8117 www.claytonnewmexico.net/ucleader.html ucleader@plateautel.net

Dulce Jicarilla Chieftain (1.3M) PO Box 507 Dulce NM 87528 **Phn:** 575-759-4223 **Fax:** 575-759-1393 jicarillachieftain@yahoo.com

Espanola Rio Grande Sun (11.5M) PO Box 790 Espanola NM 87532 **Phn:** 505-753-2126 **Fax:** 505-753-2140 www.riograndesun.com rgsun@cybermesa.com

Farmington San Juan Sun (15.0M) PO Box 450 Farmington NM 87499 **Phn:** 505-325-4545 **Fax:** 505-564-4630 www.daily-times.com croberts@daily-times.com

Fort Sumner De Baca County News (1.4M) PO Box 448 Fort Sumner NM 88119 **Phn:** 575-355-2462 **Fax:** 575-355-7253 www.debacanews.com pecospub@plateautel.net

Grants Cibola Co Beacon (3.5M) 523 W Santa Fe Ave Grants NM 87020 **Phn:** 505-287-4411 **Fax:** 505-287-7822 www.cibolabeacon.com editor@cibolabeacon.com

Jal Jal Record (1.5M) PO Box Y Jal NM 88252 **Phn:** 575-395-2516 **Fax:** 575-395-3079 jalrecordonline.com tjr@jalrecord.net

Las Cruces Las Cruces Bulletin (21.0M) 840 N Telshor Blvd Ste E Las Cruces NM 88011 **Phn:** 575-524-8061 **Fax:** 575-526-4621 www.lascrucesbulletin.com editor@lascrucesbulletin.com

Moriarty Mountain View Telegraph (6.5M) PO Box 2225 Moriarty NM 87035 **Phn:** 505-823-7100 **Fax:** 505-823-7107 www.mvtelegraph.com editor@mvtelegraph.com

Rio Rancho The Observer (23.5M) PO Box 15878 Rio Rancho NM 87174 **Phn:** 505-892-8080 **Fax:** 505-892-5719 www.rrobserver.com editor@rrobserver.com

Ruidoso Ruidoso News (6.0M) PO Box 128 Ruidoso NM 88355 **Phn:** 575-257-4001 **Fax:** 575-257-7053 www.ruidosonews.com tvestal@ruidosonews.com

Santa Fe Santa Fe Reporter (26.0M) 132 E Marcy St Santa Fe NM 87501 **Phn:** 505-988-5541 **Fax:** 505-988-5348 www.sfreporter.com editor@sfreporter.com

Santa Rosa Guadalupe Communicator (2.2M) PO Box 403 Santa Rosa NM 88435 **Phn:** 575-472-3555 **Fax:** 575-472-5555 comsilvercom@plateautel.net

Socorro El Defensor-Chieftain (4.5M) 200 Winkler St Socorro NM 87801 **Phn:** 575-835-0520 **Fax:** 575-835-1837 www.dchieftain.com editorial@dchieftain.com

Socorro Mountain Mail (2.7M) PO Box 62 Socorro NM 87801 **Phn:** 575-835-2030 **Fax:** 575-835-3998 mountainmaileditor@yahoo.com

Taos Taos News (11.0M) PO Box 3737 Taos NM 87571 **Phn:** 575-758-2241 **Fax:** 575-758-9647 www.taosnews.com editor@taosnews.com

Truth or Consequences Sierra County Sentinel (5.0M) PO Box 351 Truth or Consequences NM 87901 **Phn:** 575-894-3088 **Fax:** 575-894-3998 www.gpkmedia.com sentinel@gpkmedia.com

Truth or Consequences The Herald (4.6M) PO Box 752 Truth or Consequences NM 87901 **Phn:** 575-894-2143 **Fax:** 575-894-7824 www.heraldpub.com herald@riolink.com

Tucumcari Quay County Sun (3.7M) 902 S 1st St Tucumcari NM 88401 **Phn:** 575-461-1952 **Fax:** 575-461-1965 www.qcsunonline.com

NEW YORK

Adams Jefferson County Journal (2.8M) PO Box 68 Adams NY 13605 **Phn:** 315-232-2141 **Fax:** 315-232-4586 jcjesfucn@citlink.net

Addison Addison Post (6.4M) 42 Main St # 101 Addison NY 14801 **Phn:** 607-359-2238 **Fax:** 607-359-2283 www.myaddisonpost.com

Akron Akron Bugle (1.9M) 67 Main St Akron NY 14001 **Phn:** 716-542-9615 www.akronbugle.com news@akronbugle.com

Albany Metroland (40.0M) 419 Madison Ave Albany NY 12210 **Phn:** 518-463-2500 **Fax:** 518-463-3726 metroland.net sleon@metroland.net

Alden Alden Advertiser (3.7M) 13200 Broadway St Alden NY 14004 **Phn:** 716-937-9226 aldenadvertiser@rochester.rr.com

Alexandria Bay Thousand Islands Sun (6.7M) PO Box 277 Alexandria Bay NY 13607 **Phn:** 315-482-2581 **Fax:** 315-482-6315

Alfred Alfred Sun (1.0M) PO Box 811 Alfred NY 14802 **Phn:** 607-587-8110 alfredsun.news@gmail.com

Altamont Altamont Enterprise (6.3M) PO Box 654 Altamont NY 12009 **Phn:** 518-861-5005 **Fax:** 518-861-5105 www.altamontenterprise.com mhale-spencer@altamontenterprise.com

Amityville Amityville Record (2.9M) 85 Broadway Ste A Amityville NY 11701 **Phn:** 631-264-0077 **Fax:** 631-264-5310 www.amityvillerecord.com acjnews@rcn.com

NEW MEXICO WEEKLY NEWSPAPERS

Amsterdam Courier-Standard-Enterprise (4.0M) 1 Venner Rd Amsterdam NY 12010 **Phn:** 518-843-1100 **Fax:** 518-843-6580 www.recordernews.com geoff@recordernews.com

Arcade Arcade Herald (5.0M) 223 Main St Arcade NY 14009 **Phn:** 585-492-2525 **Fax:** 585-492-2667 www.mywnynews.com heraldnews@roadrunner.com

Arkville Catskill Mountain News (4.0M) PO Box 515 Arkville NY 12406 **Phn:** 845-586-2601 **Fax:** 845-586-2366 www.catskillmountainnews.com news@catskillmountainnews.com

Astoria Queens Gazette (90.0M) 4216 34th Ave Astoria NY 11101 **Phn:** 718-361-6161 **Fax:** 718-784-7552 www.qgazette.com qgazette@aol.com

Auburn Skaneateles Journal (5.5M) 25 Dill St Auburn NY 13021 **Phn:** 315-253-5311 **Fax:** 315-253-6031 auburnpub.com/skaneateles news@skaneatelesjournal.com

Averill Park The Advertiser (48.0M) PO Box 70 Averill Park NY 12018 **Phn:** 518-674-2841 **Fax:** 518-674-8680 www.crwnewspapers.net articles@theadvertiser.us

Babylon Babylon Beacon (3.4M) 65 Deer Park Ave Ste 2 Babylon NY 11702 **Phn:** 631-587-5612 **Fax:** 631-587-0198 www.babylonbeacon.com acjnews@rcn.com

Ballston Spa Ballston Journal (2.2M) PO Box 319 Ballston Spa NY 12020 **Phn:** 518-877-7160 **Fax:** 518-877-7824

Bath Courier-Advocate (11.0M) 10 W Steuben St Bath NY 14810 **Phn:** 607-776-2121 **Fax:** 607-776-3967

Bayside Schneps Publications (80.0M) 3815 Bell Blvd Bayside NY 11361 **Phn:** 718-224-5863 **Fax:** 718-224-5441 www.queenscourier.com queenscourier@queenscourier.com

Bayside Times/Ledger Newspapers (45.0M) 4102 Bell Blvd Bayside NY 11361 **Phn:** 718-229-0300 **Fax:** 718-225-7117 www.timesledger.com timesledgernews@cnglocal.com

Bedford Hills Record-Review (4.0M) PO Box 455 Bedford Hills NY 10507 **Phn:** 914-244-0533 **Fax:** 914-244-0537 www.record-review.com recordreview@optonline.net

Bethpage Bethpage Tribune (2.0M) PO Box 399 Bethpage NY 11714 **Phn:** 516-681-0440 **Fax:** 516-681-9354 www.bethpagetribune.com

Boonville Boonville Herald (4.4M) PO Box 372 Boonville NY 13309 **Phn:** 315-942-4449 **Fax:** 315-942-4440 www.boonvilleherald.com boonherald@aol.com

Bridgehampton Dan's Papers (69.0M) PO Box 630 Bridgehampton NY 11932 **Phn:** 631-537-0500 **Fax:** 631-537-3330 www.danshamptons.com editor@danspapers.com

Bronx Bronx Times Reporter (57.0M) 900 E 132nd St Bronx NY 10454 **Phn:** 718-597-1116 **Fax:** 718-518-0038 www.yournabe.com bronxtimes@aol.com

Bronx Co-Op City Times (50.0M) 2049 Bartow Ave Rm 21 Bronx NY 10475 **Phn:** 718-320-3375 **Fax:** 718-320-2595

Bronx Hagedorn Communications (39.3M) 135 Dreiser Loop Bronx NY 10475 **Phn:** 718-320-3071 prod@hagnews.com

Bronx Metro North Media (53.0M) PO Box 1252 Bronx NY 10471 **Phn:** 718-543-5200 **Fax:** 718-543-4206 bxny@aol.com

Bronx Norwood News (15.0M) 3400 Reservoir Oval E Bronx NY 10467 **Phn:** 718-324-4998 **Fax:** 718-324-2917 www.bronxmall.com/norwoodnews norwoodnews@norwoodnews.org

Bronx Riverdale Press (14.0M) 6155 Broadway Bronx NY 10471 **Phn:** 718-543-6065 **Fax:** 718-548-4038 www.riverdalepress.com newsroom@riverdalepress.com

Brooklyn Brooklyn Spectator (9.0M) 8723 3rd Ave Brooklyn NY 11209 **Phn:** 718-238-6600 **Fax:** 718-238-6630

Brooklyn Brooklyn View (135.0M) 1821 Schenectady Ave Brooklyn NY 11234 **Phn:** 718-209-7850 **Fax:** 718-209-7859 thebrooklynview@yahoo.com

Brooklyn Canarsie Courier (5.0M) 1142 E 92nd St Brooklyn NY 11236 **Phn:** 718-257-0600 **Fax:** 718-272-0870 www.canarsiecourier.com canarsiec@aol.com

Brooklyn Courier-Life Inc. (390.0M) 1 Metrotech Ctr Brooklyn NY 11201 **Phn:** 718-615-2500 **Fax:** 718-615-3835

Brooklyn EWA Publications (588.0M) 2446 E 65th St Brooklyn NY 11234 **Phn:** 718-763-7034 **Fax:** 718-763-7035 editman1000@yahoo.com

Brooklyn Greenpoint Gazette (5.5M) 597 Manhattan Ave Brooklyn NY 11222 **Phn:** 718-389-6067 **Fax:** 718-349-3471 www.greenpointnews.com jeff@greenpointnews.com

Brooklyn Home Reporter (11.0M) 8723 3rd Ave Brooklyn NY 11209 **Phn:** 718-238-6600 **Fax:** 718-238-6630 editorial@homereporternews.com

Brooklyn Spring Creek Sun (10.5M) 1540 Van Siclen Ave Ste 4 Brooklyn NY 11239 **Phn:** 718-642-2718 **Fax:** 718-642-7301

Brooklyn The Brooklyn Paper (259.0M) 1 Metrotech Ctr N # 1001 Brooklyn NY 11201 **Phn:** 718-260-4504 www.brooklynpaper.com newsroom@cnglocal.com

Buffalo Bee Publications (37.0M) PO Box 150 Buffalo NY 14217 **Phn:** 716-632-4700 **Fax:** 716-633-8601 www.beenews.com dsherman@beenews.com

Buffalo Riverside Review (14.5M) 215 Military Rd Buffalo NY 14207 **Phn:** 716-877-8400 **Fax:** 716-877-8742 www.buffaloreview.com rich@buffaloreview.com

Buffalo Rocket Publications (34.0M) 2507 Delaware Ave Buffalo NY 14216 **Phn:** 716-873-2594 **Fax:** 716-873-0809

Buffalo Southtowns Citizen (6.5M) 169 Delaware Ave Buffalo NY 14202 **Phn:** 716-662-0001 **Fax:** 716-667-3002

Callicoon Sullivan County Democrat (8.3M) PO Box 308 Callicoon NY 12723 **Phn:** 845-887-5200 **Fax:** 845-887-5386 www.sc-democrat.com info@sc-democrat.com

Cambridge Cambridge Eagle (4.4M) PO Box 493 Cambridge NY 12816 **Phn:** 518-677-5158 **Fax:** 518-677-8323 www.theeaglenewspaper.com news@theeaglenewspaper.com

Camden Queen Central News (7.6M) 20 Main St Camden NY 13316 **Phn:** 315-245-1849 **Fax:** 315-245-1880 www.queencentral.com qcn1974@aol.com

Canandaigua Messenger Post Media (86.0M) 73 Buffalo St Canandaigua NY 14424 **Phn:** 585-394-0770 **Fax:** 585-394-4160 www.mpnnow.com messenger@messengerpostmedia.com

Canastota Cazenovia Republican (2.8M) PO Box 301 Canastota NY 13032 **Phn:** 315-697-7142 **Fax:** 315-434-8883 www.cazenoviarepublican.com editor@cazenoviarepublican.com

Canastota Madison County Eagle (8.7M) 114 Canal St Canastota NY 13032 **Phn:** 315-697-7142 **Fax:** 315-434-8883 www.eaglenewsonline.com

Canton St. Lawrence Plaindealer (3.5M) 1 Main St Ste 103 Canton NY 13617 **Phn:** 315-386-8521 **Fax:** 315-386-8887 pdealer@ogd.com

NEW YORK WEEKLY NEWSPAPERS

Carmel Putnam County Courier (4.8M) PO Box 220 Carmel NY 10512 **Phn:** 845-225-3633 **Fax:** 845-225-1914 www.putnamcountycourier.com

Carthage Republican Tribune (2.8M) PO Box 549 Carthage NY 13619 **Phn:** 315-493-1270 **Fax:** 315-493-1271 news.crt@lowville.com

Center Moriches The Press (3.0M) PO Box 1187 Center Moriches NY 11934 **Phn:** 631-878-7600 **Fax:** 631-878-5898

Chatham Chatham Courier (4.6M) PO Box 355 Chatham NY 12037 **Phn:** 518-392-5151 **Fax:** 518-392-7322 newjerseyhills.com eparker@recordernewspapers.com

Cheektowaga Cheektowaga Times (4.0M) 343 Maryvale Dr Cheektowaga NY 14225 **Phn:** 716-892-5323 **Fax:** 716-892-4925

Chester Straus Newspapers (27.0M) 20 West Ave Ste 201 Chester NY 10918 **Phn:** 845-469-9000 **Fax:** 845-469-9001 strausnews.com editor.pn@strausnews.com

Clinton Clinton Courier (1.8M) PO Box 294 Clinton NY 13323 **Phn:** 315-853-3490 **Fax:** 315-853-3522 clintoncourier.com courierads@verizon.net

Cobleskill Cobleskill Times-Journal (6.0M) PO Box 339 Cobleskill NY 12043 **Phn:** 518-234-2515 **Fax:** 518-234-7898 timesjournalonline.com tjournalnews@yahoo.com

Cold Spring Putnam County News & Recorder (4.2M) PO Box 185 Cold Spring NY 10516 **Phn:** 845-265-2468 **Fax:** 845-265-2144 www.pcnr.com editor@pcnr.com

Conklin Country Courier (1.3M) PO Box 208 Conklin NY 13748 **Phn:** 607-775-0472 **Fax:** 607-775-5863 wecoverthetowns.com deinstein@stny.rr.com

Conklin Windsor Standard (1.3M) PO Box 208 Conklin NY 13748 **Phn:** 607-775-0472 **Fax:** 607-775-5863 wecoverthetowns.com deinstein@stny.rr.com

Cooperstown Cooperstown Crier (2.5M) 21 Railroad Ave Ste 25 Cooperstown NY 13326 **Phn:** 607-547-9493 **Fax:** 607-547-1109 coopercrier.com crier@csdsl.net

Cooperstown Freeman's Journal (2.5M) PO Box 890 Cooperstown NY 13326 **Phn:** 607-547-6103 **Fax:** 607-547-6080 jimk@allotsego.com

Cooperstown Hometown Oneonta (9.7M) PO Box 890 Cooperstown NY 13326 **Phn:** 607-547-6103 **Fax:** 607-547-6080 jimk@allotsego.com

Cornwall Cornwall Local (3.3M) PO Box 518 Cornwall NY 12518 **Phn:** 845-534-7771 **Fax:** 845-534-3855

Corona Queens Times (75.0M) 4808 111th St Corona NY 11368 **Phn:** 718-592-2196 **Fax:** 718-592-2174 www.queenstimes.com editor@queenstimes.com

Cross River Lewisboro Ledger (2.1M) PO Box 188 Cross River NY 10518 **Phn:** 914-763-8821 www.lewisboroledger.com ledger@acorn-online.com

Croton On Hudson The Gazette (3.0M) PO Box 810 Croton On Hudson NY 10520 **Phn:** 914-271-2088 **Fax:** 914-271-4219 thegazette.us@gmail.com

Cuba Patriot & Free Press (5.0M) 34 Water St Cuba NY 14727 **Phn:** 585-968-2580 **Fax:** 585-968-2622 www.cubapatriot.com mail@cubapatriot.com

Dansville Genesee County Express (2.8M) 113 Main St Dansville NY 14437 **Phn:** 585-335-2271 **Fax:** 585-335-6957 www.dansvilleonline.com colleenmahoney@dansvilleonline.com

Delhi Delaware County Times (1.7M) 56 Main St Delhi NY 13753 **Phn:** 607-746-2176 **Fax:** 607-746-3135

Delmar Spotlight LLC (53.0M) PO Box 100 Delmar NY 12054 **Phn:** 518-439-4949 **Fax:** 518-439-0609 www.spotlightnews.com news@spotlightnews.com

Deposit Deposit Courier (2.2M) 24 Laurel Bank Ave Deposit NY 13754 **Phn:** 607-467-3600 **Fax:** 607-467-5330 cprinthilton@tds.net

Dobbs Ferry Rivertowns Enterprise (6.2M) PO Box 330 Dobbs Ferry NY 10522 **Phn:** 914-478-2787 **Fax:** 914-478-2863 rivertownsnews@optonline.net

Dundee The Observer (2.1M) PO Box 127 Dundee NY 14837 **Phn:** 607-243-7600 **Fax:** 607-243-5833 www.observer-review.com theobserver@citlink.net

Dundee Watkins Glen Review/Express (3.0M) PO Box 120 Dundee NY 14837 **Phn:** 607-535-1500 **Fax:** 607-535-2500 www.observer-review.com theobserver@citlink.net

East Aurora East Aurora Advertiser (4.4M) 710 Main St East Aurora NY 14052 **Phn:** 716-652-0320 **Fax:** 716-652-8383 www.mywnynews.com eanews@eastaurorany.com

East Aurora Elma Review (1.2M) 710 Main St East Aurora NY 14052 **Phn:** 716-652-0320 **Fax:** 716-652-8383 www.mywnynews.com eanews@eastaurorany.com

East Hampton East Hampton Star (15.0M) PO Box 5002 East Hampton NY 11937 **Phn:** 631-324-0002 **Fax:** 631-324-7943 www.easthamptonstar.com editor@easthamptonstar.com

East Hampton The Independent (25.0M) 74 Montauk Hwy Unit 19 East Hampton NY 11937 **Phn:** 631-324-2500 **Fax:** 631-324-6496 www.indyeastend.com news@indyeastend.com

Elizabethtown Denton Publications (80.0M) 14 Hand Ave Elizabethtown NY 12932 **Phn:** 518-873-6368 **Fax:** 518-873-6360 www.denpubs.com

Ellenville Shawangunk Journal (3.5M) PO Box 669 Ellenville NY 12428 **Phn:** 845-647-9190 **Fax:** 845-647-8713 www.shawangunkjournal.com info@gunkjournal.com

Elmont Elmont Herald (3.0M) PO Box 30095 Elmont NY 11003 **Phn:** 516-437-1731 www.elmontherald.com elmontherald@aol.com

Far Rockaway The Wave (13.0M) PO Box 930097 Far Rockaway NY 11693 **Phn:** 718-634-4000 **Fax:** 718-945-0913 www.rockawave.com editor@rockawave.com

Farmingdale South Bay's Neighbor (255.0M) 565 Broadhollow Rd Ste 3 Farmingdale NY 11735 **Phn:** 631-226-2636 **Fax:** 631-226-2680 www.theneighbornewspapers.com editorsb@southbaynews.com

Floral Park Nassau Border Papers (29.0M) PO Box 20227 Floral Park NY 11002 **Phn:** 516-775-2700 **Fax:** 516-775-7605

Fulton Fulton Patriot Advertiser (5.7M) 67 S 2nd St Fulton NY 13069 **Phn:** 315-592-2459 **Fax:** 315-598-6618 scotsmanpress.com

Fulton The Valley News (8.1M) 117 Oneida St Fulton NY 13069 **Phn:** 315-598-6397 www.valleynewsonline.com editor@valleynewsonline.com

Garden City Oyster Bay Guardian (6.0M) 2 Endo Blvd Garden City NY 11530 **Phn:** 516-922-4215 **Fax:** 516-922-4227 www.oysterbayguardian.com scolten@oysterbayguardian.com

Garden City Richner Communications (77.4M) 2 Endo Blvd Garden City NY 11530 **Phn:** 516-569-4000 **Fax:** 516-569-4942 www.liherald.com execeditor@liherald.com

Geneseo Livingston County News (6.0M) 122 Main St Geneseo NY 14454 **Phn:** 585-243-0296 **Fax:** 585-243-0348 thelcn.com news@livingstonnews.com

Ghent The Columbia Paper (5.0M) PO Box 482 Ghent NY 12075 **Phn:** 518-392-1122 **Fax:** 866-530-3749 www.columbiapaper.com

Glen Cove Gold Coast Gazette (4.0M) 57 Glen St Ste 1 Glen Cove NY 11542 **Phn:** 516-671-2360 **Fax:** 516-671-2361 www.goldcoastgazette.net mail@goldcoastgazette.net

Glen Cove Record-Pilot (6.0M) 70 Glen St Ste 260 Glen Cove NY 11542 **Phn:** 516-759-5940 **Fax:** 516-759-2675 www.antonnews.com glencove@antonnews.com

Glens Falls The Chronicle (30.0M) 15 Ridge St Glens Falls NY 12801 **Phn:** 518-792-1126 **Fax:** 518-793-1587 readthechronicle.com chronicle@loneoak.com

Goshen Goshen Independent (2.3M) PO Box A Goshen NY 10924 **Phn:** 845-294-6111 **Fax:** 845-294-0532 indynews@frontiernet.net

Gouverneur Gouverneur Tribune-Press (4.0M) 74 Trinity Ave Gouverneur NY 13642 **Phn:** 315-287-2100 **Fax:** 315-287-2397 gouverneurtribune.com tribunepress@verizon.net

Grand Island Island Dispatch (1.2M) 1859 Whitehaven Rd Grand Island NY 14072 **Phn:** 716-773-7676 **Fax:** 716-773-7190 www.wnypapers.com dispatch@wnypapers.com

Granville Manchester Newspapers (51.0M) PO Box 330 Granville NY 12832 **Phn:** 518-642-1234 **Fax:** 518-642-1344 manchesternewspapers.com lakesfreepress@manchesternewspapers.com

Great Neck Great Neck Record (7.0M) 25 Cuttermill Rd Great Neck NY 11021 **Phn:** 516-482-4490 **Fax:** 516-482-4491 www.antonnews.com greatneck@antonnews.com

Greene Paden Publishing (3.5M) PO Box 566 Greene NY 13778 **Phn:** 607-656-4511 **Fax:** 607-656-8544 hometownnews@frontiernet.net

Greenwich Greenwich Journal & Salem Press (1.8M) PO Box 185 Greenwich NY 12834 **Phn:** 518-692-2266 **Fax:** 518-692-2589 journalpress@verizon.net

Greenwood Lake Greenwood Lake News (5.0M) PO Box 1117 Greenwood Lake NY 10925 **Phn:** 845-477-2575 **Fax:** 845-477-2577

Hamburg Sun & Erie Co. Independent (10.0M) 141 Buffalo St Hamburg NY 14075 **Phn:** 716-649-4040 **Fax:** 716-649-3231 www.thesunnews.net news@thesunnews.net

Hamilton Mid-York Weekly (8.0M) PO Box 318 Hamilton NY 13346 **Phn:** 315-824-2150 **Fax:** 315-824-4220 www.uticaod.com/midyorkweekly rjohns@uticaod.com

Hancock Hancock Herald (2.4M) PO Box 519 Hancock NY 13783 **Phn:** 607-637-3591 **Fax:** 607-637-4383 www.hancockherald.com hancockherald@hancock.net

Hempstead Beacon Newspapers (24.0M) 5 Centre St Hempstead NY 11550 **Phn:** 516-481-5400 **Fax:** 516-481-8773 thebeaconnews5@aol.com

Hicksville Litmore Publishing (58.0M) 81 E Barclay St Hicksville NY 11801 **Phn:** 516-931-0012 **Fax:** 516-931-0027 www.gcnews.com editor@gcnews.com

Highland Falls News Of The Highlands (2.7M) 4 Webb Ln Highland Falls NY 10928 **Phn:** 845-446-4519 **Fax:** 845-446-0532

Honeoye Honeoye Herald (1.2M) PO Box 648 Honeoye NY 14471 **Phn:** 585-229-2147

Hornell Hornell Spectator (14.5M) 85 Canisteo St Hornell NY 14843 **Phn:** 607-324-1425 **Fax:** 607-324-2317

Howard Beach Forum South (60.0M) 10205 159th Ave Howard Beach NY 11414 **Phn:** 718-845-3221 **Fax:** 718-738-7645 forumnewsgroup.blogspot.com forumsouth@aol.com

NEW YORK WEEKLY NEWSPAPERS

Hudson Bleezarde Publishing (4.2M) PO Box 635 Hudson NY 12534 **Phn:** 518-756-2030 **Fax:** 518-756-8555

Huntington Long Islander Newspapers (33.5M) 149 Main St Unit A Huntington NY 11743 **Phn:** 631-427-7000 **Fax:** 631-427-5820 longislandernews.com info@longislandernews.com

Island Park South Shore Tribune (64.0M) 4 California Pl N Island Park NY 11558 **Phn:** 516-431-5628 **Fax:** 516-431-5990 www.litribune.com info@litribune.com

Ithaca Ithaca Times (22.0M) PO Box 27 Ithaca NY 14851 **Phn:** 607-277-7000 **Fax:** 607-277-1012 www.ithaca.com editor@ithacatimes.com

Kingston Ulster Publishing (5.5M) PO Box 3329 Kingston NY 12402 **Phn:** 845-334-8200 **Fax:** 845-334-8809 www.ulsterpublishing.com woodstocktimes@ulsterpublishing.com

Lackawanna Front Page Group (15.0M) 2703 S Park Ave Lackawanna NY 14218 **Phn:** 716-823-8222 **Fax:** 716-821-0550

Lake Placid Lake Placid News (4.2M) 6179 Sentinel Rd Lake Placid NY 12946 **Phn:** 518-523-4401 **Fax:** 518-523-1351 www.lakeplacidnews.com news@lakeplacidnews.com

Lockport Journal-Register (1.9M) 170 Main St Lockport NY 14094 **Phn:** 585-798-1400 **Fax:** 716-439-9249

Locust Valley The Leader (3.9M) PO Box 468 Locust Valley NY 11560 **Phn:** 516-676-1434 **Fax:** 516-676-1414 www.theleaderonline.com

Long Island City Woodside Herald (16.0M) PO Box 7097 Long Island City NY 11101 **Phn:** 718-729-3772 **Fax:** 718-729-8614

Lowville Journal & Republican (5.0M) 7567 S State St Lowville NY 13367 **Phn:** 315-376-3525 **Fax:** 315-376-4136 generalnews@lowville.com

Macedon Times of Wayne County (12.5M) PO Box 608 Macedon NY 14502 **Phn:** 315-986-4300 **Fax:** 315-986-7271 www.thetimesofwaynecounty.com waynetimes@aol.com

Mahopac Putnam County Press (12.0M) PO Box 608 Mahopac NY 10541 **Phn:** 845-628-8400 putnampress@aol.com

Maspeth Queens Ledger (150.0M) PO Box 780376 Maspeth NY 11378 **Phn:** 718-639-7000 **Fax:** 718-429-1234 www.queensledger.com news@queensledger.com

Massapequa Park Massapequa Post (4.5M) 1045B Park Blvd Massapequa Park NY 11762 **Phn:** 516-798-5100 **Fax:** 516-798-5296 www.massapequapost.com acjnews@rcn.com

Mattituck Suffolk Times (12.0M) PO Box 1500 Mattituck NY 11952 **Phn:** 631-298-3200 **Fax:** 631-298-3287 suffolktimes.timesreview.com mail@timesreview.com

Mattituck The News-Review (5.0M) PO Box 1500 Mattituck NY 11952 **Phn:** 631-298-3200 **Fax:** 631-298-3287 www.timesreview.com mail@timesreview.com

Mechanicville The Express (2.8M) PO Box 608 Mechanicville NY 12118 **Phn:** 518-664-3335 **Fax:** 518-664-5997 theexpressweeklynews.com info.expresspaper@gmail.com

Merrick L & M Publications (14.0M) 1840 Merrick Ave Merrick NY 11566 **Phn:** 516-378-5320 **Fax:** 516-378-0287 www.liherald.com

Mexico Oswego Co. Weeklies (33.0M) PO Box 129 Mexico NY 13114 **Phn:** 315-963-7813 **Fax:** 315-963-4087 www.oswegocountyweeklies.com ocweekly@cnymail.com

Middletown The Gazette (9.0M) PO Box 2046 Middletown NY 10940 **Phn:** 845-858-2123 **Fax:** 845-858-8484 www.recordonline.com dmedenbach@th-record.com

Millerton Millerton News (2.0M) PO Box AD Millerton NY 12546 **Phn:** 518-789-4401 **Fax:** 518-789-9247 www.tricornernews.com editor@millertonnews.com

Mineola Anton Newspapers (52.0M) PO Box 1578 Mineola NY 11501 **Phn:** 516-747-8282 **Fax:** 516-742-5867 www.antonnews.com mineola@antonnews.com

Moravia Republican-Register (1.0M) PO Box 591 Moravia NY 13118 **Phn:** 315-497-1551

Nanuet Rockland County Times (12.0M) 119 Main St Nanuet NY 10954 **Phn:** 845-627-1414 **Fax:** 845-627-1411 www.rocklandtimes.com editor@rocklandcountytimes.com

Naples Naples Record (1.4M) PO Box 370 Naples NY 14512 **Phn:** 585-374-5260 **Fax:** 585-374-8590 news@naplesrecord.com

Narrowsburg The River Reporter (4.5M) PO Box 150 Narrowsburg NY 12764 **Phn:** 845-252-7414 **Fax:** 845-252-3298 riverreporter.com editor@riverreporter.com

New Paltz New Paltz Times (4.6M) 257 Main St New Paltz NY 12561 **Phn:** 845-255-7000 **Fax:** 845-255-7005 www.ulsterpublishing.com newpaltztimes@ulsterpublishing.com

New Rochelle Westchester Guardian (15.0M) PO Box 8 New Rochelle NY 10801 **Phn:** 914-632-2540 **Fax:** 914-633-0806 www.westchesterguardian.com whyteditor@gmail.com

New Windsor The Sentinel (6.0M) 36 Merline Ave New Windsor NY 12553 **Phn:** 845-562-1218 **Fax:** 845-562-1254 www.thesentinel-online.com sentinelnews@thesentineloc.com

New York Downtown Express (50.0M) 145 Avenue Of The Americas Ph 1 New York NY 10013 **Phn:** 212-229-1890 **Fax:** 212-229-2790 www.downtownexpress.com news@downtownexpress.com

New York Manhattan Media (57.0M) 72 Madison Ave Fl 11 New York NY 10016 **Phn:** 212-268-8600 **Fax:** 212-268-2935 www.manhattanmedia.com editorial@manhattanmedia.com

New York NY Town & Village (8.5M) 20 W 22nd St Ste 1411 New York NY 10010 **Phn:** 212-777-6611 **Fax:** 212-777-1535 editor@townvillage.net

New York Resident Publications (160.0M) 28 E 28th St Fl 9N New York NY 10016 **Phn:** 212-993-9417 www.resident.com pamelaj@resident.com

New York The New York Observer (50.0M) 321 W 44th St Fl 6 New York NY 10036 **Phn:** 212-755-2400 **Fax:** 212-688-4889 www.observer.com editorial@observer.com

New York The Villager (26.0M) 145 Avenue Of The Americas Ph 1 New York NY 10013 **Phn:** 212-229-1890 **Fax:** 212-229-2790 www.thevillager.com editor@thevillager.com

New York Village Voice (253.0M) 36 Cooper Sq New York NY 10003 **Phn:** 212-475-3300 **Fax:** 212-475-8944 www.villagevoice.com

Newark Newark Courier-Gazette (3.6M) 613 S Main St Newark NY 14513 **Phn:** 315-331-1000 **Fax:** 315-331-1053

Newburgh Times Community Newspapers (8.0M) 300 Stony Brook Ct Ste B Newburgh NY 12550 **Phn:** 845-561-0170 **Fax:** 845-561-3967 www.timescommunitypapers.com editor@tcnewspapers.com

Norwich The Gazette (2.4M) PO Box 151 Norwich NY 13815 **Phn:** 607-334-3276 **Fax:** 607-334-8273

Ogdensburg Canton Rural News (13.0M) PO Box 409 Ogdensburg NY 13669 **Phn:** 315-393-1000 **Fax:** 315-393-5108

Ogdensburg The Advance News (11.0M) PO Box 409 Ogdensburg NY 13669 **Phn:** 315-393-1000 **Fax:** 315-393-5108 www.ogd.com

Oneida Indian Country Today (125.0M) 2037 Dream Catcher Plz Oneida NY 13421 **Phn:** 315-829-8355 **Fax:** 315-829-8393 indiancountrytodaymedianetwork.com editor@ictmn.com

Oneida Rome Observer (11.0M) PO Box 120 Oneida NY 13421 **Phn:** 315-338-6160 **Fax:** 315-338-6158 www.romeobserver.com editorial@mohawkvalleymedia.com

Owego Tioga Co Courier (2.4M) 59 Church St Owego NY 13827 **Phn:** 607-687-0108 **Fax:** 607-687-9065

Palmyra Palmyra Courier-Journal (2.7M) 628 E Main St Ste C Palmyra NY 14522 **Phn:** 315-597-6655 **Fax:** 315-597-6947

Patchogue Long Island Advance (11.0M) PO Box 780 Patchogue NY 11772 **Phn:** 631-475-1000 **Fax:** 631-475-1565 advletters@optonline.net

Pelham Norway Times (7.0M) PO Box 8454 Pelham NY 10803 **Phn:** 914-819-0070 **Fax:** 914-819-0072

Pelham Pelham Weekly (2.1M) 225 Fifth Ave Pelham NY 10803 **Phn:** 914-738-8717 **Fax:** 914-738-9608 www.pelhamplus.com maggieklein@pelhamweekly.com

Penn Yan The Chronicle-Express (3.9M) 138 Main St Penn Yan NY 14527 **Phn:** 315-536-4422 **Fax:** 315-536-0682 www.chronicle-express.com news@chronicle-express.com

Perry Perry Herald (0.9M) 7851 State Route 39 Perry NY 14530 **Phn:** 585-237-6310 **Fax:** 585-237-6868 perryherald@frontiernet.net

Port Chester Hometown Media (38.0M) 200 William St Port Chester NY 10573 **Phn:** 914-653-1000 **Fax:** 914-653-5000 www.hometwn.com news@hometwn.com

Port Chester Westmore News (3.5M) 38 Broad St Port Chester NY 10573 **Phn:** 914-939-6864 **Fax:** 914-939-6877 www.westmorenews.com editor@westmorenews.com

Port Washington Port Washington News (8.0M) 270 Main St Ste 1 Port Washington NY 11050 **Phn:** 516-767-0035 **Fax:** 516-767-0036 www.antonnews.com portwashingtonnews@antonnews.com

Potsdam North Country This Week (10.5M) PO Box 975 Potsdam NY 13676 **Phn:** 315-265-1000 **Fax:** 315-268-8701 northcountrynow.com news@northcountrynow.com

Red Creek The Lakeshore News (3.5M) PO Box 199 Red Creek NY 13143 **Phn:** 315-754-6229 **Fax:** 315-754-6431 www.wayuga.com editor@wayuga.com

Rego Park Queens Chronicle (160.0M) PO Box 747769 Rego Park NY 11374 **Phn:** 718-205-8000 **Fax:** 718-205-0150 www.qchron.com mailbox@qchron.com

Ridgewood Times Newsweekly (27.0M) PO Box 299 Ridgewood NY 11386 **Phn:** 718-821-7500 **Fax:** 718-456-0120 www.timesnewsweekly.com info@timesnewsweekly.com

Riverhead Suffolk Life Papers (570.0M) PO Box 167 Riverhead NY 11901 **Phn:** 631-369-0800 **Fax:** 631-591-5190 www.suffolklife.com news@suffolklife.com

Rochester City Newspaper (40.0M) 250 Goodman St N Rochester NY 14607 **Phn:** 585-244-3329 **Fax:** 585-244-1126 www.rochestercitynewspaper.com

Rocky Point The North Shore Sun (5.0M) PO Box 5539 Rocky Point NY 11778 **Phn:** 631-744-0404 **Fax:** 631-744-2640 northshoresun.timesreview.com pboody@timesreview.com

Sag Harbor Sag Harbor Express (2.5M) PO Box 1620 Sag Harbor NY 11963 **Phn:** 631-725-1700 **Fax:** 631-725-1584 sagharborexpress.sagharborpublishing.com/shexpress info@sagharboronline.com

Salamanca County Chronicle (5.0M) PO Box 535 Salamanca NY 14779 **Phn:** 716-938-9425 **Fax:** 716-938-9435

Saratoga Springs Community News (28.0M) 20 Lake Ave Saratoga Springs NY 12866 **Phn:** 518-583-8729 **Fax:** 518-587-7750 www.cnweekly.com cnews@saratogian.com

Saugerties Saugerties Post-Star (2.5M) 858 Route 212 Saugerties NY 12477 **Phn:** 845-246-4985 **Fax:** 845-246-5108 www.poststarnews.com bgomez@hvc.rr.com

Sayville Islip Bulletin (3.0M) PO Box 367 Sayville NY 11782 **Phn:** 631-589-6200 **Fax:** 631-589-3246 islipbulletin.net scnibletter@optonline.net

Sayville Suffolk Co. News (15.0M) PO Box 367 Sayville NY 11782 **Phn:** 631-589-6200 **Fax:** 631-589-3246

Scarsdale Scarsdale Inquirer (6.5M) PO Box 418 Scarsdale NY 10583 **Phn:** 914-725-2500 **Fax:** 914-725-1552 lleavitt@scarsdalenews.com

Setauket Times-Beacon Record Newspapers (50.0M) PO Box 707 Setauket NY 11733 **Phn:** 631-751-7744 **Fax:** 631-751-4165 www.tbrnewspapers.com desk@tbrnewspapers.com

Shelter Island Shelter Island Reporter (3.2M) PO Box 756 Shelter Island NY 11964 **Phn:** 631-749-1000 **Fax:** 631-749-0144 www.timesreview.com mail@sireporter.com

Sherburne Sherburne News (1.9M) PO Box 711 Sherburne NY 13460 **Phn:** 607-674-6071 **Fax:** 607-674-5065 sherburnenews.net thesherburnenews@gmail.com

Shirley South Shore Press (45.0M) PO Box 431 Shirley NY 11967 **Phn:** 631-878-7800 **Fax:** 631-878-7805 sspress2000@aol.com

Sidney Tri-Town News (5.0M) PO Box 208 Sidney NY 13838 **Phn:** 607-563-3526 **Fax:** 607-563-8999 www.tritownnews.com ttnews@tritownnews.com

Smithtown ESP Publications (31.0M) PO Box 925 Smithtown NY 11787 **Phn:** 631-265-3500 **Fax:** 631-265-3504 messenger127e@aol.com

Smithtown Mid Island News (2.2M) PO Box 805 Smithtown NY 11787 **Phn:** 631-265-2100 **Fax:** 631-265-6237

Smithtown Smithtown News Inc. (37.0M) PO Box 805 Smithtown NY 11787 **Phn:** 631-265-2100 **Fax:** 631-265-6237 info@smithtownnews.com

Speculator Hamilton Co. Express (3.3M) PO Box 166 Speculator NY 12164 **Phn:** 800-453-6397 www.hamiltoncountyexpress.com editor@hamiltoncountyexpress.com

Spencerport Westside News Inc. (33.0M) PO Box 106 Spencerport NY 14559 **Phn:** 585-352-3411 **Fax:** 585-352-4811 www.westsidenewsny.com editor@westsidenewsny.com

Springville Springville Journal (10.0M) 41 E Main St Ste A Springville NY 14141 **Phn:** 716-592-4550 **Fax:** 716-592-4663 www.springvillejournal.com info@springvillejournal.com

Stamford Mountain Eagle (3.0M) PO Box 278 Stamford NY 12167 **Phn:** 607-652-5252 **Fax:** 607-652-5253

NEW YORK WEEKLY NEWSPAPERS

Syosset Long Island Press (65.0M) 575 Underhill Blvd Ste 210 Syosset NY 11791 **Phn:** 516-284-3300 **Fax:** 516-284-3310 www.longislandpress.com

Syracuse Eagle Newspapers (51.0M) 2501 James St Ste 100 Syracuse NY 13206 **Phn:** 315-434-8889 **Fax:** 315-434-8883 www.eaglenewsonline.com newsroom@eaglenewsonline.com

Syracuse Syracuse New Times (40.0M) 1415 W Genesee St Syracuse NY 13204 **Phn:** 315-422-7011 **Fax:** 315-422-1721 syracusenewtimes.com editorial@syracusenewtimes.com

Trumansburg Finger Lakes Community Papers (7.0M) PO Box 714 Trumansburg NY 14886 **Phn:** 607-387-3181 **Fax:** 607-387-9421 www.ithaca.com editor@flcn.org

Tupper Lake Free Press & Herald (4.0M) 136 Park St Tupper Lake NY 12986 **Phn:** 518-359-2166 **Fax:** 518-359-2295

Vestal The Reporter (2.4M) 500 Clubhouse Rd Vestal NY 13850 **Phn:** 607-724-2360 **Fax:** 607-724-2311 www.thereportergroup.org rachel@thereportergroup.org

Wading River The Community Journal (7.0M) PO Box 619 Wading River NY 11792 **Phn:** 631-929-8882 **Fax:** 631-929-4560 bernadettesbudd@aol.com

Walton Walton Reporter (5.1M) PO Box 338 Walton NY 13856 **Phn:** 607-865-4131 **Fax:** 607-865-8689 www.waltonreporter.com

Wappingers Falls Beacon Free Press (7.5M) 84 E Main St Wappingers Falls NY 12590 **Phn:** 845-297-3723 **Fax:** 845-297-6810 newsplace@aol.com

Wappingers Falls Southern Dutchess News (7.5M) 84 E Main St Wappingers Falls NY 12590 **Phn:** 845-297-3723 **Fax:** 845-297-6810 newsplace@aol.com

Warsaw Warsaw's Country Courier (2.0M) 11 S Main St Warsaw NY 14569 **Phn:** 585-786-3080 **Fax:** 585-786-3083 www.mywnynews.com news@couriercountry.com

Warwick Warwick Valley Dispatch (3.0M) PO Box 594 Warwick NY 10990 **Phn:** 845-986-2216 **Fax:** 845-987-1180 www.wvdispatch.com editor@wvdispatch.com

Washingtonville Orange County Post (2.6M) 17 Goshen Ave Washingtonville NY 10992 **Phn:** 845-496-3611 **Fax:** 845-496-1715

Waterville Waterville Times (2.6M) PO Box C Waterville NY 13480 **Phn:** 315-841-4105 **Fax:** 315-841-4104 www.watervilleny.com watervilletimes@citlink.net

Webster Wayne County Mail (2.4M) 46 North Ave Webster NY 14580 **Phn:** 585-671-1533 **Fax:** 585-671-7067 wcmail@empirestateweeklies.com

Webster Webster Herald (4.2M) 46 North Ave Webster NY 14580 **Phn:** 585-671-1533 **Fax:** 585-671-7067 websterherald@empirestateweeklies.com

West Nyack Rockland Review (20.0M) 26 Snake Hill Rd West Nyack NY 10994 **Phn:** 845-727-4114 **Fax:** 845-727-4944 www.rocklandreviewnews.com rocklandreview@optonline.net

West Winfield West Winfield Star (1.4M) PO Box 6 West Winfield NY 13491 **Phn:** 315-822-3001

Westfield Westfield Republican (1.4M) PO Box 38 Westfield NY 14787 **Phn:** 716-326-3163 **Fax:** 716-326-3165 www.westfieldrepublican.com

White Plains Review Press (5.5M) 1 Gannett Dr White Plains NY 10604 **Phn:** 914-694-9300 **Fax:** 914-696-8396 www.lohud.com

White Plains White Plains Times (25.0M) 31 Mamaroneck Ave Ste 514 White Plains NY 10601 **Phn:** 914-421-1904 **Fax:** 914-287-2099

Whitestone Queens Tribune (171.0M) 15050 14th Rd Ste 2 Whitestone NY 11357 **Phn:** 718-357-7400 **Fax:** 718-357-9417 www.queenstribune.com news@queenstribune.com

Williamson Sun & Record (3.5M) PO Box 31 Williamson NY 14589 **Phn:** 315-589-4421 **Fax:** 315-589-8433 www.sunandrecord.com recsun@rochester.rr.com

Windham Windham Journal (1.7M) PO Box 128 Windham NY 12496 **Phn:** 518-734-4400 **Fax:** 518-734-5179

Yonkers Martinelli Publications (52.0M) 40 Larkin Plz Yonkers NY 10701 **Phn:** 914-965-4000 **Fax:** 914-965-2892

Yorktown Heights North County News (10.0M) 1520 Front St Yorktown Heights NY 10598 **Phn:** 914-962-4748 **Fax:** 914-962-6763

NORTH CAROLINA

Ahoskie Roanoke News Herald (6.3M) PO Box 1325 Ahoskie NC 27910 **Phn:** 252-332-2123 **Fax:** 252-332-3940 www.roanoke-chowannewsherald.com cal.bryant@r-cnews.com

Albemarle Stanly News & Press (10.0M) PO Box 488 Albemarle NC 28002 **Phn:** 704-982-2121 **Fax:** 704-983-7999 thesnaponline.com

Andrews Andrews Journal (2.8M) PO Box 250 Andrews NC 28901 **Phn:** 828-321-4271 **Fax:** 828-321-5890 www.theandrewsjournal.com news@theandrewsjournal.com

Angier Angier Independent (2.5M) PO Box 878 Angier NC 27501 **Phn:** 919-639-4913 **Fax:** 919-639-0289 news@angierindependent.com

Archdale Archdale Trinity News (3.6M) 210 Church Ave Archdale NC 27262 **Phn:** 336-434-2716 **Fax:** 336-434-6983 www.atnonline.net

Asheboro The Randolph Guide (3.2M) PO Box 1044 Asheboro NC 27204 **Phn:** 336-625-5576 **Fax:** 336-625-1228

Asheville Mountain Xpress (28.0M) PO Box 144 Asheville NC 28802 **Phn:** 828-251-1333 **Fax:** 828-251-1311 www.mountainx.com news@mountainx.com

Asheville Pisgah Mountain News (14.0M) PO Box 2090 Asheville NC 28802 **Phn:** 828-210-6075 **Fax:** 828-681-5377 www.citizen-times.com cmorrison@citizen-times.com

Asheville Tribune Papers (25.0M) PO Box 5615 Asheville NC 28813 **Phn:** 828-277-1760 **Fax:** 866-923-0774 www.tribunepapers.com tribuneeditor@bellsouth.net

Belhaven Beaufort-Hyde News (3.5M) PO Box 99 Belhaven NC 27810 **Phn:** 252-943-2688 **Fax:** 252-943-3299 aharne@ncweeklies.com

Belmont Banner News (3.0M) PO Box 589 Belmont NC 28012 **Phn:** 704-825-0104 **Fax:** 704-825-0894

Benson News in Review (4.5M) PO Box 9 Benson NC 27504 **Phn:** 919-894-2112 **Fax:** 919-894-1069 fobnews@aol.com

Black Mountain Black Mountain News (3.2M) PO Box 9 Black Mountain NC 28711 **Phn:** 828-669-8727 **Fax:** 828-669-8619 www.blackmountainnews.com jennifer@blackmountainnews.com

Boone Avery Journal-Times (4.0M) PO Box 1815 Boone NC 28607 **Phn:** 828-733-2448 **Fax:** 828-733-0639 www.averyjournal.com news@averyjournal.com

Boone The Blowing Rocket (3.5M) PO Box 1815 Boone NC 28607 **Phn:** 828-264-6397 **Fax:** 828-262-0282 www.blowingrocket.com office@blowingrocket.com

NORTH CAROLINA WEEKLY NEWSPAPERS

Boone The Mountain Times (14.0M) PO Box 1815 Boone NC 28607 **Phn:** 828-264-6397 **Fax:** 828-262-0282 www.mountaintimes.com frank@mountaintimes.com

Boone Watauga Democrat (9.0M) 474 Industrial Park Dr Boone NC 28607 **Phn:** 828-264-3612 **Fax:** 828-262-0282 www.wataugademocrat.com newspaper@wataugademocrat.com

Brevard The Transylvania Times (8.5M) PO Box 32 Brevard NC 28712 **Phn:** 828-883-8156 **Fax:** 828-883-8158 transylvaniatimes.com

Bryson City Smoky Mountain Times (4.0M) PO Box 730 Bryson City NC 28713 **Phn:** 828-488-2189 **Fax:** 828-488-0315 www.thesmokymountaintimes.com news@thesmokymountaintimes.com

Burgaw Post & Voice (5.0M) PO Box 955 Burgaw NC 28425 **Phn:** 910-259-9111 **Fax:** 910-259-9112 www.post-voice.com posteditor@post-voice.com

Burlington Rock Creek Record (16.0M) 4213 S Church St Burlington NC 27215 **Phn:** 336-449-7064 www.news-record.com

Burnsville Times-Journal (6.4M) PO Box 280 Burnsville NC 28714 **Phn:** 828-682-2120 **Fax:** 828-682-3701

Carolina Beach Island Gazette (8.0M) PO Box 183 Carolina Beach NC 28428 **Phn:** 910-458-8156 **Fax:** 910-458-0267 www.islandgazette.net islandgazette@aol.com

Cashiers Crossroads Chronicle (3.0M) PO Box 1040 Cashiers NC 28717 **Phn:** 828-743-5101 **Fax:** 828-743-4173 www.crossroadschronicle.com news@crossroadschronicle.com

Chadbourn News Times (8.4M) 114 E 1st Ave Chadbourn NC 28431 **Phn:** 910-654-3762

Chapel Hill Chapel Hill News (25.0M) 505 W Franklin St Chapel Hill NC 27516 **Phn:** 919-932-2000 **Fax:** 919-968-4953 www.chapelhillnews.com mschultz@nando.com

Charlotte Mecklenburg Times (1.0M) 1611 E 7th St Charlotte NC 28205 **Phn:** 704-377-6221 **Fax:** 704-377-4258 mecktimes.com editor@mecktimes.com

Charlotte Mint Hill Times (5.0M) PO Box 690577 Charlotte NC 28227 **Phn:** 704-573-4606

Charlotte South Charlotte Weekly (45.0M) 1421 Orchard Lake Dr Unit C Charlotte NC 28270 **Phn:** 704-849-2261 **Fax:** 704-849-2504 www.thecharlotteweekly.com editor@thecharlotteweekly.com

Charlotte Union County Weekly (19.0M) 1421 Orchard Lake Dr Unit C Charlotte NC 28270 **Phn:** 704-849-2261 **Fax:** 704-849-2504 www.unioncountyweekly.com news@unioncountyweekly.com

Chatham Lake Norman Times (9.6M) PO Box 111 Chatham NC 24531 **Phn:** 704-664-2882 **Fax:** 704-664-2852 womackpublishing.com

Cherryville Cherryville Eagle (2.8M) PO Box 699 Cherryville NC 28021 **Phn:** 704-435-6752 **Fax:** 704-435-8293

Clayton Clayton News-Star (5.2M) PO Box 157 Clayton NC 27528 **Phn:** 919-553-7234 **Fax:** 919-553-5858 www.claytonnewsstar.com felicia.gressette@newsobserver.com

Clemmons Clemmons Courier (2.1M) PO Box 765 Clemmons NC 27012 **Phn:** 336-766-4126 **Fax:** 336-766-7350 www.clemmonscourier.net courier9@bellsouth.net

Columbus Polk Co. News-Journal (1.5M) PO Box 576 Columbus NC 28722 **Phn:** 828-894-3220 news@upstatenewspapers.com

Concord Concord Standard (18.0M) 24 Cabarrus Ave E Ste 100 Concord NC 28025 **Phn:** 704-723-6923 **Fax:** 704-723-6924

Creedmoor Butner-Creedmoor News (5.3M) PO Box 726 Creedmoor NC 27522 **Phn:** 919-528-2393 **Fax:** 919-528-0288 www.granvilleonline.com bcnews@mindspring.com

Davidson Herald Weekly (27.0M) 209 Delburg St Davidson NC 28036 **Phn:** 704-766-2100 **Fax:** 704-992-0801 www.huntersvilleherald.com editor@huntersvilleherald.com

Denton Denton Orator (2.8M) PO Box 1546 Denton NC 27239 **Phn:** 336-859-3131 **Fax:** 336-859-9656 www.dentonorator.com dentonorator@triad.rr.com

Durham Indy Week (45.0M) PO Box 2690 Durham NC 27715 **Phn:** 919-286-1972 **Fax:** 919-286-4274 www.indyweek.com editors@indyweek.com

Edenton The Chowan Herald (4.0M) PO Box 207 Edenton NC 27932 **Phn:** 252-482-4418 **Fax:** 252-482-4410

Elizabethtown Bladen Journal (4.8M) PO Box 70 Elizabethtown NC 28337 **Phn:** 910-862-4163 **Fax:** 910-862-6602 www.bladenjournal.com cvincent@civitasmedia.com

Elkin The Tribune (5.8M) 214 E Main St Elkin NC 28621 **Phn:** 336-835-1513 **Fax:** 336-835-8742 elkintribune.com ndibagno@heartlandpublications.com

Farmville Farmville Enterprise (2.6M) PO Box 247 Farmville NC 27828 **Phn:** 252-753-4126 **Fax:** 252-753-4127

Franklin Franklin Press (9.2M) PO Box 350 Franklin NC 28744 **Phn:** 828-524-2010 **Fax:** 828-524-8821 www.thefranklinpress.com news@thefranklinpress.com

Franklin Macon County News (13.0M) 107 Highlands Rd Franklin NC 28734 **Phn:** 828-369-6767 **Fax:** 828-369-2700 www.maconnews.com editor@maconnews.com

Fremont News-Leader (2.0M) PO Box 158 Fremont NC 27830 **Phn:** 919-242-6301 **Fax:** 919-936-2065 www.newsleadernow.com news@newsleadernow.com

Fuquay Varina Cleveland Post (6.5M) 209 E Vance St Fuquay Varina NC 27526 **Phn:** 919-552-5675 **Fax:** 919-552-7564 wakecountycommunitynewspapers.com

Gatesville Gates County Index (2.7M) PO Box 146 Gatesville NC 27938 **Phn:** 252-357-0960 **Fax:** 252-357-0973

Graham Alamance News (6.5M) PO Box 431 Graham NC 27253 **Phn:** 336-228-7851

Greensboro Rhinoceros Times (48.0M) PO Box 9023 Greensboro NC 27429 **Phn:** 336-763-4170 **Fax:** 336-464-2698 www.rhinotimes.com john@rhinotimes.com

Grifton The Times-Leader (2.6M) PO Box 369 Grifton NC 28530 **Phn:** 252-524-4376 **Fax:** 252-524-3312

Havelock Havelock News (2.6M) PO Box 777 Havelock NC 28532 **Phn:** 252-444-1999 **Fax:** 252-447-0897 www.havenews.com havenews@havenews.com

Hayesville Clay County Progress (3.7M) PO Box 483 Hayesville NC 28904 **Phn:** 828-389-8431 **Fax:** 828-389-9997 www.claycountyprogress.com news@claycountyprogress.com

Hayesville Smoky Mountain Sentinel (24.0M) PO Box 870 Hayesville NC 28904 **Phn:** 828-389-8338 **Fax:** 828-389-3955

Hendersonville Hendersonville Tribune (8.0M) PO Box 2801 Hendersonville NC 28793 **Phn:** 828-697-2932 **Fax:** 828-693-1873 www.thetribunepapers.com tribuneeditor@bellsouth.net

Hertford Perquimans Weekly (2.2M) 111 W Market St Hertford NC 27944 **Phn:** 252-426-5728 **Fax:** 252-426-4625 perquimansweekly@ncweeklies.com

Hickory Focus Newspaper (38.0M) PO Box 1721 Hickory NC 28603 **Phn:** 828-322-1036 www.focusnewspaper.com focus1721@embarqmail.com

High Point Thomasville Times (5.8M) PO Box 1009 High Point NC 27261 **Phn:** 336-472-9500 **Fax:** 336-472-6692 www.tvilletimes.com editor@tvilletimes.com

Highlands The Highlander (4.0M) PO Box 249 Highlands NC 28741 **Phn:** 828-526-4114 **Fax:** 828-526-3658 www.highlandsnews.com news@highlandsnews.com

Hillsborough News of Orange County (3.3M) PO Box 580 Hillsborough NC 27278 **Phn:** 919-732-2171 **Fax:** 919-732-4852 www.newsoforange.com editorial@newsoforange.com

Hope Mills The Sandspur (25.0M) 5449 Trade St Hope Mills NC 28348 **Phn:** 910-426-7787 www.fayobserver.com/location/hopemills editor@sandspuronline.com

Jamestown Jamestown News (2.8M) PO Box 307 Jamestown NC 27282 **Phn:** 336-841-4933 **Fax:** 336-841-4953 www.womacknewspapers.com/jamestownnews jamestownnews@northstate.net

Kannapolis Kannapolis Citizen (6.5M) PO Box 720 Kannapolis NC 28082 **Phn:** 704-933-3450 **Fax:** 704-639-0003 kannapoliscitizen.com news@salisburypost.com

Kenansville Duplin Times (17.0M) PO Box 69 Kenansville NC 28349 **Phn:** 910-296-0239 **Fax:** 910-296-9545 theduplintimes.com gscott@ncweeklies.com

Kenly Kenly News (3.0M) PO Box 39 Kenly NC 27542 **Phn:** 919-284-2295 **Fax:** 919-284-6397 kenlynews.com rstewart@kenlynews.com

Kernersville Kernersville News (27.0M) PO Box 337 Kernersville NC 27285 **Phn:** 336-993-2161 **Fax:** 336-993-0931 www.kernersvillenews.com news@kernersvillenews.com

King Weekly Independent (1.8M) PO Box 545 King NC 27021 **Phn:** 336-983-3109 **Fax:** 336-983-8203

Kings Mountain Kings Mtn. Herald (5.3M) PO Box 769 Kings Mountain NC 28086 **Phn:** 704-739-7496 **Fax:** 704-739-0611

Kinston Jones Post (2.8M) PO Box 129 Kinston NC 28502 **Phn:** 252-527-3191 **Fax:** 252-527-9407

La Grange Weekly Gazette (1.5M) 108 S Caswell St La Grange NC 28551 **Phn:** 252-566-3028 **Fax:** 252-566-5318

Lillington Harnett County News (3.0M) PO Box 939 Lillington NC 27546 **Phn:** 910-893-5121 **Fax:** 910-893-6128 www.mydailyrecord.com editor@harnettcountynews.com

Lincolnton Lincoln Times-News (8.0M) PO Box 40 Lincolnton NC 28093 **Phn:** 704-735-3034 **Fax:** 704-735-3996 www.lincolntimesnews.com news@lincolntimesnews.com

Littleton Lake Gaston Gazette (2.7M) 378 Lizard Creek Rd Littleton NC 27850 **Phn:** 252-586-2700 **Fax:** 252-586-3522 www.lakegastongazette-observer.com news@lakegastongazette-observer.com

Littleton Littleton Observer (3.0M) PO Box 100 Littleton NC 27850 **Phn:** 252-586-6397 **Fax:** 252-586-6875

Louisburg Franklin Times (9.2M) PO Box 119 Louisburg NC 27549 **Phn:** 919-496-6503 **Fax:** 919-496-1689 www.thefranklintimes.com news@thefranklintimes.com

NORTH CAROLINA WEEKLY NEWSPAPERS

Manteo Coastland Times (9.0M) PO Box 400 Manteo NC 27954 **Phn:** 252-473-2105 **Fax:** 252-473-1515

Marshall News-Record & Sentinel (6.6M) PO Box 369 Marshall NC 28753 **Phn:** 828-649-1075 **Fax:** 828-649-9426 www.citizen-times.com/sentinel editor@newsrecordandsentinel.com

Marshville The Home News (3.0M) PO Box 100 Marshville NC 28103 **Phn:** 704-624-5068 **Fax:** 704-624-2371 homenewseditor@aol.com

Matthews Matthews Record (12.0M) 1534 Woody Creek Rd Matthews NC 28105 **Phn:** 704-443-0017 **Fax:** 704-443-0031

Mebane Mebane Enterprise (2.4M) 106 N Fourth St Mebane NC 27302 **Phn:** 919-563-3555 **Fax:** 919-563-9242 www.aconews.com/mebane_enterprise mebenter@mebtel.net

Mocksville Davie County Enterprise (9.1M) PO Box 99 Mocksville NC 27028 **Phn:** 336-751-2120 **Fax:** 336-751-9760 www.ourdavie.com ernews@davie-enterprise.com

Mooresville Mooresville Tribune (5.6M) PO Box 300 Mooresville NC 28115 **Phn:** 704-664-5554 **Fax:** 704-664-3614 www.mooresvilletribune.com dgowing@mooresvilletribune.com

Morehead City Carteret County News Times (11.0M) PO Box 1679 Morehead City NC 28557 **Phn:** 252-726-7081 **Fax:** 252-726-6016 www.carolinacoastonline.com walter@thenewstimes.com

Morganton News Herald (7.8M) PO Box 280 Morganton NC 28680 **Phn:** 828-437-2161 **Fax:** 828-437-5372 www.morganton.com news@morganton.com

Mount Airy Surrey Scene (17.0M) 319 N Renfro St Mount Airy NC 27030 **Phn:** 336-786-4141 **Fax:** 336-789-2816 www.mtairynews.com jpeters@mtairynews.com

Mount Olive Mt. Olive Tribune (5.0M) PO Box 667 Mount Olive NC 28365 **Phn:** 919-658-9456 **Fax:** 919-658-9559 www.mountolivetribune.com editor@mountolivetribune.com

Murphy Cherokee Scout (9.0M) 89 Sycamore St Murphy NC 28906 **Phn:** 828-837-5122 **Fax:** 828-837-5832 www.cherokeescout.com news@cherokeescout.com

Murphy WNC Sentinel (5.0M) 1162 Andrews Rd Ste E Murphy NC 28906 **Phn:** 828-837-6397 **Fax:** 828-835-8337

Nags Head Outer Banks Sentinel (10.0M) PO Box 546 Nags Head NC 27959 **Phn:** 252-480-2234 **Fax:** 252-480-1146 www.obsentinel.com editor@obsentinel.com

Nashville Nashville Graphic (4.5M) 203 W Washington St Nashville NC 27856 **Phn:** 252-459-7101 **Fax:** 252-459-3052 www.nashvillegraphic.com news@nashvillegraphic.com

Newland Avery Post (5.0M) PO Box 1056 Newland NC 28657 **Phn:** 828-733-1407 **Fax:** 828-733-1408 averypost@yahoo.com

North Wilkesboro Wilkes Journal Patriot (15.2M) PO Box 70 North Wilkesboro NC 28659 **Phn:** 336-838-4117 **Fax:** 336-838-9864 www.journalpatriot.com wilkesjp@wilkes.net

Oak Ridge Northwest Observer (13.0M) PO Box 268 Oak Ridge NC 27310 **Phn:** 336-644-7035 **Fax:** 336-644-7006 www.nwobserver.com advertising@nwobserver.com

Oriental Pamlico News (3.7M) PO Box 510 Oriental NC 28571 **Phn:** 252-249-1555 **Fax:** 252-249-0857 thepamliconews.com

Oxford Oxford Public Ledger (13.0M) PO Box 643 Oxford NC 27565 **Phn:** 919-693-2646 **Fax:** 919-693-3704 opl@earthlink.net

Pilot Mountain The Pilot (4.5M) PO Box 223 Pilot Mountain NC 27041 **Phn:** 336-368-2222 **Fax:** 336-368-2244

Plymouth Roanoke Beacon (4.0M) PO Box 726 Plymouth NC 27962 **Phn:** 252-793-2123 **Fax:** 252-793-5365 news@roanokebeacon.com

Princeton News Leader (1.8M) PO Box 7 Princeton NC 27569 **Phn:** 919-936-9891 **Fax:** 919-936-2065 www.princetonleadernow.com news@newsleadernow.com

Raeford The News-Journal (4.5M) PO Box 550 Raeford NC 28376 **Phn:** 910-875-2121 **Fax:** 910-875-7256 www.thenews-journal.com ken@thenews-journal.com

Raleigh Cary News (50.0M) 1100 Situs Ct Ste 100 Raleigh NC 27606 **Phn:** 919-460-2600 **Fax:** 919-460-6034 www.carynews.com john.frank@nando.com

Red Springs Red Springs Citizen (2.6M) PO Box 72 Red Springs NC 28377 **Phn:** 910-843-4631 **Fax:** 910-843-8171 www.redspringscitizen.com rscitizen@embarqmail.com

Reidsville Madison Messenger (7.3M) PO Box 2157 Reidsville NC 27323 **Phn:** 336-548-6047 **Fax:** 336-548-2853 www.godanriver.com slawson@reidsvillereview.com

Reidsville Reidsville Review (3.3M) PO Box 2157 Reidsville NC 27323 **Phn:** 336-349-4331 **Fax:** 336-349-4320 www.godanriver.com news@reidsvillereview.com

Robbinsville The Graham Star (3.5M) PO Box 69 Robbinsville NC 28771 **Phn:** 828-479-3383 **Fax:** 828-479-1044 www.grahamstar.com editor@grahamstar.com

Roxboro The Courier Times (9.1M) PO Box 311 Roxboro NC 27573 **Phn:** 336-599-0162 **Fax:** 336-597-2773 www.personcountylife.com ctimes@roxboro-courier.com

Saint Pauls St. Pauls Review (3.2M) PO Box 265 Saint Pauls NC 28384 **Phn:** 910-865-4179 **Fax:** 910-865-4995 stpaulsreview.com ddouglas@heartlandpublications.com

Scotland Neck Commonwealth Progress (3.0M) 611 Main St Scotland Neck NC 27874 **Phn:** 252-826-2111 **Fax:** 252-826-2110

Selma Selma News (5.0M) PO Box 10 Selma NC 27576 **Phn:** 919-965-4343 **Fax:** 919-284-6397 theselmanews.com rstewart@kenlynews.com

Shallotte Brunswick Beacon (17.0M) PO Box 2558 Shallotte NC 28459 **Phn:** 910-754-6890 **Fax:** 910-754-5407 www.brunswickbeacon.com editor@brunswickbeacon.com

Shallotte Brunswick Co. News (8.0M) PO Box 1279 Shallotte NC 28459 **Phn:** 910-754-8662 brunswicknews@atmc.net

Siler City Chatham News Publishing (9.0M) PO Box 290 Siler City NC 27344 **Phn:** 919-663-3232 **Fax:** 919-663-4042 www.thechathamnews.com rigsbee@thechathamnews.com

Smithfield The Herald (36.5M) 228 E Market St Smithfield NC 27577 **Phn:** 919-836-5703 **Fax:** 919-989-7093 www.smithfieldherald.com sbolejack@newsobserver.com

Snow Hill The Standard Laconic (3.5M) PO Box 128 Snow Hill NC 28580 **Phn:** 252-747-3883 **Fax:** 252-747-7656 standardlaconic@ncweeklies.com

Southern Pines Southern Pines Pilot (16.5M) PO Box 58 Southern Pines NC 28388 **Phn:** 910-692-7271 **Fax:** 910-692-9382 www.thepilot.com hlyons@thepilot.com

Southport State Port Pilot (7.8M) 114 E Moore St Southport NC 28461 **Phn:** 910-457-4568 **Fax:** 910-457-9427 www.stateportpilot.com pilot@stateportpilot.com

Sparta Alleghany News (4.1M) PO Box 8 Sparta NC 28675 **Phn:** 336-372-8999 **Fax:** 336-372-5707 www.alleghanynews.com news@alleghanynews.com

Spring Hope Spring Hope Enterprise (3.5M) PO Box 399 Spring Hope NC 27882 **Phn:** 252-478-3651 **Fax:** 252-478-3075 springhopeenterprise.com shecommunitynews@yahoo.com

Spruce Pine Mitchell News-Journal (5.6M) PO Box 339 Spruce Pine NC 28777 **Phn:** 828-765-2071 **Fax:** 828-765-1616 www.mitchellnews.com editor@mitchellnews.com

Swansboro Tideland News (3.2M) PO Box 1000 Swansboro NC 28584 **Phn:** 910-326-5066 **Fax:** 910-326-1165 www.carolinacoastonline.com jimmy@tidelandnews.com

Sylva Sylva Herald & Ruralite (6.4M) PO Box 307 Sylva NC 28779 **Phn:** 828-586-2611 **Fax:** 828-586-2637 www.thesylvaherald.com news@thesylvaherald.com

Tabor City Tabor-Loris Tribune (3.0M) PO Box 67 Tabor City NC 28463 **Phn:** 910-653-3153 **Fax:** 910-653-5818 tabor-loris.com news@tabor-loris.com

Taylorsville Taylorsville Times (7.2M) PO Box 279 Taylorsville NC 28681 **Phn:** 828-632-2532 **Fax:** 828-632-8233 taylorsvilletimes.com taylorsvilletimes@taylorsvilletimes.com

Troy Montgomery Herald (6.0M) PO Box 466 Troy NC 27371 **Phn:** 910-576-6051 **Fax:** 910-576-1050 www.montgomeryherald.com sendnews@montgomeryherald.com

Wadesboro Anson Record (1.9M) 123 E Martin St # 400 Wadesboro NC 28170 **Phn:** 704-694-2161 **Fax:** 704-694-7060 www.ansonrecord.com acavenaugh@civitasmedia.com

Wake Forest The Wake Weekly (10.0M) PO Box 1919 Wake Forest NC 27588 **Phn:** 919-556-3182 **Fax:** 919-556-2233 www.wakeweekly.com editor@wakeweekly.com

Wallace Pender Chronicle (6.0M) PO Box 699 Wallace NC 28466 **Phn:** 910-259-2504 **Fax:** 910-259-6277

Walnut Cove The Stokes News (8.0M) PO Box 647 Walnut Cove NC 27052 **Phn:** 336-591-8191 **Fax:** 336-591-4379 thestokesnews.com cvaden@thestokesnews.com

Warrenton Warren Record (5.8M) PO Box 70 Warrenton NC 27589 **Phn:** 252-257-3341 **Fax:** 252-257-1413 www.southhillenterprise.com/warrenton news@warrenrecord.com

Waynesville Haywood County News (19.0M) 449 Pigeon St Waynesville NC 28786 **Phn:** 828-452-1471 www.citizen-times.com news@citizen-times.com

Waynesville Smoky Mountain News (16.0M) PO Box 629 Waynesville NC 28786 **Phn:** 828-452-4251 **Fax:** 828-452-3585 www.smokymountainnews.com info@smokymountainnews.com

Waynesville The Mountaineer (13.0M) PO Box 129 Waynesville NC 28786 **Phn:** 828-452-0661 **Fax:** 828-452-0665 themountaineer.villagesoup.com news@themountaineer.com

West Jefferson Jefferson Post (6.0M) PO Box 808 West Jefferson NC 28694 **Phn:** 336-846-7164 **Fax:** 336-846-7165 www.jeffersonpost.com editorial@jeffersonpost.com

Whiteville The News Reporter (10.5M) PO Box 707 Whiteville NC 28472 **Phn:** 910-642-4104 **Fax:** 910-642-1856 www.whiteville.com leshigh@whiteville.com

Williamston The Enterprise (5.1M) 106 W Main St Williamston NC 27892 **Phn:** 252-792-1181 **Fax:** 252-792-1921 lavar@nccox.com

Williamston The Weekly Herald (1.0M) PO Box 387 Williamston NC 27892 **Phn:** 252-792-1181 **Fax:** 252-792-1921 weeklyherald@nccox.com

Windsor Bertie Ledger Advance (4.5M) PO Box 69 Windsor NC 27983 **Phn:** 252-794-3185 **Fax:** 252-794-2835

Wrightsville Beach Lumina News (5.0M) PO Box 1110 Wrightsville Beach NC 28480 **Phn:** 910-256-6569 **Fax:** 910-256-6512 www.luminanews.com marimar@luminanews.com

Yadkinville Yadkin Ripple (5.3M) PO Box 7 Yadkinville NC 27055 **Phn:** 336-679-2341 **Fax:** 336-679-2340 www.yadkinripple.com cclark@elkintribune.com

Yanceyville Caswell Messenger (4.8M) PO Box 100 Yanceyville NC 27379 **Phn:** 336-694-4145 **Fax:** 336-694-5637 www.caswellmessenger.com caswellnews@caswellmessenger.com

Zebulon Eastern Wake News (6.9M) PO Box 1167 Zebulon NC 27597 **Phn:** 919-269-6101 **Fax:** 919-269-8383 www.easternwakenews.com jwhitfie@nando.com

NORTH DAKOTA

Ashley Ashley Tribune (1.7M) 115 W Main St Ashley ND 58413 **Phn:** 701-288-3531 **Fax:** 701-288-3532 www.centraldakotanews.com redhead@drtel.net

Beach Billings County Pioneer (0.3M) PO Box 156 Beach ND 58621 **Phn:** 701-872-3755 **Fax:** 701-872-3756

Beach Golden Valley News (1.2M) PO Box 156 Beach ND 58621 **Phn:** 701-872-3755 **Fax:** 701-872-3756

Belcourt Turtle Mountain Times (1.8M) PO Box 1270 Belcourt ND 58316 **Phn:** 701-477-6670 **Fax:** 701-477-6875 thetimes@utma.com

Beulah Beulah Beacon (2.6M) 324 2nd Ave NE Beulah ND 58523 **Phn:** 701-873-4381 **Fax:** 701-873-2383 www.bhgnews.com news@bhgnews.com

Beulah Center Republican (0.7M) 324 2nd Ave NE Beulah ND 58523 **Phn:** 701-873-4381 **Fax:** 701-873-2383 www.bhgnews.com news@bhgnews.com

Bottineau Bottineau Courant (3.0M) PO Box 29 Bottineau ND 58318 **Phn:** 701-228-2605 **Fax:** 701-228-5864 courant@utma.com

Bowbells Burke County Tribune (1.4M) PO Box 40 Bowbells ND 58721 **Phn:** 701-377-2626 **Fax:** 701-377-2717 www.cndnews.com tribune@nccray.net

Bowman Bowman County Pioneer (1.6M) PO Box F Bowman ND 58623 **Phn:** 701-523-5623 **Fax:** 701-523-3441 pioneernews@ndsupernet.com

Cando Towner County Record Herald (2.5M) PO Box 519 Cando ND 58324 **Phn:** 701-968-3223 **Fax:** 701-968-3345

Carrington Foster County Independent (3.2M) PO Box 138 Carrington ND 58421 **Phn:** 701-652-3181 **Fax:** 701-652-3286 fosterconews@daktel.com

Casselton Cass County Reporter (3.1M) PO Box 190 Casselton ND 58012 **Phn:** 701-347-4493 **Fax:** 701-347-4495 www.ccreporter.com news@ccreporter.com

Cavalier Cavalier Chronicle (2.4M) PO Box 520 Cavalier ND 58220 **Phn:** 701-265-8844 **Fax:** 701-265-8089 cavchronicle.com

Cooperstown Griggs County Courier (1.6M) PO Box 525 Cooperstown ND 58425 **Phn:** 701-797-3331 **Fax:** 701-797-3476

Crosby The Journal (2.9M) PO Box E Crosby ND 58730 **Phn:** 701-965-6088 **Fax:** 701-965-6089 www.journaltrib.com journal@crosbynd.com

NORTH CAROLINA WEEKLY NEWSPAPERS

Drayton Valley News (1.0M) PO Box 309 Drayton ND 58225 **Phn:** 701-360-3005 www.valleynv.com valleynv@polarcomm.com

Edgeley Edgeley Mail (1.0M) PO Box 278 Edgeley ND 58433 **Phn:** 701-493-2261

Elgin Carson Press & Grant County News (1.0M) PO Box 100 Elgin ND 58533 **Phn:** 701-584-2900 www.grantcountynews.net gcn@westriv.com

Ellendale Dickey County Leader (1.9M) PO Box 9 Ellendale ND 58436 **Phn:** 701-349-3222 **Fax:** 701-349-3229

Enderlin Enderlin Independent (1.5M) 209 4th Ave Enderlin ND 58027 **Phn:** 701-437-3131 www.enderlinindependent.com enderlinindependent@mlgc.com

Finley Steele County Press (1.2M) PO Box 475 Finley ND 58230 **Phn:** 701-524-1640 **Fax:** 701-524-2221 ldefrang@ncppub.com

Fordville Ness Press Inc (3.0M) PO Box 157 Fordville ND 58231 **Phn:** 701-229-3641 **Fax:** 701-229-3217 nesspres@polarcomm.com

Gackle Tri County News (0.8M) PO Box 214 Gackle ND 58442 **Phn:** 701-485-3550 **Fax:** 701-485-3551 tcnews@daktel.com

Garrison Mclean County Independent (3.0M) PO Box 309 Garrison ND 58540 **Phn:** 701-463-2201 **Fax:** 701-463-7487 www.bhgnews.com editors@bhgnews.com

Glen Ullin Glen Ullin Times (0.9M) PO Box 668 Glen Ullin ND 58631 **Phn:** 701-348-3325

Grafton Walsh County Record (3.8M) 402 Hill Ave Grafton ND 58237 **Phn:** 701-352-0641 **Fax:** 701-352-1502 www.wcrecord.com

Hankinson News Monitor (1.8M) PO Box 190 Hankinson ND 58041 **Phn:** 701-242-7696 **Fax:** 701-242-7406 www.wahpetondailynews.com monitor@rrt.net

Harvey Harvey Herald-Press (5.0M) 913 Lincoln Ave Harvey ND 58341 **Phn:** 701-324-4646

Hazen Hazen Star (2.5M) PO Box 508 Hazen ND 58545 **Phn:** 701-748-2255 www.bhgnews.com news@bhgnews.com

Hebron Hebron Herald (1.1M) PO Box 9 Hebron ND 58638 **Phn:** 701-878-4494 hherald@westriv.com

Hettinger Adams County Record (1.6M) PO Box 749 Hettinger ND 58639 **Phn:** 701-567-2424 **Fax:** 701-567-2425 acrnews@ndsupernet.com

Hillsboro Hillsboro Banner (1.3M) PO Box 39 Hillsboro ND 58045 **Phn:** 701-636-4241 **Fax:** 701-636-4245 hbanner1.wordpress.com hbanner@rrv.net

Jamestown Sun Country (21.0M) PO Box 1760 Jamestown ND 58402 **Phn:** 701-252-3120 **Fax:** 701-952-0025 www.jamestownsun.com news@jamestownsun.com

Jamestown The Prairie Post (18.5M) PO Box 1760 Jamestown ND 58402 **Phn:** 701-952-2796 **Fax:** 701-952-0025 news@jamestownsun.com

Kenmare Kenmare News (1.8M) PO Box 896 Kenmare ND 58746 **Phn:** 701-385-4275 **Fax:** 701-385-4395 www.kenmarend.com news@kenmarend.com

Killdeer Dunn County Herald (1.4M) PO Box 609 Killdeer ND 58640 **Phn:** 701-764-5312 **Fax:** 701-764-5049 edunn@ndsupernet.com

Kulm Kulm Messenger (1.0M) PO Box J Kulm ND 58456 **Phn:** 701-647-2411

Lakota Lakota American (1.6M) PO Box 507 Lakota ND 58344 **Phn:** 701-247-2482 lamerican@polarcomm.com

Lamoure La Moure Chronicle (1.3M) PO Box 196 Lamoure ND 58458 **Phn:** 701-883-5393 **Fax:** 701-883-5076 chronicl@drtel.net

Langdon Cavalier County Republican (2.1M) 618 3rd St Langdon ND 58249 **Phn:** 701-256-5311 **Fax:** 701-256-5841 ccr@utma.com

Linton Emmons County Record (2.8M) PO Box 38 Linton ND 58552 **Phn:** 701-254-4537 **Fax:** 701-254-4909 www.centraldakotanews.com info@lintonnd.com

Lisbon Ransom County Gazette (6.1M) PO Box 473 Lisbon ND 58054 **Phn:** 701-683-4128 **Fax:** 701-683-4129 www.rcgazette.com info@rcgazette.com

Litchville Litchville Bulletin (1.1M) PO Box 46 Litchville ND 58461 **Phn:** 701-762-4267 bulletin@drtel.net

Mandan Mandan News (1.8M) 2401 46th Ave SE Ste 201 Mandan ND 58554 **Phn:** 701-663-1164 **Fax:** 701-255-2312 mandan-news.com editor@mandan-news.com

Mayville Traill County Tribune (2.5M) PO Box 567 Mayville ND 58257 **Phn:** 701-788-3281 **Fax:** 701-788-3287 traillcotribune.wordpress.com tribune@tctribune.net

McClusky McClusky Gazette (0.9M) PO Box 457 McClusky ND 58463 **Phn:** 701-363-2492 **Fax:** 701-363-2698 www.bhgnews.com news@bhgnews.com

McClusky McLean County Journal (1.0M) PO Box 619 McClusky ND 58463 **Phn:** 701-363-2492 **Fax:** 701-363-2698 www.bhgnews.com news@bhgnews.com

Milnor Milnor Teller (2.3M) PO Box 247 Milnor ND 58060 **Phn:** 701-427-9472 **Fax:** 701-427-9492 info@thescteller.com

Minnewaukan Benson County Farmers Press (2.5M) PO Box 98 Minnewaukan ND 58351 **Phn:** 701-473-5436 **Fax:** 701-473-5736 www.bensoncountynews.com farmerspress@gondtc.com

Mohall Renville County Farmer (1.4M) PO Box 98 Mohall ND 58761 **Phn:** 701-756-6363 **Fax:** 701-756-7136 www.cndnews.com rcf1@ndak.net

Napoleon Napolean Homestead (1.7M) PO Box 29 Napoleon ND 58561 **Phn:** 701-754-2212 www.napoleonnd.com homestead@napoleonnd.com

New England The Herald (2.0M) PO Box 517 New England ND 58647 **Phn:** 701-579-4530 **Fax:** 701-579-4180 therald@ndsupernet.com

New Rockford The Transcript (3.0M) PO Box 752 New Rockford ND 58356 **Phn:** 701-947-2417 **Fax:** 701-947-2418 transcript@stellarnet.com

New Salem New Salem Journal (1.4M) PO Box 416 New Salem ND 58563 **Phn:** 701-843-7567 **Fax:** 701-843-7623 www.smalltownpapers.com

New Town Mountrail Co. Record (1.2M) PO Box 730 New Town ND 58763 **Phn:** 701-627-4829 **Fax:** 701-627-4021 www.bhgnews.com mcrecord@restel.net

New Town New Town News (1.5M) PO Box 730 New Town ND 58763 **Phn:** 701-627-4829 **Fax:** 701-627-4021 www.bhgnews.com ntnews@restel.net

Oakes Oakes Times (1.4M) PO Box 651 Oakes ND 58474 **Phn:** 701-742-2361 **Fax:** 701-742-2207 oakestms@drtel.net

Park River Walsh County Press (2.5M) PO Box 49 Park River ND 58270 **Phn:** 701-284-6333 **Fax:** 701-284-6091

Rolla Turtle Mountain Star (4.2M) PO Box 849 Rolla ND 58367 **Phn:** 701-477-6495 **Fax:** 701-477-3182 www.smalltownpapers.com tmstar@utma.com

Rugby Pierce County Tribune (2.7M) PO Box 385 Rugby ND 58368 **Phn:** 701-776-5252 **Fax:** 701-776-2159 www.thepiercecountytribune.com pctrugby@gondtc.com

Stanley Mountrail County Promoter (2.3M) PO Box 99 Stanley ND 58784 **Phn:** 701-628-2333 **Fax:** 701-628-2694 www.mountrailcountypromoter.com promoter@midstatetel.com

Steele Steele Ozone Press (1.4M) PO Box 350 Steele ND 58482 **Phn:** 701-475-2513 sop@bektel.com

Tioga Tioga Tribune (1.5M) PO Box 700 Tioga ND 58852 **Phn:** 701-664-2222 **Fax:** 701-664-3333 www.journaltrib.com tribune@tiogand.com

Towner Mouse River Journal (1.8M) PO Box 268 Towner ND 58788 **Phn:** 701-537-5610 **Fax:** 701-537-5493 msrvrjnl@ndak.net

Underwood Underwood News (0.7M) PO Box 340 Underwood ND 58576 **Phn:** 701-462-8126 **Fax:** 701-462-8128 www.bhgnews.com news@bhgnews.com

Velva Velva Area Voice (1.0M) PO Box 630 Velva ND 58790 **Phn:** 701-338-2599 **Fax:** 701-338-2705 www.bhgnews.com yournews@srt.com

Walhalla Walhalla Mountaineer (1.1M) PO Box 497 Walhalla ND 58282 **Phn:** 701-549-2580 mtneer@utma.com

Washburn Leader News (2.5M) PO Box 340 Washburn ND 58577 **Phn:** 701-462-8126 **Fax:** 701-462-8128 www.bhgnews.com news@bhgnews.com

Watford City McKenzie County Farmer (2.8M) PO Box 587 Watford City ND 58854 **Phn:** 701-842-2351 **Fax:** 701-842-2352 www.watfordcitynd.com mcf@watfordcitynd.com

West Fargo West Fargo Pioneer (3.0M) PO Box 457 West Fargo ND 58078 **Phn:** 701-282-2443 **Fax:** 701-282-9248 www.westfargopioneer.com news@westfargopioneer.com

Westhope Westhope Standard (0.8M) PO Box 267 Westhope ND 58793 **Phn:** 701-245-6461 www.cndnews.com standard@srt.com

Williston Plains Reporter (13.0M) PO Box 1447 Williston ND 58802 **Phn:** 701-572-2165 **Fax:** 701-572-1965 editor@willistonherald.com

Wishek Wishek Star (1.7M) PO Box 275 Wishek ND 58495 **Phn:** 701-452-2331 **Fax:** 701-452-2340 www.centraldakotanews.com wishekstar@gmail.com

OHIO

Ada Ada Herald (2.8M) PO Box 117 Ada OH 45810 **Phn:** 419-634-6055 **Fax:** 419-634-0912 www.adaherald.com alehman@adaherald.com

Akron Akron Suburbanite (33.0M) 3577 S Arlington Rd Ste B Akron OH 44312 **Phn:** 330-899-2872 **Fax:** 330-896-7633 www.thesuburbanite.com gary.brown@cantonrep.com

Akron Jackson Suburbanite (12.5M) 3577 S Arlington Rd Ste B Akron OH 44312 **Phn:** 330-899-2872 **Fax:** 330-896-7633 www.thesuburbanite.com erin.pustay@thesuburbanite.com

Akron South Side News Leader (23.0M) 3075 Smith Rd Ste 204 Akron OH 44333 **Phn:** 330-665-9595 **Fax:** 330-665-9590 www.akron.com editor@akron.com

Akron West Side Leader (43.0M) 3075 Smith Rd Ste 204 Akron OH 44333 **Phn:** 330-665-9595 **Fax:** 330-665-9590 www.akron.com editor@akron.com

Amherst Amherst News Times (2.5M) PO Box 67 Amherst OH 44001 **Phn:** 440-988-2801 **Fax:** 440-988-2802 theamherstnewstimes.com news@theoberlinnews.com

Andover Pymatuning Area News (2.2M) PO Box 458 Andover OH 44003 **Phn:** 440-293-6097 **Fax:** 440-293-7374 www.gazettenews.com pymatuningnews@gazettenews.com

Antwerp Antwerp Bee-Argus (1.0M) PO Box 1065 Antwerp OH 45813 **Phn:** 419-258-8161 **Fax:** 419-258-9365 antwerpbeeargus.com antwerpbeeargus@frontier.com

Archbold Archbold Buckeye (3.2M) 207 N Defiance St Archbold OH 43502 **Phn:** 419-445-4466 www.archboldbuckeye.com

Archbold Farmland News (3.5M) PO Box 240 Archbold OH 43502 **Phn:** 419-445-9456 **Fax:** 419-445-4444 www.farmlandnews.com news@farmlandnews.com

Athens Athens News (18.0M) 14 N Court St Ste 1 Athens OH 45701 **Phn:** 740-594-8219 **Fax:** 740-592-5695 www.athensnews.com news@athensnews.com

Attica Attica Hub (4.4M) PO Box 516 Attica OH 44807 **Phn:** 419-426-3491 **Fax:** 419-426-2003 www.atticahub.com copy@atticahub.com

Avon Lake North Ridgeville Press (3.5M) PO Box 300 Avon Lake OH 44012 **Phn:** 440-930-5923 **Fax:** 440-933-7904 2presspapers.northcoastnow.com news@2presspapers.com

Avon Lake The Press (9.0M) PO Box 300 Avon Lake OH 44012 **Phn:** 440-933-5100 **Fax:** 440-933-7904 2presspapers.northcoastnow.com editor@2presspapers.com

Avon Lake West Life (7.5M) PO Box 300 Avon Lake OH 44012 **Phn:** 440-871-5797 **Fax:** 440-871-3824 www.westlifenews.com editor@westlifenews.com

Baltimore Towne Crier (30.0M) PO Box 38 Baltimore OH 43105 **Phn:** 740-344-7555 **Fax:** 740-344-3555 www.fairfieldtownecrier.com freedomptg@roadrunner.com

Barberton Barberton Herald (7.9M) PO Box 830 Barberton OH 44203 **Phn:** 330-753-1068 **Fax:** 330-753-1021 www.barbertonherald.com news@barbertonherald.com

Barnesville Barnesville Enterprise (4.5M) PO Box 30 Barnesville OH 43713 **Phn:** 740-425-1912 **Fax:** 740-425-2545

Batavia Clermont Sun (3.0M) PO Box 366 Batavia OH 45103 **Phn:** 513-732-2511 **Fax:** 513-732-6344 www.clermontsun.com clermontsun@fuse.net

Bay Village Gottschalk Publishing (19.0M) PO Box 40216 Bay Village OH 44140 **Phn:** 440-356-0920 **Fax:** 440-356-0515 thetimes@cavtel.net

Bellville Star & Tri-Forks Press (2.1M) 107 Main St Bellville OH 44813 **Phn:** 419-886-2291 **Fax:** 419-886-2704

Bluffton Bluffton News (2.9M) PO Box 49 Bluffton OH 45817 **Phn:** 419-358-8010 **Fax:** 419-358-5027 blufftonnews.com editor@blufftonnews.com

Bluffton North Baltimore News (0.6M) 101 N Main St Bluffton OH 45817 **Phn:** 419-358-8010 **Fax:** 419-358-8020 nbnews@northbaltimorenews.com

Boardman Town Crier Newspapers (20.0M) 240 Franklin St Se Boardman OH 44512 **Phn:** 330-629-6200 www.towncrieronline.com awilson@towncrieronline.com

Brecksville Gazette Newspaper (10.0M) 7014 Mill Rd Brecksville OH 44141 **Phn:** 440-526-7977 **Fax:** 440-526-7114 www.gazette-news.com production1@gazette-news.com

Brookville Brookville Star (6.5M) PO Box 100 Brookville OH 45309 **Phn:** 937-833-2545 www.brookvillestar.net news@brookvillestar.net

Bryan The Countyline (21.0M) PO Box 471 Bryan OH 43506 **Phn:** 419-636-1111 **Fax:** 419-636-8937 countylineads@bryantimes.com

Buckeye Lake Buckeye Lake Beacon (14.8M) PO Box 1542 Buckeye Lake OH 43008 **Phn:** 740-928-5541 **Fax:** 740-928-7960 www.buckeyelakebeacon.net charlesprince@buckeyelakebeacon.net

Cadiz Harrison News-Herald (6.5M) 144 S Main St Ste 1 Cadiz OH 43907 **Phn:** 740-942-2118 **Fax:** 740-942-4667 www.harrisonnewsherald.com newsroom@harrisonnewsherald.com

Caldwell Journal & Noble Co. Leader (4.5M) PO Box 315 Caldwell OH 43724 **Phn:** 740-732-2341 **Fax:** 740-732-7288

Cambridge New Concord Leader (1.2M) PO Box 10 Cambridge OH 43725 **Phn:** 740-439-3531 **Fax:** 740-432-6219 newsroom@daily-jeff.com

Cambridge Village Reporter (1.0M) PO Box 10 Cambridge OH 43725 **Phn:** 740-685-2073

Carey Progressor-Times Inc (4.0M) PO Box 37 Carey OH 43316 **Phn:** 419-396-7567 **Fax:** 419-396-7527 theprogressortimes.com news@theprogressortimes.com

Carrollton Free Press Standard (8.5M) PO Box 37 Carrollton OH 44615 **Phn:** 330-627-5591 **Fax:** 330-627-3195 www.freepressstandard.com fps44615@yahoo.com

Chagrin Falls Chagrin Valley Publishing (30.0M) 525 E Washington St Chagrin Falls OH 44022 **Phn:** 440-247-5335 **Fax:** 440-247-5615 www.chagrinvalleytoday.com editor@chagrinvalleytimes.com

Chardon Geauga County Maple Leaf (3.0M) PO Box 1166 Chardon OH 44024 **Phn:** 440-285-2013 **Fax:** 440-285-2015 www.geaugamapleleaf.com info@geaugamapleleaf.com

Chesterland Chesterland News (6.4M) 8389 Mayfield Rd Ste B-6 Chesterland OH 44026 **Phn:** 440-729-7667 **Fax:** 440-729-8140 chesterlandnews.com ads@chesterlandnews.com

Cincinnati CIN Weekly (65.0M) 312 Elm St Fl 18 Cincinnati OH 45202 **Phn:** 513-768-6000 **Fax:** 513-768-8340 cinweekly.cincinnati.com cwashburn@enquirer.com

Cincinnati City Beat (53.0M) 811 Race St Fl 5 Cincinnati OH 45202 **Phn:** 513-665-4700 **Fax:** 513-665-4369 citybeat.com dcross@citybeat.com

Cincinnati Community Press (72.0M) 5556 Cheviot Rd Ste A Cincinnati OH 45247 **Phn:** 513-923-3111 **Fax:** 513-923-1806 news.communitypress.com memral@communitypress.com

Cincinnati Pulse (18.0M) 600 Vine St Ste 106 Cincinnati OH 45202 **Phn:** 513-241-9906 **Fax:** 513-241-7235

Cincinnati Valley Courier (2.2M) 260 Avalon St Cincinnati OH 45216 **Phn:** 513-821-4575 **Fax:** 513-761-3304

Cleveland Call & Post (34.0M) PO Box 6237 Cleveland OH 44101 **Phn:** 216-791-7600 **Fax:** 216-451-0404

Cleveland Cleveland Scene (90.0M) 1468 W 9th St Ste 805 Cleveland OH 44113 **Phn:** 216-241-7550 **Fax:** 216-802-7212 www.clevescene.com eburnett@clevescene.com

Clyde Clyde Enterprise (1.7M) PO Box 29 Clyde OH 43410 **Phn:** 419-547-9194 **Fax:** 419-547-4614 clydeenterprise.com clydenews@bizwoh.rr.com

Coldwater Mercer County Chronicle (3.0M) PO Box 105 Coldwater OH 45828 **Phn:** 419-678-2324 **Fax:** 419-678-4659

Columbia Station The Rural-Urban Record (10.0M) PO Box 966 Columbia Station OH 44028 **Phn:** 440-236-8982 **Fax:** 440-236-9198 www.server-jbmultimedia.net/Rural-UrbanRecord news@rural-urbanrecord.com

OHIO WEEKLY NEWSPAPERS

Columbus Columbus Alive (46.0M) PO Box 1289 Columbus OH 43216 **Phn:** 614-221-2449 **Fax:** 614-461-8746 www.columbusalive.com brian@columbusalive.com

Columbus Columbus Messenger Company (100.0M) 3500 Sullivant Ave Columbus OH 43204 **Phn:** 614-272-5422 **Fax:** 614-272-0684 www.columbusmessenger.com eastside@columbusmessenger.com

Columbus Suburban News Publications (293.0M) PO Box 29912 Columbus OH 43229 **Phn:** 614-785-1199 **Fax:** 614-842-4760 columbuslocalnews.com snpnews@columbusmediaenterprises.com

Continental Continental News Review (1.0M) PO Box 995 Continental OH 45831 **Phn:** 419-596-3897 **Fax:** 419-596-3888

Covington Stillwater Advertiser (11.0M) PO Box 69 Covington OH 45318 **Phn:** 937-473-2028 **Fax:** 937-473-2500 www.arenspub.com ywelbaum@gmail.com

Crestline Crestline Advocate (2.3M) PO Box 226 Crestline OH 44827 **Phn:** 419-683-3355 **Fax:** 419-683-0175 crestlineadvocate@yahoo.com

Dalton Dalton Gazette (1.4M) PO Box 495 Dalton OH 44618 **Phn:** 330-828-8401

Dayton Dayton City Paper (23.0M) 322 S Patterson Blvd Dayton OH 45402 **Phn:** 937-222-8855 www.daytoncitypaper.com contactus@daytoncitypaper.com

Dayton Dayton Weekly News (30.0M) 118 Salem Ave Dayton OH 45406 **Phn:** 937-223-8060 **Fax:** 937-223-9664 www.daytonweeklynews.com daytonweek@aol.com

Dayton Oakwood Register (10.0M) PO Box 572 Dayton OH 45409 **Phn:** 937-294-2662 **Fax:** 937-294-8375 www.oakwoodregister.com oakwoodregister@aol.com

Dayton Times Community Papers (78.0M) 3120 Woodman Dr Ste A Dayton OH 45420 **Phn:** 937-294-7000 **Fax:** 937-294-2981 www.tcnewsnet.com jgraue@civitasmedia.com

Delta Delta Atlas (2.0M) 212 Main St Delta OH 43515 **Phn:** 419-822-3231 **Fax:** 419-822-3289

Deshler Deshler Flag (1.5M) 107 E Main St Ste A Deshler OH 43516 **Phn:** 419-278-2816

Dresden Dresden Transcript (5.5M) PO Box 105 Dresden OH 43821 **Phn:** 740-754-1608 **Fax:** 740-754-1609

Eaton The Register-Herald (7.2M) 200 Eaton Lewisburg Rd Ste 105 Eaton OH 45320 **Phn:** 937-456-5553 **Fax:** 937-456-3558 www.registerherald.com info@registerherald.com

Edgerton Edgerton Earth (1.2M) 178 N Michigan Ave Edgerton OH 43517 **Phn:** 419-298-2369 **Fax:** 419-386-2829 edgertonearth.com edgertonearth@edgertonearth.com

Englewood Englewood Independent (4.0M) 69 N Dixie Dr Ste E Englewood OH 45322 **Phn:** 937-836-2619 **Fax:** 937-836-1940 www.tcnewsnet.com rnunnari@tcnewsnet.com

Fostoria The Focus (12.0M) 112 N Main St Fostoria OH 44830 **Phn:** 419-435-6397 **Fax:** 419-435-0101 fostoriafocus.com news@fostoriafocus.com

Fredericktown Knox County Citizen (1.4M) PO Box 240 Fredericktown OH 43019 **Phn:** 740-848-4032 **Fax:** 740-848-4104

Garrettsville Weekly Villager (13.0M) PO Box 331 Garrettsville OH 44231 **Phn:** 330-527-5761 **Fax:** 330-527-5145 weeklyvillager.com news@weeklyvillager.com

Georgetown The News Democrat (4.0M) PO Box 21169 Georgetown OH 45121 **Phn:** 937-378-6161 **Fax:** 937-378-2004 www.newsdemocrat.com info@newsdemocrat.com

Granville Granville Sentinel (2.4M) PO Box 357 Granville OH 43023 **Phn:** 740-587-3397 **Fax:** 740-587-3398 www.newarkadvocate.com mshearer@nncogannett.com

Greenville The Early Bird (22.4M) 5312 Sebring Warner Rd Greenville OH 45331 **Phn:** 937-548-3330 **Fax:** 937-548-3376 www.bluebagmedia.com flfoutz@earlybirdpaper.com

Greenwich Enterprise Review (14.0M) PO Box 7 Greenwich OH 44837 **Phn:** 419=935-0184 **Fax:** 419-933-2031

Harrison Harrison Press (5.4M) PO Box 610 Harrison OH 45030 **Phn:** 513-367-4582 **Fax:** 513-367-4593 hpresseditor@cinci.rr.com

Hartville Hartville News (2.9M) PO Box 428 Hartville OH 44632 **Phn:** 330-877-9345 **Fax:** 330-877-1364 knowlespress@sbcglobal.net

Heath Heath News (4.5M) PO Box 2010 Heath OH 43056 **Phn:** 740-522-8566 **Fax:** 740-522-8578 heathnews@aol.com

Hicksville Hicksville News-Tribune (2.5M) 147 E High St Hicksville OH 43526 **Phn:** 419-542-7764 **Fax:** 419-542-7370 www.hicksvillenewstribune.com newstrib@cros.net

Huber Heights Huber Heights Courier (9.0M) 7089 Taylorsville Rd Huber Heights OH 45424 **Phn:** 937-236-4990 **Fax:** 937-236-4176 www.hhcourier.com gsmart@tcnewsnet.com

Jackson Jackson Co. Times-Journal (5.8M) PO Box 270 Jackson OH 45640 **Phn:** 740-286-2187 **Fax:** 740-286-5854 www.JacksonCountyDaily.com jhughes@timesjournal.com

Jackson Telegram (6.0M) PO Box 667 Jackson OH 45640 **Phn:** 740-286-3604 **Fax:** 740-286-0167 skeller@jcbipaper.com

Jefferson Gazette Newspapers (13.0M) PO Box 166 Jefferson OH 44047 **Phn:** 440-576-9115 **Fax:** 440-576-4337 www.gazettenews.com gazette@gazettenews.com

Jefferson Gazette Newspapers (31.0M) PO Box 166 Jefferson OH 44047 **Phn:** 440-428-0790 **Fax:** 440-428-0786 gazettenews.com tribune@gazettenews.com

Johnstown Johnstown Independent (2.4M) 55 S Main St Ste E Johnstown OH 43031 **Phn:** 614-855-2774 **Fax:** 614-855-2857 www.thisweeknews.com mkuhlman@thisweeknews.com

Lebanon Western Star (23.0M) 200 Harmon Ave Lebanon OH 45036 **Phn:** 513-932-3010 **Fax:** 513-932-6056 www.todayspulse.com warrencountynews@coxohio.com

Leipsic Leipsic Messenger (1.4M) 117 E Main St Leipsic OH 45856 **Phn:** 419-943-2590

Lewis Center Grove City Record (3.5M) PO Box 608 Lewis Center OH 43035 **Phn:** 614-875-2307 **Fax:** 614-875-6028 www.thisweeknews.com editorial@thisweeknews.com

Lewis Center ThisWeek Newspapers (307.0M) 7801 N Central Dr Lewis Center OH 43035 **Phn:** 740-888-6100 **Fax:** 740-888-6006 www.thisweeknews.com editorial@thisweeknews.com

Liberty Center The Liberty Press (1.2M) PO Box 6 Liberty Center OH 43532 **Phn:** 419-533-2401

Liberty Township Fairfield Echo (22.0M) 7378 Liberty One Dr Liberty Township OH 45044 **Phn:** 513-755-5060 www.todayspulse.com butlercountynews@coxohio.com

London Madison Press (20.0M) PO Box 390 London OH 43140 **Phn:** 740-852-1616 **Fax:** 740-852-1620 www.madison-press.com news@madison-press.com

Loudonville Loudonville Times (2.5M) 255 W Main St Loudonville OH 44842 **Phn:** 419-994-5600 **Fax:** 419-994-5826 www.theloudonvilletimes.com jbrewer@times-gazette.com

Louisville Louisville Herald (3.0M) PO Box 170 Louisville OH 44641 **Phn:** 330-875-5610 **Fax:** 330-875-4475 www.louisvilleherald.com theherald@mac.com

Loveland Community Press (113.0M) 394 Wards Corner Rd Ste 170 Loveland OH 45140 **Phn:** 513-248-8600 **Fax:** 513-248-1938 communitypress.cincinnati.com espangler@communitypress.com

Manchester Manchester Signal (3.5M) 414 E 7th St Manchester OH 45144 **Phn:** 937-549-2800 **Fax:** 937-549-3611

Marblehead Peninsula News (1.8M) PO Box 206 Marblehead OH 43440 **Phn:** 419-798-4899 **Fax:** 419-798-1263

Mc Arthur Vinton Co Courier (2.1M) PO Box 468 Mc Arthur OH 45651 **Phn:** 740-596-5393 **Fax:** 740-596-4226

McConnelsville Morgan County Herald (5.0M) PO Box 268 McConnelsville OH 43756 **Phn:** 740-962-3377 **Fax:** 740-962-6861 www.mchnews.com newsroom@mchnews.com

Miamisburg Franklin Chronicle (8.0M) 230 S 2nd St Miamisburg OH 45342 **Phn:** 937-866-3331 **Fax:** 937-866-6011

Miamisburg Germantown Press (2.7M) PO Box 108 Miamisburg OH 45343 **Phn:** 937-855-2300

Miamisburg Miamisburg News (6.5M) PO Box 108 Miamisburg OH 45343 **Phn:** 937-866-3331 **Fax:** 937-866-6011 steve.sandlin@miamivalleynewspapers.com

Miamisburg Springboro Star Press (12.0M) 230 S 2nd St Miamisburg OH 45342 **Phn:** 937-866-3331 **Fax:** 937-866-6011

Millbury Press Newspapers (34.0M) PO Box 169 Millbury OH 43447 **Phn:** 419-836-2221 **Fax:** 419-836-1319 www.presspublications.com news@presspublications.com

Millersburg Holmes County Hub (4.4M) PO Box 151 Millersburg OH 44654 **Phn:** 330-674-1811 **Fax:** 330-674-3780 hub@the-daily-record.com

Minerva Press-News (2.2M) PO Box 304 Minerva OH 44657 **Phn:** 330-868-5222 **Fax:** 330-868-3273

Minerva The News Leader (3.9M) PO Box 304 Minerva OH 44657 **Phn:** 330-868-5222 **Fax:** 330-868-3273 www.tnl-news.com newsleader@the-review.com

Minster Community Post (6.8M) PO Box 155 Minster OH 45865 **Phn:** 419-628-2369 **Fax:** 419-628-4712 www.minstercommunitypost.com publisher@nktelco.net

Montpelier Montpelier Leader (1.8M) 319 W Main St Montpelier OH 43543 **Phn:** 419-485-3113 **Fax:** 419-485-3114

Montpelier Village Reporter (1.9M) 115 Broad St Montpelier OH 43543 **Phn:** 419-485-4851 www.thevillagereporter.com publisher@thevillagereporter.com

Mount Gilead Morrow Co. Independent (1.0M) PO Box 149 Mount Gilead OH 43338 **Phn:** 419-946-3010 **Fax:** 419-947-7241

Mount Gilead Morrow County Sentinel (4.8M) PO Box 149 Mount Gilead OH 43338 **Phn:** 419-946-3010 **Fax:** 419-947-7241 www.morrowcountysentinel.com editor@newscolorpress.com

Mount Orab Brown County Press (16.5M) 219 S High St Mount Orab OH 45154 **Phn:** 937-444-3441 **Fax:** 937-444-2652 browncountypress.com

New Lexington Perry Co Tribune (3.8M) 389 Lincoln Park Dr New Lexington OH 43764 **Phn:** 740-342-4121 **Fax:** 740-342-4131 www.perrydaily.com news@perrytribune.com

New London New London Record (2.4M) PO Box 146 New London OH 44851 **Phn:** 419-929-3411 **Fax:** 419-929-8210 www.sdgnewsgroup.com record@sdgnewsgroup.com

New Washington New Washington Herald (1.6M) PO Box 367 New Washington OH 44854 **Phn:** 419-492-2133 **Fax:** 419-492-2128 www.theheraldinc.com

Newcomerstown Newcomerstown News (3.5M) PO Box 30 Newcomerstown OH 43832 **Phn:** 740-498-7117 **Fax:** 740-498-5624

Niles The Review Newspapers (3.0M) 1123 W Park Ave Niles OH 44446 **Phn:** 330-544-5500 **Fax:** 330-544-5511 thereviewnewspapers.com mail@thereviewnewspapers.com

Oak Harbor The Exponent (2.0M) PO Box 70 Oak Harbor OH 43449 **Phn:** 419-898-5361 **Fax:** 419-898-0501

Oberlin Oberlin News Tribune (3.5M) PO Box 29 Oberlin OH 44074 **Phn:** 440-775-1611 **Fax:** 440-774-2167 www.ourtownsnews.com news@theoberlinnews.com

Ontario Tribune-Courier (2.4M) PO Box 127 Ontario OH 44862 **Phn:** 419-529-2847 www.tribune-courier.com news@tribune-courier.com

Ottawa Putnam County Sentinel (6.0M) PO Box 149 Ottawa OH 45875 **Phn:** 419-523-5709 **Fax:** 419-523-3512 putnamsentinel.com news@putnamsentinel.com

Ottawa Putnam County Vidette (1.1M) PO Box 149 Ottawa OH 45875 **Phn:** 419-659-2173 **Fax:** 419-659-2760

Oxford Oxford Press (3.7M) 15 S Beech St Oxford OH 45056 **Phn:** 513-523-4139 **Fax:** 513-523-1935 www.oxfordpress.com

Pataskala Pataskala Post (11.1M) PO Box 722 Pataskala OH 43062 **Phn:** 740-964-6226 **Fax:** 740-964-6335 home.earthlink.net/~pataskalapost

Pataskala Pataskala Standard (5.2M) 22 1st St SW Pataskala OH 43062 **Phn:** 740-927-2991 **Fax:** 740-927-2930 www.newarkadvocate.com cmmcdonald@nncogannett.com

Paulding Paulding Progress (4.2M) PO Box 180 Paulding OH 45879 **Phn:** 419-399-4015 **Fax:** 419-399-4030 www.progressnewspaper.org progress@progressnewspaper.org

Perrysburg Welch Publishing (33.0M) 117 E 2nd St Perrysburg OH 43551 **Phn:** 419-874-4491 **Fax:** 419-874-7311 perrysburg.com messenger@perrysburg.com

Port Clinton The Beacon (17.0M) 205 SE Catawba Rd Ste G Port Clinton OH 43452 **Phn:** 419-732-2154 **Fax:** 419-734-5382 www.thebeacon.net angie@thebeacon.net

Portsmouth Community Common (39.0M) PO Box 1191 Portsmouth OH 45662 **Phn:** 740-353-1151 **Fax:** 740-353-5848 www.communitycommon.com news@communitycommon.com

Richwood Richwood Gazette (2.5M) PO Box 187 Richwood OH 43344 **Phn:** 740-943-2214 **Fax:** 740-943-3595

Ripley Ripley Bee (1.3M) PO Box 97 Ripley OH 45167 **Phn:** 937-392-4321 **Fax:** 937-392-0317 info@ripleybee.com

OHIO WEEKLY NEWSPAPERS

Spencerville The Journal News (2.1M) PO Box 8 Spencerville OH 45887 **Phn:** 419-647-4981 **Fax:** 419-647-4778 www.spencervillejournalnews.com thejournalnews@midohio.twcbc.com

Stow Record Publishing (25.0M) 1619 Commerce Dr Stow OH 44224 **Phn:** 440-688-0088 **Fax:** 440-688-1588 www.recordpub.com editor@recordpub.com

Struthers Hometown Journal (6.0M) 32 State St Ste 204 Struthers OH 44471 **Phn:** 330-755-2155 hometownjournal.biz news@hometownjournal.biz

Sugarcreek The Budget (19.5M) PO Box 249 Sugarcreek OH 44681 **Phn:** 330-852-4634 **Fax:** 330-852-4421 www.thebudgetnewspaper.com localnews@thebudgetnewspaper.com

Sunbury Sunbury News (3.2M) PO Box 59 Sunbury OH 43074 **Phn:** 740-965-3891 **Fax:** 740-965-3992 www.sunburynews.com snnews@sunburynews.com

Swanton Swanton Enterprise (1.9M) PO Box 180 Swanton OH 43558 **Phn:** 419-826-3580 **Fax:** 419-335-2030 fcnews.org tsenews@civitasmedia.com

Tipp City Enon Messenger (2.0M) 1455 W Main St Tipp City OH 45371 **Phn:** 937-845-3861 **Fax:** 936-845-3577 www.tcnewsnet.com jgraue@civitasmedia.com

Tipp City Vandalia Drummer News (5.0M) 1455 W Main St Tipp City OH 45371 **Phn:** 937-890-6030 **Fax:** 937-890-9153 www.tcnewsnet.com

Toledo Herald Newspapers (10.0M) PO Box 8830 Toledo OH 43623 **Phn:** 419-885-9222 **Fax:** 419-885-0764 theheraldpapers.com

Toledo Toledo Free Press (115.0M) 605 Monroe St Toledo OH 43604 **Phn:** 419-241-1700 **Fax:** 419-241-8828 www.toledofreepress.com mmiller@toledofreepress.com

Troy Record Herald (5.5M) 224 S Market St Troy OH 45373 **Phn:** 937-440-5275 www.weeklyrecordherald.com jnevins@tdnpublishing.com

Utica Utica Herald (2.3M) PO Box 515 Utica OH 43080 **Phn:** 740-892-2771 theuticaherald@aol.com

Valley View Sun Newspapers (355.0M) 5510 Cloverleaf Pkwy Valley View OH 44125 **Phn:** 216-986-2600 **Fax:** 216-986-2380 www.neohiomediagroup.com

Vermilion Vermilion Photojournal (3.0M) PO Box 23 Vermilion OH 44089 **Phn:** 440-967-5268 **Fax:** 440-967-2535 info@vermilion-news.com

Versailles Versailles Policy (2.4M) 308 N West St Versailles OH 45380 **Phn:** 937-526-9131 **Fax:** 937-526-9891 vpolicy@embarqmail.com

Wauseon Fulton County Expositor (13.0M) PO Box 376 Wauseon OH 43567 **Phn:** 419-335-2010 **Fax:** 419-335-2030 fcnews.org fcenews@civitasmedia.com

Waverly News-Watchman (4.7M) PO Box 151 Waverly OH 45690 **Phn:** 740-947-2149 **Fax:** 740-947-1344 www.pikecountydaily.com news@newswatchman.com

Wellington Wellington Enterprise (3.0M) 119 W Herrick Ave Wellington OH 44090 **Phn:** 440-647-3171 **Fax:** 440-647-3172 thewellingtonenterprise.com

West Alexandria Twin Valley Publications (8.0M) PO Box 24 West Alexandria OH 45381 **Phn:** 937-839-4733 **Fax:** 937-839-5351 onlinetvp.com twinvpub@infinet.com

West Union The Peoples Defender (7.4M) PO Box 308 West Union OH 45693 **Phn:** 937-544-2391 **Fax:** 937-544-2298 www.peoplesdefender.com info@peoplesdefender.com

West Unity Village Reporter (3.3M) PO Box 377 West Unity OH 43570 **Phn:** 419-272-2413 **Fax:** 419-924-5240 www.thevillagereporter.com publisher@thevillagereporter.com

Wheelersburg The Scioto Voice (3.6M) PO Box 400 Wheelersburg OH 45694 **Phn:** 740-574-8494 **Fax:** 740-574-2329 www.thesciotovoice.com info@thesciotovoice.com

Willard The Times-Junction (3.8M) PO Box 368 Willard OH 44890 **Phn:** 419-935-0184 **Fax:** 419-933-2031 sdgnewsgroup.com

Willshire Photo Star (11.0M) PO Box B Willshire OH 45898 **Phn:** 419-495-2696 **Fax:** 419-495-2143

Woodsfield Monroe County Beacon (5.0M) PO Box 70 Woodsfield OH 43793 **Phn:** 740-472-0734 **Fax:** 740-472-0735 www.mcbeacon.com monroecountybeacon@sbcglobal.net

Yellow Springs Yellow Springs News (1.8M) PO Box 187 Yellow Springs OH 45387 **Phn:** 937-767-7373 **Fax:** 937-767-2254 ysnews.com ysnews@ysnews.com

Youngstown Boardman News (9.0M) 8302 Southern Blvd Ste 2 Youngstown OH 44512 **Phn:** 330-758-6397 **Fax:** 330-758-2658 bnews@zoominternet.net

OKLAHOMA

Allen Allen Advocate (1.4M) PO Box 465 Allen OK 74825 **Phn:** 580-857-2687 **Fax:** 580-857-2573 allennews@aol.com

Antlers Antlers American (2.7M) PO Box 578 Antlers OK 74523 **Phn:** 580-298-3314 **Fax:** 580-298-3316 www.theantlersamerican.com ed.antlers.amer@sbcglobal.net

Apache Apache News (1.2M) PO Box 778 Apache OK 73006 **Phn:** 580-588-3862 wrightapachenews@aol.com

Arnett Denson Publishing (1.3M) PO Box 236 Arnett OK 73832 **Phn:** 580-885-7788

Atoka Atoka County Times (4.2M) PO Box 330 Atoka OK 74525 **Phn:** 580-889-3319 **Fax:** 580-889-2300 actatoka@atoka.net

Barnsdall Bigheart Times (1.8M) PO Box 469 Barnsdall OK 74002 **Phn:** 918-847-2916 **Fax:** 918-847-2654 www.barnsdalltimes.com louise@bighearttimes.com

Beaver The Herald Democrat (2.0M) PO Box 490 Beaver OK 73932 **Phn:** 580-625-3241 **Fax:** 580-625-4269

Bethany The Tribune (3.5M) PO Box 40 Bethany OK 73008 **Phn:** 405-789-1962 **Fax:** 405-789-4253

Bixby Bixby Bulletin (10.0M) 103 N Cabaniss Ave Bixby OK 74008 **Phn:** 918-366-4655 **Fax:** 918-366-4642 southcountyleader.com/bixbybulletin news@bixbybulletin.com

Blackwell Journal-Tribune (2.0M) PO Box 760 Blackwell OK 74631 **Phn:** 580-363-3370 **Fax:** 580-363-4415

Blanchard Blanchard News (3.0M) PO Box 60 Blanchard OK 73010 **Phn:** 405-485-2311 **Fax:** 405-485-2310 theblanchardnews.com blanchardnews@pldi.net

Boise City Boise City News (1.7M) PO Box 278 Boise City OK 73933 **Phn:** 580-544-2222 **Fax:** 580-544-3281 www.boisecitynews.org bcnews@ptsi.net

Bristow Bristow News (3.2M) PO Box 840 Bristow OK 74010 **Phn:** 918-367-2282 **Fax:** 918-367-2724 bristownews@sbcglobal.net

Bristow Bristow Record Citizen (3.5M) PO Box 840 Bristow OK 74010 **Phn:** 918-367-2282 **Fax:** 918-367-2724 bristownews@sbcglobal.net

Broken Arrow Neighbor Newspapers (29.0M) 524 S Main St Broken Arrow OK 74012 **Phn:** 918-259-7500 **Fax:** 918-259-7580

OKLAHOMA WEEKLY NEWSPAPERS

Buffalo Harper County Journal (1.2M) PO Box 289 Buffalo OK 73834 **Phn:** 580-735-2526 **Fax:** 580-735-2527 hcjbuffalo@yahoo.com

Cache County Times (1.4M) PO Box 3 Cache OK 73527 **Phn:** 580-357-8200 **Fax:** 580-353-6646

Canton Canton Times (1.0M) PO Box 578 Canton OK 73724 **Phn:** 580-886-2221 **Fax:** 580-886-3320 bcpub@pldi.net

Carnegie Carnegie Herald (1.6M) PO Box 129 Carnegie OK 73015 **Phn:** 580-654-1443 **Fax:** 580-654-1608 www.carnegieherald.com news@carnegieherald.com

Chandler Lincoln County News (4.1M) PO Box 248 Chandler OK 74834 **Phn:** 405-258-1818 **Fax:** 405-258-1824

Chelsea Chelsea Reporter (2.0M) PO Box 6 Chelsea OK 74016 **Phn:** 918-789-2331 **Fax:** 918-789-2333 chelsea_reporter@sbcglobal.net

Cherokee Messenger-Republican (2.5M) PO Box 245 Cherokee OK 73728 **Phn:** 580-596-3344 **Fax:** 580-596-2959

Cheyenne Cheyenne Star (1.8M) PO Box 250 Cheyenne OK 73628 **Phn:** 580-497-3324 **Fax:** 580-497-3516 www.cheyennestar.com cheystar@dobsonteleco.com

Cleveland Cleveland American (2.8M) PO Box 68 Cleveland OK 74020 **Phn:** 918-358-2553 **Fax:** 918-358-2182 www.theclevelandamerican.com clevelandnews@sbcglobal.net

Coalgate Record Register (2.4M) 602 E Lafayette Ave Coalgate OK 74538 **Phn:** 580-927-2355 **Fax:** 580-927-3800 coalgaterecordregister.com coalgaterec@aol.com

Comanche Comanche Times (1.3M) PO Box 580 Comanche OK 73529 **Phn:** 580-439-6500

Cordell Cordell Beacon (3.2M) PO Box 220 Cordell OK 73632 **Phn:** 580-832-3333 **Fax:** 580-832-3335 www.cordellbeacon.com thebeacon@cordellbeacon.com

Corn Washita County Enterprise (1.0M) PO Box 68 Corn OK 73024 **Phn:** 580-343-2513

Cushing Cushing Citizen (2.0M) 202 N Harrison Ave Cushing OK 74023 **Phn:** 918-285-5555 **Fax:** 918-285-5556 www.cushingcitizen.com editor@cushingcitizen.com

Cyril Cyril News (1.2M) PO Box 10 Cyril OK 73029 **Phn:** 580-464-2410

Davenport Davenport New Era (1.5M) PO Box 700 Davenport OK 74026 **Phn:** 918-377-2259

Davis Davis News (1.8M) PO Box 98 Davis OK 73030 **Phn:** 580-369-2807 **Fax:** 580-369-2574 davispaper@sbcglobal.net

Drumright Drumright Gusher (1.3M) 129 E Broadway St Drumright OK 74030 **Phn:** 918-352-2284 news@drumrightgusher.com

Durant Bryan County Star (0.6M) 301 W Arkansas St Durant OK 74701 **Phn:** 580-924-6499 **Fax:** 580-924-7685

Eakly Country Connection (2.0M) PO Box 206 Eakly OK 73033 **Phn:** 405-797-3648 **Fax:** 405-797-3663 connectionnews@hotmail.com

El Reno El Reno Tribune (5.0M) PO Box 9 El Reno OK 73036 **Phn:** 405-262-5180 **Fax:** 405-262-3541 www.ertribune.com rdyer@elrenotribune.com

Elgin Comanche Co. Chronicle (2.5M) PO Box 415 Elgin OK 73538 **Phn:** 580-492-6397 **Fax:** 580-492-6398 www.comanchecountychronicle.com

Eufaula Lake Eufaula Publishing (6.4M) PO Box 689 Eufaula OK 74432 **Phn:** 918-689-2191 **Fax:** 918-689-2377

Fairfax Fairfax Chief (1.7M) 153 E Elm St Fairfax OK 74637 **Phn:** 918-642-3814 **Fax:** 918-642-1376

Fairland The American (2.0M) PO Box 339 Fairland OK 74343 **Phn:** 918-676-3484 **Fax:** 918-256-7100 vdj@cableone.net

Fairview Fairview Republican (2.9M) PO Box 497 Fairview OK 73737 **Phn:** 580-227-4439 **Fax:** 580-227-4430 www.fairviewrepublican.com info@fairviewrepublican.com

Fletcher Fletcher Herald (0.8M) PO Box 469 Fletcher OK 73541 **Phn:** 580-549-6045

Frederick Frederick Leader (1.0M) 304 W Grand Ave Frederick OK 73542 **Phn:** 580-335-2188 **Fax:** 580-335-2047 www.myfrederickleader.com rwallace@civitasmedia.com

Frederick Frederick Press (2.3M) 117 N 9th St Frederick OK 73542 **Phn:** 580-335-3893 **Fax:** 580-335-5400 frederickpress.net press@pldi.net

Freedom Freedom Call (0.5M) 1166 Main St Freedom OK 73842 **Phn:** 580-621-3578 **Fax:** 580-621-3472

Garber Garber-Billings News (0.8M) PO Box 5 Garber OK 73738 **Phn:** 580-863-2240 gbnews@pldi.net

Geary Geary Star (1.4M) 114 W Main St Geary OK 73040 **Phn:** 405-884-2424 thegearystar@pldi.net

Grandfield Big Pasture News (1.2M) PO Box 508 Grandfield OK 73546 **Phn:** 580-479-5757 **Fax:** 580-479-5232

Granite Granite Enterprise (1.2M) PO Box 128 Granite OK 73547 **Phn:** 580-535-4505 **Fax:** 325-436-7076

Hartshorne Hartshorne Sun (1.8M) PO Box 330 Hartshorne OK 74547 **Phn:** 918-297-2577 hhsun@sbcglobal.net

Haskell Haskell News (2.1M) PO Box 158 Haskell OK 74436 **Phn:** 918-482-5619 hasnews@valornet.com

Healdton Herald Company (2.8M) PO Box 250 Healdton OK 73438 **Phn:** 580-229-0147 **Fax:** 580-229-0132

Heavener Heavener Ledger (4.0M) PO Box 38 Heavener OK 74937 **Phn:** 918-653-2425 **Fax:** 918-653-7305 www.smalltownpapers.com

Hennessey Hennessey Clipper (1.7M) PO Box 338 Hennessey OK 73742 **Phn:** 405-853-4888 **Fax:** 405-853-4890 barb@hennesseyclipper.com

Henryetta Henryetta Free-Lance (2.2M) PO Box 848 Henryetta OK 74437 **Phn:** 918-652-3311 **Fax:** 918-652-7347 www.myspace.com/henryettafreelance

Henryetta Tulledega Times (0.6M) 308 N 6th St Henryetta OK 74437 **Phn:** 918-652-0935

Hinton Hinton Record (0.9M) PO Box 959 Hinton OK 73047 **Phn:** 405-542-6644 **Fax:** 405-542-3120

Hobart Democrat-Chief (3.2M) PO Box 432 Hobart OK 73651 **Phn:** 580-726-3333 **Fax:** 580-726-3431 dcnews@att.net

Holdenville Holdenville News (2.0M) PO Box 751 Holdenville OK 74848 **Phn:** 405-379-5411 **Fax:** 405-379-5413 holdenvillenews@itlnet.net

Hollis Hollis News (2.0M) PO Box 709 Hollis OK 73550 **Phn:** 580-688-3376 **Fax:** 580-688-2261 hollisnews@pldi.net

Hominy Hominy News Progress (1.5M) PO Box 38 Hominy OK 74035 **Phn:** 918-885-2101 **Fax:** 918-885-4596 hominynews2@gmail.com

Hooker Hooker Advance (1.2M) PO Box 367 Hooker OK 73945 **Phn:** 580-652-2476 advance@ptsi.net

Hugo Choctaw Co. Times (2.5M) 128 E Jackson St Hugo OK 74743 **Phn:** 580-326-7511 **Fax:** 580-326-6397 editor@sbcglobal.net

Idabel McCurtain County News (1.8M) 107 S Central Ave Idabel OK 74745 **Phn:** 580-584-6210 **Fax:** 580-286-2208 paper@mccurtain.com

Idabel Southeast Times (2.4M) 110 S Central Ave Idabel OK 74745 **Phn:** 580-286-2628 **Fax:** 580-286-3818 thellis@valliant.net

Inola Inola Independent (1.6M) PO Box 999 Inola OK 74036 **Phn:** 918-543-8786

Jay Delaware County Journal (3.3M) PO Box 1050 Jay OK 74346 **Phn:** 918-253-4322 **Fax:** 918-253-4380

Kingfisher Times & Free Press (4.0M) PO Box 209 Kingfisher OK 73750 **Phn:** 405-375-3220 **Fax:** 405-375-3222 kingfisherpress.net kfrtimes@pldi.net

Konawa Konawa Leader (2.0M) PO Box 157 Konawa OK 74849 **Phn:** 580-925-3187 konawa.net konawaleader@sbcglobal.net

Laverne Laverne Leader Tribune (1.4M) PO Box 370 Laverne OK 73848 **Phn:** 580-921-3391 **Fax:** 580-921-3392

Lindsay Lindsay News (2.5M) PO Box 768 Lindsay OK 73052 **Phn:** 405-756-4461 **Fax:** 405-756-2729 www.cableprinting.com gina@cableprinting.com

Lone Grove Lone Grove Ledger (1.2M) PO Box 577 Lone Grove OK 73443 **Phn:** 580-657-6492 lgledger@cableone.net

Madill Madill Record (4.6M) PO Box 529 Madill OK 73446 **Phn:** 580-795-3355 **Fax:** 580-795-3530 madillrecord.net recordeditorial@sbcglobal.net

Mangum Mangum Star-News (2.0M) 121 S Oklahoma Ave Mangum OK 73554 **Phn:** 580-782-3321 **Fax:** 580-782-2198 mangumstarnews.net mangumstarnews@sbcglobal.net

Marietta Marietta Monitor (3.1M) PO Box 330 Marietta OK 73448 **Phn:** 580-276-3255 **Fax:** 580-276-2118 monitor@sbcglobal.net

Marlow Marlow Review (3.7M) PO Box 153 Marlow OK 73055 **Phn:** 580-658-6657 **Fax:** 580-658-6659 www.marlowreview.com mreview@cableone.net

Maysville Garvin Co News Star (2.3M) PO Box 617 Maysville OK 73057 **Phn:** 405-867-4457 **Fax:** 405-867-5115 www.gcnews-star.com news@gcnews-star.com

Medford Medford Patriot Star (1.4M) PO Box 49 Medford OK 73759 **Phn:** 580-395-2212 **Fax:** 580-395-2907

Medford Wakita Herald (1.4M) PO Box 49 Medford OK 73759 **Phn:** 580-395-2212 **Fax:** 580-395-2907

Meeker The Meeker News (1.4M) PO Box 686 Meeker OK 74855 **Phn:** 405-279-2363 **Fax:** 405-279-3850

Miami Picher Tribune (2.8M) 14 1st Ave NW Miami OK 74354 **Phn:** 918-542-5533 **Fax:** 918-542-1903 news.staff@miaminewsrecord.com

Mooreland Mooreland Leader (1.1M) PO Box 137 Mooreland OK 73852 **Phn:** 580-994-5410 **Fax:** 580-994-5409 leader@pldi.net

Morris Morris News (0.8M) PO Box 113 Morris OK 74445 **Phn:** 918-733-4898

Mountain View Mountain View News (1.2M) PO Box 488 Mountain View OK 73062 **Phn:** 580-347-2231 www.themountainviewnews.com news@westok.net

Muskogee Ft. Gibson Times (1.5M) PO Box 1968 Muskogee OK 74402 **Phn:** 918-684-2921 **Fax:** 918-684-2865

Mustang Mustang News (4.5M) PO Box 828 Mustang OK 73064 **Phn:** 405-376-4571 **Fax:** 405-376-5312 www.mustangnews.info bjones@mustangnews.info

Newcastle Newcastle Pacer (1.6M) PO Box 429 Newcastle OK 73065 **Phn:** 405-387-5277 **Fax:** 405-387-9863 www.newcastlepacer.com news@newcastlepacer.com

Newkirk Newkirk Herald Journal (1.6M) PO Box 131 Newkirk OK 74647 **Phn:** 580-362-2140 newkirkherald.com news@newkirkherald.com

Norman Moore American (8.0M) 215 E Comanche St Norman OK 73069 **Phn:** 405-321-1800 **Fax:** 405-366-3516 mooreamerican.com

Nowata Nowata Star (2.6M) PO Box 429 Nowata OK 74048 **Phn:** 918-273-2446 **Fax:** 918-273-0537 nowatastar@sbcglobal.net

Okarche Okarche Chieftain (0.6M) PO Box 468 Okarche OK 73762 **Phn:** 405-373-1616 **Fax:** 405-373-1636 okarchechieftain@sbcglobal.net

Okeene Okeene Record (1.2M) PO Box 664 Okeene OK 73763 **Phn:** 580-822-4401 **Fax:** 580-822-3051 bcpub@pldi.net

Okemah Okemah News Leader (2.9M) PO Box 191 Okemah OK 74859 **Phn:** 918-623-0123 **Fax:** 918-623-0124 okemahnewsleader.com roger@okemahnewsleader.com

Okemah Okemah News Leader (2.9M) PO Box 191 Okemah OK 74859 **Phn:** 918-623-0123 **Fax:** 918-623-0124 okemahnewsleader.com roger@okemahnewsleader.com

Oklahoma City Capitol Hill Beacon (1.3M) 124 SW 25th St Oklahoma City OK 73109 **Phn:** 405-232-4151 **Fax:** 405-235-0818 capitolhillbeacon@coxinet.net

Oklahoma City Midcity Advocate (8.0M) 718 N Broadway Ave Oklahoma City OK 73102 **Phn:** 405-605-6062

Oklahoma City Oklahoma City Friday (8.5M) PO Box 20340 Oklahoma City OK 73156 **Phn:** 405-755-3311 **Fax:** 405-755-3315 okcfriday.com roseokcfriday@aol.com

Oklahoma City Oklahoma Gazette (46.0M) PO Box 54649 Oklahoma City OK 73154 **Phn:** 405-528-6000 **Fax:** 405-528-4600 www.okgazette.com info@tierramediagroup.com

Oologah Oologah Lake Leader (2.8M) PO Box 1175 Oologah OK 74053 **Phn:** 918-443-2428 **Fax:** 918-443-2429 oologahonline.com oologahlakeleader@sbcglobal.net

Pawhuska Journal-Capitol (2.0M) PO Box 238 Pawhuska OK 74056 **Phn:** 918-287-1590 **Fax:** 918-287-1804 www.pawhuskajournalcapital.com

Pawnee Pawnee Chief (3.0M) PO Box 370 Pawnee OK 74058 **Phn:** 918-762-2552 **Fax:** 918-762-2554 news@pawneechief.net

Perkins Perkins Journal (2.7M) PO Box 667 Perkins OK 74059 **Phn:** 405-547-2411 **Fax:** 405-547-2419 www.thejournalok.com news@thejournalok.com

Piedmont Piedmont Gazette (1.1M) PO Box 146 Piedmont OK 73078 **Phn:** 405-373-1616 **Fax:** 405-373-1636 piedmontgazette@sbcglobal.net

Prague Prague Times Herald (2.5M) PO Box U Prague OK 74864 **Phn:** 405-567-3933 **Fax:** 405-567-3934 praguetimes@brightok.net

Purcell Purcell Register (4.0M) PO Box 191 Purcell OK 73080 **Phn:** 405-527-2126 **Fax:** 405-527-3299 www.purcellregister.com purcellregister@gmail.com

OKLAHOMA WEEKLY NEWSPAPERS

Ringling Ringling Eagle (1.2M) PO Box 626 Ringling OK 73456 **Phn:** 580-662-2221

Rush Springs Rush Springs Gazette (1.2M) PO Box 597 Rush Springs OK 73082 **Phn:** 580-476-2525 **Fax:** 580-476-2526 rsgazette@sbcglobal.net

Ryan Ryan Leader (1.0M) PO Box 220 Ryan OK 73565 **Phn:** 580-757-2281 curtisplant@sbcglobal.net

Sallisaw Sequoyah County Times (5.0M) 111 N Oak St Sallisaw OK 74955 **Phn:** 918-775-4433 **Fax:** 918-775-3023 www.sequoyahcountytimes.com news@seqcotimes.com

Sayre Sayre Record (2.6M) 112 E Main St Sayre OK 73662 **Phn:** 580-928-5540 **Fax:** 580-928-5547 sayrerecord@cableone.net

Seiling Dewey Co. Record (13.0M) PO Box 117 Seiling OK 73663 **Phn:** 580-922-4296 **Fax:** 580-922-7777 dcpub@pldi.net

Sentinel Sentinel Leader (1.4M) PO Box 69 Sentinel OK 73664 **Phn:** 580-393-4348 **Fax:** 580-393-4349 sleader@pldi.net

Shattuck Northwest Oklahoman (1.5M) PO Box 460 Shattuck OK 73858 **Phn:** 580-938-2533 **Fax:** 580-938-5240

Shawnee Shawnee American (0.1M) PO Box 1592 Shawnee OK 74802 **Phn:** 405-275-1000

Shawnee Shawnee County Democrat (0.2M) PO Box 367 Shawnee OK 74802 **Phn:** 405-273-8888 **Fax:** 405-275-6473 demcop@sbcglobal.net

Shidler Shidler Review (1.0M) PO Box 6 Shidler OK 74652 **Phn:** 918-793-3841 **Fax:** 918-793-3842

Snyder Kiowa County Democrat (1.8M) PO Box 305 Snyder OK 73566 **Phn:** 580-569-2684 **Fax:** 580-569-2640

Spiro Spiro Graphic (3.2M) PO Box 190 Spiro OK 74959 **Phn:** 918-962-2075 **Fax:** 918-962-3531 spirographic@sbcglobal.net

Stigler Stigler News Sentinel (4.0M) PO Box 549 Stigler OK 74462 **Phn:** 918-967-4655 **Fax:** 918-967-4289 www.stiglernews.com

Stilwell Democrat Journal (5.0M) PO Box 508 Stilwell OK 74960 **Phn:** 918-696-2228 **Fax:** 918-696-7066

Stroud Stroud American (2.1M) PO Box 400 Stroud OK 74079 **Phn:** 918-968-2581 **Fax:** 918-968-3864 stroudamerican@brightok.net

Sulphur Sulphur Times Democrat (3.9M) PO Box 131 Sulphur OK 73086 **Phn:** 580-622-2102 **Fax:** 580-622-2937 www.sulphurtimes.com jcjohn@sulphurtimes.com

Taloga Taloga Times Advocate (0.8M) PO Box 68 Taloga OK 73667 **Phn:** 580-328-5619

Tecumseh Countywide & Sun (2.0M) PO Box 38 Tecumseh OK 74873 **Phn:** 405-598-3793 **Fax:** 405-598-3891 countywidenews.com editor@countywidenews.com

Thomas Thomas Tribune (1.4M) PO Box 10 Thomas OK 73669 **Phn:** 580-661-3525 thomastribune@pldi.net

Tishomingo Capital Democrat (2.9M) PO Box 520 Tishomingo OK 73460 **Phn:** 580-371-2356 **Fax:** 580-371-9648 capital_democrat@yahoo.com

Tonkawa Tonkawa News (1.8M) PO Box 250 Tonkawa OK 74653 **Phn:** 580-628-2532 **Fax:** 580-628-4044 tonkawanews@cableone.net

Tulsa Urban Tulsa Weekly (35.0M) PO Box 50499 Tulsa OK 74150 **Phn:** 918-592-5550 **Fax:** 918-592-5970 www.urbantulsa.com urbantulsa@urbantulsa.com

Tuttle Tuttle Times (1.4M) PO Box 180 Tuttle OK 73089 **Phn:** 405-381-3173 **Fax:** 405-381-2997 www.mustangpaper.com tuttletimes@sbcglobal.net

Valliant The Valliant Leader (2.0M) PO Box 89 Valliant OK 74764 **Phn:** 580-933-4579 **Fax:** 580-933-4900 valeader@valliant.net

Vian Vian Tenkiller News (3.0M) PO Box 750 Vian OK 74962 **Phn:** 918-773-8000 **Fax:** 918-773-8745 viannews.com news@bigbasinllc.com

Walters Walters Herald (2.9M) PO Box 247 Walters OK 73572 **Phn:** 580-875-3326 **Fax:** 580-875-3150 wherald@sbcglobal.net

Watonga Watonga Republican (2.9M) PO Box 30 Watonga OK 73772 **Phn:** 580-623-4922 **Fax:** 580-623-4925 sendnews@wrnews.net

Waurika Waurika News-Democrat (1.2M) 111 E Broadway Ave Waurika OK 73573 **Phn:** 580-228-2316 **Fax:** 580-228-3647 waurikanewsdemocrat.com

Waynoka Woods County Enterprise (1.0M) 1543 Main St Waynoka OK 73860 **Phn:** 580-824-2171 **Fax:** 580-824-2172 wcepaper@pldi.net

Weleetka The Weleetkan (1.0M) PO Box 427 Weleetka OK 74880 **Phn:** 405-786-2224 **Fax:** 405-786-4343 weleetkan@sbcglobal.net

Westville Westville Reporter (2.6M) PO Box 550 Westville OK 74965 **Phn:** 918-723-5445 **Fax:** 918-723-5511

Wetumka Hughes County Times (2.4M) PO Box 38 Wetumka OK 74883 **Phn:** 405-452-3294 **Fax:** 405-452-3329 hughescountytimes@sbcglobal.net

Wewoka Wewoka Times (1.2M) PO Box 61 Wewoka OK 74884 **Phn:** 405-257-3341 **Fax:** 405-257-3342 www.wewokatimes.com events@seminoleproducer.com

Wilburton Latimer Co. News Tribune (2.4M) PO Box 10 Wilburton OK 74578 **Phn:** 918-465-2321 **Fax:** 918-465-3011 lcnt@att.net

Wilburton Tri-Co. Publications (4.0M) PO Box 606 Wilburton OK 74578 **Phn:** 918-465-3851 **Fax:** 918-465-2170

Wynnewood Wynnewood Gazette (1.7M) PO Box 309 Wynnewood OK 73098 **Phn:** 405-665-4333 **Fax:** 405-665-4334 wynnewoodgazette@sbcglobal.net

Yukon Yukon Review (7.2M) PO Box 851400 Yukon OK 73085 **Phn:** 405-354-5264 **Fax:** 405-350-3044 www.yukonreview.net conrad@yukonreview.net

OREGON

Baker City The Record-Courier (2.5M) PO Box 70 Baker City OR 97814 **Phn:** 541-523-5353 www.therconline.com news@therconline.com

Bandon Western World (3.1M) PO Box 248 Bandon OR 97411 **Phn:** 541-347-2423 **Fax:** 541-347-2424 theworldlink.com/bandon news@theworldlink.com

Bend Bend Weekly (7.0M) 61396 S Hwy 9 # 223 Bend OR 97702 **Phn:** 541-330-5886 **Fax:** 541-330-5669 bendweekly.com

Brookings Curry Coastal Pilot (6.2M) PO Box 700 Brookings OR 97415 **Phn:** 541-469-3123 **Fax:** 541-469-4679 www.currypilot.com mail@currypilot.com

Brownsville Brownsville Times (1.0M) PO Box 278 Brownsville OR 97327 **Phn:** 541-466-5311 **Fax:** 541-466-5312 thetimes089@centurytel.net

Burns Burns Times Herald (3.0M) 355 N Broadway Ave Burns OR 97720 **Phn:** 541-573-2022 **Fax:** 541-573-3915 burnstimesherald.info editor@burnstimesherald.info

OREGON WEEKLY NEWSPAPERS

Canby Canby Herald (5.1M) 241 N Grant St Canby OR 97013 **Phn:** 503-266-6831 **Fax:** 503-266-6836 www.pamplinmedia.com jbaker@canbyherald.com

Cannon Beach Cannon Beach Gazette (3.2M) PO Box 888 Cannon Beach OR 97110 **Phn:** 503-738-5561 **Fax:** 503-436-1562 www.dailyastorian.com/your_town/cannon_beach pwebb@dailyastorian.com

Cave Junction Illinois Valley News (3.5M) PO Box 1370 Cave Junction OR 97523 **Phn:** 541-592-2541 **Fax:** 541-592-4330 www.illinois-valley-news.com dan@illinois-valley-news.com

Clatskanie The Clatskanie Chief (2.3M) PO Box 8 Clatskanie OR 97016 **Phn:** 503-728-3350 www.clatskaniechiefnews.com chief@clatskanie.com

Condon The Times-Journal (1.5M) PO Box 746 Condon OR 97823 **Phn:** 541-384-2421 **Fax:** 541-384-2411 www.smalltownpapers.com times-journal@jncable.com

Coquille The Sentinel (2.3M) PO Box 400 Coquille OR 97423 **Phn:** 541-396-3191 **Fax:** 541-396-3624 coquillevalleysentinel@yahoo.com

Cottage Grove Cottage Grove Sentinel (5.1M) PO Box 35 Cottage Grove OR 97424 **Phn:** 541-942-3325 **Fax:** 541-942-3328 www.cgsentinel.com cgnews@cgsentinel.com

Creswell Creswell Chronicle (1.1M) PO Box 428 Creswell OR 97426 **Phn:** 541-895-2197 **Fax:** 541-895-2361 www.thecreswellchronicle.com info@thecreswellchronicle.com

Dallas Polk Co. Itemizer Observer (6.8M) PO Box 108 Dallas OR 97338 **Phn:** 503-623-2373 **Fax:** 503-623-2395 www.polkio.com ionews@eaglenewspapers.com

Drain Drain Enterprise (1.3M) PO Box 26 Drain OR 97435 **Phn:** 541-836-2241 **Fax:** 541-836-2243 www.orenews.com drainenterprise@earthlink.net

Eagle Point Upper Rogue Independent (2.0M) PO Box 900 Eagle Point OR 97524 **Phn:** 541-826-7700 **Fax:** 541-826-1340

Enterprise Wallowa County Chieftain (4.2M) PO Box 338 Enterprise OR 97828 **Phn:** 541-426-4567 **Fax:** 541-426-3921 wallowa.com editor@wallowa.com

Estacada Estacada News (2.0M) PO Box 549 Estacada OR 97023 **Phn:** 503-630-3241 **Fax:** 503-630-5840 www.pamplinmedia.com editor@estacadanews.com

Eugene Eugene Weekly (40.0M) 1251 Lincoln St Eugene OR 97401 **Phn:** 541-484-0519 **Fax:** 541-484-4044 www.eugeneweekly.com

Florence Siuslaw News (6.4M) PO Box 10 Florence OR 97439 **Phn:** 541-997-3441 **Fax:** 541-997-7979 www.thesiuslawnews.com pressreleases@thesiuslawnews.com

Forest Grove Forest Grove News-Times (6.0M) PO Box 408 Forest Grove OR 97116 **Phn:** 503-357-3181 **Fax:** 503-359-8456 www.pamplinmedia.com news@fgnewstimes.com

Gold Beach Curry County Reporter (2.8M) PO Box 766 Gold Beach OR 97444 **Phn:** 541-247-6643 **Fax:** 541-247-6644 www.currycountyreporter.com currycountyreporter@gmail.com

Gresham Gresham Outlook (10.0M) PO Box 747 Gresham OR 97030 **Phn:** 503-665-2181 **Fax:** 503-665-2187 www.pamplinmedia.com todell@theoutlookonline.com

Halfway Hells Canyon Journal (1.2M) PO Box 646 Halfway OR 97834 **Phn:** 541-742-7900 **Fax:** 541-742-7933

Heppner Heppner Gazette-Times (2.0M) PO Box 337 Heppner OR 97836 **Phn:** 541-676-9228 **Fax:** 541-676-9211 www.heppner.net/Gazette editor@rapidserve.net

Hermiston Hermiston Herald (3.1M) 333 E Main St Hermiston OR 97838 **Phn:** 800-522-0255 **Fax:** 541-567-1764 www.hermistonherald.com editor@hermistonherald.com

Hillsboro Courier-Mail (20.0M) PO Box 588 Hillsboro OR 97123 **Phn:** 503-648-1131 **Fax:** 503-648-9191

Hillsboro Forest Grove Leader (16.5M) 150 SE 3rd Ave Hillsboro OR 97123 **Phn:** 503-648-1131 **Fax:** 503-294-4191 mbutler@hillsboroargus.com

Hillsboro Hillsboro Argus (4.5M) 150 SE 3rd Ave Hillsboro OR 97123 **Phn:** 503-648-1131 **Fax:** 503-294-4191 www.oregonlive.com/argus news@hillsboroargus.com

Hood River Hood River News (5.8M) PO Box 390 Hood River OR 97031 **Phn:** 541-386-1234 **Fax:** 541-386-6796 www.hoodrivernews.com kneumann-rea@hoodrivernews.com

Jefferson Jefferson Review (0.9M) PO Box 330 Jefferson OR 97352 **Phn:** 541-327-1776 **Fax:** 541-327-2241 www.jeffersonreview.net

John Day Blue Mountain Eagle (3.0M) 195 N Canyon Blvd John Day OR 97845 **Phn:** 541-575-0710 **Fax:** 541-575-1244 www.bluemountaineagle.com editor@bluemountaineagle.com

Junction City Tri-County News (2.5M) PO Box 340 Junction City OR 97448 **Phn:** 541-998-3877 **Fax:** 541-998-3878

Keizer Keizertimes (3.0M) 142 Chemawa Rd N Keizer OR 97303 **Phn:** 503-390-1051 **Fax:** 503-390-8023 keizertimes.com kt@keizertimes.com

Lake Oswego Lake Oswego Review (8.0M) PO Box 548 Lake Oswego OR 97034 **Phn:** 503-635-8811 **Fax:** 503-635-8817 www.pamplinmedia.com mforbes@lakeoswegoreview.com

Lake Oswego West Linn Tidings (4.0M) PO Box 548 Lake Oswego OR 97034 **Phn:** 503-635-8811 **Fax:** 503-635-8817 www.lakeoswegoreview.com email@commnewspapers.com

Lake Oswego Wilsonville Spokesman (3.4M) 400 2nd St Lake Oswego OR 97034 **Phn:** 503-635-8811 pamplinmedia.com lhall@wilsonvillespokesman.com

Lakeview Lake County Examiner (2.6M) 739 N 2nd St Lakeview OR 97630 **Phn:** 541-947-3378 **Fax:** 541-947-4359 www.lakecountyexam.com news@lakecountyexam.com

Lebanon Lebanon Express (3.0M) 90 E Grant St Lebanon OR 97355 **Phn:** 541-258-3151 **Fax:** 541-259-3569 www.lebanon-express.com lebanon.express@lee.net

Lincoln City The News Guard (6.2M) PO Box 848 Lincoln City OR 97367 **Phn:** 541-994-2178 **Fax:** 541-994-7613 thenewsguard.com info@thenewsguard.com

Madras Madras Pioneer (4.0M) 345 SE 5th St Madras OR 97741 **Phn:** 541-475-2275 **Fax:** 541-475-3710 pamplinmedia.com smatheny@madraspioneer.com

Manzanita North Coast Citizen (1.3M) PO Box 355 Manzanita OR 97130 **Phn:** 503-368-6397 **Fax:** 503-368-7400 northcoastcitizen.com dfisher@northcoastcitizen.com

McKenzie Bridge McKenzie River Reflections (1.0M) 59059 Old McKenzie Hwy McKenzie Bridge OR 97413 **Phn:** 541-822-3358 **Fax:** 541-663-4550 mckenzieriverreflectionsnewspaper.com rivref@aol.com

McMinnville News Register (10.5M) PO Box 727 McMinnville OR 97128 **Phn:** 503-472-5114 **Fax:** 503-472-9151 www.newsregister.com sbagwell@newsregister.com

Mill City Independent Press (1.2M) PO Box 108 Mill City OR 97360 **Phn:** 503-897-4216 **Fax:** 503-897-2428 mcipnews@aol.com

Milton Freewater Valley Herald (12.0M) PO Box 664 Milton Freewater OR 97862 **Phn:** 541-938-6688 **Fax:** 541-938-6689

Molalla Molalla Pioneer (3.3M) 217 E Main St Molalla OR 97038 **Phn:** 503-829-2301 **Fax:** 503-829-2317 www.pamplinmedia.com psavage@molallapioneer.com

Myrtle Creek Douglas County Mail (2.2M) PO Box 729 Myrtle Creek OR 97457 **Phn:** 541-863-5233 **Fax:** 541-863-5234

Myrtle Point Myrtle Point Herald (2.1M) PO Box 606 Myrtle Point OR 97458 **Phn:** 541-572-2717 **Fax:** 541-572-2828 www.orenews.com myrtlepointherald@gmail.com

Newberg Newberg Graphic (5.5M) 500 E Hancock St Newberg OR 97132 **Phn:** 503-538-2181 **Fax:** 503-538-1632 www.pamplinmedia.com gallen@newberggraphic.com

Newport News-Times (11.0M) PO Box 965 Newport OR 97365 **Phn:** 541-265-8571 **Fax:** 541-265-3103 www.newportnewstimes.com editor@newportnewstimes.com

Oakridge Dead Mountain Echo (0.8M) PO Box 900 Oakridge OR 97463 **Phn:** 541-782-4241 **Fax:** 541-782-3323 lroberts@efn.org

Pendleton Pendleton Record (1.0M) PO Box 69 Pendleton OR 97801 **Phn:** 541-276-2853 **Fax:** 541-278-2916 www.smalltownpapers.com penrecor@uci.net

Port Orford Port Orford News (1.2M) PO Box 5 Port Orford OR 97465 **Phn:** 541-332-2361 **Fax:** 541-332-8101 www.portorfordnews.net portorfordnews@gmail.com

Portland Pamplin Media (65.0M) PO Box 22109 Portland OR 97269 **Phn:** 503-684-0360 **Fax:** 503-620-3433 www.pamplinmedia.com clent@commnewspapers.com

Portland Portland Mercury (40.0M) 115 SW Ash St Ste 600 Portland OR 97204 **Phn:** 503-294-0840 **Fax:** 503-294-0844 www.portlandmercury.com news@portlandmercury.com

Portland Portland Tribune (40.0M) PO Box 22109 Portland OR 97269 **Phn:** 503-226-6397 **Fax:** 503-546-0727 www.portlandtribune.com mgarber@theoutlookonline.com

Portland Willamette Week (90.0M) 2220 NW Quimby St Portland OR 97210 **Phn:** 503-243-2122 **Fax:** 503-243-1115 wweek.com web@wweek.com

Prineville Central Oregonian (4.2M) 558 N Main St Prineville OR 97754 **Phn:** 541-447-6205 **Fax:** 541-447-1754 pamplinmedia.com news@centraloregonian.com

Redmond Redmond Spokesman (4.7M) PO Box 788 Redmond OR 97756 **Phn:** 541-548-2184 **Fax:** 541-548-3203 www.redmondspokesmanonline.com news@redmondspokesman.com

Reedsport Umpqua Post (2.0M) PO Box 145 Reedsport OR 97467 **Phn:** 541-271-7474 **Fax:** 541-271-2821 theworldlink.com/reedsport les.bowen@theworldlink.com

Rogue River Rogue River Press (2.0M) PO Box 1485 Rogue River OR 97537 **Phn:** 541-582-1707 **Fax:** 541-582-1201 www.rogueriverpress.com rrpress@rogueriverpress.com

Saint Helens St. Helens Chronicle (5.1M) PO Box 1153 Saint Helens OR 97051 **Phn:** 503-397-0116 **Fax:** 503-397-4093 news@thechronicleonline.com

Sandy Sandy Post (3.0M) PO Box 68 Sandy OR 97055 **Phn:** 503-668-5548 **Fax:** 503-668-0748 www.pamplinmedia.com editor@sandypost.com

Scappoose The South County Spotlight (4.5M) 33548 Edward Ln Ste 110 Scappoose OR 97056 **Phn:** 503-543-6387 **Fax:** 503-543-6380 www.pamplinmedia.com news@spotlightnews.net

Seaside Seaside Signal (3.6M) PO Box 848 Seaside OR 97138 **Phn:** 503-738-5561 **Fax:** 503-738-9285 www.dailyastorian.com pwebb@dailyastorian.com

Sheridan Sheridan Sun (2.6M) PO Box 68 Sheridan OR 97378 **Phn:** 503-843-2312 **Fax:** 503-843-3830 www.smalltownpapers.com news@sheridansun.com

Silverton Appeal-Tribune (8.2M) PO Box 35 Silverton OR 97381 **Phn:** 503-873-8385 **Fax:** 503-873-8064 www.statesmanjournal.com/section/silverton online@statesmanjournal.com

Sisters The Nugget (7.5M) PO Box 698 Sisters OR 97759 **Phn:** 541-549-9941 www.nuggetnews.com editor@nuggetnews.com

Stayton Stayton Mail (10.0M) PO Box 400 Stayton OR 97383 **Phn:** 503-769-6338 **Fax:** 503-769-6207 www.statesmanjournal.com/section/stayton smnews@salem.gannett.com

Sweet Home The New Era (7.5M) PO Box 39 Sweet Home OR 97386 **Phn:** 541-367-2135 **Fax:** 541-367-2137 sweethomenews.com news@sweethomenews.com

Tillamook Headlight Herald (7.5M) PO Box 444 Tillamook OR 97141 **Phn:** 503-842-7535 **Fax:** 503-842-8842 tillamookheadlightherald.com mfbell@countrymedia.net

Vale Malheur Enterprise (1.8M) PO Box 310 Vale OR 97918 **Phn:** 541-473-3377 **Fax:** 541-473-3268

Veneta West Lane News (2.0M) PO Box 188 Veneta OR 97487 **Phn:** 541-935-1882

Waldport South Lincoln County News (4.4M) 215 SW Highway 101 Waldport OR 97394 **Phn:** 541-563-6397 **Fax:** 541-563-6597 www.southlincolncountynews.com publisher@newsportnewstimes.com

Warrenton Columbia Press (1.5M) PO Box 130 Warrenton OR 97146 **Phn:** 503-861-3331 www.thecolumbiapress.com editor@thecolumbiapress.com

Woodburn Woodburn Independent (4.2M) 650 N 1st St Woodburn OR 97071 **Phn:** 503-981-3441 **Fax:** 503-981-1253 www.pamplinmedia.com lkeefer@woodburnindependent.com

PENNSYLVANIA

Albion Albion News (4.0M) PO Box 7 Albion PA 16401 **Phn:** 814-756-4133 **Fax:** 814-756-5643 news@albionnews.com

Allentown Lehigh Valley News Group (54.0M) 951 Marcon Blvd Ste 4 Allentown PA 18109 **Phn:** 610-266-7720 **Fax:** 610-266-7715

Allentown The Press (23.0M) 1633 N 26th St Ste 6 Allentown PA 18104 **Phn:** 610-740-0944 **Fax:** 610-740-0947 www.lehighvalleypress.com pwillistein@tnonline.com

Ardmore King of Prussia Courier (6.6M) 311 E Lancaster Ave Ardmore PA 19003 **Phn:** 610-642-4300 **Fax:** 610-964-1346 www.mainlinemedianews.com sgreenspon@mainlinemedianews.com

Ardmore Main Line Newspapers (46.0M) PO Box 70 Ardmore PA 19003 **Phn:** 610-642-4300 **Fax:** 610-642-9704 mainlinemedianews.com sgreenspon@mainlinemedianews.com

Ashland Schuylkill Saturday (4.5M) 533 Centre St Ashland PA 17921 **Phn:** 570-875-6397 **Fax:** 570-875-4386

Aspinwall The Herald (4.5M) 101 Emerson Ave Ste 13 Aspinwall PA 15215 **Phn:** 412-782-2121 **Fax:** 412-782-1195 triblive.com tmcgee@tribweb.com

Bala Cynwyd City Suburban News (17.0M) PO Box 17 Bala Cynwyd PA 19004 **Phn:** 610-667-6623 **Fax:** 610-667-6624 www.issuu.com/citysuburbannews citysuburbannews@mac.com

Barnesboro Star Courier (5.8M) PO Box 1158 Barnesboro PA 15714 **Phn:** 814-948-6210 **Fax:** 814-948-7563

Bath The Home News (3.5M) PO Box 39 Bath PA 18014 **Phn:** 610-923-0382 **Fax:** 610-923-0383 www.homenewspa.com info@homenewspa.com

Bedford Bedford Inquirer (0.7M) PO Box 671 Bedford PA 15522 **Phn:** 814-623-1151 **Fax:** 814-623-5055 www.bedfordgazette.com gazetteeditor@embarqmail.com

Bethlehem Bethlehem Press (10.0M) 308 E 3rd St Frnt Bethlehem PA 18015 **Phn:** 610-625-2121 **Fax:** 610-625-2126 bethlehem.thelehighvalleypress.com pwillistein@tnonline.com

Blairsville Blairsville Dispatch (19.0M) 116 E Market St Blairsville PA 15717 **Phn:** 724-459-6100 **Fax:** 724-459-7366 triblive.com/news/indiana jhimler@tribweb.com

Bradford Bradford Journal (5.5M) PO Box 17 Bradford PA 16701 **Phn:** 814-362-6563 bradfordjournal.com bradfordjournal@atlanticbb.net

Bristol Bristol Pilot (5.0M) PO Box 232 Bristol PA 19007 **Phn:** 215-788-1682 **Fax:** 215-788-6328 www.buckslocalnews.com pilot@ingnews.com

Brookville Jeffersonian Democrat (4.5M) PO Box 498 Brookville PA 15825 **Phn:** 814-849-5339 **Fax:** 814-849-4333 www.thecourierexpress.com jeffdem@windstream.net

Butler Eagle (10.0M) PO Box 271 Butler PA 16003 **Phn:** 724-794-6797 **Fax:** 724-794-5694

Canton Indep. Sentinel/Troy Gazette Register (2.7M) PO Box 128 Canton PA 17724 **Phn:** 570-673-5151 **Fax:** 570-673-5152 cisnews@frontiernet.net

Carbondale Carbondale News (6.5M) 41 N Church St Carbondale PA 18407 **Phn:** 570-282-3300 **Fax:** 570-282-3950

Clarion The Clarion News (6.0M) PO Box 647 Clarion PA 16214 **Phn:** 814-226-7000 **Fax:** 814-226-4088 www.theclarionnews.com rsherman.theclarionnews@gmail.com

Clarks Summit Abington Journal (3.5M) 211 S State St Clarks Summit PA 18411 **Phn:** 570-587-1148

Claysville Weekly Recorder (3.4M) PO Box F Claysville PA 15323 **Phn:** 724-350-0127 **Fax:** 724-663-3698 www.weekly-recorder.com recorder@pulsenet.com

Conshohocken Conshohocken Recorder (3.5M) 700 Fayette St Conshohocken PA 19428 **Phn:** 610-828-4600

Coudersport Tioga Publishing (7.0M) PO Box 29 Coudersport PA 16915 **Phn:** 814-274-8044 **Fax:** 814-274-8120 www.potterleaderenterprise.com donaldgilliland@yahoo.com

Cranberry Twp Eagle Printing (20.0M) 83 Dutilh Rd Cranberry Twp PA 16066 **Phn:** 724-776-4270 **Fax:** 724-776-0211

Delta Delta Star (4.8M) PO Box 47 Delta PA 17314 **Phn:** 717-456-5692

Dillsburg Dillsburg Banner (3.9M) 31 S Baltimore St Dillsburg PA 17019 **Phn:** 717-432-3456 **Fax:** 717-432-1518 www.dillsburgbanner.net dillsburgbanner@dillsburgbanner.net

Doylestown Doylestown Patriot (4.0M) PO Box 2103 Doylestown PA 18901 **Phn:** 215-340-9811 **Fax:** 215-340-1306 www.buckslocalnews.com advance@buckslocalnews.com

Drexel Hill Press Publishing (17.0M) 3245 Garrett Rd Drexel Hill PA 19026 **Phn:** 610-259-4141

Dushore Sullivan Review (7.0M) PO Box 305 Dushore PA 18614 **Phn:** 570-928-8403 **Fax:** 570-928-8006 sully@epix.net

Ebensburg MainLine Newspapers (16.0M) PO Box 777 Ebensburg PA 15931 **Phn:** 814-472-4110 **Fax:** 814-472-2275 www.MainLineNewspapers.com mainlinenews@verizon.net

Ellwood City Valley Tribune (21.0M) PO Box 471 Ellwood City PA 16117 **Phn:** 724-758-5573 **Fax:** 724-758-2410

Emlenton Progress News (15.0M) PO Box A Emlenton PA 16373 **Phn:** 724-867-1112 **Fax:** 724-867-1356

Emporium Cameron County Echo (3.5M) PO Box 308 Emporium PA 15834 **Phn:** 814-486-3711 **Fax:** 814-486-0990

Ephrata Ephrata Review (9.0M) PO Box 527 Ephrata PA 17522 **Phn:** 717-733-6397 **Fax:** 717-733-6058 ephratareview.com afasnacht.eph@lnpnews.com

Exton Suburban Advertiser (16.0M) 575 Exton Cmns Exton PA 19341 **Phn:** 610-363-2815

Forest City Forest City News (3.0M) 636 Main St Forest City PA 18421 **Phn:** 570-785-3800 **Fax:** 570-785-9840 www.forestcitynews.com fcnews@nep.net

Fort Washington Montgomery Newspapers (88.0M) 290 Commerce Dr Fort Washington PA 19034 **Phn:** 215-542-0200 **Fax:** 215-643-9475 www.montgomerynews.com bwilson@journalregister.com

Greencastle Greencastle Echo Pilot (3.0M) PO Box 159 Greencastle PA 17225 **Phn:** 717-597-2164 **Fax:** 717-597-3754

Grove City Allied News (5.0M) PO Box 190 Grove City PA 16127 **Phn:** 724-458-5010 **Fax:** 724-458-1609 alliednews.com alliednewspaper@gmail.com

Hamburg Hamburg Item (3.2M) 12 S 4th St Hamburg PA 19526 **Phn:** 610-562-7515 **Fax:** 610-562-4644 www.berksmontnews.com ssingley@berksmontnews.com

Hamburg Kutztown Patriot (4.0M) 12 S 4th St Hamburg PA 19526 **Phn:** 610-683-7343 **Fax:** 610-562-4644 www.berksmontnews.com lmitchell@berksmontnews.com

Harrisburg Paxton Herald (15.0M) 101 Lincoln St Harrisburg PA 17112 **Phn:** 717-545-9540 **Fax:** 717-657-3523 www.thepaxtonherald.com

Hawley The News-Eagle (2.9M) 8 Silk Milk Dr Ste 101 Hawley PA 18428 **Phn:** 570-226-4547 **Fax:** 570-226-4548 www.neagle.com advertising@neagle.com

Hellertown The Valley Voice (4.0M) PO Box 147 Hellertown PA 18055 **Phn:** 610-838-2066 **Fax:** 610-838-2239 valleyvoice@verizon.net

Holmes Town Talk News (84.0M) 1914 Parker Ave Holmes PA 19043 **Phn:** 610-583-4432 **Fax:** 610-583-0503 www.towntalknews.com cparker@delconewsnetwork.com

Hughesville The Luminary (2.0M) PO Box 266 Hughesville PA 17737 **Phn:** 570-584-0111 **Fax:** 570-584-5399 www.muncyluminary.com news@muncyluminary.com

Hummelstown The Sun-News (6.0M) 40 W Main St Ste 102 Hummelstown PA 17036 **Phn:** 717-566-3251 **Fax:** 717-566-6196 news.thesunontheweb.com news@thesunontheweb.com

PENNSYLVANIA WEEKLY NEWSPAPERS

Hunlock Creek The Suburban News (10.0M) 5724 Main Rd Hunlock Creek PA 18621 **Phn:** 570-477-5000 **Fax:** 570-477-3000

Johnsonburg Johnsonburg Press (2.0M) 517 Market St Johnsonburg PA 15845 **Phn:** 814-965-2503 **Fax:** 814-965-2504

Kelton Chester County Press (15.0M) PO Box 150 Kelton PA 19346 **Phn:** 610-869-5553 **Fax:** 610-869-9628 www.chestercounty.com shoffman@chestercounty.com

Kennett Square Hershey Chronicle (4.0M) 112 E State St Kennett Square PA 19348 **Phn:** 717-533-2900 **Fax:** 717-531-2561

Kennett Square The Kennett Paper (5.0M) 112 E State St Kennett Square PA 19348 **Phn:** 610-444-6590 **Fax:** 610-444-4931 www.kennettpaper.com kennettpaper@gmail.com

Lahaska Bucks County Herald (25.0M) PO Box 685 Lahaska PA 18931 **Phn:** 215-794-1096 **Fax:** 215-794-1109 buckscountyherald.com bridget@buckscountyherald.com

Lancaster Sunday News (99.0M) PO Box 1328 Lancaster PA 17608 **Phn:** 717-291-8788 **Fax:** 717-291-4950 lancasteronline.com sunnews@lnpnews.com

Lansdale Courier News Weekly (60.0M) 616 S Broad St Lansdale PA 19446 **Phn:** 267-663-6300 **Fax:** 267-663-6303 www.buxmontmedia.com editorial@buxmontmedia.com

Lititz Lititz Record Express (8.0M) PO Box 366 Lititz PA 17543 **Phn:** 717-626-2191 **Fax:** 717-626-1210 lititzrecord.com sseeber.eph@lnpnews.com

Martinsburg Morrisons Cove Herald (6.5M) PO Box 165 Martinsburg PA 16662 **Phn:** 814-793-2144 **Fax:** 814-793-4882

Mc Connellsburg Fulton County News (6.1M) PO Box 635 Mc Connellsburg PA 17233 **Phn:** 717-485-4513 **Fax:** 717-485-5187 www.fultoncountynews.com fultoncountynews@comcast.net

Mc Kees Rocks Suburban Gazette (8.3M) 421 Locust St Mc Kees Rocks PA 15136 **Phn:** 412-331-2645

Mc Murray The Almanac (58.0M) 395 Valleybrook Rd # 2 Mc Murray PA 15317 **Phn:** 724-941-7725 **Fax:** 724-941-8685 www.thealmanac.net pvhorn@thealmanac.net

Mercersburg Mercersburg Journal (8.4M) PO Box 239 Mercersburg PA 17236 **Phn:** 717-328-3223 mj2@cvn.net

Meyersdale The New Republic (5.0M) PO Box 239 Meyersdale PA 15552 **Phn:** 814-634-8321 **Fax:** 814-634-5556

Middleburg Snyder County Times (15.8M) PO Box 356 Middleburg PA 17842 **Phn:** 570-837-6065 **Fax:** 570-837-0776 www.thesnydercountytimes.com scuc@ptd.net

Middletown Press & Journal (8.4M) 20 S Union St Middletown PA 17057 **Phn:** 717-944-4628 **Fax:** 717-944-2083 www.pressandjournal.com info@pressandjournal.com

Mifflinburg Mifflinburg Telegraph (0.8M) PO Box 189 Mifflinburg PA 17844 **Phn:** 570-966-2255 **Fax:** 570-966-0062 mifflinburgtelegraph.com heidi@mifflinburgtelegraph.com

Mifflintown Juniata Sentinel (5.8M) PO Box 127 Mifflintown PA 17059 **Phn:** 717-436-8206 **Fax:** 717-436-5174 csmith@juniata-sentinel.com

Milford Pike County Dispatch (6.5M) PO Box 186 Milford PA 18337 **Phn:** 570-296-6641 **Fax:** 570-296-2610 suedl@ptd.net

Milford Tri-State Observer (5.0M) 113 7th St # 99 Milford PA 18337 **Phn:** 570-828-1212

Millersburg Upper Dauphin Sentinel (9.2M) PO Box 250 Millersburg PA 17061 **Phn:** 717-692-4737 **Fax:** 717-692-2420 www.Sentinelnow.com news@sentinelnow.com

Montrose The Independent (3.7M) 466 S Main St Montrose PA 18801 **Phn:** 570-278-6397 **Fax:** 570-278-4305 www.independentweekender.com indynews@independentweekender.com

Morgantown Tri County Record (21.5M) 150 Morview Blvd # 201 Morgantown PA 19543 **Phn:** 610-286-0162 **Fax:** 610-286-6358 www.tricountyrecord.com editor@tricountyrecord.com

Moscow The Villager (5.0M) RR 6 Box 6321 Moscow PA 18444 **Phn:** 570-842-8789 **Fax:** 570-842-9841

Mount Pleasant Mount Pleasant Journal (6.0M) 23 S Church St Mount Pleasant PA 15666 **Phn:** 724-547-5722 **Fax:** 724-542-4923

Mountain Top Mountain Top Eagle (1.8M) PO Box 10 Mountain Top PA 18707 **Phn:** 570-474-6397 **Fax:** 570-474-9272 www.mteagle.com

Munhall Valley Mirror (5.2M) 3910 Main St Munhall PA 15120 **Phn:** 412-462-0626 **Fax:** 412-462-1847 valleymirror@comcast.net

Murrysville Penn Franklin News (3.0M) PO Box 73 Murrysville PA 15668 **Phn:** 724-327-3471 **Fax:** 724-325-4591 www.penn-franklin.com news@penn-franklin.com

New Bethlehem The Leader Vindicator (4.8M) PO Box 158 New Bethlehem PA 16242 **Phn:** 814-275-3131 **Fax:** 814-275-3531 www.thecourierexpress.com jwalzak@thecourierexpress.com

New Bloomfield Advance Publications (10.0M) PO Box 130 New Bloomfield PA 17068 **Phn:** 717-582-4305 **Fax:** 717-582-7933 www.pennlive.com/perry-county-times editor@perrycountytimes.com

New Wilmington The Globe Leader (2.0M) PO Box 257 New Wilmington PA 16142 **Phn:** 724-946-8098 **Fax:** 724-946-2097 www.globe-leader.com globepaper@aol.com

Newtown Advance of Bucks Co (6.0M) PO Box 910 Newtown PA 18940 **Phn:** 215-968-2244 **Fax:** 215-968-3501 www.buckslocalnews.com advance@ingnews.com

Newtown Progress Newspapers (57.0M) PO Box 1695 Newtown PA 18940 **Phn:** 215-675-8250

Northern Cambria Star-Courier (4.1M) PO Box 1158 Northern Cambria PA 15714 **Phn:** 814-948-6210 **Fax:** 814-948-7563 hwww.mainlinenewspapers.com mainlinenews@verizon.net

Orbisonia Valley Log (2.4M) PO Box 219 Orbisonia PA 17243 **Phn:** 814-447-5506 **Fax:** 814-447-3050

Oxford The Oxford Tribune (3.0M) 10 S 3rd St Ste 2 Oxford PA 19363 **Phn:** 610-932-8530 **Fax:** 610-932-2808

Philadelphia Acme Newspapers (34.0M) PO Box 18971 Philadelphia PA 19119 **Phn:** 215-848-8792

Philadelphia Chestnut Hill Local (7.7M) 8434 Germantown Ave Philadelphia PA 19118 **Phn:** 215-248-8800 **Fax:** 215-248-8814 chestnuthilllocal.com/blog pete@chestnuthilllocal.com

Philadelphia City Paper (75.0M) 123 Chestnut St Fl 3 Philadelphia PA 19106 **Phn:** 215-735-8444 **Fax:** 215-735-8535 www.citypaper.net editorial@citypaper.net

Philadelphia Juniata News (10.0M) PO Box 15336 Philadelphia PA 19111 **Phn:** 215-435-3909 **Fax:** 215-739-9290 juniatapress@comcast.net

Philadelphia Olney Times (22.0M) 6001 N 5th St Philadelphia PA 19120 **Phn:** 215-424-0700

Philadelphia The Leader (26.0M) 2385 W Cheltenham Ave Ste 182 Philadelphia PA 19150 **Phn:** 215-885-4111 **Fax:** 215-885-0226

Philadelphia The Review (20.0M) 6220 Ridge Ave Philadelphia PA 19128 **Phn:** 215-483-7300 **Fax:** 215-483-2073 www.montgomerynews.com/roxborough_review review@ingnews.com

Philadelphia The Weekly (128.0M) 1500 Sansom St Ste 300 Philadelphia PA 19102 **Phn:** 215-563-7400 **Fax:** 215-563-0620 www.philadelphiaweekly.com aince@philadelphiaweekly.com

Philadelphia Westside Weekly (15.0M) PO Box 19437 Philadelphia PA 19143 **Phn:** 215-474-7411 **Fax:** 215-474-9378 westsidepa.com westsidepa@aol.com

Pittsburgh Gateway Newspapers (51.0M) 460 Rodi Rd Pittsburgh PA 15235 **Phn:** 412-856-7400 **Fax:** 412-856-7954 triblive.com kpalmiero@tribweb.com

Pittsburgh Gateway Press-West (32.0M) 1964 Greentree Rd Pittsburgh PA 15220 **Phn:** 412-388-5800 **Fax:** 412-388-0900 www.gatewaynewspapers.com kpalmiero@tribweb.com

Pittsburgh Pittsburgh City Paper (70.0M) 650 Smithfield St Ste 2200 Pittsburgh PA 15222 **Phn:** 412-316-3342 **Fax:** 412-316-3388 www.pghcitypaper.com cdeitch@pghcitypaper.com

Pittsburgh South Pittsburgh Reporter (10.0M) PO Box 4285 Pittsburgh PA 15203 **Phn:** 412-481-0266 **Fax:** 412-488-8011 sopghreporter.com news@sopghreporter.com

Pittston Sunday Dispatch (14.0M) 109 New St Pittston PA 18640 **Phn:** 570-655-1418 **Fax:** 570-602-0183

Port Royal The Times (4.0M) PO Box 419 Port Royal PA 17082 **Phn:** 717-527-2213 **Fax:** 717-527-2787 www.timesnewspaper.com thetimes@nmax.net

Pottstown Boyertown Area Times (5.0M) 24 N Hanover St Pottstown PA 19464 **Phn:** 610-970-3218 **Fax:** 610-369-0233 www.berksmontnews.com rblanchard@berksmontnews.com

Pottstown The Southern Berks News (5.5M) 24 N Hanover St Pottstown PA 19464 **Phn:** 610-367-6041 **Fax:** 610-369-0233 www.berksmontnews.com ethiel@berksmontnews.com

Punxsutawney Jefferson Neighbors (7.5M) PO Box 444 Punxsutawney PA 15767 **Phn:** 814-938-8740 **Fax:** 814-938-3794 zlantz@punxsutawneyspirit.com

Red Hill Hearthstone Town & Country (4.8M) PO Box 462 Red Hill PA 18076 **Phn:** 215-679-5060 **Fax:** 215-679-5077 www.upvnews.com hearthnews@netcarrier.com

Reedsville The County Observer (5.2M) PO Box 575 Reedsville PA 17084 **Phn:** 717-667-1113 **Fax:** 717-667-1115 editor@countyo.com

Renovo The Record (2.7M) 12423 Renovo Rd Renovo PA 17764 **Phn:** 570-923-1500 **Fax:** 570-923-1572 www.recordclct.com clintoncountyrecord@comcast.net

Robesonia West Berks Crier (2.0M) 130 E Ruth Ave Robesonia PA 19551 **Phn:** 610-693-8471

Saxton Broad Top Bulletin (3.3M) PO Box 188 Saxton PA 16678 **Phn:** 814-635-2851

Schuylkill Haven South Schuykill News (3.8M) PO Box 178 Schuylkill Haven PA 17972 **Phn:** 570-385-3120 **Fax:** 570-385-0725

Scottdale Laurel Group (22.0M) 228 Pittsburgh St Scottdale PA 15683 **Phn:** 724-887-7400 **Fax:** 724-887-5115

Scranton The Arlington Suburban (8.0M) 149 Penn Ave Scranton PA 18503 **Phn:** 570-348-9185 **Fax:** 570-348-9135 www.abingtonsuburban.com

Scranton Triboro Banner (7.2M) 149 Penn Ave Scranton PA 18503 **Phn:** 570-348-9185 **Fax:** 570-207-3448 www.triborobanner.com

Sharon Hubbard Press (2.5M) PO Box 51 Sharon PA 16146 **Phn:** 724-981-6100 **Fax:** 724-981-5116

Shippensburg Shippensburg Sentinel (11.0M) 79 W King St Shippensburg PA 17257 **Phn:** 717-530-2444 **Fax:** 717-530-0310 www.cumberlink.com frontdoor@cumberlink.com

Shippensburg The News-Chronicle (5.2M) PO Box 100 Shippensburg PA 17257 **Phn:** 717-532-4101 **Fax:** 717-532-3020

Souderton Perkasie News-Herald (7.0M) 673 E Broad St Souderton PA 18964 **Phn:** 215-257-6839 **Fax:** 215-723-8779 www.perkasienewsherald.com

Souderton Souderton Independent (7.0M) PO Box 64459 Souderton PA 18964 **Phn:** 215-723-4801 **Fax:** 215-723-8779 www.soudertonindependent.com emorris@montgomerynews.com

Strasburg Strasburg News (1.1M) PO Box 160 Strasburg PA 17579 **Phn:** 717-687-7721 **Fax:** 717-687-6551 homsherprinting@aol.com

Susquehanna Susquehanna County Transcript (6.0M) 36 Exchange St Susquehanna PA 18847 **Phn:** 570-853-3134 **Fax:** 570-853-4707 www.susquehannatranscript.com susqtran@epix.net

Swarthmore The Swarthmorean (2.4M) PO Box 59 Swarthmore PA 19081 **Phn:** 610-543-0900 **Fax:** 610-543-3790 www.swarthmorean.com editor@swarthmorean.com

Tionesta The Forest Press (5.2M) PO Box 366 Tionesta PA 16353 **Phn:** 814-755-4900 **Fax:** 814-755-4429 forestpress1@yahoo.com

Trevose Broad Street Newspapers (102.0M) 2512 Metropolitan Dr Trevose PA 19053 **Phn:** 215-355-9009 **Fax:** 215-355-4857

Tunkhannock Wyoming Co. Press Examiner (5.5M) PO Box 59 Tunkhannock PA 18657 **Phn:** 570-836-2123 **Fax:** 570-836-3378 www.wcexaminer.com news@wcexaminer.com

Valley View The Citizen-Standard (4.0M) PO Box 147 Valley View PA 17983 **Phn:** 570-682-9081 **Fax:** 570-682-8734 citizenstandard.com news@citizenstandard.com

Vandergrift Buttermilk Falls Co (28.0M) 143 Washington Ave Vandergrift PA 15690 **Phn:** 724-567-5656 **Fax:** 724-568-3818 buttermilkfalls@comcast.net

Venetia Community Press (1.1M) PO Box 148 Venetia PA 15367 **Phn:** 724-942-1300

Waynesburg Greene County Messenger (10.0M) 95 E High St Ste 107 Waynesburg PA 15370 **Phn:** 724-852-2251 **Fax:** 724-852-2271 www.heraldstandard.com/gcm info@greenecountymessenger.com

Weedville Bennetts Valley News (1.0M) PO Box 158 Weedville PA 15868 **Phn:** 814-787-4454

Wellsboro Wellsboro Gazette (6.7M) PO Box 118 Wellsboro PA 16901 **Phn:** 570-724-2287 **Fax:** 570-724-2278 www.tiogapublishing.com nkennedy@tiogapublishing.com

West Chester Ledger Newspapers (27.0M) 250 N Bradford Ave West Chester PA 19382 **Phn:** 717-786-2992 **Fax:** 717-786-8679

West Chester Local News Inc. (52.0M) 250 N Bradford Ave West Chester PA 19382 **Phn:** 610-696-1775 **Fax:** 610-430-1194 www.dailylocal.com news@dailylocal.com

West Grove Avon Grove Sun (4.5M) 50 Railroad Ave Ste 4 West Grove PA 19390 **Phn:** 610-869-8300 **Fax:** 610-869-4746 www.pa8newsgroup.com agsun@kennettpaper.com

West Newton The Times Sun (3.5M) 205 E Main St West Newton PA 15089 **Phn:** 724-872-6800 **Fax:** 724-872-6801 timessun@comcast.net

Westfield Free Press Courier (2.5M) 202 E Main St Westfield PA 16950 **Phn:** 814-367-2230 **Fax:** 814-367-5092 www.tiogapublishing.com sharon@tiogapublishing.com

White Haven The Journal-Herald (1.8M) 211 Main St White Haven PA 18661 **Phn:** 570-443-9131

Wilkes Barre Dallas Post (10.0M) 15 N Main St Wilkes Barre PA 18701 **Phn:** 570-675-5211 **Fax:** 570-675-3650 www.mydallaspost.com dmartin@mydallaspost.com

Wyalusing The Rocket-Courier (5.0M) PO Box 187 Wyalusing PA 18853 **Phn:** 570-746-1217 **Fax:** 570-746-7737 www.rocket-courier.com rocket@epix.net

Wynnewood Main Line Suburban Life (18.0M) 311 E Lancaster Ave Wynnewood PA 19096 **Phn:** 610-896-9555 **Fax:** 610-896-9560 www.mainlinemedianews.com sgreenspon@mainlinemedianews.com

Yardley Yardley News (5.5M) PO Box 334 Yardley PA 19067 **Phn:** 215-493-2794 **Fax:** 215-321-0527 www.bryalocalnews.com yardley@ingnews.com

York Weekly Record (15.0M) 1891 Loucks Rd York PA 17408 **Phn:** 717-771-2000 **Fax:** 717-771-2009 www.inyork.com/community weekly@ydr.com

RHODE ISLAND

Block Island Block Island Times (3.0M) PO Box 278 Block Island RI 02807 **Phn:** 401-466-2222 **Fax:** 401-466-8804 block-island.villagesoup.com tips@blockislandtimes.com

Bristol Bristol Phoenix (6.0M) PO Box 90 Bristol RI 02809 **Phn:** 401-253-6000 **Fax:** 401-253-6055 www.eastbayri.com

Bristol East Bay Newspapers (17.0M) PO Box 90 Bristol RI 02809 **Phn:** 401-253-6000 **Fax:** 401-434-9469 www.eastbayri.com mhayes@eastbaynewspapers.com

Bristol Times Gazette (3.2M) 1 Bradford St Bristol RI 02809 **Phn:** 401-245-6000 **Fax:** 401-253-6055 www.eastbayri.com

Coventry Coventry Courier (1.0M) 45 Reservoir Rd Coventry RI 02816 **Phn:** 401-826-4250 **Fax:** 401-826-4255 www.ricentral.com jryan@ricentral.com

East Greenwich Pendulum (3.1M) 580 Main St East Greenwich RI 02818 **Phn:** 401-884-4662 **Fax:** 401-884-9819 www.ricentral.com mgreen@ricentral.com

East Providence Barrington Times (5.0M) 1027 Waterman Ave East Providence RI 02914 **Phn:** 401-434-7210 **Fax:** 401-434-9469 www.eastbayri.com

Greenville Observer Publications (19.0M) 592 Putnam Pike Ste 2 Greenville RI 02828 **Phn:** 401-949-2700 **Fax:** 401-949-2420 www.valleybreeze.com news@valleybreeze.com

Jamestown Jamestown Press (6.0M) 45 Narragansett Ave Jamestown RI 02835 **Phn:** 401-423-3200 **Fax:** 401-423-1661 www.jamestownpress.com news@jamestownpress.com

Lincoln Valley Breeze Papers (50.2M) 6 Blackstone Valley Pl # 204 Lincoln RI 02865 **Phn:** 401-334-9555 **Fax:** 401-334-9994 www.valleybreeze.com news@valleybreeze.com

Newport Newport Mercury (10.0M) 180 Malbone Rd Newport RI 02840 **Phn:** 401-380-2371 **Fax:** 401-849-3306 www.newportri.com/newportmercury editor@newportmercury.com

Newport Newport This Week (10.0M) 86 Broadway Newport RI 02840 **Phn:** 401-847-7766 **Fax:** 401-846-4974 www.newportthisweek.com news@newportthisweek.com

North Kingstown The Standard Times (5.0M) 13 W Main St North Kingstown RI 02852 **Phn:** 401-294-4576 **Fax:** 401-294-9736 www.ricentral.com

Providence Providence Phoenix (68.0M) 150 Chestnut St Providence RI 02903 **Phn:** 401-273-6397 **Fax:** 401-273-0920 thephoenix.com letters@phx.com

Tiverton Sakonnet Times (6.4M) 1745 Main Rd Tiverton RI 02878 **Phn:** 401-683-1000 **Fax:** 401-537-9155 www.eastbayri.com

Wakefield Chariho Times (3.2M) PO Box 232 Wakefield RI 02880 **Phn:** 401-789-9744 **Fax:** 401-789-1550 www.ricentral.com mwunsch@ricentral.com

Wakefield Independent Newspapers (4.7M) PO Box 5679 Wakefield RI 02880 **Phn:** 401-789-6000 **Fax:** 401-792-9176 www.independentri.com newsroom@scindependent.com

Wakefield Naragansett Times (5.6M) PO Box 232 Wakefield RI 02880 **Phn:** 401-789-9744 **Fax:** 401-789-1550 www.ricentral.com mwunsch@ricentral.com

Warwick Beacon Communications (21.0M) 1944 Warwick Ave Warwick RI 02889 **Phn:** 401-732-3100 **Fax:** 401-732-3110 warwickonline.com johnh@rhodybeat.com

Westerly Pawcatuck Press (8.0M) 56 Main St Westerly RI 02891 **Phn:** 401-348-1000 **Fax:** 401-348-5080 www.thewesterlysun.com

Woonsocket Neighbors (32.0M) 75 Main St Woonsocket RI 02895 **Phn:** 401-767-8535

SOUTH CAROLINA

Abbeville Abbeville Press & Banner (7.5M) PO Box 769 Abbeville SC 29620 **Phn:** 864-366-5461 **Fax:** 864-366-5463 henrybannercorp@charter.net

Bamberg Advertizer-Herald (5.8M) PO Box 929 Bamberg SC 29003 **Phn:** 803-245-5204 **Fax:** 803-245-3900 www.advertizerherald.com ahpublisher@bellsouth.net

Barnwell People Sentinel (8.5M) PO Box 1255 Barnwell SC 29812 **Phn:** 803-259-3501 **Fax:** 803-259-2703 www.thepeoplesentinel.com laura.mckenzie@morris.com

Belton Belton News Chronicle (3.9M) PO Box 606 Belton SC 29627 **Phn:** 864-338-6124 **Fax:** 864-338-1109 www.bhpnc.com elaine@bhpnc.com

Bennettsville Marlboro Herald Advocate (6.8M) PO Box 656 Bennettsville SC 29512 **Phn:** 843-479-3815 **Fax:** 843-479-7671 www.heraldadvocate.com news@heraldadvocate.com

Bishopville Lee County Observer (3.5M) PO Box 567 Bishopville SC 29010 **Phn:** 803-484-9431 **Fax:** 803-484-5055

Blacksburg Blacksburg Times (2.8M) PO Box 155 Blacksburg SC 29702 **Phn:** 864-839-2621 **Fax:** 864-839-5710

Camden Chronicle-Independent (8.8M) PO Box 1137 Camden SC 29021 **Phn:** 803-432-6157 **Fax:** 803-432-7609 www.chronicle-independent.com editor@ci-camden.com

Charleston Charleston City Paper (40.0M) 1049 Morrison Dr Ste B Charleston SC 29403 **Phn:** 843-577-5304 **Fax:** 843-576-0380 www.charlestoncitypaper.com editor@charlestoncitypaper.com

SOUTH CAROLINA WEEKLY NEWSPAPERS

Cheraw The Cheraw Chronicle (8.0M) 114 Front St Cheraw SC 29520 **Phn:** 843-537-5261 **Fax:** 843-537-4518 www.thecherawchronicle.com

Chester The News & Reporter (7.0M) PO Box 250 Chester SC 29706 **Phn:** 803-385-3177 **Fax:** 803-581-2518 www.onlinechester.com editor@onlinechester.com

Clinton Clinton Chronicle (3.5M) PO Box 180 Clinton SC 29325 **Phn:** 864-833-1900 **Fax:** 864-833-1902 www.clintonchronicle.com circulation@clintonchronicle.com

Columbia Columbia Star (14.5M) PO Box 5955 Columbia SC 29250 **Phn:** 803-771-0219 www.thecolumbiastar.com pamc@thecolumbiastar.com

Columbia Free Times (35.0M) 1534 Main St Columbia SC 29201 **Phn:** 803-765-0707 **Fax:** 803-765-0727 www.free-times.com editor@free-times.com

Columbia Northeast News (10.0M) PO Box 25278 Columbia SC 29224 **Phn:** 803-865-5563 **Fax:** 803-865-5560 thenortheastnews@aol.com

Conway Horry Independent (6.0M) PO Box 740 Conway SC 29528 **Phn:** 843-248-6671 **Fax:** 843-248-6024 www.myhorrynews.com kathy.ropp@myhorrynews.com

Conway Myrtle Beach Herald (4.0M) PO Box 740 Conway SC 29528 **Phn:** 843-236-4810 **Fax:** 843-448-4860 www.myhorrynews.com charles.perry@myhorrynews.com

Daniel Island Daniel Island News (8.0M) 225 Seven Farms Dr Ste 108 Daniel Island SC 29492 **Phn:** 843-856-1999 **Fax:** 843-856-8555 thedanielislandnews.com sdetar@thedanielislandnews.com

Darlington News & Press (6.0M) PO Box 513 Darlington SC 29540 **Phn:** 843-393-3811 **Fax:** 843-393-6811

Dillon Dillon Herald (7.4M) PO Box 1288 Dillon SC 29536 **Phn:** 843-774-3311 **Fax:** 843-841-1930 www.thedillonherald.com jd@thedillonherald.com

Easley Easley Progress (9.5M) PO Box 709 Easley SC 29641 **Phn:** 864-855-0355 **Fax:** 864-855-6825 www.theeasleyprogress.com ladamson@civitasmedia.com

Easley Pickens Sentinel (7.0M) PO Box 709 Easley SC 29641 **Phn:** 864-855-0355 **Fax:** 864-855-6825 www.pickenssentinel.com pedwards@civitasmedia.com

Easley Powdersville Post (6.7M) PO Box 709 Easley SC 29641 **Phn:** 864-855-0355 **Fax:** 864-855-6825 www.theeasleyprogress.com ladamson@civitasmedia.com

Edgefield Edgefield Advertiser (2.6M) PO Box 628 Edgefield SC 29824 **Phn:** 803-637-3540 **Fax:** 803-637-0602 www.edgefieldadvertiser.com news@edgefieldadvertiser.com

Edgefield Edgefield Citizen-News (3.3M) PO Box 448 Edgefield SC 29824 **Phn:** 803-637-5306 **Fax:** 803-637-5661

Florence The News Journal (26.0M) 312 Railroad Ave Florence SC 29506 **Phn:** 843-667-9656 **Fax:** 843-661-7102 www.florencenewsjournal.com bharrison@florencenewsjournal.com

Fort Mill Ft. Mill Times (6.8M) 124 Main St Fort Mill SC 29715 **Phn:** 803-547-2353 **Fax:** 803-547-2321 www.fortmilltimes.com news@fortmilltimes.com

Gaffney Cherokee Chronicle Inc. (7.0M) PO Box 729 Gaffney SC 29342 **Phn:** 864-488-1016 **Fax:** 864-488-1443 www.thecherokeechronicle.com

Gaffney Gaffney Ledger (9.5M) PO Box 670 Gaffney SC 29342 **Phn:** 864-489-1131 **Fax:** 864-487-7667 www.gaffneyledger.com editor@gaffneyledger.com

Georgetown Georgetown Times (9.0M) PO Box 2778 Georgetown SC 29442 **Phn:** 843-546-4148 **Fax:** 843-546-2395 www.gtowntimes.com news@gtowntimes.com

Greenville Journal Watchdog (45.0M) 148 River St Ste 120 Greenville SC 29601 **Phn:** 864-467-9070 **Fax:** 864-467-9809 www.journalwatchdog.com news@greenvillejournal.com

Greenville The Beat (15.0M) PO Box 26924 Greenville SC 29616 **Phn:** 864-233-7760

Greenville Tribune Times (37.0M) PO Box 1688 Greenville SC 29602 **Phn:** 864-298-4295 **Fax:** 864-298-4395 www.greenvilleonline.com/tribune-times rdekett@greenvillenews.com

Greer Greer Citizen (11.0M) 105 Victoria St Greer SC 29651 **Phn:** 864-877-2076 **Fax:** 864-877-3563 greercitizen.com fitz@greercitizen.com

Hampton Hampton County Guardian (4.5M) PO Box 625 Hampton SC 29924 **Phn:** 803-943-4645 **Fax:** 803-943-9365 www.hamptoncountyguardian.com news@hamptoncountyguardian.com

Hartsville The Messenger (7.5M) PO Box 1865 Hartsville SC 29551 **Phn:** 843-332-6545 **Fax:** 843-332-1341 www.scnow.com themessenger@hartsvillemessenger.com

Hemingway The Weekly Observer (3.4M) PO Box 309 Hemingway SC 29554 **Phn:** 843-317-6397 **Fax:** 843-558-9601 www.scnow.com/observer news@scnow.com

Irmo Lake Murray News (9.0M) PO Box 175 Irmo SC 29063 **Phn:** 803-772-5584 **Fax:** 803-772-7795 lakemurraynews@aol.com

Kershaw Kershaw News-Era (3.2M) PO Box 398 Kershaw SC 29067 **Phn:** 803-475-6095 newsera@comporium.net

Kingstree The News (4.8M) PO Box 574 Kingstree SC 29556 **Phn:** 843-355-6397 **Fax:** 843-355-6530 www.kingstreenews.com thenews@ftc-i.net

Lake City Lake City News & Post (3.3M) PO Box 429 Lake City SC 29560 **Phn:** 843-394-3571 **Fax:** 843-394-5057 www.scnow.com newsandpost@florencenews.com

Lake Wylie Lake Wylie Pilot (11.0M) 8 Executive Ct Lake Wylie SC 29710 **Phn:** 803-831-8166 **Fax:** 803-831-0660 www.lakewyliepilot.com news@lakewyliepilot.com

Lancaster Lancaster News (13.5M) PO Box 640 Lancaster SC 29721 **Phn:** 803-283-1133 **Fax:** 803-285-5079 www.thelancasternews.com news@thelancasternews.com

Landrum The News Leader (2.4M) PO Box 9 Landrum SC 29356 **Phn:** 864-457-3337 **Fax:** 864-457-5231 news@upstatenewspapers.com

Laurens Laurens County Advertiser (8.0M) PO Box 490 Laurens SC 29360 **Phn:** 864-984-2586 **Fax:** 864-984-4039 www.laurenscountyadvertiser.net news@lcadvertiser.com

Leesville The Twin City News (4.8M) PO Box 2529 Leesville SC 29070 **Phn:** 803-532-6203 **Fax:** 803-532-6204 bbkyzer@mindspring.com

Lexington Lexington County Chronicle (8.0M) PO Box 9 Lexington SC 29071 **Phn:** 803-359-7633 **Fax:** 803-359-2936 lexingtonchronicle.com lexchron@windstream.net

Loris Loris Scene (6.5M) 4103 Main St Loris SC 29569 **Phn:** 843-756-1447 **Fax:** 843-756-7800 www.lorissc.com lsnews@sccoast.net

Manning Manning Times (3.7M) PO Box 190 Manning SC 29102 **Phn:** 803-435-8422 **Fax:** 803-435-4189 www.clarendontoday.com

Marion The Star & Enterprise (12.0M) PO Box 880 Marion SC 29571 **Phn:** 843-423-2050 **Fax:** 843-423-2542 www.scnow.com/starandenterprise starandenterprise@scnow.com

Mc Cormick McCormick Messenger (2.7M) PO Box 1807 Mc Cormick SC 29835 **Phn:** 864-852-3311 **Fax:** 864-852-3528 mccmess@wctel.net

Moncks Corner Berkeley Independent (9.5M) PO Box 427 Moncks Corner SC 29461 **Phn:** 843-761-6397 **Fax:** 843-899-6996 www.berkeleyind.com jwatts@journalscene.com

Mount Pleasant Moultrie News (32.0M) 1250 Fairmont Ave Mount Pleasant SC 29464 **Phn:** 843-849-1778 **Fax:** 843-958-7490 www.moultrienews.com editor@moultrienews.com

Newberry Observer-Herald-News (6.2M) PO Box 558 Newberry SC 29108 **Phn:** 803-276-0625 **Fax:** 803-276-1517 www.newberryobserver.com news@newberryobserver.com

Ninety Six Star & Beacon (3.0M) PO Box 327 Ninety Six SC 29666 **Phn:** 864-543-3444 **Fax:** 864-543-3440

North Augusta The Star (3.8M) 404 E Martintown Rd # 2 North Augusta SC 29841 **Phn:** 803-279-2793 **Fax:** 803-278-4070 www.northaugustastar.com editor@northaugustastar.com

North Charleston North Charleston News (12.0M) PO Box 60580 North Charleston SC 29419 **Phn:** 843-744-8000 **Fax:** 843-744-5505 hanahancom@aol.com

North Myrtle Beach North Myrtle Beach Times (16.0M) PO Box 725 North Myrtle Beach SC 29597 **Phn:** 843-249-3525 **Fax:** 843-249-7012 nmbtimes.com nmbtimes@sc.rr.com

Pageland Pageland Progressive-Journal (3.2M) PO Box 218 Pageland SC 29728 **Phn:** 843-672-2358 **Fax:** 843-672-5593 www.pagelandprogressive.com editor@pagelandprogressive.com

Pawleys Island The Coastal Observer (5.0M) PO Box 1170 Pawleys Island SC 29585 **Phn:** 843-237-8438 **Fax:** 843-235-0084 www.coastalobserver.com cswenson@coastalobserver.com

Ridgeland Sun Times Inc (2.4M) PO Box 1030 Ridgeland SC 29936 **Phn:** 843-726-6161 **Fax:** 843-726-8661 jaspercountysun.com news@jaspercountysun.com

Saint George The Eagle-Record (3.1M) PO Box 278 Saint George SC 29477 **Phn:** 843-563-3121 **Fax:** 843-563-5355 theeaglerecord.com eagle_record@bellsouth.net

Saint Matthews Calhoun Times (2.0M) PO Box 176 Saint Matthews SC 29135 **Phn:** 803-874-3137 **Fax:** 803-874-1588

Saluda Saluda Standard-Sentinel (4.5M) PO Box 668 Saluda SC 29138 **Phn:** 864-445-2527 **Fax:** 864-445-8679 www.saludastandard-sentinel.com sentinel@saludasc.com

Spartanburg Inman Times (3.8M) PO Box 5211 Spartanburg SC 29304 **Phn:** 864-472-9548 **Fax:** 864-472-5398

Summerville Goose Creek Gazette (13.0M) PO Box 715 Summerville SC 29484 **Phn:** 843-873-9424 **Fax:** 843-572-0312 www.ourgazette.com jwatts@journalscene.com

Summerville Journal-Scene (9.0M) PO Box 715 Summerville SC 29484 **Phn:** 843-873-9424 **Fax:** 843-873-9432 www.journalscene.com jwatts@journalscene.com

Travelers Rest Travelers Rest Monitor (3.0M) PO Box 247 Travelers Rest SC 29690 **Phn:** 864-836-6820 **Fax:** 864-836-8048 trnews@bellsouth.net

Walhalla Keowee Courier (2.5M) PO Box 528 Walhalla SC 29691 **Phn:** 864-638-5856 **Fax:** 864-638-5857 keoweecourier@bellsouth.net

Walterboro Press & Standard (29.0M) 1025 Bells Hwy Walterboro SC 29488 **Phn:** 843-549-2586 **Fax:** 843-549-2446 thepress@lowcountry.com

Walterboro The Dispatch (2.1M) PO Box 2201 Walterboro SC 29488 **Phn:** 843-549-1754 **Fax:** 843-549-9181

Ware Shoals The Observer (3.0M) PO Box 176 Ware Shoals SC 29692 **Phn:** 864-456-7772 **Fax:** 864-456-7122

Westminster Westminster News (2.5M) PO Box 278 Westminster SC 29693 **Phn:** 864-647-5404 **Fax:** 864-647-5405 westminstersc.com/news westnews@bellsouth.net

Williamston The Journal (4.1M) PO Box 369 Williamston SC 29697 **Phn:** 864-847-7361 **Fax:** 864-847-9879 www.thejournalonline.com editor@thejournalonline.com

Winnsboro Herald-Independent (5.0M) PO Box 90 Winnsboro SC 29180 **Phn:** 803-635-4016 **Fax:** 803-635-2948 www.heraldindependent.com pedwards@civitasmedia.com

Woodruff Hometown News (35.0M) PO Box 249 Woodruff SC 29388 **Phn:** 864-476-3513 **Fax:** 864-476-3511

York Enquirer-Herald (3.0M) 23 E Liberty St York SC 29745 **Phn:** 803-684-9903 **Fax:** 803-628-0300 www.enquirerherald.com jbecknell@heraldonline.com

SOUTH DAKOTA

Alcester Alcester Union & Hudsonite (0.9M) PO Box 227 Alcester SD 57001 **Phn:** 605-934-2640 **Fax:** 605-934-2096 www.ahenews.com publisher@ahenews.com

Alexandria Alexandria Herald (0.7M) PO Box 456 Alexandria SD 57311 **Phn:** 605-239-4521 ementerprise@triotel.net

Arlington Arlington Sun (1.3M) PO Box 370 Arlington SD 57212 **Phn:** 605-983-5491 **Fax:** 605-983-5715 www.rfdnewsgroup.com asn@mchsi.com

Avon Avon Clarion (1.0M) PO Box 345 Avon SD 57315 **Phn:** 605-286-3919 **Fax:** 605-286-3507 avonclarion@hotmail.com

Belle Fourche Butte County Post (2.0M) 614 State St Belle Fourche SD 57717 **Phn:** 605-892-2528 **Fax:** 605-892-2529 www.rapidcityjournal.com/buttecountypost bcpnews@lee.net

Belle Fourche Lawrence Co Journal (1.9M) 614 State St Belle Fourche SD 57717 **Phn:** 605-578-3305 **Fax:** 605-578-2023 www.rapidcityjournal.com news@rapidcityjournal.com

Belle Fourche Valley Irrigator (1.2M) 614 State St Belle Fourche SD 57717 **Phn:** 605-456-2585 **Fax:** 605-456-2587

Beresford Beresford Republic (1.5M) PO Box 111 Beresford SD 57004 **Phn:** 605-763-2006 republic@bmtc.net

Beresford Centerville Journal (0.7M) PO Box 111 Beresford SD 57004 **Phn:** 605-763-2006 **Fax:** 605-763-5503

Bison Bison Courier (0.9M) PO Box 429 Bison SD 57620 **Phn:** 605-244-7199 **Fax:** 605-244-7198 courier@sdplains.com

SOUTH CAROLINA WEEKLY NEWSPAPERS

Bonesteel Bonesteel Enterprise (0.4M) PO Box 170 Bonesteel SD 57317 **Phn:** 605-654-2678 **Fax:** 605-244-9926 davidp@gwtc.net

Brandon Garretson Weekly (1.4M) PO Box 257 Brandon SD 57005 **Phn:** 605-594-6315 **Fax:** 605-594-3442

Bridgewater Bridgewater Tribune (0.7M) PO Box 250 Bridgewater SD 57319 **Phn:** 605-729-2251 **Fax:** 605-425-2547 tschwans@triotel.net

Britton Britton Journal (1.8M) PO Box 69 Britton SD 57430 **Phn:** 605-448-2281 **Fax:** 605-448-2282 www.marshallcountyjournal.com journal@brittonsd.com

Britton Langford Bugle (0.8M) PO Box 69 Britton SD 57430 **Phn:** 605-448-2281 **Fax:** 605-448-2282 journal@brittonsd.com

Bryant Bryant Dakotan (0.6M) PO Box 127 Bryant SD 57221 **Phn:** 605-628-2551 dakotan@datatruck.com

Buffalo Nations Center News (1.2M) PO Box 107 Buffalo SD 57720 **Phn:** 605-375-3228 **Fax:** 605-375-3615 ncn@sdplains.com

Burke Burke Gazette (1.3M) PO Box 359 Burke SD 57523 **Phn:** 605-775-2612 burkegaz@gwtc.net

Canistota Anderson Publications (3.1M) PO Box 128 Canistota SD 57012 **Phn:** 605-296-3181 **Fax:** 605-296-3289 andersonpubl@unitelsd.com

Canton Sioux Valley News (4.0M) PO Box 255 Canton SD 57013 **Phn:** 605-764-2000 **Fax:** 605-764-6397

Castlewood Hamlin County Republican (0.9M) PO Box 50 Castlewood SD 57223 **Phn:** 605-793-2293 **Fax:** 605-793-9140

Centerville Centerville Journal (0.7M) PO Box H Centerville SD 57014 **Phn:** 605-763-2006 **Fax:** 605-763-5503

Chamberlain Central Dakota Times (3.0M) PO Box 125 Chamberlain SD 57325 **Phn:** 605-234-0266 **Fax:** 605-234-1266 centraldakotatimes.org cdt@midstatesd.net

Clark Clark County Courier (2.5M) 119 1st Ave E Clark SD 57225 **Phn:** 605-532-3654 **Fax:** 605-532-5424 courier@itctel.com

Clear Lake Clear Lake Courier (1.5M) PO Box 830 Clear Lake SD 57226 **Phn:** 605-874-2499 **Fax:** 605-874-2642 clprint@itctel.com

Corsica Douglas Co. Publishing (2.5M) PO Box 45 Corsica SD 57328 **Phn:** 605-946-5489 **Fax:** 605-946-5179 globe@siouxvalley.net

Custer Custer County Chronicle (1.9M) PO Box 551 Custer SD 57730 **Phn:** 605-673-2217 **Fax:** 605-673-3321 www.custercountynews.com custerchronicle@gwtc.net

De Smet De Smet News (1.4M) PO Box 69 De Smet SD 57231 **Phn:** 605-854-3331 **Fax:** 605-854-9977

Dell Rapids Dell Rapids Tribune (4.0M) PO Box 99 Dell Rapids SD 57022 **Phn:** 605-428-5441 **Fax:** 605-428-5992 www.dellrapidsinfo.com plalley@argusleader.com

Eagle Butte West River Eagle (2.2M) PO Box 210 Eagle Butte SD 57625 **Phn:** 605-964-2100 **Fax:** 605-964-2110 www.westrivereagle.com wreagle@westrivereagle.com

Edgemont Edgemont Herald Tribune (1.0M) PO Box 660 Edgemont SD 57735 **Phn:** 605-662-7201 **Fax:** 605-662-7202 www.edgemonttribune.com tribune@gwtc.net

Elk Point Leader Courier (1.8M) PO Box 310 Elk Point SD 57025 **Phn:** 605-356-2632 **Fax:** 605-356-3626 leader1@iw.net

Elkton Elkton Record (3.4M) PO Box K Elkton SD 57026 **Phn:** 605-542-4831 **Fax:** 605-542-1306 www.rfdnewsgroup.com ern@itctel.com

Emery Emery Enterprise (0.6M) PO Box 244 Emery SD 57332 **Phn:** 605-449-4420 **Fax:** 605-449-4430 ementerprise@triotel.net

Estelline Estelline Journal (0.9M) PO Box 159 Estelline SD 57234 **Phn:** 605-873-2475 **Fax:** 605-793-9140

Eureka Northwest Blade (1.4M) PO Box 797 Eureka SD 57437 **Phn:** 605-284-2631 **Fax:** 605-284-2632 acmehl@valleytel.net

Faith Faith Independent (1.1M) PO Box 38 Faith SD 57626 **Phn:** 605-967-2161 **Fax:** 605-967-2160 faithind@faithsd.com

Faulkton Faulk County Record (1.6M) PO Box 68 Faulkton SD 57438 **Phn:** 605-598-6525 **Fax:** 605-598-4355 www.faulkcountyrecord.com

Flandreau Moody County Enterprise (2.4M) PO Box 71 Flandreau SD 57028 **Phn:** 605-997-3725 **Fax:** 605-997-3194 www.moodycountyenterprise.com mce6@mcisweb.com

Freeman Freeman Courier (1.4M) PO Box 950 Freeman SD 57029 **Phn:** 605-925-7033 **Fax:** 605-925-4684 www.freemansd.com courier@gwtc.net

Geddes Charles Mix County News (0.7M) PO Box 257 Geddes SD 57342 **Phn:** 605-337-2571 cmcountynews@midstatesd.net

Gettysburg Potter County News (1.9M) 110 S Exene St Gettysburg SD 57442 **Phn:** 605-765-2464 **Fax:** 605-765-2465 www.pottercountynews.com pcnews@venturecomm.net

Gregory Gregory Times Advocate (2.5M) PO Box 378 Gregory SD 57533 **Phn:** 605-835-8089 **Fax:** 605-835-8467

Groton Groton Independent (1.2M) PO Box 588 Groton SD 57445 **Phn:** 877-791-2074 www.grotonsd.net news@grotonsd.net

Hayti Hamlin Herald Enterprise (0.9M) PO Box 207 Hayti SD 57241 **Phn:** 605-783-3636 **Fax:** 605-793-9140

Highmore Highmore Herald (1.5M) PO Box 435 Highmore SD 57345 **Phn:** 605-852-2927 hiherald@sbtc.net

Hill City Prevailer News (1.0M) PO Box 266 Hill City SD 57745 **Phn:** 605-574-2538 **Fax:** 605-574-4409 prevailer@goldenwest.net

Hot Springs Hot Springs Star (2.3M) PO Box 1000 Hot Springs SD 57747 **Phn:** 605-745-4170 **Fax:** 605-745-3161 www.rapidcityjournal.com/hotspringsstar hsstar@lee.net

Hoven Hoven Review (0.9M) PO Box 37 Hoven SD 57450 **Phn:** 605-948-2110 **Fax:** 605-948-2578 hoven@sbtc.net

Howard Miner County Pioneer (2.1M) PO Box 220 Howard SD 57349 **Phn:** 605-772-5644

Ipswich Ipswich Tribune (1.6M) PO Box 7 Ipswich SD 57451 **Phn:** 605-426-6471 **Fax:** 605-426-6202 news.iptribune@midconetwork.com

Irene Tri-County News (0.6M) PO Box 6 Irene SD 57037 **Phn:** 605-263-3339 **Fax:** 605-263-2425

Isabel Isabel Dakotan (0.7M) PO Box 207 Isabel SD 57633 **Phn:** 605-466-2258 dakotan@lakotanetwork.com

Kadoka Kadoka Press (1.2M) PO Box 309 Kadoka SD 57543 **Phn:** 605-837-2259 **Fax:** 605-837-2312 press@kadokatelco.com

Lake Andes Lake Andes Wave (0.5M) PO Box 369 Lake Andes SD 57356 **Phn:** 605-384-5616 **Fax:** 605-384-5955 thelakeandeswave.com announcer@hcinet.net

Lake Preston Lake Preston Times (1.0M) PO Box 368 Lake Preston SD 57249 **Phn:** 605-847-4421

Lemmon Lemmon Leader (1.6M) PO Box 180 Lemmon SD 57638 **Phn:** 605-374-3751 **Fax:** 605-374-5295 leader@sdplains.com

Lennox Lennox Independent (1.8M) PO Box 76 Lennox SD 57039 **Phn:** 605-647-2284 **Fax:** 605-647-2218 lennoxnews.com editor@lennoxnews.com

Leola McPherson County Herald (0.6M) PO Box 170 Leola SD 57456 **Phn:** 605-439-3131 **Fax:** 605-439-5315 herald@valleytel.net

Marion Marion Record (1.0M) PO Box 298 Marion SD 57043 **Phn:** 605-648-3821 **Fax:** 605-648-3920 mrecord@gwtc.net

Martin Bennett Co Booster (2.4M) PO Box 610 Martin SD 57551 **Phn:** 605-685-6866

Mc Laughlin News-Messenger (1.4M) PO Box 788 Mc Laughlin SD 57642 **Phn:** 605-823-4490 **Fax:** 605-823-4632

Menno Hutchinson Herald (1.2M) PO Box 506 Menno SD 57045 **Phn:** 605-387-5158 **Fax:** 605-387-5148 hherald@gwtc.net

Milbank Grant County Review (4.0M) PO Box 390 Milbank SD 57252 **Phn:** 605-432-4516 **Fax:** 605-432-5042

Miller Hand Co. Publishing (3.0M) PO Box 196 Miller SD 57362 **Phn:** 605-853-3575 **Fax:** 605-853-2478 www.themillerpress.com news@themillerpress.com

Mission Todd County Tribune (2.0M) PO Box 229 Mission SD 57555 **Phn:** 605-856-4469 **Fax:** 605-856-2428 www.tribnews.info tribnews@gwtc.net

Mobridge Mobridge Tribune (2.8M) PO Box 250 Mobridge SD 57601 **Phn:** 605-845-3646 **Fax:** 605-845-7659 www.mobridgetribune.com news@mobridgetribune.com

Murdo Murdo Coyote (0.6M) PO Box 465 Murdo SD 57559 **Phn:** 605-669-2271 **Fax:** 605-669-2744 mcoyote@gwtc.net

New Underwood New Underwood Post (1.2M) PO Box 426 New Underwood SD 57761 **Phn:** 605-754-6466 nupost@gwtc.net

North Sioux City Two Rivers Times (1.1M) PO Box 1340 North Sioux City SD 57049 **Phn:** 605-232-3539 **Fax:** 605-232-3679

Onida Onida Watchman (1.0M) PO Box 245 Onida SD 57564 **Phn:** 605-258-2604 **Fax:** 605-258-2572 www.onidawatchman.com watchman@venturecomm.net

Parker The New Era (1.6M) 225 N Main St Parker SD 57053 **Phn:** 605-297-4419 **Fax:** 605-297-4015 ncppub.com sebeling@ncppub.com

Parkston Parkston Advance (1.2M) PO Box J Parkston SD 57366 **Phn:** 605-928-3111 www.parkstonadvance.com advance@santel.net

Philip Pioneer Review (1.8M) PO Box 788 Philip SD 57567 **Phn:** 605-859-2516 **Fax:** 605-859-2410 www.pioneer-review.com ads@pioneer-review.com

Plankinton South Dakota Mail (1.0M) PO Box 367 Plankinton SD 57368 **Phn:** 605-942-7770 sdmail@siouxvalley.net

Platte Platte Enterprise (2.0M) PO Box 546 Platte SD 57369 **Phn:** 605-337-3101 **Fax:** 605-337-3433 eprise@midstatesd.net

Pollock Prairie Pioneer (1.9M) PO Box 218 Pollock SD 57648 **Phn:** 605-889-2320 **Fax:** 605-889-2361 www.centraldakotanews.com pioneer@valleytel.net

SOUTH DAKOTA WEEKLY NEWSPAPERS

Presho Lyman County Herald (1.0M) PO Box 518 Presho SD 57568 **Phn:** 605-895-6397 **Fax:** 605-895-6377 www.lcherald.com news@lcherald.com

Redfield Redfield Press (2.7M) PO Box 440 Redfield SD 57469 **Phn:** 605-472-0822 **Fax:** 605-472-3634 www.redfieldpress.com editor.redpress@midconetwork.com

Rosholt Rosholt Review (0.8M) PO Box 136 Rosholt SD 57260 **Phn:** 605-537-4276 **Fax:** 605-537-4858 review@tnics.com

Salem Salem Special (2.4M) PO Box 220 Salem SD 57058 **Phn:** 605-425-2361 **Fax:** 605-425-2547 tschwans@triotel.net

Scotland Scotland Journal (1.0M) PO Box 388 Scotland SD 57059 **Phn:** 605-583-4419 **Fax:** 605-583-4406 scotnews@gwtc.net

Selby Selby Record (1.1M) PO Box 421 Selby SD 57472 **Phn:** 605-649-7866 selbyrec@sbtc.net

Sisseton Sisseton Courier (3.0M) PO Box 169 Sisseton SD 57262 **Phn:** 605-698-7642 **Fax:** 605-698-3641 www.sissetoncourier.com news@sissetoncourier.com

Springfield Springfield Times (0.7M) PO Box 465 Springfield SD 57062 **Phn:** 605-369-2441 times@gwtc.net

Sturgis Black Hills Press (2.7M) PO Box 69 Sturgis SD 57785 **Phn:** 605-347-2503 **Fax:** 605-347-2321

Sturgis Meade County Times (1.9M) 1022 Main St Sturgis SD 57785 **Phn:** 605-347-2503 **Fax:** 605-347-2321 www.rapidcityjournal.com/meadecountytimes news@rapidcityjournal.com

Timber Lake Timber Lake Topic (1.5M) PO Box 10 Timber Lake SD 57656 **Phn:** 605-865-3546 **Fax:** 605-865-3787 www.timberlakesouthdakota.com timtopic@lakotanetwork.com

Tripp Tripp Star-Ledger (0.5M) PO Box D Tripp SD 57376 **Phn:** 605-928-3111 www.parkstonadvance.com advance@santel.net

Tyndall Tyndall Tribune (1.6M) PO Box 520 Tyndall SD 57066 **Phn:** 605-589-3242 ttribune@byelectric.com

Vermillion Broadcaster Press (3.0M) 201 W Cherry St Vermillion SD 57069 **Phn:** 605-624-2695 **Fax:** 605-624-2696 www.plaintalk.net david.lias@plaintalk.net

Wagner Announcer/Wagner Post (8.2M) PO Box 187 Wagner SD 57380 **Phn:** 605-384-5616 **Fax:** 605-384-5955 www.thewagnerpost.com announcer@hcinet.net

Wall Pennington County Courant (1.0M) PO Box 435 Wall SD 57790 **Phn:** 605-279-2565 **Fax:** 605-279-2965 courant@gwtc.net

Waubay Waubay Clipper (0.8M) PO Box 47 Waubay SD 57273 **Phn:** 605-947-4501

Webster Reporter & Farmer (3.3M) PO Box 30 Webster SD 57274 **Phn:** 605-345-3356 **Fax:** 605-345-3739 www.reporterandfarmer.com suhrs@reporterandfarmer.com

Wessington Springs True Dakotan (1.4M) PO Box 358 Wessington Springs SD 57382 **Phn:** 605-539-1281 **Fax:** 605-539-9315

White Lake Standard Publishing (1.0M) PO Box 216 White Lake SD 57383 **Phn:** 605-207-0029 **Fax:** 855-303-3153 standardpubl@midstatesd.net

White River Mellette County News (0.5M) PO Box F White River SD 57579 **Phn:** 605-259-3642 **Fax:** 605-259-3497 www.trib-news.com mcnews@gwtc.net

Wilmot Wilmot Enterprise (1.0M) PO Box 6 Wilmot SD 57279 **Phn:** 605-938-4651 **Fax:** 605-938-4683 wilnews@tnics.com

Winner Winner Advocate (2.7M) 125 W 3rd St Winner SD 57580 **Phn:** 605-842-1481 **Fax:** 605-842-1979 winner@gwtc.net

Woonsocket Woonsocket News (1.4M) PO Box 218 Woonsocket SD 57385 **Phn:** 605-796-4221

Yankton Town & Country News (14.0M) PO Box 56 Yankton SD 57078 **Phn:** 605-665-7811 **Fax:** 605-665-1721 www.yankton.net gary.wood@yankton.net

Yankton Yankton County Observer (3.0M) PO Box 98 Yankton SD 57078 **Phn:** 605-665-0484 **Fax:** 605-665-5582 www.ycobserver.com news@ycobserver.com

TENNESSEE

Alamo Crockett Times (4.0M) PO Box 160 Alamo TN 38001 **Phn:** 731-696-4558 **Fax:** 731-696-4550 www.thecrocketttimes.com thetimes@crockettnet.com

Ashland City Ashland City Times (6.0M) PO Box 158 Ashland City TN 37015 **Phn:** 615-792-4230 **Fax:** 615-792-3671 www.tennessean.com actimes@mtcngroup.com

Bartlett Bartlett Express (7.0M) 2850 Stage Village Cv Ste 5 Bartlett TN 38134 **Phn:** 901-388-1500 **Fax:** 901-529-7687

Benton Polk County News (3.5M) PO Box 129 Benton TN 37307 **Phn:** 423-338-2818 **Fax:** 423-338-4574 www.polknewsonline.com editor@polknewsonline.com

Bolivar Bolivar Bulletin-Times (5.2M) PO Box 152 Bolivar TN 38008 **Phn:** 731-658-3691 **Fax:** 731-658-7222

Brownsville States Graphic (5.2M) PO Box 59 Brownsville TN 38012 **Phn:** 731-772-1172 **Fax:** 731-772-5451 statesgraphic.com communitynews@statesgraphic.com

Byrdstown Pickett County Press (2.1M) PO Box 268 Byrdstown TN 38549 **Phn:** 931-864-3675 **Fax:** 931-864-3695 www.pickettcountypress.com pickettpress@twlakes.net

Camden Camden Chronicle (4.0M) PO Box 899 Camden TN 38320 **Phn:** 731-584-7200 **Fax:** 731-584-4943 www.magicvalleypublishing.com bentonco@usit.net

Carthage Carthage Courier (5.3M) PO Box 239 Carthage TN 37030 **Phn:** 615-735-1110 **Fax:** 615-735-0635 www.carthagecourier.com news@carthagecourier.com

Celina Citizen Statesman (2.6M) 801 E Lake Ave Celina TN 38551 **Phn:** 931-243-2235 **Fax:** 931-243-2232 www.citizen-statesman.com p.dixon@livingstonenterprise.net

Centerville Hickman County Times (5.6M) PO Box 100 Centerville TN 37033 **Phn:** 931-729-4283 **Fax:** 931-729-4282 hctimes@centerville.net

Chattanooga Chattanooga Pulse (8.0M) PO Box 4070 Chattanooga TN 37405 **Phn:** 423-648-7857 **Fax:** 423-648-7860 chattanoogapulse.com info@chattanoogapulse.com

Chattanooga Hamilton County Herald (3.8M) 1412 McCallie Ave Chattanooga TN 37404 **Phn:** 423-648-9841 **Fax:** 423-648-9844 www.hamiltoncountyherald.com editor@hamiltoncountyherald.com

Cleveland Bradley News Weekly (22.0M) 240 Oak St NW Cleveland TN 37311 **Phn:** 423-472-2882 **Fax:** 423-472-2135

Clinton Clinton Courier News (5.1M) PO Box 270 Clinton TN 37717 **Phn:** 865-457-2515 **Fax:** 865-457-1586 www.hometownclinton.com editor@hometownclinton.com

TENNESSEE WEEKLY NEWSPAPERS

Collierville Collierville Herald (4.0M) PO Box 427 Collierville TN 38027 **Phn:** 901-853-2241 **Fax:** 901-853-8507 www.colliervilleherald.net publisher@colliervilleherald.net

Cottontown White House Watch (27.0M) 110 Green Acres Rd Cottontown TN 37048 **Phn:** 615-838-7108 www.checkyourwatch.com

Covington The Covington Leader (7.8M) PO Box 529 Covington TN 38019 **Phn:** 901-476-7116 **Fax:** 901-476-0373 www.covingtonleader.com news@covingtonleader.com

Crossville Crossville Chronicle (16.0M) PO Box 449 Crossville TN 38557 **Phn:** 931-484-5145 **Fax:** 931-456-7683 crossville-chronicle.com reportnews@crossville-chronicle.com

Dayton The Herald-News (13.7M) PO Box 286 Dayton TN 37321 **Phn:** 423-775-6111 **Fax:** 423-775-8218 rheaheraldnews.com news@rheaheraldnews.com

Dickson Dickson Herald (7.5M) PO Box 587 Dickson TN 37056 **Phn:** 615-446-2811 **Fax:** 615-446-5560 www.tennessean.com/section/dickson dhnews@mtcngroup.com

Dover Stewart-Houston Times (6.0M) PO Box 425 Dover TN 37058 **Phn:** 931-232-5421 **Fax:** 931-232-8224 www.thestewarthoustontimes.com rstevens@theleafchronicle.com

Dunlap Dunlap Tribune (3.2M) PO Box 487 Dunlap TN 37327 **Phn:** 423-949-2505 **Fax:** 423-949-5297

Dyer Tri-City Reporter (1.8M) PO Box 266 Dyer TN 38330 **Phn:** 731-692-3506 **Fax:** 731-692-4844 www.tricityreporter.com news@tricityreporter.net

Dyersburg State Gazette (17.0M) PO Box 808 Dyersburg TN 38025 **Phn:** 731-287-1555 **Fax:** 731-287-1551 www.stategazette.com crimel@stategazette.com

Erwin The Record (4.7M) PO Box 700 Erwin TN 37650 **Phn:** 423-743-4112 **Fax:** 423-743-6125

Fairview Fairview Observer (1.7M) PO Box 506 Fairview TN 37062 **Phn:** 615-799-8565 **Fax:** 615-799-8728 www.tennessean.com fvoeditor@mtcngroup.com

Farragut Farragutpress (15.0M) 11863 Kingston Pike Farragut TN 37934 **Phn:** 865-675-6397 **Fax:** 865-675-1675 www.farragutpress.com editor@farragutpress.com

Fayetteville Elk Valley Times (9.0M) PO Box 9 Fayetteville TN 37334 **Phn:** 931-433-6151 **Fax:** 931-433-6040 www.elkvalleytimes.com evtpub@lcs.net

Franklin Franklin Review Appeal (1.7M) 121 2nd Ave N Franklin TN 37064 **Phn:** 615-771-5400 **Fax:** 615-771-5409 www.tennessean.com wam@tennessean.com

Franklin Williamson Herald (22.0M) PO Box 681359 Franklin TN 37068 **Phn:** 615-790-6465 **Fax:** 615-790-7551 www.williamsonherald.com doneil@williamsonherald.com

Gainesboro Jackson County Sentinel (3.3M) PO Box 37 Gainesboro TN 38562 **Phn:** 931-268-9725 **Fax:** 931-268-4339

Gallatin Gallatin Newspaper (8.0M) 156 N Water Ave Gallatin TN 37066 **Phn:** 615-452-4940 **Fax:** 615-452-4919 www.thegallatinnews.com

Gallatin The News-Examiner (11.0M) 1 Examiner Ct Gallatin TN 37066 **Phn:** 615-452-2561 **Fax:** 615-452-9110 www.tennessean.com gnenews@mtcngroup.com

Germantown Collierville Independent (13.0M) 7508 Capital Dr Ste 2 Germantown TN 38138 **Phn:** 901-755-7387 **Fax:** 901-755-0827 suburbancommunitynews.com grahamreview@yahoo.com

Germantown Germantown News (7.5M) 7545 North St Germantown TN 38138 **Phn:** 901-754-0337 **Fax:** 901-754-2961 www.germantownnews.com news@germantownnews.com

Germantown Shelby Sun Times (35.0M) 7508 Capital Dr Germantown TN 38138 **Phn:** 901-755-7386 **Fax:** 901-755-0827 suburbancommunitynews.com connersst@gmail.com

Hartsville Hartsville Vidette (2.3M) PO Box 47 Hartsville TN 37074 **Phn:** 615-374-3556 **Fax:** 615-374-4002 www.hartsvillevidette.com thevidette@bellsouth.net

Henderson Chester County Independent (5.0M) PO Box 306 Henderson TN 38340 **Phn:** 731-989-4624 **Fax:** 731-989-5008 www.chestercountyindependent.com swhaley@chestercountyindependent.com

Hendersonville Star-News (18.5M) PO Box 68 Hendersonville TN 37077 **Phn:** 615-824-8480 **Fax:** 615-824-3126

Hohenwald Lewis County Herald (3.6M) PO Box 69 Hohenwald TN 38462 **Phn:** 931-796-3191 **Fax:** 931-796-2153 www.lewisherald.com lewisherald@bellsouth.net

Humboldt The Chronicle (3.0M) PO Box 448 Humboldt TN 38343 **Phn:** 731-784-2531 **Fax:** 731-784-2533 www.hchronicle.net news@hchronicle.net

Huntingdon Carroll Co News Leader (6.8M) PO Box 888 Huntingdon TN 38344 **Phn:** 731-986-2253 **Fax:** 731-986-3585 www.magicvalleypublishing.com dennisr@usit.net

Jamestown Fentress Courier (5.4M) PO Box 1198 Jamestown TN 38556 **Phn:** 931-879-4040 **Fax:** 931-879-7716 fentresscouriernews.com fencourier@twlakes.net

Jefferson City Standard Banner (6.5M) PO Box 310 Jefferson City TN 37760 **Phn:** 865-475-2081 **Fax:** 865-475-8539 www.standardbanner.com news@standardbanner.com

Johnson City News & Neighbor (31.0M) PO Box 5006 Johnson City TN 37602 **Phn:** 423-979-1300 **Fax:** 423-979-1307 www.jcnewsandneighbor.com news@jcnewsandneighbor.com

Jonesborough Herald & Tribune (4.6M) PO Box 277 Jonesborough TN 37659 **Phn:** 423-753-3136 **Fax:** 423-753-6528 www.heraldandtribune.com news@heraldandtribune.com

Kingston Roane Newspapers (10.0M) PO Box 610 Kingston TN 37763 **Phn:** 865-376-3481 **Fax:** 865-376-1945 www.roanecounty.com

Kingston Springs South Cheatham Advocate (4.7M) PO Box 208 Kingston Springs TN 37082 **Phn:** 615-952-5554 **Fax:** 615-952-9625 www.scadvocate.com scadvocate@aol.com

Knoxville Knoxville Focus (19.0M) PO Box 18377 Knoxville TN 37928 **Phn:** 865-686-9970 **Fax:** 865-686-9966 www.knoxfocus.com editor@knoxfocus.com

Knoxville Metro Pulse (30.0M) 602 S Gay St 2nd flr Knoxville TN 37902 **Phn:** 865-522-5399 **Fax:** 865-522-2955 www.metropulse.com editor@metropulse.com

La Follette Advance-Sentinel (0.7M) PO Box 1261 La Follette TN 37766 **Phn:** 423-562-8468 **Fax:** 423-566-7060 www.lafollettepress.com stories@lafollettepress.com

La Follette La Follette Press (8.5M) 225 N 1st St La Follette TN 37766 **Phn:** 423-562-8468 **Fax:** 423-566-7060 www.lafollettepress.com stories@lafollettepress.com

Lafayette Macon Co. Chronicle (3.5M) 109 Public Sq Lafayette TN 37083 **Phn:** 615 688-6397 **Fax:** 615 688-2474 www.maconcountychronicle.com

Lafayette Macon County Times (4.1M) PO Box 129 Lafayette TN 37083 **Phn:** 615-666-2440 **Fax:** 615-666-4909 www.maconcountytimes.com tcryar@civitasmedia.com

Lawrenceburg Lawrence County Advocate (15.2M) PO Box 308 Lawrenceburg TN 38464 **Phn:** 931-762-1726 **Fax:** 931-762-7874 lawcoadv@bellsouth.net

Lawrenceburg The Democrat Union (17.0M) PO Box 685 Lawrenceburg TN 38464 **Phn:** 931-762-2222 **Fax:** 931-762-4191 duadv@bellsouth.net

Lebanon The Wilson Post (9.3M) PO Box 857 Lebanon TN 37088 **Phn:** 615-444-6008 **Fax:** 615-444-6018 www.wilsonpost.com news@wilsonpost.com

Lenoir City News-Herald (7.8M) PO Box 310 Lenoir City TN 37771 **Phn:** 865-986-6581 **Fax:** 865-988-3261 news-herald.net greg.wilkerson@news-herald.net

Lewisburg Marshall Co. Tribune (8.0M) 111 W Commerce Lewisburg TN 37091 **Phn:** 931-359-1188 **Fax:** 931-359-1847 www.marshalltribune.com khall@marshalltribune.com

Lexington Lexington Progress (8.0M) 508 S Broad St Lexington TN 38351 **Phn:** 731-968-6397 **Fax:** 731-968-9560 www.lexingtonprogress.com news@lexingtonprogress.com

Linden Buffalo River Review (3.0M) PO Box 914 Linden TN 37096 **Phn:** 931-589-2169 **Fax:** 931-589-3858 www.buffaloriverreview.com brreview@tds.net

Livingston Livingston Enterprise (5.5M) PO Box 129 Livingston TN 38570 **Phn:** 931-823-1274 **Fax:** 931-268-9125 www.livingstonenterprise.net

Livingston Overton County News (5.5M) PO Box 479 Livingston TN 38570 **Phn:** 931-823-6485 **Fax:** 931-823-6486 www.overtoncountynews.com news@overtoncountynews.com

Lynchburg Moore County News (1.6M) PO Box 500 Lynchburg TN 37352 **Phn:** 931-759-7302

Madison Madison Messenger (8.0M) PO Box 626 Madison TN 37116 **Phn:** 615-868-0475 **Fax:** 615-860-2797

Manchester Manchester Times (6.5M) 300 N Spring St Manchester TN 37355 **Phn:** 931-728-7577 **Fax:** 931-728-7614 www.manchestertimes.com mtpub@lcs.net

Manchester Saturday Independent (4.0M) PO Box 630 Manchester TN 37349 **Phn:** 931-728-9040 **Fax:** 931-723-0121 tsinews.com dailyliving@tsinews.com

Martin Weakley County Press (5.3M) PO Box 410 Martin TN 38237 **Phn:** 731-587-3144 **Fax:** 731-587-3147 www.nwtntoday.com editor@wcpnews.com

Maryville Blount Today (20.0M) 318 S Washington St Maryville TN 37804 **Phn:** 865-981-9101 **Fax:** 865-981-9114 www.blounttoday.com gardner@blounttoday.com

Maynardville Union News Leader (3.0M) 3755 Maynardville Hwy Maynardville TN 37807 **Phn:** 865-992-3392 **Fax:** 865-992-6861 www.unionnewsleader.com enewspaper@aol.com

Mc Kenzie McKenzie Banner (6.0M) PO Box 100 Mc Kenzie TN 38201 **Phn:** 731-352-3323 **Fax:** 731-352-3322 www.mckenziebanner.com banner@mckenziebanner.com

Mc Minnville Southern Standard (9.0M) PO Box 150 Mc Minnville TN 37111 **Phn:** 931-473-2191 **Fax:** 931-473-6823 www.southernstandard.com standard@blomand.net

Memphis Cordova Beacon (3.0M) PO Box 34967 Memphis TN 38184 **Phn:** 901-388-1597

Memphis North Shelby Times (63.0M) 3518 N Watkins St Memphis TN 38127 **Phn:** 901-358-8034 **Fax:** 901-358-8039

Memphis Silver Star News (28.0M) 3019 Park Ave Memphis TN 38114 **Phn:** 901-452-8828 **Fax:** 901-452-1656

Milan Milan Mirror Exchange (5.5M) PO Box 549 Milan TN 38358 **Phn:** 731-686-1632 **Fax:** 731-686-9005 www.milanmirrorexchange.com victor@milanmirrorexchange.com

Millington The Millington Star (6.0M) 6834 Church St Millington TN 38053 **Phn:** 901-872-2286 **Fax:** 901-872-2965 millington-news.com thomasmstar@yahoo.com

Mount Juliet Mt. Juliet News (3.2M) 2596 N Mount Juliet Rd Mount Juliet TN 37122 **Phn:** 615-754-6397 **Fax:** 615-754-6398 mtjulietnews@tds.net

Mount Juliet The Chronicle (11.5M) PO Box 647 Mount Juliet TN 37121 **Phn:** 615-754-6111 **Fax:** 615-754-8203 www.thechronicleofmtjuliet.com

Mount Juliet The Messenger (8.0M) 11509 Lebanon Rd Mount Juliet TN 37122 **Phn:** 615-868-0475 **Fax:** 615-860-2797

Mountain City The Tomahawk (5.3M) PO Box 90 Mountain City TN 37683 **Phn:** 423-727-6121 **Fax:** 423-727-4833 www.thetomahawk.com editor@thetomahawk.com

Nashville GCA Publishing (32.0M) 2323 Crestmoor Rd Nashville TN 37215 **Phn:** 615-298-1500 **Fax:** 615-298-1015 www.gcanews.com news@gcanews.com

Nashville Nashville Ledger (19.0M) 814 Church St Ste 200 Nashville TN 37203 **Phn:** 615-254-5522 **Fax:** 615-254-5525 www.nashvilleledger.com lgraves@nashvilleledger.com

Nashville Nashville Record (2.0M) 1100 Broadway Nashville TN 37203 **Phn:** 615-664-2300 **Fax:** 615-664-2301

Nashville Nashville Scene (50.0M) 210 12th Ave S Ste 100 Nashville TN 37203 **Phn:** 615-244-7989 **Fax:** 615-254-4743 www.nashvillescene.com editor@nashvillescene.com

Oneida Independent-Herald (5.0M) 19391 Alberta St Oneida TN 37841 **Phn:** 423-569-6343 **Fax:** 423-569-9566 www.ihoneida.com bengarrett@highland.net

Oneida Scott County News (5.0M) PO Box 4399 Oneida TN 37841 **Phn:** 423-569-8351 **Fax:** 423-569-4500 scnoneida.com scn@highland.net

Parsons The News Leader (4.0M) PO Box 340 Parsons TN 38363 **Phn:** 731-847-6354 **Fax:** 731-847-9120 www.readtheleader.com thenewsleader@netease.net

Pigeon Forge The Star Journal (3.0M) PO Box 898 Pigeon Forge TN 37868 **Phn:** 865-428-3811

Pikeville Bledsonian Banner (3.2M) PO Box 370 Pikeville TN 37367 **Phn:** 423-447-2996 **Fax:** 423-447-2997

Portland Portland Leader (3.1M) 109 S Broadway St Portland TN 37148 **Phn:** 615-325-9241 **Fax:** 615-325-9243 www.portlandleader.net editor@portlandleader.net

Portland Portland Progressive (2.7M) PO Box 427 Portland TN 37148 **Phn:** 615-325-3001 **Fax:** 615-325-7005

Powell Powell Post (17.0M) PO Box 1098 Powell TN 37849 **Phn:** 865-938-7678 **Fax:** 865-938-7679

Pulaski Giles Free Press (7.0M) PO Box 308 Pulaski TN 38478 **Phn:** 931-363-3544 **Fax:** 931-363-4312

Pulaski Pulaski Citizen (7.0M) PO Box 308 Pulaski TN 38478 **Phn:** 931-363-3544 **Fax:** 931-363-4319 www.pulaskicitizen.com cary.malone@pulaskicitizen.com

TENNESSEE WEEKLY NEWSPAPERS

Ripley Lauderdale Co. Enterprise (5.0M) PO Box 289 Ripley TN 38063 **Phn:** 731-635-1771 **Fax:** 731-635-2111 enterprisenewspaper@hotmail.com

Ripley The Lauderdale Voice (4.1M) PO Box 249 Ripley TN 38063 **Phn:** 731-635-1238 **Fax:** 731-635-3394 voicet@bellsouth.net

Rogersville Rogersville Review (12.0M) PO Box 100 Rogersville TN 37857 **Phn:** 423-272-7422 **Fax:** 423-272-7889 review@xtn.net

Savannah The Courier (8.7M) PO Box 340 Savannah TN 38372 **Phn:** 731-925-6397 **Fax:** 731-925-6310

Selmer Independent-Appeal (7.5M) PO Box 220 Selmer TN 38375 **Phn:** 731-645-5346 **Fax:** 731-645-3591 www.independentappeal.com submissions@independentappeal.com

Sevierville Valley Voice (8.0M) 3708 Wears Valley Rd Sevierville TN 37862 **Phn:** 865-908-5873

Seymour Seymour Herald (3.0M) 500 Maryville Hwy Seymour TN 37865 **Phn:** 865-577-6609 **Fax:** 865-577-6791 heraldnewstn.com info@seymourherald.com

Seymour Tri-County Times (2.5M) PO Box 130 Seymour TN 37865 **Phn:** 865-577-5935 **Fax:** 865-577-9896 www.tctimes.com news@tctimes.com

Smithville Middle Tennessee Times (3.0M) 206 E Public Sq Smithville TN 37166 **Phn:** 615-597-2100 **Fax:** 615-597-4119

Smithville Smithville Review (4.5M) PO Box 247 Smithville TN 37166 **Phn:** 615-597-5485 **Fax:** 615-597-5489 www.smithvillereview.com sreview@dtccom.net

Somerville East Shelby Review (1.9M) PO Box 519 Somerville TN 38068 **Phn:** 901-465-4042 **Fax:** 901-465-5493

Somerville Fayette County Review (5.1M) PO Box 519 Somerville TN 38068 **Phn:** 901-465-4042 **Fax:** 901-465-5493 suburbancommunitynews.com

Somerville Fayette Falcon (4.9M) PO Box 39 Somerville TN 38068 **Phn:** 901-465-3567 **Fax:** 901-465-3568 fcfalcon@bellsouth.net

South Pittsburg Jasper Journal (3.4M) PO Box 765 South Pittsburg TN 37380 **Phn:** 423-837-6312 **Fax:** 423-837-8715 marioncountynews.net mcnews@marioncountynews.net

South Pittsburg South Pittsburgh Hustler (2.4M) PO Box 765 South Pittsburg TN 37380 **Phn:** 423-837-6312 **Fax:** 423-837-8715 marioncountynews.net mcnews@marioncountynews.net

Sparta Sparta Expositor (5.0M) PO Box 179 Sparta TN 38583 **Phn:** 931-836-3284 **Fax:** 931-836-3948 www.myspartanews.com kim@myspartanews.com

Spencer Mountain View News (2.2M) PO Box 441 Spencer TN 38585 **Phn:** 931-946-3678 **Fax:** 931-946-3677

Springfield Robertson County Times (10.0M) PO Box 637 Springfield TN 37172 **Phn:** 615-384-3567 **Fax:** 615-384-1221 www.tennessean.com rctnews@mtcngroup.com

Sweetwater The Advocate & Democrat (5.0M) PO Box 389 Sweetwater TN 37874 **Phn:** 423-337-7101 **Fax:** 423-337-5932 advocateanddemocrat.com editor@advocateanddemocrat.com

Tazewell Claiborne Progress (7.0M) PO Box 40 Tazewell TN 37879 **Phn:** 423-626-3222 **Fax:** 423-626-6868 www.middlesborodailynews.com dcaldwell@civitasmedia.com

Tiptonville Lake County Banner (3.4M) 315 Church St Tiptonville TN 38079 **Phn:** 731-253-6666 **Fax:** 731-253-6667 www.lakecountybanner.com jone8191@bellsouth.net

Tracy City Grundy County Herald (5.1M) PO Box 189 Tracy City TN 37387 **Phn:** 931-592-2781 **Fax:** 931-592-9241 www.grundycountyherald.com gcherald@lcs.net

Trenton The Gazette (5.5M) PO Box 7 Trenton TN 38382 **Phn:** 731-855-1711 **Fax:** 731-855-9587 www.nwtntoday.com danny@trentongazette.com

Tullahoma Coffee Co Journal (8.3M) PO Box 400 Tullahoma TN 37388 **Phn:** 931-455-4545 **Fax:** 931-455-9299

Tullahoma The News (9.0M) PO Box 400 Tullahoma TN 37388 **Phn:** 931-455-4545 **Fax:** 931-455-9299 www.tullahomanews.com

Waverly Waverly News-Democrat (4.0M) PO Box 626 Waverly TN 37185 **Phn:** 931-296-2426 **Fax:** 931-296-5156 www.thenews-democrat.com newsdemocrat@bellsouth.net

Waynesboro Wayne County News (6.9M) PO Box 156 Waynesboro TN 38485 **Phn:** 931-722-5429

Winchester Herald-Chronicle (9.3M) 906 Dinah Shore Blvd Winchester TN 37398 **Phn:** 931-967-2272 **Fax:** 931-967-2299 www.heraldchronicle.com whcnews@lcs.net

Woodbury Cannon Courier (4.3M) 210 W Water St Woodbury TN 37190 **Phn:** 615-563-2512 **Fax:** 615-563-2519 www.cannoncourier.com news@cannoncourier.com

TEXAS

Albany Albany News (1.5M) PO Box 2139 Albany TX 76430 **Phn:** 325-762-2201 **Fax:** 325-762-3201 www.thealbanynews.net news@thealbanynews.net

Aledo Community News (2.6M) PO Box 1031 Aledo TX 76008 **Phn:** 817-441-7661 **Fax:** 817-441-5419 www.community-news.com news@community-news.com

Alice Nueces County Record Star (6.0M) 405 E Main St Alice TX 78333 **Phn:** 361-664-6588 **Fax:** 361-767-8827 www.recordstar.com ofelia.hunter@aliceechonews.com

Alice Orange Grove Journal (1.4M) 405 E Main St Alice TX 78332 **Phn:** 361-664-6588

Alpine Alpine Avalanche (4.5M) PO Box 719 Alpine TX 79831 **Phn:** 432-837-3334 **Fax:** 432-837-7181 www.alpineavalanche.com

Alvarado Alvarado Post (2.8M) 110 S Spears St Alvarado TX 76009 **Phn:** 817-790-8717 **Fax:** 817-783-7606 www.waxahachietx.com a.schwaderer@waxahachietx.com

Alvin Alvin Sun & Advertiser (30.0M) 570 Dula St Alvin TX 77511 **Phn:** 281-331-4421 **Fax:** 281-331-4424 www.alvinsun.net alvinsun@swbell.net

Alvord Alvord Gazette (1.5M) PO Box 7 Alvord TX 76225 **Phn:** 940-427-2112 **Fax:** 940-427-5997

Anahuac The Progress (2.1M) PO Box 100 Anahuac TX 77514 **Phn:** 409-267-6131 **Fax:** 409-267-4157 www.thevindicator.com/anahuac_progress theprogress@theanahuacprogress.com

Andrews Andrews County News (3.4M) 210 E Broadway St Andrews TX 79714 **Phn:** 432-523-2085 **Fax:** 432-523-9492 www.andrewscountynews.com news@basinbroadband.com

Angleton The Bulletin (6.0M) PO Box 2426 Angleton TX 77516 **Phn:** 978-849-5407 bulletin-ol.com

Anna Anna-Melissa Tribune (1.5M) PO Box 578 Anna TX 75409 **Phn:** 903-482-5253 **Fax:** 903-482-5656 amtrib.com news@amtrib.com

Anson Western Observer (1.2M) 1120 W Court Plz Anson TX 79501 **Phn:** 325-823-3253 **Fax:** 325-823-2957 westobserver@sbcglobal.net

TEXAS WEEKLY NEWSPAPERS

Aransas Pass Aransas Pass Progress (3.0M) PO Box 2100 Aransas Pass TX 78335 **Phn:** 361-758-5391 **Fax:** 361-758-5393 www.aransaspassprogress.com news@aransaspassprogress.com

Aransas Pass Ingleside Index (1.2M) PO Box 2100 Aransas Pass TX 78335 **Phn:** 361-758-5391 **Fax:** 361-758-5393 www.aransaspassprogress.com/the_ingleside_index publisher@theinglesideindex.com

Archer City Archer County News (1.5M) PO Box 1250 Archer City TX 76351 **Phn:** 940-574-4569 **Fax:** 940-574-4234 www.archercountynews.com archernews@yahoo.com

Aspermont Stonewall County Courier (1.0M) PO Box 808 Aspermont TX 79502 **Phn:** 940-989-3621 **Fax:** 940-989-3620 courier@westex.net

Atlanta Atlanta Citizens Journal (4.3M) 306 W Main St Atlanta TX 75551 **Phn:** 903-796-7133 **Fax:** 903-796-3294 www.news-journal.com gstratton@news-journal.com

Aubrey The Town Charter (1.2M) 5099 Highway 377 S # 200 Aubrey TX 76227 **Phn:** 940-365-4600

Austin Austin Chronicle (90.0M) PO Box 49066 Austin TX 78765 **Phn:** 512-454-5766 **Fax:** 512-458-6910 www.austinchronicle.com

Austin Oak Hill Gazette (4.5M) 7200 W Highway 71 Ste B Austin TX 78735 **Phn:** 512-301-0123 **Fax:** 512.287.5350 oakhillgazette.com editorial@oakhillgazette.com

Austin Texas Observer (7.0M) 307 W 7th St Austin TX 78701 **Phn:** 512-477-0746 **Fax:** 512-474-1175 www.texasobserver.org editors@texasobserver.org

Austin The Westlake Picayune (3.8M) PO Box 160790 Austin TX 78716 **Phn:** 512-327-2990 **Fax:** 512-328-6470 westlakepicayune.com news@westlake-picayune.com

Austin West Austin News (3.2M) 5407 Parkcrest Dr Ste 101 Austin TX 78731 **Phn:** 512-459-4070 **Fax:** 512-206-0704 www.westaustinnews.com publisher@westaustinnews.com

Azle Azle News (4.0M) 321 W Main St Azle TX 76020 **Phn:** 817-270-3340 **Fax:** 817-270-5300 www.azlenews.net publisher@azlenews.net

Ballinger Ballinger Ledger (2.3M) 806 Hutchins Ave Ballinger TX 76821 **Phn:** 325-365-3501 **Fax:** 325-365-5389

Bandera Bandera Bulletin (3.5M) PO Box 697 Bandera TX 78003 **Phn:** 830-796-3718 **Fax:** 830-796-4885 www.banderabulletin.com news@banderabulletin.com

Bartlett Tribune Progress (1.8M) PO Box 50 Bartlett TX 76511 **Phn:** 254-527-4424 **Fax:** 254-527-4333 newslady01@sbcglobal.net

Bastrop Bastrop Advertiser (5.7M) PO Box 459 Bastrop TX 78602 **Phn:** 512-321-2557 **Fax:** 512-321-1680 bastropadvertiser.com news@bastropadvertiser.com

Bay City The Tribune (5.2M) PO Box 2450 Bay City TX 77404 **Phn:** 979-245-5555 **Fax:** 979-244-5908 baycitytribune.com news@baycitytribune.com

Beaumont Beaumont Journal (20.0M) PO Box 3071 Beaumont TX 77704 **Phn:** 409-833-3311 **Fax:** 409-838-2865 www.beaumontenterprise.com localnews@beaumontenterprise.com

Beaumont The Examiner (25.0M) 795 Willow St Beaumont TX 77701 **Phn:** 409-832-1400 **Fax:** 409-832-6222 theexaminer.com mail@theexaminer.com

Beeville Beeville Bee-Picayune (5.0M) PO Box 10 Beeville TX 78104 **Phn:** 361-358-2550 **Fax:** 361-358-5323 www.mysoutex.com news@mysoutex.com

Bellaire Village News & Southwest News (40.0M) 5160 Spruce St Bellaire TX 77401 **Phn:** 713-668-9293 **Fax:** 713-668-9453 www.village-southwest-news.com mynews@village-southwest-news.com

Bellville Bellville Times (4.4M) PO Box 98 Bellville TX 77418 **Phn:** 979-865-3131 **Fax:** 979-865-3132

Belton Belton Journal (5.0M) PO Box 180 Belton TX 76513 **Phn:** 254-939-5754 **Fax:** 254-939-2333 www.beltonjournal.com editor@beltonjournal.com

Big Lake Big Lake Wildcat (1.1M) PO Box 946 Big Lake TX 76932 **Phn:** 325-884-2215 **Fax:** 325-884-5771 www.mybiglake.com editor@mybiglake.com

Big Sandy Big Sandy Journal (1.2M) PO Box 897 Big Sandy TX 75755 **Phn:** 903-636-4351 **Fax:** 903-636-5091 bshjournal@aol.com

Blanco Blanco County News (2.8M) PO Box 429 Blanco TX 78606 **Phn:** 830-833-4812 **Fax:** 830-833-4246 blancocnews.com news@blanconews.com

Boerne Boerne Star (6.0M) 941 N School St Boerne TX 78006 **Phn:** 830-249-2441 **Fax:** 830-249-4607 www.boernestar.com news@boernestar.com

Bonham Bonham Journal (8.5M) 2501 N Center St Bonham TX 75418 **Phn:** 903-583-2200 **Fax:** 903-583-9459 www.bonhamjournal.com

Booker Booker News (1.2M) PO Box 807 Booker TX 79005 **Phn:** 806-658-4732 **Fax:** 806-658-4424

Bowie Bowie News (4.5M) PO Box 831 Bowie TX 76230 **Phn:** 940-872-2247 **Fax:** 940-872-4812 bowienewsinc.com bnews@sbcglobal.net

Brackettville Brackett News (1.1M) PO Box 466 Brackettville TX 78832 **Phn:** 830-563-2852 **Fax:** 830-563-9538 thebrackettnews.com tbnews@sbcglobal.net

Brady Brady Standard (3.0M) PO Box 1151 Brady TX 76825 **Phn:** 325-597-2959 **Fax:** 325-597-1434 www.bradystandard.com bsh@centex.net

Breckenridge Breckenridge American (3.4M) PO Box 871 Breckenridge TX 76424 **Phn:** 254-559-5412 **Fax:** 254-559-3491 www.breckenridgeamerican.com editor@breckenridgeamerican.com

Bremond Bremond Press (1.2M) PO Box 490 Bremond TX 76629 **Phn:** 254-746-7033 **Fax:** 254-746-7089 bremondpress@earthlink.net

Bridgeport Bridwell Publishing (3.0M) PO Box 1150 Bridgeport TX 76426 **Phn:** 940-683-4021 **Fax:** 940-683-3841 www.bridgeportindex.com bridwellk@bridgeportindex.com

Brookshire Times Tribune (1.2M) PO Box 1549 Brookshire TX 77423 **Phn:** 281-934-4949 **Fax:** 281-934-2012

Brownfield Brownfield News (3.0M) PO Box 1272 Brownfield TX 79316 **Phn:** 806-637-4535 **Fax:** 806-637-3795 www.brownfieldonline.com news@brownfieldonline.com

Buffalo Buffalo Press (2.0M) PO Box B Buffalo TX 75831 **Phn:** 903-322-4248 **Fax:** 903-322-4023 www.leoncountytoday.com buffalopress@gmail.com

Buna Buna Beacon (8.0M) PO Box 1557 Buna TX 77612 **Phn:** 409-994-2218 **Fax:** 409-994-0228 bunabeacon@sbcglobal.net

Burkburnett Informer Star (2.9M) 417 Avenue C Burkburnett TX 76354 **Phn:** 940-569-2191 **Fax:** 940-569-0704 burknews@burknews.com

Burleson Star Group (16.0M) PO Box 909 Burleson TX 76097 **Phn:** 817-295-0486 **Fax:** 817-295-5278 www.burlesonstar.net burlesonstar@thestargroup.com

Burnet Burnet Bulletin (3.2M) PO Box 160 Burnet TX 78611 **Phn:** 512-756-6136 **Fax:** 512-756-8911 burnetbulletin.com roy.bode@highlandernews.com

Burnet Citizens Gazette (2.0M) PO Box 430 Burnet TX 78611 **Phn:** 512-756-6640 cgazette@tstar.net

Caldwell Burleson County Tribune (4.2M) 306 W Highway 21 Caldwell TX 77836 **Phn:** 979-567-3286 **Fax:** 979-567-7898 www.bctribune.com news@bctribune.com

Cameron Cameron Herald (4.1M) PO Box 1230 Cameron TX 76520 **Phn:** 254-697-6671 **Fax:** 254-697-4902 www.cameronherald.com herald@cameronherald.com

Cameron Thorndale Champion (1.2M) PO Box 1230 Cameron TX 76520 **Phn:** 254-697-6671 **Fax:** 254-697-4902 www.cameronherald.com/thorndale tdchamp@vvm.com

Canadian Canadian Record (2.0M) PO Box 898 Canadian TX 79014 **Phn:** 806-323-6461 **Fax:** 806-323-5738 www.canadianrecord.com

Canton Canton Herald (6.0M) 103 E Tyler St Canton TX 75103 **Phn:** 903-567-4000 **Fax:** 903-567-6076 www.vanzandtnewspapers.com vznews@aol.com

Canyon Canyon News (4.3M) 1500 5th Ave Canyon TX 79015 **Phn:** 806-655-7121 **Fax:** 806-655-0823 www.myplainview.com/canyon news@canyonnews.com

Canyon Lake Canyon Lake Week (1.0M) 1850 Old Sattler Rd Canyon Lake TX 78132 **Phn:** 830-899-3137

Canyon Lake Times Guardian (3.0M) PO Box 1614 Canyon Lake TX 78133 **Phn:** 830-907-3882 **Fax:** 830-964-2771

Carrizo Springs Carrizo Springs Javelin (2.2M) PO Box 1046 Carrizo Springs TX 78834 **Phn:** 830-876-2318 **Fax:** 830-876-2620 www.carrizospringsjavelin.com csjavelin@yahoo.com

Carthage Panola Watchman (6.1M) 109 W Panola St Carthage TX 75633 **Phn:** 903-693-7888 **Fax:** 903-693-5857 www.news-journal.com/panola news@panolawatchman.com

Castroville News-Bulletin Times (5.0M) PO Box 1547 Castroville TX 78009 **Phn:** 830-538-2556 **Fax:** 830-931-3450

Cedar Park Hill Country News (17.5M) PO Box 1777 Cedar Park TX 78630 **Phn:** 512-259-4449 **Fax:** 512-259-8889 www.hillcountrynews.com editor@hillcountrynews.com

Center Light & Champion (5.0M) PO Box 1989 Center TX 75935 **Phn:** 936-598-3377 **Fax:** 936-598-6394 lightandchampion.com

Centerville Centerville News (2.0M) PO Box 97 Centerville TX 75833 **Phn:** 903-536-2015 **Fax:** 903-536-2329 cnews@tconline.net

Chandler Brownsboro Statesman (1.6M) PO Box 1228 Chandler TX 75758 **Phn:** 903-849-3333 **Fax:** 903-849-3308 www.c-bstatesman.com editor@c-bstatesman.com

Childress Childress Index (3.4M) PO Box 1210 Childress TX 79201 **Phn:** 940-937-2525 **Fax:** 940-937-2239 www.childressindex.com index@chipshot.net

Clarendon The Clarendon Enterprise (1.6M) PO Box 1110 Clarendon TX 79226 **Phn:** 806-874-2259 **Fax:** 806-874-2423 www.clarendonlive.com news@clarendononline.com

Clarksville Clarksville Times (3.0M) PO Box 1018 Clarksville TX 75426 **Phn:** 903-427-5616 **Fax:** 903-427-3068 www.clarksvillenews.net theclarksvilletimes@gmail.com

Claude Claude News (3.2M) PO Box 778 Claude TX 79019 **Phn:** 806-226-4500 www.claudenews.com editor@claudenews.com

TEXAS WEEKLY NEWSPAPERS

Cleveland Cleveland Advocate (4.5M) PO Box 1628 Cleveland TX 77328 **Phn:** 281-592-2626 **Fax:** 281-592-2629 www.yourhoustonnews.com clevelandadvocate@hcnonline.com

Clifton Clifton Record (3.0M) PO Box 353 Clifton TX 76634 **Phn:** 254-675-3336 **Fax:** 254-675-4090 www.cliftonrecord.com news@cliftonrecord.com

Clyde Journal-Review Publishing (4.5M) PO Box 979 Clyde TX 79510 **Phn:** 325-893-4244 **Fax:** 325-893-2780 www.clydenewspaper.com clydejournal@earthlink.net

Coleman Chronicle & Democrat-Voice (3.1M) PO Box 840 Coleman TX 76834 **Phn:** 325-625-4128 **Fax:** 325-625-4129 www.colemannews.com dvoice@web-access.net

Colorado City Colorado City Record (4.0M) PO Box 92 Colorado City TX 79512 **Phn:** 325-728-3413 **Fax:** 325-728-3414 ccitynews.net coloradorecord@yahoo.com

Columbus Colorado County Citizen (4.0M) PO Box 548 Columbus TX 78934 **Phn:** 979-732-2304 **Fax:** 979-732-8804 www.coloradocountycitizen.com editor@coloradocountycitizen.com

Columbus Columbus Banner-Press (5.0M) PO Box 490 Columbus TX 78934 **Phn:** 979-732-6243 **Fax:** 979-732-6245

Comanche Comanche Chief (4.2M) PO Box 927 Comanche TX 76442 **Phn:** 325-356-2636 **Fax:** 325-356-5380 www.thecomanchechief.com comanchechief@htcomp.net

Comfort Comfort News (1.5M) PO Box 218 Comfort TX 78013 **Phn:** 830-995-3634 **Fax:** 830-995-2075 dukecomfort@hctc.net

Conroe The Bulletin (20.0M) PO Box 2219 Conroe TX 77305 **Phn:** 936-539-2200 www.thebulletin.com

Cooper Cooper Review (2.1M) PO Box 430 Cooper TX 75432 **Phn:** 903-395-2175 **Fax:** 903-395-0424 www.cooperreview.com news@cooperreview.com

Coppell Citizens Advocate (5.0M) PO Box 557 Coppell TX 75019 **Phn:** 972-462-8192 **Fax:** 972-304-0203 citizensadvocate2000@yahoo.com

Copperas Cove Cove Herald (8.0M) 102 Cove Ter Copperas Cove TX 76522 **Phn:** 254-547-2770 **Fax:** 254-547-7039 www.kdhnews.com/copperascove

Copperas Cove Leader-Press (4.0M) PO Box 370 Copperas Cove TX 76522 **Phn:** 254-547-4207 **Fax:** 254-542-3299 www.coveleaderpress.com news@coveleaderpress.com

Crane Crane News (1.7M) 401 S Gaston St Crane TX 79731 **Phn:** 432-558-3541 **Fax:** 432-558-2676

Crockett Houston Co Courier (5.8M) PO Box 551 Crockett TX 75835 **Phn:** 936-544-2238 **Fax:** 936-544-4088 www.HoustonCountyCourier.com news@houstoncountycourier.com

Crowell Foard County News (1.5M) PO Box 489 Crowell TX 79227 **Phn:** 940-684-1355 **Fax:** 940-684-1700

Crystal City Zavala County Sentinel (2.5M) 202 E Nueces St Crystal City TX 78839 **Phn:** 830-374-3465 **Fax:** 830-374-5771

Cuero Cuero Record (5.6M) PO Box 351 Cuero TX 77954 **Phn:** 361-275-3464 **Fax:** 361-275-3131 cuerorecord.com elizabeth@cuerorecord.com

Daingerfield The Bee (2.8M) PO Box M Daingerfield TX 75638 **Phn:** 903-645-3948 **Fax:** 903-645-3731

Dalhart Dalhart Texan (1.7M) 410 Denrock Ave Dalhart TX 79022 **Phn:** 806-244-4511 **Fax:** 806-244-2395 www.thedalharttexan.com manager@thedalharttexan.com

Dallas Dallas Observer (110.0M) PO Box 190289 Dallas TX 75219 **Phn:** 214-757-9000 **Fax:** 214-757-8593 www.dallasobserver.com

Dallas Park Cities News (5.0M) 8115 Preston Rd Ste 575 Dallas TX 75225 **Phn:** 214-369-7570 **Fax:** 214-369-7736 www.parkcitiesnews.com pcn@parkcitiesnews.com

Dallas Park Cities People (6.5M) 750 North Saint Paul St # 2100 Dallas TX 75201 **Phn:** 214-739-2244 **Fax:** 214-363-6948 www.parkcitiespeople.com editor@peoplenewspapers.com

De Leon De Leon Free Press (2.0M) PO Box 320 De Leon TX 76444 **Phn:** 254-893-6868 **Fax:** 254-893-3550 deleonfreepress.com

Decatur Wise County Messenger (8.0M) PO Box 149 Decatur TX 76234 **Phn:** 940-627-5987 **Fax:** 940-627-1004 www.wcmessenger.com news@wcmessenger.com

Dell City Hudspeth County Herald (0.8M) PO Box 659 Dell City TX 79837 **Phn:** 915-964-2426 hcherald@dellcity.com

Denver City Denver City Press (1.8M) PO Box 1240 Denver City TX 79323 **Phn:** 806-592-2141 **Fax:** 806-592-8233 www.dcpressonline.com dcpress@midtech.net

Deport Thunder Prairie Publishing (3.0M) PO Box 98 Deport TX 75435 **Phn:** 903-652-4205 **Fax:** 903-652-6041

Devine Devine News (3.8M) PO Box 508 Devine TX 78016 **Phn:** 830-665-2211 **Fax:** 830-663-3686 www.devinenews.com news@devinenews.com

Diboll The Free Press (3.6M) 207 N Temple Dr Diboll TX 75941 **Phn:** 936-829-1801 **Fax:** 936-829-3321 www.dibollfreepress.com news@dibollfreepress.com

Dimmitt Castro County News (2.1M) PO Box 67 Dimmitt TX 79027 **Phn:** 806-647-3123 **Fax:** 806-647-3112

Driftwood News-Dispatch (2.0M) PO Box 227 Driftwood TX 78619 **Phn:** 512-842-1117 **Fax:** 512-847-1590

Dublin Dublin Citizen (2.3M) 938 N Patrick St Dublin TX 76446 **Phn:** 254-445-2515 **Fax:** 254-445-4116 www.dublincitizen.com publisher@dublincitizen.com

Dumas Moore County News-Press (4.0M) PO Box 757 Dumas TX 79029 **Phn:** 806-935-4111 **Fax:** 806-935-2348 www.moorenews.com newspress@moorenews.com

Eagle Lake Eagle Lake Headlight (2.2M) PO Box 67 Eagle Lake TX 77434 **Phn:** 979-234-5521 **Fax:** 979-234-5522 www.eaglelakeheadlight.com eaglelakeheadlight@sbcglobal.net

Eagle Pass Eagle Pass News-Guide (4.3M) PO Box 764 Eagle Pass TX 78853 **Phn:** 830-773-2309 **Fax:** 830-773-3398 epnewsguide@sbcglobal.net

Eastland Eastland Co. Newspapers (5.6M) PO Box 29 Eastland TX 76448 **Phn:** 254-629-1707 **Fax:** 254-629-2092

Eden The Eden Echo (1.1M) PO Box 1069 Eden TX 76837 **Phn:** 325-869-3561 **Fax:** 325-869-5652

Edinburg Edinburg Review (2.0M) 320 W University Dr Edinburg TX 78539 **Phn:** 956-383-2705 **Fax:** 956-383-3172

Edna Chronicle-Journal (8.0M) 306 N Wells St Edna TX 77957 **Phn:** 830-393-2111 **Fax:** 830-393-9012

Edna Jackson Co. Herald-Tribune (3.5M) 306 N Wells St Edna TX 77957 **Phn:** 361-782-3547 **Fax:** 361-782-6002 jacksonconews.com clundstrom@jacksonconews.com

El Campo El Campo Leader-News (6.0M) PO Box 1180 El Campo TX 77437 **Phn:** 979-543-3363 **Fax:** 979-543-0097 www.leader-news.com leader@leader-news.com

Eldorado Eldorado Success (1.1M) PO Box 1115 Eldorado TX 76936 **Phn:** 325-853-3125 **Fax:** 325-853-3378 myeldorado.net success@myeldorado.net

Electra Electra Star-News (2.0M) PO Box 1192 Electra TX 76360 **Phn:** 940-495-2149 **Fax:** 940-495-2627

Elgin Elgin Courier (3.3M) PO Box 631 Elgin TX 78621 **Phn:** 512-285-3333 **Fax:** 512-285-9406 www.elgincourier.com elgincourier@elgincourier.com

Emory Rains County Leader (2.8M) PO Box 127 Emory TX 75440 **Phn:** 903-473-2653 **Fax:** 903-473-0050 rainscountyleader.com rainsleader@earthlink.net

Fairfield The Fairfield Recorder (3.2M) 101 E Commerce St Fairfield TX 75840 **Phn:** 903-389-3334 **Fax:** 903-389-8255 www.thefairfieldrecorder.net news@thefairfieldrecorder.com

Falfurrias Falfurrias Facts (2.6M) PO Box 619 Falfurrias TX 78355 **Phn:** 361-325-2200 falfacts@yahoo.com

Farmersville C&S Media (3.8M) PO Box 512 Farmersville TX 75442 **Phn:** 972-784-6397 **Fax:** 972-782-7023 www.farmersvilletimes.com news@farmersvilletimes.com

Farwell State Line Tribune (1.4M) PO Box 255 Farwell TX 79325 **Phn:** 806-481-3681 www.statelinetribune.com tribune@plateautel.net

Ferris The Ellis Co. Press (3.0M) 208 S Central St Ferris TX 75125 **Phn:** 972-544-2369 **Fax:** 972-544-8150 www.elliscountypress.com charles@elliscountypress.com

Flatonia Flatonia Argus (1.3M) PO Box 468 Flatonia TX 78941 **Phn:** 361-865-3510 www.flatoniaargus.com newspaper@flatoniaargus.com

Floresville Wilson County News (12.0M) 1012 C St Floresville TX 78114 **Phn:** 830-216-4519 **Fax:** 830-393-3219 wilsoncountynews.com editor@wilsoncountynews.com

Flower Mound Argyle Messenger (10.0M) 3121 Cross Timbers Rd Flower Mound TX 75028 **Phn:** 972-724-3280 **Fax:** 972-724-2420

Flower Mound Flower Mound Courier (11.0M) 3121 Cross Timbers Rd Flower Mound TX 75028 **Phn:** 972-724-3280 **Fax:** 972-724-2420

Floydada Floyd County Hesperian (2.8M) 201 W California St Ste A Floydada TX 79235 **Phn:** 806-983-3737 **Fax:** 806-983-3141 www.hesperianbeacononline.com fchb.editor@yahoo.com

Forney Forney Messenger (3.3M) PO Box 936 Forney TX 75126 **Phn:** 972-564-3121 **Fax:** 972-552-3599 www.forneymessengerinc.com messengernews@sbcglobal.net

Fort Davis Mountain Dispatch (1.6M) PO Box 1097 Fort Davis TX 79734 **Phn:** 432-426-3077 **Fax:** 432-426-3844 dispatch@mztv.net

Fort Stockton Ft. Stockton Pioneer (3.5M) PO Box 1528 Fort Stockton TX 79735 **Phn:** 432-336-2281 **Fax:** 432-336-6432 www.fortstocktonpioneer.com pioneer@fspioneer.com

Fort Worth Fort Worth Weekly (50.0M) 3311 Hamilton Ave Fort Worth TX 76107 **Phn:** 817-321-9700 **Fax:** 817-335-9575 www.fwweekly.com feedback@fwweekly.com

Fort Worth Suburban Newspapers (30.0M) 7820 Wyatt Dr Fort Worth TX 76108 **Phn:** 817-246-2473 **Fax:** 817-246-2474 suburbannews@sbcglobal.net

Franklin Franklin News Weekly (1.2M) 107 E Decherd St Franklin TX 77856 **Phn:** 979-828-1520 **Fax:** 979-828-1525 franklinnewsweekly@gmail.com

TEXAS WEEKLY NEWSPAPERS

Frankston Frankston Citizen (1.9M) PO Box 188 Frankston TX 75763 **Phn:** 903-876-2218 **Fax:** 903-876-4974 www.frankstoncitizen.com news@frankstoncitizen.com

Fredericksburg Standard-Radio Post (9.8M) PO Box 1639 Fredericksburg TX 78624 **Phn:** 830-997-2155 **Fax:** 830-990-0036 www.fredericksburgstandard.com fbgnews@fredericksburgstandard.com

Freer Freer Press (1.5M) PO Box 567 Freer TX 78357 **Phn:** 361-394-7402 **Fax:** 361-394-5386

Friona Friona Star (2.0M) 916 Main St Friona TX 79035 **Phn:** 806-250-2211 **Fax:** 806-250-5127 www.frionaonline.com frionastar@wtrt.net

Frisco Little Elm Journal (1.4M) 407 W Eldorado Pkwy # 17 Frisco TX 75034 **Phn:** 972-398-4200 starlocalmedia.com/littleelmjournal tglaze@starlocalnews.com

Fritch The Eagle Press (1.3M) PO Box 1810 Fritch TX 79036 **Phn:** 806-857-2123

Garrison Garrison News (1.4M) PO Box 278 Garrison TX 75946 **Phn:** 936-347-2575 **Fax:** 936-347-3203

Gatesville Messenger/Star-Forum (4.5M) PO Box 799 Gatesville TX 76528 **Phn:** 254-865-5212 **Fax:** 254-865-2361 www.gatesvillemessenger.com editor@gatesvillemessenger.com

Georgetown Sunday Sun (9.0M) PO Box 39 Georgetown TX 78627 **Phn:** 512-930-4824 **Fax:** 512-863-2474

Georgetown Williamson County Sun (9.0M) PO Box 39 Georgetown TX 78627 **Phn:** 512-930-4824 **Fax:** 512-863-2474

Giddings Giddings Times & News (6.8M) PO Box 947 Giddings TX 78942 **Phn:** 979-542-2222

Gilmer Gilmer Mirror (4.5M) PO Box 250 Gilmer TX 75644 **Phn:** 903-843-2503 **Fax:** 903-843-5123 www.gilmermirror.com gilmermirror@aol.com

Gladewater Gladewater Mirror (2.0M) PO Box 1549 Gladewater TX 75647 **Phn:** 903-845-2235 **Fax:** 903-845-2237 www.gladewatermirror.com gstratton@news-journal.com

Glen Rose Glen Rose Reporter (3.0M) PO Box 2009 Glen Rose TX 76043 **Phn:** 254-897-2282 **Fax:** 254-897-9423 www.yourglenrosetx.com news@theglenrosereporter.com

Goldthwaite Goldthwaite Eagle (2.7M) PO Box 249 Goldthwaite TX 76844 **Phn:** 325-648-2244 **Fax:** 325-648-2024 goldthwaiteeagle.com goldnews@centex.net

Goliad Texan Express (2.0M) PO Box 1 Goliad TX 77963 **Phn:** 361-645-2330 **Fax:** 361-645-2812 www.mysoutex.com

Gonzales Gonzales Inquirer (4.0M) PO Box 616 Gonzales TX 78629 **Phn:** 830-672-2861 **Fax:** 830-672-7029 www.gonzalesinquirer.com news@gonzalesinquirer.com

Gorman Gorman Progress (1.0M) PO Box 68 Gorman TX 76454 **Phn:** 254-734-2410 **Fax:** 254-734-2799 gprogress@txbusiness.com

Graford Lake Country Sun (2.1M) 617 N Fm 2353 Unit 4 Graford TX 76449 **Phn:** 940-779-3040 **Fax:** 940-779-3064 www.lakecountrysun.com editor@lakecountrysun.com

Graham The Graham Leader (5.2M) PO Box 600 Graham TX 76450 **Phn:** 940-549-7800 **Fax:** 940-549-4364 www.grahamleader.com editor@grahamleader.com

Granbury Hood County News (11.0M) PO Box 879 Granbury TX 76048 **Phn:** 817-573-7066 **Fax:** 817-279-8371 www.hcnews.com editor@hcnews.com

Grand Saline Edgewood Enterprise (1.1M) PO Box 608 Grand Saline TX 75140 **Phn:** 903-962-4275 **Fax:** 903-962-3660 www.smalltownpapers.com

Grand Saline Grand Saline Sun (2.0M) PO Box 608 Grand Saline TX 75140 **Phn:** 903-962-4275 **Fax:** 903-962-3660 www.grandsalinesun.com wcallaway@grandsalinesun.com

Grandview Grandview Tribune (1.2M) 104 E Criner St Grandview TX 76050 **Phn:** 817-866-3391 **Fax:** 817-866-3869

Grapeland Grapeland Messenger (2.3M) PO Box 99 Grapeland TX 75844 **Phn:** 936-687-2424 grapelandmessenger@yahoo.com

Greenville Commerce Journal (2.8M) 2305 King St Greenville TX 75401 **Phn:** 903-455-4220 **Fax:** 903-455-6281 commercejournal.com wmorrison@heraldbanner.com

Groesbeck Groesbeck Journal (4.0M) PO Box 440 Groesbeck TX 76642 **Phn:** 254-729-5103 **Fax:** 254-729-8310 www.groesbeckjournal.com groesbeckads@gmail.com

Groom Groom News (1.2M) PO Box 460 Groom TX 79039 **Phn:** 806-248-7333

Gun Barrel City Cedar Creek Pilot (5.3M) 1012 W Main St Ste 105 Gun Barrel City TX 75156 **Phn:** 903-887-8051 **Fax:** 903-887-8225 news@cedarcreekpilot.com

Hale Center Hale Center American (0.8M) PO Box 1030 Hale Center TX 79041 **Phn:** 806-839-2312 **Fax:** 806-839-9901

Hallettsville Tribune-Herald (4.2M) PO Box 427 Hallettsville TX 77964 **Phn:** 361-798-2481 **Fax:** 361-798-9902 tribuneherald@sbcglobal.net

Hamilton Hamilton Herald-News (2.8M) PO Box 833 Hamilton TX 76531 **Phn:** 254-386-3145 **Fax:** 254-386-3001 TheHamiltonHerald-News.com kmiller@thehamiltonherald-news.com

Hamlin Hamlin Herald (1.1M) 350 S Central Ave Hamlin TX 79520 **Phn:** 325-576-3606 www.ashnews.com

Harker Heights Evening Star (5.0M) PO Box 2405 Harker Heights TX 76548 **Phn:** 254-699-3998 **Fax:** 254-699-1725

Hart Hart Beat (0.5M) PO Box 350 Hart TX 79043 **Phn:** 806-938-2640 **Fax:** 806-938-2216 hbeat@amaonline.com

Haskell Haskell Free Press (2.0M) PO Box 555 Haskell TX 79521 **Phn:** 940-864-2686 **Fax:** 940-864-2687 hfp@valornet.com

Hearne Robertson Co. News (6.0M) 120 W 3rd St Hearne TX 77859 **Phn:** 979-279-3411 **Fax:** 979-279-5401 www.robconews.com dennis@robconews.com

Hebbronville Hebbronville View (1.2M) PO Box 310 Hebbronville TX 78361 **Phn:** 361-527-4272 **Fax:** 361-527-5271 hebview@yahoo.com

Hebbronville The Enterprise (1.5M) PO Box 759 Hebbronville TX 78361 **Phn:** 361-527-3261 **Fax:** 361-527-4545

Helotes Helotes Echo (14.0M) 14743 Old Bandera Rd Unit 1 Helotes TX 78023 **Phn:** 210-695-3613 **Fax:** 210-695-9151 www.helotesecho.com echoeditor@satx.rr.com

Hemphill Sabine County Reporter (3.0M) PO Box 700 Hemphill TX 75948 **Phn:** 409-787-2172 **Fax:** 409-787-4300 reporter1@windstream.net

Henderson Rusk County News (6.5M) PO Box 30 Henderson TX 75653 **Phn:** 903-657-2501 **Fax:** 903-657-2452

Henrietta Clay County Leader (3.1M) PO Drawer 10 Henrietta TX 76365 **Phn:** 940-538-4333 **Fax:** 940-538-4542 claycountyleader.com news@claycountyleader.com

Hewitt Hometown News (4.5M) PO Box 1 Hewitt TX 76643 **Phn:** 254-753-3871 **Fax:** 254-753-3884 hometown@jonesprint.com

Hico Hico News-Review (1.1M) PO Box D Hico TX 76457 **Phn:** 254-796-4325 **Fax:** 254-796-2548 www.thehiconewsreview.com hiconews@gmail.com

Highlands Star Courier (8.0M) PO Box 405 Highlands TX 77562 **Phn:** 281-328-9605 starcouriernews.com grafik2@aol.com

Hillsboro Hillsboro Reporter (5.0M) PO Box 569 Hillsboro TX 76645 **Phn:** 254-582-3431 **Fax:** 254-582-3800 hillsbororeporter.com ads@hillsbororeporter.com

Hondo Anvil Herald (5.5M) PO Box 400 Hondo TX 78861 **Phn:** 830-426-3346 **Fax:** 830-426-3348 www.hondoanvilherald.com editor@hondoanvilherald.com

Honey Grove Weekly Gazette (1.5M) PO Box 165 Honey Grove TX 75446 **Phn:** 903-378-3558 **Fax:** 903-378-3588 www.honeygroveweeklygazette.com hgwcnews@sbcglobal.net

Horizon City West Texas County Courier (10.0M) 15344 Werling Ct Horizon City TX 79928 **Phn:** 915-852-3235 **Fax:** 915-852-0123 www.wtxcc.com

Houston Houston Press (116.0M) 1621 Milam St Ste 100 Houston TX 77002 **Phn:** 713-280-2400 **Fax:** 713-280-2496 www.houstonpress.com margaret.downing@houstonpress.com

Houston Northeast News (30.0M) 5327 Aldine Mail Rd Houston TX 77039 **Phn:** 281-449-9945 **Fax:** 713-977-1188 nenewsroom.com nenewsroom@aol.com

Houston The Potpourri (42.0M) 21901 Tomball Pkwy Ste 500 Houston TX 77070 **Phn:** 281-378-1080 **Fax:** 281-320-2005 www.yourhoustonnews.com/tomball rkent@hcnonline.com

Hubbard Hubbard City News (1.5M) PO Box 492 Hubbard TX 76648 **Phn:** 254-562-2868 **Fax:** 254-562-3121

Hutto Hutto News (6.6M) PO Box 1040 Hutto TX 78634 **Phn:** 512-578-5229 **Fax:** 512-352-2227 www.thehuttonews.com newsdesk@thehuttonews.com

Idalou Idalou Beacon (0.9M) PO Box 887 Idalou TX 79329 **Phn:** 806-892-2233

Ingram West Kerr Current (1.5M) 107 Highway 39 Ste A Ingram TX 78025 **Phn:** 830-367-3501 **Fax:** 830-367-3064 wkcurrent.com wkcurrent@classicnet.net

Iowa Park Iowa Park Leader (2.7M) PO Box 430 Iowa Park TX 76367 **Phn:** 940-592-4431 www.iowaparkleader.com dhamilton@iowaparkleader.com

Irving Irving Journal (19.0M) 207 Mandalay Canal Irving TX 75039 **Phn:** 469-893-1780 https://www.facebook.com/IrvingOnline jmartinez@irvingonline.com

Irving Irving Rambler (7.0M) PO Box 177731 Irving TX 75017 **Phn:** 214-675-6493 www.irvingrambler.com john@irvingrambler.com

Jacksboro Jack County Herald (2.5M) PO Box 70 Jacksboro TX 76458 **Phn:** 940-567-2616 **Fax:** 940-567-2071 www.jacksboronewspapers.com editor@jacksboronewspapers.com

Jacksboro Jacksboro Gazette-News (2.5M) PO Box 70 Jacksboro TX 76458 **Phn:** 940-567-2616 **Fax:** 940-567-2071 www.jacksboronewspapers.com editor@jacksboronewspapers.com

TEXAS WEEKLY NEWSPAPERS

Jasper Jasper News Boy (6.0M) 702 S Jasper Jasper TX 75951 **Phn:** 409-384-3441 **Fax:** 409-384-8803 www.beaumontenterprise.com/jasper tkelly@hearstnp.com

Jefferson Jefferson Jimplecute (2.5M) 205 W Austin St Jefferson TX 75657 **Phn:** 903-665-2462 **Fax:** 903-655-3303

Jewett Jewett Messenger (1.7M) PO Box 155 Jewett TX 75846 **Phn:** 903-626-4296 **Fax:** 903-626-5248 jmessenger46@sbcglobal.net

Johnson City Record Courier (1.5M) PO Box 205 Johnson City TX 78636 **Phn:** 830-868-7181 **Fax:** 830-868-7182 www.jcrecordcourier.com jcrecordcourier@verizon.net

Junction Junction Eagle (2.0M) 215 N 6th St Junction TX 76849 **Phn:** 325-446-2610 **Fax:** 325-446-4025 www.junctioneagle.com editor@junctioneagle.com

Karnes City The Countywide (3.0M) 110 S Market St Karnes City TX 78118 **Phn:** 830-780-3924 **Fax:** 830-780-3711 www.mysoutex.com

Katy Katy Times (7.5M) 5319 E 5th St Katy TX 77493 **Phn:** 281-391-3141 **Fax:** 281-391-2030 KatyTimes.com news@katytimes.com

Kaufman Kaufman Herald (4.0M) PO Box 460 Kaufman TX 75142 **Phn:** 972-932-2171 **Fax:** 972-932-2172 www.kaufmanherald.com mlewis@kaufmanherald.com

Keller Keller Citizen (30.0M) PO Box 615 Keller TX 76244 **Phn:** 817-431-2231 **Fax:** 817-431-5534 www.star-telegram.com/kellercitizen amurray@star-telegram.com

Kerens Kerens Tribune (1.0M) 104 SE 1st St Kerens TX 75144 **Phn:** 903-396-2261 **Fax:** 903-396-2728 kteditor07@yahoo.com

Kermit Winkler County News (3.8M) PO Box A Kermit TX 79745 **Phn:** 432-586-2561 **Fax:** 432-586-2562 gfreepress@sbcglobal.net

Kilgore Bullard Banner News (1.0M) PO Box 1210 Kilgore TX 75663 **Phn:** 903-894-9306 **Fax:** 903-894-9308 www.bullardnews.com news@bullardnews.com

Kingsville Duval Co Picture (2.2M) PO Box 1071 Kingsville TX 78364 **Phn:** 361-279-3313 **Fax:** 361-279-2530 poncho2010@netscape.net

Kingsville Kingsville Journal (6.4M) 1429 S 6th St Kingsville TX 78363 **Phn:** 361-595-4414 **Fax:** 361-595-4514

Kingsville Kingsville Record (6.0M) PO Box 951 Kingsville TX 78363 **Phn:** 361-592-4304 **Fax:** 361-592-1015 www.kingsvillerecord.net

Kingwood Observer Newspapers (68.0M) 1117 Kingwood Dr Kingwood TX 77339 **Phn:** 281-359-2799 **Fax:** 281-359-0017 www.yourhoustonnews.com/kingwood observereditor@hcnonline.com

Kirbyville Kirbyville Banner (3.6M) 104 N Kellie Ave Kirbyville TX 75956 **Phn:** 409-423-2696 **Fax:** 409-423-4793 kbanner@sbcglobal.net

Knox City Knox County News (1.5M) PO Box 188 Knox City TX 79529 **Phn:** 940-657-3142

Kress Kress Chronicle (0.4M) 7580 FM 145 Kress TX 79052 **Phn:** 806-684-2586 **Fax:** 806-684-2456 kresschronicle@midplains.coop

La Feria La Feria News (5.0M) PO Box 999 La Feria TX 78559 **Phn:** 956-797-9920 **Fax:** 956-797-9921 thelaferianews.com laferianews@aol.com

La Grange The Fayette County Record (5.5M) PO Box 400 La Grange TX 78945 **Phn:** 979-968-3155 **Fax:** 979-968-6767 www.fayettecountyrecord.com fayettecountyrecord@verizon.net

La Vernia La Vernia News (1.6M) 112 E Chihuahua St La Vernia TX 78121 **Phn:** 830-779-3751

Lago Vista North Lake Travis Log (5.6M) PO Box 4910 Lago Vista TX 78645 **Phn:** 512-267-4449 **Fax:** 512-267-4464 northlaketravislog.com news@nltlog.com

Lakeway Lake Travis View (3.7M) 107 Ranch Road 620 S Ste 114 Lakeway TX 78734 **Phn:** 512-263-1100 **Fax:** 512-263-3583 laketravisview.com news@ltview.com

Lamesa Lamesa Press-Reporter (3.7M) PO Box 710 Lamesa TX 79331 **Phn:** 806-872-2177 **Fax:** 806-872-2623 pressreporter.com editor@pressreporter.com

Lampasas Lampasas Dispatch Record (4.0M) PO Box 631 Lampasas TX 76550 **Phn:** 512-556-6262 **Fax:** 512-556-3278 www.lampasasdispatchrecord.com news@lampasas.com

Leonard Leonard Graphic (1.8M) PO Box 1347 Leonard TX 75452 **Phn:** 903-587-2850 **Fax:** 903-587-0927 www.theleonardgraphic.com graphiceditor@theleonardgraphic.com

Levelland Levelland News-Press (5.0M) PO Box 1628 Levelland TX 79336 **Phn:** 806-894-3121 **Fax:** 806-894-7957 levellandnews.net levellandnews@valornet.com

Lexington Lexington Leader (2.0M) PO Box 547 Lexington TX 78947 **Phn:** 979-773-3022 **Fax:** 979-773-4125 www.lexingtonleader.com editor@lexingtonleader.com

Liberty Liberty Gazette (9.1M) PO Box 1908 Liberty TX 77575 **Phn:** 936-336-6416 **Fax:** 936-336-9400 mail@libertygazette.com

Liberty Liberty Vindicator (5.3M) PO Box 9189 Liberty TX 77575 **Phn:** 936-336-3611 **Fax:** 936-336-3345 www.thevindicator.com

Liberty Hill The Liberty Hill Independent (1.5M) PO Box 639 Liberty Hill TX 78642 **Phn:** 512-778-5577 **Fax:** 512-515-6536

Lindale Lindale News & Times (2.5M) PO Box 1559 Lindale TX 75771 **Phn:** 903-882-8880 **Fax:** 903-882-8234 news-journal.com rbrack@news-journal.com

Linden Cass County Sun (1.2M) PO Box 779 Linden TX 75563 **Phn:** 903-756-7396 **Fax:** 903-756-3038

Littlefield Lamb County Leader News (3.0M) PO Box 310 Littlefield TX 79339 **Phn:** 806-385-4481 **Fax:** 806-385-4640 leadernews@valornet.com

Livingston Polk Co. Publishing (31.0M) PO Box 1276 Livingston TX 77351 **Phn:** 936-327-4357 **Fax:** 936-327-7156 www.easttexasnews.com polknews@gmail.com

Llano Llano County Journal (4.0M) 507 Bessemer Ave Llano TX 78643 **Phn:** 325-248-0682 **Fax:** 325-248-0621 llanocj.com newscopy@llanocj.com

Llano The Llano News (3.4M) PO Box 187 Llano TX 78643 **Phn:** 325-247-4433 **Fax:** 325-247-3338 www.llanonews.com thenews@verizon.net

Lockhart Lockhart Post Register (4.1M) PO Box 929 Lockhart TX 78644 **Phn:** 512-398-4886 **Fax:** 512-398-6144 post-register.com kathibliss@post-register.com

Longview East Texas Review (10.0M) PO Box 12473 Longview TX 75607 **Phn:** 903-236-0406 www.easttexasreview.com joycelyne@easttexasreview.com

Luling Luling Newsboy-Signal (2.0M) PO Box 352 Luling TX 78648 **Phn:** 830-875-2116 **Fax:** 830-875-2124 slulingnewsboy@austin.rr.com

Lumberton Hardin Co News (17.0M) 522 N Main St Lumberton TX 77657 **Phn:** 409-755-4912 **Fax:** 409-755-7731 www.beaumontenterprise.com/hardincountynews localnews@beaumontenterprise.com

Mabank The Monitor (5.0M) PO Box 48 Mabank TX 75147 **Phn:** 903-887-4511 **Fax:** 903-887-4510 www.themonitor.net publisher@themonitor.net

Madisonville Madisonville Meteor (3.4M) PO Box 999 Madisonville TX 77864 **Phn:** 936-348-3505 **Fax:** 936-348-3338 www.madisonvillemeteor.com editor@madisonvillemeteor.com

Malakoff Malakoff News (2.4M) 815 E Royall Blvd Ste 6 Malakoff TX 75148 **Phn:** 903-489-0531 **Fax:** 903-489-2543 malakoffnews.net malnews@embarqmail.com

Mansfield Mansfield News-Mirror (4.5M) PO Box 337 Mansfield TX 76063 **Phn:** 817-473-4451 **Fax:** 817-473-0730 www.star-telegram.com arogers@star-telegram.com

Marble Falls Horseshoe Bay Beacon (3.0M) PO Box 4845 Marble Falls TX 78657 **Phn:** 830-598-6740 **Fax:** 830-598-8685 thebeacon@nctv.com

Marble Falls Kingsland Current (1.0M) PO Box 1000 Marble Falls TX 78654 **Phn:** 325-388-2343

Marble Falls The Highlander (5.8M) PO Box 1000 Marble Falls TX 78654 **Phn:** 830-693-4367 **Fax:** 830-693-3650 highlandernews.com newscopy@highlandernews.com

Marble Falls The Picayune (26.0M) PO Box 10 Marble Falls TX 78654 **Phn:** 830-693-7152 **Fax:** 830-693-3085 www.dailytrib.com

Marfa Big Bend Sentinel (3.0M) PO Box P Marfa TX 79843 **Phn:** 432-729-4342 www.bigbendnow.com editor@bigbendnow.com

Marlin Marlin Democrat (2.8M) PO Box 112 Marlin TX 76661 **Phn:** 254-883-2554 **Fax:** 254-883-6553 www.marlindemocrat.com democrat@marlindemocrat.com

Mart Mart Messenger (1.9M) 105 S Pearl St Mart TX 76664 **Phn:** 254-876-3939 **Fax:** 254-876-3942 martmessenger@yahoo.com

Mason Mason County News (2.7M) PO Box 1729 Mason TX 76856 **Phn:** 325-347-5757 **Fax:** 325-347-5668 www.masoncountynews.com mcnnews@hctc.net

Matador Motley County Tribune (1.3M) PO Box 490 Matador TX 79244 **Phn:** 806-347-2400 **Fax:** 806-347-2774

Mc Gregor Mc Gregor Mirror (2.2M) PO Box 415 Mc Gregor TX 76657 **Phn:** 254-840-2091 www.mcgregormirror.com staff@mcgregormirror.com

McAllen Valley Newspapers (123.0M) 1811 N 23rd St McAllen TX 78501 **Phn:** 956-682-2423 **Fax:** 956-630-6371 www.yourvalleyvoice.com brad@valleytowncrier.com

Memphis Hall Co. Herald (1.8M) 617 W Main St Memphis TX 79245 **Phn:** 806-259-2441 chris@myhallcounty.com

Menard Menard News (1.4M) PO Box 248 Menard TX 76859 **Phn:** 325-396-2243 **Fax:** 325-396-2739

Mercedes Mercedes Enterprise (2.2M) PO Box 657 Mercedes TX 78570 **Phn:** 956-565-2425 **Fax:** 956-565-2570 mercedesenterprise@sbcglobal.net

Meridian Bosque Co News (1.4M) PO Box 343 Meridian TX 76665 **Phn:** 254-435-6333 **Fax:** 254-435-6335

Merkel Merkel Mail (1.3M) PO Box 428 Merkel TX 79536 **Phn:** 325-928-5712 **Fax:** 325-928-5899 merkelmail@cmaaccess.net

Miami Miami Chief (0.6M) PO Box 396 Miami TX 79059 **Phn:** 806-868-2521 **Fax:** 806-868-6051 themiamichief@yahoo.com

TEXAS WEEKLY NEWSPAPERS

Midlothian Today Newspapers (33.0M) 4431 Blackchamp Rd Midlothian TX 76065 **Phn:** 972-298-4211 **Fax:** 972-298-6369

Miles Messenger Publications (1.1M) PO Box 307 Miles TX 76861 **Phn:** 325-468-3611

Mineola Mineola Monitor (3.4M) PO Box 210 Mineola TX 75773 **Phn:** 903-569-2442 **Fax:** 903-569-6836 www.themineolamonitor.com dnewman@themineolamonitor.com

Mission Progress Times (7.0M) 1217 N Conway Ave Mission TX 78572 **Phn:** 956-585-4893 **Fax:** 956-585-2304 www.progresstimes.net news@progresstimes.net

Monahans The Monahans News (3.0M) 107 W 2nd St Monahans TX 79756 **Phn:** 432-943-4313 **Fax:** 432-943-4314 editor@monahansnews.net

Morton Morton Tribune (1.2M) PO Box 1016 Morton TX 79346 **Phn:** 806-266-5576 **Fax:** 806-266-8841 mortontribune@aol.com

Moulton Moulton Eagle (1.3M) PO Box G Moulton TX 77975 **Phn:** 361-596-4871 moultoneagle@sbcglobal.net

Mount Vernon Mt. Vernon Optic-Herald (3.1M) PO Box 1199 Mount Vernon TX 75457 **Phn:** 903-537-2228 **Fax:** 903-537-2227 www.mt-vernon.com optic@mt-vernon.com

Muenster Muenster Enterprise (1.8M) PO Box 190 Muenster TX 76252 **Phn:** 940-759-4311 **Fax:** 940-759-4110 jfelderhoff@ntin.net

Muleshoe Muleshoe Journal (2.0M) PO Box 449 Muleshoe TX 79347 **Phn:** 806-272-4536 **Fax:** 806-272-3567 www.muleshoejournal.com editor@muleshoejournal.com

Munday Munday Courier (1.5M) PO Box 130 Munday TX 76371 **Phn:** 940-422-4314 **Fax:** 940-422-4333 www.themundaycourier.com mcourier@westex.net

Naples The Monitor (2.5M) PO Box 39 Naples TX 75568 **Phn:** 903-897-2281 **Fax:** 903-897-2095 themonitor@valornet.com

Navasota Navasota Examiner (5.0M) PO Box 751 Navasota TX 77868 **Phn:** 936-825-6484 **Fax:** 936-825-2230 www.navasotaexaminer.com editor@navasotaexaminer.com

Needville Gulf Coast Tribune (1.4M) PO Box 488 Needville TX 77461 **Phn:** 979-793-6560 **Fax:** 979-793-4260 gctribune@consolidated.net

New Boston Westward Communications (14.4M) 129 E North St Frnt New Boston TX 75570 **Phn:** 903-628-5801 newbostonnews.com

New Ulm New Ulm Enterprise (1.4M) PO Box 128 New Ulm TX 78950 **Phn:** 979-992-3351 **Fax:** 979-992-3352

Newton Newton County News (2.4M) PO Box 65 Newton TX 75966 **Phn:** 409-379-2416 www.newtonnews.com

Nixon Cow Country Courier (0.9M) PO Box 200 Nixon TX 78140 **Phn:** 830-582-1740 **Fax:** 830-582-2123 wscott@gvec.net

Nocona Nocona News (2.2M) PO Box 539 Nocona TX 76255 **Phn:** 940-825-3201 **Fax:** 940-825-3202 tracymesler@yahoo.com

Normangee Normangee Star (1.4M) PO Box 97 Normangee TX 77871 **Phn:** 936-396-3391 **Fax:** 936-396-2478 www.normangeestar.net publisher@texasbb.com

Odonnell O'Donnell Index-Press (0.6M) PO Box 457 Odonnell TX 79351 **Phn:** 806-428-3591 **Fax:** 806-428-3360 kelseymimi@hotmail.com

Olney Olney Enterprise (2.6M) PO Box 577 Olney TX 76374 **Phn:** 940-564-5558 **Fax:** 940-564-3992 www.olneyenterprise.com editor@olneyenterprise.com

Olton Olton Enterprise (1.1M) PO Box 1075 Olton TX 79064 **Phn:** 806-285-2631 **Fax:** 806-285-2632

Orange Orange County News (22.0M) 1507 W Park Ave Orange TX 77630 **Phn:** 409-883-4388 **Fax:** 409-886-3907 www.beaumontenterprise.com/news/orangecounty localnews@beaumontenterprise.com

Ozona Ozona Stockman (1.8M) PO Box 370 Ozona TX 76943 **Phn:** 325-392-2551 **Fax:** 325-392-2439 publisher@ozonastockman.com

Paducah Paducah Post (1.2M) PO Box E Paducah TX 79248 **Phn:** 806-492-3585

Palacios Palacios Beacon (2.2M) PO Box 817 Palacios TX 77465 **Phn:** 361-972-3009 **Fax:** 361-972-2610 www.palaciosbeacon.com palaciosbeacon@gmail.com

Panhandle Panhandle Herald (1.9M) PO Box 429 Panhandle TX 79068 **Phn:** 806-537-3634 www.panhandleherald.com shaun@panhandleherald.com

Pasadena Community Newspapers (45.0M) PO Box 6192 Pasadena TX 77506 **Phn:** 713-477-0221 **Fax:** 713-477-4172 www.yourhoustonnews.com/pasadena jmolony@hcnonline.com

Pasadena Deer Park Broadcaster (11.0M) 102 Shaver St Pasadena TX 77506 **Phn:** 713-477-0221 www.yourhoustonnews.com/deer_park jmolony@hcnonline.com

Pearland Friendswood Journal (9.0M) PO Box 1830 Pearland TX 77588 **Phn:** 281-485-2785 **Fax:** 281-485-4464 www.yourhoustonnews.com/friendswood thejournal@hcnonline.com

Pearland Pearland Journal (20.6M) PO Box 1830 Pearland TX 77588 **Phn:** 281-485-2785 **Fax:** 281-485-4464 www.yourhoustonnews.com/pearland pfjournals@hcnonline.com

Pearland Wood Land Publishing (15.0M) 2404 Park Ave Pearland TX 77581 **Phn:** 281-485-7501 **Fax:** 281-485-6397

Pearsall Frio-Nueces Current (3.4M) PO Box 1208 Pearsall TX 78061 **Phn:** 830-334-3644 **Fax:** 830-334-3647 frio-nuecescurrent.com currenteditor@att.net

Pecos Pecos Enterprise (2.0M) 324 S Cedar St Pecos TX 79772 **Phn:** 432-445-5475 **Fax:** 432-445-4321 www.pecos.net/news

Perryton Perryton Herald (3.4M) PO Box 989 Perryton TX 79070 **Phn:** 806-435-3631 **Fax:** 806-435-2420

Pharr Advance News Journal (8.7M) 1101 N Cage Blvd Ste 1C Pharr TX 78577 **Phn:** 956-783-0036 **Fax:** 956-787-8824 advancenews@aol.com

Pilot Point Post Signal (1.8M) PO Box 249 Pilot Point TX 76258 **Phn:** 940-686-2169 **Fax:** 940-686-2437 www.postsignal.com postsignal@earthlink.net

Pittsburg Pittsburg Gazette (3.4M) 112 Quitman St Pittsburg TX 75686 **Phn:** 903-856-6629 **Fax:** 903-856-0510 www.campcountynow.com

Plano Frisco Enterprise (16.0M) 624 Krona Dr Ste 170 Plano TX 75074 **Phn:** 972-398-4200 **Fax:** 972-801-3203

Plano Mesquite News (36.0M) 624 Krona Dr Ste 170 Plano TX 75074 **Phn:** 972-398-4200 **Fax:** 972-398-4470 starlocalmedia.com/mesquitenews rmann@starlocalmedia.com

Plano Rowlett Lakeshore Times (5.0M) 624 Krona Dr Ste 170 Plano TX 75074 **Phn:** 972-398-4200 **Fax:** 972-398-4470 starlocalmedia.com/rowlettlakeshoretimes kgreen@starlocalmedia.com

Plano Star Community Newspapers (8.5M) 624 Krona Dr Ste 170 Plano TX 75074 **Phn:** 972-398-4200 **Fax:** 972-398-4470 starlocalmedia.com/lewisvilleleader galdaz@starlocalmedia.com

Plano Turtle Creek News (23.0M) PO Box 864134 Plano TX 75075 **Phn:** 214-887-0737 turtlecreeknews.net chris@turtlecreeknews.com

Pleasanton Pleasanton Express (8.4M) PO Box 880 Pleasanton TX 78064 **Phn:** 830-569-4967 **Fax:** 830-569-6100 www.pleasantonexpress.com sbrown@pleasantonexpress.com

Port Aransas South Jetty (5.6M) PO Box 1117 Port Aransas TX 78373 **Phn:** 361-749-5131 **Fax:** 361-749-5137 www.portasouthjetty.com southjetty@centurytel.net

Port Isabel South Padre Press (4.8M) PO Box 308 Port Isabel TX 78578 **Phn:** 956-943-5545 **Fax:** 956-943-4782

Port Lavaca Port Lavaca Wave (4.5M) PO Box 88 Port Lavaca TX 77979 **Phn:** 361-552-9788 **Fax:** 361-552-3108 portlavacawave.com newsroom@plwave.com

Post Post Dispatch (1.6M) 123 E Main St Post TX 79356 **Phn:** 806-495-2816 **Fax:** 806-495-2059 thepostdispatchonline.com thepostcitydispatch@gmail.com

Pottsboro Pottsboro Press (1.9M) PO Box 817 Pottsboro TX 75076 **Phn:** 903-814-4152 **Fax:** 903-892-2344

Pottsboro Pottsboro Sun (1.5M) PO Box 554 Pottsboro TX 75076 **Phn:** 903-327-3870 pottsborosun@gmail.com

Pottsboro Pottsboro Sun (1.5M) PO Box 554 Pottsboro TX 75076 **Phn:** 903-327-3870 **Fax:** 903-364-2276 pottsborosun@gmail.com

Presidio The Presidio International (1.0M) PO Box 1898 Presidio TX 79845 **Phn:** 432-229-3877 www.bigbendnow.com international@bigbendnow.com

Quanah Quanah Tribune-Chief (1.5M) 310 Mercer St Quanah TX 79252 **Phn:** 940-663-5333 **Fax:** 940-663-5073

Quinlan Quinlan-Tawakoni News (3.6M) PO Box 3100 Quinlan TX 75474 **Phn:** 903-356-2311 **Fax:** 903-356-3770 www.vanzandtnewspapers.com vznews@aol.com

Quitaque Valley Tribune (1.0M) PO Box 478 Quitaque TX 79255 **Phn:** 806-455-1101

Quitman Wood County Democrat (3.0M) PO Box 308 Quitman TX 75783 **Phn:** 903-763-4522 **Fax:** 903-763-2313 www.thewoodcountydemocrat.com news@thewoodcountydemocrat.com

Ralls Crosby Co. News (0.6M) PO Box 1115 Ralls TX 79357 **Phn:** 806-253-0211

Rankin Rankin News (0.7M) PO Box 445 Rankin TX 79778 **Phn:** 432-693-2873

Raymondville Chronicle News (3.1M) PO Box 369 Raymondville TX 78580 **Phn:** 956-689-2421 **Fax:** 956-689-6915 www.raymondvillechroniclenews.com chroniclenews@msn.com

Refugio Refugio County Press (2.8M) PO Box 200 Refugio TX 78377 **Phn:** 361-526-2397 **Fax:** 361-526-2398 www.mysoutex.com

Rio Grande City Rio Grande Herald (4.0M) 100 S Corpus Christi St Ste 3 Rio Grande City TX 78582 **Phn:** 956-487-2819 **Fax:** 956-488-8252

Robert Lee Observer/Enterprise (2.0M) PO Box 1329 Robert Lee TX 76945 **Phn:** 325-453-2433 **Fax:** 325-453-4643 o-e@wcc.net

TEXAS WEEKLY NEWSPAPERS

Rockdale Rockdale Reporter (4.9M) PO Box 552 Rockdale TX 76567 **Phn:** 512-446-5838 **Fax:** 512-446-5317 www.rockdalereporter.com mike@rockdalereporter.com

Rockport Coastal Bend Herald (5.0M) PO Box 1448 Rockport TX 78381 **Phn:** 361-729-1828 **Fax:** 361-729-9060 www.theheraldonline.com theherald@the-i.net

Rockport Rockport Pilot (5.3M) PO Box 730 Rockport TX 78381 **Phn:** 361-729-9900 **Fax:** 361-729-8903 www.rockportpilot.com editorial@rockportpilot.com

Rocksprings Texas Mohair Weekly (1.2M) PO Box 287 Rocksprings TX 78880 **Phn:** 830-683-3130 **Fax:** 830-683-3230 tmw@swtexas.net

Rockwall Rockwall Co News (4.3M) PO Box 819 Rockwall TX 75087 **Phn:** 972-722-3099 **Fax:** 972-563-0340 www.rockwallcountynews.com rcn.news@yahoo.com

Rosebud Rosebud News (1.9M) PO Box 516 Rosebud TX 76570 **Phn:** 254-583-7811 **Fax:** 254-583-2493 www.marlindemocrat.com/rosebud democrat@marlindemocrat.com

Rotan Advance Star Record (1.4M) PO Box A Rotan TX 79546 **Phn:** 325-735-2562 **Fax:** 325-735-2230

Round Rock Pflugerville Pflag (7.2M) 1015 S Mays St Ste 101 Round Rock TX 78664 **Phn:** 512-251-2220 **Fax:** 512-251-6221 pflugervillepflag.com news@pflugervillepflag.com

Round Rock Round Rock Leader (7.5M) PO Box 459 Round Rock TX 78680 **Phn:** 512-255-5827 **Fax:** 512-255-3733 www.statesman.com editor@rrleader.com

Rusk The Cherokeean-Herald (3.4M) PO Box 475 Rusk TX 75785 **Phn:** 903-683-2257 **Fax:** 903-683-5104 www.thecherokeean.com news@mediactr.com

Saint Jo St. Jo Tribune (1.0M) PO Box 160 Saint Jo TX 76265 **Phn:** 940-995-2586

Salado Salado Village Voice (1.5M) PO Box 587 Salado TX 76571 **Phn:** 254-947-5321 **Fax:** 254-947-9479 www.saladovillagevoice.com news@saladovillagevoice.com

San Antonio Neighbors Newspapers (143.0M) PO Box 2171 San Antonio TX 78297 **Phn:** 210-250-3325 **Fax:** 210-250-3305 kdavis@express-news.net

San Antonio Prime Time Newspapers (159.0M) PO Box 2171 San Antonio TX 78297 **Phn:** 210-250-3385 **Fax:** 210-453-3362 www.primetimenewspapers.com dcr@primetimenewspapers.com

San Antonio San Antonio Current (47.0M) 915 Dallas St San Antonio TX 78215 **Phn:** 210-227-0044 **Fax:** 210-227-6611 sacurrent.com cenlow@sacurrent.com

San Antonio Southside Reporter (79.0M) 2203 S Hackberry San Antonio TX 78210 **Phn:** 210-534-8848 **Fax:** 210-534-7134 www.mysanantonio.com jmaccormack@express-news.net

San Augustine San Augustine Tribune (3.5M) PO Box 539 San Augustine TX 75972 **Phn:** 936-275-2181 **Fax:** 936-275-0572 www.sanaugustinetribune.com mail@sanaugustinetribune.com

San Benito San Benito News (3.5M) PO Box 1791 San Benito TX 78586 **Phn:** 956-399-2436 **Fax:** 956-399-2430

San Saba San Saba News & Star (2.7M) PO Box 815 San Saba TX 76877 **Phn:** 325-372-5115 **Fax:** 325-372-3973 www.sansabanews.com sabanews@centex.net

Sanger Sanger Courier (2.0M) PO Box 160 Sanger TX 76266 **Phn:** 940-458-7429 **Fax:** 940-458-3681

Schulenburg Schulenburg Sticker (2.9M) PO Box 160 Schulenburg TX 78956 **Phn:** 979-743-3450 **Fax:** 979-743-4609 stickereditor@cmaaccess.com

Seagoville The Suburbia News (1.3M) PO Box 130 Seagoville TX 75159 **Phn:** 972-287-3277 **Fax:** 972-287-3278 www.suburbianews.com seagonews@sbcglobal.net

Sealy The Sealy News (4.0M) Po Box 480 Sealy TX 77474 **Phn:** 979-885-3562 **Fax:** 979-885-3564 www.sealynews.com editor@sealynews.com

Seminole Seminole Sentinel (2.2M) PO Box 1200 Seminole TX 79360 **Phn:** 432-758-3667 **Fax:** 432-758-2136 www.seminolesentinel.com news@seminolesentinel.com

Seymour Baylor County Banner (2.4M) PO Box 912 Seymour TX 76380 **Phn:** 940-889-2616 **Fax:** 940-889-3610 baylorbanner.com banner@srcaccess.net

Shamrock County Star News (2.4M) 212 N Main St Shamrock TX 79079 **Phn:** 806-256-2070 **Fax:** 806-256-2071 www.countystarnews.com jeff@countystarnews.com

Shiner Shiner Gazette (2.6M) PO Box 727 Shiner TX 77984 **Phn:** 361-594-3346 **Fax:** 361-594-2655 shinergazette@sbcglobal.net

Silsbee Silsbee Bee (6.0M) PO Box 547 Silsbee TX 77656 **Phn:** 409-385-5278 **Fax:** 409-385-5270 www.silsbeebee.com editor@silsbeebee.com

Silverton Briscoe County News (0.9M) PO Box 130 Silverton TX 79257 **Phn:** 806-823-2333 **Fax:** 806-823-2528

Sinton San Patricio Publishing (9.0M) PO Box B Sinton TX 78387 **Phn:** 361-364-1270 **Fax:** 361-364-3833 sanpatpublishing.com editor@sanpatpublishing.com

Slaton Slaton Slatonite (2.4M) PO Box 667 Slaton TX 79364 **Phn:** 806-828-6201 **Fax:** 806-828-6202

Smithville Smithville Times (3.1M) PO Box 659 Smithville TX 78957 **Phn:** 512-237-4655 **Fax:** 512-237-5443 smithvilletimes.com news@smithvilletimes.com

Sonora Devils River News (1.5M) 228 E Main St Sonora TX 76950 **Phn:** 325-387-2507 **Fax:** 325-387-5691

South Padre Island Coastal Current (25.0M) PO Box 2429 South Padre Island TX 78597 **Phn:** 956-761-9341 **Fax:** 956-761-1436

Southlake Alliance Publications (82.0M) 1721 E Southlake Blvd Southlake TX 76092 **Phn:** 817-329-7700 **Fax:** 817-329-7724

Southlake Colleyville Courier (9.0M) 1721 E Southlake Blvd Southlake TX 76092 **Phn:** 817-329-7700 **Fax:** 817-329-7724

Southlake Grapevine Courier (11.0M) 1721 E Southlake Blvd Southlake TX 76092 **Phn:** 817-329-7700 **Fax:** 817-329-7724

Spearman Hansford Co. Reporter-Statesman (1.7M) 213 Main St Spearman TX 79081 **Phn:** 806-659-3434 **Fax:** 806-398-9080 www.spearmanreporter.com reporter@spearmanreporter.com

Springtown Springtown Epigraph (2.7M) PO Box 557 Springtown TX 76082 **Phn:** 817-220-7217 **Fax:** 817-523-4457 www.springtown-epigraph.net opinion@azlenews.net

Spur Texas Spur (1.4M) PO Box 430 Spur TX 79370 **Phn:** 806-271-3381 **Fax:** 806-271-3966 www.thetexasspur.com cindi@thetexasspur.com

Stafford Fort Bend Star (62.0M) 4655 Techniplex Dr Ste 300 Stafford TX 77477 **Phn:** 281-690-4200 **Fax:** 281-690-4250 www.fortbendstar.com starnews@fortbendstar.com

Stanton The Messenger (1.5M) PO Box 1488 Stanton TX 79782 **Phn:** 432-756-2090 mcmessenger@crcom.net

Stratford Stratford Star (1.2M) PO Box 8 Stratford TX 79084 **Phn:** 806-366-5885

Sugar Land Fort Bend Sun (62.0M) 13815 Southwest Fwy Sugar Land TX 77478 **Phn:** 281-242-1812 **Fax:** 281-242-1891 www.yourhoustonnews.com/fort_bend fbeditor@hcnonline.com

Sulphur Springs Hopkins County Echo (0.7M) 401 Church St Sulphur Springs TX 75482 **Phn:** 903-885-8663 **Fax:** 903-885-8768 editor@ssecho.com

Tahoka Lynn Co News (1.5M) PO Box 1170 Tahoka TX 79373 **Phn:** 806-561-4888 **Fax:** 806-561-6308 lcn1tahoka@poka.com

Tatum Trammel Trace Tribune (1.0M) PO Box 544 Tatum TX 75691 **Phn:** 903-947-2518 www.smalltownpapers.com

Teague Teague Chronicle (2.5M) PO Box 631 Teague TX 75860 **Phn:** 254-739-2141 **Fax:** 254-739-2144 www.teaguechronicle.com teaguechronicle@glade.net

The Woodlands The Villager (39.7M) 1600 Lake Front Cir Ste 190 The Woodlands TX 77380 **Phn:** 281-378-1040 **Fax:** 281-363-3299 www.yourhoustonnews.com/woodlands cdominguez@hcnonline.com

Three Rivers The Progress (3.3M) PO Box 848 Three Rivers TX 78071 **Phn:** 361-786-3022 **Fax:** 361-786-3671 www.mysoutex.com

Throckmorton Throckmorton Tribune (1.2M) PO Box 935 Throckmorton TX 76483 **Phn:** 940-849-0147 **Fax:** 940-849-0149

Timpson Timpson News (2.0M) PO Box 740 Timpson TX 75975 **Phn:** 936-254-3618 **Fax:** 936-254-3206 ttnfreeh@sbcglobal.net

Tomball Tomball Magnolia Tribune (54.0M) 517 W Main St Tomball TX 77375 **Phn:** 281-255-6397 **Fax:** 281-255-3082 www.tribunenews.com editor@tribunenews.com

Trenton Trenton Tribune (1.3M) PO Box 43 Trenton TX 75490 **Phn:** 903-989-2325 trentontribune@texoma.net

Tulia Tulia Herald (3.0M) PO Box 87 Tulia TX 79088 **Phn:** 806-995-3535 **Fax:** 806-995-3536

Tuscola The Journal (0.9M) PO Box 339 Tuscola TX 79562 **Phn:** 325-572-3716

Uvalde Uvalde Leader-News (5.5M) 110 N East St Uvalde TX 78801 **Phn:** 830-278-3335 **Fax:** 830-278-9191 www.uvaldeleadernews.com cgarnett@uvaldeleadernews.com

Valley Mills Valley Mills Progress (0.7M) PO Box 448 Valley Mills TX 76689 **Phn:** 254-932-6450

Van Alstyne Van Alstyne Leader (2.5M) PO Box 578 Van Alstyne TX 75495 **Phn:** 903-482-5253 **Fax:** 903-482-5656 www.vanalstyneleader.net rwilliams@vanalstyneleader.com

Van Horn Van Horn Advocate (1.0M) PO Box 8 Van Horn TX 79855 **Phn:** 432-283-2003 **Fax:** 432-283-7334 www.vanhornadvocate.com lsimpson@vanhornadvocate.com

Vega Vega Enterprise (0.8M) PO Box 130 Vega TX 79092 **Phn:** 806-267-2230 **Fax:** 806-267-2889

Vidor Vidor Vidorian (1.5M) PO Box 1236 Vidor TX 77670 **Phn:** 409-769-5428 **Fax:** 409-769-2600 rluker@ih2000.net

Waco Suburban Courier (1.0M) 2816 N 19th St # C Waco TX 76708 **Phn:** 254-754-3511 **Fax:** 254-754-3541 thecitizencourier.com editor@texraymedia.com

Waco The Citizen Courier (2.1M) 2816 N 19th St #C Waco TX 76708 **Phn:** 254-754-3511 **Fax:** 254-754-3541 thecitizencourier.com editor@texraymedia.com

Waller Waller Times (4.0M) PO Box 509 Waller TX 77484 **Phn:** 936-372-9448 **Fax:** 936-372-5534

Wallis Wallis News Review (1.2M) PO Box 668 Wallis TX 77485 **Phn:** 979-478-6412 **Fax:** 979-478-2198 www.wallisnews.com johnny@wallisnews.com

Waxahachie Ellis County Chronicle (1.4M) PO Box 877 Waxahachie TX 75168 **Phn:** 972-617-6397 **Fax:** 972-937-1139 www.waxahachietx.com joann@wninews.com

Waxahachie Ennis Journal (6.5M) PO Box 877 Waxahachie TX 75168 **Phn:** 972-872-9565 **Fax:** 972-872-9573 www.waxahachietx.com

Waxahachie Midlothian Mirror (2.2M) PO Box 877 Waxahachie TX 75168 **Phn:** 972-775-3322 **Fax:** 972-937-1139 www.waxahachietx.com neal.white@wninews.com

Webster Clear Lake Citizen (30.0M) 100 E NASA Rd 1 Ste 105 Webster TX 77598 **Phn:** 281-674-1406 **Fax:** 281-332-6901 citizen@hcnonline.com

Weimar Weimar Mercury (3.5M) PO Box 277 Weimar TX 78962 **Phn:** 979-725-9595 **Fax:** 979-725-9051 www.weimarmercury.com mercury@weimarmercury.com

Wellington Wellington Leader (1.9M) PO Box 992 Wellington TX 79095 **Phn:** 806-447-2550 **Fax:** 806-447-2463 wellingtonleader@valornet.com

Weslaco Mid-Valley Town Crier (25.0M) 401 S Iowa Ave Weslaco TX 78596 **Phn:** 956-969-2543 **Fax:** 956-968-0855 www.midvalleytowncrier.com johng@mvtcnews.com

West West News (3.1M) PO Box 38 West TX 76691 **Phn:** 254-826-3718 **Fax:** 254-826-3719

West Columbia Brazoria County News (11.0M) PO Box 488 West Columbia TX 77486 **Phn:** 979-345-3127 **Fax:** 979-345-5308 www.brazoriacountynews.org

Wharton Journal-Spectator (5.0M) PO Box 111 Wharton TX 77488 **Phn:** 979-532-8840 **Fax:** 979-532-8845 www.journal-spectator.com kmagee@journal-spectator.com

Wheeler Wheeler Times (1.1M) PO Box 1080 Wheeler TX 79096 **Phn:** 806-826-3123 wtimes@centramedia.net

White Deer White Deer News (2.0M) PO Box 728 White Deer TX 79097 **Phn:** 806-883-4881 thewhitedeernews@hotmail.com

White Oak Independent (1.2M) PO Box 445 White Oak TX 75693 **Phn:** 903-845-5349

Whitehouse Tri County Leader (2.4M) PO Box 1067 Whitehouse TX 75791 **Phn:** 903-839-2353 **Fax:** 903-839-8519 www.tricountyleader.com news@tricountyleader.com

Whitesboro Whitesboro News-Record (3.0M) PO Box 68 Whitesboro TX 76273 **Phn:** 903-564-3565 **Fax:** 903-564-9655 www.whitesboronews.com news@whitesboronews.com

Whitewright Whitewright Sun (1.2M) PO Box 218 Whitewright TX 75491 **Phn:** 903-364-2276 **Fax:** 903-364-2480 www.whitewrightsun.com whitewrightsun@cableone.net

Wills Point Van Zandt News (7.0M) PO Box 60 Wills Point TX 75169 **Phn:** 903-873-2525 **Fax:** 903-873-4321 www.vanzandtnewspapers.com vznews@aol.com

Wills Point Wills Point Chronicle (4.6M) PO Box 60 Wills Point TX 75169 **Phn:** 903-873-2525 **Fax:** 903-873-4321 www.vanzandtnewspapers.com vznews@aol.com

Wimberley Holly Media Group (8.0M) PO Box 49 Wimberley TX 78676 **Phn:** 512-847-2202 **Fax:** 512-847-9054 hollymedia.newspaperdirect.com

TEXAS WEEKLY NEWSPAPERS

Winnie The Hometown Press (2.0M) PO Box 801 Winnie TX 77665 **Phn:** 409-296-9988 **Fax:** 409-296-9987

Winnsboro Winnsboro News (4.2M) PO Box 87 Winnsboro TX 75494 **Phn:** 903-342-5247 **Fax:** 903-342-3266 winnsboronews@suddenlinkmail.com

Winters Winters Enterprise (1.6M) PO Box 34 Winters TX 79567 **Phn:** 325-754-4958 **Fax:** 325-754-4628

Wolfe City Wolfe City Mirror (1.0M) PO Box F Wolfe City TX 75496 **Phn:** 903-496-7297 **Fax:** 903-496-2421 www.wolfecitymirror.com hgwcnews@sbcglobal.net

Wylie C & S Media Publications (10.0M) PO Box 369 Wylie TX 75098 **Phn:** 972-442-5515 **Fax:** 972-442-4318 www.csmediatexas.com news@wylienews.com

Yoakum Yoakum Herald-Times (2.6M) PO Box 798 Yoakum TX 77995 **Phn:** 361-293-5266 **Fax:** 361-293-5267 heraldtimes@sbcglobal.net

Yorktown Yorktown News View (2.5M) PO Box 398 Yorktown TX 78164 **Phn:** 361-564-2242 **Fax:** 361-564-9290 cuerorecord.com glennrea@cuerorecord.com

Zapata Zapata County News (2.5M) 2765 US Highway 83 Zapata TX 78076 **Phn:** 956-765-6931 **Fax:** 956-765-9058 zapatanews@sbcglobal.net

UTAH

Beaver Beaver Press (1.1M) PO Box 351 Beaver UT 84713 **Phn:** 435-438-2891 **Fax:** 435-438-8804

Blanding Blue Mtn. Panorama (1.5M) PO Box 636 Blanding UT 84511 **Phn:** 435-678-3635 **Fax:** 435-678-3902

Bountiful Davis Clipper (10.0M) PO Box 267 Bountiful UT 84011 **Phn:** 801-295-2251 **Fax:** 801-295-3044 www.davisclipper.com tgunn@davisclipper.com

Brigham City Box Elder News Journal (5.8M) PO Box 370 Brigham City UT 84302 **Phn:** 435-723-3471 **Fax:** 435-723-5421 www.benewsjournal.com editor@benewsjournal.com

Castle Dale Emery County Progress (2.3M) PO Box 589 Castle Dale UT 84513 **Phn:** 435-381-2431 **Fax:** 435-381-5431 www.ecprogress.com editor@ecprogress.com

Coalville Summit County Bee (1.6M) PO Box 7 Coalville UT 84017 **Phn:** 435-336-5501

Delta Millard Chronicle-Progress (3.1M) PO Box 249 Delta UT 84624 **Phn:** 435-864-2400

Delta Millard Co. Gazette (5.0M) 347 W Main St Delta UT 84624 **Phn:** 435-864-4050

Gunnison Gunnison Valley Gazette (1.0M) PO Box 143 Gunnison UT 84634 **Phn:** 435-528-5178 **Fax:** 435-528-5179

Heber City Wasatch Wave (4.4M) 165 S 100 W Heber City UT 84032 **Phn:** 435-654-1471 **Fax:** 435-654-5085 www.wasatchwave.com editor@wasatchwave.com

Hurricane Cedar City Review (14.0M) PO Box 292 Hurricane UT 84737 **Phn:** 435-586-5678 **Fax:** 435-635-7800

Kanab Southern Utah News (2.5M) 245 S 200 E Kanab UT 84741 **Phn:** 435-644-2900 **Fax:** 435-644-2926 www.sunews.net sunews@kanab.net

Magna Magna Times (4.7M) 8980 W 2700 S Magna UT 84044 **Phn:** 801-250-5656 **Fax:** 801-250-5685

Magna West Valley News (4.0M) 8980 W 2700 S Magna UT 84044 **Phn:** 801-250-5656 **Fax:** 801-250-5685 www.oquirrhtimes.com info@oquirrhtimes.com

Manti Sanpete Messenger (2.7M) 35 S Main St Manti UT 84642 **Phn:** 435-835-4241 **Fax:** 435-835-1493 news.sanpetemessenger.com news@sanpetemessenger.com

Moab Times-Independent (3.7M) PO Box 129 Moab UT 84532 **Phn:** 435-259-7525 **Fax:** 435-259-7741 www.moabtimes.com editor@moabtimes.com

Monticello San Juan Record (2.2M) PO Box 879 Monticello UT 84535 **Phn:** 435-587-2277 **Fax:** 435-587-3377 sjrnews.com sjrnews@frontiernet.net

Morgan Morgan County News (2.1M) PO Box 190 Morgan UT 84050 **Phn:** 801-829-3451 **Fax:** 801-829-4073 morgannewspaper.com news@morgannewspaper.com

Mount Pleasant The Pyramid (2.6M) 49 W Main St Mount Pleasant UT 84647 **Phn:** 435-462-2134 **Fax:** 435-462-2459 pyramid@heraldextra.com

Nephi Nephi Times-News (1.7M) PO Box 77 Nephi UT 84648 **Phn:** 435-623-0525 **Fax:** 435-623-4735 www.nephitimesnews.com editor@nephitimesnews.com

Park City Park Record (7.5M) PO Box 3688 Park City UT 84060 **Phn:** 435-649-9014 **Fax:** 435-649-4942 www.parkrecord.com editor@parkrecord.com

Payson Payson Chronicle (1.9M) PO Box 361 Payson UT 84651 **Phn:** 801-465-9221 **Fax:** 801-465-7876

Price Sun Advocate (5.4M) 845 E Main St Price UT 84501 **Phn:** 435-637-0732 **Fax:** 435-637-2716 www.sunadvocate.com editor@sunad.com

Provo Spanish Fork Press (3.2M) PO Box 717 Provo UT 84603 **Phn:** 801-798-1011 **Fax:** 801-798-1131 www.heraldextra.com jtolman@heraldextra.com

Richfield Richfield Reaper (6.1M) PO Box 730 Richfield UT 84701 **Phn:** 435-896-5476 **Fax:** 435-896-8123 www.richfieldreaper.com reapered@richfieldreaper.com

Roosevelt Uintah Basin Standard (8.0M) 268 S Main St Roosevelt UT 84066 **Phn:** 435-722-5131 **Fax:** 435-722-4140 www.ubmedia.biz/ubstandard ubs@ubstandard.com

Salt Lake City City Weekly (60.0M) 248 S Main St Salt Lake City UT 84101 **Phn:** 801-575-7003 **Fax:** 801-575-6106 www.cityweekly.net/utah editor@cityweekly.net

Springville Springville Herald (2.9M) 230 E 400 S Ste 1 Springville UT 84663 **Phn:** 801-489-5651 **Fax:** 801-489-7021 www.heraldextra.com artcity@avpro.com

Tooele Transcript-Bulletin (8.0M) PO Box 390 Tooele UT 84074 **Phn:** 435-882-0050 **Fax:** 435-882-6123 tooeleonline.com tbp@tooeletranscript.com

Tremonton The Leader (3.0M) 119 E Main St Tremonton UT 84337 **Phn:** 435-257-5182 **Fax:** 435-257-6175 www.tremontonleader.com

Vernal Vernal Express (5.0M) 60 East 100 North Vernal UT 84078 **Phn:** 435-789-3511 **Fax:** 435-789-8690 www.ubmedia.biz/vernal editor@vernal.com

Wendover Wendover Times (6.7M) PO Box 2716 Wendover UT 84083 **Phn:** 435-665-2563 **Fax:** 435-665-7966 www.wendovertimes.com news@wendovertimes.com

VERMONT

Barre The World (28.0M) 403 US Route 302 Barre VT 05641 **Phn:** 802-479-2582 **Fax:** 802-479-7916 www.vt-world.com editor@vt-world.com

Barton The Chronicle (7.9M) PO Box 660 Barton VT 05822 **Phn:** 802-525-3531 **Fax:** 802-525-3200 www.bartonchronicle.com news@bartonchronicle.com

Bellows Falls The Town Crier (13.0M) PO Box 459 Bellows Falls VT 05101 **Phn:** 802-463-9591 **Fax:** 802-463-9818 mwinters@reformer.com

Bradford Journal-Opinion (4.5M) PO Box 378 Bradford VT 05033 **Phn:** 802-222-5281 **Fax:** 802-222-5438 www.jonews.com editor@jonews.com

Burlington Seven Days (34.0M) PO Box 1164 Burlington VT 05402 **Phn:** 802-864-5684 **Fax:** 802-865-1015 www.7dvt.com andy@sevendaysvt.com

Charlotte Charlotte News (2.7M) PO Box 251 Charlotte VT 05445 **Phn:** 802-425-4949 www.thecharlottenews.org news@charlottenewsvt.com

Chester The Message (20.0M) PO Box 759 Chester VT 05143 **Phn:** 802-875-4790 **Fax:** 802-875-4792 messagefortheweek.net message@vermontel.net

Colchester Colchester Sun (7.4M) 462 Hegeman Ave Ste 105 Colchester VT 05446 **Phn:** 802-651-6882 **Fax:** 802-651-9635 www.colchestersun.com news@colchestersun.com

Colchester Essex Reporter (8.5M) 462 Hegeman Ave Ste 105 Colchester VT 05446 **Phn:** 802-651-6882 **Fax:** 802-651-9635 www.essexreporter.com news@essexreporter.com

Enosburg Falls County Courier (3.7M) PO Box 398 Enosburg Falls VT 05450 **Phn:** 802-933-4375 **Fax:** 802-933-4907 www.thecountycourier.com

Granville Northshire Free Press (8.0M) PO Box 330 Granville NY 12832 **Phn:** 518-642-1234 **Fax:** 518-642-1344 www.manchesternewspapers.com

Hardwick Hardwick Gazette (2.7M) PO Box 367 Hardwick VT 05843 **Phn:** 802-472-6521 **Fax:** 802-472-6522 news@thehardwickgazette.com

Killington Mountain Times (10.0M) PO Box 183 Killington VT 05751 **Phn:** 802-422-2399 **Fax:** 802-422-2395 www.mountaintimes.info editor@mountaintimes.info

Manchester Center Manchester Journal (10.5M) 51 Memorial Ave Manchester Center VT 05255 **Phn:** 802-362-2222 **Fax:** 802-362-5327 www.manchesterjournal.com news@manchesterjournal.com

Manchester Center VT News Guide (16.0M) PO Box 1265 Manchester Center VT 05255 **Phn:** 802-362-3535 **Fax:** 802-362-5368

Middlebury Addison County Independent (8.1M) PO Box 31 Middlebury VT 05753 **Phn:** 802-388-4944 www.addisonindependent.com news@addisonindependent.com

Middlebury Rutland Tribune (11.0M) 16 Creek Rd Ste 5A Middlebury VT 05753 **Phn:** 802-775-4221 **Fax:** 518-873-6360 www.denpubs.com

Middlebury The Valley Voice (8.8M) 656 Exchange St Middlebury VT 05753 **Phn:** 802-388-6366 **Fax:** 802-388-6368

Middlebury The Vermont Eagle (15.0M) 16 Creek Rd Ste 5A Middlebury VT 05753 **Phn:** 802-388-6397 **Fax:** 518-873-6360 www.denpubs.com theeagle@addison-eagle.com

Middlebury Vermont Times (8.0M) 16 Creek Rd Ste 5A Middlebury VT 05753 **Phn:** 802-985-2400 www.denpubs.com

Milton Milton Independent (6.0M) PO Box 163 Milton VT 05468 **Phn:** 802-893-2028 **Fax:** 802-893-7467 www.miltonindy.com courtney@miltonindependent.com

Morrisville News & Citizen (3.0M) PO Box 369 Morrisville VT 05661 **Phn:** 802-888-2212 **Fax:** 802-888-2173 www.newsandcitizen.com

VERMONT WEEKLY NEWSPAPERS

Morrisville The Transcript (15.4M) PO Box 369 Morrisville VT 05661 **Phn:** 802-888-2212 **Fax:** 802-888-2173 www.newsandcitizen.com news@newsandcitizen.com

Northfield The Northfield News (1.7M) 7 S Main St Ste D Northfield VT 05663 **Phn:** 802-485-6397 www.thenorthfieldnews.com northfieldnewsads@gmail.com

Randolph The Herald of Randolph (6.0M) PO Box 309 Randolph VT 05060 **Phn:** 802-728-3232 **Fax:** 802-728-9275 www.ourherald.com editor@ourherald.com

Rutland Sam's Good News (10.5M) 162 N Main St Ste 8 Rutland VT 05701 **Phn:** 802-773-4040 **Fax:** 802-775-1074 www.samsgoodnews.com editor@samsgoodnews.com

Shelburne Shelburne News (4.4M) PO Box 752 Shelburne VT 05482 **Phn:** 802-985-3091 **Fax:** 802-985-5403 www.shelburnenews.com news@windridgepublishing.com

South Burlington The Other Paper (7.0M) PO Box 2032 South Burlington VT 05407 **Phn:** 802-864-6670 **Fax:** 802-864-3379 www.otherpapersbvt.com news@otherpapersbvt.com

South Hero Islander (6.0M) PO Box 212 South Hero VT 05486 **Phn:** 802-372-5600 **Fax:** 802-372-3025 www.lakechamplainislander.com islander@vermontislander.com

Springfield Springfield Reporter (2.0M) 151 Summer St Springfield VT 05156 **Phn:** 802-885-2246 **Fax:** 802-885-9821 reporter@vermontel.net

Stowe Stowe Reporter (5.3M) PO Box 489 Stowe VT 05672 **Phn:** 802-253-2101 **Fax:** 802-253-8332 www.stowetoday.com news@stowereporter.com

Waitsfield The Valley Reporter (3.7M) PO Box 119 Waitsfield VT 05673 **Phn:** 802-496-3928 **Fax:** 802-496-4703 www.valleyreporter.com news@valleyreporter.com

West Dover Deerfield Valley News (3.5M) PO Box 310 West Dover VT 05356 **Phn:** 802-464-3388 **Fax:** 802-464-7255 www.dvalnews.com news@vermontmedia.com

Williston Williston Observer (7.0M) PO Box 1158 Williston VT 05495 **Phn:** 802-872-9000 www.willistonobserver.com editor@willistonobserver.com

Winooski Vermont Guardian (10.0M) PO Box 335 Winooski VT 05404 **Phn:** 802-861-4880 **Fax:** 802-861-6388 www.vermontguardian.com

Woodstock Vermont Standard (12.0M) PO Box 88 Woodstock VT 05091 **Phn:** 802-457-1313 **Fax:** 802-457-3639 www.thevermontstandard.com pcamp@thevermontstandard.com

VIRGINIA

Abingdon Washington County News (6.0M) PO Box 399 Abingdon VA 24212 **Phn:** 276-228-6611 **Fax:** 276-228-7260 www.tricities.com/swvatoday jsage@wythenews.com

Alexandria Alexandria Times (20.0M) 110 S Pitt St Apt 2 Alexandria VA 22314 **Phn:** 703-739-0001 **Fax:** 703-739-0120 alextimes.com dperkins@alextimes.com

Alexandria Connection Newspapers (147.0M) 1606 King St Alexandria VA 22314 **Phn:** 703-821-5050 **Fax:** 703-917-0991 www.connectionnewspapers.com smauren@connectionnewspapers.com

Alexandria Metro Herald (42.0M) 901 N Washington St Ste 603 Alexandria VA 22314 **Phn:** 703-548-8891 **Fax:** 703-739-1542 www.metroherald.com pjr@metroherald.com

Alexandria Mount Vernon Voice (12.0M) PO Box 15572 Alexandria VA 22309 **Phn:** 703-360-0080 **Fax:** 703-360-0087 www.mountvernonvoice.com mountvernonvoice@aol.com

Altavista Altavista Journal (6.4M) PO Box 630 Altavista VA 24517 **Phn:** 434-369-6688 **Fax:** 434-369-6689 www.wpcva.com/altavista nrjournal@altavistajournal.com

Amelia Court House Amelia Bulletin Monitor (10.5M) PO Box 123 Amelia Court House VA 23002 **Phn:** 804-561-3655 **Fax:** 804-561-2065 www.ameliamonitor.com contactus@ameliamonitor.com

Amherst Nelson County Times (4.0M) PO Box 90 Amherst VA 24521 **Phn:** 434-946-7195 **Fax:** 434-946-2684

Amherst New Era-Progress (4.8M) PO Box 90 Amherst VA 24521 **Phn:** 434-946-7195 **Fax:** 434-946-2684

Appomattox Times-Virginian (4.0M) PO Box 2097 Appomattox VA 24522 **Phn:** 434-352-8215 **Fax:** 434-352-2216 www.timesvirginian.com news@timesvirginian.com

Ashland Herald Progress (8.0M) 11159 Air Park Rd Ste 1 Ashland VA 23005 **Phn:** 804-798-9031 **Fax:** 804-752-2338 www.herald-progress.com hpnews@herald-progress.com

Bedford Bedford Bulletin (8.5M) PO Box 331 Bedford VA 24523 **Phn:** 540-586-8612 **Fax:** 540-586-0834 www.bedfordbulletin.com news@bedfordbulletin.com

Big Stone Gap The Post (5.0M) PO Box 250 Big Stone Gap VA 24219 **Phn:** 276-523-1141 **Fax:** 276-523-1175 www.thecoalfieldprogress.com jenay@coalfield.com

Blackstone Courier-Record (6.5M) PO Box 460 Blackstone VA 23824 **Phn:** 434-292-3019 **Fax:** 434-292-5966 www.courier-record.com news@courier-record.com

Bowling Green The Caroline Progress (4.0M) PO Box 69 Bowling Green VA 22427 **Phn:** 804-633-5005 **Fax:** 804-633-6740 www.carolineprogress.com cpeditor@lcs.net

Brookneal The Union Star (3.0M) PO Box 180 Brookneal VA 24528 **Phn:** 434-376-2795 **Fax:** 434-376-2676 www.theunionstar.com news@theunionstar.com

Charlottesville C-Ville Weekly (20.0M) 308 E Main St Charlottesville VA 22902 **Phn:** 434-817-2749 **Fax:** 434-817-2758 www.c-ville.com editor@c-ville.com

Charlottesville Rural Virginian (12.0M) PO Box 9030 Charlottesville VA 22906 **Phn:** 434-978-7216 **Fax:** 434-978-7204 www.dailyprogress.com/ruralvirginian rv@dailyprogress.com

Charlottesville The Hook (21.0M) 100 2nd St NW Ste A Charlottesville VA 22902 **Phn:** 434-295-8700 **Fax:** 434-295-8097 www.readthehook.com stuart@readthehook.com

Chase City The News Progress (5.7M) PO Box 337 Chase City VA 23924 **Phn:** 434-374-2451 **Fax:** 434-374-2074 www.thenewsprogress.com dallas@thenewsprogress.com

Chatham Chatham Star-Tribune (9.0M) PO Box 111 Chatham VA 24531 **Phn:** 434-432-2791 **Fax:** 434-432-4033 www.chathamstartribune.com news@chathamstartribune.com

Chester Village News (12.0M) PO Box 2397 Chester VA 23831 **Phn:** 804-751-0421 **Fax:** 804-751-9155 www.villagenewsonline.com info@villagepublishing.com

Christiansburg Main Street Newspapers (19.0M) PO Box 6261 Christiansburg VA 24068 **Phn:** 540-382-6171 **Fax:** 540-382-3009

VIRGINIA WEEKLY NEWSPAPERS

Clarksville Mecklenburg Sun (19.0M) PO Box 997 Clarksville VA 23927 **Phn:** 434-374-8152 **Fax:** 434-374-8153

Clintwood Dickenson Star (6.4M) PO Box 707 Clintwood VA 24228 **Phn:** 276-926-8816 **Fax:** 276-926-8827 www.thecoalfieldprogress.com jlester@coalfield.com

Crewe Crewe Journal (7.5M) PO Box 108 Crewe VA 23930 **Phn:** 434-645-7534 **Fax:** 434-645-1848 cbjournal@meckcom.net

Drakes Branch Charlotte Gazette (3.4M) PO Box 214 Drakes Branch VA 23937 **Phn:** 434-568-3341 **Fax:** 434-568-3731 gazette@kinex.net

Elkton The Valley Banner (4.2M) PO Box 126 Elkton VA 22827 **Phn:** 540-298-9444 **Fax:** 540-298-2560 www.shenvalleynow.com vbnews@comcast.net

Emporia Independent-Messenger (5.0M) 111 Baker St Emporia VA 23847 **Phn:** 434-634-4153 **Fax:** 434-634-0783 www.independentmessenger.com news@imnewspaper.com

Falls Church Falls Church News Press (30.0M) 200 Little Falls St # 508 Falls Church VA 22046 **Phn:** 703-532-3267 **Fax:** 703-342-0347 www.fcnp.com fcnp@fcnp.com

Farmville Farmville Herald (7.1M) PO Box 307 Farmville VA 23901 **Phn:** 434-392-4151 **Fax:** 434-392-3366 www.farmvilleherald.com editor@farmvilleherald.com

Fincastle Fincastle Herald (7.0M) PO Box 127 Fincastle VA 24090 **Phn:** 540-473-2741 **Fax:** 540-473-2742 www.ourvalley.org fincastle@ourvalley.org

Floyd Floyd Press (4.6M) PO Box 155 Floyd VA 24091 **Phn:** 540-745-2127 **Fax:** 540-745-2123 www.swvatoday.com news@floydpress.com

Franklin Tidewater News (8.8M) PO Box 497 Franklin VA 23851 **Phn:** 757-562-3187 **Fax:** 757-562-6795 www.tidewaternews.com editor@tidewaternews.com

Galax Galax Gazette (8.4M) PO Box 68 Galax VA 24333 **Phn:** 276-236-5178 **Fax:** 276-236-0756 www.galaxgazette.com news@galaxgazette.com

Gate City Scott County Virginia Star (6.5M) PO Box 218 Gate City VA 24251 **Phn:** 276-386-6300 **Fax:** 276-386-2354 www.virginiastar.net news@virginiastar.org

Gloucester Gazette-Journal (12.5M) PO Box 2060 Gloucester VA 23061 **Phn:** 804-693-3101 **Fax:** 804-693-7844 www.gazettejournal.net info@gazettejournal.net

Grundy Virginia Mountaineer (8.2M) PO Box 2040 Grundy VA 24614 **Phn:** 276-935-2123 **Fax:** 276-935-2125 www.virginiamountaineer.com virginiamountaineer@gmail.com

Harrisonburg Shenandoah Journal (1.7M) PO Box 2068 Harrisonburg VA 22801 **Phn:** 540-879-9222 **Fax:** 540-879-9028

Heathsville Northumberland Echo (3.0M) 7072 Northumberland Hwy Heathsville VA 22473 **Phn:** 804-580-3444 **Fax:** 804-580-6826 www.northumberlandecho.com nnneditor@lcs.net

Herndon Herndon Publishing (54.0M) PO Box 109 Herndon VA 20172 **Phn:** 703-437-5886 **Fax:** 703-834-3142

Hillsville The Carroll News (6.7M) PO Box 487 Hillsville VA 24343 **Phn:** 276-728-7311 **Fax:** 276-728-4119 www.thecarrollnews.com aworrell@civitasmedia.com

Hopewell Hopewell News (6.0M) PO Box 481 Hopewell VA 23860 **Phn:** 804-458-8511 **Fax:** 804-458-7556 www.hopewellnews.com editor@hopewellnews.com

Independence The Declaration (4.2M) PO Box 70 Independence VA 24348 **Phn:** 276-773-2222 **Fax:** 276-773-2287

Kilmarnock Rappahannock Record (8.1M) PO Box 400 Kilmarnock VA 22482 **Phn:** 804-435-1701 **Fax:** 804-435-2632 www.rrecord.com mail@rrecord.com

King George The Journal (7.0M) PO Box 409 King George VA 22485 **Phn:** 540-775-2024 **Fax:** 540-775-4099 www.journalpress.com news@journalpress.com

Lebanon Lebanon News (5.7M) PO Box 1268 Lebanon VA 24266 **Phn:** 276-889-2112 **Fax:** 276-889-5017 www.thelebanonnews.com

Leesburg Leesburg Today (46.0M) PO Box 591 Leesburg VA 20178 **Phn:** 703-771-8800 **Fax:** 703-771-8833 www.leesburgtoday.com editor@leesburgtoday.com

Leesburg Loudon Times-Mirror (63.0M) 9 E Market St Leesburg VA 20176 **Phn:** 703-777-1111 **Fax:** 703-771-0036 ltmeditor@timespapers.com

Leesburg Times Community Newspapers (392.0M) 9 E Market St Leesburg VA 20176 **Phn:** 703-437-5400 **Fax:** 703-437-6019 scahill@fairfaxtimes.com

Lexington The News Gazette (9.7M) PO Box 1153 Lexington VA 24450 **Phn:** 540-463-3113 **Fax:** 540-464-6397 www.thenews-gazette.com

Louisa Goochland Courier (7.0M) PO Box 464 Louisa VA 23093 **Phn:** 804-556-5950 **Fax:** 804-556-5951 www.thecentralvirginian.com tcvregnews@lcs.net

Louisa The Central Virginian (7.8M) PO Box 464 Louisa VA 23093 **Phn:** 540-967-0368 **Fax:** 540-967-3847 www.thecentralvirginian.com tcveditor@lcs.net

Luray Page News & Courier (7.7M) PO Box 707 Luray VA 22835 **Phn:** 540-743-5123 **Fax:** 540-743-4779 ShenValleyNow.com editor@pagenewspaper.com

Madison Madison County Eagle (4.3M) PO Box 325 Madison VA 22727 **Phn:** 540-948-5121 **Fax:** 540-948-3045 www.dailyprogress.com/madisonnews news@madison-news.com

Marion Smyth Co. News & Messenger (5.0M) PO Box 640 Marion VA 24354 **Phn:** 276-783-5121 **Fax:** 276-783-9713 www.swvatoday.com sportern@wythenews.com

McLean Sun Gazette (70.0M) 6704 Old McLean Village Dr McLean VA 22101 **Phn:** 703-738-2520 **Fax:** 703-738-2530 www.sungazette.net smccaffrey@sungazette.net

Mechanicsville Goochland Gazette (13.0M) PO Box 1118 Mechanicsville VA 23111 **Phn:** 804-556-3135 **Fax:** 804-556-4237 www.timesdispatch.com/goochlandgazette mkinser@mechlocal.com

Mechanicsville Mechanicsville Local (25.0M) PO Box 1118 Mechanicsville VA 23111 **Phn:** 804-746-1235 **Fax:** 804-730-0476 www.timesdispatch.com/mechlocal mkinser@mechlocal.com

Monterey The Recorder (5.3M) PO Box 10 Monterey VA 24465 **Phn:** 540-468-2147 **Fax:** 540-468-2048 www.therecorderonline.com recorder@htcnet.org

Montross Westmoreland News (4.5M) PO Box 699 Montross VA 22520 **Phn:** 804-493-8096 **Fax:** 804-493-8009 www.westmorelandnews.net wmnews@lcs.net

Norfolk The Flagship (40.0M) 1510 Gilbert St Bldg N-21 Norfolk VA 23511 **Phn:** 757-322-2685 www.norfolknavyflagship.com news@flagshipnews.com

Norton Coalfield Progress (7.8M) PO Box 380 Norton VA 24273 **Phn:** 276-679-1101 **Fax:** 276-679-5922 www.thecoalfieldprogress.com jenay@coalfield.com

Orange Orange County Review (7.0M) 146 Byrd St Orange VA 22960 **Phn:** 540-672-1266 **Fax:** 540-672-7481 www.dailyprogress.com/orangenews jpoole@orangenews.com

Pearisburg Virginian-Leader (6.1M) 511 Mountain Lake Ave Pearisburg VA 24134 **Phn:** 540-921-3434 **Fax:** 540-921-2563 www.virginianleader.com office@virginianleader.com

Pennington Gap Powell Valley News (7.5M) PO Box 459 Pennington Gap VA 24277 **Phn:** 276-546-1210 **Fax:** 276-546-5468

Powhatan Midlothian Exchange (25.0M) PO Box 10 Powhatan VA 23139 **Phn:** 804-598-4305 **Fax:** 804-598-7757 www.timesdispatch.com/midlothianexchange editor@midlothianexchange.com

Powhatan Powhatan Today (4.2M) PO Box 10 Powhatan VA 23139 **Phn:** 804-598-4305 **Fax:** 804-598-7757 www.timesdispatch.com/powhatantoday mkinser@mechlocal.com

Richlands Clinch Valley News (3.9M) PO Box 818 Richlands VA 24641 **Phn:** 276-988-4770 **Fax:** 276-988-3815 www.richlands-news-press.com jtalbert@richlands-news-press.com

Richlands Richlands News Press (5.0M) PO Box 818 Richlands VA 24641 **Phn:** 276-963-1081 **Fax:** 276-963-0202 www.tricities.com/swvatoday jtalbert@richlands-news-press.com

Richlands Tazewell County Free Press (12.7M) PO Box 1205 Richlands VA 24641 **Phn:** 276-963-0127

Richmond Hampton Roads Voice (20.0M) 205 E Clay St Richmond VA 23219 **Phn:** 804-644-9060 **Fax:** 804-644-5617 www.voicenewspaper.com

Richmond Henrico Citizen (17.0M) 6924 Lakeside Ave # 307 Richmond VA 23228 **Phn:** 804-262-1700 **Fax:** 804-262-7731 henricocitizen.com citizen@henricocitizen.com

Richmond Style Weekly (42.0M) 1313 E Main St Ste 103 Richmond VA 23219 **Phn:** 804-358-0825 **Fax:** 804-355-9089 styleweekly.com info@styleweekly.com

Rocky Mount Franklin News-Post (8.5M) PO Box 250 Rocky Mount VA 24151 **Phn:** 540-483-5113 **Fax:** 540-483-8013 www.thefranklinnewspost.com fnpcharles@franklinnews-post.com

Rustburg The Lynchburg Ledger (7.0M) PO Box 519 Rustburg VA 24588 **Phn:** 434-332-2845

Saint Paul Clinch Valley Times (2.0M) PO Box 817 Saint Paul VA 24283 **Phn:** 276-762-7671 **Fax:** 276-762-0929 cvtimes@verizon.net

Salem Times Register (4.0M) PO Box 1125 Salem VA 24153 **Phn:** 540-389-9355 **Fax:** 540-389-2930

Salem Vinton Messenger (3.1M) PO Box 1125 Salem VA 24153 **Phn:** 540-389-9355 **Fax:** 540 389-2930 www.ourvalley.org vintonmessenger@mainstreetnewspapers.com

Smithfield The Smithfield Times (6.4M) PO Box 366 Smithfield VA 23431 **Phn:** 757-357-3288 **Fax:** 757-357-0404 www.smithfieldtimes.com news@smithfieldtimes.com

South Boston Gazette-Virginian (9.0M) PO Box 524 South Boston VA 24592 **Phn:** 434-572-3945 **Fax:** 434-572-1173 www.gazettevirginian.com gazette@gazettevirginian.com

South Boston News & Record (5.5M) PO Box 100 South Boston VA 24592 **Phn:** 434-572-2929 **Fax:** 434-572-2920 www.thenewsrecord.com mail@thenewsrecord.com

South Hill South Hill Enterprise (8.5M) 914 W Danville St South Hill VA 23970 **Phn:** 434-447-3178 **Fax:** 434-447-5931 www.southhillenterprise.com editor@southhillenterprise.com

Stafford Stafford County Sun (20.0M) PO Box 1400 Stafford VA 22555 **Phn:** 540-659-4466 **Fax:** 540-659-0039 www.staffordcountysun.com info@staffordcountysun.com

Stanardsville Greene County Record (3.0M) PO Box 66 Stanardsville VA 22973 **Phn:** 434-985-2315 **Fax:** 434-985-8356 www.dailyprogress.com/greenenews enewstips@greene-news.com

Stuart The Enterprise (5.9M) PO Box 348 Stuart VA 24171 **Phn:** 276-694-3101 **Fax:** 276-694-5110 www.theenterprise.net mail@theenterprise.net

Sutherland The Monitor (10.0M) PO Box 399 Sutherland VA 23885 **Phn:** 804-733-8636 **Fax:** 804-732-6322

Tappahannock Rappahannock Times (5.1M) PO Box 1025 Tappahannock VA 22560 **Phn:** 804-443-2200 **Fax:** 804-443-9684 raptimes@verizon.net

Tasley Gannett Newspapers (10.0M) PO Box 288 Tasley VA 23441 **Phn:** 757-787-1200 **Fax:** 757-787-2370 www.delmarvanow.com crobinson@smgpo.gannett.com

Urbanna Southside Sentinel (5.5M) PO Box 549 Urbanna VA 23175 **Phn:** 804-758-2328 **Fax:** 804-758-5896 www.ssentinel.com editor@ssentinel.com

Victoria Victoria Dispatch (3.4M) PO Box 40 Victoria VA 23974 **Phn:** 434-696-5550 **Fax:** 434-696-2958

Wakefield Sussex-Surry Dispatch (9.0M) 228 Fleetwood Ave Wakefield VA 23888 **Phn:** 757-899-3551 **Fax:** 757-899-7312 www.sussexsurrydispatch.com dmmonitor@earthlink.net

Warrenton Culpeper Times (15.0M) 39 Culpeper St Warrenton VA 20186 **Phn:** 540-347-4222 **Fax:** 540-349-8676 www.northernvatimes.com/culpeper asherman@timespapers.com

Warrenton Fauquier Citizen (9.5M) PO Box 631 Warrenton VA 20188 **Phn:** 540-347-5522 **Fax:** 540-349-8676

Warrenton Fauquier Times-Democrat (17.4M) 39 Culpeper St Warrenton VA 20186 **Phn:** 540-347-5522 **Fax:** 540-349-8676 www.fauquier.com bwalsh@timespapers.com

Warsaw Northern Neck News (9.0M) PO Box 8 Warsaw VA 22572 **Phn:** 804-333-6397 **Fax:** 804-333-0033 www.northernnecknews.com

Washington Rappahannock News (3.2M) PO Box 59 Washington VA 22747 **Phn:** 540-675-3338 **Fax:** 540-675-3088 www.rappnews.com editor@rappnews.com

West Point Tidewater Review (4.4M) PO Box 271 West Point VA 23181 **Phn:** 804-843-2282 **Fax:** 804-843-4404 www.tidewaterreview.com mail@tidewaterreview.com

Williamsburg Virginia Gazette (19.0M) 216 Ironbound Rd Williamsburg VA 23188 **Phn:** 757-220-1736 **Fax:** 757-220-1665 www.vagazette.com editor@vagazette.com

Winchester Warren Sentinel (5.9M) 2 N Kent St Winchester VA 22601 **Phn:** 540-635-4174 **Fax:** 540-635-7478 thewarrensentinel.com

Wirtz Smith Mountain Eagle (3.8M) 1650 Scruggs Rd Wirtz VA 24184 **Phn:** 540-297-1222 **Fax:** 540-719-5200 www.smithmountaineagle.com news@smithmountaineagle.com

Woodstock Free Press (4.3M) PO Box 777 Woodstock VA 22664 **Phn:** 540-459-4000 **Fax:** 540-459-7493

Woodstock Shenandoah Herald (5.2M) PO Box 507 Woodstock VA 22664 **Phn:** 540-459-4078 **Fax:** 540-459-4077 www.dnronline.com kirkwood@dnronline.com

Wytheville Bland Co. Messenger (2.0M) 460 W Main St Wytheville VA 24382 **Phn:** 276-228-6611 **Fax:** 276-228-7260 www.swvatoday.com jsage@wythenews.com

Wytheville Wytheville Enterprise (6.5M) 460 W Main St Wytheville VA 24382 **Phn:** 276-228-6611 **Fax:** 276-228-7260 www.swvatoday.com jsage@wythenews.com

VIRGINIA WEEKLY NEWSPAPERS

Yorktown Town Crier (5.0M) PO Box 978 Yorktown VA 23692 **Phn:** 757-898-7225 **Fax:** 757-890-0119 www.yorktowncrier.com

WASHINGTON

Anacortes Anacortes American (3.3M) 901 6th St Anacortes WA 98221 **Phn:** 360-293-3122 **Fax:** 360-293-5000 www.goanacortes.com news@goanacortes.com

Bainbridge Island Bainbridge Review (3.0M) PO Box 10817 Bainbridge Island WA 98110 **Phn:** 206-842-6613 **Fax:** 206-842-5867 www.bainbridgereview.com

Battle Ground The Reflector (28.0M) PO Box 2020 Battle Ground WA 98604 **Phn:** 360-687-5151 **Fax:** 360-687-5162 www.thereflector.com steve@thereflector.com

Belfair Belfair Herald (10.0M) PO Box 250 Belfair WA 98528 **Phn:** 360-275-6680 **Fax:** 360-275-2107 www.masoncounty.com pr@masoncounty.com

Bellingham Cascadia Weekly (18.0M) PO Box 2833 Bellingham WA 98227 **Phn:** 360-647-8200 www.cascadiaweekly.com editor@cascadiaweekly.com

Blaine The Northern Light (10.3M) 225 Marine Dr Ste 200 Blaine WA 98230 **Phn:** 360-332-1777 **Fax:** 360-332-2777 www.thenorthernlight.com editor@thenorthernlight.com

Brewster Quad City Herald (2.6M) PO Box 37 Brewster WA 98812 **Phn:** 509-689-2507 **Fax:** 509-682-4209 www.qcherald.com editor@lakechelanmirror.com

Burien Ballard News-Tribune (10.0M) 14006 1st Ave S # B Burien WA 98168 **Phn:** 206-783-1244 **Fax:** 206-789-2455 www.westseattleherald.com kenr@robinsonnews.com

Burien Robinson Newspapers (46.0M) 14006 1st Ave S # B Burien WA 98168 **Phn:** 206-388-1850 **Fax:** 206-388-1851 www.westseattleherald.com hteditor@robinsonnews.com

Burien West Seattle Herald (10.0M) 14006 1st Ave S # B Burien WA 98168 **Phn:** 206-708-1378 www.westseattleherald.com wseditor@robinsonnews.com

Camas Camas Post Record (10.0M) PO Box 1013 Camas WA 98607 **Phn:** 360-834-2141 **Fax:** 360-834-3423 www.camaspostrecord.com heather.acheson@camaspostrecord.com

Cashmere Cashmere Valley Record (1.6M) 201 Cottage Ave Ste 4 Cashmere WA 98815 **Phn:** 509-782-3781 **Fax:** 509-782-9074 www.cashmerevalleyrecord.com record@cashmerevalleyrecord.com

Cathlamet Wahkiakum County Eagle (1.6M) PO Box 368 Cathlamet WA 98612 **Phn:** 360-795-3391 **Fax:** 360-795-3983 waheagle.com ernelson@teleport.com

Chehalis DeVaul Publishing (14.0M) 429 N Market Blvd Chehalis WA 98532 **Phn:** 360-748-6848 **Fax:** 360-748-6841 www.devaulpublishing.com fdevaul@devaulpublishing.com

Chelan Lake Chelan Mirror (2.9M) PO Box 249 Chelan WA 98816 **Phn:** 509-682-2213 **Fax:** 509-682-4209 lakechelanmirror.com editor@lakechelanmirror.com

Cheney Cheney Free Press (2.0M) 1616 W 1st St Cheney WA 99004 **Phn:** 509-235-6184 **Fax:** 509-235-2887 cheneyfreepress.com cfp@cheneyfreepress.com

Chewelah The Independent (2.2M) PO Box 5 Chewelah WA 99109 **Phn:** 509-935-8422 **Fax:** 509-935-8426 theindependent@centurytel.net

Cle Elum Northern Kittitas Co. Tribune (3.5M) PO Box 308 Cle Elum WA 98922 **Phn:** 509-674-2511 **Fax:** 509-674-5571 nkctribune.com tribune@nkctribune.com

Colfax Whitman Co. Gazette (4.3M) PO Box 770 Colfax WA 99111 **Phn:** 509-397-4333 **Fax:** 509-397-4527 www.wcgazette.com gazette@colfax.com

Colville Statesman-Examiner (6.5M) PO Box 271 Colville WA 99114 **Phn:** 509-684-4567 **Fax:** 509-684-3849 www.statesmanexaminer.com publisher@statesmanexaminer.com

Connell Franklin County Graphic (2.7M) PO Box 160 Connell WA 99326 **Phn:** 509-234-3181 **Fax:** 509-234-3182

Coulee City News Standard (0.8M) PO Box 488 Coulee City WA 99115 **Phn:** 509-632-5402 **Fax:** 509-632-5732 www.smalltownpapers.com

Coupeville South Whidbey Record (5.3M) PO Box 1200 Coupeville WA 98239 **Phn:** 360-221-5300 **Fax:** 888-478-2126 www.southwhidbeyrecord.com

Coupeville Whidbey Examiner (2.0M) PO Box 445 Coupeville WA 98239 **Phn:** 360-678-8060 **Fax:** 360-678-6073 whidbeyexaminer.com news@whidbeyexaminer.com

Coupeville Whidbey News-Times (8.0M) PO Box 1200 Coupeville WA 98239 **Phn:** 360-675-6611 **Fax:** 360-679-2695 www.whidbeynewstimes.com editor@whidbeynewstimes.com

Davenport Davenport Times (2.2M) PO Box 66 Davenport WA 99122 **Phn:** 509-725-0101 **Fax:** 509-725-0009 davenporttimes@centurytel.net

Dayton Dayton Chronicle (1.7M) PO Box 6 Dayton WA 99328 **Phn:** 509-382-2221 **Fax:** 509-382-1546

Deer Park Deer Park Tribune (12.0M) 104 N Main St Deer Park WA 99006 **Phn:** 509-276-5043 **Fax:** 509-276-2041 www.dptribune.biz tom@dptribune.com

East Wenatchee Empire Press (1.0M) 832 Valley Mall Pkwy Ste D East Wenatchee WA 98802 **Phn:** 509-886-8668 **Fax:** 509-884-3554 empire-press.com weekly@empire-press.com

Eastsound The Island's Sounder (3.0M) PO Box 758 Eastsound WA 98245 **Phn:** 360-376-4500 **Fax:** 360-376-4501 www.islandssounder.com editor@islandssounder.com

Eatonville The Dispatch (10.0M) PO Box 248 Eatonville WA 98328 **Phn:** 360-832-4411 **Fax:** 360-832-4972 www.dispatchnews.com dispatchnews@yahoo.com

Enumclaw Enumclaw Courier Herald (14.0M) PO Box 157 Enumclaw WA 98022 **Phn:** 360-825-2555 **Fax:** 360-825-1092 www.courierherald.com editor@courierherald.com

Ephrata Grant County Journal (3.0M) PO Box 998 Ephrata WA 98823 **Phn:** 509-754-4636 **Fax:** 509-754-0996 news@gcjournal.net

Everett Weekly Herald (74.0M) 1213 California St Everett WA 98201 **Phn:** 425-339-3030 www.weeklyherald.com

Federal Way Federal Way Mirror (30.0M) 31919 1st Ave S # 10 Federal Way WA 98003 **Phn:** 253-925-5565 **Fax:** 253-925-5750 www.federalwaymirror.com publisher@fedwaymirror.com

Ferndale Ferndale Record (2.5M) PO Box 38 Ferndale WA 98248 **Phn:** 360-384-1411 **Fax:** 360-384-1417 ferndalerecord.com news@ferndalerecord.com

Fife Tacoma Weekly (40.0M) 2588 Pacific Hwy Fife WA 98424 **Phn:** 253-922-5317 **Fax:** 253-922-5305 www.tacomaweekly.com news@tacomaweekly.com

Forks Forks Forum (5.0M) PO Box 300 Forks WA 98331 **Phn:** 360-374-3311 **Fax:** 360-374-5739 www.forksforum.com editor@forksforum.com

WASHINGTON WEEKLY NEWSPAPERS

Friday Harbor The Journal (4.0M) PO Box 519 Friday Harbor WA 98250 **Phn:** 360-378-5128 www.sanjuanjournal.com editor@sanjuanjournal.com

Gig Harbor Peninsula Gateway (13.0M) PO Box 407 Gig Harbor WA 98335 **Phn:** 253-851-9921 **Fax:** 253-851-3939 www.gateline.com gatewayeditor@gateline.com

Goldendale Goldendale Sentinel (3.0M) 117 W Main St Goldendale WA 98620 **Phn:** 509-773-3777 **Fax:** 509-773-4737 www.goldendalesentinel.com sentinelnews@goldendalesentinel.com

Grand Coulee The Star (4.8M) PO Box 150 Grand Coulee WA 99133 **Phn:** 509-633-1350 **Fax:** 509-633-3828 www.grandcoulee.com star@grandcoulee.com

Grandview Grandview Herald (2.2M) 107 Division St Grandview WA 98930 **Phn:** 509-882-3712 **Fax:** 509-882-2833

Issaquah The Issaquah Press (17.0M) PO Box 1328 Issaquah WA 98027 **Phn:** 425-392-6434 **Fax:** 425-391-1541 www.issaquahpress.com news@isspress.com

La Conner Channel Town Press (2.0M) PO Box 575 La Conner WA 98257 **Phn:** 360-466-3315 **Fax:** 360-466-1195

Lake Stevens Lake Stevens Journal (12.0M) PO Box 896 Lake Stevens WA 98258 **Phn:** 425-334-9252 **Fax:** 425-334-9239 www.lakestevensjournal.com news@lakestevensjournal.com

Leavenworth Leavenworth Echo (2.5M) PO Box 39 Leavenworth WA 98826 **Phn:** 509-548-5286 **Fax:** 509-548-4789 leavenworthecho.com echo@leavenworthecho.com

Liberty Lake Liberty Lake Splash (7.0M) PO Box 363 Liberty Lake WA 99019 **Phn:** 509-242-7752 **Fax:** 509-927-2190 www.libertylakesplash.com editor@libertylakesplash.com

Long Beach Chinook Observer (7.4M) PO Box 427 Long Beach WA 98631 **Phn:** 360-642-8181 **Fax:** 360-642-8105 www.chinookobserver.com editor@chinookobserver.com

Lopez Island Islands Weekly (7.8M) PO Box 758 Lopez Island WA 98261 **Phn:** 360-468-4242 **Fax:** 360-468-4900 www.islandsweekly.com publisher@islandsweekly.net

Lynden Lynden Tribune (7.0M) PO Box 153 Lynden WA 98264 **Phn:** 360-354-4444 **Fax:** 360-354-4445 lyndentribune.com editor@lyndentribune.com

Maple Valley Voice of the Valley (17.5M) PO Box 307 Maple Valley WA 98038 **Phn:** 425-432-9696 **Fax:** 425-432-0701 www.voiceofthevalley.com news@voiceofthevalley.com

Marysville Marysville Globe (12.0M) PO Box 145 Marysville WA 98270 **Phn:** 360-659-1300 **Fax:** 360-658-0350 www.marysvilleglobe.com sfrank@marysvilleglobe.com

Mercer Island Mercer Island Reporter (5.0M) 3047 78th Ave SE #207 Mercer Island WA 98040 **Phn:** 206-232-1215 **Fax:** 206-232-1284 www.mi-reporter.com editor@mi-reporter.com

Monroe Monroe Monitor (3.0M) PO Box 399 Monroe WA 98272 **Phn:** 360-794-7116 **Fax:** 360-794-6202 www.monroemonitor.com editor@monroemonitor.com

Montesano Montesano Vidette (3.5M) PO Box 671 Montesano WA 98563 **Phn:** 360-249-3311 **Fax:** 360-249-5636 www.thevidette.com editor@thevidette.com

Morton East County Journal (3.0M) 278 W Main St Morton WA 98356 **Phn:** 360-496-5993 **Fax:** 360-496-5110 www.devaulpublishing.com/eastcounty

Mount Vernon Courier Times (9.3M) PO Box 578 Mount Vernon WA 98273 **Phn:** 360-424-3251 **Fax:** 360-428-0400 www.goskagit.com weeklyeditor@skagitpublishing.com

Mount Vernon The Argus (12.5M) PO Box 578 Mount Vernon WA 98273 **Phn:** 360-424-3251 **Fax:** 360-428-0400 www.goskagit.com weeklyeditor@skagitpublishing.com

Mukilteo Edmonds Beacon (10.0M) 806 5th St Mukilteo WA 98275 **Phn:** 425-347-1711 **Fax:** 425-347-6077 edmondsbeacon.villagesoup.com publisher@yourbeacon.net

Mukilteo Mukilteo Beacon (10.0M) 806 5th St Mukilteo WA 98275 **Phn:** 425-347-5634 **Fax:** 425-347-6077 mukilteobeacon.villagesoup.com mukilteoeditor@yourbeacon.net

Newport Newport Miner (5.0M) PO Box 349 Newport WA 99156 **Phn:** 509-447-2433 **Fax:** 509-447-9222 pendoreillerivervalley.com theminer@povn.com

Ocean Shores North Coast News (2.5M) PO Box 272 Ocean Shores WA 98569 **Phn:** 360-289-2441 **Fax:** 360-289-9306

Odessa Odessa Record (1.3M) PO Box 458 Odessa WA 99159 **Phn:** 509-982-2632 **Fax:** 509-982-2651 therecord@odessaoffice.com

Omak Omak Chronicle (6.2M) PO Box 553 Omak WA 98841 **Phn:** 509-826-1110 **Fax:** 509-826-5819 www.omakchronicle.com omaknews@eaglenewspapers.com

Oroville Gazette-Tribune (2.6M) PO Box 250 Oroville WA 98844 **Phn:** 509-476-3602 **Fax:** 509-476-3054 www.gazette-tribune.com gt@gazette-tribune.com

Othello The Othello Outlook (1.6M) 125 First Ave Othello WA 99344 **Phn:** 509-488-3342 **Fax:** 509-488-3345 othellooutlook.com editor@othellooutlook.com

Pomeroy East Washingtonian (1.6M) PO Box 70 Pomeroy WA 99347 **Phn:** 509-843-1313 **Fax:** 509-843-3911 e-dub@pomeroy-wa.com

Port Orchard Port Orchard Independent (16.0M) PO Box 27 Port Orchard WA 98366 **Phn:** 360-876-4414 **Fax:** 360-876-4458 www.portorchardindependent.com admin@portorchardindependent.com

Port Townsend Pt. Townsend Leader (10.0M) PO Box 552 Port Townsend WA 98368 **Phn:** 360-385-2900 **Fax:** 360-385-3422 www.ptleader.com

Poulsbo North Kitsap Herald (13.0M) PO Box 278 Poulsbo WA 98370 **Phn:** 360-779-4464 **Fax:** 360-779-8276 www.northkitsapherald.com publisher@northkitsapherald.com

Prosser Prosser Record-Bulletin (3.2M) PO Box 750 Prosser WA 99350 **Phn:** 509-786-1711 **Fax:** 509-786-1779 www.recordbulletin.com debrichards@recordbulletin.com

Puyallup Puyallup Herald (21.0M) 822 E Main Puyallup WA 98372 **Phn:** 253-841-2481 **Fax:** 253-840-8249 www.thenewstribune.com/puyallup editor@puyallupherald.com

Quincy Quincy Valley Post Register (1.9M) PO Box 217 Quincy WA 98848 **Phn:** 509-787-4511 **Fax:** 509-787-2682 www.qvpr.com editor@qvpr.com

Raymond Willapa Harbor Herald (5.3M) PO Box 706 Raymond WA 98577 **Phn:** 360-942-3466 **Fax:** 360-942-3487 www.flannerypubs.com flanneryads@yahoo.com

Republic News-Miner (2.2M) PO Box 438 Republic WA 99166 **Phn:** 509-775-3558 republicnewsminer@hotmail.com

Ritzville Ritzville Adams County Journal (2.4M) 216 W Railroad Ave Ritzville WA 99169 **Phn:** 509-659-1020 **Fax:** 509-659-0842 www.ritzvillejournal.com

Royal City South County Sun (1.1M) 138 Camelia St # B Royal City WA 99357 **Phn:** 509-346-9723 **Fax:** 509-346-1469

Seattle Pacific Publishing (84.0M) 4000 Aurora Ave N Ste 100 Seattle WA 98103 **Phn:** 206-461-1325 www.pacificpublishing.com lindy@pacificpublishing.com

Seattle Seattle Weekly (100.0M) 1008 Western Ave Ste 300 Seattle WA 98104 **Phn:** 206-623-0500 **Fax:** 206-467-4377 www.seattleweekly.com letters@seattleweekly.com

Seattle Western Viking (4.0M) PO Box 70408 Seattle WA 98127 **Phn:** 206-784-4617 **Fax:** 206-784-4856 www.norway.org

Sequim Sequim Gazette (8.0M) PO Box 1750 Sequim WA 98382 **Phn:** 360-683-3311 **Fax:** 360-683-6670 www.sequimgazette.com editor@sequimgazette.com

Shelton Shelton County Journal (10.0M) PO Box 430 Shelton WA 98584 **Phn:** 360-426-4412 www.masoncounty.com adam@masoncounty.com

Silverdale Bremerton Patriot (13.0M) 3888 NW Randall Way Ste 100 Silverdale WA 98383 **Phn:** 360-308-9161 **Fax:** 360-782-1583 www.bremertonpatriot.com editor@bremertonpatriot.com

Silverdale Central Kitsap Reporter (17.0M) 3888 NW Randall Way Ste 100 Silverdale WA 98383 **Phn:** 360-308-9161 **Fax:** 360-308-9363 www.centralkitsapreporter.com editor@centralkitsapreporter.com

Snohomish Snohomish County Tribune (29.0M) PO Box 499 Snohomish WA 98291 **Phn:** 360-568-4121 **Fax:** 360-568-1484 www.snoho.com editor.tribune@snoho.com

Snoqualmie Snoqualmie Valley Record (4.5M) PO Box 300 Snoqualmie WA 98065 **Phn:** 425-888-2311 **Fax:** 425-888-2427 www.valleyrecord.com

South Bend Pacific County Press (2.0M) 115 W Robert Budsh Dr South Bend WA 98586 **Phn:** 360-875-6805 **Fax:** 360-875-6802 www.pacificcountypress.com news@pacificcountypress.com

Spokane The Inlander (50.0M) 9 S Washington St Ste 400 Spokane WA 99201 **Phn:** 509-325-0634 **Fax:** 509-325-0638 www.inlander.com tedm@inlander.com

Spokane Valley Valley News Herald (10.0M) PO Box 142020 Spokane Valley WA 99214 **Phn:** 509-924-2440 **Fax:** 509-927-1154 vnh@onemain.com

Stanwood Stanwood/Camano News (18.2M) PO Box 999 Stanwood WA 98292 **Phn:** 360-629-2155 **Fax:** 360-629-4211 www.scnews.com frontdesk@scnews.com

Stevenson Skamania County Pioneer (2.6M) PO Box 219 Stevenson WA 98648 **Phn:** 509-427-8444 **Fax:** 509-427-4229 scpioneer@gorge.net

Toppenish Review Independent (6.0M) PO Box 511 Toppenish WA 98948 **Phn:** 509-865-4055 **Fax:** 509-865-2655 yvpub.com news@yvpub.com

Twisp Methow Valley News (3.4M) PO Box 97 Twisp WA 98856 **Phn:** 509-997-7011 **Fax:** 509-997-3277 www.methowvalleynews.com editor@methowvalleynews.com

Vashon Vashon-Maury Island Beachcomber (3.8M) PO Box 447 Vashon WA 98070 **Phn:** 206-463-9195 **Fax:** 206-463-6122 www.vashonbeachcomber.com njohnson@vashonbeachcomber.com

Waitsburg The Times (1.7M) PO Box 97 Waitsburg WA 99361 **Phn:** 509-337-6631 **Fax:** 509-337-6045 www.waitsburgtimes.com editor@waitsburgtimes.com

Westport South Beach Bulletin (5.2M) PO Box 1395 Westport WA 98595 **Phn:** 360-268-0736 southbeachbulletin@comcast.net

White Salmon The Enterprise (2.8M) PO Box 218 White Salmon WA 98672 **Phn:** 509-493-2112 **Fax:** 509-493-2399 www.whitesalmonenterprise.com jburkhardt@eaglenewspapers.com

Wilbur Wilbur Register (1.7M) PO Box 186 Wilbur WA 99185 **Phn:** 509-647-5551 **Fax:** 509-647-5552

Winlock Lewis County News (12.0M) PO Box 10 Winlock WA 98596 **Phn:** 360-785-3151 flannerypubs.com

Woodinville Woodinville Weekly (19.1M) PO Box 587 Woodinville WA 98072 **Phn:** 425-483-0606 **Fax:** 425-486-7593 www.nwnews.com editor@woodinville.com

Yelm Nisqually Valley News (4.0M) PO Box 597 Yelm WA 98597 **Phn:** 360-458-2681 **Fax:** 360-458-5741 yelmonline.com yelmnews@yelmonline.com

WEST VIRGINIA

Beckley Post Report (20.0M) PO Box 2398 Beckley WV 25802 **Phn:** 304-255-4400 **Fax:** 304-255-4427

Berkeley Springs The Morgan Messenger (5.2M) PO Box 567 Berkeley Springs WV 25411 **Phn:** 304-258-1800 **Fax:** 304-258-8441 morganmessenger.com news@morganmessenger.com

Bridgeport Bridgeport News (9.0M) 1400 Johnson Ave Ste 2L Bridgeport WV 26330 **Phn:** 304-842-8840 **Fax:** 304-842-8842

Buckhannon The Record Delta (5.0M) PO Box 550 Buckhannon WV 26201 **Phn:** 304-472-2800 **Fax:** 304-472-0537 www.therecorddelta.com news@recorddeltaonline.com

Charles Town Spirit Of Jefferson (4.8M) PO Box 966 Charles Town WV 25414 **Phn:** 304-725-2046 **Fax:** 304-728-6856 www.spiritofjefferson.com editor@spiritofjefferson.com

Clay Clay County Free Press (3.0M) PO Box 180 Clay WV 25043 **Phn:** 304-587-4250 **Fax:** 304-647-5767 www.claycountyfreepress.com news@claycountyfreepress.com

Culloden Cabell Standard (1.5M) PO Box 467 Culloden WV 25510 **Phn:** 304-743-1222 **Fax:** 304-562-6214

Franklin Pendleton Times (5.5M) PO Box 906 Franklin WV 26807 **Phn:** 304-358-2304

Gilbert Gilbert Times (3.0M) PO Box 1135 Gilbert WV 25621 **Phn:** 304-664-8225 **Fax:** 304-664-8239

Glenville Democrat and Pathfinder (3.5M) 108 N Court St Glenville WV 26351 **Phn:** 304-462-7309 **Fax:** 304-462-7300 www.glenvillenews.com glenvillenews@gmail.com

Grafton Mountain Statesman (3.3M) PO Box 218 Grafton WV 26354 **Phn:** 304-265-3333 **Fax:** 304-265-3342 www.mountainstatesman.com gftemail@aol.com

Grantsville Calhoun Chronicle (3.4M) PO Box 400 Grantsville WV 26147 **Phn:** 304-354-6917 www.calhounchronicle.com contact@calhounchronicle.com

Hamlin Lincoln Journal Inc. (17.0M) PO Box 308 Hamlin WV 25523 **Phn:** 304-824-5101 **Fax:** 304-824-5210 lincolnjournalinc.com lincolnjournal@zoominternet.net

Harrisville Pennsboro News (4.3M) PO Box 241 Harrisville WV 26362 **Phn:** 304-643-4947 **Fax:** 304-643-4717 news@ritchiecountynews.com

Harrisville Ritchie Gazette (3.8M) PO Box 215 Harrisville WV 26362 **Phn:** 304-643-2221 **Fax:** 304-643-2156 gazette@zoominternet.net

Hinton Hinton News (4.3M) PO Box 1000 Hinton WV 25951 **Phn:** 304-466-0005 hinton1000@aol.com

Hurricane Hurricane Breeze (1.3M) PO Box 310 Hurricane WV 25526 **Phn:** 304-562-9881

WASHINGTON WEEKLY NEWSPAPERS

Iaeger The Industrial News (2.5M) PO Box 180 Iaeger WV 24844 **Phn:** 304-938-2142

Kingwood Preston County Journal (5.5M) PO Box 587 Kingwood WV 26537 **Phn:** 304-329-0090 **Fax:** 304-329-2450

Lewisburg Mountain Messenger (4.0M) PO Box 429 Lewisburg WV 24901 **Phn:** 304-647-5724 **Fax:** 304-647-5767 mountainmessenger.com ads@mountainmessenger.com

Lewisburg Valley Ranger (27.0M) PO Box 471 Lewisburg WV 24901 **Phn:** 304-645-1206 **Fax:** 304-645-7104

Madison Coal Valley News (5.0M) 350 Main St Madison WV 25130 **Phn:** 304-369-1165 **Fax:** 304-369-1166 www.coalvalleynews.com jbyers@civitasmedia.com

Marlinton The Pocahontas Times (4.9M) 206 8th St Marlinton WV 24954 **Phn:** 304-799-4973 **Fax:** 304-799-6466 www.pocahontastimes.com jsgraham@pocahontastimes.com

Montgomery Montgomery Herald (2.5M) 406 Lee St Montgomery WV 25136 **Phn:** 304-469-3373 **Fax:** 304-469-4105 www.montgomery-herald.com ckeenan@register-herald.com

Moorefield Moorefield Examiner (4.8M) PO Box 380 Moorefield WV 26836 **Phn:** 304-530-6397 **Fax:** 304-530-6400 www.moorefieldexaminer.com news@moorefieldexaminer.com

Mullens Mullens Advocate (2.0M) 212 Moran Ave Mullens WV 25882 **Phn:** 304-294-4144 mullensadvocate@yahoo.com

New Cumberland Hancock County Courier (2.2M) PO Box 547 New Cumberland WV 26047 **Phn:** 304-564-3131 **Fax:** 304-564-3867 hcourier@frontier.com

New Martinsville Wetzel Chronicle (5.0M) PO Box 289 New Martinsville WV 26155 **Phn:** 304-455-3300 **Fax:** 304-455-1275 www.wetzelchronicle.com editor@wetzelchronicle.com

Oak Hill The Fayette Tribune (3.0M) PO Box 139 Oak Hill WV 25901 **Phn:** 304-469-3373 **Fax:** 304-469-4105 www.fayettetribune.com ckeenan@register-herald.com

Parsons The Parsons Advocate (3.8M) PO Box 345 Parsons WV 26287 **Phn:** 304-478-3533 **Fax:** 304-478-1086 www.parsonsadvocate.com

Petersburg Grant County Press (4.6M) PO Box 39 Petersburg WV 26847 **Phn:** 304-257-1844 **Fax:** 304-257-1691 www.grantcountypress.com news@grantcountypress.com

Philippi Barbour Democrat (5.3M) PO Box 459 Philippi WV 26416 **Phn:** 304-457-2222 **Fax:** 304-457-2235 barbourdemocratwv.com news@barbourdemocratwv.com

Pineville The Independent Herald (6.0M) PO Box 100 Pineville WV 24874 **Phn:** 304-732-6060 **Fax:** 304-732-8228

Princeton Princeton Times (3.0M) PO Box 1199 Princeton WV 24740 **Phn:** 304-425-8191 **Fax:** 304-487-1632 www.bdtonline.com/cnhi/bdtonline/princeton news@bdtonline.com

Ravenswood Jackson Star News (4.0M) PO Box 10 Ravenswood WV 26164 **Phn:** 304-372-4222 **Fax:** 304-372-5544 www.jacksonnewspapers.com editor@jacksonnewspapers.com

Ripley The Jackson Herald (7.0M) PO Box 31 Ripley WV 25271 **Phn:** 304-372-4222 **Fax:** 304-372-5544 www.jacksonnewspapers.com editor@jacksonnewspapers.com

Romney Hampshire Review (6.2M) PO Box 1036 Romney WV 26757 **Phn:** 304-822-3871 **Fax:** 304-822-4487 www.hampshirereview.com

Saint Marys West Central Publishing (3.3M) PO Box 27 Saint Marys WV 26170 **Phn:** 304-684-2424 **Fax:** 304-684-2426 news@oracleandleader.com

Shepherdstown Shepherdstown Chronicle (2.0M) PO Box 2088 Shepherdstown WV 25443 **Phn:** 304-876-3380 **Fax:** 304-876-1957 www.shepherdstownchronicle.com edit@shepherdstownchronicle.com

Shinnston Shinnston News Journal (3.7M) PO Box 187 Shinnston WV 26431 **Phn:** 304-592-1030 **Fax:** 304-592-0603 newsandjournal@yahoo.com

Sistersville Tyler Star-News (3.5M) PO Box 191 Sistersville WV 26175 **Phn:** 304-652-4141 **Fax:** 304-652-1454 www.tylerstarnews.com editor@tylerstarnews.com

Spencer Roane County Reporter (2.3M) 210 E Main St Spencer WV 25276 **Phn:** 304-927-2360 **Fax:** 304-927-2361 www.thetimesrecord.net dhedges@thetimesrecord.net

Spencer The Times-Record (3.5M) 210 E Main St Spencer WV 25276 **Phn:** 304-927-2360 **Fax:** 304-927-2361 www.thetimesrecord.net dhedges@thetimesrecord.net

Summersville Nicholas Chronicle (8.0M) PO Box 503 Summersville WV 26651 **Phn:** 304-872-2251 **Fax:** 304-872-2254 nicholaschronicle.com editor@nicholaschronicle.com

Sutton Braxton Citizens News (6.5M) PO Box 516 Sutton WV 26601 **Phn:** 304-765-5193 **Fax:** 304-765-2754 www.bcn-news.com editor@bcn-news.com

Sutton Braxton Democrat (5.0M) 201 2nd St Sutton WV 26601 **Phn:** 304-765-5555 braxton@mountain.net

Union Monroe Watchman (4.0M) PO Box 179 Union WV 24983 **Phn:** 304-772-3016 **Fax:** 304-772-4421 watchman2@earthlink.net

Webster Springs Webster Echo (3.0M) 219 Back Fork St Webster Springs WV 26288 **Phn:** 304-847-5828 **Fax:** 304-847-5991

Webster Springs Webster Republican (1.9M) 219 Back Fork St Webster Springs WV 26288 **Phn:** 304-847-5828 **Fax:** 304-847-5991

Welch Welch News (5.7M) PO Box 569 Welch WV 24801 **Phn:** 304-436-3144 **Fax:** 304-436-3146 welchnews@frontiernet.net

Wellsburg Brooke Co Review (2.0M) PO Box 591 Wellsburg WV 26070 **Phn:** 304-737-0946 **Fax:** 304-737-0297 brookereviewnews@comcast.net

West Union Herald Record (2.7M) 202 E Main St West Union WV 26456 **Phn:** 304-873-1600

Weston Weston Democrat (7.0M) PO Box 968 Weston WV 26452 **Phn:** 304-269-1600 **Fax:** 304-269-4035 www.westondemocrat.com news@westondemocrat.com

WISCONSIN

Abbotsford TP Printing Co (3.0M) PO Box 677 Abbotsford WI 54405 **Phn:** 715-223-2342 **Fax:** 715-223-3505 www.centralwinews.com/tribune tp@tpprinting.com

Adams Adams-Friendship Times-Reporter (3.5M) PO Box 99 Adams WI 53910 **Phn:** 608-339-7844 **Fax:** 608-339-3903 afnewspapers.com

Amery Amery Free Press (5.0M) PO Box 424 Amery WI 54001 **Phn:** 715-268-8101 **Fax:** 715-268-5300

Appleton Post-Gazette (7.4M) PO Box 59 Appleton WI 54912 **Phn:** 920-532-0054 **Fax:** 920-532-0057

Argyle Pecatonica Valley Leader (1.8M) PO Box 220 Argyle WI 53504 **Phn:** 608-543-9500 **Fax:** 608-543-9011 blade@tds.net

WISCONSIN WEEKLY NEWSPAPERS

Augusta Augusta Area Times (1.5M) PO Box 465 Augusta WI 54722 **Phn:** 715-286-2655 **Fax:** 715-597-2705

Baldwin Baldwin Bulletin (2.2M) PO Box 76 Baldwin WI 54002 **Phn:** 715-684-2484 **Fax:** 715-684-4937 www.baldwin-bulletin.com pehaw@baldwin-telecom.net

Balsam Lake Ledger Publications (8.0M) PO Box 129 Balsam Lake WI 54810 **Phn:** 715-485-3121 **Fax:** 715-485-3037 pcledger@lakeland.ws

Barron Barron News-Shield (4.3M) PO Box 100 Barron WI 54812 **Phn:** 715-537-3117 **Fax:** 715-537-5640 www.news-shield.com newsshield@chibardun.net

Berlin Berlin Journal Co. (8.0M) PO Box 10 Berlin WI 54923 **Phn:** 920-361-1515 **Fax:** 920-361-1518

Black Earth News Sickle Arrow (2.8M) PO Box 286 Black Earth WI 53515 **Phn:** 608-767-3655 **Fax:** 608-767-2222 www.newspubinc.com nsa@newspubinc.com

Black River Falls Jackson Co. Chronicle (2.1M) 34 S 1st St Black River Falls WI 54615 **Phn:** 715-284-0085 **Fax:** 715-284-0087 lacrossetribune.com/jacksoncochronicle news@jacksoncountychronicle.com

Black River Falls The Banner Journal (4.5M) 409 E Main St Black River Falls WI 54615 **Phn:** 715-284-4304 **Fax:** 715-284-4634 news@bannerjournal.com

Blair Blair Press (1.4M) PO Box 187 Blair WI 54616 **Phn:** 608-989-2531 www.blairpress.com blairprs@triwest.net

Bloomer Bloomer Advance (3.0M) PO Box 25 Bloomer WI 54724 **Phn:** 715-568-3100 **Fax:** 715-568-3111 www.bloomeradvance.com badvance@bloomer.net

Boscobel Boscobel Dial (5.8M) 901 Wisconsin Ave Boscobel WI 53805 **Phn:** 608-375-4458 **Fax:** 608-375-2369 www.swnews4u.com dialeditor@boscobeldial.net

Brillion Brillion News (2.2M) 425 W Ryan St Brillion WI 54110 **Phn:** 920-756-2222 **Fax:** 920-756-2701 www.mybrillionnews.com editor@thebrillionnews.com

Brodhead Independent-Register (9.0M) 922 W Exchange St Brodhead WI 53520 **Phn:** 608-897-2193 **Fax:** 608-897-4137 www.indreg.com paper@indreg.com

Burlington Southern Lakes Newspapers (4.8M) 700 N Pine St Burlington WI 53105 **Phn:** 262-763-3511 **Fax:** 262-763-2238 www.southernlakesnewspapers.com newsdept@standardpress.com

Cadott Cadott Sentinel (1.5M) PO Box 70 Cadott WI 54727 **Phn:** 715-289-4978

Cambridge Cambridge News (1.7M) PO Box 8 Cambridge WI 53523 **Phn:** 608-423-3213 **Fax:** 608-423-7802 www.hngnews.com cambridge.deerfield@hngnews.com

Campbellsport Campbellsport News (2.3M) 101 N Fond du Lac Ave Campbellsport WI 53010 **Phn:** 920-533-8338 **Fax:** 920-533-5579 www.thecampbellsportnews.com frontdesk@thecampbellsportnews.com

Cashton Cashton Record (1.3M) PO Box 100 Cashton WI 54619 **Phn:** 608-654-7330 **Fax:** 608-654-7324 cashtonrecord@centurytel.net

Cedarburg Ozaukee County News Graphic (10.0M) PO Box 47 Cedarburg WI 53012 **Phn:** 262-375-5100 **Fax:** 262-375-5107 www.gmtoday.com drank@conleynet.com

Chetek The Chetek Alert (3.7M) PO Box 5 Chetek WI 54728 **Phn:** 715-924-4118 **Fax:** 715-924-4122 www.chetekalert.com chetekalert@citypapers.com

Chilton Chilton Times Journal (5.0M) PO Box 227 Chilton WI 53014 **Phn:** 920-849-4551 **Fax:** 920-849-4651 www.chiltontimesjournal.com timesjournal@charter.net

Clinton Clinton Topper (1.7M) PO Box 443 Clinton WI 53525 **Phn:** 608-676-4111 **Fax:** 608-676-4664 theclintontopper@aol.com

Clinton Sharon Reporter (0.9M) PO Box 443 Clinton WI 53525 **Phn:** 608-676-4111

Clintonville Country Post East (2.0M) 17 9th St Clintonville WI 54929 **Phn:** 715-823-3151 **Fax:** 715-823-7479

Cochrane Buffalo Co Journal (1.1M) PO Box 40 Cochrane WI 54622 **Phn:** 608-248-2451 **Fax:** 608-248-2422 recorder@mwt.net

Cochrane Cochrane City Recorder (2.0M) PO Box 40 Cochrane WI 54622 **Phn:** 608-248-2451 **Fax:** 608-248-2422 recorder@mwt.net

Colfax Colfax Messenger (1.5M) PO Box 517 Colfax WI 54730 **Phn:** 715-962-3535 **Fax:** 715-962-3413 www.dewittmedia.com messenger@dewittmedia.com

Columbus Columbus Journal (2.0M) PO Box 188 Columbus WI 53925 **Phn:** 920-623-3160 **Fax:** 920-623-9383 www.wiscnews.com/columbusjournal pscharf@capitalnewspapers.com

Cornell Cornell & Lake Holcombe Courier (1.8M) PO Box 546 Cornell WI 54732 **Phn:** 715-239-6688 **Fax:** 715-239-6200

Cottage Grove Herald Independent (2.3M) 213 W Cottage Grove Rd Ste 9 Cottage Grove WI 53527 **Phn:** 608-839-1544 **Fax:** 608-839-8750 www.hngnews.com herald-independent@hngnews.com

Crandon Forest Republican (2.7M) 103 S Hazeldell Ave Crandon WI 54520 **Phn:** 715-478-3315 **Fax:** 715-478-5385 www.florence-forestnews.com news@forestrepublican.com

Cuba City Tri-County Press (2.6M) PO Box 869 Cuba City WI 53807 **Phn:** 608-744-2107 **Fax:** 608-744-2108 tcpnews@yousq.net

Cumberland Cumberland Advocate (2.7M) PO Box 637 Cumberland WI 54829 **Phn:** 715-822-4469 **Fax:** 715-822-4451 www.cumberland-advocate.com news@cumberland-advocate.com

Darlington Republican Journal (3.5M) 316 Main St Darlington WI 53530 **Phn:** 608-776-4425 **Fax:** 608-776-4301 myrjonline.com repjournal@yahoo.com

De Forest De Forest Times Tribune (2.8M) PO Box 585 De Forest WI 53532 **Phn:** 608-846-5576 **Fax:** 608-846-5757 hngnews.com deforest@hngnews.com

Deerfield Independent (1.1M) PO Box 27 Deerfield WI 53531 **Phn:** 608-764-5515 **Fax:** 608-764-8214 www.hngnews.com/cambridge_deerfield cambridge.deerfield@hngnews.com

Delavan Delavan Enterprise (5.0M) 1102 Ann St Delavan WI 53115 **Phn:** 262-728-3411 **Fax:** 262-728-6844 news.mywalworthcounty.com delavaneditor@southernlakesnewspapers.com

Delavan This Week (48.0M) PO Box 366 Delavan WI 53115 **Phn:** 262-728-5505 **Fax:** 262-728-5706 www.walworthcountytoday.com onlineeditor@communityshoppers.com

Dodgeville Dodgeville Chronicle (5.7M) 106 W Merrimac St Dodgeville WI 53533 **Phn:** 608-935-2331 **Fax:** 608-935-9531

Durand Durand Courier-Wedge (4.2M) 103 W Main St Durand WI 54736 **Phn:** 715-672-4252 **Fax:** 715-672-4254 thewedge@nelson-tel.net

Eagle River Vilas County News (11.0M) PO Box 1929 Eagle River WI 54521 **Phn:** 715-479-4421 **Fax:** 715-479-6242 www.vcnewsreview.com erpub@nnex.net

East Troy East Troy News (1.4M) 2100 Church St East Troy WI 53120 **Phn:** 262-642-7451 **Fax:** 262-642-5934 www.southernlakesnewspapers.com etnews@easttroynews.com

East Troy East Troy Times (1.7M) PO Box 274 East Troy WI 53120 **Phn:** 262-642-7837 **Fax:** 262-642-2409 www.easttroytimes.net editor@easttroytimes.net

Eau Claire The Country Today (22.0M) 701 S Farwell St Eau Claire WI 54701 **Phn:** 715-833-9275 **Fax:** 715-858-7307 www.thecountrytoday.com thecountrytoday@ecpc.com

Edgerton Edgerton Reporter (3.0M) 21 N Henry St Edgerton WI 53534 **Phn:** 608-884-3367 **Fax:** 608-884-8187

Elkhorn Elkhorn Independent (1.9M) 812 N Wisconsin St Elkhorn WI 53121 **Phn:** 262-723-2250 **Fax:** 262-723-7424 news.mywalworthcounty.com tlamb@southernlakesnewspapers.com

Ellsworth Pierce County Herald (4.6M) 126 S Chestnut St Ellsworth WI 54011 **Phn:** 715-273-4334 **Fax:** 715-273-4335 www.piercecountyherald.com pcheditor@rivertowns.net

Elroy The Messenger of Juneau Co. (2.9M) 229 Main St Elroy WI 53929 **Phn:** 608-462-4902 **Fax:** 608-462-4903 betwrites@msn.com

Evansville Evansville Review (5.4M) PO Box 77 Evansville WI 53536 **Phn:** 608-882-5220 **Fax:** 608-882-5221

Fennimore Fennimore Times (1.6M) 1150 Lincoln Ave Fennimore WI 53809 **Phn:** 608-822-3912 **Fax:** 608-822-3916 www.swnews4u.com timeseditor@tds.net

Florence Florence Mining News (2.2M) PO Box 79 Florence WI 54121 **Phn:** 715-528-3276 **Fax:** 715-528-5976 www.florence-forestnews.com upnorth2@borderlandnet.net

Frederic Inter-County Leader (8.0M) PO Box 490 Frederic WI 54837 **Phn:** 715-327-4236 **Fax:** 715-327-4117 www.the-leader.net leadernewsroom@gmail.com

Gays Mills Independent & Scout (2.1M) PO Box 188 Gays Mills WI 54631 **Phn:** 608-735-4413 **Fax:** 608-735-4419 indnews@mwt.net

Germantown Express News (233.0M) W130N10437 Washington Dr Germantown WI 53022 **Phn:** 262-238-6397 **Fax:** 262-242-9450 discoverhometown.com news@discoverhometown.com

Glenwood City Tribune Press Reporter (2.9M) PO Box 38 Glenwood City WI 54013 **Phn:** 715-265-4646 **Fax:** 715-265-7496

Glidden Glidden Enterprise (1.4M) PO Box 128 Glidden WI 54527 **Phn:** 715-264-3481

Grantsburg Burnett County Sentinel (2.5M) PO Box 397 Grantsburg WI 54840 **Phn:** 715-463-2341 **Fax:** 715-463-5138 www.presspubs.com/burnett todd@burnettcountysentinel.com

Green Bay De Pere Journal (3.4M) PO Box 23430 Green Bay WI 54305 **Phn:** 920-336-4221 **Fax:** 920-336-1646 www.greenbaypressgazette.com

Green Bay Denmark Press (2.7M) PO Box 23430 Green Bay WI 54305 **Phn:** 920-863-2154 **Fax:** 920-863-8652

Hammond Central St. Croix News (1.4M) PO Box 208 Hammond WI 54015 **Phn:** 715-796-2356 **Fax:** 715-796-2355

Hartland Lake Country Publications (16.0M) 810 Cardinal Ln Ste 210 Hartland WI 53029 **Phn:** 262-367-3272 **Fax:** 262-367-7414 www.livinglakecountry.com lakenews@jcpgroup.com

WISCONSIN WEEKLY NEWSPAPERS

Hayward Sawyer County Record (7.0M) PO Box 919 Hayward WI 54843 **Phn:** 715-634-4881 **Fax:** 715-634-8191 haywardwi.com

Hillsboro Sentry-Enterprise (1.8M) PO Box 469 Hillsboro WI 54634 **Phn:** 608-489-2264 **Fax:** 608-489-2348 sentry@mwt.net

Horicon Horicon Reporter (1.6M) 411 E Lake St Horicon WI 53032 **Phn:** 920-485-2016 **Fax:** 920-485-4820

Hudson Hudson Star-Observer (7.5M) 226 Locust St Ste 1 Hudson WI 54016 **Phn:** 715-386-9333 **Fax:** 715-386-9891   www.hudsonstarobserver.com hsoeditor@rivertowns.net

Hurley Iron County Miner (2.7M) 216 Copper St Hurley WI 54534 **Phn:** 715-561-3405 **Fax:** 715-561-3799 ironcountyminer@yahoo.com

Iola Manawa Advocate (0.6M) PO Box 235 Iola WI 54945 **Phn:** 715-445-6397

Juneau Dodge County Independent News (1.5M) PO Box 167 Juneau WI 53039 **Phn:** 920-386-2421 **Fax:** 920-386-2422

Kaukauna Times-Villager (5.5M) PO Box 229 Kaukauna WI 54130 **Phn:** 920-759-2000 **Fax:** 920-759-7344 wrightstownspirit.com editor@timesvillager.com

Kewaskum Kewaskum Statesman (3.4M) PO Box 98 Kewaskum WI 53040 **Phn:** 262-626-2626 **Fax:** 262-247-0610   www.thestatesmanwi.com andrew@thestatesmanwi.com

Kewaunee Kewaunee Co. News (5.6M) PO Box 86 Kewaunee WI 54216 **Phn:** 920-487-2222 **Fax:** 920-487-3194   www.greenbaypressgazette.com editorial@gokewauneecounty.com

Kiel Tri-County News (4.6M) PO Box 237 Kiel WI 53042 **Phn:** 920-894-2828 **Fax:** 920-894-2161 www.iwantthenews.com marks@deltapublications.com

Ladysmith Ladysmith News (5.7M) PO Box 189 Ladysmith WI 54848 **Phn:** 715-532-5591 **Fax:** 715-532-6644   www.ladysmithnews.com editor@ladysmithnews.com

Lake Geneva The Regional News (5.0M) PO Box 937 Lake Geneva WI 53147 **Phn:** 262-248-4444 **Fax:** 262-248-4476   www.lakegenevanews.net jhalverson@lakegenevanews.net

Lake Mills Lake Mills Leader (2.4M) PO Box 310 Lake Mills WI 53551 **Phn:** 920-648-2334 **Fax:** 920-648-8187 hngnews.com lakemillsleader@hngnews.com

Lancaster Grant Herald Independent (3.8M) PO Box 310 Lancaster WI 53813 **Phn:** 608-723-2151 **Fax:** 608-723-7272 lannews@tds.net

Lodi Lodi Enterprise (2.6M) PO Box 16 Lodi WI 53555 **Phn:** 608-592-3261 **Fax:** 608-592-3866 hngnews.com lodi@hngnews.com

Loyal Tribune-Record-Gleaner (3.7M) PO Box 187 Loyal WI 54446 **Phn:** 715-255-8531 **Fax:** 715-255-8357

Madison Isthmus (64.0M) 101 King St Madison WI 53703 **Phn:** 608-251-5627 **Fax:** 608-251-2165 www.thedailypage.com edit@isthmus.com

Manitowoc Lakeshore Chronicle (32.0M) 902 Franklin St Manitowoc WI 54220 **Phn:** 920-684-4433 **Fax:** 920-686-2103 www.htrnews.com htrnews@htrnews.com

Marion Marion Advertiser (2.9M) PO Box 268 Marion WI 54950 **Phn:** 715-754-5444

Mauston Juneau County Star-Times (2.8M) PO Box 220 Mauston WI 53948 **Phn:** 608-847-7341 **Fax:** 608-847-4867   www.wiscnews.com   jcst-editorial@capitalnewspapers.com

Mayville Dodge Co. Pionier (4.0M) PO Box 271 Mayville WI 53050 **Phn:** 920-387-2211 **Fax:** 920-387-5515 dodgecountypionier.com editor@dodgecountypionier.com

Mc Farland McFarland Thistle (1.2M) 5124 Farwell St Mc Farland WI 53558 **Phn:** 608-838-6435 **Fax:** 608-838-4927   www.hngnews.com mcfarland@hngnews.com

Medford Medford Star News (6.4M) PO Box 180 Medford WI 54451 **Phn:** 715-748-2626 **Fax:** 715-748-2699   www.centralwinews.com starnews@centralwinews.com

Mellen Weekly Record (1.3M) PO Box 678 Mellen WI 54546 **Phn:** 715-274-3131

Menomonie Dunn County News (4.3M) PO Box 40 Menomonie WI 54751 **Phn:** 715-235-3411 **Fax:** 715-235-0936   chippewa.com/dunnconnect barbara.lyon@lee.net

Merrill Foto News (16.4M) 807 E 1st St Merrill WI 54452 **Phn:** 715-536-7121 **Fax:** 715-539-3686 www.merrillfotonews.com clueck@jcpgroup.com

Middleton Middleton Times Tribune (3.3M) PO Box 620006 Middleton WI 53562 **Phn:** 608-836-1601 **Fax:** 608-836-3759   www.middletontimes.com mgeiger@newspubinc.com

Milton Milton Courier (3.3M) PO Box 69 Milton WI 53563 **Phn:** 608-868-2442 **Fax:** 608-868-4664 mcourier@miltoncourier.net

Milwaukee Milwakee Courier (60.0M) PO Box 06279 Milwaukee WI 53206 **Phn:** 414-449-4860 **Fax:** 414-449-4872   www.milwaukeecourier.org milwaukeecourier@aol.com

Milwaukee Shepherd Express (62.0M) 207 E Buffalo St Ste 410 Milwaukee WI 53202 **Phn:** 414-276-2222 **Fax:** 414-276-3312   www.expressmilwaukee.com editor@shepex.com

Mineral Point Democrat-Tribune (1.4M) 334 High St Mineral Point WI 53565 **Phn:** 608-987-2141 **Fax:** 608-987-4163

Minocqua Lakeland Times (13.0M) PO Box 790 Minocqua WI 54548 **Phn:** 715-356-5236 **Fax:** 715-358-2121   www.lakelandtimes.com editor@lakelandtimes.com

Mondovi Mondovi Herald-News (3.5M) PO Box 67 Mondovi WI 54755 **Phn:** 715-926-4970 **Fax:** 715-926-4928 mheditor@media-md.net

Montello Marquette County Tribune (3.8M) PO Box 188 Montello WI 53949 **Phn:** 608-297-2424 **Fax:** 608-297-9293   www.marquettecountytribune.com marquettetribune@newspubinc.com

Mosinee Mosinee Times (2.6M) 407 3rd St Mosinee WI 54455 **Phn:** 715-693-2300 **Fax:** 715-693-1574 motimes@mtc.net

Mount Horeb Mt. Horeb Mail (2.7M) 114 E Main St Mount Horeb WI 53572 **Phn:** 608-437-5553 **Fax:** 608-437-3443   www.newspubinc.com mhmail@newspubinc.com

Mukwonago Mukwonago Chief (4.5M) PO Box 204 Mukwonago WI 53149 **Phn:** 262-363-4045 **Fax:** 262-367-7414

Muscoda Muscoda Progressive (2.0M) PO Box 247 Muscoda WI 53573 **Phn:** 608-739-3550

Neenah News-Record (20.0M) 307 S Commercial St Ste 202 Neenah WI 54956 **Phn:** 920-729-6620 **Fax:** 920-729-6626   www.wisinfo.com athompson@postcrescent.com

Neillsville Clark County Press (4.2M) PO Box 149 Neillsville WI 54456 **Phn:** 715-743-2600 **Fax:** 715-743-5460 ccpress@tds.net

New Glarus Belleville Recorder (1.6M) PO Box 65 New Glarus WI 53574 **Phn:** 608-424-3232

New Glarus Post Messenger Recorder (3.5M) PO Box 65 New Glarus WI 53574 **Phn:** 608-527-5252 **Fax:** 608-527-5285   www.newspubinc.com pmreditor@newspubinc.com

New London New London Press-Star (2.8M) PO Box 283 New London WI 54961 **Phn:** 920-982-4321 **Fax:** 920-982-7672

New Richmond The News (5.0M) PO Box 338 New Richmond WI 54017 **Phn:** 715-246-6881 **Fax:** 715-246-7117   www.newrichmond-news.com nrneditor@rivertowns.net

Oconto Oconto County Reporter (4.7M) PO Box 200 Oconto WI 54153 **Phn:** 920-834-4242 **Fax:** 920-834-4878   www.greenbaypressgazette.com editorial@goocontocounty.com

Oconto Falls Oconto County Times-Herald (22.0M) PO Box 128 Oconto Falls WI 54154 **Phn:** 920-848-3427 **Fax:** 920-848-3430

Ontario County Line (1.3M) PO Box 7 Ontario WI 54651 **Phn:** 608-337-4232 **Fax:** 608-337-4658 www.thecountyline.net countyline@centurytel.net

Oostburg Lake Shore Weekly (4.0M) PO Box 700200 Oostburg WI 53070 **Phn:** 920-564-3153

Oostburg Tri-County Messenger (11.0M) 329 S 6th St Oostburg WI 53070 **Phn:** 920-564-6880 **Fax:** 920-564-6881   www.tricountymessenger.com bschanen4@ozaukeepress.com

Oregon Oregon Observer (4.0M) 125 N Main St Oregon WI 53575 **Phn:** 608-835-6677 **Fax:** 608-835-0130 www.oregonobserver.com oregonobserver@wcinet.com

Orfordville Orfordville Journal/News (0.9M) 310 Willow St Orfordville WI 53576 **Phn:** 608-879-2211 www.orfordville.com journalnews@orfordville.com

Osceola The Sun (2.1M) PO Box 248 Osceola WI 54020 **Phn:** 715-294-2314 **Fax:** 715-755-3314 www.presspubs.com/osceola editor@osceolasun.com

Osseo Tri-County News (1.5M) PO Box 460 Osseo WI 54758 **Phn:** 715-597-3313 **Fax:** 715-597-2705

Park Falls Park Falls Herald (3.4M) PO Box 410 Park Falls WI 54552 **Phn:** 715-762-4940 **Fax:** 715-762-2757 www.pricecountydaily.com smergen@thephillipsbee.com

Peshtigo Peshtigo Times (11.0M) PO Box 187 Peshtigo WI 54157 **Phn:** 715-582-4541 **Fax:** 715-582-4662 www.peshtigotimes.net news@peshtigotimes.com

Phillips Phillips Bee (4.4M) 115 N Lake Ave Phillips WI 54555 **Phn:** 715-339-3036 **Fax:** 715-339-4300 www.pricecountydaily.com news@thephillipsbee.com

Pittsville Pittsville Record (2.4M) 8265 Main St Pittsville WI 54466 **Phn:** 715-884-2314

Platteville Platteville Journal (4.2M) PO Box 266 Platteville WI 53818 **Phn:** 608-348-3006 **Fax:** 608-348-7979 www.swnews4u.com journaleditor@centurytel.net

Plymouth Plymouth Review (7.0M) 113 E Mill St Plymouth WI 53073 **Phn:** 920-893-6411 **Fax:** 920-893-5505 www.plymouth-review.com reply@plymouth-review.com

Plymouth Sheboygan Falls News (2.3M) 113 E Mill St Plymouth WI 53073 **Phn:** 920-467-6591 **Fax:** 920-893-5505 www.plymouth-review.com reply@plymouth-review.com

Port Washington Ozaukee Press (9.0M) PO Box 249 Port Washington WI 53074 **Phn:** 262-284-3494 **Fax:** 262-284-0067   ozaukeepress.com news@ozaukeepress.com

Portage Wisconsin Dells Events (2.3M) PO Box 470 Portage WI 53901 **Phn:** 608-254-8327 **Fax:** 608-254-8328 www.wiscnews.com/wisconsindellsevents wdenews@capitalnewspapers.com

Poynette Poynette Press (1.7M) PO Box 37 Poynette WI 53955 **Phn:** 608-635-2565 **Fax:** 608-635-4542 hngnews.com poynette@hngnews.com

Prairie Du Chien The Courier Press (4.0M) PO Box 149 Prairie Du Chien WI 53821 **Phn:** 608-326-2441 **Fax:** 608-326-2443 pdccourier.com howenews@mhtc.net

Prescott Prescott Journal (3.6M) PO Box 157 Prescott WI 54021 **Phn:** 715-262-5454 **Fax:** 715-262-5474 prescottjournal.net news@prescottjournal.net

Random Lake The Sounder (2.9M) PO Box 346 Random Lake WI 53075 **Phn:** 920-994-9244 **Fax:** 920-994-4817 www.thesounder.com editor@thesounder.com

Reedsburg Times Press (1.2M) PO Box 269 Reedsburg WI 53959 **Phn:** 608-524-4336 **Fax:** 608-524-4337 www.wiscnews.com rtp-news@capitalnewspapers.com

Rice Lake Rice Lake Chronotype (9.5M) PO Box 30 Rice Lake WI 54868 **Phn:** 715-234-2121 **Fax:** 715-234-5232 www.ricelakeonline.com newsroom@chronotype.com

Richland Center Richland Observer (4.0M) PO Box 31 Richland Center WI 53581 **Phn:** 608-647-6141 **Fax:** 608-647-6143

Ripon Commonwealth-Press (3.8M) PO Box 344 Ripon WI 54971 **Phn:** 920-748-3017 **Fax:** 920-748-3028 www.riponpress.com ians@riponprinters.com

River Falls River Falls Journal (4.0M) PO Box 25 River Falls WI 54022 **Phn:** 715-425-1561 **Fax:** 715-425-5666 www.riverfallsjournal.com rfjeditor@rivertowns.net

Sauk City Sauk Prairie Eagle (1.7M) PO Box 670 Sauk City WI 53583 **Phn:** 608-643-0118 **Fax:** 608-643-0120 www.wiscnews.com spe-editorial@capitalnewspapers.com

Sauk City Sauk Prairie Star (2.5M) PO Box 606 Sauk City WI 53583 **Phn:** 608-643-3444 **Fax:** 608-643-4988 www.newspubinc.com mikesps@newspubinc.com

Shell Lake Washburn Co Register (1.8M) PO Box 455 Shell Lake WI 54871 **Phn:** 715-468-2314 www.wcregisteronline.com wcregister@centurytel.net

Sparta Monroe County Democrat (5.0M) PO Box 252 Sparta WI 54656 **Phn:** 608-269-3186 **Fax:** 608-269-6876 www.spartanewspapers.com sadtad@centurytel.net

Sparta Sparta Herald (4.7M) PO Box 252 Sparta WI 54656 **Phn:** 608-269-3186 **Fax:** 608-269-6876 www.spartanewspapers.com sadtad@centurytel.net

Spooner Spooner Advocate (4.7M) PO Box 338 Spooner WI 54801 **Phn:** 715-635-2181 **Fax:** 715-635-2186 www.spooneradvocate.com news@spooneradvocate.com

Spring Green Home News (2.0M) PO Box 39 Spring Green WI 53588 **Phn:** 608-588-2508 **Fax:** 608-588-3536

Spring Valley Sun-Argus (1.1M) PO Box 69 Spring Valley WI 54767 **Phn:** 715-698-3995 **Fax:** 715-698-2952 mygatewaynews.com editor@mygatewaynews.com

Stanley Stanley Republican (2.6M) PO Box 185 Stanley WI 54768 **Phn:** 715-644-3319 **Fax:** 715-644-5452

Stevens Point Portage Co. Gazette (5.5M) PO Box 146 Stevens Point WI 54481 **Phn:** 715-343-8045 **Fax:** 715-343-8048 www.pcgazette.com pcgazette@g2a.net

Stoughton Courier-Hub (4.1M) 135 W Main St Ste 102 Stoughton WI 53589 **Phn:** 608-873-6671 **Fax:** 608-873-3473 www.stoughtonnews.com stoughtoneditor@wcinet.com

WISCONSIN WEEKLY NEWSPAPERS

Sturgeon Bay Door County Advocate (9.0M) PO Box 130 Sturgeon Bay WI 54235 **Phn:** 920-743-3321 **Fax:** 920-743-8908 www.doorcountyadvocate.com advocate@doorcountyadvocate.com

Sun Prairie The Star (5.2M) PO Box 645 Sun Prairie WI 53590 **Phn:** 608-837-2521 **Fax:** 608-825-4460 hngnews.com sunprairie@hngnews.com

Superior Superior Telegram (8.2M) 1226 Ogden Ave Superior WI 54880 **Phn:** 715-395-5000 **Fax:** 715-395-5002 www.superiortelegram.com editorial@superiortelegram.com

Thorp Thorp Courier (2.7M) PO Box 487 Thorp WI 54771 **Phn:** 715-669-5525 **Fax:** 715-669-5596 thorpcourier@centurytel.net

Tomah Journal/Monitor-Herald (10.0M) PO Box 190 Tomah WI 54660 **Phn:** 608-372-4123 **Fax:** 608-372-2791 lacrossetribune.com/tomahjournal chardie@rivervalleynewspapers.com

Tomahawk Tomahawk Leader (8.8M) PO Box 345 Tomahawk WI 54487 **Phn:** 715-453-2151 **Fax:** 715-453-1865 www.tomahawkleader.com news@tomahawkleader.com

Turtle Lake Turtle Lake Times (1.3M) PO Box 88 Turtle Lake WI 54889 **Phn:** 715-986-4675 **Fax:** 715-986-2363 halcopress@yahoo.com

Twin Lakes Wetosha Report (7.0M) 147 E Main St Twin Lakes WI 53181 **Phn:** 262-877-2813 **Fax:** 262-877-3619 www.mykenoshacounty.com annette@westoshareport.com

Valders Valders Journal (2.5M) PO Box 400 Valders WI 54245 **Phn:** 920-775-4431 **Fax:** 920-775-4474 vjournal@lakefield.net

Verona Fitchburg Star (7.6M) 133 Enterprise Dr Verona WI 53593 **Phn:** 608-845-9559 **Fax:** 608-845-0130 www.connectfitchburg.com fitchburgstar@wcinet.com

Verona Verona Press (2.5M) 133 Enterprise Dr Verona WI 53593 **Phn:** 608-845-9559 **Fax:** 608-845-9550 www.connectverona.com veronapress@wcinet.com

Viola Epitaph News (1.1M) PO Box 295 Viola WI 54664 **Phn:** 608-627-1830 **Fax:** 608-627-1838 epitaph@mwt.net

Viroqua Vernon County Broadcaster (6.0M) PO Box 472 Viroqua WI 54665 **Phn:** 608-637-3137 **Fax:** 608-637-8557 lacrossetribune.com/vernonbroadcaster matt.johnson@lee.net

Washburn Washburn County Journal (3.5M) PO Box 637 Washburn WI 54891 **Phn:** 715-373-5500 **Fax:** 715-373-5546

Waterloo Waterloo Courier (2.4M) PO Box 6 Waterloo WI 53594 **Phn:** 920-478-2188 **Fax:** 920-478-3618 www.hngnews.com wmcourier@hngnews.com

Waukesha CNI Newspapers (74.0M) 1741 Dolphin Dr Ste A Waukesha WI 53186 **Phn:** 414-224-2100 **Fax:** 262-446-6646 www.waukeshanow.com news@cninow.com

Waukesha Oconomowoc Enterprise (5.5M) PO Box B Waukesha WI 53186 **Phn:** 262-567-5511 **Fax:** 262-542-9024 www.gmtoday.com webmaster@conleynet.com

Waunakee Waunakee Tribune (3.5M) PO Box 128 Waunakee WI 53597 **Phn:** 608-849-5227 **Fax:** 608-849-4225 hngnews.com waunakee@hngnews.com

Waupaca Iola Herald (1.1M) 600 Industrial Dr Waupaca WI 54981 **Phn:** 715-445-6397

Waupaca Waupaca County Post (8.0M) PO Box 152 Waupaca WI 54981 **Phn:** 715-258-5546 **Fax:** 715-258-8162

Waupaca Weyauwega Chronicle (2.8M) PO Box 152 Waupaca WI 54981 **Phn:** 920-867-2158 **Fax:** 920-867-3316

Waupun Waupun Neighbors (8.0M) PO Box 111 Waupun WI 53963 **Phn:** 920-324-5555 **Fax:** 920-324-8582

Wausau City Pages (17.0M) PO Box 942 Wausau WI 54402 **Phn:** 715-845-5171 **Fax:** 715-848-5887 www.thecitypages.com tammy@thecitypages.com

Wautoma Waushara Argus (6.9M) PO Box 838 Wautoma WI 54982 **Phn:** 920-787-3334 **Fax:** 920-787-2883 www.wausharaargus.com argus@wausharaargus.com

West Bend Hartford Times Press (13.3M) 100 S th Ave West Bend WI 53095 **Phn:** 262-306-5000 **Fax:** 262-338-1984 www.gmtoday.com timespress@conleynet.com

West Salem River Valley Newspapers (4.2M) PO Box 140 West Salem WI 54669 **Phn:** 608-786-1950 **Fax:** 608-786-1670 www.rivervalleynewspapers.com randy.erickson@lee.net

Westby Westby Times (2.0M) PO Box 28 Westby WI 54667 **Phn:** 608-634-4317 **Fax:** 608-634-6499 lacrossetribune.com/westbytimes thetimes@mwt.net

Whitehall Trempealeau County Times (2.9M) PO Box 95 Whitehall WI 54773 **Phn:** 715-538-4765 **Fax:** 715-538-4540 scott@trempcotimes.com

Whitewater Palmyra Enterprise (1.2M) PO Box 327 Whitewater WI 53190 **Phn:** 262-473-3363 **Fax:** 262-473-5635

Whitewater Whitewater Register (3.0M) PO Box 327 Whitewater WI 53190 **Phn:** 262-473-3363 **Fax:** 262-473-5635 www.mywalworthcounty.com enadolski@standardpress.com

Winneconne Winneconne News (11.0M) PO Box 370 Winneconne WI 54986 **Phn:** 920-582-4541 **Fax:** 920-582-4417 www.rogersprintingsolutions.com winneconnenews@rogerspublishing.com

Winter Sawyer County Gazette (2.0M) PO Box 99 Winter WI 54896 **Phn:** 715-266-2511 gazette@centurytel.net

Withee O-W Enterprise (1.1M) PO Box F Withee WI 54498 **Phn:** 715-229-2103 **Fax:** 715-229-2104 news@o-wenterprise.com

Wittenberg Wittenberg Enterprise (1.9M) 702 S Grandview St Wittenberg WI 54499 **Phn:** 715-253-2737 **Fax:** 715-253-2700

Woodville Woodville Leader (0.8M) 102 Trient Dr Woodville WI 54028 **Phn:** 715-698-2401 **Fax:** 715-698-2952 mygatewaynews.com editor@mygatewaynews.com

WYOMING

Afton Star Valley Independent (4.2M) PO Box 129 Afton WY 83110 **Phn:** 307-885-5727 **Fax:** 307-885-5742 www.starvalleyindependent.com svi@silverstar.com

Basin Republican-Rustler (1.3M) PO Box 640 Basin WY 82410 **Phn:** 307-568-2458 **Fax:** 307-568-2459 www.basinrepublican-rustler.com breditor@tctwest.net

Buffalo Buffalo Bulletin (4.3M) PO Box 730 Buffalo WY 82834 **Phn:** 307-684-2223 **Fax:** 307-684-7431 buffalobulletin.com editor@buffalobulletin.com

Casper Casper Journal (4.8M) PO Box 80 Casper WY 82602 **Phn:** 307-265-3870 **Fax:** 866-265-3870 www.casperjournal.com

Cheyenne The Sentinel (5.2M) 307 E 20th St Cheyenne WY 82001 **Phn:** 307-632-5666 **Fax:** 307-632-1554 www.warrensentinel.com wsgraphics@warrensentinel.com

Cody Cody Enterprise (7.5M) PO Box 1090 Cody WY 82414 **Phn:** 307-587-2231 **Fax:** 307-587-5208 www.codyenterprise.com office@codyenterprise.com

Douglas Douglas Budget (4.2M) 310 E Center St Douglas WY 82633 **Phn:** 307-358-2965 **Fax:** 307-358-2926 www.douglas-budget.com publisher@douglas-budget.com

Dubois Dubois Frontier (1.4M) PO Box 980 Dubois WY 82513 **Phn:** 307-455-2525 **Fax:** 307-455-3163 www.duboisfrontier.com duboisfrontier@wyoming.com

Evanston Uinta County Herald (3.0M) 849 Front St Ste 101 Evanston WY 82930 **Phn:** 307-789-6560 **Fax:** 307-789-2700 www.uintacountyherald.com editor@uintacountyherald.com

Glenrock Glenrock Independent (0.9M) PO Box 339 Glenrock WY 82637 **Phn:** 307-436-2211 **Fax:** 307-436-8803 www.douglas-budget.com/glenrock budget@netcommander.com

Green River Green River Star (3.2M) PO Box 580 Green River WY 82935 **Phn:** 307-875-3103 **Fax:** 307-875-8778 www.greenriverstar.com grstar@sweetwaterhsa.com

Greybull Greybull Standard (1.7M) 614 Greybull Ave Greybull WY 82426 **Phn:** 307-765-4485 **Fax:** 307-765-4486 www.greybullstandard.com

Guernsey Gazette (0.5M) 40 S Wyoming Guernsey WY 82214 **Phn:** 307-836-2021 www.guernseygazette.com ggeditor@guernseygazette.com

Jackson Jackson Hole News&Guide (9.4M) PO Box 7445 Jackson WY 83002 **Phn:** 307-733-2047 **Fax:** 307-733-2138 www.jhnewsandguide.com editor@jhnewsandguide.com

Jackson Planet Jackson Hole (12.0M) PO Box 3249 Jackson WY 83001 **Phn:** 307-732-0299 **Fax:** 307-732-0996 www.planetjh.com editor@planetjh.com

Kemmerer Kemmerer Gazette (1.9M) PO Box 30 Kemmerer WY 83101 **Phn:** 307-877-3347 **Fax:** 307-877-3736 www.kemmerergazette.com editor@kemmerergazette.com

Lingle Lingle Guide (0.5M) 228 Main St Lingle WY 82223 **Phn:** 307-837-2255 **Fax:** 307-532-2283

Lovell Lovell Chronicle (2.1M) PO Box 787 Lovell WY 82431 **Phn:** 307-548-2217 **Fax:** 307-548-2218 www.lovellchronicle.com lcnews@tctwest.net

Lusk Lusk Herald (1.5M) PO Box 30 Lusk WY 82225 **Phn:** 307-334-2867 **Fax:** 307-334-2514 www.luskherald.com lhads@luskherald.com

Lyman Bridger Valley Pioneer (1.8M) 317 Bradshaw St # 2 Lyman WY 82937 **Phn:** 307-787-3229 **Fax:** 307-787-6795 www.bridgervalleypioneer.com news@bridgervalleypioneer.com

Moorcroft Moorcroft Leader (1.0M) PO Box 67 Moorcroft WY 82721 **Phn:** 307-756-3371 **Fax:** 307-756-9827 mleader@collinscom.net

Newcastle News-Letter-Journal (2.3M) PO Box 40 Newcastle WY 82701 **Phn:** 307-746-2777 **Fax:** 307-746-2660 www.newslj.com editor@newslj.com

Pine Bluffs Pine Bluffs Post (1.2M) PO Box 68 Pine Bluffs WY 82082 **Phn:** 307-245-3763 **Fax:** 307-245-3325 www.pinebluffspost.com news@pinebluffspost.com

Pinedale Pinedale Roundup (3.5M) PO Box 100 Pinedale WY 82941 **Phn:** 307-367-2123 **Fax:** 307-367-6623 www.pinedaleroundup.com editor@pinedaleroundup.com

Pinedale Sublette Examiner (2.3M) PO Box 1539 Pinedale WY 82941 **Phn:** 307-367-3203 **Fax:** 307-367-3209 www.sublettteexaminer.com editor@sublettteexaminer.com

Powell Powell Tribune (4.6M) PO Box 70 Powell WY 82435 **Phn:** 307-754-2221 **Fax:** 307-754-4873 www.powelltribune.com info@powelltribune.com

WYOMING WEEKLY NEWSPAPERS

Saratoga Saratoga Sun (1.7M) PO Box 489 Saratoga WY 82331 **Phn:** 307-326-8311 **Fax:** 307-326-5108 www.saratogasun.com info@saratogasun.com

Shoshoni Shoshoni Pioneer (0.6M) PO Box 420 Shoshoni WY 82649 **Phn:** 307-876-2627

Sundance Sundance Times (1.7M) PO Box 400 Sundance WY 82729 **Phn:** 307-283-3411 **Fax:** 307-283-3332 www.sundancetimes.com web@sundancetimes.com

Thermopolis Thermopolis Independent Record (2.5M) PO Box 31 Thermopolis WY 82443 **Phn:** 307-864-2328 **Fax:** 307-864-5711 thermopir.com news@thermopir.com

Torrington Torrington Telegram (2.8M) PO Box 1058 Torrington WY 82240 **Phn:** 307-532-2184 **Fax:** 307-532-2283 www.torringtontelegram.com jeff@torringtontelegram.com

Upton Weston County Gazette (1.1M) PO Box 526 Upton WY 82730 **Phn:** 307-468-2642 **Fax:** 307-468-2397 gazette@rtconnect.net

Wheatland Platte County Record-Times (2.8M) 1007 8th St Wheatland WY 82201 **Phn:** 307-322-2627 **Fax:** 307-322-9612 www.pcrecordtimes.com pceditor@pcrecordtimes.com

Wright High Plains Sentinel (1.4M) PO Box 457 Wright WY 82732 **Phn:** 307-464-0262 **Fax:** 307-464-1349

BLACK WEEKLY NEWSPAPERS

ALABAMA

Birmingham Birmingham Times (17.3M) 115 3rd Ave W Birmingham AL 35204 **Phn:** 205-251-5158 **Fax:** 205-323-2294 www.birminghamtimesonline.com

Demopolis The Demopolis Times (2.0M) 315 E Jefferson St Demopolis AL 36732 **Phn:** 334-289-4017 **Fax:** 334-289-4019 www.demopolistimes.com editor@demopolistimes.com

Eutaw Greene Co Democrat (4.3M) PO Box 598 Eutaw AL 35462 **Phn:** 205-372-3373 **Fax:** 205-372-2243

Huntsville Speakin' Out News (31.0M) 115 Wholesale Ave NE Huntsville AL 35811 **Phn:** 256-551-1020 **Fax:** 256-551-0607 www.speakinoutnews.info wsmoth3193@aol.com

Mobile Mobile Beacon/Alabama Citizen (7.0M) PO Box 1407 Mobile AL 36633 **Phn:** 251-479-0629 **Fax:** 251-479-0610 mobilebeaconinc@bellsouth.net

Montgomery Montgomery-Tuskegee Times (15.0M) PO Box 9133 Montgomery AL 36108 **Phn:** 334-280-2444 **Fax:** 334-280-2454 adixon711@aol.com

Tuskegee Tuskegee News (75.0M) 103 S Main St Tuskegee AL 36083 **Phn:** 334-727-3020 **Fax:** 334-727-7700 www.thetuskegeenews.com guynrhodes@bellsouth.net

ARIZONA

Phoenix Arizona Informant (15.0M) 1746 E Madison St Ste 2 Phoenix AZ 85034 **Phn:** 602-257-9300 **Fax:** 602-257-0547 www.arizonainformantnewspaper.com

CALIFORNIA

Bakersfield News Observer (17.0M) PO Box 3624 Bakersfield CA 93385 **Phn:** 661-324-9466 **Fax:** 661-324-9472 www.ognsc.com observernews@gmail.com

Compton Compton Bulletin (75.0M) PO Box 4248 Compton CA 90224 **Phn:** 310-635-6776 **Fax:** 310-635-4045 www.thebulletinweekly.com news@thebulletinweekly.com

Fresno California Advocate (33.0M) 1555 E Street Fresno CA 93706 **Phn:** 559-268-0941 **Fax:** 559-268-0943 www.caladvocate.com newsroom@caladvocate.com

Los Angeles Herald Dispatch Newspaper Group (89.3M) 4053 Marlton Ave Los Angeles CA 90008 **Phn:** 323-291-9486 **Fax:** 323-291-2123

Los Angeles L.A. Sentinel (20.0M) 3800 Crenshaw Blvd Los Angeles CA 90008 **Phn:** 323-299-3800 **Fax:** 323-299-3896 www.lasentinel.net

Los Angeles LA Watts Times (25.5M) PO Box 761338 Los Angeles CA 90076 **Phn:** 213-251-5700 **Fax:** 213-251-5720 www.lawattstimes.com comments@lawattstimes.com

Los Angeles Our Weekly (10.0M) 8732 S Western Ave Los Angeles CA 90047 **Phn:** 323-905-1300 **Fax:** 323-753-0456 www.ourweekly.com info@ourweekly.com

Los Angeles Wave Newspapers (150.0M) 4201 Wilshire Blvd Ste 600 Los Angeles CA 90010 **Phn:** 323-556-5720 **Fax:** 323-556-5704 www.wavenewspapers.com

Oakland The Oakland Post (8.0M) 405 14th St Ste 1215 Oakland CA 94612 **Phn:** 510-287-8200 **Fax:** 510-287-8247 www.postnewsgroup.net

Oxnard Tri-County Sentry (10.0M) PO Box 20515 Oxnard CA 93034 **Phn:** 805-486-8430 **Fax:** 805-486-3650 www.tricountysentry.com sentry1234@aol.com

Pasadena Pasadena Journal-News (7.5M) 1541 N Lake Ave Ste A Pasadena CA 91104 **Phn:** 626-798-3972 **Fax:** 626-798-3282 www.pasadenajournal.com pasjour@pacbell.net

Riverside Black Voice News (7.0M) PO Box 1581 Riverside CA 92502 **Phn:** 951-682-6070 **Fax:** 951-276-0877 www.blackvoicenews.com pressrelease@blackvoicenews.com

Sacramento Sacramento Observer (49.3M) PO Box 209 Sacramento CA 95812 **Phn:** 916-452-4781 **Fax:** 916-452-7744 www.sacobserver.com

San Bernardino American News (6.0M) PO Box 7010 San Bernardino CA 92411 **Phn:** 909-889-7677 **Fax:** 909-889-2882 sbamerican.com samerisam1@earthlink.net

San Bernardino Westside Story (5.0M) 577 N D St Ste 112H San Bernardino CA 92401 **Phn:** 909-384-8131 **Fax:** 909-884-0584 www.westsidestorynewspaper.com mail@westsidestorynewspaper.com

San Diego Voice & Viewpoint (25.0M) PO Box 120095 San Diego CA 92112 **Phn:** 619-266-2233 **Fax:** 619-266-0533

San Francisco San Francisco Bay View (15.3M) 4917 3rd St San Francisco CA 94124 **Phn:** 415-671-0789 www.sfbayview.com editor@sfbayview.com

San Francisco Sun Reporter Group (178.0M) 1791 Bancroft Ave San Francisco CA 94124 **Phn:** 415-671-1000 **Fax:** 415-671-1005 www.sunreporter.com sunmedia97@aol.com

COLORADO

Denver Denver Weekly News (10.0M) PO Box 5008 Denver CO 80217 **Phn:** 303-292-5158 **Fax:** 303-292-5344 dwnews2@yahoo.com

CONNECTICUT

Hartford Inquiring News (125.0M) PO Box 400276 Hartford CT 06140 **Phn:** 860-983-7587 **Fax:** 860-206-7587 www.inqnews.com inquirernews@aol.com

Hartford Northend Agents (40.0M) PO Box 2308 Hartford CT 06146 **Phn:** 860-522-1888 **Fax:** 860-286-0316 www.northendagentsnewspaper.com northendagents@aol.com

New Haven Inner-City News (35.0M) 50 Fitch St New Haven CT 06515 **Phn:** 203-387-0354 **Fax:** 203-387-2684 www.innercityonline.com babz@penfieldcomm.com

DISTRICT OF COLUMBIA

Washington Washington Informer (64.5M) 3117 Martin Luther King Jr Ave SE Washington DC 20032 **Phn:** 202-561-4100 **Fax:** 202-574-3785 www.washingtoninformer.com news@washingtoninformer.com

Washington Washington Sun (55.0M) 830 Kennedy St NW Ste B2 Washington DC 20011 **Phn:** 202-882-1021 **Fax:** 202-882-9817 thewashingtonsun@aol.com

FLORIDA

Fort Lauderdale South Florida Times (25.0M) 3020 NE 32nd Ave Ste 200 Fort Lauderdale FL 33308 **Phn:** 954-356-9360 **Fax:** 954-356-9395 browardtimes.com

Fort Lauderdale Westside Gazette (30.0M) PO Box 5304 Fort Lauderdale FL 33310 **Phn:** 954-525-1489 **Fax:** 954-525-1861 www.thewestsidegazette.com pamlewis@bellsouth.net

Fort Myers Community Voice (12.0M) 3046 Lafayette St Fort Myers FL 33916 **Phn:** 239-337-4444 **Fax:** 239-334-8289

Jacksonville Florida Star (2.5M) PO Box 40629 Jacksonville FL 32203 **Phn:** 904-766-8834 **Fax:** 904-765-1673 www.thefloridastar.com info@thefloridastar.com

Jacksonville Jacksonville Free Press (43.5M) PO Box 43580 Jacksonville FL 32203 **Phn:** 904-634-1993 **Fax:** 904-765-3803 www.jacksonvillefreepress.com jfreepress@aol.com

Miami Miami Times (26.6M) 900 NW 54th St Miami FL 33127 **Phn:** 305-757-1147 **Fax:** 305-757-5770 www.miamitimesonline.com miamiteditorial@bellsouth.net

Orlando Florida Sun Review (10.0M) PO Box 2348 Orlando FL 32802 **Phn:** 407-423-1156 **Fax:** 407-849-1286 www.floridasunreview.com sunreview@aol.com

Orlando Orlando Times (10.0M) PO Box 555339 Orlando FL 32855 **Phn:** 407-841-3052 **Fax:** 407-849-0434 www.orlando-times.com news@orlando-times.com

Orlando The Advocate (10.0M) 30 Coburn Ave Orlando FL 32805 **Phn:** 407-648-1162 **Fax:** 407-649-8702

Pensacola New American Press (37.7M) PO Box 13626 Pensacola FL 32591 **Phn:** 850-432-8410 **Fax:** 850-434-5023

Pensacola Pensacola Voice (37.5M) 213 E Yonge St Pensacola FL 32503 **Phn:** 850-434-6963 **Fax:** 850-469-8745 www.pensacolavoice.com info@pensacolavoice.com

Pensacola Pensacola's Independent Voice (16.0M) PO Box 19076 Pensacola FL 32523 **Phn:** 850-473-6633 **Fax:** 850-473-6634 indpvoice@aol.com

Saint Petersburg Weekly Challenger (20.0M) 2500 Dr Martin Luther King Jr St S Ste Saint Petersburg FL 33705 **Phn:** 727-896-2922 **Fax:** 727-823-2568 www.theweeklychallenger.com editor@theweeklychallenger.com

Tallahassee Capital Outlook (16.3M) 1363 E Tennessee St Tallahassee FL 32308 **Phn:** 850-877-0105 **Fax:** 850-877-5110 capitaloutlook.com/wordpress pressreleases@capitaloutlook.com

Tampa Daytona Times (90.0M) 5207 E Washington St Tampa FL 33619 **Phn:** 813-620-1300 **Fax:** 813-628-0713

Tampa Florida Courier (90.0M) 5207 E Washington St Tampa FL 33619 **Phn:** 813-620-1300 **Fax:** 813-628-0713 flcourier.com news@flcourier.com

Tampa Florida Sentinel-Bulletin (25.5M) PO Box 3363 Tampa FL 33601 **Phn:** 813-248-1921 **Fax:** 813-248-4507 www.flsentinel.com editor@flsentinel.com

West Palm Beach Palm Beach Gazette (3.0M) PO Box 18469 West Palm Beach FL 33416 **Phn:** 561-844-5501 **Fax:** 561-844-5551

GEORGIA

Albany Southwest Georgian (19.7M) PO Box 1943 Albany GA 31702 **Phn:** 229-436-2156 **Fax:** 229-435-6860 www.albanysouthwestgeorgian.com asearles@bellsouth.net

Atlanta Atlanta Daily World (4.0M) 145 Auburn Ave NE Atlanta GA 30303 **Phn:** 404-659-1110 **Fax:** 404-659-4988 www.atlantadailyworld.com publisher@atlantadailyworld.com

Atlanta Atlanta Inquirer (56.1M) PO Box 92367 Atlanta GA 30314 **Phn:** 404-523-6086 **Fax:** 404-523-6088 www.atlinq.com news@atlinq.com

Atlanta Atlanta Voice (40.0M) 633 Pryor St SW Atlanta GA 30312 **Phn:** 404-524-6426 **Fax:** 404-523-7853 www.theatlantavoice.com info@theatlantavoice.com

Augusta Augusta Focus (5.0M) 1143 Laney Walker Blvd Augusta GA 30901 **Phn:** 706-722-7327 **Fax:** 706-724-8432 www.augustafocus.com

Augusta Metro Courier (28.8M) PO Box 2385 Augusta GA 30903 **Phn:** 706-724-6556 **Fax:** 706-722-7104

Columbus Columbus Times (20.0M) PO Box 2845 Columbus GA 31902 **Phn:** 706-324-0401 **Fax:** 706-596-0657 www.columbustimes.com

Decatur The Champion (23.0M) PO Box 1347 Decatur GA 30031 **Phn:** 404-373-7779 **Fax:** 404-373-3903 www.championnewspaper.com Kathy@dekalbchamp.com

Macon Macon Courier (17.4M) PO Box 4423 Macon GA 31208 **Phn:** 478-746-5605 **Fax:** 478-742-4274

Savannah Savannah Herald (12.0M) PO Box 486 Savannah GA 31402 **Phn:** 912-232-4505 **Fax:** 912-231-0018 www.savannahherald.net news@savannahherald.net

Savannah Savannah Tribune (15.0M) PO Box 2066 Savannah GA 31402 **Phn:** 912-233-6128 **Fax:** 912-233-6140 www.savannahtribune.com sharon@savannahtribune.com

Union City Atlanta News Leader (35.0M) 4405 Mall Blvd Ste 521 Union City GA 30291 **Phn:** 770-969-7711 **Fax:** 770-969-7811 atlmet@bellsouth.net

ILLINOIS
Chicago Chicago Crusader (88.0M) 6429 S King Dr Chicago IL 60637 **Phn:** 773-752-2500 **Fax:** 773-752-2817 www.chgocrusader.com crusaderil@aol.com

Chicago Chicago Defender (45.0M) 4445 S King Dr Chicago IL 60653 **Phn:** 312-225-2400 **Fax:** 312-225-9231 www.chicagodefender.com submissions@chicagodefender.com

Chicago Citizen Newspaper Group (5 editions) (125.0M) 806 E 78th St Chicago IL 60619 **Phn:** 773-783-1251 **Fax:** 773-783-1301 citizen_newsroom@yahoo.com

Chicago Final Call (40.0M) 734 W 79th St Chicago IL 60620 **Phn:** 773-602-1230 www.finalcall.com

Chicago Independent Bulletin (59.7M) 500 N Michigan Ave Ste 300 Chicago IL 60611 **Phn:** 312-321-6485 **Fax:** 312-396-4185 Bulletinnewspaper@comcast.net

Chicago N'Digo (130.0M) 19 N Sangamon St Chicago IL 60607 **Phn:** 312-822-0202 **Fax:** 312-421-1147 www.ndigo.com

Chicago South Shore Scene (80.0M) PO Box 490085 Chicago IL 60649 **Phn:** 773-363-0441 **Fax:** 773-363-2911 vwinsteadsr@aol.com

Chicago Windy City Word (20.0M) 5090 W Harrison St Chicago IL 60644 **Phn:** 773-378-0261 **Fax:** 773-378-2408 www.windycityword.com windycityword02@yahoo.com

Decatur African-American Voice (2 editions) (9.8M) 625 E Wood St Decatur IL 62523 **Phn:** 217-423-2231 **Fax:** 217-423-5860

East Saint Louis E. St. Louis Monitor (8.8M) PO Box 2137 East Saint Louis IL 62202 **Phn:** 618-271-0468 **Fax:** 618-271-8443

INDIANA
Fort Wayne Frost Illustrated (8.5M) 3121 S Calhoun St Fort Wayne IN 46807 **Phn:** 260-745-0552 **Fax:** 260-745-9503 www.frostillustrated.com frostnews@aol.com

Gary Gary Crusader (41.7M) 1549 Broadway Gary IN 46407 **Phn:** 219-885-4357 **Fax:** 219-883-3317 www.chgocrusader.com crusaderil@aol.com

Indianapolis Indiana Herald (15.0M) PO Box 88449 Indianapolis IN 46208 **Phn:** 317-923-8291 **Fax:** 317-923-8292 www.indianaherald.com herald1@earthlink.net

Indianapolis Indianapolis Recorder (11.6M) PO Box 18499 Indianapolis IN 46218 **Phn:** 317-924-5143 **Fax:** 317-924-5148 www.indianapolisrecorder.com newsroom@indyrecorder.com

Muncie Muncie Times (5.0M) 1304 N Dr MLK Dir Muncie IN 47303 **Phn:** 765-741-0037 **Fax:** 765-741-0040 themuncietimes@comcast.net

BLACK WEEKLY NEWSPAPERS
KANSAS
Kansas City Kansas State Dispatch (27.0M) PO Box 12462 Kansas City KS 66112 **Phn:** 913-299-0001 **Fax:** 913-287-4506 www.minoritypressserviceinc.com ksglobe@sbcglobal.net

Kansas City Missouri State Post (27.0M) PO Box 414662 Kansas City MO 64141 **Phn:** 816-561-7500 **Fax:** 913-287-4506 www.minoritypressserviceinc.com mspost@sbcglobal.net

KENTUCKY
Lexington Key Newsjournal (5.0M) PO Box 23321 Lexington KY 40523 **Phn:** 859-373-9428 www.lextown.info editorial@keynewsjournal.com

Louisville Louisville Defender (2.7M) PO Box 2557 Louisville KY 40201 **Phn:** 502-772-2591 **Fax:** 502-775-8655 loudefender@aol.com

LOUISIANA
Alexandria Alexandria News Weekly (10.0M) 1746 Mason St Alexandria LA 71301 **Phn:** 318-443-7664 **Fax:** 318-487-1827

Baton Rouge Weekly Press (7.5M) PO Box 74485 Baton Rouge LA 70874 **Phn:** 225-775-2002 **Fax:** 225-775-4216 www.theweeklypress.com theweeklypress@yahoo.com

Monroe Monroe Dispatch (15.5M) PO Box 4823 Monroe LA 71211 **Phn:** 318-325-2858 **Fax:** 318-387-3001

Monroe Monroe Free Press (16.5M) PO Box 4717 Monroe LA 71211 **Phn:** 318-388-1310 **Fax:** 318-388-2911 www.monroefreepress.com rooseveltwright@prodigy.net

New Orleans Louisiana Weekly (10.0M) PO Box 8628 New Orleans LA 70182 **Phn:** 504-282-3705 **Fax:** 504-282-3773 www.louisianaweekly.com

New Orleans The New Orleans Tribune (7.0M) 2317 Esplanade Ave New Orleans LA 70119 **Phn:** 505-945-0771 **Fax:** 505-949-4129 www.neworleanstribune.com

Shreveport Shreveport Sun (7.0M) PO Box 3915 Shreveport LA 71133 **Phn:** 318-631-6222 **Fax:** 318-635-2822 sunweekly@aol.com

MARYLAND
Baltimore Afro-American Newspaper (18.0M) 2519 N Charles St Baltimore MD 21218 **Phn:** 410-554-8200 **Fax:** 877-570-9297 www.afro.com editor@afro.com

Baltimore Baltimore Times Papers (3 editions) (41.4M) 2513 N Charles St Baltimore MD 21218 **Phn:** 410-366-3900 **Fax:** 410-243-1627 www.btimes.com btimes@btimes.com

MASSACHUSETTS
Boston Bay State Banner (11.6M) 23 Drydock Ave Boston MA 02210 **Phn:** 617-261-4600 **Fax:** 617-261-2346 www.baystatebanner.com mbm@b-banner.com

MICHIGAN
Detroit MI Chronicle/MI FrontPAGE (44.3M) 479 Ledyard St Detroit MI 48201 **Phn:** 313-963-5522 **Fax:** 313-963-8788 www.michronicleonline.com chronicle4@aol.com

Detroit Michigan Citizen (60.1M) 1055 Trumbull St Detroit MI 48216 **Phn:** 313-963-8282 **Fax:** 313-963-8285 michigancitizen.com editor@michigancitizen.com

Ecorse Ecorse Telegram (12.5M) PO Box 29085 Ecorse MI 48229 **Phn:** 313-928-2955 **Fax:** 313-928-3014

Grand Rapids Grand Rapids Times (6.0M) PO Box 7258 Grand Rapids MI 49510 **Phn:** 616-245-8737 **Fax:** 616-245-1026 staff@grtimes.com

MINNESOTA
Minneapolis Insight News (35.5M) 1815 Bryant Ave N Minneapolis MN 55411 **Phn:** 612-588-1313 **Fax:** 612-588-2031 www.insightnews.com info@insightnews.com

Minneapolis One Nation News (20.0M) 2751 Hennepin Ave # 12 Minneapolis MN 55408 **Phn:** 612-861-9006 **Fax:** 612-869-8597 www.onenationnews.com info@onenationnews.com

Minneapolis Spokesman-Recorder (26.0M) 3744 4th Ave S Minneapolis MN 55409 **Phn:** 612-827-4021 **Fax:** 612-827-0577 www.spokesman-recorder.com jfreeman@spokesman-recorder.com

MISSISSIPPI
Fayette Fayette Chronicle (2.2M) PO Box 536 Fayette MS 39069 **Phn:** 601-786-3661 **Fax:** 601-786-3661

Jackson Jackson Advocate (17.0M) PO Box 3708 Jackson MS 39207 **Phn:** 601-948-4122 **Fax:** 601-948-4125 www.jacksonadvocate.com jadvocat@aol.com

Jackson Mississippi Link (16.1M) PO Box 11307 Jackson MS 39283 **Phn:** 601-896-0084 **Fax:** 601-896-0091 www.mississippilink.net editor@mississippilink.com

MISSOURI
Kansas City Kansas City Globe (10.0M) 615 E 29th St Kansas City MO 64109 **Phn:** 816-531-5253 **Fax:** 816-531-5256 kcglobe@swbell.net

Kansas City The Call (16.5M) PO Box 410477 Kansas City MO 64141 **Phn:** 816-842-3804 **Fax:** 816-842-4420 www.kccall.com kccallnews@hotmail.com

Saint Louis Metro Evening Whirl (49.7M) PO Box 8055 Saint Louis MO 63156 **Phn:** 678-778-2616 thewhirlonline.com info@thewhirlonline.com

Saint Louis Metro Sentinel Journal (35.0M) 2900 N Market St Saint Louis MO 63106 **Phn:** 314-531-2101 **Fax:** 314-531-4442 merosentineljournal.com metrosentinel@sbcglobal.net

Saint Louis St. Louis American (70.0M) 4242 Lindell Blvd Saint Louis MO 63108 **Phn:** 314-533-8000 **Fax:** 314-533-0038 www.stlamerican.com cking@stlamerican.com

Saint Louis St. Louis Argus (33.0M) 4595 Dr Martin Luther King Dr Saint Louis MO 63113 **Phn:** 314-531-1323 **Fax:** 314-531-1324

NEBRASKA
Omaha Omaha Star (30.0M) PO Box 11128 Omaha NE 68111 **Phn:** 402-346-4041 **Fax:** 402-346-4064 www.omahastarinc.com marguerita@omahastarinc.com

NEVADA
Las Vegas Sentinel-Voice (6.5M) 900 E Charleston Blvd Las Vegas NV 89104 **Phn:** 702-380-8100 **Fax:** 702-380-8102 lvsvrelease@yahoo.com

NEW JERSEY
Jersey City Urban Times News (30.0M) 529 Bergen Ave Box A43 Jersey City NJ 07304 **Phn:** 201-451-4131 **Fax:** 201-915-0498

NEW YORK
Brooklyn Afro Times (199.0M) 1195 Atlantic Ave Brooklyn NY 11216 **Phn:** 718-636-9119 **Fax:** 718-857-9115 www.challenge-group.com challengegroup@yahoo.com

Brooklyn New York Daily Challenge (81.6M) 1195 Atlantic Ave Brooklyn NY 11216 **Phn:** 718-636-9119 **Fax:** 718-857-9115 www.challenge-group.com Challengegroup@yahoo.com

Brooklyn The New American (60.1M) 1195 Atlantic Ave Brooklyn NY 11216 **Phn:** 718-636-9119 **Fax:** 718-857-9115 www.challenge-group.com challengegroup@yahoo.com

Buffalo Buffalo Challenger (11.0M) 1337 Jefferson Ave Buffalo NY 14208 **Phn:** 716-897-0442 **Fax:** 716-897-3307 challengercn.com

Buffalo Buffalo Criterion (10.0M) 623 William St Buffalo NY 14206 **Phn:** 716-882-9570 **Fax:** 716-882-9570 www.buffalocriterion.com criterion@apollo3.com

Mount Vernon Westchester Co. Press (12.5M) 29 W 4th St Mount Vernon NY 10550 **Phn:** 914-684-0006 **Fax:** 914-699-2633

New York African-American Observer (69.0M) 483 10th Ave Rm 310 New York NY 10018 **Phn:** 212-586-4141 **Fax:** 212-586-4272 blacknewswatch@aol.com

New York Black Star News (50.0M) 11 Broadway Ste 519 New York NY 10004 **Phn:** 212-481-7745 www.blackstarnews.com

New York New York Amsterdam News (36.0M) 2340 Frederick Douglass Blvd New York NY 10027 **Phn:** 212-932-7400 **Fax:** 212-932-7467 www.amsterdamnews.com kfm@amsterdamnews.com

New York New York Beacon (84.4M) 237 W 37th St Rm 802 New York NY 10018 **Phn:** 212-213-8585 **Fax:** 212-213-6291 www.newyorkbeacon.com newyorkbeacon@yahoo.com

Newburgh Hudson Valley Press (31.8M) PO Box 2160 Newburgh NY 12550 **Phn:** 845-562-1313 **Fax:** 845-562-1348 www.hvpress.net news@hvpress.net

NORTH CAROLINA

Charlotte Charlotte Post (20.4M) PO Box 30144 Charlotte NC 28230 **Phn:** 704-376-0496 **Fax:** 704-342-2160 www.thecharlottepost.com herb.white@thecharlottepost.com

Durham Carolina Times (6.0M) PO Box 3825 Durham NC 27702 **Phn:** 919-682-2913 **Fax:** 919-688-8434 thecarolinatimes@cs.com

Durham Triangle Tribune (15.3M) 115 Market St Ste 360H Durham NC 27701 **Phn:** 919-688-9408 **Fax:** 919-688-2740 www.triangletribune.com editor@triangletribune.com

Greensboro Carolina Peacemaker (5.0M) PO Box 20853 Greensboro NC 27420 **Phn:** 336-274-6210 **Fax:** 336-273-5103 www.carolinapeacemaker.com editor@carolinapeacemaker.com

Raleigh The Carolinian (15.1M) PO Box 25308 Raleigh NC 27611 **Phn:** 919-834-5558 **Fax:** 919-832-3243

Wilmington Greater Diversity News (5.0M) PO Box 1679 Wilmington NC 28402 **Phn:** 910-762-1337 **Fax:** 910-763-6304 www.greaterdiversity.com kgrear@greaterdiversity.com

Wilmington Wilmington Journal (11.0M) PO Box 1020 Wilmington NC 28402 **Phn:** 910-762-5502 **Fax:** 910-343-1334 www.wilmingtonjournal.com wilmjourn@aol.com

Winston Salem The Chronicle (10.0M) PO Box 1636 Winston Salem NC 27102 **Phn:** 336-722-8624 **Fax:** 336-723-9173 www.wschronicle.com news@wschronicle.com

OHIO

Akron The Reporter (35.0M) PO Box 2042 Akron OH 44309 **Phn:** 330-535-7061 **Fax:** 330-535-7333 reporter14@juno.com

Cincinnati Cincinnati Herald (16.0M) 3440 Burnet Ave Ste 130 Cincinnati OH 45229 **Phn:** 513-961-3331 **Fax:** 513-961-0304 www.thecincinnatiherald.com newsthecincinnatiherald@yahoo.com

BLACK WEEKLY NEWSPAPERS

Cleveland City News (70.0M) 4423 Renaissance Pkwy Cleveland OH 44128 **Phn:** 216-591-1900 www.citynewsohio.com editorial@citynewsohio.com

Cleveland Columbus Call & Post (18.0M) 11800 Shaker Blvd Cleveland OH 44120 **Phn:** 614-224-8123 **Fax:** 614-224-8517 www.callandpost.com info@call-post.com

Cleveland East Side Daily News (20.0M) 11400 Woodland Ave Cleveland OH 44104 **Phn:** 216-721-1674 **Fax:** 216-231-7945 esdn1@yahoo.com

Toledo Toledo Journal (22.1M) 3021 Douglas Rd Toledo OH 43606 **Phn:** 419-472-4521 www.thetoledojournal.com toljour@aol.com

Youngstown Buckeye Review (5.3M) 1201 Belmont Ave Youngstown OH 44504 **Phn:** 330-743-2250 **Fax:** 330-746-2340 www.buckeyereview.com

OKLAHOMA

Oklahoma City Black Chronicle (30.0M) PO Box 17498 Oklahoma City OK 73136 **Phn:** 405-424-4695 **Fax:** 405-424-6708 www.blackchronicle.com alindsey@blackchronicle.com

Tulsa Oklahoma Eagle (4.0M) PO Box 3267 Tulsa OK 74101 **Phn:** 918-582-7124 **Fax:** 918-582-8905

OREGON

Portland Portland Observer (37.0M) PO Box 3137 Portland OR 97208 **Phn:** 503-288-0033 **Fax:** 503-288-0015 www.portlandobserver.com charlesw@portlandobserver.com

Portland The Skanner (10.5M) PO Box 5455 Portland OR 97228 **Phn:** 503-285-5555 **Fax:** 503-285-2900 www.theskanner.com info@theskanner.com

PENNSYLVANIA

Philadelphia Philadelphia Sun (40.0M) 6661 Germantown Ave Philadelphia PA 19119 **Phn:** 215-848-7864 **Fax:** 215-848-7893 www.philasun.com taesun@philasun.com

Philadelphia Philadelphia Tribune (14.2M) 520 S 16th St Philadelphia PA 19146 **Phn:** 215-893-4050 **Fax:** 215-735-3612 www.phillytrib.com/tribune info@phillytrib.com

Philadelphia Scoop USA (60.0M) PO Box 14013 Philadelphia PA 19122 **Phn:** 215-232-5974 **Fax:** 215-236-2945 www.scoopusanewspaper.com

Pittsburgh New Pittsburgh Courier (20.0M) 315 E Carson St Pittsburgh PA 15219 **Phn:** 412-481-8302 **Fax:** 412-481-1360 www.newpittsburghcourieronline.com webmaster@newpittsburghcourieronline.com

RHODE ISLAND

Providence Providence American (11.0M) PO Box 5859 Providence RI 02903 **Phn:** 401-475-6480 **Fax:** 401-475-6254 www.theprovidenceamerican.com peterwells@theprovidenceamerican.com

SOUTH CAROLINA

Beaufort Gullah Sentinel (6.0M) 909 Bladen St Beaufort SC 29902 **Phn:** 843-982-0500 **Fax:** 843-982-0631 www.gullahnewspaper.net gullah@thegullahnews.net

Charleston Charleston Chronicle (6.0M) PO Box 20548 Charleston SC 29403 **Phn:** 843-723-2785 **Fax:** 843-577-6099 chaschron@aol.com

Columbia Black News (75.0M) PO Box 11128 Columbia SC 29211 **Phn:** 803-799-5252 **Fax:** 803-799-7709 www.scblacknews.com scbnews@aol.com

Columbia Carolina Panorama (15.0M) PO Box 11205 Columbia SC 29211 **Phn:** 803-256-4015 **Fax:** 803-256-6732 www.carolinapanorama.net cpanorama@aol.com

Florence Community Times (36.0M) PO Box 4197 Florence SC 29502 **Phn:** 843-667-1818 **Fax:** 843-662-9880 www.scafricanamericannews.com dsmith7716@aol.com

TENNESSEE

Memphis Mid-South Tribune (24.4M) PO Box 2272 Memphis TN 38101 **Phn:** 901-728-5001 **Fax:** 901-728-5006 www.blackinformationhighway.com mstnews@prodigy.net

Memphis Tri-State Defender (24.0M) 124 G E Patterson Ave Memphis TN 38103 **Phn:** 901-523-1818 **Fax:** 901-523-1820 www.tri-statedefender.com editorial@tri-statedefender.com

Nashville Chattanooga Courier (18.0M) PO Box 90182 Nashville TN 37209 **Phn:** 615-292-9150 **Fax:** 615-292-9056 pridepublishinggroup.com npnews@comcast.net

Nashville Knoxville Enlightener (24.0M) PO Box 90182 Nashville TN 37209 **Phn:** 615-292-9150 **Fax:** 615-292-9056 pridenewspapergroup.com npnews@comcast.net

Nashville Murfreesboro Vision (12.0M) PO Box 90182 Nashville TN 37209 **Phn:** 615-292-9150 **Fax:** 615-292-9056 pridepublishinggroup.net npnews@comcast.net

Nashville Nashville Pride (36.0M) PO Box 90182 Nashville TN 37209 **Phn:** 615-292-9150 **Fax:** 615-292-9056 pridenewspapergroup.com npnews@comcast.net

Nashville Tennessee Tribune (40.0M) 1501 Jefferson St Nashville TN 37208 **Phn:** 615-321-3268 **Fax:** 615-321-0409 www.TNtribune.com JaniceMalone@gmail.com

TEXAS

Austin Nokoa-The Observer (8.0M) PO Box 1131 Austin TX 78767 **Phn:** 512-499-8713 **Fax:** 512-499-8740 nokoanewspaper.com akwasievans@gmail.com

Austin The Villager (6.0M) 1213 N I H 35 Austin TX 78702 **Phn:** 512-476-0082 **Fax:** 512-476-0179 www.theaustinvillager.com vil3202@aol.com

Dallas Dallas Examiner (10.2M) 1516 Corinth St Dallas TX 75215 **Phn:** 214-428-3446 **Fax:** 214-428-3451 www.dallasexaminer.com newsdesk@dallasexaminer.com

Dallas Dallas Post Tribune (5.9M) PO Box 763939 Dallas TX 75376 **Phn:** 214-946-7678 **Fax:** 214-946-6823 posttrib@airmail.net

Dallas Dallas Weekly (13.5M) PO Box 151789 Dallas TX 75315 **Phn:** 214-428-8958 **Fax:** 214-428-2807 www.dallasweekly.com jmuhammad@dallasweekly.com

Ft Worth La Vida News/Black Voice (39.7M) PO Box 751 Ft Worth TX 76101 **Phn:** 817-543-2095 **Fax:** 817-274-8023 newsdesk@lavidanewstheblackvoice.com

Houston African Amer. News & Issues (315.0M) 6130 Wheatley St Houston TX 77091 **Phn:** 713-692-1892 **Fax:** 713-692-1183 www.aframnews.com news@aframnews.com

Houston Forward Times (64.6M) PO Box 8346 Houston TX 77288 **Phn:** 713-526-4727 **Fax:** 713-526-3170 www.forwardtimes.com forwardtimes@forwardtimes.com

Houston Houston Defender (15.0M) PO Box 8005 Houston TX 77288 **Phn:** 713-663-6996 **Fax:** 713-663-7116

Lubbock Southwest Digest (3.9M) 902 E 28th St Lubbock TX 79404 **Phn:** 806-762-3612 **Fax:** 806-762-4605 www.southwestdigest.com swdigest@sbcglobal.net

Plano North Dallas Gazette (5.8M) PO Box 940226 Plano TX 75094 **Phn:** 972-516-4191 **Fax:** 972-509-9058 www.northdallasgazette.com editor@northdallasgazette.com

San Antonio San Antonio Informer (6.8M) 333 S Hackberry San Antonio TX 78203 **Phn:** 210-227-8300 **Fax:** 210-223-4111 sainformer@sbcglobal.net

San Antonio San Antonio Observer (16.0M) PO Box 200226 San Antonio TX 78220 **Phn:** 210-212-6397 **Fax:** 210-271-0441 www.saobserver.com

VIRGINIA

Charlottesville Charlottesville Tribune (10.2M) PO Box 3428 Charlottesville VA 22903 **Phn:** 434-979-0373 Tribune54@gmail.com

Lynchburg Piedmont Area Journal (15.0M) PO Box 1256 Lynchburg VA 24505 **Phn:** 434-845-3431 **Fax:** 434-845-1485

Norfolk New Journal & Guide (25.0M) PO Box 209 Norfolk VA 23501 **Phn:** 757-543-6531 **Fax:** 757-543-7620 www.thenewjournalandguide.com njguide@gmail.com

Richmond Free Press (28.0M) PO Box 27709 Richmond VA 23261 **Phn:** 804-644-0496 **Fax:** 804-643-7519 www.richmondfreepress.com news@richmondfreepress.com

Richmond Richmond Voice (35.2M) 205 E Clay St Richmond VA 23219 **Phn:** 804-644-9060 **Fax:** 804-644-5617 www.voicenewspaper.com richmond.voice@verizon.net

Roanoke Roanoke Tribune (6.1M) PO Box 6021 Roanoke VA 24017 **Phn:** 540-343-0326 **Fax:** 540-343-7366

WASHINGTON

Seattle Facts-News (15.0M) PO Box 22015 Seattle WA 98122 **Phn:** 206-324-0552 **Fax:** 206-324-1007

Seattle Seattle Medium/Tacoma True Citizen (30.0M) PO Box 22047 Seattle WA 98122 **Phn:** 206-323-3070 **Fax:** 206-322-6518 www.seattlemedium.com chrisb@mediumnews.net

Seattle The Skanner (20.0M) PO Box 94473 Seattle WA 98124 **Phn:** 206-233-9888 www.theskanner.com seattle@theskanner.com

WISCONSIN

Madison Madison Times (8.5M) 313 W Beltline Hwy Ste 120 Madison WI 53713 **Phn:** 608-270-9470 **Fax:** 608-270-9472 www.themadisontimes.com news@madtimes.com

Milwaukee Community Journal (40.0M) 3612 N Dr Martin Luther King Dr Milwaukee WI 53212 **Phn:** 414-265-5300 **Fax:** 414-265-1536 www.communityjournal.net editorial@communityjournal.net

Milwaukee Milwaukee Courier/Southeastern Star (100.0M) 2003 W Capitol Dr Milwaukee WI 53206 **Phn:** 414-449-4860 **Fax:** 414-449-4872 www.milwaukeecourier.org milwaukeecourier@aol.com

Milwaukee Milwaukee Times (20.0M) 1936 N Dr Martin Luther King Dr Milwaukee WI 53212 **Phn:** 414-263-5088 **Fax:** 414-263-4445 www.milwtimes.com miltimes@gmail.com

HISPANIC WEEKLY NEWSPAPERS

ARIZONA

Phoenix La Voz (66.0M) 200 E Van Buren St Phoenix AZ 85004 **Phn:** 602-444-3800 **Fax:** 602-253-9022 www.azcentral.com/lavoz

Phoenix Prensa Hispana (65.0M) 809 E Washington St Ste 209 Phoenix AZ 85034 **Phn:** 602-256-2443 **Fax:** 602-256-2644 www.prensahispanaaz.com

Yuma Bajo El Sol (33.0M) PO Box 271 Yuma AZ 85366 **Phn:** 928-783-3333 **Fax:** 928-782-7369 www.bajoelsol.com

ARKANSAS

Fayetteville Noticias Libres (8.0M) 212 N East Ave Fayetteville AR 72701 **Phn:** 479-571-6430 **Fax:** 479-684-5571 www.laprensanwa.com

Little Rock El Latino (4.8M) 201 E Markham St Ste 200 Little Rock AR 72201 **Phn:** 501-374-0853 **Fax:** 501-375-3623 www.ellatinoarkansas.com el-latino@arktimes.com

CALIFORNIA

Bakersfield El Mexicalo (15.0M) 931 Niles St Bakersfield CA 93305 **Phn:** 661-323-9334 **Fax:** 661-323-6951 elmexicalo@sbcglobal.net

Bakersfield El Popular (24.0M) 208 Truxtun Ave Bakersfield CA 93301 **Phn:** 661-398-1000 **Fax:** 661-325-1351 www.elpopularnews.com pub@elpopularnews.com

Chula Vista La Prensa San Diego (27.6M) 651 3rd Ave Ste C Chula Vista CA 91910 **Phn:** 619-425-7400 **Fax:** 619-425-7402 www.laprensa-sandiego.org laprensa@ix.netcom.com

El Centro Adelante (10.0M) 205 N 8th St El Centro CA 92243 **Phn:** 760-337-3400 **Fax:** 760-337-4078 www.ivpressonline.com/adelantevalle pdale@ivpressonline.com

Escondido Hispanos Unidos (26.0M) PO Box 462016 Escondido CA 92046 **Phn:** 760-740-9561 **Fax:** 760-737-3035 www.hispanosnews.com editor@hispanosnews.com

Fresno Vida En El Valle (5 editions) (163.0M) 1626 E St Fresno CA 93706 **Phn:** 559-441-6780 **Fax:** 559-441-6790 www.vidaenelvalle.com jesparza@vidaenelvalle.com

Indio El Informador (18.0M) PO Box 2526 Indio CA 92202 **Phn:** 760-342-7558 **Fax:** 760-342-2918 www.elinformadordelvalle.com

Indio La Prensa Hispana (46.5M) PO Box 2509 Indio CA 92202 **Phn:** 760-342-2565 **Fax:** 760-342-1036 www.thehispanicpress.com laprehis@aol.com

Los Angeles Eastern Group (11 titles) (102.0M) 111 South Avenue 59 Los Angeles CA 90042 **Phn:** 323-341-7970 **Fax:** 323-341-7976 www.egpnews.com editorial@egpnews.com

Los Angeles Hoy (200.0M) 202 W 1st St Fl 2 Los Angeles CA 90012 **Phn:** 213-237-3001 **Fax:** 213-237-4928 www.hoyinternet.com rmena@hoyllc.com

Los Angeles La Voz Libre (44.5M) PO Box 20599 Los Angeles CA 90006 **Phn:** 213-488-0271 **Fax:** 213-488-0278 amprada@pacbell.net

Modesto Vida En El Valle (30.0M) 1325 H St Modesto CA 95354 **Phn:** 209-238-4634 **Fax:** 209-238-4641 www.vidaenelvalle.com oruiz@vidaenelvalle.com

Oakland El Mundo (9.7M) 405 14th St Ste 1215 Oakland CA 94612 **Phn:** 510-287-8200 **Fax:** 510-287-8247

Oxnard Vida (35.0M) 130 Palm Dr Ste B Oxnard CA 93030 **Phn:** 805-483-1008 **Fax:** 805-483-6233

Porterville Noticiero Semanal (23.6M) PO Box 151 Porterville CA 93258 **Phn:** 559-784-5000 **Fax:** 559-784-5245 www.noticierosemanal.com recorder@portervillerecorder.com

Riverside La Prensa (65.0M) 3450 14th St Riverside CA 92501 **Phn:** 909-806-3206 www.laprensaenlinea.com oramirez@pe.com

Sacramento El Hispano (20.0M) PO Box 2856 Sacramento CA 95812 **Phn:** 916-442-0267 **Fax:** 916-442-2818

Salinas El Sol (12.0M) 123 W Alisal St Salinas CA 93901 **Phn:** 831-754-4272 **Fax:** 831-757-1006 www.thecalifornian.com arieger@thecalifornian.com

San Diego El Latino (72.6M) PO Box 120550 San Diego CA 92112 **Phn:** 619-426-1491 **Fax:** 619-426-3206 www.ellatinoonline.com

San Diego Enlace (83.6M) PO Box 120191 San Diego CA 92112 **Phn:** 619-293-2914 **Fax:** 619-260-5088 www.mienlace.com

San Francisco El Bohemio News (22.5M) 3288 Mission St # 116 San Francisco CA 94110 **Phn:** 415-970-8850 **Fax:** 415-469-9481 www.bohemionews.com

San Francisco El Mensajero (112.0M) 333 Valencia St Ste 410 San Francisco CA 94103 **Phn:** 415-206-7230 **Fax:** 415-206-7238 www.elmensajero.com

San Francisco El Reportero (20.0M) 2601 Mission St Ste 105 San Francisco CA 94110 **Phn:** 415-648-3711 **Fax:** 415-648-3721 www.elreporterosf.com reporteronews@aol.com

San Jose El Observador (19.7M) PO Box 1990 San Jose CA 95109 **Phn:** 408-938-1700 **Fax:** 408-938-1705 www.el-observador.com spanish.editor@el-observador.com

San Jose La Oferta (22.6M) 1376 N 4th St Ste 200 San Jose CA 95112 **Phn:** 408-436-7850 **Fax:** 408-436-7861 www.laoferta.com info@laoferta.com

San Ysidro Ahora Now (20.0M) 601 E San Ysidro Blvd Ste 180 San Ysidro CA 92173 **Phn:** 619-428-2277 **Fax:** 619-428-0871 www.ahoranow.com ahoranow2008@hotmail.com

Santa Ana Azteca News (42.0M) 810 N Broadway Santa Ana CA 92701 **Phn:** 714-972-9912 **Fax:** 714-973-8117 www.aztecanews.com info@aztecanews.com

Santa Ana Excelsior (51.5M) 523 N Grand Ave Santa Ana CA 92701 **Phn:** 714-796-4300 **Fax:** 714-796-4319 www.ocexcelsior.com corozco@ocregister.com

Santa Ana Miniondas (35.0M) 2025 S Main St Santa Ana CA 92707 **Phn:** 714-668-1010 **Fax:** 714-668-1013 www.miniondas.com miniondas@miniondas.com

Torrance Impacto USA (241.0M) 21250 Hawthorne Blvd #170 Torrance CA 90503 **Phn:** 866-642-8476 www.impactousa.com jose.fuentes@impactousa.com

Visalia El Sol (11.8M) 330 N West St Visalia CA 93291 **Phn:** 559-735-3200 **Fax:** 559-733-0826

COLORADO

Aurora El Hispano (20.0M) 1200 Del Mar Pkwy Aurora CO 80010 **Phn:** 303-340-0303 **Fax:** 303-340-0330 www.elhispanonewspaper.com hispano@roes.net

Colorado Springs Hispania News (15.0M) PO Box 15116 Colorado Springs CO 80935 **Phn:** 719-540-0220 **Fax:** 719-540-0599 www.hispanianews.com editor@hispanianews.com

Denver La Voz Nueva (20.8M) 4047 Tejon St Denver CO 80211 **Phn:** 303-936-8556 **Fax:** 720-889-2455 www.lavozcolorado.com news@lavozcolorado.com

Glendale El Semanario (25.0M) PO Box 460428 Glendale CO 80246 **Phn:** 303-672-0800 **Fax:** 303-298-8654 www.elsemanario.net semanario@aol.com

CONNECTICUT

Bethel El Canillita (90.0M) PO Box 845 Bethel CT 06801 **Phn:** 203-798-2120 **Fax:** 203-778-5304 www.elcanillita.com

DISTRICT OF COLUMBIA

Silver Spring Washington Hispanic (64.0M) 8455 Colesville Rd Ste 700 Silver Spring MD 20910 **Phn:** 202-667-8881 **Fax:** 202-667-8902 www.washingtonhispanic.com info@washingtonhispanic.com

Washington El Pregonero (31.0M) PO Box 4464 Washington DC 20017 **Phn:** 202-281-2440 **Fax:** 202-281-2448 www.elpreg.org cartas@elpreg.org

Washington El Tiempo Latino (58.8M) 1150 15th St NW Washington DC 20071 **Phn:** 202-334-9100 **Fax:** 202-496-3599 www.eltiempolatino.com alberto@eltiempolatino.com

FLORIDA

Fort Lauderdale El Sentinel (90.0M) 200 E Las Olas Blvd Fort Lauderdale FL 33301 **Phn:** 954-356-4560 **Fax:** 954-356-4559 www.southflorida.elsentinel.com letters@sun-sentinel.com

Hialeah La Voz de la Calle (30.0M) PO Box 3187 Hialeah FL 33013 **Phn:** 305-687-5555 **Fax:** 305-681-0500 www.lavozdelacalle.net lavozdelacalle@bellsouth.net

Longwood La Prensa (45.0M) 685 S Ronald Reagan Blvd Ste 200 Longwood FL 32750 **Phn:** 407-767-0070 **Fax:** 407-215-7214 www.impre.com/laprensafl

Miami El Especial (25.0M) 175 Fontainebleau Blvd Ste 2J2 Miami FL 33172 **Phn:** 305-225-3742 **Fax:** 305-223-6049 www.elespecial.com news@elespecial.com

Miami El Nuevo Patria (30.0M) PO Box 2 Miami FL 33135 **Phn:** 305-530-8787 **Fax:** 305-698-0022 www.elnuevopatria.us

Miami El Venezolano (20.0M) 8390 NW 53rd St Ste 318 Miami FL 33166 **Phn:** 305-717-3206 **Fax:** 305-717-3250 www.el-venezolano.net

Miami Libre (10.0M) 2700 SW 8th St Miami FL 33135 **Phn:** 305-643-2947 **Fax:** 305-649-2767 www.libreonline.com

Orlando El Sentinel (66.2M) 633 N Orange Ave Orlando FL 32801 **Phn:** 407-650-6472 **Fax:** 407-420-6212 www.sun-sentinel.com/elsentinel dramirez@elsentinel.com

Sarasota 7 Dias (17.7M) 2555 Porter Lake Dr Ste 107 Sarasota FL 34240 **Phn:** 941-341-0000 **Fax:** 941-343-0013 www.7dias.us info@7dias.us

Tampa La Gaceta (20.0M) PO Box 5536 Tampa FL 33675 **Phn:** 813-248-3921 **Fax:** 813-247-5357 www.lagacetanewspaper.com Lagaceta@tampabay.rr.com

Tampa Nuevo Siglo (25.0M) 7137 N Armenia Ave Ste B Tampa FL 33604 **Phn:** 813-932-7181 www.nuevosiglotampa.com n.siglo@verizon.net

West Palm Beach El Latino Semanal (39.0M) 4404 Georgia Ave West Palm Beach FL 33405 **Phn:** 561-835-4913 **Fax:** 561-655-5059 www.ellatino.com

West Palm Beach Semanario Accion (25.0M) PO Box 6726 West Palm Beach FL 33405 **Phn:** 561-586-4108 **Fax:** 561-586-2838 www.semanarioaccion.net semanario@hotmail.com

GEORGIA

Atlanta Mundo Hispanico (71.5M) PO Box 13808 Atlanta GA 30329 **Phn:** 404-881-0441 **Fax:** 404-881-6085 www.mundohispanico.com rcervantes@mundohispanico.com

Dalton El Informador (10.0M) 308 S Thornton Ave Dalton GA 30720 **Phn:** 706-272-7725 **Fax:** 706-272-7713 www.elinformadoronline.com elinformador@daltoncitizen.com

Doraville Atlanta Latino (24.0M) 2865 Amwiler Rd Ste 100 Doraville GA 30360 **Phn:** 770-416-7570 **Fax:** 770-416-7991 www.atlantalatino.com

ILLINOIS

Arlington Heights Reflejos (35.0M) 155 E Algonquin Rd Arlington Heights IL 60005 **Phn:** 847-806-1111 **Fax:** 847-806-1112 www.reflejos.com ganas@reflejos.com

Chicago Extra Newspapers (55.8M) 3906 W North Ave Chicago IL 60647 **Phn:** 773-252-3534 **Fax:** 773-252-6031 www.extranews.net info@extranews.net

Chicago La Raza (191.0M) 6001 N Clark St Chicago IL 60660 **Phn:** 773-273-2900 **Fax:** 773-273-2927 www.laraza.com

Cicero El Dia (45.0M) 5718 W Cermak Rd Cicero IL 60804 **Phn:** 708-652-6397 **Fax:** 708-652-8360 www.eldianews.com eldia@eldianews.com

Cicero El Imparcial (11.6M) 3116 S Austin Blvd Cicero IL 60804 **Phn:** 708-656-9800 **Fax:** 866-415-6776

Cicero Lawndale News (200.0M) 5533 W 25th St Cicero IL 60804 **Phn:** 708-656-6400 **Fax:** 708-656-2433 www.lawndalenews.com Ashmar.Mandou@lawndalenews.com

Crystal Lake El Conquistador (14.0M) PO Box 250 Crystal Lake IL 60039 **Phn:** 815-459-4040 **Fax:** 815-459-5640 www.elconquistadornews.com

IOWA

Des Moines El Latino (5.0M) 3318 Cambridge St Des Moines IA 50313 **Phn:** 515-266-3399 **Fax:** 515-266-5820 www.latinonewspaper.com info@latinonewspaper.com

Perry El Enfoque (5.0M) PO Box 145 Perry IA 50220 **Phn:** 515-360-3985 www.elenfoque.com elenfoque@aol.com

KANSAS

Garden City La Semana (2.5M) PO Box 958 Garden City KS 67846 **Phn:** 620-275-8500 **Fax:** 620-275-5165 lasemana@gctelegram.com

MASSACHUSETTS

Boston El Mundo (30.0M) 408 S Huntington Ave Boston MA 02130 **Phn:** 617-522-5060 **Fax:** 617-524-5886 www.elmundoboston.com

Boston El Planeta (50.0M) 126 Brookline Ave Ste 3 Boston MA 02215 **Phn:** 617-232-0996 **Fax:** 617-933-7677 www.elplaneta.com editor@elplaneta.com

Roxbury La Semana (15.0M) 903 Albany St Roxbury MA 02119 **Phn:** 617-427-6212 **Fax:** 617-427-6227

MICHIGAN

Detroit El Central (14.0M) 4124 W Vernor Hwy Detroit MI 48209 **Phn:** 313-841-0100 **Fax:** 313-841-0155 elcentral1@aol.com

Detroit Latino Press (19.8M) 6301 Michigan Ave Detroit MI 48210 **Phn:** 313-361-3000 **Fax:** 313-361-3001 www.latinodetroit.com

Grand Rapids El Vocero Hispano (18.5M) 2818 Vineland Ave SE Grand Rapids MI 49508 **Phn:** 616-246-6023 **Fax:** 616-246-1228

MINNESOTA

Minneapolis Gente de MN/La Prensa de MN (30.0M) 1516 E Lake St Ste 200 Minneapolis MN 55407 **Phn:** 612-729-5900 **Fax:** 612-729-5999 www.lcnmedia.com juancarlos@lcnmedia.com

HISPANIC WEEKLY NEWSPAPERS

MISSOURI

Kansas City Dos Mundos (10.0M) 902A Southwest Blvd Kansas City MO 64108 **Phn:** 816-221-4747 **Fax:** 816-221-4894 www.dosmundos.com newsstaff@dosmundos.com

NEVADA

Las Vegas El Mundo (35.5M) 760 N Eastern Ave Ste 110 Las Vegas NV 89101 **Phn:** 702-649-8553 **Fax:** 702-649-7429 www.elmundo.net editorial@elmundo.net

Las Vegas El Tiempo (41.2M) PO Box 70 Las Vegas NV 89125 **Phn:** 702-387-5214 **Fax:** 702-387-2981 www.eltiempolv.com hamaya@reviewjournal.com

Reno Ahora (8.6M) 743 S Virginia St Reno NV 89501 **Phn:** 775-323-6811 **Fax:** 775-323-6995 www.ahoranews.com ahoranewspaper@hotmail.com

NEW JERSEY

Elizabeth Mensaje (52.0M) 614 Franklin St Elizabeth NJ 07206 **Phn:** 908-355-8835 **Fax:** 908-527-9160

Jersey City El Nuevo Hudson (58.2M) 30 Journal Sq Jersey City NJ 07306 **Phn:** 201-217-2473 **Fax:** 201-217-2455 elnuevohudson.com margaret.schmidt@jjournal.com

Newark El Nuevo Coqui (15.0M) 258 Clifton Ave Newark NJ 07104 **Phn:** 973-481-3233 **Fax:** 973-481-6807 glorin@optonline.net

Union City Continental News (38.0M) 212 48th St Union City NJ 07087 **Phn:** 201-864-9505 **Fax:** 201-864-9456 continews@aol.com

Union City El Especial (76.0M) 3510 Bergenline Ave Ste 3 Union City NJ 07087 **Phn:** 201-348-1959 **Fax:** 201-348-3385 www.elespecial.com news@elespecial.com

Vineland Nuestra Comunidad (15.0M) 891 E Oak Rd Vineland NJ 08360 **Phn:** 856-563-5206 **Fax:** 856-563-5308

NEW MEXICO

Albuquerque El Hispano News (10.0M) PO Box 986 Albuquerque NM 87103 **Phn:** 505-243-6161 **Fax:** 505-842-5464

Santa Fe La Voz de Nuevo Mexico (14.1M) PO Box 2048 Santa Fe NM 87504 **Phn:** 505-986-3062 **Fax:** 505-471-3119 www.santafenewmexican.com rrivera@sfnewmexican.com

NEW YORK

Brentwood Nueva Americana (55.0M) 990 Suffolk Ave Brentwood NY 11717 **Phn:** 631-231-6222 **Fax:** 631-231-6435 nuameric@aol.com

Hempstead La Tribuna Hispana (82.0M) 48 Main St Fl 2 Hempstead NY 11550 **Phn:** 516-486-6457 **Fax:** 516-292-3972 www.latribunahispana.com editorial@latribunahispana.com

Long Island City Resumen (27.0M) 4741 37th St Long Island City NY 11101 **Phn:** 718-899-8603 www.resumen.8m.net rojas123@aol.com

New York Hora Hispana (250.0M) 450 W 33rd St New York NY 10001 **Phn:** 212-210-2036 **Fax:** 212-643-7818

New York Impacto Latin News (55.0M) 252 W 38th St Rm 901 New York NY 10018 **Phn:** 212-807-0400 **Fax:** 212-807-0408 www.impactony.com Jason@ImpactoNY.com

New York La Voz Hispana (68.1M) 159 E 116th St Fl 2 New York NY 10029 **Phn:** 212-348-2100 **Fax:** 212-348-4469 www.lavozhispana.com discomundo@gmail.com

North Baldwin Noticia Hispanoamericana (38.0M) 636 Seaman Ave North Baldwin NY 11510 **Phn:** 516-223-5678 **Fax:** 516-377-6551 www.noticiang.com news@noticiany.com

Woodside Ecuador News (43.0M) 6403 Roosevelt Ave Fl 2 Woodside NY 11377 **Phn:** 718-205-7014 **Fax:** 718-205-2250 www.ecuanews.net ecuanews@inch.com

NORTH CAROLINA

Charlotte La Noticia (26.0M) 5936 Monroe Rd Charlotte NC 28212 **Phn:** 704-568-6966 **Fax:** 704-568-8936 www.lanoticia.com editor@lanoticia.com

Hendersonville La Voz Independiente (10.0M) 1104 Patton St Hendersonville NC 28792 **Phn:** 828-687-1132 www.lavozindependiente.com

Raleigh La Conexion (20.0M) PO Box 228 Raleigh NC 27602 **Phn:** 919-832-1225 **Fax:** 919-856-0164 www.laconexionusa.com pjaramillo@laconexionusa.com

Winston Salem Que Pasa (74.9M) PO Box 12876 Winston Salem NC 27117 **Phn:** 336-784-9004 **Fax:** 336-714-2891 www.quepasamedia.com

OHIO

Cincinnati La Jornada Latina (10.6M) 4412 Carver Woods Dr Ste 200 Cincinnati OH 45242 **Phn:** 513-891-1000 **Fax:** 513-769-1015 www.tsjnews.com simon@tsjnews.com

Columbus Fronteras (10.0M) 34 S 3rd St Columbus OH 43215 **Phn:** 614-461-5227 **Fax:** 614-461-7580 www.dispatchespanol.com

Columbus La Voz Hispana (20.0M) 3552 Sullivant Ave Columbus OH 43204 **Phn:** 614-274-5505 **Fax:** 614-245-0559 www.lavozhispana.net lavozh@yahoo.com

Toledo La Prensa Nacional (44.0M) PO Box 9416 Toledo OH 43697 **Phn:** 419-870-6565 www.laprensa1.com latinoprensa@yahoo.com

OKLAHOMA

Oklahoma City El Latino (20.0M) 8870 S Western Ave Oklahoma City OK 73139 **Phn:** 405-632-1934 **Fax:** 405-635-3440 ellatinonews@hotmail.com

Oklahoma City El Nacional (16.2M) 300 SW 25th St Oklahoma City OK 73109 **Phn:** 405-632-4531 **Fax:** 405-632-4533 www.noticiasoklahoma.com/noticias nacional@coxinet.net

OREGON

Portland El Hispanic News (20.0M) PO Box 306 Portland OR 97207 **Phn:** 503-228-3139 **Fax:** 503-228-3384 www.hispnews.com jcortez@elhispanicnews.com

PENNSYLVANIA

Allentown El Torero (4.0M) PO Box 4311 Allentown PA 18105 **Phn:** 610-435-6608 **Fax:** 610-435-4884

Philadelphia Al Dia (55.5M) 1500 John F Kennedy Blvd Ste 525 Philadelphia PA 19102 **Phn:** 215-569-4666 news.aldiainc.com editor@aldiainc.com

Philadelphia El Sol Latino (25.0M) 198 W Chew Ave Philadelphia PA 19120 **Phn:** 215-424-1200 **Fax:** 215-424-6064 www.elsoln1.com

Upper Darby El Hispano (48.0M) 8605 W Chester Pike Upper Darby PA 19082 **Phn:** 610-789-5512 **Fax:** 610-789-5524 www.el-hispano.com ALopez5268@aol.com

TENNESSEE

Memphis La Prensa Latina (37.0M) 995 S Yates Rd Ste 3 Memphis TN 38119 **Phn:** 901-751-2100 **Fax:** 901-751-1202 www.laprensalatina.com info@laprensalatina.com

TEXAS

Abilene Hispanic Guide (6.0M) PO Box 2135 Abilene TX 79604 **Phn:** 325-672-7531

Amarillo El Mensajero (3.0M) PO Box 895 Amarillo TX 79105 **Phn:** 806-371-7084 **Fax:** 806-371-7090 lmensajero@aol.com

Amarillo La Voz Hispana (4.5M) PO Box 10194 Amarillo TX 79116 **Phn:** 806-220-2869 **Fax:** 806-220-2619 www.lavozamarillo.net lavoz@suddenlinkmail.com

Austin Ahora Si (30.3M) 305 S Congress Ave Austin TX 78704 **Phn:** 512-912-2500 **Fax:** 512-912-2551 www.ahorasi.com jvillicana@ahorasi.com

Austin El Mundo (35.0M) PO Box 6519 Austin TX 78762 **Phn:** 512-476-8636 **Fax:** 512-476-6402 www.elmundonewspaper.com info@elmundonewspaper.com

Dallas El Extra (28.8M) PO Box 270432 Dallas TX 75227 **Phn:** 214-309-0990 **Fax:** 214-309-0204 www.elextranewspaper.com

Dallas El Heraldo News (26.5M) 4532 Columbia Ave Dallas TX 75226 **Phn:** 214-827-9700 **Fax:** 214-827-8200 www.elheraldonews.com jim@elheraldonews.com

Dallas El Hispano News (29.0M) 2102 Empire Central Dallas TX 75235 **Phn:** 214-357-2186 **Fax:** 214-357-2195 www.elhispanonews.com

Dallas El Lider USA (90.0M) 1813 Balboa Pl # 200 Dallas TX 75224 **Phn:** 214-942-4580 **Fax:** 214-942-0624 www.elliderusa.com

Dallas Novedades News (38.4M) 121 S Zang Blvd Dallas TX 75208 **Phn:** 214-943-2932 **Fax:** 214-943-7352 www.novedadesnews.com spuertojr@novedadesnews.com

Eagle Pass News Gram (11.0M) 2543 Del Rio Blvd Eagle Pass TX 78852 **Phn:** 830-773-8610 **Fax:** 830-773-1641 www.thenewsgramonline.net elgram@hilconet.com

El Paso El Paso Y Mas (48.8M) PO Box 20 El Paso TX 79999 **Phn:** 915-546-6100 **Fax:** 915-546-6415 www.elpasotimes.com bmoore@elpasotimes.com

Fort Worth Diario la Estrella (24.3M) 400 W 7th St Fort Worth TX 76102 **Phn:** 817-390-7180 **Fax:** 817-390-7280 www.diariolaestrella.com rcaballero@diariolaestrella.com

Fort Worth El Informador Hispano (30.1M) PO Box 163661 Fort Worth TX 76161 **Phn:** 817-626-8624 **Fax:** 817-626-1855

Fort Worth Panorama de Nuevos Horizontes (15.2M) 3501 Williams Rd Fort Worth TX 76116 **Phn:** 817-560-0188 **Fax:** 817-560-2317 www.panorama-news.com

Houston El Dia (13.0M) 6120 Tarnef Dr Ste 110 Houston TX 77074 **Phn:** 713-772-8900 **Fax:** 713-772-8999 www.eldianet.com

Houston La Informacion (84.0M) 6065 Hillcroft St Ste 400B Houston TX 77081 **Phn:** 713-272-0100 **Fax:** 713-272-0011 www.lainformacion.us lina.martinez@lainformacion.us

Houston La Voz (91.1M) 4747 Southwest Fwy Houston TX 77027 **Phn:** 713-362-8100 **Fax:** 713-362-2531 www.chron.com/news/spanish aurora.losada@chron.com

Houston Rumbo de Houston (100.0M) 9950 Westpark Dr Ste 118 Houston TX 77063 **Phn:** 713-579-3700 **Fax:** 713-579-3751 www.rumbonet.com editorial@rumbonet.com

Houston Semana (140.0M) PO Box 742149 Houston TX 77274 **Phn:** 713-774-4652 **Fax:** 713-774-4666 semananews.net

Jacksonville La Opinion (10.0M) PO Box 8340 Jacksonville TX 75766 **Phn:** 903-586-0827 **Fax:** 903-586-7016 laopinion@suddenlinkmail.com

Lubbock El Editor (4.0M) PO Box 11250 Lubbock TX 79408 **Phn:** 806-763-3841 **Fax:** 806-741-1110 www.eleditor.com eleditor@sbcglobal.net

HISPANIC WEEKLY NEWSPAPERS

Lubbock West TX Hispanic News (4.0M) PO Box 24 Lubbock TX 79408 **Phn:** 806-747-3467 **Fax:** 806-747-3524

McAllen El Extra (25.0M) PO Box 3267 McAllen TX 78502 **Phn:** 956-683-4000 **Fax:** 956-683-4401

McAllen El Periodico USA (26.5M) 801 E Fir Ave McAllen TX 78501 **Phn:** 956-631-5628 **Fax:** 956-631-0832 www.elperiodicousa.com jose@spanishprint.com

McAllen Rumbo de Valle (45.0M) 311 S Broadway St # B McAllen TX 78501 **Phn:** 956-683-3800 **Fax:** 956-633-3801 www.rumbonet.com editorial@rumbonet.com

Presidio International (1.0M) PO Box 1898 Presidio TX 79845 **Phn:** 432-229-3877 **Fax:** 432-729-4601

San Antonio Conexion (50.0M) PO Box 2171 San Antonio TX 78297 **Phn:** 210-250-2525 **Fax:** 210-250-2570 www.conexionsa.com news@conexionsa.com

San Antonio El Starous News (8.6M) PO Box 200226 San Antonio TX 78220 **Phn:** 210-212-6397 **Fax:** 210-212-0441 www.saobserver.com taylor2039@aol.com

San Antonio La Prensa/La Prensita (62.5M) 318 S Flores St San Antonio TX 78204 **Phn:** 210-242-7900 **Fax:** 210-242-7901 www.laprensasa.com

San Antonio Rumbo de San Antonio (50.0M) 115 E Travis St Ste 333 San Antonio TX 78205 **Phn:** 210-581-3500 **Fax:** 210-581-3669 www.rumbonet.com editorial@rumbonet.com

UTAH

Sandy Mundo Hispano (10.0M) 9131 Monroe Plaza Way Ste C Sandy UT 84070 **Phn:** 801-569-3338 **Fax:** 801-352-9638

WASHINGTON

Everett La Raza de Noroeste (24.0M) 1213 California St Everett WA 98201 **Phn:** 425-673-6633 **Fax:** 425-339-3190 www.nuestronoroeste.com joconnor@heraldnet.com

Wenatchee El Mundo (17.2M) PO Box 2231 Wenatchee WA 98807 **Phn:** 509-663-5737 **Fax:** 509-663-6957 www.elmundonews.net martha@elmundous.com

WISCONSIN

Madison La Comunidad (30.0M) 1117 S Park St Madison WI 53715 **Phn:** 608-255-2805 **Fax:** 608-255-2803 www.lcnews.org

HISPANIC DAILY NEWSPAPERS

CALIFORNIA

Bonita El Mexicano (20M) 4045 Bonita Rd Ste 207 Bonita CA 91902 **Phn:** 619-267-6010 **Fax:** 619-267-5965 www.el-mexicano.com.mx   Email: yelopez@el-mexicano.com.mx

Los Angeles La Opinion (126M) 700 S Flower St Ste 3000 Los Angeles CA 90017 **Phn:** 213-622-8332 **Fax:** 213-896-2171 www.laopinion.com

FLORIDA

Miami Diario Las Americas (69.1M) 888 Brickell Ave 5th flr Miami FL 33131 **Phn:** 305-633-3341 **Fax:** 305-635-7668 www.diariolasamericas.com

Miami El Nuevo Herald (85M) 3511 NW 91 Ave Miami FL 33172 **Phn:** 305-376-3535 **Fax:** 305-376-2150 www.elnuevoherald.com   Email: perspectiva@elnuevoherald.com

GEORGIA

Norcross La Vision (59M) 1394 Indian Trail Lilburn Rd Ste 202 Norcross GA 30093 **Phn:** 770-963-7521 **Fax:** 770-963-7218 www.lavisionnewspaper.com   Email: editor@lavisionnewspaper.com

ILLINOIS

Chicago Hoy (60M) 435 N Michigan Ave Fl 22 Chicago IL 60611 **Phn:** 312-527-8400 **Fax:** 312-527-8471 www.vivelohoy.com

NEW YORK

Brooklyn El Diario/La Prensa (50M) 1 Metrotech Ctr Fl 18 Brooklyn NY 11201 **Phn:** 212-807-4600 **Fax:** www.impre.com/eldiariony

Brooklyn Hoy (Online only) (50M) 1 Metrotech Ctr Fl 18 Brooklyn NY 11201 **Phn:** 212-244-2327 **Fax:** www.impre.com/hoynyc

TEXAS

Brownsville El Bravo (50M) 1144 Lincoln St Ste C Brownsville TX 78521 **Phn:** 956-542-5800 **Fax:** 956-542-6023   www.elbravo.com.mx   Email: geome29@hotmail.com

Brownsville El Nuevo Heraldo (7.4M) 1135 E Van Buren St Brownsville TX 78520 **Phn:** 956-542-4301 **Fax:** 956-542-0840   www.elnuevoheraldo.com   Email: dmaldonado@brownsvilleherald.com

Dallas Al Dia (43.1M) 508 Young St Fl 2 Dallas TX 75202 **Phn:** 469-977-3600 **Fax:** 469-977-3601 www.aldiatx.com Email: acarbajal@aldiatx.com

El Paso El Diario (20.5M) 1801 Texas Ave El Paso TX 79901 **Phn:** 915-772-1043 **Fax:** 915-225-1430 www.diariousa.com Email: newsroom@diariousa.com

Laredo El Tiempo de Laredo (17M) PO Box 2129 Laredo TX 78044 **Phn:** 956-728-2500 **Fax:** 956-724-3036   www.lmtonline.com   Email: rmontoya@lmtonline.com

NETWORK HEADQUARTERS

ABC 77 W 66th St, New York NY 10023 **Phn:** 212-456-7777

American Public Television 55 Summer St 4th flr., Boston MA 02110 **Phn:** 617-338-4455

CBN/Christian Broadcasting Net 977 Centerville Tpk, Virginia Beach VA 23463 **Phn:** 757-226-7000

CBS 51 W 52nd St, New York NY 10019 **Phn:** 212-975-4321

Corporation Public Broadcasting 401 9th St NW, Washington DC 20004 **Phn:** 202-879-9600

Educational Broadcasting Corp. 450 W 33rd St, New York NY 10001 **Phn:** 212-560-1313

Fox Broadcasting Co. 10201 W Pico Blvd, Los Angeles CA 90035 **Phn:** 310-369-1000

ION Media Networks 601 Clearwater Park Rd, W. Plm Bch. FL 33401 **Phn:** 561-659-4122

Mas Musica Teve 3310 Keller Springs Rd #105, Carrollton TX 75006 **Phn:** 972-503-6800

myNetwork TV 1211 Ave of Americas, New York NY 10036 **Phn:** 212-301-3000

Natl. Educ. Telecomms. Assn. PO Box 50008, Columbia SC 29250 **Phn:** 803-799-5517

NBC 30 Rockefeller Plz, New York NY 10112 **Phn:** 212-664-4444

PBS 2100 Crystal Dr, Arlington VA 22202 **Phn:** 703-739-5000

Telefutura TV Network 1900 NW 89th Pl, Miami FL 33172 **Phn:** 305-421-1900

Telemundo 2470 W 8th Ave, Hialeah FL 33010 **Phn:** 305-884-8200

The CW 4000 Warner Blvd, Burbank CA 91522 **Phn:** 818-977-5000

Trinity Broadcasting Network PO Box A, Santa Ana CA 92711 **Phn:** 714-832-2950

Univision Network 9405 NW 41st St, Miami FL 33178 **Phn:** 305-471-3900

NEWS SERVICES

ABC News 47 W 66 St, New York NY 10023 **Phn:** 212-456-2700

AccuWeather Inc. 385 Science Park Dr, State College PA 16803 **Phn:** 814-235-8600

Agence France-Presse 1500 K St NW #600, Washington DC 20005 **Phn:** 202-289-0700

AllAfrica Media 920 M St SE, Washington DC 20005 **Phn:** 202-546-0777

AP Broadcast News 1825 K St NW, Washington DC 20006 **Phn:** 202-736-1100

Bloomberg Television 731 Lexington Ave, New York NY 10022 **Phn:** 212-318-2000

British Information Svcs. 845 3rd Ave, New York NY 10022 **Phn:** 212-745-0277

C-SPAN 400 N Capitol St NW Ste 650, Wash. DC 20001 **Phn:** 202-737-3220

Capitol TV News 1629 S Street, Sacramento CA 95811 **Phn:** 916-446-7890

CBS News Network 524 W 57th St, New York NY 10019 **Phn:** 212-975-2881

TV NETWORKS & SERVICES

Church of LDS 15 E South Temple St, SLC UT 84150 **Phn:** 801-240-2205

CNBC 900 Sylvan Ave, Englewood Cliffs NJ 07632 **Phn:** 201-735-2622

CNN One CNN Center, Atlanta GA 30303 **Phn:** 404-827-1500

Feature Story News 1730 Rhode Isl Ave NW #405, Wash. DC 20036 **Phn:** 202-296-9012

Fox News 1211 Ave of Americas, New York NY 10036 **Phn:** 212-301-3000

Hollywood News Svc PO Box 55624, Sherman Oaks CA 91413 **Phn:** 818-986-8168

Kyodo News Service 747 3rd Ave #1803, New York NY 10017 **Phn:** 212-508-5440

Mountain News Corp 50 Vashell Way #400, Orinda CA 94563 **Phn:** 925-254-4456

MSNBC 1 MSNBC Plaza, Secaucus NJ 07094 **Phn:** 201-583-5000

NBC Network News 30 Rockefeller Plz, New York NY 10112 **Phn:** 212-664-4444

News Broadcast Network 75 Broad St 15th flr, New York NY 10004 **Phn:** 800-920-6397

Potomac Television 1510 H St NW #202, Washington DC 20005 **Phn:** 202-783-6464

Reuters America Inc. 1333 H St NW Ste 505, Washington DC 20005 **Phn:** 202-898-8300

Sidebar News International PO Box 612, Scotch Plains NJ 07076 **Phn:** 908-322-8343

Sports Network 2200 Byberry Rd #200, Hatboro PA 19040 **Phn:** 215-441-8444

Washington News Network 400 N Capitol St NW Ste G-50, Wash. DC 20001 **Phn:** 202-628-4000

PROGRAMMING SERVICES

A&E (Arts & Entertainment) 235 E 45th St, New York NY 10017 **Phn:** 212-210-1400

AMC (American Movie Classics) 200 Jericho Quadrangle, Jericho NY 11753 **Phn:** 516-803-3000

AmericanLife TV 650 Massachusetts Ave NW, Wash DC 20001 **Phn:** 202-289-6633

Animal Planet 1 Discovery Pl, Silver Spring MD 20910 **Phn:** 240-662-2000

Auto Channel 332 W Broadway #1604, Louisville KY 40202 **Phn:** 502-992-0200

BBC America PO Box 6266, Florence KY 41022 **Phn:** 859-342-4070

BET (Black Entertainment TV) 1235 W St NE, Washington DC 20018 **Phn:** 202-608-2000

Boating Channel PO Box 1148, Sag Harbor NY 11963 **Phn:** 631-725-4440

Bravo Network 30 Rockefeller Plz, New York NY 10112 **Phn:** 212-664-4444

Cartoon Network 1050 Techwood Dr, Atlanta GA 30318 **Phn:** 404-885-2263

Cinemax 1100 Ave of Americas, New York NY 10036 **Phn:** 212-512-1000

CMT (Country Music TV) 330 Commerce St, Nashville TN 37201 **Phn:** 615-335-8400

Comedy Central 1775 Broadway, New York NY 10019 **Phn:** 212-767-8600

Courtroom TV Net 600 3rd Ave Fl 2, New York NY 10016 **Phn:** 212-973-2800

Crime Channel 42335 Washington St #F371, Palm Desert CA 92211 **Phn:** 760-360-6151

Discovery Channel 1 Discovery Pl, Silver Spring MD 20910 **Phn:** 240-662-2000

Disney Channel 3800 W Alameda Ave, Burbank CA 91505 **Phn:** 818-569-7500

Do It Yourself Net 9721 Sherrill Blvd, Knoxville TN 37932 **Phn:** 865-694-2700

E! Entertainment TV 5750 Wilshire Blvd, Los Angeles CA 90036 **Phn:** 323-954-2400

ESPN 545 Middle St, Bristol CT 06010 **Phn:** 860-766-2000

EWTN (Catholic) 5817 Old Leeds Rd, Birmingham AL 35210 **Phn:** 205-271-2900

Family Channel 500 S Buena Vista St, Burbank CA 91521 **Phn:** 818-460-6363

FamilyNet 6350 W Freeway, Fort Worth TX 76116 **Phn:** 817-737-4011

Food Network 75 9th Ave 2nd flr, New York NY 10011 **Phn:** 212-398-8836

FX Networks 1440 S Sepulveda Blvd, Los Angeles CA 90025 **Phn:** 310-444-8135

Galavision (Spanish) 605 3rd Ave Fl 26, New York NY 10158 **Phn:** 212-455-5300

Game Show Network 2150 Colorado Ave, Santa Monica CA 90404 **Phn:** 310-255-6800

Golf Channel 7580 Commerce Ctr Dr, Orlando FL 32819 **Phn:** 407-345-4653

Great American Country 49 Music Sq W #301, Nashville TN 37203 **Phn:** 615-327-7525

Hallmark Channel 12700 Ventura Blvd # 200, Studio City CA 91604 **Phn:** 818-755-2400

HGTV 9721 Sherrill Blvd, Knoxville TN 37932 **Phn:** 865-694-2700

History Channel 235 E 45th St, New York NY 10017 **Phn:** 212-210-1400

Home Box Office 1100 Ave of Americas, New York NY 10036 **Phn:** 212-512-1000

Home Improvement Network 3441 Baker St, San Diego CA 92117 **Phn:** 858-273-0572

Home Shopping Network 1 HSN Dr, St Petersburg FL 33729 **Phn:** 727-872-1000

Inspiration Network 7910 Crescent Executive Dr, Charlotte NC 28217 **Phn:** 704-525-9800

International Networks 4100 E Dry Creek Rd, Centennial CO 80122 **Phn:** 917-934-1587

Jewish Television Network 13743 Ventura Bvd/200, Sherman Oaks CA 91423 **Phn:** 818-789-5891

Lifetime Television 309 W 49th St, New York NY 10019 **Phn:** 212-424-7000

MTV Latino 1111 Lincoln Rd Fl 6, Miami FL 33139 **Phn:** 305-535-3700

MTV Network 1515 Broadway, New York NY 10036 **Phn:** 212-258-8000

National Geographic Channel 1145 17th St NW, Washington DC 20036 **Phn:** 202-912-6500

NFL Network 280 Park Ave flr 17, New York NY 10017 **Phn:** 212-450-2000

Nickelodeon 1515 Broadway, New York NY 10036 **Phn:** 212-258-8000

Oasis TV 1875 Century Park E #600, L.A. CA 90067 **Phn:** 310-553-4300

Outdoor Channel 43445 Business Pk. Dr #103, Temecula CA 92590 **Phn:** 800-770-5750

Outdoor Life Network 281 Tresser Blvd, Stamford CT 06901 **Phn:** 203-406-2500

Ovation TV 2800 28th St #240, Santa Monica CA 90405 **Phn:** 800-682-8466

Oxygen Media 75 9th Ave, New York NY 10011 **Phn:** 212-651-2000

Pentagon Channel 601 N Fairfax St, Alexandria VA 22314 **Phn:** 703-428-0265

Playboy TV 2706 Media Ctr Dr, Los Angeles CA 90065 **Phn:** 323-276-4000

Praise TV PO Box 428, Safety Harbor FL 34695 **Phn:** 727-536-0036

QVC 1200 Wilson Dr, West Chester PA 19380 **Phn:** 484-701-1000

RAI Italian TV 32 Ave of Americas, New York NY 10013 **Phn:** 212-468-2500

Sci-Fi Channel 30 Rockefeller Plz, New York NY 10112 **Phn:** 212-413-5000

Showtime 1633 Broadway, New York NY 10019 **Phn:** 212-708-1600

Speed Channel 9711 Southern Pines Blvd, Charlotte NC 28273 **Phn:** 704-731-2222

Spike TV 1775 Broadway, New York NY 10019 **Phn:** 212-767-4001

TLC The Learning Channel 1 Discovery Pl, Silver Spring MD 20910 **Phn:** 240-662-2000

TNT Turner Network TV 1050 Techwood Dr NW, Atlanta GA 30318 **Phn:** 404-827-1717

Travel Channel 1 Discovery Pl, Silver Spring MD 20910 **Phn:** 240-662-2000

TV Asia 76 National Rd, Edison NJ 08817 **Phn:** 732-650-1100

TV Guide Channel 7140 S Lewis, Tulsa OK 74136 **Phn:** 918-488-4000

TV Japan 100 Broadway 15th flr, New York NY 10005 **Phn:** 212-262-3377

TV Land 1515 Broadway, New York NY 10036 **Phn:** 212-258-7579

USA Networks 30 Rockefeller Plz, New York NY 10112 **Phn:** 212-644-4444

VH1 1515 Broadway, New York NY 10036 **Phn:** 212-846-7840

WE (Women's Entertainment) 200 Jericho Quadrangle, Jericho NY 11753 **Phn:** 516-803-3000

Weather Channel 300 Interstate N Pkwy, Atlanta GA 30339 **Phn:** 770-226-0000

Worship Network 28059 US Hwy 19 N #300, Clearwater FL 33761 **Phn:** 727-536-0036

ALABAMA

Birmingham: WABM (MY) 651 Beacon Pkwy W Ste 105 Birmingham AL 35209 **Phn:** 205-943-2168 **Fax:** 205-290-2114 www.wabm68.com **Email:** programming@wabm68.com

Birmingham: WBIQ (PBS) 2112 11th Ave S Ste 400 Birmingham AL 35205 **Phn:** 205-328-8756 **Fax:** 205-251-2192 www.aptv.org **Email:** lcourington@aptv.org

Birmingham: WBMA (ABC) 800 Concourse Pkwy Ste 200 Birmingham AL 35244 **Phn:** 205-403-3340 **Fax:** 205-982-3942 www.abc3340.com **Email:** newstip@abc3340.com

Birmingham: WBRC (FOX) PO Box 6 Birmingham AL 35201 **Phn:** 205-322-6666 **Fax:** 205-583-4356 www.myfoxal.com **Email:** newstip@wbrc.com

Birmingham: WIAT (CBS) 2075 Golden Crest Dr Birmingham AL 35209 **Phn:** 205-322-4200 **Fax:** 205-320-2722 www.cbs42.com **Email:** newsrelease@cbs42.com

Birmingham: WPXH (ION) 2085 Golden Crest Dr Birmingham AL 35209 **Phn:** 205-870-4404 **Fax:** 205-870-0544 iontelevision.com **Email:** debraperry@ionmedia.com

Birmingham: WTTO (CW) 651 Beacon Pkwy W Ste 105 Birmingham AL 35209 **Phn:** 205-943-2168 **Fax:** 205-290-2114 www.wtto21.com **Email:** programming@wtto21.com

Birmingham: WVTM (NBC) 1732 Valley View Dr Birmingham AL 35209 **Phn:** 205-933-1313 **Fax:** 205-323-3314 www.alabamas13.com **Email:** newstips@alabamas13.com

Dothan: WDFX (FOX) 2221 Ross Clark Cir Dothan AL 36301 **Phn:** 334-794-2424 **Fax:** 334-794-0034 dothanconnect.revrocket.us **Email:** jrodriguez@myfox34.tv

Dothan: WDHN (ABC) PO Box 6237 Dothan AL 36302 **Phn:** 334-793-1818 **Fax:** 334-793-2623 dothanfirst.com **Email:** kenc@wdhn.com

Dothan: WJJN (IND) 4106 Ross Clark Cir Dothan AL 36303 **Phn:** 334-671-1753 **Fax:** 334-677-6923 www.wjjn.net

Dothan: WTVY (CBS) 285 N Foster St Dothan AL 36303 **Phn:** 334-792-3195 **Fax:** 334-712-7452 www.wtvy.com **Email:** newsstaff@wtvy.com

Florence: WBCF (IND) PO Box 1316 Florence AL 35631 **Phn:** 256-764-8170 www.wbcf.com **Email:** news@wbcf.com

Florence: WXFL (IND) PO Box 1316 Florence AL 35631 **Phn:** 256-764-8170 www.wbcf.com **Email:** benji@wbcf.com

Gadsden: WTJP (REL) 313 Rosedale St Gadsden AL 35901 **Phn:** 256-546-8860 **Fax:** 256-543-8623 www.tbn.org **Email:** ghodges@tbn.org

Huntsville: WAAY (ABC) 1000 Monte Sano Blvd SE Huntsville AL 35801 **Phn:** 256-533-3131 **Fax:** 256-533-5191 www.waaytv.com **Email:** newsroom@waaytv.com

Huntsville: WAFF (NBC) 1414 Memorial Pkwy NW Huntsville AL 35801 **Phn:** 256-533-4848 **Fax:** 256-534-4101 www.waff.com **Email:** news@waff.com

Huntsville: WHDF (CW) 200 Andrew Jackson Way NE Huntsville AL 35801 **Phn:** 256-536-1550 **Fax:** 256-536-8286 www.thevalleyscw.tv **Email:** dstafford@thevalleyscw.tv

Huntsville: WHNT (CBS) PO Box 19 Huntsville AL 35804 **Phn:** 256-533-1919 **Fax:** 256-536-9468 whnt.com

Huntsville: WZDX (FOX) 1309 Memorial Pkwy NW Huntsville AL 35801 **Phn:** 256-533-5454 **Fax:** 256-533-5315 www.fox54.com **Email:** news@fox54.com

TV STATIONS

Mobile: WALA (FOX) 1501 Satchel Paige Dr Mobile AL 36606 **Phn:** 251-434-1010 **Fax:** 251-434-1023 www.fox10tv.com **Email:** lpate@fox10tv.com

Mobile: WBPG (CW) 1501 Satchel Paige Dr Mobile AL 36606 **Phn:** 251-434-1010 **Fax:** 251-434-1023 www.wfnatv.com **Email:** bcashen@fox10tv.com

Mobile: WJTC (IND) 661 Azalea Rd Mobile AL 36609 **Phn:** 251-602-1544 **Fax:** 251-602-1550 www.utv44.com **Email:** local15@local15tv.com

Mobile: WKRG (CBS) 555 Broadcast Dr Mobile AL 36606 **Phn:** 251-479-5555 **Fax:** 251-662-3071 www.wkrg.com **Email:** producers@wkrg.com

Mobile: WMPV (REL) 1668 W I65 Service Rd S Mobile AL 36693 **Phn:** 251-661-2101 www.tbn.org **Email:** wmpv@tbn.org

Mobile: WPMI (NBC) 661 Azalea Rd Mobile AL 36609 **Phn:** 251-602-1500 **Fax:** 251-602-1550 www.local15tv.com **Email:** local15@local15tv.com

Montgomery: WAKA (CBS) 3020 Eastern Blvd Montgomery AL 36116 **Phn:** 334-271-8888 **Fax:** 334-244-7859 www.waka.com **Email:** rmartin@waka.com

Montgomery: WBMM (CW) 3251 Harrison Rd Montgomery AL 36109 **Phn:** 334-270-3200 **Fax:** 334-271-2972 www.cwmontgomery.com **Email:** rmartin@waka.com

Montgomery: WCOV (FOX) 1 Wcov Ave Montgomery AL 36111 **Phn:** 334-288-7020 **Fax:** 334-288-5414 wcov.com **Email:** paul@wcov.com

Montgomery: WMCF (REL) 300 Mendel Pkwy W Montgomery AL 36117 **Phn:** 334-272-0045 **Fax:** 334-277-6635

Montgomery: WNCF (ABC) 3251 Harrison Rd Montgomery AL 36109 **Phn:** 334-270-3200 **Fax:** 334-271-6348 www.wncftv.com **Email:** rmartin@waka.com

Montgomery: WRJM (MY) 4266 Lomac St Montgomery AL 36106 **Phn:** 334-670-6766 **Fax:** 334-670-6717

Montgomery: WSFA (NBC) 12 E Delano Ave Montgomery AL 36105 **Phn:** 334-288-1212 **Fax:** 334-613-8303 www.wsfa.com **Email:** news@wsfa.com

Phenix City: WYBU (REL) PO Box 579 Phenix City AL 36868 **Phn:** 334-298-5916 **Fax:** 334-297-1557 www.wybu.org **Email:** vthompson@ctntv.net

Tuscaloosa: WVUA (IND) PO Box 870172 Tuscaloosa AL 35487 **Phn:** 205-348-7000 **Fax:** 205-348-7002 www.wvuatv.com **Email:** news@wvuatv.com

ALASKA

Anchorage: KAKM (PBS) 3877 University Dr Anchorage AK 99508 **Phn:** 907-550-8400 **Fax:** 907-550-8401 www.alaskapublic.org

Anchorage: KDMD (ION) 1310 E 66th Ave Anchorage AK 99518 **Phn:** 907-562-5363 **Fax:** 907-562-5346 www.kdmd.tv

Anchorage: KIMO (ABC) 2700 E Tudor Rd Anchorage AK 99507 **Phn:** 907-561-1313 **Fax:** 907-561-8934 www.youralaskalink.com **Email:** news@youralaskalink.com

Anchorage: KJUD (ABC) 2700 E Tudor Rd Anchorage AK 99507 **Phn:** 907-586-3145 **Fax:** 907-463-3041 www.youralaskalink.com **Email:** news@youralaskalink.com

Anchorage: KTBY (FOX) 2700 E Tudor Rd Anchorage AK 99507 **Phn:** 907-274-0404 **Fax:** 907-264-5180 www.youralaskalink.com **Email:** news@youralaskalink.com

Anchorage: KTUU (NBC) 701 E Tudor Rd Ste 220 Anchorage AK 99503 **Phn:** 907-762-9202 **Fax:** 907-561-0874 www.ktuu.com **Email:** news_desk@ktuu.com

Anchorage: KTVA (CBS) 3330 Arctic Blvd Ste 206 Anchorage AK 99503 **Phn:** 907-646-2100 **Fax:** 907-646-2166 www.ktva.com **Email:** 11news@ktva.com

Anchorage: KYES (MY) 3700 Woodland Dr Ste 800 Anchorage AK 99517 **Phn:** 907-248-5937 **Fax:** 907-339-3889 www.kyes.com

Bethel: KYUK (PBS) PO Box 468 Bethel AK 99559 **Phn:** 907-543-3131 **Fax:** 907-543-3130 kyuk.org **Email:** angela@kyuk.org

Fairbanks: KATN (ABC) 516 2nd Ave Ste 400 Fairbanks AK 99701 **Phn:** 907-452-2125 **Fax:** 907-561-8934 www.youralaskalink.com **Email:** news@youralaskalink.com

Fairbanks: KFXF (FOX) 3650 Braddock St Fairbanks AK 99701 **Phn:** 907-452-3697 **Fax:** 907-456-3428 www.tvtv.com **Email:** ox@tvtv.com

Fairbanks: KTVF (NBC) 3528 International St Fairbanks AK 99701 **Phn:** 907-458-1800 **Fax:** 907-458-1820 www.webcenter11.com **Email:** montebowen@ktvf11.com

Fairbanks: KUAC (PBS) PO Box 755620 Fairbanks AK 99775 **Phn:** 907-474-7491 **Fax:** 907-474-5064 kuac.org **Email:** jerry@kuac.org

Fairbanks: KXD (CBS) 3650 Braddock St Fairbanks AK 99701 **Phn:** 907-452-3697 **Fax:** 907-456-3428 www.cbsnews13.com **Email:** news@cbsnews13.com

Juneau: KATH (NBC) 3161 Channel Dr Ste 1A Juneau AK 99801 **Phn:** 907-586-8384 **Fax:** 907-586-8394 www.kath.tv **Email:** news@kath.tv

Juneau: KTOO (PBS) 360 Egan Dr Juneau AK 99801 **Phn:** 907-586-1670 **Fax:** 907-586-2561 www.ktoo.org **Email:** news@ktoo.org

Juneau: KXLJ (CBS) 1105 W 9th St Juneau AK 99801 **Phn:** 907-586-2455 cbssoutheastak.com **Email:** andy.tierney@cbssoutheastak.com

Ketchikan: KUBD (IND) 2208 Tongass Ave Ketchikan AK 99901 **Phn:** 907-225-4613 www.cbssoutheastak.com **Email:** andy.tierney@cbssoutheastak.com

North Pole: KJNP (REL) 2501 Mission Rd North Pole AK 99705 **Phn:** 907-488-2216 **Fax:** 907-488-5246 www.mosquitonet.com~kjnp **Email:** kjnp@mosquitonet.com

Sitka: KTNL (CBS) 520 Lake St Sitka AK 99835 **Phn:** 907-747-5749 **Fax:** 907-747-8440 cbssoutheastak.com **Email:** andy.tierney@cbssoutheastak.com

ARIZONA

Douglas: KFTU (SPN) 1111 N G Ave Douglas AZ 85607 **Phn:** 520-805-1773 **Fax:** 520-805-1768 www.univision.com **Email:** ktvassignment@univision.net

Flagstaff: KFPH (SPN) 2158 N 4th St Flagstaff AZ 86004 **Phn:** 928-527-1300 **Fax:** 928-527-1394 www.univision.com **Email:** rjpineda@univision.net

Phoenix: KAET (PBS) 555 N Central Ave Ste 500 Phoenix AZ 85004 **Phn:** 480-965-8888 **Fax:** 480-965-1000 www.azpbs.org **Email:** eight@asu.edu

Phoenix: KASW (CW) 5555 N 7th Ave Phoenix AZ 85013 **Phn:** 480-661-6161 **Fax:** 602-207-3477 www.azfamily.com **Email:** demetress_hall@azfamily.com

Phoenix: KAZT (IND) 4343 E Camelback Rd Ste 130 Phoenix AZ 85018 **Phn:** 602-977-7700 **Fax:** 602-224-2214 www.aztv.com **Email:** programming@aztv.com

Phoenix: KNXV (ABC) 515 N 44th St Phoenix AZ 85008 **Phn:** 602-273-1500 **Fax:** 602-685-6363 www.abc15.com **Email:** myaznews@abc15.com

Phoenix: KPAZ (REL) 3551 E McDowell Rd Phoenix AZ 85008 **Phn:** 602-273-1477 **Fax:** 602-267-9427 www.tbn.org **Email:** ovalero@tbn.org

Phoenix: KPHO (CBS) 4016 N Black Canyon Hwy Phoenix AZ 85017 **Phn:** 602-264-1000 **Fax:** 602-650-5545 www.kpho.com **Email:** kphoactionbutton@cbs5az.com

Phoenix: KPNX (NBC) 200 E Van Buren St Phoenix AZ 85004 **Phn:** 602-257-1212 **Fax:** 602-257-6619 www.azcentral.com12news **Email:** assignmentdesk@12news.com

Phoenix: KPPX (ION) 2777 E Camelback Rd Ste 101 Phoenix AZ 85016 **Phn:** 602-340-1466 **Fax:** 602-808-8664 www.iontelevision.com

Phoenix: KSAZ (FOX) 511 W Adams St Phoenix AZ 85003 **Phn:** 602-257-1234 **Fax:** 602-262-0181 www.myfoxphoenix.com **Email:** fox10.desk@foxtv.com

Phoenix: KTAZ (SPN) 4625 S 33rd Pl Phoenix AZ 85040 **Phn:** 602-648-3900 **Fax:** 602-648-3970 msnlatino.telemundo.com **Email:** aldo.contreras@nbcuni.com

Phoenix: KTVK (IND) 5555 N 7th Ave Phoenix AZ 85013 **Phn:** 602-207-3333 **Fax:** 602-207-3477 www.azfamily.com **Email:** demetress_hall@azfamily.com

Phoenix: KTVW (SPN) 6006 S 30th St Phoenix AZ 85042 **Phn:** 602-243-3333 **Fax:** 602-232-3679 www.univision.com **Email:** vluna@univision.net

Phoenix: KUTP (MY) 511 W Adams St Phoenix AZ 85003 **Phn:** 602-257-1234 **Fax:** 602-262-0181 www.my45.com

Tucson: KGUN (ABC) 7280 E Rosewood St Tucson AZ 85710 **Phn:** 520-722-5486 **Fax:** 520-733-7050 www.kgun9.com **Email:** news@kgun9.com

Tucson: KHRR (SPN) 5151 W Broadway # 600 Tucson AZ 85716 **Phn:** 520-396-2600 **Fax:** 520-396-2640 msnlatino.telemundo.com

Tucson: KMSB (FOX) 1855 N 6th Ave Tucson AZ 85705 **Phn:** 520-770-1123 **Fax:** 520-629-7185 www.tucsonnewsnow.com **Email:** kmsb-programming@tucsonnewsnow.com

Tucson: KOLD (CBS) 7831 N Business Park Dr Tucson AZ 85743 **Phn:** 520-744-1313 **Fax:** 520-744-5233 www.tucsonnewsnow.com **Email:** dbush@tucsonnewsnow.com

Tucson: KTTU (MY) 1855 N 6th Ave Tucson AZ 85705 **Phn:** 520-770-1123 **Fax:** 520-629-7185 www.tucsonnewsnow.com **Email:** eturner@tucsonnewsnow.com

Tucson: KUAT (PBS) PO Box 210067 Tucson AZ 85721 **Phn:** 520-621-5828 **Fax:** 520-621-3360 tv.azpm.org

Tucson: KUVE (SPN) 2301 N Forbes Blvd Ste 103 Tucson AZ 85745 **Phn:** 520-204-1246 **Fax:** 520-204-1247 www.univision.com **Email:** vluna@univision.net

Tucson: KVOA (NBC) PO Box 5188 Tucson AZ 85703 **Phn:** 520-792-2270 **Fax:** 520-884-4644 www.kvoa.com **Email:** newstips@kvoa.com

Tucson: KWBA (CW) 7280 E Rosewood St Tucson AZ 85710 **Phn:** 520-722-5486 **Fax:** 520-290-7636 **Email:** news@kgun9.com

Yuma: KECY (FOX) 1965 S 4th Ave Ste B Yuma AZ 85364 **Phn:** 928-539-9990 **Fax:** 928-343-0218 yourtvfamily.com **Email:** news@kecytv.com

Yuma: KSWT (CBS) 1301 S 3rd Ave Yuma AZ 85364 **Phn:** 928-782-5113 **Fax:** 928-782-9411 www.kswt.com **Email:** snunez@kswt.com

Yuma: KYMA (NBC) 1385 S Pacific Ave Yuma AZ 85365 **Phn:** 928-782-1111 **Fax:** 928-782-5229 www.kyma.com **Email:** eromero@kyma.com

ARIZONA TV STATIONS
ARKANSAS

Conway: KETS (PBS) 350 S Donaghey Ave Conway AR 72034 **Phn:** 501-682-2386 **Fax:** 501-682-4122 www.aetn.org **Email:** info@aetn.org

Fayetteville: KFTA (FOX) 15 S Block Ave Ste 101 Fayetteville AR 72701 **Phn:** 479-571-5100 **Fax:** 479-571-8900 nwahomepage.comcontentmyfox24 **Email:** news@knwa.com

Fayetteville: KNWA (NBC) 15 S Block Ave Ste 101 Fayetteville AR 72701 **Phn:** 479-571-5100 **Fax:** 479-571-8900 nwahomepage.com **Email:** news@knwa.com

Fort Smith: KFSM (CBS) 318 N 13th St Fort Smith AR 72901 **Phn:** 479-783-3131 **Fax:** 888-369-2515 5newsonline.com **Email:** news@kfsm.com

Fort Smith: KHBS (ABC) 2415 N Albert Pike Ave Fort Smith AR 72904 **Phn:** 479-783-4040 **Fax:** 479-785-5375 www.4029tv.com **Email:** programming@4029tv.com

Fort Smith: KKYK (IND) 510 N Greenwood Ave Fort Smith AR 72901 **Phn:** 479-785-4600 **Fax:** 479-785-4844

Fort Smith: KPBI (IND) 510 N Greenwood Ave Fort Smith AR 72901 **Phn:** 479-785-4600 **Fax:** 479-785-4844 metvnetwork.com

Fort Smith: KXUN (SPN) 510 N Greenwood Ave Fort Smith AR 72901 **Phn:** 479-785-4600 **Fax:** 479-785-4844 metvnetwork.com

Jonesboro: KAIT (ABC) PO Box 790 Jonesboro AR 72403 **Phn:** 870-931-8888 **Fax:** 870-933-8058 www.kait8.com **Email:** news8@kait8.com

Little Rock: KARK (NBC) 1401 W Capitol Ave Ste 104 Little Rock AR 72201 **Phn:** 501-376-4444 **Fax:** 501-375-1961 arkansasmatters.com **Email:** news4@kark.com

Little Rock: KASN (CW) 10800 Colonel Glenn Rd Little Rock AR 72204 **Phn:** 501-225-0038 **Fax:** 501-225-0428 www.cwarkansas.com **Email:** news@fox16.com

Little Rock: KATV (ABC) PO Box 77 Little Rock AR 72203 **Phn:** 501-324-7777 **Fax:** 501-324-7852 www.katv.com **Email:** newsroom@katv.com

Little Rock: KLRT (FOX) 10800 Colonel Glenn Rd Little Rock AR 72204 **Phn:** 501-223-0016 **Fax:** 501-227-0855 www.fox16.com **Email:** news@fox16.com

Little Rock: KTHV (CBS) 720 Izard St Little Rock AR 72201 **Phn:** 501-376-1111 **Fax:** 501-376-1645 www.thv11.com **Email:** news@todaysthv.com

Little Rock: KVTJ (REL) 701 Napa Valley Dr Little Rock AR 72211 **Phn:** 501-223-2525 **Fax:** 501-221-3837 www.vtntv.com **Email:** tish.kemp@vtntv.com

Little Rock: KVTN (REL) 701 Napa Valley Dr Little Rock AR 72211 **Phn:** 501-223-2525 **Fax:** 501-221-3837 www.vtntv.com **Email:** tish.kemp@vtntv.com

Rogers: KHOG (ABC) 2809 Ajax Ave Ste 200 Rogers AR 72758 **Phn:** 479-631-4029 **Fax:** 479-878-6077 www.4029tv.com **Email:** programming@4029tv.com

CALIFORNIA

Bakersfield: KABE (SPN) 5801 Truxtun Ave Bakersfield CA 93309 **Phn:** 661-324-0031 **Fax:** 661-334-2685 www.univision.com

Bakersfield: KBAK (CBS) 1901 Westwind Dr Bakersfield CA 93301 **Phn:** 661-327-7955 **Fax:** 661-861-9810 www.bakersfieldnow.com **Email:** news@bakersfieldnow.com

Bakersfield: KERO (ABC) 321 21st St Bakersfield CA 93301 **Phn:** 661-637-2323 **Fax:** 661-323-5538 www.turnto23.com **Email:** elaina.rusk@kero.com

Bakersfield: KGET (NBC) 2120 L St Bakersfield CA 93301 **Phn:** 661-283-1700 **Fax:** 661-283-1843 www.kerngoldenempire.com **Email:** michaeltrihey@kget.com

Bakersfield: KUVI (CW) 5801 Truxtun Ave Bakersfield CA 93309 **Phn:** 661-324-0045 **Fax:** 661-334-2685

Bishop: KSRW (IND) 1280 N Main St Ste J Bishop CA 93514 **Phn:** 760-873-5329 **Fax:** 760-873-5328 www.sierrawave.net **Email:** bkessler@sierrawave.net

Brisbane: KTSF (IND) 100 Valley Dr Brisbane CA 94005 **Phn:** 415-468-2626 **Fax:** 415-468-5724 www.ktsf.com **Email:** newstip@ktsftv.com

Burbank: KNBC (NBC) 3000 W Alameda Ave Burbank CA 91523 **Phn:** 818-840-4444 **Fax:** 818-840-3535 www.nbclosangeles.com

Burbank: KPXN (ION) 2600 W Olive Ave Ste 900 Burbank CA 91505 **Phn:** 818-563-1005 **Fax:** 818-524-1999 www.iontelevision.com

Burbank: KRCA (SPN) 1845 W Empire Ave Burbank CA 91504 **Phn:** 818-563-5722 **Fax:** 818-558-4232 www.krca62.tv **Email:** cking@lbimedia.com

Burbank: KSDX (SPN) 1845 W Empire Ave Burbank CA 91504 **Phn:** 818-729-5300 **Fax:** 818-729-5678 www.lbimedia.com **Email:** bperez@lbimedia.com

Burbank: KVEA (SPN) 3000 W Alameda Ave Burbank CA 91523 **Phn:** 818-260-5700 **Fax:** 818-260-5730 www.telemundo52.com **Email:** noticierotelemundo52@nbcuni.com

Burbank: KWHY (SPN) 3000 W Alameda Ave Burbank CA 91523 **Phn:** 818-260-5700 **Fax:** 818-260-5730 www.kwhy.com **Email:** fatima.goncalves@nbcuni.com

Chico: KHSL (CBS) 3460 Silverbell Rd Chico CA 95973 **Phn:** 530-342-0141 **Fax:** 530-342-2405 www.actionnewsnow.com **Email:** news@khsltv.com

Chico: KNVN (NBC) 3460 Silverbell Rd Chico CA 95973 **Phn:** 530-893-2424 **Fax:** 530-342-2405 www.actionnewsnow.com **Email:** news@knvn.com

Chico: KRVU (MY) 300 Main St Chico CA 95928 **Phn:** 530-893-1234 **Fax:** 530-893-1091 www.my21.tv **Email:** doug@fox30.com

Chula Vista: XEWT (SPN) 637 3rd Ave Ste B Chula Vista CA 91910 **Phn:** 619-585-9398 **Fax:** 619-585-9463 www.xewt12.com

Clovis: KAIL (MY) 1590 Alluvial Ave Clovis CA 93611 **Phn:** 559-299-9753 **Fax:** 559-299-1523 www.kail.tv **Email:** promotions@kail.tv

El Centro: KVYE (SPN) 1803 N Imperial Ave El Centro CA 92243 **Phn:** 760-482-7777 **Fax:** 760-482-0099 www.kvyetv.com **Email:** aretana@entravision.com

Eureka: KAEF (ABC) 540 E St Eureka CA 95501 **Phn:** 707-444-2323 **Fax:** 707-445-9451 www.krcrtv.comkaef **Email:** traffic@krcrtv.com

Eureka: KBVU (FOX) 540 E St Eureka CA 95501 **Phn:** 707-444-2323 **Fax:** 707-445-9451 www.krcrtv.com **Email:** mdare@esteembroadcasting.com

Eureka: KEET (PBS) PO Box 13 Eureka CA 95502 **Phn:** 707-445-0813 www.keet.org **Email:** letters@keet-tv.org

Eureka: KIEM (NBC) 5650 S Broadway St Eureka CA 95503 **Phn:** 707-443-3123 **Fax:** 707-442-1459 kiem-tv.com **Email:** kiem-tv@humboldt1.com

Eureka: KVIQ (CBS) 730 7th St Ste 201 Eureka CA 95501 **Phn:** 707-443-6666 **Fax:** 707-441-0111 www.eurekatelevision.tv **Email:** terri.jensen@eurekatelevision.tv

Fresno: KFRE (CW) 5111 E McKinley Ave Fresno CA 93727 **Phn:** 559-435-5900 **Fax:** 559-255-9626 www.kmph-kfre.com **Email:** mtorres@kmph.com

Fresno: KFSN (ABC) 1777 G St Fresno CA 93706 **Phn:** 559-442-1170 **Fax:** 559-266-5024 abclocal.go.comkfsn **Email:** kfsndesk@abc.com

CALIFORNIA TV STATIONS

Fresno: KFTV (SPN) 3239 W Ashlan Ave Fresno CA 93722 **Phn:** 559-222-2121 **Fax:** 559-222-0917 www.univision.com

Fresno: KGMC (IND) 706 W Herndon Ave Fresno CA 93650 **Phn:** 559-435-7000 **Fax:** 559-435-3201 www.cocolatv.com **Email:** info@cocolatv.com

Fresno: KGPE (CBS) 4880 N 1st St Fresno CA 93726 **Phn:** 559-222-2411 **Fax:** 559-225-5305 www.yourcentralvalley.com **Email:** programming@cbs47.tv

Fresno: KJEO (IND) 706 W Herndon Ave Fresno CA 93650 **Phn:** 559-435-3200 **Fax:** 559-435-3201 www.kjeotv.com **Email:** terell@cocolatv.com

Fresno: KMPH (FOX) 5111 E McKinley Ave Fresno CA 93727 **Phn:** 559-255-2600 **Fax:** 559-255-9626 www.kmph.com

Fresno: KNSO (SPN) 30 E River Park Pl W Ste 200 Fresno CA 93720 **Phn:** 559-252-5101 **Fax:** 559-252-2747 www.holaciudad.comf **Email:** info@holaciudad.com

Fresno: KNXT (REL) 1550 N Fresno St Fresno CA 93703 **Phn:** 559-488-7440 **Fax:** 559-488-7444 www.knxt.tv **Email:** rosamaria@dioceseoffresno.org

Fresno: KSEE (NBC) 5035 E McKinley Ave Fresno CA 93727 **Phn:** 559-454-2424 **Fax:** 559-454-2496 www.yourcentralvalley.com **Email:** newsdesk@ksee.com

Fresno: KTFF (SPN) 6715 N Palm Ave Ste 201 Fresno CA 93704 **Phn:** 559-439-6100 **Fax:** 559-439-5950 www.univision.com **Email:** gersanchez@univision.net

Fresno: KVPT (PBS) 1544 Van Ness Ave Fresno CA 93721 **Phn:** 559-266-1800 **Fax:** 559-650-1880 valleypbs.org

Glendale: KABC (ABC) 500 Circle Seven Dr Glendale CA 91201 **Phn:** 818-863-7777 **Fax:** 818-863-7080 abclocal.go.comkabc **Email:** viewer.mail.kabc.tv@abc.com

Los Angeles: KBEH (SPN) 5757 W Century Blvd Ste 490 Los Angeles CA 90045 **Phn:** 310-216-0063 **Fax:** 310-216-0663 www.canal63.com **Email:** linette.rodriguez@herobroadcasting.com

Los Angeles: KCET (PBS) 4401 W Sunset Blvd Los Angeles CA 90027 **Phn:** 323-666-6500 www.kcet.org **Email:** contact@kcet.org

Los Angeles: KCOP (MY) 1999 S Bundy Dr Los Angeles CA 90025 **Phn:** 310-584-2000 **Fax:** 310-584-2024 www.myfoxla.com

Los Angeles: KFTR (SPN) 5999 Center Dr Los Angeles CA 90045 **Phn:** 310-410-8900 **Fax:** 310-348-3493 www.univision.com

Los Angeles: KJLA (SPN) 2323 Corinth Ave Los Angeles CA 90064 **Phn:** 310-943-5288 **Fax:** 310-943-5299 www.kjla.com **Email:** info@kjla.com

Los Angeles: KLCS (PBS) 1061 W Temple St Los Angeles CA 90012 **Phn:** 213-241-4000 **Fax:** 213-481-1019 www.klcs.org **Email:** jenifer.flores@lausd.net

Los Angeles: KMEX (SPN) 5999 Center Dr Los Angeles CA 90045 **Phn:** 310-216-3434 **Fax:** 310-348-3493 losangeles.univision.com

Los Angeles: KNLA (SPN) 5757 Wilshire Blvd Ste 470 Los Angeles CA 90036 **Phn:** 323-469-5638 **Fax:** 323-469-2193 **Email:** bholton@loop.com

Los Angeles: KSCI (IND) 1990 S Bundy Dr Ste 850 Los Angeles CA 90025 **Phn:** 310-478-1818 **Fax:** 310-442-2388 www.la18.tv **Email:** info@la18.tv

Los Angeles: KTLA (CW) 5800 W Sunset Blvd Los Angeles CA 90028 **Phn:** 323-460-5502 **Fax:** 323-460-5333 ktla.com **Email:** ktlastoryideas@tribune.com

Los Angeles: KTTV (FOX) 1999 S Bundy Dr Los Angeles CA 90025 **Phn:** 310-584-2000 **Fax:** 310-584-2024 www.myfoxla.com

Modesto: KAZV (IND) 2731 Iowa Ave Modesto CA 95358 **Phn:** 209-577-0743 **Fax:** 209-577-0401

Modesto: KCSO (SPN) 142 N 9th St Ste 8 Modesto CA 95350 **Phn:** 209-576-3301 **Fax:** 209-575-4547 www.kcso33.com **Email:** pschafer@kcso33.com

Monterey: KSMS (SPN) 67 Garden Ct Monterey CA 93940 **Phn:** 831-373-6767 **Fax:** 831-373-6700 www.ksmstv.com **Email:** cthomas@entravision.com

Oakland: KICU (IND) 2 Jack London Sq Oakland CA 94607 **Phn:** 510-834-1212 www.ktvu.com **Email:** newstips@ktvu.com

Oakland: KTVU (FOX) 2 Jack London Sq Oakland CA 94607 **Phn:** 510-834-1212 **Fax:** 510-451-2610 www.ktvu.com **Email:** newstips@ktvu.com

Palm Desert: KDFX (FOX) 42650 Melanie Pl Palm Desert CA 92211 **Phn:** 760-773-0342 **Fax:** 760-773-5128 www.kesq.com **Email:** newsline3@kesq.com

Palm Desert: KESQ (ABC) 42650 Melanie Pl Palm Desert CA 92211 **Phn:** 760-773-0342 **Fax:** 760-773-5128 www.kesq.com **Email:** newsline3@kesq.com

Palm Desert: KMIR (NBC) 72920 Parkview Dr Palm Desert CA 92260 **Phn:** 760-568-3636 **Fax:** 760-341-7029 www.kmir6.com **Email:** news@kmir6.com

Palm Desert: KPSE (MY) 72920 Parkview Dr Palm Desert CA 92260 **Phn:** 760-568-3636 **Fax:** 760-341-7029 www.my13palmsprings.com

Palm Desert: KRET (IND) 41625 Eclectic St Ste J1 Palm Desert CA 92260 **Phn:** 760-674-8550 **Fax:** 760-674-8490

Palm Desert: KVER (SPN) 41601 Corporate Way Palm Desert CA 92260 **Phn:** 760-341-5837 **Fax:** 760-341-0951 www.kvertv.com **Email:** echiabra@entravision.com

Palo Alto: KMTP (PBS) 1010 Corporation Way Palo Alto CA 94303 **Phn:** 650-254-1233

Rancho Cordova: KSPX (ION) 3352 Mather Field Rd Rancho Cordova CA 95670 **Phn:** 916-368-2929 **Fax:** 916-368-0225 www.iontelevision.com **Email:** leeroberts@ionmedia.com

Redding: KCVU (FOX) 755 Auditorium Dr Redding CA 96001 **Phn:** 530-243-7777 **Fax:** 530-243-0217 www.krcrtv.com **Email:** news@krcrtv.com

Redding: KIXE (PBS) 603 N Market St Redding CA 96003 **Phn:** 530-243-5493 **Fax:** 530-243-7443 www.kixe.org **Email:** rkeenan@kixe.org

Redding: KRCR (ABC) 755 Auditorium Dr Redding CA 96001 **Phn:** 530-243-7777 **Fax:** 530-243-0217 www.krcrtv.com **Email:** news@krcrtv.com

Redwood City: KKPX (ION) 660 Price Ave Ste B Redwood City CA 94063 **Phn:** 650-261-1370 **Fax:** 650-261-1293 www.iontelevision.com **Email:** andreaking@ionmedia.com

Rohnert Park: KRCB (PBS) 5850 Labath Ave Rohnert Park CA 94928 **Phn:** 707-584-2000 **Fax:** 707-585-1363 krcb.org **Email:** viewer@krcb.org

Sacramento: KCRA (NBC) 3 Television Cir Sacramento CA 95814 **Phn:** 916-446-3333 **Fax:** 916-441-4050 www.kcra.com **Email:** newstips@kcra.com

Sacramento: KQCA (MY) 58 Television Cir Sacramento CA 95814 **Phn:** 916-447-5858 **Fax:** 916-441-4050 www.kcra.commy58 **Email:** kcranewstips@thekcrachannel.com

Sacramento: KTFK (SPN) 1710 Arden Way Sacramento CA 95815 **Phn:** 916-927-1900 **Fax:** 916-614-1906 www.univision.com **Email:** kuvsnews@univision.net

Sacramento: KTXL (FOX) 4655 Fruitridge Rd Sacramento CA 95820 **Phn:** 916-454-4422 **Fax:** 916-739-0559 fox40.com **Email:** fox40news@tribune.com

Sacramento: KUVS (SPN) 1710 Arden Way Sacramento CA 95815 **Phn:** 916-927-1900 **Fax:** 916-614-1906 www.univision.com **Email:** kuvsnews@univision.net

Sacramento: KVIE (PBS) 2030 W El Camino Ave Ste 100 Sacramento CA 95833 **Phn:** 916-929-5843 www.kvie.org **Email:** member@kvie.org

Sacramento: KXTV (ABC) 400 Broadway Sacramento CA 95818 **Phn:** 916-441-2345 **Fax:** 916-447-6107 www.news10.net **Email:** comments@news10.net

Salinas: KCBA (FOX) 1550 Moffett St Salinas CA 93905 **Phn:** 831-422-3500 **Fax:** 831-422-6448 www.kionrightnow.com **Email:** newstips@kionrightnow.com

Salinas: KION (CBS) 1550 Moffett St Salinas CA 93905 **Phn:** 831-784-1702 **Fax:** 831-422-6448 www.kionrightnow.com **Email:** newstips@kionrightnow.com

Salinas: KSBW (NBC) 238 John St Salinas CA 93901 **Phn:** 831-758-8888 **Fax:** 831-422-0124 www.ksbw.com **Email:** newsdirector@ksbw.com

San Bernardino: KVCR (PBS) 701 S Mount Vernon Ave San Bernardino CA 92410 **Phn:** 909-384-4444 **Fax:** 909-885-2116 kvcr.org **Email:** bholland@kvcr.org

San Diego: KBNT (SPN) 5770 Ruffin Rd San Diego CA 92123 **Phn:** 858-576-1919 **Fax:** 858-435-1503 www.univisionsandiego.com **Email:** lsandoval@entravision.com

San Diego: KFMB (CBS) 7677 Engineer Rd San Diego CA 92111 **Phn:** 858-571-8888 **Fax:** 858-560-0627 www.cbs8.com **Email:** news8@kfmb.com

San Diego: KGTV (ABC) 4600 Air Way San Diego CA 92102 **Phn:** 858-237-1010 **Fax:** 619-527-0369 www.10news.com **Email:** sean_kennedy@10news.com

San Diego: KNSD (NBC) 225 Broadway Ste 100 San Diego CA 92101 **Phn:** 619-231-3939 **Fax:** 619-578-0202 www.nbcsandiego.com **Email:** limsandiegonewstips@nbcuni.com

San Diego: KPBS (PBS) 5200 Campanile Dr San Diego CA 92182 **Phn:** 619-594-1515 **Fax:** 619-594-3787 www.kpbs.org **Email:** news@kpbs.org

San Diego: KSWB (FOX) 7191 Engineer Rd San Diego CA 92111 **Phn:** 858-492-9269 **Fax:** 858-573-6600 fox5sandiego.com **Email:** ssalgado@tribune.com

San Diego: KUSI (IND) 4575 Viewridge Ave San Diego CA 92123 **Phn:** 858-571-5151 **Fax:** 858-576-9317 www.kusi.com **Email:** news@kusi.com

San Diego: XETV (CW) 8253 Ronson Rd San Diego CA 92111 **Phn:** 858-279-6666 **Fax:** 858-279-0061 www.sandiego6.com **Email:** newstips@sandiego6.com

San Diego: XHAS (SPN) 5770 Ruffin Rd San Diego CA 92123 **Phn:** 858-874-3320 **Fax:** 858-435-1504 www.telemundo33.com **Email:** mwilder@entravision.com

San Francisco: KBCW (CW) 855 Battery St San Francisco CA 94111 **Phn:** 415-765-8144 **Fax:** 415-765-8844 cwsanfrancisco.cbslocal.com **Email:** newsdesk@kpix.com

San Francisco: KDTV (SPN) 50 Fremont St Fl 41 San Francisco CA 94105 **Phn:** 415-538-8000 **Fax:** 415-538-8002 www.univision.com **Email:** noticias14@univision.net

San Francisco: KGO (ABC) 900 Front St San Francisco CA 94111 **Phn:** 415-954-7777 **Fax:** 415-956-6402 abclocal.go.comkgo **Email:** abc7listens@kgo-tv.com

San Francisco: KOFY (IND) 2500 Marin St San Francisco CA 94124 **Phn:** 415-821-2020 **Fax:** 415-821-9158 www.kofytv.com **Email:** askkofy@kofytv.com

San Francisco: KPIX (CBS) 855 Battery St San Francisco CA 94111 **Phn:** 415-765-8610 **Fax:** 415-765-8916 sanfrancisco.cbslocal.com **Email:** kpixnewsmanagers@cbs.com

San Francisco: KQED (PBS) 2601 Mariposa St San Francisco CA 94110 **Phn:** 415-864-2000 **Fax:** 415-553-2241 www.kqed.org **Email:** tv@kqed.org

San Francisco: KRON (MY) 1001 Van Ness Ave San Francisco CA 94109 **Phn:** 415-441-4444 **Fax:** 415-561-8136 www.kron.com **Email:** 4listens@kron.com

San Francisco: KUNO (SPN) 1700 Montgomery St Ste 400 San Francisco CA 94111 **Phn:** 415-398-4242 **Fax:** 415-352-1800 www.ktnc.com **Email:** ventas@ktnc.com

San Jose: KNTV (NBC) 2450 N 1st St San Jose CA 95131 **Phn:** 408-432-6221 **Fax:** 408-432-4425 www.nbcbayarea.com

San Jose: KSTS (SPN) 2450 N 1st St San Jose CA 95131 **Phn:** 408-944-4848 www.telemundoareadelabahia.com **Email:** noticias@telemundoareadelabahia.com

San Jose: KTEH (PBS) 1585 Schallenberger Rd San Jose CA 95131 **Phn:** 408-795-5400 **Fax:** 408-995-5446 www.kqed.org **Email:** tv@kqed.org

San Luis Obispo: KSBY (NBC) 1772 Calle Joaquin San Luis Obispo CA 93405 **Phn:** 805-541-6666 **Fax:** 805-597-8520 www.ksby.com **Email:** news@ksby.com

San Mateo: KCSM (PBS) 1700 W Hillsdale Blvd San Mateo CA 94402 **Phn:** 650-574-6586 **Fax:** 650-524-6975 kcsm.org **Email:** tv@kcsm.net

Santa Ana: KDOC (IND) 625 N Grand Ave Santa Ana CA 92701 **Phn:** 949-442-9800 **Fax:** 949-261-5956 www.kdoctv.net **Email:** info@kdoc.tv

Santa Ana: KOCE (PBS) PO Box 25113 Santa Ana CA 92799 **Phn:** 714-241-4100 **Fax:** 714-668-9689 www.pbssocal.org **Email:** comments@pbssocal.org

Santa Barbara: KEYT (ABC) 730 Miramonte Dr Santa Barbara CA 93109 **Phn:** 805-882-3933 **Fax:** 805-882-3934 www.keyt.com **Email:** assignmentdesk@keyt.com

Santa Maria: KCOY (CBS) 1211 W McCoy Ln Santa Maria CA 93455 **Phn:** 805-925-1200 **Fax:** 805-349-9965 www.kcoy.com **Email:** news12@kcoy.com

Santa Maria: KKFX (FOX) 1211 W McCoy Ln Santa Maria CA 93455 **Phn:** 805-925-1200 **Fax:** 805-349-9965 www.kcoy.com **Email:** news12@kcoy.com

Santa Maria: KPMR (SPN) 1467 Fairway Dr Santa Maria CA 93455 **Phn:** 805-685-3800 **Fax:** 805-685-6892 www.kpmrtv.com **Email:** gquiroz@entravision.com

Santa Maria: KTAS (SPN) PO Box 172 Santa Maria CA 93456 **Phn:** 805-928-7700 **Fax:** 805-928-8606 **Email:** ktastv@fix.net

Santa Maria: KTSB (SPN) 1467 Fairway Dr Santa Maria CA 93455 **Phn:** 805-685-3800 **Fax:** 805-685-6892 www.univision.com **Email:** gquiroz@entravision.com

Santa Rosa: KFTY (IND) 533 Mendocino Ave Santa Rosa CA 95401 **Phn:** 707-526-5050 **Fax:** 707-526-7429

Studio City: KCAL (CBS) 4200 Radford Ave Studio City CA 91604 **Phn:** 818-655-2000 **Fax:** 818-655-2221 losangeles.cbslocal.com **Email:** kcbstvnews@cbs.com

Studio City: KCBS (CBS) 4200 Radford Ave Studio City CA 91604 **Phn:** 818-655-2000 **Fax:** 818-655-2221 losangeles.cbslocal.com **Email:** kcbstvnews@cbs.com

Thousand Palms: KPSP (CBS) 31276 Dunham Way Thousand Palms CA 92276 **Phn:** 760-343-5700 **Fax:** 760-343-5793 www.kesq.com **Email:** bsmith@kesq.com

CALIFORNIA TV STATIONS

Victorville: KHIZ (IND) 15605 Village Dr Victorville CA 92394 **Phn:** 760-241-6464 **Fax:** 760-241-0056 www.khiztv.com

West Sacramento: KMAX (CW) 2713 Kovr Dr West Sacramento CA 95605 **Phn:** 916-374-1313 **Fax:** 916-374-1304 sacramento.cbslocal.com **Email:** news@kovt.com

West Sacramento: KOVR (CBS) 2713 Kovr Dr West Sacramento CA 95605 **Phn:** 916-374-1313 **Fax:** 916-374-1304 cbs13.com

COLORADO

Arvada: KRMT (REL) 12014 W 64th Ave Arvada CO 80004 **Phn:** 303-423-4141 **Fax:** 303-424-0571

Aurora: KPXC (ION) 3001 S Jamaica Ct Ste 200 Aurora CO 80014 **Phn:** 303-751-5959 **Fax:** 303-751-5993 www.iontelevision.com

Colorado Springs: KGHB (SPN) 118 N Tejon St Ste 210 Colorado Springs CO 80903 **Phn:** 719-632-2943 **Fax:** 719-632-8220 www.entravision.com

Colorado Springs: KKTV (CBS) 3100 N Nevada Ave Colorado Springs CO 80907 **Phn:** 719-634-2844 **Fax:** 719-634-3741 www.kktv.com **Email:** news@kktv.com

Colorado Springs: KRDO (ABC) 399 S 8th St Colorado Springs CO 80905 **Phn:** 719-632-1515 **Fax:** 719-575-0487 www.krdo.com **Email:** krdonews@krdo.com

Colorado Springs: KWHD (SPN) 1710 Briargate Blvd Ste 423 Colorado Springs CO 80920 **Phn:** 303-799-8853 **Fax:** 303-792-5303 lesea.com **Email:** dsmith@lesea.com

Colorado Springs: KXRM (FOX) 560 Wooten Rd Colorado Springs CO 80915 **Phn:** 719-596-2100 **Fax:** 719-591-1844 www.fox21news.com **Email:** news@kxrm.com

Denver: KBDI (PBS) 2900 Welton St Ste 100 Denver CO 80205 **Phn:** 303-296-1212 **Fax:** 303-296-6650 www.cpt12.org **Email:** bhaug@kbdi.org

Denver: KCEC (SPN) 1907 Mile High Stadium Wt Cir Denver CO 80204 **Phn:** 303-832-0050 **Fax:** 303-832-3410 www.somosnoticiascolorado.com **Email:** lcollins@entravision.com

Denver: KCNC (CBS) 1044 Lincoln St Denver CO 80203 **Phn:** 303-861-4444 **Fax:** 303-830-6380 denver.cbslocal.com **Email:** jmontgomery@cbs.com

Denver: KDEN (SPN) 1120 Lincoln St Ste 800 Denver CO 80203 **Phn:** 303-832-0402 **Fax:** 303-832-0777 **Email:** targuello@telemundo.com

Denver: KDVR (FOX) 100 E Speer Blvd Denver CO 80203 **Phn:** 303-595-3131 **Fax:** 303-566-7631 kdvr.com

Denver: KMGH (ABC) 123 E Speer Blvd Denver CO 80203 **Phn:** 303-832-7777 **Fax:** 303-832-0119 www.thedenverchannel.com

Denver: KRMA (PBS) 1089 Bannock St Denver CO 80204 **Phn:** 303-892-6666 **Fax:** 303-620-5600 www.rmpbs.org

Denver: KTFD (SPN) 1907 Mile High Stadium W Cir Denver CO 80204 **Phn:** 303-832-0050 **Fax:** 303-832-3410 www.somosnoticiascolorado.com **Email:** lcollins@entravision.com

Denver: KTVD (MY) 500 E Speer Blvd Denver CO 80203 **Phn:** 303-871-9999 **Fax:** 303-698-4700 www.my20denver.com **Email:** patti.dennis@9news.com

Denver: KUSA (NBC) 500 E Speer Blvd Denver CO 80203 **Phn:** 303-871-9999 **Fax:** 303-698-4700 www.9news.com **Email:** patti.dennis@9news.com

Denver: KWGN (CW) 100 E Speer Blvd Denver CO 80203 **Phn:** 303-595-3131 **Fax:** 303-566-7631 kwgn.com **Email:** greg.nieto@kdvr.com

Grand Junction: KJCT (ABC) 8 Foresight Cir Grand Junction CO 81505 **Phn:** 970-245-8880 **Fax:** 970-245-8249 www.kjct8.com **Email:** newsroom@kjct8.com

Grand Junction: KKCO (NBC) 2531 Blichman Ave Grand Junction CO 81505 **Phn:** 970-243-1111 **Fax:** 970-243-1770 www.nbc11news.com **Email:** tips@nbc11news.com

Grand Junction: KREX (CBS) 345 Hillcrest Dr Grand Junction CO 81501 **Phn:** 970-242-5000 **Fax:** 970-243-6397 www.krextv.com **Email:** news@krextv.com

Grand Junction: KRMJ (PBS) 2520 Blichman Ave Grand Junction CO 81505 **Phn:** 970-245-1818 **Fax:** 970-255-2900 www.rmpbs.org

Pueblo: KOAA (NBC) 2200 7th Ave Pueblo CO 81003 **Phn:** 719-544-5781 **Fax:** 719-295-6655 www.koaa.com **Email:** news@koaa.com

Pueblo: KTSC (PBS) 2200 Bonforte Blvd Pueblo CO 81001 **Phn:** 719-543-8800 **Fax:** 719-549-2208 www.rmpbs.org

CONNECTICUT

Hartford: WEDH (PBS) 1049 Asylum Ave Hartford CT 06105 **Phn:** 860-278-5310 **Fax:** 860-275-7403 www.cpbn.org **Email:** jwhitehead@cptv.org

Hartford: WRDM (SPN) 886 Maple Ave Hartford CT 06114 **Phn:** 860-956-1303 **Fax:** 860-956-6834 www.zgsgroup.com

Hartford: WTIC (FOX) 20 Church St Hartford CT 06103 **Phn:** 860-527-6161 **Fax:** 860-293-0178 www.ctnow.com **Email:** feedback@ctnow.com

Hartford: WTXX (CW) 20 Church St Hartford CT 06103 **Phn:** 860-527-6161 **Fax:** 860-293-0178 www.ct.com **Email:** newsteam@fox61.com

Hartford: WUVN (SPN) 1 Constitution Plz Fl 7 Hartford CT 06103 **Phn:** 860-278-1818 **Fax:** 860-278-1811 www.wuvntv.com **Email:** uarrigoitia@entravision.com

New Haven: WCTX (MY) 8 Elm St New Haven CT 06510 **Phn:** 203-782-5900 **Fax:** 203-787-9698 www.wtnh.com **Email:** news8@wtnh.com

New Haven: WTNH (ABC) 8 Elm St New Haven CT 06510 **Phn:** 203-784-8888 **Fax:** 203-787-9698 www.wtnh.com **Email:** news8@wtnh.com

New London: WHPX (ION) 3 Shaws Cv Ste 226 New London CT 06320 **Phn:** 860-444-2626 **Fax:** 860-440-2601 www.iontelevision.com **Email:** deborahreed-iler@ionmedia.com

New London: WPXQ (ION) 3 Shaws Cv Ste 226 New London CT 06320 **Phn:** 860-444-2626 **Fax:** 860-440-2601 www.iontelevision.com **Email:** deborahreed-iler@ionmedia.com

Rocky Hill: WFSB (CBS) 333 Capital Blvd Rocky Hill CT 06067 **Phn:** 860-728-3333 **Fax:** 860-728-0263 www.wfsb.com **Email:** wfsb@wfsb.com

West Hartford: WVIT (NBC) 1422 New Britain Ave West Hartford CT 06110 **Phn:** 860-521-3030 **Fax:** 860-521-4860 www.nbcconnecticut.com **Email:** tips@nbcconnecticut.com

DISTRICT OF COLUMBIA

Washington: WDCA (MY) 5151 Wisconsin Ave NW Fl 2 Washington DC 20016 **Phn:** 202-244-5151 **Fax:** 202-895-3132 www.my20dc.com **Email:** wttg.desk@foxtv.com

Washington: WDCW (CW) 2121 Wisconsin Ave NW Ste 350 Washington DC 20007 **Phn:** 202-965-5050 **Fax:** 202-965-0050 dc50tv.com **Email:** kbelle@tribune.com

Washington: WFDC (SPN) 101 Constitution Ave NW Ste L100 Washington DC 20001 **Phn:** 202-522-8640 **Fax:** 202-898-1960 www.tvwfdc.com **Email:** kmendez@entravision.com

Washington: WHUT (PBS) 2222 4th St NW Washington DC 20059 **Phn:** 202-806-3200 **Fax:** 202-806-3300 www.whut.org

Washington: WMDO (SPN) 101 Constitution Ave NW Ste L100 Washington DC 20001 **Phn:** 202-522-8640 **Fax:** 202-898-1960 www.univisiondc.com **Email:** eclavijo@entravision.com

Washington: WRC (NBC) 4001 Nebraska Ave NW Washington DC 20016 **Phn:** 202-885-4000 **Fax:** 202-885-4104 www.nbcwashington.com **Email:** news4pr@nbcuni.com

Washington: WTTG (FOX) 5151 Wisconsin Ave NW Fl 1 Washington DC 20016 **Phn:** 202-244-5151 **Fax:** 202-895-3132 www.myfoxdc.com **Email:** fox5tips@wttg.com

Washington: WUSA (CBS) 4100 Wisconsin Ave NW Washington DC 20016 **Phn:** 202-895-5999 **Fax:** 202-364-4973 www.wusa9.com **Email:** 9news@wusatv9.com

FLORIDA

Altamonte Springs: WVEN (SPN) 523 Douglas Ave Altamonte Springs FL 32714 **Phn:** 407-774-2626 **Fax:** 407-774-3384 www.wventv.com **Email:** iberrios@entravision.com

Cape Coral: WFTX (FOX) 621 SW Pine Island Rd Cape Coral FL 33991 **Phn:** 239-574-3636 **Fax:** 239-574-4803 www.fox4now.com **Email:** news@fox4now.com

Clearwater: WCLF (REL) PO Box 6922 Clearwater FL 33758 **Phn:** 727-535-5622 **Fax:** 727-531-2497 www.ctnonline.com **Email:** comments@ctntv.net

Clearwater: WXPX (ION) 14444 66th St N Clearwater FL 33764 **Phn:** 727-479-1053 **Fax:** 727-479-1180 www.iontelevision.com

Cocoa: WBCC (PBS) 1519 Clearlake Rd Cocoa FL 32922 **Phn:** 321-433-7110 **Fax:** 321-433-7154 www.wbcctv.org **Email:** wbcc@brevardcc.edu

Daytona Beach: WDSC (PBS) PO Box 9245 Daytona Beach FL 32120 **Phn:** 386-506-4415 **Fax:** 386-506-4427

Doral: WAMI (SPN) 9405 NW 41st St Doral FL 33178 **Phn:** 305-471-3944 **Fax:** 305-471-3948 www.univision.com **Email:** aramos@univision.net

Doral: WBFS (MY) 8900 NW 18th Ter Doral FL 33172 **Phn:** 305-621-3333 **Fax:** 305-477-3040

Doral: WFOR (CBS) 8900 NW 18th Ter Doral FL 33172 **Phn:** 305-591-4444 **Fax:** 305-477-3040 miami.cbslocal.com **Email:** wfornews@wfor.cbs.com

Doral: WGEN (SPN) 1800 NW 94th Ave Doral FL 33172 **Phn:** 305-860-2544 **Fax:** 305-471-0122 www.mundofox8miami.com

Doral: WLTV (SPN) 9405 NW 41st St Doral FL 33178 **Phn:** 305-471-3900 **Fax:** 305-471-4236 www.univision.com **Email:** lfrocha@univision.net

Fort Lauderdale: WSFL (CW) 200 E Las Olas Blvd Fl 11 Fort Lauderdale FL 33301 **Phn:** 954-627-7300 **Fax:** 954-355-5200 www.sfltv.net **Email:** feedback@sfltv.net

Fort Myers: WBBH (NBC) 3719 Central Ave Fort Myers FL 33901 **Phn:** 239-939-2020 **Fax:** 239-939-3244 www.nbc-2.com **Email:** newstips@nbc-2.com

Fort Myers: WGCU (PBS) 10501 Fgcu Blvd S Fort Myers FL 33965 **Phn:** 239-590-2300 **Fax:** 239-590-2520 wgcu.org **Email:** wgcunews@wgcu.org

Fort Myers: WINK (CBS) 2824 Palm Beach Blvd Fort Myers FL 33916 **Phn:** 239-334-1111 **Fax:** 239-338-4383 www.winknews.com **Email:** assignments@winktv.com

Fort Myers: WXCW (CW) 2824 Palm Beach Blvd Fort Myers FL 33916 **Phn:** 239-479-5500 **Fax:** 239-479-5592 **Email:** jim.schwartzel@cw6mail.com

DC TV STATIONS

Fort Myers: WZVN (ABC) 3719 Central Ave Fort Myers FL 33901 **Phn:** 239-939-2020 **Fax:** 239-939-3244 www.abc-7.com **Email:** newstips@abc-7.com

Fort Pierce: WTCE (REL) 3601 N 25th St Fort Pierce FL 34946 **Phn:** 772-489-2701 **Fax:** 772-489-6833 www.wtce.tv

Gainesville: WCJB (ABC) 6220 NW 43rd St Gainesville FL 32653 **Phn:** 352-377-2020 **Fax:** 352-371-0747 www.wcjb.com **Email:** tv20news@wcjb.com

Gainesville: WGFL (CBS) 1703 NW 80th Blvd Gainesville FL 32606 **Phn:** 352-332-1128 **Fax:** 352-332-1506 www.mygtn.tv **Email:** news@mygtn.tv

Gainesville: WMYG (MY) 1703 NW 80th Blvd Gainesville FL 32606 **Phn:** 352-332-1128 **Fax:** 352-332-8480 www.mygtn.tv **Email:** sedwards@mygtn.tv

Gainesville: WUFT (PBS) PO Box 118405 Gainesville FL 32611 **Phn:** 352-392-5551 **Fax:** 352-392-5720 www.wuft.org

Hollywood: WHFT (REL) 3324 Pembroke Rd Hollywood FL 33021 **Phn:** 954-962-1700 **Fax:** 954-962-2817 www.tbn.org **Email:** whft@tbn.org

Jacksonville: WAWS (FOX) 11700 Central Pkwy Unit 2 Jacksonville FL 32224 **Phn:** 904-642-3030 **Fax:** 904-642-5665 www.fox30jax.com **Email:** programming@fox30online.com

Jacksonville: WCWJ (CW) 9117 Hogan Rd Jacksonville FL 32216 **Phn:** 904-641-1700 **Fax:** 904-642-7201 yourjax.com **Email:** dhall@yourjax.com

Jacksonville: WJCT (PBS) 100 Festival Park Ave Jacksonville FL 32202 **Phn:** 904-353-7770 **Fax:** 904-358-6352 www.wjct.org **Email:** kfeagins@wjct.org

Jacksonville: WJEB (REL) 3101 Emerson Expy Jacksonville FL 32207 **Phn:** 904-399-8413 **Fax:** 904-399-8423 www.wjeb.org **Email:** joy@wjeb.org

Jacksonville: WJXT (CBS) 4 Broadcast Pl Jacksonville FL 32207 **Phn:** 904-399-4000 **Fax:** 904-393-9822 www.news4jax.com **Email:** alert@news4jax.com

Jacksonville: WJXX (ABC) 1070 E Adams St Jacksonville FL 32202 **Phn:** 904-354-1212 **Fax:** 904-633-8899 www.firstcoastnews.com **Email:** news@firstcoastnews.com

Jacksonville: WTEV (CBS) 11700 Central Pkwy Jacksonville FL 32224 **Phn:** 904-642-3030 **Fax:** 904-642-5665 www.actionnewsjax.com **Email:** news@actionnewsjax.com

Jacksonville: WTLV (NBC) 1070 E Adams St Jacksonville FL 32202 **Phn:** 904-354-1212 **Fax:** 904-633-8899 www.firstcoastnews.com **Email:** news@firstcoastnews.com

Lake Mary: WOFL (FOX) 35 Skyline Dr Lake Mary FL 32746 **Phn:** 407-644-3535 **Fax:** 407-741-5189 www.myfoxorlando.com **Email:** news@foxwofl.com

Lake Mary: WOGX (FOX) 35 Skyline Dr Lake Mary FL 32746 **Phn:** 407-644-3535 **Fax:** 407-741-5189 www.wogx.com **Email:** news@foxwofl.com

Lake Mary: WRBW (MY) 35 Skyline Dr Lake Mary FL 32746 **Phn:** 407-644-3535 **Fax:** 407-741-5189 www.my65orlando.com **Email:** news@foxwofl.com

Lake Mary: WTGL (REL) 31 Skyline Dr Lake Mary FL 32746 **Phn:** 407-215-6745 **Fax:** 407-215-6789 www.tv45.org **Email:** info@tv45.org

Melbourne: WOTF (SPN) 739 North Dr Ste C Melbourne FL 32934 **Phn:** 321-254-4343 **Fax:** 321-254-9343 www.univision.com

Miami: WLRN (PBS) 172 NE 15th St Miami FL 33132 **Phn:** 305-995-1717 **Fax:** 305-995-2299 wlrn.org **Email:** info@wlrn.org

Midway: WTLH (FOX) PO Box 949 Midway FL 32343 **Phn:** 850-576-4990 **Fax:** 850-576-0200 www.myfoxtallahassee.com **Email:** fox49@fox49.com

Midway: WTXL (ABC) 1620 Commerce Blvd Midway FL 32343 **Phn:** 850-893-3127 **Fax:** 850-575-7838 www.wtxl.com **Email:** abc27news@wtxl.tv

Miramar: WSCV (SPN) 15000 SW 27th St Miramar FL 33027 **Phn:** 305-888-5151 **Fax:** 954-622-6107 www.telemundo51.com **Email:** reporte@telemundo51.com

Miramar: WTVJ (NBC) 15000 SW 27th St Miramar FL 33027 **Phn:** 954-622-6000 **Fax:** 954-622-6107 www.nbcmiami.com **Email:** wtvjnews@nbc.com

North Bay Village: WSVN (FOX) 1401 79th Street Cswy North Bay Village FL 33141 **Phn:** 305-751-6692 **Fax:** 305-795-2746 www.wsvn.com **Email:** newsdesk@wsvn.com

North Miami: WPBT (PBS) 14901 NE 20th Ave North Miami FL 33181 **Phn:** 305-949-8321 **Fax:** 305-949-9772 www.wpbt2.org **Email:** programming@channel2.org

Orlando: WACX (REL) PO Box 608040 Orlando FL 32860 **Phn:** 407-263-4040 www.wacxtv.com

Orlando: WFTV (ABC) 490 E South St Orlando FL 32801 **Phn:** 407-841-9000 **Fax:** 407-481-2891 www.wftv.com **Email:** kevin.oliver@wftv.com

Orlando: WHLV (REL) 4525 Vineland Rd Ste 210 Orlando FL 32811 **Phn:** 407-423-5200 www.tbn.org **Email:** whlv@tbn.org

Orlando: WKMG (CBS) 4466 N John Young Pkwy Orlando FL 32804 **Phn:** 407-521-1200 **Fax:** 407-298-2122 www.clickorlando.com **Email:** newstips@clickorlando.com

Orlando: WMFE (PBS) 11510 E Colonial Dr Orlando FL 32817 **Phn:** 407-273-2300 www.wmfe.org **Email:** wmfenews@wmfe.org

Orlando: WOPX (ION) 7091 Grand National Dr Ste 100 Orlando FL 32819 **Phn:** 407-370-5600 **Fax:** 407-363-1759 www.iontelevision.com **Email:** connyfiala@ionmedia.com

Orlando: WRDQ (IND) 490 E South St Orlando FL 32801 **Phn:** 407-841-9000 **Fax:** 407-481-2891 www.wftv.com **Email:** mark.boyle@wftv.com

Orlando: WTMO (SPN) 1650 Sand Lake Rd Ste 340 Orlando FL 32809 **Phn:** 407-888-2288 **Fax:** 407-888-3486 www.zgsgroup.com

Palm Beach Gardens: WPBF (ABC) 3970 RCA Blvd Ste 7007 Palm Beach Gardens FL 33410 **Phn:** 561-694-2525 **Fax:** 561-625-0538 www.wpbf.com **Email:** wpbfnews@hearst.com

Palm Springs: WFGC (REL) 1900 S Congress Ave Ste A Palm Springs FL 33406 **Phn:** 561-642-3361 **Fax:** 561-967-5961 www.wfgctelevision.com **Email:** gm@wfgc.com

Panama City: WCAY (IND) 8317 Front Beach Rd Ste 23 Panama City FL 32407 **Phn:** 850-234-2773 **Fax:** 850-234-1179 www.tripsmarter.com **Email:** localnews@tripsmarter.com

Panama City: WJHG (NBC) 8195 Front Beach Rd Panama City FL 32407 **Phn:** 850-234-7777 **Fax:** 850-234-5771 www.wjhg.com **Email:** news@wjhg.com

Panama City: WMBB (ABC) 613 Harrison Ave Panama City FL 32401 **Phn:** 850-769-2313 **Fax:** 850-872-0922 www.wmbb.com **Email:** news@wmbb.com

Panama City: WPGX (FOX) 700 W 23rd St #C-28 Panama City FL 32405 **Phn:** 850-215-6500 **Fax:** 850-784-1773 **Email:** dramos@wpgxfox28.com

FLORIDA TV STATIONS

Pembroke Park: WPLG (ABC) 3401 Hallandale Beach Blvd Pembroke Park FL 33023 **Phn:** 954-364-2500 **Fax:** 954-364-2935 www.local10.com **Email:** bpohovey@wplg.com

Pensacola: WBQP (IND) 3101 N R St Pensacola FL 32505 **Phn:** 850-433-1210 **Fax:** 850-433-2537 www.wbqp.com **Email:** wbqp@wbqp.com

Pensacola: WEAR (ABC) 4990 Mobile Hwy Pensacola FL 32506 **Phn:** 850-456-3333 **Fax:** 850-455-8972 www.weartv.com **Email:** news@weartv.com

Pensacola: WFGX (MY) 4990 Mobile Hwy Pensacola FL 32506 **Phn:** 850-456-3333 **Fax:** 850-455-8972 www.wfgxtv.com **Email:** comments@weartv.com

Pensacola: WHBR (REL) 6500 Pensacola Blvd Pensacola FL 32505 **Phn:** 850-473-8633 **Fax:** 850-473-8631 www.whbr.org **Email:** dmayo@whbr.org

Pensacola: WSRE (PBS) 1000 College Blvd Pensacola FL 32504 **Phn:** 850-484-1200 **Fax:** 850-484-1255 www.wsre.org

Punta Gorda: WRXY (REL) 40000 Horseshoe Rd Punta Gorda FL 33982 **Phn:** 239-543-7200 **Fax:** 239-543-6800 www.ctn10.com **Email:** paullodato@wrxytv.com

Riviera Beach: WBWP (SPN) 7354 Central Industrial Dr Ste 110 Riviera Beach FL 33404 **Phn:** 561-863-0417 **Fax:** 561-863-0418 www.canal57.com **Email:** uzal@msn.com

Saint Petersburg: WTOG (CW) 365 105th Ter NE Saint Petersburg FL 33716 **Phn:** 727-576-4444 **Fax:** 727-570-4458 cwtampa.cbslocal.com **Email:** cw44@wtogtv.com

Saint Petersburg: WTSP (CBS) 11450 Gandy Blvd N Saint Petersburg FL 33702 **Phn:** 727-577-1010 **Fax:** 727-576-6924 www.wtsp.com

Sarasota: WWSB (ABC) 1477 10th St Sarasota FL 34236 **Phn:** 941-552-0777 **Fax:** 941-923-8709 www.mysuncoast.com **Email:** news@mysuncoast.com

Sunrise: WPXM (ION) 13801 NW 14th St Sunrise FL 33323 **Phn:** 954-703-1921 **Fax:** 954-858-1848 www.iontelevision.com **Email:** jamesjanuszka@ionmedia.com

Sunrise: WPXP (ION) 13801 NW 14th St Sunrise FL 33323 **Phn:** 954-703-1921 **Fax:** 954-858-1848 www.iontelevision.com

Tallahassee: WCTV (CBS) 1801 Halstead Blvd Tallahassee FL 32309 **Phn:** 850-893-6666 **Fax:** 850-668-3851 www.wctv.tv **Email:** news@wctv.tv

Tallahassee: WFSU (PBS) 1600 Red Barber Plz Tallahassee FL 32310 **Phn:** 850-487-3170 **Fax:** 850-487-3093 www.wfsu.org **Email:** wfsu-tv@mailer.fsu.edu

Tallahassee: WTWC (NBC) 8440 Deer Lk S Tallahassee FL 32312 **Phn:** 850-893-4140 **Fax:** 850-893-6974 www.wtwc40.com **Email:** clemon@wtwc40.com

Tampa: WEDU (PBS) 1300 N Boulevard Tampa FL 33607 **Phn:** 813-254-9338 **Fax:** 813-253-0826 www.wedu.org **Email:** pwebb@wedu.org

Tampa: WFLA (NBC) PO Box 1410 Tampa FL 33601 **Phn:** 813-228-8888 **Fax:** 813-225-2770 www.wfla.com **Email:** news@wfla.com

Tampa: WFTS (ABC) 4045 N Himes Ave Tampa FL 33607 **Phn:** 813-354-2828 **Fax:** 813-870-2828 www.abcactionnews.com **Email:** newstips@wfts.com

Tampa: WFTT (SPN) 2610 W Hillsborough Ave Tampa FL 33614 **Phn:** 813-872-6262 **Fax:** 813-998-3608 www.univision.com **Email:** lgonzalez@entravision.com

Tampa: WMOR (IND) 7201 E Hillsborough Ave Tampa FL 33610 **Phn:** 813-626-3232 **Fax:** 813-626-1961 www.mor-tv.com **Email:** dvlawrence@hearst.com

Tampa: WTTA (MY) 7622 Bald Cypress Pl Tampa FL 33614 **Phn:** 813-886-9882 **Fax:** 813-880-8100 www.great38.com **Email:** promotions@mytvtampabay.com

Tampa: WTVT (FOX) 3213 W Kennedy Blvd Tampa FL 33609 **Phn:** 813-876-1313 **Fax:** 813-871-3135 www.myfoxtampabay.com **Email:** news@wtvt.com

Tampa: WUSF (PBS) 4202 E Fowler Ave Stop TVB100 Tampa FL 33620 **Phn:** 813-905-6900 **Fax:** 813-974-4806 www.wusf.usf.edu **Email:** news@wusf.org

Tampa: WVEA (SPN) 2610 W Hillsborough Ave Tampa FL 33614 **Phn:** 813-872-6262 **Fax:** 813-998-3660 www.wveatv.com **Email:** lgonzalez@entravision.com

West Palm Beach: WFLX (FOX) 1100 Banyan Blvd West Palm Beach FL 33401 **Phn:** 561-845-2929 **Fax:** 561-842-5642 www.wflx.com **Email:** fox29morningnews@wflx.com

West Palm Beach: WPEC (CBS) 1100 Fairfield Dr West Palm Beach FL 33407 **Phn:** 561-844-1212 **Fax:** 561-842-1212 www.cbs12.com **Email:** newstips@cbs12.com

West Palm Beach: WPTV (NBC) 1100 Banyan Blvd West Palm Beach FL 33401 **Phn:** 561-655-5455 **Fax:** 561-653-5719 www.wptv.com **Email:** newstips@wptv.com

West Palm Beach: WTCN (MY) 1700 Palm Beach Lakes Blvd Ste 150 West Palm Beach FL 33401 **Phn:** 561-681-3434 wearewestpalm.com **Email:** rbutterfield@sbgnet.com

West Palm Beach: WTVX (CW) 1700 Palm Beach Lakes Blvd Ste 150 West Palm Beach FL 33401 **Phn:** 561-681-3434 wearewestpalm.com **Email:** info@wtvx.com

West Palm Beach: WXEL (PBS) PO Box 6607 West Palm Beach FL 33405 **Phn:** 561-737-8000 www.wxel.org **Email:** info@wxel.org

Winter Park: WESH (NBC) 1021 N Wymore Rd Winter Park FL 32789 **Phn:** 407-645-2222 **Fax:** 407-539-7948 www.wesh.com **Email:** wesh2news@gmail.com

Winter Park: WKCF (CW) 1021 N Wymore Rd Winter Park FL 32789 **Phn:** 407-645-2222 www.wesh.comcw18 **Email:** wesh2news@gmail.com

GEORGIA

Albany: WALB (NBC) 1709 Stuart Ave Albany GA 31707 **Phn:** 229-446-1010 **Fax:** 229-446-4000 www.walb.com **Email:** news@walb.com

Albany: WFXL (FOX) PO Box 4050 Albany GA 31706 **Phn:** 229-435-3100 **Fax:** 229-903-8240 www.mysouthwestga.com **Email:** jmcwilliams@wfxl.com

Athens: WNEG (CBS) 120 Hooper St Athens GA 30602 **Phn:** 706-886-0032 **Fax:** 706-282-5001

Atlanta: WAGA (FOX) 1551 Briarcliff Rd NE Atlanta GA 30306 **Phn:** 404-875-5555 **Fax:** 404-898-0238 www.myfoxatlanta.com

Atlanta: WATL (MY) 1 Monroe Pl NE Atlanta GA 30324 **Phn:** 404-881-3600 **Fax:** 404-881-3635 www.myatltv.com **Email:** news@11alive.com

Atlanta: WGCL (CBS) 425 14th St NW Atlanta GA 30318 **Phn:** 404-325-4646 **Fax:** 404-327-3004 www.cbsatlanta.com **Email:** cbs46news@cbs46.com

Atlanta: WGTV (PBS) 260 14th St NW Atlanta GA 30318 **Phn:** 404-685-2400 **Fax:** 404-685-2602 www.gpb.org **Email:** ask@gpb.org

Atlanta: WPBA (PBS) 740 Bismark Rd NE Atlanta GA 30324 **Phn:** 678-686-0321 **Fax:** 678-686-0356 www.pba.org

Atlanta: WSB (ABC) 1601 W Peachtree St NE Atlanta GA 30309 **Phn:** 404-897-7000 **Fax:** 404-897-7370 www.wsbtv.com **Email:** talk2us@wsbtv.com

Atlanta: WUPA (CW) 2700 Northeast Expy NE Atlanta GA 30345 **Phn:** 404-325-6929 **Fax:** 404-728-4624 cwatlanta.cbslocal.com **Email:** info@cwatlantatv.com

Atlanta: WUVG (SPN) 3350 Peachtree Rd NE Ste 1250 Atlanta GA 30326 **Phn:** 404-926-2300 **Fax:** 404-926-2320 atlanta.univision.com **Email:** noticias34atlanta@univision.net

Atlanta: WXIA (NBC) 1 Monroe Pl NE Atlanta GA 30324 **Phn:** 404-892-1611 **Fax:** 404-881-0675 www.11alive.com **Email:** news@11alive.com

Augusta: WAGT (NBC) 1336 Augusta West Parkway Augusta GA 30909 **Phn:** 706-826-0026 **Fax:** 706-724-4028 www.nbc26.tv **Email:** mrosen@nbc26.tv

Augusta: WFXG (FOX) 3933 Washington Rd Augusta GA 30907 **Phn:** 706-650-5400 **Fax:** 706-650-8411 www.wfxg.com **Email:** foxit2us@wfxg.com

Augusta: WJBF (ABC) 1001 Reynolds St Augusta GA 30901 **Phn:** 706-722-6664 **Fax:** 706-722-0022 www.wjbf.com **Email:** mrosen@wjbf.com

Augusta: WRDW (CBS) PO Box 1212 Augusta GA 30903 **Phn:** 803-278-1212 **Fax:** 803-442-4561 www.wrdw.com **Email:** newsroom@wrdw.com

Brunswick: WPXC (ION) 7434 Blythe Island Hwy Brunswick GA 31523 **Phn:** 912-267-0021 **Fax:** 912-261-9582 www.iontelevision.com **Email:** nancyoconnor@ionmedia.com

Columbus: WLTZ (NBC) 6140 Buena Vista Rd Columbus GA 31907 **Phn:** 706-561-3838 **Fax:** 706-221-3889 www.wltz.com **Email:** wltz@wltz.com

Columbus: WRBL (CBS) 1350 13th Ave Columbus GA 31901 **Phn:** 706-323-3333 **Fax:** 706-323-0841 www.wrbl.com **Email:** news@wrbl.com

Columbus: WTVM (ABC) PO Box 1848 Columbus GA 31902 **Phn:** 706-324-6471 **Fax:** 706-327-0179 www.wtvm.com **Email:** newsrelease@wtvm.com

Columbus: WXTX (FOX) PO Box 1848 Columbus GA 31902 **Phn:** 706-324-6471 **Fax:** 706-327-0179 www.wtvm.com **Email:** jmcdowell@wxtx.com

Cordele: WSST (IND) 112 S 7th St Cordele GA 31015 **Phn:** 229-273-0001 **Fax:** 229-273-8894 www.wsst.com **Email:** wsst_dt@bellsouth.net

Decatur: WHSG (REL) 1550 Agape Way Decatur GA 30035 **Phn:** 404-288-1156 **Fax:** 404-288-5613 www.tbn.org **Email:** dcasoria@tbn.org

Macon: WGNM (REL) 178 Steven Dr Macon GA 31210 **Phn:** 478-474-8400 **Fax:** 478-474-4777 wgnm.com **Email:** gm@wgnm.com

Macon: WGXA (FOX) PO Box 340 Macon GA 31202 **Phn:** 478-745-2424 **Fax:** 478-745-6057 www.newscentralga.com **Email:** marcnash@fox24.com

Macon: WMAZ (CBS) 1314 Gray Hwy Macon GA 31211 **Phn:** 478-752-1313 **Fax:** 478-752-1429 www.13wmaz.com **Email:** eyewitnessnews@13wmaz.com

Macon: WMGT (NBC) PO Box 4328 Macon GA 31208 **Phn:** 478-745-4141 **Fax:** 478-742-2626 www.41nbc.com **Email:** news@41nbc.com

Macon: WPGA (ABC) 1691 Forsyth St Macon GA 31201 **Phn:** 478-745-5858 **Fax:** 478-745-5800 www.wpga58.com **Email:** dhart@wpga.tv

Marietta: WPXA (ION) 200 Cobb Pkwy N Ste 114 Marietta GA 30062 **Phn:** 770-919-0575 **Fax:** 770-919-9621 www.iontelevision.com

Moultrie: WSWG (NBC) PO Box 1987 Moultrie GA 31776 **Phn:** 229-985-1340 **Fax:** 229-985-7549 www.wswg.tv **Email:** henry.brigmond@wswgtv.com

Norcross: WATC (IND) 1862 Enterprise Dr Norcross GA 30093 **Phn:** 770-300-9828 **Fax:** 770-300-9838 watc.tv **Email:** creative1atlanta@aol.com

Savannah: WGSA (CW) 401 Mall Blvd Ste 201B Savannah GA 31406 **Phn:** 912-692-8000 **Fax:** 912-692-0400

Savannah: WJCL (ABC) 10001 Abercorn St Savannah GA 31406 **Phn:** 912-925-0022 **Fax:** 912-921-2235 www.thecoastalsource.com **Email:** breakingnews@thecoastalsource.com

Savannah: WSAV (NBC) 1430 E Victory Dr Savannah GA 31404 **Phn:** 912-651-0300 **Fax:** 912-651-0320 www.wsav.com **Email:** mail@wsav.com

Savannah: WTGS (FOX) 10001 Abercorn St Savannah GA 31406 **Phn:** 912-925-0022 **Fax:** 912-921-2235 www.thecoastalsource.com **Email:** breakingnews@thecoastalsource.com

Savannah: WTOC (CBS) PO Box 8086 Savannah GA 31412 **Phn:** 912-234-1111 **Fax:** 912-232-4945 www.wtoc.com **Email:** newsrelease@wtoc.com

HAWAII

Honolulu: KAAH (REL) 1152 Smith St Honolulu HI 96817 **Phn:** 808-521-5826 **Fax:** 808-599-6238 www.tbn.org **Email:** kaah@tbn.org

Honolulu: KBFD (IND) 1188 Bishop St Ph 1 Honolulu HI 96813 **Phn:** 808-521-8066 **Fax:** 808-521-5233 www.kbfd.com

Honolulu: KFVE (MY) 420 Waiakamilo Rd Ste 205 Honolulu HI 96817 **Phn:** 808-847-3246 **Fax:** 808-845-3616 www.k5thehometeam.com **Email:** news8@khnl.com

Honolulu: KGMB (CBS) 420 Waiakamilo Rd Ste 205 Honolulu HI 96817 **Phn:** 808-847-3246 **Fax:** 808-845-3616 www.hawaiinewsnow.com **Email:** news@hawaiinewsnow.com

Honolulu: KHET (PBS) 2350 Dole St Honolulu HI 96822 **Phn:** 808-973-1000 **Fax:** 808-973-1090 www.pbshawaii.org **Email:** email@pbshawaii.org

Honolulu: KHNL (NBC) 420 Waiakamilo Rd Ste 205 Honolulu HI 96817 **Phn:** 808-847-3246 **Fax:** 808-845-3616 www.hawaiinewsnow.com **Email:** news@hawaiinewsnow.com

Honolulu: KHON (FOX) 88 Piikoi St 1st Fl Honolulu HI 96814 **Phn:** 808-591-2222 **Fax:** 808-593-2418 www.khon2.com **Email:** news@khon2.com

Honolulu: KIKU (IND) 737 Bishop St Ste 1430 Honolulu HI 96813 **Phn:** 808-847-2021 **Fax:** 808-841-3326 kikutv.com **Email:** pkihara@kikutv.com

Honolulu: KITV (ABC) 801 S King St Ste 100 Honolulu HI 96813 **Phn:** 808-535-0400 **Fax:** 808-536-8993 www.kitv.com **Email:** news@kitv.com

Honolulu: KPXO (ION) 875 Waimanu St Ste 630 Honolulu HI 96813 **Phn:** 808-591-1275 **Fax:** 808-591-1409 www.iontelevision.com **Email:** jeffreymaguire@ionmedia.com

Honolulu: KWHE (REL) 1188 Bishop St Ste 502 Honolulu HI 96813 **Phn:** 808-538-1414 **Fax:** 808-526-0326 www.kwhe.com **Email:** kwhe@lesea.com

IDAHO

Boise: KAID (PBS) 1455 N Orchard St Boise ID 83706 **Phn:** 208-373-7220 **Fax:** 208-373-7245 idahoptv.org **Email:** idptv@idahoptv.org

Boise: KBOI (CBS) 140 N 16th St Boise ID 83702 **Phn:** 208-472-2222 **Fax:** 208-472-2211 www.kboi2.com **Email:** dryder@kbcitv.com

Boise: KTVB (NBC) 5407 W Fairview Ave Boise ID 83706 **Phn:** 208-375-7277 **Fax:** 208-375-7770 www.ktvb.com **Email:** ktvbnews@ktvb.com

Idaho Falls: KIDK (CBS) 1915 N Yellowstone Hwy Idaho Falls ID 83401 **Phn:** 208-522-5100 **Fax:** 208-522-5103 www.localnews8.com **Email:** newsdesk@localnews8.com

Idaho Falls: KIFI (ABC) 1915 N Yellowstone Hwy Idaho Falls ID 83401 **Phn:** 208-525-8888 **Fax:** 208-529-2443 www.localnews8.com **Email:** newsdesk@localnews8.com

Lewiston: KLEW (CBS) 2626 17th St Lewiston ID 83501 **Phn:** 208-746-2636 **Fax:** 208-746-4819 www.klewtv.com **Email:** info@klewtv.com

Moscow: KUID (PBS) PO Box 443101 Moscow ID 83844 **Phn:** 208-885-1226 **Fax:** 208-885-5711 idahoptv.org **Email:** kuid-office@idahoptv.org

Nampa: KIVI (ABC) 1866 E Chisholm Dr Nampa ID 83687 **Phn:** 208-336-0500 **Fax:** 208-381-6681 www.kivitv.com **Email:** news@idahoonyourside.com

Nampa: KNIN (FOX) 1866 E Chisholm Dr Nampa ID 83687 **Phn:** 208-336-0500 **Fax:** 208-381-6682 www.kivitv.com **Email:** news@idahoonyourside.com

Nampa: KTRV (FOX) 1 6th St N Nampa ID 83687 **Phn:** 208-466-1200 **Fax:** 208-461-4861 www.fox12idaho.com

Pocatello: KPVI (NBC) 902 E Sherman St Pocatello ID 83201 **Phn:** 208-232-6666 **Fax:** 208-234-3650 www.kpvi.com **Email:** newsroom@kpvi.com

Twin Falls: KMVT (CBS) 1100 Blue Lakes Blvd N Twin Falls ID 83301 **Phn:** 208-733-1100 **Fax:** 208-734-1074 www.kmvt.com **Email:** jmartin@kmvt.com

Twin Falls: KSAW (ABC) 834 Falls Ave Ste 2110 Twin Falls ID 83301 **Phn:** 208-734-6022 **Fax:** 208-734-4787 ksawtv.com **Email:** news@todays6.com

Twin Falls: KTFT (NBC) 834 Falls Ave Ste 1020 Twin Falls ID 83301 **Phn:** 208-734-6064 **Fax:** 208-734-3981 www.ktvb.comon-tvktft **Email:** breakingnews@ktvb.com

Twin Falls: KXTF (FOX) 1061 Blue Lakes Blvd N Twin Falls ID 83301 **Phn:** 208-733-0035 **Fax:** 208-234-3650 www.kxtf.com **Email:** newsroom@kpvi.com

ILLINOIS

Carbondale: WSIU (PBS) 1100 Lincoln Dr Ste 1003 Carbondale IL 62901 **Phn:** 618-453-4343 **Fax:** 618-453-6186 www.wsiu.org **Email:** trina.thomas@wsiu.org

Carterville: WSIL (ABC) 1416 Country Aire Dr Carterville IL 62918 **Phn:** 618-985-2333 **Fax:** 618-985-6482 www.wsiltv.com

Champaign: WBUI (CW) 1704 S Neil St Ste D Champaign IL 61820 **Phn:** 217-403-9927 **Fax:** 217-403-1007 www.foxillinois.com

Champaign: WCCU (FOX) 1704 S Neil St Ste D Champaign IL 61820 **Phn:** 217-403-9927 **Fax:** 217-403-1007 www.foxillinois.com

Champaign: WCFN (MY) PO Box 20 Champaign IL 61824 **Phn:** 217-356-8333 **Fax:** 217-373-3663 illinoishomepage.net **Email:** news@wcia.com

Champaign: WCIA (CBS) 509 S Neil St Champaign IL 61820 **Phn:** 217-356-8333 **Fax:** 217-373-3663 illinoishomepage.net **Email:** news@wcia.com

Champaign: WICD (ABC) 250 S Country Fair Dr Champaign IL 61821 **Phn:** 217-351-8500 **Fax:** 217-351-6134 www.wicd15.com **Email:** news@wicd15.com

Charleston: WEIU (PBS) 600 Lincoln Ave Charleston IL 61920 **Phn:** 217-581-5956 **Fax:** 217-581-6650 www.weiu.net **Email:** weiu@weiu.net

Chicago: WBBM (CBS) 22 W Washington St Chicago IL 60602 **Phn:** 312-899-2222 **Fax:** 312-849-7200 chicago.cbslocal.com **Email:** vebouchard@cbs.com

Chicago: WCIU (IND) 26 N Halsted St Chicago IL 60661 **Phn:** 312-705-2600 **Fax:** 312-705-2656 www.wciu.com

Chicago: WCPX (ION) 333 S Desplaines St Ste 101 Chicago IL 60661 **Phn:** 312-376-8520 **Fax:** 312-575-8735 www.iontelevision.com **Email:** richardlindsey@ionmedia.com

Chicago: WFLD (FOX) 205 N Michigan Ave Lowr LL1 Chicago IL 60601 **Phn:** 312-565-5532 **Fax:** 312-819-1332 www.myfoxchicago.com **Email:** news@foxchicago.com

Chicago: WGBO (SPN) 541 N Fairbanks Ct Ste 1100 Chicago IL 60611 **Phn:** 312-670-1000 **Fax:** 312-494-6496 chicago.univision.com **Email:** univisionchicag@tv.univision.com

Chicago: WGN (CW) 2501 W Bradley Pl Chicago IL 60618 **Phn:** 773-528-2311 **Fax:** 773-528-6050 wgntv.com **Email:** wgntvinfo@tribune.com

Chicago: WLS (ABC) 190 N State St Chicago IL 60601 **Phn:** 312-750-7777 **Fax:** 312-899-8019 abclocal.go.comwls **Email:** wls-tv.website@abc.com

Chicago: WMAQ (NBC) 454 N Columbus Dr Chicago IL 60611 **Phn:** 312-836-5555 **Fax:** 312-527-5925 www.nbcchicago.com

Chicago: WMEU (IND) 26 N Halsted St Chicago IL 60661 **Phn:** 312-705-2600 **Fax:** 312-705-2656 www.wciu.com

Chicago: WPWR (MY) 205 N Michigan Ave Chicago IL 60601 **Phn:** 312-565-5532 **Fax:** 773-276-1717 www.my50chicago.com **Email:** news@foxchicago.com

Chicago: WSNS (SPN) 454 N Columbus Dr Fl 1 Chicago IL 60611 **Phn:** 312-836-3000 **Fax:** 312-836-3232 www.telemundochicago.com

Chicago: WTTW (PBS) 5400 N Saint Louis Ave Chicago IL 60625 **Phn:** 773-583-5000 **Fax:** 773-509-5302 www.wttw.com **Email:** chicagotonight@wttw.com

Chicago: WWME (IND) 26 N Halsted St Chicago IL 60661 **Phn:** 312-705-2600 **Fax:** 312-705-2656 metvnetwork.com

Chicago: WXFT (SPN) 541 N Fairbanks Ct Ste 1100 Chicago IL 60611 **Phn:** 312-670-1000 **Fax:** 312-494-6496 www.univision.com

Chicago: WYCC (PBS) 6258 S Union Ave Chicago IL 60621 **Phn:** 773-224-3300 **Fax:** 773-783-2906 www.wycc.org **Email:** csyperek@wycc.org

Decatur: WAND (NBC) 904 W South Side Dr Decatur IL 62521 **Phn:** 217-424-2500 **Fax:** 217-424-2583 www.wandtv.com **Email:** news@wandtv.com

East Peoria: WAOE (MY) 2907 Springfield Rd East Peoria IL 61611 **Phn:** 309-674-5900 **Fax:** 309-674-5959 my59.tv **Email:** dbrown@loop.com

East Peoria: WEEK (NBC) 2907 Springfield Rd East Peoria IL 61611 **Phn:** 309-698-2525 **Fax:** 309-674-5959 www.cinewsnow.com **Email:** news25@week.com

East Peoria: WHOI (ABC) 2907 Springfield Rd East Peoria IL 61611 **Phn:** 309-698-2525 **Fax:** 309-674-5959 www.cinewsnow.com **Email:** news25@week.com

Marion: WTCT (REL) PO Box 1010 Marion IL 62959 **Phn:** 618-997-4700 **Fax:** 618-993-9778 www.tct.tv **Email:** tcttoday@tct.tv

Moline: WQAD (ABC) 3003 Park 16th St Moline IL 61265 **Phn:** 309-764-8888 **Fax:** 309-736-3306 wqad.com **Email:** news@wqad.com

Moline: WQPT (PBS) 3800 Avenue Of The Cities Ste 101 Moline IL 61265 **Phn:** 309-764-2400 **Fax:** 309-764-2410 www.wqpt.org **Email:** wqpt@wiu.edu

Oreana: WLCF (REL) 5647 Jordan Rd Oreana IL 62554 **Phn:** 217-468-2048 www.wlcftv.net

Ottawa: WWTO (REL) 420 E Stevenson Rd Ottawa IL 61350 **Phn:** 815-434-2700 **Fax:** 815-434-2458 www.tbn.org

Peoria: WMBD (CBS) 3131 N University St Peoria IL 61604 **Phn:** 309-688-3131 **Fax:** 309-686-8658 centralillinoisproud.com **Email:** rickm@wmbd.com

Peoria: WTVP (PBS) 101 State St Peoria IL 61602 **Phn:** 309-677-4747 **Fax:** 309-677-4730 www.wtvp.org **Email:** linda.miller@wtvp.org

Peoria: WYZZ (FOX) 3131 N University St Peoria IL 61604 **Phn:** 309-688-3131 **Fax:** 309-686-8658 centralillinoisproud.com **Email:** news@wmbd.com

Quincy: KHQA (CBS) 301 S 36th St Quincy IL 62301 **Phn:** 217-222-6200 **Fax:** 217-222-5078 www.connecttristates.com **Email:** news7@khqa.com

Quincy: WGEM (NBC) 513 Hampshire St Frnt Quincy IL 62301 **Phn:** 217-228-6600 **Fax:** 217-224-5786 www.wgem.com **Email:** news@wgem.com

Quincy: WTJR (REL) 222 N 6th St Quincy IL 62301 **Phn:** 217-228-1616 www.wtjr.org **Email:** tv16@wtjr.org

Rock Island: WHBF (CBS) 231 18th St Rock Island IL 61201 **Phn:** 309-786-5441 **Fax:** 309-788-3642 www.whbf.com **Email:** newsroom@cbs4qc.com

Rockford: WIFR (CBS) PO Box 123 Rockford IL 61105 **Phn:** 815-987-5300 **Fax:** 815-987-5333 www.wifr.com **Email:** dave.smith@wifr.com

Rockford: WQRF (FOX) 1917 N Meridian Rd Rockford IL 61101 **Phn:** 815-963-5413 **Fax:** 815-963-0029 mystateline.com **Email:** newsdesk@wtvo.com

Rockford: WREX (NBC) PO Box 530 Rockford IL 61105 **Phn:** 815-335-2213 **Fax:** 815-335-2297 www.wrex.com **Email:** news@wrex.com

Rockford: WTVO (ABC) 1917 N Meridian Rd Rockford IL 61101 **Phn:** 815-963-5413 **Fax:** 815-963-0029 mystateline.com **Email:** newsdesk@wtvo.com

Skokie: KPIF (CW) 3654 Jarvis Ave Skokie IL 60076 **Phn:** 208-237-5743 **Fax:** 208-237-5768

Springfield: WICS (ABC) 2680 E Cook St Springfield IL 62703 **Phn:** 217-753-5620 **Fax:** 217-753-5681 www.wics.com **Email:** news@wics.com

Springfield: WQEC (PBS) PO Box 6248 Springfield IL 62708 **Phn:** 217-483-7887 **Fax:** 217-483-1112 www.networkknowledge.tv

Springfield: WRSP (FOX) 3003 Old Rochester Rd Springfield IL 62703 **Phn:** 217-523-8855 **Fax:** 217-523-4410 www.foxillinois.com

Springfield: WSEC (PBS) PO Box 6248 Springfield IL 62708 **Phn:** 217-483-7887 **Fax:** 217-483-1112 www.networkknowledge.tv **Email:** wmorris@wsec.tv

Tinley Park: WJYS (IND) 18600 Oak Park Ave Tinley Park IL 60477 **Phn:** 708-633-0001 **Fax:** 708-633-0040 www.wjys.tv **Email:** mco@wjysgtv62.net

Urbana: WILL (PBS) 300 N Goodwin Ave Urbana IL 61801 **Phn:** 217-333-1070 **Fax:** 217-244-2656 will.illinois.edu **Email:** bculkeen@illinois.edu

INDIANA

Bloomington: WTIU (PBS) 1229 E 7th St Bloomington IN 47405 **Phn:** 812-855-5900 **Fax:** 812-855-1177 indianapublicmedia.org **Email:** wtiu@indiana.edu

ILLINOIS TV STATIONS

Clarksville: WNDA (NBC) 220 Potters Ln Clarksville IN 47129 **Phn:** 812-949-9843 **Fax:** 812-949-5056 www.indiana9.com **Email:** news@indiana9.com

Elkhart: WNIT (PBS) PO Box 3434 Elkhart IN 46515 **Phn:** 574-675-9648 **Fax:** 574-262-8497 www.wnit.org **Email:** wnit@wnit.org

Evansville: WEVV (CBS) 44 Main St Evansville IN 47708 **Phn:** 812-464-4444 **Fax:** 812-465-4559 www.wevv.com **Email:** info@wevv.com

Evansville: WFIE (NBC) PO Box 1414 Evansville IN 47701 **Phn:** 812-426-1414 **Fax:** 812-428-2228 www.14news.com **Email:** sgalloway@14news.com

Evansville: WNIN (PBS) 405 Carpenter St Evansville IN 47708 **Phn:** 812-423-2973 **Fax:** 812-428-7548 www.wnin.org **Email:** brheinhardt@wnin.org

Evansville: WTSN (IND) 300 SE Riverside Dr # 100 Evansville IN 47713 **Phn:** 812-759-8191 **Fax:** 812-465-4559 www.wtsntv.com

Evansville: WTVW (FOX) 477 Carpenter St Evansville IN 47708 **Phn:** 812-424-7777 **Fax:** 812-421-7289 tristatehomepage.com **Email:** newstips@wtvw.com

Fort Wayne: WANE (CBS) 2915 W State Blvd Fort Wayne IN 46808 **Phn:** 260-424-1515 **Fax:** 260-424-6054 www.wane.com **Email:** scott.murray@wane.com

Fort Wayne: WFFT (IND) 3707 Hillegas Rd Fort Wayne IN 46808 **Phn:** 260-471-5555 **Fax:** 260-484-4331 fortwaynehomepage.net **Email:** dball@wfft.com

Fort Wayne: WFWA (PBS) 2501 E Coliseum Blvd Fort Wayne IN 46805 **Phn:** 260-484-8839 **Fax:** 260-482-3632 www.wfwa.org **Email:** programming@wfwa.org

Fort Wayne: WISE (NBC) 3401 Butler Rd Fort Wayne IN 46808 **Phn:** 260-483-8111 **Fax:** 260-484-8240 www.indianasnewscenter.com **Email:** newsroom@indianasnewscenter.com

Fort Wayne: WPTA (ABC) 3401 Butler Rd Fort Wayne IN 46808 **Phn:** 260-483-8111 **Fax:** 260-484-8240 www.indianasnewscenter.com **Email:** newsroom@indianasnewscenter.com

Greenwood: WCLJ (REL) 2528 US Highway 31 S Greenwood IN 46143 **Phn:** 317-535-5542 **Fax:** 317-535-8584 www.tbn.org **Email:** wclj@tbn.org

Henderson: WEHT (ABC) 800 Marywood Dr Henderson IN 42420 **Phn:** 800-879-8542 **Fax:** 270-827-0561 www.tristatehomepage.com **Email:** bfreeman@tristatehomepage.com

Indianapolis: WFYI (PBS) 1630 N Meridian St Ste 2105 Indianapolis IN 46202 **Phn:** 317-636-2020 **Fax:** 317-283-6645 www.wfyi.org

Indianapolis: WIIH (SPN) 1950 N Meridian St Indianapolis IN 46202 **Phn:** 317-824-9444 **Fax:** 317-956-8849 www.univision.com

Indianapolis: WIPX (ION) 2441 Production Dr Ste 104 Indianapolis IN 46241 **Phn:** 317-486-0633 **Fax:** 317-486-0298 www.iontelevision.com **Email:** johnkowalke@ionmedia.com

Indianapolis: WISH (CBS) 1950 N Meridian St Indianapolis IN 46202 **Phn:** 317-923-8888 **Fax:** 317-931-2242 www.wishtv.com **Email:** newsdesk@wishtv.com

Indianapolis: WNDY (MY) 1950 N Meridian St Indianapolis IN 46202 **Phn:** 317-923-8888 **Fax:** 317-931-2242 www.myndytv.com **Email:** newsdesk@wishtv.com

Indianapolis: WRTV (ABC) 1330 N Meridian St Indianapolis IN 46202 **Phn:** 317-635-9788 **Fax:** 317-269-1445 www.theindychannel.com **Email:** todd_connor@wrtv.com

Indianapolis: WTHR (NBC) 1000 N Meridian St Indianapolis IN 46204 **Phn:** 317-636-1313 **Fax:** 317-632-6720 www.wthr.com **Email:** newsdesk@wthr.com

Indianapolis: WTTV (CW) 6910 Network Pl Indianapolis IN 46278 **Phn:** 317-632-5900 **Fax:** 317-715-6251 indianas4.com **Email:** rgordon@tribune.com

Indianapolis: WXIN (FOX) 6910 Network Pl Indianapolis IN 46278 **Phn:** 317-632-5900 **Fax:** 317-687-6556 fox59.com **Email:** fox59news@fox59.com

Marion: WSOT (REL) 2172 W Chapel Pike Marion IN 46952 **Phn:** 765-668-1014 **Fax:** 765-671-2151 www.sunnycrestbaptist.orgwsot-tv.html **Email:** jason.stepp@sunnycrestbaptist.org

Merrillville: WYIN (PBS) 8625 Indiana Pl Merrillville IN 46410 **Phn:** 219-756-5656 **Fax:** 219-755-4312 www.lakeshoreptv.com **Email:** news@lakeshoreptv.com

Mishawaka: WBND (ABC) 3665 Park Pl W Ste 200 Mishawaka IN 46545 **Phn:** 574-243-4321 **Fax:** 574-243-4326 www.abc57.com **Email:** news57@abc57.com

Mishawaka: WMYS (MY) 3665 Park Pl W Mishawaka IN 46545 **Phn:** 574-243-4316 **Fax:** 574-243-4326 mymichianatv.com

Mishawaka: WSBT (CBS) 1301 E Douglas Rd Mishawaka IN 46545 **Phn:** 574-233-3141 **Fax:** 574-289-0622 www.wsbt.com **Email:** wsbtnews@wsbt.com

Muncie: WIPB (PBS) 1111 North McKinley Ave Muncie IN 47306 **Phn:** 765-285-1249 **Fax:** 765-285-5548 www.wipb.org **Email:** arapp@bsu.edu

Noblesville: WHMB (IND) 10511 Greenfield Ave Noblesville IN 46060 **Phn:** 317-773-5050 **Fax:** 317-776-4051 www.whmbtv.com **Email:** whmb@lesea.com

Richmond: WKOI (REL) PO Box 1057 Richmond IN 47375 **Phn:** 765-935-2390 www.tbn.org **Email:** wkoi@tbn.org

South Bend: WCWW (CW) 53550 Generations Dr South Bend IN 46635 **Phn:** 574-243-4321 **Fax:** 574-243-4326 www.thecw25.com

South Bend: WHME (REL) 61300 Ironwood Rd South Bend IN 46614 **Phn:** 574-291-8200 **Fax:** 574-291-9043 www.whme.com **Email:** asumrall@lesea.com

South Bend: WNDU (NBC) PO Box 1616 South Bend IN 46634 **Phn:** 574-284-3000 **Fax:** 574-284-3022 www.wndu.com **Email:** newscenter16@wndu.com

South Bend: WSJV (FOX) PO Box 28 South Bend IN 46624 **Phn:** 574-679-9758 **Fax:** 574-522-7609 www.fox28.com **Email:** fox28news@fox28.com

Terre Haute: WFXW (FOX) PO Box 9268 Terre Haute IN 47808 **Phn:** 812-238-3838 **Fax:** 812-696-2000 mywabashvalley.com **Email:** news@wtwo.com

Terre Haute: WTHI (CBS) PO Box 9606 Terre Haute IN 47808 **Phn:** 812-232-9481 **Fax:** 812-232-3694 www.wthitv.com **Email:** news10@wthitv.com

Terre Haute: WTWO (NBC) PO Box 9268 Terre Haute IN 47808 **Phn:** 812-696-2121 **Fax:** 812-696-2000 mywabashvalley.com **Email:** news@wtwo.com

Vincennes: WVUT (PBS) 1200 N 2nd St Vincennes IN 47591 **Phn:** 812-888-4345 **Fax:** 812-882-2237 wvut.org **Email:** newscenter22@wvut.org

West Lafayette: WLFI (CBS) 2605 Yeager Rd West Lafayette IN 47906 **Phn:** 765-463-1800 **Fax:** 765-463-7979 www.wlfi.com **Email:** newsroom@wlfi.com

IOWA

Ankeny: KCWI (CW) 2701 SE Convenience Blvd Ste 1 Ankeny IA 50021 **Phn:** 515-964-2323 **Fax:** 515-965-6900 www.kcwi23.com

Cedar Rapids: KCRG (ABC) PO Box 816 Cedar Rapids IA 52406 **Phn:** 319-398-8422 **Fax:** 319-368-8505 www.kcrg.com **Email:** newsreleases@kcrg.com

Cedar Rapids: KFXA (FOX) 600 Old Marion Rd NE Ste 2 Cedar Rapids IA 52402 **Phn:** 319-395-9060 **Fax:** 319-395-0113 www.fox28iowa.com **Email:** news@fox28iowa.com

Cedar Rapids: KGAN (CBS) PO Box 3131 Cedar Rapids IA 52406 **Phn:** 319-395-9060 **Fax:** 319-395-0113 www.cbs2iowa.com **Email:** news@cbs2iowa.com

Cedar Rapids: KPXR (ION) 1957 Blairs Ferry Rd NE Ste 350 Cedar Rapids IA 52402 **Phn:** 319-378-1260 **Fax:** 319-378-0076 www.iontelevision.com **Email:** vikkisteele@ionmedia.com

Davenport: KGCW (CW) 937 E 53rd St Ste D Davenport IA 52807 **Phn:** 563-386-1818 **Fax:** 563-386-8543 www.kgcwtv.com

Davenport: KLJB (FOX) 937 E 53rd St Ste D Davenport IA 52807 **Phn:** 563-386-1818 **Fax:** 563-386-8543 www.kljb.com **Email:** qandc@kljb.com

Davenport: KWQC (NBC) 805 Brady St Davenport IA 52803 **Phn:** 563-383-7000 **Fax:** 563-383-7131 www.kwqc.com **Email:** bmarsoun@kwqc.com

Des Moines: KCCI (CBS) 888 9th St Des Moines IA 50309 **Phn:** 515-247-8888 **Fax:** 515-244-0202 www.kcci.com **Email:** dbusiek@hearst.com

Des Moines: KDSM (FOX) 4023 Fleur Dr Des Moines IA 50321 **Phn:** 515-287-1717 **Fax:** 515-287-0064 www.kdsm17.com **Email:** programming@kdsm17.com

Des Moines: WHO (NBC) 1801 Grand Ave Des Moines IA 50309 **Phn:** 515-242-3500 **Fax:** 515-242-3796 whotv.com **Email:** news@whotv.com

Dubuque: KFXB (REL) 744 Main St Dubuque IA 52001 **Phn:** 563-690-1704 **Fax:** 563-557-9383 www.kfxb.net **Email:** ctnofiowa@mchsi.com

Johnston: KDIN (PBS) PO Box 6450 Johnston IA 50131 **Phn:** 515-242-3100 **Fax:** 515-242-4112 www.iptv.org **Email:** programming@iptv.org

Marshalltown: KDAO (IND) PO Box 538 Marshalltown IA 50158 **Phn:** 641-752-4122 **Fax:** 641-752-5121 kdao.com **Email:** kdao@kdao.com

Mason City: KIMT (CBS) 112 N Pennsylvania Ave Mason City IA 50401 **Phn:** 641-423-2540 **Fax:** 641-421-2675 www.kimt.com **Email:** news@kimt.com

Ottumwa: KYOU (FOX) 820 W 2nd St Ottumwa IA 52501 **Phn:** 641-684-5415 **Fax:** 641-682-5173 www.kyoutv.com

Sioux City: KCAU (ABC) 625 Douglas St Sioux City IA 51101 **Phn:** 712-277-2345 **Fax:** 712-277-3733 www.kcautv.com **Email:** news@kcautv.com

Sioux City: KTIV (NBC) 3135 Floyd Blvd Sioux City IA 51108 **Phn:** 712-239-4100 **Fax:** 712-239-3025 www.ktiv.com **Email:** ktivnews@ktiv.com

Urbandale: KFPX (ION) 4570 114th St Urbandale IA 50322 **Phn:** 515-331-3939 **Fax:** 515-331-1312 www.iontelevision.com **Email:** marshatheis@ionmedia.com

Waterloo: KWWL (NBC) 500 E 4th St Waterloo IA 50703 **Phn:** 319-291-1200 **Fax:** 319-291-1233 www.kwwl.com **Email:** kwwlnews@kwwl.com

West Branch: KWKB (CW) 1547 Baker Ave West Branch IA 52358 **Phn:** 319-643-5952 **Fax:** 319-643-3124 www.kwkb.com

West Des Moines: WOI (ABC) 3903 Westown Pkwy West Des Moines IA 50266 **Phn:** 515-457-9645 **Fax:** 515-457-1025 www.myabc5.com **Email:** news@myabc5.com

KANSAS

Bunker Hill: KOOD (PBS) 604 Elm St Bunker Hill KS 67626 **Phn:** 785-483-6990 **Fax:** 785-483-4605 www.pbs.orgshptv **Email:** shptv@shptv.org

Fairway: KPXE (ION) 4220 Shawnee Mission Pkwy Ste 110B Fairway KS 66205 **Phn:** 913-722-0798 www.iontelevision.com

Fairway: KSMO (MY) 4500 Shawnee Mission Pkwy Fairway KS 66205 **Phn:** 913-677-5555 **Fax:** 913-677-7243 www.kctv5.com **Email:** newsdesk@kctv5.com

Pittsburg: KOAM (CBS) PO Box 659 Pittsburg KS 66762 **Phn:** 417-624-0233 **Fax:** 417-624-3158 www.koamtv.com **Email:** news@koamtv.com

Topeka: KSNT (NBC) 6835 NW Hwy 24 Topeka KS 66618 **Phn:** 785-582-4000 **Fax:** 785-582-4783 www.kansasfirstnews.com **Email:** 27news@kansasfirstnews.com

Topeka: KTKA (ABC) 6835 NW Hwy 24 Topeka KS 66618 **Phn:** 785-582-4000 **Fax:** 785-582-4783 www.ktka.com **Email:** 27news@kansasfirstnews.com

Topeka: KTMJ (FOX) 6835 NW Highway 24 Topeka KS 66618 **Phn:** 785-582-4000 **Fax:** 785-582-5283 www.ksnt.com **Email:** 27news@ksnt.com

Topeka: KTWU (PBS) 1700 SW College Ave Topeka KS 66621 **Phn:** 785-670-1111 **Fax:** 785-670-1112 www.ktwu.org **Email:** ktwu-press@washburn.edu

Topeka: WIBW (CBS) 631 SW Commerce Pl Topeka KS 66615 **Phn:** 785-272-6397 **Fax:** 785-272-1363 www.wibw.com **Email:** 13news@wibw.com

Wichita: KAKE (ABC) 1500 N West St Wichita KS 67203 **Phn:** 316-943-4221 **Fax:** 316-943-5374 www.kake.com **Email:** news@kake.com

Wichita: KMTW (MY) 316 N West St Wichita KS 67203 **Phn:** 316-942-2424 **Fax:** 316-942-8927 www.mytvwichita.com **Email:** michellecleaton@foxkansas.com

Wichita: KPTS (PBS) 320 W 21st St N Wichita KS 67203 **Phn:** 316-838-3090 **Fax:** 316-838-8586 www.kpts.org **Email:** news@kpts.org

Wichita: KSAS (FOX) 316 N West St Wichita KS 67203 **Phn:** 316-942-2424 **Fax:** 316-942-8927 www.foxkansas.com **Email:** askfox@fox.com

Wichita: KSCW (CW) 2815 E 37th St N Wichita KS 67219 **Phn:** 316-838-1212 **Fax:** 316-831-6193 www.kansascw.comkscw **Email:** news@kwch.com

Wichita: KSNW (NBC) 833 N Main St Wichita KS 67203 **Phn:** 316-265-3333 **Fax:** 316-292-1195 www.ksn.com **Email:** news@ksn.com

Wichita: KWCH (CBS) 2815 E 37th St N Wichita KS 67219 **Phn:** 316-838-1212 **Fax:** 316-831-6193 www.kwch.com **Email:** news@kwch.com

KENTUCKY

Beattyville: WLJC (REL) PO Box Y Beattyville KY 41311 **Phn:** 606-464-3600 www.wljc.com **Email:** wljc@wljc.com

Bowling Green: WBKO (ABC) 2727 Russellville Rd Bowling Green KY 42101 **Phn:** 270-781-1313 **Fax:** 270-782-6156 www.wbko.com **Email:** gene.birk@wbko.com

Bowling Green: WKYU (PBS) 1906 College Heights Blvd # 11034 Bowling Green KY 42101 **Phn:** 270-745-2400 **Fax:** 270-745-2084 wkyu.lunchbox.pbs.org **Email:** wkyutv@wku.edu

Bowling Green: WNKY (NBC) 325 Emmett Ave Bowling Green KY 42101 **Phn:** 270-781-2140 **Fax:** 270-842-7140 www.wnky.net **Email:** gerald.keith@wnky.net

Frenchburg: WUPX (ION) 2166 McCausey Rdg Frenchburg KY 40322 **Phn:** 606-768-9282 **Fax:** 606-768-9278 www.iontelevision.com **Email:** latonyapettit@ionmedia.com

Hazard: WYMT (CW) 199 Black Gold Blvd Hazard KY 41701 **Phn:** 606-436-5757 **Fax:** 606-439-3760 www.wkyt.comwymtnews **Email:** newstip@wkyt.com

Hopkinsville: WKAG (IND) 1616 E 9th St Hopkinsville KY 42240 **Phn:** 270-885-4300 **Fax:** 270-886-5882

Lexington: WDKY (FOX) 836 E Euclid Ave Ste 201 Lexington KY 40502 **Phn:** 859-269-5656 **Fax:** 859-293-1578 www.foxlexington.com **Email:** mbartlett@foxlexington.com

Lexington: WKLE (PBS) 600 Cooper Dr Lexington KY 40502 **Phn:** 859-258-7000 **Fax:** 859-258-7399 www.ket.org **Email:** viewerservices@ket.org

Lexington: WKYT (CBS) 2851 Winchester Rd Lexington KY 40509 **Phn:** 859-299-0411 **Fax:** 859-293-1578 www.wkyt.com **Email:** newsrelease@wkyt.com

Lexington: WLEX (NBC) PO Box 1457 Lexington KY 40588 **Phn:** 859-259-1818 **Fax:** 859-254-2217 www.lex18.com **Email:** wlextv@wlextv.com

Lexington: WTVQ (ABC) 6940 Man O War Blvd Lexington KY 40509 **Phn:** 859-294-3636 **Fax:** 859-293-0539 www.wtvq.com **Email:** news36@wtvq.com

Louisville: WAVE (NBC) 725 S Floyd St Louisville KY 40203 **Phn:** 502-585-2201 **Fax:** 502-561-4105 www.wave3.com **Email:** newsrelease@wave3tv.com

Louisville: WBKI (CW) 6100 Dutchmans Ln Ste 701 Louisville KY 40205 **Phn:** 502-809-3400 **Fax:** 502-266-6262 www.wbki.tv **Email:** mjjaspan@wbki.tv

Louisville: WBNA (ION) 3701 Fern Valley Rd Louisville KY 40219 **Phn:** 502-964-2121 **Fax:** 502-966-9692 www.iontelevision.com

Louisville: WDRB (FOX) 624 W Muhammad Ali Blvd Louisville KY 40203 **Phn:** 502-584-6441 **Fax:** 502-568-6751 www.wdrb.com **Email:** news@wdrb.com

Louisville: WHAS (ABC) 520 W Chestnut St Louisville KY 40202 **Phn:** 502-582-7711 **Fax:** 502-585-5992 www.whas11.com **Email:** assign@whas-tv.com

Louisville: WLKY (CBS) 1918 Mellwood Ave Louisville KY 40206 **Phn:** 502-893-3671 **Fax:** 502-896-0725 www.wlky.com **Email:** newstips@wlky.com

Louisville: WMYO (FOX) 624 W Muhammad Ali Blvd Louisville KY 40203 **Phn:** 502-585-0811 **Fax:** 502-568-6751 www.wdrb.com **Email:** news@wdrb.com

Paducah: WPSD (NBC) 100 Television Ln Paducah KY 42003 **Phn:** 270-415-1900 **Fax:** 270-415-1981 www.wpsdlocal6.com **Email:** lbarrett@wpsdtv.com

LOUISIANA

Alexandria: KALB (NBC) 605 Washington St Alexandria LA 71301 **Phn:** 318-445-2456 **Fax:** 318-449-4594 www.kalb.com **Email:** news@kalb.com

Alexandria: KBCA (CW) 1777 Jackson St Alexandria LA 71301 **Phn:** 318-487-4120 **Fax:** 337-896-2681 yourcwtv.compartnersalexandria

Alexandria: KLAX (ABC) 1811 England Dr Alexandria LA 71303 **Phn:** 318-473-0031 **Fax:** 318-442-9728 klax-tv.com **Email:** bzimmerman@klax-tv.com

Alexandria: WNTZ (FOX) 4615 Parliament Dr Ste 103 Alexandria LA 71303 **Phn:** 318-443-4700 **Fax:** 318-443-4899 www.fox48tv.com **Email:** sharon@fox48tv.com

Baton Rouge: WAFB (CBS) 844 Government St Baton Rouge LA 70802 **Phn:** 225-383-9999 **Fax:** 225-379-7880 www.wafb.com **Email:** nsimonette@wafb.com

Baton Rouge: WBRL (CW) 10000 Perkins Rd Baton Rouge LA 70810 **Phn:** 225-819-0010 **Fax:** 225-768-9293 www.fox44.com

Baton Rouge: WBRZ (ABC) 1650 Highland Rd Baton Rouge LA 70802 **Phn:** 225-387-2222 **Fax:** 225-336-2246 www.wbrz.com **Email:** news@wbrz.com

Baton Rouge: WGMB (FOX) 10000 Perkins Rd Baton Rouge LA 70810 **Phn:** 225-769-0044 **Fax:** 225-768-9293 www.fox44.com **Email:** david.daquin@nbc33tv.com

Baton Rouge: WLPB (PBS) 7733 Perkins Rd Baton Rouge LA 70810 **Phn:** 225-767-5660 **Fax:** 225-767-4421 www.lpb.org **Email:** comments@lpb.org

Baton Rouge: WVLA (NBC) 10000 Perkins Rd Baton Rouge LA 70810 **Phn:** 225-766-3233 **Fax:** 225-768-9293 www.nbc33tv.com **Email:** news@nbc33tv.com

Carencro: KLWB (ABC) 3501 NW Evangeline Trwy Carencro LA 70520 **Phn:** 337-896-1600 **Fax:** 337-896-2681 lafayette.thistv.com **Email:** nancy@delta-network.com

Houma: KFOL (IND) 1202 Saint Charles St Houma LA 70360 **Phn:** 985-876-3456 **Fax:** 985-853-1856 bayoutimelive.com **Email:** news10@htv10.tv

Lafayette: KADN (FOX) 123 N Easy St Lafayette LA 70506 **Phn:** 337-237-1500 **Fax:** 337-237-2237 www.kadn.com **Email:** cajunmitch@msn.com

Lafayette: KATC (ABC) PO Box 63333 Lafayette LA 70596 **Phn:** 337-235-3333 **Fax:** 337-232-5282 www.katc.com **Email:** news@katctv.com

Lafayette: KLFY (CBS) PO Box 90665 Lafayette LA 70509 **Phn:** 337-981-4823 **Fax:** 337-981-6533 www.klfy.com **Email:** news@klfy.com

Lake Charles: KPLC (NBC) 320 Division St Lake Charles LA 70601 **Phn:** 337-439-9071 **Fax:** 337-439-9905 www.kplctv.com **Email:** aderouen@kplctv.com

Lake Charles: KVHP (FOX) 129 W Prien Lake Rd Lake Charles LA 70601 **Phn:** 337-474-1316 **Fax:** 337-477-6795 www.watchfox29.com **Email:** sduplechian@watchfox.com

Metairie: WGNO (ABC) 1 Galleria Blvd Ste 850 Metairie LA 70001 **Phn:** 504-525-3838 **Fax:** 504-619-6332 wgno.com **Email:** news@wgno.com

Metairie: WLAE (PBS) 3330 N Causeway Blvd Ste 345 Metairie LA 70002 **Phn:** 504-830-3700 **Fax:** 504-840-9838 www.wlae.com

Metairie: WNOL (CW) 1 Galleria Blvd Ste 850 Metairie LA 70001 **Phn:** 504-525-3838 **Fax:** 504-619-6332 wgno.comnola38 **Email:** news@wgno.com

Metairie: WPXL (ION) 3900 Veterans Blvd Ste 202 Metairie LA 70002 **Phn:** 504-887-9795 **Fax:** 504-887-1518 www.iontelevision.com

Metairie: WYES (PBS) 111 Veterans Memorial Blvd Ste 250 Metairie LA 70005 **Phn:** 504-486-5511 **Fax:** 504-840-9954 www.wyes.org **Email:** info@wyes.org

Monroe: KAQY (ABC) 1400 Oliver Rd Monroe LA 71201 **Phn:** 318-325-3011 **Fax:** 318-322-8774 www.kaqy11.com

Monroe: KNOE (CBS) 1400 Oliver Rd Monroe LA 71201 **Phn:** 318-388-8888 **Fax:** 318-325-3405 www.knoe.com **Email:** news@knoe.com

Morgan City: KWBJ (IND) 608 Michigan St Morgan City LA 70380 **Phn:** 985-384-6960 **Fax:** 985-385-1916 www.kwbj.net **Email:** gaprice@atvci.net

New Orleans: WDSU (NBC) 846 Howard Ave New Orleans LA 70113 **Phn:** 504-679-0600 **Fax:** 504-679-0733 www.wdsu.com **Email:** newsdesk@wdsu.com

LOUISIANA TV STATIONS

New Orleans: WHNO (IND) 839 Saint Charles Ave Ste 309 New Orleans LA 70130 **Phn:** 504-681-0120 **Fax:** 504-681-0180 www.whno.com **Email:** whno@lesea.com

New Orleans: WUPL (CW) 1024 N Rampart St New Orleans LA 70116 **Phn:** 504-529-4444 **Fax:** 504-529-6472 www.wwltv.com **Email:** pressrelease@wwltv.com

New Orleans: WVUE (FOX) 1025 S Jefferson Davis Pkwy New Orleans LA 70125 **Phn:** 504-486-6161 **Fax:** 504-483-1543 www.fox8live.com **Email:** fox8news@fox8tv.net

New Orleans: WWL (CBS) 1024 N Rampart St New Orleans LA 70116 **Phn:** 504-529-4444 **Fax:** 504-529-6472 www.wwltv.com **Email:** pressrelease@wwltv.com

Opelousas: KDCG (IND) 2897 S Union St Opelousas LA 70570 **Phn:** 337-948-7267 **Fax:** 337-948-9040 www.kdcg.com

Shreveport: KMSS (FOX) 3519 Jewella Ave Shreveport LA 71109 **Phn:** 318-631-5677 **Fax:** 318-631-4194 www.kmsstv.com **Email:** info@kmsstv.com

Shreveport: KPXJ (CW) 312 E Kings Hwy Shreveport LA 71104 **Phn:** 318-861-5800 **Fax:** 318-219-4680 www.ktbs.com **Email:** pressreleases@ktbs.com

Shreveport: KSHV (MY) 3519 Jewella Ave Shreveport LA 71109 **Phn:** 318-631-4545 **Fax:** 318-621-9688 www.kshv.com

Shreveport: KSLA (CBS) 1812 Fairfield Ave Shreveport LA 71101 **Phn:** 318-222-1212 **Fax:** 318-677-6705 www.ksla.com **Email:** ksla@ksla.com

Shreveport: KTAL (NBC) 3150 N Market St Shreveport LA 71107 **Phn:** 318-629-6000 **Fax:** 318-629-7171 arklatexhomepage.com **Email:** ktal@ktalnews.tv

Shreveport: KTBS (ABC) 312 E Kings Hwy Shreveport LA 71104 **Phn:** 318-861-5800 **Fax:** 318-219-4680 www.ktbs.com **Email:** news@ktbs.com

West Monroe: KARD (FOX) 200 Pavilion Rd West Monroe LA 71292 **Phn:** 318-323-1972 **Fax:** 318-807-0588 myarklamiss.com **Email:** cgiles@nbc10news.net

West Monroe: KMCT (REL) 701 Parkwood Dr West Monroe LA 71291 **Phn:** 318-322-1399 **Fax:** 318-323-3783 thevoicenetwork.tv **Email:** kalbritton@thevoicenetwork.tv

West Monroe: KTVE (NBC) 200 Pavilion Rd West Monroe LA 71292 **Phn:** 318-323-1972 **Fax:** 318-807-0588 myarklamiss.com **Email:** cgiles@nbc10news.net

MAINE

Auburn: WMTW (ABC) PO Box 8 Auburn ME 04212 **Phn:** 207-782-1800 **Fax:** 207-782-2165 www.wmtw.com **Email:** wmtw@wmtw.com

Bangor: WABI (CBS) 35 Hildreth St Bangor ME 04401 **Phn:** 207-947-8321 **Fax:** 207-942-0016 wabi.tv **Email:** wabi@wabi.tv

Bangor: WLBZ (NBC) 329 Mount Hope Ave Bangor ME 04401 **Phn:** 207-942-4821 **Fax:** 207-942-2109 www.wlbz2.com **Email:** newscenter2@wlbz2.com

Bangor: WVII (ABC) 371 Target Cir Bangor ME 04401 **Phn:** 207-945-6457 **Fax:** 207-945-6864 www.foxbangor.com **Email:** news@foxbangor.com

Glenburn: WBGR (ION) 2881 Ohio St Lot 6 Glenburn ME 04401 **Phn:** 207-947-3300 **Fax:** 866-236-2320 wbgr.com

Lewiston: WMEB (PBS) 1450 Lisbon St Lewiston ME 04240 **Phn:** 207-783-9101 **Fax:** 207-783-5193 www.mpbn.net **Email:** webmaster@mpbn.net

Portland: WCSH (NBC) 1 Congress Sq Portland ME 04101 **Phn:** 207-828-6666 **Fax:** 207-828-6630 www.wcsh6.com **Email:** newscenter@wcsh6.com

Portland: WGME (CBS) 81 Northport Dr Portland ME 04103 **Phn:** 207-797-1313 **Fax:** 207-878-7482 www.wgme.com **Email:** tvmail@wgme.com

Portland: WPFO (FOX) 233 Oxford St Ste 35 Portland ME 04101 **Phn:** 207-828-0023 **Fax:** 207-347-7323 www.myfoxmaine.com **Email:** newsroom@myfoxmaine.com

Presque Isle: WAGM (CBS) 12 Brewer Rd Presque Isle ME 04769 **Phn:** 207-764-4461 **Fax:** 207-764-6397 wagmtv.com **Email:** lthomas@wagmtv.com

Westbrook: WPME (MY) 4 Ledgeview Dr Westbrook ME 04092 **Phn:** 207-774-0051 **Fax:** 207-774-6849 www.ourmaine.com **Email:** wpme@ourmaine.com

Westbrook: WPXT (CW) 4 Ledgeview Dr Westbrook ME 04092 **Phn:** 207-774-0051 **Fax:** 207-774-6849 www.ourmaine.com **Email:** wpxt@ourmaine.com

MARYLAND

Baltimore: WBAL (NBC) 3800 Hooper Ave Baltimore MD 21211 **Phn:** 410-467-3000 **Fax:** 410-338-6526 www.wbaltv.com **Email:** newstips@wbaltv.com

Baltimore: WBFF (FOX) 2000 W 41st St Baltimore MD 21211 **Phn:** 410-467-4545 **Fax:** 410-467-5093 www.foxbaltimore.com **Email:** news@foxbaltimore.com

Baltimore: WJZ (CBS) 3725 Malden Ave Baltimore MD 21211 **Phn:** 410-466-0013 **Fax:** 410-578-0642 baltimore.cbslocal.com **Email:** newsroom@wjz.com

Baltimore: WMAR (ABC) 6400 York Rd Baltimore MD 21212 **Phn:** 410-377-2222 **Fax:** 410-377-5321 www.abc2news.com **Email:** newsroom@wmar.com

Baltimore: WNUV (CW) 2000 W 41st St Baltimore MD 21211 **Phn:** 410-467-4545 **Fax:** 410-467-5093 www.cwbaltimore.com **Email:** news@foxbaltimore.com

Baltimore: WUTB (MY) 4820 Seton Dr Ste M Baltimore MD 21215 **Phn:** 410-358-2400 **Fax:** 410-764-7232 www.my24wutb.com

Hagerstown: WHAG (NBC) 13 E Washington St Hagerstown MD 21740 **Phn:** 301-797-4400 **Fax:** 301-745-4093 your4state.com **Email:** mkraham@nbc25.com

Owings Mills: WMPB (PBS) 11767 Owings Mills Blvd Owings Mills MD 21117 **Phn:** 410-356-5600 www.mpt.org **Email:** directconnection@mpt.org

Salisbury: WBOC (CBS) 1729 N Salisbury Blvd Salisbury MD 21801 **Phn:** 410-749-1111 **Fax:** 410-742-5190 www.wboc.com **Email:** news@wboc.com

Salisbury: WMDT (ABC) PO Box 4009 Salisbury MD 21803 **Phn:** 410-742-4747 **Fax:** 410-749-4777 www.wmdt.com **Email:** freddie_mitchell@wmdt.com

MASSACHUSETTS

Allston: WBPX (ION) 1120 Soldiers Field Rd Allston MA 02134 **Phn:** 617-787-6868 **Fax:** 617-787-4004 www.iontelevision.com

Allston: WBZ (CBS) 1170 Soldiers Field Rd Allston MA 02134 **Phn:** 617-787-7000 **Fax:** 617-254-6383 boston.cbslocal.com **Email:** newstips@cbs4boston.com

Allston: WSBK (IND) 1170 Soldiers Field Rd Allston MA 02134 **Phn:** 617-787-7000 **Fax:** 617-254-6383 boston.cbslocal.com **Email:** prassist@boston.cbs.com

Boston: WGBH (PBS) 1 Guest St Boston MA 02135 **Phn:** 617-300-5400 **Fax:** 617-300-1031 www.wgbh.org **Email:** feedback@wgbh.org

Boston: WHDH (NBC) 7 Bulfinch Pl Boston MA 02114 **Phn:** 617-725-0777 **Fax:** 617-723-6117 www1.whdh.com **Email:** newstips@whdh.com

Boston: WLVI (CW) 7 Bulfinch Pl Boston MA 02114 **Phn:** 647-248-5400 **Fax:** 617-248-5386 www.cw56.com **Email:** program_feedback@whdh.com

Dedham: WFXT (FOX) 25 Fox Dr Dedham MA 02026 **Phn:** 781-467-2525 **Fax:** 781-467-7213 www.myfoxboston.com **Email:** harry.seeto@foxtv.com

Hudson: WUTF (SPN) 71 Parmenter Rd Hudson MA 01749 **Phn:** 978-562-0660 **Fax:** 978-562-1166 www.univision.com **Email:** mgodin@entravision.com

Needham: WCVB (ABC) 5 Tv Pl Needham MA 02494 **Phn:** 781-449-0400 **Fax:** 781-433-4510 www.wcvb.com **Email:** ahoffman@hearst.com

Needham: WUNI (SPN) 33 4th Ave Needham MA 02494 **Phn:** 781-433-2727 **Fax:** 781-433-2750 www.wunitv.com **Email:** alexvl@entravision.com

Needham: WUTH (SPN) 33 4th Ave Needham MA 02494 **Phn:** 781-433-2727 **Fax:** 781-433-2750 www.entravision.com

Springfield: WGBY (PBS) 44 Hampden St Springfield MA 01103 **Phn:** 413-781-2801 **Fax:** 413-731-5093 www.wgby.org **Email:** feedback@wgby.org

Springfield: WGGB (ABC) 1300 Liberty St Springfield MA 01104 **Phn:** 413-733-4040 **Fax:** 413-788-7640 www.wggb.com **Email:** newstips@wggb.com

Springfield: WSHM (CBS) 1 Monarch Pl Ste 300 Springfield MA 01144 **Phn:** 413-736-4333 **Fax:** 413-523-4934 www.cbs3springfield.com **Email:** news@cbs3springfield.com

Springfield: WWLP (NBC) PO Box 2210 Springfield MA 01102 **Phn:** 413-786-2200 **Fax:** 413-377-2261 www.wwlp.com **Email:** news@wwlp.com

MICHIGAN

Alpena: WBKB (CBS) 1390 N Bagley St Alpena MI 49707 **Phn:** 989-356-3434 **Fax:** 989-356-4188 www.wbkb11.com **Email:** christya@wbkb11.com

Ann Arbor: WPXD (ION) 3975 Varsity Dr Ann Arbor MI 48108 **Phn:** 734-973-7900 **Fax:** 734-973-7906 www.iontelevision.com **Email:** helenskinner@ionmedia.tv

Cadillac: WFQX (FOX) PO Box 282 Cadillac MI 49601 **Phn:** 231-775-9813 **Fax:** 231-775-2731 www.mifox32.com **Email:** news@mifox32.com

Cadillac: WWTV (CBS) PO Box 627 Cadillac MI 49601 **Phn:** 231-775-3478 **Fax:** 231-775-2731 www.9and10news.com **Email:** news@9and10news.com

Clinton Township: WADL (IND) 35000 Adell Dr Clinton Township MI 48035 **Phn:** 586-790-3838 **Fax:** 586-790-3841 www.wadldetroit.com **Email:** lewis@wadldetroit.com

Clio: WBSF (CW) 2225 W Willard Rd Clio MI 48420 **Phn:** 810-687-1000 **Fax:** 810-687-9612 www.minbcnews.com **Email:** news@nbc25.net

Clio: WEYI (NBC) 2225 W Willard Rd Clio MI 48420 **Phn:** 810-687-1000 **Fax:** 810-687-4925 www.minbcnews.com **Email:** news@nbc25.net

Detroit: WDIV (NBC) 550 W Lafayette Blvd Detroit MI 48226 **Phn:** 313-222-0444 **Fax:** 313-222-0592 www.clickondetroit.com **Email:** editorial@clickondetroit.com

East Lansing: WKAR (PBS) 283 Communication Arts And Sci East Lansing MI 48824 **Phn:** 517-432-9527 **Fax:** 517-353-7124 wkar.org **Email:** webmaster@wkar.org

Flint: WFUM (PBS) 303 E Kearsley St Flint MI 48502 **Phn:** 810-762-3028 **Fax:** 810-233-6017 michigantelevision.org **Email:** production@michigantelevision.org

Flint: WJRT (ABC) 2302 Lapeer Rd Flint MI 48503 **Phn:** 810-233-3130 **Fax:** 810-257-2812 www.abc12.com **Email:** abc12news@abc12.com

Flint: WSMH (FOX) 3463 W Pierson Rd # G Flint MI 48504 **Phn:** 810-785-8866 **Fax:** 810-785-8963 www.wsmh.com **Email:** promotions@wsmh.com

Grand Rapids: WGVU (PBS) 301 Fulton St W Grand Rapids MI 49504 **Phn:** 616-331-6666 www.wgvu.org

Grand Rapids: WOOD (NBC) 120 College Ave SE Grand Rapids MI 49503 **Phn:** 616-456-8888 **Fax:** 616-456-9169 www.woodtv.com

Grand Rapids: WOTV (ABC) 120 College Ave SE Grand Rapids MI 49503 **Phn:** 616-456-8888 **Fax:** 616-456-9169 www.wotv4women.com **Email:** wotv@wotv.com

Grand Rapids: WXMI (FOX) 3117 Plaza Dr NE Grand Rapids MI 49525 **Phn:** 616-364-8722 **Fax:** 616-364-8506 fox17online.com **Email:** news@wxmi.com

Grand Rapids: WXSP (MY) 120 College Ave SE Grand Rapids MI 49503 **Phn:** 616-456-8888 **Fax:** 616-771-9676 www.wxsp.com

Grand Rapids: WZPX (ION) 2610 Horizon Dr SE Ste E Grand Rapids MI 49546 **Phn:** 616-222-6443 **Fax:** 616-493-2677 www.iontelevision.com **Email:** tinahill@ionmedia.com

Grand Rapids: WZZM (ABC) 645 3 Mile Rd NW Grand Rapids MI 49544 **Phn:** 616-785-1313 **Fax:** 616-784-8367 www.wzzm13.com **Email:** news@wzzm13.com

Ishpeming: WBKP (ABC) 1705 Ash St Ste 5 Ishpeming MI 49849 **Phn:** 906-204-2436 **Fax:** 906-204-2433 abc10up.com **Email:** news@abc10up.com

Kalamazoo: WLLA (REL) PO Box 3157 Kalamazoo MI 49003 **Phn:** 269-345-6421 **Fax:** 269-345-5665 www.wlla.com

Kalamazoo: WWMT (CBS) 590 W Maple St Kalamazoo MI 49008 **Phn:** 269-388-3333 **Fax:** 269-388-8322 www.wwmt.com **Email:** desk@wwmt.com

Lansing: WHTV (MY) 2820 E Saginaw St Lansing MI 48912 **Phn:** 517-372-9497 **Fax:** 517-372-9499 www.my18.tv **Email:** info@my18.tv

Lansing: WILX (NBC) 500 American Rd Lansing MI 48911 **Phn:** 517-393-0110 **Fax:** 517-393-9180 www.wilx.com **Email:** news@wilx.com

Lansing: WLAJ (ABC) 2820 East Saginaw St Lansing MI 48912 **Phn:** 517-372-8282 **Fax:** 517-372-1507 www.wlns.comcategory254337wlaj **Email:** newstips@wlns.com

Lansing: WLNS (CBS) 2820 E Saginaw St Lansing MI 48912 **Phn:** 517-372-8282 **Fax:** 517-372-1507 www.wlns.com **Email:** newstips@wlns.com

Lansing: WSYM (FOX) 600 W Saint Joseph St Lansing MI 48933 **Phn:** 517-484-7747 **Fax:** 517-393-9180 www.fox47news.com **Email:** 47today@fox47news.com

Marquette: WNMU (PBS) 1401 Presque Isle Ave Marquette MI 49855 **Phn:** 906-227-1300 **Fax:** 906-227-2905 wnmutv.nmu.edu **Email:** tv13@nmu.edu

Mount Pleasant: WCMU (PBS) 1999 E Campus Dr Mount Pleasant MI 48859 **Phn:** 989-774-3105 **Fax:** 989-774-4427 www.wcmu.org **Email:** nicho1d@cmich.edu

Negaunee: WLUC (NBC) 177 US Highway 41 E Negaunee MI 49866 **Phn:** 906-475-4161 **Fax:** 906-475-5070 www.uppermichiganssource.com **Email:** tv6news@wluctv6.com

Saginaw: WAQP (REL) 2865 Trautner Dr Saginaw MI 48604 **Phn:** 989-249-5969 **Fax:** 989-249-1220 www.tct-net.org

Saginaw: WNEM (CBS) 107 N Franklin St Saginaw MI 48607 **Phn:** 989-755-8191 **Fax:** 989-758-2111 www.wnem.com **Email:** wnem@wnem.com

Southfield: WJBK (FOX) PO Box 2000 Southfield MI 48037 **Phn:** 248-557-2000 **Fax:** 248-557-1199 www.myfoxdetroit.com **Email:** fox2newsdesk@foxtv.com

Southfield: WKBD (CW) 26905 W 11 Mile Rd Southfield MI 48033 **Phn:** 248-355-7000 **Fax:** 248-359-7494 cwdetroit.cbslocal.com **Email:** web@wkbdtv.com

Southfield: WMYD (MY) 27777 Franklin Rd Ste 1220 Southfield MI 48034 **Phn:** 248-355-2020 **Fax:** 248-355-0368 www.tv20detroit.com **Email:** s.norat-phillips@tv20detroit.com

Southfield: WWJ (CBS) 26905 W 11 Mile Rd Southfield MI 48033 **Phn:** 248-355-7000 detroit.cbslocal.com **Email:** web@wwjtv.com

Southfield: WXYZ (ABC) PO Box 789 Southfield MI 48037 **Phn:** 248-827-7777 **Fax:** 248-827-9444 www.wxyz.com **Email:** talkback@wxyz.com

Traverse City: WGTU (ABC) 8513 E Traverse Hwy Traverse City MI 49684 **Phn:** 231-946-2900 **Fax:** 231-946-1600 www.upnorthlive.com **Email:** newsroom@upnorthlive.com

Traverse City: WPBN (NBC) 8513 E Traverse Hwy Traverse City MI 49684 **Phn:** 231-947-7770 **Fax:** 231-947-0354 www.upnorthlive.com **Email:** newsroom@upnorthlive.com

University Center: WDCQ (PBS) 1961 Delta Rd University Center MI 48710 **Phn:** 989-686-9362 **Fax:** 989-686-0155 www3.delta.edubroadcasting **Email:** wdcq@delta.edu

Wixom: WTVS (PBS) 1 Clover Ct Wixom MI 48393 **Phn:** 248-305-3788 **Fax:** 248-305-3990 www.dptv.org **Email:** email@dptv.org

MINNESOTA

Alexandria: KSAX (ABC) PO Box 189 Alexandria MN 56308 **Phn:** 320-763-5729 **Fax:** 320-763-4627 kstp.com **Email:** gennewstips@kstp.com

Appleton: KWCM (PBS) 120 W Schlieman Ave Appleton MN 56208 **Phn:** 320-289-2622 **Fax:** 320-289-2634 www.pioneer.org **Email:** yourtv@pioneer.org

Austin: KAAL (ABC) 1701 10th Pl NE Austin MN 55912 **Phn:** 507-437-6666 **Fax:** 507-437-7443 kaaltv.com **Email:** news@kaaltv.com

Austin: KSMQ (PBS) 2000 8th Ave NW Austin MN 55912 **Phn:** 507-433-0678 **Fax:** 507-433-0670 www.ksmq.org **Email:** ksmq@ksmq.org

Bemidji: KAWE (PBS) 1500 Birchmont Dr NE Bemidji MN 56601 **Phn:** 218-751-3407 **Fax:** 218-751-3142 www.lakelandptv.org **Email:** dweimann@lptv.org

Big Lake: KPXM (ION) 22601 176th St NW Big Lake MN 55309 **Phn:** 763-263-8666 **Fax:** 763-263-6600 www.iontelevision.com

Duluth: KBJR (NBC) 246 S Lake Ave Duluth MN 55802 **Phn:** 218-720-9600 **Fax:** 218-720-9660 www.northlandsnewscenter.com **Email:** fcc_newsroom@northlandsnewscenter.com

Duluth: KDLH (CBS) 246 S Lake Ave Duluth MN 55802 **Phn:** 218-720-9600 **Fax:** 218-720-9660 www.northlandsnewscenter.com **Email:** news3@kdlh.com

Duluth: KQDS (FOX) 2001 London Rd Duluth MN 55812 **Phn:** 218-728-1622 **Fax:** 218-728-8932 www.fox21online.com **Email:** fox21news@kqdsfox21.tv

Duluth: WDIO (ABC) PO Box 16897 Duluth MN 55816 **Phn:** 218-727-6864 **Fax:** 218-727-2318 www.wdio.com **Email:** news@wdio.com

Duluth: WDSE (PBS) 632 Niagara Ct Duluth MN 55811 **Phn:** 218-724-8568 **Fax:** 218-724-4269 www.wdse.org **Email:** email@wdse.org

Eden Prairie: KMSP (FOX) 11358 Viking Dr Eden Prairie MN 55344 **Phn:** 952-944-9999 **Fax:** 952-942-0455 www.myfoxtwincities.com **Email:** fox9news@foxtv.com

Eden Prairie: WFTC (MY) 11358 Viking Dr Eden Prairie MN 55344 **Phn:** 952-944-9999 **Fax:** 952-942-0455 www.my29tv.com **Email:** fox9news@foxtv.com

Minneapolis: KARE (NBC) 8811 Highway 55 Minneapolis MN 55427 **Phn:** 763-546-1111 **Fax:** 763-546-8606 www.kare11.com **Email:** news@kare11.com

Minneapolis: KSTC (IND) 3415 University Ave SE Minneapolis MN 55414 **Phn:** 651-646-4500 **Fax:** 651-642-4409 www.kstc45.com **Email:** assignmentdesk@kstp.com

Minneapolis: KSTP (ABC) 3415 University Ave SE Minneapolis MN 55414 **Phn:** 651-646-5555 **Fax:** 651-642-4409 kstp.com **Email:** gennewstips@kstp.com

Minneapolis: WCCO (CBS) 90 S 11th St Minneapolis MN 55403 **Phn:** 612-339-4444 **Fax:** 612-330-2767 minnesota.cbslocal.com **Email:** wcconewstips@wcco.cbs.com

Minneapolis: WUMN (SPN) 250 Marquette Ave Ste 540 Minneapolis MN 55401 **Phn:** 612-455-3960 **Fax:** 612-746-3014 www.wumn13.com

North Mankato: KEYC (CBS) 1570 Lookout Dr North Mankato MN 56003 **Phn:** 507-625-7905 **Fax:** 507-625-5745 www.keyc.com **Email:** keycnews@keyc.com

Rochester: KTTC (NBC) 6301 Bandel Rd NW Ste A Rochester MN 55901 **Phn:** 507-288-4444 **Fax:** 507-288-6278 www.kttc.com **Email:** news@kttc.com

Rochester: KXLT (FOX) 6301 Bandel Rd NW Ste 47 Rochester MN 55901 **Phn:** 507-252-4747 **Fax:** 507-288-6278 www.myfox47.com **Email:** news@fox47kxlt.com

Saint Paul: KTCA (PBS) 172 4th St E Saint Paul MN 55101 **Phn:** 651-222-1717 **Fax:** 651-229-1282 www.tpt.org

Saint Paul: WUCW (CW) 1640 Como Ave Saint Paul MN 55108 **Phn:** 651-646-2300 **Fax:** 651-646-1220 www.thecwtc.com **Email:** promotions@thecwtc.com

MISSISSIPPI

Biloxi: WLOX (ABC) 208 Debuys Rd Biloxi MS 39531 **Phn:** 228-896-1313 **Fax:** 228-896-2596 www.wlox.com **Email:** news@wlox.com

Columbus: WCBI (CBS) PO Box 271 Columbus MS 39703 **Phn:** 662-327-4444 **Fax:** 662-328-5222 www.wcbi.com

Greenville: WABG (ABC) PO Box 1243 Greenville MS 38702 **Phn:** 662-332-0949 **Fax:** 662-378-3055 www.wabg.com **Email:** newsroom@wabg.com

Greenville: WXVT (CBS) 3015 E Reed Rd Greenville MS 38703 **Phn:** 662-334-1500 **Fax:** 662-378-8122 www.wxvt.com **Email:** abrasier@wxvt.com

Gulfport: WXXV (FOX) PO Box 2500 Gulfport MS 39505 **Phn:** 228-832-2525 **Fax:** 228-832-4442 www.wxxv25.com **Email:** promotions@wxxv25.com

Hattiesburg: WDAM (NBC) PO Box 16269 Hattiesburg MS 39404 **Phn:** 601-544-4730 **Fax:** 601-584-9302 www.wdam.com **Email:** info@wdam.com

Hattiesburg: WHLT (CBS) 5912 U S Highway 49 Ste A Hattiesburg MS 39401 **Phn:** 601-545-2077 **Fax:** 601-545-3589 www.whlt.com **Email:** wbabbidge@whlt.com

Jackson: WAPT (ABC) PO Box 10297 Jackson MS 39289 **Phn:** 601-922-1607 **Fax:** 601-922-8993 www.wapt.com **Email:** news@wapt.com

Jackson: WDBD (FOX) 715 S Jefferson St Jackson MS 39201 **Phn:** 601-948-3333 **Fax:** 601-922-0268 www.msnewsnow.com **Email:** news@wlbt.com

MINNESOTA TV STATIONS

Jackson: WJTV (CBS) 1820 Tv Rd Jackson MS 39204 **Phn:** 601-372-6311 **Fax:** 601-372-8798 www.wjtv.com **Email:** rrussell@wjtv.com

Jackson: WLBT (NBC) 715 S Jefferson St Jackson MS 39201 **Phn:** 601-948-3333 **Fax:** 601-355-7830 www.msnewsnow.com **Email:** news@wlbt.com

Jackson: WMAB (PBS) 3825 Ridgewood Rd Jackson MS 39211 **Phn:** 601-432-6565 **Fax:** 601-432-6932 www.mpbonline.org

Jackson: WMAV (PBS) 3825 Ridgewood Rd Jackson MS 39211 **Phn:** 601-432-6565 **Fax:** 601-432-6932 www.mpbonline.org **Email:** communications@mpbonline.org

Jackson: WRBJ (CW) 745 N State St Jackson MS 39202 **Phn:** 601-974-5700 **Fax:** 601-974-5719 www.wrbj.tv **Email:** renella@roberts-companies.com

Meridian: WGBC (NBC) 1151 Crestview Cir Meridian MS 39301 **Phn:** 601-485-3030 **Fax:** 601-693-9889 wgbctv.com **Email:** programming@wgbctv.com

Meridian: WMDN (CBS) 1151 Crestview Cir Meridian MS 39301 **Phn:** 601-693-2424 **Fax:** 601-693-7126 www.wgbctv.com **Email:** rdenton@wmdn.net

Meridian: WTOK (ABC) 815 23rd Ave Meridian MS 39301 **Phn:** 601-693-1441 **Fax:** 601-483-6759 www.wtok.com **Email:** news@wtok.com

Tupelo: WLOV (FOX) PO Box 1732 Tupelo MS 38802 **Phn:** 662-842-2227 **Fax:** 662-620-1128 www.wlov.com **Email:** manager@wlov.com

Tupelo: WTVA (NBC) PO Box 350 Tupelo MS 38802 **Phn:** 662-842-7620 **Fax:** 662-620-1128 www.wtva.com **Email:** news@wtva.com

MISSOURI

Cape Girardeau: KBSI (FOX) 806 Enterprise St Cape Girardeau MO 63703 **Phn:** 573-334-1223 **Fax:** 573-334-1208 www.kbsi23.com **Email:** amuster@kbsi.sbgnet.com

Cape Girardeau: KFVS (CBS) 310 Broadway St Ste 1 Cape Girardeau MO 63701 **Phn:** 573-335-1212 **Fax:** 573-335-7723 www.kfvs.com **Email:** mlittle@kfvs12.com

Cape Girardeau: WDKA (MY) 806 Enterprise St Cape Girardeau MO 63703 **Phn:** 573-334-1223 **Fax:** 573-334-1208 www.mywdka.com **Email:** amuster@kbsi.sbgnet.com

Columbia: KMIZ (ABC) 501 Business Loop 70 E Columbia MO 65201 **Phn:** 573-449-0917 **Fax:** 573-875-7078 www.abc17news.com **Email:** news@kmiz.com

Columbia: KOMU (NBC) 5550 Highway 63 S Columbia MO 65201 **Phn:** 573-882-8888 **Fax:** 573-884-5353 www.komu.com **Email:** news@komu.com

Columbia: KQFX (FOX) 501 Business Loop 70 E Columbia MO 65201 **Phn:** 573-449-0917 **Fax:** 573-449-6271 www.abc17news.com **Email:** news@kmiz.com

Jefferson City: KNLJ (REL) 311 W Dunklin St Jefferson City MO 65101 **Phn:** 573-896-5105 **Fax:** 573-896-0251 www.knlj.tv **Email:** knljtv@yahoo.com

Jefferson City: KRCG (CBS) PO Box 659 Jefferson City MO 65102 **Phn:** 573-896-5144 **Fax:** 573-896-5193 www.connectmidmissouri.com **Email:** news@krcg.com

Joplin: KODE (ABC) 1928 W 13th St Joplin MO 64801 **Phn:** 417-623-7260 **Fax:** 417-623-2268 fourstateshomepage.com **Email:** leisha@kode12.tv

Joplin: KSNF (NBC) 1502 S Cleveland Ave Joplin MO 64801 **Phn:** 417-625-0294 **Fax:** 417-782-2417 www.fourstateshomepage.com **Email:** leisha@kode12.tv

Kansas City: KCPT (PBS) 125 E 31st St Kansas City MO 64108 **Phn:** 816-756-3580 **Fax:** 816-931-2500 www.kcpt.org **Email:** nick_haines@kcpt.org

Kansas City: KCTV (CBS) PO Box 5555 Kansas City MO 64128 **Phn:** 913-677-5555 **Fax:** 913-677-7243 www.kctv5.com **Email:** newsdesk@kctv5.com

Kansas City: KCWE (CW) 6455 Winchester Ave Kansas City MO 64133 **Phn:** 816-221-2900 **Fax:** 816-421-4163 www.kmbc.comkcwetv **Email:** tholderby@hearst.com

Kansas City: KMBC (ABC) 6455 Winchester Ave Kansas City MO 64133 **Phn:** 816-221-9999 **Fax:** 816-421-4163 www.kmbc.com **Email:** news@kmbc.com

Kansas City: KMCI (NBC) 4720 Oak St Kansas City MO 64112 **Phn:** 816-753-4141 **Fax:** 816-932-4145 38thespot.com **Email:** desk@kshb.com

Kansas City: KSHB (NBC) 4720 Oak St Kansas City MO 64112 **Phn:** 816-753-4141 **Fax:** 816-932-4145 www.kshb.com **Email:** desk@kshb.com

Kansas City: WDAF (FOX) 3030 Summit St Kansas City MO 64108 **Phn:** 816-753-4567 **Fax:** 816-561-4181 fox4kc.com **Email:** news@wdaftv4.com

Kirksville: KTVO (ABC) 15518 US Highway 63 Kirksville MO 63501 **Phn:** 660-627-3333 **Fax:** 660-627-4766 www.heartlandconnection.com **Email:** news@ktvo.com

Saint Joseph: KQTV (ABC) PO Box 8369 Saint Joseph MO 64508 **Phn:** 816-364-2222 **Fax:** 816-232-7505 stjoechannel.com **Email:** news@kq2.com

Saint Joseph: KTAJ (REL) 4402 S 40th St # A Saint Joseph MO 64503 **Phn:** 816-364-1616 **Fax:** 816-364-6729 www.tbn.org **Email:** ktaj@tbn.org

Saint Louis: KDNL (ABC) 1215 Cole St Saint Louis MO 63106 **Phn:** 314-436-3030 www.abcstlouis.com **Email:** info@abcstlouis.com

Saint Louis: KETC (PBS) 3655 Olive St Saint Louis MO 63108 **Phn:** 314-512-9000 **Fax:** 314-512-9005 ninenet.org **Email:** letters@ketc.org

Saint Louis: KMOV (CBS) 1 S Memorial Dr Ste 1 Saint Louis MO 63102 **Phn:** 314-621-4444 **Fax:** 314-621-4775 www.kmov.com **Email:** desk@kmov.com

Saint Louis: KNLC (REL) PO Box 924 Saint Louis MO 63188 **Phn:** 314-436-2424 **Fax:** 314-436-2434 knlc.tv **Email:** vanderson@nlecstl.org

Saint Louis: KPLR (CW) 2250 Ball Dr Saint Louis MO 63146 **Phn:** 314-447-1111 **Fax:** 314-213-7440 kplr11.com

Saint Louis: KSDK (NBC) 1000 Market St Saint Louis MO 63101 **Phn:** 314-444-5125 **Fax:** 314-444-5164 www.ksdk.com **Email:** newstips@ksdk.com

Saint Louis: KTVI (FOX) 2250 Ball Dr Saint Louis MO 63146 **Phn:** 314-447-1111 **Fax:** 314-213-7440 fox2now.com **Email:** ktvinews@tvstl.com

Saint Louis: WAZE (CW) 1408 N Kingshighway Blvd Ste 300 Saint Louis MO 63113 **Phn:** 812-425-1900 **Fax:** 812-423-3405

Saint Louis: WRBU (MY) 1408 N Kingshighway Blvd Ste 300 Saint Louis MO 63113 **Phn:** 314-367-4600 **Fax:** 314-367-0174 www.roberts-companies.com

Springfield: KOLR (CBS) 2650 E Division St Springfield MO 65803 **Phn:** 417-862-1010 **Fax:** 417-866-6397 ozarksfirst.com **Email:** dwasson@kolr10.com

Springfield: KOZK (PBS) 901 S National Ave Springfield MO 65897 **Phn:** 417-836-3500 **Fax:** 417-836-3569 www.optv.org

Springfield: KSFX (FOX) 2650 E Division St Springfield MO 65803 **Phn:** 417-862-2727 **Fax:** 417-866-6397 ozarksfirst.com **Email:** doliver@kolr10.com

Springfield: KSPR (ABC) 999 W Sunshine St Springfield MO 65807 **Phn:** 417-831-1234 **Fax:** 417-831-9358 www.kspr.com **Email:** jsmall@kspr.com

Springfield: KYTV (NBC) 999 W Sunshine St Springfield MO 65807 **Phn:** 417-268-3000 **Fax:** 417-268-3364 **Email:** newsproducers@ky3.com www.ky3.com

Warrensburg: KMOS (PBS) Univ Central Mo Wood 11 Warrensburg MO 64093 **Phn:** 660-543-4155 **Fax:** 660-543-8863 www.kmos.org **Email:** kmos@kmos.org

MONTANA

Billings: KHMT (FOX) 445 S 24th St W Billings MT 59102 **Phn:** 406-652-4743 **Fax:** 406-652-6963 yourbigsky.com **Email:** szoldowski@ksvi.com

Billings: KSVI (ABC) 445 S 24th St W Billings MT 59102 **Phn:** 406-652-4743 **Fax:** 406-652-6963 yourbigsky.com **Email:** szoldowski@ksvi.com

Billings: KTVQ (CBS) 3203 3rd Ave N Billings MT 59101 **Phn:** 406-252-5611 **Fax:** 406-869-2249 www.montanasnewsstation.com **Email:** news@ktvq.com

Billings: KULR (NBC) 2045 Overland Ave Billings MT 59102 **Phn:** 406-656-8000 **Fax:** 406-655-2688 www.kulr8.com **Email:** news@kulr.com

Black Eagle: KFBB (ABC) 3200 Old Havre Hwy Black Eagle MT 59414 **Phn:** 406-453-4377 **Fax:** 406-453-3226 www.kfbb.com **Email:** newsroom@kfbb.com

Bozeman: KBZK (CBS) 90 Television Way Bozeman MT 59718 **Phn:** 406-586-3280 **Fax:** 406-586-4135 www.kbzk.com **Email:** z7tips@kbzk.com

Bozeman: KUSM (PBS) PO Box 173340 Bozeman MT 59717 **Phn:** 406-994-3437 **Fax:** 406-994-6545 montanapbs.org

Butte: KTVM (NBC) PO Box 3118 Butte MT 59701 **Phn:** 406-494-7603 **Fax:** 406-494-2572 www.nbcmontana.comktvm **Email:** news@ktvm.com

Butte: KWYB (ABC) 3825 Harrison Ave # B Butte MT 59701 **Phn:** 406-782-7185 **Fax:** 406-723-9269 www.abcfoxmontana.com **Email:** newsroom@maxmontana.com

Butte: KXLF (CBS) 1003 S Montana St Butte MT 59701 **Phn:** 406-496-8400 **Fax:** 406-782-8906 www.kxlf.comhome **Email:** kxlf@kxlf.com

Glendive: KXGN (NBC) 210 S Douglas St Glendive MT 59330 **Phn:** 406-377-3377 **Fax:** 406-365-2181 www.kxgn.com **Email:** newsdesk@kxgn.com

Great Falls: KRTV (CBS) PO Box 2989 Great Falls MT 59403 **Phn:** 406-791-5400 **Fax:** 406-791-5479 www.krtv.com **Email:** krtvnews@krtv.com

Great Falls: KTGF (IND) PO Box 169 Great Falls MT 59403 **Phn:** 406-761-8816 **Fax:** 406-454-3484 www.ktgftv.com **Email:** familytv@gmail.com

Helena: KBGF (NBC) PO Box 6125 Helena MT 59604 **Phn:** 406-771-1666 **Fax:** 406-771-1667 www.beartoothnbc.com **Email:** gpace@ktvh.com

Helena: KTVH (NBC) 100 W Lyndale Ave Ste A Helena MT 59601 **Phn:** 406-457-1212 **Fax:** 406-442-5106 www.beartoothnbc.com **Email:** news@beartoothnbc.com

Kalispell: KCFW (NBC) 401 1st Ave E Kalispell MT 59901 **Phn:** 406-755-5239 **Fax:** 406-752-8002 www.nbcmontana.comkcfw **Email:** news@kcfw.com

Missoula: KECI (NBC) PO Box 5268 Missoula MT 59806 **Phn:** 406-721-2063 **Fax:** 406-721-6791 www.nbcmontana.comkeci **Email:** news@keci.com

Missoula: KPAX (CBS) 1049 W Central Ave Missoula MT 59801 **Phn:** 406-542-4400 **Fax:** 406-543-7127 www.kpax.com **Email:** kajnews@kpax.com

MISSOURI TV STATIONS

Missoula: KTMF (ABC) 2200 Stephens Ave Missoula MT 59801 **Phn:** 406-542-8900 **Fax:** 406-728-4800 www.abcmontana.com **Email:** sarahg@maxmontana.com

NEBRASKA

Hastings: KHAS (NBC) 6475 Osborne Dr W Hastings NE 68901 **Phn:** 402-463-1321 **Fax:** 402-463-6551 www.khastv.com **Email:** news5@khastv.com

Kearney: KHGI (ABC) PO Box 220 Kearney NE 68848 **Phn:** 308-743-2494 **Fax:** 308-743-2660 www.nebraska.tv **Email:** news@nebraska.tv

Kearney: KTVG (FOX) PO Box 220 Kearney NE 68848 **Phn:** 308-384-1717 **Fax:** 308-743-2660 www.foxnebraska.com **Email:** news@nebraska.tv

Lincoln: KLKN (ABC) 3240 S 10th St Lincoln NE 68502 **Phn:** 402-434-8000 **Fax:** 402-436-2236 www.klkntv.com **Email:** lvanhoosen@klkntv.com

Lincoln: KOLN (CBS) 840 N 40th St Lincoln NE 68503 **Phn:** 402-467-4321 **Fax:** 402-467-9208 www.1011now.com **Email:** desk@kolnkgin.com

Lincoln: KUON (PBS) 1800 N 33rd St Lincoln NE 68503 **Phn:** 402-472-3611 **Fax:** 402-472-1785 www.netnebraska.org **Email:** tv@netnebraska.org

North Platte: KNOP (NBC) PO Box 749 North Platte NE 69103 **Phn:** 308-532-2222 **Fax:** 308-532-9579 www.knopnews2.com **Email:** knop@knoptv.com

Omaha: KETV (ABC) 2665 Douglas St Omaha NE 68131 **Phn:** 402-345-7777 **Fax:** 402-978-8931 www.ketv.com **Email:** news@ketv.com

Omaha: KMTV (CBS) 10714 Mockingbird Dr Omaha NE 68127 **Phn:** 402-592-3333 **Fax:** 402-592-4714 www.kmtv.com **Email:** news@action3news.com

Omaha: KPTM (FOX) 4625 Farnam St Omaha NE 68132 **Phn:** 402-558-4200 **Fax:** 402-554-4279 www.kptm.com **Email:** news42@kptm.com

Omaha: KXVO (CW) 4625 Farnam St Omaha NE 68132 **Phn:** 402-554-1500 **Fax:** 402-554-4279 www.kxvo.com **Email:** contact15@kxvo.com

Omaha: WOWT (NBC) 3501 Farnam St Omaha NE 68131 **Phn:** 402-346-6666 **Fax:** 402-233-7888 www.wowt.com **Email:** sixonline@wowt.com

NEVADA

Henderson: KVVU (FOX) 25 Tv 5 Dr Henderson NV 89014 **Phn:** 702-435-5555 **Fax:** 702-436-2507 www.fox5vegas.com **Email:** 5newsdesk@kvvu.com

Las Vegas: KBLR (SPN) 450 Freeman Ave Ste 310 Las Vegas NV 89106 **Phn:** 702-258-0039 **Fax:** 702-258-0556 www.telemundolasvegas.com

Las Vegas: KINC (SPN) 500 Pilot Rd Ste D Las Vegas NV 89119 **Phn:** 702-434-0015 **Fax:** 702-434-0527 www.univision.com

Las Vegas: KLAS (CBS) 3228 Channel 8 Dr Las Vegas NV 89109 **Phn:** 702-792-8888 **Fax:** 702-792-2977 www.8newsnow.com **Email:** eneilson@klastv.com

Las Vegas: KLVX (PBS) 3050 E Flamingo Rd Las Vegas NV 89121 **Phn:** 702-799-1010 **Fax:** 702-799-5586 www.vegaspbs.org **Email:** mjohnson@vegaspbs.org

Las Vegas: KSNV (NBC) 1500 Foremaster Ln Las Vegas NV 89101 **Phn:** 702-642-3333 **Fax:** 702-657-3152 www.mynews3.com **Email:** news3@mynews3.com

Las Vegas: KTNV (ABC) 3355 S Valley View Blvd Las Vegas NV 89102 **Phn:** 702-876-1313 **Fax:** 702-876-2237 www.ktnv.com **Email:** desk@ktnv.com

Las`Vegas: KVCW (CW) 3830 S Jones Blvd Las Vegas NV 89103 **Phn:** 702-382-2121 **Fax:** 702-952-4676 www.thecwlasvegas.tv **Email:** promotions@thecwlasvegas.tv

Las Vegas: KVMY (MY) 3830 S Jones Blvd Las Vegas NV 89103 **Phn:** 702-382-2121 **Fax:** 702-952-4676 www.mylvtv.com **Email:** rdixon@mylvtv.com

Reno: KAME (MY) 4920 Brookside Ct Reno NV 89502 **Phn:** 775-856-2121 **Fax:** 775-856-2116 www.foxreno.com **Email:** steve.cummings@coxtv.com

Reno: KNPB (PBS) 1670 N Virginia St Reno NV 89503 **Phn:** 775-784-4555 **Fax:** 775-784-1438 www.knpb.org **Email:** programming@knpb.org

Reno: KNVV (SPN) 300 S Wells Ave Ste 12 Reno NV 89502 **Phn:** 775-333-1017 **Fax:** 775-333-9046 www.entravision.com **Email:** vcody@entravision.com

Reno: KOLO (ABC) 4850 Ampere Dr Reno NV 89502 **Phn:** 775-858-8888 **Fax:** 775-858-8855 www.kolotv.com **Email:** news@kolotv.com

Reno: KREN (SPN) 300 S Wells Ave Ste 12 Reno NV 89502 **Phn:** 775-333-1017 **Fax:** 775-333-9046 www.univisionreno.com

Reno: KRNV (NBC) 1790 Vassar St Reno NV 89502 **Phn:** 775-322-4444 **Fax:** 775-785-1206 www.mynews4.com **Email:** news@mynews4.com

Reno: KRXI (FOX) 4920 Brookside Ct Reno NV 89502 **Phn:** 775-856-1100 **Fax:** 775-856-2116 www.foxreno.com **Email:** steve.cummings@coxtv.com

Reno: KTVN (CBS) 4925 Energy Way Reno NV 89502 **Phn:** 775-858-2222 **Fax:** 775-861-4246 www.ktvn.com **Email:** producers@ktvn.com

NEW HAMPSHIRE

Derry: WBIN (IND) 11 A St Derry NH 03038 **Phn:** 603-845-1000 **Fax:** 603-434-8627 wbintv.com

Durham: WENH (PBS) 268 Mast Rd Durham NH 03824 **Phn:** 603-868-1100 **Fax:** 603-868-7552 www.nhptv.org **Email:** themailbox@nhptv.org

Manchester: WMUR (ABC) 100 South Commercial St Manchester NH 03101 **Phn:** 603-669-9999 **Fax:** 603-641-9005 www.wmur.com **Email:** storyideas@thewmurchannel.com

NEW JERSEY

Egg Harbor Township: WMCN (IND) 6575 Delilah Rd Ste 3B Egg Harbor Township NJ 08234 **Phn:** 609-569-7280 **Fax:** 609-569-7295

Fort Lee: WNJU (SPN) 2200 Fletcher Ave Ste 35 Fort Lee NJ 07024 **Phn:** 201-969-4247 **Fax:** 201-969-4120 www.telemundo47.com **Email:** manuel.martinez@nbcuni.com

Linwood: WMGM (NBC) 1601 New Rd Linwood NJ 08221 **Phn:** 609-927-4440 **Fax:** 609-926-8875 www.nbc40.net **Email:** news@nbc40.net

Newfield: WUVP (SPN) 4449 Delsea Dr Newfield NJ 08344 **Phn:** 856-691-6565 **Fax:** 856-690-3558 **Email:** noticias65@univision.net

Teaneck: WXTV (SPN) 500 Frank W Burr Blvd Ste 19 Teaneck NJ 07666 **Phn:** 201-287-4141 **Fax:** 201-287-9427 univision41.univision.com **Email:** cschwarz@univision.net

Trenton: WNJT (PBS) PO Box 777 Trenton NJ 08625 **Phn:** 609-777-5000 **Fax:** 609-633-2927

West Caldwell: WMBC (IND) 99 Clinton Rd West Caldwell NJ 07006 **Phn:** 973-852-0300 **Fax:** 973-808-5516 wmbctv.com **Email:** news@wmbctv.com

NEW MEXICO

Albuquerque: KASA (FOX) 13 Broadcast Plz SW Albuquerque NM 87104 **Phn:** 505-243-2285 **Fax:** 505-842-8483 www.kasa.com

Albuquerque: KASY (MY) 8341 Washington St NE Albuquerque NM 87113 **Phn:** 505-797-1919 **Fax:** 505-938-4401 www.my50.tv **Email:** steve.wroski@my50.tv

Albuquerque: KAZQ (REL) 4501 Montgomery Blvd NE Albuquerque NM 87109 **Phn:** 505-884-8355 **Fax:** 505-883-1229 kazq32.org **Email:** rfranks@kazq32.org

Albuquerque: KCHF (IND) PO Box 4338 Albuquerque NM 87196 **Phn:** 505-473-1111 **Fax:** 505-345-5669 www.sonbroadcasting.cc **Email:** info@sonbroadcasting.cc

Albuquerque: KLUZ (SPN) 2725 Broadbent Pkwy NE Ste E Albuquerque NM 87107 **Phn:** 505-342-4141 **Fax:** 505-344-8714 www.univision.com **Email:** acontreras@entravision.com

Albuquerque: KNAT (REL) 1510 Coors Blvd NW Albuquerque NM 87121 **Phn:** 505-836-6585 **Fax:** 505-831-8725 www.tbn.org **Email:** knat@tbn.org

Albuquerque: KNME (PBS) 1130 University Blvd NE Albuquerque NM 87102 **Phn:** 505-277-2121 **Fax:** 505-277-5967 www.newmexicopbs.org **Email:** fjoachim@newmexicopbs.org

Albuquerque: KOAT (ABC) 3801 Carlisle Blvd NE Albuquerque NM 87107 **Phn:** 505-884-7777 **Fax:** 505-884-6354 www.koat.com **Email:** koatdesk@hearst.com

Albuquerque: KOB (NBC) 4 Broadcast Plz SW Albuquerque NM 87104 **Phn:** 505-243-4411 **Fax:** 505-764-2456 www.kob.com **Email:** news@kob.com

Albuquerque: KRQE (CBS) 13 Broadcast Plz SW Albuquerque NM 87104 **Phn:** 505-243-2285 **Fax:** 505-842-8483 www.krqe.com **Email:** newsdesk@krqe.com

Albuquerque: KTEL (SPN) PO Box 30068 Albuquerque NM 87190 **Phn:** 505-884-5353 **Fax:** 505-889-8390 www.telemundo.com

Albuquerque: KWBQ (CW) 8341 Washington St NE Albuquerque NM 87113 **Phn:** 505-797-1919 **Fax:** 505-344-1145 www.newmexicoscw.tv **Email:** steve.wroski@newmexicoscw.tv

Las Cruces: KRWG (PBS) PO Box 30001 Las Cruces NM 88003 **Phn:** 575-646-2222 **Fax:** 575-646-1924 krwg.org **Email:** feedback@nmsu.edu

Portales: KENW (PBS) 1500 S Ave K Portales NM 88130 **Phn:** 575-562-2112 **Fax:** 575-562-2590 kenw.org **Email:** kenwtv@enmu.edu

Roswell: KBIM (CBS) 214 N Main St Roswell NM 88201 **Phn:** 575-622-2120 **Fax:** 575-623-6606 www.krqe.com **Email:** newsdesk@krqe.com

NEW YORK

Albany: WNYT (NBC) 715 N Pearl St Albany NY 12204 **Phn:** 518-436-4791 **Fax:** 518-434-0659 wnyt.com **Email:** newstips@wnyt.com

Albany: WTEN (ABC) 341 Northern Blvd Albany NY 12204 **Phn:** 518-436-4822 **Fax:** 518-426-4792 www.news10.com **Email:** news@news10.com

Albany: WXXA (FOX) 28 Corporate Cir Albany NY 12203 **Phn:** 518-862-2323 **Fax:** 518-862-0930 www.fox23news.com

Binghamton: WBGH (NBC) 203 Ingraham Hill Rd Binghamton NY 13903 **Phn:** 607-771-3434 **Fax:** 607-723-6403 www.binghamtonhomepage.com **Email:** news@nc34.com

Binghamton: WIVT (ABC) 203 Ingraham Hill Rd Binghamton NY 13903 **Phn:** 607-771-3434 **Fax:** 607-723-6403 www.newschannel34.com **Email:** news@newschannel34.com

NEW MEXICO TV STATIONS

Binghamton: WSKG (PBS) PO Box 3000 Binghamton NY 13902 **Phn:** 607-729-0100 **Fax:** 607-729-7328 www.wskg.org **Email:** mail@wskg.org

Buffalo: WGRZ (NBC) 259 Delaware Ave Buffalo NY 14202 **Phn:** 716-849-2222 **Fax:** 716-849-7602 www.WGRZ.com **Email:** news@wgrz.com

Buffalo: WIVB (CBS) 2077 Elmwood Ave Buffalo NY 14207 **Phn:** 716-874-4410 **Fax:** 716-874-8173 www.wivb.com **Email:** chris.musial@wivb.com

Buffalo: WKBW (ABC) 7 Broadcast Plz Buffalo NY 14202 **Phn:** 716-845-6100 **Fax:** 716-856-8784 www.wkbw.com **Email:** news@wkbw.com

Buffalo: WNED (PBS) PO Box 1263 Buffalo NY 14240 **Phn:** 716-845-7000 **Fax:** 716-845-7036 www.wned.org

Buffalo: WNLO (CW) 2077 Elmwood Ave Buffalo NY 14207 **Phn:** 716-874-4410 **Fax:** 716-874-8173 www.cw23.com **Email:** newsroom@wivb.com

Buffalo: WNYO (MY) 699 Hertel Ave Ste 100 Buffalo NY 14207 **Phn:** 716-875-4949 **Fax:** 716-875-4919 www.mytvbuffalo.com **Email:** programming@mytvbuffalo.com

Buffalo: WPXJ (ION) 726 Exchange St Ste 605 Buffalo NY 14210 **Phn:** 716-852-1818 **Fax:** 716-852-8288 www.iontelevision.com **Email:** barbaralipka@ionmedia.com

Buffalo: WUTV (FOX) 699 Hertel Ave Ste 100 Buffalo NY 14207 **Phn:** 716-447-3200 **Fax:** 716-875-4919 www.wutv29.com **Email:** comments@sbgi.net

Champlain: WWBI (ION) 732 Prospect St Champlain NY 12919 **Phn:** 518-297-2727 **Fax:** 518-298-3210 www.iontelevision.com **Email:** wwbitv27@hotmail.com

Corning: WYDC (FOX) 33 E Market St Corning NY 14830 **Phn:** 607-937-5000 **Fax:** 607-937-4019 wydc-tv.com **Email:** jmattison@wydctv.com

East Syracuse: WSPX (ION) 6508 Basile Rowe # B East Syracuse NY 13057 **Phn:** 315-414-0178 **Fax:** 315-414-0482 www.iontelevision.com **Email:** margomccaffery@ionmedia.com

East Syracuse: WSYR (ABC) 5904 Bridge St East Syracuse NY 13057 **Phn:** 315-446-9999 **Fax:** 315-446-9283 www.9wsyr.com **Email:** assignmentdesk@9wsyr.com

Elmira: WETM (NBC) 101 E Water St Elmira NY 14901 **Phn:** 607-733-5518 **Fax:** 607-733-4739 www.mytwintiers.com **Email:** wetmnewswriters@wetmtv.com

Guilderland: WYPX (ION) 1 Charles Blvd Ste 5 Guilderland NY 12084 **Phn:** 518-464-0143 **Fax:** 518-464-0633 www.iontelevision.com **Email:** reneeosterlitz@ionmedia.com

Horseheads: WENY (ABC) 474 Old Ithaca Rd Horseheads NY 14845 **Phn:** 607-739-3636 **Fax:** 607-796-6171 www.weny.com **Email:** news36@weny.com

Johnson City: WBNG (CBS) 560 Columbia Dr Johnson City NY 13790 **Phn:** 607-729-8812 **Fax:** 607-729-4022 www.wbng.com **Email:** wbng@wbngtv.com

Melville: WLNY (IND) 270 S Service Rd Melville NY 11747 **Phn:** 631-777-8855 **Fax:** 631-420-4822 newyork.cbslocal.com **Email:** wcbstvnewstips@cbs.com

New York: WABC (ABC) 7 Lincoln Sq New York NY 10023 **Phn:** 212-456-7000 **Fax:** 212-456-2381 abclocal.go.comwabc **Email:** eyewitness@abc.com

New York: WCBS (CBS) 524 W 57th St New York NY 10019 **Phn:** 212-975-4321 **Fax:** 212-975-9387 newyork.cbslocal.com **Email:** wcbstvwebteam@cbs.com

New York: WLIW (PBS) 450 Wt 33rd St New York NY 10001 **Phn:** 212-560-8021 www.wliw.org **Email:** programming@wliw.org

New York: WNBC (NBC) 30 Rockefeller Plz New York NY 10112 **Phn:** 212-664-4444 **Fax:** 212-664-2994 www.nbcnewyork.com **Email:** tips@nbcnewyork.com

New York: WNET (PBS) 825 8th Ave Fl 14 New York NY 10019 **Phn:** 212-560-1313 **Fax:** 212-560-1314 www.thirteen.org **Email:** web@thirteen.org

New York: WNYE (PBS) 1 Centre St Fl 27 New York NY 10007 **Phn:** 212-669-3000 www.nyc.govhtmlmediahtmlhomehome.shtml **Email:** submissions@media.nyc.gov

New York: WNYW (FOX) 205 E 67th St New York NY 10065 **Phn:** 212-452-5555 **Fax:** 212-452-5563 www.myfoxny.com **Email:** jim.driscoll@foxtv.com

New York: WPIX (CW) 220 E 42nd St New York NY 10017 **Phn:** 212-949-1100 **Fax:** 212-210-2591 wpix.com

New York: WPXN (ION) 810 7th Ave Fl 31 New York NY 10019 **Phn:** 212-603-8432 **Fax:** 212-664-5918 www.iontelevision.com

New York: WTBY (REL) 111 E 15th St New York NY 10003 **Phn:** 212-777-2120 **Fax:** 212-777-0405 www.tbn.org **Email:** wtby@tbn.org

Orchard Park: WNYB (REL) 5775 Big Tree Rd Orchard Park NY 14127 **Phn:** 716-662-2659 **Fax:** 716-667-2499 www.tct.tv **Email:** wnyb@tct.tv

Plattsburgh: WCFE (PBS) 1 Sesame St Plattsburgh NY 12901 **Phn:** 518-563-9770 **Fax:** 518-561-1928 mountainlake.org

Plattsburgh: WPTZ (NBC) 5 Television Dr Plattsburgh NY 12901 **Phn:** 518-561-5555 **Fax:** 518-561-1201 www.wptz.com **Email:** program@wptz.com

Rochester: WHAM (ABC) 4225 W Henrietta Rd Rochester NY 14623 **Phn:** 585-334-8700 **Fax:** 585-334-8719 www.13wham.com **Email:** news@13wham.com

Rochester: WHEC (NBC) 191 East Ave Rochester NY 14604 **Phn:** 585-546-5670 **Fax:** 585-546-5688 www.whec.com

Rochester: WROC (CBS) 201 Humboldt St Rochester NY 14610 **Phn:** 585-288-8400 **Fax:** 585-288-1505 rochesterhomepage.net **Email:** newsroom@rochesterhomepage.net

Rochester: WUHF (FOX) 201 Humboldt St Rochester NY 14610 **Phn:** 585-288-8400 **Fax:** 585-288-1505 rochesterhomepage.net **Email:** newsroom@rochesterhomepage.net

Rochester: WXXI (PBS) 280 State St Rochester NY 14614 **Phn:** 585-325-7500 **Fax:** 585-258-0335 www.wxxi.org **Email:** newsroom@wxxi.org

Rye Brook: WRNN (IND) 800 Westchester Ave Ste S640 Rye Brook NY 10573 **Phn:** 914-417-2700 **Fax:** 914-696-0276 www.rnntv.com **Email:** comments@rnntv.com

Schenectady: WCWN (CW) 1400 Balltown Rd Schenectady NY 12309 **Phn:** 518-381-4900 **Fax:** 518-381-3770 www.cwalbany.com

Schenectady: WNYA (MY) 17 Fern Ave Schenectady NY 12306 **Phn:** 518-381-3751 **Fax:** 518-381-3740 wnyt.com **Email:** newstips@wnyt.com

Schenectady: WRGB (CBS) 1400 Balltown Rd Schenectady NY 12309 **Phn:** 518-346-6666 **Fax:** 518-346-6249 www.cbs6albany.com **Email:** news@cbs6albany.com

Secaucus: WWOR (MY) 9 Broadcast Plz Secaucus NJ 07094 **Phn:** 201-348-0009 **Fax:** 201-330-3844 www.my9nj.com

Syracuse: WCNY (PBS) PO Box 2400 Syracuse NY 13220 **Phn:** 315-453-2424 **Fax:** 315-451-8824 www.wcny.org **Email:** wcny_online@wcny.org

Syracuse: WNYS (MY) 1000 James St Syracuse NY 13203 **Phn:** 315-472-6800 **Fax:** 315-471-8889 www.my43.tv **Email:** programming@my43.tv

Syracuse: WSTM (NBC) 1030 James St Syracuse NY 13203 **Phn:** 315-477-9400 **Fax:** 315-474-5122 www.cnycentral.com **Email:** news@wstm.com

Syracuse: WSYT (FOX) 1000 James St Syracuse NY 13203 **Phn:** 315-472-6800 **Fax:** 315-471-8889 www.foxsyracuse.com **Email:** programming@wsyt68.com

Syracuse: WTVH (CBS) 1030 James St Syracuse NY 13203 **Phn:** 315-477-9400 **Fax:** 315-474-5122 www.cnycentral.com **Email:** news@cnycentral.com

Troy: WMHT (PBS) 4 Global Vw Troy NY 12180 **Phn:** 518-880-3400 **Fax:** 518-880-3409 www.wmht.org

Utica: WFXV (FOX) 5956 Smith Hill Rd Utica NY 13502 **Phn:** 315-797-5220 **Fax:** 315-797-5409 cnyhomepage.com **Email:** smerren@wutr.tv

Utica: WKTV (NBC) 5936 Smith Hill Rd Utica NY 13502 **Phn:** 315-733-0404 **Fax:** 315-733-4893 www.wktv.com **Email:** smcmurray@wktv.com

Utica: WUTR (ABC) 5956 Smith Hill Rd Utica NY 13502 **Phn:** 315-797-5220 **Fax:** 315-797-5409 cnyhomepage.com **Email:** smerren@wutr.tv

Vestal: WICZ (FOX) 4600 Vestal Pkwy E Vestal NY 13850 **Phn:** 607-770-4040 **Fax:** 607-798-7950 www.wicz.com **Email:** jhorn@wicz.com

Wainscott: WVVH (IND) PO Box 769 Wainscott NY 11975 **Phn:** 212-935-4613 **Fax:** 212-935-4449 www.wvvh.com **Email:** info@wvvh.com

Watertown: WNYF (FOX) 120 Arcade St Watertown NY 13601 **Phn:** 315-788-3800 **Fax:** 315-788-3787 www.wwnytv.com **Email:** fox28@wwnytv.net

Watertown: WPBS (PBS) 1056 Arsenal St Watertown NY 13601 **Phn:** 315-782-3142 **Fax:** 315-782-2491 www.wpbstv.org **Email:** lbrown@wpbstv.org

Watertown: WWNY (CBS) 120 Arcade St Watertown NY 13601 **Phn:** 315-788-3800 **Fax:** 315-788-3787 www.wwnytv.com **Email:** news@wwnytv.net

Watertown: WWTI (ABC) 1222 Arsenal St Watertown NY 13601 **Phn:** 315-785-8850 **Fax:** 315-779-8921 www.informnny.com **Email:** news@myabc50.com

NORTH CAROLINA

Asheville: WLOS (ABC) 110 Technology Dr Asheville NC 28803 **Phn:** 828-684-1340 **Fax:** 828-651-4618 www.wlos.com **Email:** news@wlos.com

Asheville: WMYA (MY) 110 Technology Dr Asheville NC 28803 **Phn:** 864-297-1313 **Fax:** 864-297-8085 www.my40.tv **Email:** news@wlos.com

Charlotte: WAXN (IND) PO Box 34665 Charlotte NC 28234 **Phn:** 704-338-9999 **Fax:** 704-335-4736 www.wsoctv.com **Email:** assignment@wsoc-tv.com

Charlotte: WBTV (CBS) 1 Julian Price Pl Charlotte NC 28208 **Phn:** 704-374-3500 **Fax:** 704-374-3671 www.wbtv.com **Email:** assignmentdesk@wbtv.com

Charlotte: WCCB (FOX) 1 Television Pl Charlotte NC 28205 **Phn:** 704-372-1800 **Fax:** 704-632-7540 www.foxcharlotte.com **Email:** wccb@foxcharlotte.com

Charlotte: WCNC (NBC) 1001 Woodridge Center Dr Charlotte NC 28217 **Phn:** 704-329-3636 **Fax:** 704-357-4975 www.wcnc.com **Email:** news@wcnc.com

Charlotte: WJZY (CW) 3501 Performance Rd Charlotte NC 28214 **Phn:** 704-398-0046 **Fax:** 704-393-8407 www.myfoxcarolinas.com **Email:** info@wjzy.com

NEW YORK TV STATIONS

Charlotte: WMYT (MY) 3501 Performance Rd Charlotte NC 28214 **Phn:** 704-398-0046 **Fax:** 704-393-8407 www.wmyt12.com **Email:** info@wmyt12.com

Charlotte: WSOC (ABC) PO Box 34665 Charlotte NC 28234 **Phn:** 704-338-9999 **Fax:** 704-335-4736 www.wsoctv.com **Email:** public@wsoc-tv.com

Charlotte: WTVI (PBS) 3242 Commonwealth Ave Charlotte NC 28205 **Phn:** 704-372-2442 **Fax:** 704-335-1358 www.wtvi.org **Email:** rberry@wtvi.org

Durham: WRAZ (FOX) 512 S Mangum St Ste 100 Durham NC 27701 **Phn:** 919-595-5050 **Fax:** 919-821-8541 www.fox50.com **Email:** jstanley@fox50.com

Durham: WTVD (ABC) 411 Liberty St Durham NC 27701 **Phn:** 919-683-1111 **Fax:** 919-687-4373 abclocal.go.comwtvd **Email:** rob.elmore@abc.com

Greensboro: WCWG (CW) 2A Pai Park Greensboro NC 27409 **Phn:** 336-307-4900 **Fax:** 336-307-4950 triad20.com **Email:** production@wcwg20.com

Greensboro: WFMY (CBS) 1615 Phillips Ave Greensboro NC 27405 **Phn:** 336-379-9369 **Fax:** 336-230-0971 www.digtriad.com **Email:** assignmentdesk@wfmy.com

Greensboro: WGPX (ION) 1114 N Ohenry Blvd Greensboro NC 27405 **Phn:** 336-272-9227 **Fax:** 336-272-9298 www.iontelevision.com

Greensboro: WLXI (REL) 2109 Patterson St Greensboro NC 27407 **Phn:** 336-855-5610 www.tct-net.org **Email:** wlxi@tct.tv

Greenville: WNCT (CBS) 3221 Evans St Greenville NC 27834 **Phn:** 252-355-8500 **Fax:** 252-355-8566 www.wnct.com **Email:** newsdesk@wnct.com

Hickory: WHKY (IND) PO Box 1059 Hickory NC 28603 **Phn:** 828-322-5115 **Fax:** 828-485-5558 www.whky.com **Email:** whky@whky.com

High Point: WGHP (FOX) 2005 Francis St High Point NC 27263 **Phn:** 336-841-8888 **Fax:** 336-841-5169 myfox8.com **Email:** news@wghp.com

Lumber Bridge: WFPX (ION) PO Box 62 Lumber Bridge NC 28357 **Phn:** 919-827-4801 **Fax:** 919-876-1415 www.iontelevision.com **Email:** michellebarnhill@ionmedia.com

New Bern: WCTI (ABC) 225 Glenburnie Dr New Bern NC 28560 **Phn:** 252-638-1212 **Fax:** 252-637-4141 www.wcti12.com **Email:** news@wcti12.com

New Bern: WEPX (ION) 1301 S Glenburnie Rd New Bern NC 28562 **Phn:** 252-636-2550 **Fax:** 252-633-7851 www.iontelevision.com

New Bern: WFXI (FOX) 225 Glenburnie Dr New Bern NC 28560 **Phn:** 252-638-1212 **Fax:** 252-637-4141 www.fox8fox14.com **Email:** news@wcti12.com

New Bern: WYDO (FOX) 225 Glenburnie Dr New Bern NC 28560 **Phn:** 252-638-1212 **Fax:** 252-636-6855 www.fox8fox14.com **Email:** news@wcti12.com

Raleigh: WLFL (CW) 3012 Highwoods Blvd Ste 101 Raleigh NC 27604 **Phn:** 919-872-9535 **Fax:** 919-878-3697 www.raleighcw.com

Raleigh: WNCN (NBC) 1205 Front St Raleigh NC 27609 **Phn:** 919-836-1717 **Fax:** 919-836-1687 www.wncn.com **Email:** newstips@wncn.com

Raleigh: WRAL (CBS) 2619 Western Blvd Raleigh NC 27606 **Phn:** 919-821-8555 **Fax:** 919-821-8541 www.wral.com **Email:** assignmentdesk@wral.com

Raleigh: WRDC (MY) 3012 Highwoods Blvd Ste 101 Raleigh NC 27604 **Phn:** 919-872-2854 **Fax:** 919-878-6588 www.myrdctv.com

Raleigh: WRPX (ION) 3209 Gresham Lake Rd Ste 151 Raleigh NC 27615 **Phn:** 919-876-1642 **Fax:** 919-876-1415 www.iontelevision.com **Email:** michellebarnhill@ionmedia.com

Raleigh: WUVC (SPN) 900 Ridgefield Dr Ste 100 Raleigh NC 27609 **Phn:** 919-872-7440 **Fax:** 919-878-4029 www.univision.com

Research Triangle Park: WUNC (PBS) PO Box 14900 Research Triangle Park NC 27709 **Phn:** 919-549-7000 **Fax:** 919-549-7043 www.unctv.org **Email:** mlewis@unctv.org

Washington: WITN (NBC) PO Box 468 Washington NC 27889 **Phn:** 252-946-3131 **Fax:** 252-946-0558 www.witn.com **Email:** desk@witn.com

Wilmington: WECT (NBC) 322 Shipyard Blvd Wilmington NC 28412 **Phn:** 910-791-8070 **Fax:** 910-791-9535 www.wect.com **Email:** wect@wect.com

Wilmington: WILM (CBS) 3333 Wrightsville Ave Ste G Wilmington NC 28403 **Phn:** 910-798-0000 **Fax:** 910-798-0001 www.wilm-tv.com **Email:** psa@wilm-tv.com

Wilmington: WSFX (FOX) 322 Shipyard Blvd Wilmington NC 28412 **Phn:** 910-791-8070 **Fax:** 910-202-0493 www.wsfx.com

Wilmington: WWAY (ABC) 615 N Front St Wilmington NC 28401 **Phn:** 910-762-8581 **Fax:** 910-341-7926 www.wwaytv3.com **Email:** jjones@wwaytv3.com

Winston Salem: WMYV (MY) 3500 Myer Lee Dr Winston Salem NC 27101 **Phn:** 336-274-4848 **Fax:** 336-723-8217 www.my48.tv **Email:** jpruitt@sbgnet.com

Winston Salem: WXII (NBC) 700 Coliseum Dr Winston Salem NC 27106 **Phn:** 336-721-9944 **Fax:** 336-721-0856 www.wxii12.com **Email:** newstips@wxii12.com

Winston Salem: WXLV (ABC) 3500 Myer Lee Dr Winston Salem NC 27101 **Phn:** 336-722-4545 **Fax:** 336-723-8217 www.abc45.com **Email:** jpruitt@sbgnet.com

NORTH DAKOTA

Bismarck: KBMY (ABC) 1811 N 15th St Bismarck ND 58501 **Phn:** 701-223-1700 **Fax:** 701-223-1985 www.abc17.tv

Bismarck: KFYR (NBC) PO Box 1738 Bismarck ND 58502 **Phn:** 701-255-5757 **Fax:** 701-255-8244 www.kfyrtv.com **Email:** news@kfyrtv.com

Bismarck: KNDX (FOX) PO Box 4026 Bismarck ND 58502 **Phn:** 701-355-0026 **Fax:** 701-250-7244 fox26.tv **Email:** mbecker@fox26.tv

Bismarck: KXMB (CBS) 1811 N 15th St Bismarck ND 58501 **Phn:** 701-223-9197 **Fax:** 701-223-1985 www.kxnet.com **Email:** tgerhardt@kxnet.com

Dickinson: KQCD (NBC) 373 21st St E Dickinson ND 58601 **Phn:** 701-483-7777 **Fax:** 701-483-8231 www.kqcd.com **Email:** news@kqcd.com

Dickinson: KXMA (CBS) 1625 W Villard St Dickinson ND 58601 **Phn:** 701-483-1400 www.kxnet.com **Email:** tgerhardt@kxnet.com

Fargo: KFME (PBS) 207 5th St N Fargo ND 58102 **Phn:** 701-241-6900 **Fax:** 701-239-7650 www.prairiepublic.org **Email:** dthompson@prairiepublic.org

Fargo: KVLY (NBC) 1350 21st Ave S Fargo ND 58103 **Phn:** 701-282-0444 **Fax:** 701-282-0743 www.valleynewslive.com **Email:** mail@valleynewslive.com

Fargo: KVRR (FOX) PO Box 9115 Fargo ND 58106 **Phn:** 701-277-1515 **Fax:** 701-277-9656

Fargo: KXJB (CBS) 1350 21st Ave S Fargo ND 58103 **Phn:** 701-282-0444 **Fax:** 701-282-0743 valleynewslive.com **Email:** mail@valleynewslive.com

Fargo: WDAY (ABC) 301 8th St S Fargo ND 58103 **Phn:** 701-237-6500 **Fax:** 701-241-5358 www.wday.com **Email:** jnelson@wday.com

Grand Forks: WDAZ (ABC) 2220 S Washington St Grand Forks ND 58201 **Phn:** 701-775-2511 **Fax:** 701-746-4507 www.wdaz.com **Email:** news@wdaz.com

Minot: KMOT (NBC) 1800 16th St SW Minot ND 58701 **Phn:** 701-852-4101 **Fax:** 701-838-6781 www.kmot.com **Email:** news@kmot.com

Minot: KXMC (CBS) PO Box 1617 Minot ND 58702 **Phn:** 701-852-2104 **Fax:** 701-838-1050 www.kxnet.com **Email:** jolson@kxmcnews.com

Minot: KXND (FOX) 605 31st Ave SW Ste A Minot ND 58701 **Phn:** 701-858-0024 **Fax:** 701-838-8473 fox24.tv

Williston: KUMV (NBC) 602 Main St Williston ND 58801 **Phn:** 701-572-4676 **Fax:** 701-572-0118 www.kumv.com **Email:** news@kumv.com

Williston: KXMD (CBS) 1802 13th Ave W Williston ND 58801 **Phn:** 701-572-2345 **Fax:** 701-572-0658 www.kxnet.com **Email:** jolson@kxmcnews.com

OHIO

Akron: WAX (IND) PO Box 2170 Akron OH 44309 **Phn:** 330-673-2323 **Fax:** 330-673-0301 **Email:** sheri@wnir.com

Athens: WOUB (PBS) 9 S College St Athens OH 45701 **Phn:** 740-593-1771 **Fax:** 740-593-9599 woub.org **Email:** news@woub.org

Bowling Green: WBGU (PBS) 245 Troup Ave Bowling Green OH 43402 **Phn:** 419-372-2700 **Fax:** 419-372-7048 www.wbgu.org **Email:** wbgufeedback@bgsu.edu

Castalia: WGGN (REL) PO Box 247 Castalia OH 44824 **Phn:** 419-684-5311 **Fax:** 419-684-5378 www.wggn.tv

Cincinnati: WBQC (IND) 7737 Reinhold Dr Cincinnati OH 45237 **Phn:** 513-681-3800 **Fax:** 513-351-8898 www.wbqc.com **Email:** info@wbqc.com

Cincinnati: WCET (PBS) 1223 Central Pkwy Cincinnati OH 45214 **Phn:** 513-381-4033 **Fax:** 513-381-7520 www.cetconnect.org **Email:** comments@cetconnect.org

Cincinnati: WCPO (ABC) 1720 Gilbert Ave Cincinnati OH 45202 **Phn:** 513-721-9900 **Fax:** 513-721-7717 www.wcpo.com **Email:** newsdesk@wcpo.com

Cincinnati: WKRC (CBS) 1906 Highland Ave Cincinnati OH 45219 **Phn:** 513-763-5500 **Fax:** 513-421-3820 www.local12.com **Email:** local12@local12.com

Cincinnati: WLWT (NBC) 1700 Young St Cincinnati OH 45202 **Phn:** 513-412-5000 **Fax:** 513-412-6121 www.wlwt.com

Cincinnati: WSTR (MY) 5177 Fishwick Dr Cincinnati OH 45216 **Phn:** 513-641-4400 **Fax:** 513-242-2633 www.star64.tv **Email:** rwhite@sbgnet.com

Cincinnati: WXIX (FOX) 635 W 7th St Ste 200 Cincinnati OH 45203 **Phn:** 513-421-1919 **Fax:** 513-421-3022 www.fox19.com **Email:** desk@fox19.com

Cleveland: WBNX (CW) PO Box 91660 Cleveland OH 44101 **Phn:** 440-843-5555 **Fax:** 440-842-5597 www.wbnx.com **Email:** jwerth@wbnx.com

Cleveland: WEWS (ABC) 3001 Euclid Ave Cleveland OH 44115 **Phn:** 216-431-5555 **Fax:** 216-431-3666 www.newsnet5.com **Email:** newsdesk@wews.com

Cleveland: WJW (FOX) 5800 S Marginal Rd Cleveland OH 44103 **Phn:** 216-431-8888 **Fax:** 216-391-9559 fox8.com **Email:** kevin.salyer@fox8.com

Cleveland: WKYC (NBC) 1333 Lakeside Ave E Cleveland OH 44114 **Phn:** 216-344-3333 **Fax:** 216-344-3314 www.wkyc.com **Email:** news@wkyc.com

Cleveland: WOIO (CBS) 1717 E 12th St Cleveland OH 44114 **Phn:** 216-771-1943 **Fax:** 216-436-5460 www.19actionnews.com **Email:** 19tips@woio.com

Cleveland: WQHS (SPN) 2861 W Ridgewood Dr Cleveland OH 44134 **Phn:** 440-888-0061 **Fax:** 440-888-7023 www.univision.com

Cleveland: WUAB (MY) 1717 E 12th St Cleveland OH 44114 **Phn:** 216-771-1943 **Fax:** 216-436-5460 43theblock.com **Email:** dsalamone@woio.com

Cleveland: WVIZ (PBS) 1375 Euclid Ave Ste LL Cleveland OH 44115 **Phn:** 216-916-6100 **Fax:** 216-916-6101 www.wviz.org

Cleveland: WVPX (ION) 1333 Lakeside Ave E Cleveland OH 44114 **Phn:** 216-344-7465 **Fax:** 216-344-7430 www.iontelevision.com **Email:** latonyapettit@ionmedia.com

Columbus: WBNS (CBS) 770 Twin Rivers Dr Columbus OH 43215 **Phn:** 614-460-3700 **Fax:** 614-460-2891 www.10tv.com **Email:** john.cardenas@10tv.com

Columbus: WCMH (NBC) 3165 Olentangy River Rd Columbus OH 43202 **Phn:** 614-263-4444 **Fax:** 614-263-0166 www.nbc4i.com **Email:** newsdesk@nbc4i.com

Columbus: WOSU (PBS) 2400 Olentangy River Rd Columbus OH 43210 **Phn:** 614-292-9678 **Fax:** 614-688-3343 www.wosu.org **Email:** newsroom@wosu.org

Columbus: WSFJ (REL) 3948 Townsfair Way Ste 220 Columbus OH 43219 **Phn:** 614-416-6080 **Fax:** 614-416-6345 www.tbn.org

Columbus: WSYX (ABC) 1261 Dublin Rd Columbus OH 43215 **Phn:** 614-481-6666 **Fax:** 614-481-6624 www.columbusnewscenter.com **Email:** webmaster@wsyx6.com

Columbus: WTTE (FOX) 1261 Dublin Rd Columbus OH 43215 **Phn:** 614-481-6666 **Fax:** 614-481-6624 www.myfox28columbus.com **Email:** news@wsyx6.com

Columbus: WWHO (CW) 1160 Dublin Rd Ste 400 Columbus OH 43215 **Phn:** 614-485-5300 **Fax:** 614-485-5339 www.cwcolumbus.com

Dayton: WHIO (CBS) 1414 Wilmington Ave Dayton OH 45420 **Phn:** 937-259-2111 **Fax:** 937-259-2005 www.whiotv.com **Email:** 7online@whiotv.com

Dayton: WKEF (ABC) 45 Broadcast Plz Dayton OH 45417 **Phn:** 937-263-4500 **Fax:** 937-268-5265 www.abc22now.com **Email:** comments@abc22now.com

Dayton: WPTD (PBS) 110 S Jefferson St Dayton OH 45402 **Phn:** 937-220-1600 **Fax:** 937-220-1642 www.thinktv.org

Dayton: WRCX (ION) 708 W Hillcrest Ave Dayton OH 45406 **Phn:** 937-275-7677 **Fax:** 937-277-3698 www.wrcxtv40.com **Email:** anthony@wrcxtv40.com

Dayton: WRGT (FOX) 45 Broadcast Plz Dayton OH 45417 **Phn:** 937-263-4500 **Fax:** 937-268-2332 abc.daytonsnewssource.com **Email:** comments@daytonsnewssource.com

Kent: WNEO (PBS) PO Box 5191 Kent OH 44240 **Phn:** 330-677-4549 **Fax:** 330-678-0688 www.westernreservepublicmedia.org **Email:** programs@westernreservepublicmedia.org

Lima: WLIO (NBC) 1424 Rice Ave Lima OH 45805 **Phn:** 419-228-8835 **Fax:** 419-225-6109 www.wlio.com

Lima: WOHL (FOX) PO Box 1689 Lima OH 45802 **Phn:** 419-228-8835 **Fax:** 419-289-7091

Lima: WTLW (REL) 1844 Baty Rd Lima OH 45807 **Phn:** 419-339-4444 **Fax:** 419-339-1736 wtlw.com **Email:** traffic@wtlw.com

Moraine: WBDT (CW) 4595 S Dixie Dr Moraine OH 45439 **Phn:** 937-293-2101 www.daytonscw.com **Email:** email@daytonscw.com

Moraine: WDTN (NBC) 4595 S Dixie Dr Moraine OH 45439 **Phn:** 937-293-2101 **Fax:** 937-296-7147 www.wdtn.com **Email:** newstips@wdtn.com

Ontario: WMFD (IND) 2900 Park Ave W Ontario OH 44906 **Phn:** 419-529-5900 **Fax:** 419-529-2319 www.wmfd.com **Email:** newsroom@wmfd.com

Portsmouth: WQCW (CW) 800 Gallia St Ste 430 Portsmouth OH 45662 **Phn:** 740-353-3391 **Fax:** 304-344-9719 www.tristatescw.com

Steubenville: WTOV (NBC) 9 Red Donley Plz Steubenville OH 43952 **Phn:** 740-282-9999 **Fax:** 740-282-0439 www.wtov9.com **Email:** newsdesk@wtov.com

Toledo: WGTE (PBS) PO Box 30 Toledo OH 43614 **Phn:** 419-380-4600 **Fax:** 419-380-4710 www.wgte.orgwgte **Email:** public_relations@wgte.pbs.org

Toledo: WLMB (REL) 825 Capital Commons Dr Toledo OH 43615 **Phn:** 419-720-9562 **Fax:** 419-720-9563 www.wlmb.com **Email:** info@wlmb.com

Toledo: WNWO (NBC) 300 S Byrne Rd Toledo OH 43615 **Phn:** 419-535-0024 **Fax:** 419-535-8936 www.northwestohio.com **Email:** jblue@wnwo.com

Toledo: WTOL (CBS) 730 N Summit St Toledo OH 43604 **Phn:** 419-248-1111 **Fax:** 419-244-7104 www.toledonewsnow.com **Email:** news@toledonewsnow.com

Toledo: WTVG (ABC) 4247 Dorr St Toledo OH 43607 **Phn:** 419-531-1313 **Fax:** 419-534-3898 www.13abc.com **Email:** wtvg.news@13abc.com

Toledo: WUPW (FOX) 730 N Summit St Toledo OH 43604 **Phn:** 419-244-3600 **Fax:** 419-244-7104 www.toledonewsnow.com **Email:** news@toledonewsnow.com

Youngstown: WFMJ (NBC) 101 W Boardman St Youngstown OH 44503 **Phn:** 330-744-8611 **Fax:** 330-742-2472 www.wfmj.com **Email:** 21newsnow@wfmj.com

Youngstown: WKBN (CBS) 3930 Sunset Blvd Youngstown OH 44512 **Phn:** 330-782-1144 **Fax:** 330-782-5261 www.wkbn.com **Email:** assignment@wkbn.com

Youngstown: WYFX (FOX) 3944 Sunset Blvd Youngstown OH 44512 **Phn:** 330-782-1144 **Fax:** 330-782-5261 www.wkbn.com **Email:** assignment@wkbn.com

Zanesville: WHIZ (NBC) 629 Downard Rd Zanesville OH 43701 **Phn:** 740-452-5431 **Fax:** 740-452-6553 www.whiznews.com **Email:** jbullock@whizmediagroup.com

OKLAHOMA

Broken Arrow: KDOR (REL) 2120 N Yellowood Ave Broken Arrow OK 74012 **Phn:** 918-250-0777 **Fax:** 918-461-8817 www.tbn.org **Email:** kdor@tbn.org

Lawton: KSWO (ABC) PO Box 708 Lawton OK 73502 **Phn:** 580-355-7000 **Fax:** 580-355-0059 www.kswo.com **Email:** 7news@kswo.com

Oklahoma City: KAUT (CW) 444 E Britain Rd Oklahoma City OK 73114 **Phn:** 405-424-4444 **Fax:** 405-478-6264

Oklahoma City: KETA (PBS) 7403 N Kelley Ave Oklahoma City OK 73111 **Phn:** 405-848-8501 **Fax:** 405-841-9226 www.oeta.tv **Email:** info@oeta.tv

Oklahoma City: KFOR (NBC) 444 E Britton Rd Oklahoma City OK 73114 **Phn:** 405-424-4444 **Fax:** 405-478-6337 kfor.com **Email:** jesse.wells@kfor.com

Oklahoma City: KOCB (CW) 1228 E Wilshire Blvd Oklahoma City OK 73111 **Phn:** 405-478-3434 **Fax:** 405-475-9120 www.cwokc.com **Email:** csnow@sbgnet.com

Oklahoma City: KOCO (ABC) 1300 E Britton Rd Oklahoma City OK 73131 **Phn:** 405-478-3000 **Fax:** 405-478-6675 www.koco.com **Email:** desk@koco.com

Oklahoma City: KOKH (FOX) 1228 E Wilshire Blvd Oklahoma City OK 73111 **Phn:** 405-843-2525 **Fax:** 405-475-9120 www.okcfox.com **Email:** kokhnews@sbgnet.com

Oklahoma City: KOPX (ION) 13424 Railway Dr Oklahoma City OK 73114 **Phn:** 405-751-6800 **Fax:** 405-751-6867 www.iontelevision.com **Email:** philipbrooks@ionmedia.com

Oklahoma City: KTBO (REL) 1600 E Hefner Rd Oklahoma City OK 73131 **Phn:** 405-848-1414 www.tbn.org **Email:** ktbo@tbn.org

Oklahoma City: KTUZ (SPN) 5101 S Shields Blvd Oklahoma City OK 73129 **Phn:** 405-429-5061 **Fax:** 405-616-5511 www.ktuztv.com **Email:** armando.r@tylermedia.com

Oklahoma City: KUOK (SPN) 5101 S Shields Blvd Oklahoma City OK 73129 **Phn:** 405-616-5530 **Fax:** 405-616-5511 www.univisionok.com **Email:** armando.r@tylermedia.com

Oklahoma City: KWTV (CBS) 7401 N Kelley Ave Oklahoma City OK 73111 **Phn:** 405-843-6641 **Fax:** 405-841-9989 www.news9.com

Tulsa: KGEB (IND) 7777 S Lewis Ave Tulsa OK 74171 **Phn:** 918-488-5300 **Fax:** 918-495-7388 www.kgeb.net **Email:** kgeb@oru.edu

Tulsa: KJRH (NBC) 3701 S Peoria Ave Tulsa OK 74105 **Phn:** 918-743-2222 **Fax:** 918-748-1436 www.kjrh.com **Email:** news@kjrh.com

Tulsa: KMYT (MY) 2625 S Memorial Dr Tulsa OK 74129 **Phn:** 918-491-0023 **Fax:** 918-388-0516 www.fox23.com **Email:** ning@fox23.com

Tulsa: KOKI (FOX) 2625 S Memorial Dr Tulsa OK 74129 **Phn:** 918-491-0023 **Fax:** 918-388-0516 www.fox23.com **Email:** ning@fox23.com

Tulsa: KOTV (CBS) 302 S Frankfort Ave Tulsa OK 74120 **Phn:** 918-732-6000 **Fax:** 918-732-6185 www.newson6.com **Email:** newsdesk@newson6.net

Tulsa: KQCW (CW) 302 S Frankfort Ave Tulsa OK 74120 **Phn:** 918-732-6000 www.tulsacw.com **Email:** mystory@newson6.net

Tulsa: KTPX (ION) 5800 E Skelly Dr Ste 101 Tulsa OK 74135 **Phn:** 918-664-1044 **Fax:** 918-664-1483 www.iontelevision.com

Tulsa: KTUL (ABC) PO Box 8 Tulsa OK 74101 **Phn:** 918-445-8888 **Fax:** 918-445-9359 www.ktul.com **Email:** pbaldwin@ktul.com

Tulsa: KWHB (IND) 8835 S Memorial Dr Tulsa OK 74133 **Phn:** 918-254-4701 **Fax:** 918-254-5614 www.kwhb.com **Email:** kkrebbs@lesea.com

Yukon: KSBI (IND) 9802 N Morgan Rd Yukon OK 73099 **Phn:** 405-631-7335 **Fax:** 405-631-7367 www.ksbitv.com **Email:** programming@ksbitv.com

OREGON

Beaverton: KPDX (IND) 14975 NW Greenbrier Pkwy Beaverton OR 97006 **Phn:** 503-906-1249 **Fax:** 503-548-6920 www.kptv.com **Email:** webstaff@kpdx.com

Beaverton: KPTV (FOX) 14975 NW Greenbrier Pkwy Beaverton OR 97006 **Phn:** 503-906-1249 **Fax:** 503-548-6920 www.kptv.com **Email:** kptvnews@kptv.com

Beaverton: KRCW (CW) 10255 SW Arctic Dr Beaverton OR 97005 **Phn:** 503-644-3232 **Fax:** 503-626-3576 www.portlandscw32.com **Email:** news@nw32.com

OKLAHOMA TV STATIONS

Bend: KFXO (FOX) PO Box 6038 Bend OR 97708 **Phn:** 541-382-7220 **Fax:** 541-382-1616

Bend: KOHD (ABC) 63049 Lower Meadow Dr Bend OR 97701 **Phn:** 541-749-5151 kohd.com **Email:** gfair@zolomedia.com

Bend: KTVZ (NBC) PO Box 6038 Bend OR 97708 **Phn:** 541-383-2121 **Fax:** 541-382-1616 www.ktvz.com **Email:** stories@ktvz.com

Coos Bay: KCBY (CBS) PO Box 1156 Coos Bay OR 97420 **Phn:** 541-269-1111 **Fax:** 541-269-7464 www.kcby.com **Email:** kcby@kcby.com

Dallas: KWVT (IND) 17980 Brown Rd Dallas OR 97338 **Phn:** 503-930-7728 www.kwvtsalem.com **Email:** info@kwvtsalem.com

Eugene: KEVU (MY) 2940 Chad Dr Eugene OR 97408 **Phn:** 541-683-2525 **Fax:** 541-683-8016 www.oregonsfox.biz **Email:** info@oregonsfox.com

Eugene: KEZI (ABC) PO Box 7009 Eugene OR 97401 **Phn:** 541-485-5611 **Fax:** 541-343-9664 kezi.com **Email:** newsdesk@kezi.com

Eugene: KLSR (FOX) 2940 Chad Dr Eugene OR 97408 **Phn:** 541-683-3434 **Fax:** 541-683-8016 www.myfoxeugene.com

Eugene: KVAL (CBS) 4575 Blanton Rd Eugene OR 97405 **Phn:** 541-342-4961 **Fax:** 541-342-5436 www.kval.com **Email:** kval13news@kval.com

Medford: KDRV (ABC) 1090 Knutson Ave Medford OR 97504 **Phn:** 541-773-1212 **Fax:** 541-776-0659 kdrv.com **Email:** newsdesk@kdrv.com

Medford: KFBI (MY) 1236 N Riverside Ave Medford OR 97501 **Phn:** 541-245-5244 **Fax:** 541-245-5247 www.kfbimy48.com

Medford: KMVU (FOX) 820 Crater Lake Ave Ste 105 Medford OR 97504 **Phn:** 541-772-2600 **Fax:** 541-772-7364 roguelocal.wix.comfox26medford

Medford: KOBI (NBC) 125 S Fir St Medford OR 97501 **Phn:** 541-779-5555 **Fax:** 541-779-5018 localnewscomesfirst.com **Email:** newsrelease@kobi5.com

Medford: KSYS (PBS) 28 S Fir St Ste 200 Medford OR 97501 **Phn:** 541-779-0808 **Fax:** 541-779-2178 www.soptv.org **Email:** jriley@soptv.org

Medford: KTVL (CBS) 1440 Rossanley Dr Medford OR 97501 **Phn:** 541-773-7373 **Fax:** 541-245-5705 www.ktvl.com **Email:** ktvl@ktvl.com

Portland: KATU (ABC) 2153 NE Sandy Blvd Portland OR 97232 **Phn:** 503-231-4200 **Fax:** 503-231-4263 www.katu.com **Email:** thedesk@katu.com

Portland: KGW (NBC) 1501 SW Jefferson St Portland OR 97201 **Phn:** 503-226-5000 **Fax:** 503-226-5059 www.kgw.com **Email:** newsdesk@kgw.com

Portland: KOIN (CBS) 222 SW Columbia St Portland OR 97201 **Phn:** 503-464-0600 **Fax:** 503-464-0806 www.koin.com **Email:** news@koin.com

Portland: KOPB (PBS) 7140 SW Macadam Ave Portland OR 97219 **Phn:** 503-244-9900 **Fax:** 503-293-1919 www.opb.org **Email:** opbnews@opb.org

Portland: KPXG (ION) 811 SW Naito Pkwy Ste 100 Portland OR 97204 **Phn:** 503-222-2221 **Fax:** 503-222-4613 www.iontelevision.com

Portland: KUPN (SPN) 2153 NE Sandy Blvd Portland OR 97232 **Phn:** 503-231-4222 **Fax:** 503-963-2628 www.kunptv.com **Email:** noticias@kunptv.com

Roseburg: KPIC (CBS) PO Box 1345 Roseburg OR 97470 **Phn:** 541-672-4481 **Fax:** 541-672-4482 www.kpic.com **Email:** kpic4news@kpic.com

Springfield: KMTR (NBC) 3825 International Ct Springfield OR 97477 **Phn:** 541-746-1600 **Fax:** 541-747-3429 www.kmtr.com **Email:** newsdesk@kmtr.com

PENNSYLVANIA

Allentown: WBPH (IND) 813 N Fenwick St Allentown PA 18109 **Phn:** 610-433-4400 **Fax:** 610-433-8251 www.wbph.org **Email:** huber@nni.com

Allentown: WFMZ (IND) 300 E Rock Rd Allentown PA 18103 **Phn:** 610-797-4530 **Fax:** 610-791-9994 www.wfmz.com **Email:** news@wfmz.com

Altoona: WTAJ (CBS) 5000 6th Ave Ste 1 Altoona PA 16602 **Phn:** 814-942-1010 **Fax:** 814-946-4763 wearecentralpa.com **Email:** gill@wtajtv.com

Bala Cynwyd: WCAU (NBC) 10 Monument Rd Bala Cynwyd PA 19004 **Phn:** 610-668-5510 **Fax:** 610-668-3700 www.nbcphiladelphia.com **Email:** tips@nbcphiladelphia.com

Bethlehem: WLVT (PBS) 123 Sesame St Bethlehem PA 18015 **Phn:** 610-867-4677 **Fax:** 610-867-3544 www.wlvt.org

Chambersburg: WJAL (IND) 262 Swamp Fox Rd Chambersburg PA 17202 **Phn:** 717-375-4000 **Fax:** 717-375-4052 www.wjal.com

Erie: WFXP (FOX) 8455 Peach St Erie PA 16509 **Phn:** 814-864-2400 **Fax:** 814-864-1704 yourerie.com **Email:** lbaxter@wjettv.com

Erie: WICU (NBC) 3514 State St Erie PA 16508 **Phn:** 814-454-5201 **Fax:** 814-454-3753 www.erietvnews.com **Email:** news@wicu12.com

Erie: WJET (ABC) 8455 Peach St Erie PA 16509 **Phn:** 814-864-2400 **Fax:** 814-864-1704 yourerie.com **Email:** lbaxter@wjettv.com

Erie: WQLN (PBS) 8425 Peach St Erie PA 16509 **Phn:** 814-864-3001 **Fax:** 814-864-4077 www.wqln.org **Email:** dmiller@wqln.org

Erie: WSEE (CBS) 3514 State St Erie PA 16508 **Phn:** 814-455-7575 **Fax:** 814-454-2564 www.erietvnews.com **Email:** news@wicu12.com

Harrisburg: WHP (CBS) 3300 N 6th St Harrisburg PA 17110 **Phn:** 717-238-2100 **Fax:** 717-238-4903 www.local21news.com **Email:** news@local21news.com

Harrisburg: WHTM (ABC) 3235 Hoffman St Box 5860 Harrisburg PA 17110 **Phn:** 717-236-2727 **Fax:** 717-236-1263 www.abc27.com **Email:** news@abc27.com

Harrisburg: WITF (PBS) 4801 Lindle Rd Harrisburg PA 17111 **Phn:** 717-704-3000 **Fax:** 717-704-3678 www.witf.org **Email:** news@witf.org

Harrisburg: WLYH (CW) 3300 N 6th St Harrisburg PA 17110 **Phn:** 717-238-2100 **Fax:** 717-238-4903 www.cw15.com **Email:** news@cbs21.com

Hazleton: WYLN (IND) 1057 E 10th St Hazleton PA 18201 **Phn:** 570-459-1869 **Fax:** 570-459-1625 www.wylntv.com **Email:** wylnlateedition@hotmail.com

Johnstown: WATM (ABC) 1450 Scalp Ave Johnstown PA 15904 **Phn:** 814-266-8088 **Fax:** 814-266-7749 www.abc23.com **Email:** jream@fox8tv.com

Johnstown: WJAC (NBC) 49 Old Hickory Ln Johnstown PA 15905 **Phn:** 814-255-7600 **Fax:** 814-255-7658 www.wjactv.com **Email:** news@wjactv.com

Johnstown: WWCP (FOX) 1450 Scalp Ave Johnstown PA 15904 **Phn:** 814-266-8088 **Fax:** 814-266-7749 www.fox8tv.com **Email:** jream@fox8tv.com

Lancaster: WGAL (NBC) 1300 Columbia Ave Lancaster PA 17603 **Phn:** 717-393-5851 **Fax:** 717-295-7457 www.wgal.com **Email:** news8@wgal.com

Moosic: WNEP (ABC) 16 Montage Mountain Rd Moosic PA 18507 **Phn:** 570-346-7474 **Fax:** 570-341-1344 wnep.com **Email:** news@wnep.com

Philadelphia: KYW (CBS) 1555 Hamilton St Philadelphia PA 19130 **Phn:** 215-977-5300 **Fax:** 215-977-5658 philadelphia.cbslocal.com **Email:** tips@kyw.com

Philadelphia: WFPA (SPN) 1700 Market St Ste 1550 Philadelphia PA 19103 **Phn:** 215-568-2800 **Fax:** 215-568-2865 www.univision.com

Philadelphia: WHYY (PBS) 150 N 6th St Philadelphia PA 19106 **Phn:** 215-351-1200 **Fax:** 215-351-3352 www.whyy.org **Email:** newsroom@whyy.org

Philadelphia: WPHL (MY) 5001 Wynnefield Ave Philadelphia PA 19131 **Phn:** 215-878-1700 **Fax:** 215-879-3665 myphl17.com

Philadelphia: WPPX (ION) 3901B Main St Ste 301 Philadelphia PA 19127 **Phn:** 215-482-4770 **Fax:** 215-482-4777 www.iontelevision.com **Email:** mariaalpohoritis@ionmedia.com

Philadelphia: WPSG (CW) 1555 Hamilton St Philadelphia PA 19130 **Phn:** 215-977-5700 **Fax:** 215-977-5658 cwphilly.cbslocal.com **Email:** newsdesk@cbs3.com

Philadelphia: WPVI (ABC) 4100 City Ave Philadelphia PA 19131 **Phn:** 215-878-9700 **Fax:** 215-581-4530 abclocal.go.comwpvi **Email:** cyber6@abc.com

Philadelphia: WTXF (FOX) 330 Market St Philadelphia PA 19106 **Phn:** 215-925-2929 **Fax:** 215-982-5494 www.myfoxphilly.com **Email:** newsdesk@fox29.com

Philadelphia: WYBE (PBS) 8200 Ridge Ave Philadelphia PA 19128 **Phn:** 215-483-3900 **Fax:** 215-483-6908 www.mindtv.org **Email:** feedback@mindtv.org

Pittsburgh: KDKA (CBS) 420 Fort Duquesne Blvd # 100 Pittsburgh PA 15222 **Phn:** 412-575-2200 **Fax:** 412-575-2871 cwpittsburgh.cbslocal.com **Email:** newsdesk@kdka.com

Pittsburgh: WBGN (IND) 975 Greentree Rd Pittsburgh PA 15220 **Phn:** 412-922-9576 **Fax:** 412-921-6937 www.wbgn.com **Email:** debbie@wbgn.com

Pittsburgh: WPCW (CW) 420 Fort Duquesne Blvd # 100 Pittsburgh PA 15222 **Phn:** 412-575-2200 **Fax:** 412-575-2871 cwpittsburgh.cbslocal.com **Email:** newsdesk@kdka.com

Pittsburgh: WPGH (FOX) 750 Ivory Ave Pittsburgh PA 15214 **Phn:** 412-931-5300 www.wpgh53.com **Email:** promotions@wpgh53.com

Pittsburgh: WPMY (MY) 750 Ivory Ave Pittsburgh PA 15214 **Phn:** 412-931-5300 www.mypittsburghtv.com **Email:** programming@wpgh53.com

Pittsburgh: WPXI (NBC) 4145 Evergreen Rd Pittsburgh PA 15214 **Phn:** 412-237-1100 **Fax:** 412-237-4900 www.wpxi.com **Email:** assignments@wpxi.com

Pittsburgh: WQED (PBS) 4802 5th Ave Ste 1 Pittsburgh PA 15213 **Phn:** 412-622-1300 **Fax:** 412-622-6413 www.wqed.org **Email:** webmaster@wqed.org

Pittsburgh: WTAE (ABC) 400 Ardmore Blvd Pittsburgh PA 15221 **Phn:** 412-242-4300 **Fax:** 412-244-4628 www.wtae.com **Email:** news@wtae.com

Pittston: WVIA (PBS) 100 Wvia Way Pittston PA 18640 **Phn:** 570-344-1244 **Fax:** 570-655-1180 www.wvia.org **Email:** psa@wvia.org

Plains: WOLF (FOX) 1181 Highway 315 Blvd Plains PA 18702 **Phn:** 570-970-5600 **Fax:** 570-970-5601 www.myfoxnepa.com **Email:** myphl17@fox56.com

Plains: WQMY (MY) 1181 Highway 315 Blvd Plains PA 18702 **Phn:** 570-970-5600 **Fax:** 570-970-5601 www.myfoxnepa.com **Email:** myfoxnepa@fox56.com

PENNSYLVANIA TV STATIONS

Plains: WSWB (CW) 1181 Highway 315 Blvd Plains PA 18702 **Phn:** 570-970-5600 **Fax:** 570-970-5601 www.myfoxnepa.com **Email:** lgreenwald@fox56.com

Reading: WTVE (IND) 1729 N 11th St Reading PA 19604 **Phn:** 610-921-9181 **Fax:** 914-696-0279 www.wtve.com **Email:** newsdesk@fios1news.com

Red Lion: WGCB (IND) PO Box 88 Red Lion PA 17356 **Phn:** 717-246-1681 **Fax:** 717-244-9316 www.wgcbtv.com **Email:** jpeeling@wgcbtv.com

Scranton: WQPX (ION) 409 Lackawanna Ave Ste 700 Scranton PA 18503 **Phn:** 570-344-6400 **Fax:** 570-344-3303 www.iontelevision.com **Email:** reginalanzo@ionmedia.com

University Park: WPSU (PBS) 238 Outreach Bldg University Park PA 16802 **Phn:** 814-865-3333 **Fax:** 814-865-3145 www.wpsu.org **Email:** wpsu@psu.edu

Wall: WKBS (IND) 1 Signal Hill Dr Wall PA 15148 **Phn:** 412-824-3930 **Fax:** 412-824-5442 www.ctvn.org **Email:** info@ctvn.org

Wilkes Barre: WBRE (NBC) 62 S Franklin St Wilkes Barre PA 18701 **Phn:** 570-823-2828 **Fax:** 570-829-0440 pahomepage.com **Email:** newsdesk@pahomepage.com

Wilkes Barre: WYOU (CBS) 62 S Franklin St Wilkes Barre PA 18701 **Phn:** 570-823-2828 **Fax:** 570-829-0440 pahomepage.com **Email:** newsdesk@pahomepage.com

York: WPMT (FOX) 2005 S Queen St York PA 17403 **Phn:** 717-843-0043 **Fax:** 717-845-6655 fox43.com **Email:** news@fox43.com

RHODE ISLAND

Cranston: WJAR (NBC) 23 Kenney Dr Cranston RI 02920 **Phn:** 401-455-9100 **Fax:** 401-455-9140 www.turnto10.com **Email:** 10@wjar.com

Cranston: WRIW (SPN) 23 Kenney Dr Cranston RI 02920 **Phn:** 401-463-5575 www.zgsgroup.com **Email:** telemundoprovidence@gmail.com

East Providence: WNAC (FOX) 25 Catamore Blvd East Providence RI 02914 **Phn:** 401-438-7200 **Fax:** 401-431-1012 www.foxprovidence.com **Email:** desk@wpri.com

East Providence: WPRI (CBS) 25 Catamore Blvd East Providence RI 02914 **Phn:** 401-438-7200 **Fax:** 401-431-1012 www.eyewitnessnewstv.com **Email:** desk@wpri.com

Providence: WLNE (ABC) 10 Orms St Providence RI 02904 **Phn:** 401-453-8000 **Fax:** 401-331-4431 www.abc6.com **Email:** traffic@abc6.com

Providence: WLWC (CW) 275 Westminster St Ste 100 Providence RI 02903 **Phn:** 401-351-8828 **Fax:** 401-351-0222 www.thecwprov.com **Email:** tcastano@thecwprov.com

Providence: WSBE (PBS) 50 Park Ln Providence RI 02907 **Phn:** 401-222-3636 **Fax:** 401-222-3407 www.ripbs.org **Email:** public@ripbs.org

SOUTH CAROLINA

Beaufort: WJWJ (PBS) 925 Ribaut Rd Beaufort SC 29902 **Phn:** 843-524-0808 **Fax:** 843-524-1016 www.scetv.org **Email:** sjohnson@scetv.org

Charleston: WCSC (CBS) 2126 Charlie Hall Blvd Charleston SC 29414 **Phn:** 843-402-5555 **Fax:** 843-402-5744 www.live5news.com **Email:** wcscdesk@live5news.com

Columbia: WACH (FOX) 1400 Pickens St Ste 600 Columbia SC 29201 **Phn:** 803-252-5757 **Fax:** 803-212-7270 www.wach.com **Email:** news@wach.com

Columbia: WIS (NBC) 1111 Bull St Columbia SC 29201 **Phn:** 803-799-1010 **Fax:** 803-758-1278 www.wistv.com **Email:** countonwis@wistv.com

Columbia: WLTX (CBS) 6027 Garners Ferry Rd Columbia SC 29209 **Phn:** 803-776-3600 **Fax:** 803-776-1791 www.wltx.com **Email:** news19@wltx.gannett.com

Columbia: WOLO (ABC) 5807 Shakespeare Rd Columbia SC 29223 **Phn:** 803-754-7525 **Fax:** 803-691-4015 www.abccolumbia.com **Email:** eyewitnessnews@wolo.com

Columbia: WRJA (PBS) 1101 George Rogers Blvd Columbia SC 29201 **Phn:** 803-773-3545 **Fax:** 803-775-1059 www.scetv.org

Columbia: WRZB (CW) 1747 Cushman Dr Columbia SC 29204 **Phn:** 803-714-2347 **Fax:** 803-691-3848 www.roberts-companies.com

Conway: WWMB (CW) 1194 Atlantic Ave Conway SC 29526 **Phn:** 843-234-9733 **Fax:** 843-234-9739 www.carolinalive.com **Email:** feedback@wpde.com

Greenville: WGGS (REL) PO Box 1616 Greenville SC 29602 **Phn:** 864-244-1616 **Fax:** 864-292-8481 wggs16.com **Email:** traffic@wggs16.com

Greenville: WHNS (FOX) 21 Interstate Ct Greenville SC 29615 **Phn:** 864-288-2100 **Fax:** 864-987-1219 www.foxcarolina.com **Email:** whns@foxcarolina.com

Greenville: WYFF (NBC) 505 Rutherford St Greenville SC 29609 **Phn:** 864-242-4404 **Fax:** 864-240-5305 www.wyff4.com **Email:** newstips@wyff4.com

Mount Pleasant: WCBD (NBC) 210 W Coleman Blvd Mount Pleasant SC 29464 **Phn:** 843-884-2222 **Fax:** 843-884-6624 www.counton2.com **Email:** newstip@wcbd.com

Mount Pleasant: WCIV (ABC) 888 Allbritton Blvd Mount Pleasant SC 29464 **Phn:** 843-881-4444 **Fax:** 843-849-2519 www.abcnews4.com **Email:** desk@abcnews4.com

Myrtle Beach: WBTW (CBS) 101 McDonald Ct Myrtle Beach SC 29588 **Phn:** 843-317-1313 **Fax:** 843-317-1416 www.wbtw.com **Email:** skorioth@wbtw.com

Myrtle Beach: WFXB (FOX) 3364 Huger St Myrtle Beach SC 29577 **Phn:** 843-828-4300 **Fax:** 843-828-4343 www.wfxb.com **Email:** tsaghri@wfxb.com

Myrtle Beach: WMBF (ABC) 918 Frontage Rd E Myrtle Beach SC 29577 **Phn:** 843-839-7973 **Fax:** 843-839-7973 www.wmbfnews.com **Email:** news@wmbfnews.com

Myrtle Beach: WPDE (ABC) PO Box 51150 Myrtle Beach SC 29579 **Phn:** 843-234-9733 **Fax:** 843-234-9739 www.carolinalive.com **Email:** feedback@wpde.com

North Charleston: WMMP (MY) 4301 Arco Ln North Charleston SC 29418 **Phn:** 843-744-2424 **Fax:** 843-554-9649 mytvcharleston.com **Email:** programming@mytvcharleston.com

North Charleston: WTAT (FOX) 4301 Arco Ln Ste A North Charleston SC 29418 **Phn:** 843-744-2424 **Fax:** 843-554-9649 www.foxcharleston.com **Email:** programming@wtat24.com

Rock Hill: WNSC (PBS) PO Box 11766 Rock Hill SC 29731 **Phn:** 803-324-3184 **Fax:** 803-324-0580 www.scetv.org **Email:** godish@scetv.org

Spartanburg: WRET (PBS) PO Box 4069 Spartanburg SC 29305 **Phn:** 864-503-9371 **Fax:** 864-503-3615 www.scetv.org **Email:** csr@scetv.org

Spartanburg: WSPA (CBS) 250 International Dr Spartanburg SC 29303 **Phn:** 864-576-7777 **Fax:** 864-587-5430 www.wspa.com **Email:** newschannel7@wspa.com

Spartanburg: WYCW (CW) 250 International Dr Spartanburg SC 29303 **Phn:** 864-576-7777 **Fax:** 864-587-5430 www.carolinascw.com **Email:** webmaster@carolinascw.com

SOUTH DAKOTA

Rapid City: KCLO (CBS) 3615 Canyon Lake Dr Ste 5 Rapid City SD 57702 **Phn:** 605-331-1500 **Fax:** 605-348-5518 www.keloland.com **Email:** dexter@keloland.com

Rapid City: KEVN (FOX) PO Box 677 Rapid City SD 57709 **Phn:** 605-394-7777 **Fax:** 605-394-3652 www.blackhillsfox.com **Email:** news@blackhillsfox.com

Rapid City: KNBN (NBC) PO Box 9549 Rapid City SD 57709 **Phn:** 605-355-0024 **Fax:** 605-355-0564 www.newscenter1.tv **Email:** news@newscenter1.com

Rapid City: KOTA (ABC) PO Box 1760 Rapid City SD 57709 **Phn:** 605-342-2000 **Fax:** 605-721-5730 www.kotatv.com **Email:** johnpetersen@kotatv.com

Sioux City: KMEG (CBS) PO Box 3103 Sioux City SD 51102 **Phn:** 712-277-3554 **Fax:** 712-255-5250 www.siouxlandnews.com **Email:** news@siouxlandnews.com

Sioux City: KPTH (FOX) PO Box 3103 Sioux City SD 51102 **Phn:** 712-277-3554 **Fax:** 712-255-5250 www.siouxlandnews.com **Email:** news@siouxlandnews.com

Sioux Falls: KCPO (IND) PO Box 88336 Sioux Falls SD 57109 **Phn:** 605-334-0026 **Fax:** 605-334-5575 www.kcpo.tv **Email:** mail@kcpo.tv

Sioux Falls: KDLT (NBC) 3600 S Westport Ave Ste 100 Sioux Falls SD 57106 **Phn:** 605-361-5555 **Fax:** 605-361-7017 www.kdlt.com **Email:** news@kdlt.com

Sioux Falls: KELO (CBS) 501 S Phillips Ave Sioux Falls SD 57104 **Phn:** 605-336-1100 **Fax:** 605-336-0202 www.keloland.com **Email:** dexter@keloland.com

Sioux Falls: KSFY (ABC) 300 N Dakota Ave Ste 100 Sioux Falls SD 57104 **Phn:** 605-336-1300 **Fax:** 605-336-7936 www.ksfy.com **Email:** news@ksfy.com

Sioux Falls: KTTW (FOX) 2817 W 11th St Sioux Falls SD 57104 **Phn:** 605-338-0017 **Fax:** 605-338-7173 www.kttw.com **Email:** edh@kttw.com

Vermillion: KBHE (PBS) PO Box 5000 Vermillion SD 57069 **Phn:** 605-677-5861 **Fax:** 605-677-5010 www.sdpb.org **Email:** news@sdpb.org

Vermillion: KUSD (PBS) PO Box 5000 Vermillion SD 57069 **Phn:** 605-677-5861 **Fax:** 605-677-5010 www.sdpb.org **Email:** news@sdpb.org

TENNESSEE

Chattanooga: WDEF (CBS) 3300 Broad St Chattanooga TN 37408 **Phn:** 423-785-1200 **Fax:** 423-785-1273 www.wdef.com **Email:** news@wdef.com

Chattanooga: WDSI (FOX) 1101 E Main St Chattanooga TN 37408 **Phn:** 423-265-0061 **Fax:** 423-265-3636 www.myfoxchattanooga.com **Email:** rfrank@fox61tv.com

Chattanooga: WFLI (CW) 1101 E Main St Chattanooga TN 37408 **Phn:** 423-265-0061 **Fax:** 423-265-3607 **Email:** jgiddens@fox61tv.com

Chattanooga: WRCB (NBC) 900 Whitehall Rd Chattanooga TN 37405 **Phn:** 423-267-5412 **Fax:** 423-756-3148 www.wrcbtv.com **Email:** news@wrcbtv.com

Chattanooga: WTCI (PBS) 7540 Bonnyshire Dr Chattanooga TN 37416 **Phn:** 423-629-0045 **Fax:** 423-698-8557 wtcitv.org **Email:** jcrutchfield@wtcitv.org

Chattanooga: WTVC (ABC) 4279 Benton Dr Chattanooga TN 37406 **Phn:** 423-756-5500 **Fax:** 423-757-7401 www.newschannel9.com **Email:** news@newschannel9.com

Cookeville: WCTE (PBS) PO Box 2040 Cookeville TN 38502 **Phn:** 931-528-2222 **Fax:** 931-372-6284 www.wcte.org

SOUTH DAKOTA TV STATIONS

Cordova: WKNO (PBS) 7151 Cherry Farms Rd Cordova TN 38016 **Phn:** 901-458-2521 **Fax:** 901-325-6505 www.wkno.org **Email:** wknopi@wkno.org

Hendersonville: WPGD (REL) 1 Music Village Blvd Hendersonville TN 37075 **Phn:** 615-822-1243 **Fax:** 615-822-1642 www.tbn.org **Email:** wpgd@tbn.org

Jackson: WBBJ (ABC) 346 Muse St Jackson TN 38301 **Phn:** 731-424-4515 **Fax:** 731-424-9299 www.wbbjtv.com **Email:** abc7news@wbbjtv.com

Johnson City: WJHL (CBS) 338 E Main St Johnson City TN 37601 **Phn:** 423-926-2151 **Fax:** 423-926-9080 www.tricities.com **Email:** news@wjhl.com

Kingsport: WAPK (MY) 222 Commerce St Kingsport TN 37660 **Phn:** 423-246-9578 **Fax:** 423-246-1863 wapktv.com **Email:** ffalin@hvbcgroup.com

Kingsport: WKPT (ABC) 222 Commerce St Kingsport TN 37660 **Phn:** 423-246-9578 **Fax:** 423-246-1863 www.wkpttv.com **Email:** ffalin@hvbcgroup.com

Knoxville: WATE (ABC) 1306 N Broadway St Knoxville TN 37917 **Phn:** 865-637-6666 **Fax:** 865-523-3561 www.wate.com **Email:** newsroom@wate.com

Knoxville: WBIR (NBC) 1513 Hutchinson Ave Knoxville TN 37917 **Phn:** 865-637-1010 **Fax:** 865-522-7341 www.wbir.com **Email:** news@wbir.com

Knoxville: WBXX (CW) 10427 Cogdill Rd Ste 100 Knoxville TN 37932 **Phn:** 865-777-9220 **Fax:** 865-777-9221 www.wbxx.tv

Knoxville: WKOP (PBS) 1611 E Magnolia Ave Knoxville TN 37917 **Phn:** 865-595-0220 **Fax:** 865-595-0300 www.easttennesseepbs.org **Email:** programming@easttennesseepbs.org

Knoxville: WMAK (IND) 6215 Kingston Pike Ste A Knoxville TN 37919 **Phn:** 865-329-8777 **Fax:** 865-584-9098

Knoxville: WPXK (ION) 9000 Executive Park Dr Ste D300 Knoxville TN 37923 **Phn:** 865-531-4037 **Fax:** 865-531-4760 www.iontelevision.com **Email:** hollyjones@ionmedia.com

Knoxville: WTNZ (FOX) 9000 Executive Park Dr Ste D300 Knoxville TN 37923 **Phn:** 865-693-4343 **Fax:** 865-523-3561 www.wtnzfox43.com **Email:** cwhitfield@wtnzfox43.com

Knoxville: WVLT (MY) 6450 Papermill Dr Knoxville TN 37919 **Phn:** 865-450-8888 **Fax:** 865-584-1978 www.local8now.com **Email:** wvltnews@wvlt-tv.com

Kodak: WVLR (REL) 306 Kyker Ferry Rd Kodak TN 37764 **Phn:** wvlr-tv.weebly.com **Email:** comments@ctntv.net

Martin: WLJT (PBS) PO Box 966 Martin TN 38237 **Phn:** 731-881-7561 **Fax:** 731-881-7566 www.wljt.org **Email:** kcobb@wljt.org

Memphis: WHBQ (FOX) 485 S Highland St Memphis TN 38111 **Phn:** 901-320-1313 **Fax:** 901-320-1366 www.myfoxmemphis.com **Email:** news@myfoxmemphis.com

Memphis: WLMT (CW) 2701 Union Avenue Ext Memphis TN 38112 **Phn:** 901-323-2430 **Fax:** 901-452-1820 www.localmemphis.com **Email:** newsdesk@localmemphis.com

Memphis: WMC (NBC) 1960 Union Ave Memphis TN 38104 **Phn:** 901-726-0555 **Fax:** 901-278-7633 www.wmctv.com **Email:** desk@wmctv.com

Memphis: WPTY (ABC) 2701 Union Avenue Ext Memphis TN 38112 **Phn:** 901-323-2430 **Fax:** 901-452-1820 www.abc24.com **Email:** newsdesk@abc24.com

Memphis: WPXX (ION) 5050 Poplar Ave Ste 909 Memphis TN 38157 **Phn:** 901-821-8593 **Fax:** 901-821-8331 www.iontelevision.com

Memphis: WREG (CBS) 803 Channel 3 Dr Memphis TN 38103 **Phn:** 901-543-2333 **Fax:** 901-543-2167 wreg.com **Email:** news@wreg.com

Mount Juliet: WHTN (REL) 9582 Lebanon Rd Mount Juliet TN 37122 **Phn:** 615-754-0039 ctntv.org

Mount Juliet: WNPX (ION) 1281 N Mount Juliet Rd # L Mount Juliet TN 37122 **Phn:** 615-773-6100 **Fax:** 615-758-4105 www.iontelevision.com **Email:** cassandraeasley@ionmedia.com

Nashville: WKRN (ABC) 441 Murfreesboro Pike Nashville TN 37210 **Phn:** 615-369-7222 **Fax:** 615-369-7329 www.wkrn.com **Email:** news@wkrn.com

Nashville: WNAB (CW) 631 Mainstream Dr Nashville TN 37228 **Phn:** 615-259-5617 **Fax:** 615-350-5843 www.cw58.tv **Email:** news@fox17.com

Nashville: WNPT (PBS) 161 Rains Ave Nashville TN 37203 **Phn:** 615-259-9325 **Fax:** 615-248-6120 www.wnpt.org **Email:** tv8@wnpt.org

Nashville: WSMV (NBC) 5700 Knob Rd Nashville TN 37209 **Phn:** 615-353-4444 **Fax:** 615-353-2343 www.wsmv.com **Email:** news@wsmv.com

Nashville: WTVF (CBS) 474 James Robertson Pkwy Nashville TN 37219 **Phn:** 615-244-5000 **Fax:** 615-244-9883 www.newschannel5.com **Email:** newsroom@newschannel5.com

Nashville: WUXP (MY) 631 Mainstream Dr Nashville TN 37228 **Phn:** 615-259-5617 **Fax:** 615-259-5605 www.mytv30web.com **Email:** news@fox17.com

Nashville: WZTV (FOX) 631 Mainstream Dr Nashville TN 37228 **Phn:** 615-259-5617 **Fax:** 615-259-3962 www.fox17.com **Email:** news@fox17.com

TEXAS

Abilene: KRBC (NBC) 4510 S 14th St Abilene TX 79605 **Phn:** 325-692-4242 **Fax:** 325-692-8265 bigcountryhomepage.com **Email:** news@krbc.tv

Abilene: KTAB (CBS) 4510 S 14th St Abilene TX 79605 **Phn:** 325-692-5822 **Fax:** 325-691-5822 bigcountryhomepage.com **Email:** news@ktab.tv

Abilene: KTES (SPN) 4420 N Clack St Abilene TX 79601 **Phn:** 325-677-2281 **Fax:** 325-676-9231

Abilene: KTXE (ABC) 4420 N Clack St Abilene TX 79601 **Phn:** 325-677-2281 **Fax:** 325-676-9231 **Email:** fry@ktxs.com

Abilene: KTXS (ABC) PO Box 2997 Abilene TX 79604 **Phn:** 325-677-2281 **Fax:** 325-676-9231 www.ktxs.com **Email:** news@ktxs.com

Addison: KTXD (IND) 15455 Dallas Pkwy # 100 Addison TX 75001 **Phn:** 214-628-9900 **Fax:** 972-528-6895 www.ktxdtv.com **Email:** info@ktxdtv.com

Amarillo: KACV (PBS) PO Box 447 Amarillo TX 79178 **Phn:** 806-371-5222 **Fax:** 806-371-5258 www.panhandlepbs.org **Email:** panhandlepbs@actx.edu

Amarillo: KAMR (NBC) PO Box 751 Amarillo TX 79189 **Phn:** 806-383-3321 **Fax:** 806-381-0912 myhighplains.com **Email:** news@kamr.com

Amarillo: KCIT (FOX) 1015 S Fillmore St Amarillo TX 79101 **Phn:** 806-374-1414 **Fax:** 806-371-0408 www.myhighplains.com **Email:** comments@kamr.com

Amarillo: KCPN (MY) 1015 S Fillmore St Amarillo TX 79101 **Phn:** 806-374-1414 **Fax:** 806-371-0408 myhighplains.com **Email:** comments@kamr.com

Amarillo: KEYU (SPN) 1616 S Kentucky St Ste D130 Amarillo TX 79102 **Phn:** 806-359-8900

TEXAS TV STATIONS

Amarillo: KFDA (CBS) PO Box 10 Amarillo TX 79105 **Phn:** 806-383-1010 **Fax:** 806-381-9859 www.newschannel10.com **Email:** newsroom@newschannel10.com

Amarillo: KTMO (SPN) PO Box 10 Amarillo TX 79105 **Phn:** 806-383-1010 **Fax:** 806-383-7178 www.newschannel10.com **Email:** newsroom@newschannel10.com

Amarillo: KVII (ABC) 1 Broadcast Ctr Amarillo TX 79101 **Phn:** 806-373-1787 **Fax:** 806-373-6397 www.connectamarillo.com **Email:** rhazelwood@kvii.com

Arlington: KPXD (ION) 600 Six Flags Dr Ste 652 Arlington TX 76011 **Phn:** 817-633-6843 **Fax:** 817-633-3176 www.iontelevision.com **Email:** rickfetter@ionmedia.com

Austin: KAKW (SPN) 2233 W North Loop Blvd Austin TX 78756 **Phn:** 512-453-8899 **Fax:** 512-533-2874 univisionaustin.univision.com **Email:** efgarcia@univision.net

Austin: KEYE (CBS) 10700 Metric Blvd Austin TX 78758 **Phn:** 512-835-0042 **Fax:** 512-490-2111 www.keyetv.com **Email:** news@keyetv.com

Austin: KLRU (PBS) PO Box 7158 Austin TX 78713 **Phn:** 512-471-4811 **Fax:** 512-471-5561 www.klru.org **Email:** info@klru.org

Austin: KNVA (CW) 908 W Martin Luther King Jr Blvd Austin TX 78701 **Phn:** 512-478-5400 **Fax:** 512-476-1520 www.thecwaustin.com

Austin: KTBC (FOX) 119 E 10th St Austin TX 78701 **Phn:** 512-476-7777 **Fax:** 512-495-7060 www.myfoxaustin.com **Email:** news@fox7.com

Austin: KVUE (ABC) 3201 Steck Ave Austin TX 78757 **Phn:** 512-459-6521 **Fax:** 512-533-2233 www.kvue.com **Email:** news@kvue.com

Austin: KXAN (NBC) 908 W Martin Luther King Jr Blvd Austin TX 78701 **Phn:** 512-476-3636 **Fax:** 512-469-0630 www.kxan.com **Email:** news36@kxan.com

Beaumont: KBMT (ABC) 525 Interstate 10 S Beaumont TX 77701 **Phn:** 409-833-7512 **Fax:** 409-981-1564 www.12newsnow.com **Email:** 12news@kbmt-tv.com

Beaumont: KBTV (NBC) 6155 Eastex Fwy Ste 300 Beaumont TX 77706 **Phn:** 409-840-4444 **Fax:** 409-899-4639 www.fox4beaumont.com **Email:** bnixon@fox4beaumont.com

Beaumont: KFDM (CBS) PO Box 7128 Beaumont TX 77726 **Phn:** 409-892-6622 **Fax:** 409-892-7305 www.kfdm.com **Email:** news@kfdm.com

Beaumont: KUIL (FOX) 755 S 11th St Ste 270 Beaumont TX 77701 **Phn:** 409-839-4050 **Fax:** 409-839-8033 www.12newsnow.com **Email:** 12news@kbmt12.com

Brownsville: KVEO (NBC) 394 N Expressway Brownsville TX 78521 **Phn:** 956-544-2323 **Fax:** 956-544-4636 www.kveo.com **Email:** news@kveo.com

Bryan: KBTX (CW) 4141 E 29th St Bryan TX 77802 **Phn:** 979-846-7777 **Fax:** 979-846-1888 www.kbtx.com **Email:** george@kbtx.com

College Station: KAMU (PBS) 4244 Tamu College Station TX 77843 **Phn:** 979-845-5611 **Fax:** 979-845-1643 kamu.publicbroadcasting.net **Email:** jon.bennett@kamu.tamu.edu

Corpus Christi: KDF (NBC) 301 Artesian St Corpus Christi TX 78401 **Phn:** 361-886-6100 **Fax:** 361-886-6175 www.kristv.com **Email:** alesh@kristv.com

Corpus Christi: KEDT (PBS) 4455 S Padre Island Dr Ste 38 Corpus Christi TX 78411 **Phn:** 361-855-2213 **Fax:** 361-855-3877 www.kedt.org **Email:** leannewinkler@kedt.org

Corpus Christi: KIII (ABC) 5002 S Padre Island Dr Corpus Christi TX 78411 **Phn:** 361-986-8300 **Fax:** 361-986-8440 www.kiiitv.com **Email:** news@kiiitv.com

Corpus Christi: KORO (SPN) 102 N Mesquite St Corpus Christi TX 78401 **Phn:** 361-883-2823 **Fax:** 361-883-2931 www.korotv.com **Email:** rrodriguez@entravision.com

Corpus Christi: KRIS (NBC) 301 Artesian St Corpus Christi TX 78401 **Phn:** 361-886-6100 **Fax:** 361-886-6175 www.kristv.com **Email:** alesh@kristv.com

Corpus Christi: KTOV (MY) 600 Leopard St Ste 1924 Corpus Christi TX 78401 **Phn:** 361-600-3800 **Fax:** 361-882-1973 www.ktov.com **Email:** don@ktov.com

Corpus Christi: KUQI (FOX) 600 Leopard St Ste 1924 Corpus Christi TX 78401 **Phn:** 361-600-3800 **Fax:** 361-882-1973 **Email:** don@ktov.com

Corpus Christi: KZTV (CBS) 301 Artesian St Corpus Christi TX 78401 **Phn:** 361-883-7070 **Fax:** 361-884-8111 www.kztv10.com **Email:** contactus@kztv10.com

Dallas: KDAF (CW) 8001 John W Carpenter Fwy Dallas TX 75247 **Phn:** 214-252-9233 **Fax:** 214-252-3379 the33tv.com **Email:** cw33news@tribune.com

Dallas: KDFI (MY) 400 N Griffin St Dallas TX 75202 **Phn:** 214-720-4444 **Fax:** 214-720-3263 www.watchmy27.com **Email:** kdfi27@foxinc.com

Dallas: KDFW (FOX) 400 N Griffin St Dallas TX 75202 **Phn:** 214-720-4444 **Fax:** 214-720-3263 www.myfoxdfw.com **Email:** kdfw@kdfwfox4.com

Dallas: KERA (PBS) 3000 Harry Hines Blvd Dallas TX 75201 **Phn:** 214-871-1390 **Fax:** 214-754-0635 www.kera.org

Dallas: KFWD (SPN) 606 Young St Dallas TX 75202 **Phn:** 214-977-6780 **Fax:** 214-977-6544 www.kfwd.tv

Dallas: KLTJ (REL) PO Box 610546 Dallas TX 75261 **Phn:** 817-571-1229 **Fax:** 817-571-7458 www.daystar.com **Email:** partners@daystar.com

Dallas: KSTR (SPN) 2323 Bryan St Ste 1900 Dallas TX 75201 **Phn:** 214-758-2300 **Fax:** 214-758-2324 dallas.univision.com **Email:** 23@univision.net

Dallas: KTVT (CBS) 12001 N Central Expy # 1300 Dallas TX 75243 **Phn:** 817-451-1111 **Fax:** 817-496-7739 dfw.cbslocal.com **Email:** news@ktvt.com

Dallas: KUVN (SPN) 2323 Bryan St Ste 1900 Dallas TX 75201 **Phn:** 214-758-2300 **Fax:** 214-758-2324 www.univision.com

Dallas: KXTX (SPN) 3100 McKinnon St 8th Fl Dallas TX 75201 **Phn:** 817-429-5555 **Fax:** 817-654-6496 www.telemundodallas.com **Email:** jxflores@telemundo.com

Dallas: WFAA (ABC) 606 Young St Dallas TX 75202 **Phn:** 214-748-9631 **Fax:** 214-977-6585 www.wfaa.com **Email:** news8@wfaa.com

Denison: KTEN (ABC) 10 High Point Cir Denison TX 75020 **Phn:** 903-337-4000 **Fax:** 903-465-1207 www.kten.com **Email:** amaisel@kten.com

El Paso: KCOS (PBS) PO Box 26668 El Paso TX 79926 **Phn:** 915-590-1313 **Fax:** 915-594-5394 www.kcostv.org

El Paso: KDBC (CBS) 801 N Oregon St El Paso TX 79902 **Phn:** 915-496-4444 **Fax:** 915-544-0536 www.kdbc.com

El Paso: KFOX (FOX) 6004 N Mesa St El Paso TX 79912 **Phn:** 915-833-8585 **Fax:** 915-833-8973 www.kfoxtv.com **Email:** david.bennallack@cox.com

El Paso: KINT (SPN) 5426 N Mesa St El Paso TX 79912 **Phn:** 915-581-1126 **Fax:** 915-585-4642 www.kint.com **Email:** noticias26@entravision.com

El Paso: KSCE (REL) 6400 Escondido Dr El Paso TX 79912 **Phn:** 915-585-8838 kscetv.com **Email:** ksce@aol.com

El Paso: KTDO (SPN) 10033 Carnegie Ave El Paso TX 79925 **Phn:** 915-591-9595 **Fax:** 915-591-9896 **Email:** lcastaneda@zgsgroup.com

El Paso: KTSM (NBC) 801 N Oregon St El Paso TX 79902 **Phn:** 915-532-5421 **Fax:** 915-544-0536 www.ktsm.com **Email:** ktsm@whc.net

El Paso: KVIA (CW) 4140 Rio Bravo St El Paso TX 79902 **Phn:** 915-496-7777 **Fax:** 915-532-0505 www.kvia.com **Email:** kvia@kvia.com

Fort Worth: KTXA (IND) 5233 Bridge St Fort Worth TX 76103 **Phn:** 214-743-2100 **Fax:** 817-496-7739 dfw.cbslocal.com **Email:** kenf@ktvt.com

Fort Worth: KXAS (NBC) 3900 Barnett St Fort Worth TX 76103 **Phn:** 817-429-5555 **Fax:** 817-654-6325 www.nbcdfw.com **Email:** tips@nbcdfw.com

Harlingen: KGBT (CBS) 9201 W Expressway 83 Harlingen TX 78552 **Phn:** 956-366-4444 **Fax:** 956-366-4490 www.valleycentral.com **Email:** kwyatt@valleycentral.com

Harlingen: KLUJ (REL) PO Box 1647 Harlingen TX 78551 **Phn:** 956-425-4225 **Fax:** 956-412-1740 myedutv.org

Harlingen: KMBH (PBS) PO Box 2147 Harlingen TX 78551 **Phn:** 956-421-4111 **Fax:** 956-421-4150 www.kmbh.org **Email:** memberservices@kmbh.org

Houston: KETH (REL) 10902 S Wilcrest Dr Houston TX 77099 **Phn:** 281-561-5828 **Fax:** 281-561-9793 myedutv.org **Email:** keth@myedutv.org

Houston: KHOU (CBS) 1945 Allen Pkwy Houston TX 77019 **Phn:** 713-526-1111 **Fax:** 713-520-7763 www.khou.com **Email:** assignments@khou.com

Houston: KIAH (CW) 7700 Westpark Dr Houston TX 77063 **Phn:** 713-781-3939 **Fax:** 713-787-0528 newsfixnow.com **Email:** news@39online.com

Houston: KPRC (NBC) PO Box 2222 Houston TX 77252 **Phn:** 713-222-2222 **Fax:** 713-771-4930 www.click2houston.com **Email:** news2@kprc.com

Houston: KPXB (ION) 256 N Sam Houston Pkwy E Ste 49 Houston TX 77060 **Phn:** 281-820-4900 **Fax:** 281-820-3916 www.iontelevision.com **Email:** alexstroot@ionmedia.com

Houston: KRIV (FOX) 4261 Southwest Fwy Houston TX 77027 **Phn:** 713-479-2600 **Fax:** 713-479-2859 www.myfoxhouston.com **Email:** newsdesk@fox26.com

Houston: KTBU (IND) 7026 Old Katy Rd # 254 Houston TX 77024 **Phn:** 713-351-0755 **Fax:** 713-351-0756

Houston: KTMD (SPN) 1235 North Loop W Ste 125 Houston TX 77008 **Phn:** 713-974-4848 **Fax:** 713-782-5575 www.telemundohouston.com **Email:** t47promo@telemundohouston.com

Houston: KTRK (ABC) 3310 Bissonnet St Houston TX 77005 **Phn:** 713-666-0713 **Fax:** 713-668-4613 abclocal.go.comktrk **Email:** ktrkwwwnews@abc.com

Houston: KTXH (MY) 4261 Southwest Fwy Houston TX 77027 **Phn:** 713-661-2020 **Fax:** 713-479-2630 www.myfoxhouston.com

Houston: KUHT (PBS) 4343 Elgin St Houston TX 77004 **Phn:** 713-748-8888 **Fax:** 713-743-8867 www.houstonpbs.org **Email:** programming@houstonpbs.org

Houston: KXLN (SPN) 5100 Southwest Fwy Houston TX 77056 **Phn:** 713-662-4545 **Fax:** 713-965-2701 univisionhouston.univision.com **Email:** univision45@univision.net

TEXAS TV STATIONS

Houston: KZJL (SPN) 3000 Bering Dr Houston TX 77057 **Phn:** 713-315-3400 **Fax:** 713-315-3406 www.lbimedia.com **Email:** houstoninfo@lbimedia.com

Irving: KMPX (SPN) 2410 Gateway Dr Irving TX 75063 **Phn:** 972-652-2900 **Fax:** 972-652-2116 www.lbimedia.com **Email:** dallasinfo@lbimedia.com

Killeen: KNCT (PBS) PO Box 1800 Killeen TX 76540 **Phn:** 254-526-1176 **Fax:** 254-526-1850 www.knct.org **Email:** dan.hull@knct.org

Laredo: KGNS (NBC) 120 W Del Mar Blvd Laredo TX 78041 **Phn:** 956-727-8888 **Fax:** 956-727-4364 www.pro8news.com **Email:** email8@pro8news.com

Laredo: KLDO (SPN) 222 Bob Bullock Loop Laredo TX 78043 **Phn:** 956-727-0027 **Fax:** 956-728-8331 www.entravision.com **Email:** telena@entravision.com

Laredo: KVTV (CBS) 2600 Shea St Laredo TX 78040 **Phn:** 956-727-1300 **Fax:** 956-723-0474

Longview: KCEB (CW) 701 N Access Rd Longview TX 75602 **Phn:** 903-581-5656 **Email:** eddie@delta-network.com

Longview: KFXK (FOX) 701 N Access Rd Longview TX 75602 **Phn:** 903-236-0051 **Fax:** 903-753-6637 www.fox51.com **Email:** drew@fox51.com

Lubbock: KAMC (ABC) 7403 University Ave Lubbock TX 79423 **Phn:** 806-745-2828 **Fax:** 806-748-2212 everythinglubbock.com **Email:** rpoteet@klbk.com

Lubbock: KBZO (SPN) 1220 Broadway Ste 600 Lubbock TX 79401 **Phn:** 806-763-6051 **Fax:** 806-748-0216 www.kbzotv.com **Email:** ltrevino@entravision.com

Lubbock: KCBD (NBC) 5600 Avenue A Lubbock TX 79404 **Phn:** 806-744-1414 **Fax:** 806-749-1111 www.kcbd.com **Email:** 11listens@kcbd.com

Lubbock: KJTV (FOX) 9800 University Ave Lubbock TX 79423 **Phn:** 806-745-3434 **Fax:** 806-748-9387 www.myfoxlubbock.com **Email:** jklotzman@fox34.com

Lubbock: KLBK (CBS) 7403 University Ave Lubbock TX 79423 **Phn:** 806-745-2828 **Fax:** 806-748-2212 www.everythinglubbock.com **Email:** jsherwood@klbk.com

Lubbock: KLCW (CW) 9800 University Ave Lubbock TX 79423 **Phn:** 806-745-3434 **Fax:** 806-748-1949 www.lubbockcw.com **Email:** kboren@ramarcom.com

Lubbock: KMYL (MY) 9800 University Ave Lubbock TX 79423 **Phn:** 806-745-3434 **Fax:** 806-748-1949 www.mylubbocktv.com **Email:** kboren@ramarcom.com

Lubbock: KTXT (PBS) PO Box 42161 Lubbock TX 79409 **Phn:** 806-742-2209 **Fax:** 806-742-1274 www.ktxt.org

Lubbock: KXTQ (SPN) 9800 University Ave Lubbock TX 79423 **Phn:** 806-745-3434 **Fax:** 806-748-1949 **Email:** bmoran@ramarcom.com

Lufkin: KTRE (ABC) PO Box 729 Lufkin TX 75902 **Phn:** 936-853-5873 **Fax:** 936-853-3084 www.ktre.com **Email:** ktrenews@ktre.com

McAllen: KNVO (SPN) 801 N Jackson Rd McAllen TX 78501 **Phn:** 956-687-4848 **Fax:** 956-687-7784

McAllen: XERV (SPN) 4909 N McColl Rd McAllen TX 78504 **Phn:** 956-972-1117 **Fax:** 956-972-0476

McAllen: XHBR (SPN) 4904 N McColl McAllen TX 78504 **Phn:** 956-972-1117 **Fax:** 956-972-0476 www.starchannel.com **Email:** morelsa.lingoni@starchannel.com

McAllen: XHPN (SPN) 4909 N McColl Rd McAllen TX 78504 **Phn:** 956-972-1117 **Fax:** 956-972-0476 www.starchannel.com

Midland: KANG (SPN) 10313 W County Rd 117 Midland TX 76706 **Phn:** 432-563-1826 **Fax:** 432-563-0215 www.entravision.com **Email:** lmartinez@entravision.com

Midland: KMID (ABC) PO Box 60230 Midland TX 79711 **Phn:** 432-563-2222 **Fax:** 432-560-2267 www.permianbasin360.com **Email:** news@kmid.tv

Midland: KMLM (REL) PO Box 61000 Midland TX 79711 **Phn:** 432-563-0420 **Fax:** 432-563-1736 www.glc.us.com **Email:** info@glc.us.com

Midland: KOCV (PBS) PO Box 8940 Midland TX 79708 **Phn:** 432-580-0036 **Fax:** 432-563-5731 www.basinpbs.org **Email:** basinpbs@basinpbs.org

Midland: KUPB (SPN) PO Box 61907 Midland TX 79711 **Phn:** 432-563-1826 **Fax:** 432-563-0215 **Email:** lmartinez@entravision.com

Midland: KWES (NBC) PO Box 60150 Midland TX 79711 **Phn:** 432-567-9999 **Fax:** 432-567-9994 www.newswest9.com **Email:** dmarino@kwes.com

Odessa: KOSA (CBS) PO Box 4186 Odessa TX 79760 **Phn:** 432-580-5672 **Fax:** 432-580-9802 cbs7.com

Odessa: KPEJ (FOX) PO Box 11009 Odessa TX 79760 **Phn:** 432-580-0024 **Fax:** 432-337-3707 www.foxwesttexas.com **Email:** lwolf@kpejtv.com

Odessa: KWWT (IND) 1901 E 37th St Ste 207 Odessa TX 79762 **Phn:** 432-272-7514 **Email:** jameslprimm@yahoo.com

San Angelo: KIDY (FOX) 406 S Irving St San Angelo TX 76903 **Phn:** 325-655-6006 **Fax:** 325-655-8461 www.myfoxzone.com **Email:** kidy@foxsanangelo.com

San Angelo: KIDZ (MY) 406 S Irving St San Angelo TX 76903 **Phn:** 325-655-6006 **Fax:** 325-655-8461 www.myfoxzone.com **Email:** dmccoy@bayoucitybroadcasting.com

San Angelo: KLST (CBS) 2800 Armstrong St San Angelo TX 76903 **Phn:** 325-949-8800 **Fax:** 325-655-1118 conchovalleyhomepage.com **Email:** crodriguez@klst.net

San Angelo: KSAN (NBC) 2800 Armstrong St San Angelo TX 76903 **Phn:** 325-949-8800 **Fax:** 325-655-1118 conchovalleyhomepage.com

San Angelo: KXVA (FOX) 406 S Irving St San Angelo TX 76903 **Phn:** 325-655-6006 **Fax:** 325-655-8461 www.myfoxzone.com

San Antonio: KABB (FOX) 4335 NW Loop 410 San Antonio TX 78229 **Phn:** 210-366-1129 **Fax:** 210-442-6333 www.foxsanantonio.com **Email:** news@kabb.com

San Antonio: KENS (CBS) 5400 Fredericksburg Rd San Antonio TX 78229 **Phn:** 210-366-5000 **Fax:** 210-366-2716 www.kens5.com **Email:** news@kens5.com

San Antonio: KHCE (PBS) PO Box 691246 San Antonio TX 78269 **Phn:** 210-479-0123 **Fax:** 210-492-5679 www.khce.org

San Antonio: KLRN (PBS) 501 Broadway St San Antonio TX 78215 **Phn:** 210-270-9000 **Fax:** 210-270-9078 www.klrn.org **Email:** info@klrn.org

San Antonio: KMYS (MY) 4335 NW Loop 410 San Antonio TX 78229 **Phn:** 210-366-1129 **Fax:** 210-442-6333 kmys.tv **Email:** news@kabb.com

San Antonio: KPXL (ION) 6100 Bandera Rd Ste 304 San Antonio TX 78238 **Phn:** 210-682-2626 **Fax:** 210-682-3155 www.iontelevision.com **Email:** kathywilliams@ionmedia.com

San Antonio: KSAT (ABC) 1408 N Saint Marys St San Antonio TX 78215 **Phn:** 210-351-1200 **Fax:** 210-351-1310 www.ksat.com **Email:** news@ksat.com

San Antonio: KVDA (SPN) 6234 San Pedro Ave San Antonio TX 78216 **Phn:** 210-340-8860 **Fax:** 210-341-3962

San Antonio: KWEX (SPN) 411 E Durango Blvd San Antonio TX 78204 **Phn:** 210-227-4141 **Fax:** 210-227-0469 univision41.univision.com

San Antonio: WOAI (NBC) 1031 Navarro St San Antonio TX 78205 **Phn:** 210-226-4444 **Fax:** 210-224-9898 www.woai.com **Email:** newsdesk@woaitv.com

Sherman: KXII (CBS) 4201 Texoma Pkwy Sherman TX 75090 **Phn:** 903-892-8123 **Fax:** 903-892-4623 www.kxii.com **Email:** firstnews@kxii.com

Temple: KCEN (NBC) PO Box 6103 Temple TX 76503 **Phn:** 254-859-5481 **Fax:** 254-859-5831 www.kcentv.com **Email:** news@kcentv.com

Tyler: KETK (NBC) 4300 Richmond Rd Tyler TX 75703 **Phn:** 903-581-5656 **Fax:** 903-561-2459 www.ketknbc.com **Email:** nbarton@ketknbc.com

Tyler: KLTV (ABC) 105 W Ferguson St Tyler TX 75702 **Phn:** 903-597-5588 **Fax:** 903-510-7849 www.kltv.com **Email:** kboles@kltv.com

Tyler: KYTX (CBS) 2211 E Southeast Loop 323 Tyler TX 75701 **Phn:** 903-581-2211 **Fax:** 903-581-5769 www.cbs19.tv **Email:** cjobe@cbs19.tv

Victoria: KAVU (ABC) 3808 N Navarro St Victoria TX 77901 **Phn:** 361-575-2500 **Fax:** 361-575-2255 www.crossroadstoday.com **Email:** hmedrano@newscenter25.com

Victoria: KUNU (SPN) 3808 N Navarro St Victoria TX 77901 **Phn:** 361-575-2500 **Fax:** 361-575-2255 www.crossroadstoday.com **Email:** hmedrano@newscenter25.com

Victoria: KVCT (FOX) 3808 N Navarro St Victoria TX 77901 **Phn:** 361-573-1900 **Fax:** 361-575-2255 www.crossroadstoday.com **Email:** hmedrano@newscenter25.com

Waco: KWKT (FOX) 8803 Woodway Dr Waco TX 76712 **Phn:** 254-776-3844 **Fax:** 254-776-8032 www.kwkt.com **Email:** info@kwkt.com

Waco: KWTX (CW) 6700 American Plz Waco TX 76712 **Phn:** 254-776-1330 **Fax:** 254-776-4010 www.kwtx.com **Email:** news@kwtx.com

Waco: KXXV (ABC) 1909 S New Rd Waco TX 76711 **Phn:** 254-754-2525 **Fax:** 254-757-0331 www.kxxv.com **Email:** ideas@kxxv.com

Weslaco: KRGV (ABC) PO Box 5 Weslaco TX 78599 **Phn:** 956-968-5555 **Fax:** 956-973-5002 www.krgv.com **Email:** jenny@krgv.com

Wichita Falls: KAUZ (CBS) PO Box 2130 Wichita Falls TX 76307 **Phn:** 940-322-6957 **Fax:** 940-761-2354 www.newschannel6now.com **Email:** news@kauz.com

Wichita Falls: KFDX (NBC) 4500 Seymour Hwy Wichita Falls TX 76309 **Phn:** 940-691-0003 **Fax:** 940-692-1441 texomashomepage.com **Email:** kfdx@kfdx.com

Wichita Falls: KJTL (FOX) 4500 Seymour Hwy Wichita Falls TX 76309 **Phn:** 940-691-0003 **Fax:** 940-691-4856 texomashomepage.com **Email:** kfdx@kfdx.com

UTAH

Provo: KBYU (PBS) 2000 Ironton Blvd Provo UT 84606 **Phn:** 801-422-8450 **Fax:** 801-422-8478 www.kbyutv.org

Salt Lake City: KJZZ (MY) 301 W South Temple Salt Lake City UT 84101 **Phn:** 801-537-1414 **Fax:** 801-238-6414 kjzz.com **Email:** jcastro@kjzz.com

Salt Lake City: KPNZ (SPN) 150 Wright Brothers Dr Ste 520 Salt Lake City UT 84116 **Phn:** 801-519-2424 **Fax:** 801-359-1272

Salt Lake City: KSL (NBC) 55 N 300 W Ste 200 Salt Lake City UT 84101 **Phn:** 801-575-5555 **Fax:** 801-575-5561 www.ksl.com **Email:** assignment.desk@ksl.com

Salt Lake City: KSTU (FOX) 5020 Amelia Earhart Dr Salt Lake City UT 84116 **Phn:** 801-532-1300 **Fax:** 801-536-1325 fox13now.com **Email:** news@fox13now.com

Salt Lake City: KTVX (ABC) 2175 W 1700 S Salt Lake City UT 84104 **Phn:** 801-975-4444 **Fax:** 801-973-4176 www.4utah.com

Salt Lake City: KUCW (CW) 2175 W 1700 S Salt Lake City UT 84104 **Phn:** 801-975-4444 **Fax:** 801-973-4176 www.cw30.com

Salt Lake City: KUED (PBS) 101 Wasatch Dr Rm 215 Salt Lake City UT 84112 **Phn:** 801-581-7777 **Fax:** 801-585-5096 www.kued.org **Email:** askkued@kued.org

Salt Lake City: KUEN (IND) 101 Wasatch Dr Rm 215 Salt Lake City UT 84112 **Phn:** 801-581-2999 **Fax:** 801-585-6105 www.uen.orgtv **Email:** kanderson@media.utah.edu

Salt Lake City: KUPX (ION) 466 Lawndale Dr Ste C Salt Lake City UT 84115 **Phn:** 801-474-0016 **Fax:** 801-463-9667 www.iontelevision.com **Email:** jimobin@ionmedia.com

Salt Lake City: KUTV (CBS) 299 S Main St Ste 150 Salt Lake City UT 84111 **Phn:** 801-839-1234 **Fax:** 801-839-1235 www.kutv.com **Email:** newsdesk@kutv2.com

VERMONT

Brattleboro: WVBK (IND) 1300 Putney Rd Brattleboro VT 05301 **Phn:** 802-258-2200 **Fax:** 802-258-4400 www.wvbktv.com **Email:** danwvbk@comcast.net

Burlington: WCAX (CBS) PO Box 4508 Burlington VT 05406 **Phn:** 802-652-6300 **Fax:** 802-652-6399 www.wcax.com **Email:** news@wcax.com

Colchester: WETK (PBS) 204 Ethan Allen Ave Colchester VT 05446 **Phn:** 802-655-4800 **Fax:** 802-655-6593 www.vpt.org **Email:** view@vpt.org

Colchester: WFFF (FOX) 298 Mountain View Dr Colchester VT 05446 **Phn:** 802-660-9333 **Fax:** 802-660-8673 www.fox30jax.com **Email:** news@actionnewsjax.com

Colchester: WVNY (ABC) 298 Mountain View Dr Colchester VT 05446 **Phn:** 802-660-9333 **Fax:** 802-660-8673 www.mychamplainvalley.com **Email:** news@fox44now.com

White River Junction: WNNE (NBC) PO Box 1310 White River Junction VT 05001 **Phn:** 802-295-3100 **Fax:** 802-295-9056 www.wptz.comwnne **Email:** sgorin@hearst.com

VIRGINIA

Abingdon: WLFG (REL) PO Box 1867 Abingdon VA 24212 **Phn:** 888-275-9534 **Fax:** 276-676-3572 www.livingfaithtv.com **Email:** info@livingfaithtv.com

Arlington: WETA (PBS) 3939 Campbell Ave Ste 100 Arlington VA 22206 **Phn:** 703-998-2600 **Fax:** 703-998-3401 www.weta.org **Email:** info@weta.com

Arlington: WJLA (ABC) 1100 Wilson Blvd Ste 600 Arlington VA 22209 **Phn:** 703-236-9552 **Fax:** 703-236-2331 www.wjla.com **Email:** 7onyourside@wjla.com

Arlington: WZDC (SPN) 3939 Campbell Ave Ste 100 Arlington VA 22206 **Phn:** 703-820-8333 **Fax:** 703-820-1556 zgsgroup.com **Email:** info@zgsgroup.com

Bristol: WCYB (NBC) 101 Lee St Bristol VA 24201 **Phn:** 276-645-1555 **Fax:** 276-645-1554 www.wcyb.com **Email:** news@wcyb.tv

Bristol: WEMT (FOX) 101 Lee St Bristol VA 24201 **Phn:** 276-821-9296 **Fax:** 276-645-1554 www.wcyb.comfox-tri-cities

UTAH TV STATIONS

Charlottesville: WCAV (CBS) 999 2nd St SE Charlottesville VA 22902 **Phn:** 434-242-1919 **Fax:** 434-220-0398 www.newsplex.com **Email:** news@wcav.tv

Charlottesville: WHTJ (PBS) 528 E Main St Fl 2 Charlottesville VA 22902 **Phn:** 804-320-1301 **Fax:** 804-320-8729 whtj.org

Charlottesville: WVIR (NBC) 503 East Market St Charlottesville VA 22902 **Phn:** 434-220-2900 **Fax:** 434-220-2905 www.nbc29.com **Email:** newsdesk@nbc29.com

Chesapeake: WSKY (ION) 920 Corporate Ln Ste 200 Chesapeake VA 23320 **Phn:** 757-382-0004 **Fax:** 757-382-0365 www.sky4tv.com **Email:** edward@wsky4.com

Fairfax Station: WPXW (ION) 6199 Old Arrington Ln Fairfax Station VA 22039 **Phn:** 703-503-7966 **Fax:** 703-503-1225 www.iontelevision.com **Email:** fayewilliams@ionmedia.com

Falls Church: WNVC (PBS) 8101A Lee Hwy Falls Church VA 22042 **Phn:** 703-770-7100 **Fax:** 703-770-7112 www.mhznetworks.org **Email:** mhzmarketing@mhznetworks.org

Harrisonburg: WHSV (ABC) 50 N Main St Harrisonburg VA 22802 **Phn:** 540-433-9191 **Fax:** 540-433-2700 www.whsv.com **Email:** newsroom@whsv.com

Harrisonburg: WVPT (PBS) 298 Port Republic Rd Harrisonburg VA 22801 **Phn:** 540-434-5391 **Fax:** 540-434-7084 www.wvpt.net **Email:** wvptcomments@wvpt.net

Lynchburg: WSET (ABC) 2320 Langhorne Rd Lynchburg VA 24501 **Phn:** 434-528-1313 **Fax:** 434-847-8800 www.wset.com **Email:** newsdesk@wset.com

Norfolk: WGNT (CW) 720 Boush St Norfolk VA 23510 **Phn:** 757-446-1000 **Fax:** 757-399-3303 wgnt.com **Email:** cw27@wgnttv.com

Norfolk: WHRO (PBS) 5200 Hampton Blvd Norfolk VA 23508 **Phn:** 757-889-9400 **Fax:** 757-489-0007 www.whro.org **Email:** info@whro.org

Norfolk: WTKR (CBS) 720 Boush St Norfolk VA 23510 **Phn:** 757-446-1000 **Fax:** 757-446-1376 wtkr.com **Email:** desk@wtkr.com

Norfolk: WTVZ (MY) 900 Granby St Norfolk VA 23510 **Phn:** 757-622-3333 **Fax:** 757-623-1541 www.mytvz.com **Email:** comments@sbgi.net

Norfolk: WVEC (ABC) 613 Woodis Ave Norfolk VA 23510 **Phn:** 757-625-1313 **Fax:** 757-628-5855 www.wvec.com **Email:** assignments@wvec.com

Portsmouth: WAVY (NBC) 300 Wavy St Portsmouth VA 23704 **Phn:** 757-393-1010 **Fax:** 757-397-8279 www.wavy.com **Email:** newsdesk@wavy.com

Portsmouth: WVBT (FOX) 243 Wythe St Portsmouth VA 23704 **Phn:** 757-393-4343 **Fax:** 757-397-8279 www.fox43tv.com **Email:** general.manager@wavy.com

Richmond: WCVE (PBS) 23 Sesame St Richmond VA 23235 **Phn:** 804-320-1301 **Fax:** 804-320-8729 ideastations.org **Email:** jcampbell@ideastations.org

Richmond: WRIC (ABC) 301 Arboretum Pl Richmond VA 23236 **Phn:** 804-330-8888 **Fax:** 804-330-8883 www.wric.com **Email:** news@wric.com

Richmond: WRLH (FOX) 1925 Westmoreland St Richmond VA 23230 **Phn:** 804-358-3535 **Fax:** 804-230-2789 www.foxrichmond.com **Email:** comments@foxrichmond.com

Richmond: WTVR (CBS) 3301 W Broad St Richmond VA 23230 **Phn:** 804-254-3600 **Fax:** 804-254-3697 wtvr.com **Email:** newstips@wtvr.com

Richmond: WUPV (CW) 5710 Midlothian Tpke Richmond VA 23225 **Phn:** 804-230-1212 **Fax:** 804-230-7059 www.cwrichmond.tv **Email:** programming@cwrichmond.tv

Richmond: WWBT (NBC) 5710 Midlothian Tpke Richmond VA 23225 **Phn:** 804-230-1212 **Fax:** 804-230-2789 www.nbc12.com **Email:** newsroom@nbc12.com

Roanoke: WBRA (PBS) 1215 McNeil Dr SW Roanoke VA 24015 **Phn:** 540-344-0991 **Fax:** 540-344-2148 www.BlueRidgePBS.org **Email:** info@blueridgepbs.org

Roanoke: WDBJ (CBS) 2807 Hershberger Rd NW Roanoke VA 24017 **Phn:** 540-344-7000 **Fax:** 540-344-5097 www.WDBJ7.COM **Email:** news@wdbj7.com

Roanoke: WFXR (FOX) 2618 Colonial Ave SW Roanoke VA 24015 **Phn:** 540-344-2127 **Fax:** 540-345-1912 www.fox2127.com

Roanoke: WPXR (ION) 401 3rd St SW Roanoke VA 24011 **Phn:** 540-857-0038 **Fax:** 540-345-8568 www.iontelevision.com **Email:** shirleybundy@ionmedia.com

Roanoke: WSLS (NBC) PO Box 10 Roanoke VA 24022 **Phn:** 540-981-9110 **Fax:** 540-343-2059 www.wsls.com **Email:** news@wsls.com

Virginia Beach: WPXV (ION) 230 Clearfield Ave Ste 104 Virginia Beach VA 23462 **Phn:** 757-499-1261 **Fax:** 757-499-1679 www.ionmedianetworks.com **Email:** rhondanelson@ionmedia.com

Woodstock: WAZT (REL) PO Box 508 Woodstock VA 22664 **Phn:** 540-459-8810 **Fax:** 540-459-5834 www.wazt.com **Email:** roncroom@wazt.com

WASHINGTON

Bellingham: KVOS (IND) 3111 Newmarket St # 108 Bellingham WA 98226 **Phn:** 360-671-1212 **Fax:** 360-647-0824 metvnetwork.com **Email:** shlebichuk@kvos.com

Federal Way: KTBW (REL) 1909 S 341st Pl Federal Way WA 98003 **Phn:** 253-874-7420 **Fax:** 253-874-7432 www.tbn.org **Email:** ktbw@tbn.org

Kennewick: KFFX (FOX) 2509 W Falls Ave Kennewick WA 99336 **Phn:** 509-735-1700 **Fax:** 509-735-1004 www.myfoxtricities.com

Kennewick: KNDU (NBC) 3312 W Kennewick Ave Kennewick WA 99336 **Phn:** 509-737-6700 **Fax:** 509-737-6749 www.nbcrightnow.com **Email:** news@kndu.com

Kennewick: KVEW (ABC) 601 N Edison St Kennewick WA 99336 **Phn:** 509-735-8369 **Fax:** 509-735-1836 www.kvewtv.com **Email:** kvewnews@kvewtv.com

Pasco: KEPR (CBS) 2807 W Lewis St Pasco WA 99301 **Phn:** 509-547-0547 **Fax:** 509-547-5365 www.keprtv.com **Email:** newsroom@keprtv.com

Preston: KWPX (ION) PO Box 426 Preston WA 98050 **Phn:** 425-222-6010 **Fax:** 425-222-6032 www.iontelevision.com

Pullman: KWSU (PBS) PO Box 642530 Pullman WA 99164 **Phn:** 509-335-6588 www.kwsu.org **Email:** kwsutv@wsu.edu

Seattle: KCPQ (FOX) 1813 Westlake Ave N Seattle WA 98109 **Phn:** 206-674-1313 **Fax:** 206-674-1713 q13fox.com **Email:** tips@q13.com

Seattle: KCTS (PBS) 401 Mercer St Seattle WA 98109 **Phn:** 206-728-6463 **Fax:** 206-443-6691 kcts9.org

Seattle: KING (NBC) 333 Dexter Ave N Seattle WA 98109 **Phn:** 206-448-5555 **Fax:** 206-448-4525 www.king5.com **Email:** newstips@king5.com

Seattle: KIRO (CBS) 2807 3rd Ave Seattle WA 98121 **Phn:** 206-728-7777 **Fax:** 206-441-4840 www.kirotv.com **Email:** newstips@kirotv.com

Seattle: KMYQ (MY) 1813 Westlake Ave N Seattle WA 98109 **Phn:** 206-674-1313 **Fax:** 206-674-1713 www.q13fox.com **Email:** tips@q13fox.com

Seattle: KOMO (ABC) 140 4th Ave N Ste 400 Seattle WA 98109 **Phn:** 206-404-4000 **Fax:** 206-404-4422 www.komonews.com **Email:** tips@komo4news.com

Seattle: KONG (IND) 333 Dexter Ave N Seattle WA 98109 **Phn:** 206-448-5555 **Fax:** 206-448-4525 www.king5.com **Email:** newstips@king5.com

Seattle: KSTW (CW) 1000 Dexter Ave N Ste 205 Seattle WA 98109 **Phn:** 206-441-1111 **Fax:** 206-861-8915 cwseattle.cbslocal.com **Email:** cw11@kstwtv.com

Seattle: KUNS (SPN) 140 4th Ave N Seattle WA 98109 **Phn:** 206-404-5867 www.univision.com

Spokane: KAYU (FOX) 4600 S Regal St Spokane WA 99223 **Phn:** 509-448-2828 **Fax:** 509-448-3815 www.myfoxspokane.com

Spokane: KGPX (ION) 1201 W Sprague Ave Spokane WA 99201 **Phn:** 509-340-3400 **Fax:** 509-340-3417 www.iontelevision.com **Email:** ambermorales@ionmedia.com

Spokane: KHQ (NBC) PO Box 600 Spokane WA 99210 **Phn:** 509-448-6000 **Fax:** 509-448-4644 www.khq.com **Email:** q6news@khq.com

Spokane: KREM (CBS) 4103 S Regal St Spokane WA 99223 **Phn:** 509-448-2000 **Fax:** 509-448-6397 www.krem.com **Email:** newsdesk@krem.com

Spokane: KSKN (CW) 4103 S Regal St Spokane WA 99223 **Phn:** 509-448-2000 **Fax:** 509-448-6397 **Email:** dweig@krem.com

Spokane: KSPS (PBS) 3911 S Regal St Spokane WA 99223 **Phn:** 509-354-7800 **Fax:** 509-354-7757 www.ksps.org **Email:** ksps@ksps.org

Spokane: KXLY (ABC) 500 W Boone Ave Spokane WA 99201 **Phn:** 509-324-4004 **Fax:** 509-327-3932 www.kxly.com **Email:** news4@kxly.com

Tacoma: KBTC (PBS) 2320 S 19th St Tacoma WA 98405 **Phn:** 253-680-7700 **Fax:** 253-680-7725 www.kbtc.org **Email:** programming@kbtc.org

Yakima: KAPP (ABC) PO Box 10208 Yakima WA 98909 **Phn:** 509-453-0351 **Fax:** 509-453-3263 www.kapptv.com **Email:** kvewnews@kvewtv.com

Yakima: KEBB (SPN) 713 W Yakima Ave Yakima WA 98902 **Phn:** 509-452-8817 **Fax:** 509-248-7499 **Email:** hispanavision2003@yahoo.com

Yakima: KIMA (CBS) 2801 Terrace Heights Dr Yakima WA 98901 **Phn:** 509-575-0029 **Fax:** 509-575-5526 www.kimatv.com **Email:** information@kimatv.com

Yakima: KNDO (NBC) 216 W Yakima Ave Yakima WA 98902 **Phn:** 509-225-2323 **Fax:** 509-225-2330 www.nbcrightnow.com **Email:** news@kndo.com

Yakima: KYVE (PBS) 12 S 2nd St Yakima WA 98901 **Phn:** 509-452-4700 **Fax:** 509-452-4704 kcts9.org

WEST VIRGINIA

Bluefield: WVVA (NBC) PO Box 1930 Bluefield WV 24701 **Phn:** 304-325-5487 **Fax:** 304-327-5586 www.wvva.com **Email:** eschaffer@wvva.com

Bridgeport: WDTV (CBS) 5 Television Dr Bridgeport WV 26330 **Phn:** 304-848-5000 **Fax:** 304-842-4604 www.wdtv.com **Email:** news@wdtv.com

Bridgeport: WVFX (FOX) 5 Television Dr Bridgeport WV 26330 **Phn:** 304-848-5000 **Fax:** 304-842-7501 www.wdtv.comfox10.cfm **Email:** news@wdtv.com

Charleston: WCHS (ABC) 1301 Piedmont Rd Charleston WV 25301 **Phn:** 304-346-5358 **Fax:** 304-345-1849 www.wchstv.com **Email:** news@wchstv.com

Charleston: WNPB (PBS) 600 Capitol St Charleston WV 25301 **Phn:** 304-556-4900 **Fax:** 304-284-1454 wvpublic.org **Email:** feedback@wvpubcast.org

WASHINGTON TV STATIONS

Charleston: WOWK (CBS) PO Box 11848 Charleston WV 25339 **Phn:** 304-720-6550 **Fax:** 304-343-6138 www.wowktv.com **Email:** kbaker@wowktv.com

Charleston: WPBY (PBS) 600 Capitol St Charleston WV 25301 **Phn:** 304-556-4900 **Fax:** 304-556-4982 www.wvpubcast.org **Email:** feedback@wvpubcast.org

Charleston: WSWP (PBS) 600 Capitol St Charleston WV 25301 **Phn:** 304-254-7840 **Fax:** 304-254-7879 wvpublic.org

Charleston: WVAH (FOX) 1301 Piedmont Rd Charleston WV 25301 **Phn:** 304-346-5358 **Fax:** 304-345-1849 www.wvah.com **Email:** news@wvah.com

Clarksburg: WBOY (NBC) 904 W Pike St Clarksburg WV 26301 **Phn:** 304-623-3311 **Fax:** 304-623-9269 www.wboy.com **Email:** awilliams@wboy.com

Ghent: WVNS (CBS) 141 Old Cline Rd Ghent WV 25843 **Phn:** 304-787-5959 **Fax:** 304-787-2440 www.wvnstv.com **Email:** news@wvnstv.com

Huntington: WSAZ (NBC) 645 5th Ave Huntington WV 25701 **Phn:** 304-697-4780 **Fax:** 304-690-3065 www.wsaz.com **Email:** newschannel3@wsaz.com

Hurricane: WLPX (ION) 600 Prestige Park Dr # C Hurricane WV 25526 **Phn:** 304-760-1029 **Fax:** 304-760-1036 www.iontelevision.com **Email:** stevenstanley@ionmedia.com

Oak Hill: WOAY (ABC) PO Box 3001 Oak Hill WV 25901 **Phn:** 304-469-3361 **Fax:** 304-465-1420 www.woay.com **Email:** news@woay.com

Parkersburg: WTAP (NBC) 1 Television Plz Parkersburg WV 26101 **Phn:** 304-485-4588 **Fax:** 304-422-4107 www.thenewscenter.tv **Email:** news@thenewscenter.tv

Wheeling: WTRF (CBS) 96 16th St Wheeling WV 26003 **Phn:** 304-232-7777 **Fax:** 304-233-5822 www.wtrf.com **Email:** bdanehart@wtrf.com

WISCONSIN

Eau Claire: WEAU (NBC) 1907 S Hastings Way Eau Claire WI 54701 **Phn:** 715-835-1313 **Fax:** 715-832-3476 www.weau.com **Email:** news@weau.com

Eau Claire: WEUX (FOX) 3403 State Road 93 Ste 3 Eau Claire WI 54701 **Phn:** 715-831-2548 **Fax:** 715-831-2550 www.fox2548.com **Email:** news@fox25fox48.com

Eau Claire: WQOW (ABC) 5545 State Road 93 Eau Claire WI 54701 **Phn:** 715-835-1881 **Fax:** 715-831-1859 www.wqow.com **Email:** news@wqow.com

Glendale: WPXE (ION) 6161 N Flint Rd Ste F Glendale WI 53209 **Phn:** 414-247-0206 **Fax:** 414-247-1302 www.iontelevision.com

Glendale: WTPX (ION) 6161 N Flint Rd Ste F Glendale WI 53209 **Phn:** 414-247-0206 **Fax:** 414-247-1302 www.ionmedianetworks.com

Green Bay: WBAY (ABC) 115 S Jefferson St Ste 100 Green Bay WI 54301 **Phn:** 920-432-3331 **Fax:** 920-432-1190 www.wbay.com **Email:** wbay@wbay.com

Green Bay: WCWF (CW) PO Box 19011 Green Bay WI 54307 **Phn:** 920-494-8711 **Fax:** 920-494-8782 www.cw14online.com **Email:** jeff.bartel@wluk.com

Green Bay: WFRV (CBS) PO Box 19055 Green Bay WI 54307 **Phn:** 920-437-5411 **Fax:** 920-437-5769 www.wearegreenbay.com **Email:** tips@wearegreenbay.com

Green Bay: WGBA (NBC) 1391 North Rd Green Bay WI 54313 **Phn:** 920-494-2626 **Fax:** 920-494-9550 www.nbc26.com **Email:** youask@nbc26.com

Green Bay: WLUK (FOX) PO Box 19011 Green Bay WI 54307 **Phn:** 920-494-8711 **Fax:** 920-494-9109 www.fox11online.com **Email:** jeff.bartel@wluk.com

La Crosse: KQEG (IND) 505 King St Ste 221 La Crosse WI 54601 **Phn:** 608-784-0876 **Fax:** 608-784-1138 kqegtv.com **Email:** rwilson608@aol.com

La Crosse: WKBT (CBS) 141 6th St S La Crosse WI 54601 **Phn:** 608-782-4678 **Fax:** 608-782-4672 www.news8000.com **Email:** news8@wkbt.com

La Crosse: WLAX (FOX) 1305 Interchange Pl La Crosse WI 54603 **Phn:** 608-781-0025 **Fax:** 608-781-1456 www.fox2548.com **Email:** news@fox25fox48.com

La Crosse: WXOW (ABC) PO Box C-4019 La Crosse WI 54602 **Phn:** 507-895-9969 **Fax:** 507-895-6196 www.wxow.com **Email:** news19@wxow.com

Madison: WBUW (CW) 2814 Syene Rd Madison WI 53713 **Phn:** 608-270-5700 **Fax:** 608-270-5717 madisonscw.com

Madison: WHA (PBS) 821 University Ave Madison WI 53706 **Phn:** 608-263-2121 **Fax:** 608-263-9763 wpt.org **Email:** comments@wpt.org

Madison: WISC (CBS) 7025 Raymond Rd Madison WI 53719 **Phn:** 608-271-4321 **Fax:** 608-271-0800 www.channel3000.com **Email:** assignment@wisctv.com

Madison: WKOW (ABC) 5727 Tokay Blvd Madison WI 53719 **Phn:** 608-274-1234 **Fax:** 608-274-9569 www.wkow.com **Email:** news@wkowtv.com

Madison: WMSN (FOX) 7847 Big Sky Dr Madison WI 53719 **Phn:** 608-833-0047 **Fax:** 608-274-9569 www.fox47.com **Email:** news@wkowtv.com

Madison: WMTV (NBC) 615 Forward Dr Madison WI 53711 **Phn:** 608-274-1515 **Fax:** 608-271-5194 www.nbc15.com **Email:** news@nbc15.com

Milwaukee: WCGV (MY) 4041 N 35th St Milwaukee WI 53216 **Phn:** 414-442-7050 **Fax:** 414-874-1812 www.my24milwaukee.com **Email:** info@my24milwaukee.com

Milwaukee: WDJT (CBS) 809 S 60th St Milwaukee WI 53214 **Phn:** 414-777-5800 **Fax:** 414-777-5802 www.cbs58.com **Email:** newsdesk@cbs58.com

Milwaukee: WISN (ABC) 759 N 19th St Milwaukee WI 53233 **Phn:** 414-342-8812 **Fax:** 414-342-7505 www.wisn.com **Email:** wisntvnews@hearst.com

Milwaukee: WITI (FOX) 9001 N Green Bay Rd Milwaukee WI 53209 **Phn:** 414-355-6666 **Fax:** 414-586-2141 fox6now.com **Email:** fox6news@fox6now.com

Milwaukee: WMLW (IND) 809 S 60th St Milwaukee WI 53214 **Phn:** 414-777-5800 **Fax:** 414-777-5802 www.wmlw.com **Email:** slong@wciu.com

Milwaukee: WMVS (PBS) 1036 N 8th St Milwaukee WI 53233 **Phn:** 414-271-1036 **Fax:** 414-297-7536 www.mptv.org **Email:** tvviewer@matc.edu

Milwaukee: WTMJ (NBC) 720 E Capitol Dr Milwaukee WI 53212 **Phn:** 414-332-9611 **Fax:** 414-967-5378 www.todaystmj4.com **Email:** tmj4feedback@todaystmj4.com

Milwaukee: WVCY (REL) 3434 W Kilbourn Ave Milwaukee WI 53208 **Phn:** 414-935-3000 **Fax:** 414-935-3015 www.vcyamerica.org **Email:** vcy@vcyamerica.org

Milwaukee: WVTV (CW) 4041 N 35th St Milwaukee WI 53216 **Phn:** 414-442-7050 **Fax:** 414-203-2300 www.cw18milwaukee.com **Email:** info@cw18milwaukee.com

Milwaukee: WYTU (SPN) 809 S 60th St Milwaukee WI 53214 **Phn:** 414-777-5800 **Fax:** 414-777-5802 msnlatino.telemundo.com

Rhinelander: WJFW (NBC) 3217 County G Rhinelander WI 54501 **Phn:** 715-365-8812 **Fax:** 715-365-8810 www.wjfw.com **Email:** email@wjfw.com

Wausau: WAOW (ABC) 1908 Grand Ave Wausau WI 54403 **Phn:** 715-842-2251 **Fax:** 715-849-2999 www.waow.com **Email:** news@waow.com

Wausau: WFXS (FOX) 1000 3rd St Wausau WI 54403 **Phn:** 715-847-1155 **Fax:** 715-847-1156 www.myfoxwausau.com **Email:** rraff@wfxs.com

Wausau: WSAW (CBS) 1114 Grand Ave Wausau WI 54403 **Phn:** 715-845-4211 **Fax:** 715-842-0879 www.wsaw.com **Email:** news@wsaw.com

WYOMING

Casper: KFNB (FOX) 1856 Skyview Dr Casper WY 82601 **Phn:** 307-577-5923 **Fax:** 307-234-4005

Casper: KFNR (ABC) 1856 Skyview Dr Casper WY 82601 **Phn:** 307-577-5923 **Fax:** 307-234-4005

Casper: KGWC (CBS) 1856 Skyview Dr Casper WY 82601 **Phn:** 307-577-5923 **Fax:** 307-234-4005

Casper: KLWY (FOX) 1856 Skyview Dr Casper WY 82601 **Phn:** 307-577-5925 **Fax:** 307-577-5928

Casper: KTWO (ABC) 1896 Skyview Dr Casper WY 82601 **Phn:** 307-237-3711 **Fax:** 307-234-9866 www.k2tv.com **Email:** info@k2tv.com

Cheyenne: KGWN (CBS) 2923 E Lincolnway Cheyenne WY 82001 **Phn:** 307-634-7755 **Fax:** 307-638-0182 www.kgwn.tv **Email:** news@kgwn.tv

Jackson: KJWY (NBC) PO Box 7454 Jackson WY 83002 **Phn:** 307-733-2066 **Fax:** 307-235-9037 www.kjwy2.com **Email:** crahme@kjwy2.com

Mills: KCWY (NBC) PO Box 1540 Mills WY 82644 **Phn:** 307-577-0013 **Fax:** 307-235-9037 www.kcwy13.com **Email:** jehrhart@kcwy13.com

Riverton: KCWC (PBS) 2660 Peck Ave Riverton WY 82501 **Phn:** 307-856-6944 **Fax:** 307-856-3893 www.wyoptv.org **Email:** jamend@cwc.edu

ARIZONA

Douglas: KFTU (SPN) 1111 N G Ave Douglas AZ 85607 Phn: 520-805-1773 Fax: 520-805-1768 www.univision.com **Email:** ktvwassignment@univision.net

Flagstaff: KFPH (SPN) 2158 N 4th St Flagstaff AZ 86004 **Phn:** 928-527-1300 **Fax:** 928-527-1394 www.univision.com **Email:** rjpineda@univision.net

Phoenix: KTAZ (SPN) 4625 S 33rd Pl Phoenix AZ 85040 **Phn:** 602-648-3900 **Fax:** 602-648-3970 msnlatino.telemundo.com **Email:** aldo.contreras@nbcuni.com

Phoenix: KTVW (SPN) 6006 S 30th St Phoenix AZ 85042 **Phn:** 602-243-3333 **Fax:** 602-232-3679 www.univision.com **Email:** vluna@univision.net

Tucson: KHRR (SPN) 5151 W Broadway # 600 Tucson AZ 85716 **Phn:** 520-396-2600 **Fax:** 520-396-2640 msnlatino.telemundo.com

Tucson: KUVE (SPN) 2301 N Forbes Blvd Ste 103 Tucson AZ 85745 **Phn:** 520-204-1246 **Fax:** 520-204-1247 www.univision.com **Email:** vluna@univision.net

ARKANSAS

Fort Smith: KXUN (SPN) 510 N Greenwood Ave Fort Smith AR 72901 **Phn:** 479-785-4600 **Fax:** 479-785-4844 metvnetwork.com

CALIFORNIA

Bakersfield: KABE (SPN) 5801 Truxtun Ave Bakersfield CA 93309 **Phn:** 661-324-0031 **Fax:** 661-334-2685 www.univision.com

Burbank: KRCA (SPN) 1845 W Empire Ave Burbank CA 91504 **Phn:** 818-563-5722 **Fax:** 818-558-4232 www.krca62.tv **Email:** cking@lbimedia.com

Burbank: KSDX (SPN) 1845 W Empire Ave Burbank CA 91504 **Phn:** 818-729-5300 **Fax:** 818-729-5678 www.lbimedia.com **Email:** bperez@lbimedia.com

Burbank: KVEA (SPN) 3000 W Alameda Ave Burbank CA 91523 **Phn:** 818-260-5700 **Fax:** 818-260-5730 www.telemundo52.com **Email:** noticierotelemundo52@nbcuni.com

Burbank: KWHY (SPN) 3000 W Alameda Ave Burbank CA 91523 **Phn:** 818-260-5700 **Fax:** 818-260-5730 www.kwhy.com **Email:** fatima.goncalves@nbcuni.com

Chula Vista: XEWT (SPN) 637 3rd Ave Ste B Chula Vista CA 91910 **Phn:** 619-585-9398 **Fax:** 619-585-9463 www.xewt12.com

El Centro: KVYE (SPN) 1803 N Imperial Ave El Centro CA 92243 **Phn:** 760-482-7777 **Fax:** 760-482-0099 www.kvyetv.com **Email:** aretana@entravision.com

Fresno: KFTV (SPN) 3239 W Ashlan Ave Fresno CA 93722 **Phn:** 559-222-2121 **Fax:** 559-222-0917 www.univision.com

Fresno: KNSO (SPN) 30 E River Park Pl W Ste 200 Fresno CA 93720 **Phn:** 559-252-5101 **Fax:** 559-252-2747 www.holaciudad.comf **Email:** info@holaciudad.com

Fresno: KTFF (SPN) 6715 N Palm Ave Ste 201 Fresno CA 93704 **Phn:** 559-439-6100 **Fax:** 559-439-5950 www.univision.com **Email:** gersanchez@univision.net

Los Angeles: KBEH (SPN) 5757 W Century Blvd Ste 490 Los Angeles CA 90045 **Phn:** 310-216-0063 **Fax:** 310-216-0663 **Email:** linette.rodriguez@herobroadcasting.com

Los Angeles: KFTR (SPN) 5999 Center Dr Los Angeles CA 90045 **Phn:** 310-410-8900 **Fax:** 310-348-3493 www.univision.com

HISPANIC TV STATIONS

Los Angeles: KJLA (SPN) 2323 Corinth Ave Los Angeles CA 90064 **Phn:** 310-943-5288 **Fax:** 310-943-5299 www.kjla.com **Email:** info@kjla.com

Los Angeles: KMEX (SPN) 5999 Center Dr Los Angeles CA 90045 **Phn:** 310-216-3434 **Fax:** 310-348-3493 losangeles.univision.com

Los Angeles: KNLA (SPN) 5757 Wilshire Blvd Ste 470 Los Angeles CA 90036 **Phn:** 323-469-5638 **Fax:** 323-469-2193 **Email:** bholton@loop.com

Modesto: KCSO (SPN) 142 N 9th St Ste 8 Modesto CA 95350 **Phn:** 209-576-3301 **Fax:** 209-575-4547 www.kcso33.com **Email:** pschafer@kcso33.com

Monterey: KSMS (SPN) 67 Garden Ct Monterey CA 93940 **Phn:** 831-373-6767 **Fax:** 831-373-6700 www.ksmstv.com **Email:** cthomas@entravision.com

Palm Desert: KVER (SPN) 41601 Corporate Way Palm Desert CA 92260 **Phn:** 760-341-5837 **Fax:** 760-341-0951 www.kvertv.com **Email:** echiabra@entravision.com

Sacramento: KTFK (SPN) 1710 Arden Way Sacramento CA 95815 **Phn:** 916-927-1900 **Fax:** 916-614-1906 www.univision.com **Email:** kuvsnews@univision.net

Sacramento: KUVS (SPN) 1710 Arden Way Sacramento CA 95815 **Phn:** 916-927-1900 **Fax:** 916-614-1906 www.univision.com **Email:** kuvsnews@univision.net

San Diego: KBNT (SPN) 5770 Ruffin Rd San Diego CA 92123 **Phn:** 858-576-1919 **Fax:** 858-435-1503 www.univisionsandiego.com **Email:** lsandoval@entravision.com

San Diego: XHAS (SPN) 5770 Ruffin Rd San Diego CA 92123 **Phn:** 858-874-3320 **Fax:** 858-435-1504 www.telemundo33.com **Email:** mwilder@entravision.com

San Francisco: KDTV (SPN) 50 Fremont St Fl 41 San Francisco CA 94105 **Phn:** 415-538-8000 **Fax:** 415-538-8002 www.univision.com **Email:** noticias14@univision.net

San Francisco: KUNO (SPN) 1700 Montgomery St Ste 400 San Francisco CA 94111 **Phn:** 415-398-4242 **Fax:** 415-352-1800 www.ktnc.com **Email:** ventas@ktnc.com

San Jose: KSTS (SPN) 2450 N 1st St San Jose CA 95131 **Phn:** 408-944-4848 www.telemundoareadelabahia.com **Email:** noticias@telemundoareadelabahia.com

Santa Maria: KPMR (SPN) 1467 Fairway Dr Santa Maria CA 93455 **Phn:** 805-685-3800 **Fax:** 805-685-6892 www.kpmrtv.com **Email:** gquiroz@entravision.com

Santa Maria: KTAS (SPN) PO Box 172 Santa Maria CA 93456 **Phn:** 805-928-7700 **Fax:** 805-928-8606 **Email:** ktastv@fix.net

Santa Maria: KTSB (SPN) 1467 Fairway Dr Santa Maria CA 93455 **Phn:** 805-685-3800 **Fax:** 805-685-6892 www.univision.com **Email:** gquiroz@entravision.com

COLORADO

Colorado Springs: KGHB (SPN) 118 N Tejon St Ste 210 Colorado Springs CO 80903 **Phn:** 719-632-2943 **Fax:** 719-632-8220 www.entravision.com

Colorado Springs: KWHD (SPN) 1710 Briargate Blvd Ste 423 Colorado Springs CO 80920 **Phn:** 303-799-8853 **Fax:** 303-792-5303 lesea.com **Email:** dsmith@lesea.com

Denver: KCEC (SPN) 1907 Mile High Stadium Wt Cir Denver CO 80204 **Phn:** 303-832-0050 **Fax:** 303-832-3410 www.somosnoticiascolorado.com **Email:** lcollins@entravision.com

Denver: KDEN (SPN) 1120 Lincoln St Ste 800 Denver CO 80203 **Phn:** 303-832-0402 **Fax:** 303-832-0777 **Email:** targuello@telemundo.com

Denver: KTFD (SPN) 1907 Mile High Stadium W Cir Denver CO 80204 **Phn:** 303-832-0050 **Fax:** 303-832-3410 www.somosnoticiascolorado.com **Email:** lcollins@entravision.com

CONNECTICUT

Hartford: WRDM (SPN) 886 Maple Ave Hartford CT 06114 **Phn:** 860-956-1303 **Fax:** 860-956-6834 www.zgsgroup.com

Hartford: WUVN (SPN) 1 Constitution Plz Fl 7 Hartford CT 06103 **Phn:** 860-278-1818 **Fax:** 860-278-1811 www.wuvntv.com **Email:** uarrigoitia@entravision.com

DISTRICT OF COLUMBIA

Washington: WFDC (SPN) 101 Constitution Ave NW Ste L100 Washington DC 20001 **Phn:** 202-522-8640 **Fax:** 202-898-1960 www.tvwfdc.com **Email:** kmendez@entravision.com

Washington: WMDO (SPN) 101 Constitution Ave NW Ste L100 Washington DC 20001 **Phn:** 202-522-8640 **Fax:** 202-898-1960 www.univisiondc.com **Email:** eclavijo@entravision.com

FLORIDA

Altamonte Springs: WVEN (SPN) 523 Douglas Ave Altamonte Springs FL 32714 **Phn:** 407-774-2626 **Fax:** 407-774-3384 www.wventv.com **Email:** iberrios@entravision.com

Doral: WAMI (SPN) 9405 NW 41st St Doral FL 33178 **Phn:** 305-471-3944 **Fax:** 305-471-3948 www.univision.com **Email:** aramos@univision.net

Doral: WGEN (SPN) 1800 NW 94th Ave Doral FL 33172 **Phn:** 305-860-2544 **Fax:** 305-471-0122 www.mundofox8miami.com

Doral: WLTV (SPN) 9405 NW 41st St Doral FL 33178 **Phn:** 305-471-3900 **Fax:** 305-471-4236 www.univision.com **Email:** lfrocha@univision.net

Melbourne: WOTF (SPN) 739 North Dr Ste C Melbourne FL 32934 **Phn:** 321-254-4343 **Fax:** 321-254-9343 www.univision.com

Miramar: WSCV (SPN) 15000 SW 27th St Miramar FL 33027 **Phn:** 305-888-5151 **Fax:** 954-622-6107 www.telemundo51.com **Email:** reporte@telemundo51.com

Orlando: WTMO (SPN) 1650 Sand Lake Rd Ste 340 Orlando FL 32809 **Phn:** 407-888-2288 **Fax:** 407-888-3486 www.zgsgroup.com

Riviera Beach: WBWP (SPN) 7354 Central Industrial Dr Ste 110 Riviera Beach FL 33404 **Phn:** 561-863-0417 **Fax:** 561-863-0418 www.canal57.com **Email:** uzal@msn.com

Tampa: WFTT (SPN) 2610 W Hillsborough Ave Tampa FL 33614 **Phn:** 813-872-6262 **Fax:** 813-998-3608 www.univision.com **Email:** lgonzalez@entravision.com

Tampa: WVEA (SPN) 2610 W Hillsborough Ave Tampa FL 33614 **Phn:** 813-872-6262 **Fax:** 813-998-3660 www.wveatv.com **Email:** lgonzalez@entravision.com

GEORGIA

Atlanta: WUVG (SPN) 3350 Peachtree Rd NE Ste 1250 Atlanta GA 30326 **Phn:** 404-926-2300 **Fax:** 404-926-2320 atlanta.univision.com **Email:** noticias34atlanta@univision.net

ILLINOIS

Chicago: WGBO (SPN) 541 N Fairbanks Ct Ste 1100 Chicago IL 60611 **Phn:** 312-670-1000 **Fax:** 312-494-6496 chicago.univision.com **Email:** univisionchicag@tv.univision.com

Chicago: WSNS (SPN) 454 N Columbus Dr Fl 1 Chicago IL 60611 **Phn:** 312-836-3000 **Fax:** 312-836-3232 www.telemundochicago.com

Chicago: WXFT (SPN) 541 N Fairbanks Ct Ste 1100 Chicago IL 60611 **Phn:** 312-670-1000 **Fax:** 312-494-6496 www.univision.com

INDIANA

Indianapolis: WIIH (SPN) 1950 N Meridian St Indianapolis IN 46202 **Phn:** 317-824-9444 **Fax:** 317-956-8849 www.univision.com

MASSACHUSETTS

Hudson: WUTF (SPN) 71 Parmenter Rd Hudson MA 01749 **Phn:** 978-562-0660 **Fax:** 978-562-1166 www.univision.com **Email:** mgodin@entravision.com

Needham: WUNI (SPN) 33 4th Ave Needham MA 02494 **Phn:** 781-433-2727 **Fax:** 781-433-2750 www.wunitv.com **Email:** alexvl@entravision.com

Needham: WUTH (SPN) 33 4th Ave Needham MA 02494 **Phn:** 781-433-2727 **Fax:** 781-433-2750 www.entravision.com

MINNESOTA

Minneapolis: WUMN (SPN) 250 Marquette Ave Ste 540 Minneapolis MN 55401 **Phn:** 612-455-3960 **Fax:** 612-746-3014 www.wumn13.com

NEVADA

Las Vegas: KBLR (SPN) 450 Freeman Ave Ste 310 Las Vegas NV 89106 **Phn:** 702-258-0039 **Fax:** 702-258-0556 www.telemundolasvegas.com

Las Vegas: KINC (SPN) 500 Pilot Rd Ste D Las Vegas NV 89119 **Phn:** 702-434-0015 **Fax:** 702-434-0527 www.univision.com

Reno: KNVV (SPN) 300 S Wells Ave Ste 12 Reno NV 89502 **Phn:** 775-333-1017 **Fax:** 775-333-9046 www.entravision.com **Email:** vcody@entravision.com

Reno: KREN (SPN) 300 S Wells Ave Ste 12 Reno NV 89502 **Phn:** 775-333-1017 **Fax:** 775-333-9046 www.univisionreno.com

NEW JERSEY

Fort Lee: WNJU (SPN) 2200 Fletcher Ave Ste 35 Fort Lee NJ 07024 **Phn:** 201-969-4247 **Fax:** 201-969-4120 www.telemundo47.com **Email:** manuel.martinez@nbcuni.com

Newfield: WUVP (SPN) 4449 Delsea Dr Newfield NJ 08344 **Phn:** 856-691-6565 **Fax:** 856-690-3558 **Email:** noticias65@univision.net

Teaneck: WXTV (SPN) 500 Frank W Burr Blvd Ste 19 Teaneck NJ 07666 **Phn:** 201-287-4141 **Fax:** 201-287-9427 univision41.univision.com **Email:** cschwarz@univision.net

NEW MEXICO

Albuquerque: KLUZ (SPN) 2725 Broadbent Pkwy NE Ste E Albuquerque NM 87107 **Phn:** 505-342-4141 **Fax:** 505-344-8714 www.univision.com **Email:** acontreras@entravision.com

Albuquerque: KTEL (SPN) PO Box 30068 Albuquerque NM 87190 **Phn:** 505-884-5353 **Fax:** 505-889-8390 www.telemundo.com

NORTH CAROLINA

Raleigh: WUVC (SPN) 900 Ridgefield Dr Ste 100 Raleigh NC 27609 **Phn:** 919-872-7440 **Fax:** 919-878-4029 www.univision.com

OHIO

Cleveland: WQHS (SPN) 2861 W Ridgewood Dr Cleveland OH 44134 **Phn:** 440-888-0061 **Fax:** 440-888-7023 www.univision.com

HISPANIC TV STATIONS

OKLAHOMA

Oklahoma City: KTUZ (SPN) 5101 S Shields Blvd Oklahoma City OK 73129 **Phn:** 405-429-5061 **Fax:** 405-616-5511 www.ktuztv.com **Email:** armando.r@tylermedia.com

Oklahoma City: KUOK (SPN) 5101 S Shields Blvd Oklahoma City OK 73129 **Phn:** 405-616-5530 **Fax:** 405-616-5511 www.univisionok.com **Email:** armando.r@tylermedia.com

OREGON

Portland: KUPN (SPN) 2153 NE Sandy Blvd Portland OR 97232 **Phn:** 503-231-4222 **Fax:** 503-963-2628 www.kunptv.com **Email:** noticias@kunptv.com

PENNSYLVANIA

Philadelphia: WFPA (SPN) 1700 Market St Ste 1550 Philadelphia PA 19103 **Phn:** 215-568-2800 **Fax:** 215-568-2865 www.univision.com

RHODE ISLAND

Cranston: WRIW (SPN) 23 Kenney Dr Cranston RI 02920 **Phn:** 401-463-5575 www.zgsgroup.com **Email:** telemundoprovidence@gmail.com

TEXAS

Abilene: KTES (SPN) 4420 N Clack St Abilene TX 79601 **Phn:** 325-677-2281 **Fax:** 325-676-9231

Amarillo: KEYU (SPN) 1616 S Kentucky St Ste D130 Amarillo TX 79102 **Phn:** 806-359-8900

Amarillo: KTMO (SPN) PO Box 10 Amarillo TX 79105 **Phn:** 806-383-1010 **Fax:** 806-383-7178 www.newschannel10.com **Email:** newsroom@newschannel10.com

Austin: KAKW (SPN) 2233 W North Loop Blvd Austin TX 78756 **Phn:** 512-453-8899 **Fax:** 512-533-2874 univisionaustin.univision.com **Email:** efgarcia@univision.net

Corpus Christi: KORO (SPN) 102 N Mesquite St Corpus Christi TX 78401 **Phn:** 361-883-2823 **Fax:** 361-883-2931 www.korotv.com **Email:** rrodriguez@entravision.com

Dallas: KFWD (SPN) 606 Young St Dallas TX 75202 **Phn:** 214-977-6780 **Fax:** 214-977-6544 www.kfwd.tv

Dallas: KSTR (SPN) 2323 Bryan St Ste 1900 Dallas TX 75201 **Phn:** 214-758-2300 **Fax:** 214-758-2324 dallas.univision.com **Email:** 23@univision.net

Dallas: KUVN (SPN) 2323 Bryan St Ste 1900 Dallas TX 75201 **Phn:** 214-758-2300 **Fax:** 214-758-2324 www.univision.com

Dallas: KXTX (SPN) 3100 McKinnon St 8th Fl Dallas TX 75201 **Phn:** 817-429-5555 **Fax:** 817-654-6496 www.telemundodallas.com **Email:** jxflores@telemundo.com

El Paso: KINT (SPN) 5426 N Mesa St El Paso TX 79912 **Phn:** 915-581-1126 **Fax:** 915-585-4642 www.kint.com **Email:** noticias26@entravision.com

El Paso: KTDO (SPN) 10033 Carnegie Ave El Paso TX 79925 **Phn:** 915-591-9595 **Fax:** 915-591-9896 **Email:** lcastaneda@zgsgroup.com

Houston: KTMD (SPN) 1235 North Loop W Ste 125 Houston TX 77008 **Phn:** 713-974-4848 **Fax:** 713-782-5575 www.telemundohouston.com **Email:** t47promo@telemundohouston.com

Houston: KXLN (SPN) 5100 Southwest Fwy Houston TX 77056 **Phn:** 713-662-4545 **Fax:** 713-965-2701 univisionhouston.univision.com **Email:** univision45@univision.net

Houston: KZJL (SPN) 3000 Bering Dr Houston TX 77057 **Phn:** 713-315-3400 **Fax:** 713-315-3406 www.lbimedia.com **Email:** houstoninfo@lbimedia.com

Irving: KMPX (SPN) 2410 Gateway Dr Irving TX 75063 **Phn:** 972-652-2900 **Fax:** 972-652-2116 www.lbimedia.com **Email:** dallasinfo@lbimedia.com

Laredo: KLDO (SPN) 222 Bob Bullock Loop Laredo TX 78043 **Phn:** 956-727-0027 **Fax:** 956-728-8331 www.entravision.com **Email:** telena@entravision.com

Lubbock: KBZO (SPN) 1220 Broadway Ste 600 Lubbock TX 79401 **Phn:** 806-763-6051 **Fax:** 806-748-0216 www.kbzotv.com **Email:** ltrevino@entravision.com

Lubbock: KXTQ (SPN) 9800 University Ave Lubbock TX 79423 **Phn:** 806-745-3434 **Fax:** 806-748-1949 **Email:** bmoran@ramarcom.com

McAllen: KNVO (SPN) 801 N Jackson Rd McAllen TX 78501 **Phn:** 956-687-4848 **Fax:** 956-687-7784

McAllen: XERV (SPN) 4909 N McColl Rd McAllen TX 78504 **Phn:** 956-972-1117 **Fax:** 956-972-0476

McAllen: XHBR (SPN) 4904 N McColl McAllen TX 78504 **Phn:** 956-972-1117 **Fax:** 956-972-0476 www.starchannel.com **Email:** morelsa.lingoni@starchannel.com

McAllen: XHPN (SPN) 4909 N McColl Rd McAllen TX 78504 **Phn:** 956-972-1117 **Fax:** 956-972-0476 www.starchannel.com

Midland: KANG (SPN) 10313 W County Rd 117 Midland TX 76706 **Phn:** 432-563-1826 **Fax:** 432-563-0215 www.entravision.com **Email:** lmartinez@entravision.com

Midland: KUPB (SPN) PO Box 61907 Midland TX 79711 **Phn:** 432-563-1826 **Fax:** 432-563-0215 **Email:** lmartinez@entravision.com

San Antonio: KVDA (SPN) 6234 San Pedro Ave San Antonio TX 78216 **Phn:** 210-340-8860 **Fax:** 210-341-3962

San Antonio: KWEX (SPN) 411 E Durango Blvd San Antonio TX 78204 **Phn:** 210-227-4141 **Fax:** 210-227-0469 univision41.univision.com

Victoria: KUNU (SPN) 3808 N Navarro St Victoria TX 77901 **Phn:** 361-575-2500 **Fax:** 361-575-2255 www.crossroadstoday.com **Email:** hmedrano@newscenter25.com

UTAH

Salt Lake City: KPNZ (SPN) 150 Wright Brothers Dr Ste 520 Salt Lake City UT 84116 **Phn:** 801-519-2424 **Fax:** 801-359-1272

VIRGINIA

Arlington: WZDC (SPN) 3939 Campbell Ave Ste 100 Arlington VA 22206 **Phn:** 703-820-8333 **Fax:** 703-820-1556 zgsgroup.com **Email:** info@zgsgroup.com

WASHINGTON

Seattle: KUNS (SPN) 140 4th Ave N Seattle WA 98109 **Phn:** 206-404-5867 www.univision.com

Yakima: KEBB (SPN) 713 W Yakima Ave Yakima WA 98902 **Phn:** 509-452-8817 **Fax:** 509-248-7499 **Email:** hispanavision2003@yahoo.com

WISCONSIN

Milwaukee: WYTU (SPN) 809 S 60th St Milwaukee WI 53214 **Phn:** 414-777-5800 **Fax:** 414-777-5802 msnlatino.telemundo.com

RADIO GROUP OWNERS

Beasley Broadcasting Group 3033 Riviera Dr # 200, Naples FL 34103 **Phn:** 239-263-5000

Bott Radio Network 10550 Barkley St #100, Overland Park KS 66212 **Phn:** 913-642-7770

Buckley Broadcasting 166 W Putnam Ave, Greenwich CT 06830 **Phn:** 203-661-4307

CBS Radio 1515 Broadway 46th flr., New York NY 10036 **Phn:** 212-846-3939

Citadel Communications 7201 W Lake Meade # 400, Las Vegas NV 89128 **Phn:** 702-804-5200

Clear Channel Communications 200 E Basse Rd, San Antonio TX 78209 **Phn:** 210-822-2828

Cox Radio 6205 Peachtree Dunwoody Rd, Atlanta GA 30328 **Phn:** 678-645-0000

Crawford Broadcasting 725 Skippack Pike #210, Blue Bell PA 19422 **Phn:** 215-628-3500

Cumulus Broadcasting 3535 Piedmont Rd #1400, Atlanta GA 30305 **Phn:** 404-949-0700

Emmis Communications 40 Monument Cir #700, Indianapolis IN 46204 **Phn:** 317-266-0100

Entercom Communications Corp. 401 City Ave # 809, Bala Cynwyd PA 19004 **Phn:** 610-660-5610

Entravision Communications 2425 Olympic Blvd # 6000W, Santa Monica CA 90404 **Phn:** 310-447-3870

Journal Broadcast Group 720 E Capitol Dr, Milwaukee WI 53212 **Phn:** 414-332-9611

Midwest Communications PO Box 23333, Green Bay WI 54305 **Phn:** 920-435-3771

NextMedia Group 6312 S Fiddlers Green Cir #205E, Greenwood Village CO 80111 **Phn:** 303-694-9118

Radio One 5900 Princess Garden Pkwy, Lanham MD 20706 **Phn:** 301-306-1111

Regent Broadcasting 3360 Alta Mesa Dr, Redding CA 96002 **Phn:** 530-226-9500

Renda Broadcasting 900 Parish St flr 4, Pittsburgh PA 15220 **Phn:** 412-875-1800

Saga Communications 73 Kercheval #201, Grosse Pointe Farms MI 48236 **Phn:** 313-886-7070

Salem Communications 4880 Santa Rosa Rd, Camarillo CA 93012 **Phn:** 805-987-0400

Three Eagles Communications 3800 Cornhusker Hwy, Lincoln NE 68504 **Phn:** 402-466-1234

Univision Radio 3102 Oak Lawn Ave # 215, Dallas TX 75219 **Phn:** 214-525-7700

Withers Broadcasting PO Box 1508, Mount Vernon IL 62864 **Phn:** 618-242-3500

NETWORK HEADQUARTERS

ABC Radio Network 125 West End Ave 6th flr, New York NY 10023 **Phn:** 212-456-5100

AccuWeather Inc 385 Science Park Rd, State College PA 16803 **Phn:** 814-235-8600

Agrinet Farm Radio Network 104 Radio Rd, Powells Point NC 27966 **Phn:** 252-491-2414

AllAfrica Global Media 920 M St SE, Washington DC 20003 **Phn:** 202-546-0777

American Family Radio PO Box 3206, Tupelo MS 38803 **Phn:** 662-844-8888

American Urban Network 960 Penn Ave # 200, Pittsburgh PA 15222 **Phn:** 412-456-4000

Associated Press Broadcast 1825 K St NW #800, Washington DC 20006 **Phn:** 202-736-1100

Black Radio Network 166 Madison Ave, New York NY 10016 **Phn:** 212-686-6850

Bloomberg News Radio 731 Lexington Ave, New York NY 10022 **Phn:** 212-318-2000

Business TalkRadio PO Box 4826, Greenwich CT 06831 **Phn:** 203-323-7300

C-Span 400 N Capitol St NW #650, Washington DC 20001 **Phn:** 202-737-3220

CBS Radio News 524 W 57th St, New York NY 10019 **Phn:** 212-975-2021

CNN Radio Network One CNN Center, Atlanta GA 30303 **Phn:** 404-827-2750

Cox Radio 1601 W Peachtree St NE, Atlanta GA 30309 **Phn:** 404-843-5000

Eastern Public Radio PO Box 615, Kensington MD 20895 **Phn:** 301-943-2930

ESPN Radio 545 Middle St, Bristol CT 06010 **Phn:** 860-585-2000

Family Stations Radio 290 Hegenberger Rd, Oakland CA 94621 **Phn:** 510-568-6200

Fox Sports Radio 15260 Ventura Blvd #400, Sherman Oaks CA 91403 **Phn:** 818-461-8289

Hispanic Radio Networks 1126 16th St NW #350, Washington DC 20036 **Phn:** 202-637-8800

Irish Radio Network 515 Madison Ave Flr 11, New York NY 10022 **Phn:** 212-935-0606

Jones Radio Network 8200 S Akron St Ste 103, Centennial CO 80112 **Phn:** 303-784-8700

Livestock News Network PO Box 144, Brush CO 80723 **Phn:** 970-842-2902

Market Watch 201 California St 13th flr, San Francisco CA 94111 **Phn:** 415-439-6400

Medialink 708 3rd Ave, New York NY 10017 **Phn:** 212-682-8300

Metro Network News 2800 Post Oak Blvd #4000, Houston TX 77056 **Phn:** 713-407-6000

Moody Broadcasting Network 820 N LaSalle Blvd, Chicago IL 60610 **Phn:** 312-329-4433

Motor Racing Network PO Box 2801, Daytona Bch FL 32120 **Phn:** 386-947-6400

MTV Radio Network 1515 Broadway Flr 29, New York NY 10036 **Phn:** 212-846-5345

Multicultural Radio 7250 NW 58th St, Miami FL 33166 **Phn:** 786-497-3414

News Broadcast Network 75 Broad St 15th flr, New York NY 10004 **Phn:** 800-920-6397

NPR (National Public Radio) 635 Massachusetts Ave NW, Washington DC 20001 **Phn:** 202-513-2000

Premiere Radio Network 15260 Ventura Blvd # 500, Sherman Oaks CA 91403 **Phn:** 818-377-5300

PRI (Public Radio International) 100 N 6th St Ste 900A, Minneapolis MN 55403 **Phn:** 612-338-5000

Radio America 1100 N Glebe Rd, Arlington VA 22201 **Phn:** 703-302-1000

Radio Disney 500 S Buena Vista St, Burbank CA 91521 **Phn:** 818-973-4680

Radio Free Asia 2025 M St NW #300, Washington DC 20036 **Phn:** 202-530-4900

Radio Free Europe 1201 Connecticut Ave NW, Washington DC 20036 **Phn:** 202-457-6950

Reuters America 1333 H St NW #500, Washington DC 20005 **Phn:** 202-898-8300

Salem Music Network 402 BNA Dr Ste 400, Nashville TN 37217 **Phn:** 615-367-2210

Sheridan Broadcasting 960 Penn Ave # 200, Pittsburgh PA 15222 **Phn:** 412-456-4000

Sheridan Gospel Network 4025 Pleasantdale Rd # 240, Atlanta GA 30340 **Phn:** 770-416-2205

Sirius Satellite Radio 1221 Ave of Americas, New York NY 10020 **Phn:** 212-584-5100

Sports Network 2200 Byberry Rd, Hatboro PA 19040 **Phn:** 215-441-8444

Talk Radio Network PO Box 3755, Central Point OR 97502 **Phn:** 541-664-8827

United Press Int'l. 1510 H St NW, Washington DC 20005 **Phn:** 202-898-8000

United Stations Radio 1065 Ave of Americas flr 3, New York NY 10018 **Phn:** 212-869-1111

USA Radio Network 2290 Springlake Rd Ste 107, Dallas TX 75234 **Phn:** 972-484-3900

Voice of America 330 Independence Ave SW, Washington DC 20237 **Phn:** 202-203-4302

Wall Street Journal Radio 335 Madison Ave flr 18, New York NY 10017 **Phn:** 212-597-5630

Weather Channel Radio 300 Interstate North Pkwy, Atlanta GA 30339 **Phn:** 770-226-0000

Westwood One 40 W 57th St, New York NY 10019 **Phn:** 212-641-2000

WFMT Fine Arts Network 5400 N St Louis Ave, Chicago IL 60625 **Phn:** 773-279-2000

WOR Radio Network 111 Broadway, New York NY 10006 **Phn:** 212-642-4533

XM Satellite Radio 1500 Eckington Pl NE, Washington DC 20002 **Phn:** 202-380-4000

REGIONAL NETWORKS

Arkansas Radio Network 700 Wellington Hills Dr, Little Rock AR 72211 **Phn:** 501-401-0200

Brownfield Network 505 Hobbs Rd, Jefferson City MO 65109 **Phn:** 573-893-7200

Connecticut Radio Network 1 Circular Ave, Hamden CT 06514 **Phn:** 203-288-2002

Florida Public Radio Network 1600 Red Barber Plz, Tallahassee FL 32310 **Phn:** 850-487-3194

Florida Radio Network 2500 Maitland Ctr Pkwy Ste 407, Maitland FL 32751 **Phn:** 407-916-7800

Georgia News Network 1819 Peachtree Rd NE #700, Atlanta GA 30309 **Phn:** 404-607-9045

Georgia Public Radio 260 14th St NW, Atlanta GA 30318 **Phn:** 404-685-2690

Iowa Brownfield Network 505 Hobbs Rd, Jefferson City MO 65109 **Phn:** 573-893-7200

Kentucky News Network 4000 Radio Dr Ste 1, Louisville KY 40218 **Phn:** 502-479-2240

Louisiana Network 10500 Coursey Blvd #104, Baton Rouge LA 70816 **Phn:** 225-291-2727

Minnesota News Network 100 N 6th St #476A, Minneapolis MN 55403 **Phn:** 612-321-7200

Mississippi Radio Networks 6311 Ridgewood Rd, Jackson MS 39211 **Phn:** 601-957-1700

Missourinet 505 Hobbs Rd, Jefferson City MO 65109 **Phn:** 573-893-2829

North Carolina News Net 711 Hillsborough St, Raleigh NC 27603 **Phn:** 919-890-6030

North Dakota News Net 2501 13th Ave S # 201, Fargo ND 58103 **Phn:** 701-237-5000

Ohio News Network 770 Twin Rivers Dr, Columbus OH 43215 **Phn:** 614-280-3601

Oklahoma News Network/Agrinet PO Box 1000, Oklahoma City OK 73101 **Phn:** 405-858-1400

Radio Iowa 2700 Grand Ave Ste 103, Des Moines IA 50312 **Phn:** 515-282-1984

Radio Pennsylvania 4801 Lindle Rd, Harrisburg PA 17111 **Phn:** 717-232-8400

RFD Illinois Radio Net 1701 N Towanda Ave, Bloomington IL 61701 **Phn:** 309-557-2598

South Carolina News Network 3710 Landmark Dr Ste 100, Columbia SC 29204 **Phn:** 803-790-4300

South Dakota News Net PO Box 1197, Pierre SD 57501 **Phn:** 605-224-9911

Southeast AgNet 5053 NW Hwy 225A, Ocala FL 34482 **Phn:** 352-671-1909

Tennessee Radio Networks 55 Music Square W, Nashville TN 37203 **Phn:** 615-664-2400

Texas State Networks 4131 N Central Expwy #500, Dallas TX 75204 **Phn:** 214-443-6400

Virginia Radio Network 3245 Basie Rd, Richmond VA 23228 **Phn:** 804-474-0000

West Virginia Radio Corp 1251 Earl Core Rd, Morgantown WV 26505 **Phn:** 304-296-0029

Wisconsin Radio Network 222 State St # 401, Madison WI 53703 **Phn:** 608-251-3900

Wyoming Public Radio 1000 E University Ave Dept 3984, Laramie WY 82071 **Phn:** 307-766-4240

RADIO STATIONS

ALABAMA

Alabaster WQCR-AM (y) 50 Highway 26, Alabaster AL 35007 **Phn:** 205-621-8915 **Fax:** 205-621-7742 joelrivera1500am@yahoo.com

Albertville WAVU-AM (g) PO Box 190, Albertville AL 35950 **Phn:** 256-878-8575 **Fax:** 256-878-1051 www.wavuam.com wqsb@aol.com

Albertville WQSB-FM (c) PO Box 190, Albertville AL 35950 **Phn:** 256-878-8575 **Fax:** 256-878-1051 www.wqsb.com wqsb@aol.com

Andalusia WAAO-FM (c) PO Box 987, Andalusia AL 36420 **Phn:** 334-222-1166 **Fax:** 334-222-1167 www.waao.com waao@waao.com

Anniston WDNG-AM (nt) 1115 Leighton Ave, Anniston AL 36207 **Phn:** 256-236-8291 **Fax:** 256-236-8292 www.wdng.net

Anniston WGRW-FM (vq) PO Box 2555, Anniston AL 36202 **Phn:** 256-238-9990 **Fax:** 256-237-1102 www.graceradio.com jon@graceradio.com

Anniston WHMA-AM (g) 801 Noble St 30, Anniston AL 36201 **Phn:** 256-236-1880 **Fax:** 256-231-9414

Anniston WHMA-FM (c) 801 Noble St 30, Anniston AL 36201 **Phn:** 256-236-1880 **Fax:** 256-236-4480 www.whmabig95.com randijo1630@aol.com

Anniston WHOG-AM (wu) 1330 Noble St Ste 25, Anniston AL 36201 **Phn:** 256-236-6484 hog1120@aol.com

Anniston WTXO-FM (r) 801 Noble St Ste 30, Anniston AL 36201 **Phn:** 256-236-1274 **Fax:** 256-321-9414 www.rock1059.net chris@rock1059.net

Arab WAFN-FM (o) 981 N Brindlee Mountain Pkwy, Arab AL 35016 **Phn:** 256-586-9300 **Fax:** 256-586-9301 www.fun927.com funradio@otelco.net

Arab WRAB-AM (cg) PO Box 625, Arab AL 35016 **Phn:** 256-586-4123 **Fax:** 256-586-4124 wrab@otelco.net

Ashland WZZX-AM (c) 83545 Highway 9, Ashland AL 36251 **Phn:** 256-354-4600 **Fax:** 256-354-7224

Athens WHRP-FM (u) 1717 US Highway 72 E, Athens AL 35611 **Phn:** 256-830-8300 www.whrpfm.com toni.terrell@cumulus.com

Athens WKAC-AM (o) PO Box 1083, Athens AL 35612 **Phn:** 256-232-6827 **Fax:** 256-232-6828 www.wkac1080.com wkac@wkac1080.com

Athens WUMP-AM (sn) 1717 US Highway 72 E, Athens AL 35611 **Phn:** 256-830-8300 **Fax:** 256-232-6842 www.730ump.com jason.marks@cumulus.com

Athens WVNN-FM (nt) 1717 US Highway 72 E, Athens AL 35611 **Phn:** 256-830-8300 **Fax:** 256-232-6842 www.wvnn.com dale.jackson@cumulus.com

Athens WVNN-AM (nt) 1717 US Highway 72 E, Athens AL 35611 **Phn:** 256-830-8300 **Fax:** 256-232-6842 www.wvnn.com programdirector@wvnn.com

Athens WWFF-FM (c) 1717 US Highway 72 E, Athens AL 35611 **Phn:** 256-830-8300 **Fax:** 256-232-6842 www.whrpfm.com toni.terrell@cumulus.com

Athens WZYP-FM (h) 1717 US Highway 72 E, Athens AL 35611 **Phn:** 256-830-8300 **Fax:** 256-232-6842 www.wzyp.com steve.smith@cumulus.com

Auburn WANI-AM (nt) PO Box 950, Auburn AL 36831 **Phn:** 334-826-2929 **Fax:** 334-826-9151 www.wani1400.com aburcham@aunetwork.com

Auburn WAUD-AM (s) 2514 S College St Ste 104, Auburn AL 36832 **Phn:** 334-887-3401 **Fax:** 334-826-9599 waudradio.com brooke@thetiger.fm

Auburn WELL-FM (vaq) PO Box 2208, Auburn AL 36831 **Phn:** 334-705-8004 www.praise887.com

Auburn WQNR-FM (r) 2514 S College St Ste 104, Auburn AL 36832 **Phn:** 334-887-9999 **Fax:** 334-826-9599 www.katefm.com brooke@thetiger.fm

Auburn WQSI-AM (c) 2514 S College St Ste 104, Auburn AL 36832 **Phn:** 334-887-9999 **Fax:** 334-826-9599 www.wqsifm.com brooke@thetiger.fm

Auburn WTGZ-FM (r) 2514 S College St Ste 104, Auburn AL 36832 **Phn:** 334-887-9999 **Fax:** 334-826-9599 www.thetiger.fm kevin@thetiger.fm

Auburn University WEGL-FM (vr) 255 Duncan Dr, Auburn University AL 36849 **Phn:** 334-844-4057 **Fax:** 334-844-4118

Bessemer WZGX-AM (y) 3500 Jaybird Rd, Bessemer AL 35020 **Phn:** 205-428-0146 **Fax:** 205-426-3178 la10qnetwork@gmail.com

Birmingham WAGG-AM (gw) 950 22nd St N Ste 1000, Birmingham AL 35203 **Phn:** 205-322-2987 **Fax:** 205-324-6397 www.610wagg.com mary.k@coxradio.com

Birmingham WAPI-AM (nt) 244 Goodwin Crest Dr Ste 300, Birmingham AL 35209 **Phn:** 205-945-4646 **Fax:** 205-945-3999 www.100wapi.com frank.giardina@cumulus.com

Birmingham WATV-AM (gw) 3025 Kenley Way, Birmingham AL 35242 **Phn:** 205-780-2014 **Fax:** 205-780-4034 www.900goldwatv.com spstewart@watv900.com

Birmingham WAYE-AM (q) 836 Lomb Ave SW, Birmingham AL 35211 **Phn:** 205-786-9293 **Fax:** 205-786-9296 wayepd@live.com

Birmingham WBHJ-FM (h) 2700 Corporate Dr # 115, Birmingham AL 35242 **Phn:** 205-322-2987 **Fax:** 205-324-6329 www.957jamz.com dwight.stone@summitmediacorp.com

Birmingham WBHK-FM (au) 950 22nd St N Ste 1000, Birmingham AL 35203 **Phn:** 205-322-2987 **Fax:** 205-324-6329 www.987kiss.com darryl.johnson@coxradio.com

Birmingham WBHM-FM (pln) 650 11th St S, Birmingham AL 35233 **Phn:** 205-934-2606 **Fax:** 205-934-5075 www.wbhm.org info@wbhm.org

Birmingham WBPT-FM (r) 301 Beacon Pkwy W Ste 200, Birmingham AL 35209 **Phn:** 205-916-1100 **Fax:** 205-290-1061 www.birminghamseagle.com john.olsen@coxinc.com

Birmingham WDJC-FM (q) 120 Summit Pkwy Ste 200, Birmingham AL 35209 **Phn:** 205-879-3324 **Fax:** 205-802-4555 www.wdjconline.com terry@wdjconline.com

Birmingham WDXB-FM (c) 600 Beacon Pkwy W Ste 400, Birmingham AL 35209 **Phn:** 205-439-9600 **Fax:** 205-439-8390 www.1025thebull.com tomhanrahan@clearchannel.com

Birmingham WENN-AM (w) 950 22nd St N Ste 1000, Birmingham AL 35203 **Phn:** 205-322-2987 **Fax:** 205-324-6397

Birmingham WERC-AM (nt) 600 Beacon Pkwy W Ste 400, Birmingham AL 35209 **Phn:** 205-439-9600 **Fax:** 205-439-8390

Birmingham WERC-FM (nt) 600 Beacon Pkwy W Ste 400, Birmingham AL 35209 **Phn:** 205-439-9600 **Fax:** 205-439-8390 www.wercfm.com aarontrimmer@clearchannel.com

Birmingham WGIB-FM (qv) 1137 10th Pl S, Birmingham AL 35205 **Phn:** 205-323-1516 **Fax:** 205-252-5432 www.gleniris.net info@gleniris.net

Birmingham WJLD-FM (ouw) PO Box 19123, Birmingham AL 35219 **Phn:** 205-942-1776 **Fax:** 205-942-4814 www.wjldfm.com wr@wjldfm.com

Birmingham WJLD-AM (ouw) PO Box 19123, Birmingham AL 35219 **Phn:** 205-942-1776 **Fax:** 205-942-4814 www.wjldfm.com wr@wjldfm.com

Birmingham WJOX-FM (st) 244 Goodwin Crest Dr, Birmingham AL 35209 **Phn:** 205-945-4646 **Fax:** 205-945-3999 www.joxfm.com ryan@joxfm.com

Birmingham WJSR-FM (vr) 2601 Carson Rd, Birmingham AL 35215 **Phn:** 205-856-6095 **Fax:** 205-856-7702

Birmingham WKLF-AM (g) PO Box 381163, Birmingham AL 35238 **Phn:** 205-755-0980 **Fax:** 205-280-0980

Birmingham WLJR-FM (vq) 2200 Briarwood Way, Birmingham AL 35243 **Phn:** 205-776-5270 **Fax:** 205-776-5241 briarwood.orgwljr-radio jpscruggs@briarwood.org

Birmingham WMJJ-FM (a) 600 Beacon Pkwy W Ste 400, Birmingham AL 35209 **Phn:** 205-439-9600 **Fax:** 205-439-8391 www.magic96.com tomhanrahan@clearchannel.com

Birmingham WQEN-FM (h) 600 Beacon Pkwy W Ste 600, Birmingham AL 35209 **Phn:** 205-439-9600 **Fax:** 205-439-8390 www.1037theq.com keithallen@clearchannel.com

Birmingham WSPZ-AM (s) 244 Goodwin Crest Dr Ste 300, Birmingham AL 35209 **Phn:** 205-945-4646 **Fax:** 205-945-3999 www.sportstalk570.com management@espn980.com

Birmingham WUHT-FM (u) 244 Goodwin Crest Dr Ste 300, Birmingham AL 35209 **Phn:** 205-945-4646 **Fax:** 205-942-3175 www.hot1077radio.com

Birmingham WVSU-FM (vj) 800 Lakeshore Dr, Birmingham AL 35229 **Phn:** 205-726-2877 **Fax:** 205-726-4032 www.samford.edugroupswvsu wvsu@samford.edu

Birmingham WZRR-FM (r) 244 Goodwin Crest Dr Ste 300, Birmingham AL 35209 **Phn:** 205-945-4646 **Fax:** 205-945-3999 www.rock99online.com john.walker@cumulus.com

Birmingham WZZK-FM (c) 2700 Corporate Dr # 115, Birmingham AL 35242 **Phn:** 205-916-1100 **Fax:** 205-290-1061 wzzk.com paul.orr@summitmediacorp.com

Boaz WBSA-AM (g) 1525 Wills Rd, Boaz AL 35957 **Phn:** 256-593-4264 **Fax:** 256-593-4265 www.wbsaam.com 1300@wbsaam.com

Brewton WEBJ-AM (o) 301 Downing St, Brewton AL 36426 **Phn:** 251-867-5717 **Fax:** 251-867-5718

Brewton WELJ-FM (qg) PO Box 347, Brewton AL 36427 **Phn:** 251-809-1915 **Fax:** 251-809-1916

Brewton WKNU-FM (c) PO Box 468, Brewton AL 36427 **Phn:** 251-867-4824 **Fax:** 251-867-7003 wknubroadcasting@bellsouth.net

Butler WPRN-FM (c) 909 W Pushmataha St, Butler AL 36904 **Phn:** 205-459-3222 **Fax:** 205-459-4140

Calera WBYE-AM (g) PO Box 1727, Calera AL 35040 **Phn:** 205-668-1370 **Fax:** 205-668-7562

Centre WEIS-AM (cg) PO Box 297, Centre AL 35960 **Phn:** 256 927-4232 **Fax:** 256-927-6503 www.weis990am.com weisradio@tds.net

Cullman WFMH-AM (nt) 1707 Warnke Rd NW, Cullman AL 35055 **Phn:** 256-734-3271 **Fax:** 256-734-3622 flyinggdude@aol.com

ALABAMA RADIO STATIONS

Cullman WKUL-FM (c) 214 1st Ave SE, Cullman AL 35055 **Phn:** 256-734-0183 **Fax:** 256-739-2999 www.wkul.com wkul@wkul.com

Decatur WWTM-AM (st) 1209 Danville Rd SW Ste N, Decatur AL 35601 **Phn:** 256-353-1400 **Fax:** 256-353-0363 www.espn1400.info jburns@espn1400.info

Decatur WYAM-AM (y) 1301 Central Pkwy SW, Decatur AL 35601 **Phn:** 256-355-4567 **Fax:** 256-351-1234 wileywg@acninc.net

Demopolis WINL-FM (c) PO Box 938, Demopolis AL 36732 **Phn:** 334-289-9850 **Fax:** 334-289-9811 mywin98.com valerie@mywin98.com

Demopolis WXAL-AM (g) PO Box 938, Demopolis AL 36732 **Phn:** 334-289-9850 **Fax:** 334-289-9811

Demopolis WZNJ-FM (ox) PO Box 938, Demopolis AL 36732 **Phn:** 334-289-9850 **Fax:** 334-289-9811 www.znj1065.com

Dixons Mills WMBV-FM (q) PO Box 91.9, Dixons Mills AL 36736 **Phn:** 334-992-2425 **Fax:** 334-992-2637 www.moodyradiosouth.fm wmft@moody.edu

Dothan WAGF-AM (t) 4106 Ross Clark Cir, Dothan AL 36303 **Phn:** 334-671-1753 **Fax:** 334-677-6923 www.wjjn.net wtraffic@graceba.net

Dothan WAGF-FM (wg) 4106 Ross Clark Cir, Dothan AL 36303 **Phn:** 334-671-1753 **Fax:** 334-677-6923 www.wjjn.net wtraffic@graceba.net

Dothan WBBK-AM (ax) 285 N Foster St, Dothan AL 36303 **Phn:** 334-792-0047 **Fax:** 334-712-9346

Dothan WDBT-FM (nt) 3245 Montgomery Hwy Ste 1, Dothan AL 36303 **Phn:** 334-712-9233 **Fax:** 334-712-0374 newstalk1053.com ron@wdjr.com

Dothan WDJR-FM (c) 3245 Montgomery Hwy Ste 1, Dothan AL 36303 **Phn:** 334-712-9233 **Fax:** 334-712-0374 wdjr.com ron@wdjr.com

Dothan WESP-FM (c) 3245 Montgomery Hwy Ste 1, Dothan AL 36303 **Phn:** 334-712-9233 **Fax:** 334-712-0374 1025theeagle.com ron@wdjr.com

Dothan WGTF-FM (q) 107 Wanda Ct, Dothan AL 36303 **Phn:** 334-794-4770

Dothan WIZB-FM (q) 2563 Montgomery Hwy, Dothan AL 36303 **Phn:** 334-699-5672 **Fax:** 334-699-5034 alabama.thejoyfm.com

Dothan WJJN-FM (uw) 4106 Ross Clark Cir, Dothan AL 36303 **Phn:** 334-671-1753 **Fax:** 334-677-6923 www.wjjn.net wtraffic@graceba.net

Dothan WJRL-FM (st) PO Box 889, Dothan AL 36302 **Phn:** 334-792-0047 **Fax:** 334-712-9346

Dothan WKMX-FM (ah) 3245 Montgomery Hwy #1, Dothan AL 36303 **Phn:** 334-712-9233 **Fax:** 334-712-0374 www.wkmx.com

Dothan WLDA-FM (h) 285 N Foster St, Dothan AL 36303 **Phn:** 334-792-0047 **Fax:** 334-712-9346

Dothan WOOF-AM (wgt) PO Box 1427, Dothan AL 36302 **Phn:** 334-792-1149 **Fax:** 334-677-4612 www.woofradio.com woof@ala.net

Dothan WOOF-FM (a) PO Box 1427, Dothan AL 36302 **Phn:** 334-792-1149 **Fax:** 334-677-4612 www.woofradio.com woof@ala.net

Dothan WTVY-FM (c) 3245 Montgomery Hwy #1, Dothan AL 36303 **Phn:** 334-712-9233 **Fax:** 334-712-0374 www.955wtvy.com

Dothan WVOB-FM (qv) PO Box 1944, Dothan AL 36302 **Phn:** 334-671-9862 **Fax:** 334-793-4344 www.bethanybc.edu svshuemake@bethanybc.edu

Dothan WWNT-AM (nt) 1733 Highway 52 E, Dothan AL 36303 **Phn:** 334-671-0075 **Fax:** 334-671-0091 www.wwntradio.com

Elba WELB-AM (g) 20334 Highway 87, Elba AL 36323 **Phn:** 334-897-2216 **Fax:** 334-897-3694

Enterprise WVVL-FM (c) PO Box 311686, Enterprise AL 36331 **Phn:** 334-347-5621 **Fax:** 334-347-5631 www.weevil101.com wvvl@weevil101.com

Eufaula WRVX-FM (ar) PO Box 754, Eufaula AL 36072 **Phn:** 334-232-4532

Eva WRJL-FM (g) 5610 Highway 55 E, Eva AL 35621 **Phn:** 256-796-8000 **Fax:** 256-796-8515

Fairhope WABF-AM (ma) PO Box 1220, Fairhope AL 36533 **Phn:** 251-928-2384 **Fax:** 251-928-9229 www.wabf1220.net wabf1220@bellsouth.net

Fayette WLDX-AM (c) PO Box 189, Fayette AL 35555 **Phn:** 205-932-3318 www.wldx.com wldx@wldx.com

Florala WKWL-AM (g) PO Box 159, Florala AL 36442 **Phn:** 334-858-6162 wkwl.ezstream.com wkwl@alaweb.com

Florence WBCF-AM (snt) PO Box 1316, Florence AL 35631 **Phn:** 256-764-8170 **Fax:** 256-764-8340 www.wbcf.com news@wbcf.com

Florence WBCF-FM (snt) PO Box 1316, Florence AL 35631 **Phn:** 256-764-8170 **Fax:** 256-764-8340 www.wbcf.com news@wbcf.com

Florence WFIX-FM (q) PO Box 397, Florence AL 35631 **Phn:** 256-764-9964 **Fax:** 256-764-9154 www.wfix.net

Florence WLVS-FM (c) PO Box 932, Florence AL 35631 **Phn:** 256-764-8121 **Fax:** 256-764-8169 www.wxfl.com nmartin@bigriverbroadcasting.com

Florence WQLT-FM (a) PO Box 932, Florence AL 35631 **Phn:** 256-764-8121 **Fax:** 256-764-8169 www.wqlt.com nmartin@bigriverbroadcasting.com

Florence WSBM-AM (wu) PO Box 932, Florence AL 35631 **Phn:** 256-764-8121 **Fax:** 256-764-8169 www.wsbm.com nmartin@bigriverbroadcasting.com

Florence WXFL-FM (c) PO Box 932, Florence AL 35631 **Phn:** 256-764-8121 **Fax:** 256-764-8169 www.wxfl.com nmartin@bigriverbroadcasting.com

Florence WYTK-FM (s) PO Box 146, Florence AL 35631 **Phn:** 256-764-9390 **Fax:** 256-764-7760 www.939thescore.com thescore@bellsouth.net

Foley WHEP-AM (nts) PO Box 1747, Foley AL 36536 **Phn:** 251-943-7131 **Fax:** 251-943-7031 www.whep1310.com

Fort Payne WFPA-AM (nt) 1210 Johnson St E, Fort Payne AL 35967 **Phn:** 256-845-7721 **Fax:** 256-845-6593 1400wfpa.com wfpa@1400wfpa.com

Fort Payne WZOB-AM (c) PO Box 680748, Fort Payne AL 35968 **Phn:** 256-845-2810 **Fax:** 256-845-7521

Gadsden WAAX-AM (nt) 304 S 4th St, Gadsden AL 35901 **Phn:** 256-543-9229 **Fax:** 256-543-8777 www.waax570.com ricksisk@clearchannel.com

Gadsden WGAD-AM (o) PO Box 1350, Gadsden AL 35902 **Phn:** 256-546-1611 **Fax:** 256-547-9062

Gadsden WGMZ-FM (h) PO Box 517, Gadsden AL 35902 **Phn:** 256-549-0931 **Fax:** 256-543-8777 www.wgmz.com z93@clearchannel.com

Gadsden WJBY-AM (gq) PO Box 1350, Gadsden AL 35902 **Phn:** 256-546-1611 **Fax:** 256-547-9062

Gadsden WKXX-FM (a) PO Box 8405, Gadsden AL 35902 **Phn:** 256-442-3944 **Fax:** 256-442-7287 www.wkxx.com frontdesk@wkxx.com

Gadsden WMGJ-AM (wu) 815 Tuscaloosa Ave, Gadsden AL 35901 **Phn:** 256-546-4434 **Fax:** 256-546-9645 www.wmgj.com floyddonald@wmgj.com

Greenville WGYV-AM (ot) PO Box 585, Greenville AL 36037 **Phn:** 334-382-5444 wgyv.ezstream.com wkwl@alaweb.com

Greenville WKXK-FM (wu) PO Box 369, Greenville AL 36037 **Phn:** 334-382-6555 **Fax:** 334-382-7770 www.watchdognetwork.com wkxn@wkxn.com

Greenville WKXN-FM (wu) PO Box 369, Greenville AL 36037 **Phn:** 334-382-6555 **Fax:** 334-382-7770 www.wkxn.com wkxn@wkxn.com

Greenville WQZX-FM (c) 205 W Commerce St, Greenville AL 36037 **Phn:** 334-382-6633 **Fax:** 334-382-6634 www.q94.net kyle@q94.net

Gulf Shores WCSN-FM (a) PO Box 1919, Gulf Shores AL 36547 **Phn:** 251-967-1057 **Fax:** 251-967-1050 www.sunny105.com sunny105@gulftel.com

Guntersville WGSV-AM (nt) PO Box 220, Guntersville AL 35976 **Phn:** 256-582-8131 **Fax:** 256-582-4347 www.wgsv.com wgsv@wgsv.com

Guntersville WJIA-FM (vq) 5025 Spring Creek Dr, Guntersville AL 35976 **Phn:** 256-505-0885 **Fax:** 256-505-0886 www.wjia885.com

Guntersville WTWX-FM (c) PO Box 220, Guntersville AL 35976 **Phn:** 256-582-4946 **Fax:** 256-582-4347 www.wtwx.com wtwx@wtwx.com

Haleyville WJBB-AM (g) PO Box 370, Haleyville AL 35565 **Phn:** 205-486-2277 **Fax:** 205-486-3905

Haleyville WJBB-FM (c) PO Box 370, Haleyville AL 35565 **Phn:** 205-486-2277 **Fax:** 205-486-3905

Hamilton WERH-FM (r) PO Box 1119, Hamilton AL 35570 **Phn:** 205-921-3481 **Fax:** 205-921-7187 werh@sonet.net

Hamilton WERH-AM (cg) PO Box 1119, Hamilton AL 35570 **Phn:** 205-921-3481 **Fax:** 205-921-7187 werh@sonet.net

Hartselle WQAH-FM (c) PO Box 1048, Hartselle AL 35640 **Phn:** 256-773-2563 **Fax:** 256-773-6915 www.wqah.com info@wqah.com

Heflin WPIL-FM (qc) 256 Brockford Rd, Heflin AL 36264 **Phn:** 334-463-4226 **Fax:** 334-463-4232 www.wpilfm.com wpil@wpilfm.com

Huntsville WAHR-FM (a) PO Box 5287, Huntsville AL 35814 **Phn:** 256-536-1568 **Fax:** 256-536-4416 rocketcitynews.com bstephens@mystar99.com

Huntsville WBHP-AM (n) PO Box 21008, Huntsville AL 35813 **Phn:** 256-309-2400 **Fax:** 256-350-2653 www.wbhpam.com stuartlangston@clearchannel.com

Huntsville WDRM-FM (c) PO Box 21008, Huntsville AL 35813 **Phn:** 256-309-2400 **Fax:** 256-350-2653 www.wdrm.com erichwest@clearchannel.com

Huntsville WEUP-AM (wgt) 2609 Jordan Ln NW, Huntsville AL 35816 **Phn:** 256-837-9387 **Fax:** 256-837-9404 www.weupam.com churchnews@weupam.com

Huntsville WEUP-FM (u) 2609 Jordan Ln NW, Huntsville AL 35816 **Phn:** 256-837-9387 **Fax:** 256-837-9404 www.103weup.com promotions@103weup.com

Huntsville WEUV-AM (tg) 2609 Jordan Ln NW, Huntsville AL 35816 **Phn:** 256-837-9387 **Fax:** 256-837-9404 www.weupam.com churchnews@weupam.com

Huntsville WEUZ-FM (u) 2609 Jordan Ln NW, Huntsville AL 35816 **Phn:** 256-837-9387 **Fax:** 256-837-9404 www.103weup.com promotions@103weup.com

Huntsville WHOS-AM (n) PO Box 21008, Huntsville AL 35813 **Phn:** 256-309-2400 **Fax:** 256-350-2653 www.wbhpam.com stuartlangston@clearchannel.com

ALABAMA RADIO STATIONS

Huntsville WHWT-FM (h) 2084 Washington St NW, Huntsville AL 35811 **Phn:** 256-489-9498 **Fax:** 256-489-5035 www.hot1035fm.com djfreshinc@aol.com

Huntsville WJOU-FM (vq) 7000 Adventist Blvd NW, Huntsville AL 35896 **Phn:** 256-722-9990 **Fax:** 256-837-7918 www.wjou.org wjou@oakwood.edu

Huntsville WLOR-AM (wgu) 1555 The Boardwalk Ste 1, Huntsville AL 35816 **Phn:** 256-536-1568 **Fax:** 256-536-4416

Huntsville WLRH-FM (pln) Uah Campus John Wright Dr, Huntsville AL 35899 **Phn:** 256-895-9574 **Fax:** 256-830-4577 www.wlrh.org gkennedy@hiwaay.net

Huntsville WQRV-FM (a) PO Box 21008, Huntsville AL 35813 **Phn:** 256-309-2400 **Fax:** 256-350-2653 www.1003theriver.com rickbrown@clearchannel.com

Huntsville WRSA-FM (a) 8402 Memorial Pkwy SW, Huntsville AL 35802 **Phn:** 256-885-9797 **Fax:** 256-885-9796 www.lite969.com penny@lite969.com

Huntsville WRTT-FM (r) 1555 The Boardwalk # 1, Huntsville AL 35816 **Phn:** 256-536-1568 **Fax:** 256-536-4416 rocketcitynews.com jwood@therocket951.com

Huntsville WZZN-FM (s) 108 Woodson St NW, Huntsville AL 35801 **Phn:** 256-382-0724 **Fax:** 256-382-0729 www.977thezone.com

Jackson WBMH-FM (c) 4428 N College Ave, Jackson AL 36545 **Phn:** 251-246-4431 **Fax:** 251-246-1980

Jackson WHOD-FM (ah) PO Box 518, Jackson AL 36545 **Phn:** 251-246-4431 **Fax:** 251-246-1980 rcoffice@bellsouth.net

Jackson WRJX-AM (ob) PO Box 518, Jackson AL 36545 **Phn:** 251-246-4431 **Fax:** 251-246-1980 rcoffice@bellsouth.net

Jacksonville WLJS-FM (vpr) 700 Pelham Rd N, Jacksonville AL 36265 **Phn:** 256-782-5572 919fm.webs.com

Jasper WIXI-AM (c) PO Box 622, Jasper AL 35502 **Phn:** 205-384-3461 **Fax:** 205-384-3462

Jasper WLYJ-AM (g) 513 19th St W, Jasper AL 35501 **Phn:** 205-221-2222 **Fax:** 205-295-1238 joychristianradio.com radio@joychristian.com

Madison WAYH-FM (q) 9582 Madison Blvd Ste 8, Madison AL 35758 **Phn:** 256-837-9293 **Fax:** 256-772-6731 wayh.wayfm.com contact@wayfm.com

Madison WTAK-FM (r) 26869 Peoples Rd, Madison AL 35756 **Phn:** 256-309-2400 **Fax:** 256-350-2653 www.wtak.com erichwest@clearchannel.com

Mobile WABB-AM (nt) 1551 Spring Hill Ave, Mobile AL 36604 **Phn:** 251-432-5572 **Fax:** 251-438-4044 wabbam.com info@wabb.com

Mobile WBHY-AM (taq) PO Box 1328, Mobile AL 36633 **Phn:** 251-473-8488 www.goforth.org news@goforth.org

Mobile WBLX-FM (uw) 2800 Dauphin St Ste 104, Mobile AL 36606 **Phn:** 251-652-2000 **Fax:** 251-652-2001 www.thebigstation93blx.com vinny.d@cumulus.com

Mobile WDLT-FM (wu) 2800 Dauphin St Ste 104, Mobile AL 36606 **Phn:** 251-652-2000 **Fax:** 251-652-2001 www.983wdlt.com cathyb983@bellsouth.net

Mobile WGOK-AM (wu) 2800 Dauphin St Ste 104, Mobile AL 36606 **Phn:** 251-652-2000 **Fax:** 251-652-2001 www.gospel900.com felicia.allbritton@cumulus.com

Mobile WHIL-FM (vl) 4000 Dauphin St, Mobile AL 36608 **Phn:** 251-380-4685 **Fax:** 251-460-2189 apr.org aprnews@apr.org

Mobile WKSJ-FM (c) 555 Broadcast Dr 3rd Fl, Mobile AL 36606 **Phn:** 251-450-0100 **Fax:** 251-479-3418 www.95ksj.com bblack@ccmobile.com

Mobile WMOB-AM (q) PO Box 63, Mobile AL 36601 **Phn:** 251-432-1360

Mobile WMXC-FM (a) 555 Broadcast Dr 3rd Fl, Mobile AL 36606 **Phn:** 251-450-0100 **Fax:** 251-479-3418 www.litemix.com danmason@clearchannel.com

Mobile WNSP-FM (s) 1100 Dauphin St Ste E, Mobile AL 36604 **Phn:** 251-438-5460 **Fax:** 251-438-5462 www.wnsp.com ken@wnsp.com

Mobile WPMI-AM (nt) 555 Broadcast Dr 3rd Fl, Mobile AL 36606 **Phn:** 251-450-0100 **Fax:** 251-479-3418 www.newsradio710.com danmason@clearchannel.com

Mobile WRKH-FM (r) 555 Broadcast Dr 3rd Fl, Mobile AL 36606 **Phn:** 251-450-0100 **Fax:** 251-473-6662 www.961therocket.com stevepowers@clearchannel.com

Mobile WTOF-AM (nt) PO Box 63, Mobile AL 36601 **Phn:** 251-937-1110

Mobile WYOK-FM (h) 2800 Dauphin St Ste 104, Mobile AL 36606 **Phn:** 251-652-2000 **Fax:** 251-652-2001

Mobile WZEW-FM (a) 1100 Dauphin St Ste E, Mobile AL 36604 **Phn:** 251-438-5460 **Fax:** 251-438-5462 www.92zew.net zewradio@gmail.com

Monroeville WMFC-FM (o) PO Box 645, Monroeville AL 36461 **Phn:** 251-575-3281 **Fax:** 251-575-3280 wmfc@frontiernet.net

Monroeville WMFC-AM (g) PO Box 645, Monroeville AL 36461 **Phn:** 251-575-3281 **Fax:** 251-575-3280 wmfc@frontiernet.net

Montgomery WACV-AM (nt) 4101 Wall St Ste A, Montgomery AL 36106 **Phn:** 334-244-1170 **Fax:** 334-279-9563 1049thegump.com tbarber@bluewaterbroadcasting.com

Montgomery WBAM-FM (c) 4101 Wall St Ste A, Montgomery AL 36106 **Phn:** 334-244-0961 **Fax:** 334-279-9563 bamacountry.com info@buzzmontgomery.com

Montgomery WHHY-FM (h) 1 Commerce St Ste 300, Montgomery AL 36104 **Phn:** 334-240-9274 **Fax:** 334-240-9219 www.y102montgomery.com steve.smith@cumulus.com

Montgomery WHLW-FM (g) 203 Gunn Rd, Montgomery AL 36117 **Phn:** 334-274-6464 www.1043hallelujahfm.com

Montgomery WJWZ-FM (uw) 4101 Wall St Ste A, Montgomery AL 36106 **Phn:** 334-244-0961 **Fax:** 334-279-9563 979jamz.com tbarber@bluewaterbroadcasting.com

Montgomery WLBF-FM (vq) PO Box 210789, Montgomery AL 36121 **Phn:** 334-271-8900 **Fax:** 334-260-8962 www.faithbroadcasting.org mail@faithradio.org

Montgomery WLWI-AM (nt) 1 Commerce St Ste 300, Montgomery AL 36104 **Phn:** 334-240-9274 **Fax:** 334-240-9219 www.newsradio1440.com bob.wooddy@cumulus.com

Montgomery WLWI-FM (c) 1 Commerce St Ste 300, Montgomery AL 36104 **Phn:** 334-240-9274 **Fax:** 334-240-9219 www.wlwi.com bill.hardin@cumulus.com

Montgomery WMGY-AM (g) 2305 Upper Wetumpka Rd, Montgomery AL 36107 **Phn:** 334-834-3710 **Fax:** 334-834-3711 www.wmgyradio.com admin@wmgyradio.com

Montgomery WMSP-AM (snt) 1 Commerce St Ste 300, Montgomery AL 36104 **Phn:** 334-240-9274 **Fax:** 334-240-9219 www.sportsradio740.com bwooddy@cumulus.com

Montgomery WMXS-FM (a) 1 Commerce St Ste 300, Montgomery AL 36104 **Phn:** 334-240-9274 **Fax:** 334-240-9219 www.mix103.com brian.roberts@cumulus.com

Montgomery WNZZ-AM (am) 1 Commerce St Ste 300, Montgomery AL 36104 **Phn:** 334-240-9274 **Fax:** 334-240-9219 www.wnzz950.com bob.wooddy@cumulus.com

Montgomery WQKS-FM (rh) 4101 Wall St, Montgomery AL 36106 **Phn:** 334-244-0961 **Fax:** 334-279-9563 q961fm.com rpeters@bluewaterbroadcasting.com

Montgomery WVAS-FM (vj) 915 S Jackson St, Montgomery AL 36104 **Phn:** 334-229-4708 **Fax:** 334-269-4995 www.wvasfm.org ccapel@alasu.edu

Montgomery WWMG-FM (o) 203 Gunn Rd, Montgomery AL 36117 **Phn:** 334-274-6464 **Fax:** 334-274-6467 www.mymagic97.com mymagic97@gmail.com

Montgomery WXFX-FM (r) 1 Commerce St Ste 300, Montgomery AL 36104 **Phn:** 334-240-9274 **Fax:** 334-240-9219 www.wxfx.com rick1.hendrick@cumulus.com

Montgomery WZHT-FM (wu) 203 Gunn Rd, Montgomery AL 36117 **Phn:** 334-274-6464 **Fax:** 334-274-6465 www.myhot105.com darrylelliott@clearchannel.com

Moody WURL-AM (g) 2999 Radio Park Dr, Moody AL 35004 **Phn:** 205-699-9875 **Fax:** 205-640-4379 wurlradio.com wurlradio@aol.com

Normal WJAB-FM (vj) PO Box 1687, Normal AL 35762 **Phn:** 256-372-5795 **Fax:** 256-372-5907 www2.aamu.eduwjab

Opelika WKKR-FM (c) 915 Veterans Pkwy, Opelika AL 36801 **Phn:** 334-745-4656 **Fax:** 334-749-1520 www.kickerfm.com

Opelika WMXA-FM (a) 915 Veterans Pkwy, Opelika AL 36801 **Phn:** 334-745-4656 **Fax:** 334-749-1520

Opelika WZMG-AM (wg) 915 Veterans Pkwy, Opelika AL 36801 **Phn:** 334-745-4656 **Fax:** 334-749-1520 www.intouch910am.com richard.lagrand@qantumofauburn.com

Opp WAMI-AM (c) PO Box 40, Opp AL 36467 **Phn:** 334-493-3588 **Fax:** 334-493-4182 wami@oppcatv.com

Opp WAMI-FM (c) PO Box 40, Opp AL 36467 **Phn:** 334-493-3588 **Fax:** 334-493-4182 wami@oppcatv.com

Opp WOPP-AM (c) 1101 Cameron Rd, Opp AL 36467 **Phn:** 334-493-4545 **Fax:** 334-493-4546 www.wopp.com wopp@wopp.com

Oxford WANA-AM (s) 1913 Barry St # B, Oxford AL 36203 **Phn:** 256-741-6000 **Fax:** 256-741-6031 jimj@wtdrthunder.com

Oxford WSYA-FM (oa) 1913 Barry St # B, Oxford AL 36203 **Phn:** 256-741-6080 **Fax:** 256-741-6031 www.wtdrthunder.com jimj@wtdrthunder.com

Oxford WTBB-FM (q) 1500 Airport Rd, Oxford AL 36203 **Phn:** 256-831-3333 **Fax:** 256-831-5895 www.trinityoxford.org truth@trinityoxford.org

Oxford WTDR-FM (c) 1913 Barry St # B, Oxford AL 36203 **Phn:** 256-741-6000 **Fax:** 256-741-6031 www.wtdrthunder.com news@wtdrthunder.com

Oxford WVOK-FM (a) PO Box 3770, Oxford AL 36203 **Phn:** 256-835-1580 **Fax:** 256-831-1500 www.979wvok.com email@979wvok.com

Ozark WGEA-FM (cgt) 285 E Broad St, Ozark AL 36360 **Phn:** 334-774-7673 **Fax:** 334-774-6450 www.wgea.us

Ozark WOZK-AM (a) PO Box 1109, Ozark AL 36361 **Phn:** 334-774-5600

Ozark WRJM-FM (nt) 285 E Broad St, Ozark AL 36360 **Phn:** 334-774-7673 **Fax:** 334-774-6450

Pell City WFHK-AM (tc) 22 Cogswell Ave, Pell City AL 35125 **Phn:** 205-338-1430 **Fax:** 205-814-1430

Rainsville WVSM-AM (g) PO Box 339, Rainsville AL 35986 **Phn:** 256-638-2137 www.wvsmam.com wvsm@farmerstel.com

Roanoke WELR-FM (c) PO Box 710, Roanoke AL 36274 **Phn:** 334-863-4139 **Fax:** 334-863-2540 www.eagle1023.com welr@eagle1023.com

Roanoke WELR-AM (s) PO Box 710, Roanoke AL 36274 **Phn:** 334-863-4139 **Fax:** 334-863-2540 www.eagle1023.com welr@eagle1023.com

Russellville WGOL-AM (cs) 113 Washington Ave NW, Russellville AL 35653 **Phn:** 256-332-0214 www.wgolam.com

Russellville WKAX-AM (g) 113 Washington Ave NW, Russellville AL 35653 **Phn:** 256-332-0214 **Fax:** 256-332-7430

Scottsboro WKEA-FM (c) PO Box 966, Scottsboro AL 35768 **Phn:** 256-259-2341 **Fax:** 256-574-2156 www.wkeafm.com lisa@wkeafm.com

Scottsboro WMXN-FM (r) PO Box 966, Scottsboro AL 35768 **Phn:** 256-259-2341 **Fax:** 256-574-2156 www.1017Thestorm.com ron@wkeafm.com

Scottsboro WWIC-AM (c) PO Box 759, Scottsboro AL 35768 **Phn:** 256-259-1050 **Fax:** 256-575-2411 www.wwicradio.com wwic@scottsboro.org

Scottsboro WZCT-AM (g) 1111 E Willow St, Scottsboro AL 35768 **Phn:** 256-574-1330 www.scottsboro.com scottadmin@scottsboro.com

Selma WALX-FM (a) 273 Persimmon Tree Rd, Selma AL 36701 **Phn:** 334-875-7101 **Fax:** 334-875-1340

Selma WDXX-FM (c) PO Box 1055, Selma AL 36702 **Phn:** 334-875-3350 **Fax:** 334-874-6959

Selma WHBB-AM (nt) PO Box 1055, Selma AL 36702 **Phn:** 334-875-3350 **Fax:** 334-874-6959

Selma WJAM-AM (u) PO Box 1150, Selma AL 36702 **Phn:** 334-875-9360 **Fax:** 334-875-1340

Selma WMRK-FM (nt) PO Box 1150, Selma AL 36702 **Phn:** 334-244-1170 **Fax:** 334-279-9563

Selma WMRK-AM (ot) PO Box 1150, Selma AL 36702 **Phn:** 334-875-7101 **Fax:** 334-875-1340

Sheffield WBTG-AM (o) PO Box 518, Sheffield AL 35660 **Phn:** 256-381-6800 **Fax:** 256-381-6801 www.wbtgradio.com announcements@wbtgradio.com

Sheffield WBTG-FM (g) PO Box 518, Sheffield AL 35660 **Phn:** 256-381-6800 **Fax:** 256-381-6801 www.wbtgradio.com announcements@wbtgradio.com

Spanish Fort WLVV-AM (wgu) 1263 Battleship Pkwy, Spanish Fort AL 36527 **Phn:** 251-626-1090 **Fax:** 251-626-1099

Spanish Fort WNSI-AM (snt) 9945 Spanish Fort Blvd Ste G, Spanish Fort AL 36527 **Phn:** 251-625-8646 **Fax:** 251-947-2347

Spanish Fort WNSI-FM (sn) 9945 Spanish Fort Blvd Ste G, Spanish Fort AL 36527 **Phn:** 251-368-2511 **Fax:** 251-625-2842

Sylacauga WFEB-AM (snt) PO Box 358, Sylacauga AL 35150 **Phn:** 256-245-3281 **Fax:** 256-245-3050

Sylacauga WYEA-AM (h) PO Box 629, Sylacauga AL 35150 **Phn:** 256-249-4263 **Fax:** 678-399-9640 www.wyea.net info@wyea.net

Tallassee WACQ-AM (o) 320 Barnett Blvd, Tallassee AL 36078 **Phn:** 334-283-6888 www.wacqradio.com wacqradio@elmore.rr.com

Tallassee WTLS-AM (st) PO Box 780146, Tallassee AL 36078 **Phn:** 334-283-8200 **Fax:** 334-283-8622 www.1300wtls.com mbutler@1300wtls.com

Thomasville WJDB-AM (o) 30280 Highway 43, Thomasville AL 36784 **Phn:** 334-636-4438 **Fax:** 334-636-4439

Thomasville WJDB-FM (c) 30280 Highway 43, Thomasville AL 36784 **Phn:** 334-636-4438 **Fax:** 334-636-4439

Troy WRWA-FM (pl) Wallace Hall Troy Univ, Troy AL 36082 **Phn:** 334-670-3268 **Fax:** 334-670-3934 troypublicradio.org publicradio@troy.edu

Troy WTBF-AM (st) 67 W Court Sq, Troy AL 36081 **Phn:** 334-566-0300 **Fax:** 334-566-5689 www.wtbf.com wtbf@troycable.net

Troy WTBF-FM (co) 67 W Court Sq, Troy AL 36081 **Phn:** 334-566-0300 **Fax:** 334-566-5689 www.wtbf.com wtbf@troycable.net

Troy WTJB-FM (pjln) Troy State Univ, Troy AL 36082 **Phn:** 334-670-3268 publicradio.troy.edu publicradio@troy.edu

Troy WTSU-FM (pl) Univ Avenue Troy State Univ, Troy AL 36082 **Phn:** 334-670-3268 **Fax:** 334-670-3934 publicradio.troy.eduwtsu-fm publicradio@troy.edu

Tuscaloosa WACT-AM (t) 3900 11th Ave, Tuscaloosa AL 35401 **Phn:** 205-349-3200 **Fax:** 205-366-9774 www.247comedy.com

Tuscaloosa WBEI-FM (a) 142 Skyland Blvd E, Tuscaloosa AL 35405 **Phn:** 205-345-7200 **Fax:** 205-349-1715 www.b1017online.com greg.thomas@cumulus.com

Tuscaloosa WDGM-FM (o) 142 Skyland Blvd E, Tuscaloosa AL 35405 **Phn:** 205-345-7200 **Fax:** 205-349-1715 greg.thomas@cumulus.com

Tuscaloosa WFFN-FM (c) 142 Skyland Blvd E, Tuscaloosa AL 35405 **Phn:** 205-345-7200 **Fax:** 205-349-1715 www.953thebear.com monk.monk@townsquaremedia.com

Tuscaloosa WQPR-FM (plnj) PO Box 870370, Tuscaloosa AL 35487 **Phn:** 205-348-6644 **Fax:** 205-348-6648 wual.public.broadcasting.net aprnews@apr.org

Tuscaloosa WQZZ-FM (wu) 601 Greensboro Ave Ste 507, Tuscaloosa AL 35401 **Phn:** 205-345-4787 **Fax:** 205-345-4790 jwlawson@bellsouth.net

Tuscaloosa WRTR-FM (t) 3900 11th Ave, Tuscaloosa AL 35401 **Phn:** 205-344-4589 **Fax:** 205-752-4592 www.talkradio1059.com keithallen@clearchannel.com

Tuscaloosa WTBC-AM (snt) PO Box 2000, Tuscaloosa AL 35403 **Phn:** 205-758-5523 **Fax:** 205-752-9696 www.wtbc1230.com wtbc1@wtbc1230.com

Tuscaloosa WTSK-AM (wg) 142 Skyland Blvd E, Tuscaloosa AL 35405 **Phn:** 205-345-7200 **Fax:** 205-349-1715 www.790wtsk.com todd.livingston@townsquaremedia.com

Tuscaloosa WTUG-FM (wu) 142 Skyland Blvd E, Tuscaloosa AL 35405 **Phn:** 205-345-7200 **Fax:** 205-349-1715 www.wtug.com todd.livingston@townsquaremedia.com

Tuscaloosa WTXT-FM (c) 3900 11th Ave, Tuscaloosa AL 35401 **Phn:** 205-349-3200 **Fax:** 205-366-9774 www.98txt.com jaymichaels@clearchannel.com

Tuscaloosa WUAL-FM (pln) PO Box 870370, Tuscaloosa AL 35487 **Phn:** 205-348-6644 **Fax:** 205-348-6648 wual.publicbroadcasting.net aprnews@apr.org

Tuscaloosa WVUA-FM (vr) PO Box 870152, Tuscaloosa AL 35487 **Phn:** 205-348-6461 wvuafm.ua.edu wvua@sa.ua.edu

Tuscaloosa WWPG-AM (wxg) 601 Greensboro Ave Ste 507, Tuscaloosa AL 35401 **Phn:** 205-345-4787 **Fax:** 205-345-4790 jwlawson@bellsouth.net

Tuscaloosa WZBQ-FM (h) 2121 9th St Ste B, Tuscaloosa AL 35401 **Phn:** 205-344-4589 **Fax:** 205-366-9774 www.941zbq.com dlo@941zbq.com

Tuscumbia WLAY-AM (s) 509 N Main St, Tuscumbia AL 35674 **Phn:** 256-383-2525 **Fax:** 256-383-4450 www.wlaythesound.com kevinwhorton@urbanradio.fm

Tuscumbia WLAY-FM (c) 509 N Main St, Tuscumbia AL 35674 **Phn:** 256-383-2525 **Fax:** 256-383-4450 www.wlay1035.com brianrickman@urbanradio.fm

Tuscumbia WVNA-FM (r) 509 N Main St, Tuscumbia AL 35674 **Phn:** 256-383-2525 **Fax:** 256-383-4450 www.bigdog1055.com tckinkead@urbanradio.fm

Tuscumbia WVNA-AM (snt) 509 N Main St, Tuscumbia AL 35674 **Phn:** 256-383-2525 **Fax:** 256-383-4450 www.newstalkwvna.com amandanorton@urbanradio.fm

Tuscumbia WZZA-AM (wgx) 1570 Woodmont Dr, Tuscumbia AL 35674 **Phn:** 256-381-1862 **Fax:** 256-381-6006 www.wzzaradio.com news@wzzaradio.com

Tuskegee WBIL-AM (gw) 118 S Main St, Tuskegee AL 36083 **Phn:** 334-727-2100 wbil580am.com rejoice@wbil580am.com

Valley WEBT-FM (vg) 2615 64th Blvd, Valley AL 36854 **Phn:** 334-756-6923 **Fax:** 334-756-8430

Vernon WJEC-FM (g) PO Box 630, Vernon AL 35592 **Phn:** 205-695-9191 **Fax:** 205-695-9131 www.wjec1065.com info@wjec1065.com

Vernon WVSA-AM (s) PO Box 630, Vernon AL 35592 **Phn:** 205-695-9191 **Fax:** 205-695-9131 www.wjec1065.com info@wjec1065.com

Wetumpka WAPZ-AM (gxw) 2821 US Highway 231, Wetumpka AL 36093 **Phn:** 334-567-9279 **Fax:** 334-567-7971

Winfield WKXM-AM (st) PO Box 608, Winfield AL 35594 **Phn:** 205-487-3261 **Fax:** 205-487-6991 wkxm@dlis.net

Winfield WKXM-FM (o) PO Box 608, Winfield AL 35594 **Phn:** 205-487-3261 **Fax:** 205-487-6991 wkxm@dlis.net

York WSLY-FM (uw) 11474 U S Highway 11, York AL 36925 **Phn:** 205-392-5234 **Fax:** 205-392-5536

York WYLS-AM (ob) 11474 U S Highway 11, York AL 36925 **Phn:** 205-392-5234 **Fax:** 205-392-5536

ALASKA

Anchorage KAFC-FM (q) PO Box 210389, Anchorage AK 99521 **Phn:** 907-333-5282 **Fax:** 907-333-9851 kafc.org kathleen@kafc.org

Anchorage KASH-FM (c) 800 E Dimond Blvd Ste 3-370, Anchorage AK 99515 **Phn:** 907-522-1515 **Fax:** 907-743-5186 www.kashcountry1075.com mattcourtice@clearchannel.com

Anchorage KATB-FM (q) PO Box 210389, Anchorage AK 99521 **Phn:** 907-333-5282 **Fax:** 907-333-9851 www.katb.org tom@katb.org

Anchorage KBBO-FM (a) 833 Gambell St, Anchorage AK 99501 **Phn:** 907-344-4045 **Fax:** 907-522-6053 921bob.fm bill.sigmar@ohanamediagroup.com

ALASKA RADIO STATIONS

Anchorage KBFX-FM (r) 800 E Dimond Blvd Ste 3-370, Anchorage AK 99515 **Phn:** 907-522-1515 **Fax:** 907-743-5186 www.1005thefox.com joeallen@clearchannel.com

Anchorage KBRJ-FM (c) 301 Arctic Slope Ave Ste 200, Anchorage AK 99518 **Phn:** 907-344-9622 **Fax:** 907-349-7326 www.kbrj.com alaskawins@kbrj.com

Anchorage KBYR-AM (nt) 833 Gambell St, Anchorage AK 99501 **Phn:** 907-344-4045 **Fax:** 907-522-6053 www.kbyr.com

Anchorage KDBZ-FM (a) 833 Gambell St, Anchorage AK 99501 **Phn:** 907-344-4045 **Fax:** 907-522-6053

Anchorage KEAG-FM (h) 301 Arctic Slope Ave Ste 200, Anchorage AK 99518 **Phn:** 907-344-9622 **Fax:** 907-349-3299 www.kool973.com ed.riley@anchoragemediagroup.com

Anchorage KENI-AM (nt) 800 E Dimond Blvd Ste 3-370, Anchorage AK 99515 **Phn:** 907-522-1515 **Fax:** 907-743-5184 www.650keni.com markmurphy@clearchannel.com

Anchorage KFAT-FM (hu) 833 Gambell St, Anchorage AK 99501 **Phn:** 907-344-4297 **Fax:** 907-522-6053 www.kfat929.com

Anchorage KFQD-AM (nt) 301 Arctic Slope Ave Ste 200, Anchorage AK 99518 **Phn:** 907-344-9622 **Fax:** 907-349-7326 www.kfqd.com joe.campbell@anchoragemediagroup.com

Anchorage KGOT-FM (h) 800 E Dimond Blvd Ste 3-370, Anchorage AK 99515 **Phn:** 907-522-1515 **Fax:** 907-743-5186 www.kgot.com stewart@clearchannel.com

Anchorage KHAR-AM (bm) 301 Arctic Slope Ave Ste 200, Anchorage AK 99518 **Phn:** 907-344-9622 **Fax:** 907-349-7326 khar590.com joe@kfqd.com

Anchorage KLEF-FM (l) 3601 C St Ste 290, Anchorage AK 99503 **Phn:** 907-561-5556 **Fax:** 907-562-4219 www.klef.com klef@klef.com

Anchorage KMXS-FM (a) 301 Arctic Slope Ave Ste 200, Anchorage AK 99518 **Phn:** 907-344-9622 **Fax:** 907-349-7326 www.kmxs.com devan.mitchell@anchoragemediagroup.com

Anchorage KNBA-FM (e) 3600 San Jeronimo Dr Ste 480, Anchorage AK 99508 **Phn:** 907-793-3500 **Fax:** 907-793-3536 www.knba.org feedback@knba.org

Anchorage KNIK-FM (aj) 4700 Business Park Blvd Ste 44, Anchorage AK 99503 **Phn:** 907-522-1018 **Fax:** 907-522-1027 www.knik.com danny@alaskaim.com

Anchorage KRUA-FM (vr) 3211 Providence Dr, Anchorage AK 99508 **Phn:** 907-786-6800 **Fax:** 907-786-6806 www.kruaradio.org uaa_krua1@uaa.alaska.edu

Anchorage KSKA-FM (pnj) 3877 University Dr, Anchorage AK 99508 **Phn:** 907-550-8400 **Fax:** 907-550-8401 www.alaskapublic.org news@aprn.org

Anchorage KTZN-AM (s) 800 E Dimond Blvd Ste 3-370, Anchorage AK 99515 **Phn:** 907-522-1515 **Fax:** 907-743-5183 www.550thezone.com markmurphy@clearchannel.com

Anchorage KUDO-AM (nt) 4700 Business Park Blvd Ste 44, Anchorage AK 99503 **Phn:** 907-522-1018 **Fax:** 907-522-1027 www.1080theticket.com klef@klef.com

Anchorage KWHL-FM (r) 301 Arctic Slope Ave Ste 200, Anchorage AK 99518 **Phn:** 907-344-9622 **Fax:** 907-349-7326 www.kwhl.com studio@kwhl.com

Anchorage KXLW-FM (cr) 833 Gambell St, Anchorage AK 99501 **Phn:** 907-344-4045 **Fax:** 907-522-6053 www.963thewolf.com tom.oakes@ohanamediagroup.com

Anchorage KYMG-FM (a) 800 E Dimond Blvd Ste 3-370, Anchorage AK 99515 **Phn:** 907-743-5101 **Fax:** 907-743-5183 www.magic989fm.com

Barrow KBRW-FM (p) PO Box 109, Barrow AK 99723 **Phn:** 907-852-6811 **Fax:** 907-852-2274 www.kbrw.org

Barrow KBRW-AM (p) PO Box 109, Barrow AK 99723 **Phn:** 907-852-6811 **Fax:** 907-852-2274 www.kbrw.org kbrw.radio@gmail.com

Bethel KYKD-FM (q) PO Box 2428, Bethel AK 99559 **Phn:** 907-543-5953 www.vfcm.org kykd@vfcm.org

Bethel KYUK-AM (p) PO Box 468, Bethel AK 99559 **Phn:** 907-543-3131 **Fax:** 907-543-3130 kyuk.org angela@kyuk.org

Cordova KCDV-FM (a) PO Box 60, Cordova AK 99574 **Phn:** 907-424-3796 **Fax:** 907-424-3737 www.cordovaradio.com info@cordovaradio.com

Cordova KLAM-AM (cor) PO Box 60, Cordova AK 99574 **Phn:** 907-424-3796 **Fax:** 907-424-3737 www.cordovaradio.com info@cordovaradio.com

Dillingham KDLG-AM (par) PO Box 670, Dillingham AK 99576 **Phn:** 907-842-5281 **Fax:** 907-842-5645 kdlg.org kdlg@dlgsd.org

Fairbanks KAKQ-FM (a) 546 9th Ave, Fairbanks AK 99701 **Phn:** 907-450-1000 www.101magic.com 101magic@clearchannel.com

Fairbanks KCBF-AM (s) 819 1st Ave # A, Fairbanks AK 99701 **Phn:** 907-451-5910 **Fax:** 907-451-5999 www.820sports.com perry@fbxradio.com

Fairbanks KFAR-AM (t) 819 1st Ave # A, Fairbanks AK 99701 **Phn:** 907-451-5910 **Fax:** 907-451-5999 www.kfar660.com perry@fbxradio.com

Fairbanks KFBX-AM (nt) 546 9th Ave, Fairbanks AK 99701 **Phn:** 907-450-1000 **Fax:** 907-457-2128 www.970kfbx.com charlieotoole@clearchannel.com

Fairbanks KIAK-FM (c) 546 9th Ave, Fairbanks AK 99701 **Phn:** 907-450-1000 **Fax:** 907-450-1092 www.kiak.com kiak@clearchannel.com

Fairbanks KKED-FM (r) 546 9th Ave, Fairbanks AK 99701 **Phn:** 907-450-1000 www.1047theedge.com theedge@clearchannel.com

Fairbanks KSUA-FM (vr) PO Box 750113, Fairbanks AK 99775 **Phn:** 907-474-7054 **Fax:** 907-474-6314 www.ksuaradio.com ksuaprogramming@gmail.com

Fairbanks KUAC-FM (plnt) PO Box 755620, Fairbanks AK 99775 **Phn:** 907-474-7491 **Fax:** 907-474-5064 www.kuac.org jerry@kuac.org

Fairbanks KWLF-FM (h) 819 1st Ave # A, Fairbanks AK 99701 **Phn:** 907-451-5910 **Fax:** 907-451-5999 www.kwolf981.com perry@fbxradio.com

Fairbanks KXLR-FM (r) 819 1st Ave # A, Fairbanks AK 99701 **Phn:** 907-451-5910 **Fax:** 907-451-5999 www.kxlrfm.com perry@fbxradio.com

Fairbanks KYSC-FM (a) 3650 Braddock St, Fairbanks AK 99701 **Phn:** 907-455-9690 **Fax:** 907-455-4369

Galena KIYU-AM (p) PO Box 165, Galena AK 99741 **Phn:** 907-656-1488 **Fax:** 907-656-1734 www.kiyu.com raven@kiyu.org

Girdwood KEUL-FM (p) PO Box 29, Girdwood AK 99587 **Phn:** 907-754-2489 glaciercity.usKEUL keul@glaciercity.us

Glennallen KCAM-AM (cq) PO Box 249, Glennallen AK 99588 **Phn:** 907-822-5226 **Fax:** 907-822-3761 www.kcam.org kcam@kcam.org

Haines KHNS-FM (p) PO Box 1109, Haines AK 99827 **Phn:** 907-766-2020 **Fax:** 907-766-2022 www.khns.org khns@khns.org

Homer KBBI-AM (pln) 3913 Kachemak Way, Homer AK 99603 **Phn:** 907-235-7721 **Fax:** 907-235-2357 www.kbbi.org casey@kbbi.org

Homer KGTL-AM (a) PO Box 109, Homer AK 99603 **Phn:** 907-235-6000 **Fax:** 907-235-6683

Homer KPEN-FM (c) PO Box 109, Homer AK 99603 **Phn:** 907-235-6000 **Fax:** 907-235-6683

Homer KWVV-FM (a) PO Box 109, Homer AK 99603 **Phn:** 907-235-6000 **Fax:** 907-235-6683 kwavefm@xyz.net

Juneau KINY-AM (a) 3161 Channel Dr Ste 2, Juneau AK 99801 **Phn:** 907-586-3630 **Fax:** 907-463-3685 www.kinyradio.com kiny@abcstations.com

Juneau KJNO-AM (st) 3161 Channel Dr Ste 2, Juneau AK 99801 **Phn:** 907-586-3630 **Fax:** 907-463-3685

Juneau KSUP-FM (r) 3161 Channel Dr Ste 2, Juneau AK 99801 **Phn:** 907-586-3630 **Fax:** 907-463-3685

Juneau KTKU-FM (c) 3161 Channel Dr Ste 2, Juneau AK 99801 **Phn:** 907-586-3630 **Fax:** 907-463-3685 www.taku105.com

Juneau KTOO-FM (pln) 360 Egan Dr, Juneau AK 99801 **Phn:** 907-586-1670 **Fax:** 907-586-2561 www.ktoo.org ktoo@ktoo.org

Kenai KDLL-FM (pn) PO Box 2111, Kenai AK 99611 **Phn:** 907-283-8433 **Fax:** 907-283-6701 www.kdll.org news@kdllradio.org

Kenai KKIS-FM (h) 40960 Kalifornsky Beach Rd, Kenai AK 99611 **Phn:** 907-283-8700 **Fax:** 907-283-9177 radiokenai.net ericprice@radiokenai.com

Kenai KSLD-AM (s) 40960 Kalifornsky Beach Rd, Kenai AK 99611 **Phn:** 907-283-8700 **Fax:** 907-283-9177 radiokenai.net melissahutchins@radiokenai.com

Kenai KSRM-AM (nt) 40960 Kalifornsky Beach Rd, Kenai AK 99611 **Phn:** 907-283-8700 **Fax:** 907-283-9177 radiokenai.net jakethompson@radiokenai.com

Kenai KWHQ-FM (c) 40960 Kalifornsky Beach Rd, Kenai AK 99611 **Phn:** 907-283-8700 **Fax:** 907-283-9177 radiokenai.net mattwilson@radiokenai.com

Ketchikan KFMJ-FM (o) 516 Stedman St, Ketchikan AK 99901 **Phn:** 907-247-3699 **Fax:** 907-247-5365 www.alaska.fmkfmj kfmj@alaska.fm

Ketchikan KGTW-FM (c) 526 Stedman St, Ketchikan AK 99901 **Phn:** 907-225-2193 **Fax:** 907-225-0444 www.ketchikanradio.com

Ketchikan KRBD-FM (p) 1101 Copper Ridge Rd, Ketchikan AK 99901 **Phn:** 907-225-9655 **Fax:** 907-247-0808 www.krbd.org

Ketchikan KTKN-AM (ant) 526 Stedman St, Ketchikan AK 99901 **Phn:** 907-225-2193 **Fax:** 907-225-0444

Kodiak KMXT-FM (pn) 620 Egan Way, Kodiak AK 99615 **Phn:** 907-486-3181 **Fax:** 907-486-2733 www.kmxt.org gm@kmxt.org

Kodiak KRXX-FM (r) PO Box 708, Kodiak AK 99615 **Phn:** 907-486-5159 **Fax:** 907-486-3044 www.kvok.com kvok@ak.net

Kodiak KVOK-AM (ont) PO Box 708, Kodiak AK 99615 **Phn:** 907-486-5159 **Fax:** 907-486-3044 www.kvok.com kvok@ak.net

Kotzebue KOTZ-AM (p) PO Box 78, Kotzebue AK 99752 **Phn:** 907-442-3434 **Fax:** 907-442-2292 www.kotz.org jgreene@kotz.org

Naknek KAKN-FM (qnt) PO Box 214, Naknek AK 99633 **Phn:** 907-246-7492 **Fax:** 907-246-7462 www.kakn.org kakn@kakn.org

Nenana KIAM-AM (q) PO Box 474, Nenana AK 99760 **Phn:** 907-832-5426 **Fax:** 907-832-5450 www.vfcm.org alaskaradio@vfcm.org

Nome KICY-AM (g) PO Box 820, Nome AK 99762 **Phn:** 907-443-2213 **Fax:** 907-443-2344 www.kicy.org office@kicy.org

Nome KICY-FM (aq) PO Box 820, Nome AK 99762 **Phn:** 907-443-2213 **Fax:** 907-443-2344 www.kicy.org office@kicy.org

Nome KNOM-FM (q) PO Box 988, Nome AK 99762 **Phn:** 907-443-5221 **Fax:** 907-443-5757 www.knom.org rschmidt@knom.org

Nome KNOM-AM (q) PO Box 988, Nome AK 99762 **Phn:** 907-443-5221 **Fax:** 907-443-5757 www.knom.org knomhotline@gmail.com

North Pole KJNP-AM (cg) PO Box 56359, North Pole AK 99705 **Phn:** 907-488-2216 **Fax:** 907-488-5246 www.mosquitonet.com~kjnp kjnp@mosquitonet.com

North Pole KJNP-FM (zq) PO Box 56359, North Pole AK 99705 **Phn:** 907-488-2216 **Fax:** 907-488-5246 www.mosquitonet.com~kjnp kjnp@mosquitonet.com

Petersburg KFSK-FM (pnr) PO Box 149, Petersburg AK 99833 **Phn:** 907-772-3808 **Fax:** 907-772-9296 www.kfsk.org julie@kfsk.org

Petersburg KRSA-AM (cq) PO Box 650, Petersburg AK 99833 Phn: 907-772-3891 Fax: 907-772-4538

Saint Paul KUHB-FM (p) PO Box 905, Saint Paul AK 99660 **Phn:** 907-546-2254 **Fax:** 907-546-2367 www.kuhbradio.org waltgregg@kuhbradio.org

Sand Point KSDP-AM (p) PO Box 328, Sand Point AK 99661 **Phn:** 907-383-5737 **Fax:** 907-383-5271 apradio.org gm@ksdpradio.com

Sitka KCAW-FM (pn) 2 Lincoln St Ste B, Sitka AK 99835 **Phn:** 907-747-5877 **Fax:** 907-747-5977 www.kcaw.org ed@kcaw.org

Sitka KIFW-AM (a) 611 Lake St, Sitka AK 99835 **Phn:** 907-747-5439 **Fax:** 907-747-8455

Sitka KSBZ-FM (r) 611 Lake St, Sitka AK 99835 **Phn:** 907-747-6626 **Fax:** 907-747-8455

Talkeetna KTNA-FM (v) PO Box 300, Talkeetna AK 99676 **Phn:** 907-733-1700 **Fax:** 907-733-1781 ktna.org info@ktna.org

Unalaska KIAL-AM (P) PO Box 181, Unalaska AK 99685 **Phn:** 907-581-1888 **Fax:** 907-581-1634 www.kucb.org alexandra@kucb.org

Valdez KCHU-AM (p) PO Box 467, Valdez AK 99686 **Phn:** 907-835-4665 **Fax:** 907-835-2847 www.kchu.org news@kchu.org

Valdez KVAK-AM (c) PO Box 367, Valdez AK 99686 **Phn:** 907-835-5825 **Fax:** 907-835-5158 www.kvakradio.com valdeznews@gci.net

Valdez KVAK-FM (r) PO Box 367, Valdez AK 99686 **Phn:** 907-835-5825 **Fax:** 907-835-5158 www.kvakradio.com valdeznews@gci.net

Wasilla KMBQ-FM (a) 851 E Westpoint Dr Ste 301, Wasilla AK 99654 **Phn:** 907-373-0222 **Fax:** 907-376-1575 www.kmbq.com bill.sigmar@ohanamediagroup.com

Wrangell KSTK-FM (p) PO Box 1141, Wrangell AK 99929 **Phn:** 907-874-2345 **Fax:** 907-874-3293 www.kstk.org news@kstk.org

ARIZONA

Avondale KMVP-AM (g) PO Box 322, Avondale AZ 85323 **Phn:** 623-533-3213 www.gospel860.com louisbland@gospel860.com

ALASKA RADIO STATIONS

Bullhead City KFLG-FM (a) 1531 E Jill Way Ste 7, Bullhead City AZ 86426 **Phn:** 928-763-5586 **Fax:** 928-763-3775 www.kflg947.com djaeger@cameronbroadcasting.com

Bullhead City KLUK-FM (r) 2350 Miracle Mile Rd # 300, Bullhead City AZ 86442 **Phn:** 928-763-5586 **Fax:** 928-763-3775 www.lucky98fm.com requests@lucky98fm.com

Bullhead City KZZZ-AM (nt) 1531 E Jill Way Ste 7, Bullhead City AZ 86426 **Phn:** 928-763-5586 **Fax:** 928-763-3775 www.talkatoz.com djaeger@cameronbroadcasting.com

Cottonwood KKLD-FM (o) PO Box 187, Cottonwood AZ 86326 **Phn:** 928-634-2286 www.kkld.com kkld@myradioplace.com

Cottonwood KQST-FM (h) PO Box 187, Cottonwood AZ 86326 **Phn:** 928-634-2286 **Fax:** 928-634-2295 myradioplace.com q@myradioplace.com

Cottonwood KVNA-FM (a) PO Box 187, Cottonwood AZ 86326 **Phn:** 928-634-2286 **Fax:** 928-634-2295 myradioplace.com news@myradioplace.com

Cottonwood KVRD-FM (c) PO Box 187, Cottonwood AZ 86326 **Phn:** 928-634-2286 **Fax:** 928-634-2295 www.kvrdfm.com kvrd@myradioplace.com

Cottonwood KYBC-AM (a) PO Box 187, Cottonwood AZ 86326 **Phn:** 928-634-2286 **Fax:** 928-634-2295 www.1600kybc.com news@myradioplace.com

Douglas KDAP-FM (c) PO Box 1179, Douglas AZ 85608 Phn: 520-364-3484 Fax: 520-364-3483

Douglas KDAP-AM (y) PO Box 1179, Douglas AZ 85608 Phn: 520-364-3484 Fax: 520-364-3483

Douglas KRMC-FM (qy) PO Box 2520, Douglas AZ 85608 **Phn:** 520-364-5392 www.worldradionetwork.org krmc@lwrn.org

Flagstaff KAFF-FM (c) 1117 W Route 66, Flagstaff AZ 86001 **Phn:** 928-774-5231 **Fax:** 928-779-2988 kaff.gcmaz.com

Flagstaff KAFF-AM (c) 1117 W Route 66, Flagstaff AZ 86001 **Phn:** 928-774-5231 **Fax:** 928-779-2988 kaff.gcmaz.com

Flagstaff KFLX-FM (r) 2409 N 4th St Ste 101, Flagstaff AZ 86004 **Phn:** 928-779-1177 **Fax:** 928-774-5179 kflx.com stan@northlandradio.com

Flagstaff KJTA-FM (vq) 1700 N 2nd St, Flagstaff AZ 86004 **Phn:** 928-774-9514

Flagstaff KMGN-FM (r) 1117 W Route 66, Flagstaff AZ 86001 **Phn:** 928-774-5231 **Fax:** 928-779-2988 939themountain.gcmaz.com

Flagstaff KNAU-FM (pln) PO Box 5764, Flagstaff AZ 86011 **Phn:** 928-523-5628 **Fax:** 928-523-7647 www.knau.org knau@nau.edu

Flagstaff KSED-FM (c) 2409 N 4th St Ste 101, Flagstaff AZ 86004 **Phn:** 928-779-1177 **Fax:** 928-774-5179 www.koltcountry.com kolt@nazbestradio.com

Flagstaff KTMG-FM (a) 1117 W Route 66, Flagstaff AZ 86001 **Phn:** 928-774-5231 **Fax:** 928-779-2988 magic991.gcmaz.com

Flagstaff KVNA-AM (stn) 1800 S Milton Rd Ste 105, Flagstaff AZ 86001 **Phn:** 928-526-2700 www.myradioplace.com news@myradioplace.com

Flagstaff KWMX-FM (r) 2409 N 4th St Ste 101, Flagstaff AZ 86004 **Phn:** 928-779-1177 **Fax:** 928-774-5179 www.967thewolf.com wolf@nazbestradio.com

Globe KRDE-FM (c) PO Box 1660, Globe AZ 85502 **Phn:** 928-402-9222 **Fax:** 928-425-5063 www.krde.com krde@cableone.net

Green Valley KGVY-AM (no) PO Box 767, Green Valley AZ 85622 **Phn:** 520-399-1000 **Fax:** 520-399-9300 www.kgvy1080.com kgvynews@kgvy1080.com

Keams Canyon KUYI-FM (ve) PO Box 1500, Keams Canyon AZ 86034 **Phn:** 928-738-5505 **Fax:** 928-738-5501 www.kuyi.net info@kuyi.net

Kingman KAAA-AM (snt) 1880 Lucille Ave Ste 2, Kingman AZ 86401 **Phn:** 928-753-2537 **Fax:** 928-753-1551 www.talkatoz.com news@cameronbroadcasting.com

Kingman KGMN-FM (c) 812 E Beale St, Kingman AZ 86401 **Phn:** 928-753-9100 **Fax:** 928-753-1978 www.kgmn.net newshawk22@hotmail.com

Kingman KNKK-FM (a) 2535 Hualapai Mtn Rd #D, Kingman AZ 86401 **Phn:** 928-763-5586 **Fax:** 928-763-3775 www.theknack107.com

Lake Havasu City KJJJ-FM (c) PO Box 2009, Lake Havasu City AZ 86405 **Phn:** 928-855-9336 **Fax:** 928-855-9333 www.todaysbestcountryonline.com steve@kjjjfm.com

Lake Havasu City KNLB-FM (q) PO Box 747, Lake Havasu City AZ 86405 **Phn:** 928-855-9110 **Fax:** 928-453-2588 www.knlb.com info@knlb.com

Lake Havasu City KNTR-AM (nt) 1845 McCulloch Blvd N Ste A14, Lake Havasu City AZ 86403 **Phn:** 928-855-9336 **Fax:** 928-855-9333 www.kntram.com office@myradiocentral.com

Lake Havasu City KRRK-FM (r) 10 Media Center Dr, Lake Havasu City AZ 86403 **Phn:** 928-855-1051 **Fax:** 928-855-7996 mediacenter@maddog.net

Lake Havasu City KWFH-FM (q) PO Box 747, Lake Havasu City AZ 86405 **Phn:** 928-855-9110 www.kwfh.org faron@kwfh.org

Lake Havasu City KZUL-FM (a) 2068 McCulloch Blvd N, Lake Havasu City AZ 86403 **Phn:** 928-855-1051 **Fax:** 928-855-7996 maddogwireless.net baddog@maddog.net

Lakeside KDJI-AM (nt) 1838 Commerce Dr Ste A, Lakeside AZ 85929 **Phn:** 928-368-8100 **Fax:** 928-368-8108 www.whitemountainradio.com production@whitemountainradio.com

Lakeside KRFM-FM (a) 1838 Commerce Dr Ste A, Lakeside AZ 85929 **Phn:** 928-368-8100 **Fax:** 928-368-8108 965krfm.com krfmradio@gmail.com

Lakeside KSNX-FM (o) 1838 Commerce Dr Ste A, Lakeside AZ 85929 **Phn:** 928-368-8100 **Fax:** 928-368-8108

Lakeside KVSL-AM (jb) 1838 Commerce Dr Ste A, Lakeside AZ 85929 **Phn:** 928-368-8100 **Fax:** 928-368-8108 www.whitemountainradio.com production@whitemountainradio.com

Lakeside KVWM-AM (nt) 1838 Commerce Dr Ste A, Lakeside AZ 85929 **Phn:** 928-368-8100 **Fax:** 928-368-8108 www.970kvwm.com production@whitemountainradio.com

Lakeside KZUA-FM (c) 1838 Commerce Dr Ste A, Lakeside AZ 85929 **Phn:** 928-368-8100 **Fax:** 928-368-8108 www.whitemountainradio.com production@whitemountainradio.com

Mesa KDKB-FM (r) 1167 W Javelina Ave, Mesa AZ 85210 **Phn:** 480-897-9300 **Fax:** 480-897-1964 www.kdkb.com koz@kdkb.com

Miami KIKO-FM (a) 4501 Broadway, Miami AZ 85539 **Phn:** 928-425-4471 **Fax:** 928-425-9393 radiokiko@cableone.net

Miami KIKO-AM (az) 4501 Broadway, Miami AZ 85539 **Phn:** 928-425-4471 **Fax:** 928-425-9393 radiokiko@cableone.net

ARIZONA RADIO STATIONS

Miami KQSS-FM (c) PO Box 292, Miami AZ 85539 **Phn:** 928-425-7186 **Fax:** 928-425-7982 gila1019.com bill@gila1019.com

Nogales KNOG-FM (yqv) PO Box 1614, Nogales AZ 85628 **Phn:** 520-287-5206 **Fax:** 520-287-3606 www.knog.org knog@lwrn.org

Nogales KOFH-FM (y) 934 N Bejarano St Ste 2, Nogales AZ 85621 **Phn:** 520-287-3163 **Fax:** 520-287-8290

Page KPGE-AM (c) PO Box 1030, Page AZ 86040 **Phn:** 928-645-8181 **Fax:** 928-645-3347 www.lakepowelllife.com news@kxaz.com

Page KXAZ-FM (a) PO Box 1030, Page AZ 86040 **Phn:** 928-645-8181 **Fax:** 928-645-3347 www.kxaz.com news@kxaz.com

Parker KLPZ-AM (cns) 816 W 6th St, Parker AZ 85344 **Phn:** 928-669-9274 **Fax:** 928-669-9300 www.klpz1380.com

Parker KPKR-FM (r) 1713 S Kofa Ave Ste E, Parker AZ 85344 **Phn:** 928-669-9274 **Fax:** 928-669-9300 www.riverratradio.com ken@kppv.com

Payson KMOG-AM (c) 500 E Tyler Pkwy, Payson AZ 85541 **Phn:** 928-474-5214 **Fax:** 928-474-0236 www.rimcountryradio.comKMOGHome.html blaine@1420kmog.com

Phoenix KASA-AM (qy) 1445 W Baseline Rd, Phoenix AZ 85041 **Phn:** 602-276-4241 **Fax:** 602-276-8119

Phoenix KAZG-AM (o) 4343 E Camelback Rd Ste 200, Phoenix AZ 85018 **Phn:** 480-941-1007 **Fax:** 480-808-2288

Phoenix KBMB-AM (ys) 501 N 44th St Ste 425, Phoenix AZ 85008 **Phn:** 602-776-1400 **Fax:** 602-279-2921 www.espnradio710am.com nrocha@entravision.com

Phoenix KBMB-FM (ys) 501 N 44th St Ste 425, Phoenix AZ 85008 **Phn:** 602-776-1400 **Fax:** 602-279-2921 www.espnradio710am.com nrocha@entravision.com

Phoenix KDVA-FM (y) 501 N 44th St Ste 425, Phoenix AZ 85008 **Phn:** 602-776-1400 **Fax:** 602-279-2921 www.josephoenix.com dapostalides@entravision.com

Phoenix KESZ-FM (a) 4686 E Van Buren St Ste 300, Phoenix AZ 85008 **Phn:** 602-374-6000 **Fax:** 602-374-6284 www.kez999.com joepuglise@clearchannel.com

Phoenix KEXX-FM (r) 4745 N 7th St Ste 410, Phoenix AZ 85014 **Phn:** 602-648-9800 **Fax:** 602-283-0923 my1039phoenix.com

Phoenix KFLR-FM (q) 428 E Thunderbird Rd, Phoenix AZ 85022 **Phn:** 800-776-1070 www.myflr.org

Phoenix KFNX-AM (nt) 2001 N 3rd St Ste 102, Phoenix AZ 85004 **Phn:** 602-277-1100 **Fax:** 602-248-1478 www.1100kfnx.com traffic@1100kfnx.com

Phoenix KFYI-AM (nt) 4686 E Van Buren St Ste 300, Phoenix AZ 85008 **Phn:** 602-374-6120 **Fax:** 602-374-6284 www.kfyi.com kfyinews@clearchannel.com

Phoenix KGME-AM (s) 4686 E Van Buren St Ste 300, Phoenix AZ 85008 **Phn:** 602-374-6000 **Fax:** 602-374-6284 www.foxsports910.com carinaiannuzzi@clearchannel.com

Phoenix KHOT-FM (y) 4745 N 7th St Ste 140, Phoenix AZ 85014 **Phn:** 602-308-7900 **Fax:** 602-308-7979 lanueva1059.univision.com

Phoenix KHOV-FM (y) 4745 N 7th St Ste 140, Phoenix AZ 85014 **Phn:** 602-308-7900 **Fax:** 602-308-7979 lakalle1003.univision.com

Phoenix KKFR-FM (u) 4745 N 7th St Ste 410, Phoenix AZ 85014 **Phn:** 602-648-9800 **Fax:** 602-248-4402 www.power983fm.com mikey@rbgphx.com

Phoenix KKMR-FM (y) 4745 N 7th St Ste 140, Phoenix AZ 85014 **Phn:** 602-308-7900 recuerdophoenix.univision.com

Phoenix KKNT-AM (nt) 2425 E Camelback Rd Ste 570, Phoenix AZ 85016 **Phn:** 602-955-9600 **Fax:** 602-955-7860 www.960thepatriot.com jryan@salemphx.com

Phoenix KLNZ-FM (y) 501 N 44th St Ste 425, Phoenix AZ 85008 **Phn:** 602-776-1400 **Fax:** 602-279-2921 www.tricolor1035.com nrocha@entravision.com

Phoenix KMIA-AM (ys) 501 N 44th St Ste 425, Phoenix AZ 85008 **Phn:** 602-266-2005 **Fax:** 602-279-2921 www.espnradio710am.com cstrait@entravision.com

Phoenix KMIK-AM (m) 4602 E University Dr Ste 150, Phoenix AZ 85034 **Phn:** 602-381-1580 **Fax:** 602-967-0895 music.disney.com

Phoenix KMLE-FM (c) 840 N Central Ave, Phoenix AZ 85004 **Phn:** 602-452-1000 **Fax:** 602-440-6530 kmle1079.cbslocal.com andrea.burtscher@cbsradio.com

Phoenix KMXP-FM (h) 4686 E Van Buren St Ste 300, Phoenix AZ 85008 **Phn:** 602-374-6000 **Fax:** 602-374-6284 www.mix969.com ronprice@clearchannel.com

Phoenix KNIX-FM (c) 4686 E Van Buren St Ste 300, Phoenix AZ 85008 **Phn:** 602-374-6000 **Fax:** 602-374-6284 www.knixcountry.com carinaiannuzzi@clearchannel.com

Phoenix KOMR-FM (y) 4745 N 7th St Ste 140, Phoenix AZ 85014 **Phn:** 602-308-7900 **Fax:** 602-308-7979

Phoenix KOOL-FM (o) 840 N Central Ave, Phoenix AZ 85004 **Phn:** 602-452-1000 **Fax:** 602-440-6530 kool.cbslocal.com dave.shakes@cbsradio.com

Phoenix KOY-AM (ob) 4686 E Van Buren St Ste 300, Phoenix AZ 85008 **Phn:** 602-374-6000 **Fax:** 602-374-6284 www.kfyi.biz koywebmaster@clearchannel.com

Phoenix KPHX-AM (m) 824 E Washington St, Phoenix AZ 85034 **Phn:** 602-257-1351 **Fax:** 602-386-4873 www.1480kphx.com

Phoenix KPKX-FM (a) 7740 N 16th St Ste 200, Phoenix AZ 85020 **Phn:** 602-274-6200 **Fax:** 602-266-3858 987thepeak.com jriley@987thepeak.com

Phoenix KPXQ-AM (qt) 2425 E Camelback Rd Ste 570, Phoenix AZ 85016 **Phn:** 602-955-9600 www.faithtalk1360.com dzapponi@salemphx.com

Phoenix KQMR-FM (y) 4745 N 7th St Ste 140, Phoenix AZ 85014 **Phn:** 602-308-7900 **Fax:** 602-308-7979 www.univision.com

Phoenix KSLX-FM (r) 4343 E Camelback Rd Ste 200, Phoenix AZ 85018 **Phn:** 480-941-1007 **Fax:** 480-808-2288 www.kslx.com info@kslx.com

Phoenix KSUN-AM (ya) 714 N 3rd St, Phoenix AZ 85004 **Phn:** 602-252-0030 **Fax:** 602-252-4211 radiofiesta1400.wix.comradiofiesta ksun@radiofiesta.net

Phoenix KTAR-AM (snt) 5300 N Central Ave, Phoenix AZ 85012 **Phn:** 602-274-6200 **Fax:** 602-266-3858 www.620ktar.com newsradio620@ktar.com

Phoenix KVVA-FM (y) 501 N 44th St Ste 425, Phoenix AZ 85008 **Phn:** 602-776-1400 **Fax:** 602-279-2921 www.josephoenix.com cstrait@entravision.com

Phoenix KXEG-AM (q) 2800 N 44th St Ste 100, Phoenix AZ 85008 **Phn:** 602-254-5001 **Fax:** 623-245-1010 www.azchristiantalk.com info@azchristiantalk.com

Phoenix KXXT-AM (nt) 2800 N 44th St Ste 100, Phoenix AZ 85008 **Phn:** 602-254-5001 **Fax:** 623-245-1010 www.1280kxeg.com info@azchristiantalk.com

Phoenix KYOT-FM (ah) 4686 E Van Buren St Ste 300, Phoenix AZ 85008 **Phn:** 602-374-6000 **Fax:** 602-374-6263 www.eva955.com smokeyrivers@clearchannel.com

Phoenix KZON-FM (r) 840 N Central Ave, Phoenix AZ 85004 **Phn:** 602-452-1000 **Fax:** 602-440-6530 live1015phoenix.cbslocal.com dave.shakes@cbsradio.com

Phoenix KZZP-FM (h) 4686 E Van Buren St Ste 300, Phoenix AZ 85008 **Phn:** 602-374-6000 **Fax:** 602-374-6263 www.1047kissfm.com specialk@clearchannel.com

Prescott KAHM-FM (zob) PO Box 2529, Prescott AZ 86302 **Phn:** 928-445-7800 **Fax:** 928-445-5365 www.kahm.info prescott@kahm.info

Prescott KDDL-FM (c) 3755 Karicio Ln # 2C, Prescott AZ 86303 **Phn:** 928-445-8289 **Fax:** 928-442-0448 www.cattlecountryradio.com

Prescott KGCB-FM (a) 3741 Karicio Ln, Prescott AZ 86303 **Phn:** 928-776-0909 **Fax:** 928-776-1736 radioshine.org info@radioshine.org

Prescott KNOT-AM (c) 116 S Alto, Prescott AZ 86301 **Phn:** 928-445-6880 **Fax:** 928-445-6852 magic991.gcmaz.com

Prescott KYCA-AM (nt) PO Box 1631, Prescott AZ 86302 **Phn:** 928-445-1700 **Fax:** 928-445-5365 www.kyca.info prescott@kyca.info

Prescott Valley KPPV-FM (a) PO Box 26523, Prescott Valley AZ 86312 **Phn:** 928-445-8289 **Fax:** 928-442-0448 www.kppv.com ken@kppv.com

Prescott Valley KQNA-AM (snt) PO Box 26523, Prescott Valley AZ 86312 **Phn:** 928-445-8289 **Fax:** 928-442-0448 www.kqna.com promotions@kppv.com

Quartzsite KBUX-FM (z) 16031 Camel Dr, Quartzsite AZ 85346 **Phn:** 928-927-5111 kbuxradio.tripod.com kbuxradio@hotmail.com

Safford KATO-AM (snt) PO Box L, Safford AZ 85548 **Phn:** 928-428-1230 **Fax:** 928-428-1311 www.mysouthernaz.com davis@mcmurrayradio.com

Safford KWRQ-FM (a) PO Box L, Safford AZ 85548 **Phn:** 928-428-1230 **Fax:** 928-428-1311 mysouthernaz.com davis@mcmurrayradio.com

Safford KXKQ-FM (c) PO Box L, Safford AZ 85548 **Phn:** 928-428-1230 **Fax:** 928-428-1311 www.mysouthernaz.com davis@mcmurrayradio.com

Scottsdale KAJM-FM (x) 7434 E Stetson Dr Ste 255, Scottsdale AZ 85251 **Phn:** 480-994-9100 **Fax:** 480-423-8770 www.mega1043.com beau.duran@sierrah.com

Scottsdale KFNN-AM (ntk) 8145 E Evans Rd # 8, Scottsdale AZ 85260 **Phn:** 602-241-1510 **Fax:** 602-241-1540 www.moneyradio1510.com

Scottsdale KNRJ-FM (h) 7434 E Stetson Dr Ste 255, Scottsdale AZ 85251 **Phn:** 480-994-9100 **Fax:** 480-423-8770 www.azthebeat.com beauduran@gmail.com

Sedona KAZM-AM (ant) PO Box 1525, Sedona AZ 86339 **Phn:** 928-282-4154 **Fax:** 928-282-2230 www.kazmradio.com info@kazmradio.com

Sells KOHN-FM (ve) PO Box 837, Sells AZ 85634 **Phn:** 520-361-5011 **Fax:** 520-361-3931

Show Low KQAZ-FM (a) PO Box 2020, Show Low AZ 85902 **Phn:** 928-532-1010 **Fax:** 928-532-0101 www.majik101.com camden@majik101.com

Show Low KTHQ-FM (c) 391 W Deuce Of Clubs Ste C, Show Low AZ 85901 **Phn:** 928-532-1010 **Fax:** 928-532-0101 www.qcountry92.com camden@majik101.com

Show Low KWKM-FM (a) 1520 E Commerce Ste B, Show Low AZ 85901 **Phn:** 928-532-2949 **Fax:** 928-532-3176 www.kwkm.com program@kwkm.com

ARIZONA RADIO STATIONS

Sierra Vista KKYZ-FM (o) 500 E Fry Blvd Ste L10, Sierra Vista AZ 85635 **Phn:** 520-459-8201 **Fax:** 520-458-7104 www.kkyz.com jeanbarton@kwkm.com

Sierra Vista KTAN-AM (snt) PO Box 2770, Sierra Vista AZ 85636 **Phn:** 520-458-4313 **Fax:** 520-458-4317 www.cherrycreekradio.com

Sierra Vista KWCD-FM (c) PO Box 2770, Sierra Vista AZ 85636 **Phn:** 520-458-4313 **Fax:** 520-458-4317 www.cherrycreekradio.com

Sierra Vista KWRB-FM (q) 3320 E Fry Blvd, Sierra Vista AZ 85635 **Phn:** 520-452-8022 **Fax:** 520-452-0927 www.kwrb.org

Sierra Vista KZMK-FM (a) PO Box 2770, Sierra Vista AZ 85636 **Phn:** 520-458-4313 **Fax:** 520-458-4317 www.cherrycreekradio.com

Springerville KRVZ-AM (o) 1367 E Main St, Springerville AZ 85938 **Phn:** 928-333-2080 **Fax:** 928-333-2081

Tempe KBAQ-FM (pln) 2323 W 14th St, Tempe AZ 85281 **Phn:** 480-833-1122 **Fax:** 480-774-8475 kbaq.org mail@kbaq.org

Tempe KDUS-AM (s) 1900 W Carmen St, Tempe AZ 85283 **Phn:** 480-838-0400 **Fax:** 480-820-8469 nbcsportsradioam1060.com angel@nbcsportsradioam1060.com

Tempe KJZZ-FM (pnj) 2323 W 14th St, Tempe AZ 85281 **Phn:** 480-834-5627 **Fax:** 480-774-8475 www.kjzz.org news@kjzz.org

Tempe KUPD-FM (r) 1900 W Carmen St, Tempe AZ 85283 **Phn:** 480-838-0400 **Fax:** 480-820-8469 www.98kupd.com info@98kupd.com

Tuba City KGHR-FM (pe) PO Box 160, Tuba City AZ 86045 **Phn:** 928-283-5555 **Fax:** 928-283-5557

Tucson KAPR-AM (q) 3222 S Richey Ave, Tucson AZ 85713 **Phn:** 520-790-2440 **Fax:** 520-790-2937 www.kgms.com chrissy@kvoi.com

Tucson KAVV-FM (c) PO Box 18899, Tucson AZ 85731 **Phn:** 520-586-9797 www.cavefm.com you@cavefm.com

Tucson KCMT-FM (y) 3871 N Commerce Dr, Tucson AZ 85705 **Phn:** 520-407-4500 **Fax:** 520-407-4600 www.kcmt.com steve@kcmt.com

Tucson KCUB-AM (s) 575 W Roger Rd, Tucson AZ 85705 **Phn:** 520-887-1000 **Fax:** 520-887-6397 www.1290amthesource.com robert.lantz@cumulus.com

Tucson KCUZ-AM (c) PO Box 35997, Tucson AZ 85740 **Phn:** 928-428-0916 **Fax:** 928-428-7797 www.saffordradio.com

Tucson KEVT-AM (yq) 2955 E Broadway Blvd, Tucson AZ 85716 **Phn:** 520-889-8904 **Fax:** 520-889-8573

Tucson KFFN-AM (st) 7280 E Rosewood St, Tucson AZ 85710 **Phn:** 520-722-5486 **Fax:** 520-327-2260 www.espntucson.com sholly@jrn.com

Tucson KFLT-AM (q) PO Box 35300, Tucson AZ 85740 **Phn:** 520-797-3700 **Fax:** 520-742-6979

Tucson KFMA-FM (r) 3871 N Commerce Dr, Tucson AZ 85705 **Phn:** 520-407-4500 **Fax:** 520-407-4600 www.kfma.com ego@kfma.com

Tucson KFMM-FM (r) PO Box 35997, Tucson AZ 85740 **Phn:** 928-428-0916 **Fax:** 928-428-7797 saffordradio.com

Tucson KGMG-FM (o) 7280 E Rosewood St, Tucson AZ 85710 **Phn:** 520-722-5486 **Fax:** 520-327-2260 www.1063thegroove.com feedback@1063thegroove.com

Tucson KGMS-AM (q) 3222 S Richey Ave, Tucson AZ 85713 **Phn:** 520-790-2440 **Fax:** 520-790-2937 www.kgms.com chrissy@kvoi.com

Tucson KHYT-FM (r) 575 W Roger Rd, Tucson AZ 85705 **Phn:** 520-887-1000 **Fax:** 520-887-6397 www.khit1075.com herb.crowe@cumulus.com

Tucson KIIM-FM (c) 575 W Roger Rd, Tucson AZ 85705 **Phn:** 520-696-2710 **Fax:** 520-887-6397 www.kiimfm.com

Tucson KJAA-AM (tq) 3222 S Richey Ave, Tucson AZ 85713 **Phn:** 520-790-2440 **Fax:** 520-790-2937 www.kgms.com chrissy@kvoi.com

Tucson KJLL-AM (nt) 4433 E Broadway Blvd Ste 210, Tucson AZ 85711 **Phn:** 520-529-5865 **Fax:** 520-529-9324 www.tucsonsjolt.com johncscott@tucsonsjolt.com

Tucson KLPX-FM (r) 3871 N Commerce Dr, Tucson AZ 85705 **Phn:** 520-407-4500 **Fax:** 520-407-4600 www.klpx.com lmac@klpx.com

Tucson KMXZ-FM (a) 7280 E Rosewood St, Tucson AZ 85710 **Phn:** 520-722-5486 **Fax:** 520-327-2260 www.mixfm.com sholly@jrn.com

Tucson KNST-AM (snt) 3202 N Oracle Rd, Tucson AZ 85705 **Phn:** 520-618-2100 **Fax:** 520-618-2135 www.knst.com paul@knst.com

Tucson KNXN-AM (q) 3222 S Richey Ave, Tucson AZ 85713 **Phn:** 520-790-2440 **Fax:** 520-790-2937 www.kgms.com chrissy@kvoi.com

Tucson KOHT-FM (h) 3202 N Oracle Rd, Tucson AZ 85705 **Phn:** 520-618-2100 **Fax:** 520-618-2135 www.hot983.com

Tucson KQTH-FM (t) 7280 E Rosewood St, Tucson AZ 85710 **Phn:** 520-722-5486 www.1041thetruth.com bwhite@jrn.com

Tucson KRDX-FM (o) 2959 E Grant Rd, Tucson AZ 85716 **Phn:** 520-325-3054 **Fax:** 520-325-3495

Tucson KRQQ-FM (h) 3202 N Oracle Rd, Tucson AZ 85705 **Phn:** 520-618-2100 **Fax:** 520-618-2135 www.krq.com chrispickett@clearchannel.com

Tucson KSAZ-AM (am) 1011 N Craycroft Rd Ste 302, Tucson AZ 85711 **Phn:** 520-298-6880 **Fax:** 520-298-6077 amradio1@cox.net

Tucson KSZR-FM (a) 575 W Roger Rd, Tucson AZ 85705 **Phn:** 520-887-1000 **Fax:** 520-887-6397

Tucson KTKT-AM (sy) 3871 N Commerce Dr, Tucson AZ 85705 **Phn:** 520-622-6711 **Fax:** 520-624-3226

Tucson KTUC-AM (ob) 575 W Roger Rd, Tucson AZ 85705 **Phn:** 520-887-1000 **Fax:** 520-887-6397 www.ktucam.com herb.crowe@cumulus.com

Tucson KTZR-FM (y) 3202 N Oracle Rd, Tucson AZ 85705 **Phn:** 520-618-2100 **Fax:** 520-618-2165 www.lapreciosa1450.com alymasterson@clearchannel.com

Tucson KUAT-FM (pl) PO Box 210067, Tucson AZ 85721 **Phn:** 520-621-5828 **Fax:** 520-621-9105 radio.azpm.orgclassical

Tucson KUAZ-FM (pj) PO Box 210067, Tucson AZ 85721 **Phn:** 520-621-7548 **Fax:** 520-621-9105 radio.azpm.orgkuaz

Tucson KUAZ-AM (pnj) PO Box 210067, Tucson AZ 85721 **Phn:** 520-621-5828 **Fax:** 520-621-9105 radio.azpm.orgkuaz

Tucson KVOI-AM (t) 3222 S Richey Ave Ste 100, Tucson AZ 85713 **Phn:** 520-790-2440 **Fax:** 520-790-2937 www.kvoi.com chrissy@kvoi.com

Tucson KWFM-AM (o) 3202 N Oracle Rd, Tucson AZ 85705 **Phn:** 520-618-2100 **Fax:** 520-618-2135 www.iheart.com

Tucson KWMT-FM (a) 3202 N Oracle Rd, Tucson AZ 85705 **Phn:** 520-618-2100 **Fax:** 520-618-2122 www.my929.com chrispickett@clearchannel.com

Tucson KXCI-FM (vr) 220 S 4th Ave, Tucson AZ 85701 **Phn:** 520-623-1000 **Fax:** 520-623-0758 www.kxci.org amanda@kxci.org

Tucson KXEW-AM (y) 3202 N Oracle Rd, Tucson AZ 85705 **Phn:** 520-618-2100 **Fax:** 520-618-2122 www.tejano1600.com

Tucson KZLZ-FM (y) 2959 E Grant Rd, Tucson AZ 85716 **Phn:** 520-325-3054 **Fax:** 520-325-3495 www.lapoderosakzlz.com sonia@kzlzradio.com

Whiteriver KNNB-FM (v) PO Box 310, Whiteriver AZ 85941 **Phn:** 928-338-5229 **Fax:** 928-338-1744

Wickenburg KSWG-FM (c) 801 W Wickenburg Way, Wickenburg AZ 85390 **Phn:** 602-254-6644 **Fax:** 623-321-1862 kswgradio.com

Willcox KHIL-AM (c) PO Box 1250, Willcox AZ 85644 **Phn:** 520-384-4626 www.xwave1049.com marklucke@qwestoffice.net

Willcox KWCX-FM (a) PO Box 1250, Willcox AZ 85644 **Phn:** 520-384-4626 www.xwave1049.com marklucke@qwestoffice.net

Window Rock KHAC-AM (qe) PO Box 9090, Window Rock AZ 86515 **Phn:** 505-371-5587 **Fax:** 505-371-5588

Window Rock KTNN-AM (c) PO Box 2569, Window Rock AZ 86515 **Phn:** 928-871-3553 **Fax:** 928-871-3479 www.ktnnonline.com

Window Rock KWIM-FM (q) PO Box 9090, Window Rock AZ 86515 **Phn:** 505-371-5749 **Fax:** 505-371-5588 www.westernindian.org wim@westernindian.org

Window Rock KWRK-FM (c) PO Box 2569, Window Rock AZ 86515 **Phn:** 928-871-3553 **Fax:** 928-871-3479 www.ktnnonline.com troylittle@ktnnonline.com

Winslow KINO-AM (cn) PO Box K, Winslow AZ 86047 **Phn:** 928-289-3364 **Fax:** 928-289-3366 kinoradio@cableone.net

Yuma KAWC-FM (vlj) PO Box 929, Yuma AZ 85366 **Phn:** 928-317-7690 **Fax:** 928-317-7740 www.kawc.org brenda.badilla@kawc.org

Yuma KAWC-AM (p) PO Box 929, Yuma AZ 85366 **Phn:** 928-317-7690 **Fax:** 928-317-7040 www.kawc.org kim.johnson@kawc.org

Yuma KBLU-AM (snt) 755 W 28th St, Yuma AZ 85364 **Phn:** 928-344-4980 **Fax:** 928-344-4983 www.kbluam.com programming@560kblu.com

Yuma KCEC-FM (y) 670 E 32nd St Ste 12A, Yuma AZ 85365 **Phn:** 928-782-5995 **Fax:** 928-782-3874 www.campesina.net rosella.lopez@campesina.net

Yuma KCFY-FM (q) 1921 S Rail Ave Ste A, Yuma AZ 85365 **Phn:** 928-341-9730 **Fax:** 928-341-9099 www.kcfyfm.com mike@kcfyfm.com

Yuma KCYK-AM (c) 949 S Avenue B, Yuma AZ 85364 **Phn:** 928-782-4321 **Fax:** 928-343-1710 www.outlawcountry1400.com klewis@z93yuma.com

Yuma KLJZ-FM (a) 949 S Avenue B, Yuma AZ 85364 **Phn:** 928-782-4321 **Fax:** 928-343-1710 www.z93yuma.com todaysbestmusic@z93yuma.com

Yuma KQSR-FM (a) 755 W 28th St, Yuma AZ 85364 **Phn:** 928-344-4980 **Fax:** 928-344-4983 www.kqsrfm.com jeffedwards@edbroadcasters.com

Yuma KTTI-FM (c) 755 W 28th St, Yuma AZ 85364 **Phn:** 928-344-4980 **Fax:** 928-344-4983 www.kttifm.com programming@951ktti.com

Yuma KYRM-FM (vy) PO Box 5965, Yuma AZ 85366 **Phn:** 928-341-0919 **Fax:** 928-314-4141 www.kyrmradio.org kyrm@lwrn.org

ARKANSAS

Arkadelphia KDEL-FM (a) 601 S 7th St, Arkadelphia AR 71923 **Phn:** 870-246-9272 **Fax:** 870-246-5878 stephanielcollie@yahoo.com

Arkadelphia KSWH-FM (vr) HSU Box 7872, Arkadelphia AR 71999 **Phn:** 870-230-5185 **Fax:** 870-230-5046 mypulse999online.com kswh@hsu.edu

Arkadelphia KVRC-AM (b) 601 S 7th St, Arkadelphia AR 71923 **Phn:** 870-246-9272 **Fax:** 870-246-5878

Arkadelphia KYXK-FM (c) 601 S 7th St, Arkadelphia AR 71923 **Phn:** 870-246-9272 **Fax:** 870-246-5878

Barling KERX-FM (ah) 1912 Church St, Barling AR 72923 **Phn:** 479-484-7285 **Fax:** 479-484-7290 www.953therebel.com jay.james@pearsonbroadcasting.com

Barling KTTG-FM (s) 1912 Church St, Barling AR 72923 **Phn:** 479-484-7285 **Fax:** 479-484-7290 www.espnarkansas.net derek.ruscin@pearsonbroadcasting.com

Batesville KAAB-AM (h) 920 Harrison St # C, Batesville AR 72501 **Phn:** 870-793-4196 **Fax:** 870-793-5222

Batesville KBTA-AM (s) 920 Harrison St # C, Batesville AR 72501 **Phn:** 870-793-4196 **Fax:** 870-793-5222 garyb15@swbell.net

Batesville KKIK-FM (o) PO Box 2077, Batesville AR 72503 **Phn:** 870-793-4196 **Fax:** 870-793-4437 ginger@maxfm.com

Batesville KWOZ-FM (c) 920 Harrison St # C, Batesville AR 72501 **Phn:** 870-793-4196 **Fax:** 870-793-5222 www.ar1033.com

Batesville KZLE-FM (r) 920 Harrison St # C, Batesville AR 72501 **Phn:** 870-793-4196 **Fax:** 870-793-5222 www.cr93.com

Benton KEWI-AM (sno) 115 S Main St, Benton AR 72015 **Phn:** 501-778-6677 **Fax:** 501-778-7717 www.kewi690.com kewi690@yahoo.com

Berryville KTHS-FM (c) PO Box 191, Berryville AR 72616 **Phn:** 870-423-2147 **Fax:** 870-423-2146 kthsradio.com studio@kthsradio.com

Blytheville KAMJ-FM (ur) PO Box 989, Blytheville AR 72316 **Phn:** 870-762-2093 **Fax:** 870-763-8459

Blytheville KHLS-FM (c) PO Box 989, Blytheville AR 72316 **Phn:** 870-762-2093 **Fax:** 870-763-8459 www.thundercountry963.com keith@thundercountry963.com

Blytheville KLCN-AM (n) PO Box 989, Blytheville AR 72316 **Phn:** 870-762-2093 **Fax:** 870-763-8459

Blytheville KOSE-AM (r) PO Box 989, Blytheville AR 72316 **Phn:** 870-762-2093 **Fax:** 870-763-8459

Blytheville KQDD-FM (r) PO Box 989, Blytheville AR 72316 **Phn:** 870-762-2093 **Fax:** 870-763-8459

Brinkley KBRI-AM (c) Highway 70 W, Brinkley AR 72021 **Phn:** 870-734-1570 **Fax:** 870-734-1571

Camden KAMD-FM (a) 612 Fairview Rd SW, Camden AR 71701 **Phn:** 870-836-9567 **Fax:** 870-836-9500 www.yesradioworks.com helenaregood@yesradioworks.com

Camden KCAC-FM (vr) PO Box 3499, Camden AR 71711 **Phn:** 870-836-5289

Camden KCXY-FM (c) 612 Fairview Rd SW, Camden AR 71701 **Phn:** 870-836-9567 **Fax:** 870-836-9500 www.yesradioworks.com celiaschinz@yesradioworks.com

ARIZONA RADIO STATIONS

Camden KMGC-FM (gxu) 612 Fairview Rd SW, Camden AR 71701 **Phn:** 870-836-9567 **Fax:** 870-836-9500 www.yesradioworks.com danmurphy@yesradioworks.com

Cave City KVMN-FM (qv) PO Box 190, Cave City AR 72521 **Phn:** 870-283-5331 **Fax:** 870-283-3255

Cherokee Village KFCM-FM (o) PO Box 909, Cherokee Village AR 72525 **Phn:** 870-856-3249 **Fax:** 870-856-4088

Cherokee Village KOOU-FM (bo) PO Box 909, Cherokee Village AR 72525 **Phn:** 870-856-3240 **Fax:** 870-856-4088 hometownradio@centurytel.net

Clarksville KWXT-AM (cg) PO Box 215, Clarksville AR 72830 **Phn:** 479-754-3399 www.kwxt1490am.com kwxt1490am@yahoo.com

Clarksville KXIO-FM (c) 901 S Rogers St, Clarksville AR 72830 **Phn:** 479-705-1069 **Fax:** 479-754-5518 office@kxio-fmradio.com

Clinton KGFL-AM (o) PO Box 1349, Clinton AR 72031 **Phn:** 501-745-4474 **Fax:** 501-745-4084 www.infozark.netkgfl kgflkhpq@artelco.com

Clinton KHPQ-FM (c) PO Box 33, Clinton AR 72031 **Phn:** 501-745-4474 **Fax:** 501-745-4084 www.infozark.netkhpq kgflkhpq@artelco.com

Conway KASR-FM (s) 1072 Markham St, Conway AR 72032 **Phn:** 501-327-6611 **Fax:** 501-327-7920 www.kasr.com kasr@sbcglobal.net

Conway KHDX-FM (vj) 1600 Washington Ave, Conway AR 72032 **Phn:** 501-450-1339 khdx.fm khdx@hendrix.edu

Corning KBKG-FM (ah) PO Box 398, Corning AR 72422 **Phn:** 870-857-6646 **Fax:** 870-857-6795

Corning KCCB-AM (ah) PO Box 398, Corning AR 72422 **Phn:** 870-857-6646 **Fax:** 870-857-6795

Crossett KAGH-FM (c) PO Box 697, Crossett AR 71635 **Phn:** 870-364-2181 **Fax:** 870-364-2183 www.crossettradio.com kagh@windstream.net

Crossett KAGH-AM (g) PO Box 697, Crossett AR 71635 **Phn:** 870-364-2183 **Fax:** 870-364-2183 www.crossettradio.com kagh@windstream.net

Crossett KWLT-FM (r) PO Box 697, Crossett AR 71635 **Phn:** 870-364-2182 **Fax:** 870-364-2183 www.crossettradio.com kagh@windstream.net

De Queen KDQN-AM (y) PO Box 311, De Queen AR 71832 **Phn:** 870-642-2446 **Fax:** 870-642-2442 kdqn.netdefault.htm numberonecountry@yahoo.com

De Queen KDQN-FM (c) PO Box 311, De Queen AR 71832 **Phn:** 870-642-2446 **Fax:** 870-642-2442 www.kdqn.net numberonecountry@yahoo.com

El Dorado KAGL-FM (ar) 2525 N West Ave, El Dorado AR 71730 **Phn:** 870-863-6126 **Fax:** 870-863-4555 www.totalradio.com pthomas@totalradio.us

El Dorado KDMS-AM (g) 1904 W Hillsboro St, El Dorado AR 71730 **Phn:** 870-863-5121 **Fax:** 870-863-6221

El Dorado KELD-FM (o) 2525 N West Ave, El Dorado AR 71730 **Phn:** 870-863-6126 **Fax:** 870-863-4555 www.totalradio.com

El Dorado KELD-AM (nt) 2525 N West Ave, El Dorado AR 71730 **Phn:** 870-863-6126 **Fax:** 870-863-4555 www.totalradio.com

El Dorado KIXB-FM (c) 2525 N West Ave, El Dorado AR 71730 **Phn:** 870-863-6126 **Fax:** 870-863-4555 www.totalradio.com newsroom@totalradio.us

El Dorado KLBQ-FM (a) 1904 W Hillsboro St, El Dorado AR 71730 **Phn:** 870-863-5121 **Fax:** 870-863-6221

El Dorado KMLK-FM (w) 2525 N West Ave, El Dorado AR 71730 **Phn:** 870-863-6126 **Fax:** 870-863-4555 www.totalradio.com

El Dorado KMRX-FM (a) 2525 N West Ave, El Dorado AR 71730 **Phn:** 870-863-6126 **Fax:** 870-863-4555 www.totalradio.com

Fairfield Bay KFFB-FM (o) PO Box 1050, Fairfield Bay AR 72088 **Phn:** 501-723-4850 **Fax:** 501-723-4861 www.kffb.com kffb@kffb.com

Fayetteville KAKS-FM (y) 1780 W Holly St, Fayetteville AR 72703 **Phn:** 479-443-9960 **Fax:** 479-444-9670

Fayetteville KAMO-FM (c) 4209 N Frontage Rd, Fayetteville AR 72703 **Phn:** 479-521-5566 **Fax:** 479-521-0751 www.us94.com dan.hentschel@cumulus.com

Fayetteville KAYH-FM (qg) PO Box 1288, Fayetteville AR 72702 **Phn:** 479-750-7707 **Fax:** 479-927-1250 www.bottradionetwork.com sgossett@bottradionetwork.com

Fayetteville KEZA-FM (a) 2049 E Joyce Blvd Ste 101, Fayetteville AR 72703 **Phn:** 479-521-0104 **Fax:** 479-587-8255 www.magic1079.com jaysteele@clearchannel.com

Fayetteville KFAY-AM (nt) 4209 N Frontage Rd, Fayetteville AR 72703 **Phn:** 479-521-5566 **Fax:** 479-521-0751 www.newstalk1030.com anita.cowan@cumulus.com

Fayetteville KIGL-FM (r) 2049 E Joyce Blvd Ste 101, Fayetteville AR 72703 **Phn:** 479-973-9339 **Fax:** 479-587-8255 www.933theeagle.com

Fayetteville KKEG-FM (r) 4209 N Frontage Rd, Fayetteville AR 72703 **Phn:** 479-521-5566 **Fax:** 479-521-4968 www.983thekeg.com matt_miller@cumulus.com

Fayetteville KKIX-FM (c) PO Box 8190, Fayetteville AR 72703 **Phn:** 479-521-0104 **Fax:** 479-587-8255 www.kix104.com daveashcraft@clearchannel.com

Fayetteville KMCK-FM (a) 4209 N Frontage Rd, Fayetteville AR 72703 **Phn:** 479-521-5566 **Fax:** 479-521-6493 www.power1057.com anita.cowan@cumulus.com

Fayetteville KMXF-FM (a) PO Box 8190, Fayetteville AR 72703 **Phn:** 479-442-0102 **Fax:** 479-587-8255 www.hotmix1019.com daveashcraft@clearchannel.com

Fayetteville KOFC-AM (qg) PO Box 1288, Fayetteville AR 72702 **Phn:** 479-750-7707 **Fax:** 479-927-1250 www.bottradionetwork.com sgossett@bottradionetwork.com

Fayetteville KQSM-FM (c) 4209 N Frontage Rd, Fayetteville AR 72703 **Phn:** 479-521-5566 **Fax:** 479-521-0751

Fayetteville KREB-AM (s) 1780 W Holly St, Fayetteville AR 72703 **Phn:** 479-582-3776 **Fax:** 479-571-0995

Fayetteville KUAF-FM (plnj) 747 W Dickson St Ste 2, Fayetteville AR 72701 **Phn:** 479-575-2556 **Fax:** 479-575-8440 www.kuaf.org kuafinfo@uark.edu

Fayetteville KXNA-FM (r) 1780 W Holly St, Fayetteville AR 72703 **Phn:** 479-582-3776 **Fax:** 479-571-0995 www.newrock1049x.com butlerbroadcast1@aol.com

Fordyce KBJT-AM (nt) 303 N Spring St, Fordyce AR 71742 **Phn:** 870-352-7137 **Fax:** 870-352-7139 www.kbjtkq.com kbjt@windstream.net

Fordyce KQEW-FM (t) 303 N Spring St, Fordyce AR 71742 **Phn:** 870-352-7137 **Fax:** 870-352-7139 coatesmedia.com kbjt@windstream.net

Forrest City KBFC-FM (c) PO Box 707, Forrest City AR 72336 **Phn:** 870-633-1252 **Fax:** 870-633-1259 www.kbfc.com radio@arkansas.net

ARKANSAS RADIO STATIONS

Forrest City KXJK-AM (r) PO Box 707, Forrest City AR 72336 **Phn:** 870-633-1252 **Fax:** 870-633-1259 www.kxjk.com radio@arkansas.net

Fort Smith KBBQ-FM (h) 3104 S 70th St Ste 104, Fort Smith AR 72903 **Phn:** 479-452-0681 **Fax:** 479-452-0873 www.1027thevibe.com anita.cowan@cumulus.com

Fort Smith KFPW-AM (am) PO Box 908, Fort Smith AR 72902 **Phn:** 479-783-5379 **Fax:** 479-785-2638 sportshog1031.com karenpharis40@yahoo.com

Fort Smith KFPW-FM (nt) PO Box 908, Fort Smith AR 72902 **Phn:** 479-783-5379 **Fax:** 479-785-2638 kfpwam.com karen@kfpwam.com

Fort Smith KFSA-AM (g) PO Box 6210, Fort Smith AR 72906 **Phn:** 479-646-6700 **Fax:** 479-646-1373 www.kzkzfm.com kzkzfm@kzkzfm.com

Fort Smith KHGG-AM (st) PO Box 908, Fort Smith AR 72902 **Phn:** 479-288-1047 **Fax:** 479-785-2638 www.sportshog1031.com karenpharis40@yahoo.com

Fort Smith KHGG-FM (s) PO Box 908, Fort Smith AR 72902 **Phn:** 479-288-1047 **Fax:** 479-785-2638 www.sportshog1031.com karenpharis40@yahoo.com

Fort Smith KISR-FM (h) PO Box 3100, Fort Smith AR 72913 **Phn:** 479-785-2526 **Fax:** 479-782-9127 www.kisr.net gary@kisr.net

Fort Smith KKBD-FM (r) 311 Lexington Ave, Fort Smith AR 72901 **Phn:** 479-782-8888 **Fax:** 479-782-0366 www.bigdog959.com coreywinfield@clearchannel.com

Fort Smith KLSZ-FM (r) 3100 Free Ferry Rd # E, Fort Smith AR 72903 **Phn:** 479-452-0681 **Fax:** 479-452-0873 rock1007.com matt.miller2@cumulus.com

Fort Smith KMAG-FM (c) 311 Lexington Ave, Fort Smith AR 72901 **Phn:** 479-782-8888 **Fax:** 479-782-0366 www.kmag991.com robertbaldwin@clearchannel.com

Fort Smith KOMS-FM (c) 3104 S 70th St Ste 104, Fort Smith AR 72903 **Phn:** 479-452-0681 **Fax:** 479-452-0873 bigcountry1073.com productionnwa@cumulus.com

Fort Smith KQBK-FM (o) PO Box 908, Fort Smith AR 72902 **Phn:** 479-288-1047 **Fax:** 479-785-2638 sportshog1031.com karenpharis40@yahoo.com

Fort Smith KTCS-AM (g) PO Box 180188, Fort Smith AR 72918 **Phn:** 479-646-6151 **Fax:** 479-646-3509 www.ktcs.com leeyoung@ktcs.com

Fort Smith KTCS-FM (c) PO Box 180188, Fort Smith AR 72918 **Phn:** 479-646-6151 **Fax:** 479-646-3509 www.ktcs.com leeyoung@ktcs.com

Fort Smith KWHN-AM (nt) 311 Lexington Ave, Fort Smith AR 72901 **Phn:** 479-782-8888 **Fax:** 479-782-5946 www.kwhn.com daveashcraft@clearchannel.com

Fort Smith KZBB-FM (h) 311 Lexington Ave, Fort Smith AR 72901 **Phn:** 479-782-8888 **Fax:** 479-785-5946 www.kzbb.com coreywinfield@clearchannel.com

Fort Smith KZKZ-FM (q) PO Box 6210, Fort Smith AR 72906 **Phn:** 479-646-6700 **Fax:** 479-646-1373 www.kzkzfm.com kzkzfm@kzkzfm.com

Glenwood KWXI-AM (snt) PO Box 740, Glenwood AR 71943 **Phn:** 870-356-2151 **Fax:** 870-356-4684 www.kwxi.net kwxi@windstream.net

Gravette KBVA-FM (m) 1655 W Highway 72, Gravette AR 72736 **Phn:** 800-467-1065 **Fax:** 479-787-6116 www.variety1065.com kbva@variety1065.com

Harrison KCWD-FM (r) PO Box 850, Harrison AR 72602 **Phn:** 870-741-1402 **Fax:** 870-741-9702 www.kcwdradio.com kcwd@windstream.net

Harrison KHOZ-AM (h) 1111 Radio Ave, Harrison AR 72601 **Phn:** 870-741-2301 **Fax:** 870-741-3299 www.1029thez.com khozradio@khoz.com

Harrison KHOZ-FM (c) 1111 Radio Ave, Harrison AR 72601 **Phn:** 870-741-2301 **Fax:** 870-741-3299 www.1029thez.com khozradio@khoz.com

Harrison KNWA-AM (st) PO Box 850, Harrison AR 72602 **Phn:** 870-741-1402 **Fax:** 870-741-9702

Helena KFFA-AM (stc) PO Box 430, Helena AR 72342 **Phn:** 870-338-8361 **Fax:** 870-338-8332 www.kffa.com kffa@arkansas.net

Helena KFFA-FM (as) PO Box 430, Helena AR 72342 **Phn:** 870-338-8361 **Fax:** 870-338-8332 www.kffa.com kffa@arkansas.net

Helena KJIW-FM (g) 204 Moore St, Helena AR 72342 **Phn:** 870-338-2700 **Fax:** 870-338-3166 www.kjiwfm.com news@lordradio.com

Hope KHPA-FM (c) PO Box 424, Hope AR 71802 **Phn:** 870-777-8868 **Fax:** 870-777-8888 www.supercountry105.com khpafm@supercountry105.com

Hope KTPA-AM (c) PO Box 424, Hope AR 71802 **Phn:** 870-777-8868 **Fax:** 870-777-8888 www.supercountry105.com khpafm@supercountry105.com

Hope KXAR-AM (c) PO Box 424, Hope AR 71802 **Phn:** 870-777-8868 **Fax:** 870-777-8888 www.supercountry105.com khpafm@supercountry105.com

Hot Springs KBHS-AM (c) 208 Buena Vista Rd, Hot Springs AR 71913 **Phn:** 501-525-1301 **Fax:** 501-525-4344

Hot Springs KHTO-FM (h) 125 Corporate Ter, Hot Springs AR 71913 **Phn:** 501-525-9700 **Fax:** 501-525-9739 www.myhotsprings.com gterrell@usstations.com

Hot Springs KLAZ-FM (ah) 208 Buena Vista Rd, Hot Springs AR 71913 **Phn:** 501-525-1420 **Fax:** 501-525-4344 www.klaz.com

Hot Springs KLBL-FM (c) 125 Corporate Ter, Hot Springs AR 71913 **Phn:** 501-525-9700 **Fax:** 501-525-9739 gterrell@usstations.com

Hot Springs KLEZ-FM (o) 208 Buena Vista Rd, Hot Springs AR 71913 **Phn:** 501-525-4600 **Fax:** 501-525-4344

Hot Springs KLXQ-FM (r) 125 Corporate Ter, Hot Springs AR 71913 **Phn:** 501-525-9700 **Fax:** 501-525-9739 www.myhotsprings.com cdale@usstations.com

Hot Springs KQUS-FM (c) 125 Corporate Ter, Hot Springs AR 71913 **Phn:** 501-525-9700 **Fax:** 501-525-9739 www.myhotsprings.com gterrell@usstations.com

Hot Springs KZNG-AM (nt) 125 Corporate Ter, Hot Springs AR 71913 **Phn:** 501-525-9700 **Fax:** 501-525-9739 www.myhotsprings.com cdale@usstations.com

Hot Springs Village KVRE-FM (a) PO Box 8439, Hot Springs Village AR 71910 **Phn:** 501-922-5678 **Fax:** 501-922-6626 alice@kvre.com

Jonesboro KBTM-AM (nt) 403 W Parker Rd # B, Jonesboro AR 72404 **Phn:** 870-934-5000 **Fax:** 870-932-3814

Jonesboro KDEZ-FM (r) 314 Union St, Jonesboro AR 72401 **Phn:** 870-933-8800 **Fax:** 870-933-0403 eagle1005.com trey@jonesbororadiogroup.com

Jonesboro KDXY-FM (c) 314 Union St, Jonesboro AR 72401 **Phn:** 870-933-8800 **Fax:** 870-933-0403 www.thefox1049.com christie@triplefm.com

Jonesboro KFIN-FM (c) 407 W Parker Rd # B, Jonesboro AR 72404 **Phn:** 870-934-5000 **Fax:** 870-932-3814 www.kfin.com kfin@kfin.com

Jonesboro KIYS-FM (h) 407 W Parker Rd # B, Jonesboro AR 72404 **Phn:** 870-934-5000 **Fax:** 870-932-3814 www.kissjonesboro.com

Jonesboro KJBX-FM (a) 314 Union St, Jonesboro AR 72401 **Phn:** 870-933-8800 **Fax:** 870-933-0403 themix1063.com tstafford@jonesbororadiogroup.com

Jonesboro KNEA-AM (g) 407 W Parker Rd # B, Jonesboro AR 72404 **Phn:** 870-934-5000 **Fax:** 870-932-3814

Little Rock KAAY-AM (q) 700 Wellington Hills Rd, Little Rock AR 72211 **Phn:** 501-401-0200 **Fax:** 501-401-0367 www.1090kaay.com dianne.bivens@cumulus.com

Little Rock KABF-FM (wjg) 2101 Main St # 200, Little Rock AR 72206 **Phn:** 501-372-6119 **Fax:** 501-376-3952 www.kabf.org stationmanager@kabf.org

Little Rock KABZ-FM (t) 2400 Cottondale Ln, Little Rock AR 72202 **Phn:** 501-661-1037 **Fax:** 501-664-5871 www.1037thebuzz.com

Little Rock KARN-AM (nt) 700 Wellington Hills Rd, Little Rock AR 72211 **Phn:** 501-401-0200 **Fax:** 501-401-0367 karnnewsradio.com

Little Rock KARN-FM (nt) 700 Wellington Hills Rd, Little Rock AR 72211 **Phn:** 501-401-0200 **Fax:** 501-401-0367 www.karnnewsradio.com

Little Rock KDJE-FM (r) 10800 Colonel Glenn Rd, Little Rock AR 72204 **Phn:** 501-217-5000 **Fax:** 501-374-0808 www.edgelittlerock.com jeffcage@clearchannel.com

Little Rock KHKN-FM (r) 10800 Colonel Glenn Rd, Little Rock AR 72204 **Phn:** 501-217-5000 **Fax:** 501-374-0808 www.949tomfm.com tom@949tomfm.com

Little Rock KHLR-FM (x) 10800 Colonel Glenn Rd, Little Rock AR 72204 **Phn:** 501-217-5000 **Fax:** 501-374-0808 www.heartbeat1067.com mikek@signalmedia.com

Little Rock KHTE-FM (t) 400 Hardin Rd Ste 150, Little Rock AR 72211 **Phn:** 501-219-1919 **Fax:** 501-225-4610 www.965thevoice.com

Little Rock KIPR-FM (uw) 700 Wellington Hills Rd, Little Rock AR 72211 **Phn:** 501-401-0200 **Fax:** 501-401-0366 www.power923.com joe.booker@cumulus.com

Little Rock KKPT-FM (r) 2400 Cottondale Ln, Little Rock AR 72202 **Phn:** 501-664-9410 **Fax:** 501-664-5871 www.point941.com chuck@kkpt.com

Little Rock KKSP-FM (nt) 400 Hardin Rd Ste 150, Little Rock AR 72211 **Phn:** 501-219-1919 **Fax:** 501-225-4610

Little Rock KLAL-FM (h) 700 Wellington Hills Rd, Little Rock AR 72211 **Phn:** 501-401-0200 **Fax:** 501-401-0374 www.alice1077.com randy.cain@cumulus.com

Little Rock KLRE-FM (pl) 2801 S University Ave, Little Rock AR 72204 **Phn:** 501-569-8485 **Fax:** 501-569-8488 ualrpublicradio.org news@kuar.org

Little Rock KMJX-FM (c) 10800 Colonel Glenn Rd, Little Rock AR 72204 **Phn:** 501-217-5000 **Fax:** 501-228-9547 www.1051thewolf.com

Little Rock KOKY-FM (wau) 700 Wellington Hills Rd, Little Rock AR 72211 **Phn:** 501-401-0200 **Fax:** 501-401-0374 www.koky.com joe.booker@cumulus.com

Little Rock KOLL-FM (m) 400 Hardin Rd Ste 150, Little Rock AR 72211 **Phn:** 501-219-1919 **Fax:** 501-225-4610 www.fm1063theriver.com

Little Rock KPZK-AM (q) 700 Wellington Hills Rd, Little Rock AR 72211 **Phn:** 501-401-0200 **Fax:** 501-401-0366 www.1250rejoice.faithweb.com

Little Rock KPZK-FM (wg) 700 Wellington Hills Rd, Little Rock AR 72211 **Phn:** 501-401-0200 **Fax:** 501-401-0349 www.praisepage.com joe.booker@cumulus.com

Little Rock KSSN-FM (c) 10800 Colonel Glenn Rd, Little Rock AR 72204 **Phn:** 501-217-5000 **Fax:** 501-374-0808 www.kssn.com djtaylor@clearchannel.com

ARKANSAS RADIO STATIONS

Little Rock KUAR-FM (pnj) 2801 S University Ave, Little Rock AR 72204 **Phn:** 501-569-8485 **Fax:** 501-569-8488 www.kuar.org news@kuar.org

Little Rock KURB-FM (a) 700 Wellington Hills Rd, Little Rock AR 72211 **Phn:** 501-401-0200 **Fax:** 501-401-0367 www.b98.com randy.cain@cumulus.com

Magnolia KVMA-AM (c) PO Box 430, Magnolia AR 71754 **Phn:** 870-234-9901 **Fax:** 870-234-5865 www.magnoliaradio.com kvmakvmz@magnoliaradio.com

Magnolia KVMZ-FM (c) PO Box 430, Magnolia AR 71754 **Phn:** 870-234-5862 **Fax:** 870-234-5865 www.magnoliaradio.com office@magnoliaradio.com

Magnolia KZHE-FM (c) 406 W Union, Magnolia AR 71753 **Phn:** 870-234-7790 **Fax:** 870-234-7791 www.kzhe.com kzhe@magnolia-net.com

Mammoth Spring KAMS-AM (q) PO Box 193, Mammoth Spring AR 72554 **Phn:** 417-264-7211 **Fax:** 417-264-7212 www.am1290thegift.com news@kkountry.com

Mammoth Spring KAMS-FM (c) PO Box 193, Mammoth Spring AR 72554 **Phn:** 417-264-7211 **Fax:** 417-264-7212 www.kkountry.com news@kkountry.com

Marshall KCGS-AM (g) 208 Battle St, Marshall AR 72650 **Phn:** 870-448-5567 **Fax:** 870-448-5384

McGehee KVSA-AM (mc) PO Box 110, McGehee AR 71654 **Phn:** 870-222-4200 **Fax:** 870-538-3389 kvsa1220@yahoo.com

Mena KENA-AM (g) PO Box 1450, Mena AR 71953 **Phn:** 479-394-1450 **Fax:** 479-394-1459

Mena KENA-FM (c) PO Box 1450, Mena AR 71953 **Phn:** 479-394-1450 **Fax:** 479-394-1459 www.bestcountryaround.com menaradio@allegiance.tv

Mena KILX-FM (a) PO Box 1450, Mena AR 71953 **Phn:** 479-394-1450 menaradio@allegiance.tv

Mena KQOR-FM (o) PO Box 1450, Mena AR 71953 **Phn:** 479-394-1450 menaradio@aol.com

Monticello KGPQ-FM (a) 279 Midway Rte, Monticello AR 71655 **Phn:** 870-367-6854 **Fax:** 870-367-9564 pines.radio@sbcglobal.net

Monticello KHBM-FM (h) 279 Midway Rte, Monticello AR 71655 **Phn:** 870-367-6854 **Fax:** 870-367-9564 pines.radio@sbcglobal.net

Monticello KHBM-AM (m) 279 Midway Rte, Monticello AR 71655 **Phn:** 870-367-6854 **Fax:** 870-367-9564

Monticello KXSA-FM (c) 279 Midway Rte, Monticello AR 71655 **Phn:** 870-367-8528 **Fax:** 870-367-9564 pines.radio@sbcglobal.net

Morrilton KVOM-FM (c) PO Box 541, Morrilton AR 72110 **Phn:** 501-354-2484 **Fax:** 501-354-5629 www.kvom.com kvom@kvom.com

Morrilton KVOM-AM (s) PO Box 541, Morrilton AR 72110 **Phn:** 501-354-2484 **Fax:** 501-354-5629 www.espn800.com kvom@kvom.com

Mountain Home KCMH-FM (q) 126 S Church St, Mountain Home AR 72653 **Phn:** 870-425-2525 **Fax:** 870-424-2626 www.kcmhradio.org

Mountain Home KCTT-FM (o) PO Box 2010, Mountain Home AR 72654 **Phn:** 870-425-3101 **Fax:** 870-424-4314 www.ktlo.com news@ktlo.com

Mountain Home KKTZ-FM (a) 2352 Highway 62 E, Mountain Home AR 72653 **Phn:** 870-492-6022 **Fax:** 870-492-2137 www.twinlakesradio.com radio@mtnhome.com

Mountain Home KPFM-FM (c) 2352 Highway 62 B, Mountain Home AR 72653 **Phn:** 870-492-6022 **Fax:** 870-492-2137 www.twinlakesradio.com radio@mtnhome.com

Mountain Home KTLO-AM (c) PO Box 2010, Mountain Home AR 72654 **Phn:** 870-425-3101 **Fax:** 870-424-4314 www.ktlo.com news@ktlo.com

Mountain Home KTLO-FM (bz) PO Box 2010, Mountain Home AR 72654 **Phn:** 870-425-3101 **Fax:** 870-424-4314 www.ktlo.com news@ktlo.com

Nashville KBHC-AM (y) 1513 S 4th St, Nashville AR 71852 **Phn:** 870-845-3601 **Fax:** 870-845-3680

Nashville KMTB-FM (c) 1513 S 4th St, Nashville AR 71852 **Phn:** 870-845-3601 **Fax:** 870-845-3680 www.southwestarkansasradio.com operations@southwestarkansasradio.com

Nashville KNAS-FM (o) 1513 ˙S 4th St, Nashville AR 71852 **Phn:** 870-845-3601 **Fax:** 870-845-3680 www.southwestarkansasradio.com operations@southwestarkansasradio.com

Newport KNBY-AM (gt) PO Box 768, Newport AR 72112 **Phn:** 870-523-5891 **Fax:** 870-523-2967

Newport KOKR-FM (c) PO Box 768, Newport AR 72112 **Phn:** 870-523-5891 **Fax:** 870-523-2967 www.rivercountry967.com info@rivercountry967.com

North Little Rock KJBN-AM (q) 1800 Maple St, North Little Rock AR 72114 **Phn:** 501-791-1000 **Fax:** 501-791-7121

North Little Rock KLRG-AM (t) 10000 Warden Rd, North Little Rock AR 72120 **Phn:** 501-985-0880 **Fax:** 727-441-1300 www.tantalk1340.com

North Little Rock KMTL-AM (g) PO Box 6460, North Little Rock AR 72124 **Phn:** 501-835-1554 **Fax:** 479-968-1337 www.kmtl760am.com kmtl760am@sbcglobal.net

Ozark KDYN-FM (c) PO Box 1086, Ozark AR 72949 **Phn:** 479-667-4567 **Fax:** 479-667-5214 kdyn.com kdyn@centurytel.net

Ozark KDYN-AM (c) PO Box 1086, Ozark AR 72949 **Phn:** 479-667-4567 **Fax:** 479-667-5214 kdyn.com kdyn@centurytel.net

Ozark KLYR-AM (c) PO Box 1086, Ozark AR 72949 **Phn:** 479-754-3092 **Fax:** 479-667-5214 www.kdyn.com kdyn@centurytel.net

Paragould KDRS-AM (st) 400 Tower Dr, Paragould AR 72450 **Phn:** 870-236-7627 **Fax:** 870-239-4583 www.neajackfm.com brian@kdrs.com

Paragould KDRS-FM (a) 400 Tower Dr, Paragould AR 72450 **Phn:** 870-236-7627 **Fax:** 870-239-4583 www.neajackfm.com brian@kdrs.com

Pine Bluff KCAT-AM (wgx) 1207 W 6th Ave, Pine Bluff AR 71601 **Phn:** 870-534-5001 **Fax:** 870-534-7985 www.kcatam.com news@lordradio.com

Pine Bluff KUAP-FM (vu) 1200 University Dr, Pine Bluff AR 71601 **Phn:** 870-575-8951

Pocahontas KPOC-AM (sn) PO Box 508, Pocahontas AR 72455 **Phn:** 870-892-5234 **Fax:** 870-892-5235

Pocahontas KPOC-FM (a) PO Box 508, Pocahontas AR 72455 **Phn:** 870-892-5234 **Fax:** 870-892-5235

Pocahontas KRLW-AM (o) PO Box 508, Pocahontas AR 72455 **Phn:** 870-892-5234 **Fax:** 870-892-5235 kpoc-krlw@centurytel.net

Pocahontas KRLW-FM (c) PO Box 508, Pocahontas AR 72455 **Phn:** 870-892-5234 **Fax:** 870-892-5235 kpoc-krlw@centurytel.net

Rogers KURM-AM (nt) 113 E New Hope Rd, Rogers AR 72758 **Phn:** 479-633-0790 **Fax:** 479-631-9711 www.kurm.net

Rogers KURM-FM (at) 113 E New Hope Rd, Rogers AR 72758 **Phn:** 479-633-0790 **Fax:** 479-631-9711 www.kurm.net

Russellville KARV-FM (snt) 201 W 2nd St, Russellville AR 72801 **Phn:** 479-968-1184 **Fax:** 479-967-5278 cwomack@centurytel.net

Russellville KARV-AM (snt) 201 W 2nd St, Russellville AR 72801 **Phn:** 479-968-1184 **Fax:** 479-967-5278 cwomack@centurytel.net

Russellville KCAB-AM (nt) 2705 E Parkway Dr, Russellville AR 72802 **Phn:** 479-968-6816 **Fax:** 479-968-2946 www.rivertalk980.com news@rivervalleyradio.com

Russellville KCJC-FM (a) PO Box 10310, Russellville AR 72812 **Phn:** 479-968-6816 **Fax:** 479-968-2946 www.rivercountrykcjc.com

Russellville KMTC-FM (vq) PO Box 570, Russellville AR 72811 **Phn:** 479-967-7400 www.rccenter.org kmtc@rccenter.org

Russellville KVLD-FM (r) 2705 E Parkway, Russellville AR 72802 **Phn:** 479-968-6816 **Fax:** 479-968-2946 www.sharpe993.com rich@rivervalleyradio.com

Russellville KWKK-FM (a) 2705 E Parkway Dr, Russellville AR 72802 **Phn:** 479-968-6816 **Fax:** 479-968-2946 www.riverhitskwkk.com jarrettjackson@rivervalleyradio.com

Russellville KXRJ-FM (vjz) Arkansas Tech Univ Crabaugh, Russellville AR 72801 **Phn:** 479-964-0806 www.atu.edubroadcast acaton@atu.edu

Salem KSAR-FM (nc) PO Box 458, Salem AR 72576 **Phn:** 870-856-3240 **Fax:** 870-856-4408 hometownradio@centurytel.net

Searcy KAPZ-AM (nt) 111 N Spring St, Searcy AR 72143 **Phn:** 501-268-9898 **Fax:** 501-268-3838

Searcy KAWW-FM (r) 111 N Spring St, Searcy AR 72143 **Phn:** 501-268-7123 **Fax:** 501-279-2900

Searcy KFLI-FM (o) 302 E Park Ave, Searcy AR 72143 **Phn:** 501-268-1047 **Fax:** 501-305-2977

Searcy KWCK-AM (nt) 111 N Spring St, Searcy AR 72143 **Phn:** 501-268-7123 **Fax:** 501-279-2900

Searcy KWCK-FM (c) 111 N Spring St, Searcy AR 72143 **Phn:** 501-268-7123 **Fax:** 501-279-2900 www.kwck999.com grantcarey@crainmedia.com

Siloam Springs KLRC-FM (q) 110 N Broadway, Siloam Springs AR 72761 **Phn:** 479-238-8600 **Fax:** 479-238-8602 www.klrc.com

Springdale KTHS-AM (s) 2250 W Sunset Ave Ste 3, Springdale AR 72762 **Phn:** 479-303-2034 **Fax:** 479-303-2037 www.hogsportsradio.com dan@hogradio.com

Springdale KUOA-AM (s) 2250 W Sunset Ave Ste 3, Springdale AR 72762 **Phn:** 479-303-2034 **Fax:** 479-303-2037

Springdale KUOA-FM (s) 2250 W Sunset Ave Ste 3, Springdale AR 72762 **Phn:** 479-303-2034 **Fax:** 479-303-2037

State University KASU-FM (plnj) PO Box 2160, State University AR 72467 **Phn:** 870-972-2200 **Fax:** 870-972-2997 www.kasu.org gchance@astate.edu

Stuttgart KDEW-FM (c) PO Box 910, Stuttgart AR 72160 **Phn:** 870-673-1595 **Fax:** 870-673-8445 kdew973@yahoo.com

Stuttgart KWAK-AM (s) PO Box 910, Stuttgart AR 72160 **Phn:** 870-673-1595 **Fax:** 870-673-8445 kdew973@yahoo.com

Stuttgart KWAK-FM (o) PO Box 910, Stuttgart AR 72160 **Phn:** 870-673-1595 **Fax:** 870-673-8445 kdew973@yahoo.com

Texarkana KKYR-FM (c) 2324 Arkansas Blvd, Texarkana AR 71854 **Phn:** 870-772-3771 **Fax:** 870-772-0364 kkyr.com mariogarcia@townsquaremedia.com

Texarkana KMJI-FM (a) 2324 Arkansas Blvd, Texarkana AR 71854 **Phn:** 870-772-3771 **Fax:** 870-772-0364 www.magic933.com scottmills@townsquaremedia.com

Texarkana KPWW-FM (h) 2324 Arkansas Blvd, Texarkana AR 71854 **Phn:** 870-772-3771 **Fax:** 870-772-0364 power959.com wesspicher@townsquaremedia.com

Texarkana KYGL-FM (r) 2324 Arkansas Blvd, Texarkana AR 71854 **Phn:** 870-772-3771 **Fax:** 870-772-0364 kygl.com jeff.easterling@townsquaremedia.com

Warren KWRF-AM (c) 1255 N Myrtle St, Warren AR 71671 **Phn:** 870-226-2653 **Fax:** 870-226-3039

Warren KWRF-FM (c) 1255 N Myrtle St, Warren AR 71671 **Phn:** 870-226-2653 **Fax:** 870-226-3039

West Helena KAKJ-FM (wu) PO Box 2870, West Helena AR 72390 **Phn:** 870-633-9000 **Fax:** 870-572-1845 www.force2radio.com force2@sbcglobal.net

West Helena KCLT-FM (wu) PO Box 2870, West Helena AR 72390 **Phn:** 870-572-9506 **Fax:** 870-572-1845 www.force2radio.com force2@sbcglobal.net

Wynne KTRQ-FM (o) PO Box 789, Wynne AR 72396 **Phn:** 870-238-8141 **Fax:** 870-238-5997 ktrq.com radiokwyn@cablelynx.com

Wynne KWYN-AM (ct) PO Box 789, Wynne AR 72396 **Phn:** 870-238-8141 **Fax:** 870-238-5997 kwyn.com radiokwyn@cablelynx.com

Wynne KWYN-FM (c) PO Box 789, Wynne AR 72396 **Phn:** 870-238-8141 **Fax:** 870-238-5997 radiokwyn@cablelynx.com

CALIFORNIA

Alturas KCFJ-AM (ntc) PO Box 580, Alturas CA 96101 **Phn:** 530-233-3570 **Fax:** 530-233-5470

Alturas KCNO-FM (c) PO Box 580, Alturas CA 96101 **Phn:** 530-233-3570 **Fax:** 530-233-5470

Anaheim KLAA-AM (st) 2000 E Gene Autry Way, Anaheim CA 92806 **Phn:** 714-940-2500 **Fax:** 714-940-2589 www.am830klaa.com officemanager@am830klaa.com

anta Rosa KFGY-FM (c) 1410 Neotomas Ave # 200, anta Rosa CA 95405 **Phn:** 707-543-0100 **Fax:** 707-571-1097 www.froggy929.com jim@mysonomamedia.com

Arcata KHSU-FM (p) 1 Harpst St, Arcata CA 95521 **Phn:** 707-826-4807 **Fax:** 707-826-6082 www.khsu.org homepage@khsu.org

Auburn KAHI-AM (nt) 985 Lincoln Way Ste 103, Auburn CA 95603 **Phn:** 530-885-5636 **Fax:** 530-885-0166 www.kahi.com info@kahi.com

Bakersfield KAXL-FM (q) 110 S Montclair St Ste 205, Bakersfield CA 93309 **Phn:** 661-832-2800 **Fax:** 661-832-3164 kaxl.com kaxl@kaxl.com

Bakersfield KBDS-FM (y) 6313 Schirra Ct, Bakersfield CA 93313 **Phn:** 661-837-0745 **Fax:** 661-837-1612 www.campesina.com cesar.chavez@campesina.com

Bakersfield KBFP-AM (y) 1100 Mohawk St Ste 280, Bakersfield CA 93309 **Phn:** 661-322-9929 **Fax:** 661-322-7239 www.lapreciosa1053.com kennmccloud@clearchannel.com

Bakersfield KBFP-FM (y) 1100 Mohawk St Ste 280, Bakersfield CA 93309 **Phn:** 661-322-9929 **Fax:** 661-322-9239 www.lapreciosa1053.com kennmccloud@clearchannel.com

Bakersfield KCHJ-AM (y) 5100 Commerce Dr, Bakersfield CA 93309 **Phn:** 661-327-9711 **Fax:** 661-327-0797 vicente@lotusbakersfield.com

Bakersfield KCWR-FM (c) 3223 Sillect Ave, Bakersfield CA 93308 **Phn:** 661-326-1011 **Fax:** 661-328-7535

Bakersfield KDFO-FM (r) 1100 Mohawk St Ste 280, Bakersfield CA 93309 **Phn:** 661-322-9929 **Fax:** 661-322-7239 www.985thefox.com kennmccloud@clearchannel.com

Bakersfield KEBT-FM (y) 1400 Easton Dr Ste 144, Bakersfield CA 93309 **Phn:** 661-328-1410 **Fax:** 661-328-0873 www.969lacaliente.com tsnyder@americangeneralmedia.com

Bakersfield KERI-AM (q) 1400 Easton Dr Ste 144, Bakersfield CA 93309 **Phn:** 661-328-1410 **Fax:** 661-328-0873 www.keri.com tsnyder@americangeneralmedia.com

Bakersfield KERN-AM (nt) 1400 Easton Dr Ste 144, Bakersfield CA 93309 **Phn:** 661-328-1410 **Fax:** 661-328-0873 www.kernradio.com news@kernradio.com

Bakersfield KGEO-AM (st) 1400 Easton Dr Ste 144, Bakersfield CA 93309 **Phn:** 661-328-1410 **Fax:** 661-328-0873 kernradio.com jlemucchi@americangeneralmedia.com

Bakersfield KGFM-FM (a) 1400 Easton Dr Ste 144, Bakersfield CA 93309 **Phn:** 661-328-1410 **Fax:** 661-328-0873 www.kgfm.com chris@kgfm.com

Bakersfield KHTY-AM (s) 1100 Mohawk St Ste 280, Bakersfield CA 93309 **Phn:** 661-322-9929 **Fax:** 661-283-2963 www.foxsports970am.com kennmccloud@clearchannel.com

Bakersfield KISV-FM (h) 1400 Easton Dr Ste 144, Bakersfield CA 93309 **Phn:** 661-328-1410 **Fax:** 661-328-0873 www.hot941.com jreed@hot941.com

Bakersfield KIWI-FM (y) 5100 Commerce Dr, Bakersfield CA 93309 **Phn:** 661-327-9711 **Fax:** 661-327-0797

Bakersfield KKBB-FM (ox) 3651 Pegasus Dr Ste 107, Bakersfield CA 93308 **Phn:** 661-393-1900 **Fax:** 661-393-1915

Bakersfield KKXX-FM (h) 1400 Easton Dr Ste 144, Bakersfield CA 93309 **Phn:** 661-328-1410 **Fax:** 661-328-0873 www.hits931fm.com jreed@americangeneralmedia.com

Bakersfield KLLY-FM (a) 3651 Pegasus Dr Ste 107, Bakersfield CA 93308 **Phn:** 661-393-1900 **Fax:** 661-393-1915 www.klly.com

Bakersfield KNZR-AM (snt) 3651 Pegasus Dr Ste 107, Bakersfield CA 93308 **Phn:** 661-393-1900 **Fax:** 661-393-1915 www.knzr.com

Bakersfield KPSL-FM (y) 5100 Commerce Dr, Bakersfield CA 93309 **Phn:** 661-327-9711 **Fax:** 661-327-0797 concierto965.com

Bakersfield KRAB-FM (r) 1100 Mohawk St Ste 280, Bakersfield CA 93309 **Phn:** 661-322-9929 **Fax:** 661-322-7239 www.krab.com dannyspanks@clearchannel.com

Bakersfield KSMJ-FM (aj) 3651 Pegasus Dr Ste 107, Bakersfield CA 93308 **Phn:** 661-393-1900 **Fax:** 661-393-1915

Bakersfield KUZZ-AM (c) 3223 Sillect Ave, Bakersfield CA 93308 **Phn:** 661-326-1011 **Fax:** 661-328-7503 www.kuzzradio.com kuzznews@buckowens.com

Bakersfield KUZZ-FM (c) 3223 Sillect Ave, Bakersfield CA 93308 **Phn:** 661-326-1011 **Fax:** 661-328-7503 www.kuzzradio.com kuzznews@buckowens.com

Bakersfield KVMX-FM (c) 5100 Commerce Dr, Bakersfield CA 93309 **Phn:** 661-327-9711 **Fax:** 661-327-0797 www.921kix.com greg@lotusbakersfield.com

Bakersfield KWAC-AM (s) 5100 Commerce Dr, Bakersfield CA 93309 **Phn:** 661-327-9711 **Fax:** 661-327-0797

Barstow KBTW-FM (y) 125 E Fredricks St, Barstow CA 92311 **Phn:** 760-255-1316 **Fax:** 760-255-2406 dinom@radiolazer.com

Barstow KDUC-FM (h) 29000 Radio Rd, Barstow CA 92311 **Phn:** 760-256-2121 **Fax:** 760-256-5090 doscostas@yahoo.com

Barstow KDUQ-FM (h) 29000 Radio Rd, Barstow CA 92311 **Phn:** 760-256-2121 **Fax:** 760-256-5090 doscostas@yahoo.com

Barstow KHDR-FM (r) 1611 E Main St, Barstow CA 92311 **Phn:** 760-256-0326 **Fax:** 760-256-9507 highwayradio.com thehighwaystations@highwayradio.com

Barstow KHWY-FM (a) 1611 E Main St, Barstow CA 92311 **Phn:** 760-256-0326 **Fax:** 760-256-9507 www.thehighwaystations.com thehighwaystations@highwayradio.com

Barstow KHYZ-FM (a) 1611 E Main St, Barstow CA 92311 **Phn:** 760-256-0326 **Fax:** 760-256-9507 www.thehighwaystations.com thehighwaystations@highwayradio.com

Barstow KIXW-FM (c) 1611 E Main St, Barstow CA 92311 **Phn:** 760-256-0326 **Fax:** 760-256-9507 www.thehighwaystations.com thehighwaystations@highwayradio.com

Barstow KRXV-FM (a) 1611 E Main St, Barstow CA 92311 **Phn:** 760-256-0326 **Fax:** 760-256-9507 www.thehighwaystations.com thehighwaystations@highwayradio.com

Barstow KSZL-AM (snt) 29000 Radio Rd, Barstow CA 92311 **Phn:** 760-256-2121 **Fax:** 760-256-5090 doscostas@yahoo.com

Barstow KXXZ-FM (y) 29000 Radio Rd, Barstow CA 92311 **Phn:** 760-256-2121 **Fax:** 760-256-5090 doscostas@yahoo.com

Berkeley KALX-FM (v) 26 Barrows Hall Spc 5650, Berkeley CA 94720 **Phn:** 510-642-1111 kalx.berkeley.edu news@kalx.berkeley.edu

Berkeley KPFA-FM (v) 1929 Martin Luther King Jr Way, Berkeley CA 94704 **Phn:** 510-848-6767 **Fax:** 510-848-3812 www.kpfa.org news@kpfa.org

Big Bear City KBHR-FM (ar) PO Box 2979, Big Bear City CA 92314 **Phn:** 909-584-5247 **Fax:** 909-584-5347 kbhr933.com info@kbhr933.com

Bishop KBOV-AM (o) PO Box 757, Bishop CA 93515 **Phn:** 760-873-6324 **Fax:** 760-872-2639 www.kibskbov.com kibskbov@kibskbov.com

Bishop KIBS-FM (c) PO Box 757, Bishop CA 93515 **Phn:** 760-873-6324 **Fax:** 760-872-2639 www.kibskbov.com kibskbov@kibskbov.com

Bishop KSRW-FM (a) 1280 N Main St Ste J, Bishop CA 93514 **Phn:** 760-873-5329 bkessler@sierrawave.net

Bishop KWTW-FM (q) PO Box 637, Bishop CA 93515 **Phn:** 866-466-5989 **Fax:** 760-872-4155 www.kwtw.org friar@schat.com

Blythe KJMB-FM (a) 681 N 4th St, Blythe CA 92225 **Phn:** 760-922-7143 **Fax:** 760-922-2844 www.kjmbfm.com kjmbfm@hotmail.com

CALIFORNIA RADIO STATIONS

Brawley KROP-AM (c) PO Box 238, Brawley CA 92227 **Phn:** 760-344-1300 **Fax:** 760-344-1763 www.cherrycreekradio.com tdriskill@cherrycreekradio.com

Brawley KSIQ-FM (h) 120 S Plaza St, Brawley CA 92227 **Phn:** 760-344-1300 **Fax:** 760-344-1763 www.q96ksiq.com q96ksiq@yahoo.com

Burbank KBUA-FM (y) 1845 W Empire Ave, Burbank CA 91504 **Phn:** 818-729-5300 **Fax:** 818-729-5678 aquisuena.estrellatv.com pgarza@lbimedia.com

Burbank KBUE-FM (y) 1845 W Empire Ave, Burbank CA 91504 **Phn:** 818-729-5300 **Fax:** 818-729-5678 www.aquisuena.com pgarza@lbimedia.com

Burbank KDIS-AM (M) 500 S Buena Vista St, Burbank CA 91521 **Phn:** 818-955-5000 **Fax:** 818-973-4077 music.disney.com natalie.r.eig@disney.com

Burbank KFI-AM (t) 3400 W Olive Ave Ste 550, Burbank CA 91505 **Phn:** 818-559-2252 **Fax:** 818-260-9915 www.kfiam640.com kfinewsdirector@kfi640.com

Burbank KHJ-AM (y) 1845 W Empire Ave, Burbank CA 91504 **Phn:** 818-729-5300 **Fax:** 818-729-5678 laranchera.estrellatv.com info@lbimedia.com

Burbank KIIS-FM (h) 3400 W Olive Ave Ste 550, Burbank CA 91505 **Phn:** 818-566-4800 **Fax:** 818-955-8384 www.kiisfm.com johnivey@clearchannel.com

Burbank KLAC-AM (s) 3400 W Olive Ave Ste 550, Burbank CA 91505 **Phn:** 818-559-2252 **Fax:** 818-260-9961 www.am570radio.com gregashlock@clearchannel.com

Burbank KOST-FM (a) 3400 W Olive Ave Ste 550, Burbank CA 91505 **Phn:** 818-559-2252 **Fax:** 818-260-9069 www.kost1035.com kostpromo@clearchannel.com

Burbank KPWR-FM (rh) 2600 W Olive Ave Ste 850, Burbank CA 91505 **Phn:** 818-953-4200 **Fax:** 818-848-0961 www.power106.com jsteal@power106.com

Burbank KROQ-FM (ra) 5901 Venice Blvd, Burbank CA 90034 **Phn:** 323-930-1067 **Fax:** 323-931-1067 kroq.cbslocal.com tips@kroq.com

Burbank KTLK-AM (t) 3400 W Olive Ave Ste 550, Burbank CA 91505 **Phn:** 818-559-2252 **Fax:** 818-260-9961 www.ktlkam1150.com

Burbank KVVS-FM (h) 3400 W Olive Ave Ste 550, Burbank CA 91505 **Phn:** 818-559-2252 **Fax:** 818-729-2502 www.kiisfm.com

Burbank KYSR-FM (a) 3400 W Olive Ave Ste 550, Burbank CA 91505 **Phn:** 818-559-2252 **Fax:** 818-262-9047 www.987fm.com 987programming@clearchannel.com

Burbank XTRA-AM (sy) 3500 W Olive Ave Ste 250, Burbank CA 91505 **Phn:** 818-729-2605 www.wradiousa.com

Camarillo KMRO-FM (vyq) PO Box 500, Camarillo CA 93011 **Phn:** 805-482-4797 **Fax:** 805-388-5202 www.nuevavida.com

Carlsbad KCEO-AM (nt) 2888 Loker Ave E # 211, Carlsbad CA 92010 **Phn:** 760-729-1000 **Fax:** 760-931-8201 ihradio.com

Carlsbad KFSD-AM (l) 2888 Loker Ave E Ste 211, Carlsbad CA 92010 **Phn:** 760-729-1000 **Fax:** 760-931-8201 www.thesparadio.com peri@astorbroadcastgroup.com

Ceres KADV-FM (vq) 2020 Academy Pl, Ceres CA 95307 **Phn:** 209-537-1201 **Fax:** 209-537-1945 www.mypromisefm.com info@mypromisefm.com

Chico KALF-FM (c) 1459 Humboldt Rd Ste D, Chico CA 95928 **Phn:** 530-899-3600 **Fax:** 530-343-0243

Chico KBQB-FM (h) 856 Manzanita Ct, Chico CA 95926 **Phn:** 530-342-2200 **Fax:** 530-342-2260 www.927bobfm.com friendsofbob@927bobfm.com

Chico KCEZ-FM (h) 856 Manzanita Ct, Chico CA 95926 **Phn:** 530-342-2200 **Fax:** 530-342-2260 www.power102radio.com

Chico KCHO-FM (plnj) Calif State Univ, Chico CA 95929 **Phn:** 530-898-5896 **Fax:** 530-898-4348 www.kcho.org kchonews@csuchico.edu

Chico KFMF-FM (r) 1459 Humboldt Rd Ste D, Chico CA 95928 **Phn:** 530-899-3600 **Fax:** 530-343-0243

Chico KHSL-FM (c) 2654 Cramer Ln, Chico CA 95928 **Phn:** 530-345-0021 **Fax:** 530-893-2121 www.1035theblaze.com dcorbin@dcbchico.com

Chico KKXX-AM (q) 1363 Longfellow Ave, Chico CA 95926 **Phn:** 530-894-7325 **Fax:** 530-894-5372 chicochristianradio.com andrew@kkxx.net

Chico KMXI-FM (a) 2654 Cramer Ln, Chico CA 95928 **Phn:** 530-345-0021 **Fax:** 530-893-2121 www.kmxi.com dcorbin@dcbchico.com

Chico KPAY-AM (nt) 2654 Cramer Ln, Chico CA 95928 **Phn:** 530-345-0021 **Fax:** 530-893-2121 newstalk1290.wordpress.com mray@dcbchico.com

Chico KQPT-FM (a) 1459 Humboldt Rd Ste D, Chico CA 95928 **Phn:** 530-899-3600 **Fax:** 530-343-0243

Chico KRQR-FM (r) 856 Manzanita Ct, Chico CA 95926 **Phn:** 530-342-2200 **Fax:** 530-342-2260 www.zrockfm.com sbell@resultsradio.com

Chico KYIX-FM (q) 1363 Longfellow Ave, Chico CA 95926 **Phn:** 530-894-7325 **Fax:** 530-894-5372 chicochristianradio.com andrew@kkxx.net

Chico KZAP-FM (h) 1459 Humboldt Rd Ste D, Chico CA 95928 **Phn:** 530-899-3600 **Fax:** 530-343-0243 www.kpig.com pd@kpig.com

Chico KZFR-FM (v) PO Box 3173, Chico CA 95927 **Phn:** 530-895-0706 **Fax:** 530-895-0775 www.kzfr.org gm@kzfr.org

Chula Vista KSDO-AM (y) 344 F St Ste 200, Chula Vista CA 91910 **Phn:** 626-356-4230 www.nuevavida.com

Chula Vista KURS-AM (g) 296 H St Ste 300, Chula Vista CA 91910 **Phn:** 619-426-5645 **Fax:** 619-425-1000 sdgospel@att.net

Chula Vista XEXX-AM (y) 303 H St # 418, Chula Vista CA 91910 **Phn:** 619-819-5749 **Fax:** 619-819-5743 bernalhenry@aol.com

Claremont KSPC-FM (vr) 340 N College Ave, Claremont CA 91711 **Phn:** 909-621-8157 **Fax:** 909-621-8769 www.kspc.org

Colton KFRG-FM (c) 900 E Washington St Ste 315, Colton CA 92324 **Phn:** 909-825-9525 **Fax:** 909-825-0441 kfrog.cbslocal.com lee.douglas@cbsradio.com

Colton KXFG-FM (c) 900 E Washington St Ste 315, Colton CA 92324 **Phn:** 909-825-9525 **Fax:** 909-825-0441 kfrog.radio.com webmaster@kfrog.net

Concord KVHS-FM (vr) 1101 Alberta Way # S-2, Concord CA 94521 **Phn:** 925-682-5847 **Fax:** 925-609-5847 www.kvhs.com

Corona KWRM-AM (y) 210 Radio Rd, Corona CA 92879 **Phn:** 951-737-1370 **Fax:** 951-735-9572 www.kwrm1370am.com

Costa Mesa KBRT-AM (qt) 3183 Airway Ave Ste D, Costa Mesa CA 92626 **Phn:** 714-754-4450 **Fax:** 714-754-0735 www.kbrt740.com

Crescent City KCRE-FM (a) PO Box 1089, Crescent City CA 95531 **Phn:** 707-464-9561 **Fax:** 707-464-4303 www.kcrefm.com kcre@bicoastalmedia.com

Crescent City KPOD-AM (b) 1345 Northcrest Dr, Crescent City CA 95531 **Phn:** 707-464-1000 **Fax:** 707-464-4303 www.kpodfm.com kpod@bicoastalmedia.com

Crescent City KPOD-FM (c) PO Box 1089, Crescent City CA 95531 **Phn:** 707-464-3183 **Fax:** 707-464-4303 www.kpod.com kpod@bicoastalmedia.com

Davis KDVS-FM (vrj) 14 Lower Freeborn Hall, Davis CA 95616 **Phn:** 530-752-0728 **Fax:** 530-752-8548 www.kdvs.org news@kdvs.org

Dinuba KRDU-AM (qt) 597 N Alta Ave, Dinuba CA 93618 **Phn:** 559-591-1130 **Fax:** 559-591-4822 www.krdu1130.com

El Centro KGBA-FM (yq) 605 W State St, El Centro CA 92243 **Phn:** 760-352-9860 **Fax:** 760-352-1883 www.kgba.org kgba@kgba.org

El Centro KMXX-FM (y) 1803 N Imperial Ave, El Centro CA 92243 **Phn:** 760-482-7777 **Fax:** 760-482-0099 www.tricolor993.com

El Centro KSEH-FM (yh) 1803 N Imperial Ave, El Centro CA 92243 **Phn:** 760-482-7777 **Fax:** 760-482-0099 www.jose945.com gflores@entravision.com

El Centro KWST-AM (q) 1803 N Imperial Ave, El Centro CA 92243 **Phn:** 760-482-7777 **Fax:** 760-482-0099 www.esneradio.com

El Centro KXO-AM (o) PO Box 140, El Centro CA 92244 **Phn:** 760-352-1230 kxoradio.com kxoamfm@kxoradio.com

El Centro KXO-FM (a) PO Box 140, El Centro CA 92244 **Phn:** 760-352-1230 kxoradio.com kxoamfm@kxoradio.com

Eureka KATA-AM (s) 5640 S Broadway St, Eureka CA 95503 **Phn:** 707-442-2000 **Fax:** 707-443-6848 kata1340.com mathers84@yahoo.com

Eureka KEKA-FM (c) 1101 Marsh Rd, Eureka CA 95501 **Phn:** 707-442-5744 www.keka101.com

Eureka KFMI-FM (a) 5640 S Broadway St, Eureka CA 95503 **Phn:** 707-442-2000 **Fax:** 707-443-6848 power963.com eurekanews@bicoastalmedia.com

Eureka KGOE-AM (snt) 5640 S Broadway St, Eureka CA 95503 **Phn:** 707-442-2000 **Fax:** 707-443-6848 kgoe1480.com eurekanews@bicoastalmedia.com

Eureka KINS-FM (nt) 1101 Marsh Rd, Eureka CA 95501 **Phn:** 707-442-5744 www.kins1063.com

Eureka KJNY-FM (h) 728 7th St # 2A, Eureka CA 95501 **Phn:** 707-445-3699 **Fax:** 707-445-3906 www.991kissfm.com randy@kjny.net

Eureka KKHB-FM (o) 5640 S Broadway St, Eureka CA 95503 **Phn:** 707-442-2000 **Fax:** 707-443-6848 cool1055.com burlyman105@hotmail.com

Eureka KMDR-FM (r) 728 7th St # 2A, Eureka CA 95501 **Phn:** 707-445-3699 **Fax:** 707-445-3906 www.1067theedgefm.com randy@kjny.net

Eureka KRED-FM (c) 5640 S Broadway St, Eureka CA 95503 **Phn:** 707-442-2000 **Fax:** 707-443-6848 kred923.com mail@kred923.com

Eureka KWSW-AM (t) 1101 Marsh Rd, Eureka CA 95501 **Phn:** 707-442-5744 www.kwsw790.com

Ferndale KHUM-FM (a) PO Box 25, Ferndale CA 95536 **Phn:** 707-786-5104 **Fax:** 707-786-5100 khum.com info@khum.com

Ferndale KSLG-FM (r) PO Box 25, Ferndale CA 95536 **Phn:** 707-786-5104 **Fax:** 707-786-5100 kslg.com jmatthews@kslg.com

Ferndale KWPT-FM (h) PO Box 25, Ferndale CA 95536 **Phn:** 707-786-5104 **Fax:** 707-786-5100 kwpt.com caroleann@kwpt.com

CALIFORNIA RADIO STATIONS

Ferndale KXGO-FM (r) 1400 Main St, Ferndale CA 95536 **Phn:** 707-445-8104 **Fax:** 707-445-3906 kxgo.com psa@khum.com

Fort Bragg KMFB-FM (o) 101 Boatyard Dr Ste E, Fort Bragg CA 95437 **Phn:** 707-964-5307 **Fax:** 707-964-3299 www.kmfb-fm.com bobkmfb@email.com

Fort Bragg KOZT-FM (r) 110 S Franklin St, Fort Bragg CA 95437 **Phn:** 707-964-7277 **Fax:** 707-964-9536 www.kozt.com thecoast@kozt.com

Fort Bragg KSAY-FM (a) PO Box 2269, Fort Bragg CA 95437 **Phn:** 707-964-5729

Fremont KDOW-AM (nk) 39138 Fremont Blvd Fl 3, Fremont CA 94538 **Phn:** 510-713-1100 **Fax:** 510-505-1448 www.kdow.biz comments@kdow.biz

Fremont KFAX-AM (qt) 39138 Fremont Blvd Fl 3, Fremont CA 94538 **Phn:** 510-713-1100 **Fax:** 510-505-1448 www.kfax.com comments@kfax.com

Fremont KOHL-FM (v) 43600 Mission Blvd, Fremont CA 94539 **Phn:** 510-659-6221 **Fax:** 510-659-6001 www.kohlradio.com psa@kohlradio.com

Fresno KALZ-FM (a) 83 E Shaw Ave Ste 150, Fresno CA 93710 **Phn:** 559-230-4300 **Fax:** 559-230-4301 www.powertalk967.com jaybohannon@clearchannel.com

Fresno KBIF-AM (k) 3401 W Holland Ave, Fresno CA 93722 **Phn:** 559-222-0900 **Fax:** 559-222-1573 kbifkirv@aol.com

Fresno KBOS-FM (h) 83 E Shaw Ave Ste 150, Fresno CA 93710 **Phn:** 559-230-4300 **Fax:** 559-241-6011 www.b95forlife.com tonybanks@clearchannel.com

Fresno KCBL-AM (s) 83 E Shaw Ave Ste 150, Fresno CA 93710 **Phn:** 559-230-4300 **Fax:** 559-243-4301 www.foxsportsradio1340.com jaybohannon@clearchannel.com

Fresno KEZL-AM (s) 83 E Shaw Ave Ste 150, Fresno CA 93710 **Phn:** 559-230-4300 **Fax:** 559-241-6011 www.sports1340.com jeffnegrete@clearchannel.com

Fresno KFCF-FM (v) PO Box 4364, Fresno CA 93744 **Phn:** 559-233-2221 www.kfcf.org rwithers@kfcf.org

Fresno KFRR-FM (r) 1066 E Shaw Ave, Fresno CA 93710 **Phn:** 559-230-0104 **Fax:** 559-230-0177 www.newrock1041.fm jsquires@wilksfresno.com

Fresno KFSO-FM (y) 83 E Shaw Ave Ste 150, Fresno CA 93710 **Phn:** 559-230-4300 **Fax:** 559-241-6011 www.lapreciosa929.com tonybanks@clearchannel.com

Fresno KFSR-FM (v) 5201 N Maple Ave Ms Sa-119, Fresno CA 93725 **Phn:** 559-278-2598 **Fax:** 559-278-6985 kfsr.org 90.7kfsr@gmail.com

Fresno KGED-AM (t) 139 W Olive Ave, Fresno CA 93728 **Phn:** 559-233-8803 **Fax:** 559-233-8871 www.my1680.com

Fresno KGST-AM (y) 1110 E Olive Ave, Fresno CA 93728 **Phn:** 559-497-1100 **Fax:** 559-497-1125 dcrotty@lotusfresno.com

Fresno KHGE-FM (c) 83 E Shaw Ave Ste 150, Fresno CA 93710 **Phn:** 559-230-4300 **Fax:** 559-243-4301 www.1027thewolf.com nickcash@clearchannel.com

Fresno KHIT-FM (h) 1110 E Olive Ave, Fresno CA 93728 **Phn:** 559-497-1100 **Fax:** 559-497-1125 jguillen@lotusfresno.com

Fresno KIRV-AM (q) 3401 W Holland Ave, Fresno CA 93722 **Phn:** 559-222-0900 **Fax:** 559-222-1573 kbifkirv@aol.com

Fresno KJFX-FM (r) 1066 E Shaw Ave, Fresno CA 93710 **Phn:** 559-230-0104 **Fax:** 559-230-0177 www.957thefox.com carter957@wilksfresno.com

Fresno KJWL-FM (a) 1415 Fulton St, Fresno CA 93721 **Phn:** 559-497-5118 **Fax:** 559-497-9760 www.kjwl.com layne@940espnfresno.com

Fresno KKBZ-FM (h) 1110 E Olive Ave, Fresno CA 93728 **Phn:** 559-499-1051 **Fax:** 559-497-1125 www.1051theblaze.com kororke@lotusfresno.com

Fresno KLBN-FM (y) 1110 E Olive Ave, Fresno CA 93728 **Phn:** 559-490-1019 **Fax:** 59-497-1125 jguillen@lotusfresno.com

Fresno KLLE-FM (y) 1981 N Gateway Blvd # 101, Fresno CA 93727 **Phn:** 559-456-4000 **Fax:** 559-251-9555 www.univision.com jmitchell@univisionradio.com

Fresno KMAK-FM (y) 227 W Teague Ave, Fresno CA 93711 **Phn:** 559-217-9156

Fresno KMGV-FM (oh) 1071 W Shaw Ave, Fresno CA 93711 **Phn:** 559-490-5800 **Fax:** 559-490-4199 www.mega979.com jeff.davis@peakbroadcasting.com

Fresno KMJ-FM (a) 1071 W Shaw Ave, Fresno CA 93711 **Phn:** 559-490-5800 **Fax:** 559-490-5878 www.kmjnow.com skip@kmjnow.com

Fresno KMJ-AM (nt) 1071 W Shaw Ave, Fresno CA 93711 **Phn:** 559-490-5800 **Fax:** 559-490-5878 www.kmj580.com skip@kmjnow.com

Fresno KOKO-FM (u) 2775 E Shaw Ave, Fresno CA 93710 **Phn:** 559-292-9494 **Fax:** 559-294-7041 www.koko94.com hitradio@koko94.com

Fresno KQEQ-AM (d) 139 W Olive Ave, Fresno CA 93728 **Phn:** 559-499-1210 **Fax:** 559-499-1212

Fresno KRDA-FM (y) 601 W Univision Plz, Fresno CA 93704 **Phn:** 559-430-8500 **Fax:** 559-251-9555 www.univision.com anavarrete@univisionradio.com

Fresno KRZR-FM (r) 83 E Shaw Ave Ste 150, Fresno CA 93710 **Phn:** 559-230-4300 **Fax:** 559-241-6011 www.thebeat1037.com pd@krzr.com

Fresno KSJV-FM (vy) 5005 E Belmont Ave, Fresno CA 93727 **Phn:** 559-455-5777 **Fax:** 559-455-5778 www.radiobilingue.org

Fresno KSKS-FM (c) 1071 W Shaw Ave, Fresno CA 93711 **Phn:** 559-490-5800 **Fax:** 559-490-5838 www.ksks.com mac.daniels@peakbroadcasting.com

Fresno KSOF-FM (a) 83 E Shaw Ave Ste 150, Fresno CA 93710 **Phn:** 559-230-4300 **Fax:** 559-241-6011 www.softrock989.com mikebrady@clearchannel.com

Fresno KTQX-FM (vy) 5005 E Belmont Ave, Fresno CA 93727 **Phn:** 559-455-5777 **Fax:** 559-455-5778 www.radiobilingue.org

Fresno KUBO-FM (vy) 5005 E Belmont Ave, Fresno CA 93727 **Phn:** 559-455-5777 **Fax:** 559-455-5778 www.radiobilingue.org

Fresno KVPR-FM (pln) 3437 W Shaw Ave Ste 101, Fresno CA 93711 **Phn:** 559-275-0764 **Fax:** 559-275-2202 www.kvpr.org kvpr@kvpr.org

Fresno KWYE-FM (h) 1071 W Shaw Ave, Fresno CA 93711 **Phn:** 559-490-1011 **Fax:** 559-490-5889 www.y101hits.com mac.daniels@peakbroadcasting.com

Fresno KXEX-AM (y) 139 W Olive Ave, Fresno CA 93728 **Phn:** 559-233-8803 **Fax:** 559-233-8871 xco@att.net

Fullerton KBPK-FM (va) 321 E Chapman Ave, Fullerton CA 92832 **Phn:** 714-992-7165 www.kbpk-fm.com kbpk-fm@kbpk-fm.com

Glendale KFSH-FM (q) PO Box 29023, Glendale CA 91209 **Phn:** 714-520-0959 www.kfsh.com fishfeedback@thefish959.com

Glendale KKLA-FM (tq) PO Box 29023, Glendale CA 91209 **Phn:** 818-956-5552 **Fax:** 818-551-1110 www.kkla.com info@kkla.com

Glendale KLVE-FM (y) 655 N Central Ave Ste 2500, Glendale CA 91203 **Phn:** 818-500-4500 **Fax:** 818-500-4480 www.univision.com

Glendale KRCD-FM (yo) 655 N Central Ave Ste 2500, Glendale CA 91203 **Phn:** 818-500-4500 **Fax:** 818-500-4329 www.univision.com

Glendale KRCV-FM (yo) 655 N Central Ave Ste 2500, Glendale CA 91203 **Phn:** 818-500-4500 **Fax:** 818-500-4560 www.univision.com ojaramillo@univisionradio.com

Glendale KRLA-AM (t) PO Box 29023, Glendale CA 91209 **Phn:** 818-956-5552 **Fax:** 818-551-1110 www.am870theanswer.com info@krla870.com

Glendale KSCA-FM (y) 655 N Central Ave Ste 2500, Glendale CA 91203 **Phn:** 818-500-4500 **Fax:** 818-500-4329 www.univision.com

Glendale KTNQ-AM (y) 655 N Central Ave Ste 2500, Glendale CA 91203 **Phn:** 818-500-4500 **Fax:** 818-500-4307 www.univision.com

Grass Valley KNCO-AM (nt) 1255 E Main St Ste A, Grass Valley CA 95945 **Phn:** 530-272-3424 **Fax:** 530-272-2872 www.knco.com

Grass Valley KNCO-FM (a) 1255 E Main St Ste A, Grass Valley CA 95945 **Phn:** 530-477-9494 **Fax:** 530-272-2872 www.mystarradio.com greg@knco.com

Gualala KTDE-FM (a) PO Box 1557, Gualala CA 95445 **Phn:** 707-884-1000 **Fax:** 707-884-1229 ktde.com thetide@mcn.org

Hanford KIGS-AM (y) 6165 Lacey Blvd, Hanford CA 93230 **Phn:** 559-582-0361 **Fax:** 559-582-3981

Hayward KCRH-FM (v) 25555 Hesperian Blvd, Hayward CA 94545 **Phn:** 510-723-6954 **Fax:** 510-723-7155 www.kcrhradio.com programdirector@kcrhradio.com

Hesperia KVFG-FM (ho) 11920 Hesperia Rd, Hesperia CA 92345 **Phn:** 760-244-2000 **Fax:** 760-244-1198 910cbssports.cbslocal.com kimberly.martinez@cbsradio.com

Hoopa KIDE-FM (ve) PO Box 1220, Hoopa CA 95546 **Phn:** 530-625-4245

Hughson KAFY-AM (y) 4043 Geer Rd, Hughson CA 95326 **Phn:** 209-883-8760 **Fax:** 209-883-8769 www.lafavorita.net lafavorita@lafavorita.net

Hughson KBYN-FM (y) 4043 Geer Rd, Hughson CA 95326 **Phn:** 209-883-8760 **Fax:** 209-883-8769 www.lafavorita.net lafavorita@lafavorita.net

Hughson KNTO-FM (y) 4043 Geer Rd, Hughson CA 95326 **Phn:** 209-883-8760 **Fax:** 209-883-8769 www.lafavorita.net lafavorita@lafavorita.net

Inglewood KJLH-FM (wu) 161 N La Brea Ave, Inglewood CA 90301 **Phn:** 310-330-2200 **Fax:** 310-330-5555 www.kjlhradio.com

Inglewood KTYM-AM (qe) 6803 West Blvd, Inglewood CA 90302 **Phn:** 310-672-3700 **Fax:** 310-673-2259 www.ktym.com ktympublicaffairs@sbcglobal.net

Irvine KUCI-FM (v) PO Box 4362, Irvine CA 92616 **Phn:** 949-824-6868 www.kuci.org kuci@kuci.org

Joshua Tree KCDZ-FM (a) 6448 Hallee Rd Ste 5, Joshua Tree CA 92252 **Phn:** 760-366-8471 **Fax:** 760-366-2976 www.kcdzfm.com z1077fm@gmail.com

Joshua Tree KQCM-FM (h) PO Box 1437, Joshua Tree CA 92252 **Phn:** 760-362-4264 **Fax:** 760-362-4463

Joshua Tree KXCM-FM (c) PO Box 1437, Joshua Tree CA 92252 **Phn:** 760-362-4264 www.kxcmradio.com

CALIFORNIA RADIO STATIONS

Kernville KCNQ-FM (c) PO Box 2008, Kernville CA 93238 **Phn:** 760-376-4500 **Fax:** 760-376-3119 jamisonqabmedia@yahoo.com

Kernville KQAB-AM (t) PO Box 2008, Kernville CA 93238 **Phn:** 760-376-4500 **Fax:** 760-376-3119

Kernville KVLI-FM (o) PO Box 2008, Kernville CA 93238 **Phn:** 760-376-4500 **Fax:** 760-376-3119 jamisonqabmedia@yahoo.com

King City KRKC-AM (c) 1134 Broadway St, King City CA 93930 **Phn:** 831-385-5421 **Fax:** 831-385-0635 www.krkc.com bill@krkc.com

King City KRKC-FM (a) 1134 Broadway St, King City CA 93930 **Phn:** 831-385-5421 **Fax:** 831-385-0635 www.krkc.com bill@krkc.com

Lakeport KNTI-FM (a) PO Box 759, Lakeport CA 95453 **Phn:** 707-263-6113 **Fax:** 707-263-0939 www.knti.com pthomas@bicoastalmedia.com

Lakeport KQPM-FM (c) 140 N Main St, Lakeport CA 95453 **Phn:** 707-263-6113 **Fax:** 707-263-0939 www.kqpm.com

Lakeport KXBX-AM (am) PO Box 759, Lakeport CA 95453 **Phn:** 707-263-6113 **Fax:** 707-263-0939 www.kxbx.com amathews@bicoastalmedia.com

Lakeport KXBX-FM (a) PO Box 759, Lakeport CA 95453 **Phn:** 707-263-6113 **Fax:** 707-263-0939 www.kxbxfm.com mike@bicoastalmedia.com

Lakeside KECR-AM (qg) 11865 Moreno Ave, Lakeside CA 92040 **Phn:** 619-390-3481 **Fax:** 619-443-7693 www.familyradio.com billjeanne1@cox.net

Lancaster KAVL-AM (s) 352 E Avenue K4, Lancaster CA 93535 **Phn:** 661-942-1121 **Fax:** 661-723-5512 www.foxsports610.com

Lancaster KOSS-FM (a) 352 E Avenue K4 Ste B3, Lancaster CA 93535 **Phn:** 661-942-1121 **Fax:** 661-723-5512

Lancaster KTPI-AM (c) 352 E Avenue K4, Lancaster CA 93535 **Phn:** 661-942-1121 **Fax:** 661-723-5512 www.magic1340.com

Lancaster KTPI-FM (c) 352 E Avenue K4 Ste B3, Lancaster CA 93535 **Phn:** 661-942-1121 **Fax:** 661-723-5512 www.ktpi.com

Le Grand KEFR-FM (q) PO Box 52, Le Grand CA 95333 **Phn:** 209-389-4659 **Fax:** 209-389-0215 www.familyradio.com

Long Beach KFRN-AM (q) 3550 Long Beach Blvd Ste C, Long Beach CA 90807 **Phn:** 562-427-7773 **Fax:** 562-427-7723 www.familyradio.com

Long Beach KKJZ-FM (pnj) 1288 N Bellflower Blvd, Long Beach CA 90815 **Phn:** 562-985-2999 **Fax:** 562-985-2982 www.jazzandblues.org

Los Altos KFJC-FM (v) 12345 S El Monte Rd, Los Altos CA 94022 **Phn:** 650-949-7260 **Fax:** 650-948-1085 www.kfjc.org genmgr@kfjc.org

Los Angeles KABC-AM (t) 3321 S La Cienega Blvd, Los Angeles CA 90016 **Phn:** 310-840-4900 **Fax:** 310-840-4967 www.kabc.com victoria.avitia@cumulus.com

Los Angeles KAMP-FM (t) 5670 Wilshire Blvd Ste 200, Los Angeles CA 90036 **Phn:** 323-971-9710 **Fax:** 323-931-6872 amp.cbslocal.com amp@ampradio.com

Los Angeles KCBS-FM (ah) 5901 Venice Blvd, Los Angeles CA 90034 **Phn:** 323-937-9331 **Fax:** 323-931-5198 931jackfm.cbslocal.com jack@931jackfm.com

Los Angeles KDAY-FM (u) 5055 Wilshire Blvd Ste 720, Los Angeles CA 90036 **Phn:** 323-337-1600 **Fax:** 323-337-1633 www.935kday.com

Los Angeles KDLD-FM (h) 5700 Wilshire Blvd Ste 250, Los Angeles CA 90036 **Phn:** 323-900-6100 **Fax:** 323-900-6200

Los Angeles KDLE-FM (r) 5700 Wilshire Blvd Ste 250, Los Angeles CA 90036 **Phn:** 323-900-6100 **Fax:** 323-900-6200

Los Angeles KFWB-AM (n) 5670 Wilshire Blvd Ste 200, Los Angeles CA 90036 **Phn:** 323-525-0980 **Fax:** 323-930-8798 losangeles.cbslocal.com guimond@kfwb.cbs.com

Los Angeles KGIL-AM (nt) 1500 Cotner Ave, Los Angeles CA 90025 **Phn:** 310-478-5540 **Fax:** 310-445-1439 www.jazzandblues.org

Los Angeles KIRN-AM (i) 3301 Barham Blvd Ste 300, Los Angeles CA 90068 **Phn:** 323-851-5476 **Fax:** 323-512-7452 www.670amkirn.com pmozaffari@670amkirn.com

Los Angeles KKGO-FM (c) PO Box 250028, Los Angeles CA 90025 **Phn:** 310-478-5540 **Fax:** 310-445-1439 www.gocountry105.com mail@gocountry105.com

Los Angeles KLAX-FM (y) 10281 W Pico Blvd, Los Angeles CA 90064 **Phn:** 310-203-0900 **Fax:** 310-203-8989 979laraza.lamusica.com jhidalgo@sbslosangeles.com

Los Angeles KLOS-FM (r) 3321 S La Cienega Blvd, Los Angeles CA 90016 **Phn:** 310-840-4900 **Fax:** 310-840-4846 www.955klos.com

Los Angeles KLYY-FM (y) 5700 Wilshire Blvd Ste 250, Los Angeles CA 90036 **Phn:** 323-900-6100 **Fax:** 323-900-6200 www.jose975.com abecerra@entravision.com

Los Angeles KNX-AM (n) 5670 Wilshire Blvd Ste 200, Los Angeles CA 90036 **Phn:** 323-569-1070 **Fax:** 323-964-8329 losangeles.cbslocal.com knxnews@cbsradio.com

Los Angeles KRTH-FM (o) 5670 Wilshire Blvd Ste 200, Los Angeles CA 90036 **Phn:** 323-936-5784 **Fax:** 323-933-6072 kearth101.cbslocal.com promotions@kearth101.com

Los Angeles KSPN-AM (s) 800 W Olympic Blvd Ste A200, Los Angeles CA 90015 **Phn:** 213-284-7100 **Fax:** 213-284-7196 espn.go.comlos-angelesradio michael.f.thompson@espn.com

Los Angeles KSSC-FM (y) 5700 Wilshire Blvd Ste 250, Los Angeles CA 90036 **Phn:** 323-900-6100 **Fax:** 323-900-6200 www.superestrella.com kmeyer@entravision.com

Los Angeles KSSD-FM (y) 5700 Wilshire Blvd Ste 250, Los Angeles CA 90036 **Phn:** 323-900-6100 **Fax:** 323-900-6127 www.superestrella.com kmeyer@entravision.com

Los Angeles KSSE-FM (y) 5700 Wilshire Blvd Ste 250, Los Angeles CA 90036 **Phn:** 323-900-6100 **Fax:** 323-900-6127 www.superestrella.com

Los Angeles KTWV-FM (aj) 5670 Wilshire Blvd Ste 200, Los Angeles CA 90036 **Phn:** 323-937-9283 **Fax:** 323-634-0947 947thewave.cbslocal.com wave@947thewave.com

Los Angeles KUSC-FM (pl) PO Box 77913, Los Angeles CA 90007 **Phn:** 213-225-7400 **Fax:** 213-225-7410 www.kusc.org kusc@kusc.org

Los Angeles KWKU-AM (sny) 3301 Barham Blvd Ste 201, Los Angeles CA 90068 **Phn:** 323-851-5959 **Fax:** 323-512-7460 jrodriguez@kwkwradio.com

Los Angeles KWKW-AM (ys) 3301 Barham Blvd Ste 201, Los Angeles CA 90068 **Phn:** 323-851-5959 **Fax:** 323-512-7460 espn1330.com kwkw1330@aol.com

Los Angeles KXLU-FM (v) 1 Lmu Dr, Los Angeles CA 90045 **Phn:** 310-338-2866 **Fax:** 310-338-5959 www.kxlu.com lammosso@lmu.edu

Los Angeles KXOL-FM (y) 10281 W Pico Blvd, Los Angeles CA 90064 **Phn:** 310-229-3200 **Fax:** 310-203-8989 www.latino963.com pioferro@hotmail.com

Los Angeles KZMT-AM (l) PO Box 250028, Los Angeles CA 90025 **Phn:** 310-478-5540 **Fax:** 310-445-1439 www.kmozart.com kbiscaya@mountwilsoninc.com

Los Banos KLBS-AM (e) 401 Pacheco Blvd Ste A, Los Banos CA 93635 **Phn:** 209-826-0578 **Fax:** 209-826-1906 www.klbs.com pr@klbs.com

Los Banos KQLB-FM (y) 401 Pacheco Blvd, Los Banos CA 93635 **Phn:** 209-827-0123 **Fax:** 209-826-1906 www.kqlb.com sales@kqlb.com

Mammoth Lakes KMMT-FM (h) PO Box 1284, Mammoth Lakes CA 93546 **Phn:** 760-934-8888 www.kmmtradio.com kmmtradioworks@yahoo.com

Mammoth Lakes KRHV-FM (r) PO Box 1284, Mammoth Lakes CA 93546 **Phn:** 760-934-8888 **Fax:** 760-934-2429 www.kmmtradio.com kmmtradioworks@yahoo.com

Marysville KMYC-AM (nt) PO Box 669, Marysville CA 95901 **Phn:** 530-742-5555 **Fax:** 530-741-3758 www.syix.comkmyc kmyc@syix.com

Merced KABX-FM (o) 1020 W Main St, Merced CA 95340 **Phn:** 209-723-2191 **Fax:** 209-383-2950 www.975kabx.com

Merced KAMB-FM (q) 90 E 16th St, Merced CA 95340 **Phn:** 209-723-1015 **Fax:** 209-723-1945 celebrationradio.com kamb@celebrationradio.com

Merced KBKY-FM (a) 2855 G St, Merced CA 95340 **Phn:** 209-385-9994 **Fax:** 209-385-9982 sharon.nelson55@yahoo.com

Merced KBRE-FM (r) 1020 W Main St, Merced CA 95340 **Phn:** 209-723-2191 **Fax:** 209-383-2950 www.925thebear.com rgarrett@hotmail.com

Merced KHPO-FM (r) 1020 W Main St, Merced CA 95340 **Phn:** 209-723-2191 **Fax:** 209-383-2950

Merced KHTN-FM (h) 510 W 19th St, Merced CA 95340 **Phn:** 209-383-7900 **Fax:** 209-723-8461 www.hot1047fm.com hot1047email@aol.com

Merced KLOQ-FM (y) 1020 W Main St, Merced CA 95340 **Phn:** 209-723-2191 **Fax:** 209-383-2950 www.radiolobo987.com

Merced KTIQ-AM (yq) 1020 W Main St, Merced CA 95340 **Phn:** 209-723-2191 **Fax:** 209-383-2950

Merced KUBB-FM (c) 510 W 19th St, Merced CA 95340 **Phn:** 209-383-7900 **Fax:** 209-723-8461 www.kubb.com kubbemail@aol.com

Merced KYOS-AM (nt) 1020 W Main St, Merced CA 95340 **Phn:** 209-723-2191 **Fax:** 209-383-2950 www.1480kyos.com kyos@radiomerced.com

Mission Viejo KSBR-FM (vj) 28000 Marguerite Pkwy, Mission Viejo CA 92692 **Phn:** 949-582-4508 **Fax:** 949-347-9693 www.ksbr.org dkamber@saddleback.edu

Modesto KBBU-FM (y) 903 Kansas Ave Ste R, Modesto CA 95351 **Phn:** 209-526-5352

Modesto KCIV-FM (q) 1031 15th St Ste 1, Modesto CA 95354 **Phn:** 209-524-8999 **Fax:** 209-524-9088 www.bottradionetwork.com kciv@bottradionetwork.com

Modesto KESP-AM (st) 1581 Cummins Dr Ste 135, Modesto CA 95358 **Phn:** 209-766-5000 **Fax:** 209-593-7970 www.sportsradio970.com

CALIFORNIA RADIO STATIONS

Modesto KFIV-AM (nt) 2121 Lancey Dr, Modesto CA 95355 **Phn:** 209-551-1306 **Fax:** 209-551-1359 www.powertalk1360.com karafranklyn@clearchannel.com

Modesto KHKK-FM (r) 1581 Cummins Dr Ste 135, Modesto CA 95358 **Phn:** 209-766-5000 **Fax:** 209-522-2061 www.104thehawk.com 104.1thehawk@cumulus.com

Modesto KHOP-FM (a) 1581 Cummins Dr Ste 135, Modesto CA 95358 **Phn:** 209-766-5000 **Fax:** 209-522-2061 www.khop.com madden@khop.com

Modesto KJSN-FM (az) 2121 Lancey Dr, Modesto CA 95355 **Phn:** 209-551-1306 **Fax:** 209-551-1359 www.sunny102fm.com garymichaels@clearchannel.com

Modesto KMPH-AM (nt) 1192 Norwegian Ave, Modesto CA 95350 **Phn:** 209-527-8400 **Fax:** 209-526-0820 www.kmph840.com

Modesto KMRQ-FM (r) 2121 Lancey Dr, Modesto CA 95355 **Phn:** 209-551-1306 **Fax:** 209-551-1359 rock967.com donovanshort@townsquaremedia.com

Modesto KOSO-FM (a) 2121 Lancey Dr, Modesto CA 95355 **Phn:** 209-551-1306 **Fax:** 209-551-1359 www.hitradio929.com jackpaper95@gmail.com

Modesto KQOD-FM (x) 2121 Lancey Dr, Modesto CA 95355 **Phn:** 209-551-1306 **Fax:** 209-551-5319 www.mega100online.com tonybear@clearchannel.com

Modesto KRVR-FM (h) 961 N Emerald Ave Ste A, Modesto CA 95351 **Phn:** 209-544-1055 **Fax:** 209-544-8105 www.krvr.com theriver@krvr.com

Modesto KUYL-AM (q) 2121 Lancey Dr, Modesto CA 95355 **Phn:** 209-551-1306 **Fax:** 209-551-1359

Modesto KVIN-AM (m) 961 N Emerald Ave Ste A, Modesto CA 95351 **Phn:** 209-544-1055 **Fax:** 209-544-8105 kvin.net thevine@kvin.net

Modesto KWSK-AM (nt) 2121 Lancey Dr, Modesto CA 95355 **Phn:** 209-551-1306 **Fax:** 209-551-1359

Monterey KBOQ-FM (a) 60 Garden Ct Ste 300, Monterey CA 93940 **Phn:** 831-658-5200 **Fax:** 831-658-5299 www.b1039fm.com kallen@radiomontereybay.com

Monterey KCDU-FM (a) 60 Garden Ct Ste 300, Monterey CA 93940 **Phn:** 831-658-5200 **Fax:** 831-658-5299 www.1017thebeach.com thebeach1017@yahoo.com

Monterey KHIP-FM (r) 60 Garden Ct Ste 300, Monterey CA 93940 **Phn:** 831-658-5200 **Fax:** 831-658-5299 www.thehippo.com kallen@radiomontereybay.com

Monterey KIDD-AM (o) 5 Harris Ct Bldg C, Monterey CA 93940 **Phn:** 831-649-0969 **Fax:** 831-649-3335 z979fm.com bmoody@kwav.com

Monterey KKHK-FM (c) 60 Garden Ct Ste 300, Monterey CA 93940 **Phn:** 831-658-5200 **Fax:** 831-658-5299

Monterey KLOK-FM (y) 67 Garden Ct, Monterey CA 93940 **Phn:** 831-333-9735 **Fax:** 831-373-6700 www.tricolor995.com ascoby@entravision.com

Monterey KMBX-AM (q) 67 Garden Ct, Monterey CA 93940 **Phn:** 831-333-6767 **Fax:** 831-373-6700 www.jose1071.com ascoby@entravision.com

Monterey KNRY-AM (nst) 651 Cannery Row Ste 1, Monterey CA 93940 **Phn:** 831-372-1074 **Fax:** 831-372-3585

Monterey KSES-FM (y) 67 Garden Ct, Monterey CA 93940 **Phn:** 831-333-6767 **Fax:** 831-373-6700 www.jose971.com kmaciel@entravision.com

Monterey KWAV-FM (a) PO Box 1391, Monterey CA 93942 **Phn:** 831-649-0969 **Fax:** 831-649-3335 www.kwav.com bmoody@kwav.com

Monterey KYAA-AM (yt) 651 Cannery Row Ste 1, Monterey CA 93940 **Phn:** 831-372-1074 **Fax:** 831-372-3585

Monterey KYZZ-FM (ah) 5 Harris Ct Bldg C, Monterey CA 93940 **Phn:** 831-649-0969 **Fax:** 831-649-3335

Moraga KSMC-FM (vhc) PO Box 3223, Moraga CA 94575 **Phn:** 925-631-4252 www.stmarys-ca.edu/ksmc ksmc@stmarys-ca.edu

Morgan Hill KAZA-AM (yq) 1820 Cochrane Rd, Morgan Hill CA 95037 **Phn:** 408-778-8526 juansidhu@yahoo.com

Mount Shasta KNTK-FM (nt) 1934 S Mount Shasta Blvd, Mount Shasta CA 96067 **Phn:** 530-926-5946 **Fax:** 530-926-0830 www.kntk.net

Mount Shasta KZRO-FM (ro) 113 E Alma St, Mount Shasta CA 96067 **Phn:** 530-926-1332 **Fax:** 530-926-0737 www.zchannelradio.com zmail@zchannelradio.com

Napa KVON-AM (nt) 1124 Foster Rd, Napa CA 94558 **Phn:** 707-252-1440 **Fax:** 707-226-7544 www.kvon.com lsharp@winecountrybroadcasting.com

Napa KVYN-FM (a) 1124 Foster Rd, Napa CA 94558 **Phn:** 707-252-1440 **Fax:** 707-226-7544 www.993thevine.com lsharp@winecountrybroadcasting.com

National City KOCL-FM (y) 401 Mile Of Cars Way # 322, National City CA 91950 **Phn:** 619-474-9000 **Fax:** 619-474-9040

National City XLTN-FM (y) 401 Mile Of Cars Way # 370, National City CA 91950 **Phn:** 619-336-7800 **Fax:** 619-420-1092 1045radiolatina.com comentarios@104.5radiolatina.com

Needles KTOX-AM (nt) 100 Balboa St, Needles CA 92363 **Phn:** 760-326-4500 **Fax:** 760-326-6849

Nevada City KVMR-FM (v) 401 Spring St, Nevada City CA 95959 **Phn:** 530-265-9073 **Fax:** 530-265-9077 www.kvmr.org news@kvmr.org

North Hollywood KPFK-FM (pnt) 3729 Cahuenga Blvd, North Hollywood CA 91604 **Phn:** 818-985-2711 **Fax:** 818-763-7526 www.kpfk.org

Northridge KCSN-FM (pl) 18111 Nordhoff St, Northridge CA 91330 **Phn:** 818-677-3090 www.kcsn.org keith.goldstein@csun.edu

Oakdale KCBC-AM (q) 10948 Cleveland Ave, Oakdale CA 95361 **Phn:** 209-847-7700 **Fax:** 209-847-1769 www.770kcbc.com kcbcprogramming@velociter.net

Oakhurst KAAT-FM (y) 40356 Oak Park Way Ste F, Oakhurst CA 93644 **Phn:** 559-683-1031 **Fax:** 559-683-5488

Oxnard KDAR-FM (q) 500 E Esplanade Dr Ste 1500, Oxnard CA 93036 **Phn:** 805-485-8881 **Fax:** 805-656-5330 www.kdar.com jeff.hunter@kdar.com

Oxnard KLJR-FM (y) PO Box 6940, Oxnard CA 93031 **Phn:** 805-240-2070 **Fax:** 805-240-5960 terryj@radiolazer.com

Oxnard KMLA-FM (y) 355 S A St Ste 103, Oxnard CA 93030 **Phn:** 805-385-5656 **Fax:** 805-385-5690 www.lam1037.com willy@lam1037.com

Oxnard KOXR-AM (y) PO Box 6940, Oxnard CA 93031 **Phn:** 805-240-2070 **Fax:** 805-240-5960

Oxnard KSRN-FM (y) 200 S A St Ste 400, Oxnard CA 93030 **Phn:** 805-240-2070 **Fax:** 805-240-5960

Oxnard KSTN-FM (y) 200 S A St Ste 400, Oxnard CA 93030 **Phn:** 805-240-2070 **Fax:** 805-240-5960 radiolazer1029.com

Oxnard KXLM-FM (y) PO Box 6940, Oxnard CA 93031 **Phn:** 805-240-2070 **Fax:** 805-240-5960 radiolazer.com terryj@radiolazer.com

Palm Desert KESQ-AM (y) 42650 Melanie Pl, Palm Desert CA 92211 **Phn:** 760-568-6830 **Fax:** 760-568-3984 www.kesq.com ainiguez@kunamundo.com

Palm Desert KEZN-FM (a) 72915 Parkview Dr, Palm Desert CA 92260 **Phn:** 760-340-9383 **Fax:** 760-340-5756 ez103.cbslocal.com lee.douglas@cbsradio.com

Palm Desert KLOB-FM (y) 41601 Corporate Way, Palm Desert CA 92260 **Phn:** 760-341-5837 **Fax:** 760-837-3711 www.jose947.com lvasquez@entravision.com

Palm Desert KMRJ-FM (ar) 75153 Merle Dr #G, Palm Desert CA 92211 **Phn:** 760-320-4550 **Fax:** 760-341-7600 www.jammin995fm.com jammin995@markerbroadcasting.com

Palm Desert KPLM-FM (c) 75153 Merle Dr # G, Palm Desert CA 92211 **Phn:** 760-568-4550 **Fax:** 760-341-7600 www.thebig106.com kplm@dc.rr.com

Palm Desert KUNA-FM (y) 42650 Melanie Pl, Palm Desert CA 92211 **Phn:** 760-568-6830 **Fax:** 760-568-3984 ainiguez@kunamundo.com

Palm Desert KXPS-AM (st) 75-153 Merle Dr, Palm Desert CA 92211 **Phn:** 760-621-0100 **Fax:** 760-322-5493 team1010.com team1010kxps@gmail.com

Palm Springs KCLB-FM (r) 1321 N Gene Autry Trl, Palm Springs CA 92262 **Phn:** 760-322-7890 **Fax:** 760-322-5493 www.937kclb.com jennifer.shevlin@morris.com

Palm Springs KDES-FM (o) 2100 E Tahquitz Canyon Way, Palm Springs CA 92262 **Phn:** 760-325-2582 **Fax:** 760-322-3562 www.kdes.com gene@rrbroadcasting.com

Palm Springs KDGL-FM (h) 1321 N Gene Autry Trl, Palm Springs CA 92262 **Phn:** 760-322-7890 **Fax:** 760-322-5493 www.theeagle1069.com sean.flannigan@morris.com

Palm Springs KFUT-AM (y) 1321 N Gene Autry Trl, Palm Springs CA 92262 **Phn:** 760-322-7890 **Fax:** 760-322-5493 www.1270kfut.com info@desertradiogroup.com

Palm Springs KGAM-AM (snt) 2100 E Tahquitz Canyon Way, Palm Springs CA 92262 **Phn:** 760-325-2582 **Fax:** 760-322-3562 www.kgam.com stevekelly@rrbroadcasting.com

Palm Springs KJJZ-FM (j) 441 S Calle Encilia Ste 8, Palm Springs CA 92262 **Phn:** 760-320-4550 **Fax:** 760-320-3037 www.kjjz.com jimi24fitz@gmail.com

Palm Springs KKUU-FM (hx) 1321 N Gene Autry Trl, Palm Springs CA 92262 **Phn:** 760-322-7890 **Fax:** 760-322-5493 www.927kkuu.com bianca.fort@desertradiogroup.com

Palm Springs KNWH-AM (nt) 1321 N Gene Autry Trl, Palm Springs CA 92262 **Phn:** 760-322-7890 **Fax:** 760-322-5493 www.943knews.com charlie@knewsradio.com

Palm Springs KNWQ-AM (nt) 1321 N Gene Autry Trl, Palm Springs CA 92262 **Phn:** 760-322-7890 **Fax:** 760-322-5493 knewsradio.com charlie@knewsradio.com

Palm Springs KNWZ-AM (n) 1321 N Gene Autry Trl, Palm Springs CA 92262 **Phn:** 760-322-7890 **Fax:** 760-322-5493 www.943knews.com charlie@knewsradio.com

Palm Springs KPSI-AM (nt) 2100 E Tahquitz Canyon Way, Palm Springs CA 92262 **Phn:** 760-325-2582 **Fax:** 760-322-3562 www.newstalk920.com stevekelly@rrbroadcasting.com

CALIFORNIA RADIO STATIONS

Palm Springs KPSI-FM (a) 2100 E Tahquitz Canyon Way, Palm Springs CA 92262 **Phn:** 760-325-2582 **Fax:** 760-322-3562 www.mix1005.fm bradley@mix1005.fm

Palm Springs KPTR-AM (t) 2100 E Tahquitz Canyon Way, Palm Springs CA 92262 **Phn:** 760-325-2582 **Fax:** 760-322-3562 www.kptr1450.com gene@rrbroadcasting.com

Palm Springs KWXY-AM (z) 2100 E Tahquitz Canyon Way, Palm Springs CA 92262 **Phn:** 760-325-2582 **Fax:** 760-328-7814 www.kwxy.com fmichaels@rrbroadcasting.com

Palm Springs KWXY-FM (z) PO Box 5470, Palm Springs CA 92263 **Phn:** 760-328-1104 **Fax:** 760-328-7814 www.kwxy.com kwxynews@gmail.com

Palmdale KCEL-FM (y) 570 E Avenue Q9, Palmdale CA 93550 **Phn:** 661-947-3107 **Fax:** 760-373-1069 laquebuena961.com

Palmdale KGMX-FM (a) 570 E Avenue Q9, Palmdale CA 93550 **Phn:** 661-947-3107 **Fax:** 661-272-5688 www.kmix1063.com psa@highdesertbroadcasting.com

Palmdale KKZQ-FM (r) 570 E Avenue Q9, Palmdale CA 93550 **Phn:** 661-947-3107 **Fax:** 661-272-5688 www.edge100.com psa@highdesertbroadcasting.com

Palmdale KLKX-FM (r) 570 E Avenue Q9, Palmdale CA 93550 **Phn:** 661-947-3107 **Fax:** 661-272-5688 www.935thequake.com psa@highdesertbroadcasting.com

Palmdale KMVE-FM (h) 570 E Avenue Q9, Palmdale CA 93550 **Phn:** 661-947-3107 **Fax:** 760-373-1069 www.classictop401069.com

Palmdale KOSS-AM (nt) 570 E Avenue Q9, Palmdale CA 93550 **Phn:** 661-947-3107 **Fax:** 661-272-5688 www.newstalk1380.com psa@highdesertbroadcasting.com

Palmdale KQAV-FM (r) 570 E Avenue Q9, Palmdale CA 93550 **Phn:** 661-947-3107 **Fax:** 760-373-1069 www.935thequake.com

Palmdale KUTY-AM (nt) 570 E Avenue Q9, Palmdale CA 93550 **Phn:** 661-947-3107 **Fax:** 661-272-5688 www.lameramera1470.com psa@highdesertbroadcasting.com

Palmdale KWJL-AM (nt) 570 E Avenue Q9, Palmdale CA 93550 **Phn:** 661-947-3107 **Fax:** 661-272-5688

Pasadena KALI-FM (dt) 747 E Green St Ste 400, Pasadena CA 91101 **Phn:** 626-844-8882 **Fax:** 626-844-0156 www.mrbi.net

Pasadena KALI-AM (qy) 747 E Green St Ste 400, Pasadena CA 91101 **Phn:** 626-844-8882 **Fax:** 626-844-0156

Pasadena KAZN-AM (d) 747 E Green St Ste 101, Pasadena CA 91101 **Phn:** 626-568-1300 **Fax:** 626-568-3666 www.am1300.com

Pasadena KLTX-AM (qy) 136 S Oak Knoll Ave Ste 200, Pasadena CA 91101 **Phn:** 626-356-4230 **Fax:** 626-817-9851 www.nuevavida.com

Pasadena KMRB-AM (de) 747 E Green St Ste 208, Pasadena CA 91101 **Phn:** 626-773-1430 **Fax:** 626-792-8890 www.am1430.net

Pasadena KPCC-FM (pt) 1570 E Colorado Blvd, Pasadena CA 91106 **Phn:** 626-585-7000 **Fax:** 626-585-7916 www.scpr.org mail@scpr.org

Paso Robles KPRL-AM (snt) PO Box 7, Paso Robles CA 93447 **Phn:** 805-238-1230 **Fax:** 805-238-5332 www.kprl.com kprl@tcsn.net

Philo KZYX-FM (p) PO Box 1, Philo CA 95466 **Phn:** 707-895-2324 **Fax:** 707-895-2451 www.kzyx.org news@kzyx.org

Pleasanton KKDV-FM (a) 7901 Stoneridge Dr Ste 525, Pleasanton CA 94588 **Phn:** 925-455-4500 **Fax:** 925-416-1211 www.kkdv.com programming@kkdv.com

Pleasanton KKIQ-FM (a) 7901 Stoneridge Dr Ste 525, Pleasanton CA 94588 **Phn:** 925-455-4500 **Fax:** 925-416-1211 kkiq.com gm@kkiq.com

Point Reyes Station KWMR-FM (v) PO Box 1262, Point Reyes Station CA 94956 **Phn:** 415-663-8068 **Fax:** 415-663-0746 kwmr.org programming@kwmr.org

Porterville KTIP-AM (nt) 1660 N Newcomb St, Porterville CA 93257 **Phn:** 559-784-1450 **Fax:** 559-784-2482 www.ktip.com pk@ktip.com

Quincy KNLF-FM (qts) PO Box 117, Quincy CA 95971 **Phn:** 530-283-4145 **Fax:** 530-283-5135 www.knlfradio.com listener@knlfradio.com

Rancho Cucamonga KSPA-AM (c) 8729 9th St # 110, Rancho Cucamonga CA 91730 **Phn:** 909-483-1500 **Fax:** 909-483-1515 www.financialnewsandtalk.com contact@am1510kspa.com

Red Bluff KBLF-AM (mnt) PO Box 1490, Red Bluff CA 96080 **Phn:** 530-527-1490 kblfam.com calhunter@kblfam.com

Redding KESR-FM (h) 1588 Charles Dr, Redding CA 96003 **Phn:** 530-244-9700 **Fax:** 530-244-9707 www.1071bobfm.com rhealy@resultsradiomail.com

Redding KEWB-FM (h) 1588 Charles Dr, Redding CA 96003 **Phn:** 530-244-9700 **Fax:** 530-244-9707 www.power94radio.com jakeeasy@power94radio.com

Redding KFPR-FM (plnj) 603 N Market St, Redding CA 96003 **Phn:** 530-241-5246 www.kcho.org kchonews@csuchico.edu

Redding KHRD-FM (r) 1588 Charles Dr, Redding CA 96003 **Phn:** 530-244-9700 **Fax:** 530-244-9707 www.red1031.com dwilson@resultsradiomail.com

Redding KKXS-FM (st) 1588 Charles Dr, Redding CA 96003 **Phn:** 530-244-9700 **Fax:** 530-244-9707 www.xs961.com rhealy@resultsradiomail.com

Redding KLXR-AM (am) 1326 Market St, Redding CA 96001 **Phn:** 530-244-5082 **Fax:** 530-244-5698 klxr1230@yahoo.com

Redding KNCQ-FM (c) 1588 Charles Dr, Redding CA 96003 **Phn:** 530-244-9700 **Fax:** 530-244-9707 www.q97country.com

Redding KNRO-AM (snt) 3360 Alta Mesa Dr, Redding CA 96002 **Phn:** 530-226-9500 **Fax:** 530-221-4940

Redding KQMS-AM (nt) 3360 Alta Mesa Dr, Redding CA 96002 **Phn:** 530-226-9500 **Fax:** 530-221-4940 www.kqms.com jim@kqms.com

Redding KRDG-FM (o) 3360 Alta Mesa Dr, Redding CA 96002 **Phn:** 530-226-9500 **Fax:** 530-221-4940 www.koolgold1053.com

Redding KRRX-FM (r) 3360 Alta Mesa Dr, Redding CA 96002 **Phn:** 530-226-9500 **Fax:** 530-221-4940 www.106x.com clark@reddingradio.com

Redding KSHA-FM (a) 3360 Alta Mesa Dr, Redding CA 96002 **Phn:** 530-226-9500 **Fax:** 530-221-4940 kshasta.com don@kshasta.com

Redding KVIP-FM (q) 1139 Hartnell Ave, Redding CA 96002 **Phn:** 530-222-4455 **Fax:** 530-222-4484 www.kvip.org info@kvip.org

Redding KVIP-AM (q) 1139 Hartnell Ave, Redding CA 96002 **Phn:** 530-222-4455 **Fax:** 530-222-4484 www.kvip.org info@kvip.org

Redlands KCAL-FM (r) 1940 Orange Tree Ln Ste 200, Redlands CA 92374 **Phn:** 909-793-3554 **Fax:** 909-798-6627 www.kcalfm.com jparke@kcalfm.com

Redlands KMET-AM (snt) 700 E Redlands Blvd, Redlands CA 92373 **Phn:** 951-849-4644 www.kmet1490am.com kmet1490talkradio@yahoo.com

Redlands KOLA-FM (o) 1940 Orange Tree Ln Ste 200, Redlands CA 92374 **Phn:** 909-793-3554 **Fax:** 909-798-6627 www.kolafm.com gary@kolafm.com

Redlands KSGN-FM (q) 2048 Orange Tree Ln Ste 200, Redlands CA 92374 **Phn:** 909-583-2150 **Fax:** 909-583-2170 www.ksgn.com info@ksgn.com

Redway KMUD-FM (v) PO Box 135, Redway CA 95560 **Phn:** 707-923-2513 **Fax:** 707-923-2501 www.kmud.org news@kmud.org

Redway KMUE-FM (v) PO Box 135, Redway CA 95560 **Phn:** 707-923-2513 **Fax:** 707-923-2501 www.kmud.org news@kmud.org

Richmond KDIA-AM (g) 3260 Blume Dr Ste 520, Richmond CA 94806 **Phn:** 510-222-4242 **Fax:** 510-262-9054 www.kdia.com

Richmond KDYA-AM (g) 3260 Blume Dr Ste 520, Richmond CA 94806 **Phn:** 510-222-4242 **Fax:** 510-262-9054 www.gospel1190.net ministries@gospel1190.net

Ridgecrest KEDD-FM (y) 731 Balsam St, Ridgecrest CA 93555 **Phn:** 760-371-1700 **Fax:** 760-371-1824

Ridgecrest KLOA-FM (c) 731 Balsam St, Ridgecrest CA 93555 **Phn:** 760-371-1700 **Fax:** 760-371-1824 adelmanbroadcasting.com vgarcia@adelmanbroadcasting.com

Ridgecrest KLOA-AM (o) 731 Balsam St, Ridgecrest CA 93555 **Phn:** 760-371-1700 **Fax:** 760-371-1824 www.kloaam.com vgarcia@adelmanbroadcasting.com

Ridgecrest KRAJ-FM (a) 731 Balsam St, Ridgecrest CA 93555 **Phn:** 760-371-1700 **Fax:** 760-371-1824 www.theheat1009.com vgarcia@adelmanbroadcasting.com

Ridgecrest KSSI-FM (r) 1621 N Downs St, Ridgecrest CA 93555 **Phn:** 760-446-5774 **Fax:** 760-444-2729 www.kssifm.com kssirock@iwvisp.com

Ridgecrest KWDJ-AM (nt) 121 W Ridgecrest Blvd, Ridgecrest CA 93555 **Phn:** 760-384-4937 **Fax:** 760-384-4978

Ridgecrest KZIQ-FM (c) 121 W Ridgecrest Blvd, Ridgecrest CA 93555 **Phn:** 760-384-4937 **Fax:** 760-384-4978

Rio Vista KRVH-FM (v) 410 S 4th St, Rio Vista CA 94571 **Phn:** 707-374-6336 **Fax:** 707-374-6810

Riverside KDIF-AM (h) 2030 Iowa Ave Ste A, Riverside CA 92507 **Phn:** 951-684-1991 **Fax:** 951-274-4949 www.comedy1440.com

Riverside KGGI-FM (h) 2030 Iowa Ave Ste A, Riverside CA 92507 **Phn:** 951-684-1991 **Fax:** 951-784-1991 www.kggiradio.com bobridzak@clearchannel.com

Riverside KKDD-AM (m) 2030 Iowa Ave Ste A, Riverside CA 92507 **Phn:** 951-684-1991 **Fax:** 951-274-4949 music.disney.com bobridzak@clearchannel.com

Riverside KPRO-AM (q) 7351 Lincoln Ave, Riverside CA 92504 **Phn:** 951-688-1570 **Fax:** 951-688-7009 www.kpro1570.com

Riverside KUCR-FM (v) 691 Linden St, Riverside CA 92521 **Phn:** 951-827-3737 **Fax:** 951-827-3240 kucr.org

Rohnert Park KRCB-FM (pln) 5850 Labath Ave, Rohnert Park CA 94928 **Phn:** 707-584-2020 **Fax:** 707-585-1363 krcb.org

Roseville KIID-AM (m) 8265 Sierra College Blvd Ste 312, Roseville CA 95661 **Phn:** 916-780-1470 **Fax:** 916-780-1493 music.disney.com ginger.m.lundgren@disney.com

CALIFORNIA RADIO STATIONS

Sacramento KCCL-FM (h) 298 Commerce Cir, Sacramento CA 95815 **Phn:** 916-576-7333 **Fax:** 916-929-5330 1015khits.com rico@921khits.com

Sacramento KCTC-AM (s) 5345 Madison Ave, Sacramento CA 95841 **Phn:** 916-334-7777 **Fax:** 916-339-4559 www.espn1320.net writeus@espn1320.net

Sacramento KDND-FM (h) 5345 Madison Ave, Sacramento CA 95841 **Phn:** 916-334-7777 **Fax:** 916-339-4293 www.endonline.com kwong@entercom.com

Sacramento KEAR-FM (q) 4135 Northgate Blvd Ste 1, Sacramento CA 95834 **Phn:** 916-641-8191 **Fax:** 916-641-8238

Sacramento KFBK-AM (nt) 1545 River Park Dr # 500, Sacramento CA 95815 **Phn:** 916-929-5325 **Fax:** 916-929-2236 www.kfbk.com gennymclaren@clearchannel.com

Sacramento KFIA-AM (tq) 1425 River Park Dr Ste 520, Sacramento CA 95815 **Phn:** 916-924-0710 **Fax:** 916-924-1587 www.kfia.com info@kfia.com

Sacramento KFNO-FM (q) 4135 Northgate Blvd Ste 1, Sacramento CA 95834 **Phn:** 866-641-8191 **Fax:** 916-641-8238

Sacramento KGBY-FM (a) 1545 River Park Dr # 500, Sacramento CA 95815 **Phn:** 916-929-5325 **Fax:** 916-646-6864 www.kfbk.com news@kfbk.com

Sacramento KGRB-FM (y) 500 Media Pl, Sacramento CA 95815 **Phn:** 916-368-6300 **Fax:** 916-473-0143 www.adelantemediagroup.com

Sacramento KHLX-FM (or) 1440 Ethan Way Ste 200, Sacramento CA 95825 **Phn:** 916-929-5325 **Fax:** 916-929-2236 www.classic931.com paulboris@clearchannel.com

Sacramento KHTK-AM (s) 5244 Madison Ave, Sacramento CA 95841 **Phn:** 916-338-9200 **Fax:** 916-338-9208 sacramento.cbslocal.com byron.kennedy@cbsradio.com

Sacramento KHYL-FM (ox) 1545 River Park Dr #500, Sacramento CA 95815 **Phn:** 916-929-5325 **Fax:** 916-925-0118 www.v1011fm.com

Sacramento KKDO-FM (a) 5345 Madison Ave, Sacramento CA 95841 **Phn:** 916-334-7777 **Fax:** 916-339-4281 www.radio947.net feedback@radio947.net

Sacramento KKFS-FM (q) 1425 River Park Dr Ste 520, Sacramento CA 95815 **Phn:** 916-924-0710 **Fax:** 916-924-1587 www.1039thefish.com mivey@1039thefish.com

Sacramento KNCI-FM (c) 5244 Madison Ave, Sacramento CA 95841 **Phn:** 916-338-9200 **Fax:** 916-338-9208 kncifm.cbslocal.com byron.kennedy@cbsradio.com

Sacramento KNTY-FM (c) 1436 Auburn Blvd, Sacramento CA 95815 **Phn:** 916-646-4000 **Fax:** 916-925-7969 www.1019thewolf.com promotions@1019thewolf.com

Sacramento KQJK-FM (a) 1440 Ethan Way Ste 200, Sacramento CA 95825 **Phn:** 916-929-9370 www.937jackfm.com webmaster@937jackfm.com

Sacramento KRCX-FM (y) 1436 Auburn Blvd, Sacramento CA 95815 **Phn:** 916-646-4000 **Fax:** 916-646-1958 www.tricolor999.com promociones@tricolor999.com

Sacramento KRXQ-FM (r) 5345 Madison Ave # 1000, Sacramento CA 95841 **Phn:** 916-334-7777 **Fax:** 916-339-4293 www.krxq.net jfox@entercom.com

Sacramento KSAC-AM (k) 1425 River Park Dr Ste 520, Sacramento CA 95815 **Phn:** 916-924-0710 **Fax:** 916-924-1587 www.money1055.com scott.hamilton@salemcommunications.com

Sacramento KSAC-AM (g) PO Box 1228, Sacramento CA 95812 **Phn:** 916-553-3000 **Fax:** 916-553-3013

Sacramento KSEG-FM (r) 5345 Madison Ave, Sacramento CA 95841 **Phn:** 916-334-7777 **Fax:** 916-339-4559 www.eagle969.com brian@eagle969.com

Sacramento KSFM-FM (h) 280 Commerce Cir, Sacramento CA 95815 **Phn:** 916-923-6800 **Fax:** 916-929-5341 ksfm.cbslocal.com byron.kennedy@cbsradio.com

Sacramento KSSJ-FM (aj) 5345 Madison Ave, Sacramento CA 95841 **Phn:** 916-334-7777 **Fax:** 916-339-4281 www.radio947.net feedback@radio947.net

Sacramento KSTE-AM (t) 1440 Ethan Way Ste 200, Sacramento CA 95825 **Phn:** 916-929-5325 **Fax:** 916-925-6326 www.kste.com alaneisenson@clearchannel.com

Sacramento KTKZ-AM (nt) 1425 River Park Dr Ste 520, Sacramento CA 95815 **Phn:** 916-924-0710 **Fax:** 916-924-1587 www.am1380theanswer.com info@ktkz.com

Sacramento KWOD-FM (r) 5345 Madison Ave, Sacramento CA 95841 **Phn:** 916-339-5669

Sacramento KXJZ-FM (pnj) 7055 Folsom Blvd, Sacramento CA 95826 **Phn:** 916-278-8900 **Fax:** 916-278-8989 www.capradio.org info@capradio.org

Sacramento KXPR-FM (pln) 7055 Folsom Blvd, Sacramento CA 95826 **Phn:** 916-278-8900 **Fax:** 916-278-8989 www.capradio.org info@capradio.org

Sacramento KXSE-FM (y) 1436 Auburn Blvd, Sacramento CA 95815 **Phn:** 916-646-4000 **Fax:** 916-646-3237 www.jose1043.com slopez@entravision.com

Sacramento KYMX-FM (a) 280 Commerce Cir, Sacramento CA 95815 **Phn:** 916-923-6800 **Fax:** 916-923-9696 kymx.cbslocal.com bjackson@kymx.com

Sacramento KZZO-FM (a) 280 Commerce Cir, Sacramento CA 95815 **Phn:** 916-923-6800 **Fax:** 916-927-6468 now100fm.cbslocal.com chad.rufer@cbsradio.com

Salinas KDON-FM (h) 903 N Main St, Salinas CA 93906 **Phn:** 831-755-8181 **Fax:** 831-755-8193 www.kdon.com eric@kdon.com

Salinas KEXA-FM (a) 548 E Alisal St, Salinas CA 93905 **Phn:** 831-757-1910 **Fax:** 831-757-8015

Salinas KHDC-FM (v) 161 Main St Ste 4, Salinas CA 93901 **Phn:** 831-757-8039 **Fax:** 831-757-9854

Salinas KION-AM (h) 903 N Main St, Salinas CA 93906 **Phn:** 831-755-8181 **Fax:** 831-755-8193 www.1460kion.com markcarbonaro@clearchannel.com

Salinas KKMC-AM (ntq) 30 E San Joaquin St Ste 105, Salinas CA 93901 **Phn:** 831-424-5562 **Fax:** 831-424-6437 www.kkmc.com

Salinas KMJV-FM (y) PO Box 1939, Salinas CA 93902 **Phn:** 831-757-1910 **Fax:** 831-757-8015 romero_vicente@hotmail.com

Salinas KOCN-FM (or) 903 N Main St, Salinas CA 93906 **Phn:** 831-755-8181 **Fax:** 831-755-8193 www.1051kocean.com eric@kdon.com

Salinas KPRC-FM (yo) 903 N Main St, Salinas CA 93906 **Phn:** 831-755-8181 **Fax:** 831-755-8193 salinas.lapreciosa.com josevalenzuela@lapreciosa.com

Salinas KRAY-FM (y) 548 E Alisal St, Salinas CA 93905 **Phn:** 831-757-1910 **Fax:** 831-757-8015 romero_vicente@hotmail.com

Salinas KSEA-FM (y) 229 Pajaro St Ste 302D, Salinas CA 93901 **Phn:** 831-754-1469 **Fax:** 831-754-1563 www.campesina.net paco@campesina.net

Salinas KTGE-AM (y) 548 E Alisal St, Salinas CA 93905 **Phn:** 831-757-1910 **Fax:** 831-757-8015 sls.rcastro@mail.com

Salinas KTOM-FM (c) 903 N Main St, Salinas CA 93906 **Phn:** 831-755-8181 **Fax:** 831-755-8193 www.ktom.com rhondamccormack@clearchannel.com

Salinas KXSM-FM (y) 600 E Market St # 200, Salinas CA 93905 **Phn:** 831-422-5019 **Fax:** 831-422-5027 radiolazer935.com

Salinas KXZM-FM (y) 600 E Market St # 200, Salinas CA 93905 **Phn:** 831-422-5019 **Fax:** 831-422-5027 radiolazer.com

San Bernardino KAEH-FM (qy) 650 S E St, San Bernardino CA 92408 **Phn:** 909-381-0969 **Fax:** 909-381-5409

San Bernardino KCAL-AM (y) 1950 S Sunwest Ln Ste 302, San Bernardino CA 92408 **Phn:** 909-825-5020 **Fax:** 909-884-5844 lamexicana1410@radiolazer.com

San Bernardino KCXX-FM (r) 242 E Airport Dr Ste 106, San Bernardino CA 92408 **Phn:** 909-890-5904 **Fax:** 909-890-9035 www.x1039.com dirtyd@x1039.com

San Bernardino KRQB-FM (y) 1845 Business Center Dr Ste 106, San Bernardino CA 92408 **Phn:** 909-663-1961 **Fax:** 909-663-1996 quebuena961.estrellatv.com pgarza@lbimedia.com

San Bernardino KTIE-AM (t) 992 Inland Center Dr, San Bernardino CA 92408 **Phn:** 818-956-5552 **Fax:** 818-551-1710 www.590ktie.com info@am590theanswer.com

San Bernardino KVCR-FM (pn) 701 S Mount Vernon Ave, San Bernardino CA 92410 **Phn:** 909-384-4444 **Fax:** 909-885-2116 www.kvcr.org kvcrnews@gmail.com

San Bernardino KXRS-FM (y) 1950 S Sunwest Ln Ste 302, San Bernardino CA 92408 **Phn:** 909-825-5020 **Fax:** 909-884-5844 radiolazer.com

San Bernardino KXSB-FM (y) 1950 S Sunwest Ln Ste 302, San Bernardino CA 92408 **Phn:** 909-825-5020 **Fax:** 909-884-5844 radiolazer.com lazerbroadcasting@radiolazer.com

San Carlos KMKY-AM (m) 963 Industrial Rd Ste I, San Carlos CA 94070 **Phn:** 650-637-8800 music.disney.com

San Diego KBZT-FM (r) PO Box 889004, San Diego CA 92168 **Phn:** 619-297-9595 **Fax:** 619-543-1353 www.fm949sd.com gmichaels@fm949sd.com

San Diego KCBQ-AM (t) 9255 Towne Centre Dr Ste 535, San Diego CA 92121 **Phn:** 858-535-1210 **Fax:** 858-535-1212 www.kcbq.com info@kcbq.com

San Diego KEGY-FM (a) 8033 Linda Vista Rd, San Diego CA 92111 **Phn:** 858-571-7600 **Fax:** 858-571-0326 energy1037.cbslocal.com promotions@energy1037.com

San Diego KFMB-FM (a) 7677 Engineer Rd, San Diego CA 92111 **Phn:** 858-292-7600 **Fax:** 858-278-1394 www.sandiegojack.com sniff@kfmb.com

San Diego KFMB-AM (nt) 7677 Engineer Rd, San Diego CA 92111 **Phn:** 858-571-8888 **Fax:** 858-278-1394 www.760kfmb.com radiopromotions@kfmb.com

San Diego KGB-FM (r) 9660 Granite Ridge Dr, San Diego CA 92123 **Phn:** 858-292-2000 **Fax:** 858-279-9579 www.101kgb.com smoran@clearchannel.com

San Diego KHTS-FM (h) 9660 Granite Ridge Dr, San Diego CA 92123 **Phn:** 858-292-2000 **Fax:** 858-715-3333 www.channel933.com jimmysteele@clearchannel.com

CALIFORNIA RADIO STATIONS

San Diego KIFM-FM (aj) 1615 Murray Canyon Rd Ste 710, San Diego CA 92108 **Phn:** 619-291-9797 **Fax:** 619-543-1353 www.easy981.com mikev@easy981.com

San Diego KIOZ-FM (r) 9660 Granite Ridge Dr, San Diego CA 92123 **Phn:** 858-292-2000 **Fax:** 858-278-1394 www.rock1053.com shaunamoran@clearchannel.com

San Diego KLNV-FM (y) 600 W Broadway Ste 2150, San Diego CA 92101 **Phn:** 619-235-0600 **Fax:** 619-744-4300 www.univision.com

San Diego KLQV-FM (y) 600 W Broadway Ste 2150, San Diego CA 92101 **Phn:** 619-235-0600 **Fax:** 619-744-4300

San Diego KLSD-AM (s) 9660 Granite Ridge Dr, San Diego CA 92123 **Phn:** 858-292-2000 **Fax:** 858-715-3333 www.xtrasports1360.com bwilson@clearchannel.com

San Diego KMYI-FM (ahr) 9660 Granite Ridge Dr Ste 100, San Diego CA 92123 **Phn:** 858-292-2000 **Fax:** 858-715-3333 www.star941fm.com debbiewagner@clearchannel.com

San Diego KOGO-AM (nt) 9660 Granite Ridge Dr, San Diego CA 92123 **Phn:** 858-292-2000 **Fax:** 858-715-3333 www.kogo.com calbert@clearchannel.com

San Diego KPBS-FM (p) 5200 Campanile Dr, San Diego CA 92182 **Phn:** 619-594-6983 **Fax:** 619-594-3812 www.kpbs.org

San Diego KPRI-FM (a) 9710 Scranton Rd Ste 200, San Diego CA 92121 **Phn:** 858-678-0102 **Fax:** 858-320-7024 www.kprifm.com hjones@kprifm.com

San Diego KPRZ-AM (qt) 9255 Towne Centre Dr Ste 535, San Diego CA 92121 **Phn:** 858-535-1210 **Fax:** 858-535-1212 www.kprz.com heatherlloyd@kprz.com

San Diego KSDS-FM (j) 1313 Park Blvd, San Diego CA 92101 **Phn:** 619-388-3037 **Fax:** 619-388-3928 www.Jazz88.org markd@jazz88.org

San Diego KSON-FM (c) PO Box 889004, San Diego CA 92168 **Phn:** 619-291-9797 **Fax:** 619-543-1353 www.kson.com nick@kson.com

San Diego KUSS-FM (c) 9660 Granite Ridge Dr, San Diego CA 92123 **Phn:** 858-292-2000 **Fax:** 858-560-7267 www.957kissfm.com debbiewagner@clearchannel.com

San Diego KYXY-FM (a) 8033 Linda Vista Rd, San Diego CA 92111 **Phn:** 858-571-7600 **Fax:** 858-571-0326 kyxy.cbslocal.com marlo@kyxy.com

San Diego XEMO-AM (y) 5030 Camino De La Siesta Ste 403, San Diego CA 92108 **Phn:** 619-497-0600 **Fax:** 619-497-1019 www.uniradio.com contactus@uniradio.com

San Diego XHA-FM (y) 5030 Camino De La Siesta Ste 403, San Diego CA 92108 **Phn:** 619-497-0600 **Fax:** 619-497-1019 www.uniradio.com contactus@uniradio.com

San Diego XHRM-FM (a) 9660 Granite Ridge Dr Ste 200, San Diego CA 92123 **Phn:** 858-495-9100 **Fax:** 858-499-1750 www.magic925.com gwolfson@lmasandiego.com

San Diego XMOR-FM (y) 1027 10th Ave Ste C, San Diego CA 92101 **Phn:** 619-696-9902 **Fax:** 19-702-5570

San Diego XPRS-AM (sh) 6161 Cornerstone Ct E # 100, San Diego CA 92121 **Phn:** 858-535-2500 **Fax:** 858-202-0299 www.xxsportsradio.com jackevans@bcaradio.com

San Diego XTRA-FM (ry) 9660 Granite Ridge Dr Ste 200, San Diego CA 92123 **Phn:** 858-495-9100 **Fax:** 858-499-1805 www.xtrasports1150.com billlally@clearchannel.com

San Francisco KALW-FM (pn) 500 Mansell St, San Francisco CA 94134 **Phn:** 415-841-4121 **Fax:** 415-841-4125 www.kalw.org kalw@kalw.org

San Francisco KATD-AM (y) 44 Gough St # 301, San Francisco CA 94103 **Phn:** 415-978-5378 **Fax:** 415-978-5380 www.kiqi1010am.com

San Francisco KBLX-FM (a) 55 Hawthorne St Ste 900, San Francisco CA 94105 **Phn:** 415-284-1029 **Fax:** 415-764-1029 www.kblx.com kblxcomments@entercom.com

San Francisco KBRG-FM (y) 750 Battery St Ste 200, San Francisco CA 94111 **Phn:** 415-989-5765 **Fax:** 415-733-5766 www.univision.com

San Francisco KBWF-FM (s) 201 3rd St # 1200, San Francisco CA 94103 **Phn:** 415-957-0957 **Fax:** 415-356-8394 www.957thegame.com thegame@957thegame.com

San Francisco KCBS-AM (n) 865 Battery St, San Francisco CA 94111 **Phn:** 415-765-4000 **Fax:** 415-765-4080 sanfrancisco.cbslocal.com kcbsnewsdesk@cbs.com

San Francisco KDFC-FM (l) 201 3rd St Fl 12, San Francisco CA 94103 **Phn:** 415-546-8311 **Fax:** 415-546-8366 www.kdfc.com lmattson@kdfc.com

San Francisco KEST-AM (de) 145 Natoma St Ste 101, San Francisco CA 94105 **Phn:** 415-978-5378 **Fax:** 415-978-5380 www.kestradio.com kest1450@sbcglobal.net

San Francisco KFFG-FM (rh) 55 Hawthorne St Ste 1100, San Francisco CA 94105 **Phn:** 415-817-5364 **Fax:** 415-995-6867 www.kfog.com kfog@kfog.com

San Francisco KFOG-FM (r) 55 Hawthorne St Ste 1100, San Francisco CA 94105 **Phn:** 415-817-5364 **Fax:** 415-995-6867 www.kfog.com kfog@kfog.com

San Francisco KFRC-FM (h) 865 Battery St 2nd Fl, San Francisco CA 94111 **Phn:** 415-391-9970 **Fax:** 415-397-7655 sanfrancisco.cbslocal.com kcbscomments@kcbs.com

San Francisco KGO-AM (nt) 55 Hawthorne St, San Francisco CA 94105 **Phn:** 415-954-8100 **Fax:** 415-954-8686 kgoradio.com producers@kgoradio.com

San Francisco KIOI-FM (ux) 340 Townsend St Ste 5-101, San Francisco CA 94107 **Phn:** 415-975-5555 **Fax:** 415-975-5421 www.1013.com travisloughran@clearchannel.com

San Francisco KIQI-AM (y) 44 Gough St # 301, San Francisco CA 94103 **Phn:** 415-978-5378 **Fax:** 415-978-5380 www.kiqi1010am.com

San Francisco KISQ-FM (uo) 340 Townsend St, San Francisco CA 94107 **Phn:** 415-975-5555 **Fax:** 415-947-5375 www.981kissfm.com riccifiliar@clearchannel.com

San Francisco KITS-FM (r) 865 Battery St 2nd Fl, San Francisco CA 94111 **Phn:** 415-512-1053 **Fax:** 415-956-3314 live105.cbslocal.com liz@sfradio.cbs.com

San Francisco KKSF-FM (r) 340 Townsend St Ste 4, San Francisco CA 94107 **Phn:** 415-356-5500 **Fax:** 415-975-5471 www.talk910.com corycallewaert@clearchannel.com

San Francisco KKSF-AM (nt) 340 Townsend St Ste 5-101, San Francisco CA 94107 **Phn:** 415-975-5555 **Fax:** 415-538-5953 www.talk910.com corycallewaert@clearchannel.com

San Francisco KLLC-FM (a) 865 Battery St, San Francisco CA 94111 **Phn:** 415-765-4097 **Fax:** 415-781-3697 radioalice.cbslocal.com studio@radioalice.com

San Francisco KMEL-FM (u) 340 Townsend St Ste 5-106, San Francisco CA 94107 **Phn:** 415-538-1061 **Fax:** 415-538-1060 www.kmel.com

San Francisco KNBR-AM (snt) 55 Hawthorne St Ste 1100, San Francisco CA 94105 **Phn:** 415-995-6800 **Fax:** 415-995-6867 www.knbr.com lee.hammer@cumulus.com

San Francisco KNEW-AM (t) 340 Townsend St # 5-101, San Francisco CA 94107 **Phn:** 415-975-5555 **Fax:** 415-538-5953 www.960knew.com corycallewaert@clearchannel.com

San Francisco KOIT-FM (a) 201 3rd St Fl 12, San Francisco CA 94103 **Phn:** 415-777-0965 **Fax:** 415-896-0965 www.koit.com koit@koit.com

San Francisco KPOO-FM (v) PO Box 156650, San Francisco CA 94115 **Phn:** 415-346-5373 **Fax:** 415-346-5173 www.kpoo.com news@kpoo.com

San Francisco KQED-FM (pnt) 2601 Mariposa St, San Francisco CA 94110 **Phn:** 415-553-2241 **Fax:** 415-553-2118 www.kqed.org assignmentdesk@kqed.org

San Francisco KSAN-FM (r) 55 Hawthorne St Ste 1100, San Francisco CA 94105 **Phn:** 415-981-5726 **Fax:** 415-995-6867 www.1077thebone.com thebone@thebone.net

San Francisco KSFO-AM (t) 55 Hawthorne St Flr 11, San Francisco CA 94105 **Phn:** 415-398-5600 **Fax:** 415-391-3616 www.ksfo.com ruben.pimentel@cumulus.com

San Francisco KSOL-FM (y) 750 Battery St Ste 200, San Francisco CA 94111 **Phn:** 415-989-5765 **Fax:** 415-733-5766 www.univision.com mrojas@univisionradio.com

San Francisco KSQL-FM (y) 750 Battery St Ste 200, San Francisco CA 94111 **Phn:** 415-989-5765 **Fax:** 415-733-5766 www.univision.com

San Francisco KTCT-AM (s) 55 Hawthorne St Ste 1100, San Francisco CA 94105 **Phn:** 415-995-6800 **Fax:** 415-995-6867 www.knbr.com sports@knbr.com

San Francisco KTRB-AM (s) 380 Broadway # 8, San Francisco CA 94133 **Phn:** 415-362-8686 **Fax:** 415-391-6860 www.xtra860am.com suecker@ueckerassoc.com

San Francisco KVTO-AM (dei) 55 Hawthorne St Ste 900, San Francisco CA 94105 **Phn:** 415-284-1029 **Fax:** 415-764-4959 jaimea@inlanguageradio.com

San Francisco KVVF-FM (y) 750 Battery St Ste 200, San Francisco CA 94111 **Phn:** 415-989-5765 **Fax:** 415-733-5766 www.univision.com

San Francisco KVVN-AM (de) 55 Hawthorne St Ste 900, San Francisco CA 94105 **Phn:** 415-284-1029 **Fax:** 415-764-4959

San Francisco KVVZ-FM (y) 750 Battery St Ste 200, San Francisco CA 94111 **Phn:** 415-989-5765 **Fax:** 415-733-5766 www.univision.com

San Francisco KYLD-FM (h) 340 Townsend St Ste 4-949, San Francisco CA 94107 **Phn:** 415-356-0949 www.wild949.com tonyng@clearchannel.com

San Jose KBAY-FM (a) 190 Park Center Plz Ste 200, San Jose CA 95113 **Phn:** 408-287-5775 **Fax:** 408-293-3341 www.kbay.com djang@nextmediagroup.net

San Jose KCNL-FM (y) 1420 Koll Cir Ste A, San Jose CA 95112 **Phn:** 408-453-5400 **Fax:** 408-452-1330

San Jose KEZR-FM (a) 190 Park Center Plz Ste 200, San Jose CA 95113 **Phn:** 408-287-5775 **Fax:** 408-293-3341 www.mymix1065.com djang@nextmediagroup.net

San Jose KLIV-AM (n) 750 Story Rd, San Jose CA 95122 **Phn:** 408-293-8030 **Fax:** 408-995-0823 www.kliv.com gsampson@empirebroadcasting.com

San Jose KRTY-FM (c) 750 Story Rd, San Jose CA 95122 **Phn:** 408-293-8030 **Fax:** 408-293-6124 www.krty.com jstevens@empirebroadcasting.com

CALIFORNIA RADIO STATIONS

San Jose KSJO-FM (a) 2905 S King Rd, San Jose CA 95122 **Phn:** 408-440-0851 **Fax:** 408-440-0853 www.u923fm.com contact@u923fm.com

San Jose KSJS-FM (v) Hugh Gillis Hall Rm 132, San Jose CA 95192 **Phn:** 408-924-5757 **Fax:** 408-924-4558 www.ksjs.org ksjs@ksjs.org

San Jose KSJX-AM (e) 501 Wooster Ave # C, San Jose CA 95116 **Phn:** 408-280-1515 **Fax:** 408-280-1585 www.mrbi.net julier@mrbi.net

San Jose KSQQ-FM (ey) 1629 Alum Rock Ave Ste 40, San Jose CA 95116 **Phn:** 408-258-9696 **Fax:** 408-258-9770 www.ksqq.com pr@ksqq.com

San Jose KUFX-FM (r) 1420 Koll Cir Ste A, San Jose CA 95112 **Phn:** 408-452-7900 **Fax:** 408-452-8030

San Jose KZSF-AM (y) 3031 Tisch Way Ste 3, San Jose CA 95128 **Phn:** 408-247-0100 **Fax:** 408-247-4353 www.1370am.com reynasantillan@1370am.com

San Luis Obispo KCBX-FM (plnj) 4100 Vachell Ln, San Luis Obispo CA 93401 **Phn:** 805-549-8855 www.kcbx.org interact@kcbx.org

San Luis Obispo KCPR-FM (vr) Calif Polytech State Univ, San Luis Obispo CA 93407 **Phn:** 805-756-5998 kcpr.calpoly.edu generalmanagers.kcpr@gmail.com

San Luis Obispo KIQO-FM (o) 3620 Sacramento Dr # 206, San Luis Obispo CA 93401 **Phn:** 805-781-2750 **Fax:** 805-786-2828 www.q1045fm.com ksignorelli@americangeneralmedia.com

San Luis Obispo KKAL-FM (a) 3620 Sacramento Dr Ste 204, San Luis Obispo CA 93401 **Phn:** 805-781-2750 **Fax:** 805-786-2828 http:www.krush925.com kathy@americangeneralmedia.com

San Luis Obispo KKJG-FM (c) 3620 Sacramento Dr Ste 204, San Luis Obispo CA 93401 **Phn:** 805-781-2750 **Fax:** 805-781-2758 www.jugcountry.com kjug@jugcountry.com

San Luis Obispo KKJL-FM (am) PO Box 1400, San Luis Obispo CA 93406 **Phn:** 805-543-9400 **Fax:** 805-543-0787 www.kkjl1400.com carol@kjewel.net

San Luis Obispo KKJL-AM (am) PO Box 1400, San Luis Obispo CA 93406 **Phn:** 805-543-9400 **Fax:** 805-543-0787 www.fabulous1400.com carol@kjewel.net

San Luis Obispo KLFF-FM (q) PO Box 1561, San Luis Obispo CA 93406 **Phn:** 805-541-4343 **Fax:** 805-541-9101 www.klife.org info@klife.org

San Luis Obispo KPYG-FM (a) 795 Buckley Rd Ste 2, San Luis Obispo CA 93401 **Phn:** 805-786-2570 **Fax:** 805-547-9860 www.kpig.com manager@radiocentralcoast.com

San Luis Obispo KSLY-FM (c) 51 Zaca Ln Ste 100, San Luis Obispo CA 93401 **Phn:** 805-545-0101 **Fax:** 805-541-5303 sunnycountry.com jayturner@sunnycountry.com

San Luis Obispo KSTT-FM (a) 51 Zaca Ln Ste 100, San Luis Obispo CA 93401 **Phn:** 805-545-0101 **Fax:** 805-541-5303 www.kstt.com andrewcannon@edbroadcasters.com

San Luis Obispo KURQ-FM (r) 51 Zaca Ln Ste 100, San Luis Obispo CA 93401 **Phn:** 805-545-0101 **Fax:** 805-541-5303 www.newrock1073.com tristan@newrock1073.com

San Luis Obispo KVEC-AM (snt) 51 Zaca Ln Ste 100, San Luis Obispo CA 93401 **Phn:** 805-545-0101 **Fax:** 805-541-5303 www.920kvec.com king@920kvec.com

San Luis Obispo KWWV-FM (h) 795 Buckley Rd Ste 2, San Luis Obispo CA 93401 **Phn:** 805-786-2570 **Fax:** 805-547-9860 www.wild1061.com manager@radiocentralcoast.com

San Luis Obispo KXDZ-FM (h) 795 Buckley Rd Ste 2, San Luis Obispo CA 93401 **Phn:** 805-786-2570 manager@radiocentralcoast.com

San Luis Obispo KXTZ-FM (h) 795 Buckley Rd Ste 2, San Luis Obispo CA 93401 **Phn:** 805-786-2570 **Fax:** 805-547-9860 manager@radiocentralcoast.com

San Luis Obispo KZOZ-FM (r) 3620 Sacramento Dr # 206, San Luis Obispo CA 93401 **Phn:** 805-781-2750 **Fax:** 805-781-2758 www.kzoz.com drhoads@americangeneralmedia.com

San Marcos KKSM-AM (va) 1140 W Mission Rd, San Marcos CA 92069 **Phn:** 760-744-5576 www.palomar.edukksm

San Mateo KCSM-FM (pj) 1700 W Hillsdale Blvd, San Mateo CA 94402 **Phn:** 650-574-6586 **Fax:** 650-524-6975 kcsm.org alisa@kcsm.net

Santa Ana KWIZ-FM (y) 3101 W 5th St, Santa Ana CA 92703 **Phn:** 714-554-5000 **Fax:** 714-554-9362 larockola967.estrellatv.com kwizinfo@lbimedia.com

Santa Ana KWVE-FM (q) 3000 W Macarthur Blvd Ste 500, Santa Ana CA 92704 **Phn:** 714-918-6207 **Fax:** 714-918-6256 kwve.com brianperez@kwve.com

Santa Barbara KCSB-FM (v) PO Box 13401, Santa Barbara CA 93107 **Phn:** 805-893-3757 www.kcsb.org news@kcsb.org

Santa Barbara KDB-FM (l) PO Box 91660, Santa Barbara CA 93190 **Phn:** 805-966-4131 **Fax:** 805-966-4788 www.kdb.com bob@kdb.com

Santa Barbara KIST-AM (st) 414 E Cota St, Santa Barbara CA 93101 **Phn:** 805-879-8300 **Fax:** 805-879-8430 www.ktlkam.com j.d.freeman@clearchannel.com

Santa Barbara KIST-FM (y) 414 E Cota St, Santa Barbara CA 93101 **Phn:** 805-879-8300 **Fax:** 805-879-8430 www.radiobronco.com jose.fierros@rinconbroadcasting.com

Santa Barbara KJEE-FM (r) 302 W Carrillo St, Santa Barbara CA 93101 **Phn:** 805-962-4588 **Fax:** 805-963-8166 www.kjee.com kjee929@aol.com

Santa Barbara KRUZ-FM (a) 403 E Montecito St Ste A, Santa Barbara CA 93101 **Phn:** 805-966-1755 **Fax:** 805-560-6172 www.kruz.com max@cumulus.com

Santa Barbara KSBL-FM (a) 414 E Cota St, Santa Barbara CA 93101 **Phn:** 805-879-8300 **Fax:** 805-879-8430 www.ksbl.com lin.aubuchon@rinconbroadcasting.com

Santa Barbara KSPE-FM (y) 414 E Cota St, Santa Barbara CA 93101 **Phn:** 805-879-8300 **Fax:** 805-879-8430 www.radiobronco.com jose.fierros@rinconbroadcasting.com

Santa Barbara KTMS-AM (snt) 414 E Cota St, Santa Barbara CA 93101 **Phn:** 805-879-8300 **Fax:** 805-879-8430 www.990am.com lin.aubuchon@rinconbroadcasting.com

Santa Barbara KTYD-FM (r) 414 E Cota St, Santa Barbara CA 93101 **Phn:** 805-879-8300 **Fax:** 805-879-8430 www.ktyd.com keith.royer@rinconbroadcasting.com

Santa Barbara KZER-AM (y) 1330 Cacique St, Santa Barbara CA 93103 **Phn:** 805-963-7824 **Fax:** 805-965-7816

Santa Barbara KZSB-AM (nt) 1317 Santa Barbara St, Santa Barbara CA 93101 **Phn:** 805-568-1444 **Fax:** 805-966-3530

Santa Clara KKUP-FM (v) 933 Monroe St PMB 9150, Santa Clara CA 95050 **Phn:** 408-260-2999 www.kkup.org webmeister@kkup.org

Santa Clara KSCU-FM (v) 500 El Camino Real 3207, Santa Clara CA 95050 **Phn:** 408-554-4414 www.kscu.org traffic@kscu.org

Santa Clarita KHTS-AM (ant) 27225 Camp Plenty Rd Ste 8, Santa Clarita CA 91351 **Phn:** 661-298-1220 **Fax:** 661-298-2020 hometownstation.com info@hometownstation.com

Santa Cruz KFER-FM (vq) PO Box 13, Santa Cruz CA 95063 **Phn:** 831-464-8295

Santa Cruz KOMY-AM (o) 2300 Portola Dr, Santa Cruz CA 95062 **Phn:** 831-475-1080 **Fax:** 831-475-2967 komy.uncasnetworks.com

Santa Cruz KSCO-AM (nt) 2300 Portola Dr, Santa Cruz CA 95062 **Phn:** 831-475-1080 **Fax:** 831-475-2967 www.ksco.com ksconews@gmail.com

Santa Cruz KUSP-FM (p) 203 8th Ave, Santa Cruz CA 95062 **Phn:** 831-476-2800 **Fax:** 831-476-2802 www.kusp.org psa@kusp.org

Santa Cruz KZSC-FM (v) 1156 High St, Santa Cruz CA 95064 **Phn:** 831-459-2811 kzsc.org stationmanager@kzsc.org

Santa Maria KBOX-FM (a) 2325 Skyway Dr Ste J, Santa Maria CA 93455 **Phn:** 805-922-1041 **Fax:** 805-928-3069 www.1041pirateradio.com rwatson@americangeneralmedia.com

Santa Maria KIDI-FM (y) 718 E Chapel St, Santa Maria CA 93454 **Phn:** 805-928-4334 **Fax:** 805-349-2765

Santa Maria KLMM-FM (y) 312 E Mill St Ste 302, Santa Maria CA 93454 **Phn:** 805-928-9796 **Fax:** 805-928-3367 radiolazer.com

Santa Maria KPAT-FM (x) 2325 Skyway Dr Ste J, Santa Maria CA 93455 **Phn:** 805-922-1041 **Fax:** 805-928-3069 www.957thebeatfm.com rwatson@americangeneralmedia.com

Santa Maria KRAZ-FM (c) 1101 S Broadway Ste C, Santa Maria CA 93454 **Phn:** 805-922-7727 **Fax:** 805-349-0265 www.krazfm.com

Santa Maria KRQK-FM (y) 2325 Skyway Dr Ste J, Santa Maria CA 93455 **Phn:** 805-922-1041 **Fax:** 805-928-3069 www.1003laley.com estich@americangeneralmedia.com

Santa Maria KSBQ-AM (y) 312 E Mill St Ste 302, Santa Maria CA 93454 **Phn:** 805-928-9796 **Fax:** 805-928-3367

Santa Maria KSMA-AM (snt) 1101 S Broadway, Santa Maria CA 93454 **Phn:** 805-922-7727 **Fax:** 805-349-0265 www.am1440.com

Santa Maria KSNI-FM (c) 2215 Skyway Dr, Santa Maria CA 93455 **Phn:** 805-925-2582 **Fax:** 805-928-1544 www.sunnycountry.com jayturner@sunnycountry.com

Santa Maria KSYV-FM (a) 1101 S Broadway #C, Santa Maria CA 93455 **Phn:** 805-922-7727 **Fax:** 805-349-0265 www.mix96.com

Santa Maria KTAP-AM (y) 718 E Chapel St, Santa Maria CA 93454 **Phn:** 805-928-4334 **Fax:** 805-349-2765

Santa Maria KUHL-AM (snt) 1101 S Broadway Ste C, Santa Maria CA 93454 **Phn:** 805-922-7727 **Fax:** 805-349-0265 www.am1440.com

Santa Maria KXFM-FM (r) 2215 Skyway Dr, Santa Maria CA 93455 **Phn:** 805-925-2582 **Fax:** 805-928-1544 www.991thefox.com jennifergrant@edbroadcasters.com

Santa Monica KCRI-FM (p) 1900 Pico Blvd, Santa Monica CA 90405 **Phn:** 310-450-5183 **Fax:** 310-450-7172 www.kcrw mail@kcrw.org

Santa Monica KCRU-FM (p) 1900 Pico Blvd, Santa Monica CA 90405 **Phn:** 310-450-5183 **Fax:** 310-450-7172 www.kcrw.com mail@kcrw.org

Santa Monica KCRW-FM (pn) 1900 Pico Blvd, Santa Monica CA 90405 **Phn:** 310-450-5183 **Fax:** 310-450-7172 www.kcrw.com mail@kcrw.org

CALIFORNIA RADIO STATIONS

Santa Monica KMPC-AM (s) 2800 28th St Ste 308, Santa Monica CA 90405 **Phn:** 310-452-7100 **Fax:** 310-452-8010

Santa Rosa KBBF-FM (vy) PO Box 7189, Santa Rosa CA 95407 **Phn:** 707-545-8833 kbbf-fm.org info@kbbf-fm.org

Santa Rosa KJZY-FM (a) PO Box 100, Santa Rosa CA 95402 **Phn:** 707-528-4434 **Fax:** 707-527-8216 www.kjzy.com info@kjzy.com

Santa Rosa KMHX-FM (a) 1410 Neotomas Ave # 200, Santa Rosa CA 95405 **Phn:** 707-543-0100 **Fax:** 707-571-1097 www.mix1049fm.com danny@mysonomamedia.com

Santa Rosa KNOB-FM (a) 3565 Standish Ave, Santa Rosa CA 95407 **Phn:** 707-588-0707 **Fax:** 707-588-0777 winecountryradio.net bobfm@winecountryradio.net

Santa Rosa KRRS-AM (y) PO Box 2277, Santa Rosa CA 95405 **Phn:** 707-545-1460 **Fax:** 707-545-0112

Santa Rosa KRSH-FM (r) 3565 Standish Ave, Santa Rosa CA 95407 **Phn:** 707-588-0707 **Fax:** 707-588-0777 www.krsh.com bill@krsh.com

Santa Rosa KSRO-AM (snt) 1410 Neotomas Ave Ste 200, Santa Rosa CA 95405 **Phn:** 707-543-0100 **Fax:** 707-571-1097 www.ksro.com thenewguy@ksro.com

Santa Rosa KSXY-FM (h) 3565 Standish Ave, Santa Rosa CA 95407 **Phn:** 707-588-0707 **Fax:** 707-588-0777 www.allthehits.fm

Santa Rosa KTOB-AM (y) 1410 Neotomas Ave Ste 104, Santa Rosa CA 95405 **Phn:** 707-545-1460 **Fax:** 707-545-0112

Santa Rosa KVRV-FM (r) 1410 Neotomas Ave # 200, Santa Rosa CA 95405 **Phn:** 707-543-0100 **Fax:** 707-571-1097 www.977theriver.com

Santa Rosa KXFX-FM (c) 1410 Neotomas Ave Ste 200, Santa Rosa CA 95405 **Phn:** 707-543-0100 **Fax:** 707-571-1097 www.hot1017online.com

Santa Rosa KXTS-FM (y) 3565 Standish Ave, Santa Rosa CA 95407 **Phn:** 707-588-0707 **Fax:** 707-588-0777 winecountryradio.net alex@winecountryradio.net

Santa Rosa KZST-FM (a) PO Box 100, Santa Rosa CA 95402 **Phn:** 707-528-4434 **Fax:** 707-527-8216 www.kzst.com news@kzst.com

Seaside KAZU-FM (n) 100 Campus Ctr Bdg 201 Rm 315, Seaside CA 93955 **Phn:** 831-582-5298 **Fax:** 831-582-5299 www.kazu.org news@kazu.org

Sonora KKBN-FM (c) 342 S Washington St, Sonora CA 95370 **Phn:** 209-533-1450 **Fax:** 209-533-9520 www.kkbn.com jmarshall@clarkebroadcasting.com

Sonora KVML-AM (nt) 342 S Washington St, Sonora CA 95370 **Phn:** 209-533-1450 **Fax:** 209-533-9520 www.kvml.com news@clarkebroadcasting.com

Sonora KZSQ-FM (a) 342 S Washington St, Sonora CA 95370 **Phn:** 209-533-1450 **Fax:** 209-533-9520 www.kzsq.com

South Lake Tahoe KTHO-AM (st) 2520 Lake Tahoe Blvd Ste 5, South Lake Tahoe CA 96150 **Phn:** 530-543-0950 **Fax:** 530-543-1101 www.kthoradio.com ktho590@yahoo.com

Stanford KZSU-FM (v) PO Box 20190, Stanford CA 94309 **Phn:** 650-725-4868 **Fax:** 650-725-5865 kzsu.stanford.edu gm@kzsu.stanford.edu

Stockton KATM-FM (c) 3136 Boeing Way #125, Stockton CA 95206 **Phn:** 209-766-5103 **Fax:** 209-571-1033 www.katm.com

Stockton KCVR-AM (y) 6820 Pacific Ave # 3, Stockton CA 95207 **Phn:** 209-474-0154 **Fax:** 209-474-0316

Stockton KCVR-FM (y) 6820 Pacific Ave, Stockton CA 95207 **Phn:** 209-529-1900 **Fax:** 209-529-1528

Stockton KJOY-FM (a) 4643 Quail Lakes Dr Ste 100, Stockton CA 95207 **Phn:** 209-476-1230 **Fax:** 209-951-0033 www.993kjoy.com dirk.kooyman@cumulus.com

Stockton KLOC-AM (y) 6820 Pacific Ave, Stockton CA 95207 **Phn:** 209-529-1900 **Fax:** 209-529-1528 www.lafavorita.net lafavorita@lafavorita.net

Stockton KMIX-FM (y) 6820 Pacific Ave # 3, Stockton CA 95207 **Phn:** 209-474-0180 **Fax:** 209-474-0316 www.tricolor1009.com

Stockton KTSE-FM (y) 6820 Pacific Ave # 3, Stockton CA 95207 **Phn:** 209-474-0154 **Fax:** 209-474-0316 www.jose971.com

Stockton KWG-AM (q) 2280 E Weber Ave, Stockton CA 95205 **Phn:** 209-462-8307

Stockton KWIN-FM (h) 3136 Boeing Way # 125, Stockton CA 95206 **Phn:** 209-507-8500 www.kwin.com maui@kwin.com

Stockton KWNN-FM (h) 3136 Boeing Way # 125, Stockton CA 95206 **Phn:** 209-766-5000 www.kwin.com

Stockton KYCC-FM (qg) 9019 West Ln, Stockton CA 95210 **Phn:** 209-477-3690 **Fax:** 209-477-2762 www.kycc.org scott@kycc.org

Susanville KJDX-FM (c) 3015 Johnstonville Rd, Susanville CA 96130 **Phn:** 530-257-2121 **Fax:** 530-257-6955 sierradailynews.com rchambers@theradionetwork.com

Susanville KSUE-AM (nt) 3015 Johnstonville Rd, Susanville CA 96130 **Phn:** 530-257-2121 **Fax:** 530-257-6955 sierradailynews.com ruth@theradionetwork.com

Tahoma KSMH-AM (q) PO Box 180, Tahoma CA 96142 **Phn:** 530-584-5700 ihradio.com

Temecula KATY-FM (a) 27431 Enterprise Cir W # 101, Temecula CA 92590 **Phn:** 951-506-1222 **Fax:** 951-506-1213 www.1013themix.com jd@1013katy.com

Thousand Oaks KAJL-FM (a) 99 Long Ct Ste 200, Thousand Oaks CA 91360 **Phn:** 805-497-8511 **Fax:** 805-497-8514

Thousand Oaks KCLU-FM (vjnt) 60 W Olsen Rd # 4400, Thousand Oaks CA 91360 **Phn:** 805-493-3900 **Fax:** 805-493-3982 www.kclu.org jrondeau@callutheran.edu

Tulare KGEN-FM (y) 333 E San Joaquin Ave, Tulare CA 93274 **Phn:** 559-686-1370 **Fax:** 559-685-1394 kgen@sbcglobal.net

Tulare KMQA-FM (y) 1450 E Bardsley Ave, Tulare CA 93274 **Phn:** 559-687-3170 **Fax:** 559-687-3175

Turlock KCSS-FM (v) 1 University Cir, Turlock CA 95382 **Phn:** 209-667-3378 **Fax:** 209-667-3901 www.kcss.net sm@kcss.net

Ukiah KLLK-AM (nt) 1400 Kuki Ln, Ukiah CA 95482 **Phn:** 707-466-5868 **Fax:** 707-466-5852

Ukiah KMKX-FM (r) 1100B Hastings Rd, Ukiah CA 95482 **Phn:** 707-462-1483 **Fax:** 707-462-4670 www.maxrock.com info@maxrock.com

Ukiah KUKI-FM (c) 1400 Kuki Ln, Ukiah CA 95482 **Phn:** 707-466-5868 **Fax:** 707-466-5852 www.kukifm.com ukiah@bicoastalspots.com

Ukiah KUKI-AM (y) 1400 Kuki Ln, Ukiah CA 95482 **Phn:** 707-466-5868 **Fax:** 707-466-5852 www.kuki.com ukiah@bicoastalspots.com

Ukiah KWNE-FM (a) PO Box 1056, Ukiah CA 95482 **Phn:** 707-462-0945 **Fax:** 707-462-4670 www.kwine.com justin@kwine.com

Vacaville KUIC-FM (a) 555 Mason St Ste 245, Vacaville CA 95688 **Phn:** 707-446-0200 **Fax:** 707-446-0122 www.kuic.com programming@kuic.com

Van Nuys KTLW-FM (qt) 14820 Sherman Way, Van Nuys CA 91405 **Phn:** 818-779-8444 **Fax:** 818-779-8411 www.ktlw.net ktlwnews@ktlw.net

Ventura KBBY-FM (a) 1376 Walter St Ste 6, Ventura CA 93003 **Phn:** 805-642-8595 **Fax:** 805-639-0792 www.b951.com barbara.haser@cumulus.com

Ventura KCAQ-FM (h) 2284 S Victoria Ave Ste 2G, Ventura CA 93003 **Phn:** 805-289-1400 **Fax:** 805-644-7906 www.q1047.com bigbear@q1047.com

Ventura KFYV-FM (h) 2284 S Victoria Ave Ste 2G, Ventura CA 93003 **Phn:** 805-289-1400 **Fax:** 805-644-4257 www.live1055.fm psa@goldcoastbroadcasting.com

Ventura KHAY-FM (c) 1376 Walter St Ste 6, Ventura CA 93003 **Phn:** 805-642-8595 **Fax:** 805-639-0792 www.khay.com khaydave@khay.com

Ventura KOCP-FM (r) 2284 S Victoria Ave Ste 2G, Ventura CA 93003 **Phn:** 805-289-1400 **Fax:** 805-644-7906 www.rewind959.com

Ventura KRRF-FM (r) 1376 Walter St, Ventura CA 93003 **Phn:** 805-677-1063 www.1063thesurf.com charles.wolfe@cumulus.com

Ventura KVEN-AM (o) 1376 Walter St Ste 6, Ventura CA 93003 **Phn:** 805-642-8595 **Fax:** 805-639-0792 www.1450amespn.com charles.wolfe@cumulus.com

Ventura KVTA-AM (nt) 2284 S Victoria Ave Ste 2G, Ventura CA 93003 **Phn:** 805-289-1400 **Fax:** 805-644-7768 www.kvta.com tom@kvta.com

Ventura KVYB-FM (u) 1376 Walter St Ste 6, Ventura CA 93003 **Phn:** 805-642-8595 **Fax:** 805-656-5838 www.1033thevibe.com picazzo@1033thevibe.com

Victorville KATJ-FM (c) 12370 Hesperia Rd Ste 16, Victorville CA 92395 **Phn:** 760-241-1313 **Fax:** 760-241-0205 www.katcountry1007.com greg@thefox1065.com

Victorville KIXA-FM (r) 12370 Hesperia Rd Ste 16, Victorville CA 92395 **Phn:** 760-241-1313 **Fax:** 760-241-0205 thefox1065.com greg@thefox1065.com

Victorville KIXW-AM (t) 12370 Hesperia Rd Ste 16, Victorville CA 92395 **Phn:** 760-241-1313 **Fax:** 760-241-0205 www.talk960.com greg@thefox1065.com

Victorville KRSX-FM (o) 12370 Hesperia Rd Ste 16, Victorville CA 92395 **Phn:** 818-845-1027

Victorville KWRN-AM (y) 15165 Seventh St Ste D, Victorville CA 92395 **Phn:** 760-955-8722 **Fax:** 760-955-5751

Victorville KZXY-FM (a) 12370 Hesperia Rd Ste 16, Victorville CA 92395 **Phn:** 760-241-1313 **Fax:** 760-241-0205 www.y102fm.com coleenquinn@edbroadcasters.com

Visalia KARM-FM (q) 1300 S Woodland St, Visalia CA 93277 **Phn:** 559-627-5276 **Fax:** 559-627-5288 www.mypromisefm.com info@mypromisefm.com

Visalia KCRZ-FM (h) 1401 W Caldwell Ave, Visalia CA 93277 **Phn:** 559-553-1500 **Fax:** 559-627-1496 www.z1049.com randy@kjug.com

Visalia KDUV-FM (vq) 130 N Kelsey St Ste H1, Visalia CA 93291 **Phn:** 559-651-4111 **Fax:** 559-651-4115 www.spirit889.com spirit@spirit889.com

Visalia KIOO-FM (r) 1401 W Caldwell # 3, Visalia CA 93277 **Phn:** 559-553-1500 **Fax:** 559-627-1496 www.997classicrock.com askye@momentumbroadcasting.com

Visalia KJUG-FM (c) 1401 W Caldwell Ave, Visalia CA 93277 **Phn:** 559-553-1500 **Fax:** 559-627-1496 www.kjug.com studio@kjug.com

Visalia KJUG-AM (c) 1401 W Caldwell Ave, Visalia CA 93277 **Phn:** 559-553-1500 **Fax:** 559-627-1496 www.kjugam.com studio@kjug.com

Visalia KSEQ-FM (h) 617 W Tulare Ave, Visalia CA 93277 **Phn:** 559-627-9710 **Fax:** 559-627-1590 www.q97.com sterling@q97.com

Walnut KSAK-FM (vaj) 1100 N Grand Ave, Walnut CA 91789 **Phn:** 909-594-5611 **Fax:** 909-468-4449 mtrockradio.com ksak@mtsac.edu

Watsonville KPIG-FM (ar) 1110 Main St Ste 16, Watsonville CA 95076 **Phn:** 831-722-9000 **Fax:** 831-722-7548 www.kpig.com pd@kpig.com

West Sacramento KJAY-AM (i) 5030 S River Rd, West Sacramento CA 95691 **Phn:** 916-371-5101 **Fax:** 916-371-1459 kjay1430am@yahoo.com

Westminster KVNR-AM (de) 13749 Beach Blvd, Westminster CA 92683 **Phn:** 714-933-7888 **Fax:** 714-933-7808 www.littlesaigonradio.com

Yreka KSYC-FM (c) PO Box 1729, Yreka CA 96097 **Phn:** 530-842-4158 **Fax:** 530-842-7635 traffic@ksyc.net

Yuba City KKCY-FM (c) 861 Gray Ave Ste K, Yuba City CA 95991 **Phn:** 530-673-2200 **Fax:** 530-673-3010 www.kkcy.com ccarothers@resultsradiomail.com

Yuba City KMJE-FM (a) 861 Gray Ave Ste K, Yuba City CA 95991 **Phn:** 530-673-2200 **Fax:** 530-673-3010 www.gosunny.com newprod@syix.com

Yuba City KUBA-AM (n) 1479 Sanborn Rd, Yuba City CA 95993 **Phn:** 530-673-1600 **Fax:** 530-673-3010 www.kubaradio.com

COLORADO
Alamosa KALQ-FM (c) PO Box 179, Alamosa CO 81101 **Phn:** 719-589-6644 **Fax:** 719-589-0993 www.kgiwkalq.com info@kgiwkalq.com

Alamosa KASF-FM (vr) 208 Edgemont Blvd, Alamosa CO 81101 **Phn:** 719-587-7154 **Fax:** 719-587-7522 blogs.adams.edukasf kasf909fm@gmail.com

Alamosa KGIW-AM (o) PO Box 179, Alamosa CO 81101 **Phn:** 719-589-6644 **Fax:** 719-589-0993 www.kgiwkalq.com info@kgiwkalq.com

Alamosa KRZA-FM (p) 528 9th St, Alamosa CO 81101 **Phn:** 719-589-9057 **Fax:** 719-587-0032 www.krza.org news@krza.org

Aspen KAJX-FM (plnj) 110 E Hallam St Ste 134, Aspen CO 81611 **Phn:** 970-925-5259 **Fax:** 970-544-8002 www.kajx.org carolyne@aspenpublicradio.org

Aspen KNFO-FM (snt) 402 AABC Ste D, Aspen CO 81611 **Phn:** 970-925-5776 **Fax:** 970-544-9101 alwaysmountaintime.comknfo colleen@alwaysmountaintime.com

Aspen KPVW-FM (y) 20 Sunset Dr # C, Aspen CO 81621 **Phn:** 970-927-6902 **Fax:** 970-927-8001 www.denverhispanicradio.com sbernal@entravision.com

Aspen KSNO-FM (a) 225 N Mill St Ste L100, Aspen CO 81611 **Phn:** 970-925-4111 **Fax:** 970-925-7190

Aspen KSPN-FM (r) 402 Aspen Airport Business Ctr Ste D, Aspen CO 81611 **Phn:** 970-925-5776 **Fax:** 970-925-1142 alwaysmountaintime.comkspn colleen@alwaysmountaintime.com

Aspen KUUR-FM (a) PO Box 11657, Aspen CO 81612 **Phn:** 970-920-9600 **Fax:** 970-925-9245 www.aspenshines.com marcos@rodriguez.com

Aurora KBJD-AM (nt) 3131 S Vaughn Way Ste 601, Aurora CO 80014 **Phn:** 303-750-5687 **Fax:** 303-696-8063 www.710knus.com 710knus@710knus.com

CALIFORNIA RADIO STATIONS
Aurora KLTT-AM (qt) 2821 S Parker Rd #1205, Aurora CO 80014 **Phn:** 303-433-5500 **Fax:** 303-433-1555 www.670kltt.com kltt@crawfordbroadcasting.com

Aurora KLZ-AM (t) 2821 S Parker Rd # 1205, Aurora CO 80014 **Phn:** 303-433-5500 **Fax:** 303-433-1555 www.560thesource.com klz@crawfordbroadcasting.com

Aurora KNUS-AM (nt) 3131 S Vaughn Way Ste 601, Aurora CO 80014 **Phn:** 303-750-5687 **Fax:** 303-696-8063 www.710knus.com news@salemdenver.com

Aurora KRKS-AM (q) 3131 S Vaughn Way Ste 601, Aurora CO 80014 **Phn:** 303-750-5687 www.947krks.com kelly@salemdenver.com

Aurora KRKS-FM (q) 3131 S Vaughn Way Ste 601, Aurora CO 80014 **Phn:** 303-750-5687 **Fax:** 303-696-8063 www.947krks.com btaylor@salemdenver.com

Avon KKCH-FM (a) PO Box 7205, Avon CO 81620 **Phn:** 970-949-0140 **Fax:** 970-949-1464

Avon KSKE-FM (c) PO Box 7205, Avon CO 81620 **Phn:** 970-949-0140 **Fax:** 970-949-4318

Avon KTUN-FM (r) PO Box 7205, Avon CO 81620 **Phn:** 970-949-0140 **Fax:** 970-949-1464

Boulder KBCO-FM (r) 2500 Pearl St Ste 315, Boulder CO 80302 **Phn:** 303-444-5600 **Fax:** 303-449-3057 www.kbco.com brad@kbco.com

Boulder KGNU-FM (p) 4700 Walnut St, Boulder CO 80301 **Phn:** 303-449-4885 www.kgnu.org

Boulder KVCU-AM (t) Campus Box 207, Boulder CO 80309 **Phn:** 303-492-5031 **Fax:** 303-492-1369 www.radio1190.org hwarner@radio1190.org

Breckenridge KRKY-AM (c) PO Box 7069, Breckenridge CO 80424 **Phn:** 970-453-2234 **Fax:** 970-453-5425

Breckenridge KSMT-FM (r) PO Box 7069, Breckenridge CO 80424 **Phn:** 970-453-2234 **Fax:** 970-453-5425 www.ksmtradio.com ksmt@colorado.net

Breckenridge KZMV-FM (c) PO Box 7069, Breckenridge CO 80424 **Phn:** 970-453-2234 **Fax:** 970-453-5425

Burlington KNAB-AM (am) PO Box 516, Burlington CO 80807 **Phn:** 719-346-8600 **Fax:** 719-346-8656

Burlington KNAB-FM (c) PO Box 516, Burlington CO 80807 **Phn:** 719-346-8600 **Fax:** 719-346-8656

Canon City KRLN-AM (nt) 1615 Central Ave, Canon City CO 81212 **Phn:** 719-275-7488 **Fax:** 719-275-5132

Canon City KSTY-FM (c) 1615 Central Ave, Canon City CO 81212 **Phn:** 719-275-7488 **Fax:** 719-275-5132

Carbondale KDNK-FM (p) PO Box 1388, Carbondale CO 81623 **Phn:** 970-963-0139 **Fax:** 970-963-0810 www.kdnk.org news@kdnk.org

Centennial KCFP-FM (pln) 7409 S Alton Ct, Centennial CO 80112 **Phn:** 303-871-9191 www.cpr.org

Centennial KCFR-FM (pln) 7409 S Alton Ct, Centennial CO 80112 **Phn:** 303-871-9191 **Fax:** 303-733-3319 www.cpr.org

Centennial KKPC-AM (nt) 7409 S Alton Ct, Centennial CO 80112 **Phn:** 303-871-9191 **Fax:** 303-733-3319 www.cpr.org

Centennial KPRE-FM (pln) 7409 S Alton Ct, Centennial CO 80112 **Phn:** 303-871-9191 **Fax:** 303-733-3319 www.cpr.org

Centennial KPRH-FM (pln) 7409 S Alton Ct, Centennial CO 80112 **Phn:** 303-871-9191 www.cpr.org

Centennial KVOD-FM (pl) 7409 S Alton Ct, Centennial CO 80112 **Phn:** 303-871-9191 **Fax:** 303-733-3319 www.cpr.org

Colorado Springs KATC-FM (c) 6805 Corporate Dr Ste 130, Colorado Springs CO 80919 **Phn:** 719-593-2700 **Fax:** 719-593-2727 www.catcountry951.com bobby.irwin@cumulus.com

Colorado Springs KBIQ-FM (q) 7150 Campus Dr Ste 150, Colorado Springs CO 80920 **Phn:** 719-531-5438 **Fax:** 719-531-5588 www.kbiqradio.com kim@kbiqradio.com

Colorado Springs KCBR-AM (q) 5050 Edison Ave Ste 218, Colorado Springs CO 80915 **Phn:** 719-570-1530 **Fax:** 719-570-1007

Colorado Springs KCCY-FM (c) 2864 S Circle Dr Ste 150, Colorado Springs CO 80906 **Phn:** 719-540-9200 **Fax:** 719-579-0882 www.y969.com adamburnes@clearchannel.com

Colorado Springs KCME-FM (vl) 1921 N Weber St, Colorado Springs CO 80907 **Phn:** 719-578-5263 **Fax:** 719-578-1033 www.kcme.org gm@kcme.org

Colorado Springs KCMN-AM (am) 5050 Edison Ave Ste 218, Colorado Springs CO 80915 **Phn:** 719-570-1530 **Fax:** 719-570-1007

Colorado Springs KCSF-AM (s) 6805 Corporate Dr Ste 130, Colorado Springs CO 80919 **Phn:** 719-593-2700 **Fax:** 719-593-2727 www.theanimal1300.com bobby.irwin@cumulus.com

Colorado Springs KDZA-FM (r) 2864 S Circle Dr # 300, Colorado Springs CO 80906 **Phn:** 719-540-9200 www.z1079rocks.com paulkelley@clearchannel.com

Colorado Springs KEPC-FM (v) 5675 S Academy Blvd, Colorado Springs CO 80906 **Phn:** 719-502-3128 www.ppcc.edunewskepc-897-fm kepc@ppcc.edu

Colorado Springs KGFT-FM (qnt) 7150 Campus Dr Ste 150, Colorado Springs CO 80920 **Phn:** 719-531-5438 **Fax:** 719-531-5588 www.kgftradio.com mgoodyear@kbiqradio.com

Colorado Springs KIBT-FM (h) 2864 S Circle Dr Ste 150, Colorado Springs CO 80906 **Phn:** 719-540-9200 **Fax:** 719-579-0882 www.beatcolorado.com davidblack@clearchannel.com

Colorado Springs KILO-FM (r) 1805 E Cheyenne Rd, Colorado Springs CO 80905 **Phn:** 719-634-4896 **Fax:** 719-634-5837 www.kilo943.com kilostudio@kilo943.com

Colorado Springs KKFM-FM (r) 6805 Corporate Dr Ste 130, Colorado Springs CO 80919 **Phn:** 719-593-2700 **Fax:** 719-593-2727 www.kkfm.com bobby.irwin@cumulus.com

Colorado Springs KKLI-FM (a) 2864 S Circle Dr Ste 150, Colorado Springs CO 80906 **Phn:** 719-540-9200 **Fax:** 719-579-0882 www.klite1063.com davidblack@clearchannel.com

Colorado Springs KKMG-FM (h) 6805 Corporate Dr Ste 130, Colorado Springs CO 80919 **Phn:** 719-593-2700 **Fax:** 719-593-2727 www.989magicfm.com bobby.irwin@cumulus.com

Colorado Springs KKPK-FM (a) 6805 Corporate Dr Ste 130, Colorado Springs CO 80919 **Phn:** 719-593-2700 **Fax:** 719-593-2727 bobby.irwin@cumulus.com

Colorado Springs KRCC-FM (pn) 912 N Weber St, Colorado Springs CO 80903 **Phn:** 719-473-4801 **Fax:** 719-473-7863 www.krcc.org jeff@krcc.org

Colorado Springs KRDO-FM (n) 399 S 8th St, Colorado Springs CO 80905 **Phn:** 719-632-1515 **Fax:** 719-475-0815 www.krdo.com radionews@krdo.com

Colorado Springs KRDO-AM (s) 399 S 8th St, Colorado Springs CO 80905 **Phn:** 719-632-1515 **Fax:** 719-475-0815 www.krdo.com krdonews@krdo.com

COLORADO RADIO STATIONS

Colorado Springs KRXP-FM (r) 1805 E Cheyenne Rd, Colorado Springs CO 80905 **Phn:** 719-634-4896 **Fax:** 719-634-5837 www.1039rxp.com

Colorado Springs KTPL-FM (q) 1665 Briargate Blvd Ste 100, Colorado Springs CO 80920 **Phn:** 719-593-0600 **Fax:** 719-593-2399

Colorado Springs KVOR-AM (nt) 6805 Corporate Dr Ste 130, Colorado Springs CO 80919 **Phn:** 719-593-2700 **Fax:** 719-593-2727 www.kvor.com bobby.irwin@cumulus.com

Colorado Springs KVUU-FM (a) 2864 S Circle Dr Ste 150, Colorado Springs CO 80906 **Phn:** 719-540-9200 **Fax:** 719-579-0882 www.my999radio.com chrispickett@clearchannel.com

Colorado Springs KZNT-AM (nt) 7150 Campus Dr Ste 150, Colorado Springs CO 80920 **Phn:** 719-531-5438 **Fax:** 719-531-5588 www.kzntradio.com

Cortez KRTZ-FM (a) 2402 Hawkins St, Cortez CO 81321 **Phn:** 970-565-6565 **Fax:** 970-565-8567 www.krtzradio.com radio@krtzradio.com

Cortez KSJD-FM (vr) PO Box 116, Cortez CO 81321 **Phn:** 970-564-9727 **Fax:** 970-516-1927 www.ksjd.org

Craig KRAI-AM (c) 1111 W Victory Way Ste 105, Craig CO 81625 **Phn:** 970-824-6574 **Fax:** 970-826-4581 krai.com krai@krai.com

Craig KRAI-FM (a) 1111 W Victory Way Ste 105, Craig CO 81625 **Phn:** 970-824-6574 **Fax:** 970-826-4581 krai.com traffic@krai.com

Crested Butte KBUT-FM (v) PO Box 308, Crested Butte CO 81224 **Phn:** 970-349-5225 **Fax:** 970-349-6440 www.kbut.org kbut@kbut.org

Denver KALC-FM (ah) 4700 S Syracuse St Ste 1050, Denver CO 80237 **Phn:** 303-967-2700 **Fax:** 303-967-2747 www.alice1059.com mrpeterson@entercom.com

Denver KBNO-AM (y) 600 Grant St Ste 600, Denver CO 80203 **Phn:** 303-733-5266 **Fax:** 303-733-5242 www.radioquebueno.com zee@kbno.net

Denver KBPI-FM (r) 4695 S Monaco St, Denver CO 80237 **Phn:** 303-713-8000 **Fax:** 303-713-8743 www.kbpi.com nick@clearchannel.com

Denver KEZW-AM (m) 4700 S Syracuse St Ste 1050, Denver CO 80237 **Phn:** 303-967-2700 **Fax:** 303-967-2747 www.studio1430.com rc1430@comcast.net

Denver KHOW-AM (nt) 4695 S Monaco St, Denver CO 80237 **Phn:** 303-713-8000 **Fax:** 303-713-8509 www.khow.com danmandis@clearchannel.com

Denver KIMN-FM (a) 720 S Colorado Blvd # 1200N, Denver CO 80246 **Phn:** 303-832-5665 **Fax:** 303-832-7000 www.mix100.com

Denver KJMN-FM (y) 777 Grant St Fl 5, Denver CO 80203 **Phn:** 303-832-0050 **Fax:** 303-721-1435 www.jose921.com mcarrera@entravision.com

Denver KKZN-AM (st) 4695 S Monaco St, Denver CO 80237 **Phn:** 303-713-8000 **Fax:** 303-713-8424 www.am760.net donnahendricks@clearchannel.com

Denver KLDC-AM (qg) 2150 W 29th Ave Ste 300, Denver CO 80211 **Phn:** 303-433-5500 **Fax:** 303-433-1555 www.crawfordbroadcasting.com info@crawfordbroadcasting.com

Denver KLVZ-AM (ynt) 2150 W 29th Ave Ste 300, Denver CO 80211 **Phn:** 303-433-5500 **Fax:** 303-433-1555 www.crawfordbroadcasting.com info@crawfordbroadcasting.com

Denver KMXA-AM (y) 1907 Mile High Stadium W Cir, Denver CO 80204 **Phn:** 303-832-0050 **Fax:** 303-721-1435 www.965tricolor.com

Denver KOA-AM (snt) 4695 S Monaco St, Denver CO 80237 **Phn:** 303-713-8000 **Fax:** 303-713-8424 www.850koa.com patconnor@clearchannel.com

Denver KOSI-FM (a) 4700 S Syracuse St Ste 1050, Denver CO 80237 **Phn:** 303-967-2700 **Fax:** 303-967-2747 www.kosi101.com mrpeterson@entercom.com

Denver KPTT-FM (h) 4695 S Monaco St, Denver CO 80237 **Phn:** 303-713-8000 **Fax:** 303-713-8743 www.957theparty.com

Denver KQMT-FM (r) 4700 S Syracuse St Ste 1050, Denver CO 80237 **Phn:** 303-967-2700 **Fax:** 303-967-2747 www.995themountain.com sam@alice1059.com

Denver KRFX-FM (r) 4695 S Monaco St, Denver CO 80237 **Phn:** 303-713-8000 **Fax:** 303-713-8509 www.thefox.com robbynhart@clearchannel.com

Denver KTCL-FM (r) 4695 S Monaco St, Denver CO 80237 **Phn:** 303-713-8000 www.area93.com nerf@clearchannel.com

Denver KUVO-FM (pj) PO Box 2040, Denver CO 80201 **Phn:** 303-480-9272 **Fax:** 303-291-0757 www.kuvo.org denise@kuvo.org

Denver KWOF-FM (c) 1560 Broadway Ste 1100, Denver CO 80202 **Phn:** 303-832-5665 **Fax:** 303-832-7000 www.925thewolf.com begger@wilksdenver.com

Denver KXKL-FM (o) 720 S Colorado Blvd #1200N, Denver CO 80246 **Phn:** 303-832-5665 **Fax:** 303-832-7000 www.kool105.com

Denver KXPK-FM (y) 777 Grant St Fl 5, Denver CO 80203 **Phn:** 303-832-0500 **Fax:** 303-721-1435 www.denverse.com mcarrera@entravision.com

Durango KDGO-AM (t) 1911 Main Ave Ste 100, Durango CO 81301 **Phn:** 970-247-1240 **Fax:** 970-247-1771 www.kdgoradio.com bkruger@americangeneralmedia.com

Durango KDUR-FM (v) 1000 Rim Dr, Durango CO 81301 **Phn:** 970-247-7262 **Fax:** 970-247-7487 www.kdur.org kdur_pd@fortlewis.edu

Durango KIQX-FM (a) 190 Turner Dr Unit G, Durango CO 81303 **Phn:** 970-259-4444 **Fax:** 970-247-1005 www.radiodurango.com ward@radiodurango.com

Durango KIUP-AM (m) 190 Turner Dr Unit G, Durango CO 81303 **Phn:** 970-259-4444 **Fax:** 970-247-1005 www.radiodurango.com ward@radiodurango.com

Durango KPTE-FM (a) 1911 Main Ave Ste 100, Durango CO 81301 **Phn:** 970-247-1240 **Fax:** 970-247-1771 99xdurango.com bkruger@americangeneralmedia.com

Durango KRSJ-FM (c) 190 Turner Dr Unit G, Durango CO 81303 **Phn:** 970-259-4444 **Fax:** 970-247-1005 www.radiodurango.com news@radiodurango.com

Edwards KZYR-FM (r) 275 Main St # 201, Edwards CO 81632 **Phn:** 970-926-7625 **Fax:** 970-926-7635 www.kzyr.com tony@kzyr.com

Fort Collins KCSU-FM (p) Student Ctr Box 13, Fort Collins CO 80523 **Phn:** 970-491-7611 **Fax:** 970-491-1690 www.kcsufm.com rmaddock@rams.colostate.edu

Fort Morgan KFTM-AM (a) PO Box 430, Fort Morgan CO 80701 **Phn:** 970-867-5674 **Fax:** 970-542-1023 www.kftm.net wayne@kftm.net

Fort Morgan KPRB-FM (a) 220 State St # 106, Fort Morgan CO 80701 **Phn:** 970-867-7271 **Fax:** 970-867-2676 www.b106.com news@b106.com

Fort Morgan KSIR-AM (st) PO Box 917, Fort Morgan CO 80701 **Phn:** 970-867-7271 **Fax:** 970-867-2676 www.ksir.com news@ksir.com

Frisco KYSL-FM (ar) PO Box 27, Frisco CO 80443 **Phn:** 970-513-9393 **Fax:** 970-262-3677 www.krystal93.com news@krystal93.com

Glenwood Springs KGLN-AM (n) 3230 S Glen Ave Apt B, Glenwood Springs CO 81601 **Phn:** 970-945-9124 **Fax:** 970-945-5409 gabe@kmts.com

Glenwood Springs KMTS-FM (c) 3230 S Glen Ave Apt B, Glenwood Springs CO 81601 **Phn:** 970-945-9124 **Fax:** 970-945-5409 www.kmts.com kmts@kmts.com

Grand Junction KAFM-FM (vp) 1310 Ute Ave, Grand Junction CO 81501 **Phn:** 970-241-8801 kafmradio.org tedi@kafmradio.org

Grand Junction KBKL-FM (o) 315 Kennedy Ave, Grand Junction CO 81501 **Phn:** 970-242-7788 **Fax:** 970-243-0567 www.kool1079.com kool1079@cumulus.com

Grand Junction KCIC-FM (qv) 3102 E Rd, Grand Junction CO 81504 **Phn:** 970-434-4113 www.pearparkbaptistchurch.org pearpark@juno.com

Grand Junction KEKB-FM (c) 315 Kennedy Ave, Grand Junction CO 81501 **Phn:** 970-242-7788 **Fax:** 970-243-0567 kekbfm.com mackenzie.dodge@townsquaremedia.com

Grand Junction KEXO-AM (y) 315 Kennedy Ave, Grand Junction CO 81501 **Phn:** 970-242-7788 **Fax:** 970-243-0567 1230espn.com brad.larock@townsquaremedia.com

Grand Junction KJOL-AM (q) 1354 E Sherwood Dr, Grand Junction CO 81501 **Phn:** 970-254-5565 **Fax:** 970-254-5550 www.kjol.org info@kjol.org

Grand Junction KJYE-FM (a) 1360 E Sherwood Dr, Grand Junction CO 81501 **Phn:** 970-254-2100 **Fax:** 970-245-7551

Grand Junction KKNN-FM (r) 315 Kennedy Ave, Grand Junction CO 81501 **Phn:** 970-242-7788 **Fax:** 970-243-0567 95rockfm.com tommy.rocker@townsquaremedia.com

Grand Junction KMGJ-FM (a) 1360 E Sherwood Dr, Grand Junction CO 81501 **Phn:** 970-254-2100 **Fax:** 970-245-7551 www.931magic.com 931magic@gmail.com

Grand Junction KMOZ-FM (c) 1360 E Sherwood Dr, Grand Junction CO 81501 **Phn:** 970-254-2121 **Fax:** 970-245-7551 www.themoose1007.com libby@gjradio.com

Grand Junction KMSA-FM (v) 1100 North Ave, Grand Junction CO 81501 **Phn:** 970-248-1442 **Fax:** 970-248-1834 www.kmsa913.com tucci@kmsa913.com

Grand Junction KMXY-FM (a) 315 Kennedy Ave, Grand Junction CO 81501 **Phn:** 970-242-7788 **Fax:** 970-243-0567 www.mix1043fm.com roxi@townsquaremedia.com

Grand Junction KNZZ-AM (nt) 1360 E Sherwood Dr, Grand Junction CO 81501 **Phn:** 970-254-2100 **Fax:** 970-245-7551 www.1100knzz.com ken@gjradio.com

Grand Junction KRGS-AM (st) 751 Horizon Ct Ste 225, Grand Junction CO 81506 **Phn:** 970-241-6460 **Fax:** 970-241-6452

Grand Junction KRVG-FM (r) 751 Horizon Ct Ste 225, Grand Junction CO 81506 **Phn:** 970-241-6460 **Fax:** 970-241-6452 wscradio.net tom@wscradio.net

Grand Junction KSTR-FM (r) 1360 E Sherwood Dr, Grand Junction CO 81501 **Phn:** 970-254-2100 **Fax:** 970-245-7551 www.961kstr.com tom@gjradio.com

Grand Junction KTMM-AM (st) 1360 E Sherwood Dr, Grand Junction CO 81501 **Phn:** 970-254-2100 **Fax:** 970-245-7551 www.theteam1340.com jimd@gjradio.com

COLORADO RADIO STATIONS

Grand Junction KWGL-FM (r) 751 Horizon Ct Ste 225, Grand Junction CO 81506 **Phn:** 970-241-6460 **Fax:** 970-241-6452 wscradio.net tom@wscradio.net

Grand Junction KZKS-FM (c) 751 Horizon Ct Ste 225, Grand Junction CO 81506 **Phn:** 970-241-6460 **Fax:** 970-241-6452 wscradio.net tom@wscradio.net

Greeley KFKA-AM (nt) PO Box 460, Greeley CO 80632 **Phn:** 970-356-1310 **Fax:** 970-356-1314 www.1310kfka.com troy@1310kfka.com

Greeley KGRE-AM (y) 800 8th Ave St 304, Greeley CO 80631 **Phn:** 970-356-1452 **Fax:** 970-356-8522 www.tigrecolorado.com kgre@msn.com

Greeley KUNC-FM (p) 1901 56th Ave Ste 200, Greeley CO 80634 **Phn:** 970-378-2579 **Fax:** 970-378-2580 www.kunc.org news@kunc.org

Greenwood Village KEPN-AM (s) 7800 E Orchard Rd Ste 400, Greenwood Village CO 80111 **Phn:** 303-321-0950 **Fax:** 303-394-4407 www.espnradio1600.com nate.lundy@lincolnfinancialmedia.com

Greenwood Village KKFN-FM (s) 7800 E Orchard Rd Ste 400, Greenwood Village CO 80111 **Phn:** 303-321-0950 **Fax:** 303-321-3383 www.1043thefan.com

Greenwood Village KQKS-FM (h) 7800 E Orchard Rd Ste 400, Greenwood Village CO 80111 **Phn:** 303-321-0950 **Fax:** 303-321-3383 www.ks1075.com

Greenwood Village KRWZ-AM (o) 7800 E Orchard Rd Ste 400, Greenwood Village CO 80111 **Phn:** 303-321-0950 **Fax:** 303-321-3383 www.cruisinoldies950.com randy@cruisinoldies950.com

Greenwood Village KYGO-FM (c) 7800 E Orchard Rd Ste 400, Greenwood Village CO 80111 **Phn:** 303-321-0950 **Fax:** 303-321-3383 www.kygo.com

Gunnison KEJJ-FM (o) PO Box 1288, Gunnison CO 81230 **Phn:** 970-641-4000 **Fax:** 970-641-3300

Gunnison KPKE-AM (c) PO Box 1288, Gunnison CO 81230 **Phn:** 970-641-4000 **Fax:** 970-641-3300

Gunnison KVLE-FM (r) PO Box 884, Gunnison CO 81230 **Phn:** 970-641-3600 **Fax:** 970-641-4566 1060thebiz.com marty@kvleradio.com

Gunnison KWSB-FM (v) W Co State College, Gunnison CO 81231 **Phn:** 970-943-2036 **Fax:** 970-943-7069 www.kwsb.org tmaurer@western.edu

Ignacio KSUT-FM (pn) PO Box 737, Ignacio CO 81137 **Phn:** 970-563-0255 **Fax:** 970-563-0399 www.ksut.org bruce@ksut.org

Ignacio KUTE-FM (p) PO Box 737, Ignacio CO 81137 **Phn:** 970-563-0255 **Fax:** 970-563-0399 www.ksut.org bruce@ksut.org

Johnstown KHNC-AM (nt) PO Box 1750, Johnstown CO 80534 **Phn:** 970-587-5175 **Fax:** 970-587-5450 www.americanewsnet.com don@americanewsnet.com

La Junta KBLJ-AM (o) PO Box 485, La Junta CO 81050 **Phn:** 719-384-5456 **Fax:** 719-384-5450 www.cherrycreekradio.com kblj@secom.net

La Junta KTHN-FM (c) PO Box 485, La Junta CO 81050 **Phn:** 719-384-5456 **Fax:** 719-384-5450 www.cherrycreekradio.com kblj@secom.net

Lakewood KDDZ-AM (m) 12136 W Bayaud Ave Ste 125, Lakewood CO 80228 **Phn:** 303-783-0880 **Fax:** 303-761-1774 music.disney.com

Lamar KLMR-AM (c) PO Box 890, Lamar CO 81052 **Phn:** 719-336-2206 **Fax:** 719-336-7973 www.cherrycreekradio.com bguerra@cherrycreekradio.com

Lamar KLMR-FM (s) PO Box 890, Lamar CO 81052 **Phn:** 719-336-2206 **Fax:** 719-336-7973 www.cherrycreekradio.com tdriskill@cherrycreekradio.com

Lamar KVAY-FM (c) PO Box 1176, Lamar CO 81052 **Phn:** 719-336-8734 **Fax:** 719-336-5977 www.kvay.com news@kvay.com

Longmont KJJD-AM (y) 624 Main St, Longmont CO 80501 **Phn:** 303-651-1199 **Fax:** 303-651-2244

Longmont KKKK-AM (ntq) 600 S Airport Rd # B, Longmont CO 80503 **Phn:** 720-684-6708

Longmont KRCN-AM (t) 614 Kimbark St, Longmont CO 80501 **Phn:** 303-776-2323 **Fax:** 720-247-9149 1060thebiz.com marty@kvleradio.com

Longmont KSKE-AM (nt) 614 Kimbark St, Longmont CO 80501 **Phn:** 303-776-2323 **Fax:** 303-776-1377

Longmont KSXT-AM (nt) 1270 Boston Ave, Longmont CO 80501 **Phn:** 303-772-7676 **Fax:** 970-612-0137

Loveland KCOL-AM (nt) 4270 Byrd Dr, Loveland CO 80538 **Phn:** 970-461-2560 **Fax:** 970-461-0118 www.600kcol.com scottjames@clearchannel.com

Loveland KFEL-AM (q) 1576 W 1st St, Loveland CO 80537 **Phn:** 719-543-7506 **Fax:** 719-543-0432 www.thecatholicradionetwork.com

Loveland KIIX-AM (a) 4270 Byrd Dr, Loveland CO 80538 **Phn:** 970-461-2560 **Fax:** 970-461-0118 www.kiixcountry.com stuhaskell@clearchannel.com

Loveland KPAW-FM (a) 4270 Byrd Dr, Loveland CO 80538 **Phn:** 970-461-2560 **Fax:** 970-461-0118 www.1079thebear.com stuhaskell@clearchannel.com

Loveland KSME-FM (h) 4270 Byrd Dr, Loveland CO 80538 **Phn:** 970-461-2560 **Fax:** 970-461-0118 www.kissfmcolorado.com chris@kissfmcolorado.com

Loveland KXBG-FM (c) 4270 Byrd Dr, Loveland CO 80538 **Phn:** 970-461-2560 **Fax:** 970-461-0118 www.bigcountry979.com chris@kissfmcolorado.com

Monte Vista KSLV-FM (a) PO Box 631, Monte Vista CO 81144 **Phn:** 719-852-3581 **Fax:** 719-852-3583 www.kslvradio.com kslv@amigo.net

Monte Vista KSLV-AM (c) PO Box 631, Monte Vista CO 81144 **Phn:** 719-852-3581 **Fax:** 719-852-3583 www.kslvradio.com kslv@amigo.net

Montrose KBNG-FM (a) PO Box 970, Montrose CO 81402 **Phn:** 970-249-4546 **Fax:** 970-249-2229 coloradoradio.com news@coloradoradio.com

Montrose KKXK-FM (c) PO Box 970, Montrose CO 81402 **Phn:** 970-249-4546 **Fax:** 970-249-2229 coloradoradio.com news@coloradoradio.com

Montrose KRYD-FM (h) 475 Water Ave, Montrose CO 81401 **Phn:** 970-249-8989 **Fax:** 970-240-0909 krydfm.com studio@krydradio.com

Montrose KUBC-AM (nt) PO Box 970, Montrose CO 81402 **Phn:** 970-249-4546 **Fax:** 970-249-2229 coloradoradio.com news@coloradoradio.com

Pagosa Springs KWUF-FM (jb) PO Box 780, Pagosa Springs CO 81147 **Phn:** 970-264-5983 **Fax:** 970-264-5129 www.kwuf.com admin@kwuf.com

Pagosa Springs KWUF-AM (h) PO Box 780, Pagosa Springs CO 81147 **Phn:** 970-264-5983 **Fax:** 970-264-5129 www.kwuf.com admin@kwuf.com

Paonia KVNF-FM (p) PO Box 1350, Paonia CO 81428 **Phn:** 970-527-4866 **Fax:** 970-527-4865 www.kvnf.org news@kvnf.org

Pueblo KCSJ-AM (snt) 106 W 24th St, Pueblo CO 81003 **Phn:** 719-545-2080 **Fax:** 719-543-9898 www.590kcsj.com

Pueblo KNKN-FM (y) 30 N Electronic Dr, Pueblo CO 81007 **Phn:** 719-547-0411 **Fax:** 719-547-9301 radiolobo@amigo.net

Pueblo KRMX-AM (y) 30 N Electronic Dr, Pueblo CO 81007 **Phn:** 719-545-2883 **Fax:** 719-547-9301 radiolobo@amigo.net

Pueblo KRYE-FM (y) 106 W 24th St, Pueblo CO 81003 **Phn:** 720-382-9697 **Fax:** 719-562-0947

Pueblo KTSC-FM (v) 2200 Bonforte Blvd Rm 120, Pueblo CO 81001 **Phn:** 719-549-2821 **Fax:** 719-549-2120 mike.atencio@colostate-pueblo.edu

Pueblo KYRE-FM (y) 106 W 24th St, Pueblo CO 81003 **Phn:** 720-382-9697 **Fax:** 719-562-0947

Salida KBVC-FM (c) 7600 County Road 120, Salida CO 81201 **Phn:** 719-539-2575 **Fax:** 719-539-4851 www.kbvcfm.com danr@kvrh.com

Salida KSBV-FM (r) PO Box 832, Salida CO 81201 **Phn:** 719-539-9377 **Fax:** 719-539-7904 www.ksbv.net ksbvradio@chaffee.net

Salida KVRH-AM (nt) 7600 County Road 120, Salida CO 81201 **Phn:** 719-539-2575 **Fax:** 719-539-4851 www.kvrh.comkvrham.htm danr@kvrh.com

Salida KVRH-FM (ac) 7600 County Road 120, Salida CO 81201 **Phn:** 719-539-2575 **Fax:** 719-539-4851 www.kvrh.com danr@kvrh.com

Salida KWUZ-FM (h) 7600 County Road 120, Salida CO 81201 **Phn:** 719-539-2575 **Fax:** 719-539-4851 danr@kvrh.com

Steamboat Springs KBCR-AM (s) PO Box 774050, Steamboat Springs CO 80477 **Phn:** 970-879-2270 **Fax:** 970-879-1404 www.kbcr.com craig@kbcr.com

Steamboat Springs KBCR-FM (c) PO Box 774050, Steamboat Springs CO 80477 **Phn:** 970-879-2270 **Fax:** 970-879-1404 kbcr.com craig@kbcr.com

Steamboat Springs KFMU-FM (r) PO Box 772850, Steamboat Springs CO 80477 **Phn:** 970-879-5368 **Fax:** 970-879-5843

Steamboat Springs KIDN-FM (r) PO Box 772850, Steamboat Springs CO 80477 **Phn:** 970-242-7788 **Fax:** 970-870-0300 www.95rockfm.com tommy.rocker@townsquaremedia.com

Steamboat Springs KRMR-FM (c) PO Box 772850, Steamboat Springs CO 80477 **Phn:** 970-879-5368 **Fax:** 970-879-5843

Sterling KATR-FM (c) 519 W Main St, Sterling CO 80751 **Phn:** 970-521-2732 **Fax:** 970-521-2733 www.katcountry983.com wayne@kftm.net

Sterling KNNG-FM (c) PO Box 830, Sterling CO 80751 **Phn:** 970-522-1607 **Fax:** 970-522-1322

Sterling KPMX-FM (a) 117 Main St, Sterling CO 80751 **Phn:** 970-522-4800 **Fax:** 970-522-3997 www.kpmx.com news@kpmx.com

Sterling KSTC-AM (o) PO Box 830, Sterling CO 80751 **Phn:** 970-522-1607 **Fax:** 970-522-1322 bettykstc@yahoo.com

Telluride KOTO-FM (p) PO Box 1069, Telluride CO 81435 **Phn:** 970-728-4334 **Fax:** 970-728-4326 www.koto.org news@koto.org

Trinidad KCRT-AM (c) 100 Fisher Dr, Trinidad CO 81082 **Phn:** 719-846-3355 **Fax:** 719-846-4711 www.kcrtradio.com kcrt@comcast.net

Trinidad KCRT-FM (r) 100 Fisher Dr, Trinidad CO 81082 **Phn:** 719-846-3355 **Fax:** 719-846-4711 www.kcrtradio.com kcrt@comcast.net

Walsenburg KSPK-FM (cf) 516 Main St, Walsenburg CO 81089 **Phn:** 719-738-3636 **Fax:** 719-738-2010 www.kspk.com info@kspk.com

Westminster KPOF-AM (ah) 3455 W 83rd Ave, Westminster CO 80031 **Phn:** 303-428-0910 **Fax:** 303-429-0910 am91.org info@am91.org

Windsor KARS-FM (ho) 600 Main St, Windsor CO 80550 **Phn:** 970-674-2700 **Fax:** 970-686-7491 943loudwire.com george.king@townsquaremedia.com

Windsor KKAW-FM (c) PO Box 123, Windsor CO 80550 **Phn:** 815-301-3434 www.thecountrymusicstation.com kkaw@networkradio.com

Windsor KTRR-FM (a) 600 Main St, Windsor CO 80550 **Phn:** 970-674-2700 **Fax:** 970-686-7491 tri1025.com pat.kelley@townsquaremedia.com

Windsor KUAD-FM (c) 600 Main St, Windsor CO 80550 **Phn:** 970-674-2700 **Fax:** 970-686-7491 www.k99.com pat.kelley@townsquaremedia.com

Wray KRDZ-AM (o) 32992 US Highway 34, Wray CO 80758 **Phn:** 970-332-4171 **Fax:** 970-332-4172 www.krdz.com krdz@medialogicradio.com

Yuma KNEC-FM (a) 205 S Main St, Yuma CO 80759 **Phn:** 970-848-2302 **Fax:** 970-848-2240 knec@plains.net

CONNECTICUT

Berlin WPRX-AM (y) 1253 Berlin Tpk, Berlin CT 06037 **Phn:** 860-348-0667 **Fax:** 860-358-0711 www.wprx1120.net wprx1120@comcast.net

Bloomfield WDRC-AM (nt) 869 Blue Hills Ave, Bloomfield CT 06002 **Phn:** 860-243-1115 **Fax:** 860-286-8257 talkofct.com brouder@grolen.com

Bloomfield WDRC-FM (h) 869 Blue Hills Ave, Bloomfield CT 06002 **Phn:** 860-243-1115 **Fax:** 860-286-8257 www.drcfm.com gwinters@drcfm.com

Bloomfield WMMW-AM (nt) 869 Blue Hills Ave, Bloomfield CT 06002 **Phn:** 860-243-1115 **Fax:** 860-286-8257 www.talkofconnecticut.com grahamewinters@talkofconnecticut.com

Bloomfield WSNG-AM (nt) 869 Blue Hills Ave, Bloomfield CT 06002 **Phn:** 860-689-8050 **Fax:** 860-286-8257 www.talkofconnecticut.com grahamewinters@talkofconnecticut.com

Bloomfield WWCO-AM (nta) 869 Blue Hills Ave, Bloomfield CT 06002 **Phn:** 860-274-8841 **Fax:** 860-286-8257 www.talkofconnecticut.com grahamewinters@talkofconnecticut.com

Bridgeport WCUM-AM (y) 1862 Commerce Dr, Bridgeport CT 06605 **Phn:** 203-335-1450 **Fax:** 203-337-1216 www.radiocumbre.am

Bridgeport WDJZ-AM (g) 211 State St Flr 3, Bridgeport CT 06604 **Phn:** 203-367-4395 **Fax:** 203-367-4551 www.wdjzradio.com

Bridgeport WEBE-FM (a) 2 Lafayette Sq, Bridgeport CT 06604 **Phn:** 203-366-6000 **Fax:** 203-394-6000 www.webe108.com dannylyons@webe108.com

Bridgeport WICC-AM (nt) 350 Fairfield Ave # 2, Bridgeport CT 06604 **Phn:** 203-366-6000 **Fax:** 203-394-6000 www.wicc600.com danny.lyons@cumulus.com

Bridgeport WPKN-FM (v) 244 University Ave, Bridgeport CT 06604 **Phn:** 203-331-9756 www.wpkn.org gm@wpkn.org

Brookfield WDBY-FM (a) 1004 Federal Rd, Brookfield CT 06804 **Phn:** 203-775-1212 **Fax:** 203-775-7652 kicks1055.com tim.sheehan@cumulus.com

Brookfield WINE-AM (st) 1004 Federal Rd, Brookfield CT 06804 **Phn:** 203-775-1212 **Fax:** 203-775-6452

Brookfield WPUT-AM (st) 1004 Federal Rd, Brookfield CT 06804 **Phn:** 203-775-1212 **Fax:** 203-775-6452

Brookfield WRKI-FM (r) 1004 Federal Rd, Brookfield CT 06804 **Phn:** 203-775-1212 **Fax:** 203-775-6452 www.i95rock.com equest@i95rock.com

Danbury WDAQ-FM (a) 198 Main St, Danbury CT 06810 **Phn:** 203-744-4800 **Fax:** 203-778-4655 www.98q.com gm@98q.com

Danbury WFAR-FM (ve) 25 Chestnut St, Danbury CT 06810 **Phn:** 203-748-0001 **Fax:** 203-746-4262 www.radiofamilia.com wfar@radiofamilia.com

Danbury WLAD-AM (m) 198 Main St, Danbury CT 06810 **Phn:** 203-744-4800 **Fax:** 203-778-4655 www.wlad.com news@wlad.com

Danbury WREF-AM (o) 198 Main St, Danbury CT 06810 **Phn:** 203-744-4800 **Fax:** 203-778-4655 www.850wref.com feedback@b1073fm.com

Fairfield WSHU-FM (pln) 5151 Park Ave, Fairfield CT 06825 **Phn:** 203-365-6604 wshu.org

Fairfield WSTC-AM (nt) 5151 Park Ave, Fairfield CT 06825 **Phn:** 203-365-6604 www.wshu.org

Fairfield WVOF-FM (v) 1073 N Benson Rd # R, Fairfield CT 06824 **Phn:** 203-254-4144 **Fax:** 203-254-4224 www.wvof.org wvoffm@gmail.com

Farmington WRCH-FM (a) 10 Executive Dr Ste 1, Farmington CT 06032 **Phn:** 860-677-6700 **Fax:** 860-677-5483 wrch.cbslocal.com acamp@cbs.com

Farmington WTIC-AM (nt) 10 Executive Dr Ste 1, Farmington CT 06032 **Phn:** 860-677-6700 **Fax:** 860-284-9842 connecticut.cbslocal.com wticnews@cbs.com

Farmington WTIC-FM (a) 10 Executive Dr Ste 1, Farmington CT 06032 **Phn:** 860-677-6700 **Fax:** 860-284-9842 965tic.radio.com ryan.jones@cbsradio.com

Farmington WZMX-FM (h) 10 Executive Dr, Farmington CT 06032 **Phn:** 860-677-6700 **Fax:** 860-674-8427 hot937.cbslocal.com jason.ricketts@cbsradio.com

Glastonbury WMRQ-FM (r) 131 New London Tpke Ste 101, Glastonbury CT 06033 **Phn:** 860-723-6000 **Fax:** 860-657-1042 www.radio1041.fm requests@radio1041.fm

Greenwich WGCH-AM (ant) 71 Lewis St, Greenwich CT 06830 **Phn:** 203-869-1490 **Fax:** 203-869-3636 www.wgch.com tony.savino@wgch.com

Hamden WAVZ-AM (s) 495 Benham St, Hamden CT 06514 **Phn:** 203-248-8814 **Fax:** 203-281-7640 www.espnradio1300.com sarahhannon@clearchannel.com

Hamden WELI-AM (nt) 495 Benham St, Hamden CT 06514 **Phn:** 203-281-9600 **Fax:** 203-407-4652 www.960weli.com comments@weli.com

Hamden WKCI-FM (h) 495 Benham St, Hamden CT 06514 **Phn:** 203-281-9600 **Fax:** 203-281-7640 www.kc101.com jbwilde@clearchannel.com

Hamden WQAQ-FM (v) 555 New Rd, Hamden CT 06518 **Phn:** 203-582-5278 **Fax:** 203-582-5372 www.wqaq.com

Hamden WQUN-AM (ntb) 275 Mount Carmel Ave, Hamden CT 06518 **Phn:** 203-582-8984 **Fax:** 203-582-5372 www.quinnipiac.edux1353.xml ray.andrewsen@quinnipiac.edu

Hartford WCCC-FM (r) 1039 Asylum Ave, Hartford CT 06105 **Phn:** 860-525-1069 **Fax:** 860-246-9084 www.wccc.com karolyi@wccc.com

Hartford WCCC-AM (l) 1039 Asylum Ave, Hartford CT 06105 **Phn:** 860-525-1069 **Fax:** 860-246-9084 www.beethoven.com barnold@marlinbroadcasting.com

Hartford WHCN-FM (r) 10 Columbus Blvd, Hartford CT 06106 **Phn:** 860-723-6000 **Fax:** 860-493-7090 www.theriver1059.com renee3@clearchannel.com

Hartford WKND-AM (uw) 330 Main St, Hartford CT 06106 **Phn:** 860-524-0001 **Fax:** 860-548-1922

Hartford WKSS-FM (h) 10 Columbus Blvd, Hartford CT 06106 **Phn:** 860-723-6000 **Fax:** 860-723-6198 www.kiss957.com rickvaughn@clearchannel.com

Hartford WLAT-AM (y) 135 Burnside Ave, Hartford CT 06108 **Phn:** 860-524-0001 **Fax:** 860-548-1922 robbiedjtrigueno@yahoo.com

Hartford WNEZ-AM (uy) 135 Burnside Ave, Hartford CT 06108 **Phn:** 860-524-0001 **Fax:** 860-548-1922 robbiedjtrigueno@yahoo.com

Hartford WNPR-FM (pln) 1049 Asylum Ave, Hartford CT 06105 **Phn:** 860-278-5310 **Fax:** 860-275-7482 www.cpbn.org wherewelive@wnpr.org

Hartford WPKT-FM (p) 1049 Asylum Ave, Hartford CT 06105 **Phn:** 860-278-5310 **Fax:** 860-275-7482 www.cpbn.org

Hartford WPOP-AM (s) 10 Columbus Blvd, Hartford CT 06106 **Phn:** 860-723-6000 **Fax:** 860-493-7090 www.foxsportsradio1410.com lancetidwell@clearchannel.com

Hartford WQTQ-FM (vuj) 415 Granby St, Hartford CT 06112 **Phn:** 860-695-1899 uhavax.hartford.eduwqtq wqtqfm@yahoo.com

Hartford WRTC-FM (wj) 300 Summit St, Hartford CT 06106 **Phn:** 860-297-2450 **Fax:** 860-987-6214 www.wrtcfm.com wrtchartford@gmail.com

Hartford WWYZ-FM (c) 10 Columbus Blvd, Hartford CT 06106 **Phn:** 860-723-6000 **Fax:** 860-723-6159 www.country925.com cameronhendrix@clearchannel.com

Lakeville WQQQ-FM (a) PO Box 446, Lakeville CT 06039 **Phn:** 860-435-3333 **Fax:** 860-435-3334 wshu.org

Ledyard WBMW-FM (a) PO Box 357, Ledyard CT 06339 **Phn:** 860-464-1066 **Fax:** 860-464-8143 www.wbmw.com brian@wbmw.com

Ledyard WWRX-FM (u) PO Box 357, Ledyard CT 06339 **Phn:** 860-464-1077 **Fax:** 860-464-8143 www.jammin1077.com john@wbmw.com

Litchfield WZBG-FM (a) 49 Commons Dr, Litchfield CT 06759 **Phn:** 860-567-3697 **Fax:** 860-567-3292 www.973wzbg.com news@wzbg.com

Middletown WESU-FM (vrj) 45 Wyllys Ave, Middletown CT 06459 **Phn:** 860-685-7703 **Fax:** 860-704-0608 www.wesufm.org programmanager@wesufm.org

Middletown WIHS-FM (q) 1933 S Main St, Middletown CT 06457 **Phn:** 860-346-1049 **Fax:** 860-347-1049 www.wihsradio.org wihs@snet.net

Middletown WLIS-AM (ant) PO Box 1150, Middletown CT 06457 **Phn:** 860-388-1420 **Fax:** 860-347-7704 www.wliswmrd.net radio@wliswmrd.net

Middletown WMRD-AM (nta) PO Box 1150, Middletown CT 06457 **Phn:** 860-347-9673 **Fax:** 860-347-7704 www.wliswmrd.net office@wliswmrd.net

Milford WEZN-FM (a) 440 Wheelers Farms Rd Ste 302, Milford CT 06461 **Phn:** 203-783-8200 **Fax:** 203-783-8383 www.star999.com john.voket@coxradio.com

Milford WFIF-AM (q) 90 Kay Ave, Milford CT 06460 **Phn:** 203-878-5915 **Fax:** 603-434-1035 lifechangingradio.comwfif info@wfif.net

Milford WPLR-FM (r) 440 Wheelers Farms Rd Ste 302, Milford CT 06461 **Phn:** 203-783-8200 **Fax:** 203-783-8373 www.wplr.com keith.dakin@coxmg.com

Monroe WGRS-FM (pl) PO Box 920, Monroe CT 06468 **Phn:** 203-268-9667 www.wmnr.org psa@wmnr.org

Monroe WMNR-FM (pl) PO Box 920, Monroe CT 06468 **Phn:** 203-268-9667 www.wmnr.org psa@wmnr.org

New Britain WFCS-FM (vr) 1615 Stanley St, New Britain CT 06053 **Phn:** 860-832-1883 **Fax:** 860-832-3757

New Haven WADS-AM (qyv) PO Box 384, New Haven CT 06513 **Phn:** 203-777-7690 **Fax:** 203-782-3565

New Haven WYBC-FM (a) 142 Temple St Ste 203, New Haven CT 06510 **Phn:** 203-776-4118 **Fax:** 203-776-2446 www.943wybc.com sam.tilery@coxradio.com

New Haven WYBC-AM (a) 142 Temple St Ste 203, New Haven CT 06510 **Phn:** 203-776-4118 **Fax:** 203-776-2446 wybc.com programming@wybc.com

New London WCNI-FM (v) 270 Mohegan Ave, New London CT 06320 **Phn:** 860-439-2853 **Fax:** 860-439-2805 www.wcniradio.org wcni@conncoll.edu

New London WMOS-FM (h) 7 Governor Winthrop Blvd, New London CT 06320 **Phn:** 860-443-1980 **Fax:** 860-444-7970 www.1023thewolf.com thewolf@mohegansun.com

New London WNLC-FM (a) 89 Broad St, New London CT 06320 **Phn:** 860-442-5328 **Fax:** 860-442-6532 www.wnlc.com news@wich.com

New London WQGN-FM (h) 7 Governor Winthrop Blvd, New London CT 06320 **Phn:** 860-443-1980 **Fax:** 860-444-7970 www.q105.fm

New London WSUB-AM (y) 7 Governor Winthrop Blvd, New London CT 06320 **Phn:** 860-443-1980 **Fax:** 860-444-7970 www.caliente980am.com

New London WXLM-FM (snt) 7 Governor Winthrop Blvd, New London CT 06320 **Phn:** 860-443-1980 **Fax:** 860-444-7970 www.wxlm.fm

Newington WRYM-AM (y) 1056 Willard Ave, Newington CT 06111 **Phn:** 860-666-5646 **Fax:** 860-666-5647 www.wrymradio.com wmartinez@wrym840.com

Norwalk WCTZ-FM (o) 444 Westport Ave, Norwalk CT 06851 **Phn:** 203-845-3030 **Fax:** 203-845-3097 967thecoast.com

Norwalk WFOX-FM (r) 444 Westport Ave, Norwalk CT 06851 **Phn:** 203-845-3030 **Fax:** 203-845-3097 www.959thefox.com allan.lamberti@coxradio.com

Norwalk WNLK-AM (nt) 5151 Park Ave, Norwalk CT 60115 **Phn:** 815-748-1000 **Fax:** 815-748-9000 wshu.org norwalknews@yahoo.com

Norwich WCTY-FM (c) PO Box 551, Norwich CT 06360 **Phn:** 860-887-3511 **Fax:** 860-886-7649 www.wcty.com jimmy@wcty.com

Norwich WICH-AM (at) PO Box 551, Norwich CT 06360 **Phn:** 860-887-3511 wich.com acormier@hallradio.com

Norwich WKNL-FM (ah) PO Box 561, Norwich CT 06360 **Phn:** 860-887-3511 **Fax:** 860-886-7649 www.radioroxy.com jreed@hallradio.com

Plantsville WXCT-AM (ay) 440 Old Turnpike Rd, Plantsville CT 06479 **Phn:** 860-621-1754 ericksalgado1430@hotmail.com

Prospect WJMJ-FM (vlj) 15 Peach Orchard Rd, Prospect CT 06712 **Phn:** 860-242-8800 **Fax:** 203-758-7371 www.ortv.org wjmj@wjmj.org

Putnam WINY-AM (a) PO Box 231, Putnam CT 06260 **Phn:** 860-928-1350 **Fax:** 860-928-7878 www.winyradio.com news@winyradio.com

Sharon WHDD-AM (p) 67 Main St, Sharon CT 06069 **Phn:** 860-364-4640 **Fax:** 860-364-7035 robinhoodradio.com mmiles@robinhoodradio.com

Storrs WHUS-FM (v) 2110 Hillside Rd # 412, Storrs CT 06269 **Phn:** 860-486-4007 **Fax:** 860-486-2955 www.whus.org operationsmanager@whus.org

Torrington WAPJ-FM (v) 42 Water St, Torrington CT 06790 **Phn:** 860-489-9033 www.wapjfm.com wapjfm@sbcglobal.net

CONNECTICUT RADIO STATIONS

Wallingford WWEB-FM (q) 333 Christian St, Wallingford CT 06492 **Phn:** 203-697-2506

Waterbury WATR-AM (nt) 1 Broadcast Ln, Waterbury CT 06706 **Phn:** 203-755-1121 **Fax:** 203-574-3025 www.watr.com talkback@watr.com

Waterbury WFNW-AM (y) 182 Grand St Ste 215, Waterbury CT 06702 **Phn:** 203-755-4962 **Fax:** 203-755-4957 galaxia1380@yahoo.com

West Hartford WWUH-FM (v) 200 Bloomfield Ave, West Hartford CT 06117 **Phn:** 860-768-4703 **Fax:** 860-768-5701 wwuh.org wwuh@hartford.edu

West Haven WNHU-FM (vbw) 300 Boston Post Rd, West Haven CT 06516 **Phn:** 203-934-9648 **Fax:** 203-306-3073 www.newhaven.edu281164 blane@newhaven.edu

Willimantic WECS-FM (vr) 83 Windham St, Willimantic CT 06226 **Phn:** 860-465-5354 **Fax:** 860-465-5073 www.easternct.eduwecs zatowski@easternct.edu

Willimantic WILI-AM (at) 720 Main St, Willimantic CT 06226 **Phn:** 860-456-1111 **Fax:** 860-456-9501 www.wili.comam wayne@wili.com

Willimantic WILI-FM (h) 720 Main St, Willimantic CT 06226 **Phn:** 860-456-1111 **Fax:** 860-456-9501 www.wili.comfm

DELAWARE

Dover WDOV-AM (nt) 1575 McKee Rd Ste 206, Dover DE 19904 **Phn:** 302-674-1410 **Fax:** 302-674-5978 www.wdov.com ericfendt@clearchannel.com

Georgetown WGBG-FM (r) 20200 Dupont Blvd, Georgetown DE 19947 **Phn:** 302-856-2567 **Fax:** 302-856-7633 www.bigclassicrock.com wgbg@bigclassicrock.com

Georgetown WJKI-FM (r) 20200 Dupont Blvd, Georgetown DE 19947 **Phn:** 302-856-2567 **Fax:** 302-856-7633 www.bigclassicrock.com wgbg@bigclassicrock.com

Georgetown WKHI-FM (c) 20200 Dupont Blvd, Georgetown DE 19947 **Phn:** 302-856-2567 **Fax:** 302-856-7633 www.hotcountry1077.com jim@greatscottbroadcasting.com

Georgetown WZBH-FM (r) 20200 Dupont Blvd, Georgetown DE 19947 **Phn:** 302-856-2567 **Fax:** 302-856-7633 www.wzbhrocks.com sean@greatscottbroadcasting.com

Georgetown WZEB-FM (a) 20200 Dupont Blvd, Georgetown DE 19947 **Phn:** 302-856-2567 **Fax:** 302-856-7633 musicontheb.com mikeontheb@hotmail.com

Milford WAFL-FM (a) 1666 Blairs Pond Rd, Milford DE 19963 **Phn:** 302-422-7575 **Fax:** 302-422-3069 www.eagle977.com staff@eagle977.com

Milford WJWL-AM (y) 233 NE Front St, Milford DE 19963 **Phn:** 302-422-2600 **Fax:** 302-424-1630

Milford WNCL-FM (o) 1666 Blairs Pond Rd, Milford DE 19963 **Phn:** 302-422-7575 **Fax:** 302-422-3069 www.cool1013.com cool@cool1013.com

Milford WYUS-AM (y) 1666 Blairs Pond Rd, Milford DE 19963 **Phn:** 302-422-7575 **Fax:** 302-422-3069 www.wyusam.com

New Castle WDSD-FM (c) 920 W Basin Rd #400, New Castle DE 19720 **Phn:** 302.395.9800 www.wdsd.com skyphillips@clearchannel.com

New Castle WILM-AM (nt) 920 W Basin Rd Ste 400, New Castle DE 19720 **Phn:** 302-395-9800 **Fax:** 302-395-9808 www.wilm.com newsroom@wilm.com

New Castle WRDX-FM (r) 920 W Basin Rd Ste 400, New Castle DE 19720 **Phn:** 302-395-9800 **Fax:** 302-395-9808 www.929tomfm.com info@929tomfm.com

New Castle WWTX-AM (s) 920 W Basin Rd Ste 200, New Castle DE 19720 **Phn:** 302-395-9800 **Fax:** 302-395-9808 www.1290theticket.com kathrynalt@clearchannel.com

Newark WVUD-FM (v) Perkins Student Ctr, Newark DE 19716 **Phn:** 302-831-2701 **Fax:** 302-831-3592 www.wvud.org ud.wvud@gmail.com

Newark WXHL-FM (q) 179 Stanton Christiana Rd, Newark DE 19702 **Phn:** 302-731-0690 **Fax:** 302-738-3090

Rehoboth Beach WGMD-FM (nt) PO Box 530, Rehoboth Beach DE 19971 **Phn:** 302-945-2050 **Fax:** 302-945-3781 www.wgmd.com news@wgmd.com

Wilmington WDEL-AM (nt) PO Box 7492, Wilmington DE 19803 **Phn:** 302-478-2700 **Fax:** 302-479-1532 www.wdel.com wdelnews@wdel.com

Wilmington WFAI-AM (g) 704 N King St # 604, Wilmington DE 19801 **Phn:** 302-622-8895 **Fax:** 302-622-8678 www.faith1510.com steven@wjks1017.com

Wilmington WJBR-FM (a) 812 Philadelphia Pike Ste C, Wilmington DE 19809 **Phn:** 302-765-1160 **Fax:** 302-765-1192 www.wjbr.com info@wjbr.com

Wilmington WJKS-FM (u) 704 N King St # 604, Wilmington DE 19801 **Phn:** 302-622-8895 **Fax:** 302-622-8678 www.wjks1017.com

Wilmington WMPH-FM (h) 5201 Washington Blvd, Wilmington DE 19809 **Phn:** 302-762-7199 **Fax:** 302-762-7042 www.wmph.org

Wilmington WSTW-FM (ah) PO Box 7492, Wilmington DE 19803 **Phn:** 302-478-2700 **Fax:** 302-478-0100 www.wstw.com wstw@wstw.com

DISTRICT OF COLUMBIA

Washington WAMU-FM (pnt) 4000 Brandywine St NW, Washington DC 20016 **Phn:** 202-885-1200 **Fax:** 202-885-1269 wamu.org feedback@wamu.org

Washington WCSP-FM (vn) 400 N Capitol St NW Ste 650, Washington DC 20001 **Phn:** 202-737-3220 **Fax:** 202-737-5554 www.c-span.org radio@c-span.org

Washington WFED-AM (n) 3400 Idaho Ave NW Ste 200, Washington DC 20016 **Phn:** 202-895-5000 **Fax:** 202-895-5144 www.federalnewsradio.com lwolfe@federalnewsradio.com

Washington WHUR-FM (wu) 529 Bryant St NW, Washington DC 20059 **Phn:** 202-806-3500 **Fax:** 202-806-3522 www.whur.com programming@whur.com

Washington WJZW-FM (aj) 4400 Jenifer St NW, Washington DC 20015 **Phn:** 202-686-3100 **Fax:** 202-686-3064 www.smoothjazz1059.com

Washington WMAL-AM (nt) 4400 Jenifer St NW, Washington DC 20015 **Phn:** 202-686-3100 **Fax:** 202-686-3061 www.wmal.com bill.hess@cumulus.com

Washington WPFW-FM (vjn) 1819 L St NW, Washington DC 20036 **Phn:** 202-588-0999 **Fax:** 202-296-3040 www.wpfwfm.orgradio gmahdi@wpfw.org

Washington WPRS-FM (g) 3400 Idaho Ave NW, Washington DC 20016 **Phn:** 202-895-5000 **Fax:** 202-895-5016 praisedc.com

Washington WRQX-FM (a) 4400 Jenifer St NW Ste 400, Washington DC 20015 **Phn:** 202-686-3100 **Fax:** 202-686-3061 www.mix1073fm.com marco@cumulus.com

Washington WTLP-AM (n) 3400 Idaho Ave NW, Washington DC 20016 **Phn:** 202-895-5000 **Fax:** 202-895-5140 www.wtop.com mgartell@wtop.com

Washington WTOP-AM (n) 3400 Idaho Ave NW, Washington DC 20016 **Phn:** 202-895-5000 **Fax:** 202-895-5140 www.wtop.com newsroom@wtop.com

Washington WTOP-FM (n) 3400 Idaho Ave NW, Washington DC 20016 **Phn:** 202-895-5000 **Fax:** 202-895-5088 www.wtop.com joxley@wtopnews.com

Washington WWFD-AM (n) 3400 Idaho Ave NW, Washington DC 20016 **Phn:** 202-895-5000 **Fax:** 202-895-5144 www.federalnewsradio.com lwolfe@federalnewsradio.com

FLORIDA

Altamonte Springs WHIM-AM (qtg) 1188 Lake View Dr, Altamonte Springs FL 32714 **Phn:** 407-682-9494 **Fax:** 407-682-7005 www.wtln.com office@salemorlando.com

Altamonte Springs WNUE-FM (y) 523 Douglas Ave, Altamonte Springs FL 32714 **Phn:** 407-774-2626 **Fax:** 407-774-8251

Altamonte Springs WONQ-AM (y) 1355 E Altamonte Dr, Altamonte Springs FL 32701 **Phn:** 407-830-0800 **Fax:** 407-260-6100 1030lagrande.com

Altamonte Springs WORL-AM (nt) 1188 Lake View Dr, Altamonte Springs FL 32714 **Phn:** 407-682-9494 **Fax:** 407-682-7005 www.660worl.com joef@salemorlando.com

Altamonte Springs WPOZ-FM (qv) 1065 Rainer Dr, Altamonte Springs FL 32714 **Phn:** 407-869-8000 **Fax:** 407-869-0380 zradio.org zcrew@zradio.org

Altamonte Springs WRMQ-AM (q) 1355 E Altamonte Dr, Altamonte Springs FL 32701 **Phn:** 407-830-0800 **Fax:** 407-260-6100 rejoice1140.net georgearroyo@qbcflorida.com

Altamonte Springs WTLN-AM (qtg) 1188 Lake View Dr, Altamonte Springs FL 32714 **Phn:** 407-682-9494 **Fax:** 407-682-7005 www.wtln.com office@salemorlando.com

Arcadia WFLN-AM (nt) 201 Asbury St, Arcadia FL 34266 **Phn:** 863-993-1480 **Fax:** 863-993-1489 www.wflnradio.com wflnradio@aol.com

Auburndale WTWB-AM (y) 127 Glenn Rd, Auburndale FL 33823 **Phn:** 863-967-1570 www.laraza1570.com laraza1570@gmail.com

Baker WTJT-FM (qv) PO Box 189, Baker FL 32531 **Phn:** 850-537-2009

Bartow WQXM-AM (y) 1355 N Maple Ave, Bartow FL 33830 **Phn:** 305-358-5644 **Fax:** 863-519-9514 ovega@lax1460.com

Bartow WWBF-AM (os) 1130 Radio Rd, Bartow FL 33830 **Phn:** 863-533-0744 **Fax:** 863-533-8546 www.wwbf.com susan@wwbf.com

Belle Glade WBGF-FM (c) PO Box 1505, Belle Glade FL 33430 **Phn:** 561-996-2063 **Fax:** 561-996-1852

Belle Glade WSWN-AM (wg) PO Box 1505, Belle Glade FL 33430 **Phn:** 561-996-2063 **Fax:** 561-996-1852

Big Pine Key WCNK-FM (c) 30336 Overseas Hwy, Big Pine Key FL 33043 **Phn:** 305-872-9100 **Fax:** 305-872-1603 www.conchcountry.com erika@us1radio.com

Big Pine Key WWUS-FM (o) 30336 Overseas Hwy, Big Pine Key FL 33043 **Phn:** 305-872-9100 **Fax:** 305-872-1603 www.us1radio.com news@us1radio.com

Blountstown WPHK-FM (c) 20872 NE Kelley Ave, Blountstown FL 32424 **Phn:** 850-674-5101 **Fax:** 850-674-2965

Blountstown WYBT-AM (o) 20872 NE Kelley Ave, Blountstown FL 32424 **Phn:** 850-674-5101 **Fax:** 850-674-2965

Boca Raton WHSR-AM (e) 6699 N Federal Hwy Ste 200, Boca Raton FL 33487 **Phn:** 561-997-0074 **Fax:** 561-997-0476 www.whsrradio.com iynstyne@aol.com

Boca Raton WSBR-AM (k) 6699 N Federal Hwy Ste 200, Boca Raton FL 33487 **Phn:** 561-997-0074 www.wsbrradio.com iynstyne@aol.com

Boca Raton WWNN-AM (t) 1650 S Dixie Hwy 5th flr, Boca Raton FL 33432 **Phn:** 561-997-0074 **Fax:** 561-997-0476 www.wwnnradio.com karen@bbgiboca.com

Bonita Springs WGUF-FM (nt) 10915 K Nine Dr, Bonita Springs FL 34135 **Phn:** 239-495-8383 **Fax:** 239-495-0883 www.wguf989.com tr@rendabroadcasting.com

Bonita Springs WJGO-FM (ou) 10915 K Nine Dr, Bonita Springs FL 34135 **Phn:** 239-495-8383 **Fax:** 239-495-0883 www.1029bobfm.com rharris@rendabroadcasting.com

Bonita Springs WSGL-FM (a) 10915 K Nine Dr, Bonita Springs FL 34135 **Phn:** 239-495-8383 **Fax:** 239-495-0883 www.1047mixfm.com rsavage@rendabroadcasting.com

Bonita Springs WWGR-FM (c) 10915 K Nine Dr, Bonita Springs FL 34135 **Phn:** 239-495-8383 **Fax:** 239-495-0883 www.gatorcountry1019.com rsavage@rendabroadcasting.com

Boynton Beach WRMB-FM (qt) 1511 W Boynton Beach Blvd, Boynton Beach FL 33436 **Phn:** 561-737-9762 **Fax:** 561-737-9899 www.moodyradiosouthflorida.fm wrmb@moody.edu

Bradenton WWPR-AM (t) 5910 Cortez Rd W Ste 130, Bradenton FL 34210 **Phn:** 941-761-8843 **Fax:** 941-761-8683 www.1490wwpr.com manager@1490wwpr.com

Brooksville WWJB-AM (snt) PO Box 1507, Brooksville FL 34605 **Phn:** 352-796-7469 **Fax:** 352-796-5074 www.wwjb.com info@wwjb.com

Celebration WDYZ-AM (m) 610 Sycamore St Ste 220, Celebration FL 34747 **Phn:** 407-566-2033 **Fax:** 407-566-2034 music.disney.com

Clearwater WDCF-AM (snt) 706 North Myrtle Ave, Clearwater FL 33755 **Phn:** 727-441-3311 wdcf.tantalknetwork.com dave@tantalk1340.com

Clearwater WTAN-AM (snt) 706 N Myrtle Ave, Clearwater FL 33755 **Phn:** 727-441-3311 www.tantalk1340.com lola@tantalk1340.com

Clearwater WZHR-AM (t) 706 North Myrtle Ave, Clearwater FL 33755 **Phn:** 727-441-3311 wzhr.tantalknetwork.com lola@tantalk1340.com

Clewiston WAFC-AM (y) 530 E Alverdez Ave, Clewiston FL 33440 **Phn:** 863-902-0995 **Fax:** 863-983-6109 www.radiofiesta.com jesus@gladesmedia.com

Cocoa WJFP-FM (vw) 1150 King St, Cocoa FL 32922 **Phn:** 321-632-1000 **Fax:** 321-636-0000 wjfp.com

Cocoa WMEL-AM (nt) 2355 Pluckebaum Rd, Cocoa FL 32926 **Phn:** 321-631-1300 **Fax:** 321-631-9113 www.1300wmel.com wmelradiojohn@gmail.com

Cocoa WWBC-AM (qt) 1150 King St, Cocoa FL 32922 **Phn:** 321-632-1510

Coral Gables WAMR-FM (y) 800 S Douglas Rd Ste 111, Coral Gables FL 33134 **Phn:** 305-447-1140 **Fax:** 305-441-2364 www.univision.com

Coral Gables WAQI-AM (y) 800 S Douglas Rd Ste 111, Coral Gables FL 33134 **Phn:** 305-445-4040 **Fax:** 305-443-3061 www.univision.com

Coral Gables WQBA-AM (y) 800 S Douglas Rd Ste 111, Coral Gables FL 33134 **Phn:** 305-447-1140 **Fax:** 305-445-1541 www.univision.com

Coral Gables WRTO-FM (y) 800 S Douglas Rd Ste 111, Coral Gables FL 33134 **Phn:** 305-447-1140 **Fax:** 305-445-1541 www.univision.com

Coral Gables WSUA-AM (y) 2100 Coral Way Ste 200, Coral Gables FL 33145 **Phn:** 305-285-1260 **Fax:** 305-858-5907 www.caracol1260.com admin@caracolusa.com

Coral Gables WURN-AM (ynt) 2525 Ponce de Leon Blvd # 250, Coral Gables FL 33134 **Phn:** 305-446-5444 **Fax:** 786-388-3868 www.actualidadradio.com aeden@bellsouth.net

Coral Gables WVUM-FM (v) PO Box 248191, Coral Gables FL 33124 **Phn:** 305-284-3955 www.wvum.org pd@wvum.org

Crestview WAAZ-FM (c) PO Box 267, Crestview FL 32536 **Phn:** 850-682-3040 **Fax:** 850-682-5232 waazwjsb@embarqmail.com

Crestview WJSB-AM (c) PO Box 267, Crestview FL 32536 **Phn:** 850-682-3040 **Fax:** 850-682-5232

Crestview WXEI-FM (t) 3497 Melissa Ln, Crestview FL 32539 **Phn:** 877-777-9934 www.wxei.8m.com

Crystal River WRGO-FM (o) 1929 Suncoast Blvd, Crystal River FL 34428 **Phn:** 352-795-1027 **Fax:** 352-795-0002 www.wrgoradio.com info@wrgoradio.com

Davie WAVS-AM (e) 6360 SW 41st Pl, Davie FL 33314 **Phn:** 954-584-1170 **Fax:** 954-581-6441 www.wavs1170.com info@wavs1170.com

Daytona Beach WAPN-FM (q) 1508 State Ave, Daytona Beach FL 32117 **Phn:** 386-677-4272 **Fax:** 386-677-7095 www.wapn.net wapn@wapn.net

Daytona Beach WHOG-FM (r) 126 W International Speedway Blvd, Daytona Beach FL 32114 **Phn:** 386-257-1150 **Fax:** 386-238-6488 www.newsdaytonabeach.comWHOG.html whogradio_tracy@yahoo.com

Daytona Beach WKRO-FM (c) 126 W International Speedway Blvd, Daytona Beach FL 32114 **Phn:** 386-255-9300 **Fax:** 386-238-6488

Daytona Beach WNDB-AM (snt) 126 W International Speedway Blvd, Daytona Beach FL 32114 **Phn:** 386-257-1150 **Fax:** 386-238-6488 newsdaytonabeach.com

Daytona Beach WPUL-AM (t) 427 Dr Martin Luther King Blvd, Daytona Beach FL 32114 **Phn:** 386-492-2908 **Fax:** 386-254-7510 www.wpul1590.com ccherry2@aol.com

Daytona Beach WROD-AM (o) 100 Marina Point Dr, Daytona Beach FL 32114 **Phn:** 386-253-0000 **Fax:** 386-255-3178 www.DaytonaOldies.com joe@wrodam.com

Daytona Beach WVYB-FM (ah) 126 W Intl Speedway Blvd, Daytona Beach FL 32114 **Phn:** 386-255-9300 **Fax:** 386-238-6488 1033wvyb.com frank@frankandtracy.com

Defuniak Springs WAKJ-FM (q) PO Box 125, Defuniak Springs FL 32435 **Phn:** 850-892-2107 **Fax:** 866-309-6532 www.wakj.org wakjradio@gmail.com

Defuniak Springs WZEP-AM (cno) PO Box 627, Defuniak Springs FL 32435 **Phn:** 850-892-3158 **Fax:** 850-892-9675 https:sites.google.comsitewzepam1460 wzep@wzep1460.com

Deland WYND-AM (qnt) 316 Taylor Rd E, Deland FL 32724 **Phn:** 386-734-1310

Delray Beach WDJA-AM (snt) 2710 W Atlantic Ave, Delray Beach FL 33445 **Phn:** 561-278-1420 **Fax:** 561-278-7815 roybresky@msn.com

Destin WECQ-FM (h) 34 Harbor Blvd # 202, Destin FL 32549 **Phn:** 850-654-1000 **Fax:** 850-654-6510 q92online.com seanmack@apexbroadcasting.com

Destin WWAV-FM (r) 743 Harbor Blvd Ste 6, Destin FL 32541 **Phn:** 850-654-1000 **Fax:** 850-654-6510

FLORIDA RADIO STATIONS

Eastpoint WOCY-FM (c) 35 Island Dr Ste 16, Eastpoint FL 32328 **Phn:** 850-670-8450 **Fax:** 850-670-8492 www.hitz106fm.com manager@oysterradio.com

Eastpoint WOYS-FM (r) 35 Island Dr Ste 16, Eastpoint FL 32328 **Phn:** 850-670-8450 **Fax:** 850-670-8492 oysterradio.com manager@oysterradio.com

Ellenton WBRD-AM (y) PO Box 826, Ellenton FL 34222 **Phn:** 941-266-4260 **Fax:** 941-723-9831 wbrd1420am@yahoo.com

Englewood WENG-AM (nt) PO Box 2908, Englewood FL 34295 **Phn:** 941-474-3231 **Fax:** 941-475-2205 www.wengradio.com kenb@wengradio.com

Englewood WSEB-FM (q) 135 W Dearborn St, Englewood FL 34223 **Phn:** 941-475-9732 **Fax:** 941-473-7308

Estero WJBX-FM (r) 20125 S Tamiami Trl, Estero FL 33928 **Phn:** 239-495-2100 **Fax:** 239-992-8165 99xonline.com brad@bbgi.com

Estero WJPT-FM (am) 20125 S Tamiami Trl, Estero FL 33928 **Phn:** 239-495-2100 **Fax:** 239-992-8165 sunny1063.com randy@sunny1063.com

Estero WRXK-FM (r) 20125 S Tamiami Trl, Estero FL 33928 **Phn:** 239-495-2100 **Fax:** 239-992-8165 96krock.com cd@bbgi.com

Estero WWCN-AM (st) 20125 S Tamiami Trl, Estero FL 33928 **Phn:** 239-495-2100 **Fax:** 239-992-8165 www.770espn.com johnjcassio@gmail.com

Estero WXKB-FM (h) 20125 S Tamiami Trl, Estero FL 33928 **Phn:** 239-495-2100 **Fax:** 239-992-8165 www.b1039.com adam.star@bbgi.com

Fort Lauderdale WAFG-FM (vqnt) 5555 N Federal Hwy, Fort Lauderdale FL 33308 **Phn:** 954-334-5000 **Fax:** 954-771-2633

Fort Myers WARO-FM (r) 2824 Palm Beach Blvd, Fort Myers FL 33916 **Phn:** 239-337-2346 **Fax:** 239-479-5583 www.classicrock945.com

Fort Myers WAYJ-FM (q) PO Box 61275, Fort Myers FL 33906 **Phn:** 239-936-1929 **Fax:** 239-936-5433 wayj.wayfm.com contact@wayfm.com

Fort Myers WBTT-FM (hx) 13320 Metro Pkwy Ste 1, Fort Myers FL 33966 **Phn:** 239-225-4300 **Fax:** 239-225-4410 www.1055thebeat.com scrappy@1055thebeat.com

Fort Myers WCKT-FM (c) 13320 Metro Pkwy Ste 1, Fort Myers FL 33966 **Phn:** 239-225-4300 **Fax:** 239-225-4410 www.catcountry1071.com sherrigriswold@clearchannel.com

Fort Myers WCRM-AM (yu) 3548 Canal St, Fort Myers FL 33916 **Phn:** 239-332-1350 **Fax:** 239-332-8890 www.vidaradionetwork.com fvida1350@gmail.com

Fort Myers WGCU-FM (pnja) 10501 Fgcu Blvd S, Fort Myers FL 33965 **Phn:** 239-590-2500 **Fax:** 239-590-2520 wgcu.org wgcunews@wgcu.org

Fort Myers WINK-AM (nt) 2824 Palm Beach Blvd, Fort Myers FL 33916 **Phn:** 239-338-4380 **Fax:** 239-479-5579 www.925foxnews.com michael@969morefm.com

Fort Myers WINK-FM (a) 2824 Palm Beach Blvd, Fort Myers FL 33916 **Phn:** 239-337-2346 **Fax:** 239-332-0767 www.winkfm.com

Fort Myers WNOG-AM (nt) 2824 Palm Beach Blvd, Fort Myers FL 33916 **Phn:** 239-337-2346 **Fax:** 239-332-0767 www.925foxnews.com joe.schwartzel@mbimail.com

Fort Myers WOLZ-FM (o) 13320 Metro Pkwy Ste 1, Fort Myers FL 33966 **Phn:** 239-225-4300 **Fax:** 239-225-4329 www.953theriver.com

Fort Myers WTLQ-FM (y) 2824 Palm Beach Blvd, Fort Myers FL 33916 **Phn:** 239-334-1111 **Fax:** 239-334-0744 www.latino977.com hector.velazquez@fmbcradio.com

Fort Myers WTLT-FM (a) 2824 Palm Beach Blvd, Fort Myers FL 33916 **Phn:** 239-337-2346 **Fax:** 239-479-5583 www.lite937.com

Fort Myers WWCL-AM (y) PO Box 50580, Fort Myers FL 33994 **Phn:** 239-369-0344 **Fax:** 239-369-3386

Fort Myers WZJZ-FM (ha) 13320 Metro Pkwy Ste 1, Fort Myers FL 33966 **Phn:** 239-225-4300 **Fax:** 239-225-4329 www.1055thebeat.com scrappy@1055thebeat.com

Fort Pierce WJNX-AM (y) 4100 Metzger Rd, Fort Pierce FL 34947 **Phn:** 772-340-1590 **Fax:** 772-340-3245 www.lagigante1330.com

Fort Pierce WPSL-AM (st) 4100 Metzger Rd, Fort Pierce FL 34947 **Phn:** 772-340-1590 **Fax:** 772-340-3245 www.wpsl.com

Fort Pierce WQCS-FM (pln) 3209 Virginia Ave, Fort Pierce FL 34981 **Phn:** 772-465-8989 **Fax:** 772-462-4743 www.wqcs.org news@wqcs.org

Fort Pierce WSTU-AM (o) 4100 Metzger Rd, Fort Pierce FL 34947 **Phn:** 772-220-9788 **Fax:** 772-340-3245 www.wstu1450.com

Fort Walton Beach WBAU-AM (a) 21 Miracle Strip Pkwy SE, Fort Walton Beach FL 32548 **Phn:** 850-244-1400 **Fax:** 850-243-1471

Fort Walton Beach WFTW-AM (nt) 225 Hollywood Blvd NW, Fort Walton Beach FL 32548 **Phn:** 850-243-7676 **Fax:** 850-664-0203 www.wftw.com ken@wftw.com

Fort Walton Beach WKSM-FM (r) 225 Hollywood Blvd NW, Fort Walton Beach FL 32548 **Phn:** 850-243-7676 **Fax:** 850-243-6806 www.wksm.com woofy@wksm.com

Fort Walton Beach WNCV-FM (a) 225 Hollywood Blvd NW, Fort Walton Beach FL 32548 **Phn:** 850-243-7676 **Fax:** 850-243-6806 www.wncv.com bobchase@wncv.com

Fort Walton Beach WPSM-FM (aq) PO Box 10, Fort Walton Beach FL 32549 **Phn:** 850-244-7667 **Fax:** 850-244-3254 www.wpsm.com

Fort Walton Beach WTKE-FM (s) 21 Miracle Strip Pkwy SE, Fort Walton Beach FL 32548 **Phn:** 850-244-1400 **Fax:** 850-243-1471 www.theticketsportsnetwork.com

Fort Walton Beach WYZB-FM (c) 225 Hollywood Blvd NW, Fort Walton Beach FL 32548 **Phn:** 850-243-2323 **Fax:** 850-243-6806 www.wyzb.com

Fort Walton Beach WZNS-FM (h) 225 Hollywood Blvd NW, Fort Walton Beach FL 32548 **Phn:** 850-243-7676 **Fax:** 850-243-6806 www.z96.com hayden@z96.com

Gainesville WAJD-AM (m) 7120 SW 24th Ave, Gainesville FL 32607 **Phn:** 352-331-2200 **Fax:** 352-331-0401 music.disney.com

Gainesville WBXY-FM (snt) 4424 NW 13th St, Gainesville FL 32609 **Phn:** x52-375-1317 **Fax:** 352-375-6961 www.party995.com

Gainesville WDVH-AM (c) 100 NW 76th Dr Ste 2, Gainesville FL 32607 **Phn:** 352-313-3150 **Fax:** 352-313-3166

Gainesville WDVH-FM (c) 100 NW 76th Dr Ste 2, Gainesville FL 32607 **Phn:** 352-313-3150 **Fax:** 352-313-3166

Gainesville WHHZ-FM (r) 100 NW 76th Dr Ste 2, Gainesville FL 32607 **Phn:** 352-313-3150 **Fax:** 352-313-3166 www.1005thebuzz.com kevin.mangan@marcradio.com

Gainesville WHIJ-FM (q) 408 W University Ave Ste 206, Gainesville FL 32601 **Phn:** 352-351-8810 **Fax:** 352-351-8917 www.thejoyfm.com thejoyfm@thejoyfm.com

Gainesville WJLF-FM (q) 2131 NW 40th Ter Ste F, Gainesville FL 32605 **Phn:** 352-373-9553 **Fax:** 352-373-9888 www.thejoyfm.com thejoyfm@thejoyfm.com

Gainesville WKTK-FM (na) 3600 NW 43rd St Ste B, Gainesville FL 32606 **Phn:** 352-377-0985 **Fax:** 352-377-1884 www.ktk985.com cmalone@entercom.com

Gainesville WNDN-FM (r) 4020 W Newberry Rd, Gainesville FL 32607 **Phn:** 352-373-6644 www.windfm.com windfm@windfm.com

Gainesville WNDT-FM (r) 4020 W Newberry Rd Ste 100, Gainesville FL 32607 **Phn:** 352-373-6644 **Fax:** 352-375-1700 www.windfm.com hunter@windfm.com

Gainesville WPLL-FM (a) 100 NW 76th Dr, Gainesville FL 32607 **Phn:** 352-313-3150 **Fax:** 352-313-3166 www.1069pulsefm.com kevin.mangan@marcradio.com

Gainesville WRUF-FM (r) PO Box 14444, Gainesville FL 32604 **Phn:** 352-392-0771 **Fax:** 352-392-0519 www.rock104.com md@rock104.com

Gainesville WRUF-AM (snt) PO Box 14444, Gainesville FL 32604 **Phn:** 352-392-0771 **Fax:** 352-392-0519 www.wruf.com tkrynski@wruf.com

Gainesville WSKY-FM (nt) 3600 NW 43rd St Ste B, Gainesville FL 32606 **Phn:** 352-377-0985 **Fax:** 352-337-2968 www.thesky973.com jckirwan@entercom.com

Gainesville WTMG-FM (au) 100 NW 76th Dr Ste 2, Gainesville FL 32607 **Phn:** 352-313-3110 **Fax:** 352-313-3166 www.magic1013.com camellia.pflum@marcradio.com

Gainesville WTMN-AM (g) 249 W University Ave Ste B, Gainesville FL 32601 **Phn:** 352-371-1980 **Fax:** 352-338-0566

Gainesville WUFT-FM (vn) PO Box 118405, Gainesville FL 32611 **Phn:** 352-392-5551 **Fax:** 352-392-5741 www.wuft.orgfm radio@wuft.org

Gainesville WXJZ-FM (aj) 4424 NW 13th St, Gainesville FL 32609 **Phn:** 352-375-1317 **Fax:** 352-375-6961 www.wxjz.fm

Gainesville WYKS-FM (h) 7120 SW 24th Ave, Gainesville FL 32607 **Phn:** 352-331-2200 **Fax:** 352-331-0401 www.kiss1053.com doug@kiss1053.com

Green Cove Springs WAYR-AM (q) 2500 Russell Rd, Green Cove Springs FL 32043 **Phn:** 904-284-1111 **Fax:** 904-284-2501 550.wayradio.org manager@wayradio.org

Haines City WLVF-FM (gq) 810 E Hinson Ave, Haines City FL 33844 **Phn:** 863-422-9583 **Fax:** 863-422-0110 www.gospel903.org info@gospel903.com

Hernando WRZN-AM (bo) 3988 N Roscoe Rd, Hernando FL 34442 **Phn:** 352-726-7221 **Fax:** 352-726-3172

Hialeah WMYM-AM (m) 2150 W 68th St Ste 202, Hialeah FL 33016 **Phn:** 305-823-0990 **Fax:** 305-823-9322 music.disney.com

Hollywood WEDR-FM (wu) 2741 N 29th Ave, Hollywood FL 33020 **Phn:** 305-444-4404 **Fax:** 305-567-5774 www.wedr.com jerry.rushin@coxradio.com

Hollywood WFEZ-FM (a) 2741 N 29th Ave, Hollywood FL 33020 **Phn:** 305-444-4404 **Fax:** 954-847-3201 www.easy93.com gary.williams@coxinc.com

Hollywood WFLC-FM (a) 2741 N 29th Ave, Hollywood FL 33020 **Phn:** 954-584-7117 **Fax:** 954-847-3201 www.973thecoast.com tom.calococci@coxinc.com

Hollywood WHDR-FM (r) 2741 N 29th Ave, Hollywood FL 33020 **Phn:** 305-444-4404 **Fax:** 954-847-3201 www.party931.com pmt@coxradio.com

Hollywood WHQT-FM (wut) 2741 N 29th Ave, Hollywood FL 33020 **Phn:** 305-444-4404 **Fax:** 954-847-3200 www.hot105fm.com jerry.rushin@coxradio.com

FLORIDA RADIO STATIONS

Homestead WKLG-FM (a) 1460 Jefferson Dr, Homestead FL 33034 **Phn:** 305-246-1123 www.wklginc.com cs@wklginc.com

Homosassa WXOF-FM (h) 4554 S Suncoast Blvd, Homosassa FL 34446 **Phn:** 352-628-4444 **Fax:** 352-628-4450 www.thefox967.com staff@thefox967.com

Homosassa Springs WXCV-FM (a) 4554 S Suncoast Blvd, Homosassa Springs FL 34446 **Phn:** 352-628-4444 **Fax:** 352-628-4450 laura@citrus953.com

Hudson WJQB-FM (o) 13825 US Highway 19 Ste 400, Hudson FL 34667 **Phn:** 727-697-1063 **Fax:** 727-817-1063 www.trueoldies1063.com staff@trueoldies1063.com

Immokalee WAFZ-AM (y) 2105 W Immokalee Dr, Immokalee FL 34142 **Phn:** 239-657-9210 **Fax:** 888-859-9210 www.wafz.com ricardo@gladesmedia.com

Immokalee WAFZ-FM (y) 2105 W Immokalee Dr, Immokalee FL 34142 **Phn:** 239-657-9210 **Fax:** 888-859-9210 www.wafz.com kc@gladesmedia.com

Jacksonville WAPE-FM (h) 8000 Belfort Pkwy, Jacksonville FL 32256 **Phn:** 904-245-8500 **Fax:** 904-245-8501 www.wape.com tim.clarke@coxinc.com

Jacksonville WAYL-FM (q) 4190 Belfort Rd #450, Jacksonville FL 32216 **Phn:** 904-641-9626 **Fax:** 904-645-9626 fm88.org contact@fm88.org

Jacksonville WBOB-AM (snt) 4190 Belfort Rd Ste 450, Jacksonville FL 32216 **Phn:** 904-470-4615 **Fax:** 904-296-1683 www.600wbob.com charlotte@600wbob.com

Jacksonville WCGL-AM (qwg) 3890 Dunn Ave Ste 804, Jacksonville FL 32218 **Phn:** 904-766-9955 **Fax:** 904-765-9214 www.wcgl1360.com wcgl@aol.com

Jacksonville WCRJ-FM (q) 2361 Cortez Rd, Jacksonville FL 32246 **Phn:** 904-641-9626 **Fax:** 904-645-9626 fm88.org calvin@ilovethepromise.com

Jacksonville WEJZ-FM (a) 6440 Atlantic Blvd, Jacksonville FL 32211 **Phn:** 904-727-9696 **Fax:** 904-721-9322 www.wejz.com jbyard@rendabroadcasting.com

Jacksonville WFJO-FM (s) 9550 Regency Square Blvd Ste 200, Jacksonville FL 32225 **Phn:** 904-680-1050 **Fax:** 904-680-1051

Jacksonville WFKS-FM (h) 11700 Central Pkwy, Jacksonville FL 32224 **Phn:** 904-636-0507 www.979kissfm.com erinweiffenbach@clearchannel.com

Jacksonville WFXJ-AM (s) 11700 Central Pkwy, Jacksonville FL 32224 **Phn:** 904-636-0507 **Fax:** 904-997-7713 www.sportsradiojax.com

Jacksonville WFYV-FM (r) 8000 Belfort Pkwy, Jacksonville FL 32256 **Phn:** 904-245-8500 **Fax:** 904-245-8501 www.rock1045.com todd.shannon@coxradio.com

Jacksonville WGNE-FM (c) 6440 Atlantic Blvd, Jacksonville FL 32211 **Phn:** 904-727-9696 **Fax:** 904-721-9322 www.999gatorcountry.com cbeck@rendabroadcasting.com

Jacksonville WHJX-FM (u) 9550 Regency Square Blvd Ste 200, Jacksonville FL 32225 **Phn:** 904-680-1050 **Fax:** 904-680-1051 www.whjx.biz joelwiddows@msn.com

Jacksonville WJAX-AM (b) 5353 Arlington Expy, Jacksonville FL 32211 **Phn:** 904-680-1220 www.wjaxradio.com kjones@jones.edu

Jacksonville WJBT-FM (uw) 11700 Central Pkwy, Jacksonville FL 32224 **Phn:** 904-636-0507 www.wjbt.com geewiz@ccjax.com

Jacksonville WJCT-FM (plnj) 100 Festival Park Ave, Jacksonville FL 32202 **Phn:** 904-353-7770 **Fax:** 904-358-6352 www.wjct.org

Jacksonville WJFR-FM (q) 2771 Monument Rd Ste 29 # 318, Jacksonville FL 32225 **Phn:** 904-389-9088 www.familyradio.com

Jacksonville WJGL-FM (h) 8000 Belfort Pkwy, Jacksonville FL 32256 **Phn:** 904-245-8500 **Fax:** 904-245-8501 www.969theeagle.com todd.shannon@coxradio.com

Jacksonville WJGR-AM (sn) 4190 Belfort Rd Ste 450, Jacksonville FL 32216 **Phn:** 904-296-1683

Jacksonville WJSJ-FM (aj) 9550 Regency Square Blvd Ste 200, Jacksonville FL 32225 **Phn:** 904-680-1050 **Fax:** 904-680-1051 www.smoothjazz1053.com joelwiddows@msn.com

Jacksonville WJXL-AM (st) 9090 Hogan Rd, Jacksonville FL 32216 **Phn:** 904-641-1011 **Fax:** 904-641-1022 www.1010xl.com steveg@1010xl.com

Jacksonville WJXR-FM (t) PO Box 1, Jacksonville FL 32234 **Phn:** 904-259-2292 **Fax:** 904-259-4488 www.wjxr.com info@wjxr.com

Jacksonville WKTZ-FM (z) 5353 Arlington Expy Fl 4, Jacksonville FL 32211 **Phn:** 904-371-1184 wktz.jones.edu kjones@jones.edu

Jacksonville WMUV-FM (c) 6440 Atlantic Blvd, Jacksonville FL 32211 **Phn:** 904-727-9696 **Fax:** 904-721-9322 www.bull1007.com cbeck@rendabroadcasting.com

Jacksonville WMXQ-FM (am) 8000 Belfort Pkwy, Jacksonville FL 32256 **Phn:** 904-245-8500 **Fax:** 904-245-8501 www.x1029.com aaron.schachter@coxradio.com

Jacksonville WOKV-FM (nt) 8000 Belfort Pkwy, Jacksonville FL 32256 **Phn:** 904-245-8500 **Fax:** 904-245-8501 www.wokv.com news@wokv.com

Jacksonville WOKV-AM (nt) 8000 Belfort Pkwy, Jacksonville FL 32256 **Phn:** 904-245-8500 **Fax:** 904-245-8501 www.wokv.com news@wokv.com

Jacksonville WPLA-FM (r) 11700 Central Pkwy, Jacksonville FL 32224 **Phn:** 904-636-0507 **Fax:** 904-998-3070 www.1073jack.com skipk@1073jack.com

Jacksonville WQIK-FM (c) 11700 Central Pkwy, Jacksonville FL 32224 **Phn:** 904-636-0507 **Fax:** 904-636-7971 www.991wqik.com cindyspicer@clearchannel.com

Jacksonville WROO-FM (c) 11700 Central Pkwy, Jacksonville FL 32224 **Phn:** 904-642-3030 **Fax:** 904-636-0533

Jacksonville WROS-AM (qg) 5590 Rio Grande Ave, Jacksonville FL 32254 **Phn:** 904-353-1050 **Fax:** 904-353-7076 www.wros.net wros@wros.net

Jacksonville WSOL-FM (xuw) 11700 Central Pkwy, Jacksonville FL 32224 **Phn:** 904-636-0507 **Fax:** 904-997-7713 www.v1015.com kj@v1015.com

Jacksonville WSOS-FM (a) 6440 Atlantic Blvd, Jacksonville FL 32211 **Phn:** 904-727-9696 **Fax:** 904-721-9322 www.classicrock941.com breese@rendabroadcasting.com

Jacksonville WXXJ-FM (r) 8000 Belfort Pkwy, Jacksonville FL 32256 **Phn:** 904-245-8500 **Fax:** 904-245-8501 www.1075wzrx.com aaron@x1029.com

Jacksonville WYMM-AM (q) 5900 Pickettville Rd, Jacksonville FL 32254 **Phn:** 904-786-2820 **Fax:** 904-786-2661

Jacksonville WZAZ-AM (g) 4190 Belfort Rd Ste 450, Jacksonville FL 32216 **Phn:** 904-470-4707 **Fax:** 904-652-1426 www.wzaz.com manager@wzaz.com

Jacksonville WZNZ-AM (q) 4190 Belfort Rd Ste 450, Jacksonville FL 32216 **Phn:** 904-470-4630 **Fax:** 904-296-1683

Jacksonville Beach WQOP-AM (qt) PO Box 51585, Jacksonville Beach FL 32240 **Phn:** 904-241-3311 **Fax:** 904-241-1402 www.qopradio.com radioqop@aol.com

Key West WAIL-FM (r) 5450 MacDonald Ave Ste 10, Key West FL 33040 **Phn:** 305-296-7511 **Fax:** 305-296-0358 www.sun103.com deweyengstrom@clearchannel.com

Key West WEOW-FM (h) 5450 MacDonald Ave Ste 10, Key West FL 33040 **Phn:** 305-296-7511 **Fax:** 305-296-0358 www.weow927.com billbravo@clearchannel.com

Key West WIIS-FM (r) 1075 Duval St Ste C17, Key West FL 33040 **Phn:** 305-292-1133 **Fax:** 305-292-6936 www.Island107.com linda@island107.com

Key West WJIR-FM (vqa) 1209 United St, Key West FL 33040 **Phn:** 305-296-5773 **Fax:** 305-294-9547

Key West WKEY-FM (a) 5450 MacDonald Ave Ste 10, Key West FL 33040 **Phn:** 305-296-7511 **Fax:** 305-296-1155 www.key935.com kperez@clearchannel.com

Key West WKWF-AM (st) 5450 MacDonald Ave Ste 10, Key West FL 33040 **Phn:** 305-296-7511 **Fax:** 305-296-0358 www.sportsradio1600.com scotthamilton@clearchannel.com

Key West WKYZ-FM (a) 5555 College Rd, Key West FL 33040 **Phn:** 305-587-3636 www.wkyz.com info@wkyz.com

Lake City WCJX-FM (r) 1305 E Helvenston St, Lake City FL 32055 **Phn:** 386-755-9259 **Fax:** 386-755-1557

Lake City WDSR-AM (h) 2485 S Marion Ave, Lake City FL 32025 **Phn:** 386-752-1340 barry@mix943.com

Lake City WGRO-AM (c) 9206 W US Highway 90, Lake City FL 32055 **Phn:** 386-752-0960 **Fax:** 386-752-9861

Lake City WNFB-FM (a) 2485 S Marion Ave, Lake City FL 32025 **Phn:** 386-752-1340 **Fax:** 386-755-9369 northfloridanow.com wnfb@mix943.com

Lake City WQLC-FM (c) 9206 W US Highway 90, Lake City FL 32055 **Phn:** 386-755-4102 **Fax:** 386-752-9861

Lake Worth WPBR-AM (t) 1776 Lake Worth Rd Ste 201, Lake Worth FL 33460 **Phn:** 561-641-8882 **Fax:** 561-533-0607 sakpaseamerica.com

Lakeland WLKF-AM (nt) 404 W Lime St, Lakeland FL 33815 **Phn:** 863-682-8184 **Fax:** 863-683-2409 www.wlkf.com

Lakeland WONN-AM (ma) 404 W Lime St, Lakeland FL 33815 **Phn:** 863-682-8184 **Fax:** 863-683-2409 www.wonn.com

Lakeland WPCV-FM (c) 404 W Lime St, Lakeland FL 33815 **Phn:** 863-682-8184 **Fax:** 863-683-2409 wpcv.com

Lakeland WWRZ-FM (a) 404 W Lime St, Lakeland FL 33815 **Phn:** 863-682-8184 **Fax:** 863-683-2409 www.max983fm.com news@wpcv.com

Largo WHBO-AM (s) 800 8th Ave SE, Largo FL 33771 **Phn:** 813-281-1040 **Fax:** 813-281-1948 www.sportstalkflorida.com

Largo WWBA-AM (snt) 800 8th Ave SE, Largo FL 33771 **Phn:** 813-281-1040 **Fax:** 813-281-1948 www.newstalkflorida.com

Leesburg WLBE-AM (to) 32900 Radio Rd, Leesburg FL 34788 **Phn:** 352-787-7900 790wlbe@comcast.net

Live Oak WLVO-FM (r) PO Box 1061, Live Oak FL 32064 **Phn:** 386-364-1061 **Fax:** 386-362-3148

FLORIDA RADIO STATIONS

Live Oak WOLR-FM (q) PO Box 1448, Live Oak FL 32064 **Phn:** 386-935-3300   www.christianhitradio.net 913fm@email.com

Live Oak WQHL-FM (c) 1305 Helvenston St SE, Live Oak FL 32064 **Phn:** 386-362-1250 **Fax:** 386-364-3504 northflatoday.com   dean@wqhl981.com

Live Oak WQHL-AM (c) 1305 Helvenston St SE, Live Oak FL 32064 **Phn:** 386-362-1250 **Fax:** 386-364-3504 wqhl981.com   dean@wqhl981.com

Madison WMAF-AM (c) PO Box 621, Madison FL 32341 **Phn:** 850-973-3233 **Fax:** 850-973-3097 www.1230wmaf.com   countrywmaf@embarqmail.com

Maitland WFLF-AM (nt) 2500 Maitland Center Pkwy Ste 401, Maitland FL 32751 **Phn:** 407-916-7800 **Fax:** 407-661-1940   www.1045wfla.com jimpoling@clearchannel.com

Maitland WHLF-FM (snt) 2500 Maitland Center Pkwy Ste 401, Maitland FL 32751 **Phn:** 407-916-7800 **Fax:** 407-916-7407   www.1045wfla.com jimpoling@clearchannel.com

Maitland WJRR-FM (r) 2500 Maitland Center Pkwy Ste 401, Maitland FL 32751 **Phn:** 407-916-7800 **Fax:** 407-916-7407 www.wjrr.com   rickeverett@wjrr.com

Maitland WLOQ-FM (j) 2301 Lucien Way Ste 180, Maitland FL 32751 **Phn:** 407-647-5557 **Fax:** 407-647-4495

Maitland WMGF-FM (a) 2500 Maitland Center Pkwy Ste 401, Maitland FL 32751 **Phn:** 407-916-7800 **Fax:** 407-916-7407   www.magic107.com laurakam@cccorlando.com

Maitland WRUM-FM (y) 2500 Maitland Center Pkwy Ste 401, Maitland FL 32751 **Phn:** 407-916-7800 **Fax:** 407-916-7407   www.rumba100.com suheiley@rumba100.com

Maitland WTKS-FM (rt) 2500 Maitland Center Pkwy Ste 401, Maitland FL 32751 **Phn:** 407-916-7800 **Fax:** 407-916-0329   www.realradio.fm programdirector@wtks.com

Maitland WXXL-FM (h) 2500 Maitland Center Pkwy Ste 401, Maitland FL 32751 **Phn:** 407-916-7800 **Fax:** 407-916-7407   www.xl1067.com kristinluby@clearchannel.com

Maitland WYGM-AM (s) 2500 Maitland Center Pkwy Ste 401, Maitland FL 32751 **Phn:** 407-916-7800 **Fax:** 407-916-7407   www.740thegame.com rickeverett@clearchannel.com

Marathon WFFG-AM (snt) PO Box 500940, Marathon FL 33050 **Phn:** 305-743-5563 **Fax:** 305-293-4014

Marathon WGMX-FM (a) PO Box 500940, Marathon FL 33050 **Phn:** 305-743-5563 **Fax:** 305-293-4014

Marianna WJAQ-FM (c) PO Box 569, Marianna FL 32447 **Phn:** 850-482-3046 **Fax:** 850-482-3049

Marianna WTYS-AM (c) PO Box 777, Marianna FL 32447 **Phn:** 850-482-2131 **Fax:** 850-526-3687 www.wtys.cc   wtysradio@embarqmail.com

Marianna WTYS-FM (g) PO Box 777, Marianna FL 32447 **Phn:** 850-482-2131 **Fax:** 850-526-3687 www.wtys.cc   wtysradio@phonl.com

Mayo WGSG-FM (q) PO Box 644, Mayo FL 32066 **Phn:** 386-294-2525

Melbourne WAOA-FM (ah) 1800 W Hibiscus Blvd Ste 138, Melbourne FL 32901 **Phn:** 321-984-1000 **Fax:** 321-724-1565   www.wa1a.com melbourne.promotions@cumulus.com

Melbourne WBVD-FM (h) 1388 S Babcock St, Melbourne FL 32901 **Phn:** 321-821-7100 www.mykiss951.com   deano@clearchannel.com

Melbourne WCIF-FM (q) PO Box 366, Melbourne FL 32902 **Phn:** 321-725-9243   www.wcif.com info@wcif.com

Melbourne WFIT-FM (vjn) 150 W University Blvd, Melbourne FL 32901 **Phn:** 321-674-8140 **Fax:** 321-674-8139 www.wfit.org   wfit@fit.edu

Melbourne WHKR-FM (c) 1775 W Hibiscus Blvd Ste 101, Melbourne FL 32901 **Phn:** 321-984-1000 **Fax:** 321-724-1565   www.thehitkicker.com melbourne.promotions@cumulus.com

Melbourne WINT-AM (ob) 1800 W Hibiscus Blvd Ste 138, Melbourne FL 32901 **Phn:** 321-984-1000 **Fax:** 321-724-1565   www.wa1a.com melbourne.promotions@cumulus.com

Melbourne WLRQ-FM (a) 1388 S Babcock St, Melbourne FL 32901 **Phn:** 321-821-7100 **Fax:** 321-733-0904   www.literock993.com michaellowe@clearchannel.com

Melbourne WMMB-AM (nt) 1388 S Babcock St, Melbourne FL 32901 **Phn:** 321-821-7100 **Fax:** 321-733-0904 www.wmmbam.com   billmick@clearchannel.com

Melbourne WMMV-AM (nt) 1388 S Babcock St, Melbourne FL 32901 **Phn:** 321-821-7100 **Fax:** 321-733-0904 www.wmmbam.com   billmick@clearchannel.com

Melbourne WSBH-FM (or) 380 N Wickham Rd, Melbourne FL 32935 **Phn:** 321-752-9850 **Fax:** 321-254-2057 www.beach985.com   rmichaels@beach985.com

Melbourne WSJZ-FM (s) 1800 W Hibiscus Blvd Ste 138, Melbourne FL 32901 **Phn:** 321-984-1000 **Fax:** 321-724-1565   www.espn959.com melbourne.promotions@cumulus.com

Miami WACC-AM (yq) 1779 NW 28th St, Miami FL 33142   **Phn:** 305-638-9729 **Fax:** 305-635-4748 www.paxcc.org   rmcid@paxcc.org

Miami WAXY-AM (snt) 20450 NW 2nd Ave, Miami FL 33169   **Phn:** 305-521-5100 **Fax:** 305-521-1416 www.theticketmiami.com gary.aybar@lincolnfinancialmedia.com

Miami WCMQ-FM (y) 7007 NW 77th Ave, Miami FL 33166 **Phn:** 305-444-9292 **Fax:** 305-461-0987 www.clasica92fm.com   jcaride@sbsmiami.com

Miami WDNA-FM (vjy) PO Box 558636, Miami FL 33255 **Phn:** 305-662-8889 **Fax:** 305-662-1975 www.wdna.org mpelleya@wdna.org

Miami WKAT-AM (y) 2828 W Flagler St, Miami FL 33135 **Phn:** 305-503-1340 **Fax:** 305-677-7585 www.1360wkat.com

Miami WKIS-FM (c) 194 NW 187th St, Miami FL 33169 **Phn:** 305-654-1700 www.wkis.com   joe@wkis.com

Miami WLQY-AM (ey) 10800 Biscayne Blvd Ste 810, Miami FL 33161 **Phn:** 305-891-1729 **Fax:** 305-891-1583 risas@bellsouth.net

Miami WLRN-FM (pn) 172 NE 15th St, Miami FL 33132 **Phn:** 305-995-1717 **Fax:** 305-995-2221 www.wlrn.org radionews@miamiherald.com

Miami WLYF-FM (a) 20450 NW 2nd Ave, Miami FL 33169 **Phn:** 305-521-5100 **Fax:** 305-521-1413 www.litemiami.com   litefm@litemiami.com

Miami WMCU-AM (qv) 2828 W Flagler St, Miami FL 33135 **Phn:** 305-644-0800 **Fax:** 305-677-7585 www.1080theanswer.com   info@1080theanswer.com

Miami WMKL-FM (t) PO Box 561832, Miami FL 33256 **Phn:** 786-429-3606   callfm.com

Miami WMXJ-FM (o) 20450 NW 2nd Ave, Miami FL 33169 **Phn:** 305-521-5100 **Fax:** 305-521-1415 www.magicmiami.com   webmasterwmxj@wmxj.com

Miami WOCN-AM () 350 NE 71st St, Miami FL 33138 **Phn:** 305-759-7280 **Fax:** 305-759-2276

Miami WPOW-FM (h) 194 NW 187th St, Miami FL 33169 **Phn:** 305-654-1715 **Fax:** 305-770-1456 www.power96.com   jill.strada@power96.com

Miami WQAM-AM (snt) 20295 NW 2nd Ave Ste 300, Miami FL 33169 **Phn:** 305-653-6796 **Fax:** 305-770-1456 www.wqam.com   joshd@wqam.com

Miami WRHC-AM (y) 330 SW 27th Ave Ste 207, Miami FL 33135 **Phn:** 305-541-3300 **Fax:** 305-541-2013 www.cadenaazul.com

Miami WRMA-FM (y) 7007 NW 77th Ave, Miami FL 33166 **Phn:** 305-444-9292 **Fax:** 305-883-1264 romancefm.lamusica.com   jacinsbs@hotmail.com

Miami WWFE-AM (y) 330 SW 27th Ave Ste 207, Miami FL 33135 **Phn:** 305-541-3300 **Fax:** 305-541-9585 www.lapoderosa.com   info@cadenaazul.com

Miami WXDJ-FM (y) 7007 NW 77th Ave, Miami FL 33166 **Phn:** 305-533-9200 **Fax:** 305-250-4332 elzol.lamusica.com   jacinsbs@hotmail.com

Milton WEBY-AM (nt) 7179 Printers Aly, Milton FL 32583 **Phn:** 850-983-2242 **Fax:** 850-983-3231 www.1330weby.com   mikebates@1330weby.com

Milton WECM-AM (y) 6583 Berryhill Rd, Milton FL 32570 **Phn:** 850-623-1490

Miramar WBGG-FM (r) 7601 Riviera Blvd, Miramar FL 33023 **Phn:** 954-862-2000 **Fax:** 954-862-4210 www.big1059.com   rmcmillan@ccmiami.com

Miramar WHYI-FM (h) 7601 Riviera Blvd, Miramar FL 33023 **Phn:** 954-862-2000 **Fax:** 954-862-4013 www.y100.com   ejones@ccmiami.com

Miramar WINZ-AM (s) 7601 Riviera Blvd, Miramar FL 33023 **Phn:** 954-862-2000 **Fax:** 954-862-4019 www.940winz.com   kcerenzia@ccmiami.com

Miramar WIOD-AM (nt) 7601 Riviera Blvd, Miramar FL 33023 **Phn:** 954-862-2000 **Fax:** 954-862-4012 www.wiod.com   graceblazer@clearchannel.com

Miramar WMGE-FM (y) 7601 Riviera Blvd, Miramar FL 33023 **Phn:** 954-862-2000 **Fax:** 954-862-4012 www.mega949.com   rayhernandez@clearchannel.com

Miramar WMIA-FM (ah) 7601 Riviera Blvd, Miramar FL 33023 **Phn:** 954-862-2000 **Fax:** 954-862-2001 www.939mia.com   rayhernandez@clearchannel.com

Miramar WMIB-FM (y) 7601 Riviera Blvd, Miramar FL 33023 **Phn:** 954-862-2000 **Fax:** 954-862-4013 www.1035superx.com   vcurry@wmbm.com

Naples WAVV-FM (z) 11800 Tamiami Trl E, Naples FL 34113 **Phn:** 239-793-1011 **Fax:** 239-793-7000 www.wavv101.com   kennylamb@wavv101.com

Naples WCNZ-AM (t) 5043 Tamiami Trl E, Naples FL 34113 **Phn:** 239-732-9369 **Fax:** 239-732-7267 bladd@mail.com

Naples WSRX-FM (q) 3805 The Lords Way, Naples FL 34114 **Phn:** 239-775-8950 **Fax:** 239-774-5889 praisefm895@msn.com

New Smyrna Beach WKTO-FM (q) 900 Old Mission Rd, New Smyrna Beach FL 32168 **Phn:** 386-427-1095 **Fax:** 386-427-8970 wkto.net   carol@wkto.net

New Smyrna Beach WSBB-AM (q) 229 Canal St, New Smyrna Beach FL 32168 **Phn:** 386-428-9091 **Fax:** 386-428-1924   skipdiegel@wsbbradio.com

North Miami WMBM-AM (gwt) 13242 NW 7th Ave, North Miami FL 33168 **Phn:** 305-769-1100 **Fax:** 305-769-9975 www.wmbm.com   trobinson@wmbm.com

North Miami Beach WSRF-AM (exg) 1510 NE 162nd St, North Miami Beach FL 33162 **Phn:** 305-940-1580 **Fax:** 305-947-8050 www.wsrf.com   info@wsrf.com

FLORIDA RADIO STATIONS

Ocala WAQV-FM (q) 3343 E Silver Springs Blvd, Ocala FL 34470 **Phn:** 352-351-8810 **Fax:** 352-351-8917 www.thejoyfm.com thejoyfm@thejoyfm.com

Ocala WLQH-AM (m) 2830 Old Fanning Spring Rd, Ocala FL 34470 **Phn:** 352-493-4940 **Fax:** 352-493-9909

Ocala WMFQ-FM (o) 3357 SW 7th St, Ocala FL 34474 **Phn:** 352-732-0079 **Fax:** 352-622-6675 www.radio92q.com

Ocala WMOP-AM (s) PO Box 3930, Ocala FL 34478 **Phn:** 352-732-2010 **Fax:** 352-629-1614 www.floridasportstalk.fm thesportsfix@espngo1.com

Ocala WNDD-FM (r) 3602 NE 20th Pl, Ocala FL 34470 **Phn:** 352-622-9500 **Fax:** 352-622-1900 www.windfm.com windfm@windfm.com

Ocala WOCA-AM (nt) PO Box 1056, Ocala FL 34478 **Phn:** 352-732-8000 **Fax:** 352-240-3858 thesource1370.com woca@woca.com

Ocala WOGK-FM (c) 3602 NE 20th Pl, Ocala FL 34470 **Phn:** 352-622-5600 **Fax:** 352-622-3998 www.937kcountry.com kcountry93@aol.com

Ocala WTRS-FM (c) 3357 SW 7th St, Ocala FL 34474 **Phn:** 352-867-1023 **Fax:** 352-622-6675 www.mycountryfla.com

Ocala WYGC-FM (c) 3357 SW 7th St, Ocala FL 34474 **Phn:** 352-732-9877 **Fax:** 352-622-6675 www.mycountryfla.com

Ocoee WUNA-AM (y) 749 S Bluford Ave, Ocoee FL 34761 **Phn:** 407-656-9823 **Fax:** 407-656-2092

Okeechobee WOKC-AM (c) 210 NW Park St Ste 102, Okeechobee FL 34972 **Phn:** 863-467-1570 **Fax:** 863-763-3171 www.wokc.com billy@gladesmedia.com

Oldsmar WPSO-AM (ei) 109 S Bayview Blvd Ste A, Oldsmar FL 34677 **Phn:** 727-725-3500 www.wpso.com angelo@wzra48.com

Oldsmar WXYB-AM (e) 109 S Bayview Blvd Ste A, Oldsmar FL 34677 **Phn:** 727-725-5555 www.wpso.com

Orlando WAMT-AM (nt) 1160 S Semoran Blvd Ste A, Orlando FL 32807 **Phn:** 407-380-9255 **Fax:** 407-382-7565 www.newstalkflorida.com

Orlando WCFB-FM (ua) 4192 N John Young Pkwy, Orlando FL 32804 **Phn:** 321-281-2000 **Fax:** 407-290-6631 www.star945.com michael.saunders@coxinc.com

Orlando WDBO-AM (nt) 4192 N John Young Pkwy, Orlando FL 32804 **Phn:** 321-281-2000 **Fax:** 407-297-0156 www.news965.com joe.kelley@coxinc.com

Orlando WJHM-FM (u) 1800 Pembrook Dr Ste 400, Orlando FL 32810 **Phn:** 407-919-1000 **Fax:** 407-919-1136 102jamzorlando.cbslocal.com bobby.smith@cbsradio.com

Orlando WMFE-FM (pln) 11510 E Colonial Dr, Orlando FL 32817 **Phn:** 407-273-2300 www.wmfe.org newsreleases@wmfe.org

Orlando WMMO-FM (a) 4192 N John Young Pkwy, Orlando FL 32804 **Phn:** 407-422-9890 **Fax:** 407-422-6538 www.wmmo.com michael.saunders@coxmediagroup.com

Orlando WOCL-FM (r) 1800 Pembrook Dr Ste 400, Orlando FL 32810 **Phn:** 407-919-1000 1059sunnyfm.cbslocal.com rick@1059sunnyfm.com

Orlando WOKB-AM (xwg) 3765 N John Young Pkwy, Orlando FL 32804 **Phn:** 407-291-1395 **Fax:** 407-293-2870 www.wokbradio.com

Orlando WOMX-FM (a) 1800 Pembrook Dr Ste 400, Orlando FL 32810 **Phn:** 407-919-1000 **Fax:** 407-919-1138 mix1051.cbslocal.com bobby@mix1051.com

Orlando WOTS-AM (ynt) 222 Hazard St, Orlando FL 32804 **Phn:** 407-841-8282 **Fax:** 407-841-8250 www.wots1220.com wprd1440@hotmail.com

Orlando WPRD-AM (ynt) 222 Hazard St, Orlando FL 32804 **Phn:** 407-841-8282 **Fax:** 407-841-8250 www.wprd.com wprd1440@hotmail.com

Orlando WPYO-FM (u) 4192 N John Young Pkwy, Orlando FL 32804 **Phn:** 321-281-2000 **Fax:** 407-290-1302 www.power953.com stevie.demann@coxinc.com

Orlando WRLZ-AM (y) PO Box 593642, Orlando FL 32859 **Phn:** 407-345-0700 **Fax:** 407-345-1492

Orlando WSDO-AM (yq) 222 Hazard St, Orlando FL 32804 **Phn:** 407-841-8282 **Fax:** 407-841-8250 wprd1440@gmail.com

Orlando WUCF-FM (pj) PO Box 162199, Orlando FL 32816 **Phn:** 407-823-0899 **Fax:** 407-823-6364 wucf.org wucfhost@ucf.edu

Orlando WWKA-FM (c) 4192 N John Young Pkwy, Orlando FL 32804 **Phn:** 407-298-9292 **Fax:** 407-299-4947 www.k923orlando.com drew.anderssen@coxinc.com

Palatka WHIF-FM (q) 201 S Palm Ave, Palatka FL 32177 **Phn:** 386-325-3334 **Fax:** 386-325-0934 www.whif.org info@whif.org

Palatka WIYD-AM (cns) 1428 Saint Johns Ave # 200, Palatka FL 32177 **Phn:** 386-325-4556 **Fax:** 386-328-5161

Palatka WPLK-AM (o) 1428 Saint Johns Ave, Palatka FL 32177 **Phn:** 386-325-5800 **Fax:** 386-328-8725 wplk.com wplk@wplk.com

Palm Bay WEJF-FM (p) 2824 Palm Bay Rd NE # B, Palm Bay FL 32905 **Phn:** 321-722-9998 **Fax:** 321-724-0845

Palm City WCNO-FM (q) 2960 SW Mapp Rd, Palm City FL 34990 **Phn:** 772-221-1100 **Fax:** 772-221-8716 www.wcno.com

Panama City WAKT-FM (c) 118 Gwyn Dr, Panama City FL 32408 **Phn:** 850-234-8858 **Fax:** 850-234-6592 kickin1035.com melissamiller@panamacityradio.com

Panama City WDIZ-AM (s) 1834 Lisenby Ave, Panama City FL 32405 **Phn:** 850-769-1408 **Fax:** 850-769-0659 www.espn590.com toddberry@clearchannel.com

Panama City WEBZ-FM (h) 1834 Lisenby Ave, Panama City FL 32405 **Phn:** 850-769-1408 **Fax:** 850-769-0659 www.993thebeat.com toddberry@clearchannel.com

Panama City WFSY-FM (a) 1834 Lisenby Ave, Panama City FL 32405 **Phn:** 850-769-1408 **Fax:** 850-769-0659 www.sunny985.com todd@sunny985.com

Panama City WILN-FM (h) 7106 Laird St Ste 102, Panama City FL 32408 **Phn:** 850-230-5855 **Fax:** 850-230-6988 www.island106.com

Panama City WJTF-FM (q) 835A S Berthe Ave, Panama City FL 32404 **Phn:** 850-874-9900 **Fax:** 850-874-9930

Panama City WKGC-FM (p) 5230 W Highway 98, Panama City FL 32401 **Phn:** 850-873-3500 **Fax:** 850-913-3299 www.wkgc.org wkgcnews@gulfcoast.edu

Panama City WKGC-AM (p) 5230 W Highway 98, Panama City FL 32401 **Phn:** 850-873-3500 **Fax:** 850-913-3299 www.wkgc.org wkgcnews@gulfcoast.edu

Panama City WLTG-AM (nt) 3100 E 15th St, Panama City FL 32405 **Phn:** 850-784-9873 **Fax:** 850-784-6908

Panama City WPAP-FM (c) 1834 Lisenby Ave, Panama City FL 32405 **Phn:** 850-769-1408 **Fax:** 850-769-0659 www.925wpap.com toddberry@clearchannel.com

Panama City WPBH-FM (o) 1834 Lisenby Ave, Panama City FL 32405 **Phn:** 850-769-1408 **Fax:** 850-769-0659 www.sunny985.com todd@sunny985.com

Panama City WPCF-FM (cr) 7106 Laird St Ste 102, Panama City FL 32408 **Phn:** 850-230-5855 **Fax:** 850-230-6988 island106.com syoungblood@magicfl.com

Panama City WPFM-FM (h) 118 Gwyn Dr, Panama City FL 32408 **Phn:** 850-234-8858 **Fax:** 850-234-6592 www.hot1079pc.com neilknight@panamacityradio.com

Panama City WVVE-FM (a) 7106 Laird St Ste 102, Panama City FL 32408 **Phn:** 850-230-5855 **Fax:** 850-230-6988

Panama City WYOO-FM (nt) 7106 Laird St Ste 102, Panama City FL 32408 **Phn:** 850-230-5855 **Fax:** 850-230-6988 www.talkradio101.com melissa@magicfl.com

Panama City WYYX-FM (r) 7106 Laird St Ste 102, Panama City FL 32408 **Phn:** 850-230-5855 **Fax:** 850-230-6988 www.wyyx.com

Panama City Beach WASJ-FM (ah) 118 Gwyn Dr, Panama City Beach FL 32408 **Phn:** 850-234-8858 **Fax:** 850-234-6592 www.bobatthebeach.com melissamiller@panamacityradio.com

Panama City Beach WRBA-FM (r) 118 Gwyn Dr, Panama City Beach FL 32408 **Phn:** 850-234-8858 **Fax:** 850-234-6592 www.959online.com melissamiller@panamacityradio.com

Pensacola WBSR-AM (a) PO Box 19047, Pensacola FL 32523 **Phn:** 850-438-4982 **Fax:** 850-433-7932

Pensacola WCOA-AM (nt) 6565 N W St Ste 270, Pensacola FL 32505 **Phn:** 850-478-6011 **Fax:** 850-478-3971 www.wcoapensacola.com kevin.peterson@cumulus.com

Pensacola WCOA-FM (nt) 6565 N W St Ste 270, Pensacola FL 32505 **Phn:** 850-478-6011 **Fax:** 850-478-3971 www.wcoapensacola.com terry.simmons@cumulus.com

Pensacola WEGS-FM (q) 1836 E Olive Rd, Pensacola FL 32514 **Phn:** 850-475-4465 **Fax:** 850-474-9650 olivebaptist.org afarr@olivebaptist.org

Pensacola WMEZ-FM (a) 6565 North W. St, Pensacola FL 32505 **Phn:** 850-478-6011 **Fax:** 850-478-3971 softrock941.com kevin.peterson@cumulus.com

Pensacola WNVY-AM (wug) 2070 N Palafox St, Pensacola FL 32501 **Phn:** 850-435-1115 **Fax:** 864-597-0687 www.wilkinsradio.com wnvy@wilkinsradio.com

Pensacola WPCS-FM (q) PO Box 18000, Pensacola FL 32523 **Phn:** 850-479-6570 **Fax:** 850-969-1638 www.rejoice.org rbn@rejoice.org

Pensacola WPNN-AM (nt) 3801 N Pace Blvd, Pensacola FL 32505 **Phn:** 850-433-1141 **Fax:** 850-433-1142 talk790.com

Pensacola WRGV-FM (h) 6485 Pensacola Blvd, Pensacola FL 32505 **Phn:** 850-473-0400 **Fax:** 850-473-0907 www.1073now.com joelsampson@clearchannel.com

Pensacola WRNE-AM (wux) 312 E Nine Mile Rd Ste 29D, Pensacola FL 32514 **Phn:** 850-478-6000 **Fax:** 850-484-8080 www.wrne980.com info@wrne980.com

Pensacola WRRX-FM (u) 6565 N W St Ste 270, Pensacola FL 32505 **Phn:** 850-478-6011 **Fax:** 850-478-3971 mymagic106.com linda.moorer@cumulus.com

Pensacola WTKX-FM (r) 6485 Pensacola Blvd, Pensacola FL 32505 **Phn:** 850-473-0400 **Fax:** 850-473-0907 www.tk101.com joel@tk101.com

Pensacola WUWF-FM (pln) 11000 University Pkwy, Pensacola FL 32514 **Phn:** 850-474-2787 **Fax:** 850-474-3283 wuwf.org john@wuwf.org

Pensacola WVTJ-AM (gw) 2070 N Palafox St, Pensacola FL 32501 **Phn:** 850-432-3658 **Fax:** 864-597-0687 www.wilkinsradio.com wvtj@wilkinsradio.com

FLORIDA RADIO STATIONS

Pensacola WXBM-FM (c) 6565 North W. Street, Pensacola FL 32505 **Phn:** 850-478-6011 **Fax:** 850-478-3971 www.wxbm.com lynn.west@cumulus.com

Pensacola WYCT-FM (c) 7251 Plantation Rd, Pensacola FL 32504 **Phn:** 850-494-2800 **Fax:** 850-494-0778 www.catcountry987.com mhoxeng@catcountry987.com

Perry WPRY-AM (o) 872 E US Highway 27, Perry FL 32347 **Phn:** 850-223-1400 **Fax:** 850-223-3501

Pompano Beach WFTL-AM (nt) 2100 Park Central Blvd N Ste 100, Pompano Beach FL 33064 **Phn:** 954-315-1515 **Fax:** 954-315-1555 www.850wftl.com news@jamescrystal.com

Pompano Beach WMEN-AM (s) 2100 Central Park Blvd N # 100, Pompano Beach FL 33064 **Phn:** 954-315-1515 **Fax:** 954-315-1555 laparadio@aol.com

Port Charlotte WCCF-AM (nt) 24100 Tiseo Blvd Unit 10, Port Charlotte FL 33980 **Phn:** 941-206-1188 **Fax:** 941-206-9296 www.wccfam.com toddmatthews@clearchannel.com

Port Charlotte WIKX-FM (c) 24100 Tiseo Blvd Unit 10, Port Charlotte FL 33980 **Phn:** 941-206-1188 **Fax:** 941-206-9296 www.kixcountry929.com larrytimko@clearchannel.com

Port Charlotte WKII-AM (a) 24100 Tiseo Blvd Unit 10, Port Charlotte FL 33980 **Phn:** 941-639-1112 **Fax:** 941-206-9296

Port Charlotte WVIJ-FM (v) 3279 Sherwood Rd, Port Charlotte FL 33980 **Phn:** 941-624-5000 wvij.com wvij@wvij.com

Port Orange WJLH-FM (q) 4295 S Ridgewood Ave, Port Orange FL 32127 **Phn:** 386-756-9094 **Fax:** 386-760-7107 wjlu.org wjlu@wjlu.org

Port Orange WMFJ-AM (qt) 4295 S Ridgewood Ave, Port Orange FL 32127 **Phn:** 386-756-9094 www.wjlu.org wjlu@wjlu.org

Port Richey WLPJ-FM (q) 6214 Springer Dr, Port Richey FL 34668 **Phn:** 727-848-9150 **Fax:** 727-848-1233 www.thejoyfm.com thejoyfm@thejoyfm.com

Port Saint Lucie WAVW-FM (c) 3771 SE Jennings Rd, Port Saint Lucie FL 34952 **Phn:** 772-335-9300 **Fax:** 772-335-3291 www.wavw.com johnhunt@clearchannel.com

Port Saint Lucie WCZR-FM (t) 3771 SE Jennings Rd, Port Saint Lucie FL 34952 **Phn:** 772-335-9300 **Fax:** 772-335-3291 www.wzzr.com andrewbednar@clearchannel.com

Port Saint Lucie WFLM-FM (uw) PO Box 880052, Port Saint Lucie FL 34988 **Phn:** 772-460-9356 **Fax:** 772-460-2700 www.1047theflame.com management@1047theflame.com

Port Saint Lucie WQOL-FM (o) 3771 SE Jennings Rd, Port Saint Lucie FL 34952 **Phn:** 772-335-9300 **Fax:** 772-335-3291 www.oldies1037fm.com johnhunt@clearchannel.com

Port Saint Lucie WSYR-FM (a) 3771 SE Jennings Rd, Port Saint Lucie FL 34952 **Phn:** 772-335-9300 **Fax:** 772-335-3291 www.rushradio947.com brianmudd@clearchannel.com

Port Saint Lucie WZTA-AM (nt) 3771 SE Jennings Rd, Port Saint Lucie FL 34952 **Phn:** 772-335-9300 **Fax:** 772-335-3291 www.waxe1370.com heathwest@clearchannel.com

Quincy WGWD-FM (c) PO Box 919, Quincy FL 32353 **Phn:** 850-627-7086 **Fax:** 850-627-3422 monbit@tds.net

Saint Augustine WAOC-AM (s) PO Box 3847, Saint Augustine FL 32085 **Phn:** 904-797-4444 **Fax:** 904-797-3446 www.1420sports.com kris@1240news.com

Saint Augustine WFCF-FM (vjl) PO Box 1027, Saint Augustine FL 32085 **Phn:** 904-819-6449 **Fax:** 904-826-3471 www.flagler.educampus-lifecampus-facilitieswfcf.html wfcf@flagler.edu

Saint Augustine WFOY-FM (snt) PO Box 3847, Saint Augustine FL 32085 **Phn:** 904-797-4444 **Fax:** 904-797-3446 www.1023newsradio.com matt@1023newsradio.com

Saint Petersburg WDUV-FM (a) 11300 4th St N Ste 300, Saint Petersburg FL 33716 **Phn:** 727-579-2000 **Fax:** 727-579-2271 www.wduv.com ann.kelly@coxinc.com

Saint Petersburg WFTI-FM (q) 360 Central Ave Ste 1240, Saint Petersburg FL 33701 **Phn:** 727-823-1140 **Fax:** 727-823-2216 florida.thejoyfm.com thejoyfm@thejoyfm.com

Saint Petersburg WHPT-FM (r) 11300 4th St N Ste 300, Saint Petersburg FL 33716 **Phn:** 727-579-2000 **Fax:** 727-579-2662 www.theboneonline.com michael.sharkey@coxinc.com

Saint Petersburg WKES-FM (q) 5800 100th Way N, Saint Petersburg FL 33708 **Phn:** 727-391-9994 **Fax:** 727-397-6425 www.moodyradioflorida.fm ron.maxwell@moody.edu

Saint Petersburg WKZM-FM (q) PO Box 8889, Saint Petersburg FL 33738 **Phn:** 727-391-9994 **Fax:** 727-397-6425 www.moodyradioflorida.fm moodyradiooffice@moody.edu

Saint Petersburg WLLD-FM (h) 9721 Executive Center Dr N Ste 200, Saint Petersburg FL 33702 **Phn:** 727-579-1925 **Fax:** 727-578-0902 wild941.cbslocal.com christine.peters@cbsradio.com

Saint Petersburg WPOI-FM (r) 11300 4th St N Ste 300, Saint Petersburg FL 33716 **Phn:** 727-579-2000 **Fax:** 727-579-2271 www.hot1015tampabay.com tim.clarke@coxinc.com

Saint Petersburg WQYK-FM (c) 9721 Executive Center Dr N Ste 200, Saint Petersburg FL 33702 **Phn:** 727-579-1925 **Fax:** 727-563-8202 wqyk.cbslocal.com mculotta@cbs.com

Saint Petersburg WQYK-AM (s) 9721 Executive Center Dr N Ste 200, Saint Petersburg FL 33702 **Phn:** 727-579-1925 **Fax:** 727-563-8202 wqyk.cbslocal.com mculotta@cbs.com

Saint Petersburg WRBQ-FM (o) 9721 Executive Center Dr N Ste 200, Saint Petersburg FL 33702 **Phn:** 727-579-1925 **Fax:** 727-579-8888 myq105.cbslocal.com andrew.marenus@cbsradio.com

Saint Petersburg WRXB-AM (wau) 3551 42nd Ave S Ste B106, Saint Petersburg FL 33711 **Phn:** 727-865-1591 **Fax:** 727-866-1728 www.wrxb.us mediaguy@kentdgustafson.com

Saint Petersburg WSUN-FM (r) 11300 4th St N Ste 300, Saint Petersburg FL 33716 **Phn:** 727-579-2000 **Fax:** 727-579-2273 www.97xonline.com 97xcomments@97xonline.com

Saint Petersburg WTIS-AM (qt) 311 112th Ave NE, Saint Petersburg FL 33716 **Phn:** 727-576-2234 **Fax:** 727-577-3814 www.wix.comwtisam1110radio wtis1110@yahoo.com

Saint Petersburg WWMI-AM (m) 11300 4th St N Ste 143, Saint Petersburg FL 33716 **Phn:** 727-577-4500 **Fax:** 727-579-1340 music.disney.com

Saint Petersburg WWRM-FM (a) 11300 4th St N Ste 300, Saint Petersburg FL 33716 **Phn:** 727-579-2000 **Fax:** 727-579-2271 www.mymagic949.com julia.freeman@coxinc.com

Saint Petersburg WXGL-FM (h) 11300 4th St N Ste 300, Saint Petersburg FL 33716 **Phn:** 727-579-2000 **Fax:** 727-579-2662 www.1073theeagle.com 1073comments@coxtampa.com

Saint Petersburg WYUU-FM (y) 9721 Executive Center Dr N Ste 200, Saint Petersburg FL 33702 **Phn:** 866-932-9250 925maxima.cbslocal.com nio.encendio@cbsradio.com

Sarasota WCTQ-FM (c) 1779 Independence Blvd, Sarasota FL 34234 **Phn:** 941-552-4800 **Fax:** 941-552-4900 www.1065ctq.com heidi@1065ctq.com

Sarasota WDDV-FM (m) 1779 Independence Blvd, Sarasota FL 34234 **Phn:** 941-552-4800 **Fax:** 941-552-4900 www.doveradio.com eddierupp@clearchannel.com

Sarasota WJIS-FM (q) 6469 Parkland Dr, Sarasota FL 34243 **Phn:** 941-753-0401 **Fax:** 941-753-2963 www.thejoyfm.com thejoyfm@thejoyfm.com

Sarasota WLTQ-FM (a) 1779 Independence Blvd, Sarasota FL 34234 **Phn:** 941-552-4800 **Fax:** 941-552-4900 www.921thecoast.com eddierupp@clearchannel.com

Sarasota WSDV-AM (bj) 1779 Independence Blvd, Sarasota FL 34234 **Phn:** 941-552-4800 **Fax:** 941-552-4900 www.doveradio.com drewthomas@clearchannel.com

Sarasota WSMR-FM (q) 240 N Washington Blvd Ste 500, Sarasota FL 34236 **Phn:** 941-906-9767 **Fax:** 941-362-0377

Sarasota WSRZ-FM (o) 1779 Independence Blvd, Sarasota FL 34234 **Phn:** 941-552-4800 **Fax:** 941-552-4900 www.wsrz.com drew@wsrz.com

Sarasota WTMY-AM (nt) 2101 Hammock Pl, Sarasota FL 34235 **Phn:** 941-954-1280 **Fax:** 941-955-9062 www.wtmy.com

Sarasota WTZB-FM (r) 1779 Independence Blvd, Sarasota FL 34234 **Phn:** 941-552-4800 **Fax:** 941-552-4900 www.1059thebuzz.com meat@1059thebuzz.com

Sebring WITS-AM (a) 3750 US Highway 27 N Ste 1, Sebring FL 33870 **Phn:** 863-382-9999 **Fax:** 863-382-1982 www.cohanradiogroup.com cohanradiogroup@htn.net

Sebring WJCM-AM (o) 3750 US Highway 27 N Ste 1, Sebring FL 33870 **Phn:** 863-382-9999 **Fax:** 863-382-1982 www.cohanradiogroup.com cohanradiogroup@htn.net

Sebring WWLL-FM (a) 3750 US Highway 27 N Ste 1, Sebring FL 33870 **Phn:** 863-382-9999 **Fax:** 863-382-1982 www.cohanradiogroup.com cohanradiogroup@htn.net

Sebring WWOJ-FM (c) 3750 US Highway 27 N Ste 1, Sebring FL 33870 **Phn:** 863-382-9999 **Fax:** 863-382-1982 www.cohanradiogroup.com cohanradiogroup@htn.net

Sebring WWTK-AM (t) 3750 US Highway 27 N Ste 1, Sebring FL 33870 **Phn:** 863-382-9999 **Fax:** 863-382-1982 www.cohanradiogroup.com cohanradiogroup@htn.net

Starke WEAG-AM (c) 1421 S Water St, Starke FL 32091 **Phn:** 904-964-5001 ckramer@atlantic.net

Starke WEAG-FM (c) 1421 S Water St, Starke FL 32091 **Phn:** 904-964-5001 ckramer@atlantic.net

Stuart WHLG-FM (a) 1670 NW Federal Hwy, Stuart FL 34994 **Phn:** 772-692-9454 **Fax:** 772-692-0258 www.coast1013.com jroberts@coast1013.com

Summerland Key WPIK-FM (y) PO Box 420249, Summerland Key FL 33042 **Phn:** 305-745-4162 **Fax:** 305-745-4165 www.radioritmolafabulosa.com sabadoslatinos@yahoo.com

Tallahassee WAIB-FM (c) 3000 Olson Rd, Tallahassee FL 32308 **Phn:** 850-386-8004 **Fax:** 850-422-1897 1031thewolf.com jbone@opusbroadcasting.com

FLORIDA RADIO STATIONS

Tallahassee WAKU-FM (q) 3225 Hartsfield Rd, Tallahassee FL 32303 **Phn:** 850-926-9258 **Fax:** 850-562-2730 www.wave94.com mail@wave94.com

Tallahassee WANM-FM (wvj) 510 Orr Dr # 3056, Tallahassee FL 32304 **Phn:** 850-599-3083 **Fax:** 850-561-2829 www.wanm.org info@wanm.org

Tallahassee WBZE-FM (a) 3411 W Tharpe St, Tallahassee FL 32303 **Phn:** 850-201-3000 **Fax:** 850-561-8903 www.mystar98.com info@mystar98.com

Tallahassee WCVC-AM (qg) 117 12 Henderson Rd, Tallahassee FL 32312 **Phn:** 850-386-1330 **Fax:** 850-386-2138

Tallahassee WEGT-FM (r) 3000 Olson Rd, Tallahassee FL 32308 **Phn:** 850-386-8004 **Fax:** 850-422-1897 www.999hank.fm hkestenbaum@opusbroadcasting.com

Tallahassee WFLA-FM (t) 325 John Knox Rd Bldg G, Tallahassee FL 32303 **Phn:** 850-558-1455 **Fax:** 850-383-0747 www.wflafm.com jeffwolf@clearchannel.com

Tallahassee WFRF-AM (q) PO Box 181000, Tallahassee FL 32318 **Phn:** 850-201-1070 **Fax:** 850-201-1071 www.faithradio.us mailbox@faithradio.us

Tallahassee WFSQ-FM (pl) 1600 Red Barber Plz, Tallahassee FL 32310 **Phn:** 850-487-3086 **Fax:** 850-487-3293 www.wfsu.org

Tallahassee WFSU-FM (pnt) 1600 Red Barber Plz, Tallahassee FL 32310 **Phn:** 850-487-3086 **Fax:** 850-487-3093 www.wfsu.org tgomes@fsu.edu

Tallahassee WFSW-FM (p) 1600 Red Barber Plz, Tallahassee FL 32310 **Phn:** 850-487-3086 **Fax:** 850-487-3093 www.wfsu.org

Tallahassee WGLF-FM (r) 3411 W Tharpe St, Tallahassee FL 32303 **Phn:** 850-201-3000 **Fax:** 850-561-8903 www.gulf104.com victor.duncan@cumulus.com

Tallahassee WGMY-FM (a) 325 John Knox Rd Bldg G, Tallahassee FL 32303 **Phn:** 850-422-3107 **Fax:** 850-383-0747 www.1071hitmusicnow.com maverick2@clearchannel.com

Tallahassee WHBT-AM (g) 3411 W Tharpe St, Tallahassee FL 32303 **Phn:** 850-201-3000 **Fax:** 850-561-8903 www.heaven1410.com docd@cumulus.com

Tallahassee WHBX-FM (u) 3411 W Tharpe St, Tallahassee FL 32303 **Phn:** 850-201-3000 **Fax:** 850-561-8903 www.961jamz.com joe.bullard@cumulus.com

Tallahassee WHTF-FM (h) 3000 Olson Rd, Tallahassee FL 32308 **Phn:** 850-386-8004 **Fax:** 850-422-1897 www.hot1049.com hkestenbaum@opusbroadcasting.com

Tallahassee WMGY-FM (a) 325 John Knox Rd, Tallahassee FL 32303 **Phn:** 850-422-3107 **Fax:** 850-383-0747 www.1071hitmusicnow.com jeffwolf@clearchannel.com

Tallahassee WNLS-AM (s) 325 John Knox Rd Bldg G, Tallahassee FL 32303 **Phn:** 850-422-3107 **Fax:** 850-383-0747 www.1270theteam.com jeffwolf@clearchannel.com

Tallahassee WQTL-FM (o) 3000 Olson Rd, Tallahassee FL 32308 **Phn:** 850-386-8004 **Fax:** 850-422-1897 hkestenbaum@opusbroadcasting.com

Tallahassee WTAL-AM (nt) 1363 E Tennessee St, Tallahassee FL 32308 **Phn:** 850-877-0105 **Fax:** 850-877-5110 www.wtal1450.com

Tallahassee WTNT-FM (c) 325 John Knox Rd Bldg G, Tallahassee FL 32303 **Phn:** 850-422-3107 **Fax:** 850-383-0747 www.949tnt.com maverick2@clearchannel.com

Tallahassee WTSM-FM (s) 435 Saint Francis St, Tallahassee FL 32301 **Phn:** 850-561-8400 **Fax:** 850-224-1553 www.979espnradio.com tom@979espnradio.com

Tallahassee WVFS-FM (v) 420 Diffenbaugh Bldg, Tallahassee FL 32306 **Phn:** 850-644-3871 **Fax:** 850-644-8753 www.wvfs.fsu.edu news@wvfs.fsu.edu

Tallahassee WWLD-FM (u) 3411 W Tharpe St, Tallahassee FL 32303 **Phn:** 850-201-3000 **Fax:** 850-561-8903 www.blazin1023.com info@blazin1023.com

Tallahassee WXSR-FM (r) 325 John Knox Rd Bldg G, Tallahassee FL 32303 **Phn:** 850-422-3107 **Fax:** 850-383-0747 www.x1015.com lisajrice@clearchannel.com

Tampa WAMA-AM (y) 4107 W Spruce St # 200, Tampa FL 33607 **Phn:** 813-374-9075 **Fax:** 813-374-9102 www.laley1550.com info@laley1550.com

Tampa WBTP-FM (u) 4002 W Gandy Blvd, Tampa FL 33611 **Phn:** 813-839-9393 **Fax:** 813-839-5969 www.957thebeat.com kimcusmano@clearchannel.com

Tampa WBVM-FM (q) 717 S Dale Mabry Hwy, Tampa FL 33609 **Phn:** 813-289-8040 **Fax:** 813-282-3580 www.spiritfm905.com contact@spiritfm905.com

Tampa WDAE-AM (st) 4002 W Gandy Blvd, Tampa FL 33611 **Phn:** 813-839-9393 **Fax:** 813-831-3299 www.620wdae.com tampadigital@clearchannel.com

Tampa WFLA-AM (nt) 4002 W Gandy Blvd, Tampa FL 33611 **Phn:** 813-832-1000 **Fax:** 813-832-1090 www.970wfla.com

Tampa WFLZ-FM (h) 4002 W Gandy Blvd, Tampa FL 33611 **Phn:** 813-839-9393 **Fax:** 813-832-1090 www.933flz.com kimcusmano@clearchannel.com

Tampa WFUS-FM (c) 4002 W Gandy Blvd, Tampa FL 33611 **Phn:** 813-839-9393 **Fax:** 813-831-6397 www.us1035.com travisdaily@clearchannel.com

Tampa WGUL-AM (t) 5211 W Laurel St Ste 101, Tampa FL 33607 **Phn:** 813-639-1903 **Fax:** 813-639-1272 www.860wgul.com cgould@salemtampa.com

Tampa WHNZ-AM (nt) 4002 W Gandy Blvd, Tampa FL 33611 **Phn:** 813-839-9393 **Fax:** 813-831-6397 www.whnz.com gordonbyrd@clearchannel.com

Tampa WLCC-AM (y) 5211 W Laurel St # 101, Tampa FL 33607 **Phn:** 813-639-1903 www.760radioluz.com barb@salemtampa.com

Tampa WLSS-AM (nt) 5211 W Laurel St Ste 101, Tampa FL 33607 **Phn:** 941-363-0930 **Fax:** 941-639-1272 www.wlssradio.com cgould@salemtampa.com

Tampa WMNF-FM (p) 1210 E Dr Martin Luther King Jr Blvd, Tampa FL 33603 **Phn:** 813-238-8001 www.wmnf.org newsroom@wmnf.org

Tampa WMTX-FM (a) 4002 W Gandy Blvd, Tampa FL 33611 **Phn:** 813-839-9393 **Fax:** 813-839-5969 www.tampabaysmix.com kristyknight@clearchannel.com

Tampa WQBN-AM (y) 5203 N Armenia Ave, Tampa FL 33603 **Phn:** 813-871-1333 **Fax:** 813-876-1333 joyce.cordero@gmail.com

Tampa WTBN-AM (q) 5211 W Laurel St Ste 101, Tampa FL 33607 **Phn:** 813-639-1903 **Fax:** 13-639-1272 www.letstalkfaith.com tammyb@salemtampa.com

Tampa WTMP-FM (y) 407 N Howard Ave Ste 200, Tampa FL 33606 **Phn:** 813-259-9867 **Fax:** 813-254-9867 www.bahiatampa.com

Tampa WTMP-AM (y) 407 N Howard Ave Ste 200, Tampa FL 33606 **Phn:** 813-259-9867 **Fax:** 813-254-9867 www.bahiatampa.com

Tampa WTWD-AM (q) 5211 W Laurel St Ste 101, Tampa FL 33607 **Phn:** 813-639-1903 **Fax:** 813-639-1272 www.bayword.com tammyb@salemtampa.com

Tampa WUSF-FM (p) 4202 E Fowler Ave Stop WRB219, Tampa FL 33620 **Phn:** 813-974-8700 **Fax:** 813-974-5016 www.wusf.usf.edu news@wusf.org

Tampa WXTB-FM (r) 4002 W Gandy Blvd, Tampa FL 33611 **Phn:** 813-839-9393 **Fax:** 813-831-5969 www.98ROCK.com bigrig@clearchannel.com

Tavernier WCTH-FM (c) 93351 Overseas Hwy, Tavernier FL 33070 **Phn:** 305-852-9085 **Fax:** 305-852-2304 www.thundercountry.com doughitchcock@clearchannel.com

Tavernier WFKZ-FM (h) 93351 Overseas Hwy, Tavernier FL 33070 **Phn:** 305-852-9085 **Fax:** 305-852-2304 www.sun103.com deweyengstrom@clearchannel.com

Tavernier WKEZ-FM (z) 93351 Overseas Hwy, Tavernier FL 33070 **Phn:** 305-852-9085 **Fax:** 305-852-2304

Titusville WPGS-AM (tno) 805 N Dixie Ave, Titusville FL 32796 **Phn:** 321-383-1000 wpgs840@aol.com

Titusville WPIO-FM (v) 505 Josephine St, Titusville FL 32796 **Phn:** 321-267-3000 **Fax:** 321-264-9370

Vero Beach WGYL-FM (a) 1235 16th St, Vero Beach FL 32960 **Phn:** 772-567-0937 **Fax:** 772-562-4747 www.thebreeze.fm news@wttbam.com

Vero Beach WJKD-FM (ah) 1235 16th St, Vero Beach FL 32960 **Phn:** 772-567-0937 **Fax:** 772-562-4747 www.997jackfm.com news@wttbam.com

Vero Beach WOSN-FM (a) 1235 16th St, Vero Beach FL 32960 **Phn:** 772-567-0937 **Fax:** 772-562-4747 www.wosnfm.com news@wttbam.com

Vero Beach WSCF-FM (q) 6767 20th St, Vero Beach FL 32966 **Phn:** 772-569-0919 **Fax:** 772-562-4892 www.wscf.com martha@wscf.com

Vero Beach WTTB-AM (nt) 1235 16th St, Vero Beach FL 32960 **Phn:** 772-567-0937 **Fax:** 772-562-4747 www.wttbam.com news@wttbam.com

W Palm Beach WZZR-FM (t) 3071 Continental Dr, W Palm Beach FL 33407 **Phn:** 561-616-6600 www.wzzr.com andrewbednar@clearchannel.com

West Palm Beach WAFC-FM (y) 2326 S Congress Ave Ste 2A, West Palm Beach FL 33406 **Phn:** 561-721-9950 **Fax:** 561-721-9973 www.wafcfm.com brian@gladesmedia.com

West Palm Beach WAYF-AM (q) 800 Northpoint Pkwy Ste 881, West Palm Beach FL 33407 **Phn:** 561-881-1929 **Fax:** 561-840-1929 wayf.wayfm.com jim@wayfm.com

West Palm Beach WBZT-AM (nt) 3071 Continental Dr, West Palm Beach FL 33407 **Phn:** 561-616-6600 **Fax:** 561-616-6677 www.wbzt.com jimhedwards@clearchannel.com

West Palm Beach WEAT-FM (a) 701 Northpoint Pkwy Ste 500, West Palm Beach FL 33407 **Phn:** 561-686-9505 **Fax:** 561-689-4043 sunny1043.radio.com joconnell@cbs.com

West Palm Beach WIRK-FM (m) 701 Northpoint Pkwy Ste 500, West Palm Beach FL 33407 **Phn:** 561-616-4777 **Fax:** 561-868-1111 www.wirk.com kailey.mills@palmbeach-broadcasting.com

West Palm Beach WJNO-AM (nt) 3071 Continental Dr, West Palm Beach FL 33407 **Phn:** 561-616-6600 **Fax:** 561-616-6643 www.wjno.com ethanbriner@clearchannel.com

West Palm Beach WKGR-FM (r) 3071 Continental Dr, West Palm Beach FL 33407 **Phn:** 561-616-6600 **Fax:** 561-616-6677 www.gaterrocks.com andypreston@clearchannel.com

West Palm Beach WLDI-FM (ah) 3071 Continental Dr, West Palm Beach FL 33407 **Phn:** 561-616-6600 **Fax:** 561-616-6643 www.wild955.com ethanbriner@clearchannel.com

West Palm Beach WMBX-FM (h) 701 Northpoint Pkwy Ste 500, West Palm Beach FL 33407 **Phn:** 561-616-4777 **Fax:** 561-868-1111 www.thex1023.com tara.davis@palmbeach-broadcasting.com

West Palm Beach WOLL-FM (oh) 3071 Continental Dr, West Palm Beach FL 33407 **Phn:** 561-616-6600 **Fax:** 561-616-6643 www.1055online.com ethanbriner@clearchannel.com

West Palm Beach WPSP-AM (y) 5730 Corporate Way Ste 210, West Palm Beach FL 33407 **Phn:** 561-681-9777 **Fax:** 561-687-3398

West Palm Beach WRLX-FM (a) 3071 Continental Dr, West Palm Beach FL 33407 **Phn:** 561-616-6600 **Fax:** 561-616-6677

West Palm Beach WRMF-FM (a) 477 S Rosemary Ave Ste 302, West Palm Beach FL 33401 **Phn:** 561-868-1100 **Fax:** 561-868-1111 www.wrmf.com ehamma@wrmf.com

West Palm Beach WWRF-AM (y) 2326 S Congress Ave Ste 2A, West Palm Beach FL 33406 **Phn:** 561-721-9950 **Fax:** 561-721-9973 www.la1380.com la1380@radiofiesta.com

Winter Haven WHNR-AM (y) 1505 Dundee Rd, Winter Haven FL 33884 **Phn:** 863-299-1141 **Fax:** 863-293-6397 mail@whnr1360.com

Winter Haven WSIR-AM (ug) 665 Lake Howard Dr SW, Winter Haven FL 33880 **Phn:** 863-295-9411 **Fax:** 863-401-9365 www.familyradio1490.com

Winter Park WPRK-FM (v) 1000 Holt Ave # 2745, Winter Park FL 32789 **Phn:** 407-646-2241 wprk.org wprkfm@rollins.edu

Zolfo Springs WZSP-FM (y) 7891 US Highway 17 S, Zolfo Springs FL 33890 **Phn:** 863-494-4111 **Fax:** 863-494-4443 www.lazeta.fm info@lazeta.fm

Zolfo Springs WZZS-FM (c) 7891 US Highway 17 S, Zolfo Springs FL 33890 **Phn:** 863-494-4111 **Fax:** 863-494-4443 www.bull.fm info@bull.fm

GEORGIA

Albany WALG-AM (nt) 1104 W Broad Ave, Albany GA 31707 **Phn:** 229-888-5000 **Fax:** 229-888-6018 www.1590walg.com boomer.lee@cumulus.com

Albany WEGC-FM (a) 1104 W Broad Ave, Albany GA 31707 **Phn:** 229-888-5000 **Fax:** 229-888-6018 www.mix1077albany.com april.bailey@cumulus.com

Albany WGPC-AM (s) 1104 W Broad Ave, Albany GA 31707 **Phn:** 229-888-5000 **Fax:** 229-435-9059 april.bailey@cumulus.com

Albany WJAD-FM (r) 1104 W Broad Ave, Albany GA 31707 **Phn:** 229-888-5000 **Fax:** 229-888-6018 www.rock103albany.com kelly.carpenter@cumulus.com

Albany WJIZ-FM (wu) 809 S Westover Blvd, Albany GA 31707 **Phn:** 229-439-9704 **Fax:** 229-439-1509 www.wjiz.com

Albany WJYZ-AM (wg) 809 S Westover Blvd, Albany GA 31707 **Phn:** 229-439-9704 **Fax:** 229-439-1509 www.wjyz.com

Albany WKAK-FM (c) 1104 W Broad Ave, Albany GA 31707 **Phn:** 229-888-5000 **Fax:** 229-888-5960 www.kcountry104.com roger.russell@cumulus.com

Albany WMRZ-FM (ax) 809 S Westover Blvd, Albany GA 31707 **Phn:** 229-439-9704 **Fax:** 229-439-1509 www.kissalbany.com

FLORIDA RADIO STATIONS

Albany WNUQ-FM (h) 1104 W Broad Ave, Albany GA 31707 **Phn:** 229-888-5000 **Fax:** 229-888-6018 www.q102albany.com roger.russell@cumulus.com

Albany WOBB-FM (c) 809 S Westover Blvd, Albany GA 31707 **Phn:** 229-439-9704 **Fax:** 229-439-1509 www.b100wobb.com caseycarter@clearchannel.com

Albany WQVE-FM (wu) 1104 W Broad Ave, Albany GA 31707 **Phn:** 229-888-5000 **Fax:** 229-888-5960 www.wqvealbany.com roger.russell@cumulus.com

Albany WRAK-FM (r) 809 S Westover Blvd, Albany GA 31707 **Phn:** 229-439-9704 **Fax:** 229-439-1509 www.973hitmusicnow.com

Albany WZBN-FM (uh) 1104 W Broad Ave, Albany GA 31707 **Phn:** 229-888-5000 **Fax:** 229-888-5960 www.wqvealbany.com roger.russell@cumulus.com

Alma WAJQ-FM (c) PO Box F, Alma GA 31510 **Phn:** 912-632-1000

Alma WAJQ-AM (g) PO Box F, Alma GA 31510 **Phn:** 912-632-1000

Americus WDEC-FM (a) PO Box 727, Americus GA 31709 **Phn:** 229-924-6500 **Fax:** 229-928-2337 www.americusradio.com stevelashley@mchsi.com

Americus WISK-FM (c) PO Box 727, Americus GA 31709 **Phn:** 229-924-6500 **Fax:** 229-928-2337 www.americusradio.com radiojimweaver@yahoo.com

Americus WISK-AM (o) PO Box 727, Americus GA 31709 **Phn:** 229-924-6500 **Fax:** 229-928-2337 www.americusradio.com doones1974@live.com

Appling WQRX-AM (gy) PO Box 510, Appling GA 30802 **Phn:** 706-309-9610 **Fax:** 706-309-9669 www.gnnradio.org

Athens WUGA-FM (plnj) 1197 S Lumpkin St Rm 138, Athens GA 30602 **Phn:** 706-542-9842 **Fax:** 706-542-6718 www.wuga.org wuga@uga.edu

Athens WUOG-FM (v) PO Box 2065, Athens GA 30612 **Phn:** 706-542-7100 **Fax:** 706-542-0070 wuog.org affairs@wuog.org

Atlanta WABE-FM (pln) 740 Bismark Rd NE, Atlanta GA 30324 **Phn:** 678-686-0321 **Fax:** 678-686-0356 wabe.org

Atlanta WAEC-AM (q) 1465 Northside Dr NW Ste 218, Atlanta GA 30318 **Phn:** 404-355-8600 **Fax:** 404-355-4156 love860.com

Atlanta WAFS-AM (y) 2970 Peachtree Rd NW Ste 700, Atlanta GA 30305 **Phn:** 770-290-8950 **Fax:** 770-209-8910 adam.asher@salematlanta.com

Atlanta WALR-FM (a) 1601 W Peachtree St NE, Atlanta GA 30309 **Phn:** 404-897-7500 **Fax:** 404-897-7363 www.kiss104fm.com tony.kidd@coxinc.com

Atlanta WALR-AM (s) 3535 Piedmont Rd NE Ste 14-1200, Atlanta GA 30305 **Phn:** 404-688-0068 **Fax:** 404-995-4045 scottmcfarlane@680thefan.com

Atlanta WAMJ-FM (ox) 101 Marietta St NW 12th Fl, Atlanta GA 30303 **Phn:** 404-765-9750 **Fax:** 404-688-7686 majicatl.com ldunbar@radio-one.com

Atlanta WAOK-AM (nt) 1201 Peachtree St NE Ste 800, Atlanta GA 30361 **Phn:** 404-898-8900 **Fax:** 404-898-8915 atlanta.cbslocal.com shelice.smith@cbsradio.com

Atlanta WBTS-FM (h) 1601 W Peachtree St NE, Atlanta GA 30309 **Phn:** 404-897-7500 **Fax:** 404-897-7363 www.955thebeat.com lee.cagle@coxradio.com

Atlanta WBZY-FM (y) 1819 Peachtree Rd NE Ste 700, Atlanta GA 30309 **Phn:** 404-875-8080 **Fax:** 404-367-1111 www.elpatron1053.com stevengarza@clearchannel.com

Atlanta WCLK-FM (pj) 111 James P Brawley Dr SW, Atlanta GA 30314 **Phn:** 404-880-8273 **Fax:** 404-880-8869 www.wclk.com wclkfm@cau.edu

Atlanta WCNN-AM (s) 3535 Piedmont Rd NE Ste 14-1200, Atlanta GA 30305 **Phn:** 404-688-0068 **Fax:** 404-995-4045 www.680thefan.com scottmcfarlane@680thefan.com

Atlanta WDWD-AM (M) 900 Circle 75 Pkwy SE Ste 1320, Atlanta GA 30339 **Phn:** 770-541-7472 **Fax:** 770-980-9457 music.disney.com

Atlanta WFSH-FM (g) 2970 Peachtree Rd NW Ste 700, Atlanta GA 30305 **Phn:** 404-365-0970 **Fax:** 404-816-0748 www.thefishatlanta.com kevin@thefishatlanta.com

Atlanta WGKA-AM (nt) 2970 Peachtree Rd NW Ste 700, Atlanta GA 30305 **Phn:** 404-995-7300 **Fax:** 404-816-0748 www.talk920.com mikem@thefishatlanta.com

Atlanta WGST-AM (ys) 1819 Peachtree Rd NE Ste 700, Atlanta GA 30309 **Phn:** 404-367-0640 **Fax:** 404-367-6401 www.espndeportesatlanta.com chriseast@clearchannel.com

Atlanta WHTA-FM (uwx) 101 Marietta St NW 12th Fl, Atlanta GA 30303 **Phn:** 404-765-9750 **Fax:** 404-688-7686 hotspotatl.com

Atlanta WJSP-FM (pln) 260 14th St NW, Atlanta GA 30318 **Phn:** 404-685-2690 **Fax:** 404-685-2684 www.gpb.org

Atlanta WKHX-FM (c) 780 Johnson Ferry Road NE, Atlanta GA 30342 **Phn:** 404-497-4700 www.wkhx.com jenn.fallin@cumulus.com

Atlanta WLTA-AM (qnt) 2970 Peachtree Rd NW Ste 700, Atlanta GA 30305 **Phn:** 404-995-7300 **Fax:** 404-816-0748 www.faithtalk970.com adam.asher@salematlanta.com

Atlanta WNIV-AM (tq) 2970 Peachtree Rd NW Ste 700, Atlanta GA 30305 **Phn:** 404-995-7300 www.faithtalk970.com adam.asher@salematlanta.com

Atlanta WNNX-FM (r) 780 Johnson Ferry Rd NE Ste 500, Atlanta GA 30342 **Phn:** 404-497-4700 **Fax:** 404-497-4745 www.99x.com programminghelp@99x.com

Atlanta WPZE-FM (g) 101 Marietta St NW 12th Fl, Atlanta GA 30303 **Phn:** 404-765-9750 **Fax:** 404-688-7686 mypraiseatl.com

Atlanta WQXI-AM (snt) 210 Interstate N Cir # 100, Atlanta GA 30339 **Phn:** 404-261-2970 **Fax:** 404-365-9026 www.790thezone.com rick.mack@lincolnfinancialmedia.com

Atlanta WRAS-FM (vr) PO Box 4048, Atlanta GA 30302 **Phn:** 404-651-2240 **Fax:** 404-463-9535 www.wras.org 88news@gmail.com

Atlanta WREK-FM (v) 350 Ferst Dr NW # 2224, Atlanta GA 30332 **Phn:** 404-894-2468 **Fax:** 404-894-6872 www.wrek.org news.director@wrek.org

Atlanta WRFG-FM (v) 1083 Austin Ave NE, Atlanta GA 30307 **Phn:** 404-523-3471 **Fax:** 404-523-8990 www.wrfg.org office@wrfg.org

Atlanta WSB-AM (snt) 1601 W Peachtree St NE, Atlanta GA 30309 **Phn:** 404-897-7500 **Fax:** 404-897-7363 www.wsbradio.com pete.spriggs@coxradio.com

Atlanta WSB-FM (an) 1601 W Peachtree St NE, Atlanta GA 30309 **Phn:** 404-897-7500 **Fax:** 404-897-7363 www.b985.com dan.kearney@coxradio.com

Atlanta WSRV-FM (h) 1601 W Peachtree St NE, Atlanta GA 30309 **Phn:** 404-897-7500 **Fax:** 404-897-7363 www.971theriver.com dave.clapper@coxradio.com

Atlanta WSTR-FM (ha) 3350 Peachtree Rd NE Ste 1800, Atlanta GA 30326 **Phn:** 404-261-2970 **Fax:** 404-365-9026 www.star94.com rstadler@star94.com

GEORGIA RADIO STATIONS

Atlanta WUBL-FM (c) 1819 Peachtree Rd NE Ste 700, Atlanta GA 30309 **Phn:** 404-875-8080 www.949thebull.com

Atlanta WUMJ-FM (g) 101 Marietta St NW 12th Fl, Atlanta GA 30303 **Phn:** 404-765-9750 **Fax:** 404-688-7686

Atlanta WVEE-FM (wu) 1201 Peachtree St NE Ste 800, Atlanta GA 30361 **Phn:** 404-898-8900 **Fax:** 404-898-8909 v103.cbslocal.com tbrown@cbs.com

Atlanta WWLG-FM (h) 1819 Peachtree Rd NE Ste 700, Atlanta GA 30309 **Phn:** 404-875-8080 **Fax:** 404-367-1105 www.radio1057.com rickvaughn@clearchannel.com

Atlanta WWPW-FM (h) 1819 Peachtree Rd NE Ste 700, Atlanta GA 30309 **Phn:** 404-875-8080 **Fax:** 404-367-1153 www.power961.com rickvaughn@clearchannel.com

Atlanta WWVA-FM (h) 1819 Peachtree Rd NE Ste 700, Atlanta GA 30309 **Phn:** 404-607-1336 **Fax:** 404-367-1105 www.wildatlanta.com micolrankin@clearchannel.com

Atlanta WWWE-AM (y) 1465 Northside Dr NW Ste 218, Atlanta GA 30318 **Phn:** 404-355-8600 **Fax:** 404-355-4156 www.bbgi.com email@bbgi.com

Atlanta WWWQ-FM (h) 780 Johnson Ferry Rd NE Ste 500, Atlanta GA 30342 **Phn:** 404-497-4700 **Fax:** 404-497-4735 www.q100atlanta.com therese.campanelli@cumulus.com

Atlanta WYAY-FM (o) 780 Johnson Ferry Road NE, Atlanta GA 30342 **Phn:** 404-497-4700 www.allnews1067.com newsroom@allnews1067.com

Atlanta WYZE-AM (wg) 1111 Boulevard SE, Atlanta GA 30312 **Phn:** 404-622-7802 **Fax:** 404-622-6767 www.wyzeradio.com wyzepressmail@bellsouth.net

Atlanta WZGC-FM (s) 1201 Peachtree St NE Ste 800, Atlanta GA 30361 **Phn:** 404-898-8900 **Fax:** 404-898-8916 atlanta.cbslocal.com

Augusta WAKB-FM (wu) PO Box 1584, Augusta GA 30903 **Phn:** 803-279-2330 **Fax:** 803-279-8149 www.1009magic.com vperry@perrybroadcasting.net

Augusta WBBQ-FM (a) 2743 Perimeter Pkwy Ste 100-300, Augusta GA 30909 **Phn:** 706-396-6000 **Fax:** 706-396-6010 www.wbbq.com augustapsa@clearchannel.com

Augusta WCHZ-FM (r) 4051 Jimmie Dyess Pkwy, Augusta GA 30909 **Phn:** 706-396-7000 **Fax:** 706-396-7100 www.95rock.com chuck@95rock.com

Augusta WDRR-FM (h) 4051 Jimmie Dyess Pkwy, Augusta GA 30909 **Phn:** 706-396-7000 **Fax:** 706-396-7092 www.ilovebobfm.com

Augusta WEKL-FM (r) 2743 Perimeter Pkwy Ste 100-300, Augusta GA 30909 **Phn:** 706-396-6000 **Fax:** 706-396-6010 www.eagle1057.com cliffbennett@clearchannel.com

Augusta WFAM-AM (qt) 552 Laney Walker Boulevard Ext, Augusta GA 30901 **Phn:** 706-722-6077 **Fax:** 706-722-7066 www.wilkinsradio.com wfam@wilkinsradio.com

Augusta WGAC-FM (nt) 4051 Jimmie Dyess Pkwy, Augusta GA 30909 **Phn:** 706-396-7000 **Fax:** 706-396-7100 www.wgac.com newstips@wgac.com

Augusta WGAC-AM (nt) 4051 Jimmie Dyess Pkwy, Augusta GA 30909 **Phn:** 706-396-7000 **Fax:** 706-396-7100 www.wgac.com

Augusta WGUS-FM (g) 4051 Jimmie Dyess Pkwy, Augusta GA 30909 **Phn:** 706-396-7000 **Fax:** 706-396-7100 www.1027wgus.com

Augusta WHHD-FM (a) 4051 Jimmie Dyess Pkwy, Augusta GA 30909 **Phn:** 706-396-7000 **Fax:** 706-396-7100 www.hd983.com mail@hd983.com

Augusta WIBL-FM (c) 2743 Perimeter Pkwy Ste 100-300, Augusta GA 30909 **Phn:** 706-396-6000 **Fax:** 706-396-6010 www.1077thebull.com augustapsa@clearchannel.com

Augusta WKSP-FM (wxo) 2743 Perimeter Pkwy Ste 100-300, Augusta GA 30909 **Phn:** 706-396-6000 **Fax:** 706-396-6010 www.963kissfm.com fattz@963kissfm.com

Augusta WKXC-FM (c) 4051 Jimmie Dyess Pkwy, Augusta GA 30909 **Phn:** 706-396-7000 **Fax:** 706-396-7100 www.kicks99.com tgentry@kicks99.com

Augusta WKZK-AM (wx) PO Box 1454, Augusta GA 30903 **Phn:** 706-738-9191 **Fax:** 706-481-8442 www.wkzk.net

Augusta WPRW-FM (u) 2743 Perimeter Pkwy Ste 100-300, Augusta GA 30909 **Phn:** 706-396-6000 **Fax:** 706-396-6010 www.power107.net minnesotafattz@clearchannel.com

Augusta WRDW-AM (snt) 4051 Jimmie Dyess Pkwy, Augusta GA 30909 **Phn:** 706-396-7000 **Fax:** 706-396-7100 www.wrdwam.com ab@wrdwam.com

Augusta WYNF-AM (c) 2743 Perimeter Pkwy Ste 100-300, Augusta GA 30909 **Phn:** 706-396-6000 **Fax:** 706-396-6010 www.espncsra.com travisdylan@clearchannel.com

Austell WAOS-AM (y) 5815 Westside Rd, Austell GA 30106 **Phn:** 770-944-0900 **Fax:** 770-944-9794

Austell WLBA-AM (y) 5815 Westside Rd, Austell GA 30106 **Phn:** 770-944-0900

Austell WXEM-AM (y) 5815 Westside Rd, Austell GA 30106 **Phn:** 770-944-0900 **Fax:** 770-944-9794

Bainbridge WBGE-FM (rq) 521 S Scott St, Bainbridge GA 39819 **Phn:** 229-246-1960 **Fax:** 229-246-9995 sowegalive.com livecrew@rockin1063.com

Bainbridge WMGR-AM (am) PO Box 930, Bainbridge GA 39818 **Phn:** 229-246-1650 **Fax:** 229-246-1403 www.wmgr.net wmgr@wmgr.net

Barnesville WBAF-AM (c) 645 Forsyth St, Barnesville GA 30204 **Phn:** 770-358-1090

Baxley WBYZ-FM (c) PO Box 390, Baxley GA 31515 **Phn:** 912-367-3000 **Fax:** 912-367-9779 www.wbyz94.com peggy@wbyz94.com

Baxley WUFE-AM (o) PO Box 390, Baxley GA 31515 **Phn:** 912-367-3000 **Fax:** 912-367-9779 www.bigwufe.com peggy@wbyz94.com

Bethlehem WIMO-AM (nt) PO Box 565, Bethlehem GA 30620 **Phn:** 578-963-5482 **Fax:** 678-963-5483 wimoradio.com smitchell@wimoradio.com

Bloomingdale WYFS-FM (q) 156 Falcon Ln, Bloomingdale GA 31302 **Phn:** 877-554-8226 www.bbnradio.org

Blue Ridge WPPL-FM (c) PO Box 938, Blue Ridge GA 30513 **Phn:** 706-632-9775 **Fax:** 706-632-5922 www.mountaincountryradio.com wppl@mountaincountryradio.com

Bogart WGAU-AM (nt) 1010 Tower Pl, Bogart GA 30622 **Phn:** 706-549-1340 **Fax:** 706-546-0441 www.1340wgau.com matt.caesar@coxradio.com

Bogart WGMG-FM (a) 1010 Tower Pl, Bogart GA 30622 **Phn:** 706-549-6222 **Fax:** 706-546-0441 www.magic1021.com jerry.arnold@coxinc.com

Bogart WMSL-FM (q) 2121 Ruth Jackson Rd, Bogart GA 30622 **Phn:** 770-725-8890 **Fax:** 678-753-0088 wmsl.fm

Bogart WNGC-FM (c) 1010 Tower Pl, Bogart GA 30622 **Phn:** 706-549-6222 **Fax:** 706-546-0441 www.1061wngc.com scott@southernbroadcasting.com

Bogart WPUP-FM (r) 1010 Tower Pl, Bogart GA 30622 **Phn:** 706-549-6222 **Fax:** 706-353-1967

Bogart WRFC-AM (s) 1010 Tower Pl, Bogart GA 30622 **Phn:** 706-549-6222 www.960theref.com david.johnston@coxradio.com

Bremen WGMI-AM (g) 613 Tallapoosa St W, Bremen GA 30110 **Phn:** 770-537-0840 **Fax:** 770-537-0220 www.wgmiradio.com wgmi1440@yahoo.com

Brunswick WBGA-FM (au) 3833 US Highway 82, Brunswick GA 31523 **Phn:** 912-267-1025 **Fax:** 912-264-5462

Brunswick WFNS-AM (s) 7515 Blythe Island Hwy, Brunswick GA 31523 **Phn:** 912-264-6251 **Fax:** 912-285-3877 www.thefansportsradio.com thefansportsradio@yahoo.com

Brunswick WGIG-AM (nt) 3833 US Highway 82, Brunswick GA 31523 **Phn:** 912-267-1025 **Fax:** 912-264-5462 www.1440wgig.net ryfun@adelphia.net

Brunswick WHFX-FM (r) 3833 US Highway 82, Brunswick GA 31523 **Phn:** 912-267-1025 **Fax:** 912-264-5462

Brunswick WMOG-AM (snt) 3833 US Highway 82, Brunswick GA 31523 **Phn:** 912-267-1025 **Fax:** 912-264-5462 www.1490wmog.net

Brunswick WRJY-FM (c) 185 Benedict Rd, Brunswick GA 31520 **Phn:** 912-261-1000 **Fax:** 912-265-8391 www.thewave1041.com joewilliesousa@thewave1041.com

Brunswick WSFN-AM (s) 7515 Blythe Island Hwy, Brunswick GA 31523 **Phn:** 912-264-6251 **Fax:** 912-264-9991 www.thefansportsradio.com thefansportsradio@yahoo.com

Brunswick WWSN-FM (a) 3833 US Highway 82, Brunswick GA 31523 **Phn:** 912-267-1025 **Fax:** 912-264-5462

Brunswick WXMK-FM (ha) 185 Benedict Rd, Brunswick GA 31520 **Phn:** 912-261-1000 **Fax:** 912-265-8391 www.magic1059.com info@magic1059.com

Brunswick WYNR-FM (c) 3833 US Highway 82, Brunswick GA 31523 **Phn:** 912-267-1025 **Fax:** 912-264-5462 1025wynr.net

Cairo WGRA-AM (nt) 644 Hall Rd, Cairo GA 39828 **Phn:** 229-377-4392 **Fax:** 229-377-4564 www.wgra.net jeff@wgra.net

Calhoun WEBS-AM (o) 427 S Wall St, Calhoun GA 30701 **Phn:** 706-629-1110 **Fax:** 706-629-7092 webscalhoun.com communitynews@webscalhoun.com

Calhoun WJTH-AM (c) PO Box 1119, Calhoun GA 30703 **Phn:** 706-629-6397 **Fax:** 706-629-8463 www.wjth.com am900@wjth.com

Calhoun WJTH-FM (c) PO Box 1119, Calhoun GA 30703 **Phn:** 706-629-6397 **Fax:** 706-629-8463 www.wjth.com am900@wjth.com

Canton WCHK-AM (y) PO Box 1290, Canton GA 30169 **Phn:** 770-479-2101 **Fax:** 770-479-1134

Carrollton WBTR-FM (c) 102 Parkwood Cir, Carrollton GA 30117 **Phn:** 770-832-9685 **Fax:** 770-830-1027 www.gradickcommunications.com cworthington@newstalk1330.com

Carrollton WCKS-FM (a) 102 Parkwood Cir, Carrollton GA 30117 **Phn:** 770-834-5477 **Fax:** 770-830-1027 www.gradickcommunications.com cworthington@newstalk1330.com

GEORGIA RADIO STATIONS

Carrollton WKNG-FM (qg) 102 Parkwood Cir, Carrollton GA 30117 **Phn:** 770-834-5477 **Fax:** 770-830-1027 www.rejoice891.com cworthington@newstalk1330.com

Carrollton WLBB-AM (nt) 808 Newnan Rd, Carrollton GA 30117 **Phn:** 678-601-1330 **Fax:** 678-601-8256 www.gradickcommunications.com cworthington@newstalk1330.com

Cartersville WBHF-AM (snt) 7 N Wall St, Cartersville GA 30120 **Phn:** 770-386-1450 **Fax:** 770-382-5390 www.wbhfradio.org news@wbhfradio.org

Cartersville WCCV-FM (q) PO Box 1000, Cartersville GA 30120 **Phn:** 770-387-0917 **Fax:** 770-387-2856 www.ibn.org onair@ibn.org

Cartersville WYXC-AM (nt) 1410 HIghway 411 NE, Cartersville GA 30121 **Phn:** 770-382-1306

Cedartown WGAA-AM (scn) PO Box 167, Cedartown GA 30125 **Phn:** 770-748-1340 **Fax:** 770-748-4539 www.wgaaradio.com chasitye@wgaaradio.com

Clarkesville WCHM-AM (nt) 683 Grant St Ste U, Clarkesville GA 30523 **Phn:** 706-839-1490 **Fax:** 706-754-5034 www.wchmradio.com

Claxton WCLA-AM (q) 316 N River St, Claxton GA 30417 **Phn:** 912-739-9252 **Fax:** 912-739-0050 www.wclaradio.net radioevans@bellsouth.net

Clayton WGHC-AM (at) PO Box 1149, Clayton GA 30525 **Phn:** 706-782-4251 **Fax:** 706-782-4252 rabunradio@windstream.net

Clayton WRBN-FM (a) PO Box 1149, Clayton GA 30525 **Phn:** 706-782-1041 **Fax:** 706-243-6173 sky104.com sky104wrbn@gmail.com

Cleveland WRWH-AM (nt) PO Box 181, Cleveland GA 30528 **Phn:** 706-865-3181 **Fax:** 706-865-0421 www.wrwh.com info@wrwh.com

Columbus WAGH-FM (wu) PO Box 687, Columbus GA 31902 **Phn:** 706-576-3000 **Fax:** 706-576-3010 www.mymagic101.com derrickgreene@clearchannel.com

Columbus WBFA-FM (u) 1501 13th Ave, Columbus GA 31901 **Phn:** 706-576-3000 **Fax:** 706-576-3010 www.thebeatcolumbus.com jennifernewman@clearchannel.com

Columbus WCGQ-FM (a) 1820 Wynnton Rd, Columbus GA 31906 **Phn:** 706-327-1217 **Fax:** 706-596-4600 www.q1073.com dave@q1073.com

Columbus WDAK-AM (t) 1501 13th Ave, Columbus GA 31901 **Phn:** 706-576-3000 **Fax:** 706-576-3005 www.newsradio540.com scottmiller@newsradio540.com

Columbus WEAM-AM (s) PO Box 1998, Columbus GA 31902 **Phn:** 706-576-3565 **Fax:** 706-576-3683

Columbus WEAM-FM (g) 2203 Wynnton Rd, Columbus GA 31906 **Phn:** 706-576-3565 **Fax:** 706-653-9676

Columbus WFXE-FM (wu) PO Box 1998, Columbus GA 31902 **Phn:** 706-576-3565 **Fax:** 706-576-3683 www.foxie105fm.com foxie1049@aol.com

Columbus WGSY-FM (a) PO Box 687, Columbus GA 31902 **Phn:** 706-576-3000 **Fax:** 706-576-3010 www.sunny100.com gregfitzgerald@clearchannel.com

Columbus WIOL-FM (s) PO Box 1998, Columbus GA 31902 **Phn:** 706-576-3565 **Fax:** 706-576-3683 foxie1049@aol.com

Columbus WKCN-FM (c) 1820 Wynnton Rd, Columbus GA 31906 **Phn:** 706-327-1217 **Fax:** 706-596-4600 www.ilovekissin.com jbrannan@pmbbroadcasting.com

Columbus WKZJ-FM (au) PO Box 1998, Columbus GA 31902 **Phn:** 706-576-3565 **Fax:** 706-576-3683 cconner@dbicolumbus.com

Columbus WOKS-AM (wu) PO Box 1998, Columbus GA 31902 **Phn:** 706-576-3565 **Fax:** 706-576-3683

Columbus WRCG-AM (sn) 1820 Wynnton Rd, Columbus GA 31906 **Phn:** 706-327-1217 **Fax:** 706-596-4600 pmbbroadcasting.com jbrannan@pmbbroadcasting.com

Columbus WRLD-FM (o) 1820 Wynnton Rd, Columbus GA 31906 **Phn:** 706-327-1217 **Fax:** 706-596-4600 pmbbroadcasting.com ahaynes@pmbbroadcasting.com

Columbus WSHE-AM (g) PO Box 687, Columbus GA 31902 **Phn:** 706-576-3000 **Fax:** 706-576-3010 www.am1270radio.com wshe@morrisbb.net

Columbus WSTH-FM (c) 1501 13th Ave, Columbus GA 31901 **Phn:** 706-576-3000 **Fax:** 706-576-3005 www.mysouth1061.com jennifernewman@clearchannel.com

Columbus WVRK-FM (r) 1501 13th Ave, Columbus GA 31901 **Phn:** 706-576-3000 **Fax:** 706-576-3010 www.rock103columbus.com robcater@clearchannel.com

Commerce WJJC-AM (c) PO Box 379, Commerce GA 30529 **Phn:** 706-335-3155 **Fax:** 706-335-1905 www.wjjc.net wjjc@windstream.net

Cornelia WCON-FM (cg) PO Box 100, Cornelia GA 30531 **Phn:** 706-778-2241 **Fax:** 706-778-0576 www.wconfm.com bfoster@wconfm.com

Cornelia WCON-AM (m) PO Box 100, Cornelia GA 30531 **Phn:** 706-778-2241 **Fax:** 706-778-0576 wconam.com bfoster@wconfm.com

Covington WGFS-AM (i) 1151 Hendrick St SW, Covington GA 30014 **Phn:** 770-786-1430 **Fax:** 770-784-9892

Cumming WWEV-FM (q) PO Box 248, Cumming GA 30028 **Phn:** 770-781-9150 **Fax:** 770-781-5003 victory915.com wwev@wwev.org

Dahlonega WZTR-FM (r) 1376 Ben Higgins Rd, Dahlonega GA 30533 **Phn:** 706-867-9542 **Fax:** 706-864-4364 www.thunder1043fm.com info@thunder1043fm.com

Dalton WBLJ-AM (snt) 613 Silver Cir, Dalton GA 30721 **Phn:** 706-278-5511 **Fax:** 706-278-9917 www.wblj1230.com

Dalton WDAL-AM (y) PO Box 1284, Dalton GA 30722 **Phn:** 706-278-5511 **Fax:** 706-226-8766 dhernandez@ngaradio.com

Dalton WTTI-AM (g) PO Box 1953, Dalton GA 30722 **Phn:** 706-277-5188 **Fax:** 706-277-7180 www.wttiradio.com troyhall2408@windstream.net

Dalton WYYU-FM (a) 613 Silver Cir, Dalton GA 30721 **Phn:** 706-278-5511 **Fax:** 706-278-9917 www.mixx1045.com lgibson@ngaradio.com

Donalsonville WSEM-AM (cgt) Hwy 91 N, Donalsonville GA 39845 **Phn:** 229-524-5123 **Fax:** 229-524-2265 kevin@live1019.com

Douglas WDMG-AM (nt) 1931 Ga Highway 32 E, Douglas GA 31533 **Phn:** 912-389-0995 **Fax:** 912-383-8552 wrdoradio@windstream.net

Douglas WDMG-FM (h) 1931 Ga Highway 32 E, Douglas GA 31533 **Phn:** 912-389-0995 **Fax:** 912-383-8552 www.979thebigdog.com bstraffic@windstream.net

Douglas WOKA-AM (g) 1310 Walker St W, Douglas GA 31533 **Phn:** 912-384-8153 **Fax:** 912-383-6328 www.dixiecountry.com production@atc.cc

Douglas WOKA-FM (c) 1310 Walker St W, Douglas GA 31533 **Phn:** 912-384-8153 **Fax:** 912-383-6328 www.dixiecountry.com dixiecountry@accessatc.net

Douglasville WDCY-AM (q) 8451 S Cherokee Blvd Ste B, Douglasville GA 30134 **Phn:** 770-920-1520 **Fax:** 770-920-4600 www.wordchristianbroadcasting.com

Douglasville WNEA-AM (gq) 8451 S Cherokee Blvd Ste B, Douglasville GA 30134 **Phn:** 770-920-1520 **Fax:** 770-920-4600 www.wordchristianbroadcasting.com

Dublin WDBN-FM (r) 807 Bellevue Ave, Dublin GA 31021 **Phn:** 478-272-4422 **Fax:** 478-275-4657

Dublin WKKZ-FM (ah) PO Box 967, Dublin GA 31040 **Phn:** 478-272-9270 **Fax:** 78-275-3592 www.wkkz927.com

Dublin WMCG-FM (c) PO Box 130, Dublin GA 31040 **Phn:** 478-272-4422 **Fax:** 478-275-4657 www.1049wmcg.com

Dublin WMLT-AM (ug) 807 Bellevue Ave, Dublin GA 31021 **Phn:** 478-272-4422 **Fax:** 478-275-4657 1330wmlt.com

Dublin WQZY-FM (c) PO Box 130, Dublin GA 31040 **Phn:** 478-272-4422 **Fax:** 478-275-4657 wqzy.com lea@wqzy.com

Dublin WXLI-AM (c) PO Box 967, Dublin GA 31040 **Phn:** 478-272-9270 **Fax:** 478-275-3592

Duluth WLKQ-FM (y) 1176 Satellite Blvd Bldg 400 # 230, Duluth GA 30096 **Phn:** 770-623-8772 **Fax:** 770-623-4722 www.laraza1023.com

Eastman WUFF-AM (c) 855 College St, Eastman GA 31023 **Phn:** 478-374-3437 **Fax:** 478-374-3585 wuffradio@yahoo.com

Eastman WUFF-FM (c) 855 College St, Eastman GA 31023 **Phn:** 478-374-3437 **Fax:** 478-374-3585 wolfcountry975.com wuffradio@yahoo.com

Eatonton WKVQ-AM (am) PO Box 3965, Eatonton GA 31024 **Phn:** 706-485-8792 **Fax:** 706-485-3555

Elberton WSGC-AM (o) PO Box 340, Elberton GA 30635 **Phn:** 706-283-1400 **Fax:** 706-283-8710 www.wsgcradio.com wsgc@elbertonradio.com

Elberton WSGC-FM (c) PO Box 340, Elberton GA 30635 **Phn:** 706-283-1400 **Fax:** 706-283-8710 www.elbertonradio.com wsgc@elbertonradio.com

Ellenwood WIGO-AM (gq) 2424 Old Rex Morrow Rd, Ellenwood GA 30294 **Phn:** 404-361-1570 **Fax:** 404-366-9772 www.wigoam.com mgamble@sgnthelight.com

Fitzgerald WBHB-AM (o) 601 W Roanoke Dr, Fitzgerald GA 31750 **Phn:** 229-423-2077 **Fax:** 229-423-8313

Fitzgerald WKZZ-FM (a) 601 W Roanoke Dr, Fitzgerald GA 31750 **Phn:** 229-423-2077 **Fax:** 229-423-8313

Fitzgerald WRDO-FM (h) 601 W Roanoke Dr, Fitzgerald GA 31750 **Phn:** 229-423-2077 **Fax:** 229-423-8313 wrdoradio@windstream.net

Gainesville WBCX-FM (v) 500 Washington St SE, Gainesville GA 30501 **Phn:** 770-538-4744 **Fax:** 770-538-4558 wbcx@brenau.edu

Gainesville WDUN-FM (nt) PO Box 10, Gainesville GA 30503 **Phn:** 770-532-9921 **Fax:** 770-532-0506 www.wdun.com joel.williams@jacobsmedia.net

Gainesville WDUN-AM (snt) PO Box 10, Gainesville GA 30503 **Phn:** 770-532-9921 **Fax:** 770-532-0506 www.wdun.com joel.williams@jacobsmedia.net

Gainesville WGGA-AM (am) PO Box 10, Gainesville GA 30503 **Phn:** 770-532-9921 **Fax:** 770-532-0506 www.1240theticket.com news@jacobsmedia.net

Gainesville WGTJ-AM (g) PO Box 907038, Gainesville GA 30501 **Phn:** 770-297-7485 **Fax:** 770-297-8030 www.glory1330.com mail@glory1330.com

Greensboro WDDK-FM (a) 1271 E Broad St Ste B, Greensboro GA 30642 **Phn:** 706-453-4140

GEORGIA RADIO STATIONS

Griffin WHIE-AM (cnt) PO Box G, Griffin GA 30224 **Phn:** 770-227-9451 **Fax:** 770-229-2291

Griffin WKEU-AM (ot) PO Box 997, Griffin GA 30224 **Phn:** 770-227-5507 **Fax:** 770-229-2291 wkeuradio.com wkeu@aol.com

Griffin WMVV-FM (q) PO Box 2020, Griffin GA 30224 **Phn:** 770-229-2020 **Fax:** 770-229-4820 www.wmvv.com

Grovetown WBLR-AM (y) 2278 Wortham Ln, Grovetown GA 30813 **Phn:** 706-309-9610 **Fax:** 706-309-9669

Grovetown WGPH-FM (q) 2278 Wortham Ln, Grovetown GA 30813 **Phn:** 706-309-9610 **Fax:** 706-309-9669

Grovetown WKTM-AM (y) 2278 Wortham Ln, Grovetown GA 30813 **Phn:** 706-309-9610 **Fax:** 706-309-9669

Grovetown WLPE-FM (q) 2278 Wortham Ln, Grovetown GA 30813 **Phn:** 706-309-9610 **Fax:** 706-309-9669

Hartwell WKLY-AM (cnt) PO Box 636, Hartwell GA 30643 **Phn:** 706-376-2233 **Fax:** 706-376-3100 www.wklyradio.com wklyradio@hartcom.net

Hawkinsville WCEH-AM (c) PO Box 1398, Hawkinsville GA 31036 **Phn:** 478-892-9061 **Fax:** 478-892-9063

Hawkinsville WQXZ-FM (o) PO Box 1398, Hawkinsville GA 31036 **Phn:** 478-892-9061 **Fax:** 478-892-9063

Hawkinsville WRPG-FM (nt) PO Box 90, Hawkinsville GA 31036 **Phn:** 478-971-0103 **Fax:** 478-971-2136

Hazlehurst WVOH-AM (g) 546 Baxley Hwy, Hazlehurst GA 31539 **Phn:** 912-375-4511 **Fax:** 912-375-4512 www.wvohradio.com wvoh@wvohradio.com

Hazlehurst WVOH-FM (c) PO Box 645, Hazlehurst GA 31539 **Phn:** 912-375-4511 **Fax:** 912-375-4512 www.wvohradio.com wvoh93@yahoo.com

Helen WZGA-FM (a) PO Box 256, Helen GA 30545 **Phn:** 706-878-1051 www.georgia105.com studio@georgia105.com

Hinesville WGML-AM (gw) PO Box 615, Hinesville GA 31310 **Phn:** 912-368-3399 **Fax:** 912-368-4191 www.phodd.orgwgml.html wgml99@yahoo.com

Hinesville WOAH-FM (u) 951 EG Miles Pkwy, Hinesville GA 31313 **Phn:** 912-408-1063 www.woah1063.com

Hinesville WTHG-FM (r) PO Box 29, Hinesville GA 31310 **Phn:** 912-368-9258 **Fax:** 912-368-5526

Irwinton WVKX-FM (uxw) PO Box 569, Irwinton GA 31042 **Phn:** 478-946-3445 **Fax:** 478-946-2406 love1037@windstream.net

Jackson WJGA-FM (wgr) PO Box 878, Jackson GA 30233 **Phn:** 770-775-3151 **Fax:** 770-775-3153

Jackson WKKP-AM (g) PO Box 878, Jackson GA 30233 **Phn:** 770-775-3151 **Fax:** 770-775-3153

Jasper WJLA-FM (gc) 134 S Main St, Jasper GA 30143 **Phn:** 706-276-2016 **Fax:** 706-635-1018 www.wljaradio.com byron@wljaradio.com

Jasper WLJA-FM (cg) 134 S Main St, Jasper GA 30143 **Phn:** 706-276-2016 **Fax:** 678-454-9350 www.wljaradio.com byron@wljaradio.com

Jasper WPGY-AM (o) 134 S Main St, Jasper GA 30143 **Phn:** 706-276-2016 **Fax:** 706-635-1018 randy@wljaradio.com

Jasper WYYZ-AM (cng) PO Box 1390, Jasper GA 30143 **Phn:** 706-692-4100 **Fax:** 706-692-4012 wyyz_1490am@yahoo.com

Jesup WIFO-FM (c) PO Box 647, Jesup GA 31598 **Phn:** 912-427-3711 **Fax:** 912-530-7717 www.bigdogcountry.com cwhubbard@bellsouth.net

Jesup WLOP-AM (c) PO Box 647, Jesup GA 31598 **Phn:** 912-427-3711 **Fax:** 912-530-7717

Kingsland WKBX-FM (c) 111 North Grove Blvd, Kingsland GA 31548 **Phn:** 912-729-6106 **Fax:** 912-729-4106 kbay1063.com

La Fayette WQCH-AM (c) PO Box 746, La Fayette GA 30728 **Phn:** 706-638-3276 **Fax:** 706-638-3896 www.wqch.net info@wqch.net

Lagrange WLAG-AM (st) 304 E Broome St, Lagrange GA 30240 **Phn:** 706-845-1023 **Fax:** 706-845-8642 www.eagle1023.com welr@eagle1023.com

Lagrange WOAK-FM (vq) 1921 Hamilton Rd, Lagrange GA 30241 **Phn:** 706-884-2950 **Fax:** 706-882-7729 www.woak.com woak@woak.org

Lawrenceville WPLO-AM (yo) 239 Ezzard St, Lawrenceville GA 30046 **Phn:** 770-237-9897 **Fax:** 770-237-8769 www.radiomex610atlanta.com

Lindale WROM-AM (gh) PO Box 99, Lindale GA 30147 **Phn:** 706-234-1237 **Fax:** 706-234-8043

Louisville WPEH-FM (c) PO Box 425, Louisville GA 30434 **Phn:** 478-625-7248 **Fax:** 478-625-7249 wpeh@classicsouth.net

Louisville WPEH-AM (c) PO Box 425, Louisville GA 30434 **Phn:** 478-625-7248 **Fax:** 478-625-7249 wpeh@classicsouth.net

Lumber City WMOC-FM (q) PO Box 520, Lumber City GA 31549 **Phn:** 912-363-4502 **Fax:** 912-363-2106 www.wmoc887fm.com wmoc887@yahoo.com

Lyons WBBT-AM (wx) PO Box 629, Lyons GA 30436 **Phn:** 912-526-8122 **Fax:** 912-526-9155

Lyons WLYU-FM (c) PO Box 629, Lyons GA 30436 **Phn:** 912-526-8122 **Fax:** 912-526-9155 toombsnow.comy-101radio.html barney@toombsnow.com

Macon WAYS-FM (o) 544 Mulberry St Ste 500, Macon GA 31201 **Phn:** 478-746-6286 **Fax:** 478-742-8061

Macon WBML-AM (gq) PO Box 6298, Macon GA 31208 **Phn:** 478-743-5453 **Fax:** 478-743-9265

Macon WDDO-AM (wg) 544 Mulberry St Ste 500, Macon GA 31201 **Phn:** 478-746-6286 **Fax:** 478-742-8061 willie.collins@cumulus.com

Macon WDEN-FM (c) 544 Mulberry St Ste 500, Macon GA 31201 **Phn:** 478-746-6286 **Fax:** 478-741-8811 www.wden.com

Macon WEBL-FM (c) 7080 Industrial Hwy, Macon GA 31216 **Phn:** 478-781-1063 **Fax:** 478-781-6711 www.newcountry965.com

Macon WFXM-FM (au) 6174 Ga Highway 57, Macon GA 31217 **Phn:** 478-745-3301 **Fax:** 478-742-2293

Macon WIBB-FM (uw) 7080 Industrial Hwy, Macon GA 31216 **Phn:** 478-781-1063 **Fax:** 478-781-6711 www.wibb.com thomasbacote@clearchannel.com

Macon WIFN-FM (s) 544 Mulberry St Ste 500, Macon GA 31201 **Phn:** 478-746-6286 **Fax:** 478-742-8061

Macon WLCG-AM (g) 7080 Industrial Hwy, Macon GA 31216 **Phn:** 478-781-1063 **Fax:** 478-781-6711 chriswilliams@clearchannel.com

Macon WLZN-FM (x) 544 Mulberry St Ste 500, Macon GA 31201 **Phn:** 478-746-6286 **Fax:** 478-749-1393 www.blazin923.com gentleman.george@cumulus.com

Macon WMAC-AM (nt) 544 Mulberry St Ste 500, Macon GA 31201 **Phn:** 478-746-6286 **Fax:** 478-742-8061 www.wmac-am.com chris.krok@cumulus.com

Macon WMGB-FM (h) 544 Mulberry St Ste 500, Macon GA 31201 **Phn:** 478-746-6286 **Fax:** 478-742-8061 www.allthehitsb951.com joe.browning@cumulus.com

Macon WNEX-AM (nt) 1691 Forsyth St, Macon GA 31201 **Phn:** 478-745-5858 **Fax:** 478-745-0500

Macon WPEZ-FM (a) 544 Mulberry St Ste 500, Macon GA 31201 **Phn:** 478-746-6286 **Fax:** 478-742-8061 www.z937.com

Macon WPGA-AM (m) 1691 Forsyth St, Macon GA 31201 **Phn:** 478-745-5858 **Fax:** 478-745-0500 music.disney.com

Macon WPGA-FM (a) 1691 Forsyth St, Macon GA 31201 **Phn:** 478-745-5858 **Fax:** 478-745-0500 phil@wpga.tv

Macon WQBZ-FM (r) 7080 Industrial Hwy, Macon GA 31216 **Phn:** 478-781-1063 **Fax:** 478-781-6711 www.Q106.fm thomasbacote@clearchannel.com

Macon WQMJ-FM (wx) 6174 Ga Highway 57, Macon GA 31217 **Phn:** 478-745-3301 **Fax:** 478-742-2293

Macon WRBV-FM (uw) 7080 Industrial Hwy, Macon GA 31216 **Phn:** 478-781-1063 **Fax:** 478-781-6711

Macon WXKO-AM (g) 6174 Ga Highway 57, Macon GA 31217 **Phn:** 478-745-3301 **Fax:** 478-742-2293

Macon WZCH-FM (h) 7080 Industrial Hwy, Macon GA 31216 **Phn:** 478-781-1063 **Fax:** 478-781-6711 johnlund@clearchannel.com

Madison WYTH-AM (m) 1281 Eatonton Rd, Madison GA 30650 **Phn:** 706-342-1250 **Fax:** 706-342-1752

McRae WYIS-AM (nt) PO Box 247, McRae GA 31055 **Phn:** 229-868-5611 **Fax:** 229-868-7552

McRae WYSC-FM (a) PO Box 247, McRae GA 31055 **Phn:** 229-868-5611 **Fax:** 229-868-7552

Metter WBMZ-FM (o) PO Box 238, Metter GA 30439 **Phn:** 912-685-2136 **Fax:** 912-685-2137

Metter WHCG-AM (g) PO Box 238, Metter GA 30439 **Phn:** 912-685-2136 **Fax:** 912-685-2137 wbmz@pineland.net

Milledgeville WKGQ-AM (ug) 156 Lake Laurel Rd NE, Milledgeville GA 31061 **Phn:** 478-453-9406 **Fax:** 478-453-3298 z97mail@yahoo.com

Milledgeville WKZR-FM (c) PO Box 519, Milledgeville GA 31059 **Phn:** 478-452-0586 **Fax:** 478-452-5886 www.country102fm.com mail@country102fm.com

Milledgeville WMGZ-FM (a) PO Box 832, Milledgeville GA 31059 **Phn:** 478-453-9406 **Fax:** 478-453-3298 www.z97.fm wmgz.z97@gmail.com

Milledgeville WMVG-AM (s) 1250 W Charlton St, Milledgeville GA 31061 **Phn:** 478-452-0586 **Fax:** 478-452-5886 www.country102fm.com mail@country102fm.com

Monroe WKUN-AM (g) PO Box 649, Monroe GA 30655 **Phn:** 770-267-0923 **Fax:** 770-342-8135 www.wmoqfm.com1490.html leslane@wmoqfm.com

Monroe WMOQ-FM (c) PO Box 649, Monroe GA 30655 **Phn:** 770-267-0923 **Fax:** 706-342-8135 www.wmoqfm.com julio_@wmoqfm.com

Montezuma WMNZ-AM (scn) PO Box 610, Montezuma GA 31063 **Phn:** 478-472-8386 **Fax:** 478-472-8296

Moultrie WMTM-FM (o) PO Box 788, Moultrie GA 31776 **Phn:** 229-985-1300 **Fax:** 229-890-0905 jim@cruisin94.com

Moultrie WMTM-AM (g) PO Box 788, Moultrie GA 31776 **Phn:** 229-985-1300 **Fax:** 229-890-0905 jim@cruisin94.com

Newnan WCOH-AM (s) 154 Boone Dr, Newnan GA 30263 **Phn:** 770-683-7234 **Fax:** 770-683-9846 www.foxsports1400.com johnlund@clearchannel.com

GEORGIA RADIO STATIONS

Newnan WMGP-FM (a) 154 Boone Dr, Newnan GA 30263 **Phn:** 770-683-7234 **Fax:** 770-683-9846 www.magic981.com johnlund@clearchannel.com

Newnan WVCC-AM (nt) 154 Boone Dr, Newnan GA 30263 **Phn:** 770-683-7234 **Fax:** 770-683-9846 www.720thevoice.com blainesaunders@clearchannel.com

Rockmart WZOT-AM (g) 602 W Elm St, Rockmart GA 30153 **Phn:** 770-684-7848

Rome WATG-FM (o) 2 Mount Alto Rd SW, Rome GA 30165 **Phn:** 706-378-8040 www.theridge957.com davis.elizabeth@comcast.net

Rome WLAQ-AM (snt) 2 Mount Alto Rd SW, Rome GA 30165 **Phn:** 706-232-7767 **Fax:** 706-295-9225 www.wlaq1410.com wlaq@comcast.net

Rome WQTU-FM (ar) 20 John Davenport Dr NW, Rome GA 30165 **Phn:** 706-291-9496 **Fax:** 706-235-7107 www.q102rome.com randyq@south107.com

Rome WRGA-AM (nt) 20 John Davenport Dr NW, Rome GA 30165 **Phn:** 706-291-9496 **Fax:** 706-235-7107 www.wrgarome.com randyq@south107.com

Rome WTSH-FM (c) 20 John Davenport Dr NW, Rome GA 30165 **Phn:** 706-291-9496 **Fax:** 706-235-7107 www.south107.com south107@aol.com

Rossville WJOC-AM (t) 805 Chickamauga Ave Frnt, Rossville GA 30741 **Phn:** 706-861-0800 **Fax:** 706-861-2299 wjoc.com wjoc1490@aol.com

Royston WBIC-AM (n) 259 Turner St, Royston GA 30662 **Phn:** 706-246-0059 **Fax:** 706-245-0890

Sandersville WSNT-FM (c) PO Box 150, Sandersville GA 31082 **Phn:** 478-552-5182 **Fax:** 478-553-0800 www.waco100fm.com

Sandersville WSNT-AM (s) PO Box 150, Sandersville GA 31082 **Phn:** 478-552-5182 **Fax:** 478-553-0800

Savannah WAEV-FM (h) 245 Alfred St, Savannah GA 31408 **Phn:** 912-964-7794 **Fax:** 912-964-9414 www.973kissfm.com info@973kissfm.com

Savannah WBMQ-AM (nt) 214 Television Cir, Savannah GA 31406 **Phn:** 912-961-9000 **Fax:** 912-961-7070 www.wbmq.net gil.jones@cumulus.com

Savannah WEAS-FM (wu) 214 Television Cir, Savannah GA 31406 **Phn:** 912-961-9000 **Fax:** 912-961-7070 www.e93fm.com lg@cumulus.com

Savannah WGCO-FM (o) 401 Mall Blvd Ste 101D, Savannah GA 31406 **Phn:** 912-351-9830 **Fax:** 912-352-4821 www.big983.com cbeverly@adventureradio.fm

Savannah WHCJ-FM (v) PO Box 20484, Savannah GA 31404 **Phn:** 912-356-2399 **Fax:** 912-356-2041 whcj@savannahstate.edu

Savannah WIXV-FM (r) 214 Television Cir, Savannah GA 31406 **Phn:** 912-961-9000 **Fax:** 912-961-7070 www.rockofsavannah.net don.scott@cumulus.com

Savannah WJCL-FM (c) 214 Television Cir, Savannah GA 31406 **Phn:** 912-961-9000 **Fax:** 912-961-7070 www.kix96.com boomer.lee@cumulus.com

Savannah WJLG-AM (g) 214 Television Cir, Savannah GA 31406 **Phn:** 912-961-9000 **Fax:** 912-961-7070

Savannah WLVH-FM (uw) 245 Alfred St, Savannah GA 31408 **Phn:** 912-964-7794 **Fax:** 912-964-9414 www.love1011.com community@love1011.com

Savannah WQBT-FM (u) 245 Alfred St, Savannah GA 31408 **Phn:** 912-964-7794 **Fax:** 912-964-9414 www.941thebeat.com info@941thebeat.com

Savannah WRHQ-FM (ar) 1102 E 52nd St, Savannah GA 31404 **Phn:** 912-234-1053 **Fax:** 912-354-6600 www.wrhq.com qualityrock@wrhq.com

Savannah WSGA-FM (a) PO Box 13980, Savannah GA 31416 **Phn:** 912-691-1934 **Fax:** 912-368-5526 joelwiddows@msn.com

Savannah WSOK-AM (wg) 245 Alfred St, Savannah GA 31408 **Phn:** 912-964-7794 **Fax:** 912-964-9414 www.1230wsok.com elarry@1230wsok.com

Savannah WSSJ-FM (ug) PO Box 13980, Savannah GA 31416 **Phn:** 912-691-1934 **Fax:** 912-368-5526 myjoy100.com

Savannah WTKS-AM (nt) 245 Alfred St, Savannah GA 31408 **Phn:** 912-964-7794 **Fax:** 912-964-9414 www.newsradio1290wtks.com sherylcollison@clearchannel.com

Savannah WTYB-FM (u) 214 Television Cir, Savannah GA 31406 **Phn:** 912-961-9000 **Fax:** 912-961-7070 www.magic1039fm.com lg@cumulus.com

Savannah WYKZ-FM (a) 245 Alfred St, Savannah GA 31408 **Phn:** 912-964-7794 **Fax:** 912-964-9414 www.987theriver.com mark@987theriver.com

Savannah WZAT-FM (a) 214 Television Cir, Savannah GA 31406 **Phn:** 912-961-9000 **Fax:** 912-961-7070

Scottdale WATB-AM (i) 3589 N Decatur Rd, Scottdale GA 30079 **Phn:** 404-508-1420 **Fax:** 404-508-8930 benv@mrbi.net

Senoia WEKS-FM (c) PO Box 925, Senoia GA 30276 **Phn:** 770-599-1923 925fmthebear.com

Statesboro WHKN-FM (c) PO Box 348, Statesboro GA 30459 **Phn:** 912-764-5446 **Fax:** 912-764-8827 georgiaeaglestatesboro.combest-country-949 information@georgiaeaglemedia.com

Statesboro WMCD-FM (a) PO Box 958, Statesboro GA 30459 **Phn:** 912-764-5446 **Fax:** 912-764-8827 statesboro365.com

Statesboro WPMX-FM (a) PO Box 958, Statesboro GA 30459 **Phn:** 912-764-5446 **Fax:** 912-764-8827 statesboro365.com

Statesboro WSYL-AM (c) PO Box 958, Statesboro GA 30459 **Phn:** 912-764-5446 **Fax:** 912-764-8827 georgiaeaglestatesboro.comkool-1490 information@georgiaeaglemedia.com

Statesboro WVGS-FM (v) PO Box 8016, Statesboro GA 30460 **Phn:** 912-681-0877 **Fax:** 912-681-0822

Statesboro WWNS-AM (ns) PO Box 958, Statesboro GA 30459 **Phn:** 912-764-5446 **Fax:** 912-764-8827 www.statesboro365.com information@georgiaeaglemedia.com

Statesboro WZBX-FM (c) PO Box 958, Statesboro GA 30459 **Phn:** 912-764-5446 **Fax:** 912-764-8827 statesboro365.com

Summerville WZQZ-AM (am) PO Box 735, Summerville GA 30747 **Phn:** 706-857-5555 **Fax:** 706-857-2006

Suwanee WNSY-FM (y) 1176 Satellite Blvd NW Ste 200, Suwanee GA 30024 **Phn:** 770-623-8772 **Fax:** 770-623-4722 www.laraza1023.com

Swainsboro WEDB-FM (ha) 2 Radio Loop, Swainsboro GA 30401 **Phn:** 478-237-1590 **Fax:** 478-237-3559 www.radiojones.com bobbydjd@yahoo.com

Swainsboro WJAT-AM (snt) 2 Radio Loop, Swainsboro GA 30401 **Phn:** 478-237-1590 **Fax:** 478-237-3559

Swainsboro WXRS-AM (o) 2 Radio Loop, Swainsboro GA 30401 **Phn:** 478-237-1590 **Fax:** 478-237-3559

Swainsboro WXRS-FM (c) 2 Radio Loop, Swainsboro GA 30401 **Phn:** 478-237-1590 **Fax:** 478-237-3559

Tallapoosa WKNG-AM (c) PO Box 655, Tallapoosa GA 30176 **Phn:** 770-573-7244 **Fax:** 404-551-2709 www.gradickcommunications.com cworthington@newstalk1330.com

Tennille WJFL-FM (a) PO Box 36, Tennille GA 31089 **Phn:** 478-553-1019 **Fax:** 478-553-1123 www.wjfl.com wjfl@wjfl.com

Thomaston WTGA-FM (a) PO Box 550, Thomaston GA 30286 **Phn:** 706-647-7121 **Fax:** 706-647-7122

Thomaston WTGA-AM (cgt) PO Box 550, Thomaston GA 30286 **Phn:** 706-647-7121 **Fax:** 706-647-7122 www.fun101fm.com wtga@fun101fm.com

Thomasville WHGH-AM (wu) 19 Pall Bearer Rd, Thomasville GA 31792 **Phn:** 229-228-4124 **Fax:** 229-225-9508

Thomasville WJEP-AM (q) PO Box 90, Thomasville GA 31799 **Phn:** 229-228-5683 **Fax:** 229-436-0544

Thomasville WPAX-AM (ma) PO Box 129, Thomasville GA 31799 **Phn:** 229-226-1240 **Fax:** 229-226-1361 www.wpaxradio.com lenrob@rose.net

Thomasville WPAX-FM (ma) PO Box 129, Thomasville GA 31799 **Phn:** 229-226-1240 **Fax:** 229-226-1361 www.wpaxradio.com lenrob@rose.net

Thomasville WTUF-FM (c) PO Box 129, Thomasville GA 31799 **Phn:** 229-225-1063 **Fax:** 229-226-1361 www.wtufradio.com lenrob@rose.net

Thomson WTHO-FM (c) 788 Cedar Rock Rd, Thomson GA 30824 **Phn:** 706-595-5122 **Fax:** 706-595-3021 wtho@classicsouth.net

Thomson WTWA-AM (jb) 788 Cedar Rock Rd, Thomson GA 30824 **Phn:** 706-595-1561 **Fax:** 706-595-3021

Tifton WPLH-FM (p) PO Box 36, Tifton GA 31793 **Phn:** 229-386-7158

Tifton WTIF-AM (ct) 458 Virginia Ave N, Tifton GA 31794 **Phn:** 229-382-1340 **Fax:** 229-386-8658

Toccoa WEPC-FM (vq) PO Box 780, Toccoa GA 30577 **Phn:** 706-282-6030 **Fax:** 706-282-6090 toccoafallsradio.org radio@myfavoritestation.net

Toccoa WNEG-AM (am) PO Box 1159, Toccoa GA 30577 **Phn:** 706-886-2191 **Fax:** 706-282-0189 www.wnegradio.com wneg@windstream.net

Toccoa Falls WLET-AM (ntg) PO Box 780, Toccoa Falls GA 30598 **Phn:** 706-282-6030 **Fax:** 706-282-6090 www.toccoafallsradio.org radio@myfavoritestation.net

Toccoa Falls WRAF-FM (vq) PO Box 780, Toccoa Falls GA 30598 **Phn:** 706-282-6030 **Fax:** 706-282-6090 www.toccoafallsradio.org radio@myfavoritestation.net

Trenton WKWN-AM (nt) 12544 N Main St, Trenton GA 30752 **Phn:** 706-657-7594 **Fax:** 706-657-6767

Tucker WGUN-AM (qt) 2901 Mountain Industrial Blvd, Tucker GA 30084 **Phn:** 770-491-7748 **Fax:** 770-491-3019

Tyrone WFDR-FM (q) 1175 Senoia Rd, Tyrone GA 30290 **Phn:** 770-487-4500 **Fax:** 770-486-6400 georgia.thejoyfm.com

Tyrone WVFJ-FM (q) 1175 Senoia Rd Ste E, Tyrone GA 30290 **Phn:** 770-487-4500 **Fax:** 770-486-6400 georgia.thejoyfm.com

Valdosta WAAC-FM (c) 2973 US Highway 84 W, Valdosta GA 31601 **Phn:** 229-242-4513 **Fax:** 229-247-7676

Valdosta WAFT-FM (q) 215 Waft Hill Ln, Valdosta GA 31602 **Phn:** 229-244-5180 **Fax:** 229-242-8808 www.waft.org mail@waft.org

Valdosta WGOV-AM (ot) PO Box 5739, Valdosta GA 31603 **Phn:** 229-242-4513 **Fax:** 229-247-7676

Valdosta WKAA-FM (c) 1711 Ellis Dr, Valdosta GA 31601 **Phn:** 229-244-8642 **Fax:** 229-242-7620

Valdosta WQPW-FM (a) 1711 Ellis Dr, Valdosta GA 31601 **Phn:** 229-244-8642 **Fax:** 229-242-7620

Valdosta WSFB-AM (z) 118 N Patterson St, Valdosta GA 31601 **Phn:** 229-263-4373 **Fax:** 229-263-7693 scottjames29@hotmail.com

Valdosta WSTI-FM (u) 1711 Ellis Dr, Valdosta GA 31601 **Phn:** 229-244-8642 **Fax:** 229-242-7620

Valdosta WVGA-FM (nt) 1711 Ellis Dr, Valdosta GA 31601 **Phn:** 229-244-8642 **Fax:** 229-242-7620

Valdosta WVLD-AM (nt) 1711 Ellis Dr, Valdosta GA 31601 **Phn:** 229-244-8642 **Fax:** 229-249-0991

Valdosta WVVS-FM (vr) 1500 N Patterson St, Valdosta GA 31698 **Phn:** 229-333-5662 www.valdosta.edu jahallsw@valdosta.edu

Valdosta WWRQ-FM (r) 1711 Ellis Dr, Valdosta GA 31601 **Phn:** 229-244-8642 **Fax:** 229-242-7620 kpelkowski@blackcrow.fm

Valdosta WXHT-FM (h) 1711 Ellis Dr, Valdosta GA 31601 **Phn:** 229-244-8642 **Fax:** 229-242-7620 myhot1027.com jmathews@blackcrow.fm

Vidalia WTCQ-FM (a) PO Box 900, Vidalia GA 30475 **Phn:** 912-537-9202 **Fax:** 912-537-4477 southeastgeorgiatoday.com jfoskey@vidaliacommunications.com

Vidalia WVOP-AM (nt) PO Box 900, Vidalia GA 30475 **Phn:** 912-537-9202 **Fax:** 912-537-4477 southeastgeorgiatoday.com helen@vidaliacommunications.com

Vidalia WYUM-FM (c) PO Box 900, Vidalia GA 30475 **Phn:** 912-537-9202 **Fax:** 912-537-4477 southeastgeorgiatoday.com zfowler@vidaliacommunications.com

Warner Robins WRWR-AM (n) 1350 Radio Loop, Warner Robins GA 31088 **Phn:** 478-923-3416 **Fax:** 478-923-3236 www.wrwr.com news@wrwr.com

Waycross WKUB-FM (c) PO Box 1472, Waycross GA 31502 **Phn:** 912-449-3391 **Fax:** 912-449-6284 wkub@almatel.net

Waycross WWUF-FM (o) PO Box 1472, Waycross GA 31502 **Phn:** 912-449-3391 **Fax:** 912-449-6284 classichitsradioonline.com wkub@almatel.net

West Point WCJM-FM (c) 705 4th Ave, West Point GA 31833 **Phn:** 706-645-2991 **Fax:** 706-645-3364 www.wcjmthebull.com

Young Harris WACF-FM (r) 1352 Main St Ste 6, Young Harris GA 30582 **Phn:** 706-379-9770 **Fax:** 706-379-3004

HAWAII

Aiea KLHT-AM (q) 98-1016 Komo Mai Dr, Aiea HI 96701 **Phn:** 808-524-1040 www.klight.org klhtradio@gmail.com

Hanalei KAQA-FM (vqe) PO Box 825, Hanalei HI 96714 **Phn:** 808-826-7774 **Fax:** 808-826-7977 www.kkcr.org kkcr@kkcr.org

Hanalei KKCR-FM (vqe) PO Box 825, Hanalei HI 96714 **Phn:** 808-826-7774 **Fax:** 808-826-7977 kkcr@kkcr.org

Hilo KAGB-FM (e) 688 Kinoole St, Hilo HI 96720 **Phn:** 808-935-6858 **Fax:** 808-969-7949

Hilo KAOY-FM (e) 1145 Kilauea Ave, Hilo HI 96720 **Phn:** 808-935-5461 **Fax:** 808-935-7761 www.kwxx.com sales@kwxx.com

Hilo KAPA-FM (e) 913 Kanoelehua Ave, Hilo HI 96720 **Phn:** 808-961-0651 **Fax:** 808-935-0396 www.kaparadio.com studio@kaparadio.com

Hilo KCIF-FM (q) PO Box 1066, Hilo HI 96721 **Phn:** 808-982-4356 **Fax:** 808-966-6439 www.kcifhawaii.org keepchristinfocus@kcifradio.com

Hilo KHBC-AM (a) 688 Kinoole St Ste 112, Hilo HI 96720 **Phn:** 808-959-5700 **Fax:** 808-959-5800 www.khbcradio.com scott@konafm.com

Hilo KHLO-AM (s) 913 Kanoelehua Ave, Hilo HI 96720 **Phn:** 808-961-0651 **Fax:** 808-935-0396 jpacheco@pacificradiogroup.com

Hilo KHWI-FM (a) 688 Kinoole St Ste 112, Hilo HI 96720 **Phn:** 808-959-5700 **Fax:** 808-959-5800 www.khbcradio.com scott@konafm.com

Hilo KKBG-FM (ae) 913 Kanoelehua Ave, Hilo HI 96720 **Phn:** 808-961-0651 **Fax:** 808-935-0396 www.kbigfm.com studio@kbigfm.com

Hilo KKON-AM (s) 913 Kanoelehua Ave, Hilo HI 96720 **Phn:** 808-961-0651 **Fax:** 808-934-8008 www.espnhawaii.com

Hilo KLUA-FM (u) 688 Kinoole St, Hilo HI 96720 **Phn:** 808-935-6858 **Fax:** 808-969-7949

Hilo KNWB-FM (ah) 1145 Kilauea Ave, Hilo HI 96720 **Phn:** 808-935-5461 **Fax:** 808-935-7761 www.b97hawaii.com psa@b97hawaii.com

Hilo KPUA-AM (tns) 1145 Kilauea Ave, Hilo HI 96720 **Phn:** 808-935-5461 **Fax:** 808-935-7761 www.kpua.net news@kpua.net

Hilo KPVS-FM (u) 913 Kanoelehua Ave, Hilo HI 96720 **Phn:** 808-298-2328 **Fax:** 808-935-0396

Hilo KWXX-FM (ae) 1145 Kilauea Ave, Hilo HI 96720 **Phn:** 808-935-5461 **Fax:** 808-935-7761 www.kwxx.com sales@kwxx.com

Honolulu KAIM-FM (q) 1160 N King St, Honolulu HI 96817 **Phn:** 808-533-0065 **Fax:** 808-524-2104 www.thefishhawaii.com jwaters@salemhawaii.com

Honolulu KBIG-FM (a) 913 Kanoelehua Ave, Honolulu HI 96720 **Phn:** 808-961-065 www.kbigfm.com keith@kbigfm.com

Honolulu KCCN-FM (e) 900 Fort Street Mall Ste 700, Honolulu HI 96813 **Phn:** 808-536-2728 **Fax:** 808-536-2528 www.kccnfm100.com patti.milburn@coxradio.com

Honolulu KDDB-FM (h) 765 Amana St Ste 200, Honolulu HI 96814 **Phn:** 808-947-1500 **Fax:** 808-947-1506 www.1027dabomb.net lilly.yamachika@vrehawaii.com

Honolulu KDNN-FM (e) 650 Iwilei Rd Ste 400, Honolulu HI 96817 **Phn:** 808-550-9200 **Fax:** 808-550-9504 www.island985.com hrhawaii@clearchannel.com

Honolulu KGMZ-FM (o) 1160 N King St, Honolulu HI 96817 **Phn:** 808-533-0065 **Fax:** 808-524-2104 oldies1079honolulu.com

Honolulu KGU-FM (qt) 1160 N King St, Honolulu HI 96817 **Phn:** 808-533-0065 **Fax:** 808-524-2104 www.995theword.com jwaters@salemhawaii.com

Honolulu KHBZ-AM (t) 650 Iwilei Rd Ste 400, Honolulu HI 96817 **Phn:** 808-550-9200 **Fax:** 808-550-9288 www.kikiradio.com stevennorstrom@clearchannel.com

Honolulu KHCM-AM (c) 1160 N King St, Honolulu HI 96817 **Phn:** 808-533-0065 **Fax:** 808-524-2104

Honolulu KHCM-FM (c) 1160 N King St, Honolulu HI 96817 **Phn:** 808-533-0065 **Fax:** 808-524-2104 www.975countrykhcm.com

Honolulu KHNR-AM (nt) 1160 N King St, Honolulu HI 96817 **Phn:** 808-533-0065 **Fax:** 808-524-2104 www.khnr.com jwaters@salemhawaii.com

Honolulu KHPR-FM (p) 738 Kaheka St Ste 101, Honolulu HI 96814 **Phn:** 808-955-8821 www.hawaiipublicradio.org news@hawaiipublicradio.org

Honolulu KHVH-AM (nt) 650 Iwilei Rd Ste 400, Honolulu HI 96817 **Phn:** 808-550-9200 **Fax:** 808-550-9288 www.khvhradio.com stevennorstrom@clearchannel.com

Honolulu KIKI-FM (h) 650 Iwilei Rd Ste 400, Honolulu HI 96817 **Phn:** 808-550-9200 **Fax:** 808-550-9288 www.939jamz.com jamiehyatt@clearchannel.com

Honolulu KINE-FM (a) 900 Fort Street Mall Ste 700, Honolulu HI 96813 **Phn:** 808-275-1000 **Fax:** 808-536-2528 www.hawaiian105.com kimo.akane@coxradio.com

Honolulu KIPO-FM (pnj) 738 Kaheka St Ste 101, Honolulu HI 96814 **Phn:** 808-955-8821 **Fax:** 808-946-3863 www.hawaiipublicradio.org news@hawaiipublicradio.org

Honolulu KKEA-AM (s) 900 Fort Street Mall Ste 700, Honolulu HI 96813 **Phn:** 808-536-3624 **Fax:** 808-548-0608 www.espn1420am.com

Honolulu KKNE-AM (e) 900 Fort Street Mall Ste 700, Honolulu HI 96813 **Phn:** 808-275-1000 **Fax:** 808-536-2528 www.am940hawaii.com kimo.akane@coxinc.com

Honolulu KKUA-FM (p) 738 Kaheka St Ste 101, Honolulu HI 96814 **Phn:** 808-955-8821 **Fax:** 808-946-3863 www.hawaiipublicradio.org mail@hawaiipublicradio.org

Honolulu KNDI-AM (eq) 1734 S King St, Honolulu HI 96826 **Phn:** 808-946-2844 **Fax:** 808-947-3531 www.kndi.com kndiradio@hawaii.rr.com

Honolulu KORL-FM (aj) 900 Fort Street Mall Ste 450, Honolulu HI 96813 **Phn:** 808-538-1180 **Fax:** 808-538-9548 www.hhawaiimedia.com

Honolulu KPHI-AM (e) 900 Fort Street Mall Ste 450, Honolulu HI 96813 **Phn:** 808-538-1180 **Fax:** 808-536-9548 www.hhawaiimedia.com gh5512@aol.com

Honolulu KPHW-FM (h) 900 Fort Street Mall Ste 700, Honolulu HI 96813 **Phn:** 808-275-1000 **Fax:** 808-275-1196 www.power1043.com kc@power1043.com

Honolulu KPOI-FM (r) 1000 Bishop St # 200, Honolulu HI 96813 **Phn:** 808-947-1500 **Fax:** 808-947-1506 www.kpoifm.com 1059kpoi@gmail.com

Honolulu KQMQ-FM (h) 1000 Bishop St # 200, Honolulu HI 96813 **Phn:** 808-947-1500 **Fax:** 808-947-1506 www.931dapaina.com fredrico@ohanabroadcast.com

Honolulu KREA-AM (de) 1839 S King St, Honolulu HI 96826 **Phn:** 808-955-2295 **Fax:** 808-947-0844

Honolulu KRTR-AM (z) 900 Fort Street Mall Ste 700, Honolulu HI 96813 **Phn:** 808-275-1000 **Fax:** 808-536-2528 www.650amhawaii.com

Honolulu KRTR-FM (a) 900 Fort Street Mall Ste 700, Honolulu HI 96813 **Phn:** 808-275-1000 **Fax:** 808-536-2528 www.krater96.com patti.milburn@summitmediacorp.com

Honolulu KSSK-AM (a) 650 Iwilei Rd Ste 400, Honolulu HI 96817 **Phn:** 808-550-9200 **Fax:** 808-550-9288 www.ksskradio.com jamiehyatt@clearchannel.com

Honolulu KSSK-FM (a) 650 Iwilei Rd Ste 400, Honolulu HI 96817 **Phn:** 808-550-9200 **Fax:** 808-550-9288 www.ksskradio.com jamiehyatt@clearchannel.com

Honolulu KTUH-FM (v) 2445 Campus Rd # 203, Honolulu HI 96822 **Phn:** 808-956-5288 www.ktuh.org gm@ktuh.org

Honolulu KUCD-FM (r) 650 Iwilei Rd Ste 400, Honolulu HI 96817 **Phn:** 808-550-9200 **Fax:** 808-550-9288 www.star1019.com jamiehyatt@clearchannel.com

Honolulu KUMU-AM (t) 1000 Bishop St # 200, Honolulu HI 96813 **Phn:** 808-947-1500 **Fax:** 808-947-1506 www.kumu.com fredrico@ohanabroadcast.com

Honolulu KUMU-FM (a) 1000 Bishop St # 200, Honolulu HI 96813 **Phn:** 808-947-1500 **Fax:** 808-947-1506 www.kumu.com fredrico@ohanabroadcast.com

Honolulu KWAI-AM (nts) 100 N Beretania St Ste 401, Honolulu HI 96817 **Phn:** 808-523-3868 **Fax:** 808-531-6532 kwai1080am.com

Honolulu KZOO-AM (e) 2454 S Beretania St Ste 203, Honolulu HI 96826 **Phn:** 808-947-5966 **Fax:** 808-946-5966 www.kzoohawaii.com

Kahului KJKS-FM (a) 311 Ano St, Kahului HI 96732 **Phn:** 808-877-5566 **Fax:** 808-871-0666 www.kissfmmaui.com

Kahului KJMD-FM (h) 311 Ano St, Kahului HI 96732 **Phn:** 808-877-5566 **Fax:** 808-877-2888 www.dajam983.com studio@dajam983.com

Kahului KLHI-FM (ar) 311 Ano St, Kahului HI 96732 **Phn:** 808-877-5566 **Fax:** 808-871-0666 www.native925.com studio@native925.com

Kahului KMVI-AM (s) 311 Ano St, Kahului HI 96732 **Phn:** 808-877-5566 **Fax:** 808-871-0666 www.espn550.com

Kahului KNUI-AM (a) 311 Ano St, Kahului HI 96732 **Phn:** 808-877-5566 **Fax:** 808-871-0666

Kahului KPMW-FM (h) 230 Hana Hwy Ste 2, Kahului HI 96732 **Phn:** 808-871-6251 **Fax:** 808-871-5670

Kahului KPOA-FM (e) 311 Ano St, Kahului HI 96732 **Phn:** 808-877-5566 **Fax:** 808-871-0666 www.kpoa.com alakai@kpoa.com

Kailua Kona KLEO-FM (a) 75-5852 Alii Dr Ste B1-B-2, Kailua Kona HI 96740 **Phn:** 808-329-6633 **Fax:** 808-326-7886 www.kbigfm.com

Kihei KONI-FM (o) 300 Ohukai Rd Ste C318, Kihei HI 96753 **Phn:** 808-875-8866 **Fax:** 808-875-8870 hhawaiimedia.net j.carroll@hhawaiimedia.com

Kihei KRKH-FM (r) 300 Ohukai Rd Ste C318, Kihei HI 96753 **Phn:** 808-875-8866 **Fax:** 808-875-8870 hhawaiimedia.net j.carroll@hhawaiimedia.com

Lihue KFMN-FM (a) PO Box 1566, Lihue HI 96766 **Phn:** 808-246-1197 **Fax:** 808-246-9697 john.wada@fm97radio.com

Lihue KITH-FM (he) 4334 Rice St Ste 204B, Lihue HI 96766 **Phn:** 808-246-4444 www.island989.com kith@hhawaiimedia.com

Lihue KQNG-FM (a) PO Box 1748, Lihue HI 96766 **Phn:** 808-245-9527 **Fax:** 808-245-3563 www.kongradio.com kong@kongradio.com

Lihue KQNG-AM (snt) PO Box 1748, Lihue HI 96766 **Phn:** 808-245-9527 **Fax:** 808-245-3563 www.kongradio.com kong@kongradio.com

Lihue KSHK-FM (r) PO Box 1748, Lihue HI 96766 **Phn:** 808-245-9527 www.shaka103.com kong@kongradio.com

Lihue KSRF-FM (ae) PO Box 1201, Lihue HI 96766 **Phn:** 808-245-9527 www.surf959fm.com kong@kongradio.com

Lihue KTOH-FM (c) 4334 Rice St Ste 204B, Lihue HI 96766 **Phn:** 808-246-4444 hhawaiimedia.com gh5512@aol.com

Lihue KUAI-AM (ae) PO Box 1748, Lihue HI 96766 **Phn:** 808-245-9527 kong@kongradio.com

HAWAII RADIO STATIONS

Wailuku KAOI-AM (snt) PO Box 1437, Wailuku HI 96793 **Phn:** 808-244-9145 **Fax:** 808-244-8247 www.kaoifm.com kaoi@kaoi.net

Wailuku KAOI-FM (ar) PO Box 1437, Wailuku HI 96793 **Phn:** 808-244-9145 **Fax:** 808-244-8247 www.kaoifm.com info@kaoifm.com

Wailuku KDLX-FM (c) PO Box 1437, Wailuku HI 96793 **Phn:** 808-244-9145 **Fax:** 808-244-8247 vremaui.com kaoi@kaoi.net

IDAHO

Blackfoot KCVI-FM (r) PO Box 699, Blackfoot ID 83221 **Phn:** 208-785-1400 **Fax:** 208-785-0184 kbear.fm tisa@kbear.fm

Blackfoot KTHK-FM (c) PO Box 699, Blackfoot ID 83221 **Phn:** 208-785-1400 **Fax:** 208-782-1084 www.1055thehawk.com

Boise KAWO-FM (c) 827 E Park Blvd Ste 100, Boise ID 83712 **Phn:** 208-344-6363 **Fax:** 208-385-7385 www.wow1043.com lisa.adams@peakbroadcasting.com

Boise KBOI-AM (nt) 1419 W Bannock St, Boise ID 83702 **Phn:** 208-336-3670 **Fax:** 208-336-3734 www.670kboi.com news@kboi.com

Boise KBSU-AM (pj) 1910 University Dr, Boise ID 83725 **Phn:** 208-426-3663 **Fax:** 208-344-6631 boisestatepublicradio.org kbsxnewsroom@boisestate.edu

Boise KBSU-FM (pln) 1910 University Dr, Boise ID 83725 **Phn:** 208-426-3663 **Fax:** 208-344-6631 boisestatepublicradio.org nprnews91@yahoo.com

Boise KBXL-FM (q) 1440 S Weideman Ave, Boise ID 83709 **Phn:** 208-377-3790 **Fax:** 208-377-3792 www.941thevoice.com david@myfamilyradio.com

Boise KCID-AM (yq) PO Box 714, Boise ID 83701 **Phn:** 208-629-4869 salyluzradio.com

Boise KCIX-FM (a) 827 E Park Blvd Ste 100, Boise ID 83712 **Phn:** 208-344-6363 **Fax:** 208-947-9707 www.mix106radio.com boisepsa@peakbroadcasting.com

Boise KFXD-FM (c) 827 Park Blvd Ste 100, Boise ID 83712 **Phn:** 208-344-6363 **Fax:** 208-344-1134 www.kfxd.com kevin.godwin@peakbroadcasting.com

Boise KGEM-AM (am) 5257 W Fairview Ave Ste 260, Boise ID 83706 **Phn:** 208-344-3511 **Fax:** 208-947-6765 www.journalbroadcastgroup.com mmcglynn@journalbroadcastgroup.com

Boise KIDO-AM (nt) 827 Park Blvd Ste 100, Boise ID 83712 **Phn:** 208-344-6363 **Fax:** 208-344-1134 www.kidoam.com kevin.miller@peakbroadcasting.com

Boise KIZN-FM (c) 1419 W Bannock St, Boise ID 83702 **Phn:** 208-336-3670 **Fax:** 208-336-3734 www.kizn.com kissin92@kizn.com

Boise KJOT-FM (r) 5257 W Fairview Ave Ste 260, Boise ID 83706 **Phn:** 208-344-3511 **Fax:** 208-947-6765 www.varietyrocks.com varietyrock1051@gmail.com

Boise KKGL-FM (r) 1419 W Bannock St, Boise ID 83702 **Phn:** 208-336-3670 **Fax:** 208-336-3734 www.96-9theeagle.com scott.souhrada@cumulus.com

Boise KQFC-FM (c) 1419 W Bannock St, Boise ID 83702 **Phn:** 208-336-3670 **Fax:** 208-336-3734 www.98kqfc.com hank@nashfm979.com

Boise KQXR-FM (r) 5257 W Fairview Ave Ste 260, Boise ID 83706 **Phn:** 208-344-3511 **Fax:** 208-947-6765 www.xrock.com jnicolato@journalbroadcastgroup.com

Boise KRVB-FM (a) 5257 W Fairview Ave Ste 260, Boise ID 83706 **Phn:** 208-344-3511 **Fax:** 208-947-6765 www.riverinteractive.com mmcglynn@journalbroadcastgroup.com

Boise KSAS-FM (h) 827 E Park Blvd Ste 201, Boise ID 83712 **Phn:** 208-344-6363 **Fax:** 208-385-7385 www.1033kissfm.com kekeluv@gmail.com

Boise KSPD-AM (qt) 1440 S Weideman Ave, Boise ID 83709 **Phn:** 208-377-3790 **Fax:** 208-377-3792 www.myfamilyradio.com info@myfamilyradio.com

Boise KTHI-FM (h) 5257 W Fairview Ave Ste 260, Boise ID 83706 **Phn:** 208-344-3511 **Fax:** 208-947-6765 www.khits.fm rowilliams@jrn.com

Boise KTIK-AM (s) 1419 W Bannock St, Boise ID 83702 **Phn:** 208-336-3670 **Fax:** 208-336-3734 www.ktik.com

Boise KWEI-AM (y) 1156 N Orchard St, Boise ID 83706 **Phn:** 208-367-1859 **Fax:** 208-383-9170 kweiradio.com

Boise KWEI-FM (y) 1156 N Orchard St, Boise ID 83706 **Phn:** 208-367-1859 **Fax:** 208-383-9170 kweiradio.com

Boise KXLT-FM (a) 827 Park Blvd Ste 100, Boise ID 83712 **Phn:** 208-344-6363 **Fax:** 208-344-1134 www.liteonline.com lisa.adams@peakbroadcasting.com

Boise KZMG-FM (h) 1419 W Bannock St, Boise ID 83702 **Phn:** 208-336-3670 **Fax:** 208-336-3734 www.kzmg.com ken.weaver@cumulus.com

Caldwell KBGN-AM (q) 3303 E Chicago St, Caldwell ID 83605 **Phn:** 208-459-3635 www.kbgnradio.com kbgn@kbgnradio.com

Caldwell KTSY-FM (q) 16115 S Montana Ave, Caldwell ID 83607 **Phn:** 208-459-5879 **Fax:** 208-459-3144 895ktsy.org family@ktsy.org

Grangeville KORT-FM (c) PO Box 510, Grangeville ID 83530 **Phn:** 208-983-1230 **Fax:** 208-983-2744

Grangeville KORT-AM (c) PO Box 510, Grangeville ID 83530 **Phn:** 208-983-1230 **Fax:** 208-983-2744

Idaho Falls KBJX-FM (a) 1327 E 17th St, Idaho Falls ID 83404 **Phn:** 208-529-6926 **Fax:** 208-529-6927 www.b106.com jj@b106.com

Idaho Falls KBLI-AM (nt) 400 W Sunnyside Rd, Idaho Falls ID 83402 **Phn:** 208-785-1400 **Fax:** 208-785-0184 www.eastidahonews.com mike@klce.com

Idaho Falls KBLY-AM (nt) 400 W Sunnyside Rd, Idaho Falls ID 83402 **Phn:** 208-785-1400 **Fax:** 208-785-0184 www.eastidahonews.com mike@klce.com

Idaho Falls KFTZ-FM (a) 400 W Sunnyside Rd, Idaho Falls ID 83402 **Phn:** 208-523-3722 **Fax:** 208-525-2575 www.z103.fm onair@z103.com

Idaho Falls KGTM-FM (o) 1327 E 17th St, Idaho Falls ID 83404 **Phn:** 208-529-6926 **Fax:** 208-529-6927

Idaho Falls KID-AM (snt) 1406 Commerce Way, Idaho Falls ID 83401 **Phn:** 208-524-5900 **Fax:** 208-522-9696 590kid.com neal@590kid.com

Idaho Falls KID-FM (c) 1406 Commerce Way, Idaho Falls ID 83401 **Phn:** 208-524-5900 **Fax:** 208-522-9696 961thebull.com catfish@richbroadcasting.com

Idaho Falls KLCE-FM (a) 1190 E Lincoln Rd, Idaho Falls ID 83221 **Phn:** 208-523-3722 **Fax:** 208-525-2575 www.klce.com paul@klce.com

Idaho Falls KQEO-FM (h) 854 Lindsay Blvd, Idaho Falls ID 83402 **Phn:** 208-522-1101 **Fax:** 208-522-6110 www.arrow107.com keith@sandhillradio.com

Idaho Falls KQPI-FM (c) 854 Lindsay Blvd, Idaho Falls ID 83402 **Phn:** 208-522-1101 **Fax:** 208-522-6110 www.99kupi.com contactus@kupi99.com

Idaho Falls KSNA-FM (a) 854 Lindsay Blvd, Idaho Falls ID 83402 **Phn:** 208-522-1101 **Fax:** 208-522-6110 www.100myfm.com contactus@100myfm.com

Idaho Falls KSPZ-AM (y) 854 Lindsay Blvd, Idaho Falls ID 83402 **Phn:** 208-522-1101 **Fax:** 208-522-6110

Jerome KART-AM (c) 47 N 100 W, Jerome ID 83338 **Phn:** 208-324-8182 **Fax:** 208-324-7124

Jerome KMVX-FM (s) 47 N 100 W, Jerome ID 83338 **Phn:** 208-324-8181 **Fax:** 208-324-7124

Ketchum KECH-FM (r) PO Box 2750, Ketchum ID 83340 **Phn:** 208-726-5324 **Fax:** 208-788-7119 kech95@cox-internet.com

Ketchum KSKI-FM (ar) PO Box 2158, Ketchum ID 83340 **Phn:** 208-726-5324 **Fax:** 208-788-7119 www.kski.com bobthompson@hotmail.com

Ketchum KYZK-FM (ja) PO Box 2158, Ketchum ID 83340 **Phn:** 208-726-5324 **Fax:** 208-788-7119 kech95@cox-internet.com

Lewiston KATW-FM (a) 403 Capital St, Lewiston ID 83501 **Phn:** 208-743-6564 **Fax:** 208-798-0110 catfm01.businesscatalyst.com

Lewiston KCLK-FM (o) 403 C St, Lewiston ID 83501 **Phn:** 208-743-6564 **Fax:** 208-798-0110

Lewiston KMOK-FM (c) 805 Stewart Ave, Lewiston ID 83501 **Phn:** 208-746-5056 **Fax:** 208-743-4440 kelly@idavend.com

Lewiston KOZE-FM (r) 2560 Snake River Ave, Lewiston ID 83501 **Phn:** 208-743-2502 **Fax:** 208-743-1995 leemcv@koze.com

Lewiston KOZE-AM (t) PO Box 936, Lewiston ID 83501 **Phn:** 208-743-2502 **Fax:** 208-743-1995 www.koze950.com jford@koze.com

Lewiston KRLC-AM (c) 805 Stewart Ave, Lewiston ID 83501 **Phn:** 208-743-1551 **Fax:** 208-743-4440 newsroom@idavend.com

Lewiston KVAB-FM (r) 403 C St, Lewiston ID 83501 **Phn:** 208-743-6564 **Fax:** 208-798-0110

Lewiston KVTY-FM (a) 805 Stewart Ave, Lewiston ID 83501 **Phn:** 208-743-1551 **Fax:** 208-743-4440

McCall KDZY-FM (c) PO Box 2514, McCall ID 83638 **Phn:** 208-634-3781 **Fax:** 208-634-3799 www.kdzy98.com david@myfamilyradio.com

Montpelier KVSI-AM (c) PO Box 340, Montpelier ID 83254 **Phn:** 208-847-1450 **Fax:** 208-847-1451 kvsi.com kvsi@dcdi.net

Moscow KCLX-AM (c) PO Box 8849, Moscow ID 83843 **Phn:** 208-882-2551 **Fax:** 208-883-3571

Moscow KMAX-AM (t) PO Box 8849, Moscow ID 83843 **Phn:** 208-882-2551 **Fax:** 208-883-3571 gary@inlandradio.com

Moscow KRAO-FM (a) PO Box 8849, Moscow ID 83843 **Phn:** 208-882-2551 **Fax:** 208-883-3571 gary@inlandradio.com

Moscow KRPL-AM (ob) PO Box 8849, Moscow ID 83843 **Phn:** 208-882-2551 **Fax:** 208-883-3571 gary@inlandradio.com

Moscow KUOI-FM (v) PO Box 444272, Moscow ID 83844 **Phn:** 208-885-2218 **Fax:** 208-885-2222 kuoi.org shawno@kuoi.org

Moscow KZFN-FM (h) PO Box 8849, Moscow ID 83843 **Phn:** 208-882-2551 **Fax:** 208-883-3571 shad@inlandradio.com

Moscow KZZL-FM (c) PO Box 8849, Moscow ID 83843 **Phn:** 208-882-2551 **Fax:** 208-883-3571 gary@inlandradio.com

Mountain Home KMHI-AM (c) PO Box 704, Mountain Home ID 83647 **Phn:** 208-587-8424 **Fax:** 208-587-8425 impactradiogroup.com alvin@impactradiogroup.com

Nampa KDBI-FM (y) 3307 Caldwell Blvd Ste 101, Nampa ID 83651 **Phn:** 208-463-2900 **Fax:** 208-406-8750

IDAHO RADIO STATIONS

Nampa KQLZ-FM (y) 5660 E Franklin Rd Ste 200, Nampa ID 83687 **Phn:** 208-465-9966 **Fax:** 208-465-2922 www.1007lapoderosa.com mikey@impactradiogroup.com

Orofino KLER-AM (c) PO Box 32, Orofino ID 83544 **Phn:** 208-476-5702 klerproduction@kler-radio.com

Orofino KLER-FM (a) PO Box 32, Orofino ID 83544 **Phn:** 208-476-5702 **Fax:** 208-476-5703

Osburn KWAL-AM (c) PO Box 828, Osburn ID 83849 **Phn:** 208-752-1141 **Fax:** 208-753-5111 kwalradio@suddenlinkmail.com

Pocatello KLLP-AM (a) 259 E Center St, Pocatello ID 83201 **Phn:** 208-524-5900 **Fax:** 208-232-1240 star985.com dusty@star98radio.com

Pocatello KMGI-FM (r) PO Box 40, Pocatello ID 83204 **Phn:** 208-233-2121 **Fax:** 208-234-7682 www.102kmgi.com news@102kmgi.com

Pocatello KOUU-AM (c) PO Box 97, Pocatello ID 83204 **Phn:** 208-234-1290 **Fax:** 208-234-9451 www.kouu.com

Pocatello KPKY-FM (r) 259 E Center St, Pocatello ID 83201 **Phn:** 208-233-1133 **Fax:** 208-232-1240 949therock.com scott@949therock.com

Pocatello KRTK-AM (q) 1633 Olympus Dr, Pocatello ID 83201 **Phn:** 208-237-9500 www.calvarychapel.com krtk@calvarychapel.com

Pocatello KSEI-AM (s) PO Box 40, Pocatello ID 83204 **Phn:** 208-233-2121 **Fax:** 208-234-7682 www.930espn.com news@102kmgi.com

Pocatello KWIK-AM (nt) PO Box 998, Pocatello ID 83204 **Phn:** 208-233-1133 **Fax:** 208-232-1240 jeffevans@gapbroadcasting.com

Pocatello KZBQ-FM (c) PO Box 97, Pocatello ID 83204 **Phn:** 208-234-1290 **Fax:** 208-234-9451 www.kzbq.com

Preston KACH-AM (o) 1633 N Radio Station Rd, Preston ID 83263 **Phn:** 208-852-1340 **Fax:** 208-852-1342 www.kachradio.com kach@plmw.com

Rexburg KBYI-FM (pln) 102 Rgs Bldg Byu, Rexburg ID 83460 **Phn:** 208-496-2907 **Fax:** 208-496-2912 www.byui.edukbyi kbyi@byui.edu

Rupert KBAR-AM (ont) 120 S 300 W, Rupert ID 83350 **Phn:** 208-436-4757 **Fax:** 208-436-3050

Rupert KFTA-AM (y) 120 S 300 W, Rupert ID 83350 **Phn:** 208-436-4757 **Fax:** 208-436-3050 www.lafantastica970.com kfta970am@yahoo.com

Saint Maries KOFE-AM (oh) PO Box 278, Saint Maries ID 83861 **Phn:** 208-245-1240 **Fax:** 208-245-6525

Salmon KSRA-FM (ac) 315 Riverfront Dr, Salmon ID 83467 **Phn:** 208-756-2218 **Fax:** 208-756-2098 www.ksrafm.com ksraradio@ksrafm.com

Salmon KSRA-AM (ac) 315 Riverfront Dr, Salmon ID 83467 **Phn:** 208-756-2218 **Fax:** 208-756-2098 ksraradio@ksrafm.com

Sandpoint KBFI-AM (snt) 327 S Marion Ave, Sandpoint ID 83864 **Phn:** 208-263-2179 **Fax:** 208-265-5440 www.953kpnd.com dylanb@953kpnd.com

Sandpoint KIBR-FM (c) 327 S Marion Ave, Sandpoint ID 83864 **Phn:** 208-263-2179 **Fax:** 208-265-5440 www.953kpnd.com mikeb@953kpnd.com

Sandpoint KICR-FM (c) 327 S Marion Ave, Sandpoint ID 83864 **Phn:** 208-263-2179 **Fax:** 208-265-5440 dylanb@953kpnd.com

Sandpoint KPND-FM (r) 327 S Marion Ave, Sandpoint ID 83864 **Phn:** 208-263-2179 **Fax:** 208-265-5440 www.953kpnd.com dylanb@953kpnd.com

Sandpoint KSPT-AM (snt) 327 S Marion Ave, Sandpoint ID 83864 **Phn:** 208-263-2179 **Fax:** 208-265-5440 www.953kpnd.com mikeb@953kpnd.com

Soda Springs KITT-FM (c) PO Box 101, Soda Springs ID 83276 **Phn:** 208-547-2500 **Fax:** 208-547-4593 kitt_radio@yahoo.com

Twin Falls KAWZ-FM (q) PO Box 391, Twin Falls ID 83303 **Phn:** 208-734-4357 **Fax:** 208-736-1958

Twin Falls KAYN-FM (c) 21361 Highway 30, Twin Falls ID 83301 **Phn:** 208-735-8300 **Fax:** 208-733-4196 www.106thecanyon.com

Twin Falls KEZJ-FM (c) PO Box 1259, Twin Falls ID 83303 **Phn:** 208-733-7512 **Fax:** 208-733-7525 kezj.com janicedegner@gapbroadcasting.com

Twin Falls KIKX-FM (r) 21361 Highway 30, Twin Falls ID 83301 **Phn:** 208-735-8300 **Fax:** 208-733-4196 www.kikx1047.com

Twin Falls KKMV-FM (c) 3219 Laurelwood Dr, Twin Falls ID 83301 **Phn:** 208-436-4757 **Fax:** 208-436-3050 www.kat106.com kzdxblastoff@yahoo.com

Twin Falls KLIX-AM (nt) 415 Park Ave, Twin Falls ID 83301 **Phn:** 208-733-7512 **Fax:** 208-733-7525 newsradio1310.com janicedegner@townsquaremedia.com

Twin Falls KLIX-FM (s) PO Box 1259, Twin Falls ID 83303 **Phn:** 208-733-7512 **Fax:** 208-733-7525 kool965.com bradweiser@gapbroadcasting.com

Twin Falls KTPZ-FM (h) 21361 Highway 30, Twin Falls ID 83301 **Phn:** 208-735-8300 **Fax:** 208-733-4196 www.ktpz927.com

Twin Falls KZDX-FM (a) 953 Blue Lakes Blvd N, Twin Falls ID 83301 **Phn:** 208-436-4757 **Fax:** 208-436-3050 www.thebuzz999.com kzdxblastoff@yahoo.com

ILLINOIS

Aledo WRMJ-FM (c) PO Box 187, Aledo IL 61231 **Phn:** 309-582-5666 **Fax:** 309-582-5667 www.wrmj.com john@wrmj.com

Alton WBGZ-AM (nt) PO Box 615, Alton IL 62002 **Phn:** 618-465-3535 **Fax:** 618-465-3546 www.wbgzradio.com wbgz@wbgzradio.com

Anna WIBH-AM (c) 330 S Main St, Anna IL 62906 **Phn:** 618-833-9424 **Fax:** 618-833-9091 www.wibhradio.com onair@wibhradio.com

Aurora WBIG-AM (nts) 620 N Eola Rd, Aurora IL 60502 **Phn:** 630-851-5200 **Fax:** 630-851-5286 www.wbig1280.com ryangatenby@wbig1280.com

Aurora WERV-FM (h) 1884 Plain Ave, Aurora IL 60502 **Phn:** 630-898-1580 **Fax:** 630-898-2463 www.959theriver.com jbass@nextmediachicago.com

Ava WXAN-FM (g) 9077 Ava Rd, Ava IL 62907 **Phn:** 618-426-3308 **Fax:** 618-426-3310 www.mysoutherngospel.net wxangm@yahoo.com

Beardstown WKXQ-FM (af) 108 E Main St, Beardstown IL 62618 **Phn:** 217-323-1790 **Fax:** 217-323-1705 www.wkxqfm.com larry.bostwick@gmail.com

Beardstown WRMS-FM (c) 108 E Main St, Beardstown IL 62618 **Phn:** 217-323-1790 **Fax:** 217-323-1705 wrmsfm@casscomm.com

Beardstown WVIL-FM (s) 108 E Main St, Beardstown IL 62618 **Phn:** 217-323-1790 **Fax:** 217-323-1705 www.wvilfm.com larry.bostwick@gmail.com

Benton WQRL-FM (o) PO Box 818, Benton IL 62812 **Phn:** 618-435-8100 **Fax:** 618-435-8102 www.wqrlradio.com info@wqrlradio.com

Berkeley WJJG-AM (nta) 5629 Saint Charles Rd Ste 208, Berkeley IL 60163 **Phn:** 708-493-1530 www.wjjgam1530.com

ILLINOIS RADIO STATIONS

Bloomington WBBE-FM (a) 520 N Center St, Bloomington IL 61701 **Phn:** 309-834-1100 **Fax:** 309-834-4390 www.bob979.com grant@connoisseurmedia.com

Bloomington WBNQ-FM (a) 236 Greenwood Ave, Bloomington IL 61704 **Phn:** 309-829-1221 **Fax:** 309-827-8071 wbnq.com davis@wbnq.com

Bloomington WBWN-FM (c) 236 Greenwood Ave, Bloomington IL 61704 **Phn:** 309-829-1221 **Fax:** 309-827-8071 wbwn.com dan@wbwn.com

Bloomington WESN-FM (p) PO Box 2900, Bloomington IL 61702 **Phn:** 309-556-2638 **Fax:** 309-556-2949 www.wesn.org881 wesn@iwu.edu

Bloomington WIHN-FM (r) 520 N Center St, Bloomington IL 61701 **Phn:** 309-834-1100 **Fax:** 309-834-4390 www.967irock.com chandler@967irock.com

Bloomington WJBC-FM (nt) 236 Greenwood Ave, Bloomington IL 61704 **Phn:** 309-829-1221 **Fax:** 309-827-8071 wjbc.com news@wjbc.com

Bloomington WJBC-AM (nt) 236 Greenwood Ave, Bloomington IL 61704 **Phn:** 309-829-1221 **Fax:** 309-827-8071 wjbc.com news@wjbc.com

Bloomington WVMG-FM (a) 520 N Center St, Bloomington IL 61701 **Phn:** 309-834-1100 **Fax:** 309-834-4390

Bourbonnais WONU-FM (v) 1 University Ave, Bourbonnais IL 60914 **Phn:** 815-939-5330 **Fax:** 815-939-5087 www.shine.fm shine@olivet.edu

Bourbonnais WVLI-FM (o) PO Box 758, Bourbonnais IL 60914 **Phn:** 815-933-9287 **Fax:** 815-933-8696 rivervalleyradio.net mick@rivervalleyradio.net

Cairo WKRO-AM (u) PO Box 311, Cairo IL 62914 **Phn:** 618-734-1490 **Fax:** 618-734-0884 djman75@hotmail.com

Canton WBYS-AM (snt) 1000 E Linn St, Canton IL 61520 **Phn:** 309-647-1560 **Fax:** 309-647-1563 www.wbysradio.com wbysnews@yahoo.com

Canton WCDD-FM (h) 1000 E Linn St, Canton IL 61520 **Phn:** 309-647-1560 **Fax:** 309-647-1563 www.cd1079.net bj.stone@prairiecommunications.net

Carbondale WDBX-FM (p) 224 N Washington St, Carbondale IL 62901 **Phn:** 618-529-5900 www.wdbx.org wdbx911@yahoo.com

Carbondale WSIU-FM (plnj) 1100 Lincoln Dr # 1003, Carbondale IL 62901 **Phn:** 618-453-4343 **Fax:** 618-453-6186 www.wsiu.org

Carlinville WIBI-FM (q) PO Box 140, Carlinville IL 62626 **Phn:** 217-854-4800 **Fax:** 217-854-4810 www.wibi.org wibi@wibi.org

Carlinville WTSG-FM (g) PO Box 140, Carlinville IL 62626 **Phn:** 217-854-4851 **Fax:** 217-854-4810

Carmi WROY-AM (o) PO Box 400, Carmi IL 62821 **Phn:** 618-382-4161 **Fax:** 618-382-4162 www.wrul.com

Carmi WRUL-FM (c) PO Box 400, Carmi IL 62821 **Phn:** 618-382-4161 **Fax:** 618-382-4162 www.wrul.com

Carterville WCIL-FM (h) 1431 Country Aire Dr, Carterville IL 62918 **Phn:** 618-985-4843 **Fax:** 618-985-6529 www.cilfm.com jonnyq@riverradio.net

Carterville WCIL-AM (nt) 1431 Country Aire Dr, Carterville IL 62918 **Phn:** 618-985-4843 **Fax:** 618-985-6529 www.wjpf.com tomm@riverradio.net

Carterville WJPF-AM (nt) 1431 Country Aire Dr, Carterville IL 62918 **Phn:** 618-985-4843 **Fax:** 618-985-6529 www.wjpf.com tomm@riverradio.net

Carterville WOOZ-FM (c) 1431 Country Aire Dr, Carterville IL 62918 **Phn:** 618-985-4843 **Fax:** 618-985-6529 www.z100fm.com tracym@riverradio.net

Carterville WUEZ-FM (a) 1431 Country Aire Dr, Carterville IL 62918 **Phn:** 618-985-4843 **Fax:** 618-985-6529 www.magic951.com stevef@riverradio.net

Carterville WXLT-FM (s) 1431 Country Aire Dr, Carterville IL 62918 **Phn:** 618-985-4843 **Fax:** 618-985-6529 www.1035espn.com gary@riverradio.net

Carthage WCAZ-AM (nt) PO Box 498, Carthage IL 62321 **Phn:** 217-357-3128 **Fax:** 217-357-2014 www.wcazam990.com wcaz@wcazam990.com

Centralia WIBV-FM (c) PO Box 1626, Centralia IL 62801 **Phn:** 618-249-6025 www.wibv102.com wibv@wibv102.com

Centralia WILY-AM (o) PO Box 528, Centralia IL 62801 **Phn:** 618-533-5700 **Fax:** 618-533-5737 www.myspace.comwily1210 wily1210@gmail.com

Centralia WRXX-FM (a) PO Box 528, Centralia IL 62801 **Phn:** 618-533-5700 **Fax:** 618-533-5737 wrxx@mvn.net

Champaign WBCP-AM (wgu) 904 N 4th St Ste D, Champaign IL 61820 **Phn:** 217-359-1580 **Fax:** 217-359-1583 www.wbcp1580.com wbcpradio@sbcglobal.net

Champaign WBGL-FM (q) 4101 Fieldstone Rd, Champaign IL 61822 **Phn:** 217-359-8232 **Fax:** 217-359-7374 www.wbgl.org wbgl@wbgl.org

Champaign WCFF-FM (a) 2603 W Bradley Ave, Champaign IL 61821 **Phn:** 217-352-1040 **Fax:** 217-352-1256 www.925thechief.com abeck@illiniradio.com

Champaign WCFL-FM (q) 4101 Fieldstone Rd, Champaign IL 61822 **Phn:** 866.917.9245 **Fax:** 217.359.7374 www.wbgl.org wbgl@wbgl.org

Champaign WDWS-AM (nt) PO Box 3939, Champaign IL 61826 **Phn:** 217-351-5300 **Fax:** 217-351-5385 www.wdws.com talk@wdws.com

Champaign WEFT-FM (p) PO Box 1223, Champaign IL 61824 **Phn:** 217-359-9338 weft.org weft@weft.org

Champaign WGKC-FM (r) 4112C Fieldstone Rd, Champaign IL 61822 **Phn:** 217-367-1195 **Fax:** 217-367-3291 www.wgkc.net ken.cunningham@sjbroadcasting.com

Champaign WHMS-FM (a) PO Box 3939, Champaign IL 61826 **Phn:** 217-351-5300 **Fax:** 217-351-5385 www.whms.com literock@whms.com

Champaign WIXY-FM (c) 2603 W Bradley Ave, Champaign IL 61821 **Phn:** 217-355-2222 **Fax:** 217-352-1256 www.wixy.com jdrake@mix945.com

Champaign WLFH-FM (t) 4112C Fieldstone Rd, Champaign IL 61822 **Phn:** 217-367-1195 **Fax:** 217-367-3291 www.myconnectfm.com ken.cunningham@sjbroadcasting.com

Champaign WLRW-FM (a) 2603 W Bradley Ave, Champaign IL 61821 **Phn:** 217-352-4141 **Fax:** 217-352-1256 www.mix945.com jdrake@mix945.com

Champaign WPCD-FM (vr) 2400 W Bradley Ave, Champaign IL 61821 **Phn:** 217-351-2450 parkland.eduwpcd wpcdradio@parkland.edu

Champaign WPGU-FM (r) 512 E Green St, Champaign IL 61820 **Phn:** 217-337-3100 **Fax:** 217-337-3162 the217.comwpgu producer@the217.com

Champaign WQQB-FM (h) 4112C Fieldstone Rd, Champaign IL 61822 **Phn:** 217-367-1195 **Fax:** 217-367-3291 www.wqqb.com josh.laskowski@sjbroadcasting.com

Champaign WSJK-FM (t) 4112C Fieldstone Rd, Champaign IL 61822 **Phn:** 217-367-1195 **Fax:** 217-367-3291 www.myconnectfm.com ken.cunningham@sjbroadcasting.com

Champaign WXTT-FM (h) 2603 W Bradley Ave, Champaign IL 61821 **Phn:** 217-352-4141 **Fax:** 217-352-1256 www.extra921.com abeck@illiniradio.com

Champaign WYXY-FM (c) 2603 W Bradley Ave, Champaign IL 61821 **Phn:** 217-352-4141 **Fax:** 217-352-1256 www.extra921.com abeck@illiniradio.com

Charleston WEIC-AM (g) 2560 W State St, Charleston IL 61920 **Phn:** 217-345-2148 www.weic1270.org weic1270@consolidated.net

Charleston WEIU-FM (vlj) 600 Lincoln Ave # 1521, Charleston IL 61920 **Phn:** 217-581-5956 **Fax:** 217-581-6650 weiu.net weiu@weiu.net

Charleston WRJM-AM (n) 2560 W State St, Charleston IL 61920 **Phn:** 217-345-2148 **Fax:** 217-689-2277 www.wrjmdailynews.com rjm1955@gmail.com

Chicago WAIT-AM (q) 5625 N Milwaukee Ave, Chicago IL 60646 **Phn:** 773-774-0850 www.thepromise850.com

Chicago WBBM-AM (n) 180 N Stetson Ave Ste 1100, Chicago IL 60601 **Phn:** 312-297-7800 **Fax:** 312-297-7822 chicago.cbslocal.com wbbmnewsradiotips@cbsradio.com

Chicago WBBM-FM (h) 180 N Stetson Ave Ste 963, Chicago IL 60601 **Phn:** 312-861-9600 **Fax:** 312-729-3816 chicago.cbslocal.com wbbmnewsradiotips@cbsradio.com

Chicago WBEZ-FM (pnj) 848 E Grand Ave, Chicago IL 60611 **Phn:** 312-948-4600 www.wbez.org news@chicagopublicradio.org

Chicago WBGX-AM (tg) 5956 S Michigan Ave, Chicago IL 60637 **Phn:** 773-752-1570 **Fax:** 773-752-2242 www.gospel1570.com

Chicago WCEV-AM (eqg) 5356 W Belmont Ave, Chicago IL 60641 **Phn:** 773-282-6700 **Fax:** 773-282-0123 www.wcev1450.com wcev@wcev1450.com

Chicago WCFJ-AM (ue) 5625 N Milwaukee Ave, Chicago IL 60646 **Phn:** 773-792-1121 **Fax:** 773-792-2904 www.accessradiochicago.com mpinski@newswebradio.net

Chicago WCFS-FM (a) 180 N Stetson Ave Ste 1059, Chicago IL 60601 **Phn:** 312-240-7900 **Fax:** 312-565-3181

Chicago WCKG-FM (t) 180 N Stetson Ave Ste 1059, Chicago IL 60601 **Phn:** 312-240-7900 **Fax:** 312-565-3181

Chicago WCPQ-FM (t) 6012 S Pulaski Rd, Chicago IL 60629 **Phn:** 773-767-1000 **Fax:** 773-767-1100 www.chicagoprogressivetalk.com web@newswebradio.net

Chicago WCPT-AM (t) 5475 N Milwaukee Ave, Chicago IL 60630 **Phn:** 773-792-0400 **Fax:** 773-792-0082 www.chicagosprogressivetalk.com web@newswebradio.net

Chicago WCPT-FM (t) 5475 N Milwaukee Ave, Chicago IL 60630 **Phn:** 773-792-0400 **Fax:** 773-792-0082 www.chicagosprogressivetalk.com web@newswebradio.net

Chicago WCPY-FM (t) 6012 S Pulaski Rd, Chicago IL 60629 **Phn:** 773-767-1000 **Fax:** 773-767-1100 www.chicagoprogressivetalk.com web@newswebradio.net

Chicago WCRX-FM (v) 33 E Congress Pkwy Ste 700, Chicago IL 60605 **Phn:** 312-344-8155 **Fax:** 312-344-8007 www.colum.eduAcademicsRadioWCRX tkwiecinski@colum.edu

Chicago WDRV-FM (r) 875 N Michigan Ave Ste 1510, Chicago IL 60611 **Phn:** 312-274-9710 **Fax:** 312-274-1304 www.wdrv.com kvoltmer@wdrv.com

Chicago WFMT-FM (l) 5400 N Saint Louis Ave, Chicago IL 60625 **Phn:** 773-279-2000 **Fax:** 773-279-2199 www.wfmt.com

ILLINOIS RADIO STATIONS

Chicago WGCI-FM (wu) 233 N Michigan Ave Ste 2800, Chicago IL 60601 **Phn:** 312-540-2000 **Fax:** 312-938-4477 www.wgci.com tywansley@wgci.com

Chicago WGN-AM (snt) 435 N Michigan Ave, Chicago IL 60611 **Phn:** 312-222-4700 **Fax:** 312-222-5165 www.wgnradio.com tips@wgnradio.com

Chicago WGRB-AM (g) 233 N Michigan Ave Ste 2700, Chicago IL 60601 **Phn:** 312-540-2000 **Fax:** 312-938-7335 www.inspiration1390.com sonyablakey@clearchannel.com

Chicago WHPK-FM (v) 5706 S University Ave, Chicago IL 60637 **Phn:** 773-702-8289 **Fax:** 773-702-7718 www.whpk.org pd@whpk.org

Chicago WIIT-FM (vw) 3201 S State St, Chicago IL 60616 **Phn:** 312-567-3087 **Fax:** 312-567-7042 radio.iit.edu wiit@iit.edu

Chicago WILV-FM (ma) 130 E Randolph St Ste 2780, Chicago IL 60601 **Phn:** 312-297-5100 **Fax:** 312-297-5155 www.wilv.com bpeck@wilv.com

Chicago WJMK-FM (r) 180 N Stetson Ave Ste 900, Chicago IL 60601 **Phn:** 312-870-6400 **Fax:** 312-977-1859 khitschicago.cbslocal.com promotions@khitschicago.com

Chicago WKIF-FM (a) 6012 S Pulaski Rd, Chicago IL 60629 **Phn:** 773-767-1000 **Fax:** 773-767-1100

Chicago WKSC-FM (h) 233 N Michigan Ave Ste 2800, Chicago IL 60601 **Phn:** 312-540-2000 **Fax:** 312-938-7334 www.1035kissfm.com

Chicago WLEY-FM (y) 150 N Michigan Ave Ste 1040, Chicago IL 60601 **Phn:** 312-920-9500 **Fax:** 312-920-9515 laley1079.com ecastro@sbschicago.com

Chicago WLIT-FM (a) 233 N Michigan Ave Ste 2800, Chicago IL 60601 **Phn:** 312-540-2000 **Fax:** 312-938-5444 www.939myfm.com

Chicago WLS-FM (o) 190 N State St Fl 8, Chicago IL 60601 **Phn:** 312-984-9923 **Fax:** 312-984-5357 www.947wls.com wlsfm.programdirector@947wls.com

Chicago WLS-AM (nt) 190 N State St, Chicago IL 60601 **Phn:** 312-984-0890 **Fax:** 312-984-5305 wlsam.com tracy.slutzkin@wlsam.com

Chicago WLUP-FM (r) 222 Merchandise Mart Plz, Chicago IL 60654 **Phn:** 312-245-1200 **Fax:** 312-527-3620 www.wlup.com

Chicago WLUW-FM (v) 1032 W Sheridan Rd, Chicago IL 60660 **Phn:** 773-508-8080 **Fax:** 773-508-8082 wluw.org wluw-fm@luc.edu

Chicago WMBI-FM (q) 820 N La Salle Dr, Chicago IL 60610 **Phn:** 312-329-4300 **Fax:** 312-329-4468 www.moodyradiochicago.fm wmbi@moody.edu

Chicago WMBI-AM (y) 820 N La Salle Dr, Chicago IL 60610 **Phn:** 312-329-4300 **Fax:** 312-329-4468 www.moodyradiochicago.fm wmbi@moody.edu

Chicago WMVP-AM (s) 190 N State St Fl 7, Chicago IL 60601 **Phn:** 312-980-1000 **Fax:** 312-980-1010 espn.go.comchicagoradio

Chicago WNDZ-AM (y) 5625 N Milwaukee Ave, Chicago IL 60646 **Phn:** 773-792-1121 **Fax:** 773-792-2904 www.accessradiochicago.com

Chicago WNUA-FM (y) 233 N Michigan Ave Ste 2800, Chicago IL 60601 **Phn:** 312-540-2000 **Fax:** 312-938-0692 www.955elpatron.com earljones@clearchannel.com

Chicago WNVR-AM (e) 3656 W Belmont Ave, Chicago IL 60618 **Phn:** 773-588-6300 **Fax:** 773-267-4913 www.polskieradio.com jtrzos@polskieradio.com

Chicago WOJO-FM (y) 625 N Michigan Ave # 300, Chicago IL 60611 **Phn:** 312-981-1800 **Fax:** 312-981-1840 www.univision.com jerryryan@univisionradio.com

Chicago WPPN-FM (y) 625 N Michigan Ave # 300, Chicago IL 60611 **Phn:** 312-981-1800 **Fax:** 312-981-1840 pasionchicago.univision.com jerryryan@univisionradio.com

Chicago WRDZ-AM (m) 190 N State St, Chicago IL 60601 **Phn:** 312-683-1300 music.disney.com cathleen.a.wolfe@abc.com

Chicago WRTO-AM (ynt) 625 N Michigan Ave # 300, Chicago IL 60611 **Phn:** 312-981-1800 **Fax:** 312-981-1840 www.univision.com

Chicago WSBC-AM (ey) 5625 N Milwaukee Ave, Chicago IL 60646 **Phn:** 773-792-1121 **Fax:** 773-792-2904 www.accessradiochicago.com jmurillo@newswebradio.net

Chicago WSCR-AM (st) 180 N Stetson Ave Ste 1000, Chicago IL 60601 **Phn:** 312-729-3967 **Fax:** 312-245-6143 chicago.cbslocal.com comments@670thescore.com

Chicago WTMX-FM (a) 130 E Randolph St Ste 2700, Chicago IL 60601 **Phn:** 312-946-1019 **Fax:** 312-946-4747 www.wtmx.com swiencek@hubbardradio.com

Chicago WUSN-FM (c) 180 N Stetson Ave Ste 1000, Chicago IL 60601 **Phn:** 312-649-0099 **Fax:** 312-856-9586 us995.cbslocal.com jeff@cbsradio.com

Chicago WVAZ-FM (wu) 233 N Michigan Ave Ste 2700, Chicago IL 60601 **Phn:** 312-540-2000 **Fax:** 312-938-7335 www.v103.com loyallistener@v103.com

Chicago WVIV-FM (y) 625 N Michigan Ave # 300, Chicago IL 60611 **Phn:** 312-981-1800 **Fax:** 312-981-1840 www.univision.com

Chicago WVIX-FM (y) 625 N Michigan Ave # 300, Chicago IL 60611 **Phn:** 312-981-1800 **Fax:** 312-981-1840 www.univision.com dlevy@univisionradio.com

Chicago WVON-AM (nt) 1000 E 87th St, Chicago IL 60619 **Phn:** 773-247-6200 **Fax:** 773-768-0372 www.wvon.com info@wvon.com

Chicago WWDV-FM (h) 875 N Michigan Ave Ste 1510, Chicago IL 60611 **Phn:** 312-274-9710 **Fax:** 312-274-1304 www.wdrv.com kvoltmer@wdrv.com

Chicago WXRT-FM (a) 180 N Stetson Ave Ste 1000, Chicago IL 60601 **Phn:** 312-649-0099 **Fax:** 312-240-7973 wxrt.cbslocal.com xrtcomments@wxrt.com

Chicago WZRD-FM (v) 5500 N Saint Louis Ave, Chicago IL 60625 **Phn:** 773-442-4586 **Fax:** 773-442-4900 wzrdchicago.org stationmanager@wzrdchicago.org

Chicago Heights WCGO-AM (ob) 222 Vollmer Rd, Chicago Heights IL 60411 **Phn:** 847-475-1590 1590wcgo.com

Clinton WHOW-AM (ntf) 2980 US Highway 51, Clinton IL 61727 **Phn:** 217-935-9590 **Fax:** 217-935-9909

Crest Hill WCCQ-FM (c) 2410 Caton Farm Rd Unit B, Crest Hill IL 60403 **Phn:** 815-556-0100 **Fax:** 815-577-9231 www.wccq.com rgregory@nextmediachicago.com

Crest Hill WJOL-AM (snt) 2410 Caton Farm Rd Unit B, Crest Hill IL 60403 **Phn:** 815-556-0100 **Fax:** 815-577-9231 www.wjol.com scottslocum@wjol.com

Crest Hill WRXQ-FM (r) 2410 Caton Farm Rd Unit B, Crest Hill IL 60403 **Phn:** 815-556-0100 **Fax:** 815-577-9231 www.wrxq.com ppendergast@nextmediachicago.com

Crest Hill WSSR-FM (a) 2410 Caton Farm Rd, Crest Hill IL 60403 **Phn:** 815-556-0100 **Fax:** 815-577-9231 www.star967.net ppendergast@nextmediachicago.com

Crystal Lake WZSR-FM (a) 8800 Rte 14, Crystal Lake IL 60012 **Phn:** 815-459-7000 **Fax:** 815-459-7027 www.star105.com stew@star105.com

Danville WDAN-AM (snt) 1501 N Washington Ave, Danville IL 61832 **Phn:** 217-442-1700 **Fax:** 217-431-1489 vermilioncountyfirst.com billpickett@neuhoffmedia.com

Danville WDNL-FM (a) 1501 N Washington Ave, Danville IL 61832 **Phn:** 217-442-1700 **Fax:** 217-431-1489 www.wdnlfm.com kenkirby@neuhoffmedia.com

Danville WITY-AM (af) PO Box 142, Danville IL 61834 **Phn:** 217-446-1312 **Fax:** 217-446-1314 www.wityradio.com news@wityradio.com

Danville WKZS-FM (c) PO Box 67, Danville IL 61834 **Phn:** 765-793-4823 **Fax:** 765-793-4644 www.kisscountryradio.com info@kisscountryradio.com

Danville WRHK-FM (r) 1501 N Washington Ave, Danville IL 61832 **Phn:** 217-442-1700 **Fax:** 217-431-1489 vermilioncountyfirst.com billpickett@neuhoffmedia.com

Decatur WCZQ-FM (u) 337 N Water St, Decatur IL 62523 **Phn:** 217-373-1055 **Fax:** 217-423-9764 www.hot1055.com

Decatur WDZ-AM (s) 250 N Water St Ste 100, Decatur IL 62523 **Phn:** 217-428-1050 **Fax:** 217-423-9764

Decatur WDZQ-FM (c) 250 N Water St Ste 100, Decatur IL 62523 **Phn:** 217-423-9744 **Fax:** 217-423-9764 www.95q.com toby@95q.com

Decatur WEJT-FM (a) 410 N Water St Ste B, Decatur IL 62523 **Phn:** 217-428-4487 **Fax:** 217-428-4501 www.decaturradio.com tnickerson@cromwellradio.com

Decatur WJMU-FM (v) 1184 W Main St, Decatur IL 62522 **Phn:** 217-424-6377 **Fax:** 217-424-3993 www.millikin.eduacademicscascommunicationwjmuPages wjmu@millikin.edu

Decatur WSOY-AM (nt) 250 N Water St Ste 100, Decatur IL 62523 **Phn:** 217-423-9744 **Fax:** 217-423-9764 www.wsoyam.com news@wsoyam.com

Decatur WSOY-FM (a) 250 N Water St Ste 100, Decatur IL 62523 **Phn:** 217-423-9744 **Fax:** 217-423-9764 www.y103.com markhanson@neuhoffmedia.com

Decatur WYDS-FM (h) 410 N Water St Ste B, Decatur IL 62523 **Phn:** 217-428-4487 **Fax:** 217-428-4501 www.decaturradio.com tnickerson@cromwellradio.com

Decatur WZNX-FM (r) 410 N Water St Ste B, Decatur IL 62523 **Phn:** 217-428-4487 **Fax:** 217-428-4501 www.decaturradio.com tnickerson@cromwellradio.com

Decatur WZUS-FM (t) 410 N Water St Ste B, Decatur IL 62523 **Phn:** 217-428-4487 **Fax:** 217-428-4501 www.decaturradio.com tnickerson@cromwellradio.com

Dekalb WDKB-FM (a) 2201 N 1st St Ste 95, Dekalb IL 60115 **Phn:** 815-758-0950 **Fax:** 815-758-6226 www.b95fm.com kenmisch@b95fm.com

Dekalb WLBK-FM (ntf) 2410 Sycamore Rd Ste C, Dekalb IL 60115 **Phn:** 815-748-1000 **Fax:** 815-748-9000 wlbkradio.com wlbk-news@nelsonmultimedia.net

Dekalb WLBK-AM (ntf) 2410 Sycamore Rd Ste C, Dekalb IL 60115 **Phn:** 815-748-1000 **Fax:** 815-748-9000 wlbkradio.com scottz@nelsonmultimedia.net

Dekalb WNIJ-FM (pnt) 801 N 1st St, Dekalb IL 60115 **Phn:** 815-753-9000 **Fax:** 815-753-9938 www.wnij.org wnijnews@hotmail.com

Dekalb WNIQ-FM (pln) 801 N 1st St, Dekalb IL 60115 **Phn:** 815-753-9000 **Fax:** 815-753-9938 www.northernpublicradio.org nprnews@niu.edu

Dekalb WNIU-FM (pl) 801 N 1st St, Dekalb IL 60115 **Phn:** 815-753-9000 **Fax:** 815-753-9938 www.northernpublicradio.org nprnews@niu.edu

ILLINOIS RADIO STATIONS

Dekalb WNIW-FM (pln) 801 N 1st St, Dekalb IL 60115 **Phn:** 815-753-9000 **Fax:** 815-753-9938 www.northernpublicradio.org sstephens@niu.edu

Dennison WKZI-AM (q) 18889 N 2350th St, Dennison IL 62423 **Phn:** 217-826-9673 www.wordpower.us wkzi@rr1.net

Dennison WPFR-AM (q) 18889 N 2350th St, Dennison IL 62423 **Phn:** 217-826-9673 www.wordpower.us wpfr@joink.com

Dennison WPFR-FM (q) 18889 N 2350th St, Dennison IL 62423 **Phn:** 217-826-9673 www.wordpower.us wpfr@joink.com

Dixon WIXN-AM (fo) 1460 S College Ave, Dixon IL 61021 **Phn:** 815-288-3341 **Fax:** 815-284-1017 www.myrockriverradio.com nmahan@nrgmedia.com

Dixon WLLT-FM (a) 260 II Route 2, Dixon IL 61021 **Phn:** 815-284-1077

Dixon WRCV-FM (c) 1460 S College Ave, Dixon IL 61021 **Phn:** 815-288-3341 **Fax:** 815-284-1017 www.myrockriverradio.com avannatta@nrgmedia.com

Dixon WSEY-FM (o) 1460 S College Ave, Dixon IL 61021 **Phn:** 815-288-3341 **Fax:** 815-284-1017 www.myrockriverradio.com aknickrehm@nrgmedia.com

Du Quoin WDQN-AM (ac) PO Box 190, Du Quoin IL 62832 **Phn:** 618-542-3894 **Fax:** 618-542-4514 wdqnradio@onecliq.net

East Moline WDLM-FM (q) PO Box 149, East Moline IL 61244 **Phn:** 309-234-5111 **Fax:** 309-234-5114 www.moodyradioqc.fm

East Moline WDLM-AM (q) PO Box 149, East Moline IL 61244 **Phn:** 309-234-5111 **Fax:** 309-234-5114 www.moodyradioqc.fm wdlm@moody.edu

Edwardsville WSIE-FM (pj) Campus Box 1773, Edwardsville IL 62026 **Phn:** 618-650-2228 **Fax:** 618-650-2233 wsie.org wsie887@siue.edu

Effingham WCRA-AM (nt) 405 S Banker St Ste 201, Effingham IL 62401 **Phn:** 217-342-4141 **Fax:** 217-342-4143 www.cromwellradio.com mphillips@cromwellradio.com

Effingham WCRC-FM (c) 405 S Banker St Ste 201, Effingham IL 62401 **Phn:** 217-342-4141 **Fax:** 217-342-4143 www.cromwellradio.com wcrc@wcrc957.com

Effingham WHQQ-FM (a) 405 S Banker St, Effingham IL 62401 **Phn:** 217-342-4141 **Fax:** 217-342-4143 www.effinghamradio.com tjamison@cromwellradio.com

Effingham WKJT-FM (c) PO Box 988, Effingham IL 62401 **Phn:** 217-347-5518 **Fax:** 217-347-5519 www.kjcountry.com info@thexradio.com

Effingham WXEF-FM (a) PO Box 988, Effingham IL 62401 **Phn:** 217-347-5518 **Fax:** 217-347-5519 www.thexradio.com info@thexradio.com

Elgin WEPS-FM (vlj) 355 E Chicago St, Elgin IL 60120 **Phn:** 847-888-5000 **Fax:** 847-888-0272 www.wpr.org

Elgin WRMN-AM (nt) 14 Douglas Ave, Elgin IL 60120 **Phn:** 847-741-7700 **Fax:** 847-888-4227 www.wrmn1410.com rickjakle@jakle.com

Elk Grove Village WIND-AM (nt) 25 Northwest Point Blvd Ste 400, Elk Grove Village IL 60007 **Phn:** 847-437-5200 **Fax:** 847-956-5040 www.560wind.com mbrown@salemradiochicago.com

Elk Grove Village WYLL-AM (q) 25 Northwest Point Blvd Ste 400, Elk Grove Village IL 60007 **Phn:** 847-956-5030 **Fax:** 847-956-5040 www.wyll.com jreisman@salemradiochicago.com

Elmhurst WRSE-FM (v) 190 S Prospect Ave, Elmhurst IL 60126 **Phn:** 630-617-3729

Elsah WTPC-FM (v) Principia College, Elsah IL 62028 **Phn:** 618-374-4934

Evanston WNUR-FM (vjr) 1877 Campus Dr, Evanston IL 60208 **Phn:** 847-491-7101 **Fax:** 847-467-2058 www.wnur.org gm@wnur.org

Fairfield WFIW-AM (nt) PO Box 310, Fairfield IL 62837 **Phn:** 618-842-2159 **Fax:** 618-847-5907 www.wfiwradio.com wfiwnews@fairfieldwireless.net

Fairfield WFIW-FM (a) PO Box 310, Fairfield IL 62837 **Phn:** 618-842-2159 **Fax:** 618-847-5907 www.wfiwradio.com wfiwwokz@fairfieldwireless.net

Fairfield WOKZ-FM (c) PO Box 310, Fairfield IL 62837 **Phn:** 618-842-2159 **Fax:** 618-847-5907 www.wfiwradio.com wfiwwokz@fairfieldwireless.net

Farmer City WWHP-FM (c) 407 N Main St, Farmer City IL 61842 **Phn:** 309-928-9876 **Fax:** 309-928-3708 www.wwhp.com wwhp@farmwagon.com

Flora WNOI-FM (a) PO Box 368, Flora IL 62839 **Phn:** 618-662-8331 **Fax:** 618-662-2407 www.wnoi.com info@wnoi.com

Freeport WFPS-FM (c) PO Box 807, Freeport IL 61032 **Phn:** 815-235-7191 **Fax:** 815-235-4318 www.wekz.com

Freeport WFRL-AM (a) PO Box 807, Freeport IL 61032 **Phn:** 815-235-7191 **Fax:** 815-235-4318 www.wekz.com

Freeport WQLF-FM (h) PO Box 807, Freeport IL 61032 **Phn:** 815-235-7191 **Fax:** 815-235-4318 www.wekz.com

Galesburg WAAG-FM (c) PO Box 1227, Galesburg IL 61402 **Phn:** 309-342-5131 **Fax:** 309-342-0619 www.fm95online.com fm95@fm95online.com

Galesburg WGIL-AM (fnt) 154 E Simmons St, Galesburg IL 61401 **Phn:** 309-342-5131 **Fax:** 309-342-0840 www.wgil.com wgil@wgil.com

Galesburg WKAY-FM (a) PO Box 1227, Galesburg IL 61402 **Phn:** 309-342-5131 **Fax:** 309-342-0840 www.1053kfm.com kfm@1053kfm.com

Galesburg WLSR-FM (r) PO Box 1227, Galesburg IL 61402 **Phn:** 309-342-5131 **Fax:** 309-342-0840 www.thelaseronline.com thelaser@thelaseronline.com

Galesburg WVKC-FM (v) PO Box 245, Galesburg IL 61402 **Phn:** 309-341-7266 **Fax:** 309-341-7090

Gibson City WGCY-FM (z) PO Box 192, Gibson City IL 60936 **Phn:** 217-784-8661 **Fax:** 217-784-8677 www.wgcyradio.com jimkillian@hotmail.com

Glen Ellyn WDCB-FM (vj) 425 Fawell Blvd, Glen Ellyn IL 60137 **Phn:** 630-942-4200 **Fax:** 630-942-2788 www.wdcb.org news@wdcb.org

Godfrey WLCA-FM (vr) 5800 Godfrey Rd, Godfrey IL 62035 **Phn:** 618-468-4940 **Fax:** 618-466-7458 wlcafm.com mlemons@lc.edu

Greenville WGEL-FM (c) PO Box 277, Greenville IL 62246 **Phn:** 618-664-3300 **Fax:** 618-664-3318 www.wgel.com tom@wgel.com

Greenville WGRN-FM (v) 315 E College Ave, Greenville IL 62246 **Phn:** 618-664-6789 wgrn.net

Harrisburg WEBQ-FM (a) 701 S Commercial St, Harrisburg IL 62946 **Phn:** 618-252-6307 **Fax:** 618-252-2366 webqradio.com webq@yourclearwave.com

Harrisburg WEBQ-AM (c) 701 S Commercial St, Harrisburg IL 62946 **Phn:** 618-253-7282 **Fax:** 618-252-2366 webq@yourclearwave.com

Havana WDUK-FM (c) 901 N Promenade St, Havana IL 62644 **Phn:** 309-543-3331

Hoopeston WHPO-FM (c) 912 S Dixie Hwy, Hoopeston IL 60942 **Phn:** 217-283-7744 **Fax:** 217-283-6090 www.whporadio.com whpo@whporadio.com

Jacksonville WEAI-FM (h) PO Box 1180, Jacksonville IL 62651 **Phn:** 217-245-7171 **Fax:** 217-245-6711 wlds.com weai@weai.com

Jacksonville WJIL-AM (a) PO Box 1055, Jacksonville IL 62651 **Phn:** 217-245-5119 **Fax:** 217-245-1596 www.wjvofm.com 1029wjil@gmail.com

Jacksonville WJVO-FM (c) PO Box 1055, Jacksonville IL 62651 **Phn:** 217-245-5119 **Fax:** 217-245-1596 www.wjvofm.com sarahwjvo@mchsi.com

Jacksonville WLDS-AM (ntf) PO Box 1180, Jacksonville IL 62651 **Phn:** 217-245-7171 **Fax:** 217-245-6711 www.wlds.com wlds@wlds.com

Joliet WCSF-FM (va) 500 Wilcox St, Joliet IL 60435 **Phn:** 815-740-3217 **Fax:** 815-740-4285 www.stfrancis.educontenttheedge wcsf@stfrancis.edu

Joliet WJCH-FM (q) 13 Fairlane Dr, Joliet IL 60435 **Phn:** 815-725-1331 www.familyradio.com

Kankakee WKAN-AM (t) 70 Meadowview Ctr Ste 400, Kankakee IL 60901 **Phn:** 815-935-9555 **Fax:** 815-935-9593 www.wkan.com wkan@staradio.com

Kankakee WXNU-FM (c) 70 Meadowview Ctr Ste 400, Kankakee IL 60901 **Phn:** 815-935-9555 **Fax:** 815-935-9593 www.xcountry1065.com

Kankakee WYKT-FM (o) 70 Meadowview Ctr Ste 400, Kankakee IL 60901 **Phn:** 815-935-9555 **Fax:** 815-724-1025 www.kat1055.com production1@staradio.com

Kewanee WGEN-AM (nt) PO Box 266, Kewanee IL 61443 **Phn:** 309-853-4471 **Fax:** 309-853-4474 www.regionaldailynews.com

Kewanee WJRE-FM (a) PO Box 266, Kewanee IL 61443 **Phn:** 309-853-4471 **Fax:** 309-853-4474 www.regionaldailynews.com

Kewanee WKEI-AM (nt) PO Box 266, Kewanee IL 61443 **Phn:** 309-853-4471 **Fax:** 309-853-4474 www.regionaldailynews.com

Kewanee WYEC-FM (a) PO Box 266, Kewanee IL 61443 **Phn:** 309-853-4471 **Fax:** 309-853-4474 www.regionaldailynews.com

La Grange WLTL-FM (vr) 100 S Brainard Ave, La Grange IL 60525 **Phn:** 708-482-9585 **Fax:** 708-482-7051

Lake Forest WMXM-FM (vr) 555 N Sheridan Rd, Lake Forest IL 60045 **Phn:** 847-735-5220 **Fax:** 847-735-6291 wmxm.org hehnca@lakeforest.edu

Lawrenceville WAKO-FM (ac) PO Box 210, Lawrenceville IL 62439 **Phn:** 618-943-3354 **Fax:** 618-943-4173 www.wakoradio.com

Lawrenceville WAKO-AM (ac) PO Box 210, Lawrenceville IL 62439 **Phn:** 618-943-3354 **Fax:** 618-943-4173 www.wakoradio.com

Lincoln WLLM-AM (gt) 800 S Postville Dr, Lincoln IL 62656 **Phn:** 217-735-9735 **Fax:** 217-735-9736 www.wllmradio.com wllmam@juno.com

Lincoln WLNX-FM (vhr) 300 Keokuk St, Lincoln IL 62656 **Phn:** 217-732-3495 **Fax:** 217-732-8859 www.wlnxradio.com

Litchfield WAOX-FM (a) PO Box 10, Litchfield IL 62056 **Phn:** 217-532-2085 **Fax:** 217-532-2431 www.waox.com waox@waoxradio.com

Litchfield WSMI-FM (cfn) PO Box 10, Litchfield IL 62056 **Phn:** 217-324-5921 **Fax:** 217-532-2431 www.wsmiradio.com wsmi@wsmiradio.com

Litchfield WSMI-AM (cft) PO Box 10, Litchfield IL 62056 **Phn:** 217-324-5921 **Fax:** 217-532-2431 www.wsmiradio.com news@wsmiradio.com

Loves Park WGSL-FM (q) PO Box 2730, Loves Park IL 61132 **Phn:** 815-654-1200 **Fax:** 815-282-7779

ILLINOIS RADIO STATIONS

Loves Park WQFL-FM (q) PO Box 2730, Loves Park IL 61132 **Phn:** 815-654-1200 **Fax:** 815-282-7779

Macomb WIUM-FM (pln) 1 University Cir, Macomb IL 61455 **Phn:** 309-298-1873 **Fax:** 309-298-2133 www.tristatesradio.com publicradio@wiu.edu

Macomb WIUS-FM (var) 326 Sallee Hall, Macomb IL 61455 **Phn:** 309-298-3217 www.wiu.eduusersmiwius wius@wiu.edu

Macomb WJEQ-FM (r) 1034 W Jackson, Macomb IL 61455 **Phn:** 309-833-2121 **Fax:** 309-836-3291 www.wjeqfm.com radio@prestigeradio.com

Macomb WKAI-FM (h) 1034 W Jackson, Macomb IL 61455 **Phn:** 309-833-2121 **Fax:** 309-833-3921 www.wkaifm.com radio@prestigeradio.com

Macomb WLMD-FM (c) 1034 W Jackson, Macomb IL 61455 **Phn:** 309-833-2121 **Fax:** 309-833-3291 www.wlmdfm.com radio@prestigeradio.com

Macomb WLRB-AM (am) 1034 W Jackson, Macomb IL 61455 **Phn:** 309-833-2121 **Fax:** 309-833-3921 www.prestigeradio.com radio@prestigeradio.com

Macomb WMQZ-FM (o) 1034 W Jackson, Macomb IL 61455 **Phn:** 309-833-2121 **Fax:** 309-836-3291 wmqzfm.com radio@prestigeradio.com

Macomb WNLF-FM (r) 1034 W Jackson, Macomb IL 61455 **Phn:** 309-833-2121 **Fax:** 309-836-3291 wnlffm.com radio@prestigeradio.com

Marion WBVN-FM (q) PO Box 1126, Marion IL 62959 **Phn:** 618-997-1500 www.wbvn.org wbvn@wbvn.org

Marion WDDD-FM (c) PO Box 127, Marion IL 62959 **Phn:** 618-997-8123 **Fax:** 618-993-2319 www.mywithersradio.comw3d robert.guy@mvn.net

Marion WDDD-AM (st) PO Box 127, Marion IL 62959 **Phn:** 618-997-8123 **Fax:** 618-993-2319 janet.jensen@mvn.net

Marion WFRX-AM (am) PO Box 127, Marion IL 62959 **Phn:** 618-997-8123 **Fax:** 618-993-2319 robert.guy@mvn.net

Marion WGGH-AM (qg) PO Box 340, Marion IL 62959 **Phn:** 618-993-8102 **Fax:** 618-997-2307 www.wggh.net webmaster@wggh.net

Marion WHET-FM (c) PO Box 127, Marion IL 62959 **Phn:** 618-997-8123 **Fax:** 618-993-2319 www.mywithersradio.combear

Marion WTAO-FM (r) PO Box 127, Marion IL 62959 **Phn:** 618-997-8123 www.105tao.com janet.jensen@mvn.net

Marion WVZA-FM (h) PO Box 127, Marion IL 62959 **Phn:** 618-997-8123 **Fax:** 618-993-2319

Marshall WMMC-FM (a) PO Box 158, Marshall IL 62441 **Phn:** 217-826-8017 **Fax:** 217-826-8519 wmmc106@aol.com

Mattoon WCBH-FM (h) 209 Lake Land Blvd, Mattoon IL 61938 **Phn:** 217-235-5624 **Fax:** 217-235-6624 www.1043theparty.com cfloyd@cromwellradio.com

Mattoon WLBH-FM (a) PO Box 322, Mattoon IL 61938 **Phn:** 217-234-6464 **Fax:** 217-234-6019

Mattoon WLBH-AM (ah) PO Box 322, Mattoon IL 61938 **Phn:** 217-234-6464 **Fax:** 217-234-6019

Mattoon WLKL-FM (v) 5001 Lake Land Blvd, Mattoon IL 61938 **Phn:** 217-234-5373

Mattoon WMCI-FM (c) 209 Lake Land Blvd, Mattoon IL 61938 **Phn:** 217-235-5624 **Fax:** 217-235-6624 www.myradiolink.com cfloyd@cromwellradio.com

Mattoon WWGO-FM (h) 209 Lake Land Blvd, Mattoon IL 61938 **Phn:** 217-235-5624 **Fax:** 217-235-6624 classichits921.com cfloyd@cromwellradio.com

McLeansboro WMCL-AM (c) RR 1 Box 46A, McLeansboro IL 62859 **Phn:** 618-643-2311 **Fax:** 618-643-3299

Mendota WMKB-FM (r) 4756 E 4th Rd, Mendota IL 61342 **Phn:** 815-538-7500 **Fax:** 815-538-7505 www.theclassicrockexperience.com info@wmkbradio.com

Metropolis KLUE-FM (h) 6120 Waldo Church Rd, Metropolis IL 62960 **Phn:** 618-564-9836 **Fax:** 618-564-3202 stratemeyer@hotmail.com www.stratemeyermedia.com

Metropolis WMOK-AM (c) PO Box 720, Metropolis IL 62960 **Phn:** 618-524-9209 **Fax:** 618-524-3133

Metropolis WTHQ-AM (nt) 6120 Waldo Church Rd, Metropolis IL 62960 **Phn:** 618-564-9836 **Fax:** 618-564-3202 stratemeyer@hotmail.com

Monmouth WAIK-AM (snt) 55 Public Sq, Monmouth IL 61462 **Phn:** 309-734-9452 **Fax:** 309-734-3276 www.1590waik.com waiknews@yahoo.com

Monmouth WMOI-FM (a) PO Box 885, Monmouth IL 61462 **Phn:** 309-734-9452 **Fax:** 309-734-3276 www.977wmoi.com

Monmouth WRAM-AM (c) PO Box 885, Monmouth IL 61462 **Phn:** 309-734-9452 **Fax:** 309-734-3276 www.1330wram.com waiknews@yahoo.com

Morris WCSJ-AM (nt) 219 W Washington St, Morris IL 60450 **Phn:** 815-941-1000 **Fax:** 815-941-9300 www.wcsjfm.com wspy-news@nelsonmultimedia.net

Morris WCSJ-FM (nt) 219 W Washington St, Morris IL 60450 **Phn:** 815-941-1000 **Fax:** 815-941-9300 www.wcsjfm.com jackd@nelsonmultimedia.net

Morris WJDK-FM (a) 219 W Washington St, Morris IL 60450 **Phn:** 815-941-1000 **Fax:** 815-941-9300 www.wjdkfm.com wcsj-news@nelsonmultimedia.net

Mount Carmel WSJD-FM (r) 328 N Market St, Mount Carmel IL 62863 **Phn:** 618-262-4102 **Fax:** 618-262-4103

Mount Carmel WVJC-FM (v) 2200 College Dr, Mount Carmel IL 62863 **Phn:** 618-262-8989 **Fax:** 618-262-7317 myweb.iecc.eduwvjc peachk@iecc.edu

Mount Carmel WVMC-AM (s) 328 N Market St, Mount Carmel IL 62863 **Phn:** 618-262-4102 **Fax:** 618-262-4103 wsjd@live.com

Mount Vernon WMIX-AM (s) PO Box 1508, Mount Vernon IL 62864 **Phn:** 618-242-3500 **Fax:** 618-242-2490 www.wmixsports.com wmixnews@mvn.net

Mount Vernon WMIX-FM (c) PO Box 1508, Mount Vernon IL 62864 **Phn:** 618-242-3500 **Fax:** 618-242-2490 www.wmixsports.com wmixnews@mvn.net

Mt Zion WDKR-FM (o) 120 W Wildwood Dr, Mt Zion IL 62549 **Phn:** 217-864-4141

Mt Zion WXFM-FM (a) 120 W Wildwood Dr, Mt Zion IL 62549 **Phn:** 217-864-4141

Murphysboro WINI-AM (nt) 10519 Hwy 149 # A, Murphysboro IL 62966 **Phn:** 618-684-2128 **Fax:** 618-687-4318 www.newstalk1420wini.com wini@newstalk1420wini.com

Naperville WKQX-FM (r) PO Box 5502, Naperville IL 60654 **Phn:** 312-527-8348 **Fax:** 312-527-5682 www.q101.com

Naperville WONC-FM (vr) PO Box 3063, Naperville IL 60566 **Phn:** 630-637-8989 www.wonc.org feedback@wonc.org

Nashville WNSV-FM (a) 186 E Saint Louis St, Nashville IL 62263 **Phn:** 618-327-4444 **Fax:** 618-327-3716

Normal WGLT-FM (pjn) Campus Box 8910, Normal IL 61790 **Phn:** 309-438-2255 **Fax:** 309-438-7870 wglt.org wglt@ilstu.edu

Normal WRPW-FM (nt) 108 Boeykens Pl, Normal IL 61761 **Phn:** 309-888-4496 **Fax:** 309-452-9677 www.cities929.com robert@cities929.com

Normal WYST-FM (c) 108 Boeykens Pl, Normal IL 61761 **Phn:** 309-888-4496 **Fax:** 309-452-9677 www.1077thebull.com jroberts@greatplainsmedia.us

Northbrook WEEF-AM (e) 4320 Dundee Rd, Northbrook IL 60062 **Phn:** 847-498-3350 **Fax:** 847-498-5743 goga@polskieradio.com

Northbrook WKTA-AM (re) 4320 Dundee Rd, Northbrook IL 60062 **Phn:** 847-498-3350 **Fax:** 847-498-5743

Oak Park WPNA-AM (e) 408 S Oak Park Ave, Oak Park IL 60302 **Phn:** 708-848-8980 **Fax:** 708-848-9220 www.wpna1490am.com email@wpna1490am.com

Oglesby WAJK-FM (a) 1 Broadcast Ln, Oglesby IL 61348 **Phn:** 815-223-3100 **Fax:** 815-223-3095 www.wajk.com programdirector@993wajk.com

Oglesby WKOT-FM (o) 1 Broadcast Ln, Oglesby IL 61348 **Phn:** 815-223-3100 **Fax:** 815-223-3095 www.wkot.com

Oglesby WLPO-AM (nt) 1 Broadcast Ln, Oglesby IL 61348 **Phn:** 815-223-3100 **Fax:** 815-223-3095 www.wlpo.net programdirector@wlpoamandfm.com

Olney WIKK-FM (rh) PO Box L, Olney IL 62450 **Phn:** 618-393-2156 **Fax:** 618-392-4536 www.freedom929.com mishipman@forchtbroadcasting.com

Olney WPTH-FM (q) 817 Orchard Dr, Olney IL 62450 **Phn:** 618-863-2765

Olney WSEI-FM (h) PO Box L, Olney IL 62450 **Phn:** 618-393-2156 **Fax:** 618-392-4536 www.freedom929.com mishipman@forchtbroadcasting.com

Olney WVLN-AM (st) PO Box L, Olney IL 62450 **Phn:** 618-393-2156 **Fax:** 618-392-4536 www.freedom929.com maweiler@forchtbroadcasting.com

Ottawa WCMY-AM (nt) 216 W Lafayette St, Ottawa IL 61350 **Phn:** 815-434-6050 **Fax:** 815-434-5311 www.ottawaradio.net

Ottawa WRKX-FM (a) 216 W Lafayette St, Ottawa IL 61350 **Phn:** 815-434-6050

Park Ridge WMTH-FM (v) 2601 Dempster St, Park Ridge IL 60068 **Phn:** 847-692-8484 **Fax:** 847-692-8499

Paxton WPXN-FM (o) 361 N Railroad Ave, Paxton IL 60957 **Phn:** 217-379-9796 **Fax:** 217-379-4334 www.wpxnradio.com news@wpxnradio.com

Pekin WBNH-FM (q) 1919 Mayflower Dr, Pekin IL 61554 **Phn:** 309-636-8850 **Fax:** 877-631-8850 www.wbnh.org wbnh@wbnh.org

Peoria WCBU-FM (pln) 1501 W Bradley Ave, Peoria IL 61625 **Phn:** 309-677-3690 **Fax:** 309-677-3462 www.wcbufm.org wcbu@bradley.edu

Peoria WCIC-FM (vq) 3902 Barring Trce, Peoria IL 61615 **Phn:** 309-692-9242 **Fax:** 309-692-9241 www.wcicfm.org wcic@wcicfm.org

Peoria WDQX-FM (r) 4234 N Brandywine Dr Ste D, Peoria IL 61614 **Phn:** 309-686-0101 **Fax:** 309-686-0111 www.1023maxfm.com studio@1023maxfm.com

Peoria WFYR-FM (c) 120 Eaton St, Peoria IL 61603 **Phn:** 309-676-5000 **Fax:** 309-676-2600 973rivercountry.com shelly.andeen@cumulus.com

Peoria WGLO-FM (ar) 120 Eaton St, Peoria IL 61603 **Phn:** 309-676-5000 **Fax:** 309-676-2600 955glo.com matt.bahan@cumulus.com

Peoria WHPI-FM (ah) 2006 W Altorfer Dr, Peoria IL 61615 **Phn:** 309-686-0101 **Fax:** 309-686-0111 jack1011.com mrea@ampillinois.com

Peoria WIRL-AM (c) 331 Fulton St Ste 1200, Peoria IL 61602 **Phn:** 309-637-3700 **Fax:** 309-673-9562 www.1290wirl.com courtneylynne@1290wirl.com

Peoria WIXO-FM (r) 120 Eaton St, Peoria IL 61603 **Phn:** 309-676-5000 **Fax:** 309-676-2600 1057thexrocks.com matt.bahan@cumulus.com

Peoria WMBD-AM (nt) 331 Fulton St Ste 1200, Peoria IL 61602 **Phn:** 309-637-3700 **Fax:** 309-673-9562 www.1470wmbd.com shaunnewell@1470wmbd.com

Peoria WPBG-FM (o) 331 Fulton St Ste 1200, Peoria IL 61602 **Phn:** 309-637-3700 **Fax:** 309-673-9562 www.933thedrive.com rickhirschmann@jmpradio.com

Peoria WPEO-AM (q) PO Box 1, Peoria IL 61650 **Phn:** 309-698-9736 **Fax:** 309-698-9740 www.wpeo.com wpeo@wpeo.com

Peoria WPIA-FM (h) 2006 W Altorfer Dr, Peoria IL 61615 **Phn:** 309-691-0101 **Fax:** 309-692-0111 kisspeoria.com megana@ampillinois.com

Peoria WSWT-FM (a) 331 Fulton St Ste 1200, Peoria IL 61602 **Phn:** 309-637-3700 **Fax:** 309-694-2233 www.literock107.com randyrundle@literock107.com

Peoria WVEL-AM (q) 120 Eaton St, Peoria IL 61603 **Phn:** 309-676-5000 **Fax:** 309-676-2600 wvel.com robert.caruth@cumulus.com

Peoria WWCT-FM (ar) 2006 W Altorfer Dr, Peoria IL 61615 **Phn:** 309-686-0101 **Fax:** 309-686-0111 mrea@ampillinois.com

Peoria WXCL-FM (c) 331 Fulton St 12th Fl, Peoria IL 61602 **Phn:** 309-637-3700 www.1049thewolf.com cindyaustin@1049thewolf.com

Peoria WZPN-FM (s) 2006 W Altorfer Dr, Peoria IL 61615 **Phn:** 309-686-0101 **Fax:** 309-686-0111 mrea@ampillinois.com

Peoria WZPW-FM (h) 120 Eaton St, Peoria IL 61603 **Phn:** 309-676-5000 **Fax:** 309-676-2600 powerpeoria.com amanda.king@cumulus.com

Peru WALS-FM (c) 3905 Progress Blvd, Peru IL 61354 **Phn:** 815-224-2100 **Fax:** 815-224-2066 www.walls102.com

Peru WBZG-FM (r) 3905 Progress Blvd, Peru IL 61354 **Phn:** 815-224-2100 **Fax:** 815-224-2066 www.wbzg.net wbzg@studstillmedia.com

Peru WGLC-FM (c) 3905 Progress Blvd, Peru IL 61354 **Phn:** 815-224-2100 **Fax:** 815-224-2066 www.wglc.net wglc@studstillmedia.com

Peru WIVQ-FM (h) 3905 Progress Blvd, Peru IL 61354 **Phn:** 815-224-2100 **Fax:** 815-224-2066 www.qhitmusic.com q@studstillmedia.com

Peru WSPL-AM (s) 3905 Progress Blvd, Peru IL 61354 **Phn:** 815-224-2100 **Fax:** 815-224-2066 www.am1250wspl.com wspl@studstillmedia.com

Peru WSTQ-FM (h) 3905 Progress Blvd, Peru IL 61354 **Phn:** 815-224-2100 **Fax:** 815-224-2066 www.qhitmusic.com q@studstillmedia.com

Peru WYYS-FM (a) 3905 Progress Blvd, Peru IL 61354 **Phn:** 815-224-2100 **Fax:** 815-224-2066 www.classichits106.com wyys@studstillmedia.com

Pittsfield WBBA-FM (ntc) PO Box 312, Pittsfield IL 62363 **Phn:** 217-285-5975 **Fax:** 217-285-5977 www.wbbaradio.com wbba@wbbaradio.com

Plano WSPY-AM (an) 1 Broadcast Ctr, Plano IL 60545 **Phn:** 630-552-1000 **Fax:** 630-552-9300 wspyam.com wspy-news@nelsonmultimedia.net

Plano WSQR-AM (c) 1 Broadcast Ctr, Plano IL 60545 **Phn:** 815-899-1000 **Fax:** 630-552-9300 nelsonmultimedia.net bethp@nelsonmultimedia.net

Pontiac WJEZ-FM (a) 315 N Mill St, Pontiac IL 61764 **Phn:** 815-844-6101 **Fax:** 815-842-6515 wjez.com tom.meredith@cumulus.com

Princeton WRVY-FM (r) PO Box 69, Princeton IL 61356 **Phn:** 309-364-4411 www.wzoe.com

Princeton WZOE-AM (snt) PO Box 69, Princeton IL 61356 **Phn:** 815-875-8014 www.wzoe.com

Princeton WZOE-FM (o) PO Box 69, Princeton IL 61356 **Phn:** 815-875-8014 www.wzoeradio.com

Quincy KGRC-FM (h) 329 Maine St, Quincy IL 62301 **Phn:** 217-224-4102 **Fax:** 217-224-4133 www.real929.com kgrc@staradio.com

Quincy KRRY-FM (h) 408 N 24th St, Quincy IL 62301 **Phn:** 217-223-5292 **Fax:** 217-223-5299 y101radio.com dennis.oliver@townsquaremedia.com

Quincy KWBZ-FM (o) 1645 Highway 104 Ste G, Quincy IL 62305 **Phn:** 217-224-4653 **Fax:** 217-885-3233 www.oldiessuperstation.com

Quincy KZZK-FM (r) 329 Maine St, Quincy IL 62301 **Phn:** 217-224-4102 **Fax:** 217-224-4133 www.kzzk.com mmoyers@staradio.com

Quincy WCOY-FM (c) 329 Maine St, Quincy IL 62301 **Phn:** 217-224-4102 **Fax:** 217-224-4133 www.wcoy.com wcoy@staradio.com

Quincy WGCA-FM (q) 535 Maine St Ste 10, Quincy IL 62301 **Phn:** 217-224-9422 **Fax:** 217-228-0504 www.wgca.org themix@wgca.org

Quincy WGEM-AM (snt) PO Box 80, Quincy IL 62306 **Phn:** 217-228-6600 **Fax:** 217-228-6670 www.wgem.com news@wgem.com

Quincy WGEM-FM (cnt) PO Box 80, Quincy IL 62306 **Phn:** 217-228-6600 **Fax:** 217-228-6670 www.wgem.com news@wgem.com

Quincy WPWQ-FM (o) 1645 Highway 104 Ste G, Quincy IL 62305 **Phn:** 217-224-4653 **Fax:** 217-885-3233 www.oldiessuperstation.com wpwq106@adams.net

Quincy WQCY-FM (h) 329 Maine St, Quincy IL 62301 **Phn:** 217-224-4102 **Fax:** 217-224-4133 www.1039thefox.com sboll@staradio.com

Quincy WQUB-FM (v) 1800 College Ave, Quincy IL 62301 **Phn:** 217-228-5410 **Fax:** 217-228-5616 www.stlpublicradio.orgquincy news@stlpublicradio.org

Quincy WTAD-AM (snt) 329 Maine St, Quincy IL 62301 **Phn:** 217-224-4102 **Fax:** 217-224-4133 www.wtad.com mgriffith@staradio.com

Ramsey WJLY-FM (q) RR 2 Box 51A, Ramsey IL 62080 **Phn:** 618-423-2082 **Fax:** 618-423-2394 www.wjly.org wjly@frontiernet.net

Ramsey WTRH-FM (t) RR 2 Box 51A, Ramsey IL 62080 **Phn:** 618-423-2082 **Fax:** 618-423-2394 www.wjly.org wjly@frontiernet.net

River Grove WRRG-FM (v) 2000 5th Ave, River Grove IL 60171 **Phn:** 708-583-3110 www.wrrg.org wrrg@hotmail.com

Robinson WTAY-AM (asn) PO Box 245, Robinson IL 62454 **Phn:** 618-544-2191 **Fax:** 618-544-3621 www.wtyefm.com wtaywtye@yahoo.com

Robinson WTYE-FM (ant) PO Box 245, Robinson IL 62454 **Phn:** 618-544-2191 **Fax:** 618-544-3621 www.wtyefm.com wtaywtye@yahoo.com

Rochelle WRHL-AM (nt) PO Box 177, Rochelle IL 61068 **Phn:** 815-562-7001 **Fax:** 815-562-7002 www.wrhl.net jmlvoice@wrhl.net

Rochelle WRHL-FM (a) PO Box 177, Rochelle IL 61068 **Phn:** 815-562-7001 **Fax:** 815-562-7002 www.wrhl.net jmlvoice@wrhl.net

Rock Island WVIK-FM (pln) 3808 8th Ave, Rock Island IL 61201 **Phn:** 309-794-7500 **Fax:** 309-794-1236 www.wvik.org news@wvik.org

Rockford WFEN-FM (q) 4721 S Main St, Rockford IL 61102 **Phn:** 815-964-9336 **Fax:** 815-964-0550 www.wfen.org sky@wfen.org

Rockford WKGL-FM (r) 3901 Brendenwood Rd, Rockford IL 61107 **Phn:** 815-399-2233 **Fax:** 815-484-2432 www.967theeagle.net becky.riojas@cumulus.com

Rockford WLUV-AM (c) 2272 Elmwood Rd, Rockford IL 61103 **Phn:** 815-877-9588 **Fax:** 815-877-9649 joesalvi2000@yahoo.com

Rockford WNTA-AM (snt) 2830 Sandy Hollow Rd, Rockford IL 61109 **Phn:** 815-874-7861 **Fax:** 815-874-2202 www.nta.fm kennyd58@aol.com

Rockford WROK-AM (nt) 3901 Brendenwood Rd, Rockford IL 61107 **Phn:** 815-399-2233 **Fax:** 815-484-2432 www.1440wrok.com scot.bertram@cumulus.com

Rockford WRTB-FM (r) 2830 Sandy Hollow Rd, Rockford IL 61109 **Phn:** 815-874-7861 **Fax:** 815-874-2202 www.953bobfm.com

Rockford WXRX-FM (r) 2830 Sandy Hollow Rd, Rockford IL 61109 **Phn:** 815-874-7861 **Fax:** 815-874-2202 www.wxrx.com doublet@wxrx.com

Rockford WXXQ-FM (c) 3901 Brendenwood Rd, Rockford IL 61107 **Phn:** 815-399-2233 **Fax:** 815-484-2432 www.q985online.com qcrew@q985online.com

Rockford WZOK-FM (ah) 3901 Brendenwood Rd, Rockford IL 61107 **Phn:** 815-399-2233 **Fax:** 815-484-2432 www.97zokonline.com sweet.lenny@cumulus.com

Romeoville WLRA-FM (v) 500 Independence Blvd, Romeoville IL 60446 **Phn:** 815-836-5214 **Fax:** 815-838-9149

Salem WJBD-FM (a) PO Box 70, Salem IL 62881 **Phn:** 618-548-2000 **Fax:** 618-548-2079 www.wjbdradio.com news@wjbdradio.com

Salem WJBD-AM (c) PO Box 70, Salem IL 62881 **Phn:** 618-548-2000 **Fax:** 618-548-2079 www.wjbdradio.com news@wjbdradio.com

Savanna WCCI-FM (c) PO Box 310, Savanna IL 61074 **Phn:** 815-273-7757 **Fax:** 815-273-2760 www.wcciradio.com newssports@wcciradio.com

Sparta WHCO-AM (snt) 1230 W Broadway St, Sparta IL 62286 **Phn:** 618-443-2121 **Fax:** 618-443-2280 realcountry1230.com news@realcountry1230.com

Springfield WABZ-FM (a) 3501 E Sangamon Ave, Springfield IL 62707 **Phn:** 217-753-5400 **Fax:** 217-753-7902 www.abefm.com jaddams@capitolradiogroup.com

Springfield WCVS-FM (r) 3055 S 4th St, Springfield IL 62703 **Phn:** 217-528-3033 **Fax:** 217-528-5348 www.wcvs.com davecomstock@neuhoffmedia.com

Springfield WDBR-FM (h) 3501 E Sangamon Ave, Springfield IL 62707 **Phn:** 217-753-5400 **Fax:** 217-753-7902 www.wdbr.com jaddams@capitolradiogroup.com

Springfield WFMB-FM (c) 3055 S 4th St, Springfield IL 62703 **Phn:** 217-528-3033 **Fax:** 217-528-5348 www.wfmb.com jessicaross@neuhoffmedia.com

Springfield WFMB-AM (st) 3055 S 4th St, Springfield IL 62703 **Phn:** 217-528-3033 **Fax:** 217-528-5348 www.sportsradio1450.com sportsradio1450@sportsradio1450.com

Springfield WLCE-FM (r) PO Box 460, Springfield IL 62705 **Phn:** 217-629-7077 **Fax:** 217-629-7952 www.alice.fm alice@alice.fm

Springfield WLUJ-FM (q) 600 W Mason St, Springfield IL 62702 **Phn:** 217-528-2300 **Fax:** 217-528-2400 www.wluj.org comments@wluj.org

Springfield WMAY-AM (nt) PO Box 460, Springfield IL 62705 **Phn:** 217-629-7077 **Fax:** 217-629-7952 www.wmay.com wmay@wmay.com

Springfield WNNS-FM (a) PO Box 460, Springfield IL 62705 **Phn:** 217-629-7077 **Fax:** 217-629-7952 www.wnns.com

Springfield WQLZ-FM (r) PO Box 460, Springfield IL 62705 **Phn:** 217-629-7077 **Fax:** 217-629-7952 www.wqlz.com wqlz@wqlz.com

Springfield WQNA-FM (v) 2201 Toronto Rd, Springfield IL 62712 **Phn:** 217-529-5431 **Fax:** 217-529-7861 www.wqna.org

Springfield WQQL-FM (o) 3501 E Sangamon Ave, Springfield IL 62707 **Phn:** 217-753-5400 **Fax:** 217-753-7902 cool939.com anelson@capitolradiogroup.com

Springfield WTAX-AM (fnt) 3501 E Sangamon Ave, Springfield IL 62707 **Phn:** 217-753-5400 **Fax:** 217-753-7902 www.wtax.com wtaxnews@wtax.com

Springfield WUIS-FM (plnj) 1 University Plz, Springfield IL 62703 **Phn:** 217-206-6516 **Fax:** 217-206-6527 wuis.org wuis@uis.edu

Springfield WXAJ-FM (h) 3055 S 4th St, Springfield IL 62703 **Phn:** 217-528-3033 **Fax:** 217-528-5348 www.997kissfm.com jessicaross@neuhoffmedia.com

Springfield WYMG-FM (r) 3501 E Sangamon Ave, Springfield IL 62707 **Phn:** 217-753-5400 **Fax:** 217-753-7902 wymg.com jane@wymg.com

Sterling WSDR-AM (nt) 3101 Freeport Rd, Sterling IL 61081 **Phn:** 815-625-3400 **Fax:** 815-625-6940 www.rockriverradio.com wsdr1240@theramp.net

Sterling WSSQ-FM (a) 3101 Freeport Rd, Sterling IL 61081 **Phn:** 815-625-3400 **Fax:** 815-625-6940 www.rockriverradio.com wsdr1240@theramp.net

Sterling WZZT-FM (h) 3101 Freeport Rd, Sterling IL 61081 **Phn:** 815-625-3400 **Fax:** 815-625-6940 www.rockriverradio.com wsdr1240@theramp.net

Summit Argo WARG-FM (vr) 7329 W 63rd St, Summit Argo IL 60501 **Phn:** 708-728-8368 **Fax:** 708-728-3155

Taylorville WMKR-FM (c) PO Box 169, Taylorville IL 62568 **Phn:** 217-824-3395 **Fax:** 217-824-3301 www.taylorvilledailynews.comwmkr.php news@taylorvilledailynews.com

Taylorville WRAN-FM (a) PO Box 169, Taylorville IL 62568 **Phn:** 217-824-3395 **Fax:** 217-824-3301 www.taylorvilledailynews.comwran.php wran983@randyradio.com

Taylorville WTIM-FM (nt) PO Box 169, Taylorville IL 62568 **Phn:** 217-824-3395 **Fax:** 217-824-3301 www.taylorvilledailynews.comwtim.php wtim@randyradio.com

Urbana WILL-FM (pn) 300 N Goodwin Ave, Urbana IL 61801 **Phn:** 217-333-7300 **Fax:** 217-333-7151 will.illinois.edu dperry@uiuc.edu

Urbana WILL-AM (pl) 300 N Goodwin Ave, Urbana IL 61801 **Phn:** 217-333-7300 **Fax:** 217-333-7151 www.will.illinois.edu willamfm@uiuc.edu

Vandalia WKRV-FM (a) 232 S 4th St, Vandalia IL 62471 **Phn:** 618-283-2325 **Fax:** 618-283-1503 www.vandaliaradio.com wkrv@sbcglobal.net

Vandalia WPMB-AM (ob) 232 S 4th St, Vandalia IL 62471 **Phn:** 618-283-2325 **Fax:** 618-283-1503 www.vandaliaradio.com tstapleton@cromwellradio.com

Watseka WFAV-FM (c) 202 E Walnut St, Watseka IL 60970 **Phn:** 815-933-9287 **Fax:** 815-933-8696 rivervalleyradio.net tim@rivervalleyradio.net

Watseka WGFA-AM (nt) 1973 E 1950 North Rd, Watseka IL 60970 **Phn:** 815-432-4955 **Fax:** 815-432-4957 www.wgfaradio.com 941fm@wgfaradio.com

Watseka WGFA-FM (af) 1973 E 1950 North Rd, Watseka IL 60970 **Phn:** 815-432-4955 **Fax:** 815-432-4957 www.wgfaradio.com 941fm@wgfaradio.com

Watseka WIVR-FM (c) 202 E Walnut St, Watseka IL 60970 **Phn:** 815-933-9287 **Fax:** 815-933-8696 rivervalleyradio.net tim@rivervalleyradio.net

Waukegan WKRS-AM (snt) 3250 Belvidere Rd, Waukegan IL 60085 **Phn:** 847-336-7900 **Fax:** 847-336-1523 www.wkrs.com jcornell@nextmediachicago.com

Waukegan WXLC-FM (a) 3250 Belvidere Rd, Waukegan IL 60085 **Phn:** 847-336-7900 **Fax:** 847-336-1523 www.1023xlc.com hjohns@nextmediachicago.com

Wheaton WETN-FM (v) 501 College Ave, Wheaton IL 60187 **Phn:** 630-752-5074 **Fax:** 630-752-5286 www.wheaton.eduwetn wetn@wheaton.edu

Winnetka WNTH-FM (v) 385 Winnetka Ave, Winnetka IL 60093 **Phn:** 847-784-2322 www.wnth.org wnth@newtrier.k12.il.us

INDIANA

Anderson WGNR-FM (q) 1920 W 53rd St, Anderson IN 46013 **Phn:** 888-877-9467 **Fax:** 765-642-4033 www.mbn.org wgnr@moody.edu

Anderson WHPL-FM (q) 1920 W 53rd St, Anderson IN 46013 **Phn:** 888-877-9467 **Fax:** 765-642-4033

Anderson WQME-FM (q) 1100 E 5th St, Anderson IN 46012 **Phn:** 765-641-4349 **Fax:** 765-641-3825 www.wqme.com news@wqme.com

Angola WEAX-FM (v) 1 University Ave, Angola IN 46703 **Phn:** 260-665-4288 www.88xradio.com hornbacherj@trine.edu

Angola WLKI-FM (a) PO Box 999, Angola IN 46703 **Phn:** 260-665-9554 **Fax:** 260-665-9064 www.wlki.com wlki@wlki.com

Batesville WRBI-FM (c) PO Box 201, Batesville IN 47006 **Phn:** 812-934-5111 **Fax:** 812-934-2765 www.wrbiradio.com wrbi@wrbiradio.com

Bedford WBIW-AM (snt) PO Box 1307, Bedford IN 47421 **Phn:** 812-275-7555 **Fax:** 812-279-8046 www.wbiw.com comments@wbiw.com

Bedford WPHZ-FM (a) 424 Heltonville Rd W, Bedford IN 47421 **Phn:** 812-275-7555 **Fax:** 812-279-8046 www.wphz.com

Bedford WQRJ-FM (o) PO Box 1307, Bedford IN 47421 **Phn:** 812-275-7555 **Fax:** 812-279-8046 www.superoldies.net comments@superoldies.net

Bedford WQRK-FM (o) PO Box 1307, Bedford IN 47421 **Phn:** 812-275-7555 **Fax:** 812-279-8046 www.superoldies.net comments@superoldies.net

Berne WZBD-FM (a) PO Box 4050, Berne IN 46711 **Phn:** 260-589-9300 **Fax:** 260-589-8045 www.wzbd.com wzbd@onlyinternet.net

Bloomington WBWB-FM (h) 304 S State Road 446, Bloomington IN 47401 **Phn:** 812-336-8000 **Fax:** 812-336-7000 www.wbwb.com kev@wbwb.com

Bloomington WCLS-FM (r) 5858 W State Road 46, Bloomington IN 47404 **Phn:** 812-935-7400 **Fax:** 812-935-7404 www.wclsfm.com wclsfm@smithville.net

Bloomington WFHB-FM (r) PO Box 1973, Bloomington IN 47402 **Phn:** 812-323-1200 **Fax:** 812-323-0320 www.wfhb.org news@wfhb.org

Bloomington WFIU-FM (pljn) 1229 E 7th St, Bloomington IN 47405 **Phn:** 812-855-1357 **Fax:** 812-855-5600 indianapublicmedia.orgradio wfiu@indiana.edu

Bloomington WGCL-AM (nt) 120 W 7th St Ste 400, Bloomington IN 47404 **Phn:** 812-332-3366 **Fax:** 812-331-4570 www.wgclradio.com comments@wgclradio.com

Bloomington WHCC-FM (c) PO Box 7797, Bloomington IN 47407 **Phn:** 812-336-8000 **Fax:** 812-336-7000 www.whcc105.com rick@whcc105.com

Bloomington WMYJ-AM (q) 2723 N Walnut St, Bloomington IN 47404 **Phn:** 812-335-9500 **Fax:** 812-335-8800 www.spirit95fm.com jim@spirit95fm.com

Bloomington WVNI-FM (q) PO Box 1628, Bloomington IN 47402 **Phn:** 812-335-9500 **Fax:** 812-335-8880 www.spirit95fm.com spirit95@spirit95fm.com

Boonville WBNL-AM (z) PO Box 270, Boonville IN 47601 **Phn:** 812-897-2080 **Fax:** 812-897-2130 www.radio1540.net rturpen@radio1540.net

Carmel WHJE-FM (vr) 520 E Main St, Carmel IN 46032 **Phn:** 317-571-4055 **Fax:** 317-571-4066 www.whje.com whje@ccs.k12.in.us

Clarksville WNDA-AM (gnt) PO Box 2623, Clarksville IN 47131 **Phn:** 502-584-2400 www.newstalk1570.com choffman@wkyitv.com

Columbia City WJHS-FM (vr) 600 N Whitley St, Columbia City IN 46725 **Phn:** 260-248-8915 www.wjhs915.org walkerzoltekkd@wccsonline.com

Columbus WCSI-AM (nt) PO Box 1789, Columbus IN 47202 **Phn:** 812-372-4448 **Fax:** 812-372-1061 www.wcsiradio.com wcsi@wcsiradio.com

Columbus WKKG-FM (c) PO Box 1789, Columbus IN 47202 **Phn:** 812-372-4448 **Fax:** 812-372-1061 www.wkkg.com studio@wkkg.com

Columbus WRZQ-FM (a) 825 Washington St Ste 1A, Columbus IN 47201 **Phn:** 812-379-1077 **Fax:** 812-375-2555 www.qmix.com news@qmix.com

Columbus WWWY-FM (r) 3212 Washington St, Columbus IN 47203 **Phn:** 812-372-4448 **Fax:** 812-372-1061 www.y106.com tonyahaze@y106.com

Columbus WYGB-FM (c) 825 Washington St, Columbus IN 47201 **Phn:** 812-378-1003 **Fax:** 812-375-2555 www.korncountry.com qmix@qmix.com

Connersville WIFE-AM (o) PO Box 619, Connersville IN 47331 **Phn:** 765-825-6411 **Fax:** 765-825-2411 www.superoldies1580.com news@wifefm.com

Connersville WIFE-FM (c) PO Box 619, Connersville IN 47331 **Phn:** 765-825-6411 **Fax:** 765-825-2411 www.wifefm.com news@wifefm.com

Corydon WOCC-AM (o) PO Box 838, Corydon IN 47112 **Phn:** 812-738-9622 **Fax:** 812-738-1676

Covington WSKL-FM (o) PO Box 67, Covington IN 47932 **Phn:** 765-793-5665 **Fax:** 765-793-4644 www.koololdies.net

Crawfordsville WCDQ-FM (c) PO Box 603, Crawfordsville IN 47933 **Phn:** 765-362-8200 **Fax:** 765-364-1550 www.wcdqfm.com dapeach@forchtbroadcasting.com

INDIANA RADIO STATIONS

Crawfordsville WCVL-AM (o) PO Box 603, Crawfordsville IN 47933 **Phn:** 765-362-8200 **Fax:** 765-364-1550 www.wcvlam.com dapeach@forchtbroadcasting.com

Crawfordsville WIMC-FM (r) PO Box 603, Crawfordsville IN 47933 **Phn:** 765-362-8200 **Fax:** 765-364-1550 www.crawfordsvilleradio.com dapeach@forchtbroadcasting.com

Crawfordsville WNDY-FM (v) 301 W Wabash Ave, Crawfordsville IN 47933 **Phn:** 765-361-6240 **Fax:** 765-361-6437 www3.wabash.eduorgswndy

Decatur WJZI-AM (j) PO Box 530, Decatur IN 46733 **Phn:** 260-724-7161 **Fax:** 260-490-9614 www.wjzi.com

Elkhart WFRN-FM (q) PO Box 307, Elkhart IN 46515 **Phn:** 574-875-5166 **Fax:** 574-875-6662 wfrn.com events@wfrn.com

Elkhart WTRC-AM (nt) 421 S 2nd St, Elkhart IN 46516 **Phn:** 574-389-5100 **Fax:** 574-389-5101

Elkhart WVPE-FM (v) 2424 California Rd, Elkhart IN 46514 **Phn:** 574-262-5660 **Fax:** 574-262-5700 www.wvpe.org wvpe@wvpe.org

Evansville WABX-FM (r) 1162 Mount Auburn Rd, Evansville IN 47720 **Phn:** 812-424-8284 **Fax:** 812-426-7928 www.wabx.net

Evansville WBJW-FM (q) PO Box 4164, Evansville IN 47724 **Phn:** 800-264-5550 **Fax:** 812-768-5552 www.thywordnetwork.org

Evansville WDKS-FM (h) 117 SE 5th St, Evansville IN 47708 **Phn:** 812-425-4226 **Fax:** 812-428-5895 1061evansville.com ryano@1061evansville.com

Evansville WEJK-FM (h) PO Box 3848, Evansville IN 47736 **Phn:** 812-424-8284 **Fax:** 812-426-7928 www.1071jackfm.com rjames@southcentralmedia.com

Evansville WEOA-AM (uw) 915 Main St Ste 1, Evansville IN 47708 **Phn:** 812-424-8864 **Fax:** 812-424-9946 weoa_1@yahoo.com

Evansville WGAB-AM (gq) 2601 S Boeke Rd, Evansville IN 47714 **Phn:** 812-479-5342 **Fax:** 812-474-0483 www.faith1180.com

Evansville WGBF-AM (nt) 117 SE 5th St, Evansville IN 47708 **Phn:** 812-425-4226 **Fax:** 812-421-0005 newstalk1280.com bobby.gates@townsquaremedia.com

Evansville WGBF-FM (r) 117 SE 5th St, Evansville IN 47708 **Phn:** 812-425-4226 **Fax:** 812-421-0005 103gbfrocks.com sandman@103gbfrocks.com

Evansville WIKY-FM (a) PO Box 3848, Evansville IN 47736 **Phn:** 812-424-8284 **Fax:** 812-426-7928 www.wiky.com

Evansville WKDQ-FM (c) 117 SE 5th St, Evansville IN 47708 **Phn:** 812-425-4226 **Fax:** 812-421-0005 wkdq.com jonp@wkdq.com

Evansville WLFW-FM (c) PO Box 3848, Evansville IN 47736 **Phn:** 812-424-8284 **Fax:** 812-426-7928 www.935thewolf.com

Evansville WNIN-FM (pln) 405 Carpenter St, Evansville IN 47708 **Phn:** 812-423-2973 **Fax:** 812-428-7548 www.wnin.org info@wnin.org

Evansville WPSR-FM (v) 5400 N 1st Ave, Evansville IN 47710 **Phn:** 812-435-8241

Evansville WSTO-FM (h) PO Box 3848, Evansville IN 47736 **Phn:** 812-421-9696 **Fax:** 812-421-3273 www.hot96.com jeff@hot96.com

Evansville WSWI-AM (vr) 8600 University Blvd, Evansville IN 47712 **Phn:** 812-464-1927 **Fax:** 812-461-5261 www.820theedge.com theedgepromotions@gmail.com

Evansville WUEV-FM (v) 1800 Lincoln Ave, Evansville IN 47714 **Phn:** 812-488-2022 **Fax:** 812-488-2320 www.evansville.eduwuev wuevfm@evansville.edu

Evansville WVHI-AM (q) 114 NW Martin Luther King Jr Blvd, Evansville IN 47708 **Phn:** 812-425-2221 **Fax:** 812-425-2078 www.j5.wvhi.com krista@wvhi.com

Fort Wayne WAJI-FM (a) 347 W Berry St Ste 600, Fort Wayne IN 46802 **Phn:** 260-423-3676 **Fax:** 260-422-5266 www.waji.com dan@waji.com

Fort Wayne WBCL-FM (q) 1025 W Rudisill Blvd, Fort Wayne IN 46807 **Phn:** 260-745-0576 **Fax:** 260-745-2001 www.wbcl.org newspc@wbcl.org

Fort Wayne WBNI-FM (plnj) 3204 Clairmont Ct, Fort Wayne IN 46808 **Phn:** 260-452-1189 **Fax:** 260-452-1188 www.nipr.fm

Fort Wayne WBTU-FM (c) 2100 Goshen Rd Ste 232, Fort Wayne IN 46808 **Phn:** 260-482-9288 **Fax:** 260-482-8655 www.us933.us phil.becker@oasisradiogroup.com

Fort Wayne WBYR-FM (r) 1005 Production Rd, Fort Wayne IN 46808 **Phn:** 260-471-5100 **Fax:** 260-471-5224 www.989thebear.com

Fort Wayne WFCV-AM (q) 3737 Lake Ave Ste 2, Fort Wayne IN 46805 **Phn:** 260-423-2337 **Fax:** 260-423-6355 www.bottradionetwork.com wfcv@bottradionetwork.com

Fort Wayne WGAW-AM (nt) 2100 Goshen Rd Ste 232, Fort Wayne IN 46808 **Phn:** 260-482-9288 **Fax:** 260-482-8655 www.1063joefm.com

Fort Wayne WGL-FM (am) 2000 Lower Huntington Rd, Fort Wayne IN 46819 **Phn:** 260-747-1511 **Fax:** 260-747-3999 www.wglradio.com jj@summitcityradio.com

Fort Wayne WGL-AM (a) 2000 Lower Huntington Rd, Fort Wayne IN 46819 **Phn:** 260-747-1511 **Fax:** 260-747-3999 www.wglradio.com jj@summitcityradio.com

Fort Wayne WGLL-AM (snt) 2000 Lower Huntington Rd, Fort Wayne IN 46819 **Phn:** 260-747-5100 **Fax:** 260-747-3999 jj@rock104radio.com

Fort Wayne WJFX-FM (h) 2100 Goshen Rd Ste 232, Fort Wayne IN 46808 **Phn:** 260-482-9288 **Fax:** 260-482-8655 www.hot1079online.com phil.becker@oasisradiogroup.com

Fort Wayne WKJG-AM (s) 2915 Maples Rd, Fort Wayne IN 46816 **Phn:** 260-447-5511 **Fax:** 260-447-7546

Fort Wayne WLAB-FM (q) 6600 N Clinton St, Fort Wayne IN 46825 **Phn:** 260-483-8236 **Fax:** 260-482-7707 www.star883.com

Fort Wayne WLDE-FM (o) 347 W Berry St Ste 600, Fort Wayne IN 46802 **Phn:** 260-423-3676 **Fax:** 260-422-5266 www.wlde.com ltobin@wlde.com

Fort Wayne WLYV-AM (qt) 4618 E State Blvd # 200, Fort Wayne IN 46815 **Phn:** 260-436-9598 **Fax:** 260-432-6179 www.redeemerradio.com info@redeemerradio.com

Fort Wayne WMEE-FM (h) 2915 Maples Rd, Fort Wayne IN 46816 **Phn:** 260-447-5511 **Fax:** 260-447-7546 www.wmee.com jimmy@wmee.com

Fort Wayne WNHT-FM (u) 2000 Lower Huntington Rd, Fort Wayne IN 46819 **Phn:** 260-747-1511 **Fax:** 260-747-3999 www.wild963.com shady@summitcityradio.com

Fort Wayne WNUY-FM (snt) 4714 Parnell Ave, Fort Wayne IN 46825 **Phn:** 260-469-2412 **Fax:** 260-484-3504

Fort Wayne WOWO-AM (snt) 2915 Maples Rd, Fort Wayne IN 46816 **Phn:** 260-447-5511 **Fax:** 260-447-7546 www.wowo.com news@wowo.com

Fort Wayne WOWO-FM (r) 2915 Maples Rd, Fort Wayne IN 46816 **Phn:** 260-447-5511 **Fax:** 260-471-5224 wowo.com wrecker@wowo.com

Fort Wayne WQHK-FM (c) 2915 Maples Rd, Fort Wayne IN 46816 **Phn:** 260-447-5511 **Fax:** 260-447-7546 www.k105fm.com dmichaels@federatedmedia.com

Fort Wayne WXKE-FM (r) 2000 Lower Huntington Rd, Fort Wayne IN 46819 **Phn:** 260-747-1511 **Fax:** 260-747-3999 www.rock104radio.com doc@rock104radio.com

Frankfort WILO-AM (nt) 1401 W Barner St, Frankfort IN 46041 **Phn:** 765-659-3338 **Fax:** 765-659-3338 www.wilo.us rk@kasparradio.com

Frankfort WSHW-FM (fa) PO Box 545, Frankfort IN 46041 **Phn:** 765-659-3338 www.shine99.com pddir@kasparradio.com

Franklin WFCI-FM (vr) 101 Branigin Blvd, Franklin IN 46131 **Phn:** 317-738-8205

Franklin WFDM-FM (nt) 645 Industrial Dr, Franklin IN 46131 **Phn:** 317-736-4040 **Fax:** 317-736-4781 www.freedom95.us info@freedom959.com

Franklin WXLW-AM (s) 645 Industrial Dr, Franklin IN 46131 **Phn:** 317-736-4040 **Fax:** 317-736-4781 www.freedom95.us info@xl950.com

French Lick WFLQ-FM (c) PO Box 100, French Lick IN 47432 **Phn:** 812-936-9100 **Fax:** 812-936-9495 www.wflq.com wflqfm@smithville.net

Gary WGVE-FM (v) 1800 E 35th Ave, Gary IN 46409 **Phn:** 219-962-9483 **Fax:** 219-962-3726

Goshen WGCS-FM (v) 1700 S Main St, Goshen IN 46526 **Phn:** 574-535-7488 **Fax:** 574-535-7293 www.globeradio.org globe@goshen.edu

Goshen WKAM-AM (y) 930 E Lincoln Ave, Goshen IN 46528 **Phn:** 574-533-1460 **Fax:** 574-534-3698

Greencastle WGRE-FM (v) 609 S Locust St, Greencastle IN 46135 **Phn:** 765-658-4642 **Fax:** 765-658-4455 www.wgre.org wgre@depauw.edu

Greencastle WREB-FM (c) 2468 W County Road 25 N, Greencastle IN 46135 **Phn:** 812-882-6060 **Fax:** 812-885-2604 www.originalcompany.com wreb@originalcompany.com

Greensburg WTRE-AM (c) 1217 W Park Rd, Greensburg IN 47240 **Phn:** 812-663-3000 **Fax:** 812-663-8355 www.wtrecommunity.com sandybiddinger@yahoo.com

Hammond WJOB-AM (snt) 6405 Olcott St, Hammond IN 46320 **Phn:** 219-844-1230 **Fax:** 219-989-8516 www.wjob1230.com jed@heyregion.com

Hammond WPXW-FM (u) 6336 Calumet Ave, Hammond IN 46324 **Phn:** 312-649-2420 **Fax:** 312-642-0728 www.power92chicago.com

Hammond WSRB-FM (ua) 6336 Calumet Ave, Hammond IN 46324 **Phn:** 219-933-4455 **Fax:** 219-933-0323 www.soul1063radio.com karenr@crawfordbroadcasting.com

Hammond WYCA-FM (gw) 6336 Calumet Ave, Hammond IN 46324 **Phn:** 219-933-4455 **Fax:** 219-933-0323 www.rejoice102.com

Howe WHWE-FM (v) PO Box 240, Howe IN 46746 **Phn:** 260-562-2131 **Fax:** 260-562-3678

Huntingburg WBDC-FM (c) PO Box 330, Huntingburg IN 47542 **Phn:** 812-683-4144 **Fax:** 812-683-5891 www.wbdc.us mailbox@wbdc.us

Indianapolis WBDG-FM (vr) 1200 N Girls School Rd, Indianapolis IN 46214 **Phn:** 317-988-7122 **Fax:** 317-988-7311 www.wayne.k12.in.usbdwbdg

INDIANA RADIO STATIONS

Indianapolis WBRI-AM (q) 4802 E 62nd St, Indianapolis IN 46220 **Phn:** 317-255-5484 **Fax:** 317-255-8592 www.wilkinsradio.com wbri@wilkinsradio.com

Indianapolis WEDJ-FM (y) 1800 N Meridian St Ste 603, Indianapolis IN 46202 **Phn:** 317-924-1071 **Fax:** 317-924-7766 www.wedjfm.com bart@wedjfm.com

Indianapolis WEDM-FM (vh) 9651 E 21st St, Indianapolis IN 46229 **Phn:** 317-532-6301 **Fax:** 317-532-6199

Indianapolis WFBQ-FM (r) 6161 Fall Creek Rd, Indianapolis IN 46220 **Phn:** 317-257-7565 **Fax:** 317-254-9619 www.q95.com rickgreen@clearchannel.com

Indianapolis WFMS-FM (c) 6810 N Shadeland Ave, Indianapolis IN 46220 **Phn:** 317-842-9550 **Fax:** 317-577-3361 www.wfms.com info@wfms.com

Indianapolis WFNI-AM (s) 40 Monument Cir Ste 400, Indianapolis IN 46204 **Phn:** 317-261-1070 **Fax:** 317-684-2004 www.wibc.com steve@wibc.com

Indianapolis WFYI-FM (pln) 1630 N Meridian St, Indianapolis IN 46202 **Phn:** 317-636-2020 www.wfyi.org

Indianapolis WHHH-FM (uw) 21 E Saint Joseph St, Indianapolis IN 46204 **Phn:** 317-266-9600 **Fax:** 317-328-3870 indyhiphop.com cwilliams@radio-one.com

Indianapolis WIBC-AM (nt) 40 Monument Cir Ste 400, Indianapolis IN 46204 **Phn:** 317-266-9422 **Fax:** 317-684-2021 www.wibc.com steve@wibc.com

Indianapolis WICR-FM (vlj) 1400 E Hanna Ave, Indianapolis IN 46227 **Phn:** 317-788-3280 **Fax:** 317-788-3490 wicr.uindy.edu wicr@uindy.edu

Indianapolis WJJK-FM (ha) 6810 N Shadeland Ave, Indianapolis IN 46220 **Phn:** 317-842-9550 **Fax:** 317-577-3361 www.1045jackfm.com

Indianapolis WKLU-FM (r) 8120 KNUE Rd, Indianapolis IN 46250 **Phn:** 317-841-1019 **Fax:** 317-841-5167

Indianapolis WLHK-FM (c) 40 Monument Cir Ste 600, Indianapolis IN 46204 **Phn:** 317-266-9700 **Fax:** 317-684-2017 www.hankfm.com brichards@indy.emmis.com

Indianapolis WNDE-AM (st) 6161 Fall Creek Rd, Indianapolis IN 46220 **Phn:** 317-257-7565 www.wnde.com rickgreen@clearchannel.com

Indianapolis WNOU-FM (h) 21 E Saint Joseph St, Indianapolis IN 46204 **Phn:** 317-266-9600 **Fax:** 317-261-4664 radionowindy.com cpruitt@radio-one.com

Indianapolis WNTR-FM (a) 9245 N Meridian St Ste 300, Indianapolis IN 46260 **Phn:** 317-816-4000 **Fax:** 317-816-4004 www.my1079online.com

Indianapolis WNTS-AM (y) 4800 E Raymond St, Indianapolis IN 46203 **Phn:** 317-359-5591

Indianapolis WRWM-FM (t) 6810 N Shadeland Ave, Indianapolis IN 46220 **Phn:** 317-842-9550 **Fax:** 317-577-3361 i94hits.com jay.michaels@cumulus.com

Indianapolis WRZX-FM (r) 6161 Fall Creek Rd, Indianapolis IN 46220 **Phn:** 317-257-7565 **Fax:** 317-465-9103 www.x103.com rickgreen@clearchannel.com

Indianapolis WSYW-AM (y) 1800 N Meridian St Ste 603, Indianapolis IN 46202 **Phn:** 317-924-1071 **Fax:** 317-924-7766 www.laquebuena810am.com manuel@wedjfm.com

Indianapolis WTLC-AM (wg) 21 E Saint Joseph St, Indianapolis IN 46204 **Phn:** 317-266-9600 **Fax:** 317-328-3870 praiseindy.com abrown@radio-one.com

Indianapolis WTLC-FM (xw) 21 E Saint Joseph St, Indianapolis IN 46204 **Phn:** 317-266-9600 **Fax:** 317-328-3870 tlcnaptown.com abrown@radio-one.com

Indianapolis WTTS-FM (ar) 407 Fulton St Ste 92, Indianapolis IN 46202 **Phn:** 317-972-9887 **Fax:** 317-972-9886 wttsfm.com brad@wttsfm.com

Indianapolis WXNT-AM (s) 9245 N Meridian St Ste 300, Indianapolis IN 46260 **Phn:** 317-816-4000 **Fax:** 317-816-4035 www.cbssports1430.com

Indianapolis WYXB-FM (a) 40 Monument Cir Ste 600, Indianapolis IN 46204 **Phn:** 317-684-1057 **Fax:** 317-684-2021 www.b1057.com dwood@indy.emmis.com

Indianapolis WZPL-FM (a) 9245 N Meridian St Ste 300, Indianapolis IN 46260 **Phn:** 317-816-4000 **Fax:** 317-816-4080 www.wzpl.com jammons@entercom.com

Jasper WAXL-FM (a) PO Box 1009, Jasper IN 47547 **Phn:** 812-683-1215 **Fax:** 812-683-5891 www.waxl.us mailbox@waxl.us

Jasper WITZ-AM (a) PO Box 167, Jasper IN 47547 **Phn:** 812-482-2131 **Fax:** 812-482-9609 www.witzamfm.com news@witzamfm.com

Jasper WITZ-FM (a) PO Box 167, Jasper IN 47547 **Phn:** 812-482-2131 **Fax:** 812-482-9609 www.witzamfm.com news@witzamfm.com

Jasper WQKZ-FM (c) PO Box 167, Jasper IN 47547 **Phn:** 812-367-1884 **Fax:** 812-482-9609 www.witzamfm.com news@witzamfm.com

Jasper WRZR-FM (r) PO Box 1009, Jasper IN 47547 **Phn:** 812-634-9232 **Fax:** 812-482-3696 www.dcbroadcasting.com mailbox@wrzr.us

Kendallville WAWK-FM (o) 931 East Ave Ste A, Kendallville IN 46755 **Phn:** 260-347-2400 **Fax:** 260-347-2524 www.955fmthehawk.com don@wawk.com

Kendallville WAWK-AM (o) 931 East Ave Ste A, Kendallville IN 46755 **Phn:** 260-347-2400 **Fax:** 260-347-2524 www.955fmthehawk.com don@wawk.com

Knightstown WKPW-FM (hr) 8149 W US Highway 40, Knightstown IN 46148 **Phn:** 765-345-9070 **Fax:** 765-345-7977 www.wkpwfm.com wkpw@wkpwfm.com

Knox WKVI-FM (a) 400 W Culver Rd, Knox IN 46534 **Phn:** 574-772-6241 **Fax:** 574-772-5920 www.wkvi.com mary@wkvi.com

Knox WKVI-AM (a) 400 W Culver Rd, Knox IN 46534 **Phn:** 574-772-6241 **Fax:** 574-772-5920 www.wkvi.com mary@wkvi.com

Kokomo WIOU-AM (snt) PO Box 2208, Kokomo IN 46904 **Phn:** 765-453-1212 **Fax:** 765-455-3882 svlamar76@aol.com

Kokomo WMYK-FM (r) PO Box 2208, Kokomo IN 46904 **Phn:** 765-455-9850 **Fax:** 765-455-3882 www.rock985.com classicrock985@sbcglobal.net

Kokomo WWKI-FM (c) 519 N Main St, Kokomo IN 46901 **Phn:** 765-459-4191 **Fax:** 765-456-1111 www.wwki.com wwki@cumulus.com

Kokomo WZWZ-FM (a) PO Box 2208, Kokomo IN 46904 **Phn:** 765-453-1212 **Fax:** 765-455-3882 www.kzrx921.com jimlowe@clearchannel.com

La Porte WCOE-FM (c) 1700 Lincolnway Pl Ste 8, La Porte IN 46350 **Phn:** 219-362-5290 **Fax:** 219-324-7418 www.wcoefm.com denny@wcoefm.com

La Porte WLOI-AM (b) 1700 Lincolnway Pl Ste 8, La Porte IN 46350 **Phn:** 219-362-6144 **Fax:** 219-324-7418

Lafayette WASK-FM (o) 3575 McCarty Ln, Lafayette IN 47905 **Phn:** 765-447-2186 **Fax:** 765-448-4452 www.wask.com mcgarvey@wask.com

Lafayette WAZY-FM (h) 3824 S 18th St, Lafayette IN 47909 **Phn:** 765-474-1410 **Fax:** 765-474-3442 www.wazy.com ric@wazy.com

Lafayette WBPE-FM (a) 3824 S 18th St, Lafayette IN 47909 **Phn:** 765-474-1410 **Fax:** 765-474-3442 www.wbpefm.com judy@artisticradio.com

Lafayette WKHY-FM (r) 3575 McCarty Ln, Lafayette IN 47905 **Phn:** 765-447-2186 **Fax:** 765-448-4452 www.wkhy.com strange@wkhy.com

Lafayette WKOA-FM (c) 3575 McCarty Ln, Lafayette IN 47905 **Phn:** 765-447-2186 **Fax:** 765-448-4452 www.wkoa.com shamus@wkoa.com

Lafayette WSHP-FM (h) 3824 S 18th St, Lafayette IN 47909 **Phn:** 765-474-1410 **Fax:** 765-474-3442 www.957therocket.com

Lafayette WXXB-FM (h) 3575 McCarty Ln, Lafayette IN 47905 **Phn:** 765-448-1566 **Fax:** 765-448-1348 www.b1029.com logan@b1029.com

Lagrange WTHD-FM (c) PO Box 263, Lagrange IN 46761 **Phn:** 260-463-8500 **Fax:** 260-463-8580 www.wthd.net wthd@wthd.net

Lawrenceburg WSCH-FM (c) 20 E High St, Lawrenceburg IN 47025 **Phn:** 812-537-0944 **Fax:** 812-537-5735 www.eaglecountryonline.com mike@eaglecountryonline.com

Lawrenceburg WXCH-FM (c) 20 E High St, Lawrenceburg IN 47025 **Phn:** 812-537-0944 **Fax:** 812-537-5735 www.eaglecountryonline.com mike@eaglecountryonline.com

Logansport WHZR-FM (c) PO Box 103, Logansport IN 46947 **Phn:** 574-722-1037 **Fax:** 574-739-1037 www.indianasbestradio.com wsalnewsroom@gmail.com

Logansport WLHM-FM (h) PO Box 103, Logansport IN 46947 **Phn:** 574-722-4000 **Fax:** 574-722-4010 www.indianasbestradio.com wsalnewsroom@gmail.com

Logansport WSAL-AM (at) PO Box 103, Logansport IN 46947 **Phn:** 574-722-4000 **Fax:** 574-722-4010 www.indianasbestradio.com wsalnewsroom@gmail.com

Madison WIKI-FM (c) 2604 Michigan Rd, Madison IN 47250 **Phn:** 812-273-3139 **Fax:** 812-265-4536 www.953wiki.com

Madison WORX-FM (a) PO Box 95, Madison IN 47250 **Phn:** 812-265-3322 **Fax:** 812-273-5509 www.worxradio.com thebestmusic@worxradio.com

Madison WXGO-AM (o) PO Box 95, Madison IN 47250 **Phn:** 812-265-3322 **Fax:** 812-273-5509 www.worxradio.com thebestmusic@worxradio.com

Marion WBAT-AM (nt) 820 S Pennsylvania St, Marion IN 46953 **Phn:** 765-664-6239 **Fax:** 765-662-0730 www.wbat.com wbat@comteck.com

Marion WCJC-FM (c) 820 S Pennsylvania St, Marion IN 46953 **Phn:** 765-664-6239 **Fax:** 765-662-0730 www.wcjc.com wcjc@comteck.com

Marion WMRI-AM (m) PO Box 1538, Marion IN 46952 **Phn:** 765-664-7396 **Fax:** 765-668-6767 www.wmri.com news@wbat.com

Marion WXXC-FM (h) PO Box 839, Marion IN 46952 **Phn:** 765-664-7396 **Fax:** 765-668-6767 www.1069wxxc.com news@wbat.com

Martinsville WCBK-FM (c) PO Box 1577, Martinsville IN 46151 **Phn:** 765-342-3394 **Fax:** 765-342-5020

Michigan City WEFM-FM (ao) 1903 Springland Ave, Michigan City IN 46360 **Phn:** 219-879-8201 **Fax:** 219-879-8202 wefmr@yahoo.com

Michigan City WIMS-AM (snt) 720 Franklin St, Michigan City IN 46360 **Phn:** 219-879-9810 **Fax:** 219-879-9813 www.wimsradio.com ric@wimsradio.com

INDIANA RADIO STATIONS

Mishawaka WAOR-FM (r) 237 W Edison Rd, Mishawaka IN 46545 **Phn:** 574-258-5483 **Fax:** 574-258-0930 www.waor.com 953@waor.com

Mishawaka WBYT-FM (c) 237 W Edison Rd Ste 200, Mishawaka IN 46545 **Phn:** 574-258-5483 **Fax:** 574-258-0930 www.b100.com jesse@b100.com

Mishawaka WNIL-AM (qt) 237 W Edison Rd, Mishawaka IN 46545 **Phn:** 574-258-5483 **Fax:** 574-258-0930 mighty1290.com bwilliams@federatedmedia.com

Mishawaka WRBR-FM (r) 237 W Edison Rd Ste 200, Mishawaka IN 46545 **Phn:** 574-258-5483 **Fax:** 574-258-0930 www.wrbr.com rstryker@wrbr.com

Mishawaka WSBT-AM (nts) 1301 E Douglas Rd, Mishawaka IN 46545 **Phn:** 574-233-3141 **Fax:** 574-239-4231 www.wsbtradio.com bmontgomery@wsbt.com

Mishawaka WYPW-FM (hu) 237 W Edison Rd, Mishawaka IN 46545 **Phn:** 888-737-6244 **Fax:** 574-258-0930

Mishawaka WZOC-FM (o) 1301 E Douglas Rd, Mishawaka IN 46545 **Phn:** 574-233-3141 **Fax:** 574-289-7382 www.oldies943fm.com bgamble@wsbt.com

Monticello WMRS-FM (a) 132 N Main St, Monticello IN 47960 **Phn:** 574-583-8933 www.wmrsradio.com brandi@wmrsradio.com

Mount Vernon WRCY-AM (c) 7109 Upton Rd, Mount Vernon IN 47620 **Phn:** 812-838-4484 **Fax:** 812-882-7770 www.originalcompany.com news@originalcompany.com

Mount Vernon WYFX-FM (s) 7109 Upton Rd, Mount Vernon IN 47620 **Phn:** 812-838-4484 **Fax:** 812-882-7770 www.originalcompany.com wyfx@originalcompany.com

Muncie WBSB-FM (plnj) Ball State Univ, Muncie IN 47306 **Phn:** 765-285-5888 **Fax:** 765-285-6397 www.bsu.edu\ipr ipr@bsu.edu

Muncie WBST-FM (plnj) Ball State Univ, Muncie IN 47306 **Phn:** 765-285-5888 **Fax:** 765-285-6397 www.bsu.edu\ipr ipr@bsu.edu

Muncie WERK-FM (o) 800 E 29th St, Muncie IN 47302 **Phn:** 765-288-4403 **Fax:** 765-288-0429 www.werkradio.com jay.garrison@bybradio.com

Muncie WHBU-AM (nt) 800 E 29th St, Muncie IN 47302 **Phn:** 765-288-4403 **Fax:** 765-288-0429 www.1240whbu.com steve.lindell@bybradio.com

Muncie WHTI-FM (r) 800 E 29th St, Muncie IN 47302 **Phn:** 765-378-2080 **Fax:** 765-378-2090 www.maxrocks.net jay.garrison@woofboom.com

Muncie WHTY-FM (r) 800 E 29th St, Muncie IN 47302 **Phn:** 765-378-2080 **Fax:** 765-378-2090 www.maxrocks.net jay.garrison@woofboom.com

Muncie WLBC-FM (a) 800 E 29th St, Muncie IN 47302 **Phn:** 765-288-4403 **Fax:** 765-288-0429 www.wlbc.com steve.lindell@bybradio.com

Muncie WURK-FM (o) 800 E 29th St, Muncie IN 47302 **Phn:** 765-288-4403 **Fax:** 765-288-0429

Muncie WXFN-AM (s) 800 E 29th St, Muncie IN 47302 **Phn:** 765-288-4403 **Fax:** 765-288-0429 jay.garrison@bybradio.com

New Albany WNAS-FM (vh) 1020 Vincennes St, New Albany IN 47150 **Phn:** 812-981-7621 **Fax:** 812-949-6926 www.wnas.org

New Castle WLTI-AM (am) PO Box 690, New Castle IN 47362 **Phn:** 765-529-2600 **Fax:** 765-529-1688 www.wmdh.com

New Castle WMDH-FM (c) PO Box 690, New Castle IN 47362 **Phn:** 765-529-2600 **Fax:** 765-529-1688 www.wmdh.com

North Manchester WBKE-FM (v) Mc Box 19, North Manchester IN 46962 **Phn:** 260-982-5424 **Fax:** 260-982-5043 wbke.manchester.edu dan@wrsw.net

Notre Dame WSND-FM (v) 315 Lafortune Student Ctr, Notre Dame IN 46556 **Phn:** 574-631-7342 **Fax:** 574-631-3653 wsnd.nd.edu wsnd@nd.edu

Oxford WIBN-FM (o) PO Box 25, Oxford IN 47971 **Phn:** 765-385-2373 **Fax:** 765-385-2374

Paoli WSEZ-AM (o) PO Box 26, Paoli IN 47454 **Phn:** 812-723-4484 **Fax:** 812-723-4966

Paoli WUME-FM (a) PO Box 26, Paoli IN 47454 **Phn:** 812-723-4484 **Fax:** 812-723-4966

Pendleton WEEM-FM (v) 1 Arabian Dr, Pendleton IN 46064 **Phn:** 765-778-2161 **Fax:** 765-778-0605 www.917weem.org jpetrey@smadison.k12.in.us

Peru WARU-AM (c) PO Box 1010, Peru IN 46970 **Phn:** 765-473-4448 **Fax:** 765-473-4449 waru@sbcglobal.net

Peru WARU-FM (c) PO Box 1010, Peru IN 46970 **Phn:** 765-473-4448 **Fax:** 765-473-4449 www.mitunes1019.com waru@mitunes1019.com

Plymouth WTCA-AM (o) 112 W Washington St, Plymouth IN 46563 **Phn:** 574-936-4096 **Fax:** 574-936-6776 am1050.com wtca@am1050.com

Portland WPGW-FM (c) 1891 W State Road 67, Portland IN 47371 **Phn:** 260-726-8729 **Fax:** 260-726-4311 wpgw@jayco.net

Portland WPGW-AM (a) 1891 W State Road 67, Portland IN 47371 **Phn:** 260-726-8729 **Fax:** 260-726-4311 wpgw@jayco.net

Princeton WRAY-FM (c) PO Box 8, Princeton IN 47670 **Phn:** 812-386-1250 **Fax:** 812-386-6249 www.wrayradio.com cliff@wrayradio.com

Princeton WRAY-AM (nt) PO Box 8, Princeton IN 47670 **Phn:** 812-386-1250 **Fax:** 812-386-6249 www.wrayradio.com wray@wrayradio.com

Rensselaer WLQI-FM (a) PO Box D, Rensselaer IN 47978 **Phn:** 219-866-4104 **Fax:** 219-866-5106

Rensselaer WPUM-FM (vr) PO Box 651, Rensselaer IN 47978 **Phn:** 219-866-6000 www.saintjoe.edu\wpum sallyn@saintjoe.edu

Rensselaer WRIN-AM (o) PO Box D, Rensselaer IN 47978 **Phn:** 219-866-5105 **Fax:** 219-866-5106

Richmond WECI-FM (v) 801 National Rd W # 45, Richmond IN 47374 **Phn:** 765-983-1246 **Fax:** 765-983-1641 www.weciradio.org news.director.weci@gmail.com

Richmond WFMG-FM (a) PO Box 1646, Richmond IN 47375 **Phn:** 765-962-6533 **Fax:** 765-966-1499

Richmond WHON-AM (nt) 2626 Tingler Rd, Richmond IN 47374 **Phn:** 765-962-1595 **Fax:** 765-966-4824 1017thepoint.com jeffl@kicks96.com

Richmond WKBV-AM (nt) PO Box 1646, Richmond IN 47375 **Phn:** 765-962-6533 **Fax:** 765-966-1499 g1013.com rickduncan@g1013.com

Richmond WQLK-FM (c) 2626 Tingler Rd W, Richmond IN 47374 **Phn:** 765-962-1595 **Fax:** 765-966-4824 www.kicks96.com jeffl@kicks96.com

Rochester WROI-FM (o) 110 E 8th St, Rochester IN 46975 **Phn:** 574-223-6059 **Fax:** 574-223-2238 www.wroifm.com wroi@rtcol.com

Salem WSLM-FM (cft) PO Box 385, Salem IN 47167 **Phn:** 812-883-5750 **Fax:** 812-883-2797 www.wslmradio.webs.com wslm@blueriver.net

Salem WSLM-AM (sh) PO Box 385, Salem IN 47167 **Phn:** 812-883-5750 **Fax:** 812-883-2797 www.wslmradio.com wslmradio@gmail.com

Scottsburg WMPI-FM (c) PO Box 270, Scottsburg IN 47170 **Phn:** 812-752-5612 **Fax:** 812-752-2345 www.i1053online.com jross@i1053.com

Seymour WJAA-FM (r) 1531 W Tipton St, Seymour IN 47274 **Phn:** 812-523-3343 **Fax:** 812-523-5116 www.wjaa.net radio@wjaa.net

Seymour WZZB-AM (ant) PO Box 806, Seymour IN 47274 **Phn:** 812-522-1390 **Fax:** 812-522-9541

Shelbyville WSVX-FM (snt) 2356 N Morristown Rd, Shelbyville IN 46176 **Phn:** 317-398-2200 **Fax:** 317-392-3292 www.wsvx.com shuber@wsvx.com

South Bend WDND-AM (s) 3371 Cleveland Road Ext Ste 300, South Bend IN 46628 **Phn:** 574-273-9300 **Fax:** 574-273-9090 rob@u93.com

South Bend WHME-FM (q) 61300 Ironwood Rd, South Bend IN 46614 **Phn:** 574-291-8200 **Fax:** 574-291-9043 www.whmefm.com

South Bend WHPZ-FM (q) 61300 Ironwood Rd, South Bend IN 46614 **Phn:** 574-291-8200 **Fax:** 574-291-9043 www.pulsefm.com pulse@lesea.com

South Bend WNDV-FM (h) 3371 Cleveland Road Ext Ste 300, South Bend IN 46628 **Phn:** 574-273-9300 **Fax:** 574-273-9090 www.u93.com

South Bend WNSN-FM (a) 202 S Michigan St Ste 300, South Bend IN 46601 **Phn:** 574-233-3141 **Fax:** 574-239-4231 www.sunny1015.com roberts@sunny1015.com

South Bend WSMM-FM (a) 3371 Cleveland Road Ext Ste 300, South Bend IN 46628 **Phn:** 574-273-9300 **Fax:** 574-273-9090 www.stream1023.com arthur@artisticradio.com

South Bend WUBS-FM (g) PO Box 3931, South Bend IN 46619 **Phn:** 574-287-4700 www.wubs.org revwilliams@wubs.org

Sullivan WNDI-FM (c) 556 E State Road 54, Sullivan IN 47882 **Phn:** 812-268-6322 **Fax:** 812-268-6652

Sullivan WNDI-AM (c) 556 E State Road 54, Sullivan IN 47882 **Phn:** 812-268-6322 **Fax:** 812-268-6652

Terre Haute WFNB-FM (ah) 925 Wabash Ave # 300, Terre Haute IN 47807 **Phn:** 317-384-2953 **Fax:** 317-684-6533 www.emmis.com ir@emmis.com

Terre Haute WIBQ-FM (nt) 824 S 3rd St, Terre Haute IN 47807 **Phn:** 812-232-4161 **Fax:** 812-234-9999 www.wibqfm.com bill.cain@mwcradio.com

Terre Haute WISU-FM (vju) 221 N 6th St, Terre Haute IN 47809 **Phn:** 812-237-3248 **Fax:** 812-237-3241 www.indstate.edu\sycmedia mslizewski@sycamores.indstate.edu

Terre Haute WMGI-FM (h) 824 S 3rd St, Terre Haute IN 47807 **Phn:** 812-232-4161 **Fax:** 812-234-9999 mymixfm.com webmaster@1007mixfm.com

Terre Haute WMHD-FM (v) 5500 Wabash Ave, Terre Haute IN 47803 **Phn:** 812-872-6923 **Fax:** 812-872-6926 wmhdradio.org manager@wmhdradio.org

Terre Haute WPRS-AM (nt) 824 S 3rd St, Terre Haute IN 47807 **Phn:** 812-232-4161 **Fax:** 812-234-9999 www.wprsam.com steve.hall@mwcradio.com

Terre Haute WSDX-AM (s) 1301 Ohio St, Terre Haute IN 47807 **Phn:** 812-234-9770 **Fax:** 812-238-1576 www.1130thefan.com ir@emmis.com

Terre Haute WTHI-FM (c) PO Box 9606, Terre Haute IN 47808 **Phn:** 812-232-9481 **Fax:** 812-234-0089 www.hi99.com jconner@wthi.emmis.com

Terre Haute WWVR-FM (r) PO Box 9606, Terre Haute IN 47808 **Phn:** 812-232-9481 **Fax:** 812-234-0089 www.1055theriver.com jconner@wthi.emmis.com

Union City WJYW-FM (qv) PO Box 445, Union City IN 47390 **Phn:** 937-968-5633 **Fax:** 937-968-3320 www.889joyfm.com office@889joyfm.com

Upland WTUR-FM (q) 236 W Reade Ave, Upland IN 46989 **Phn:** 765-998-5263 **Fax:** 765-998-4810 wtur@taylor.edu

Valparaiso WAKE-AM (n) 2755 Sager Rd, Valparaiso IN 46383 **Phn:** 219-462-6111 **Fax:** 219-462-4880 www.wakeradio.com

Valparaiso WLJE-FM (c) 2755 Sager Rd, Valparaiso IN 46383 **Phn:** 219-462-8125 **Fax:** 219-462-4880 www.indiana105.com admin@indiana105.com

Valparaiso WVUR-FM (v) 1809 Chapel Dr, Valparaiso IN 46383 **Phn:** 219-464-5383 thesource95.com thesource95@gmail.com

Valparaiso WXRD-FM (r) 2755 Sager Rd, Valparaiso IN 46383 **Phn:** 219-462-6111 **Fax:** 219-462-4880 www.xrock1039.com

Valparaiso WZVN-FM (a) 2755 Sager Rd, Valparaiso IN 46383 **Phn:** 219-462-6111 **Fax:** 219-462-4880 www.z1071.com admin@indiana105.com

Vevay WKID-FM (c) 118 W Main St, Vevay IN 47043 **Phn:** 812-427-9590 **Fax:** 812-427-2492

Vincennes WAOV-AM (snt) PO Box 242, Vincennes IN 47591 **Phn:** 812-882-6060 **Fax:** 812-885-2604 www.originalcompany.com news@originalcompany.com

Vincennes WBTO-FM (r) PO Box 242, Vincennes IN 47591 **Phn:** 812-882-6060 **Fax:** 812-882-7770 www.originalcompany.com marklange@originalcompany.com

Vincennes WFML-FM (c) PO Box 882, Vincennes IN 47591 **Phn:** 812-254-6761 **Fax:** 812-254-3940 www.wfml.net braddeetz@wfml.net

Vincennes WQTY-FM (c) PO Box 242, Vincennes IN 47591 **Phn:** 812-882-6060 **Fax:** 812-885-2604 www.originalcompany.com wqty@originalcompany.com

Vincennes WUZR-FM (o) PO Box 242, Vincennes IN 47591 **Phn:** 812-882-6060 **Fax:** 812-885-2604 www.originalcompany.com wuzr@originalcompany.com

Vincennes WVUB-FM (p) 1200 N 2nd St, Vincennes IN 47591 **Phn:** 812-888-4347 **Fax:** 812-882-2237 blazer911wvub.com wvub@vinu.edu

Vincennes WZDM-FM (a) PO Box 242, Vincennes IN 47591 **Phn:** 812-882-6060 **Fax:** 812-885-2604 www.originalcompany.com wzdm@originalcompany.com

Wabash WJOT-AM (o) 1360 S Wabash St, Wabash IN 46992 **Phn:** 260-563-1161 **Fax:** 260-563-0883 wjot@comteck.com

Wabash WJOT-FM (o) 1360 S Wabash St, Wabash IN 46992 **Phn:** 260-563-1161 **Fax:** 260-563-0883 wjot@comteck.com

Wabash WKUZ-FM (a) PO Box 342, Wabash IN 46992 **Phn:** 260-563-4111 **Fax:** 260-563-4425 www.wkuz.com sonia@wkuz.com

Warsaw WAWC-FM (a) 216 W Market St, Warsaw IN 46580 **Phn:** 574-372-3064 **Fax:** 574-267-2230 www.willie1035.com cmarsh@lakecityradio.com

Warsaw WLZQ-FM (a) PO Box 2020, Warsaw IN 46581 **Phn:** 260-482-8500 **Fax:** 574-268-077 www.wlzq.com q101@wlzq.com

INDIANA RADIO STATIONS

Warsaw WMYQ-FM (a) PO Box 2020, Warsaw IN 46581 **Phn:** 800-398-5788 www.myq101.com news@myq101.com

Warsaw WRSW-FM (oh) 216 W Market St Ste 1, Warsaw IN 46580 **Phn:** 574-372-3064 **Fax:** 574-267-2230 www.wrsw.net jmichaels@lakecityradio.com

Warsaw WRSW-AM (s) 216 W Market St Ste 1, Warsaw IN 46580 **Phn:** 574-372-3064 **Fax:** 574-267-2230 www.espnwarsaw.com roger@wrsw.net

Washington WAMW-AM (m) 800 W National Hwy, Washington IN 47501 **Phn:** 812-254-6761 **Fax:** 812-254-3940 www.wamwamfm.com don@wamwamfm.com

Washington WAMW-FM (a) 800 W National Hwy, Washington IN 47501 **Phn:** 812-254-6761 **Fax:** 812-254-3940 www.wamwamfm.com brad@wamwamfm.com

Washington WWBL-FM (c) 3 E Van Trees, Washington IN 47501 **Phn:** 812-254-4300 **Fax:** 812-254-4361 www.originalcompany.com johnszink@originalcompany.com

West Lafayette WBAA-FM (pl) 712 3rd St, West Lafayette IN 47907 **Phn:** 765-494-5920 **Fax:** 765-496-1542 wbaa.org news@wbaa.org

West Lafayette WBAA-AM (pnt) 712 3rd St, West Lafayette IN 47907 **Phn:** 765-494-5920 **Fax:** 765-496-1542 wbaa.org news@wbaa.org

Winchester WZZY-FM (a) 112 W Washington St, Winchester IN 47394 **Phn:** 765-962-6533 **Fax:** 765-966-1499 www.todaysmusicmix.com johnrose@g1013.com

IOWA

Albia KIIC-FM (c) PO Box 654, Albia IA 52531 **Phn:** 641-932-2112 **Fax:** 641-932-2113 kiicradio.com joe@kiicradio.com

Algona KLGA-AM (c) PO Box 160, Algona IA 50511 **Phn:** 515-295-2475 **Fax:** 515-295-3851 bketchum@nrgmedia.com

Algona KLGA-FM (a) PO Box 160, Algona IA 50511 **Phn:** 515-295-2475 **Fax:** 515-295-3851 bketchum@nrgmedia.com

Ames KASI-AM (m) 415 Main St Ste 102, Ames IA 50010 **Phn:** 515-232-1430 **Fax:** 515-232-1439 www.1430kasi.com trentrice@clearchannel.com

Ames KCCQ-FM (r) 415 Main St, Ames IA 50010 **Phn:** 515-232-1430 **Fax:** 515-232-1439 www.newrock1051.com carolkisling@clearchannel.com

Ames KTPR-FM (plnj) 2022 Communications Bldg ISU, Ames IA 50011 **Phn:** 515-725-1700 **Fax:** 515-725-1714 iowapublicradio.org news@iowapublicradio.org

Ames KURE-FM (v) 1199 Friley Hall Ia State U, Ames IA 50012 **Phn:** 515-294-4332 www.kure.stuorg.iastate.edu press@kure885.org

Ames WOI-FM (p) 2022 Communications Bldg ISU, Ames IA 50011 **Phn:** 515-725-1700 **Fax:** 515-725-1714 iowapublicradio.org news@iowapublicradio.org

Ames WOI-AM (pln) 2022 Communications Bldg ISU, Ames IA 50011 **Phn:** 515-725-1700 **Fax:** 515-725-1714 iowapublicradio.org news@iowapublicradio.org

Atlantic KJAN-AM (bma) PO Box 389, Atlantic IA 50022 **Phn:** 712-243-3920 **Fax:** 712-243-3937 www.kjan.com kjan@metc.net

Atlantic KSOM-FM (c) 413 Chestnut St, Atlantic IA 50022 **Phn:** 712-243-6885 **Fax:** 712-243-1691 www.965ksom.com mandy@iowasuperstation.com

Atlantic KSWI-FM (a) 413 Chestnut St, Atlantic IA 50022 **Phn:** 712-243-6885 **Fax:** 712-243-1691 ks957.com tori@iowasuperstation.com

Bloomfield KOJY-FM (h) 22620 195th St, Bloomfield IA 52537 **Phn:** 641-722-3008 **Fax:** 641-722-3009

Boone KWBG-AM (cnt) 724 Story St Ste 201, Boone IA 50036 **Phn:** 515-432-2046 **Fax:** 515-432-1448 www.kwbg.com kwbgnews@nrgmedia.com

Burlington KBKB-FM (c) 610 N 4th St Ste 310, Burlington IA 52601 **Phn:** 319-752-2701 **Fax:** 319-752-5287 www.1017thebull.com drew@1017thebull.com

Burlington KBKB-AM (s) 610 N 4th St Ste 310, Burlington IA 52601 **Phn:** 319-752-5402 **Fax:** 319-752-5287 www.1360kbkb.com johnp@burlingtonradio.com

Burlington KBUR-AM (nt) 610 N 4th St Ste 300, Burlington IA 52601 **Phn:** 319-752-5402 **Fax:** 319-752-4715 www.kbur.com info@kbur.com

Burlington KDMG-FM (c) 610 N 4th St Ste 300, Burlington IA 52601 **Phn:** 319-752-5402 **Fax:** 319-752-4715 www.bigcountry1031.com bigcountry1031@bigcountry1031.com

Burlington KGRS-FM (a) 610 N 4th St Ste 310, Burlington IA 52601 **Phn:** 319-752-2701 **Fax:** 319-752-5287 thenewmix.com jason@thenewmix.com

Burlington KKMI-FM (a) 610 N 4th St Ste 300, Burlington IA 52601 **Phn:** 319-752-5402 **Fax:** 319-752-4715 www.935kkmi.com scottm@935kkmi.com

Burlington WQKQ-FM (r) 610 N 4th St Ste 300, Burlington IA 52601 **Phn:** 319-752-5402 **Fax:** 319-752-4715 www.kq92rocks.com johnp@burlingtonradio.com

Carroll KCIM-AM (ant) PO Box 886, Carroll IA 51401 **Phn:** 712-792-4321 **Fax:** 712-792-6667 www.1380kcim.com kcim@carrollbroadcasting.com

Carroll KIKD-FM (c) 1119 Plaza Dr, Carroll IA 51401 **Phn:** 712-792-4321 **Fax:** 712-792-6667 www.kick1067.com kikd@carrollbroadcasting.com

Carroll KKRL-FM (a) PO Box 886, Carroll IA 51401 **Phn:** 712-792-4321 **Fax:** 712-792-6667 www.1380kcim.com kcim@carrollbroadcasting.com

Cedar Falls KCNZ-AM (ns) PO Box 248, Cedar Falls IA 50613 **Phn:** 319-277-1918 **Fax:** 319-277-5202 www.1650thefan.com jim@1650thefan.com

Cedar Falls KCVM-FM (a) 721 Shirley St, Cedar Falls IA 50613 **Phn:** 319-277-1918 **Fax:** 319-277-5202 935themix.com themix@935themix.com

Cedar Falls KDNZ-AM (s) PO Box 248, Cedar Falls IA 50613 **Phn:** 319-277-1918 **Fax:** 319-277-5202 www.1650thefan.com jesse@1650thefan.com

Cedar Falls KHKE-FM (p) Univ Of N Iowa, Cedar Falls IA 50614 **Phn:** 319-273-6400 **Fax:** 319-273-2682 iowapublicradio.org info@iowapublicradio.org

Cedar Falls KUNI-FM (pln) Univ Of N Iowa, Cedar Falls IA 50614 **Phn:** 319-273-6400 **Fax:** 319-273-2682 iowapublicradio.org info@iowapublicradio.org

Cedar Rapids KCCK-FM (pjn) 6301 Kirkwood Blvd SW, Cedar Rapids IA 52404 **Phn:** 319-398-5446 **Fax:** 319-398-5492 www.kcck.org bobs@kcck.org

Cedar Rapids KDAT-FM (a) 425 2nd St SE Ste 450, Cedar Rapids IA 52401 **Phn:** 319-365-9431 **Fax:** 319-363-8062 www.kdat.com kdat@kdat.com

Cedar Rapids KGYM-AM (s) 1110 26th Ave SW, Cedar Rapids IA 52404 **Phn:** 319-363-2061 **Fax:** 319-363-2948 www.kgymradio.com info@1600espn.com

Cedar Rapids KHAK-FM (c) 425 2nd St SE Ste 450, Cedar Rapids IA 52401 **Phn:** 319-365-9431 **Fax:** 319-363-8062 www.khak.com khak@khak.com

Cedar Rapids KMJM-AM (s) 600 Old Marion Rd NE Ste 1, Cedar Rapids IA 52402 **Phn:** 319-395-0530 **Fax:** 319-393-9527 www.1360kmjm.com newsroom@wmtradio.com

Cedar Rapids KMRY-AM (bm) 1957 Blairs Ferry Rd NE, Cedar Rapids IA 52402 **Phn:** 319-393-1450 **Fax:** 319-393-1407 www.kmryradio.com kmry@kmryradio.com

Cedar Rapids KRNA-FM (r) 425 2nd St SE Ste 450, Cedar Rapids IA 52401 **Phn:** 319-365-9431 **Fax:** 319-363-8062 www.krna.com greg.sher@cumulus.com

Cedar Rapids KZIA-FM (h) 1110 26th Ave SW, Cedar Rapids IA 52404 **Phn:** 319-363-2061 **Fax:** 319-363-2948 www.kzia.com info@kzia.com

Cedar Rapids WMT-FM (c) 600 Old Marion Rd NE, Cedar Rapids IA 52402 **Phn:** 319-395-0530 **Fax:** 319-393-9600 www.965kisscountry.com newsroom@wmtradio.com

Cedar Rapids WMT-AM (nts) 600 Old Marion Rd NE, Cedar Rapids IA 52402 **Phn:** 319-395-0530 **Fax:** 319-393-9600 www.wmtradio.com newsroom@wmtradio.com

Centerville KCOG-AM (a) 402 N 12th St, Centerville IA 52544 **Phn:** 641-437-4242 **Fax:** 641-856-3337

Centerville KMGO-FM (c) 402 N 12th St, Centerville IA 52544 **Phn:** 641-437-4242 **Fax:** 641-856-3337 www.kmgo.com kmgofm@lisco.net

Charles City KCHA-FM (a) 207 N Main St, Charles City IA 50616 **Phn:** 641-228-1000 **Fax:** 641-228-1200 www.kchafm.com chrisberg@northiowabroadcasting.com

Charles City KCHA-AM (a) 207 N Main St, Charles City IA 50616 **Phn:** 641-228-1000 **Fax:** 641-228-1200 www.kchaam.com chrisberg@northiowabroadcasting.com

Charles City KCZE-FM (c) 207 N Main St, Charles City IA 50616 **Phn:** 641-228-1000 **Fax:** 641-228-1200 www.951thebull.com chrisberg@northiowabroadcasting.com

Cherokee KCHE-AM (h) PO Box 141, Cherokee IA 51012 **Phn:** 712-225-2511 **Fax:** 712-225-2513 www.kcheradio.com news@kcheradio.com

Cherokee KCHE-FM (a) PO Box 141, Cherokee IA 51012 **Phn:** 712-225-2511 **Fax:** 712-225-2513 www.kcheradio.com kche1@ncn.net

Clarinda KRSS-FM (q) 1500 S 14th St, Clarinda IA 51632 **Phn:** 660-736-4321 **Fax:** 660-736-5789 krss.me sethhiggins@gmail.com

Clinton KCLN-AM (ob) 1853 442nd Ave, Clinton IA 52732 **Phn:** 563-243-1390 **Fax:** 563-242-4567

Clinton KMCN-FM (c) 1853 442nd Ave, Clinton IA 52732 **Phn:** 563-243-1390 **Fax:** 563-242-4567 931mac.com mail@voiceofmuscatine.com

Clinton KROS-AM (a) PO Box 518, Clinton IA 52733 **Phn:** 563-242-1252 **Fax:** 563-242-4825 www.krosradio.com contactus@krosradio.com

Council Bluffs KIWR-FM (vr) 2700 College Rd, Council Bluffs IA 51503 **Phn:** 712-325-3254 **Fax:** 712-325-3391 www.897theriver.com stephaniedoty@897theriver.com

Council Bluffs KLNG-AM (qg) 120 S 35th St Ste 2, Council Bluffs IA 51501 **Phn:** 712-323-0100 **Fax:** 712-323-0022 www.wilkinsradio.com klng@wilkinsradio.com

Cresco KCZQ-FM (a) 116 1st Ave W, Cresco IA 52136 **Phn:** 563-547-1000 **Fax:** 563-547-2200

Creston KSIB-AM (c) PO Box 426, Creston IA 50801 **Phn:** 641-782-2155 **Fax:** 641-782-6963 ksibradio.com news@ksibradio.com

Creston KSIB-FM (c) PO Box 426, Creston IA 50801 **Phn:** 641-782-2155 **Fax:** 641-782-6963 ksibradio.com news@ksibradio.com

Davenport KALA-FM (vju) 518 W Locust St, Davenport IA 52803 **Phn:** 563-333-6219 **Fax:** 563-333-6218 web.sau.edukala kala@sau.edu

Davenport KBEA-FM (h) 1229 Brady St, Davenport IA 52803 **Phn:** 563-326-2541 **Fax:** 563-326-1819 www.b100.net brian.scott@cumulus.com

Davenport KBOB-FM (c) 1229 Brady St, Davenport IA 52803 **Phn:** 563-326-2541 **Fax:** 563-326-1819 www.rock1049.net dave.levora@cumulus.com

Davenport KCQQ-FM (r) 3535 E Kimberly Rd, Davenport IA 52807 **Phn:** 563-344-7000 **Fax:** 563-344-7007 www.q106online.com qcpsa@clearchannel.com

Davenport KJOC-AM (o) 1229 Brady St, Davenport IA 52803 **Phn:** 563-326-2541 **Fax:** 563-326-1819 darren.pitra@cumulus.com

Davenport KMXG-FM (a) 3535 E Kimberly Rd, Davenport IA 52807 **Phn:** 563-344-7000 **Fax:** 563-344-7007 www.mix96online.com jimohara@clearchannel.com

Davenport KQCS-FM (a) 1229 Brady St, Davenport IA 52803 **Phn:** 563-326-2541 **Fax:** 563-326-1819 www.star935fm.com darren.pitra@cumulus.com

Davenport KUUL-FM (h) 3535 E Kimberly Rd, Davenport IA 52807 **Phn:** 563-344-7101 **Fax:** 563-344-7007 www.1013kissfm.com todd@1013kissfm.com

Davenport WFXN-AM (snc) 3535 E Kimberly Rd, Davenport IA 52807 **Phn:** 563-344-7000 **Fax:** 563-344-7016 www.wfxnthefox.com ronevans@clearchannel.com

Davenport WLLR-FM (c) 3535 E Kimberly Rd, Davenport IA 52807 **Phn:** 563-344-7000 **Fax:** 563-344-7016 www.1037wllr.com jimohara@clearchannel.com

Davenport WOC-AM (nt) 3535 E Kimberly Rd, Davenport IA 52807 **Phn:** 563-344-7000 **Fax:** 563-344-7065 www.woc1420.com news@woc1420.com

Davenport WXLP-FM (r) 1229 Brady St, Davenport IA 52803 **Phn:** 563-326-2541 **Fax:** 563-326-1819 www.97x.com marissa.soliz@cumulus.com

Decorah KDEC-AM (am) PO Box 27, Decorah IA 52101 **Phn:** 563-382-4251 **Fax:** 563-382-9540 www.kdecradio.net kdec@kdecradio.net

Decorah KDEC-FM (a) PO Box 27, Decorah IA 52101 **Phn:** 563-382-4251 **Fax:** 563-382-9540 www.kdecradio.net kdec@kdecradio.net

Decorah KVIK-FM (o) 501 W Water St, Decorah IA 52101 **Phn:** 563-382-5845 **Fax:** 563-382-5581 www.kvikradio.com kvik@kvikradio.com

Decorah KWLC-AM (v) 700 College Dr, Decorah IA 52101 **Phn:** 563-387-1240 **Fax:** 563-387-2158 www.luther.edukwlc kwlcam@luther.edu

Denison KDSN-AM (c) PO Box 670, Denison IA 51442 **Phn:** 712-263-3141 **Fax:** 712-263-2088 www.kdsnradio.com info@kdsnradio.com

Denison KDSN-FM (a) PO Box 670, Denison IA 51442 **Phn:** 712-263-3141 **Fax:** 712-263-2088 www.kdsnradio.com info@kdsnradio.com

Des Moines KAZR-FM (r) 1416 Locust St, Des Moines IA 50309 **Phn:** 515-280-1350 **Fax:** 515-280-3011 www.lazer1033.com ryan@lazer1033.com

Des Moines KDFR-FM (q) PO Box 57023, Des Moines IA 50317 **Phn:** 515-262-0449 www.familyradio.com

Des Moines KDPS-FM (v) 1800 Grand Ave, Des Moines IA 50309 **Phn:** 515-242-7723 **Fax:** 515-242-7598

Des Moines KDRB-FM (h) 2141 Grand Ave, Des Moines IA 50312 **Phn:** 515-245-8900 **Fax:** 515-245-8904 www.thebusfm.com comments@thebusfm.com

Des Moines KIOA-FM (o) 1416 Locust St, Des Moines IA 50309 **Phn:** 515-280-1350 **Fax:** 515-280-3011 www.kioa.com programming@kioa.com

Des Moines KJMC-FM (u) 1169 25th St, Des Moines IA 50311 **Phn:** 515-279-1811 **Fax:** 515-279-1802 kjmcfm@mchsi.com

Des Moines KKDM-FM (h) 2141 Grand Ave, Des Moines IA 50312 **Phn:** 515-245-8900 **Fax:** 515-245-8904 www.1075kissfm.com gregchance@clearchannel.com

Des Moines KLTI-FM (a) 1416 Locust St, Des Moines IA 50309 **Phn:** 515-280-1350 **Fax:** 515-280-3011 www.lite1041.com jdelvaux@desmoinesradiogroup.com

Des Moines KPSZ-AM (q) 1416 Locust St, Des Moines IA 50309 **Phn:** 515-280-1350 **Fax:** 515-280-3011 www.praise940.com mmcdowell@desmoinesradiogroup.com

Des Moines KPTL-FM (a) 2141 Grand Ave, Des Moines IA 50312 **Phn:** 515-245-8900 **Fax:** 515-245-8904 www.capital1063.com gregchance@clearchannel.com

Des Moines KRNT-AM (bom) 1416 Locust St, Des Moines IA 50309 **Phn:** 515-280-1350 **Fax:** 515-280-3011 1350krnt.com jdelvaux@desmoinesradiogroup.com

Des Moines KSTZ-FM (a) 1416 Locust St, Des Moines IA 50309 **Phn:** 515-280-1350 **Fax:** 515-280-3011 www.star1025.com jwright@desmoinesradiogroup.com

Des Moines KXNO-AM (s) 2141 Grand Ave, Des Moines IA 50312 **Phn:** 515-245-8900 **Fax:** 515-245-8904 www.kxno.com jimboyd@clearchannel.com

Des Moines WHO-AM (nt) 2141 Grand Ave, Des Moines IA 50312 **Phn:** 515-245-8900 **Fax:** 515-245-8904 www.whoradio.com jimboyd@clearchannel.com

Des Moines WSUI-AM (pn) 2111 Grand Ave Ste 100, Des Moines IA 50312 **Phn:** 515-725-1700 **Fax:** 515-725-1714 iowapublicradio.org info@iowapublicradio.org

Dubuque KATF-FM (a) PO Box 659, Dubuque IA 52004 **Phn:** 563-690-0800 **Fax:** 563-588-0858 www.katfm.com katfm@katfm.com

Dubuque KDTH-AM (m) PO Box 659, Dubuque IA 52004 **Phn:** 563-690-0800 **Fax:** 563-690-0858 www.kdth.com kdth@kdth.com

Dubuque KGRR-FM (r) PO Box 659, Dubuque IA 52004 **Phn:** 563-690-0800 **Fax:** 563-588-0858 www.973therock.com johnrhodes@kgrr.com

Dubuque KLYV-FM (h) 5490 Saratoga Rd, Dubuque IA 52002 **Phn:** 563-557-1040 **Fax:** 563-583-4535 chris.farber@cumulus.com

Dubuque KXGE-FM (r) 5490 Saratoga Rd, Dubuque IA 52002 **Phn:** 563-557-1040 **Fax:** 563-583-4535 eagle102rocks.com jeff.robb@cumulus.com

Dubuque WDBQ-AM (nt) 5490 Saratoga Rd, Dubuque IA 52002 **Phn:** 563-557-1040 **Fax:** 563-583-4535 www.wdbqam.com ken.peiffer@cumulus.com

Dubuque WDBQ-FM (o) 5490 Saratoga Rd, Dubuque IA 52002 **Phn:** 563-557-1040 **Fax:** 563-583-4535 www.myq1075.com jolene.kilcoyne@cumulus.com

Dubuque WJOD-FM (c) 5490 Saratoga Rd, Dubuque IA 52002 **Phn:** 563-557-1040 **Fax:** 563-583-4535 www.103wjod.com ken.peiffer@cumulus.com

Dubuque WVRE-FM (c) PO Box 659, Dubuque IA 52004 **Phn:** 563-690-0800 **Fax:** 563-588-5688 www.1011theriver.com

Dyersville KDST-FM (c) 1931 20th Ave SE, Dyersville IA 52040 **Phn:** 563-875-8193 **Fax:** 563-875-6001 kdst993@iowatelecom.net

IOWA RADIO STATIONS

Eagle Grove KJYL-FM (q) PO Box 325, Eagle Grove IA 50533 **Phn:** 515-448-4588 **Fax:** 515-448-5267 www.kjyl.org kjyl@kjyl.org

Elkader KADR-AM (a) PO Box 990, Elkader IA 52043 **Phn:** 563-245-1400 **Fax:** 563-245-1402 www.kctn.com kctn@alpinecom.net

Elkader KCTN-FM (c) PO Box 990, Elkader IA 52043 **Phn:** 563-245-1400 **Fax:** 563-245-1402 www.kctn.com kctn@alpinecom.net

Estherville KILR-FM (c) PO Box 453, Estherville IA 51334 **Phn:** 712-362-2644 **Fax:** 712-362-5951 kilrradio.com kilrradio@hotmail.com

Estherville KILR-AM (nt) PO Box 453, Estherville IA 51334 **Phn:** 712-362-2644 **Fax:** 712-362-5951 kilrradio.com kilrnews@yourstarnet.net

Fairfield KHOE-FM (vl) 1000 N 4th St, Fairfield IA 52557 **Phn:** 641-469-5463 www.khoe.org khoe@mum.edu

Fairfield KKFD-FM (r) PO Box 648, Fairfield IA 52556 **Phn:** 641-472-4191 **Fax:** 641-472-2071 www.exploreseiowa.com news@fairfieldiowaradio.com

Fairfield KMCD-AM (nt) PO Box 648, Fairfield IA 52556 **Phn:** 641-472-4191 **Fax:** 641-472-2071 www.exploreseiowa.com news@fairfieldiowaradio.com

Forest City KHAM-FM (a) PO Box 308, Forest City IA 50436 **Phn:** 641-585-1073 **Fax:** 641-585-2990 www.kiow.com news@kiow.com

Forest City KIOW-FM (ac) PO Box 308, Forest City IA 50436 **Phn:** 641-585-1073 **Fax:** 641-585-2990 www.kiow.com news@kiow.com

Fort Dodge KIAQ-FM (c) 200 N 10th St, Fort Dodge IA 50501 **Phn:** 515-955-5656 **Fax:** 515-955-5844 yourfortdodge.com jmccarthy@ftdodge.threeeagles.com

Fort Dodge KKEZ-FM (ar) 200 N 10th St, Fort Dodge IA 50501 **Phn:** 515-955-5656 **Fax:** 515-955-4250 yourfortdodge.com bknight@ftdodge.threeeagles.com

Fort Dodge KTLB-FM (h) 200 N 10th St, Fort Dodge IA 50501 **Phn:** 515-955-5656 **Fax:** 515-955-5844 threeeagles.com jmccarthy@ftdodge.threeeagles.com

Fort Dodge KVFD-AM (on) 200 N 10th St, Fort Dodge IA 50501 **Phn:** 515-955-5656 **Fax:** 515-955-5844 www.threeeagles.com jmccarthy@ftdodge.threeeagles.com

Fort Dodge KWMT-AM (c) 200 N 10th St, Fort Dodge IA 50501 **Phn:** 515-955-5656 **Fax:** 515-955-5844 www.kwmt.com dmurley@ftdodge.threeeagles.com

Fort Dodge KZLB-FM (a) 200 N 10th St, Fort Dodge IA 50501 **Phn:** 515-576-7334 **Fax:** 515-955-5844 www.yourfortdodge.com sgossweiler@threeeagles.com

Grinnell KDIC-FM (v) 1115 8th Ave, Grinnell IA 50112 **Phn:** 641-269-3328 kdic.grinnell.edu kdic88.5@gmail.com

Grinnell KGRN-AM (a) PO Box 660, Grinnell IA 50112 **Phn:** 641-236-6106 **Fax:** 641-236-8896 www.myiowainfo.com kgrnnews@iowatelecom.net

Hampton KLMJ-FM (c) PO Box 495, Hampton IA 50441 **Phn:** 641-456-5656 **Fax:** 641-456-5655 www.klmj.com klmj@klmj.com

Hampton KQCR-FM (a) PO Box 495, Hampton IA 50441 **Phn:** 641-456-5656 **Fax:** 641-456-5655 www.kqcr.fm kqcr@kqcr.com

Harlan KNOD-FM (o) 902 Chatburn Ave, Harlan IA 51537 **Phn:** 712-755-3883 **Fax:** 712-755-7511 www.knodfm.com knodnews@harlannet.com

Humboldt KHBT-FM (r) PO Box 217, Humboldt IA 50548 **Phn:** 515-332-4100 **Fax:** 515-332-2723 thebolt@nrgmedia.com

Independence KQMG-AM (st) PO Box 221, Independence IA 50644 **Phn:** 319-334-3300 **Fax:** 319-334-6158

Independence KQMG-FM (a) PO Box 221, Independence IA 50644 **Phn:** 319-334-3300 **Fax:** 319-334-6158

Indianola KSTM-FM (v) 701 N C St, Indianola IA 50125 **Phn:** 515-961-1747 **Fax:** 515-961-1674

Iowa City KCJJ-AM (ant) PO Box 2118, Iowa City IA 52244 **Phn:** 319-354-1242 **Fax:** 319-354-1921 www.1630kcjj.com kcjjam@gmail.com

Iowa City KKRQ-FM (h) 1 Stephen Atkins Dr, Iowa City IA 52240 **Phn:** 319-354-9500 **Fax:** 319-354-9504 www.kkrq.com jaycapron@clearchannel.com

Iowa City KRUI-FM (v) 379 Iowa Memorial Un, Iowa City IA 52242 **Phn:** 319-335-9525 krui.fm krui@uiowa.edu

Iowa City KSUI-FM (pl) 710 S Clinton St, Iowa City IA 52240 **Phn:** 319-335-5730 **Fax:** 319-335-6116 iowapublicradio.org news@iowapublicradio.org

Iowa City KXIC-AM (nt) 1 Stephen Atkins Dr, Iowa City IA 52240 **Phn:** 319-354-9500 **Fax:** 319-354-9504 www.kxic.com news@kxic.com

Iowa Falls KIFG-AM (h) 406 Stevens St, Iowa Falls IA 50126 **Phn:** 641-648-4281 **Fax:** 641-648-4765 www.kifgradio.com kifg@iafalls.com

Iowa Falls KIFG-FM (a) PO Box 640, Iowa Falls IA 50126 **Phn:** 641-648-4281 **Fax:** 641-648-4606 www.kifgradio.com kifg@iafalls.com

Keokuk KOKX-AM (a) PO Box 427, Keokuk IA 52632 **Phn:** 319-524-5410 **Fax:** 319-524-7275 www.keokukradio.com gmkokx@mchsi.com

Keokuk KOKX-FM (o) PO Box 427, Keokuk IA 52632 **Phn:** 319-524-5410 **Fax:** 319-524-7275 www.keokukradio.com gmkokx@mchsi.com

Keokuk KRNQ-FM (r) PO Box 427, Keokuk IA 52632 **Phn:** 319-524-5410 **Fax:** 319-524-7275 www.keokukradio.com krnq963@mchsi.com

Keokuk WCEZ-FM (r) PO Box 427, Keokuk IA 52632 **Phn:** 319-524-5410 **Fax:** 319-524-7275 www.keokukradio.com krnq963@mchsi.com

Knoxville KNIA-AM (c) PO Box 31, Knoxville IA 50138 **Phn:** 641-842-3161 **Fax:** 641-842-5606 www.kniakrls.com kniakrls@kniakrls.com

Knoxville KRLS-FM (nto) PO Box 31, Knoxville IA 50138 **Phn:** 641-842-3161 **Fax:** 641-842-5606 www.kniakrls.com jmbutler@kniakrls.com

Le Mars KLEM-AM (a) 37 2nd Ave NW, Le Mars IA 51031 **Phn:** 712-546-4121 **Fax:** 712-546-9672 www.klem1410.com klem@premieronline.net

Manchester KMCH-FM (snc) PO Box 497, Manchester IA 52057 **Phn:** 563-927-6249 **Fax:** 563-927-4372 www.kmch.com mix947@kmch.com

Maquoketa KMAQ-FM (am) PO Box 940, Maquoketa IA 52060 **Phn:** 563-652-2426 **Fax:** 563-652-6210 www.kmaq.com kmaq@kmaq.com

Maquoketa KMAQ-AM (c) PO Box 940, Maquoketa IA 52060 **Phn:** 563-652-2426 **Fax:** 563-652-6210 www.kmaq.com kmaq@kmaq.com

Marshalltown KDAO-AM (m) PO Box 538, Marshalltown IA 50158 **Phn:** 641-752-4122 **Fax:** 641-752-5121 www.kdao.com kdao@kdao.com

Marshalltown KDAO-FM (a) PO Box 538, Marshalltown IA 50158 **Phn:** 641-752-4122 **Fax:** 641-752-5121 www.kdao.com kdao@kdao.com

Marshalltown KFJB-AM (nt) PO Box 698, Marshalltown IA 50158 **Phn:** 641-753-3361 **Fax:** 641-752-7201 www.1230kfjb.com news@marshalltownbroadcasting.com

Marshalltown KXIA-FM (c) 123 W Main St, Marshalltown IA 50158 **Phn:** 641-753-3361 **Fax:** 641-752-7201 www.kixweb.com office@marshalltownbroadcasting.com

Mason City KCMR-FM (v) 600 1st St NW, Mason City IA 50401 **Phn:** 641-424-9300 **Fax:** 641-424-9301

Mason City KGLO-AM (nt) 341 S Yorktown Pike, Mason City IA 50401 **Phn:** 641-423-1300 **Fax:** 641-423-2906 tfleming@kglo.threeeagles.com

Mason City KIAI-FM (c) 341 S Yorktown Pike, Mason City IA 50401 **Phn:** 641-423-1300 **Fax:** 641-423-2906

Mason City KLKK-FM (r) 31 1st St NE, Mason City IA 50401 **Phn:** 641-421-7744 **Fax:** 641-421-7755 www.klkkfm.com klkk@klkkfm.com

Mason City KLSS-FM (a) 341 S Yorktown Pike, Mason City IA 50401 **Phn:** 641-423-1300 **Fax:** 641-423-2906 www.klssradio.com rfisher@klss.threeeagles.com

Mason City KRIB-AM (o) 341 S Yorktown Pike, Mason City IA 50401 **Phn:** 641-423-1300 **Fax:** 641-423-2906 rfisher@klss.threeeagles.com

Mason City KSMA-FM (h) 31 1st St NE, Mason City IA 50401 **Phn:** 641-421-7744 **Fax:** 641-421-7755 www.987kisscountry.com jbrooks@northiowabroadcasting.com

Mason City KYTC-FM (c) 341 S Yorktown Pike, Mason City IA 50401 **Phn:** 641-423-1300 **Fax:** 641-423-2906 www.discovernorthiowa.com jallen@masoncity.threeeagles.com

Mount Pleasant KILJ-FM (c) 2411 Radio Dr, Mount Pleasant IA 52641 **Phn:** 319-385-8728 **Fax:** 319-385-4517 www.kilj.com kiljradio@kilj.com

Mount Pleasant KILJ-AM (o) 2411 Radio Dr, Mount Pleasant IA 52641 **Phn:** 319-385-8728 **Fax:** 319-385-4517 www.kilj.com kiljradio@kilj.com

Mount Vernon KRNL-FM (v) 810 Commons Cir SW, Mount Vernon IA 52314 **Phn:** 319-895-4431 orgs.cornellcollege.edukrnl mzhorne@cornellcollege.edu

Muscatine KMCS-FM (m) 3218 Mulberry Ave, Muscatine IA 52761 **Phn:** 563-263-2442 **Fax:** 563-263-9206 www.voiceofmuscatine.com mail@voiceofmuscatine.com

Muscatine KWPC-AM (a) 3218 Mulberry Ave, Muscatine IA 52761 **Phn:** 563-263-2442 **Fax:** 563-263-9206 www.voiceofmuscatine.com mail@voiceofmuscatine.com

Newton KCOB-FM (c) 1801 N 13th Ave E Ste 100, Newton IA 50208 **Phn:** 641-792-5262 **Fax:** 641-792-8403 www.myiowainfo.com info@kcobradio.com

Newton KCOB-AM (c) 1801 N 13th Ave E Ste 100, Newton IA 50208 **Phn:** 641-792-5262 **Fax:** 641-792-8403 www.myiowainfo.com info@kcobradio.com

Newton KRTI-FM (a) 1801 N 13th Ave E, Newton IA 50208 **Phn:** 641-792-5262 **Fax:** 641-792-8403 www.myiowainfo.com info@kcobradio.com

Norwalk KWKY-AM (q) PO Box 160, Norwalk IA 50211 **Phn:** 515-223-1150 **Fax:** 515-981-0840 www.iowacatholicradio.com contact@iowacatholicradio.com

Oelwein KOEL-AM (ntc) 2502 S Frederick Ave, Oelwein IA 50662 **Phn:** 319-283-1234 **Fax:** 319-283-3615 www.koel.com koelam@koel.com

Oskaloosa KBOE-FM (c) PO Box 380, Oskaloosa IA 52577 **Phn:** 641-673-3493 **Fax:** 641-673-3495 www.kboeradio.com news@kboeradio.com

IOWA RADIO STATIONS

Oskaloosa KBOE-AM (c) PO Box 380, Oskaloosa IA 52577 **Phn:** 641-673-3493 **Fax:** 641-673-3495 www.kboeradio.com news@kboeradio.com

Oskaloosa KIGC-FM (v) 201 Trueblood Ave, Oskaloosa IA 52577 **Phn:** 641-673-1095 **Fax:** 641-673-1396

Ottumwa KBIZ-AM (nt) 416 E Main St, Ottumwa IA 52501 **Phn:** 641-684-5563 **Fax:** 641-684-5832 www.kbizam.com info@ottumwaradio.com

Ottumwa KKSI-FM (r) 416 E Main St, Ottumwa IA 52501 **Phn:** 641-684-5563 **Fax:** 641-684-5832 www.kissclassicrock.com info@ottumwaradio.com

Ottumwa KLEE-AM (o) 601 W 2nd St Ste 1, Ottumwa IA 52501 **Phn:** 641-682-8711 **Fax:** 641-682-8482 kleeamottumwa.webs.com schuyler@tomfmottumwa.com

Ottumwa KOTM-FM (h) 601 W 2nd St Ste 1, Ottumwa IA 52501 **Phn:** 641-682-8711 **Fax:** 641-682-8482 www.kotm.com schuyler@tomfmottumwa.com

Ottumwa KRKN-FM (c) 416 E Main St, Ottumwa IA 52501 **Phn:** 641-684-5563 **Fax:** 641-684-5832 www.krknnewcountry.com info@ottumwaradio.com

Ottumwa KTWA-FM (a) 416 E Main St, Ottumwa IA 52501 **Phn:** 641-684-5563 **Fax:** 641-684-5832 www.ktwafm.com info@ottumwaradio.com

Pella KCUI-FM (v) 812 University St, Pella IA 50219 **Phn:** 641-628-5263 **Fax:** 641-628-5316

Perry KDLS-AM (m) 22560 141st Dr, Perry IA 50220 **Phn:** 515-465-5357 **Fax:** 515-465-3952

Perry KDLS-FM (y) 22560 141st Dr, Perry IA 50220 **Phn:** 515-465-5357 **Fax:** 515-465-3952 laley105@yahoo.com

Perry KGRA-FM (c) 22562 141st Dr, Perry IA 50220 **Phn:** 515-465-5357 **Fax:** 515-465-3952

Perry KKRF-FM (c) 22562 141st Dr, Perry IA 50220 **Phn:** 515-523-1107 **Fax:** 515-465-3952

Red Oak KCSI-FM (c) PO Box 465, Red Oak IA 51566 **Phn:** 712-623-2584 **Fax:** 712-623-2583 www.kcsifm.com kcsi@kcsifm.com

Red Oak KOAK-AM (c) PO Box 465, Red Oak IA 51566 **Phn:** 712-623-2584 **Fax:** 712-623-2583 kcsi@kcsifm.com

Sheldon KIWA-FM (r) 411 9th St, Sheldon IA 51201 **Phn:** 712-324-2597 **Fax:** 712-324-2340 www.kiwaradio.com newstips@kiwaradio.com

Sheldon KIWA-AM (cnt) 411 9th St, Sheldon IA 51201 **Phn:** 712-324-2597 **Fax:** 712-324-2340 www.kiwaradio.com newstips@kiwaradio.com

Shenandoah KMA-AM (ct) 290 N Elm St, Shenandoah IA 51601 **Phn:** 712-246-5270 **Fax:** 712-246-5275 www.kmaland.com kmaradio@kmaland.com

Shenandoah KYFR-AM (q) PO Box 286, Shenandoah IA 51601 **Phn:** 712-246-5151

Sioux Center KDCR-FM (v) 498 4th Ave NE, Sioux Center IA 51250 **Phn:** 712-722-0885 **Fax:** 712-722-6244 www.kdcr.dordt.edu kdcr@dordt.edu

Sioux Center KIHK-FM (c) PO Box 298, Sioux Center IA 51250 **Phn:** 712-722-1090 **Fax:** 712-722-1102 www.ksoufm.com caukes@siouxcountyradio.com

Sioux Center KSOU-FM (a) PO Box 298, Sioux Center IA 51250 **Phn:** 712-722-1090 **Fax:** 712-722-1102 www.ksoufm.com caukes@siouxcountyradio.com

Sioux Center KSOU-AM (q) PO Box 298, Sioux Center IA 51250 **Phn:** 712-722-1090 **Fax:** 712-722-1102 www.ksoufm.com caukes@siouxcountyradio.com

Sioux City KGLI-FM (h) 1113 Nebraska St, Sioux City IA 51105 **Phn:** 712-258-5595 **Fax:** 712-252-2430 www.kg95.com

Sioux City KKMA-FM (a) 2000 Indian Hills Dr, Sioux City IA 51104 **Phn:** 712-239-2100 **Fax:** 712-239-3346 www.kool995.com smckenzie@powelliowa.com

Sioux City KKYY-FM (c) 2000 Indian Hills Dr, Sioux City IA 51104 **Phn:** 712-239-2100 **Fax:** 712-239-3345 www.y1013.net

Sioux City KMNS-AM (nt) PO Box 3009, Sioux City IA 51102 **Phn:** 712-258-5595 **Fax:** 712-252-2430 www.620kmns.com ericbishop2@clearchannel.com

Sioux City KMSC-FM (v) 1501 Morningside Ave, Sioux City IA 51106 **Phn:** 712-274-5665 **Fax:** 712-274-5664 www.listen.tofusion88 kmsc@morningside.edu

Sioux City KQNU-FM (a) 2000 Indian Hills Dr, Sioux City IA 51104 **Phn:** 712-239-2100 **Fax:** 712-239-3346 www.q102online.com moose@q102online.com

Sioux City KSCJ-AM (nt) 2000 Indian Hills Dr, Sioux City IA 51104 **Phn:** 712-239-2100 **Fax:** 712-239-3346 www.kscj.com dbullock@powelliowa.com

Sioux City KSEZ-FM (r) PO Box 3009, Sioux City IA 51102 **Phn:** 712-258-5595 **Fax:** 712-252-2430 www.z98rocks.com

Sioux City KSFT-FM (ar) 1113 Nebraska St, Sioux City IA 51105 **Phn:** 712-258-5595 **Fax:** 712-252-2430 www.1071kissfm.com robpowers@clearchannel.com

Sioux City KSUX-FM (c) 2000 Indian Hills Dr, Sioux City IA 51104 **Phn:** 712-239-2100 **Fax:** 712-239-3346 www.ksux.com

Sioux City KTFC-FM (q) 1534 Buchanan Ave, Sioux City IA 51106 **Phn:** 712-252-4621

Sioux City KTFG-FM (qn) 1534 Buchanan Ave, Sioux City IA 51106 **Phn:** 712-252-4621

Sioux City KTFJ-AM (qnt) 4110 Floyd Blvd, Sioux City IA 51108 **Phn:** 712-239-0311

Sioux City KWIT-FM (plnj) 4647 Stone Ave, Sioux City IA 51106 **Phn:** 712-274-6406 **Fax:** 712-274-6411 www.kwit.org mindy.thompson@witcc.edu

Sioux City KWSL-AM (s) PO Box 3009, Sioux City IA 51102 **Phn:** 712-258-5595 **Fax:** 712-252-2430 www.1470kwsl.com ericbishop2@clearchannel.com

Spencer KICD-AM (nt) 2600 Highway Blvd, Spencer IA 51301 **Phn:** 712-262-1240 **Fax:** 712-262-2076 www.kicdam.com rlong@spencerradiogroup.com

Spencer KICD-FM (c) PO Box 260, Spencer IA 51301 **Phn:** 712-262-1240 **Fax:** 712-262-2076 www.cd1077fm.com rlong@spencerradiogroup.com

Spencer KLLT-FM (z) PO Box 260, Spencer IA 51301 **Phn:** 712-262-3300 **Fax:** 712-262-2076 lite1049.com lite1049@ncn.net

Spencer KUYY-FM (a) 2303 W 18th St, Spencer IA 51301 **Phn:** 712-264-1074 **Fax:** 712-264-1077 www.y1013.net

Spirit Lake KUOO-FM (a) PO Box 528, Spirit Lake IA 51360 **Phn:** 712-336-5800 **Fax:** 712-336-1634 www.kuooradio.com news@kuooradio.com

Spirit Lake KUQQ-FM (r) PO Box 528, Spirit Lake IA 51360 **Phn:** 712-336-5800 **Fax:** 712-336-1634 www.kuqqfm.com news@kuooradio.com

Storm Lake KAYL-AM (y) PO Box 1037, Storm Lake IA 50588 **Phn:** 712-732-3520 **Fax:** 712-732-1746 www.stormlakeradio.com

Storm Lake KAYL-FM (a) PO Box 1037, Storm Lake IA 50588 **Phn:** 712-732-3520 **Fax:** 712-732-1746 www.stormlakeradio.com

Storm Lake KBVU-FM (r) 610 W 4th St, Storm Lake IA 50588 **Phn:** 712-749-1234 web.bvu.eduorganizationskbvu kbvu@bvu.edu

Storm Lake KKIA-FM (c) PO Box 1037, Storm Lake IA 50588 **Phn:** 712-732-3520 **Fax:** 712-732-1746 www.stormlakeradio.com

Tama KZAT-FM (ar) PO Box 357, Tama IA 52339 **Phn:** 641-484-5958 **Fax:** 641-484-5962 www.kzat.com kzat@kzat.com

Urbandale KGGO-FM (r) 4143 109th St, Urbandale IA 50322 **Phn:** 515-331-9200 **Fax:** 515-331-9292 www.kggo.com bob.odell@cumulus.com

Urbandale KHKI-FM (c) 4143 109th St, Urbandale IA 50322 **Phn:** 515-331-9200 **Fax:** 515-331-9292 www.nashfm973.com

Urbandale KJJY-FM (c) 4143 109th St, Urbandale IA 50322 **Phn:** 515-331-9200 **Fax:** 515-331-9292 www.kjjy.com bob.odell@cumulus.com

Urbandale KWQW-FM (snt) 4143 109th St, Urbandale IA 50322 **Phn:** 515-331-9200 **Fax:** 515-331-9292 www.983wowfm.com

Washington KCII-FM (am) PO Box 524, Washington IA 52353 **Phn:** 319-653-2113 **Fax:** 319-653-3500 www.kciiradio.com kcii@kciiradio.com

Washington KCII-AM (o) PO Box 524, Washington IA 52353 **Phn:** 319-653-2113 **Fax:** 319-653-3500 www.kciiradio.com kcii@kciiradio.com

Waterloo KBBG-FM (vw) 918 Newell St, Waterloo IA 50703 **Phn:** 319-234-1441 **Fax:** 319-234-6182 www.kbbgfm.org realmanagement@kbbg.org

Waterloo KBBG-AM (ynt) 918 Newell St, Waterloo IA 50703 **Phn:** 319-235-1515 **Fax:** 319-234-6182 www.kbbgfm.org

Waterloo KCRR-FM (r) 501 Sycamore St Ste 300, Waterloo IA 50703 **Phn:** 319-833-4800 **Fax:** 319-833-4866 www.kcrr.com kcrr@kcrr.com

Waterloo KFMW-FM (r) 514 Jefferson St, Waterloo IA 50701 **Phn:** 319-234-2200 **Fax:** 319-234-0149 www.rock108.com cross@rock108.com

Waterloo KKHQ-FM (h) 501 Sycamore St Ste 300, Waterloo IA 50703 **Phn:** 319-833-4800 **Fax:** 319-833-4866 www.q923.net santini@q923.net

Waterloo KNWS-FM (q) 4880 Texas St, Waterloo IA 50702 **Phn:** 319-296-1975 **Fax:** 319-296-1977 www.life1019.com info@life1019.com

Waterloo KNWS-AM (q) 4880 Texas St, Waterloo IA 50702 **Phn:** 319-296-1975 **Fax:** 319-296-1977 www.life1019.com info@life1019.com

Waterloo KOEL-FM (c) 501 Sycamore St Ste 300, Waterloo IA 50703 **Phn:** 319-833-4800 **Fax:** 319-833-4866 www.k985.com

Waterloo KWLO-AM (mb) 514 Jefferson St, Waterloo IA 50701 **Phn:** 319-234-2200 **Fax:** 319-233-4946 tim@radiogroup.net

Waterloo KXEL-AM (nt) 514 Jefferson St, Waterloo IA 50701 **Phn:** 319-234-2200 **Fax:** 319-233-4946 www.kxel.com news@kxel.com

Waterloo KXGM-AM (q) 3232 Osage Rd, Waterloo IA 50703 **Phn:** 319-236-5700 **Fax:** 319-236-8777 www.extremegracemedia.org studio@891thespirit.com

Waukee KPUL-FM (aqr) 33365 335th St, Waukee IA 50263 **Phn:** 515-987-9995 **Fax:** 515-987-9808 pulse995.com info@pulse995.com

Waukon KHPP-AM (o) 14 W Main St, Waukon IA 52172 **Phn:** 563-568-3476 **Fax:** 563-568-3391 josh@kneiradio.com

Waukon KNEI-AM (s) 14 W Main St, Waukon IA 52172 **Phn:** 563-568-3476 **Fax:** 563-568-3391

Waukon KNEI-FM (c) 14 W Main St, Waukon IA 52172 **Phn:** 563-568-3476 **Fax:** 563-568-3391 www.kneiradio.com knei@kneiradio.com

Waverly KWAR-FM (v) 100 Wartburg Blvd, Waverly IA 50677 **Phn:** 319-352-8209 **Fax:** 319-352-8610 www.wartburgcircuit.orgKWAR899 pamela.ohrt@wartburg.edu

Waverly KWAY-AM (c) PO Box 307, Waverly IA 50677 **Phn:** 319-352-3550 **Fax:** 319-352-3601 www.kwayradio.com traffic@kwayradio.com

Waverly KWAY-FM (h) PO Box 307, Waverly IA 50677 **Phn:** 319-352-3550 **Fax:** 319-352-3601 www.kwayradio.com traffic@kwayradio.com

Webster City KQWC-FM (a) PO Box 550, Webster City IA 50595 **Phn:** 515-832-1570 **Fax:** 515-832-2079 www.kqradio.com ppowers@nrgmedia.com

Webster City KQWC-AM (a) PO Box 550, Webster City IA 50595 **Phn:** 515-832-1570 **Fax:** 515-832-2079 www.kqradio.com ppowers@nrgmedia.com

West Burlington KCPS-AM (ts) 205 S Gear Ave Ste 1, West Burlington IA 52655 **Phn:** 319-754-6698 **Fax:** 319-754-8899 www.kcpsradio.com kcps@aol.com

KANSAS

Abilene KABI-AM (am) PO Box 80, Abilene KS 67410 **Phn:** 785-823-1111 **Fax:** 785-823-2034 www.ksal.com bob.protzman@salinamediagroup.com

Abilene KJRL-FM (q) PO Box 14, Abilene KS 67410 **Phn:** 785-263-7200 **Fax:** 785-263-3876 www.kjil1057.com radioforlife@kjil.com

Abilene KSAJ-FM (o) PO Box 80, Abilene KS 67410 **Phn:** 785-823-1111 **Fax:** 785-823-2034

Arkansas City KACY-FM (r) 106 N Summit St, Arkansas City KS 67005 **Phn:** 620-442-1102 **Fax:** 620-442-8102 www.kacy.fm kacyrocks@kacy.fm

Arkansas City KSOK-AM (c) 334 E Radio Ln, Arkansas City KS 67005 **Phn:** 620-442-5400 **Fax:** 620-442-5401 www.ksokradio.com ksok@ksokradio.com

Arkansas City KSOK-FM (c) 334 E Radio Ln, Arkansas City KS 67005 **Phn:** 620-442-5400 **Fax:** 620-442-5401 www.ksokradio.com ksok@ksokradio.com

Atchison KAIR-AM (snc) PO Box G, Atchison KS 66002 **Phn:** 913-367-1470 **Fax:** 913-367-7021 www.kairfm.com kairradio@gmail.com

Atchison KAIR-FM (c) PO Box G, Atchison KS 66002 **Phn:** 913-367-1470 **Fax:** 913-367-7021 www.kairfm.com airjasondj@hotmail.com

Baldwin City KNBU-FM (crv) PO Box 65, Baldwin City KS 66006 **Phn:** 785-594-4509

Belleville KREP-FM (c) 2307 US Highway 81, Belleville KS 66935 **Phn:** 785-527-2266 **Fax:** 785-527-5919 kr-92@nckcn.com

Beloit KVSV-AM (a) PO Box 7, Beloit KS 67420 **Phn:** 785-738-2206 **Fax:** 785-738-2208 www.kvsvradio.com news@kvsvradio.com

Brewster KGCR-FM (q) PO Box 9, Brewster KS 67732 **Phn:** 785-694-2877 **Fax:** 785-694-2875 www.kgcr.org kgcr@kgcr.org

Burlington KSNP-FM (r) PO Box 233, Burlington KS 66839 **Phn:** 620-364-8807 **Fax:** 620-364-2047 www.977thedawg.com

Chanute KINZ-FM (h) 702 N Plummer Ave, Chanute KS 66720 **Phn:** 620-431-3700 **Fax:** 620-431-1943 www.kinz.biz

IOWA RADIO STATIONS

Chanute KKOY-AM (nt) 702 N Plummer Ave, Chanute KS 66720 **Phn:** 620-431-3700 **Fax:** 620-431-4643

Chanute KKOY-FM (a) 702 N Plummer Ave, Chanute KS 66720 **Phn:** 620-431-3700 **Fax:** 620-431-4643 www.kkoy.com

Clay Center KCLY-FM (acg) 1815 Meadowlark Rd, Clay Center KS 67432 **Phn:** 785-632-5661 **Fax:** 785-632-5662 www.kclyradio.com news@kclyradio.com

Clay Center KFRM-AM (nt) 1815 Meadowlark Rd, Clay Center KS 67432 **Phn:** 785-632-5661 **Fax:** 785-632-5662 www.kfrm.com kbauer@kfrm.com

Coffeyville KGGF-AM (snt) PO Box 1087, Coffeyville KS 67337 **Phn:** 620-251-3800 **Fax:** 620-251-9210 www.radioresultsgroup.com kggf.newsinfo@sbcglobal.net

Coffeyville KGGF-FM (a) PO Box 1087, Coffeyville KS 67337 **Phn:** 620-251-3800 **Fax:** 620-251-9210 www.radioresultsgroup.com kggf.newsinfo@sbcglobal.net

Coffeyville KKRK-FM (r) 306 W 8th St, Coffeyville KS 67337 **Phn:** 620-251-3800 **Fax:** 620-251-9210 www.radioresultsgroup.com kggf.newsinfo@sbcglobal.net

Coffeyville KUSN-FM (c) PO Box 1087, Coffeyville KS 67337 **Phn:** 620-251-3800 **Fax:** 620-251-9210 www.radioresultsgroup.com kggf.newsinfo@sbcglobal.net

Colby KRDQ-FM (a) 1065 S Range Ave, Colby KS 67701 **Phn:** 785-462-3305 **Fax:** 785-462-3307 kxxxkqls@rockingmradio.com

Colby KXXX-AM (c) 1065 S Range Ave, Colby KS 67701 **Phn:** 785-462-3305 **Fax:** 785-462-3307 kxxxkqls@rockingmradio.com

Concordia KCKS-FM (a) PO Box 629, Concordia KS 66901 **Phn:** 785-243-1414

Concordia KNCK-AM (ob) PO Box 629, Concordia KS 66901 **Phn:** 785-243-1414

Concordia KVCO-FM (v) 2221 Campus Dr, Concordia KS 66901 **Phn:** 785-243-4444 **Fax:** 785-243-1043

Dodge City KAHE-FM (o) 2601 Central Ave Ste C, Dodge City KS 67801 **Phn:** 620-225-8080 **Fax:** 620-225-6655 bnugen@rockingmradio.com

Dodge City KDCC-AM (vst) 3004 N 14th Ave, Dodge City KS 67801 **Phn:** 620-225-6720 **Fax:** 620-225-0918

Dodge City KGNO-AM (nt) 2601 Central Ave Ste C, Dodge City KS 67801 **Phn:** 620-225-8080 **Fax:** 620-225-6655 bnugen@rockingmradio.com

Dodge City KZRD-FM (r) 2601 Central Ave Ste C, Dodge City KS 67801 **Phn:** 620-225-8080 **Fax:** 620-225-6655

El Dorado KBTL-FM (v) 901 S Haverhill Rd, El Dorado KS 67042 **Phn:** 316-733-3881

Emporia KANS-FM (a) 918 Graham St, Emporia KS 66801 **Phn:** 620-343-9393 www.ksradio.com lisavega@ksradio.com

Emporia KFFX-FM (a) PO Box 968, Emporia KS 66801 **Phn:** 620-342-1400 **Fax:** 620-342-0804 www.kvoe.com kvoe@kvoe.com

Emporia KVOE-AM (a) PO Box 968, Emporia KS 66801 **Phn:** 620-342-1400 **Fax:** 620-342-0804 www.kvoe.com kvoe@kvoe.com

Emporia KVOE-FM (c) PO Box 968, Emporia KS 66801 **Phn:** 620-342-1400 **Fax:** 620-342-0804 www.kvoe.com kvoe@kvoe.com

Eureka KOTE-FM (c) PO Box 350, Eureka KS 67045 **Phn:** 620-583-7414 **Fax:** 620-583-7233 www.kotefm.com steve@kotefm.com

Fort Scott KMDO-AM (oh) PO Box 72, Fort Scott KS 66701 **Phn:** 620-223-4500 **Fax:** 620-223-5662 www.kombfm.com deb@kombfm.com

Fort Scott KOMB-FM (oh) PO Box 72, Fort Scott KS 66701 **Phn:** 620-223-4500 **Fax:** 620-223-5662 www.kombfm.com tim@kombfm.com

Garden City KANZ-FM (p) 210 N 7th St, Garden City KS 67846 **Phn:** 620-275-7444 **Fax:** 620-275-7496 www.hppr.org mhaslett@hppr.org

Garden City KBUF-AM (cfn) 1402 E Kansas Ave, Garden City KS 67846 **Phn:** 620-276-2366 **Fax:** 620-276-3568

Garden City KIUL-AM (snt) 609 E Kansas Plz, Garden City KS 67846 **Phn:** 620-276-3251 **Fax:** 620-276-3649 www.kiulradio.com

Garden City KKJQ-FM (c) 1402 E Kansas Ave, Garden City KS 67846 **Phn:** 620-276-2366 **Fax:** 620-276-3568

Garden City KSKZ-FM (a) 1402 E Kansas Ave, Garden City KS 67846 **Phn:** 620-276-2366 **Fax:** 620-276-3568 www.wksradio.com jamesjanda@wksradio.com

Garden City KSSA-FM (y) 1402 E Kansas Ave, Garden City KS 67846 **Phn:** 620-276-2366 **Fax:** 620-276-3568 www.wksradio.com

Garden City KWKR-FM (r) 1402 E Kansas Ave, Garden City KS 67846 **Phn:** 620-276-2366 **Fax:** 620-276-3568 www.wksradio.com jamesjanda@wksradio.com

Garden City KZNA-FM (p) 210 N 7th St, Garden City KS 67846 **Phn:** 620-275-7444 **Fax:** 620-275-7496 www.hppr.org programming@hppr.org

Glen Elder KDNS-FM (c) PO Box 88, Glen Elder KS 67446 **Phn:** 785-545-3220 **Fax:** 785-545-3191 www.kdcountry94.com kdnskzdy@nckcn.com

Glen Elder KZDY-FM (o) PO Box 88, Glen Elder KS 67446 **Phn:** 785-545-3220 www.z963thelake.com

Goodland KKCI-FM (a) 3023 W 31st St Box 569, Goodland KS 67735 **Phn:** 785-899-2309 **Fax:** 785-899-3062 www.kloe.com

Goodland KLOE-AM (sntf) 3023 W 31st St Box 569, Goodland KS 67735 **Phn:** 785-899-2309 **Fax:** 785-899-3062 www.kloe.com

Goodland KWGB-FM (c) 3023 W 31st St Box 569, Goodland KS 67735 **Phn:** 785-899-2309 **Fax:** 785-899-3062 www.nwksradio.com sacha@rockingmradio.com

Great Bend KBGL-FM (o) 1200 Baker Ave, Great Bend KS 67530 **Phn:** 620-792-3647 **Fax:** 620-792-3649

Great Bend KHOK-FM (c) 1200 Baker Ave, Great Bend KS 67530 **Phn:** 620-792-3647 **Fax:** 620-792-3649 www.khokfm.com

Great Bend KNNS-AM (s) 5501 10th St, Great Bend KS 67530 **Phn:** 620-792-7108 **Fax:** 620-792-7051

Great Bend KSOB-FM (h) 5501 10th St, Great Bend KS 67530 **Phn:** 620-792-7108 **Fax:** 620-792-7051

Great Bend KVGB-AM (nt) PO Box 609, Great Bend KS 67530 **Phn:** 620-792-3647 **Fax:** 620-792-3649 www.kvgbam.com

Great Bend KVGB-FM (r) PO Box 609, Great Bend KS 67530 **Phn:** 620-792-3647 **Fax:** 620-792-3649 www.eagleradio.net rick.nulton@eagleradio.net

Great Bend KZRS-FM (a) 5501 10th St, Great Bend KS 67530 **Phn:** 316-792-7108 **Fax:** 316-792-7051

Hays KAYS-AM (o) PO Box 6, Hays KS 67601 **Phn:** 785-625-2578 **Fax:** 785-625-3632

Hays KFIX-FM (r) PO Box 6, Hays KS 67601 **Phn:** 785-625-2578 **Fax:** 785-625-3632 www.kfix.com studio@kfix.com

KANSAS RADIO STATIONS

Hays KHAZ-FM (c) PO Box 6, Hays KS 67601 **Phn:** 785-625-2578 **Fax:** 785-625-3632 t.lynd@eagleradio.net

Hays KJLS-FM (a) PO Box 6, Hays KS 67601 **Phn:** 785-625-2578 **Fax:** 785-625-3632

Hays KKQY-FM (c) PO Box 6, Hays KS 67601 **Phn:** 785-625-2578 **Fax:** 785-625-3632 hayspost.com admin@hayspost.com

Hays KPRD-FM (q) 205 E 7th St Ste 218, Hays KS 67601 **Phn:** 785-628-6300 **Fax:** 785-628-6389 www.kprd.org kprd@kprd.org

Hiawatha KNZA-FM (c) PO Box 104, Hiawatha KS 66434 **Phn:** 785-547-3461 **Fax:** 785-547-9900 www.knzafm.com knza@rainbowtel.net

Hutchinson KHCC-FM (pln) 815 N Walnut St Ste 300, Hutchinson KS 67501 **Phn:** 620-662-6646 www.radiokansas.org comments@radiokansas.org

Hutchinson KHCD-FM (pln) 815 N Walnut St Ste 300, Hutchinson KS 67501 **Phn:** 620-662-6646 www.radiokansas.org kbaker@radiokansas.org

Hutchinson KHMY-FM (a) 825 N Main, Hutchinson KS 67501 **Phn:** 620-662-4486 **Fax:** 620-662-5357 www.khmyfm.com khmy@cox.net

Hutchinson KHUT-FM (c) PO Box 1036, Hutchinson KS 67504 **Phn:** 620-662-4486 **Fax:** 620-662-5357 www.hutchinsonscountrystation.com mark.trotman@eagleradio.net

Hutchinson KSKU-FM (a) 106 N Main St, Hutchinson KS 67501 **Phn:** 620-665-5758 **Fax:** 620-665-6655 latino.myspace.comkskuhitradio aaron@adastra.kscoxmail.com

Hutchinson KWBW-AM (snt) 825 N Main St, Hutchinson KS 67501 **Phn:** 620-662-4486 **Fax:** 620-662-5357 www.bwradio.biz info@bwradio.biz

Hutchinson KWHK-FM (o) 106 N Main St, Hutchinson KS 67501 **Phn:** 620-665-5758 **Fax:** 620-665-6655 aaron@adastra.kscoxmail.com

Hutchinson KXKU-FM (c) 106 N Main St, Hutchinson KS 67501 **Phn:** 620-665-5758 **Fax:** 620-665-6655 aaron@adastra.kscoxmail.com

Independence KIND-AM (r) 122 W Myrtle St, Independence KS 67301 **Phn:** 620-331-3000 **Fax:** 620-331-8008

Independence KIND-FM (a) 122 W Myrtle St, Independence KS 67301 **Phn:** 620-331-3000 **Fax:** 620-331-8008

Iola KIKS-FM (a) PO Box 710, Iola KS 66749 **Phn:** 620-365-3151 **Fax:** 620-365-5431 www.iolaradio.com radiostation@iolaradio.com

Junction City KJCK-AM (nt) PO Box 789, Junction City KS 66441 **Phn:** 785-762-5525 **Fax:** 785-762-5387 www.kjck.com mark.ediger@eagleradio.net

Junction City KJCK-FM (h) PO Box 789, Junction City KS 66441 **Phn:** 785-762-5525 **Fax:** 785-762-5387 www.kjck.com mark.ediger@eagleradio.net

Junction City KQLA-FM (ah) PO Box 789, Junction City KS 66441 **Phn:** 785-762-5525 **Fax:** 785-762-5387 www.kjck.com office@eagleradio.net

Kansas City KCNW-AM (q) 4535 Metropolitan Ave, Kansas City KS 66106 **Phn:** 913-384-1380 **Fax:** 913-236-9470 www.wilkinsradio.com kcnw@wilkinsradio.com

Kansas City KCZZ-AM (y) 1701 S 55th St, Kansas City KS 66106 **Phn:** 913-287-7994 **Fax:** 913-287-5881 www.reyesmediagroup.com ereyes@reyesmediagroup.com

Lawrence KANU-FM (plnj) 1120 W 11th St, Lawrence KS 66044 **Phn:** 785-864-4530 **Fax:** 785-864-5278 www.kpr.ku.edu rhunter@ku.edu

Lawrence KJHK-FM (v) 1301 Jayhawk Blvd, Lawrence KS 66045 **Phn:** 785-864-4745 kjhkarea51.org kjhkprogramming@ku.edu

Lawrence KLWN-AM (nt) 3125 W 6th St, Lawrence KS 66049 **Phn:** 785-843-1320 **Fax:** 785-841-5941 www.klwn.com trobisch@gpmnow.com

Lawrence KLZR-FM (a) 3125 W 6th St, Lawrence KS 66049 **Phn:** 785-843-1320 **Fax:** 785-841-5924 www.1059kissfm.com tlevrault@gpmnow.com

Lawrence KMXN-FM (c) 3125 W 6th St, Lawrence KS 66049 **Phn:** 785-843-1320 **Fax:** 785-841-5924 www.bull929.com trobisch@gpmnow.com

Leavenworth KKLO-AM (q) 481 Muncie Rd, Leavenworth KS 66048 **Phn:** 913-351-1410

Liberal KLDG-FM (c) 1410 N Western Ave, Liberal KS 67901 **Phn:** 620-624-3891 **Fax:** 620-624-7885 www.kscbnews.net joe@kscb.net

Liberal KSCB-AM (nt) 1410 N Western Ave, Liberal KS 67901 **Phn:** 620-624-3891 **Fax:** 620-624-9472 www.kscbnews.net mail@kscb.net

Liberal KSCB-FM (a) 1410 N Western Ave, Liberal KS 67901 **Phn:** 620-624-3891 **Fax:** 620-624-7885 www.kscbnews.net psa@kscb.net

Liberal KSMM-FM (y) 150 Plaza Dr Ste J, Liberal KS 67901 **Phn:** 620-624-8156 **Fax:** 620-624-4606 ksmmproduction@gmail.com

Liberal KZQD-FM (yq) PO Box 1893, Liberal KS 67905 **Phn:** 620-626-8282 **Fax:** 620-626-8080 www.kzqdradiolibertad.com radiolibertad@sbcglobal.net

Manhattan KACZ-FM (h) 2414 Casement Rd, Manhattan KS 66502 **Phn:** 785-776-1350 **Fax:** 785-539-1000 z963.com rwartell@1350kman.com

Manhattan KHCA-FM (q) PO Box 1471, Manhattan KS 66505 **Phn:** 785-537-9595 **Fax:** 785-537-2955 www.angel95fm.com angel95fm@hotmail.com

Manhattan KMAN-AM (snt) 2414 Casement Rd, Manhattan KS 66502 **Phn:** 785-776-1350 **Fax:** 785-539-1000 www.1350kman.com news@1350kman.com

Manhattan KMKF-FM (r) PO Box 1350, Manhattan KS 66505 **Phn:** 785-776-1350 **Fax:** 785-539-1000 www.purerock.com dubs@purerock.com

Manhattan KSDB-FM (vr) 105 Kedzie Hall Ks State U, Manhattan KS 66506 **Phn:** 785-532-0919 **Fax:** 785-532-5484 www.wildcat919.com wildcat919@gmail.com

Manhattan KXBZ-FM (c) 2414 Casement Rd, Manhattan KS 66502 **Phn:** 785-776-1350 **Fax:** 785-539-1000 www.b1047.com rwartell@1350kman.com

Marysville KNDY-FM (c) 937 Jayhawk Rd, Marysville KS 66508 **Phn:** 785-562-2361 **Fax:** 785-562-2188 www.kndyradio.com yourcountrystation@gmail.com

Marysville KNDY-AM (c) 937 Jayhawk Rd, Marysville KS 66508 **Phn:** 785-562-2361 **Fax:** 785-562-2188 www.kndyradio.com yourcountrystation@gmail.com

McPherson KBBE-FM (a) 411 E Euclid St, McPherson KS 67460 **Phn:** 620-241-1504 **Fax:** 620-241-3196 www.midkansasradio.com oldies96.7@midkansasradio.com

McPherson KNGL-AM (t) PO Box 1069, McPherson KS 67460 **Phn:** 620-241-1504 **Fax:** 620-241-3196 www.midkansasradio.com news@midkansasradio.com

Medicine Lodge KREJ-FM (q) 301 S Main St, Medicine Lodge KS 67104 **Phn:** 620-886-3537 www.krejksns.org

Mission KCFX-FM (r) 5800 Foxridge Dr Ste 600, Mission KS 66202 **Phn:** 913-514-3000 **Fax:** 913-514-3004 www.101thefox.net dan.mcclintock@cumulus.com

Mission KCHZ-FM (h) 5800 Foxridge Dr Ste 600, Mission KS 66202 **Phn:** 913-514-3000 **Fax:** 913-514-3004 www.957thevibe.com brodie@cumulus.com

Mission KCJK-FM (a) 5800 Foxridge Dr Ste 600, Mission KS 66202 **Phn:** 913-514-3000 **Fax:** 913-514-3009 www.1051jackfm.com mornings@1051jackfm.com

Mission KCMO-FM (o) 5800 Foxridge Dr Ste 600, Mission KS 66202 **Phn:** 913-514-3000 **Fax:** 913-514-3004 www.949kcmo.com mornings@1051jackfm.com

Mission KCMO-AM (t) 5800 Foxridge Dr Ste 600, Mission KS 66202 **Phn:** 913-514-3000 **Fax:** 913-514-3004 www.kcmotalkradio.com andy.barnett@cumulus.com

Mission KCSP-AM (st) 7000 Squibb Rd Ste 200, Mission KS 66202 **Phn:** 913-744-3600 **Fax:** 913-744-3700 www.610sports.com

Mission KMBZ-AM (nt) 7000 Squibb Rd Ste 200, Mission KS 66202 **Phn:** 913-744-3600 **Fax:** 913-744-3700 www.kmbz.com news@kmbz.com

Mission KQRC-FM (r) 7000 Squibb Rd Ste 200, Mission KS 66202 **Phn:** 913-744-3600 **Fax:** 913-744-3700 www.989therock.com bedwards@entercom.com

Mission KRBZ-FM (r) 7000 Squibb Rd Ste 200, Mission KS 66202 **Phn:** 913-744-3600 **Fax:** 913-744-3721 www.965thebuzz.com lazlo@entercom.com

Mission KUDL-FM (a) 7000 Squibb Rd, Mission KS 66202 **Phn:** 913-744-3600 **Fax:** 913-744-3721 www.997thepoint.com jraines@entercom.com

Mission KXTR-AM (l) 7000 Squibb Rd, Mission KS 66202 **Phn:** 913-744-3600 **Fax:** 913-677-8981 blogs.jccc.eduradiobach askbach@radiobach.com

Mission WDAF-FM (c) 7000 Squibb Rd Ste 200, Mission KS 66202 **Phn:** 913-744-3600 **Fax:** 913-744-3700 www.1065thewolf.com wpoe@entercom.com

North Newton KBCU-FM (vj) 300 E 27th St, North Newton KS 67117 **Phn:** 316-284-5273 **Fax:** 316-284-5286 www.bethelks.eduKBCU

Norton KQNK-FM (oh) 17038 Kqnk Rd, Norton KS 67654 **Phn:** 785-877-3378 **Fax:** 785-877-3379 www.kqnk.com kqnk@ruraltel.net

Norton KQNK-AM (oh) 17038 Kqnk Rd, Norton KS 67654 **Phn:** 785-877-3378 **Fax:** 785-877-3379 www.kqnk.com kqnk@ruraltel.net

Ottawa KOFO-AM (c) PO Box 16, Ottawa KS 66067 **Phn:** 785-242-1220 **Fax:** 785-242-1442 www.kofo.com kofo@kofo.com

Ottawa KTJO-FM (v) 1001 S Cedar St Box 10, Ottawa KS 66067 **Phn:** 785-242-5200

Overland Park KCTE-AM (t) 6721 W 121st St, Overland Park KS 66209 **Phn:** 913-344-1500 **Fax:** 913-344-1599 www.1510.com chadboeger@810whb.com

Overland Park KLJC-FM (q) 8717 W 110th St # 480, Overland Park KS 66210 **Phn:** 816-331-8700 **Fax:** 816-331-3497 life885.com

Overland Park WHB-AM (st) 6721 W 121st St, Overland Park KS 66209 **Phn:** 913-344-1563 **Fax:** 913-344-1599 www.810whb.com info@810whb.com

Parsons KLKC-AM (nt) PO Box 853, Parsons KS 67357 **Phn:** 620-421-6400 **Fax:** 620-421-5570 www.sekinfo.com

Parsons KLKC-FM (a) PO Box 853, Parsons KS 67357 **Phn:** 620-421-6400 **Fax:** 620-421-5570 www.sekinfo.com

Phillipsburg KKAN-AM (m) PO Box 548, Phillipsburg KS 67661 **Phn:** 785-543-2151 **Fax:** 785-543-2152 www.kkankqma.com bobyates@kkankqma.com

Phillipsburg KQMA-FM (m) PO Box 548, Phillipsburg KS 67661 **Phn:** 785-543-2151 **Fax:** 785-543-2152 www.kkankqma.com bobyates@kkankqma.com

Pittsburg KBZI-FM (r) 1162 E Highway 126, Pittsburg KS 66762 **Phn:** 620-231-7200 **Fax:** 620-231-3321

Pittsburg KHST-FM (r) 412 N Locust St, Pittsburg KS 66762 **Phn:** 620-232-5993 **Fax:** 620-232-5550 mycountry1017.com

Pittsburg KKOW-FM (c) 1162 E Highway 126, Pittsburg KS 66762 **Phn:** 620-231-7200 **Fax:** 620-231-3321 www.kkowfm.com kkow@kkowradio.com

Pittsburg KKOW-AM (c) 1162 E Highway 126, Pittsburg KS 66762 **Phn:** 620-231-7200 **Fax:** 620-231-3321 www.kkowradio.com kkow@kkowradio.com

Pittsburg KRPS-FM (plnj) PO Box 899, Pittsburg KS 66762 **Phn:** 620-235-4288 **Fax:** 620-235-4290 www.krps.org krps@pittstate.edu

Pittsburg KSEK-AM (s) 202 E Centennial Dr # B-2, Pittsburg KS 66762 **Phn:** 620-232-9912 **Fax:** 620-232-9915

Pittsburg KSEK-FM (r) 202 E Centennial Dr # B-2, Pittsburg KS 66762 **Phn:** 620-232-9912 **Fax:** 620-232-9915

Pittsburg KWXD-FM (o) 412 N Locust St, Pittsburg KS 66762 **Phn:** 620-232-5993 **Fax:** 620-232-5550 www.1035x.net

Pratt KMMM-AM (ont) PO Box 486, Pratt KS 67124 **Phn:** 620-672-5581 **Fax:** 620-672-5583 www.superhits1290.com lcoss@rockingmradio.com

Russell KCAY-FM (a) PO Box 666, Russell KS 67665 **Phn:** 785-483-3121 **Fax:** 785-483-6511 www.krsl.com mike@krsl.com

Russell KRSL-AM (a) PO Box 666, Russell KS 67665 **Phn:** 785-483-3121 **Fax:** 785-483-6511 www.krsl.com comments@krsl.com

Salina KBLS-FM (a) PO Box 80, Salina KS 67402 **Phn:** 785-823-1111 **Fax:** 785-823-2034 www.sunny1025.com john.anderson@sunny1025.com

Salina KINA-AM (t) 1825 S Ohio St, Salina KS 67401 **Phn:** 785-825-4631 **Fax:** 785-825-4600

Salina KSAL-FM (a) PO Box 80, Salina KS 67402 **Phn:** 785-823-1111 **Fax:** 785-823-2034 www.1049classichits.com todd.pittenger@morris.com

Salina KSAL-AM (nt) PO Box 80, Salina KS 67402 **Phn:** 785-823-1111 **Fax:** 785-823-2034 www.ksallink.com todd.pittenger@salinamediagroup.com

Salina KSKG-FM (c) 1825 S Ohio St, Salina KS 67401 **Phn:** 785-825-4631 **Fax:** 785-825-4600

Salina KUOB-FM (ah) 641 W Cloud St, Salina KS 67401 **Phn:** 785-827-2100 **Fax:** 785-827-3503

Salina KVOB-FM (r) 641 W Cloud St, Salina KS 67401 **Phn:** 785-827-2100 **Fax:** 785-827-3503

Salina KYEZ-FM (c) PO Box 80, Salina KS 67402 **Phn:** 785-823-1111 **Fax:** 785-823-2034 www.y937.com todd.pittenger@morris.com

Salina KZUH-FM (s) 641 W Cloud St, Salina KS 67401 **Phn:** 785-827-2100 **Fax:** 785-827-3503

Seneca KMZA-FM (cns) PO Box 92, Seneca KS 66538 **Phn:** 785-336-6166 **Fax:** 785-336-3600 www.kmzafm.com kmza@bbwi.net

Shawnee Mission KCCV-FM (q) 10550 Barkley St Ste 112, Shawnee Mission KS 66212 **Phn:** 913-642-7600 **Fax:** 913-642-2424 www.bottradionetwork.com kccv@bottradionetwork.com

Shawnee Mission KCCV-AM (q) 10550 Barkley St Ste 112, Shawnee Mission KS 66212 **Phn:** 913-642-7600 **Fax:** 913-642-2424 www.bottradionetwork.com kccv@bottradionetwork.com

Topeka KCVT-FM (qnt) 534 S Kansas Ave Ste 930, Topeka KS 66603 **Phn:** 785-233-9250 **Fax:** 785-233-9260 www.bottradionetwork.com kcvt@bottradionetwork.com

Topeka KDVV-FM (r) 825 S Kansas Ave Fl 1, Topeka KS 66612 **Phn:** 785-272-2122 **Fax:** 785-272-6219 www.v100rocks.com

Topeka KMAJ-FM (a) 825 S Kansas Ave Fl 1, Topeka KS 66612 **Phn:** 785-272-2122 **Fax:** 785-272-6219 www.kmaj.com debbie.walsh@cumulus.com

Topeka KMAJ-AM (snt) 825 S Kansas Ave Fl 1, Topeka KS 66612 **Phn:** 785-272-2122 **Fax:** 785-272-6219

Topeka KTOP-FM (c) 825 S Kansas Ave # 100, Topeka KS 66612 **Phn:** 785-272-2122 **Fax:** 785-272-6219 www.ktopcountry.com bobby.hapgood@cumulus.com

Topeka KTOP-AM (m) 825 S Kansas Ave # 100, Topeka KS 66612 **Phn:** 785-272-2122 **Fax:** 785-272-6219 ktop1490.com forrest@v100rocks.com

Topeka KTPK-FM (c) 2121 SW Chelsea Dr, Topeka KS 66614 **Phn:** 785-273-1069 **Fax:** 785-273-0123 Countrylegends1069fm.com robb@countrylegends1069.com

Topeka KWIC-FM (h) 825 S Kansas Ave Fl 1, Topeka KS 66612 **Phn:** 785-272-2122 **Fax:** 785-272-6219 www.eagle993.com debbie.walsh@cumulus.com

Topeka WIBW-FM (c) 1210 SW Executive Dr, Topeka KS 66615 **Phn:** 785-272-3456 **Fax:** 785-228-7282 www.94country.com keith@94country.com

Topeka WIBW-AM (nt) 1210 SW Executive Dr, Topeka KS 66615 **Phn:** 785-272-3456 **Fax:** 785-228-7282 www.wibwnewsnow.com shawn.wheat@morris.com

Ulysses KULY-AM (cn) 2917 S Colorado St, Ulysses KS 67880 **Phn:** 620-356-1420 **Fax:** 620-356-3635

Wellington KKLE-AM (snt) PO Box 249, Wellington KS 67152 **Phn:** 620-326-3341 **Fax:** 620-326-8512 www.kkle.com kley@sutv.com

Wellington KLEY-AM (snt) PO Box 249, Wellington KS 67152 **Phn:** 620-326-3341 **Fax:** 620-326-8512 www.kleyam.com kley@sutv.com

Wellington KWME-FM (o) PO Box 249, Wellington KS 67152 **Phn:** 620-326-3341 **Fax:** 620-326-8512 www.kwme.com kley@sutv.com

Wichita KCFN-FM (q) 720 N Murray St, Wichita KS 67212 **Phn:** 316-831-9111 **Fax:** 316-831-9119

Wichita KDGS-FM (h) 2120 N Woodlawn St Ste 352, Wichita KS 67208 **Phn:** 316-685-2121 **Fax:** 316-685-3408 www.power939.com gwilliams@entercom.com

Wichita KEYN-FM (o) 2120 N Woodlawn St Ste 352, Wichita KS 67208 **Phn:** 316-685-2121 **Fax:** 316-685-3408 www.keyn.com jack@keyn.com

Wichita KFBZ-FM (ar) 2120 N Woodlawn St Ste 352, Wichita KS 67208 **Phn:** 316-685-2121 **Fax:** 316-685-3408 www.1053thebuzz.com dhayes@entercom.com

Wichita KFDI-FM (c) 4200 N Old Lawrence Rd, Wichita KS 67219 **Phn:** 316-838-9141 **Fax:** 316-838-3607 www.kfdi.com emccart@journalbroadcastgroup.com

Wichita KFH-AM (t) 2120 N Woodlawn St Ste 352, Wichita KS 67208 **Phn:** 316-685-2121 **Fax:** 316-685-3408 www.kfhradio.com tony@kfhradio.com

Wichita KFH-FM (t) 2120 N Woodlawn St Ste 352, Wichita KS 67208 **Phn:** 316-685-2121 **Fax:** 316-685-3408 www.kfhradio.com tony@kfhradio.com

Wichita KFTI-AM (c) 4200 N Old Lawrence Rd, Wichita KS 67219 **Phn:** 316-838-9141 **Fax:** 316-838-3607 www.trueoldies1070.com emccart@journalbroadcastgroup.com

Wichita KFXJ-FM (r) 4200 N Old Lawrence Rd, Wichita KS 67219 **Phn:** 316-838-9141 **Fax:** 316-838-3607 www.1045thefox.com emccart@journalbroadcastgroup.com

Wichita KGSO-AM (s) 1632 S Maize Rd Ste 100, Wichita KS 67209 **Phn:** 316-721-8484 **Fax:** 316-721-8276 www.kgso.com gsteckline@maanradio.com

Wichita KIBB-FM (a) 1938 N Woodlawn St Ste 150, Wichita KS 67208 **Phn:** 316-558-8800 **Fax:** 316-558-8802 www.971bobfm.com pjames@connoisseurwichita.com

Wichita KICT-FM (r) 4200 N Old Lawrence Rd, Wichita KS 67219 **Phn:** 316-838-9141 **Fax:** 316-838-3607 www.t95.com emccart@journalbroadcastgroup.com

Wichita KMUW-FM (pn) 3317 E 17th St N, Wichita KS 67208 **Phn:** 316-978-6789 **Fax:** 316-978-3946 www.kmuw.org info@kmuw.org

Wichita KNSS-AM (nt) 2120 N Woodlawn St Ste 352, Wichita KS 67208 **Phn:** 316-685-2121 **Fax:** 316-685-3314 www.knssradio.com news@knssradio.com

Wichita KRBB-FM (a) 9323 E 37th St N, Wichita KS 67226 **Phn:** 316-494-6600 **Fax:** 316-494-6730 www.b98fm.com dave@b98fm.com

Wichita KSGL-AM (qa) 3337 W Central Ave, Wichita KS 67203 **Phn:** 316-942-3231 **Fax:** 316-942-9314 www.ksgl.com am900@ksgl.com

Wichita KTHR-FM (r) 9323 E 37th St N, Wichita KS 67226 **Phn:** 316-494-6600 **Fax:** 316-494-6730 www.1073thebrew.com dickharlow@clearchannel.com

Wichita KTLI-FM (q) 125 N Market St Ste 1900, Wichita KS 67202 **Phn:** 316-303-9999 **Fax:** 316-303-9900

Wichita KVWF-FM (c) 1938 N Woodlawn St Ste 150, Wichita KS 67208 **Phn:** 316-558-8800 **Fax:** 316-558-8802 www.wichitawolf.com pjames@connoisseurwichita.com

Wichita KYQQ-FM (y) 4200 N Old Lawrence Rd, Wichita KS 67219 **Phn:** 316-838-9141 **Fax:** 316-838-3607 www.radiolobo1065.com bbrannigan@kfdi.com

Wichita KZCH-FM (h) 9323 E 37th St N, Wichita KS 67226 **Phn:** 316-494-6600 www.channel963.com wichitanews@clearchannel.com

Wichita KZSN-FM (c) 9323 E 37th St N, Wichita KS 67226 **Phn:** 316-494-6600 **Fax:** 316-494-6730 www.1021thebull.com brianjennings@clearchannel.com

KENTUCKY

Albany WANY-AM (c) PO Box 400, Albany KY 42602 **Phn:** 606-387-5186 **Fax:** 606-387-6595

Albany WANY-FM (c) PO Box 400, Albany KY 42602 **Phn:** 606-387-5186 **Fax:** 606-387-6595 wanyradio@hotmail.com

Ashland WYHY-AM (c) 3027 Lester Ln, Ashland KY 41102 **Phn:** 606-928-3778 **Fax:** 606-928-1659

Barbourville WKKQ-FM (a) 222 Daniel Boone Dr, Barbourville KY 40906 **Phn:** 606-546-4128 **Fax:** 606-546-4138

Barbourville WYWY-AM (g) 222 Daniel Boone Dr, Barbourville KY 40906 **Phn:** 606-546-4128 **Fax:** 606-546-4138

KENTUCKY RADIO STATIONS

Bardstown WBRT-AM (c) 106 S 3rd St, Bardstown KY 40004 **Phn:** 502-348-3943 **Fax:** 502-348-4043 www.wbrtcountry.com info@wbrtradio.com

Beattyville WLJC-FM (g) PO Box Y, Beattyville KY 41311 **Phn:** 606-464-3600 www.wljc.com wljc@wljc.com

Benton WCBL-FM (o) PO Box 387, Benton KY 42025 **Phn:** 270-527-3102 **Fax:** 270-527-5606 www.wcblradio.com wcbl@bellsouth.net

Benton WCBL-AM (c) PO Box 387, Benton KY 42025 **Phn:** 270-527-3102 **Fax:** 270-527-5606 www.wcblradio.com wcbl@bellsouth.net

Bowling Green WBGN-AM (snt) 1919 Scottsville Rd, Bowling Green KY 42104 **Phn:** 270-843-3333 **Fax:** 270-843-0454 www.1340wbgn.com sportsguys@1340wbgn.com

Bowling Green WBVR-FM (c) 1919 Scottsville Rd, Bowling Green KY 42104 **Phn:** 270-843-3333 **Fax:** 270-843-0454 www.beaverfm.com mthomas@beaverfm.com

Bowling Green WCVK-FM (q) PO Box 539, Bowling Green KY 42102 **Phn:** 270-781-7326 **Fax:** 270-781-8005 www.christianfamilyradio.com donna@christianfamilyradio.com

Bowling Green WDNS-FM (r) PO Box 930, Bowling Green KY 42102 **Phn:** 270-781-2121 **Fax:** 270-842-0232 www.wdnsfm.com alan@wdnsfm.com

Bowling Green WGGC-FM (c) PO Box 70163, Bowling Green KY 42102 **Phn:** 270-782-9595 **Fax:** 270-783-8665 www.wggc.com darrin@wggc.com

Bowling Green WKCT-AM (nt) PO Box 930, Bowling Green KY 42102 **Phn:** 270-781-2121 **Fax:** 270-842-0232 www.93wkct.com

Bowling Green WKLX-FM (h) 1823 McIntosh St Ste 107, Bowling Green KY 42104 **Phn:** 270-842-4487 **Fax:** 270-783-8829 www.bowlinggreensam.com tonyrose@commonwealthbroadcasting.com

Bowling Green WKYU-FM (pln) 1906 College Heights Blvd # 11035, Bowling Green KY 42101 **Phn:** 270-745-5489 **Fax:** 270-745-6272 www.wkyufm.org wkyufm@wku.edu

Bowling Green WLYE-FM (c) 1919 Scottsville Rd, Bowling Green KY 42104 **Phn:** 270-843-3333 **Fax:** 270-843-0454 www.willie941.com mthomas@beaverfm.com

Bowling Green WQGY-FM (h) 1919 Scottsville Rd, Bowling Green KY 42104 **Phn:** 270-843-3333

Bowling Green WTJW-AM (h) 1919 Scottsville Rd, Bowling Green KY 42104 **Phn:** 270-843-3333

Bowling Green WUHU-FM (a) 1919 Scottsville Rd, Bowling Green KY 42104 **Phn:** 270-843-3333 **Fax:** 270-843-0454 www.allhitwuhu107.com kirk@allhitwuhu107.com

Bowling Green WWHR-FM (vr) Western Ky Univ, Bowling Green KY 42101 **Phn:** 270-745-5439 revolution.fm info@revolution.fm

Brandenburg WMMG-FM (c) PO Box 505, Brandenburg KY 40108 **Phn:** 270-422-3961 **Fax:** 270-422-3464 wmmg935@bbtel.com

Brandenburg WMMG-AM (c) PO Box 505, Brandenburg KY 40108 **Phn:** 270-422-3961 **Fax:** 270-422-3464 wmmg935@bbtel.com

Burkesville WKYR-FM (c) PO Box 340, Burkesville KY 42717 **Phn:** 270-433-7191 **Fax:** 270-433-7195 wkyr@mchsi.com

Cadiz WHVO-AM (o) PO Box 1900, Cadiz KY 42211 **Phn:** 270-886-1480 **Fax:** 270-886-6286 www.oldies1480.com bmann@wkdzradio.com

Cadiz WKDZ-FM (c) PO Box 1900, Cadiz KY 42211 **Phn:** 270-522-3232 **Fax:** 270-522-1110 www.wkdzradio.com awatts@wkdzradio.com

Cadiz WKDZ-AM (nt) PO Box 1900, Cadiz KY 42211 **Phn:** 270-522-3232 **Fax:** 270-522-1110 www.wkdzradio.com wkdz@wkdzradio.com

Calvert City WCCK-FM (c) PO Box 1116, Calvert City KY 42029 **Phn:** 270-395-5133 **Fax:** 270-395-5231 wcck@freelandbroadcasting.com

Campbellsville WCKQ-FM (a) PO Box 1053, Campbellsville KY 42719 **Phn:** 270-789-2401 **Fax:** 270-789-1450 www.myq104.com wckq@commonwealthbroadcasting.com

Campbellsville WGRK-FM (c) PO Box 1053, Campbellsville KY 42719 **Phn:** 270-789-1464 **Fax:** 270-789-1450 kcountry1057.com wgrk@commonwealthbroadcasting.com

Campbellsville WGRK-AM (c) PO Box 1053, Campbellsville KY 42719 **Phn:** 270-789-1464 **Fax:** 270-789-1450 www.kcountry1057.com wgrk@commonwealthbroadcasting.com

Campbellsville WTCO-AM (s) PO Box 1053, Campbellsville KY 42719 **Phn:** 270-789-2401 **Fax:** 270-789-1450 www.wtcosports.com rcollins@commonwealthbroadcasting.com

Campbellsville WVLC-FM (c) PO Box 4190, Campbellsville KY 42719 **Phn:** 270-789-4998 **Fax:** 270-789-4584 www.wvlc.com bigdawg@wvlc.com

Central City WNES-AM (c) PO Box 471, Central City KY 42330 **Phn:** 270-754-3000 **Fax:** 270-754-3710

Central City WQXQ-FM (a) PO Box 471, Central City KY 42330 **Phn:** 270-754-3000 **Fax:** 270-754-3710

Columbia WAIN-FM (c) 1521 Liberty Rd, Columbia KY 42728 **Phn:** 270-384-2135 **Fax:** 270-384-6722 www.935wain.com wain@keybroadcasting.net

Columbia WAIN-AM (o) 1521 Liberty Rd, Columbia KY 42728 **Phn:** 270-384-2135 **Fax:** 270-384-6722

Columbia WHVE-FM (a) PO Box 927, Columbia KY 42728 **Phn:** 270-384-7979 **Fax:** 270-384-6244 www.ridingthewave.com thewave@ridingthewave.com

Corbin WCTT-AM (am) 821 Adams Rd, Corbin KY 40701 **Phn:** 606-528-4717 **Fax:** 606-528-4487

Corbin WCTT-FM (a) 821 Adams Rd, Corbin KY 40701 **Phn:** 606-528-4717 **Fax:** 606-528-4487 t1073.com

Corbin WKDP-AM (nt) 821 Adams Rd, Corbin KY 40701 **Phn:** 606-528-6617 **Fax:** 606-528-4487 www.kdcountry995.com

Corbin WKDP-FM (c) 821 Adams Rd, Corbin KY 40701 **Phn:** 606-528-6617 **Fax:** 606-528-4487 www.kdcountry995.com

Covington WCVG-AM (y) 135 W 38th St, Covington KY 41015 **Phn:** 859-291-2255

Cumberland WCPM-AM (qc) 101 Keller St, Cumberland KY 40823 **Phn:** 606-589-4623 www.wcpmradio.com wcpmradio@windstream.net

Cynthiana WCYN-AM (o) 111 Court St, Cynthiana KY 41031 **Phn:** 859-234-1004 **Fax:** 859-234-1425 www.wcyn.com chris.winkle@wcyn.com

Danville WDFB-AM (gq) 3596 Alum Springs Rd, Danville KY 40422 **Phn:** 859-236-9333 **Fax:** 859-236-3348 wdfb.com wdfb@wdfb.org

Danville WDFB-FM (vq) 3596 Alum Springs Rd, Danville KY 40422 **Phn:** 859-236-9333 **Fax:** 859-236-3348 www.wdfb.com wdfb@wdfb.org

Danville WHBN-AM (c) 2063 Shakertown Rd, Danville KY 40422 **Phn:** 859-734-4321 **Fax:** 859-734-5786 hometownlive.net hometownnews@bellsouth.net

Danville WHIR-AM (nt) 2063 Shakertown Rd, Danville KY 40422 **Phn:** 859-236-2711 **Fax:** 859-236-1461 hometownlive.net hometownnews@bellsouth.net

Danville WRNZ-FM (a) 2063 Shakertown Rd, Danville KY 40422 **Phn:** 859-236-2711 **Fax:** 859-236-1461 hometownlive.net hometownnews@bellsouth.net

Dry Ridge WNKR-FM (c) PO Box 182, Dry Ridge KY 41035 **Phn:** 859-824-9106 **Fax:** 859-824-9835 wnkrproduction@fuse.net

Elizabethtown WAKY-FM (o) PO Box 2087, Elizabethtown KY 42702 **Phn:** 502-584-9259 www.waky1035.com rbell@waky1035.com

Elizabethtown WIEL-AM (s) 611 W Poplar St Ste C2, Elizabethtown KY 42701 **Phn:** 270-763-0800 **Fax:** 270-769-6349

Elizabethtown WKMO-FM (c) 611 W Poplar St Ste C2, Elizabethtown KY 42701 **Phn:** 270-763-0800 **Fax:** 270-769-6349

Elizabethtown WLVK-FM (c) PO Box 2087, Elizabethtown KY 42702 **Phn:** 270-766-1035 **Fax:** 270-769-1052 www.bigcat1055.com rbell@waky1035.com

Elizabethtown WQXE-FM (a) 233 W Dixie Ave, Elizabethtown KY 42701 **Phn:** 270-737-8000 **Fax:** 270-737-7229 www.wqxe.com quicksie@wqxe.com

Elizabethtown WRZI-FM (r) 611 W Poplar St Ste C2, Elizabethtown KY 42701 **Phn:** 270-763-0800 **Fax:** 270-769-6349 www.1073thepoint.com news@commonwealthbroadcasting.com

Elizabethtown WTHX-FM (s) 611 W Poplar St Ste C2, Elizabethtown KY 42701 **Phn:** 270-763-0800 **Fax:** 270-769-6349

Elizabethtown WULF-FM (c) 233 W Dixie Ave, Elizabethtown KY 42701 **Phn:** 270-765-0943 **Fax:** 270-737-7229 www.943wulf.com

Elizabethtown WXAM-AM (s) 611 W Poplar St Ste C2, Elizabethtown KY 42701 **Phn:** 270-358-4707 **Fax:** 270-358-4755

Elkton WEKT-AM (g) PO Box 577, Elkton KY 42220 **Phn:** 270-265-5636 **Fax:** 270-265-5637 wektam1070@yahoo.com

Falmouth WIDS-AM (g) PO Box 50, Falmouth KY 41040 **Phn:** 859-472-1075 **Fax:** 859-472-2875 www.wiok.com wiok@fuse.net

Falmouth WIOK-FM (gq) PO Box 50, Falmouth KY 41040 **Phn:** 859-472-1075 **Fax:** 859-472-2875 www.wiok.com wiok@fuse.net

Falmouth WYGH-AM (q) PO Box 50, Falmouth KY 41040 **Phn:** 859-472-1075 **Fax:** 859-472-2875 www.wiok.com wiok@fuse.net

Flemingsburg WFLE-FM (c) 334 Recreation Park Rd, Flemingsburg KY 41041 **Phn:** 606-849-4433 **Fax:** 606-845-9353

Flemingsburg WFLE-AM (g) 334 Recreation Park Rd, Flemingsburg KY 41041 **Phn:** 606-849-4433 **Fax:** 606-845-9353

Frankfort WCND-AM (o) 115 W Main St, Frankfort KY 40601 **Phn:** 502-875-1130 **Fax:** 502-875-1225

Frankfort WFKY-FM (c) 115 W Main St, Frankfort KY 40601 **Phn:** 502-875-1130 **Fax:** 502-875-1225 www.myfroggyville.com cricket@capcityradio.com

Frankfort WFKY-AM (o) 115 W Main St, Frankfort KY 40601 **Phn:** 502-875-1130 **Fax:** 502-875-1225

Frankfort WKED-FM (a) 115 W Main St, Frankfort KY 40601 **Phn:** 502-875-1130 **Fax:** 502-875-1225

Frankfort WKYW-AM (c) 115 W Main St, Frankfort KY 40601 **Phn:** 502-875-1130 **Fax:** 502-875-1225

KENTUCKY RADIO STATIONS

Frankfort WSTV-FM (ah) 115 W Main St, Frankfort KY 40601 **Phn:** 502-875-1130 **Fax:** 502-875-1225 www.star1037.com kaytlin@capcityradio.com

Franklin WFKN-AM (c) 103 N High St, Franklin KY 42134 **Phn:** 270-586-4481 **Fax:** 270-586-6031 kpyles@franklinfavorite.com

Fulton WFUL-AM (oam) 8807 State Route 166 E, Fulton KY 42041 **Phn:** 270-472-1270 **Fax:** 270-472-1189

Glasgow WCDS-AM (s) PO Box 457, Glasgow KY 42142 **Phn:** 270-651-6050 **Fax:** 270-651-7666

Glasgow WCLU-AM (ma) PO Box 1628, Glasgow KY 42142 **Phn:** 270-651-9149 **Fax:** 270-651-9222 wcluradio.com henryroyse@wcluradio.com

Glasgow WCLU-FM (a) PO Box 1628, Glasgow KY 42142 **Phn:** 270-651-9149 **Fax:** 270-651-9222 wcluradio.com news@wcluradio.com

Glasgow WHHT-FM (a) PO Box 457, Glasgow KY 42142 **Phn:** 270-651-6050 **Fax:** 270-651-7666

Glasgow WOVO-FM (o) 113 W Public Sq Ste 400, Glasgow KY 42141 **Phn:** 270-651-6050 **Fax:** 270-651-7666 www.my1053.com rex1053@yahoo.com

Glasgow WPTQ-FM (r) PO Box 457, Glasgow KY 42142 **Phn:** 270-651-6060 **Fax:** 270-651-7666 www.1037thepoint.net

Grayson WGOH-AM (c) PO Box 487, Grayson KY 41143 **Phn:** 606-474-5144 **Fax:** 606-474-7777 www.wgohwugo.com mail@wgohwugo.com

Grayson WUGO-FM (a) PO Box 487, Grayson KY 41143 **Phn:** 606-474-5144 **Fax:** 606-474-7777 www.wgohwugo.com mail@wgohwugo.com

Hardin WAAJ-FM (q) PO Box 281, Hardin KY 42048 **Phn:** 270-437-4095 **Fax:** 270-437-4098

Hardin WVHM-FM (q) PO Box 281, Hardin KY 42048 **Phn:** 270-437-4095 **Fax:** 270-437-4098 www.hmiradio.com info@hmiradio.com

Hardinsburg WXBC-FM (ac) PO Box 104, Hardinsburg KY 40143 **Phn:** 270-756-1043 **Fax:** 270-756-1086 www.wxbc1043.com wxbc@bbtel.com

Harlan WFSR-AM (g) PO Box 818, Harlan KY 40831 **Phn:** 606-573-1470 **Fax:** 606-573-1473 www.wtuk1051.com wtuk-wfsr@harlanonline.net

Harlan WHLN-AM (o) PO Box 898, Harlan KY 40831 **Phn:** 606-573-2540 **Fax:** 606-573-7557 whln@harlanonline.net

Harlan WTUK-FM (c) PO Box 818, Harlan KY 40831 **Phn:** 606-573-1470 **Fax:** 606-573-1473 www.wtuk1051.com wtuk-wfsr@harlanonline.net

Harold WIFX-FM (ua) 98 Church Rd, Harold KY 41635 **Phn:** 606-633-9430 **Fax:** 606-478-9439 www.foxy943.com wifx@foxy943.com

Harold WXKZ-FM (ro) 98 Church Rd, Harold KY 41635 **Phn:** 606-478-1200 **Fax:** 606-478-1050 adam@gearheart.com

Harold WXLR-FM (r) 98 Church Rd, Harold KY 41635 **Phn:** 606-478-1200 **Fax:** 606-478-4202

Hartford WAIA-AM (st) 314 S Main St, Hartford KY 42347 **Phn:** 270-298-3268 **Fax:** 270-298-9326

Hartford WXMZ-FM (r) 314 S Main St, Hartford KY 42347 **Phn:** 270-298-3268 **Fax:** 270-298-9326

Hazard WJMD-FM (qg) PO Box 7001, Hazard KY 41702 **Phn:** 606-439-3358 **Fax:** 606-439-3371 www.wjmd104.com wjmd@windstream.net

Hazard WKIC-AM (h) PO Box 7428, Hazard KY 41702 **Phn:** 606-436-2121 **Fax:** 606-436-4172 www.wsgs.com wsgs@windstream.net

Hazard WSGS-FM (c) PO Box 7428, Hazard KY 41702 **Phn:** 606-436-2121 **Fax:** 606-436-4172 www.wsgs.com wsgs@windstream.net

Henderson WSON-AM (m) PO Box 418, Henderson KY 42419 **Phn:** 270-826-3923 **Fax:** 270-826-7572

Highland Heights WNKU-FM (r) N KY Univ 301 Landrum, Highland Heights KY 41099 **Phn:** 859-572-6500 **Fax:** 859-572-6604 www.wnku.org radio@wnku.org

Hindman WKCB-FM (r) PO Box 864, Hindman KY 41822 **Phn:** 606-785-3129 **Fax:** 606-785-0106 www.wkcb.com

Hindman WKCB-AM (q) PO Box 864, Hindman KY 41822 **Phn:** 606-785-3129 **Fax:** 606-785-0106

Hopkinsville WHOP-AM (nt) PO Box 709, Hopkinsville KY 42241 **Phn:** 270-885-5331 **Fax:** 270-885-2688 www.whopam.com jesisk@forchtbroadcasting.com

Hopkinsville WHOP-FM (a) PO Box 709, Hopkinsville KY 42241 **Phn:** 270-885-5331 **Fax:** 270-885-2688 www.lite987whop.com jesisk@forchtbroadcasting.com

Hopkinsville WNKJ-FM (q) PO Box 1029, Hopkinsville KY 42241 **Phn:** 270-886-9655 **Fax:** 270-885-7210 www.wnkj.org wnkj@wnkj.org

Horse Cave WLOC-AM (cg) PO Box 98, Horse Cave KY 42749 **Phn:** 270-786-4400 **Fax:** 270-786-4402 www.wloconline.com wloc@scrtc.com

Irvine WIRV-AM (nt) PO Box 281, Irvine KY 40336 **Phn:** 606-723-5138 **Fax:** 606-723-5180 www.wirvam.com

Jackson WEKG-AM (ct) 1501 Hargis Ln Ste 2, Jackson KY 41339 **Phn:** 606-666-7531 **Fax:** 606-666-4946 www.wjsnfm.com kdavidson@wjsnfm.com

Jackson WJSN-FM (ct) 1501 Hargis Ln Ste 2, Jackson KY 41339 **Phn:** 606-666-7531 **Fax:** 606-666-4946

Jackson WMTC-AM (g) 1036 Highway 541, Jackson KY 41339 **Phn:** 606-666-5006 **Fax:** 888-510-3334 wp.mountaingospel.org studio@mountaingospel.org

Jackson WMTC-FM (q) 1036 Highway 541, Jackson KY 41339 **Phn:** 606-666-5006 **Fax:** 888-510-3334 wp.mountaingospel.org studio@mountaingospel.org

Jamestown WJKY-AM (cg) PO Box 800, Jamestown KY 42629 **Phn:** 270-866-3487 **Fax:** 270-866-2060 lakercountry.com

Jamestown WJRS-FM (cg) PO Box 800, Jamestown KY 42629 **Phn:** 270-866-3487 **Fax:** 270-866-2060 lakercountry.com

Jenkins WKVG-AM (g) PO Box 1474, Jenkins KY 41537 **Phn:** 606-832-4655 **Fax:** 606-832-4656

Keavy WVCT-FM (v) 968 W City Dam Rd, Keavy KY 40737 **Phn:** 606-528-4671 earthly_raisin@yahoo.com

Kevil WGCF-FM (vqa) 1112 Kentucky Ave, Kevil KY 42053 **Phn:** 270-462-3020 www.afa.net

Lebanon WLBN-AM (tm) 253 W Main St, Lebanon KY 40033 **Phn:** 270-692-3126 **Fax:** 270-692-6003 www.1590wlbn.com acolley@commonwealthbroadcasting.com

Lebanon WLSK-FM (a) 253 W Main St, Lebanon KY 40033 **Phn:** 270-692-3126 **Fax:** 270-692-6003 www.lebanonmike.com cmattingly@commonwealthbroadcasting.com

Leitchfield WKHG-FM (a) 2160 Brandenburg Rd, Leitchfield KY 42754 **Phn:** 270-259-5692 **Fax:** 270-259-5693 www.k105.com news@k105.com

Leitchfield WMTL-AM (c) 2160 Brandenburg Rd, Leitchfield KY 42754 **Phn:** 270-259-3165 **Fax:** 270-259-5693 news@k105.com

Lexington WBTF-FM (u) 401 W Main St Ste 301, Lexington KY 40507 **Phn:** 859-233-1515 **Fax:** 859-233-1517 www.1079thebeat.com info@1079thebeat.com

Lexington WBUL-FM (c) 2601 Nicholasville Rd, Lexington KY 40503 **Phn:** 859-422-1000 **Fax:** 859-422-1038 www.wbul.com michaeljordan@clearchannel.com

Lexington WBVX-FM (a) 401 W Main St Ste 301, Lexington KY 40507 **Phn:** 859-233-1515 www.b92fm.com charlie@b92fm.com

Lexington WCDA-FM (a) 401 W Main St Ste 301, Lexington KY 40507 **Phn:** 859-233-1515 **Fax:** 859-233-1517 www.your1063.com cruz@your1063.com

Lexington WGKS-FM (a) 401 W Main St Ste 301, Lexington KY 40507 **Phn:** 859-233-1515 **Fax:** 859-233-1517 www.969kissfm.com info@969kissfm.com

Lexington WKQQ-FM (r) 2601 Nicholasville Rd, Lexington KY 40503 **Phn:** 859-422-1000 **Fax:** 859-422-1038 www.wkqq.com dennisdillon@clearchannel.com

Lexington WLAP-AM (snt) 2601 Nicholasville Rd, Lexington KY 40503 **Phn:** 859-422-1000 **Fax:** 859-422-1038 www.wlap.com michaeljordan@clearchannel.com

Lexington WLKT-FM (h) 2601 Nicholasville Rd, Lexington KY 40503 **Phn:** 859-422-1000 **Fax:** 859-422-1038 www.1045thecat.com michaeljordan@clearchannel.com

Lexington WLTO-FM (h) 300 W Vine St, Lexington KY 40507 **Phn:** 859-253-5900 **Fax:** 859-253-5940 www.hot102.net tabatha73@yahoo.com

Lexington WLXG-AM (s) 401 W Main St Ste 301, Lexington KY 40507 **Phn:** 859-233-1515 **Fax:** 859-233-1517 www.wlxg.com

Lexington WLXO-FM (c) 401 W Main St Ste 301, Lexington KY 40507 **Phn:** 859-233-1515 **Fax:** 859-233-1517 www.hank961.com comments@hank961.com

Lexington WLXX-FM (c) 300 W Vine St Ste 3, Lexington KY 40507 **Phn:** 859-253-5900 **Fax:** 859-253-5940 www.wlxxthebear.com steve.bearance@cumulus.com

Lexington WMJR-AM (q) 195 Moore Dr, Lexington KY 40503 **Phn:** 859-278-0894 **Fax:** 859-278-0426 realliferadio.com info@realliferadio.com

Lexington WMKJ-FM (o) 2601 Nicholasville Rd, Lexington KY 40503 **Phn:** 859-422-1000 **Fax:** 859-422-1038 dennisdillon@clearchannel.com

Lexington WMXL-FM (a) 2601 Nicholasville Rd, Lexington KY 40503 **Phn:** 859-422-1000 **Fax:** 859-422-1038 www.mymix945.com michaeljordan@clearchannel.com

Lexington WRFL-FM (v) 777 University Sta, Lexington KY 40506 **Phn:** 859-257-4636 **Fax:** 859-323-1039 wrfl.fm news@wrfl.fm

Lexington WUKY-FM (pr) 340 McVey Hall, Lexington KY 40506 **Phn:** 859-257-3221 **Fax:** 859-257-6291 www.wuky.org wukynews@hotmail.com

Lexington WVLK-FM (r) 300 W Vine St, Lexington KY 40507 **Phn:** 859-253-5900 **Fax:** 859-253-5940 wvlkfm.com scott.johnson@cumulus.com

Lexington WVLK-AM (snt) 300 W Vine St, Lexington KY 40507 **Phn:** 859-253-5900 **Fax:** 859-253-5948 www.wvlkam.com scott.johnson@cumulus.com

Lexington WXZZ-FM (r) 300 W Vine St, Lexington KY 40507 **Phn:** 859-253-5900 **Fax:** 859-253-5940 zrock103.com

Liberty WKDO-AM (c) PO Box 990, Liberty KY 42539 **Phn:** 606-787-7331 **Fax:** 606-787-2166 wkdo98.7@hotmail.com

KENTUCKY RADIO STATIONS

Liberty WKDO-FM (c) PO Box 990, Liberty KY 42539 **Phn:** 606-787-7331 **Fax:** 606-787-2166 wkdo98.7@hotmail.com

London WANV-FM (o) 534 Tobacco Rd, London KY 40741 **Phn:** 606-864-2148 trhouse@forchtbroadcasting.com

London WFTG-AM (nt) 534 Tobacco Rd, London KY 40741 **Phn:** 606-864-2148 **Fax:** 606-864-0645 www.sam1039.com teharris@forchtbroadcasting.com

London WGWM-AM (g) 948 Moriah Church Rd, London KY 40741 **Phn:** 606-878-0980

London WWEL-FM (c) 534 Tobacco Rd, London KY 40741 **Phn:** 606-864-2148 **Fax:** 606-864-0645 www.sam1039.com dabegley@forchtbroadcasting.com

London WYGE-FM (q) 201 E 2nd St, London KY 40741 **Phn:** 606-877-1326 **Fax:** 606-864-3702

Louisville WAMZ-FM (c) 4000 Radio Dr Ste 1, Louisville KY 40218 **Phn:** 502-479-2222 www.wamz.com coyote@wamz.com

Louisville WDJX-FM (h) 520 S 4th St 2nd Fl, Louisville KY 40202 **Phn:** 502-625-1220 **Fax:** 502-625-1253 www.wdjx.com jminton@mainlinelouisville.com

Louisville WFIA-AM (tq) 9960 Corporate Campus Dr Ste 3600, Louisville KY 40223 **Phn:** 502-339-9470 **Fax:** 502-423-3139 www.wfia-fm.com gkramer@salemradiogroup.com

Louisville WFIA-FM (qt) 9960 Corporate Campus Dr Ste 3600, Louisville KY 40223 **Phn:** 502-339-9470 **Fax:** 502-423-3139 www.wfia-fm.com gkramer@salemradiogroup.com

Louisville WFPK-FM (pa) 619 S 4th St, Louisville KY 40202 **Phn:** 502-814-6500 **Fax:** 502-814-6599 www.wfpk.org sowen@wfpk.org

Louisville WFPL-FM (pjnt) 619 S 4th St, Louisville KY 40202 **Phn:** 502-814-6500 **Fax:** 502-814-6599 www.wfpl.org rhowlett@wfpl.org

Louisville WGTK-AM (nt) 9960 Corporate Campus Dr Ste 3600, Louisville KY 40223 **Phn:** 502-339-9470 **Fax:** 502-423-3139 www.970wgtk.com dreichel@salemradiogroup.com

Louisville WGZB-FM (wu) 520 S 4th St 2nd Fl, Louisville KY 40202 **Phn:** 502-625-1220 **Fax:** 502-625-1257 www.b96jams.com

Louisville WHAS-AM (nt) 4000 Radio Dr Ste 1, Louisville KY 40218 **Phn:** 502-479-2222 **Fax:** 502-479-2308 www.whas.com info@whas.com

Louisville WKJK-AM (nt) 4000 Radio Dr Ste 1, Louisville KY 40218 **Phn:** 502-479-2222 www.talkradio1080.com jimfenn@clearchannel.com

Louisville WKRD-AM (s) 4000 Radio Dr Ste 1, Louisville KY 40218 **Phn:** 502-479-2222 www.790krd.com jimfenn@clearchannel.com

Louisville WLCR-AM (q) 3600 Goldsmith Ln, Louisville KY 40220 **Phn:** 502-451-9527 www.wlcr.org vince@wlcr.net

Louisville WLGX-FM (a) 4000 Radio Dr Ste 1, Louisville KY 40218 **Phn:** 502-479-2222 www.genxlouisville.com jonathanshuford@clearchannel.com

Louisville WLLV-AM (wg) 2001 W Broadway Ste 13, Louisville KY 40203 **Phn:** 502-776-1240 **Fax:** 502-776-1250

Louisville WLOU-AM (wjx) 2001 W Broadway Ste 13, Louisville KY 40203 **Phn:** 502-776-1240 **Fax:** 502-776-1250

Louisville WLRS-FM (t) 520 S 4th St 2nd Fl, Louisville KY 40202 **Phn:** 502-625-1220 www.easyrock1051.com easyrock1051@gmail.com

Louisville WMJM-FM (u) 520 S 4th St 2nd Fl, Louisville KY 40202 **Phn:** 502-625-1220 **Fax:** 502-625-1253 www.1013online.com vsickles@mainlinelouisville.com

Louisville WQKC-AM (c) 9900 Corporate Campus Dr Ste 2600, Louisville KY 40223 **Phn:** 502-992-0939 **Fax:** 502-992-0862

Louisville WQMF-FM (r) 4000 Radio Dr Ste 1, Louisville KY 40218 **Phn:** 502-479-2222 www.wqmf.com webweasel@wqmf.com

Louisville WQNU-FM (c) 612 S 4th St Ste 100, Louisville KY 40202 **Phn:** 502-589-4800 **Fax:** 502-681-3010 www.newcountryq1031.com shane.collins@summitmediacorp.com

Louisville WRKA-FM (o) 612 S 4th St Ste 100, Louisville KY 40202 **Phn:** 502-589-4800 **Fax:** 502-561-3010 www.countrylegends1039.com shane.collins@summitmediacorp.com

Louisville WSFR-FM (r) 612 S 4th St Ste 100, Louisville KY 40202 **Phn:** 502-589-4800 **Fax:** 502-681-0111 www.1077theeagle.com shane.collins@summitmediacorp.com

Louisville WTFX-FM (r) 4000 Radio Dr Ste 1, Louisville KY 40218 **Phn:** 502-479-2222 **Fax:** 502-479-2233 www.foxrocks.com charliesteele@clearchannel.com

Louisville WUOL-FM (v) 619 S 4th St, Louisville KY 40202 **Phn:** 502-814-6500 **Fax:** 502-814-6599 www.wuol.org info@wuol.org

Louisville WVEZ-FM (a) 612 S 4th St Ste 100, Louisville KY 40202 **Phn:** 502-589-4800 **Fax:** 502-515-3820 www.lite1069.com shane.collins@coxmg.com

Louisville WXMA-FM (a) 520 S 4th St 2nd Fl, Louisville KY 40202 **Phn:** 502-625-1220 **Fax:** 502-625-1258 www.themaxfm.com themaxfm@gmail.com

Louisville WZKF-FM (h) 4000 Radio Dr Ste 1, Louisville KY 40218 **Phn:** 502-479-2222 www.989radionow.com jonathanshuford@clearchannel.com

Madisonville WFMW-AM (c) PO Box 338, Madisonville KY 42431 **Phn:** 270-821-4096 **Fax:** 270-821-5954 www.wfmw.net news@wfmw.net

Madisonville WKTG-FM (r) PO Box 338, Madisonville KY 42431 **Phn:** 270-821-4096 **Fax:** 270-821-5954 www.wktg.com wktg@wktg.com

Madisonville WSOF-FM (q) PO Box 1246, Madisonville KY 42431 **Phn:** 270-825-3004 **Fax:** 270-825-3005 www.wsof.org comments@wsof.org

Madisonville WTTL-AM (st) 265 S Main St, Madisonville KY 42431 **Phn:** 270-821-1310 **Fax:** 270-825-3260 bcardwell@commonwealthbroadcasting.com

Madisonville WWKY-FM (o) PO Box 1310, Madisonville KY 42431 **Phn:** 270-825-9779 **Fax:** 270-825-3260

Madisonville WYMV-FM (a) 265 S Main St, Madisonville KY 42431 **Phn:** 270-821-1310 **Fax:** 270-825-3260 bcardwell@commonwealthbroadcasting.com

Manchester WTBK-FM (r) 107 Dickenson St, Manchester KY 40962 **Phn:** 606-598-7588 **Fax:** 606-598-7598 wtbkradio.com wtbkradio@yahoo.com

Marion WMJL-FM (o) PO Box 68, Marion KY 42064 **Phn:** 270-965-2271

Marion WMJL-AM (o) PO Box 68, Marion KY 42064 **Phn:** 270-965-2271

Martin WMDJ-FM (co) PO Box 1530, Martin KY 41649 **Phn:** 606-874-8005 **Fax:** 606-874-0057 fm100wmdj@mikrotec.com

Mayfield WYMC-AM (ma) PO Box V, Mayfield KY 42066 **Phn:** 270-247-1430 **Fax:** 270-247-1825 mywymc.com radio@wymcradio.com

Mayking WTCW-AM (c) PO Box 288, Mayking KY 41837 **Phn:** 606-633-4434 **Fax:** 606-633-4445 www.1039thebulldog.com wxkq@yahoo.com

Mayking WXKQ-FM (c) PO Box 288, Mayking KY 41837 **Phn:** 606-633-4434 **Fax:** 606-633-4445 www.1039thebulldog.com wxkq@yahoo.com

Maysville WFTM-AM (a) PO Box 100, Maysville KY 41056 **Phn:** 606-564-3361 **Fax:** 606-564-4291 www.wftm.net wftmsales@maysvilleky.net

Maysville WFTM-FM (h) PO Box 100, Maysville KY 41056 **Phn:** 606-564-3361 **Fax:** 606-564-4291 www.wftm.net wftmnews@maysvilleky.net

McCarr WHJC-AM (g) 156 Radio Hill St, McCarr KY 41544 **Phn:** 606-427-7261 **Fax:** 606-427-7260

McCarr WVKM-FM (a) 156 Radio Hill St, McCarr KY 41544 **Phn:** 606-427-7261 **Fax:** 606-427-7260

McDaniels WBFI-FM (qvnt) PO Box 2, McDaniels KY 40152 **Phn:** 270-257-2689 **Fax:** 270-257-8344 wbfiradio@yahoo.com

Middlesboro WANO-AM (c) PO Box 823, Middlesboro KY 40965 **Phn:** 606-337-9528 **Fax:** 606-248-9391 www.1230wano.com wanocountry@gmail.com

Middlesboro WFXY-AM (c) PO Box 823, Middlesboro KY 40965 **Phn:** 606-248-9399 **Fax:** 606-248-9391 www.1490wfxy.com wfxyproduction@gmail.com

Middlesboro WMIK-FM (q) PO Box 608, Middlesboro KY 40965 **Phn:** 606-248-5842 **Fax:** 606-248-7660 radiog2@bellsouth.net

Middlesboro WMIK-AM (g) PO Box 608, Middlesboro KY 40965 **Phn:** 606-248-5842 **Fax:** 606-248-7660 radiog2@bellsouth.net

Middlesboro WRIL-FM (arc) PO Box 1846, Middlesboro KY 40965 **Phn:** 606-248-6565 **Fax:** 606-248-6569 www.thebig1063.com brian@thebig1063.com

Monticello WFLW-AM (g) 150 Worsham Ln, Monticello KY 42633 **Phn:** 606-348-8427

Monticello WKYM-FM (r) PO Box 696, Monticello KY 42633 **Phn:** 606-348-7083 www.wkym.com news@wkym.com

Monticello WMKZ-FM (c) 105 Highway 3106, Monticello KY 42633 **Phn:** 606-348-3393 **Fax:** 606-348-3330 www.wmkz.com studio@z93country.com

Morehead WIVY-FM (a) PO Box 963, Morehead KY 40351 **Phn:** 606-784-9966 **Fax:** 606-674-6700

Morehead WMKY-FM (pln) 150 University Blvd Box 903, Morehead KY 40351 **Phn:** 606-783-2001 **Fax:** 606-783-2335 wmky.org

Morganfield WMSK-FM (c) PO Box 369, Morganfield KY 42437 **Phn:** 270-389-1550 **Fax:** 270-389-1553 www.wmskamfm.com wmsk@bellsouth.net

Morganfield WMSK-AM (c) PO Box 369, Morganfield KY 42437 **Phn:** 270-389-1550 **Fax:** 270-389-1553 www.wmskamfm.com wmsk@bellsouth.net

Morgantown WLBQ-AM (co) 210 N Main St, Morgantown KY 42261 **Phn:** 502-526-3321 wlbqam@bellsouth.net

Mount Sterling WMST-AM (co) 22 W Main St, Mount Sterling KY 40353 **Phn:** 859-498-1150 **Fax:** 859-498-7930 www.wmstradio.com dan@wmstradio.com

Murray WFGE-FM (c) 1500 Diuguid Dr, Murray KY 42071 **Phn:** 270-753-2400 **Fax:** 270-753-9434 www.froggy103.com scott@forevercomm.com

Murray WKMS-FM (pn) 2018 University Sta, Murray KY 42071 **Phn:** 270-809-4359 **Fax:** 270-809-4667 www.wkms.org msu.wkmsnews@murraystate.edu

KENTUCKY RADIO STATIONS

Murray WNBS-AM (cnt) 1500 Diuguid Dr, Murray KY 42071 **Phn:** 270-753-2400 **Fax:** 270-753-9434 www.1340wnbs.com scott@forevercomm.com

Murray WOFC-AM (s) 1500 Diuguid Dr, Murray KY 42071 **Phn:** 270-753-2400 **Fax:** 270-753-9434

Murray WRKY-AM (s) 1500 Diuguid Dr, Murray KY 42071 **Phn:** 270-753-2400 **Fax:** 270-753-9434

Owensboro WBIO-FM (c) 1115 Tamarack Rd Ste 500, Owensboro KY 42301 **Phn:** 270-683-5200 **Fax:** 270-688-0108 www.owensbororadio.com melford@cromwellradio.com

Owensboro WBKR-FM (c) 3301 Frederica St, Owensboro KY 42301 **Phn:** 270-683-1558 **Fax:** 270-685-2500 wbkr.com moon@wbkr.com

Owensboro WKCM-AM (g) 1115 Tamarack Rd Ste 500, Owensboro KY 42301 **Phn:** 270-683-5200 **Fax:** 270-688-0108 www.owensbororadio.com jmorgan@cromwellradio.com

Owensboro WKCM-FM (oh) 1115 Tamarack Rd Ste 500, Owensboro KY 42301 **Phn:** 270-683-5200 **Fax:** 270-688-0108 www.owensbororadio.com bstacy@cromwellradio.com

Owensboro WLME-FM (o) 1115 Tamarack Rd Ste 500, Owensboro KY 42301 **Phn:** 270-683-5200 **Fax:** 270-688-0108 www.owensbororadio.com bstacy@cromwellradio.com

Owensboro WOMI-AM (nt) 3301 Frederica St, Owensboro KY 42301 **Phn:** 270-683-1558 **Fax:** 270-685-2500 1490womi.com chad@wbkr.com

Owensboro WTCJ-FM (h) 1115 Tamarack Rd Ste 500, Owensboro KY 42301 **Phn:** 270-683-5200 **Fax:** 270-688-0108 www.cromwellradio.com mchaney@cromwellradio.com

Owensboro WTCJ-AM (ob) 1115 Tamarack Rd Ste 500, Owensboro KY 42301 **Phn:** 270-683-5200 **Fax:** 270-688-0108 www.owensbororadio.com tmehringer@cromwellradio.com

Owensboro WVJS-AM (m) 1115 Tamarack Rd Ste 500, Owensboro KY 42301 **Phn:** 270-683-5200 **Fax:** 270-688-0108 www.owensbororadio.com aspalding@cromwellradio.com

Owensboro WXCM-FM (r) 1115 Tamarack Rd Ste 500, Owensboro KY 42301 **Phn:** 270-683-5200 **Fax:** 270-688-0108 www.owensbororadio.com jmorgan@cromwellradio.com

Owingsville WKCA-FM (c) PO Box 1010, Owingsville KY 40360 **Phn:** 606-674-2266 **Fax:** 606-674-6700

Paducah WDDJ-FM (h) 6000 Bristol Dr, Paducah KY 42003 **Phn:** 270-534-9690 **Fax:** 270-554-4613 electric969.com pd@electric969.com

Paducah WDXR-AM (ua) PO Box 2397, Paducah KY 42002 **Phn:** 270-554-8255 **Fax:** 270-554-5468

Paducah WGKY-FM (cg) 1700 N 8th St, Paducah KY 42001 **Phn:** 270-538-5251 **Fax:** 270-415-0599 www.959wgky.com

Paducah WJLI-FM (a) 1211 Kentucky Ave # 191, Paducah KY 42003 **Phn:** 270-442-0098 www.radiojelli.com onair@radiojelli.com

Paducah WKYQ-FM (c) PO Box 2397, Paducah KY 42002 **Phn:** 270-554-0093 **Fax:** 270-554-5468 wkyq.com pd@wkyq.com

Paducah WKYX-AM (nt) PO Box 2397, Paducah KY 42002 **Phn:** 270-554-8255 **Fax:** 270-554-5468 www.wkyx.com news@wkyx.com

Paducah WLLE-FM (c) PO Box 2397, Paducah KY 42002 **Phn:** 270-554-0093 **Fax:** 270-554-5468 www.willieradio.com joejackson@wkyx.com

Paducah WNGO-AM (st) PO Box 2397, Paducah KY 42002 **Phn:** 270-554-8255 **Fax:** 270-554-5468 www.wkyx.com

Paducah WQQR-FM (r) PO Box 2397, Paducah KY 42002 **Phn:** 270-534-9690 **Fax:** 270-554-5468 www.wqqr.com news@wkyx.com

Paducah WREZ-FM (a) PO Box 7501, Paducah KY 42002 **Phn:** 270-538-5251 **Fax:** 270-415-0599 www.1055thecat.com rlambert@withersradio.net

Paducah WRIK-AM (tn) 1211 Kentucky Ave # 191, Paducah KY 42003 **Phn:** 270-442-0098 onair@radiojelli.com

Paducah WZZL-FM (hr) PO Box 7501, Paducah KY 42002 **Phn:** 270-538-5251 **Fax:** 270-415-0599 www.wzzl.com rlambert@withersradio.net

Paintsville WKLW-FM (a) PO Box 1407, Paintsville KY 41240 **Phn:** 606-789-6664 **Fax:** 606-789-6669 wklw.com comments@wklw.com

Paintsville WKYH-AM (nt) PO Box 597, Paintsville KY 41240 **Phn:** 606-789-5311 **Fax:** 859-789-7200 www.wkyham.com wkyh600@yahoo.com

Paintsville WSIP-AM (nt) 124 Main St, Paintsville KY 41240 **Phn:** 606-789-5311 **Fax:** 606-789-7200 www.kokosuniverse.comradio_stationswsip.htm spberkhimer@keybroadcasting.net

Paintsville WSIP-FM (c) 124 Main St, Paintsville KY 41240 **Phn:** 606-789-5311 **Fax:** 606-789-7200 www.wsipfm.com

Pikeville WDHR-FM (c) PO Box 2200, Pikeville KY 41502 **Phn:** 606-437-4051 **Fax:** 606-432-2809 www.wdhr.com

Pikeville WEKB-AM (o) PO Box 2200, Pikeville KY 41502 **Phn:** 606-432-8103 **Fax:** 606-432-2809 www.myoldiesradio.com info@ekbradio.com

Pikeville WLSI-AM (c) PO Box 2200, Pikeville KY 41502 **Phn:** 606-437-4051 **Fax:** 606-432-2809 www.900wlsi.com waltmay@ekbradio.com

Pikeville WPKE-FM (h) PO Box 2200, Pikeville KY 41502 **Phn:** 606-437-4051 **Fax:** 606-432-2809 www.wpke.com

Pikeville WXCC-FM (c) PO Box 2200, Pikeville KY 41502 **Phn:** 304-235-3600 **Fax:** 304-235-8118 www.1069wxxc.com studio@1069wxxc.com

Pikeville WZLK-FM (r) PO Box 2200, Pikeville KY 41502 **Phn:** 606-437-4051 **Fax:** 606-432-2809 www.1075zrock.com

Pippa Passes WWJD-FM (vqa) 100 Purpose Rd, Pippa Passes KY 41844 **Phn:** 606-368-6131 **Fax:** 606-368-6017

Prestonsburg WDOC-AM (gnt) PO Box 345, Prestonsburg KY 41653 **Phn:** 606-886-2338 **Fax:** 606-886-1026 q95prod@bellsouth.net

Prestonsburg WQHY-FM (h) PO Box 345, Prestonsburg KY 41653 **Phn:** 606-886-8409 **Fax:** 606-886-1026 www.q95fm.net q95prod@bellsouth.net

Princeton WAVJ-FM (a) PO Box 270, Princeton KY 42445 **Phn:** 270-365-2072 **Fax:** 270-365-2073 bcardwell@commonwealthbroadcasting.com

Princeton WPKY-AM (st) PO Box 270, Princeton KY 42445 **Phn:** 270-365-2072 **Fax:** 270-365-2073

Renfro Valley WRVK-AM (cnt) PO Box 7, Renfro Valley KY 40473 **Phn:** 606-256-2146 **Fax:** 606-256-9146 www.wrvk1460.com manager@wrvk1460.com

Richmond WCBR-AM (g) PO Box 570, Richmond KY 40476 **Phn:** 859-623-1235 **Fax:** 859-623-7094 www.wcbr1110.com wcbrdavid@bellsouth.net

Richmond WCYO-FM (c) 128 Big Hill Ave, Richmond KY 40475 **Phn:** 859-623-1386 **Fax:** 859-623-1341 www.wcyofm.com

Richmond WEKH-FM (pln) 521 Lancaster Ave, Richmond KY 40475 **Phn:** 859-622-1660 **Fax:** 859-622-6276 www.weku.fm weku@eku.edu

Richmond WEKU-FM (pln) 521 Lancaster Ave, Richmond KY 40475 **Phn:** 859-622-1660 **Fax:** 859-622-6276 www.weku.fm weku@eku.edu

Richmond WEKY-AM (nt) 128 Big Hill Ave, Richmond KY 40475 **Phn:** 859-623-1340 **Fax:** 859-623-1341 www.wekyam.com davidandkathycox@aol.com

Richmond WKXO-AM (ont) 128 Big Hill Ave, Richmond KY 40475 **Phn:** 859-623-1340 **Fax:** 859-623-1341 www.wkxoam.com

Richmond WLFX-FM (r) 128 Big Hill Ave, Richmond KY 40475 **Phn:** 859-623-1386 **Fax:** 859-623-1341 wlfxfm.com ron@wcyofm.com

Russellville WRUS-AM (nt) PO Box 1740, Russellville KY 42276 **Phn:** 270-726-2471 **Fax:** 270-726-3095 www.wrusam.com mack@logantele.com

Scottsville WLCK-AM (q) PO Box 158, Scottsville KY 42164 **Phn:** 270-237-3149 **Fax:** 270-237-3533 darrin@wggc.com

Scottsville WVLE-FM (c) PO Box 158, Scottsville KY 42164 **Phn:** 270-237-3148 **Fax:** 270-237-3533

Somerset WKEQ-FM (r) PO Box 740, Somerset KY 42502 **Phn:** 606-678-5151 **Fax:** 606-678-2026 www.q97rock.com rodzimmerman@somersetradio.com

Somerset WLLK-FM (a) PO Box 740, Somerset KY 42502 **Phn:** 606-678-5151 **Fax:** 606-678-2026 www.lake1023.com rodzimmerman@somersetradio.com

Somerset WSEK-FM (c) PO Box 740, Somerset KY 42502 **Phn:** 606-678-5151 **Fax:** 606-678-2026 www.k93country.com paulamolen@somersetradio.com

Somerset WSFC-AM (snt) PO Box 740, Somerset KY 42502 **Phn:** 606-678-5151 **Fax:** 606-678-2026 www.wsfcam.com rodzimmerman@somersetradio.com

Somerset WTHL-FM (qy) PO Box 1423, Somerset KY 42502 **Phn:** 606-679-6300 **Fax:** 606-679-1342

Somerset WTLO-AM (b) 290 Wtlo Rd, Somerset KY 42503 **Phn:** 606-678-8151 **Fax:** 606-678-8152 wtloam.com mitarter@forchtbroadcasting.com

South Shore WOKE-FM (g) PO Box 926, South Shore KY 41175 **Phn:** 606-932-2223 **Fax:** 606-932-6132

Stanton WBFC-AM (g) PO Box 577, Stanton KY 40380 **Phn:** 606-663-6631 **Fax:** 606-663-2267 www.wbfcam.com william@wbfcam.com

Stanton WSKV-FM (c) PO Box 610, Stanton KY 40380 **Phn:** 606-663-2811 **Fax:** 606-663-2895 www.wskvfm.com wskv@wskvfm.com

Tompkinsville WKWY-FM (cg) 341 Radio Station Rd, Tompkinsville KY 42167 **Phn:** 270-487-6119 **Fax:** 270-487-8462 kixcountry@windstream.net

Tompkinsville WTKY-AM (cg) 341 Radio Station Rd, Tompkinsville KY 42167 **Phn:** 270-487-6119 **Fax:** 270-487-8462 kixcountry@windstream.net

Tompkinsville WTKY-FM (cg) 341 Radio Station Rd, Tompkinsville KY 42167 **Phn:** 270-487-6119 **Fax:** 270-487-8462 kixcountry@windstream.net

Tompkinsville WVFB-FM (cg) 341 Radio Station Rd, Tompkinsville KY 42167 **Phn:** 270-487-6119 **Fax:** 270-487-8462 kixcountry@windstream.net

Tyner WWAG-FM (c) 1731 Highway 1071, Tyner KY 40486 **Phn:** 606-287-9924 1079fm@prtcnet.org

Vanceburg WKKS-FM (cg) PO Box 10, Vanceburg KY 41179 **Phn:** 606-796-3031 **Fax:** 606-796-6186

Vanceburg WKKS-AM (c) PO Box 10, Vanceburg KY 41179 **Phn:** 606-796-3031 **Fax:** 606-796-6186

Versailles WCGW-AM (g) 3950 Lexington Rd, Versailles KY 40383 **Phn:** 859-873-8844 **Fax:** 859-873-1318 www.wcgwam.com benson.gregory@cbslradio.com

Versailles WJMM-FM (q) 3950 Lexington Rd, Versailles KY 40383 **Phn:** 859-264-9700 **Fax:** 859-264-9705 www.wjmm.com bruce.edwards@cbslradio.com

Versailles WLRT-AM (t) 3950 Lexington Rd, Versailles KY 40383 **Phn:** 859-264-9700 **Fax:** 859-264-9705

West Libert WRLV-FM (c) PO Box 338, West Libert KY 41472 **Phn:** 606-349-6125 **Fax:** 606-349-6129 radio41472@yahoo.com

West Liberty WCBJ-FM (r) 129 College St, West Liberty KY 41472 **Phn:** 606-668-9225 **Fax:** 606-743-9557

West Liberty WLKS-AM (o) PO Box 338, West Liberty KY 41472 **Phn:** 606-743-1029 **Fax:** 606-743-9557

West Liberty WLKS-FM (c) PO Box 338, West Liberty KY 41472 **Phn:** 606-743-1029 **Fax:** 606-743-9557

West Liberty WMOR-AM (c) PO Box 338, West Liberty KY 41472 **Phn:** 606-784-4141 **Fax:** 606-743-9557

West Liberty WQXX-FM (a) PO Box 338, West Liberty KY 41472 **Phn:** 606-784-4141 **Fax:** 606-743-9557

West Liberty WRLV-AM (c) PO Box 338, West Liberty KY 41472 **Phn:** 606-349-6125 **Fax:** 606-349-6129

Whitesburg WMMT-FM (p) 91 Madison Ave, Whitesburg KY 41858 **Phn:** 606-633-0108 **Fax:** 606-633-1009 www.wmmt.org wmmtfm@appalshop.org

Whitley City WHAY-FM (c) PO Box 69, Whitley City KY 42653 **Phn:** 606-376-2218 **Fax:** 606-376-5146 www.hay98.com whayradio@highland.net

Williamsburg WEKC-AM (gq) 402 Main St, Williamsburg KY 40769 **Phn:** 606-549-3000 **Fax:** 606-539-0916 wekcradio.org wekc@wekcradio.org

Williamsburg WEKX-FM (r) 522 Main St, Williamsburg KY 40769 **Phn:** 606-549-1027 **Fax:** 606-549-5565

Williamsburg WEZJ-AM (nt) 522 Main St, Williamsburg KY 40769 **Phn:** 606-549-2285 **Fax:** 606-549-5565

Williamsburg WEZJ-FM (c) 522 Main St, Williamsburg KY 40769 **Phn:** 606-549-2285 **Fax:** 606-549-5565 dpestes@bellsouth.net

LOUISIANA

Alexandria KBCE-FM (wu) 1605 Murray St Ste 111, Alexandria LA 71301 **Phn:** 318-445-0800 **Fax:** 318-445-1445

Alexandria KDBS-AM (s) 1115 Texas Ave, Alexandria LA 71301 **Phn:** 318-445-1234 **Fax:** 318-473-7231 www.espn1410.com taylor@cenlabroadcasting.com

Alexandria KEDG-FM (u) 1115 Texas Ave, Alexandria LA 71301 **Phn:** 318-445-1234 **Fax:** 318-445-7231

Alexandria KJMJ-AM (q) 601 Washington St, Alexandria LA 71301 **Phn:** 888-408-0201 **Fax:** 318-449-9954 radiomaria.us

Alexandria KKST-FM (u) 1115 Texas Ave, Alexandria LA 71301 **Phn:** 318-445-1234 **Fax:** 318-473-1960 www.kiss987.fm jaykiss106@aol.com

Alexandria KQID-FM (h) 1115 Texas Ave, Alexandria LA 71301 **Phn:** 318-445-1234 **Fax:** 318-473-1960 www.q93fm.com beaurichards@hotmail.com

Alexandria KRRV-FM (c) 1115 Texas Ave, Alexandria LA 71301 **Phn:** 318-445-1234 **Fax:** 318-473-1960 www.krrvonline.com

Alexandria KSYL-AM (nt) 1115 Texas Ave, Alexandria LA 71301 **Phn:** 318-445-1234 **Fax:** 318-473-7231 www.ksyl.com

Alexandria KTTP-AM (g) 3419 Hynson St, Alexandria LA 71303 **Phn:** 318-445-5206 **Fax:** 318-445-5207 kttpam1110@aol.com

Alexandria KZMZ-FM (r) 1115 Texas Ave, Alexandria LA 71301 **Phn:** 318-445-1234 **Fax:** 318-473-1960 www.969rocks.com pat@cenlabroadcasting.com

Amite WABL-AM (ct) PO Box 787, Amite LA 70422 **Phn:** 985-748-8385 **Fax:** 985-748-3918

Angola KLSP-FM (v) La State Penitentiary, Angola LA 70712 **Phn:** 225-655-4411

Baton Rouge KDDK-FM (y) 263 3rd St Ste 703, Baton Rouge LA 70801 **Phn:** 225-344-2882 www.kddkfm.com kddk1055@att.net

Baton Rouge KLSU-FM (vr) B-39 Hodges Hall LSU Campus, Baton Rouge LA 70893 **Phn:** 225-578-5578 **Fax:** 225-578-0579 www.lsureveille.comklsu stationmanager@tigers.lsu.edu

Baton Rouge KNXX-FM (r) PO Box 2231, Baton Rouge LA 70821 **Phn:** 225-388-9898 **Fax:** 225-499-9800 www.countrylegends1049.com dave.dunaway@gbcradio.com

Baton Rouge KQXL-FM (wu) 650 Wooddale Blvd, Baton Rouge LA 70806 **Phn:** 225-926-1106 **Fax:** 225-928-1606 q106dot5.com jmichael.wxok@cumulus.com

Baton Rouge KRVE-FM (a) 5555 Hilton Ave Ste 500, Baton Rouge LA 70808 **Phn:** 225-231-1860 **Fax:** 225-231-1879 www.961theriver.com samnorth@clearchannel.com

Baton Rouge WBRH-FM (vj) 2825 Government St, Baton Rouge LA 70806 **Phn:** 225-383-3243 **Fax:** 225-379-7685

Baton Rouge WDGL-FM (r) 929 Government St B, Baton Rouge LA 70802 **Phn:** 225-388-9898 **Fax:** 225-383-3700 www.eagle981.com dave.dunaway@gbcradio.com

Baton Rouge WEMX-FM (wu) 650 Wooddale Blvd, Baton Rouge LA 70806 **Phn:** 225-926-1106 **Fax:** 225-928-1606 www.max94one.com

Baton Rouge WFMF-FM (h) 5555 Hilton Ave Ste 500, Baton Rouge LA 70808 **Phn:** 225-231-1860 **Fax:** 225-231-1879 www.wfmf.com kevincampbell@clearchannel.com

Baton Rouge WIBR-AM (nts) 650 Wooddale Blvd, Baton Rouge LA 70806 **Phn:** 225-926-1106 **Fax:** 225-928-1606

Baton Rouge WJBO-AM (snt) 5555 Hilton Ave Ste 500, Baton Rouge LA 70808 **Phn:** 225-231-1860 **Fax:** 225-231-1879 www.wjbo.com kevin@wjbo.com

Baton Rouge WJFM-FM (qg) PO Box 262550, Baton Rouge LA 70826 **Phn:** 225-768-7000 **Fax:** 225-769-2244 www.jsm.org

Baton Rouge WNXX-FM (s) 929 Government St B, Baton Rouge LA 70802 **Phn:** 225-388-9898 www.1045espn.com dave.dunaway@gbcradio.com

Baton Rouge WPFC-AM (q) 6943 Titian Ave, Baton Rouge LA 70806 **Phn:** 225-926-6550

Baton Rouge WRKF-FM (pl) 3050 Valley Creek Dr, Baton Rouge LA 70808 **Phn:** 225-926-3050 **Fax:** 225-926-3105 www.wrkf.org david@wrkf.org

Baton Rouge WTGE-FM (c) PO Box 2231, Baton Rouge LA 70821 **Phn:** 225-388-9898 **Fax:** 225-499-9800

Baton Rouge WXOK-AM (wgx) 650 Wooddale Blvd, Baton Rouge LA 70806 **Phn:** 225-926-1106 **Fax:** 225-928-1606

Baton Rouge WYNK-FM (c) 5555 Hilton Ave Ste 500, Baton Rouge LA 70808 **Phn:** 225-231-1860 **Fax:** 225-231-1879 www.wynkcountry.com

Baton Rouge WYPY-FM (c) 929 Government St, Baton Rouge LA 70802 **Phn:** 225-388-9898 **Fax:** 225-499-9800 www.newcountry1007.com dave.dunaway@gbcradio.com

Bogalusa WBOX-AM (c) PO Box 280, Bogalusa LA 70429 **Phn:** 985-732-4288 wboxamfm@bellsouth.net

Bogalusa WBOX-FM (c) PO Box 280, Bogalusa LA 70429 **Phn:** 985-732-4288 wboxamfm@bellsouth.net

Bogalusa WIKC-AM (q) PO Box 638, Bogalusa LA 70429 **Phn:** 985-732-4190 **Fax:** 985-732-7594 wikc@bellsouth.net

Bossier City KIOU-AM (qg) 2438 E Texas St Ste 7, Bossier City LA 71111 **Phn:** 318-752-2115 www.wilkinsradio.com janet@wilkinsradio.com

Bossier City KMJJ-FM (wu) PO Box 5459, Bossier City LA 71171 **Phn:** 318-549-8500 **Fax:** 318-549-8505 www.997kmjj.com kmjj@cumulus.com

Bossier City KRMD-FM (c) 270 Plaza Loop, Bossier City LA 71111 **Phn:** 318-549-8500 **Fax:** 318-549-8505 www.krmd.com krmd@cumulus.com

Bossier City KRMD-AM (s) PO Box 5459, Bossier City LA 71171 **Phn:** 318-549-8500 **Fax:** 318-549-8505 www.supertalk1340.com

Bossier City KVMA-FM (ua) 270 Plaza Loop, Bossier City LA 71111 **Phn:** 318-549-8500 **Fax:** 318-549-8505 www.magic1029fm.com

Corpus Christi KYRK-FM (r) 101 N Shoreline Blvd # 303, Corpus Christi TX 78401 **Phn:** 361-334-4963 **Fax:** 361-334-4964 www.1065theshark.com scott@1065theshark.com

Coushatta KRRP-AM (s) 163 Catfish Bend Rd, Coushatta LA 71019 **Phn:** 318-932-6704

Covington WUUU-FM (c) 307 S Jefferson Ave, Covington LA 70433 **Phn:** 985-892-3661 **Fax:** 985-892-3372

Crowley KAJN-FM (g) PO Box 1469, Crowley LA 70527 **Phn:** 337-783-1560 **Fax:** 337-783-1674 www.kajn.com barryt@kajn.com

Donaldsonville KKAY-AM (o) 706 Railroad Ave, Donaldsonville LA 70346 **Phn:** 225-473-6397 globalradiokkay.com hoyler@frontiernet.net

Eunice KBON-FM (m) 109 S 2nd St, Eunice LA 70535 **Phn:** 337-546-0007 **Fax:** 337-546-0097 kbon.com paul@kbon.com

Eunice KEUN-AM (c) PO Box 1055, Eunice LA 70535 **Phn:** 337-457-3041 **Fax:** 337-457-3081

Eunice KEUN-FM (c) PO Box 1055, Eunice LA 70535 **Phn:** 337-457-3041 **Fax:** 337-457-3081

Ferriday KFNV-FM (o) PO Box 1510, Ferriday LA 71334 **Phn:** 318-757-1071 **Fax:** 318-757-7689 kfnvfm.com kfnv@bellsouth.net

Ferriday KWTG-FM (c) PO Box 1510, Ferriday LA 71334 **Phn:** 318-757-4200 **Fax:** 318-757-7689 radioeddie107@yahoo.com

Grambling KGRM-FM (vw) PO Box 4254, Grambling LA 71245 **Phn:** 318-274-6343 **Fax:** 318-274-3245 www.gram.edulifecampus%20mediakgrm evansjb@gram.edu

Gretna WLNO-AM (q) 401 Whitney Ave Ste 160, Gretna LA 70056 **Phn:** 504-362-9800 **Fax:** 504-362-5541 www.wlno.com jwhitehurst@communicom.com

LOUISIANA RADIO STATIONS

Hammond KSLU-FM (plnj) Slu Box 10783, Hammond LA 70402 **Phn:** 985-549-2330 **Fax:** 985-549-3960 www.kslu.org kslu@selu.edu

Hammond WFPR-AM (c) 200 E Thomas St, Hammond LA 70401 **Phn:** 985-345-0060 **Fax:** 985-542-9377

Hammond WHMD-FM (c) 200 E Thomas St, Hammond LA 70401 **Phn:** 985-345-0060 **Fax:** 985-542-9377

Hammond WKSY-FM (a) 200 E Thomas St, Hammond LA 70401 **Phn:** 985-345-0060

Hammond WTGG-AM (o) 200 E Thomas St, Hammond LA 70401 **Phn:** 985-345-0060 **Fax:** 985-542-9377

Houma KCIL-FM (ac) PO Box 2068, Houma LA 70361 **Phn:** 985-851-1020 **Fax:** 985-872-4403 www.c967.com

Houma KJIN-AM (s) PO Box 2068, Houma LA 70361 **Phn:** 985-851-1020 **Fax:** 985-872-4403

Houma KMYO-FM (o) 120 Prevost Dr, Houma LA 70364 **Phn:** 985-851-1020

Houma KXOR-FM (r) 120 Prevost Dr, Houma LA 70364 **Phn:** 985-851-1020 **Fax:** 985-872-4403 www.la1063.com

Jena KJNA-FM (c) PO Box 2750, Jena LA 71342 **Phn:** 318-992-4155

Lafayette KFTE-FM (r) 1749 Bertrand Dr, Lafayette LA 70506 **Phn:** 337-233-6000 **Fax:** 337-234-7360 planet965.com scott.perrin@regentcomm.com

Lafayette KFXZ-FM (aj) 3225 Ambassador Caffery Pkwy, Lafayette LA 70506 **Phn:** 337-993-5500 **Fax:** 337-993-5510 jimmiecole@gmail.com

Lafayette KFXZ-AM (c) 3225 Ambassador Caffery Pkwy, Lafayette LA 70506 **Phn:** 337-993-5500 **Fax:** 337-993-5510 jimmiecole@gmail.com

Lafayette KJCB-AM (wu) 604 Saint John St, Lafayette LA 70501 **Phn:** 337-233-4262 **Fax:** 337-235-9681

Lafayette KMDL-FM (c) 1749 Bertrand Dr, Lafayette LA 70506 **Phn:** 337-232-2242 **Fax:** 337-234-7360 973thedawg.com mike.grimsley@regentcomm.com

Lafayette KNEK-FM (wu) 202 Galbert Rd, Lafayette LA 70506 **Phn:** 337-232-1311 **Fax:** 337-233-3779 www.knek.com jackson.brown@cumulus.com

Lafayette KNEK-AM (wu) 202 Galbert Rd, Lafayette LA 70506 **Phn:** 337-232-1311 **Fax:** 337-233-3779 www.knek.com jackson.brown@cumulus.com

Lafayette KPEL-FM (nt) 1749 Bertrand Dr, Lafayette LA 70506 **Phn:** 337-233-6000 **Fax:** 337-233-2989 kpel965.com bernie@kpel965.com

Lafayette KPEL-AM (snt) 1749 Bertrand Dr, Lafayette LA 70506 **Phn:** 337-233-6000 **Fax:** 337-233-2989 espn1420.com kevin@espn1420.com

Lafayette KQIS-FM (a) PO Box 60571, Lafayette LA 70596 **Phn:** 337-783-2521 **Fax:** 337-783-5744 www.kqis.com

Lafayette KRDJ-FM (r) 202 Galbert Rd, Lafayette LA 70506 **Phn:** 337-232-1311 rock937fm.com lance.knoll@cumulus.com

Lafayette KRKA-FM (h) 1749 Bertrand Dr, Lafayette LA 70506 **Phn:** 337-233-6000 **Fax:** 337-234-7360 1079ishot.com dave@1079ishot.com

Lafayette KROF-AM (t) 1749 Bertrand Dr, Lafayette LA 70506 **Phn:** 337-233-6000 **Fax:** 337-234-7360 talkradio960.com bernie.lee@townsquaremedia.com

Lafayette KRRQ-FM (uw) 202 Galbert Rd, Lafayette LA 70506 **Phn:** 337-232-1311 **Fax:** 337-233-3779 www.krrq.com jackson.brown@cumulus.com

Lafayette KRVS-FM (plj) PO Box 42171, Lafayette LA 70504 **Phn:** 337-482-5787 **Fax:** 337-482-6101 www.krvs.org jmeriwether@krvs.org

Lafayette KSMB-FM (h) 202 Galbert Rd, Lafayette LA 70506 **Phn:** 337-232-1311 **Fax:** 337-233-3779 www.ksmb.com bobby.novosad@cumulus.com

Lafayette KTDY-FM (a) 1749 Bertrand Dr, Lafayette LA 70506 **Phn:** 337-233-6000 **Fax:** 337-234-7360 999ktdy.com debbie@999ktdy.com

Lafayette KVOL-AM (st) 3225 Ambassador Caffery Pkwy, Lafayette LA 70506 **Phn:** 337-993-5500 **Fax:** 337-993-5510 deltamediacorp.com missy@delta-network.com

Lafayette KXKC-FM (c) 202 Galbert Rd, Lafayette LA 70506 **Phn:** 337-232-1311 **Fax:** 337-233-3779 www.nashfm991.com jeni@kxkc.com

Lafayette KYMK-FM (wx) 3225 Ambassador Caffery Pkwy, Lafayette LA 70506 **Phn:** 337-993-5500 **Fax:** 337-993-5510 jimmiecole@gmail.com

Lake Charles KAOK-AM (nt) 425 Broad St, Lake Charles LA 70601 **Phn:** 337-439-3300 **Fax:** 337-436-7278 www.kaok.com eric.nielson@cumulus.com

Lake Charles KBIU-FM (a) 425 Broad St, Lake Charles LA 70601 **Phn:** 337-439-3300 **Fax:** 337-433-7701 www.kbiu.com eric.nielson@cumulus.com

Lake Charles KHLA-FM (o) 900 N Lake Shore Dr, Lake Charles LA 70601 **Phn:** 337-436-9929 **Fax:** 337-433-1603 929thelake.com garyshannon@townsquaremedia.com

Lake Charles KJEF-AM (ec) 900 N Lake Shore Dr, Lake Charles LA 70601 **Phn:** 337-433-1641 **Fax:** 337-433-2999 cajunradio.com mikesoileau@townsquaremedia.com

Lake Charles KJMH-FM (u) 900 N Lake Shore Dr, Lake Charles LA 70601 **Phn:** 337-433-1641 **Fax:** 337-433-2999 107jamz.com eriktee@gapbroadcasting.com

Lake Charles KKGB-FM (r) 425 Broad St, Lake Charles LA 70601 **Phn:** 337-439-3300 **Fax:** 337-433-7701 www.kkgb.com eric.nielson@cumulus.com

Lake Charles KLCL-AM (c) 900 N Lake Shore Dr, Lake Charles LA 70601 **Phn:** 337-433-1641 **Fax:** 337-433-2999 cajunradio.com mikesoileau@townsquaremedia.com

Lake Charles KNGT-FM (c) 900 N Lake Shore Dr, Lake Charles LA 70601 **Phn:** 337-433-1641 **Fax:** 337-433-0838 gator995.com donrivers@townsquaremedia.com

Lake Charles KQLK-FM (hu) 425 Broad St, Lake Charles LA 70601 **Phn:** 337-439-3300 **Fax:** 337-433-7701 www.kqlk.com eric.nielson@cumulus.com

Lake Charles KTSR-FM (h) 900 N Lake Shore Dr, Lake Charles LA 70601 **Phn:** 337-433-1641 **Fax:** 337-433-2999

Lake Charles KXZZ-AM (s) 425 Broad St, Lake Charles LA 70601 **Phn:** 337-439-3300 **Fax:** 337-433-7701 www.kxzz1580am.com eric.nielson@cumulus.com

Lake Charles KYKZ-FM (c) 425 Broad St, Lake Charles LA 70601 **Phn:** 337-439-3300 **Fax:** 337-433-7701 www.kykz.com eric.nielson@cumulus.com

Lake Charles KZWA-FM (ua) 305 Enterprise Blvd, Lake Charles LA 70601 **Phn:** 337-491-9955 **Fax:** 337-433-8097

Larose KLEB-AM (ec) PO Box 1350, Larose LA 70373 **Phn:** 985-798-7792 **Fax:** 985-798-7793 www.klrzfm.com klrz@mobiletel.com

Larose KLRZ-FM (ec) PO Box 1350, Larose LA 70373 **Phn:** 985-798-7792 **Fax:** 985-798-7793 www.klrzfm.com klrz@viscom.net

Leesville KJAE-FM (c) PO Box 1323, Leesville LA 71496 **Phn:** 337-238-5523 **Fax:** 337-238-9283 www.kjae935.com

Leesville KLLA-AM (o) 101 Lees Ln, Leesville LA 71446 **Phn:** 337-239-3402 **Fax:** 337-238-9283 www.kjae935.com sales@kjae935.com

Leesville KROK-FM (a) 168 Kvvp Dr, Leesville LA 71446 **Phn:** 337-537-9292 **Fax:** 337-537-4152 www.krok.com doug@krok.com

Leesville KUMX-FM (a) 168 Kvvp Dr, Leesville LA 71446 **Phn:** 337-537-9000 **Fax:** 337-537-4152

Leesville KVVP-FM (c) 168 Kvvp Dr, Leesville LA 71446 **Phn:** 337-537-5887 **Fax:** 337-537-4152 www.todayscountry1057.com kvvp@kvvp.com

Many KTHP-FM (c) 605 San Antonio Ave, Many LA 71449 **Phn:** 409-787-1039 www.bdcradio.com cezernack@bellsouth.net

Many KWLV-FM (c) 605 San Antonio Ave, Many LA 71449 **Phn:** 318-256-5177 **Fax:** 318-256-0950 www.bdcradio.com kwlv@bellsouth.net

Marksville KAPB-FM (c) PO Box 7, Marksville LA 71351 **Phn:** 318-253-5272 **Fax:** 318-253-5262 kapbfm@yahoo.com

Marrero KKNO-AM (g) 980 Avenue A, Marrero LA 70072 **Phn:** 504-347-7775 **Fax:** 504-347-7440 www.kkno750am.com

Metairie KAGY-AM (r) 4401 Veterans Blvd, Metairie LA 70006 **Phn:** 504-657-5249

Metairie KGLA-AM (y) 3850 N Causeway Blvd Ste 454, Metairie LA 70002 **Phn:** 504-799-3420 **Fax:** 504-799-3434 www.tropical1540.com info@kgla.tv

Metairie KXMG-FM (y) 3850 N Causeway Blvd # 830, Metairie LA 70002 **Phn:** 504-832-3555 www.mega1075fm.com

Metairie WASO-AM (nts) 3313 Kingman St, Metairie LA 70006 **Phn:** 504-888-8255 www.hottalkradio.com

Metairie WFNO-AM (y) 3841 Veterans Blvd # 201, Metairie LA 70002 **Phn:** 504-832-3555 **Fax:** 504-830-7200

Metairie WIST-AM (q) PO Box 8386, Metairie LA 70011 **Phn:** 504-885-4690 **Fax:** 504-885-4671

Metairie WPRF-FM (q) 3500 N Causeway Blvd Ste 400, Metairie LA 70002 **Phn:** 504-834-7095 **Fax:** 504-834-7096

Metairie WTIX-FM (o) 4539 N I 10 Service Rd W, Metairie LA 70006 **Phn:** 504-454-9000 **Fax:** 504-454-9002 wtixfm.com pressrelease@wtixfm.com

Metairie WVOG-AM (gq) 2730 Loumor Ave, Metairie LA 70001 **Phn:** 504-831-6941 **Fax:** 504-831-2647 www.600wvog.com wvog@bellsouth.net

Minden KASO-AM (am) 410 Lakeshore Dr, Minden LA 71055 **Phn:** 318-377-1240 **Fax:** 318-377-4619 www.kbef.com mark@kbef.com

Minden KBEF-FM (q) 410 Lakeshore Dr, Minden LA 71055 **Phn:** 318-377-1240 **Fax:** 318-377-4619 www.kbef.com mark@kbef.com

Monroe KBMQ-FM (q) PO Box 3265, Monroe LA 71210 **Phn:** 318-387-1230 **Fax:** 318-387-8856 kbmq.org

Monroe KEDM-FM (plnj) 401 Bayou Dr # 205, Monroe LA 71201 **Phn:** 318-342-5556 **Fax:** 318-342-5570 www.kedm.org news@kedm.org

Monroe KJLO-FM (c) 1109 Hudson Ln, Monroe LA 71201 **Phn:** 318-388-2323 **Fax:** 318-388-0569 www.kjlo.com jreynolds@bayou.com

Monroe KJMG-FM (wu) 1109 Hudson Ln, Monroe LA 71201 **Phn:** 318-388-2323 **Fax:** 318-388-0569

LOUISIANA RADIO STATIONS

Monroe KLIC-AM (qt) PO Box 3265, Monroe LA 71210 **Phn:** 318-387-1230 **Fax:** 318-387-8856 www.klic1230.com gm@887fm.org

Monroe KLIP-FM (or) 1109 Hudson Ln, Monroe LA 71201 **Phn:** 318-388-2323 **Fax:** 318-388-0569 www.la105.com gman@bayou.com

Monroe KMLB-AM (snt) 1109 Hudson Ln, Monroe LA 71201 **Phn:** 318-388-2323 **Fax:** 318-388-0569 www.kmlb.com gman@bayou.com

Monroe KMYY-FM (c) 1200 N 18th St Ste D, Monroe LA 71201 **Phn:** 318-387-3922 **Fax:** 318-322-4585 www.923thewolf.com 923thewolf@gmail.com

Monroe KNOE-FM (h) PO Box 4067, Monroe LA 71211 **Phn:** 318-388-8888 **Fax:** 318-325-3405 www.starradiomonroe.com knoe.cisco@gmail.com

Monroe KNOE-AM (snt) PO Box 4067, Monroe LA 71211 **Phn:** 318-388-8888 **Fax:** 318-325-3405

Monroe KQLQ-FM (o) 1200 N 18th St Ste D, Monroe LA 71201 **Phn:** 318-387-3922 **Fax:** 318-322-4585 www.hot1031.com hot1031@opusbroadcasting.com

Monroe KRJO-AM (au) 1109 Hudson Ln, Monroe LA 71201 **Phn:** 318-388-2323 **Fax:** 318-388-0569

Monroe KRVV-FM (wu) 1109 Hudson Ln, Monroe LA 71201 **Phn:** 318-388-2323 **Fax:** 318-388-0569 www.thebeat.net

Monroe KXRR-FM (r) 1200 N 18th St Ste D, Monroe LA 71201 **Phn:** 318-387-3922 **Fax:** 318-322-4585 www.rock106kxrr.com

Monroe KXUL-FM (vr) 401 Bayou Dr 130 Stubbs Hall, Monroe LA 71209 **Phn:** 318-342-5986 kxul.com

Monroe KZRZ-FM (a) 1200 N 18th St Ste D, Monroe LA 71201 **Phn:** 318-387-3922 **Fax:** 318-322-4585 www.sunny983.com sunny983@opusbroadcasting.com

Moreauville KLIL-FM (o) PO Box 365, Moreauville LA 71355 **Phn:** 318-985-2929 **Fax:** 318-985-2995 klil@kricket.net

Morgan City KBZE-FM (wu) 1320 Victor II Blvd Ste 101, Morgan City LA 70380 **Phn:** 985-385-6266 **Fax:** 985-385-6268 www.kbze.com howard@kbze.com

Morgan City KFRA-AM (wu) 1320 Victor II Blvd, Morgan City LA 70380 **Phn:** 337-924-7100 www.1390kfra.com howard@kbze.com

Morgan City KMRC-AM (r) 409 Duke St, Morgan City LA 70380 **Phn:** 985-384-1430

Morgan City KQKI-FM (c) PO Box 847, Morgan City LA 70381 **Phn:** 985-395-2853 **Fax:** 985-395-5094 www.kqki.com pcook@cp-tel.net

Natchitoches KCIJ-FM (h) 213 Renee St, Natchitoches LA 71457 **Phn:** 318-354-4000 **Fax:** 214-377-4200 www.106kcij.com sales.mgmt@eliteradiogroup.com

Natchitoches KDBH-FM (a) 400 Jefferson St, Natchitoches LA 71457 **Phn:** 318-352-9696 **Fax:** 318-357-9595 www.bdcradio.com rhonda@bdcradio.com

Natchitoches KNOC-AM (nt) 213 Renee St, Natchitoches LA 71457 **Phn:** 318-354-4000 **Fax:** 318-352-9598 www.1450knocradio.com

Natchitoches KNWD-FM (v) 109 Kyser Hall Nsu, Natchitoches LA 71497 **Phn:** 318-357-4523 knwdradio@gmail.com

Natchitoches KSBH-FM (c) 213 Renee St, Natchitoches LA 71457 **Phn:** 318-354-4000 **Fax:** 214-377-4200

Natchitoches KZBL-FM (o) 400 Jefferson St, Natchitoches LA 71457 **Phn:** 318-352-9696 **Fax:** 318-357-9595 www.bdcradio.com rb.leach-bdc@suddenlinkmail.com

New Iberia KANE-AM (o) 145B W Main St, New Iberia LA 70560 **Phn:** 337-365-3434 **Fax:** 337-365-9117 www.kane1240.com kane@kane1240.com

New Orleans KKND-FM (u) 201 Saint Charles Ave Ste 201, New Orleans LA 70170 **Phn:** 504-581-7002 **Fax:** 504-566-4857 www.power1029.com

New Orleans KMEZ-FM (wu) 201 Saint Charles Ave Ste 201, New Orleans LA 70170 **Phn:** 504-581-7002 **Fax:** 504-566-4857 www.oldschool1067.com lbj.kmez@cumulus.com

New Orleans WBSN-FM (q) 3939 Gentilly Blvd, New Orleans LA 70126 **Phn:** 504-816-8000 **Fax:** 504-816-8580 www.lifesongs.com onair@lifesongs.com

New Orleans WEZB-FM (ah) 400 Poydras St Ste 900, New Orleans LA 70130 **Phn:** 504-593-6376 **Fax:** 504-593-2203 www.b97.com jammer@b97.com

New Orleans WKBU-FM (r) 400 Poydras St Ste 1000, New Orleans LA 70130 **Phn:** 504-593-6376 **Fax:** 504-593-2203 www.bayou957.com kat@bayou957.com

New Orleans WLMG-FM (ah) 400 Poydras St Ste 900, New Orleans LA 70130 **Phn:** 504-593-6376 **Fax:** 504-593-2204 www.magic1019.com ssuter@entercom.com

New Orleans WNOE-FM (c) 929 Howard Ave, New Orleans LA 70113 **Phn:** 504-679-7300 **Fax:** 504-679-7343 www.wnoe.com eddie@wnoe.com

New Orleans WODT-AM (s) 929 Howard Ave, New Orleans LA 70113 **Phn:** 504-679-7300 **Fax:** 504-679-7345 sportsradio1280am@clearchannel.com

New Orleans WQUE-FM (wu) 929 Howard Ave, New Orleans LA 70113 **Phn:** 504-679-7300 **Fax:** 504-679-7345 www.q93.com angelawatson@clearchannel.com

New Orleans WRBH-FM (v) 3606 Magazine St, New Orleans LA 70115 **Phn:** 504-899-1144 **Fax:** 504-899-1165 www.wrbh.org natalia@wrbh.org

New Orleans WRNO-FM (t) 929 Howard Ave, New Orleans LA 70113 **Phn:** 504-679-7300 **Fax:** 504-679-7343 www.wrno.com news@wrno.com

New Orleans WSHO-AM (qat) 365 Canal St Ste 1175, New Orleans LA 70130 **Phn:** 504-527-0800 **Fax:** 504-527-0881 www.wsho.com wsho@wsho.com

New Orleans WTUL-FM (v) Tulane University Box 5069, New Orleans LA 70118 **Phn:** 504-865-5887 www.wtulneworleans.com gm@wtulneworleans.com

New Orleans WWL-FM (nt) 400 Poydras St Ste 1000, New Orleans LA 70130 **Phn:** 504-593-6376 **Fax:** 504-593-2144 www.wwl.com dkcohen@entercom.com

New Orleans WWL-AM (snt) 400 Poydras St Ste 1000, New Orleans LA 70130 **Phn:** 504-593-6376 **Fax:** 504-593-2144 www.wwl.com dkcohen@entercom.com

New Orleans WWNO-FM (pln) 2000 Lakeshore Dr, New Orleans LA 70122 **Phn:** 504-280-7000 **Fax:** 504-280-6061 www.wwno.org wwno@uno.edu

New Orleans WWOZ-FM (pjx) PO Box 51840, New Orleans LA 70151 **Phn:** 504-568-1239 **Fax:** 504-558-9332 www.wwoz.org feedback@wwoz.org

New Orleans WWWL-FM (st) 400 Poydras St # 800, New Orleans LA 70130 **Phn:** 504-593-6376 **Fax:** 504-593-1850 cclaus@entercom.com

New Orleans WYLD-FM (wu) 929 Howard Ave, New Orleans LA 70113 **Phn:** 504-679-7300 **Fax:** 504-679-7345 www.wyldfm.com adberry@wyldfm.com

New Orleans WYLD-AM (g) 929 Howard Ave, New Orleans LA 70113 **Phn:** 504-679-7300 **Fax:** 504-679-7345 www.am940.com rayromero@clearchannel.com

New Roads KCLF-AM (wgu) 803 Parent St, New Roads LA 70760 **Phn:** 225-638-6821 **Fax:** 225-638-6882 rgremillion@bellsouth.net

Oak Grove KWCL-FM (o) 230 E Main St, Oak Grove LA 71263 **Phn:** 318-428-9670 **Fax:** 318-428-2476 kwcl@bellsouth.net

Opelousas KOGM-FM (a) PO Box 1150, Opelousas LA 70571 **Phn:** 337-942-2633 **Fax:** 337-942-2635 kslokogm@bellsouth.net

Opelousas KSLO-AM (c) PO Box 1150, Opelousas LA 70571 **Phn:** 337-942-2633 **Fax:** 337-942-2635 kslokogm@bellsouth.net

Pineville KBKK-FM (c) 92 W Shamrock Ave, Pineville LA 71360 **Phn:** 318-487-1035 **Fax:** 318-487-1045 www.la103.com

Pineville KEZP-FM (o) 92 W Shamrock Ave, Pineville LA 71360 **Phn:** 318-487-1035 **Fax:** 318-487-1045 www.la103.com

Pineville KLAA-FM (c) 92 W Shamrock Ave, Pineville LA 71360 **Phn:** 318-487-1035 **Fax:** 318-487-4419 www.la103.com

Pineville KWDF-AM (g) 3735 Rigolette Rd, Pineville LA 71360 **Phn:** 318-640-4373 **Fax:** 318-640-5971 www.wilkinsradio.com denise@wilkinsradio.com

Port Allen KPAE-FM (q) 13028 Highway 190 W, Port Allen LA 70767 **Phn:** 225-627-4578 **Fax:** 225-627-4970 www.soundradio.org wpaefm@telepak.net

Ruston KLPI-FM (vr) PO Box 8638, Ruston LA 71272 **Phn:** 318-257-4851 klpi.latech.edu music@891klpi.com

Ruston KNBB-FM (st) PO Box 430, Ruston LA 71273 **Phn:** 318-255-5000 **Fax:** 318-255-5084 www.espn977.com espn977@gmail.com

Ruston KPCH-FM (oa) PO Box 430, Ruston LA 71273 **Phn:** 318-255-5000 **Fax:** 318-255-5084

Ruston KRUS-AM (wg) PO Box 430, Ruston LA 71273 **Phn:** 318-255-5000 **Fax:** 318-255-5084 radio1234@gmail.com

Ruston KXKZ-FM (c) PO Box 430, Ruston LA 71273 **Phn:** 318-255-5000 **Fax:** 318-255-5084 www.z1075fm.com z1075fm@bayou.com

Shreveport KBCL-AM (q) 316 Gregg St, Shreveport LA 71104 **Phn:** 318-861-1070 www.kbclthebridge.org kbcl_radio@bellsouth.net

Shreveport KBSA-FM (vljn) PO Box 5250, Shreveport LA 71135 **Phn:** 318-798-0102 **Fax:** 318-798-0107 www.redriverradio.org wbeckett@lsus.edu

Shreveport KDAQ-FM (plnj) PO Box 5250, Shreveport LA 71135 **Phn:** 318-798-0102 **Fax:** 318-798-0107 www.redriverradio.org karcher@lsus.edu

Shreveport KDKS-FM (wu) 208 N Thomas Dr, Shreveport LA 71107 **Phn:** 318-222-3122 **Fax:** 318-459-1493 www.kdks.fm qeradio@aol.com

Shreveport KEEL-AM (nt) 6341 W Port Ave, Shreveport LA 71129 **Phn:** 318-688-1130 **Fax:** 318-688-8574 710keel.com erinmccarty@townsquaremedia.com

Shreveport KLKL-FM (o) 208 N Thomas Dr, Shreveport LA 71107 **Phn:** 318-222-3122 **Fax:** 318-459-1493 www.klkl.fm jj@radiogroupshreveport.com

Shreveport KLSA-FM (plnj) PO Box 5250, Shreveport LA 71135 **Phn:** 318-798-0102 **Fax:** 318-798-0107 www.redriverradio.org kpoling@lsus.edu

Shreveport KOKA-AM (wg) 208 N Thomas Dr, Shreveport LA 71107 **Phn:** 318-222-3122 **Fax:** 318-459-1493 www.koka.am

Shreveport KRUF-FM (h) 6341 W Port Ave, Shreveport LA 71129 **Phn:** 318-688-1130 **Fax:** 318-688-8574 k945.com erinmccarty@gapbroadcasting.com

Shreveport KSCL-FM (v) 2911 Centenary Blvd, Shreveport LA 71104 **Phn:** 318-869-5296 **Fax:** 318-869-5294 extra.centenary.edukscl ksclnews@gmail.com

Shreveport KSYB-AM (wg) PO Box 7685, Shreveport LA 71137 **Phn:** 318-222-2744 **Fax:** 318-425-7507 www.amistadradiogroup.com info@amistadradiogroup.com

Shreveport KSYR-FM (a) 208 N Thomas Dr, Shreveport LA 71107 **Phn:** 318-222-3122 **Fax:** 318-459-1493

Shreveport KTAL-FM (r) 208 N Thomas Dr, Shreveport LA 71107 **Phn:** 318-222-3122 www.98rocks.fm nuke@98rocks.fm

Shreveport KTUX-FM (r) 6341 Westport Ave, Shreveport LA 71129 **Phn:** 318-688-1130 **Fax:** 318-687-8574 therockstation99x.com paulcannell@townsquaremedia.com

Shreveport KVKI-FM (a) 6341 W Port Ave, Shreveport LA 71129 **Phn:** 318-688-1130 **Fax:** 318-688-8574 965kvki.com erinbristol@gapbroadcasting.com

Shreveport KWKH-AM (c) 6341 Westport Ave, Shreveport LA 71129 **Phn:** 318-688-1130 **Fax:** 318-688-8574 1130thetiger.com chrisevans@townsquaremedia.com

Shreveport KXKS-FM (c) 6341 W Port Ave, Shreveport LA 71129 **Phn:** 318-688-1130 **Fax:** 318-688-8574 mykisscountry937.com garymccoy@townsquaremedia.com

Slidell WGSO-AM (nt) 2250 Gause Blvd E Ste 205, Slidell LA 70461 **Phn:** 985-639-3820 **Fax:** 985-639-3869 wgso.com harry@wgso.com

Slidell WSLA-AM (snt) PO Box 1175, Slidell LA 70459 **Phn:** 985-643-1560 **Fax:** 985-649-9822 wslaradio.com wsla1560@bellsouth.net

Springhill KTKC-FM (o) 226 N Main St, Springhill LA 71075 **Phn:** 318-539-6000 **Fax:** 318-539-6002 www.ktkcfm.com

Sulphur KEZM-AM (s) 113 E Napoleon St, Sulphur LA 70663 **Phn:** 337-527-3611 kezmonline.com

Ville Platte KVPI-FM (o) PO Box J, Ville Platte LA 70586 **Phn:** 337-363-2124 **Fax:** 337-363-3574 www.oldies925.com

Ville Platte KVPI-AM (o) PO Box J, Ville Platte LA 70586 **Phn:** 337-363-2124 **Fax:** 337-363-3574 oldies925@gmail.com

Vivian KNCB-FM (c) PO Box 1072, Vivian LA 71082 **Phn:** 318-375-3278 **Fax:** 318-375-3329 kncb@centurytel.net

Vivian KNCB-AM (cq) PO Box 1072, Vivian LA 71082 **Phn:** 318-375-3278 **Fax:** 318-375-3329 kncb@centurytel.net

West Monroe KHLL-FM (q) 704 Trenton St Ste C, West Monroe LA 71291 **Phn:** 318-322-1009 www.hillradio.com mail@hillradio.com

Winnfield KVCL-FM (c) 304 Kvcl Rd, Winnfield LA 71483 **Phn:** 318-628-5822 **Fax:** 318-628-7355 kvclradio.com rhonda@bdcradio.com

Winnsboro KMAR-FM (c) PO Box 312, Winnsboro LA 71295 **Phn:** 318-435-5141 **Fax:** 318-435-5749

MAINE

Auburn WEZR-AM (n) 555 Center St, Auburn ME 04210 **Phn:** 207-784-5868 **Fax:** 207-514-8444 www.ez1240.com news@gleasonmedia.com

Augusta WABK-FM (h) 125 Community Dr # 201, Augusta ME 04330 **Phn:** 207-623-9000 **Fax:** 207-623-9007 www.big104fm.com wabk@blueberrybroadcasting.com

LOUISIANA RADIO STATIONS

Augusta WEBB-FM (c) 56 Western Ave # 1, Augusta ME 04330 **Phn:** 207-623-4735 **Fax:** 207-626-5948 www.b985.fm andy.capwell@townsquaremedia.com

Augusta WFAU-AM (s) 150 Whitten Rd, Augusta ME 04330 **Phn:** 207-623-9000 **Fax:** 207-623-9007 jackobrien@blueberrybroadcasting.com

Augusta WJZN-AM (a) 56 Western Ave Ste 13, Augusta ME 04330 **Phn:** 207-623-4735 **Fax:** 207-626-5948 koolam.com mac.dickson@townsquaremedia.com

Augusta WMDR-AM (q) 160 Riverside Dr, Augusta ME 04330 **Phn:** 207-622-9467 **Fax:** 207-623-2874 lightoflife.infonews wwwa@adelphia.net

Augusta WMME-FM (h) 56 Western Ave Ste 13, Augusta ME 04330 **Phn:** 207-623-4735 **Fax:** 207-626-5948 www.92moose.fm mac.dickson@townsquaremedia.com

Augusta WTOS-FM (r) 150 Whitten Rd, Augusta ME 04330 **Phn:** 207-623-9000 **Fax:** 207-623-9007 www.wtosfm.com jackobrien@blueberrybroadcasting.com

Augusta WTVL-AM (am) 56 Western Ave Ste 13, Augusta ME 04330 **Phn:** 207-623-4735 **Fax:** 207-626-5948 koolam.com al.perry@townsquaremedia.com

Augusta WVQM-FM (t) 125 Community Dr # 201, Augusta ME 04330 **Phn:** 207-623-9000 **Fax:** 207-623-9007 www.wvomfm.com jackobrien@blueberrybroadcasting.com

Bangor WAEI-AM (s) 184 Target Cir, Bangor ME 04401 **Phn:** 207-947-9100 **Fax:** 207-942-8039

Bangor WAEI-FM (s) 184 Target Cir, Bangor ME 04401 **Phn:** 207-947-9100 **Fax:** 207-942-8039

Bangor WBFB-FM (c) 184 Target Cir, Bangor ME 04401 **Phn:** 207-947-9100 **Fax:** 207-942-8039 www.thenewbear.com pauldupuis@blueberrybroadcasting.com

Bangor WGUY-FM (o) 184 Target Cir, Bangor ME 04401 **Phn:** 207-947-9100 **Fax:** 207-942-8039

Bangor WHCF-FM (q) PO Box 5000, Bangor ME 04402 **Phn:** 207-947-2751 **Fax:** 207-947-0010 www.whcffm.com info@whcffm.com

Bangor WHSN-FM (vr) 1 College Cir, Bangor ME 04401 **Phn:** 207-941-7116 **Fax:** 207-947-3987 www.whsn-fm.com whsn@nescom.edu

Bangor WKIT-FM (r) PO Box 1929, Bangor ME 04402 **Phn:** 207-990-2800 **Fax:** 207-990-2444 www.wkitfm.com wkit@zoneradio.com

Bangor WKSQ-FM (a) 184 Target Cir, Bangor ME 04401 **Phn:** 207-947-9100 **Fax:** 207-942-8039 wksqfm.com

Bangor WMEH-FM (pln) 65 Texas Ave, Bangor ME 04401 **Phn:** 207-941-1010 **Fax:** 207-942-2857 www.mpbn.net radionews@mpbn.net

Bangor WVOM-FM (nt) 184 Target Cir, Bangor ME 04401 **Phn:** 207-947-9100 **Fax:** 207-942-8039 www.wvomfm.com jackobrien@blueberrybroadcasting.com

Bangor WZLO-AM (s) 861 Broadway, Bangor ME 04401 **Phn:** 207-942-6200 **Fax:** 207-990-2444 www.wzlofm.com wzlo@zoneradio.com

Bath WJTO-AM (bjz) PO Box 308, Bath ME 04530 **Phn:** 207-443-6671 www.wjto.com bobthemusicman7@aol.com

Brewer WBZN-FM (h) 49 Acme Rd, Brewer ME 04412 **Phn:** 207-989-5631 **Fax:** 207-989-5685 z1073.com arlen.jameson@townsquaremedia.com

Brewer WDEA-AM (ob) PO Box 100, Brewer ME 04412 **Phn:** 207-989-5631 **Fax:** 207-989-5685 wdea.am fred.miller@townsquaremedia.com

Brewer WEZQ-FM (a) PO Box 100, Brewer ME 04412 **Phn:** 207-989-5631 **Fax:** 207-989-5685 929theticket.com dale.duff@townsquaremedia.com

Brewer WQCB-FM (c) 49 Acme Rd Ste 1, Brewer ME 04412 **Phn:** 207-989-5631 **Fax:** 207-989-5685 q1065.fm darin.ingersoll@townsquaremedia.com

Brewer WWMJ-FM (r) PO Box 100, Brewer ME 04412 **Phn:** 207-989-5631 **Fax:** 207-989-5685 i95rocks.com fred.miller@townsquaremedia.com

Brunswick WBOR-FM (v) Bowdoin College, Brunswick ME 04011 **Phn:** 207-725-3210 wbor.org wbor@bowdoin.edu

Calais WALZ-FM (h) 637 Main St, Calais ME 04619 **Phn:** 207-454-7545 **Fax:** 207-454-3062 www.wqdy.fm wqdy@wqdy.fm

Calais WCRQ-FM (a) 637 Main St, Calais ME 04619 **Phn:** 207-454-7545 **Fax:** 207-454-3062 www.wcrqfm.com onair@wcrqfm.com

Calais WQDY-FM (h) 637 Main St, Calais ME 04619 **Phn:** 207-454-7545 **Fax:** 207-454-3062 www.wqdy.fm tom@wqdy.fm

Caribou WCXU-FM (ant) 152 E Green Ridge Rd, Caribou ME 04736 **Phn:** 207-473-7513 **Fax:** 207-472-3221 channelxradio.com channelxradio@yahoo.com

Caribou WCXX-FM (ant) 152 E Green Ridge Rd, Caribou ME 04736 **Phn:** 207-473-7513 **Fax:** 207-472-3221 channelxradio.com channelxradio@yahoo.com

Caribou WFST-AM (q) PO Box 600, Caribou ME 04736 **Phn:** 207-492-6000 **Fax:** 207-493-3268 www.wfst.net wfst@wfst.net

Dover Foxcroft WDME-FM (r) PO Box 473, Dover Foxcroft ME 04426 **Phn:** 207-564-2642 **Fax:** 207-564-8905

Dover Foxcroft WZON-FM (snt) PO Box 473, Dover Foxcroft ME 04426 **Phn:** 207-564-2642 **Fax:** 207-564-8905 www.wzonthepulse.com thepulse@zoneradio.com

East Orland WERU-FM (p) PO Box 170, East Orland ME 04431 **Phn:** 207-469-6600 **Fax:** 207-469-8961 weru.org info@weru.org

Ellsworth WNSX-FM (r) PO Box 1171, Ellsworth ME 04605 **Phn:** 207-667-0002 **Fax:** 207-667-0627

Farmington WKTJ-FM (a) 121 Broadway, Farmington ME 04938 **Phn:** 207-778-3400 **Fax:** 207-778-3000 www.993ktj.com wktj@wktj.com

Farmington WUMF-FM (rv) 111 South St, Farmington ME 04938 **Phn:** 207-778-7352 wumf.umf.maine.edu 100.1wumf@gmail.com

Freeport WMSJ-FM (q) PO Box 287, Freeport ME 04032 **Phn:** 207-865-3448 **Fax:** 207-865-1763 www.positive.fm

Houlton WHOU-FM (a) PO Box 40, Houlton ME 04730 **Phn:** 207-532-3600 **Fax:** 207-521-0056 www.whoufm.com manager@whoufm.com

Kennebunk WBYA-FM (r) 169 Port Rd, Kennebunk ME 04043 **Phn:** 207-967-0993 **Fax:** 207-967-8671

Lewiston WRBC-FM (v) 31 Frye St, Lewiston ME 04240 **Phn:** 207-777-7532 abacus.bates.eduwrbc lmorse@gwi.net

Millinocket WSYY-AM (s) PO Box 1240, Millinocket ME 04462 **Phn:** 207-723-9657 www.themountain949.com jtalbott@themountain949.com

Millinocket WSYY-FM (a) PO Box 1240, Millinocket ME 04462 **Phn:** 207-723-9657 www.themountain949.com jtalbott@themountain949.com

Norway WKTQ-AM (st) PO Box 72, Norway ME 04268 **Phn:** 207-743-5911 **Fax:** 207-743-5913 www.wtme.com news@gleasonmedia.com

Norway WOXO-FM (cs) PO Box 72, Norway ME 04268 **Phn:** 207-743-5911 **Fax:** 207-743-5913 www.oxocountry.com news@gleasonmedia.com

Norway WTBM-FM (cs) PO Box 72, Norway ME 04268 **Phn:** 207-743-5911 **Fax:** 207-743-5913 www.woxo.com news@gleasonmedia.com

Norway WTME-AM (qn) PO Box 72, Norway ME 04268 **Phn:** 207-743-5911 **Fax:** 207-743-5913 www.wtme.com news@gleasonmedia.com

Orono WMEB-FM (v) 5748 Memorial Un, Orono ME 04469 **Phn:** 207-581-4340 **Fax:** 207-581-4343 www.wmeb.fm murph@maine.edu

Orrington WJCX-FM (qnt) 154 River Rd, Orrington ME 04474 **Phn:** 207-991-9555 www.ccbangor.org

Portland WBLM-FM (r) 1 City Ctr, Portland ME 04101 **Phn:** 207-774-6364 **Fax:** 207-774-8707 www.wblm.com herb.ivy@townsquaremedia.com

Portland WBQQ-FM (c) 477 Congress St, Portland ME 04101 **Phn:** 207-797-0780 **Fax:** 207-774-4390 wtht.nh1media.com sbennett@binradio.com

Portland WBQX-FM (l) 477 Congress St, Portland ME 04210 **Phn:** 207-967-0993 **Fax:** 207-774-4390 wbqx.nh1media.com

Portland WCLZ-FM (ar) 420 Western Ave, Portland ME 04106 **Phn:** 207-774-4561 **Fax:** 207-774-3788 www.989wclz.com wclz@989wclz.com

Portland WCYY-FM (r) 1 City Ctr, Portland ME 04101 **Phn:** 207-774-6364 **Fax:** 207-774-8707 www.wcyy.com mike.sambrook@townsquaremedia.com

Portland WFNK-FM (c) 477 Congress St Ste 3A, Portland ME 04101 **Phn:** 207-797-0780 **Fax:** 207-797-0368 wfnk.nh1media.com pcollins@binradio.com

Portland WHOM-FM (a) 1 City Ctr, Portland ME 04101 **Phn:** 207-774-6364 **Fax:** 207-774-8707 www.949whom.com herb.ivy@townsquaremedia.com

Portland WHXR-FM (r) 477 Congress St Ste 3B, Portland ME 04101 **Phn:** 207-797-0780 **Fax:** 207-774-4390 whxr.nh1media.com

Portland WJAE-AM (st) 779 Warren Ave, Portland ME 04103 **Phn:** 207-773-9695 **Fax:** 207-761-4406 www.thebigjab.com shoe@thebigjab.com

Portland WJBQ-FM (h) 1 City Ctr Stop 22, Portland ME 04101 **Phn:** 207-774-6364 **Fax:** 207-774-8707 www.wjbq.com psa.portland@cumulus.com

Portland WJJB-AM (st) 779 Warren Ave, Portland ME 04103 **Phn:** 207-773-9695 **Fax:** 207-761-4406 www.thebigjab.com shoe@thebigjab.com

Portland WJJB-FM (st) 779 Warren Ave, Portland ME 04103 **Phn:** 207-773-9695 **Fax:** 207-761-4406 www.thebigjab.com shoe@thebigjab.com

Portland WLAM-AM (s) 477 Congress St Ste 3A, Portland ME 04101 **Phn:** 207-797-0780 **Fax:** 207-797-0368

Portland WLOB-AM (nt) 779 Warren Ave, Portland ME 04103 **Phn:** 207-773-9695 **Fax:** 207-761-4406 www.wlobradio.com newstalkwlob@yahoo.com

Portland WLVP-AM (t) 477 Congress St Ste 3B, Portland ME 04101 **Phn:** 207-797-0780 **Fax:** 207-253-1929

Portland WMEA-FM (plj) 309 Marginal Way, Portland ME 04101 **Phn:** 207-874-6570 **Fax:** 207-761-0318 www.mpbn.net radionews@mpbn.net

MAINE RADIO STATIONS

Portland WMPG-FM (v) 96 Falmouth St, Portland ME 04103 **Phn:** 207-780-4943 www.wmpg.org stationmanager@wmpg.org

Portland WRED-FM (h) 779 Warren Ave, Portland ME 04103 **Phn:** 207-773-9695 **Fax:** 207-761-4406 www.thebigjab.com shoe@thebigjab.com

Portland WTHT-FM (x) 477 Congress St Ste 3A, Portland ME 04101 **Phn:** 207-797-0780 **Fax:** 207-797-0368 www.999thewolf.com sbennett@binradio.com

Presque Isle WBPW-FM (c) 551 Main St, Presque Isle ME 04769 **Phn:** 207-769-6600 **Fax:** 207-764-5274 bigcountry969.com mark.shaw@townsquaremedia.com

Presque Isle WEGP-AM (t) PO Box 4088, Presque Isle ME 04769 **Phn:** 207-762-6700 **Fax:** 207-762-3319

Presque Isle WOZI-FM (r) 551 Main St, Presque Isle ME 04769 **Phn:** 207-769-6600 **Fax:** 207-764-5274 www.1019therock.com mark.shaw@townsquaremedia.com

Presque Isle WQHR-FM (a) 551 Main St, Presque Isle ME 04769 **Phn:** 207-769-6600 **Fax:** 207-764-5274 q961.com mark.shaw@townsquaremedia.com

Presque Isle WUPI-FM (v) 181 Main St, Presque Isle ME 04769 **Phn:** 207-768-9742

Rockland WMCM-FM (c) 15 Payne Ave, Rockland ME 04841 **Phn:** 207-594-9400 **Fax:** 207-594-2234

Rockland WQSS-FM (r) 15 Payne Ave, Rockland ME 04841 **Phn:** 207-594-9400 **Fax:** 207-594-2234

Rockland WRKD-AM (s) 15 Payne Ave, Rockland ME 04841 **Phn:** 207-594-9400 **Fax:** 207-594-2234

Skowhegan WCTB-FM (h) PO Box 159, Skowhegan ME 04976 **Phn:** 207-474-5171 **Fax:** 207-474-3299 riverrocks@gmail.com

Skowhegan WSKW-AM (s) PO Box 159, Skowhegan ME 04976 **Phn:** 207-474-5171 **Fax:** 207-474-3299

South Portland WBAE-AM (am) 420 Western Ave, South Portland ME 04106 **Phn:** 207-774-4561 **Fax:** 207-774-3788 am1490thebay.com news@560wgan.com

South Portland WGAN-AM (nt) 420 Western Ave, South Portland ME 04106 **Phn:** 207-774-4561 **Fax:** 207-761-7765 www.560wgan.com news@560wgan.com

South Portland WMGX-FM (h) 420 Western Ave, South Portland ME 04106 **Phn:** 207-774-4561 **Fax:** 207-774-3788 coast931.com rkirshbaum@portlandradiogroup.com

South Portland WPOR-FM (c) 420 Western Ave, South Portland ME 04106 **Phn:** 207-774-4561 **Fax:** 207-774-3788 www.wpor.com wpor@wpor.com

South Portland WVAE-AM (am) 420 Western Ave, South Portland ME 04106 **Phn:** 207-774-4561 **Fax:** 207-774-3788 www.am1400and1490.com news@560wgan.com

South Portland WYNZ-FM (o) 420 Western Ave, South Portland ME 04106 **Phn:** 207-774-4561 **Fax:** 207-774-3788 rewind1009.com cmac@portlandradiogroup.com

South Portland WZAN-AM (t) 420 Western Ave, South Portland ME 04106 **Phn:** 207-774-4561 **Fax:** 207-774-3788 www.970wzan.com news@560wgan.com

Topsham WBCI-FM (qt) 122 Main St, Topsham ME 04086 **Phn:** 207-725-9224 **Fax:** 207-725-2686 lifechangingradio.comwbci info@wbci.fm

Waterville WMHB-FM (v) 4000 Mayflower Hl, Waterville ME 04901 **Phn:** 207-859-5454 www.wmhb.org info@wmhb.org

MARYLAND

Aberdeen WAMD-AM (qt) 400 Hiobs Ln, Aberdeen MD 21001 **Phn:** 410-272-4400 **Fax:** 410-575-6890

Annapolis WBIS-AM (kn) 1610 West St Ste 209, Annapolis MD 21401 **Phn:** 410-269-0700

Annapolis WFSI-FM (q) 918 Chesapeake Ave, Annapolis MD 21403 **Phn:** 410-268-6200

Annapolis WNAV-AM (ant) PO Box 6726, Annapolis MD 21401 **Phn:** 410-263-1430 **Fax:** 410-268-5360 www.wnav.com news@wnav.com

Annapolis WRNR-FM (r) 112 Main St Ste 3, Annapolis MD 21401 **Phn:** 410-626-0103 **Fax:** 410-267-7634 www.wrnr.com bobw@wrnr.com

Baltimore WBAL-AM (snt) 3800 Hooper Ave, Baltimore MD 21211 **Phn:** 410-467-3000 **Fax:** 410-338-6491 www.wbal.com news@wbal.com

Baltimore WBJC-FM (pl) 6776 Reisterstown Rd Ste 202, Baltimore MD 21215 **Phn:** 410-580-5800 www.wbjc.

Baltimore WCAO-AM (gw) 711 W 40th St Ste 350, Baltimore MD 21211 **Phn:** 410-366-7600 **Fax:** 410-467-0011 www.heaven600.com lsmichaels@wcao.com

Baltimore WERQ-FM (wu) 1705 Whitehead Rd, Baltimore MD 21207 **Phn:** 410-332-4600 **Fax:** 410-944-7989 92q.com neke92@aol.com

Baltimore WIYY-FM (r) 3800 Hooper Ave, Baltimore MD 21211 **Phn:** 410-467-3000 **Fax:** 410-338-6526 www.98online.com dshill@hearst.com

Baltimore WJFK-AM (snt) 1423 Clarkview Rd Ste 100, Baltimore MD 21209 **Phn:** 410-828-7722 **Fax:** 410-821-2031 www.1300wjfk.com

Baltimore WJZ-FM (s) 1423 Clarkview Rd Ste 100, Baltimore MD 21209 **Phn:** 410-828-1057 **Fax:** 410-821-8256 baltimore.cbslocal.com dave.labrozzi@cbsradio.com

Baltimore WLIF-FM (m) 1423 Clarkview Rd Ste 100, Baltimore MD 21209 **Phn:** 410-296-1019 **Fax:** 410-821-5482 1019litefm.cbslocal.com greg.carpenter@cbsradio.com

Baltimore WOLB-AM (wnt) 1705 Whitehead Rd, Baltimore MD 21207 **Phn:** 410-332-4600 **Fax:** 410-944-7201 wolbbaltimore.com apayne@radio-one.com

Baltimore WPOC-FM (c) 711 W 40th St Ste 350, Baltimore MD 21211 **Phn:** 410-366-7600 **Fax:** 410-235-3899 www.wpoc.com megstevens@clearchannel.com

Baltimore WQSR-FM (o) 711 W 40th St, Baltimore MD 21211 **Phn:** 410-366-7900 **Fax:** 410-235-3899 www.1027jackfm.com hartleyadkins@clearchannel.com

Baltimore WTMD-FM (vr) 8000 York Rd, Baltimore MD 21252 **Phn:** 410-704-8938 **Fax:** 410-704-2609 www.wtmd.org wtmd@towson.edu

Baltimore WWIN-AM (wg) 1705 Whitehead Rd, Baltimore MD 21207 **Phn:** 410-332-4600 **Fax:** 410-944-7989 mybaltimorespirit.com lyoung@radio-one.com

Baltimore WWIN-FM (we) 1705 Whitehead Rd, Baltimore MD 21207 **Phn:** 410-332-4600 **Fax:** 410-944-2473 magicbaltimore.com kwynder@radio-one.com

Baltimore WWMX-FM (a) 1423 Clarkview Rd Ste 100, Baltimore MD 21209 **Phn:** 410-825-1065 **Fax:** 410-321-4548 mix1065fm.cbslocal.com dave.labrozzi@cbsradio.com

Baltimore WYPR-FM (p) 2216 N Charles St, Baltimore MD 21218 **Phn:** 410-235-1660 **Fax:** 410-235-1161 wypr.org fsmith@wypr.org

MARYLAND RADIO STATIONS

Baltimore WZFT-FM (h) 711 W 40th St Ste 350, Baltimore MD 21211 **Phn:** 410-366-7600 **Fax:** 410-235-3899 www.z1043.com jerryhouston@clearchannel.com

Bel Air WHFC-FM (v) 401 Thomas Run Rd, Bel Air MD 21015 **Phn:** 410-836-4151 www.whfc911.org whfc@harford.edu

Cambridge WAAI-FM (c) 2 Bay St, Cambridge MD 21613 **Phn:** 410-228-4800 **Fax:** 410-228-0130 www.mtslive.com news@mtslive.com

Cambridge WCEM-FM (a) 2 Bay St, Cambridge MD 21613 **Phn:** 410-228-4800 **Fax:** 410-228-0130 www.mtslive.com theheat@mtslive.com

Cambridge WCEM-AM (oa) 2 Bay St, Cambridge MD 21613 **Phn:** 410-228-4800 **Fax:** 410-228-0130 www.mtslive.com news@mtslive.com

Cambridge WTDK-FM (o) 2 Bay St, Cambridge MD 21613 **Phn:** 410-228-4800 **Fax:** 410-228-0130 www.mtslive.com news@mtslive.com

Chestertown WCTR-AM (a) 231 Flatland Rd, Chestertown MD 21620 **Phn:** 410-778-1530 **Fax:** 410-778-4800 www.wctr.com kcollins@wctr.com

College Park WMUC-FM (v) 3130 S Campus Dining Hall, College Park MD 20742 **Phn:** 301-314-7868 www.wmuc.umd.edu wmucnewsdirector@gmail.com

Cumberland WCBC-AM (nt) PO Box 1290, Cumberland MD 21501 **Phn:** 301-724-5000 **Fax:** 301-722-8336 wcbcradio.com info@wcbcradio.com

Cumberland WCBC-FM (o) PO Box 1290, Cumberland MD 21501 **Phn:** 301-724-5000 **Fax:** 301-722-8336 wcbcradio.com info@wcbcradio.com

Cumberland WDZN-FM (m) PO Box 477, Cumberland MD 21501 **Phn:** 301-724-6000 **Fax:** 301-724-0617 music.disney.com

Cumberland WKGO-FM (a) 350 Byrd Ave, Cumberland MD 21502 **Phn:** 301-722-6666 **Fax:** 301-722-0945 www.go106.com richcornwell@go106.com

Cumberland WQZK-FM (r) 15 Industrial Blvd E, Cumberland MD 21502 **Phn:** 301-759-1005 www.941qzk.com aryan@wvradio.com

Cumberland WTBO-AM (s) 350 Byrd Ave, Cumberland MD 21502 **Phn:** 301-722-6666 **Fax:** 301-722-0945 www.foxsportsradio1450.com

Denton WKDI-AM (q) PO Box 309, Denton MD 21629 **Phn:** 410-479-2288 **Fax:** 410-479-5188

Easton WCEI-FM (a) 306 Port St, Easton MD 21601 **Phn:** 410-822-3301 **Fax:** 410-822-0576 www.wceiradio.com stacie@wceiradio.com

Easton WEMD-AM (bz) 306 Port St, Easton MD 21601 **Phn:** 410-822-3301 **Fax:** 410-822-0576 www.wceiradio.com stacie@wceiradio.com

Easton WINX-FM (c) 306 Port St, Easton MD 21601 **Phn:** 410-822-3301 **Fax:** 410-822-0576 www.winxfm.com stacie@wceiradio.com

Elkton WOEL-FM (q) PO Box 246, Elkton MD 21922 **Phn:** 410-392-3225 **Fax:** 410-392-3229

Emmitsburg WMTB-FM (v) 16300 Old Emmitsburg Rd, Emmitsburg MD 21727 **Phn:** 301-447-5239 wmtb@msmary.edu

Frederick WAFY-FM (a) 5742 Industry Ln, Frederick MD 21704 **Phn:** 301-620-7700 **Fax:** 301-696-0509 www.key103radio.com tommy@manningbroadcastinginc.com

Frederick WFMD-AM (nt) 5966 Grove Hill Rd, Frederick MD 21703 **Phn:** 301-663-4181 **Fax:** 301-682-8018 www.wfmd.com news@wfmd.com

Frederick WFRE-FM (c) 5966 Grove Hill Rd, Frederick MD 21703 **Phn:** 301-663-4337 **Fax:** 301-682-8018 www.wfre.com dianahgibson@clearchannel.com

Frostburg WFRB-AM (a) 242 Finzel Rd, Frostburg MD 21532 **Phn:** 301-689-8871 **Fax:** 301-689-8880 richcornwell@go106.com

Frostburg WFRB-FM (c) 242 Finzel Rd, Frostburg MD 21532 **Phn:** 301-689-8871 **Fax:** 301-689-8880 www.wfrb.com richcornwell@go106.com

Frostburg WFWM-FM (v) Frostburg State Univ, Frostburg MD 21532 **Phn:** 301-687-4143 **Fax:** 301-687-7040 www.wfwm.org wfwm@frostburg.edu

Georgetown WOCQ-FM (h) 20200 Dupont Blvd, Georgetown MD 19947 **Phn:** 302-856-2567 **Fax:** 302-856-7633 www.oc104.com

Glen Burnie WFBR-AM (q) 159 8th Ave NW, Glen Burnie MD 21061 **Phn:** 410-761-1590

Grantsville WPCL-FM (gq) PO Box 540, Grantsville MD 21536 **Phn:** 301-895-3292 **Fax:** 301-895-3293

Hagerstown WARK-AM (st) 880 Commonwealth Ave, Hagerstown MD 21740 **Phn:** 301-733-4500 **Fax:** 301-733-0040

Hagerstown WDLD-FM (hr) 1250 Maryland Ave, Hagerstown MD 21740 **Phn:** 301-797-7300 **Fax:** 301-797-2659 www.wild967.fm artieshultz@mix95.com

Hagerstown WHAG-AM (am) 1250 Maryland Ave, Hagerstown MD 21740 **Phn:** 301-797-7300 **Fax:** 301-797-2659

Hagerstown WJEJ-AM (z) 1135 Haven Rd, Hagerstown MD 21742 **Phn:** 301-739-2326 **Fax:** 301-797-7408 www.wjejradio.com wjej@myactv.net

Hagerstown WQCM-FM (r) 1250 Maryland Ave, Hagerstown MD 21740 **Phn:** 301-797-7300 **Fax:** 301-797-2659 www.wqcmfm.com mholder@mlbroadcasting.net

Hagerstown WWEG-FM (h) 880 Commonwealth Ave, Hagerstown MD 21740 **Phn:** 301-733-4500 **Fax:** 301-733-0040 www.1069theeagle.com kevin@1069theeagle.com

Halethorpe WRBS-FM (q) 3500 Commerce Dr, Halethorpe MD 21227 **Phn:** 410-247-4100 www.951shinefm.com info@951shinefm.com

Havre de Grace WJSS-AM (jb) 1605 Level Rd, Havre de Grace MD 21078 **Phn:** 410-939-0800 **Fax:** 410-939-2156 www.wjss1330.com wjss@comcast.net

Havre de Grace WXCY-FM (c) PO Box 269, Havre de Grace MD 21078 **Phn:** 410-939-1100 **Fax:** 410-939-1104 www.wxcyfm.com

Hunt Valley WZBA-FM (ar) 11350 McCormick Rd Ste 701, Hunt Valley MD 21031 **Phn:** 410-771-8484 **Fax:** 410-771-1616 www.thebayonline.com askthepd@thebayonline.com

Lanham WHFS-AM (t) 4200 Parliament Pl Ste 300, Lanham MD 20706 **Phn:** 301-731-1580 whfs.cbslocal.com gregory.edger@cbsradio.com

Lanham WLZL-FM (y) 4200 Parliament Pl Ste 300, Lanham MD 20706 **Phn:** 301-306-0991 **Fax:** 301-731-0431 elzolradio.cbslocal.com juan.romero@cbsradio.com

Lanham WOL-AM (wnt) 5900 Princess Garden Pkwy, Lanham MD 20706 **Phn:** 301-306-1111 **Fax:** 301-306-9540 woldcnews.com

Lanham WPGC-FM (h) 4200 Parliament Pl Ste 300, Lanham MD 20706 **Phn:** 301-731-1580 wpgc.cbslocal.com jason.kidd@cbsradio.com

Lanham WTGB-FM (a) 4200 Parliament Pl Ste 300, Lanham MD 20706 **Phn:** 301-683-0947 **Fax:** 301-918-2354 947freshfm.cbslocal.com steve.davis@947freshfm.com

Lanham WYCB-AM (wgu) 5900 Princess Garden Pkwy Ste 800, Lanham MD 20706 **Phn:** 301-306-1111 **Fax:** 301-306-9540 myspiritdc.com rthompson@radio-one.com

Laurel WILC-AM (y) 13499 Baltimore Ave Ste 200, Laurel MD 20707 **Phn:** 301-419-2122 **Fax:** 301-419-2409 www.holaciudad.com info@holaciudad.com

Mechanicsville WKIK-FM (c) 28095 Three Notch Rd Ste 2B, Mechanicsville MD 20659 **Phn:** 301-870-5550 www.country1029wkik.com frank@somdradio.com

Mechanicsville WKIK-AM (c) 28095 Three Notch Rd Ste 2B, Mechanicsville MD 20659 **Phn:** 301-870-5550 wkikfm@aol.com

Mechanicsville WMDM-FM (o) 28095 Three Notch Rd Ste 2B, Mechanicsville MD 20659 **Phn:** 301-870-5550

Mechanicsville WPTX-AM (nt) 28095 Three Notch Rd Ste 2B, Mechanicsville MD 20659 **Phn:** 301-870-5550 wsmdfm@aol.com

Mechanicsville WSMD-FM (or) 28095 Three Notch Rd Ste 2B, Mechanicsville MD 20659 **Phn:** 301-870-5550 www.star983.com patrick@somdradio.com

Mechanicsville WYRX-FM (r) 28095 Three Notch Rd Ste 2B, Mechanicsville MD 20659 **Phn:** 301-870-5550 wsmdfm@aol.com

Mountain Lake Park WKHJ-FM (a) PO Box 2337, Mountain Lake Park MD 21550 **Phn:** 301-334-4272 **Fax:** 301-334-2152 1045khj.com office@wkhj.com

Ocean City WOCM-FM (r) 117 49th St, Ocean City MD 21842 **Phn:** 410-723-3683 ocean98.com bulldog@ocean98.com

Pikesville WCBM-AM (nt) 1726 Reisterstown Rd Ste 117, Pikesville MD 21208 **Phn:** 410-580-6800 **Fax:** 410-580-6810 www.wcbm.com am680@wcbm.com

Potomac WCTN-AM (y) 7825 Tuckerman Ln Ste 211, Potomac MD 20854 **Phn:** 301-299-7026 **Fax:** 301-299-5301 950wctn@gmail.com

Princess Anne WESM-FM (pjn) Umes Backbone Rd, Princess Anne MD 21853 **Phn:** 410-651-8001 **Fax:** 410-651-8005 www.wesm913.org wesm913@umes.edu

Princess Anne WOLC-FM (q) PO Box 130, Princess Anne MD 21853 **Phn:** 410-543-9652 **Fax:** 410-651-9652 www.wolc.org wolc@wolc.org

Rockville WASH-FM (a) 1801 Rockville Pike Ste 601, Rockville MD 20852 **Phn:** 240-747-2800 www.washfm.com dcpsa@clearchannel.com

Rockville WBIG-FM (o) 1801 Rockville Pike Ste 602, Rockville MD 20852 **Phn:** 240-747-2700 www.wbig.com billcahill@clearchannel.com

Rockville WIHT-FM (h) 1801 Rockville Pike Ste 603, Rockville MD 20852 **Phn:** 240-747-2700 **Fax:** 240-747-3700 www.hot995.com dcpsa@clearchannel.com

Rockville WMZQ-FM (c) 1801 Rockville Pike Fl 5, Rockville MD 20852 **Phn:** 240-747-2700 **Fax:** 240-747-3700 www.wmzq.com megstevens@wmzq.com

Rockville WTEM-AM (st) 1801 Rockville Pike Ste 405, Rockville MD 20852 **Phn:** 301-230-3500 **Fax:** 240-430-2742 www.espn980.com glasgowd@redskins.com

Rockville WTNT-AM (nt) 1801 Rockville Pike Ste 405, Rockville MD 20852 **Phn:** 301-231-7798 **Fax:** 301-231-9889 sportstalk570.com management@espn980.com

Rockville WWDC-FM (r) 1801 Rockville Pike Ste 405, Rockville MD 20852 **Phn:** 240-747-2700 **Fax:** 240-747-3700 www.DC101.com roche@dc101.com

Rockville WWRC-AM (t) 1801 Rockville Pike Ste 402, Rockville MD 20852 **Phn:** 301-231-7798 **Fax:** 301-231-9889 kathylennhoff@clearchannel.com

Salisbury WDIH-FM (q) PO Box 186, Salisbury MD 21803 **Phn:** 410-860-5000

Salisbury WDKZ-FM (h) 351 Tilghman Rd, Salisbury MD 21804 **Phn:** 410-742-1923 **Fax:** 410-742-2329 www.kiss959fm.com matthewderrick@clearchannel.com

Salisbury WICO-FM (c) PO Box 909, Salisbury MD 21803 **Phn:** 410-219-3500 **Fax:** 410-548-1543 www.catcountryradio.com catcountry@catcountryradio.com

Salisbury WICO-AM (nt) PO Box 909, Salisbury MD 21803 **Phn:** 410-219-3500 **Fax:** 410-548-1543 www.wicoam.com wico@wicoam.com

Salisbury WJDY-AM (st) 351 Tilghman Rd, Salisbury MD 21804 **Phn:** 410-742-1923 **Fax:** 410-742-2329 www.foxsports1470.com randallscott2@clearchannel.com

Salisbury WKTT-FM (c) PO Box 909, Salisbury MD 21803 **Phn:** 410-219-3500 **Fax:** 410-548-1543 www.catcountryradio.com catcountry@catcountryradio.com

Salisbury WLBW-FM (o) 351 Tilghman Rd, Salisbury MD 21804 **Phn:** 410-742-1923

Salisbury WQHQ-FM (a) 351 Tilghman Rd, Salisbury MD 21804 **Phn:** 410-742-1923 **Fax:** 410-742-2329 www.q105fm.com joshwolff@clearchannel.com

Salisbury WQJZ-FM (aj) PO Box 909, Salisbury MD 21803 **Phn:** 410-219-3500 **Fax:** 410-548-1543 www.971thewave.com wave@971thewave.com

Salisbury WSBY-FM (u) 351 Tilghman Rd, Salisbury MD 21804 **Phn:** 410-742-1923 **Fax:** 410-742-2329 www.mymagic989.com susangroves@clearchannel.com

Salisbury WSCL-FM (pln) PO Box 2596, Salisbury MD 21802 **Phn:** 410-543-6895 **Fax:** 410-548-3000 www.publicradiodelmarva.net dwroeck@salisbury.edu

Salisbury WSDL-FM (pn) PO Box 2596, Salisbury MD 21802 **Phn:** 410-543-6895 **Fax:** 410-548-3000 www.publicradiodelmarva.net dwroeck@salisbury.edu

Salisbury WTGM-AM (st) 351 Tilghman Rd, Salisbury MD 21804 **Phn:** 410-742-1923 **Fax:** 410-742-2329 www.foxsports1470.com justinthomas@clearchannel.com

Salisbury WWFG-FM (c) 351 Tilghman Rd, Salisbury MD 21804 **Phn:** 410-742-1923 **Fax:** 410-742-2329 www.froggy999.com dickraymond@froggy999.com

Salisbury WZKT-FM (c) PO Box 909, Salisbury MD 21803 **Phn:** 410-219-3500 **Fax:** 410-548-1543 www.catcountryradio.com catcountry@catcountryradio.com

Silver Spring WACA-AM (yt) 11141 Georgia Ave Ste 310, Silver Spring MD 20902 **Phn:** 301-942-3500 **Fax:** 301-942-7798 www.radioamerica.net cabina@radioamerica.net

Silver Spring WKYS-FM (wu) 8515 Georgia Ave Flr 9, Silver Spring MD 20910 **Phn:** 301-306-1111 **Fax:** 301-306-9540 kysdc.com aleinwand@radio-one.com

Silver Spring WMET-AM (q) 8121 Georgia Ave #806, Silver Spring MD 20910 **Phn:** 877-636-1160 **Fax:** 301-585-1682 grnonline.com steve@grnonline.com

Silver Spring WMMJ-FM (wau) 8515 Georgia Ave Flr 9, Silver Spring MD 20910 **Phn:** 301-306-1111 **Fax:** 301-306-9540 mymajicdc.com cbullock@radio-one.com

Suitland WWGB-AM (yug) 5210 Auth Rd Ste 500, Suitland MD 20746 **Phn:** 301-899-1444 **Fax:** 301-899-7244 www.wwgb.com radio@wwgb.com

MARYLAND RADIO STATIONS

Takoma Park WGTS-FM (v) 7600 Flower Ave, Takoma Park MD 20912 **Phn:** 301-891-4200 **Fax:** 301-270-9191 wgts.org wgts@wgts.org

Thurmont WTHU-AM (snt) 10 Radio Ln, Thurmont MD 21788 **Phn:** 301-271-2188 **Fax:** 301-271-2158 www.wthu.org

Towson WNST-AM (s) 1550 Hart Rd, Towson MD 21286 **Phn:** 410-821-9678 **Fax:** 410-828-4698 www.wnst.net info@wnst.net

Westminster WTTR-AM (o) 101 WTTR Ln, Westminster MD 21158 **Phn:** 410-848-5511 **Fax:** 410-876-5095 www.wttr.com info@wttr.com

Williamsport WCRH-FM (q) PO Box 439, Williamsport MD 21795 **Phn:** 301-582-0282 **Fax:** 301-582-2707 wcrh.org wcrh@wcrh.org

Worton WKHS-FM (v) 25301 Lambs Meadow Rd, Worton MD 21678 **Phn:** 410-778-4249 **Fax:** 410-778-3802 www.wkhsradio.org wkhsradio@gmail.com

MASSACHUSETTS

Allston WBZ-AM (nt) 1170 Soldiers Field Rd, Allston MA 02134 **Phn:** 617-787-7000 **Fax:** 617-787-7060 boston.cbslocal.com wbzradionews@wbz.com

Amherst WAMH-FM (v) Ac #1907 Campus Ctr, Amherst MA 01002 **Phn:** 413-542-2224 wamh.amherst.edu wamh@amherst.edu

Amherst WFCR-FM (plnj) 131 County Cir, Amherst MA 01003 **Phn:** 413-545-0100 **Fax:** 413-545-2546 www.nepr.net radio@nepr.net

Amherst WMUA-FM (vxj) 105 Campus Ctr, Amherst MA 01003 **Phn:** 413-545-2876 **Fax:** 413-545-0682 www.wmua.org manager@wmua.org

Amherst WNNZ-AM (pn) 131 County Cir, Amherst MA 01003 **Phn:** 413-545-0100 **Fax:** 413-545-2546 www.nepr.net radio@nepr.net

Amherst WNNZ-FM (pn) 131 County Cir, Amherst MA 01003 **Phn:** 413-545-0100 **Fax:** 413-545-2546 www.nepr.net radio@nepr.net

Andover WPAA-FM (v) 180 Main St, Andover MA 01810 **Phn:** 978-749-4384 **Fax:** 978-749-4123 wpaa@aol.com

Auburndale WNTN-AM (m) 143 Rumford Ave, Auburndale MA 02466 **Phn:** 617-969-1550 www.wntn.com info@wntn.com

Beverly WBOQ-FM (o) 8 Enon St, Beverly MA 01915 **Phn:** 978-927-1049 **Fax:** 978-921-2635 www.northshore1049.com charlie@northshore1049.com

Boston WBMX-FM (a) 83 Leo M Birmingham Pkwy, Boston MA 02135 **Phn:** 617-746-1300 **Fax:** 617-746-1395 mix1041.cbslocal.com mmullaney@mix1041.com

Boston WBUR-FM (pnt) 890 Commonwealth Ave, Boston MA 02215 **Phn:** 617-353-0909 **Fax:** 617-353-4747 www.wbur.org wburnews@wbur.org

Boston WBUR-AM (pnt) 890 Commonwealth Ave, Boston MA 02215 **Phn:** 617-353-0909 **Fax:** 617-353-4747 www.wbur.org wburnews@wbur.org

Boston WBZ-FM (s) 83 Leo M Birmingham Pkwy, Boston MA 02135 **Phn:** 617-746-1400 **Fax:** 617-746-1408 boston.cbslocal.com mike.thomas@cbsradio.com

Boston WERS-FM (a) 120 Boylston St, Boston MA 02116 **Phn:** 617-824-8890 **Fax:** 617-824-8804 www.wers.org info@wers.org

Boston WGBH-FM (plnj) PO Box 200, Boston MA 02134 **Phn:** 617-300-2000 **Fax:** 617-300-1025 www.wgbh.org newsevents@wgbh.org

Boston WRBB-FM (v) 360 Huntington Ave, Boston MA 02115 **Phn:** 617-373-4338 **Fax:** 617-373-5095 wrbbradio.org news@wrbbradio.org

Boston WUNR-AM (ey) 160 N Washington St, Boston MA 02114 **Phn:** 617-367-9003 **Fax:** 617-367-2265

Bridgewater WBIM-FM (v) 109 Campus Ctr, Bridgewater MA 02325 **Phn:** 508-697-1303 wbim@bridgew.edu

Brighton WAAF-FM (r) 20 Guest St Ste 300, Brighton MA 02135 **Phn:** 617-779-5400 **Fax:** 617-779-5484 www.waaf.com rvaleri@entercom.com

Brighton WEEI-FM (a) 20 Guest St Fl 3, Brighton MA 02135 **Phn:** 617-779-3400 **Fax:** 617-779-3555 www.weei.com jwolfe@entercom.com

Brighton WEEI-AM (st) 20 Guest St Ste 300, Brighton MA 02135 **Phn:** 617-779-3500 **Fax:** 617-779-3557 www.weei.com jwolfe@entercom.com

Brighton WODS-FM (h) 83 Leo M Birmingham Pkwy, Brighton MA 02135 **Phn:** 617-787-7500 **Fax:** 617-787-7523 1033amradio.cbslocal.com dmason@boston.cbs.com

Brighton WRKO-AM (nt) 20 Guest St Ste 300, Brighton MA 02135 **Phn:** 617-779-3400 **Fax:** 617-779-3555 www.wrko.com jbrown@entercom.com

Brighton WZLX-FM (r) 83 Leo M Birmingham Pkwy, Brighton MA 02135 **Phn:** 617-746-5100 **Fax:** 617-746-5102 wzlx.cbslocal.com mikethomas@wzlx.com

Brockton WMSX-AM (y) 288 Linwood St, Brockton MA 02301 **Phn:** 508-587-5454 **Fax:** 508-587-1950 molinahbone@aol.com

Brockton WXBR-AM (nt) 60 Main St, Brockton MA 02301 **Phn:** 508-525-4550 wxbr1460.com

Cambridge WHRB-FM (njl) 389 Harvard St, Cambridge MA 02138 **Phn:** 617-495-4818 www.whrb.org psa@whrb.org

Cambridge WJIB-AM (bzj) 443 Concord Ave, Cambridge MA 02138 **Phn:** 617-868-7400 wjib740.com

Cambridge WMBR-FM (v) 3 Ames St, Cambridge MA 02142 **Phn:** 617-253-4000 wmbr.org management@wmbr.org

Cambridge WRCA-AM (ey) 552 Massachusetts Ave Ste 201, Cambridge MA 02139 **Phn:** 617-492-3300 **Fax:** 617-492-2800 www.1330wrca.com wrca1330@aol.com

Charlestown WAMG-AM (s) 529 Main St Ste 200, Charlestown MA 02129 **Phn:** 617-830-1000 **Fax:** 617-242-8176 espn.go.comboston

Charlestown WLLH-AM (s) 529 Main St Ste 200, Charlestown MA 02129 **Phn:** 617-830-1000 **Fax:** 617-242-8176 espn.go.comboston

Chelsea WESX-AM (y) 90 Everett Ave, Chelsea MA 02150 **Phn:** 617-884-4500 **Fax:** 617-884-4515 www.wesx1230am.com

Chelsea WJDA-AM (y) 90 Everett Ave Ste 5, Chelsea MA 02150 **Phn:** 617-884-4500 **Fax:** 617-884-4515 www.wjda1300am.com arivas5906@aol.com

Deerfield WGAJ-FM (v) Deerfield Academy, Deerfield MA 01342 **Phn:** 413-774-1539 **Fax:** 413-772-1100

Dorchester WBOS-FM (ar) 55 William T Morrissey Blvd, Dorchester MA 02125 **Phn:** 617-822-9600 **Fax:** 617-822-6759 www.myradio929.com kwest@myradio929.com

Dorchester WKLB-FM (c) 55 William T Morrissey Blvd, Dorchester MA 02125 **Phn:** 617-822-9600 **Fax:** 617-822-6671 www.wklb.com jwillis@wklb.com

MASSACHUSETTS RADIO STATIONS

Dorchester WMJX-FM (a) 55 William T Morrissey Blvd, Dorchester MA 02125 **Phn:** 617-822-9600 **Fax:** 617-822-6571 www.magic1067.com coterry@magic1067.com

Dorchester WROR-FM (a) 55 William T Morrissey Blvd, Dorchester MA 02125 **Phn:** 617-822-9600 **Fax:** 617-822-6471 www.wror.com bknight@wror.com

Dorchester WUMB-FM (p) 100 William T Morrissey Blvd, Dorchester MA 02125 **Phn:** 617-287-6900 **Fax:** 617-287-6916 www.wumb.org wumb@umb.edu

Dudley WNRC-FM (v) PO Box 5000, Dudley MA 01571 **Phn:** 508-213-2157 wnrc.nichols.edu wnrc@nichols.edu

East Longmeadow WAQY-FM (r) 45 Fisher Ave, East Longmeadow MA 01028 **Phn:** 413-525-4141 **Fax:** 413-525-4334 www.rock102.com gzenobi@springfieldrocks.com

East Longmeadow WLZX-FM (r) 45 Fisher Ave, East Longmeadow MA 01028 **Phn:** 413-525-4141 **Fax:** 413-525-4334 www.lazer993.com rcressman@lazer993.com

Fairhaven WBSM-AM (nt) 22 Sconticut Neck Rd, Fairhaven MA 02719 **Phn:** 508-993-1767 **Fax:** 508-999-1420 www.wbsm.com news@wbsm.com

Fairhaven WFHN-FM (h) 22 Sconticut Neck Rd, Fairhaven MA 02719 **Phn:** 508-999-6690 **Fax:** 508-999-1420 www.fun107.com jr.reitz@townsquaremedia.com

Fitchburg WPKZ-AM (st) 762 Water St, Fitchburg MA 01420 **Phn:** 978-343-3766 **Fax:** 978-345-6397 wpkz.net

Fitchburg WXPL-FM (v) 160 Pearl St, Fitchburg MA 01420 **Phn:** 978-665-3692 **Fax:** 978-665-3693

Framingham WDJM-FM (vr) 100 State St Ste 512, Framingham MA 01702 **Phn:** 508-626-4622 **Fax:** 508-626-4939

Framingham WSRO-AM (nt) 100 Mount Wayte Ave, Framingham MA 01702 **Phn:** 508-424-2568 www.wsro.com

Gardner WJOE-AM (t) 362 Green St, Gardner MA 01440 **Phn:** 978-632-1340 **Fax:** 78-630-3011 www.wgaw1340.com

Gardner WNYN-FM (r) 362 Green St, Gardner MA 01440 **Phn:** 978-630-8700 **Fax:** 978-630-3011

Great Barrington WSBS-AM (a) 425 Stockbridge Rd, Great Barrington MA 01230 **Phn:** 413-528-0860 **Fax:** 413-528-2162 www.wsbs.com jesse@wsbs.com

Greenfield WHAI-FM (a) 81 Woodard Rd, Greenfield MA 01301 **Phn:** 413-774-4301 **Fax:** 413-773-5637 www.whai.com nick@whai.com

Greenfield WHMQ-AM (ant) 81 Woodard Rd, Greenfield MA 01301 **Phn:** 413-774-4301 **Fax:** 413-773-5637 www.whmp.com dan@whai.com

Haverhill WLKC-FM (a) 30 How St, Haverhill MA 01830 **Phn:** 978-374-4733 **Fax:** 978-373-8023 www.wxrv.com mphipps@wxrv.com

Haverhill WXRV-FM (a) 30 How St, Haverhill MA 01830 **Phn:** 978-374-4733 **Fax:** 978-373-8023 www.wxrv.com cmorrell@wxrv.com

Holyoke WCCH-FM (v) 303 Homestead Ave, Holyoke MA 01040 **Phn:** 413-552-2488

Hyannis WCIB-FM (ar) 154 Barnstable Rd, Hyannis MA 02601 **Phn:** 508-778-2888 **Fax:** 508-778-9651 www.cool102.com news@95wxtk.com

Hyannis WCOD-FM (a) 154 Barnstable Rd, Hyannis MA 02601 **Phn:** 508-778-2888 **Fax:** 508-778-9651 www.106wcod.com news@95wxtk.com

Hyannis WEII-FM (st) 154 Barnstable Rd, Hyannis MA 02601 **Phn:** 508-778-2888 **Fax:** 508-778-9651 www.963weii.com news@95wxtk.com

Hyannis WFCC-FM (l) 737 W Main St, Hyannis MA 02601 **Phn:** 508-771-1224 **Fax:** 508-775-2605 www.wfcc.com wfcc@capecodbroadcasting.com

Hyannis WFQR-FM (a) 243 South St, Hyannis MA 02601 **Phn:** 508-778-8000 www.frankplaysitall.com

Hyannis WFRQ-FM (a) 243 South St, Hyannis MA 02601 **Phn:** 508-778-8000

Hyannis WKPE-FM (c) 737 W Main St, Hyannis MA 02601 **Phn:** 508-771-1224 **Fax:** 508-775-2605 www.capecountry104.com waynewhite@capecodbroadcasting.com

Hyannis WOCN-FM (am) 737 W Main St, Hyannis MA 02601 **Phn:** 508-771-1224 **Fax:** 508-775-2605 www.ocean1047.com news@capecodbroadcasting.com

Hyannis WPXC-FM (ra) 243 South St, Hyannis MA 02601 **Phn:** 508-778-8000 www.pixy103.com

Hyannis WQRC-AM (a) 737 W Main St, Hyannis MA 02601 **Phn:** 508-771-1224 **Fax:** 508-775-2605 www.wqrc.com news@capecodbroadcasting.com

Hyannis WXTK-FM (nt) 154 Barnstable Rd, Hyannis MA 02601 **Phn:** 508-778-2888 **Fax:** 508-778-9651 www.95wxtk.com news@95wxtk.com

Lowell WCAP-AM (nt) 243 Central St, Lowell MA 01852 **Phn:** 978-454-0404 **Fax:** 978-458-9124 www.980wcap.com ryan@980wcap.com

Lowell WUML-FM (vr) 1 University Ave, Lowell MA 01854 **Phn:** 978-934-4975 www.wuml.org md@wuml.org

Lynn WFNX-FM (r) 25 Exchange St Ste 1, Lynn MA 01901 **Phn:** 781-595-6200 **Fax:** 781-595-6567 wfnx.com promotions@wfnx.com

Marshfield WATD-FM (ao) 130 Enterprise Dr, Marshfield MA 02050 **Phn:** 781-837-1169 **Fax:** 781-837-1825 959watd.com watdnews@gmail.com

Medford WJMN-FM (h) 10 Cabot Rd Ste 302, Medford MA 02155 **Phn:** 781-663-2500 **Fax:** 781-290-0722 www.jamn945.com anthonyalfano@clearchannel.com

Medford WKOX-AM (y) 10 Cabot Rd Ste 302, Medford MA 02155 **Phn:** 781-396-1430 **Fax:** 781-391-3064 www.mia1430.com jeffreyoar@clearchannel.com

Medford WMFO-FM (v) PO Box 65, Medford MA 02155 **Phn:** 617-627-3800 www.wmfo.org wmfo@wmfo.org

Medford WXKS-AM (y) 10 Cabot Rd Ste 302, Medford MA 02155 **Phn:** 781-396-1430 **Fax:** 781-391-3064 www.kiss108.com anthonyalfano@clearchannel.com

Medford WXKS-FM (y) 10 Cabot Rd Ste 302, Medford MA 02155 **Phn:** 781-396-1430 **Fax:** 781-391-3064 www.kiss108.com anthonyalfano@clearchannel.com

Methuen WCCM-AM (nt) 462 Merrimack St, Methuen MA 01844 **Phn:** 978-683-7171 **Fax:** 978-687-1180 www.1110wccmam.com info@1110wccmam.com

Methuen WNNW-AM (y) 462 Merrimack St, Methuen MA 01844 **Phn:** 978-686-9966 **Fax:** 978-687-1180 www.power800am.com

Milford WMRC-AM (a) 258 Main St Ste 301, Milford MA 01757 **Phn:** 508-473-1490 **Fax:** 508-478-2200 www.wmrcdailynews.com edcentral1490@yahoo.com

Milton WMLN-FM (var) 1071 Blue Hill Ave, Milton MA 02186 **Phn:** 617-333-0311

Needham WBNW-AM (nk) 144 Gould St Ste 155, Needham MA 02494 **Phn:** 781-474-5180 **Fax:** 781-433-0002 www.moneymattersboston.com

New Bedford WJFD-FM (ey) 651 Orchard St #300, New Bedford MA 02744 **Phn:** 508-997-2929 **Fax:** 508-990-3893 wjfd.com claudia@wjfd.com

New Bedford WNBH-AM (s) 888 Purchase St Unit 212, New Bedford MA 02740 **Phn:** 508-979-8003 **Fax:** 508-979-8009 www.hallradio.com twall@hallradio.com

Newburyport WNBP-AM (amj) 1 Merrimac St Ste 14, Newburyport MA 01950 **Phn:** 978-462-1450 **Fax:** 978-462-0333 www.wnbp.com carl@wnbp.com

Norfolk WDIS-AM (nt) 100 Pond St, Norfolk MA 02056 **Phn:** 508-384-8255 **Fax:** 508-384-1530 www.wdisam.com wdismgmt@aol.com

North Adams WJJW-FM (v) 375 Church St, North Adams MA 01247 **Phn:** 413-662-5405

North Adams WNAW-AM (a) PO Box 707, North Adams MA 01247 **Phn:** 413-663-6567 **Fax:** 413-662-2143 www.wnaw.com

North Dartmouth WSMU-FM (v) 285 Old Westport Rd, North Dartmouth MA 02747 **Phn:** 508-999-8149 wsmu@umassd.edu

North Easton WSHL-FM (v) 320 Washington St, North Easton MA 02357 **Phn:** 508-565-1919

North Quincy WEZE-AM (qt) 500 Victory Rd, North Quincy MA 02171 **Phn:** 617-328-0880 **Fax:** 617-328-0375 www.wezeradio.com patr@salemradioboston.com

North Quincy WROL-AM (q) 500 Victory Rd Ste 14, North Quincy MA 02171 **Phn:** 617-328-0880 **Fax:** 617-328-0375 www.wrolboston.com patr@salemradioboston.com

Northampton WEIB-FM (aj) 8 N King St, Northampton MA 01060 **Phn:** 413-585-1112 **Fax:** 413-585-9138 www.weibfm.com

Northampton WHMP-AM (nt) 15 Hampton Ave, Northampton MA 01060 **Phn:** 413-586-7400 **Fax:** 413-585-0927 www.whmp.com dvozella@whmp.com

Northampton WHNP-AM (nt) 15 Hampton Ave, Northampton MA 01060 **Phn:** 413-586-7400 **Fax:** 413-585-0927 www.whmp.com dvozella@whmp.com

Northampton WOZQ-FM (v) 100 Elm St # 106, Northampton MA 01063 **Phn:** 413-585-4956 **Fax:** 413-585-2075 sophia.smith.eduwozq wozq@email.smith.edu

Northampton WPVQ-FM (c) 100 Main St, Northampton MA 01060 **Phn:** 413-774-2322 **Fax:** 413-774-4963 www.bear953.com dvozella@whmp.com

Northampton WRSI-FM (ar) 15 Hampton Ave, Northampton MA 01060 **Phn:** 413-586-7400 **Fax:** 413-585-0927 www.wrsi.com monte@wrsi.com

Northampton WRSY-FM (a) 15 Hampton Ave, Northampton MA 01060 **Phn:** 413-586-7400 **Fax:** 413-585-0927 www.wrsi.com monte@wrsi.com

Northfield WNMH-FM (v) 206 Main St, Northfield MA 01360 **Phn:** 413-498-3603 wnmh.nmhschool.org wnmh_md@nmhschool.org

Orange WJDF-FM (ah) PO Box 973, Orange MA 01364 **Phn:** 978-544-0957 **Fax:** 978-544-2131 www.wjdf.com jay@wjdf.com

Palmer WARE-AM (o) 3 Converse St Ste 101, Palmer MA 01069 **Phn:** 413-289-2300 **Fax:** 413-289-2323 www.realoldies1250.net manager@realoldies1250.net

Paxton WSRS-FM (a) 96 Stereo Ln, Paxton MA 01612 **Phn:** 508-757-9696 **Fax:** 508-757-1779 www.wsrs.com kevinjohnson@clearchannel.com

Paxton WTAG-AM (snt) 96 Stereo Ln, Paxton MA 01612 **Phn:** 508-795-0580 **Fax:** 508-757-7279 www.wtag.com news@wtag.com

Pittsfield WBEC-FM (a) 211 Jason St, Pittsfield MA 01201 **Phn:** 413-499-3333 **Fax:** 413-442-1590 www.live959.com traffic@live959.com

Pittsfield WBEC-AM (snt) 211 Jason St, Pittsfield MA 01201 **Phn:** 413-499-3333 **Fax:** 413-442-1590 www.live959.com traffic@live959.com

Pittsfield WBRK-AM (am) 100 North St, Pittsfield MA 01201 **Phn:** 413-442-1553 **Fax:** 413-445-5294 www.wbrk.com wbrk@wbrk.com

Pittsfield WBRK-FM (a) 100 North St, Pittsfield MA 01201 **Phn:** 413-442-1553 **Fax:** 413-445-5294 www.wbrk.com wbrk@wbrk.com

Pittsfield WUPE-AM (a) 211 Jason St, Pittsfield MA 01201 **Phn:** 413-499-3333 **Fax:** 413-442-1590 www.wupe.com news@wupe.com

Pittsfield WUPE-FM (a) 211 Jason St, Pittsfield MA 01201 **Phn:** 413-499-3333 **Fax:** 413-442-1590 www.wupe.com news@wupe.com

Plymouth WPLM-FM (a) 17 Columbus Rd, Plymouth MA 02360 **Phn:** 508-746-1390 **Fax:** 508-830-1128 easy991.com patriciac@easy991.com

Provincetown WOMR-FM (p) PO Box 975, Provincetown MA 02657 **Phn:** 508-487-2619 **Fax:** 508-487-5524 www.womr.org info@womr.org

Quincy WWDJ-AM (y) 500 Victory Rd, Quincy MA 02171 **Phn:** 617-328-0880 **Fax:** 617-328-0375 salemradioboston.com patr@salemradioboston.com

Quincy WWZN-AM (nt) 308 Victory Rd Ste 8, Quincy MA 02171 **Phn:** 617-237-1200 **Fax:** 617-237-1177 www.revolutionboston.com

Salem WMWM-FM (v) 352 Lafayette St, Salem MA 01970 **Phn:** 978-542-8500 www.wmwmsalem.com wmwmsalem@gmail.com

Sheffield WBSL-FM (v) 245 N Undermountain Rd, Sheffield MA 01257 **Phn:** 413-229-1927 www.berkshireschool.org

Somerset WHTB-AM (te) 1 Home St, Somerset MA 02725 **Phn:** 508-678-9727 **Fax:** 508-673-0310 hector@wsar.com

Somerset WSAR-AM (snt) 1 Home St, Somerset MA 02725 **Phn:** 508-678-9727 **Fax:** 508-673-0310 www.wsar.com news@wsar.com

South Hadley WMHC-FM (v) Blanchard Student Ctr, South Hadley MA 01075 **Phn:** 413-538-2044 **Fax:** 413-538-2431 www.wmhcradio.org

South Hamilton WNSH-AM (y) PO Box 242, South Hamilton MA 01982 **Phn:** 978-954-1282 **Fax:** 978-468-1954 www.viva1570.com radioviva1570@gmail.com

Springfield WACE-AM (eqy) PO Box 1, Springfield MA 01101 **Phn:** 413-594-6654 www.waceradio.com wace@waceradio.com

Springfield WAIC-FM (v) 1000 State St, Springfield MA 01109 **Phn:** 413-205-3941

Springfield WHYN-AM (snt) 1331 Main St Ste 4, Springfield MA 01103 **Phn:** 413 536-1105 **Fax:** 413-734-4434 www.whyn.com brad@whyn.com

Springfield WHYN-FM (a) 1331 Main St Ste 4, Springfield MA 01103 **Phn:** 413-781-1011 **Fax:** 413-734-4434 www.mix931.com danielle@mix931.com

Springfield WMAS-AM (ab) 1000 W Columbus Ave, Springfield MA 01105 **Phn:** 413-737-1414 **Fax:** 413-737-1488 www.947wmas.com susanwmas@aol.com

Springfield WMAS-FM (a) 1000 W Columbus Ave, Springfield MA 01105 **Phn:** 413-737-1414 **Fax:** 413-737-1488 www.947wmas.com susanwmas@aol.com

MASSACHUSETTS RADIO STATIONS

Springfield WNEK-FM (v) 1215 Wilbraham Rd, Springfield MA 01119 **Phn:** 413-782-1582 **Fax:** 413-796-2111

Springfield WPKX-FM (c) 1331 Main St Ste 400, Springfield MA 01103 **Phn:** 413-781-1011 **Fax:** 413-858-1958 www.mykix1009.com kera@mykix1009.com

Springfield WRNX-FM (c) 1331 Main St Ste 4, Springfield MA 01103 **Phn:** 413-781-1011 www.mykix1009.com kera@mykix1009.com

Springfield WSCB-FM (v) 263 Alden St, Springfield MA 01109 **Phn:** 413-748-3712 **Fax:** 413-748-3473

Springfield WTCC-FM (v) 1 Armory Sq, Springfield MA 01105 **Phn:** 413-755-6822 **Fax:** 413-755-6305 www.wtccfm.org

Sudbury WYAJ-FM (v) 390 Lincoln Rd, Sudbury MA 01776 **Phn:** 978-443-9961 **Fax:** 978-443-8824

Vineyard Haven WMVY-FM (r) PO Box 1148, Vineyard Haven MA 02568 **Phn:** 508-693-5000 **Fax:** 508-693-8211 www.mvyradio.com news@mvyradio.com

Waltham WBRS-FM (v) 415 South St, Waltham MA 02453 **Phn:** 781-736-4786 www.wbrs.org news@wbrs.org

Webster WGFP-AM (c) 27 Douglas Rd, Webster MA 01570 **Phn:** 508-943-9400 **Fax:** 508-943-0405 www.coolcountry940.com mike@coolcountry940.com

Wellesley Hills WZLY-FM (v) 106 Central St, Wellesley Hills MA 02481 **Phn:** 781-283-2791 www.wzly.net wzly@wellesley.edu

West Barnstable WKKL-FM (v) 2240 Iyannough Rd, West Barnstable MA 02668 **Phn:** 508-375-4030 **Fax:** 508-375-4063 wkkl247@yahoo.com

West Springfield WACM-AM (y) 34 Sylvan St, West Springfield MA 01089 **Phn:** 413-781-5200 **Fax:** 413-734-2240 www.wacmpopular1490.com

West Springfield WSPR-AM (y) 34 Sylvan St, West Springfield MA 01089 **Phn:** 413-781-5200 **Fax:** 413-734-2240 jrizza@davidsonmediagroup.com

Westfield WSKB-FM (v) 577 Western Ave, Westfield MA 01085 **Phn:** 413-572-5579 **Fax:** 413-572-5625 wskb895.wordpress.com wskbgm@yahoo.com

Woods Hole WCAI-FM (pnt) PO Box 82, Woods Hole MA 02543 **Phn:** 508-548-9600 **Fax:** 508-548-5517 capeandislands.org wcai@capeandislands.org

Woods Hole WNAN-FM (pnt) PO Box 82, Woods Hole MA 02543 **Phn:** 508-548-9600 **Fax:** 508-548-5517 www.wgbh.orgcainan cainan@wgbh.org

Worcester WCHC-FM (v) 1 College St, Worcester MA 01610 **Phn:** 508-793-2475 college.holycross.eduwchc wchc@g.holycross.edu

Worcester WCRN-AM (t) 82 Franklin St Fl 1, Worcester MA 01608 **Phn:** 508-792-5803 **Fax:** 508-770-0659 www.wcrnradio.com tony@wcrnradio.com

Worcester WCUW-FM (vm) 910 Main St, Worcester MA 01610 **Phn:** 508-753-1012 www.wcuw.org wcuw@wcuw.org

Worcester WICN-FM (plj) 50 Portland St, Worcester MA 01608 **Phn:** 508-752-0700 **Fax:** 508-752-7518 www.wicn.org johnk@wicn.org

Worcester WNEB-AM (q) 70 James St Ste 201, Worcester MA 01603 **Phn:** 508-831-9863

Worcester WORC-AM (y) 122 Green St Ste 2R, Worcester MA 01604 **Phn:** 508-791-2111 **Fax:** 508-752-6897

Worcester WORC-FM (o) 250 Commercial St Ste 500, Worcester MA 01608 **Phn:** 508-752-1045 **Fax:** 508-793-0824 www.oldies989.com adam.webster@cumulus.com

Worcester WVEI-AM (s) 179 Moreland St, Worcester MA 01609 **Phn:** 508-752-5611 **Fax:** 508-752-1006 www.weei.com doldread@entercom.com

Worcester WVNE-AM (qt) 70 James St Ste 201, Worcester MA 01603 **Phn:** 508-831-9863 lifechangingradio.comwvne info@wvne.net

Worcester WWFX-FM (r) 250 Commercial St Ste 530, Worcester MA 01608 **Phn:** 508-752-1045 **Fax:** 508-770-9964 www.pikefm.com

Worcester WXLO-FM (a) 250 Commercial St Ste 500, Worcester MA 01608 **Phn:** 508-752-1045 **Fax:** 508-793-0824 www.wxlo.com

Worthington WWNH-AM (q) PO Box 87, Worthington MA 01098 **Phn:** 603-742-8575 www.loveradio.net

MICHIGAN

Adrian WABJ-AM (nt) 121 W Maumee St, Adrian MI 49221 **Phn:** 517-265-1500 **Fax:** 517-263-4525

Adrian WBZV-FM (r) 121 W Maumee St, Adrian MI 49221 **Phn:** 517-265-9500 **Fax:** 517-263-4525

Adrian WLEN-FM (a) PO Box 687, Adrian MI 49221 **Phn:** 517-263-1039 **Fax:** 517-265-5362 www.wlen.com info@wlen.com

Adrian WQTE-FM (c) 121 W Maumee St, Adrian MI 49221 **Phn:** 517-265-9500 **Fax:** 517-263-4525

Adrian WVAC-FM (v) 110 S Madison St, Adrian MI 49221 **Phn:** 517-264-4154 **Fax:** 517-264-3331

Alma WFYC-AM (s) PO Box 665, Alma MI 48801 **Phn:** 989-463-3175 **Fax:** 989-463-6674

Alma WMLM-AM (c) 4170 N State Rd, Alma MI 48801 **Phn:** 989-463-4013 **Fax:** 989-463-4014 vbongard@winntelwb.coop

Alma WQAC-FM (vr) 614 W Superior St, Alma MI 48801 **Phn:** 989-463-7301 **Fax:** 989-463-7277 www.wqac.org staff@wqac.org

Alma WQBX-FM (a) PO Box 665, Alma MI 48801 **Phn:** 989-463-3175 **Fax:** 989-463-6674

Alpena WATZ-FM (c) 123 Prentiss St, Alpena MI 49707 **Phn:** 989-354-8400 **Fax:** 989-354-3436 www.watz.com watz@watz.com

Alpena WATZ-AM (tc) 123 Prentiss St, Alpena MI 49707 **Phn:** 989-354-8400 **Fax:** 989-354-3436 www.watz.com watz@watz.com

Alpena WHSB-FM (h) 1491 M 32 W, Alpena MI 49707 **Phn:** 989-354-4611 **Fax:** 989-354-4014 www.alpenanow.com thebay@truenorthradionetwork.com

Alpena WWTH-FM (a) 1491 M 32 W, Alpena MI 49707 **Phn:** 989-354-4611 **Fax:** 989-354-4014 www.alpenanow.com thewave@truenorthradionetwork.com

Ann Arbor WAAM-AM (nt) 4230 Packard St, Ann Arbor MI 48108 **Phn:** 734-971-1600 **Fax:** 734-973-2916 www.waamradio.com linda@waamradio.com

Ann Arbor WCBN-FM (v) 530 Sab Univ Of Mi, Ann Arbor MI 48109 **Phn:** 734-647-4122 www.wcbn.org programming@wcbn.org

Ann Arbor WDEO-AM (qnt) PO Box 374, Ann Arbor MI 48106 **Phn:** 734-930-5200 **Fax:** 734-930-3101 www.avemariaradio.net tloewe@avemariaradio.net

Ann Arbor WLBY-AM (t) 1100 Victors Way Ste 100, Ann Arbor MI 48108 **Phn:** 734-302-8100 www.1290wlby.com chris.ammel@cumulus.com

Ann Arbor WQKL-FM (a) 1100 Victors Way Ste 100, Ann Arbor MI 48108 **Phn:** 734-302-8100 **Fax:** 734-213-7508 www.annarbors107one.com chris@annarbors107one.com

MICHIGAN RADIO STATIONS

Ann Arbor WTKA-AM (st) 1100 Victors Way Ste 100, Ann Arbor MI 48108 **Phn:** 734-302-8100 **Fax:** 734-213-7508 www.wtka.com brian.cowan@cumulus.com

Ann Arbor WUOM-FM (p) 535 W William St Ste 110, Ann Arbor MI 48103 **Phn:** 734-764-9210 **Fax:** 734-647-3488 www.michiganradio.org michigan.radio@umich.edu

Ann Arbor WWWW-FM (c) 1100 Victors Way Ste 100, Ann Arbor MI 48108 **Phn:** 734-302-8100 **Fax:** 734-213-7508 www.w4country.com scott.meier@cumulus.com

Bad Axe WLEW-AM (c) 935 S Van Dyke Rd, Bad Axe MI 48413 **Phn:** 989-269-9931 **Fax:** 989-269-9702 www.thumbnet.net wlewradio@gmail.com

Bad Axe WLEW-FM (h) 935 S Van Dyke Rd, Bad Axe MI 48413 **Phn:** 989-269-9931 **Fax:** 989-269-9702 www.thumbnet.net wlew@avci.net

Battle Creek WBCK-AM (c) 390 Golden Ave, Battle Creek MI 49015 **Phn:** 269-963-5555 **Fax:** 269-963-5185

Battle Creek WBCK-FM (nt) 390 Golden Ave, Battle Creek MI 49015 **Phn:** 269-963-5555 **Fax:** 269-963-5185 www.wbckfm.com bcnews@cumulus.com

Battle Creek WBXX-FM (a) 390 Golden Ave, Battle Creek MI 49015 **Phn:** 269-963-5555 **Fax:** 269-963-5185 www.mix1049online.com bcnews@cumulus.com

Battle Creek WNWN-FM (c) 70 W Michigan Ave # 700, Battle Creek MI 49017 **Phn:** 269-968-1991 **Fax:** 269-968-1881 wincountry.com pj.lacey@mwcradio.com

Battle Creek WOLY-AM (gq) 15074 6 12 Mile Rd, Battle Creek MI 49014 **Phn:** 269-965-1515

Beaverton WMRX-FM (ao) PO Box 428, Beaverton MI 48612 **Phn:** 989-631-1490 **Fax:** 989-631-6357 wmpxwmrx.com wmpx@ejourney.com

Benton Harbor WHFB-FM (c) 2100 Fairplain Ave, Benton Harbor MI 49022 **Phn:** 269-925-9300 **Fax:** 574-239-4231 www.realcountry999.com montgom@wsbt.com

Benton Harbor WHIT-FM (h) 580 E Napier Ave, Benton Harbor MI 49022 **Phn:** 269-925-1111 **Fax:** 269-925-1011 www.hitradio1550.com golson@wsjm.com

Benton Harbor WYTZ-FM (c) 580 E Napier Ave, Benton Harbor MI 49022 **Phn:** 269-925-1111 **Fax:** 269-925-1011 975ycountry.com spatzer@theradiostations.com

Berrien Springs WAUS-FM (pl) Andrews U Howard Ctr, Berrien Springs MI 49104 **Phn:** 269-471-3400 **Fax:** 269-471-3804 www.waus.org waus@andrews.edu

Big Rapids WBRN-AM (snt) 18720 16 Mile Rd, Big Rapids MI 49307 **Phn:** 231-796-7000 **Fax:** 231-796-7951 www.wbrn.com news@bigrapidsradionetwork.com

Big Rapids WWBR-FM (c) 18720 16 Mile Rd, Big Rapids MI 49307 **Phn:** 231-796-7000 **Fax:** 231-796-7951 www.bigcountry1009.com brian@bigrapidsradionetwork.com

Big Rapids WYBR-FM (ha) 18720 16 Mile Rd, Big Rapids MI 49307 **Phn:** 231-796-7000 **Fax:** 231-796-7951 www.wybr.com diane@bigrapidsradionetwork.com

Burton WCRZ-FM (a) 3338 E Bristol Rd, Burton MI 48529 **Phn:** 810-743-1080 **Fax:** 810-742-5170 wcrz.com jaypatrick@wcrz.com

Burton WFNT-AM (ob) 3338 E Bristol Rd, Burton MI 48529 **Phn:** 810-742-1470 **Fax:** 810-742-5170 wfnt dan.foley@townsquaremedia.com

Burton WQUS-FM (r) 3338 E Bristol Rd, Burton MI 48529 **Phn:** 810-743-1080 **Fax:** 810-742-5170 us103.com jaypatrick@wcrz.com

Burton WRCL-FM (h) 3338 E Bristol Rd, Burton MI 48529 **Phn:** 810-743-1080 **Fax:** 810-742-5170 club937.com clay@club937.com

Burton WWBN-FM (r) 3338 E Bristol Rd # G, Burton MI 48529 **Phn:** 810-743-1080 **Fax:** 810-742-5170 banana1015.com tony@banana1015.com

Cadillac WATT-AM (nt) PO Box 520, Cadillac MI 49601 **Phn:** 231-775-1263 **Fax:** 231-779-2844 bill.michaels@106khq.com

Cadillac WKAD-FM (s) PO Box 520, Cadillac MI 49601 **Phn:** 231-775-1263 **Fax:** 231-779-2844 www.937fmtheticket.com traffic@mix96cadillac.com

Cadillac WLXV-FM (a) 7825 S Mackinaw Trail, Cadillac MI 49601 **Phn:** 231-775-1263 **Fax:** 231-779-2844 www.mix96cadillac.com traffic@mix96cadillac.com

Caro WIDL-FM (a) PO Box 106, Caro MI 48723 **Phn:** 989-672-1360 **Fax:** 989-673-0256

Caro WKYO-AM (c) PO Box 106, Caro MI 48723 **Phn:** 989-672-1360 **Fax:** 989-673-0256

Charlotte WLCM-AM (q) PO Box 338, Charlotte MI 48813 **Phn:** 517-543-8200 **Fax:** 517-543-7779 wlcmradio.com jeff.frank@cbsradio.com

Cheboygan WAVC-FM (c) 1356 Mackinaw Ave, Cheboygan MI 49721 **Phn:** 877-627-2341 **Fax:** 231-627-7000 www.1029bigcountry.com nikki@1029bigcountry.com

Cheboygan WCBY-AM (zm) 1356 Mackinaw Ave, Cheboygan MI 49721 **Phn:** 231-627-2341 **Fax:** 231-627-7000 bigmichael@nsbroadcasting.com

Cheboygan WCKC-FM (r) 1356 Mackinaw Ave, Cheboygan MI 49721 **Phn:** 231-627-2341 **Fax:** 231-627-7000 www.classicrockthebear.com del@nsbroadcasting.com

Cheboygan WGFM-FM (r) 1356 Mackinaw Ave, Cheboygan MI 49721 **Phn:** 231-627-2341 **Fax:** 231-922-3633 rock105.fm info@nsbroadcasting.com

Cheboygan WGFN-FM (r) 1356 Mackinaw Ave, Cheboygan MI 49721 **Phn:** 231-627-2341 **Fax:** 231-627-7000 www.classicrockthebear.com del@nsbroadcasting.com

Cheboygan WJZJ-FM (r) 1356 Mackinaw Ave, Cheboygan MI 49721 **Phn:** 231-627-2341 **Fax:** 231-627-7000 jonir@nsbroadcasting.com

Cheboygan WLJZ-FM (r) 1356 Mackinaw Ave, Cheboygan MI 49721 **Phn:** 231-627-2341 **Fax:** 231-627-7000 jonir@nsbroadcasting.com

Cheboygan WMKC-FM (c) 1356 Mackinaw Ave, Cheboygan MI 49721 **Phn:** 231-627-2341 **Fax:** 231-627-7000 www.1029bigcountry.com nikki@1029bigcountry.com

Clinton Township WUFL-AM (q) 42669 Garfield Rd Ste 328, Clinton Township MI 48038 **Phn:** 586-263-1030 www.myflr.org

Coldwater WTVB-AM (h) 182 N Angola Rd, Coldwater MI 49036 **Phn:** 517-279-1590 **Fax:** 517-279-4695 www.wtvbam.com ken.delaney@mwcradio.com

Dearborn WHFR-FM (v) 5101 Evergreen Rd, Dearborn MI 48128 **Phn:** 313-845-9676 **Fax:** 313-317-4034 whfr.fm whfr-nd@hfcc.edu

Detroit WCHB-AM (ntg) 3250 Franklin St, Detroit MI 48207 **Phn:** 313-259-2000 **Fax:** 313-259-7011 wchbnewsdetroit.com kstinehour@radio-one.com

Detroit WCSX-FM (r) 1 Radio Plaza St, Detroit MI 48220 **Phn:** 248-398-9470 **Fax:** 248-586-3042 www.wcsx.com feedback@wcsx.com

Detroit WDET-FM (pja) 4600 Cass Ave, Detroit MI 48201 **Phn:** 313-577-4146 **Fax:** 313-577-1300 wdet.org wdetfm@wdet.org

Detroit WDMK-FM (au) 3250 Franklin St, Detroit MI 48207 **Phn:** 313-259-2000 **Fax:** 313-259-7011 kissdetroit.com

Detroit WDRJ-AM (wqg) 2994 E Grand Blvd, Detroit MI 48202 **Phn:** 313-871-1440 **Fax:** 313-871-6088

Detroit WDRQ-FM (h) 3011 W Grand Blvd Ste 800, Detroit MI 48202 **Phn:** 313-871-9300 **Fax:** 313-872-0190 www.931dougfm.com ronald.smerigan@cumulus.com

Detroit WDVD-FM (a) 3011 W Grand Blvd Ste 800, Detroit MI 48202 **Phn:** 313-871-3030 **Fax:** 313-872-0190 www.963wdvd.com

Detroit WEXL-AM (gq) 12300 Radio Pl, Detroit MI 48228 **Phn:** 313-272-1340 www.wexl1340.com station@wmuz.com

Detroit WHTD-FM (au) 3250 Franklin St, Detroit MI 48207 **Phn:** 313-259-2000 **Fax:** 313-259-7011 hothiphopdetroit.com kstinehour@radio-one.com

Detroit WJLB-FM (wu) 645 Griswold St Ste 633, Detroit MI 48226 **Phn:** 313-965-2000 **Fax:** 313-965-1729 www.fm98wjlb.com wjlb@fm98wjlb.com

Detroit WJR-AM (snt) 3011 W Grand Blvd Ste 800, Detroit MI 48202 **Phn:** 313-875-4440 **Fax:** 313-875-9022 www.760wjr.com

Detroit WMGC-FM (a) 1 Radio Plaza St, Detroit MI 48220 **Phn:** 248-547-0101 **Fax:** 248-542-8800 www.detroitsports1051.com feedback@detroitsports1051.com

Detroit WMUZ-FM (qt) 12300 Radio Pl, Detroit MI 48228 **Phn:** 313-272-3434 www.wmuz.com station@wmuz.com

Detroit WRDT-AM (q) 12300 Radio Pl, Detroit MI 48228 **Phn:** 313-272-3434 www.wrdt560.com station@wmuz.com

East Lansing WDBM-FM (v) 234 Wilson Rd, East Lansing MI 48825 **Phn:** 517-884-8900 **Fax:** 517-355-6552 impact89fm.org manager@impact89fm.org

East Lansing WKAR-FM (pl) 283 Communication Arts And Sci, East Lansing MI 48824 **Phn:** 517-432-9527 **Fax:** 517-353-7124 www.wkar.org mail@wkar.org

East Lansing WKAR-AM (pnt) 283 Communication Arts And Sci, East Lansing MI 48824 **Phn:** 517-432-9527 **Fax:** 517-353-7124 www.wkar.org mail@wkar.org

Escanaba WCHT-AM (nt) 524 Ludington St Ste 300, Escanaba MI 49829 **Phn:** 906-789-9700 www.wchtradio.com rrnews@radioresultsnetwork.com

Escanaba WCMM-FM (c) 524 Ludington St Ste 300, Escanaba MI 49829 **Phn:** 906-789-9700 **Fax:** 906-789-9701 www.wcmmradio.com countrymoose@radioresultsnetwork.com

Escanaba WDBC-AM (ob) 604 Ludington St, Escanaba MI 49829 **Phn:** 906-786-3800 **Fax:** 906-789-9959 kmbbroadcasting.com wykxinfo@yahoo.com

Escanaba WGKL-FM (o) 524 Ludington St Ste 300, Escanaba MI 49829 **Phn:** 906-789-9700 **Fax:** 906-789-9701 www.wgklradio.com rrnews@radioresultsnetwork.com

Escanaba WGLQ-FM (a) 524 Ludington St Ste 300, Escanaba MI 49829 **Phn:** 906-789-9700 www.wglqradio.com rrnews@radioresultsnetwork.com

Escanaba WYKX-FM (c) 604 Ludington St, Escanaba MI 49829 **Phn:** 906-786-3800 **Fax:** 906-789-9959 kmbbroadcasting.comwykx wykxinfo@yahoo.com

Farmington Hills WDFN-AM (st) 27675 Halsted Rd, Farmington Hills MI 48331 **Phn:** 248-324-5800 **Fax:** 248-848-0312 www.wdfn.com

MICHIGAN RADIO STATIONS

Farmington Hills WDTW-FM (r) 27675 Halsted Rd, Farmington Hills MI 48331 **Phn:** 248-324-5800 **Fax:** 248-848-0312 www.thedrocks.com jaytowers@clearchannel.com

Farmington Hills WKQI-FM (h) 27675 Halsted Rd, Farmington Hills MI 48331 **Phn:** 248-324-5800 **Fax:** 248-848-0312 www.channel955.com tonytravatto@clearchannel.com

Farmington Hills WMXD-FM (auo) 27675 Halsted Rd, Farmington Hills MI 48331 **Phn:** 248-324-5800 **Fax:** 248-848-0316 www.mix923fm.com contact@mix923fm.com

Farmington Hills WNIC-FM (a) 27675 Halsted Rd, Farmington Hills MI 48331 **Phn:** 248-324-5800 **Fax:** 248-848-0312 www.fresh100.com shannonbomia@clearchannel.com

Farmington Hills WXYT-FM (s) 31555 W 14 Mile Rd Ste 102, Farmington Hills MI 48334 **Phn:** 248-855-5100 **Fax:** 248-855-1302 detroit.cbslocal.com james.powers@cbsradio.com

Ferndale WDTK-AM (t) 2 Radio Plaza St, Ferndale MI 48220 **Phn:** 248-581-1234 **Fax:** 248-581-1231 www.wdtkam.com

Ferndale WLQV-AM (q) 2 Radio Plaza St, Ferndale MI 48220 **Phn:** 248-581-1234 **Fax:** 248-581-1231 www.faithtalk1500.com diannes@salemdetroit.com

Ferndale WOMC-FM (h) 2201 Woodward Hts, Ferndale MI 48220 **Phn:** 248-581-2200 **Fax:** 248-546-5446 womc.cbslocal.com tim.roberts@cbsradio.com

Ferndale WRIF-FM (r) 1 Radio Plaza St, Ferndale MI 48220 **Phn:** 248-547-0101 **Fax:** 248-586-3030 www.wrif.com mpennington@greatermediadetroit.com

Ferndale WYCD-FM (c) 2201 Woodward Hts, Ferndale MI 48220 **Phn:** 248-581-2200 **Fax:** 248-546-5446 wycd.cbslocal.com troberts@wycd.com

Flint WDZZ-FM (wu) 6317 Taylor Dr, Flint MI 48507 **Phn:** 810-238-7300 **Fax:** 810-743-2500 www.wdzz.com amie.burke@cumulus.com

Flint WFBE-FM (c) 4511 Miller Rd Ste 9, Flint MI 48507 **Phn:** 810-720-9510 **Fax:** 810-720-9513 www.b95.fm april.rose@cumulus.com

Flint WFLT-AM (wg) 317 S Averill Ave, Flint MI 48506 **Phn:** 810-762-1420 **Fax:** 810-239-7134 wflt1420am@aol.com

Flint WOWE-FM (wu) 126 W Kearsley St, Flint MI 48502 **Phn:** 810-234-4335 **Fax:** 810-234-7286

Flint WRSR-FM (r) 6317 Taylor Dr, Flint MI 48507 **Phn:** 810-720-9510 **Fax:** 810-720-9513 www.classicfox.com rock@classicfox.com

Flint WSNL-AM (qa) 5210 S Saginaw Rd, Flint MI 48507 **Phn:** 810-694-4146 **Fax:** 810-694-0661 www.wsnlradio.com info@cbslradio.com

Flint WTRX-AM (st) 4511 Miller Rd Ste 9, Flint MI 48507 **Phn:** 810-720-9510 **Fax:** 810-720-9513 www.wtrxsports.com april.rose@cumulus.com

Flint WWCK-AM (t) 6317 Taylor Dr, Flint MI 48507 **Phn:** 810-238-7300 **Fax:** 810-238-7310 www.supertalk1570.com jerry.noble@cumulus.com

Flint WWCK-FM (h) 6317 Taylor Dr, Flint MI 48507 **Phn:** 810-238-7300 **Fax:** 810-238-7310 www.wwck.com michael.macdonald@cumulus.com

Frankfort WBNZ-FM (a) 1532 Forrester Rd, Frankfort MI 49635 **Phn:** 231-352-6374 **Fax:** 231-947-7201

Gaylord WMJZ-FM (o) PO Box 1766, Gaylord MI 49734 **Phn:** 989-732-2341 **Fax:** 989-732-6202 radioeagle.com kent@radioeagle.com

Gaylord WOLW-FM (q) PO Box 695, Gaylord MI 49734 **Phn:** 989-732-6274 www.thepromisefm.com jana@ncradio.org

Gaylord WPHN-AM (q) PO Box 695, Gaylord MI 49734 **Phn:** 989-732-6274 **Fax:** 989-732-8171 www.ncradio.org glake@ncradio.org

Gaylord WSRT-FM (a) 440 W Main St Ste C, Gaylord MI 49735 **Phn:** 231-546-4485 **Fax:** 231-947-7002

Gladwin WGDN-FM (c) 3601 Woods Rd, Gladwin MI 48624 **Phn:** 989-426-1031 www.103country.com win@103country.com

Gladwin WGDN-AM (q) 3601 Woods Rd, Gladwin MI 48624 **Phn:** 989-426-1031 www.103country.com win@103country.com

Grand Haven WGHN-FM (a) 1 S Harbor Dr Ste L1, Grand Haven MI 49417 **Phn:** 616-842-8110 **Fax:** 616-842-4350 www.wghn.com ron@wghn.com

Grand Haven WGHN-AM (a) 1 S Harbor Dr Ste L1, Grand Haven MI 49417 **Phn:** 616-842-8110 **Fax:** 616-842-4350 www.wghn.com walt@wghn.com

Grand Rapids WAYG-FM (vq) 1159 E Beltline Ave NE, Grand Rapids MI 49525 **Phn:** 888-525-8830 **Fax:** 616-942-7078 www.way.fm way@way.fm

Grand Rapids WAYK-FM (q) 1159 E Beltline Ave NE, Grand Rapids MI 49525 **Phn:** 888-525-8830 **Fax:** 616-942-7078 www.way.fm way@way.fm

Grand Rapids WBBL-FM (s) 60 Monroe Center St NW, Grand Rapids MI 49503 **Phn:** 616-744-8461 **Fax:** 774-0351

Grand Rapids WBCT-FM (c) 77 Monroe Center St NW Ste 1000, Grand Rapids MI 49503 **Phn:** 616-459-1919 **Fax:** 616-732-3330 www.b93.com reese@b93.com

Grand Rapids WBFX-FM (r) 77 Monroe Center St NW Ste 1000, Grand Rapids MI 49503 **Phn:** 616-459-1919 **Fax:** 616-242-9373 www.1013thebrew.com mattwalker@clearchannel.com

Grand Rapids WCSG-FM (vq) 1159 E Beltline Ave NE, Grand Rapids MI 49525 **Phn:** 616-942-1500 **Fax:** 616-942-7078 www.wcsg.org wcsg@wcsg.org

Grand Rapids WFGR-FM (o) 50 Monroe Ave NW Ste 500, Grand Rapids MI 49503 **Phn:** 616-451-4800 **Fax:** 616-451-0113 wfgr.com russ.hines@townsquaremedia.com

Grand Rapids WFUR-AM (q) PO Box 1808, Grand Rapids MI 49501 **Phn:** 616-451-9387 **Fax:** 616-451-8460 wfuramfm.com wfuramfm@sbcglobal.net

Grand Rapids WFUR-FM (q) PO Box 1808, Grand Rapids MI 49501 **Phn:** 616-451-9387 **Fax:** 616-451-8460 wfuramfm.com wfuramfm@sbcglobal.net

Grand Rapids WGRD-FM (r) 50 Monroe Ave NW Ste 500, Grand Rapids MI 49503 **Phn:** 616-451-4800 **Fax:** 616-451-0113 wgrd.com russ.hines@townsquaremedia.com

Grand Rapids WGVU-AM (pnj) 301 Fulton St W, Grand Rapids MI 49504 **Phn:** 616-331-6666 **Fax:** 616-331-6625 www.wgvu.org

Grand Rapids WHTS-FM (a) 60 Monroe Center St NW, Grand Rapids MI 49503 **Phn:** 616-774-8461 **Fax:** 616-774-0351 www.1053hotfm.com beau.derek@cumulus.com

Grand Rapids WJRW-AM (nt) 60 Monroe Center St NW, Grand Rapids MI 49503 **Phn:** 616-744-8461 **Fax:** 616-774-0351 www.1340wjrw.com news@wjrwam.com

Grand Rapids WKLQ-FM (r) 60 Monroe Center St NW Ste 300, Grand Rapids MI 49503 **Phn:** 616-774-8461 **Fax:** 616-774-2491

Grand Rapids WLAV-FM (r) 60 Monroe Center St NW Ste 300, Grand Rapids MI 49503 **Phn:** 616-456-5461 **Fax:** 616-451-3299 www.wlav.com rob.brandt@cumulus.com

Grand Rapids WLHT-FM (a) 50 Monroe Ave NW Ste 500, Grand Rapids MI 49503 **Phn:** 616-451-4800 **Fax:** 616-451-0113 mychannel957.com russ.hines@townsquaremedia.com

Grand Rapids WMAX-FM (a) 77 Monroe Center St NW Ste 1000, Grand Rapids MI 49503 **Phn:** 616-459-1919 **Fax:** 616-732-3331 www.espn961.com michaelallen2@clearchannel.com

Grand Rapids WMFN-AM (kn) 2422 Burton St SE, Grand Rapids MI 49546 **Phn:** 616-451-0551 **Fax:** 616-451-0565 www.birach.com sima@birach.com

Grand Rapids WMJH-AM (am) 2422 Burton St SE, Grand Rapids MI 49546 **Phn:** 616-451-0551 **Fax:** 616-451-0565 www.birach.com sima@birach.com

Grand Rapids WNWZ-AM (a) 50 Monroe Ave NW Ste 500, Grand Rapids MI 49503 **Phn:** 616-451-4800 **Fax:** 616-451-0113 Funny1410am.com russ.hines@townsquaremedia.com

Grand Rapids WOOD-AM (nt) 77 Monroe Center St NW Ste 1000, Grand Rapids MI 49503 **Phn:** 616-459-1919 **Fax:** 616-732-3330 www.woodradio.com

Grand Rapids WOOD-FM (a) 77 Monroe Center St NW Ste 1000, Grand Rapids MI 49503 **Phn:** 616-459-1919 **Fax:** 616-732-3330 www.westmichiganstar.com kellyiris@clearchannel.com

Grand Rapids WPRR-FM (p) 3777 44th St, Grand Rapids MI 49512 **Phn:** 616-656-2619 **Fax:** 616-656-2158 www.publicrealityradio.org info@publicrealityradio.org

Grand Rapids WPRR-AM (p) 3777 44th St, Grand Rapids MI 49512 **Phn:** 616-656-2619 **Fax:** 616-656-2158 www.publicrealityradio.org info@publicrealityradio.org

Grand Rapids WSNX-FM (h) 77 Monroe Center St NW Ste 1000, Grand Rapids MI 49503 **Phn:** 616-459-1919 **Fax:** 616-732-3331 www.1045snx.com eob@wsnx.com

Grand Rapids WTKG-AM (t) 77 Monroe Center St NW Ste 1000, Grand Rapids MI 49503 **Phn:** 616-459-1919 **Fax:** 616-242-6599 www.wtkg.com

Grand Rapids WTNR-FM (c) 60 Monroe Center St NW, Grand Rapids MI 49503 **Phn:** 616-774-8461 **Fax:** 616-774-0351 www.thunder945.com marcus.bradman@cumulus.com

Grand Rapids WTRV-FM (a) 50 Monroe Ave NW Ste 500, Grand Rapids MI 49503 **Phn:** 616-451-4800 **Fax:** 616-451-0113 rivergrandrapids.com russ.hines@townsquaremedia.com

Grand Rapids WYCE-FM (v) 711 Bridge St NW, Grand Rapids MI 49504 **Phn:** 616-459-4788 **Fax:** 616-459-3970 www.grcmc.orgradio comments@wyce.org

Grand Rapids WYGR-AM (y) PO Box 9591, Grand Rapids MI 49509 **Phn:** 616-452-8589 **Fax:** 616-248-0176 www.wygr.net roberts@wygr.net

Grayling WGRY-FM (c) 6514 Old Lake Rd, Grayling MI 49738 **Phn:** 989-348-6171 **Fax:** 989-348-6181 www.gannonbroadcasting.com radio@i2k.net

Grayling WGRY-AM (a) 6514 Old Lake Rd, Grayling MI 49738 **Phn:** 989-348-6171 **Fax:** 989-348-6181 www.gannonbroadcasting.com billgannon@i2k.net

Grayling WQON-FM (a) 6514 Old Lake Rd, Grayling MI 49738 **Phn:** 989-348-6171 **Fax:** 989-348-6181 www.gannonbroadcasting.com radio@i2k.net

Greenville WGLM-FM (atn) 9181 SW Greenville Rd, Greenville MI 48838 **Phn:** 616-754-1063 **Fax:** 616-619-6138 www.m1063.com office@m1063.com

MICHIGAN RADIO STATIONS

Greenville WSCG-AM (nt) PO Box 340, Greenville MI 48838 **Phn:** 616-754-3656 **Fax:** 616-754-2390

Hancock WKMJ-FM (an) 326 Quincy St, Hancock MI 49930 **Phn:** 906-482-3700 **Fax:** 906-482-1540 www.themix93.com rick@wmpl920.com

Hancock WMPL-AM (snt) PO Box 547, Hancock MI 49930 **Phn:** 906-482-1330 **Fax:** 906-482-1540

Hastings WBCH-AM (nt) PO Box 88, Hastings MI 49058 **Phn:** 269-945-3414 **Fax:** 269-945-3470 www.wbch.com wbch@wbch.com

Hastings WBCH-FM (c) PO Box 88, Hastings MI 49058 **Phn:** 269-945-3414 **Fax:** 269-945-3470 www.wbch.com wbch@wbch.com

Highland Park WHPR-FM (vx) 160 Victor St, Highland Park MI 48203 **Phn:** 313-868-6612 **Fax:** 313-868-8725 www.fm881whpr.com

Hillsdale WCSR-FM (asn) PO Box 273, Hillsdale MI 49242 **Phn:** 517-437-4444 **Fax:** 517-437-7461 www.radiohillsdale.com wcsrinc@comcast.net

Hillsdale WCSR-AM (a) PO Box 273, Hillsdale MI 49242 **Phn:** 517-437-4444 **Fax:** 517-437-7461 www.radiohillsdale.com wcsrinc@comcast.net

Holland WHTC-AM (nt) 87 Central Ave, Holland MI 49423 **Phn:** 616-392-3121 **Fax:** 616-392-8066 www.whtc.com whtcstudio@whtc.com

Holland WTHS-FM (v) PO Box 9000, Holland MI 49422 **Phn:** 616-395-7878 wths.hope.edu wths@hope.edu

Holland WYVN-FM (h) 87 Central Ave, Holland MI 49423 **Phn:** 616-392-3121 **Fax:** 616-392-8066 www.927thevan.com whtcstudio@whtc.com

Holt WJXQ-FM (r) 2495 Cedar St # 106, Holt MI 48842 **Phn:** 517-699-0111 **Fax:** 517-699-1880 www.q106fm.com webmaster.wjxq@q106fm.com

Holt WJZL-FM (j) 2495 Cedar St # 106, Holt MI 48842 **Phn:** 517-699-0111 **Fax:** 517-699-1880

Holt WLMI-FM (o) 2495 Cedar St # 106, Holt MI 48842 **Phn:** 517-699-0111 **Fax:** 517-699-1880 929wlmi.com aimee.sedik@mwcradio.com

Holt WVIC-FM (ah) 2495 Cedar St # 106, Holt MI 48842 **Phn:** 517-699-0111 **Fax:** 517-699-1880 www.941theedge.com jay.morris@mwcradio.com

Houghton WCCY-AM (ob) 313 E Montezuma Ave, Houghton MI 49931 **Phn:** 906-482-7700 **Fax:** 906-482-7751 www.wccy.com houghtonradio@up.net

Houghton WGGL-FM (pln) PO Box 65, Houghton MI 49931 **Phn:** 906-487-1911 **Fax:** 906-487-1913 minnesota.publicradio.org newsroom@mpr.org

Houghton WHKB-FM (a) 313 E Montezuma Ave, Houghton MI 49931 **Phn:** 906-482-7700 **Fax:** 906-482-7751 www.kbear102.com kreport@up.net

Houghton WMTU-FM (v) 1703 Townsend Dr, Houghton MI 49931 **Phn:** 906-487-2333 wmtu.mtu.edu gm@mtu.edu

Houghton WOLV-FM (h) 313 E Montezuma Ave, Houghton MI 49931 **Phn:** 906-482-7700 **Fax:** 906-482-7751 www.thewolf.com kreport@up.net

Howell WHMI-FM (oh) PO Box 935, Howell MI 48844 **Phn:** 517-546-0860 **Fax:** 517-546-1758 whmi.com news@whmi.com

Indian River WIDG-AM (q) PO Box 1109, Indian River MI 49749 **Phn:** 231-238-0811 **Fax:** 231-238-0803 suzanneh@baragamail.com

Interlochen WIAA-FM (pln) PO Box 199, Interlochen MI 49643 **Phn:** 231-276-4400 **Fax:** 231-276-4417 ipr.interlochen.org ipr@interlochen.org

Iron Mountain WHTO-FM (o) 212 W J St, Iron Mountain MI 49801 **Phn:** 906-774-5731 **Fax:** 906-774-4542 hootselvis@yahoo.com

Iron Mountain WIMK-FM (r) 101 Kent St, Iron Mountain MI 49801 **Phn:** 906-774-4321 **Fax:** 906-774-7799 www.uprockradio.com prodguy@uplogon.com

Iron Mountain WJNR-FM (c) 212 W J St, Iron Mountain MI 49801 **Phn:** 906-774-5731 **Fax:** 906-774-4542 www.frogcountry.com trisha@frogcountry.com

Iron Mountain WMIQ-AM (snt) 101 Kent St, Iron Mountain MI 49801 **Phn:** 906-774-4321 **Fax:** 906-774-7799 www.wmiq.net talk1450wmiq@uplogon.com

Iron Mountain WOBE-FM (o) 212 W J St, Iron Mountain MI 49801 **Phn:** 906-774-5731 **Fax:** 906-774-4542 classichitsb100fm.com trisha@frogcountry.com

Iron Mountain WUPK-FM (r) 101 Kent St, Iron Mountain MI 49801 **Phn:** 906-774-1318 **Fax:** 906-774-7799 www.rockthebear.com prodguy@uplogon.com

Iron Mountain WZNL-FM (a) 101 Kent St, Iron Mountain MI 49801 **Phn:** 906-774-4321 **Fax:** 906-774-7799 wznl.tripod.com star943@uplogon.com

Iron River WIKB-AM (o) 809 W Genesee St, Iron River MI 49935 **Phn:** 906-265-5104 **Fax:** 906-265-3486 www.wikb.com wikb@wikb.com

Iron River WIKB-FM (o) 809 W Genesee St, Iron River MI 49935 **Phn:** 906-265-5104 **Fax:** 906-265-3486 www.wikb.com wikb@sbcglobal.net

Ironwood WIMI-FM (a) 222 S Lawrence St, Ironwood MI 49938 **Phn:** 906-932-2411 **Fax:** 906-932-2485 www.wimifm.com wjmswimi@chartermi.net

Ironwood WJMS-AM (ct) 222 S Lawrence St, Ironwood MI 49938 **Phn:** 906-932-2411 **Fax:** 906-932-2485 www.wjmsam.com wjmswimi@chartermi.net

Ironwood WUPM-FM (a) 209 Harrison St, Ironwood MI 49938 **Phn:** 906-932-5234 **Fax:** 906-932-1548 https:www.facebook.comWUPMRadio wupm@wupm-whry.com

Jackson WIBM-AM (s) 1700 Glenshire Dr, Jackson MI 49201 **Phn:** 517-787-9546 **Fax:** 517-787-7517 wkhm.com mdaly@wkhm.com

Jackson WKHM-AM (snt) 1700 Glenshire Dr, Jackson MI 49201 **Phn:** 517-787-9546 **Fax:** 517-787-7517 www.wkhm.com jamie@k1053.com

Jackson WKHM-FM (a) 1700 Glenshire Dr, Jackson MI 49201 **Phn:** 517-787-9546 **Fax:** 517-787-7517 www.k1053.com jamie@k1053.com

Kalamazoo WIDR-FM (v) 1501 Faunce Student Services Bldg, Kalamazoo MI 49008 **Phn:** 269-387-6301 widr.gm@gmail.com

Kalamazoo WKDS-FM (v) 606 E Kilgore Rd, Kalamazoo MI 49001 **Phn:** 269-337-0200 **Fax:** 269-337-0251

Kalamazoo WKFR-FM (h) 4154 Jennings Dr, Kalamazoo MI 49048 **Phn:** 269-344-0111 **Fax:** 269-344-4223 www.wkfr.com glen.dillon@cumulus.com

Kalamazoo WKMI-AM (nt) 4154 Jennings Dr, Kalamazoo MI 49048 **Phn:** 269-344-0111 **Fax:** 269-344-4223 www.wkmi.com bensonshow@cumulus.com

Kalamazoo WKPR-AM (q) PO Box 1808, Kalamazoo MI 49004 **Phn:** 616-451-9387 **Fax:** 616-451-8460

Kalamazoo WKZO-AM (nt) 4200 W Main St, Kalamazoo MI 49006 **Phn:** 269-345-7121 **Fax:** 269-345-1436 www.wkzo.com lori.moore@wkzo.com

Kalamazoo WKZO-FM (nt) 4200 W Main St, Kalamazoo MI 49006 **Phn:** 269-345-7121 **Fax:** 269-345-1436 www.wkzo.com amy.burrow@mwcradio.com

Kalamazoo WMUK-FM (plnj) 1903 W Michigan Ave, Kalamazoo MI 49008 **Phn:** 269-387-5715 **Fax:** 269-387-4630 www.wmuk.org webmaster@wmuk.org

Kalamazoo WNWN-AM (u) 4200 W Main St, Kalamazoo MI 49006 **Phn:** 269-345-7121 **Fax:** 269-345-1436 www.go955.com amy.burrow@mwcradio.com

Kalamazoo WQLR-AM (s) 4200 W Main St, Kalamazoo MI 49006 **Phn:** 269-345-7121 **Fax:** 269-345-1436 www.1660thefan.com jay.morris@mwcradio.com

Kalamazoo WQSN-AM (s) 4200 W Main St, Kalamazoo MI 49006 **Phn:** 269-349-1660 **Fax:** 269-345-1436 www.1660thefan.com

Kalamazoo WRKR-FM (r) 4154 Jennings Dr, Kalamazoo MI 49048 **Phn:** 269-344-0111 **Fax:** 269-344-4223 www.wrkr.com mike.mckelly@cumulus.com

Kalamazoo WVFM-FM (r) 4200 W Main St, Kalamazoo MI 49006 **Phn:** 269-345-7121 **Fax:** 269-345-1436 myfm1065.com

Lansing WFMK-FM (a) 3420 Pinetree Rd, Lansing MI 48911 **Phn:** 517-394-7272 **Fax:** 517-394-3391 www.99wfmk.com chris.tyler@cumulus.com

Lansing WHZZ-FM (h) 600 W Cavanaugh Rd, Lansing MI 48910 **Phn:** 517-393-1320 **Fax:** 517-393-0882 www.1017mikefm.com scott@1017mikefm.com

Lansing WILS-AM (am) 600 W Cavanaugh Rd, Lansing MI 48910 **Phn:** 517-393-1320 **Fax:** 517-393-0882 www.1320wils.com scott@1017mikefm.com

Lansing WITL-FM (c) 3420 Pinetree Rd, Lansing MI 48911 **Phn:** 517-393-7272 **Fax:** 517-394-3391 www.witl.com studio@witl.com

Lansing WJIM-AM (nt) 3420 Pinetree Rd, Lansing MI 48911 **Phn:** 517-394-7272 **Fax:** 517-394-3565 www.wjimam.com bigshowproducer@gmail.com

Lansing WJIM-FM (h) 3420 Pinetree Rd, Lansing MI 48911 **Phn:** 517-394-7272 **Fax:** 517-394-3565 www.wjimam.com bigshowproducer@gmail.com

Lansing WLNZ-FM (vjx) 400 N Capitol Ave, Lansing MI 48933 **Phn:** 517-483-1710 **Fax:** 517-483-1894 www.lcc.eduradio wlnzlyn@yahoo.com

Lansing WMMQ-FM (r) 3420 Pinetree Rd, Lansing MI 48911 **Phn:** 517-394-7272 **Fax:** 517-394-3391 www.wmmq.com deb@wmmq.com

Lansing WQHH-FM (wu) 600 W Cavanaugh Rd, Lansing MI 48910 **Phn:** 517-393-1320 **Fax:** 517-393-0882 www.power965fm.com cindytuck@macdonaldbroadcasting.com

Lansing WVFN-AM (st) 3420 Pinetree Rd, Lansing MI 48911 **Phn:** 517-394-7272 **Fax:** 517-394-3391 www.thegame730am.com

Lansing WXLA-AM (wx) 600 W Cavanaugh Rd, Lansing MI 48910 **Phn:** 517-393-1320 **Fax:** 517-393-0882 traffic@1017mikefm.com

Lapeer WMPC-AM (qg) PO Box 104, Lapeer MI 48446 **Phn:** 810-664-6211 **Fax:** 810-664-5361 www.wmpc.org

Ludington WKLA-AM (nt) 5941 W US Highway 10, Ludington MI 49431 **Phn:** 231-843-3438 **Fax:** 231-843-1886

Ludington WKLA-FM (a) 5941 W US Highway 10, Ludington MI 49431 **Phn:** 231-843-3438 **Fax:** 231-843-1886

Ludington WKZC-FM (c) 5941 W US Highway 10, Ludington MI 49431 **Phn:** 231-843-3438 **Fax:** 231-843-1886

Ludington WMLQ-FM (a) PO Box 855, Ludington MI 49431 **Phn:** 231-843-0941 **Fax:** 231-843-9411 97-coastfm.com

MICHIGAN RADIO STATIONS

Ludington WMOM-FM (a) 206 E Ludington Ave, Ludington MI 49431 **Phn:** 231-845-9666 **Fax:** 231-845-9332 www.wmom.fm news@wmom.fm

Ludington WWKR-FM (r) 5399 W Wallace Ln, Ludington MI 49431 **Phn:** 231-843-0941 **Fax:** 231-843-9411 www.94k-rock.com studio@94k-rock.com

Manistee WMTE-FM (o) 52 Greenbush St, Manistee MI 49660 **Phn:** 231-723-0010 **Fax:** 231-723-9908

Manistee WMTE-AM (nt) 52 Greenbush St, Manistee MI 49660 **Phn:** 231-723-9906 **Fax:** 231-723-9908

Manistique WTIQ-AM (o) PO Box 220, Manistique MI 49854 **Phn:** 906-341-8444 **Fax:** 906-341-6222 www.wtiqradio.com rrnnews@radioresultsnetwork.com

Marquette WDMJ-AM (nt) 1009 W Ridge St Ste A, Marquette MI 49855 **Phn:** 906-225-1313 **Fax:** 906-225-1324

Marquette WFXD-FM (c) 3060 US Highway 41 W, Marquette MI 49855 **Phn:** 906-228-6800 **Fax:** 906-228-8128 wfxd.com todd@toddnoordyk.com

Marquette WHWL-FM (q) 130 Carmen Dr, Marquette MI 49855 **Phn:** 906-249-1423 **Fax:** 906-249-4042 whwl.net whwl@whwl.net

Marquette WIAN-AM (nt) 1009 W Ridge St Ste A, Marquette MI 49855 **Phn:** 906-225-1313 **Fax:** 906-225-1324 wjpd@wjpd.com

Marquette WJPD-FM (c) 1009 W Ridge St Ste A, Marquette MI 49855 **Phn:** 906-225-1313 **Fax:** 906-225-1324 www.wjpd.com news@wjpd.com

Marquette WKQS-FM (a) 3060 US Highway 41 W, Marquette MI 49855 **Phn:** 906-228-6800 **Fax:** 906-228-8128 wkqsfm.com todd@toddnoordyk.com

Marquette WMQT-FM (a) 121 N Front St Ste A, Marquette MI 49855 **Phn:** 906-225-9100 **Fax:** 906-225-5577 www.wmqt.com wmqt@wmqt.com

Marquette WNGE-FM (o) 1009 W Ridge St Ste A, Marquette MI 49855 **Phn:** 906-225-1313 **Fax:** 906-225-1324 wjpd@wjpd.com

Marquette WNMU-FM (plnj) 1401 Presque Isle Ave, Marquette MI 49855 **Phn:** 906-227-2600 **Fax:** 906-227-2905 wnmufm.org fmnews@nmu.edu

Marquette WQXO-AM (bo) 3060 US Highway 41 W, Marquette MI 49855 **Phn:** 906-228-6800 **Fax:** 906-228-8128 wqxo.com todd@toddnoordyk.com

Marquette WRUP-FM (r) 3060 US Highway 41 W, Marquette MI 49855 **Phn:** 906-228-6800 **Fax:** 906-228-8128 wrup.com todd@toddnoordyk.com

Marquette WUPX-FM (vr) 1204 University Ctr, Marquette MI 49855 **Phn:** 906-227-1844 www.wupx.com stationmanager@wupx.com

Marquette WZAM-AM (s) 121 N Front St Ste A, Marquette MI 49855 **Phn:** 906-225-9100 **Fax:** 906-225-5577 www.espn970.com casey@espn970.com

Menominee WAGN-AM (nt) 413 10th Ave, Menominee MI 49858 **Phn:** 906-863-5551 **Fax:** 906-863-5679 baycitiesradio.net kenconners@baycitiesradio.net

Menominee WHYB-FM (o) 413 10th Ave, Menominee MI 49858 **Phn:** 906-863-5551 **Fax:** 715-732-0125 baycitiesradio.net kenconners@baycitiesradio.net

Menominee WLST-FM (c) 413 10th Ave, Menominee MI 49858 **Phn:** 906-863-5551 **Fax:** 906-863-5679 baycitiesradio.net kenconners@baycitiesradio.net

Menominee WMAM-AM (s) 413 10th Ave, Menominee MI 49858 **Phn:** 906-863-5551 **Fax:** 715-732-0125 baycitiesradio.net kenconners@baycitiesradio.net

Menominee WSFQ-FM (a) 413 10th Ave, Menominee MI 49858 **Phn:** 906-863-5551 **Fax:** 715-732-0125 baycitiesradio.net kenconners@baycitiesradio.net

Midland WMPX-AM (am) PO Box 1689, Midland MI 48641 **Phn:** 989-631-1490 **Fax:** 989-631-6357 wmpxwmrx.com wmpx@ejourney.com

Midland WUGN-FM (q) 510 E Isabella Rd, Midland MI 48640 **Phn:** 989-631-7060 **Fax:** 989-631-4825 www.myflr.org

Monroe WTWR-FM (h) 14 S Monroe St, Monroe MI 48161 **Phn:** 734-242-6600 **Fax:** 734-242-6599 my983.com ryan.nutter@cumulus.com

Mount Pleasant WCFX-FM (h) 5847 Venture Way, Mount Pleasant MI 48858 **Phn:** 989-772-4173 **Fax:** 989-773-1236 www.wcfx.com becca@wcfx.com

Mount Pleasant WCMU-FM (plnj) 1999 E Campus Dr, Mount Pleasant MI 48859 **Phn:** 989-774-3105 **Fax:** 989-774-4427 www.wcmu.org david.nicholas@cmich.edu

Mount Pleasant WCZY-FM (zh) 4895 E Wing Rd, Mount Pleasant MI 48858 **Phn:** 989-772-9664 **Fax:** 989-773-5000 www.wczy.net wczy@wczy.net

Mount Pleasant WMHW-FM (vr) 340 Moore Hall Cen Mi Univ, Mount Pleasant MI 48859 **Phn:** 989-774-7287 **Fax:** 989-774-2426 www.wmhw.org

Mount Pleasant WMMI-AM (t) 4895 E Wing Rd, Mount Pleasant MI 48858 **Phn:** 989-772-9664 **Fax:** 989-773-5000 wczy.net wczy@wczy.net

Muskegon Heights WLCS-FM (o) 3375 Merriam St Ste 201, Muskegon Heights MI 49444 **Phn:** 231-830-0176 **Fax:** 231-830-0194

Muskegon Heights WODJ-AM (s) 3375 Merriam St Ste 201, Muskegon Heights MI 49444 **Phn:** 231-830-0176 **Fax:** 231-830-0194

Muskegon Heights WVIB-FM (ua) 3375 Merriam St, Muskegon Heights MI 49444 **Phn:** 231-830-0176 **Fax:** 231-830-0194 www.v100fm.com

Newberry WMJT-FM (ant) PO Box 486, Newberry MI 49868 **Phn:** 906-293-1400 **Fax:** 906-293-5161 kent@radioeagle.com

Newberry WNBY-AM (c) PO Box 501, Newberry MI 49868 **Phn:** 906-293-3221 **Fax:** 906-293-8275 www.1450wnby.com travis@wnby.net

Newberry WNBY-FM (o) PO Box 501, Newberry MI 49868 **Phn:** 906-293-3221 **Fax:** 906-293-8275 www.oldies93fm.com travis@wnby.net

Niles WSMK-FM (h) 925 N 5th St, Niles MI 49120 **Phn:** 269-683-4343 **Fax:** 269-683-7759 www.wsmkradio.com mtaylor@wsmkradio.com

Norton Shores WKBZ-AM (nt) 3565 Green St, Norton Shores MI 49444 **Phn:** 231-733-2600 **Fax:** 231-733-7461 www.newstalk1090.com markdixon@clearchannel.com

Norton Shores WMRR-FM (r) 3565 Green St, Norton Shores MI 49444 **Phn:** 231-733-2600 **Fax:** 231-733-7461 www.rock1017fm.com timfeagan@clearchannel.com

Norton Shores WMUS-FM (c) 3565 Green St, Norton Shores MI 49444 **Phn:** 231-733-2600 **Fax:** 231-733-7461 www.107mus.com markdixon@clearchannel.com

Norton Shores WSHZ-FM (a) 3565 Green St, Norton Shores MI 49444 **Phn:** 231-733-2600 **Fax:** 231-739-9037 www.westmichiganstar.com tonybrooks@clearchannel.com

Olivet WOCR-FM (v) 320 S Main St, Olivet MI 49076 **Phn:** 269-749-7398 **Fax:** 269-749-7695

Ontonagon WUPY-FM (c) PO Box 265, Ontonagon MI 49953 **Phn:** 906-884-9668 **Fax:** 906-884-4985 www.wupy101.com wupy@jamadots.com

Otsego WQXC-FM (o) PO Box 80, Otsego MI 49078 **Phn:** 269-692-6851 **Fax:** 269-692-6861 www.wqxc.com overhuel@wqxc.com

Otsego WZUU-FM (r) PO Box 80, Otsego MI 49078 **Phn:** 269-692-6851 **Fax:** 269-692-6861 www.wzuu.com scottybud@wzuu.com

Owosso WJSZ-FM (r) 103 N Washington St, Owosso MI 48867 **Phn:** 989-725-1925 **Fax:** 989-725-7925 www.z925.com studio@z925.com

Petoskey WJML-AM (nt) 2175 Click Rd, Petoskey MI 49770 **Phn:** 231-348-5000 www.wjml.com news@wjml.com

Petoskey WJNL-AM (nt) 2175 Click Rd, Petoskey MI 49770 **Phn:** 231-348-5000 www.wjml.com news@wjml.com

Petoskey WKHQ-FM (h) PO Box 286, Petoskey MI 49770 **Phn:** 231-347-8713 **Fax:** 231-347-8782 www.106khq.com bill.michaels@106khq.com

Petoskey WLXT-FM (a) PO Box 286, Petoskey MI 49770 **Phn:** 231-347-8713 **Fax:** 231-347-8782 www.lite96.com tmac@106khq.com

Petoskey WMBN-AM (a) PO Box 286, Petoskey MI 49770 **Phn:** 231-347-8713 **Fax:** 231-347-9920 www.1340amwmbn.com bill@1340amtheticket.com

Petoskey WMKT-AM (nt) PO Box 286, Petoskey MI 49770 **Phn:** 231-347-8713 **Fax:** 231-347-8782 www.wmktthetalkstation.com bill.michaels@106khq.com

Pittsford WPCJ-FM (vq) 9400 E Beecher Rd, Pittsford MI 49271 **Phn:** 517-523-3427 66.133.129.5~freedomfarmWPCJ.html wpcj@freedomfarm.info

Plainwell WAKV-AM (ob) 213 Gilkey St, Plainwell MI 49080 **Phn:** 269-685-2438 980am@net-link.net

Port Huron WBTI-FM (a) 808 Huron Ave, Port Huron MI 48060 **Phn:** 810-982-9000 **Fax:** 810-987-9380 www.wbti.com bcoburn@radiofirst.net

Port Huron WGRT-FM (a) 624 Grand River Ave, Port Huron MI 48060 **Phn:** 810-987-3200 **Fax:** 810-987-3325 www.wgrt.com news@wgrt.com

Port Huron WHLS-AM (o) 808 Huron Ave, Port Huron MI 48060 **Phn:** 810-982-9000 **Fax:** 810-987-9380 www.whls.net

Port Huron WHLX-AM (a) 808 Huron Ave, Port Huron MI 48060 **Phn:** 810-982-9000 **Fax:** 810-987-9380 www.whls.net

Port Huron WNFR-FM (q) 2865 Maywood Dr, Port Huron MI 48060 **Phn:** 810-985-3260 **Fax:** 810-985-7712 www.wnradio.com info@wnradio.com

Port Huron WPHM-AM (snt) 808 Huron Ave, Port Huron MI 48060 **Phn:** 810-982-9000 **Fax:** 810-987-9380 www.wphm.net pmiller@radiofirst.net

Port Huron WSAQ-FM (c) 808 Huron Ave, Port Huron MI 48060 **Phn:** 810-982-9000 **Fax:** 810-987-9380 www.wsaq.com lsmith@radiofirst.net

Port Huron WSGR-FM (vr) 323 Erie St, Port Huron MI 48060 **Phn:** 810-989-5564

Prudenville WTWS-FM (c) PO Box 468, Prudenville MI 48651 **Phn:** 989-366-5364 **Fax:** 989-366-6200 www.ilovethetwister.com

Prudenville WUPS-FM (h) PO Box 468, Prudenville MI 48651 **Phn:** 989-366-5364 **Fax:** 989-366-6200 www.wups.com wupsfm@yahoo.com

Rochester WXOU-FM (v) 69 Oakland Ctr, Rochester MI 48309 **Phn:** 248-370-4273 www.wxou.org wxou@wxou.org

Saginaw WCEN-FM (c) 1795 Tittabawassee Rd, Saginaw MI 48604 **Phn:** 989-752-3456 **Fax:** 989-754-5046 www.945themoose.com jim@945themoose.com

MICHIGAN RADIO STATIONS

Saginaw WGER-FM (a) 1795 Tittabawassee Rd, Saginaw MI 48604 **Phn:** 989-752-3456 **Fax:** 989-754-5046 www.mix1063fm.com

Saginaw WHNN-FM (o) 1740 Champagne Dr N, Saginaw MI 48604 **Phn:** 989-776-2100 **Fax:** 989-776-2121 www.whnn.com

Saginaw WILZ-FM (r) 1740 Champagne Dr N, Saginaw MI 48604 **Phn:** 989-776-2100 **Fax:** 989-767-6541 www.wheelz.fm stan.parman@cumulus.com

Saginaw WIOG-FM (h) 1740 Champagne Dr N, Saginaw MI 48604 **Phn:** 989-776-2100 **Fax:** 989-776-2121 www.wiog.com rachel.geddes@cumulus.com

Saginaw WKCQ-FM (c) 2000 Whittier St, Saginaw MI 48601 **Phn:** 989-752-8161 **Fax:** 989-752-8102 www.98fmkcq.com wkcq@chartermi.net

Saginaw WKQZ-FM (r) 1740 Champagne Dr N, Saginaw MI 48604 **Phn:** 989-776-2100 **Fax:** 989-776-2121 www.z93kqz.com lynn.roberts@cumulus.com

Saginaw WMJO-FM (h) PO Box 1776, Saginaw MI 48605 **Phn:** 989-752-8161 **Fax:** 989-752-8102 www.973joefm.com admin@973joefm.com

Saginaw WNEM-AM (snt) 107 N Franklin St, Saginaw MI 48607 **Phn:** 989-755-8191 **Fax:** 989-758-2111 www.wnem.com wnem@wnem.com

Saginaw WSAM-AM (m) PO Box 1776, Saginaw MI 48605 **Phn:** 989-752-8161 **Fax:** 989-752-8102 www.thebay104fm.com

Saginaw WSGW-AM (nt) 1795 Tittabawassee Rd, Saginaw MI 48604 **Phn:** 989-752-3456 **Fax:** 989-754-5046 www.wsgw.com news@wsgw.com

Saginaw WSGW-FM (snt) 1795 Tittabawassee Rd, Saginaw MI 48604 **Phn:** 989-752-3456 **Fax:** 989-754-5046 www.wsgw.com news@wsgw.com

Saginaw WTLZ-FM (wu) 1795 Tittabawassee Rd, Saginaw MI 48604 **Phn:** 989-752-3456 **Fax:** 989-754-5046 www.kisswtlz.com yvonne@kisswtlz.com

Saint Johns WWSJ-AM (g) 1363 W Parks Rd Box 451, Saint Johns MI 48879 **Phn:** 989-224-7911 **Fax:** 989-224-4683 www.joy1580.com communitynews@joy1580.com

Saint Joseph WCNF-FM (c) PO Box 107, Saint Joseph MI 49085 **Phn:** 269-925-1111 **Fax:** 269-925-1011 www.983thecoast.com news@wsjm.com

Saint Joseph WIRX-FM (r) PO Box 107, Saint Joseph MI 49085 **Phn:** 269-925-1111 **Fax:** 269-925-1011 www.wirx.com juli@wirx.com

Saint Joseph WSJM-AM (nt) PO Box 107, Saint Joseph MI 49085 **Phn:** 269-925-1111 **Fax:** 269-925-1011 www.wsjm.com mike@wsjm.com

Saint Joseph WSJM-FM (nt) PO Box 107, Saint Joseph MI 49085 **Phn:** 269-925-1111 **Fax:** 269-925-1011 www.wsjm.com

Sandusky WBGV-FM (c) 19 S Elk St, Sandusky MI 48471 **Phn:** 810-648-2700 **Fax:** 810-648-3242 www.sanilacbroadcasting.com boba@sanilacbroadcasting.com

Sandusky WMIC-AM (c) 19 S Elk St, Sandusky MI 48471 **Phn:** 810-648-2700 **Fax:** 810-648-3242 www.sanilacbroadcasting.com renaed@sanilacbroadcasting.com

Sandusky WTGV-FM (a) 19 S Elk St, Sandusky MI 48471 **Phn:** 810-648-2700 **Fax:** 810-648-3242 www.sanilacbroadcasting.com renaed@sanilacbroadcasting.com

Sault Sainte Marie WIHC-FM (r) 1402 Ashmun St, Sault Sainte Marie MI 49783 **Phn:** 906-635-0995 **Fax:** 906-635-1216 www.classicrockthebear.com tim@classicrockthebear.com

Sault Sainte Marie WKNW-AM (snt) 1402 Ashmun St, Sault Sainte Marie MI 49783 **Phn:** 906-635-0995 **Fax:** 906-635-1216

Sault Sainte Marie WLSO-FM (v) 680 W Easterday Ave, Sault Sainte Marie MI 49783 **Phn:** 906-635-2107 **Fax:** 906-635-2111

Sault Sainte Marie WSOO-AM (a) PO Box 1230, Sault Sainte Marie MI 49783 **Phn:** 906-632-2231 **Fax:** 906-632-4411 www.1230wsoo.com

Sault Sainte Marie WSUE-FM (r) PO Box 1230, Sault Sainte Marie MI 49783 **Phn:** 906-632-2231 **Fax:** 906-632-4411 www.rock101.net webmaster@rock101.net

Sault Sainte Marie WYSS-FM (h) 1402 Ashmun St, Sault Sainte Marie MI 49783 **Phn:** 906-635-0995 **Fax:** 906-635-1216 www.yesfm.net tomewing@charter.net

South Haven WCSY-FM (aj) 11637 M-140 Hwy # B, South Haven MI 49090 **Phn:** 269-637-6397 **Fax:** 269-637-2675 www.wcsy.com paul@wcsy.com

South Haven WHIT-AM (o) 510 Williams St, South Haven MI 49090 **Phn:** 269-637-6397 **Fax:** 269-637-2675 golson@wirx.com

Southfield WNZK-AM (e) 21700 Northwestern Hwy Ste 1190, Southfield MI 48075 **Phn:** 248-557-3500 **Fax:** 248-557-2950 www.wnzk.com sima@birach.com

Southfield WPON-AM (ot) 21700 Northwestern Hwy Ste 1190, Southfield MI 48075 **Phn:** 248-557-3500 **Fax:** 248-557-2950 www.wpon.com

Southfield WWJ-AM (n) 26495 American Dr, Southfield MI 48034 **Phn:** 248-455-7200 **Fax:** 248-304-4970 detroit.cbslocal.com wwjnewsroom@cbsradio.com

Southfield WXYT-AM (st) 26455 American Dr, Southfield MI 48034 **Phn:** 248-327-2900 **Fax:** 248-356-5470 detroit.cbslocal.com jessica.shaw@cbsradio.com

Spring Arbor KTGG-AM (v) 106 E Main St, Spring Arbor MI 49283 **Phn:** 517-750-6540 **Fax:** 517-750-6619 malachi@arbor.edu

Spring Arbor WSAE-FM (a) 106 E Main St, Spring Arbor MI 49283 **Phn:** 517-750-6540 **Fax:** 517-750-6619 home.fm info@home.fm

Sturgis WMSH-FM (o) PO Box 7080, Sturgis MI 49091 **Phn:** 269-651-2383 **Fax:** 269-659-1111 www.trueoldies993.com wmsh@wmshradio.com

Sturgis WMSH-AM (s) PO Box 7080, Sturgis MI 49091 **Phn:** 269-651-2383 **Fax:** 269-659-1111

Tawas City WIOS-AM (a) PO Box 549, Tawas City MI 48764 **Phn:** 989-362-3417 **Fax:** 989-362-4544 www.wkjc.com wkjc@wkjc.com

Tawas City WKJC-FM (c) 523 Meadow Rd, Tawas City MI 48763 **Phn:** 989-362-3417 **Fax:** 989-362-4544 www.wkjc.com wkjc@wkjc.com

Tawas City WKJZ-FM (h) 523 Meadow Rd, Tawas City MI 48763 **Phn:** 989-362-3417 **Fax:** 989-362-4544 www.hitsfm.net wkjc@wkjc.com

Tawas City WQLB-FM (r) 523 Meadow Rd, Tawas City MI 48763 **Phn:** 989-362-3417 **Fax:** 989-362-4544 www.hitsfm.net wkjc@wkjc.com

Three Rivers WLKM-FM (ar) 59750 Constantine Rd, Three Rivers MI 49093 **Phn:** 269-278-1815 **Fax:** 269-273-7975 www.wlkm.com info@wlkm.com

Three Rivers WRCI-AM (c) 59750 Constantine Rd, Three Rivers MI 49093 **Phn:** 269-278-1815 **Fax:** 269-273-7975 www.wlkm.com info@wlkm.com

Traverse City WCCW-AM (st) PO Box 427, Traverse City MI 49685 **Phn:** 231-946-6211 **Fax:** 231-946-1914 brianh@wccw.fm

Traverse City WCCW-FM (o) 300 E Front St Ste 450, Traverse City MI 49684 **Phn:** 231-946-6211 **Fax:** 231-946-1914 www.wccw.fm daveg@wccw.fm

Traverse City WFCX-FM (h) 1020 Hastings St Ste 102, Traverse City MI 49686 **Phn:** 231-947-0003 **Fax:** 231-947-7002 www.943thefoxfm.com charlie@wklt.com

Traverse City WFDX-FM (h) 1020 Hastings St Ste 102, Traverse City MI 49686 **Phn:** 231-947-0003 **Fax:** 231-947-7002 www.943thefoxfm.com charlie@wklt.com

Traverse City WJZQ-FM (aj) 300 E Front St #450, Traverse City MI 49684 **Phn:** 231-946-6211 **Fax:** 231-946-1914 z93hits.com ronpritchard@z93hits.com

Traverse City WKLT-FM (r) 1020 Hastings St Ste 102, Traverse City MI 49686 **Phn:** 231-947-0003 **Fax:** 231-947-7002 wklt.com rcoates@wklt.com

Traverse City WKLZ-FM (r) 1020 Hastings St Ste 102, Traverse City MI 49686 **Phn:** 231-947-0003 **Fax:** 231-947-7002 www.wklt.com charlie@wklt.com

Traverse City WLDR-FM (c) 13999 S West Bay Shore Dr, Traverse City MI 49684 **Phn:** 231-947-3220 **Fax:** 231-947-7201 sunnycountry1019@gmail.com

Traverse City WLJN-FM (q) PO Box 1400, Traverse City MI 49685 **Phn:** 231-946-1400 **Fax:** 231-946-3959 www.wljn.com info@wljn.com

Traverse City WLJN-AM (q) PO Box 1400, Traverse City MI 49685 **Phn:** 231-946-1400 **Fax:** 231-946-3959 www.wljn.com info@wljn.com

Traverse City WNMC-FM (v) 1701 E Front St, Traverse City MI 49686 **Phn:** 231-995-2562 www.wnmc.org wnmc@nmc.edu

Traverse City WTCM-AM (t) 314 E Front St, Traverse City MI 49684 **Phn:** 231-947-7675 **Fax:** 231-929-3988 www.wtcmradio.com wtcm@wtcmradio.com

Traverse City WTCM-FM (c) 314 E Front St, Traverse City MI 49684 **Phn:** 231-947-7675 **Fax:** 231-929-3988 www.wtcmi.com wtcm@wtcmradio.com

Troy WCAR-AM (s) PO Box 4905, Troy MI 48099 **Phn:** 734-525-1111 **Fax:** 734-525-3608 www.nbcsportsradiodetroit.com

Twin Lake WBLU-FM (plnj) 300 E Crystal Lake Rd, Twin Lake MI 49457 **Phn:** 231-894-2616 www.bluelake.org radio@bluelake.org

Warren WPHS-FM (v) 30333 Hoover Rd, Warren MI 48093 **Phn:** 586-698-4501 **Fax:** 586-751-3755 wphs891.weebly.com

Ypsilanti WEMU-FM (pjnx) PO Box 980350, Ypsilanti MI 48198 **Phn:** 734-487-2229 **Fax:** 734-487-1015 www.wemu.org wemu@emich.edu

Ypsilanti WSDS-AM (cy) 580 W Clark Rd, Ypsilanti MI 48198 **Phn:** 734-484-1480 **Fax:** 734-484-5313 www.wsds1480.com wsds@explosiva1480.com

Zeeland WGNB-FM (q) PO Box 40, Zeeland MI 49464 **Phn:** 616-772-7300 **Fax:** 616-772-9663 www.moodyradiowestmichigan.fm wgnb@moody.edu

Zeeland WJQK-FM (q) 425 Centerstone Ct, Zeeland MI 49464 **Phn:** 616-931-9930 **Fax:** 616-931-1280 jq99.com traffic@jq99.com

Zeeland WPNW-AM (t) 425 Centerstone Ct # 1, Zeeland MI 49464 **Phn:** 616-931-9930 **Fax:** 616-931-1280 www.1260thepledge.com traffic@jq99.com

MINNESOTA

Ada KRJB-FM (cnt) 312 W Main St, Ada MN 56510 **Phn:** 218-784-2844 **Fax:** 218-784-3749 www.krjbradio.com krjbada@loretel.net

MINNESOTA RADIO STATIONS

Aitkin KFGI-FM (r) PO Box 140, Aitkin MN 56431 **Phn:** 218-927-2100 **Fax:** 218-927-4090 www.redrockradiobrainerd.com kkinradio@embarqmail.com

Aitkin KKIN-FM (c) PO Box 140, Aitkin MN 56431 **Phn:** 218-927-2344 **Fax:** 218-927-4090 www.kkinradio.com kkinradio@embarqmail.com

Aitkin KKIN-AM (am) PO Box 140, Aitkin MN 56431 **Phn:** 218-927-2344 **Fax:** 218-927-4090 www.kkinradio.com kkinradio@embarqmail.com

Aitkin KLKS-FM (a) PO Box 140, Aitkin MN 56431 **Phn:** 218-927-2100 **Fax:** 218-927-4090 www.redrockradiobrainerd.com kkinradio@embarqmail.com

Aitkin WWWI-AM (r) PO Box 140, Aitkin MN 56431 **Phn:** 218-927-2100 **Fax:** 218-927-4090 www.redrockradiobrainerd.com kkinradio@embarqmail.com

Aitkin WWWI-FM (o) PO Box 140, Aitkin MN 56431 **Phn:** 218-927-2100 **Fax:** 218-927-4090 www.redrockradiobrainerd.com kkinradio@embarqmail.com

Albany KASM-AM (ct) PO Box 160, Albany MN 56307 **Phn:** 320-845-2184 **Fax:** 320-845-2187 www.kasmradio.com kasm1150am@albanytel.com

Albany KDDG-FM (c) PO Box 160, Albany MN 56307 **Phn:** 320-845-2184 **Fax:** 320-845-2187

Albert Lea KATE-AM (ntm) 1633 W Main St, Albert Lea MN 56007 **Phn:** 507-373-2338 **Fax:** 507-373-4736 www.myalbertlea.com rmithuen@albertlea.threeeagles.com

Albert Lea KCPI-FM (h) 1633 W Main St, Albert Lea MN 56007 **Phn:** 507-373-2338 **Fax:** 507-373-4736 www.myalbertlea.com rmithuen@kaus.threeeagles.com

Albert Lea KQPR-FM (r) PO Box 1106, Albert Lea MN 56007 **Phn:** 507-373-9600 **Fax:** 507-373-9045 www.power96rocker.com kqpr@power96rocker.com

Alexandria KIKV-FM (c) 604 3rd Ave W, Alexandria MN 56308 **Phn:** 320-762-2154 **Fax:** 320-762-2156 www.kikvradio.com 100.7@kikvfm.com

Alexandria KULO-FM (o) PO Box 1024, Alexandria MN 56308 **Phn:** 320-762-2154 **Fax:** 320-762-2156 www.cool943.com dvagle@kikvfm.com

Alexandria KXRA-FM (r) 1312 Broadway, Alexandria MN 56308 **Phn:** 320-763-3131 **Fax:** 320-763-5641 www.voiceofalexandria.com thefolks@kxra.com

Alexandria KXRA-AM (nt) 1312 Broadway, Alexandria MN 56308 **Phn:** 320-763-3131 **Fax:** 320-763-5641 www.voiceofalexandria.com thefolks@kxra.com

Alexandria KXRZ-FM (a) PO Box 69, Alexandria MN 56308 **Phn:** 320-763-3131 **Fax:** 320-763-5641 www.kxra.com thefolks@kxra.com

Austin KAUS-FM (c) 18431 State Highway 105, Austin MN 55912 **Phn:** 507-437-7666 **Fax:** 507-437-7669 www.myaustinminnesota.com news@kaus.threeeagles.com

Austin KAUS-AM (nt) 18431 State Highway 105, Austin MN 55912 **Phn:** 507-437-7666 **Fax:** 507-437-7669 www.myaustinminnesota.com news@kaus.threeeagles.com

Bemidji KBHP-FM (c) PO Box 1656, Bemidji MN 56619 **Phn:** 218-444-1500 **Fax:** 218-751-8091 www.kb101fm.com

Bemidji KBLB-FM (c) PO Box 1656, Bemidji MN 56619 **Phn:** 218-828-1244 **Fax:** 218-828-1119 www.todaysbestcountry.com b933@brainerd.net

Bemidji KBSB-FM (v) 1500 Birchmont Dr NE, Bemidji MN 56601 **Phn:** 218-755-4120 **Fax:** 218-755-4119

Bemidji KBUN-AM (s) PO Box 1656, Bemidji MN 56619 **Phn:** 218-444-1500 **Fax:** 218-751-8091

Bemidji KCRB-FM (pl) PO Box 578, Bemidji MN 56619 **Phn:** 218-751-8864 **Fax:** 218-751-8640 minnesota.publicradio.org ngrosfield@mpr.org

Bemidji KKBJ-AM (nt) 2115 Washington Ave S, Bemidji MN 56601 **Phn:** 218-751-7777 **Fax:** 218-759-0658 kkbjam.com

Bemidji KKBJ-FM (a) 2115 Washington Ave S, Bemidji MN 56601 **Phn:** 218-751-7777 **Fax:** 218-759-0658 www.kkbj.com

Bemidji KKZY-FM (a) PO Box 1656, Bemidji MN 56619 **Phn:** 218-444-1500 **Fax:** 218-751-8091

Bemidji KNBJ-FM (p) PO Box 578, Bemidji MN 56619 **Phn:** 218-751-8864 **Fax:** 218-751-8640 minnesota.publicradio.org ngrosfield@mpr.org

Bemidji WBJI-FM (c) 2115 Washington Ave S, Bemidji MN 56601 **Phn:** 218-251-7777 **Fax:** 218-759-0658 www.wbji.com dvoss@kkbj.com

Bemidji WJJY-FM (a) PO Box 1656, Bemidji MN 56619 **Phn:** 218-828-1244 **Fax:** 218-828-1119 www.1067wjjy.com wakeup@1067wjjy.com

Benson KBMO-AM (a) 105 13th St N, Benson MN 56215 **Phn:** 320-843-3290 **Fax:** 320-843-3955 kscr@info-link.net

Blue Earth KBEW-AM (ntc) PO Box 278, Blue Earth MN 56013 **Phn:** 507-526-2181 **Fax:** 507-526-7468 www.kbew98country.com kbew@bevcomm.net

Blue Earth KBEW-FM (c) PO Box 278, Blue Earth MN 56013 **Phn:** 507-526-2181 **Fax:** 507-526-7468 www.kbew98country.com kbew@bevcomm.net

Blue Earth KJLY-FM (q) PO Box 72, Blue Earth MN 56013 **Phn:** 507-526-3233 **Fax:** 507-526-3235 www.kjly.com kjly@kjly.com

Brainerd KLIZ-FM (r) PO Box 746, Brainerd MN 56401 **Phn:** 218-828-1244 **Fax:** 218-828-1119 www.theloon.com kliz_1075@hotmail.com

Brainerd KLIZ-AM (t) PO Box 746, Brainerd MN 56401 **Phn:** 218-828-1244 **Fax:** 218-828-1119 www.kliz.com dannywild@kliz.com

Brainerd KLLZ-FM (r) PO Box 746, Brainerd MN 56401 **Phn:** 218-829-1075 **Fax:** 218-828-1119 theloon.com kliz_1075@hotmail.com

Brainerd KUAL-FM (o) PO Box 746, Brainerd MN 56401 **Phn:** 218-828-1244 **Fax:** 218-828-1119 www.cool1035.com email@cool1035.com

Brainerd KVBR-AM (kt) PO Box 746, Brainerd MN 56401 **Phn:** 218-828-1244 **Fax:** 218-828-1119 www.brainerdradio.netkvbr dannywild@theloon.com

Buffalo KRWC-AM (nt) PO Box 267, Buffalo MN 55313 **Phn:** 763-682-4444 **Fax:** 763-682-3542 www.krwc1360.com info@krwc1360.com

Cloquet WKLK-AM (ob) 1104 Cloquet Ave, Cloquet MN 55720 **Phn:** 218-879-4534 **Fax:** 218-879-1962 msenarighi@aol.com

Cloquet WKLK-FM (r) 1104 Cloquet Ave, Cloquet MN 55720 **Phn:** 218-879-4534 **Fax:** 218-879-1962

Collegeville KNSR-FM (pn) PO Box 7011, Collegeville MN 56321 **Phn:** 320-363-7702 **Fax:** 320-363-4948 minnesota.publicradio.org jlegore@mpr.org

Collegeville KSJR-FM (pl) PO Box 7011, Collegeville MN 56321 **Phn:** 320-363-7702 **Fax:** 320-363-4948 minnesota.publicradio.org newsroom@mpr.org

Crookston KROX-AM (nta) PO Box 620, Crookston MN 56716 **Phn:** 218-281-1140 **Fax:** 218-281-5036 www.kroxam.com krox@rrv.net

Detroit Lakes KBOT-FM (a) PO Box 746, Detroit Lakes MN 56502 **Phn:** 218-847-5624 **Fax:** 218-847-7657 www.catchthewave1041.com jeff@1340kdlm.com

Detroit Lakes KDLM-AM (snt) PO Box 746, Detroit Lakes MN 56502 **Phn:** 218-847-5624 **Fax:** 218-847-7657 www.1340kdlm.com news@1340kdlm.com

Detroit Lakes KRCQ-FM (c) PO Box 556, Detroit Lakes MN 56502 **Phn:** 218-847-2001 **Fax:** 218-847-2271

Duluth KAOD-FM (r) 501 S Lake Ave Ste 200, Duluth MN 55802 **Phn:** 218-728-9500 **Fax:** 218-723-1499 www.95kqds.com kq95@redrockradio.org

Duluth KBAJ-FM (r) 501 S Lake Ave Ste 200, Duluth MN 55802 **Phn:** 218-728-9500 **Fax:** 218-723-1499 www.redrockradio.org

Duluth KBMX-FM (a) 14 E Central Entrance, Duluth MN 55811 **Phn:** 218-727-4500 **Fax:** 218-727-9356 mix108.com laura@mix108.com

Duluth KDAL-AM (am) 11 E Superior St # 300, Duluth MN 55802 **Phn:** 218-722-4321 **Fax:** 218-722-5423 www.kdal610.com

Duluth KDAL-FM (a) 715 E Central Entrance, Duluth MN 55811 **Phn:** 218-722-4321 **Fax:** 218-722-5423 www.96rockon.com mark.fleischer@mwcradio.com

Duluth KDNW-FM (vq) 1101 E Central Entrance, Duluth MN 55811 **Phn:** 218-722-6700 **Fax:** 218-722-1092 life973.com

Duluth KHQG-FM (r) 715 E Central Entrance, Duluth MN 55811 **Phn:** 218-722-4321 **Fax:** 218-722-5423

Duluth KKCB-FM (c) 14 E Central Entrance, Duluth MN 55811 **Phn:** 218-727-4500 **Fax:** 218-727-9356 kkcb.com cathykates@kkcb.com

Duluth KLDJ-FM (o) 14 E Central Entrance, Duluth MN 55811 **Phn:** 218-727-4500 **Fax:** 218-727-9356 kool1017.com

Duluth KQDS-FM (r) 501 S Lake Ave Ste 200, Duluth MN 55802 **Phn:** 218-728-9500 **Fax:** 218-723-1499 www.95kqds.com kq95@redrockradio.org

Duluth KQDS-AM (t) 501 S Lake Ave Ste 200, Duluth MN 55802 **Phn:** 218-728-9500 **Fax:** 218-723-1499 www.95kqds.com kq95@redrockradio.org

Duluth KTCO-FM (c) 11 E Superior St #380, Duluth MN 55802 **Phn:** 218-722-4321 **Fax:** 218-722-5423 ktcofm.com

Duluth KUMD-FM (pa) 1201 Ordean Ct #H130, Duluth MN 55812 **Phn:** 218-726-7181 **Fax:** 218-726-6571 www.kumd.org kumd@kumd.org

Duluth KZIO-FM (r) 501 S Lake Ave Ste 200, Duluth MN 55802 **Phn:** 218-728-9500 **Fax:** 218-723-1499 94xrocks.com 94x@94xrocks.com

Duluth WDSM-AM (st) 715 E Central Entrance, Duluth MN 55811 **Phn:** 218-722-4321 **Fax:** 218-722-5423

Duluth WEBC-AM (nt) 14 E Central Entrance, Duluth MN 55811 **Phn:** 218-727-4500 **Fax:** 218-727-9356 webc560.com booth@kfan.com

Duluth WGEE-AM (m) 715 E Central Entrance, Duluth MN 55811 **Phn:** 218-722-4321 **Fax:** 218-722-5423

Duluth WIRR-FM (pln) 207 W Superior St Ste 224, Duluth MN 55802 **Phn:** 218-722-9411 **Fax:** 218-720-4900 minnesota.publicradio.org newsroom@mpr.org

Duluth WJRF-FM (q) 4604 Airpark Blvd, Duluth MN 55811 **Phn:** 218-722-2727 www.refugeradio.com info@refugeradio.com

Duluth WWAX-FM (h) 501 S Lake Ave Ste 200, Duluth MN 55802 **Phn:** 218-728-9500 **Fax:** 218-723-1499 nu92.fm nu92@nu92.fm

MINNESOTA RADIO STATIONS

Duluth WWJC-AM (q) 1120 E McCuen St, Duluth MN 55808 **Phn:** 218-626-2738 www.wwjc.com radio@wwjc.com

Duluth WXXZ-FM (r) 501 S Lake Ave Ste 200, Duluth MN 55802 **Phn:** 218-728-9500 **Fax:** 218-723-1499 www.redrockradio.org

Eagan WWTC-AM (nt) 2110 Cliff Rd, Eagan MN 55122 **Phn:** 651-405-8800 **Fax:** 651-405-8222 www.am1280thepatriot.com comments@am1280thepatriot.com

Eden Prairie KTNF-AM (t) 11320 Valley View Rd, Eden Prairie MN 55344 **Phn:** 952-946-8885 **Fax:** 952-946-0888 www.am950radio.com chad@am950radio.com

Edina KHTC-FM (uh) 5300 Edina Industrial Blvd Ste 200, Edina MN 55439 **Phn:** 952-842-7200 **Fax:** 952-842-1048

Ely WELY-AM (o) 133 E Chapman St, Ely MN 55731 **Phn:** 218-365-4444 **Fax:** 218-365-3657 www.wely.com welydj@wely.com

Ely WELY-FM (o) 133 E Chapman St, Ely MN 55731 **Phn:** 218-365-4444 **Fax:** 218-365-3657 www.wely.com

Eveleth KRBT-AM (nt) PO Box 650, Eveleth MN 55734 **Phn:** 218-741-5922 **Fax:** 218-741-7302

Eveleth WEVE-FM (a) PO Box 650, Eveleth MN 55734 **Phn:** 218-741-5922 **Fax:** 218-741-7302 weve.redrockradioeveleth.com tranger@redrockradio.org

Fairmont KFMC-FM (r) PO Box 491, Fairmont MN 56031 **Phn:** 507-235-5595 **Fax:** 507-235-5973 www.kfmc.com woodyw@kfmc.com

Fairmont KSUM-AM (c) PO Box 491, Fairmont MN 56031 **Phn:** 507-235-5595 **Fax:** 507-235-5973 www.ksum.com woodyw@kfmc.com

Faribault KDHL-AM (snt) 601 Central Ave N, Faribault MN 55021 **Phn:** 507-334-0061 **Fax:** 507-334-7057 www.kdhlradio.com gordy.kosfeld@cumulus.com

Faribault KQCL-FM (r) 601 Central Ave N, Faribault MN 55021 **Phn:** 507-334-0061 **Fax:** 507-334-7057 www.power96radio.com mike.eiler@cumulus.com

Fergus Falls KBRF-AM (ct) PO Box 495, Fergus Falls MN 56538 **Phn:** 218-736-7596 **Fax:** 218-736-2836 www.lakesradio.net contactus@lakesradio.net

Fergus Falls KJJK-FM (c) PO Box 495, Fergus Falls MN 56538 **Phn:** 218-736-7596 **Fax:** 218-736-2836 www.bestcountryaround.com lakesradio@prtel.com

Fergus Falls KJJK-AM (o) PO Box 495, Fergus Falls MN 56538 **Phn:** 218-736-7596 **Fax:** 218-736-2836 lakesradio.net sweds@lakesradio.net

Fergus Falls KZCR-FM (r) PO Box 495, Fergus Falls MN 56538 **Phn:** 218-736-7596 **Fax:** 218-736-2836 www.lakesradio.net contactus@lakesradio.net

Forest Lake WLKX-FM (aq) 15226 W Freeway Dr NE, Forest Lake MN 55025 **Phn:** 651-464-6796 **Fax:** 651-464-3638

Fosston KKCQ-FM (c) PO Box 180, Fosston MN 56542 **Phn:** 218-435-1919 **Fax:** 218-435-1480 www.yourqfm.com info@yourqfm.com

Fosston KKCQ-AM (ot) PO Box 180, Fosston MN 56542 **Phn:** 218-435-1919 **Fax:** 218-435-1480 www.kkcqradio.blogspot.com laura@kkcqradio.com

Fosston KKEQ-FM (q) PO Box 180, Fosston MN 56542 **Phn:** 218-435-1919 **Fax:** 218-435-1480 www.yourqfm.com info@yourqfm.com

Glenwood KMGK-FM (a) PO Box 241, Glenwood MN 56334 **Phn:** 320-634-5358 **Fax:** 320-634-5359 www.kmgk1071.com nestor@kmgk1071.com

Golden Valley WLOL-AM (q) 7575 Golden Valley Rd Ste 310N, Golden Valley MN 55417 **Phn:** 612-643-4110 **Fax:** 612-546-4444 www.relevantradio.com info@relevantradio.com

Grand Marais WTIP-FM (pra) PO Box 1005, Grand Marais MN 55604 **Phn:** 218-387-1070 **Fax:** 218-387-1120 www.wtip.org wtip@boreal.org

Grand Rapids KAXE-FM (p) 260 NE 2nd St, Grand Rapids MN 55744 **Phn:** 218-326-1234 **Fax:** 218-326-1235 www.kaxe.org kaxeboard@kaxe.org

Grand Rapids KGPZ-FM (c) PO Box 447, Grand Rapids MN 55744 **Phn:** 218-327-3339 **Fax:** 218-327-3425 www.kgpzfm.com kgpz@paulbunyan.net

Grand Rapids KMFY-FM (a) PO Box 597, Grand Rapids MN 55744 **Phn:** 218-999-0969 **Fax:** 218-999-5609 www.kozyradio.com kozykmfypd@paulbunyan.net

Grand Rapids KOZY-AM (o) PO Box 597, Grand Rapids MN 55744 **Phn:** 218-999-5699 **Fax:** 218-999-5609 www.kozyradio.com kozykmfypd@paulbunyan.net

Hastings KDWA-AM (nt) 514 Vermillion St, Hastings MN 55033 **Phn:** 651-437-1460 **Fax:** 651-438-3042 www.kdwa.com news@kdwa.com

Hibbing KMFG-FM (r) 807 W 37th St, Hibbing MN 55746 **Phn:** 218-263-7531 **Fax:** 218-263-6112 mwcradio.com

Hibbing WMFG-FM (o) 807 W 37th St, Hibbing MN 55746 **Phn:** 218-263-7531 **Fax:** 218-263-6112 mwcradio.com webmaster@wmfgfm.com

Hibbing WMFG-AM (st) 807 W 37th St, Hibbing MN 55746 **Phn:** 218-263-7531 **Fax:** 218-263-6112 mwcradio.com

Hibbing WNMT-AM (snt) 807 W 37th St, Hibbing MN 55746 **Phn:** 218-263-7531 **Fax:** 218-263-6112 www.wnmtradio.com

Hibbing WTBX-FM (a) 807 W 37th St, Hibbing MN 55746 **Phn:** 218-263-7531 **Fax:** 218-263-6112 www.wtbx.com

Hibbing WUSZ-FM (c) 807 W 37th St, Hibbing MN 55746 **Phn:** 218-263-7531 **Fax:** 218-263-6112 www.radiousa.com scott.hanson@radiousa.com

Hutchinson KARP-FM (c) PO Box 366, Hutchinson MN 55350 **Phn:** 320-587-2140 **Fax:** 320-587-5158 www.karpradio.com

Hutchinson KDUZ-AM (nt) PO Box 366, Hutchinson MN 55350 **Phn:** 320-587-2140 **Fax:** 320-587-5158 www.kduz.com info@kduz.com

International Falls KBHW-FM (q) PO Box 433, International Falls MN 56649 **Phn:** 218-285-7398 **Fax:** 218-285-7419 www.psalmfm.com email@psalmfm.org

International Falls KGHS-AM (o) 519 3rd St, International Falls MN 56649 **Phn:** 218-283-3481 **Fax:** 218-283-3087 www.ksdmradio.com production@ksdmradio.com

International Falls KSDM-FM (c) 519 3rd St, International Falls MN 56649 **Phn:** 218-283-3481 **Fax:** 218-283-3087 www.ksdmradio.com dennis@ksdmradio.com

Jackson KKOJ-AM (c) PO Box 29, Jackson MN 56143 **Phn:** 507-847-5400 **Fax:** 507-847-5745 www.kkoj.com info@kkoj.com

Jackson KRAQ-FM (or) PO Box 29, Jackson MN 56143 **Phn:** 507-847-5400 **Fax:** 507-847-5745 www.kkoj.com kkoj@rconnect.com

Litchfield KLFD-AM (m) 234 N Sibley Ave, Litchfield MN 55355 **Phn:** 320-693-3281 **Fax:** 320-693-3283 www.klfd1410.com pam@klfd1410.com

Little Falls KFML-FM (oa) 16405 Haven Rd, Little Falls MN 56345 **Phn:** 320-632-2992 **Fax:** 320-632-2571 www.fallsradio.com coreyfink@fallsradio.com

Little Falls KLTF-AM (ntf) 16405 Haven Rd, Little Falls MN 56345 **Phn:** 320-632-2992 **Fax:** 320-632-2571 www.fallsradio.com ads@fallsradio.com

Little Falls WYRQ-FM (csf) 16405 Haven Rd, Little Falls MN 56345 **Phn:** 320-632-2992 **Fax:** 320-632-2571 www.fallsradio.com al@fallsradio.com

Long Prairie KEYL-AM (c) PO Box 187, Long Prairie MN 56347 **Phn:** 320-732-2164 **Fax:** 320-732-2284

Long Prairie KXDL-FM (o) PO Box 187, Long Prairie MN 56347 **Phn:** 320-732-2164 **Fax:** 320-732-2284 www.kxdlhotrodradio.com hotrodfm@rea-alp.com

Luverne KLQL-FM (cf) PO Box 599, Luverne MN 56156 **Phn:** 507-283-4444 **Fax:** 507-283-4445 www.oursiouxland.com info@luverne.threeeagles.com

Luverne KQAD-AM (a) 1140 150th Ave, Luverne MN 56156 **Phn:** 507-283-4444 **Fax:** 507-283-4445 www.oursiouxland.com mcrosby@luverne.threeeagles.com

Madison KLQP-FM (c) PO Box 70, Madison MN 56256 **Phn:** 320-598-7301 **Fax:** 320-598-7955 www.klqpfm.com klqpfm@farmerstel.net

Mahnomen KRJM-FM (nto) PO Box 420, Mahnomen MN 56557 **Phn:** 218-935-5355 **Fax:** 218-935-9020 www.krjmradio.com krjm@arvig.net

Mankato KATO-FM (c) PO Box 1420, Mankato MN 56002 **Phn:** 507-345-5364 www.minnesota93.com terrycooley@radiomankato.com

Mankato KDOG-FM (h) 59346 Madison Ave, Mankato MN 56002 **Phn:** 507-345-4537 www.hot967.fm jobailey@radiomankato.com

Mankato KHRS-FM (r) PO Box 1420, Mankato MN 56002 **Phn:** 507-345-4537 **Fax:** 507-345-5364 jobailey@radiomankato.com

Mankato KMSU-FM (plnj) 1536 Warren St # 205, Mankato MN 56001 **Phn:** 507-389-5678 **Fax:** 507-389-1705 www.mnsu.edukmsufm james.gullickson@mnsu.edu

Mankato KRRW-FM (c) PO Box 1420, Mankato MN 56002 **Phn:** 507-375-3386 **Fax:** 507-345-5364 www.967kdog.com dwaynemegaw@radiomankato.com

Mankato KTOE-AM (ant) PO Box 1420, Mankato MN 56002 **Phn:** 507-345-4537 **Fax:** 507-345-5364 www.katoinfo.comlinder_radioktoeindex.php jobailey@radiomankato.com

Mankato KXAC-FM (a) PO Box 1420, Mankato MN 56002 **Phn:** 507-345-4537 **Fax:** 507-345-5364

Mankato KXLP-FM (r) PO Box 1420, Mankato MN 56002 **Phn:** 507-345-4537 **Fax:** 507-345-5364 www.94kxlp.com jobailey@radiomankato.com

Mankato KYSM-AM (st) PO Box 1420, Mankato MN 56002 **Phn:** 507-345-4537 **Fax:** 507-345-5364 www.mygreatermankato.com jobailey@radiomankato.com

Marshall KARL-FM (c) PO Box 61, Marshall MN 56258 **Phn:** 507-532-2282 **Fax:** 507-532-3739 www.marshallradio.net info@marshallradio.net

Marshall KARZ-FM (r) 1414 E College Dr, Marshall MN 56258 **Phn:** 507-532-2282 **Fax:** 507-532-3739 marshallradio.net info@marshallradio.net

Marshall KKCK-FM (h) 1414 E College Dr, Marshall MN 56258 **Phn:** 507-532-2282 **Fax:** 507-532-3739 www.997kkck.com info@marshallradio.net

MINNESOTA RADIO STATIONS

Marshall KMHL-AM (snt) 1414 E College Dr, Marshall MN 56258 **Phn:** 507-532-2282 **Fax:** 507-532-3739 marshallradio.net info@marshallradio.net

Minneapolis KBEM-FM (pj) 1555 James Ave N, Minneapolis MN 55411 **Phn:** 612-668-1735 **Fax:** 612-668-1766 jazz88.mpls.k12.mn.us jenny.odden@mpls.k12.mn.us

Minneapolis KDIZ-AM (m) 2000 Elm St SE, Minneapolis MN 55414 **Phn:** 612-617-4000 **Fax:** 612-676-8214 music.disney.com

Minneapolis KDWB-FM (h) 1600 Utica Ave S Ste 400, Minneapolis MN 55416 **Phn:** 952-417-3000 **Fax:** 952-417-3001 www.kdwb.com promo@kdwb.com

Minneapolis KEEY-FM (c) 1600 Utica Ave S Ste 400, Minneapolis MN 55416 **Phn:** 952-417-3000 **Fax:** 952-417-3001 www.k102.com k102studio@clearchannel.com

Minneapolis KFAI-FM (v) 1808 Riverside Ave Ste 300, Minneapolis MN 55454 **Phn:** 612-341-3144 **Fax:** 612-341-4281 www.kfai.org newsdepartment@kfai.org

Minneapolis KFAN-AM (snt) 1600 Utica Ave S Ste 400, Minneapolis MN 55416 **Phn:** 952-417-3000 **Fax:** 952-417-3001 www.kfan.com chadabbott@clearchannel.com

Minneapolis KFXN-AM (s) 1600 Utica Ave S Ste 400, Minneapolis MN 55416 **Phn:** 952-417-3000 **Fax:** 952-417-3001 www.thescore1035.com chadabbott@clearchannel.com

Minneapolis KMNV-AM (y) 1516 E Lake St Ste 200, Minneapolis MN 55407 **Phn:** 612-729-5900 **Fax:** 612-729-5999 vidaysabor.net conectando@vidaysabor.net

Minneapolis KNOF-FM (gq) 910 Elliot Ave, Minneapolis MN 55404 **Phn:** 651-645-8271

Minneapolis KQQL-FM (o) 1600 Utica Ave S Ste 400, Minneapolis MN 55416 **Phn:** 952-417-3000 **Fax:** 952-417-3001 www.kool108.com koolonline@clearchannel.com

Minneapolis KQRS-FM (r) 2000 Elm St SE, Minneapolis MN 55414 **Phn:** 612-617-4000 **Fax:** 612-623-9292 www.92kqrs.com

Minneapolis KSTP-AM (nt) 3415 University Ave SE, Minneapolis MN 55414 **Phn:** 651-647-1500 **Fax:** 651-647-2904 1500espn.com

Minneapolis KSTP-FM (a) 3415 University Ave SE, Minneapolis MN 55414 **Phn:** 651-642-4141 **Fax:** 651-647-2904 www.ks95.com events@ks95.com

Minneapolis KTCZ-FM (ar) 1600 Utica Ave S Ste 400, Minneapolis MN 55416 **Phn:** 952-417-3000 **Fax:** 952-417-3001 www.cities97.com ericdeneui@clearchannel.com

Minneapolis KTLK-FM (nt) 1600 Utica Ave S Ste 500, Minneapolis MN 55416 **Phn:** 952-417-3000 **Fax:** 952-417-3001 www.twincitiesnewstalk.com andrewlee@clearchannel.com

Minneapolis KTMY-FM (t) 3415 University Ave SE, Minneapolis MN 55414 **Phn:** 651-642-4107 **Fax:** 651-647-2901 mytalk1071.com adaniels@mytalk1071.com

Minneapolis KUOM-FM (pr) 330 21st Ave S Ste 610, Minneapolis MN 55455 **Phn:** 612-625-3500 **Fax:** 612-625-2112 www.radiok.org stationmanager@radiok.org

Minneapolis KUOM-AM (pr) 330 21st Ave S Ste 610, Minneapolis MN 55455 **Phn:** 612-625-3500 **Fax:** 612-625-2112 www.radiok.org music@radiok.org

Minneapolis KXXR-FM (r) 2000 Elm St SE, Minneapolis MN 55414 **Phn:** 612-617-4000 **Fax:** 612-676-8293 www.93x.com mail@93x.com

Minneapolis KZJK-FM (a) 625 2nd Ave S Ste 200, Minneapolis MN 55402 **Phn:** 612-370-0611 **Fax:** 612-370-0683 1041jackfm.cbslocal.com rob.morris@cbsradio.com

Minneapolis WCCO-AM (ntm) 625 2nd Ave S Ste 200, Minneapolis MN 55402 **Phn:** 612-370-0611 **Fax:** 612-370-0159 minnesota.cbslocal.com newstips@wccoradio.com

Minneapolis WDGY-AM (y) 2619 E Lake St, Minneapolis MN 55406 **Phn:** 612-729-3776 **Fax:** 612-724-0437 www.radiorey630am.com felicia@radiorey630am.com

Minneapolis WGVX-FM (r) 2000 Elm St SE, Minneapolis MN 55414 **Phn:** 612-617-4000 **Fax:** 612-676-8293 www.love105.fm love105comments@gmail.com

Minneapolis WGVY-FM (r) 2000 Elm St SE, Minneapolis MN 55414 **Phn:** 612-617-4000 **Fax:** 612-676-8292 www.love105.fm love105comments@gmail.com

Minneapolis WGVZ-FM (m) 2000 Elm St SE, Minneapolis MN 55414 **Phn:** 612-617-4000 **Fax:** 612-676-8293 www.love105.fm love105comments@gmail.com

Minneapolis WLTE-FM (c) 625 2nd Ave S Ste 200, Minneapolis MN 55402 **Phn:** 612-370-0611 **Fax:** 612-370-0683 buzn1029.cbslocal.com kris.cegla@cbsradio.com

Minneapolis WREY-AM (y) 2619 E Lake St, Minneapolis MN 55406 **Phn:** 612-729-3776 **Fax:** 612-724-0437 www.radiorey630am.com felicia@radiorey630am.com

Montevideo KDMA-AM (nt) PO Box 513, Montevideo MN 56265 **Phn:** 320-269-8815 **Fax:** 320-269-8449 kdmanews.com kdmanews@gmail.com

Montevideo KKRC-FM (o) PO Box 513, Montevideo MN 56265 **Phn:** 320-269-8815 **Fax:** 320-269-8449 kdmanews.com ashley@kdmanews.com

Montevideo KMGM-FM (r) PO Box 513, Montevideo MN 56265 **Phn:** 320-269-8815 **Fax:** 320-269-8449 kdmanews.com kdmanews@gmail.com

Moorhead KCCM-FM (pl) 901 8th St S, Moorhead MN 56562 **Phn:** 218-299-3666 **Fax:** 218-299-3418 minnesota.publicradio.org dgunderson@mpr.org

Mora KBEK-FM (ao) PO Box 136, Mora MN 55051 **Phn:** 320-679-6955 **Fax:** 320-679-2348 www.kbek.com kbek@besttimes.com

Morris KKOK-FM (c) PO Box 533, Morris MN 56267 **Phn:** 320-589-3131 **Fax:** 320-589-2715 www.kmrskkok.com kmrskkok@fedtel.net

Morris KMRS-AM (snt) PO Box 533, Morris MN 56267 **Phn:** 320-589-3131 **Fax:** 320-589-2715 www.kmrskkok.com kmrskkok@fedtel.net

Morris KUMM-FM (vr) 600 E 4th St, Morris MN 56267 **Phn:** 320-589-6076 **Fax:** 320-589-6084 www.kumm.org kummnews@gmail.com

New Prague KCHK-AM (c) 25821 Langford Ave, New Prague MN 56071 **Phn:** 952-758-2571 **Fax:** 952-758-3170 www.kchkradio.net production@kchkradio.net

New Prague KRDS-FM (o) 25821 Langford Ave, New Prague MN 56071 **Phn:** 952-758-2571 **Fax:** 952-758-3170 www.kchkradio.net production@kchkradio.net

New Ulm KNUJ-AM (cnt) PO Box 368, New Ulm MN 56073 **Phn:** 507-359-2921 **Fax:** 507-359-4520 www.knuj.net knuj@knuj.net

New Ulm KNUJ-FM (a) PO Box 368, New Ulm MN 56073 **Phn:** 507-359-2921 **Fax:** 507-359-4520 www.knuj.net news@knuj.net

North Mankato KEEZ-FM (a) 1807 Lee Blvd, North Mankato MN 56003 **Phn:** 507-345-4646 **Fax:** 507-345-3299 www.myz99.com rzens@mankato.threeeagles.com

North Mankato KRBI-FM (r) 1807 Lee Blvd, North Mankato MN 56003 **Phn:** 507-345-4646 **Fax:** 507-345-3299 www.river105.com ddose@mankato.threeeagles.com

North Mankato KYSM-FM (c) 1807 Lee Blvd, North Mankato MN 56003 **Phn:** 507-345-4646 **Fax:** 507-345-4675 www.country103.com ddose@mankato.threeeagles.com

Northfield KYMN-AM (am) 200 Division St S Ste 260, Northfield MN 55057 **Phn:** 507-645-5695 **Fax:** 507-645-9768 kymnradio.net contact@kymnradio.net

Ortonville KDIO-AM (ct) 47 2nd St NW Ste 103, Ortonville MN 56278 **Phn:** 605-432-5516 **Fax:** 605-432-4231 www.kphrfm.com kdio@bigstoneradio.com

Osakis KBHL-FM (q) PO Box 247, Osakis MN 56360 **Phn:** 320-859-3000 **Fax:** 320-859-3010 www.praisefm.org mail@praisefm.org

Osakis KBHZ-FM (q) PO Box 247, Osakis MN 56360 **Phn:** 320-859-3000 **Fax:** 320-859-3010 www.praisefm.org mail@praisefm.org

Owatonna KOWZ-FM (af) 255 Cedardale Dr SE, Owatonna MN 55060 **Phn:** 507-444-9224 **Fax:** 507-444-9080 www.kowzfm.com craigs@kowzonline.com

Owatonna KRFO-FM (c) 245 18th St SE Ste 2, Owatonna MN 55060 **Phn:** 507-451-2250 **Fax:** 507-214-1422 www.krforadio.com krfo@cumulus.com

Owatonna KRFO-AM (ont) 245 18th St SE Ste 2, Owatonna MN 55060 **Phn:** 507-451-2250 **Fax:** 507-214-1422 www.krforadio.com mike.eiler@cumulus.com

Owatonna KRUE-FM (a) 255 Cedardale Dr SE, Owatonna MN 55060 **Phn:** 507-444-9224 **Fax:** 507-444-9080 www.kowzonline.com krue@krue92.com

Park Rapids KDKK-FM (am) PO Box 49, Park Rapids MN 56470 **Phn:** 218-732-3306 **Fax:** 218-732-3307 www.kkradionetwork.com kprmkdkk@unitelc.com

Park Rapids KPRM-AM (t) PO Box 49, Park Rapids MN 56470 **Phn:** 218-732-3306 **Fax:** 218-732-3307 www.kkradionetwork.com kprmkdkk@unitelc.com

Park Rapids KXKK-FM (c) PO Box 49, Park Rapids MN 56470 **Phn:** 218-732-3306 **Fax:** 218-732-3307

Pequot Lakes KCFB-FM (q) PO Box 409, Pequot Lakes MN 56472 **Phn:** 320-252-4214 mcbiradio.org

Pequot Lakes KTIG-FM (tq) PO Box 409, Pequot Lakes MN 56472 **Phn:** 218-568-4422 **Fax:** 218-568-5950 mcbiradio.org

Perham KPRW-FM (a) PO Box 363, Perham MN 56573 **Phn:** 218-346-4800 www.lakesradio.net kprw@eot.com

Pine City WCMP-FM (c) 15429 Pokegama Lake Rd, Pine City MN 55063 **Phn:** 320-629-7575 **Fax:** 320-629-3933 redrockonair.com jesselogan@redrockonair.com

Pine City WCMP-AM (nm) 15429 Pokegama Lake Rd, Pine City MN 55063 **Phn:** 320-629-7575 **Fax:** 320-629-3933 redrockonair.com jesselogan@redrockonair.com

Pipestone KISD-FM (o) PO Box 456, Pipestone MN 56164 **Phn:** 507-825-4282 **Fax:** 507-825-3364 www.christensenbroadcasting.com kisd@kisdradio.com

Pipestone KJOE-FM (cnt) PO Box 456, Pipestone MN 56164 **Phn:** 507-825-4282 www.christensenbroadcasting.com kjoe@kjoeradio.com

Pipestone KLOH-AM (nt) PO Box 456, Pipestone MN 56164 **Phn:** 507-825-4282 **Fax:** 507-825-3364 www.christensenbroadcasting.com kloh@klohradio.com

MINNESOTA RADIO STATIONS

Plymouth WCTS-AM (q) 900 Forestview Ln N, Plymouth MN 55441 **Phn:** 763-417-8270 **Fax:** 763-417-8278 www.wctsradio.com

Preston KFIL-FM (cf) 300 Saint Paul St SW, Preston MN 55965 **Phn:** 507-765-3856 **Fax:** 507-765-2738 www.kfilradio.com kvgo104@centurytel.net

Preston KFIL-AM (nt) 300 Saint Paul St SW, Preston MN 55965 **Phn:** 507-765-3856 **Fax:** 507-765-2738 www.kfilradio.com kvgo104@centurytel.net

Preston KVGO-FM (o) PO Box 370, Preston MN 55965 **Phn:** 507-765-3856 **Fax:** 507-765-2738

Ramsey KBGY-FM (y) 14443 Armstrong Blvd NW, Ramsey MN 55303 **Phn:** 763-412-4626 **Fax:** 763-412-4691 www.lamerabuena.net djtiger_lamerabuena@hotmail.com

Ramsey KLCI-FM (c) 14443 Armstrong Blvd NW, Ramsey MN 55303 **Phn:** 763-450-7777 **Fax:** 763-412-4687 www.dothebob.com howard@dothebob.com

Red Wing KCUE-AM (snt) 474 Guernsey Ln, Red Wing MN 55066 **Phn:** 651-388-7151 **Fax:** 651-388-7153 1250kcue.com

Red Wing KLCH-FM (a) 474 Guernsey Ln, Red Wing MN 55066 **Phn:** 651-388-7151 **Fax:** 651-388-7153 www.lakehits95.com

Red Wing KWNG-FM (h) 474 Guernsey Ln, Red Wing MN 55066 **Phn:** 651-388-7151 **Fax:** 651-388-7153 www.kwng.com thughes@kwng.com

Redwood Falls KLGR-FM (o) PO Box 65, Redwood Falls MN 56283 **Phn:** 507-637-2989 **Fax:** 507-637-5347 www.myklgr.com klgr@mchsi.com

Redwood Falls KLGR-AM (c) PO Box 65, Redwood Falls MN 56283 **Phn:** 507-637-2989 **Fax:** 507-637-5347 www.myklgr.com klgr@mchsi.com

Rochester KFSI-FM (q) 4016 28th St SE, Rochester MN 55904 **Phn:** 507-289-8585 **Fax:** 507-529-4017 www.kfsi.org shine@kfsi.org

Rochester KLCX-FM (o) 122 4th St SW, Rochester MN 55902 **Phn:** 507-286-1010 **Fax:** 507-286-9370 www.klcxfm.com jeff@klcxfm.com

Rochester KLSE-FM (pl) 206 S Broadway Ste 735, Rochester MN 55904 **Phn:** 507-282-0910 **Fax:** 507-282-2107 minnesota.publicradio.org ccross@mpr.org

Rochester KMFX-FM (c) 1530 Greenview Dr SW Ste 200, Rochester MN 55902 **Phn:** 507-288-3888 **Fax:** 507-288-7815 www.1025thefox.com jessicademsky@clearchannel.com

Rochester KMSE-FM (v) 206 S Broadway Ste 735, Rochester MN 55904 **Phn:** 507-282-0910 **Fax:** 507-282-2107 minnesota.publicradio.org ccross@mpr.org

Rochester KNXR-FM (ajm) 1620 Greenview Dr SW Ste 101, Rochester MN 55902 **Phn:** 507-288-7700 **Fax:** 507-288-4531

Rochester KOLM-AM (st) 122 4th St SW, Rochester MN 55902 **Phn:** 507-286-1010 **Fax:** 507-286-9370 www.1520theticket.com brent.ackerman@cumulus.com

Rochester KRCH-FM (r) 1530 Greenview Dr SW Ste 200, Rochester MN 55902 **Phn:** 507-288-3888 **Fax:** 507-288-7815 www.laser1017.com mclark@clearchannel.com

Rochester KROC-AM (nt) 122 4th St SW, Rochester MN 55902 **Phn:** 507-286-1010 **Fax:** 507-286-9370 www.kroc.com troy@kroc.com

Rochester KROC-FM (h) 122 4th St SW, Rochester MN 55902 **Phn:** 507-286-1010 **Fax:** 507-286-9370 www.kroc.com brent@kroc.com

Rochester KWEB-AM (st) 1530 Greenview Dr SW Ste 200, Rochester MN 55902 **Phn:** 507-288-3888 **Fax:** 507-288-7815 www.fan1270.com greghenn@clearchannel.com

Rochester KWWK-FM (c) 122 4th St SW, Rochester MN 55902 **Phn:** 507-286-1010 **Fax:** 507-286-9370 www.quickcountry.com alanreed@quickcountry.com

Rochester KYBA-FM (a) 122 4th St SW, Rochester MN 55902 **Phn:** 507-286-1010 **Fax:** 507-286-9370 www.y105fm.com feedback@y105fm.com

Rochester KZSE-FM (pn) 206 S Broadway Ste 735, Rochester MN 55904 **Phn:** 507-282-0910 **Fax:** 507-282-2107 minnesota.publicradio.org newsroom@mpr.org

Roseau KCAJ-FM (ant) 107 Center St W, Roseau MN 56751 **Phn:** 218-463-3360 wild102fm.com info@wild102fm.com

Roseau KRWB-AM (r) 30817 County Road 28, Roseau MN 56751 **Phn:** 218-386-3024 **Fax:** 218-386-3090 www.1410krwb.com kq92@mncable.net

Saint Cloud KCLD-FM (h) PO Box 1458, Saint Cloud MN 56302 **Phn:** 320-251-1450 **Fax:** 320-251-8952 www.1047kcld.com jjholiday@1047kcld.com

Saint Cloud KCML-FM (a) 619 W Saint Germain St, Saint Cloud MN 56301 **Phn:** 320-251-1450 **Fax:** 320-251-8952 www.lite999.com

Saint Cloud KLZZ-FM (r) 640 Lincoln Ave SE, Saint Cloud MN 56304 **Phn:** 320-257-7207 **Fax:** 320-251-1855 1037theloon.com sloan@1037theloon.com

Saint Cloud KMXK-FM (a) 640 Lincoln Ave SE, Saint Cloud MN 56304 **Phn:** 320-251-4422 **Fax:** 320-251-1855 mix949.com peterk@mix949.com

Saint Cloud KNSI-AM (nt) PO Box 1458, Saint Cloud MN 56302 **Phn:** 320-251-1450 **Fax:** 320-251-8952 knsiradio.com news@1450knsi.com

Saint Cloud KVSC-FM (v) 720 4th Ave S # 27, Saint Cloud MN 56301 **Phn:** 320-308-3053 **Fax:** 320-308-5337 www.kvsc.org info@kvsc.org

Saint Cloud KXSS-AM (st) 640 Lincoln Ave SE, Saint Cloud MN 56304 **Phn:** 320-251-4422 **Fax:** 320-251-1855 1390thefan.com thefanman@1390thefan.com

Saint Cloud KZPK-FM (c) PO Box 1458, Saint Cloud MN 56302 **Phn:** 320-251-1450 **Fax:** 320-251-8952 www.wildcountry99.com jsowada@leightonbroadcasting.com

Saint Cloud WJON-AM (nt) 640 Lincoln Ave SE, Saint Cloud MN 56304 **Phn:** 320-251-4422 **Fax:** 320-251-1855 wjon.com jim@wjon.com

Saint Cloud WWJO-FM (c) 640 Lincoln Ave SE, Saint Cloud MN 56304 **Phn:** 320-251-4422 **Fax:** 320-251-1855 98country.com pete@98country.com

Saint Paul KCMP-FM (p) 480 Cedar St, Saint Paul MN 55101 **Phn:** 651-290-1500 minnesota.publicradio.org

Saint Paul KKMS-AM (qt) 2110 Cliff Rd, Saint Paul MN 55122 **Phn:** 651-405-8800 **Fax:** 651-405-8222 www.kkms.com comments@kkms.com

Saint Paul KNOW-FM (pn) 480 Cedar St, Saint Paul MN 55101 **Phn:** 651-290-1500 **Fax:** 651-290-1224 minnesota.publicradio.org newsroom@mpr.org

Saint Paul KSJN-FM (pln) 480 Cedar St, Saint Paul MN 55101 **Phn:** 651-290-1500 **Fax:** 651-290-1224 minnesota.publicradio.org msteil@mpr.org

Saint Paul KTIS-FM (q) 3003 Snelling Ave N, Saint Paul MN 55113 **Phn:** 651-631-5000 **Fax:** 651-631-5084 myktis.com feedback@ktis.fm

Saint Paul KYCR-AM (k) 2110 Cliff Rd, Saint Paul MN 55122 **Phn:** 651-289-8800 **Fax:** 651-405-8222 www.business1570.com comments@business1570.com

Saint Paul WMCN-FM (vrj) 1600 Grand Ave, Saint Paul MN 55105 **Phn:** 651-696-6082 www.macalester.edu/wmcn wmcn@macalester.edu

Sauk Rapids KKJM-FM (q) PO Box 547, Sauk Rapids MN 56379 **Phn:** 320-251-1780 **Fax:** 320-257-1624 www.spirit929.com friends@spirit929.com

Sauk Rapids WBHR-AM (s) PO Box 366, Sauk Rapids MN 56379 **Phn:** 320-252-6200 **Fax:** 320-252-9367 www.660wbhr.com tim@rockin101.com

Sauk Rapids WHMH-FM (r) PO Box 366, Sauk Rapids MN 56379 **Phn:** 320-252-6200 **Fax:** 320-252-9367 www.rockin101.com mail@rockin101.com

Sauk Rapids WMIN-AM (st) PO Box 366, Sauk Rapids MN 56379 **Phn:** 320-252-6200 **Fax:** 320-252-9367 www.1010wmin.com

Sauk Rapids WVAL-AM (c) PO Box 366, Sauk Rapids MN 56379 **Phn:** 320-252-6200 **Fax:** 320-252-9367 www.800wval.com mark.a.hoppe@tricountybroadcasting.com

St Louis Park KKXL-AM (s) 1600 Utica Ave S Ste 400, St Louis Park MN 55416 **Phn:** 952-417-3000 **Fax:** 952-417-3001 www.kfan.com chadabbott@clearchannel.com

Stillwater KLBB-AM (tm) 104 Main St N Ste 100, Stillwater MN 55082 **Phn:** 651-439-5006 **Fax:** 651-439-5015 www.klbbradio.com

Thief River Falls KKAQ-AM (cn) PO Box 40, Thief River Falls MN 56701 **Phn:** 218-681-4900 **Fax:** 218-681-3717 www.trfradio.com ktrf@mncable.net

Thief River Falls KKDQ-FM (c) PO Box 40, Thief River Falls MN 56701 **Phn:** 218-681-4900 **Fax:** 218-681-3717 www.trfradio.com ktrf@mncable.net

Thief River Falls KSRQ-FM (var) 1101 Highway 1 E, Thief River Falls MN 56701 **Phn:** 218-683-8588 **Fax:** 218-681-0774 radionorthland.org ksrq@northlandcollege.edu

Thief River Falls KTRF-AM (nt) PO Box 40, Thief River Falls MN 56701 **Phn:** 218-681-1230 **Fax:** 218-681-3717 www.trfradio.com ktrf@mncable.net

Wadena KKWS-FM (c) PO Box 551, Wadena MN 56482 **Phn:** 218-631-1803 **Fax:** 218-631-4557 www.superstationk106.com rick@kwadknsp.com

Wadena KNSP-AM (cn) PO Box 551, Wadena MN 56482 **Phn:** 218-631-1803 **Fax:** 218-631-4557 www.superstationk106.com rick@kwadknsp.com

Wadena KSKK-FM (a) 11 Bryant Ave SE, Wadena MN 56482 **Phn:** 218-631-3441 **Fax:** 218-631-3414 www.kkradionetwork.com kskk@eot.com

Wadena KWAD-AM (c) PO Box 551, Wadena MN 56482 **Phn:** 218-631-1803 **Fax:** 218-631-4557 www.superstationk106.com rick@kwadknsp.com

Walker KAKK-AM (o) PO Box 1022, Walker MN 56484 **Phn:** 218-547-4000 **Fax:** 218-547-4001 kqkkkakk@eot.com

Walker KQKK-FM (h) PO Box 1022, Walker MN 56484 **Phn:** 218-547-4000 **Fax:** 218-547-4001 www.kkradionetwork.com kqkkkakk@eot.com

Warroad KKWQ-FM (c) PO Box 69, Warroad MN 56763 **Phn:** 218-386-3024 **Fax:** 218-386-3090 www.kq92.com kq92@mncable.net

Willmar KDJS-AM (o) 730 NE Hwy 71 Service Dr, Willmar MN 56201 **Phn:** 320-231-1600 **Fax:** 320-235-7010 www.k-musicradio.com rryan@k-musicradio.com

Willmar KDJS-FM (c) 730 NE Hwy 71 Service Dr, Willmar MN 56201 **Phn:** 320-231-1600 **Fax:** 320-235-7010 www.k-musicradio.com rryan@k-musicradio.com

Willmar KKLN-FM (r) 1605 1st St S Ste B16, Willmar MN 56201 **Phn:** 320-235-1194 **Fax:** 320-235-6894 www.kkln.com info@kkln.com

Willmar KOLV-FM (c) PO Box 838, Willmar MN 56201 **Phn:** 320-235-3535 **Fax:** 320-235-9111 www.bigcountry100.com bob@bigcountry100.com

Willmar KQIC-FM (a) PO Box 838, Willmar MN 56201 **Phn:** 320-235-3535 **Fax:** 320-235-9111 www.yourq102.com ben@yourq102.com

Willmar KRVY-FM (r) PO Box 380, Willmar MN 56201 **Phn:** 320-231-1600 **Fax:** 320-235-7010 www.k-musicradio.com csmdrhanson@yahoo.com

Willmar KWLM-AM (nt) 1340 N 7th St, Willmar MN 56201 **Phn:** 320-235-1340 **Fax:** 320-235-9111 www.kwlm.com askus@kwlm.com

Windom KDOM-AM (c) PO Box 218, Windom MN 56101 **Phn:** 507-831-3908 **Fax:** 507-831-3913 www.kdomradio.com kdomnews@windomnet.com

Windom KDOM-FM (c) PO Box 218, Windom MN 56101 **Phn:** 507-831-3908 **Fax:** 507-831-3913 www.kdomradio.com kdomnews@windomnet.com

Winona KAGE-AM (nt) PO Box 767, Winona MN 55987 **Phn:** 507-452-4000 **Fax:** 507-452-9494 www.winonaradio.com jristow@winonaradio.com

Winona KAGE-FM (a) PO Box 767, Winona MN 55987 **Phn:** 507-452-4000 **Fax:** 507-452-9494 www.winonaradio.com jristow@winonaradio.com

Winona KHME-FM (a) PO Box 767, Winona MN 55987 **Phn:** 507-452-4000 **Fax:** 507-452-9494 www.winonaradio.com plundquist@winonaradio.com

Winona KQAL-FM (vjr) PO Box 5838, Winona MN 55987 **Phn:** 507-453-2222 **Fax:** 507-457-5226 www.kqal.org kqalfm@winona.edu

Winona KWNO-AM (snt) PO Box 767, Winona MN 55987 **Phn:** 507-452-4000 **Fax:** 507-452-9494 www.winonaradio.com bob@winonaradio.com

Winona KWNO-FM (c) PO Box 767, Winona MN 55987 **Phn:** 507-452-4000 **Fax:** 507-452-9494 www.winonaradio.com bob@winonaradio.com

Worthington KAUR-FM (vjr) 1450 Collegeway, Worthington MN 56187 **Phn:** 605-335-6666 minnesota.publicradio.org msteil@mpr.org

Worthington KITN-FM (s) 28779 County Highway 35, Worthington MN 56187 **Phn:** 507-376-6165 **Fax:** 507-376-5071 contactus@935thebreeze.com

Worthington KRSW-FM (pl) 1450 Collegeway, Worthington MN 56187 **Phn:** 507-372-2904 minnesota.publicradio.org msteil@mpr.org

Worthington KWOA-AM (nt) 28779 County Highway 35, Worthington MN 56187 **Phn:** 507-376-6165 **Fax:** 507-376-5071 www.kwoa.com info@myradioworks.net

MISSISSIPPI

Aberdeen WWZQ-AM (nt) 1053 S Meridian St, Aberdeen MS 39730 **Phn:** 662-256-9726 **Fax:** 662-256-9725 www.fm95radio.com fm95@fm95radio.com

Amory WAFM-FM (o) PO Box 458, Amory MS 38821 **Phn:** 662-256-9726 **Fax:** 662-256-9725 www.fm95radio.com fm95@fm95radio.com

Amory WAMY-AM (stn) PO Box 458, Amory MS 38821 **Phn:** 662-256-9726 **Fax:** 662-256-9725 fm95radio.com fm95@fm95radio.com

Batesville WBLE-FM (c) PO Box 1528, Batesville MS 38606 **Phn:** 662-563-4664 **Fax:** 662-563-9002

Batesville WHKL-FM (o) PO Box 1528, Batesville MS 38606 **Phn:** 662-563-4664 **Fax:** 662-563-9002

MINNESOTA RADIO STATIONS

Bay Saint Louis WBSL-AM (xw) 1190 Hollywood Blvd, Bay Saint Louis MS 39520 **Phn:** 228-467-1190 **Fax:** 228-467-3525 ihatchett@bellsouth.net

Belzoni WELZ-AM (wg) PO Box 299, Belzoni MS 39038 **Phn:** 662-247-1744 **Fax:** 662-247-1745 www.power107.org power107@power107.org

Biloxi WBUV-FM (u) 286 Debuys Rd, Biloxi MS 39531 **Phn:** 228-388-2323 **Fax:** 228-388-2362 www.newsradio1049fm.com kippgreggory@clearchannel.com

Biloxi WKNN-FM (c) 286 Debuys Rd, Biloxi MS 39531 **Phn:** 228-388-2323 **Fax:** 228-388-2362 k99fm.com kellybennett@clearchannel.com

Biloxi WMJY-FM (a) 286 Debuys Rd, Biloxi MS 39531 **Phn:** 228-388-2323 **Fax:** 228-388-2362 www.magic937.com kellybennett@clearchannel.com

Biloxi WQFX-AM (wg) 336 Rodenberg Ave, Biloxi MS 39531 **Phn:** 228-374-9739 wqfxradio@bellsouth.net

Biloxi WQYZ-FM (g) 286 Debuys Rd, Biloxi MS 39531 **Phn:** 228-388-2323 **Fax:** 228-388-2362 www.925fmthebeat.com walterbrown@clearchannel.com

Booneville WBIP-AM (c) PO Box 356, Booneville MS 38829 **Phn:** 662-728-0200 **Fax:** 662-728-2572 wbipam@yahoo.com

Brookhaven WBKN-FM (c) 104 N First St, Brookhaven MS 39601 **Phn:** 601-833-9210 **Fax:** 601-833-6221

Brookhaven WCHJ-AM (wg) PO Box 177, Brookhaven MS 39602 **Phn:** 601-823-9006 **Fax:** 601-823-0503 victory1470wchj.com victory1470wchj@birch.net

Brookhaven WDXO-FM (o) 110 W Monticello St, Brookhaven MS 39601 **Phn:** 601-587-9363 **Fax:** 601-587-9401

Brookhaven WMJU-FM (a) PO Box 711, Brookhaven MS 39602 **Phn:** 601-833-9210 **Fax:** 601-833-6221

Brookhaven WOEG-AM (g) 110 W Monticello St, Brookhaven MS 39601 **Phn:** 601-587-9363 **Fax:** 601-587-9401

Brookhaven WRQO-FM (c) 110 W Monticello St, Brookhaven MS 39601 **Phn:** 601-835-5005 **Fax:** 601-587-9401 supertalk.fm rbyrd@telesouth.com

Canton WMGO-AM (mn) PO Box 182, Canton MS 39046 **Phn:** 601-859-2373 **Fax:** 601-859-2664 www.wmgoradio.com jlou1@prodigy.net

Centreville WPAE-FM (q) PO Box 1390, Centreville MS 39631 **Phn:** 601-645-6515 **Fax:** 601-645-9122 www.soundradio.org wpaefm@telepak.net

Clarksdale WAID-FM (wu) PO Box 780, Clarksdale MS 38614 **Phn:** 662-627-2281 **Fax:** 662-624-2900

Clarksdale WKDJ-FM (c) 112 Leflore Ave, Clarksdale MS 38614 **Phn:** 662-627-2281 **Fax:** 662-624-2900

Clarksdale WROX-AM (gw) PO Box 1450, Clarksdale MS 38614 **Phn:** 662-627-1450 **Fax:** 662-621-1176 www.wroxradio.com manager@wroxradio.com

Cleveland WCLD-AM (gw) PO Box 780, Cleveland MS 38732 **Phn:** 662-843-4091 **Fax:** 662-843-9805

Cleveland WCLD-FM (wu) PO Box 780, Cleveland MS 38732 **Phn:** 662-843-4091 **Fax:** 662-843-9805

Cleveland WKXY-FM (c) 201 E Sunflower Rd Ste 5, Cleveland MS 38732 **Phn:** 662-843-3392 **Fax:** 662-846-9002 www.kix921.com larry@deltaradio.net

Cleveland WMJW-FM (c) PO Box 780, Cleveland MS 38732 **Phn:** 662-843-4091 **Fax:** 662-843-9805

Clinton WHJT-FM (q) PO Box 4048, Clinton MS 39058 **Phn:** 601-925-3458 **Fax:** 601-925-3337 star93fm.com

Columbia WCJU-AM (wg) PO Box 472, Columbia MS 39429 **Phn:** 601-736-2616 **Fax:** 601-736-2617

Columbia WFFF-FM (a) PO Box 550, Columbia MS 39429 **Phn:** 601-736-1360 **Fax:** 601-736-1361 wfffradio@yahoo.com

Columbia WFFF-AM (c) PO Box 550, Columbia MS 39429 **Phn:** 601-736-1360 **Fax:** 601-736-1361 wfffradio@yahoo.com

Columbia WJDR-FM (c) PO Box 351, Columbia MS 39429 **Phn:** 601-731-2298 **Fax:** 601-736-2617 www.wjdrfm.com wjdr@wjdrfm.com

Columbus WABG-AM (xt) 699 Matson Rd, Columbus MS 39205 **Phn:** 662-455-1688 www.awesomeam.com wabgawesomeradio@yahoo.com

Columbus WJWF-AM (s) 200 6th St N Ste 205, Columbus MS 39701 **Phn:** 662-327-1183 **Fax:** 662-328-1122

Columbus WKOR-AM (g) 200 6th St N Ste 205, Columbus MS 39701 **Phn:** 662-327-1183 **Fax:** 662-328-1122

Columbus WKOR-FM (c) 200 6th St N Ste 205, Columbus MS 39701 **Phn:** 662-327-1183 **Fax:** 662-328-1122 www.k949.net greg.benefield@cumulus.com

Columbus WMBC-FM (h) 200 6th St N Ste 205, Columbus MS 39701 **Phn:** 662-327-1183 **Fax:** 662-328-1122

Columbus WMUW-FM (vr) 1100 College St 1619, Columbus MS 39701 **Phn:** 662-329-7254 **Fax:** 662-329-7250 www.muw.eduwmuw wmuw@muw.edu

Columbus WMXU-FM (u) 200 6th St N Ste 205, Columbus MS 39701 **Phn:** 662-327-1183 **Fax:** 662-328-1122 www.mymix1061.com greg.benefield@cumulus.com

Columbus WSMS-FM (r) 200 6th St N Ste 205, Columbus MS 39701 **Phn:** 662-327-1183 **Fax:** 662-328-1122 www.999thefoxrocks.com greg.benefield@cumulus.com

Columbus WSSO-AM (s) 200 6th St N Ste 205, Columbus MS 39701 **Phn:** 662-327-1183 **Fax:** 662-328-1122

Columbus WTWG-AM (g) 1910 14th Ave N, Columbus MS 39701 **Phn:** 662-328-1050 **Fax:** 662-328-1054 wtwg1050@yahoo.com

Corinth WKCU-AM (g) 1608 S Johns St, Corinth MS 38834 **Phn:** 662-286-8451 **Fax:** 662-286-8452

Corinth WXRZ-FM (t) 1608 S Johns St, Corinth MS 38834 **Phn:** 662-286-8451 **Fax:** 662-286-8452 supertalk.fm programming@supertalk.fm

Flora WYAB-FM (nt) 740 Highway 49 Ste R, Flora MS 39071 **Phn:** 601-879-0093 **Fax:** 601-427-0088 www.wyab.com info@wyab.com

French Camp WFCA-FM (g) 40 Mecklin Ave, French Camp MS 39745 **Phn:** 662-547-6414 **Fax:** 662-547-9451 www.wfcafm108.com events@wfcafm108.com

Greenville WBAD-FM (wju) PO Box 4426, Greenville MS 38704 **Phn:** 662-335-9265 **Fax:** 662-335-5538

Greenville WDMS-FM (c) 1383 Pickett St, Greenville MS 38703 **Phn:** 662-334-4559 **Fax:** 662-332-1315 wdms@bellsouth.net

Greenville WESY-AM (wgx) PO Box 5804, Greenville MS 38704 **Phn:** 662-378-9405 **Fax:** 662-335-5538

Greenville WIQQ-FM (a) 1399 E Reed Rd, Greenville MS 38703 **Phn:** 662-378-2617 **Fax:** 662-378-8341 www.q102.net newsroom@deltaradio.net

Greenville WLTM-FM (z) 1399 E Reed Rd, Greenville MS 38703 **Phn:** 662-378-2617 **Fax:** 662-378-8341 lite979.net newsroom@deltaradio.net

MISSISSIPPI RADIO STATIONS

Greenville WNIX-AM (o) PO Box 1816, Greenville MS 38702 **Phn:** 662-378-2617 **Fax:** 662-378-8341

Greenwood WGNG-FM (wu) PO Box 1801, Greenwood MS 38935 **Phn:** 662-453-1646 **Fax:** 662-453-7002 wgnl@bellsouth.net

Greenwood WGNL-FM (wu) PO Box 1801, Greenwood MS 38935 **Phn:** 662-453-1643 **Fax:** 662-453-7002

Greenwood WGRM-AM (g) 1110 Wright St, Greenwood MS 38930 **Phn:** 662-453-1240 **Fax:** 662-453-1241

Greenwood WGRM-FM (ao) 1110 Wright St, Greenwood MS 38930 **Phn:** 662-453-1240 **Fax:** 662-453-1241

Greenwood WTCD-FM (nt) 3192 Browning Road 520, Greenwood MS 38930 **Phn:** 662-453-2174 **Fax:** 662-455-5733 supertalk.fm marshall@supertalk.fm

Greenwood WYMX-FM (r) PO Box 1686, Greenwood MS 38935 **Phn:** 662-453-2174 **Fax:** 662-455-5733

Gulfport WAOY-FM (aq) 12280 Ashley Dr, Gulfport MS 39503 **Phn:** 228-831-3020 **Fax:** 228-831-4540

Gulfport WCPR-FM (ar) 1909 E Pass Rd Ste D11, Gulfport MS 39507 **Phn:** 228-388-2001 **Fax:** 228-896-9736 979cprrocks.com bwest@msmediaradio.com

Gulfport WGCM-FM (o) 10250 Lorraine Rd, Gulfport MS 39503 **Phn:** 228-896-5500 **Fax:** 228-896-0458 www.coast102.com pat@coast102.com

Gulfport WHGO-FM (r) 1909 E Pass Rd Ste D11, Gulfport MS 39507 **Phn:** 228-388-2001 **Fax:** 228-896-9114

Gulfport WJZD-FM (autx) 10211 Southpark Dr, Gulfport MS 39503 **Phn:** 228-896-5307 **Fax:** 228-896-5703 www.wjzd.com info@wjzd.com

Gulfport WROA-AM (z) 10250 Lorraine Rd, Gulfport MS 39503 **Phn:** 228-896-5500 **Fax:** 228-896-0458

Gulfport WTNI-AM (s) 1909 E Pass Rd Ste D11, Gulfport MS 39507 **Phn:** 228-388-2001 **Fax:** 228-896-9114 kcurley@msmediaradio.com

Gulfport WUJM-FM (s) 1909 E Pass Rd Ste D11, Gulfport MS 39507 **Phn:** 228-388-2001 **Fax:** 228-896-9114 www.967thechamp.com kcurley@cableone.net

Gulfport WXBD-FM (s) 1909 E Pass Rd Ste D11, Gulfport MS 39507 **Phn:** 228-388-2001 **Fax:** 228-896-9114 www.967thechamp.com

Gulfport WXYK-FM (h) 1909 E Pass Rd Ste D11, Gulfport MS 39507 **Phn:** 228-388-2001 **Fax:** 228-896-9736 www.1071themonkey.net bwest@msmediaradio.com

Gulfport WZKX-FM (c) 10250 Lorraine Rd, Gulfport MS 39503 **Phn:** 228-896-5500 **Fax:** 228-896-0458 KICKER108.COM irma.n.aviles@abc.com

Gulfport WZNF-FM (r) 10250 Lorraine Rd, Gulfport MS 39503 **Phn:** 228-896-5500 **Fax:** 228-896-0458 www.z95fm.com bryan@z95fm.com

Hattiesburg WFOR-AM (s) 6555 Highway 98 W # 8, Hattiesburg MS 39402 **Phn:** 601-296-9800 **Fax:** 601-296-9838 jacksonwalker@clearchannel.com

Hattiesburg WJKX-FM (uw) 6555 Highway 98 W # 8, Hattiesburg MS 39402 **Phn:** 601-296-9800 **Fax:** 601-296-9838 www.102jkx.com contact@102jkx.com

Hattiesburg WJMG-FM (wu) 1204 Kinnard St, Hattiesburg MS 39401 **Phn:** 601-544-1941 **Fax:** 601-544-1947

Hattiesburg WMXI-FM (snt) 7501 U S Highway 49, Hattiesburg MS 39402 **Phn:** 601-264-0443 **Fax:** 601-264-5733 wmxi.com

Hattiesburg WNSL-FM (h) 6555 Highway 98 W # 8, Hattiesburg MS 39402 **Phn:** 601-296-9800 **Fax:** 601-582-5481 www.sl100.com contact@sl100.com

Hattiesburg WORV-AM (wg) 1204 Kinnard St, Hattiesburg MS 39401 **Phn:** 601-544-1941 **Fax:** 601-544-1947

Hattiesburg WUSM-FM (vj) 118 College Dr # 10045, Hattiesburg MS 39406 **Phn:** 601-266-4287 www.southernmissradio.com wusm@usm.edu

Hattiesburg WXRR-FM (r) PO Box 16596, Hattiesburg MS 39404 **Phn:** 601-544-0095 **Fax:** 601-545-8199 www.rock104fm.com rock104@rock104fm.com

Hattiesburg WZLD-FM (u) 6555 Highway 98 W # 8, Hattiesburg MS 39402 **Phn:** 601-296-9800 **Fax:** 601-296-9838 www.wild1063.com denisebrooks@clearchannel.com

Holly Springs WKRA-AM (gw) 1400 Highway 4 E # C, Holly Springs MS 38635 **Phn:** 662-252-1110 **Fax:** 662-252-2739

Holly Springs WKRA-FM (wx) PO Box 398, Holly Springs MS 38635 **Phn:** 662-252-6692 **Fax:** 662-252-2739

Holly Springs WURC-FM (wvj) 150 Rust Ave, Holly Springs MS 38635 **Phn:** 662-252-5881 **Fax:** 662-252-8869 www.wurc.org dmoyo@rustcollege.edu

Houston WCPC-AM (cgw) 1189 N Jackson St, Houston MS 38851 **Phn:** 662-456-3071 www.wilkinsradio.com wcpc@wilkinsradio.com

Indianola WNLA-AM (wg) PO Box 667, Indianola MS 38751 **Phn:** 662-887-1380 **Fax:** 662-887-1396 gospel1380.com wnlaamfm@bellsouth.net

Iuka WADI-FM (c) 121 E Front St, Iuka MS 38852 **Phn:** 662-423-9533

Iuka WFXO-FM (r) 311 W Eastport St, Iuka MS 38852 **Phn:** 662-423-2369 www.rock1059.net prod983@cableone.net

Jackson WFMM-FM (t) 6311 Ridgewood Rd, Jackson MS 39211 **Phn:** 601-957-1700 **Fax:** 601-956-5228 www.supertalk.fm programming@supertalk.fm

Jackson WFMN-FM (snt) 6311 Ridgewood Rd, Jackson MS 39211 **Phn:** 601-957-1700 **Fax:** 601-957-2389 supertalk.fm bwallace@telesouth.com

Jackson WHLH-FM (wg) 1375 Beasley Rd, Jackson MS 39206 **Phn:** 601-982-1062 **Fax:** 601-362-1905 www.hallelujah955.com kennywindham@clearchannel.com

Jackson WJDX-AM (s) 1375 Beasley Rd, Jackson MS 39206 **Phn:** 601-982-1062 **Fax:** 601-362-8270 www.wjdx.com randybell@clearchannel.com

Jackson WJMI-FM (u) PO Box 9446, Jackson MS 39286 **Phn:** 601-957-1300 **Fax:** 601-956-0516 www.wjmi.com production@wjmi.com

Jackson WJNT-AM (nt) PO Box 9446, Jackson MS 39286 **Phn:** 601-957-1150 **Fax:** 601-956-0516 www.wjnt.com

Jackson WJSU-FM (pj) PO Box 18450, Jackson MS 39217 **Phn:** 601-979-2285 **Fax:** 601-979-2878 www.wjsu.org gina.p.carter@jsums.edu

Jackson WMPN-FM (plnj) 3825 Ridgewood Rd, Jackson MS 39211 **Phn:** 601-432-6565 **Fax:** 601-432-6806 www.mpbonline.org

Jackson WMPR-FM (vwg) 1018 Pecan Park Cir, Jackson MS 39209 **Phn:** 601-948-5835 **Fax:** 601-948-6162 www.wmpr901.com frontoffice@wmpr901.com

Jackson WMSI-FM (c) 1375 Beasley Rd, Jackson MS 39206 **Phn:** 601-982-1062 **Fax:** 601-362-8270 www.miss103.com rickadams@clearchannel.com

Jackson WOAD-FM (wg) PO Box 9446, Jackson MS 39286 **Phn:** 601-957-1300 **Fax:** 601-956-0516 www.woad.com kwebb1234@aol.com

Jackson WOAD-AM (gw) PO Box 9446, Jackson MS 39286 **Phn:** 601-957-1300 **Fax:** 601-956-0516 www.woad.com

Jackson WQJQ-FM (o) PO Box 31999, Jackson MS 39286 **Phn:** 601-982-1062 **Fax:** 601-362-1905 www.wjdxfm.com jankaym@aol.com

Jackson WRBJ-FM (u) 745 N State St, Jackson MS 39202 **Phn:** 601-974-5700 **Fax:** 601-974-5719

Jackson WRXW-FM (r) 222 Beasley Rd, Jackson MS 39206 **Phn:** 601-957-3000 www.rock939.com

Jackson WSTZ-FM (r) 1375 Beasley Rd, Jackson MS 39206 **Phn:** 601-982-1062 **Fax:** 601-362-1905 www.z106.com mikebridges@clearchannel.com

Jackson WTWZ-AM (c) 4611 Terry Rd Ste C, Jackson MS 39212 **Phn:** 601-346-0074 **Fax:** 601-346-0896 wtwzradio.com am1120@wtwzradio.com

Jackson WWJK-FM (a) 222 Beasley Rd, Jackson MS 39206 **Phn:** 601-957-3000 **Fax:** 601-956-0370

Jackson WZRX-AM (t) 1375 Beasley Rd, Jackson MS 39206 **Phn:** 601-995-1490 **Fax:** 601-981-9093 www.1590wzrx.com radioair@bellsouth.net

Kosciusko WKOZ-AM (on) PO Box 1700, Kosciusko MS 39090 **Phn:** 662-289-1340 **Fax:** 662-289-7907 www.breezynews.com breezy@boswellmedia.net

Kosciusko WLIN-FM (aq) PO Box 1700, Kosciusko MS 39090 **Phn:** 662-289-1050 **Fax:** 662-289-7907 www.breezynews.com breezy@boswellmedia.net

Laurel WAML-AM (gnq) PO Box 6226, Laurel MS 39441 **Phn:** 601-425-0011

Laurel WBBN-FM (c) PO Box 6408, Laurel MS 39441 **Phn:** 601-544-0095 **Fax:** 601-545-8199 www.b95country.com b95@b95country.com

Laurel WKZW-FM (a) PO Box 6408, Laurel MS 39441 **Phn:** 601-544-0095 **Fax:** 601-545-8199 www.kz943.com kz943@kz943.com

Laurel WMLC-AM (s) PO Box 6226, Laurel MS 39441 **Phn:** 601-425-0011

Laurel WXHB-FM (g) PO Box 6408, Laurel MS 39441 **Phn:** 601-544-0095 **Fax:** 601-425-4171 www.wxhbfm.com wxhb@wxhbfm.com

Lexington WAGR-FM (co) 100 Radio Rd, Lexington MS 39095 **Phn:** 662-834-1025 **Fax:** 662-834-1254

Lexington WXTN-AM (wg) 100 Radio Rd, Lexington MS 39095 **Phn:** 662-834-1025 **Fax:** 662-834-1254

Lorman WPRL-FM (v) 1000 Alcorn Dr # 269, Lorman MS 39096 **Phn:** 601-877-6290 www.wprl.org cedmond@alcorn.edu

Louisville WLSM-FM (c) PO Box 279, Louisville MS 39339 **Phn:** 662-773-3481 **Fax:** 662-773-3482

Lucedale WRBE-AM (cg) PO Box 827, Lucedale MS 39452 **Phn:** 601-947-8151 **Fax:** 601-947-8152 www.wrberadio.com

Lucedale WRBE-FM (cg) PO Box 827, Lucedale MS 39452 **Phn:** 601-947-8151 **Fax:** 601-947-8152 www.wrberadio.com

Marks WQMA-AM (o) 1820 W Marks Rd, Marks MS 38646 **Phn:** 662-326-3555 **Fax:** 662-796-3003 www.q1520radio.com jason@q1520radio.com

McComb WAKH-FM (c) PO Box 1649, McComb MS 39649 **Phn:** 601-684-4116 **Fax:** 601-684-4654 k106.net

MISSISSIPPI RADIO STATIONS

McComb WAKK-AM (wu) PO Box 1649, McComb MS 39649 **Phn:** 601-684-4116 **Fax:** 601-684-4654 sandlow@telepak.net

McComb WAPF-AM (snt) PO Box 1649, McComb MS 39649 **Phn:** 601-684-4116 **Fax:** 601-684-4654

McComb WAZA-FM (o) PO Box 1649, McComb MS 39649 **Phn:** 601-684-4116 **Fax:** 601-684-4654

McComb WZFL-FM (uog) PO Box 1649, McComb MS 39649 **Phn:** 601-684-4116 **Fax:** 601-684-4654

Meridian WALT-AM (t) PO Box 5797, Meridian MS 39302 **Phn:** 601-693-3434 **Fax:** 601-483-0826 dee@radiopeople.net

Meridian WHTU-FM (u) 4307 Highway 39 N, Meridian MS 39301 **Phn:** 601-693-2381 **Fax:** 601-485-2972

Meridian WJDQ-FM (a) 3436 Old Hwy 45N, Meridian MS 39301 **Phn:** 601-693-2661 **Fax:** 601-483-0826 www.q101radio.net leetaylor@q101radio.net

Meridian WJXM-FM (u) 3436 Highway 45 N, Meridian MS 39301 **Phn:** 601-693-2661 **Fax:** 601-483-0826 www.1057thebeat.com diane@wokk.com

Meridian WKZB-FM (h) 3436 Highway 45 N, Meridian MS 39301 **Phn:** 601-693-2661 **Fax:** 601-483-0826

Meridian WMLV-FM (a) 3436 Highway 45 N, Meridian MS 39301 **Phn:** 601-693-2661 **Fax:** 601-483-0826

Meridian WMOX-AM (ct) PO Box 5184, Meridian MS 39302 **Phn:** 601-693-1891 **Fax:** 601-483-1010 www.wmox.net wmoxradio@wmox.net

Meridian WMSO-FM (c) 4307 Highway 39 N, Meridian MS 39301 **Phn:** 601-693-2381 **Fax:** 601-485-2972 www.miss101.com

Meridian WNBN-AM (wgt) 266 23rd St, Meridian MS 39301 **Phn:** 601-483-3401 **Fax:** 601-483-3411 frankrack@netzero.com

Meridian WOKK-FM (c) PO Box 5797, Meridian MS 39302 **Phn:** 601-693-2661 **Fax:** 601-483-0826 www.wokk.com newsroom@wokk.com

Meridian WYHL-AM (gq) 4307 Highway 39 N, Meridian MS 39301 **Phn:** 601-693-2381 **Fax:** 601-485-2972

Meridian WZKS-FM (ux) 4307 Highway 39 N, Meridian MS 39301 **Phn:** 601-693-2381 **Fax:** 601-485-2972 www.1041kissfm.com

Natchez KTGV-FM (u) 2 Oferrall St, Natchez MS 39120 **Phn:** 601-442-4895 **Fax:** 601-446-8260 margaretperkins@bellsouth.net

Natchez WKSO-FM (a) PO Box 768, Natchez MS 39121 **Phn:** 601-442-4895 **Fax:** 601-446-8260 listenupyall.com margaretperkins@bellsouth.net

Natchez WMIS-AM (wgx) 20 E Franklin St, Natchez MS 39120 **Phn:** 601-442-2522 **Fax:** 601-446-9918 wmiswtyj@bellsouth.net

Natchez WNAT-AM (snt) PO Box 768, Natchez MS 39121 **Phn:** 601-442-4895 **Fax:** 601-446-8260 margaretperkins@bellsouth.net

Natchez WQNZ-FM (c) PO Box 768, Natchez MS 39121 **Phn:** 601-442-4895 **Fax:** 601-446-8260 listenupyall.com margaretperkins@bellsouth.net

Natchez WTYJ-FM (wux) 20 E Franklin St, Natchez MS 39120 **Phn:** 601-442-2522 **Fax:** 601-446-9918 wmiswtyj@bellsouth.net

New Albany WNAU-AM (o) PO Box 808, New Albany MS 38652 **Phn:** 662-534-8133 **Fax:** 662-538-4183

Ocean Springs WOSM-FM (g) 4720 Radio Rd, Ocean Springs MS 39564 **Phn:** 228-875-9031 **Fax:** 228-875-6461

Oxford WOXD-FM (o) 302 Highway 7 S, Oxford MS 38655 **Phn:** 662-234-9631 **Fax:** 662-236-5390 www.bullseye955.com production@bullseye955.com

Oxford WQLJ-FM (a) PO Box 1077, Oxford MS 38655 **Phn:** 662-236-0093 **Fax:** 662-234-5155 q937@telesouth.com

Oxford WTNM-FM (t) 461 Highway 6 W, Oxford MS 38655 **Phn:** 662-236-0093 **Fax:** 662-234-5155 supertalk.fm tanyatsupertalk@comcast.net

Pascagoula WPMP-AM (t) 5115 Telephone Rd, Pascagoula MS 39567 **Phn:** 228-762-5683 **Fax:** 228-762-1222

Philadelphia WHOC-AM (cnt) 1016 W Beacon St, Philadelphia MS 39350 **Phn:** 601-656-7102 **Fax:** 601-656-1491

Philadelphia WWSL-FM (a) 1016 W Beacon St, Philadelphia MS 39350 **Phn:** 601-656-7102 **Fax:** 601-656-1491

Picayune WRJW-AM (cg) PO Box 907, Picayune MS 39466 **Phn:** 601-798-4835 **Fax:** 601-798-9755 www.wrjwradio.com wrjwradio@bellsouth.net

Ridgeland WIIN-AM (m) 265 Highpoint Dr, Ridgeland MS 39157 **Phn:** 601-956-0102 **Fax:** 601-978-3980 gwenr@radiopeople.net

Ridgeland WJKK-FM (a) 265 Highpoint Dr, Ridgeland MS 39157 **Phn:** 601-956-0102 **Fax:** 601-978-3980 www.mix987.com dave@mix987.com

Ridgeland WKXI-FM (au) 731 S Pear Orchard Rd Ste 27, Ridgeland MS 39157 **Phn:** 601-957-1300 **Fax:** 601-956-0516 www.wkxi.com

Ridgeland WSFZ-AM (s) 571 Highway 51 Ste H, Ridgeland MS 39157 **Phn:** 601-605-6656 **Fax:** 601-605-6646 www.supersport930.com info@supersport930.com

Ridgeland WUSJ-FM (c) 265 Highpoint Dr, Ridgeland MS 39157 **Phn:** 601-956-0102 **Fax:** 601-978-3980 www.us963.com gwenr@radiopeople.net

Ridgeland WYOY-FM (h) 265 Highpoint Dr, Ridgeland MS 39157 **Phn:** 601-956-0102 **Fax:** 601-978-3980 www.y101.com gwenr@radiopeople.net

Ripley WKZU-FM (c) PO Box 572, Ripley MS 38663 **Phn:** 662-837-1023 **Fax:** 662-837-2994 www.classicradiofm.com wkzu@aol.com

Ripley WSKK-FM (h) PO Box 572, Ripley MS 38663 **Phn:** 662-837-1023 **Fax:** 662-837-2994 www.classicradiofm.com

Senatobia WSAO-AM (wqg) PO Box 190, Senatobia MS 38668 **Phn:** 662-562-4445 **Fax:** 662-562-9881 jrer1140@aol.com

Southaven WVIM-FM (o) 230 Goodman Rd E Ste 2-202, Southaven MS 38671 **Phn:** 901-272-0008 www.rebel953.com

Starkville WACR-FM (ua) 608 Yellow Jacket Dr, Starkville MS 39759 **Phn:** 662-338-5424 **Fax:** 662-338-5436 www.wacr1053.com markmaharrey@urbanradio.fm

Starkville WAJV-FM (g) 608 Yellow Jacket Dr, Starkville MS 39759 **Phn:** 662-338-5424 **Fax:** 662-338-5436 www.joy989.com markmaharrey@urbanradio.fm

Starkville WLZA-FM (a) PO Box 884, Starkville MS 39760 **Phn:** 662-324-9601 **Fax:** 662-324-7400 961wlza.com

Starkville WMSU-FM (h) 608 Yellow Jacket Dr, Starkville MS 39759 **Phn:** 662-338-5424 **Fax:** 662-338-5436 www.power92jamz.net

Starkville WROB-AM (g) 201 Academy Rd Ste 4, Starkville MS 39759 **Phn:** 662-494-1450 **Fax:** 662-494-9762 dsmothers@telesouth.com

Tupelo WAFR-FM (q) PO Box 3206, Tupelo MS 38803 **Phn:** 662-844-8888 www.afa.netradio msanders@afa.net

Tupelo WBVV-FM (g) PO Box 3300, Tupelo MS 38803 **Phn:** 662-842-1067 **Fax:** 662-844-2887

Tupelo WCNA-FM (r) PO Box 2116, Tupelo MS 38803 **Phn:** 662-842-9595 **Fax:** 662-842-9568

Tupelo WELO-AM (m) PO Box 410, Tupelo MS 38802 **Phn:** 662-842-7658 **Fax:** 662-842-0197 msradiogroup.com scott@msradiogroup.com

Tupelo WESE-FM (wu) 5026 Cliff Gookin Blvd, Tupelo MS 38801 **Phn:** 662-842-1067 **Fax:** 662-842-0725 www.power925jamz.com markmaharrey@urbanradio.fm

Tupelo WFTA-FM (a) PO Box 2116, Tupelo MS 38803 **Phn:** 662-842-1019 **Fax:** 662-842-9568

Tupelo WKMQ-AM (t) PO Box 3300, Tupelo MS 38803 **Phn:** 662-842-1067 **Fax:** 662-842-0725 rickstevens@urbanradio.fm

Tupelo WSEL-FM (gu) PO Box 3788, Tupelo MS 38803 **Phn:** 662-489-0297

Tupelo WSYE-FM (a) PO Box 410, Tupelo MS 38802 **Phn:** 662-842-7658 **Fax:** 662-842-0197 www.sunny933fm.com

Tupelo WTUP-AM (so) PO Box 3300, Tupelo MS 38803 **Phn:** 662-842-1067 **Fax:** 662-842-0725 rickstevens@urbanradio.fm

Tupelo WWKZ-FM (h) 5026 Cliff Gookin Blvd, Tupelo MS 38801 **Phn:** 662-842-1067 **Fax:** 662-842-0725 www.kz103.com

Tupelo WWMS-FM (c) 2214 S Gloster St, Tupelo MS 38801 **Phn:** 662-842-7658 **Fax:** 662-842-0197 sportsdriveradio.commiss98 spencer@msradiogroup.com

Tupelo WWZD-FM (c) 5026 Cliff Gookin Blvd, Tupelo MS 38801 **Phn:** 662-842-1067 **Fax:** 662-842-0725 www.wizard106.com markmaharrey@urbanradio.fm

Tupelo WZLQ-FM (r) PO Box 410, Tupelo MS 38802 **Phn:** 662-842-7658 **Fax:** 662-842-0197 www.z985.net

Tylertown WTYL-AM (c) 930 Union Rd, Tylertown MS 39667 **Phn:** 601-876-2105 **Fax:** 601-876-9551

Tylertown WTYL-FM (c) 930 Union Rd, Tylertown MS 39667 **Phn:** 601-876-2105 **Fax:** 601-876-9551

University WUMS-FM (vr) 201 Bishop Hall, University MS 38677 **Phn:** 662-915-5503 **Fax:** 662-915-5703

Vicksburg WBBV-FM (cn) 1601 N Frontage Rd # E, Vicksburg MS 39180 **Phn:** 601-636-2340 **Fax:** 601-638-0869

Vicksburg WQBC-AM (snt) PO Box 820483, Vicksburg MS 39182 **Phn:** 601-636-1108 www.wqbc.net

Vicksburg WRTM-FM (wx) PO Box 820583, Vicksburg MS 39182 **Phn:** 601-636-7944 radioair@bellsouth.net

Walnut WLRC-AM (qg) PO Box 37, Walnut MS 38683 **Phn:** 662-223-4071 **Fax:** 662-223-4072 www.wlrcradio.com

Waynesboro WABO-AM (r) PO Box 507, Waynesboro MS 39367 **Phn:** 601-735-4331 **Fax:** 601-735-4332 www.105wabo.com

Waynesboro WABO-FM (r) PO Box 507, Waynesboro MS 39367 **Phn:** 601-735-4331 **Fax:** 601-735-4332 www.105wabo.com

West Point WKBB-FM (nt) 413 N Forest St, West Point MS 39773 **Phn:** 662-494-1450 **Fax:** 662-494-9762 supertalk.fm tanyatsupertalk@comcast.net

Wiggins WIGG-AM (c) PO Box 723, Wiggins MS 39577 **Phn:** 601-928-7281 **Fax:** 601-528-5011

Winona WONA-AM (c) 1006 S Applegate St, Winona MS 38967 **Phn:** 662-283-1570 **Fax:** 662-283-1520 hawg95.com wonafm@gmail.com

Winona WONA-FM (c) 1006 S Applegate St, Winona MS 38967 **Phn:** 662-283-1570 **Fax:** 662-283-1520 wonafm@gmail.com

Yazoo City WBYP-FM (cg) PO Box 130, Yazoo City MS 39194 **Phn:** 662-746-7676 **Fax:** 662-746-1525 www.power107.org power107@power107.org

MISSOURI

Ava KKOZ-AM (cn) PO Box 386, Ava MO 65608 **Phn:** 417-683-4193 **Fax:** 417-683-4192 www.kkoz.com

Ava KKOZ-FM (cn) PO Box 386, Ava MO 65608 **Phn:** 417-683-4193 **Fax:** 417-683-4192 www.kkoz.com

Bethany KAAN-FM (cn) PO Box 447, Bethany MO 64424 **Phn:** 660-425-6380 **Fax:** 660-425-8148 www.northwestmoinfo.com dschmitz@regionalradio.com

Bethany KAAN-AM (of) PO Box 447, Bethany MO 64424 **Phn:** 660-425-6380 **Fax:** 660-425-8148 www.northwestmoinfo.com dschmitz@regionalradio.com

Bolivar KYOO-FM (c) 205 N Pike Ave, Bolivar MO 65613 **Phn:** 417-326-5257 **Fax:** 417-326-5900 kyooradio.com

Bolivar KYOO-AM (c) 205 N Pike Ave, Bolivar MO 65613 **Phn:** 417-326-5257 **Fax:** 417-326-5900 kyooradio.com

Boonville KWJK-FM (ah) 1600 Radio Hill Rd, Boonville MO 65233 **Phn:** 660-882-6686 **Fax:** 660-882-6687 www.931jack.fm jackfm@cebridge.net

Boonville KWRT-AM (cnt) 1600 Radio Hill Rd, Boonville MO 65233 **Phn:** 660-882-6686 **Fax:** 660-882-6688 www.1370kwrt.com kwrt@classicnet.net

Branson KLFC-FM (q) PO Box 2030, Branson MO 65615 **Phn:** 417-334-5532 **Fax:** 417-335-2437 www.klfcradio.com news@klfcradio.com

Branson KOMC-AM (g) 202 Courtney St, Branson MO 65616 **Phn:** 417-334-6003 **Fax:** 417-334-7141 www.hometowndailynews.com mikegreeley@krzk.com

Branson KOMC-FM (a) 202 Courtney St, Branson MO 65616 **Phn:** 417-334-6003 **Fax:** 417-334-7141 www.hometowndailynews.com haroldsmith@krzk.com

Branson KRZK-FM (c) 202 Courtney St, Branson MO 65616 **Phn:** 417-334-6003 **Fax:** 417-334-7141 www.hometowndailynews.com haroldsmith@krzk.com

Brookfield KFMZ-AM (a) 107 S Main St, Brookfield MO 64628 **Phn:** 660-258-3383 **Fax:** 660-258-7307 bestbroadcastgroup.com kfmz@bestbroadcastgroup.com

Brookfield KZBK-FM (a) 107 S Main St, Brookfield MO 64628 **Phn:** 660-258-3383 **Fax:** 660-258-7307 www.kzbkradio.com kzbk@shighway.com

Brookline KADI-AM (q) 5431 W Sunshine St, Brookline MO 65619 **Phn:** 417-831-0995 **Fax:** 417-831-4026 www.1340bigtalker.com station.manager@kadi.com

Brookline KADI-FM (q) 5431 W Sunshine St, Brookline MO 65619 **Phn:** 417-831-0995 **Fax:** 417-831-4026 www.99hitfm.com rod@99hitfm.com

Butler KMAM-AM (c) 800 E Nursery St, Butler MO 64730 **Phn:** 660-679-4191 **Fax:** 660-679-4193 www.921kmoe.com fm92@embarqmail.com

Butler KMOE-FM (c) 800 E Nursery St, Butler MO 64730 **Phn:** 660-679-4191 **Fax:** 660-679-4193 www.921kmoe.com fm92@embarqmail.com

MISSISSIPPI RADIO STATIONS

California KRLL-AM (c) PO Box 307, California MO 65018 **Phn:** 573-796-3139 **Fax:** 573-796-4131

Camdenton KCVJ-FM (qnt) PO Box 800, Camdenton MO 65020 **Phn:** 573-346-3200 **Fax:** 573-346-1010 www.spiritfm.org

Camdenton KCVO-FM (q) PO Box 800, Camdenton MO 65020 **Phn:** 573-346-3200 **Fax:** 573-346-1010 www.spiritfm.org

Cameron KKWK-FM (a) PO Box 643, Cameron MO 64429 **Phn:** 816-632-6661 **Fax:** 816-632-1334 www.northwestmoinfo.com chrisw@regionalradio.com

Cameron KMRN-AM (c) PO Box 643, Cameron MO 64429 **Phn:** 816-632-6661 **Fax:** 816-632-1334 www.northwestmoinfo.com dschmitz@regionalradio.com

Cape Girardeau KAML-AM (s) 324 Broadway St, Cape Girardeau MO 63701 **Phn:** 573-335-8291 **Fax:** 573-335-4806 www.1470kmal.com eriks@riverradio.net

Cape Girardeau KAPE-AM (nt) 901 S. Kingshighway, Cape Girardeau MO 63703 **Phn:** 573-339-7000 **Fax:** 573-651-4100 www.kaperadio1550.com news@withersradio.net

Cape Girardeau KCGQ-FM (r) 324 Broadway St, Cape Girardeau MO 63701 **Phn:** 573-335-8291 **Fax:** 573-335-4806 www.realrock993.com realrock@riverradio.net

Cape Girardeau KEZS-FM (c) 324 Broadway St, Cape Girardeau MO 63701 **Phn:** 573-335-8291 **Fax:** 573-335-4806 www.k103fm.com k103@riverradio.net

Cape Girardeau KGIR-AM (st) 324 Broadway St, Cape Girardeau MO 63701 **Phn:** 573-335-8291 **Fax:** 573-335-4806 www.kgir.com eriks@riverradio.net

Cape Girardeau KGMO-FM (r) PO Box 558, Cape Girardeau MO 63702 **Phn:** 573-339-7000 **Fax:** 573-339-1550 www.kgmo.com alex@kgmo.com

Cape Girardeau KLSC-FM (a) 324 Broadway St, Cape Girardeau MO 63701 **Phn:** 573-335-8291 **Fax:** 573-335-4806 www.929theriver.com theriver@riverradio.net

Cape Girardeau KRCU-FM (plnj) 1 University Plz, Cape Girardeau MO 63701 **Phn:** 573-651-5070 **Fax:** 573-651-5071 krcu.org comments@krcu.org

Cape Girardeau KREZ-FM (a) 901 S Kingshighway St, Cape Girardeau MO 63703 **Phn:** 573-339-7000 **Fax:** 573-651-4100 www.softrock1047.com news@withersradio.net

Cape Girardeau KSIM-AM (nt) 324 Broadway St, Cape Girardeau MO 63701 **Phn:** 573-335-8291 **Fax:** 573-335-4806 www.1400ksim.com

Cape Girardeau KWKZ-FM (c) 753 Enterprise St, Cape Girardeau MO 63703 **Phn:** 573-334-7800 **Fax:** 573-334-7440 www.kwkz.com cuz@kwkz.com

Cape Girardeau KYRX-FM (h) PO Box 558, Cape Girardeau MO 63702 **Phn:** 573-339-7000 **Fax:** 573-651-4100 www.withersradio.net rlambert@withersradio.net

Cape Girardeau KZIM-AM (nt) PO Box 1610, Cape Girardeau MO 63702 **Phn:** 573-335-8291 **Fax:** 573-335-4806 www.960kzim.com kzim@riverradio.net

Cape Girardeau WKIB-FM (a) 901 S Kingshighway, Cape Girardeau MO 63703 **Phn:** 573-339-7000 **Fax:** 573-339-4100 www.mix965.net news@withersradio.net

Carrollton KAOL-AM (nt) 102 N Mason St, Carrollton MO 64633 **Phn:** 660-542-0404 **Fax:** 660-542-3152 kaolradio.com news@kmzu.com

Carrollton KMZU-FM (cnt) 102 N Mason St, Carrollton MO 64633 **Phn:** 660-542-0404 **Fax:** 660-542-0420 www.kmzu.com news@kmzu.com

Carrollton KRLI-FM (c) 102 N Mason St, Carrollton MO 64633 **Phn:** 660-542-0404 krlicountry.com

Carthage KDMO-AM (am) PO Box 426, Carthage MO 64836 **Phn:** 417-358-6054 news@cbciradio.com

Carthage KMXL-FM (a) 221 E 4th St, Carthage MO 64836 **Phn:** 417-358-6054 **Fax:** 417-358-1278 www.951mikefm.com news@cbciradio.com

Centralia KMFC-FM (q) 1249 E Highway 22, Centralia MO 65240 **Phn:** 573-682-5525 **Fax:** 573-682-2744 www.kmfc.com info@kmfc.com

Charleston KCHR-AM (cnt) 205 E Commercial St, Charleston MO 63834 **Phn:** 573-683-6044

Chillicothe KCHI-AM (ont) 421 Washington St, Chillicothe MO 64601 **Phn:** 660-646-4173 **Fax:** 660-646-2868 www.kchi.com kchi@greenhills.net

Chillicothe KCHI-FM (ont) 421 Washington St, Chillicothe MO 64601 **Phn:** 660-646-4173 www.kchi.com kchi@greenhills.net

Clinton KDKD-FM (c) PO Box 448, Clinton MO 64735 **Phn:** 660-885-6141 **Fax:** 660-885-4801 www.westcentralmoinfo.com bob@kdkd.net

Clinton KDKD-AM (o) PO Box 448, Clinton MO 64735 **Phn:** 660-885-6141 **Fax:** 660-885-4801 www.westcentralmoinfo.com dlee@kdkd.net

Clinton KXEA-FM (h) PO Box 448, Clinton MO 64735 **Phn:** 660-885-6141 **Fax:** 660-885-4801 www.westcentralmoinfo.com bob@kdkd.net

Columbia KBIA-FM (pln) 409 Jesse Hall U Of Mo, Columbia MO 65211 **Phn:** 573-882-3431 **Fax:** 573-882-2636 www.kbia.org dunnm@missouri.edu

Columbia KBXR-FM (r) 503 Old 63 N, Columbia MO 65201 **Phn:** 573-449-4141 **Fax:** 573-449-7770 www.bxr.com 1023bxr@gmail.com

Columbia KCLR-FM (c) 3215 Lemone Industrial Blvd Ste 200, Columbia MO 65201 **Phn:** 573-875-1099 **Fax:** 573-875-2439 www.clear99.com andyt@zrgmail.com

Columbia KCMQ-FM (r) 3215 Lemone Industrial Blvd Ste 200, Columbia MO 65201 **Phn:** 573-875-1099 **Fax:** 573-875-2439 kcmq.com cynthias@zrgmail.com

Columbia KCOU-FM (vr) 101-F Pershing U Of Mo, Columbia MO 65201 **Phn:** 573-882-7820 kcou.fm gm@kcou.fm

Columbia KFRU-AM (nt) 503 Old 63 N, Columbia MO 65201 **Phn:** 573-449-4141 **Fax:** 573-449-7770 www.kfru.com brian.wilson@cumulus.com

Columbia KOPN-FM (v) 915 E Broadway, Columbia MO 65201 **Phn:** 573-874-1139 **Fax:** 573-499-1662 kopn.org mail@kopn.org

Columbia KOQL-FM (h) 503 Old 63 N, Columbia MO 65201 **Phn:** 573-449-1061 **Fax:** 573-449-7770 www.q1061.com d.larimer@cumulus.com

Columbia KPLA-FM (a) 503 Old 63 N, Columbia MO 65201 **Phn:** 573-449-4141 **Fax:** 573-449-7770 www.kpla.com chris.kellogg@cumulus.com

Columbia KSSZ-FM (t) 3215 Lemone Industrial Blvd Ste 200, Columbia MO 65201 **Phn:** 573-875-1099 **Fax:** 573-875-2439 theeagle939.com cynthias@zrgmail.com

Columbia KTGR-AM (s) 3215 Lemone Industrial Blvd Ste 200, Columbia MO 65201 **Phn:** 573-875-1099 **Fax:** 573-875-2439 ktgr.com cosmo@zrgmail.com

Columbia KTXY-FM (a) 3215 Lemone Industrial Blvd Ste 200, Columbia MO 65201 **Phn:** 573-875-1099 **Fax:** 573-875-2439 y107.com y107@zrgmail.com

Columbia KWWC-FM (vjx) PO Box 2114, Columbia MO 65215 **Phn:** 573-876-7272 **Fax:** 573-876-2330 www.stephens.edukwwc

Dexter KDEX-AM (c) PO Box 249, Dexter MO 63841 **Phn:** 573-624-3545 **Fax:** 573-624-9926 kdex1@sbcglobal.net

MISSOURI RADIO STATIONS

Dexter KDEX-FM (c) PO Box 249, Dexter MO 63841 **Phn:** 573-624-3545 **Fax:** 573-624-9926 kdex1@sbcglobal.net

East Prairie KYMO-AM (jb) PO Box 130, East Prairie MO 63845 **Phn:** 573-649-3597 **Fax:** 573-649-3983

East Prairie KYMO-FM (o) PO Box 130, East Prairie MO 63845 **Phn:** 573-649-3597 **Fax:** 573-649-3983

El Dorado Springs KESM-AM (c) 200 Radio Ln, El Dorado Springs MO 64744 **Phn:** 417-876-2741 **Fax:** 417-876-2743 www.kesmradio.com kesm@kesmradio.com

El Dorado Springs KESM-FM (c) 200 Radio Ln, El Dorado Springs MO 64744 **Phn:** 417-876-2741 **Fax:** 417-876-2743 www.kesmradio.com kesm@kesmradio.com

Excelsior Springs KEXS-AM (q) 201 N Industrial Park Rd, Excelsior Springs MO 64024 **Phn:** 816-630-1090 www.thecatholicradionetwork.com info@thecatholicradionetwork.com

Farmington KREI-AM (nt) PO Box 461, Farmington MO 63640 **Phn:** 573-756-6476 **Fax:** 573-756-9127 www.mymoinfo.com dickw@regionalradio.com

Farmington KTJJ-FM (c) PO Box 461, Farmington MO 63640 **Phn:** 573-756-6476 **Fax:** 573-756-1110 www.mymoinfo.com tamip@j98.com

Farmington KYLS-FM (c) 900 E Karsch Blvd, Farmington MO 63640 **Phn:** 573-701-9590 **Fax:** 573-701-9696

Festus KJFF-AM (nts) PO Box 368, Festus MO 63028 **Phn:** 636-937-7642 **Fax:** 636-937-3636 www.mymoinfo.com kmooney@j98.com

Fulton KFAL-AM (c) 1805 Westminster Ave, Fulton MO 65251 **Phn:** 573-642-3341 **Fax:** 573-642-3343 kfalthebig900.com jeremyw@zrgmail.com

Hannibal KHMO-AM (nt) 119 N 3rd St, Hannibal MO 63401 **Phn:** 573-221-3450 **Fax:** 573-221-5331 www.khmoam.com bill.shuler@townsquaremedia.com

Harrison KBCN-FM (c) 100 Bluebird St, Harrison MO 72601 **Phn:** 870-743-1157 **Fax:** 870-743-1168

Harrison KMAC-FM (a) 100 Bluebird St, Harrison MO 72601 **Phn:** 870-743-1157 **Fax:** 870-743-1168

Hollister KOZO-FM (gq) 301 Gibson Rd, Hollister MO 65672 **Phn:** 417-339-3388 **Fax:** 417-339-3410 www.oasisnetwork.org mail@oasisnetwork.org

Houston KBTC-AM (c) PO Box 230, Houston MO 65483 **Phn:** 417-967-3353 **Fax:** 417-967-2281 www.bigcountry99.com traffic@bigcountry99.com

Houston KUNQ-FM (c) PO Box 230, Houston MO 65483 **Phn:** 417-967-3353 **Fax:** 417-967-2281 www.bigcountry99.com news@bigcountry99.com

Independence KCWJ-AM (q) 18920 E Valley View Pkwy # C, Independence MO 64055 **Phn:** 816-313-0049 **Fax:** 816-313-1036 www.kcwj.org

Jackson KUGT-AM (qt) 1301 Woodland Dr, Jackson MO 63755 **Phn:** 573-243-0649 **Fax:** 573-243-0640 www.jacksonmo.comorgsKUGT.html

Jefferson City KATI-FM (c) 3109 S 10 Mile Dr, Jefferson City MO 65109 **Phn:** 573-893-5696 **Fax:** 573-893-4137 kat943.com

Jefferson City KBBM-FM (r) 3605 Country Club Dr, Jefferson City MO 65109 **Phn:** 573-449-4141

Jefferson City KJMO-FM (o) 3605 Country Club Dr, Jefferson City MO 65109 **Phn:** 573-893-5100 **Fax:** 573-893-8330 www.kjmo.com chris.kellogg@cumulus.com

Jefferson City KLIK-AM (nt) 1002 Diamond Ridge # 400, Jefferson City MO 65109 **Phn:** 573-893-5100 **Fax:** 573-893-8330 www.klik1240.com kevin.joyce@cumulus.com

Jefferson City KWOS-AM (nt) 3109 S 10 Mile Dr, Jefferson City MO 65109 **Phn:** 573-893-5696 **Fax:** 573-893-4137 kwos.com russd@zrgmail.com

Joplin KBTN-FM (c) 2510 W 20th St, Joplin MO 64804 **Phn:** 417-781-1313 **Fax:** 417-781-1316 kbtnradio.com

Joplin KCAR-FM (r) 2510 W 20th St, Joplin MO 64804 **Phn:** 417-781-1313 **Fax:** 417-781-1316 star1043joplin.com

Joplin KIXQ-FM (c) 2702 E 32nd St, Joplin MO 64804 **Phn:** 417-624-1025 **Fax:** 417-781-6842 www.kix1025.com chade@zrgmail.com

Joplin KJMK-FM (r) 2702 E 32nd St, Joplin MO 64804 **Phn:** 417-624-1025 **Fax:** 417-781-6842 www.939classichits.com chade@zrgmail.com

Joplin KKLL-AM (qg) 831 S Moffet Ave, Joplin MO 64801 **Phn:** 417-781-1100 hereshelpnet.org

Joplin KMOQ-FM (h) 2510 W 20th St, Joplin MO 64804 **Phn:** 417-781-1313 **Fax:** 417-781-1316 matt@ami-joplin.com

Joplin KQYX-AM (nt) 2510 W 20th St, Joplin MO 64804 **Phn:** 417-781-1313 **Fax:** 417-781-1316 1450thescore.com jennisom@ami-joplin.com

Joplin KSYN-FM (h) 2702 E 32nd St, Joplin MO 64804 **Phn:** 417-624-1025 **Fax:** 417-781-6842 www.ksyn925.com chade@zrgmail.com

Joplin KXDG-FM (r) 2702 E 32nd St, Joplin MO 64804 **Phn:** 417-624-1025 **Fax:** 417-781-6842 www.bigdog979.com chade@zrgmail.com

Joplin KXMS-FM (vl) 3950 Newman Rd, Joplin MO 64801 **Phn:** 417-625-9356 www.mssu.edukxms kxms@mssu.edu

Joplin KZRG-AM (nt) 2702 E 32nd St, Joplin MO 64804 **Phn:** 417-624-1025 **Fax:** 417-781-6842 www.1310kzrg.com chade@zrgmail.com

Joplin KZYM-AM (t) 2702 E 32nd St, Joplin MO 64804 **Phn:** 417-624-1025 **Fax:** 417-781-6842 www.1230thetalker.com chade@zrgmail.com

Kaiser KLOZ-FM (a) 160 Highway 42, Kaiser MO 65047 **Phn:** 573-348-1958 **Fax:** 573-348-1923 mix927.com mike@mix927.com

Kaiser KQUL-FM (o) 160 Highway 42, Kaiser MO 65047 **Phn:** 573-348-1958 **Fax:** 573-348-1923

Kansas City KBEQ-FM (c) 508 Westport Rd Ste 202, Kansas City MO 64111 **Phn:** 816-753-4000 **Fax:** 816-753-4045 www.q104kc.com mkennedy@wilkskc.com

Kansas City KCKC-FM (a) 508 Westport Rd Ste 202, Kansas City MO 64111 **Phn:** 816-753-4000 **Fax:** 816-753-4045 www.alice102.com tom@alice102.com

Kansas City KCUR-FM (pjn) 4825 Troost Ave Ste 202, Kansas City MO 64110 **Phn:** 816-235-1551 **Fax:** 816-235-2865 www.kcur.org kcur@umkc.edu

Kansas City KFKF-FM (c) 508 Westport Rd Ste 202, Kansas City MO 64111 **Phn:** 816-753-4000 **Fax:** 816-753-4045 www.kfkf.com dalec@kfkf.com

Kansas City KGGN-AM (gu) 1734 E 63rd St Ste 600, Kansas City MO 64110 **Phn:** 816-333-0092 **Fax:** 816-363-8120 www.kggnam.com

Kansas City KKFI-FM (pj) PO Box 32250, Kansas City MO 64171 **Phn:** 816-931-3122 **Fax:** 816-931-7078 www.kkfi.org

Kansas City KMXV-FM (h) 508 Westport Rd Ste 202, Kansas City MO 64111 **Phn:** 816-753-4000 **Fax:** 816-753-4045 www.mix93.com ponch@mix93.com

Kansas City KPHN-AM (m) 1100 Main St Ste 1950, Kansas City MO 64105 **Phn:** 816-221-0206 **Fax:** 816-221-1050 music.disney.com

Kansas City KPRS-FM (wu) 11131 Colorado Ave, Kansas City MO 64137 **Phn:** 816-763-2040 **Fax:** 816-966-1055 www.kprs.com beth@kprs.com

Kansas City KPRT-AM (wg) 11131 Colorado Ave, Kansas City MO 64137 **Phn:** 816-763-2040 **Fax:** 816-966-1055 www.kprt.com myrond@kprs.com

Kennett KBOA-FM (am) PO Box 509, Kennett MO 63857 **Phn:** 573-888-4616 **Fax:** 573-888-4890 www.kboaradio.com

Kennett KBOA-AM (nt) PO Box 509, Kennett MO 63857 **Phn:** 573-888-4616 **Fax:** 573-888-6693 www.kboaradio.com

Kennett KCRV-FM (oa) PO Box 509, Kennett MO 63857 **Phn:** 573-888-4616 **Fax:** 573-888-4890

Kennett KCRV-AM (c) PO Box 509, Kennett MO 63857 **Phn:** 573-888-4616 **Fax:** 573-888-4890

Kennett KMIS-AM (s) PO Box 509, Kennett MO 63857 **Phn:** 573-888-4616 **Fax:** 573-888-4890 www.kmisradio.com

Kennett KTMO-FM (c) PO Box 509, Kennett MO 63857 **Phn:** 573-888-4616 **Fax:** 573-888-4890 www.ktmoradio.com paige@semoradio.com

Kirksville KHGN-FM (vq) PO Box 800, Kirksville MO 63501 **Phn:** 573-346-3200 **Fax:** 573-346-1010 www.lifechangingradio.org khgn@kvmo.net

Kirksville KIRX-AM (o) PO Box 130, Kirksville MO 63501 **Phn:** 660-665-9841 **Fax:** 660-665-0711 www.1450kirx.com kirx@cableone.net

Kirksville KLTE-FM (q) 3 Crown Dr Ste 100, Kirksville MO 63501 **Phn:** 660-627-5583 **Fax:** 660-665-8900 www.bottradionetwork.com klte@bottradionetwork.com

Kirksville KRXL-FM (r) PO Box 130, Kirksville MO 63501 **Phn:** 660-665-9841 **Fax:** 660-665-0711 www.945thex.com krxl@cableone.net

Kirksville KTRM-FM (vr) Truman State Univ, Kirksville MO 63501 **Phn:** 660-785-4506 **Fax:** 660-785-7261 tmn.truman.eduktrm ktrm88.7@gmail.com

Kirksville KTUF-FM (c) PO Box 130, Kirksville MO 63501 **Phn:** 660-665-9841 **Fax:** 660-665-0711 www.937ktuf.com ktuf@cableone.net

Lake Saint Louis KFNS-FM (s) 1000 Lake St Louis Blvd # 110, Lake Saint Louis MO 63387 **Phn:** 636-695-2300 www.viperrocks.com cdavison@kfns.com

Lebanon KBNN-AM (nt) PO Box 1112, Lebanon MO 65536 **Phn:** 417-532-9111 **Fax:** 417-588-4191 www.myozarksonline.com kjel@regionalradio.com

Lebanon KCLQ-FM (c) 18785 Finch Rd, Lebanon MO 65536 **Phn:** 417-532-2962 **Fax:** 417-532-5184 www.1079thecoyote.com dan@kclq.com

Lebanon KJEL-FM (c) PO Box 1112, Lebanon MO 65536 **Phn:** 417-532-9111 **Fax:** 417-588-4191 www.myozarksonline.com kjel@regionalradio.com

Lebanon KLWT-AM (q) 18785 Finch Rd, Lebanon MO 65536 **Phn:** 417-532-2962 **Fax:** 417-532-5184 brian@kclq.com

Liberty KCXL-AM (nt) 310 S La Frenz Rd, Liberty MO 64068 **Phn:** 816-792-1140 **Fax:** 816-792-8258 www.kcxl.com kcxl@kc.rr.com

Liberty KWJC-FM (vq) 500 College Hl, Liberty MO 64068 **Phn:** 816-415-7594 **Fax:** 816-415-5027

Louisiana KJFM-FM (c) PO Box 438, Louisiana MO 63353 **Phn:** 573-754-5102 **Fax:** 573-754-5544 kjfmeagle102.net kjfmradioeagle102@yahoo.com

MISSOURI RADIO STATIONS

Macon KLTI-AM (c) 32968 US Highway 63, Macon MO 63552 **Phn:** 660-385-1560 **Fax:** 660-385-7090 www.kltiradio.com klti@bestbroadcastgroup.com

Marble Hill KMHM-FM (g) RR 1 Box 266E, Marble Hill MO 63764 **Phn:** 573-238-1041 **Fax:** 573-238-0104

Marshall KMMO-AM (c) PO Box 128, Marshall MO 65340 **Phn:** 660-886-7422 **Fax:** 660-886-6291

Marshall KMMO-FM (c) PO Box 128, Marshall MO 65340 **Phn:** 660-886-7422 **Fax:** 660-886-6291

Marshall KMVC-FM (v) 500 E College St, Marshall MO 65340 **Phn:** 660-831-4193

Maryville KNIM-AM (n) PO Box 278, Maryville MO 64468 **Phn:** 660-582-2151 **Fax:** 660-582-3211 www.nodawaybroadcasting.com traffic@nodawaybroadcasting.com

Maryville KNIM-FM (r) PO Box 278, Maryville MO 64468 **Phn:** 660-582-2151 **Fax:** 660-582-3211 www.nodawaybroadcasting.com jim.cronin@nodawaybroadcasting.com

Maryville KXCV-FM (plnj) 800 University Dr, Maryville MO 64468 **Phn:** 660-562-1164 **Fax:** 660-562-1832 www.kxcv.org pholley@nwmissouri.edu

Memphis KMEM-FM (c) PO Box 121, Memphis MO 63555 **Phn:** 660-465-7225 **Fax:** 660-465-2626 www.kmemfm.com newstips@kmemfm.com

Mexico KJAB-FM (q) 621 W Monroe St, Mexico MO 65265 **Phn:** 573-581-8606 **Fax:** 573-581-9655 www.kjab.com kjab@kjab.com

Mexico KWWR-FM (c) PO Box 475, Mexico MO 65265 **Phn:** 573-581-5500 **Fax:** 573-581-1801 www.country96.com news@radiogetsresults.net

Mexico KXEO-AM (a) PO Box 475, Mexico MO 65265 **Phn:** 573-581-2340 **Fax:** 573-581-1801 kxeo.com

Mission KMJK-FM (uo) 5800 Foxridge Dr Ste 600, Mission MO 66202 **Phn:** 913-514-3000 **Fax:** 913-312-0296 www.magic1073.com brian.goeke@cumulus.com

Moberly KIRK-FM (a) PO Box 619, Moberly MO 65270 **Phn:** 660-263-6999 **Fax:** 660-269-8811 centralmoinfo.com kresnews@regionalradio.com

Moberly KRES-FM (c) PO Box 619, Moberly MO 65270 **Phn:** 660-263-1600 **Fax:** 660-269-8811 www.regionalradio.com kresnews@regionalradio.com

Moberly KWIX-AM (nt) PO Box 619, Moberly MO 65270 **Phn:** 660-263-1600 **Fax:** 660-269-8811 regionalradio.com kwixam@regionalradio.com

Moberly KZZT-FM (o) PO Box 128, Moberly MO 65270 **Phn:** 660-263-9390 **Fax:** 660-263-8800 bestbroadcastgroup.com kzzt@bestbroadcastgroup.com

Monett KKBL-FM (a) PO Box 109, Monett MO 65708 **Phn:** 417-235-6041 **Fax:** 417-235-6388 www.krmo.com blewis@radiotalon.com

Monett KRMO-AM (c) PO Box 109, Monett MO 65708 **Phn:** 417-235-6041 **Fax:** 417-235-6388 www.krmo.com jgandy@radiotalon.com

Monett KSWM-AM (nt) PO Box 109, Monett MO 65708 **Phn:** 417-235-6041 **Fax:** 417-235-6388 www.kswm940.com

Montgomery City KMCR-FM (a) 205 E Norman St, Montgomery City MO 63361 **Phn:** 573-564-2275 **Fax:** 573-564-8036 sunny1039.com rich@sunny1039.com

Mountain Grove KELE-FM (c) 800 Hubbard St, Mountain Grove MO 65711 **Phn:** 417-926-4650 **Fax:** 417-926-7604 production@925thegrove.com

Mountain Grove KOZX-FM (h) 800 Hubbard St, Mountain Grove MO 65711 **Phn:** 417-926-4650 **Fax:** 417-962-3303

Mountain View KUPH-FM (ah) 6962 US Highway 60, Mountain View MO 65548 **Phn:** 417-934-1000 **Fax:** 417-934-2565 www.ozarkareanetwork.com crystalc@ozarkradionetwork.com

Neosho KNEO-FM (qg) 10827 E Highway 86, Neosho MO 64850 **Phn:** 417-451-5636 **Fax:** 417-451-1891 www.kneo.org kneo@kneo.org

Nevada KNEM-AM (c) PO Box 447, Nevada MO 64772 **Phn:** 417-667-3113 **Fax:** 417-667-9797 www.knemknmo.com news@knemknmo.com

Nevada KNMO-FM (c) PO Box 447, Nevada MO 64772 **Phn:** 417-667-3113 **Fax:** 417-667-9797 www.knemknmo.com news@knemknmo.com

Osage Beach KMYK-FM (r) PO Box 225, Osage Beach MO 65065 **Phn:** 573-348-2772 **Fax:** 573-348-2779 www.935rocksthelake.com info@krmsradio.com

Osage Beach KRMS-AM (nt) PO Box 225, Osage Beach MO 65065 **Phn:** 573-348-2772 **Fax:** 573-348-2779 www.krmsradio.com ken@krmsradio.com

Park Hills KDBB-FM (r) PO Box 36, Park Hills MO 63601 **Phn:** 573-431-1000 **Fax:** 573-431-0850 b104fm.com jason@b104fm.com

Park Hills KFMO-AM (c) PO Box 36, Park Hills MO 63601 **Phn:** 573-431-2000 **Fax:** 573-431-0850 kfmo.com jason@b104fm.com

Parkville KGSP-FM (v) 8700 NW River Park Dr, Parkville MO 64152 **Phn:** 816-741-6326 **Fax:** 816-741-4911 kgsp.park.edu

Perryville KBDZ-FM (nc) PO Box 344, Perryville MO 63775 **Phn:** 573-547-8005 **Fax:** 573-883-2866 www.suntimesnews.com news@suntimesnews.com

Point Lookout KCOZ-FM (plnj) College Of The Ozarks, Point Lookout MO 65726 **Phn:** 417-334-6411 **Fax:** 417-335-2618

Poplar Bluff KAHR-FM (a) 932 County Road 448, Poplar Bluff MO 63901 **Phn:** 573-686-3700 **Fax:** 573-686-1713 www.foxradionetwork.com

Poplar Bluff KDFN-AM (o) 932 County Road 448, Poplar Bluff MO 63901 **Phn:** 573-686-3700 **Fax:** 573-686-1713 www.foxradionetwork.com

Poplar Bluff KFEB-FM (h) 932 County Road 448, Poplar Bluff MO 63901 **Phn:** 573-686-3700 **Fax:** 573-686-1713 www.foxradionetwork.com

Poplar Bluff KJEZ-FM (r) 1015 W Pine St, Poplar Bluff MO 63901 **Phn:** 573-785-0881 **Fax:** 573-785-0646 z95thebone.net johnr@riverradio.net

Poplar Bluff KKLR-FM (c) 1015 W Pine St, Poplar Bluff MO 63901 **Phn:** 573-785-0881 **Fax:** 573-785-0646 www.clear94.com clear94@riverradio.net

Poplar Bluff KLID-AM (o) 102 N 11th St, Poplar Bluff MO 63901 **Phn:** 573-686-1600 www.klidradio.com jerry@klidradio.com

Poplar Bluff KLUH-FM (q) PO Box 1313, Poplar Bluff MO 63902 **Phn:** 573-686-1663 **Fax:** 573-686-7703 dcmliferadio.org info@dcmliferadio.org

Poplar Bluff KOEA-FM (c) 932 County Road 448, Poplar Bluff MO 63901 **Phn:** 573-686-3700 **Fax:** 573-686-1713 www.foxradionetwork.com

Poplar Bluff KOKS-FM (q) 2773 Barron Rd, Poplar Bluff MO 63901 **Phn:** 573-686-5080 **Fax:** 573-686-5544

Poplar Bluff KOTC-AM (t) 932 County Road 448, Poplar Bluff MO 63901 **Phn:** 573-686-3700 **Fax:** 573-686-1713 www.foxradionetwork.com

Poplar Bluff KPPL-FM (ch) 932 County Road 448, Poplar Bluff MO 63901 **Phn:** 573-686-3700 **Fax:** 573-686-1713 www.foxradionetwork.com

Poplar Bluff KWOC-AM (nt) 1015 W Pine St, Poplar Bluff MO 63901 **Phn:** 573-785-0881 **Fax:** 573-785-0646 www.kwoc.com kwoc@riverradio.net

Poplar Bluff KXOQ-FM (r) 932 County Road 448, Poplar Bluff MO 63901 **Phn:** 573-686-3700 **Fax:** 573-686-1713 www.foxradionetwork.com

Quincy KICK-FM (c) 408 N 24th St, Quincy MO 62301 **Phn:** 217-223-5292 **Fax:** 573-221-5331 www.979kickfm.com brian.myles@townsquaremedia.com

Richmond KAYX-FM (q) 111 W Main St, Richmond MO 64085 **Phn:** 816-470-9925 **Fax:** 816-470-8925 www.bottradionetwork.com kayx@bottradionetwork.com

Richmond KLEX-AM (q) 111 W Main St, Richmond MO 64085 **Phn:** 816-470-9925 **Fax:** 816-470-8925 www.bottradionetwork.com kayx@bottradionetwork.com

Rolla KDAA-FM (a) PO Box 727, Rolla MO 65402 **Phn:** 573-364-2525 **Fax:** 573-364-5161 www.resultsradioonline.com kttrkznn@fidmail.com

Rolla KKID-FM (r) 1415 Forum Dr, Rolla MO 65401 **Phn:** 573-364-4433 **Fax:** 573-364-8385

Rolla KMNR-FM (v) 113 University Ctr W, Rolla MO 65401 **Phn:** 573-341-4272

Rolla KMST-FM (p) 400 W 14th St, Rolla MO 65409 **Phn:** 573-341-4386 **Fax:** 573-341-4889 www.kmst.org kmst@mst.edu

Rolla KTTR-FM (snt) PO Box 727, Rolla MO 65402 **Phn:** 573-364-2525 **Fax:** 573-364-5161 www.resultsradioonline.com kttrkznn@fidmail.com

Rolla KTTR-AM (snt) PO Box 727, Rolla MO 65402 **Phn:** 573-364-2525 **Fax:** 573-364-5161 www.resultsradioonline.com kttrkznn@fidmail.com

Rolla KXMO-FM (o) PO Box 727, Rolla MO 65402 **Phn:** 573-364-2525 **Fax:** 573-364-5161 www.resultsradioonline.com officemresultsradio@yahoo.com

Rolla KZNN-FM (c) PO Box 727, Rolla MO 65402 **Phn:** 573-364-2525 **Fax:** 573-364-5161 www.resultsradioonline.com kznnpd@yahoo.com

Saint Charles KCLC-FM (vj) 209 S Kingshighway St, Saint Charles MO 63301 **Phn:** 636-949-4890 www.891thewood.com fm891@lindenwood.edu

Saint Joseph KESJ-AM (s) PO Box 8550, Saint Joseph MO 64508 **Phn:** 816-233-8881 **Fax:** 816-279-8280 www.1550espn.com dave.riggert@eagleradio.net

Saint Joseph KFEQ-AM (sntf) 4104 Country Ln, Saint Joseph MO 64506 **Phn:** 816-233-8881 **Fax:** 816-279-8280 www.680kfeq.com barry.birr@eagleradio.net

Saint Joseph KGNM-FM (aq) 2414 S Leonard Rd, Saint Joseph MO 64503 **Phn:** 816-233-2577 **Fax:** 816-233-2374 kgnm.webs.com kgnm@stjoelive.com

Saint Joseph KGNM-AM (aq) 2414 S Leonard Rd, Saint Joseph MO 64503 **Phn:** 816-233-2577 **Fax:** 816-233-2374 kgnm.webs.com kgnm@stjoelive.com

Saint Joseph KKJO-FM (a) 4104 Country Lane, Saint Joseph MO 64506 **Phn:** 816-233-8881 **Fax:** 816-279-8280 www.kjo1055.com gregg.lynn@eagleradio.net

Saint Joseph KSJQ-FM (c) PO Box 8550, Saint Joseph MO 64508 **Phn:** 816-233-8881 **Fax:** 816-279-8280 www.qcountry927.com

MISSOURI RADIO STATIONS

Saint Louis KATZ-AM (wg) 1001 Highlands Plaza Dr W Ste 110, Saint Louis MO 63110 **Phn:** 314-333-8000 **Fax:** 314-333-8200 www.hallelujah1600.com katzam@clearchannel.com

Saint Louis KDHX-FM (p) 3504 Magnolia Ave, Saint Louis MO 63118 **Phn:** 314-664-3955 **Fax:** 314-664-1020 kdhx.org connect@kdhx.org

Saint Louis KEZK-FM (a) 1220 Olive St Flr 3, Saint Louis MO 63103 **Phn:** 314-531-0000 **Fax:** 314-969-7638 fresh1025.cbslocal.com marty.linck@cbsradio.com

Saint Louis KFNS-AM (st) 8045 Big Bend Blvd Ste 200, Saint Louis MO 63119 **Phn:** 314-962-0590 **Fax:** 314-962-7576 www.590theman.com cdavison@kfns.com

Saint Louis KFTK-FM (t) 401 S 18th St # 800, Saint Louis MO 63103 **Phn:** 314-231-9710 **Fax:** 314-621-3000 www.971talk.com jaallen@stl.emmis.com

Saint Louis KFUO-AM (tq) 85 Founders Ln, Saint Louis MO 63105 **Phn:** 314-505-7800 **Fax:** 314-725-3801 www.kfuo.org gduncan@kfuo.org

Saint Louis KFUO-FM (l) 85 Founders Ln, Saint Louis MO 63105 **Phn:** 314-725-0099 **Fax:** 314-725-3801 www.classic99.com rklemm@classic99.com

Saint Louis KIHT-FM (r) 401 S 18th St # 800, Saint Louis MO 63103 **Phn:** 314-621-4106 **Fax:** 314-621-3000 www.k-hits.com rick@stl.emmis.com

Saint Louis KJSL-AM (nqt) 10845 Olive Blvd Ste 160, Saint Louis MO 63141 **Phn:** 314-878-3600 **Fax:** 314-656-3608 www.truthtalk630.com

Saint Louis KLOU-FM (o) 1001 Highlands Plaza Dr W Ste 100, Saint Louis MO 63110 **Phn:** 314-333-8000 **Fax:** 314-333-8300 www.klou.com klou@clearchannel.com

Saint Louis KMJM-FM (uw) 1001 Highlands Plaza Dr W Ste 100, Saint Louis MO 63110 **Phn:** 314-333-8000 **Fax:** 314-333-8300 www.kmjm.com kmjm@clearchannel.com

Saint Louis KMOX-AM (snt) 1 S Memorial Dr Fl 3, Saint Louis MO 63102 **Phn:** 314-621-2345 **Fax:** 314-444-1867 stlouis.cbslocal.com kmox@kmox.com

Saint Louis KPNT-FM (r) 401 S 18th St # 800, Saint Louis MO 63103 **Phn:** 314-231-1057 **Fax:** 314-621-3000 www.1057thepoint.com tommythepointpd@stl.emmis.com

Saint Louis KRFT-AM (s) 8045 Big Bend Blvd Ste 200, Saint Louis MO 63119 **Phn:** 314-962-0590 **Fax:** 314-962-7576 www.kfns.com dgreene@kfns.com

Saint Louis KSD-FM (c) 1001 Highlands Plaza Dr W Ste 100, Saint Louis MO 63110 **Phn:** 314-333-8000 **Fax:** 314-333-8300 www.937thebull.com ksd@clearchannel.com

Saint Louis KSHE-FM (r) 401 S 18th St Ste 101, Saint Louis MO 63103 **Phn:** 314-621-0095 **Fax:** 314-621-3428 www.kshe95.com feedback@kshe95.com

Saint Louis KSIV-AM (ntq) 1750 S Brentwood Blvd Ste 811, Saint Louis MO 63144 **Phn:** 314-961-1320 **Fax:** 314-961-7562 www.bottradionetwork.com ksiv@bottradionetwork.com

Saint Louis KSIV-FM (nqt) 1750 S Brentwood Blvd Ste 811, Saint Louis MO 63144 **Phn:** 314-961-1320 **Fax:** 314-961-7562 www.bottradionetwork.com ksiv@bottradionetwork.com

Saint Louis KSLZ-FM (h) 1001 Highlands Plaza Dr W Ste 100, Saint Louis MO 63110 **Phn:** 314-333-8000 **Fax:** 314-333-8200 www.z1077.com kslz@clearchannel.com

Saint Louis KSTL-AM (gw) 10845 Olive Blvd Ste 160, Saint Louis MO 63141 **Phn:** 314-878-3600 **Fax:** 314-656-3608 www.shine690.com

Saint Louis KTRS-AM (nt) 638 West Port Plz, Saint Louis MO 63146 **Phn:** 314-453-5500 **Fax:** 314-453-9807 www.ktrs.com caspernews@townsquaremedia.com

Saint Louis KWMU-FM (pln) 1 University Blvd, Saint Louis MO 63121 **Phn:** 314-516-5968 **Fax:** 314-516-6397 kwmu.org news@stlpublicradio.org .

Saint Louis KWUR-FM (v) 1 Brookings Dr Box 1205, Saint Louis MO 63130 **Phn:** 314-935-5952 **Fax:** 314-935-8833 kwur.com gm@kwur.com

Saint Louis KXEN-AM (q) 5615 Pershing Ave # 112, Saint Louis IL 63112 **Phn:** 314-454-0400 **Fax:** 314-448-4999 www.kxen1010am.com info@kxen1010am.com

Saint Louis KYKY-FM (a) 1220 Olive St Flr 3, Saint Louis MO 63103 **Phn:** 314-531-0000 **Fax:** 314-531-9855 y98.cbslocal.com marty.linck@cbsradio.com

Saint Louis WARH-FM (a) 11647 Olive Blvd, Saint Louis MO 63141 **Phn:** 314-983-6000 **Fax:** 314-994-9447 www.1065thearch.com kevin@1065thearch.com

Saint Louis WEW-AM (y) 2740 Hampton Ave, Saint Louis MO 63139 **Phn:** 314-781-9397 **Fax:** 314-781-8545 www.wewradio.com wewradio@aol.com

Saint Louis WFUN-FM (ua) 9666 Olive Blvd Ste 610, Saint Louis MO 63132 **Phn:** 314-989-9550 **Fax:** 314-989-9551 oldschool955.com

Saint Louis WHHL-FM (ha) 9666 Olive Blvd Ste 610, Saint Louis MO 63132 **Phn:** 314-989-9550 **Fax:** 314-989-9551 hot1041stl.com

Saint Louis WIL-FM (c) 11647 Olive Blvd, Saint Louis MO 63141 **Phn:** 314-983-6000 **Fax:** 314-994-9421 www.wil92.com greg.mozingo@wil92.com

Saint Louis WRYT-AM (q) 4424 Hampton Ave, Saint Louis MO 63109 **Phn:** 314-752-7000 www.covenantnet.net covenantnetwork@juno.com

Saint Louis WSDD-FM (wx) 1001 Highlands Plaza Dr W, Saint Louis MO 63110 **Phn:** 314-333-8000 **Fax:** 314-333-8200 www.wild1049stl.com wild1049stl@clearchannel.com

Saint Louis WSDZ-AM (m) 1978 Innerbelt Business Center Dr, Saint Louis MO 63114 **Phn:** 314-428-4023 **Fax:** 314-428-9119 music.disney.com

Saint Louis WXOS-FM (s) 11647 Olive Blvd, Saint Louis MO 63141 **Phn:** 314-983-6000

Saint Robert KFLW-FM (h) 555 Marshall Dr, Saint Robert MO 65584 **Phn:** 573-336-5359 **Fax:** 573-336-7619 www.kflw989.com manager@ozarkmedia.com

Sainte Genevieve KSGM-AM (cnt) PO Box 428, Sainte Genevieve MO 63670 **Phn:** 573-883-2980 **Fax:** 573-883-2866 www.ksgm980.com news@suntimesnews.com

Salem KSMO-AM (csn) 800 S Main St, Salem MO 65560 **Phn:** 573-729-6117 **Fax:** 573-729-7337 www.ksmoradio.com info@ksmoradio.com

Sedalia KDRO-AM (c) 301 S Ohio Ave, Sedalia MO 65301 **Phn:** 660-826-5000 **Fax:** 660-826-5557 www.kdro.com charlie@kdro.com

Sedalia KPOW-FM (r) 301 S Ohio Ave, Sedalia MO 65301 **Phn:** 660-826-5005 **Fax:** 660-826-5557 www.power977.com sales@bennemedia.com

Sedalia KSDL-FM (a) 2209 S Limit Ave, Sedalia MO 65301 **Phn:** 660-826-1050 **Fax:** 660-827-5072 923bobfm.com doug.allen@townsquaremedia.com

Sedalia KSIS-AM (t) 2209 S Limit Ave, Sedalia MO 65301 **Phn:** 660-826-1050 **Fax:** 660-827-5072 www.ksisradio.com doug.allen@townsquaremedia.com

Sedalia KXKX-FM (c) 2209 S Limit Ave, Sedalia MO 65301 **Phn:** 660-826-1050 **Fax:** 660-827-5072 www.kxkx.com doug.allen@townsquaremedia.com

Sikeston KBXB-FM (c) 1 Industrial Dr, Sikeston MO 63801 **Phn:** 573-471-2000 www.b979.net gdavis@withersradio.net

Sikeston KRHW-AM (c) PO Box 907, Sikeston MO 63801 **Phn:** 573-471-2000

Springfield KBFL-FM (m) 3000 E Chestnut Expy, Springfield MO 65802 **Phn:** 417-862-3751 **Fax:** 417-869-7675 radiospringfield.com manager@radiospringfield.com

Springfield KGBX-FM (a) 1856 S Glenstone Ave, Springfield MO 65804 **Phn:** 417-890-5555 **Fax:** 417-890-5050 www.kgbx.com marybrown@clearchannel.com

Springfield KGMY-AM (s) 1856 S Glenstone Ave, Springfield MO 65804 **Phn:** 417-890-5555 **Fax:** 417-890-5050 www.espn1400.com brianedwards@clearchannel.com

Springfield KKLH-FM (r) 2453 E Elm St, Springfield MO 65802 **Phn:** 417-886-5677 **Fax:** 417-886-2155 www.hot967fm.com kluchs@nrgmedia.com

Springfield KOMG-FM (c) 2453 E Elm St, Springfield MO 65802 **Phn:** 417-886-5677 **Fax:** 417-886-2155 www.hot967fm.com kluchs@nrgmedia.com

Springfield KOSP-FM (o) 2453 E Elm St, Springfield MO 65802 **Phn:** 417-886-5677 **Fax:** 417-886-2155 www.929thebeat.com garfield@mwfmarketing.fm

Springfield KQRA-FM (r) 2453 E Elm St, Springfield MO 65802 **Phn:** 417-886-5677 **Fax:** 417-886-2155 www.hot967fm.com kluchs@nrgmedia.com

Springfield KSCV-FM (q) 1111 S Glenstone Ave Ste 3-102, Springfield MO 65804 **Phn:** 417-864-0901 **Fax:** 417-862-7263 www.bottradionetwork.com pschneider@bottradionetwork.com

Springfield KSGF-FM (nt) PO Box 2180, Springfield MO 65801 **Phn:** 417-865-6614 **Fax:** 417-865-9643 www.ksgf.com lwright@journalbroadcastgroup.com

Springfield KSGF-AM (nt) PO Box 2180, Springfield MO 65801 **Phn:** 417-865-6614 **Fax:** 417-865-9643 www.ksgf.com lwright@journalbroadcastgroup.com

Springfield KSMU-FM (pln) 901 S National Ave, Springfield MO 65897 **Phn:** 417-836-5878 **Fax:** 417-836-5889 www.ksmu.org ksmu@missouristate.edu

Springfield KSPW-FM (h) 2330 W Grand St, Springfield MO 65802 **Phn:** 417-862-9965 **Fax:** 417-865-9643 www.power965.com vknight@journalbroadcastgroup.com

Springfield KSWF-FM (c) 1856 S Glenstone Ave, Springfield MO 65804 **Phn:** 417-890-5555 **Fax:** 417-823-8505 www.1005thewolf.com studio@1005thewolf.com

Springfield KTOZ-FM (r) 1856 S Glenstone Ave, Springfield MO 65804 **Phn:** 417-890-5555 **Fax:** 417-890-5050 www.alice955.com tonymatteo@clearchannel.com

Springfield KTTS-FM (c) PO Box 2180, Springfield MO 65801 **Phn:** 417-447-1822 **Fax:** 417-865-9643 www.ktts.com vknight@journalbroadcastgroup.com

Springfield KTXR-FM (a) PO Box 3925, Springfield MO 65808 **Phn:** 417-862-3751 **Fax:** 417-869-7675 radiospringfield.com manager@radiospringfield.com

Springfield KWFC-FM (q) PO Box 8900, Springfield MO 65801 **Phn:** 417-869-0891 **Fax:** 417-866-7525 www.kwfc.org news@kwfc.org

Springfield KWND-FM (vq) 2550 S Campbell Ave Ste 100, Springfield MO 65807 **Phn:** 417-889-0883 **Fax:** 417-886-8656 88.3thewind.com sue@kwnd.com

Springfield KWTO-FM (s) PO Box 3793, Springfield MO 65808 **Phn:** 417-862-5600 **Fax:** 417-869-7675 www.jock987.net manager@radiospringfield.com

Springfield KWTO-AM (snt) PO Box 3793, Springfield MO 65808 **Phn:** 417-862-5600 **Fax:** 417-869-7675 radiospringfield.com manager@radiospringfield.com

Springfield KXUS-FM (r) 1856 S Glenstone Ave, Springfield MO 65804 **Phn:** 417-890-5555 **Fax:** 417-890-5050 www.us97.com paulkelley@clearchannel.com

Springfield KZRQ-FM (r) 2330 W Grand St, Springfield MO 65802 **Phn:** 417-865-6614 **Fax:** 417-865-9643 www.1067theriver.com rhansen@journalbroadcastgroup.com

Stockton KRWP-FM (c) PO Box 1070, Stockton MO 65785 **Phn:** 417-276-5253 **Fax:** 417-276-2255 ed.koca@cumulus.com

Sullivan KTUI-FM (sc) PO Box 99, Sullivan MO 63080 **Phn:** 573-468-5101 **Fax:** 573-468-5440 www.fidelitycommunications.comktui john@ktui.com

Sullivan KTUI-AM (nt) PO Box 99, Sullivan MO 63080 **Phn:** 573-468-5101 **Fax:** 573-468-5884 www.fidelitycommunications.comktui info@ktui.com

Trenton KGOZ-FM (c) 804 Main St, Trenton MO 64683 **Phn:** 660-359-2727 **Fax:** 660-359-4126

Trenton KTTN-AM (a) 804 Main St, Trenton MO 64683 **Phn:** 660-359-2261 **Fax:** 660-359-4126 www.kgozfm.com kttnamfm@grm.net

Trenton KTTN-FM (r) PO Box 307, Trenton MO 64683 **Phn:** 660-359-2261 **Fax:** 660-359-4126 www.kgozfm.com

Versailles KTKS-FM (c) PO Box 409, Versailles MO 65084 **Phn:** 573-378-5669 **Fax:** 573-378-6640 lakeradio.com ks95@lakeradio.net

Warrensburg KOKO-AM (o) PO Box 398, Warrensburg MO 64093 **Phn:** 660-747-9191 **Fax:** 660-747-5611 www.kwkj.com ghassler@kwkj.com

Warrensburg KTBG-FM (pj) Wood 11 Cmsu, Warrensburg MO 64093 **Phn:** 660-543-4130 **Fax:** 660-543-8863 www.ktbg.fm jhart@ktbg.fm

Warrensburg KWKJ-FM (h) PO Box 398, Warrensburg MO 64093 **Phn:** 660-747-9191 **Fax:** 660-747-5611 www.kwkj.com koko@kwkj.com

Warrenton KFAV-FM (c) PO Box 220, Warrenton MO 63383 **Phn:** 636-456-3311 **Fax:** 636-456-8767 www.kfav.com bevw@socket.net

Warrenton KWRE-AM (c) PO Box 220, Warrenton MO 63383 **Phn:** 636-377-2300 **Fax:** 636-456-8767 www.kwre.com kwrekfav@socket.net

Warsaw KAYQ-FM (c) PO Box 1420, Warsaw MO 65355 **Phn:** 660-438-7343 **Fax:** 660-438-7159 kayqtraffic@embarqmail.com

Washington KLPW-AM (nt) PO Box 623, Washington MO 63090 **Phn:** 636-583-4606 **Fax:** 636-583-1644 www.klpw.com marcy@klpw.com

Washington KLPW-FM (c) PO Box 623, Washington MO 63090 **Phn:** 636-583-4606 **Fax:** 636-583-1644 www.klpw.com marcy@klpw.com

Washington KSLQ-FM (a) 511 W 5th St, Washington MO 63090 **Phn:** 636-239-6800 www.kslq.co delta@kslq.com

Washington KWMO-AM (t) 511 W 5th St, Washington MO 63090 **Phn:** 636-239-6800 **Fax:** 636-239-3200

Waynesville KFBD-FM (r) PO Box D, Waynesville MO 65583 **Phn:** 573-336-4913 **Fax:** 573-336-2222 www.myozarksonline.com kjpw@regionalradio.com

Waynesville KIIK-AM (s) PO Box D, Waynesville MO 65583 **Phn:** 573-336-4913 **Fax:** 573-336-2222 www.myozarksonline.com medwards@regionalradio.com

Waynesville KJPW-AM (t) PO Box D, Waynesville MO 65583 **Phn:** 573-336-4913 **Fax:** 573-336-2222 www.myozarksonline.com kjpw@regionalradio.com

Waynesville KOZQ-AM (snt) PO Box D, Waynesville MO 65583 **Phn:** 573-336-4913 **Fax:** 573-336-2222 www.myozarksonline.com kjpw@regionalradio.com

Waynesville KOZQ-FM (r) PO Box D, Waynesville MO 65583 **Phn:** 573-336-4913 **Fax:** 573-336-2222 www.myozarksonline.com medwards@regionalradio.com

West Plains KBMV-FM (a) PO Box 107, West Plains MO 65775 **Phn:** 417-255-2548 **Fax:** 417-255-2907 thepoint@centurytel.net

West Plains KHOM-FM (c) PO Box 107, West Plains MO 65775 **Phn:** 417-255-2548 **Fax:** 417-255-2907 www.threeriversdailynews.com khom@centurytel.net

West Plains KKDY-FM (c) 983 E US Highway 160, West Plains MO 65775 **Phn:** 417-256-1025 **Fax:** 417-256-2208 www.kkdy.com news@ozarkradionetwork.com

West Plains KSPQ-FM (r) 983 E US Highway 160, West Plains MO 65775 **Phn:** 417-256-3131 **Fax:** 417-256-2208 www.ozarkareanetwork.com crystalc@ozarkradionetwork.com

West Plains KUKU-FM (ons) 983 E US Highway 160, West Plains MO 65775 **Phn:** 417-469-2500 **Fax:** 417-256-2208 ozarkareanetwork.com news@ozarkradionetwork.com

West Plains KUKU-AM (nt) 983 E US Highway 160, West Plains MO 65775 **Phn:** 417-469-2500 **Fax:** 417-256-2208 www.ozarkareanetwork.com crystalc@ozarkradionetwork.com

West Plains KWPM-AM (nt) 983 E US Highway 160, West Plains MO 65775 **Phn:** 417-256-3131 **Fax:** 417-256-2208 www.ozarkareanetwork.com crystalc@ozarkradionetwork.com

MONTANA

Anaconda KANA-AM (o) 105 Main St, Anaconda MT 59711 **Phn:** 406-563-8011 **Fax:** 406-494-5534 mail@magic97.mobi

Anaconda KGLM-FM (a) 105 Main St, Anaconda MT 59711 **Phn:** 406-563-8011 **Fax:** 406-494-5534 mail@magic97.mobi

Baker KFLN-AM (c) PO Box 790, Baker MT 59313 **Phn:** 406-778-3371 **Fax:** 406-778-3373 www.newellbroadcasting.com kfln@newellbroadcasting.com

Baker KJMM-AM (r) PO Box 790, Baker MT 59313 **Phn:** 406-778-3371 **Fax:** 406-778-3373

Belgrade KCMM-FM (qh) 2050 Amsterdam Rd, Belgrade MT 59714 **Phn:** 406-388-4281 **Fax:** 406-388-1700

Belgrade KGVW-AM (q) 2050 Amsterdam Rd, Belgrade MT 59714 **Phn:** 406-388-4281 **Fax:** 406-388-1700

Billings KBBB-FM (a) PO Box 1276, Billings MT 59103 **Phn:** 406-248-7827 **Fax:** 406-252-9577

Billings KBLG-AM (s) 2075 Central Ave Ste 5, Billings MT 59102 **Phn:** 406-652-8400 **Fax:** 406-652-4899 kblg910.com jseymour@connoisseurmedia.com

Billings KBUL-AM (nt) 27 N 27th St, Billings MT 59101 **Phn:** 406-248-7827 **Fax:** 406-252-9577 newstalk955.com donoylear@townsquaremedia.com

Billings KCTR-FM (c) 27 N 27th St, Billings MT 59101 **Phn:** 406-248-7827 **Fax:** 406-252-9577 catcountry1029.com donoylear@townsquaremedia.com

Billings KEMC-FM (pln) 1500 University Dr, Billings MT 59101 **Phn:** 406-657-2941 **Fax:** 406-657-2977 www.ypradio.org mail@ypradio.org

Billings KGHL-FM (c) 222 N 32nd St Ste 1001, Billings MT 59101 **Phn:** 406-238-1000 **Fax:** 406-238-1038 www.985thewolf.com pete.benedetti@benedettimedia.com

Billings KGHL-AM (c) 222 N 32nd St Ste 1001, Billings MT 59101 **Phn:** 406-238-1000 **Fax:** 406-238-1038 www.mighty790.com ntyler@northernbroadcasting.com

Billings KKBR-FM (h) 27 N 27th St Flr 23, Billings MT 59101 **Phn:** 406-248-7827 **Fax:** 406-252-9577 popcrush971.com donoylear@townsquaremedia.com

Billings KMHK-FM (r) PO Box 1276, Billings MT 59103 **Phn:** 406-248-7827 **Fax:** 406-252-9577 kmhk.com kmhk955@yahoo.com

Billings KPLN-FM (a) 101 Grand Ave, Billings MT 59101 **Phn:** 406-248-7777 **Fax:** 406-248-8577 www.planet1067.com planet@planet1067.com

Billings KQBL-FM (r) 222 N 32nd St Ste 1001, Billings MT 59101 **Phn:** 406-238-1000 **Fax:** 406-238-1038 benedettimedia.com pete.benedetti@benedettimedia.com

Billings KRKX-FM (r) 2075 Central Ave, Billings MT 59102 **Phn:** 406-248-7777 www.941ksky.com

Billings KRPM-FM (c) 222 N 32nd St, Billings MT 59101 **Phn:** 406-238-1000 **Fax:** 406-238-1038

Billings KRSQ-FM (h) 222 N 32nd St Fl 10, Billings MT 59101 **Phn:** 406-238-1000 **Fax:** 406-238-1038 www.hot1019.com

Billings KRZN-FM (r) 2075 Central Ave Ste 5, Billings MT 59102 **Phn:** 406-248-7777 963thezone.com

Billings KURL-AM (q) PO Box 30315, Billings MT 59107 **Phn:** 406-245-3121 **Fax:** 406-245-0822 www.kurlradio.com news@kurlradio.com

Billings KWMY-FM (h) 101 Grand Ave, Billings MT 59101 **Phn:** 406-248-7777 **Fax:** 406-248-8577 www.my1059.com cmaxwell@connoisseurmedia.com

Billings KYYA-AM (nt) 2075 Central Ave, Billings MT 59102 **Phn:** 406-652-8400 **Fax:** 406-652-4899 newstalk730.com jseymour@connoisseurmedia.com

Bozeman KBOZ-FM (c) PO Box 20, Bozeman MT 59719 **Phn:** 406-587-9999 **Fax:** 406-587-5855

Bozeman KBOZ-AM (nt) PO Box 20, Bozeman MT 59719 **Phn:** 406-587-9999 **Fax:** 406-587-5855

Bozeman KBZM-FM (r) 8274 Huffine Ln, Bozeman MT 59718 **Phn:** 406-582-1045 **Fax:** 406-582-0388 www.montanassuperstation.com jbalding@kbzm.com

Bozeman KGLT-FM (v) Msu Box 174240, Bozeman MT 59717 **Phn:** 406-994-3001 **Fax:** 406-994-1987 www.kglt.net

Bozeman KISN-FM (h) 125 W Mendenhall St, Bozeman MT 59715 **Phn:** 406-586-2343 **Fax:** 406-587-2202 bozemanskissfm.com chadwick@gapbroadcasting.com

Bozeman KKQX-FM (r) 8274 Huffine Ln, Bozeman MT 59718 **Phn:** 406-582-1045 **Fax:** 406-582-0388 www.montanassuperstation.com jbalding@kbzm.com

Bozeman KMMS-FM (r) 125 W Mendenhall St Ste 1, Bozeman MT 59715 **Phn:** 406-586-2343 **Fax:** 406-587-2202 mooseradio.com michellewolfe@townsquaremedia.com

MONTANA RADIO STATIONS

Bozeman KMMS-AM (nt) 125 W Mendenhall St Ste 1, Bozeman MT 59715 **Phn:** 406-586-2343 **Fax:** 406-587-2202 kmmsam.com chris@kmmsam.com

Bozeman KOBB-AM (a) PO Box 20, Bozeman MT 59719 **Phn:** 406-587-9999 **Fax:** 406-587-5855

Bozeman KOBB-FM (o) PO Box 20, Bozeman MT 59719 **Phn:** 406-587-9999 **Fax:** 406-587-5855

Bozeman KOZB-FM (r) PO Box 20, Bozeman MT 59719 **Phn:** 406-587-9999 **Fax:** 406-587-5855

Bozeman KXLB-FM (c) 125 W Mendenhall St, Bozeman MT 59715 **Phn:** 406-586-2343 **Fax:** 406-587-2202 xlcountry.com erinphillips@gapbroadcasting.com

Bozeman KZMY-FM (a) 125 W Mendenhall St, Bozeman MT 59715 **Phn:** 406-586-2343 **Fax:** 406-587-2202 my1035.com erinphillips@townsquaremedia.com

Butte KAAR-FM (c) 750 Dewey Blvd Ste 1, Butte MT 59701 **Phn:** 406-494-4442 **Fax:** 406-494-6020 www.925kaar.com cackerman@cherrycreekradio.com

Butte KMBR-FM (r) 750 Dewey Blvd Ste 1, Butte MT 59701 **Phn:** 406-494-4442 **Fax:** 406-494-6020 www.955kmbr.com cackerman@cherrycreekradio.com

Butte KMSM-FM (v) 1301 W Park St, Butte MT 59701 **Phn:** 406-496-4601

Butte KOPR-FM (a) PO Box 3389, Butte MT 59702 **Phn:** 406-494-4777 **Fax:** 406-494-5534

Butte KXTL-AM (ot) 750 Dewey Blvd Ste 1, Butte MT 59701 **Phn:** 406-494-4442 **Fax:** 406-494-6020 www.kxtl.com cackerman@cherrycreekradio.com

Deer Lodge KBCK-AM (c) 302 Missouri Ave, Deer Lodge MT 59722 **Phn:** 406-846-1100 **Fax:** 406-846-1636

Deer Lodge KQRV-FM (c) 302 Missouri Ave, Deer Lodge MT 59722 **Phn:** 406-846-1100

Dillon KBEV-FM (a) 610 N Montana St, Dillon MT 59725 **Phn:** 406-683-2800 **Fax:** 406-683-9480 www.kdbm-kbev.com joann@kdbm-kbev.com

Dillon KDBM-AM (c) 610 N Montana St Ste 5, Dillon MT 59725 **Phn:** 406-683-2800 **Fax:** 406-683-9480 www.kdbm-kbev.com joann@kdbm-kbev.com

Forsyth KIKC-AM (o) PO Box 1140, Forsyth MT 59327 **Phn:** 406-346-2711 **Fax:** 406-346-2712

Forsyth KIKC-FM (c) PO Box 1140, Forsyth MT 59327 **Phn:** 406-346-2711 **Fax:** 406-346-2712 newsdesk@kxgn.com

Glasgow KLAN-FM (a) PO Box 671, Glasgow MT 59230 **Phn:** 406-228-9336 **Fax:** 406-228-9338 www.kltz.com kltz@kltz.com

Glasgow KLTZ-AM (c) PO Box 671, Glasgow MT 59230 **Phn:** 406-228-9336 **Fax:** 406-228-9338 www.kltz.com kltz@kltz.com

Glendive KDZN-FM (c) 210 S Douglas St, Glendive MT 59330 **Phn:** 406-377-3377 **Fax:** 406-365-2181 www.kxgn.com newsdesk@kxgn.com

Glendive KGLE-AM (q) PO Box 931, Glendive MT 59330 **Phn:** 406-377-3331 **Fax:** 406-377-3332 www.kgle.org kgle@midrivers.com

Glendive KXGN-AM (a) 210 S Douglas St, Glendive MT 59330 **Phn:** 406-377-3377 **Fax:** 406-365-2181 www.kxgn.com kxgnkdzn@midrivers.com

Great Falls KAAK-FM (h) 20 3rd St N Ste 231, Great Falls MT 59401 **Phn:** 406-761-7600 **Fax:** 406-761-5511

Great Falls KEIN-AM (a) PO Box 1239, Great Falls MT 59403 **Phn:** 406-761-1310 **Fax:** 406-454-3775

Great Falls KGPR-FM (pln) 2100 16th Ave S, Great Falls MT 59405 **Phn:** 406-268-3739 **Fax:** 406-268-3736 kgpr.msugf.edu info@kgpr.org

Great Falls KIKF-FM (c) 1300 Central Ave W, Great Falls MT 59404 **Phn:** 406-761-2800 **Fax:** 406-727-7218 www.1049wolf.com

Great Falls KLFM-FM (rh) PO Box 3309, Great Falls MT 59403 **Phn:** 406-761-7600 **Fax:** 406-727-6753 corywells@cherrycreekradio.com

Great Falls KMON-FM (c) 20 3rd St N Ste 231, Great Falls MT 59401 **Phn:** 406-761-7600 **Fax:** 406-761-5511

Great Falls KMON-AM (cfn) 20 3rd St N Ste 231, Great Falls MT 59401 **Phn:** 406-761-7600 **Fax:** 406-761-5511 rkorb@cherrycreekradio.com

Great Falls KQDI-FM (r) 1300 Central Ave W, Great Falls MT 59404 **Phn:** 406-761-2800 **Fax:** 406-727-7218 www.q106rocks.com jsenst@staradio.com

Great Falls KQDI-AM (nt) 1300 Central Ave W, Great Falls MT 59403 **Phn:** 406-761-2800 **Fax:** 406-727-7218 www.newstalk1450.com jsenst@staradio.com

Great Falls KVVR-FM (a) PO Box 3309, Great Falls MT 59403 **Phn:** 406-761-7600 **Fax:** 406-761-5511 www.kvvr.com rkorb@cherrycreekradio.com

Great Falls KXGF-AM (st) PO Box 3129, Great Falls MT 59403 **Phn:** 406-727-7211 **Fax:** 406-727-7218

Hamilton KLYQ-AM (nt) PO Box 660, Hamilton MT 59840 **Phn:** 406-363-3010 **Fax:** 406-363-6436 klyq.com contact@klyq.com

Hardin KHDN-AM (nt) PO Box 230, Hardin MT 59034 **Phn:** 406-665-2828 **Fax:** 406-665-2131 www.bigskyradio.net rich@bigskyradio.net

Havre KGFC-FM (q) PO Box 2426, Havre MT 59501 **Phn:** 406-265-5845 **Fax:** 406-265-8860 www.ynop.org info@ynop.org

Havre KOJM-AM (a) 2210 31st St N, Havre MT 59501 **Phn:** 406-265-7841 **Fax:** 406-265-8855 www.kojm.com nmb@nmbi.com

Havre KPQX-FM (c) 2210 31st St N, Havre MT 59501 **Phn:** 406-265-7841 **Fax:** 406-265-8855 www.kpqx.com nmb@nmbi.com

Havre KRYK-FM (a) 2210 31st St N, Havre MT 59501 **Phn:** 406-265-7841 **Fax:** 406-265-8855 www.kryk.com nmb@nmbi.com

Havre KXEI-FM (q) PO Box 2426, Havre MT 59501 **Phn:** 406-265-5845 **Fax:** 406-265-8860 www.ynop.org psa@ynop.org

Helena KBLL-AM (nt) 110 E Broadway St, Helena MT 59601 **Phn:** 406-442-4490 **Fax:** 406-442-7356 www.kbllradio.com kbllam@cherrycreekradio.com

Helena KBLL-FM (c) 110 E Broadway St, Helena MT 59601 **Phn:** 406-442-4490 **Fax:** 406-442-7356 www.kbllradio.com kbllfm@cherrycreekradio.com

Helena KCAP-AM (snt) 110 E Broadway St, Helena MT 59601 **Phn:** 406-442-4490 **Fax:** 406-442-7356 www.kcap.com tcronen@cherrycreekradio.com

Helena KHKR-FM (c) PO Box 4111, Helena MT 59604 **Phn:** 406-442-4490 **Fax:** 406-442-7356 www.khkr.com tcronen@cherrycreekradio.com

Helena KKGR-AM (o) 1400 11th Ave Ste 10, Helena MT 59601 **Phn:** 406-443-5237 **Fax:** 406-442-6161

Helena KMTX-AM (h) PO Box 1183, Helena MT 59624 **Phn:** 406-442-0400 **Fax:** 406-442-0491

Helena KMTX-FM (a) PO Box 1183, Helena MT 59624 **Phn:** 406-442-0400 **Fax:** 406-442-0491

Helena KZMT-FM (r) 110 E Broadway St, Helena MT 59601 **Phn:** 406-442-4490 **Fax:** 406-442-7356 www.kzmt.com sevans@cherrycreekradio.com

Kalispell KALS-FM (q) 106 Cooperative Way Ste 102, Kalispell MT 59901 **Phn:** 406-752-5257 **Fax:** 406-752-3416 www.kals.com kals@kals.com

Kalispell KBBZ-FM (ar) PO Box 5409, Kalispell MT 59903 **Phn:** 406-755-8700 **Fax:** 406-755-8770 www.kbbz.com brew@1051cool.com

Kalispell KDBR-FM (c) PO Box 5409, Kalispell MT 59903 **Phn:** 406-755-8700 **Fax:** 406-755-8770 www.kdbr.com thebear@beebroadcasting.com

Kalispell KHNK-FM (c) PO Box 5409, Kalispell MT 59903 **Phn:** 406-755-8700 **Fax:** 406-755-8770 www.myhank.com hank@myhank.com

Kalispell KJJR-AM (nt) PO Box 5409, Kalispell MT 59903 **Phn:** 406-756-5557 www.kjjr.com kjjr@beebroadcasting.com

Kalispell KOFI-AM (nto) 317 1st Ave, Kalispell MT 59901 **Phn:** 406-755-6690 **Fax:** 406-752-5078 www.kofiradio.com info@kofiradio.com

Kalispell KZMN-FM (r) PO Box 608, Kalispell MT 59903 **Phn:** 406-755-6690 **Fax:** 406-752-5078 www.monster1039.com djmusic@monster1039.com

Laurel KBSR-AM (sna) PO Box 248, Laurel MT 59044 **Phn:** 406-665-2828 www.bigskyradio.net rich@bigskyradio.net

Lewistown KLCM-FM (r) 620 NE Main St, Lewistown MT 59457 **Phn:** 406-535-3441 **Fax:** 406-535-3495 www.kxlo-klcm.com news@kxlo-klcm.com

Lewistown KXLO-AM (c) 620 NE Main St, Lewistown MT 59457 **Phn:** 406-535-3441 **Fax:** 406-535-3495 www.kxlo-klcm.com news@kxlo-klcm.com

Libby KLCB-AM (c) PO Box 730, Libby MT 59923 **Phn:** 406-293-6234 **Fax:** 406-293-6235 www.klcb-ktny.com klcb@frontiernet.net

Libby KTNY-FM (ah) PO Box 730, Libby MT 59923 **Phn:** 406-293-6234 **Fax:** 406-293-6235 www.klcb-ktny.com klcb@frontiernet.net

Livingston KPRK-AM (or) PO Box 1340, Livingston MT 59047 **Phn:** 406 222-1340 **Fax:** 406 222-1341

Malta KMMR-FM (m) PO Box 1073, Malta MT 59538 **Phn:** 406-654-2472 **Fax:** 406-654-2506 www.kmmrfm.com kmmrfm@itstriangle.com

Miles City KATL-AM (a) PO Box 700, Miles City MT 59301 **Phn:** 406-234-7700 **Fax:** 406-234-7783 www.katlradio.com katlradio@katlradio.com

Miles City KMTA-AM (a) 508 Main St, Miles City MT 59301 **Phn:** 406-234-5626 **Fax:** 406-874-7000 www.kyuskmta.com newsdesk@kxgn.com

Miles City KYUS-FM (a) 508 Main St, Miles City MT 59301 **Phn:** 406-234-5626 **Fax:** 406-874-7000 www.kyuskmta.com newsdesk@kxgn.com

Missoula KBAZ-FM (r) 3250 S Reserve St # 200, Missoula MT 59801 **Phn:** 406-728-9300 **Fax:** 406-542-2329 963theblaze.com kc@963theblaze.com

Missoula KBGA-FM (vr) University Ctr # 208, Missoula MT 59812 **Phn:** 406-243-6758 **Fax:** 406-243-6428

Missoula KBQQ-FM (o) 1600 North Ave W Ste 101, Missoula MT 59801 **Phn:** 406-728-5000 **Fax:** 406-721-3020 www.b1067.net mweber@cherrycreekradio.com

Missoula KDTR-FM (r) 2425 W Central Ave Ste 203, Missoula MT 59801 **Phn:** 406-721-6800 www.trail1033.com robert@montanaradio.com

Missoula KGGL-FM (c) 1600 North Ave, Missoula MT 59803 **Phn:** 406-728-1450 **Fax:** 406-721-3020 www.eagle93.com

Missoula KGRZ-AM (st) PO Box 4106, Missoula MT 59806 Phn: 406-728-1450 Fax: 406-721-3020

Missoula KGVO-AM (snt) 3250 S Reserve St # 200, Missoula MT 59801 Phn: 406-728-9300 Fax: 406-542-2329 newstalkkgvo.com kgvonewsroom@townsquaremedia.com

Missoula KHKM-FM (c) 1600 North Ave, Missoula MT 59803 Phn: 406-728-5000 Fax: 406-721-3020 www.thehawkclassiccountry.com tom@thehawkclassiccountry.com

Missoula KKVU-FM (a) 2425 W Central Ave Ste 203, Missoula MT 59801 Phn: 406-721-6800 Fax: 406-329-1850 www.u1045.com leah@montanaradio.com

Missoula KMPT-AM (t) 3250 S Reserve St # 200, Missoula MT 59801 Phn: 406-728-9300 Fax: 406-542-2329

Missoula KMSO-FM (a) 725 Strand Ave, Missoula MT 59801 Phn: 406-542-1025 Fax: 406-721-1036 www.moclub.com news@mtnbdc.com

Missoula KSCY-FM (c) 2425 W Central Ave Ste 203, Missoula MT 59801 Phn: 406-582-1045 Fax: 406-582-0388

Missoula KUFM-FM (plj) 32 Campus Dr, Missoula MT 59812 Phn: 406-243-4931 Fax: 406-243-3299 www.kufm.org news@mtpr.org

Missoula KXDR-FM (a) 1600 North Ave, Missoula MT 59803 Phn: 406-728-5000 Fax: 406-721-3020 www.1067starfm.com

Missoula KYLT-AM (t) PO Box 4106, Missoula MT 59806 Phn: 406-728-5000 Fax: 406-721-3020

Missoula KYSS-FM (c) 3250 S Reserve St # 200, Missoula MT 59801 Phn: 406-728-9300 Fax: 406-542-2329 kyssfm.com realcountry@kyssfm.com

Missoula KZOQ-FM (r) 1600 North Ave W, Missoula MT 59801 Phn: 406-728-5000 Fax: 406-721-3020 www.z100missoula.com

Plentywood KATQ-AM (c) 112 E 3rd Ave, Plentywood MT 59254 Phn: 406-765-1480 Fax: 406-765-2357 katqradio.com katq@nemont.net

Plentywood KATQ-FM (r) 112 E 3rd Ave, Plentywood MT 59254 Phn: 406-765-1480 Fax: 406-765-2357 katqradio.com katq@nemont.net

Polson KERR-AM (c) 36581 N Reservoir Rd, Polson MT 59860 Phn: 406-883-5255 Fax: 406-883-4441 www.750kerr.com kerrnews@750kerr.com

Red Lodge KMXE-FM (r) PO Box 1678, Red Lodge MT 59068 Phn: 406-446-1199 Fax: 406-446-1978 www.fm99mtn.com fm99office@starband.net

Scobey KCGM-FM (c) PO Box 220, Scobey MT 59263 Phn: 406-487-2293 Fax: 406-487-5922 kcgm@nemontel.net

Shelby KSEN-AM (os) 830 Oilfield Ave, Shelby MT 59474 Phn: 406-434-5241 Fax: 406-434-2122 ksenam.com ksen@gapbroadcasting.com

Shelby KZIN-FM (c) 830 Oilfield Ave, Shelby MT 59474 Phn: 406-434-5241 Fax: 406-434-2122 k96fm.com annejames@townsquaremedia.com

Sidney KGCX-FM (r) 213 2nd Ave SW, Sidney MT 59270 Phn: 406-433-5429 Fax: 406-433-5430 newsdesk@kxgn.com

Sidney KTHC-FM (a) 120 E Main St Ste 13, Sidney MT 59270 Phn: 406-433-5090 Fax: 406-433-5095 www.kthcradio.com

Wolf Point KVCK-FM (c) 324 Main St Ste 1, Wolf Point MT 59201 Phn: 406-653-1900 Fax: 406-653-1909 kvckradio.com kvck@nemont.net

MONTANA RADIO STATIONS

Wolf Point KVCK-AM (h) 324 Main St Ste 1, Wolf Point MT 59201 Phn: 406-653-1900 Fax: 406-653-1909 kvckradio.com kvck@nemont.net

NEBRASKA

Ainsworth KBRB-AM (ac) PO Box 285, Ainsworth NE 69210 Phn: 402-387-1400 Fax: 402-387-2624 www.kbrbradio.com kbrb@sscg.net

Ainsworth KBRB-FM (ac) PO Box 285, Ainsworth NE 69210 Phn: 402-387-1400 Fax: 402-387-2624 www.kbrbradio.com kbrb@sscg.net

Alliance KAAQ-FM (c) PO Box 600, Alliance NE 69301 Phn: 308-762-1400 Fax: 308-762-7804 www.panhandlepost.com

Alliance KCOW-AM (ont) PO Box 600, Alliance NE 69301 Phn: 308-762-1400 Fax: 308-762-7804 www.panhandlepost.com

Beatrice KWBE-AM (fan) PO Box 10, Beatrice NE 68310 Phn: 402-228-5923 Fax: 402-228-3704 www.kwbe.com kwbe@diodecom.net

Broken Bow KBBN-FM (r) PO Box 409, Broken Bow NE 68822 Phn: 308-872-5881 Fax: 308-872-3284 www.kbbn.com

Broken Bow KCNI-AM (c) PO Box 409, Broken Bow NE 68822 Phn: 308-872-5881 Fax: 308-872-3284 www.kbbn.com

Chadron KCNB-FM (a) PO Box 1117, Chadron NE 69337 Phn: 308-432-2060 Fax: 308-432-2059 www.panhandlepost.com

Chadron KCSR-AM (c) 226 Bordeaux St, Chadron NE 69337 Phn: 308-432-5545 Fax: 308-432-5601 www.chadrad.com kcsr@chadrad.com

Chadron KQSK-FM (c) PO Box 1117, Chadron NE 69337 Phn: 308-432-2060 Fax: 308-432-2059 www.doubleqcountry.com

Columbus KJSK-AM (snt) 1418 25th St, Columbus NE 68601 Phn: 402-564-2866 Fax: 402-564-1999 www.mycentralnebraska.com kjsk@megavision.com

Columbus KKOT-FM (h) 1418 25th St, Columbus NE 68601 Phn: 402-564-2866 Fax: 402-564-2867 sgossweiler@threeeagles.com

Columbus KLIR-FM (a) 1418 25th St, Columbus NE 68601 Phn: 402-564-2866 Fax: 402-564-1999 klir@columbus.threeeagles.com

Columbus KTLX-FM (vq) 2200 25th St Ste 1, Columbus NE 68601 Phn: 402-564-8548 Fax: 402-562-6003

Columbus KTTT-AM (nt) 1418 25th St, Columbus NE 68601 Phn: 402-564-2866 Fax: 402-564-2867

Columbus KZEN-FM (c) 1418 25th St, Columbus NE 68601 Phn: 402-564-2866 Fax: 402-564-2867 newskzen@kzen.threeeagles.com

Crete KDNE-FM (vr) 1014 Boswell Ave, Crete NE 68333 Phn: 402-826-8677 www.doane.edufacstaffmediakdne kdne@doane.edu

Fairbury KGMT-AM (a) 414 4th St, Fairbury NE 68352 Phn: 402-729-3382 Fax: 402-729-3446 www.kutt995.com kuttnews@diodecom.net

Fairbury KUTT-FM (c) 414 4th St, Fairbury NE 68352 Phn: 402-729-3382 Fax: 402-729-3446 www.kutt995.com kutt@diodecom.net

Falls City KLZA-FM (a) PO Box 101, Falls City NE 68355 Phn: 402-245-6010 Fax: 402-245-6040 www.sunny1013.com sunny1013fm@hotmail.com

Falls City KTNC-AM (o) 1602 Stone St, Falls City NE 68355 Phn: 402-245-2453 Fax: 402-245-6040 www.ktncradio.com ktnc@sentco.net

Fremont KFMT-FM (r) PO Box 669, Fremont NE 68026 Phn: 402-721-1340 Fax: 402-721-5023 myfremontradio.com dmeyer@myfremontradio.com

Fremont KHUB-AM (snt) PO Box 669, Fremont NE 68026 Phn: 402-721-1340 Fax: 402-721-5023 myfremontradio.com dmeyer@myfremontradio.com

Gordon KSDZ-FM (ch) PO Box 390, Gordon NE 69343 Phn: 308-282-2500 Fax: 308-282-0061 www.ksdzfm.com thetwister@ksdzfm.com

Grand Island KRGI-AM (nt) 3205 W North Front St, Grand Island NE 68803 Phn: 308-381-1430 Fax: 308-382-6701 newsacrossnebraska.com

Grand Island KRGI-FM (c) 3205 W North Front St, Grand Island NE 68803 Phn: 308-381-1430 Fax: 308-382-6701 www.hometownfamilyradio.com news@hometownfamilyradio.com

Grand Island KRGY-FM (a) 3205 W North Front St, Grand Island NE 68803 Phn: 308-381-1430 Fax: 308-382-6701 www.hometownfamilyradio.com news@hometownfamilyradio.com

Grand Island KROR-FM (r) PO Box 5108, Grand Island NE 68802 Phn: 308-381-1077 Fax: 308-384-8900 www.rock1015.com tmarshall@nrgmedia.com

Grand Island KSYZ-FM (a) 3532 W Capital Ave, Grand Island NE 68803 Phn: 308-381-1077 Fax: 308-384-8900 1077theisland.com

Hastings KCNT-FM (v) PO Box 1024, Hastings NE 68902 Phn: 402-461-2580 Fax: 402-461-2507 members.tripod.com~KCNT_FM kcntfm@cccneb.edu

Hastings KFKX-FM (vr) 710 N Turner Ave, Hastings NE 68901 Phn: 402-461-7367 Fax: 402-461-7480

Hastings KHAS-AM (a) PO Box 726, Hastings NE 68902 Phn: 402-462-5101 Fax: 402-461-3866 hastingslink.com news@khasradio.com

Hastings KICS-AM (s) PO Box 726, Hastings NE 68902 Phn: 402-462-5101 Fax: 402-461-3866 espnsuperstation.com news@khasradio.com

Hastings KLIQ-FM (a) 500 E J St, Hastings NE 68901 Phn: 402-461-4922 Fax: 402-461-3866 www.kliqfm.com thebreeze@kliqfm.com

Holdrege KMTY-FM (o) PO Box 465, Holdrege NE 68949 Phn: 308-995-4020 Fax: 308-995-2202 plainsreporter.k2radio.net randy@highplainsradio.net

Holdrege KUVR-AM (a) PO Box 465, Holdrege NE 68949 Phn: 308-995-4122 Fax: 308-995-2202 newsacrossnebraska.com randy@highplainsradio.net

Kearney KGFW-AM (t) PO Box 669, Kearney NE 68848 Phn: 308-698-2100 Fax: 308-237-0312 kgfw.com saltmaier@nrgmedia.com

Kearney KKPR-FM (o) PO Box 130, Kearney NE 68848 Phn: 308-236-9900 Fax: 308-234-6781 www.kkpr.com generalmanager@kkpr.com

Kearney KLPR-FM (vjr) Univ Of NE, Kearney NE 68849 Phn: 308-865-8217 mcluhan.unk.eduklpr scholwinem@unk.edu

Kearney KQKY-FM (h) 2223 Central Ave, Kearney NE 68847 Phn: 308-698-2100 Fax: 308-698-2112 www.kqky.com swhite@nrgmedia.com

Kearney KRNY-FM (c) 2223 Central Ave, Kearney NE 68847 Phn: 308-698-2100 Fax: 308-237-0312 www.krny.com swhite@nrgmedia.com

Kearney KXPN-AM (st) PO Box 130, Kearney NE 68848 Phn: 308-236-9900 Fax: 308-234-6781 www.espnsuperstation.com generalmanager@espnsuperstation.com

Lexington KRVN-AM (c) PO Box 880, Lexington NE 68850 Phn: 308-324-2371 Fax: 308-324-5786 www.krvn.com krvnam@krvn.com

NEBRASKA RADIO STATIONS

Lexington KRVN-FM (c) PO Box 880, Lexington NE 68850 **Phn:** 308-324-2371 **Fax:** 308-324-5786 www.krvn.com dlane@krvn.com

Lincoln KBBK-FM (a) 4343 O St, Lincoln NE 68510 **Phn:** 402-475-4567 **Fax:** 402-479-1411 www.b1073.com salbertsen@broadcasthouse.com

Lincoln KCVN-FM (q) 233 S 13th St Ste 1520, Lincoln NE 68508 **Phn:** 402-465-8850 **Fax:** 402-465-8852 www.bottradionetwork.com klcv@bottradionetwork.com

Lincoln KFGE-FM (c) 4343 O St, Lincoln NE 68510 **Phn:** 402-475-4567 **Fax:** 402-479-1411 www.froggy981.com andyr@broadcasthouse.com

Lincoln KFOR-AM (nt) 3800 Cornhusker Hwy, Lincoln NE 68504 **Phn:** 402-466-1234 **Fax:** 402-467-4095 www.kfor1240.com mtaylor@threeeagles.com

Lincoln KFRX-FM (h) 3800 Cornhusker Hwy, Lincoln NE 68504 **Phn:** 402-466-1234 **Fax:** 402-467-4095 www.kfrxfm.com

Lincoln KIBZ-FM (r) 3800 Cornhusker Hwy, Lincoln NE 68504 **Phn:** 402-466-1234 **Fax:** 402-467-4095 www.kibz.com blaze@kibz.com

Lincoln KLCV-FM (qt) 233 S 13th St Ste 1520, Lincoln NE 68508 **Phn:** 402-465-8850 **Fax:** 402-465-8852 www.bottradionetwork.com klcv@bottradionetwork.com

Lincoln KLIN-AM (nt) 4343 O St, Lincoln NE 68510 **Phn:** 402-475-4567 **Fax:** 402-479-1412 www.klin.com jbishop@broadcasthouse.com

Lincoln KLMS-AM (s) 3800 Cornhusker Hwy, Lincoln NE 68504 **Phn:** 402-466-1234 **Fax:** 402-467-4095 www.espn1480.com cgoforth@threeeagles.com

Lincoln KLNC-FM (h) 4343 O St, Lincoln NE 68510 **Phn:** 402-475-4567 **Fax:** 402-479-1411 www.1053wow.com salbertsen@broadcasthouse.com

Lincoln KRNU-FM (v) PO Box 880466, Lincoln NE 68588 **Phn:** 402-472-3054 **Fax:** 402-472-8403 krnu.unl.edu krnu@unl.edu

Lincoln KROA-FM (q) PO Box 30345, Lincoln NE 68503 **Phn:** 888-627-1020 www.mybridgeradio.net email@mybridgeradio.net

Lincoln KTGL-FM (r) 3800 Cornhusker Hwy, Lincoln NE 68504 **Phn:** 402-466-1234 **Fax:** 402-467-4095 www.ktgl.com clinville@ktgl.com

Lincoln KUCV-FM (plnj) 1800 N 33rd St, Lincoln NE 68503 **Phn:** 402-472-3611 **Fax:** 402-472-2403 netnebraska.org dkellogg@netnebraska.org

Lincoln KZKX-FM (c) 3800 Cornhusker Hwy, Lincoln NE 68504 **Phn:** 402-466-1234 **Fax:** 402-489-9607 www.kzkx.com jp@kzkx.com

Lincoln KZUM-FM (v) 941 O St Ste 1025, Lincoln NE 68508 **Phn:** 402-474-5086 **Fax:** 402-474-5091 www.kzum.org gm@kzum.org

McCook KBRL-AM (t) PO Box 333, McCook NE 69001 **Phn:** 308-345-5400 **Fax:** 308-345-4720 www.plainsreporter.com openline@highplainsradio.net

McCook KFNF-FM (c) 1811 W O St, McCook NE 69001 **Phn:** 308-345-5400 **Fax:** 308-345-4720 plainsreporter.k2radio.net kfnf@kicx.net

McCook KICX-FM (a) 1811 W O St, McCook NE 69001 **Phn:** 308-345-5400 **Fax:** 308-345-4720 www.plainsreporter.com rich@highplainsradio.net

McCook KIOD-FM (c) PO Box 939, McCook NE 69001 **Phn:** 308-345-1981 **Fax:** 308-345-7202 newsacrossnebraska.com

McCook KNGN-AM (q) 38005 Road 717, McCook NE 69001 **Phn:** 308-345-2006 **Fax:** 308-345-2052 www.kngn.org jim@kngn.org

McCook KQHK-FM (r) PO Box 333, McCook NE 69001 **Phn:** 308-345-5400 **Fax:** 308-345-4720 www.plainsreporter.com openline@highplainsradio.net

McCook KSWN-FM (h) PO Box 939, McCook NE 69001 **Phn:** 308-345-1100 **Fax:** 308-345-7202 newsacrossnebraska.com

Nebraska City KNCY-FM (c) 814 Central Ave, Nebraska City NE 68410 **Phn:** 402-873-3348 **Fax:** 402-873-7882 www.kncycountry.com kncy@kncycountry.com

Nebraska City KNCY-AM (c) 814 Central Ave, Nebraska City NE 68410 **Phn:** 402-873-3348 **Fax:** 402-873-7882 www.kncycountry.com nateg@kncycountry.com

Norfolk KEXL-FM (a) PO Box 789, Norfolk NE 68702 **Phn:** 402-371-0780 **Fax:** 402-371-6303 www.literock97.com susan@wjag.com

Norfolk KNEN-FM (r) PO Box 747, Norfolk NE 68702 **Phn:** 402-379-3300 **Fax:** 402-379-3008 www.94rock.fm 94rock@94rock.fm

Norfolk KPNO-FM (q) 109 S 2nd St, Norfolk NE 68701 **Phn:** 402-379-3677 **Fax:** 402-379-3662

Norfolk KQKX-FM (c) PO Box 789, Norfolk NE 68702 **Phn:** 402-371-0780 **Fax:** 402-371-6303 jsteffen@kexl.com

Norfolk KUSO-FM (c) PO Box 747, Norfolk NE 68702 **Phn:** 402-371-0100 **Fax:** 402-371-0050 www.us92.com news@us92.com

Norfolk WJAG-AM (nt) PO Box 789, Norfolk NE 68702 **Phn:** 402-371-0780 **Fax:** 402-371-6303 wjag.com susan@wjag.com

North Platte KELN-FM (a) PO Box 248, North Platte NE 69103 **Phn:** 308-532-1120 **Fax:** 308-532-0458 www.northplattepost.com

North Platte KJLT-FM (q) PO Box 709, North Platte NE 69103 **Phn:** 308-532-5515 **Fax:** 308-532-5516 www.kjlt.org kjlt@kjlt.org

North Platte KJLT-AM (q) PO Box 709, North Platte NE 69103 **Phn:** 308-532-5515 **Fax:** 308-532-5516 www.kjlt.org kjlt@kjlt.org

North Platte KODY-AM (nt) PO Box 1085, North Platte NE 69103 **Phn:** 308-534-6650 **Fax:** 308-534-6651 plainsreporter.k2radio.net tlama@huskeradio.com

North Platte KOOQ-AM (s) PO Box 248, North Platte NE 69103 **Phn:** 308-532-1120 **Fax:** 308-532-0458 www.northplattepost.com

North Platte KXNP-FM (c) PO Box 1085, North Platte NE 69103 **Phn:** 308-534-6650 **Fax:** 308-534-6651 huskeradio.com gkeltz@huskeradio.com

O'Neill KMMJ-AM (q) 128 S 4th St, O'Neill NE 68763 **Phn:** 888-920-5665 www.kmmj.org kmmj@kmmj.org

Ogallala KMCX-FM (c) PO Box 509, Ogallala NE 69153 **Phn:** 308-284-3633 **Fax:** 308-284-3517 www.kmcx.com johnmarquis@clearchannel.com

Ogallala KOGA-AM (o) PO Box 509, Ogallala NE 69153 **Phn:** 308-284-3633 **Fax:** 308-284-3517 www.930koga.com johnmarquis@clearchannel.com

Ogallala KOGA-FM (r) PO Box 509, Ogallala NE 69153 **Phn:** 308-284-3633 **Fax:** 308-284-3517 www.997thelake.com davebradley@clearchannel.com

Omaha KBBX-FM (y) 11128 John Galt Blvd Ste 25, Omaha NE 68137 **Phn:** 402-884-0968 **Fax:** 402-884-4754 www.radiolobo977.com mschoonover@connoisseurmedia.com

Omaha KCRO-AM (qt) 11717 Burt St Ste 202, Omaha NE 68154 **Phn:** 402-422-1600 **Fax:** 402-422-1602 www.kcro.com public@kcro.com

Omaha KEZO-FM (r) 5030 N 72nd St, Omaha NE 68134 **Phn:** 402-592-5300 **Fax:** 402-898-5487 www.z92.com jessica@z92.com

Omaha KFAB-AM (nt) 5010 Underwood Ave, Omaha NE 68132 **Phn:** 402-561-2000 **Fax:** 402-556-8937 www.kfab.com tomstanton@clearchannel.com

Omaha KFFF-FM (c) 5010 Underwood Ave, Omaha NE 68132 **Phn:** 402-561-2000 **Fax:** 402-556-8937 www.wolfradio933.com heathhedstrom@clearchannel.com

Omaha KGBI-FM (q) 11717 Burt St Ste 202, Omaha NE 68154 **Phn:** 402-422-1600 **Fax:** 402-422-1602 www.kgbifm.com kgbi@kgbifm.com

Omaha KGOR-FM (o) 5010 Underwood Ave, Omaha NE 68132 **Phn:** 402-561-2000 **Fax:** 402-556-9999 www.kgor.com tomstanton@clearchannel.com

Omaha KIOS-FM (pln) 3230 Burt St, Omaha NE 68131 **Phn:** 402-557-2777 **Fax:** 402-557-2559 www.kios.org news@kios.org

Omaha KKAR-AM (t) 5011 Capitol Ave, Omaha NE 68132 **Phn:** 402-342-2000 **Fax:** 402-827-5293 www.mighty1290koil.com nnelkin@nrgmedia.com

Omaha KKCD-FM (hr) 5030 N 72nd St, Omaha NE 68134 **Phn:** 402-592-5300 **Fax:** 402-592-6605 www.cd1059.com jspector@journalbroadcastgroup.com

Omaha KOIL-AM (snt) 5011 Capitol Ave, Omaha NE 68132 **Phn:** 402-342-2000 **Fax:** 402-342-6146 1620thezone.com nnelkin@nrgmedia.com

Omaha KOOO-FM (ar) 5011 Capitol Ave, Omaha NE 68132 **Phn:** 402-342-2000 **Fax:** 402-342-5874 www.whatever1019.com kkohls@nrgmedia.com

Omaha KOPW-FM (h) 5011 Capitol Ave, Omaha NE 68132 **Phn:** 402-342-2000 **Fax:** 402-342-5874 www.power1069fm.com aruback@nrgmedia.com

Omaha KOTK-AM (qy) 11717 Burt St Ste 202, Omaha NE 68154 **Phn:** 402-422-1600 **Fax:** 402-422-1602 www.1420kotk.com anunez@salemomaha.com

Omaha KOZN-AM (s) 5011 Capitol Ave, Omaha NE 68132 **Phn:** 402-342-2000 **Fax:** 402-342-5874 www.1620thezone.com nnelkin@nrgmedia.com

Omaha KQBW-FM (r) 5010 Underwood Ave, Omaha NE 68132 **Phn:** 402-561-2000 www.961kissonline.com erikjohnson3@clearchannel.com

Omaha KQCH-FM (h) 10714 Mockingbird Dr, Omaha NE 68127 **Phn:** 402-592-5300 **Fax:** 402-898-5487 www.channel941.com mtodd@journalbroadcastgroup.com

Omaha KQKQ-FM (h) 5011 Capitol Ave, Omaha NE 68132 **Phn:** 402-342-2000 **Fax:** 402-342-6146 www.q985fm.com jenny@q985fm.com

Omaha KSRZ-FM (an) 5030 N 72nd St, Omaha NE 68134 **Phn:** 402-592-5300 **Fax:** 402-898-5487 www.104star.com jpmiller@journalbroadcastgroup.com

Omaha KTWI-FM (c) 5010 Underwood Ave, Omaha NE 68132 **Phn:** 402-561-2000 **Fax:** 402-556-8937 www.wolfradio933.com erikjohnson3@clearchannel.com

Omaha KVNO-FM (p) 6001 Dodge St Unit 200, Omaha NE 68182 **Phn:** 402-559-5866 **Fax:** 402-554-2440 www.kvno.org dbuckingham@unomaha.edu

Omaha KVSS-FM (q) 13326 A St, Omaha NE 68114 **Phn:** 402-571-0200 **Fax:** 402-571-0833 www.spiritcatholicradio.com kvss@kvss.com

Omaha KXKT-FM (c) 5010 Underwood Ave, Omaha NE 68132 **Phn:** 402-561-2000 **Fax:** 402-556-8937 www.TheKat.com ej@thekat.com

Omaha KXSP-AM (s) 10714 Mockingbird Dr, Omaha NE 68127 **Phn:** 402-592-5300 **Fax:** 402-898-5487 www.am590espnradio.com kowens@jrn.com

Oneill KBRX-AM (r) PO Box 150, Oneill NE 68763 **Phn:** 402-336-1612 **Fax:** 402-336-3585 www.kbrx.com news@kbrx.com

Oneill KBRX-FM (c) PO Box 150, Oneill NE 68763 **Phn:** 402-336-1612 **Fax:** 402-336-3585 www.kbrx.com scott@kbrx.com

Oneill KGRD-FM (q) 128 S 4th St, Oneill NE 68763 **Phn:** 402-336-3886 www.goodnewsgreatmusic.org email@goodnewsgreatmusic.org

Ord KNLV-AM (o) 205 S 16th St, Ord NE 68862 **Phn:** 308-728-3263 **Fax:** 308-728-3264 www.knlvradio.com knlvnews@yahoo.com

Ord KNLV-FM (c) 205 S 16th St, Ord NE 68862 **Phn:** 308-728-3263 **Fax:** 308-728-3264 www.knlvradio.com knlvnews@yahoo.com

Scottsbluff KBFZ-FM (o) PO Box 1263, Scottsbluff NE 69363 **Phn:** 308-632-5667 **Fax:** 308-635-1905

Scottsbluff KCMI-FM (q) 209 E 15th St, Scottsbluff NE 69361 **Phn:** 308-632-5264 **Fax:** 308-635-0104 kcmifm.org contact@kcmifm.com

Scottsbluff KETT-FM (r) PO Box 1263, Scottsbluff NE 69363 **Phn:** 308-632-5667 **Fax:** 308-635-1905

Scottsbluff KHYY-FM (c) PO Box 1263, Scottsbluff NE 69363 **Phn:** 308-632-5667 **Fax:** 308-635-1905

Scottsbluff KMOR-FM (r) PO Box 1263, Scottsbluff NE 69363 **Phn:** 308-632-5667 **Fax:** 308-635-1905

Scottsbluff KNEB-FM (c) PO Box 239, Scottsbluff NE 69363 **Phn:** 308-632-7121 **Fax:** 308-635-1079 www.kneb.com kmooney@kneb.com

Scottsbluff KNEB-AM (nt) PO Box 239, Scottsbluff NE 69363 **Phn:** 308-632-7121 **Fax:** 308-635-1079 www.kneb.com dernest@kneb.com

Scottsbluff KOAQ-AM (o) PO Box 1263, Scottsbluff NE 69363 **Phn:** 308-635-2690 **Fax:** 308-635-1905

Scottsbluff KOLT-AM (snt) PO Box 1263, Scottsbluff NE 69363 **Phn:** 308-635-1320 **Fax:** 308-635-1905

Scottsbluff KOLT-FM (c) PO Box 1263, Scottsbluff NE 69363 **Phn:** 308-632-5667 **Fax:** 308-635-1905 www.koltcountry.com kolt@nazbestradio.com

Sidney KSID-AM (c) PO Box 37, Sidney NE 69162 **Phn:** 308-254-5803 **Fax:** 308-254-5901 www.ksidradio.com dave@ksidradio.com

Sidney KSID-FM (ar) PO Box 37, Sidney NE 69162 **Phn:** 308-254-5803 **Fax:** 308-254-5901 www.ksidradio.com dave@ksidradio.com

Superior KRFS-AM (c) 630 W 8th St, Superior NE 68978 **Phn:** 402-879-4741

Superior KRFS-FM (c) 630 W 8th St, Superior NE 68978 **Phn:** 402-879-4741

Valentine KVSH-AM (arc) 126 W 3rd St, Valentine NE 69201 **Phn:** 402-376-2400 **Fax:** 402-376-2402 kvsh.com mike@kvsh.com

Wayne KCTY-FM (c) PO Box 413, Wayne NE 68787 **Phn:** 402-375-3700 **Fax:** 402-375-5402 www.waynedailynews.com ktch@ktch.com

Wayne KTCH-AM (c) PO Box 413, Wayne NE 68787 **Phn:** 402-375-3700 **Fax:** 402-375-5402 www.waynedailynews.com ktch@ktch.com

West Point KTIC-AM (cf) PO Box 84, West Point NE 68788 **Phn:** 402-372-5423 **Fax:** 402-372-5425 www.kticam.com dlane@kticradio.com

NEBRASKA RADIO STATIONS

West Point KTIC-FM (c) PO Box 84, West Point NE 68788 **Phn:** 402-372-5423 **Fax:** 402-372-5425 www.kticam.com tharrington@kticradio.com

York KAWL-AM (o) 1309 Road 11, York NE 68467 **Phn:** 402-362-4433 **Fax:** 402-362-6501 www.ktmxfm.com kawl@kawlam.com

York KTMX-FM (a) 1309 Road 11, York NE 68467 **Phn:** 402-362-4433 **Fax:** 402-362-6501 www.hitsandfavorites.com kawl@kawlam.com

NEVADA

Carson City KCMY-AM (c) 1960 Idaho St, Carson City NV 89701 **Phn:** 775-884-8000 **Fax:** 775-882-3961

Carson City KKFT-FM (t) 1960 Idaho St, Carson City NV 89701 **Phn:** 775-884-8000 **Fax:** 775-882-3961 www.991fmtalk.com jerry@991fmtalk.com

Carson City KNIS-FM (q) 6363 Hwy 50 East, Carson City NV 89701 **Phn:** 775-883-5647 www.pilgrimradio.com info@pilgrimradio.com

Elko KEBG-AM (c) 1750 Manzanita Dr Ste 1, Elko NV 89801 **Phn:** 775-777-1196 **Fax:** 775-777-9587 rubyradio.fm news@rubyradio.fm

Elko KELK-AM (a) 1800 Idaho St, Elko NV 89801 **Phn:** 775-738-1240 **Fax:** 775-753-5556 www.elkoradio.com

Elko KHIX-FM (a) 1750 Manzanita Dr Ste 1, Elko NV 89801 **Phn:** 775-777-1196 **Fax:** 775-777-9587 www.bigcountry.fm news@rubyradio.fm

Elko KLKO-FM (r) 1800 Idaho St, Elko NV 89801 **Phn:** 775-738-1240 **Fax:** 775-753-5556 www.elkoradio.com

Elko KOYT-FM (r) 1750 Manzanita Dr Ste 1, Elko NV 89801 **Phn:** 775-777-1196 **Fax:** 775-777-9587 rubyradio.fm news@rubyradio.fm

Elko KRJC-FM (c) 1250 Lamoille Hwy Ste 1045, Elko NV 89801 **Phn:** 775-738-9895 **Fax:** 775-753-8085 www.krjc.com julie@krjc.com

Elko KTSN-AM (snt) 1250 Lamoille Hwy Ste 1045, Elko NV 89801 **Phn:** 775-738-9895 **Fax:** 775-753-8085

Ely KDSS-FM (c) 501 Aultman St Ste 2, Ely NV 89301 **Phn:** 775-289-6474 **Fax:** 775-289-6531 kdssfm@sbcglobal.net

Fallon KKTU-FM (a) 1155 Gummow Dr, Fallon NV 89406 **Phn:** 775-423-2243 **Fax:** 775-423-8889 www.kvlvradio.com kvlv@phonewave.net

Fallon KVLV-AM (c) 1155 Gummow Dr, Fallon NV 89406 **Phn:** 775-423-2243 **Fax:** 775-423-8889 www.kvlvradio.com kvlv@phonewave.net

Las Vegas KBAD-AM (st) 8755 W Flamingo Rd, Las Vegas NV 89147 **Phn:** 702-876-1460 **Fax:** 702-876-6685 www.werlv.com espnradio1100@gmail.com

Las Vegas KCEP-FM (wv) 330 W Washington Ave, Las Vegas NV 89106 **Phn:** 702-648-0104 **Fax:** 702-647-0803 kcep.power88lv.com power88@power88lv.com

Las Vegas KCYE-FM (c) 1455 E Tropicana Ave Ste 800, Las Vegas NV 89119 **Phn:** 702-730-0300 **Fax:** 702-736-8447 www.kcye.com justin.chase@bbgilv.com

Las Vegas KDOX-AM (nt) 150 Spectrum Blvd, Las Vegas NV 89101 **Phn:** 702-258-0285 **Fax:** 702-258-7570 www.foxnews1280.com jdawes@smiradio.com

Las Vegas KDWN-AM (snt) 1456 E Tropicana Ave Ste 800, Las Vegas NV 89119 **Phn:** 702-730-0300 **Fax:** 702-262-5639 www.kdwn.com news@kdwn.com

Las Vegas KENO-AM (ns) 8755 W Flamingo Rd, Las Vegas NV 89147 **Phn:** 702-876-1460 **Fax:** 702-876-6685 www.espn1100.com espnradio1100@gmail.com

Las Vegas KFRH-FM (h) 6725 Via Austi Pkwy # 200, Las Vegas NV 89119 **Phn:** 702-546-5000 www.1043now.com

Las Vegas KISF-FM (y) 6767 W Tropicana Ave Ste 102, Las Vegas NV 89103 **Phn:** 702-284-6400 **Fax:** 702-284-6403 www.univision.com joseramonbravo@univision.com

Las Vegas KJUL-FM (a) 150 Spectrum Blvd, Las Vegas NV 89101 **Phn:** 702-258-0285 **Fax:** 702-258-7570 www.kjul1047.com scott@smiradio.com

Las Vegas KKLZ-FM (r) 1455 E Tropicana Ave Ste 800, Las Vegas NV 89119 **Phn:** 702-730-0300 **Fax:** 702-736-8447 www.963kklz.com justin.chase@bbgilv.com

Las Vegas KKVV-AM (qt) 3185 S Highland Dr Ste 13, Las Vegas NV 89109 **Phn:** 702-731-5588 **Fax:** 702-731-5851 www.kkvv.com kkvvradio@kkvv.com

Las Vegas KLAV-AM (nt) 6655 W Sahara Ave #C216, Las Vegas NV 89146 **Phn:** 702-796-1230 **Fax:** 702-853-2597 www.klav1230am.com robin.covey@lvradio.com

Las Vegas KLSQ-AM (y) 6767 W Tropicana Ave Ste 102, Las Vegas NV 89103 **Phn:** 702-284-6400 **Fax:** 702-284-6403 www.univision.com

Las Vegas KLUC-FM (h) 7255 S Tenaya Way # 100, Las Vegas NV 89113 **Phn:** 702-253-9800 **Fax:** 702-889-7373 kluc.cbslocal.com cat@kluc.com

Las Vegas KMXB-FM (a) 7255 S Tenaya Way # 100, Las Vegas NV 89113 **Phn:** 702-257-9400 **Fax:** 702-257-2936 mix941fm.cbslocal.com charese.fruge@cbsradio.com

Las Vegas KNPR-FM (pnt) 1289 S Torrey Pines Dr, Las Vegas NV 89146 **Phn:** 702-258-9895 **Fax:** 702-258-5646 www.knpr.org info@knpr.org

Las Vegas KOAS-FM (aj) 1455 E Tropicana Ave Ste 800, Las Vegas NV 89119 **Phn:** 702-784-4000 **Fax:** 702-784-4040 www.1057theoasis.com cory.cuddeback@bbgilv.com

Las Vegas KOMP-FM (r) 8755 W Flamingo Rd, Las Vegas NV 89147 **Phn:** 702-876-1460 **Fax:** 702-876-6685 www.komp.com komp@komp.com

Las Vegas KPLV-FM (h) 2880 Meade Ave Ste 250, Las Vegas NV 89102 **Phn:** 702-238-7300 **Fax:** 702-732-4890 www.my931.com

Las Vegas KQRT-FM (y) 500 Pilot Rd Ste D, Las Vegas NV 89119 **Phn:** 702-597-3070 **Fax:** 702-507-1084 www.entravision.com croman@entravision.com

Las Vegas KRGT-FM (y) 6767 W Tropicana Ave Ste 102, Las Vegas NV 89103 **Phn:** 702-284-6400 **Fax:** 702-284-6475 www.univision.com

Las Vegas KRRN-FM (hy) 500 Pilot Rd Ste D, Las Vegas NV 89119 **Phn:** 323-900-6100 www.jose927.com croman@entravision.com

Las Vegas KSHP-AM (st) 2400 S Jones Blvd Ste 3, Las Vegas NV 89146 **Phn:** 702-221-1200 **Fax:** 702-221-2285 www.kshp.com mail@kshp.com

Las Vegas KSNE-FM (a) 2880 Meade Ave Ste 250, Las Vegas NV 89102 **Phn:** 702-238-7300 **Fax:** 702-732-4890 www.sunny1065.com tomchase@clearchannel.com

Las Vegas KSOS-FM (q) 2201 S 6th St, Las Vegas NV 89104 **Phn:** 702-731-5452 www.sosradio.net info@sosradio.net

Las Vegas KUNV-FM (vj) 4505 S Maryland Pkwy, Las Vegas NV 89154 **Phn:** 702-895-0065 **Fax:** 702-895-0068 kunv.org kim.linzy@unlv.edu

Las Vegas KVEG-FM (xh) 3999 Las Vegas Blvd S Ste K, Las Vegas NV 89119 **Phn:** 702-736-6161 **Fax:** 702-736-2986 www.kvegas.com

Las Vegas KVGS-FM (au) 1455 E Tropicana Ave Ste 800, Las Vegas NV 89119 **Phn:** 702-784-4000 **Fax:** 702-784-4040 www.1079bob.com cory.cuddeback@bbgilv.com

Las Vegas KWID-FM (y) 3755 W Flamingo Rd, Las Vegas NV 89102 **Phn:** 702-238-7300 **Fax:** 702-732-4890

Las Vegas KWNR-FM (c) 2880 Meade Ave Ste 250, Las Vegas NV 89102 **Phn:** 702-238-7300 **Fax:** 702-732-4890 www.955thebull.com

Las Vegas KWWN-AM (s) 8755 W Flamingo Rd, Las Vegas NV 89147 **Phn:** 702-876-1460 **Fax:** 702-876-6685 www.espn1100.com

Las Vegas KXNT-AM (nt) 6655 W Sahara Ave Ste D110, Las Vegas NV 89146 **Phn:** 702-889-7300 **Fax:** 702-889-7384 lasvegas.cbslocal.com joe.gillespie@cbsradio.com

Las Vegas KXPT-FM (r) 8755 W Flamingo Rd, Las Vegas NV 89147 **Phn:** 702-876-1460 **Fax:** 702-876-6685 www.point97.com info@point97.com

Las Vegas KXTE-FM (r) 7255 South Tenaya Way # 1000, Las Vegas NV 89113 **Phn:** 702-257-1075 **Fax:** 702-889-7595 x1075lasvegas.cbslocal.com charese.fruge@cbsradio.com

Pahrump KNYE-FM (o) 1230 Dutch Ford St, Pahrump NV 89048 **Phn:** 775-537-6100 **Fax:** 775-751-6193 www.knye.com knye@knye.com

Reno KBUL-FM (c) 595 E Plumb Ln, Reno NV 89502 **Phn:** 775-789-6700 **Fax:** 775-789-6767 www.kbul.com jay.schell@cumulus.com

Reno KBZZ-AM (s) 961 Matley Ln Ste 120, Reno NV 89502 **Phn:** 775-829-1964 **Fax:** 775-825-3183 www.renosportsradio.com dcook@renomediagroup.com

Reno KDOT-FM (r) 2900 Sutro St, Reno NV 89512 **Phn:** 775-329-9261 **Fax:** 775-323-1450 www.kdot.com javep@kdot.com

Reno KHIT-AM (s) 2900 Sutro St, Reno NV 89512 **Phn:** 775-329-9261 **Fax:** 775-323-1450 kena@lotusradio.com

Reno KJZS-FM (aj) 300 E 2nd St Ste 1400, Reno NV 89501 **Phn:** 775-333-0123 **Fax:** 775-322-7361 www.smoothjazzreno.com amattingly@wilksreno.com

Reno KKOH-AM (nt) 595 E Plumb Ln, Reno NV 89502 **Phn:** 775-789-6700 **Fax:** 775-789-6767 www.kkoh.com news@kkoh.com

Reno KLCA-FM (a) 961 Matley Ln Ste 120, Reno NV 89502 **Phn:** 775-829-1964 **Fax:** 775-825-3183 www.alice965.com

Reno KMXW-FM (r) 300 E 2nd St Ste 1400, Reno NV 89501 **Phn:** 775-333-0123 **Fax:** 775-322-7361 www.renosmix.com

Reno KNEV-FM (a) 595 E Plumb Ln, Reno NV 89502 **Phn:** 775-789-6700 **Fax:** 775-789-6767 www.magic95.com doug.daniels@cumulus.com

Reno KODS-FM (or) 961 Matley Ln Ste 120, Reno NV 89502 **Phn:** 775-829-1964 **Fax:** 775-825-3183 www.river1037.com beej@alice965.com

Reno KOLC-FM (a) 961 Matley Ln Ste 120, Reno NV 89502 **Phn:** 775-829-1964 **Fax:** 775-825-3183 www.littlecity973.com info@littlecity973.com

Reno KOZZ-FM (r) 2900 Sutro St, Reno NV 89512 **Phn:** 775-329-9261 **Fax:** 775-323-1450 www.kozzradio.com max@lotusradio.com

Reno KPLY-AM (s) 2900 Sutro St, Reno NV 89512 **Phn:** 775-329-9261 **Fax:** 775-323-1450 kena@lotusradio.com

NEVADA RADIO STATIONS

Reno KRNO-FM (r) 961 Matley Ln Ste 120, Reno NV 89502 **Phn:** 775-829-1964 **Fax:** 775-825-3183 www.sunny1069.com info@sunny1069.com

Reno KRNV-FM (y) 300 S Wells Ave Ste 12, Reno NV 89502 **Phn:** 775-333-1017 **Fax:** 775-333-9046 www.tricolor1021.com vcody@entravision.com

Reno KTHX-FM (ar) 300 E 2nd St Ste 1400, Reno NV 89501 **Phn:** 775-333-0123 **Fax:** 775-322-7361 www.kthxfm.com rob@kthxfm.com

Reno KUNR-FM (plnj) Mail Stop 0294 Univ Of Nevada, Reno NV 89557 **Phn:** 775-682-6300 **Fax:** 775-327-5386 www.kunr.org news@kunr.org

Reno KURK-FM (h) 300 E 2nd St Ste 1400, Reno NV 89501 **Phn:** 775-333-0123 **Fax:** 775-322-7361 www.929thebandit.com aperini@wilksreno.com

Reno KUUB-FM (c) 2900 Sutro St, Reno NV 89512 **Phn:** 775-329-9261 **Fax:** 775-323-1450 dane@lotusradio.com

Reno KWYL-FM (h) 595 E Plumb Ln, Reno NV 89502 **Phn:** 775-789-6700 **Fax:** 775-789-6767 www.wild1029.com r.boogie@cumulus.com

Reno KXEQ-AM (y) 225 Linden St, Reno NV 89502 **Phn:** 775-827-1111 **Fax:** 775-827-2082

Reno KZTQ-FM (a) 961 Matley Ln Ste 120, Reno NV 89502 **Phn:** 775-829-1964 **Fax:** 775-825-3183 www.bob937.com webmaster@bob937.com

Stateline KOWL-AM (snt) 276 Kingsbury Grade # 203, Stateline NV 89449 **Phn:** 775-580-7130 **Fax:** 775-580-7131 www.krltfm.com steve@krltfm.com

Wadsworth KRNG-FM (qr) PO Box 490, Wadsworth NV 89442 **Phn:** 775-575-7777 www.renegaderadio.org email@renegaderadio.org

Winnemucca KELY-AM (nt) PO Box 1400, Winnemucca NV 89446 **Phn:** 775-289-2077 **Fax:** 775-289-6997

Winnemucca KWNA-AM (o) PO Box 1400, Winnemucca NV 89446 **Phn:** 775-623-5203 **Fax:** 775-625-1011 kwnaradio@gmail.com

Winnemucca KWNA-FM (c) PO Box 1400, Winnemucca NV 89446 **Phn:** 775-623-5203 **Fax:** 775-625-1011 kwnanews@gmail.com

Zephyr Cove KRLT-FM (a) PO Box 11101, Zephyr Cove NV 89448 **Phn:** 775-580-7130 www.krltfm.com steve@krltfm.com

NEW HAMPSHIRE

Berlin WMOU-AM (a) 297 Pleasant St, Berlin NH 03570 **Phn:** 603-752-1230 **Fax:** 603-788-3636

Bow WLKZ-FM (o) 501 South St, Bow NH 03304 **Phn:** 603-545-0777 **Fax:** 603-545-0781 www.thehawkrocks.com jtyler@greateasternradio.com

Bow WTPL-FM (nts) 501 South St Ste 301A, Bow NH 03304 **Phn:** 603-545-0777 **Fax:** 603-545-0781 www.wtplfm.com news@wtplfm.com

Concord WEVH-FM (pln) 2 Pillsbury St Fl 6, Concord NH 03301 **Phn:** 603-228-8910 **Fax:** 603-224-6052 www.nhpr.org

Concord WEVO-FM (pln) 2 Pillsbury St Ste 600, Concord NH 03301 **Phn:** 603-228-8910 **Fax:** 603-224-6052 www.nhpr.org

Concord WVNH-FM (q) 37 Redington Rd, Concord NH 03301 **Phn:** 603-227-0911 www.wvnh.org info@nhgr.org

Conway WBNC-AM (n) PO Box 2008, Conway NH 03818 **Phn:** 603-356-8870 **Fax:** 603-356-8875 conwaymagic.com office@conwaymagic.com

Conway WMWV-FM (a) PO Box 2008, Conway NH 03818 **Phn:** 603-356-8870 **Fax:** 603-356-8875 www.wmwv.com office@wmwv.com

Conway WVMJ-FM (a) PO Box 2008, Conway NH 03818 **Phn:** 603-356-8870 **Fax:** 603-356-8875 conwaymagic.com office@conwaymagic.com

Derry WDER-AM (q) 8 Lawrence Rd, Derry NH 03038 **Phn:** 603-437-9337 **Fax:** 603-434-1035 lifechangingradio.comwder info@wder.com

Dover WBYY-FM (a) PO Box 400, Dover NH 03821 **Phn:** 603-742-0987 **Fax:** 603-742-0448 www.987thebay.com thegreat987@ttlc.net

Dover WOKQ-FM (c) PO Box 576, Dover NH 03821 **Phn:** 603-749-9750 **Fax:** 603-749-1459 www.wokq.com mail@wokq.com

Dover WPKQ-FM (c) PO Box 576, Dover NH 03821 **Phn:** 603-749-9750 **Fax:** 603-749-1459 www.wokq.com don.briand@cumulus.com

Dover WSAK-FM (r) PO Box 576, Dover NH 03821 **Phn:** 603-749-2766 **Fax:** 603-749-6589 www.shark1053.com shark.mail@cumulus.com

Dover WSHK-FM (r) PO Box 576, Dover NH 03821 **Phn:** 603-749-2776 **Fax:** 603-749-1459 shark1053.com shark.mail@cumulus.com

Dover WTSN-AM (snt) PO Box 400, Dover NH 03821 **Phn:** 603-742-1270 **Fax:** 603-742-0448 www.wtsnam1270.com mike@wtsnam1270.com

Durham WUNH-FM (v) U Of Nh Union Bldg, Durham NH 03824 **Phn:** 603-862-2222 www.wunh.org program@wunh.org

Exeter WPEA-FM (v) 20 Main St, Exeter NH 03833 **Phn:** 603-777-4414 exeter.edustudent_life9671.aspx wpea@exeter.edu

Franklin WFTN-AM (ob) PO Box 941, Franklin NH 03235 **Phn:** 603-934-2500 **Fax:** 603-934-2933 amy@mix941fm.com

Franklin WFTN-FM (a) PO Box 941, Franklin NH 03235 **Phn:** 603-934-2500 **Fax:** 603-934-2933 www.mix941fm.com amy@mix941fm.com

Franklin WPNH-AM (a) PO Box 99, Franklin NH 03235 **Phn:** 888-536-9764 **Fax:** 603-934-2933 jefff@mix941fm.com

Franklin WPNH-FM (r) PO Box 99, Franklin NH 03235 **Phn:** 603-536-2500 **Fax:** 603-934-2933 www.wpnhfm.com annie@wpnhfm.com

Franklin WSCY-FM (c) PO Box 99, Franklin NH 03235 **Phn:** 603-934-2500 **Fax:** 603-934-2933 www.wscy.com joyce@wscy.com

Gilford WJYY-FM (h) PO Box 7326, Gilford NH 03249 **Phn:** 603-224-8486 **Fax:** 603-528-5185 wjyy.nh1media.com adukette@binradio.com

Gilford WWHQ-FM (r) 25 Country Club Rd, Gilford NH 03249 **Phn:** 603-524-1323 **Fax:** 603-528-5185

Hanover WDCR-AM (r) 6176 Robinson Hall, Hanover NH 03755 **Phn:** 603-646-3313 **Fax:** 603-643-7655 www.wfrd.com whelan.j.boyd.13@dartmouth.edu

Hanover WFRD-FM (r) 6176 Robinson Hall, Hanover NH 03755 **Phn:** 603-646-3313 **Fax:** 603-643-7655 www.wfrd.com christopher.zhao.13@dartmouth.edu

Henniker WNEC-FM (v) 196 Bridge St, Henniker NH 03242 **Phn:** 603-428-2278

Keene WINQ-FM (c) 69 Stanhope Ave, Keene NH 03431 **Phn:** 603-352-9230 **Fax:** 603-357-3926 987wink.com bcox@monadnockradiogroup.com

Keene WKBK-AM (snt) 69 Stanhope Ave, Keene NH 03431 **Phn:** 603-352-9230 **Fax:** 603-357-3926 wkbkradio.com bcox@monadnockradiogroup.com

Keene WKNE-FM (nt) 69 Stanhope Ave, Keene NH 03431 **Phn:** 603-352-9230 **Fax:** 603-357-3926 wkne.com shamel@monadnockradiogroup.com

Keene WKNH-FM (vr) 226 Main St, Keene NH 03435 **Phn:** 603-358-2421 wknh.tumblr.com wknhkeene@gmail.com

Keene WZBK-AM (a) 69 Stanhope Ave, Keene NH 03431 **Phn:** 603-352-9230 **Fax:** 603-357-3926 www.musicofyourlife.com dmitchell@monadnockradiogroup.com

Laconia WEMJ-AM (snt) PO Box 7326, Laconia NH 03247 **Phn:** 603-524-1323 **Fax:** 603-528-5185

Laconia WEZS-AM (nt) 277 Union Ave Ste 205, Laconia NH 03246 **Phn:** 603-524-6288 www.wezs.com staff@wezs.com

Laconia WNHW-FM (c) PO Box 7326, Laconia NH 03247 **Phn:** 603-524-1323 **Fax:** 603-528-5185 wnhw.nh1media.com

Lebanon WGXL-FM (a) 31 Hanover St Ste 4, Lebanon NH 03766 **Phn:** 603-448-1400 **Fax:** 603-448-1755 www.wgxl.com bfranklin@greateasternradio.com

Lebanon WMXR-FM (c) 31 Hanover St Ste 4, Lebanon NH 03766 **Phn:** 603-448-1400 **Fax:** 603-448-1755 www.maxx939.com wcaswell@uppervalleyradio.com

Lebanon WUVR-AM (nt) 103 Hanover St, Lebanon NH 03766 **Phn:** 603-448-0500 www.wntk.com info@wntk.com

Lebanon WVRR-FM (r) 31 Hanover St Ste 4, Lebanon NH 03766 **Phn:** 603-448-1400 **Fax:** 603-448-1755

Lebanon WXXK-FM (c) 31 Hanover St Ste 4, Lebanon NH 03766 **Phn:** 603-448-1400 **Fax:** 603-448-5231 www.kixx.com wcaswell@uppervalleyradio.com

Littleton WLTN-AM (o) 15 Main St Ste 3E, Littleton NH 03561 **Phn:** 603-444-3911 **Fax:** 603-444-7186

Littleton WLTN-FM (a) 15 Main St Ste 3E, Littleton NH 03561 **Phn:** 603-444-3911 **Fax:** 603-444-7186 mix967@adelphia.net

Littleton WMTK-FM (r) PO Box 106, Littleton NH 03561 **Phn:** 603-444-5106 **Fax:** 603-444-1205

Manchester WFEA-AM (a) 500 North Commercial St, Manchester NH 03101 **Phn:** 603-669-5777 **Fax:** 603-668-3299 www.wfea1370.com raydionh@wzid.com

Manchester WGIR-AM (snt) 195 McGregor St Ste 810, Manchester NH 03102 **Phn:** 603-625-6915 **Fax:** 603-625-9255 www.nhnewsnetwork610.com jeffpierce@clearchannel.com

Manchester WGIR-FM (r) 195 McGregor St Ste 810, Manchester NH 03102 **Phn:** 603-625-6915 **Fax:** 603-625-9255 www.rock101fm.com laura@morningbuzz.com

Manchester WMLL-FM (r) 500 North Commercial St, Manchester NH 03101 **Phn:** 603-669-5777 **Fax:** 603-668-3299 www.965themill.com raydionh@wzid.com

Manchester WZID-FM (a) 500 North Commercial St, Manchester NH 03101 **Phn:** 603-669-5777 **Fax:** 603-668-3299 wzid.com raydionh@wzid.com

Nashua WFNQ-FM (h) 20 Industrial Park Dr, Nashua NH 03062 **Phn:** 603-889-1063 **Fax:** 603-882-0688 wfnq.nh1media.com cgarrett@binradio.com

Nashua WNNH-FM (o) 20 Industrial Park Dr Ste 1, Nashua NH 03062 **Phn:** 603-225-1160 **Fax:** 603-225-5938

Nashua WWHK-FM (r) 20 Industrial Park Dr Ste 1, Nashua NH 03062 **Phn:** 603-225-1160 **Fax:** 603-225-5938

NEW HAMPSHIRE RADIO STATIONS

New London WNTK-FM (t) PO Box 2295, New London NH 03257 **Phn:** 603-448-0500 **Fax:** 603-526-2824 www.wntk.com info@wntk.com

New London WNTK-AM (t) PO Box 2295, New London NH 03257 **Phn:** 603-448-0500 **Fax:** 603-448-6601

New London WSCS-FM (v) 541 Main St, New London NH 03257 **Phn:** 603-526-3493 **Fax:** 603-526-3452 www.colby-sawyer.edu/wscs wscs@colby-sawyer.edu

Newport WCNL-AM (c) 11 Main St, Newport NH 03773 **Phn:** 603-863-0080 **Fax:** 603-448-6601 www.country1010.com steve@country1010.com

Portsmouth WERZ-FM (ahr) 815 Lafayette Rd, Portsmouth NH 03801 **Phn:** 603-436-7300 **Fax:** 603-430-9415 www.z107fm.com jefferypierce@clearchannel.com

Portsmouth WHEB-FM (r) 815 Lafayette Rd, Portsmouth NH 03801 **Phn:** 603-436-7300 **Fax:** 603-430-9415 www.wheb.com laura@morningbuzz.com

Portsmouth WMYF-AM (s) 815 Lafayette Rd, Portsmouth NH 03801 **Phn:** 603-436-7300 **Fax:** 603-430-9415 www.sportsanimalnh.com jefferypierce@clearchannel.com

Portsmouth WQSO-FM (nt) 815 Lafayette Rd, Portsmouth NH 03801 **Phn:** 603-436-7300 **Fax:** 603-430-9415 www.newsradio967.com jeffpierce@clearchannel.com

Portsmouth WSKX-FM (h) 815 Lafayette Rd, Portsmouth NH 03801 **Phn:** 603-436-7300 **Fax:** 603-430-9415 www.953thecoast.com jefferypierce@clearchannel.com

Rochester WMEX-FM (a) 1 Wakefield St Ste 302, Rochester NH 03867 **Phn:** 603-335-6600 **Fax:** 603-299-0325

West Lebanon WHDQ-FM (r) 106 N Main St, West Lebanon NH 03784 **Phn:** 603-298-0332 **Fax:** 603-298-7554 www.theqrocks.com

West Lebanon WTSL-AM (snt) 106 N Main St, West Lebanon NH 03784 **Phn:** 603-298-0332 **Fax:** 603-448-1755 www.wtsl.com comments@wtsl.com

West Lebanon WTSV-AM (sn) 106 N Main St, West Lebanon NH 03784 **Phn:** 603-542-7735 **Fax:** 603-542-8721

West Lebanon WXLF-FM (c) 8 Glen Rd, West Lebanon NH 03784 **Phn:** 603-298-0123 **Fax:** 603-298-0150 wxlf.nh1media.com

West Lebanon WZLF-FM (c) 8 Glen Rd, West Lebanon NH 03784 **Phn:** 603-298-0123 **Fax:** 603-298-0150 wxlf.nh1media.com adukette@binradio.com

Winchester WYRY-FM (c) 30 Warwick Rd Ste 10, Winchester NH 03470 **Phn:** 603-239-8200 **Fax:** 603-239-6203 www.wyry.com spatrik@wyry.com

Wolfeboro WASR-AM (anm) PO Box 900, Wolfeboro NH 03894 **Phn:** 603-569-1420 **Fax:** 603-569-1900 www.wasr.net mail@wasr.net

NEW JERSEY

Atlantic City WAJM-FM (v) 1400 N Albany Ave, Atlantic City NJ 08401 **Phn:** 609-343-7300

Burlington WIFI-AM (g) 2035 Columbus Rd, Burlington NJ 08016 **Phn:** 609-499-4800 **Fax:** 609-499-4905

Camden WTMR-AM (q) 2775 Mount Ephraim Ave, Camden NJ 08104 **Phn:** 856-962-8000 **Fax:** 856-962-8004

Cedar Knolls WDHA-FM (r) 55 Horsehill Rd, Cedar Knolls NJ 07927 **Phn:** 973-538-1250 **Fax:** 973-538-3060 www.wdhafm.com ckay@greatermedianj.com

Cedar Knolls WMTR-AM (o) 55 Horsehill Rd, Cedar Knolls NJ 07927 **Phn:** 973-538-1250 **Fax:** 973-538-3060 www.wmtram.com cedwards@wmtr-wdha.com

Cedar Knolls WWTR-AM (d) 55 Horsehill Rd, Cedar Knolls NJ 07927 **Phn:** 973-538-1250 **Fax:** 973-538-3060 ebcmusic.com

Ewing WTSR-FM (vr) PO Box 7718, Ewing NJ 08628 **Phn:** 609-771-3200 **Fax:** 609-637-5113 wtsr.org wtsr@wtsr.org

Flemington WCVH-FM (v) 84 State Route 31, Flemington NJ 08822 **Phn:** 908-782-9595

Franklin WHCY-FM (h) 45 Ed Mitchell Ave, Franklin NJ 07416 **Phn:** 973-827-2525 **Fax:** 973-827-2135 www.max1063.com bobdunphy@clearchannel.com

Franklin WNNJ-FM (r) 45 Ed Mitchell Ave, Franklin NJ 07416 **Phn:** 973-827-2525 **Fax:** 973-827-2135 www.wnnj.com

Franklin WNNJ-AM (o) 45 Ed Mitchell Ave, Franklin NJ 07416 **Phn:** 973-827-2525 **Fax:** 973-827-2135

Franklin WSUS-FM (a) 45 Ed Mitchell Ave, Franklin NJ 07416 **Phn:** 973-827-2525 **Fax:** 973-827-2135 www.wsus1023.com

Galloway WLFR-FM (v) 101 Vera King Farris Dr, Galloway NJ 08205 **Phn:** 609-652-4781 www.wlfr.fm wlfroffice@stockton.edu

Glassboro WGLS-FM (v) 201 Mullica Hill Rd, Glassboro NJ 08028 **Phn:** 856-863-9457 **Fax:** 856-256-4704 wgls.rowan.edu wgls@rowan.edu

Hackettstown WNTI-FM (p) 400 Jefferson St, Hackettstown NJ 07840 **Phn:** 908-852-4545 www.wnti.org lewisj01@centenarycollege.edu

Hackettstown WRNJ-AM (ant) 100 Route 46, Hackettstown NJ 07840 **Phn:** 908-850-1000 **Fax:** 908-852-8000 wrnjradio.com playton@wrnj.com

Hasbrouck Heights WMCA-AM (wtq) 777 Terrace Ave Ste 602, Hasbrouck Heights NJ 07604 **Phn:** 201-298-5700 **Fax:** 201-298-5797 www.wmca.com contact@nycradio.com

Jersey City WFMU-FM (v) PO Box 2011, Jersey City NJ 07303 **Phn:** 201-521-1416 www.wfmu.org terre@wfmu.org

Lake Como WRAT-FM (r) 1731 Main St, Lake Como NJ 07719 **Phn:** 732-681-3800 **Fax:** 732-681-5995 www.wrat.com carl@wrat.com

Lincroft WBJB-FM (pj) 765 Newman Springs Rd, Lincroft NJ 07738 **Phn:** 732-224-2470 www.wbjb.org comments@wbjb.org

Linwood WGYM-AM (nt) 1601 New Rd, Linwood NJ 08221 **Phn:** 609-653-1400 **Fax:** 609-601-0450

Linwood WJSE-FM (r) 1601 New Rd, Linwood NJ 08221 **Phn:** 609-653-1400 **Fax:** 609-927-5712

Linwood WMGM-FM (r) 1601 New Rd, Linwood NJ 08221 **Phn:** 609-653-1400 **Fax:** 609-601-0450 www.1037wmgm.com

Linwood WOND-AM (nt) 1601 New Rd, Linwood NJ 08221 **Phn:** 609-653-1400 **Fax:** 609-601-0450

Linwood WTAA-AM (y) 1601 New Rd, Linwood NJ 08221 **Phn:** 609-653-1400 **Fax:** 609-601-0450

Linwood WTKU-AM (oh) 1601 New Rd, Linwood NJ 08221 **Phn:** 609-601-1100 **Fax:** 609-601-0450

Linwood WTKU-FM (o) 1601 New Rd, Linwood NJ 08221 **Phn:** 609-601-1100 **Fax:** 609-601-0450 www.kool983.com

Madison WMNJ-FM (v) 36 Madison Ave, Madison NJ 07940 **Phn:** 973-408-4753

NEW JERSEY RADIO STATIONS

Mahwah WRPR-FM (v) 505 Ramapo Valley Rd, Mahwah NJ 07430 **Phn:** 201-825-7998 **Fax:** 201-327-9036 www.ramapo.edu/wrpr-fm wrpr@ramapo.edu

Manahawkin WJRZ-FM (o) PO Box 1000, Manahawkin NJ 08050 **Phn:** 609-597-1100 **Fax:** 609-597-4400 www.magicvariety.com szarnowski@greatermedianj.com

Manahawkin WYRS-FM (q) PO Box 730, Manahawkin NJ 08050 **Phn:** 609-978-1678 **Fax:** 609-597-4146 www.wyrs.org info@wyrs.org

Millville WMVB-AM (m) 415 N High St, Millville NJ 08332 **Phn:** 856-327-8800 **Fax:** 856-327-0408

Millville WSNJ-AM (bm) 415 N High St, Millville NJ 08332 **Phn:** 856-327-8800 **Fax:** 856-327-0408 www.wsnjam.com corky@wsnjam.com

Montclair WMSC-FM (v) Montclair State Univ, Montclair NJ 07043 **Phn:** 973-655-4257 **Fax:** 973-655-7433 wmscradio.com gm@wmscradio.com

Morristown WJSV-FM (vr) 50 Early St, Morristown NJ 07960 **Phn:** 973-292-2168

Neptune WBBO-FM (r) 2355 W Bangs Ave, Neptune NJ 07753 **Phn:** 732-774-4755 **Fax:** 732-774-7315 b985radio.com ajc@presscommradio.com

Neptune WBHX-FM (oa) 2355 W Bangs Ave, Neptune NJ 07753 **Phn:** 732-774-4755 **Fax:** 732-774-7315 1071radio.com dant@breezeradio.com

Neptune WHTG-FM (r) 2355 W Bangs Ave, Neptune NJ 07753 **Phn:** 732-774-4755 **Fax:** 732-774-7315 www.hit106.com dpellegrino@presscommradio.com

Neptune WHTG-AM (ob) 2355 W Bangs Ave, Neptune NJ 07753 **Phn:** 732-774-4755 **Fax:** 732-774-4974 www.1410amradio.com johnf@presscommradio.com

Neptune WWZY-FM (oa) 2355 W Bangs Ave, Neptune NJ 07753 **Phn:** 732-774-4755 **Fax:** 732-774-4974 www.breezeradio.com dant@breezeradio.com

New Brunswick WRSU-FM (v) 126 College Ave, New Brunswick NJ 08901 **Phn:** 732-932-7800 **Fax:** 732-932-1768 wrsu.rutgers.edu news@wrsu.edu

Newark WBGO-FM (pj) 54 Park Pl, Newark NJ 07102 **Phn:** 973-624-8880 **Fax:** 973-824-8888 www.wbgo.org ddoyle@wbgo.org

Northfield WENJ-FM (s) 950 Tilton Rd Ste 200, Northfield NJ 08225 **Phn:** 609-645-9797 www.973espn.com nj1015@nj1015.com

Northfield WFPG-FM (a) 950 Tilton Rd Ste 200, Northfield NJ 08225 **Phn:** 609-645-9797 **Fax:** 609-272-9228 www.literock969.com gary.guida@mrgnj.com

Northfield WJPH-FM (q) 950 Tilton Rd Ste 101, Northfield NJ 08225 **Phn:** 609-861-3700 www.praise899.org letters@praise899.org

Northfield WPUR-FM (c) 950 Tilton Rd Ste 200, Northfield NJ 08225 **Phn:** 609-645-9797 **Fax:** 609-272-9228 www.catcountry1073.com joe.kelly@townsquaremedia.com

Northfield WSJO-FM (aj) 950 Tilton Rd Ste 200, Northfield NJ 08225 **Phn:** 609-645-9797 www.sojo1049.com eric.johnson@mrgnj.com

Ocean City WIBG-AM (aq) 3328 Simpson Ave, Ocean City NJ 08226 **Phn:** 609-398-7575 **Fax:** 609-398-3736 www.wibg.com

Paterson WWRV-AM (qy) PO Box 2908, Paterson NJ 07509 **Phn:** 973-881-8700 **Fax:** 973-881-8324 radiovision.net dtirado@radiovision.net

Pemberton WBZC-FM (v) 601 Pemberton Browns Mills Rd, Pemberton NJ 08068 **Phn:** 609-894-8900 **Fax:** 609-894-9440 www.z889.org bholcomb@bcc.edu

Piscataway WVPH-FM (v) 100 Behmer Rd, Piscataway NJ 08854 **Phn:** 732-981-0153 www.wvphradio.bravehost.com wvph@pway.org

Plainfield WKMB-AM (q) 120 W 7th St Ste 201, Plainfield NJ 07060 **Phn:** 908-822-1515

Pleasantville WAIV-FM (aj) 8025 Black Horse Pike Ste 100, Pleasantville NJ 08232 **Phn:** 609-484-8444 **Fax:** 609-646-6331 www.951wayv.com rgarcia@equitycommunications.net

Pleasantville WAYV-FM (h) 8025 Black Horse Pike Ste 100, Pleasantville NJ 08232 **Phn:** 609-484-8444 **Fax:** 609-646-6331 www.951wayv.com 951wayv@gmail.com

Pleasantville WEZW-FM (z) 8025 Black Horse Pike Ste 100, Pleasantville NJ 08232 **Phn:** 609-484-8444 **Fax:** 609-646-6331 easy931.com easy931@gmail.com

Pleasantville WMID-AM (am) 8025 Black Horse Pike Ste 100, Pleasantville NJ 08232 **Phn:** 609-484-8444 **Fax:** 609-646-6331 www.classicoldieswmid.com rgarcia@equitycommunications.net

Pleasantville WSNQ-FM (h) 8025 Black Horse Pike Ste 100, Pleasantville NJ 08232 **Phn:** 609-484-8444 **Fax:** 609-646-6331 www.993kiss.fm rgarcia@equitycommunications.net

Pleasantville WTTH-FM (ua) 8025 Black Horse Pike Ste 100, Pleasantville NJ 08232 **Phn:** 609-484-8444 **Fax:** 609-646-6331 www.961wtth.com swray@hotmail.com

Pleasantville WZBZ-FM (h) 8025 Black Horse Pike Ste 100, Pleasantville NJ 08232 **Phn:** 609-484-8444 **Fax:** 609-646-6331 www.993kiss.fm info@951wayv.com

Pleasantville WZXL-FM (r) 8025 Black Horse Pike Ste 100, Pleasantville NJ 08232 **Phn:** 609-484-8444 **Fax:** 609-646-6331 www.wzxl.com steve@wzxl.com

Pompton Lakes WGHT-AM (on) PO Box 316, Pompton Lakes NJ 07442 **Phn:** 973-839-1500 www.wghtradio.com jimmy.howes@ghtradio.com

Princeton WBYN-AM (gq) 619 Alexander Rd Fl 3, Princeton NJ 08540 **Phn:** 609-454-4185 TheLightradio.com ddecker@thelightradio.com

Princeton WCHR-AM (q) 619 Alexander Rd Fl 3, Princeton NJ 08540 **Phn:** 609-454-4185 www.wchram.net jwhite@wchram.net

Princeton WHWH-AM (nt) 619 Alexander Rd, Princeton NJ 08540 **Phn:** 609-419-0300 **Fax:** 609-419-0143

Princeton WPRB-FM (jl) 30 Bloomberg Hall, Princeton NJ 08544 **Phn:** 609-258-3655 **Fax:** 609-258-1806 www.wprb.com manager@wprb.com

Princeton WPST-FM (hr) 619 Alexander Rd, Princeton NJ 08540 **Phn:** 609-419-0300 **Fax:** 609-419-0143 www.wpst.com dmckay@wpst.com

Sergeantsville WDVR-FM (v) PO Box 191, Sergeantsville NJ 08557 **Phn:** 609-397-1620 **Fax:** 609-397-5991 www.wdvrfm.org napp2@comcast.net

Somerset WCTC-AM (nt) 78 Veronica Ave, Somerset NJ 08873 **Phn:** 732-249-2600 **Fax:** 732-249-9010 www.wctcam.com bbaron@greatermedianj.com

Somerset WMGQ-FM (a) 78 Veronica Ave, Somerset NJ 08873 **Phn:** 732-249-2600 **Fax:** 732-249-9010 www.magic983.com bjohnson@greatermedianj.com

South Orange WSOU-FM (v) 400 S Orange Ave, South Orange NJ 07079 **Phn:** 973-761-9768 **Fax:** 973-761-7593 www.wsou.net wsounews@gmail.com

Teaneck WFDU-FM (v) 1000 River Rd # T-WFDU, Teaneck NJ 07666 **Phn:** 201-692-2806 **Fax:** 201-692-2807 alpha.fdu.edu/wfdu/wfdufmhome.html barrys@fdu.edu

Teaneck WVNJ-AM (nt) 1086 Teaneck Rd Ste 4F, Teaneck NJ 07666 **Phn:** 201-837-0400 **Fax:** 201-837-9664 www.wvnj.com wvnj1160am@aol.com

Toms River WADB-AM (o) 8 Robbins St # 201, Toms River NJ 08753 **Phn:** 848-221-8000 **Fax:** 848-221-8090 www.wobmam.com steve.ardolina@townsquaremedia.com

Toms River WCHR-FM (r) 8 Robbins St # 201, Toms River NJ 08753 **Phn:** 848-221-8000 **Fax:** 848-221-8090 www.1057thehawk.com wendy.wesley@mrgnj.com

Toms River WJLK-FM (a) 8 Robbins St # 201, Toms River NJ 08753 **Phn:** 848-221-8000 **Fax:** 848-221-8090 www.943thepoint.com steve.ardolina@townsquaremedia.com

Toms River WOBM-AM (o) 8 Robbins St # 201, Toms River NJ 08753 **Phn:** 848-221-8000 **Fax:** 848-221-8090 www.wobmam.com steve.ardolina@townsquaremedia.com

Toms River WOBM-FM (a) 8 Robbins St # 201, Toms River NJ 08753 **Phn:** 848-221-8000 **Fax:** 848-221-8090 www.wobm.com wobmnews@wobm.com

Trenton WBUD-AM (not) PO Box 5698, Trenton NJ 08638 **Phn:** 609-771-8181 **Fax:** 609-406-7956 www.nj1015.com eric.johnson@mrgnj.com

Trenton WIMG-AM (wgu) PO Box 9078, Trenton NJ 08650 **Phn:** 609-695-1300 **Fax:** 609-278-1588 www.wimg1300.com vennie@wimg1300.com

Trenton WKXW-FM (ot) PO Box 5698, Trenton NJ 08638 **Phn:** 609-771-8181 **Fax:** 609-771-0581 www.nj1015.com nj1015@nj1015.com

Trenton WNJT-FM (pntj) PO Box 777, Trenton NJ 08625 **Phn:** 609-777-5000

Trenton WRRC-FM (v) 2083 Lawrenceville Rd, Trenton NJ 08648 **Phn:** 609-896-5369

Trenton WWFM-FM (pl) PO Box B, Trenton NJ 08690 **Phn:** 609-587-8989 **Fax:** 609-570-3863 www.wwfm.org info@wwfm.org

Union WKNJ-FM (v) 1000 Morris Ave, Union NJ 07083 **Phn:** 908-737-0450 **Fax:** 908-737-0445 smchugh@kean.edu

Vineland WMIZ-AM (y) 632 Maurice River Pkwy, Vineland NJ 08360 **Phn:** 856-692-8888 **Fax:** 856-696-2568 www.wmizradio.com chemple@aol.com

Vineland WVLT-FM (o) 632 Maurice River Pkwy, Vineland NJ 08360 **Phn:** 856-692-8888 **Fax:** 856-696-2568 www.wvlt.com chemple@aol.com

Wayne WPSC-FM (v) 300 Pompton Rd, Wayne NJ 07470 **Phn:** 973-720-3319 www.wpradio887.org wpsc@wpunj.edu

West Long Branch WMCX-FM (v) 400 Cedar Ave, West Long Branch NJ 07764 **Phn:** 732-571-3482 **Fax:** 732-263-5145 wmcx.com wmcxpd@monmouth.edu

Wildwood WCMC-AM (a) 3010 New Jersey Ave, Wildwood NJ 08260 **Phn:** 609-522-1416 **Fax:** 609-729-9264

Wildwood WCZT-FM (a) 3208 Pacific Ave, Wildwood NJ 08260 **Phn:** 609-522-1987 **Fax:** 609-522-3666 www.987thecoast.com news@coastalbroadcasting.com

Zarephath WAWZ-FM (q) PO Box 9058, Zarephath NJ 08890 **Phn:** 732-469-0991 **Fax:** 732-469-2115 www.star991.com info@star991.com

NEW MEXICO

Alamogordo KINN-AM (ant) PO Box 1848, Alamogordo NM 88311 **Phn:** 575-434-1414 **Fax:** 575-434-2213 ktalk@bbiradio.net

NEW MEXICO RADIO STATIONS

Alamogordo KNMZ-FM (s) PO Box 2710, Alamogordo NM 88311 **Phn:** 575-437-1505 **Fax:** 575-437-5566 www.snmradio.com

Alamogordo KQEL-FM (oh) PO Box 1848, Alamogordo NM 88311 **Phn:** 575-434-1414 **Fax:** 575-434-2213

Alamogordo KRSY-AM (snt) PO Box 2710, Alamogordo NM 88311 **Phn:** 575-437-1505 **Fax:** 575-437-5566 www.snmradio.com krsy@snmradio.com

Alamogordo KRSY-FM (c) PO Box 2710, Alamogordo NM 88311 **Phn:** 575-437-1505 **Fax:** 575-437-5566 www.snmradio.com krsy@snmradio.com

Alamogordo KYEE-FM (h) PO Box 1848, Alamogordo NM 88311 **Phn:** 575-434-1414 **Fax:** 575-434-2213

Alamogordo KZZX-FM (c) PO Box 1848, Alamogordo NM 88311 **Phn:** 575-434-1414 **Fax:** 575-434-2213 kzzx@bbiradio.net

Albuquerque KABG-FM (o) 4125 Carlisle Blvd NE, Albuquerque NM 87107 **Phn:** 505-878-0980 **Fax:** 505-878-0098 www.big985.com srufail@americangeneralmedia.com

Albuquerque KABQ-AM (t) 5411 Jefferson St NE Ste 100, Albuquerque NM 87109 **Phn:** 505-830-6400 **Fax:** 505-830-6543 www.abqtalk.com chuckhammond@clearchannel.com

Albuquerque KABQ-FM (c) 5411 Jefferson St NE Ste 100, Albuquerque NM 87109 **Phn:** 505-830-6400 **Fax:** 505-830-6543 www.classiccountry981.com tonymanero@clearchannel.com

Albuquerque KAGM-FM (u) 4125 Carlisle Blvd NE, Albuquerque NM 87107 **Phn:** 505-878-0980 **Fax:** 505-878-0098 www.power1067.com

Albuquerque KAJZ-FM (hx) 8009 Marble Ave NE, Albuquerque NM 87110 **Phn:** 505-262-1142 **Fax:** 505-262-9211

Albuquerque KANW-FM (wv) 2020 Coal Ave SE, Albuquerque NM 87106 **Phn:** 505-242-7163 www.kanw.com brasher@aps.edu

Albuquerque KBQI-FM (r) 5411 Jefferson St NE Ste 100, Albuquerque NM 87109 **Phn:** 505-830-6400 **Fax:** 505-830-6543 www.bigi1079.com chuckhammond@clearchannel.com

Albuquerque KBZU-FM (r) 500 4th St NW, Albuquerque NM 87102 **Phn:** 505-767-6700 **Fax:** 505-767-6767 william.harris@cumulus.com

Albuquerque KDAZ-AM (ntq) PO Box 4338, Albuquerque NM 87196 **Phn:** 505-345-7373 **Fax:** 505-345-5669 www.am730.cc dan@am730.cc

Albuquerque KDEF-AM (s) 10424 Edith Blvd NE, Albuquerque NM 87113 **Phn:** 505-888-1150 **Fax:** 505-883-7323

Albuquerque KDLW-FM (h) 4125 Carlisle Blvd NE, Albuquerque NM 87107 **Phn:** 505-878-0980 **Fax:** 505-878-0098 z1067.com z1063radio@gmail.com

Albuquerque KDRF-FM (h) 500 4th St NW, Albuquerque NM 87102 **Phn:** 505-767-6700 **Fax:** 505-767-6767 www.ed.fm

Albuquerque KHFM-FM (l) 4125 Carlisle Blvd NE, Albuquerque NM 87107 **Phn:** 505-878-0980 **Fax:** 505-878-0098 www.classicalkhfm.com bstevens@americangeneralmedia.com

Albuquerque KIOT-FM (r) 8009 Marble Ave NE, Albuquerque NM 87110 **Phn:** 505-254-7100 **Fax:** 505-254-7106 www.coyote1025.com

Albuquerque KJFA-FM (y) 8009 Marble Ave NE, Albuquerque NM 87110 **Phn:** 505-262-1142 **Fax:** 505-254-7106

Albuquerque KKIM-AM (qt) 4125 Carlisle Blvd NE, Albuquerque NM 87107 **Phn:** 505-878-0980 **Fax:** 505-878-0098 www.mykkim.com srufail@americangeneralmedia.com

Albuquerque KKNS-AM (nt) 1606 Central Ave SE Ste 104, Albuquerque NM 87106 **Phn:** 505-255-5015 **Fax:** 505-262-4792 vcamino@elcaminocomm.com

Albuquerque KKOB-AM (snt) 500 4th St NW, Albuquerque NM 87102 **Phn:** 505-767-6700 **Fax:** 505-767-6767 www.770kkob.com pat.frisch@cumulus.com

Albuquerque KKOB-FM (a) 500 4th St NW, Albuquerque NM 87102 **Phn:** 505-767-6700 **Fax:** 505-767-6767 www.kobfm.com

Albuquerque KKRG-FM (aj) 8009 Marble Ave NE, Albuquerque NM 87110 **Phn:** 505-262-1142 **Fax:** 505-254-7106

Albuquerque KKSS-FM (h) 8009 Marble Ave NE, Albuquerque NM 87110 **Phn:** 505-262-1142 **Fax:** 505-254-7106 www.mykiss973.com djlopez@univisionradio.com

Albuquerque KLVO-FM (y) 4125 Carlisle Blvd NE, Albuquerque NM 87107 **Phn:** 505-878-0980 **Fax:** 505-878-0098 www.radiolobo.net srufail@americangeneralmedia.com

Albuquerque KLYT-FM (cq) 4001 Osuna Rd NE, Albuquerque NM 87109 **Phn:** 505-344-9146 **Fax:** 505-344-9193 www.mystaticradio.com studio@mystaticradio.com

Albuquerque KMGA-FM (a) 500 4th St NW Ste 500, Albuquerque NM 87102 **Phn:** 505-767-6700 **Fax:** 505-767-9199 www.995magicfm.com kmga@cumulus.com

Albuquerque KNKT-FM (qah) 4001 Osuna Rd NE, Albuquerque NM 87109 **Phn:** 505-344-9146 **Fax:** 505-344-9193 www.knkt.com knkt@calvaryabq.org

Albuquerque KNML-AM (s) 500 4th St NW, Albuquerque NM 87102 **Phn:** 505-767-6700 **Fax:** 505-767-6711 www.610thesportsanimal.com 610.knml@cumulus.com

Albuquerque KPEK-FM (am) 5411 Jefferson St NE Ste 100, Albuquerque NM 87109 **Phn:** 505-830-6400 **Fax:** 505-830-6491 www.1003thepeak.com ryan@clearchannel.com

Albuquerque KRST-FM (c) 500 4th St NW, Albuquerque NM 87102 **Phn:** 505-767-6700 **Fax:** 505-767-6767 www.923krst.com

Albuquerque KRZY-AM (y) 2725 Broadbent Pkwy NE Ste F, Albuquerque NM 87107 **Phn:** 505-342-4141 **Fax:** 505-344-0891 www.tricolor1450.com mwilder@entravision.com

Albuquerque KRZY-FM (y) 2725 Broadbent Pkwy NE Ste F, Albuquerque NM 87107 **Phn:** 505-342-4141 **Fax:** 505-345-6407 www.jose1059.com mwilder@entravision.com

Albuquerque KSYU-FM (wx) 5411 Jefferson St NE Ste 100, Albuquerque NM 87109 **Phn:** 505-830-6400 **Fax:** 505-830-6543 ryan@clearchannel.com

Albuquerque KTBL-AM (t) 500 4th St NW, Albuquerque NM 87102 **Phn:** 505-767-6700 **Fax:** 505-767-6767 www.1050talk.com pat.frisch@cumulus.com

Albuquerque KTEG-FM (r) 5411 Jefferson St NE Ste 100, Albuquerque NM 87109 **Phn:** 505-830-6400 **Fax:** 505-830-6543 www.1041theedge.com tonymanero@clearchannel.com

Albuquerque KUNM-FM (pnt) MSC06 3520 Onate Hall, Albuquerque NM 87131 **Phn:** 505-277-4806 **Fax:** 505-277-8004 www.kunm.org news@kunm.org

Albuquerque KZRR-FM (r) 5411 Jefferson St NE Ste 100, Albuquerque NM 87109 **Phn:** 505-830-6400 **Fax:** 505-830-6543 www.94rock.com kzrr@94rock.com

Artesia KEND-FM (r) 317 W Quay Ave, Artesia NM 88210 **Phn:** 575-746-2751 **Fax:** 575-748-3748 www.pecosvalleybroadcasting.com news@ksvpradio.com

Artesia KPZE-FM (y) 317 W Quay Ave, Artesia NM 88210 **Phn:** 575-746-2751 **Fax:** 575-748-3748 www.kpze.com news@ksvpradio.com

Artesia KSVP-AM (nt) 317 W Quay Ave, Artesia NM 88210 **Phn:** 575-746-2751 **Fax:** 575-748-3748 www.ksvpradio.com news@pvbcradio.com

Artesia KTZA-FM (c) 317 W Quay Ave, Artesia NM 88210 **Phn:** 575-746-2751 **Fax:** 575-748-3748 www.pecosvalleybroadcasting.com news@ksvpradio.com

Belen KARS-AM (y) 208 N 2nd St, Belen NM 87002 **Phn:** 505-864-3024 **Fax:** 505-864-2719 www.americangeneralmedia.com srufail@americangeneralmedia.com

Carlsbad KAMQ-AM (s) PO Box 1538, Carlsbad NM 88221 **Phn:** 575-887-7563 **Fax:** 575-887-7000 carlsbadradio.com don@carlsbadradio.com

Carlsbad KATK-AM (ob) PO Box 1538, Carlsbad NM 88221 **Phn:** 575-887-7563 **Fax:** 575-887-7000 carlsbadradio.com don@carlsbadradio.com

Carlsbad KATK-FM (c) PO Box 1538, Carlsbad NM 88221 **Phn:** 575-887-7563 **Fax:** 575-887-7000 carlsbadradio.com don@carlsbadradio.com

Carlsbad KCCC-AM (ot) 930 N Canal St, Carlsbad NM 88220 **Phn:** 575-887-5521 **Fax:** 575-885-5481

Carlsbad KCDY-FM (a) PO Box 1538, Carlsbad NM 88221 **Phn:** 575-887-7563 **Fax:** 575-887-7000 carlsbadradio.com don@carlsbadradio.com

Chama KZRM-FM (h) PO Box 307, Chama NM 87520 **Phn:** 575-756-1617 **Fax:** 575-756-1317 www.kzrmradio.com production@kzrmradio.com

Clayton KLMX-AM (cy) PO Box 547, Clayton NM 88415 **Phn:** 575-374-2555 **Fax:** 575-374-2557

Clovis KCLV-FM (c) PO Box 1907, Clovis NM 88102 **Phn:** 575-763-4401 **Fax:** 575-769-2564 www.kclvsports.com chase@kclvsports.com

Clovis KCLV-AM (c) PO Box 1907, Clovis NM 88102 **Phn:** 575-763-4401 **Fax:** 575-769-2564 www.kclvsports.com chase@kclvsports.com

Clovis KICA-AM (cg) 1000 Sycamore St, Clovis NM 88101 **Phn:** 575-762-6200 **Fax:** 575-762-8800

Clovis KICA-FM (r) 1000 Sycamore St, Clovis NM 88101 **Phn:** 575-762-6200 **Fax:** 575-762-8800

Clovis KKYC-FM (c) 1000 Sycamore St, Clovis NM 88101 **Phn:** 575-762-6200 **Fax:** 575-762-8800

Clovis KTQM-FM (a) PO Box 869, Clovis NM 88102 **Phn:** 575-762-4411 **Fax:** 575-769-0197 www.ktqm.com ktqm@plateautel.net

Clovis KWKA-AM (o) PO Box 869, Clovis NM 88102 **Phn:** 575-762-4411 **Fax:** 575-769-0197 ktqm@plateautel.net

Corrales KSVA-AM (q) PO Box 2378, Corrales NM 87048 **Phn:** 505-890-0800 **Fax:** 505-890-0808

Deming KDEM-FM (a) PO Box 470, Deming NM 88031 **Phn:** 575-546-9011 **Fax:** 575-546-9342 www.demingradio.com radio@demingradio.com

Deming KOTS-AM (cy) PO Box 470, Deming NM 88031 **Phn:** 575-546-9011 **Fax:** 575-546-9342 www.demingradio.com radio@demingradio.com

Dulce KCIE-FM (v) PO Box 603, Dulce NM 87528 **Phn:** 575-759-3681 **Fax:** 575-759-9140

NEW MEXICO RADIO STATIONS

Espanola KDCE-AM (y) 403 W Pueblo Dr, Espanola NM 87532 **Phn:** 505-753-2201 **Fax:** 505-753-8685 kdceradio.com tomas@kdceradio.com

Espanola KYBR-FM (y) 403 W Pueblo Dr, Espanola NM 87532 **Phn:** 505-753-2201 **Fax:** 505-753-8685 www.radiooso.com

Farmington KAZX-FM (h) PO Box 6030, Farmington NM 87499 **Phn:** 505-325-1716 **Fax:** 505-325-6797 www.star1029.com billkruger@clearchannel.com

Farmington KCQL-AM (s) 200 E Broadway, Farmington NM 87401 **Phn:** 505-325-1716 **Fax:** 505-325-6797 www.sports1340.com stevebortstein@clearchannel.com

Farmington KDAG-FM (r) 200 E Broadway, Farmington NM 87401 **Phn:** 505-325-1716 **Fax:** 505-325-6797 www.969thedogrocks.com randyburton@clearchannel.com

Farmington KENN-AM (tn) 212 W Apache St, Farmington NM 87401 **Phn:** 505-325-3541 **Fax:** 505-327-5796 www.kennradio.com bkruger@americangeneralmedia.com

Farmington KISZ-FM (c) 212 W Apache St, Farmington NM 87401 **Phn:** 505-325-3541 **Fax:** 505-327-5796 www.kisscountry.net bkruger@americangeneralmedia.com

Farmington KKFG-FM (o) 200 E Broadway, Farmington NM 87401 **Phn:** 505-325-1716 **Fax:** 505-325-6797 www.kool1045.com sherrycurry@clearchannel.com

Farmington KNDN-AM (e) 1515 W Main St, Farmington NM 87401 **Phn:** 505-325-1996 kgober@basinbroadcasting.com

Farmington KNMI-FM (q) 2103 W Main St, Farmington NM 87401 **Phn:** 505-327-4357 **Fax:** 505-325-9035 www.verticalradio.org email@verticalradio.org

Farmington KPCL-FM (gq) PO Box 232, Farmington NM 87499 **Phn:** 505-327-7202 **Fax:** 505-327-2163 www.kpcl.org kpcl@kpcl.org

Farmington KRWN-FM (r) 212 W Apache St, Farmington NM 87401 **Phn:** 505-325-3541 **Fax:** 505-327-5796 www.krwn.com cheryl@krwn.com

Farmington KSJE-FM (vl) 4601 College Blvd, Farmington NM 87402 **Phn:** 505-566-3377 **Fax:** 505-566-3385 www.ksje.com ksje@sanjuancollege.edu

Farmington KTRA-FM (c) 200 E Broadway, Farmington NM 87401 **Phn:** 505-325-1716 **Fax:** 505-325-6797 www.102ktra.com daveschaefer@clearchannel.com

Farmington KVFC-AM (nt) 212 W Apache, Farmington NM 87401 **Phn:** 505-325-3541 **Fax:** 505-327-5796 www.KVFCRadio.com

Farmington KWYK-FM (ha) 1515 W Main St, Farmington NM 87401 **Phn:** 505-325-1996 **Fax:** 505-327-2019 www.kwykradio.com morningshow@kwykradio.com

Gallup KFMQ-FM (r) 1632 S Second St, Gallup NM 87301 **Phn:** 505-863-9391 **Fax:** 505-863-9393 blassaucedo@clearchannel.com

Gallup KFXR-FM (c) 1632 S Second St, Gallup NM 87301 **Phn:** 520-674-3200 **Fax:** 505-863-9393 tedfoster@clearchannel.com

Gallup KGAK-AM (e) 401 E Coal Ave, Gallup NM 87301 **Phn:** 505-863-4444 **Fax:** 505-722-7381

Gallup KGLP-FM (pjn) 705 Gurley Ave, Gallup NM 87301 **Phn:** 505-863-7626 **Fax:** 505-863-7633 www.kglp.org kglpradio@kglp.org

Gallup KGLX-FM (c) 1632 S Second St, Gallup NM 87301 **Phn:** 505-863-9391 **Fax:** 505-863-9393 tedfoster@clearchannel.com

Gallup KKOR-FM (h) PO Box 420, Gallup NM 87305 **Phn:** 505-863-6851 **Fax:** 505-863-2429 www.gallupradio.com news@gallupradio.com

Gallup KXTC-FM (h) 1632 S Second St, Gallup NM 87301 **Phn:** 505-863-9391 **Fax:** 505-863-9393

Gallup KXXI-FM (r) PO Box 420, Gallup NM 87305 **Phn:** 505-863-6851 **Fax:** 505-863-2429 www.gallupradio.com news@gallupradio.com

Gallup KYVA-AM (cns) PO Box 420, Gallup NM 87305 **Phn:** 505-863-6851 **Fax:** 505-863-2429 www.gallupradio.com news@gallupradio.com

Gallup KYVA-FM (or) PO Box 420, Gallup NM 87305 **Phn:** 505-863-6851 **Fax:** 505-863-2429 www.gallupradio.com news@gallupradio.com

Grants KDSK-FM (a) 733 E Roosevelt Ave, Grants NM 87020 **Phn:** 505-285-5598 **Fax:** 505-285-5575 www.kdsk.com

Grants KMIN-AM (o) 733 E Roosevelt Ave, Grants NM 87020 **Phn:** 505-285-5598 **Fax:** 505-285-5575 www.kmin980.com

Hobbs KEJL-FM (r) 619 N Turner, Hobbs NM 88240 **Phn:** 575-397-4969 hobbsradio.comeagle harry@1radiosquare.com

Hobbs KIXN-FM (c) 619 N Turner St, Hobbs NM 88240 **Phn:** 575-397-4969 **Fax:** 575-393-4310 www.1radiosquare.com harry@1radiosquare.com

Hobbs KLMA-FM (y) PO Box 457, Hobbs NM 88241 **Phn:** 575-391-9650 **Fax:** 575-397-9373 www.klmaradio.com klmaradio@leaco.net

Hobbs KPER-FM (c) 619 N Turner, Hobbs NM 88241 **Phn:** 575-397-4969 **Fax:** 575-397-6088 www.hobbsradio.comkper harry@1radiosquare.com

Hobbs KPZA-FM (y) 619 N Turner St, Hobbs NM 88240 **Phn:** 575-397-4969 **Fax:** 575-393-4310 www.kpzafm.com mail@1radiosquare.com

Hobbs KYKK-AM (nt) 1423 W Bender, Hobbs NM 88240 **Phn:** 575-393-1551 **Fax:** 575-397-6088 hobbsradio.com

Hobbs KZOR-FM (a) 619 N Turner St, Hobbs NM 88240 **Phn:** 575-397-4969 **Fax:** 575-393-4310 www.kzorfm.com mail@1radiosquare.com

Las Cruces KGRT-FM (c) PO Box 968, Las Cruces NM 88004 **Phn:** 575-525-9298 **Fax:** 575-525-9419 www.kgrt.com radiolc@kgrt.com

Las Cruces KHQT-FM (h) PO Box 968, Las Cruces NM 88004 **Phn:** 575-525-9298 **Fax:** 575-525-9419 www.hot103.fm radiolc@kgrt.com

Las Cruces KKVS-FM (y) 1355 California Ave, Las Cruces NM 88001 **Phn:** 575-525-9298 **Fax:** 575-525-9419 www.vista.fm a.lumeyer@kgrt.com

Las Cruces KMVR-FM (a) 101 Perkins Dr, Las Cruces NM 88005 **Phn:** 575-527-1111 **Fax:** 575-527-1100 www.mymagic105.com msmith@bravomic.com

Las Cruces KOBE-AM (snt) 101 Perkins Dr, Las Cruces NM 88005 **Phn:** 575-527-1111 **Fax:** 575-527-1100 b1450.com

Las Cruces KRUX-FM (vr) PO Box 30004 Corbett Center, Las Cruces NM 88003 **Phn:** 575-646-4640 **Fax:** 575-646-5219 www.kruxradio.com kruxnews@nmsu.edu

Las Cruces KRWG-FM (plnj) PO Box 3000, Las Cruces NM 88003 **Phn:** 575-646-2222 www.krwg.org krwgfm@nmsu.edu

Las Cruces KSNM-AM (t) PO Box 968, Las Cruces NM 88004 **Phn:** 575-525-9298 **Fax:** 575-525-9419 www.ksnm570.am newsdesk@kgrt.com

Las Cruces KVLC-FM (o) 101 Perkins Dr, Las Cruces NM 88005 **Phn:** 575-527-1111 **Fax:** 575-527-1100 www.101gold.com

Las Vegas KFUN-AM (cy) PO Box 700, Las Vegas NM 87701 **Phn:** 505-425-6766 **Fax:** 505-425-6767 www.kfunonline.com jpbaca1946@kfunonline.com

Las Vegas KLVF-FM (a) PO Box 700, Las Vegas NM 87701 **Phn:** 505-425-6766 **Fax:** 505-425-6767 jpbaca1946@yahoo.com

Las Vegas KNMX-AM (y) 304 S Grand Ave, Las Vegas NM 87701 **Phn:** 505-425-5669 **Fax:** 505-425-3557 www.lvnmradio.com mog87701@aol.com

Lovington KLEA-AM (a) PO Box 877, Lovington NM 88260 **Phn:** 575-396-2244 **Fax:** 575-396-3355 susanklea@gmail.com

Lovington KLEA-FM (o) PO Box 877, Lovington NM 88260 **Phn:** 575-396-2244 **Fax:** 575-396-3355 www.oldies1017.com

Lovington KTUM-FM (r) 916 West Ave D, Lovington NM 88260 **Phn:** 575-396-0499 **Fax:** 575-396-8349 www.1071thenerve.com thenerve@mtdradio.com

Portales KENW-FM (p) 52 Broadcast Ctr, Portales NM 88130 **Phn:** 575-562-2112 **Fax:** 575-562-2590 www.kenw.org

Portales KSEL-AM (n) 42437 US 70, Portales NM 88130 **Phn:** 575-359-1759 **Fax:** 575-359-0724

Portales KSEL-FM (c) 42437 US 70, Portales NM 88130 **Phn:** 575-359-1759 **Fax:** 575-359-0724 www.kselcountry.com radio@kselcountry.com

Portales KSMX-FM (a) 42437 US 70, Portales NM 88130 **Phn:** 575-359-1759 **Fax:** 575-359-0724 www.heymix.com info@heymix.com

Raton KRTN-AM (a) PO Box 638, Raton NM 87740 **Phn:** 575-445-3652 **Fax:** 575-445-2911 krtn@bacavalley.com

Roswell KBCQ-AM (h) PO Box 670, Roswell NM 88202 **Phn:** 575-622-6450 **Fax:** 575-622-9041 www.am1230kbcq.com

Roswell KBIM-FM (a) PO Box 1953, Roswell NM 88202 **Phn:** 575-623-9100 **Fax:** 575-623-4775 www.kbim949.com kevin@kbimradio.com

Roswell KBIM-AM (nt) PO Box 1953, Roswell NM 88202 **Phn:** 575-623-9100 **Fax:** 575-623-4775 www.kbim949.com kevin@kbimradio.com

Roswell KCRX-AM (o) 200 W 1st St, Roswell NM 88203 **Phn:** 575-622-1432

Roswell KMOU-FM (c) PO Box 670, Roswell NM 88202 **Phn:** 575-622-6450 **Fax:** 575-622-9041 www.1047kmou.com

Roswell KRDD-AM (yh) PO Box 1615, Roswell NM 88202 **Phn:** 575-623-8111 krddam@yahoo.com

Roswell KSFX-FM (r) PO Box 670, Roswell NM 88202 **Phn:** 575-622-6450 **Fax:** 575-622-9041 www.1005ksfx.com

Ruidoso KBUY-AM (o) 1096 Mechem Dr Ste 230, Ruidoso NM 88345 **Phn:** 575-258-2222 **Fax:** 575-258-2224

Ruidoso KIDX-FM (r) 1086 Mechem Dr Ste A, Ruidoso NM 88345 **Phn:** 575-258-9922 **Fax:** 575-258-2363 www.kidxradio.com kidx@mtdradio.com

Ruidoso KNMB-FM (a) 1086 Mechem Dr, Ruidoso NM 88345 **Phn:** 575-258-9922 **Fax:** 575-258-2363 www.mymix967.com mix@mtdradio.com

Ruidoso KRUI-AM (nt) 1086 Mechem Dr, Ruidoso NM 88345 **Phn:** 575-258-9922 **Fax:** 575-258-2363 www.1490krui.com krui@mtdradio.com

Ruidoso KWES-AM (s) 1096 Mechem Dr Ste 230, Ruidoso NM 88345 **Phn:** 575-258-2222 **Fax:** 575-258-2224

Ruidoso KWES-FM (c) 1096 Mechem Dr Ste 230, Ruidoso NM 88345 **Phn:** 575-258-2222 **Fax:** 575-258-2224

Ruidoso KWMW-FM (c) 1086 Mechem Dr, Ruidoso NM 88345 **Phn:** 575-258-9922 **Fax:** 575-258-2363 www.105radio.com w105@mtdradio.com

Santa Fe KBAC-FM (ar) 2502 Camino Entrada Ste C, Santa Fe NM 87507 **Phn:** 505-471-1067 **Fax:** 505-473-2667 www.santafe.comkbac ira@santafe.com

Santa Fe KLBU-FM (j) 2502 Camino Entrada Ste C, Santa Fe NM 87507 **Phn:** 505-471-1067 www.huttonbroadcasting.com ira@huttonbroadcasting.com

Santa Fe KQBA-FM (c) 2502 Camino Entrada, Santa Fe NM 87507 **Phn:** 505-471-1067 **Fax:** 505-473-2667 www.santafe.comoutlaw chrisd@santafe.com

Santa Fe KSFR-FM (pj) PO Box 31366, Santa Fe NM 87594 **Phn:** 505-428-1527 **Fax:** 505-424-8938 www.ksfr.org info@ksfr.org

Santa Fe KSWV-AM (y) 102 Taos St, Santa Fe NM 87505 **Phn:** 505-989-7441 **Fax:** 505-989-7607

Santa Fe KTRC-AM (nt) 2502 Camino Entrada, Santa Fe NM 87507 **Phn:** 505-471-1067 **Fax:** 505-473-2667 www.santafe.comktrc talk@talk1260.com

Santa Fe KVSF-AM (s) 2502 Camino Entrada Ste C, Santa Fe NM 87507 **Phn:** 505-471-1067 **Fax:** 505-473-2667 www.santafe.com

Santa Rosa KIVA-FM (h) 2818 Historic Route 66, Santa Rosa NM 88435 **Phn:** 575-472-5777 kssrradio@yahoo.com

Santa Rosa KSSR-AM (acy) 2818 Historic Route 66, Santa Rosa NM 88435 **Phn:** 575-472-5777 kssrradio@yahoo.com

Silver City KNFT-AM (snt) 1560 N Corbin St, Silver City NM 88061 **Phn:** 575-538-3396 **Fax:** 575-388-1759 www.silvercityradio.com

Silver City KNFT-FM (c) 1560 N Corbin St, Silver City NM 88061 **Phn:** 575-538-3396 **Fax:** 575-388-1759 www.silvercityradio.com

Silver City KPSA-FM (or) 1560 N Corbin St, Silver City NM 88061 **Phn:** 575-388-1958 **Fax:** 575-388-5000 silvercityradio.com

Silver City KSCQ-FM (ah) 1560 N Corbin St, Silver City NM 88061 **Phn:** 575-538-3396 **Fax:** 575-388-1759 silvercityradio.com

Socorro KMXQ-FM (c) PO Box 699, Socorro NM 87801 **Phn:** 575-835-1286 **Fax:** 575-835-2015

Taos KKIT-FM (r) 125 Camino De La Merced, Taos NM 87571 **Phn:** 575-758-4491 **Fax:** 575-758-4452 www.kkitthemountain.com production@kxmt.com

Taos KKTC-FM (c) 125 Camino De La Merced, Taos NM 87571 **Phn:** 575-758-4491 **Fax:** 575-758-4452 darren@kxmt.com

Taos KTAO-FM (r) PO Box 1844, Taos NM 87571 **Phn:** 575-758-5826 **Fax:** 575-758-8430 ktaos.comblog info@ktaos.com

Taos KVOT-AM (nt) 125 Camino De La Merced, Taos NM 87571 **Phn:** 575-758-4491 **Fax:** 575-758-4452 www.1340kvot.com francina@kxmt.com

Taos KXMT-FM (y) 125 Camino De La Merced, Taos NM 87571 **Phn:** 575-758-4491 **Fax:** 575-758-4452 www.kxmt.com

NEW MEXICO RADIO STATIONS

Truth Or Consequences KCHS-AM (c) PO Box 351, Truth Or Consequences NM 87901 **Phn:** 575-894-2400 **Fax:** 575-894-3998 www.gpkmedia.com kchs@gpkmedia.com

Tucumcari KQAY-FM (a) PO Box 668, Tucumcari NM 88401 **Phn:** 575-461-0522 **Fax:** 575-461-0092

Tucumcari KTNM-AM (c) PO Box 668, Tucumcari NM 88401 **Phn:** 575-461-0522 **Fax:** 575-461-0092 ktnmkqay@yahoo.com

NEW YORK

Albany WAMC-FM (ptn) PO Box 66600, Albany NY 12206 **Phn:** 518-465-5233 **Fax:** 518-432-0991 www.wamc.org news@wamc.org

Albany WCDB-FM (v) 1400 Washington Ave, Albany NY 12222 **Phn:** 518-442-5234 **Fax:** 518-442-4366 www.wcdbfm.com programdirector@wcdbfm.com

Albany WDCD-AM (q) 4243 Albany St, Albany NY 12205 **Phn:** 518-862-1540 **Fax:** 518-862-1545 www.1540wdcd.com richleighton.djr@gmail.com

Albany WDDY-AM (m) 52 Corporate Cir Ste K, Albany NY 12203 **Phn:** 518-464-1311 **Fax:** 518-464-4185 music.disney.com

Albany WPTR-FM (q) 4243 Albany St, Albany NY 12205 **Phn:** 518-862-1540 **Fax:** 518-862-1545 www.967wptr.com victoriavandewal.djr@gmail.com

Albany WVCR-FM (vr) 515 Loudon Rd, Albany NY 12211 **Phn:** 518-783-6751 **Fax:** 518-782-6498 www.wvcr.com jkelly@siena.edu

Alfred WALF-FM (v) 1 Saxon Dr, Alfred NY 14802 **Phn:** 607-871-2287 www.walf.fm

Alfred WETD-FM (v) 10 Upper Campus Dr, Alfred NY 14802 **Phn:** 607-587-2907 www.wetd.fm wetd@alfredstate.edu

Amagansett WBAZ-FM (a) PO Box 7162, Amagansett NY 11930 **Phn:** 631-267-7800 **Fax:** 631-267-1018 www.wbaz.com dave@wbaz.com

Amagansett WBEA-FM (h) 249 Montauk Hwy, Amagansett NY 11930 **Phn:** 631-267-7800 **Fax:** 631-267-1018 www.beach1017.com johngovia@gmail.com

Amagansett WEHM-FM (a) PO Box 7162, Amagansett NY 11930 **Phn:** 631-267-7800 **Fax:** 631-267-1018 www.wehm.com info@wehm.com

Amsterdam WCSS-AM (bm) 135 Guy Park Ave, Amsterdam NY 12010 **Phn:** 518-843-2500 **Fax:** 518-842-0315

Amsterdam WVTL-AM (z) 5816 State Highway 30, Amsterdam NY 12010 **Phn:** 518-843-9284 **Fax:** 518-843-5225 wvtlfm.com jason@rosergroup.com

Amsterdam WVTL-FM (z) 5816 State Highway 30, Amsterdam NY 12010 **Phn:** 518-843-9284 **Fax:** 518-843-5225 wvtlfm.com jason@rosergroup.com

Auburn WDWN-FM (vr) 197 Franklin St, Auburn NY 13021 **Phn:** 315-255-1743 **Fax:** 315-255-2690 www.wdwn.fm wdwn@hotmail.com

Avon WYSL-AM (snt) PO Box 236, Avon NY 14414 **Phn:** 585-346-3000 **Fax:** 585-346-0450 www.wysl1040.com news@wysl1040.com

Baldwinsville WBXL-FM (v) 29 E Oneida St, Baldwinsville NY 13027 **Phn:** 315-638-6010

Baldwinsville WFBL-AM (o) PO Box 1050, Baldwinsville NY 13027 **Phn:** 315-635-3971 **Fax:** 315-635-3490 www.cnytalkradio.com j.carucci@lmgiradio.com

Baldwinsville WSEN-FM (h) PO Box 1050, Baldwinsville NY 13027 **Phn:** 315-635-3971 **Fax:** 315-635-3490 www.wsenfm.com d.wagner@lmgiradio.com

Batavia WBTA-AM (amn) 113 Main St Ste 1, Batavia NY 14020 **Phn:** 585-344-1490 **Fax:** 585-344-1441 www.wbta1490.com feedback@wbta1490.com

Batavia WGCC-FM (v) 1 College Rd, Batavia NY 14020 **Phn:** 585-343-0055 www.wgcc-fm.com cmplatt@genesee.edu

Bath WABH-AM (o) PO Box 72, Bath NY 14810 **Phn:** 607-776-3326 **Fax:** 607-776-6161

Bath WCIK-FM (qnv) PO Box 506, Bath NY 14810 **Phn:** 607-776-4151 **Fax:** 607-776-6929 www.fln.org

Bath WVIN-FM (a) PO Box 72, Bath NY 14810 **Phn:** 607-776-3326 **Fax:** 607-776-6161 wvinsales@stny.rr.com

Beacon WBNR-AM (as) PO Box 310, Beacon NY 12508 **Phn:** 845-838-6000 **Fax:** 845-838-2109 www.hvradionet.com bowens@pamal.com

Beacon WHUD-FM (a) PO Box 310, Beacon NY 12508 **Phn:** 845-838-6800 **Fax:** 845-838-2109 www.whud.com sguzman@pamal.com

Beacon WLNA-AM (am) PO Box 310, Beacon NY 12508 **Phn:** 845-838-6800 **Fax:** 845-838-2109 www.hvradionet.com bowens@pamal.com

Beacon WSPK-FM (h) PO Box 310, Beacon NY 12508 **Phn:** 845-831-8000 **Fax:** 845-838-2109 www.k104online.com smac@k104online.com

Binghamton WAAL-FM (r) PO Box 414, Binghamton NY 13902 **Phn:** 607-772-8400 **Fax:** 607-772-9806 www.991thewhale.com randy.horton@townsquaremedia.com

Binghamton WHRW-FM (v) PO Box 2000, Binghamton NY 13902 **Phn:** 607-777-2139 **Fax:** 607-777-6501 www.whrwfm.org pd@whrwfm.org

Binghamton WHWK-FM (c) PO Box 414, Binghamton NY 13902 **Phn:** 607-772-8400 **Fax:** 607-772-9806 www.981thehawk.com marybeth.walsh@townsquaremedia.com

Binghamton WNBF-AM (nt) PO Box 414, Binghamton NY 13902 **Phn:** 607-772-8400 **Fax:** 607-772-9806 www.wnbf.com roger.neel@townsquaremedia.com

Binghamton WSKG-FM (pln) PO Box 3000, Binghamton NY 13902 **Phn:** 607-729-0100 **Fax:** 607-729-7328 www.wskg.org wskgcomment@wskg.org

Binghamton WSQX-FM (pnj) PO Box 3000, Binghamton NY 13902 **Phn:** 607-729-0100 **Fax:** 607-729-7328

Binghamton WWYL-FM (h) 59 Court St Ste 100, Binghamton NY 13901 **Phn:** 607-772-8400 **Fax:** 607-772-9806 www.wild104fm.com matt.johnson@cumulus.com

Binghamton WYOS-AM (t) PO Box 414, Binghamton NY 13902 **Phn:** 607-772-8850 **Fax:** 607-772-9806

Brentwood WXBA-FM (v) 1st & 5th Aves Ross Bldg, Brentwood NY 11717 **Phn:** 631-434-2581

Brockport WASB-AM (q) 6675 4th Section Rd, Brockport NY 14420 **Phn:** 585-637-7040

Brockport WBSU-FM (v) 135 Seymour UN, Brockport NY 14420 **Phn:** 585-395-2580 **Fax:** 585-395-5334 www.891thepoint.com

Brockport WRSB-AM (q) 6675 4th Section Rd, Brockport NY 14420 **Phn:** 585-637-7040

Bronx WFUV-FM (vp) Fordham Univ, Bronx NY 10458 **Phn:** 718-817-4550 **Fax:** 718-365-9815 www.wfuv.org thefolks@wfuv.org

Brooklyn WKRB-FM (v) 2001 Oriental Blvd, Brooklyn NY 11235 **Phn:** 718-368-4572 **Fax:** 718-368-4776 www.wkrb.org gm@wkrb.org

NEW YORK RADIO STATIONS

Brooklyn WNSW-AM (y) PO Box 200012, Brooklyn NY 11220 **Phn:** 718-491-1430 **Fax:** 908-436-1431 www.radiocanticonuevo.com ericksalgado1430@hotmail.com

Buffalo WBBF-AM (g) 1420 Main St, Buffalo NY 14209 **Phn:** 716-783-7522 **Fax:** 716-783-7526

Buffalo WBEN-AM (nt) 500 Corporate Pkwy Ste 200, Buffalo NY 14226 **Phn:** 716-843-0600 **Fax:** 716-832-3080 www.wben.com tpuckett@entercom.com

Buffalo WBFO-FM (pjn) 3435 Main St Bldg 33, Buffalo NY 14214 **Phn:** 716-829-6000 **Fax:** 716-829-2277 www.wbfo.org news@wbfo.org

Buffalo WBLK-FM (wu) 14 Lafayette Sq Ste 1300, Buffalo NY 14203 **Phn:** 716-852-9393 **Fax:** 716-852-9290 wblk.com chris.reynolds@townsquaremedia.com

Buffalo WBNY-FM (pr) 1300 Elmwood Ave, Buffalo NY 14222 **Phn:** 716-878-3080 **Fax:** 716-878-6600 www.buffalostate.eduwbny wbnygm@gmail.com

Buffalo WBUF-FM (o) 14 Lafayette Sq Ste 1300, Buffalo NY 14203 **Phn:** 716-852-7444 **Fax:** 716-852-9290 929jackfm.com john.lassman@townsquaremedia.com

Buffalo WDCX-AM (e) 625 Delaware Ave Ste 308, Buffalo NY 14202 **Phn:** 716-883-3010 **Fax:** 716-883-3606 www.wdcxam.com info@wdcxradio.com

Buffalo WDCX-FM (q) 625 Delaware Ave Ste 308, Buffalo NY 14202 **Phn:** 716-883-3010 **Fax:** 716-883-3606 www.wdcxfm.com info@wdcxradio.com

Buffalo WECK-AM (c) 29 Genesee St, Buffalo NY 14203 **Phn:** 716-783-9325 **Fax:** 716-783-9120

Buffalo WEDG-FM (r) 50 James E Casey Dr, Buffalo NY 14206 **Phn:** 716-881-4555 **Fax:** 716-888-9773 www.wedg.com john.hager@cumulus.com

Buffalo WGR-AM (snt) 500 Corporate Pkwy Ste 200, Buffalo NY 14226 **Phn:** 716-843-0600 **Fax:** 716-832-3080 www.wgr550.com adavis@wgr550.com

Buffalo WGRF-FM (r) 50 James E Casey Dr, Buffalo NY 14206 **Phn:** 716-881-4555 **Fax:** 716-884-2931 www.97rock.com john.hager@cumulus.com

Buffalo WHLD-AM (g) 1420 Main St, Buffalo NY 14209 **Phn:** 716-783-7522 **Fax:** 716-783-7526 www.totallygospel.com johnyoung@totallygospel.com

Buffalo WHTT-FM (rh) 50 James E Casey Dr, Buffalo NY 14206 **Phn:** 716-881-4555 **Fax:** 716-885-6104 www.whtt.com joe.siragusa@cumulus.com

Buffalo WJYE-FM (a) 14 Lafayette Sq Ste 1200, Buffalo NY 14203 **Phn:** 716-852-7444 **Fax:** 716-852-0537 961joyfm.com richard.chiaino@townsquaremedia.com

Buffalo WKSE-FM (h) 500 Corporate Pkwy Ste 200, Buffalo NY 14226 **Phn:** 716-843-0600 **Fax:** 716-832-3297 www.kiss985.com soneil@entercom.com

Buffalo WLKK-FM (r) 500 Corporate Pkwy Ste 200, Buffalo NY 14226 **Phn:** 716-843-0600 **Fax:** 716-823-3297 www.1077thelake.com

Buffalo WNED-AM (pn) PO Box 1263, Buffalo NY 14240 **Phn:** 716-845-7000 **Fax:** 716-845-7043 www.wned.org news@wned.org

Buffalo WNED-FM (pl) PO Box 1263, Buffalo NY 14240 **Phn:** 716-845-7000 **Fax:** 716-845-7043 www.wned.org

Buffalo WTSS-FM (a) 500 Corporate Pkwy Ste 200, Buffalo NY 14226 **Phn:** 716-843-0600 **Fax:** 716-832-3080 www.mystar1025.com sueoneil@mystar1025.com

Buffalo WUFO-AM (wg) 89 Lasalle Ave, Buffalo NY 14214 **Phn:** 716-834-1080 **Fax:** 716-837-1438 www.wufoam.com lpettigrew@wufoam.com

Buffalo WWKB-AM (o) 500 Corporate Pkwy Ste 200, Buffalo NY 14226 **Phn:** 716-843-0600 **Fax:** 716-832-3080 www.kb1520.com kcarr@entercom.com

Buffalo WWWS-AM (u) 500 Corporate Pkwy Ste 200, Buffalo NY 14226 **Phn:** 716-843-0600 **Fax:** 716-871-0930 www.am1400solidgoldsoul.com soneil@entercom.com

Buffalo WYRK-FM (c) 14 Lafayette Sq Ste 1200, Buffalo NY 14203 **Phn:** 716-852-7444 **Fax:** 716-852-0537 wyrk.com wendy.lynn@regentcomm.com

Buskirk WNGN-FM (gq) 65 King Rd, Buskirk NY 12028 **Phn:** 518-686-0975

Canton WSLU-FM (p) Saint Lawrence Univ, Canton NY 13617 **Phn:** 315-229-5356 **Fax:** 315-229-5373 www.northcountrypublicradio.org radio@ncpr.org

Cazenovia WITC-FM (v) 22 Sullivan St, Cazenovia NY 13035 **Phn:** 315-655-7154

Central Islip WLIE-AM (y) 990 Motor Pkwy, Central Islip NY 11722 **Phn:** 631-569-4294 **Fax:** 631-761-8649 www.wlie540am.com smusgrave@mercurycapitalpartners.com

Champlain WCHP-AM (q) 137 Rapids Rd, Champlain NY 12919 **Phn:** 518-298-2800 **Fax:** 518-298-2604 wchp.com wchp@primelink1.net

Cherry Valley WJIV-FM (q) 1668 County Highway 50, Cherry Valley NY 13320 **Phn:** 607-264-3062 **Fax:** 607-264-8277 www.wjivradio.com wjiv@hughes.net

Clinton WHCL-FM (v) 198 College Hill Rd, Clinton NY 13323 **Phn:** 315-859-4200 www.whcl.org

Cobleskill WSDE-AM (nt) PO Box 608, Cobleskill NY 12043 **Phn:** 518-234-3400 **Fax:** 518-234-4567 www.1190wsde.com localnews@1190wsde.com

Cohoes WBAR-FM (q) 30 Park Ave, Cohoes NY 12047 **Phn:** 518-237-1330 www.aliveradionetwork.com events@aliveradionetwork.com

Cohoes WHAZ-AM (q) 30 Park Ave, Cohoes NY 12047 **Phn:** 518-237-1330 **Fax:** 518-235-4468 www.aliveradionetwork.com events@aliveradionetwork.com

Cohoes WHAZ-FM (q) 30 Park Ave, Cohoes NY 12047 **Phn:** 518-237-1330 **Fax:** 518-235-4468 www.aliveradionetwork.com events@aliveradionetwork.com

Cohoes WMNV-FM (q) 30 Park Ave, Cohoes NY 12047 **Phn:** 518-237-1330 **Fax:** 518-235-4468 www.aliveradionetwork.com events@aliveradionetwork.com

Cohoes WMYY-FM (q) 30 Park Ave, Cohoes NY 12047 **Phn:** 518-237-1330 **Fax:** 518-235-4468 www.aliveradionetwork.com events@aliveradionetwork.com

Corning WCBA-AM (a) 21 E Market St Ste 101, Corning NY 14830 **Phn:** 607-937-8181 **Fax:** 607-962-1138

Corning WCEB-FM (vr) 1 Academic Dr, Corning NY 14830 **Phn:** 607-962-9360

Corning WENI-FM (a) 21 E Market St Ste 101, Corning NY 14830 **Phn:** 607-937-8181 **Fax:** 607-962-1138 magic927977.net wenyfranklyspeaking@gmail.com

Corning WENY-AM (nt) 21 E Market St Ste 101, Corning NY 14830 **Phn:** 607-937-8181 **Fax:** 607-962-1138

Corning WENY-FM (a) 21 E Market St Ste 101, Corning NY 14830 **Phn:** 607-937-8181 **Fax:** 607-962-1138 www.magic927977.com wenyfranklyspeaking@gmail.com

Corning WGMM-FM (o) 21 E Market St Ste 101, Corning NY 14830 **Phn:** 607-937-8181 **Fax:** 607-962-1138

Cortland WSUC-FM (v) Graham Ave Brockway Hall Sun, Cortland NY 13045 **Phn:** 607-753-2936 web.cortland.eduwsuc wsucsecretary@yahoo.com

Dansville WDNY-AM (ob) 195 Main St, Dansville NY 14437 **Phn:** 585-335-2273 **Fax:** 585-335-9677 www.wdnyradio.com wdny@frontiernet.net

Dansville WDNY-FM (sna) 195 Main St, Dansville NY 14437 **Phn:** 585-335-9677 **Fax:** 585-335-9677 www.wdnyradio.com wdny@frontiernet.net

Dundee WFLR-AM (c) 30 Main St, Dundee NY 14837 **Phn:** 607-243-7158 www.fingerlakesdailynews.com abishop@flradiogroup.com

Dunkirk WBKX-FM (c) PO Box 209, Dunkirk NY 14048 **Phn:** 716-366-1410 **Fax:** 716-366-1416 www.wbkxcountry.com news@wdoe1410.com

Dunkirk WDOE-AM (a) PO Box 209, Dunkirk NY 14048 **Phn:** 716-366-1410 **Fax:** 716-366-1416 www.chautauquatoday.com news@wdoe1410.com

East Syracuse WSIV-AM (wgq) 7095 Myers Rd, East Syracuse NY 13057 **Phn:** 315-656-2231 **Fax:** 315-656-2259

East Syracuse WVOA-FM (m) 7095 Myers Rd, East Syracuse NY 13057 **Phn:** 315-656-2231 **Fax:** 315-656-2259 www.wvoaradio.com programming@wvoaradio.com

Elmira WECW-FM (v) 1 Park Pl, Elmira NY 14901 **Phn:** 607-735-1885

Elmira WEHH-AM (a) 1705 Lake St, Elmira NY 14901 **Phn:** 607-733-5626 **Fax:** 607-733-5627 rjp-ppmg@stny.rr.com

Elmira WELM-AM (s) 1705 Lake St, Elmira NY 14901 **Phn:** 607-733-5626 **Fax:** 607-733-5627 www.welm1410.com rjp-ppmg@stny.rr.com

Elmira WLVY-FM (h) 1705 Lake St, Elmira NY 14901 **Phn:** 607-733-5626 **Fax:** 607-733-5627 www.94rockfm.com playlist@stny.rr.com

Elmira WNGZ-FM (r) 2205 College Ave, Elmira NY 14903 **Phn:** 607-732-4400 **Fax:** 607-732-7774 www.wngz.com smitty.oloughlin@bybradio.com

Elmira WNKI-FM (ah) 2205 College Ave, Elmira NY 14903 **Phn:** 607-732-4400 **Fax:** 607-732-7774 www.wink106.com scott.free@bybradio.com

Elmira WOKN-FM (c) 1705 Lake St, Elmira NY 14901 **Phn:** 607-733-5626 **Fax:** 607-733-5627 995woknelmira.com

Elmira WPGI-FM (c) 2205 College Ave, Elmira NY 14903 **Phn:** 607-732-4400 **Fax:** 607-732-7774 www.bigpigfm.com scott.free@bybradio.com

Elmira WPIE-AM (sc) 1705 Lake St, Elmira NY 14901 **Phn:** 607-733-5626 **Fax:** 607-733-5627 tmallinson@gmail.com

Elmira WWLZ-AM (nt) 2205 College Ave, Elmira NY 14903 **Phn:** 607-732-4400 **Fax:** 607-732-7774 www.wwlzam820.com sandy.swan@bybradio.com

Endwell WLTB-FM (a) 3215 E Main St Ste 2, Endwell NY 13760 **Phn:** 607-748-9131 **Fax:** 607-748-0061 www.magic1017fm.com info@magic1017fm.com

Farmingdale WBZO-FM (o) 234 Airport Plaza Blvd Ste 5, Farmingdale NY 11735 **Phn:** 631-770-4200 **Fax:** 631-770-0101 www.b103.com wiseman@b103.com

Farmingdale WHLI-AM (om) 234 Airport Plaza Blvd Ste 5, Farmingdale NY 11735 **Phn:** 631-770-4200 **Fax:** 631-770-0101 www.whli.com paul@whli.com

Farmingdale WIGX-FM (ah) 234 Airport Plaza Blvd Ste 5, Farmingdale NY 11735 **Phn:** 631-770-4200 **Fax:** 631-770-0101

Farmingdale WKJY-FM (a) 234 Airport Plaza Blvd Ste 5, Farmingdale NY 11735 **Phn:** 631-770-4200 **Fax:** 631-770-0101 www.k983.com steve@kjoy.com

Floral Park WLIR-FM (ar) 20 Nassau St, Floral Park NY 11001 **Phn:** 516-495-8504 **Fax:** 631-648-2510 wlir.fm

Fredonia WCVF-FM (v) 115 McEwan Hall Suny, Fredonia NY 14063 **Phn:** 716-673-3420 **Fax:** 716-673-3427 www.wdvl895.com fredoniaradio@gmail.com

Garden City WHPC-FM (v) 1 Education Dr, Garden City NY 11530 **Phn:** 516-572-7438 **Fax:** 516-572-7831 www.ncc.eduwhpc whpc@ncc.edu

Geneseo WGSU-FM (v) 1 College Cir, Geneseo NY 14454 **Phn:** 585-245-5488 **Fax:** 585-245-5240 www.geneseo.edu~wgsu wgsumd@geneseo.edu

Geneva WAUB-AM (nt) 3568 Lenox Rd, Geneva NY 14456 **Phn:** 315-781-7000 **Fax:** 315-781-7077 www.fingerlakesdailynews.com tbaker@flradiogroup.com

Geneva WCGR-FM (an) 3568 Lenox Rd, Geneva NY 14456 **Phn:** 315-781-7000 **Fax:** 315-781-7077 www.fingerlakesdailynews.com news@flradiogroup.com

Geneva WEOS-FM (pjn) 300 Pulteney St, Geneva NY 14456 **Phn:** 315-781-3456 **Fax:** 315-781-3916 www.weos.org cotterill@hws.edu

Geneva WFLK-FM (c) PO Box 1017, Geneva NY 14456 **Phn:** 315-781-1101 **Fax:** 315-781-6666 www.k1017.com

Geneva WGVA-AM (t) 3568 Lenox Rd, Geneva NY 14456 **Phn:** 315-781-1240 **Fax:** 315-781-7077 www.fingerlakesdailynews.com tbaker@flradiogroup.com

Geneva WLLW-FM (r) 3568 Lenox Rd, Geneva NY 14456 **Phn:** 315-781-7000 **Fax:** 315-781-7700 kparadise@flradiogroup.com

Geneva WNYR-FM (a) 3568 Lenox Rd, Geneva NY 14456 **Phn:** 315-781-7000 **Fax:** 315-781-7077 www.fingerlakesdailynews.com wnyr@flradiogroup.com

Geneva WSFW-AM (nt) 3568 Lenox Rd, Geneva NY 14456 **Phn:** 315-781-7000 **Fax:** 315-781-7007 www.fingerlakesdailynews.com

Gloversville WENT-AM (a) PO Box 831, Gloversville NY 12078 **Phn:** 518-725-7175 **Fax:** 518-725-7177 www.am1340went.com went@capital.net

Greenvale WCWP-FM (v) 720 Northern Blvd, Greenvale NY 11548 **Phn:** 516-299-2626 **Fax:** 516-299-2767 www.wcwp.org

Hamilton WRCU-FM (v) 13 Oak Dr, Hamilton NY 13346 **Phn:** 315-228-7901 www.wrcufm.com wrcugeneralmanager@gmail.com

Hartsdale WFAF-FM (r) 365 Secor Rd, Hartsdale NY 10530 **Phn:** 914-693-2400 **Fax:** 914-693-0000 www.wfasfm.com jolana.smith@cumulus.com

Hartsdale WFAS-AM (nt) 365 Secor Rd, Hartsdale NY 10530 **Phn:** 914-693-2400 **Fax:** 914-693-4489 www.wfasam.com robby.bridges@cumulus.com

Hartsdale WFAS-FM (a) 365 Secor Rd, Hartsdale NY 10530 **Phn:** 914-693-2400 **Fax:** 914-693-0000 www.wfasfm.com jolana.smith@cumulus.com

Hempstead WRHU-FM (v) 1000 Fulton Ave, Hempstead NY 11550 **Phn:** 516-463-5667 **Fax:** 516-463-5668 www.wrhu.org dadingles@aol.com

Herkimer WVHC-FM (v) 100 Reservoir Rd, Herkimer NY 13350 **Phn:** 315-866-0300 wvhc@herkimer.edu

Herkimer WXUR-FM (o) 566 Baum Rd, Herkimer NY 13350 **Phn:** 315-266-0250 **Fax:** 315-266-0291 927thedrive.net wxur@hotmail.com

Homer WXHC-FM (o) PO Box 386, Homer NY 13077 **Phn:** 607-749-9942 **Fax:** 607-749-2374 www.wxhc.com johneves@wxhc.com

Hornell WKPQ-FM (a) 1484 Beech St, Hornell NY 14843 **Phn:** 607-324-1596 **Fax:** 607-324-4800

Hornell WLEA-AM (nt) 5942 County Route 64, Hornell NY 14843 **Phn:** 607-324-1480 **Fax:** 607-324-5415 www.am1480wlea.com newsroom@wlea.net

Horseheads WLNL-AM (q) 3134 Lake Rd, Horseheads NY 14845 **Phn:** 607-737-9208

Horseheads WMTT-FM (r) 734 Chemung St, Horseheads NY 14845 **Phn:** 607-795-0795 **Fax:** 607-795-1095 www.themetrocks.com shimes@themetrocks.com

Hudson WCTW-FM (a) 5620 State Route 9G, Hudson NY 12534 **Phn:** 518-828-5006 **Fax:** 518-828-1080

Hudson WZCR-FM (o) 5620 State Route 9G, Hudson NY 12534 **Phn:** 518-828-5006 **Fax:** 518-828-1080 www.oldies935.com billwilliams@clearchannel.com

Ilion WNRS-AM (s) PO Box 927, Ilion NY 13357 **Phn:** 315-866-9200 **Fax:** 315-866-6906 wxur@hotmail.com

Ithaca WHCU-AM (snt) 1751 Hanshaw Rd, Ithaca NY 14850 **Phn:** 607-257-6400 **Fax:** 607-257-6497 whcuradio.com callinger@cyradiogroup.com

Ithaca WICB-FM (v) 118 Park Hall Ithaca Coll, Ithaca NY 14850 **Phn:** 607-274-1040 **Fax:** 607-274-1061 www.wicb.org news@wicb.org

Ithaca WIII-FM (r) 1751 Hanshaw Rd, Ithaca NY 14850 **Phn:** 607-257-6400 **Fax:** 607-257-6497 www.i100rocks.com callinger@cyradiogroup.com

Ithaca WNYY-AM (t) 1751 Hanshaw Rd, Ithaca NY 14850 **Phn:** 607-257-6400 **Fax:** 607-257-6497 wnyyradio.com cosadchey@cyradiogroup.com

Ithaca WQNY-FM (c) 1751 Hanshaw Rd, Ithaca NY 14850 **Phn:** 607-257-6400 **Fax:** 607-257-6497 1037qcountry.com cosadchey@cyradiogroup.com

Ithaca WVBR-FM (r) 957 Mitchell St # B, Ithaca NY 14850 **Phn:** 607-273-4000 **Fax:** 607-273-4069 www.wvbr.com gm@wvbr.com

Ithaca WYXL-FM (a) 1751 Hanshaw Rd, Ithaca NY 14850 **Phn:** 607-257-6400 **Fax:** 607-257-6497 www.literock973.com news@cyradiogroup.com

Jamestown WHUG-FM (c) PO Box 1139, Jamestown NY 14702 **Phn:** 716-487-1151 **Fax:** 716-664-9326 www.whug.com

Jamestown WJTN-AM (nt) 2 Orchard Rd, Jamestown NY 14701 **Phn:** 716-487-1151 **Fax:** 716-664-9326 www.wjtn.com larry@radiojamestown.com

Jamestown WKSN-AM (t) PO Box 1139, Jamestown NY 14702 **Phn:** 716-487-1151 **Fax:** 716-664-9326 www.wksn.com

Jamestown WQFX-FM (r) 2 Orchard Rd, Jamestown NY 14701 **Phn:** 716-487-1151 **Fax:** 716-664-9326 www.wqfx1031.com terry@radiojamestown.com

Jamestown WWSE-FM (a) PO Box 1139, Jamestown NY 14702 **Phn:** 716-487-1151 **Fax:** 716-664-9326 www.se933.com

Jeffersonville WJFF-FM (pln) PO Box 546, Jeffersonville NY 12748 **Phn:** 845-482-4141 **Fax:** 845-482-9533 www.wjffradio.org wjff@wjffradio.org

Johnson City WCDW-FM (o) 101 Main St Ste 1, Johnson City NY 13790 **Phn:** 607-772-1005 **Fax:** 607-772-2945 www.cool1067.coolesthits.com

Kingston WKNY-AM (a) 718 Broadway, Kingston NY 12401 **Phn:** 845-331-1490 **Fax:** 845-331-9569 www.1490wkny.com lindarosnerwkny@yahoo.com

Lake Katrine WFGB-FM (q) PO Box 777, Lake Katrine NY 12449 **Phn:** 845-336-6199 **Fax:** 845-336-7205 www.SoundofLife.org conniev@soundoflife.org

Lancaster WXRL-AM (c) PO Box 170, Lancaster NY 14086 **Phn:** 716-681-1313 **Fax:** 716-681-7172 www.wxrl.com wxrl@aol.com

Latham WAJZ-FM (wua) 6 Johnson Rd, Latham NY 12110 **Phn:** 518-786-6600 **Fax:** 518-786-6669 jamz963.com charlie@jamz963.com

Latham WFLY-FM (h) 6 Johnson Rd, Latham NY 12110 **Phn:** 518-786-6600 **Fax:** 518-786-6669 www.fly92.com ally@fly92.com

Latham WGY-AM (nat) 1203 Troy Schenectady Rd Ste 201, Latham NY 12110 **Phn:** 518-452-4800 **Fax:** 518-452-4813 www.wgy.com josh@wgy.com

Latham WHRL-FM (r) 1203 Troy Schenectady Rd Ste 201, Latham NY 12110 **Phn:** 518-452-4800 **Fax:** 518-452-4870 www.pyx106.com johncooper@clearchannel.com

Latham WKKF-FM (h) 1203 Troy Schenectady Rd Ste 201, Latham NY 12110 **Phn:** 518-452-4800 **Fax:** 518-452-4813 www.kiss1023.com randymccarten@clearchannel.com

Latham WKLI-FM (az) 6 Johnson Rd, Latham NY 12110 **Phn:** 518-786-6600 **Fax:** 518-786-6610 www.albanymagic.com jscott@albanybroadcasting.com

Latham WOFX-AM (st) 1203 Troy Schenectady Rd, Latham NY 12110 **Phn:** 518-452-4800 **Fax:** 518-452-4855 www.foxsports980.com wofx@clearchannel.com

Latham WPYX-FM (r) 1203 Troy Schenectady Rd Ste 201, Latham NY 12110 **Phn:** 518-452-4800 **Fax:** 518-452-4855 www.pyx106.com johncooper@clearchannel.com

Latham WROW-AM (nt) 6 Johnson Rd, Latham NY 12110 **Phn:** 518-786-6600 **Fax:** 518-786-6659 albanymagic.com

Latham WRVE-FM (ra) 1203 Troy Schenectady Rd Ste 201, Latham NY 12110 **Phn:** 518-452-4800 **Fax:** 518-452-4855 www.995theriver.com randymccarten@clearchannel.com

Latham WTRY-FM (o) 1203 Troy Schenectady Rd, Latham NY 12110 **Phn:** 518-452-4800 **Fax:** 518-452-4813 www.oldies983.com johncooper@clearchannel.com

Latham WYJB-FM (ar) 6 Johnson Rd, Latham NY 12110 **Phn:** 518-786-6600 **Fax:** 518-786-6610 b95.com

Latham WZMR-FM (r) 6 Johnson Rd, Latham NY 12110 **Phn:** 518-786-6600 **Fax:** 518-786-6610 www.albanyedge.com jsenecal@albanybroadcasting.com

Liberty WDNB-FM (n) 1987 State Route 52 Ste 9, Liberty NY 12754 **Phn:** 845-292-7535 **Fax:** 845-292-7529 thunder102.com msakell@boldgoldmedia.com

Lockport WLVL-AM (ntb) PO Box 477, Lockport NY 14095 **Phn:** 716-433-5944 **Fax:** 716-433-6588 www.wlvl.com wlvl@wlvl.com

Lowville WBRV-FM (c) 7606 N State St, Lowville NY 13367 **Phn:** 315-376-7500 **Fax:** 315-376-8549 themoose.net sales@themoose.net

Lowville WBRV-AM (c) 7606 N State St, Lowville NY 13367 **Phn:** 315-376-7500 **Fax:** 315-376-8549

Lowville WLLG-FM (c) 7606 N State St, Lowville NY 13367 **Phn:** 315-376-7500 **Fax:** 315-376-8549 themoose.net sales@themoose.net

Malone WICY-AM (o) 86 Porter Rd, Malone NY 12953 **Phn:** 518-483-1100 **Fax:** 518-483-1382 www.oldiesradioonline.com

NEW YORK RADIO STATIONS

Malone WVNV-FM (c) 86 Porter Rd, Malone NY 12953 **Phn:** 518-483-1100 **Fax:** 518-483-1382 www.country965.com drew@country965.com

Malone WYUL-FM (h) 86 Porter Rd, Malone NY 12953 **Phn:** 518-483-1100 **Fax:** 518-483-1356 www.947hits.com drew@947hits.com

Malta WABY-FM (ob) 100 Saratoga Village Blvd Ste 21, Malta NY 12020 **Phn:** 518-899-3000 **Fax:** 518-899-3057 www.saratogamoon.com wabymoon@aol.com

Malta WQAR-FM (a) 100 Saratoga Village Blvd Ste 21, Malta NY 12020 **Phn:** 518-899-3000 **Fax:** 518-899-3057

Malta WUAM-AM (ob) 100 Saratoga Village Blvd Ste 21, Malta NY 12020 **Phn:** 518-899-3000 **Fax:** 518-899-3057 jhmeaney@aol.com

Malta WVKZ-AM (snt) 100 Saratoga Village Blvd Ste 21, Malta NY 12020 **Phn:** 518-899-3000 **Fax:** 518-899-3057 www.trueoldies1240.com scott@trueoldieschannel.com

Marcy WFRG-FM (c) 9418 River Rd, Marcy NY 13403 **Phn:** 315-768-9500 **Fax:** 315-736-0720 bigfrog104.com news@wibx950.com

Marcy WIBX-AM (snt) 9418 River Rd, Marcy NY 13403 **Phn:** 315-768-9500 **Fax:** 315-736-0720 wibx950.com news@wibx950.com

Marcy WLZW-FM (a) 9418 River Rd, Marcy NY 13403 **Phn:** 315-768-9500 **Fax:** 315-736-0720 lite987.com eric.meier@townsquaremedia.com

Marcy WODZ-FM (o) 9418 River Rd, Marcy NY 13403 **Phn:** 315-768-9500 **Fax:** 315-736-0720 961wodz.com david.wheeler@townsquaremedia.com

Massena WMSA-AM (o) PO Box 210, Massena NY 13662 **Phn:** 315-769-3333 **Fax:** 315-769-3299 www.1340wmsa.com news@1340wmsa.com

Massena WRCD-FM (r) PO Box 210, Massena NY 13662 **Phn:** 315-769-3333 **Fax:** 315-769-3299 www.1015thefox.com community@1015thefox.com

Massena WVLF-FM (a) PO Box 210, Massena NY 13662 **Phn:** 315-769-3333 **Fax:** 315-769-3299 www.mymix961.com community@mymix961.com

Massena WYBG-AM (at) PO Box 298, Massena NY 13662 **Phn:** 315-764-0554 **Fax:** 315-764-0118 www.wybg1050.com wybgradio@nnymail.com

Medford WLVG-FM (a) 3241 Route 112 Ste 7 # 2, Medford NY 11763 **Phn:** 631-451-1039 **Fax:** 631-451-0891

Medford WRCN-FM (rh) 3241 Route 112 Ste 7, Medford NY 11763 **Phn:** 631-451-1039 **Fax:** 631-451-0891 www.wrcn.com

Mineola WTHE-AM (wgu) 260 E 2nd St, Mineola NY 11501 **Phn:** 516-742-1520 **Fax:** 516-742-2878 www.wthe1520am.com nygospelradio@aol.com

Monticello WSUL-FM (a) PO Box 983, Monticello NY 12701 **Phn:** 845-794-9898 **Fax:** 845-794-0125

Monticello WVOS-AM (c) 198 Bridgeville Rd, Monticello NY 12701 **Phn:** 845-794-9898 **Fax:** 845-794-0125 www.wvosfm.com mail@wvosfm.com

Monticello WVOS-FM (a) 198 Bridgeville Rd, Monticello NY 12701 **Phn:** 845-794-9898 **Fax:** 845-794-0125 www.wvosfm.com mail@wvosfm.com

New Hartford WIXT-AM (s) 39 Kellogg Rd, New Hartford NY 13413 **Phn:** 315-797-1330 **Fax:** 315-738-1073 espnur.com elevine@galaxycommunications.com

New Hartford WKLL-FM (r) 39 Kellogg Rd, New Hartford NY 13413 **Phn:** 315-797-1330 **Fax:** 315-738-1073 www.krock.com kgaluppo@galaxycommunications.com

New Hartford WKRH-FM (r) 39 Kellogg Rd, New Hartford NY 13479 **Phn:** 315-797-1330 **Fax:** 315-738-1073 syracuse.krock.com

New Hartford WOUR-FM (r) 39 Kellogg Rd, New Hartford NY 13413 **Phn:** 315-797-1330 **Fax:** 315-738-1073 wour.com askwour@wour.com

New Hartford WRNY-AM (s) 39 Kellogg Rd, New Hartford NY 13413 **Phn:** 315-797-1330 **Fax:** 315-738-1073 mgriswold@galaxycommunications.com

New Hartford WTLB-AM (am) 39 Kellogg Rd, New Hartford NY 13413 **Phn:** 315-797-1330 **Fax:** 315-738-1073 jburke@galaxycommunications.com

New Hartford WUMX-FM (a) 39 Kellogg Rd, New Hartford NY 13413 **Phn:** 315-797-1330 **Fax:** 315-738-1073 www.mix1025.com askmix@mix1025.com

New Paltz WFNP-AM (vr) Suny Sub 413, New Paltz NY 12561 **Phn:** 845-257-3094 **Fax:** 845-257-3099 wfnp.org wfnpnews@gmail.com

New Rochelle WVIP-AM (a) 1 Broadcast Plz, New Rochelle NY 10801 **Phn:** 914-636-1460 **Fax:** 914-636-2900 www.wvox.com info@wvox.com

New Rochelle WVOX-AM (nt) 1 Broadcast Plz, New Rochelle NY 10801 **Phn:** 914-636-1460 **Fax:** 914-636-2900 www.wvox.com don@wvox.com

New Windsor WGNY-AM (o) 661 Little Britain Rd, New Windsor NY 12553 **Phn:** 845-561-2131 **Fax:** 845-561-2138 www.foxradio.net

New Windsor WGNY-FM (a) 661 Little Britain Rd, New Windsor NY 12553 **Phn:** 845-561-2131 **Fax:** 845-561-2138 foxradio.net

New York WABC-AM (nt) 2 Penn Plz Fl 17, New York NY 10121 **Phn:** 212-613-3800 **Fax:** 212-268-5730 www.wabcradio.com leslie.slender@cumulus.com

New York WADO-AM (ynt) 485 Madison Ave Fl 3, New York NY 10022 **Phn:** 212-310-6000 **Fax:** 212-310-6095 www.univision.com

New York WAXQ-FM (r) 32 Avenue Of The Americas, New York NY 10013 **Phn:** 212-377-7900 **Fax:** 212-302-7814 www.q1043.com ericwellman@clearchannel.com

New York WBAI-FM (v) 120 Wall St Ste 1002, New York NY 10005 **Phn:** 212-209-2800 **Fax:** 212-747-1698 www.wbai.org jsantiago@wbai.org

New York WBBR-AM (nk) 731 Lexington Ave, New York NY 10022 **Phn:** 212-318-2350 **Fax:** 917-369-5653 www.bloomberg.com release@bloomberg.net

New York WBLS-FM (wu) 3 Park Ave, New York NY 10016 **Phn:** 212-447-1000 **Fax:** 212-447-5791 www.wbls.com cynthia@wbls.com

New York WCBS-AM (n) 524 W 57th St, New York NY 10019 **Phn:** 212-975-4321 **Fax:** 212-975-1907 newyork.cbslocal.com

New York WCBS-FM (a) 345 Hudson St Fl 10, New York NY 10014 **Phn:** 212-242-6190 **Fax:** 212-975-1907 wcbsfm.cbslocal.com brian.thomas@cbsradio.com

New York WEPN-AM (s) 2 Penn Plz Fl 17, New York NY 10121 **Phn:** 212-615-3200 espn.go.comnewyorkradioindex jeff.skopin@espnradio.disney.com

New York WFAN-AM (s) 345 Hudson St 10th Fl, New York NY 10014 **Phn:** 212-315-7000 **Fax:** 212-352-2471 newyork.cbslocal.com espitz@wfan.com

New York WHCR-FM (wvy) 160 Convent Ave, New York NY 10031 **Phn:** 212-650-7481 **Fax:** 212-650-5736 www.whcr.org generalmanager@whcr.org

New York WHTZ-FM (h) 32 Avenue of the Americas, New York NY 10013 **Phn:** 212-377-7900 **Fax:** 212-239-2308 www.z100.com ccny-communities@clearchannel.com

New York WINS-AM (n) 345 Hudson St Fl 10, New York NY 10014 **Phn:** 212-315-7090 **Fax:** 212-489-7034 newyork.cbslocal.com mevorach@wins.com

New York WKCR-FM (v) 2920 Broadway 2612, New York NY 10027 **Phn:** 212-854-9920 www.studentaffairs.columbia.eduwkcr news@wkcr.org

New York WKTU-FM (h) 32 Avenue Of The Americas Bldg 1, New York NY 10013 **Phn:** 212-377-7900 **Fax:** 212-549-0762 www.ktu.com

New York WLIB-AM (wq) 641 Avenue Of The Americas Fl 4, New York NY 10011 **Phn:** 212-447-1000 **Fax:** 212-447-5791 www.wlib.com info@wlib.com

New York WLTW-FM (a) 32 Avenue Of The Americas, New York NY 10013 **Phn:** 212-377-7900 **Fax:** 212-603-4684 www.1067litefm.com litefmfeedback@clearchannel.com

New York WNYC-AM (pnt) 160 Varick St Fl 7, New York NY 10013 **Phn:** 646-829-4000 www.wnyc.org newsroom@wnyc.org

New York WNYC-FM (pl) 160 Varick St Fl 7, New York NY 10013 **Phn:** 646-829-4000 www.wnyc.org newsroom@wnyc.org

New York WNYE-FM (v) 1 Centre St Fl 28, New York NY 10007 **Phn:** 212-669-7400 www.nyc.govhtmlmediahtmlradioradio.shtml submissions@media.nyc.gov

New York WNYU-FM (v) 5 University Pl Bsmt 11, New York NY 10003 **Phn:** 212-998-1660 wnyu.org news@wnyu.org

New York WOR-AM (nt) 111 Broadway Fl 3, New York NY 10006 **Phn:** 212-642-4500 **Fax:** 212-642-4486 www.wor710.com jillkempton@clearchannel.com

New York WPAT-AM (y) 26 W 56th St, New York NY 10019 **Phn:** 212-246-9393 **Fax:** 212-664-1922

New York WPAT-FM (y) 26 W 56th St, New York NY 10019 **Phn:** 212-246-9393 **Fax:** 212-664-1922 www.931amor.com info@931amor.com

New York WPLJ-FM (ah) 2 Penn Plz Fl 17, New York NY 10121 **Phn:** 212-613-8900 **Fax:** 212-613-8956 www.plj.com comments@plj.com

New York WQBU-FM (y) 485 Madison Ave Fl 3, New York NY 10022 **Phn:** 212-310-6000 **Fax:** 212-888-3694 www.univision.com

New York WQEW-AM (m) 2 Penn Plz, New York NY 10121 **Phn:** 212-760-1560 **Fax:** 212-613-3868 music.disney.com

New York WQHT-FM (h) 395 Hudson St Fl 7, New York NY 10014 **Phn:** 212-229-9797 **Fax:** 212-929-8559 www.Hot97.com hot97@hot97.com

New York WQXR-FM (l) 160 Varick St Flr 8, New York NY 10013 **Phn:** 212-633-7600 **Fax:** 212-633-7666 www.wqxr.org

New York WRXP-FM (r) 395 Hudson St, New York NY 10014 **Phn:** 212-352-1019 **Fax:** 212-929-8559 www.newrock1019.com

New York WSKQ-FM (y) 26 W 56th St, New York NY 10019 **Phn:** 212-541-9200 **Fax:** 212-541-6904 lamega.lamusica.com jtorres@sbsnewyork.com

New York WWFS-FM (a) 345 Hudson St Fl 10, New York NY 10014 **Phn:** 212-489-1027 **Fax:** 212-489-1263 fresh1027.cbslocal.com

New York WWPR-FM (wx) 32 Avenue Of The Americas Bldg 1, New York NY 10013 **Phn:** 212-377-7900 **Fax:** 212-549-0832 www.power1051fm.com

New York WWRL-AM (wge) 333 7th Ave Rm 1401, New York NY 10001 **Phn:** 212-631-0800 **Fax:** 212-239-7203 www.wwrl1600.com adriane@wwrl1600.com

NEW YORK RADIO STATIONS

Newark WACK-AM (snt) PO Box 1420, Newark NY 14513 **Phn:** 315-331-1420 **Fax:** 315-331-7101 www.1420wack.com 1420wack@rochester.rr.com

Newark WUUF-FM (c) 187 Vienna Rd, Newark NY 14513 **Phn:** 716-482-9667 **Fax:** 315-331-7101 www.bigdog1035.com bigdogfm@rochester.rr.com

Norwich WBKT-FM (c) 25 S Broad St, Norwich NY 13815 **Phn:** 607-432-1030 **Fax:** 607-432-6909 www.wbktfm.com george.wells@townsquaremedia.com

Norwich WKXZ-FM (h) 25 S Broad St, Norwich NY 13815 **Phn:** 607-432-1030 **Fax:** 607-432-6909 www.wkxzfm.com george.wells@townsquaremedia.com

Nyack WNYK-FM (v) 1 S Boulevard # 406, Nyack NY 10960 **Phn:** 845-358-1828

Ogdensburg WGIX-FM (o) 2315 Knox St, Ogdensburg NY 13669 **Phn:** 315-393-1100 **Fax:** 315-393-6673

Ogdensburg WNCQ-FM (c) 1 Bridge Plz Ste 204, Ogdensburg NY 13669 **Phn:** 315-393-1220 **Fax:** 315-393-3974 www.q1029.com john@q1029.com

Ogdensburg WPAC-FM (r) 1 Bridge Plz Ste 204, Ogdensburg NY 13669 **Phn:** 315-393-1220 **Fax:** 315-393-3974 yesfm.com john@q1029.com

Ogdensburg WSLB-AM (t) 1 Bridge Plz Ste 204, Ogdensburg NY 13669 **Phn:** 315-393-1120 **Fax:** 315-393-6673

Ogdensburg WYSX-FM (h) 1 Bridge Plz Ste 204, Ogdensburg NY 13669 **Phn:** 315-393-1220 **Fax:** 315-393-3974 www.yesfm.com john@q1029.com

Olean WGGO-AM (am) 231 N Union St, Olean NY 14760 **Phn:** 716-945-1590 **Fax:** 716-945-1515

Olean WHDL-AM (o) 3163 Nys Route 417, Olean NY 14760 **Phn:** 716-372-0161 **Fax:** 716-372-0164 mark.thompson@bybradio.com

Olean WMXO-FM (a) 231 N Union St, Olean NY 14760 **Phn:** 716-375-1015 **Fax:** 716-375-7705 www.themixwmxo.com wqrw93radio@yahoo.com

Olean WOEN-AM (t) 231 N Union St, Olean NY 14760 **Phn:** 716-375-1015 **Fax:** 716-375-7705 aaron@mix1015online.com

Olean WPIG-FM (c) 3163 Nys Route 417, Olean NY 14760 **Phn:** 716-372-0161 **Fax:** 716-372-0164 www.wpig.com john.morton@bybradio.com

Olean WQRS-FM (r) 231 N Union St, Olean NY 14760 **Phn:** 716-945-1590 **Fax:** 716-945-1515 qrock@atlanticbbn.net

Oneida WMCR-FM (a) 237 Genesee St, Oneida NY 13421 **Phn:** 315-363-6050 j.johnson@lmgiradio.com

Oneida WMCR-AM (a) 237 Genesee St, Oneida NY 13421 **Phn:** 315-363-6050 j.johnson@lmgiradio.com

Oneonta WCHN-AM (a) 34 Chestnut St, Oneonta NY 13820 **Phn:** 607-432-1030 **Fax:** 607-432-6909 cnynews.com george.wells@townsquaremedia.com

Oneonta WDLA-AM (abo) 34 Chestnut St, Oneonta NY 13820 **Phn:** 607-432-1030 **Fax:** 607-432-6909 cnynews.com george.wells@townsquaremedia.com

Oneonta WDOS-AM (c) 34 Chestnut St, Oneonta NY 13820 **Phn:** 607-432-1030 **Fax:** 607-432-6909 cnynews.com george.wells@townsquaremedia.com

Oneonta WONY-FM (v) Alumni Hall Suny, Oneonta NY 13820 **Phn:** 607-436-2712 organizations.oneonta.eduwony wonynews@gmail.com

Oneonta WRHO-FM (v) 1 Hartwick Dr, Oneonta NY 13820 **Phn:** 607-431-4555 **Fax:** 607-431-4556 wrhofm.com wrho@hartwick.edu

Oneonta WSRK-FM (a) 34 Chestnut St, Oneonta NY 13820 **Phn:** 607-432-1030 **Fax:** 607-432-8952 wsrkfm.com george.wells@townsquaremedia.com

Oneonta WZOZ-FM (r) 34 Chestnut St, Oneonta NY 13820 **Phn:** 607-432-1030 **Fax:** 607-432-6909 wzozfm.com wsrknews@yahoo.com

Oswego WNYO-FM (vru) 98 Hewitt UN, Oswego NY 13126 **Phn:** 315-312-2101 www.wnyo.org wnyo@wnyo.org

Oswego WRVO-FM (p) 7060 State Route 104, Oswego NY 13126 **Phn:** 315-312-3690 **Fax:** 315-312-3174 www.wrvo.fm news@wrvo.fm

Patchogue WALK-FM (a) 66 Colonial Dr, Patchogue NY 11772 **Phn:** 631-475-5200 **Fax:** 631-475-0159 www.walkradio.com jnewport@walkradio.com

Patchogue WALK-AM (a) 66 Colonial Dr, Patchogue NY 11772 **Phn:** 631-475-5200 **Fax:** 631-475-0159 www.1370walk.com walknews@walkradio.com

Penfield WBER-FM (vr) 2596 Baird Rd, Penfield NY 14526 **Phn:** 585-419-8190 **Fax:** 585-419-8191 wber.monroe.edu wber@monroe.edu

Penn Yan WYLF-AM (am) 100 Main St Ste 104, Penn Yan NY 14527 **Phn:** 315-536-0850 **Fax:** 315-536-3299 wylf@airxcess.net

Plattsburgh WIRY-AM (a) 4712 State Route 9, Plattsburgh NY 12901 **Phn:** 518-563-1340 **Fax:** 518-563-1343 www.wiry.com wiry@wiry.com

Plattsburgh WQKE-FM (v) 65 Broad St, Plattsburgh NY 12901 **Phn:** 518-564-2727

Pomona WLIM-AM (yq) 1551 Route 202, Pomona NY 10970 **Phn:** 845-354-4917 **Fax:** 845-354-4917 www.polskieradio.com goga@polskieradio.com

Pomona WRCR-AM (ant) 5 Provident Bank Park Dr, Pomona NY 10970 **Phn:** 845-362-5070 **Fax:** 845-362-5073 www.wrcr.com info@wrcr.com

Pomona WRKL-AM (e) 1551 Route 202, Pomona NY 10970 **Phn:** 845-354-2000 **Fax:** 845-354-4917 www.polskieradio.com radio@polskieradio.com

Potsdam WAIH-FM (v) 9050 Barrington Dr, Potsdam NY 13676 **Phn:** 315-267-4888 www.theway903.com hohjk192@potsdam.edu

Potsdam WPDM-AM (ao) PO Box 348, Potsdam NY 13676 **Phn:** 315-265-5510 **Fax:** 315-265-4040

Potsdam WSNN-FM (a) PO Box 348, Potsdam NY 13676 **Phn:** 315-265-5510 **Fax:** 315-265-4040

Potsdam WTSC-FM (v) PO Box 8743, Potsdam NY 13699 **Phn:** 315-268-7658 radio.clarkson.edu wtsc911@gmail.com

Poughkeepsie WALL-AM (m) 2 Pendell Rd, Poughkeepsie NY 12601 **Phn:** 845-471-1500 **Fax:** 845-454-1204 music.disney.com

Poughkeepsie WBWZ-FM (r) 20 Tucker Dr, Poughkeepsie NY 12603 **Phn:** 845-471-2300 **Fax:** 845-471-2683 www.rock933.com chrismarino@clearchannel.com

Poughkeepsie WCZX-FM (a) PO Box 416, Poughkeepsie NY 12602 **Phn:** 845-471-1500 **Fax:** 845-454-1204 www.mix97fm.com newsroom@pendellrd.com

Poughkeepsie WELG-FM (a) 20 Tucker Dr, Poughkeepsie NY 12603 **Phn:** 845-471-2300 **Fax:** 845-471-2683 www.1450wkip.com stevegiuttari@clearchannel.com

Poughkeepsie WEOK-AM (nt) 2 Pendell Rd, Poughkeepsie NY 12601 **Phn:** 845-471-1500 **Fax:** 845-454-1204 music.disney.com

Poughkeepsie WFKP-FM (h) 20 Tucker Dr, Poughkeepsie NY 12603 **Phn:** 845-471-2300 **Fax:** 845-471-2683 www.kissfmhv.com terryodonnell@clearchannel.com

Poughkeepsie WHUC-AM (c) 20 Tucker Dr, Poughkeepsie NY 12603 **Phn:** 845-471-2300 **Fax:** 845-471-2683 www.wrwdcountry.com billwilliams@clearchannel.com

Poughkeepsie WJIP-AM (nt) 20 Tucker Dr, Poughkeepsie NY 12603 **Phn:** 845-471-2300 **Fax:** 845-471-2683 www.1450wkip.com chrismarino@clearchannel.com

Poughkeepsie WKIP-AM (nt) 20 Tucker Dr, Poughkeepsie NY 12603 **Phn:** 845-471-2300 **Fax:** 845-471-2683 www.1450wkip.com rickknight@clearchannel.com

Poughkeepsie WKXP-FM (c) 2 Pendell Rd, Poughkeepsie NY 12601 **Phn:** 845-471-1500 **Fax:** 845-454-1204 www.hudsonvalleycountry.com newsroom@pendellrd.com

Poughkeepsie WPDH-FM (r) PO Box 416, Poughkeepsie NY 12602 **Phn:** 845-471-1500 **Fax:** 845-454-1204 www.wpdh.com newsroom@pendellrd.com

Poughkeepsie WPKF-FM (h) 20 Tucker Dr, Poughkeepsie NY 12603 **Phn:** 845-471-2300 **Fax:** 845-471-2683 www.kissfmjams.com kenyagipson@clearchannel.com

Poughkeepsie WRNQ-FM (a) 20 Tucker Dr, Poughkeepsie NY 12603 **Phn:** 845-471-2300 **Fax:** 845-471-2683 www.lite921.com terryodonnell@clearchannel.com

Poughkeepsie WRRB-FM (r) 2 Pendell Rd, Poughkeepsie NY 12601 **Phn:** 845-471-1500 **Fax:** 845-454-1204 www.wrrv.com andrew.boris@cumulus.com

Poughkeepsie WRRV-FM (r) 2 Pendell Rd, Poughkeepsie NY 12601 **Phn:** 845-471-1500 **Fax:** 845-454-1204 www.wrrv.com wrrv@wrrv.com

Poughkeepsie WRWC-FM (c) 20 Tucker Dr, Poughkeepsie NY 12603 **Phn:** 845-471-2300 **Fax:** 845-471-2683 www.wrwdcountry.com chrismarino@clearchannel.com

Poughkeepsie WRWD-FM (c) 20 Tucker Dr, Poughkeepsie NY 12603 **Phn:** 845-471-2300 **Fax:** 845-471-2683 www.wrwdfm.com stevegiuttari@clearchannel.com

Poughkeepsie WVKR-FM (v) 124 Raymond Ave Box 726, Poughkeepsie NY 12604 **Phn:** 845-437-5475 www.wvkr.org newsdirector@wvkr.org

Poughkeepsie WZAD-FM (o) 2 Pendell Rd, Poughkeepsie NY 12601 **Phn:** 845-471-1500 **Fax:** 845-454-1204 www.mix97fm.com newsroom@pendellrd.com

Pulaski WSCP-AM (r) PO Box 640, Pulaski NY 13142 **Phn:** 315-298-3185 **Fax:** 315-298-6181 gdennis@galaxycommunications.com

Queensbury WCKM-FM (o) 238 Bay Rd, Queensbury NY 12804 **Phn:** 518-761-9890 **Fax:** 518-761-9893 www.wckm.com danminer@rrggf.com

Queensbury WCQL-FM (r) 238 Bay Rd, Queensbury NY 12804 **Phn:** 518-761-9890 **Fax:** 518-761-9893 www.wcql.com johnpratt@rrggf.com

Queensbury WENU-AM (am) 89 Everts Ave, Queensbury NY 12804 **Phn:** 518-793-7733 **Fax:** 518-793-0838

Queensbury WFFG-FM (c) 89 Everts Ave, Queensbury NY 12804 **Phn:** 518-793-7733 **Fax:** 518-793-0838 www.froggy107.com ksullivan@adirondackbroadcasting.com

Queensbury WKBE-FM (a) 89 Everts Ave, Queensbury NY 12804 **Phn:** 518-793-7733 www.thepointontheweb.com jpowell@albanybroadcasting.com

Queensbury WNYQ-FM (a) 89 Everts Ave, Queensbury NY 12804 **Phn:** 518-793-7733 **Fax:** 518-793-0838 www.classichitswnyq.com ksullivan@adirondackbroadcasting.com

Queensbury WWSC-AM (snt) 238 Bay Rd, Queensbury NY 12804 **Phn:** 518-761-9890 **Fax:** 518-761-9893 talk1450wwsc.com alan@talk1450wwsc.com

Red Hook WKZE-FM (r) 7392 S Broadway, Red Hook NY 12571 **Phn:** 845-758-9810 **Fax:** 845-758-9819 www.wkze.com info@wkze.com

Riverhead WRIV-AM (ma) PO Box 1390, Riverhead NY 11901 **Phn:** 631-727-1390 **Fax:** 631-369-9748

Rochester WBEE-FM (c) 70 Commercial St, Rochester NY 14614 **Phn:** 585-423-2900 **Fax:** 585-325-5139 www.wbee.com jspinder@entercom.com

Rochester WBZA-FM (r) 70 Commercial St, Rochester NY 14614 **Phn:** 585-423-2900 **Fax:** 585-325-5139 www.rochesterbuzz.com bbarnett@entercom.com

Rochester WCMF-FM (r) 100 Chestnut St Ste 1700, Rochester NY 14604 **Phn:** 585-423-2900 www.wcmf.com bbarnett@entercom.com

Rochester WDKX-FM (wu) 683 E Main St, Rochester NY 14605 **Phn:** 585-262-2050 **Fax:** 585-262-2626 www.wdkx.com wdkx@wdkx.com

Rochester WDVI-FM (a) 100 Chestnut St Ste 1700, Rochester NY 14604 **Phn:** 585-454-4884 **Fax:** 585-454-5081 www.mydrivefm.com juliedepasquale@clearchannel.com

Rochester WFXF-FM (h) 100 Chestnut St Ste 1700, Rochester NY 14604 **Phn:** 585-454-3942 **Fax:** 585-454-5081 www.951thebrew.com whamnews@clearchannel.com

Rochester WHAM-AM (nt) 100 Chestnut St Ste 1700, Rochester NY 14604 **Phn:** 585-454-4884 **Fax:** 585-454-5081 www.wham1180.com whamnews@clearchannel.com

Rochester WHTK-AM (snt) 100 Chestnut St Ste 1700, Rochester NY 14604 **Phn:** 585-454-4884 **Fax:** 585-454-5081 www.whtk.com davelefrois@clearchannel.com

Rochester WHTK-FM (st) 100 Chestnut St Ste 1700, Rochester NY 14604 **Phn:** 585-454-4884 **Fax:** 585-454-5081 www.whtk.com davelefrois@clearchannel.com

Rochester WIRQ-FM (v) 260 Cooper Rd, Rochester NY 14617 **Phn:** 585-336-3065 **Fax:** 585-336-2929

Rochester WITR-FM (v) 32 Lomb Memorial Dr, Rochester NY 14623 **Phn:** 585-475-2000 **Fax:** 585-475-4988 witr.rit.edu news@witr.rit.edu

Rochester WJZR-FM (wju) 1237 E Main St Ste E, Rochester NY 14609 **Phn:** 585-288-5020

Rochester WKGS-FM (hw) 100 Chestnut St Ste 1700, Rochester NY 14604 **Phn:** 585-232-8870 **Fax:** 585-454-5081 www.kiss1067.com aj@clearchannel.com

Rochester WLGZ-FM (a) 2494 Browncroft Blvd, Rochester NY 14625 **Phn:** 585-222-4000 **Fax:** 585-264-1165 www.legends1027.com mshuttleworth@legends1027.com

Rochester WPXY-FM (h) 70 Commercial St, Rochester NY 14614 **Phn:** 585-423-2900 www.98pxy.com danger@entercom.com

Rochester WRCI-FM (q) 2494 Browncroft Blvd, Rochester NY 14625 **Phn:** 585-264-1027 **Fax:** 585-264-1165

Rochester WRMM-FM (a) 28 E Main St, Rochester NY 14614 **Phn:** 585-399-5700 **Fax:** 585-399-5750 www.warm1013.com stan@warm1013.com

Rochester WROC-AM (s) 70 Commercial St, Rochester NY 14614 **Phn:** 585-423-2900 **Fax:** 585-423-2947 www.sportsradio950espn.com smunn@entercom.com

Rochester WRUR-FM (v) PO Box 277356, Rochester NY 14627 **Phn:** 585-275-9787 www.wrur.org

Rochester WVOR-FM (a) 100 Chestnut St Ste 1700, Rochester NY 14604 **Phn:** 585-454-3942 **Fax:** 585-454-5081 www.radiosunny.com juliedepasquale@clearchannel.com

Rochester WXXI-FM (pl) PO Box 30021, Rochester NY 14603 **Phn:** 585-325-7500 interactive.wxxi.org newsroom@wxxi.org

Rochester WXXI-AM (pj) PO Box 30021, Rochester NY 14603 **Phn:** 585-325-7500 wxxi.orgradioam newsroom@wxxi.org

Rochester WZNE-FM (r) 28 E Main St Ste 800, Rochester NY 14614 **Phn:** 585-399-5700 **Fax:** 585-399-5750 thezone941.com nik@thezone941.com

Ronkonkoma WBZB-FM (kt) 3075 Veterans Memorial Hwy Ste 201, Ronkonkoma NY 11779 **Phn:** 631-648-2500 **Fax:** 631-648-2510

Ronkonkoma WDRE-FM (hu) 3075 Veterans Memorial Hwy Ste 201, Ronkonkoma NY 11779 **Phn:** 631-648-2500 **Fax:** 631-648-2510 lanuevafiesta.mfbiz.com johnc@jvcbroadcasting.com

Sag Harbor WLNG-FM (on) PO Box 2000, Sag Harbor NY 11963 **Phn:** 631-725-2300 **Fax:** 631-725-5897 www.wlng.com info@wlng.com

Saint Bonaventure WSBU-FM (v) PO Box O, Saint Bonaventure NY 14778 **Phn:** 716-375-2307 **Fax:** 716-375-2583 wsbufm.net wsbufm@sbu.edu

Saranac Lake WLPW-FM (r) PO Box 211, Saranac Lake NY 12983 **Phn:** 518-891-1544 **Fax:** 518-891-1545 www.theclassicrock105.com

Saranac Lake WNBZ-AM (nt) PO Box 211, Saranac Lake NY 12983 **Phn:** 518-891-1544 **Fax:** 518-891-1545 www.wnbz.com news@wnbz.com

Saranac Lake WRGR-FM (r) PO Box 211, Saranac Lake NY 12983 **Phn:** 518-891-1544 **Fax:** 518-891-1545 www.theclassicrock105.com

Saranac Lake WYZY-FM (a) PO Box 211, Saranac Lake NY 12983 **Phn:** 518-891-1544 **Fax:** 518-891-1545

Saratoga Springs WSPN-FM (v) 815 N Broadway, Saratoga Springs NY 12866 **Phn:** 518-580-5787 www.skidmore.edustudentorgswspn wspn@skidmore.edu

Schenectady WGNA-FM (c) 1241 Kings Rd, Schenectady NY 12303 **Phn:** 518-881-1515 **Fax:** 518-881-1516 wgna.com jake@wgna.com

Schenectady WQBJ-FM (r) 1241 Kings Rd, Schenectady NY 12303 **Phn:** 518-881-1515 **Fax:** 518-881-1516

Schenectady WQBK-FM (r) 1241 Kings Rd, Schenectady NY 12303 **Phn:** 518-881-1515 **Fax:** 518-881-1516 Q103Albany.com wes.styles@townsquaremedia.com

Schenectady WQSH-FM (ah) 1241 Kings Rd, Schenectady NY 12303 **Phn:** 518-881-1515 **Fax:** 518-881-1516 hot991.com jamie.tanchyk@townsquaremedia.com

Schenectady WRUC-FM (v) 807 Union St, Schenectady NY 12308 **Phn:** 518-388-6151 **Fax:** 518-388-6790 wruc.union.eduwruc wruc@union.edu

Schenectady WTMM-AM (s) 1241 Kings Rd, Schenectady NY 12303 **Phn:** 518-881-1515 **Fax:** 518-881-1516 1045theteam.com stephen.giuttari@townsquaremedia.com

Sidney WCDO-FM (a) 75 Main St, Sidney NY 13838 **Phn:** 607-563-3588 **Fax:** 607-563-7805 wcdo@wcdofm.com

Sidney WCDO-AM (a) 75 Main St, Sidney NY 13838 **Phn:** 607-563-3588 **Fax:** 607-563-7805

Springville WSPQ-AM (st) 51 Franklin St, Springville NY 14141 **Phn:** 716-592-9500 **Fax:** 716-592-9522 arrowflinger80@yahoo.com

Staten Island WSIA-FM (vjr) 2800 Victory Blvd, Staten Island NY 10314 **Phn:** 718-982-3050 **Fax:** 718-982-3052 wsia.csi.cuny.edu gm@wsia.fm

Stony Brook WUSB-FM (v) Stony Brook Un # 266, Stony Brook NY 11794 **Phn:** 631-632-6498 **Fax:** 631-632-7182 wusb.fm psa@wusb.fm

Syracuse WAER-FM (pjn) 795 Ostrom Ave, Syracuse NY 13210 **Phn:** 315-443-4021 **Fax:** 315-443-2148 waer.org waer@syr.edu

Syracuse WAQX-FM (r) 1064 James St, Syracuse NY 13203 **Phn:** 315-472-0200 **Fax:** 315-472-1146 www.95x.com

Syracuse WBBS-FM (c) 500 Plum St Ste 100, Syracuse NY 13204 **Phn:** 315-448-1047 **Fax:** 315-472-6160 www.b1047.net billdrace@clearchannel.com

Syracuse WCNY-FM (pl) PO Box 2400, Syracuse NY 13220 **Phn:** 315-453-2424 **Fax:** 315-451-8824 www.wcny.org

Syracuse WHEN-AM (s) 500 Plum St Ste 100, Syracuse NY 13204 **Phn:** 315-472-9797 **Fax:** 315-472-2323 www.power620.com kennydees@clearchannel.com

Syracuse WJPZ-FM (v) 316 Waverly Ave, Syracuse NY 13210 **Phn:** 315-443-4689 **Fax:** 315-443-4379

Syracuse WKRL-FM (r) 235 Walton St, Syracuse NY 13202 **Phn:** 315-472-9111 **Fax:** 315-472-1888 www.krock.com

Syracuse WMHR-FM (q) 4044 Makyes Rd, Syracuse NY 13215 **Phn:** 315-469-5051 www.marshillnetwork.org

Syracuse WNTQ-FM (h) 1064 James St, Syracuse NY 13203 **Phn:** 315-472-0200 **Fax:** 315-478-5625 www.93q.com phil.spevak@cumulus.com

Syracuse WOLF-AM (m) 401 W Kirkpatrick St, Syracuse NY 13204 **Phn:** 315-472-0222 **Fax:** 315-478-7745 music.disney.com

Syracuse WOLF-FM (m) 401 W Kirkpatrick St, Syracuse NY 13204 **Phn:** 315-472-0222 **Fax:** 315-478-7745 www.movin100.com sclark@movin100.com

Syracuse WPHR-FM (u) 500 Plum St # 400, Syracuse NY 13204 **Phn:** 315-472-9797 **Fax:** 315-472-2323 www.power620.com kennydees@clearchannel.com

Syracuse WSGO-AM (b) 235 Walton St, Syracuse NY 13202 **Phn:** 315-472-9111 **Fax:** 315-472-1888 elevine@galaxycommunications.com

Syracuse WSKO-AM (s) 1064 James St, Syracuse NY 13203 **Phn:** 315-472-0200 **Fax:** 315-472-1146 www.thescore1260.com phil.spevak@cumulus.com

Syracuse WSYR-AM (nt) 500 Plum St Ste 100, Syracuse NY 13204 **Phn:** 315-472-9797 **Fax:** 315-472-2323 www.wsyr.com wsyrnews@clearchannel.com

Syracuse WTKV-FM (r) 235 Walton St, Syracuse NY 13202 **Phn:** 315-472-9111 **Fax:** 315-472-1888 tk99.net asktk@tk99.net

Syracuse WTKW-FM (r) 235 Walton St, Syracuse NY 13202 **Phn:** 315-472-9111 **Fax:** 315-472-1888 tk99.net asktk@tk99.net

Syracuse WTLA-AM (a) 235 Walton St, Syracuse NY 13202 **Phn:** 315-472-9111 **Fax:** 315-472-1888 mgriswold@galaxycommunications.com

Syracuse WWHT-FM (h) 500 Plum St Ste 100, Syracuse NY 13204 **Phn:** 315-472-9797 **Fax:** 315-466-1079 www.hot1079.com richlauber@clearchannel.com

Syracuse WWLF-AM (m) 401 W Kirkpatrick St, Syracuse NY 13204 **Phn:** 315-472-0222 **Fax:** 315-478-7745 www.movin100.com sclark@movin100.com

Syracuse WXTL-FM (t) 1064 James St, Syracuse NY 13203 **Phn:** 315-472-0200 **Fax:** 315-472-1146 www.1059thebigtalker.com phil.spevak@cumulus.com

Syracuse WYYY-FM (a) 500 Plum St Ste 100, Syracuse NY 13204 **Phn:** 315-472-9797 **Fax:** 315-472-6160 www.y94fm.com joeldelmonico@clearchannel.com

Syracuse WZUN-FM (r) 235 Walton St, Syracuse NY 13202 **Phn:** 315-472-9111 **Fax:** 315-472-1888 www.thesunnyspot.com asksunny@thesunnyspot.com

Troy WMHT-FM (pl) 4 Global Vw, Troy NY 12180 **Phn:** 518-880-3400 **Fax:** 518-880-3409 www.wmht.org email@wmht.org

Troy WRPI-FM (v) 1 Wrpi Plz, Troy NY 12180 **Phn:** 518-276-2648 **Fax:** 518-276-2360 www.wrpi.org

Utica WADR-AM (as) 239 Genesee St Ste 500, Utica NY 13501 **Phn:** 315-797-0803 **Fax:** 315-797-7813

Utica WBGK-FM (c) 185 Genesee St Ste 1601, Utica NY 13501 **Phn:** 315-734-9245 **Fax:** 315-624-9245 www.bugcountry.com

Utica WBUG-FM (c) 185 Genesee St Ste 1601, Utica NY 13501 **Phn:** 315-734-9245 **Fax:** 315-624-9245 www.bugcountry.com

Utica WOKR-FM (h) 239 Genesee St Ste 500, Utica NY 13501 **Phn:** 315-797-0803 **Fax:** 315-797-7813

Utica WPNR-FM (v) 1600 Burrstone Rd, Utica NY 13502 **Phn:** 315-792-3066 **Fax:** 315-792-3292 www.utica.edustudentactivitiesorganizationswpnr wpnr@utica.edu

Utica WSKS-FM (h) 185 Genesee St Ste 1601, Utica NY 13501 **Phn:** 315-734-9245 **Fax:** 315-797-7813 www.cnykiss.com shaun@cnykiss.com

Utica WSKU-FM (h) 185 Genesee St Ste 1601, Utica NY 13501 **Phn:** 315-734-9245 **Fax:** 315-624-9245 www.cnykiss.com

Utica WUTQ-AM (s) 239 Genesee St Fl 5, Utica NY 13501 **Phn:** 315-797-0803 **Fax:** 315-797-7813

Vestal WBBI-FM (r) 320 N Jensen Rd, Vestal NY 13850 **Phn:** 607-584-5800 **Fax:** 607-584-5900 www.oldies969fm.com jimfree@clearchannel.com

Vestal WENE-AM (s) 320 N Jensen Rd Ste 8, Vestal NY 13850 **Phn:** 607-584-5800 **Fax:** 607-584-5900 www.foxsports1430.com jonscaptura@clearchannel.com

Vestal WINR-AM (am) 320 N Jensen Rd Ste 8, Vestal NY 13850 **Phn:** 607-584-5800 **Fax:** 607-584-5900 www.oldies969fm.com jimfree@clearchannel.com

Vestal WKGB-FM (r) 320 N Jensen Rd Ste 8, Vestal NY 13850 **Phn:** 607-584-5800 **Fax:** 607-584-5900 www.925kgb.com

Vestal WMRV-FM (h) 320 N Jensen Rd Ste 8, Vestal NY 13850 **Phn:** 607-584-5800 **Fax:** 607-584-5900 www.radionow1057.com jimfree@clearchannel.com

Vestal WMXW-FM (a) 320 N Jensen Rd, Vestal NY 13850 **Phn:** 607-584-5800 **Fax:** 607-584-5900 www.mix103.com jamie.thompson@cumulus.com

Walton WDHI-FM (o) 188 Radio Station Rd, Walton NY 13856 **Phn:** 607-865-4321 **Fax:** 607-865-4189 www.wdhifm.com george.wells@townsquaremedia.com

Walton WDLA-FM (c) 188 Radio Station Rd, Walton NY 13856 **Phn:** 607-865-4321 **Fax:** 607-865-4189 www.wdlafm.com george.wells@townsquaremedia.com

Warsaw WCJW-AM (cf) 3258 Merchant Rd, Warsaw NY 14569 **Phn:** 585-786-8131 **Fax:** 585-786-2241 www.wcjw.com wcjw@wcjw.com

Watertown WATN-AM (nt) 199 Wealtha Ave, Watertown NY 13601 **Phn:** 315-782-1240 **Fax:** 315-782-0312 www.gisco.netwatn jim_leven@commbroadcasters.com

Watertown WBDI-FM (h) 199 Wealtha Ave, Watertown NY 13601 **Phn:** 315-782-1240 **Fax:** 315-782-0312 ewise2.comtheborder.fm jim_leven@commbroadcasters.com

Watertown WBDR-FM (h) 199 Wealtha Ave, Watertown NY 13601 **Phn:** 315-782-1240 **Fax:** 315-782-0312 www.theborder.fm jim_leven@commbroadcasters.com

Watertown WCIZ-FM (h) 134 Mullin St, Watertown NY 13601 **Phn:** 315-788-0790 **Fax:** 315-788-4379 www.z93.fm

Watertown WFRY-FM (c) 134 Mullin St, Watertown NY 13601 **Phn:** 315-788-0790 **Fax:** 315-788-4379 www.froggy97.com

Watertown WNER-AM (s) 134 Mullin St, Watertown NY 13601 **Phn:** 315-788-0790 **Fax:** 315-788-4379 www.wner1410.com

Watertown WOTT-FM (r) 199 Wealtha Ave, Watertown NY 13601 **Phn:** 315-786-9552 **Fax:** 315-782-0312 www.94rockwott.com jim_leven@commbroadcasters.com

Watertown WTNY-AM (ant) 134 Mullin St, Watertown NY 13601 **Phn:** 315-788-0790 **Fax:** 315-788-4379 www.790wtny.com

Watertown WTOJ-FM (a) 199 Wealtha Ave, Watertown NY 13601 **Phn:** 315-755-1031 **Fax:** 315-782-0312 jim_leven@commbroadcasters.com

Wellsville WJQZ-FM (h) 82 Railroad Ave, Wellsville NY 14895 **Phn:** 585-593-6070 **Fax:** 585-593-6212 oldiesz103.topcities.com oldiesz103@yahoo.com

Wellsville WLSV-AM (c) 82 Railroad Ave, Wellsville NY 14895 **Phn:** 585-593-6070 **Fax:** 585-593-6212 www.wlsv.com

Wellsville WZKZ-FM (c) 3012 Eastside Ave, Wellsville NY 14895 **Phn:** 585-593-9553 **Fax:** 585-593-9554

West Babylon WBAB-FM (r) 555 Sunrise Hwy, West Babylon NY 11704 **Phn:** 631-587-1023 **Fax:** 631-587-1282 www.wbab.com wbab@wbab.com

West Babylon WBLI-FM (h) 555 Sunrise Hwy, West Babylon NY 11704 **Phn:** 631-669-9254 **Fax:** 631-376-0812 www.wbli.com wbli@wbli.com

West Babylon WGBB-AM (k) 404 Route 109, West Babylon NY 11704 **Phn:** 516-623-1240 **Fax:** 516-955-9422 www.am1240wgbb.com

West Babylon WHFM-FM (r) 555 Sunrise Hwy, West Babylon NY 11704 **Phn:** 631-587-1023 **Fax:** 631-587-1282 www.wbab.com wbab@wbab.com

West Seneca WJJL-AM (o) 920 Union Rd, West Seneca NY 14224 **Phn:** 716-674-9555 **Fax:** 716-674-0400 wjjl.com radio1440@roadrunner.com

White Plains WXPK-FM (a) 56 Lafayette Ave Ste 370, White Plains NY 10603 **Phn:** 914-397-0127 **Fax:** 914-397-0129 www.1071thepeak.com cherrmann@1071thepeak.com

Whitehall WNYV-FM (aco) PO Box 141, Whitehall NY 12887 **Phn:** 518-499-2438 wvnrwnyv@yahoo.com

Windham WRIP-FM (ao) PO Box 979, Windham NY 12496 **Phn:** 518-734-4747 **Fax:** 518-734-9147 wrip979.com wrip@mhcable.com

Woodstock WDST-FM (ar) PO Box 367, Woodstock NY 12498 **Phn:** 845-679-7600 **Fax:** 845-679-5395 www.wdst.com buff@wdst.com

NORTH CAROLINA

Ahoskie WRCS-AM (wg) 443 Nc Highway 42 W, Ahoskie NC 27910 **Phn:** 252-332-3101 **Fax:** 252-332-3103 wrcs@embarqmail.com

Albemarle WSPC-AM (nt) PO Box 549, Albemarle NC 28002 **Phn:** 704-983-1580 **Fax:** 704-983-1436 www.1010wspc.com mattsmith@1010wspc.com

Albemarle WZKY-AM (o) PO Box 549, Albemarle NC 28002 **Phn:** 704-983-1580 **Fax:** 704-983-1436 www.1010wspc.com leonradio@hotmail.com

Asheboro WKXR-AM (c) 1119 Eastview Dr, Asheboro NC 27203 **Phn:** 336-625-2187 **Fax:** 336-626-9292 www.wkxr.com wkxr@atomic.net

Asheville WCQS-FM (pljn) 73 Broadway St, Asheville NC 28801 **Phn:** 828-210-4800 **Fax:** 828-210-4801 www.wcqs.org dhurand@wcqs.org

Asheville WISE-AM (s) 1190 Patton Ave, Asheville NC 28806 **Phn:** 828-259-9695 **Fax:** 828-253-5619 espnasheville.com bmcclement@avlradio.com

Asheville WKJV-AM (gq) 70 Adams Hill Rd, Asheville NC 28806 **Phn:** 828-252-1380 **Fax:** 828-259-9427 www.wkjv.com wkjvradio@cleaninter.net

Asheville WKSF-FM (c) 13 Summerlin Dr, Asheville NC 28806 **Phn:** 828-257-2700 **Fax:** 828-255-7850 www.99kisscountry.com jeffdavis@clearchannel.com

Asheville WMXF-AM (a) 13 Summerlin Dr, Asheville NC 28806 **Phn:** 828-257-2700 **Fax:** 828-255-7850 www.wwnc.com brian@wwnc.com

Asheville WOXL-FM (o) 1190 Patton Ave, Asheville NC 28806 **Phn:** 828-259-9695 **Fax:** 828-253-5619 mix965asheville.com bmcclement@avlradio.com

Asheville WPEK-AM (t) 13 Summerlin Dr, Asheville NC 28806 **Phn:** 828-257-2700 **Fax:** 828-255-7850 www.880therevolution.com brianhall@clearchannel.com

Asheville WQNQ-FM (r) 13 Summerlin Dr, Asheville NC 28806 **Phn:** 828-257-2700 **Fax:** 828-255-7850 www.star1043.com josh@star1043.com

Asheville WQNS-FM (r) 13 Summerlin Dr, Asheville NC 28806 **Phn:** 828-257-2700 **Fax:** 828-255-7850 www.rock104rocks.com rickrice@clearchannel.com

Asheville WSKY-AM (gqt) 40 Westgate Pkwy Ste F, Asheville NC 28806 **Phn:** 828-251-2000 **Fax:** 864-597-0687 www.wilkinsradio.com wsky@wilkinsradio.com

Asheville WWNC-AM (nt) 13 Summerlin Dr, Asheville NC 28806 **Phn:** 828-253-3835 **Fax:** 828-255-7850 www.wwnc.com brian@wwnc.com

Belmont WCGC-AM (q) 6021 W Wilkinson Blvd, Belmont NC 28012 **Phn:** 704-825-2812 **Fax:** 704-825-2127

Benson WPYB-AM (cg) PO Box 215, Benson NC 27504 **Phn:** 919-894-1130 **Fax:** 919-894-1530

Black Mountain WFGW-AM (nq) PO Box 159, Black Mountain NC 28711 **Phn:** 828-669-8477 **Fax:** 828-298-0117 www.wfgw.org

Black Mountain WMIT-FM (nq) PO Box 159, Black Mountain NC 28711 **Phn:** 828-285-8477 **Fax:** 828-298-0117 www.1069thelight.org thankyou@brb.org

NORTH CAROLINA RADIO STATIONS

Boiling Springs WGWG-FM (vlj) PO Box 876, Boiling Springs NC 28017 **Phn:** 704-406-3525 **Fax:** 704-406-4338 152.44.63.252wgwg info@wgwg.org

Boone WASU-FM (vjl) Appalachian State Univ, Boone NC 28608 **Phn:** 828-262-3170

Boone WATA-AM (ant) 738 Blowing Rock Rd, Boone NC 28607 **Phn:** 828-264-2411 **Fax:** 828-264-2412 www.wataradio.com john@wataradio.com

Boone WECR-FM (a) 738 Blowing Rock Rd, Boone NC 28607 **Phn:** 828-264-2411 **Fax:** 828-264-2412 www.wecr1023.com

Boone WZJS-FM (c) 738 Blowing Rock Rd, Boone NC 28607 **Phn:** 828-264-2411 **Fax:** 828-264-2412 www.goblueridge.net

Brevard WSQL-AM (ntm) 62 W Main St, Brevard NC 28712 **Phn:** 828-877-5252 **Fax:** 828-877-5253 www.wsqlradio.com news@wsqlradio.com

Burlington WBAG-AM (snt) 1745 Burch Bridge Rd, Burlington NC 27217 **Phn:** 336-226-1150 **Fax:** 336-226-1180 www.wbag1150.com wbag@bellsouth.net

Burlington WPCM-AM (t) 1109 Tower Dr, Burlington NC 27215 **Phn:** 336-584-0126 **Fax:** 336-584-0739 www.920wpcm.com wpcm@curtismedia.com

Burlington WZTK-FM (t) 1109 Tower Dr, Burlington NC 27215 **Phn:** 336-584-0126 **Fax:** 336-584-0739

Burnsville WKYK-AM (c) PO Box 744, Burnsville NC 28714 **Phn:** 828-682-3510 **Fax:** 828-682-6227 www.ourlocalcommunityonline.com 940@wkyk.com

Burnsville WTOE-AM (a) PO Box 744, Burnsville NC 28714 **Phn:** 828-682-3798 **Fax:** 828-682-6227 www.ourlocalcommunityonline.com 1470@wtoe.com

Canton WPTL-AM (c) PO Box 909, Canton NC 28716 **Phn:** 828-648-3576 **Fax:** 828-648-3577 wptlradio.net admin@wptlradio.net

Chadbourn WVOE-AM (wgx) 1528 Old US Highway 74, Chadbourn NC 28431 **Phn:** 910-654-5621 **Fax:** 910-654-4385

Chapel Hill WCHL-AM (nt) 88 Vilcom Center Dr Ste 130, Chapel Hill NC 27514 **Phn:** 919-933-4165 **Fax:** 919-968-3748 www.chapelboro.com rnortham@wchl.com

Chapel Hill WUNC-FM (pln) 120 Friday Center Dr, Chapel Hill NC 27517 **Phn:** 919-445-9150 **Fax:** 919-966-5955 www.wunc.org news@wunc.org

Chapel Hill WXYC-FM (v) 5210 Carolina Un, Chapel Hill NC 27599 **Phn:** 919-962-7768 www.wxyc.org psa@wxyc.org

Charlotte WAVO-AM (a) 5732 N Tryon St, Charlotte NC 28213 **Phn:** 704-596-4900 **Fax:** 704-596-6939 1150wavo.com station@1150wavo.com

Charlotte WBAV-FM (au) 1520 South Blvd Ste 300, Charlotte NC 28203 **Phn:** 704-522-1103 **Fax:** 704-227-8985 v1019.cbslocal.com tlavery@cbs.com

Charlotte WBCN-AM (nt) 1520 South Blvd Ste 300, Charlotte NC 28203 **Phn:** 704-319-9369 **Fax:** 704-335-0631 dj@wfnz.com

Charlotte WBT-FM (nt) 1 Julian Price Pl, Charlotte NC 28208 **Phn:** 704-374-3500 **Fax:** 704-374-3830 www.wbt.com pr@wbt.com

Charlotte WBT-AM (nt) 1 Julian Price Pl, Charlotte NC 28208 **Phn:** 704-374-3500 **Fax:** 704-374-3830 www.wbt.com pr@wbt.com

Charlotte WEND-FM (r) 801 Woodridge Center Dr, Charlotte NC 28217 **Phn:** 704-714-9444 **Fax:** 704-372-3208 www.1065.com jackdaniel@clearchannel.com

Charlotte WFAE-FM (pnj) 8801 J M Keynes Dr Ste 91, Charlotte NC 28262 **Phn:** 704-549-9323 **Fax:** 704-547-8851 www.wfae.org wfae@wfae.org

Charlotte WFNZ-AM (s) 1520 South Blvd Ste 300, Charlotte NC 28203 **Phn:** 704-319-9369 **Fax:** 704-319-3933 charlotte.cbslocal.com djstout@cbs.com

Charlotte WGAS-AM (q) PO Box 16048, Charlotte NC 28297 **Phn:** 704-393-1540 **Fax:** 704-393-1527 www.wordnet.org

Charlotte WGFY-AM (m) 1100 S Tryon St Ste 210, Charlotte NC 28203 **Phn:** 704-377-2223 **Fax:** 704-373-2245 music.disney.com

Charlotte WHQC-FM (uh) 801 Wood Ridge Center Dr, Charlotte NC 28217 **Phn:** 704-714-9444 **Fax:** 704-371-3239 www.channel961.com anthonytesta@clearchannel.com

Charlotte WHVN-AM (q) 5732 N Tryon St, Charlotte NC 28213 **Phn:** 704-596-4900 **Fax:** 704-596-6939

Charlotte WKKT-FM (c) 801 Woodridge Center Dr, Charlotte NC 28217 **Phn:** 704-714-9444 **Fax:** 704-372-3208 www.969thekat.com tylerreese@clearchannel.com

Charlotte WKQC-FM (h) 1520 South Blvd Ste 300, Charlotte NC 28203 **Phn:** 704-372-1103 **Fax:** 704-523-1047 k1047.cbslocal.com jreynolds@cbs.com

Charlotte WLNK-FM (a) 1 Julian Price Pl, Charlotte NC 28208 **Phn:** 704-374-3500 **Fax:** 704-374-3830 www.1079thelink.com

Charlotte WLYT-FM (a) 801 Woodridge Center Dr, Charlotte NC 28217 **Phn:** 704-714-9444 **Fax:** 704-372-3208 www.1029thelake.com brucelogan@clearchannel.com

Charlotte WNKS-FM (h) 1520 South Blvd Ste 300, Charlotte NC 28203 **Phn:** 704-522-1103 **Fax:** 704-344-8237 kiss951.cbslocal.com jreynolds@cbs.com

Charlotte WNOW-AM (y) 4321 Stuart Andrew Blvd Ste B, Charlotte NC 28217 **Phn:** 704-665-9355 www.wnow-am.com smiller@davidsonmediagroup.com

Charlotte WNOW-FM (y) 4321 Stuart Andrew Blvd Ste B, Charlotte NC 28217 **Phn:** 704-665-9355

Charlotte WOGR-AM (g) PO Box 16408, Charlotte NC 28297 **Phn:** 704-393-1540 **Fax:** 704-393-1527 www.wordnet.org info@wordnet.org

Charlotte WOLS-FM (y) 4801 E Independence Blvd, Charlotte NC 28212 **Phn:** 704-442-7277 **Fax:** 704-405-3173

Charlotte WPEG-FM (uw) 1520 South Blvd Ste 300, Charlotte NC 28203 **Phn:** 704-522-1103 **Fax:** 704-227-8979 power98fm.cbslocal.com tlavery@cbs.com

Charlotte WQNC-FM (u) 8809 Lenox Pointe Dr Unit A, Charlotte NC 28273 **Phn:** 704-548-7800 **Fax:** 704-548-7810 oldschool1053.com gweiss@radio-one.com

Charlotte WRFX-FM (r) 801 Woodridge Center Dr, Charlotte NC 28217 **Phn:** 704-714-9444 **Fax:** 704-372-3208 www.wrfx.com jeffkent@clearchannel.com

Charlotte WSOC-FM (c) 1520 South Blvd Ste 300, Charlotte NC 28203 **Phn:** 704-522-1103 **Fax:** 704-529-1037 thenew1037.cbslocal.com djstout@cbs.com

Charlotte WTIX-AM (h) 5732 N Tryon St, Charlotte NC 28213 **Phn:** 843-665-1230

Charlotte WXRC-FM (h) 1515 Mockingbird Ln Ste 205, Charlotte NC 28209 **Phn:** 704-527-0957 **Fax:** 704-527-2720 www.957theride.com dave@957theride.com

Claremont WPIR-FM (vg) PO Box 909, Claremont NC 28610 **Phn:** 828-459-9803 **Fax:** 828-459-9805

Clinton WCLN-AM (o) 118 E Main St, Clinton NC 28328 **Phn:** 910-864-5028 **Fax:** 910-864-6270 www.oldies1170.com grandpas@oldies1170.com

Columbus WJFJ-AM (ag) 11 Courthouse St, Columbus NC 28722 **Phn:** 828-894-5858 **Fax:** 828-894-2957 www.wjfjradio.com wjfj@windstream.net

Cullowhee WWCU-FM (vh) G-3 Old Sub Wc University, Cullowhee NC 28723 **Phn:** 828-227-3533 www.wwcufm.com dconnelly@wcu.edu

Dallas WCRU-AM (q) PO Box 477, Dallas NC 28034 **Phn:** 704-922-5960 **Fax:** 704-922-6998

Dallas WSGE-FM (ax) 201 Highway 321 S, Dallas NC 28034 **Phn:** 704-922-6552 www.wsge.org hall.cathis@gaston.edu

Davidson WDAV-FM (vl) PO Box 8890, Davidson NC 28035 **Phn:** 704-894-8900 **Fax:** 704-894-2997 www.wdav.org wdav@davidson.edu

Dobson WCOK-AM (g) PO Box 797, Dobson NC 27017 **Phn:** 336-372-5700 gbiradio.org wcoksparta@yahoo.com

Dobson WYZD-AM (g) PO Box 797, Dobson NC 27017 **Phn:** 336-356-1560 gbiradio.org wyzdradio@yahoo.com

Dunn WCKB-AM (qg) PO Box 789, Dunn NC 28335 **Phn:** 910-892-3133 **Fax:** 910-892-3135 www.wckb780.com wckb@wckb780.com

Durham WNCU-FM (pjn) PO Box 19875, Durham NC 27707 **Phn:** 919-530-7445 **Fax:** 919-530-5031 www.wncu.org kpierce@nccu.edu

Durham WXDU-FM (v) PO Box 90689, Durham NC 27708 **Phn:** 919-684-2957 www.wxdu.org wxdu@duke.edu

Edenton WBXB-FM (g) PO Box 765, Edenton NC 27932 **Phn:** 252-482-8680 **Fax:** 252-482-4260

Elizabeth City WCNC-AM (y) PO Box 1246, Elizabeth City NC 27906 **Phn:** 252-335-4379 **Fax:** 252-338-5275 www.ecri.net psa@ecri.net

Elizabeth City WKJX-FM (a) PO Box 1246, Elizabeth City NC 27906 **Phn:** 252-338-0196 **Fax:** 252-338-5275

Elizabeth City WRVS-FM (p) 1704 Weeksville Rd Box 800, Elizabeth City NC 27909 **Phn:** 252-335-3517 **Fax:** 252-335-3946 www.ecsu.eduwrvs wrvs899@mail.ecsu.edu

Elizabeth City WZBO-AM (y) PO Box 1246, Elizabeth City NC 27906 **Phn:** 252-338-0196 **Fax:** 252-338-5275 www.ecri.net psa@ecri.net

Elizabethtown WBLA-AM (g) 996 Helen St, Elizabethtown NC 28337 **Phn:** 910-862-3184 **Fax:** 910-862-2692

Elkin WIFM-FM (ah) PO Box 1038, Elkin NC 28621 **Phn:** 336-835-2511 **Fax:** 336-835-5248 www.wifmradio.com info@wifmradio.com

Elon College WSOE-FM (v) Campus Box 2700, Elon College NC 27244 **Phn:** 336-278-7210 org.elon.eduwsoe wsoe@elon.edu

Fairmont WFMO-AM (gwy) PO Box 668, Fairmont NC 28340 **Phn:** 910-628-6781 **Fax:** 910-628-6648

Fairmont WSTS-FM (g) PO Box 668, Fairmont NC 28340 **Phn:** 910-628-6781 **Fax:** 910-628-6648 www.wstsfm.com catoe@wstsfm.com

Fayetteville WAGR-AM (gw) 1338 Bragg Blvd, Fayetteville NC 28301 **Phn:** 910-483-6111 **Fax:** 910-483-6601

Fayetteville WAZZ-AM (am) 508 Person St, Fayetteville NC 28301 **Phn:** 910-486-2055 **Fax:** 910-323-5635 www.am1490wazz.com mac@bbgi.com

NORTH CAROLINA RADIO STATIONS

Fayetteville WCCG-FM (au) 115 Gillespie St, Fayetteville NC 28301 **Phn:** 910-484-4932 **Fax:** 910-485-5192 www.wccg1045fm.com

Fayetteville WCLN-FM (q) 996 Helen St, Fayetteville NC 28303 **Phn:** 910-864-5028 **Fax:** 910-864-6270 www.christian107.com

Fayetteville WFLB-FM (o) PO Box 530, Fayetteville NC 28302 **Phn:** 910-486-4114 **Fax:** 910-323-5635 965bobfm.com stoney@965bobfm.com

Fayetteville WFNC-AM (nt) 1009 Drayton Rd, Fayetteville NC 28303 **Phn:** 910-864-5222 **Fax:** 910-864-3065 www.wfnc640am.com jim.cooke@cumulus.com

Fayetteville WFNC-FM (nt) 1009 Drayton Rd, Fayetteville NC 28303 **Phn:** 910-864-5222 **Fax:** 910-864-3065 www.wfnc640am.com jim.cooke@cumulus.com

Fayetteville WFSS-FM (vjw) 1200 Murchison Rd, Fayetteville NC 28301 **Phn:** 910-672-1381 **Fax:** 910-672-1964 www.wfss.org jross@uncfsu.edu

Fayetteville WGQR-FM (g) 996 Helen St, Fayetteville NC 28303 **Phn:** 910-864-5028 **Fax:** 910-864-6270 www.wgqr1057.com

Fayetteville WIDU-AM (gw) 145 Rowan St # A3, Fayetteville NC 28301 **Phn:** 910-483-6111 **Fax:** 910-483-6601 www.widuradio.com

Fayetteville WKML-FM (c) 508 Person St, Fayetteville NC 28301 **Phn:** 910-486-4114 **Fax:** 910-483-0669 www.wkml.com country@wkml.com

Fayetteville WMGU-FM (o) 1009 Drayton Rd, Fayetteville NC 28303 **Phn:** 910-864-5222 **Fax:** 910-864-3065 www.magic1069.com greg.sher@cumulus.com

Fayetteville WQSM-FM (a) 1009 Drayton Rd, Fayetteville NC 28303 **Phn:** 910-864-5222 **Fax:** 910-864-3065 www.Q98FM.com jeff.davis@cumulus.com

Fayetteville WRCQ-FM (r) 1009 Drayton Rd, Fayetteville NC 28303 **Phn:** 910-864-5222 **Fax:** 910-864-3065 www.rock103rocks.com kelvin.culbreth@cumulus.com

Fayetteville WUKS-FM (ua) 508 Person St, Fayetteville NC 28301 **Phn:** 910-486-4114 **Fax:** 910-486-6720 www.kiss1077.com taylor@kiss1077.com

Fayetteville WZFX-FM (wu) 508 Person St, Fayetteville NC 28301 **Phn:** 910-486-4114 **Fax:** 910-486-6720 www.foxy99.com promotions@foxy99.com

Fayetteville WZKB-FM (q) 996 Helen St, Fayetteville NC 28303 **Phn:** 910-864-5028 **Fax:** 910-864-6270 www.christian107.com jccoello@hotmail.com

Forest City WAGY-AM (c) PO Box 280, Forest City NC 28043 **Phn:** 828-245-9887 **Fax:** 828-245-9880

Forest City WWOL-AM (g) 1381 W Main St, Forest City NC 28043 **Phn:** 828-245-0078 **Fax:** 828-245-8528 wwol780.com wwol@wwol780.com

Franklin WFSC-AM (o) 180 Radio Hill Rd, Franklin NC 28734 **Phn:** 828-524-4418 **Fax:** 828-524-2788 www.1050wfsc.com newsradio@gacaradio.com

Franklin WNCC-FM (c) PO Box 470, Franklin NC 28744 **Phn:** 828-524-4418 **Fax:** 828-524-2788 1050wfsc.com franklinradio@gacaradio.com

Franklin WPFJ-AM (q) 185 Franklin Plaza Dr, Franklin NC 28734 **Phn:** 828-369-5033 **Fax:** 828-369-3197

Goldsboro WAGO-FM (q) PO Box 1895, Goldsboro NC 27533 **Phn:** 252-747-8887 **Fax:** 252-747-7888 www.gomixradio.org wago@gomixradio.org

Goldsboro WEQR-FM (c) 2581 US Highway 70 W, Goldsboro NC 27530 **Phn:** 919-736-1150 **Fax:** 919-736-3876 www.facebook.comQ97.7FM

Goldsboro WFMC-AM (wgu) 2581 US Highway 70 W, Goldsboro NC 27530 **Phn:** 919-736-1150 **Fax:** 919-736-3876 www.730wfmc.com cbowden@curtismedia.com

Goldsboro WGBR-AM (nt) 2581 US Highway 70 W, Goldsboro NC 27530 **Phn:** 919-736-1150 **Fax:** 919-736-3876 curtismedia.com bjohnston@curtismedia.com

Goldsboro WSSG-AM (g) 116 W Mulberry St, Goldsboro NC 27530 **Phn:** 919-734-1300

Goldsboro WZRU-FM (q) PO Box 1895, Goldsboro NC 27533 **Phn:** 252-747-8887 www.gomixradio.org wago@gomixradio.org

Granite Falls WYCV-AM (g) PO Box 486, Granite Falls NC 28630 **Phn:** 828-396-3361 **Fax:** 828-396-9193 www.gospel9.com wycvradio@charter.net

Greensboro WEAL-AM (g) 7819 National Service Rd Ste 401, Greensboro NC 27409 **Phn:** 336-605-5200 **Fax:** 336-605-0138 www.1510weal.com scole@entercom.com

Greensboro WGBT-FM (y) 2B Pai Park, Greensboro NC 27409 **Phn:** 336-822-2000 **Fax:** 336-887-0104 www.945wpti.com richmcmillan@rushradio945.comÿ

Greensboro WJMH-FM (wu) 7819 National Service Rd Ste 401, Greensboro NC 27409 **Phn:** 336-605-5200 **Fax:** 336-605-5219 www.102jamz.com kscales@entercom.com

Greensboro WKRR-FM (r) 192 E Lewis St, Greensboro NC 27406 **Phn:** 336-274-8042 **Fax:** 336-274-1629 www.rock92.com bwheeler@dbcradio.com

Greensboro WKZL-FM (h) 192 E Lewis St, Greensboro NC 27406 **Phn:** 336-274-8042 **Fax:** 336-274-1629 www.1075kzl.com jgoodman@dbcradio.com

Greensboro WMAG-FM (a) 2B Pai Park, Greensboro NC 27409 **Phn:** 336-822-2000 **Fax:** 336-887-0104 www.995wmag.com jeffcushman@clearchannel.com

Greensboro WMKS-FM (h) 2B Pai Park, Greensboro NC 27409 **Phn:** 336-822-2000 **Fax:** 336-887-0104 www.1057now.com triadviewpoints@clearchannel.com

Greensboro WNAA-FM (wv) 302 Crosby Hall, Greensboro NC 27411 **Phn:** 336-334-7936 **Fax:** 336-334-7960 wnaa-online.ncat.edu tonyb@ncat.edu

Greensboro WPAW-FM (c) 7819 National Service Rd Ste 401, Greensboro NC 27409 **Phn:** 336-605-5200 **Fax:** 336-605-5221 www.931wolfcountry.com rbliss@entercom.com

Greensboro WPET-AM (g) 7819 National Service Rd Ste 401, Greensboro NC 27409 **Phn:** 336-605-5200 **Fax:** 336-387-7206 www.wpetam950.com jcompton@entercom.com

Greensboro WQFS-FM (v) 5800 W Friendly Ave, Greensboro NC 27410 **Phn:** 336-316-2352 www.guilford.eduwqfs wqfsnews@gmail.com

Greensboro WQMG-FM (wu) 7819 National Service Rd Ste 401, Greensboro NC 27409 **Phn:** 336-605-5200 **Fax:** 336-605-0138 www.wqmg.com scole@entercom.com

Greensboro WSMW-FM (r) 7819 National Service Rd Ste 401, Greensboro NC 27409 **Phn:** 336-605-5200 **Fax:** 336-387-7206 www.987simon.com seansellers@987simon.com

Greensboro WTQR-FM (c) 2B Pai Park, Greensboro NC 27409 **Phn:** 336-822-2000 **Fax:** 336-887-0104 www.wtqr.com wtqr@wtqr.com

Greensboro WUAG-FM (v) Taylor Bldg Univ Of Nc, Greensboro NC 27412 **Phn:** 336-334-4308 wuag.net wuag@uncg.edu

Greensboro WVBZ-FM (r) 2B Pai Park, Greensboro NC 27409 **Phn:** 336-822-2000 **Fax:** 336-887-0104 www.ihaveabuzz.com alanchapman@clearchannel.com

Greenville WDLX-AM (t) PO Box 3333, Greenville NC 27836 **Phn:** 252-317-1250 www.pirateradio930.com troy@pirateradio1250.com

Greenville WGHB-AM (st) PO Box 3333, Greenville NC 27836 **Phn:** 252-317-1250 www.pirateradio1250.com ellerbe@pirateradio1250.com

Greenville WNBU-FM (nt) 408 W Arlington Blvd Ste 101C, Greenville NC 27834 **Phn:** 252-355-1037 **Fax:** 252-355-2234 maddawg@ibxmedia.com

Greenville WNCT-FM (h) 2929 Radio Station Rd, Greenville NC 27834 **Phn:** 252-757-0011 **Fax:** 252-757-0286 www.1070wnct.com live@1070wnct.com

Greenville WNCT-AM (ox) 2929 Radio Station Rd, Greenville NC 27834 **Phn:** 252-757-0011 **Fax:** 252-757-0286 www.1070wnct.com live@1070wnct.com

Greenville WOOW-AM (gy) 405 Evans St, Greenville NC 27858 **Phn:** 252-757-0365 **Fax:** 252-757-1793

Greenville WRHD-FM (h) 407 W Arlington Blvd # 101-C, Greenville NC 27834 **Phn:** 252-355-8822 **Fax:** 252-355-2234 www.thundercountryonline.com henry@ibxmedia.com

Greenville WRHT-FM (c) 408 W Arlington Blvd Ste 101C, Greenville NC 27834 **Phn:** 252-355-1037 **Fax:** 252-355-2234 www.thundercountryonline.com maddawg@ibxmedia.com

Greenville WTIB-FM (t) 408 W Arlington Blvd Ste 101C, Greenville NC 27834 **Phn:** 252-355-1037 **Fax:** 252-355-2234 www.wtibfm.com henry@ibxmedia.com

Greenville WZMB-FM (vr) Mendenhall Student Ctr, Greenville NC 27834 **Phn:** 252-328-4751 **Fax:** 252-328-4773 www.ecu.eduwzmb wzmb@ecu.edu

Hamlet WKDX-AM (q) PO Box 827, Hamlet NC 28345 **Phn:** 910-582-1997 **Fax:** 910-582-1920 www.wkdx.net wkdxthespirit@yahoo.com

Henderson WIZS-AM (c) PO Box 1299, Henderson NC 27536 **Phn:** 252-492-3001 **Fax:** 252-492-3002 www.wizs.com wizs@vance.net

Hendersonville WHKP-AM (ntz) PO Box 2470, Hendersonville NC 28793 **Phn:** 828-693-9061 **Fax:** 828-696-9329 www.whkp.com 1450@whkp.com

Hendersonville WTZQ-AM (am) PO Box 462, Hendersonville NC 28793 **Phn:** 828-692-1600 **Fax:** 828-697-1416 www.wtzq.com 1600@wtzq.com

Hickory WAIZ-AM (o) PO Box 938, Hickory NC 28603 **Phn:** 828-466-2551 **Fax:** 828-464-9662 www.mytotalradio.com dave@957theride.com

Hickory WHKY-AM (nt) PO Box 1059, Hickory NC 28603 **Phn:** 828-322-1290 **Fax:** 828-322-8256 www.whky.com news@whky.com

High Point WBLO-AM (st) PO Box 5663, High Point NC 27262 **Phn:** 336-887-0983 **Fax:** 336-887-3055

High Point WGOS-AM (ty) 6223 Old Mendenhall Rd, High Point NC 27263 **Phn:** 336-434-5024 **Fax:** 336-434-6018 cadenaradialnuevavida.com javierfzb@hotmail.com

High Point WIST-FM (y) PO Box 5663, High Point NC 27262 **Phn:** 336-887-0983 **Fax:** 336-887-3055 larazalaraza.com programming@norsanmultimedia.com

Highlands WHLC-FM (z) PO Box 1889, Highlands NC 28741 **Phn:** 828-526-1045 **Fax:** 828-526-4900 www.whlc.com info@whlc.com

NORTH CAROLINA RADIO STATIONS

Jacksonville WJCV-AM (g) PO Box 1216, Jacksonville NC 28541 **Phn:** 910-347-6141 **Fax:** 910-347-1290 www.wjcv.com michael-b-wjcv@ec.rr.com

Kannapolis WRKB-AM (g) PO Box 8146, Kannapolis NC 28081 **Phn:** 704-983-1460 **Fax:** 704-857-0680 www.fordbroadcasting.com carl@fordbroadcasting.com

Kannapolis WRNA-AM (g) PO Box 8146, Kannapolis NC 28081 **Phn:** 704-857-1101 **Fax:** 704-857-0680 www.fordbroadcasting.com carl@fordbroadcasting.com

Kill Devil Hills WCXL-FM (a) PO Box 1897, Kill Devil Hills NC 27948 **Phn:** 252-480-4655 **Fax:** 252-441-4827 www.beach104.com bob@beach104.com

King WKTE-AM (cg) PO Box 465, King NC 27021 **Phn:** 336-983-3111 **Fax:** 336-368-1090

Kinston WELS-FM (g) PO Box 3384, Kinston NC 28502 **Phn:** 252-523-5151 **Fax:** 252-523-9357

Kinston WELS-AM (g) PO Box 3384, Kinston NC 28502 **Phn:** 252-523-5151 **Fax:** 252-523-9357

Laurinburg WEWO-AM (nt) PO Box 788, Laurinburg NC 28353 **Phn:** 910-276-1460 **Fax:** 910-276-9787

Laurinburg WLNC-AM (oa) PO Box 1748, Laurinburg NC 28353 **Phn:** 910-276-1300 **Fax:** 910-276-1319 www.wlncradio.com wlncradio@carolina.net

Lenoir WJRI-AM (snt) PO Box 1678, Lenoir NC 28645 **Phn:** 828-758-1033 **Fax:** 828-757-3300 www.foothillsradio.com crockett@kicksradio.com

Lenoir WKGX-AM (c) PO Box 1678, Lenoir NC 28645 **Phn:** 828-758-1033 **Fax:** 828-757-3300 www.foothillsradio.com crockett@kicksradio.com

Lenoir WKVS-FM (c) PO Box 1678, Lenoir NC 28645 **Phn:** 828-758-1033 **Fax:** 828-757-3300 www.foothillsradio.com crockett@kicksradio.com

Lexington WLXN-AM (snt) 200 Radio Dr, Lexington NC 27292 **Phn:** 336-248-2716 **Fax:** 336-248-2800 www.wlxn.com stacy@majic941.com

Lexington WTHZ-FM (a) 200 Radio Dr, Lexington NC 27292 **Phn:** 336-248-2716 **Fax:** 336-248-2800 www.majic941.com stacy@majic941.com

Lincolnton WCSL-AM (o) PO Box 430, Lincolnton NC 28093 **Phn:** 704-735-8071 **Fax:** 704-732-9567 www.hrnb.com info@hrnb.com

Lincolnton WLON-AM (o) PO Box 430, Lincolnton NC 28093 **Phn:** 704-732-8011 **Fax:** 704-732-9567

Louisburg WKXU-FM (c) PO Box 463, Louisburg NC 27549 **Phn:** 919-496-3105 **Fax:** 919-496-5864

Louisburg WYRN-AM (c) PO Box 463, Louisburg NC 27549 **Phn:** 919-496-3105 **Fax:** 919-496-5864

Marion WBRM-AM (c) 147 N Garden St, Marion NC 28752 **Phn:** 828-652-9500 **Fax:** 828-652-9700

Marshall WHBK-AM (cg) 1055 Skyway Dr, Marshall NC 28753 **Phn:** 828-649-3914 **Fax:** 828-649-2869

Mayodan WLOE-AM (ntq) PO Box 279, Mayodan NC 27027 **Phn:** 336-627-9563 **Fax:** 336-548-4636 www.wloewmyn.com info@rockinghamcountyradio.com

Mayodan WMYN-AM (qtn) PO Box 279, Mayodan NC 27027 **Phn:** 336-427-9696 **Fax:** 336-548-4636 www.wloewmyn.com info@rockinghamcountyradio.com

Monroe WIXE-AM (c) 1700 Buena Vista Rd, Monroe NC 28112 **Phn:** 704-289-2525 **Fax:** 704-289-1416 www.wixe1190.com archiewixe1190@gmail.com

Mooresville WHIP-AM (o) 2432 Hwy 115 N, Mooresville NC 28115 **Phn:** 704-664-9447 **Fax:** 704-664-5551 www.carolinascene.comwwhip

Morganton WCIS-AM (g) PO Box 1806, Morganton NC 28680 **Phn:** 828-584-3176

Morganton WMNC-AM (c) PO Box 969, Morganton NC 28680 **Phn:** 828-437-0521 **Fax:** 828-433-8855 www.bigdawg92fm.com wmnc@bellsouth.net

Morganton WMNC-FM (c) PO Box 969, Morganton NC 28680 **Phn:** 828-437-0521 **Fax:** 828-433-8855 www.bigdawg92fm.com wmnc@bellsouth.net

Mount Airy WPAQ-AM (c) PO Box 907, Mount Airy NC 27030 **Phn:** 336-786-6111 **Fax:** 336-789-7792 www.wpaq740.com info@wpaq740.com

Mount Airy WSYD-AM (cg) PO Box 1678, Mount Airy NC 27030 **Phn:** 336-786-2147 **Fax:** 336-789-9858 www.wsyd1300.com

Mount Olive WDJS-AM (nq) PO Box 479, Mount Olive NC 28365 **Phn:** 919-658-9751 **Fax:** 919-658-4894

Murfreesboro WDLZ-FM (r) PO Box 38, Murfreesboro NC 27855 **Phn:** 252-398-4111 **Fax:** 252-398-3581 firstmediaradio.com

Murfreesboro WWDR-AM (ug) PO Box 38, Murfreesboro NC 27855 **Phn:** 252-398-4111 **Fax:** 252-398-3581 firstmediaradio.com al@bestradioaround.com

Murphy WCNG-FM (a) 195 Hampton Church Rd, Murphy NC 28906 **Phn:** 828-837-9264 **Fax:** 828-837-5509

Murphy WCVP-AM (c) PO Box 280, Murphy NC 28906 **Phn:** 828-837-2151 **Fax:** 828-837-9264

Murphy WKRK-AM (c) 427 Hill St, Murphy NC 28906 **Phn:** 828-837-4332 **Fax:** 828-837-8610 www.1320am.com

Nags Head WERX-FM (o) PO Box 1418, Nags Head NC 27959 **Phn:** 252-441-1024 **Fax:** 252-441-2109 www.1025theshark.com marko@ecri.net

Nags Head WOBR-FM (r) 2422 S Wrightsville Ave, Nags Head NC 27959 **Phn:** 252-441-1024 **Fax:** 252-449-8956 www.wobr.com curtis@ecri.net

Nags Head WOBX-FM (nt) PO Box 1418, Nags Head NC 27959 **Phn:** 252-441-1024 **Fax:** 252-441-2109 www.wobx.net curtis@ecri.net

Nags Head WRSF-FM (c) PO Box 1418, Nags Head NC 27959 **Phn:** 252-441-1024 **Fax:** 252-449-8354 www.dixie1057.com ray@ecri.net

New Bern WANG-AM (o) 1361 Colony Dr, New Bern NC 28562 **Phn:** 252-447-3333 **Fax:** 252-514-0377

New Bern WEGG-AM (g) 233 Middle St Ste 207, New Bern NC 28560 **Phn:** 252-633-2143

New Bern WERO-FM (h) 1361 Colony Dr, New Bern NC 28562 **Phn:** 252-639-7900 **Fax:** 252-639-7979 www.bob933.com hollywood@bob933.com

New Bern WIKS-FM (wu) 207 Glenburnie Dr, New Bern NC 28560 **Phn:** 252-633-1500 **Fax:** 252-633-0718 1019online.com teresaterry@1019online.com

New Bern WMGV-FM (a) 207 Glenburnie Dr, New Bern NC 28560 **Phn:** 252-633-1500 **Fax:** 252-633-0718 www.v1033.com colleen@v1033.com

New Bern WNBB-FM (c) 233 Middle St Ste 107B, New Bern NC 28560 **Phn:** 252-638-8500 **Fax:** 252-638-8597 www.bear979.com

New Bern WNBR-FM (c) 233 Middle St Ste 107B, New Bern NC 28560 **Phn:** 252-638-8500 **Fax:** 252-638-8597

New Bern WNOS-AM (s) 1202 Pollock St, New Bern NC 28560 **Phn:** 252-633-1490 **Fax:** 888-878-5251 www.rfenc.com info@rfenc.com

New Bern WQSL-FM (ah) 1361 Colony Dr, New Bern NC 28562 **Phn:** 252-639-7900 **Fax:** 252-639-7979 www.carolinatouch.com lweiss@nextmediagroup.net

New Bern WQZL-FM (r) 1361 Colony Dr, New Bern NC 28562 **Phn:** 252-639-7900 **Fax:** 252-639-7979 www.carolinaspurerock.com lweiss@nextmediagroup.net

New Bern WRNS-FM (c) 1361 Colony Dr, New Bern NC 28562 **Phn:** 252-639-7900 **Fax:** 252-639-7979 www.wrns.com tommy@wrns.com

New Bern WRNS-AM (g) 1361 Colony Dr, New Bern NC 28562 **Phn:** 252-639-7900 **Fax:** 252-639-7979 www.wrns.com tommy@wrns.com

New Bern WSFL-FM (r) 207 Glenburnie Dr, New Bern NC 28560 **Phn:** 252-633-1500 **Fax:** 252-633-0718 www.wsfl.com bruce@wsfl.com

New Bern WSSM-FM (o) 1361 Colony Dr, New Bern NC 28562 **Phn:** 252-639-7900 **Fax:** 252-639-7979

New Bern WSTK-FM (g) 233 Middle St Ste 207, New Bern NC 28560 **Phn:** 252-633-2143

New Bern WTEB-FM (pln) 800 College Ct, New Bern NC 28562 **Phn:** 252-638-3434 **Fax:** 252-638-3538 www.publicradioeast.org golsen@publicradioeast.org

New Bern WXNR-FM (r) 207 Glenburnie Dr, New Bern NC 28560 **Phn:** 252-633-1500 **Fax:** 252-633-0718 995thex.com cindymiller@wsfl.com

New Bern WXQR-FM (r) 1361 Colony Dr, New Bern NC 28562 **Phn:** 252-639-7900 **Fax:** 252-639-7979 www.carolinaspurerock.com lweiss@nextmediagroup.net

Newland WECR-AM (c) 1281 Newland Hwy, Newland NC 28657 **Phn:** 828-733-0188 **Fax:** 828-733-0189 wecr1023.com tom@wecr1023.com

Newland WXIT-AM (nt) 1281 Newland Hwy, Newland NC 28657 **Phn:** 828-733-0188 **Fax:** 828-733-0189 wecrglory1130.wordpress.com wecr@bellsouth.net

Newport WJNC-AM (snt) PO Box 70, Newport NC 28570 **Phn:** 252-247-6343 **Fax:** 252-247-7343 www.wtkf107.com news@thetalkstation.com

Newport WOTJ-FM (q) 520 Roberts Rd, Newport NC 28570 **Phn:** 252-223-4600 www.fbnradio.com fbn@fbnradio.com

Newport WTKF-FM (nts) PO Box 70, Newport NC 28570 **Phn:** 252-247-6343 **Fax:** 252-247-7343 www.wtkf107.com news@thetalkstation.com

Newton WNNC-AM (a) PO Box 430, Newton NC 28658 **Phn:** 828-464-4041 **Fax:** 828-464-9662 www.mytotalradio.com

North Wilkesboro WKBC-FM (a) PO Box 938, North Wilkesboro NC 28659 **Phn:** 336-667-2221 **Fax:** 336-667-3677

North Wilkesboro WKBC-AM (c) PO Box 938, North Wilkesboro NC 28659 **Phn:** 336-667-2221 **Fax:** 336-667-3677

Oxford WLUS-FM (c) PO Box 1603, Oxford NC 27565 **Phn:** 919-693-7900 **Fax:** 919-693-9585 www.us983.com chrismichaels@lakesmediallc.com

Pineville WGCD-AM (wxqg) 9349 China Grove Church Rd, Pineville NC 28134 **Phn:** 980-297-7256 **Fax:** 980-297-7248 www.wgivcharlotte.com mikerobinson@wgiv.net

Pineville WGIV-AM (wx) 9349 China Grove Church Rd, Pineville NC 28134 **Phn:** 980-297-7256 **Fax:** 980-297-7248 www.wgivcharlotte.com mikerobinson@wgiv.net

NORTH CAROLINA RADIO STATIONS

Pineville WGIV-FM (wx) 9349 China Grove Church Rd, Pineville NC 28134 **Phn:** 980-297-7256 **Fax:** 980-297-7248 www.wgivcharlotte.com mikerobinson@wgiv.net

Pineville WYPJ-FM (wxqg) 9349 China Grove Church Rd, Pineville NC 28134 **Phn:** 980-297-7256 **Fax:** 980-297-7248 www.wgivcharlotte.com mikerobinson@wgiv.net

Pisgah Forest WGCR-AM (tg) 3232 Hendersonville Hwy, Pisgah Forest NC 28768 **Phn:** 828-884-9427 wgcr.net admin@wgcr.net

Raeford WMFA-AM (gq) 1085 E Central Ave, Raeford NC 28376 **Phn:** 910-875-6225 **Fax:** 910-875-3220 wmfa1400@yahoo.com

Raleigh WAUG-AM (wgu) 1315 Oakwood Ave, Raleigh NC 27610 **Phn:** 919-516-4750 **Fax:** 919-516-4087 www.mywaug.com

Raleigh WBBB-FM (r) 3012 Highwoods Blvd Ste 201, Raleigh NC 27604 **Phn:** 919-876-3831 **Fax:** 919-876-9213 www.radio961.com jnachlis@curtismedia.com

Raleigh WCLY-AM (ys) 3100 Highwoods Blvd Ste 140, Raleigh NC 27604 **Phn:** 919-890-6299

Raleigh WDCG-FM (h) 3100 Smoketree Ct Ste 700, Raleigh NC 27604 **Phn:** 919-878-1500 **Fax:** 919-876-2929 www.g105.com randi@g105.com

Raleigh WDNC-AM (snt) 3100 Highwoods Blvd Ste 140, Raleigh NC 27604 **Phn:** 919-890-6302 **Fax:** 919-510-6146

Raleigh WDNZ-AM (nt) 3012 Highwoods Blvd Ste 200, Raleigh NC 27604 **Phn:** 919-790-9392 **Fax:** 919-790-6654

Raleigh WDUR-AM (s) 3305 Durham Dr Ste 111, Raleigh NC 27603 **Phn:** 919-329-9810 **Fax:** 919-329-9803 trianglesportstalk.com

Raleigh WETC-AM (y) 3305 Durham Dr Ste 111, Raleigh NC 27603 **Phn:** 919-772-1717 **Fax:** 919-772-1718 laregia540am@bellsouth.net

Raleigh WFXC-FM (wu) 8001 Creedmoor Rd Ste 101, Raleigh NC 27613 **Phn:** 919-863-4800 **Fax:** 919-848-4724 foxync.com

Raleigh WFXK-FM (wu) 8001 Creedmoor Rd # 100, Raleigh NC 27613 **Phn:** 919-863-4800 **Fax:** 919-848-4724 foxync.com

Raleigh WKIX-FM (h) 4601 Six Forks Rd # 520, Raleigh NC 27609 **Phn:** 919-875-9100 **Fax:** 919-510-6990 www.KIX1029.com

Raleigh WKNC-FM (wv) PO Box 8607, Raleigh NC 27695 **Phn:** 919-515-2401 **Fax:** 919-515-5133 wknc.org gm@wknc.org

Raleigh WKSL-FM (a) 3100 Smoketree Ct Ste 700, Raleigh NC 27604 **Phn:** 919-878-1500 **Fax:** 919-876-2929 www.939kissfm.com chrisshebel@clearchannel.com

Raleigh WNNL-FM (g) 8001 Creedmoor Rd Ste 101, Raleigh NC 27613 **Phn:** 919-848-9736 **Fax:** 919-848-4724 thelightnc.com kclark@radio-one.com

Raleigh WPJL-AM (q) PO Box 27946, Raleigh NC 27611 **Phn:** 919-834-6401 **Fax:** 919-832-1240

Raleigh WPTF-AM (nt) 3012 Highwoods Blvd Ste 200, Raleigh NC 27604 **Phn:** 919-790-9392 **Fax:** 919-790-8369 www.wptf.com

Raleigh WQDR-FM (c) 3012 Highwoods Blvd Ste 201, Raleigh NC 27604 **Phn:** 919-876-6464 **Fax:** 919-790-8893 www.wqdr.net lmckay@curtismedia.com

Raleigh WQOK-FM (u) 8001 Creedmoor Rd Ste 101, Raleigh NC 27613 **Phn:** 919-848-9736 **Fax:** 919-848-4724 hiphopnc.com gweiss@radio-one.com

Raleigh WRAL-FM (a) 3100 Highwoods Blvd Ste 140, Raleigh NC 27604 **Phn:** 919-890-6101 **Fax:** 919-890-6146 www.wralfm.com mixonline@wralfm.com

Raleigh WRBZ-AM (s) 4601 Six Forks Rd Ste 520, Raleigh NC 27609 **Phn:** 919-875-9100 **Fax:** 919-510-6990 www.espntriangle.com

Raleigh WRDU-FM (r) 3100 Smoketree Ct Ste 700, Raleigh NC 27604 **Phn:** 919-878-1500 **Fax:** 919-876-8578 www.wrdu.com rachaellotter@clearchannel.com

Raleigh WRVA-FM (a) 3100 Smoketree Ct Ste 700, Raleigh NC 27604 **Phn:** 919-878-1500 **Fax:** 919-876-2929 www.wrdu.com rachaellotter@clearchannel.com

Raleigh WSHA-FM (vj) 118 E South St, Raleigh NC 27601 **Phn:** 919-546-8430 **Fax:** 919-546-8315 www.shawu.eduwshahome wsha@shawu.edu

Raleigh WTKK-FM (t) 3100 Smoketree Ct Ste 700, Raleigh NC 27604 **Phn:** 919-878-1500 **Fax:** 919-876-2929 www.1061fmtalk.com briantaylor@clearchannel.com

Raleigh WYMY-FM (y) 3012 Highwoods Blvd, Raleigh NC 27604 **Phn:** 919-790-9392 **Fax:** 919-790-8996 www.laley969.com

Red Springs WTEL-AM (g) PO Box 711, Red Springs NC 28377 **Phn:** 910-843-5946 **Fax:** 910-843-8694

Roanoke Rapds WRTG-AM (Hits) PO Box 910, Roanoke Rapds NC 27870 **Phn:** 252-536-3115 **Fax:** 252-538-0378 www.thegreat98fm.com cj@bestradioaround.com

Roanoke Rapids WCBT-AM (s) PO Box 910, Roanoke Rapids NC 27870 **Phn:** 252-536-3115 **Fax:** 252-538-0378 firstmediaradio.com cj@bestradioaround.com

Roanoke Rapids WPTM-FM (c) PO Box 910, Roanoke Rapids NC 27870 **Phn:** 252-536-3115 **Fax:** 252-538-0378 www.wptm1023.com haskinsal@yahoo.com

Roanoke Rapids WSMY-AM (gu) PO Box 910, Roanoke Rapids NC 27870 **Phn:** 252-536-3115 **Fax:** 252-538-0378 firstmediaradio.com al@bestradioaround.com

Roanoke Rapids WTRG-FM (o) PO Box 910, Roanoke Rapids NC 27870 **Phn:** 252-536-3115 **Fax:** 252-538-0378 firstmediaradio.com cj@bestradioaround.com

Roanoke Rapids WWDW-FM (a) PO Box 910, Roanoke Rapids NC 27870 **Phn:** 252-536-3115 firstmediaradio.com al@bestradioaround.com

Robbinsville WCVP-FM (c) PO Box 756, Robbinsville NC 28771 **Phn:** 828-479-8080 **Fax:** 828-479-2296

Rockingham WAYN-AM (a) PO Box 519, Rockingham NC 28380 **Phn:** 910-895-4041 **Fax:** 910-895-4993

Rockingham WJSG-FM (cq) 180 Airport Rd, Rockingham NC 28379 **Phn:** 910-895-3787 **Fax:** 910-895-8811 www.g104fm.com g104fm@g104.com

Rockingham WLWL-AM (cgq) 275 River Rd, Rockingham NC 28379 **Phn:** 910-997-2526 **Fax:** 910-997-2527

Rocky Mount WDWG-FM (c) 12714 E Nc Highway 97, Rocky Mount NC 27803 **Phn:** 252-442-8092 **Fax:** 252-977-6664 www.bigdawg985.com mbinkley@firstmedianc.com

Rocky Mount WEED-AM (nta) 115 N Church St, Rocky Mount NC 27804 **Phn:** 252-937-7400 **Fax:** 252-443-5977 soul92_2000@yahoo.com

Rocky Mount WPWZ-FM (h) 12714 E Nc Highway 97, Rocky Mount NC 27803 **Phn:** 252-442-8092 **Fax:** 252-977-6664 powerhits95.com dperkins@firstmedianc.com

Rocky Mount WRMT-AM (s) 12714 E Nc Highway 97, Rocky Mount NC 27803 **Phn:** 252-442-8091 **Fax:** 252-977-6664 mbinkley@firstmedianc.com

Rocky Mount WRSV-FM (wu) 115 N Church St, Rocky Mount NC 27804 **Phn:** 252-937-6111 **Fax:** 252-443-5977 wrsv-fm.tritondigitalmedia.com chuckjohnson9210@gmail.com

Rocky Mount WZAX-FM (h) 12714 E Nc Highway 97, Rocky Mount NC 27803 **Phn:** 252-442-8092 **Fax:** 252-977-6664 www.jammin993.com dperkins@firstmedianc.com

Roxboro WKRX-FM (c) PO Box 1176, Roxboro NC 27573 **Phn:** 336-599-0266 **Fax:** 336-599-9411 radioroxboro.com radiod@aol.com

Roxboro WRXO-AM (c) PO Box 1176, Roxboro NC 27573 **Phn:** 336-599-0266 **Fax:** 336-599-9411 radioroxboro.com radiod@aol.com

Rutherfordton WCAB-AM (cnt) PO Box 511, Rutherfordton NC 28139 **Phn:** 828-287-3356 **Fax:** 828-287-7182 www.wcab59.com

Salisbury WSAT-AM (os) 1525 Jake Alexander Blvd W, Salisbury NC 28147 **Phn:** 704-633-0621 **Fax:** 704-636-2955 1280wsat.com

Salisbury WSTP-AM (nt) PO Box 4157, Salisbury NC 28145 **Phn:** 704-636-3811 **Fax:** 704-637-1490 www.1490wstp.com newsradio1490@yahoo.com

Sanford WDCC-FM (vr) 1105 Kelly Dr, Sanford NC 27330 **Phn:** 919-718-7257 **Fax:** 919-718-7429 www.wdccfm.com bfreeman@cccc.edu

Sanford WFJA-FM (o) PO Box 3457, Sanford NC 27331 **Phn:** 919-775-3525 **Fax:** 919-775-4503 www.classichitsandoldies.comv2 news@wfjaradio.com

Sanford WLHC-FM (z) 102 S Steele St Ste 301, Sanford NC 27330 **Phn:** 919-775-1031 **Fax:** 919-775-1397 www.life1031.com wlhc@life1031.com

Sanford WWGP-AM (c) PO Box 3457, Sanford NC 27331 **Phn:** 919-775-3525 **Fax:** 919-775-4503 wfja@richardfeindel.com

Sanford WXKL-AM (wgx) PO Box 1290, Sanford NC 27331 **Phn:** 919-774-1080 **Fax:** 919-774-1118

Scotland Neck WYAL-AM (g) 25539 Hwy 125, Scotland Neck NC 27874 **Phn:** 252-826-3066

Shallotte WVCB-AM (gq) PO Box 314, Shallotte NC 28459 **Phn:** 910-754-4512 **Fax:** 910-754-3461

Shelby WADA-AM (c) 1511 W Dixon Blvd, Shelby NC 28152 **Phn:** 704-482-1390 **Fax:** 704-482-4680

Shelby WGNC-AM (o) PO Box 1590, Shelby NC 28151 **Phn:** 704-868-8222 **Fax:** 704-482-4680 netoldies@aol.com

Siler City WNCA-AM (ay) PO Box 429, Siler City NC 27344 **Phn:** 919-742-2135 **Fax:** 919-663-2843

Smithfield WMPM-AM (qt) PO Box 57, Smithfield NC 27577 **Phn:** 919-934-2434 **Fax:** 919-989-6388 www.1270wmpm.com lynda@1270wmpm.com

Smithfield WTSB-AM (nt) PO Box 90, Smithfield NC 27577 **Phn:** 919-934-6789 **Fax:** 919-934-6824 wtsbradio.com info@wtsbradio.com

Southern Pines WEEB-AM (snt) PO Box 1855, Southern Pines NC 28388 **Phn:** 910-692-7440 **Fax:** 910-692-7372 www.weeb990.com steve@weeb990.com

Southern Pines WIOZ-AM (am) 200 Short Rd, Southern Pines NC 28387 **Phn:** 910-692-2107 **Fax:** 910-692-6849 www.wioz.com rich@star1025fm.com

Southern Pines WIOZ-FM (r) 200 Short Rd, Southern Pines NC 28387 **Phn:** 910-692-2107 **Fax:** 910-692-6849 www.star1025fm.com walker@star1025fm.com

Spindale WGMA-AM (g) PO Box 805, Spindale NC 28160 **Phn:** 828-287-5150

Spindale WNCW-FM (p) PO Box 804, Spindale NC 28160 **Phn:** 828-287-8000 **Fax:** 828-287-8012 www.wncw.org info@wncw.org

Statesville WAME-AM (am) 212 Signal Hill Dr, Statesville NC 28625 **Phn:** 704-872-0550 **Fax:** 704-872-5547

Statesville WSIC-AM (nt) 1117 Radio Rd, Statesville NC 28677 **Phn:** 704-872-6345 **Fax:** 704-873-6921 www.wsicweb.com news@wsicweb.com

Tabor City WTAB-AM (cg) PO Box 127, Tabor City NC 28463 **Phn:** 910-653-2131 **Fax:** 910-653-5146 www.wtabradio.com wtab@wtabradio.com

Tarboro WCPS-AM (gwx) 1406 Saint Andrew St, Tarboro NC 27886 **Phn:** 252-824-7878 **Fax:** 252-824-7818

Taylorsville WACB-AM (m) 133 E Main Ave, Taylorsville NC 28681 **Phn:** 828-632-4621 **Fax:** 828-632-9081 wacbwtlk@applecitybroadcasting.com

Taylorsville WTLK-AM (g) 133 E Main Ave, Taylorsville NC 28681 **Phn:** 828-632-4214 **Fax:** 828-632-9081 wacbwtlk@applecitybroadcasting.com

Valdese WSVM-AM (cgo) PO Box 99, Valdese NC 28690 **Phn:** 828-874-0000 **Fax:** 828-874-2123

Wadesboro WADE-AM (qa) 65 Radio Tower Rd, Wadesboro NC 28170 **Phn:** 704-695-1060 **Fax:** 704-695-1495

Wake Forest WCPE-FM (lv) PO Box 897, Wake Forest NC 27588 **Phn:** 919-556-5178 **Fax:** 919-556-9273 theclassicalstation.org curtis@theclassicalstation.org

Wanchese WFMZ-FM (r) 637 Harbor Rd, Wanchese NC 27981 **Phn:** 252-475-1888 **Fax:** 252-475-1881 www.classichits1049.com classichits@maxradionc.com

Wanchese WOBX-AM (qg) PO Box 340, Wanchese NC 27981 **Phn:** 252-473-5402 **Fax:** 252-473-5838

Wanchese WVOD-FM (r) 637 Harbor Rd, Wanchese NC 27981 **Phn:** 252-475-1888 **Fax:** 252-475-1881 www.991thesound.com matt@maxradionc.com

Wanchese WYND-FM (c) 637 Harbor Rd, Wanchese NC 27981 **Phn:** 252-475-1888 **Fax:** 252-475-1881

Wanchese WZPR-FM (s) 637 Harbor Rd, Wanchese NC 27981 **Phn:** 252-475-1888 **Fax:** 252-475-1881

Warrenton WARR-AM (og) PO Box 611, Warrenton NC 27589 **Phn:** 252-257-5557 **Fax:** 252-257-5988 warr1520@embarqmail.com

West Jefferson WKSK-AM (c) PO Box 729, West Jefferson NC 28694 **Phn:** 336-246-6001 www.580wksk.com wksk@skybest.com

Whiteville WENC-AM (wgx) 108 Radio Station Rd, Whiteville NC 28472 **Phn:** 910-642-2133 **Fax:** 910-642-5981

Whiteville WTXY-AM (nt) PO Box 1038, Whiteville NC 28472 **Phn:** 910-642-8214 **Fax:** 910-640-1540 www.wtxy1540.com kendall@wtxy1540.com

Wilkesboro WWWC-AM (g) PO Box 580, Wilkesboro NC 28697 **Phn:** 336-838-1241 **Fax:** 336-838-9040 www.12403wc.com onair@12403wc.com

Williamston WIAM-AM (gq) PO Box 591, Williamston NC 27892 **Phn:** 252-792-4161 **Fax:** 252-809-0039

Wilmington WAAV-AM (snt) 3233 Burnt Mill Dr, Wilmington NC 28403 **Phn:** 910-763-9977 **Fax:** 910-762-0456 980waav.com brian.sims@cumulus.com

Wilmington WAZO-FM (h) 25 N Kerr Ave Ste C, Wilmington NC 28405 **Phn:** 910-791-3088 **Fax:** 910-791-0112 www.z1075.com matt@z1075.com

NORTH CAROLINA RADIO STATIONS

Wilmington WBNE-FM (r) 122 Cinema Dr, Wilmington NC 28403 **Phn:** 910-772-6300 **Fax:** 910-772-6310

Wilmington WGNI-FM (a) 3233 Burnt Mill Dr, Wilmington NC 28403 **Phn:** 910-763-9977 **Fax:** 910-763-0201 www.wgni.com brian.sims@cumulus.com

Wilmington WHQR-FM (pln) 254 N Front St Ste 300, Wilmington NC 28401 **Phn:** 910-343-1640 **Fax:** 910-251-8693 www.whqr.org whqr@whqr.org

Wilmington WKXB-FM (o) 25 N Kerr Ave, Wilmington NC 28405 **Phn:** 910-791-3088 **Fax:** 910-791-0112 www.jammin999fm.com sb@cbc-sunrise.com

Wilmington WKXS-FM (uw) 3233 Burnt Mill Dr, Wilmington NC 28403 **Phn:** 910-763-9977 **Fax:** 910-762-0456 www.945thehawkradio.com brian.sims@cumulus.com

Wilmington WLSG-AM (g) PO Box 957, Wilmington NC 28402 **Phn:** 910-763-2452 **Fax:** 910-763-6578 www.godscountry1340.com church@life905.com

Wilmington WLTT-FM (nt) 122 Cinema Dr, Wilmington NC 28403 **Phn:** 910-772-6300 **Fax:** 910-772-6310 portcityradio.com aimee.b@hometownwilmington.com

Wilmington WMFD-AM (s) 25 N Kerr Ave Ste C, Wilmington NC 28405 **Phn:** 910-791-3088 **Fax:** 910-791-0112 www.am630.net am630@live.com

Wilmington WMNX-FM (wu) 3233 Burnt Mill Dr, Wilmington NC 28403 **Phn:** 910-763-6511 **Fax:** 910-763-5926 www.coast973.com brian.sims@cumulus.com

Wilmington WNTB-FM (nt) 122 Cinema Dr, Wilmington NC 28403 **Phn:** 910-772-6300 **Fax:** 910-772-6310

Wilmington WRQR-FM (r) 25 N Kerr Ave Ste C, Wilmington NC 28405 **Phn:** 910-791-3088 **Fax:** 910-791-0112

Wilmington WUIN-FM (a) 122 Cinema Dr, Wilmington NC 28403 **Phn:** 910-772-6300 **Fax:** 910-772-6310 www.983thepenguin.com penguinrequests@hometownwilmington.com

Wilmington WWQQ-FM (c) 3233 Burnt Mill Dr, Wilmington NC 28403 **Phn:** 910-763-9977 **Fax:** 910-762-0456 www.wwqq101.com brian.sims@cumulus.com

Wilson WGTM-AM (wg) PO Box 3837, Wilson NC 27895 **Phn:** 252-243-2188 **Fax:** 252-237-8813

Wilson WVOT-AM (g) 2860 Ward Blvd # B, Wilson NC 27893 **Phn:** 252-243-1420 **Fax:** 252-291-5000

Winston Salem WBFJ-AM (aq) 1249 N Trade St, Winston Salem NC 27101 **Phn:** 336-721-1560 www.wbfj.org live@wbfj.fm

Winston Salem WBFJ-FM (v) 1249 N Trade St, Winston Salem NC 27101 **Phn:** 336-721-1560 **Fax:** 336-777-1032

Winston Salem WFDD-FM (p) PO Box 8850, Winston Salem NC 27109 **Phn:** 336-758-8850 **Fax:** 336-758-5193 www.wfdd.org wfdd@wfu.edu

Winston Salem WMFR-AM (nt) 875 W 5th St, Winston Salem NC 27101 **Phn:** 336-777-3900 **Fax:** 336-777-3915 www.triadsports.com comments@triadsports.com

Winston Salem WPIP-AM (q) 4135 Thomasville Rd, Winston Salem NC 27107 **Phn:** 336-785-0527 **Fax:** 336-785-0529 www.bereanbaptistwsnc.org wpip880am@triad.rr.com

Winston Salem WPOL-AM (q) 4405 Providence Ln, Winston Salem NC 27106 **Phn:** 336-759-0363 **Fax:** 336-759-0366 www.sgnthelight.com

Winston Salem WSGH-AM (y) 4015 Brownsboro Rd, Winston Salem NC 27106 **Phn:** 336-759-0524 **Fax:** 336-759-9327 www.radiolamovidita.com lucysaucedo@radiolamovidita.com

Winston Salem WSJS-AM (nt) 875 W 5th St, Winston Salem NC 27101 **Phn:** 336-777-3900 **Fax:** 336-777-3915 www.wsjs.com kfeltes@curtismedia.com

Winston Salem WSML-AM (st) 875 W 5th St, Winston Salem NC 27101 **Phn:** 336-777-3900 **Fax:** 336-777-3915 www.triadsports.com kfeltes@curtismedia.com

Winston Salem WSNC-FM (wvj) 601 M L K Jr Dr, Winston Salem NC 27110 **Phn:** 336-750-2324 **Fax:** 336-750-2329 jenkinse@wssu.edu

Winston Salem WTRU-AM (q) 4405 Providence Ln Ste D, Winston Salem NC 27106 **Phn:** 336-759-0363 **Fax:** 336-759-0366 www.wtru.com info@wtru.com

Yanceyville WYNC-AM (qn) PO Box 670, Yanceyville NC 27379 **Phn:** 336-694-7343 **Fax:** 336-694-7514 wync@embarqmail.com

NORTH DAKOTA

Bismarck KBMR-AM (c) 3500 E Rosser Ave, Bismarck ND 58501 **Phn:** 701-255-1234 **Fax:** 701-222-1131 www.kbmr.com jimlowe@clearchannel.com

Bismarck KBYZ-FM (r) 1830 N 11th St, Bismarck ND 58501 **Phn:** 701-663-9600 **Fax:** 701-663-8790 www.965thefox.com kbyz@cumulus.com

Bismarck KCND-FM (plnj) 1814 N 15th St, Bismarck ND 58501 **Phn:** 701-224-1700 **Fax:** 701-224-0555 www.prairiepublic.orgradio info@prairiepublic.org

Bismarck KDKT-AM (s) 547 S 7th St # 166, Bismarck ND 58504 **Phn:** 701-873-2215 **Fax:** 701-873-2363 www.foxsports1410.com info@foxsports1410.com

Bismarck KFYR-AM (snta) PO Box 2156, Bismarck ND 58502 **Phn:** 701-255-1234 **Fax:** 701-222-1131 www.kfyr.com kfyr@clearchannel.com

Bismarck KQDY-FM (c) 3500 E Rosser Ave, Bismarck ND 58501 **Phn:** 701-255-1234 **Fax:** 701-222-1131 www.kqdy.com jimlowe@clearchannel.com

Bismarck KSSS-FM (r) 3500 E Rosser Ave, Bismarck ND 58501 **Phn:** 701-255-1234 **Fax:** 701-222-1131 www.1015.fm rock101@clearchannel.com

Bismarck KXMR-AM (s) 3500 E Rosser Ave, Bismarck ND 58501 **Phn:** 701-255-1234 **Fax:** 701-222-1131 www.espn710am.com kxmr@clearchannel.com

Bismarck KYYY-FM (h) 3500 E Rosser Ave, Bismarck ND 58501 **Phn:** 701-255-1234 **Fax:** 701-222-1131 www.y93.fm y93@y93.fm

Bottineau KBTO-FM (c) PO Box 28, Bottineau ND 58318 **Phn:** 701-228-5151 **Fax:** 701-228-2483 sunnyradio@hotmail.com

Bowman KPOK-AM (c) PO Box 829, Bowman ND 58623 **Phn:** 701-523-3883 **Fax:** 701-523-3885 www.kpokradio.com kpok@kpokradio.com

Carrington KDAK-AM (c) PO Box 50, Carrington ND 58421 **Phn:** 701-652-3151 **Fax:** 701-652-2916

Devils Lake KDLR-AM (nt) PO Box 190, Devils Lake ND 58301 **Phn:** 701-662-2161 **Fax:** 701-662-2222 www.lrradioworks.com kdlrkdvl@stellarnet.com

Devils Lake KDVL-FM (o) PO Box 190, Devils Lake ND 58301 **Phn:** 701-662-2161 **Fax:** 701-662-2222 www.lrradioworks.com kdlrkdvl@gondtc.com

Devils Lake KQZZ-FM (r) PO Box 190, Devils Lake ND 58301 **Phn:** 701-662-2161 **Fax:** 701-662-2222 www.lrradioworks.com kzzyfm@gondtc.com

Devils Lake KZZY-FM (c) PO Box 190, Devils Lake ND 58301 **Phn:** 701-662-7563 **Fax:** 701-662-7564 www.lrradioworks.com kzzyfm@gondtc.com

NORTH DAKOTA RADIO STATIONS

Dickinson KCAD-FM (c) 11291 39th St SW, Dickinson ND 58601 **Phn:** 701-227-1876 **Fax:** 701-483-1959 www.roughridercountry.net

Dickinson KDIX-AM (ao) 119 2nd Ave W, Dickinson ND 58601 **Phn:** 701-225-5133 **Fax:** 701-225-4136 kdix.net kdix@kdix.net

Dickinson KLTC-AM (cnt) 11291 39th St SW, Dickinson ND 58601 **Phn:** 701-227-1876 **Fax:** 701-483-1959

Dickinson KZRX-FM (a) 11291 39th St SW, Dickinson ND 58601 **Phn:** 701-227-1876 **Fax:** 701-483-1959 www.kzrx921.com

Fargo KBVB-FM (h) 1020 25th St S, Fargo ND 58103 **Phn:** 701-237-5346 **Fax:** 701-237-0980 www.bob95fm.com studio@bob95fm.com

Fargo KDSU-FM (p) 207 5th St N, Fargo ND 58102 **Phn:** 701-241-6900 **Fax:** 701-239-7650 www.prairiepublic.org dthompson@prairiepublic.org

Fargo KEGK-FM (o) 64 Broadway N, Fargo ND 58102 **Phn:** 701-356-1156 **Fax:** 701-356-1155 www.youreagle1069.com boe@gpimonline.com

Fargo KFAB-FM (c) 1020 25th St S, Fargo ND 58103 **Phn:** 701-237-5346 **Fax:** 701-235-4042 www.kfab.com garysadlemyer@hotmail.com

Fargo KFBN-FM (vq) PO Box 107, Fargo ND 58107 **Phn:** 701-298-8877 www.kfbn.org heaven887@cableone.net

Fargo KFGO-AM (snt) 1020 25th St S, Fargo ND 58103 **Phn:** 701-237-5346 **Fax:** 701-237-0980 www.kfgo.com news@kfgo.com

Fargo KFJM-FM (p) 207 5th St N, Fargo ND 58102 **Phn:** 701-241-6900 **Fax:** 701-239-7650 www.prairiepublic.org dthompson@prairiepublic.org

Fargo KFNW-FM (q) 5702 52nd Ave S, Fargo ND 58104 **Phn:** 701-282-5910 **Fax:** 701-282-5781 life979.com kfnw@kfnw.org

Fargo KFNW-AM (q) 5702 52nd Ave S, Fargo ND 58104 **Phn:** 701-282-5910 **Fax:** 701-282-5781 life979.com kfnw@kfnw.org

Fargo KLTA-FM (a) 2720 7th Ave S, Fargo ND 58103 **Phn:** 701-237-4500 **Fax:** 701-235-9082 www.big987.com scotty@big987.com

Fargo KMJO-FM (h) 1020 25th St S, Fargo ND 58103 **Phn:** 701-237-5346 **Fax:** 701-298-3770 nancyodney@radiofargomoorhead.com

Fargo KPFX-FM (r) 2720 7th Ave S, Fargo ND 58103 **Phn:** 701-237-4500 **Fax:** 701-235-9082 www.1079thefox.com moose.johnson@1079thefox.com

Fargo KQWB-FM (r) 2720 7th Ave S, Fargo ND 58103 **Phn:** 701-237-4500 **Fax:** 701-235-9082 www.q1051rocks.com gunner@q1051rocks.com

Fargo KQWB-AM (s) PO Box 9919, Fargo ND 58106 **Phn:** 701-237-4500 **Fax:** 701-235-9082

Fargo KRWK-FM (r) 1020 25th St S, Fargo ND 58103 **Phn:** 701-237-5346 **Fax:** 701-235-4042 www.rock102online.com nancyodney@radiofargomoorhead.com

Fargo KUND-FM (p) 207 5th St N, Fargo ND 58102 **Phn:** 701-241-6900 **Fax:** 701-239-7650 www.prairiepublic.org dthompson@prairiepublic.org

Fargo KVOX-FM (c) PO Box 9919, Fargo ND 58106 **Phn:** 701-237-5346 **Fax:** 701-237-0980 www.froggyweb.com lilly.pad@froggyweb.com

Fargo KVOX-AM (snt) 1020 25th St S, Fargo ND 58103 **Phn:** 701-237-5346 **Fax:** 701-237-0980 www.740thefan.com nancyodney@radiofargomoorhead.com

Fargo WDAY-AM (nt) 301 8th St S, Fargo ND 58103 **Phn:** 701-237-6500 **Fax:** 701-241-5373 wday.com ejohnson@wday.com

Fargo WDAY-FM (h) 1020 25th St S, Fargo ND 58103 **Phn:** 701-237-5346 **Fax:** 701-237.0980 www.y94.com studio@y94.com

Fargo WZFG-AM (nt) 64 Broadway N, Fargo ND 58102 **Phn:** 701-356-1156

Grafton KAUJ-FM (o) 856 W 12th St, Grafton ND 58237 **Phn:** 701-352-0431 **Fax:** 701-352-0436 kxpoaj@polarcomm.com

Grafton KXPO-AM (c) 856 W 12th St, Grafton ND 58237 **Phn:** 701-352-0431 **Fax:** 701-352-0436 www.walshcountydailynews.com kxponews@polarcomm.com

Grand Forks KCNN-AM (snt) PO Box 13638, Grand Forks ND 58208 **Phn:** 701-775-4611 **Fax:** 701-772-0540 www.kcnn.com dsanden@kcnn.com

Grand Forks KJKJ-FM (r) 505 University Ave, Grand Forks ND 58203 **Phn:** 701-746-1417 **Fax:** 701-746-1410 www.kjkj.com brianrivers@clearchannel.com

Grand Forks KKXL-FM (h) 505 University Ave, Grand Forks ND 58203 **Phn:** 701-746-1417 **Fax:** 701-746-1410 www.xl93.com rickacker@clearchannel.com

Grand Forks KNOX-AM (nt) PO Box 13638, Grand Forks ND 58208 **Phn:** 701-775-4611 **Fax:** 701-772-0540 www.knoxradio.com live@knoxradio.com

Grand Forks KNOX-FM (c) PO Box 13638, Grand Forks ND 58208 **Phn:** 701-775-4611 **Fax:** 701-772-0540 knoxradio.com jt@knoxradio.com

Grand Forks KQHT-FM (ah) 505 University Ave, Grand Forks ND 58203 **Phn:** 701-746-1417 **Fax:** 701-746-1410 www.961thefox.com brianrivers@clearchannel.com

Grand Forks KSNR-FM (o) 505 University Ave, Grand Forks ND 58203 **Phn:** 701-746-1417 **Fax:** 701-746-1410 www.thecatfm.com daveandrews@clearchannel.com

Grand Forks KUND-AM (pn) PO Box 8117, Grand Forks ND 58202 **Phn:** 701-777-2577 **Fax:** 701-777-2810

Grand Forks KYCK-FM (c) PO Box 13638, Grand Forks ND 58208 **Phn:** 701-775-4611 **Fax:** 701-772-0540 www.97kyck.com live@97kyck.com

Grand Forks KZLT-FM (a) PO Box 13638, Grand Forks ND 58208 **Phn:** 701-775-4611 **Fax:** 701-772-0540 www.literock1043.com jt@literock1043.com

Harvey KHND-AM (rnt) PO Box 6, Harvey ND 58341 **Phn:** 701-324-4848 **Fax:** 701-324-2043 www.khnd1470.com studio@khnd1470.com

Hettinger KNDC-AM (c) PO Box 151, Hettinger ND 58639 **Phn:** 701-567-2421 **Fax:** 701-567-4636 www.kndcradio.com kndc1490@ndsupernet.com

Jamestown KQDJ-AM (nt) PO Box 1170, Jamestown ND 58402 **Phn:** 701-252-1400 **Fax:** 701-252-1402

Jamestown KSJB-AM (cnt) PO Box 5180, Jamestown ND 58402 **Phn:** 701-252-3570 **Fax:** 701-252-1277 www.ksjbam.com bweatherly@ksjbam.com

Jamestown KSJZ-FM (ah) PO Box 5180, Jamestown ND 58402 **Phn:** 701-252-3570 **Fax:** 701-252-1277 news@ksjbam.com

Jamestown KXGT-FM (o) PO Box 1170, Jamestown ND 58402 **Phn:** 701-252-1400 **Fax:** 701-252-1402

Jamestown KYNU-FM (c) PO Box 1170, Jamestown ND 58402 **Phn:** 701-252-1400 **Fax:** 701-252-1402

Langdon KAOC-FM (c) 1403 3rd St, Langdon ND 58249 **Phn:** 701-256-1080 **Fax:** 701-256-1081 www.maverick105fm.com kndkkicksbs@utma.com

Langdon KNDK-FM (a) PO Box 30, Langdon ND 58249 **Phn:** 701-256-1080 **Fax:** 701-256-1081 www.myborderland.comkndkfm.html kndkmw@utma.com

Langdon KNDK-AM (cnt) PO Box 30, Langdon ND 58249 **Phn:** 701-256-1080 **Fax:** 701-256-1081 kndkam.myborderland.com kndkmw@utma.com

Langdon KYTZ-FM (a) 1403 3rd St, Langdon ND 58249 **Phn:** 701-256-1080 **Fax:** 701-256-1081 www.maverick105fm.com kndkkicksbs@utma.com

Lisbon KQLX-FM (c) 1206 Main St, Lisbon ND 58054 **Phn:** 701-356-9790 **Fax:** 701-356-9792 greatplainslive.netgpimkqlx_com kqlx@kqlx.com

Lisbon KQLX-AM (cn) 1206 Main St, Lisbon ND 58054 **Phn:** 701-356-9790 **Fax:** 701-356-9792 greatplainslive.netgpimkqlx_com kqlx@kqlx.com

Mandan KACL-FM (o) 4303 Memorial Hwy, Mandan ND 58554 **Phn:** 701-250-6602 **Fax:** 701-250-6632 www.cool987fm.com jj.hemingway@townsquaremedia.com

Mandan KKCT-FM (h) 4303 Memorial Hwy, Mandan ND 58554 **Phn:** 701-250-6602 **Fax:** 701-663-8790 www.hot975fm.com mia.amini@townsquaremedia.com

Mandan KLXX-AM (t) 4303 Memorial Hwy, Mandan ND 58554 **Phn:** 701-250-6602 **Fax:** 701-250-6632 supertalk1270.com larry.leblanc@townsquaremedia.com

Mandan KNDR-FM (q) 1400 3rd St NE, Mandan ND 58554 **Phn:** 701-663-2345 **Fax:** 701-663-2347 kndr.fm kndr@midconetwork.com

Mandan KUSB-FM (c) 4303 Memorial Hwy, Mandan ND 58554 **Phn:** 701-250-6602 **Fax:** 701-663-8790 www.1033uscountry.com larry.leblanc@townsquaremedia.com

Mayville KMAV-AM (s) PO Box 216, Mayville ND 58257 **Phn:** 701-786-2335 **Fax:** 701-786-2268 kmav.com news@kmav.com

Mayville KMAV-FM (c) PO Box 216, Mayville ND 58257 **Phn:** 701-786-2335 **Fax:** 701-786-2268 www.kmav.com news@kmav.com

Mayville KMSR-AM (s) PO Box 216, Mayville ND 58257 **Phn:** 701-786-2335 **Fax:** 701-786-2268 kmav.com news@kmav.com

Minot KCJB-AM (ntc) PO Box 10, Minot ND 58702 **Phn:** 701-852-4646 **Fax:** 701-852-1390 www.kcjb910.com rickstensby@clearchannel.com

Minot KHRT-AM (g) PO Box 1210, Minot ND 58702 **Phn:** 701-852-3789 **Fax:** 701-852-8498 www.khrt.com production@khrt.com

Minot KHRT-FM (q) PO Box 1210, Minot ND 58702 **Phn:** 701-852-3789 **Fax:** 701-852-8498 www.khrt.com production@khrt.com

Minot KIZZ-FM (a) 1000 20th Ave SW, Minot ND 58701 **Phn:** 701-852-4646 **Fax:** 701-852-1390 www.z94radio.com allisonbostow@clearchannel.com

Minot KMXA-FM (a) 1000 20th Ave SW, Minot ND 58701 **Phn:** 701-852-4646 **Fax:** 701-852-1390 www.mix999fm.com rickstensby@clearchannel.com

Minot KRRZ-AM (str) 1000 20th Ave SW, Minot ND 58701 **Phn:** 701-852-4646 **Fax:** 701-852-1390 www.oldies1390.com rickstensby@clearchannel.com

Minot KYYX-FM (c) PO Box 10, Minot ND 58702 **Phn:** 701-852-4646 **Fax:** 701-852-1390 www.97kicksfm.com rickstensby@clearchannel.com

Minot KZPR-FM (r) 1000 20th Ave SW, Minot ND 58701 **Phn:** 701-852-4646 **Fax:** 701-852-1390 www.1053thefox.com allisonbostow@clearchannel.com

Oakes KDDR-AM (c) 412 Main Ave Ste 2, Oakes ND 58474 **Phn:** 701-742-2187 **Fax:** 701-742-2009 kddr@drtel.net

Rugby KZZJ-AM (cn) 230 Highway 2 SE, Rugby ND 58368 **Phn:** 701-776-5254 **Fax:** 701-776-6154 www.kzzj.com kzzj@kzzj.com

Saint Michael KABU-FM (v) 7889 Highway 57, Saint Michael ND 58370 **Phn:** 701-766-4095 **Fax:** 701-766-4068

Tioga KTGO-AM (ct) PO Box 457, Tioga ND 58852 **Phn:** 701-664-3322

Valley City KOVC-AM (cn) 136 Central Ave N, Valley City ND 58072 **Phn:** 701-845-1490 **Fax:** 701-845-1245

Valley City KQDJ-FM (a) PO Box 994, Valley City ND 58072 **Phn:** 701-845-1490 **Fax:** 701-845-1245 www.newsdakota.com

Williston KDSR-FM (a) 910 E Broadway, Williston ND 58801 **Phn:** 701-572-4478 **Fax:** 701-572-1419 newsdesk@kxgn.com

Williston KEYZ-AM (cn) 410 6th St E, Williston ND 58801 **Phn:** 701-572-5371 **Fax:** 701-572-7511 www.keyzradio.com scotth@nccray.net

Williston KYYZ-FM (c) PO Box 2048, Williston ND 58802 **Phn:** 701-572-5371 **Fax:** 701-572-7511 shaugen@cherrycreekradio.com

OHIO

Ada WONB-FM (vohj) 525 S Main St, Ada OH 45810 **Phn:** 419-772-1194 **Fax:** 419-772-2794 www.onu.eduwonb wonb@onu.edu

Akron WAKR-AM (sno) 1795 W Market St, Akron OH 44313 **Phn:** 330-869-9800 **Fax:** 330-869-9750 www.akronnewsnow.com news@rcrg.net

Akron WAPS-FM (vpj) 65 Steiner Ave, Akron OH 44301 **Phn:** 330-761-3099 **Fax:** 330-761-3103 www.913thesummit.com billgruber@913thesummit.com

Akron WJMP-AM (st) PO Box 2170, Akron OH 44309 **Phn:** 330-673-2323 **Fax:** 330-673-0301 traffic@wnir.com

Akron WNIR-FM (nt) PO Box 2170, Akron OH 44309 **Phn:** 330-673-2323 **Fax:** 330-673-0301 www.wnir.com news@wnir.com

Akron WONE-FM (r) 1795 W Market St, Akron OH 44313 **Phn:** 330-869-9800 **Fax:** 330-869-9750 www.wone.net tdaugherty@wone.net

Akron WQMX-FM (c) 1795 W Market St, Akron OH 44313 **Phn:** 330-869-9800 **Fax:** 330-869-9750 www.wqmx.com swilson@wqmx.com

Akron WZIP-FM (vu) 302 Buchtel Mall, Akron OH 44325 **Phn:** 330-972-7105 **Fax:** 330-972-5521 www.wzip.fm wzip@uakron.edu

Alliance WDJQ-FM (h) PO Box 2356, Alliance OH 44601 **Phn:** 330-450-9250 **Fax:** 330-821-0379 www.q92radio.com

Alliance WDPN-AM (am) PO Box 2356, Alliance OH 44601 **Phn:** 330-821-1111 **Fax:** 330-821-0379 johnstewartradio@gmail.com

Alliance WRMU-FM (vjr) 1972 Clark Ave, Alliance OH 44601 **Phn:** 330-823-2414 **Fax:** 330-829-4913

Archbold WMTR-FM (ah) 303 12 N Defiance St, Archbold OH 43502 **Phn:** 419-445-9050 **Fax:** 419-445-3531 www.961wmtr.com wmtr@rtecexpress.net

Ashland WFXN-FM (r) 1197 US Highway 42, Ashland OH 44805 **Phn:** 419-289-2605 **Fax:** 419-289-0304 www.wfxnthefox.com erichansen@clearchannel.com

Ashland WNCO-FM (c) 1197 US Highway 42, Ashland OH 44805 **Phn:** 419-289-2605 **Fax:** 419-289-0304 www.wncofm.com ronaldcolman@clearchannel.com

Ashland WNCO-AM (nt) 1197 US Highway 42, Ashland OH 44805 **Phn:** 419-289-2605 **Fax:** 419-289-0304 www.wncoam.com ronaldcolman@clearchannel.com

Ashland WRDL-FM (vr) 401 College Ave, Ashland OH 44805 **Phn:** 419-289-5157 **Fax:** 419-289-5329

Ashtabula WFUN-AM (snt) 3226 Jefferson Rd, Ashtabula OH 44004 **Phn:** 440-993-2126 **Fax:** 440-992-2658 www.espn970wfun.com danaschulte@mediaone-group.com

Ashtabula WFXJ-FM (r) 3226 Jefferson Rd, Ashtabula OH 44004 **Phn:** 440-993-2126 **Fax:** 440-992-2658 www.thefox1075.com danaschulte@mediaone-group.com

Ashtabula WREO-FM (a) 3226 Jefferson Rd, Ashtabula OH 44004 **Phn:** 440-993-2126 **Fax:** 440-992-2658 www.star97.com danaschulte@mediaone-group.com

Ashtabula WYBL-FM (c) 3226 Jefferson Rd, Ashtabula OH 44004 **Phn:** 440-993-2126 **Fax:** 440-992-2658 danaschulte@mediaone-group.com

Ashtabula WZOO-FM (a) 3226 Jefferson Rd, Ashtabula OH 44004 **Phn:** 440-993-2126 **Fax:** 440-992-2658 www.magicoldies1025.com danaschulte@mediaone.com

Athens WATH-AM (snt) PO Box 210, Athens OH 45701 **Phn:** 740-593-6651 **Fax:** 740-594-3488 www.970wath.com twilliams@wxtq.com

Athens WOUB-FM (plj) 9 S College St, Athens OH 45701 **Phn:** 740-593-1771 **Fax:** 740-593-0240 woub.orgradio radio@woub.org

Athens WOUB-AM (pnt) 9 S College St, Athens OH 45701 **Phn:** 740-593-4554 **Fax:** 740-593-0240 woub.org radio@woub.org

Athens WXTQ-FM (a) PO Box 210, Athens OH 45701 **Phn:** 740-593-6651 **Fax:** 740-594-3488 wxtq.com twilliams@wxtq.com

Barnesville WBNV-FM (a) 175 E Main St, Barnesville OH 43713 **Phn:** 740-425-9268 **Fax:** 740-484-4430 www.yourradioplace.com avcnews@yourradioplace.com

Bellaire WOMP-AM (nt) PO Box 448, Bellaire OH 43906 **Phn:** 740-676-5661 **Fax:** 740-676-2742

Bellaire WYJK-FM (h) 56325 High Ridge Rd, Bellaire OH 43906 **Phn:** 740-676-5661 **Fax:** 740-676-2742 www.wyjkfm.com

Bellefontaine WBLL-AM (snt) 1501 Road 235, Bellefontaine OH 43311 **Phn:** 937-592-1045 www.peakofohio.com btipple@wpko.com

Bellefontaine WPKO-FM (a) 1501 Road 235, Bellefontaine OH 43311 **Phn:** 937-592-1045 www.peakofohio.com cwilkinson@wpko.com

Belpre WCVV-FM (q) PO Box 405, Belpre OH 45714 **Phn:** 740-423-5895 **Fax:** 740-423-9951 wcvv@juno.com

Berea WBWC-FM (v) 275 Eastland Rd, Berea OH 44017 **Phn:** 440-826-2145 **Fax:** 440-826-3426 www.wbwc.com news@wbwc.com

Blue Ash WCIN-AM (wou) 4445 Lake Forest Dr Ste 420, Blue Ash OH 45242 **Phn:** 513-281-7180 **Fax:** 513-281-5678 www.oldies1480.net garys@oldies1480.net

Bowling Green WBGU-FM (vjw) Bowling Green State U, Bowling Green OH 43403 **Phn:** 419-372-8657 wbgufm.com

Brecksville WCRF-FM (qv) 9756 Barr Rd, Brecksville OH 44141 **Phn:** 440-526-1111 **Fax:** 440-526-1319 www.mbn.org wcrf@moody.edu

Bryan WBNO-FM (r) 12810 State Route 34, Bryan OH 43506 **Phn:** 419-636-3175 **Fax:** 419-636-4570 www.wbno-wqct.com wbno@wbno-wqct.com

Bryan WLZZ-FM (c) 5691 State Route 15 Ste B, Bryan OH 43506 **Phn:** 419-633-1045 **Fax:** 419-633-1047 www.wlzzradio.com wlzz@wlzzradio.com

Bryan WQCT-AM (ob) 12810 State Route 34, Bryan OH 43506 **Phn:** 419-636-3175 **Fax:** 419-636-4570 www.wbno-wqct.com wbno@wbno-wqct.com

Bucyrus WBCO-AM (a) PO Box 1140, Bucyrus OH 44820 **Phn:** 419-562-2222 **Fax:** 419-562-0520 wbcowqel.com wbeard@wbcowqel.com

Bucyrus WQEL-FM (sno) PO Box 1140, Bucyrus OH 44820 **Phn:** 419-562-2222 **Fax:** 419-562-0520 wbcowqel.com wbeard@wbcowqel.com

Cambridge WCMJ-FM (a) PO Box 338, Cambridge OH 43725 **Phn:** 740-432-5605 **Fax:** 740-432-1991 www.wcmj.com avcnews@yourradioplace.com

Cambridge WILE-FM (nt) PO Box 338, Cambridge OH 43725 **Phn:** 740-432-5605 **Fax:** 740-432-1991 yourradioplace.com info@yourradioplace.com

Cambridge WWKC-FM (c) PO Box 338, Cambridge OH 43725 **Phn:** 740-432-5605 **Fax:** 740-432-1991 www.wwkc.com avcnews@yourradioplace.com

Canton WCER-AM (q) 4537 22nd St NW, Canton OH 44708 **Phn:** 330-478-6655 **Fax:** 330-478-6651

Canton WHBC-AM (nt) 550 Market Ave S, Canton OH 44702 **Phn:** 330-456-7166 **Fax:** 330-456-7199 www.whbc.com pcook@whbc.com

Canton WHBC-FM (a) 550 Market Ave S, Canton OH 44702 **Phn:** 330-456-7166 **Fax:** 330-471-1894 www.mix941.com pcook@whbc.com

Canton WNPQ-FM (q) 3969 Convenience Cir NW Ste 205, Canton OH 44718 **Phn:** 330-492-9590 **Fax:** 330-492-3702 www.thelight959.com tom@thelight959.com

Castalia WGGN-FM (q) PO Box 247, Castalia OH 44824 **Phn:** 419-684-5311 **Fax:** 419-684-5378 www.fm977.net

Castalia WJKW-FM (q) PO Box 247, Castalia OH 44824 **Phn:** 740-592-9879 www.wjkw.net wjkw@cfbroadcast.net

Celina WCSM-FM (a) PO Box 492, Celina OH 45822 **Phn:** 419-586-5134 **Fax:** 419-586-3814 www.wcsmradio.com wcsm@bright.net

Celina WCSM-AM (snt) PO Box 492, Celina OH 45822 **Phn:** 419-586-5133 **Fax:** 419-586-3814 www.wcsmradio.com suebrunswick@wcsmradio.com

Celina WKKI-FM (a) PO Box 322, Celina OH 45822 **Phn:** 419-586-7715 **Fax:** 419-586-1074 www.k943.com psa@wkki.net

Chagrin Falls WKHR-FM (vbj) 17425 Snyder Rd, Chagrin Falls OH 44023 **Phn:** 440-543-9646 www.wkhr.org info@wkhr.org

Chillicothe WBEX-AM (nt) PO Box 94, Chillicothe OH 45601 **Phn:** 740-773-3000 **Fax:** 740-774-4494 www.wbex.com newsroom@wkkj.com

Chillicothe WCHI-AM (a) 45 W Main St, Chillicothe OH 45601 **Phn:** 740-773-3000 **Fax:** 740-774-4494 www.comedy1350.com newsroom@wkkj.com

Chillicothe WKKJ-FM (c) 45 W Main St, Chillicothe OH 45601 **Phn:** 740-773-3000 **Fax:** 740-774-4494 www.wkkj.com danlatham@clearchannel.com

Cincinnati WAKW-FM (qa) PO Box 24126, Cincinnati OH 45224 **Phn:** 513-542-9259 **Fax:** 513-542-9333 www.mystar933.com wakw@eos.net

OHIO RADIO STATIONS

Cincinnati WCKY-AM (s) 8044 Montgomery Rd Ste 650, Cincinnati OH 45236 **Phn:** 513-686-8300 **Fax:** 513-333-4245 www.espn1530.com tonybender@clearchannel.com

Cincinnati WCVX-AM (q) 635 W 7th St Ste 400, Cincinnati OH 45203 **Phn:** 513-533-2500 **Fax:** 513-533-2528 wcvx.com comments@wcvx.com

Cincinnati WDBZ-AM (wt) 705 Central Ave Ste 200, Cincinnati OH 45202 **Phn:** 513-679-6000 **Fax:** 513-679-6014 thebuzzcincy.com jtolliver@radio-one.com

Cincinnati WDJO-AM (o) 635 W 7th St Ste 203, Cincinnati OH 45203 **Phn:** 513-281-7180 **Fax:** 513-281-5678 www.oldies1480.net garys@oldies1480.net

Cincinnati WEBN-FM (r) 8044 Montgomery Rd Ste 650, Cincinnati OH 45236 **Phn:** 513-686-8300 **Fax:** 513-665-9700 www.webn.com webn@clearchannel.com

Cincinnati WFTK-FM (t) 4805 Montgomery Rd Ste 100, Cincinnati OH 45212 **Phn:** 513-241-9898 **Fax:** 513-241-6689 www.supertalkfm965.com angie.irick@cumulus.com

Cincinnati WGRR-FM (o) 2060 Reading Rd, Cincinnati OH 45202 **Phn:** 513-241-9898 **Fax:** 513-241-6689 www.wgrr.com keith.mitchell@cumulus.com

Cincinnati WGUC-FM (pl) 1223 Central Pkwy, Cincinnati OH 45214 **Phn:** 513-241-8282 www.wguc.org wguc@wguc.org

Cincinnati WIZF-FM (uw) 705 Central Ave Ste 200, Cincinnati OH 45202 **Phn:** 513-679-6000 **Fax:** 513-679-6014 wiznation.com ejgreig@radio-one.com

Cincinnati WKFS-FM (h) 8044 Montgomery Rd Ste 650, Cincinnati OH 45236 **Phn:** 513-686-8300 **Fax:** 513-333-4245 www.kiss107.com jare@kiss107.com

Cincinnati WKRC-AM (t) 8044 Montgomery Rd Ste 650, Cincinnati OH 45236 **Phn:** 513-686-8300 **Fax:** 513-333-4245 www.55krc.com tbender@55krc.com

Cincinnati WKRQ-FM (a) 2060 Reading Rd, Cincinnati OH 45202 **Phn:** 513-699-5102 **Fax:** 513-699-5460 www.wkrq.com blair@hubbardinteractive.com

Cincinnati WLW-AM (snt) 8044 Montgomery Rd Ste 650, Cincinnati OH 45236 **Phn:** 513-686-8300 **Fax:** 513-333-4245 www.700wlw.com jeffhenderson@clearchannel.com

Cincinnati WMUB-FM (pnj) 1223 Central Pkwy, Cincinnati OH 45214 **Phn:** 513-352-9170 **Fax:** 513-241-8456 www.wmub.org wvxu@wvxu.org

Cincinnati WREW-FM (a) 2060 Reading Rd, Cincinnati OH 45202 **Phn:** 513-699-5102 **Fax:** 513-699-5000 www.949cincinnati.com lthal@hubbardinteractive.com

Cincinnati WRRM-FM (a) 4805 Montgomery Rd Ste 300, Cincinnati OH 45212 **Phn:** 513-241-9898 **Fax:** 513-241-6689 www.warm98.com keith.mitchell@cumulus.com

Cincinnati WSAI-AM (s) 8044 Montgomery Rd Ste 650, Cincinnati OH 45236 **Phn:** 513-686-8300 **Fax:** 513-333-4245 www.foxsports1360.com tonybender@clearchannel.com

Cincinnati WUBE-FM (c) 2060 Reading Rd, Cincinnati OH 45202 **Phn:** 513-699-5105 **Fax:** 513-699-5460 www.b105.com cmello@hubbardinteractive.com

Cincinnati WVXU-FM (pjb) 1223 Central Pkwy, Cincinnati OH 45214 **Phn:** 513-352-9170 **Fax:** 513-241-8456 www.wvxu.org wvxu@wvxu.org

Cincinnati WYGY-FM (c) 2060 Reading Rd, Cincinnati OH 45202 **Phn:** 513-699-5103 **Fax:** 513-699-5460 www.theworldwidewolf.com cmello@hubbardinteractive.com

Cleveland WABQ-AM (wg) 8000 Euclid Ave, Cleveland OH 44103 **Phn:** 216-231-8005 **Fax:** 216-231-9803

Cleveland WCCD-AM (g) 3130 Mayfield Rd, Cleveland OH 44118 **Phn:** 216-320-0000 **Fax:** 216-397-0987

Cleveland WCLV-FM (l) 26501 Renaissance Pkwy, Cleveland OH 44128 **Phn:** 216-464-0900 **Fax:** 216-464-2206 www.wclv.com wclv@wclv.com

Cleveland WCPN-FM (pnj) 1375 Euclid Ave, Cleveland OH 44115 **Phn:** 216-916-6100 **Fax:** 216-916-6090 www.wcpn.org

Cleveland WCSB-FM (v) 2121 Euclid Ave # 956, Cleveland OH 44115 **Phn:** 216-687-3523 www.wcsb.org gm@wcsb.org

Cleveland WDOK-FM (a) 1041 Huron Rd, Cleveland OH 44115 **Phn:** 216-861-0100 new102.cbslocal.com dave.popovich@cbsradio.com

Cleveland WENZ-FM (u) 6555 Carnegie Ave #100, Cleveland OH 44103 **Phn:** 216-579-1111 **Fax:** 216-771-4164 zhiphopcleveland.com

Cleveland WERE-AM (nt) 2510 Saint Clair Ave NE, Cleveland OH 44114 **Phn:** 216-579-1111 **Fax:** 216-771-4164 newstalkcleveland.com elogan@radio-one.com

Cleveland WJMO-AM (wg) 6555 Carnegie Ave # 100, Cleveland OH 44103 **Phn:** 216-579-1111 **Fax:** 216-771-4164 praisecleveland.com

Cleveland WKRK-FM (st) 1041 Huron Rd E, Cleveland OH 44115 **Phn:** 216-861-0100 **Fax:** 216-696-0385 cleveland.cbslocal.com andy.roth@cbsradio.com

Cleveland WNCX-FM (r) 1041 Huron Rd E, Cleveland OH 44115 **Phn:** 216-861-0100 **Fax:** 216-696-0385 wncx.cbslocal.com info@wncx.com

Cleveland WQAL-FM (a) 1041 Huron Rd, Cleveland OH 44115 **Phn:** 216-696-0123 **Fax:** 216-363-7104 q104.cbslocal.com skippy@q104.com

Cleveland WRUW-FM (v) 11220 Bellflower Rd, Cleveland OH 44106 **Phn:** 216-368-2208 www.wruw.org gm@wruw.org

Cleveland WZAK-FM (wu) 6555 Carnegie Ave # 100, Cleveland OH 44103 **Phn:** 216-579-1111 **Fax:** 216-771-4164 wzakcleveland.com

Clyde WHVT-FM (q) PO Box 273, Clyde OH 43410 **Phn:** 419-547-8254 **Fax:** 567-855-0001 www.cleanair.fm gene@ibmradio.com

Columbus WBNS-FM (s) 605 S Front St Fl 3, Columbus OH 43215 **Phn:** 614-460-3850 **Fax:** 614-460-3757 www.971thefan.com dave.vanstone@radiohio.com

Columbus WBNS-AM (s) 605 S Front St Fl 3, Columbus OH 43215 **Phn:** 614-460-3850 **Fax:** 614-460-3757 www.971thefan.com dave.vanstone@radiohio.com

Columbus WBWR-FM (r) 2323 W 5th Ave Ste 200, Columbus OH 43204 **Phn:** 614-486-6101 **Fax:** 614-487-2559 www.thebrew1057.com lauralee@clearchannel.com

Columbus WCBE-FM (pn) 540 Jack Gibbs Blvd, Columbus OH 43215 **Phn:** 614-365-5555 **Fax:** 614-365-5060 www.wcbe.org wcbe-news@wcbe.org

Columbus WCKX-FM (uw) 350 E 1st Ave Ste 100, Columbus OH 43201 **Phn:** 614-487-1444 **Fax:** 614-487-5862 mycolumbuspower.com

Columbus WCOL-FM (c) 2323 W 5th Ave Ste 200, Columbus OH 43204 **Phn:** 614-486-6101 **Fax:** 614-487-2555 www.wcol.com stacieraterman@clearchannel.com

Columbus WHOK-FM (c) 2400 Corporate Exchange Dr # 200, Columbus OH 43231 **Phn:** 614-227-9696 www.k95.fm

Columbus WJYD-FM (u) 350 E 1st Ave Ste 100, Columbus OH 43201 **Phn:** 614-487-1444 **Fax:** 614-487-5862 mycolumbusmagic.com

Columbus WJZA-FM (aj) 4401 Carriage Hill Ln, Columbus OH 43220 **Phn:** 614-451-2191 **Fax:** 614-451-1831 rewindcolumbus.com michelle.hurley@columbusradiogroup.com

Columbus WLVQ-FM (ar) 280 N High St Fl 10, Columbus OH 43215 **Phn:** 614-227-9696 **Fax:** 614-461-1059 www.qfm96.com joeshow@qfm96.com

Columbus WLZT-FM (o) 2323 W 5th Ave Ste 200, Columbus OH 43204 **Phn:** 614-486-6101 **Fax:** 614-487-2559 www.oldies933fm.com michaelmccoy@clearchannel.com

Columbus WMNI-AM (am) 1458 Dublin Rd, Columbus OH 43215 **Phn:** 614-481-7800 **Fax:** 614-481-8070 www.wmni.com hfish@nabco-inc.com

Columbus WNCI-FM (h) 2323 W 5th Ave Ste 200, Columbus OH 43204 **Phn:** 614-487-3550 **Fax:** 614-487-3553 www.wnci.com michaelmccoy@clearchannel.com

Columbus WNKK-FM (c) 2400 Corporate Exchange Dr # 200, Columbus OH 43231 **Phn:** 614-227-9696 www.k95.fm

Columbus WODB-FM (h) 4401 Carriage Hill Ln, Columbus OH 43220 **Phn:** 614-451-2191 **Fax:** 614-451-1831 rewindcolumbus.com michelle.hurley@columbusradiogroup.com

Columbus WOSU-FM (p) 2400 Olentangy River Rd, Columbus OH 43210 **Phn:** 614-292-9678 **Fax:** 614-292-0513 www.wosu.org news@wosu.org

Columbus WOSU-AM (p) 2400 Olentangy River Rd, Columbus OH 43210 **Phn:** 614-292-9678 **Fax:** 614-292-0513 www.wosu.org news@wosu.org

Columbus WRFD-AM (qt) 8101 N High St Ste 360, Columbus OH 43235 **Phn:** 614-885-0880 **Fax:** 614-885-6322 www.wrfd.com mail@wrfd.com

Columbus WRKZ-AM (r) 1458 Dublin Rd, Columbus OH 43215 **Phn:** 614-481-7800 **Fax:** 614-481-8070 www.theblitz.com hfish@nabco-inc.com

Columbus WRXS-FM (r) 2323 W 5th Ave Ste 200, Columbus OH 43204 **Phn:** 614-486-6101 **Fax:** 614-487-2559 www.x1067.com lauralee@clearchannel.com

Columbus WSNY-FM (a) 4401 Carriage Hill Ln, Columbus OH 43220 **Phn:** 614-451-2191 **Fax:** 614-451-1831 sunny95.com

Columbus WTDA-FM (a) 1458 Dublin Rd, Columbus OH 43215 **Phn:** 614-481-7800 **Fax:** 614-481-8070 www.1039wtda.com hfish@nabco-inc.com

Columbus WTVN-AM (nt) 2323 W 5th Ave Ste 200, Columbus OH 43204 **Phn:** 614-486-6101 **Fax:** 614-487-2555 www.610wtvn.com newsroom@wtvn.com

Columbus WVKO-FM (y) 74 S 4th St, Columbus OH 43215 **Phn:** 614-469-1930 **Fax:** 614-224-6208

Columbus WVMX-FM (a) 4401 Carriage Hill Ln, Columbus OH 43220 **Phn:** 614-451-2191 **Fax:** 614-451-1831

Columbus WVSG-AM (q) 4673 Winterset Dr, Columbus OH 43220 **Phn:** 614-459-4820 **Fax:** 714-845-0411 www.stgabrielradio.com

Columbus WWCD-FM (r) 1036 S Front St, Columbus OH 43206 **Phn:** 614-221-9923 **Fax:** 614-227-0021 cd1025.com webmaster@cd1025.com

Columbus WXMG-FM (x) 350 E 1st Ave Ste 100, Columbus OH 43201 **Phn:** 614-487-1444 **Fax:** 614-487-5862 mycolumbusmagic.com jeffwilson@radio-one.com

Columbus WYTS-AM (st) 2323 W 5th Ave Ste 200, Columbus OH 43204 **Phn:** 614-486-6101 **Fax:** 614-487-2555 www.am1230wyts.com daveman@clearchannel.com

OHIO RADIO STATIONS

Conneaut WGOJ-FM (q) PO Box 725, Conneaut OH 44030 **Phn:** 440-593-1055 wgoj-christian-radio.com wgoj@suite224.net

Conneaut WWOW-AM (o) 229 Broad St, Conneaut OH 44030 **Phn:** 440-593-2233 www.1360wwow.com wshanleaf@aol.com

Coshocton WTNS-AM (c) 114 N 6th St, Coshocton OH 43812 **Phn:** 740-622-1560 **Fax:** 740-622-7940 wtnsnewsroom@sbcglobal.net

Coshocton WTNS-FM (a) 114 N 6th St, Coshocton OH 43812 **Phn:** 740-622-1560 **Fax:** 740-622-7940 wtnsnewsroom@sbcglobal.net

Dayton WCWT-FM (v) 500 E Franklin St, Dayton OH 45459 **Phn:** 937-439-3557 **Fax:** 937-439-3574

Dayton WDAO-AM (uwx) 1012 W 3rd St, Dayton OH 45402 **Phn:** 937-222-9326 **Fax:** 937-461-6100

Dayton WDHT-FM (x) 717 E David Rd, Dayton OH 45429 **Phn:** 937-294-5858 **Fax:** 937-297-5233 www.hot1029.com pdhot1029@gmail.com

Dayton WDKF-FM (h) 101 Pine St Ste 300, Dayton OH 45402 **Phn:** 937-224-1137 **Fax:** 937-224-5015 www.channeldayton.com stevekramer@clearchannel.com

Dayton WDSJ-FM (c) 101 Pine St Ste 300, Dayton OH 45402 **Phn:** 937-224-1137 **Fax:** 937-224-3667 www.big1065.com jeffstevens@clearchannel.com

Dayton WFCJ-FM (q) PO Box 937, Dayton OH 45449 **Phn:** 937-866-2471 **Fax:** 937-866-2062 www.wfcj.com

Dayton WGTZ-FM (ha) 717 E David Rd, Dayton OH 45429 **Phn:** 937-294-5858 **Fax:** 937-297-5233 www.fly929.com bwaldo@mainlinedayton.com

Dayton WHIO-AM (nt) 1414 Wilmington Ave, Dayton OH 45420 **Phn:** 937-259-2111 **Fax:** 937-259-2168 www.newstalkradiowhio.com nick.roberts@coxradio.com

Dayton WHKO-FM (c) 1414 Wilmington Ave, Dayton OH 45420 **Phn:** 937-259-2111 **Fax:** 937-259-2168 www.k99online.com nick.roberts@coxradio.com

Dayton WING-AM (snt) 717 E David Rd, Dayton OH 45429 **Phn:** 937-294-5858 **Fax:** 937-297-5233 www.wingam.com daytonsports@yahoo.com

Dayton WIZE-AM (ob) 101 Pine St Ste 300, Dayton OH 45402 **Phn:** 937-224-1137 **Fax:** 937-224-5015 tonytilford@clearchannel.com

Dayton WLQT-FM (c) 101 Pine St Ste 300, Dayton OH 45402 **Phn:** 937-224-1137 **Fax:** 937-224-5015 www.hotcountryb945.com brianmichaels@clearchannel.com

Dayton WMMX-FM (a) 101 Pine St, Dayton OH 45402 **Phn:** 937-224-1137 **Fax:** 937-224-3667 www.mix1077.com jeffstevens@clearchannel.com

Dayton WONE-AM (s) 101 Pine St Ste 300, Dayton OH 45402 **Phn:** 937-224-1137 **Fax:** 937-224-5015 www.wone.com tonytilford@clearchannel.com

Dayton WQRP-FM (q) 917 E Central Ave, Dayton OH 45449 **Phn:** 937-865-5900

Dayton WROU-FM (uw) 717 E David Rd, Dayton OH 45429 **Phn:** 937-294-5858 **Fax:** 937-297-5233 www.921wrou.com

Dayton WTUE-FM (r) 101 Pine St Ste 300, Dayton OH 45402 **Phn:** 937-224-1137 **Fax:** 937-224-3667 www.wtue.com tonytilford@clearchannel.com

Dayton WWSU-FM (v) 3640 Colonel Glenn Hwy, Dayton OH 45435 **Phn:** 937-775-5554 wwsu1069.com gm@wwsu1069.com

Dayton WXEG-FM (r) 101 Pine St Ste 300, Dayton OH 45402 **Phn:** 937-224-1137 **Fax:** 937-224-5015 www.newrock1039.com stevekramer@clearchannel.com

Dayton WZLR-FM (r) 1414 Wilmington Ave, Dayton OH 45420 **Phn:** 937-259-2111 **Fax:** 937-259-2168 www.953theeagle.com nick.roberts@coxradio.com

Defiance WDFM-FM (a) 2110 Radio Dr, Defiance OH 43512 **Phn:** 419-782-9336 **Fax:** 419-784-0306 www.mix981fm.com ricksmall@clearchannel.com

Defiance WONW-AM (snt) 2110 Radio Dr, Defiance OH 43512 **Phn:** 419-782-8126 **Fax:** 419-784-4154 www.wonw1280.com bobmclimans@clearchannel.com

Defiance WZOM-FM (c) 2110 Radio Dr, Defiance OH 43512 **Phn:** 419-782-8126 **Fax:** 419-784-4154 www.1057thebull.com josh@1057thebull.com

Delaware WSLN-FM (v) 61 S Sandusky St, Delaware OH 43015 **Phn:** 740-368-2912 **Fax:** 740-368-3649 radio.owu.edu wslnoffice@gmail.com

Delphos WDOH-FM (a) 111 E 2nd St, Delphos OH 45833 **Phn:** 419-692-3963 **Fax:** 419-692-5896 www.literock1071.com bobulm3963@gmail.com

Dover WJER-AM (a) 646 Boulevard St, Dover OH 44622 **Phn:** 330-343-7755 **Fax:** 330-364-4538 www.wjer.com wjer@wjer.com

Elyria WEOL-AM (ns) PO Box 4006, Elyria OH 44036 **Phn:** 440-322-3761 **Fax:** 440-284-3189 www.weol.com cadams@weol.com

Elyria WJTB-AM (wug) 105 Lake Ave, Elyria OH 44035 **Phn:** 440-327-1844 **Fax:** 440-322-8942

Elyria WNWV-FM (aj) PO Box 4006, Elyria OH 44036 **Phn:** 440-322-3761 **Fax:** 440-236-3299 1073thewave.net news@rcrg.net

Fairfield WCNW-AM (gq) 8686 Michael Ln, Fairfield OH 45014 **Phn:** 513-829-7700

Fairfield WNLT-FM (q) 8686 Michael Ln, Fairfield OH 45014 **Phn:** 513-829-7700

Findlay WBUK-FM (o) PO Box 1507, Findlay OH 45839 **Phn:** 419-422-4545 **Fax:** 419-422-6736 www.wbuk.com ericsiewert@1063thefox.com

Findlay WBVI-FM (a) PO Box 1624, Findlay OH 45839 **Phn:** 419-422-9284 **Fax:** 419-435-6611 www.wbvi.com production@wfob.com

Findlay WFIN-AM (nt) PO Box 1507, Findlay OH 45839 **Phn:** 419-422-4545 **Fax:** 419-422-6736 www.wfin.com wfin@wfin.com

Findlay WKXA-FM (ar) PO Box 1507, Findlay OH 45839 **Phn:** 419-422-4545 **Fax:** 419-422-6736 www.wkxa.com wkxa@wkxa.com

Fostoria WFOB-AM (an) PO Box 1157, Fostoria OH 44830 **Phn:** 419-435-1430 **Fax:** 419-435-6611 www.wfob.com production@wfob.com

Fremont WFRO-FM (a) 1281 N River Rd, Fremont OH 43420 **Phn:** 419-332-8218 **Fax:** 419-333-8226 www.wfroradio.com tomklein@basbroadcasting.com

Fremont WOHF-FM (r) 1281 N River Rd, Fremont OH 43420 **Phn:** 419-332-8218 **Fax:** 419-333-8226 wohf.basohio.com tomklein@basbroadcasting.com

Gahanna WCVO-FM (q) 881 E Johnstown Rd, Gahanna OH 43230 **Phn:** 614-289-5700 **Fax:** 614-289-5796 www.1049theriver.com theriver@1049theriver.com

Gallipolis WJEH-AM (am) 117 Portsmouth Rd, Gallipolis OH 45631 **Phn:** 740-446-3543 **Fax:** 740-446-3001

Gallipolis WNTO-FM (h) 117 Portsmouth Rd, Gallipolis OH 45631 **Phn:** 740-446-3543 **Fax:** 740-446-3001

Gambier WKCO-FM (v) PO Box 312, Gambier OH 43022 **Phn:** 740-427-5411 **Fax:** 740-427-5413 wkco.kenyon.eduwkco wkco@kenyon.edu

Geneva WKKY-FM (c) 95 W Main St, Geneva OH 44041 **Phn:** 440-466-9559 **Fax:** 440-466-3138 www.wkky.com wkky@wkky.com

Georgetown WOXY-FM (a) 8354 Fryer Rd, Georgetown OH 45121 **Phn:** 937-377-2211 **Fax:** 937-377-2200 bryan@woxy.com

Granville WDUB-FM (v) Denison Univ, Granville OH 43023 **Phn:** 740-587-5775

Greenfield WVNU-FM (a) PO Box 329, Greenfield OH 45123 **Phn:** 937-981-5050 **Fax:** 937-981-2107 www.wvnu.com pat@wvnu.com

Greenville WTGR-FM (c) PO Box 176, Greenville OH 45331 **Phn:** 937-548-5085 **Fax:** 937-548-5089 www.wtgr.com scott@wtgr.com

Hamilton WHSS-FM (vr) 1111 Eaton Ave, Hamilton OH 45013 **Phn:** 513-887-4818

Hamilton WMOH-AM (snt) 2081 Fairgrove Ave, Hamilton OH 45011 **Phn:** 513-863-1111 **Fax:** 513-863-6856 www.wmoh.com stevevaughn@wmoh.com

Hillsboro WSRW-AM (a) 5765 Sr 247, Hillsboro OH 45133 **Phn:** 937-393-1590 **Fax:** 937-393-1611 www.buckeyecountry105.com news@buckeyecountry105.com

Hillsboro WSRW-FM (c) PO Box 9, Hillsboro OH 45133 **Phn:** 937-393-1590 **Fax:** 937-393-1611 www.buckeyecountry105.com news@buckeyecountry105.com

Holland WPOS-FM (q) PO Box 457, Holland OH 43528 **Phn:** 419-865-9767 proclaimfm.com office@wposfm.com

Independence WAKS-FM (a) 6200 Oak Tree Blvd, Independence OH 44131 **Phn:** 216-520-2600 **Fax:** 216-901-8133 www.kisscleveland.com feedback@waks.com

Independence WFHM-FM (q) 4 Summit Park Dr Ste 150, Independence OH 44131 **Phn:** 216-901-0921 **Fax:** 216-901-5517 www.955thefish.com mark@955thefish.com

Independence WGAR-FM (c) 6200 Oak Tree Blvd, Independence OH 44131 **Phn:** 216-520-2600 **Fax:** 216-524-2600 www.wgar.com feedback@wgar.com

Independence WHK-AM (nt) 4 Summit Park Dr Ste 150, Independence OH 44131 **Phn:** 216-901-0921 **Fax:** 216-901-5517 www.whkradio.com

Independence WHKZ-AM (t) 4 Summit Park Dr Ste 150, Independence OH 44131 **Phn:** 216-901-0921 **Fax:** 216-901-5517 www.whkradio.com mharchar@salemcleveland.com

Independence WMJI-FM (o) 6200 Oak Tree Blvd, Independence OH 44131 **Phn:** 216-520-2600 **Fax:** 216-524-5600 www.wmji.com chip@wmji.com

Independence WMMS-FM (r) 6200 Oak Tree Blvd, Independence OH 44131 **Phn:** 216-520-2600 **Fax:** 216-901-8169 www.wmms.com feedback@wmms.com

Independence WMVX-FM (a) 6200 Oak Tree Blvd, Independence OH 44131 **Phn:** 216-520-2600 **Fax:** 216-901-8133 www.1065thelake.com feedback@1065thelake.com

Independence WTAM-AM (snt) 6200 Oak Tree Blvd, Independence OH 44131 **Phn:** 216-520-2600 www.wtam.com news@wtam.com

Jackson WCJO-FM (c) PO Box 667, Jackson OH 45640 **Phn:** 740-286-3023 **Fax:** 740-286-6679 rburtrand@jcbiradio.com

OHIO RADIO STATIONS

Jackson WKOV-FM (a) PO Box 667, Jackson OH 45640 **Phn:** 740-286-3023 **Fax:** 740-286-6679 jmossbarger@jcbiradio.com

Jackson WYPC-AM (am) PO Box 667, Jackson OH 45640 **Phn:** 740-286-3023 **Fax:** 740-286-6679 jmossbarger@jcbiradio.com

Jackson WYRO-FM (r) 295 E Main St, Jackson OH 45640 **Phn:** 740-286-3023 **Fax:** 740-286-6679 jpelletier@jcbiradio.com

Kent WKSU-FM (pln) 1613 E Summit St, Kent OH 44242 **Phn:** 330-672-3114 **Fax:** 330-672-4107 www.wksu.org letters@wksu.org

Kenton WKTN-FM (a) PO Box 213, Kenton OH 43326 **Phn:** 419-675-2355 **Fax:** 419-673-1096 www.wktn.com wktn@kenton.com

Lakewood WKTX-AM (oe) 11906 Madison Ave, Lakewood OH 44107 **Phn:** 216-221-0330 **Fax:** 216-221-3638

Lancaster WLOH-AM (o) 2686 N Columbus St Ste 101, Lancaster OH 43130 **Phn:** 740-653-4373 **Fax:** 740-653-0702 www.wloh.net news@wloh.net

Lima WCIT-AM (s) 57 Town Sq, Lima OH 45801 **Phn:** 419-331-1600 **Fax:** 419-228-5085 www.940wcit.com

Lima WEGE-FM (r) 57 Town Sq, Lima OH 45801 **Phn:** 419-331-1600 **Fax:** 419-228-5085 www.1049theeagle.com phil@cmgroup.co

Lima WFGF-FM (c) 57 Town Sq, Lima OH 45801 **Phn:** 419-331-1600 **Fax:** 419-228-5085 921thefrog.com jp@cmgroup.co

Lima WIMA-AM (nt) 667 W Market St, Lima OH 45801 **Phn:** 419-223-2060 **Fax:** 419-229-3888 www.1150wima.com jasonaldrich@clearchannel.com

Lima WIMT-FM (c) 667 W Market St, Lima OH 45801 **Phn:** 419-223-2060 **Fax:** 419-229-3888 www.t102.com reneescott@clearchannel.com

Lima WMLX-FM (a) 667 W Market St, Lima OH 45801 **Phn:** 419-223-2060 **Fax:** 419-229-3888 www.mix1033.com reneescott@clearchannel.com

Lima WTGN-FM (q) 1600 Elida Rd, Lima OH 45805 **Phn:** 419-227-2525 **Fax:** 419-222-5438 witnessingthegoodnews.org wtgn@wcoil.com

Lima WWSR-FM (s) 57 Town Sq, Lima OH 45801 **Phn:** 419-331-1600 **Fax:** 419-228-5085 www.931thefan.com aaron@cmgroup.co

Lima WZRX-FM (r) 667 W Market St, Lima OH 45801 **Phn:** 419-223-2060 **Fax:** 419-229-3888 www.wzrxfm.com reneescott@clearchannel.com

Logan WKNA-FM (c) PO Box 429, Logan OH 43138 **Phn:** 740-385-2151 **Fax:** 740-385-4022 sblazer@hotmail.com

Logan WLGN-FM (c) PO Box 429, Logan OH 43138 **Phn:** 740-385-2151 **Fax:** 740-385-4022 sblazer@hotmail.com

Manchester WAGX-FM (oa) PO Box 492, Manchester OH 45144 **Phn:** 606-564-8474

Mansfield WMAN-AM (snt) 1400 Radio Ln, Mansfield OH 44906 **Phn:** 419-529-2211 **Fax:** 419-529-2516 www.wmanfm.com rustycates@clearchannel.com

Mansfield WSWR-FM (o) 1400 Radio Ln, Mansfield OH 44906 **Phn:** 419-529-2211 **Fax:** 419-529-2516 www.my100fm.com erichansen@clearchannel.com

Mansfield WVMC-FM (vq) 500 Logan Rd, Mansfield OH 44907 **Phn:** 419-756-5651 **Fax:** 419-756-7470

Mansfield WYHT-FM (h) 1400 Radio Ln, Mansfield OH 44906 **Phn:** 419-529-2211 **Fax:** 419-529-2516 www.wyht.com erichansen@clearchannel.com

Marietta WCMO-FM (vr) 215 5th St, Marietta OH 45750 **Phn:** 740-376-4804 **Fax:** 740-376-4807 www.marietta.edu~wcmofm sinclaij@marietta.edu

Marietta WJAW-AM (s) 925 Lancaster St, Marietta OH 45750 **Phn:** 740-373-1490 **Fax:** 740-373-1717 www.wmoa1490.com jwharff@wmoa1490.com

Marietta WMOA-AM (as) PO Box 690, Marietta OH 45750 **Phn:** 740-373-1490 **Fax:** 740-373-1717 www.wmoa1490.com news@wmoa1490.com

Marietta WMRT-FM (vlj) 215 5th St, Marietta OH 45750 **Phn:** 740-376-4800 **Fax:** 740-376-4807 wmrtfm.com wmrt@marietta.edu

Marion WMRN-FM (cn) 1330 N Main St, Marion OH 43302 **Phn:** 740-383-1131 **Fax:** 740-387-8173 www.buckeyecountry943.com

Marion WMRN-AM (nt) 1330 N Main St, Marion OH 43302 **Phn:** 740-383-1131 **Fax:** 740-387-8173 www.wmrn.com

Marion WYNT-FM (oh) 1330 N Main St, Marion OH 43302 **Phn:** 740-383-1131 **Fax:** 740-387-8173 www.majic959.com pauljames@clearchannel.com

Massillon WTIG-AM (s) PO Box 38, Massillon OH 44648 **Phn:** 330-837-9900 **Fax:** 330-837-9844 www.espn990.com espn990@gmail.com

Middleport WMPO-AM (s) PO Box 71, Middleport OH 45760 **Phn:** 740-992-6485 **Fax:** 740-992-6486 office@wyvk.com

Middleport WYVK-FM (a) PO Box 71, Middleport OH 45760 **Phn:** 740-992-6485 **Fax:** 740-992-6486 www.wyvk.com office@wyvk.com

Middletown WPFB-FM (c) 4505 Central Ave, Middletown OH 45044 **Phn:** 513-422-3625 **Fax:** 513-424-9732

Middletown WPFB-AM (nt) 4505 Central Ave, Middletown OH 45044 **Phn:** 513-422-3625 **Fax:** 513-424-9732

Milan WKFM-FM (c) 10327 US Highway 250 N, Milan OH 44846 **Phn:** 419-609-5961 **Fax:** 419-609-2679 wkfm.northcoastnow.com mjeffries@wkfm.com

Milan WLKR-AM (o) 10327 US Highway 250 N, Milan OH 44846 **Phn:** 419-609-5961 **Fax:** 419-609-2679 wlkr.northcoastnow.com bforthofer@wkfm.com

Milan WLKR-FM (a) 10327 US Highway 250 N, Milan OH 44846 **Phn:** 419-609-5961 **Fax:** 419-609-2679 wlkr.northcoastnow.com wlkr@wlkrradio.com

Millersburg WKLM-FM (a) 7409 Private Road 341, Millersburg OH 44654 **Phn:** 330-674-1953 **Fax:** 330-674-9556

Morrow WLMH-FM (v) 605 Welch Rd, Morrow OH 45152 **Phn:** 513-899-3884

Mount Vernon WMVO-AM (o) 17421 Coshocton Rd, Mount Vernon OH 43050 **Phn:** 740-397-1000 **Fax:** 740-392-9300 www.wmvo.com davebevington@basbroadcasting.com

Mount Vernon WNZR-FM (q) 800 Martinsburg Rd, Mount Vernon OH 43050 **Phn:** 740-392-9090 **Fax:** 740-392-9155 wnzr.fm wnzr@mvnu.edu

Mount Vernon WQIO-FM (a) 17421 Coshocton Rd, Mount Vernon OH 43050 **Phn:** 740-397-1000 **Fax:** 740-392-9300 wqio.basohio.com curtisnewland@basbroadcasting.com

Napoleon WNDH-FM (a) 709 N Perry St, Napoleon OH 43545 **Phn:** 419-592-8060 **Fax:** 419-592-1085 www.wndh1031.com wndh@clearchannel.com

Nelsonville WAIS-AM (ntc) 15751 US Highway 33, Nelsonville OH 45764 **Phn:** 740-753-4094 **Fax:** 740-753-4965

New Concord WMCO-FM (v) 163 Stormont St, New Concord OH 43762 **Phn:** 740-826-8907 **Fax:** 740-826-6122 www.orbitmediaonline.com wmcomusicdepartment@gmail.com

New Lexington WWJM-FM (a) 210 S Jackson St, New Lexington OH 43764 **Phn:** 740-342-1988 **Fax:** 740-342-1036 www.wwjm.com wwjm@aol.com

New Philadelphia WTUZ-FM (c) 2424 E High Ave, New Philadelphia OH 44663 **Phn:** 330-339-2222 **Fax:** 330-339-5930 www.wtuz.com news@wtuz.com

Newark WCLT-AM (nt) PO Box 5150, Newark OH 43058 **Phn:** 740-345-4004 **Fax:** 740-345-5775 www.wclt.com wclt@wclt.com

Newark WCLT-FM (c) PO Box 5150, Newark OH 43058 **Phn:** 740-345-4004 **Fax:** 740-345-5775 www.wclt.com wclt@wclt.com

Newark WHTH-AM (nt) PO Box 1057, Newark OH 43058 **Phn:** 740-522-8171 **Fax:** 740-522-8174 www.wnko.com studio@wnko.com

Newark WNKO-FM (o) PO Box 1057, Newark OH 43058 **Phn:** 740-522-8171 **Fax:** 740-522-8174 www.wnko.com studio@wnko.com

North Canton WARF-AM (s) 7755 Freedom Ave NW, North Canton OH 44720 **Phn:** 330-836-4700 **Fax:** 330-492-1350 www.sportsradio1350.com

North Canton WHLO-AM (nt) 7755 Freedom Ave NW, North Canton OH 44720 **Phn:** 330-836-4700 **Fax:** 330-836-5321 www.640whlo.com keithkennedy@clearchannel.com

North Canton WHOF-FM (a) 7755 Freedom Ave NW, North Canton OH 44720 **Phn:** 330-492-4700 **Fax:** 330-492-1350 www.my1017.com keithkennedy@clearchannel.com

North Canton WKDD-FM (a) 7755 Freedom Ave NW, North Canton OH 44720 **Phn:** 330-836-4700 **Fax:** 330-492-1350 www.wkdd.com danlankford@clearchannel.com

North Canton WRQK-FM (h) 7755 Freedom Ave NW, North Canton OH 44720 **Phn:** 330-492-4700 **Fax:** 330-492-5633 www.wrqk.com

Oberlin WDLW-AM (o) PO Box 277, Oberlin OH 44074 **Phn:** 440-775-1380 **Fax:** 440-774-1336 woblwdlw.com woblwdlw@yahoo.com

Oberlin WOBC-FM (v) 135 W Lorain St, Oberlin OH 44074 **Phn:** 440-775-8107 www.wobc.org wobc@oberlin.edu

Oberlin WOBL-AM (c) PO Box 277, Oberlin OH 44074 **Phn:** 440-774-1320 **Fax:** 440-774-1336 woblwdlw.com woblwdlw@yahoo.com

Ontario WRGM-AM (s) 2900 Park Ave W, Ontario OH 44906 **Phn:** 419-529-5900 **Fax:** 419-529-2319 www.wrgm.com newsroom@wmfd.com

Ontario WVNO-FM (a) 2900 Park Ave W, Ontario OH 44906 **Phn:** 419-529-5900 **Fax:** 419-529-2319 www.wvno.com newsroom@wmfd.com

Owensville WOBO-FM (vbc) PO Box 338, Owensville OH 45160 **Phn:** 513-724-3999 www.wobofm.com

Painesville WBKC-AM (nl) 1 Radio Pl, Painesville OH 44077 **Phn:** 440-352-1460 **Fax:** 440-352-8194

Piketon WXZQ-FM (h) PO Box 820, Piketon OH 45661 **Phn:** 740-947-0059 **Fax:** 740-947-4600

Piqua WPTW-AM (o) 1625 Covington Ave, Piqua OH 45356 **Phn:** 937-773-3513 **Fax:** 937-773-4345 www.1570wptw.com rick@muzzybroadcasting.net

Portsmouth WNXT-FM (a) PO Box 1228, Portsmouth OH 45662 **Phn:** 740-353-1161 **Fax:** 740-353-3191 www.wnxtradio.com wnxtradio@yahoo.com

OHIO RADIO STATIONS

Portsmouth WNXT-AM (sn) PO Box 1228, Portsmouth OH 45662 **Phn:** 740-353-1161 **Fax:** 740-353-3191 wnxtradio@yahoo.com

Portsmouth WPAY-FM (c) 1009 Gallia St, Portsmouth OH 45662 **Phn:** 740-353-5176 **Fax:** 740-353-1715

Portsmouth WPAY-AM (nt) 1009 Gallia St, Portsmouth OH 45662 **Phn:** 740-353-5176 **Fax:** 740-353-1715

Portsmouth WZZZ-FM (r) 602 Chillicothe St, Portsmouth OH 45662 **Phn:** 740-353-1979 **Fax:** 740-353-3191 www.wzzz.com classicrock1075thebreeze@yahoo.com

Rushville WLRY-FM (v) PO Box 220, Rushville OH 43150 **Phn:** 740-536-0885 **Fax:** 740-536-1885 www.wlry.org mikewlry@gmail.com

Sandusky WCPZ-FM (a) 1640 Cleveland Rd, Sandusky OH 44870 **Phn:** 419-625-1010 **Fax:** 419-625-1348 wcpz.basohio.com randyhugg@basbroadcasting.com

Sandusky WLEC-AM (m) 1640 Cleveland Rd, Sandusky OH 44870 **Phn:** 419-625-1010 **Fax:** 419-625-1348 www.wlec.com steveshoffner@basbroadcasting.com

Sandusky WMJK-FM (c) 1640 Cleveland Rd, Sandusky OH 44870 **Phn:** 419-625-1010 **Fax:** 419-625-1348 coast1009.com randyhugg@basbroadcasting.com

Sidney WMVR-FM (a) 2929 W Russell Rd, Sidney OH 45365 **Phn:** 937-492-1270 **Fax:** 937-498-2277 www.hits1055.com loretta@hits1055.com

Springfield WEEC-FM (q) 2265 Troy Rd, Springfield OH 45504 **Phn:** 937-399-7837 **Fax:** 937-399-7802 www.weec.org info@weec.org

Springfield WUSO-FM (vq) PO Box 720, Springfield OH 45501 **Phn:** 937-327-7026 **Fax:** 937-327-6340 www.wuso.org gm@wuso.org

Steubenville WDIG-AM (u) 4039 Sunset Blvd, Steubenville OH 43952 **Phn:** 740-264-1760 **Fax:** 740-264-5035

Steubenville WOGH-FM (c) 320 Market St, Steubenville OH 43952 **Phn:** 740-283-4747 **Fax:** 740-283-3655 www.froggyland.com prothfuss@keymarketradio.com

Streetsboro WSTB-FM (vr) PO Box 2542, Streetsboro OH 44241 **Phn:** 330-626-4906 www.rock889.org rlong@rockets.sparcc.org

Tiffin WHEI-FM (v) 310 E Market St, Tiffin OH 44883 **Phn:** 419-448-2283 **Fax:** 419-448-2705

Tiffin WTTF-AM (ao) 310 E Market St, Tiffin OH 44883 **Phn:** 419-447-2212 **Fax:** 419-447-1709 www.wttf.com rsnyder@basbroadcasting.com

Toledo WCKY-FM (c) 125 S Superior St, Toledo OH 43604 **Phn:** 419-244-8321 **Fax:** 419-244-7631 www.1037wcky.com jayharris@1037wcky.com

Toledo WCWA-AM (nt) 124 N Summit St, Toledo OH 43604 **Phn:** 419-244-8321 **Fax:** 419-244-2483 www.1230foxsports.com tomriggs@clearchannel.com

Toledo WGTE-FM (pln) 1270 S Detroit Ave, Toledo OH 43614 **Phn:** 419-380-4600 **Fax:** 419-380-4710 www.wgte.org management@wgte.pbs.org

Toledo WIMX-FM (uw) 720 Water St, Toledo OH 43604 **Phn:** 419-244-8261 **Fax:** 419-244-9261 www.mix957.net brandibrown@urbanradio.fm

Toledo WIOT-FM (r) 125 S Superior St, Toledo OH 43604 **Phn:** 419-244-8321 **Fax:** 419-244-7631 www.wiot.com scottsands@clearchannel.com

Toledo WJUC-FM (gu) PO Box 351450, Toledo OH 43635 **Phn:** 419-861-9582 **Fax:** 419-861-2866 www.thejuice1073.com wcharleswelch@aol.com

Toledo WJZE-FM (uw) 720 Water St, Toledo OH 43604 **Phn:** 419-244-6354 **Fax:** 419-244-8261 www.mix957.net brandibrown@urbanradio.fm

Toledo WKKO-FM (c) 3225 Arlington Ave, Toledo OH 43614 **Phn:** 419-725-5700 **Fax:** 419-389-5172 www.k100country.com k100@k100country.com

Toledo WLQR-AM (s) 3225 Arlington Ave, Toledo OH 43614 **Phn:** 419-725-5700 **Fax:** 419-389-5172 1065theticket.com norm.wamer@cumulus.com

Toledo WRQN-FM (h) 3225 Arlington Ave, Toledo OH 43614 **Phn:** 419-725-5700 **Fax:** 419-725-5893 www.935wrqn.com ron.finn@cumulus.com

Toledo WRVF-FM (a) 125 S Superior St, Toledo OH 43604 **Phn:** 419-244-8321 **Fax:** 419-244-7631 www.1015theriver.com nathan@wspd.com

Toledo WRWK-FM (o) 3225 Arlington Ave, Toledo OH 43614 **Phn:** 419-725-5700 **Fax:** 419-389-5172 www.1065thezone.com ryan.young@cumulus.com

Toledo WSPD-AM (nt) 125 S Superior St, Toledo OH 43604 **Phn:** 419-244-8321 **Fax:** 419-244-7631 www.wspd.com toledonewsroom@clearchannel.com

Toledo WVKS-FM (h) 125 S Superior St, Toledo OH 43604 **Phn:** 419-244-8321 **Fax:** 419-244-7631 www.925kissfm.com kissfm@925kissfm.com

Toledo WWWM-FM (a) 3225 Arlington Ave, Toledo OH 43614 **Phn:** 419-725-5700 **Fax:** 419-389-5172 www.star105toledo.com tanya.redway@cumulus.com

Toledo WXKR-FM (r) 3225 Arlington Ave, Toledo OH 43614 **Phn:** 419-725-5700 **Fax:** 419-389-5172 www.wxkr.com dan.mcclintock@cumulus.com

Toledo WXTS-FM (v) 2400 Collingwood Blvd, Toledo OH 43620 **Phn:** 419-244-6875

Toledo WXUT-FM (v) 2801 W Bancroft St Ms 118, Toledo OH 43606 **Phn:** 419-530-4172 **Fax:** 419-530-2210 www.wxut.com allison.dow@utoledo.edu

University Heights WJCU-FM (v) 20700 N Park Blvd, University Heights OH 44118 **Phn:** 216-397-4437 www.wjcu.org wjcu.info@gmail.com

Upper Sandusky WXML-FM (q) PO Box 158, Upper Sandusky OH 43351 **Phn:** 419-294-2900 **Fax:** 419-294-1786 www.newvision.fm contactus@newvision.fm

Van Wert WERT-AM (am) PO Box 487, Van Wert OH 45891 **Phn:** 419-238-1220 **Fax:** 419-238-2578 www.vanwert.comwert wert@bright.net

Van Wert WKSD-FM (as) 9070 Mendon Rd, Van Wert OH 45891 **Phn:** 419-238-1220 **Fax:** 419-238-2578 www.vanwert.comwert wert@bright.net

Warren WANR-AM (o) PO Box 1798, Warren OH 44482 **Phn:** 330-394-7700

Washington Court House WCHO-FM (cb) 1535 N North St, Washington Court House OH 43160 **Phn:** 740-335-0941 **Fax:** 740-335-6869 www.buckeyecountry105.com news@buckeyecountry105.com

Washington Court House WCHO-AM (c) 1535 N North St, Washington Court House OH 43160 **Phn:** 740-335-0941 **Fax:** 740-335-6869 www.wchoam.com news@buckeyecountry105.com

Waverly WXIC-AM (qg) PO Box 227, Waverly OH 45690 **Phn:** 740-947-2166 **Fax:** 740-947-4600

Waverly WXIZ-FM (c) PO Box 227, Waverly OH 45690 **Phn:** 740-947-2166 **Fax:** 740-947-4600

West Union WAOL-FM (a) PO Box 103, West Union OH 45693 **Phn:** 937-544-9722 **Fax:** 937-544-5523 www.c103.fm kensmith@c103.fm

West Union WRAC-FM (hc) PO Box 103, West Union OH 45693 **Phn:** 937-544-9722 **Fax:** 937-544-5523 www.c103.fm kensmith@c103.fm

Westerville WOBN-FM (v) Otterbein College, Westerville OH 43081 **Phn:** 614-823-1557 ocwobn.otterbein.edu

Westerville WUFM-FM (q) PO Box 1887, Westerville OH 43086 **Phn:** 614-839-7100 **Fax:** 614-839-1329 radiou.com radiou@radiou.com

Wilberforce WCSU-FM (p) PO Box 1004, Wilberforce OH 45384 **Phn:** 937-376-9278 **Fax:** 937-376-6015 www.wcsufm.org wcsu@centralstate.edu

Willoughby WELW-AM (o) PO Box 1330, Willoughby OH 44096 **Phn:** 440-946-1330 **Fax:** 440-953-0320 www.welw.com email@welw.com

Wooster WCWS-FM (vhr) Wishart Hall Coll Of Wooster, Wooster OH 44691 **Phn:** 330-263-2240 **Fax:** 330-263-2690 woo91.sites.wooster.edu wcws@wooster.edu

Wooster WKVX-AM (o) 186 S Hillcrest Dr, Wooster OH 44691 **Phn:** 330-264-5122 **Fax:** 330-264-3571 www.wqkt.com events@wqkt.com

Wooster WQKT-FM (sc) 186 S Hillcrest Dr, Wooster OH 44691 **Phn:** 330-264-5122 **Fax:** 330-264-3571 www.wqkt.com contact@wqkt.com

Wooster WQKT-AM (o) 186 S Hillcrest Dr, Wooster OH 44691 **Phn:** 330-264-5122 **Fax:** 330-264-3571 www.wqkt.com contact@wqkt.com

Xenia WBZI-AM (c) 23 E 2nd St, Xenia OH 45385 **Phn:** 866-372-3531 www.myclassiccountry.com myclassiccountry@myclassiccountry.com

Xenia WKFI-AM (c) 486 W 2nd St, Xenia OH 45385 **Phn:** 866-372-3531 **Fax:** 937-372-3508 www.myclassiccountry.com myclassiccountry@myclassiccountry.com

Yellow Springs WYSO-FM (p) 795 Livermore St, Yellow Springs OH 45387 **Phn:** 937-767-6420 **Fax:** 937-769-1382 wyso.org wyso@wyso.org

Youngstown WASN-AM (wqg) 20 W Federal St # T-2, Youngstown OH 44503 **Phn:** 330-744-5115 **Fax:** 330-744-4020 www.1500wasn.com skip@ytownradio.com

Youngstown WBBG-FM (o) 7461 South Ave, Youngstown OH 44512 **Phn:** 330-965-0057 **Fax:** 330-729-9991 www.oldies1061radio.com jeffkelly@clearchannel.com

Youngstown WBBW-AM (st) 4040 Simon Rd, Youngstown OH 44512 **Phn:** 330-783-1000 **Fax:** 330-783-0060 www.wbbw.com rick.parrish@cumulus.com

Youngstown WGFT-AM (t) 20 W Federal St # T-2, Youngstown OH 44503 **Phn:** 330-744-5115 **Fax:** 330-744-4020 www.1330wgft.com skip@ytownradio.com

Youngstown WHOT-FM (h) 4040 Simon Rd, Youngstown OH 44512 **Phn:** 330-783-1000 **Fax:** 330-783-0060 www.hot101.com win@hot101.com

Youngstown WKBN-AM (nt) 7461 South Ave, Youngstown OH 44512 **Phn:** 330-729-9990 **Fax:** 330-729-9991 www.570wkbn.com jimmichaels@clearchannel.com

Youngstown WMXY-FM (a) 7461 South Ave, Youngstown OH 44512 **Phn:** 330-965-0057 **Fax:** 330-965-8277

Youngstown WNCD-FM (r) 7461 South Ave, Youngstown OH 44512 **Phn:** 330-965-0057 **Fax:** 330-729-9991 www.933fmthewolf.com jeffkelly@clearchannel.com

Youngstown WNIO-AM (b) 7461 South Ave, Youngstown OH 44512 **Phn:** 330-965-0057 **Fax:** 330-729-9991 www.sportsradio1390.com markfrench@clearchannel.com

Youngstown WQXK-FM (c) 4040 Simon Rd, Youngstown OH 44512 **Phn:** 330-783-1000 **Fax:** 330-783-0060 www.k105country.com

Youngstown WRBP-FM (u) 20 W Federal St # T2, Youngstown OH 44503 **Phn:** 330-744-5115 **Fax:** 330-744-4020 jamz1019.com skip@ytownradio.com

Youngstown WSOM-AM (ob) 4040 Simon Rd, Youngstown OH 44512 **Phn:** 330-783-1000 **Fax:** 330-783-0060 www.600wsom.com rick.parrish@cumulus.com

Youngstown WWIZ-FM (r) 4040 Simon Rd, Youngstown OH 44512 **Phn:** 330-783-1000 **Fax:** 330-783-0060 www.realrock104.com rick.parrish@cumulus.com

Youngstown WYFM-FM (rh) 4040 Simon Rd, Youngstown OH 44512 **Phn:** 330-783-1000 **Fax:** 330-783-0060 www.y-103.com win@y103.com

Youngstown WYSU-FM (pljn) 1 University Plz, Youngstown OH 44555 **Phn:** 330-941-3363 **Fax:** 330-941-1501 wysu.org sexton@wysu.org

Zanesville WHIZ-FM (ar) 629 Downard Rd, Zanesville OH 43701 **Phn:** 740-452-5431 **Fax:** 740-452-6553 www.whiznews.com ebrooks@whizmediagroup.com

Zanesville WHIZ-AM (a) 629 Downard Rd, Zanesville OH 43701 **Phn:** 740-452-5431 **Fax:** 740-452-6553 www.whiznews.com jbullock@whizmediagroup.com

Zanesville WYBZ-FM (o) PO Box 669, Zanesville OH 43702 **Phn:** 740-453-6004 **Fax:** 740-453-5865 www.wybz.com

OKLAHOMA

Ada KADA-AM (st) PO Box 609, Ada OK 74821 **Phn:** 580-332-1212 **Fax:** 580-332-0128 www.kadaradio.net kada@wilnet1.com

Ada KADA-FM (a) PO Box 609, Ada OK 74821 **Phn:** 580-332-1212 **Fax:** 580-332-0128 www.kadaradio.net kada@wilnet1.com

Ada KIMY-FM (g) PO Box 1343, Ada OK 74821 **Phn:** 580-623-4777

Ada KTGS-FM (gq) PO Box 1343, Ada OK 74821 **Phn:** 580-332-0902 **Fax:** 580-332-0922 www.thegospelstation.com email@thegospelstation.com

Ada KTLS-FM (r) PO Box 609, Ada OK 74821 **Phn:** 580-332-1212 **Fax:** 580-332-0128 www.ktlsradio.com score@cableone.net

Ada KXFC-FM (r) PO Box 609, Ada OK 74821 **Phn:** 580-332-2211 **Fax:** 580-436-1629 www.kxfcradio.com score@cableone.net

Ada KYKC-FM (c) PO Box 609, Ada OK 74821 **Phn:** 580-436-1616 **Fax:** 580-436-1671 www.kykc.net kykc@cableone.net

Altus KEYB-FM (c) PO Box 1077, Altus OK 73522 **Phn:** 580-482-1555 **Fax:** 580-482-8353 www.keyb.net tracie@keyb.net

Altus KQTZ-FM (a) 212 W Cypress St, Altus OK 73521 **Phn:** 580-482-1450 **Fax:** 580-482-3420 www.kwhw.com

Altus KRKZ-FM (r) PO Box 577, Altus OK 73522 **Phn:** 580-482-1450 **Fax:** 580-482-3420 www.kwhw.com mward@kwhw.com

Altus KWHW-AM (c) 212 W Cypress St, Altus OK 73521 **Phn:** 580-482-1450 **Fax:** 580-482-3420 www.kwhw.com mward@kwhw.com

Alva KALV-AM (o) 45180 Hughes Rd, Alva OK 73717 **Phn:** 580-327-1430 **Fax:** 580-327-1433

Ardmore KHKC-FM (c) PO Box 1487, Ardmore OK 73402 **Phn:** 580-226-9797 **Fax:** 580-226-5113 thebigstation.net

OHIO RADIO STATIONS

Ardmore KICM-FM (c) PO Box 1487, Ardmore OK 73402 **Phn:** 580-226-9797 **Fax:** 580-226-5113 thebigstation.net bill@kicm.com

Ardmore KKAJ-FM (c) 1205 Northglen St, Ardmore OK 73401 **Phn:** 580-226-0421 **Fax:** 580-226-0464 www.kkaj.com terry@sokradio.com

Ardmore KMAD-AM (c) PO Box 1487, Ardmore OK 73402 **Phn:** 580-226-9797 **Fax:** 580-226-5113 thebigstation.net

Ardmore KTRX-FM (r) 1205 Northglen St, Ardmore OK 73401 **Phn:** 580-226-0421 **Fax:** 580-226-0464 www.texomarocks.com news@sokradio.com

Ardmore KVSO-AM (s) 1205 Northglen St, Ardmore OK 73401 **Phn:** 580-226-0421 **Fax:** 580-226-0464 www.kvso.com michael@sokradio.com

Ardmore KYNZ-FM (a) 1205 Northglen St, Ardmore OK 73401 **Phn:** 580-226-0421 **Fax:** 580-226-0464 www.kynz.com news@sokradio.com

Atoka KEOR-AM (g) PO Box 810, Atoka OK 74525 **Phn:** 580-889-6300 **Fax:** 580-889-9308 gospelradio@yahoo.com

Bartlesville KRIG-FM (c) PO Box 1100, Bartlesville OK 74005 **Phn:** 918-336-1001 **Fax:** 918-336-6939 www.bartlesvilleradio.com radio@bartlesvilleradio.com

Bartlesville KWON-AM (nt) PO Box 1100, Bartlesville OK 74005 **Phn:** 918-336-1001 **Fax:** 918-336-6939 www.bartlesvilleradio.com charlie@bartlesvilleradio.com

Bartlesville KYFM-FM (a) PO Box 1100, Bartlesville OK 74005 **Phn:** 918-336-1001 **Fax:** 918-336-6939 www.bartlesvilleradio.com radio@bartlesvilleradio.com

Bristow KREK-FM (c) PO Box 1280, Bristow OK 74010 **Phn:** 918-367-5501

Broken Bow KKBI-FM (c) PO Box 1016, Broken Bow OK 74728 **Phn:** 580-584-3388 **Fax:** 580-584-3341 www.kkbifm.com

Broken Bow KQIB-FM (a) PO Box 1016, Broken Bow OK 74728 **Phn:** 580-584-3388 **Fax:** 580-584-3341 www.kkbifm.com kkbi@pine-net.com

Chickasha KWCO-FM (h) 627 W Chickasha Ave, Chickasha OK 73018 **Phn:** 405-224-1560 **Fax:** 405-224-2890

Claremore KRSC-FM (va) 1701 W Will Rogers Blvd, Claremore OK 74017 **Phn:** 918-343-7670 **Fax:** 918-343-7952 www.rsu.edursuradio requestline@rsu.edu

Cushing KUSH-AM (c) 3818 E Main, Cushing OK 74023 **Phn:** 918-225-0922 **Fax:** 918-225-0925 www.1600kush.com kushradio@yahoo.com

Duncan KDDQ-FM (a) 1701 W Pine Ave, Duncan OK 73533 **Phn:** 580-255-1350 **Fax:** 580-470-9993 kddqfm.com joyc@kjmz.com

Duncan KKEN-FM (c) 1701 W Pine Ave, Duncan OK 73533 **Phn:** 580-255-1350 **Fax:** 580-470-9993 www.kickincountry971.com tony@kjmz.com

Duncan KPNS-AM (nt) 1701 W Pine Ave, Duncan OK 73533 **Phn:** 580-255-1350 **Fax:** 580-470-9993

Durant KLBC-FM (c) PO Box 190, Durant OK 74702 **Phn:** 580-924-3100 **Fax:** 580-920-1426 www.klbcfm.com bob@klbcfm.com

Durant KSEO-AM (q) PO Box 190, Durant OK 74702 **Phn:** 580-924-3100 **Fax:** 580-920-1426 toddt@netcommander.com

Durant KSSU-FM (v) 1405 N 4th Ave PMB 4129, Durant OK 74701 **Phn:** 580-745-2906 **Fax:** 580-745-3311

Edmond KCSC-FM (pl) 100 N University Dr, Edmond OK 73034 **Phn:** 405-974-3333 **Fax:** 405-974-3844 www.kcscfm.com kcscfm@uco.edu

El Reno KZUE-AM (y) 2715 S Radio Rd, El Reno OK 73036 **Phn:** 405-262-1460 kzue@aol.com

Elk City KECO-FM (c) 220 S Pioneer Rd, Elk City OK 73644 **Phn:** 580-225-9696 **Fax:** 580-225-9699 www.kecofm.com bbrewerkeco@cableone.net

Elk City KXOO-FM (q) PO Box 945, Elk City OK 73648 **Phn:** 580-225-5966 **Fax:** 580-225-9699 www.kxoofm.com kxoo@cableone.net

Enid KCRC-AM (s) PO Box 952, Enid OK 73702 **Phn:** 580-237-1390 **Fax:** 580-242-1390

Enid KGWA-AM (nt) 1710 W Willow Rd Ste 300, Enid OK 73703 **Phn:** 580-234-4230 **Fax:** 580-234-2971 www.kofm.com dsmith@kofm.com

Enid KNID-FM (c) PO Box 952, Enid OK 73702 **Phn:** 580-237-1390 **Fax:** 580-242-1390 www.knid.com rroggow@knid.com

Enid KOFM-FM (c) 1710 W Willow Rd Ste 300, Enid OK 73703 **Phn:** 580-234-4230 **Fax:** 580-234-2971 www.kofm.com aclepper@kofm.com

Enid KXLS-FM (a) PO Box 952, Enid OK 73702 **Phn:** 580-237-1390 **Fax:** 580-242-1390 rroggow@knid.com

Eufaula KTNT-FM (c) PO Box 956, Eufaula OK 74432 **Phn:** 918-689-3663 **Fax:** 918-689-5451 www.kfoxradio.com kfox_1025@live.com

Frederick KTAT-AM (h) PO Box 1088, Frederick OK 73542 **Phn:** 580-335-3874 **Fax:** 580-335-7659 kybe959@pldi.net

Frederick KYBE-FM (c) PO Box 1088, Frederick OK 73542 **Phn:** 580-335-5923 **Fax:** 580-335-7659 www.coyotenews.com kybe959@pldi.net

Grove KGLC-FM (nq) PO Box 451750, Grove OK 74345 **Phn:** 918-542-1818

Grove KGVE-FM (c) PO Box 451749, Grove OK 74345 **Phn:** 918-786-2211 **Fax:** 918-786-2284

Grove KVIS-AM (nq) PO Box 451750, Grove OK 74345 **Phn:** 918-542-1818

Guymon KGYN-AM (c) PO Box 130, Guymon OK 73942 **Phn:** 580-338-1210 **Fax:** 580-338-8255 www.kgynradio.com

Guymon KKBS-FM (r) PO Box 1756, Guymon OK 73942 **Phn:** 580-338-5493 **Fax:** 580-338-0717 www.kkbs.com kkbs@kkbs.com

Hobart KTIJ-FM (h) 1515 N Broadway, Hobart OK 73651 **Phn:** 580-726-5656 **Fax:** 580-726-2222 chadfuchs@itlnet.net

Hobart KTJS-AM (cnt) PO Box 311, Hobart OK 73651 **Phn:** 580-726-5656 **Fax:** 580-726-2222 chadfuchs@itlnet.net

Hugo KIHN-AM (co) PO Box 430, Hugo OK 74743 **Phn:** 580-326-6411 **Fax:** 580-326-7921

Hugo KITX-FM (c) 1600 W Jackson St, Hugo OK 74743 **Phn:** 580-326-2555 **Fax:** 580-326-2623 www.k955.com will@k955.com

Idabel KBEL-FM (c) PO Box 418, Idabel OK 74745 **Phn:** 580-286-6642 **Fax:** 580-286-6643 www.kbelradio.com kbel976@yahoo.com

Idabel KBEL-AM (s) PO Box 418, Idabel OK 74745 **Phn:** 580-286-6642 **Fax:** 580-286-6643

Langston KALU-FM (v) Langston Univ Box 1500, Langston OK 73050 **Phn:** 405-466-2924

Lawton KBZQ-FM (a) PO Box 6888, Lawton OK 73506 **Phn:** 580-357-9950 **Fax:** 580-357-9995 hitsandfavorites.com kbzq@sbcglobal.net

OKLAHOMA RADIO STATIONS

Lawton KCCU-FM (pln) 2800 W Gore Blvd, Lawton OK 73505 **Phn:** 888-454-7800 **Fax:** 580-581-5571 www.kccu.org kccu@cameron.edu

Lawton KJMZ-FM (u) 1525 SE Flower Mound Rd, Lawton OK 73501 **Phn:** 580-355-1050 **Fax:** 580-355-1056 www.kjmz.com joyc@kjmz.com

Lawton KKRX-AM (uo) 1525 SE Flower Mound Rd, Lawton OK 73501 **Phn:** 580-355-1050 **Fax:** 580-355-1056 www.kkrx.com joyc@kjmz.com

Lawton KLAW-FM (c) 626 SW D Ave, Lawton OK 73501 **Phn:** 580-581-3600 **Fax:** 580-357-2880 klaw.com frankseres@townsquaremedia.com

Lawton KMGZ-FM (h) 1421 NW Great Plains Blvd Ste C, Lawton OK 73505 **Phn:** 580-536-9530 **Fax:** 580-536-3299 www.magic953.com gm@kmgz.com

Lawton KVRW-FM (h) 626 SW D Ave, Lawton OK 73501 **Phn:** 580-581-3600 **Fax:** 580-357-2880 my1073fm.com nancymace@townsquaremedia.com

Lawton KXCA-AM (s) 1525 SE Flower Mound Rd, Lawton OK 73501 **Phn:** 580-355-1050 **Fax:** 580-355-1056 theticket1380.com tony@kjmz.com

Lawton KZCD-FM (r) 626 SW D Ave, Lawton OK 73501 **Phn:** 580-581-3600 **Fax:** 580-357-2880 z94.com critter@townsquaremedia.com

Lindsay KBLP-FM (c) 204 S Main St, Lindsay OK 73052 **Phn:** 405-756-4438 **Fax:** 405-756-2040 www.kblpradio.com

Marlow KFXI-FM (c) 1101 N Highway 81, Marlow OK 73055 **Phn:** 580-658-9292 **Fax:** 580-658-2561

McAlester KMCO-FM (c) PO Box 1068, McAlester OK 74502 **Phn:** 918-423-1460 **Fax:** 918-423-7119 www.mcalesterradio.com info@mcalesterradio.com

McAlester KNED-AM (c) PO Box 1068, McAlester OK 74502 **Phn:** 918-423-1460 **Fax:** 918-423-7119 www.mcalesterradio.com info@mcalesterradio.com

McAlester KTMC-FM (r) PO Box 1068, McAlester OK 74502 **Phn:** 918-426-1050 **Fax:** 918-423-7119 www.mcalesterradio.com info@mcalesterradio.com

McAlester KTMC-AM (ob) PO Box 1068, McAlester OK 74502 **Phn:** 918-426-1050 **Fax:** 918-423-7119 www.mcalesterradio.com info@mcalesterradio.com

Moore KMSI-FM (q) 120 SW 4th St, Moore OK 73160 **Phn:** 405-794-5674 **Fax:** 405-794-5112 www.oasisnetwork.org mail@oasisnetwork.org

Norman KGOU-FM (pnj) 860 Van Vleet Oval, Norman OK 73019 **Phn:** 405-325-3388 **Fax:** 405-325-7129 www.kgou.org news@kgou.org

Norman KREF-AM (snt) 2020 Alameda St, Norman OK 73071 **Phn:** 405-321-1400 **Fax:** 405-321-6820 www.kref.com tjperry@kref.com

Oklahoma City KATT-FM (r) 4045 NW 64th St Ste 600, Oklahoma City OK 73116 **Phn:** 405-848-0100 **Fax:** 405-843-5288 www.katt.com brad.reed@cumulus.com

Oklahoma City KEBC-AM (s) PO Box 1000, Oklahoma City OK 73101 **Phn:** 405-840-5271 **Fax:** 405-840-5808 www.1340thegame.com davidgarrett@clearchannel.com

Oklahoma City KHBZ-FM (a) 1900 NW Expressway Ste 1000, Oklahoma City OK 73118 **Phn:** 405-840-5271 **Fax:** 405-858-5333 www.947thebrew.com tomtravis@clearchannel.com

Oklahoma City KJYO-FM (h) PO Box 1000, Oklahoma City OK 73101 **Phn:** 405-858-1400 **Fax:** 405-858-5333 www.kj103fm.com mikemccoy@clearchannel.com

Oklahoma City KKNG-FM (c) 5101 S Shields Blvd, Oklahoma City OK 73129 **Phn:** 405-616-5500 **Fax:** 405-616-5505 www.kkng.com info@kkng.com

Oklahoma City KKWD-FM (h) 4045 NW 64th St Ste 600, Oklahoma City OK 73116 **Phn:** 405-848-0100 **Fax:** 405-843-5288 www.wild1049hd.com

Oklahoma City KMGL-FM (a) 400 E Britton Rd, Oklahoma City OK 73114 **Phn:** 405-478-5104 **Fax:** 405-475-7021 www.magic104.com steve.o@tylermedia.com

Oklahoma City KOCY-AM (m) 5101 S Shields Blvd, Oklahoma City OK 73129 **Phn:** 405-616-5500 **Fax:** 405-616-5505 tylermedia.com kevin.c@tylermedia.com

Oklahoma City KOKC-AM (nt) 400 E Britton Rd, Oklahoma City OK 73114 **Phn:** 405-478-5104 **Fax:** 405-475-7021 www.kokcradio.com kevin.c@tylermedia.com

Oklahoma City KOMA-FM (o) 400 E Britton Rd, Oklahoma City OK 73114 **Phn:** 405-478-5104 **Fax:** 405-475-7021 www.komaradio.com kent.j@tylermedia.com

Oklahoma City KQCV-AM (q) 1919 N Broadway Ave, Oklahoma City OK 73103 **Phn:** 405-521-0800 **Fax:** 405-521-1391 www.bottradionetwork.com kqcv@bottradionetwork.com

Oklahoma City KQCV-FM (q) 1919 N Broadway Ave, Oklahoma City OK 73103 **Phn:** 405-521-0800 **Fax:** 405-521-1391 www.bottradionetwork.com kqcv@bottradionetwork.com

Oklahoma City KQOB-FM (h) 4045 NW 64th St Ste 600, Oklahoma City OK 73116 **Phn:** 405-848-0100 **Fax:** 405-843-5288 www.969bobfm.com larry.bastida@cumulus.com

Oklahoma City KRMP-AM (ua) 1528 NE 23rd St, Oklahoma City OK 73111 **Phn:** 405-427-5877 **Fax:** 405-424-6708 www.thetouch1140.com kperry@kvsp.com

Oklahoma City KRXO-FM (r) 400 E Britton Rd, Oklahoma City OK 73114 **Phn:** 405-478-5104 **Fax:** 405-478-0448 www.krxo.com buddy.w@tylermedia.com

Oklahoma City KTLR-AM (t) 5101 S Shields Blvd, Oklahoma City OK 73129 **Phn:** 405-616-5500 **Fax:** 405-616-5505 www.ktlr.com mike.m@tylermedia.com

Oklahoma City KTLV-AM (gqw) 3336 SE 67th St, Oklahoma City OK 73135 **Phn:** 405-672-3886 **Fax:** 405-672-5858 www.ktlv1220.com ktlv1220@aol.com

Oklahoma City KTOK-AM (nt) PO Box 1000, Oklahoma City OK 73101 **Phn:** 405-840-5271 **Fax:** 405-858-1435 www.ktok.com leematthews@clearchannel.com

Oklahoma City KTST-FM (c) 50 Penn Pl Ste 1000, Oklahoma City OK 73118 **Phn:** 405-840-5271 **Fax:** 405-858-5333 www.thetwister.com billhurley@clearchannel.com

Oklahoma City KTUZ-FM (y) 5101 S Shields Blvd, Oklahoma City OK 73129 **Phn:** 405-616-5500 **Fax:** 405-616-0328 www.ktuz.com gabriel.o@tylermedia.com

Oklahoma City KVSP-AM (wxu) 1528 NE 23rd St, Oklahoma City OK 73111 **Phn:** 405-427-5877 **Fax:** 405-424-6708 www.kvsp.com kperry@kvsp.com

Oklahoma City KVSP-FM (u) 1528 NE 23rd St, Oklahoma City OK 73111 **Phn:** 405-247-6682 **Fax:** 405-247-1051 www.kvsp.com tmonday@perrybroadcasting.net

Oklahoma City KXXY-FM (c) PO Box 1000, Oklahoma City OK 73101 **Phn:** 405-840-5271 **Fax:** 405-858-1106 www.kxy.com breed@clearchannel.com

Oklahoma City KYIS-FM (a) 4045 NW 64th St Ste 600, Oklahoma City OK 73116 **Phn:** 405-848-0100 **Fax:** 405-843-5288 www.kyis.com

Oklahoma City WKY-AM (y) 4045 NW 64th St Ste 600, Oklahoma City OK 73116 **Phn:** 405-848-0100 **Fax:** 405-843-5288 www.laindomable.com

Oklahoma City WWLS-AM (st) 4045 NW 64th St Ste 600, Oklahoma City OK 73116 **Phn:** 405-848-0100 **Fax:** 405-843-5288 www.thesportsanimal.com

Oklahoma City WWLS-FM (c) 4045 NW 64th St Ste 600, Oklahoma City OK 73116 **Phn:** 405-848-0100 **Fax:** 405-843-5288 www.thesportsanimal.com

Okmulgee KOKL-AM (c) 100 E 7th St, Okmulgee OK 74447 **Phn:** 918-756-3646 **Fax:** 918-756-1800 kokl.net news@kokl.net

Pawhuska KPGM-AM (q) 129 W Main, Pawhuska OK 74056 **Phn:** 918-287-1145 **Fax:** 918-287-1473 www.bartlesvilleradio.com kpgm@bartlesvilleradio.com

Ponca City KIXR-FM (a) 3924 Santa Fe St, Ponca City OK 74601 **Phn:** 580-765-5491 **Fax:** 580-762-8329 www.kixr.com kixr@kixr.com

Ponca City KLOR-FM (o) PO Box 2509, Ponca City OK 74602 **Phn:** 580-765-2485 **Fax:** 580-767-1103 www.eteamradio.com klor@eteamradio.com

Ponca City KLVV-FM (aq) PO Box 14, Ponca City OK 74602 **Phn:** 580-767-1400 **Fax:** 580-765-1700 www.klvv.com mail@klvv.com

Ponca City KOKB-AM (c) PO Box 2509, Ponca City OK 74602 **Phn:** 580-765-2485 **Fax:** 580-767-1103 www.eteamradio.com billc@eteamradio.com

Ponca City KOKP-AM (t) PO Box 2509, Ponca City OK 74602 **Phn:** 580-765-2485 **Fax:** 580-767-1103 www.eteamradio.com bill@eteamradio.com

Ponca City KPNC-FM (c) PO Box 2509, Ponca City OK 74602 **Phn:** 580-765-2485 **Fax:** 580-767-1103 www.eteamradio.com kpnc@eteamradio.com

Ponca City WBBZ-AM (a) PO Box 588, Ponca City OK 74602 **Phn:** 580-765-6607 **Fax:** 580-765-6611 www.wbbz.com wbbz@wbbz.com

Poteau KPRV-AM (a) PO Box 368, Poteau OK 74953 **Phn:** 918-647-3221 **Fax:** 918-647-5092 www.kprvpoteau.com kprv@windstream.net

Poteau KPRV-FM (c) PO Box 368, Poteau OK 74953 **Phn:** 918-647-3221 **Fax:** 918-647-5092 www.kprvpoteau.com kprv@windstream.net

Shawnee KGFF-AM (h) PO Box 9, Shawnee OK 74802 **Phn:** 405-273-4390 **Fax:** 405-273-4530 www.kgff.com mike@kgff.com

Shawnee KIRC-FM (c) 2 E Main St, Shawnee OK 74801 **Phn:** 405-878-1803 **Fax:** 405-878-0162

Shawnee KSLE-FM (or) 2 E Main St, Shawnee OK 74801 **Phn:** 405-878-0077 **Fax:** 405-878-0162 kirc1059@aol.com

Shawnee KWSH-AM (c) 2 E Main St, Shawnee OK 74801 **Phn:** 405-382-1260 **Fax:** 405-382-0128 kirc1059@aol.com

Stillwater KGFY-FM (c) 408 E Thomas Ave, Stillwater OK 74075 **Phn:** 405-372-7800 **Fax:** 405-372-6969 stillwaterradio.net buyradio@aol.com

Stillwater KOSU-FM (pln) 303 Paul Miller Building, Stillwater OK 74078 **Phn:** 405-744-6352 **Fax:** 405-744-9970 kosu.org

Stillwater KSPI-AM (snt) PO Box 1269, Stillwater OK 74076 **Phn:** 405-372-7800 **Fax:** 405-372-6969 stillwaterradio.net buyradio@aol.com

Stillwater KSPI-FM (a) PO Box 1269, Stillwater OK 74076 **Phn:** 405-372-7800 **Fax:** 405-372-6969 stillwaterradio.net buyradio@aol.com

Stillwater KVRO-FM (o) PO Box 1269, Stillwater OK 74076 **Phn:** 405-372-7800 **Fax:** 405-372-6969 stillwaterradio.net buyradio@aol.com

Sulphur KIXO-FM (c) 1507 W Broadway Ave, Sulphur OK 73086 **Phn:** 580-658-9292 **Fax:** 580-658-2561

Tahlequah KEOK-FM (c) 5686 S Muskogee Ave, Tahlequah OK 74464 **Phn:** 918-456-2511 **Fax:** 918-456-3231 www.lakescountry1021.com ralph@ktlq1350.com

Tahlequah KTLQ-AM (c) 5686 S Muskogee Ave, Tahlequah OK 74464 **Phn:** 918-456-2511 **Fax:** 918-456-3231 www.lakescountry1021.com ralph@ktlq1350.com

Tonkawa KAYE-FM (vr) 1220 E Grand Ave, Tonkawa OK 74653 **Phn:** 580-628-6446 **Fax:** 580-628-6209

Tulsa KAKC-AM (kt) 2625 S Memorial Dr, Tulsa OK 74129 **Phn:** 918-388-5100 www.1300thebuzz.com chrisplank@clearchannel.com

Tulsa KBEZ-FM (a) 7030 S Yale Ave Ste 711, Tulsa OK 74136 **Phn:** 918-496-9336 **Fax:** 918-496-1937 www.929bobfm.com jblack@jrn.com

Tulsa KBIX-AM (s) 2448 E 81st St Ste 5500, Tulsa OK 74137 **Phn:** 918-492-2660 **Fax:** 918-492-8840

Tulsa KCFO-AM (q) 5800 E Skelly Dr Ste 150, Tulsa OK 74135 **Phn:** 918-622-0970 **Fax:** 918-622-0985 www.kcfo.com

Tulsa KCXR-FM (q) 2448 E 81st St Ste 5500, Tulsa OK 74137 **Phn:** 918-492-2660 **Fax:** 918-492-8840 kxoj.com kxoj@kxoj.com

Tulsa KEMX-FM (q) 2448 E 81st St Ste 5500, Tulsa OK 74137 **Phn:** 918-492-2660 **Fax:** 918-492-8840 kxoj.com

Tulsa KFAQ-AM (nt) 4590 E 29th St, Tulsa OK 74114 **Phn:** 918-743-7814 **Fax:** 918-743-6462 www.1170kfaq.com bgann@jrn.com

Tulsa KGTO-AM (wx) 7030 S Yale Ave Ste 302, Tulsa OK 74136 **Phn:** 918-494-9886 **Fax:** 918-494-9683 www.perrybroadcasting.net

Tulsa KHHT-FM (h) 7030 S Yale Ave Ste 711, Tulsa OK 74136 **Phn:** 918-492-2020 **Fax:** 918-496-2681 www.khits.com jblack@jrn.com

Tulsa KHTT-FM (h) 4590 E 29th St, Tulsa OK 74114 **Phn:** 918-743-7814 **Fax:** 918-743-7613 www.khits.com cthompson@jrn.com

Tulsa KIZS-FM (y) 2625 S Memorial Dr, Tulsa OK 74129 **Phn:** 918-388-3738 **Fax:** 918-388-5400 www.1015lapreciosa.com doncristi@clearchannel.com

Tulsa KJMM-FM (uw) 7030 S Yale Ave Ste 302, Tulsa OK 74136 **Phn:** 918-494-9886 **Fax:** 918-494-9683 www.kjmm.com traffic@kjmm.com

Tulsa KJSR-FM (r) 7136 S Yale Ave Ste 500, Tulsa OK 74136 **Phn:** 918-493-3434 **Fax:** 918-493-2376 www.rock103tulsa.com dena.fletcher@coxinc.com

Tulsa KMOD-FM (r) 2625 S Memorial Dr, Tulsa OK 74129 **Phn:** 918-664-2810 **Fax:** 918-665-0555 www.kmod.com doncristi@clearchannel.com

Tulsa KMYZ-FM (r) 2448 E 81st, Tulsa OK 74137 **Phn:** 918-492-2660 www.edgetulsa.com studio@edgetulsa.com

Tulsa KNYD-FM (q) PO Box 1924, Tulsa OK 74101 **Phn:** 918-455-5693 www.oasisnetwork.org mail@oasisnetwork.org

Tulsa KQLL-FM (c) 2625 S Memorial Dr, Tulsa OK 74129 **Phn:** 918-388-5100 **Fax:** 918-388-5400 www.1061thetwister.com jonathanshuford@clearchannel.com

Tulsa KRAV-FM (a) 7136 S Yale Ave Ste 500, Tulsa OK 74136 **Phn:** 918-491-9696 **Fax:** 918-493-5385 www.mix96tulsa.com dena.fletcher@coxinc.com

OKLAHOMA RADIO STATIONS

Tulsa KRMG-AM (nt) 7136 S Yale Ave Ste 500, Tulsa OK 74136 **Phn:** 918-493-7400 **Fax:** 918-493-5345 www.krmg.com drew.anderssen@coxradio.com

Tulsa KRMG-FM (nt) 7136 S Yale Ave Ste 500, Tulsa OK 74136 **Phn:** 918-493-7400 **Fax:** 918-493-5345 www.krmg.com drew.anderssen@coxradio.com

Tulsa KTBT-FM (h) 2625 S Memorial Dr, Tulsa OK 74129 **Phn:** 918-388-5100 **Fax:** 918-665-0555 www.921thebeat.com corbinpierce@clearchannel.com

Tulsa KTBZ-AM (s) 2625 S Memorial Dr, Tulsa OK 74129 **Phn:** 918-664-2810 **Fax:** 918-665-0555 www.buzztulsa.com plank@1430thebuzz.com

Tulsa KTSO-FM (o) 2448 E 81st St Ste 5500, Tulsa OK 74137 **Phn:** 918-492-2660 **Fax:** 918-492-8840 941thebreeze.com studio@941thebreeze.com

Tulsa KVOO-FM (c) 4590 E 29th St, Tulsa OK 74114 **Phn:** 918-743-7814 **Fax:** 918-743-6462 www.kvoo.com bgann@journalbroadcastgroup.com

Tulsa KWEN-FM (c) 7136 S Yale Ave Ste 500, Tulsa OK 74136 **Phn:** 918-494-9500 **Fax:** 918-493-2889 www.k95tulsa.com steve.hunter@coxinc.com

Tulsa KWGS-FM (pn) 800 Tucker Dr, Tulsa OK 74104 **Phn:** 918-631-2577 **Fax:** 918-631-3695 www.kwgs.org public@publicmediatulsa.org

Tulsa KXBL-FM (c) 4590 E 29th St, Tulsa OK 74114 **Phn:** 918-743-7814 **Fax:** 918-743-7613 www.bigcountry995.com bgann@journalbroadcastgroup.com

Tulsa KXOJ-FM (q) 2448 E 81st St Ste 5500, Tulsa OK 74137 **Phn:** 918-492-2660 **Fax:** 918-492-8840 kxoj.com kxoj@kxoj.com

Tulsa KYAL-AM (s) 2448 E 81st St Ste 5500, Tulsa OK 74137 **Phn:** 918-492-2660 **Fax:** 918-492-8840 sportsanimalradio.com studio@sportsanimaltulsa.com

Vinita KGND-AM (st) PO Box 961, Vinita OK 74301 **Phn:** 918-256-2255 **Fax:** 918-256-2633 kito@kitofm.com

Vinita KITO-FM (st) PO Box 961, Vinita OK 74301 **Phn:** 918-256-2255 **Fax:** 918-256-2633 kito@kitofm.com

Weatherford KCDL-FM (r) 10040 Highway 54, Weatherford OK 73096 **Phn:** 580-772-5939 **Fax:** 580-772-1590 www.kcdl.com todd@wrightwradio.com

Weatherford KCLI-AM (nt) 10040 N Hwy 54, Weatherford OK 73096 **Phn:** 580-772-5939 **Fax:** 580-772-1590 www.newstalkkcli.com

Weatherford KWEY-FM (c) 10040 Highway 54, Weatherford OK 73096 **Phn:** 580-772-5939 **Fax:** 580-772-1590 www.kwey.com news@wrightwradio.com

Weatherford KWEY-AM (c) 10040 Highway 54, Weatherford OK 73096 **Phn:** 580-772-5939 **Fax:** 580-772-1590 www.kwey.com

Woodward KMZE-FM (as) 2728 Williams Ave, Woodward OK 73801 **Phn:** 580-256-4101 www.z92online.com smiller@k101online.com

Woodward KSIW-AM (st) PO Box 1600, Woodward OK 73802 **Phn:** 580-256-1450 **Fax:** 580-254-9103 www.woodwardradio.com cciradio@sbcglobal.net

Woodward KWDQ-FM (r) PO Box 1600, Woodward OK 73802 **Phn:** 580-254-9102 **Fax:** 580-254-9103 www.woodwardradio.com cciradio@sbcglobal.net

Woodward KWFX-FM (c) PO Box 1600, Woodward OK 73802 **Phn:** 580-256-1450 **Fax:** 580-254-9103 www.woodwardradio.com cciradio@sbcglobal.net

Woodward KWOX-FM (c) 2728 Williams Ave, Woodward OK 73801 **Phn:** 580-256-4101 **Fax:** 580-256-3825 www.k101online.com kgrice@k101online.com

OREGON

Albany KEJO-AM (st) 2840 Marion St SE, Albany OR 97322 **Phn:** 541-926-8628 www.kejoam.com billlundun@bicoastalmedia.com

Albany KGAL-AM (nt) PO Box 749, Albany OR 97321 **Phn:** 541-451-5425 **Fax:** 541-451-5429 www.kgal.com forum@kgal.com

Albany KHPE-FM (q) PO Box 278, Albany OR 97321 **Phn:** 541-926-2233 **Fax:** 541-926-3925 www.hope1079.com randy@hope1079.com

Albany KLOO-FM (r) 2840 Marion St SE, Albany OR 97322 **Phn:** 541-926-8628 **Fax:** 541-928-1261 www.kloo.com debistarr@bicoastalmedia.com

Albany KLOO-AM (nt) 2840 Marion St SE, Albany OR 97322 **Phn:** 541-926-8628 **Fax:** 541-928-1261 www.news1340.com billlundun@bicoastalmedia.com

Albany KRKT-FM (c) 2840 Marion St SE, Albany OR 97322 **Phn:** 541-926-8628 **Fax:** 541-928-1261 www.krkt.com scottschuler@bicoastalmedia.com

Albany KSHO-AM (am) PO Box 749, Albany OR 97321 **Phn:** 541-451-5425 **Fax:** 541-451-5429 www.ksho.net news@kgall.com

Albany KTHH-AM (c) 2840 Marion St SE, Albany OR 97322 **Phn:** 541-926-8628 **Fax:** 541-928-1261 www.990thelegend.com scottschuler@bicoastalmedia.com

Albany KWIL-AM (q) PO Box 278, Albany OR 97321 **Phn:** 541-926-2233 **Fax:** 541-926-3925 www.kwilforchrist.com pauldelury@kwil790.com

Ashland KSOR-FM (pln) 1250 Siskiyou Blvd, Ashland OR 97520 **Phn:** 541-552-6301 **Fax:** 541-552-8565 www.ijpr.org christim@sou.edu

Astoria KCYS-FM (c) PO Box 1258, Astoria OR 97103 **Phn:** 503-717-9643 **Fax:** 503-717-9578 www.newhitcountry.com kcys@gowebway.com

Astoria KMUN-FM (plnj) PO Box 269, Astoria OR 97103 **Phn:** 503-325-0010 **Fax:** 503-325-3956 coastradio.org info@coastradio.org

Bend KBND-AM (nt) PO Box 5037, Bend OR 97708 **Phn:** 541-382-5263 **Fax:** 541-388-0456 www.kbnd.com talk@kbnd.com

Bend KBNW-AM (nt) 854 NE 4th St, Bend OR 97701 **Phn:** 541-383-3825 **Fax:** 541-383-3403 www.newsradiocentraloregon.com news@horizonbroadcastinggroup.com

Bend KICE-AM (st) 705 SW Bonnett Way Ste 1100, Bend OR 97702 **Phn:** 541-388-3300 **Fax:** 541-389-7885 www.espn940.com mflanagan@bendradiogroup.com

Bend KLRR-FM (a) PO Box 5037, Bend OR 97708 **Phn:** 541-382-5263 **Fax:** 541-388-0456 www.clear1017.fm clear@clear1017.fm

Bend KLTW-FM (a) 854 NE 4th St, Bend OR 97701 **Phn:** 541-383-3825 **Fax:** 541-383-3403 www.lite957.com news@horizonbroadcastinggroup.com

Bend KMGX-FM (a) 345 SW Cyber Dr Ste 101, Bend OR 97702 **Phn:** 541-388-3300 **Fax:** 541-388-3303 www.kmgx.com

Bend KMTK-FM (c) PO Box 5037, Bend OR 97708 **Phn:** 541-382-5263 **Fax:** 541-388-0456 www.mountain997.com country@mountain997.com

Bend KNLR-FM (aq) PO Box 7408, Bend OR 97708 **Phn:** 541-389-8873 **Fax:** 541-389-5291 www.knlr.com info@knlr.com

Bend KQAK-FM (o) 854 NE 4th St, Bend OR 97701 **Phn:** 541-383-3825 **Fax:** 541-383-3403 www.kqakfm.com news@horizonbroadcastinggroup.com

OREGON RADIO STATIONS

Bend KRCO-AM (c) 854 NE 4th St, Bend OR 97701 **Phn:** 541-447-6770 **Fax:** 541-383-3403 www.krcoam.com news@horizonbroadcastinggroup.com

Bend KRXF-FM (r) 705 SW Bonnett Way Ste 1100, Bend OR 97702 **Phn:** 541-388-3300 **Fax:** 541-389-7885 www.929online.com mflanagan@bendradiogroup.com

Bend KSJJ-FM (c) 345 SW Cyber Dr Ste 101, Bend OR 97702 **Phn:** 541-388-3300 **Fax:** 541-389-7885 www.ksjj1029.com rl@bendradiogroup.com

Bend KTWS-FM (r) PO Box 5037, Bend OR 97708 **Phn:** 541-382-5263 **Fax:** 541-388-0456 www.thetwins.com alvarez@thetwins.com

Bend KWLZ-FM (r) 854 NE 4th St, Bend OR 97701 **Phn:** 541-383-3825 **Fax:** 541-383-3403 www.newsradiocentraloregon.com kbnw1340@horizonbroadcastinggroup.com

Bend KWPK-FM (a) 854 NE 4th St, Bend OR 97701 **Phn:** 541-383-3825 **Fax:** 541-383-3403 www.thepeak1041.com news@horizonbroadcastinggroup.com

Bend KXIX-FM (h) 705 SW Bonnett Way Ste 1100, Bend OR 97702 **Phn:** 541-388-3300 **Fax:** 541-389-7885 www.power94.fm mflanagan@bendradiogroup.com

Brookings KURY-AM (a) PO Box 1029, Brookings OR 97415 **Phn:** 541-469-2111 **Fax:** 541-469-6397 www.kuryradio.com

Brookings KURY-FM (a) PO Box 1029, Brookings OR 97415 **Phn:** 541-469-2111 **Fax:** 541-469-6397 www.kuryradio.com

Burns KQHC-FM (h) PO Box 877, Burns OR 97720 **Phn:** 541-573-2055 **Fax:** 541-573-5223

Burns KZZR-AM (cnt) PO Box 877, Burns OR 97720 **Phn:** 541-573-2055 **Fax:** 541-573-5223

Coos Bay KBBR-AM (nt) PO Box 180, Coos Bay OR 97420 **Phn:** 541-267-2121 **Fax:** 541-267-5229 www.1340kbbr.com

Coos Bay KDCQ-FM (h) PO Box 478, Coos Bay OR 97420 **Phn:** 541-269-0929 **Fax:** 541-269-9376 kdcq.com stephanie@kdock929.com

Coos Bay KHSN-AM (s) PO Box 180, Coos Bay OR 97420 **Phn:** 541-267-2121 **Fax:** 541-267-5229 www.khsn1230.com

Coos Bay KJMX-FM (o) PO Box 180, Coos Bay OR 97420 **Phn:** 541-267-2121 **Fax:** 541-267-5229 news@kjmxfm.com mobrien@bicoastalmedia.com

Coos Bay KOOS-FM (h) PO Box 180, Coos Bay OR 97420 **Phn:** 541-267-2121 **Fax:** 541-267-5229 www.power1073.com eford@bicoastalmedia.com

Coos Bay KTEE-FM (a) PO Box 180, Coos Bay OR 97420 **Phn:** 541-267-2121 **Fax:** 541-267-5229 www.ktee.com mobrien@bicoastalmedia.com

Coos Bay KYSJ-FM (j) 580 Kingwood Ave, Coos Bay OR 97420 **Phn:** 541-266-8531 **Fax:** 541-267-0114 www.lighthouseradio.com rick@lighthouseradio.com

Coos Bay KYTT-FM (q) 580 Kingwood Ave, Coos Bay OR 97420 **Phn:** 541-269-2022 **Fax:** 541-267-0114 www.lighthouseradio.com rick@lighthouseradio.com

Coquille KBDN-FM (c) PO Box 180, Coquille OR 97423 **Phn:** 541-267-2121 **Fax:** 541-267-5229 www.kbdn.com mobrien@bicoastalmedia.com

Coquille KSHR-FM (c) PO Box 180, Coquille OR 97423 **Phn:** 541-267-2121 **Fax:** 541-267-5229 www.kshr.com mobrien@bicoastalmedia.com

Coquille KWRO-AM (nt) PO Box 180, Coquille OR 97423 **Phn:** 541-267-2121 **Fax:** 541-267-5229 www.kwro.com mobrien@bicoastalmedia.com

Corvallis KBVR-FM (vju) 210 Memorial Un E, Corvallis OR 97331 **Phn:** 541-737-6323 kbvr.com

Cottage Grove KNND-AM (c) 321 E Main St, Cottage Grove OR 97424 **Phn:** 541-942-2468 **Fax:** 541-942-5797 www.knndweb.com cameron@knnd.com

Dallas KWIP-AM (y) PO Box 469, Dallas OR 97338 **Phn:** 503-623-0245 **Fax:** 503-623-6733 www.kwip.com lucy@kwip.com

Enterprise KWVR-AM (snt) 220 W Main St, Enterprise OR 97828 **Phn:** 541-426-4577 **Fax:** 541-426-4578 kwvrradio.net kwvrron@gmail.com

Enterprise KWVR-FM (c) 220 W Main St, Enterprise OR 97828 **Phn:** 541-426-4577 **Fax:** 541-426-4578 kwvrradio.net kwvrradio@gmail.com

Eugene KDUK-FM (h) 1500 Valley River Dr Ste 350, Eugene OR 97401 **Phn:** 541-284-3600 **Fax:** 541-484-5769 www.kduk.com larryrogers@bicoastalmedia.com

Eugene KEHK-FM (a) 1200 Executive Pkwy Ste 440, Eugene OR 97401 **Phn:** 541-284-8500 **Fax:** 541-485-4070 www.starfm1023.com maverick@starfm1023.com

Eugene KEUG-FM (ah) 925 Country Club Rd Ste 200, Eugene OR 97401 **Phn:** 541-484-9400 **Fax:** 541-344-9424 www.1055bobfm.com

Eugene KFLY-FM (r) 1500 Valley River Dr Ste 350, Eugene OR 97401 **Phn:** 541-284-3600 **Fax:** 541-484-5769 www.kflyfm.com larryrogers@bicoastalmedia.com

Eugene KKNU-FM (c) 925 Country Club Rd Ste 200, Eugene OR 97401 **Phn:** 541-484-9400 **Fax:** 541-344-9424 www.kknu.com jim@kknu.fm

Eugene KKNX-AM (hsn) 1142 Willagillespie Rd, Eugene OR 97401 **Phn:** 541-342-1012 **Fax:** 541-342-6201 www.radio84.com john@radio84.com

Eugene KLCC-FM (pjn) 136 W 8th Ave, Eugene OR 97401 **Phn:** 541-463-6000 **Fax:** 541-463-6046 www.klcc.org news@klcc.org

Eugene KMGE-FM (a) 925 Country Club Rd Ste 200, Eugene OR 97401 **Phn:** 541-484-9400 **Fax:** 541-344-9424 www.kmge.fm john@kmge.fm

Eugene KNRQ-FM (r) 1200 Executive Pkwy Ste 440, Eugene OR 97401 **Phn:** 541-284-8500 www.nrq.com al@nrq.com

Eugene KODZ-FM (o) 1500 Valley River Dr Ste 350, Eugene OR 97401 **Phn:** 541-284-3600 **Fax:** 541-484-5769 www.kool991.com eugenepsa@bicoastalmedia.com

Eugene KPNW-AM (nt) 1500 Valley River Dr # 350, Eugene OR 97401 **Phn:** 541-485-1120 **Fax:** 541-484-5769 www.kpnw.com billlundun@bicoastalmedia.com

Eugene KRVM-FM (r) 1574 Coburg Rd # 237, Eugene OR 97401 **Phn:** 541-790-6686 **Fax:** 541-790-6688 www.krvm.org webmaster@krvm.org

Eugene KSCR-AM (s) 1200 Executive Pkwy Ste 440, Eugene OR 97401 **Phn:** 541-284-8500 **Fax:** 541-485-0969 www.953thescore.com al@nrq.com

Eugene KUGN-AM (nt) 1200 Executive Pkwy Ste 440, Eugene OR 97401 **Phn:** 541-284-8500 **Fax:** 541-485-0969 www.kugn.com mark.raney@cumulus.com

Eugene KUJZ-FM (s) 1200 Executive Pkwy Ste 440, Eugene OR 97401 **Phn:** 541-284-8500 **Fax:** 541-485-0969 www.953thescore.com al@nrq.com

Eugene KWAX-FM (pl) 75 Centennial Loop, Eugene OR 97401 **Phn:** 541-345-0800 www.kwax.com inquiry@kwax.com

Eugene KWVA-FM (vu) PO Box 3157, Eugene OR 97403 **Phn:** 541-346-4091 **Fax:** 541-346-0648 kwva.uoregon.edu kwva@gladstone.uoregon.edu

Eugene KZEL-FM (r) 1200 Executive Pkwy Ste 440, Eugene OR 97401 **Phn:** 541-284-8500 **Fax:** 541-485-0969 www.96kzel.com mark@96kzel.com

Florence KCST-FM (ac) PO Box 20000, Florence OR 97439 **Phn:** 541-997-9136 **Fax:** 541-997-9165 www.kcfmradio.com ccates@kcst.com

Florence KCST-AM (zb) PO Box 20000, Florence OR 97439 **Phn:** 541-997-9136 **Fax:** 541-997-9165 www.kcfmradio.com radiowaves@kcst.com

Gold Beach KGBR-FM (ar) PO Box 787, Gold Beach OR 97444 **Phn:** 541-247-7211 **Fax:** 541-247-4155 www.kgbr.com

Grants Pass KAJO-AM (am) 888 Rogue River Hwy, Grants Pass OR 97527 **Phn:** 541-476-6608 **Fax:** 541-476-4018 www.kajo.com kajo@kajo.com

Grants Pass KLDR-FM (r) 888 Rogue River Hwy, Grants Pass OR 97527 **Phn:** 541-474-7292 **Fax:** 541-476-4018 www.kldr.com kldr@kldr.com

Happy Valley KKPZ-AM (qt) 9700 SE Eastview Dr, Happy Valley OR 97086 **Phn:** 503-242-1950 **Fax:** 503-242-0155 www.kkpz.com info@kkpz.com

Hermiston KOHU-AM (cnt) PO Box 145, Hermiston OR 97838 **Phn:** 541-567-6500 **Fax:** 541-567-6068

Hermiston KQFM-FM (r) PO Box 145, Hermiston OR 97838 **Phn:** 541-567-6500 **Fax:** 541-567-6068

Hillsboro KUIK-AM (snt) PO Box 566, Hillsboro OR 97123 **Phn:** 503-640-1360 **Fax:** 503-640-6108 www.kuik.com spencer@kuik.com

Hood River KCGB-FM (h) PO Box 360, Hood River OR 97031 **Phn:** 541-386-1511 **Fax:** 541-386-7155 www.gorgeradio.com mbailey@bicoastalmedia.com

Hood River KIHR-AM (c) PO Box 360, Hood River OR 97031 **Phn:** 541-386-1511 **Fax:** 541-386-7155 www.gorgeradio.com plaroque@bicoastalmedia.com

Jacksonville KAPL-AM (ntq) PO Box 1090, Jacksonville OR 97530 **Phn:** 541-899-5275 www.kaplradio.com kaplradio@gmail.com

John Day KJDY-AM (c) PO Box 399, John Day OR 97845 **Phn:** 541-575-1400 **Fax:** 541-575-2313

John Day KJDY-FM (c) PO Box 399, John Day OR 97845 **Phn:** 541-575-1400 **Fax:** 541-575-2313 kjdy@centurytel.net

Klamath Falls KAGO-AM (nt) PO Box 339, Klamath Falls OR 97601 **Phn:** 541-882-8833 **Fax:** 541-882-8836 www.mybasin.com

Klamath Falls KAGO-FM (ar) PO Box 339, Klamath Falls OR 97601 **Phn:** 541-882-8833 **Fax:** 541-882-8836 www.mybasin.com

Klamath Falls KBUG-FM (qc) PO Box 111, Klamath Falls OR 97601 **Phn:** 541-884-8167 **Fax:** 541-884-8226

Klamath Falls KFLS-FM (c) 1338 Oregon Ave, Klamath Falls OR 97601 **Phn:** 541-882-4656 **Fax:** 541-884-2845 www.klamathradio.com bob@klamathradio.com

Klamath Falls KFLS-AM (sn) 1338 Oregon Ave, Klamath Falls OR 97601 **Phn:** 541-882-4656 **Fax:** 541-884-2845 www.klamathradio.com bob@klamathradio.com

Klamath Falls KKJX-AM (c) PO Box 339, Klamath Falls OR 97601 **Phn:** 541-882-8833 **Fax:** 541-882-8836

Klamath Falls KKRB-FM (a) PO Box 1450, Klamath Falls OR 97601 **Phn:** 541-882-4656 **Fax:** 541-884-2845 www.klamathradio.com carol@klamathradio.com

Klamath Falls KLAD-FM (c) PO Box 339, Klamath Falls OR 97601 **Phn:** 541-882-8833 **Fax:** 541-882-8836 www.mybasin.com rob@mybasin.com

OREGON RADIO STATIONS

Klamath Falls KLAD-AM (s) PO Box 339, Klamath Falls OR 97601 **Phn:** 541-882-8833 **Fax:** 541-882-8836 www.mybasin.com rob@mybasin.com

Klamath Falls KRAT-FM (o) PO Box 235, Klamath Falls OR 97601 **Phn:** 541-884-8167

La Grande KBKR-AM (nt) 2510 Cove Ave, La Grande OR 97850 **Phn:** 541-963-4121 **Fax:** 541-963-3117 www.supertalk1490.com supertalk@eoni.com

La Grande KCMB-FM (c) 1009 Adams Ave Ste C, La Grande OR 97850 **Phn:** 541-963-3405 **Fax:** 541-963-5090 myeasternoregon.com randy@elkhornmediagroup.com

La Grande KEOL-FM (vr) 1 University Blvd, La Grande OR 97850 **Phn:** 541-962-3698 www.eou.edukeol 91.7keol@gmail.com

La Grande KKBC-FM (o) 2510 Cove Ave, La Grande OR 97850 **Phn:** 541-523-4431 www.yourboomerradio.com

La Grande KLBM-AM (nt) 2510 Cove Ave, La Grande OR 97850 **Phn:** 541-963-4121 **Fax:** 541-963-3117 supertalk@eoni.com

La Grande KRJT-FM (o) 2510 Cove Ave, La Grande OR 97850 **Phn:** 541-963-4121 **Fax:** 541-963-3117 www.yourboomerradio.com

La Grande KUBQ-FM (h) 2510 Cove Ave, La Grande OR 97850 **Phn:** 541-963-4121 **Fax:** 541-963-3117 987kubq.com mail@987kubq.com

La Grande KWRL-FM (a) 1009 Adams Ave Ste C, La Grande OR 97850 **Phn:** 541-963-7911 **Fax:** 541-963-5090 myeasternoregon.com tracy@elkhornmediagroup.com

Lakeview KQIK-AM (oc) 629 Center St, Lakeview OR 97630 **Phn:** 541-947-3351 **Fax:** 541-947-2309

Lakeview KQIK-FM (a) 629 Center St, Lakeview OR 97630 **Phn:** 541-947-3351 **Fax:** 541-947-3375

McMinnville KLYC-AM (ao) PO Box 1099, McMinnville OR 97128 **Phn:** 503-472-1260 **Fax:** 503-472-3243 klyc@viclink.com

McMinnville KSLC-FM (vr) 900 SE Baker St, McMinnville OR 97128 **Phn:** 503-883-2550 www.linfield.edukslcfm.html

Medford KAKT-FM (c) 1438 Rossanley Dr, Medford OR 97501 **Phn:** 541-779-1550 **Fax:** 541-776-2360 www.thewolf1051.com bbishop@radiomedford.com

Medford KBOY-FM (r) 1438 Rossanley Dr, Medford OR 97501 **Phn:** 541-779-1550 **Fax:** 541-776-2360 www.957kboy.com

Medford KCMX-AM (nt) 1438 Rossanley Dr, Medford OR 97501 **Phn:** 541-779-1550 **Fax:** 541-776-2360 www.kcmxam.com gemineye@radiomedford.com

Medford KCMX-FM (a) 1438 Rossanley Dr, Medford OR 97501 **Phn:** 541-779-1550 **Fax:** 541-776-2360 www.lite102.com graneiri@radiomedford.com

Medford KCNA-FM (o) 511 Rossanley Dr, Medford OR 97501 **Phn:** 541-772-0322 **Fax:** 541-772-4233 www.1027thedrive.com rcharles@opusradio.com

Medford KDOV-FM (ntq) 1236 Disk Dr Ste E, Medford OR 97501 **Phn:** 541-776-5368 www.thedove.us thedove@thedove.us

Medford KEZX-AM (t) 511 Rossanley Dr, Medford OR 97501 **Phn:** 541-772-0322 **Fax:** 541-772-4233 www.sportsradio730.com rcharles@opusradio.com

Medford KGAY-FM (s) 1438 Rossanley Dr, Medford OR 97501 **Phn:** 541-779-1550 **Fax:** 541-776-2360 jmussio@radiomedford.com

Medford KIFS-FM (h) 3624 Avion Dr, Medford OR 97504 **Phn:** 541-772-4170 **Fax:** 541-858-5416 www.107kiss.com gemineyemayers@bicoastalmedia.com

Medford KLDZ-FM (o) 3624 Avion Dr, Medford OR 97504 **Phn:** 541-774-1324 **Fax:** 541-857-0326 www.kool1035.com donhurley@bicoastalmedia.com

Medford KMED-AM (nt) 3624 Avion Dr, Medford OR 97504 **Phn:** 541-774-1324 **Fax:** 541-858-5416 www.kmed.com bill@billmeyershow.com

Medford KROG-FM (a) 511 Rossanley Dr, Medford OR 97501 **Phn:** 541-772-0322 **Fax:** 541-772-4233 www.969therogue.com

Medford KRTA-AM (ys) 511 Rossanley Dr, Medford OR 97501 **Phn:** 541-772-0322 **Fax:** 541-772-4233 opusradio.com dean@opusradio.com

Medford KRWQ-FM (c) 3624 Avion Dr, Medford OR 97504 **Phn:** 541-772-4170 **Fax:** 541-858-5416 www.q1003.com larryneal@bicoastalmedia.com

Medford KTMT-FM (a) 1438 Rossanley Dr, Medford OR 97501 **Phn:** 541-779-1550 **Fax:** 541-776-2360 radiomedford.com graneiri@radiomedford.com

Medford KZZE-FM (r) 3624 Avion Dr, Medford OR 97504 **Phn:** 541-772-4170 **Fax:** 541-858-5416 www.kzze.com donhurley@bicoastalmedia.com

Newport KBCH-AM (am) PO Box 1430, Newport OR 97365 **Phn:** 541-265-2266 **Fax:** 541-265-6397 www.kbcham.com news@ybcradio.com

Newport KCRF-FM (r) PO Box 1430, Newport OR 97365 **Phn:** 541-265-2266 **Fax:** 541-265-6397 www.kcrffm.com news@ybcradio.com

Newport KCUP-AM (o) PO Box 456, Newport OR 97365 **Phn:** 541-265-5000 **Fax:** 541-265-9576 www.kcup.net info@kcup.net

Newport KNCU-FM (c) PO Box 1430, Newport OR 97365 **Phn:** 541-265-2266 **Fax:** 541-265-6397 www.u92fm.com news@ybcradio.com

Newport KNPT-AM (nt) PO Box 1430, Newport OR 97365 **Phn:** 541-265-2266 **Fax:** 541-265-6397 www.knptam.com news@ybcradio.com

Newport KPPT-FM (r) PO Box 456, Newport OR 97365 **Phn:** 541-265-5000 **Fax:** 541-265-9576 www.bossfmradio.net info@bossradio.net

Newport KSHL-FM (c) PO Box 1180, Newport OR 97365 **Phn:** 541-265-6477 **Fax:** 541-265-6478 www.kshl.com info@kshl.com

Newport KYTE-FM (a) PO Box 1430, Newport OR 97365 **Phn:** 541-265-2266 **Fax:** 541-265-6397 www.kytefm.com news@ybcradio.com

Ontario KSRV-AM (c) PO Box 129, Ontario OR 97914 **Phn:** 541-889-8651 **Fax:** 541-889-8733

Ontario KSRV-FM (c) PO Box 129, Ontario OR 97914 **Phn:** 541-889-8651 **Fax:** 541-889-8733 www.961bobfm.com bob@impactradiogroup.com

Pendleton KTIX-AM (snt) 2003 NW 56th St, Pendleton OR 97801 **Phn:** 541-278-2500 **Fax:** 541-276-1480

Pendleton KUMA-AM (nt) 2003 NW 56th St, Pendleton OR 97801 **Phn:** 541-276-1511 **Fax:** 541-276-1480 www.mycolumbiabasin.com jjford@uci.net

Pendleton KWVN-FM (a) 2003 NW 56th St, Pendleton OR 97801 **Phn:** 541-276-1511 **Fax:** 541-276-1480 www.mycolumbiabasin.com

Portland KBNP-AM (ntk) 278 SW Arthur St, Portland OR 97201 **Phn:** 503-223-6769 **Fax:** 503-223-4305 www.kbnp.com contact@kbnp.com

Portland KBOO-FM (v) 20 SE 8th Ave, Portland OR 97214 **Phn:** 503-231-8032 **Fax:** 503-231-7145 kboo.fm amnews@kboo.org

Portland KBPS-FM (pl) 515 NE 15th Ave, Portland OR 97232 **Phn:** 503-916-5828 www.allclassical.org music.info@allclassical.org

Portland KBVM-FM (q) PO Box 5888, Portland OR 97228 **Phn:** 503-285-5200 **Fax:** 503-285-3322 www.kbvm.fm

Portland KFBW-FM (or) 4949 SW Macadam Ave, Portland OR 97239 **Phn:** 503-802-1600 www.theriver1059.com chrissargent@clearchannel.com

Portland KFIS-FM (q) 6400 SE Lake Rd Ste 350, Portland OR 97222 **Phn:** 503-786-0600 **Fax:** 503-786-1551 www.1041thefish.com

Portland KFXX-AM (s) 0700 SW Bancroft St, Portland OR 97239 **Phn:** 503-223-1441 **Fax:** 503-223-6909 www.1080thefan.com jaustin@entercom.com

Portland KGDD-AM (y) 5110 SE Stark St, Portland OR 97215 **Phn:** 503-234-5550 **Fax:** 503-234-5583 www.lagrande.mx contact@bustosmedia.com

Portland KGON-FM (r) 0700 SW Bancroft St, Portland OR 97239 **Phn:** 503-223-1441 **Fax:** 503-223-6909 www.kgon.com asteinbeck@entercom.com

Portland KINK-FM (ar) 1211 SW 5th Ave 6th Flr, Portland OR 97204 **Phn:** 503-517-6200 **Fax:** 503-517-6100 www.kink.fm chris@kink.fm

Portland KKAD-AM (nt) 6605 SE Lake Rd, Portland OR 97222 **Phn:** 503-228-5523 **Fax:** 503-294-0074 www.1550kkad.com jwinter@kpam.com

Portland KKCW-FM (a) 4949 SW Macadam Ave, Portland OR 97239 **Phn:** 503-323-6400 **Fax:** 503-323-6662 www.k103.com tommyaustin@clearchannel.com

Portland KKRZ-FM (h) 4949 SW Macadam Ave, Portland OR 97239 **Phn:** 503-226-0100 **Fax:** 503-295-9281 www.z100portland.com geoffowens@clearchannel.com

Portland KLTH-FM (h) 4949 SW Macadam Ave, Portland OR 97239 **Phn:** 503-243-1067 **Fax:** 503-323-6660 www.portlandoldies.com

Portland KMHD-FM (vj) 7140 SW Macadam Ave, Portland OR 97219 **Phn:** 503-244-9900 www.kmhd.org

Portland KNRK-FM (r) 0700 SW Bancroft St, Portland OR 97239 **Phn:** 503-223-1441 **Fax:** 503-223-6909 www.947.fm mhamilton@entercom.com

Portland KOOR-AM (h) 5110 SE Stark St, Portland OR 97215 **Phn:** 503-234-5550 **Fax:** 503-234-5583 russianradio7.com russianradio7@gmail.com

Portland KOPB-FM (plnj) 7140 SW Macadam Ave, Portland OR 97219 **Phn:** 503-293-1905 **Fax:** 503-293-1919 www.opb.org opbnews@opb.org

Portland KPAM-AM (nt) 6605 SE Lake Rd, Portland OR 97222 **Phn:** 503-223-4321 **Fax:** 503-294-0074 www.kpam.com jwinter@kpam.com

Portland KPDQ-FM (q) 6400 SE Lake Rd Ste 350, Portland OR 97222 **Phn:** 503-786-0600 **Fax:** 503-786-1551 www.kpdq.com justin@kpdq.com

Portland KPDQ-AM (g) 6400 SE Lake Rd Ste 350, Portland OR 97222 **Phn:** 503-786-0600 **Fax:** 503-786-1551 www.truetalk800.com justin@kpdq.com

Portland KQAC-AM (pl) 515 NE 15th Ave, Portland OR 97232 **Phn:** 503-916-5828

Portland KRRC-FM (v) 3203 SE Woodstock Blvd, Portland OR 97202 **Phn:** 503-771-1112

Portland KRSK-FM (ah) 0700 SW Bancroft St, Portland OR 97239 **Phn:** 503-223-1441 **Fax:** 503-223-6909 www.1051thebuzz.com jhutchison@entercom.com

Portland KSZN-AM (or) 5110 SE Stark St, Portland OR 97215 **Phn:** 503-234-5550 www.bustosmedia.com contact@bustosmedia.com

Portland KUFO-AM (t) 1211 SW 5th Ave 6th Flr, Portland OR 97204 **Phn:** 503-517-6000 **Fax:** 503-517-6100 www.freedom970.com events@freedom970.com

Portland KUPL-FM (c) 1211 SW 5th Ave, Portland OR 97204 **Phn:** 503-517-6000 **Fax:** 503-517-6401 www.987thebull.com scott.mahalick@alphabroadcasting.com

Portland KWJJ-FM (c) 0700 SW Bancroft St, Portland OR 97239 **Phn:** 503-223-1441 **Fax:** 503-223-6909 www.thewolfonline.com mmoore@entercom.com

Portland KXJM-FM (h) 4949 SW Macadam Ave, Portland OR 97239 **Phn:** 503-323-6400 **Fax:** 503-323-6660 www.wild1075portland.com

Portland KXL-FM (nt) 1211 SW 5th Ave 6th Flr, Portland OR 97204 **Phn:** 503-517-6000 **Fax:** 503-517-6100 www.kxl.com rebecca.marshall@alphabroadcasting.com

Portland KYCH-FM (a) 0700 SW Bancroft St, Portland OR 97239 **Phn:** 503-226-9791 **Fax:** 503-242-0142 www.charliefm.com mhamilton@947.fm

Reedsport KDUN-AM (ot) 136 N 7th St, Reedsport OR 97467 **Phn:** 541-271-1030 **Fax:** 541-271-5140 www.kdune.com kdune@kdune.com

Roseburg KKMX-FM (a) 1445 W Harvard Ave, Roseburg OR 97471 **Phn:** 541-672-6641 **Fax:** 541-673-7598 www.541radio.com randy@bciradio.com

Roseburg KQEN-AM (snt) 1445 W Harvard Ave, Roseburg OR 97471 **Phn:** 541-672-6641 **Fax:** 541-673-7598 www.541radio.com country@bciradio.com

Roseburg KRSB-FM (s) 1445 W Harvard Ave, Roseburg OR 97471 **Phn:** 541-672-6641 **Fax:** 541-673-7598 www.541radio.com country@bciradio.com

Roseburg KSKR-FM (s) 1445 W Harvard Ave, Roseburg OR 97471 **Phn:** 541-672-6641 **Fax:** 541-673-7598 www.541radio.com randy@bciradio.com

Roseburg KSKR-AM (s) 1445 W Harvard Ave, Roseburg OR 97471 **Phn:** 541-672-6641 **Fax:** 541-673-7598 www.541radio.com randy@bciradio.com

Saint Helens KOHI-AM (c) 36200 Pittsburg Rd Ste D, Saint Helens OR 97051 **Phn:** 503-397-1600 www.am1600kohi.com kohi.radio@gmail.com

Salem KBZY-AM (a) 2659 Commercial St SE Ste 204, Salem OR 97302 **Phn:** 503-362-1490 **Fax:** 503-362-6545 www.kbzy.com dittmanr@kbzy.com

Salem KPJC-AM (qt) 3190 Lancaster Dr NE, Salem OR 97305 **Phn:** 503-316-1220

Salem KYKN-AM (nt) PO Box 1430, Salem OR 97308 **Phn:** 503-390-3014 **Fax:** 503-390-3728 1430kykn.com mfrith@1430kykn.com

Seaside KCBZ-FM (a) PO Box 354, Seaside OR 97138 **Phn:** 503-738-8668 **Fax:** 503-738-8778 www.musicmatters949.com calbrady@pacbell.net

Springfield KORE-AM (qt) 2080 Laura St, Springfield OR 97477 **Phn:** 541-747-5673 www.koreradio.com kore@koreradio.com

Sweet Home KFIR-AM (nt) PO Box 720, Sweet Home OR 97386 **Phn:** 541-367-5115 **Fax:** 541-367-5233 www.kfir720am.com info@kfir720am.com

The Dalles KACI-FM (o) 719 E 2nd St # 203, The Dalles OR 97058 **Phn:** 541-296-2211 **Fax:** 541-296-2213 www.gorgeradio.com gleblanc@bicoastalmedia.com

The Dalles KACI-AM (nt) 719 E 2nd St # 203, The Dalles OR 97058 **Phn:** 541-296-2211 **Fax:** 541-296-2213 www.gorgeradio.com mbailey@bicoastalmedia.com

The Dalles KLCK-AM (t) PO Box 1023, The Dalles OR 97058 **Phn:** 541-296-9102 **Fax:** 541-298-7775 klck1400.com info@haystackbroadcasting.com

The Dalles KMSW-FM (r) 719 E 2nd St # 203, The Dalles OR 97058 **Phn:** 541-296-2211 **Fax:** 541-296-2213 www.gorgeradio.com gary@bicoastalmedia.com

The Dalles KODL-AM (ah) PO Box 1488, The Dalles OR 97058 **Phn:** 541-296-2101 **Fax:** 541-296-3766 www.kodl.com newsroom@kodl.com

The Dalles KYYT-FM (cn) PO Box 1023, The Dalles OR 97058 **Phn:** 541-296-9102 **Fax:** 541-298-7775

Tigard KEX-AM (nt) 13333 SW 68th Parkway, Tigard OR 97223 **Phn:** 503-323-6400 **Fax:** 503-323-6660 www.1190kex.com melissaives@clearchannel.com

Tigard KPOJ-AM (nt) 13333 SW 68th Parkway, Tigard OR 97223 **Phn:** 503-323-6400 **Fax:** 503-323-6660 www.foxsportsradio620.com

Tillamook KTIL-AM (t) 170 3rd St W, Tillamook OR 97141 **Phn:** 503-842-4422 **Fax:** 503-842-2755 www.ktil-radio.com shaena@ktil-radio.com

Tillamook KTIL-FM (m) 170 3rd St W, Tillamook OR 97141 **Phn:** 503-842-4422 **Fax:** 503-842-2755 www.ktil-radio.com shaena@ktil-radio.com

Waldport KORC-AM (o) PO Box 495, Waldport OR 97394 **Phn:** 541-563-5100 **Fax:** 541-563-5116 www.korcam820.com larry@korcam820.com

Warm Springs KWSO-FM (v) PO Box 489, Warm Springs OR 97761 **Phn:** 541-553-1968 **Fax:** 541-553-3348 www.kwso.org kwsonews@wstribes.org

Warrenton KAST-AM (nt) 285 SW Main Ct Ste 200, Warrenton OR 97146 **Phn:** 503-861-6620 **Fax:** 503-861-6630 www.kast1370.com collin.mcdonnell@ohanamediagroup.com

Warrenton KCRX-FM (r) 285 SW Main Ct Ste 200, Warrenton OR 97146 **Phn:** 503-861-6620 **Fax:** 503-861-6630 www.1023kcrx.com

Warrenton KKEE-AM (s) 285 SW Main Ct Ste 200, Warrenton OR 97146 **Phn:** 503-861-6620 **Fax:** 503-861-6630

Warrenton KVAS-FM (c) 285 SW Main Ct Ste 200, Warrenton OR 97146 **Phn:** 503-861-6620 **Fax:** 503-861-6630 www.eaglecountry1039.com

Wilsonville KXPD-AM (y) 8532 SW Saint Helens Dr Ste 100, Wilsonville OR 97070 **Phn:** 971-224-2260 **Fax:** 971-224-2270

Winston KGRV-AM (q) PO Box 1598, Winston OR 97496 **Phn:** 541-679-8185 **Fax:** 541-679-6456

Woodburn KCKX-AM (y) 1665 James St, Woodburn OR 97071 **Phn:** 503-769-1460 **Fax:** 503-981-3561 www.lapantera940.com

Woodburn KSND-FM (y) PO Box 158, Woodburn OR 97071 **Phn:** 503-981-9400 **Fax:** 503-981-3561 www.lapantera940.com

Woodburn KWBY-AM (y) 1665 James St, Woodburn OR 97071 **Phn:** 503-981-9400 **Fax:** 503-981-3561 www.lapantera940.com

PENNSYLVANIA

Aliquippa WKPL-FM (o) 131 Pleasant Dr Ste 5U, Aliquippa PA 15001 **Phn:** 724-378-1271 **Fax:** 724-378-4653 danthony@keymarketradio.com

Aliquippa WOGF-FM (c) 131 Pleasant Dr Ste 5U, Aliquippa PA 15001 **Phn:** 724-378-1271 **Fax:** 724-378-4653 www.froggyland.com danthony@keymarketradio.com

Aliquippa WOHI-AM (obt) 131 Pleasant Dr Ste 5U, Aliquippa PA 15001 **Phn:** 724-378-1271 **Fax:** 724-378-4653

Allentown WHOL-AM (y) 1125 Colorado St, Allentown PA 18103 **Phn:** 610-434-4801 www.holaenturadio.com holaradionoticias@holaenturadio.com

Allentown WJCS-FM (qnt) PO Box 8900, Allentown PA 18105 **Phn:** 610-791-7262 **Fax:** 610-797-6922

Allentown WMUH-FM (p) 2400 Chew St, Allentown PA 18104 **Phn:** 484-664-3456 www.muhlenberg.eduwmuh wmuh@muhlenberg.edu

Altoona WBRX-FM (r) 2513 6th Ave, Altoona PA 16602 **Phn:** 814-943-6112 **Fax:** 814-944-9782 www.mymix947.com chrisforshey@gmail.com

Altoona WBXQ-FM (r) 2513 6th Ave, Altoona PA 16602 **Phn:** 814-943-6112 **Fax:** 814-944-9782 www.wbxq.com diane@theradiocampus.com

Altoona WKMC-AM (am) 2513 6th Ave, Altoona PA 16602 **Phn:** 814-224-7501 **Fax:** 814-944-9782 www.wkmcam.com chris@wrta.com

Altoona WRTA-AM (nt) 2513 6th Ave, Altoona PA 16602 **Phn:** 814-943-6112 **Fax:** 814-944-9782 www.wrta.com

Aston WPWA-AM (gq) 12 Kent Rd, Aston PA 19014 **Phn:** 610-358-1400 **Fax:** 610-358-1845 www.wpwa.net amarily@wpwa.net

Avoca WCDL-AM (a) 957 Broadcast Ctr, Avoca PA 18641 **Phn:** 570-414-1943 **Fax:** 570-414-1944

Avoca WNAK-AM (z) 957 Broadcast Ctr, Avoca PA 18641 **Phn:** 570-414-1943 **Fax:** 570-414-1944

Bala Cynwyd WBEB-FM (a) 225 E City Ave Ste 200, Bala Cynwyd PA 19004 **Phn:** 610-667-8400 **Fax:** 610-667-6795 www.b101radio.com webmaster@b101radio.com

Bala Cynwyd WBEN-FM (ha) 1 Bala Plz Ste 424, Bala Cynwyd PA 19004 **Phn:** 610-771-0957 **Fax:** 610-771-9690 www.ilikebenfm.com questions@ilikebenfm.com

Bala Cynwyd WDAS-FM (wu) 111 Presidential Blvd Ste 100, Bala Cynwyd PA 19004 **Phn:** 610-784-3333 **Fax:** 610-784-2098 www.wdasfm.com lorainemorrill@clearchannel.com

Bala Cynwyd WDAS-AM (wg) 111 Presidential Blvd Ste 100, Bala Cynwyd PA 19004 **Phn:** 610-784-3333 **Fax:** 610-784-2098 www.wdasfm.com loraineballardmorrill@clearchannel.com

Bala Cynwyd WHAT-AM (st) 25 Bala Ave Ste 202, Bala Cynwyd PA 19004 **Phn:** 484-562-0516 **Fax:** 484-562-0552

Bala Cynwyd WIOQ-FM (h) 111 Presidential Blvd Ste 100, Bala Cynwyd PA 19004 **Phn:** 610-784-3333 **Fax:** 610-784-2020 www.q102.com richardlewis@clearchannel.com

Bala Cynwyd WIP-AM (st) 2 Bala Plz Ste 700, Bala Cynwyd PA 19004 **Phn:** 610-949-7800 **Fax:** 610-949-7889 philadelphia.cbslocal.com wippromotions@cbsradio.com

Bala Cynwyd WISX-FM (a) 111 Presidential Blvd Ste 100, Bala Cynwyd PA 19004 **Phn:** 610-784-3333 **Fax:** 610-784-2098 www.mixphiladelphia.com richardlewis@clearchannel.com

Bala Cynwyd WMGK-FM (ah) 1 Bala Plz Ste 339, Bala Cynwyd PA 19004 **Phn:** 610-667-8500 **Fax:** 610-664-9610 www.wmgk.com theoffice@wmgk.com

PENNSYLVANIA RADIO STATIONS

Bala Cynwyd WMMR-FM (r) 1 Bala Plz Ste 424, Bala Cynwyd PA 19004 **Phn:** 610-771-0933 **Fax:** 610-771-9667 www.wmmr.com programdirector@wmmr.com

Bala Cynwyd WNWR-AM (eyt) 200 Monument Rd Ste 6, Bala Cynwyd PA 19004 **Phn:** 610-664-6780 **Fax:** 610-664-8529 www.wnwr.com information@wnwr.com

Bala Cynwyd WOGL-FM (o) 2 Bala Plz Ste 800, Bala Cynwyd PA 19004 **Phn:** 610-668-5900 **Fax:** 610-668-5998 wogl.cbslocal.com questions@wogl.com

Bala Cynwyd WPEN-AM (s) 1 Bala Plz Ste 429, Bala Cynwyd PA 19004 **Phn:** 610-667-8500 **Fax:** 610-771-9692 www.975thefanatic.com mnahigian@975thefanatic.com

Bala Cynwyd WPEN-FM (s) 1 Bala Plz Ste 429, Bala Cynwyd PA 19004 **Phn:** 610-667-8500 **Fax:** 610-771-9692 www.975thefanatic.com mnahigian@975thefanatic.com

Bala Cynwyd WPHI-FM (h) 2 Bala Plz Ste 700, Bala Cynwyd PA 19004 **Phn:** 610-538-1100 **Fax:** 610-949-7889 hot1079philly.com bmorris@radio-one.com

Bala Cynwyd WPHT-AM (nt) 2 Bala Plz Ste 800, Bala Cynwyd PA 19004 **Phn:** 610-668-5800 **Fax:** 610-668-5888 philadelphia.cbslocal.com thebigtalker1210@cbsradio.com

Bala Cynwyd WRDW-FM (h) 555 E City Ave Ste 330, Bala Cynwyd PA 19004 **Phn:** 610-667-9000 www.wired965.com dan.hunt@wired965.com

Bala Cynwyd WRFF-AM (hr) 111 Presidential Blvd Ste 100, Bala Cynwyd PA 19004 **Phn:** 610-784-3333 **Fax:** 610-784-2021 www.radio1045.com johnallers@clearchannel.com

Bala Cynwyd WRNB-FM (wx) 2 Bala Plz Ste 700, Bala Cynwyd PA 19004 **Phn:** 610-276-1100 **Fax:** 610-276-1139 oldschool1003.com elroysmith@radio-one.com

Bala Cynwyd WUSL-FM (wu) 111 Presidential Blvd Ste 100, Bala Cynwyd PA 19004 **Phn:** 610-784-3333 **Fax:** 610-784-2075 www.power99.com lorainemorrill@clearchannel.com

Bala Cynwyd WWDB-AM (kt) 555 E City Ave Ste 330, Bala Cynwyd PA 19004 **Phn:** 610-667-9000 **Fax:** 610-667-5978 www.wwdbam.com thalloran@wwdbam.com

Bala Cynwyd WXTU-FM (c) 555 E City Ave Ste 330, Bala Cynwyd PA 19004 **Phn:** 610-667-9000 **Fax:** 610-667-5978 www.wxtu.com shelly.easton@wxtu.com

Beaver Falls WBVP-AM (snt) PO Box 719, Beaver Falls PA 15010 **Phn:** 724-846-4100 **Fax:** 724-843-7771 www.wbvp-wmba.com 1230@wbvp-wmba.com

Beaver Falls WGEV-FM (vq) Geneva College, Beaver Falls PA 15010 **Phn:** 724-847-6678 www.wgev.net thughes@geneva.edu

Beaver Falls WMBA-AM (nt) PO Box 719, Beaver Falls PA 15010 **Phn:** 724-846-4100 **Fax:** 724-843-7771 www.wbvp-wmba.com 1230@wbvp-wmba.com

Bedford WAYC-AM (a) PO Box 1, Bedford PA 15522 **Phn:** 814-623-1000 **Fax:** 814-623-9692 johncesscomm@embarqmail.com

Bedford WAYC-FM (a) PO Box 1, Bedford PA 15522 **Phn:** 814-623-1000 **Fax:** 814-623-9692 johncesscomm@embarqmail.com

Bedford WBFD-AM (o) PO Box 1, Bedford PA 15522 **Phn:** 814-623-1000 **Fax:** 814-623-9692 geoengland@embarqmail.com

Bedford WBVE-FM (r) PO Box 1, Bedford PA 15522 **Phn:** 814-623-1000 **Fax:** 814-623-9692 johncesscomm@embarqmail.com

Bethlehem WCTO-FM (c) 2158 Avenue C Ste 100, Bethlehem PA 18017 **Phn:** 610-266-7600 **Fax:** 610-231-0400 www.catcountry96.com sam.malone@cumulus.com

Bethlehem WGPA-AM (mnt) 528 N New St, Bethlehem PA 18018 **Phn:** 610-866-8074 **Fax:** 610-866-9381 wgpasunny1100.com wgpasunny1100@yahoo.com

Bethlehem WLEV-FM (a) 2158 Avenue C Ste 100, Bethlehem PA 18017 **Phn:** 610-266-7600 **Fax:** 610-231-0400 www.wlevradio.com

Bethlehem WLVR-FM (v) 39 University Dr, Bethlehem PA 18015 **Phn:** 610-758-4187 www.wlvr.org inwlvr@lehigh.edu

Bloomsburg WBUQ-FM (vr) 400 E 2nd St, Bloomsburg PA 17815 **Phn:** 570-389-4686 **Fax:** 570-389-2718 jdjs.webs.comWBUQ 91wbuq@gmail.com

Bloomsburg WFYY-FM (h) 246 W Main St, Bloomsburg PA 17815 **Phn:** 570-784-5500 **Fax:** 570-784-1004

Bloomsburg WHLM-AM (s) 124 E Main St, Bloomsburg PA 17815 **Phn:** 570-784-1200 **Fax:** 570-784-6060 www.whlm.com joewhlm@aol.com

Bloomsburg WHLM-FM (r) 124 E Main St, Bloomsburg PA 17815 **Phn:** 570-784-1200 **Fax:** 570-784-6060 www.whlm.com joewhlm@aol.com

Boyertown WBYN-FM (h) 280 Mill St, Boyertown PA 19512 **Phn:** 610-369-7777 **Fax:** 610-369-7780 www.wbynfm.com info@wbynfm.com

Bradford WBRR-FM (o) PO Box 545, Bradford PA 16701 **Phn:** 814-368-4141 **Fax:** 814-368-3180 www.wbrrfm.com dfredeen@wesb.com

Bradford WESB-AM (a) PO Box 545, Bradford PA 16701 **Phn:** 814-368-4141 **Fax:** 814-368-3180 www.wesb.com 1490@wesb.com

Brookhaven WVCH-AM (q) PO Box A, Brookhaven PA 19015 **Phn:** 610-279-9000 **Fax:** 610-279-9002 www.wvch.com charcos@juno.com

Brookville WMKX-FM (r) 51 Pickering St, Brookville PA 15825 **Phn:** 814-849-8100 **Fax:** 814-849-4585 www.megarock.fm

Brownsville WASP-AM (o) 123 Blaine Rd, Brownsville PA 15417 **Phn:** 724-938-2000 **Fax:** 724-938-7824

Brownsville WFGI-AM (c) 123 Blaine Rd, Brownsville PA 15417 **Phn:** 724-938-2000 **Fax:** 724-938-7824 www.froggyland.com danthony@keymarketradio.com

Brownsville WOGG-FM (c) 123 Blaine Rd, Brownsville PA 15417 **Phn:** 724-938-2000 **Fax:** 724-938-7824 www.froggyland.com jhaywood@keymarketradio.com

Brownsville WPKL-FM (o) 123 Blaine Rd, Brownsville PA 15417 **Phn:** 724-938-2000 **Fax:** 724-938-7824 classichitsradioonline.com danthony@keymarketradio.com

Brownsville WYJK-AM (o) 123 Blaine Rd, Brownsville PA 15417 **Phn:** 724-938-2000 **Fax:** 724-938-7824 classichitsradioonline.com

Burnham WCHX-FM (rns) 114 N Logan Blvd, Burnham PA 17009 **Phn:** 717-242-1055 **Fax:** 717-242-3764 www.chx105.com wchx@chx105.com

Burnham WKVA-AM (o) 114 N Logan Blvd, Burnham PA 17009 **Phn:** 717-242-1495 **Fax:** 717-242-3764 www.wkva920.com kvatoday@wkva920.com

Butler WBUT-AM (c) 252 Pillow St, Butler PA 16001 **Phn:** 724-287-5778 **Fax:** 724-282-9188 www.wbut.com frontdesk@bcrnetwork.com

Butler WISR-AM (nnt) 252 Pillow St, Butler PA 16001 **Phn:** 724-283-1500 **Fax:** 724-283-3005 www.wisr680.com frontdesk@bcrnetwork.com

Butler WLER-FM (r) 252 Pillow St, Butler PA 16001 **Phn:** 724-287-5778 **Fax:** 724-283-3005 www.wbut.com frontdesk@bcrnetwork.com

California WVCS-FM (v) 428 Hickory St, California PA 15419 **Phn:** 724-938-4330 **Fax:** 724-938-5959

Camp Hill WCAT-FM (c) 515 S 32nd St, Camp Hill PA 17011 **Phn:** 717-635-7000 **Fax:** 717-635-7551 www.red1023.com rich.creeger@cumulus.com

Camp Hill WQXA-FM (ar) 515 S 32nd St, Camp Hill PA 17011 **Phn:** 717-635-7000 **Fax:** 717-635-7551 www.1057thex.com chris.james@cumulus.com

Camp Hill WQXA-AM (c) 515 S 32nd St, Camp Hill PA 17011 **Phn:** 717-635-7000 **Fax:** 717-635-7551

Camp Hill WWII-AM (q) 8 W Main St, Camp Hill PA 17011 **Phn:** 717-731-9944 **Fax:** 717-731-4002 www.720therock.com tsullivan720@yahoo.com

Carlisle WDCV-FM (v) Dickinson Coll Box 1773, Carlisle PA 17013 **Phn:** 717-245-1444 www2.dickinson.edustorgwdcv wdcvfm@gmail.com

Carlisle WEEO-AM (c) 180 York Rd, Carlisle PA 17013 **Phn:** 717-243-1200 **Fax:** 717-243-1277 www.wioo.com wioo@pa.net

Carlisle WHYL-AM (a) 1703 Walnut Bottom Rd, Carlisle PA 17015 **Phn:** 717-249-1717 **Fax:** 717-258-4638 whylradio.com dennis@whylradio.com

Carlisle WIOO-AM (c) 180 York Rd, Carlisle PA 17013 **Phn:** 717-243-1200 **Fax:** 717-243-1277 www.wioo.com wioo@pa.net

Chambersburg WCHA-AM (snt) 25 Penncraft Ave Ste 425, Chambersburg PA 17201 **Phn:** 717-263-0813 **Fax:** 717-263-9649 www.trueoldies800and1410.com ralexander@mlbroadcasting.net

Chambersburg WIKZ-FM (a) 25 Penncraft Ave, Chambersburg PA 17201 **Phn:** 717-263-0813 **Fax:** 717-263-9649 www.mix95.com mix95.1@mix95.com

Chester WDNR-FM (v) 1 University Pl Box 1000, Chester PA 19013 **Phn:** 610-499-4439 **Fax:** 610-499-4387 www2.widener.eduWDNR-895-Radio wdnr895@mail.widener.edu

Clarion WCCR-FM (h) PO Box 688, Clarion PA 16214 **Phn:** 814-226-4500 **Fax:** 814-226-5898 www.clarioncountydailynews.com clarionradio@comcast.net

Clarion WWCH-AM (cn) PO Box 688, Clarion PA 16214 **Phn:** 814-226-4500 **Fax:** 814-226-5898 www.clarioncountydailynews.com clarionradio@comcast.net

Clearfield WOKW-FM (a) PO Box 589, Clearfield PA 16830 **Phn:** 814-765-4955 **Fax:** 814-765-7038 www.wokw.com news@wokw.com

Connellsville WLSW-FM (a) PO Box 763, Connellsville PA 15425 **Phn:** 724-628-2800 **Fax:** 724-628-7380 www.musicpower104.com wlswmgr@hotmail.com

Conshohocken WPPZ-FM (wg) 1000 River Rd Ste 400, Conshohocken PA 19428 **Phn:** 610-276-1100 **Fax:** 610-276-1139 praisephilly.com elroysmith@radio-one.com

Corry WWCB-AM (zos) 418 N Center St, Corry PA 16407 **Phn:** 814-664-8694 **Fax:** 814-664-8695

Coudersport WFRM-AM (cnt) 9 S Main St, Coudersport PA 16915 **Phn:** 814-274-8600 **Fax:** 814-274-0760

Coudersport WFRM-FM (a) 9 S Main St, Coudersport PA 16915 **Phn:** 814-274-8600 **Fax:** 814-274-0760 whks@verizon.net

Danville WPGM-AM (q) PO Box 236, Danville PA 17821 **Phn:** 570-275-1570 **Fax:** 570-275-4071 www.wpgmfm.org

Danville WPGM-FM (q) 8 E Market St, Danville PA 17821 **Phn:** 570-275-1570 **Fax:** 570-275-4071 www.wpgmfm.org

Doylestown WCOJ-AM (q) PO Box 798, Doylestown PA 18901 **Phn:** 215-345-1570 **Fax:** 215-345-1946 holyspiritradio.org 1570am@holyspiritradio.org

Doylestown WISP-AM (q) PO Box 798, Doylestown PA 18901 **Phn:** 215-345-1570 **Fax:** 215-345-1946 www.holyspiritradio.org 1570am@holyspiritradio.org

Du Bois WCED-AM (st) 12 W Long Ave Ste 100, Du Bois PA 15801 **Phn:** 814-375-5260 **Fax:** 814-372-1420 www.1420wced.com news@1420wced.com

Du Bois WDBA-FM (q) 28 W Scribner Ave, Du Bois PA 15801 **Phn:** 814-371-1330 **Fax:** 814-375-5650

Du Bois WDSN-FM (an) 12 W Long Ave, Du Bois PA 15801 **Phn:** 814-375-5260 **Fax:** 814-375-5262 www.sunny106.fm news@sunny1065.fm

Du Bois WOWQ-FM (c) 801 E Dubois Ave, Du Bois PA 15801 **Phn:** 814-371-6100 **Fax:** 814-371-7724 www.q102radio.fm wowq@comcast.net

DuBois WCPA-AM (o) 801 E Dubois Ave, DuBois PA 15801 **Phn:** 814-765-5541 **Fax:** 814-765-6333

DuBois WQYX-FM (a) 801 E Dubois Ave, DuBois PA 15801 **Phn:** 814-765-5541 **Fax:** 814-765-6333

Dushore WGMF-AM (c) PO Box 230, Dushore PA 18614 **Phn:** 570-928-7200 **Fax:** 570-928-2100 www.gem104.com bensmith@gem104.com

Dushore WNKZ-FM (a) PO Box 230, Dushore PA 18614 **Phn:** 570-928-7200 **Fax:** 570-928-2100

East Stroudsburg WESS-FM (v) E Stroudsburg Univ, East Stroudsburg PA 18301 **Phn:** 570-422-3512 **Fax:** 570-422-3615 www.esu.eduwess wess@esu.edu

Easton WEEX-AM (s) 107 Paxinosa Rd W, Easton PA 18040 **Phn:** 610-258-6155 **Fax:** 610-253-3384 www.espnlv.com

Easton WEST-AM (y) 436 Northampton St, Easton PA 18042 **Phn:** 610-250-9557 **Fax:** 610-250-9675 www.whol1600.com tonyrodriguez@hola1600.com

Easton WODE-FM (o) 107 Paxinosa Rd W, Easton PA 18040 **Phn:** 610-258-6155 **Fax:** 610-253-3384 www.999thehawk.com

Ebensburg WHPA-FM (o) 104 S Center St, Ebensburg PA 15931 **Phn:** 814-472-4060 **Fax:** 814-472-7390

Ebensburg WNCC-AM (o) 104 S Center St, Ebensburg PA 15931 **Phn:** 814-472-4060 **Fax:** 814-472-9370

Edinboro WFSE-FM (vr) U Of Pa Faculty Anx 110, Edinboro PA 16444 **Phn:** 814-732-2641

Elizabethtown WPDC-AM (s) 1051 Dairy Ln, Elizabethtown PA 17022 **Phn:** 717-367-1600

Elizabethtown WWEC-FM (v) 1 Alpha Dr, Elizabethtown PA 17022 **Phn:** 717-361-1413 wwec.fm wwec@etown.edu

Emporium WLEM-AM (c) 145 E 4th St, Emporium PA 15834 **Phn:** 814-486-3712 **Fax:** 814-486-1772 www.theriver989.com wlemwqky@yahoo.com

Emporium WQKY-FM (a) 145 E 4th St, Emporium PA 15834 **Phn:** 814-486-3712 **Fax:** 814-486-1772 www.theriver989.com theriver989@yahoo.com

Ephrata WIOV-AM (snt) 44 Bethany Rd, Ephrata PA 17522 **Phn:** 717-738-1191 **Fax:** 717-738-1661 www.wiov985.com hr.harrisburg@cumulus.com

Ephrata WIOV-FM (c) 44 Bethany Rd, Ephrata PA 17522 **Phn:** 717-738-1191 **Fax:** 717-738-1661 www.wiov.com rich.creeger@cumulus.com

Erie WERG-FM (v) 109 University Sq, Erie PA 16541 **Phn:** 814-459-9374 www.wergfm.com laprice002@gannon.edu

Erie WFNN-AM (s) 1 Boston Store Pl, Erie PA 16501 **Phn:** 814-461-1000 **Fax:** 814-461-1500 www.sportsradio1330.com barryandjim@jetradio1400.com

Erie WJET-AM (nt) 1 Boston Store Pl, Erie PA 16501 **Phn:** 814-461-1000 **Fax:** 814-874-0011 jetradio1400.com barryandjim@jetradio1400.com

Erie WMCE-FM (v) 501 E 38th St, Erie PA 16546 **Phn:** 814-824-2294 wmce.mercyhurst.edu dgeary@mercyhurst.edu

Erie WPSE-AM (kn) 4071 College Dr, Erie PA 16563 **Phn:** 814-898-6495

Erie WQHZ-FM (hr) 471 Robison Rd W, Erie PA 16509 **Phn:** 814-868-5355 **Fax:** 814-868-1876 www.z1023online.com jim.riley@cumulus.com

Erie WQLN-FM (plnj) 8425 Peach St, Erie PA 16509 **Phn:** 814-864-3001 **Fax:** 814-864-4077 www.wqln.org dmiller@wqln.org

Erie WRIE-AM (s) 471 Robison Rd W, Erie PA 16509 **Phn:** 814-868-5355 **Fax:** 814-868-1876 www.am1260thescore.com chuck.priestap@cumulus.com

Erie WRKT-FM (r) 1 Boston Store Pl, Erie PA 16501 **Phn:** 814-461-1000 **Fax:** 814-461-1500 www.rocket101.com rocket@rocket101.com

Erie WRTS-FM (h) 1 Boston Store Pl, Erie PA 16501 **Phn:** 814-461-1000 **Fax:** 814-455-6000 www.star104.com

Erie WTWF-FM (c) 1 Boston Store Pl, Erie PA 16501 **Phn:** 814-461-1000 **Fax:** 814-874-0011 www.939thewolf.com greg@connoisseurerie.com

Erie WXBB-FM (a) 1 Boston Store Pl, Erie PA 16501 **Phn:** 814-461-1000 **Fax:** 814-874-0011 www.947bobfm.com

Erie WXKC-FM (a) 471 Robison Rd W, Erie PA 16509 **Phn:** 814-868-5355 **Fax:** 814-868-1876 www.classy100.com ron.arlen@cumulus.com

Erie WXTA-FM (c) 471 Robison Rd, Erie PA 16509 **Phn:** 814-868-5355 **Fax:** 814-868-1876 www.country98wxta.com jim.riley@cumulus.com

Everett WSKE-FM (c) PO Box 133, Everett PA 15537 **Phn:** 814-652-2600 **Fax:** 814-652-9347 wske@penn.com

Everett WZSK-AM (nt) PO Box 133, Everett PA 15537 **Phn:** 814-652-2600 **Fax:** 814-652-9347 wzsk@penn.com

Exeter WITK-AM (o) 944 Exeter Ave, Exeter PA 18643 **Phn:** 570-344-1221 **Fax:** 570-344-0996 www.wilkinsradio.com witk@wilkinsradio.com

Franklin WGYI-FM (c) 484 Allegheny Blvd Ste A, Franklin PA 16323 **Phn:** 814-724-1111 **Fax:** 814-333-9628 www.froggyfun.com kylehendricks44@gmail.com

Franklin WGYY-FM (c) 484 Allegheny Blvd Ste A, Franklin PA 16323 **Phn:** 814-724-1111 **Fax:** 814-333-9628 www.froggyfun.com amy.sasfai@gmail.com

Franklin WOXX-FM (a) 1411 Liberty St, Franklin PA 16323 **Phn:** 814-432-2188 **Fax:** 414-437-9372

Franklin WUUZ-FM (r) 1411 Liberty St, Franklin PA 16323 **Phn:** 814-432-2188 **Fax:** 414-437-9372 www.mywuzz.com amy.sasfai@gmail.com

Gettysburg WGET-AM (ans) 1560 Fairfield Rd, Gettysburg PA 17325 **Phn:** 717-334-3101 **Fax:** 717-334-5822 www.espnradio1320.com

Gettysburg WGTY-FM (c) PO Box 3179, Gettysburg PA 17325 **Phn:** 717-334-3101 **Fax:** 717-334-5822 www.wgty.com news@wgty.com

Gettysburg WZBT-FM (v) Gettysburg Coll Box 435, Gettysburg PA 17325 **Phn:** 717-337-6315

Gibsonia WWNL-AM (q) 5316 William Flynn Hwy Ste 3N, Gibsonia PA 15044 **Phn:** 724-443-4844 www.wilkinsradio.com wwnl@wilkinsradio.com

Grantham WVMM-FM (q) PO Box 3058, Grantham PA 17027 **Phn:** 717-691-6081

Greencastle WAYZ-FM (c) PO Box 788, Greencastle PA 17225 **Phn:** 717-597-9200 **Fax:** 717-597-9210 www.wayz.com info@wayz.com

Greencastle WCBG-AM (snt) PO Box 788, Greencastle PA 17225 **Phn:** 717-597-9200 **Fax:** 717-597-9210

Greencastle WPPT-FM (c) PO Box 788, Greencastle PA 17225 **Phn:** 717-597-9200 **Fax:** 717-597-9210

Greensburg WHJB-FM (or) 2000 Tower Way # 2040, Greensburg PA 15601 **Phn:** 724-216-1200 **Fax:** 724-216-1201 www.whjbfm.com tmichaels@rendabroadcasting.com

Greenville WTGP-FM (v) 75 College Ave, Greenville PA 16125 **Phn:** 724-589-2210 **Fax:** 724-589-2010

Grove City WSAJ-FM (v) 100 Campus Dr, Grove City PA 16127 **Phn:** 724-458-3304 www.wsaj.com feedback@wsaj.com

Hanover WHVR-AM (c) PO Box 234, Hanover PA 17331 **Phn:** 717-637-3831 **Fax:** 717-637-9006

Harrisburg WHGB-AM (s) 2300 Vartan Way, Harrisburg PA 17110 **Phn:** 717-238-1041 **Fax:** 717-234-4842 www.espnradio1400.com john.odea@cumulus.com

Harrisburg WHKF-FM (h) 600 Corporate Cir, Harrisburg PA 17110 **Phn:** 717-540-8800 **Fax:** 717-540-8814 www.993kissfm.com jtbosch@clearchannel.com

Harrisburg WHP-AM (nt) 600 Corporate Cir, Harrisburg PA 17110 **Phn:** 717-540-8800 **Fax:** 717-540-9271 www.whp580.com news@whp580.com

Harrisburg WITF-FM (plnt) 4801 Lindle Rd, Harrisburg PA 17111 **Phn:** 717-704-3000 **Fax:** 717-704-3659 www.witf.org news@witf.org

Harrisburg WKBO-AM (q) 600 Corporate Cir, Harrisburg PA 17110 **Phn:** 717-540-8800 **Fax:** 717-540-8814 www.oneheartministries.comfortress_1230am_wkbo.htm oneheartministries@verizon.net

Harrisburg WNNK-FM (ah) 2300 Vartan Way, Harrisburg PA 17110 **Phn:** 717-238-1041 **Fax:** 717-238-7780 www.wink104.com john.odea@cumulus.com

Harrisburg WRBT-FM (c) 600 Corporate Cir, Harrisburg PA 17110 **Phn:** 717-540-8800 **Fax:** 717-671-9973 www.bob949.com webmaster@bobradio.com

Harrisburg WRVV-FM (a) 600 Corporate Cir, Harrisburg PA 17110 **Phn:** 717-540-8800 **Fax:** 717-540-9268 www.theriver973.com wrvv@river973.com

Harrisburg WTKT-AM (s) 600 Corporate Cir, Harrisburg PA 17110 **Phn:** 717-540-8800 **Fax:** 717-540-8814 www.1460theticket.com 1460theticket@1460theticket.com

Harrisburg WTPA-FM (r) 2300 Vartan Way, Harrisburg PA 17110 **Phn:** 717-238-1041 **Fax:** 717-234-7780

Harrisburg WWKL-FM (h) 2300 Vartan Way, Harrisburg PA 17110 **Phn:** 717-238-1041 **Fax:** 717-234-7780 www.hot935fm.com jenna.clay@cumulus.com

Harrisburg WZCY-FM (c) 2300 Vartan Way # 130, Harrisburg PA 17110 **Phn:** 717-238-1041 www.zcountry1067.com ron.giovanniello@cumulus.com

Hazleton WAZL-AM (m) 8 W Broad St, Hazleton PA 18201 **Phn:** 570-445-1490 **Fax:** 570-501-1112

Hellam WARM-FM (a) 5989 Susquehanna Plaza Dr, Hellam PA 17406 **Phn:** 717-764-1155 **Fax:** 717-252-4708 www.warm103.com bobby.d@cumulus.com

Hellam WSOX-FM (o) 5989 Susquehanna Plaza Dr, Hellam PA 17406 **Phn:** 717-764-1155 **Fax:** 717-252-4708 www.961wsox.com bobby.d@cumulus.com

PENNSYLVANIA RADIO STATIONS

Hermitage WLLF-FM (o) 2030 Pine Hollow Blvd, Hermitage PA 16148 **Phn:** 724-346-4113 **Fax:** 724-981-4545 www.967theriver.com rick.parrish@cumulus.com

Hermitage WPIC-AM (nts) 2030 Pine Hollow Blvd, Hermitage PA 16148 **Phn:** 724-346-4113 **Fax:** 724-981-4545 www.790wpic.com bob.greenburg@cumulus.com

Hollidaysburg WALY-FM (o) 1 Forever Dr, Hollidaysburg PA 16648 **Phn:** 814-941-9800 **Fax:** 814-943-2754 www.waly1039.com bob@waly1039.com

Hollidaysburg WFBG-AM (nt) 1 Forever Dr, Hollidaysburg PA 16648 **Phn:** 814-941-9800 **Fax:** 814-941-7198 www.wfbg.com charlie@wfbg.com

Hollidaysburg WFGY-FM (c) 1 Forever Dr, Hollidaysburg PA 16648 **Phn:** 814-941-9800 **Fax:** 814-941-7198 www.froggyradio.com kelliegreen@froggyradio.com

Hollidaysburg WRKY-FM (r) 1 Forever Dr, Hollidaysburg PA 16648 **Phn:** 814-941-9800 **Fax:** 814-943-2754 www.rocky1049.com tommy@rocky1049.com

Hollidaysburg WVAM-AM (s) 1 Forever Dr, Hollidaysburg PA 16648 **Phn:** 814-941-9800 **Fax:** 814-941-7198 www.wvamam.com charlie@wfbg.com

Hollidaysburg WWOT-FM (h) 1 Forever Dr, Hollidaysburg PA 16648 **Phn:** 814-941-9800 **Fax:** 814-943-2754 www.hot92and100.com tdeitz@96key.com

Honesdale WDNH-FM (ah) 575 Grove St, Honesdale PA 18431 **Phn:** 570-253-1616 **Fax:** 570-253-6297 www.boldgoldlakeregion.com gschmitt@boldgoldmedia.com

Honesdale WPSN-AM (nt) 575 Grove St, Honesdale PA 18431 **Phn:** 570-253-1616 **Fax:** 570-253-6297 www.boldgoldlakeregion.com gschmitt@boldgoldmedia.com

Honesdale WYCY-FM (h) 575 Grove St, Honesdale PA 18431 **Phn:** 570-253-1616 **Fax:** 570-253-6297 www.boldgoldlakeregion.com gschmitt@boldgoldmedia.com

Hunlock Creek WRGN-FM (q) 2457 State Route 118, Hunlock Creek PA 18621 **Phn:** 570-477-3688 **Fax:** 570-477-2310 www.wrgn.com wrgn@epix.net

Huntingdon WKVR-FM (vr) 1700 Moore St Box 1005, Huntingdon PA 16652 **Phn:** 814-641-9587

Indiana WCCS-AM (a) 840 Philadelphia St Ste 100, Indiana PA 15701 **Phn:** 724-465-4700 **Fax:** 724-349-6842 www.1160wccs.com jdecesare@rendabroadcasting.com

Indiana WDAD-AM (ot) 840 Philadelphia St Ste 100, Indiana PA 15701 **Phn:** 724-465-4700 **Fax:** 724-349-6842 www.wdadradio.com nruffner@rendabroadcasting.com

Indiana WLCY-FM (c) 840 Philadelphia St Ste 100, Indiana PA 15701 **Phn:** 724-465-4700 **Fax:** 724-349-6842 www.country1063fm.com nruffner@rendabroadcasting.com

Indiana WQMU-FM (hr) 840 Philadelphia St Ste 100, Indiana PA 15701 **Phn:** 724-465-4700 **Fax:** 724-349-6842 www.u92radio.com jsmathers@rendabroadcasting.com

Jersey Shore WJSA-FM (q) 262 Allegheny St Ste 4, Jersey Shore PA 17740 **Phn:** 570-398-7200 **Fax:** 570-398-7201 www.wjsaradio.com wjsaradio@aol.com

Jersey Shore WJSA-AM (q) 262 Allegheny St Ste 4, Jersey Shore PA 17740 **Phn:** 570-398-7200 **Fax:** 570-398-7201 www.wjsaradio.com mail@wjsaradio.com

Johnstown WBHV-AM (s) 970 Tripoli St, Johnstown PA 15902 **Phn:** 814-534-8975 **Fax:** 814-266-9212

Johnstown WCCL-FM (o) 970 Tripoli St, Johnstown PA 15902 **Phn:** 814-534-8975 **Fax:** 814-534-8979 cool101online.com nferrara@resultsradiopa.com

Johnstown WFGI-FM (c) 109 Plaza Dr, Johnstown PA 15905 **Phn:** 814-255-4186 **Fax:** 814-255-6145 www.myfroggy95.com lmosby@myfroggy95.com

Johnstown WFRJ-FM (q) 2714 William Penn Ave # 5, Johnstown PA 15909 **Phn:** 814-322-3144

Johnstown WKYE-FM (a) 109 Plaza Dr, Johnstown PA 15905 **Phn:** 814-255-4186 **Fax:** 814-255-6145 www.96key.com jmichaels@96key.com

Johnstown WLKH-FM (q) 109 Plaza Dr, Johnstown PA 15905 **Phn:** 814-255-4186 **Fax:** 814-255-6145

Johnstown WNTJ-AM (nt) 109 Plaza Dr, Johnstown PA 15905 **Phn:** 814-255-4186 **Fax:** 814-255-6145 bossfrog@myfroggy95.com

Johnstown WNTW-AM (nt) 109 Plaza Dr, Johnstown PA 15905 **Phn:** 814-255-4186 **Fax:** 814-255-6145 www.ntjnetwork.com tdeitz@96key.com

Johnstown WRKW-FM (r) 109 Plaza Dr, Johnstown PA 15905 **Phn:** 814-255-4186 **Fax:** 814-255-6145 www.rocky99.com mstevens@rocky99.com

Kane WXMT-FM (c) 29 S Fraley St, Kane PA 16735 **Phn:** 814-837-9564 **Fax:** 814-975-1078

Kittanning WTYM-AM (o) 114 S Jefferson St, Kittanning PA 16201 **Phn:** 724-543-1380 **Fax:** 724-543-1140

Lafayette Hill WFIL-AM (qt) 117 Ridge Pike, Lafayette Hill PA 19444 **Phn:** 610-941-9560 **Fax:** 610-828-8879 www.wfil.com wfil@wfil.com

Lafayette Hill WNTP-AM (t) 117 Ridge Pike, Lafayette Hill PA 19444 **Phn:** 610-940-0990 **Fax:** 610-828-8879 www.wntp.com contactus@wntp.com

Lancaster WDAC-FM (q) PO Box 3022, Lancaster PA 17604 **Phn:** 717-284-4123 **Fax:** 717-284-1000 www.wdac.com postmaster@wdac.com

Lancaster WFNM-FM (var) PO Box 3220, Lancaster PA 17604 **Phn:** 717-291-4096 **Fax:** 717-358-4437 wfnm.org dan.lewis@fandm.edu

Lancaster WLAN-AM (t) 1685 Crown Ave Ste 100, Lancaster PA 17601 **Phn:** 717-295-9700 **Fax:** 717-295-7329 www.1390wlan.com

Lancaster WLAN-FM (h) 1685 Crown Ave Ste 100, Lancaster PA 17601 **Phn:** 717-295-9700 **Fax:** 717-295-7329 www.fm97.com billmead@clearchannel.com

Lancaster WLCH-FM (vy) 453 S Lime St #D, Lancaster PA 17602 **Phn:** 717-295-7996 **Fax:** 717-295-7759 wlchradio.org cgaldamez@sacapa.org

Lancaster WLPA-AM (sn) PO Box 4368, Lancaster PA 17604 **Phn:** 717-653-0800 **Fax:** 717-653-0122 www.wlpa.com suesen@hallradio.com

Lancaster WROZ-FM (a) PO Box 4368, Lancaster PA 17604 **Phn:** 717-653-0800 **Fax:** 717-653-0122 www.roseradio.com wroz@hallradio.com

Lansdale WNPV-AM (ant) PO Box 1440, Lansdale PA 19446 **Phn:** 215-855-8211 **Fax:** 215-368-0180 www.wnpv1440.com phunt@wnpv1440.com

Lansford WLSH-AM (z) PO Box D, Lansford PA 18232 **Phn:** 570-645-3123 **Fax:** 570-645-2159 www.wmgh.com businessoffice@wmgh.com

Lansford WMGH-FM (a) PO Box D, Lansford PA 18232 **Phn:** 570-668-2992 **Fax:** 570-645-2159 www.wmgh.com businessoffice@wmgh.com

Latrobe WCNS-AM (os) 400 Unity St Ste 200, Latrobe PA 15650 **Phn:** 724-537-3338 **Fax:** 724-539-9798 www.1480wcns.com mailbox@wcnsradio.com

Latrobe WQTW-AM (o) PO Box 208, Latrobe PA 15650 **Phn:** 724-532-1778 **Fax:** 724-532-1779

Lebanon WLBR-AM (nt) RR 72, Lebanon PA 17046 **Phn:** 717-272-7651 **Fax:** 717-274-0161

Lebanon WQIC-FM (a) North Rte 72, Lebanon PA 17046 **Phn:** 717-272-7651 **Fax:** 717-274-0161

Levittown WBCB-AM (stb) 200 Magnolia Dr, Levittown PA 19054 **Phn:** 215-949-1490 **Fax:** 215-949-3671 www.wbcb1490.com wendy@wbcb1490.com

Lewisburg WGRC-FM (q) 101 Armory Blvd, Lewisburg PA 17837 **Phn:** 570-523-1190 **Fax:** 570-523-1114 www.wgrc.com email@wgrc.com

Lewisburg WVBU-FM (vr) Bucknell Univ Box C-3956, Lewisburg PA 17837 **Phn:** 570-577-1174 www.wvbu.com wvbumd@yahoo.com

Lewistown WIEZ-AM (nt) PO Box 667, Lewistown PA 17044 **Phn:** 717-248-6757 **Fax:** 717-248-6759 new.wiez.com news@merfradio.com

Lewistown WLAK-FM (a) 12 E Market St Fl 2, Lewistown PA 17044 **Phn:** 717-248-6757 **Fax:** 717-248-6759 new.merfradio.com news@merfradio.com

Lewistown WMRF-FM (a) PO Box 667, Lewistown PA 17044 **Phn:** 717-248-6757 **Fax:** 717-248-6759 new.merfradio.com marylee@merfradio.com

Lewistown WVNW-FM (c) PO Box 911, Lewistown PA 17044 **Phn:** 717-242-1493 **Fax:** 717-242-3764 star967.com wvnw@star967.com

Lock Haven WBPZ-AM (o) 21 E Main St, Lock Haven PA 17745 **Phn:** 570-748-4038 **Fax:** 570-748-0092

Manheim WJTL-FM (q) 1875 Junction Rd, Manheim PA 17545 **Phn:** 717-392-3690 **Fax:** 717-459-3710 wjtl.com contact@wjtl.com

Manheim WKZF-FM (r) 1996 Auction Rd, Manheim PA 17545 **Phn:** 717-653-0800 **Fax:** 717-653-0122 www.927kzf.com webmaster@927kzf.com

Mansfield WDKC-FM (c) PO Box 1015, Mansfield PA 16933 **Phn:** 570-662-9000 **Fax:** 570-324-1015 kc101@frontier.com

Mansfield WNTE-FM (vrh) Mansfield Univ South Hall, Mansfield PA 16933 **Phn:** 570-662-4653 www.wnte.com

Martinsburg WJSM-FM (g) 724 Rebecca Furnace Rd, Martinsburg PA 16662 **Phn:** 814-793-2188 **Fax:** 814-793-9727 www.wjsm.com wjsmradio@gmail.com

Martinsburg WJSM-AM (q) 724 Rebecca Furnace Rd, Martinsburg PA 16662 **Phn:** 814-793-2188 **Fax:** 814-793-9727 www.wjsm.com wjsmradio@gmail.com

McElhattan WQBR-FM (c) PO Box 135, McElhattan PA 17748 **Phn:** 570-769-2327 **Fax:** 570-769-7746 www.bear999.com bear@kcnet.org

Meadville WARC-FM (v) 520 N Main St, Meadville PA 16335 **Phn:** 814-332-3376 sites.allegheny.eduwarc warc@allegheny.edu

Meadville WFRA-FM (m) 900 Water St, Meadville PA 16335 **Phn:** 14-432-2188 **Fax:** 414-437-9372 myantsnetwork.com wmgwboss@yahoo.com

Meadville WMGW-AM (st) 900 Water St, Meadville PA 16335 **Phn:** 814-724-1111 **Fax:** 814-333-9628 myantsnetwork.com wmgwboss@yahoo.com

Meadville WMVL-FM (sr) PO Box 846, Meadville PA 16335 **Phn:** 814-337-8440 **Fax:** 814-333-2562 www.cool1017online.com

Meadville WTIV-AM (nt) 900 Water St, Meadville PA 16335 **Phn:** 814-432-2188 **Fax:** 317-736-4781 myantsnetwork.com wmgwboss@yahoo.com

Meadville WXXO-FM (a) 900 Water St, Meadville PA 16335 **Phn:** 814-724-1111 **Fax:** 814-333-9628

Mexico WJUN-AM (s) PO Box 209, Mexico PA 17056 **Phn:** 717-436-2135 **Fax:** 717-436-8155 wjun@nmax.net

Mexico WJUN-FM (c) PO Box 209, Mexico PA 17056 **Phn:** 717-436-2135 **Fax:** 717-436-8155 wjun925.com wjun@nmax.net

Mexico WLZS-FM (o) Old Route 22 East, Mexico PA 17056 **Phn:** 717-436-2135 **Fax:** 717-436-8155 wheels1061.com wheels@wheels1061.com

Meyersdale WQZS-FM (o) PO Box 218, Meyersdale PA 15552 **Phn:** 814-634-9111 **Fax:** 814-634-0882 helenwahl27@hotmail.com

Millersburg WQLV-FM (a) PO Box 158, Millersburg PA 17061 **Phn:** 717-692-9758 **Fax:** 717-692-2080 www.wqlvfm.com bob@wqlvfm.com

Millersville WIXQ-FM (v) Millersville Univ, Millersville PA 17551 **Phn:** 717-872-3518 **Fax:** 717-872-3383 www.wixq.com comments@wixq.com

Montrose WPEL-AM (g) PO Box 248, Montrose PA 18801 **Phn:** 570-278-2811 **Fax:** 570-278-1442 www.wpel.org mail@wpel.org

Montrose WPEL-FM (q) PO Box 248, Montrose PA 18801 **Phn:** 570-278-2811 **Fax:** 570-278-1442 www.wpel.org mail@wpel.org

Nanticoke WSFX-FM (v) Luzerne Co Comm College, Nanticoke PA 18634 **Phn:** 570-740-0634 **Fax:** 570-740-0605

New Castle WJST-AM (s) 219 Savannah Gardner Rd, New Castle PA 16101 **Phn:** 724-654-5502 jthomas95@yahoo.com

New Castle WKST-AM (nt) 219 Savannah Gardner Rd, New Castle PA 16101 **Phn:** 724-654-5502 www.wkst.com khlebovy@foreverradio.com

New Castle WWGY-FM (c) 219 Savannah Gardner Rd, New Castle PA 16101 **Phn:** 724-654-5502 **Fax:** 724-654-3101 jthomas95@yahoo.com

New Kensington WGBN-AM (gw) 560 7th St, New Kensington PA 15068 **Phn:** 724-337-3588 **Fax:** 724-337-1318 wgbn.net

New Wilmington WWNW-FM (vhr) Westminster Coll Box 89, New Wilmington PA 16142 **Phn:** 724-946-7242 **Fax:** 724-946-7070 www.westminster.eduacadcommradio titanradio@westminster.edu

Norristown WNAP-AM (wg) 2311 Old Arch Rd, Norristown PA 19401 **Phn:** 610-272-7600 **Fax:** 610-272-5793 www.wnap1110am.com fred@wnap1110am.com

North Versailles WKFB-AM (m) 1918 Lincoln Hwy, North Versailles PA 15137 **Phn:** 412-823-7000

North Versailles WKHB-AM (m) 1918 Lincoln Hwy, North Versailles PA 15137 **Phn:** 412-823-7000

Oil City WKQW-AM (s) 806 C Grandview Rd, Oil City PA 16301 **Phn:** 814-676-8254 **Fax:** 814-677-4272 www.venangocountydailynews.com kqwtraffic@usachoice.net

Oil City WKQW-FM (a) 806 C Grandview Rd, Oil City PA 16301 **Phn:** 814-676-8254 **Fax:** 814-677-4272 www.venangocountydailynews.com kqwtraffic@usachoice.net

Olean WVTT-FM (c) 1 Bluebird Sq, Olean NY 14760 **Phn:** 716-372-9564 bigboblive.com news@colonialme.com

Palmyra WWSM-AM (c) 277 Gravel Hill Rd, Palmyra PA 17078 **Phn:** 717-272-1510 **Fax:** 717-832-0209 www.wwsm.us news@wwsm.us

Philadelphia KYW-AM (n) 400 Market St Fl 9, Philadelphia PA 19106 **Phn:** 215-238-2000 **Fax:** 215-238-4657 philadelphia.cbslocal.com newstips@kyw1060info.com

Philadelphia WEMG-AM (y) 1341 N Delaware Ave Ste 509, Philadelphia PA 19125 **Phn:** 215-426-1900 **Fax:** 215-426-1550 davidsonmediagroup.com jyoung@davidsonmediagroup.com

Philadelphia WHYY-FM (tnl) 150 N 6th St, Philadelphia PA 19106 **Phn:** 215-351-1200 **Fax:** 215-351-3352 www.whyy.org newsroom@whyy.org

Philadelphia WKDU-FM (vr) 3210 Chestnut St, Philadelphia PA 19104 **Phn:** 215-895-5920 www.wkdu.org program@wkdu.org

Philadelphia WPHE-AM (nty) PO Box 46325, Philadelphia PA 19160 **Phn:** 215-291-7532 **Fax:** 215-739-1337 www.radiosalvacion.com

Philadelphia WRTI-FM (jl) 1509 Cecil B Moore Ave 3rd Fl, Philadelphia PA 19121 **Phn:** 215-204-8405 **Fax:** 215-204-7027 www.wrti.org programming@wrti.org

Philadelphia WURD-AM (wt) 1341 N Delaware Ave Ste 300, Philadelphia PA 19125 **Phn:** 215-425-7875 **Fax:** 215-634-6003 900amwurd.com 900amwurd@wurdradio.com

Philadelphia WXPN-FM (par) 3025 Walnut St, Philadelphia PA 19104 **Phn:** 215-898-6677 **Fax:** 215-898-0707 www.xpn.org wxpndesk@xpn.org

Pittsburgh KDKA-AM (nt) 1 Gateway Ctr, Pittsburgh PA 15229 **Phn:** 412-575-2200 **Fax:** 412-575-2845 pittsburgh.cbslocal.com radionews@kdka.com

Pittsburgh KQV-AM (n) 650 Smithfield St, Pittsburgh PA 15222 **Phn:** 412-562-5900 **Fax:** 412-562-5903 www.kqv.com kqvnews@kqv.com

Pittsburgh WBGG-AM (s) 200 Fleet St 4th Fl, Pittsburgh PA 15220 **Phn:** 412-937-1441 **Fax:** 412-937-0323 www.970espn.com davidedgar@clearchannel.com

Pittsburgh WBZW-FM (h) 651 Holiday Dr, Pittsburgh PA 15220 **Phn:** 412-920-9400 **Fax:** 412-920-9444

Pittsburgh WDSY-FM (c) 651 Holiday Dr Ste 2, Pittsburgh PA 15220 **Phn:** 412-920-9400 **Fax:** 412-920-9444 y108.cbslocal.com mark.anderson@cbsradio.com

Pittsburgh WDUQ-FM (pnj) 600 Forbes Ave, Pittsburgh PA 15219 **Phn:** 412-396-6030 **Fax:** 412-396-5061

Pittsburgh WDVE-FM (r) 200 Fleet St Ste 400, Pittsburgh PA 15220 **Phn:** 412-937-1441 **Fax:** 412-937-0323 www.dve.com elunch@dve.com

Pittsburgh WEAE-AM (s) 400 Ardmore Blvd, Pittsburgh PA 15221 **Phn:** 412-731-1250 **Fax:** 412-244-4596 espn.com

Pittsburgh WESA-FM (p) 67 Bedford Sq, Pittsburgh PA 15203 **Phn:** 412-381-9131 **Fax:** 412-381-9126 wesa.fm news@wesa.fm

Pittsburgh WJAS-AM (ob) 900 Parish St Ste 300, Pittsburgh PA 15220 **Phn:** 412-875-4800 **Fax:** 412-875-9970 www.1320wjas.com rantill@1320wjas.com

Pittsburgh WKST-FM (h) 200 Fleet St 4th Fl, Pittsburgh PA 15220 **Phn:** 412-937-1441 **Fax:** 412-937-0323 www.961kiss.com ginasuiter@clearchannel.com

Pittsburgh WLTJ-FM (a) 650 Smithfield St Ste 2200, Pittsburgh PA 15222 **Phn:** 412-316-3342 **Fax:** 412-316-3388 www.q929fm.com qfeedback@q929fm.com

Pittsburgh WMNY-AM (kt) 900 Parish St 3rd Fl, Pittsburgh PA 15220 **Phn:** 412-875-4800 **Fax:** 412-875-9474 www.wmnyradio.com rantill@rendabroadcasting.com

Pittsburgh WOGI-FM (c) 100 Ryan Ct # 98, Pittsburgh PA 15205 **Phn:** 412-279-5400 **Fax:** 412-279-5500 www.froggyland.com danthony@keymarketradio.com

Pittsburgh WORD-FM (q) 7 Parkway Ctr Ste 625, Pittsburgh PA 15220 **Phn:** 412-937-1500 **Fax:** 412-937-1576 www.wordfm.com word@wordfm.com

Pittsburgh WPGB-FM (nt) 200 Fleet St 4th Fl, Pittsburgh PA 15220 **Phn:** 412-937-1441 **Fax:** 412-937-0323 www.wpgb.com davidedgar@clearchannel.com

Pittsburgh WPIT-AM (q) 7 Parkway Ctr Ste 625, Pittsburgh PA 15220 **Phn:** 412-937-1500 **Fax:** 412-937-1576 www.wpitam.com word2@wordfm.com

Pittsburgh WPTS-FM (v) 411 William Pitt Un, Pittsburgh PA 15260 **Phn:** 412-648-7990 **Fax:** 412-648-7988 www.wpts.pitt.edu wpts@pitt.edu

Pittsburgh WQED-FM (pl) 4802 5th Ave Ste 1, Pittsburgh PA 15213 **Phn:** 412-622-1300 **Fax:** 412-622-1488 www.wqed.orgfm

Pittsburgh WRCT-FM (v) 5000 Forbes Ave, Pittsburgh PA 15213 **Phn:** 412-621-0728 www.wrct.org info@wrct.org

Pittsburgh WRRK-FM (ah) 650 Smithfield St Ste 2200, Pittsburgh PA 15222 **Phn:** 412-316-3342 **Fax:** 412-316-3388 www.bobfm969.com feedback@bobfm969.com

Pittsburgh WSHH-FM (a) 900 Parish St 3rd Fl, Pittsburgh PA 15220 **Phn:** 412-875-4800 **Fax:** 412-875-9970 www.wshh.com rantill@wshh.com

Pittsburgh WWCS-AM (m) 400 Ardmore Blvd, Pittsburgh PA 15221 **Phn:** 412-244-4586 **Fax:** 412-244-4409 music.disney.com

Pittsburgh WWSW-FM (o) 200 Fleet St 4th Fl, Pittsburgh PA 15220 **Phn:** 412-937-1441 **Fax:** 412-937-0323 www.3wsradio.com davidedgar@clearchannel.com

Pittsburgh WXDX-FM (r) 200 Fleet St 4th Fl, Pittsburgh PA 15220 **Phn:** 412-937-1441 **Fax:** 412-937-0323 www.1059thex.com mosh@wxdx.com

Pittsburgh WZPT-FM (a) 651 Holiday Dr Ste 310, Pittsburgh PA 15220 **Phn:** 412-920-9400 **Fax:** 412-920-9444 starpittsburgh.cbslocal.com mark.anderson@cbsradio.com

Pittston WBZU-AM (nt) 305 Route 315 Hwy, Pittston PA 18640 **Phn:** 570-883-9800 **Fax:** 570-883-9851 www.wilknewsradio.com shenry@entercom.com

Pittston WDMT-FM (h) 305 Route 315 Hwy, Pittston PA 18640 **Phn:** 570-883-9850 **Fax:** 570-883-9851 www.themountain985.com feedbackwdmt@102themountain.com

Pittston WGGY-FM (c) 305 Route 315 Hwy, Pittston PA 18640 **Phn:** 570-883-1111 **Fax:** 570-883-1360 www.froggy101.com feedbackwggy@entercom.com

Pittston WILK-AM (snt) 305 Route 315 Hwy, Pittston PA 18640 **Phn:** 570-883-9800 **Fax:** 570-883-9851 www.wilknewsradio.com nkman@entercom.com

Pittston WILK-FM (nt) 305 Route 315 Hwy, Pittston PA 18640 **Phn:** 570-883-9800 **Fax:** 570-883-9851 www.wilknewsradio.com nkman@entercom.com

Pittston WKRF-FM (h) 305 Route 315 Hwy, Pittston PA 18640 **Phn:** 570-883-9800 **Fax:** 570-883-9851 www.985krz.com modonnell@entercom.com

Pittston WKRZ-FM (h) 305 Route 315 Hwy, Pittston PA 18640 **Phn:** 570-883-9850 **Fax:** 570-883-9851 www.wkrz.com jwydra@entercom.com

Pittston WKZN-AM (nt) 305 Route 315 Hwy, Pittston PA 18640 **Phn:** 570-883-9800 **Fax:** 570-883-9851 www.wilknewsradio.com nancy@wilknewsradio.com

PENNSYLVANIA RADIO STATIONS

Port Allegany WHKS-FM (a) 42 N Main St, Port Allegany PA 16743 **Phn:** 814-642-7004 **Fax:** 814-642-9491 www.whksradio.com whks@verizon.net

Pottstown WPAZ-AM (o) 224 Maugers Mill Rd, Pottstown PA 19464 **Phn:** 610-326-4000 **Fax:** 610-326-7984

Pottsville WAVT-FM (h) 212 S Centre St Ste 1, Pottsville PA 17901 **Phn:** 570-622-1360 **Fax:** 570-622-2822 www.t102radio.com deb@pbcradio.com

Pottsville WPAM-AM (r) 1450 Lawtons Hl, Pottsville PA 17901 **Phn:** 570-622-1450 **Fax:** 570-622-4690

Pottsville WPPA-AM (a) PO Box 540, Pottsville PA 17901 **Phn:** 570-622-1360 **Fax:** 570-622-2822 wpparadio.com news@pbcradio.com

Punxsutawney WECZ-AM (am) 904 N Main St, Punxsutawney PA 15767 **Phn:** 814-938-6000 **Fax:** 814-938-4237 www.rendabroadcasting.com jhill@rendabroadcasting.com

Punxsutawney WKQL-FM (r) 904 N Main St, Punxsutawney PA 15767 **Phn:** 814-938-6000 **Fax:** 814-938-4237 www.kool1033fm.com jhill@rendabroadcasting.com

Punxsutawney WPXZ-FM (ar) 904 N Main St, Punxsutawney PA 15767 **Phn:** 814-938-6000 **Fax:** 814-938-4237 www.wpxz1041fm.com mcarroll@rendabroadcasting.com

Punxsutawney WYTR-FM (o) 904 N Main St, Punxsutawney PA 15767 **Phn:** 814-938-6000 **Fax:** 814-938-4237 jhill@rendabroadcasting.com

Reading WEEU-AM (at) 34 N 4th St, Reading PA 19601 **Phn:** 610-376-7335 **Fax:** 610-376-7756 www.weeu.com weeu@weeu.com

Reading WRAW-AM (o) 1265 Perkiomen Ave, Reading PA 19602 **Phn:** 610-376-6671 **Fax:** 610-376-1270 www.1340wraw.com alburke@wrfy.com

Reading WRFY-FM (rh) 1265 Perkiomen Ave, Reading PA 19602 **Phn:** 610-376-6671 **Fax:** 610-376-1270 www.y102reading.com al@wrfy.com

Reading WXAC-FM (vr) 1621 N 13th St, Reading PA 19604 **Phn:** 610-921-7545 wxac.squarespace.com wxac@albright.edu

Renovo WZYY-FM (r) 240 11th St, Renovo PA 17764 **Phn:** 570-923-9106

Ridgway WDDH-FM (c) 14902 Boot Jack Rd, Ridgway PA 15853 **Phn:** 814-772-9700 **Fax:** 814-772-9750 www.houndcountry.com becky@houndcountry.com

Ridgway WKBI-FM (a) PO Box O, Ridgway PA 15853 **Phn:** 814-834-2821 **Fax:** 814-772-9750 www.wkbiradio.com info@wkbiradio.com

Ridgway WKBI-AM (am) PO Box O, Ridgway PA 15853 **Phn:** 814-772-9700 **Fax:** 814-772-9750 www.wkbiradio.com info@wkbiradio.com

Sarver WAVL-AM (q) 120 Beale Rd, Sarver PA 16055 **Phn:** 724-295-2000 **Fax:** 724-295-9009 www.liberty910.com

Sayre WATS-AM (a) 204 Desmond St, Sayre PA 18840 **Phn:** 570-888-7745 **Fax:** 570-888-9005 www.choice102.com sherie@choice102.com

Sayre WAVR-FM (a) 204 Desmond St, Sayre PA 18840 **Phn:** 570-888-7745 **Fax:** 570-888-9005 www.watswavr.com chuckc@choice102.com

Schnecksville WXLV-FM (v) 4525 Education Park Dr, Schnecksville PA 18078 **Phn:** 610-799-4141 www.wxlvradio.com bbeard@lccc.edu

Scranton WBAX-AM (s) 149 Penn Ave Ste 1, Scranton PA 18503 **Phn:** 570-207-8599 **Fax:** 570-346-6038 www.nepasespnradio.com elogan@shamrocknepa.com

Scranton WEJL-AM (s) 149 Penn Ave, Scranton PA 18503 **Phn:** 570-207-8599 **Fax:** 570-346-6038 www.nepasespnradio.com elogan@shamrocknepa.com

Scranton WEZX-FM (r) 149 Penn Ave Ste 1, Scranton PA 18503 **Phn:** 570-346-6555 **Fax:** 570-346-6038 www.rock107.com ruthmiller107@msn.com

Scranton WICK-AM (o) 1049 N Sekol Ave, Scranton PA 18504 **Phn:** 570-344-1221 **Fax:** 570-344-0996

Scranton WQFM-FM (o) 149 Penn Ave Ste 1, Scranton PA 18503 **Phn:** 570-346-6555 **Fax:** 570-346-6038 www.newcoolfm.com elogan@shamrocknepa.com

Scranton WQFN-FM (o) 149 Penn Ave, Scranton PA 18503 **Phn:** 570-346-6555 **Fax:** 570-346-6038 www.newcoolfm.com elogan@shamrocknepa.com

Scranton WUSR-FM (vrj) 800 Linden St, Scranton PA 18510 **Phn:** 570-941-4279 www.wusrfm.com wusrfm@scranton.edu

Scranton WWRR-FM (a) 1049 N Sekol Ave, Scranton PA 18504 **Phn:** 570-344-1221 **Fax:** 570-344-0996 boldgoldradionepa.com bspinelli@boldgoldmedia.com

Scranton WYCK-AM (o) 1049 N Sekol Ave, Scranton PA 18504 **Phn:** 570-344-1221 **Fax:** 570-344-0996 bspinelli@boldgoldmedia.com

Selinsgrove WLGL-FM (c) PO Box 90, Selinsgrove PA 17870 **Phn:** 570-374-8819 **Fax:** 570-374-9856 b983.com smarx@ptd.net

Selinsgrove WQSU-FM (v) 514 University Ave, Selinsgrove PA 17870 **Phn:** 570-372-4030 **Fax:** 570-372-2757 www.susqu.eduwqsu-fm wqsunews@gmail.com

Selinsgrove WWBE-FM (c) PO Box 90, Selinsgrove PA 17870 **Phn:** 570-374-8819 **Fax:** 570-374-7444 www.bigcountrynow.com bigcountryrequest@hotmail.com

Selinsgrove WYGL-AM (c) PO Box 90, Selinsgrove PA 17870 **Phn:** 570-374-8819 **Fax:** 570-374-7444

Selinsgrove WYGL-FM (c) 450 Route 204, Selinsgrove PA 17870 **Phn:** 570-374-8819 **Fax:** 570-374-7444 983b.com cpierson@ptd.net

Shippensburg WSYC-FM (vr) 1871 Old Main Dr 3rd Fl, Shippensburg PA 17257 **Phn:** 717-532-6006 **Fax:** 717-477-4024 clubs.ship.eduWSYC wsycgm@ship.edu

Slippery Rock WRSK-FM (v) PO Box C-211, Slippery Rock PA 16057 **Phn:** 724-738-2931 wrsk@sru.edu

State College WBLF-AM (snt) 315 S Atherton St, State College PA 16801 **Phn:** 814-272-1320 wblfproduction@yahoo.com

State College WBUS-FM (r) 2551 Park Center Blvd, State College PA 16801 **Phn:** 814-237-9800 **Fax:** 814-237-2477 www.thebus.net businfo@thebus.net

State College WJOW-FM (r) 315 S Atherton St, State College PA 16801 **Phn:** 814-272-1320 **Fax:** 814-272-3291 1059qwikrock.com

State College WMAJ-FM (a) 2551 Park Center Blvd, State College PA 16801 **Phn:** 814-237-9800 **Fax:** 814-237-2477 jer477@gmail.com

State College WOWY-FM (o) 160 Clearview Ave, State College PA 16803 **Phn:** 814-238-5085 **Fax:** 814-238-7932 wowyonline.com wowyonline@gmail.com

State College WQWK-AM (s) 2551 Park Center Blvd, State College PA 16801 **Phn:** 814-237-9800 **Fax:** 814-237-2477 www.1450espnradio.com wmaj@comcast.net

State College WQWK-FM (r) 2551 Park Center Blvd, State College PA 16801 **Phn:** 814-237-9800 **Fax:** 814-237-2477

State College WRSC-AM (snt) 2551 Park Center Blvd, State College PA 16801 **Phn:** 814-237-9800 **Fax:** 814-237-2477

State College WTLR-FM (q) 2020 Cato Ave, State College PA 16801 **Phn:** 814-237-9857 cpci.org wtlrnews@cpci.org

State College WZWW-FM (a) 863 Benner Pike # 200, State College PA 16801 **Phn:** 814-231-0953 **Fax:** 814-231-0950 www.3wzradio.com nancy@3wz.com

Stroudsburg WSBG-FM (a) 22 S 6th St, Stroudsburg PA 18360 **Phn:** 570-421-2100 **Fax:** 570-421-2040 www.935sbg.com rbauman@935sbg.com

Stroudsburg WVPO-AM (nt) 22 S 6th St, Stroudsburg PA 18360 **Phn:** 570-421-2100 **Fax:** 570-421-2040

Sunbury WEGH-FM (h) PO Box 1070, Sunbury PA 17801 **Phn:** 570-286-5838 **Fax:** 570-743-7837 www.eagle107.com newsroom@wkok.com

Sunbury WKOK-AM (n) PO Box 1070, Sunbury PA 17801 **Phn:** 570-286-5838 **Fax:** 570-743-7837 www.wqkx.com drewk@wqkx.com

Sunbury WMLP-AM (t) PO Box 1070, Sunbury PA 17801 **Phn:** 570-286-5838 **Fax:** 570-743-7837 www.wqkx.com1380_WMLP sbartlett@wkok.com

Sunbury WQKX-FM (a) PO Box 1070, Sunbury PA 17801 **Phn:** 570-286-5838 **Fax:** 570-743-7837 www.wkok.com haddon@wqkx.com

Sunbury WVLY-FM (a) PO Box 1070, Sunbury PA 17801 **Phn:** 570-286-5838 **Fax:** 570-743-7837 newsroom@wkok.com

Swarthmore WSRN-FM (v) 500 College Ave, Swarthmore PA 19081 **Phn:** 610-328-8340 www.wsrnfm.org

Troy WHGL-FM (c) PO Box 100, Troy PA 16947 **Phn:** 570-297-0100 **Fax:** 570-297-3193 www.wiggle100.com mikepowers@wiggle100.com

Troy WTTC-AM (o) 1233 Redington Ave, Troy PA 16947 **Phn:** 570-268-9882 **Fax:** 570-297-3193

Troy WTTC-FM (o) 1233 Redington Ave, Troy PA 16947 **Phn:** 570-268-9882 **Fax:** 570-297-3193 www.953thebridge.com thebridgefm@frontiernet.net

Troy WTZN-AM (s) PO Box 100, Troy PA 16947 **Phn:** 570-297-0100 **Fax:** 570-297-3193 www.wtzn.com trueoldieschannel@wtzn.com

Tyrone WTRN-AM (z) 101 Washington Ave, Tyrone PA 16686 **Phn:** 814-684-3200 **Fax:** 814-684-1220 www.wtrn.net amnnet@aol.com

Uniontown WMBS-AM (am) 44 S Mount Vernon Ave, Uniontown PA 15401 **Phn:** 724-438-3900 **Fax:** 724-438-2406 www.wmbs590.com news@wmbs590.com

University Park WKPS-FM (v) 125 Hub Robeson Ctr, University Park PA 16802 **Phn:** 814-865-9577 **Fax:** 814-865-2751 thelion.fm lion-officers@psu.edu

Villanova WXVU-FM (v) 800 E Lancaster Ave, Villanova PA 19085 **Phn:** 610-519-7200 **Fax:** 610-519-7956 www.wxvufm.com villanova.radio@gmail.com

Warminster WRDV-FM (v) PO Box 2012, Warminster PA 18974 **Phn:** 215-674-8002 www.wrdv.org info@wrdv.org

Warren WKNB-FM (c) PO Box 824, Warren PA 16365 **Phn:** 814-723-1310 **Fax:** 814-723-3356 www.kibcoradio.com info@kibcoradio.com

Warren WNAE-AM (an) PO Box 824, Warren PA 16365 **Phn:** 814-723-1310 **Fax:** 814-723-3356 www.kibcoradio.com info@kibcoradio.com

Warren WRRN-FM (o) PO Box 824, Warren PA 16365 **Phn:** 814-723-1310 **Fax:** 814-723-3356 www.kibcoradio.com info@kibcoradio.com

Washington WJPA-AM (orn) 98 S Main St, Washington PA 15301 **Phn:** 724-222-2110 **Fax:** 724-228-2299 www.wjpa.com news@wjpa.com

Washington WJPA-FM (orn) 98 S Main St, Washington PA 15301 **Phn:** 724-222-2110 **Fax:** 724-228-2299 www.wjpa.com pete@wjpa.com

Washington WNJR-FM (vr) 60 S Lincoln St, Washington PA 15301 **Phn:** 724-223-6039 https:sakai.washjeff.eduwikiwnjrHome.html programming@wnjr.org

Waterford WCTL-FM (q) 10912 Route 19 N, Waterford PA 16441 **Phn:** 814-796-6000 **Fax:** 814-796-3200 www.wctl.org afrase@wctl.org

Waynesburg WANB-AM (c) 369 Tower Rd, Waynesburg PA 15370 **Phn:** 724-627-5555 **Fax:** 724-627-4021

Waynesburg WANB-FM (c) 369 Tower Rd, Waynesburg PA 15370 **Phn:** 724-627-5555 **Fax:** 724-627-4021

Waynesburg WCYJ-FM (vr) 51 W College St, Waynesburg PA 15370 **Phn:** 724-852-3310 wcyjfm@waynesburg.edu

Wellsboro WLIH-FM (q) PO Box 97, Wellsboro PA 16901 **Phn:** 570-724-4272 **Fax:** 570-724-2302 www.wlih.com info@wlih.com

Wellsboro WNBQ-FM (a) PO Box 98, Wellsboro PA 16901 **Phn:** 570-724-1490 **Fax:** 570-724-6971 www.wnbt.net wnbt@ynt.net

Wellsboro WNBT-AM (am) PO Box 98, Wellsboro PA 16901 **Phn:** 570-724-1490 **Fax:** 570-724-6971 www.wnbt.net wnbt@ynt.net

Wellsboro WNBT-FM (ah) PO Box 98, Wellsboro PA 16901 **Phn:** 570-724-1490 **Fax:** 570-724-6971 www.wnbt.net wnbt@ynt.net

West Chester WCHE-AM (nt) 105 W Gay St Frnt, West Chester PA 19380 **Phn:** 610-692-3131 **Fax:** 610-692-3133 www.wche1520.com jay@wche1520.com

White Oak WEDO-AM (t) 1985 Lincoln Way Ste 4, White Oak PA 15131 **Phn:** 412-664-4431 **Fax:** 412-664-1236 www.wedo810.com wedoradio@comcast.net

Whitehall WAEB-AM (nt) 1541 Alta Dr Ste 400, Whitehall PA 18052 **Phn:** 610-434-1742 **Fax:** 610-434-3808 www.790waeb.com craigstevens@clearchannel.com

Whitehall WAEB-FM (h) 1541 Alta Dr Ste 400, Whitehall PA 18052 **Phn:** 610-434-1742 **Fax:** 610-434-3808 www.b104.com jeffhurley@clearchannel.com

Whitehall WKAP-AM (o) 1541 Alta Dr Ste 400, Whitehall PA 18052 **Phn:** 610-434-1742 **Fax:** 610-434-3808 mandyschnell@clearchannel.com

Whitehall WZZO-FM (r) 1541 Alta Dr Ste 400, Whitehall PA 18052 **Phn:** 610-434-1742 **Fax:** 610-434-6288 www.951zzo.com craigstevens@clearchannel.com

Wilkes Barre WARM-AM (snt) 600 Baltimore Dr Ste 3, Wilkes Barre PA 18702 **Phn:** 570-824-9000 **Fax:** 570-820-0520 www.warm590.com jeanne.kerr@cumulus.com

Wilkes Barre WBHD-FM (h) 600 Baltimore Dr, Wilkes Barre PA 18702 **Phn:** 570-824-9000 **Fax:** 570-820-0520 www.97bht.com jeanne.kerr@cumulus.com

Wilkes Barre WBHT-FM (h) 600 Baltimore Dr, Wilkes Barre PA 18702 **Phn:** 570-824-9000 **Fax:** 570-820-0520 www.97bht.com jeanne.kerr@cumulus.com

Wilkes Barre WBSX-FM (c) 600 Baltimore Dr Ste 2, Wilkes Barre PA 18702 **Phn:** 570-824-9000 **Fax:** 570-820-0520 www.979x.com jeanne.kerr@cumulus.com

PENNSYLVANIA RADIO STATIONS

Wilkes Barre WCLH-FM (v) 84 W South St, Wilkes Barre PA 18766 **Phn:** 570-408-5907 wclh.org wclhpd@gmail.com

Wilkes Barre WMGS-FM (a) 600 Baltimore Dr, Wilkes Barre PA 18702 **Phn:** 570-824-9000 **Fax:** 570-820-0520 www.magic93fm.com stan.phillips@cumulus.com

Wilkes Barre WRKC-FM (v) 133 N Franklin St, Wilkes Barre PA 18701 **Phn:** 570-208-5821 wrkc.kings.edu wrkc@kings.edu

Wilkes Barre WSJR-FM (c) 600 Baltimore Dr, Wilkes Barre PA 18702 **Phn:** 570-824-9000 **Fax:** 570-820-0520 www.jr937.us brian.hughes@cumulus.com

Williamsport WBLJ-FM (c) 1559 W 4th St, Williamsport PA 17701 **Phn:** 570-327-1400 **Fax:** 570-327-8156 www.bill95.com ericwhite@clearchannel.com

Williamsport WBYL-FM (c) 1559 W 4th St, Williamsport PA 17701 **Phn:** 570-327-1400 **Fax:** 570-327-8156 www.bill95.com ericwhite@clearchannel.com

Williamsport WBZD-FM (o) 1685 Four Mile Dr, Williamsport PA 17701 **Phn:** 570-323-8200 **Fax:** 570-323-5075 www.wbzd.com ted.minier@bybradio.com

Williamsport WCXR-FM (r) 1685 Four Mile Dr, Williamsport PA 17701 **Phn:** 570-323-8200 **Fax:** 570-323-5075 www.wzxr.com john.finn@bybradio.com

Williamsport WILQ-FM (c) 1685 Four Mile Dr Ste 2, Williamsport PA 17701 **Phn:** 570-323-8200 **Fax:** 570-323-5075 www.wilq.com john.finn@bybradio.com

Williamsport WKSB-FM (a) 1559 W 4th St, Williamsport PA 17701 **Phn:** 570-327-1400 **Fax:** 570-327-8156 www.kiss1027fm.com ericwhite@clearchannel.com

Williamsport WLYC-AM (s) 460 Market St # 310, Williamsport PA 17701 **Phn:** 570-327-1300 **Fax:** 570-327-5565 espnwilliamsport.com

Williamsport WPTC-FM (v) 1 College Ave, Williamsport PA 17701 **Phn:** 570-320-2400 **Fax:** 570-320-2423 www.pct.eduwptc wptc@pct.edu

Williamsport WRAK-AM (snt) 1559 W 4th St, Williamsport PA 17701 **Phn:** 570-327-1400 **Fax:** 570-327-8156 www.wrak.com ksawyer@clearchannel.com

Williamsport WRKK-AM (nt) 1559 W 4th St, Williamsport PA 17701 **Phn:** 570-327-1400 **Fax:** 570-327-8156 www.wrak.com ksawyer@clearchannel.com

Williamsport WRLC-FM (v) 700 College Pl, Williamsport PA 17701 **Phn:** 570-321-4060 www.lycoming.eduorgswrlc ossjust@lycoming.edu

Williamsport WRVH-FM (a) 1685 Four Mile Dr, Williamsport PA 17701 **Phn:** 570-323-8200 **Fax:** 570-327-9138

Williamsport WVRT-FM (a) 1559 W 4th St, Williamsport PA 17701 **Phn:** 570-327-1400 **Fax:** 570-327-8156 www.v97fm.com ericwhite@clearchannel.com

Williamsport WVRZ-FM (a) 1559 W 4th St, Williamsport PA 17701 **Phn:** 570-327-1400 **Fax:** 570-327-8156 www.variety977.com ericwhite@clearchannel.com

Williamsport WWPA-AM (nt) 1685 Four Mile Dr Ste 2, Williamsport PA 17701 **Phn:** 570-323-8200 ted.minier@bybradio.com

Williamsport WZXR-FM (r) 1685 Four Mile Dr Ste 2, Williamsport PA 17701 **Phn:** 570-323-8200 **Fax:** 570-323-5075 www.wzxr.com john.finn@bybradio.com

York WOYK-AM (s) PO Box 20249, York PA 17402 **Phn:** 717-840-0355

York WSBA-AM (snt) 5989 Susquehanna Plaza Dr, York PA 17406 **Phn:** 717-764-1155 **Fax:** 717-252-4708 www.newsradio910.com wsbanews@cumulus.com

York WVYC-FM (vr) 399 Country Club Rd, York PA 17405 **Phn:** 717-815-1932 wvyc.ycp.edu news@wvyc.org

York WYCR-FM (h) 221 W Philadelphia St # 116, York PA 17401 **Phn:** 717-792-0098 **Fax:** 717-637-9006 www.thepeak985.com info@thepeak985.com

York WYYC-AM (qt) 1545 N Queen St, York PA 17404 **Phn:** 717-848-4418 www.wilkinsradio.com wyyc@wilkinsradio.com

PUERTO RICO

Aguadilla WABA-AM (y) PO Box 188, Aguadilla PR 00605 **Phn:** 787-891-1230 **Fax:** 787-882-2282 www.waba850.com waba850am@yahoo.com

Arecibo WMIA-AM (y) PO Box 1055, Arecibo PR 00613 **Phn:** 787-878-1275

Bayamon WXLX-FM (y) PO Box 15390, Bayamon PR 00956 **Phn:** 787-785-9390 **Fax:** 787-785-9377 www.lax.fm

Guayanilla WOIZ-AM (y) PO Box 561130, Guayanilla PR 00656 **Phn:** 787-835-1130 **Fax:** 787-835-3130 www.radioantillas.4t.com radioantillas@yahoo.com

Guaynabo WEGM-FM (y) PO Box 949, Guaynabo PR 00970 **Phn:** 787-622-9700 **Fax:** 787-622-9477 www.lamega.fm rogie@sbspuertorico.com

Guaynabo WIOB-FM (y) PO Box 949, Guaynabo PR 00970 **Phn:** 787-622-9700 **Fax:** 787-622-9477 lrivera@sbspuertorico.com

Humacao WALO-AM (y) PO Box 9230, Humacao PR 00792 **Phn:** 787-852-1240 **Fax:** 787-852-1280 waloradio.com walo1240@yahoo.com

Salinas WHOY-AM (y) PO Box 1148, Salinas PR 00751 **Phn:** 787-824-3420 **Fax:** 787-824-8054

San German WSOL-AM (y) 220 Ave Los Atleticos De San Ger, San German PR 00683 **Phn:** 787-892-2975 **Fax:** 787-264-1090

San Juan WBMJ-AM (yq) 1409 Ave Ponce De Leon, San Juan PR 00907 **Phn:** 787-724-1190 **Fax:** 787-722-4395 therockradio.org programming@therockradio.org

San Juan WCMN-FM (y) PO Box 363222, San Juan PR 00936 **Phn:** 787-878-0070 **Fax:** 787-880-1112 tocadeto.com noticias@notiuno.com

San Juan WCMN-AM (y) PO Box 363222, San Juan PR 00936 **Phn:** 787-773-7474 **Fax:** 787-880-1112 noticias@notiuno.com

San Juan WIVV-AM (yq) 1409 Ave Ponce De Leon, San Juan PR 00907 **Phn:** 787-724-1190 **Fax:** 787-722-4395 therockradio.org programming@therockradio.org

San Juan WLUZ-AM (y) PO Box 9394, San Juan PR 00908 **Phn:** 787-729-1600 **Fax:** 787-723-8685 ttrelles@yahoo.com

San Juan WMNT-AM (y) 1305 Delta Caparra Ter, San Juan PR 00920 **Phn:** 787-783-8810 **Fax:** 787-781-7647

Yauco WKFE-AM (y) PO Box 533, Yauco PR 00698 **Phn:** 787-856-1320 **Fax:** 787-856-4420

RHODE ISLAND

Bristol WQRI-FM (vr) 1 Old Ferry Rd, Bristol RI 02809 **Phn:** 401-254-3283 **Fax:** 401-254-3355 wqri.rwu.edu generalmanager_wqri@hawks.rwu.edu

Exeter WCNX-AM (c) 400 South County Trl Ste A105, Exeter RI 02822 **Phn:** 401-294-9274 **Fax:** 401-294-4034 1180wcnx.com wcri@classical959.com

Exeter WCRI-FM (l) 400 South County Trl Ste A105, Exeter RI 02822 **Phn:** 401-294-9274 **Fax:** 401-294-4034 www.classical959.com wcri@classical959.com

Kingston WRIU-FM (vjl) 326 Memorial UN, Kingston RI 02881 **Phn:** 401-874-4949 **Fax:** 401-874-4349 www.wriu.org comments@wriu.org

Newport WADK-AM (nt) PO Box 367, Newport RI 02840 **Phn:** 401-846-1540 **Fax:** 401-846-1598 www.wadk.com art@wadk.com

Newport WJZS-FM (ja) PO Box 367, Newport RI 02840 **Phn:** 401-846-1540 **Fax:** 401-846-1598 www.wadk.com lmcguire@wadk.com

North Providence WPMZ-AM (y) 1270 Mineral Spring Ave, North Providence RI 02904 **Phn:** 401-726-8413 **Fax:** 401-726-8649 www.poder1110.com info@poder1110.com

Pawtucket WDDZ-FM (m) 203 Concord St Unit 453, Pawtucket RI 02860 **Phn:** 401-722-0839 **Fax:** 401-722-1459 music.disney.com

Portsmouth WJHD-FM (v) 285 Corys Ln, Portsmouth RI 02871 **Phn:** 401-683-2000 **Fax:** 401-683-5888

Providence WALE-AM (ynt) 1185 N Main St, Providence RI 02904 **Phn:** 401-521-0990 **Fax:** 401-521-5077

Providence WARL-AM (s) 127 Dorrance St Ste 5, Providence RI 02903 **Phn:** 401-521-5945 **Fax:** 401-521-5878 www.1320warlradio.com

Providence WBRU-FM (r) 88 Benevolent St, Providence RI 02906 **Phn:** 401-272-9550 **Fax:** 401-272-9278 wbru.com promotions@wbru.com

Providence WCTK-FM (c) 75 Oxford St Ste 402, Providence RI 02905 **Phn:** 401-467-4366 **Fax:** 401-941-2795 www.wctk.com studio@wctk.com

Providence WDOM-FM (vr) 549 River Ave, Providence RI 02918 **Phn:** 401-865-2460 **Fax:** 401-865-2822 wdomdj@yahoo.com

Providence WELH-FM (vjy) PO Box 1930, Providence RI 02912 **Phn:** 401-421-8100 www.bsrlive.com news.director@bsrlive.com

Providence WHJJ-AM (nt) 75 Oxford St # 302, Providence RI 02905 **Phn:** 401-781-9979 **Fax:** 401-781-9329 www.920whjj.com billgeorge@clearchannel.com

Providence WHJY-FM (r) 75 Oxford St Ste 302A, Providence RI 02905 **Phn:** 401-781-9979 **Fax:** 401-781-9329 www.94hjy.com charles@94hjy.com

Providence WLKW-AM (s) 75 Oxford St Ste 402, Providence RI 02905 **Phn:** 401-467-4366 **Fax:** 401-941-2795 twall@hallradio.com

Providence WRNI-AM (p) 1 Union Sta Ste 6, Providence RI 02903 **Phn:** 401-351-2800 **Fax:** 401-351-0246 ripr.org news@ripr.org

Providence WSNE-FM (a) 75 Oxford St Ste 302A, Providence RI 02905 **Phn:** 401-781-9979 **Fax:** 401-781-9329 www.coast933.com

Providence WWBB-FM (o) 75 Oxford St, Providence RI 02905 **Phn:** 401-781-9979 **Fax:** 401-781-9329 www.b101.com feedback@b101.com

Riverside WEAN-FM (s) 1502 Wampanoag Trl, Riverside RI 02915 **Phn:** 401-433-4200 **Fax:** 401-433-5967 www.630wpro.com

Riverside WPRO-FM (h) 1502 Wampanoag Trl, Riverside RI 02915 **Phn:** 401-433-4200 www.92profm.com

Riverside WPRO-AM (snt) 1502 Wampanoag Trl, Riverside RI 02915 **Phn:** 401-433-4200 www.630wpro.com craig.schwalb@cumulus.com

Riverside WPRV-AM (k) 1502 Wampanoag Trl, Riverside RI 02915 **Phn:** 401-433-4200 **Fax:** 401-433-5967 www.790business.com craig.schwalb@cumulus.com

Riverside WWKX-FM (h) 1502 Wampanoag Trl, Riverside RI 02915 **Phn:** 401-433-4200 **Fax:** 401-725-8609 www.hot1063.com davey.morris@cumulus.com

Riverside WWLI-FM (a) 1502 Wampanoag Trl, Riverside RI 02915 **Phn:** 401-433-4200 www.literock105fm.com brian.demay@cumulus.com

Smithfield WJMF-FM (vr) 1150 Douglas Pike, Smithfield RI 02917 **Phn:** 401-232-6150 www.wjmfradio.com wjfm@bryant.edu

Warwick WARV-AM (qt) 19 Luther Ave, Warwick RI 02886 **Phn:** 401-737-0700 **Fax:** 401-737-1604 lifechangingradio.comwarv info@warv.net

Westerly WBLQ-FM (vr) PO Box 2175, Westerly RI 02891 **Phn:** 401-322-1743 **Fax:** 401-322-1645 www.wblq.net chris@wblq.net

Woonsocket WNRI-AM (nt) 786 Diamond Hill Rd, Woonsocket RI 02895 **Phn:** 401-769-0600 **Fax:** 401-762-0442 www.wnri.com jeff.gamache@wnri.com

Woonsocket WOON-AM (mnt) 985 Park Ave, Woonsocket RI 02895 **Phn:** 401-762-1240 **Fax:** 401-769-8232 www.onworldwide.com email@onworldwide.com

SOUTH CAROLINA

Abbeville WZLA-FM (o) 112 N Main St, Abbeville SC 29620 **Phn:** 864-366-5785 **Fax:** 864-366-9391 z93oldies.com z93@wctel.net

Allendale WDOG-FM (cwu) PO Box 442, Allendale SC 29810 **Phn:** 803-584-3500 **Fax:** 803-584-0202 www.bigdogradio.com wdog935@aol.com

Allendale WDOG-AM (c) PO Box 442, Allendale SC 29810 **Phn:** 803-584-3500 **Fax:** 803-584-0202 www.bigdogradio.com wdog935@aol.com

Anderson WAIM-AM (nt) 2203 Old Williamston Rd, Anderson SC 29621 **Phn:** 864-226-1511 **Fax:** 864-226-1513 waim.us waimrd@carol.net

Anderson WRIX-AM (g) 102 E Shockley Ferry Rd, Anderson SC 29624 **Phn:** 864-225-9999 **Fax:** 864-224-0260

Anderson WRIX-FM (t) 102 E Shockley Ferry Rd, Anderson SC 29624 **Phn:** 864-224-6733 **Fax:** 864-224-0260 www.wrixfm103.com garywrix@yahoo.com

Barnwell WIIZ-FM (u) PO Box 814, Barnwell SC 29812 **Phn:** 803-259-9797 **Fax:** 803-541-9700 www.wiizfm.com thewiz@wiiz979.com

Beaufort WAGP-FM (q) PO Box 119, Beaufort SC 29901 **Phn:** 843-525-1859 www.wagp.net info@wagp.net

Beaufort WJWJ-FM (pln) 925 Ribaut Rd, Beaufort SC 29902 **Phn:** 843-524-0808 www.scetv.org

Beaufort WVGB-AM (wg) 806 Monson St, Beaufort SC 29902 **Phn:** 843-524-4700 **Fax:** 843-524-1329 945thecoast.com karl@945thecoast.com

Bennettsville WBSC-AM (rgt) 226 Radio Rd, Bennettsville SC 29512 **Phn:** 843-479-7121 **Fax:** 843-479-4474

Bishopville WAGS-AM (c) 142 Wags Dr, Bishopville SC 29010 **Phn:** 803-484-5415 www.wagsradio.com wagsradio@sc.rr.com

Camden WCAM-AM (o) PO Box 753, Camden SC 29021 **Phn:** 803-438-9002 **Fax:** 803-408-2288 www.kool1027.com wpubradio@bellsouth.net

Camden WEAF-AM (s) 1709 Lyndhurst Dr, Camden SC 29020 **Phn:** 803-432-8717

Camden WPUB-FM (o) PO Box 753, Camden SC 29021 **Phn:** 803-438-9002 **Fax:** 803-408-2288 www.kool1027.com wpubradio@bellsouth.net

Cayce WLXC-FM (au) 1801 Charleston Hwy Ste J, Cayce SC 29033 **Phn:** 803-796-9975 **Fax:** 803-739-1072 kiss-1031.com doug.williams@cumulus.com

Cayce WNKT-FM (s) 1801 Charleston Hwy Ste J, Cayce SC 29033 **Phn:** 843-277-1200 **Fax:** 843-277-1212

Charleston WAVF-FM (h) 2294 Clements Ferry Rd, Charleston SC 29492 **Phn:** 843-972-1100 **Fax:** 843-972-1200 www.1017chuckfm.com bryan@apexbroadcasting.com

Charleston WCKN-FM (c) 2294 Clements Ferry Rd, Charleston SC 29492 **Phn:** 843-972-1100 **Fax:** 843-972-1200 www.kickin925.com bryan@apexbroadcasting.com

Charleston WCOO-FM (r) 59 Windermere Blvd, Charleston SC 29407 **Phn:** 843-225-1055 www.1055thebridge.com

Charleston WJKB-AM (s) 60 Markfield Dr Ste 4, Charleston SC 29407 **Phn:** 843-763-6631 **Fax:** 843-766-1239 www.charlestonsportsradio.com ted@kirkmanbroadcasting.com

Charleston WMXZ-FM (u) 2294 Clements Ferry Rd, Charleston SC 29492 **Phn:** 843-972-1100 **Fax:** 843-972-1200 993thebox.com

Charleston WQNT-AM (s) 60 Markfield Dr Ste 4, Charleston SC 29407 **Phn:** 843-763-6631 **Fax:** 843-766-1239 www.charlestonsportsradio.com ted@kirkmanbroadcasting.com

Charleston WQSC-AM (nt) 60 Markfield Dr Ste 4, Charleston SC 29407 **Phn:** 843-763-6631 **Fax:** 843-766-1239 www.wqsc1340.com ted@kirkmanbroadcasting.com

Charleston WTMZ-AM (s) 60 Markfield Dr Ste 4, Charleston SC 29407 **Phn:** 843-763-6631 **Fax:** 843-766-1239 www.charlestonsportsradio.com ted@kirkmanbroadcasting.com

Charleston WWIK-FM (o) 60 Markfield Dr Ste 4, Charleston SC 29407 **Phn:** 843-763-6631 **Fax:** 843-766-1239 www.989funfm.com ted@kirkmanbroadcasting.com

Charleston WXST-FM (ua) 2294 Clements Ferry Rd, Charleston SC 29492 **Phn:** 843-972-1100 **Fax:** 843-972-1200 www.star997.com michaelt@star997.com

Charleston WYBB-FM (r) 59 Windermere Blvd, Charleston SC 29407 **Phn:** 843-769-4799 **Fax:** 843-769-4797 www.my98rock.com newavecohn@aol.com

Cheraw WCRE-FM (o) PO Box 160, Cheraw SC 29520 **Phn:** 843-537-7887 **Fax:** 843-537-7307 www.myfm939.com janepigg@gmail.com

Chester WRBK-FM (v) PO Box 15, Chester SC 29706 **Phn:** 803-581-9030 **Fax:** 803-581-9932

Clemson WAHT-AM (gw) PO Box 1560, Clemson SC 29633 **Phn:** 864-654-4004 **Fax:** 864-654-3300

Clemson WCCP-FM (s) 202 Lawrence Rd, Clemson SC 29631 **Phn:** 864-654-4004 **Fax:** 864-654-3300 www.wccpfm.com chris@wccpfm.com

Clemson WSBF-FM (v) 315 Hendrix Student Ctr, Clemson SC 29634 **Phn:** 864-656-4010 **Fax:** 864-656-4011 wsbf.net gm@wsbf.net

Clinton WPCC-AM (snt) PO Box 1455, Clinton SC 29325 **Phn:** 864-833-1410 **Fax:** 864-833-2467 www.sportsradio1410wpcc.com wpcc@bellsouth.net

Columbia WARQ-FM (r) 1900 Pineview Dr, Columbia SC 29209 **Phn:** 803-695-8600 **Fax:** 803-695-8605 www.warq.com mlee@innercitysc.com

Columbia WCOS-FM (c) 316 Greystone Blvd, Columbia SC 29210 **Phn:** 803-343-1100 **Fax:** 803-256-5255 www.975wcos.com davidwaterman@clearchannel.com

SOUTH CAROLINA RADIO STATIONS

Columbia WCOS-AM (qg) 316 Greystone Blvd, Columbia SC 29210 **Phn:** 803-343-1100 **Fax:** 803-256-5255 www.hallelujah1400.com davidwaterman@clearchannel.com

Columbia WGCV-AM (wg) 2440 Millwood Ave, Columbia SC 29205 **Phn:** 803-939-9530 **Fax:** 803-799-1620 www.wgcv.net tjamison@wfmv.com

Columbia WHXT-FM (u) 1900 Pineview Dr, Columbia SC 29209 **Phn:** 803-695-8600 **Fax:** 803-695-8605 www.hot1039fm.com spatterson@innercitysc.com

Columbia WISW-AM (snt) PO Box 5106, Columbia SC 29250 **Phn:** 803-796-7600 www.wisradio.com

Columbia WLJK-FM (plj) 1101 George Rogers Blvd, Columbia SC 29201 **Phn:** 803-737-3200 **Fax:** 803-737-3552 www.scetv.org

Columbia WLTR-FM (pln) 1101 George Rogers Blvd, Columbia SC 29201 **Phn:** 803-737-3200 **Fax:** 803-737-3552 www.scetv.org gasque@scetv.org

Columbia WLTY-FM (a) 316 Greystone Blvd, Columbia SC 29210 **Phn:** 803-343-1100 **Fax:** 803-748-9267 www.967stevefm.com ljsmith@clearchannel.com

Columbia WMFX-FM (r) 1900 Pineview Dr, Columbia SC 29209 **Phn:** 803-776-1013 **Fax:** 803-695-8605 www.fox102.com dstewart@innercitysc.com

Columbia WMHK-FM (q) PO Box 3122, Columbia SC 29230 **Phn:** 803-754-5400 www.wmhk.com wmhk@wmhk.com

Columbia WNOK-FM (h) 316 Greystone Blvd, Columbia SC 29210 **Phn:** 803-343-1100 **Fax:** 803-799-4367 www.wnok.com ljsmith@clearchannel.com

Columbia WOIC-AM (uw) 1900 Pineview Dr, Columbia SC 29209 **Phn:** 803-776-1013 **Fax:** 803-695-8605 www.woic.com programming@woic.com

Columbia WOMG-FM (o) PO Box 5106, Columbia SC 29250 **Phn:** 803-223-6985 **Fax:** 803-796-5502 www.womg.com tj.mckay@cumulus.com

Columbia WQXL-AM (q) 2440 Millwood Ave, Columbia SC 29205 **Phn:** 803-779-7911 **Fax:** 803-799-1620

Columbia WSCI-FM (pln) 1101 George Rogers Blvd, Columbia SC 29201 **Phn:** 803-737-3200 **Fax:** 803-737-3552 www.etvradio.org gasque@scetv.org

Columbia WTCB-FM (a) PO Box 5106, Columbia SC 29250 **Phn:** 803-796-7600 **Fax:** 803-926-1067 www.b106fm.com wtcb@b106fm.com

Columbia WUSC-FM (v) 1400 Greene St, Columbia SC 29225 **Phn:** 803-777-5468 **Fax:** 803-777-6482 wusc.sc.edu wuscsm@sc.edu

Columbia WVOC-AM (snt) 316 Greystone Blvd, Columbia SC 29210 **Phn:** 803-343-1100 **Fax:** 803-376-4815 www.wvoc.com news@wvoc.com

Columbia WWDM-FM (wu) 1900 Pineview Dr, Columbia SC 29209 **Phn:** 803-695-8600 **Fax:** 803-695-8605 www.thebigdm.com cconnors@innercitysc.com

Columbia WXBT-AM (s) 316 Greystone Blvd, Columbia SC 29210 **Phn:** 803-343-1100 **Fax:** 803-779-9727 www.560theteam.com ljsmith@clearchannel.com

Columbia WZMJ-FM (s) 1900 Pineview Dr, Columbia SC 29209 **Phn:** 803-776-1013 **Fax:** 803-695-8697 www.espncolumbia.com

Conway WPJS-AM (wg) PO Box 961, Conway SC 29528 **Phn:** 843-248-6365 **Fax:** 843-248-2890

Easley WELP-AM (q) 100 Cross Hill Rd, Easley SC 29640 **Phn:** 864-855-9300 **Fax:** 864-597-0687 www.wilkinsradio.com welp@wilkinsradio.com

Florence WBZF-FM (g) 2014 N Irby St, Florence SC 29501 **Phn:** 843-661-5000 **Fax:** 843-661-0888 www.glory985.com david.williams@cumulus.com

Florence WCMG-FM (ua) 2014 N Irby St, Florence SC 29501 **Phn:** 843-661-5000 **Fax:** 843-661-0888 www.943thedam.com matt.scurry@cumulus.com

Florence WDAR-FM (a) 181 E Evans St Ste 311, Florence SC 29506 **Phn:** 843-667-4600 **Fax:** 843-673-7390 www.sunny1055online.com

Florence WDSC-AM (g) 181 E Evans St Ste 311, Florence SC 29506 **Phn:** 843-667-4600 **Fax:** 843-673-7390 cap226@hotmail.com

Florence WEGX-FM (c) 181 E Evans St Ste 311, Florence SC 29506 **Phn:** 843-667-4600 **Fax:** 843-673-7390 www.eagle929online.com brothermud@aol.com

Florence WHLZ-FM (c) 2014 N Irby St, Florence SC 29501 **Phn:** 843-661-5000 **Fax:** 843-661-0888 www.whlz1005.com matt.scurry@cumulus.com

Florence WJMX-FM (h) 181 E Evans St Ste 311, Florence SC 29506 **Phn:** 843-667-4600 **Fax:** 843-673-7390 www.103xonline.com

Florence WJMX-AM (snt) 181 E Evans St Ste 311, Florence SC 29506 **Phn:** 843-667-4600 **Fax:** 843-673-7390 www.newstalk970online.com newstalk970@gmail.com

Florence WMXT-FM (r) 2014 N Irby St, Florence SC 29501 **Phn:** 843-661-5000 **Fax:** 843-661-0888 1021thefox.com matt.scurry@cumulus.com

Florence WRZE-FM (h) 181 E Evans St # 311, Florence SC 29506 **Phn:** 843-667-4600 **Fax:** 843-673-7390

Florence WWFN-FM (s) 2014 N Irby St, Florence SC 29501 **Phn:** 843-661-5000 **Fax:** 843-661-0888 www.thefanfm.com matt.scurry@cumulus.com

Florence WWRK-AM (g) 181 E Evans St Ste 311, Florence SC 29506 **Phn:** 843-667-4600 **Fax:** 843-673-7390 cap226@hotmail.com

Florence WYNN-AM (gw) 2014 N Irby St, Florence SC 29501 **Phn:** 843-661-5000 **Fax:** 843-661-0888 www.wynn1063.com gerald.mcswain@cumulus.com

Florence WYNN-FM (wu) 2014 N Irby St, Florence SC 29501 **Phn:** 843-661-5000 **Fax:** 843-661-0888 www.wynn1063.com gerald.mcswain@cumulus.com

Florence WZTF-FM (u) 181 E Evans St Ste 311, Florence SC 29506 **Phn:** 843-667-4600 **Fax:** 843-673-7390 www.theflo1029.com denis103x@gmail.com

Fountain Inn WFIS-AM (st) PO Box 156, Fountain Inn SC 29644 **Phn:** 864-963-5991 **Fax:** 864-963-5992

Gaffney WEAC-AM (t) PO Box 1210, Gaffney SC 29342 **Phn:** 864-489-9066 **Fax:** 864-489-9069

Gaffney WFGN-AM (wgu) PO Box 1388, Gaffney SC 29342 **Phn:** 864-489-9430 **Fax:** 864-489-9440

Georgetown WGTN-AM (o) PO Box 1400, Georgetown SC 29442 **Phn:** 843-903-9962 **Fax:** 843-903-1797 www.wgtnradio.com crystal@wezv.com

Georgetown WLMC-AM (wgut) 2508 Highmarket St, Georgetown SC 29440 **Phn:** 843-546-1400 **Fax:** 843-546-6821 www.wlmcradio.com wlmcradio@aol.com

Greenville WESC-FM (c) PO Box 100, Greenville SC 29602 **Phn:** 864-242-4660 **Fax:** 864-271-3830 www.wescfm.com

Greenville WFBC-FM (h) 25 Garlington Rd, Greenville SC 29615 **Phn:** 864-271-9200 **Fax:** 864-242-1567 www.b937.com tias@entercom.com

Greenville WGVL-AM (s) 6119 White Horse Rd Ste 16, Greenville SC 29611 **Phn:** 864-220-1115 **Fax:** 864-220-1120

Greenville WHZT-FM (h) 220 N Main St Ste 402, Greenville SC 29601 **Phn:** 864-232-9810 **Fax:** 864-370-3403 www.hot981.com jet@hot981.com

Greenville WJMZ-FM (wu) 220 N Main St Ste 402, Greenville SC 29601 **Phn:** 864-235-1073 **Fax:** 864-370-3403 www.1073jamz.com karolyn.mulvaney@summitmediacorp.com

Greenville WLFJ-AM (q) 2420 Wade Hampton Blvd, Greenville SC 29615 **Phn:** 864-292-6040 www.christiantalk660.com gary.miller@hisradio.net

Greenville WMUU-FM (z) 920 Wade Hampton Blvd, Greenville SC 29609 **Phn:** 864-242-6240 **Fax:** 864-370-3829 www.wmuu.com

Greenville WMYI-FM (a) PO Box 100, Greenville SC 29602 **Phn:** 864-235-1025 **Fax:** 864-242-1025 www.wmyi.com stevegeofferies@clearchannel.com

Greenville WOLI-FM (y) 225 S Pleasantburg Dr, Greenville SC 29607 **Phn:** 864-751-0113 **Fax:** 863-223-1553 www.woli-am.com jyoung@davidsonmediagroup.com

Greenville WOLT-FM (os) 225 S Pleasantburg Dr Ste B3, Greenville SC 29607 **Phn:** 864-751-0113 www.wolt-fm.com

Greenville WORD-AM (nt) 25 Garlington Rd, Greenville SC 29615 **Phn:** 864-271-9200 **Fax:** 864-242-1567 www.newsradioword.com bmclain@entercom.com

Greenville WPLS-FM (vr) 3300 Poinsett Hwy, Greenville SC 29613 **Phn:** 864-294-3045 fuwpls.wordpress.com wplsfurman@gmail.com

Greenville WROQ-FM (r) 25 Garlington Rd, Greenville SC 29615 **Phn:** 864-271-9200 **Fax:** 864-242-1567 www.wroq.com mhendrix@entercom.com

Greenville WSPA-FM (a) 25 Garlington Rd, Greenville SC 29615 **Phn:** 864-271-9200 **Fax:** 864-242-1567 www.magic989online.com tias@entercom.com

Greenville WSSL-FM (c) 101 N Main St Ste 1000, Greenville SC 29601 **Phn:** 864-242-1005 **Fax:** 864-271-3830 www.wsslfm.com kixlayton@clearchannel.com

Greenville WTBI-AM (gq) 3931 White Horse Rd, Greenville SC 29611 **Phn:** 864-295-2145 **Fax:** 864-295-6313 tbc.scwtbi wtbi@tabernacleministries.org

Greenville WTPT-FM (r) 25 Garlington Rd, Greenville SC 29615 **Phn:** 864-271-9200 **Fax:** 864-242-1567 www.newrock933.com mhendrix@entercom.com

Greenville WYRD-FM (cq) 25 Garlington Rd, Greenville SC 29615 **Phn:** 864-271-9200 **Fax:** 864-242-1567 www.newsradioword.com bmclain@entercom.com

Greenville WYRD-AM (nt) 25 Garlington Rd, Greenville SC 29615 **Phn:** 864-271-9200 **Fax:** 864-242-1567 www.newsradioword.com ejenson@entercom.com

Greenwood WCZZ-AM (o) 210 Montague Ave, Greenwood SC 29649 **Phn:** 864-223-4300 **Fax:** 864-223-4096 dave@sunny103-5.com

Greenwood WLMA-AM (wg) 1220 Bypass 72 NE, Greenwood SC 29649 **Phn:** 864-229-7984 **Fax:** 864-229-5896 www.wlma.net wlma@wlma.net

Greenwood WZSN-FM (a) 210 Montague Ave, Greenwood SC 29649 **Phn:** 864-223-4300 **Fax:** 864-223-4096 www.sunny103-5.com sunny@sunny103-5.com

Greer WCKI-AM (g) PO Box 905, Greer SC 29652 **Phn:** 864-877-8458 **Fax:** 864-877-8459 www.catholicradiosc.com info@catholicradiosc.com

Greer WPJM-AM (gw) 305 N Tryon St, Greer SC 29651 **Phn:** 864-877-1112 **Fax:** 864-877-0342 www.800wpjm.com

Hampton WBHC-FM (c) PO Box 607, Hampton SC 29924 **Phn:** 803-943-2831 **Fax:** 803-943-5450

Hilton Head Island WFXH-AM (st) 1 Saint Augustine Pl, Hilton Head Island SC 29928 **Phn:** 843-785-9569 **Fax:** 843-842-3369

SOUTH CAROLINA RADIO STATIONS

Hilton Head Island WFXH-FM (r) 1 Saint Augustine Pl, Hilton Head Island SC 29928 **Phn:** 843-785-9569 **Fax:** 843-842-3369 www.rock1061.com cbeverly@adventureradio.fm

Hilton Head Island WGZO-FM (h) 1 Saint Augustine Pl, Hilton Head Island SC 29928 **Phn:** 843-785-9569 **Fax:** 843-842-3369 www.1031thedrive.com skeith@adventureradio.fm

Hilton Head Island WGZR-FM (c) 1 Saint Augustine Pl, Hilton Head Island SC 29928 **Phn:** 843-785-9569 **Fax:** 843-842-3369 www.bob1069.com billie@bob1069.com

Hilton Head Island WLOW-FM (am) 1 Saint Augustine Pl, Hilton Head Island SC 29928 **Phn:** 843-785-9569 **Fax:** 843-842-3369 www.y1079online.com skeith@adventureradio.fm

Holly Hill WJBS-AM (cg) PO Box 1087, Holly Hill SC 29059 **Phn:** 803-496-5352 **Fax:** 803-496-2526 wjbsam@yahoo.com

Irmo WIGL-FM (wu) PO Box 537, Irmo SC 29063 **Phn:** 803-536-1710 **Fax:** 803-531-1089

Johnston WKSX-FM (o) PO Box I, Johnston SC 29832 **Phn:** 803-275-4444 **Fax:** 803-275-3185

Ladson WKCL-FM (qg) PO Box 809, Ladson SC 29456 **Phn:** 843-553-8740 **Fax:** 843-553-0636 www.915wkcl.com wkcl@msn.com

Lancaster WAGL-AM (go) PO Box 28, Lancaster SC 29721 **Phn:** 803-283-8431 **Fax:** 803-286-4702 www.waglradio.com waglradio@comporium.net

Laurens WLBG-AM (snt) PO Box 1289, Laurens SC 29360 **Phn:** 864-984-3544 **Fax:** 864-984-3545 www.wlbg.com mail@wlbg.com

Loris WLSC-AM (nt) PO Box 578, Loris SC 29569 **Phn:** 843-808-4437 **Fax:** 801-838-3262 www.tigerradio.com info@wlscradio.com

Manning WYMB-AM (st) 517 Sunset Dr, Manning SC 29102 **Phn:** 843-661-5000 **Fax:** 843-661-0888

Marion WJAY-AM (wg) PO Box 1020, Marion SC 29571 **Phn:** 843-423-1140 **Fax:** 843-423-2829

Mount Pleasant WEZL-FM (c) 950 Houston Northcutt Blvd Ste 201, Mount Pleasant SC 29464 **Phn:** 843-884-2534 **Fax:** 843-884-1218 www.wezl.com billwest@clearchannel.com

Mount Pleasant WLTQ-AM (y) 950 Houston Northcutt Blvd Ste 201, Mount Pleasant SC 29464 **Phn:** 843-884-2534 **Fax:** 843-884-1218

Mount Pleasant WRFQ-FM (r) 950 Houston Northcutt Blvd Ste 201, Mount Pleasant SC 29464 **Phn:** 843-884-2534 **Fax:** 843-884-1218 www.q1045.com steveburke@clearchannel.com

Mount Pleasant WSCC-FM (nt) 950 Houston Northcutt Blvd Ste 201, Mount Pleasant SC 29464 **Phn:** 843-884-2534 **Fax:** 843-884-1218 www.943wsc.com kelly@943wsc.com

Mount Pleasant WXLY-FM (o) 950 Houston Northcutt Blvd Ste 201, Mount Pleasant SC 29464 **Phn:** 843-884-2534 **Fax:** 843-884-1218 www.y1025.com news@wscfm.com

Murrells Inlet WDAI-FM (u) 11640 Highway 17 Byp, Murrells Inlet SC 29576 **Phn:** 843-651-7869 **Fax:** 843-651-9123 www.985kissfm.net david.lewis@cumulus.com

Murrells Inlet WHSC-AM (s) 11640 Highway 17 Byp, Murrells Inlet SC 29576 **Phn:** 843-651-7869 **Fax:** 843-651-9123 david.lewis@cumulus.com

Murrells Inlet WJXY-FM (h) 11640 Highway 17 Byp, Murrells Inlet SC 29576 **Phn:** 843-651-7869 **Fax:** 843-651-9123 www.teammyrtlebeach.com radiogm@aol.com

Murrells Inlet WSEA-FM (h) 11640 Highway 17 Byp, Murrells Inlet SC 29576 **Phn:** 843-651-7869 **Fax:** 843-651-9123 www.hot100fm.com brodie.hot@cumulus.com

Murrells Inlet WSYN-FM (o) 11640 Highway 17 Byp, Murrells Inlet SC 29576 **Phn:** 843-651-7869 **Fax:** 843-651-3197

Murrells Inlet WXJY-FM (a) 11640 Highway 17 Byp, Murrells Inlet SC 29576 **Phn:** 843-651-7869 **Fax:** 843-651-3197 david.lewis@cumulus.com

Murrells Inlet WYAK-FM (c) 11640 Highway 17 Byp, Murrells Inlet SC 29576 **Phn:** 843-651-7869 **Fax:** 843-651-3197

Myrtle Beach WEZV-FM (z) PO Box 2830, Myrtle Beach SC 29578 **Phn:** 843-903-9962 **Fax:** 843-903-1797 www.wezv.com sedota@wezv.com

Myrtle Beach WGTN-FM (a) PO Box 2830, Myrtle Beach SC 29578 **Phn:** 843-903-9962 **Fax:** 843-903-1797 www.wezv.com

Myrtle Beach WGTR-FM (c) 4841 Highway 17 Byp S, Myrtle Beach SC 29577 **Phn:** 843-293-0107 **Fax:** 843-293-1717 www.gator1079.com

Myrtle Beach WKZQ-FM (r) 1016 Ocala St, Myrtle Beach SC 29577 **Phn:** 843-448-1041 **Fax:** 843-626-2508 www.wkzq.net

Myrtle Beach WLQB-FM (y) 4841 Highway 17 Byp S, Myrtle Beach SC 29577 **Phn:** 843-293-0107 **Fax:** 843-293-1717

Myrtle Beach WMYB-FM (a) 1016 Ocala St, Myrtle Beach SC 29577 **Phn:** 843-448-1041 **Fax:** 843-626-5988 www.star921.net awilson@nextmediagroup.net

Myrtle Beach WQSD-FM (r) 4841 Highway 17 Byp S, Myrtle Beach SC 29577 **Phn:** 843-293-0107 **Fax:** 843-293-1717 www.rock107mb.com

Myrtle Beach WRNN-AM (nt) 1016 Ocala St, Myrtle Beach SC 29577 **Phn:** 843-448-1041 **Fax:** 843-626-5988

Myrtle Beach WRNN-FM (nt) 1016 Ocala St, Myrtle Beach SC 29577 **Phn:** 843-448-1041 **Fax:** 843-626-5988 www.wrnn.net dpriest@nextmediagroup.net

Myrtle Beach WWXM-FM (h) 4841 Highway 17 Byp S, Myrtle Beach SC 29577 **Phn:** 843-293-0107 **Fax:** 843-293-1717 mix977online.com

Myrtle Beach WYAV-FM (r) 1016 Ocala St, Myrtle Beach SC 29577 **Phn:** 843-448-1041 **Fax:** 843-626-5988 www.wave104.net awilson@nextmediagroup.net

Myrtle Beach WYEZ-FM (or) PO Box 2830, Myrtle Beach SC 29578 **Phn:** 843-903-9962 **Fax:** 843-903-1797 www.movin945.net will@movin945.net

Myrtle Beach WYNA-FM (o) 3926 Wesley St Ste 301, Myrtle Beach SC 29579 **Phn:** 843-903-9962 **Fax:** 843-903-1797 1049bobfm.com blue@1049bobfm.com

Newberry WKDK-AM (anos) PO Box 753, Newberry SC 29108 **Phn:** 803-276-2957 **Fax:** 803-276-3337 www.wkdk.com contactus@wkdk.com

Newberry WKMG-AM (wuo) 1840 Glenn Street Ext, Newberry SC 29108 **Phn:** 803-405-0111

North Augusta WAEG-FM (aj) 6025 Broadcast Dr, North Augusta SC 29841 **Phn:** 803-279-2330 www.923smoothjazz.com

North Augusta WAFJ-FM (q) 102 Lecompte Ave, North Augusta SC 29841 **Phn:** 803-819-3125 **Fax:** 803-819-3129 www.wafj.com sue@wafj.com

North Augusta WFXA-FM (wu) 104 Bennett Ln, North Augusta SC 29841 **Phn:** 803-279-2330 **Fax:** 803-279-8149

North Augusta WTHB-AM (wg) 411 Radio Station Rd, North Augusta SC 29841 **Phn:** 803-279-2330 **Fax:** 803-279-8149 praise969.com vperry@perrybroadcasting.net

North Augusta WTHB-FM (gh) 411 Radio Station Rd, North Augusta SC 29841 **Phn:** 803-279-2330 **Fax:** 803-279-8149 praise969.com dforbes@perrybroadcasting.net

North Charleston WIWF-FM (c) 4230 Faber Place Dr Ste 100, North Charleston SC 29405 **Phn:** 843-277-1200 **Fax:** 843-277-1212

North Charleston WMGL-FM (uw) 4230 Faber Place Dr Ste 100, North Charleston SC 29405 **Phn:** 843-277-1200 **Fax:** 843-277-1212 www.magic1017.com terry.base@cumulus.com

North Charleston WPAL-FM (u) 2045 Spaulding Dr, North Charleston SC 29406 **Phn:** 843-974-6001 **Fax:** 843-974-6002

North Charleston WSSX-FM (h) 4230 Faber Place Dr Ste 100, North Charleston SC 29405 **Phn:** 843-277-1200 **Fax:** 843-277-1212 www.95sx.com

North Charleston WTMA-AM (nt) 4230 Faber Place Dr Ste 100, North Charleston SC 29405 **Phn:** 843-277-1200 **Fax:** 843-277-1212 www.wtma.com fred.storey@cumulus.com

North Charleston WWWZ-FM (wu) 4230 Faber Place Dr Ste 100, North Charleston SC 29405 **Phn:** 843-277-1200 **Fax:** 843-277-1212 www.z93jamz.com terry.base@cumulus.com

North Charleston WZJY-AM (y) 5081 Rivers Ave, North Charleston SC 29406 **Phn:** 843-529-1185 **Fax:** 843-974-6002 www.elsol980.com

North Myrtle Beach WVCO-FM (o) PO Box 4487, North Myrtle Beach SC 29582 **Phn:** 843-663-9400 www.949thesurf.com

Orangeburg WGFG-FM (c) 200 Regional Pkwy # C-200, Orangeburg SC 29118 **Phn:** 803-536-1710 **Fax:** 803-531-1089 www.catcountry1053.com radiojimweaver@yahoo.com

Orangeburg WORG-FM (a) 1675 Chestnut St, Orangeburg SC 29115 **Phn:** 803-516-8400 **Fax:** 803-516-0704 www.worg.com worg@worg.com

Orangeburg WPJK-AM (gw) 175 Cannon Bridge Rd, Orangeburg SC 29115 **Phn:** 803-534-4848

Orangeburg WQKI-FM (ux) 200 Regional Pkwy # C-200, Orangeburg SC 29118 **Phn:** 803-536-1710 **Fax:** 803-531-1089 wqki@miller.fm

Orangeburg WSSB-FM (wv) PO Box 7619, Orangeburg SC 29117 **Phn:** 803-536-8585 **Fax:** 803-516-4700 www.wssb903fm.org wssb@scsu.edu

Rock Hill WBZK-AM (g) 400 Pineview St, Rock Hill SC 29730 **Phn:** 803-325-1533 **Fax:** 803-325-7937

Rock Hill WRHI-AM (nt) PO Box 307, Rock Hill SC 29731 **Phn:** 803-324-1340 **Fax:** 803-324-2860 www.wrhi.com newsroom@wrhi.com

Rock Hill WRHI-FM (c) PO Box 307, Rock Hill SC 29731 **Phn:** 803-324-1340 **Fax:** 803-324-2860 www.fm107.com newsroom@wrhi.com

Rock Hill WRHM-FM (c) PO Box 307, Rock Hill SC 29731 **Phn:** 803-286-1071 **Fax:** 803-324-2860 www.fm107.com newsroom@wrhi.com

Rock Hill WVSZ-FM (c) PO Box 307, Rock Hill SC 29731 **Phn:** 803-324-0943 www.fm107.com

Saint Stephen WTUA-FM (wg) 4013 Byrnes Dr, Saint Stephen SC 29479 **Phn:** 843-567-2091 **Fax:** 843-567-3088

Spartanburg WASC-AM (wu) PO Box 5686, Spartanburg SC 29304 **Phn:** 864-585-1530 **Fax:** 864-573-7790

Spartanburg WSPG-AM (st) 340 Garner Rd, Spartanburg SC 29303 **Phn:** 864-573-1400 **Fax:** 864-573-8699 www.espnspartanburg.com mhauser@espnspartanburg.com

Sumter WDKD-AM (nt) 51 Commerce St, Sumter SC 29150 **Phn:** 803-775-2321 **Fax:** 803-773-4856 tmiller55@aol.com

Sumter WDXY-AM (snt) 51 Commerce St, Sumter SC 29150 **Phn:** 803-775-2321 **Fax:** 803-773-4856 vgraham@miller.fm

Sumter WIBZ-FM (o) PO Box 1269, Sumter SC 29151 **Phn:** 803-775-2321 **Fax:** 803-773-4856

Sumter WSIM-FM (c) 51 Commerce St, Sumter SC 29150 **Phn:** 803-775-2321 **Fax:** 803-773-4856 www.star937.com dbaker@miller.fm

Sumter WWHM-AM (c) 51 Commerce St, Sumter SC 29150 **Phn:** 803-775-2321 **Fax:** 803-773-4856 dbaker@miller.fm

Sumter WWKT-FM (wu) 51 Commerce St, Sumter SC 29150 **Phn:** 803-775-2321 **Fax:** 803-773-4856 www.katcountry993.net dbaker@miller.fm

Thompsonville WWBD-FM (r) 2423 Walker Swinton Rd, Thompsonville SC 29161 **Phn:** 843-678-9393 **Fax:** 843-661-0555 www.baddog947.com

Timmonsville WHYM-AM (m) 2423 Walker Swinton Rd, Timmonsville SC 29161 **Phn:** 843-678-9393 **Fax:** 843-661-0555 dbaker@miller.fm

Timmonsville WOLH-AM (m) 2423 Walker Swinton Rd, Timmonsville SC 29161 **Phn:** 843-678-9393 **Fax:** 843-661-0555 tmiller55@aol.com

Union WBCU-AM (cn) 210 E Main St, Union SC 29379 **Phn:** 864-427-2411 **Fax:** 864-429-2975 www.wbcuradio.com chris@wbcuradio.com

Walhalla WGOG-FM (o) PO Box 10, Walhalla SC 29691 **Phn:** 864-638-3616 **Fax:** 864-638-6810 www.wgog.com gary@wgog.com

Walterboro WALI-FM (c) 724 S Jefferies Blvd, Walterboro SC 29488 **Phn:** 843-549-1543 **Fax:** 843-549-2711

West Columbia WFMV-FM (quw) PO Box 2355, West Columbia SC 29171 **Phn:** 803-939-9530 **Fax:** 803-939-9469 columbiainspiration.com tonyg@wfmv.com

West Columbia WLJI-FM (ugw) PO Box 2355, West Columbia SC 29171 **Phn:** 803-939-9530 **Fax:** 803-939-9469 columbiainspiration.com athomas@wfmv.com

SOUTH DAKOTA

Aberdeen KBFO-FM (a) PO Box 1930, Aberdeen SD 57402 **Phn:** 605-229-3632 **Fax:** 605-229-4849 brian.lundquist@hubcityradio.com

Aberdeen KGIM-AM (s) PO Box 1930, Aberdeen SD 57402 **Phn:** 605-229-3632 **Fax:** 605-229-4849 doc@hubcityradio.com

Aberdeen KGIM-FM (c) PO Box 1930, Aberdeen SD 57402 **Phn:** 605-229-3632 **Fax:** 605-229-4849

Aberdeen KNBZ-FM (a) PO Box 1930, Aberdeen SD 57402 **Phn:** 605-229-3632 **Fax:** 605-229-4849 phcountry@hubcityradio.com

Aberdeen KSDN-FM (h) PO Box 1930, Aberdeen SD 57402 **Phn:** 605-229-3632 **Fax:** 605-229-4849 www.hubcityradio.com doc@hubcityradio.com

Aberdeen KSDN-AM (ans) PO Box 1930, Aberdeen SD 57402 **Phn:** 605-229-3632 **Fax:** 605-229-4849 www.hubcityradio.com nikkikrenz@hubcityradio.com

SOUTH CAROLINA RADIO STATIONS

Belle Fourche KBFS-AM (csn) PO Box 787, Belle Fourche SD 57717 **Phn:** 605-892-2571 **Fax:** 605-892-2573 www.kbfs.com kbfs@mato.com

Belle Fourche KYDT-FM (cs) PO Box 787, Belle Fourche SD 57717 **Phn:** 605-892-2571 **Fax:** 605-892-2573 www.kydt.com kbfs@mato.com

Brookings KBRK-AM (m) 227 22nd Ave S, Brookings SD 57006 **Phn:** 605-692-1430 **Fax:** 605-692-6434 www.brookingsradio.com kjjqnews@brookings.net

Brookings KBRK-FM (a) 227 22nd Ave S, Brookings SD 57006 **Phn:** 605-692-1430 **Fax:** 605-692-4441 www.brookingsradio.com kjjqnews@brookings.net

Brookings KDBX-FM (r) 227 22nd Ave S, Brookings SD 57006 **Phn:** 605-692-1430 **Fax:** 605-692-6434 brookingsradio.com kjjqnews@brookings.net

Brookings KJJQ-AM (snt) 227 22nd Ave S, Brookings SD 57006 **Phn:** 605-692-1430 **Fax:** 605-692-6434 brookingsradio.com kjjqnews@brookings.net

Brookings KKQQ-FM (c) 227 22nd Ave S, Brookings SD 57006 **Phn:** 605-692-9125 **Fax:** 605-692-6434 www.kcountry102.com brad@kcountry102.com

Brookings KSDJ-FM (vr) PO Box 2815, Brookings SD 57007 **Phn:** 605-688-5559 **Fax:** 605-688-4973 ksdjradio.com ksdj@live.com

Chamberlain KPLO-FM (c) PO Box 317, Chamberlain SD 57325 **Phn:** 605-734-4000 **Fax:** 605-734-6634 www.drgnews.com news@dakotaradiogroup.com

Deadwood KDSJ-AM (on) 745 Main St, Deadwood SD 57732 **Phn:** 605-578-1826 **Fax:** 605-578-1827 www.kdsj980.com kdsj@knology.net

Hot Springs KFCR-AM (a) PO Box 611, Hot Springs SD 57747 **Phn:** 605-745-3637 **Fax:** 605-745-3517

Hot Springs KZMX-FM (c) PO Box 611, Hot Springs SD 57747 **Phn:** 605-745-3637 **Fax:** 605-745-3517

Hot Springs KZMX-AM (c) PO Box 611, Hot Springs SD 57747 **Phn:** 605-745-3637 **Fax:** 605-745-3517

Huron KIJV-AM (nt) 1726 Dakota Ave S, Huron SD 57350 **Phn:** 605-352-8621 **Fax:** 605-352-0911 www.performance-radio.com smartin@kokk.com

Huron KOKK-AM (cf) 1726 Dakota Ave S, Huron SD 57350 **Phn:** 605-352-8621 **Fax:** 605-352-0911 www.performance-radio.com news@kokk.com

Huron KXLG-FM (c) 1726 Dakota Ave S, Huron SD 57350 **Phn:** 605-352-8621 **Fax:** 605-352-0911 www.performance-radio.com news@kokk.com

Huron KZKK-FM (a) 1726 Dakota Ave S, Huron SD 57350 **Phn:** 605-352-8621 **Fax:** 605-352-0911 www.performance-radio.com janet@kokk.com

Lemmon KBJM-AM (c) PO Box 540, Lemmon SD 57638 **Phn:** 605-374-5747 **Fax:** 605-374-5332 www.kbjm.com kbjm1400@sdplains.com

Madison KJAM-FM (cn) 101 S Egan Ave, Madison SD 57042 **Phn:** 605-256-4514 **Fax:** 605-256-6477 www.amazingmadison.com pnordling@madison.threeeagles.com

Madison KJAM-AM (a) 101 S Egan Ave, Madison SD 57042 **Phn:** 605-256-4514 **Fax:** 605-256-6477 www.amazingmadison.com pnordling@madison.threeeagles.com

McLaughlin KLND-FM (ve) 11420 Sd Highway 63, McLaughlin SD 57642 **Phn:** 605-823-4661 **Fax:** 605-823-4660 zbolts@hotmail.com

Milbank KMSD-AM (nt) PO Box 1005, Milbank SD 57252 **Phn:** 605-432-5516 **Fax:** 605-432-4231 www.kphrfm.com kmsd@bigstoneradio.com

Mitchell KMIT-FM (c) 501 S Ohlman St Ste 1, Mitchell SD 57301 **Phn:** 605-996-9667 **Fax:** 605-996-0013 www.kmit.com kmit@kmit.com

Mitchell KORN-AM (nt) 319 N Main St, Mitchell SD 57301 **Phn:** 605-996-1490 **Fax:** 605-996-6680 www.1490korn.com kornstudio@kornq107.com

Mitchell KQRN-FM (a) 319 N Main St, Mitchell SD 57301 **Phn:** 605-996-1490 **Fax:** 605-996-6680 www.q107radio.com kornstudio@kornq107.com

Mitchell KUQL-FM (o) PO Box 520, Mitchell SD 57301 **Phn:** 605-996-9667 **Fax:** 605-996-0013 www.kool98.com cj@kool98.com

Mobridge KMLO-FM (c) PO Box 400, Mobridge SD 57601 **Phn:** 605-845-3654 **Fax:** 605-845-5094 www.drgnews.com johnschreier@amfmradio.biz

Mobridge KOLY-FM (a) PO Box 400, Mobridge SD 57601 **Phn:** 605-845-3654 **Fax:** 605-845-5094 www.drgnews.com news@dakotaradiogroup.com

Mobridge KOLY-AM (am) PO Box 400, Mobridge SD 57601 **Phn:** 605-845-3654 **Fax:** 605-845-5094 www.drgnews.com news@dakotaradiogroup.com

Pierre KCCR-AM (a) 106 W Capitol Ave, Pierre SD 57501 **Phn:** 605-224-1240 **Fax:** 605-945-4270 www.todayskccr.com steve@todayskccr.com

Pierre KGFX-FM (r) PO Box 1197, Pierre SD 57501 **Phn:** 605-224-8686 **Fax:** 605-224-8984 www.dakotaradiogroup.com news@dakotaradiogroup.com

Pierre KGFX-AM (ntf) PO Box 1197, Pierre SD 57501 **Phn:** 605-224-8686 **Fax:** 605-224-8984 www.drgnews.com news@dakotaradiogroup.com

Pierre KLXS-FM (c) 106 W Capitol Ave, Pierre SD 57501 **Phn:** 605-224-1240 **Fax:** 605-945-4270 www.pierrecountry.com steve@todayskccr.com

Rapid City KFXS-FM (r) PO Box 2480, Rapid City SD 57709 **Phn:** 605-343-6161 **Fax:** 605-343-9012 www.newrushmoreradio.comkfxs liagreen@newrushmoreradio.com

Rapid City KIQK-FM (c) 3601 Canyon Lake Dr Ste 1, Rapid City SD 57702 **Phn:** 605-343-0888 **Fax:** 605-342-3075 www.kick104.com

Rapid City KKLS-AM (o) 660 Flormann St # 1000, Rapid City SD 57701 **Phn:** 605-343-6161 **Fax:** 605-343-9012 www.newrushmoreradio.comkkls liagreen@newrushmoreradio.com

Rapid City KKMK-FM (a) PO Box 2480, Rapid City SD 57709 **Phn:** 605-343-6161 **Fax:** 605-343-9012 www.newrushmoreradio.com kurt@939themix.com

Rapid City KLMP-FM (qt) 1853 Fountain Plaza Dr, Rapid City SD 57702 **Phn:** 605-342-6822 **Fax:** 605-342-0854 klmp.com klmp@klmp.com

Rapid City KOTA-AM (ant) 518 Saint Joseph St, Rapid City SD 57701 **Phn:** 605-342-2000 **Fax:** 605-342-7305 www.kotaradio.com

Rapid City KOUT-FM (c) PO Box 2480, Rapid City SD 57709 **Phn:** 605-343-6161 **Fax:** 605-343-9012 www.newrushmoreradio.comkout houston@katradio.com

Rapid City KQRQ-FM (h) PO Box 1760, Rapid City SD 57709 **Phn:** 605-342-2000 **Fax:** 605-342-7305 www.q923radio.com rick@dberadio.com

Rapid City KRCS-FM (h) 660 Flormann St # 1000, Rapid City SD 57701 **Phn:** 605-343-6161 **Fax:** 605-343-9012 www.newrushmoreradio.comkrcs jay@hot931.com

Rapid City KSLT-FM (q) 1853 Fountain Plaza Dr, Rapid City SD 57702 **Phn:** 605-342-6822 **Fax:** 605-342-0854 www.kslt.com

Rapid City KSQY-FM (r) 3601 Canyon Lake Dr Ste 1, Rapid City SD 57702 **Phn:** 605-343-0888 **Fax:** 605-342-3075 www.951ksky.com studio@951ksky.com

Rapid City KTEQ-FM (v) 501 E Saint Joseph St, Rapid City SD 57701 **Phn:** 605-394-2233 www.hpcnet.orgkteq kteq@sdsmt.edu

Rapid City KTOQ-AM (nt) 3601 Canyon Lake Dr Ste 1, Rapid City SD 57702 **Phn:** 605-343-0888 **Fax:** 605-342-3075

Rapid City KZLK-FM (a) 518 Saint Joseph St, Rapid City SD 57701 **Phn:** 605-342-2000 **Fax:** 605-342-7305 www.she1063.com she1063@dberadio.com

Sioux Falls KCSD-FM (pl) 1101 W 22nd St, Sioux Falls SD 57105 **Phn:** 605-331-6690 www.sdpb.org joe.tlustos@state.sd.us

Sioux Falls KELO-AM (snt) 500 S Phillips Ave, Sioux Falls SD 57104 **Phn:** 605-331-5350 **Fax:** 605-336-0415 www.kelo.com

Sioux Falls KELO-FM (a) 500 S Phillips Ave, Sioux Falls SD 57104 **Phn:** 605-331-5350 **Fax:** 605-336-0415 www.kelofm.com craig.hodgson@bybradio.com

Sioux Falls KIKN-FM (c) 5100 S Tennis Ln Ste 200, Sioux Falls SD 57108 **Phn:** 605-361-0300 **Fax:** 605-361-5410 www.kikn.com jay@kikn.com

Sioux Falls KKLS-FM (h) 5100 S Tennis Ln, Sioux Falls SD 57108 **Phn:** 605-361-0300 **Fax:** 605-361-5410 www.hot1047.com andy@hot1047.com

Sioux Falls KMXC-FM (a) 5100 S Tennis Ln Ste 200, Sioux Falls SD 57108 **Phn:** 605-361-0300 **Fax:** 605-339-2735 www.mix97-3.com don.jacobs@townsquaremedia.com

Sioux Falls KNWC-AM (q) 6300 S Tallgrass Ave, Sioux Falls SD 57108 **Phn:** 605-339-1270 **Fax:** 605-339-1271 www.life965.fm knwc@knwc.org

Sioux Falls KNWC-FM (q) 6300 S Tallgrass Ave, Sioux Falls SD 57108 **Phn:** 605-339-1270 **Fax:** 605-339-1271 www.life965.fm knwc@knwc.org

Sioux Falls KRRO-FM (r) 500 S Phillips Ave, Sioux Falls SD 57104 **Phn:** 605-331-5350 **Fax:** 605-336-0415 www.krro.com

Sioux Falls KRSD-FM (pln) 2001 S Summit Ave Box 737, Sioux Falls SD 57197 **Phn:** 605-335-6666 **Fax:** 605-335-1259 minnesota.publicradio.org newsroom@mpr.org

Sioux Falls KSOO-AM (nt) 5100 S Tennis Ln, Sioux Falls SD 57108 **Phn:** 605-361-0300 **Fax:** 605-339-2735 www.ksoo.com don.jacobs@townsquaremedia.com

Sioux Falls KSQB-AM (s) 500 S Phillips Ave, Sioux Falls SD 57104 **Phn:** 605-331-5350 **Fax:** 605-336-0415

Sioux Falls KSQB-FM (a) 500 S Phillips Ave, Sioux Falls SD 57104 **Phn:** 605-331-5350 **Fax:** 605-336-0415 www.q957.com

Sioux Falls KTWB-FM (c) 500 S Phillips Ave, Sioux Falls SD 57104 **Phn:** 605-331-5350 **Fax:** 605-336-0415 www.ktwb.com

Sioux Falls KWSF-FM (c) 500 S Phillips Ave, Sioux Falls SD 57104 **Phn:** 605-331-5350 **Fax:** 605-336-0415 www.q957.com

Sioux Falls KWSN-AM (s) 500 S Phillips Ave, Sioux Falls SD 57104 **Phn:** 605-331-5350 **Fax:** 605-336-0415 www.kwsn.com craig.hodgson@bybradio.com

Sioux Falls KXQL-FM (o) 500 S Phillips Ave, Sioux Falls SD 57104 **Phn:** 605-331-5350 **Fax:** 605-336-0415 q957.com

Sioux Falls KXRB-AM (c) 5100 S Tennis Ln Ste 200, Sioux Falls SD 57108 **Phn:** 605-361-0300 **Fax:** 605-361-5410 www.kxrb.com randy@kxrb.com

SOUTH DAKOTA RADIO STATIONS

Sioux Falls KYBB-FM (r) 5100 S Tennis Ln Ste 200, Sioux Falls SD 57108 **Phn:** 605-361-0300 **Fax:** 605-339-2735 www.b1027.com crash@b1027.com

Sisseton KBWS-FM (c) 509 Veterans Ave, Sisseton SD 57262 **Phn:** 605-432-5516 **Fax:** 605-432-4231 www.kphrfm.com kbwsstudio@venturecomm.net

Spearfish KBHU-FM (var) 1200 University St Unit 9003, Spearfish SD 57799 **Phn:** 605-642-6265 **Fax:** 605-642-6762 www.thebuzzfm.net thebuzzfm@gmail.com

Spearfish KDDX-FM (r) 2827 E Colorado Blvd, Spearfish SD 57783 **Phn:** 605-642-7800 **Fax:** 605-642-7849 www.xrock.fm jfk@dberadio.com

Spearfish KZZI-FM (c) 2827 E Colorado Blvd, Spearfish SD 57783 **Phn:** 605-642-5747 **Fax:** 605-642-7849 www.myeaglecountry.com eagle@dberadio.com

Sturgis KBHB-AM (foc) 1612 Junction Ave Ste 1, Sturgis SD 57785 **Phn:** 605-347-4455 **Fax:** 605-347-5120 www.newrushmoreradio.comkbhb info@kbhbradio.com

Vermillion KAOR-FM (vr) 414 E Clark St, Vermillion SD 57069 **Phn:** 605-677-5477 **Fax:** 605-677-4250

Vermillion KBHE-FM (p) PO Box 5000, Vermillion SD 57069 **Phn:** 605-394-2551 www.sdpb.org joe.tlustos@state.sd.us

Vermillion KESD-FM (pln) PO Box 5000, Vermillion SD 57069 **Phn:** 605-688-4191 www.sdpb.org joe.tlustos@state.sd.us

Vermillion KUSD-FM (plnj) PO Box 5000, Vermillion SD 57069 **Phn:** 605-677-5861 **Fax:** 605-677-5010 www.sdpb.org susan.hanson@state.sd.us

Watertown KDLO-FM (c) 921 9th Ave SE, Watertown SD 57201 **Phn:** 605-886-8444 **Fax:** 605-886-9306 www.mywatertownsd.com kwatnews@watertown.threeeagles.com

Watertown KIXX-FM (a) 921 9th Ave SE, Watertown SD 57201 **Phn:** 605-886-8444 **Fax:** 605-886-9306 www.mywatertownsd.com kwatnews@watertown.threeeagles.com

Watertown KKSD-FM (o) 921 9th Ave SE, Watertown SD 57201 **Phn:** 605-886-8444 **Fax:** 605-886-9306 www.mywatertownsd.com kwatnews@watertown.threeeagles.com

Watertown KPHR-FM (r) 508 Jenson Ave SE, Watertown SD 57201 **Phn:** 605-884-3548 **Fax:** 605-884-3549 www.bigstoneradio.com jeffkurtz@bigstoneradio.com

Watertown KSDR-AM (t) 921 9th Ave SE, Watertown SD 57201 **Phn:** 605-886-5747 **Fax:** 605-886-9306 www.mywatertownsd.com cpowers@brookings.net

Watertown KSDR-FM (c) 921 9th Ave SE, Watertown SD 57201 **Phn:** 605-886-8444 **Fax:** 605-886-9306 www.mywatertownsd.com brorvick@watertown.threeeagles.com

Watertown KWAT-AM (ntf) 921 9th Ave SE, Watertown SD 57201 **Phn:** 605-886-8444 **Fax:** 605-886-9306 www.mywatertownsd.com kwatnews@watertown.threeeagles.com

Winner KWYR-AM (c) PO Box 491, Winner SD 57580 **Phn:** 605-842-3333 **Fax:** 605-842-3875 www.kwyr.com sschramm@gwtc.net

Winner KWYR-FM (a) PO Box 491, Winner SD 57580 **Phn:** 605-842-3333 **Fax:** 605-842-3875 www.kwyr.com kwyrnews@gwtc.net

Yankton KKYA-FM (c) PO Box 628, Yankton SD 57078 **Phn:** 605-665-7892 **Fax:** 605-665-0818 www.kk93.com davelee@kk93.com

Yankton KVHT-FM (a) 210 W 3rd St, Yankton SD 57078 **Phn:** 605-665-2600 **Fax:** 605-665-8875 www.kvht.com news@kvht.com

Yankton KVTK-AM (s) 210 W 3rd St, Yankton SD 57078 **Phn:** 605-665-2600 **Fax:** 605-665-8875 www.kvtk.com sports@kvht.com

Yankton KYNT-AM (ta) PO Box 628, Yankton SD 57078 **Phn:** 605-665-7892 **Fax:** 605-665-0818 www.kynt1450.com cdykstra@kynt1450.com

Yankton WNAX-AM (cf) 1609 E Highway 50, Yankton SD 57078 **Phn:** 605-665-7442 **Fax:** 605-665-8788 www.wnax.com oster@wnax.com

Yankton WNAX-FM (c) 1609 E Highway 50, Yankton SD 57078 **Phn:** 605-665-7442 **Fax:** 605-665-8788 www.thewolf1041.com holst@wnax.com

TENNESSEE

Alcoa WBCR-AM (nq) PO Box 130, Alcoa TN 37701 **Phn:** 865-984-1470 **Fax:** 865-983-0890 www.truthradio.tv gm@truthradio.tv

Ardmore WSLV-AM (gc) PO Box 96, Ardmore TN 38449 **Phn:** 931-427-2178 **Fax:** 931-427-2179 www.wslvradio.com wslv@ardmore.net

Ashland City WQSV-AM (cg) PO Box 619, Ashland City TN 37015 **Phn:** 615-792-6789 **Fax:** 615-792-7795 www.wqsvam790.com

Athens WJSQ-FM (c) PO Box 986, Athens TN 37371 **Phn:** 423-745-1000 **Fax:** 423-745-2000

Athens WLAR-AM (c) PO Box 986, Athens TN 37371 **Phn:** 423-745-1000 **Fax:** 423-745-2000

Athens WYXI-AM (tm) PO Box 1390, Athens TN 37371 **Phn:** 423-745-1390 www.wyxi.net wyxi@bellsouth.net

Benton WBIN-AM (gq) 108 Lifestyle Way, Benton TN 37307 **Phn:** 423-338-2864 craig@craigharding.com

Bolivar WBOL-AM (a) 123 W Market St, Bolivar TN 38008 **Phn:** 731-658-3690 **Fax:** 731-658-3408 www.wojg.com tracy.shaw@wojg.com

Bolivar WMOD-FM (c) PO Box 438, Bolivar TN 38008 **Phn:** 731-658-4320 wmodradio.com news@wmodradio.com

Bolivar WOJG-FM (gw) PO Box 191, Bolivar TN 38008 **Phn:** 731-658-3690 **Fax:** 731-658-3408 www.wojg.com tracy.shaw@wojg.com

Bristol WHCB-FM (vtq) PO Box 2061, Bristol TN 37621 **Phn:** 423-878-6279 **Fax:** 423-878-6520 www.whcbradio.org appedu@yahoo.com

Bristol WIGN-AM (qt) PO Box 68, Bristol TN 37621 **Phn:** 276-591-5800 **Fax:** 276-591-5278 wignam.com manager@wignam.com

Bristol WPWT-AM (vt) PO Box 2061, Bristol TN 37621 **Phn:** 423-878-6279 **Fax:** 423-878-6520 www.powertalk870.com

Brownsville WNWS-AM (wg) PO Box 198, Brownsville TN 38012 **Phn:** 731-772-3700

Brownsville WTBG-FM (cnt) PO Box 198, Brownsville TN 38012 **Phn:** 731-772-3700

Camden WFWL-AM (g) 117 Vicksburg Ave, Camden TN 38320 **Phn:** 731-584-7570 **Fax:** 731-584-7553 www.wrjbradio.com wfwlwrjbprod@bellsouth.net

Camden WRJB-FM (a) 117 Vicksburg Ave, Camden TN 38320 **Phn:** 731-584-7570 **Fax:** 731-584-7553 www.wrjbradio.com jrlane@bellsouth.net

Carthage WRKM-AM (st) PO Box 179, Carthage TN 37030 **Phn:** 615-735-1350 **Fax:** 615-735-0381 www.1041theranch.net

Carthage WUCZ-FM (c) PO Box 179, Carthage TN 37030 **Phn:** 615-735-1350 **Fax:** 615-735-1351 www.1041theranch.com dennis@1041theranch.net

TENNESSEE RADIO STATIONS

Centerville WNKX-FM (c) PO Box 280, Centerville TN 37033 **Phn:** 931-729-5192 **Fax:** 931-729-5467 www.countrykix96.com mail@countrykix96.com

Chattanooga WALV-FM (s) 1305 Carter St, Chattanooga TN 37402 **Phn:** 423-242-7656 **Fax:** 423-472-5290 www.brewerradio.com jessicab@brewerradio.com

Chattanooga WBDX-FM (aq) PO Box 9396, Chattanooga TN 37412 **Phn:** 423-892-1200 **Fax:** 423-892-1633 www.j103.com info@j103.com

Chattanooga WDEF-FM (a) 2615 Broad St Ste A, Chattanooga TN 37408 **Phn:** 423-321-6200 **Fax:** 423-321-6264 www.sunny923.com bbarker@wdefradio.com

Chattanooga WDEF-AM (snt) 2615 Broad St Ste A, Chattanooga TN 37408 **Phn:** 423-321-6200 **Fax:** 423-321-6264 foxsportschattanooga.com bbarker@wdefradio.com

Chattanooga WDOD-AM (am) 2615 Broad St Ste A, Chattanooga TN 37408 **Phn:** 423-321-6200 **Fax:** 423-321-6270 www.hits96.com dhoward@wdefradio.com

Chattanooga WDOD-FM (h) 2615 Broad St Ste A, Chattanooga TN 37408 **Phn:** 423-321-6200 **Fax:** 423-321-6270 www.hits96.com dhoward@wdefradio.com

Chattanooga WDYN-FM (vq) 1815 Union Ave, Chattanooga TN 37404 **Phn:** 423-493-4382 **Fax:** 423-493-4526 www.wdyn.com wdyn@wdyn.com

Chattanooga WFLI-AM (g) 621 O Grady Dr, Chattanooga TN 37419 **Phn:** 423-821-3555 **Fax:** 423-821-3557 benns@mindspring.com

Chattanooga WGOW-FM (t) PO Box 11202, Chattanooga TN 37401 **Phn:** 423-756-6141 **Fax:** 423-266-1652 www.wgow.com

Chattanooga WGOW-AM (nt) PO Box 11202, Chattanooga TN 37401 **Phn:** 423-756-6141 **Fax:** 423-266-3629

Chattanooga WJTT-FM (wu) 1305 Carter St, Chattanooga TN 37402 **Phn:** 423-265-9494 **Fax:** 423-266-2335 www.power94.com jay@power94.com

Chattanooga WLLJ-FM (q) PO Box 9396, Chattanooga TN 37412 **Phn:** 423-892-1200 www.j103.com jocks@j103.com

Chattanooga WLMR-AM (q) 3809 Ringgold Rd, Chattanooga TN 37412 **Phn:** 423-624-4200 www.wilkinsradio.com wlmr@wilkinsradio.com

Chattanooga WMBW-FM (vq) PO Box 73026, Chattanooga TN 37407 **Phn:** 423-629-8900 **Fax:** 423-629-0021 www.mbn.org wmbw@moody.edu

Chattanooga WMPZ-FM (wg) 1305 Carter St, Chattanooga TN 37402 **Phn:** 423-265-9494 **Fax:** 423-266-2335 www.groove93.com

Chattanooga WNLD-FM (c) 7413 Old Lee Hwy, Chattanooga TN 37421 **Phn:** 423-892-3333 **Fax:** 423-899-7224 www.us101country.com

Chattanooga WNOO-AM (wug) PO Box 5597, Chattanooga TN 37412 **Phn:** 423-698-8617 **Fax:** 423-698-8796 www.wnooradio.com wnoo@epbinternet.com

Chattanooga WOGT-FM (c) PO Box 11202, Chattanooga TN 37401 **Phn:** 423-756-6141 **Fax:** 423-266-1652 1079bigfm.com randy.price@cumulus.com

Chattanooga WRXR-FM (r) 7413 Old Lee Hwy, Chattanooga TN 37421 **Phn:** 423-892-3333 **Fax:** 423-899-7224 www.rock105.com gatorharrison@clearchannel.com

Chattanooga WSKZ-FM (r) PO Box 11202, Chattanooga TN 37401 **Phn:** 423-756-6141 **Fax:** 423-266-3629 www.wskz.com

Chattanooga WUSY-FM (c) 7413 Old Lee Hwy, Chattanooga TN 37421 **Phn:** 423-892-3333 **Fax:** 423-899-7224 www.us101country.com kylecroft@clearchannel.com

Chattanooga WUTC-FM (pn) 615 McCallie Ave Dept 1151, Chattanooga TN 37403 **Phn:** 423-425-4756 **Fax:** 423-425-2379 www.wutc.org mark-colbert@utc.edu

Chattanooga WUUS-FM (h) PO Box 4743, Chattanooga TN 37405 **Phn:** 423-643-2212 **Fax:** 423-643-2215

Church Hill WEYE-FM (c) 439 Richmond St, Church Hill TN 37642 **Phn:** 423-357-5601 www.eagle1043fm.com dsandz@yahoo.com

Church Hill WMCH-AM (g) PO Box 128, Church Hill TN 37642 **Phn:** 423-357-5601 **Fax:** 423-357-3635 www.wmch.us wmchradio@yahoo.com

Clarksville WCVQ-FM (a) 1640 Old Russellville Pike, Clarksville TN 37043 **Phn:** 931-648-7720 **Fax:** 931-648-7769 www.q108.com lee@clarksvillenow.com

Clarksville WEGI-AM (h) 1640 Old Russellville Pike, Clarksville TN 37043 **Phn:** 931-648-7720 **Fax:** 931-648-7769 eagle943.com lee@5starradio.com

Clarksville WEGI-FM (r) 1640 Old Russellville Pike, Clarksville TN 37043 **Phn:** 931-648-7720 **Fax:** 931-648-7769 eagle943.com lee@5starradio.com

Clarksville WJQI-AM (q) 1640 Old Russellville Pike, Clarksville TN 37043 **Phn:** 931-648-7720 **Fax:** 931-648-7769

Clarksville WJZM-AM (snt) PO Box 648, Clarksville TN 37041 **Phn:** 931-645-6414 **Fax:** 931-551-8432 www.wjzm.com 14jzm@wjzm.com

Clarksville WKFN-AM (st) 1640 Old Russellville Pike, Clarksville TN 37043 **Phn:** 931-648-7720 **Fax:** 931-648-7769 5starradio.com

Clarksville WVVR-FM (h) 1640 Old Russellville Pike, Clarksville TN 37043 **Phn:** 931-648-7720 **Fax:** 931-648-7769 beaver1003.com katie@5starradio.com

Clarksville WZZP-FM (r) 1640 Old Russellville Pike, Clarksville TN 37043 **Phn:** 931-648-7720 **Fax:** 931-648-7769 z975.com jrod@z975.com

Cleveland WBAC-AM (nos) 2640 Ralph Buckner Blvd NE, Cleveland TN 37311 **Phn:** 423-242-7656 **Fax:** 423-472-5290

Cleveland WCLE-AM (g) 1860 Executive Park NW Ste E, Cleveland TN 37312 **Phn:** 423-472-6700 **Fax:** 423-476-4686 www.1570wcle.com info@mymix1041.com

Cleveland WCLE-FM (a) 1860 Executive Park Dr, Cleveland TN 37312 **Phn:** 423-472-6700 **Fax:** 423-476-4686 mix104.info info@mymix1041.com

Cleveland WPLZ-FM (nt) 2640 Ralph Buckner Blvd NE, Cleveland TN 37311 **Phn:** 423-265-9494 **Fax:** 423-266-2335 www.catcountry953.com

Clinton WGAP-AM (t) PO Box 329, Clinton TN 37717 **Phn:** 865-457-1380 **Fax:** 865-457-4440 www.wgapradio.com wysh@wyshradio.com

Clinton WYSH-AM (c) PO Box 329, Clinton TN 37717 **Phn:** 865-457-1380 **Fax:** 865-457-4440 www.wyshradio.com wysh@wyshradio.com

Collegedale WSMC-FM (pln) PO Box 370, Collegedale TN 37315 **Phn:** 423-236-2905 **Fax:** 423-236-1905 https:www.southern.eduwsmc wsmc@southern.edu

Columbia WKOM-FM (o) PO Box 1377, Columbia TN 38402 **Phn:** 931-388-3636 **Fax:** 931-381-1017

Columbia WKRM-AM (a) PO Box 1377, Columbia TN 38402 **Phn:** 931-388-3636 **Fax:** 931-381-1017

Columbia WMCP-AM (c) PO Box 711, Columbia TN 38402 **Phn:** 931-388-3241 **Fax:** 931-381-2510

Columbia WMRB-AM (gw) 1116 W 7th St, Columbia TN 38401 **Phn:** 931-381-7100 **Fax:** 931-381-0088

Cookeville WATX-AM (snt) 259 S Willow Ave, Cookeville TN 38501 **Phn:** 931-528-6064 **Fax:** 931-520-1590 cookevillesnewstalk.com information@stonecomradio.com

Cookeville WBXE-FM (r) 259 S Willow Ave, Cookeville TN 38501 **Phn:** 931-528-6064 **Fax:** 931-520-1590 rock937online.com greg@stonecomradio.com

Cookeville WGIC-FM (h) 698 S Willow Ave, Cookeville TN 38501 **Phn:** 931-526-2131 **Fax:** 931-528-8400 www.kissfm985.com freakyd@gpmnow.com

Cookeville WGSQ-FM (c) 698 S Willow Ave, Cookeville TN 38501 **Phn:** 931-526-7144 **Fax:** 931-528-8400 www.countrygiant.com channel7@gpmnow.com

Cookeville WHUB-AM (c) 698 S Willow Ave, Cookeville TN 38501 **Phn:** 931-526-2131 **Fax:** 931-528-8400

Cookeville WKXD-FM (c) 259 S Willow Ave, Cookeville TN 38501 **Phn:** 931-528-6064 **Fax:** 931-520-1590 www.1069kicksfm.com information@stonecomradio.com

Cookeville WLQK-FM (ar) 259 S Willow Ave, Cookeville TN 38501 **Phn:** 931-528-6064 **Fax:** 931-520-1590 www.literock959.com

Cookeville WPTN-AM (o) 698 S Willow Ave, Cookeville TN 38501 **Phn:** 931-526-7144 **Fax:** 931-528-8400

Cookeville WTTU-FM (v) PO Box 5113, Cookeville TN 38505 **Phn:** 931-372-3169 **Fax:** 931-372-6225 www.tntech.eduwttu rwitcher@tntech.edu

Cordova WKNO-FM (pln) 7151 Cherry Farms Rd, Cordova TN 38016 **Phn:** 901-458-2521 **Fax:** 901-325-6506 www.wknofm.org radio@wkno.org

Covington WKBL-AM (c) 101 Wkbl Dr, Covington TN 38019 **Phn:** 901-476-7129 **Fax:** 901-476-7120 us51country.com

Covington WKBQ-FM (a) 101 Wkbl Dr, Covington TN 38019 **Phn:** 901-476-7129 **Fax:** 901-476-7120 www.us51country.com

Cowan WZYX-AM (o) PO Box 398, Cowan TN 37318 **Phn:** 931-967-7471 **Fax:** 931-962-1440 wzyxradio@cafes.net

Crossville WAEW-AM (nt) 961 Miller Ave, Crossville TN 38555 **Phn:** 931-707-1102 **Fax:** 931-707-1220 www.waewradio.com

Crossville WCSV-AM (s) 961 Miller Ave, Crossville TN 38555 **Phn:** 931-707-1102 **Fax:** 931-707-1220 www.1490wcsv.com

Crossville WOFE-AM (c) 37 South Dr, Crossville TN 38555 **Phn:** 931-484-1057 **Fax:** 931-707-0580

Crossville WOWF-FM (c) 961 Miller Ave, Crossville TN 38555 **Phn:** 931-707-1102 **Fax:** 931-707-1220 www.1025wowcountry.com news@pegbroadcasting.com

Crossville WPBX-FM (h) 961 Miller Ave, Crossville TN 38555 **Phn:** 931-707-1102 **Fax:** 931-707-1220 www.mix993.net christy.lewis@pegbroadcasting.com

Dayton WDNT-AM (snt) PO Box 1235, Dayton TN 37321 **Phn:** 423-285-6441 www.rheacountyradio.com comments@rheacountyradio.com

Dickson WDKN-AM (c) 106 E College St, Dickson TN 37055 **Phn:** 615-446-0752 **Fax:** 615-446-9681

Dunlap WSDQ-AM (c) 1446 Main St, Dunlap TN 37327 **Phn:** 423-949-5805 **Fax:** 423-949-5143 wsdq@bledsoe.net

Dyersburg WASL-FM (a) PO Box 100, Dyersburg TN 38025 **Phn:** 731-285-1339 **Fax:** 731-287-0100

TENNESSEE RADIO STATIONS

Dyersburg WTNV-FM (r) 2555 Burks Pl, Dyersburg TN 38024 **Phn:** 731-285-1339 **Fax:** 731-287-0100 www.eagle973.net jaredmims08@yahoo.com

Dyersburg WTRO-AM (o) PO Box 100, Dyersburg TN 38025 **Phn:** 731-285-1339 **Fax:** 731-287-0100

Elizabethton WBEJ-AM (c) 510 Broad St, Elizabethton TN 37643 **Phn:** 423-542-2184 **Fax:** 423-542-3192 www.wbej.com wbej@planetc.com

Englewood WENR-AM (cg) PO Box 809, Englewood TN 37329 **Phn:** 423-263-5555 **Fax:** 423-263-2555

Erwin WEMB-AM (c) PO Box 280, Erwin TN 37650 **Phn:** 423-743-6123 www.wemb.com wembnews@hotmail.com

Erwin WXIS-FM (h) 101 Riverview Rd, Erwin TN 37650 **Phn:** 423-743-6123 **Fax:** 423-743-6122 www.923jamzfm.com

Etowah WCPH-AM (m) PO Box 676, Etowah TN 37331 **Phn:** 423-263-5555 **Fax:** 423-263-2555 wcphradio@yahoo.com

Fayetteville WBXR-AM (tq) 2926 Huntsville Hwy Ste D, Fayetteville TN 37334 **Phn:** 931-433-7017 www.wilkinsradio.com wbxr@wilkinsradio.com

Fayetteville WEKR-AM (cg) 76 Molino Rd, Fayetteville TN 37334 **Phn:** 931-433-3545 **Fax:** 931-438-0620

Fayetteville WYTM-FM (ac) PO Box 717, Fayetteville TN 37334 **Phn:** 931-433-1531 **Fax:** 931-433-4110

Franklin WAKM-AM (cs) 222 Mallory Station Rd, Franklin TN 37067 **Phn:** 615-794-1594 **Fax:** 615-794-1595 www.wakmworldwide.com wakm950@comcast.net

Franklin WAY-FM (qm) 1095 W McEwen Dr, Franklin TN 37067 **Phn:** 615-261-9293 **Fax:** 615-261-3967 www.wayfm.com waym@wayfm.com

Gallatin WHIN-AM (c) PO Box 1685, Gallatin TN 37066 **Phn:** 615-451-0450 **Fax:** 615-452-9446 www.whinradio.com whinam@comcast.net

Gallatin WMRO-AM (o) PO Box 1445, Gallatin TN 37066 **Phn:** 615-451-2131

Gallatin WVCP-FM (or) Ramer Bldg # 101, Gallatin TN 37066 **Phn:** 615-230-3618 **Fax:** 615-230-4803 www.wvcp.net howard.espravnik@volstate.edu

Gray WGOC-AM (c) PO Box 8668, Gray TN 37615 **Phn:** 423-477-1000 **Fax:** 423-477-4747 www.wgoc.com bill.meade@cumulus.com

Gray WJCW-AM (nt) PO Box 8668, Gray TN 37615 **Phn:** 423-477-1000 **Fax:** 423-477-4747 www.wjcw.com bill.meade@cumulus.com

Gray WKOS-FM (o) PO Box 8668, Gray TN 37615 **Phn:** 423-477-1000 **Fax:** 423-477-4747 www.greatcountry1049.com john.patrick@cumulus.com

Gray WQUT-FM (r) PO Box 8668, Gray TN 37615 **Phn:** 423-477-1000 **Fax:** 423-477-4747 www.wqut.com john.patrick@cumulus.com

Gray WXSM-AM (s) PO Box 8668, Gray TN 37615 **Phn:** 423-477-1000 **Fax:** 423-477-4747 www.640wxsm.com bob.lawrence@cumulus.com

Greeneville WGRV-AM (c) PO Box 278, Greeneville TN 37744 **Phn:** 423-638-4147 **Fax:** 423-638-1979 www.greeneville.comwgrv wgrv@greeneville.com

Greeneville WIKQ-FM (c) PO Box 278, Greeneville TN 37744 **Phn:** 423-639-1831 **Fax:** 423-638-1979 www.greeneville.comwikq wikq@greeneville.com

Greeneville WSMG-AM (ar) PO Box 278, Greeneville TN 37744 **Phn:** 423-638-3188 **Fax:** 423-638-1979 www.greeneville.comwsmg wsmg@greeneville.com

Henderson WFHU-FM (var) 158 E Main St, Henderson TN 38340 **Phn:** 731-989-6749 www.fhu.edufm91 rmeans@fhu.edu

Hohenwald WMLR-AM (c) 184 Switzerland Rd, Hohenwald TN 38462 **Phn:** 931-796-5967 **Fax:** 931-796-7353 donhaney@yahoo.com

Huntingdon WVHR-FM (c) 215 Baker Rd, Huntingdon TN 38344 **Phn:** 731-986-0242 **Fax:** 731-986-8557

Jackson WDXI-AM (nt) PO Box 3845, Jackson TN 38303 **Phn:** 731-424-1310 **Fax:** 731-424-1321 kool103fm@yahoo.com

Jackson WFGZ-FM (q) 25 Stonebrook Pl # G-322, Jackson TN 38305 **Phn:** 731-664-9497 **Fax:** 731-645-6197 www.gracebroadcasting.com

Jackson WFKX-FM (wuh) 111 W Main St, Jackson TN 38301 **Phn:** 731-427-9616 **Fax:** 731-427-9302

Jackson WHHM-FM (a) 111 W Main St, Jackson TN 38301 **Phn:** 731-427-9616 **Fax:** 731-427-9302

Jackson WJAK-AM (s) 111 W Main St, Jackson TN 38301 **Phn:** 731-427-9616 **Fax:** 731-427-9302

Jackson WMXX-FM (o) PO Box 3845, Jackson TN 38303 **Phn:** 731-424-1310 **Fax:** 731-424-1321 www.kool103.com

Jackson WNWS-FM (sn) 207 W Lafayette St, Jackson TN 38301 **Phn:** 731-423-8316 **Fax:** 731-423-8304 wnws.point5digital.com keith@wnws.com

Jackson WOGY-FM (c) 122 Radio Rd, Jackson TN 38301 **Phn:** 731-427-3316 **Fax:** 731-427-4576 www.froggy1041.com pollywogg@forevertn.com

Jackson WSIB-FM (q) 25 Stonebrook Pl # G-322, Jackson TN 38305 **Phn:** 731-645-6165 **Fax:** 731-661-9064 www.gracebroadcasting.com

Jackson WTJS-AM (nt) 122 Radio Rd, Jackson TN 38301 **Phn:** 731-427-3316 **Fax:** 731-427-4576 www.wtjs.com rhaney@forevertn.com

Jackson WTKB-FM (c) 25 Stonebrook Pl # G322, Jackson TN 38305 **Phn:** 731-664-9497 **Fax:** 731-855-1600 www.gracebroadcasting.com

Jackson WTNE-AM (ant) 25 Stonebrook Pl # G-322, Jackson TN 38305 **Phn:** 731-663-2327 **Fax:** 731-663-2427 www.gracebroadcasting.com gminyard@gracebroadcasting.com

Jackson WTNE-FM (a) 25 Stonebrook Pl # G-322, Jackson TN 38305 **Phn:** 731-664-9497 **Fax:** 731-855-1600 www.gracebroadcasting.com

Jackson WWGM-FM (gq) 25 Stonebrook Pl # G-322, Jackson TN 38305 **Phn:** 731-663-2327 **Fax:** 731-663-2427 www.gracebroadcasting.com

Jackson WWYN-FM (c) 111 W Main St, Jackson TN 38301 **Phn:** 731-427-9616 **Fax:** 731-427-9302

Jackson WYNU-FM (ar) 122 Radio Rd, Jackson TN 38301 **Phn:** 731-427-3316 **Fax:** 731-427-4576 www.rock923.net request@rock923.net

Jackson WZDQ-FM (r) 111 W Main St, Jackson TN 38301 **Phn:** 731-427-9616 **Fax:** 731-427-9302

Jamestown WCLC-FM (gq) PO Box 1509, Jamestown TN 38556 **Phn:** 931-879-8188 **Fax:** 931-879-1733 www.newlife105.com info@newlife105.com

Jamestown WDEB-FM (c) PO Box 69, Jamestown TN 38556 **Phn:** 931-879-8164 **Fax:** 931-879-7437

Jamestown WDEB-AM (c) PO Box 69, Jamestown TN 38556 **Phn:** 931-879-8164 **Fax:** 931-879-7437

Jamestown WGSN-FM (q) PO Box 1509, Jamestown TN 38556 **Phn:** 877-947-6907 **Fax:** 931-879-1733 www.wgsnradio.com info@wgsnradio.com

Jasper WWAM-AM (gt) PO Box 279, Jasper TN 37347 **Phn:** 423-942-1700 **Fax:** 423-942-1701

Jefferson City WJFC-AM (c) PO Box 430, Jefferson City TN 37760 **Phn:** 865-475-3825 **Fax:** 865-475-3800 www.wjfcradio.com

Johnson City WETB-AM (g) PO Box 4127, Johnson City TN 37602 **Phn:** 423-928-7131 **Fax:** 423-928-8392 wetb@mounet.com

Johnson City WETS-FM (plnj) PO Box 70630, Johnson City TN 37614 **Phn:** 423-439-6440 **Fax:** 423-439-6449 www.wets.org

Kingsport WKTP-AM (a) 222 Commerce St, Kingsport TN 37660 **Phn:** 423-246-9578 **Fax:** 423-247-9836 www.wkptam.com charlie@wkptradio.com

Kingsport WOPI-AM (o) 222 Commerce St, Kingsport TN 37660 **Phn:** 423-246-9578 **Fax:** 23-247-9836 www.wopi.com charlie@wkptradio.com

Kingsport WRZK-FM (r) 222 Commerce St, Kingsport TN 37660 **Phn:** 423-246-9578 **Fax:** 423-247-9836 www.wrzk.com scott@wrzk.com

Kingsport WTFM-FM (a) 222 Commerce St, Kingsport TN 37660 **Phn:** 423-246-9578 **Fax:** 423-247-9836 www.wtfm.com charlie@hvbcgroup.com

Kingsport WVEK-FM (ro) 222 Commerce St, Kingsport TN 37660 **Phn:** 423-246-9578 **Fax:** 423-247-9836 www.wvekfm.com classichits1027@live.com

Knoxville WATO-AM (ob) 517 N Watt Rd, Knoxville TN 37934 **Phn:** 865-675-4105 **Fax:** 865-675-4859

Knoxville WCYQ-FM (c) 1533 Amherst Rd, Knoxville TN 37909 **Phn:** 865-824-1021 **Fax:** 865-824-1881 www.q100country.com rbailey@journalbroadcastgroup.com

Knoxville WDVX-FM (vbm) PO Box 27568, Knoxville TN 37927 **Phn:** 865-544-1029 www.wdvx.com mail@wdvx.com

Knoxville WETR-AM (nt) 1621 E Magnolia Ave, Knoxville TN 37917 **Phn:** 865-525-0620 **Fax:** 865-521-8923 www.talkradio760.com info@talkradio760.com

Knoxville WFIV-FM (a) 517 N Watt Rd, Knoxville TN 37934 **Phn:** 865-675-4105 **Fax:** 865-675-4859 www.myi105.com

Knoxville WIFA-AM (q) 818 N Cedar Bluff Rd # 102, Knoxville TN 37923 **Phn:** 865-690-0101 **Fax:** 865-531-2006 www.1240radio.com zabrina@1240radio.com

Knoxville WIMZ-FM (r) 1100 Sharps Ridge Rd, Knoxville TN 37917 **Phn:** 865-525-6000 **Fax:** 865-525-2000 www.wimz.com rchambers@sccradio.com

Knoxville WITA-AM (q) 2914 Sanderson Rd, Knoxville TN 37921 **Phn:** 865-588-2974 **Fax:** 865-588-6720 www.1490wita.com cjohnsonwita1490@bellsouth.net

Knoxville WIVK-FM (c) PO Box 11167, Knoxville TN 37939 **Phn:** 865-588-6511 **Fax:** 865-588-3725 www.wivk.com alison@wivk.com

Knoxville WJXB-FM (a) PO Box 27100, Knoxville TN 37927 **Phn:** 865-525-6000 **Fax:** 865-525-2000 www.b975.com terry@southcentralmedia.com

Knoxville WKCE-AM (s) 802 S Central St, Knoxville TN 37902 **Phn:** 865-546-4653

Knoxville WKHT-FM (h) 1533 Amherst Rd, Knoxville TN 37909 **Phn:** 865-824-1021 **Fax:** 865-824-1881 www.hot1045.net cprotzman@journalbroadcastgroup.com

Knoxville WKTI-AM (st) 1533 Amherst Rd, Knoxville TN 37909 **Phn:** 865-824-1021 **Fax:** 865-824-1881 www.studio1040.com cprotzman@journalbroadcastgroup.com

TENNESSEE RADIO STATIONS

Knoxville WKXV-AM (qg) 5106 Middlebrook Pike, Knoxville TN 37921 **Phn:** 865-558-0900 **Fax:** 865-588-5848

Knoxville WLOD-AM (c) 517 N Watt Rd, Knoxville TN 37934 **Phn:** 865-675-4105 **Fax:** 865-675-4859

Knoxville WNFZ-FM (r) PO Box 27100, Knoxville TN 37927 **Phn:** 865-525-6000 **Fax:** 865-525-2000 www.943thex.com scox@southcentralmedia.com

Knoxville WNML-AM (s) PO Box 11167, Knoxville TN 37939 **Phn:** 865-588-6511 **Fax:** 865-588-3725 www.sportsanimal99.com mickey.dearstone@cumulus.com

Knoxville WNOX-FM (nt) PO Box 11167, Knoxville TN 37939 **Phn:** 865-588-6511 **Fax:** 865-588-3725 987NewsTalk.com wnox.news@cumulus.com

Knoxville WOKI-FM (o) 4711 Old Kingston Pike, Knoxville TN 37919 **Phn:** 865-588-6511 **Fax:** 865-588-3725 www.987newstalk.com

Knoxville WQJK-FM (a) PO Box 27100, Knoxville TN 37927 **Phn:** 865-525-6000 **Fax:** 865-525-2000 www.jackfmknoxville.com terry@southcentralmedia.com

Knoxville WRJZ-AM (q) 1621 E Magnolia Ave, Knoxville TN 37917 **Phn:** 865-525-0620 **Fax:** 865-521-8923 www.wrjz.com dclabo@wrjz.com

Knoxville WUOT-FM (plnj) 209 Comm Bldg Univ Of Tn, Knoxville TN 37996 **Phn:** 865-974-5375 **Fax:** 865-946-1781 www.wuot.org newsroom@wuot.org

Knoxville WUTK-FM (vr) P103 Andy Holt Twr, Knoxville TN 37996 **Phn:** 865-974-2229 **Fax:** 865-974-2814 www.wutkradio.com pgross@utk.edu

Knoxville WVLZ-AM (st) 802 S Central St, Knoxville TN 37902 **Phn:** 865-546-4653

Knoxville WWST-FM (h) 1533 Amherst Rd, Knoxville TN 37909 **Phn:** 865-824-1021 **Fax:** 865-824-1881 www.star1021fm.com richbailey@journalbroadcastgroup.com

Knoxville WYLV-FM (q) 1621 E Magnolia Ave, Knoxville TN 37917 **Phn:** 865-521-8910 **Fax:** 865-521-8923 www.wrjz.com dclabo@wrjz.com

Kodak WPFT-FM (rh) 196 W Dumplin Valley Rd, Kodak TN 37764 **Phn:** 865-932-6002 **Fax:** 865-932-0167 easttennesseeradio.com

Kodak WSEV-AM (a) 196 W Dumplin Valley Rd, Kodak TN 37764 **Phn:** 865-932-6002 **Fax:** 865-429-2601 www.easttennesseeradio.com

La Follette WLAF-AM (cg) PO Box 1409, La Follette TN 37766 **Phn:** 423-562-3557 **Fax:** 423-562-5764 wlaf@bellsouth.net

La Follette WTNQ-FM (c) PO Box 1530, La Follette TN 37766 **Phn:** 423-566-1310 **Fax:** 865-562-0105

Lafayette WEEN-AM (g) 231 Chaffin Rd, Lafayette TN 37083 **Phn:** 615-666-2169 **Fax:** 615-666-8056 www.wlct.com wlct@nctc.com

Lafayette WLCT-FM (c) 231 Chaffin Rd, Lafayette TN 37083 **Phn:** 615-666-2169 **Fax:** 615-666-8056 www.wlct.com wlct@nctc.com

Lawrenceburg WDXE-FM (rh) 29 Public Sq, Lawrenceburg TN 38464 **Phn:** 931-762-4411 **Fax:** 931-762-4789 www.wdxe.com jack@wdxe.com

Lawrenceburg WDXE-AM (c) 29 Public Sq, Lawrenceburg TN 38464 **Phn:** 931-762-4411 **Fax:** 931-762-4789 www.wdxe.com jack@wdxe.com

Lawrenceburg WLLX-FM (c) PO Box 156, Lawrenceburg TN 38464 **Phn:** 931-762-6200 www.wlxonline.com wlxnews@bellsouth.net

Lawrenceburg WWLX-AM (c) PO Box 156, Lawrenceburg TN 38464 **Phn:** 931-762-6200

Lebanon WANT-FM (c) PO Box 399, Lebanon TN 37088 **Phn:** 615-449-3699 **Fax:** 615-443-4235 www.wantfm.com info@wantfm.com

Lebanon WCOR-AM (c) PO Box 399, Lebanon TN 37088 **Phn:** 615-449-3699 **Fax:** 615-443-4235 www.wantfm.com info@wantfm.com

Lebanon WFMQ-FM (vlj) 1 Cumberland Sq, Lebanon TN 37087 **Phn:** 615-444-2562 **Fax:** 615-444-2569

Lenoir City WKZX-FM (y) PO Box 340, Lenoir City TN 37771 **Phn:** 865-986-9850 wkzx@aol.com

Lenoir City WLIL-AM (c) 14542 El Camino Ln, Lenoir City TN 37771 **Phn:** 865-986-7536 wlilcountry.com wlilcountry@aol.com

Lewisburg WAXO-AM (c) 217 W Commerce St, Lewisburg TN 37091 **Phn:** 931-359-6641 **Fax:** 931-270-9290 www.waxo.com waxo@waxo.com

Lewisburg WJJM-FM (c) PO Box 2025, Lewisburg TN 37091 **Phn:** 931-359-4511 **Fax:** 931-270-9556 www.wjjm.com wjjm@wjjm.com

Lewisburg WJJM-AM (c) PO Box 2025, Lewisburg TN 37091 **Phn:** 931-359-4511 **Fax:** 931-270-9556 www.wjjm.com wjjm@wjjm.com

Lexington WDXL-AM (g) PO Box 279, Lexington TN 38351 **Phn:** 731-968-3500 **Fax:** 731-968-0380

Lexington WZLT-FM (c) PO Box 279, Lexington TN 38351 **Phn:** 731-968-3500 **Fax:** 731-968-0380

Livingston WLIV-FM (c) PO Box 359, Livingston TN 38570 **Phn:** 931-823-1226 **Fax:** 931-823-6005

Livingston WLIV-AM (c) PO Box 359, Livingston TN 38570 **Phn:** 931-823-1226 **Fax:** 931-823-6005

Madison WYFN-AM (q) PO Box 747, Madison TN 37116 **Phn:** 615-868-4458

Madisonville WRKQ-AM (st) PO Box 489, Madisonville TN 37354 **Phn:** 423-442-1446 www.wrkq.net monroe.radio@live.com

Manchester WFTZ-FM (a) PO Box 1015, Manchester TN 37349 **Phn:** 931-728-3458 **Fax:** 931-723-1099 www.fantasyradio.com avdotson@fantasyradio.com

Manchester WMSR-FM (or) 1030 Oakdale St, Manchester TN 37355 **Phn:** 931-728-3526 **Fax:** 931-728-3527 www.thunder1320.com wmsr@thunder1320.com

Manchester WMSR-AM (or) 1030 Oakdale St, Manchester TN 37355 **Phn:** 931-728-3526 **Fax:** 931-728-3527 www.thunder1320.com wmsr@thunder1320.com

Martin WCDZ-FM (o) PO Box 318, Martin TN 38237 **Phn:** 731-587-9595 **Fax:** 731-587-5079 wcdzradio.com programming@wcmt.com

Martin WCMT-FM (a) PO Box 318, Martin TN 38237 **Phn:** 731-587-9526 **Fax:** 731-587-5079 www.wcmt.com

Martin WCMT-AM (nt) PO Box 318, Martin TN 38237 **Phn:** 731-587-9526 **Fax:** 731-587-5079 www.wcmt.com programming@wcmt.com

Martin WQAK-FM (r) PO Box 318, Martin TN 38237 **Phn:** 731-885-0051 **Fax:** 731-885-0250 www.wcmt.com newsroom@unioncityradio.com

Martin WUTM-FM (v) 220 Gooch Hall, Martin TN 38238 **Phn:** 731-881-7095 **Fax:** 531-881-7550 www.utm.eduorganizationswutm wutm@utm.edu

McMinnville WAKI-AM (t) 230 W Colville St, McMinnville TN 37110 **Phn:** 931-473-9253 **Fax:** 931-473-4149

McMinnville WBMC-AM (cg) PO Box 759, McMinnville TN 37111 **Phn:** 931-473-9253 **Fax:** 931-473-4149

McMinnville WCPI-FM (v) PO Box 728, McMinnville TN 37111 **Phn:** 931-506-9274 **Fax:** 931-507-1005

McMinnville WKZP-FM (a) PO Box 759, McMinnville TN 37111 **Phn:** 931-473-2104 **Fax:** 931-473-4149

McMinnville WTRZ-FM (c) PO Box 759, McMinnville TN 37111 **Phn:** 931-507-2855 **Fax:** 931-473-4149

Memphis KJMS-FM (wu) 2650 Thousand Oaks Blvd Ste 4100, Memphis TN 38118 **Phn:** 901-259-1300 **Fax:** 901-259-6451 www.myv101.com frankgilbert@clearchannel.com

Memphis KWAM-AM (nt) 5495 Murray Rd, Memphis TN 38119 **Phn:** 901-261-4200 **Fax:** 901-261-4210 www.kwam990.com info@kwam990.com

Memphis KXHT-FM (uw) 6080 Mount Moriah Road Ext, Memphis TN 38115 **Phn:** 901-375-9324 **Fax:** 901-375-4117 www.hot1071.com

Memphis WBBP-AM (g) 369 E GE Patterson Ave, Memphis TN 38126 **Phn:** 901-278-7878 **Fax:** 901-332-1707 bbless.org publicrelations@bbless.org

Memphis WCRV-AM (q) 6401 Poplar Ave Ste 640, Memphis TN 38119 **Phn:** 901-763-4640 **Fax:** 901-763-4920 www.bottradionetwork.com sgossett@bottradionetwork.com

Memphis WDIA-AM (wx) 2650 Thousand Oaks Blvd Ste 4100, Memphis TN 38118 **Phn:** 901-259-1300 **Fax:** 901-259-6451 www.mywdia.com jefflee@clearchannel.com

Memphis WEGR-FM (r) 2650 Thousand Oaks Blvd Ste 4100, Memphis TN 38118 **Phn:** 901-259-1300 **Fax:** 901-259-6449 www.rock103.com dannybowen@clearchannel.com

Memphis WEVL-FM (v) PO Box 40952, Memphis TN 38174 **Phn:** 901-528-0560 wevl.org prmmgr@wevl.org

Memphis WGKX-FM (c) 5629 Murray Rd, Memphis TN 38119 **Phn:** 901-682-1106 **Fax:** 901-767-9531 www.kix106.com

Memphis WHAL-FM (g) 2650 Thousand Oaks Blvd Ste 4100, Memphis TN 38118 **Phn:** 901-259-1300 **Fax:** 901-529-9557 www.hallelujahfm.com

Memphis WHBQ-AM (s) 6080 Mount Moriah Road Ext, Memphis TN 38115 **Phn:** 901-375-9324 **Fax:** 901-795-4454 www.sports56whbq.com

Memphis WHBQ-FM (r) 6080 Mount Moriah Road Ext, Memphis TN 38115 **Phn:** 901-375-9324 **Fax:** 901-375-4117 www.q1075.com

Memphis WHRK-FM (wu) 2650 Thousand Oaks Blvd Ste 4100, Memphis TN 38118 **Phn:** 901-259-1300 **Fax:** 901-259-6449 www.k97fm.com devinsteel@clearchannel.com

Memphis WKIM-FM (nt) 5629 Murray Rd, Memphis TN 38119 **Phn:** 901-682-1106 **Fax:** 901-767-9531 www.newstalkfm989.com

Memphis WKQK-FM (o) 1835 Moriah Woods Blvd Ste 1, Memphis TN 38117 **Phn:** 901-384-5900 **Fax:** 901-767-6076 www.941kqk.com bcarson@941kqk.com

Memphis WLOK-AM (wgt) 363 S 2nd St, Memphis TN 38103 **Phn:** 901-527-9565 **Fax:** 901-528-0335 www.wlok.com wlokradio@aol.com

Memphis WMC-AM (s) 1835 Moriah Woods Blvd Ste 1, Memphis TN 38117 **Phn:** 901-384-5900 **Fax:** 901-767-6076 www.wmc79.com dfuller@entercom.com

Memphis WMC-FM (a) 1835 Moriah Woods Blvd Ste 1, Memphis TN 38117 **Phn:** 901-384-5900 **Fax:** 901-767-6076 www.fm100memphis.com fm100memphis@fm100memphis.com

TENNESSEE RADIO STATIONS

Memphis WMFS-AM (s) 1835 Moriah Woods Blvd, Memphis TN 38117 **Phn:** 901-384-5900 **Fax:** 901-767-6076 cdebardelaben@entercom.com

Memphis WMFS-FM (s) 1835 Moriah Woods Blvd, Memphis TN 38117 **Phn:** 901-384-5900 **Fax:** 901-767-6076 www.espn929.com bcarson@entercom.com

Memphis WMPS-AM (r) 6080 Mount Moriah Road Ext, Memphis TN 38115 **Phn:** 901-375-9324 **Fax:** 901-375-4117 radiosuperhero.com

Memphis WMQM-AM (qt) 3704 Whittier Rd, Memphis TN 38108 **Phn:** 901-327-2500 **Fax:** 901-327-2777 wmqm1600.com askwwcr@wwcr.com

Memphis WOWW-AM (m) 6080 Mount Moriah Road Ext, Memphis TN 38115 **Phn:** 901-375-9324 **Fax:** 901-375-4117 music.disney.com

Memphis WRBO-FM (ox) 5629 Murray Rd, Memphis TN 38119 **Phn:** 901-682-1106 **Fax:** 901-680-0457 www.soulclassics.com earle.augustus@cumulus.com

Memphis WREC-AM (nt) 2650 Thousand Oaks Blvd Ste 4100, Memphis TN 38118 **Phn:** 901-259-1300 **Fax:** 901-259-6449 www.600wrec.com news@600wrec.com

Memphis WRVR-FM (a) 1835 Moriah Woods Blvd Ste 1, Memphis TN 38117 **Phn:** 901-384-5900 **Fax:** 901-767-6076 www.1045theriver.com river104@wrvr.com

Memphis WUMR-FM (vjw) 3745 Central Ave, Memphis TN 38152 **Phn:** 901-678-3176 **Fax:** 901-678-4331

Memphis WXMX-FM (r) 5629 Murray Rd, Memphis TN 38119 **Phn:** 901-682-1106 **Fax:** 901-680-0482 www.981themax.com

Memphis WYPL-FM (vn) 3030 Poplar Ave, Memphis TN 38111 **Phn:** 901-415-2752 **Fax:** 901-323-7902 www.memphislibrary.orgwypl

Morristown WBGQ-FM (a) PO Box 519, Morristown TN 37815 **Phn:** 423-235-4640 www.wbgqfm.com radiomanone@hotmail.com

Morristown WCRK-AM (a) PO Box 220, Morristown TN 37815 **Phn:** 423-586-9101 **Fax:** 423-587-2866 www.wcrk.com ed@wcrk.com

Morristown WJDT-FM (c) PO Box 519, Morristown TN 37815 **Phn:** 423-235-4640 www.wjdtfm.com wjdtprogramdirector@gmail.com

Morristown WMTN-AM (c) PO Box 220, Morristown TN 37815 **Phn:** 423-586-9101 **Fax:** 423-587-2866 www.wmtnradio.com ed@wcrk.com

Mount Pleasant WXRQ-AM (g) PO Box 31, Mount Pleasant TN 38474 **Phn:** 931-379-3119 **Fax:** 931-379-3129 wxrq@yahoo.com

Mountain City WMCT-AM (cg) PO Box 396, Mountain City TN 37683 **Phn:** 423-727-6701 **Fax:** 423-727-9454 www.wmctradio.net wmct@wmctradio.net

Murfreesboro WGNS-AM (snt) 306 S Church St, Murfreesboro TN 37130 **Phn:** 615-893-5373 **Fax:** 615-867-6397 www.wgnsradio.com bart@wgnsradio.com

Murfreesboro WMOT-FM (pj) Mtsu Po Box 3, Murfreesboro TN 37132 **Phn:** 615-898-2800 **Fax:** 615-898-2774 www.wmot.org mosborne@mtsu.edu

Murfreesboro WMTS-FM (vr) 1301 E Main St, Murfreesboro TN 37132 **Phn:** 615-898-2636 **Fax:** 615-898-5682 www.wmts.org manager@wmts.org

Nashville WAMB-AM (bm) 1617 Lebanon Pike Ste 100, Nashville TN 37210 **Phn:** 615-889-1960 **Fax:** 615-902-9108 www.wambradio.com harrywamb@bellsouth.net

Nashville WBOZ-FM (g) 402 Bna Dr Ste 400, Nashville TN 37217 **Phn:** 615-367-2210 **Fax:** 615-367-0758 vdillard@salemmusicnetwork.com

Nashville WBUZ-FM (r) 1824 Murfreesboro Pike, Nashville TN 37217 **Phn:** 615-399-1029 **Fax:** 615-361-9873 www.1029thebuzz.com programdirector@cromwellradio.com

Nashville WCJK-FM (o) 504 Rosedale Ave, Nashville TN 37211 **Phn:** 615-259-4567 **Fax:** 615-259-4594 www.963jackfm.com

Nashville WFFI-FM (g) 402 Bna Dr Ste 400, Nashville TN 37217 **Phn:** 615-367-2210 **Fax:** 615-367-0758 www.94fmthefish.net info@salemmusicnetwork.com

Nashville WFSK-FM (vj) 1000 17th Ave N, Nashville TN 37208 **Phn:** 615-329-8754 **Fax:** 615-329-8711 www.wfskfm.org skay@fisk.edu

Nashville WGFX-FM (st) 10 Music Circle E, Nashville TN 37203 **Phn:** 615-321-1067 www.1045thezone.com

Nashville WJXA-FM (a) PO Box 40506, Nashville TN 37204 **Phn:** 615-259-9393 **Fax:** 615-259-4594 www.mix929.com kim@mix929.com

Nashville WKDA-AM (y) 1617 Lebanon Pike, Nashville TN 37210 **Phn:** 615-889-1960 **Fax:** 615-902-9108

Nashville WKDF-FM (c) 10 Music Circle E, Nashville TN 37203 **Phn:** 615-321-1067 www.103wkdf.com

Nashville WLAC-AM (snt) 55 Music Sq W, Nashville TN 37203 **Phn:** 615-664-2400 **Fax:** 615-664-2410 www.wlac.com programming@wlac.com

Nashville WNAH-AM (wq) 44 Music Sq E Ste 101, Nashville TN 37203 **Phn:** 615-254-7611 **Fax:** 615-256-6553 www.wnah.com

Nashville WNFN-FM (s) 10 Music Cir E, Nashville TN 37203 **Phn:** 615-321-1067 **Fax:** 615-321-5771

Nashville WNQM-AM (q) 1300 Wwcr Ave, Nashville TN 37218 **Phn:** 615-255-1300 **Fax:** 615-255-1311 www.1300wnqm.com

Nashville WNRQ-FM (r) 55 Music Sq W, Nashville TN 37203 **Phn:** 615-664-2400 **Fax:** 615-687-9797 www.1059therock.com mud@clearchannel.com

Nashville WNSG-AM (g) 209 10th Ave S Ste 342, Nashville TN 37203 **Phn:** 615-242-1411 **Fax:** 615-242-3823

Nashville WNSR-AM (s) 810 Dominican Dr, Nashville TN 37228 **Phn:** 615-844-1039 **Fax:** 615-777-2284 nashvillesportsoriginal.com info@wnsr.com

Nashville WPLN-FM (pl) 630 Mainstream Dr, Nashville TN 37228 **Phn:** 615-760-2903 **Fax:** 615-760-2905 www.wpln.org

Nashville WPRT-FM (h) 1824 Murfreesboro Pike, Nashville TN 37217 **Phn:** 615-399-1029 **Fax:** 615-361-9873 cromwellradio.com thanson@cromwellradio.com

Nashville WQQK-FM (wu) 10 Music Cir E, Nashville TN 37203 **Phn:** 615-321-1067 **Fax:** 615-321-5771 www.92qnashville.com ernie.allen@cumulus.com

Nashville WQZQ-AM (g) 1824 Murfreesboro Rd, Nashville TN 37217 **Phn:** 615-399-1029 **Fax:** 931-647-6925 www.wqzq.com jhampton@cromwellradio.com

Nashville WQZQ-FM (g) 1824 Murfreesboro Rd, Nashville TN 37217 **Phn:** 615-399-1029 **Fax:** 931-647-6925 thelightnashville.com jhampton@cromwellradio.com

Nashville WRLT-FM (r) 1310 Clinton St Ste 200, Nashville TN 37203 **Phn:** 615-242-5600 **Fax:** 615-523-2153 lightning100.com kcoes@wrlt.com

Nashville WRQQ-FM (a) 10 Music Cir E, Nashville TN 37203 **Phn:** 615-321-1067 **Fax:** 615-321-5771 www.star97.net michael.dickey@cumulus.com

Nashville WRVU-FM (vrj) PO Box 9100, Nashville TN 37235 **Phn:** 615-322-3691 **Fax:** 615-343-2582 www.wrvu.org wrvugm@gmail.com

Nashville WRVW-FM (h) 55 Music Sq W, Nashville TN 37203 **Phn:** 615-664-2400 **Fax:** 615-664-2434 www.1075theriver.com brianmack@clearchannel.com

Nashville WSIX-FM (c) 55 Music Sq W, Nashville TN 37203 **Phn:** 615-664-2400 **Fax:** 615-664-2410 www.wsix.com andielynne@clearchannel.com

Nashville WSM-AM (c) 2804 Opryland Dr, Nashville TN 37214 **Phn:** 615-889-6595 **Fax:** 615-458-2445 www.wsmonline.com tom@wsmonline.com

Nashville WSM-FM (c) 10 Music Cir E, Nashville TN 37203 **Phn:** 615-321-1067 **Fax:** 615-321-5771 www.955thewolf.com jerry.minshall@cumulus.com

Nashville WUBT-FM (u) 55 Music Sq W, Nashville TN 37203 **Phn:** 615-664-2400 **Fax:** 615-664-2410 www.1011thebeat.com pamelaaniese@clearchannel.com

Nashville WVOL-AM (wxo) 1320 Brick Church Pike, Nashville TN 37207 **Phn:** 615-226-9510 **Fax:** 615-226-0709 www.wvol1470.com wvol1470@aol.com

Nashville WVRY-FM (g) 402 Bna Dr Ste 400, Nashville TN 37217 **Phn:** 615-367-2210 **Fax:** 615-367-0758 www.solidgospel105.com

Nashville WWTN-FM (snt) 10 Music Cir E, Nashville TN 37203 **Phn:** 615-321-1067 **Fax:** 615-321-5771 www.997wtn.com brian.wilson@cumulus.com

Newport WLIK-AM (o) 640 W Highway 25 70, Newport TN 37821 **Phn:** 423-623-3095 **Fax:** 423-623-3096 wlik.net wlik@wlik.net

Newport WNPC-AM (g) 377 Graham St, Newport TN 37821 **Phn:** 423-623-8743 **Fax:** 423-623-0545 www.923wnpc.com ray@923wnpc.com

Newport WNPC-FM (cn) 377 Graham St, Newport TN 37821 **Phn:** 423-623-8743 **Fax:** 423-623-0545 www.923wnpc.com ray@923wnpc.com

Oneida WBNT-FM (ac) PO Box 4370, Oneida TN 37841 **Phn:** 423-569-8598 **Fax:** 423-569-5572 www.hive105.com wbnt@highland.net

Oneida WOCV-AM (t) PO Box 4370, Oneida TN 37841 **Phn:** 423-569-8598 **Fax:** 423-569-5572 www.hive105.com wbnt@highland.net

Paris WAKQ-FM (h) 206 N Brewer St, Paris TN 38242 **Phn:** 731-642-7100 **Fax:** 731-644-9367 www.kf99kq105.com thailey@wenkwtpr.com

Paris WLZK-FM (a) 110 India Rd, Paris TN 38242 **Phn:** 731-644-9455 **Fax:** 731-644-9421 www.wmufradio.comWLZK.html wlzk@bellsouth.net

Paris WMUF-FM (c) 110 India Rd, Paris TN 38242 **Phn:** 731-644-9455 **Fax:** 731-644-9421 www.wmufradio.com wmuf@bellsouth.net

Paris WMUF-AM (c) 110 India Rd, Paris TN 38242 **Phn:** 731-644-9455 **Fax:** 731-644-9421 www.wmufradio.com wmuf@bellsouth.net

Paris WTPR-FM (o) 206 N Brewer St, Paris TN 38242 **Phn:** 731-642-7100 www.wenkwtpr.com thailey@wenkwtpr.com

Paris WTPR-AM (o) 206 N Brewer St, Paris TN 38242 **Phn:** 731-642-7100 **Fax:** 731-644-9367 www.wenkwtpr.com thailey@wenkwtpr.com

Parsons WKJQ-FM (c) PO Box 576, Parsons TN 38363 **Phn:** 731-847-3011 **Fax:** 731-847-4600

Parsons WKJQ-AM (g) PO Box 576, Parsons TN 38363 **Phn:** 731-847-3011 **Fax:** 731-847-4600

Pikeville WUAT-AM (cg) PO Box 128, Pikeville TN 37367 **Phn:** 423-447-2906 **Fax:** 423-447-7309 www.wuatradio.com wuat@bledsoe.net

Portland WQKR-AM (snto) 100 Main St Ste 201, Portland TN 37148 **Phn:** 615-325-3250 **Fax:** 615-325-0803 www.wqkr.com lee@wqkr.com

Portland WQKR-FM (snto) 100 Main St Ste 201, Portland TN 37148 **Phn:** 615-325-3250 **Fax:** 615-325-0803 www.wqkr.com lee@wqkr.com

Pulaski WKSR-AM (o) 104 S 2nd St, Pulaski TN 38478 **Phn:** 931-363-2505 **Fax:** 931-424-3157 www.wksr.com wksrnews@wksr.com

Pulaski WKSR-FM (c) PO Box 738, Pulaski TN 38478 **Phn:** 931-363-2505 **Fax:** 931-424-3157 www.wksr.com jack@wdxe.com

Ripley WTRB-AM (cn) PO Box 410, Ripley TN 38063 **Phn:** 731-635-1570 **Fax:** 731-635-9722

Rogersville WRGS-AM (cns) 211 Burem Rd, Rogersville TN 37857 **Phn:** 423-272-3900 **Fax:** 423-272-0328 www.wrgsradio.com stationmanager@wrgsradio.com

Rogersville WRGS-FM (cns) 211 Burem Rd, Rogersville TN 37857 **Phn:** 423-272-3900 **Fax:** 423-272-0328 www.wrgsradio.com stationmanager@wrgsradio.com

Savannah WKWX-FM (c) PO Box 40, Savannah TN 38372 **Phn:** 731-925-9600 **Fax:** 731-925-8828

Savannah WORM-AM (o) PO Box 550, Savannah TN 38372 **Phn:** 731-925-4981

Savannah WORM-FM (c) PO Box 550, Savannah TN 38372 **Phn:** 731-925-4981

Sevierville WSEV-AM (c) 415 Middle Creek Rd, Sevierville TN 37862 **Phn:** 865-453-2844 **Fax:** 865-429-2601 www.easttennesseeradio.com

Sewanee WUTS-FM (v) 735 University Ave, Sewanee TN 37383 **Phn:** 931-598-1112 www.wutsfm.org wuts@sewanee.edu

Shelbyville WLIJ-AM (c) PO Box 7, Shelbyville TN 37162 **Phn:** 931-684-1514 **Fax:** 931-684-3956

Smithville WJLE-FM (cg) 2606 McMinnville Hwy, Smithville TN 37166 **Phn:** 615-597-4265 **Fax:** 615-597-6025 www.wjle.com wjle@dtccom.net

Smithville WJLE-AM (cg) 2606 McMinnville Hwy, Smithville TN 37166 **Phn:** 615-597-4265 **Fax:** 615-597-6025 www.wjle.com wjle@dtccom.net

South Pittsburg WEPG-AM (c) PO Box 8, South Pittsburg TN 37380 **Phn:** 423-837-0747 **Fax:** 423-837-2974

Sparta WRKK-FM (r) 520 N Spring St, Sparta TN 38583 **Phn:** 931-836-1055 **Fax:** 931-836-2320

Sparta WSMT-AM (cg) 520 N Spring St, Sparta TN 38583 **Phn:** 931-836-1055 **Fax:** 931-836-2320

Sparta WTZX-AM (o) 520 N Spring St, Sparta TN 38583 **Phn:** 931-836-1055 **Fax:** 931-836-2320

Springfield WDBL-AM (nt) PO Box 909, Springfield TN 37172 **Phn:** 615-384-9744 **Fax:** 615-384-9746 www.wsgi1100.com wsgi1100@yahoo.com

Springfield WSGI-AM (cg) PO Box 909, Springfield TN 37172 **Phn:** 615-384-9744 **Fax:** 615-384-9746 www.wsgi1100.com wsgi1100@yahoo.com

Sweetwater WDEH-AM (g) PO Box 330, Sweetwater TN 37874 **Phn:** 423-744-8080 **Fax:** 423-337-5026

Sweetwater WLOD-FM (o) PO Box 330, Sweetwater TN 37874 **Phn:** 423-337-5025 **Fax:** 423-337-5026

Tazewell WNTT-AM (c) PO Box 95, Tazewell TN 37879 **Phn:** 423-626-4203 **Fax:** 423-626-3040 www.wntt1250am.com news@wntt1250am.com

TENNESSEE RADIO STATIONS

Tracy City WSGM-FM (gnt) PO Box 1269, Tracy City TN 37387 **Phn:** 931-592-7777 **Fax:** 931-592-7778 wsgmfm@hotmail.com

Tullahoma WJIG-AM (q) 2214 N Jackson St, Tullahoma TN 37388 **Phn:** 931-455-7426 **Fax:** 931-455-7438

Union City WENK-AM (ons) 1729 Nailling Dr, Union City TN 38261 **Phn:** 731-885-1240 **Fax:** 731-885-3405 www.wenkwtpr.com thailey@wenkwtpr.com

Union City WWKF-FM (h) 1729 Nailling Dr, Union City TN 38261 **Phn:** 731-885-1240 **Fax:** 731-885-3405 www.kf99kq105.comk thailey@kf99kq105.com

Wartburg WECO-AM (cs) PO Box 100, Wartburg TN 37887 **Phn:** 423-346-3900 **Fax:** 423-346-7686 www.wecoradio.com wecoradio@highland.net

Wartburg WECO-FM (cs) PO Box 100, Wartburg TN 37887 **Phn:** 423-346-3900 **Fax:** 423-346-7686 www.wecoradio.com wecoradio@highland.net

Waynesboro WWON-AM (o) PO Box 999, Waynesboro TN 38485 **Phn:** 931-722-3631

Winchester WCDT-AM (c) 1201 S College St, Winchester TN 37398 **Phn:** 931-967-2201 www.wcdt1340.com newsfirst@bellsouth.net

Woodbury WBRY-AM (cg) PO Box 7, Woodbury TN 37190 **Phn:** 615-563-2313 **Fax:** 615-563-6229 www.wbry.com askus@wbry.com

TEXAS

Abilene KABW-FM (c) 4400 Buffalo Gap Rd # 1200, Abilene TX 79606 **Phn:** 325-437-9596 **Fax:** 325-673-1819 www.wolfabilene.com richarddoud@doudmediagroup.com

Abilene KACU-FM (pln) PO Box 27820, Abilene TX 79699 **Phn:** 325-674-2441 **Fax:** 325-674-2417 www.kacu.org info@kacu.org

Abilene KATX-FM (c) PO Box 2482, Abilene TX 79604 **Phn:** 254-629-2621 **Fax:** 254-629-8520

Abilene KBCY-FM (c) 2525 S Danville Dr, Abilene TX 79605 **Phn:** 325-793-9700 **Fax:** 325-692-1576 www.kbcy.com kelly.jay@cumulus.com

Abilene KCDD-FM (h) 2525 S Danville Dr, Abilene TX 79605 **Phn:** 325-793-9700 **Fax:** 325-692-1576 www.power103.com ronnie.baird@cumulus.com

Abilene KEAN-FM (c) 3911 S 1st St, Abilene TX 79605 **Phn:** 325-676-7711 **Fax:** 325-676-3851 keanradio.com rudyfernandez@gapbroadcasting.com

Abilene KEAS-AM (c) PO Box 2482, Abilene TX 79604 **Phn:** 254-629-2621 **Fax:** 254-629-8520

Abilene KEYJ-FM (r) 3911 S 1st St, Abilene TX 79605 **Phn:** 325-676-7711 **Fax:** 325-676-3851 keyj.com karenhines@townsquaremedia.com

Abilene KFGL-FM (r) 3911 S 1st St, Abilene TX 79605 **Phn:** 325-676-5100 **Fax:** 325-676-3851 koolfmabilene.com landonking@townsquaremedia.com

Abilene KGNZ-FM (q) 542 Butternut St, Abilene TX 79602 **Phn:** 325-673-3045 **Fax:** 325-672-7938 www.kgnz.com kgnzpsa@kgnz.com

Abilene KHXS-FM (r) 2525 S Danville Dr, Abilene TX 79605 **Phn:** 325-793-9700 **Fax:** 325-692-1576 www.102thebear.com ronnie.baird@cumulus.com

Abilene KKHR-FM (y) 402 Cypress St Ste 510, Abilene TX 79601 **Phn:** 325-672-5442 **Fax:** 325-672-6128 www.radioabilene.com

Abilene KORQ-FM (c) 4400 Buffalo Gap Rd # 1200, Abilene TX 79606 **Phn:** 325-437-9596 **Fax:** 325-673-1819 www.qabilene.com richarddoud@doudmediagroup.com

Abilene KSLI-AM (t) 3911 S 1st St, Abilene TX 79605 **Phn:** 325-676-7711 **Fax:** 325-676-3851

Abilene KTLT-FM (r) 2525 S Danville Dr, Abilene TX 79605 **Phn:** 325-793-9700 **Fax:** 325-692-1576

Abilene KULL-FM (o) 3911 S 1st St, Abilene TX 79605 **Phn:** 325-676-7711 **Fax:** 325-676-3851 mix925abilene.com david.wheaton@townsquaremedia.com

Abilene KWKC-AM (nt) 402 Cypress St Ste 510, Abilene TX 79601 **Phn:** 325-673-1455 **Fax:** 325-672-6128 www.radioabilene.com

Abilene KYYW-AM (c) 3911 S 1st St, Abilene TX 79605 **Phn:** 325-676-7711 **Fax:** 325-676-3851 classiccountry1470.com karenhines@gapbroadcasting.com

Abilene KZQQ-AM (snt) 402 Cypress St Ste 510, Abilene TX 79601 **Phn:** 325-672-5442 **Fax:** 325-672-6128 www.radioabilene.com

Alice KOPY-FM (y) PO Box 731, Alice TX 78333 **Phn:** 361-664-1884 **Fax:** 361-664-1886 claroradio@yahoo.com

Alice KOPY-AM (c) PO Box 731, Alice TX 78333 **Phn:** 361-664-1884 **Fax:** 361-664-1886 jenbc13130@yahoo.com

Alice KUKA-FM (c) PO Box 731, Alice TX 78333 **Phn:** 361-664-1884 **Fax:** 361-664-1886 www.kukaradio.com

Alpine KALP-FM (c) PO Box 9650, Alpine TX 79831 **Phn:** 432-837-2144 **Fax:** 432-837-3984 www.bigbendradio.com ray@bigbendradio.com

Alpine KVLF-AM (z) PO Box 779, Alpine TX 79831 **Phn:** 432-837-2144 **Fax:** 432-837-3984 www.bigbendradio.com ray@bigbendradio.com

Alvin KACC-FM (vh) 3110 Mustang Rd, Alvin TX 77511 **Phn:** 281-756-3766 **Fax:** 281-756-3885 www.kaccradio.com mossman@kaccradio.com

Amarillo KACV-FM (vr) PO Box 447, Amarillo TX 79178 **Phn:** 806-371-5222 **Fax:** 806-371-5258 www.kacvfm.org kacvfm90@actx.edu

Amarillo KARX-FM (r) 301 S Polk St Ste 100, Amarillo TX 79101 **Phn:** 806-342-5200 **Fax:** 806-342-5202 www.957thekar.com karx957@hotmail.com

Amarillo KATP-FM (c) 6214 SW 34th Ave, Amarillo TX 79109 **Phn:** 806-355-9777 **Fax:** 806-355-5832 blakefm.com rickandrews@townsquaremedia.com

Amarillo KBZD-FM (yo) 5200 E Amarillo Blvd, Amarillo TX 79107 **Phn:** 806-355-1044 **Fax:** 806-457-0642

Amarillo KGNC-AM (nt) PO Box 710, Amarillo TX 79105 **Phn:** 806-355-9801 **Fax:** 806-354-8779 www.kgncam.com kgncam@kgnc.com

Amarillo KGNC-FM (c) PO Box 710, Amarillo TX 79105 **Phn:** 806-355-9801 **Fax:** 806-354-8779 www.kgncfm.com kgnc@kgnc.com

Amarillo KGRW-FM (y) 3639 Wolflin Ave, Amarillo TX 79102 **Phn:** 505-762-5031 **Fax:** 806-457-0642

Amarillo KIXZ-AM (ny) 6214 SW 34th Ave, Amarillo TX 79109 **Phn:** 806-355-9777 **Fax:** 806-355-5832 voiceofamarillo.com jamesguthrie@townsquaremedia.com

Amarillo KMXJ-FM (a) 6214 SW 34th Ave, Amarillo TX 79109 **Phn:** 806-355-9777 **Fax:** 806-355-5832 mix941kmxj.com rickandrews@townsquaremedia.com

Amarillo KPRF-FM (h) 6214 SW 34th Ave, Amarillo TX 79109 **Phn:** 806-355-9777 **Fax:** 806-355-5832 987jackfm.com rickandrews@townsquaremedia.com

Amarillo KPUR-AM (st) 301 S Polk St Ste 100, Amarillo TX 79101 **Phn:** 806-342-5200 **Fax:** 806-342-5202 jack.light@cumulus.com

TEXAS RADIO STATIONS

Amarillo KPUR-FM (c) 301 S Polk St Ste 100, Amarillo TX 79101 **Phn:** 806-342-5200 **Fax:** 806-342-5202 www.kpur107.com craig.vaughn@cumulus.com

Amarillo KQFX-FM (y) 3639 Wolflin Ave, Amarillo TX 79102 **Phn:** 806-355-1044 **Fax:** 806-457-0642

Amarillo KQIZ-FM (h) 301 S Polk St Ste 100, Amarillo TX 79101 **Phn:** 806-342-5200 **Fax:** 806-342-5202 www.931thebeat.com

Amarillo KTNZ-AM (y) 3639 Wolflin Ave, Amarillo TX 79102 **Phn:** 806-355-1044 **Fax:** 806-457-0642

Amarillo KXSS-FM (h) 6214 SW 34th St, Amarillo TX 79109 **Phn:** 806-355-9777 **Fax:** 806-355-5832 kissfm969.com skipstow@townsquaremedia.com

Amarillo KZIP-AM (y) 3639 Wolflin Ave, Amarillo TX 79102 **Phn:** 806-355-1044 **Fax:** 806-457-0642

Amarillo KZRK-AM (s) 301 S Polk St Ste 100, Amarillo TX 79101 **Phn:** 806-342-5200 **Fax:** 806-342-5202

Amarillo KZRK-FM (r) 301 S Polk St Ste 100, Amarillo TX 79101 **Phn:** 806-342-5200 **Fax:** 806-342-5202 www.amarillosrockstation.com

Andrews KACT-AM (c) PO Box 524, Andrews TX 79714 **Phn:** 432-523-2845 **Fax:** 432-523-5671 www.kactradio.com kact1055@windstream.net

Andrews KACT-FM (c) PO Box 524, Andrews TX 79714 **Phn:** 432-523-2845 **Fax:** 432-523-5671 www.kactradio.com kact1055@windstream.net

Arlington KESN-FM (s) 400 E Las Colinas Blvd Ste 1033, Arlington TX 76006 **Phn:** 214-258-2800 espn.go.comdallasradio barry.vigoda@espn.com

Arlington KMKI-AM (m) 2221 E Lamar Blvd Ste 300, Arlington TX 76006 **Phn:** 817-695-1333 **Fax:** 817-695-3556 music.disney.com pamela.j.ketel@disney.com

Arlington KSCS-FM (c) 2221 E Lamar Blvd Ste 300, Arlington TX 76006 **Phn:** 817-640-1963 **Fax:** 817-695-0014 www.kscs.com cari.swartzell@cumulus.com

Austin KAMX-FM (a) 4301 Westbank Dr Ste B-350, Austin TX 78746 **Phn:** 512-327-9595 **Fax:** 512-329-6255 www.mix947.com catthomas@entercom.com

Austin KASE-FM (c) 3601 S Congress Ave Bldg F, Austin TX 78704 **Phn:** 512-684-7300 **Fax:** 512-684-7441 www.kase101.com garywalsh@clearchannel.com

Austin KAZI-FM (vwj) 8906 Wall St Ste 203, Austin TX 78754 **Phn:** 512-836-9544 **Fax:** 512-836-9563 www.kazifm.org marion@kazifm.org

Austin KBPA-FM (m) 8309 N I H 35, Austin TX 78753 **Phn:** 512-832-4000 **Fax:** 512-832-4071 www.1035bobfm.com krash@hibob.com

Austin KFIT-AM (gy) PO Box 160158, Austin TX 78716 **Phn:** 512-328-8400 **Fax:** 512-328-8437 gospel1060.com

Austin KFMK-FM (a) 3601 S Congress Ave Bldg F, Austin TX 78704 **Phn:** 512-684-7300 **Fax:** 512-684-7441 www.thebeatatx.com jayshannon@clearchannel.com

Austin KGSR-FM (r) 8309 N I H 35, Austin TX 78753 **Phn:** 512-832-4000 **Fax:** 512-832-4071 www.kgsr.com bwalden@emmisaustin.com

Austin KHFI-FM (h) 3601 S Congress Ave Bldg F, Austin TX 78704 **Phn:** 512-684-7300 **Fax:** 512-684-7441 www.967kissfm.com jayshannon@clearchannel.com

Austin KIXL-AM (qt) 11615 Angus Rd Ste 102, Austin TX 78759 **Phn:** 512-390-5495 **Fax:** 512-241-0510 www.relevantradio.com info@relevantradio.com

Austin KJCE-AM (t) 4301 Westbank Dr Ste B-350, Austin TX 78746 **Phn:** 512-327-9595 **Fax:** 512-329-6257 www.talkradio1370am.com smkerr@entercom.com

Austin KKMJ-FM (a) 4301 Westbank Dr Ste B-350, Austin TX 78746 **Phn:** 512-327-9595 **Fax:** 512-684-0984 www.majic.com catthomas@entercom.com

Austin KLBJ-AM (snt) 8309 N I H 35, Austin TX 78753 **Phn:** 512-832-4000 **Fax:** 512-832-4081 www.newsradioklbj.com newsroom@emmisaustin.com

Austin KLBJ-FM (r) 8309 N I H 35, Austin TX 78753 **Phn:** 512-832-4000 **Fax:** 512-832-4081 www.klbjfm.com chase@emmisaustin.com

Austin KMFA-FM (vl) 3001 N Lamar Blvd Ste 100, Austin TX 78705 **Phn:** 512-476-5632 **Fax:** 512-474-7463 www.kmfa.org info@kmfa.org

Austin KPEZ-FM (q) 3601 S Congress Ave Bldg F, Austin TX 78704 **Phn:** 512-684-7300 **Fax:** 512-684-7441 www.thebeatatx.com jayshannon@clearchannel.com

Austin KROX-FM (r) 8309 N I H 35, Austin TX 78753 **Phn:** 512-832-4000 **Fax:** 512-832-4071 www.101x.com lawless@krox.com

Austin KUT-FM (p) 1 University Sta Stop A0704, Austin TX 78712 **Phn:** 512-471-1631 **Fax:** 512-471-3700 kut.org edonahue@kut.org

Austin KVET-AM (s) 3601 S Congress Ave, Austin TX 78704 **Phn:** 512-684-7300 **Fax:** 512-684-7441 www.am1300thezone.com jonmadani@clearchannel.com

Austin KVET-FM (c) 3601 S Congress Ave, Austin TX 78704 **Phn:** 512-684-7300 **Fax:** 512-684-7441 www.kvet.com garywalsh@clearchannel.com

Austin KVRX-FM (v) PO Box D, Austin TX 78713 **Phn:** 512-471-5106 www.kvrx.org kvrx@kvrx.org

Austin KZNX-AM (y) 1050 E 11th St Ste 300, Austin TX 78702 **Phn:** 512-346-8255 **Fax:** 512-692-0599 www.radiomujer.com.mx

Ballinger KRUN-AM (c) PO Box 230, Ballinger TX 76821 **Phn:** 325-365-5500 **Fax:** 325-365-3407 www.krunam.com krun1400@hotmail.com

Bay City KKHA-FM (c) 1713 7th St, Bay City TX 77414 **Phn:** 979-323-7771 **Fax:** 979-319-4163 www.yoursoutheasttexas.com lee@kyyk.com

Bay City KMKS-FM (c) PO Box 789, Bay City TX 77404 **Phn:** 979-244-4242 **Fax:** 979-245-0107 www.kmks.com kmks@kmks.com

Baytown KWWJ-AM (wg) 4638 Decker Dr, Baytown TX 77520 **Phn:** 281-837-8777 **Fax:** 281-424-7588 www.kwwj.org kwwj1360@yahoo.com

Beaumont KAYD-FM (c) 775 S 11th St # 102, Beaumont TX 77701 **Phn:** 409-951-2500 **Fax:** 409-833-9296 www.kayd.com j.bernard@cumulus.com

Beaumont KBED-AM (y) 775 S 11th St # 102, Beaumont TX 77701 **Phn:** 409-951-2500 **Fax:** 09-833-9296

Beaumont KCOL-FM (o) PO Box 5488, Beaumont TX 77726 **Phn:** 409-896-5555 **Fax:** 409-896-5500 www.cool925.com haroldmann@clearchannel.com

Beaumont KIKR-AM (s) 775 S 11th St # 102, Beaumont TX 77701 **Phn:** 409-951-2500 **Fax:** 409-833-9296

Beaumont KIOC-FM (r) PO Box 5488, Beaumont TX 77726 **Phn:** 409-896-5555 **Fax:** 409-896-5599 www.bigdog106.com bigdog106@clearchannel.com

Beaumont KKMY-FM (a) PO Box 5488, Beaumont TX 77726 **Phn:** 409-896-5555 **Fax:** 409-896-5599 www.kiss1045fm.com

Beaumont KLVI-AM (nt) 2885 Interstate 10 E, Beaumont TX 77702 **Phn:** 409-896-5555 **Fax:** 409-896-5599 www.klvi.com jimlove@clearchannel.com

Beaumont KOLE-AM (nt) 27 Sawyer St, Beaumont TX 77702 **Phn:** 409-835-1340 **Fax:** 409-832-5686

Beaumont KQXY-FM (h) 775 S 11th St # 102, Beaumont TX 77701 **Phn:** 409-833-9421 **Fax:** 409-833-9296 www.kqxy.com qmorningcrew@aol.com

Beaumont KRCM-AM (nt) 27 Sawyer St, Beaumont TX 77702 **Phn:** 409-835-1340 rhm1975@gmail.com

Beaumont KSTB-FM (c) 775 S 11th St # 102, Beaumont TX 77701 **Phn:** 409-951-2500 **Fax:** 409-833-9296

Beaumont KTCX-FM (u) 775 S 11th St # 102, Beaumont TX 77701 **Phn:** 409-951-2500 **Fax:** 409-833-9296 www.ktcx.com adrian.scott@cumulus.com

Beaumont KVLU-FM (plnj) PO Box 10064, Beaumont TX 77710 **Phn:** 409-880-8164 www.kvlu.org byron.balentine@lamar.edu

Beaumont KYKR-FM (c) PO Box 5488, Beaumont TX 77726 **Phn:** 409-896-5555 **Fax:** 409-896-5599 www.kykr.com haroldmann@clearchannel.com

Beaumont KZZB-AM (gw) 2531 Calder St, Beaumont TX 77702 **Phn:** 409-833-0990 **Fax:** 409-833-0995

Beeville KRXB-FM (r) 110 E Bowie St, Beeville TX 78102 **Phn:** 361-358-4941 **Fax:** 361-358-0601 krxbfm@sbcglobal.net

Beeville KTKO-FM (c) 2300 S Washington St, Beeville TX 78102 **Phn:** 361-358-1490 **Fax:** 361-358-7814

Big Spring KBST-FM (c) 608 Johnson St, Big Spring TX 79720 **Phn:** 432-267-6391 **Fax:** 432-267-1579 kbst.com kbstnews@kbst.com

Big Spring KBST-AM (snt) 608 Johnson St, Big Spring TX 79720 **Phn:** 432-267-6391 **Fax:** 432-267-1579 kbst.com kbstnews@kbst.com

Big Spring KBTS-FM (r) 608 Johnson, Big Spring TX 79720 **Phn:** 432 267-6391 **Fax:** 432-267-1579 www.943fuse.com kbstnews@kbst.com

Big Spring KBYG-AM (oy) 2801 Wasson Rd, Big Spring TX 79720 **Phn:** 432-263-6351 **Fax:** 432-263-8223 www.kbygradio.com

Bonham KFYN-AM (c) 506 N Main St, Bonham TX 75418 **Phn:** 903-583-3151 **Fax:** 903-583-2728 1420thewarrior.com wanda@1420thewarrior.com

Borger KQTY-FM (cg) PO Box 165, Borger TX 79008 **Phn:** 806-273-7533 **Fax:** 806-273-3727 www.kqtyradio.com kqtyradio@yahoo.com

Borger KQTY-AM (cg) PO Box 165, Borger TX 79008 **Phn:** 806-273-7533 **Fax:** 806-273-3727 www.kqtyradio.net kqtyradio@yahoo.com

Bowie KNTX-AM (o) PO Box 1080, Bowie TX 76230 **Phn:** 940-872-2288 **Fax:** 940-872-1228 www.kntxradio.com onair@kntxradio.com

Brady KNEL-FM (c) PO Box 630, Brady TX 76825 **Phn:** 325-597-2119 **Fax:** 325-597-1925 www.knelradio.com knel@airmail.net

Brady KNEL-AM (or) PO Box 630, Brady TX 76825 **Phn:** 325-597-2119 **Fax:** 325-597-1925 www.knelradio.com knel@airmail.net

Brenham KHTZ-FM (a) 530 W Main St, Brenham TX 77833 **Phn:** 979-836-9411 **Fax:** 979-836-9435

Brenham KLTR-FM (a) 530 W Main St, Brenham TX 77833 **Phn:** 979-836-9411 **Fax:** 979-836-9435 www.litefm941.com lorihenderson01@hotmail.com

Brenham KTTX-FM (c) PO Box 1280, Brenham TX 77834 **Phn:** 979-836-3655 **Fax:** 979-830-8141 www.ktex.com mail@ktex.com

TEXAS RADIO STATIONS

Brenham KWHI-AM (ct) PO Box 1280, Brenham TX 77834 **Phn:** 979-836-3655 **Fax:** 979-830-8141 www.kwhi.com mail@kwhi.com

Brownsville KBNR-FM (vqy) PO Box 5480, Brownsville TX 78523 **Phn:** 956-542-6933 **Fax:** 956-542-0523 www.radiokbnr.org

Brownsville KHKZ-FM (a) 901 E Pike Blvd, Brownsville TX 78520 **Phn:** 956-973-9202 **Fax:** 956-973-9355 www.kiss1063.net jaycantu@clearchannel.com

Brownwood KBUB-FM (vq) PO Box 1549, Brownwood TX 76804 **Phn:** 325-646-3420

Brownwood KBWD-AM (a) PO Box 280, Brownwood TX 76804 **Phn:** 325-646-3505 **Fax:** 325-646-2220 www.koxe.com upfront@koxe.com

Brownwood KHPU-FM (q) 1000 Fisk Ave, Brownwood TX 76801 **Phn:** 325-649-8119 **Fax:** 325-649-8947

Brownwood KOXE-FM (c) 300 Carnegie St, Brownwood TX 76801 **Phn:** 325-646-3505 **Fax:** 325-646-2220 www.koxe.com upfront@koxe.com

Brownwood KPSM-FM (q) PO Box 1549, Brownwood TX 76804 **Phn:** 325-646-5993 **Fax:** 325-643-9772 www.kpsm.net kpsmfm@gmail.com

Brownwood KQBZ-FM (a) 600 Fisk Ave, Brownwood TX 76801 **Phn:** 325-646-3535 www.wendleebroadcasting.com samcoursey@wendlee.com

Brownwood KSTA-AM (c) PO Box 100, Brownwood TX 76804 **Phn:** 325-646-3535 **Fax:** 325-646-5347 www.wendleebroadcasting.com ksta1000@gmail.com

Brownwood KXCT-FM (r) PO Box 100, Brownwood TX 76804 **Phn:** 325-646-3535 **Fax:** 325-646-5347

Brownwood KXYL-FM (nt) 600 Fisk Ave, Brownwood TX 76801 **Phn:** 325-646-3535 **Fax:** 325-646-5347 www.wendleebroadcasting.com newstalk@wendlee.com

Brownwood KXYL-AM (nt) 600 Fisk Ave, Brownwood TX 76801 **Phn:** 325-646-3535 **Fax:** 325-646-5347 www.wendleebroadcasting.com newstalk@wendlee.com

Bryan KAGC-AM (q) PO Box 3248, Bryan TX 77805 **Phn:** 979-695-9595 **Fax:** 979-695-1933 kagc1510.com kagcradio@suddenlinkmail.com

Bryan KAGC-FM (c) 1716 Briarcrest Dr Ste 150, Bryan TX 77802 **Phn:** 979-268-9696 www.aggie96.com jennifer@aggie96.com

Bryan KAGG-FM (c) 1716 Briarcrest Dr Ste 150, Bryan TX 77802 **Phn:** 979-846-5597 **Fax:** 979-268-9090 www.aggie96.com

Bryan KAPN-FM (a) 1240 E Villa Maria Rd, Bryan TX 77802 **Phn:** 979-776-1240 brazosradio.com

Bryan KBXT-FM (h) 1240 E Villa Maria Rd, Bryan TX 77802 **Phn:** 979-776-1240 **Fax:** 979-776-0123 1019thebeatfm.com

Bryan KJXJ-FM (r) 1240 E Villa Maria Rd, Bryan TX 77802 **Phn:** 979-776-1240 **Fax:** 979-776-6074 www.1039jackfm.com chris.kiske@brazosradio.com

Bryan KKYS-FM (a) 1716 Briarcrest Dr Ste 150, Bryan TX 77802 **Phn:** 979-846-5597 **Fax:** 979-268-9090 www.mix1047.com mikegatons@clearchannel.com

Bryan KNDE-FM (h) PO Box 3248, Bryan TX 77805 **Phn:** 979-695-9595 **Fax:** 979-695-1933 www.candy95.com radio@bryanbroadcasting.com

Bryan KNFX-FM (r) 1716 Briarcrest Dr Ste 150, Bryan TX 77802 **Phn:** 979-846-5597 **Fax:** 979-268-9090 www.995thefox.com kcwheeler@995thefox.com

Bryan KORA-FM (c) 1240 E Villa Maria Rd, Bryan TX 77802 **Phn:** 979-776-1240 **Fax:** 979-767-0123 983korafm.com roger@brazosradio.com

Bryan KTAM-AM (y) 1240 E Villa Maria Rd, Bryan TX 77802 **Phn:** 979-776-1240 **Fax:** 979-776-0123 www.brazosradio.com sweetc@brazosradio.com

Bryan KVJM-FM (y) 1716 Briarcrest Dr Ste 150, Bryan TX 77802 **Phn:** 979-846-5597 **Fax:** 979-268-9090 www.kissfm1031.com jimharrington@clearchannel.com

Bryan KZNE-AM (s) PO Box 3248, Bryan TX 77805 **Phn:** 979-695-9595 **Fax:** 979-695-1933 www.kzne.com radio@wtaw.com

Bryan WTAW-AM (snt) PO Box 3248, Bryan TX 77805 **Phn:** 979-695-9595 **Fax:** 979-695-1933 www.bryanbroadcasting.com radio@bryanbroadcasting.com

Cameron KMIL-FM (cy) PO Box 832, Cameron TX 76520 **Phn:** 254-697-6633 **Fax:** 254-697-6330 www.kmil.com kmil@kmil.com

Canyon KWTS-FM (v) Wtamu Box 61514, Canyon TX 79016 **Phn:** 806-651-2911 **Fax:** 806-651-2818 www.wtamu.edukwts kwtsgm@gmail.com

Carthage KGAS-AM (g) 215 S Market St, Carthage TX 75633 **Phn:** 903-693-6668 **Fax:** 903-693-7188 www.easttexastoday.com info@kgasradio.com

Carthage KGAS-FM (c) 215 S Market St, Carthage TX 75633 **Phn:** 903-693-6668 **Fax:** 903-693-7188 www.easttexastoday.com info@kgasradio.com

Center KDET-AM (c) PO Box 930, Center TX 75935 **Phn:** 936-598-3304 **Fax:** 936-598-9537 radiodmack@cs.com

Center KQBB-FM (c) PO Box 930, Center TX 75935 **Phn:** 936-598-3304 **Fax:** 936-598-9537 radiodmack@cs.com

Childress KCTX-FM (c) PO Box 540, Childress TX 79201 **Phn:** 940-937-6989 **Fax:** 940-937-6551 kctxradio@gmail.com

Clarendon KEFH-FM (a) PO Box 370, Clarendon TX 79226 **Phn:** 806-874-9930 **Fax:** 806-874-4411 www.kool993.net kefh@kool993.net

College Station KAMU-FM (plnj) 4244 Tamu, College Station TX 77843 **Phn:** 979-845-5611 **Fax:** 979-845-1643 kamu.publicbroadcasting.net cwallace@kamu.tamu.edu

College Station KEOS-FM (v) PO Box 78, College Station TX 77841 **Phn:** 979-779-5367 **Fax:** 979-779-7259 www.keos.org keos@keos.org

Colleyville KNOR-FM (y) 4201 Pool Rd, Colleyville TX 76034 **Phn:** 817-868-2900 **Fax:** 817-868-2116

Colleyville KZZA-FM (y) 4201 Pool Rd, Colleyville TX 76034 **Phn:** 817-868-2900 **Fax:** 817-868-2116 www.casa1067.com dallasinfo@lbimedia.com

Colorado City KAUM-FM (c) PO Box 990, Colorado City TX 79512 **Phn:** 325-728-5224

Colorado City KVMC-AM (c) PO Box 990, Colorado City TX 79512 **Phn:** 325-728-5224 kvmckaum.blogspot.com kvmckaum@sbcglobal.net

Columbus KULM-FM (c) PO Box 111, Columbus TX 78934 **Phn:** 979-732-5766 **Fax:** 979-732-6377 www.kulmradio.com

Comanche KCOM-AM (c) 218 N Austin St, Comanche TX 76442 **Phn:** 325-356-2558 **Fax:** 325-356-3120

Comanche KYOX-FM (c) 218 N Austin St, Comanche TX 76442 **Phn:** 325-356-3090 **Fax:** 325-356-3120

Commerce KETR-FM (pn) PO Box 4504, Commerce TX 75429 **Phn:** 903-886-5848 **Fax:** 903-886-5850 www.ketr.org news@ketr.org

Conroe KVST-FM (c) 1212 S Frazier St, Conroe TX 77301 **Phn:** 936-788-1035 **Fax:** 936-788-2525 www.kstarcountry.com promotions@kstarcountry.com

Conroe KYOK-AM (wg) 300 Bryant Rd, Conroe TX 77303 **Phn:** 936-441-1140 **Fax:** 936-788-1140

Corpus Christi KBNJ-FM (vq) PO Box 270068, Corpus Christi TX 78427 **Phn:** 361-855-0975 **Fax:** 361-855-0977 www.kbnj.org kbnj@lwrn.org

Corpus Christi KBSO-FM (c) 701 Benys Rd, Corpus Christi TX 78408 **Phn:** 361-826-5250 www.badlandsfm.com

Corpus Christi KCCT-AM (o) PO Box 5278, Corpus Christi TX 78465 **Phn:** 361-289-0999 **Fax:** 361-289-0810

Corpus Christi KCTA-AM (q) 1602 S Brownlee Blvd, Corpus Christi TX 78404 **Phn:** 361-882-7711 **Fax:** 361-882-3038 www.kctaradio.com kctaradio@yahoo.com

Corpus Christi KEDT-FM (plnj) 4455 S Padre Island Dr Ste 38, Corpus Christi TX 78411 **Phn:** 361-855-2213 **Fax:** 361-855-3877 www.kedt.org leannewinkler@kedt.org

Corpus Christi KEYS-AM (nt) 2117 Leopard St, Corpus Christi TX 78408 **Phn:** 361-883-3516 **Fax:** 361-882-9767 www.1440keys.com

Corpus Christi KFTX-FM (c) 1520 S Port Ave, Corpus Christi TX 78405 **Phn:** 361-883-5987 **Fax:** 361-883-3648

Corpus Christi KKBA-FM (a) 2117 Leopard St, Corpus Christi TX 78408 **Phn:** 361-883-3516 **Fax:** 361-882-9767 927kbay.com bartallison@msn.com

Corpus Christi KKPN-FM (a) 826 S Padre Island Dr, Corpus Christi TX 78416 **Phn:** 361-814-3800 **Fax:** 361-855-3770 www.planet1023.com

Corpus Christi KKTX-AM (nt) 501 Tupper Ln, Corpus Christi TX 78417 **Phn:** 361-289-0111 **Fax:** 361-289-6670 www.1360kktx.com frankedwards@clearchannel.com

Corpus Christi KLHB-FM (y) 1300 Antelope St, Corpus Christi TX 78401 **Phn:** 361-883-1600 **Fax:** 361-883-9303

Corpus Christi KLTG-FM (a) 1733 S Brownlee Blvd, Corpus Christi TX 78404 **Phn:** 361-883-1600 **Fax:** 361-888-5685 www.thebeach965fm.com

Corpus Christi KLUX-FM (q) 1200 Lantana St, Corpus Christi TX 78407 **Phn:** 361-289-2487 **Fax:** 361-289-1420 www.klux.org mrivera@goccn.org

Corpus Christi KMIQ-FM (y) 2209 N Padre Island Dr, Corpus Christi TX 78408 **Phn:** 361-855-0975 **Fax:** 361-855-0977 carloslopezmagic@yahoo.com

Corpus Christi KMJR-FM (y) 1300 Antelope St, Corpus Christi TX 78401 **Phn:** 361-183-1600 **Fax:** 361-888-5685

Corpus Christi KMXR-FM (o) 501 Tupper Ln, Corpus Christi TX 78417 **Phn:** 361-289-0111 **Fax:** 361-289-5035 www.939online.com kmxr@clearchannel.com

Corpus Christi KNCN-FM (r) 501 Tupper Ln, Corpus Christi TX 78417 **Phn:** 361-289-0111 **Fax:** 361-289-6670 www.c101.com c101@clearchannel.com

Corpus Christi KOUL-FM (c) 1300 Antelope St, Corpus Christi TX 78401 **Phn:** 361-883-1600 **Fax:** 361-888-5685

Corpus Christi KPRX-FM (r) 826 S Padre Island Dr, Corpus Christi TX 78416 **Phn:** 361-814-3800 **Fax:** 361-855-3770

TEXAS RADIO STATIONS

Corpus Christi KRYS-FM (c) 501 Tupper Ln, Corpus Christi TX 78417 **Phn:** 361-289-0111 **Fax:** 361-289-5035 www.k99country.com bigfrank@k99country.com

Corpus Christi KSAB-FM (y) 501 Tupper Ln, Corpus Christi TX 78417 **Phn:** 361-289-0111 **Fax:** 361-289-5035 www.ksabfm.com ksab@clearchannel.com

Corpus Christi KUNO-AM (y) 501 Tupper Ln, Corpus Christi TX 78417 **Phn:** 361-289-0111 **Fax:** 361-289-5035 www.1400kuno.com danpena@clearchannel.com

Corpus Christi KZFM-FM (h) 2117 Leopard St, Corpus Christi TX 78408 **Phn:** 361-883-3516 **Fax:** 361-882-9767 www.hotz95.com

Corsicana KAND-AM (cnt) PO Box 2298, Corsicana TX 75151 **Phn:** 903-874-7421 **Fax:** 903-874-0789 www.kandradio.com peter@kandradio.com

Crockett KIVY-FM (c) 102 S 5th St, Crockett TX 75835 **Phn:** 936-544-2171 **Fax:** 936-544-4891 www.kivy.com

Crockett KIVY-AM (nt) 102 S 5th St, Crockett TX 75835 **Phn:** 936-544-2171 **Fax:** 936-544-4891 www.kivy.com kivy@kivy.com

Dalhart KXIT-AM (c) PO Box 1359, Dalhart TX 79022 **Phn:** 806-249-4747 www.kxit.com kxitamfm@xit.net

Dalhart KXIT-FM (o) PO Box 1359, Dalhart TX 79022 **Phn:** 806-249-4747 www.kxit.com kxitamfm@xit.net

Dallas KATH-AM (R) 8828 N Stemmons Fwy # 106, Dallas TX 75247 **Phn:** 214-951-0132 **Fax:** 214-951-8622 www.grnonline.com davepalmer@grnonline.com

Dallas KBFB-FM (u) 13331 Preston Rd Ste 1180, Dallas TX 75240 **Phn:** 972-331-5400 **Fax:** 972-331-5560 thebeatdfw.com

Dallas KDBN-FM (r) 3500 Maple Ave Ste 1600, Dallas TX 75219 **Phn:** 214-526-7400 **Fax:** 214-525-2525 www.933thebone.com john.foxx@cumulus.com

Dallas KDFT-AM (qy) 5801 Marvin D Love Fwy Ste 409, Dallas TX 75237 **Phn:** 972-572-1540 **Fax:** 972-572-1263 www.kdft540.com kdft-kmny@mrbi.net

Dallas KDGE-FM (r) 14001 Dallas Pkwy Ste 300, Dallas TX 75240 **Phn:** 214-866-8000 **Fax:** 214-866-8101 www.kdge.com webguy@kdge.com

Dallas KDMX-FM (a) 14001 Dallas Pkwy Ste 300, Dallas TX 75240 **Phn:** 214-866-8000 **Fax:** 214-866-8588 www.1029now.com

Dallas KDXX-AM (y) 7700 John W Carpenter Fwy, Dallas TX 75247 **Phn:** 214-525-0400 **Fax:** 214-631-1196 www.univision.com

Dallas KEGL-FM (r) 14001 Dallas Pkwy Ste 300, Dallas TX 75240 **Phn:** 214-866-8000 **Fax:** 214-866-8101 www.kegl.com jacobcarty@clearchannel.com

Dallas KERA-FM (pna) 3000 Harry Hines Blvd, Dallas TX 75201 **Phn:** 214-871-1390 **Fax:** 214-754-0635 www.kera.org

Dallas KESS-FM (y) 7700 John W Carpenter Fwy, Dallas TX 75247 **Phn:** 214-525-0400 **Fax:** 214-631-1196 www.univision.com

Dallas KFLC-AM (y) 7700 John W Carpenter Fwy, Dallas TX 75247 **Phn:** 214-525-0400 **Fax:** 214-631-1196 www.univision.com

Dallas KFXR-AM (n) 14001 Dallas Pkwy Ste 300, Dallas TX 75240 **Phn:** 214-866-8000 **Fax:** 214-866-8400

Dallas KFZO-FM (y) 7700 John W Carpenter Fwy, Dallas TX 75247 **Phn:** 214-525-0400 **Fax:** 214-631-1196 www.univision.com

Dallas KGGR-AM (wgq) 5787 S Hampton Rd Ste 285, Dallas TX 75232 **Phn:** 972-572-5447 **Fax:** 214-330-6133 www.kggram.com

Dallas KHKS-FM (h) 14001 Dallas Pkwy Ste 300, Dallas TX 75240 **Phn:** 214-866-8000 **Fax:** 214-866-8501 www.1061kissfm.com billythekidd@1061kissfm.com

Dallas KHVN-AM (wg) 5787 S Hampton Rd Ste 285, Dallas TX 75232 **Phn:** 214-331-5486 **Fax:** 214-331-1908 khvnam.com rwashley@yahoo.com

Dallas KJKK-FM (h) 4131 N Central Expy Ste 1000, Dallas TX 75204 **Phn:** 214-525-7000 **Fax:** 214-688-7775 jackontheweb.cbslocal.com jack@cbsradio.com

Dallas KJON-AM (qy) 8828 N Stemmons Fwy # 106, Dallas TX 75247 **Phn:** 214-951-0132 **Fax:** 214-951-8622 www.grnonline.com davepalmer@grnonline.com

Dallas KKDA-FM (wu) 1230 River Bend Dr Ste 150, Dallas TX 75247 **Phn:** 214-583-1430 **Fax:** 214-638-5316 www.myk104.com community@k104fm.com

Dallas KKDA-AM (wu) 1230 River Bend Dr Ste 150, Dallas TX 75247 **Phn:** 214-583-1400 **Fax:** 214-638-5316 traffic@k104fm.com

Dallas KKGM-AM (wgq) 5787 S Hampton Rd Ste 108, Dallas TX 75232 **Phn:** 214-337-5700 **Fax:** 214-337-5707 www.kkgmam.com paul.hughes@kkgmam.com

Dallas KKLF-AM (nt) 3090 Olive St # 400, Dallas TX 75219 **Phn:** 214-526-2400 **Fax:** 214-523-2732 www.klif.com

Dallas KLIF-AM (nt) 3090 Olive St W # 400, Dallas TX 75219 **Phn:** 214-526-2400 **Fax:** 214-520-4343 klif.com dan.bennett@cumulus.com

Dallas KLNO-FM (y) 7700 John W Carpenter Fwy, Dallas TX 75247 **Phn:** 214-525-0400 **Fax:** 214-631-1196 www.univision.com

Dallas KLUV-FM (o) 4131 N Central Expy Ste 1000, Dallas TX 75204 **Phn:** 214-526-7000 kluv.cbslocal.com

Dallas KMVK-FM (y) 4131 N Central Expy Ste 1000, Dallas TX 75204 **Phn:** 214-525-7000 **Fax:** 214-525-7150 lagrande1075.cbslocal.com jennifer.marquez@cbsradio.com

Dallas KNON-FM (v) PO Box 710909, Dallas TX 75371 **Phn:** 214-828-9500 www.knon.org news@knon.org

Dallas KPLX-FM (c) 3500 Maple Ave Ste 1600, Dallas TX 75219 **Phn:** 214-526-2400 **Fax:** 214-520-4343 www.995thewolf.com wolf@995thewolf.com

Dallas KRLD-AM (nt) 4131 N Central Expy Ste 500, Dallas TX 75204 **Phn:** 214-525-7000 **Fax:** 214-525-7372 dfw.cbslocal.com programdirector@1053thefan.com

Dallas KSOC-FM (u) 13331 Preston Rd Ste 1180, Dallas TX 75240 **Phn:** 972-331-5400 **Fax:** 972-331-5560 oldschool945.com oldschool945@radio-one.com

Dallas KTCK-AM (s) 3500 Maple Ave Ste 1600, Dallas TX 75219 **Phn:** 214-526-7400 **Fax:** 214-525-2525 www.theticket.com jeff.catlin@cumulus.com

Dallas KTDK-FM (s) 3500 Maple Ave # 1310, Dallas TX 75219 **Phn:** 214-526-7400 **Fax:** 214-525-2525 www.theticket.com jeff.catlin@cumulus.com

Dallas KTNO-AM (qy) 5787 S Hampton Rd Ste 340, Dallas TX 75232 **Phn:** 214-330-5866 **Fax:** 214-330-9885 www.ktnoam.com hugo.gamboa@klty.com

Dallas KVIL-FM (a) 4131 N Central Expy Ste 1000, Dallas TX 75204 **Phn:** 214-525-7000 **Fax:** 214-525-7157 kvil.cbslocal.com ron.harrell@cbsradio.com

Dallas KVTT-FM (v) 11061 Shady Trl, Dallas TX 75229 **Phn:** 214-351-6655

Dallas KXEZ-FM (c) 12225 Greenville Ave Ste 359, Dallas TX 75243 **Phn:** 972-633-0953 **Fax:** 972-396-1643 www.kxez.com info@kxez.com

Dallas KZPS-FM (r) 14001 Dallas Pkwy Ste 300, Dallas TX 75240 **Phn:** 214-866-8000 **Fax:** 214-866-8688 www.lonestar925.com dondavis@clearchannel.com

Dallas WBAP-AM (nt) 3090 Olive St # 400, Dallas TX 75219 **Phn:** 214-526-2400 www.wbap.com

Dallas WRR-FM (l) PO Box 159001, Dallas TX 75315 **Phn:** 214-670-8888 **Fax:** 214-670-8394 www.wrr101.com padams@wrr101.com

Del Rio KDLK-FM (c) PO Box 1489, Del Rio TX 78841 **Phn:** 830-775-9583 **Fax:** 830-774-4009 www.kdlk.com helen@kdlk.com

Del Rio KTDR-FM (h) 307 E 8th St, Del Rio TX 78840 **Phn:** 830-775-6291 **Fax:** 830-775-6545

Del Rio KWMC-AM (or) 903 E Cortinas St, Del Rio TX 78840 **Phn:** 830-775-3544 kwmc1490@wcsonline.net

Denison KJIM-AM (abo) 4367 Woodlawn Rd, Denison TX 75021 **Phn:** 903-893-1197

Denison KMAD-FM (r) 101 E Main St Ste 255, Denison TX 75021 **Phn:** 903-463-6800 **Fax:** 903-463-9816 www.madrock1025.com hmcmonigle@nextmediagroup.net

Denison KMKT-FM (c) 101 E Main St Ste 255, Denison TX 75021 **Phn:** 903-463-6800 **Fax:** 903-463-9816 www.931kmkt.com hmcmonigle@nextmediagroup.net

Dimmitt KDHN-AM (c) 704 W Cleveland St, Dimmitt TX 79027 **Phn:** 806-647-4161 **Fax:** 806-647-4715 kdhn1984@yahoo.com

Dumas KDDD-FM (o) PO Box 555, Dumas TX 79029 **Phn:** 806-935-4141 **Fax:** 806-935-3836 www.kddd953fm.com

Dumas KDDD-AM (cf) PO Box 396, Dumas TX 79029 **Phn:** 806-935-4141 **Fax:** 806-935-3836

Eagle Pass KEPS-AM (y) PO Box 1123, Eagle Pass TX 78853 **Phn:** 830-773-9247 **Fax:** 830-773-9500

Eagle Pass KINL-FM (a) PO Box 1123, Eagle Pass TX 78853 **Phn:** 830-773-9247 **Fax:** 830-773-9500 www.power927.net

Edinburg KOIR-FM (qy) 4300 S US Highway 281, Edinburg TX 78539 **Phn:** 956-380-3435 **Fax:** 956-380-8156 radioesperanza.com correo@radioesperanza.com

El Campo KULP-AM (cnt) PO Box 390, El Campo TX 77437 **Phn:** 979-543-3303 **Fax:** 979-543-1546 www.kulpradio.com contact01@kulpradio.com

El Paso KAMA-AM (y) 2211 E Missouri Ave Ste S300, El Paso TX 79903 **Phn:** 915-544-9797 **Fax:** 915-544-1247 univisionamerica.univision.com

El Paso KBNA-FM (y) 2211 E Missouri Ave Ste S300, El Paso TX 79903 **Phn:** 915-544-9797 **Fax:** 915-544-1247 kbna975.univision.com

El Paso KELP-AM (qt) 6900 Commerce Ave, El Paso TX 79915 **Phn:** 915-779-0016 **Fax:** 915-779-6641 www.kelpradio.com kelpradio@gmail.com

El Paso KELP-FM (qt) 6900 Commerce Ave, El Paso TX 79915 **Phn:** 915-779-0016 **Fax:** 915-779-6641 www.kelpradio.com kelpradio@gmail.com

El Paso KHEY-AM (st) 4045 N Mesa St, El Paso TX 79902 **Phn:** 915-351-5400 **Fax:** 915-351-3101 www.khey1380.com billtole@clearchannel.com

El Paso KHEY-FM (c) 4045 N Mesa St, El Paso TX 79902 **Phn:** 915-351-5400 **Fax:** 915-351-3101 www.khey.com bobcatbrown@clearchannel.com

El Paso KHRO-AM (o) 5426 N Mesa St, El Paso TX 79912 **Phn:** 915-581-1126 **Fax:** 915-585-4642 www.fox1150.com iponce@entravision.com

TEXAS RADIO STATIONS

El Paso KINT-FM (y) 5426 N Mesa St, El Paso TX 79912 **Phn:** 915-581-1126 **Fax:** 915-585-4642 www.jose939.com iponce@entravision.com

El Paso KLAQ-FM (r) 4180 N Mesa St, El Paso TX 79902 **Phn:** 915-544-8864 **Fax:** 915-544-9536 klaq.com bdubow@regentcomm.com

El Paso KOFX-FM (o) 5426 N Mesa St, El Paso TX 79912 **Phn:** 915-581-1126 **Fax:** 915-585-4642 www.923thefox.com dcandelaria@entravision.com

El Paso KPAS-FM (q) PO Box 371010, El Paso TX 79937 **Phn:** 915-851-3382 **Fax:** 915-851-4360

El Paso KPRR-FM (h) 4045 N Mesa St, El Paso TX 79902 **Phn:** 915-351-5400 **Fax:** 915-351-3101 www.kprr.com pattidiaz@clearchannel.com

El Paso KQBA-AM (y) 2211 E Missouri Ave Ste S300, El Paso TX 79903 **Phn:** 915-544-9797 **Fax:** 915-544-1247 www.univision.com

El Paso KROD-AM (st) 4180 N Mesa St, El Paso TX 79902 **Phn:** 915-544-8864 **Fax:** 915-544-9536 krod.com jwalker@krod.com

El Paso KROL-FM (q) 6900 Commerce Ave, El Paso TX 79915 **Phn:** 915-779-0016 **Fax:** 915-779-6641

El Paso KSII-FM (a) 4180 N Mesa St, El Paso TX 79902 **Phn:** 915-544-9550 **Fax:** 915-532-3334 kisselpaso.com monika@ksii.com

El Paso KSVE-AM (y) 5426 N Mesa St, El Paso TX 79912 **Phn:** 915-581-1126 **Fax:** 915-585-4642 www.jose939.com iponce@entravision.com

El Paso KTEP-FM (plnj) 500 W University Ave # 203, El Paso TX 79968 **Phn:** 915-747-5152 **Fax:** 915-747-5641 www.ktep.org ktep@utep.edu

El Paso KTSM-AM (nt) 4045 N Mesa St, El Paso TX 79902 **Phn:** 915-351-5400 **Fax:** 915-351-3101 www.ktsmradio.com mikeryan3@clearchannel.com

El Paso KTSM-FM (a) 4045 N Mesa St, El Paso TX 79902 **Phn:** 915-351-5400 **Fax:** 915-351-3101 www.sunny999fm.com billtole@clearchannel.com

El Paso KVER-FM (yvq) PO Box 12008, El Paso TX 79913 **Phn:** 915-544-9190 **Fax:** 915-544-9193 www.kver.org kver@lwrn.org

El Paso KVIV-AM (qy) 6060 Surety Dr Ste 100, El Paso TX 79905 **Phn:** 915-565-2999 **Fax:** 915-562-3156 www.kviv1340.com info@kviv1340.com

El Paso KYSE-FM (y) 5426 N Mesa St, El Paso TX 79912 **Phn:** 915-581-1126 **Fax:** 915-585-4642 www.elgato947.com sfleming@entravision.com

Fairfield KNES-FM (c) PO Box 347, Fairfield TX 75840 **Phn:** 903-389-5637 **Fax:** 903-389-7172 texas99-1.com texas99@texas99.com

Falfurrias KPSO-FM (cy) 304 E Rice St, Falfurrias TX 78355 **Phn:** 361-325-2112

Farwell KIJN-AM (q) PO Box 458, Farwell TX 79325 **Phn:** 806-481-3318 **Fax:** 806-481-3835 www.angelfire.combizKIJN kijn@email.com

Farwell KIJN-FM (q) PO Box 458, Farwell TX 79325 **Phn:** 806-481-3318 **Fax:** 806-481-3835 www.angelfire.combizKIJN kijn@email.com

Floresville KWCB-FM (vy) 1905 10th St, Floresville TX 78114 **Phn:** 830-393-6116 **Fax:** 830-393-3817 www.wilsoncountynews.comkwcb kwcb89fm@yahoo.com

Floydada KFLP-AM (cf) PO Box 658, Floydada TX 79235 **Phn:** 806-983-5704 **Fax:** 806-983-5705 www.kflp.net kflp@kflp.net

Floydada KFLP-FM (c) PO Box 658, Floydada TX 79235 **Phn:** 806-983-5704 **Fax:** 806-983-5705 www.kflp.net kflp@kflp.net

Fort Stockton KFST-AM (cy) 954 S US Highway 385, Fort Stockton TX 79735 **Phn:** 432-336-2228 **Fax:** 432-336-5834 www.kfstradio.com kfst@sbcglobal.net

Fort Stockton KFST-FM (a) 954 S US Highway 385, Fort Stockton TX 79735 **Phn:** 432-336-2228 **Fax:** 432-336-5834 www.kfstradio.com kfst@sbcglobal.net

Fort Worth KFWR-FM (c) 115 W 3rd St, Fort Worth TX 76102 **Phn:** 817-332-0959 www.921hankfm.com

Fort Worth KTCU-FM (vlj) Tcu Box 298020, Fort Worth TX 76129 **Phn:** 817-257-7631 **Fax:** 817-257-7637 www.ktcu.net ktcu@tcu.edu

Fort Worth KTFW-FM (c) 115 W 3rd St, Fort Worth TX 76102 **Phn:** 817-332-0959 **Fax:** 817-348-8373 www.921hankfm.com

Fredericksburg KEEP-FM (arc) PO Box 311, Fredericksburg TX 78624 **Phn:** 830-997-2197 **Fax:** 830-997-2198

Fredericksburg KFAN-FM (r) PO Box 311, Fredericksburg TX 78624 **Phn:** 830-997-2197 **Fax:** 830-997-2198 www.kfanfmradio.com txradio@ktc.com

Fredericksburg KNAF-AM (ct) PO Box 311, Fredericksburg TX 78624 **Phn:** 830-997-2197 **Fax:** 830-997-2198

Gainesville KGAF-AM (c) PO Box 368, Gainesville TX 76241 **Phn:** 940-665-5546 **Fax:** 940-665-1580

Gonzales KCTI-AM (cns) 615 Saint Paul St, Gonzales TX 78629 **Phn:** 830-672-3631 **Fax:** 830-672-9603 www.kcti1450.com egon@kcti1450.com

Graham KLXK-FM (c) 620 Oak St, Graham TX 76450 **Phn:** 940-549-1330 **Fax:** 940-549-8628 programming@kwkq-kswa.com

Graham KROO-AM (o) 620 Oak St, Graham TX 76450 **Phn:** 940-549-1330 **Fax:** 940-549-8628 www.hitsandfavorites.com programming@kwkq-kswa.com

Graham KSWA-AM (a) 620 Oak St, Graham TX 76450 **Phn:** 940-549-1330 **Fax:** 940-549-8628 programming@kwkq-kswa.com

Graham KWKQ-FM (r) 620 Oak St, Graham TX 76450 **Phn:** 940-549-1330 **Fax:** 940-549-8628 programming@kwkq-kswa.com

Grand Prairie KRNB-FM (wx) 621 NW 6th St, Grand Prairie TX 75050 **Phn:** 972-263-9911 **Fax:** 972-558-0010 www.krnb.com community@krnb.com

Greenville KGVL-AM (c) PO Box 1015, Greenville TX 75403 **Phn:** 903-455-1400 **Fax:** 903-455-5485

Greenville KIKT-FM (c) PO Box 1015, Greenville TX 75403 **Phn:** 903-455-1400 **Fax:** 903-455-5485

Hamilton KCLW-AM (c) PO Box 631, Hamilton TX 76531 **Phn:** 254-386-8804 **Fax:** 866-348-6792 www.kclw.com

Harker Heights KIIZ-FM (uw) PO Box 2469, Harker Heights TX 76548 **Phn:** 254-699-5000 www.kiiz.com

Harlingen KMBH-FM (plnj) PO Box 2147, Harlingen TX 78551 **Phn:** 956-421-4111 www.kmbh.org memberservices@kmbh.org

Haskell KVRP-AM (c) PO Box 1118, Haskell TX 79521 **Phn:** 940-864-8505 **Fax:** 940-864-8001 www.kvrp.com kvrp@kvrp.com

Haskell KVRP-FM (c) PO Box 1118, Haskell TX 79521 **Phn:** 940-864-8505 **Fax:** 940-864-8001 www.kvrp.com kvrp@kvrp.com

Hereford KNNK-FM (gz) PO Box 1635, Hereford TX 79045 **Phn:** 806-363-1005 **Fax:** 806-364-0226 knnk@wtrt.net

Hereford KPAN-AM (c) PO Box 1757, Hereford TX 79045 **Phn:** 806-364-1860 **Fax:** 806-364-5814 www.kpanradio.com chip@kpanradio.com

Hereford KPAN-FM (c) PO Box 1757, Hereford TX 79045 **Phn:** 806-364-1860 **Fax:** 806-364-5814 www.kpanradio.com josie@kpanradio.com

Hillsboro KHBR-AM (c) PO Box 569, Hillsboro TX 76645 **Phn:** 254-582-3431 **Fax:** 254-582-3800 khbrhillsboro.com info@khbrhillsboro.com

Hondo KCWM-AM (c) PO Box 447, Hondo TX 78861 **Phn:** 830-741-5296 **Fax:** 830-426-3368 kcwm.net kcwm@aol.com

Hooks KZRB-FM (u) 710 W Avenue A, Hooks TX 75561 **Phn:** 903-547-3223 **Fax:** 903-547-3095 kzrb@txk.net

Houston KBME-AM (st) 2000 West Loop S Ste 300, Houston TX 77027 **Phn:** 713-212-8000 **Fax:** 713-212-8950 www.sports790.com bryanerickson@clearchannel.com

Houston KBXX-FM (h) 24 Greenway Plz Ste 900, Houston TX 77046 **Phn:** 713-623-2108 **Fax:** 713-300-5751 theboxhouston.com tthomas@radio-one.com

Houston KCOH-AM (wu) 5011 Almeda Rd, Houston TX 77004 **Phn:** 713-522-1001 **Fax:** 713-521-0769 www.kcohradio.com info@kcohradio.com

Houston KEYH-AM (y) 3000 Bering Dr, Houston TX 77057 **Phn:** 713-315-3400 **Fax:** 713-315-3506 www.lbimedia.com info@lbimedia.com

Houston KFNC-FM (s) 9801 Westheimer Rd Ste 700, Houston TX 77042 **Phn:** 713-266-1000 **Fax:** 713-954-2344 espn975.com david.tepper@gowmedia.com

Houston KGBC-AM (q) 1302 N Shepherd Dr, Houston TX 77008 **Phn:** 409-744-1540 **Fax:** 409-740-0944

Houston KGLK-FM (h) 1990 Post Oak Blvd Ste 2300, Houston TX 77056 **Phn:** 713-963-1200 **Fax:** 713-622-5457 www.houstoneagle.com scott.sparks@coxinc.com

Houston KGOL-AM (ey) 5821 Southwest Fwy Ste 600, Houston TX 77057 **Phn:** 713-349-9880 **Fax:** 713-349-9365 entravision.com

Houston KHCB-FM (q) 2424 South Blvd, Houston TX 77098 **Phn:** 713-520-7900 www.khcb.org email@khcb.org

Houston KHCB-AM (q) 2424 South Blvd, Houston TX 77098 **Phn:** 713-520-5200 www.khcb.org email@khcb.org

Houston KHJK-FM (r) 9801 Westheimer Rd Ste 700, Houston TX 77042 **Phn:** 713-266-1000 **Fax:** 713-954-2344

Houston KHJZ-FM (aj) 24 Greenway Plz Ste 1900, Houston TX 77046 **Phn:** 713-881-5100 **Fax:** 713-881-5999 mix965houston.cbslocal.com bob.neumann@mix965houston.com

Houston KHMX-FM (a) 24 Greenway Plz Ste 1900, Houston TX 77046 **Phn:** 713-881-5100 mix965houston.cbslocal.com bob.neumann@mix965houston.com

Houston KHPT-FM (r) 1990 Post Oak Blvd Ste 2300, Houston TX 77056 **Phn:** 713-963-1200 **Fax:** 713-993-9300 www.1069thezone.com johnny.chiang@coxinc.com

Houston KIKK-AM (kn) 24 Greenway Plz Ste 1900, Houston TX 77046 **Phn:** 713-881-5957 **Fax:** 713-881-5999 houston.cbslocal.com ryan.mccredden@cbsradio.com

Houston KILT-AM (s) 24 Greenway Plz Ste 1900, Houston TX 77046 **Phn:** 713-881-5100 **Fax:** 713-881-5459 houston.cbslocal.com laurareynolds@sportsradio610.com

TEXAS RADIO STATIONS

Houston KILT-FM (c) 24 Greenway Plz Ste 1900, Houston TX 77046 **Phn:** 713-881-5100 **Fax:** 713-881-5450 thebull.cbslocal.com greg.frey@cbsradio.com

Houston KIOX-FM (y) 3000 Bering Dr, Houston TX 77057 **Phn:** 713-315-3400 **Fax:** 713-315-3506 www.kioxradio.com

Houston KJOJ-AM (qty) 3000 Bering Dr, Houston TX 77057 **Phn:** 713-315-3400 **Fax:** 713-315-3506 www.lbimedia.com houstoninfo@lbimedia.com

Houston KJOJ-FM (y) 3000 Bering Dr, Houston TX 77057 **Phn:** 713-315-3400 **Fax:** 713-315-3405 www.laraza.fm

Houston KKBQ-FM (c) 1990 Post Oak Blvd Ste 2300, Houston TX 77056 **Phn:** 713-963-1200 **Fax:** 713-993-9300 www.thenew93q.com lisa.riha@coxradio.com

Houston KKHH-FM (h) 24 Greenway Plz Ste 1900, Houston TX 77046 **Phn:** 713-881-5100 www.gradickcommunications.com madams@cbs.com

Houston KKHT-FM (q) 6161 Savoy Dr Ste 1200, Houston TX 77036 **Phn:** 713-260-3600 **Fax:** 713-260-3628 www.kkht.com chuckj@kkht.com

Houston KKRW-FM (r) 2000 West Loop S Ste 300, Houston TX 77027 **Phn:** 713-212-8000 **Fax:** 713-212-8937 www.937thearrow.com stevefixx@clearchannel.com

Houston KLAT-AM (cy) 5100 Southwest Fwy, Houston TX 77056 **Phn:** 713-965-2400 **Fax:** 713-965-2401 www.univision.com

Houston KLOL-FM (y) 24 Greenway Plz Ste 1900, Houston TX 77046 **Phn:** 713-881-5100 **Fax:** 713-881-5598 klol.cbslocal.com liliana.ary@cbsradio.com

Houston KLTN-FM (y) 5100 Southwest Fwy, Houston TX 77056 **Phn:** 713-965-2400 **Fax:** 713-965-2401 www.univision.com

Houston KLVL-AM (qy) 1302 N Shepherd Dr, Houston TX 77008 **Phn:** 713-868-5559 **Fax:** 713-868-9631 www.sigabroadcasting.com sigabroadcasting@gmail.com

Houston KMIC-AM (m) 3120 Southwest Fwy Ste 610, Houston TX 77098 **Phn:** 713-552-1590 **Fax:** 713-552-1588 music.disney.com

Houston KMJQ-FM (wux) 24 Greenway Plz Ste 900, Houston TX 77046 **Phn:** 713-623-2108 myhoustonmajic.com dabernethy@radio-one.com

Houston KNTE-FM (y) 3000 Bering Dr, Houston TX 77057 **Phn:** 713-315-3400 whorton@lbimedia.com

Houston KNTT-FM (nt) 6161 Savoy Dr Ste 1200, Houston TX 77036 **Phn:** 713-260-3600 **Fax:** 713-260-3628 www.1070knth.com

Houston KODA-FM (a) 2000 West Loop S Ste 300, Houston TX 77027 **Phn:** 713-212-8000 **Fax:** 713-212-8953 www.sunny99.com markkopelman@clearchannel.com

Houston KOVE-FM (y) 5100 Southwest Fwy, Houston TX 77056 **Phn:** 713-965-2400 **Fax:** 713-965-2401 www.univision.com

Houston KPFT-FM (p) 419 Lovett Blvd, Houston TX 77006 **Phn:** 713-526-4000 **Fax:** 713-526-5750 www.kpft.org

Houston KPRC-AM (st) 2000 West Loop S Ste 300, Houston TX 77027 **Phn:** 713-212-8000 **Fax:** 713-212-8950 www.kprcradio.com ramonrobles@clearchannel.com

Houston KQBU-FM (y) 5100 Southwest Fwy, Houston TX 77056 **Phn:** 713-965-2400 **Fax:** 13-965-2401 www.univision.com

Houston KQQK-FM (y) 3000 Bering Dr, Houston TX 77057 **Phn:** 713-315-3400 **Fax:** 713-315-3506 elnorte.estrellatv.com greyes@lbimedia.com

Houston KQUE-AM (y) 3000 Bering Dr, Houston TX 77057 **Phn:** 713-315-3400 **Fax:** 713-315-3506

Houston KRBE-FM (h) 9801 Westheimer Rd Ste 700, Houston TX 77042 **Phn:** 713-266-1000 **Fax:** 713-954-2344 www.104krbe.com leslie.whittle@cumulus.com

Houston KROI-FM (q) 24 Greenway Plz Ste 900, Houston TX 77046 **Phn:** 713-623-2108 **Fax:** 713-622-7785 praisehouston.com jmccruse@radio-one.com

Houston KSEV-AM (st) 11451 Katy Fwy Ste 215, Houston TX 77079 **Phn:** 281-588-4800 ksevradio.com

Houston KSHJ-AM (q) 11511 Katy Fwy # 301, Houston TX 77079 **Phn:** 832-786-4500 **Fax:** 832-786-4501 grnonline.com joe@grnonline.com

Houston KTBZ-FM (r) 2000 West Loop S Ste 300, Houston TX 77027 **Phn:** 713-212-8000 **Fax:** 713-212-8945 www.thebuzz.com marcsherman@clearchannel.com

Houston KTEK-AM (q) 6161 Savoy Dr Ste 1200, Houston TX 77036 **Phn:** 713-260-3600 **Fax:** 713-260-3628 www.ktek.com chuckj@kkht.com

Houston KTHT-FM (c) 1900 Post Oak Blvd # 2300, Houston TX 77056 **Phn:** 713-963-1200 **Fax:** 713-993-9300 www.countrylegends971.com johnny.chiang@coxradio.com

Houston KTJM-FM (y) 3000 Bering Dr, Houston TX 77057 **Phn:** 713-315-3400 **Fax:** 713-315-3506 www.laraza.fm whorton@lbimedia.com

Houston KTMR-AM (qy) 1302 N Shepherd Dr, Houston TX 77008 **Phn:** 713-868-5559 **Fax:** 713-868-9631 www.sigabroadcasting.com sigabroadcasting@gmail.com

Houston KTRH-AM (ns) 2000 West Loop S Ste 300, Houston TX 77027 **Phn:** 713-212-8740 **Fax:** 713-212-8958 www.ktrh.com rogerhudson@clearchannel.com

Houston KTRU-FM (v) 6100 Main St, Houston TX 77005 **Phn:** 713-348-4098 ktru.org ktru@ktru.org

Houston KTSU-FM (vj) 3100 Cleburne St, Houston TX 77004 **Phn:** 713-313-7591 **Fax:** 713-313-7479 www.ktsufm.org thomas_gx@tsu.edu

Houston KUHF-FM (pln) 4343 Elgin St, Houston TX 77004 **Phn:** 713-743-0887 **Fax:** 713-743-0868 www.kuhf.org news@kuhf.org

Houston KYND-AM (qye) PO Box 19886, Houston TX 77224 **Phn:** 281-373-1520

Houston KYST-AM (y) 7322 Southwest Fwy Ste 500, Houston TX 77074 **Phn:** 713-779-9292 **Fax:** 713-779-1651

Humble KSBJ-FM (q) 1722 Treble Dr, Humble TX 77338 **Phn:** 281-446-5725 **Fax:** 281-540-2198 www.ksbj.org frontdesk@ksbj.org

Huntsville KHVL-AM (o) PO Box 330, Huntsville TX 77342 **Phn:** 936-295-2651 **Fax:** 936-295-8201 ksam1017.com steveeverett@ksam1017.com

Huntsville KSAM-FM (c) PO Box 330, Huntsville TX 77342 **Phn:** 936-295-2651 **Fax:** 936-295-8201 ksam1017.com ksamnews@yahoo.com

Huntsville KSHU-FM (vlj) PO Box 2207, Huntsville TX 77341 **Phn:** 936-294-3939 **Fax:** 936-294-1888 www.kshu.org rtf_news@shsu.edu

Irving KAAM-AM (ab) 3201 Royalty Row, Irving TX 75062 **Phn:** 972-445-1700 **Fax:** 972-438-6574 www.kaamradio.com kaam@kaamradio.com

Irving KLTY-FM (a) 6400 N Belt Line Rd Ste 120, Irving TX 75063 **Phn:** 972-870-9949 www.klty.com onair@klty.com

Irving KPXI-FM (q) 6400 N Belt Line Rd Ste 110, Irving TX 75063 **Phn:** 972-870-9949 www.thewordfm.com

Irving KSKY-AM (nt) 6400 N Belt Line Rd Ste 110, Irving TX 75063 **Phn:** 972-870-9949 www.660amtheanswer.com

Irving KWRD-FM (qt) 6400 N Belt Line Rd Ste 110, Irving TX 75063 **Phn:** 972-870-9949 www.thewordfm.com

Jacksonville KBJS-FM (q) PO Box 193, Jacksonville TX 75766 **Phn:** 903-586-5257 **Fax:** 903-586-4986 www.kbjs.org

Jacksonville KDVE-FM (y) PO Box 1648, Jacksonville TX 75766 **Phn:** 903-586-2527 **Fax:** 903-663-9492 bullboyroy@yahoo.com

Jacksonville KEBE-AM (y) PO Box 1648, Jacksonville TX 75766 **Phn:** 903-586-2527 **Fax:** 903-663-9492 bullboyroy@yahoo.com

Jasper KCOX-AM (nt) PO Box 2008, Jasper TX 75951 **Phn:** 409-384-4500 **Fax:** 409-384-4525 www.1027ktxj.com request@1027ktxj.com

Jasper KJAS-FM (a) 765 Hemphill St, Jasper TX 75951 **Phn:** 409-384-2626 **Fax:** 409-383-1979 www.kjas.com press@kjas.com

Jasper KTXJ-AM (g) PO Box 2008, Jasper TX 75951 **Phn:** 409-384-4500 **Fax:** 409-384-4525 www.1027ktxj.com request@1027ktxj.com

Keene KJCR-FM (q) 304 N College Dr, Keene TX 76059 **Phn:** 817-202-6788 **Fax:** 817-202-6790

Kerrville KERV-AM (ob) 2125 Sidney Baker St, Kerrville TX 78028 **Phn:** 830-896-1230 **Fax:** 830-792-4142

Kerrville KMBL-AM (c) 2125 Sidney Baker St, Kerrville TX 78028 **Phn:** 830-896-1230 **Fax:** 830-792-4142

Kerrville KOOK-FM (o) 2125 Sidney Baker St, Kerrville TX 78028 **Phn:** 830-896-1230 **Fax:** 830-792-4142 www.revfmradio.com

Kerrville KRNH-FM (c) 3505 Fredericksburg Rd, Kerrville TX 78028 **Phn:** 830-896-4990 923theranch.com

Kerrville KRVL-FM (r) 2125 Sidney Baker St, Kerrville TX 78028 **Phn:** 830-896-1230 **Fax:** 830-895-8770 www.revfmradio.com diane@krvl.com

Kilgore KDOK-AM (o) PO Box 1008, Kilgore TX 75663 **Phn:** 903-643-7711 **Fax:** 903-643-8272 www.kdokradio.com kdok1240@aol.com

Kilgore KTPB-FM (pl) 814 E Main St, Kilgore TX 75662 **Phn:** 903-983-8625

Killeen KNCT-FM (pl) PO Box 1800, Killeen TX 76540 **Phn:** 254-526-1176 **Fax:** 254-526-1850 www.knct.org knct@knct.org

Killeen KRMY-AM (g) 314 N 2nd St, Killeen TX 76541 **Phn:** 254-628-7070 **Fax:** 254-634-5263

Kingsville KTAI-FM (vrco) 700 University Blvd, Kingsville TX 78363 **Phn:** 361-593-5824 **Fax:** 361-593-3406 www.tamuk.eduktai ktai91.1@hotmail.com

La Grange KBUK-FM (c) PO Box 609, La Grange TX 78945 **Phn:** 979-968-3173 **Fax:** 979-968-6196 www.kvlgkbuk.com kvlgkbuk@kvlgkbuk.com

La Grange KVLG-AM (c) PO Box 609, La Grange TX 78945 **Phn:** 979-968-3173 **Fax:** 979-968-6196 www.kvlgkbuk.com kvlgkbuk@kvlgkbuk.com

Lamesa KPET-AM (c) PO Box 1188, Lamesa TX 79331 **Phn:** 806-872-6511 **Fax:** 806-872-6514

TEXAS RADIO STATIONS

Lampasas KACQ-FM (c) 505 N Key Ave, Lampasas TX 76550 **Phn:** 512-556-6193 **Fax:** 512-556-2197 www.lampasasradio.com management@lampasasradio.com

Lampasas KCYL-AM (c) 505 N Key Ave, Lampasas TX 76550 **Phn:** 512-556-6193 **Fax:** 512-556-2197 www.lampasasradio.com management@lampasasradio.com

Laredo KBDR-FM (y) 107 Calle Del Norte Ste 107, Laredo TX 78041 **Phn:** 956-725-1000 **Fax:** 956-794-9155 www.laley1005.com

Laredo KBNL-FM (qy) PO Box 2425, Laredo TX 78044 **Phn:** 956-724-9211 **Fax:** 956-724-9919 www.kbnl.org kbnl@lwrn.org

Laredo KHOY-FM (vy) 1901 Corpus Christi St, Laredo TX 78043 **Phn:** 956-722-4167 **Fax:** 956-722-4464 www.khoy.org khoy@khoy.org

Laredo KJBZ-FM (y) 6402 N Bartlett Ave Ste 1, Laredo TX 78041 **Phn:** 956-726-9393 **Fax:** 956-724-9915 restrada@krrg.com

Laredo KLAR-AM (ynt) PO Box 2517, Laredo TX 78044 **Phn:** 956-723-1300 **Fax:** 956-723-9539

Laredo KLNT-AM (c) 107 Calle Del Norte Ste 107, Laredo TX 78041 **Phn:** 956-725-1490 **Fax:** 956-794-9171

Laredo KNEX-FM (h) 107 Calle Del Norte # 212, Laredo TX 78041 **Phn:** 956-725-1000 **Fax:** 956-794-9171 www.hot1061.com aserna@rcommunications.com

Laredo KQUR-FM (h) 107 Calle Del Norte Ste 107, Laredo TX 78041 **Phn:** 956-725-1000 **Fax:** 956-794-9155

Laredo KRRG-FM (ah) 6402 N Bartlett Ave Ste 1, Laredo TX 78041 **Phn:** 956-724-9800 **Fax:** 956-724-9815

Laredo XEAS-AM (y) 1510 Calle Del Norte Ste 2, Laredo TX 78041 **Phn:** 956-727-3670 **Fax:** 956-727-3680

Laredo XERT-AM (y) 1510 Calle Del Norte Ste 2, Laredo TX 78041 **Phn:** 956-727-3670 **Fax:** 956-727-3680

Laredo XHMW-FM (y) 1510 Calle Del Norte Ste 2, Laredo TX 78041 **Phn:** 956-727-3670 **Fax:** 956-727-3680

Laredo XHRT-FM (y) 1510 Calle Del Norte Ste 2, Laredo TX 78041 **Phn:** 956-727-3670 **Fax:** 956-727-3680

Levelland KLVT-AM (c) PO Box 967, Levelland TX 79336 **Phn:** 806-894-3134 **Fax:** 806-894-3135 www.klvtradio.com office@klvtradio.com

Levelland KZZN-AM (c) PO Box 967, Levelland TX 79336 **Phn:** 806-894-3134 **Fax:** 806-894-3135

Liberty KSHN-FM (aco) 2099 Sam Houston St, Liberty TX 77575 **Phn:** 936-336-5793 **Fax:** 936-336-5250 www.kshnfm.com news@kshn.com

Livingston KETX-FM (rh) 115 Radio Rd, Livingston TX 77351 **Phn:** 936-327-8916 **Fax:** 936-327-8477 www.923theeagle.com

Longview KFRO-FM (h) 3400 W Marshall Ave # 307, Longview TX 75608 **Phn:** 903-663-2477 **Fax:** 903-663-9492 www.mybreezefm.com sherris@wallerbroadcasting.com

Longview KJTX-FM (gq) PO Box 150508, Longview TX 75615 **Phn:** 903-759-1243 **Fax:** 903-759-9725 www.kjtx1045fm.com kjtxlr@juno.com

Longview KLJT-FM (h) 481 E Loop 281, Longview TX 75605 **Phn:** 903-586-2527 **Fax:** 903-663-9492 www.mybreezefm.com brain@mybreezefm.com

Longview KYKX-FM (c) 4408 Hwy 259 N, Longview TX 75605 **Phn:** 903-663-9800 **Fax:** 903-663-1022 www.kykx.com gnimmons@etradiogroup.com

Lubbock KAIQ-FM (y) 1220 Broadway Ste 600, Lubbock TX 79401 **Phn:** 806-763-6051 **Fax:** 806-744-8363 www.tricolor955.com ltrevino@entravision.com

Lubbock KAMY-FM (q) 7204 Joliet Ave Ste 4, Lubbock TX 79423 **Phn:** 806-794-1766 **Fax:** 806-798-3251

Lubbock KBTE-FM (h) 33 Briercroft Office Park, Lubbock TX 79412 **Phn:** 806-762-3000 **Fax:** 806-770-5363 www.1049thebeat.com

Lubbock KBZO-AM (y) 1220 Broadway Ste 600, Lubbock TX 79401 **Phn:** 806-763-6051 **Fax:** 806-744-8363 www.espn1460am.com ltrevino@entravision.com

Lubbock KDAV-AM (o) 1714 Buddy Holly Ave, Lubbock TX 79401 **Phn:** 806-744-5859 **Fax:** 806-744-5888 www.kdav.orgkdav emery@kdav.org

Lubbock KFMX-FM (r) 4413 82nd St Ste 300, Lubbock TX 79424 **Phn:** 806-798-7078 **Fax:** 806-798-7052 kfmx.com voodoo@kfmx.com

Lubbock KFYO-AM (snt) 4413 82nd St Ste 300, Lubbock TX 79424 **Phn:** 806-798-7078 **Fax:** 806-798-7052 kfyo.com news@kfyo.com

Lubbock KJAK-FM (q) PO Box 6490, Lubbock TX 79493 **Phn:** 806-745-6677 **Fax:** 806-745-8140 www.kjak.com kjak@kjak.com

Lubbock KJTV-AM (nt) PO Box 3757, Lubbock TX 79452 **Phn:** 806-745-3434 **Fax:** 806-748-2470 cheinz@ramarcom.com

Lubbock KKAM-AM (s) 4413 82nd St Ste 300, Lubbock TX 79424 **Phn:** 806-798-7078 **Fax:** 806-798-7052 1340thefan.com robertsnyder@townsquaremedia.com

Lubbock KKCL-FM (o) 4413 82nd St Ste 300, Lubbock TX 79424 **Phn:** 806-798-7078 **Fax:** 806-783-9067 98kool.com landonking@gapbroadcasting.com

Lubbock KLLL-FM (c) 33 Briercroft Office Park, Lubbock TX 79412 **Phn:** 806-762-3000 **Fax:** 806-762-8419 www.klll.com jscott@klll.com

Lubbock KLZK-FM (a) PO Box 3757, Lubbock TX 79452 **Phn:** 806-745-3434 **Fax:** 806-748-2470 www.973yesfm.com rcreighton@ramarcom.com

Lubbock KMMX-FM (h) 33 Briercroft Office Park, Lubbock TX 79412 **Phn:** 806-762-3000 **Fax:** 806-770-5363 www.kmmx.com info@mix100.net

Lubbock KOHM-FM (pl) 1901 University # 603B, Lubbock TX 79410 **Phn:** 806-742-3100 **Fax:** 806-742-3716 kttz.org

Lubbock KONE-FM (r) 33 Briercroft Office Park, Lubbock TX 79412 **Phn:** 806-762-3000 **Fax:** 806-762-8419 www.rock101.fm sean@rock101.fm

Lubbock KQBR-FM (c) 4413 82nd St Ste 300, Lubbock TX 79424 **Phn:** 806-798-7078 **Fax:** 806-798-7052 995blakefm.com scottphillips@townsquaremedia.com

Lubbock KRFE-AM (z) 6602 Martin L King Blvd, Lubbock TX 79404 **Phn:** 806-745-1197 **Fax:** 806-745-1088 www.am580lubbock.com shane@westtexasmedia.com

Lubbock KTTU-FM (s) 9800 University Ave, Lubbock TX 79452 **Phn:** 806-745-3434 **Fax:** 806-748-2470 www.doublet1043.com jlent@ramarcom.com

Lubbock KXTQ-FM (y) PO Box 3757, Lubbock TX 79452 **Phn:** 806-745-3434 **Fax:** 806-748-2470 www.magic937.fm cheinz@ramarcom.com

Lubbock KZII-FM (h) 4413 82nd St Ste 300, Lubbock TX 79424 **Phn:** 806-798-7078 **Fax:** 806-798-7052 1025kiss.com ethandometrius@townsquaremedia.com

Lufkin KAFX-FM (a) 1216 S 1st St, Lufkin TX 75901 **Phn:** 936-639-4455 **Fax:** 936-639-5540 kfox95.com danpatrick@gapbroadcasting.com

Lufkin KAVX-FM (vt) PO Box 151340, Lufkin TX 75915 **Phn:** 936-639-5673 **Fax:** 936-639-5677 www.kavx.org 919kavx@kavx.org

Lufkin KRBA-AM (cg) 121 S Cotton Sq, Lufkin TX 75904 **Phn:** 936-634-6661 **Fax:** 936-632-5722 yatesmedia.com

Lufkin KSFA-AM (nt) 1216 S 1st St, Lufkin TX 75901 **Phn:** 936-639-4455 **Fax:** 936-632-5957 ksfa860.com tamikoonce@gapbroadcasting.com

Lufkin KSML-AM (y) 121 S Cotton Sq, Lufkin TX 75904 **Phn:** 936-634-4584 **Fax:** 936-632-5722 yatesmedia.com radioman@yatesmedia.com

Lufkin KTBQ-FM (r) 1216 S 1st St, Lufkin TX 75901 **Phn:** 936-639-4455 **Fax:** 936-639-5540 q1077.com tamijones@townsquaremedia.com

Lufkin KVLL-FM (a) 1216 S 1st St, Lufkin TX 75901 **Phn:** 936-639-4455 **Fax:** 936-639-5540 my947.com tamikoonce@townsquaremedia.com

Lufkin KYBI-FM (a) 121 S Cotton Sq, Lufkin TX 75904 **Phn:** 936-634-4584 **Fax:** 936-632-5722 www.kybiradio.com radioman@yatesmedia.com

Lufkin KYKS-FM (c) 1216 S 1st St, Lufkin TX 75901 **Phn:** 936-639-4455 **Fax:** 936-639-5540 kicks105.com dannymerrell@gapbroadcasting.com

Madisonville KMVL-FM (c) 102 W Main St, Madisonville TX 77864 **Phn:** 936-348-9200 **Fax:** 936-348-9201 www.kmvl.net kmvl@sbcglobal.net

Madisonville KMVL-AM (am) 102 W Main St, Madisonville TX 77864 **Phn:** 936-348-9200 **Fax:** 936-348-9201 www.kmvl.net kmvl@kmvl.net

Malakoff KCKL-FM (c) PO Box 489, Malakoff TX 75148 **Phn:** 903-489-1238 **Fax:** 903-489-2671 www.kcklfm.com thoward@kcklfm.com

Malakoff KLVQ-AM (g) PO Box 489, Malakoff TX 75148 **Phn:** 903-489-1238 **Fax:** 903-489-2671 www.kcklfm.comklvq thoward@kcklfm.com

Marble Falls KHLE-AM (a) 5526 Highway 281 N, Marble Falls TX 78654 **Phn:** 830-693-5551 **Fax:** 830-693-5107

Marble Falls KHRC-FM (c) 5526 Highway 281 N, Marble Falls TX 78654 **Phn:** 830-693-5551 **Fax:** 830-693-5107

Marion KBIB-AM (qy) 290 N Santa Clara Rd, Marion TX 78124 **Phn:** 830-914-2083

Marshall KBWC-FM (wv) 711 Wiley Ave, Marshall TX 75670 **Phn:** 903-927-3266

McAllen KBTQ-FM (u) 200 S 10th St Ste 600, McAllen TX 78501 **Phn:** 956-631-5499 **Fax:** 956-631-0090 recuerdo961.univision.com

McAllen KFRQ-FM (r) 801 N Jackson Rd, McAllen TX 78501 **Phn:** 956-687-4848 **Fax:** 956-661-6082 www.q945therock.com aduran@entravision.com

McAllen KGBT-AM (y) 200 S 10th St Ste 600, McAllen TX 78501 **Phn:** 956-631-5499 **Fax:** 956-631-0090 www.univision.com

McAllen KGBT-FM (y) 200 S 10th St Ste 600, McAllen TX 78501 **Phn:** 956-631-5499 **Fax:** 956-631-0090 www.univision.com lagueraruby@univision.com

McAllen KIBL-AM (qy) PO Box 252, McAllen TX 78505 **Phn:** 956-686-6382 **Fax:** 956-686-2999

McAllen KJAV-FM (a) 1201 N Jackson Rd Ste 900, McAllen TX 78501 **Phn:** 866-470-5225 www.valleyjack.com

McAllen KKPS-FM (y) 801 N Jackson Rd, McAllen TX 78501 **Phn:** 956-661-6000 **Fax:** 956-661-6081 995lanueva.com

McAllen KNVO-FM (y) 801 N Jackson Rd, McAllen TX 78501 **Phn:** 956-661-6000 **Fax:** 956-661-6081 www.jose1011.com anthonyacosta@entravision.com

McAllen KSOX-AM (s) 1201 N Jackson Rd Ste 900, McAllen TX 78501 **Phn:** 956-992-8895 **Fax:** 956-992-8897

McAllen KTUE-AM (yq) PO Box 252, McAllen TX 78505 **Phn:** 956-686-6382

McAllen KUBR-AM (yq) PO Box 252, McAllen TX 78505 **Phn:** 956-781-5528 **Fax:** 956-686-2999

McAllen KURV-AM (snt) PO Box 3037, McAllen TX 78502 **Phn:** 956-992-8895 **Fax:** 956-992-8897 www.kurv.com talk@kurv.com

McAllen KVLY-FM (a) 801 N Jackson Rd, McAllen TX 78501 **Phn:** 956-661-6000 **Fax:** 956-661-6081 www.mix1079.net

McKinney KLAK-FM (a) 1700 Redbud Blvd Ste 185, McKinney TX 75069 **Phn:** 972-542-9755 **Fax:** 972-838-1330 www.975klak.com johnnyb@975klak.com

Memphis KLSR-FM (c) 114 N 7th St, Memphis TX 79245 **Phn:** 806-259-3511 **Fax:** 806-259-2397 klsr105fm@arn.net

Merkel KMXO-AM (qy) PO Box 523, Merkel TX 79536 **Phn:** 325-928-3060 **Fax:** 325-928-4683 www.kmxoradiofe.com zacarias@kmxoradiofe.com

Mesquite KEOM-FM (v) 2600 Motley Dr Ste 300, Mesquite TX 75150 **Phn:** 972-882-7560 **Fax:** 972-882-7569 www.keom.fm keom@mesquiteisd.org

Midland KBAT-FM (h) 11300 State Highway 191 # 2, Midland TX 79707 **Phn:** 432-563-5636 **Fax:** 432-563-3823 www.kbat.com kevin.chase@townsquaremedia.com

Midland KHKX-FM (c) 3303 N Midkiff Rd Ste 115, Midland TX 79705 **Phn:** 432-520-9912 **Fax:** 432-520-0112 www.kicks99.net kpeterson@westtexasradio.net

Midland KLPF-AM (q) 1903 S Lamesa Rd, Midland TX 79701 **Phn:** 432-682-5476 **Fax:** 432-684-5588 grnonline.com luisds@grnonline.com

Midland KMCM-FM (o) PO Box 9400, Midland TX 79708 **Phn:** 432-520-9912 **Fax:** 432-520-0112 www.97gold.com harold@brazosradio.com

Midland KMMZ-FM (a) PO Box 60375, Midland TX 79711 **Phn:** 432-563-2266 **Fax:** 432-563-2288

Midland KMND-AM (s) 11300 State Highway 191 # 2, Midland TX 79707 **Phn:** 432-563-9300 **Fax:** 432-563-3823 www.kmnd.com gary.hinterlong@townsquaremedia.com

Midland KNFM-FM (c) 11300 State Highway 191 # 2, Midland TX 79707 **Phn:** 432-563-5636 **Fax:** 432-563-3823 www.lonestar92.com gwen.mccown@townsquaremedia.com

Midland KODM-FM (a) 11300 State Highway 191 # 2, Midland TX 79707 **Phn:** 432-561-9809 **Fax:** 432-563-3823 www.kodm.com kodm@cumulus.com

Midland KQRX-FM (r) 3303 N Midkiff Rd Ste 115, Midland TX 79705 **Phn:** 432-520-9912 **Fax:** 432-520-0112 www.rock951online.com kpeterson@westtexasradio.net

Midland KRIL-AM (c) 11300 State Highway 191 # 2, Midland TX 79707 **Phn:** 432-563-5499 **Fax:** 432-563-5541

Midland KTXC-FM (y) PO Box 60403, Midland TX 79711 **Phn:** 432-570-6670 **Fax:** 432-567-9992 bdawson@kwes.com

Midland KVDG-FM (q) 1903 S Lamesa Rd, Midland TX 79701 **Phn:** 432-682-5476 **Fax:** 432-684-5588 grnonline.com faustino@grnonline.com

Midland KWEL-AM (t) 310 W Wall St Ste 104, Midland TX 79701 **Phn:** 432-620-9393 **Fax:** 432-620-9591 www.kwel.com

Midland KZBT-FM (h) 11300 State Highway 191 # 2, Midland TX 79707 **Phn:** 432-563-9300 **Fax:** 432-563-3823 www.b93.net dale.harris@townsquaremedia.com

Mineola KMOO-FM (c) PO Box 628, Mineola TX 75773 **Phn:** 903-569-3823 **Fax:** 903-569-6641 www.kmoo.com news@kmoo.com

Mount Pleasant KALK-FM (a) PO Box 990, Mount Pleasant TX 75456 **Phn:** 903-572-8726 **Fax:** 903-572-7232 www.easttexasradio.com nscooper@easttexasradio.com

Mount Pleasant KIMP-AM (nc) PO Box 990, Mount Pleasant TX 75456 **Phn:** 903-572-8726 **Fax:** 903-572-7232 www.easttexasradio.com nscooper@easttexasradio.com

Mount Pleasant KSCN-FM (c) PO Box 990, Mount Pleasant TX 75456 **Phn:** 903-572-8726 **Fax:** 903-572-7232 www.easttexasradio.com moose@easttexasradio.com

Muleshoe KMUL-AM (y) 600 W 8th St, Muleshoe TX 79347 **Phn:** 806-272-4273 **Fax:** 806-272-5067

Muleshoe KMUL-FM (c) 600 W 8th St, Muleshoe TX 79347 **Phn:** 806-272-4273 **Fax:** 806-272-5067

Nacogdoches KSAU-FM (vjr) PO Box 13048, Nacogdoches TX 75962 **Phn:** 936-468-4000 **Fax:** 936-468-1331 www2.sfasu.edu/ksau ksau@sfasu.edu

New Boston KLBW-AM (gq) 1198 Daniels Chapel Rd, New Boston TX 75570 **Phn:** 903-628-2561 thelight1530@yahoo.com

New Boston KNBO-AM (g) 1198 Daniels Chapel Rd, New Boston TX 75570 **Phn:** 903-628-2561

New Braunfels KGNB-AM (nt) 1540 Loop 337, New Braunfels TX 78130 **Phn:** 830-625-7311 **Fax:** 830-625-7336 kgnb.am

New Braunfels KNBT-FM (c) 1540 Loop 337, New Braunfels TX 78130 **Phn:** 830-625-7311 **Fax:** 830-625-7336 knbt.fm

Odessa KCHX-FM (a) 1330 E 8th St Ste 207, Odessa TX 79761 **Phn:** 432-563-9102 **Fax:** 432-580-9102 www.mymix1067.com gtijerina@icabroadcasting.com

Odessa KCRS-AM (nt) 1330 E 8th St Ste 207, Odessa TX 79761 **Phn:** 432-563-9102 **Fax:** 432-580-9102 www.newstalkkcrs.com newstalkkcrs@icabroadcasting.com

Odessa KCRS-FM (h) 1330 E 8th St Ste 207, Odessa TX 79761 **Phn:** 432-563-9102 **Fax:** 432-580-9102 www.1033kissfm.net nrodriguez@icabroadcasting.com

Odessa KFZX-FM (r) 1330 E 8th St Ste 207, Odessa TX 79761 **Phn:** 432-563-9102 **Fax:** 432-580-9102 www.classicrock102.net gtijerina@icabroadcasting.com

Odessa KMRK-FM (c) 1330 E 8th St Ste 207, Odessa TX 79761 **Phn:** 432-563-9102 **Fax:** 432-580-9102 www.mycountry961.com

Odessa KOCV-FM (vl) 201 W University Blvd, Odessa TX 79764 **Phn:** 432-335-6340

Odessa KOZA-AM (y) 1319 S Crane Ave, Odessa TX 79763 **Phn:** 432-333-1227 **Fax:** 432-435-0064

Odessa KQLM-FM (y) 1319 S Crane Ave, Odessa TX 79763 **Phn:** 432-333-1227 **Fax:** 432-435-0064 www.q108fm.com benjaminv@kqlm.com

Orange KOGT-AM (c) PO Box 1667, Orange TX 77631 **Phn:** 409-883-4381 **Fax:** 409-883-7996 www.kogt.com gstelly@gt.rr.com

Ozona KYXX-FM (c) 917 Shefield, Ozona TX 76943 **Phn:** 325-392-9100 **Fax:** 325-392-9150 eligio@krvl.com

Palestine KNET-AM (c) PO Box 3649, Palestine TX 75802 **Phn:** 903-729-6077 **Fax:** 903-729-4742 www.youreasttexas.com news@kyyk.com

Palestine KYYK-FM (c) PO Box 3649, Palestine TX 75802 **Phn:** 903-729-6077 **Fax:** 903-729-4742 www.youreasttexas.com lee@kyyk.com

Pampa KGRO-AM (a) PO Box 1779, Pampa TX 79066 **Phn:** 806-669-6809 **Fax:** 806-669-0662 www.kgrokomxradio.com dgsweather@hotmail.com

Pampa KOMX-FM (c) PO Box 1779, Pampa TX 79066 **Phn:** 806-669-6809 **Fax:** 806-669-0662 www.kgrokomxradio.com production@kgrokomxradio.com

Paris KBUS-FM (r) 2810 Pine Mill Rd, Paris TX 75460 **Phn:** 903-785-1068 **Fax:** 903-785-7176 www.easttexasradio.com davejohnson@easttexasradio.com

Paris KCCS-AM (vj) 2400 Clarksville St, Paris TX 75460 **Phn:** 903-782-0792

Paris KOYN-FM (c) 2810 Pine Mill Rd, Paris TX 75460 **Phn:** 903-785-1068 **Fax:** 903-785-7176 www.easttexasradio.com mallory@easttexasradio.com

Paris KPLT-AM (c) 2810 Pine Mill Rd, Paris TX 75460 **Phn:** 903-785-1068 **Fax:** 903-785-7176 www.easttexasradio.com bobh@easttexasradio.com

Paris KPLT-FM (a) 2810 Pine Mill Rd, Paris TX 75460 **Phn:** 903-785-1068 **Fax:** 903-785-7176 www.easttexasradio.com davejohnson@easttexasradio.com

Pecos KIUN-AM (cy) PO Box 469, Pecos TX 79772 **Phn:** 432-445-2497 **Fax:** 432-445-4092 www.98xfm.com

Pecos KPTX-FM (c) PO Box 469, Pecos TX 79772 **Phn:** 432-445-2497 **Fax:** 432-445-4092 www.98xfm.com

Perryton KEYE-FM (a) PO Box 630, Perryton TX 79070 **Phn:** 806-435-5458 **Fax:** 806-435-5393 www.keye.net keye@keye.net

Perryton KEYE-AM (c) PO Box 630, Perryton TX 79070 **Phn:** 806-435-5458 **Fax:** 806-435-5393 www.keye.net keye@keye.net

Perryton KXDJ-FM (c) PO Box 830, Perryton TX 79070 **Phn:** 806-648-2650 www.kxdjradio.com

Plainview KKYN-FM (c) PO Box 1478, Plainview TX 79073 **Phn:** 806-296-2771 **Fax:** 806-293-5732 www.kkyn.net bobd@plainviewradio.com

Plainview KREW-AM (o) PO Box 1420, Plainview TX 79073 **Phn:** 806-296-2771 **Fax:** 806-293-5732

Plainview KRIA-FM (y) PO Box 1420, Plainview TX 79073 **Phn:** 806-296-2771 **Fax:** 806-293-5732

Plainview KVOP-AM (m) PO Box 1420, Plainview TX 79073 **Phn:** 806-296-2771 **Fax:** 806-293-5732

Plano KHYI-FM (c) PO Box 940670, Plano TX 75094 **Phn:** 972-633-0953 **Fax:** 972-633-0957 www.khyi.com josh@khyi.com

Prairie View KPVU-FM (wvj) PO Box 519, Prairie View TX 77446 **Phn:** 936-261-3750 **Fax:** 936-261-3769 www.pvamu.edu/kpvu cdbrooks@pvamu.edu

Robstown KINE-AM (yq) 115 W Avenue D, Robstown TX 78380 **Phn:** 361-289-8877 **Fax:** 361-289-7722

TEXAS RADIO STATIONS

Rockdale KRXT-FM (c) 1095 W US Highway 79, Rockdale TX 76567 **Phn:** 512-446-6985 **Fax:** 512-446-6987 www.krxt985.com krxt@krxt985.com

Rusk KTLU-AM (o) PO Box 475, Rusk TX 75785 **Phn:** 903-683-2257 **Fax:** 903-683-5104 kwrw@mediactr.com

Rusk KWRW-FM (o) PO Box 475, Rusk TX 75785 **Phn:** 903-683-2258 **Fax:** 903-683-5104

San Angelo KCLL-FM (y) 2824 Sherwood Way, San Angelo TX 76901 **Phn:** 325-949-2112 **Fax:** 325-944-0851 www.kcll-fm.com info@kcll-fm.com

San Angelo KCRN-FM (q) PO Box 32, San Angelo TX 76902 **Phn:** 325-655-6917 **Fax:** 325-655-7806 www.kcrn.org kcrn@kcrn.org

San Angelo KCRN-AM (q) PO Box 32, San Angelo TX 76902 **Phn:** 325-655-6917 **Fax:** 325-655-7806 www.kcrn.org kcrn@kcrn.org

San Angelo KDCD-FM (c) 3434 Sherwood Way, San Angelo TX 76901 **Phn:** 325-947-0899 **Fax:** 325-947-0996 www.kdcdradio.com sstark@lonestar-mdx.com

San Angelo KELI-FM (ah) 1301 S Abe St, San Angelo TX 76903 **Phn:** 325-655-7161 **Fax:** 325-658-7377 www.magic987.com boomerkingston@townsquaremedia.com

San Angelo KGKL-FM (c) PO Box 1878, San Angelo TX 76902 **Phn:** 325-655-7161 **Fax:** 325-658-7377 www.975kgkl.com boomerkingston@townsquaremedia.com

San Angelo KGKL-AM (nt) PO Box 1878, San Angelo TX 76902 **Phn:** 325-655-7161 **Fax:** 325-658-7377 www.960kgkl.com boomer.kingston@townsquaremedia.com

San Angelo KIXY-FM (ah) PO Box 2191, San Angelo TX 76902 **Phn:** 325-949-2112 **Fax:** 325-944-0851 www.kixyfm.com davidcarr@kixyfm.com

San Angelo KKCN-FM (c) PO Box 1878, San Angelo TX 76902 **Phn:** 325-655-6171 **Fax:** 325-658-7377

San Angelo KKSA-AM (snt) PO Box 2191, San Angelo TX 76902 **Phn:** 325-949-2112 **Fax:** 325-944-0851 www.kksa-am.com jeffrottman@kksa-am.com

San Angelo KMDX-FM (ahr) 3434 Sherwood Way, San Angelo TX 76901 **Phn:** 325-947-0899 **Fax:** 325-947-0996 www.themixonline.com awright@lonestar-mdx.com

San Angelo KNRX-FM (r) 1301 S Abe St, San Angelo TX 76903 **Phn:** 325-655-7161 **Fax:** 325-658-7377 www.965therock.com boomerkingston@townsquaremedia.com

San Angelo KSJT-FM (yst) 209 W Beauregard Ave, San Angelo TX 76903 **Phn:** 325-655-1717 **Fax:** 325-657-0601 nikkibkyzz@yahoo.com

San Angelo KWFR-FM (r) 2824 Sherwood Way, San Angelo TX 76901 **Phn:** 325-949-3333 **Fax:** 325-944-0851 www.kwfrfm.com

San Antonio KAHL-AM (t) 8023 Vantage Dr Ste 840, San Antonio TX 78230 **Phn:** 210-341-1310 **Fax:** 210-341-1777 www.call1310.com info@call1310.com

San Antonio KAJA-FM (c) 6222 W Ih 10, San Antonio TX 78201 **Phn:** 210-736-9700 **Fax:** 210-735-8811 www.kj97.com sheilagarcia@clearchannel.com

San Antonio KBBT-FM (h) 12451 Network Blvd, San Antonio TX 78249 **Phn:** 210-610-4300 **Fax:** 210-804-7820 www.univision.com

San Antonio KCHL-AM (gw) 1211 W Hein Rd, San Antonio TX 78220 **Phn:** 210-333-0050 **Fax:** 210-333-0081 www.kchl.org

San Antonio KCOR-AM (y) 1777 NE Loop 410 Ste 400, San Antonio TX 78217 **Phn:** 210-821-6548 **Fax:** 210-804-7825 www.univision.com dwilson@univisionradio.com

San Antonio KCYY-FM (c) 8122 Datapoint Dr Ste 600, San Antonio TX 78229 **Phn:** 210-615-5400 **Fax:** 210-615-5300 www.y100fm.com jeff.garrison@coxinc.com

San Antonio KDRY-AM (q) 16414 San Pedro Ave Ste 575, San Antonio TX 78232 **Phn:** 210-545-1100 www.kdry.com am1100@kdry.com

San Antonio KEDA-AM (nty) 510 S Flores St, San Antonio TX 78204 **Phn:** 210-226-5254 **Fax:** 210-227-7937 www.kedaradio.com kedakid@aol.com

San Antonio KGSX-FM (y) 1777 NE Loop 410 Ste 400, San Antonio TX 78217 **Phn:** 210-821-6548 www.univision.com

San Antonio KISS-FM (r) 8122 Datapoint Dr Ste 600, San Antonio TX 78229 **Phn:** 210-615-5400 **Fax:** 210-615-5331 www.kissrocks.com randy.bonillas@coxinc.com

San Antonio KJMA-FM (q) 3308 Broadway #401, San Antonio TX 78209 **Phn:** 210-579-9844 **Fax:** 210-821-5052 www.grnonline.com richard@grnonline.com

San Antonio KJXK-FM (a) 4050 Eisenhauer Rd, San Antonio TX 78218 **Phn:** 210-654-5100 **Fax:** 210-855-5056 www.hellojack.com mlandis@bordermedia.com

San Antonio KKYX-AM (c) 8122 Datapoint Dr Ste 600, San Antonio TX 78229 **Phn:** 210-615-5400 **Fax:** 210-615-5300 www.kkyx.com doug.bennett@coxradio.com

San Antonio KLEY-FM (y) 4050 Eisenhauer Rd, San Antonio TX 78218 **Phn:** 210-654-5100 **Fax:** 210-855-5076 bmpradio.com sgranato@bmpradio.com

San Antonio KLTO-FM (r) 1777 NE Loop 410 Ste 400, San Antonio TX 78217 **Phn:** 210-804-6900 **Fax:** 210-804-7844 www.univision.com dwilson@univisionradio.com

San Antonio KLUP-AM (t) 9601 McAllister Fwy Ste 1200, San Antonio TX 78216 **Phn:** 210-344-8481 **Fax:** 210-340-1213 www.klup.com baron@salemsanantonio.com

San Antonio KONO-FM (o) 8122 Datapoint Dr Ste 600, San Antonio TX 78229 **Phn:** 210-615-5400 **Fax:** 210-615-5300 www.kono1011.com steve.casanova@coxradio.com

San Antonio KONO-AM (o) 8122 Datapoint Dr Ste 500, San Antonio TX 78229 **Phn:** 210-615-5400 **Fax:** 210-615-5300 www.kono1011.com roger.allen@coxradio.com

San Antonio KPAC-FM (pl) 8401 Datapoint Dr Ste 800, San Antonio TX 78229 **Phn:** 210-614-8977 **Fax:** 210-614-8983 www.tpr.org news@tpr.org

San Antonio KPWT-FM (t) 8122 Datapoint Dr Ste 600, San Antonio TX 78229 **Phn:** 210-615-5400 **Fax:** 210-615-5300 power1067fm.com adam.michaels@coxradio.com

San Antonio KQXT-FM (a) 6222 W Ih 10, San Antonio TX 78201 **Phn:** 210-736-9700 **Fax:** 210-735-8811 www.q1019.com tonytravatto@clearchannel.com

San Antonio KROM-FM (y) 1777 NE Loop 410 Ste 400, San Antonio TX 78217 **Phn:** 210-821-6548 **Fax:** 210-804-7825 www.univision.com nperez@univisionradio.com

San Antonio KRPT-FM (t) 6222 W Ih 10, San Antonio TX 78201 **Phn:** 210-736-9700 **Fax:** 210-785-2665 www.sanantonioiswild.com chasemurphy@clearchannel.com

San Antonio KRTU-FM (vlj) 1 Trinity Pl, San Antonio TX 78212 **Phn:** 210-999-8917 web.krtu.org krtu@trinity.edu

San Antonio KSAH-AM (y) 4050 Eisenhauer Rd, San Antonio TX 78218 **Phn:** 210-654-5100 **Fax:** 210-855-5076 bmpradio.com sgranato@bmpradio.com

San Antonio KSLR-AM (q) 9601 McAllister Fwy Ste 1200, San Antonio TX 78216 **Phn:** 210-344-8481 **Fax:** 210-340-1213 www.kslr.com barry@salemsanantonio.com

San Antonio KSMG-FM (a) 8122 Datapoint Dr Ste 600, San Antonio TX 78229 **Phn:** 210-615-5400 **Fax:** 210-615-5331 www.magic1053.com dan.lawrie@coxinc.com

San Antonio KSTX-FM (pn) 8401 Datapoint Dr Ste 800, San Antonio TX 78229 **Phn:** 210-614-8977 **Fax:** 210-614-8983 www.tpr.org news@tpr.org

San Antonio KSYM-FM (vrc) 1300 San Pedro Ave, San Antonio TX 78212 **Phn:** 210-486-1373 www.alamo.edusacksym psaksym@hotmail.com

San Antonio KTFM-FM (uo) 4050 Eisenhauer Rd, San Antonio TX 78218 **Phn:** 210-654-5100 **Fax:** 210-855-5076 www.ktfm.com bbilleck@bordermedia.com

San Antonio KTKR-AM (snt) 6222 W Ih 10, San Antonio TX 78201 **Phn:** 210-736-9700 **Fax:** 210-735-8811 www.ticket760.com marlenetrevino@clearchannel.com

San Antonio KTSA-AM (nt) 4050 Eisenhauer Rd, San Antonio TX 78218 **Phn:** 210-654-5100 **Fax:** 210-855-5076 www.ktsa.com ktsanews@bmpradio.com

San Antonio KXTN-FM (y) 1777 NE Loop 410 Ste 400, San Antonio TX 78217 **Phn:** 210-829-1075 **Fax:** 210-804-7825 www.kxtn.com jonramirez@univisionradio.com

San Antonio KXXM-FM (h) 6222 W Ih 10, San Antonio TX 78201 **Phn:** 210-736-9700 **Fax:** 210-735-8811 www.mix961.com tonytravatto@clearchannel.com

San Antonio KZDC-AM (st) 4050 Eisenhauer Rd, San Antonio TX 78218 **Phn:** 210-654-5100 **Fax:** 210-855-5056 bmpradio.com gmartin@bordermedia.com

San Antonio KZEP-FM (r) 6222 NW I H 10, San Antonio TX 78201 **Phn:** 210-736-9700 **Fax:** 210-225-5736 www.kzep.com craig_chambers@kzep.com

San Antonio WOAI-AM (snt) 6222 W Ih 10, San Antonio TX 78201 **Phn:** 210-736-9700 **Fax:** 210-785-2665 www.woai.com jimforsyth@clearchannel.com

San Marcos KTSW-FM (vr) 601 University Dr # OM-106, San Marcos TX 78666 **Phn:** 512-245-3485 **Fax:** 512-245-3732 ktsw.txstate.edu ktswnews@txstate.edu

San Saba KNVR-AM (ob) PO Box 126, San Saba TX 76877 **Phn:** 325-372-5225 **Fax:** 325-372-3817 www.sansabaradio.com production@sansabaradio.com

Seguin KWED-AM (c) 609 E Court St, Seguin TX 78155 **Phn:** 830-379-2234 **Fax:** 830-379-2238 www.seguintoday.com news@kwed1580.com

Seminole KIKZ-AM (cy) 105 NW 11th St, Seminole TX 79360 **Phn:** 432-758-5878 **Fax:** 432-758-5474

Seminole KSEM-FM (c) 105 NW 11th St, Seminole TX 79360 **Phn:** 432-758-5878 **Fax:** 432-758-5474

Seymour KSEY-AM (y) 1 Radio Ln, Seymour TX 76380 **Phn:** 940-889-2637 www.radioksey.com fmksey@aol.com

Seymour KSEY-FM (nt) 1 Radio Ln, Seymour TX 76380 **Phn:** 940-889-2637 www.radioksey.com fmksey@aol.com

Snyder KLYD-FM (c) PO Box 1008, Snyder TX 79550 **Phn:** 325-573-9322 **Fax:** 325-573-7445 ksnyradio.com dink@ksnyradio.com

Snyder KSNY-AM (c) PO Box 1008, Snyder TX 79550 **Phn:** 325-573-9322 **Fax:** 325-573-7445 ksnyradio.com

TEXAS RADIO STATIONS

Snyder KSNY-FM (c) PO Box 1008, Snyder TX 79550 **Phn:** 325-573-9322 **Fax:** 325-573-7445 ksnyradio.com dink@ksnyradio.com

Sonora KHOS-FM (c) 680 Highway 277 S, Sonora TX 76950 **Phn:** 325-387-3553 **Fax:** 325-387-3554 khoskyxx@verizon.net

Stephenville KCUB-FM (r) 471 N Harbin Dr Ste 102, Stephenville TX 76401 **Phn:** 254-968-7459 **Fax:** 254-968-6258

Stephenville KSTV-AM (y) 3209 W Washington St, Stephenville TX 76401 **Phn:** 254-968-2141 **Fax:** 254-968-6221 www.thecrustychicken2.comkstvradio troy.stark@gmail.com

Stephenville KSTV-FM (c) 3209 W Washington St, Stephenville TX 76401 **Phn:** 254-968-2141 **Fax:** 254-968-6221 www.thecrustychicken2.comkstvradio troy.stark@gmail.com

Sulphur Springs KSCH-FM (c) 930 Gilmer St, Sulphur Springs TX 75482 **Phn:** 903-885-1546 **Fax:** 903-885-1101 www.easttexasradio.com dkirkpatrick@easttexasradio.com

Sulphur Springs KSST-AM (am) PO Box 284, Sulphur Springs TX 75483 **Phn:** 903-885-3111 **Fax:** 903-885-4160

Sweetwater KXOX-AM (c) PO Box 570, Sweetwater TX 79556 **Phn:** 325-236-6655 **Fax:** 325-235-4391

Sweetwater KXOX-FM (c) PO Box 570, Sweetwater TX 79556 **Phn:** 325-236-6655 **Fax:** 325-235-4391

Temple KLTD-FM (h) 608 Moody Ln, Temple TX 76504 **Phn:** 254-773-5252 **Fax:** 254-773-0115 k1017fm.com jamie.garrett@townsquaremedia.com

Temple KOOC-FM (a) 608 Moody Ln, Temple TX 76504 **Phn:** 254-773-5252 **Fax:** 254-773-0115 www.myb106.com john.medina@townsquaremedia.com

Temple KSSM-FM (u) 608 Moody Ln, Temple TX 76504 **Phn:** 254-773-5252 **Fax:** 254-773-0115 www.mykiss1031.com jj.jackson@townsquaremedia.com

Temple KTEM-AM (nt) 608 Moody Ln, Temple TX 76504 **Phn:** 254-773-5252 **Fax:** 254-773-0115 ktemnews.com john.medina@townsquaremedia.com

Temple KUSJ-FM (c) 608 Moody Ln, Temple TX 76504 **Phn:** 254-773-5252 **Fax:** 254-773-0115 us105fm.com jamie.garrett@townsquaremedia.com

Terrell KPYK-AM (zb) PO Box 157, Terrell TX 75160 **Phn:** 972-524-5795 www.kpyk.com

Texarkana KBYB-FM (h) 615 Olive St, Texarkana TX 75501 **Phn:** 903-793-4671 **Fax:** 903-792-4261 www.1017hotfm.com info@texarkanaradio.com

Texarkana KCAR-AM (c) 1323 College Dr, Texarkana TX 75503 **Phn:** 903-427-3861 **Fax:** 903-427-5524

Texarkana KCMC-AM (st) 615 Olive St, Texarkana TX 75501 **Phn:** 903-793-4671 **Fax:** 903-792-4261 texarkanaradio.com scott@texarkanaradio.com

Texarkana KEWL-FM (o) 1323 College Dr, Texarkana TX 75503 **Phn:** 903-793-1100 **Fax:** 903-794-4717

Texarkana KFYX-FM (c) 615 Olive St, Texarkana TX 75501 **Phn:** 903-793-4671 **Fax:** 903-792-4261 www.1017bobfm.com

Texarkana KGAP-FM (o) 1323 College Dr, Texarkana TX 75503 **Phn:** 903-427-3861 **Fax:** 903-427-5524

Texarkana KKTK-AM (s) 3446 B Summerhill Road, Texarkana TX 75503 **Phn:** 903-255-7935 **Fax:** 903-255-7942 www.foxsportstexarkana.com info@foxsportstexarkana.com

Texarkana KPGG-FM (c) 1323 College Dr, Texarkana TX 75503 **Phn:** 903-793-1109 **Fax:** 903-794-4717

Texarkana KTFS-AM (nt) 615 Olive St, Texarkana TX 75501 **Phn:** 903-793-4671 **Fax:** 903-792-4261 texarkanaradio.com scott@texarkanaradio.com

Texarkana KTOY-FM (au) 615 Olive St, Texarkana TX 75501 **Phn:** 903-793-4671 **Fax:** 903-792-4261 www.ktoy1047.com billybland@texarkanaradio.com

Texarkana KTXK-FM (pln) 2500 N Robison Rd, Texarkana TX 75501 **Phn:** 903-838-4541 **Fax:** 903-832-5030 ktxk.org ktxktc@yahoo.com

Tyler KAJK-FM (t) 212 Old Grande Blvd Ste B100, Tyler TX 75703 **Phn:** 903-759-2329 **Fax:** 903-759-5189

Tyler KAZE-FM (h) 212 Old Grande Blvd Ste B100, Tyler TX 75703 **Phn:** 903-759-2329 www.theblaze.fm

Tyler KBLZ-FM (u) 212 Old Grande Blvd Ste B100, Tyler TX 75703 **Phn:** 903-581-5259 **Fax:** 903-939-3473 www.theblaze.fm

Tyler KCUL-FM (y) PO Box 7820, Tyler TX 75711 **Phn:** 903-581-9966 **Fax:** 903-534-5300 www.lainvasora.fm dlaborde@etradiogroup.com

Tyler KCUL-AM (g) PO Box 7820, Tyler TX 75711 **Phn:** 903-581-9966 **Fax:** 903-534-5300 www.theranch.fm dlaborde@etradiogroup.com

Tyler KEES-AM (t) 1001 E Southeast Loop 323 Ste 455, Tyler TX 75701 **Phn:** 903-593-2519 **Fax:** 903-597-4141 pgleiser@ktbb.com

Tyler KFRO-AM (qt) 210 S Broadway Ave, Tyler TX 75702 **Phn:** 903-663-9800 **Fax:** 903-663-1022 gnimmons@etradiogroup.com

Tyler KGLD-AM (o) 2737 S Broadway Ave Ste 101, Tyler TX 75701 **Phn:** 903-526-1330 **Fax:** 903-593-4918 www.kgld.org kgldradio@yahoo.com

Tyler KGLY-FM (q) PO Box 8525, Tyler TX 75711 **Phn:** 903-593-5863 **Fax:** 903-593-2663 www.encouragementfm.com

Tyler KISX-FM (h) 3810 Brookside Dr, Tyler TX 75701 **Phn:** 903-581-0606 **Fax:** 903-581-2011 hot1073jamz.com jeffevans@gapbroadcasting.com

Tyler KKTX-FM (r) 3810 Brookside Dr, Tyler TX 75701 **Phn:** 903-581-0606 **Fax:** 903-581-2011 classicrock961.com don.jones@townsquaremedia.com

Tyler KKUS-FM (c) PO Box 7820, Tyler TX 75711 **Phn:** 903-581-9966 **Fax:** 903-534-5300 theranch.fm gnimmons@etradiogroup.com

Tyler KNUE-FM (c) 3810 Brookside Dr, Tyler TX 75701 **Phn:** 903-581-0606 **Fax:** 903-581-2011 knue.com johnnylathrop@gapbroadcasting.com

Tyler KOOI-FM (a) PO Box 7820, Tyler TX 75711 **Phn:** 903-581-9966 **Fax:** 903-534-5300 www.kooi.com sunny@kooi.com

Tyler KOYE-FM (y) 210 S Broadway Ave, Tyler TX 75702 **Phn:** 903-581-9966 **Fax:** 903-534-5300 www.lainvasora.fm

Tyler KTBB-AM (snt) 1001 E Southeast Loop 323 Ste 455, Tyler TX 75701 **Phn:** 903-593-2519 **Fax:** 903-597-8378 www.ktbb.com news@ktbb.com

Tyler KTBB-FM (nt) 1001 E Southeast Loop 323 Ste 455, Tyler TX 75701 **Phn:** 903-593-2519 **Fax:** 903-597-4141 www.ktbb.com

Tyler KTYL-FM (a) 3810 Brookside Dr, Tyler TX 75701 **Phn:** 903-581-0606 **Fax:** 903-581-2011 mix931fm.com luckylarry@mix931fm.com

Tyler KYZS-AM (st) 1001 E Southeast Loop 323 Ste 455, Tyler TX 75701 **Phn:** 903-593-2519 **Fax:** 903-597-8378 ktbb.com news@ktbb.com

Tyler KZEY-AM (u) 4296 County Road 427, Tyler TX 75704 **Phn:** 903-593-1744 **Fax:** 903-593-2666

Uvalde KBNU-FM (c) 935 E Main St, Uvalde TX 78801 **Phn:** 830-278-3693 **Fax:** 830-278-2329 www.kbnu.fm kbradioranch@hotmail.com

Uvalde KUVA-FM (y) PO Box 758, Uvalde TX 78802 **Phn:** 830-278-2555 **Fax:** 830-278-9461 www.uvalderadio.com news@uvalderadio.com

Uvalde KVOU-AM (ob) PO Box 758, Uvalde TX 78802 **Phn:** 830-278-2555 **Fax:** 830-278-9461 www.uvalderadio.com news@uvalderadio.com

Uvalde KVOU-FM (c) PO Box 758, Uvalde TX 78802 **Phn:** 830-278-2555 **Fax:** 830-278-9461 www.uvalderadio.com mariointhemorning@uvalderadio.com

Vernon KVWC-AM (c) PO Box 1419, Vernon TX 76385 **Phn:** 940-552-6221 **Fax:** 940-553-4222 www.kvwc.com kvwc@kvwc.com

Vernon KVWC-FM (c) PO Box 1419, Vernon TX 76385 **Phn:** 940-552-6221 **Fax:** 940-553-4222 www.kvwc.com kvwc@kvwc.com

Victoria KBAR-FM (h) 3613 N Main St, Victoria TX 77901 **Phn:** 361-576-6111 **Fax:** 361-572-0014 cindycox@suddenlinkmail.com

Victoria KHMC-FM (y) 2001 E Sabine St Ste 101, Victoria TX 77901 **Phn:** 361-575-9533 **Fax:** 361-575-9502 www.majic95fm.com majictejano@yahoo.com

Victoria KITE-FM (o) PO Box 3487, Victoria TX 77903 **Phn:** 361-576-6111 **Fax:** 361-572-0014

Victoria KIXS-FM (c) 107 N Star Dr, Victoria TX 77904 **Phn:** 361-573-0777 **Fax:** 361-578-0059 kixs.com joeburris@gapbroadcasting.com

Victoria KLUB-FM (r) 107 N Star Dr, Victoria TX 77904 **Phn:** 361-573-0777 **Fax:** 361-578-0059 1069therock.com jefflyon@gapbroadcasting.com

Victoria KNAL-AM (a) PO Box 3487, Victoria TX 77903 **Phn:** 361-576-6111 **Fax:** 361-572-0014

Victoria KQVT-FM (ay) PO Box 3325, Victoria TX 77903 **Phn:** 361-573-0777 **Fax:** 361-578-0059 www.kqvt.com adamwest@townsquaremedia.com

Victoria KVIC-FM (a) PO Box 3487, Victoria TX 77903 **Phn:** 361-576-6111 **Fax:** 361-572-0014 cindycox@suddenlinkmail.com

Victoria KVNN-AM (nt) PO Box 3487, Victoria TX 77903 **Phn:** 361-576-6111 **Fax:** 361-572-0014

Waco KBBW-AM (qt) 1019 Washington Ave, Waco TX 76701 **Phn:** 254-757-1010 **Fax:** 254-752-5339 www.1010kbw.com info@1010kbw.com

Waco KBCT-FM (c) 4701 W Waco Dr, Waco TX 76710 **Phn:** 254-399-9450 www.kbct.com info@kbct.com

Waco KBGO-FM (o) 314 W State Highway 6, Waco TX 76712 **Phn:** 254-776-3900 **Fax:** 254-399-8134 www.kbgo.com dewaynewells@clearchannel.com

Waco KBRQ-FM (r) 314 W Highway 6, Waco TX 76712 **Phn:** 254-776-3900 **Fax:** 254-751-0097 www.1025thebear.com brenthenslee@clearchannel.com

Waco KLFX-FM (r) 314 W State Highway 6, Waco TX 76712 **Phn:** 254-699-5000 **Fax:** 254-761-6371 www.1073rocks.com brenthenslee@clearchannel.com

Waco KLRK-FM (a) 5501 Bagby Ave, Waco TX 76711 **Phn:** 254-772-0930 **Fax:** 254-753-0499

Waco KRQX-AM (c) 220 S 2nd St Apt 2B2, Waco TX 76701 **Phn:** 254-772-0930 **Fax:** 254-753-0499

Waco KRZI-AM (s) 5501 Bagby Ave, Waco TX 76711 **Phn:** 254-772-0930 **Fax:** 254-753-0499 www.1660espn.com smoaky@1660espn.com

Waco KWBU-FM (p) 1 Bear Pl # 9729, Waco TX 76798 **Phn:** 254-710-3472 **Fax:** 254-710-3874 www.kwbu.org carla@kwbu.org

Waco KWOW-FM (y) 6401 Cobbs Dr, Waco TX 76710 **Phn:** 254-772-6104 **Fax:** 254-776-0642 www.laley104.com

Waco KWTX-FM (h) 314 W State Highway 6, Waco TX 76712 **Phn:** 254-776-3900 **Fax:** 254-399-8134 www.975online.com evanarmstrong@clearchannel.com

Waco KWTX-AM (nt) 314 W State Highway 6, Waco TX 76712 **Phn:** 254-776-3900 **Fax:** 254-776-3917 www.newstalk1230.com evanarmstrong@clearchannel.com

Waco WACO-FM (c) 314 W State Highway 6, Waco TX 76712 **Phn:** 254-776-3900 **Fax:** 254-399-8134 www.waco100.com zackowen@clearchannel.com

Waxahachie KBEC-AM (c) 711 Ferris Ave, Waxahachie TX 75165 **Phn:** 972-923-1390 **Fax:** 972-935-0871 www.kbec.com kenr@kbec.com

Weatherford KYQX-FM (vb) 1612 S Main St, Weatherford TX 76086 **Phn:** 817-341-2337 **Fax:** 817-596-9842 www.qxfm.com

Weslaco KBFM-FM (h) 901 E Pike Blvd, Weslaco TX 78596 **Phn:** 956-973-1041 **Fax:** 956-973-9355 www.wild104.net billysantiago@clearchannel.com

Weslaco KQXX-FM (o) 901 E Pike Blvd, Weslaco TX 78596 **Phn:** 956-973-9202 **Fax:** 956-973-9355 www.1055thex.com billysantiago@clearchannel.com

Weslaco KRGE-AM (yq) PO Box 1290, Weslaco TX 78599 **Phn:** 956-968-7777 **Fax:** 956-968-5143 www.tigrecolorado.com lindc13@yahoo.com

Weslaco KTEX-FM (c) 901 E Pike Blvd, Weslaco TX 78596 **Phn:** 956-973-9202 **Fax:** 956-973-9355 www.ktex.net billysantiago@clearchannel.com

Weslaco KVNS-AM (nt) 901 E Pike Blvd, Weslaco TX 78596 **Phn:** 956-973-9202 **Fax:** 956-973-9355 www.newstalk1700.net jaycantu@clearchannel.com

Weslaco WSFE-AM (st) 901 E Pike Blvd, Weslaco TX 78596 **Phn:** 956-973-1041 **Fax:** 956-973-9355 www.foxsports1700.com billysantiago@clearchannel.com

West Lake Hills KHHL-FM (y) 912 S Capital Of Texas Hwy Ste 400, West Lake Hills TX 78746 **Phn:** 512-390-5539 **Fax:** 512-314-7742

West Lake Hills KXBT-FM (h) 912 S Capital Of Texas Hwy Ste 400, West Lake Hills TX 78746 **Phn:** 512-327-9595 **Fax:** 512-314-7742 www.925trueoldies.com jwolf@bordermedia.com

West Lake Hills KXXS-FM (y) 912 S Capital Of Texas Hwy Ste 400, West Lake Hills TX 78746 **Phn:** 512-416-1100 **Fax:** 512-317-7742

Wharton KANI-AM (wqg) PO Box 350, Wharton TX 77488 **Phn:** 979-532-3800 **Fax:** 979-532-8510 kaniam1500@yahoo.com

Wichita Falls KBZS-FM (r) 2525 Kell Blvd Ste 200, Wichita Falls TX 76308 **Phn:** 940-763-1111 **Fax:** 940-322-3166 1063thebuzz.com lizryan@gapbroadcasting.com

Wichita Falls KLUR-FM (c) 4302 Call Field Rd Ste D, Wichita Falls TX 76308 **Phn:** 940-691-2311 **Fax:** 940-696-2255 www.klur.com lindy.parr@cumulus.com

Wichita Falls KMOC-FM (q) PO Box 41, Wichita Falls TX 76307 **Phn:** 940-767-3303 **Fax:** 940-723-5807 www.kmocfm.com

TEXAS RADIO STATIONS

Wichita Falls KNIN-FM (h) 2525 Kell Blvd Ste 200, Wichita Falls TX 76308 **Phn:** 940-763-1111 **Fax:** 940-322-3166 929nin.com lizryan@gapbroadcasting.com

Wichita Falls KQXC-FM (h) 4302 Call Field Rd, Wichita Falls TX 76308 **Phn:** 940-691-2311 **Fax:** 940-696-2255 www.thehot1039.com lindy.parr@cumulus.com

Wichita Falls KWFB-FM (a) 719 Scott Ave Ste 1009, Wichita Falls TX 76301 **Phn:** 940-322-1009 **Fax:** 940-767-3299 bobradio.fm dana@bobradio.fm

Wichita Falls KWFS-AM (nt) 2525 Kell Blvd Ste 200, Wichita Falls TX 76308 **Phn:** 940-763-1111 **Fax:** 940-322-3166 newstalk1290.com lizryan@gapbroadcasting.com

Wichita Falls KWFS-FM (c) 2525 Kell Blvd Ste 200, Wichita Falls TX 76308 **Phn:** 940-763-1111 **Fax:** 940-322-3166 1023blakefm.com drew.bartlett@townsquaremedia.com

Wichita Falls KYYI-FM (r) 4302 Call Field Rd, Wichita Falls TX 76308 **Phn:** 940-691-2311 **Fax:** 940-696-2255 www.bear104.com lindy.parr@cumulus.com

Winnsboro KWNS-FM (cg) 215 Market St, Winnsboro TX 75494 **Phn:** 903-342-3501

UTAH

Cedar City KCIN-FM (c) 5 N Main St Ste 209, Cedar City UT 84720 **Phn:** 435-867-8156 **Fax:** 435-673-8900 www.bigkickincountry.com bkomarek@cherrycreekradio.com

Cedar City KSUB-AM (nta) 5 N Main St Ste 209, Cedar City UT 84720 **Phn:** 435-867-8156 **Fax:** 435-586-4444 www.ksub590.com bkomarek@cherrycreekradio.com

Cedar City KSUU-FM (vh) 351 W University Blvd, Cedar City UT 84720 **Phn:** 435-865-8224 **Fax:** 435-865-8352 www.power91radio.com

Delta KNAK-AM (st) PO Box 636, Delta UT 84624 **Phn:** 435-864-5111

Heber City KTMP-AM (c) 216 N Main St, Heber City UT 84032 **Phn:** 435-654-0740 **Fax:** 435-654-9261

Logan KBLQ-FM (a) 810 W 200 N, Logan UT 84321 **Phn:** 435-752-1390 **Fax:** 435-752-1392 www.q92.fm

Logan KBNZ-FM (c) PO Box 6280, Logan UT 84341 **Phn:** 435-752-1390 **Fax:** 435-752-1392 kent@cvradio.com

Logan KGNT-FM (h) PO Box 3369, Logan UT 84323 **Phn:** 435-752-1390 **Fax:** 435-752-1392 www.kool.fm shauna@cvradio.com

Logan KKEX-FM (c) 810 W 200 N, Logan UT 84321 **Phn:** 435-752-1390 **Fax:** 435-752-1392 www.kix96fm.com lynn@cvradio.com

Logan KLGN-AM (am) PO Box 3369, Logan UT 84323 **Phn:** 435-752-1390 **Fax:** 435-752-1392 1390klgn.com dave@cvradio.com

Logan KUSU-FM (plnt) 8505 Old Main Hl, Logan UT 84322 **Phn:** 435-797-3138 **Fax:** 435-797-3150 www.upr.org

Logan KVFX-FM (h) 810 W 200 N, Logan UT 84321 **Phn:** 435-752-1390 **Fax:** 435-752-1392 www.utahsvfx.com james@cvradio.com

Logan KVNU-AM (snt) PO Box 267, Logan UT 84323 **Phn:** 435-752-5141 **Fax:** 435-753-5555 www.610kvnu.com jennie@cvradio.com

Logan KYLZ-FM (c) PO Box 6280, Logan UT 84341 **Phn:** 435-752-1390 **Fax:** 435-752-1392 kent@cvradio.com

Manti KLGL-FM (h) PO Box 40, Manti UT 84642 **Phn:** 435-835-7301 **Fax:** 435-835-2250 midutahradio.comklgl jdfox@midutahradio.com

Manti KMTI-AM (c) PO Box 40, Manti UT 84642 **Phn:** 435-835-7301 **Fax:** 435-835-2250 midutahradio.comkmti jdfox@midutahradio.com

Moab KCYN-FM (c) PO Box 1119, Moab UT 84532 **Phn:** 435-259-1035 **Fax:** 435-259-1037 www.kcynfm.com traffic@kcynfm.com

North Salt Lake KXOL-AM (on) 80 S Redwood Rd Ste 211, North Salt Lake UT 84054 **Phn:** 801-936-0812 **Fax:** 801-936-0670

Ogden KWCR-FM (v) 2188 University Cir, Ogden UT 84408 **Phn:** 801-626-6450 departments.weber.edukwcr weberfm@gmail.com

Orem KQMB-AM (a) 1454 W Business Park Dr, Orem UT 84058 **Phn:** 801-224-1400

Orem KSRR-AM (a) 1454 W Business Park Dr, Orem UT 84058 **Phn:** 801-224-1400

Park City KPCW-FM (vn) PO Box 1372, Park City UT 84060 **Phn:** 435-649-9004 **Fax:** 435-645-9063 kpcw.org radionews@kpcw.org

Price KARB-FM (c) PO Box 875, Price UT 84501 **Phn:** 435-637-1167 **Fax:** 435-637-1177 www.castlecountryradio.com news@koal.net

Price KOAL-AM (nt) PO Box 875, Price UT 84501 **Phn:** 435-637-1167 **Fax:** 435-637-1177 www.castlecountryradio.com news@koal.net

Provo KBYU-FM (pl) 701 E University Pkwy, Provo UT 84602 **Phn:** 801-422-3552 **Fax:** 801-422-0922 www.classical89.org eric.glissmeyer@byu.edu

Provo KEYY-AM (q) 307 S 1600 W, Provo UT 84601 **Phn:** 801-374-5210 www.keyradio.org mail@keyradio.org

Richfield KCYQ-FM (c) 390 E Annabella Rd, Richfield UT 84701 **Phn:** 435-896-4456 **Fax:** 435-896-9333 midutahradio.comkcyq jdfox@midutahradio.com

Richfield KSVC-AM (t) 390 E Annabella Rd, Richfield UT 84701 **Phn:** 435-896-4456 **Fax:** 435-896-9333 midutahradio.comksvc

Roosevelt KIFX-FM (a) 2242 E 1000 S, Roosevelt UT 84066 **Phn:** 435-722-5011 **Fax:** 435-722-5012 www.stormpc.comFoxFoxLink.htm radio@ubtanet.com

Roosevelt KNEU-AM (c) 2242 E 1000 S, Roosevelt UT 84066 **Phn:** 435-722-5011 **Fax:** 435-722-5012 www.stormpc.comFoxCntryLink.htm radio@ubtanet.com

Saint George KDXU-AM (snt) 750 W Ridge View Dr, Saint George UT 84770 **Phn:** 435-673-3579 **Fax:** 435-673-8900 www.newstalk890.com pgardner@cherrycreekradio.com

Saint George KPLD-FM (r) PO Box 910580, Saint George UT 84791 **Phn:** 435-628-3643 **Fax:** 435-673-1210 www.planet941.com

Saint George KREC-FM (a) 750 W Ridge View Dr, Saint George UT 84770 **Phn:** 435-673-3579 **Fax:** 435-673-8900 www.star98online.com

Saint George KUNF-AM (ob) 750 W Ridge View Dr, Saint George UT 84770 **Phn:** 435-673-3579 **Fax:** 435-673-8900 www.sportsradio1210.com mmcgary@cherrycreekradio.com

Salt Lake City KBEE-FM (a) 434 Bearcat Dr, Salt Lake City UT 84115 **Phn:** 801-485-6700 **Fax:** 801-485-6611 www.b987.com

Salt Lake City KBER-FM (r) 434 Bearcat Dr, Salt Lake City UT 84115 **Phn:** 801-485-6700 **Fax:** 801-487-5369 www.kber.com

Salt Lake City KBZN-FM (a) 257 E 200 S Ste 400, Salt Lake City UT 84111 **Phn:** 801-364-9836 **Fax:** 801-364-8068 www.kbzn.com kelly@kbzn.com

Salt Lake City KDUT-FM (y) 2722 S Redwood Rd Ste 1, Salt Lake City UT 84119 **Phn:** 801-908-8777 **Fax:** 801-908-8782 kdut.radiolagrande.com acadenas@adelantemediagroup.com

Salt Lake City KDYL-AM (o) 3606 S 500 W, Salt Lake City UT 84115 **Phn:** 801-262-5624 **Fax:** 801-266-1510 www.kdylam.com kdyl@kdylam.com

Salt Lake City KENZ-FM (r) 434 Bearcat Dr, Salt Lake City UT 84115 **Phn:** 801-485-6700 **Fax:** 801-832-1019 www.1019theend.com

Salt Lake City KJMY-FM (r) 2801 Decker Lake Dr, Salt Lake City UT 84119 **Phn:** 801-908-1300 **Fax:** 801-908-1415 www.my995fm.com

Salt Lake City KJQS-AM (s) 434 Bearcat Dr, Salt Lake City UT 84115 **Phn:** 801-485-6700 **Fax:** 801-487-5369 www.kjzz.com sgarrard@kjzz.com

Salt Lake City KJZZ-AM (s) 301 W South Temple, Salt Lake City UT 84101 **Phn:** 801-537-1414 www.kjzz.com jcastro@kjzz.com

Salt Lake City KLO-AM (t) 257 E 200 S Ste 400, Salt Lake City UT 84111 **Phn:** 801-364-9836 **Fax:** 801-364-8068 www.kloradio.com rob@kloradio.com

Salt Lake City KNRS-FM (nt) 2801 Decker Lake Dr, Salt Lake City UT 84119 **Phn:** 801-908-1300 **Fax:** 801-908-1310 www.knrs.com news@knrs.com

Salt Lake City KODJ-FM (o) 2801 Decker Lake Dr, Salt Lake City UT 84119 **Phn:** 801-908-1300 **Fax:** 801-908-1310 www.oldies941.com jeffcochran@clearchannel.com

Salt Lake City KOSY-FM (a) 2801 Decker Lake Dr, Salt Lake City UT 84119 **Phn:** 801-908-1300 **Fax:** 801-908-1310 www.rock1065.com jeffcochran@clearchannel.com

Salt Lake City KOVO-AM (s) 515 S 700 E Ste 1C, Salt Lake City UT 84102 **Phn:** 801-524-2600

Salt Lake City KRCL-FM (v) 1971 W North Temple, Salt Lake City UT 84116 **Phn:** 801-363-1818 **Fax:** 801-533-9136 www.krcl.org troyw@krcl.org

Salt Lake City KRSP-FM (r) 55 N 300 W, Salt Lake City UT 84101 **Phn:** 801-575-5555 **Fax:** 801-526-1074 www.1035thearrow.com

Salt Lake City KSFI-FM (a) 55 N 300 W, Salt Lake City UT 84101 **Phn:** 801-575-5555 **Fax:** 801-526-1070 www.fm100.com

Salt Lake City KSL-AM (nt) 55 N 300 W Ste 200, Salt Lake City UT 84101 **Phn:** 801-526-1036 **Fax:** 801-575-7329 www.ksl.com radio.news@ksl.com

Salt Lake City KSL-FM (n) 55 N 300 W Ste 200, Salt Lake City UT 84101 **Phn:** 801-575-5555 www.ksl.com klarue@ksl.com

Salt Lake City KSOP-FM (c) PO Box 25548, Salt Lake City UT 84125 **Phn:** 801-972-1043 **Fax:** 801-974-0868 www.ksopcountry.com

Salt Lake City KUBL-FM (c) 434 Bearcat Dr, Salt Lake City UT 84115 **Phn:** 801-485-6700 **Fax:** 801-487-5369 www.kbull93.com

Salt Lake City KUDD-FM (h) 515 S 100 E # 1C, Salt Lake City UT 84102 **Phn:** 801-524-2600 **Fax:** 801-412-6041 www.mix1079fm.com

Salt Lake City KUDE-FM (a) 515 S 100 E # 1C, Salt Lake City UT 84102 **Phn:** 801-524-2600 mix1079fm.com

Salt Lake City KUER-FM (plnj) 101 Wasatch Dr Rm 270, Salt Lake City UT 84112 **Phn:** 801-581-6625 **Fax:** 801-581-5426 www.kuer.org news@kuer.org

Salt Lake City KUUU-FM (h) 515 S 700 E # 1C, Salt Lake City UT 84102 **Phn:** 801-524-2600 **Fax:** 801-364-1811 www.u92online.com djerockalypze@bwaymedia.com

Salt Lake City KXRK-FM (r) 515 S 700 E Ste 1C, Salt Lake City UT 84102 **Phn:** 801-524-2600 **Fax:** 801-364-1811 www.x96.com

Salt Lake City KZHT-FM (h) 2801 Decker Lake Dr, Salt Lake City UT 84119 **Phn:** 801-908-1300 **Fax:** 801-908-1310 www.971zht.com jeffmccartney@clearchannel.com

Salt Lake City KZNS-AM (s) 515 S 700 E Ste 1C, Salt Lake City UT 84102 **Phn:** 801-524-2600 **Fax:** 801-364-1811 www.1280thezone.com sgarrard@kjzz.com

South Jordan KTKK-AM (t) 10348 S Redwood Rd, South Jordan UT 84095 **Phn:** 801-253-4883 **Fax:** 801-253-9085 www.k-talk.com webmaster@k-talk.com

St George KXBN-FM (h) 750 W Ridge View Dr, St George UT 84770 **Phn:** 435-673-3579 **Fax:** 435-673-8900 www.b92fmonline.com tnesmith@cherrycreekradio.com

St George KZNU-AM (s) 619 S Bluff St, St George UT 84770 **Phn:** 435-628-3643 **Fax:** 435-673-1210 www.foxnews1450.com

St. George KONY-FM (c) 619 S Bluff St Tower 1 # 300, St. George UT 84770 **Phn:** 435-628-3643 **Fax:** 435-673-1210 www.999konycountry.com kony@infowest.com

Vernal KLCY-FM (c) PO Box 307, Vernal UT 84078 **Phn:** 435-789-1059 **Fax:** 435-789-6977 klcy.com janet@klcy.com

Vernal KVEL-AM (snt) PO Box 307, Vernal UT 84078 **Phn:** 435-789-0920 **Fax:** 435-789-6977

Washington KZHK-FM (or) 204 Playa Della Rosita, Washington UT 84780 **Phn:** 435-628-3643 **Fax:** 435-673-1210 www.959thehawk.com randy@canyonmedia.net

West Valley City KSOP-AM (c) 1285 West 2320 South, West Valley City UT 84119 **Phn:** 801-972-1043 **Fax:** 801-974-0868 www.cc1370.com gentlemanjim@ksopcountry.com

VERMONT

Barre WORK-FM (a) 41 Jacques St, Barre VT 05641 **Phn:** 802-476-4168 **Fax:** 802-479-5893 www.1071frankfm.com

Barre WSNO-AM (nt) 41 Jacques St, Barre VT 05641 **Phn:** 802-476-4168 **Fax:** 802-479-5893 www.wsno1450.com jseverance@greateasternradio.com

Barre WWFY-FM (c) 41 Jacques St, Barre VT 05641 **Phn:** 802-476-4168 **Fax:** 802-479-5893 www.froggy1009.com wcaswell@greateasternradio.com

Bennington WBTN-AM (nt) 407 Harwood Hill Rd, Bennington VT 05201 **Phn:** 802-442-6321 **Fax:** 802-442-3112 www.wbtnam.org info@wbtnam.org

Brattleboro WKVT-AM (nt) 458 Williams St, Brattleboro VT 05301 **Phn:** 802-254-2343 **Fax:** 802-254-6683 www.wkvt.com pc@wkvt.com

Brattleboro WKVT-FM (r) 458 Williams St, Brattleboro VT 05301 **Phn:** 802-254-2343 **Fax:** 802-254-6683 www.wkvt.com psa@wkvt.com

Brattleboro WTSA-FM (ahn) PO Box 819, Brattleboro VT 05302 **Phn:** 802-254-4577 **Fax:** 802-257-4644 www.wtsa.net news@wtsa.net

Brattleboro WTSA-AM (st) PO Box 819, Brattleboro VT 05302 **Phn:** 802-254-4577 **Fax:** 802-257-4644 www.wtsa.net news@wtsa.net

Bridport WCLX-FM (r) 802-759-5002, Bridport VT 05734 **Phn:** 802-759-5002 **Fax:** 509-752-4105 www.farmfreshradio.com kathy@wclxfm.com

Burlington WBTZ-FM (ar) PO Box 4489, Burlington VT 05406 **Phn:** 802-658-1230 **Fax:** 802-862-0786 www.999thebuzz.com mailbag@999thebuzz.com

Burlington WIZN-FM (r) PO Box 4489, Burlington VT 05406 **Phn:** 802-658-1230 **Fax:** 802-862-0786 www.wizn.com wizn@wizn.com

Burlington WJOY-AM (zo) PO Box 4489, Burlington VT 05406 **Phn:** 802-658-1230 **Fax:** 802-862-0786 www.wjoy.com ddubonnet@hallradio.com

Burlington WKOL-FM (o) PO Box 4489, Burlington VT 05406 **Phn:** 802-658-1230 **Fax:** 802-862-0786 www.wkol.com kool105@hallradio.com

Burlington WOKO-FM (c) PO Box 4489, Burlington VT 05406 **Phn:** 802-658-1230 **Fax:** 802-862-0786 www.woko.com woko@hallradio.com

Burlington WRUV-FM (vj) Billings Student Ctr, Burlington VT 05405 **Phn:** 802-656-0796 www.uvm.edu~wruv wruv@wruv.org

Castleton WIUV-FM (vr) 86 Seminary St, Castleton VT 05735 **Phn:** 802-468-1264 www.castleton.educampuswiuv wiuv@castleton.edu

Colchester WEZF-FM (a) 265 Hegeman Ave, Colchester VT 05446 **Phn:** 802-655-0093 **Fax:** 802-655-1993 www.star929.com jenniferfoxx@star929.com

Colchester WVMT-AM (snt) PO Box 620, Colchester VT 05446 **Phn:** 802-655-1620 **Fax:** 802-655-1329 www.newstalk620wvmt.com talk@newstalk620wvmt.com

Colchester WVPS-FM (plnj) 365 Troy Ave, Colchester VT 05446 **Phn:** 802-655-9451 www.vpr.net news@vpr.net

Colchester WWPV-FM (vr) 1 Winooski Park, Colchester VT 05439 **Phn:** 802-654-2334 www.wwpv.org wwpv@smcvt.edu

Colchester WXXX-FM (h) PO Box 620, Colchester VT 05446 **Phn:** 802-655-9550 **Fax:** 802-655-1329 www.95triplex.com 95triplex@95triplex.com

Derby WIKE-AM (c) 3422 US Route 5, Derby VT 05829 **Phn:** 802-766-9236 **Fax:** 802-766-8067 www.1490wike.com wcaswell@greateasternradio.com

Derby WMOO-FM (a) 3422 US Route 5, Derby VT 05829 **Phn:** 802-766-9236 **Fax:** 802-766-8067 www.moo92.com

East Poultney WVNR-AM (aco) PO Box 568, East Poultney VT 05741 **Phn:** 802-287-9031 wvnrwnyv@yahoo.com

Essex WGLY-FM (q) PO Box 8310, Essex VT 05451 **Phn:** 802-878-8885 **Fax:** 802-879-6835 thelightradio.net

Johnson WJSC-FM (v) 337 College HI, Johnson VT 05656 **Phn:** 802-635-1355

Lyndonville WGMT-FM (a) PO Box 97, Lyndonville VT 05851 **Phn:** 802-626-9800 **Fax:** 802-626-8500 www.magic977.com magic977@gmail.com

Manchester WEQX-FM (r) PO Box 1027, Manchester VT 05254 **Phn:** 802-362-4800 **Fax:** 802-362-5555 www.weqx.com eqx@weqx.com

Middlebury WRMC-FM (v) PO Box 29, Middlebury VT 05753 **Phn:** 802-443-2471 **Fax:** 802-443-5108 wrmc.middlebury.edu wrmc911@gmail.com

Middlebury WVTK-FM (h) 63 Maple St Ste 9, Middlebury VT 05753 **Phn:** 802-388-7563 www.921wvtk.com bruce@921wvtk.com

Montpelier WDOT-FM (ar) 169 River St, Montpelier VT 05602 **Phn:** 802-223-2396 **Fax:** 802-223-1520 www.pointfm.com feedback@pointfm.com

Montpelier WNCS-FM (a) 169 River St, Montpelier VT 05602 **Phn:** 802-223-2396 **Fax:** 802-223-1520 www.pointfm.com feedback@pointfm.com

Montpelier WRJT-FM (ar) 169 River St, Montpelier VT 05602 **Phn:** 802-223-2396 **Fax:** 802-223-1520 www.pointfm.com feedback@pointfm.com

Montpelier WSKI-AM (o) 169 River St, Montpelier VT 05602 **Phn:** 802-223-5275 **Fax:** 802-223-1520

Morrisville WLVB-FM (c) PO Box 94, Morrisville VT 05661 **Phn:** 802-888-4294 **Fax:** 802-888-8523 wlvb@radiovermont.com

Northfield WNUB-FM (v) 158 Harmon Dr, Northfield VT 05663 **Phn:** 802-485-2483 **Fax:** 802-485-2565 www.norwich.eduaboutwnub.html

Plainfield WGDR-FM (v) PO Box 336, Plainfield VT 05667 **Phn:** 802-454-7762 www.wgdr.org wgdr@goddard.edu

Randolph WCVR-FM (r) 62 Radio Dr, Randolph VT 05060 **Phn:** 802-728-4411 **Fax:** 802-728-4013 www.champrocks.com

Randolph Center WVTC-FM (v) Vt Tech Coll, Randolph Center VT 05061 **Phn:** 802-728-1550 www.wvtc.net mpotter-jacobus@vtc.edu

Rutland WEBK-FM (c) 67 Merchants Row, Rutland VT 05701 **Phn:** 802-775-7500 **Fax:** 802-775-7555 www.catcountryvermont.com

Rutland WFTF-FM (q) 2 Meadow Ln, Rutland VT 05701 **Phn:** 802-773.2863

Rutland WJAN-FM (c) PO Box 30, Rutland VT 05702 **Phn:** 802-775-7500 **Fax:** 802-775-7555 www.catcountryvermont.com

Rutland WJEN-FM (c) 67 Merchants Row, Rutland VT 05701 **Phn:** 802-775-7500 **Fax:** 802-775-7555 www.catcountryvermont.com

Rutland WJJR-FM (a) 67 Merchants Row, Rutland VT 05701 **Phn:** 802-775-7500 **Fax:** 802-775-7555 www.wjjr.net

Rutland WSYB-AM (snt) 67 Merchants Row, Rutland VT 05701 **Phn:** 802-775-7500 **Fax:** 802-775-7555 www.wsyb1380am.com cmeeks@catamountradio.com

Rutland WTHK-FM (r) 1 Scale Ave Ste 84, Rutland VT 05701 **Phn:** 802-464-1111 **Fax:** 802-747-0553 www.101thefox.com

Rutland WZRT-FM (h) 67 Merchants Row, Rutland VT 05701 **Phn:** 802-775-7500 **Fax:** 802-775-7555 z971.com dgrembowicz@catamountradio.com

Saint Johnsbury WKXH-FM (c) PO Box 249, Saint Johnsbury VT 05819 **Phn:** 802-748-2345 **Fax:** 802-748-2361 www.kix1055.com

Saint Johnsbury WSTJ-AM (am) PO Box 249, Saint Johnsbury VT 05819 **Phn:** 802-748-1340 **Fax:** 802-748-2361

South Burlington WCAT-AM (snt) 372 Dorset St, South Burlington VT 05403 **Phn:** 802-863-1010 **Fax:** 802-861-7256 foxsportsvermont.com

South Burlington WFAD-AM (s) 372 Dorset St, South Burlington VT 05403 **Phn:** 802-863-1010 **Fax:** 802-861-7256 foxsportsvermont.com joannad@champlainradio.com

South Burlington WRSA-AM (s) 372 Dorset St, South Burlington VT 05403 **Phn:** 802-863-1010 **Fax:** 802-861-7256 foxsportsvermont.com

VERMONT RADIO STATIONS

South Burlington WUSX-FM (c) 372 Dorset St, South Burlington VT 05403 **Phn:** 802-863-1010 **Fax:** 802-861-7256 www.cruisin937.com bobrowevt@gmail.com

South Burlington WWMP-FM (ah) 372 Dorset St, South Burlington VT 05403 **Phn:** 802-863-1010 **Fax:** 802-861-7256 mp103.com ronniek@champlainradio.com

Springfield WCFR-AM (o) 19 Main St, Springfield VT 05156 **Phn:** 802-885-1480 www.wcfram1480.com

Waterbury WCVT-FM (l) 9 Stowe St, Waterbury VT 05676 **Phn:** 802-244-1764 **Fax:** 802-244-1771 wcvt@classicvermont.com

Waterbury WDEV-AM (nsa) PO Box 550, Waterbury VT 05676 **Phn:** 802-244-7321 **Fax:** 802-244-1771 www.wdevradio.com wdev@radiovermont.com

Waterbury WDEV-FM (sa) PO Box 550, Waterbury VT 05676 **Phn:** 802-244-7321 **Fax:** 802-244-1771 www.wdevradio.com wdev@radiovermont.com

Wells River WTWN-AM (q) PO Box 757, Wells River VT 05081 **Phn:** 802-757-3311 **Fax:** 802-757-2774 www.wtwnradio.com studio@wykr.com

Wells River WYKR-FM (c) 1047 Route 302, Wells River VT 05081 **Phn:** 802-757-2773 **Fax:** 802-757-2774 www.wykr.com studio@wykr.com

VIRGINIA

Altavista WKDE-FM (c) 290 Frazier Rd, Altavista VA 24517 **Phn:** 434-369-5588 **Fax:** 434-369-1632 www.kdcountry.com info@kdcountry.com

Altavista WKDE-AM (n) PO Box 390, Altavista VA 24517 **Phn:** 434-369-5588 **Fax:** 434-369-1632

Amherst WAMV-AM (co) PO Box 1420, Amherst VA 24521 **Phn:** 434-946-9000 **Fax:** 434-946-2201

Arlington WAVA-AM (q) 1901 N Moore St Ste 200, Arlington VA 22209 **Phn:** 703-807-2266 **Fax:** 703-807-2248 www.wava.com comment@wava.com

Arlington WAVA-FM (q) 1901 N Moore St Ste 200, Arlington VA 22209 **Phn:** 703-807-2266 **Fax:** 703-807-2248 www.wava.com comment@wava.com

Arlington WETA-FM (pln) 3939 Campbell Ave Ste 100, Arlington VA 22206 **Phn:** 703-998-2600 **Fax:** 703-998-3401 www.weta.org

Ashland WHAN-AM (nt) 11337 Ashcake Rd, Ashland VA 23005 **Phn:** 804-798-1010 **Fax:** 804-798-7933

Bassett WZBB-FM (c) 10899 Virginia Ave, Bassett VA 24055 **Phn:** 540-489-9999 www.supercountryonline.com traffic@wzbbfm.com

Blacksburg WKEX-AM (st) PO Box 889, Blacksburg VA 24063 **Phn:** 540-951-9791 **Fax:** 540-961-2021 espnblacksburg.com wkexam@yahoo.com

Blacksburg WUVT-FM (v) 350 Squires Student Ctr, Blacksburg VA 24061 **Phn:** 540-231-9880 www.wuvt.vt.edu

Blackstone WBBC-FM (c) PO Box 300, Blackstone VA 23824 **Phn:** 434-292-4146 **Fax:** 434-292-7669 www.bobcatcountryradio.com

Blackstone WKLV-AM (s) PO Box 300, Blackstone VA 23824 **Phn:** 434-292-4146 **Fax:** 434-525-4876 wbbc@bobcatcountryradio.com

Bristol WAEZ-FM (h) PO Box 1389, Bristol VA 24203 **Phn:** 276-669-8112 **Fax:** 276-669-0541 www.electric949.com

Bristol WFHG-FM (nt) PO Box 1389, Bristol VA 24203 **Phn:** 276-669-8112 **Fax:** 276-669-0541 www.supertalkwfhg.com comments@supertalkwfhg.com

Bristol WFHG-AM (snt) PO Box 1389, Bristol VA 24203 **Phn:** 276-669-8112 **Fax:** 276-669-0541

Bristol WTZR-FM (r) PO Box 1389, Bristol VA 24203 **Phn:** 276-669-8112 **Fax:** 276-669-0541 www.zrock993.com jay@zrock993.com

Bristol WXBQ-FM (c) PO Box 1389, Bristol VA 24203 **Phn:** 276-669-8112 **Fax:** 276-669-0541 wxbq.com billhagy@wxbq.com

Bristol WZAP-AM (q) PO Box 369, Bristol VA 24203 **Phn:** 276-669-6950 **Fax:** 276-669-0794 www.wzapradio.com wzapradio@aol.com

Broadway WBTX-AM (g) PO Box 337, Broadway VA 22815 **Phn:** 540-896-8933 **Fax:** 540-896-1448 www.positive-radio.com wbtx@positive-radio.com

Broadway WLTK-FM (aq) PO Box 337, Broadway VA 22815 **Phn:** 540-896-8933 **Fax:** 540-896-1448 www.klove.com

Brookneal WODI-AM (oq) 1230 Radio Rd, Brookneal VA 24528 **Phn:** 434-376-1230 **Fax:** 434-376-9634

Cedar Bluff WYRV-AM (g) PO Box 70, Cedar Bluff VA 24609 **Phn:** 276-964-9619 **Fax:** 276-964-9610

Charlottesville WBNN-FM (c) PO Box 7111, Charlottesville VA 22906 **Phn:** 434-983-6621 **Fax:** 434-983-6772 www.bigcountry1053.com mail@bigcountry1053.com

Charlottesville WCHV-AM (nt) 1150 Pepsi Pl Ste 300, Charlottesville VA 22901 **Phn:** 434-978-4408 **Fax:** 434-978-1109 www.wchv.com mneeley@cvillestations.com

Charlottesville WCNR-FM (a) 1140 Rose Hill Dr, Charlottesville VA 22903 **Phn:** 434-220-2300 **Fax:** 434-220-2304 www.1061thecorner.com brad@1061thecorner.com

Charlottesville WCYK-FM (c) 1150 Pepsi Pl Ste 300, Charlottesville VA 22901 **Phn:** 434-978-4408 **Fax:** 434-978-0723 www.hitkicker997.com sgaines@cvillestations.com

Charlottesville WHTE-FM (h) 1150 Pepsi Pl Ste 300, Charlottesville VA 22901 **Phn:** 434-978-4408 **Fax:** 434-978-1109 www.1019hot.com pj@1019hot.com

Charlottesville WINA-AM (nt) 1140 Rose Hill Dr, Charlottesville VA 22903 **Phn:** 434-220-2300 **Fax:** 434-220-2304 www.wina.com news@wina.com

Charlottesville WKAV-AM (st) 1150 Pepsi Pl Ste 300, Charlottesville VA 22901 **Phn:** 434-978-4408 **Fax:** 434-978-0723 www.wkav.com jthomas@cvillestations.com

Charlottesville WKTR-AM (s) PO Box 7111, Charlottesville VA 22906 **Phn:** 434-985-8585 **Fax:** 434-985-7369

Charlottesville WNRN-FM (vru) 2250 Old Ivy Rd Ste 2, Charlottesville VA 22903 **Phn:** 434-971-4096 **Fax:** 434-971-6562 www.wnrn.org info@wnrn.org

Charlottesville WQMZ-FM (ha) 1140 Rose Hill Dr, Charlottesville VA 22903 **Phn:** 434-220-2300 **Fax:** 434-220-2304 literockz951.com mail@literockz951.com

Charlottesville WTJU-FM (plr) PO Box 400811, Charlottesville VA 22904 **Phn:** 434-924-0885 **Fax:** 434-924-8996 wtju.net wtju@virginia.edu

Charlottesville WUVA-FM (uw) 1928 Arlington Blvd Ste 312, Charlottesville VA 22903 **Phn:** 434-817-6880 **Fax:** 434-817-6884 www.92.7kissfm.com programming@92.7kissfm.com

Charlottesville WVAX-AM (s) 1140 Rose Hill Dr, Charlottesville VA 22903 **Phn:** 434-220-2300 **Fax:** 434-220-2304 www.wvax.com jim@charlottesvilleradiogroup.com

Charlottesville WWTJ-FM (a) 1150 Pepsi Pl Ste 300, Charlottesville VA 22901 **Phn:** 434-978-4408 **Fax:** 434-978-1109

VIRGINIA RADIO STATIONS

Charlottesville WWWV-FM (r) 1140 Rose Hill Dr, Charlottesville VA 22903 **Phn:** 434-220-2300 **Fax:** 434-220-2304 www.3wv.com pstone@3wv.com

Charlottesville WZGN-FM (r) 1150 Pepsi Pl Ste 300, Charlottesville VA 22901 **Phn:** 434-978-4408 **Fax:** 434-978-1109

Chase City WJYK-AM (qt) 7925 Highway Forty Seven, Chase City VA 23924 **Phn:** 434-372-0803

Chatham WKBY-AM (wg) 12932 US Highway 29, Chatham VA 24531 **Phn:** 434-432-8108 **Fax:** 434-432-1523 sweetlois@hotmail.com

Chesapeake WAFX-FM (r) 870 Greenbrier Cir Ste 399, Chesapeake VA 23320 **Phn:** 757-366-9900 **Fax:** 757-366-0022 1069thefox.com dtaylor@tciradio.net

Chesapeake WFOS-FM (xob) 1617 Cedar Rd, Chesapeake VA 23322 **Phn:** 757-547-1036 **Fax:** 757-547-0160 www.cpschools.comdepartmentsradio richard.babb@cpschools.com

Chesapeake WJOI-AM (a) 870 Greenbrier Cir Ste 399, Chesapeake VA 23320 **Phn:** 757-366-9906 **Fax:** 757-366-0022 abrown@tciradio.net

Chesapeake WNOR-FM (r) 870 Greenbrier Cir Ste 399, Chesapeake VA 23320 **Phn:** 757-366-9900 **Fax:** 757-366-0022 www.fm99.com

Chester WGGM-AM (q) 4301 W Hundred Rd, Chester VA 23831 **Phn:** 804-717-2000 **Fax:** 804-717-2009

Chilhowie WXMY-AM (c) PO Box 5555, Chilhowie VA 24319 **Phn:** 276-685-1810 1600wxmy@gmail.com

Churchville WNLR-AM (qa) PO Box 400, Churchville VA 24421 **Phn:** 540-885-8600 **Fax:** 540-886-8624 www.wnlr1150.com wnlr@nlministries.org

Clintwood WDIC-FM (o) 2298 Rose Rdg, Clintwood VA 24228 **Phn:** 276-835-8626 **Fax:** 276-835-8627 www.wdicradio.com wdic@wdicradio.com

Clintwood WDIC-AM (c) 2298 Rose Rdg, Clintwood VA 24228 **Phn:** 276-835-8626 **Fax:** 276-835-8627 www.wdicradio.com wdic@wdicradio.com

Covington WIQO-FM (c) PO Box 710, Covington VA 24426 **Phn:** 540-962-1133 www.lynchburgradiogroup.com edgeradio850@yahoo.com

Covington WKEY-AM (o) PO Box 710, Covington VA 24426 **Phn:** 540-962-1133 www.lynchburgradiogroup.com edgeradio850@yahoo.com

Covington WXCF-FM (a) PO Box 710, Covington VA 24426 **Phn:** 540-962-1133 **Fax:** 540-962-4401

Covington WXCF-AM (c) PO Box 710, Covington VA 24426 **Phn:** 540-962-1133 **Fax:** 540-962-4401

Crewe WSVS-AM (c) PO Box 47, Crewe VA 23930 **Phn:** 434-645-7734 **Fax:** 434-645-1701 www.wsvsam.com wsvs@wsvsam.com

Culpeper WPRZ-FM (q) 219 E Davis St # 220, Culpeper VA 22701 **Phn:** 540-727-9779 wprz.org info@wprz.org

Danville WAKG-FM (c) PO Box 1629, Danville VA 24543 **Phn:** 434-797-4290 **Fax:** 434-797-3918 www.wakg.com wakg@wakg.com

Danville WBTM-AM (at) PO Box 1629, Danville VA 24543 **Phn:** 434-793-4411 **Fax:** 434-797-3918 www.wbtmdanville.com hutch@wbtm1330.com

Danville WDVA-AM (q) 1 Radio Ln, Danville VA 24541 **Phn:** 434-797-1250 **Fax:** 434-797-1255 wdvaradio@gmail.com

Edinburg WOTC-FM (vq) 408 Stoney Creek Rd, Edinburg VA 22824 **Phn:** 540-984-8998

Emporia WEVA-AM (a) 705 Washington St, Emporia VA 23847 **Phn:** 434-634-2133 **Fax:** 434-634-5050 www.wevaradio.com info@wevaradio.com

Fairfax WDCT-AM (q) 3251 Old Lee Hwy Ste 506, Fairfax VA 22030 **Phn:** 703-273-4000

Fairfax WJFK-FM (t) 4200 Parliment Pl # 300, Fairfax VA 22030 **Phn:** 703-691-1900 **Fax:** 703-385-0189 washington.cbslocal.com cnkinard@cbs.com

Fairlawn WBRW-FM (r) 7080 Lee Hwy, Fairlawn VA 24141 **Phn:** 540-731-6000 **Fax:** 540-633-2998 www.1053thebear.com

Fairlawn WFNR-AM (nts) 7080 Lee Hwy, Fairlawn VA 24141 **Phn:** 540-731-6000 **Fax:** 540-731-6074 www.710wfnr.com

Fairlawn WFNR-FM (h) 7080 Lee Hwy, Fairlawn VA 24141 **Phn:** 540-633-5330 **Fax:** 540-731-6074 www.allthehitshot100.com

Fairlawn WPSK-FM (c) 7080 Lee Hwy, Fairlawn VA 24141 **Phn:** 540-731-6000 **Fax:** 540-731-6074

Fairlawn WRAD-AM (am) 7080 Lee Hwy, Fairlawn VA 24141 **Phn:** 540-731-6000 **Fax:** 540-633-2998 scott.stevens@cumulus.com

Fairlawn WWBU-FM (c) 7080 Lee Hwy, Fairlawn VA 24141 **Phn:** 540-731-6000 **Fax:** 540-731-6075

Falls Church WFAX-AM (q) 161 Hillwood Ave Ste B, Falls Church VA 22046 **Phn:** 703-532-1220 **Fax:** 703-533-7572 www.wfax.com wfax@wfax.com

Falls Church WUST-AM (we) 2131 Crimmins Ln, Falls Church VA 22043 **Phn:** 703-532-0400 **Fax:** 703-532-5033 www.wust1120.com contactwust@wust1120.com

Farmville WFLO-FM (a) PO Box 367, Farmville VA 23901 **Phn:** 434-392-4195 **Fax:** 434-392-1823 www.wflo.net news@wflo.net

Farmville WFLO-AM (cnt) PO Box 367, Farmville VA 23901 **Phn:** 434-392-4195 **Fax:** 434-392-1823 www.wflo.net news@wflo.net

Farmville WPAK-AM (q) PO Box 494, Farmville VA 23901 **Phn:** 434-392-8114

Farmville WVHL-FM (c) 116 North St, Farmville VA 23901 **Phn:** 434-392-9393 **Fax:** 434-392-6091 www.wvhl.net sm@wvhl.net

Ferrum WFFC-FM (v) PO Box 1000, Ferrum VA 24088 **Phn:** 540-365-4482 www2.ferrum.eduwffc clogan@ferrum.edu

Floyd WGFC-AM (cg) PO Box 495, Floyd VA 24091 **Phn:** 540-745-9811 **Fax:** 540-745-9812 www.wgfcradio.com wgfc@wgfcradio.com

Forest WBLT-AM (s) PO Box 348, Forest VA 24551 **Phn:** 434-534-6100 **Fax:** 434-534-6101 www.espninva.com randy@espninva.com

Forest WMNA-FM (s) PO Box 348, Forest VA 24551 **Phn:** 434-534-6100 **Fax:** 434-534-6101 www.espninva.com ashley@espninva.com

Franklin WLQM-AM (gu) PO Box 735, Franklin VA 23851 **Phn:** 757-562-3135 **Fax:** 757-562-2345 wlqm@wlqmradio.com

Franklin WLQM-FM (c) PO Box 735, Franklin VA 23851 **Phn:** 757-562-3135 **Fax:** 757-562-2345 wlqm@wlqmradio.com

Fredericksburg WBQB-FM (ah) 1914 Mimosa St, Fredericksburg VA 22405 **Phn:** 540-373-7721 **Fax:** 540-899-3879 www.b1015.com ted@wfvaradio.com

Fredericksburg WFLS-FM (c) 616 Amelia St, Fredericksburg VA 22401 **Phn:** 540-374-5000 **Fax:** 540-374-5525 www.wfls.com pjohnson@starradiogroup.com

Fredericksburg WFVA-AM (m) 1914 Mimosa St, Fredericksburg VA 22405 **Phn:** 540-373-7721 **Fax:** 540-899-3879 www.newstalk1230.net ted@newstalk1230.net

Fredericksburg WGRQ-FM (o) 4414 Lafayette Blvd Ste 100, Fredericksburg VA 22408 **Phn:** 540-891-9696 **Fax:** 540-891-1656 www.959wgrq.com tcooper@959wgrq.com

Fredericksburg WGRX-FM (c) 4414 Lafayette Blvd Ste 100, Fredericksburg VA 22408 **Phn:** 540-891-9696 **Fax:** 540-891-1656 www.thunder1045.com tcooper@959wgrq.com

Fredericksburg WWUZ-FM (r) 616 Amelia St, Fredericksburg VA 22401 **Phn:** 540-373-1500 **Fax:** 540-374-5525 www.969therock.com pjohnson@starradiogroup.com

Fredericksburg WWVB-FM (h) 616 Amelia St, Fredericksburg VA 22401 **Phn:** 540-374-5000 **Fax:** 540-374-5525 www.WFLS.com pjohnson@starradiogroup.com

Front Royal WFTR-AM (c) PO Box 192, Front Royal VA 22630 **Phn:** 540-635-4121 **Fax:** 540-635-9387

Front Royal WZRV-FM (o) 1106 Elm St, Front Royal VA 22630 **Phn:** 540-635-4121 **Fax:** 540-635-9387 www.theriver953online.com

Galax WBRF-FM (cn) PO Box 838, Galax VA 24333 **Phn:** 276-236-9273 **Fax:** 276-236-7198 www.blueridgecountry98.com debby@blueridgecountry98.com

Galax WWWJ-AM (ag) PO Box 270, Galax VA 24333 **Phn:** 276-236-2921 **Fax:** 276-236-2922

Gate City WGAT-AM (cg) 117 West Jackson St # 203, Gate City VA 24251 **Phn:** 276-386-7025 **Fax:** 276-386-7026

Gloucester WXGM-AM (ob) PO Box 634, Gloucester VA 23061 **Phn:** 804-693-2105 **Fax:** 804-693-2182 www.xtra99.com news@xtra99.com

Gloucester WXGM-FM (a) PO Box 634, Gloucester VA 23061 **Phn:** 804-693-2105 **Fax:** 804-693-2182 www.xtra99.com office@xtra99.com

Gretna WMNA-AM (ct) PO Box 730, Gretna VA 24557 **Phn:** 434-656-1234 **Fax:** 434-656-1236 wmna730@hotmail.com

Grundy WMJD-FM (a) 1011 Radio Dr, Grundy VA 24614 **Phn:** 276-935-7227 **Fax:** 276-935-2587 www.wmjd.org

Grundy WNRG-AM (c) 1011 Radio Dr, Grundy VA 24614 **Phn:** 276-935-7227 **Fax:** 276-935-2587

Hampden Sydney WWHS-FM (vh) PO Box 606, Hampden Sydney VA 23943 **Phn:** 434-223-6009

Hampton WHOV-FM (v) Hampton Univ, Hampton VA 23668 **Phn:** 757-727-5711

Hampton WTJZ-AM (wq) 553 Michigan Dr, Hampton VA 23669 **Phn:** 757-723-1270

Harrisonburg WACL-FM (r) 207 University Blvd, Harrisonburg VA 22801 **Phn:** 540-434-1777 **Fax:** 540-432-9968 www.98rockme.com steveknupp@clearchannel.com

Harrisonburg WAZR-FM (h) 207 University Blvd, Harrisonburg VA 22801 **Phn:** 540-434-1777 **Fax:** 540-432-9968 www.937now.com chuckpeterson@clearchannel.com

Harrisonburg WBOP-FM (c) PO Box 2460, Harrisonburg VA 22801 **Phn:** 540-432-1063 **Fax:** 540-433-9267 www.955wbop.com scott@969wsig.com

Harrisonburg WEMC-FM (vql) 983 Reservoir St, Harrisonburg VA 22801 **Phn:** 540-568-6221 **Fax:** 540-568-3814 www.wmra.org wmra@jmu.edu

Harrisonburg WHBG-AM (snt) PO Box 752, Harrisonburg VA 22803 **Phn:** 540-434-0331

Harrisonburg WJDV-FM (a) PO Box 752, Harrisonburg VA 22803 **Phn:** 540-434-0331 www.fresh961.com ian@valleyradio.com

Harrisonburg WKCI-AM (nt) 207 University Blvd, Harrisonburg VA 22801 **Phn:** 540-343-1777 **Fax:** 540-432-9968 www.wkcyam.com sknupp@clearchannel.com

Harrisonburg WKCY-AM (nt) 207 University Blvd, Harrisonburg VA 22801 **Phn:** 540-434-1777 **Fax:** 540-432-9968 www.wkcyam.com steveknupp@clearchannel.com

Harrisonburg WKCY-FM (c) 207 University Blvd, Harrisonburg VA 22801 **Phn:** 540-434-1777 **Fax:** 540-432-9968 www.kcycountry.com chuckpeterson@clearchannel.com

Harrisonburg WKDW-AM (c) 207 University Blvd, Harrisonburg VA 22801 **Phn:** 540-886-2376 **Fax:** 540-885-8662 www.wkdwam.com sknupp@clearchannel.com

Harrisonburg WMRA-FM (pln) 983 Reservoir St, Harrisonburg VA 22801 **Phn:** 540-568-6221 www.wmra.org

Harrisonburg WMXH-FM (a) 130 University Blvd Ste B, Harrisonburg VA 22801 **Phn:** 540-801-1057 **Fax:** 540-564-2873 easyradioinc.com stardust1057@easyradioinc.com

Harrisonburg WQPO-FM (h) PO Box 752, Harrisonburg VA 22803 **Phn:** 540-434-0331 **Fax:** 540-434-7087 www.q101online.com news@valleyradio.com

Harrisonburg WSIG-FM (c) PO Box 2460, Harrisonburg VA 22801 **Phn:** 540-432-1063 **Fax:** 540-433-9267 www.realcountrywsig.com

Harrisonburg WSVA-AM (nt) PO Box 752, Harrisonburg VA 22803 **Phn:** 540-434-0331 **Fax:** 540-432-0129 www.wsvaonline.com wsva@valleyradio.com

Harrisonburg WSVO-FM (a) 207 University Blvd, Harrisonburg VA 22801 **Phn:** 540-434-1777 **Fax:** 540-432-9968 www.mix931online.com chuckpeterson@clearchannel.com

Harrisonburg WXJM-FM (vr) 6801 Jmu, Harrisonburg VA 22807 **Phn:** 540-568-6878 wxjm.org wxjm@jmu.edu

Hillsville WHHV-AM (gq) PO Box 648, Hillsville VA 24343 **Phn:** 276-728-9114 **Fax:** 276-728-9968 www.whhvradio.com whhv@whhvradio.com

Kilmarnock WKWI-FM (a) PO Box 819, Kilmarnock VA 22482 **Phn:** 804-435-1414 **Fax:** 804-435-0484 office@1017bayfm.com

Lebanon WLRV-AM (c) PO Box 939, Lebanon VA 24266 **Phn:** 276-889-1380 **Fax:** 276-889-1388 www.wlrv.com radio@wlrv.com

Lebanon WXLZ-AM (c) PO Box 1299, Lebanon VA 24266 **Phn:** 276-889-1073 **Fax:** 276-889-3677 www.wxlz.net wxlz1073@bvu.net

Lebanon WXLZ-FM (c) PO Box 1299, Lebanon VA 24266 **Phn:** 276-889-1073 **Fax:** 276-889-3677 www.wxlz.net wxlz1073@bvu.net

Lexington WLUR-FM (v) 204 W Washington St, Lexington VA 24450 **Phn:** 540-458-4017 **Fax:** 540-458-4079 wlur.wlu.edu

Lexington WREL-AM (cn) 392 E Midland Trl, Lexington VA 24450 **Phn:** 540-463-2161 **Fax:** 540-463-9524 3wzfm.webs.com 96.7@3wzfm.com

Lexington WWZW-FM (a) 392 E Midland Trl, Lexington VA 24450 **Phn:** 540-463-2161 **Fax:** 540-463-9524 3wzfm.webs.com 96.7@3wzfm.com

Luray WRAA-AM (c) 1057 US Highway 211 W, Luray VA 22835 **Phn:** 540-743-5167 **Fax:** 540-743-5168 www.1330wraa.com

Lynchburg WBRG-AM (snt) PO Box 1079, Lynchburg VA 24505 **Phn:** 434-632-7207 wbrgradio.com manager@wbrgradio.com

Lynchburg WILA-AM (wx) 1209 McKinney Ave, Lynchburg VA 24502 **Phn:** 434-792-2133 **Fax:** 434-792-2134

Lynchburg WLLL-AM (wg) PO Box 11375, Lynchburg VA 24506 **Phn:** 434-385-9555 **Fax:** 434-385-6073 www.wlllradio.com wlllam930@aol.com

Lynchburg WLNI-FM (st) 19-C Wadsworth St, Lynchburg VA 24501 **Phn:** 434-845-3698 **Fax:** 434-455-0987 wlni.com

Lynchburg WRVL-FM (vqn) 1971 University Blvd, Lynchburg VA 24502 **Phn:** 434-582-3688 **Fax:** 434-582-2994 www.wrvlfm.com victoryfm@liberty.edu

Lynchburg WTTX-FM (g) 22226 Timberlake Rd, Lynchburg VA 24502 **Phn:** 877-569-1071 **Fax:** 434-237-1025

Lynchburg WYYD-FM (c) 3305 Old Forest Rd, Lynchburg VA 24501 **Phn:** 434-385-8298 **Fax:** 434-385-7279 www.newcountry1079.com ripwooten@clearchannel.com

Lynchburg WZZI-FM (st) PO Box 11798, Lynchburg VA 24506 **Phn:** 434-845-3698 **Fax:** 434-845-2063 www.foxsportsradio.com babbott@centennialbroadcasting.com

Lynchburg WZZU-FM (r) PO Box 11798, Lynchburg VA 24506 **Phn:** 434-845-3698 **Fax:** 434-845-2063 centennialbroadcasting.com production@centennialbroadcasting.com

Marion WMEV-AM (g) 1041 Radio Hill Rd, Marion VA 24354 **Phn:** 276-783-3151 **Fax:** 276-783-3152 www.fm94.com fm94@smyth.net

Marion WMEV-FM (c) 1041 Radio Hill Rd, Marion VA 24354 **Phn:** 276-783-3151 **Fax:** 276-783-3152 www.fm94.com fm94@fm94.com

Marion WOLD-FM (a) PO Box 1047, Marion VA 24354 **Phn:** 540-783-7100 **Fax:** 276-783-2064

Marion WZVA-FM (h) 114 W Main St, Marion VA 24354 **Phn:** 276-783-4042 **Fax:** 276-783-2120

Martinsville WCBX-AM (st) PO Box 192, Martinsville VA 24114 **Phn:** 276-638-5235 **Fax:** 276-638-6089 wcbxwodywfic@yahoo.com

Martinsville WHEE-AM (ct) PO Box 3551, Martinsville VA 24115 **Phn:** 276-632-2152 **Fax:** 276-632-4500 martinsvillemedia.com bill@martinsvillemedia.com

Martinsville WMVA-AM (a) PO Box 3551, Martinsville VA 24115 **Phn:** 276-632-2152 **Fax:** 276-632-4500 martinsvillemedia.com bill@martinsvillemedia.com

Martinsville WODY-AM (s) PO Box 192, Martinsville VA 24112 **Phn:** 276-638-5205 **Fax:** 276-638-6089 www.espnsouthside.com wcbxwodywfic@yahoo.com

Monterey WVLS-FM (v) PO Box 431, Monterey VA 24465 **Phn:** 540-468-1234 **Fax:** 540-468-1233

Narrows WNRV-AM (c) PO Box 99, Narrows VA 22124 **Phn:** 540-921-0166 **Fax:** 540-343-2306 www.wnrvbluegrassradio.com info@wnrvbluegrassradio.com

Norfolk WCDG-FM (a) 1003 Norfolk Sq, Norfolk VA 23502 **Phn:** 757-466-0009 **Fax:** 757-466-7043 www.now105.com mattderrick@clearchannel.com

Norfolk WGPL-AM (g) 645 Church St Ste 400, Norfolk VA 23510 **Phn:** 757-622-4600 **Fax:** 757-624-6515 jujoyner@gmail.com

Norfolk WHRO-FM (pl) 5200 Hampton Blvd, Norfolk VA 23508 **Phn:** 757-889-9400 **Fax:** 757-489-0007 www.whro.org info@whro.org

Norfolk WJCD-FM (wx) 1003 Norfolk Sq, Norfolk VA 23502 **Phn:** 757-466-0009 **Fax:** 757-466-7043 www.kissva.com mattderrick@clearchannel.com

Norfolk WKUS-FM (uo) 1003 Norfolk Sq, Norfolk VA 23502 **Phn:** 757-466-0009 **Fax:** 757-466-7043 www.kissfmvirginia.com

Norfolk WNIS-AM (nt) 999 Waterside Dr Ste 500, Norfolk VA 23510 **Phn:** 757-640-8500 **Fax:** 757-622-6397 www.wnis.com bobmatthews@sinclairstations.com

Norfolk WNSB-FM (jv) 700 Park Ave Ste 129, Norfolk VA 23504 **Phn:** 757-823-9672 https:www.nsu.edupresidentwnsbindex wgbrockington@nsu.edu

Norfolk WOWI-FM (wu) 1003 Norfolk Sq, Norfolk VA 23502 **Phn:** 757-466-0009 **Fax:** 757-466-9523 www.103jamz.com 103jamz@clearchannel.com

Norfolk WPCE-AM (wgq) 645 Church St Ste 400, Norfolk VA 23510 **Phn:** 757-622-4600 **Fax:** 757-624-6515 walterbrickhouse@yahoo.com

Norfolk WPYA-FM (ar) 999 Waterside Dr Ste 500, Norfolk VA 23510 **Phn:** 757-640-8500 **Fax:** 757-640-8552 sinclairstations.com lisasin@sinclairstations.com

Norfolk WROX-FM (h) 999 Waterside Dr Ste 500, Norfolk VA 23510 **Phn:** 757-640-8500 **Fax:** 757-640-8552 96x.fm info@96x.fm

Norfolk WTAR-AM (snt) 999 Waterside Dr Ste 500, Norfolk VA 23510 **Phn:** 757-640-8500 **Fax:** 757-640-8552 www.funny850.com

Norfolk WUSH-FM (c) 999 Waterside Dr Ste 500, Norfolk VA 23510 **Phn:** 757-640-8500 **Fax:** 757-640-8552 us106.comus jaymichaels@sinclairstations.com

Norfolk WVXX-AM (yh) 700 Monticello Ave Ste 301, Norfolk VA 23510 **Phn:** 757-627-9899 **Fax:** 757-627-0123 www.selecta1050.com ahindlin@yahoo.com

Norfolk WYRM-AM (q) 700 Monticello Ave Ste 305, Norfolk VA 23510 **Phn:** 757-622-9256 **Fax:** 757-622-9253 j5.wyrmradio.com wyrm1110@hotmail.com

Norton WAXM-FM (c) 724 Park Ave NW, Norton VA 24273 **Phn:** 276-679-1901 **Fax:** 276-679-1198 www.waxm.com 93.5@waxm.com

Norton WLSD-AM (g) 724 Park Ave NW, Norton VA 24273 **Phn:** 276-523-1700 **Fax:** 276-679-1198 93.5@waxm.com

Onley WESR-AM (nt) PO Box 460, Onley VA 23418 **Phn:** 757-787-3200 **Fax:** 757-787-3819 shoredailynews.com will@wesr.net

Onley WESR-FM (a) PO Box 460, Onley VA 23418 **Phn:** 757-787-3200 **Fax:** 757-787-3819 wesr.net will@wesr.net

Orange WCVA-AM (m) PO Box 271, Orange VA 22960 **Phn:** 540-825-3900 **Fax:** 540-672-0282

Orange WJMA-FM (c) PO Box 271, Orange VA 22960 **Phn:** 540-672-1000 **Fax:** 540-672-0282 www.wjmafm.com

Orange WOJL-FM (a) PO Box 271, Orange VA 22960 **Phn:** 540-672-1000 **Fax:** 540-672-0282 www.1055samfm.com news@wjmafm.com

Petersburg WVST-FM (ju) PO Box 9067, Petersburg VA 23806 **Phn:** 804-524-6725 **Fax:** 804-524-5826 www.vsu.eduwvst jwilliamson@vsu.edu

Pound WDXC-FM (c) 12548 Orby Cantrell Hwy, Pound VA 24279 **Phn:** 276-796-5411 **Fax:** 276-796-5412 www.wdxcfm.com wdxc102fm@windstream.net

VIRGINIA RADIO STATIONS

Pulaski WBLB-AM (gq) PO Box 150, Pulaski VA 24301 **Phn:** 540-980-3411 **Fax:** 540-980-8320 wblb1340am@verizon.net

Radford WVRU-FM (v) PO Box 6973, Radford VA 24142 **Phn:** 540-831-6059 **Fax:** 540-831-5893 www.wvru.org aclaud@radford.edu

Richlands WGTH-AM (qg) PO Box 370, Richlands VA 24641 **Phn:** 276-964-2502 **Fax:** 276-964-4500 www.wgth.net ron@wgth.net

Richlands WGTH-FM (qg) PO Box 370, Richlands VA 24641 **Phn:** 276-964-2502 **Fax:** 276-964-4500 www.wgth.net wgth@wgth.net

Richmond WARV-FM (o) 300 Arboretum Pl Ste 590, Richmond VA 23236 **Phn:** 804-327-9902 **Fax:** 804-327-9911 mmurphy@mainlinerichmond.com

Richmond WBBT-FM (o) 300 Arboretum Pl Ste 590, Richmond VA 23236 **Phn:** 804-327-9902 **Fax:** 804-327-9911 www.bigoldies1073.com mmurphy@mainlinerichmond.com

Richmond WBTJ-FM (wx) 3245 Basie Rd, Richmond VA 23228 **Phn:** 804-474-0000 **Fax:** 804-474-0092 www.1065thebeat.com ruthjones@clearchannel.com

Richmond WCDX-FM (wu) 2809 Emerywood Pkwy Ste 300, Richmond VA 23294 **Phn:** 804-672-9299 **Fax:** 804-672-9314 ipowerrichmond.com janderson@radio-one.com

Richmond WCVE-FM (plnj) 23 Sesame St, Richmond VA 23235 **Phn:** 804-320-1301 **Fax:** 804-320-8729 ideastations.org wfarrar@ideastations.org

Richmond WDYL-FM (r) 812 Moorefield Park Dr Ste 300, Richmond VA 23236 **Phn:** 804-330-5700 **Fax:** 804-330-4079 www.hot1009.com melissa.chase@coxinc.com

Richmond WDZY-AM (m) 413 Stuart Cir Unit 110, Richmond VA 23220 **Phn:** 804-353-7200 **Fax:** 804-353-2633 music.disney.com angela.garza@disney.com

Richmond WFTH-AM (qw) 227 E Belt Blvd Ste C, Richmond VA 23224 **Phn:** 804-233-0765 **Fax:** 804-233-3725

Richmond WKHK-FM (c) 812 Moorefield Park Dr Ste 300, Richmond VA 23236 **Phn:** 804-330-5700 **Fax:** 804-330-4079 www.k95country.com bob.willoughby@coxradio.com

Richmond WKJM-FM (u) 2809 Emerywood Pkwy Ste 300, Richmond VA 23294 **Phn:** 804-672-9299 **Fax:** 804-672-9314 kissrichmond.com apayne@radio-one.com

Richmond WKJS-FM (a) 2809 Emerywood Pkwy Ste 300, Richmond VA 23294 **Phn:** 804-672-9299 **Fax:** 804-672-9314 kissrichmond.com janderson@radio-one.com

Richmond WKLR-FM (r) 812 Moorefield Park Dr Ste 300, Richmond VA 23236 **Phn:** 804-330-5700 **Fax:** 804-330-4079 www.rock965klr.com buddy.vanarsdale@summitmediacorp.com

Richmond WLEE-AM (t) 308 W Broad St, Richmond VA 23220 **Phn:** 804-643-0990 **Fax:** 804-474-5070 www.wlee990.am bflynn@davidsonmediagroup.com

Richmond WLFV-FM (c) 300 Arboretum Pl Ste 590, Richmond VA 23236 **Phn:** 804-327-9902 **Fax:** 804-327-9911 www.931thewolf.com mmurphy@mainlinerichmond.com

Richmond WMXB-FM (a) 812 Moorefield Park Dr Ste 300, Richmond VA 23236 **Phn:** 804-330-5700 **Fax:** 804-330-4079 www.1037river.com melissa.chase@coxinc.com

Richmond WPZZ-FM (wu) 2809 Emerywood Pkwy Ste 300, Richmond VA 23294 **Phn:** 804-672-9299 **Fax:** 804-672-9316 praiserichmond.com rebaker@radio-one.com

Richmond WREJ-AM (q) 308 W Broad St, Richmond VA 23220 **Phn:** 804-643-0990 **Fax:** 804-474-5070 www.rejoice1540.com wrej@davidsonmediagroup.com

Richmond WRNL-AM (s) 3245 Basie Rd, Richmond VA 23228 **Phn:** 804-474-0000 **Fax:** 804-474-0092 www.sportsradio910.com michaelclifford@clearchannel.com

Richmond WRVA-AM (nt) 3245 Basie Rd, Richmond VA 23228 **Phn:** 804-474-0000 www.1140wrva.com jimmybarrett@1140wrva.com

Richmond WRVQ-FM (h) 3245 Basie Rd, Richmond VA 23228 **Phn:** 804-474-0000 **Fax:** 804-474-0090 www.q94radio.com amykusmin@clearchannel.com

Richmond WRXL-FM (r) 3245 Basie Rd, Richmond VA 23228 **Phn:** 804-474-0000 **Fax:** 804-474-0102 www.xl102richmond.com dustinmatthews@clearchannel.com

Richmond WTOX-AM (t) 306 W Broad St, Richmond VA 23220 **Phn:** 804-643-0990 **Fax:** 804-474-5070

Richmond WTPS-AM (wnt) 2809 Emerywood Pkwy Ste 300, Richmond VA 23294 **Phn:** 804-672-9299 urbanpetersburg.com cllawrence@radio-one.com

Richmond WTVR-FM (a) 3245 Basie Rd, Richmond VA 23228 **Phn:** 804-474-0000 **Fax:** 804-474-0092 www.lite98.com deannamalone@clearchannel.com

Richmond WVNZ-AM (y) 308 W Broad St, Richmond VA 23220 **Phn:** 804-643-0990 **Fax:** 804-643-4990 www.selecta1320.com jjacobs@davidsonmediagroup.com

Richmond WWLB-FM (a) 300 Arboretum Pl Ste 590, Richmond VA 23236 **Phn:** 804-327-9902 **Fax:** 804-327-9911 www.989liberty.com mmurphy@mainlinerichmond.com

Richmond WXGI-AM (s) 701 German School Rd, Richmond VA 23225 **Phn:** 804-233-7666 **Fax:** 804-233-7681 www.espn950am.com espn950am@redskins.com

Roanoke WFIR-AM (nt) 3934 Electric Rd, Roanoke VA 24018 **Phn:** 540-345-1511 **Fax:** 540-342-2270 wfir960.com news@wfir960.com

Roanoke WISE-FM (pln) 3520 Kingsbury Cir, Roanoke VA 24014 **Phn:** 276-328-0300 www.wvtf.org tdehner@siue.edu

Roanoke WJJS-FM (a) 3807 Brandon Ave SW Ste 2350, Roanoke VA 24018 **Phn:** 540-725-1220 **Fax:** 540-725-1245 www.wjjs.com

Roanoke WJJX-FM (h) 3807 Brandon Ave SW Ste 2350, Roanoke VA 24018 **Phn:** 540-725-1220 **Fax:** 540-725-1245 www.wjjs.com nicky@wjjs.com

Roanoke WKBA-AM (gq) 2043 10th St NE, Roanoke VA 24012 **Phn:** 540-343-5597 **Fax:** 540-345-4064 www.wkbaradio.com wkba@cox.net

Roanoke WKPA-AM (wg) 2043 10th St NE, Roanoke VA 24012 **Phn:** 540-343-5597 **Fax:** 540-345-4064 www.wkbaradio.com wkba@cox.net

Roanoke WRIS-AM (q) PO Box 6099, Roanoke VA 24017 **Phn:** 540-342-1410 **Fax:** 540-342-5952 wris.cc

Roanoke WROV-FM (r) 3807 Brandon Ave SW Ste 2350, Roanoke VA 24018 **Phn:** 540-725-1220 **Fax:** 540-725-1245 www.rovrocks.com wrov@clearchannel.com

Roanoke WSFF-FM (h) 3807 Brandon Ave SW Ste 2350, Roanoke VA 24018 **Phn:** 540-725-1220 **Fax:** 540-725-1245 www.1061stevefm.com stevencross@clearchannel.com

Roanoke WSLC-FM (c) 3934 Electric Rd, Roanoke VA 24018 **Phn:** 540-387-0237 **Fax:** 540-389-0837 www.949starcountry.com bsharp@949starcountry.com

Roanoke WSLQ-FM (a) 3934 Electric Rd, Roanoke VA 24018 **Phn:** 540-387-0234 **Fax:** 540-389-0837 www.q99fm.com kscott@q99fm.com

Roanoke WSNV-FM (a) 3807 Brandon Ave SW Ste 2350, Roanoke VA 24018 **Phn:** 540-725-1220 **Fax:** 540-725-1245 www.sunny935.com sunny@mysunnyfm.com

Roanoke WSNZ-FM (a) 3807 Brandon Ave SW Ste 2350, Roanoke VA 24018 **Phn:** 540-725-1220 **Fax:** 540-725-1245 www.mysunnyfm.com stevencross@clearchannel.com

Roanoke WTOY-AM (wug) 504 23rd St NW, Roanoke VA 24017 **Phn:** 540-344-9869 **Fax:** 540-344-0976 wtoyradio@aol.com

Roanoke WVBE-FM (h) 3934 Electric Rd, Roanoke VA 24018 **Phn:** 540-774-9200 **Fax:** 540-774-5667 www.vibe100.com info@vibe100.com

Roanoke WVBE-AM (us) 3934 Electric Rd, Roanoke VA 24018 **Phn:** 540-774-9200 **Fax:** 540-774-5667

Roanoke WVMP-FM (r) 210 1st St SW Ste 240, Roanoke VA 24011 **Phn:** 540-344-2800 **Fax:** 540-344-4001 www.1015themusicplace.com

Roanoke WVTF-FM (plnj) 3520 Kingsbury Cir, Roanoke VA 24014 **Phn:** 540-989-8900 **Fax:** 540-776-2727 www.wvtf.org wvtf@vt.edu

Roanoke WWWR-AM (st) 1848 Clay St SE, Roanoke VA 24013 **Phn:** 540-343-7109 **Fax:** 540-343-2306

Roanoke WXLK-FM (h) 3934 Electric Rd, Roanoke VA 24018 **Phn:** 540-774-9200 **Fax:** 540-774-5667 www.k92radio.com

Rocky Mount WYTI-AM (cg) 275 Glennwood Dr, Rocky Mount VA 24151 **Phn:** 540-483-9955 **Fax:** 540-483-7802 www.wytiradio.com wyti@wytiradio.com

Smithfield WKGM-AM (ntq) PO Box 339, Smithfield VA 23431 **Phn:** 757-357-9546 **Fax:** 757-365-0412

South Boston WSBV-AM (g) PO Box 778, South Boston VA 24592 **Phn:** 434-572-4418 **Fax:** 434-572-9245 www.wsbvsouthboston.com

South Hill WSHV-AM (g) 26256 Highway Forty Seven, South Hill VA 23970 **Phn:** 434-447-8218 **Fax:** 434-447-8041

Staunton WTON-FM (a) PO Box 1085, Staunton VA 24402 **Phn:** 540-885-5188 **Fax:** 540-885-1240

Staunton WTON-AM (s) PO Box 1085, Staunton VA 24402 **Phn:** 540-885-5188 **Fax:** 540-885-1240

Stuart WHEO-AM (cnt) 3824 Wayside Rd, Stuart VA 24171 **Phn:** 276-694-3114 **Fax:** 276-694-2241 www.wheo.info 1270am@wheo.info

Tappahannock WRAR-FM (a) PO Box 1023, Tappahannock VA 22560 **Phn:** 804-443-4321 **Fax:** 804-443-1055 realradio804.com contact@realradio804.com

Vienna WKCW-AM (hn) 320 Maple Ave E, Vienna VA 22180 **Phn:** 540-351-0101 **Fax:** 540-351-0606 www.wkcw1420am.com

Virginia Beach WFMI-FM (g) 4801 Columbus St Ste 400, Virginia Beach VA 23462 **Phn:** 757-490-9364 **Fax:** 757-490-2524 www.rejoice1009.com

Virginia Beach WGH-FM (c) 5589 Greenwich Rd Ste 200, Virginia Beach VA 23462 **Phn:** 757-671-1000 **Fax:** 757-671-1010 www.eagle97.com jshomby@eagle97.com

Virginia Beach WGH-AM (s) 5589 Greenwich Rd Ste 200, Virginia Beach VA 23462 **Phn:** 757-671-1000 **Fax:** 757-490-8973 www.star1310.com theboss@star1310.com

Virginia Beach WJLZ-FM (q) 3500 Virginia Beach Blvd Ste 201, Virginia Beach VA 23452 **Phn:** 757-498-9632 **Fax:** 757-498-8609 currentfm.com info@currentfm.com

Virginia Beach WNVZ-FM (h) 236 Clearfield Ave Ste 206, Virginia Beach VA 23462 **Phn:** 757-497-2000 **Fax:** 757-518-8372 www.z104.com mklein@entercom.com

Virginia Beach WPTE-FM (a) 236 Clearfield Ave Ste 206, Virginia Beach VA 23462 **Phn:** 757-497-2000 **Fax:** 757-518-8379 www.pointradio.com

Virginia Beach WVBW-FM (a) 5589 Greenwich Rd Ste 200, Virginia Beach VA 23462 **Phn:** 757-671-1000 **Fax:** 757-671-1010 www.929thewave.com theboss@929thewave.com

Virginia Beach WVHT-FM (h) 5589 Greenwich Rd Ste 200, Virginia Beach VA 23462 **Phn:** 757-671-1000 **Fax:** 757-671-1010 www.hot1005.com theboss@hot1005.com

Virginia Beach WVKL-FM (x) 236 Clearfield Ave Ste 206, Virginia Beach VA 23462 **Phn:** 757-497-2000 www.957rnb.com dlondon@entercom.com

Virginia Beach WWDE-FM (a) 236 Clearfield Ave Ste 206, Virginia Beach VA 23462 **Phn:** 757-497-2000 **Fax:** 757-456-5458 www.thenew1013.com dlondon@entercom.com

Warrenton WKDL-AM (t) 7351 Hunton St, Warrenton VA 20187 **Phn:** 703-330-8244 **Fax:** 703-331-4706 www.730wtnt.com kelly@metroradioinc.com

Warsaw WNNT-FM (c) 194 Islington Rd, Warsaw VA 22572 **Phn:** 804-333-4900 **Fax:** 804-333-4531

Williamsburg WBQK-FM (l) 4732 Longview Rd # 2201, Williamsburg VA 23188 **Phn:** 757-565-1079 **Fax:** 757-565-7094 wbach.net music@wbach.net

Williamsburg WCWM-FM (v) PO Box 8793, Williamsburg VA 23187 **Phn:** 757-221-3287 wcwm.blogs.wm.edu tcvanluling@email.wm.edu

Williamsburg WMBG-AM (a) 1005 Richmond Rd, Williamsburg VA 23185 **Phn:** 757-229-7400 www.wmbgradio.com info@wmbgradio.com

Williamsburg WTYD-FM (r) 5000 New Point Rd Ste 2201, Williamsburg VA 23188 **Phn:** 757-565-1079 **Fax:** 757-565-7094 www.tideradio.com music@tideradio.com

Winchester WFQX-FM (r) 510 Pegasus Ct, Winchester VA 22602 **Phn:** 540-662-5101 **Fax:** 540-662-8610 www.993thefox.com davidmiller@clearchannel.com

Winchester WINC-FM (snt) PO Box 3300, Winchester VA 22604 **Phn:** 540-667-2224 **Fax:** 540-722-3295 www.winc.fm rallen@winc.fm

Winchester WKSI-FM (h) 510 Pegasus Ct, Winchester VA 22602 **Phn:** 540-662-5101 **Fax:** 540-662-8610 www.kiss983.com rickythomas@clearchannel.com

Winchester WMRE-AM (st) 510 Pegasus Ct, Winchester VA 22602 **Phn:** 540-662-5101 **Fax:** 540-662-8610 www.sportstalk1550.com davidmiller@clearchannel.com

Winchester WTFX-AM (s) 510 Pegasus Ct, Winchester VA 22602 **Phn:** 540-662-5101 www.sportstalk1550.com davidmiller@clearchannel.com

Winchester WTRM-FM (q) PO Box 3438, Winchester VA 22604 **Phn:** 540-869-4997 **Fax:** 540-869-7173 www.southernlight.us office@southernlight.us

Winchester WUSQ-FM (c) 510 Pegasus Ct, Winchester VA 22602 **Phn:** 540-662-5101 **Fax:** 540-662-8610 www.wusq.com davidmiller@clearchannel.com

Winchester WWRT-FM (r) PO Box 3300, Winchester VA 22604 **Phn:** 540-667-2224 **Fax:** 540-722-3295

VIRGINIA RADIO STATIONS

Winchester WXBN-FM (r) PO Box 3300, Winchester VA 22604 **Phn:** 540-667-2224 **Fax:** 540-722-3295 www.rockthebone.com

Winchester WXVA-FM (h) 510 Pegasus Ct, Winchester VA 22602 **Phn:** 540-662-5101 **Fax:** 540-662-8610 www.983kissfm.com derrickcole@clearchannel.com

Wise WNVA-AM (gq) 214 Walnut Dr SE, Wise VA 24293 **Phn:** 276-328-2244

Wise WNVA-FM (ac) 214 Walnut Dr SE, Wise VA 24293 **Phn:** 276-328-2244

Wytheville WLOY-AM (t) PO Box 1247, Wytheville VA 24382 **Phn:** 276-228-3185 **Fax:** 276-228-9261 www.threeriversmedia.net office@threeriversmedia.net

Wytheville WXBX-FM (o) PO Box 1247, Wytheville VA 24382 **Phn:** 276-228-3185 **Fax:** 276-228-9261 www.wxbx.com office@threeriversmedia.net

Wytheville WYVE-AM (cn) PO Box 1247, Wytheville VA 24382 **Phn:** 276-228-3185 **Fax:** 276-228-9261 www.wyve.com office@threeriversmedia.net

WASHINGTON

Aberdeen KBKW-AM (nt) PO Box 1198, Aberdeen WA 98520 **Phn:** 360-533-3000 **Fax:** 360-532-1456 kbkw.com info@jodesha.com

Aberdeen KDUX-FM (r) 1308 Coolidge Rd, Aberdeen WA 98520 **Phn:** 360-533-1320 **Fax:** 360-532-0935 www.kdux.com donna@kdux.com

Aberdeen KJET-FM (a) PO Box 1198, Aberdeen WA 98520 **Phn:** 360-533-3000 **Fax:** 360-532-1456 www.jodesha.com info@jodesha.com

Aberdeen KSWW-FM (a) PO Box 1198, Aberdeen WA 98520 **Phn:** 360-533-3000 **Fax:** 360-532-1456 www.jodesha.com info@jodesha.com

Aberdeen KWOK-AM (st) 1308 Coolidge Rd, Aberdeen WA 98520 **Phn:** 360-533-1320 **Fax:** 360-532-0935 donna@kdux.com

Aberdeen KXRO-AM (nt) 1308 Coolidge Rd, Aberdeen WA 98520 **Phn:** 360-533-1320 **Fax:** 360-532-0935 www.kxro.com pat@kdux.com

Aberdeen KXXK-FM (c) 1308 Coolidge Rd, Aberdeen WA 98520 **Phn:** 360-533-1320 **Fax:** 360-532-0935 www.kix953.com donna.rosi@morris.com

Auburn KDDS-FM (y) 1400 W Main St, Auburn WA 98001 **Phn:** 253-735-9700 **Fax:** 253-735-7424

Auburn KGRG-FM (vr) 12401 SE 320th St, Auburn WA 98092 **Phn:** 253-833-9111 www.kgrg.com

Bellevue KBCS-FM (v) 3000 Landerholm Cir SE, Bellevue WA 98007 **Phn:** 425-564-6195 kbcs.fm sonya.green@kbcs.fm

Bellevue KIXI-AM (o) 3650 131st Ave SE Ste 550, Bellevue WA 98006 **Phn:** 425-653-9462 **Fax:** 425-653-1088 www.kixi.com marck@kixi.com

Bellevue KKNW-AM (n) 3650 131st Ave SE Ste 550, Bellevue WA 98006 **Phn:** 425-373-5536 **Fax:** 425-373-5548 www.1150kknw.com cindyg@1150kknw.com

Bellevue KQMV-FM (h) 3650 131st Ave SE Ste 550, Bellevue WA 98006 **Phn:** 425-653-9462 movin925.com info@movin925.fm

Bellevue KRWM-FM (a) 3650 131st Ave SE Ste 550, Bellevue WA 98006 **Phn:** 425-373-5545 **Fax:** 425-653-1199 www.warm1069.com marck@warm1069.com

Bellevue KWJZ-FM (j) 3650 131st Ave SE Ste 550, Bellevue WA 98006 **Phn:** 425-373-5536 **Fax:** 425-373-5548 www.click989.com

Bellingham KAFE-FM (a) 2219 Yew Street Rd, Bellingham WA 98229 **Phn:** 360-734-9790 **Fax:** 360-733-4551 www.kafe.com kafe@kafe.com

Bellingham KBAI-AM (ab) 2219 Yew Street Rd, Bellingham WA 98229 **Phn:** 360-734-9790 **Fax:** 360-733-4551 www.930kbai.com kbaipd@cascaderadiogroup.com

Bellingham KGMI-AM (snt) 2219 Yew Street Rd, Bellingham WA 98229 **Phn:** 360-734-9790 **Fax:** 360-733-4551 www.kgmi.com kgmi@kgmi.com

Bellingham KISM-FM (r) 2219 Yew Street Rd, Bellingham WA 98229 **Phn:** 360-734-9790 **Fax:** 360-733-4551 www.kism.com kism@kism.com

Bellingham KPUG-AM (snt) 2219 Yew Street Rd, Bellingham WA 98229 **Phn:** 360-734-9790 **Fax:** 360-733-4551 www.kpug1170.com thezone@kpug1170.com

Bellingham KUGS-FM (v) 700 Viking Union Bldg, Bellingham WA 98225 **Phn:** 360-650-4771 **Fax:** 360-650-6507 as.wwu.edukugs kugs.newsdirector@wwu.edu

Bellingham KZAZ-FM (plnj) PO Box 642530, Bellingham WA **Phn:** 800-842-8991 **Fax:** 509-335-6577 www.nwpr.org nwpr@wsu.edu

Blaine KARI-AM (q) 4840 Lincoln Rd, Blaine WA 98230 **Phn:** 360-371-5500 **Fax:** 360-371-7617 www.kari55.com gary@kari55.com

Centralia KCED-FM (v) 600 Centralia College Blvd, Centralia WA 98531 **Phn:** 360-736-9391

Centralia KELA-AM (snt) 1635 S Gold St, Centralia WA 98531 **Phn:** 360-736-3321 **Fax:** 360-736-0150 www.kelaam.com stevegeorge@bicoastalmedia.com

Centralia KITI-FM (ah) 1133 Kresky Ave, Centralia WA 98531 **Phn:** 360-736-1355 **Fax:** 360-736-4761 www.Live95.com mshannon@live95.com

Centralia KITI-AM (o) 1133 Kresky Ave, Centralia WA 98531 **Phn:** 360-736-1355 **Fax:** 360-736-4761 www.1420kiti.com dshannon@live95.com

Centralia KMNT-FM (c) 1635 S Gold St, Centralia WA 98531 **Phn:** 360-736-3321 **Fax:** 360-736-0150 www.kmnt.com

Chehalis KACS-FM (v) 2451 NE Kresky Ave Unit A, Chehalis WA 98532 **Phn:** 360-740-9436 **Fax:** 360-740-9415 www.kacs.org kacs@kacs.org

Chelan KOZI-AM (ant) PO Box 819, Chelan WA 98816 **Phn:** 509-682-4033 **Fax:** 509-682-4035 www.kozi.com jay@kozi.com

Chelan KOZI-FM (ant) PO Box 819, Chelan WA 98816 **Phn:** 509-682-4033 **Fax:** 509-682-4035 www.kozi.com jay@kozi.com

Cheney KEWU-FM (v) 104 Rtv Bldg, Cheney WA 99004 **Phn:** 509-359-4226 **Fax:** 509-359-4841 www.ewu.educaleprogramsfilmkewu.xml jazz@mail.ewu.edu

College Place KGTS-FM (vq) 204 S College Ave, College Place WA 99324 **Phn:** 509-527-2991 **Fax:** 509-527-2611 www.plr.org

Colville KCRK-FM (a) PO Box 111, Colville WA 99114 **Phn:** 509-684-5032 **Fax:** 509-684-5034 www.kcvl.com news@kcvl.com

Colville KCVL-AM (c) PO Box 111, Colville WA 99114 **Phn:** 509-684-5032 **Fax:** 509-684-5034 www.kcvl.com news@kcvl.com

Ellensburg KCWU-FM (vr) 400 E University Way, Ellensburg WA 98926 **Phn:** 509-963-2283 **Fax:** 509-963-1688 www.881theburg.com news@cwu.edu

Ellensburg KXLE-AM (snt) 1311 Vantage Hwy, Ellensburg WA 98926 **Phn:** 509-925-1488 **Fax:** 509-962-7882

WASHINGTON RADIO STATIONS

Ellensburg KXLE-FM (c) 1311 Vantage Hwy, Ellensburg WA 98926 **Phn:** 509-925-1488 **Fax:** 509-962-7882 www.kxleradio.com kxle@elltel.net

Ephrata KTBI-AM (q) 55 Alder St NW # 3, Ephrata WA 98823 **Phn:** 509-754-2000 www.ktbi.com ktbi@ktbi.com

Ephrata KULE-AM (t) 910 Basin St SW, Ephrata WA 98823 **Phn:** 509-754-4661 **Fax:** 509-754-4110

Ephrata KULE-FM (c) 910 Basin St SW, Ephrata WA 98823 **Phn:** 509-754-4661 **Fax:** 509-754-4110

Ephrata KZML-FM (y) 910 Basin St SW, Ephrata WA 98823 **Phn:** 509-754-4661 **Fax:** 509-754-4110

Everett KRKO-AM (st) 2707 Colby Ave Ste 1380, Everett WA 98201 **Phn:** 425-304-1381 **Fax:** 425-304-1382 www.everettpost.com andrew.skotdal@krko.com

Ferndale KRPI-AM (q) PO Box 3213, Ferndale WA 98248 **Phn:** 360-384-5117 **Fax:** 360-380-4202 www.krpiradio.com grace@krpiradio.com

Forks KBDB-FM (h) PO Box 450, Forks WA 98331 **Phn:** 360-374-6233 **Fax:** 360-374-6852

Forks KBIS-AM (h) PO Box 450, Forks WA 98331 **Phn:** 360-374-6233 **Fax:** 360-374-6852

Grand Coulee KEYG-AM (c) PO Box K, Grand Coulee WA 99133 **Phn:** 509-633-2020 **Fax:** 509-633-1014 www.kxa937.comkeygam.html nwheeler@nwi.net

Grand Coulee KEYG-FM (o) PO Box K, Grand Coulee WA 99133 **Phn:** 509-633-2020 **Fax:** 509-633-1014 www.keyg985.com keygprod@aol.com

Granger KDNA-FM (vy) PO Box 800, Granger WA 98932 **Phn:** 509-854-1900 **Fax:** 509-854-2223 www.kdna.org

Kelso KLOG-AM (hn) PO Box 90, Kelso WA 98626 **Phn:** 360-636-0110 **Fax:** 360-577-6949 klog.com news@klog.com

Kelso KUKN-FM (c) PO Box 90, Kelso WA 98626 **Phn:** 360-636-0110 **Fax:** 360-577-6949 kukn.com news@klog.com

Kennewick KALE-AM (s) 4304 W 24th Ave # 200, Kennewick WA 99338 **Phn:** 509-783-0783 **Fax:** 509-735-8627 www.am960.com

Kennewick KBLD-FM (q) 412 S Vancouver St, Kennewick WA 99336 **Phn:** 509-736-2086 **Fax:** 509-736-9599 www.kbld.com

Kennewick KEGX-FM (r) 830 N Columbia Center Blvd Ste B2, Kennewick WA 99336 **Phn:** 509-783-0783 **Fax:** 509-735-8627 www.eagle1065.com

Kennewick KIOK-FM (c) 830 N Columbia Center Blvd Ste B2, Kennewick WA 99336 **Phn:** 509-783-0783 **Fax:** 509-735-8627 949thewolfpack.com

Kennewick KKSR-FM (h) 830 N Columbia Center Blvd Ste B2, Kennewick WA 99336 **Phn:** 509-783-0783 **Fax:** 509-735-8627

Kennewick KNLT-FM (o) 830 N Columbia Center Blvd Ste B2, Kennewick WA 99336 **Phn:** 509-783-0783 **Fax:** 509-735-8627 www.knlt.com

Kennewick KTCR-AM (c) 4304 W 24th Ave # 200, Kennewick WA 99338 **Phn:** 509-783-0783 **Fax:** 509-735-8627 www.1390thetractor.com

Kirkland KBLE-AM (q) PO Box 2482, Kirkland WA 98083 **Phn:** 425-867-2340 www.sacredheartradio.org info@sacredheartradio.org

Lakewood KLAY-AM (nt) 10025 Lakewood Dr SW Ste B, Lakewood WA 98499 **Phn:** 253-581-0324 **Fax:** 253-581-0326 www.klay1180.com klay1180@blarg.net

Leavenworth KOHO-FM (h) 7475 Koho Pl, Leavenworth WA 98826 **Phn:** 509-548-1011 **Fax:** 509-548-3222 www.kohoradio.com traffic@kozi.com

Longview KBAM-AM (c) 1130 14th Ave, Longview WA 98632 **Phn:** 360-425-1500 **Fax:** 360-423-1554 www.kbamcountry.com greg@bicoastalmedia.com

Longview KEDO-AM (ont) 1130 14th Ave, Longview WA 98632 **Phn:** 360-425-1500 **Fax:** 360-423-1554 www.threeriversradio.com greg@bicoastalmedia.com

Longview KLYK-FM (a) 1130 14th Ave, Longview WA 98632 **Phn:** 360-425-1500 **Fax:** 360-423-1554 bicoastalmedia.com greg@bicoastalmedia.com

Longview KRQT-FM (r) 1130 14th Ave, Longview WA 98632 **Phn:** 360-425-1500 **Fax:** 360-423-1554 www.bicoastalmedia.com greg@bicoastalmedia.com

Lynden KWPZ-FM (q) 1843 Front St, Lynden WA 98264 **Phn:** 360-354-5596 **Fax:** 360-354-7517 www.praise1065.com comments@praise1065.com

Moses Lake KBSN-AM (m) PO Box B, Moses Lake WA 98837 **Phn:** 509-765-3441 **Fax:** 509-766-0273

Moses Lake KDRM-FM (a) PO Box B, Moses Lake WA 98837 **Phn:** 509-765-3441 **Fax:** 509-766-0273 jp1470@hotmail.com

Moses Lake KWIQ-AM (s) 11768 Kittleson Rd NE, Moses Lake WA 98837 **Phn:** 509-765-1761 **Fax:** 509-765-8901 www.kkrt.com gary.patrick@morris.com

Moses Lake KWIQ-FM (c) 11768 Kittleson Rd NE, Moses Lake WA 98837 **Phn:** 509-765-1761 **Fax:** 509-765-8901 www.kwiq.com gary.patrick@morris.com

Mount Vernon KAPS-AM (c) 2029 Freeway Dr, Mount Vernon WA 98273 **Phn:** 360-424-7676 **Fax:** 360-424-1660 www.kapsradio.com kapsradio@gmail.com

Mount Vernon KBRC-AM (sna) PO Box 250, Mount Vernon WA 98273 **Phn:** 360-424-1430 **Fax:** 360-424-1660 www.kbrcradio.com kbrcradio@gmail.com

Mount Vernon KSVR-FM (v) 2405 E College Way, Mount Vernon WA 98273 **Phn:** 360-416-7711 www.ksvr.org mail@ksvr.org

Olympia KAOS-FM (v) 2700 Evergreen Pkwy NW CAB 101, Olympia WA 98505 **Phn:** 360-867-6888 www.kaosradio.org kaos@evergreen.edu

Olympia KGY-AM (ant) PO Box 1249, Olympia WA 98507 **Phn:** 360-943-1240 **Fax:** 360-352-1222 www.kgyradio.com news@kgyradio.com

Olympia KGY-FM (c) 1700 Marine Dr NE, Olympia WA 98501 **Phn:** 360-943-1240 **Fax:** 360-352-1222 www.kgyradio.com news@kgyradio.com

Olympia KRXY-FM (ah) 2124 Pacific Ave SE, Olympia WA 98506 **Phn:** 360-236-1010 **Fax:** 360-236-1133 945Roxy.com krxy@krxy.com

Olympia KXXO-FM (a) PO Box 7937, Olympia WA 98507 **Phn:** 360-943-9937 **Fax:** 360-352-3643 www.mixx96.com news@mixx96.com

Omak KNCW-FM (c) PO Box 151, Omak WA 98841 **Phn:** 509-826-0100 **Fax:** 509-826-3929 www.komw.net info@komw.net

Omak KOMW-AM (nt) PO Box 151, Omak WA 98841 **Phn:** 509-826-0100 **Fax:** 509-826-3929 www.komw.net news@komw.net

Omak KZBE-FM (a) PO Box 151, Omak WA 98841 **Phn:** 509-826-0100 **Fax:** 509-826-3929 www.komw.net news@komw.net

Pasco KEYW-FM (a) 2621 W A St, Pasco WA 99301 **Phn:** 509-547-9791 **Fax:** 509-547-8509 keyw.com pauldrake@gapbroadcasting.com

Pasco KFLD-AM (nt) 2621 W A St, Pasco WA 99301 **Phn:** 509-547-9791 **Fax:** 509-547-8509 newstalk870.am johnmckay@townsquaremedia.com

Pasco KOLU-FM (q) PO Box 2734, Pasco WA 99302 **Phn:** 509-547-2062 **Fax:** 509-544-0340 www.kolu.com

Pasco KOLW-FM (o) 2621 W A St, Pasco WA 99301 **Phn:** 509-547-9791 **Fax:** 509-547-8509 www.975coolfm.com barrylong@gapbroadcasting.com

Pasco KONA-AM (nt) 2823 W Lewis St, Pasco WA 99301 **Phn:** 509-547-1618 **Fax:** 509-546-2678 www.610kona.com dshannon@cherrycreekradio.com

Pasco KONA-FM (a) 2823 W Lewis St, Pasco WA 99301 **Phn:** 509-547-1618 **Fax:** 509-546-2678 www.mix1053.com tpeterson@cherrycreekradio.com

Pasco KORD-FM (c) 2621 W A St, Pasco WA 99301 **Phn:** 509-547-9791 **Fax:** 509-547-8509 1027kord.com pauldrake@gapbroadcasting.com

Pasco KRCW-FM (y) 508 W Lewis St, Pasco WA 99301 **Phn:** 509-545-0700 **Fax:** 509-543-4100 www.campesina.com

Pasco KXRX-FM (r) 2621 W A St, Pasco WA 99301 **Phn:** 509-547-9791 **Fax:** 509-547-8509 97rockonline.com adamlamberd@townsquaremedia.com

Pasco KZHR-FM (y) 2823 W Lewis St, Pasco WA 99301 **Phn:** 509-547-1618 **Fax:** 509-546-2678 www.kzhr.com

Port Angeles KONP-AM (nt) PO Box 1450, Port Angeles WA 98362 **Phn:** 360-457-1450 **Fax:** 360-457-9114 www.konp.com info@konp.com

Port Orchard KITZ-AM (nt) 1700 SE Mile Hill Dr Ste 243, Port Orchard WA 98366 **Phn:** 360-876-1400 **Fax:** 360-876-7920 www.kitz1400.com news@kitz1400.com

Prosser KLES-FM (y) 1227 Hillcrest Dr, Prosser WA 99350 **Phn:** 509-786-1310 **Fax:** 509-786-6814

Pullman KHTR-FM (r) PO Box 1, Pullman WA 99163 **Phn:** 509-332-6551 **Fax:** 509-332-5151

Pullman KQQQ-AM (nt) PO Box 1, Pullman WA 99163 **Phn:** 509-332-6551 **Fax:** 509-332-5151

Pullman KWSU-AM (pln) PO Box 642530, Pullman WA 99164 **Phn:** 509-335-6500 **Fax:** 509-335-6577 www.nwpr.org nwpr@wsu.edu

Pullman KZUU-FM (vrj) Wa State U Cub Rm 311, Pullman WA 99164 **Phn:** 509-335-2208 kzuu.wsu.edu kzuu@wsu.edu

Seattle KBKS-FM (h) 351 Elliott Ave W Ste 300, Seattle WA 98119 **Phn:** 206-494-2000 **Fax:** 206-286-2376 www.kissfmseattle.com tyler@kissfmseattle.com

Seattle KEXP-FM (vr) 113 Dexter Ave N, Seattle WA 98109 **Phn:** 206-520-5800 **Fax:** 206-520-5899 www.kexp.org info@kexp.org

Seattle KGNW-AM (tq) 2201 6th Ave Ste 1500, Seattle WA 98121 **Phn:** 206-443-8200 **Fax:** 206-777-1133 www.kgnw.com webmaster@kgnw.com

Seattle KHHO-AM (s) 645 Elliott Ave W # 400, Seattle WA 98119 **Phn:** 206-494-2000 **Fax:** 206-286-2376 www.sportsradiokjr.com programming@kjram.com

Seattle KING-FM (l) 10 Harrison St Ste 100, Seattle WA 98109 **Phn:** 206-691-2981 **Fax:** 206-691-2982 www.king.org

Seattle KIRO-FM (snt) 1820 Eastlake Ave E, Seattle WA 98102 **Phn:** 206-726-7000 **Fax:** 206-726-5446 mynorthwest.com newsdesk@973kiro.com

Seattle KIRO-AM (s) 1820 Eastlake Ave E, Seattle WA 98102 **Phn:** 206-726-7000 **Fax:** 206-726-5446 mynorthwest.com newsdesk@973kiro.com

Seattle KISW-FM (r) 1100 Olive Way Ste 1650, Seattle WA 98101 **Phn:** 206-285-7625 **Fax:** 206-215-9355 www.KISW.com bthorpe@kisw.com

Seattle KJAQ-FM (r) 1000 Dexter Ave N Ste 100, Seattle WA 98109 **Phn:** 206-805-0965 **Fax:** 206-805-0911 jackseattle.cbslocal.com jim.trapp@cbsradio.com

Seattle KJR-FM (h) 645 Elliott Ave W # 400, Seattle WA 98119 **Phn:** 206-494-2000 **Fax:** 206-286-2376 www.957kjr.com jennygudmundson@clearchannel.com

Seattle KJR-AM (s) 645 Elliott Ave W Ste 400, Seattle WA 98119 **Phn:** 206-494-2000 **Fax:** 206-286-2376 www.sportsradiokjr.com programming@kjram.com

Seattle KKBW-FM (r) 645 Elliott Ave W Ste 400, Seattle WA 98119 **Phn:** 206-494-2000 **Fax:** 206-653-5507 www.thebrew1049.com johnpeake@clearchannel.com

Seattle KKMO-AM (y) 2201 6th Ave Ste 1500, Seattle WA 98121 **Phn:** 206-443-8200 **Fax:** 206-777-1133 www.radiosol1360.comUC

Seattle KKOL-AM (kt) 2201 6th Ave Ste 1500, Seattle WA 98121 **Phn:** 206-443-8200 **Fax:** 206-777-1133 www.kkol.com daved@salemradioseattle.com

Seattle KKWF-FM (c) 1100 Olive Way Ste 1650, Seattle WA 98101 **Phn:** 206-285-7625 www.seattlewolf.com seapa@entercom.com

Seattle KLFE-AM (qtg) 2201 6th Ave Ste 1500, Seattle WA 98121 **Phn:** 206-443-8200 **Fax:** 206-777-1133 www.freedom1590.com chuck@kgnw.com

Seattle KMPS-FM (c) PO Box 24888, Seattle WA 98124 **Phn:** 206-805-0941 **Fax:** 206-805-0911 kmps.cbslocal.com ed.hill@cbsradio.com

Seattle KMTT-FM (r) 1100 Olive Way Ste 1650, Seattle WA 98101 **Phn:** 206-233-1037 **Fax:** 206-233-8979 www.themountainseattle.com drichards@entercom.com

Seattle KNBQ-FM (c) 351 Elliott Ave W Ste 300, Seattle WA 98119 **Phn:** 206-494-2000 **Fax:** 206-286-2376 www.1029nowhits.com

Seattle KNDD-FM (r) 1100 Olive Way Ste 1650, Seattle WA 98101 **Phn:** 206-622-3251 **Fax:** 206-682-8349 www.1077theend.com gmichaels@entercom.com

Seattle KNHC-FM (vh) 10750 30th Ave NE, Seattle WA 98125 **Phn:** 206-252-3800 **Fax:** 206-252-3805 www.c895.org

Seattle KNTS-AM (tq) 2201 6th Ave Ste 1500, Seattle WA 98121 **Phn:** 206-443-8200 **Fax:** 206-777-1133

Seattle KOMO-AM (nt) 140 4th Ave N Ste 400, Seattle WA 98109 **Phn:** 206-404-5666 **Fax:** 206-404-3646 www.komonews.com tips@komo4news.com

Seattle KPLZ-FM (a) 140 4th Ave N Ste 340, Seattle WA 98109 **Phn:** 206-404-4000 www.star1015.com starcomment@fisherradio.com

Seattle KPTK-AM (nt) 1000 Dexter Ave N Ste 100, Seattle WA 98109 **Phn:** 206-805-1090 **Fax:** 206-805-0932 seattle.cbslocal.com steve.sandmeyer@cbsradio.com

Seattle KRIZ-AM (wu) 2600 S Jackson St, Seattle WA 98144 **Phn:** 206-323-3070 **Fax:** 206-322-6518 www.ztwins.com ztwins@aol.com

Seattle KTTH-AM (nk) 1820 Eastlake Ave E, Seattle WA 98102 **Phn:** 206-726-7000 **Fax:** 206-726-7001 mynorthwest.com newsdesk@973kiro.com

Seattle KUBE-FM (h) 645 Elliott Ave W STe 400, Seattle WA 98119 **Phn:** 206-494-2000 **Fax:** 206-286-2376 www.kube93.com ericpowers@kube93.com

Seattle KUOW-FM (pn) 4518 University Way NE Ste 310, Seattle WA 98105 **Phn:** 206-543-2710 www.kuow.org newsroom@kuow.org

Seattle KVI-AM (nt) 140 4th Ave N Ste 340, Seattle WA 98109 **Phn:** 206-404-4000 **Fax:** 206-404-3648 www.kvi.com 570kvi@fisherradio.com

Seattle KXPA-AM (ye) 114 Lakeside Ave, Seattle WA 98122 **Phn:** 206-292-7800 **Fax:** 206-292-2140 www.kxpa.com

Seattle KYIZ-AM (wug) 2600 S Jackson St, Seattle WA 98144 **Phn:** 206-323-3070 **Fax:** 206-322-6518 www.ztwins.com gametime@ztwins.com

Seattle KZIZ-AM (wg) 2600 S Jackson St, Seattle WA 98144 **Phn:** 206-323-3070 **Fax:** 206-322-6518 www.ztwins.com ztwins@aol.com

Seattle KZOK-FM (r) 1000 Dexter Ave N Ste 100, Seattle WA 98109 **Phn:** 206-805-1025 **Fax:** 206-805-0911 kzok.cbslocal.com carey.curelop@cbsradio.com

Shelton KMAS-FM (sn) PO Box 760, Shelton WA 98584 **Phn:** 360-426-1030 **Fax:** 360-427-5268 kmasnewsradio.com kmasnews@kmas.com

Shelton KMAS-AM (sn) PO Box 760, Shelton WA 98584 **Phn:** 360-426-1030 **Fax:** 360-427-5268 kmasnewsradio.com kmasnews@kmas.com

Shoreline KCIS-AM (qt) 19303 Fremont Ave N, Shoreline WA 98133 **Phn:** 206-546-7350 **Fax:** 206-289-7792 www.kcisradio.com news@kcisradio.com

Shoreline KCMS-FM (aq) 19303 Fremont Ave N, Shoreline WA 98133 **Phn:** 206-546-7350 **Fax:** 206-546-7372 www.spirit1053.com news@spirit1053.com

Spokane KAGU-FM (va) 502 E Boone Ave, Spokane WA 99258 **Phn:** 509-328-4220

Spokane KBBD-FM (a) 1601 E 57th Ave, Spokane WA 99223 **Phn:** 509-448-1000 **Fax:** 509-448-7015 www.1039bobfm.com mskot@radiospokane.com

Spokane KCDA-FM (a) 808 E Sprague Ave, Spokane WA 99202 **Phn:** 509-242-2400 **Fax:** 509-242-1160 www.1031kcda.com mattauclair@clearchannel.com

Spokane KDRK-FM (c) 1601 E 57th Ave, Spokane WA 99223 **Phn:** 509-448-1000 **Fax:** 509-448-7015 www.catcountry94.com

Spokane KEEH-FM (q) PO Box 19039, Spokane WA 99219 **Phn:** 509-456-4870 **Fax:** 509-838-4882 www.plr.org

Spokane KEYF-AM (a) 1601 E 57th Ave, Spokane WA 99223 **Phn:** 509-448-1000 **Fax:** 509-448-7015

Spokane KEYF-FM (o) 1601 E 57th Ave, Spokane WA 99223 **Phn:** 509-448-1000 **Fax:** 509-448-7015 1011fmSpokane.com mskot@radiospokane.com

Spokane KEZE-FM (c) 500 W Boone Ave, Spokane WA 99201 **Phn:** 509-324-4200 **Fax:** 509-324-8992 www.thebig999coyotecountry.com

Spokane KGA-AM (nt) 1601 E 57th Ave, Spokane WA 99223 **Phn:** 509-448-1000 **Fax:** 509-448-7015 www.1510kga.com thowell@radiospokane.com

Spokane KHTQ-FM (r) 500 W Boone Ave, Spokane WA 99201 **Phn:** 208-664-9271 **Fax:** 208-667-0945 www.rock945.com

Spokane KISC-FM (a) 808 E Sprague Ave, Spokane WA 99202 **Phn:** 509-242-2400 **Fax:** 509-242-1160 www.kiss981.com michaellacrosse@clearchannel.com

Spokane KIXZ-AM (c) 808 E Sprague Ave, Spokane WA 99202 **Phn:** 509-242-2400 **Fax:** 509-242-1160

Spokane KJRB-AM (c) 1601 E 57th Ave, Spokane WA 99223 **Phn:** 509-448-1000 **Fax:** 509-448-7015 www.790kjrb.com

Spokane KKZX-FM (r) 808 E Sprague Ave, Spokane WA 99202 **Phn:** 509-242-2400 **Fax:** 509-242-1160 www.989kkzx.com calhall@clearchannel.com

Spokane KMBI-AM (q) 5408 S Freya St, Spokane WA 99223 **Phn:** 509-448-2555 **Fax:** 509-448-6855 www.mbn.org kmbi@moody.edu

Spokane KMBI-FM (q) 5408 S Freya St, Spokane WA 99223 **Phn:** 509-448-2555 **Fax:** 509-448-6855 www.mbn.org kmbi@moody.edu

Spokane KPBX-FM (plnj) 2319 N Monroe St, Spokane WA 99205 **Phn:** 509-328-5729 **Fax:** 509-328-5764 www.kpbx.org kpbx@kpbx.org

Spokane KPTQ-AM (t) 808 E Sprague Ave, Spokane WA 99202 **Phn:** 509-242-2400 **Fax:** 509-242-1160 www.1280foxsports.com jasonmccollim@clearchannel.com

Spokane KQNT-AM (nt) 808 E Sprague Ave, Spokane WA 99202 **Phn:** 509-242-2400 **Fax:** 509-242-1160 www.590kqnt.com calhall@clearchannel.com

Spokane KQQB-FM (h) 505 W Riverside Ave # 101, Spokane WA 99201 **Phn:** 509-252-8440 **Fax:** 509-252-8453

Spokane KSBN-AM (nk) 7 S Howard St Ste 430, Spokane WA 99201 **Phn:** 509-838-4000 **Fax:** 509-838-4800 www.ksbn.net ksbn@ksbn.net

Spokane KSFC-FM (plnj) 2319 N Monroe St, Spokane WA 99205 **Phn:** 509-328-5729 **Fax:** 509-328-5764 www.ksfc.org kpbx@kpbx.org

Spokane KTSL-FM (q) 1212 N Washington St Ste 124, Spokane WA 99201 **Phn:** 509-326-9500 **Fax:** 509-326-1560

Spokane KVNI-AM (o) 500 W Boone Ave, Spokane WA 99201 **Phn:** 208-664-9271 **Fax:** 208-667-0945 www.kvni.com

Spokane KXLX-AM (s) 500 W Boone Ave, Spokane WA 99201 **Phn:** 509-324-4000 **Fax:** 509-324-8992 www.kxly.comsports news4@kxly.com

Spokane KXLY-FM (a) 500 W Boone Ave, Spokane WA 99201 **Phn:** 509-324-4000 **Fax:** 509-324-8992 www.spokanesriver.com

Spokane KXLY-AM (nt) 500 W Boone Ave, Spokane WA 99201 **Phn:** 509-324-4200 **Fax:** 509-324-8992 www.kxly.com news4@kxly.com

Spokane KZBD-FM (r) 1601 E 57th Ave, Spokane WA 99223 **Phn:** 509-448-1000 **Fax:** 509-448-7015 now1057fm.com

Spokane KZZU-FM (h) 500 W Boone Ave, Spokane WA 99201 **Phn:** 509-324-4200 **Fax:** 509-324-8992 www.kzzu.com kenho@kzzu.com

Stanwood KWLE-AM (snt) 26910 92nd Ave NW #C5 PMB 235, Stanwood WA 98292 **Phn:** 360-293-3141 **Fax:** 360-293-9463 www.1340thewhale.com jdella@1340thewhale.com

Tacoma KPLU-FM (pjn) 12180 Park Ave S, Tacoma WA 98447 **Phn:** 253-535-7758 **Fax:** 253-535-8332 www.kplu.org news@kplu.org

Tacoma KUPS-FM (vr) 1500 N Warner St, Tacoma WA 98416 **Phn:** 253-879-3288 www.kups.net info@kups.net

Vancouver KBMS-AM (u) PO Box 251, Vancouver WA 98666 **Phn:** 360-699-1881 avjkbms@aol.com

Walla Walla KGDC-AM (nts) 30 W Main St Ste 303, Walla Walla WA 99362 **Phn:** 509-525-7878 rfazzari@kgdcradio.com

Walla Walla KHSS-FM (q) 30 W Main St Ste 303, Walla Walla WA 99362 **Phn:** 509-525-7878 www.khssradio.com rfazzari@kgdcradio.com

Walla Walla KTEL-AM (o) 13 12 E Main St Ste 202, Walla Walla WA 99362 **Phn:** 509-522-1383 **Fax:** 509-522-0211 www.mycolumbiabasin.com joertel@cappsbroadcastgroup.com

Walla Walla KUJ-AM (snt) 45 S Campbell Rd, Walla Walla WA 99362 **Phn:** 509-527-1000 **Fax:** 509-529-5534 www.kujam.com

Walla Walla KWCW-FM (v) 200 Boyer Ave, Walla Walla WA 99362 **Phn:** 509-527-5285 www.kwcw.net

Walla Walla KWHT-FM (c) 13 12 E Main St Ste 202, Walla Walla WA 99362 **Phn:** 509-522-1383 **Fax:** 509-522-0211 www.mycolumbiabasin.com stayseejc@yahoo.com

Wenatchee KAAP-FM (r) 231 N Wenatchee Ave, Wenatchee WA 98801 **Phn:** 509-665-6565 **Fax:** 509-663-1150 www.applefm.com dbernstein@cherrycreekradio.com

Wenatchee KKRT-AM (s) PO Box 79, Wenatchee WA 98807 **Phn:** 509-663-5186 **Fax:** 509-663-8779 www.kkrt.com gary.patrick@morris.com

Wenatchee KKRV-FM (c) PO Box 79, Wenatchee WA 98807 **Phn:** 509-663-5186 **Fax:** 509-663-8779 www.kkrv.com gary.patrick@morris.com

Wenatchee KPLW-FM (q) 606 N Western Ave, Wenatchee WA 98801 **Phn:** 509-665-6641 **Fax:** 509-665-3126 www.plr.org

Wenatchee KPQ-FM (h) 231 N Wenatchee Ave, Wenatchee WA 98801 **Phn:** 509-665-6565 **Fax:** 509-663-1150 www.thequake1021.com

Wenatchee KPQ-AM (nt) 231 N Wenatchee Ave, Wenatchee WA 98801 **Phn:** 509-665-6565 **Fax:** 509-663-1150 www.kpq.com newswenatchee@cherrycreekradio.com

Wenatchee KWLN-FM (y) 32 N Mission St Unit B2, Wenatchee WA 98801 **Phn:** 509-663-5186 www.lanuevaradio.com jlhigh@morris.com

Wenatchee KWNC-AM (sn) 231 N Wenatchee Ave, Wenatchee WA 98801 **Phn:** 509-787-4461

Wenatchee KWWW-FM (h) 231 N Wenatchee Ave, Wenatchee WA 98801 **Phn:** 509-665-6565 **Fax:** 509-663-1150 www.kw3.com connor@cherrycreekradio.com

Wenatchee KWWX-FM (r) 231 N Wenatchee Ave, Wenatchee WA 98801 **Phn:** 509-665-6565

Wenatchee KWWX-AM (y) 231 N Wenatchee Ave, Wenatchee WA 98801 **Phn:** 509-665-6565

Wenatchee KYSN-FM (c) 231 N Wenatchee Ave, Wenatchee WA 98801 **Phn:** 509-665-6565 **Fax:** 509-663-1150 www.kysn.com

Wenatchee KZPH-FM (r) 231 N Wenatchee Ave, Wenatchee WA 98801 **Phn:** 509-665-6565 **Fax:** 509-663-1150 www.therock1067.com

Yakima KARY-FM (o) 1200 Chesterly Dr Ste 160, Yakima WA 98902 **Phn:** 509-248-2900 **Fax:** 509-452-9661 www.cherryfm.com

Yakima KATS-FM (r) 4010 Summitview Ave Ste 200, Yakima WA 98908 **Phn:** 509-972-3461 **Fax:** 509-972-3540 katsfm.com katsfm@gmail.com

Yakima KBBO-AM (snt) 1200 Chesterly Dr Ste 160, Yakima WA 98902 **Phn:** 509-248-2900 **Fax:** 509-452-9661 talk980kusa.com deweyb@yakimaradiogroup.com

Yakima KDBL-FM (c) 4010 Summitview Ave, Yakima WA 98908 **Phn:** 509-972-3461 **Fax:** 509-972-3540 929thebull.com

Yakima KFFM-FM (h) 4010 Summitview Ave, Yakima WA 98908 **Phn:** 509-972-3461 **Fax:** 509-972-3540 kffm.com rikmikals@townsquaremedia.com

Yakima KHHK-FM (u) 1200 Chesterly Dr Ste 160, Yakima WA 98902 **Phn:** 509-248-2900 **Fax:** 509-452-9661 www.newhot997.com

Yakima KIT-AM (nt) 4010 Summitview Ave Ste 200, Yakima WA 98908 **Phn:** 509-972-3461 **Fax:** 509-972-3540 newstalkkit.com daveettl@townsquaremedia.com

Yakima KMMG-FM (y) 706 Butterfield Rd, Yakima WA 98901 **Phn:** 509-457-1000 **Fax:** 509-452-0541

Yakima KQSN-FM (y) 4010 Summitview Ave Ste 200, Yakima WA 98908 **Phn:** 509-972-3461 **Fax:** 509-972-3540 www.lapreciosa.com

Yakima KRSE-FM (a) 1200 Chesterly Dr Ste 160, Yakima WA 98902 **Phn:** 509-248-2900 **Fax:** 509-452-9661 www.1057bobfm.com bob.fm@hotmail.com

Yakima KUSA-AM (t) 1200 Chesterly Dr Ste 160, Yakima WA 98902 **Phn:** 509-248-2900 **Fax:** 509-452-9661 talk980kusa.com deweyb@yakimaradiogroup.com

Yakima KUTI-AM (s) 4010 Summitview Ave, Yakima WA 98908 **Phn:** 509-972-3461 **Fax:** 509-972-3540 1460espnyakima.com mikebastinelli@townsquaremedia.com

Yakima KXDD-FM (c) 1200 Chesterly Dr Ste 160, Yakima WA 98902 **Phn:** 509-248-2900 **Fax:** 509-452-9661 www.1041kxdd.com

Yakima KYAK-AM (q) PO Box 130, Yakima WA 98907 **Phn:** 509-452-5925 www.kyak.com kyak@kyak.com

Yakima KYPL-FM (q) PO Box 9306, Yakima WA 98909 **Phn:** 509-527-2991 **Fax:** 509-527-2611 www.plr.org

Yakima KYXE-AM (y) PO Box 2888, Yakima WA 98907 **Phn:** 509-457-1000 **Fax:** 509-452-0541

Yakima KZTA-FM (y) PO Box 2888, Yakima WA 98907 **Phn:** 509-457-1000 **Fax:** 509-452-0541

Yakima KZTB-FM (y) 706 Butterfield Rd, Yakima WA 98901 **Phn:** 509-457-1000 **Fax:** 509-452-0541

Yakima KZTS-AM (y) PO Box 2888, Yakima WA 98907 **Phn:** 509-457-1000 **Fax:** 509-452-0541

WEST VIRGINIA

Beckley WAXS-FM (a) 306 S Kanawha St, Beckley WV 25801 **Phn:** 304-253-7000 **Fax:** 304-255-1044 www.groovy94.com

Beckley WCIR-FM (a) 306 S Kanawha St, Beckley WV 25801 **Phn:** 304-253-7000 **Fax:** 304-255-1044 www.103cir.com rickrizer@radiocitywv.com

Beckley WIWS-AM (o) 306 S Kanawha St, Beckley WV 25801 **Phn:** 304-253-7000 **Fax:** 304-255-1044 rickrizer@radiocitywv.com

Beckley WJLS-AM (g) PO Box 5499, Beckley WV 25801 **Phn:** 304-253-7311 **Fax:** 304-253-3466 www.wjls.com jeffreyjoe@wjls.com

Beckley WJLS-FM (c) PO Box 5499, Beckley WV 25801 **Phn:** 304-253-7311 **Fax:** 304-253-3466 www.wjls.com jeffreyjoe@wjls.com

Beckley WTNJ-FM (c) 306 S Kanawha St, Beckley WV 25801 **Phn:** 304-253-7000 **Fax:** 304-255-1044 www.wtnjfm.com jayq@radiocitywv.com

Beckley WWNR-AM (nt) 306 S Kanawha St, Beckley WV 25801 **Phn:** 304-253-7000 **Fax:** 304-255-1044 www.wwnrradio.com jayq@radiocitywv.com

Berkeley Springs WCST-AM (c) 440 Radio Station Ln, Berkeley Springs WV 25411 **Phn:** 304-258-1010 **Fax:** 304-258-1976 c929@comcast.net

Berkeley Springs WDHC-FM (c) 440 Radio Station Ln, Berkeley Springs WV 25411 **Phn:** 304-258-1010 **Fax:** 304-258-1976 www.wdhc.com

Bethany WVBC-FM (v) Campus Box 55, Bethany WV 26032 **Phn:** 304-829-7564 www.bethanywv.edu psutherl@bethanywv.edu

Bluefield WAMN-AM (s) PO Box 6350, Bluefield WV 24701 **Phn:** 304-327-9266 **Fax:** 304-325-8058

Bluefield WBDY-AM (s) 900 Bluefield Ave, Bluefield WV 24701 **Phn:** 304-327-7114 **Fax:** 304-325-7850 ken@adventureradio.com

Bluefield WHAJ-FM (a) 900 Bluefield Ave, Bluefield WV 24701 **Phn:** 304-327-7114 **Fax:** 304-325-7850 www.j1045.com ken@adventureradio.com

Bluefield WHIS-AM (nt) 900 Bluefield Ave, Bluefield WV 24701 **Phn:** 304-327-7114 **Fax:** 304-325-7850 www.whistalkradio.com

Bluefield WHKX-FM (c) 900 Bluefield Ave, Bluefield WV 24701 **Phn:** 304-325-2250 **Fax:** 304-325-7850 www.kickscountry.com joe@adventureradio.com

Bluefield WHQX-FM (c) 900 Bluefield Ave, Bluefield WV 24701 **Phn:** 304-325-2250 **Fax:** 304-325-7850 www.kickscountry.com joe@adventureradio.com

Bluefield WKEZ-AM (o) 900 Bluefield Ave, Bluefield WV 24701 **Phn:** 304-327-7114 **Fax:** 304-325-7850

Bluefield WKOY-FM (r) 900 Bluefield Ave, Bluefield WV 24701 **Phn:** 304-327-7114 **Fax:** 304-325-7850 www.theeaglefm.com brock@adventureradio.com

Bluefield WKQY-FM (o) 900 Bluefield Ave, Bluefield WV 24701 **Phn:** 304-327-7114 **Fax:** 304-325-7850 www.theeaglefm.com brock@adventureradio.com

Bluefield WTZE-AM (nt) 900 Bluefield Ave, Bluefield WV 24701 **Phn:** 304-327-7114 **Fax:** 304-325-7850

Bluefield WWYO-AM (cm) PO Box 647, Bluefield WV 24701 **Phn:** 304-327-5651

Bridgeport WDCI-FM (a) PO Box 360, Bridgeport WV 26330 **Phn:** 304-848-5000 **Fax:** 304-842-7501 joliverio@wdtv.com

Buckhannon WBTQ-FM (a) 189 Wbuc Rd, Buckhannon WV 26201 **Phn:** 304-636-1300 **Fax:** 304-472-1528 www.935btq.com rhenline@wvradio.com

Buckhannon WVWC-FM (vr) 59 College Ave, Buckhannon WV 26201 **Phn:** 304-473-8292 **Fax:** 304-472-2571 www.wvwc.educampusc92

Charleston WBES-AM (s) PO Box 871, Charleston WV 25323 **Phn:** 304-744-7020 **Fax:** 304-744-8562 news@wqbe.com

Charleston WCHS-AM (nt) 1111 Virginia St E, Charleston WV 25301 **Phn:** 304-342-8131 **Fax:** 304-344-4745 www.58wchs.com jjenkins@wvradio.com

Charleston WKAZ-FM (o) 1111 Virginia St E, Charleston WV 25301 **Phn:** 304-342-8131 **Fax:** 304-344-4745 www.1073jackfm.com

Charleston WKAZ-AM (g) 1111 Virginia St E, Charleston WV 25301 **Phn:** 304-342-8131 **Fax:** 304-344-4745

Charleston WKWS-FM (c) 1111 Virginia St E, Charleston WV 25301 **Phn:** 304-342-8131 **Fax:** 304-344-4745 www.961thewolf.com janthony@wvradio.com

Charleston WQBE-FM (c) PO Box 871, Charleston WV 25323 **Phn:** 304-744-7020 **Fax:** 304-744-8562 www.wqbe.com news@wqbe.com

Charleston WRVZ-FM (h) 1111 Virginia St E, Charleston WV 25301 **Phn:** 304-342-8131 **Fax:** 304-344-4745 www.987thebeat.com wwoods@wvradio.com

Charleston WSWW-FM (st) 1111 Virginia St E, Charleston WV 25301 **Phn:** 304-342-8131 **Fax:** 304-344-4745 www.3ws957.com

WEST VIRGINIA RADIO STATIONS

Charleston WVAF-FM (a) 1111 Virginia St E, Charleston WV 25301 **Phn:** 304-342-8131 **Fax:** 304-344-4745 www.v100.fm jk@wvradio.com

Charleston WVPN-FM (plnj) 600 Capitol St, Charleston WV 25301 **Phn:** 304-556-4900 **Fax:** 304-556-4960

Charleston WVSR-FM (h) PO Box 871, Charleston WV 25323 **Phn:** 304-744-7020 **Fax:** 304-744-8562 www.electric102.com wade@electric102.com

Charleston WVTS-FM (nt) 4250 Washington St W, Charleston WV 25313 **Phn:** 304-744-7020 **Fax:** 304-744-8562

Charleston WVTS-AM (nt) PO Box 871, Charleston WV 25323 **Phn:** 304-744-7020 **Fax:** 304-744-8562 dave@wqbe.com

Dunmore WVMR-AM (vc) RR 1 Box 139, Dunmore WV 24934 **Phn:** 304-799-6004 **Fax:** 304-799-7444 www.alleghenymountainradio.org ewamr@frontier.com

Elkins WBUC-AM (t) PO Box 1337, Elkins WV 26241 **Phn:** 304-636-1300 **Fax:** 304-636-2200

Elkins WDNE-AM (c) PO Box 1337, Elkins WV 26241 **Phn:** 304-636-1300 **Fax:** 304-636-2200 wdne@wvradio.com

Elkins WDNE-FM (c) PO Box 1337, Elkins WV 26241 **Phn:** 304-636-1300 **Fax:** 304-636-2200 wdnefm.com wdne@wvradio.com

Elkins WELK-FM (a) 228 Randolph Ave, Elkins WV 26241 **Phn:** 304-636-8800 **Fax:** 304-636-8801 947welk.com

Fairmont WGIE-FM (c) 1489 Locust Ave Ste D, Fairmont WV 26554 **Phn:** 304-367-0823 **Fax:** 304-367-1885 www.froggycountry.net laura@froggycountry.net

Fairmont WGYE-FM (c) 1489 Locust Ave Ste C, Fairmont WV 26554 **Phn:** 304-363-8888 **Fax:** 304-367-1885 www.froggycountry.net laura@froggycountry.net

Fairmont WMMN-AM (snt) 450 Leonard Ave, Fairmont WV 26554 **Phn:** 304-366-3700 **Fax:** 304-366-3706 www.920wmmn.com

Fairmont WOBG-AM (am) 1489 Locust Ave Ste D, Fairmont WV 26554 **Phn:** 304-367-0823 **Fax:** 304-367-1885 froggycountry.net laura@froggycountry.net

Fairmont WOBG-FM (sr) 1489 Locust Ave Ste D, Fairmont WV 26554 **Phn:** 304-367-0823 **Fax:** 304-367-1885 froggycountry.wix.com laura@froggycountry.net

Fairmont WPDX-FM (c) 59 Mountain Park Dr, Fairmont WV 26554 **Phn:** 304-624-6425 **Fax:** 304-363-3852

Fairmont WPDX-AM (gc) 59 Mountain Park Dr, Fairmont WV 26554 **Phn:** 304-363-3851 **Fax:** 304-363-3852

Fairmont WRLF-FM (r) 450 Leonard Ave, Fairmont WV 26554 **Phn:** 304-366-3700 **Fax:** 304-366-3706 nlfantasia@wrlf.com

Fairmont WTCS-AM (nt) PO Box 1549, Fairmont WV 26555 **Phn:** 304-366-3700 **Fax:** 304-366-3706 nlfantasia@wrlf.com

Fairmont WXKX-AM (s) 1489 Locust Ave Ste D, Fairmont WV 26554 **Phn:** 304-624-1400 **Fax:** 304-624-1402 laura@froggycountry.net

Fairmont WZST-FM (a) 450 Leonard Ave, Fairmont WV 26554 **Phn:** 304-366-3700 **Fax:** 304-366-3706 nlfantasia@wrlf.com

Fisher WELD-FM (c) 126 Kessel Rd, Fisher WV 26818 **Phn:** 304-538-6062 **Fax:** 304-538-7032

Fisher WELD-AM (c) 126 Kessel Rd, Fisher WV 26818 **Phn:** 304-538-6062 **Fax:** 304-538-7032 weld@hardynet.com

Grafton WLOL-FM (q) PO Box 2, Grafton WV 26354 **Phn:** 304-265-2200 www.lolradio.org info@lolradio.org

Grafton WVUS-AM (q) PO Box 2, Grafton WV 26354 **Phn:** 304-265-2200 www.lolradio.org info@lolradio.org

Hinton WMTD-FM (r) PO Box 1000, Hinton WV 25951 **Phn:** 304-253-7000 **Fax:** 304-255-1044 www.radioam1380.com shane.boone@radioam1380.com

Hinton WMTD-AM (r) PO Box 1000, Hinton WV 25951 **Phn:** 304-253-7000 **Fax:** 304-255-1044 www.radioam1380.com shane.boone@radioam1380.com

Huntington WAMX-FM (r) 134 4th Ave, Huntington WV 25701 **Phn:** 304-525-7788 **Fax:** 304-525-3299 www.1063thebrew.com x1063@x1063.com

Huntington WBVB-FM (o) 134 4th Ave, Huntington WV 25701 **Phn:** 304-525-7788 **Fax:** 304-525-3299 www.oldies971.com b97fm@clearchannel.com

Huntington WCMI-AM (s) PO Box 1150, Huntington WV 25713 **Phn:** 304-523-8401 **Fax:** 304-523-4848

Huntington WCMI-FM (r) PO Box 1150, Huntington WV 25713 **Phn:** 304-523-8401 **Fax:** 304-523-4848 www.planet927.com reeves@kindredcom.net

Huntington WDGG-FM (c) PO Box 1150, Huntington WV 25713 **Phn:** 304-523-8401 **Fax:** 304-523-4848 www.937thedawg.com studio@937thedawg.com

Huntington WEMM-FM (g) 703 3rd Ave, Huntington WV 25701 **Phn:** 304-525-5141 **Fax:** 304-525-0748 www.wemmfm.com

Huntington WIRO-AM (nt) 134 4th Ave, Huntington WV 25701 **Phn:** 304-525-7788 **Fax:** 304-525-7861 www.800wvhu.com news@800wvhu.com

Huntington WKEE-FM (a) 134 4th Ave, Huntington WV 25701 **Phn:** 304-525-7788 **Fax:** 304-525-3299 www.kee100.com jimdavis@clearchannel.com

Huntington WLRX-FM (ua) 134 4th Ave, Huntington WV 25701 **Phn:** 304-525-7788 **Fax:** 304-525-7861 judycornett@clearchannel.com

Huntington WMEJ-FM (q) PO Box 7575, Huntington WV 25777 **Phn:** 740-867-5333

Huntington WMGA-FM (a) 555 5th Ave #K, Huntington WV 25701 **Phn:** 304-523-8401 **Fax:** 304-523-4848 www.hits979.com studio@hits979.com

Huntington WMUL-FM (vp) 1 John Marshall Dr, Huntington WV 25755 **Phn:** 304-696-6640 **Fax:** 304-696-3232 www.marshall.eduwmul wmulnews@gmail.com

Huntington WRVC-AM (snt) PO Box 1150, Huntington WV 25713 **Phn:** 304-523-8401 **Fax:** 304-523-4848 www.supertalk941.com studio@huntingtonsupertalk.com

Huntington WRWB-AM (g) 703 3rd Ave, Huntington WV 25701 **Phn:** 304-525-5141 **Fax:** 304-525-0748

Huntington WTCR-FM (c) 134 4th Ave, Huntington WV 25701 **Phn:** 304-525-7788 **Fax:** 304-525-6281 www.wtcr.com judyeaton@clearchannel.com

Huntington WTCR-AM (s) 134 4th Ave, Huntington WV 25701 **Phn:** 304-525-7788 **Fax:** 304-525-3299 www.foxsports1420.com jim.davis@clearchannel.com

Huntington WVHU-AM (nt) 134 4th Ave, Huntington WV 25701 **Phn:** 304-525-7788 **Fax:** 304-525-7861 www.800wvhu.com

Huntington WXBW-FM (c) 555 5th Ave # K, Huntington WV 25701 **Phn:** 304-523-8401 **Fax:** 304-523-8045 www.bigbuck1015.com

Kingwood WFSP-AM (g) PO Box 567, Kingwood WV 26537 **Phn:** 304-329-1780 **Fax:** 304-329-1781 www.prestoncounty.comwfsp wfsp@wvdsl.net

Kingwood WFSP-FM (am) PO Box 567, Kingwood WV 26537 **Phn:** 304-329-1780 **Fax:** 304-329-1781 www.prestoncounty.comwfsp wfsp@wvdsl.net

Kingwood WKMM-FM (c) 106 E Main St, Kingwood WV 26537 **Phn:** 304-329-0967 **Fax:** 304-329-2131 www.wkmmfm.com wkmmfm@yahoo.com

Lewisburg WRLB-FM (g) PO Box 1727, Lewisburg WV 24901 **Phn:** 304-647-3606 radiogreenbrier.com awilliams@wron.net

Logan WVOW-AM (a) 204 Main St Ste 201, Logan WV 25601 **Phn:** 304-752-5080 **Fax:** 304-752-5711

Logan WVOW-FM (a) 204 Main St Ste 201, Logan WV 25601 **Phn:** 304-752-5080 **Fax:** 304-752-5711

Martinsburg WEPM-AM (s) 1606 W King St, Martinsburg WV 25401 **Phn:** 304-263-8868 **Fax:** 304-263-8906 wepm.com greg@prettymanbroadcasting.com

Martinsburg WICL-FM (c) 1606 W King St, Martinsburg WV 25401 **Phn:** 304-263-8868 **Fax:** 304-263-8906 www.bigdawgfm.com marc@prettymanbroadcasting.com

Martinsburg WLTF-FM (z) 1606 W King St, Martinsburg WV 25401 **Phn:** 304-263-8868 **Fax:** 304-263-8906 www.lite975.com mikem@prettymanbroadcasting.com

Martinsburg WRNR-AM (snt) PO Box 709, Martinsburg WV 25402 **Phn:** 304-263-6586 **Fax:** 304-263-3082 www.talkradiowrnr.com info@talkradiowrnr.com

Morgantown WAJR-FM (nt) 1251 Earl L Core Rd, Morgantown WV 26505 **Phn:** 304-296-0029 **Fax:** 304-296-3876 www.wajr.com wajr@wvradio.com

Morgantown WAJR-AM (snt) 1251 Earl L Core Rd, Morgantown WV 26505 **Phn:** 304-296-0029 **Fax:** 304-296-3876 www.wajr.com wajr@wvradio.com

Morgantown WCLG-FM (r) PO Box 885, Morgantown WV 26507 **Phn:** 304-292-2222 **Fax:** 304-291-1111 www.wclg.com

Morgantown WCLG-AM (o) PO Box 885, Morgantown WV 26507 **Phn:** 304-292-2222 **Fax:** 304-291-1111 www.wclg.com

Morgantown WKKW-FM (c) 1251 Earl L Core Rd, Morgantown WV 26505 **Phn:** 304-296-0029 **Fax:** 304-296-3876 www.wkkwfm.com nzsprts@aol.com

Morgantown WVAQ-FM (h) 1251 Earl L Core Rd, Morgantown WV 26505 **Phn:** 304-296-0029 **Fax:** 304-296-3876 www.wvaq.com lneff@wvradio.com

Morgantown WWVU-FM (v) PO Box 6446, Morgantown WV 26506 **Phn:** 304-293-3329 **Fax:** 304-293-7363 u92.wvu.edu kharriso@wvu.edu

Moundsville WRKP-FM (q) 2002 1st St, Moundsville WV 26041 **Phn:** 304-845-1052 **Fax:** 304-845-1054

Mount Clare WBRB-FM (c) 1065 Radio Park Dr, Mount Clare WV 26408 **Phn:** 304-623-6546 **Fax:** 304-623-6547 www.1013thebear.com tjones@wvradio.com

Mount Clare WFBY-FM (r) 1065 Radio Park Dr, Mount Clare WV 26408 **Phn:** 304-623-6546 **Fax:** 304-623-6547 www.wfby.com metronews@aol.com

Mount Clare WWLW-FM (a) 1065 Radio Park Dr, Mount Clare WV 26408 **Phn:** 304-623-6546 **Fax:** 304-623-6547 www.wvmagic.com

New Martinsville WETZ-FM (c) PO Box 10, New Martinsville WV 26155 **Phn:** 304-455-1111 **Fax:** 304-455-6170

New Martinsville WETZ-AM (snt) PO Box 10, New Martinsville WV 26155 **Phn:** 304-455-1111 **Fax:** 304-455-1170

New Martinsville WYMJ-FM (o) PO Box 10, New Martinsville WV 26155 **Phn:** 304-455-1111 **Fax:** 304-455-6170

Oak Hill WOAY-AM (q) 240 Central Ave, Oak Hill WV 25901 **Phn:** 304-465-0534 **Fax:** 304-465-1486 www.woayradio.com info@woayradio.com

Parkersburg WADC-AM (am) 5 Rosemar Cir, Parkersburg WV 26104 **Phn:** 304-485-4565 **Fax:** 304-424-6955

Parkersburg WGGE-FM (c) 5 Rosemar Cir, Parkersburg WV 26104 **Phn:** 304-485-4565 **Fax:** 304-424-6955 froggy99.net

Parkersburg WHBR-FM (r) 5 Rosemar Cir, Parkersburg WV 26104 **Phn:** 304-485-4565 **Fax:** 304-424-6955 www.thebearrocks.net bigric@resultsradiowv.com

Parkersburg WRZZ-FM (r) 5 Rosemar Cir, Parkersburg WV 26104 **Phn:** 304-485-4565 **Fax:** 304-424-6955 z106.net bigric@resultsradiowv.com

Parkersburg WVNT-AM (m) 5 Rosemar Cir, Parkersburg WV 26104 **Phn:** 304-485-4565 **Fax:** 304-424-6955 bguthrie@resultsradiowv.com

Parkersburg WXIL-FM (h) 5 Rosemar Cir, Parkersburg WV 26104 **Phn:** 304-485-4565 **Fax:** 304-424-6955 95xil.com requests@95xil.com

Petersburg WQWV-FM (a) PO Box 55, Petersburg WV 26847 **Phn:** 304-257-4432 **Fax:** 304-257-9733

Philippi WQAB-FM (vha) PO Box 2097, Philippi WV 26416 **Phn:** 304-457-6271 **Fax:** 304-457-6367 www.ab.eduperforming_artswqab

Point Pleasant WBGS-AM (g) 303 8th St, Point Pleasant WV 25550 **Phn:** 304-675-2763 **Fax:** 304-675-2771 production@wbyg.com

Point Pleasant WBYG-FM (c) 303 8th St, Point Pleasant WV 25550 **Phn:** 304-675-2763 www.wbyg.com wbyg@wbyg.com

Princeton WAEY-AM (g) PO Box 5588, Princeton WV 24740 **Phn:** 304-425-2151 **Fax:** 304-487-2016

Princeton WSTG-FM (a) PO Box 5588, Princeton WV 24740 **Phn:** 304-425-2151 **Fax:** 304-487-2016 www.star95.com

Rainelle WRRL-AM (gnt) 507 Main St, Rainelle WV 25962 **Phn:** 304-438-8537

Ripley WCEF-FM (c) PO Box 798, Ripley WV 25271 **Phn:** 304-372-9800 **Fax:** 304-372-9811 www.c98.com studio@thebull983.com

Romney WVSB-FM (vc) 301 E Main St, Romney WV 26757 **Phn:** 304-822-4838 **Fax:** 304-822-4896 gpark@access.k12.wv.us

Roncecerte WKCJ-FM (h) 276 Seneca Trl, Roncecerte WV 24970 **Phn:** 304-645-1400 **Fax:** 304-647-4802 www.wron.comWKCJ radio@wron.net

Roncecerte WRON-FM (c) 276 Seneca Trl, Roncecerte WV 24970 **Phn:** 304-645-1400 **Fax:** 304-647-4802 www.wron.com radio@wron.net

Roncecerte WRON-AM (nt) 276 Seneca Trl, Roncecerte WV 24970 **Phn:** 304-645-1400 **Fax:** 304-647-4802 www.wron.com mkidd@wron.net

Roncecerte WSLW-AM (a) 276 Seneca Trl, Roncecerte WV 24970 **Phn:** 304-645-1400 **Fax:** 304-647-4802 www.wron.comWSLW radio@wron.net

Rupert WYKM-AM (cg) PO Box 627, Rupert WV 25984 **Phn:** 304-392-6003 **Fax:** 304-392-5352

WEST VIRGINIA RADIO STATIONS

Saint Albans WJYP-AM (q) 100 Kanawha Ter, Saint Albans WV 25177 **Phn:** 304-722-3308 **Fax:** 304-727-1300

Saint Albans WKLC-FM (r) 100 Kanawha Ter, Saint Albans WV 25177 **Phn:** 304-722-3308 **Fax:** 304-727-1300 www.wklc.com krisbrown@wklc.com

Saint Albans WMXE-FM (h) 100 Kanawha Ter, Saint Albans WV 25177 **Phn:** 304-722-3308 **Fax:** 304-727-1300 www.wmxe.net mixstudio@wmxe.net

Saint Albans WSCW-AM (c) 100 Kanawha Ter, Saint Albans WV 25177 **Phn:** 304-722-3308 **Fax:** 304-727-1300 classiccountry1410.com

Saint Marys WRRR-FM (a) PO Box 374, Saint Marys WV 26170 **Phn:** 304-684-3400 **Fax:** 304-684-9241 www.hitsandfavorites.com samyoho@literock93r.com

Saint Marys WXCR-FM (r) PO Box 374, Saint Marys WV 26170 **Phn:** 304-684-3400 **Fax:** 304-684-9241 samyoho@literock93r.com

Shepherdstown WSHC-FM (vr) PO Box 5000, Shepherdstown WV 25443 **Phn:** 304-876-5134 **Fax:** 304-876-5405 www.897wshc.org wshc@shepherd.edu

Spencer WVRC-AM (g) PO Box 622, Spencer WV 25276 **Phn:** 304-927-3760 **Fax:** 304-927-2877 larry@wvrcfm.com

Spencer WVRC-FM (c) PO Box 622, Spencer WV 25276 **Phn:** 304-927-3760 **Fax:** 304-927-2877 www.wvrcfm.com contact@wvrcfm.com

Summersville WCWV-FM (a) 713 Main St, Summersville WV 26651 **Phn:** 304-872-5202 **Fax:** 304-872-6904 www.wcwv929.com wcwv@wcwv929.com

Sutton WAFD-FM (cg) 180 Main St, Sutton WV 26601 **Phn:** 304-765-7373 **Fax:** 304-765-7836 www.wafdfm.com lisa@summitmediawv.com

Sutton WDBS-FM (c) 180 Main St, Sutton WV 26601 **Phn:** 304-765-7373 **Fax:** 304-765-7836 www.theboss97fm.com info@theboss97fm.com

Sutton WKQV-FM (r) 180 Main St, Sutton WV 26601 **Phn:** 304-765-7373 **Fax:** 304-765-7836 www.105kqv.com mail@105kqv.com

Sutton WSGB-AM (h) 180 Main St, Sutton WV 26601 **Phn:** 304-765-7373 **Fax:** 304-765-7836 www.summitmediawv.com al@theboss97fm.com

Sutton WVAR-FM (h) 180 Main St, Sutton WV 26601 **Phn:** 304-765-7373 **Fax:** 304-765-7836 www.summitmediawv.com al@summitmediawv.com

Vienna WDMX-FM (o) PO Box 5559, Vienna WV 26105 **Phn:** 304-295-6070 **Fax:** 304-295-4389 www.mymix100.com

Vienna WHNK-AM (c) PO Box 5559, Vienna WV 26105 **Phn:** 304-295-6070 **Fax:** 304-295-4389 www.hank1450.com

Vienna WLTP-AM (snt) PO Box 5559, Vienna WV 26105 **Phn:** 304-295-6070 **Fax:** 304-295-4389 www.newstalk910wltp.com chuckpoet@clearchannel.com

Vienna WNUS-FM (c) PO Box 5559, Vienna WV 26105 **Phn:** 304-295-4389 **Fax:** 304-295-4389 www.107nus.com rodneyortiz@clearchannel.com

Vienna WRVB-FM (h) PO Box 5559, Vienna WV 26105 **Phn:** 304-295-6070 **Fax:** 304-295-4389 www.102theriver.com

Weirton WEIR-AM (nt) 2307 Pennsylvania Ave, Weirton WV 26062 **Phn:** 304-723-1444 **Fax:** 304-723-1688 weirsports.net jvavrek@1063theriver.com

Welch WELC-FM (a) 18385 Coal Heritage Rd, Welch WV 24801 **Phn:** 304-436-2131 **Fax:** 304-436-2132

Welch WELC-AM (a) 18385 Coal Heritage Rd, Welch WV 24801 **Phn:** 304-436-2131 **Fax:** 304-436-2132

West Liberty WGLZ-FM (vr) 208 University Dr CUB 143, West Liberty WV 26074 **Phn:** 304-336-8508 wglzradio.com wglz@westliberty.edu

Weston WHAW-AM (c) 300 Harrison Ave, Weston WV 26452 **Phn:** 304-269-5555 **Fax:** 304-269-4800 www.whawradio.com whaw@aol.com

Weston WOTR-FM (c) 301 Harrison Ave, Weston WV 26452 **Phn:** 304-269-5555 **Fax:** 304-269-4800 www.wotrfm.com info@wotrfm.com

Weston WVRW-FM (o) 303 Harrison Ave, Weston WV 26452 **Phn:** 304-462-7771 **Fax:** 304-269-4800 www.wvrwfm.com info@wvrwfm.com

Wheeling WBBD-AM (ob) 1015 Main St, Wheeling WV 26003 **Phn:** 304-232-1170 **Fax:** 304-234-0041 www.247comedy.com quinn@247comedy.com

Wheeling WEGW-FM (r) 1015 Main St, Wheeling WV 26003 **Phn:** 304-232-1170 **Fax:** 304-234-0041 www.eagle1075.com chadtyson@clearchannel.com

Wheeling WKKX-AM (s) 1201 Main St Ste 100, Wheeling WV 26003 **Phn:** 304-214-1610 **Fax:** 304-214-1609 eric@wkkx.com

Wheeling WKWK-FM (a) 1015 Main St, Wheeling WV 26003 **Phn:** 304-232-1170 **Fax:** 304-234-0041 www.mix973wheeling.com

Wheeling WOVK-FM (c) 1015 Main St, Wheeling WV 26003 **Phn:** 304-232-1170 **Fax:** 304-234-0041 www.wovk.com jimelliott@clearchannel.com

Wheeling WPHP-FM (v) 1976 Park View Rd, Wheeling WV 26003 **Phn:** 304-243-0410 **Fax:** 304-243-0449

Wheeling WVLY-AM (nt) 1143 Main St Ste 3, Wheeling WV 26003 **Phn:** 304-233-9859 **Fax:** 304-214-9859 wvly.net radiomonroe@aol.com

Wheeling WWVA-AM (nt) 1015 Main St, Wheeling WV 26003 **Phn:** 304-232-1170 **Fax:** 304-234-0041 www.newsradio1170.com chadtyson@clearchannel.com

Williamson WBTH-AM (snt) 31 E 2nd Ave, Williamson WV 25661 **Phn:** 304-235-3600 **Fax:** 304-235-8118

WISCONSIN

Altoona WAXX-FM (c) 944 Harlem St, Altoona WI 54720 **Phn:** 715-832-1530 **Fax:** 715-832-5329 www.todayswaxx1045.com

Altoona WAYY-AM (nt) 944 Harlem St, Altoona WI 54720 **Phn:** 715-832-1530 **Fax:** 715-832-5329 www.wayy790.com rickroberts@midwestfamilyec.com

Altoona WDRK-FM (ah) 944 Harlem St, Altoona WI 54720 **Phn:** 715-832-1530 **Fax:** 715-832-5329 www.bobfm999.com

Altoona WEAQ-AM (st) 944 Harlem St, Altoona WI 54720 **Phn:** 715-832-1530 **Fax:** 715-832-5329 www.espn1150.com rickroberts@midwestfamilyec.com

Altoona WECL-FM (r) 944 Harlem St, Altoona WI 54720 **Phn:** 715-832-1530 **Fax:** 715-832-5329 www.929thex.com

Altoona WIAL-FM (a) 944 Harlem St, Altoona WI 54720 **Phn:** 715-832-1530 **Fax:** 715-832-5329 www.i94online.com

Amery WXCE-AM (on) PO Box 1260, Amery WI 54001 **Phn:** 715-268-7185 **Fax:** 715-268-7187

Antigo WACD-FM (a) N2237 US Highway 45 S, Antigo WI 54409 **Phn:** 715-623-4124 **Fax:** 715-627-4497 www.country106.fm country106@gmail.com

WISCONSIN RADIO STATIONS

Antigo WATK-AM (c) N2237 US Highway 45 S, Antigo WI 54409 **Phn:** 715-623-4124 **Fax:** 715-627-4497 www.watkantigo.com duff@nrgnorthwoods.com

Appleton WAPL-FM (r) PO Box 1519, Appleton WI 54912 **Phn:** 920-734-9226 **Fax:** 920-739-0494 www.wapl.com waplstudio@wcinet.com

Appleton WEMI-FM (q) 1909 W 2nd St, Appleton WI 54914 **Phn:** 920-749-9456 **Fax:** 920-749-0474 www.thefamily.net

Appleton WEMY-FM (vq) 1909 W 2nd St, Appleton WI 54914 **Phn:** 920-749-9456 **Fax:** 920-749-0474 www.thefamily.net

Appleton WHBY-AM (nt) 2800 E College Ave, Appleton WI 54915 **Phn:** 920-734-9226 **Fax:** 920-739-0494 www.whby.com whbyam@wcinet.com

Appleton WKSZ-FM (h) PO Box 1519, Appleton WI 54912 **Phn:** 920-431-0959 **Fax:** 920-431-8490 www.959kissfm.com dkane@wcinet.com

Appleton WKZG-FM (a) 2800 E College Ave, Appleton WI 54915 **Phn:** 920-734-9226 **Fax:** 920-739-0494 mykzradio.com dkane@wcinet.com

Appleton WOZZ-FM (h) 1500 N Casaloma Dr Ste 301, Appleton WI 54913 **Phn:** 920-733-4990 **Fax:** 920-733-5507 93rockon.com webmaster.wozz@wozz.com

Appleton WROE-FM (a) 1500 N Casaloma Dr Ste 301, Appleton WI 54913 **Phn:** 920-733-4990 **Fax:** 920-733-0831 www.mwcradio.com webmaster@wroe.com

Appleton WSCO-AM (s) 00 E College Ave, Appleton WI 54915 **Phn:** 920-734-9226 **Fax:** 920-739-0494 www.am1570thescore.com gbell@wcinet.com

Appleton WZOR-FM (r) PO Box 1519, Appleton WI 54912 **Phn:** 920-734-9226 **Fax:** 920-739-0494 www.razor947.com razor@wcinet.com

Ashland WATW-AM (amo) PO Box 613, Ashland WI 54806 **Phn:** 715-682-2727 **Fax:** 715-682-9338 www.watwam.com sjaegergm@charter.net

Ashland WBSZ-FM (c) 2320 Ellis Ave, Ashland WI 54806 **Phn:** 715-682-2727 **Fax:** 715-682-9338 www.wbszfm.com skiphunter@charter.net

Ashland WJJH-FM (r) PO Box 613, Ashland WI 54806 **Phn:** 715-682-2727 **Fax:** 715-682-9338 www.wjjhfm.com sjaegergm@charter.net

Ashland WNXR-FM (o) PO Box 613, Ashland WI 54806 **Phn:** 715-372-5400 **Fax:** 715-682-9338 www.wnxrfm.com kzinnecker@heartlandcomm.com

Baraboo WRPQ-AM (a) PO Box 456, Baraboo WI 53913 **Phn:** 608-356-3974 **Fax:** 608-355-9952 www.wrpq.com jeffsmith@wrpq.com

Beaver Dam WBEV-AM (at) 100 Stoddart St, Beaver Dam WI 53916 **Phn:** 920-885-4442 **Fax:** 920-885-2152 www.wbevradio.com

Beaver Dam WTLX-FM (s) 100 Stoddart St, Beaver Dam WI 53916 **Phn:** 608-245-9859 **Fax:** 920-885-2152 www.espnmadison.com jrutledge@espnmadison.com

Beaver Dam WXRO-FM (c) 100 Stoddart St, Beaver Dam WI 53916 **Phn:** 920-885-4442 **Fax:** 920-885-2152 www.wxroradio.com

Beloit WBCR-FM (v) 700 College St, Beloit WI 53511 **Phn:** 608-363-2402 **Fax:** 608-363-2718 www.beloit.eduwbcr wbcrfm@gmail.com

Beloit WGEZ-AM (o) PO Box 416, Beloit WI 53512 **Phn:** 608-365-8865 **Fax:** 608-365-8867 www.1490trueoldies.com wgezam@hotmail.com

Berlin WISS-AM (c) PO Box 71, Berlin WI 54923 **Phn:** 920-361-3551 **Fax:** 866-594-4698 www.wissradio.com tboyson@wissradio.com

Black River Falls WWIS-FM (a) W11573 Town Creek Rd, Black River Falls WI 54615 **Phn:** 715-284-4391 **Fax:** 715-284-9740 www.wwisradio.com gabby@wwisradio.com

Black River Falls WWIS-AM (ot) W11573 Town Creek Rd, Black River Falls WI 54615 **Phn:** 715-284-4391 **Fax:** 715-284-9740 www.wwisradio.com wwis@wwisradio.com

Chippewa Falls WCFW-FM (a) 318 Well St, Chippewa Falls WI 54729 **Phn:** 715-723-2257 **Fax:** 715-723-8276

Chippewa Falls WOGO-AM (q) 2396 Hallie Rd Ste 1, Chippewa Falls WI 54729 **Phn:** 715-723-1037 **Fax:** 715-723-1348 www.wogo.com mhalvo@wwib.com

Chippewa Falls WWIB-FM (a) 2396 Hallie Rd Ste 1, Chippewa Falls WI 54729 **Phn:** 715-723-1037 **Fax:** 715-723-1348 www.wwib.com wwib@wwib.com

Cleveland WLKN-FM (a) PO Box 26, Cleveland WI 53015 **Phn:** 920-693-3103 **Fax:** 920-693-3104 www.wlkn.com wlkn@wlkn.com

Denmark WGBW-AM (on) PO Box 100, Denmark WI 54208 **Phn:** 920-863-1234 **Fax:** 920-863-2710 wgbw@lsol.net

Dodgeville WDMP-FM (c) PO Box 9, Dodgeville WI 53533 **Phn:** 608-935-2302 **Fax:** 608-935-3464 www.d99point3.com kreinicke@charter.net

Dodgeville WDMP-AM (c) PO Box 9, Dodgeville WI 53533 **Phn:** 608-935-2302 **Fax:** 608-935-3464 www.d99point3.com hadz1@excite.com

Eagle River WERL-AM (nt) PO Box 309, Eagle River WI 54521 **Phn:** 715-479-4451 **Fax:** 715-479-6511 www.werlam.com

Eagle River WRJO-FM (or) PO Box 309, Eagle River WI 54521 **Phn:** 715-479-4451 **Fax:** 715-479-6511 www.wrjo.com lynnw@wrjo.com

Eau Claire WATQ-FM (c) 619 Cameron St, Eau Claire WI 54703 **Phn:** 715-830-4000 **Fax:** 715-835-9680 www.moose106.com jarejordan@clearchannel.com

Eau Claire WBIZ-FM (h) 619 Cameron St, Eau Claire WI 54703 **Phn:** 715-830-4000 **Fax:** 715-835-9680 www.z100radio.com keithedwards@clearchannel.com

Eau Claire WBIZ-AM (s) 619 Cameron St, Eau Claire WI 54703 **Phn:** 715-830-4000 **Fax:** 715-835-9680 www.sportsradio1400.com keithedwards@clearchannel.com

Eau Claire WDVM-AM (q) 1752 Brackett Ave, Eau Claire WI 54701 **Phn:** 715-855-1439 **Fax:** 715-855-1471 www.relevantradio.com info@relevantradio.com

Eau Claire WHEM-FM (q) 228 E Lowes Creek Rd, Eau Claire WI 54701 **Phn:** 715-838-9595 www.whem.com whem@whem.com

Eau Claire WISM-FM (a) 619 Cameron St, Eau Claire WI 54703 **Phn:** 715-830-4000 **Fax:** 715-835-9680 www.mix98online.com keithedwards@clearchannel.com

Eau Claire WMEQ-AM (nt) 619 Cameron St, Eau Claire WI 54703 **Phn:** 715-830-4000 **Fax:** 715-835-9680 www.wmeq.com keithedwards@clearchannel.com

Eau Claire WMEQ-FM (r) 619 Cameron St, Eau Claire WI 54703 **Phn:** 715-830-4000 **Fax:** 715-835-9680 www.rock921.com jarejordan@clearchannel.com

Eau Claire WQRB-FM (c) 619 Cameron St, Eau Claire WI 54703 **Phn:** 715-830-4000 **Fax:** 715-835-9680 www.b95radio.com mikemckay@clearchannel.com

Eau Claire WUEC-FM (plnj) 1221 W Clairemont Ave, Eau Claire WI 54701 **Phn:** 715-839-3868 www.wpr.org kallenbach@wpr.org

Fitchburg WIBA-AM (nt) 2651 S Fish Hatchery Rd, Fitchburg WI 53711 **Phn:** 608-274-5450 **Fax:** 608-274-5521 www.wiba.com timscott@clearchannel.com

Fitchburg WMAD-FM (c) 2651 S Fish Hatchery Rd, Fitchburg WI 53711 **Phn:** 608-274-5450 **Fax:** 608-274-5521 www.wmad.com

Fond Du Lac KFIZ-AM (nmt) 254 Winnebago Dr, Fond Du Lac WI 54935 **Phn:** 920-921-1071 **Fax:** 920-921-0757 kfiz.com info@kfiz.com

Fond du Lac WCLB-AM (s) 254 Winnebago Dr, Fond du Lac WI 54935 **Phn:** 920-921-1071 950thegame.com wbates@mdogmedia.com

Fond Du Lac WFDL-FM (a) 210 S Main St, Fond Du Lac WI 54935 **Phn:** 920-924-9697 **Fax:** 920-929-8865 www.wfdl.com wheels@wfdl.com

Fond Du Lac WFON-FM (a) 254 Winnebago Dr, Fond Du Lac WI 54935 **Phn:** 920-921-1071 **Fax:** 920-921-0757 www.k107.com

Fond du Lac WMBE-AM (s) 254 Winnebago Dr, Fond du Lac WI 54935 **Phn:** 920-921-1071 **Fax:** 920-921-0757 www.950thegame.com wbates@mdogmedia.com

Fond du Lac WTCX-FM (r) 210 S Main St, Fond du Lac WI 54935 **Phn:** 920-924-9697 **Fax:** 920-929-8865 www.961tcx.com owens@wtcx.com

Fort Atkinson WFAW-AM (ot) PO Box 94, Fort Atkinson WI 53538 **Phn:** 920-563-9329 **Fax:** 920-563-0315 www.940wfaw.com jvriezen@nrgmedia.com

Fort Atkinson WKCH-FM (h) PO Box 94, Fort Atkinson WI 53538 **Phn:** 262-473-9524 **Fax:** 920-563-0315 suntz@nrgmedia.com

Friendship WDKM-FM (c) 408 Hillwood Ln, Friendship WI 53934 **Phn:** 608-339-3221 **Fax:** 608-339-2403 wdkmfm.com news@wdkmfm.com

Green Bay WAUN-FM (r) 1221 Bellevue St, Green Bay WI 54302 **Phn:** 920-388-9286 **Fax:** 920-818-0263 rick@magnumbroadcasting.com

Green Bay WDUZ-AM (s) 810 Victoria St, Green Bay WI 54302 **Phn:** 920-468-4100 **Fax:** 920-468-0250 www.thefan1075.com thefan@cumulus.com

Green Bay WDUZ-FM (st) 810 Victoria St, Green Bay WI 54302 **Phn:** 920-468-4100 **Fax:** 920-468-0250 www.thefan1075.com

Green Bay WHID-FM (p) 2420 Nicolet Dr, Green Bay WI 54311 **Phn:** 920-465-2444 **Fax:** 920-465-2576 www.wpr.org reyer@wpr.org

Green Bay WIXX-FM (h) PO Box 23333, Green Bay WI 54305 **Phn:** 920-435-3771 www.wixx.com

Green Bay WJOK-AM (q) 1496 Bellevue St Ste 201, Green Bay WI 54311 **Phn:** 877-291-0123 **Fax:** 920-884-3170 www.relevantradio.com info@relevantradio.com

Green Bay WNCY-FM (c) PO Box 23333, Green Bay WI 54305 **Phn:** 920-435-3771 **Fax:** 920-444-1155 www.wncy.com duke@mwcradio.com

Green Bay WNFL-AM (nt) PO Box 23333, Green Bay WI 54305 **Phn:** 920-435-3771 **Fax:** 920-455-1155 www.wnflam.com nick.vitrano@mwcradio.com

Green Bay WOGB-FM (o) 810 Victoria St, Green Bay WI 54302 **Phn:** 920-468-4100 **Fax:** 920-468-0250 www.wogb.fm wogb@cumulus.com

Green Bay WORQ-FM (vr) 1075 Brookwood Dr # 2C, Green Bay WI 54304 **Phn:** 920-494-9010 **Fax:** 920-494-7602 www.q90fm.com gm@q90fm.com

Green Bay WPCK-FM (c) 810 Victoria St, Green Bay WI 54302 **Phn:** 920-468-4100 **Fax:** 920-236-4240 www.kicks1049.com

WISCONSIN RADIO STATIONS

Green Bay WQLH-FM (h) 810 Victoria St, Green Bay WI 54302 **Phn:** 920-468-4100 **Fax:** 920-468-0250 www.star98.net jimmy.clark@cumulus.com

Green Bay WRQE-FM (a) PO Box 23333, Green Bay WI 54305 **Phn:** 920-435-3771 **Fax:** 920-444-1155

Green Bay WTAQ-AM (n) PO Box 23333, Green Bay WI 54305 **Phn:** 920-435-3771 **Fax:** 920-444-1155 www.wtaq.com robert.kennedy@wtaq.com

Green Bay WZBY-FM (h) PO Box 23333, Green Bay WI 54305 **Phn:** 920-435-3771 **Fax:** 920-444-1155

Greenfield WISN-AM (nt) 12100 W Howard Ave, Greenfield WI 53228 **Phn:** 414-545-8900 **Fax:** 414-944-5484 www.newstalk1130.com kenherrera@clearchannel.com

Greenfield WKKV-FM (wu) 12100 W Howard Ave, Greenfield WI 53228 **Phn:** 414-321-1007 **Fax:** 414-546-9654 www.v100.com

Greenfield WMIL-FM (c) 12100 W Howard Ave, Greenfield WI 53228 **Phn:** 414-545-8900 **Fax:** 414-327-3200 www.fm106.com scottdolphin@clearchannel.com

Greenfield WOKY-AM (ma) 12100 W Howard Ave, Greenfield WI 53228 **Phn:** 414-545-5920 **Fax:** 414-546-9654 www.am920thewolf.com gregoryjon@clearchannel.com

Greenfield WRIT-FM (o) 12100 W Howard Ave, Greenfield WI 53228 **Phn:** 414-545-8900 **Fax:** 414-546-9654 www.milwaukeeoldies.com daveadams@clearchannel.com

Greenfield WRNW-FM (h) 12100 W Howard Ave, Greenfield WI 53228 **Phn:** 414-545-8900 **Fax:** 414-546-9654 www.973radionow.com daveadams@clearchannel.com

Hales Corners WMYX-FM (a) 11800 W Grange Ave, Hales Corners WI 53130 **Phn:** 414-529-1250 **Fax:** 414-529-2122 www.991themix.com jmorales@entercom.com

Hales Corners WSSP-AM (q) 11800 W Grange Ave, Hales Corners WI 53130 **Phn:** 414-529-1250 **Fax:** 414-529-2122 www.sportsradio1250.com tparker@entercom.com

Hales Corners WXSS-FM (h) 11800 W Grange Ave, Hales Corners WI 53130 **Phn:** 414-529-1250 **Fax:** 414-529-2122 www.1037kissfm.com bkelly@entercom.com

Hartford WTKM-FM (c) PO Box 270526, Hartford WI 53027 **Phn:** 262-673-3550 **Fax:** 262-673-5472 www.wtkm.com wtkm@nconnect.net

Hartford WTKM-AM (o) PO Box 270526, Hartford WI 53027 **Phn:** 262-673-3550 **Fax:** 262-673-5472 www.wtkmradio.com wtkm@nconnect.net

Hayward WHSM-FM (a) 16880 W US Highway 63, Hayward WI 54843 **Phn:** 715-634-4836 **Fax:** 715-634-8256 www.whsm.com radio@whsm.com

Hayward WHSM-AM (a) 16880 W US Highway 63, Hayward WI 54843 **Phn:** 715-634-4836 **Fax:** 715-634-8256 www.whsm.com radio@whsm.com

Hayward WRLS-FM (a) PO Box 1008, Hayward WI 54843 **Phn:** 715-634-4871 **Fax:** 715-634-3025 www.wrlsfm.com skaner@cheqnet.net

Ironwood WHRY-AM (o) 209 Harrison St, Ironwood WI 49938 **Phn:** 906-932-5234 **Fax:** 906-932-1548 https:www.facebook.comWUPMRadio wupm@wupm-whry.com

Janesville WCLO-AM (nt) PO Box 5001, Janesville WI 53547 **Phn:** 608-752-7895 **Fax:** 608-752-4438 www.wclo.com programming@wclo.com

Janesville WJVL-FM (c) PO Box 5001, Janesville WI 53547 **Phn:** 608-752-7895 **Fax:** 608-752-4438 www.wjvl.com rdailey@wclo.com

Janesville WSJY-FM (r) PO Box 2107, Janesville WI 53547 **Phn:** 608-756-0747 **Fax:** 608-242-0147 www.lite1073.com jvriezen@nrgmedia.com

Janesville WTJK-AM (s) 1 Parker Pl Ste 485, Janesville WI 53545 **Phn:** 608-758-9025 **Fax:** 608-758-9550 www.espn1380.com agannon@gkbsports.com

Janesville WWHG-FM (r) 1 Parker Pl Ste 485, Janesville WI 53545 **Phn:** 608-758-9025 **Fax:** 608-758-9550 www.1059thehog.com lclark@gkbsports.com

Kenosha WGTD-FM (pln) 3520 30th Ave, Kenosha WI 53144 **Phn:** 262-564-3800 **Fax:** 262-564-3801 www.wgtd.org coled@gtc.edu

La Crosse KCLH-FM (h) 201 State St, La Crosse WI 54601 **Phn:** 608-782-1230 **Fax:** 608-796-2506 www.classichits947.com email@classichits947.com

La Crosse KQYB-FM (c) 201 State St, La Crosse WI 54601 **Phn:** 608-782-1230 **Fax:** 608-782-1170 www.kq98.com

La Crosse WIZM-AM (nt) 201 State St, La Crosse WI 54601 **Phn:** 608-782-1230 **Fax:** 608-782-1170 www.1410wizm.com news@1410wizm.com

La Crosse WIZM-FM (h) 201 State St, La Crosse WI 54601 **Phn:** 608-782-1230 **Fax:** 608-782-1170 www.z933.com

La Crosse WKBH-FM (r) PO Box 2017, La Crosse WI 54602 **Phn:** 608-782-8335 **Fax:** 608-782-8340 www.classicrock1001.com psmith@lacrosseradiogroup.net

La Crosse WKTY-AM (st) 201 State St, La Crosse WI 54601 **Phn:** 608-782-1230 **Fax:** 608-782-1170 www.580wkty.com scott@580wkty.com

La Crosse WLFN-AM (t) PO Box 2017, La Crosse WI 54602 **Phn:** 608-782-2554 **Fax:** 608-782-8340 www.1490wlfn.com

La Crosse WLSU-FM (plnj) 1725 State St, La Crosse WI 54601 **Phn:** 608-785-8380 **Fax:** 608-785-5005 www.wpr.org wlsuwhla@uwlax.edu

La Crosse WLXR-FM (a) PO Box 2017, La Crosse WI 54602 **Phn:** 608-782-8335 **Fax:** 608-782-8340 www.wlxr.com

La Crosse WQCC-FM (c) PO Box 2017, La Crosse WI 54602 **Phn:** 608-782-8335 **Fax:** 608-782-8340 www.kicks1063.com johns@lacrosseradiogroup.net

La Crosse WRQT-FM (r) 201 State St, La Crosse WI 54601 **Phn:** 608-782-1230 **Fax:** 608-782-1170 www.957therock.com jean@957therock.com

Ladysmith WJBL-FM (o) PO Box 351, Ladysmith WI 54848 **Phn:** 715-532-5588 **Fax:** 715-532-7357 wldy-wjbl.com

Ladysmith WLDY-AM (t) PO Box 351, Ladysmith WI 54848 **Phn:** 715-532-5588 **Fax:** 715-532-7357

Lake Geneva WLKG-FM (a) 500 Interchange North, Lake Geneva WI 53147 **Phn:** 262-249-9600 **Fax:** 262-249-9630 lake961.com dave@lake961.com

Lancaster WJTY-FM (q) 341 S Washington St, Lancaster WI 53813 **Phn:** 608-723-7888 **Fax:** 608-723-4557

Madison WERN-FM (pln) 821 University Ave, Madison WI 53706 **Phn:** 608-263-3970 **Fax:** 608-263-5838 www.wpr.org corriveau@wpr.org

Madison WHFA-AM (q) 1 Point Pl Ste 50, Madison WI 53719 **Phn:** 608-833-7888 **Fax:** 608-833-7117 www.relevantradio.com jdeschepper@relevantradio.com

Madison WIBA-FM (r) PO Box 99, Madison WI 53701 **Phn:** 608-274-5450 **Fax:** 608-274-5521 www.wibafm.com mikeferris@clearchannel.com

Madison WJJO-FM (r) 730 Ray O Vac Dr, Madison WI 53711 **Phn:** 608-273-1000 **Fax:** 608-271-0400 www.wjjo.com randy.hawke@wjjo.com

Madison WJQM-FM (h) PO Box 44408, Madison WI 53744 **Phn:** 608-273-1000 **Fax:** 608-271-8182 www.madtownjamz.com garfield@midwestfamilybroadcasting.com

Madison WLMV-AM (y) PO Box 44408, Madison WI 53744 **Phn:** 608-273-1000 **Fax:** 608-271-8182 tom.walker@mwfbg.net

Madison WMGN-FM (ja) PO Box 44408, Madison WI 53744 **Phn:** 608-273-1000 **Fax:** 608-271-0400 www.magic98.com info@magic98.com

Madison WMHX-FM (ah) 7601 Ganser Way, Madison WI 53719 **Phn:** 608-826-0077 **Fax:** 608-826-1246 www.mix1051fm.com demoore@entercom.com

Madison WMMM-FM (r) 7601 Ganser Way, Madison WI 53719 **Phn:** 608-826-0077 **Fax:** 608-826-1244 www.1055triplem.com 1055triplem@entercom.com

Madison WNWC-FM (nq) 5606 Medical Cir, Madison WI 53719 **Phn:** 608-271-1025 **Fax:** 608-271-1150 wnwc.nwc.edu wnwc@nwc.edu

Madison WNWC-AM (qt) 5606 Medical Cir, Madison WI 53719 **Phn:** 608-271-1025 **Fax:** 608-271-1150 myfaithradio.com wnwc@nwc.edu

Madison WOLX-FM (o) 7601 Ganser Way, Madison WI 53719 **Phn:** 608-826-0077 **Fax:** 608-826-1244 www.wolx.com wolx@entercom.com

Madison WORT-FM (pnt) 118 S Bedford St, Madison WI 53703 **Phn:** 608-256-2001 **Fax:** 608-256-3704 www.wortfm.org newsfac@wort-fm.org

Madison WOZN-AM (nt) 730 Ray O Vac Dr, Madison WI 53711 **Phn:** 608-273-1000 **Fax:** 608-271-0400 www.madcitysportszone.com

Madison WTSO-AM (s) PO Box 99, Madison WI 53701 **Phn:** 608-274-5450 **Fax:** 608-274-5521 espn.go.com timscott@clearchannel.com

Madison WWQM-FM (c) 730 Ray O Vac Dr, Madison WI 53711 **Phn:** 608-273-1000 **Fax:** 608-271-0400 www.q106.com fletch@q106.com

Madison WWQN-FM (c) PO Box 44408, Madison WI 53744 **Phn:** 608-273-1000 **Fax:** 608-271-0400 www.q106.com tom.walker@mwfbg.net

Madison WXXM-FM (t) PO Box 99, Madison WI 53701 **Phn:** 608-274-5450 **Fax:** 608-274-5521 www.themic921.com timscott@clearchannel.com

Madison WZEE-FM (h) PO Box 99, Madison WI 53701 **Phn:** 608-274-5450 **Fax:** 608-274-5521 www.z104fm.com

Manitowoc WCUB-AM (c) PO Box 1990, Manitowoc WI 54221 **Phn:** 920-683-6800 **Fax:** 920-683-6807 www.cubradio.com jenny@cubradio.com

Manitowoc WLTU-FM (o) PO Box 1990, Manitowoc WI 54221 **Phn:** 920-683-6800 **Fax:** 920-683-6807 www.cubradio.com

Manitowoc WOMT-AM (m) PO Box 1385, Manitowoc WI 54221 **Phn:** 920-682-0351 **Fax:** 920-682-1008 www.womtradio.com info@womtradio.com

Manitowoc WQTC-FM (r) PO Box 1385, Manitowoc WI 54221 **Phn:** 920-682-0351 **Fax:** 920-682-1008 www.womtradio.com info@womtradio.com

Marshfield WDLB-AM (nt) 1714 N Central Ave, Marshfield WI 54449 **Phn:** 715-384-2191 **Fax:** 715-387-3588 www.wdlbam.com news@wdlbwosq.com

Marshfield WOSQ-FM (c) 1714 N Central Ave, Marshfield WI 54449 **Phn:** 715-384-2191 **Fax:** 715-387-3588 www.wdlbam.com news@wdlbwosq.com

WISCONSIN RADIO STATIONS

Mauston WRJC-AM (c) N5240 Fairway Ln, Mauston WI 53948 **Phn:** 608-847-6565 **Fax:** 608-847-6249 www.wrjc.com info@wrjc.com

Mauston WRJC-FM (a) N5240 Fairway Ln, Mauston WI 53948 **Phn:** 608-847-6565 **Fax:** 608-847-6249 www.wrjc.com info@wrjc.com

Mayville WMDC-FM (or) 132 N Main St, Mayville WI 53050 **Phn:** 920-387-0000 **Fax:** 920-387-2222

Medford WIGM-AM (s) PO Box 59, Medford WI 54451 **Phn:** 715-748-2566 **Fax:** 715-748-2693 www.k99wigm.com k99@k99wigm.com

Medford WKEB-FM (a) PO Box 59, Medford WI 54451 **Phn:** 715-748-2566 **Fax:** 715-748-2693 www.k99wigm.com k99@k99wigm.com

Menomonee Falls WLDB-FM (a) N72W12922 Good Hope Rd, Menomonee Falls WI 53051 **Phn:** 414-778-1933 **Fax:** 414-771-3036 www.b933fm.com stanatkinson@milwaukeeradio.com

Menomonee Falls WLUM-FM (r) N72W12922 Good Hope Rd, Menomonee Falls WI 53051 **Phn:** 414-771-1021 **Fax:** 414-771-3036 www.fm1021milwaukee.com jjackson@milwaukeeradio.com

Menomonee Falls WZTI-AM (ob) N72 W12922 Good Hope Rd, Menomonee Falls WI 53051 **Phn:** 414-771-1021 www.1290martiniradio.com stanatkinson@milwaukeeradio.com

Menomonie WDMO-FM (r) 313 Main St E, Menomonie WI 54751 **Phn:** 715-231-9500 zoestations.com wendy@zoestations.com

Merrill WJMT-AM (a) 1106 W Main St, Merrill WI 54452 **Phn:** 715-536-6262 **Fax:** 715-536-0583 www.wjmt.com

Merrill WMZK-FM (r) 120 S Mill St, Merrill WI 54452 **Phn:** 715-536-6262 **Fax:** 715-536-0583

Milladore WGNV-FM (q) PO Box 88, Milladore WI 54454 **Phn:** 715-457-2988 **Fax:** 715-457-2987 www.thefamily.net

Milwaukee KCVS-FM (q) 3434 W Kilbourn Ave, Milwaukee WI 53208 **Phn:** 414-935-3000 **Fax:** 414-935-3015 www.vcyamerica.org kcvs@vcyamerica.org

Milwaukee KVCY-FM (q) 3434 W Kilbourn Ave, Milwaukee WI 53208 **Phn:** 414-935-3000 **Fax:** 414-935-3015 www.vcyamerica.org kvcy@vcyamerica.org

Milwaukee WEGZ-FM (q) 3434 W Kilbourn Ave, Milwaukee WI 53208 **Phn:** 414-935-3000 www.vcyamerica.org wegz@vcyamerica.org

Milwaukee WFZH-FM (q) 135 S 84th St Ste 310, Milwaukee WI 53214 **Phn:** 414-258-1700 **Fax:** 414-266-5353 www.todayschristianmusic.com

Milwaukee WGLB-AM (g) 5181 N 35th St, Milwaukee WI 53209 **Phn:** 414-527-4365 **Fax:** 414-527-4367 www.wglbam1560.com wglb@wglbam1560.com

Milwaukee WHQG-FM (r) 5407 W McKinley Ave, Milwaukee WI 53208 **Phn:** 414-978-9000 **Fax:** 414-978-9001 www.1029thehog.com headhog@1029thehog.com

Milwaukee WJMR-FM (xu) 5407 W McKinley Ave, Milwaukee WI 53208 **Phn:** 414-978-9000 **Fax:** 414-978-9001 jammin983.com ljones@jammin983.com

Milwaukee WJYI-AM (qg) 5407 W McKinley Ave, Milwaukee WI 53208 **Phn:** 414-978-9478 **Fax:** 414-978-9001 www.joy1340.com ryansalzer@joy1340.com

Milwaukee WKLH-FM (r) 5407 W McKinley Ave, Milwaukee WI 53208 **Phn:** 414-978-9000 **Fax:** 414-978-9001 www.wklh.com bellini@wklh.com

Milwaukee WLWK-FM (a) 720 E Capitol Dr, Milwaukee WI 53212 **Phn:** 414-332-9611 **Fax:** 414-967-5266 www.945thelake.com jroberts@journalbroadcastgroup.com

Milwaukee WMSE-FM (vr) 1025 N Broadway, Milwaukee WI 53202 **Phn:** 414-277-7247 **Fax:** 414-277-7149 www.wmse.org wmse@msoe.edu

Milwaukee WNRG-FM (h) 5407 W McKinley Ave, Milwaukee WI 53208 **Phn:** 414-978-9000 **Fax:** 414-978-9001 energy1069.com llucas@mkeradiogrp.com

Milwaukee WTMJ-AM (snt) 720 E Capitol Dr, Milwaukee WI 53212 **Phn:** 414-332-9611 **Fax:** 414-967-5492 www.620wtmj.com jbyman@620wtmj.com

Milwaukee WUWM-FM (p) PO Box 413, Milwaukee WI 53201 **Phn:** 414-227-3355 **Fax:** 414-270-1297 www.wuwm.com wuwm@uwm.edu

Milwaukee WVCY-FM (q) 3434 W Kilbourn Ave, Milwaukee WI 53208 **Phn:** 414-935-3000 **Fax:** 414-935-3015 www.vcyamerica.org wvcyfm@vcyamerica.org

Milwaukee WVCY-AM (q) 3434 W Kilbourn Ave, Milwaukee WI 53208 **Phn:** 414-935-3000 **Fax:** 414-935-3015 www.vcyamerica.org wvcyam@vcyamerica.org

Milwaukee WYMS-FM (pu) 5312 W Vliet St, Milwaukee WI 53208 **Phn:** 414-475-8979 **Fax:** 414-773-9889 www.radiomilwaukee.org info@radiomilwaukee.org

Monroe WEKZ-AM (c) W4765 Radio Ln, Monroe WI 53566 **Phn:** 608-325-2161 **Fax:** 608-325-2164 www.wekz.com

Monroe WEKZ-FM (a) W4765 Radio Ln, Monroe WI 53566 **Phn:** 608-325-2161 **Fax:** 608-325-2164 www.wekz.com

Neillsville WCCN-AM (b) PO Box 387, Neillsville WI 54456 **Phn:** 715-743-3333 **Fax:** 715-743-2288 www.cwbradio.com

Neillsville WCCN-FM (r) PO Box 387, Neillsville WI 54456 **Phn:** 715-743-3333 **Fax:** 715-743-2288 www.cwbradio.com

New Richmond WIXK-AM (c) PO Box 8, New Richmond WI 54017 **Phn:** 715-246-2254 **Fax:** 715-246-7090 www.wixk.com jpetersen@hbi.com

Oconto WOCO-FM (zb) 3829 State Highway 22, Oconto WI 54153 **Phn:** 920-834-3540 **Fax:** 920-834-3532 woco@centurytel.net

Oconto WOCO-AM (c) 3829 State Highway 22, Oconto WI 54153 **Phn:** 920-834-3540 **Fax:** 920-834-3532 woco@centurytel.net

Onalaska KQEG-FM (o) 1407 2nd Ave N, Onalaska WI 54650 **Phn:** 608-782-8335 **Fax:** 608-782-8340 www.eagle1027.com kqegradio@yahoo.com

Oshkosh WNAM-AM (ob) 491 S Washburn St Ste 400, Oshkosh WI 54904 **Phn:** 920-426-3239 **Fax:** 920-236-1040 www.1280wnam.com dan.willis@cumulus.com

Oshkosh WOSH-AM (nt) 491 S Washburn St Ste 400, Oshkosh WI 54904 **Phn:** 920-236-1050 **Fax:** 920-231-0145 www.1490wosh.com wosh.news@cumulus.com

Oshkosh WPKR-FM (c) 491 S Washburn St Ste 400, Oshkosh WI 54904 **Phn:** 920-426-3239 **Fax:** 920-236-1040 www.thewolf.fm jonathan.krause@cumulus.com

Oshkosh WVBO-FM (o) 491 S Washburn St Ste 400, Oshkosh WI 54904 **Phn:** 920-426-3239 **Fax:** 920-236-1040 www.1039wvbo.com wvbo@cumulus.com

Oshkosh WWWX-FM (r) 491 S Washburn St Ste 400, Oshkosh WI 54904 **Phn:** 920-426-3239 **Fax:** 920-231-0145 www.fox969.com guy.dark@cumulus.com

Park Falls WCQM-FM (c) PO Box 309, Park Falls WI 54552 **Phn:** 715-762-3221 **Fax:** 715-762-2358 www.wcqm.com wcqm@pctcnet.net

Pewaukee WKSH-AM (m) W223N3251 Shady Ln, Pewaukee WI 53072 **Phn:** 262-695-9500 **Fax:** 262-691-2378 music.disney.com

Platteville KIYX-FM (h) 51 Means Dr, Platteville WI 53818 **Phn:** 608-349-2000 **Fax:** 608-349-2003 www.superhits106.com dsullivan@queenbradio.com

Platteville WGLR-FM (c) 51 Means Dr, Platteville WI 53818 **Phn:** 608-349-2000 **Fax:** 608-349-2002 www.wglr.com dsullivan@queenbradio.com

Platteville WGLR-AM (s) 51 Means Dr, Platteville WI 53818 **Phn:** 608-349-2000 **Fax:** 608-349-2003 www.wglr.com dsullivan@queenbradio.com

Platteville WPVL-FM (r) 51 Means Dr, Platteville WI 53818 **Phn:** 608-349-2000 **Fax:** 608-349-2002 x1071.com bjohnson@queenbradio.com

Platteville WPVL-AM (s) 51 Means Dr, Platteville WI 53818 **Phn:** 608-349-2000 **Fax:** 608-349-2003 dsullivan@queenbradio.com

Platteville WSUP-FM (v) 1 University Plz, Platteville WI 53818 **Phn:** 608-342-1165 **Fax:** 608-342-1290 www.uwplatt.eduorgwsup wsup.management@uwplatt.edu

Pleasant Prairie WIIL-FM (r) 8500 Green Bay Rd, Pleasant Prairie WI 53158 **Phn:** 262-694-7800 **Fax:** 262-694-7767 www.95wiil.com jp@95wiilrock.com

Pleasant Prairie WLIP-AM (nt) 8500 Green Bay Rd, Pleasant Prairie WI 53158 **Phn:** 262-694-7800 **Fax:** 262-694-7767 www.wlip.com jp@95wiilrock.com

Plover WBCV-FM (h) 2301 Plover Rd, Plover WI 54467 **Phn:** 715-341-8838 **Fax:** 715-341-9744 www.bigcheese1079.net kluchs@nrgmedia.com

Plover WGLX-FM (r) 2301 Plover Rd, Plover WI 54467 **Phn:** 715-341-8838 **Fax:** 715-341-9744 www.wglx.com wglx@nrgmedia.com

Plover WHTQ-FM (h) 2301 Plover Rd, Plover WI 54467 **Phn:** 715-341-8838 **Fax:** 715-341-9744 www.hot967fm.com kluchs@nrgmedia.com

Plover WLJY-FM (r) 2301 Plover Rd, Plover WI 54467 **Phn:** 715-341-8838 **Fax:** 715-341-9744 hot967fm.com wljy@nrgmedia.com

Plymouth WJUB-AM (qnt) PO Box 259, Plymouth WI 53073 **Phn:** 920-893-2661 **Fax:** 920-892-2706 www.1420thebreeze.com dhendrickson@jmiradio.org

Portage WDDC-FM (c) PO Box 448, Portage WI 53901 **Phn:** 608-742-1001 **Fax:** 608-742-1688 www.thunder100fm.com wendy@zoestations.com

Portage WPDR-AM (at) PO Box 448, Portage WI 53901 **Phn:** 608-742-1001 **Fax:** 608-742-1688 www.wpdr.com

Prairie Du Chien WPRE-AM (o) PO Box 90, Prairie Du Chien WI 53821 **Phn:** 608-326-2411 **Fax:** 608-326-2412 www.wpreradio.com wqpcwpre@mwt.net

Prairie Du Chien WQPC-FM (c) PO Box 90, Prairie Du Chien WI 53821 **Phn:** 608-326-2411 **Fax:** 608-326-2412 www.wqpcradio.com wqpcwprenews@mhtc.net

Racine WEZY-FM (a) 4201 Victory Ave, Racine WI 53405 **Phn:** 262-634-3311 **Fax:** 262-634-6515 www.literock921.com news@racineradio.com

Racine WRJN-AM (ant) 4201 Victory Ave, Racine WI 53405 **Phn:** 262-634-3311 **Fax:** 262-634-6515 www.wrjn.com news@racineradio.com

Reedsburg WBDL-FM (a) PO Box 349, Reedsburg WI 53959 **Phn:** 608-524-1400 **Fax:** 608-524-2474 www.magnumbroadcasting.com rick@magnumbroadcasting.com

Reedsburg WNFM-FM (c) PO Box 349, Reedsburg WI 53959 **Phn:** 608-524-1400 **Fax:** 608-524-2474 www.magnumbroadcasting.com rick@magnumbroadcasting.com

Reedsburg WRDB-AM (an) PO Box 349, Reedsburg WI 53959 **Phn:** 608-524-1400 **Fax:** 608-524-2474 www.magnumbroadcasting.com magcom@chorus.net

WISCONSIN RADIO STATIONS

Rhinelander WHDG-FM (c) 3616 Highway 47, Rhinelander WI 54501 **Phn:** 715-362-1975 **Fax:** 715-362-1973 www.whdg.com

Rhinelander WLKD-AM (s) 3616 Highway 47, Rhinelander WI 54501 **Phn:** 715-362-1975 **Fax:** 715-362-1973 www.am1570wlkd.com duff@nrgnorthwoods.com

Rhinelander WMQA-FM (a) 3616 Highway 47, Rhinelander WI 54501 **Phn:** 715-362-1975 **Fax:** 715-362-1973 www.wmqa.com

Rhinelander WOBT-AM (nos) 3616 Highway 47, Rhinelander WI 54501 **Phn:** 715-362-1975 **Fax:** 715-362-1973 www.northwoodsespnsportszone.com duff@nrgnorthwoods.com

Rhinelander WRHN-FM (an) 3616 Highway 47, Rhinelander WI 54501 **Phn:** 715-362-6140 **Fax:** 715-362-1973 www.wrhn.com

Rhinelander WRLO-FM (r) 3616 Highway 47, Rhinelander WI 54501 **Phn:** 715-362-1975 **Fax:** 715-362-1973 www.rock1053wrlo.com

Rhinelander WXPR-FM (p) 28 N Stevens St, Rhinelander WI 54501 **Phn:** 715-362-6000 **Fax:** 715-362-6007 wxpr.org ken@wxpr.org

Rice Lake WAQE-AM (c) PO Box 703, Rice Lake WI 54868 **Phn:** 715-234-9059 **Fax:** 715-234-6942

Rice Lake WAQE-FM (a) PO Box 703, Rice Lake WI 54868 **Phn:** 715-234-9059 **Fax:** 715-234-6942 www.waqe.com

Rice Lake WJMC-AM (m) PO Box 352, Rice Lake WI 54868 **Phn:** 715-234-2131 **Fax:** 715-234-6942 wjmcradio.com news@wjmcradio.com

Rice Lake WJMC-FM (c) PO Box 352, Rice Lake WI 54868 **Phn:** 715-234-2131 **Fax:** 715-234-6942 wjmcradio.com info@wjmcradio.com

Rice Lake WKFX-FM (h) PO Box 352, Rice Lake WI 54868 **Phn:** 715-736-9910 **Fax:** 715-234-6942 www.fox99.com info@fox99.com

Richland Center WRCO-AM (ac) PO Box 529, Richland Center WI 53581 **Phn:** 608-647-2111 **Fax:** 608-647-8025 www.wrco.com wrco@wrco.com

Richland Center WRCO-FM (ac) PO Box 529, Richland Center WI 53581 **Phn:** 608-647-2111 **Fax:** 608-647-8025 www.wrco.com wrco@mwt.net

Ripon WBJZ-FM (jx) 112 Watson St, Ripon WI 54971 **Phn:** 920-748-5111 **Fax:** 920-748-5530 www.magic104fm.com wbjz@hotmail.com

Ripon WRPN-FM (vr) 300 W Seward St, Ripon WI 54971 **Phn:** 920-748-8147 **Fax:** 920-748-7243 wrpn.fm@gmail.com

Ripon WRPN-AM (nt) N7502 Radio Rd, Ripon WI 54971 **Phn:** 920-748-5111 **Fax:** 920-748-5530 www.wrpnam.com wrpn@wrpnam.com

River Falls WEVR-FM (a) 178 Radio Rd, River Falls WI 54022 **Phn:** 715-425-1111

River Falls WEVR-AM (a) 178 Radio Rd, River Falls WI 54022 **Phn:** 715-425-1111

River Falls WRFW-FM (v) 410 S 3rd St, River Falls WI 54022 **Phn:** 715-425-3886 **Fax:** 715-425-3532 www.uwrf.edu/wrfw wrfwdj@gmail.com

Robinson WYTE-FM (c) PO Box 242, Robinson IL 62454 **Phn:** 715-341-8838 **Fax:** 715-341-9744 www.originalcompany.com wtye@wtyefm.com

Schofield WCLQ-FM (q) 4111 Schofield Ave Ste 10, Schofield WI 54476 **Phn:** 715-355-5151 **Fax:** 715-359-3128 www.89q.org 89q@89q.org

Shawano WJMQ-FM (c) 1456 E Green Bay St, Shawano WI 54166 **Phn:** 715-524-2194 **Fax:** 715-524-9980 frogcountry923.com wtchnews@gmail.com

Shawano WOTE-AM (am) 1456 E Green Bay St, Shawano WI 54166 **Phn:** 715-524-2194 **Fax:** 715-524-9980 1380thelounge.com wtchnews@gmail.com

Shawano WOWN-FM (o) 1456 E Green Bay St, Shawano WI 54166 **Phn:** 715-524-2194 **Fax:** 715-524-9980 www.b993.com resultsbroadcasting@gmail.com

Shawano WTCH-AM (c) 1456 E Green Bay St, Shawano WI 54166 **Phn:** 715-524-2194 **Fax:** 715-524-9980 www.wtcham960.com resultsbroadcasting@gmail.com

Sheboygan WBFM-FM (c) PO Box 27, Sheboygan WI 53082 **Phn:** 920-458-2107 **Fax:** 920-458-9775 www.b93radio.com

Sheboygan WHBL-AM (nt) PO Box 27, Sheboygan WI 53082 **Phn:** 920-458-2107 **Fax:** 920-458-9775 www.whbl.com

Sheboygan WHBZ-FM (r) PO Box 27, Sheboygan WI 53082 **Phn:** 920-458-2107 **Fax:** 920-458-9775 1065thebuzz.com webmaster.whbz@whbz.fm

Sheboygan WXER-FM (a) PO Box 27, Sheboygan WI 53082 **Phn:** 920-458-2107 **Fax:** 920-458-9775 www.1045thepoint.com

Shell Lake WCSW-AM (nt) PO Box 190, Shell Lake WI 54871 **Phn:** 715-468-9500 **Fax:** 715-468-9505

Shell Lake WGMO-FM (r) PO Box 190, Shell Lake WI 54871 **Phn:** 715-468-9500 **Fax:** 715-468-9505 www.95gmo.com

Sparta WCOW-FM (c) 113 W Oak St, Sparta WI 54656 **Phn:** 608-269-3100 **Fax:** 608-269-5170 www.cow97.com willie@stbroadcasting.com

Sparta WFBZ-FM (s) 113 W Oak St, Sparta WI 54656 **Phn:** 608-269-3100 **Fax:** 608-269-5170 www.espnlacrosse.com willie@stbroadcasting.com

Sparta WKLJ-AM (snt) 113 W Oak St, Sparta WI 54656 **Phn:** 608-269-3100 **Fax:** 608-269-5170 www.espnlacrosse.com willie@stbroadcasting.com

Stevens Point WKQH-FM (c) 500 Division St, Stevens Point WI 54481 **Phn:** 715-341-9800 **Fax:** 715-341-0000 www.b1049.com tvr979@yahoo.com

Stevens Point WSPT-FM (a) 500 Division St, Stevens Point WI 54481 **Phn:** 715-341-9800 **Fax:** 715-341-0000 www.979wspt.com scott@muzzybroadcasting.net

Stevens Point WSPT-AM (nt) 500 Division St, Stevens Point WI 54481 **Phn:** 715-341-9800 **Fax:** 715-341-0000 www.1010wspt.com scott@muzzybroadcasting.net

Stevens Point WWSP-FM (vjr) 1101 Reserve St # 105, Stevens Point WI 54481 **Phn:** 715-346-3755 **Fax:** 715-346-4012 www.uwsp.edu/wwsp

Sturgeon Bay WBDK-FM (bo) 3030 Park Dr Ste D, Sturgeon Bay WI 54235 **Phn:** 920-746-9430 **Fax:** 920-746-9433 www.doorcountydailynews.com wbdk@doorcountydailynews.com

Sturgeon Bay WDOR-AM (a) PO Box 549, Sturgeon Bay WI 54235 **Phn:** 920-743-4411 **Fax:** 920-743-2334 www.wdor.com email@wdor.com

Sturgeon Bay WDOR-FM (a) PO Box 549, Sturgeon Bay WI 54235 **Phn:** 920-743-4411 **Fax:** 920-743-2334 www.wdor.com email@wdor.com

Sturgeon Bay WPFF-FM (q) PO Box 28, Sturgeon Bay WI 54235 **Phn:** 920-743-7443 www.wpff.com bnelson@bcbradio.org

Sturgeon Bay WRKU-FM (o) 3030 Park Dr # 3, Sturgeon Bay WI 54235 **Phn:** 920-746-9430 **Fax:** 920-746-9433 www.doorcountydailynews.com klement@doorcountydailynews.com

Sturgeon Bay WRLU-FM (c) 3030 Park Dr # 3, Sturgeon Bay WI 54235 **Phn:** 920-746-9430 **Fax:** 920-746-9433 www.doorcountydailynews.com freimuth@doorcountydailynews.com

Superior KUWS-FM (pnt) 801 N 28th St, Superior WI 54880 **Phn:** 715-394-8530 **Fax:** 715-394-8404 www.wpr.org listener@wpr.org

Suring WRVM-FM (q) PO Box 212, Suring WI 54174 **Phn:** 920-842-2900 **Fax:** 920-842-2704 www.wrvmradio.org wrvm@wrvm.org

Tomah WBOG-AM (o) 1021 N Superior Ave Ste 5, Tomah WI 54660 **Phn:** 608-372-9600 **Fax:** 608-372-7566 www.koolgold1460.com

Tomah WDLS-AM (c) 1021 N Superior Ave, Tomah WI 54660 **Phn:** 608-745-0959 **Fax:** 608-374-5550 www.magnumbroadcasting.com debbied@magnumbroadcasting.com

Tomah WNNO-FM (a) 1021 N Superior Ave, Tomah WI 54660 **Phn:** 608-745-0959 **Fax:** 608-745-5771 www.magnumbroadcasting.com rick@magnumbroadcasting.com

Tomah WXYM-FM (a) 1021 N Superior Ave Ste 5, Tomah WI 54660 **Phn:** 608-372-9400 **Fax:** 608-372-7566 www.mix96wxym.com

Tomahawk WJJQ-FM (a) PO Box 10, Tomahawk WI 54487 **Phn:** 715-453-4482 **Fax:** 715-453-7169 www.wjjq.com wjjq@wjjq.com

Tomahawk WJJQ-AM (snt) PO Box 10, Tomahawk WI 54487 **Phn:** 715-453-4482 **Fax:** 715-453-7169 www.wjjq.com wjjq@wjjq.com

Viroqua WVRQ-FM (c) E7601A County Road SS, Viroqua WI 54665 **Phn:** 608-637-7200 **Fax:** 608-637-7299 greatriversnews.com news@q102wvrq.com

Viroqua WVRQ-AM (o) E7601A County Road SS, Viroqua WI 54665 **Phn:** 608-637-7200 **Fax:** 608-637-7299 greatriversnews.com news@q102wvrq.com

Watertown WTTN-AM (ys) PO Box 509, Watertown WI 53094 **Phn:** 920-261-1580 **Fax:** 920-885-2152

Waupaca WDUX-AM (c) 200 Tower Rd, Waupaca WI 54981 **Phn:** 715-258-5528 **Fax:** 715-258-7711 www.wduxradio.com mail@wdux.net

Waupaca WDUX-FM (a) 200 Tower Rd, Waupaca WI 54981 **Phn:** 715-258-5528 **Fax:** 715-258-7711 www.wduxradio.com mail@wdux.net

Waupun WFDL-AM (ob) 609 Home Ave, Waupun WI 53963 **Phn:** 920-324-4441 **Fax:** 920-324-3139 www.am1170radio.com nickr@wfdl.com

Wausau WDEZ-FM (c) 557 Scott St, Wausau WI 54403 **Phn:** 715-842-1672 **Fax:** 715-848-3158 www.wdez.com joe.cassady@mwcradio.com

Wausau WIFC-FM (h) PO Box 2048, Wausau WI 54402 **Phn:** 715-842-1672 **Fax:** 715-848-3158 www.wifc.com

Wausau WOFM-FM (o) PO Box 2048, Wausau WI 54402 **Phn:** 715-842-1672 **Fax:** 715-848-3158 www.rock947.com chris.conley@mwcradio.com

Wausau WRIG-AM (st) PO Box 2048, Wausau WI 54402 **Phn:** 715-842-1672 **Fax:** 715-848-3158 foxsportswausau.com

Wausau WSAU-AM (snt) 557 Scott St, Wausau WI 54403 **Phn:** 715-842-1672 **Fax:** 715-842-1672 www.wsau.com

Wausau WXCO-AM (s) PO Box 778, Wausau WI 54402 **Phn:** 715-845-8218 **Fax:** 715-845-6582 www.1230wxco.com stever@sunriseamfm.com

West Allis WDDW-FM (y) 1138 S 108th St, West Allis WI 53214 **Phn:** 414-325-1800 **Fax:** 414-607-1837

West Bend WBKV-AM (c) PO Box 933, West Bend WI 53095 **Phn:** 262-334-2344 **Fax:** 262-334-1512 www.wbkvam.com bob@wbkvam.com

West Bend WBWI-FM (c) PO Box 933, West Bend WI 53095 **Phn:** 262-334-2344 **Fax:** 262-334-1512 wbwifm.com

Whitehall WHTL-FM (r) PO Box 66, Whitehall WI 54773 **Phn:** 715-538-4341 **Fax:** 715-538-4360 whtlradio.com whtl@centurytel.net

Whitewater WSLD-FM (c) PO Box 709, Whitewater WI 53190 **Phn:** 608-883-6677 **Fax:** 608-883-2054 www.1045wsld.com wsld@prairiecommunications.net

Whitewater WSUW-FM (vr) 800 W Main St, Whitewater WI 53190 **Phn:** 262-472-1323 wsuw.org news@wsuw.org

Wisconsin Rapids WFHR-AM (snt) 645 25th Ave N, Wisconsin Rapids WI 54495 **Phn:** 715-424-1300 **Fax:** 715-424-1347 www.wfhr.com carl@wfhr.com

Wisconsin Rapids WRCW-FM (o) 645 25th Ave N, Wisconsin Rapids WI 54495 **Phn:** 715-424-1300 **Fax:** 715-424-1347 www.wrcwfm.com geoff@wfhr.com

WYOMING

Afton KRSV-AM (c) PO Box 1210, Afton WY 83110 **Phn:** 307-885-5778 **Fax:** 307-885-3678 krsv@silverstar.com

Afton KRSV-FM (c) PO Box 1210, Afton WY 83110 **Phn:** 307-885-5778 **Fax:** 307-885-3678 krsv@silverstar.com

Buffalo KBBS-AM (oc) 1221 Fort St, Buffalo WY 82834 **Phn:** 307-684-5126 **Fax:** 307-684-7676 www.bighornmountainradio.com kbbs@vcn.com

Buffalo KLGT-FM (c) 1221 Fort St, Buffalo WY 82834 **Phn:** 307-684-5126 **Fax:** 307-684-7676 www.bighornmountainradio.com klgt@vcn.com

Buffalo KZZS-FM (a) 1221 Fort St, Buffalo WY 82834 **Phn:** 307-684-5126 **Fax:** 307-684-7676

Casper KASS-FM (r) 218 N Wolcott St, Casper WY 82601 **Phn:** 307-265-1984 **Fax:** 307-266-3295 www.wyomingradio.com

Casper KHOC-FM (a) 218 N Wolcott St, Casper WY 82601 **Phn:** 307-265-1984 **Fax:** 307-266-3295 www.wyomingradio.com

Casper KIQZ-FM (a) 218 N Wolcott St, Casper WY 82601 **Phn:** 307-324-3315 **Fax:** 307-324-3509 kiqz@vcn.com

Casper KKTL-AM (s) 150 Nichols Ave, Casper WY 82601 **Phn:** 307-266-5252 **Fax:** 307-235-9143 am1400espn.com donovanshort@townsquaremedia.com

Casper KMGW-FM (a) 150 Nichols Ave, Casper WY 82601 **Phn:** 307-266-5252 **Fax:** 307-235-9143 rock967online.com donovanshort@townsquaremedia.com

Casper KMLD-FM (o) 218 N Wolcott St, Casper WY 82601 **Phn:** 307-265-1984 **Fax:** 307-266-3295 www.wyomingradio.com

Casper KQLT-FM (c) 218 N Wolcott St, Casper WY 82601 **Phn:** 307-265-1984 **Fax:** 307-266-3295 www.wyomingradio.com

Casper KRAL-AM (a) 218 N Wolcott St, Casper WY 82601 **Phn:** 307-324-3315 **Fax:** 307-324-3509 www.kiqz.net kiqz@vcn.com

Casper KRVK-FM (h) 150 Nichols Ave, Casper WY 82601 **Phn:** 307-266-5252 **Fax:** 307-235-9143 theriver1079.com donovanshort@townsquaremedia.com

Casper KTRS-FM (h) 150 Nichols Ave, Casper WY 82601 **Phn:** 307-266-5252 **Fax:** 307-235-9143 kisscasper.com caspernews@gapbroadcasting.com

Casper KTWO-AM (t) 150 Nichols Ave, Casper WY 82601 **Phn:** 307-266-5252 **Fax:** 307-235-9143 k2radio.com caspernews@gapbroadcasting.com

Casper KUYO-AM (qc) PO Box 50607, Casper WY 82605 **Phn:** 307-577-5896 **Fax:** 307-577-0850 www.kuyo.com sstumbo@kuyo.com

Casper KVOC-AM (s) 218 N Wolcott St, Casper WY 82601 **Phn:** 307-265-1984 **Fax:** 307-266-3295

Casper KWYY-FM (c) 150 Nichols Ave, Casper WY 82601 **Phn:** 307-266-5252 **Fax:** 307-235-9143 mycountry955.com donovanshort@townsquaremedia.com

Cheyenne KAZY-FM (a) 2109 E 10th St, Cheyenne WY 82001 **Phn:** 307-638-8921 **Fax:** 307-638-8922 www.hitsandfavorites.com traffic@1049krrr.com

Cheyenne KFBC-AM (ant) 1806 Capitol Ave, Cheyenne WY 82001 **Phn:** 307-634-4461 **Fax:** 307-632-8586 www.kfbcradio.com news@kfbcradio.com

Cheyenne KGAB-AM (nt) 1912 Capitol Ave Ste 300, Cheyenne WY 82001 **Phn:** 307-632-4400 **Fax:** 307-632-1818 kgab.com am650kgab@hotmail.com

Cheyenne KIGN-FM (r) 1912 Capitol Ave Ste 300, Cheyenne WY 82001 **Phn:** 307-632-4400 **Fax:** 307-632-1818 kingfm.com gailensprague@townsquaremedia.com

Cheyenne KJUA-AM (yo) 110 E 17th St Ste 205, Cheyenne WY 82001 **Phn:** 307-635-8787 **Fax:** 307-635-8788

Cheyenne KLEN-FM (c) 1912 Capitol Ave Ste 300, Cheyenne WY 82001 **Phn:** 307-632-4400 **Fax:** 307-632-1818 1063cowboycountry.com donovan.short@townsquaremedia.com

Cheyenne KRAE-AM (s) 2109 E 10th St, Cheyenne WY 82001 **Phn:** 307-638-8921 **Fax:** 307-638-8922 www.1049krrr.com

Cheyenne KRAN-FM (c) 2109 E 10th St, Cheyenne WY 82001 **Phn:** 307-638-8921 **Fax:** 307-638-8922

Cheyenne KRRR-FM (o) 2109 E 10th St, Cheyenne WY 82001 **Phn:** 307-638-8921 **Fax:** 307-638-8922 www.1049krrr.com traffic@1049krrr.com

Cody KCGL-FM (r) PO Box 1210, Cody WY 82414 **Phn:** 307-578-5000 **Fax:** 307-527-5045 www.theclassicrockstation.com comments@theclassicrockstation.com

Cody KODI-AM (snt) PO Box 1210, Cody WY 82414 **Phn:** 307-578-5000 **Fax:** 307-527-5045 www.mybighornbasin.com news@bhrnwy.com

Cody KTAG-FM (a) PO Box 1210, Cody WY 82414 **Phn:** 307-578-5000 **Fax:** 307-527-5045 ktag979.com

Cody KZMQ-AM (c) PO Box 1210, Cody WY 82414 **Phn:** 307-578-5000 **Fax:** 307-527-5045 www.mybighornbasin.com news@bhrnwy.com

Cody KZMQ-FM (cn) PO Box 1210, Cody WY 82414 **Phn:** 307-578-5000 **Fax:** 307-527-5045

Douglas KKTY-AM (o) PO Box 135, Douglas WY 82633 **Phn:** 307-358-3636 **Fax:** 307-358-4010 www.kktyonline.com kkty@netcommander.com

Douglas KKTY-FM (c) PO Box 135, Douglas WY 82633 **Phn:** 307-358-3636 **Fax:** 307-358-4010 www.kktyonline.com kkty@netcommander.com

Evanston KEVA-AM (c) PO Box 190, Evanston WY 82931 **Phn:** 307-789-9101 **Fax:** 307-789-8521 www.1240keva.com info@1240keva.com

Gillette KAML-FM (a) PO Box 1179, Gillette WY 82717 **Phn:** 307-686-2242 **Fax:** 307-686-7736 www.basinsradio.com news@basinsradio.com

Gillette KGWY-FM (c) PO Box 1179, Gillette WY 82717 **Phn:** 307-686-2242 **Fax:** 307-686-7736 www.basinsradio.com donc@basinsradio.com

Gillette KIML-AM (st) PO Box 1179, Gillette WY 82717 **Phn:** 307-686-2242 **Fax:** 307-686-7736 www.basinsradio.com news@basinsradio.com

Gillette KXXL-FM (r) 305 S Garner Lake Rd, Gillette WY 82718 **Phn:** 307-687-1003 **Fax:** 307-687-1006 debora@koal1061.com

Green River KFRZ-FM (c) 40 Shoshone Ave, Green River WY 82935 **Phn:** 307-875-6666 **Fax:** 307-875-5847

Green River KUGR-AM (a) 40 Shoshone Ave, Green River WY 82935 **Phn:** 307-875-6666 **Fax:** 307-875-5847 www.theradionetwork.net mail@theradionetwork.net

Green River KYCS-FM (a) 40 Shoshone Ave, Green River WY 82935 **Phn:** 307-875-6666 **Fax:** 307-875-5847 www.theradionetwork.net mail@theradionetwork.net

Jackson KJAX-FM (c) 1140 State Highway 22, Jackson WY 83001 **Phn:** 307-733-4500 **Fax:** 307-733-4760 jacksonholeradio.com jacksonholeradionews@gmail.com

Jackson KMTN-FM (a) 1140 State Highway 22, Jackson WY 83001 **Phn:** 307-733-4500 **Fax:** 307-733-4760 jacksonholeradio.com jacksonholeradionews@gmail.com

Jackson KSGT-AM (cn) 1140 State Highway 22, Jackson WY 83001 **Phn:** 307-733-4500 **Fax:** 307-733-4760 jacksonholeradio.com admin@jacksonholeradio.com

Jackson KZJH-FM (ar) 1140 State Highway 22, Jackson WY 83001 **Phn:** 307-733-4500 **Fax:** 307-733-4760 jacksonholeradionews@gmail.com

Kemmerer KMER-AM (o) PO Box 432, Kemmerer WY 83101 **Phn:** 307-877-4422 **Fax:** 307-877-5937

Lander KDLY-FM (a) 1530 Main St, Lander WY 82520 **Phn:** 307-332-5683 **Fax:** 307-332-5548 fremontcountyradio.com radio1@wyoming.com

Lander KOVE-AM (c) 1530 Main St, Lander WY 82520 **Phn:** 307-332-5683 **Fax:** 307-332-5548 fremontcountyradio.com radio1@wyoming.com

Laramie KCGY-FM (c) 3525 Soldier Springs Rd, Laramie WY 82070 **Phn:** 307-745-9242 **Fax:** 307-742-4576 y95country.com andyhoefer@gapbroadcasting.com

Laramie KHAT-FM (h) 302 S 2nd St Ste 204, Laramie WY 82070 **Phn:** 307-745-5208 **Fax:** 307-745-8570

Laramie KIMX-FM (a) 302 S 2nd St Ste 204, Laramie WY 82070 **Phn:** 307-745-5208 **Fax:** 307-745-8570 www.kimx967.comconcrete imixwyoming@gmail.com

Laramie KOWB-AM (snt) PO Box 1290, Laramie WY 82073 **Phn:** 307-745-4888 **Fax:** 307-742-4576 kowb1290.com davidsettle@townsquaremedia.com

Laramie KRQU-FM (r) 302 S 2nd St Ste 204, Laramie WY 82070 **Phn:** 307-745-5208 **Fax:** 307-745-8570

Laramie KUSZ-FM (h) 302 S 2nd St Ste 204, Laramie WY 82070 **Phn:** 307-745-5208 **Fax:** 307-745-8570

Laramie KUWR-FM (pln) 1000 E University Ave # 3984, Laramie WY 82071 **Phn:** 307-766-4240 **Fax:** 307-766-6184 wyomingpublicradio.net btwo@uwyo.edu

Loveland KOLZ-FM (c) 4270 Byrd Dr, Loveland CO 80538 **Phn:** 970-461-2560 **Fax:** 307-632-1818 www.koltfm.com stuhaskell@clearchannel.com

Newcastle KASL-AM (ac) 2208 W Main St, Newcastle WY 82701 **Phn:** 307-746-4433 **Fax:** 307-746-4435 am1240kasl.com news@kaslradio.com

Pinedale KPIN-FM (c) PO Box 2000, Pinedale WY 82941 **Phn:** 307-367-2000 www.kpinfm.com

Powell KPOW-AM (c) PO Box 968, Powell WY 82435 **Phn:** 307-754-5183 **Fax:** 307-754-9667

Riverton KTAK-FM (c) 603 E Pershing Ave, Riverton WY 82501 **Phn:** 307-856-2251 **Fax:** 307-856-0252 rivertonradio.com

Riverton KTRZ-FM (a) PO Box 808, Riverton WY 82501 **Phn:** 307-856-2922 **Fax:** 307-856-7552

Riverton KVOW-AM (nt) 603 E Pershing Ave, Riverton WY 82501 **Phn:** 307-856-2251 **Fax:** 307-856-0252 rivertonradio.com

Rock Springs KMRZ-FM (y) PO Box 2128, Rock Springs WY 82902 **Phn:** 307-362-3793 **Fax:** 307-362-8727 www.wyoradio.com

Rock Springs KQSW-FM (c) PO Box 2128, Rock Springs WY 82902 **Phn:** 307-362-3793 **Fax:** 307-362-8727 www.wyoradio.com

Rock Springs KRKK-AM (t) PO Box 2128, Rock Springs WY 82902 **Phn:** 307-362-3793 **Fax:** 307-362-8727 www.wyoradio.com

Rock Springs KSIT-FM (r) PO Box 2128, Rock Springs WY 82902 **Phn:** 307-362-3793 **Fax:** 307-362-8727 www.wyoradio.com

Sheridan KLQQ-FM (h) PO Box 5086, Sheridan WY 82801 **Phn:** 307-672-7421 **Fax:** 307-672-2933 www.sheridanmedia.com info@sheridanmedia.com

Sheridan KROE-AM (o) PO Box 5086, Sheridan WY 82801 **Phn:** 307-672-7421 **Fax:** 307-672-2933 www.sheridanmedia.com info@sheridanmedia.com

Sheridan KWYO-AM (am) PO Box 5086, Sheridan WY 82801 **Phn:** 307-672-7421 **Fax:** 307-672-2933 www.sheridanmedia.com info@sheridanmedia.com

Sheridan KYTI-FM (c) PO Box 5086, Sheridan WY 82801 **Phn:** 307-672-7421 **Fax:** 307-672-2933 www.sheridanmedia.com info@sheridanmedia.com

Sheridan KZWY-FM (ar) PO Box 5086, Sheridan WY 82801 **Phn:** 307-672-7421 **Fax:** 307-672-2933 www.sheridanmedia.com info@sheridanmedia.com

Thermopolis KTHE-AM (ao) PO Box 591, Thermopolis WY 82443 **Phn:** 307-864-2119 **Fax:** 307-864-3937

Torrington KERM-FM (c) 7060 Radio Rd, Torrington WY 82240 **Phn:** 307-532-2158 **Fax:** 307-532-2641

Torrington KGOS-AM (c) 7060 Radio Rd, Torrington WY 82240 **Phn:** 307-532-2158 **Fax:** 307-532-2641

Wheatland KYCN-AM (aco) PO Box 248, Wheatland WY 82201 **Phn:** 307-322-5926 **Fax:** 307-322-9300 kycn@communicomm.com

Wheatland KZEW-FM (a) PO Box 248, Wheatland WY 82201 **Phn:** 307-322-5926 **Fax:** 307-322-9300 www.wheatlandradio.com kzew@communicomm.com

Worland KKLX-FM (a) 1340 Radio Dr, Worland WY 82401 **Phn:** 307-347-3231 **Fax:** 307-347-4880 www.mybighornbasin.com grobertson@bhrnwy.com

Worland KWOR-AM (snt) 1340 Radio Dr, Worland WY 82401 **Phn:** 307-347-3231 **Fax:** 307-347-4880

This page left blank intentionally.

ALABAMA

Anniston WHOG-AM (wu) 1330 Noble St Ste 25, Anniston AL 36201 **Phn:** 256-236-6484 hog1120@aol.com

Birmingham WAGG-AM (gw) 950 22nd St N Ste 1000, Birmingham AL 35203 **Phn:** 205-322-2987 **Fax:** 205-324-6397 www.610wagg.com mary.k@coxradio.com

Birmingham WATV-AM (gw) 3025 Kenley Way, Birmingham AL 35242 **Phn:** 205-780-2014 **Fax:** 205-780-4034 www.900goldwatv.com spstewart@watv900.com

Birmingham WENN-AM (w) 950 22nd St N Ste 1000, Birmingham AL 35203 **Phn:** 205-322-2987 **Fax:** 205-324-6397

Birmingham WJLD-AM (ouw) PO Box 19123, Birmingham AL 35219 **Phn:** 205-942-1776 **Fax:** 205-942-4814 www.wjldfm.com wr@wjldfm.com

Birmingham WJLD-FM (ouw) PO Box 19123, Birmingham AL 35219 **Phn:** 205-942-1776 **Fax:** 205-942-4814 www.wjldfm.com wr@wjldfm.com

Dothan WAGF-FM (wg) 4106 Ross Clark Cir, Dothan AL 36303 **Phn:** 334-671-1753 **Fax:** 334-677-6923 www.wjjn.net wtraffic@graceba.net

Dothan WJJN-FM (uw) 4106 Ross Clark Cir, Dothan AL 36303 **Phn:** 334-671-1753 **Fax:** 334-677-6923 www.wjjn.net wtraffic@graceba.net

Dothan WOOF-AM (wgt) PO Box 1427, Dothan AL 36302 **Phn:** 334-792-1149 **Fax:** 334-677-4612 www.woofradio.com woof@ala.net

Florence WSBM-AM (wu) PO Box 932, Florence AL 35631 **Phn:** 256-764-8121 **Fax:** 256-764-8169 www.wsbm.com nmartin@bigriverbroadcasting.com

Gadsden WMGJ-AM (wu) 815 Tuscaloosa Ave, Gadsden AL 35901 **Phn:** 256-546-4434 **Fax:** 256-546-9645 www.wmgj.com floyddonald@wmgj.com

Greenville WKXK-FM (wu) PO Box 369, Greenville AL 36037 **Phn:** 334-382-6555 **Fax:** 334-382-7770 www.watchdognetwork.com wkxn@wkxn.com

Greenville WKXN-FM (wu) PO Box 369, Greenville AL 36037 **Phn:** 334-382-6555 **Fax:** 334-382-7770 www.wkxn.com wkxn@wkxn.com

Huntsville WEUP-AM (wgt) 2609 Jordan Ln NW, Huntsville AL 35816 **Phn:** 256-837-9387 **Fax:** 256-837-9404 www.weupam.com churchnews@weupam.com

Huntsville WLOR-AM (wgu) 1555 The Boardwalk Ste 1, Huntsville AL 35816 **Phn:** 256-536-1568 **Fax:** 256-536-4416

Mobile WBLX-FM (uw) 2800 Dauphin St Ste 104, Mobile AL 36606 **Phn:** 251-652-2000 **Fax:** 251-652-2001 www.thebigstation93blx.com vinny.d@cumulus.com

Mobile WDLT-FM (wu) 2800 Dauphin St Ste 104, Mobile AL 36606 **Phn:** 251-652-2000 **Fax:** 251-652-2001 www.983wdlt.com cathyb983@bellsouth.net

Mobile WGOK-AM (wu) 2800 Dauphin St Ste 104, Mobile AL 36606 **Phn:** 251-652-2000 **Fax:** 251-652-2001 www.gospel900.com felicia.allbritton@cumulus.com

Montgomery WJWZ-FM (uw) 4101 Wall St Ste A, Montgomery AL 36106 **Phn:** 334-244-0961 **Fax:** 334-279-9563 979jamz.com tbarber@bluewaterbroadcasting.com

Montgomery WZHT-FM (wu) 203 Gunn Rd, Montgomery AL 36117 **Phn:** 334-274-6464 **Fax:** 334-274-6465 www.myhot105.com darrylelliott@clearchannel.com

BLACK RADIO STATIONS

Opelika WZMG-AM (wg) 915 Veterans Pkwy, Opelika AL 36801 **Phn:** 334-745-4656 **Fax:** 334-749-1520 www.intouch910am.com richard.lagrand@qantumofauburn.com

Spanish Fort WLVV-AM (wgu) 1263 Battleship Pkwy, Spanish Fort AL 36527 **Phn:** 251-626-1090 **Fax:** 251-626-1099

Tuscaloosa WQZZ-FM (wu) 601 Greensboro Ave Ste 507, Tuscaloosa AL 35401 **Phn:** 205-345-4787 **Fax:** 205-345-4790 jwlawson@bellsouth.net

Tuscaloosa WTSK-AM (wg) 142 Skyland Blvd E, Tuscaloosa AL 35405 **Phn:** 205-345-7200 **Fax:** 205-349-1715 www.790wtsk.com todd.livingston@townsquaremedia.com

Tuscaloosa WTUG-FM (wu) 142 Skyland Blvd E, Tuscaloosa AL 35405 **Phn:** 205-345-7200 **Fax:** 205-349-1715 www.wtug.com todd.livingston@townsquaremedia.com

Tuscaloosa WWPG-AM (wxg) 601 Greensboro Ave Ste 507, Tuscaloosa AL 35401 **Phn:** 205-345-4787 **Fax:** 205-345-4790 jwlawson@bellsouth.net

Tuscumbia WZZA-AM (wgx) 1570 Woodmont Dr, Tuscumbia AL 35674 **Phn:** 256-381-1862 **Fax:** 256-381-6006 www.wzzaradio.com news@wzzaradio.com

Tuskegee WBIL-AM (gw) 118 S Main St, Tuskegee AL 36083 **Phn:** 334-727-2100 wbil580am.com rejoice@wbil580am.com

Wetumpka WAPZ-AM (gxw) 2821 US Highway 231, Wetumpka AL 36093 **Phn:** 334-567-9279 **Fax:** 334-567-7971

York WSLY-FM (uw) 11474 U S Highway 11, York AL 36925 **Phn:** 205-392-5234 **Fax:** 205-392-5536

ARKANSAS

El Dorado KMLK-FM (w) 2525 N West Ave, El Dorado AR 71730 **Phn:** 870-863-6126 **Fax:** 870-863-4555 www.totalradio.com

Little Rock KABF-FM (wjg) 2101 Main St # 200, Little Rock AR 72206 **Phn:** 501-372-6119 **Fax:** 501-376-3952 www.kabf.org stationmanager@kabf.org

Little Rock KIPR-FM (uw) 700 Wellington Hills Rd, Little Rock AR 72211 **Phn:** 501-401-0200 **Fax:** 501-401-0366 www.power923.com joe.booker@cumulus.com

Little Rock KOKY-FM (wau) 700 Wellington Hills Rd, Little Rock AR 72211 **Phn:** 501-401-0200 **Fax:** 501-401-0374 www.koky.com joe.booker@cumulus.com

Little Rock KPZK-FM (wg) 700 Wellington Hills Rd, Little Rock AR 72211 **Phn:** 501-401-0200 **Fax:** 501-401-0349 www.praisepage.com joe.booker@cumulus.com

Pine Bluff KCAT-AM (wgx) 1207 W 6th Ave, Pine Bluff AR 71601 **Phn:** 870-534-5001 **Fax:** 870-534-7985 www.kcatam.com news@lordradio.com

West Helena KAKJ-FM (wu) PO Box 2870, West Helena AR 72390 **Phn:** 870-633-9000 **Fax:** 870-572-1845 www.force2radio.com force2@sbcglobal.net

West Helena KCLT-FM (wu) PO Box 2870, West Helena AR 72390 **Phn:** 870-572-9506 **Fax:** 870-572-1845 www.force2radio.com force2@sbcglobal.net

CALIFORNIA

Inglewood KJLH-FM (wu) 161 N La Brea Ave, Inglewood CA 90301 **Phn:** 310-330-2200 **Fax:** 310-330-5555 www.kjlhradio.com

CONNECTICUT

Hartford WKND-AM (uw) 330 Main St, Hartford CT 06106 **Phn:** 860-524-0001 **Fax:** 860-548-1922

Hartford WRTC-FM (wj) 300 Summit St, Hartford CT 06106 **Phn:** 860-297-2450 **Fax:** 860-987-6214 www.wrtcfm.com wrtchartford@gmail.com

West Haven WNHU-FM (vbw) 300 Boston Post Rd, West Haven CT 06516 **Phn:** 203-934-9648 **Fax:** 203-306-3073 www.newhaven.edu281164 blane@newhaven.edu

DISTRICT OF COLUMBIA

Washington WHUR-FM (wu) 529 Bryant St NW, Washington DC 20059 **Phn:** 202-806-3500 **Fax:** 202-806-3522 www.whur.com programming@whur.com

FLORIDA

Belle Glade WSWN-AM (wg) PO Box 1505, Belle Glade FL 33430 **Phn:** 561-996-2063 **Fax:** 561-996-1852

Cocoa WJFP-FM (vw) 1150 King St, Cocoa FL 32922 **Phn:** 321-632-1000 **Fax:** 321-636-0000 wjfp.com

Hollywood WEDR-FM (wu) 2741 N 29th Ave, Hollywood FL 33020 **Phn:** 305-444-4404 **Fax:** 305-567-5774 www.wedr.com jerry.rushin@coxradio.com

Hollywood WHQT-FM (wut) 2741 N 29th Ave, Hollywood FL 33020 **Phn:** 305-444-4404 **Fax:** 954-847-3200 www.hot105fm.com jerry.rushin@coxradio.com

Jacksonville WCGL-AM (qwg) 3890 Dunn Ave Ste 804, Jacksonville FL 32218 **Phn:** 904-766-9955 **Fax:** 904-765-9214 www.wcgl1360.com wcgl@aol.com

Jacksonville WJBT-FM (uw) 11700 Central Pkwy, Jacksonville FL 32224 **Phn:** 904-636-0507 www.wjbt.com geewiz@ccjax.com

Jacksonville WSOL-FM (xuw) 11700 Central Pkwy, Jacksonville FL 32224 **Phn:** 904-636-0507 **Fax:** 904-997-7713 www.v1015.com kj@v1015.com

North Miami WMBM-AM (gwt) 13242 NW 7th Ave, North Miami FL 33168 **Phn:** 305-769-1100 **Fax:** 305-769-9975 www.wmbm.com trobinson@wmbm.com

Orlando WOKB-AM (xwg) 3765 N John Young Pkwy, Orlando FL 32804 **Phn:** 407-291-1395 **Fax:** 407-293-2870 www.wokbradio.com

Pensacola WNVY-AM (wug) 2070 N Palafox St, Pensacola FL 32501 **Phn:** 850-435-1115 **Fax:** 864-597-0687 www.wilkinsradio.com wnvy@wilkinsradio.com

Pensacola WRNE-AM (wux) 312 E Nine Mile Rd Ste 29D, Pensacola FL 32514 **Phn:** 850-478-6000 **Fax:** 850-484-8080 www.wrne980.com info@wrne980.com

Pensacola WVTJ-AM (gw) 2070 N Palafox St, Pensacola FL 32501 **Phn:** 850-432-3658 **Fax:** 864-597-0687 www.wilkinsradio.com wvtj@wilkinsradio.com

Port Saint Lucie WFLM-FM (uw) PO Box 880052, Port Saint Lucie FL 34988 **Phn:** 772-460-9356 **Fax:** 772-460-2700 www.1047theflame.com management@1047theflame.com

Saint Petersburg WRXB-AM (wau) 3551 42nd Ave S Ste B106, Saint Petersburg FL 33711 **Phn:** 727-865-1591 **Fax:** 727-866-1728 www.wrxb.us mediaguy@kentdgustafson.com

Tallahassee WANM-FM (wvj) 510 Orr Dr # 3056, Tallahassee FL 32304 **Phn:** 850-599-3083 **Fax:** 850-561-2829 www.wanm.org info@wanm.org

GEORGIA

Albany WJIZ-FM (wu) 809 S Westover Blvd, Albany GA 31707 **Phn:** 229-439-9704 **Fax:** 229-439-1509 www.wjiz.com

Albany WJYZ-AM (wg) 809 S Westover Blvd, Albany GA 31707 **Phn:** 229-439-9704 **Fax:** 229-439-1509 www.wjyz.com

Albany WQVE-FM (wu) 1104 W Broad Ave, Albany GA 31707 **Phn:** 229-888-5000 **Fax:** 229-888-5960 www.wqvealbany.com roger.russell@cumulus.com

Atlanta WHTA-FM (uwx) 101 Marietta St NW 12th Fl, Atlanta GA 30303 **Phn:** 404-765-9750 **Fax:** 404-688-7686 hotspotatl.com

Atlanta WVEE-FM (wu) 1201 Peachtree St NE Ste 800, Atlanta GA 30361 **Phn:** 404-898-8900 **Fax:** 404-898-8909 v103.cbslocal.com tbrown@cbs.com

Atlanta WYZE-AM (wg) 1111 Boulevard SE, Atlanta GA 30312 **Phn:** 404-622-7802 **Fax:** 404-622-6767 www.wyzeradio.com wyzepressmail@bellsouth.net

Augusta WAKB-FM (wu) PO Box 1584, Augusta GA 30903 **Phn:** 803-279-2330 **Fax:** 803-279-8149 www.1009magic.com vperry@perrybroadcasting.net

Augusta WKSP-FM (wxo) 2743 Perimeter Pkwy Ste 100-300, Augusta GA 30909 **Phn:** 706-396-6000 **Fax:** 706-396-6010 www.963kissfm.com fattz@963kissfm.com

Augusta WKZK-AM (wx) PO Box 1454, Augusta GA 30903 **Phn:** 706-738-9191 **Fax:** 706-481-8442 www.wkzk.net

Columbus WAGH-FM (wu) PO Box 687, Columbus GA 31902 **Phn:** 706-576-3000 **Fax:** 706-576-3010 www.mymagic101.com derrickgreene@clearchannel.com

Columbus WFXE-FM (wu) PO Box 1998, Columbus GA 31902 **Phn:** 706-576-3565 **Fax:** 706-576-3683 www.foxie105fm.com foxie1049@aol.com

Columbus WOKS-AM (wu) PO Box 1998, Columbus GA 31902 **Phn:** 706-576-3565 **Fax:** 706-576-3683

Hinesville WGML-AM (gw) PO Box 615, Hinesville GA 31310 **Phn:** 912-368-3399 **Fax:** 912-368-4191 www.phodd.orgwgml.html wgml99@yahoo.com

Irwinton WVKX-FM (uxw) PO Box 569, Irwinton GA 31042 **Phn:** 478-946-3445 **Fax:** 478-946-2406 love1037@windstream.net

Jackson WJGA-FM (wgr) PO Box 878, Jackson GA 30233 **Phn:** 770-775-3151 **Fax:** 770-775-3153

Lyons WBBT-AM (wx) PO Box 629, Lyons GA 30436 **Phn:** 912-526-8122 **Fax:** 912-526-9155

Macon WDDO-AM (wg) 544 Mulberry St Ste 500, Macon GA 31201 **Phn:** 478-746-6286 **Fax:** 478-742-8061 willie.collins@cumulus.com

Macon WIBB-FM (uw) 7080 Industrial Hwy, Macon GA 31216 **Phn:** 478-781-1063 **Fax:** 478-781-6711 www.wibb.com thomasbacote@clearchannel.com

Macon WQMJ-FM (wx) 6174 Ga Highway 57, Macon GA 31217 **Phn:** 478-745-3301 **Fax:** 478-742-2293

Macon WRBV-FM (uw) 7080 Industrial Hwy, Macon GA 31216 **Phn:** 478-781-1063 **Fax:** 478-781-6711

Savannah WEAS-FM (wu) 214 Television Cir, Savannah GA 31406 **Phn:** 912-961-9000 **Fax:** 912-961-7070 www.e93fm.com lg@cumulus.com

Savannah WLVH-FM (uw) 245 Alfred St, Savannah GA 31408 **Phn:** 912-964-7794 **Fax:** 912-964-9414 www.love1011.com community@love1011.com

Savannah WSOK-AM (wg) 245 Alfred St, Savannah GA 31408 **Phn:** 912-964-7794 **Fax:** 912-964-9414 www.1230wsok.com elarry@1230wsok.com

Thomasville WHGH-AM (wu) 19 Pall Bearer Rd, Thomasville GA 31792 **Phn:** 229-228-4124 **Fax:** 229-225-9508

BLACK RADIO STATIONS
ILLINOIS

Champaign WBCP-AM (wgu) 904 N 4th St Ste D, Champaign IL 61820 **Phn:** 217-359-1580 **Fax:** 217-359-1583 www.wbcp1580.com wbcpradio@sbcglobal.net

Chicago WGCI-FM (wu) 233 N Michigan Ave Ste 2800, Chicago IL 60601 **Phn:** 312-540-2000 **Fax:** 312-938-4477 www.wgci.com tywansley@wgci.com

Chicago WIIT-FM (vw) 3201 S State St, Chicago IL 60616 **Phn:** 312-567-3087 **Fax:** 312-567-7042 radio.iit.edu wiit@iit.edu

Chicago WVAZ-FM (wu) 233 N Michigan Ave Ste 2700, Chicago IL 60601 **Phn:** 312-540-2000 **Fax:** 312-938-7335 www.v103.com loyallistener@v103.com

INDIANA

Evansville WEOA-AM (uw) 915 Main St Ste 1, Evansville IN 47708 **Phn:** 812-424-8864 **Fax:** 812-424-9946 weoa_1@yahoo.com

Hammond WYCA-FM (gw) 6336 Calumet Ave, Hammond IN 46324 **Phn:** 219-933-4455 **Fax:** 219-933-0323 www.rejoice102.com

Indianapolis WHHH-FM (uw) 21 E Saint Joseph St, Indianapolis IN 46204 **Phn:** 317-266-9600 **Fax:** 317-328-3870 indyhiphop.com cwilliams@radio-one.com

Indianapolis WTLC-FM (xw) 21 E Saint Joseph St, Indianapolis IN 46204 **Phn:** 317-266-9600 **Fax:** 317-328-3870 tlcnaptown.com abrown@radio-one.com

Indianapolis WTLC-AM (wg) 21 E Saint Joseph St, Indianapolis IN 46204 **Phn:** 317-266-9600 **Fax:** 317-328-3870 praiseindy.com abrown@radio-one.com

IOWA

Waterloo KBBG-FM (vw) 918 Newell St, Waterloo IA 50703 **Phn:** 319-234-1441 **Fax:** 319-234-6182 www.kbbgfm.org realmanagement@kbbg.org

KENTUCKY

Louisville WGZB-FM (wu) 520 S 4th St 2nd Fl, Louisville KY 40202 **Phn:** 502-625-1220 **Fax:** 502-625-1257 www.b96jams.com

Louisville WLLV-AM (wg) 2001 W Broadway Ste 13, Louisville KY 40203 **Phn:** 502-776-1240 **Fax:** 502-776-1250

Louisville WLOU-AM (wjx) 2001 W Broadway Ste 13, Louisville KY 40203 **Phn:** 502-776-1240 **Fax:** 502-776-1250

LOUISIANA

Alexandria KBCE-FM (wu) 1605 Murray St Ste 111, Alexandria LA 71301 **Phn:** 318-445-0800 **Fax:** 318-445-1445

Baton Rouge KQXL-FM (wu) 650 Wooddale Blvd, Baton Rouge LA 70806 **Phn:** 225-926-1106 **Fax:** 225-928-1606 q106dot5.com jmichael.wxok@cumulus.com

Baton Rouge WEMX-FM (wu) 650 Wooddale Blvd, Baton Rouge LA 70806 **Phn:** 225-926-1106 **Fax:** 225-928-1606 www.max94one.com

Baton Rouge WXOK-AM (wgx) 650 Wooddale Blvd, Baton Rouge LA 70806 **Phn:** 225-926-1106 **Fax:** 225-928-1606

Bossier City KMJJ-FM (wu) PO Box 5459, Bossier City LA 71171 **Phn:** 318-549-8500 **Fax:** 318-549-8505 www.997kmjj.com kmjj@cumulus.com

Grambling KGRM-FM (vw) PO Box 4254, Grambling LA 71245 **Phn:** 318-274-6343 **Fax:** 318-274-3245 www.gram.edulifecampus%20mediakgrm evansjb@gram.edu

Lafayette KJCB-AM (wu) 604 Saint John St, Lafayette LA 70501 **Phn:** 337-233-4262 **Fax:** 337-235-9681

Lafayette KNEK-FM (wu) 202 Galbert Rd, Lafayette LA 70506 **Phn:** 337-232-1311 **Fax:** 337-233-3779 www.knek.com jackson.brown@cumulus.com

Lafayette KNEK-AM (wu) 202 Galbert Rd, Lafayette LA 70506 **Phn:** 337-232-1311 **Fax:** 337-233-3779 www.knek.com jackson.brown@cumulus.com

Lafayette KRRQ-FM (uw) 202 Galbert Rd, Lafayette LA 70506 **Phn:** 337-232-1311 **Fax:** 337-233-3779 www.krrq.com jackson.brown@cumulus.com

Lafayette KYMK-FM (wx) 3225 Ambassador Caffery Pkwy, Lafayette LA 70506 **Phn:** 337-993-5500 **Fax:** 337-993-5510 jimmiecole@gmail.com

Monroe KJMG-FM (wu) 1109 Hudson Ln, Monroe LA 71201 **Phn:** 318-388-2323 **Fax:** 318-388-0569

Monroe KRVV-FM (wu) 1109 Hudson Ln, Monroe LA 71201 **Phn:** 318-388-2323 **Fax:** 318-388-0569 www.thebeat.net

Morgan City KBZE-FM (wu) 1320 Victor II Blvd Ste 101, Morgan City LA 70380 **Phn:** 985-385-6266 **Fax:** 985-385-6268 www.kbze.com howard@kbze.com

Morgan City KFRA-AM (wu) 1320 Victor II Blvd, Morgan City LA 70380 **Phn:** 337-924-7100 www.1390kfra.com howard@kbze.com

New Orleans KMEZ-FM (wu) 201 Saint Charles Ave Ste 201, New Orleans LA 70170 **Phn:** 504-581-7002 **Fax:** 504-566-4857 www.oldschool1067.com lbj.kmez@cumulus.com

New Orleans WQUE-FM (wu) 929 Howard Ave, New Orleans LA 70113 **Phn:** 504-679-7300 **Fax:** 504-679-7345 www.q93.com angelawatson@clearchannel.com

New Orleans WYLD-FM (wu) 929 Howard Ave, New Orleans LA 70113 **Phn:** 504-679-7300 **Fax:** 504-679-7345 www.wyldfm.com adberry@wyldfm.com

New Roads KCLF-AM (wgu) 803 Parent St, New Roads LA 70760 **Phn:** 225-638-6821 **Fax:** 225-638-6882 rgremillion@bellsouth.net

Ruston KRUS-AM (wg) PO Box 430, Ruston LA 71273 **Phn:** 318-255-5000 **Fax:** 318-255-5084 radio1234@gmail.com

Shreveport KDKS-FM (wu) 208 N Thomas Dr, Shreveport LA 71107 **Phn:** 318-222-3122 **Fax:** 318-459-1493 www.kdks.fm qeradio@aol.com

Shreveport KOKA-AM (wg) 208 N Thomas Dr, Shreveport LA 71107 **Phn:** 318-222-3122 **Fax:** 318-459-1493 www.koka.am

Shreveport KSYB-AM (wg) PO Box 7685, Shreveport LA 71137 **Phn:** 318-222-2744 **Fax:** 318-425-7507 www.amistadradiogroup.com info@amistadradiogroup.com

MARYLAND

Baltimore WCAO-AM (gw) 711 W 40th St Ste 350, Baltimore MD 21211 **Phn:** 410-366-7600 **Fax:** 410-467-0011 www.heaven600.com lsmichaels@wcao.com

Baltimore WERQ-FM (wu) 1705 Whitehead Rd, Baltimore MD 21207 **Phn:** 410-332-4600 **Fax:** 410-944-7989 92q.com neke92@aol.com

Baltimore WOLB-AM (wnt) 1705 Whitehead Rd, Baltimore MD 21207 **Phn:** 410-332-4600 **Fax:** 410-944-7201 wolbbaltimore.com apayne@radio-one.com

Baltimore WWIN-FM (we) 1705 Whitehead Rd, Baltimore MD 21207 **Phn:** 410-332-4600 **Fax:** 410-944-2473 magicbaltimore.com kwynder@radio-one.com

Baltimore WWIN-AM (wg) 1705 Whitehead Rd, Baltimore MD 21207 **Phn:** 410-332-4600 **Fax:** 410-944-7989 mybaltimorespirit.com lyoung@radio-one.com

Lanham WOL-AM (wnt) 5900 Princess Garden Pkwy, Lanham MD 20706 **Phn:** 301-306-1111 **Fax:** 301-306-9540 woldcnews.com

Lanham WYCB-AM (wgu) 5900 Princess Garden Pkwy Ste 800, Lanham MD 20706 **Phn:** 301-306-1111 **Fax:** 301-306-9540 myspiritdc.com rthompson@radio-one.com

Silver Spring WKYS-FM (wu) 8515 Georgia Ave Flr 9, Silver Spring MD 20910 **Phn:** 301-306-1111 **Fax:** 301-306-9540 kysdc.com aleinwand@radio-one.com

Silver Spring WMMJ-FM (wau) 8515 Georgia Ave Flr 9, Silver Spring MD 20910 **Phn:** 301-306-1111 **Fax:** 301-306-9540 mymajicdc.com cbullock@radio-one.com

MICHIGAN

Detroit WDRJ-AM (wqg) 2994 E Grand Blvd, Detroit MI 48202 **Phn:** 313-871-1440 **Fax:** 313-871-6088

Detroit WJLB-FM (wu) 645 Griswold St Ste 633, Detroit MI 48226 **Phn:** 313-965-2000 **Fax:** 313-965-1729 www.fm98wjlb.com wjlb@fm98wjlb.com

Flint WDZZ-FM (wu) 6317 Taylor Dr, Flint MI 48507 **Phn:** 810-238-7300 **Fax:** 810-743-2500 www.wdzz.com amie.burke@cumulus.com

Flint WFLT-AM (wg) 317 S Averill Ave, Flint MI 48506 **Phn:** 810-762-1420 **Fax:** 810-239-7134 wflt1420am@aol.com

Flint WOWE-FM (wu) 126 W Kearsley St, Flint MI 48502 **Phn:** 810-234-4335 **Fax:** 810-234-7286

Lansing WQHH-FM (wu) 600 W Cavanaugh Rd, Lansing MI 48910 **Phn:** 517-393-1320 **Fax:** 517-393-0882 www.power965fm.com cindytuck@macdonaldbroadcasting.com

Lansing WXLA-AM (wx) 600 W Cavanaugh Rd, Lansing MI 48910 **Phn:** 517-393-1320 **Fax:** 517-393-0882 traffic@1017mikefm.com

Saginaw WTLZ-FM (wu) 1795 Tittabawassee Rd, Saginaw MI 48604 **Phn:** 989-752-3456 **Fax:** 989-754-5046 www.kisswtlz.com yvonne@kisswtlz.com

MISSISSIPPI

Bay Saint Louis WBSL-AM (xw) 1190 Hollywood Blvd, Bay Saint Louis MS 39520 **Phn:** 228-467-1190 **Fax:** 228-467-3525 ihatchett@bellsouth.net

Belzoni WELZ-AM (wg) PO Box 299, Belzoni MS 39038 **Phn:** 662-247-1744 **Fax:** 662-247-1745 www.power107.org power107@power107.org

Biloxi WQFX-AM (wg) 336 Rodenberg Ave, Biloxi MS 39531 **Phn:** 228-374-9739 wqfxradio@bellsouth.net

Brookhaven WCHJ-AM (wg) PO Box 177, Brookhaven MS 39602 **Phn:** 601-823-9006 **Fax:** 601-823-0503 victory1470wchj.com victory1470wchj@birch.net

Clarksdale WAID-FM (wu) PO Box 780, Clarksdale MS 38614 **Phn:** 662-627-2281 **Fax:** 662-624-2900

Clarksdale WROX-AM (gw) PO Box 1450, Clarksdale MS 38614 **Phn:** 662-627-1450 **Fax:** 662-621-1176 www.wroxradio.com manager@wroxradio.com

Cleveland WCLD-AM (gw) PO Box 780, Cleveland MS 38732 **Phn:** 662-843-4091 **Fax:** 662-843-9805

Cleveland WCLD-FM (wu) PO Box 780, Cleveland MS 38732 **Phn:** 662-843-4091 **Fax:** 662-843-9805

Columbia WCJU-AM (wg) PO Box 472, Columbia MS 39429 **Phn:** 601-736-2616 **Fax:** 601-736-2617

Greenville WBAD-FM (wju) PO Box 4426, Greenville MS 38704 **Phn:** 662-335-9265 **Fax:** 662-335-5538

Greenville WESY-AM (wgx) PO Box 5804, Greenville MS 38704 **Phn:** 662-378-9405 **Fax:** 662-335-5538

BLACK RADIO STATIONS

Greenwood WGNG-FM (wu) PO Box 1801, Greenwood MS 38935 **Phn:** 662-453-1646 **Fax:** 662-453-7002 wgnl@bellsouth.net

Greenwood WGNL-FM (wu) PO Box 1801, Greenwood MS 38935 **Phn:** 662-453-1643 **Fax:** 662-453-7002

Hattiesburg WJKX-FM (uw) 6555 Highway 98 W # 8, Hattiesburg MS 39402 **Phn:** 601-296-9800 **Fax:** 601-296-9838 www.102jkx.com contact@102jkx.com

Hattiesburg WJMG-FM (wu) 1204 Kinnard St, Hattiesburg MS 39401 **Phn:** 601-544-1941 **Fax:** 601-544-1947

Hattiesburg WORV-AM (wg) 1204 Kinnard St, Hattiesburg MS 39401 **Phn:** 601-544-1941 **Fax:** 601-544-1947

Holly Springs WKRA-FM (wx) PO Box 398, Holly Springs MS 38635 **Phn:** 662-252-6692 **Fax:** 662-252-2739

Holly Springs WKRA-AM (gw) 1400 Highway 4 E # C, Holly Springs MS 38635 **Phn:** 662-252-1110 **Fax:** 662-252-2739

Holly Springs WURC-FM (wvj) 150 Rust Ave, Holly Springs MS 38635 **Phn:** 662-252-5881 **Fax:** 662-252-8869 www.wurc.org dmoyo@rustcollege.edu

Houston WCPC-AM (cgw) 1189 N Jackson St, Houston MS 38851 **Phn:** 662-456-3071 www.wilkinsradio.com wcpc@wilkinsradio.com

Indianola WNLA-AM (wg) PO Box 667, Indianola MS 38751 **Phn:** 662-887-1380 **Fax:** 662-887-1396 gospel1380.com wnlaamfm@bellsouth.net

Jackson WHLH-FM (wg) 1375 Beasley Rd, Jackson MS 39206 **Phn:** 601-982-1062 **Fax:** 601-362-1905 www.hallelujah955.com kennywindham@clearchannel.com

Jackson WMPR-FM (vwg) 1018 Pecan Park Cir, Jackson MS 39209 **Phn:** 601-948-5835 **Fax:** 601-948-6162 www.wmpr901.com frontoffice@wmpr901.com

Jackson WOAD-FM (wg) PO Box 9446, Jackson MS 39286 **Phn:** 601-957-1300 **Fax:** 601-956-0516 www.woad.com kwebb1234@aol.com

Jackson WOAD-AM (gw) PO Box 9446, Jackson MS 39286 **Phn:** 601-957-1300 **Fax:** 601-956-0516 www.woad.com

Lexington WXTN-AM (wg) 100 Radio Rd, Lexington MS 39095 **Phn:** 662-834-1025 **Fax:** 662-834-1254

McComb WAKK-AM (wu) PO Box 1649, McComb MS 39649 **Phn:** 601-684-4116 **Fax:** 601-684-4654 sandlow@telepak.net

Meridian WNBN-AM (wgt) 266 23rd St, Meridian MS 39301 **Phn:** 601-483-3401 **Fax:** 601-483-3411 frankrack@netzero.com

Natchez WMIS-AM (wgx) 20 E Franklin St, Natchez MS 39120 **Phn:** 601-442-2522 **Fax:** 601-446-9918 wmiswtyj@bellsouth.net

Natchez WTYJ-FM (wux) 20 E Franklin St, Natchez MS 39120 **Phn:** 601-442-2522 **Fax:** 601-446-9918 wmiswtyj@bellsouth.net

Senatobia WSAO-AM (wqg) PO Box 190, Senatobia MS 38668 **Phn:** 662-562-4445 **Fax:** 662-562-9881 jrer1140@aol.com

Tupelo WESE-FM (wu) 5026 Cliff Gookin Blvd, Tupelo MS 38801 **Phn:** 662-842-1067 **Fax:** 662-842-0725 www.power925jamz.com markmaharrey@urbanradio.fm

Vicksburg WRTM-FM (wx) PO Box 820583, Vicksburg MS 39182 **Phn:** 601-636-7944 radioair@bellsouth.net

MISSOURI

Kansas City KPRS-FM (wu) 11131 Colorado Ave, Kansas City MO 64137 **Phn:** 816-763-2040 **Fax:** 816-966-1055 www.kprs.com beth@kprs.com

Kansas City KPRT-AM (wg) 11131 Colorado Ave, Kansas City MO 64137 **Phn:** 816-763-2040 **Fax:** 816-966-1055 www.kprt.com myrond@kprs.com

Saint Louis KATZ-AM (wg) 1001 Highlands Plaza Dr W Ste 110, Saint Louis MO 63110 **Phn:** 314-333-8000 **Fax:** 314-333-8200 www.hallelujah1600.com katzam@clearchannel.com

Saint Louis KMJM-FM (uw) 1001 Highlands Plaza Dr W Ste 100, Saint Louis MO 63110 **Phn:** 314-333-8000 **Fax:** 314-333-8300 www.kmjm.com kmjm@clearchannel.com

Saint Louis KSTL-AM (gw) 10845 Olive Blvd Ste 160, Saint Louis MO 63141 **Phn:** 314-878-3600 **Fax:** 314-656-3608 www.shine690.com

Saint Louis WSDD-FM (wx) 1001 Highlands Plaza Dr W, Saint Louis MO 63110 **Phn:** 314-333-8000 **Fax:** 314-333-8200 www.wild1049stl.com wild1049stl@clearchannel.com

NEVADA

Las Vegas KCEP-FM (wv) 330 W Washington Ave, Las Vegas NV 89106 **Phn:** 702-648-0104 **Fax:** 702-647-0803 kcep.power88lv.com power88@power88lv.com

NEW JERSEY

Hasbrouck Heights WMCA-AM (wtq) 777 Terrace Ave Ste 602, Hasbrouck Heights NJ 07604 **Phn:** 201-298-5700 **Fax:** 201-298-5797 www.wmca.com contact@nycradio.com

Trenton WIMG-AM (wgu) PO Box 9078, Trenton NJ 08650 **Phn:** 609-695-1300 **Fax:** 609-278-1588 www.wimg1300.com vennie@wimg1300.com

NEW MEXICO

Albuquerque KANW-FM (wv) 2020 Coal Ave SE, Albuquerque NM 87106 **Phn:** 505-242-7163 www.kanw.com brasher@aps.edu

Albuquerque KSYU-FM (wx) 5411 Jefferson St NE Ste 100, Albuquerque NM 87109 **Phn:** 505-830-6400 **Fax:** 505-830-6543 ryan@clearchannel.com

NEW YORK

Buffalo WBLK-FM (wu) 14 Lafayette Sq Ste 1300, Buffalo NY 14203 **Phn:** 716-852-9393 **Fax:** 716-852-9290 wblk.com chris.reynolds@townsquaremedia.com

Buffalo WUFO-AM (wg) 89 Lasalle Ave, Buffalo NY 14214 **Phn:** 716-834-1080 **Fax:** 716-837-1438 www.wufoam.com lpettigrew@wufoam.com

East Syracuse WSIV-AM (wgq) 7095 Myers Rd, East Syracuse NY 13057 **Phn:** 315-656-2231 **Fax:** 315-656-2259

Latham WAJZ-FM (wua) 6 Johnson Rd, Latham NY 12110 **Phn:** 518-786-6600 **Fax:** 518-786-6669 jamz963.com charlie@jamz963.com

Mineola WTHE-AM (wgu) 260 E 2nd St, Mineola NY 11501 **Phn:** 516-742-1520 **Fax:** 516-742-2878 www.wthe1520am.com nygospelradio@aol.com

New York WBLS-FM (wu) 3 Park Ave, New York NY 10016 **Phn:** 212-447-1000 **Fax:** 212-447-5791 www.wbls.com cynthia@wbls.com

New York WHCR-FM (wvy) 160 Convent Ave, New York NY 10031 **Phn:** 212-650-7481 **Fax:** 212-650-5736 www.whcr.org generalmanager@whcr.org

New York WLIB-AM (wq) 641 Avenue Of The Americas Fl 4, New York NY 10011 **Phn:** 212-447-1000 **Fax:** 212-447-5791 www.wlib.com info@wlib.com

New York WWPR-FM (wx) 32 Avenue Of The Americas Bldg 1, New York NY 10013 **Phn:** 212-377-7900 **Fax:** 212-549-0832 www.power1051fm.com

New York WWRL-AM (wge) 333 7th Ave Rm 1401, New York NY 10001 **Phn:** 212-631-0800 **Fax:** 212-239-7203 www.wwrl1600.com adriane@wwrl1600.com

Rochester WDKX-FM (wu) 683 E Main St, Rochester NY 14605 **Phn:** 585-262-2050 **Fax:** 585-262-2626 www.wdkx.com wdkx@wdkx.com

Rochester WJZR-FM (wju) 1237 E Main St Ste E, Rochester NY 14609 **Phn:** 585-288-5020

Rochester WKGS-FM (hw) 100 Chestnut St Ste 1700, Rochester NY 14604 **Phn:** 585-232-8870 **Fax:** 585-454-5081 www.kiss1067.com aj@clearchannel.com

NORTH CAROLINA

Ahoskie WRCS-AM (wg) 443 Nc Highway 42 W, Ahoskie NC 27910 **Phn:** 252-332-3101 **Fax:** 252-332-3103 wrcs@embarqmail.com

Chadbourn WVOE-AM (wgx) 1528 Old US Highway 74, Chadbourn NC 28431 **Phn:** 910-654-5621 **Fax:** 910-654-4385

Charlotte WPEG-FM (uw) 1520 South Blvd Ste 300, Charlotte NC 28203 **Phn:** 704-522-1103 **Fax:** 704-227-8979 power98fm.cbslocal.com tlavery@cbs.com

Fairmont WFMO-AM (gwy) PO Box 668, Fairmont NC 28340 **Phn:** 910-628-6781 **Fax:** 910-628-6648

Fayetteville WAGR-AM (gw) 1338 Bragg Blvd, Fayetteville NC 28301 **Phn:** 910-483-6111 **Fax:** 910-483-6601

Fayetteville WFSS-FM (vjw) 1200 Murchison Rd, Fayetteville NC 28301 **Phn:** 910-672-1381 **Fax:** 910-672-1964 www.wfss.org jross@uncfsu.edu

Fayetteville WIDU-AM (gw) 145 Rowan St # A3, Fayetteville NC 28301 **Phn:** 910-483-6111 **Fax:** 910-483-6601 www.widuradio.com

Fayetteville WZFX-FM (wu) 508 Person St, Fayetteville NC 28301 **Phn:** 910-486-4114 **Fax:** 910-486-6720 www.foxy99.com promotions@foxy99.com

Goldsboro WFMC-AM (wgu) 2581 US Highway 70 W, Goldsboro NC 27530 **Phn:** 919-736-1150 **Fax:** 919-736-3876 www.730wfmc.com cbowden@curtismedia.com

Greensboro WJMH-FM (wu) 7819 National Service Rd Ste 401, Greensboro NC 27409 **Phn:** 336-605-5200 **Fax:** 336-605-5219 www.102jamz.com kscales@entercom.com

Greensboro WNAA-FM (wv) 302 Crosby Hall, Greensboro NC 27411 **Phn:** 336-334-7936 **Fax:** 336-334-7960 wnaa-online.ncat.edu tonyb@ncat.edu

Greensboro WQMG-FM (wu) 7819 National Service Rd Ste 401, Greensboro NC 27409 **Phn:** 336-605-5200 **Fax:** 336-605-0138 www.wqmg.com scole@entercom.com

New Bern WIKS-FM (wu) 207 Glenburnie Dr, New Bern NC 28560 **Phn:** 252-633-1500 **Fax:** 252-633-0718 1019online.com teresaterry@1019online.com

Pineville WGCD-AM (wxqg) 9349 China Grove Church Rd, Pineville NC 28134 **Phn:** 980-297-7256 **Fax:** 980-297-7248 www.wgivcharlotte.com mikerobinson@wgiv.net

Pineville WGIV-AM (wx) 9349 China Grove Church Rd, Pineville NC 28134 **Phn:** 980-297-7256 **Fax:** 980-297-7248 www.wgivcharlotte.com mikerobinson@wgiv.net

Pineville WGIV-FM (wx) 9349 China Grove Church Rd, Pineville NC 28134 **Phn:** 980-297-7256 **Fax:** 980-297-7248 mikerobinson@wgiv.net

BLACK RADIO STATIONS

Pineville WYPJ-FM (wxqg) 9349 China Grove Church Rd, Pineville NC 28134 **Phn:** 980-297-7256 **Fax:** 980-297-7248 www.wgivcharlotte.com mikerobinson@wgiv.net

Raleigh WAUG-AM (wgu) 1315 Oakwood Ave, Raleigh NC 27610 **Phn:** 919-516-4750 **Fax:** 919-516-4087 www.mywaug.com

Raleigh WFXC-FM (wu) 8001 Creedmoor Rd Ste 101, Raleigh NC 27613 **Phn:** 919-863-4800 **Fax:** 919-848-4724 foxync.com

Raleigh WFXK-FM (wu) 8001 Creedmoor Rd # 100, Raleigh NC 27613 **Phn:** 919-863-4800 **Fax:** 919-848-4724 foxync.com

Raleigh WKNC-FM (wv) PO Box 8607, Raleigh NC 27695 **Phn:** 919-515-2401 **Fax:** 919-515-5133 wknc.org gm@wknc.org

Rocky Mount WRSV-FM (wu) 115 N Church St, Rocky Mount NC 27804 **Phn:** 252-937-6111 **Fax:** 252-443-5977 wrsv-fm.tritondigitalmedia.com chuckjohnson9210@gmail.com

Sanford WXKL-AM (wgx) PO Box 1290, Sanford NC 27331 **Phn:** 919-774-1080 **Fax:** 919-774-1118

Tarboro WCPS-AM (gwx) 1406 Saint Andrew St, Tarboro NC 27886 **Phn:** 252-824-7878 **Fax:** 252-824-7818

Whiteville WENC-AM (wgx) 108 Radio Station Rd, Whiteville NC 28472 **Phn:** 910-642-2133 **Fax:** 910-642-5981

Wilmington WKXS-FM (uw) 3233 Burnt Mill Dr, Wilmington NC 28403 **Phn:** 910-763-9977 **Fax:** 910-762-0456 www.945thehawkradio.com brian.sims@cumulus.com

Wilmington WMNX-FM (wu) 3233 Burnt Mill Dr, Wilmington NC 28403 **Phn:** 910-763-6511 **Fax:** 910-763-5926 www.coast973.com brian.sims@cumulus.com

Wilson WGTM-AM (wg) PO Box 3837, Wilson NC 27895 **Phn:** 252-243-2188 **Fax:** 252-237-8813

Winston Salem WSNC-FM (wvj) 601 M L K Jr Dr, Winston Salem NC 27110 **Phn:** 336-750-2324 **Fax:** 336-750-2329 jenkinse@wssu.edu

OHIO

Blue Ash WCIN-AM (wou) 4445 Lake Forest Dr Ste 420, Blue Ash OH 45242 **Phn:** 513-281-7180 **Fax:** 513-281-5678 www.oldies1480.net garys@oldies1480.net

Bowling Green WBGU-FM (vjw) Bowling Green State U, Bowling Green OH 43403 **Phn:** 419-372-8657 wbgufm.com

Cincinnati WDBZ-AM (wt) 705 Central Ave Ste 200, Cincinnati OH 45202 **Phn:** 513-679-6000 **Fax:** 513-679-6014 thebuzzcincy.com jtolliver@radio-one.com

Cincinnati WIZF-FM (uw) 705 Central Ave Ste 200, Cincinnati OH 45202 **Phn:** 513-679-6000 **Fax:** 513-679-6014 wiznation.com ejgreig@radio-one.com

Cleveland WABQ-AM (wg) 8000 Euclid Ave, Cleveland OH 44103 **Phn:** 216-231-8005 **Fax:** 216-231-9803

Cleveland WJMO-AM (wg) 6555 Carnegie Ave # 100, Cleveland OH 44103 **Phn:** 216-579-1111 **Fax:** 216-771-4164 praisecleveland.com

Cleveland WZAK-FM (wu) 6555 Carnegie Ave # 100, Cleveland OH 44103 **Phn:** 216-579-1111 **Fax:** 216-771-4164 wzakcleveland.com

Columbus WCKX-FM (uw) 350 E 1st Ave Ste 100, Columbus OH 43201 **Phn:** 614-487-1444 **Fax:** 614-487-5862 mycolumbuspower.com

Dayton WDAO-AM (uwx) 1012 W 3rd St, Dayton OH 45402 **Phn:** 937-222-9326 **Fax:** 937-461-6100

Dayton WROU-FM (uw) 717 E David Rd, Dayton OH 45429 **Phn:** 937-294-5858 **Fax:** 937-297-5233 www.921wrou.com

Elyria WJTB-AM (wug) 105 Lake Ave, Elyria OH 44035 **Phn:** 440-327-1844 **Fax:** 440-322-8942

Toledo WIMX-FM (uw) 720 Water St, Toledo OH 43604 **Phn:** 419-244-8261 **Fax:** 419-244-9261 www.mix957.net brandibrown@urbanradio.fm

Toledo WJZE-FM (uw) 720 Water St, Toledo OH 43604 **Phn:** 419-244-8261 **Fax:** 419-244-8261 www.mix957.net brandibrown@urbanradio.fm

Youngstown WASN-AM (wqg) 20 W Federal St # T-2, Youngstown OH 44503 **Phn:** 330-744-5115 **Fax:** 330-744-4020 www.1500wasn.com skip@ytownradio.com

OKLAHOMA

Oklahoma City KTLV-AM (gqw) 3336 SE 67th St, Oklahoma City OK 73135 **Phn:** 405-672-3886 **Fax:** 405-672-5858 www.ktlv1220.com ktlv1220@aol.com

Oklahoma City KVSP-AM (wxu) 1528 NE 23rd St, Oklahoma City OK 73111 **Phn:** 405-427-5877 **Fax:** 405-424-6708 www.kvsp.com kperry@kvsp.com

Tulsa KGTO-AM (wx) 7030 S Yale Ave Ste 302, Tulsa OK 74136 **Phn:** 918-494-9886 **Fax:** 918-494-9683 www.perrybroadcasting.net

Tulsa KJMM-FM (uw) 7030 S Yale Ave Ste 302, Tulsa OK 74136 **Phn:** 918-494-9886 **Fax:** 918-494-9683 www.kjmm.com traffic@kjmm.com

PENNSYLVANIA

Bala Cynwyd WDAS-AM (wg) 111 Presidential Blvd Ste 100, Bala Cynwyd PA 19004 **Phn:** 610-784-3333 **Fax:** 610-784-2098 www.wdasfm.com loraineballardmorrill@clearchannel.com

Bala Cynwyd WDAS-FM (wu) 111 Presidential Blvd Ste 100, Bala Cynwyd PA 19004 **Phn:** 610-784-3333 **Fax:** 610-784-2098 www.wdasfm.com lorainemorrill@clearchannel.com

Bala Cynwyd WRNB-FM (wx) 2 Bala Plz Ste 700, Bala Cynwyd PA 19004 **Phn:** 610-276-1100 **Fax:** 610-276-1139 oldschool1003.com elroysmith@radio-one.com

Bala Cynwyd WUSL-FM (wu) 111 Presidential Blvd Ste 100, Bala Cynwyd PA 19004 **Phn:** 610-784-3333 **Fax:** 610-784-2075 www.power99.com lorainemorrill@clearchannel.com

Conshohocken WPPZ-FM (wg) 1000 River Rd Ste 400, Conshohocken PA 19428 **Phn:** 610-276-1100 **Fax:** 610-276-1139 praisephilly.com elroysmith@radio-one.com

New Kensington WGBN-AM (gw) 560 7th St, New Kensington PA 15068 **Phn:** 724-337-3588 **Fax:** 724-337-1318 wgbn.net

Norristown WNAP-AM (wg) 2311 Old Arch Rd, Norristown PA 19401 **Phn:** 610-272-7600 **Fax:** 610-272-5793 www.wnap1110am.com fred@wnap1110am.com

Philadelphia WURD-AM (wt) 1341 N Delaware Ave Ste 300, Philadelphia PA 19125 **Phn:** 215-425-7875 **Fax:** 215-634-6003 900amwurd.com 900amwurd@wurdradio.com

SOUTH CAROLINA

Allendale WDOG-FM (cwu) PO Box 442, Allendale SC 29810 **Phn:** 803-584-3500 **Fax:** 803-584-0202 www.bigdogradio.com wdog935@aol.com

Beaufort WVGB-AM (wg) 806 Monson St, Beaufort SC 29902 **Phn:** 843-524-4700 **Fax:** 843-524-1329 945thecoast.com karl@945thecoast.com

Clemson WAHT-AM (gw) PO Box 1560, Clemson SC 29633 **Phn:** 864-654-4004 **Fax:** 864-654-3300

Columbia WGCV-AM (wg) 2440 Millwood Ave, Columbia SC 29205 **Phn:** 803-939-9530 **Fax:** 803-799-1620 www.wgcv.net tjamison@wfmv.com

Columbia WOIC-AM (uw) 1900 Pineview Dr, Columbia SC 29209 **Phn:** 803-776-1013 **Fax:** 803-695-8605 www.woic.com programming@woic.com

Columbia WWDM-FM (wu) 1900 Pineview Dr, Columbia SC 29209 **Phn:** 803-695-8600 **Fax:** 803-695-8605 www.thebigdm.com cconnors@innercitysc.com

Conway WPJS-AM (wg) PO Box 961, Conway SC 29528 **Phn:** 843-248-6365 **Fax:** 843-248-2890

Florence WYNN-FM (wu) 2014 N Irby St, Florence SC 29501 **Phn:** 843-661-5000 **Fax:** 843-661-0888 www.wynn1063.com gerald.mcswain@cumulus.com

Florence WYNN-AM (gw) 2014 N Irby St, Florence SC 29501 **Phn:** 843-661-5000 **Fax:** 843-661-0888 www.wynn1063.com gerald.mcswain@cumulus.com

Gaffney WFGN-AM (wgu) PO Box 1388, Gaffney SC 29342 **Phn:** 864-489-9430 **Fax:** 864-489-9440

Georgetown WLMC-AM (wgut) 2508 Highmarket St, Georgetown SC 29440 **Phn:** 843-546-1400 **Fax:** 843-546-6821 www.wlmcradio.com wlmcradio@aol.com

Greenville WJMZ-FM (wu) 220 N Main St Ste 402, Greenville SC 29601 **Phn:** 864-235-1073 **Fax:** 864-370-3403 www.1073jamz.com karolyn.mulvaney@summitmediacorp.com

Greenwood WLMA-AM (wg) 1220 Bypass 72 NE, Greenwood SC 29649 **Phn:** 864-229-7984 **Fax:** 864-229-5896 www.wlma.net wlma@wlma.net

Greer WPJM-AM (gw) 305 N Tryon St, Greer SC 29651 **Phn:** 864-877-1112 **Fax:** 864-877-0342 www.800wpjm.com

Irmo WIGL-FM (wu) PO Box 537, Irmo SC 29063 **Phn:** 803-536-1710 **Fax:** 803-531-1089

Marion WJAY-AM (wg) PO Box 1020, Marion SC 29571 **Phn:** 843-423-1140 **Fax:** 843-423-2829

Newberry WKMG-AM (wuo) 1840 Glenn Street Ext, Newberry SC 29108 **Phn:** 803-405-0111

North Augusta WFXA-FM (wu) 104 Bennett Ln, North Augusta SC 29841 **Phn:** 803-279-2330 **Fax:** 803-279-8149

North Augusta WTHB-AM (wg) 411 Radio Station Rd, North Augusta SC 29841 **Phn:** 803-279-2330 **Fax:** 803-279-8149 praise969.com vperry@perrybroadcasting.net

North Charleston WMGL-FM (uw) 4230 Faber Place Dr Ste 100, North Charleston SC 29405 **Phn:** 843-277-1200 **Fax:** 843-277-1212 www.magic1017.com terry.base@cumulus.com

North Charleston WWWZ-FM (wu) 4230 Faber Place Dr Ste 100, North Charleston SC 29405 **Phn:** 843-277-1200 **Fax:** 843-277-1212 www.z93jamz.com terry.base@cumulus.com

Orangeburg WPJK-AM (gw) 175 Cannon Bridge Rd, Orangeburg SC 29115 **Phn:** 803-534-4848

Orangeburg WSSB-FM (wv) PO Box 7619, Orangeburg SC 29117 **Phn:** 803-536-8585 **Fax:** 803-516-4700 www.wssb903fm.org wssb@scsu.edu

Saint Stephen WTUA-FM (wg) 4013 Byrnes Dr, Saint Stephen SC 29479 **Phn:** 843-567-2091 **Fax:** 843-567-3088

Spartanburg WASC-AM (wu) PO Box 5686, Spartanburg SC 29304 **Phn:** 864-585-1530 **Fax:** 864-573-7790

Sumter WWKT-FM (wu) 51 Commerce St, Sumter SC 29150 **Phn:** 803-775-2321 **Fax:** 803-773-4856 www.katcountry993.net dbaker@miller.fm

BLACK RADIO STATIONS

West Columbia WFMV-FM (quw) PO Box 2355, West Columbia SC 29171 **Phn:** 803-939-9530 **Fax:** 803-939-9469 columbiainspiration.com tonyg@wfmv.com

West Columbia WLJI-FM (ugw) PO Box 2355, West Columbia SC 29171 **Phn:** 803-939-9530 **Fax:** 803-939-9469 columbiainspiration.com athomas@wfmv.com

TENNESSEE

Bolivar WOJG-FM (gw) PO Box 191, Bolivar TN 38008 **Phn:** 731-658-3690 **Fax:** 731-658-3408 www.wojg.com tracy.shaw@wojg.com

Brownsville WNWS-AM (wg) PO Box 198, Brownsville TN 38012 **Phn:** 731-772-3700

Chattanooga WJTT-FM (wu) 1305 Carter St, Chattanooga TN 37402 **Phn:** 423-265-9494 **Fax:** 423-266-2335 www.power94.com jay@power94.com

Chattanooga WMPZ-FM (wg) 1305 Carter St, Chattanooga TN 37402 **Phn:** 423-265-9494 **Fax:** 423-266-2335 www.groove93.com

Chattanooga WNOO-AM (wug) PO Box 5597, Chattanooga TN 37412 **Phn:** 423-698-8617 **Fax:** 423-698-8796 www.wnooradio.com wnoo@epbinternet.com

Columbia WMRB-AM (gw) 1116 W 7th St, Columbia TN 38401 **Phn:** 931-381-7100 **Fax:** 931-381-0088

Jackson WFKX-FM (wuh) 111 W Main St, Jackson TN 38301 **Phn:** 731-427-9616 **Fax:** 731-427-9302

Memphis KJMS-FM (wu) 2650 Thousand Oaks Blvd Ste 4100, Memphis TN 38118 **Phn:** 901-259-1300 **Fax:** 901-259-6451 www.myv101.com frankgilbert@clearchannel.com

Memphis KXHT-FM (uw) 6080 Mount Moriah Road Ext, Memphis TN 38115 **Phn:** 901-375-9324 **Fax:** 901-375-4117 www.hot1071.com

Memphis WDIA-AM (wx) 2650 Thousand Oaks Blvd Ste 4100, Memphis TN 38118 **Phn:** 901-259-1300 **Fax:** 901-259-6451 www.mywdia.com jefflee@clearchannel.com

Memphis WHRK-FM (wu) 2650 Thousand Oaks Blvd Ste 4100, Memphis TN 38118 **Phn:** 901-259-1300 **Fax:** 901-259-6449 www.k97fm.com devinsteel@clearchannel.com

Memphis WLOK-AM (wgt) 363 S 2nd St, Memphis TN 38103 **Phn:** 901-527-9565 **Fax:** 901-528-0335 www.wlok.com wlokradio@aol.com

Memphis WUMR-FM (vjw) 3745 Central Ave, Memphis TN 38152 **Phn:** 901-678-3176 **Fax:** 901-678-4331

Nashville WNAH-AM (wq) 44 Music Sq E Ste 101, Nashville TN 37203 **Phn:** 615-254-7611 **Fax:** 615-256-6553 www.wnah.com

Nashville WQQK-FM (wu) 10 Music Cir E, Nashville TN 37203 **Phn:** 615-321-1067 **Fax:** 615-321-5771 www.92qnashville.com ernie.allen@cumulus.com

Nashville WVOL-AM (wxo) 1320 Brick Church Pike, Nashville TN 37207 **Phn:** 615-226-9510 **Fax:** 615-226-0709 www.wvol1470.com wvol1470@aol.com

TEXAS

Austin KAZI-FM (vwj) 8906 Wall St Ste 203, Austin TX 78754 **Phn:** 512-836-9544 **Fax:** 512-836-9563 www.kazifm.org marion@kazifm.org

Baytown KWWJ-AM (wg) 4638 Decker Dr, Baytown TX 77520 **Phn:** 281-837-8777 **Fax:** 281-424-7588 www.kwwj.org kwwj1360@yahoo.com

Beaumont KZZB-AM (gw) 2531 Calder St, Beaumont TX 77702 **Phn:** 409-833-0990 **Fax:** 409-833-0995

Conroe KYOK-AM (wg) 300 Bryant Rd, Conroe TX 77303 **Phn:** 936-441-1140 **Fax:** 936-788-1140

Dallas KGGR-AM (wgq) 5787 S Hampton Rd Ste 285, Dallas TX 75232 **Phn:** 972-572-5447 **Fax:** 214-330-6133 www.kggram.com

Dallas KHVN-AM (wg) 5787 S Hampton Rd Ste 285, Dallas TX 75232 **Phn:** 214-331-5486 **Fax:** 214-331-1908 khvnam.com rwashley@yahoo.com

Dallas KKDA-AM (wu) 1230 River Bend Dr Ste 150, Dallas TX 75247 **Phn:** 214-583-1400 **Fax:** 214-638-5316 traffic@k104fm.com

Dallas KKDA-FM (wu) 1230 River Bend Dr Ste 150, Dallas TX 75247 **Phn:** 214-583-1430 **Fax:** 214-638-5316 www.myk104.com community@k104fm.com

Dallas KKGM-AM (wgq) 5787 S Hampton Rd Ste 108, Dallas TX 75232 **Phn:** 214-337-5700 **Fax:** 214-337-5707 www.kkgmam.com paul.hughes@kkgmam.com

Grand Prairie KRNB-FM (wx) 621 NW 6th St, Grand Prairie TX 75050 **Phn:** 972-263-9911 **Fax:** 972-558-0010 www.krnb.com community@krnb.com

Harker Heights KIIZ-FM (uw) PO Box 2469, Harker Heights TX 76548 **Phn:** 254-699-5000 www.kiiz.com

Houston KCOH-AM (wu) 5011 Almeda Rd, Houston TX 77004 **Phn:** 713-522-1001 **Fax:** 713-521-0769 www.kcohradio.com info@kcohradio.com

Houston KMJQ-FM (wux) 24 Greenway Plz Ste 900, Houston TX 77046 **Phn:** 713-623-2108 myhoustonmajic.com dabernethy@radio-one.com

Marshall KBWC-FM (wv) 711 Wiley Ave, Marshall TX 75670 **Phn:** 903-927-3266

Prairie View KPVU-FM (wvj) PO Box 519, Prairie View TX 77446 **Phn:** 936-261-3750 **Fax:** 936-261-3769 www.pvamu.edukpvu cdbrooks@pvamu.edu

San Antonio KCHL-AM (gw) 1211 W Hein Rd, San Antonio TX 78220 **Phn:** 210-333-0050 **Fax:** 210-333-0081 www.kchl.org

Wharton KANI-AM (wqg) PO Box 350, Wharton TX 77488 **Phn:** 979-532-3800 **Fax:** 979-532-8510 kaniam1500@yahoo.com

VIRGINIA

Charlottesville WUVA-FM (uw) 1928 Arlington Blvd Ste 312, Charlottesville VA 22903 **Phn:** 434-817-6880 **Fax:** 434-817-6884 www.92.7kissfm.com programming@92.7kissfm.com

Chatham WKBY-AM (wg) 12932 US Highway 29, Chatham VA 24531 **Phn:** 434-432-8108 **Fax:** 434-432-1523 sweetlois@hotmail.com

Falls Church WUST-AM (we) 2131 Crimmins Ln, Falls Church VA 22043 **Phn:** 703-532-0400 **Fax:** 703-532-5033 www.wust1120.com contactwust@wust1120.com

Hampton WTJZ-AM (wq) 553 Michigan Dr, Hampton VA 23669 **Phn:** 757-723-1270

Lynchburg WILA-AM (wx) 1209 McKinney Ave, Lynchburg VA 24502 **Phn:** 434-792-2133 **Fax:** 434-792-2134

Lynchburg WLLL-AM (wg) PO Box 11375, Lynchburg VA 24506 **Phn:** 434-385-9555 **Fax:** 434-385-6073 www.wlllradio.com wlllam930@aol.com

Norfolk WJCD-FM (wx) 1003 Norfolk Sq, Norfolk VA 23502 **Phn:** 757-466-0009 **Fax:** 757-466-7043 www.kissva.com mattderrick@clearchannel.com

Norfolk WOWI-FM (wu) 1003 Norfolk Sq, Norfolk VA 23502 **Phn:** 757-466-0009 **Fax:** 757-466-9523 www.103jamz.com 103jamz@clearchannel.com

Norfolk WPCE-AM (wgq) 645 Church St Ste 400, Norfolk VA 23510 **Phn:** 757-622-4600 **Fax:** 757-624-6515 walterbrickhouse@yahoo.com

Richmond WBTJ-FM (wx) 3245 Basie Rd, Richmond VA 23228 **Phn:** 804-474-0000 **Fax:** 804-474-0092 www.1065thebeat.com ruthjones@clearchannel.com

Richmond WCDX-FM (wu) 2809 Emerywood Pkwy Ste 300, Richmond VA 23294 **Phn:** 804-672-9299 **Fax:** 804-672-9314 ipowerrichmond.com janderson@radio-one.com

Richmond WFTH-AM (qw) 227 E Belt Blvd Ste C, Richmond VA 23224 **Phn:** 804-233-0765 **Fax:** 804-233-3725

Richmond WPZZ-FM (wu) 2809 Emerywood Pkwy Ste 300, Richmond VA 23294 **Phn:** 804-672-9299 **Fax:** 804-672-9316 praiserichmond.com rebaker@radio-one.com

Richmond WTPS-AM (wnt) 2809 Emerywood Pkwy Ste 300, Richmond VA 23294 **Phn:** 804-672-9299 urbanpetersburg.com cllawrence@radio-one.com

Roanoke WKPA-AM (wg) 2043 10th St NE, Roanoke VA 24012 **Phn:** 540-343-5597 **Fax:** 540-345-4064 www.wkbaradio.com wkba@cox.net

Roanoke WTOY-AM (wug) 504 23rd St NW, Roanoke VA 24017 **Phn:** 540-344-9869 **Fax:** 540-344-0976 wtoyradio@aol.com

WASHINGTON

Seattle KRIZ-AM (wu) 2600 S Jackson St, Seattle WA 98144 **Phn:** 206-323-3070 **Fax:** 206-322-6518 www.ztwins.com ztwins@aol.com

Seattle KYIZ-AM (wug) 2600 S Jackson St, Seattle WA 98144 **Phn:** 206-323-3070 **Fax:** 206-322-6518 www.ztwins.com gametime@ztwins.com

Seattle KZIZ-AM (wg) 2600 S Jackson St, Seattle WA 98144 **Phn:** 206-323-3070 **Fax:** 206-322-6518 www.ztwins.com ztwins@aol.com

WISCONSIN

Greenfield WKKV-FM (wu) 12100 W Howard Ave, Greenfield WI 53228 **Phn:** 414-321-1007 **Fax:** 414-546-9654 www.v100.com

ALABAMA

Alabaster WQCR-AM (y) 50 Highway 26, Alabaster AL 35007 **Phn:** 205-621-8915 **Fax:** 205-621-7742 joelrivera1500am@yahoo.com

Bessemer WZGX-AM (y) 3500 Jaybird Rd, Bessemer AL 35020 **Phn:** 205-428-0146 **Fax:** 205-426-3178 la10qnetwork@gmail.com

Decatur WYAM-AM (y) 1301 Central Pkwy SW, Decatur AL 35601 **Phn:** 256-355-4567 **Fax:** 256-351-1234 wileywg@acninc.net

ARIZONA

Douglas KDAP-AM (y) PO Box 1179, Douglas AZ 85608 **Phn:** 520-364-3484 **Fax:** 520-364-3483

Douglas KRMC-FM (qy) PO Box 2520, Douglas AZ 85608 **Phn:** 520-364-5392 www.worldradionetwork.org krmc@lwrn.org

Nogales KNOG-FM (yqv) PO Box 1614, Nogales AZ 85628 **Phn:** 520-287-5206 **Fax:** 520-287-3606 www.knog.org knog@lwrn.org

Nogales KOFH-FM (y) 934 N Bejarano St Ste 2, Nogales AZ 85621 **Phn:** 520-287-3163 **Fax:** 520-287-8290

Phoenix KASA-AM (qy) 1445 W Baseline Rd, Phoenix AZ 85041 **Phn:** 602-276-4241 **Fax:** 602-276-8119

Phoenix KBMB-AM (ys) 501 N 44th St Ste 425, Phoenix AZ 85008 **Phn:** 602-776-1400 **Fax:** 602-279-2921 www.espnradio710am.com nrocha@entravision.com

Phoenix KBMB-FM (ys) 501 N 44th St Ste 425, Phoenix AZ 85008 **Phn:** 602-776-1400 **Fax:** 602-279-2921 www.espnradio710am.com nrocha@entravision.com

Phoenix KDVA-FM (y) 501 N 44th St Ste 425, Phoenix AZ 85008 **Phn:** 602-776-1400 **Fax:** 602-279-2921 www.josephoenix.com dapostalides@entravision.com

Phoenix KHOT-FM (y) 4745 N 7th St Ste 140, Phoenix AZ 85014 **Phn:** 602-308-7900 **Fax:** 602-308-7979 lanueva1059.univision.com

Phoenix KHOV-FM (y) 4745 N 7th St Ste 140, Phoenix AZ 85014 **Phn:** 602-308-7900 **Fax:** 602-308-7979 lakalle1003.univision.com

Phoenix KKMR-FM (y) 4745 N 7th St Ste 140, Phoenix AZ 85014 **Phn:** 602-308-7900 recuerdophoenix.univision.com

Phoenix KLNZ-FM (y) 501 N 44th St Ste 425, Phoenix AZ 85008 **Phn:** 602-776-1400 **Fax:** 602-279-2921 www.tricolor1035.com nrocha@entravision.com

Phoenix KMIA-AM (ys) 501 N 44th St Ste 425, Phoenix AZ 85008 **Phn:** 602-266-2005 **Fax:** 602-279-2921 www.espnradio710am.com cstrait@entravision.com

Phoenix KOMR-FM (y) 4745 N 7th St Ste 140, Phoenix AZ 85014 **Phn:** 602-308-7900 **Fax:** 602-308-7979

Phoenix KQMR-FM (y) 4745 N 7th St Ste 140, Phoenix AZ 85014 **Phn:** 602-308-7900 **Fax:** 602-308-7979 www.univision.com

Phoenix KSUN-AM (ya) 714 N 3rd St, Phoenix AZ 85004 **Phn:** 602-252-0030 **Fax:** 602-252-4211 radiofiesta1400.wix.comradiofiesta ksun@radiofiesta.net

Phoenix KVVA-FM (y) 501 N 44th St Ste 425, Phoenix AZ 85008 **Phn:** 602-776-1400 **Fax:** 602-279-2921 www.josephoenix.com cstrait@entravision.com

Tucson KCMT-FM (y) 3871 N Commerce Dr, Tucson AZ 85705 **Phn:** 520-407-4500 **Fax:** 520-407-4600 www.kcmt.com steve@kcmt.com

Tucson KEVT-AM (yq) 2955 E Broadway Blvd, Tucson AZ 85716 **Phn:** 520-889-8904 **Fax:** 520-889-8573

HISPANIC RADIO STATIONS

Tucson KTKT-AM (sy) 3871 N Commerce Dr, Tucson AZ 85705 **Phn:** 520-622-6711 **Fax:** 520-624-3226

Tucson KTZR-FM (y) 3202 N Oracle Rd, Tucson AZ 85705 **Phn:** 520-618-2100 **Fax:** 520-618-2165 www.lapreciosa1450.com alymasterson@clearchannel.com

Tucson KXEW-AM (y) 3202 N Oracle Rd, Tucson AZ 85705 **Phn:** 520-618-2100 **Fax:** 520-618-2122 www.tejano1600.com

Tucson KZLZ-FM (y) 2959 E Grant Rd, Tucson AZ 85716 **Phn:** 520-325-3054 **Fax:** 520-325-3495 www.lapoderosakzlz.com sonia@kzlzradio.com

Yuma KCEC-FM (y) 670 E 32nd St Ste 12A, Yuma AZ 85365 **Phn:** 928-782-5995 **Fax:** 928-782-3874 www.campesina.net rosella.lopez@campesina.com

Yuma KYRM-FM (vy) PO Box 5965, Yuma AZ 85366 **Phn:** 928-341-0919 **Fax:** 928-314-4141 www.kyrmradio.org kyrm@lwrn.org

ARKANSAS

De Queen KDQN-AM (y) PO Box 311, De Queen AR 71832 **Phn:** 870-642-2446 **Fax:** 870-642-2442 kdqn.netdefault.htm numberonecountry@yahoo.com

Fayetteville KAKS-FM (y) 1780 W Holly St, Fayetteville AR 72703 **Phn:** 479-443-9960 **Fax:** 479-444-9670

Nashville KBHC-AM (y) 1513 S 4th St, Nashville AR 71852 **Phn:** 870-845-3601 **Fax:** 870-845-3680

CALIFORNIA

Bakersfield KBDS-FM (y) 6313 Schirra Ct, Bakersfield CA 93313 **Phn:** 661-837-0745 **Fax:** 661-837-1612 www.campesina.com cesar.chavez@campesina.com

Bakersfield KBFP-AM (y) 1100 Mohawk St Ste 280, Bakersfield CA 93309 **Phn:** 661-322-9929 **Fax:** 661-322-7239 www.lapreciosa1053.com kennmccloud@clearchannel.com

Bakersfield KBFP-FM (y) 1100 Mohawk St Ste 280, Bakersfield CA 93309 **Phn:** 661-322-9929 **Fax:** 661-322-9239 www.lapreciosa1053.com kennmccloud@clearchannel.com

Bakersfield KCHJ-AM (y) 5100 Commerce Dr, Bakersfield CA 93309 **Phn:** 661-327-9711 **Fax:** 661-327-0797 vicente@lotusbakersfield.com

Bakersfield KEBT-FM (y) 1400 Easton Dr Ste 144, Bakersfield CA 93309 **Phn:** 661-328-1410 **Fax:** 661-328-0873 www.969lacaliente.com tsnyder@americangeneralmedia.com

Bakersfield KIWI-FM (y) 5100 Commerce Dr, Bakersfield CA 93309 **Phn:** 661-327-9711 **Fax:** 661-327-0797

Bakersfield KPSL-FM (y) 5100 Commerce Dr, Bakersfield CA 93309 **Phn:** 661-327-9711 **Fax:** 661-327-0797 concierto965.com

Barstow KBTW-FM (y) 125 E Fredricks St, Barstow CA 92311 **Phn:** 760-255-1316 **Fax:** 760-255-2406 dinom@radiolazer.com

Barstow KXXZ-FM (y) 29000 Radio Rd, Barstow CA 92311 **Phn:** 760-256-2121 **Fax:** 760-256-5090 doscostas@yahoo.com

Burbank KBUA-FM (y) 1845 W Empire Ave, Burbank CA 91504 **Phn:** 818-729-5300 **Fax:** 818-729-5678 aquisuena.estrellatv.com pgarza@lbimedia.com

Burbank KBUE-FM (y) 1845 W Empire Ave, Burbank CA 91504 **Phn:** 818-729-5300 **Fax:** 818-729-5678 www.aquisuena.com pgarza@lbimedia.com

Burbank KHJ-AM (y) 1845 W Empire Ave, Burbank CA 91504 **Phn:** 818-729-5300 **Fax:** 818-729-5678 laranchera.estrellatv.com info@lbimedia.com

Burbank XTRA-AM (sy) 3500 W Olive Ave Ste 250, Burbank CA 91505 **Phn:** 818-729-2605 www.wradiousa.com

Camarillo KMRO-FM (vyq) PO Box 500, Camarillo CA 93011 **Phn:** 805-482-4797 **Fax:** 805-388-5202 www.nuevavida.com

Chula Vista KSDO-AM (y) 344 F St Ste 200, Chula Vista CA 91910 **Phn:** 626-356-4230 www.nuevavida.com

Chula Vista XEXX-AM (y) 303 H St # 418, Chula Vista CA 91910 **Phn:** 619-819-5749 **Fax:** 619-819-5743 bernalhenry@aol.com

Corona KWRM-AM (y) 210 Radio Rd, Corona CA 92879 **Phn:** 951-737-1370 **Fax:** 951-735-9572 www.kwrm1370am.com

El Centro KGBA-FM (yq) 605 W State St, El Centro CA 92243 **Phn:** 760-352-9860 **Fax:** 760-352-1883 www.kgba.org kgba@kgba.org

El Centro KMXX-FM (y) 1803 N Imperial Ave, El Centro CA 92243 **Phn:** 760-482-7777 **Fax:** 760-482-0099 www.tricolor993.com

El Centro KSEH-FM (yh) 1803 N Imperial Ave, El Centro CA 92243 **Phn:** 760-482-7777 **Fax:** 760-482-0099 www.jose945.com gflores@entravision.com

Fresno KFSO-FM (y) 83 E Shaw Ave Ste 150, Fresno CA 93710 **Phn:** 559-230-4300 **Fax:** 559-241-6011 www.lapreciosa929.com tonybanks@clearchannel.com

Fresno KGST-AM (y) 1110 E Olive Ave, Fresno CA 93728 **Phn:** 559-497-1100 **Fax:** 559-497-1125 dcrotty@lotusfresno.com

Fresno KLBN-FM (y) 1110 E Olive Ave, Fresno CA 93728 **Phn:** 559-490-1019 **Fax:** 59-497-1125 jguillen@lotusfresno.com

Fresno KLLE-FM (y) 1981 N Gateway Blvd # 101, Fresno CA 93727 **Phn:** 559-456-4000 **Fax:** 559-251-9555 www.univision.com jmitchell@univisionradio.com

Fresno KMAK-FM (y) 227 W Teague Ave, Fresno CA 93711 **Phn:** 559-217-9156

Fresno KRDA-FM (y) 601 W Univision Plz, Fresno CA 93704 **Phn:** 559-430-8500 **Fax:** 559-251-9555 www.univision.com anavarrete@univisionradio.com

Fresno KSJV-FM (vy) 5005 E Belmont Ave, Fresno CA 93727 **Phn:** 559-455-5777 **Fax:** 559-455-5778 www.radiobilingue.org

Fresno KTQX-FM (vy) 5005 E Belmont Ave, Fresno CA 93727 **Phn:** 559-455-5777 **Fax:** 559-455-5778 www.radiobilingue.org

Fresno KUBO-FM (vy) 5005 E Belmont Ave, Fresno CA 93727 **Phn:** 559-455-5777 **Fax:** 559-455-5778 www.radiobilingue.org

Fresno KXEX-AM (y) 139 W Olive Ave, Fresno CA 93728 **Phn:** 559-233-8803 **Fax:** 559-233-8871 xco@att.net

Glendale KLVE-FM (y) 655 N Central Ave Ste 2500, Glendale CA 91203 **Phn:** 818-500-4500 **Fax:** 818-500-4480 www.univision.com

Glendale KRCD-FM (yo) 655 N Central Ave Ste 2500, Glendale CA 91203 **Phn:** 818-500-4500 **Fax:** 818-500-4329 www.univision.com

Glendale KRCV-FM (yo) 655 N Central Ave Ste 2500, Glendale CA 91203 **Phn:** 818-500-4500 **Fax:** 818-500-4560 www.univision.com ojaramillo@univisionradio.com

Glendale KSCA-FM (y) 655 N Central Ave Ste 2500, Glendale CA 91203 **Phn:** 818-500-4500 **Fax:** 818-500-4329 www.univision.com

HISPANIC RADIO STATIONS

Glendale KTNQ-AM (y) 655 N Central Ave Ste 2500, Glendale CA 91203 **Phn:** 818-500-4500 **Fax:** 818-500-4307 www.univision.com

Hanford KIGS-AM (y) 6165 Lacey Blvd, Hanford CA 93230 **Phn:** 559-582-0361 **Fax:** 559-582-3981

Hughson KAFY-AM (y) 4043 Geer Rd, Hughson CA 95326 **Phn:** 209-883-8760 **Fax:** 209-883-8769 www.lafavorita.net lafavorita@lafavorita.net

Hughson KBYN-FM (y) 4043 Geer Rd, Hughson CA 95326 **Phn:** 209-883-8760 **Fax:** 209-883-8769 www.lafavorita.net lafavorita@lafavorita.net

Hughson KNTO-FM (y) 4043 Geer Rd, Hughson CA 95326 **Phn:** 209-883-8760 **Fax:** 209-883-8769 www.lafavorita.net lafavorita@lafavorita.net

Los Angeles KLAX-FM (y) 10281 W Pico Blvd, Los Angeles CA 90064 **Phn:** 310-203-0900 **Fax:** 310-203-8989 979laraza.lamusica.com jhidalgo@sbslosangeles.com

Los Angeles KLYY-FM (y) 5700 Wilshire Blvd Ste 250, Los Angeles CA 90036 **Phn:** 323-900-6100 **Fax:** 323-900-6200 www.jose975.com abecerra@entravision.com

Los Angeles KSSC-FM (y) 5700 Wilshire Blvd Ste 250, Los Angeles CA 90036 **Phn:** 323-900-6100 **Fax:** 323-900-6200 www.superestrella.com kmeyer@entravision.com

Los Angeles KSSD-FM (y) 5700 Wilshire Blvd Ste 250, Los Angeles CA 90036 **Phn:** 323-900-6100 **Fax:** 323-900-6127 www.superestrella.com kmeyer@entravision.com

Los Angeles KSSE-FM (y) 5700 Wilshire Blvd Ste 250, Los Angeles CA 90036 **Phn:** 323-900-6100 **Fax:** 323-900-6127 www.superestrella.com kmeyer@entravision.com

Los Angeles KWKU-AM (sny) 3301 Barham Blvd Ste 201, Los Angeles CA 90068 **Phn:** 323-851-5959 **Fax:** 323-512-7460 jrodriguez@kwkwradio.com

Los Angeles KWKW-AM (ys) 3301 Barham Blvd Ste 201, Los Angeles CA 90068 **Phn:** 323-851-5959 **Fax:** 323-512-7460 espn1330.com kwkw1330@aol.com

Los Angeles KXOL-FM (y) 10281 W Pico Blvd, Los Angeles CA 90064 **Phn:** 310-229-3200 **Fax:** 310-203-8989 www.latino963.com pioferro@hotmail.com

Los Banos KQLB-FM (y) 401 Pacheco Blvd, Los Banos CA 93635 **Phn:** 209-827-0123 **Fax:** 209-826-1906 www.kqlb.com sales@kqlb.com

Merced KLOQ-FM (y) 1020 W Main St, Merced CA 95340 **Phn:** 209-723-2191 **Fax:** 209-383-2950 www.radiolobo987.com

Merced KTIQ-AM (yq) 1020 W Main St, Merced CA 95340 **Phn:** 209-723-2191 **Fax:** 209-383-2950

Modesto KBBU-FM (y) 903 Kansas Ave Ste R, Modesto CA 95351 **Phn:** 209-526-5352

Monterey KLOK-FM (y) 67 Garden Ct, Monterey CA 93940 **Phn:** 831-333-9735 **Fax:** 831-373-6700 www.tricolor995.com ascoby@entravision.com

Monterey KSES-FM (y) 67 Garden Ct, Monterey CA 93940 **Phn:** 831-333-6767 **Fax:** 831-373-6700 www.jose971.com kmaciel@entravision.com

Monterey KYAA-AM (yt) 651 Cannery Row Ste 1, Monterey CA 93940 **Phn:** 831-372-1074 **Fax:** 831-372-3585

Morgan Hill KAZA-AM (yq) 1820 Cochrane Rd, Morgan Hill CA 95037 **Phn:** 408-778-8526 juansidhu@yahoo.com

National City KOCL-FM (y) 401 Mile Of Cars Way # 322, National City CA 91950 **Phn:** 619-474-9000 **Fax:** 619-474-9040

National City XLTN-FM (y) 401 Mile Of Cars Way # 370, National City CA 91950 **Phn:** 619-336-7800 **Fax:** 619-420-1092 1045radiolatina.com comentarios@104.5radiolatina.com

Oakhurst KAAT-FM (y) 40356 Oak Park Way Ste F, Oakhurst CA 93644 **Phn:** 559-683-1031 **Fax:** 559-683-5488

Oxnard KLJR-FM (y) PO Box 6940, Oxnard CA 93031 **Phn:** 805-240-2070 **Fax:** 805-240-5960 terryj@radiolazer.com

Oxnard KMLA-FM (y) 355 S A St Ste 103, Oxnard CA 93030 **Phn:** 805-385-5656 **Fax:** 805-385-5690 www.lam1037.com willy@lam1037.com

Oxnard KOXR-AM (y) PO Box 6940, Oxnard CA 93031 **Phn:** 805-240-2070 **Fax:** 805-240-5960

Oxnard KSRN-FM (y) 200 S A St Ste 400, Oxnard CA 93030 **Phn:** 805-240-2070 **Fax:** 805-240-5960

Oxnard KSTN-FM (y) 200 S A St Ste 400, Oxnard CA 93030 **Phn:** 805-240-2070 **Fax:** 805-240-5960 radiolazer1029.com

Oxnard KXLM-FM (y) PO Box 6940, Oxnard CA 93031 **Phn:** 805-240-2070 **Fax:** 805-240-5960 radiolazer.com terryj@radiolazer.com

Palm Desert KESQ-AM (y) 42650 Melanie Pl, Palm Desert CA 92211 **Phn:** 760-568-6830 **Fax:** 760-568-3984 www.kesq.com ainiguez@kunamundo.com

Palm Desert KLOB-FM (y) 41601 Corporate Way, Palm Desert CA 92260 **Phn:** 760-341-5837 **Fax:** 760-837-3711 www.jose947.com lvasquez@entravision.com

Palm Desert KUNA-FM (y) 42650 Melanie Pl, Palm Desert CA 92211 **Phn:** 760-568-6830 **Fax:** 760-568-3984 ainiguez@kunamundo.com

Palm Springs KFUT-AM (y) 1321 N Gene Autry Trl, Palm Springs CA 92262 **Phn:** 760-322-7890 **Fax:** 760-322-5493 www.1270kfut.com info@desertradiogroup.com

Palmdale KCEL-FM (y) 570 E Avenue Q9, Palmdale CA 93550 **Phn:** 661-947-3107 **Fax:** 760-373-1069 laquebuena961.com

Pasadena KALI-AM (qy) 747 E Green St Ste 400, Pasadena CA 91101 **Phn:** 626-844-8882 **Fax:** 626-844-0156

Pasadena KLTX-AM (qy) 136 S Oak Knoll Ave Ste 200, Pasadena CA 91101 **Phn:** 626-356-4230 **Fax:** 626-817-9851 www.nuevavida.com

Ridgecrest KEDD-FM (y) 731 Balsam St, Ridgecrest CA 93555 **Phn:** 760-371-1700 **Fax:** 760-371-1824

Sacramento KGRB-FM (y) 500 Media Pl, Sacramento CA 95815 **Phn:** 916-368-6300 **Fax:** 916-473-0143 www.adelantemediagroup.com

Sacramento KRCX-FM (y) 1436 Auburn Blvd, Sacramento CA 95815 **Phn:** 916-646-4000 **Fax:** 916-646-1958 www.tricolor999.com promociones@tricolor999.com

Sacramento KXSE-FM (y) 1436 Auburn Blvd, Sacramento CA 95815 **Phn:** 916-646-4000 **Fax:** 916-646-3237 www.jose1043.com slopez@entravision.com

Salinas KMJV-FM (y) PO Box 1939, Salinas CA 93902 **Phn:** 831-757-1910 **Fax:** 831-757-8015 romero_vicente@hotmail.com

Salinas KPRC-FM (yo) 903 N Main St, Salinas CA 93906 **Phn:** 831-755-8181 **Fax:** 831-755-8193 salinas.lapreciosa.com josevalenzuela@lapreciosa.com

Salinas KRAY-FM (y) 548 E Alisal St, Salinas CA 93905 **Phn:** 831-757-1910 **Fax:** 831-757-8015 romero_vicente@hotmail.com

Salinas KSEA-FM (y) 229 Pajaro St Ste 302D, Salinas CA 93901 **Phn:** 831-754-1469 **Fax:** 831-754-1563 www.campesina.net paco@campesina.com

Salinas KTGE-AM (y) 548 E Alisal St, Salinas CA 93905 **Phn:** 831-757-1910 **Fax:** 831-757-8015 sls.rcastro@mail.com

Salinas KXSM-FM (y) 600 E Market St # 200, Salinas CA 93905 **Phn:** 831-422-5019 **Fax:** 831-422-5027 radiolazer935.com

Salinas KXZM-FM (y) 600 E Market St # 200, Salinas CA 93905 **Phn:** 831-422-5019 **Fax:** 831-422-5027 radiolazer.com

San Bernardino KAEH-FM (qy) 650 S E St, San Bernardino CA 92408 **Phn:** 909-381-0969 **Fax:** 909-381-5409

San Bernardino KCAL-AM (y) 1950 S Sunwest Ln Ste 302, San Bernardino CA 92408 **Phn:** 909-825-5020 **Fax:** 909-884-5844 lamexicana1410@radiolazer.com

San Bernardino KRQB-FM (y) 1845 Business Center Dr Ste 106, San Bernardino CA 92408 **Phn:** 909-663-1961 **Fax:** 909-663-1996 quebuena961.estrellatv.com pgarza@lbimedia.com

San Bernardino KXRS-FM (y) 1950 S Sunwest Ln Ste 302, San Bernardino CA 92408 **Phn:** 909-825-5020 **Fax:** 909-884-5844 radiolazer.com

San Bernardino KXSB-FM (y) 1950 S Sunwest Ln Ste 302, San Bernardino CA 92408 **Phn:** 909-825-5020 **Fax:** 909-884-5844 radiolazer.com lazerbroadcasting@radiolazer.com

San Diego KLNV-FM (y) 600 W Broadway Ste 2150, San Diego CA 92101 **Phn:** 619-235-0600 **Fax:** 619-744-4300 www.univision.com

San Diego KLQV-FM (y) 600 W Broadway Ste 2150, San Diego CA 92101 **Phn:** 619-235-0600 **Fax:** 619-744-4300

San Diego XEMO-AM (y) 5030 Camino De La Siesta Ste 403, San Diego CA 92108 **Phn:** 619-497-0600 **Fax:** 619-497-1019 www.uniradio.com contactus@uniradio.com

San Diego XHA-FM (y) 5030 Camino De La Siesta Ste 403, San Diego CA 92108 **Phn:** 619-497-0600 **Fax:** 619-497-1019 www.uniradio.com contactus@uniradio.com

San Diego XMOR-FM (y) 1027 10th Ave Ste C, San Diego CA 92101 **Phn:** 619-696-9902 **Fax:** 19-702-5570

San Diego XTRA-FM (ry) 9660 Granite Ridge Dr Ste 200, San Diego CA 92123 **Phn:** 858-495-9100 **Fax:** 858-499-1805 www.xtrasports1150.com billlally@clearchannel.com

San Francisco KATD-AM (y) 44 Gough St # 301, San Francisco CA 94103 **Phn:** 415-978-5378 **Fax:** 415-978-5380 www.kiqi1010am.com

San Francisco KBRG-FM (y) 750 Battery St Ste 200, San Francisco CA 94111 **Phn:** 415-989-5765 **Fax:** 415-733-5766 www.univision.com

San Francisco KIQI-AM (y) 44 Gough St # 301, San Francisco CA 94103 **Phn:** 415-978-5378 **Fax:** 415-978-5380 www.kiqi1010am.com

San Francisco KSOL-FM (y) 750 Battery St Ste 200, San Francisco CA 94111 **Phn:** 415-989-5765 **Fax:** 415-733-5766 www.univision.com mrojas@univisionradio.com

San Francisco KSQL-FM (y) 750 Battery St Ste 200, San Francisco CA 94111 **Phn:** 415-989-5765 **Fax:** 415-733-5766 www.univision.com

San Francisco KVVF-FM (y) 750 Battery St Ste 200, San Francisco CA 94111 **Phn:** 415-989-5765 **Fax:** 415-733-5766 www.univision.com

San Francisco KVVZ-FM (y) 750 Battery St Ste 200, San Francisco CA 94111 **Phn:** 415-989-5765 **Fax:** 415-733-5766 www.univision.com

San Jose KCNL-FM (y) 1420 Koll Cir Ste A, San Jose CA 95112 **Phn:** 408-453-5400 **Fax:** 408-452-1330

San Jose KSQQ-FM (ey) 1629 Alum Rock Ave Ste 40, San Jose CA 95116 **Phn:** 408-258-9696 **Fax:** 408-258-9770 www.ksqq.com pr@ksqq.com

San Jose KZSF-AM (y) 3031 Tisch Way Ste 3, San Jose CA 95128 **Phn:** 408-247-0100 **Fax:** 408-247-4353 www.1370am.com reynasantillan@1370am.com

Santa Ana KWIZ-FM (y) 3101 W 5th St, Santa Ana CA 92703 **Phn:** 714-554-5000 **Fax:** 714-554-9362 larockola967.estrellatv.com kwizinfo@lbimedia.com

Santa Barbara KIST-FM (y) 414 E Cota St, Santa Barbara CA 93101 **Phn:** 805-879-8300 **Fax:** 805-879-8430 www.radiobronco.com jose.fierros@rinconbroadcasting.com

Santa Barbara KSPE-FM (y) 414 E Cota St, Santa Barbara CA 93101 **Phn:** 805-879-8300 **Fax:** 805-879-8430 www.radiobronco.com jose.fierros@rinconbroadcasting.com

Santa Barbara KZER-AM (y) 1330 Cacique St, Santa Barbara CA 93103 **Phn:** 805-963-7824 **Fax:** 805-965-7816

Santa Maria KIDI-FM (y) 718 E Chapel St, Santa Maria CA 93454 **Phn:** 805-928-4334 **Fax:** 805-349-2765

Santa Maria KLMM-FM (y) 312 E Mill St Ste 302, Santa Maria CA 93454 **Phn:** 805-928-9796 **Fax:** 805-928-3367 radiolazer.com

Santa Maria KRQK-FM (y) 2325 Skyway Dr Ste J, Santa Maria CA 93455 **Phn:** 805-922-1041 **Fax:** 805-928-3069 www.1003laley.com estich@americangeneralmedia.com

Santa Maria KSBQ-AM (y) 312 E Mill St Ste 302, Santa Maria CA 93454 **Phn:** 805-928-9796 **Fax:** 805-928-3367

Santa Maria KTAP-AM (y) 718 E Chapel St, Santa Maria CA 93454 **Phn:** 805-928-4334 **Fax:** 805-349-2765

Santa Rosa KBBF-FM (vy) PO Box 7189, Santa Rosa CA 95407 **Phn:** 707-545-8833 kbbf-fm.org info@kbbf-fm.org

Santa Rosa KRRS-AM (y) PO Box 2277, Santa Rosa CA 95405 **Phn:** 707-545-1460 **Fax:** 707-545-0112

Santa Rosa KTOB-AM (y) 1410 Neotomas Ave Ste 104, Santa Rosa CA 95405 **Phn:** 707-545-1460 **Fax:** 707-545-0112

Santa Rosa KXTS-FM (y) 3565 Standish Ave, Santa Rosa CA 95407 **Phn:** 707-588-0707 **Fax:** 707-588-0777 winecountryradio.net alex@winecountryradio.net

Stockton KCVR-AM (y) 6820 Pacific Ave # 3, Stockton CA 95207 **Phn:** 209-474-0154 **Fax:** 209-474-0316

Stockton KCVR-FM (y) 6820 Pacific Ave, Stockton CA 95207 **Phn:** 209-529-1900 **Fax:** 209-529-1528

Stockton KLOC-AM (y) 6820 Pacific Ave, Stockton CA 95207 **Phn:** 209-529-1900 **Fax:** 209-529-1528 www.lafavorita.net lafavorita@lafavorita.net

Stockton KMIX-FM (y) 6820 Pacific Ave # 3, Stockton CA 95207 **Phn:** 209-474-0180 **Fax:** 209-474-0316 www.tricolor1009.com

Stockton KTSE-FM (y) 6820 Pacific Ave # 3, Stockton CA 95207 **Phn:** 209-474-0154 **Fax:** 209-474-0316 www.jose971.com

Tulare KGEN-FM (y) 333 E San Joaquin Ave, Tulare CA 93274 **Phn:** 559-686-1370 **Fax:** 559-685-1394 kgen@sbcglobal.net

HISPANIC RADIO STATIONS

Tulare KMQA-FM (y) 1450 E Bardsley Ave, Tulare CA 93274 **Phn:** 559-687-3170 **Fax:** 559-687-3175

Ukiah KUKI-AM (y) 1400 Kuki Ln, Ukiah CA 95482 **Phn:** 707-466-5868 **Fax:** 707-466-5852 www.kuki.com ukiah@bicoastalspots.com

Victorville KWRN-AM (y) 15165 Seventh St Ste D, Victorville CA 92395 **Phn:** 760-955-8722 **Fax:** 760-955-5751

COLORADO

Aspen KPVW-FM (y) 20 Sunset Dr # C, Aspen CO 81621 **Phn:** 970-927-6902 **Fax:** 970-927-8001 www.denverhispanicradio.com sbernal@entravision.com

Denver KBNO-AM (y) 600 Grant St Ste 600, Denver CO 80203 **Phn:** 303-733-5266 **Fax:** 303-733-5242 www.radioquebueno.com zee@kbno.net

Denver KJMN-FM (y) 777 Grant St Fl 5, Denver CO 80203 **Phn:** 303-832-0050 **Fax:** 303-721-1435 www.jose921.com mcarrera@entravision.com

Denver KLVZ-AM (ynt) 2150 W 29th Ave Ste 300, Denver CO 80211 **Phn:** 303-433-5500 **Fax:** 303-433-1555 www.crawfordbroadcasting.com info@crawfordbroadcasting.com

Denver KMXA-AM (y) 1907 Mile High Stadium W Cir, Denver CO 80204 **Phn:** 303-832-0050 **Fax:** 303-721-1435 www.965tricolor.com

Denver KXPK-FM (y) 777 Grant St Fl 5, Denver CO 80203 **Phn:** 303-832-0500 **Fax:** 303-721-1435 www.denverse.com mcarrera@entravision.com

Grand Junction KEXO-AM (y) 315 Kennedy Ave, Grand Junction CO 81501 **Phn:** 970-242-7788 **Fax:** 970-243-0567 1230espn.com brad.larock@townsquaremedia.com

Greeley KGRE-AM (y) 800 8th Ave St 304, Greeley CO 80631 **Phn:** 970-356-1452 **Fax:** 970-356-8522 www.tigrecolorado.com kgre@msn.com

Longmont KJJD-AM (y) 624 Main St, Longmont CO 80501 **Phn:** 303-651-1199 **Fax:** 303-651-2244

Pueblo KNKN-FM (y) 30 N Electronic Dr, Pueblo CO 81007 **Phn:** 719-547-0411 **Fax:** 719-547-9301 radiolobo@amigo.net

Pueblo KRMX-AM (y) 30 N Electronic Dr, Pueblo CO 81007 **Phn:** 719-545-2883 **Fax:** 719-547-9301 radiolobo@amigo.net

Pueblo KRYE-FM (y) 106 W 24th St, Pueblo CO 81003 **Phn:** 720-382-9697 **Fax:** 719-562-0947

Pueblo KYRE-FM (y) 106 W 24th St, Pueblo CO 81003 **Phn:** 720-382-9697 **Fax:** 719-562-0947

CONNECTICUT

Berlin WPRX-AM (y) 1253 Berlin Tpk, Berlin CT 06037 **Phn:** 860-348-0667 **Fax:** 860-358-0711 www.wprx1120.net wprx1120@comcast.net

Bridgeport WCUM-AM (y) 1862 Commerce Dr, Bridgeport CT 06605 **Phn:** 203-335-1450 **Fax:** 203-337-1216 www.radiocumbre.am

Hartford WLAT-AM (y) 135 Burnside Ave, Hartford CT 06108 **Phn:** 860-524-0001 **Fax:** 860-548-1922 robbiedjtrigueno@yahoo.com

Hartford WNEZ-AM (uy) 135 Burnside Ave, Hartford CT 06108 **Phn:** 860-524-0001 **Fax:** 860-548-1922 robbiedjtrigueno@yahoo.com

New Haven WADS-AM (qyv) PO Box 384, New Haven CT 06513 **Phn:** 203-777-7690 **Fax:** 203-782-3565

New London WSUB-AM (y) 7 Governor Winthrop Blvd, New London CT 06320 **Phn:** 860-443-1980 **Fax:** 860-444-7970 www.caliente980am.com

Newington WRYM-AM (y) 1056 Willard Ave, Newington CT 06111 **Phn:** 860-666-5646 **Fax:** 860-666-5647 www.wrymradio.com wmartinez@wrym840.com

Plantsville WXCT-AM (ay) 440 Old Turnpike Rd, Plantsville CT 06479 **Phn:** 860-621-1754 ericksalgado1430@hotmail.com

Waterbury WFNW-AM (y) 182 Grand St Ste 215, Waterbury CT 06702 **Phn:** 203-755-4962 **Fax:** 203-755-4957 galaxia1380@yahoo.com

DELAWARE

Milford WJWL-AM (y) 233 NE Front St, Milford DE 19963 **Phn:** 302-422-2600 **Fax:** 302-424-1630

Milford WYUS-AM (y) 1666 Blairs Pond Rd, Milford DE 19963 **Phn:** 302-422-7575 **Fax:** 302-422-3069 www.wyusam.com

FLORIDA

Altamonte Springs WNUE-FM (y) 523 Douglas Ave, Altamonte Springs FL 32714 **Phn:** 407-774-2626 **Fax:** 407-774-8251

Altamonte Springs WONQ-AM (y) 1355 E Altamonte Dr, Altamonte Springs FL 32701 **Phn:** 407-830-0800 **Fax:** 407-260-6100 1030lagrande.com

Auburndale WTWB-AM (y) 127 Glenn Rd, Auburndale FL 33823 **Phn:** 863-967-1570 www.laraza1570.com laraza1570@gmail.com

Bartow WQXM-AM (y) 1355 N Maple Ave, Bartow FL 33830 **Phn:** 305-358-5644 **Fax:** 863-519-9514 ovega@lax1460.com

Clewiston WAFC-AM (y) 530 E Alverdez Ave, Clewiston FL 33440 **Phn:** 863-902-0995 **Fax:** 863-983-6109 www.radiofiesta.com jesus@gladesmedia.com

Coral Gables WAMR-FM (y) 800 S Douglas Rd Ste 111, Coral Gables FL 33134 **Phn:** 305-447-1140 **Fax:** 305-441-2364 www.univision.com

Coral Gables WAQI-AM (y) 800 S Douglas Rd Ste 111, Coral Gables FL 33134 **Phn:** 305-445-4040 **Fax:** 305-443-3061 www.univision.com

Coral Gables WQBA-AM (y) 800 S Douglas Rd Ste 111, Coral Gables FL 33134 **Phn:** 305-447-1140 **Fax:** 305-445-1541 www.univision.com

Coral Gables WRTO-FM (y) 800 S Douglas Rd Ste 111, Coral Gables FL 33134 **Phn:** 305-447-1140 **Fax:** 305-445-1541 www.univision.com

Coral Gables WSUA-AM (y) 2100 Coral Way Ste 200, Coral Gables FL 33145 **Phn:** 305-285-1260 **Fax:** 305-858-5907 www.caracol1260.com admin@caracolusa.com

Coral Gables WURN-AM (ynt) 2525 Ponce de Leon Blvd # 250, Coral Gables FL 33134 **Phn:** 305-446-5444 **Fax:** 786-388-3868 www.actualidadradio.com aeden@bellsouth.net

Ellenton WBRD-AM (y) PO Box 826, Ellenton FL 34222 **Phn:** 941-266-4260 **Fax:** 941-723-9831 wbrd1420am@yahoo.com

Fort Myers WCRM-AM (yu) 3548 Canal St, Fort Myers FL 33916 **Phn:** 239-332-1350 **Fax:** 239-332-8890 www.vidaradionetwork.com fvida1350@gmail.com

Fort Myers WTLQ-FM (y) 2824 Palm Beach Blvd, Fort Myers FL 33916 **Phn:** 239-334-1111 **Fax:** 239-334-0744 www.latino977.com hector.velazquez@fmbcradio.com

Fort Myers WWCL-AM (y) PO Box 50580, Fort Myers FL 33994 **Phn:** 239-369-0344 **Fax:** 239-369-3386

Fort Pierce WJNX-AM (y) 4100 Metzger Rd, Fort Pierce FL 34947 **Phn:** 772-340-1590 **Fax:** 772-340-3245 www.lagigante1330.com

Immokalee WAFZ-AM (y) 2105 W Immokalee Dr, Immokalee FL 34142 **Phn:** 239-657-9210 **Fax:** 888-859-9210 www.wafz.com ricardo@gladesmedia.com

Immokalee WAFZ-FM (y) 2105 W Immokalee Dr, Immokalee FL 34142 **Phn:** 239-657-9210 **Fax:** 888-859-9210 www.wafz.com kc@gladesmedia.com

Maitland WRUM-FM (y) 2500 Maitland Center Pkwy Ste 401, Maitland FL 32751 **Phn:** 407-916-7800 **Fax:** 407-916-7407 www.rumba100.com suheiley@rumba100.com

Miami WACC-AM (yq) 1779 NW 28th St, Miami FL 33142 **Phn:** 305-638-9729 **Fax:** 305-635-4748 www.paxcc.org rmcid@paxcc.org

Miami WCMQ-FM (y) 7007 NW 77th Ave, Miami FL 33166 **Phn:** 305-444-9292 **Fax:** 305-461-0987 www.clasica92fm.com jcaride@sbsmiami.com

Miami WDNA-FM (vjy) PO Box 558636, Miami FL 33255 **Phn:** 305-662-8889 **Fax:** 305-662-1975 www.wdna.org mpelleya@wdna.org

Miami WKAT-AM (y) 2828 W Flagler St, Miami FL 33135 **Phn:** 305-503-1340 **Fax:** 305-677-7585 www.1360wkat.com

Miami WLQY-AM (ey) 10800 Biscayne Blvd Ste 810, Miami FL 33161 **Phn:** 305-891-1729 **Fax:** 305-891-1583 risas@bellsouth.net

Miami WRHC-AM (y) 330 SW 27th Ave Ste 207, Miami FL 33135 **Phn:** 305-541-3300 **Fax:** 305-541-2013 www.cadenaazul.com

Miami WRMA-FM (y) 7007 NW 77th Ave, Miami FL 33166 **Phn:** 305-444-9292 **Fax:** 305-883-1264 romancefm.lamusica.com jacinsbs@hotmail.com

Miami WWFE-AM (y) 330 SW 27th Ave Ste 207, Miami FL 33135 **Phn:** 305-541-3300 **Fax:** 305-541-9585 www.lapoderosa.com info@cadenaazul.com

Miami WXDJ-FM (y) 7007 NW 77th Ave, Miami FL 33166 **Phn:** 305-533-9200 **Fax:** 305-250-4332 elzol.lamusica.com jacinsbs@hotmail.com

Milton WECM-AM (y) 6583 Berryhill Rd, Milton FL 32570 **Phn:** 850-623-1490

Miramar WMGE-FM (y) 7601 Riviera Blvd, Miramar FL 33023 **Phn:** 954-862-2000 **Fax:** 954-862-4012 www.mega949.com rayhernandez@clearchannel.com

Miramar WMIB-FM (y) 7601 Riviera Blvd, Miramar FL 33023 **Phn:** 954-862-2000 **Fax:** 954-862-4013 www.1035superx.com vcurry@wmbm.com

Ocoee WUNA-AM (y) 749 S Bluford Ave, Ocoee FL 34761 **Phn:** 407-656-9823 **Fax:** 407-656-2092

Orlando WOTS-AM (ynt) 222 Hazard St, Orlando FL 32804 **Phn:** 407-841-8282 **Fax:** 407-841-8250 www.wots1220.com wprd1440@hotmail.com

Orlando WPRD-AM (ynt) 222 Hazard St, Orlando FL 32804 **Phn:** 407-841-8282 **Fax:** 407-841-8250 www.wprd.com wprd1440@hotmail.com

Orlando WRLZ-AM (y) PO Box 593642, Orlando FL 32859 **Phn:** 407-345-0700 **Fax:** 407-345-1492

Orlando WSDO-AM (yq) 222 Hazard St, Orlando FL 32804 **Phn:** 407-841-8282 **Fax:** 407-841-8250 wprd1440@gmail.com

Saint Petersburg WYUU-FM (y) 9721 Executive Center Dr N Ste 200, Saint Petersburg FL 33702 **Phn:** 866-932-9250 925maxima.cbslocal.com nio.encendio@cbsradio.com

Summerland Key WPIK-FM (y) PO Box 420249, Summerland Key FL 33042 **Phn:** 305-745-4162 **Fax:** 305-745-4165 www.radioritmolafabulosa.com sabadoslatinos@yahoo.com

Tampa WAMA-AM (y) 4107 W Spruce St # 200, Tampa FL 33607 **Phn:** 813-374-9075 **Fax:** 813-374-9102 www.laley1550.com info@laley1550.com

Tampa WLCC-AM (y) 5211 W Laurel St # 101, Tampa FL 33607 **Phn:** 813-639-1903 www.760radioluz.com barb@salemtampa.com

Tampa WQBN-AM (y) 5203 N Armenia Ave, Tampa FL 33603 **Phn:** 813-871-1333 **Fax:** 813-876-1333 joyce.cordero@gmail.com

Tampa WTMP-FM (y) 407 N Howard Ave Ste 200, Tampa FL 33606 **Phn:** 813-259-9867 **Fax:** 813-254-9867 www.bahiatampa.com

Tampa WTMP-AM (y) 407 N Howard Ave Ste 200, Tampa FL 33606 **Phn:** 813-259-9867 **Fax:** 813-254-9867 www.bahiatampa.com

West Palm Beach WAFC-FM (y) 2326 S Congress Ave Ste 2A, West Palm Beach FL 33406 **Phn:** 561-721-9950 **Fax:** 561-721-9973 www.wafcfm.com brian@gladesmedia.com

West Palm Beach WPSP-AM (y) 5730 Corporate Way Ste 210, West Palm Beach FL 33407 **Phn:** 561-681-9777 **Fax:** 561-687-3398

West Palm Beach WWRF-AM (y) 2326 S Congress Ave Ste 2A, West Palm Beach FL 33406 **Phn:** 561-721-9950 **Fax:** 561-721-9973 www.la1380.com la1380@radiofiesta.com

Winter Haven WHNR-AM (y) 1505 Dundee Rd, Winter Haven FL 33884 **Phn:** 863-299-1141 **Fax:** 863-293-6397 mail@whnr1360.com

Zolfo Springs WZSP-FM (y) 7891 US Highway 17 S, Zolfo Springs FL 33890 **Phn:** 863-494-4111 **Fax:** 863-494-4443 www.lazeta.fm info@lazeta.fm

GEORGIA

Appling WQRX-AM (gy) PO Box 510, Appling GA 30802 **Phn:** 706-309-9610 **Fax:** 706-309-9669 www.gnnradio.org

Atlanta WAFS-AM (y) 2970 Peachtree Rd NW Ste 700, Atlanta GA 30305 **Phn:** 770-290-8950 **Fax:** 770-209-8910 adam.asher@salematlanta.com

Atlanta WBZY-FM (y) 1819 Peachtree Rd NE Ste 700, Atlanta GA 30309 **Phn:** 404-875-8080 **Fax:** 404-367-1111 www.elpatron1053.com stevengarza@clearchannel.com

Atlanta WGST-AM (ys) 1819 Peachtree Rd NE Ste 700, Atlanta GA 30309 **Phn:** 404-367-0640 **Fax:** 404-367-6401 www.espndeportesatlanta.com chriseast@clearchannel.com

Atlanta WWWE-AM (y) 1465 Northside Dr NW Ste 218, Atlanta GA 30318 **Phn:** 404-355-8600 **Fax:** 404-355-4156 www.bbgi.com email@bbgi.com

Austell WAOS-AM (y) 5815 Westside Rd, Austell GA 30106 **Phn:** 770-944-0900 **Fax:** 770-944-9794

Austell WLBA-AM (y) 5815 Westside Rd, Austell GA 30106 **Phn:** 770-944-0900

Austell WXEM-AM (y) 5815 Westside Rd, Austell GA 30106 **Phn:** 770-944-0900 **Fax:** 770-944-9794

Canton WCHK-AM (y) PO Box 1290, Canton GA 30169 **Phn:** 770-479-2101 **Fax:** 770-479-1134

Dalton WDAL-AM (y) PO Box 1284, Dalton GA 30722 **Phn:** 706-278-5511 **Fax:** 706-226-8766 dhernandez@ngaradio.com

Duluth WLKQ-FM (y) 1176 Satellite Blvd Bldg 400 # 230, Duluth GA 30096 **Phn:** 770-623-8772 **Fax:** 770-623-4722 www.laraza1023.com

Grovetown WBLR-AM (y) 2278 Wortham Ln, Grovetown GA 30813 **Phn:** 706-309-9610 **Fax:** 706-309-9669

Grovetown WKTM-AM (y) 2278 Wortham Ln, Grovetown GA 30813 **Phn:** 706-309-9610 **Fax:** 706-309-9669

Lawrenceville WPLO-AM (yo) 239 Ezzard St, Lawrenceville GA 30046 **Phn:** 770-237-9897 **Fax:** 770-237-8769 www.radiomex610atlanta.com

Suwanee WNSY-FM (y) 1176 Satellite Blvd NW Ste 200, Suwanee GA 30024 **Phn:** 770-623-8772 **Fax:** 770-623-4722 www.laraza1023.com

IDAHO

Boise KCID-AM (yq) PO Box 714, Boise ID 83701 **Phn:** 208-629-4869 salyluzradio.com

Boise KWEI-FM (y) 1156 N Orchard St, Boise ID 83706 **Phn:** 208-367-1859 **Fax:** 208-383-9170 kweiradio.com

Boise KWEI-AM (y) 1156 N Orchard St, Boise ID 83706 **Phn:** 208-367-1859 **Fax:** 208-383-9170 kweiradio.com

Idaho Falls KSPZ-AM (y) 854 Lindsay Blvd, Idaho Falls ID 83402 **Phn:** 208-522-1101 **Fax:** 208-522-6110

Nampa KDBI-FM (y) 3307 Caldwell Blvd Ste 101, Nampa ID 83651 **Phn:** 208-463-2900 **Fax:** 208-406-8750

Nampa KQLZ-FM (y) 5660 E Franklin Rd Ste 200, Nampa ID 83687 **Phn:** 208-465-9966 **Fax:** 208-465-2922 www.1007lapoderosa.com mikey@impactradiogroup.com

Rupert KFTA-AM (y) 120 S 300 W, Rupert ID 83350 **Phn:** 208-436-4757 **Fax:** 208-436-3050 www.lafantastica970.com kfta970am@yahoo.com

ILLINOIS

Chicago WLEY-FM (y) 150 N Michigan Ave Ste 1040, Chicago IL 60601 **Phn:** 312-920-9500 **Fax:** 312-920-9515 laley1079.com ecastro@sbschicago.com

Chicago WMBI-AM (y) 820 N La Salle Dr, Chicago IL 60610 **Phn:** 312-329-4300 **Fax:** 312-329-4468 www.moodyradiochicago.fm wmbi@moody.edu

Chicago WNDZ-AM (y) 5625 N Milwaukee Ave, Chicago IL 60646 **Phn:** 773-792-1121 **Fax:** 773-792-2904 www.accessradiochicago.com

Chicago WNUA-FM (y) 233 N Michigan Ave Ste 2800, Chicago IL 60601 **Phn:** 312-540-2000 **Fax:** 312-938-0692 www.955elpatron.com earljones@clearchannel.com

Chicago WOJO-FM (y) 625 N Michigan Ave # 300, Chicago IL 60611 **Phn:** 312-981-1800 **Fax:** 312-981-1840 www.univision.com jerryryan@univisionradio.com

Chicago WPPN-FM (y) 625 N Michigan Ave # 300, Chicago IL 60611 **Phn:** 312-981-1800 **Fax:** 312-981-1840 pasionchicago.univision.com jerryryan@univisionradio.com

Chicago WRTO-AM (ynt) 625 N Michigan Ave # 300, Chicago IL 60611 **Phn:** 312-981-1800 **Fax:** 312-981-1840 www.univision.com

Chicago WSBC-AM (ey) 5625 N Milwaukee Ave, Chicago IL 60646 **Phn:** 773-792-1121 **Fax:** 773-792-2904 www.accessradiochicago.com jmurillo@newswebradio.net

Chicago WVIV-FM (y) 625 N Michigan Ave # 300, Chicago IL 60611 **Phn:** 312-981-1800 **Fax:** 312-981-1840 www.univision.com

Chicago WVIX-FM (y) 625 N Michigan Ave # 300, Chicago IL 60611 **Phn:** 312-981-1800 **Fax:** 312-981-1840 www.univision.com dlevy@univisionradio.com

INDIANA

Goshen WKAM-AM (y) 930 E Lincoln Ave, Goshen IN 46528 **Phn:** 574-533-1460 **Fax:** 574-534-3698

Indianapolis WEDJ-FM (y) 1800 N Meridian St Ste 603, Indianapolis IN 46202 **Phn:** 317-924-1071 **Fax:** 317-924-7766 www.wedjfm.com bart@wedjfm.com

Indianapolis WNTS-AM (y) 4800 E Raymond St, Indianapolis IN 46203 **Phn:** 317-359-5591

Indianapolis WSYW-AM (y) 1800 N Meridian St Ste 603, Indianapolis IN 46202 **Phn:** 317-924-1071 **Fax:** 317-924-7766 www.laquebuena810am.com manuel@wedjfm.com

IOWA
Perry KDLS-FM (y) 22560 141st Dr, Perry IA 50220 **Phn:** 515-465-5357 **Fax:** 515-465-3952 laley105@yahoo.com

Storm Lake KAYL-AM (y) PO Box 1037, Storm Lake IA 50588 **Phn:** 712-732-3520 **Fax:** 712-732-1746 www.stormlakeradio.com

Waterloo KBBG-AM (ynt) 918 Newell St, Waterloo IA 50703 **Phn:** 319-235-1515 **Fax:** 319-234-6182 www.kbbgfm.org

KANSAS
Garden City KSSA-FM (y) 1402 E Kansas Ave, Garden City KS 67846 **Phn:** 620-276-2366 **Fax:** 620-276-3568 www.wksradio.com

Kansas City KCZZ-AM (y) 1701 S 55th St, Kansas City KS 66106 **Phn:** 913-287-7994 **Fax:** 913-287-5881 www.reyesmediagroup.com ereyes@reyesmediagroup.com

Liberal KSMM-FM (y) 150 Plaza Dr Ste J, Liberal KS 67901 **Phn:** 620-624-8156 **Fax:** 620-624-4606 ksmmproduction@gmail.com

Liberal KZQD-FM (yq) PO Box 1893, Liberal KS 67905 **Phn:** 620-626-8282 **Fax:** 620-626-8080 www.kzqdradiolibertad.com radiolibertad@sbcglobal.net

Wichita KYQQ-FM (y) 4200 N Old Lawrence Rd, Wichita KS 67219 **Phn:** 316-838-9141 **Fax:** 316-838-3607 www.radiolobo1065.com bbrannigan@kfdi.com

KENTUCKY
Covington WCVG-AM (y) 135 W 38th St, Covington KY 41015 **Phn:** 859-291-2255

Somerset WTHL-FM (qy) PO Box 1423, Somerset KY 42502 **Phn:** 606-679-6300 **Fax:** 606-679-1342

LOUISIANA
Baton Rouge KDDK-FM (y) 263 3rd St Ste 703, Baton Rouge LA 70801 **Phn:** 225-344-2882 www.kddkfm.com kddk1055@att.net

Metairie KGLA-AM (y) 3850 N Causeway Blvd Ste 454, Metairie LA 70002 **Phn:** 504-799-3420 **Fax:** 504-799-3434 www.tropical1540.com info@kgla.tv

Metairie KXMG-FM (y) 3850 N Causeway Blvd # 830, Metairie LA 70002 **Phn:** 504-832-3555 www.mega1075fm.com

Metairie WFNO-AM (y) 3841 Veterans Blvd # 201, Metairie LA 70002 **Phn:** 504-832-3555 **Fax:** 504-830-7200

MARYLAND
Lanham WLZL-FM (y) 4200 Parliament Pl Ste 300, Lanham MD 20706 **Phn:** 301-306-0991 **Fax:** 301-731-0431 elzolradio.cbslocal.com juan.romero@cbsradio.com

Laurel WILC-AM (y) 13499 Baltimore Ave Ste 200, Laurel MD 20707 **Phn:** 301-419-2122 **Fax:** 301-419-2409 www.holaciudad.com info@holaciudad.com

Potomac WCTN-AM (y) 7825 Tuckerman Ln Ste 211, Potomac MD 20854 **Phn:** 301-299-7026 **Fax:** 301-299-5301 950wctn@gmail.com

HISPANIC RADIO STATIONS
Silver Spring WACA-AM (yt) 11141 Georgia Ave Ste 310, Silver Spring MD 20902 **Phn:** 301-942-3500 **Fax:** 301-942-7798 www.radioamerica.net cabina@radioamerica.net

Suitland WWGB-AM (yug) 5210 Auth Rd Ste 500, Suitland MD 20746 **Phn:** 301-899-1444 **Fax:** 301-899-7244 www.wwgb.com radio@wwgb.com

MASSACHUSETTS
Boston WUNR-AM (ey) 160 N Washington St, Boston MA 02114 **Phn:** 617-367-9003 **Fax:** 617-367-2265

Brockton WMSX-AM (y) 288 Linwood St, Brockton MA 02301 **Phn:** 508-587-5454 **Fax:** 508-587-1950 molinahbone@aol.com

Cambridge WRCA-AM (ey) 552 Massachusetts Ave Ste 201, Cambridge MA 02139 **Phn:** 617-492-3300 **Fax:** 617-492-2800 www.1330wrca.com wrca1330@aol.com

Chelsea WESX-AM (y) 90 Everett Ave, Chelsea MA 02150 **Phn:** 617-884-4500 **Fax:** 617-884-4515 www.wesx1230am.com

Chelsea WJDA-AM (y) 90 Everett Ave Ste 5, Chelsea MA 02150 **Phn:** 617-884-4500 **Fax:** 617-884-4515 www.wjda1300am.com arivas5906@aol.com

Medford WKOX-AM (y) 10 Cabot Rd Ste 302, Medford MA 02155 **Phn:** 781-396-1430 **Fax:** 781-391-3064 www.mia1430.com jeffreyoar@clearchannel.com

Medford WXKS-AM (y) 10 Cabot Rd Ste 302, Medford MA 02155 **Phn:** 781-396-1430 **Fax:** 781-391-3064 www.kiss108.com anthonyalfano@clearchannel.com

Medford WXKS-FM (y) 10 Cabot Rd Ste 302, Medford MA 02155 **Phn:** 781-396-1430 **Fax:** 781-391-3064 www.kiss108.com anthonyalfano@clearchannel.com

Methuen WNNW-AM (y) 462 Merrimack St, Methuen MA 01844 **Phn:** 978-686-9966 **Fax:** 978-687-1180 www.power800am.com

New Bedford WJFD-FM (ey) 651 Orchard St #300, New Bedford MA 02744 **Phn:** 508-997-2929 **Fax:** 508-990-3893 wjfd.com claudia@wjfd.com

Quincy WWDJ-AM (y) 500 Victory Rd, Quincy MA 02171 **Phn:** 617-328-0880 **Fax:** 617-328-0375 salemradioboston.com patr@salemradioboston.com

South Hamilton WNSH-AM (y) PO Box 242, South Hamilton MA 01982 **Phn:** 978-954-1282 **Fax:** 978-468-1954 www.viva1570.com radioviva1570@gmail.com

Springfield WACE-AM (eqy) PO Box 1, Springfield MA 01101 **Phn:** 413-594-6654 www.waceradio.com wace@waceradio.com

West Springfield WACM-AM (y) 34 Sylvan St, West Springfield MA 01089 **Phn:** 413-781-5200 **Fax:** 413-734-2240 www.wacmpopular1490.com

West Springfield WSPR-AM (y) 34 Sylvan St, West Springfield MA 01089 **Phn:** 413-781-5200 **Fax:** 413-734-2240 jrizza@davidsonmediagroup.com

Worcester WORC-AM (y) 122 Green St Ste 2R, Worcester MA 01604 **Phn:** 508-791-2111 **Fax:** 508-752-6897

MICHIGAN
Grand Rapids WYGR-AM (y) PO Box 9591, Grand Rapids MI 49509 **Phn:** 616-452-8589 **Fax:** 616-248-0176 www.wygr.net roberts@wygr.net

Ypsilanti WSDS-AM (cy) 580 W Clark Rd, Ypsilanti MI 48198 **Phn:** 734-484-1480 **Fax:** 734-484-5313 www.wsds1480.com wsds@explosiva1480.com

MINNESOTA
Minneapolis KMNV-AM (y) 1516 E Lake St Ste 200, Minneapolis MN 55407 **Phn:** 612-729-5900 **Fax:** 612-729-5999 vidaysabor.net conectando@vidaysabor.com

Minneapolis WDGY-AM (y) 2619 E Lake St, Minneapolis MN 55406 **Phn:** 612-729-3776 **Fax:** 612-724-0437 www.radiorey630am.com felicia@radiorey630am.com

Minneapolis WREY-AM (y) 2619 E Lake St, Minneapolis MN 55406 **Phn:** 612-729-3776 **Fax:** 612-724-0437 www.radiorey630am.com felicia@radiorey630am.com

Ramsey KBGY-FM (y) 14443 Armstrong Blvd NW, Ramsey MN 55303 **Phn:** 763-412-4626 **Fax:** 763-412-4691 www.lamerabuena.net djtiger_lamerabuena@hotmail.com

MISSOURI
Saint Louis WEW-AM (y) 2740 Hampton Ave, Saint Louis MO 63139 **Phn:** 314-781-9397 **Fax:** 314-781-8545 www.wewradio.com wewradio@aol.com

NEBRASKA
Omaha KBBX-FM (y) 11128 John Galt Blvd Ste 25, Omaha NE 68137 **Phn:** 402-884-0968 **Fax:** 402-884-4754 www.radiolobo977.com mschoonover@connoisseurmedia.com

Omaha KOTK-AM (qy) 11717 Burt St Ste 202, Omaha NE 68154 **Phn:** 402-422-1600 **Fax:** 402-422-1602 www.1420kotk.com anunez@salemomaha.com

NEVADA
Las Vegas KISF-FM (y) 6767 W Tropicana Ave Ste 102, Las Vegas NV 89103 **Phn:** 702-284-6400 **Fax:** 702-284-6403 www.univision.com joseramonbravo@univision.com

Las Vegas KLSQ-AM (y) 6767 W Tropicana Ave Ste 102, Las Vegas NV 89103 **Phn:** 702-284-6400 **Fax:** 702-284-6403 www.univision.com

Las Vegas KQRT-FM (y) 500 Pilot Rd Ste D, Las Vegas NV 89119 **Phn:** 702-597-3070 **Fax:** 702-507-1084 www.entravision.com croman@entravision.com

Las Vegas KRGT-FM (y) 6767 W Tropicana Ave Ste 102, Las Vegas NV 89103 **Phn:** 702-284-6400 **Fax:** 702-284-6475 www.univision.com

Las Vegas KRRN-FM (hy) 500 Pilot Rd Ste D, Las Vegas NV 89119 **Phn:** 323-900-6100 www.jose927.com croman@entravision.com

Las Vegas KWID-FM (y) 3755 W Flamingo Rd, Las Vegas NV 89102 **Phn:** 702-238-7300 **Fax:** 702-732-4890

Reno KRNV-FM (y) 300 S Wells Ave Ste 12, Reno NV 89502 **Phn:** 775-333-1017 **Fax:** 775-333-9046 www.tricolor1021.com vcody@entravision.com

Reno KXEQ-AM (y) 225 Linden St, Reno NV 89502 **Phn:** 775-827-1111 **Fax:** 775-827-2082

NEW JERSEY
Linwood WTAA-AM (y) 1601 New Rd, Linwood NJ 08221 **Phn:** 609-653-1400 **Fax:** 609-601-0450

Paterson WWRV-AM (qy) PO Box 2908, Paterson NJ 07509 **Phn:** 973-881-8700 **Fax:** 973-881-8324 radiovision.net dtirado@radiovision.net

Vineland WMIZ-AM (y) 632 Maurice River Pkwy, Vineland NJ 08360 **Phn:** 856-692-8888 **Fax:** 856-696-2568 www.wmizradio.com chemple@aol.com

NEW MEXICO
Albuquerque KJFA-FM (y) 8009 Marble Ave NE, Albuquerque NM 87110 **Phn:** 505-262-1142 **Fax:** 505-254-7106

Albuquerque KLVO-FM (y) 4125 Carlisle Blvd NE, Albuquerque NM 87107 **Phn:** 505-878-0980 **Fax:** 505-878-0098 www.radiolobo.net srufail@americangeneralmedia.com

Albuquerque KRZY-FM (y) 2725 Broadbent Pkwy NE Ste F, Albuquerque NM 87107 **Phn:** 505-342-4141 **Fax:** 505-345-6407 www.jose1059.com mwilder@entravision.com

Albuquerque KRZY-AM (y) 2725 Broadbent Pkwy NE Ste F, Albuquerque NM 87107 **Phn:** 505-342-4141 **Fax:** 505-344-0891 www.tricolor1450.com mwilder@entravision.com

Artesia KPZE-FM (y) 317 W Quay Ave, Artesia NM 88210 **Phn:** 575-746-2751 **Fax:** 575-748-3748 www.kpze.com news@ksvpradio.com

Belen KARS-AM (y) 208 N 2nd St, Belen NM 87002 **Phn:** 505-864-3024 **Fax:** 505-864-2719 www.americangeneralmedia.com srufail@americangeneralmedia.com

Clayton KLMX-AM (cy) PO Box 547, Clayton NM 88415 **Phn:** 575-374-2555 **Fax:** 575-374-2557

Deming KOTS-AM (cy) PO Box 470, Deming NM 88031 **Phn:** 575-546-9011 **Fax:** 575-546-9342 www.demingradio.com radio@demingradio.com

Espanola KDCE-AM (y) 403 W Pueblo Dr, Espanola NM 87532 **Phn:** 505-753-2201 **Fax:** 505-753-8685 kdceradio.com tomas@kdceradio.com

Espanola KYBR-FM (y) 403 W Pueblo Dr, Espanola NM 87532 **Phn:** 505-753-2201 **Fax:** 505-753-8685 www.radiooso.com

Hobbs KLMA-FM (y) PO Box 457, Hobbs NM 88241 **Phn:** 575-391-9650 **Fax:** 575-397-9373 www.klmaradio.com klmaradio@leaco.net

Hobbs KPZA-FM (y) 619 N Turner St, Hobbs NM 88240 **Phn:** 575-397-4969 **Fax:** 575-393-4310 www.kpzafm.com mail@1radiosquare.com

Las Cruces KKVS-FM (y) 1355 California Ave, Las Cruces NM 88001 **Phn:** 575-525-9298 **Fax:** 575-525-9419 www.vista.fm a.lumeyer@kgrt.com

Las Vegas KFUN-AM (cy) PO Box 700, Las Vegas NM 87701 **Phn:** 505-425-6766 **Fax:** 505-425-6767 www.kfunonline.com jpbaca1946@kfunonline.com

Las Vegas KNMX-AM (y) 304 S Grand Ave, Las Vegas NM 87701 **Phn:** 505-425-5669 **Fax:** 505-425-3557 www.lvnmradio.com mog87701@aol.com

Roswell KRDD-AM (yh) PO Box 1615, Roswell NM 88202 **Phn:** 575-623-8111 krddam@yahoo.com

Santa Fe KSWV-AM (y) 102 Taos St, Santa Fe NM 87505 **Phn:** 505-989-7441 **Fax:** 505-989-7607

Santa Rosa KSSR-AM (acy) 2818 Historic Route 66, Santa Rosa NM 88435 **Phn:** 575-472-5777 kssrradio@yahoo.com

Taos KXMT-FM (y) 125 Camino De La Merced, Taos NM 87571 **Phn:** 575-758-4491 **Fax:** 575-758-4452 www.kxmt.com

NEW YORK
Brooklyn WNSW-AM (y) PO Box 200012, Brooklyn NY 11220 **Phn:** 718-491-1430 **Fax:** 908-436-1431 www.radiocanticonuevo.com ericksalgado1430@hotmail.com

Central Islip WLIE-AM (y) 990 Motor Pkwy, Central Islip NY 11722 **Phn:** 631-569-4294 **Fax:** 631-761-8649 www.wlie540am.com smusgrave@mercurycapitalpartners.com

New York WADO-AM (ynt) 485 Madison Ave Fl 3, New York NY 10022 **Phn:** 212-310-6000 **Fax:** 212-310-6095 www.univision.com

HISPANIC RADIO STATIONS
New York WHCR-FM (wvy) 160 Convent Ave, New York NY 10031 **Phn:** 212-650-7481 **Fax:** 212-650-5736 www.whcr.org generalmanager@whcr.org

New York WPAT-AM (y) 26 W 56th St, New York NY 10019 **Phn:** 212-246-9393 **Fax:** 212-664-1922

New York WPAT-AM (y) 26 W 56th St, New York NY 10019 **Phn:** 212-246-9393 **Fax:** 212-664-1922 www.931amor.com info@931amor.com

New York WQBU-FM (y) 485 Madison Ave Fl 3, New York NY 10022 **Phn:** 212-310-6000 **Fax:** 212-888-3694 www.univision.com

New York WSKQ-FM (y) 26 W 56th St, New York NY 10019 **Phn:** 212-541-9200 **Fax:** 212-541-6904 lamega.lamusica.com jtorres@sbsnewyork.com

Pomona WLIM-AM (yq) 1551 Route 202, Pomona NY 10970 **Phn:** 845-354-4917 **Fax:** 845-354-4917 www.polskieradio.com goga@polskieradio.com

NORTH CAROLINA
Charlotte WNOW-FM (y) 4321 Stuart Andrew Blvd Ste B, Charlotte NC 28217 **Phn:** 704-665-9355

Charlotte WNOW-AM (y) 4321 Stuart Andrew Blvd Ste B, Charlotte NC 28217 **Phn:** 704-665-9355 www.wnow-am.com smiller@davidsonmediagroup.com

Charlotte WOLS-FM (y) 4801 E Independence Blvd, Charlotte NC 28212 **Phn:** 704-442-7277 **Fax:** 704-405-3173

Elizabeth City WCNC-AM (y) PO Box 1246, Elizabeth City NC 27906 **Phn:** 252-335-4379 **Fax:** 252-338-5275 www.ecri.net psa@ecri.net

Elizabeth City WZBO-AM (y) PO Box 1246, Elizabeth City NC 27906 **Phn:** 252-338-0196 **Fax:** 252-338-5275 www.ecri.net psa@ecri.net

Fairmont WFMO-AM (gwy) PO Box 668, Fairmont NC 28340 **Phn:** 910-628-6781 **Fax:** 910-628-6648

Greensboro WGBT-FM (y) 2B Pai Park, Greensboro NC 27409 **Phn:** 336-822-2000 **Fax:** 336-887-0104 www.945wpti.com richmcmillan@rushradio945.comÿ

Greenville WOOW-AM (gy) 405 Evans St, Greenville NC 27858 **Phn:** 252-757-0365 **Fax:** 252-757-1793

High Point WGOS-AM (ty) 6223 Old Mendenhall Rd, High Point NC 27263 **Phn:** 336-434-5024 **Fax:** 336-434-6018 cadenaradialnuevavida.com javierfzb@hotmail.com

High Point WIST-FM (y) PO Box 5663, High Point NC 27262 **Phn:** 336-887-0983 **Fax:** 336-887-3055 larazalaraza.com programming@norsanmultimedia.com

Raleigh WCLY-AM (ys) 3100 Highwoods Blvd Ste 140, Raleigh NC 27604 **Phn:** 919-890-6299

Raleigh WETC-AM (y) 3305 Durham Dr Ste 111, Raleigh NC 27603 **Phn:** 919-772-1717 **Fax:** 919-772-1718 laregia540am@bellsouth.net

Raleigh WYMY-FM (y) 3012 Highwoods Blvd, Raleigh NC 27604 **Phn:** 919-790-9392 **Fax:** 919-790-8996 www.laley969.com

Siler City WNCA-AM (ay) PO Box 429, Siler City NC 27344 **Phn:** 919-742-2135 **Fax:** 919-663-2843

Winston Salem WSGH-AM (y) 4015 Brownsboro Rd, Winston Salem NC 27106 **Phn:** 336-759-0524 **Fax:** 336-759-9327 www.radiolamovidita.com lucysaucedo@radiolamovidita.com

OHIO
Columbus WVKO-FM (y) 74 S 4th St, Columbus OH 43215 **Phn:** 614-469-1930 **Fax:** 614-224-6208

OKLAHOMA
El Reno KZUE-AM (y) 2715 S Radio Rd, El Reno OK 73036 **Phn:** 405-262-1460 kzue@aol.com

Oklahoma City KTUZ-FM (y) 5101 S Shields Blvd, Oklahoma City OK 73129 **Phn:** 405-616-5500 **Fax:** 405-616-0328 www.ktuz.com gabriel.o@tylermedia.com

Oklahoma City WKY-AM (y) 4045 NW 64th St Ste 600, Oklahoma City OK 73116 **Phn:** 405-848-0100 **Fax:** 405-843-5288 www.laindomable.com

Tulsa KIZS-FM (y) 2625 S Memorial Dr, Tulsa OK 74129 **Phn:** 918-388-3738 **Fax:** 918-388-5400 www.1015lapreciosa.com doncristi@clearchannel.com

OREGON
Dallas KWIP-AM (y) PO Box 469, Dallas OR 97338 **Phn:** 503-623-0245 **Fax:** 503-623-6733 www.kwip.com lucy@kwip.com

Medford KRTA-AM (ys) 511 Rossanley Dr, Medford OR 97501 **Phn:** 541-772-0322 **Fax:** 541-772-4233 opusradio.com dean@opusradio.com

Portland KGDD-AM (y) 5110 SE Stark St, Portland OR 97215 **Phn:** 503-234-5550 **Fax:** 503-234-5583 www.lagrande.mx contact@bustosmedia.com

Wilsonville KXPD-AM (y) 8532 SW Saint Helens Dr Ste 100, Wilsonville OR 97070 **Phn:** 971-224-2260 **Fax:** 971-224-2270

Woodburn KCKX-AM (y) 1665 James St, Woodburn OR 97071 **Phn:** 503-769-1460 **Fax:** 503-981-3561 www.lapantera940.com

Woodburn KSND-FM (y) PO Box 158, Woodburn OR 97071 **Phn:** 503-981-9400 **Fax:** 503-981-3561 www.lapantera940.com

Woodburn KWBY-AM (y) 1665 James St, Woodburn OR 97071 **Phn:** 503-981-9400 **Fax:** 503-981-3561 www.lapantera940.com

PENNSYLVANIA
Allentown WHOL-AM (y) 1125 Colorado St, Allentown PA 18103 **Phn:** 610-434-4801 www.holaenturadio.com holaradionoticias@holaenturadio.com

Bala Cynwyd WNWR-AM (eyt) 200 Monument Rd Ste 6, Bala Cynwyd PA 19004 **Phn:** 610-664-6780 **Fax:** 610-664-8529 www.wnwr.com information@wnwr.com

Easton WEST-AM (y) 436 Northampton St, Easton PA 18042 **Phn:** 610-250-9557 **Fax:** 610-250-9675 www.whol1600.com tonyrodriguez@hola1600.com

Lancaster WLCH-FM (vy) 453 S Lime St #D, Lancaster PA 17602 **Phn:** 717-295-7996 **Fax:** 717-295-7759 wlchradio.org cgaldamez@sacapa.org

Philadelphia WEMG-AM (y) 1341 N Delaware Ave Ste 509, Philadelphia PA 19125 **Phn:** 215-426-1900 **Fax:** 215-426-1550 davidsonmediagroup.com jyoung@davidsonmediagroup.com

Philadelphia WPHE-AM (nty) PO Box 46325, Philadelphia PA 19160 **Phn:** 215-291-7532 **Fax:** 215-739-1337 www.radiosalvacion.com

PUERTO RICO
Aguadilla WABA-AM (y) PO Box 188, Aguadilla PR 00605 **Phn:** 787-891-1230 **Fax:** 787-882-2282 www.waba850.com waba850am@yahoo.com

Arecibo WMIA-AM (y) PO Box 1055, Arecibo PR 00613 **Phn:** 787-878-1275

Bayamon WXLX-FM (y) PO Box 15390, Bayamon PR 00956 **Phn:** 787-785-9390 **Fax:** 787-785-9377 www.lax.fm

Guayanilla WOIZ-AM (y) PO Box 561130, Guayanilla PR 00656 **Phn:** 787-835-1130 **Fax:** 787-835-3130 www.radioantillas.4t.com radioantillas@yahoo.com

Guaynabo WEGM-FM (y) PO Box 949, Guaynabo PR 00970 **Phn:** 787-622-9700 **Fax:** 787-622-9477 www.lamega.fm rogie@sbspuertorico.com

Guaynabo WIOB-FM (y) PO Box 949, Guaynabo PR 00970 **Phn:** 787-622-9700 **Fax:** 787-622-9477 lrivera@sbspuertorico.com

Humacao WALO-AM (y) PO Box 9230, Humacao PR 00792 **Phn:** 787-852-1240 **Fax:** 787-852-1280 waloradio.com walo1240@yahoo.com

Salinas WHOY-AM (y) PO Box 1148, Salinas PR 00751 **Phn:** 787-824-3420 **Fax:** 787-824-8054

San German WSOL-AM (y) 220 Ave Los Atleticos De San Ger, San German PR 00683 **Phn:** 787-892-2975 **Fax:** 787-264-1090

San Juan WBMJ-AM (yq) 1409 Ave Ponce De Leon, San Juan PR 00907 **Phn:** 787-724-1190 **Fax:** 787-722-4395 therockradio.org programming@therockradio.org

San Juan WCMN-FM (y) PO Box 363222, San Juan PR 00936 **Phn:** 787-878-0070 **Fax:** 787-880-1112 tocadeto.com noticias@notiuno.com

San Juan WCMN-AM (y) PO Box 363222, San Juan PR 00936 **Phn:** 787-773-7474 **Fax:** 787-880-1112 noticias@notiuno.com

San Juan WIVV-AM (yq) 1409 Ave Ponce De Leon, San Juan PR 00907 **Phn:** 787-724-1190 **Fax:** 787-722-4395 therockradio.org programming@therockradio.org

San Juan WLUZ-AM (y) PO Box 9394, San Juan PR 00908 **Phn:** 787-729-1600 **Fax:** 787-723-8685 ttrelles@yahoo.com

San Juan WMNT-AM (y) 1305 Delta Caparra Ter, San Juan PR 00920 **Phn:** 787-783-8810 **Fax:** 787-781-7647

Yauco WKFE-AM (y) PO Box 533, Yauco PR 00698 **Phn:** 787-856-1320 **Fax:** 787-856-4420

RHODE ISLAND
North Providence WPMZ-AM (y) 1270 Mineral Spring Ave, North Providence RI 02904 **Phn:** 401-726-8413 **Fax:** 401-726-8649 www.poder1110.com info@poder1110.com

Providence WALE-AM (ynt) 1185 N Main St, Providence RI 02904 **Phn:** 401-521-0990 **Fax:** 401-521-5077

Providence WELH-FM (vjy) PO Box 1930, Providence RI 02912 **Phn:** 401-421-8100 www.bsrlive.com news.director@bsrlive.com

SOUTH CAROLINA
Greenville WOLI-FM (y) 225 S Pleasantburg Dr, Greenville SC 29607 **Phn:** 864-751-0113 **Fax:** 863-223-1553 www.woli-am.com jyoung@davidsonmediagroup.com

Mount Pleasant WLTQ-AM (y) 950 Houston Northcutt Blvd Ste 201, Mount Pleasant SC 29464 **Phn:** 843-884-2534 **Fax:** 843-884-1218

Myrtle Beach WLQB-FM (y) 4841 Highway 17 Byp S, Myrtle Beach SC 29577 **Phn:** 843-293-0107 **Fax:** 843-293-1717

North Charleston WZJY-AM (y) 5081 Rivers Ave, North Charleston SC 29406 **Phn:** 843-529-1185 **Fax:** 843-974-6002 www.elsol980.com

TENNESSEE
Lenoir City WKZX-FM (y) PO Box 340, Lenoir City TN 37771 **Phn:** 865-986-9850 wkzx@aol.com

Nashville WKDA-AM (y) 1617 Lebanon Pike, Nashville TN 37210 **Phn:** 615-889-1960 **Fax:** 615-902-9108

HISPANIC RADIO STATIONS
TEXAS
Abilene KKHR-FM (y) 402 Cypress St Ste 510, Abilene TX 79601 **Phn:** 325-672-5442 **Fax:** 325-672-6128 www.radioabilene.com

Alice KOPY-FM (y) PO Box 731, Alice TX 78333 **Phn:** 361-664-1884 **Fax:** 361-664-1886 claroradio@yahoo.com

Amarillo KBZD-FM (yo) 5200 E Amarillo Blvd, Amarillo TX 79107 **Phn:** 806-355-1044 **Fax:** 806-457-0642

Amarillo KGRW-FM (y) 3639 Wolflin Ave, Amarillo TX 79102 **Phn:** 505-762-5031 **Fax:** 806-457-0642

Amarillo KIXZ-AM (ny) 6214 SW 34th Ave, Amarillo TX 79109 **Phn:** 806-355-9777 **Fax:** 806-355-5832 voiceofamarillo.com jamesguthrie@townsquaremedia.com

Amarillo KQFX-FM (y) 3639 Wolflin Ave, Amarillo TX 79102 **Phn:** 806-355-1044 **Fax:** 806-457-0642

Amarillo KTNZ-AM (y) 3639 Wolflin Ave, Amarillo TX 79102 **Phn:** 806-355-1044 **Fax:** 806-457-0642

Amarillo KZIP-AM (y) 3639 Wolflin Ave, Amarillo TX 79102 **Phn:** 806-355-1044 **Fax:** 806-457-0642

Austin KFIT-AM (gy) PO Box 160158, Austin TX 78716 **Phn:** 512-328-8400 **Fax:** 512-328-8437 gospel1060.com

Austin KZNX-AM (y) 1050 E 11th St Ste 300, Austin TX 78702 **Phn:** 512-346-8255 **Fax:** 512-692-0599 www.radiomujer.com.mx

Beaumont KBED-AM (y) 775 S 11th St # 102, Beaumont TX 77701 **Phn:** 409-951-2500 **Fax:** 09-833-9296

Big Spring KBYG-AM (oy) 2801 Wasson Rd, Big Spring TX 79720 **Phn:** 432-263-6351 **Fax:** 432-263-8223 www.kbygradio.com

Brownsville KBNR-FM (vqy) PO Box 5480, Brownsville TX 78523 **Phn:** 956-542-6933 **Fax:** 956-542-0523 www.radiokbnr.org

Bryan KTAM-AM (y) 1240 E Villa Maria Rd, Bryan TX 77802 **Phn:** 979-776-1240 **Fax:** 979-776-0123 www.brazosradio.com sweetc@brazosradio.com

Bryan KVJM-FM (y) 1716 Briarcrest Dr Ste 150, Bryan TX 77802 **Phn:** 979-846-5597 **Fax:** 979-268-9090 www.kissfm1031.com jimharrington@clearchannel.com

Cameron KMIL-FM (cy) PO Box 832, Cameron TX 76520 **Phn:** 254-697-6633 **Fax:** 254-697-6330 www.kmil.com kmil@kmil.com

Colleyville KNOR-FM (y) 4201 Pool Rd, Colleyville TX 76034 **Phn:** 817-868-2900 **Fax:** 817-868-2116

Colleyville KZZA-FM (y) 4201 Pool Rd, Colleyville TX 76034 **Phn:** 817-868-2900 **Fax:** 817-868-2116 www.casa1067.com dallasinfo@lbimedia.com

Corpus Christi KLHB-FM (y) 1300 Antelope St, Corpus Christi TX 78401 **Phn:** 361-883-1600 **Fax:** 361-883-9303

Corpus Christi KMIQ-FM (y) 2209 N Padre Island Dr, Corpus Christi TX 78408 **Phn:** 361-855-0975 **Fax:** 361-855-0977 carloslopezmagic@yahoo.com

Corpus Christi KMJR-FM (y) 1300 Antelope St, Corpus Christi TX 78401 **Phn:** 361-183-1600 **Fax:** 361-888-5685

Corpus Christi KSAB-FM (y) 501 Tupper Ln, Corpus Christi TX 78417 **Phn:** 361-289-0111 **Fax:** 361-289-5035 www.ksabfm.com ksab@clearchannel.com

Corpus Christi KUNO-AM (y) 501 Tupper Ln, Corpus Christi TX 78417 **Phn:** 361-289-0111 **Fax:** 361-289-5035 www.1400kuno.com danpena@clearchannel.com

Dallas KDFT-AM (qy) 5801 Marvin D Love Fwy Ste 409, Dallas TX 75237 **Phn:** 972-572-1540 **Fax:** 972-572-1263 www.kdft540.com kdft-kmny@mrbi.net

Dallas KDXX-AM (y) 7700 John W Carpenter Fwy, Dallas TX 75247 **Phn:** 214-525-0400 **Fax:** 214-631-1196 www.univision.com

Dallas KESS-FM (y) 7700 John W Carpenter Fwy, Dallas TX 75247 **Phn:** 214-525-0400 **Fax:** 214-631-1196 www.univision.com

Dallas KFLC-AM (y) 7700 John W Carpenter Fwy, Dallas TX 75247 **Phn:** 214-525-0400 **Fax:** 214-631-1196 www.univision.com

Dallas KFZO-FM (y) 7700 John W Carpenter Fwy, Dallas TX 75247 **Phn:** 214-525-0400 **Fax:** 214-631-1196 www.univision.com

Dallas KJON-AM (qy) 8828 N Stemmons Fwy # 106, Dallas TX 75247 **Phn:** 214-951-0132 **Fax:** 214-951-8622 www.grnonline.com davepalmer@grnonline.com

Dallas KLNO-FM (y) 7700 John W Carpenter Fwy, Dallas TX 75247 **Phn:** 214-525-0400 **Fax:** 214-631-1196 www.univision.com

Dallas KMVK-FM (y) 4131 N Central Expy Ste 1000, Dallas TX 75204 **Phn:** 214-525-7000 **Fax:** 214-525-7150 lagrande1075.cbslocal.com jennifer.marquez@cbsradio.com

Dallas KTNO-AM (qy) 5787 S Hampton Rd Ste 340, Dallas TX 75232 **Phn:** 214-330-5866 **Fax:** 214-330-9885 www.ktnoam.com hugo.gamboa@klty.com

Eagle Pass KEPS-AM (y) PO Box 1123, Eagle Pass TX 78853 **Phn:** 830-773-9247 **Fax:** 830-773-9500

Edinburg KOIR-FM (qy) 4300 S US Highway 281, Edinburg TX 78539 **Phn:** 956-380-3435 **Fax:** 956-380-8156 radioesperanza.com correo@radioesperanza.com

El Paso KAMA-AM (y) 2211 E Missouri Ave Ste S300, El Paso TX 79903 **Phn:** 915-544-9797 **Fax:** 915-544-1247 univisionamerica.univision.com

El Paso KBNA-FM (y) 2211 E Missouri Ave Ste S300, El Paso TX 79903 **Phn:** 915-544-9797 **Fax:** 915-544-1247 kbna975.univision.com

El Paso KINT-FM (y) 5426 N Mesa St, El Paso TX 79912 **Phn:** 915-581-1126 **Fax:** 915-585-4642 www.jose939.com iponce@entravision.com

El Paso KQBA-AM (y) 2211 E Missouri Ave Ste S300, El Paso TX 79903 **Phn:** 915-544-9797 **Fax:** 915-544-1247 www.univision.com

El Paso KSVE-AM (y) 5426 N Mesa St, El Paso TX 79912 **Phn:** 915-581-1126 **Fax:** 915-585-4642 www.jose939.com iponce@entravision.com

El Paso KVER-FM (yvq) PO Box 12008, El Paso TX 79913 **Phn:** 915-544-9190 **Fax:** 915-544-9193 www.kver.org kver@lwrn.com

El Paso KVIV-AM (qy) 6060 Surety Dr Ste 100, El Paso TX 79905 **Phn:** 915-565-2999 **Fax:** 915-562-3156 www.kviv1340.com info@kviv1340.com

El Paso KYSE-FM (y) 5426 N Mesa St, El Paso TX 79912 **Phn:** 915-581-1126 **Fax:** 915-585-4642 www.elgato947.com sfleming@entravision.com

Falfurrias KPSO-FM (cy) 304 E Rice St, Falfurrias TX 78355 **Phn:** 361-325-2112

Floresville KWCB-FM (vy) 1905 10th St, Floresville TX 78114 **Phn:** 830-393-6116 **Fax:** 830-393-3817 www.wilsoncountynews.comkwcb kwcb89fm@yahoo.com

HISPANIC RADIO STATIONS

Fort Stockton KFST-AM (cy) 954 S US Highway 385, Fort Stockton TX 79735 **Phn:** 432-336-2228 **Fax:** 432-336-5834 www.kfstradio.com kfst@sbcglobal.net

Houston KEYH-AM (y) 3000 Bering Dr, Houston TX 77057 **Phn:** 713-315-3400 **Fax:** 713-315-3506 www.lbimedia.com info@lbimedia.com

Houston KGOL-AM (ey) 5821 Southwest Fwy Ste 600, Houston TX 77057 **Phn:** 713-349-9880 **Fax:** 713-349-9365 entravision.com

Houston KIOX-FM (y) 3000 Bering Dr, Houston TX 77057 **Phn:** 713-315-3400 **Fax:** 713-315-3506 www.kioxradio.com

Houston KJOJ-FM (y) 3000 Bering Dr, Houston TX 77057 **Phn:** 713-315-3400 **Fax:** 713-315-3405 www.laraza.fm

Houston KJOJ-AM (qty) 3000 Bering Dr, Houston TX 77057 **Phn:** 713-315-3400 **Fax:** 713-315-3506 www.lbimedia.com houstoninfo@lbimedia.com

Houston KLAT-AM (cy) 5100 Southwest Fwy, Houston TX 77056 **Phn:** 713-965-2400 **Fax:** 713-965-2401 www.univision.com

Houston KLOL-FM (y) 24 Greenway Plz Ste 1900, Houston TX 77046 **Phn:** 713-881-5100 **Fax:** 713-881-5598 klol.cbslocal.com liliana.ary@cbsradio.com

Houston KLTN-FM (y) 5100 Southwest Fwy, Houston TX 77056 **Phn:** 713-965-2400 **Fax:** 713-965-2401 www.univision.com

Houston KLVL-AM (qy) 1302 N Shepherd Dr, Houston TX 77008 **Phn:** 713-868-5559 **Fax:** 713-868-9631 www.sigabroadcasting.com sigabroadcasting@gmail.com

Houston KNTE-FM (y) 3000 Bering Dr, Houston TX 77057 **Phn:** 713-315-3400 whorton@lbimedia.com

Houston KOVE-FM (y) 5100 Southwest Fwy, Houston TX 77056 **Phn:** 713-965-2400 **Fax:** 713-965-2401 www.univision.com

Houston KQBU-FM (y) 5100 Southwest Fwy, Houston TX 77056 **Phn:** 713-965-2400 **Fax:** 13-965-2401 www.univision.com

Houston KQQK-FM (y) 3000 Bering Dr, Houston TX 77057 **Phn:** 713-315-3400 **Fax:** 713-315-3506 elnorte.estrellatv.com greyes@lbimedia.com

Houston KQUE-AM (y) 3000 Bering Dr, Houston TX 77057 **Phn:** 713-315-3400 **Fax:** 713-315-3506

Houston KTJM-FM (y) 3000 Bering Dr, Houston TX 77057 **Phn:** 713-315-3400 **Fax:** 713-315-3506 www.laraza.fm whorton@lbimedia.com

Houston KTMR-AM (qy) 1302 N Shepherd Dr, Houston TX 77008 **Phn:** 713-868-5559 **Fax:** 713-868-9631 www.sigabroadcasting.com sigabroadcasting@gmail.com

Houston KYND-AM (qye) PO Box 19886, Houston TX 77224 **Phn:** 281-373-1520

Houston KYST-AM (y) 7322 Southwest Fwy Ste 500, Houston TX 77074 **Phn:** 713-779-9292 **Fax:** 713-779-1651

Jacksonville KDVE-FM (y) PO Box 1648, Jacksonville TX 75766 **Phn:** 903-586-2527 **Fax:** 903-663-9492 bullboyroy@yahoo.com

Jacksonville KEBE-AM (y) PO Box 1648, Jacksonville TX 75766 **Phn:** 903-586-2527 **Fax:** 903-663-9492 bullboyroy@yahoo.com

Laredo KBDR-FM (y) 107 Calle Del Norte Ste 107, Laredo TX 78041 **Phn:** 956-725-1000 **Fax:** 956-794-9155 www.laley1005.com

Laredo KBNL-FM (qy) PO Box 2425, Laredo TX 78044 **Phn:** 956-724-9211 **Fax:** 956-724-9919 www.kbnl.org kbnl@lwrn.org

Laredo KHOY-FM (vy) 1901 Corpus Christi St, Laredo TX 78043 **Phn:** 956-722-4167 **Fax:** 956-722-4464 www.khoy.org khoy@khoy.org

Laredo KJBZ-FM (y) 6402 N Bartlett Ave Ste 1, Laredo TX 78041 **Phn:** 956-726-9393 **Fax:** 956-724-9915 restrada@krrg.com

Laredo KLAR-AM (ynt) PO Box 2517, Laredo TX 78044 **Phn:** 956-723-1300 **Fax:** 956-723-9539

Laredo XEAS-AM (y) 1510 Calle Del Norte Ste 2, Laredo TX 78041 **Phn:** 956-727-3670 **Fax:** 956-727-3680

Laredo XERT-AM (y) 1510 Calle Del Norte Ste 2, Laredo TX 78041 **Phn:** 956-727-3670 **Fax:** 956-727-3680

Laredo XHMW-FM (y) 1510 Calle Del Norte Ste 2, Laredo TX 78041 **Phn:** 956-727-3670 **Fax:** 956-727-3680

Laredo XHRT-FM (y) 1510 Calle Del Norte Ste 2, Laredo TX 78041 **Phn:** 956-727-3670 **Fax:** 956-727-3680

Lubbock KAIQ-FM (y) 1220 Broadway Ste 600, Lubbock TX 79401 **Phn:** 806-763-6051 **Fax:** 806-744-8363 www.tricolor955.com ltrevino@entravision.com

Lubbock KBZO-AM (y) 1220 Broadway Ste 600, Lubbock TX 79401 **Phn:** 806-763-6051 **Fax:** 806-744-8363 www.espn1460am.com ltrevino@entravision.com

Lubbock KXTQ-FM (y) PO Box 3757, Lubbock TX 79452 **Phn:** 806-745-3434 **Fax:** 806-748-2470 www.magic937.fm cheinz@ramarcom.com

Lufkin KSML-AM (y) 121 S Cotton Sq, Lufkin TX 75904 **Phn:** 936-634-4584 **Fax:** 936-632-5722 yatesmedia.com radioman@yatesmedia.com

Marion KBIB-AM (qy) 290 N Santa Clara Rd, Marion TX 78124 **Phn:** 830-914-2083

McAllen KGBT-FM (y) 200 S 10th St Ste 600, McAllen TX 78501 **Phn:** 956-631-5499 **Fax:** 956-631-0090 www.univision.com laguerararuby@univision.com

McAllen KGBT-AM (y) 200 S 10th St Ste 600, McAllen TX 78501 **Phn:** 956-631-5499 **Fax:** 956-631-0090 www.univision.com

McAllen KIBL-AM (qy) PO Box 252, McAllen TX 78505 **Phn:** 956-686-6382 **Fax:** 956-686-2999

McAllen KKPS-FM (y) 801 N Jackson Rd, McAllen TX 78501 **Phn:** 956-661-6000 **Fax:** 956-661-6081 995lanueva.com

McAllen KNVO-FM (y) 801 N Jackson Rd, McAllen TX 78501 **Phn:** 956-661-6000 **Fax:** 956-661-6081 www.jose1011.com anthonyacosta@entravision.com

McAllen KTUE-AM (yq) PO Box 252, McAllen TX 78505 **Phn:** 956-686-6382

McAllen KUBR-AM (yq) PO Box 252, McAllen TX 78505 **Phn:** 956-781-5528 **Fax:** 956-686-2999

Merkel KMXO-AM (qy) PO Box 523, Merkel TX 79536 **Phn:** 325-928-3060 **Fax:** 325-928-4683 www.kmxoradiofe.com zacarias@kmxoradiofe.com

Midland KTXC-FM (y) PO Box 60403, Midland TX 79711 **Phn:** 432-570-6670 **Fax:** 432-567-9992 bdawson@kwes.com

Muleshoe KMUL-AM (y) 600 W 8th St, Muleshoe TX 79347 **Phn:** 806-272-4273 **Fax:** 806-272-5067

Odessa KOZA-AM (y) 1319 S Crane Ave, Odessa TX 79763 **Phn:** 432-333-1227 **Fax:** 432-435-0064

Odessa KQLM-FM (y) 1319 S Crane Ave, Odessa TX 79763 **Phn:** 432-333-1227 **Fax:** 432-435-0064 www.q108fm.com benjaminv@kqlm.com

Pecos KIUN-AM (cy) PO Box 469, Pecos TX 79772 **Phn:** 432-445-2497 **Fax:** 432-445-4092 www.98xfm.com

Plainview KRIA-FM (y) PO Box 1420, Plainview TX 79073 **Phn:** 806-296-2771 **Fax:** 806-293-5732

Robstown KINE-AM (yq) 115 W Avenue D, Robstown TX 78380 **Phn:** 361-289-8877 **Fax:** 361-289-7722

San Angelo KCLL-FM (y) 2824 Sherwood Way, San Angelo TX 76901 **Phn:** 325-949-2112 **Fax:** 325-944-0851 www.kcll-fm.com info@kcll-fm.com

San Angelo KSJT-FM (yst) 209 W Beauregard Ave, San Angelo TX 76903 **Phn:** 325-655-1717 **Fax:** 325-657-0601 nikkibkyzz@yahoo.com

San Antonio KCOR-AM (y) 1777 NE Loop 410 Ste 400, San Antonio TX 78217 **Phn:** 210-821-6548 **Fax:** 210-804-7825 www.univision.com dwilson@univisionradio.com

San Antonio KEDA-AM (nty) 510 S Flores St, San Antonio TX 78204 **Phn:** 210-226-5254 **Fax:** 210-227-7937 www.kedaradio.com kedakid@aol.com

San Antonio KGSX-FM (y) 1777 NE Loop 410 Ste 400, San Antonio TX 78217 **Phn:** 210-821-6548 www.univision.com

San Antonio KLEY-FM (y) 4050 Eisenhauer Rd, San Antonio TX 78218 **Phn:** 210-654-5100 **Fax:** 210-855-5076 bmpradio.com sgranato@bmpradio.com

San Antonio KROM-FM (y) 1777 NE Loop 410 Ste 400, San Antonio TX 78217 **Phn:** 210-821-6548 **Fax:** 210-804-7825 www.univision.com nperez@univisionradio.com

San Antonio KSAH-AM (y) 4050 Eisenhauer Rd, San Antonio TX 78218 **Phn:** 210-654-5100 **Fax:** 210-855-5076 bmpradio.com sgranato@bmpradio.com

San Antonio KXTN-FM (y) 1777 NE Loop 410 Ste 400, San Antonio TX 78217 **Phn:** 210-829-1075 **Fax:** 210-804-7825 www.kxtn.com jonramirez@univisionradio.com

Seminole KIKZ-AM (cy) 105 NW 11th St, Seminole TX 79360 **Phn:** 432-758-5878 **Fax:** 432-758-5474

Seymour KSEY-AM (y) 1 Radio Ln, Seymour TX 76380 **Phn:** 940-889-2637 www.radioksey.com fmksey@aol.com

Stephenville KSTV-AM (y) 3209 W Washington St, Stephenville TX 76401 **Phn:** 254-968-2141 **Fax:** 254-968-6221 www.thecrustychicken2.comkstvradio troy.stark@gmail.com

Tyler KCUL-FM (y) PO Box 7820, Tyler TX 75711 **Phn:** 903-581-9966 **Fax:** 903-534-5300 www.lainvasora.fm dlaborde@etradiogroup.com

Tyler KOYE-FM (y) 210 S Broadway Ave, Tyler TX 75702 **Phn:** 903-581-9966 **Fax:** 903-534-5300 www.lainvasora.fm

Uvalde KUVA-FM (y) PO Box 758, Uvalde TX 78802 **Phn:** 830-278-2555 **Fax:** 830-278-9461 www.uvalderadio.com news@uvalderadio.com

Victoria KHMC-FM (y) 2001 E Sabine St Ste 101, Victoria TX 77901 **Phn:** 361-575-9533 **Fax:** 361-575-9502 www.majic95fm.com majictejano@yahoo.com

Victoria KQVT-FM (ay) PO Box 3325, Victoria TX 77903 **Phn:** 361-573-0777 **Fax:** 361-578-0059 www.kqvt.com adamwest@townsquaremedia.com

Waco KWOW-FM (y) 6401 Cobbs Dr, Waco TX 76710 **Phn:** 254-772-6104 **Fax:** 254-776-0642 www.laley104.com

Weslaco KRGE-AM (yq) PO Box 1290, Weslaco TX 78599 **Phn:** 956-968-7777 **Fax:** 956-968-5143 www.tigrecolorado.com lindc13@yahoo.com

West Lake Hills KHHL-FM (y) 912 S Capital Of Texas Hwy Ste 400, West Lake Hills TX 78746 **Phn:** 512-390-5539 **Fax:** 512-314-7742

West Lake Hills KXXS-FM (y) 912 S Capital Of Texas Hwy Ste 400, West Lake Hills TX 78746 **Phn:** 512-416-1100 **Fax:** 512-317-7742

UTAH

Salt Lake City KDUT-FM (y) 2722 S Redwood Rd Ste 1, Salt Lake City UT 84119 **Phn:** 801-908-8777 **Fax:** 801-908-8782 kdut.radiolagrande.com acadenas@adelantemediagroup.com

VIRGINIA

Norfolk WVXX-AM (yh) 700 Monticello Ave Ste 301, Norfolk VA 23510 **Phn:** 757-627-9899 **Fax:** 757-627-0123 www.selecta1050.com ahindlin@yahoo.com

Richmond WVNZ-AM (y) 308 W Broad St, Richmond VA 23220 **Phn:** 804-643-0990 **Fax:** 804-643-4990 www.selecta1320.com jjacobs@davidsonmediagroup.com

WASHINGTON

Auburn KDDS-FM (y) 1400 W Main St, Auburn WA 98001 **Phn:** 253-735-9700 **Fax:** 253-735-7424

Ephrata KZML-FM (y) 910 Basin St SW, Ephrata WA 98823 **Phn:** 509-754-4661 **Fax:** 509-754-4110

Granger KDNA-FM (vy) PO Box 800, Granger WA 98932 **Phn:** 509-854-1900 **Fax:** 509-854-2223 www.kdna.org

Pasco KRCW-FM (y) 508 W Lewis St, Pasco WA 99301 **Phn:** 509-545-0700 **Fax:** 509-543-4100 www.campesina.com

Pasco KZHR-FM (y) 2823 W Lewis St, Pasco WA 99301 **Phn:** 509-547-1618 **Fax:** 509-546-2678 www.kzhr.com

Prosser KLES-FM (y) 1227 Hillcrest Dr, Prosser WA 99350 **Phn:** 509-786-1310 **Fax:** 509-786-6814

Seattle KKMO-AM (y) 2201 6th Ave Ste 1500, Seattle WA 98121 **Phn:** 206-443-8200 **Fax:** 206-777-1133 www.radiosol1360.comUC

Seattle KXPA-AM (ye) 114 Lakeside Ave, Seattle WA 98122 **Phn:** 206-292-7800 **Fax:** 206-292-2140 www.kxpa.com

Wenatchee KWLN-FM (y) 32 N Mission St Unit B2, Wenatchee WA 98801 **Phn:** 509-663-5186 www.lanuevaradio.com jlhigh@morris.com

Wenatchee KWWX-AM (y) 231 N Wenatchee Ave, Wenatchee WA 98801 **Phn:** 509-665-6565

Yakima KMMG-FM (y) 706 Butterfield Rd, Yakima WA 98901 **Phn:** 509-457-1000 **Fax:** 509-452-0541

Yakima KQSN-FM (y) 4010 Summitview Ave Ste 200, Yakima WA 98908 **Phn:** 509-972-3461 **Fax:** 509-972-3540 www.lapreciosa.com

Yakima KYXE-AM (y) PO Box 2888, Yakima WA 98907 **Phn:** 509-457-1000 **Fax:** 509-452-0541

Yakima KZTA-FM (y) PO Box 2888, Yakima WA 98907 **Phn:** 509-457-1000 **Fax:** 509-452-0541

Yakima KZTB-FM (y) 706 Butterfield Rd, Yakima WA 98901 **Phn:** 509-457-1000 **Fax:** 509-452-0541

Yakima KZTS-AM (y) PO Box 2888, Yakima WA 98907 **Phn:** 509-457-1000 **Fax:** 509-452-0541

WISCONSIN

Madison WLMV-AM (y) PO Box 44408, Madison WI 53744 **Phn:** 608-273-1000 **Fax:** 608-271-8182 tom.walker@mwfbg.net

Watertown WTTN-AM (ys) PO Box 509, Watertown WI 53094 **Phn:** 920-261-1580 **Fax:** 920-885-2152

West Allis WDDW-FM (y) 1138 S 108th St, West Allis WI 53214 **Phn:** 414-325-1800 **Fax:** 414-607-1837

WYOMING

Cheyenne KJUA-AM (yo) 110 E 17th St Ste 205, Cheyenne WY 82001 **Phn:** 307-635-8787 **Fax:** 307-635-8788

Rock Springs KMRZ-FM (y) PO Box 2128, Rock Springs WY 82902 **Phn:** 307-362-3793 **Fax:** 307-362-8727 www.wyoradio.com